GRADUATE STUDY IN
PSYCHOLOGY

2003

American
Psychological
Association

American Psychological Association
Washington, DC

Published by
American Psychological Association
750 First Street, NE
Washington, DC 20002

www.apa.org

ISBN: 1-55798-972-9
ISSN: 0742-7220
36th edition

To order
APA Order Department
P.O. Box 92984
Washington, DC 20090-2984
Tel: (800) 374-2721, Direct: (202) 336-5510
Fax: (202) 336-5502, TDD/TTY: (202) 336-6123
Online: www.apa.org/books/
Email: order@apa.org

Printed in the United States of America

Contents

Foreword

This is the 36th edition of a book prepared to assist individuals interested in graduate study in psychology. The current edition provides information for more than 500 graduate departments, programs, and schools of psychology in the United States and Canada. The information was obtained from questionnaires sent to graduate departments and schools of psychology and was provided voluntarily. The American Psychological Association (APA) is not responsible for the accuracy of the information reported.

The purpose of this publication is to provide an information service, offering in one book information about the majority of graduate programs in psychology. Inclusion in this publication does not signify APA approval or endorsement of a graduate program; nor should it be assumed that a listing of a program in *Graduate Study in Psychology* means that its graduates are automatically qualified to sit for licensure as psychologists or are eligible for positions requiring a psychology degree.

On the other hand, programs listed in this publication have agreed to the following quality assurance provisions:

1. They have agreed to honor April 15 as the date allowed for graduate applicants to accept or reject an offer of admission and financial assistance for fall matriculation. This date adheres to national policy guidelines as stated by the Council of Graduate Schools and the Council of Graduate Departments of Psychology.

2. They have satisfied the following criteria. The program offers a graduate degree and is sponsored by a public or private higher education institution accredited by one of six regional accrediting bodies recognized by the U.S. Secretary of Education or, in the case of Canadian programs, the institution is publicly recognized by the Association of Universities and Colleges of Canada as a member in good standing, or the program indicates that it meets *all* of the following criteria:

   A. The graduate program, wherever it may be administratively housed, is publicly labeled as a psychology program in pertinent institutional catalogs and brochures.

   B. The psychology program stands as a recognizable, coherent organizational entity within the institution.

   C. There is an identifiable core of full-time psychology faculty.

   D. Psychologists have clear authority and primary responsibility for the academic core and specialty preparation, whether or not the program involves multiple administrative lines.

   E. There is an identifiable body of graduate students who are enrolled in the program for the attainment of the graduate degree offered.

   F. The program is an organized, integrated sequence of study designed by the psychology faculty responsible for the program.

   G. Programs leading to a doctoral degree require at least the equivalent of three full-time academic years of graduate study.

   H. Doctoral programs ensure appropriate breadth and depth of education and training in psychology as follows:

1) Methodology and history. Systematic preparation in scientific standards and responsibilities, research design and methodology, quantitative methods (e.g., statistics, psychometric methods), and historical foundations in psychology.

2) Foundations in psychology, including

   a. biological bases of behavior (e.g., physiological psychology, comparative psychology, neuropsychology, psychopharmacology),

   b. cognitive–affective bases of behavior (e.g., learning, memory, perception, cognition, thinking, motivation, emotion),

   c. social bases of behavior (e.g., social psychology; cultural, ethnic, and group processes; sex roles; organizational behavior), and

   d. individual differences (e.g., personality theory, human development, individual differences, abnormal psychology, psychology of women, psychology of the handicapped, psychology of the minority experience).

3) Additional preparation in the program's area of specialization, to include:

   a. knowledge and application of ethical principles and guidelines and standards as may apply to scientific and professional practice activities;

   b. supervised practicum and/or laboratory experiences appropriate to the area of practice, teaching, or research in psychology; and

   c. advanced preparation appropriate to the area of specialization.

This publication may not answer all questions you have about graduate education in psychology. Some questions you may want to direct to particular graduate departments, programs, or schools of psychology. *For more information about general policies and information related to graduate education, visit the following Web site, http://www.apa.org/ed/graduate/.*

Producing this publication involved the cooperation of many. I wish to express appreciation to all graduate departments, programs, and schools that contributed information. Also, I wish to acknowledge the work and assistance of a number of my APA colleagues in the Education Directorate, Research Office, and the Books Department who have contributed greatly to the success of this publication. Especially due recognition for coordinating the collecting and editing of information are Joan Freund and Yashica Joyner (Education Directorate); for assistance on questionnaire development, data analysis, and graphics are Jessica Kohout, PhD, Marlene Wicherski, and William Pate (Research Office); and for preparing the final document for publication, Catherine Hudson (Books Department).

Paul Nelson, PhD
Deputy Executive Director and
    Director, Office of Graduate Education and Training
Education Directorate
American Psychological Association

Considering Graduate Study

Psychology is a broad scientific discipline bridging the social and biological sciences, influenced also by such disciplines as philosophy and mathematics. Psychology's applications are similarly diverse and responsive to problem-solving in areas such as education and human development, health, family and community relations, organizations and other work environments, engineering and technology, the arts and architecture, communications, and political and judiciary systems.

Just as the discipline of psychology is broad, there are many types of graduate programs available in psychology. Thus, selecting a graduate program that is best for you requires thoughtful consideration. Because of their diversity, the American Psychological Association (APA) does not rank graduate programs. Rather, APA encourages you to think about the best match for you. Some programs are intensely focused on preparing an individual for an academic research career, while other programs focus on preparing an individual for applied research outside the university. Other programs prepare students to provide psychological services as licensed professional psychologists. Some programs bridge these various goals. Also, some programs offer a breadth of scholarly professional development in addition to a substantive focus in psychology to prepare individuals for a college teaching career in psychology. Substantive program areas of recent doctoral graduates are illustrated in Figure 1. For each department, program, or school, you are advised to review the section entitled *Orientation, Objectives, and Emphasis of Departments* for more information about various program emphases.

Figure 1.   New Doctorates in Psychology by Subfield, 2000–2001

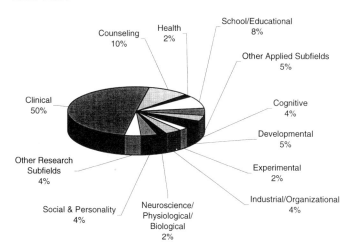

Source: Graduate Study in Psychology: 2003, APA Research Office

Accreditation in Professional Psychology

Many students ask about a program's accreditation. The APA accredits doctoral programs in health service areas of psychology but not programs in other areas of professional practice (e.g. industrial/organizational psychology). It does not accredit master's-degree programs. You should know also that accreditation applies to educational programs (i.e., doctoral programs in professional psychology) and institutions (i.e., colleges, universities, and free-standing professional schools), not to individuals. It is a system for recognizing educational quality as defined by the profession or other accrediting bodies. Graduation from an accredited school or program does not guarantee employment or licensure for individuals, although being a graduate of an accredited program may facilitate such achievement. Programs in this publication are so identified, if they are APA accredited. *For more information and the most current lists of accredited programs, see the APA Office of Program Consultation and Accreditation Web site at http://www.apa.org/ed/accred.html.*

Programs, Degrees, and Employment

Although employment in research, teaching, and human service positions is possible for those with a master's degree in psychology, the doctoral degree is generally considered the entry-level degree in psychology for the independent, licensed practice of psychology as a profession. Increasingly it is the preferred degree for college and university faculty. For specific information about employment outcomes of a program's graduates, review the section entitled *Employment of Department Graduates* in each listing.

At a broader level, Figure 2 summarizes types of settings in which graduates of master's-degree programs are employed. Some students earn a master's degree, work for a few years, then return to study for a doctorate in psychology or another field. Other students earn a master's degree as part of the doctoral program preparation. Still others bypass the master's degree and work directly on the doctorate. Doctoral programs vary in their practices and admission preferences in this regard. Thus, be sure

Figure 2.   Psychology Master's-Degree Recipients by Employment Setting: 1997

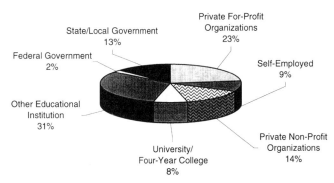

Source: 1997 Scientists and Engineers Statistical Data System, National Science Foundation

to note this preference when reviewing the programs in which you are interested.

Doctoral programs also differ in terms of the type of doctoral degree awarded. The two most common doctoral degrees are the PhD and the PsyD. A few programs in Colleges of Education may offer the EdD. The PhD is the older doctorate and is generally regarded as the research degree. Although many professional psychology programs award it, especially those in university academic departments, they typically have an emphasis on research training and the integration of that with applied or practice training. The PsyD, first awarded in the late 1960s but increasing in popularity among professional school programs, is a professional degree in psychology (similar to the MD in medicine). Programs awarding the PsyD place major emphasis on preparing their graduates for professional practice as practitioner–scholars but typically with less extensive research training. Presently, about 75% of all doctoral degrees in psychology are PhDs; of the degrees awarded in clinical psychology, however, only 60% are PhDs, with the others being PsyDs. Figure 3 gives a profile of initial employment outcomes for PhD and PsyD program graduates. *For more information about degrees, employment, and salaries in psychology, you may wish to visit the Web site of the APA Research Office at http://research.apa.org/index.html.*

Figure 3. Primary Employment Settings of 1999 PhD and PsyD Recipients in Psychology

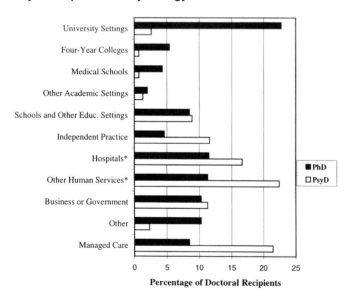

*Disproportionately high percentages are represented in these categories, as many recent graduates are still gaining experience in these organized settings prior to licensure. Also, note that "Independent Practice" numbers were relatively low, as a number of respondents to the survey were still gaining experience in organized settings prior to licensure.

Source: 1999 Doctorate Employment Survey, APA Research Office

Admission Requirements

Requirements for admission vary from program to program. Many psychology programs prefer or require significant undergraduate coursework in psychology, often the equivalent of a major or minor, while others do not. Evaluate your educational background and be realistic about your abilities and academic potential.

To assist in their evaluation of academic potential, many graduate departments require the Graduate Record Examination (GRE), and some require the Miller Analogies Test (MAT). If the programs in which you are interested require these standardized tests, you should take the GRE, GRE-Subject (Psychology), and the MAT in time for the scores to be included with your application materials.

Other criteria considered as admission factors may include previous research activity, work experience, clinically related public service, extracurricular activity, letters of recommendation, statement of goals and objectives, and an interview. Many programs rate letters of recommendation as high in importance, and an increasing number are requiring an interview. Of the departments and programs listed in this publication, 77% rated letters of recommendation as high in importance when considering students for admission. In addition, a clear statement of goals and objectives was rated as high in importance by 72% of departments and programs. Review the section entitled *Student Applications/Admissions* in this publication for information related to scores and other criteria considered.

Competition for Admission

Gaining entry into graduate school in psychology can be difficult. The number of applicants typically exceeds the number of student openings. The number of applications received by the department or school and the number of students accepted should provide a sense of the competition you can expect when applying to a particular department, program, or school. For more information, review the section entitled *Student Applications/Admissions*.

Time to Degree

Programs should be clear about the minimum number of years in full-time study (or part-time equivalent) required to complete the degree requirements. The reality of doctoral education and training is that students average 5–6 years after the bachelor's degree, some taking even longer to complete the degree. The time taken by students to complete their degrees is a result of many possible factors. One of those is the extent to which financial assistance is available.

Tuition and Financial Assistance

The cost of graduate education can be expensive. Tuition for out-of-state students in public institutions and for all students in private institutions will be higher. Many students require loans, even when working part-time to pay for their graduate education. Indeed, the amount of debt incurred by graduate students can be significant, as illustrated by Figure 4.

Figure 4. Level of Cumulative Debt Related to Graduate Education: 1999 Doctorate Recipients

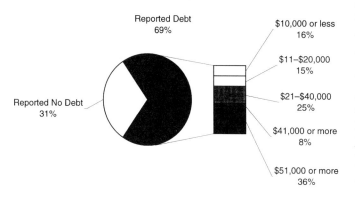

Source: 1999 Doctorate Employment Survey, APA Research Office

On the other hand, financial assistance in various forms is available to many students. Figure 4 indicates that about one third of those who earn their doctorate are debt free on graduation. Thus, you may wish to apply for a fellowship, scholarship, assistantship, or another type of financial assistance. Many fellowships and scholarships are outright grants or subsidies and require no service to the department or university. For departments and programs reporting in this publication, 44% indicated that they offer some form of fellowship or scholarship to first-year students, and 39% indicated they offered some form of fellowship or scholarship to advanced students.

Assistantships in teaching and research are also available in many programs. These are forms of employment for services in a department. Teaching assistantships may require teaching a class or assisting a professor by grading papers, acting as a laboratory assistant, and performing other such supporting work. Research assistants ordinarily work on research projects being conducted by program faculty. Among departments and programs reporting for this publication, about one half offer teaching assistantships and about one half offer research assistantships for first-year students. For advanced students, the availability of assistantships is similar, although slightly greater.

The amount of work required for fellowships, assistantships, and traineeships is expressed in hours per week. The number of hours indicated should be considered an approximation. Stipends are expressed in terms of total stipend for an academic year of nine months. Students should inquire, when receiving an offer of financial assistance, as to the amount to be given in terms of tuition remission (not requiring the student to pay tuition) versus a stipend (actual cash in hand).

For information about tuition costs and the types of assistance offered by departments and programs, review the section entitled *Financial Information/Assistance.*

Also, you may want to review information listed at the APA Education Web site at http://www.apa.org/ed/grants.html for information about scholarships, fellowships, grants, and other funding opportunities.

Application Information

An application to a department or program of study is a very important document. Make sure it represents you in the best possible manner and that you confirm (a) the deadline for filing the application, (b) what documents are required, and (c) who should receive the application. In addition, do not forget the admission fee usually required when filing an application.

Most graduate programs in psychology accept students only for fall admission. However, if you are interested in winter, spring, or summer admission, check the application information listed in this publication for the program to which you are applying. Information about application deadlines in this publication are listed in the section entitled *Application Information.*

Rules for Acceptance of Offers for Admission and Financial Aid

The Council of Graduate Schools has adopted the following policy that provides guidance to students and graduate programs regarding offers of financial support. The policy was adopted by the Council of Graduate Schools in 1965 and reaffirmed in 1992. It was endorsed by the Council of Graduate Departments of Psychology in 1981 and reaffirmed in 2000. Graduate programs and schools currently listed in the book have agreed to honor the policy. The policy reads as follows:

Acceptance of an offer of financial support (such as graduate scholarship, fellowship, traineeship, or assistantship) for the next academic year by a prospective or enrolled graduate student completes an agreement that both student and graduate school expect to honor. In that context, the conditions affecting such offers and their acceptance must be defined carefully and understood by all parties.

Students are under no obligation to respond to offers of financial support prior to April 15; earlier deadlines for acceptance of such offers violate the intent of this Resolution. In those instances in which the student accepts the offer before April 15, and subsequently desires to withdraw that acceptance, the student may submit in writing a resignation of the appointment at any time through April 15. However, an acceptance given or left in force after April 15 commits the student not to accept another offer without first obtaining a written release for the institution to which a commitment has been made. Similarly, an offer by an institution after April 15 is conditional on presentation by the student of the written release from any previously accepted offer. It is further agreed by the institutions and organizations subscribing to the above Resolution that a copy of this Resolution should accompany every scholarship, fellowship, traineeship, and assistantship offer.

Explanation of Program Listings

The following summarizes the information solicited from each program:

Contact Information

The name of the university or school, address, telephone number, fax number, e-mail, and World Wide Web address are provided. There may be more than one department in an institution that offers degrees in psychology.

Department Established

The year the department was established, the name of the department chairperson, and the number of full-time and part-time faculty members in the department are provided.

Programs and Degrees Offered

This heading highlights the program areas in which degrees are offered by the department or school, the type of degree, and the number of degrees awarded.

APA Accreditation Status

Whether a program in clinical psychology, counseling psychology, school psychology, or combined professional–scientific psychology is accredited when this publication went to press is noted. Since changes in accreditation status may occur after publication, please contact the APA Office of Program Consultation and Accreditation, or review the Web site at http://www.apa.org/ed/accred.html.

Student Applications/Admissions

This section includes information about the number of applications received by the individual program areas of departments and schools. Also listed are the number of applicants accepted into the program and the number of openings anticipated in the next year. In addition, the information reflects the median number of years required for a degree and the number of students enrolled who were dismissed or voluntarily withdrew from the program before completing their degree requirements.

Standardized tests scores and other information are presented. Scores including the Graduate Record Exam Verbal (GRE-V), Quantitative (GRE-Q), and Analytical (GRE-A); the combined GRE-V + Q score; the combined GRE-V + Q + A; and the GRE-Subject (Psychology) score are listed.

Other criteria considered as admission factors are rated according to their importance for admission. These criteria include previous research activity, work experience, clinically related public service, extracurricular activity, letters of recommendation, statement of goals and objectives, and an interview. Characteristics of students enrolled in the department or programs psychology programs are also reported.

Financial Information/Assistance

Tuition figures per year and/or per academic unit are indicated. The words "non-state residents" are used by state universities that charge more for out-of-state residents than students who reside in the state. These fees should be used as rough guidelines and are subject to change.

Teaching assistantships, research assistantships, traineeships, or fellowships and scholarships are reported. The data for each type of assistance is listed for first year and advanced. The average amount awarded to each student and the average number of hours that must be worked each week are included in the listing. Contact information for financial assistance is also listed.

In addition, this section includes information related to housing and day care. The availability of housing and day care facilities, on and off campus, is indicated.

Employment of Department Graduates

This section provides information about employment activities of graduates. Data presented by departments or schools includes information about master's- and doctoral-degree graduates, such as enrollment in psychology doctoral programs; enrollment by graduates in post-doctoral residency/fellowship programs; and employment by graduates in academic teaching or research positions; employment by graduates in business or industry, government agencies, hospitals, or other positions.

Additional Information

This section provides an opportunity to present the orientation, objectives, and emphasis of the department or school and information. Information is also presented about the special facilities or resources offered by the school or institution.

Application Information

This last section provides the addresses, deadlines, and fees for the submission of applications. There is not a common deadline for admission for programs of psychology.

2003

Graduate
Study
in
Psychology

Alabama, University of
Department of Psychology
College of Arts and Sciences
P.O. Box 870348
Tuscaloosa, AL 35487-0348
Telephone: (205) 348-5083
Fax: (205) 348-8648
E-mail: *blyman@gp.as.ua.edu*
Web: *http://www.as.ua.edu/psychology/*

Department Established:
1957. Chairperson: Robert D. Lyman. Number of Faculty: total–full-time 23, part-time 3; women–full-time 11; minority–full-time 2.

Programs and Degrees Offered:
Listed in the following order: Program area, degree type (T if terminal Master's), number awarded 7/00-6/01. Clinical-adult PhD 2, clinical-child PhD 5, clinical-psych/law PhD 5, cognitive PhD 2.

APA Accreditation: Clinical PhD: full.

Student Applications/Admissions:
Student Applications
Clinical-adult PhD—Applications 2001–2002, 30. Total applicants accepted 2001–2002, 9. New applicants enrolled 2001–2002, 7. Total enrolled 2001–2002 full-time, 23. Openings 2002–2003, 4. The Median number of years required for completion of a degree are 6. The number of students enrolled full and part-time, who were dismissed or voluntarily withdrew from this program area were 0. *Clinical-child PhD*—Applications 2001–2002, 63. Total applicants accepted 2001–2002, 7. New applicants enrolled 2001–2002, 5. Total enrolled 2001–2002 full-time, 23, part-time, 1. Openings 2002–2003, 4. The Median number of years required for completion of a degree are 6. The number of students enrolled full and part-time, who were dismissed or voluntarily withdrew from this program area were 0. *Clinical-psych/law PhD*—Applications 2001–2002, 63. Total applicants accepted 2001–2002, 4. New applicants enrolled 2001–2002, 4. Total enrolled 2001–2002 full-time, 12. Openings 2002–2003, 4. The Median number of years required for completion of a degree are 6. The number of students enrolled full and part-time, who were dismissed or voluntarily withdrew from this program area were 0. *Cognitive PhD*—Applications 2001–2002, 4. Total applicants accepted 2001–2002, 3. New applicants enrolled 2001–2002, 3. Total enrolled 2001–2002 full-time, 15. Openings 2002–2003, 3. The Median number of years required for completion of a degree are 6. The number of students enrolled full and part-time, who were dismissed or voluntarily withdrew from this program area were 0.

Admissions Requirements:
Scores: Entries appear in this order: required test or GPA, minimum score (if required), median score of students entering in 2001–2002. Doctoral Programs: GRE-V 500, 575; GRE-Q 500, 570; GRE-Analytical 500, 660; GRE-V+Q+Analytical no minimum stated; GRE-Subject(Psych) 500, 613; overall undergraduate GPA 3.0, 3.6 ; last 2 years GPA no minimum stated; psychology GPA no minimum stated; psychology GPA no minimum stated. GRE subject is preferred—500 minimum score.
Other Criteria: (importance of criteria rated low, medium, or high): GRE/MAT scores high, research experience high, work experience medium, extracurricular activity low, clinically related public service low, GPA medium, letters of recommendation high, interview high, statement of goals and objectives medium.

Student Characteristics: The following represents characteristics of students in 2001–2002 in all graduate psychology programs in the department: Female–full-time 52, part-time 1; Male–full-time 20, part-time 0; African American/Black–full-time 8, part-time 0; Hispanic/Latino(a)–full-time 0, part-time 0; Asian/Pacific Islander–full-time 1, part-time 0; American Indian/Alaska Native–full-time 0, part-time 0; Multi-ethnic–full-time 0, part-time 0; students subject to the Americans with Disabilities Act–full-time 0, part-time 0.

Financial Information/Assistance:
Tuition for Full-Time Study: *Doctoral:* State residents: per academic year $3,292; nonstate residents: per academic year $8,912.

Financial Assistance:
First Year Students: Teaching assistantships available for first-year. Average amount paid per academic year: $8,433. Average number of hours worked per week: 20. Tuition remission given: full. Research assistantships available for first-year. Average amount paid per academic year: $8,433. Average number of hours worked per week: 29. Tuition remission given: full. Fellowships and scholarships available for first-year. Average amount paid per academic year: $10,000. Tuition remission given: full.
Advanced Students: Teaching assistantships available for advanced students. Average amount paid per academic year: $8,433. Average number of hours worked per week: 20. Tuition remission given: full. Research assistantships available for advanced students. Average amount paid per academic year: $8,433. Average number of hours worked per week: 20. Tuition remission given: full. Fellowships and scholarships available for advanced students. Average amount paid per academic year: $10,000. Tuition remission given: full.
Contact Information: Of all students currently enrolled full-time, 85% benefitted from one or more of the listed financial assistance programs. For information on financial assistance, contact: Further details of assistance are provided during applicant interviews.

Internships/Practica: There are a number of practica available to graduate students. All doctoral students must take PY695/696, a teaching internship, in which the student teaches an introductory psychology class under the supervision of a faculty member. Two semesters of basic psychotherapy practicum are required of every doctoral student in clinical psychology. In this practicum, students conduct psychotherapy with four to six clients in the Department's Psychological Clinic. Students are required to complete 100 hours of direct client contact to fulfill this requirement. After basic psychotherapy practicum, doctoral clinical psychology students are required to take either one or two (depending on specialty area) advanced practica in their area of specialization. Many of these practica are housed in community service agencies (e.g., state psychiatric hospital, community mental health center, University operated treatment center for disturbed children). In addition to these formal practica, most doctoral students in the clinical program are financially supported at some time during their graduate school years through field placements in various community agencies. These students are supervised by either licensed psychologists employed by these agencies or by Department of Psychology clinical faculty. In addition to the intervention practica discussed above, all clinical doctoral students must take two of the three graduate psychological assessment courses offered. These courses have a significant practicum component, requiring that 5-10 administrations of commonly used psychological assessment instruments be conducted with Psychological Clinic clients. In addition, students in the Adult Clinical specialization must take advanced assessment and advanced intervention electives, which may have practicum components. For those doctoral students for whom a professional internship is required prior to graduation, 7 applied in 2000–2001. Of those who applied, 7 were placed in internships listed by the Association of Psychology Postdoctoral and Internship Programs (APPIC); 7 were placed in APA accredited internships.

Housing and Day Care: No on-campus housing and day care facilities are available.

Employment of Department Graduates:

Master's Degree Graduates: Of those who graduated in the academic year 2000–2001, the following categories and numbers represent the post-graduate activities and employment of master's degree graduates: Enrolled in a post-doctoral residency/fellowship (n/a), employed in independent practice (n/a).

Doctoral Degree Graduates: Of those who graduated in the academic year 2000–2001, the following categories and numbers represent the post-graduate activities and employment of doctoral degree graduates: Enrolled in a psychology doctoral program (n/a), enrolled in another graduate/professional program (n/a), enrolled in a post-doctoral residency/fellowship (6), employed in independent practice (2), employed in an academic position at a university (3), employed in an academic position at a 2-year/4-year college (1), employed in business or industry (research/consulting) (1), employed in a government agency (professional services) (1), other employment position (1).

Additional Information:

Orientation, Objectives, and Emphasis of Department: The University of Alabama doctoral program in psychology was founded in 1957 and the clinical program has been continuously accredited by the American Psychological Association since 1959. The department trains scientists and scientist-practitioners for a variety of roles: research, teaching, and applied practice. Of moderate size, the psychology department has awarded some 385 doctoral degrees, principally in the areas of clinical psychology, cognitive psychology, and mental retardation. The department has also developed innovative and successful subspecialty training programs in areas such as individual differences/mental retardation, psychology-law, and clinical-child. The doctoral programs emphasize core knowledge in the social, cognitive, developmental, and biological aspects of behavior as well as the methodological foundations necessary to scientific advancement. Students share a common core curriculum in these fundamental areas. Further, all students take additional courses designed to prepare them with the necessary knowledge and skills in their chosen specialty areas. A further objective of the department is to promote independent scholarship and professional development. Coursework is supplemented by the active collaboration of faculty and students in ongoing research projects and clinical activities. The department maintains access to a wide range of settings in which students can refine their research and applied skills.

Special Facilities or Resources: The department is housed in a modern three-story building that it shares with the Department of Mathematics. It is directly connected to the department's Psychological Clinic and the University's Computer Center. Facilities include student offices, excellent classroom and seminar space, and several research laboratories. Graduate students have access to microcomputers for research and word processing and videotaping capabilities for instruction and training. A major resource is the department's Psychological Clinic, which provides psychological assessment, referral, treatment planning, and direct intervention for a variety of clinical populations. The department's Child and Family Research Clinic serves as a specialized training and research laboratory. Both clinics include observation facilities. Also affiliated with the department is the Brewer-Porch Children's Center, a training and research facility for seriously disordered young children. The University of Alabama's Student Health Center also serves as a practicum site. Other research and clinical relationships are maintained with local psychiatric hospitals (Bryce Hospital and the Veterans Affairs Medical Center), Partlow State School (for severe developmental disabilities), the Capstone Medical Center, DCH Regional Medical Center, Family Counseling Services, Institute for Social Science Research, city and county school systems, Indian Rivers Mental Health Center, and the Taylor Hardin Forensic Center. Paid advanced training or research positions are often available in these facilities. Several faculty in the Cognitive Studies area have research grants that include student support. Some 30 adjunct faculty in diverse fields contribute to program enrichment.

Information for Students With Physical Disabilities: All facilities are handicap accessible.

Application Information:
Send to: Office of the Graduate School, University of Alabama, Box 870118, Tuscaloosa, AL 35487-0118. Students are admitted in the Fall, application deadline January 1. Deadline for the applications to the clinical program is January 1; February 1 deadline for cognitive. *Fee:* $25.

Alabama, University of, at Birmingham

Department of Psychology
School of Social and Behavioral Sciences
415 Campbell Hall
Birmingham, AL 35294-1170
Telephone: (205) 934-3850
Fax: (205) 975-6110
E-mail: *cmcfarla@uab.edu*
Web: *http://www.psy.uab.edu*

Department Established:

1969. Chairperson: Carl E. McFarland, Jr. Number of Faculty: total–full-time 28, part-time 58; women–full-time 9, part-time 16; minority–full-time 3, part-time 2.

Programs and Degrees Offered:

Listed in the following order: Program area, degree type (T if terminal Master's), number awarded 7/00-6/01. Behavioral neuroscience PhD 3, cognitive science PhD 0, developmental PhD 2, medical/clincal PhD 2.

APA Accreditation: Clinical PhD: full.

Student Applications/Admissions:

Student Applications

Behavioral neuroscience PhD—Applications 2001–2002, 9. Total applicants accepted 2001–2002, 1. New applicants enrolled 2001–2002, 1. Total enrolled 2001–2002 full-time, 9. Openings 2002–2003, 3. The Median number of years required for completion of a degree are 5. *Cognitive science PhD*—Applications 2001–2002, 4. Total enrolled 2001–2002 full-time, 2. Openings 2002–2003, 2. The number of students enrolled full and part-time, who were dismissed or voluntarily withdrew from this program area were 0. *Developmental PhD*—Applications 2001–2002, 20. Total applicants accepted 2001–2002, 4. New applicants enrolled 2001–2002, 4. Total enrolled 2001–2002 full-time, 12. Openings 2002–2003, 4. The Median number of years required for completion of a degree are 5. The number of students enrolled full and part-time, who were dismissed or voluntarily withdrew from this program area were 0. *Medical/clincal PhD*—Applications 2001–2002, 63. Total applicants accepted 2001–2002, 5. New applicants enrolled 2001–2002, 5. Total enrolled 2001–2002 full-time, 27. Openings 2002–2003, 6. The Median number of years required for completion of a degree are 6. The number of students enrolled full and part-time, who were dismissed or voluntarily withdrew from this program area were 1.

Admissions Requirements:

Scores: Entries appear in this order: required test or GPA, minimum score (if required), median score of students entering in 2001–2002. Doctoral Programs: GRE-V+Q 1150, 1240; GRE-Subject(Psych) no minimum stated; overall undergraduate GPA 3.00, 3.57; last 2 years GPA 3.20, 3.82; psychology GPA no minimum stated; psychology GPA no minimum stated.

Other Criteria: (importance of criteria rated low, medium, or high): GRE/MAT scores high, research experience high, work experience low, extracurricular activity low, clinically related public service medium, GPA high, letters of recommendation medium, interview medium, statement of goals and objectives medium.

Student Characteristics:

The following represents characteristics of students in 2001–2002 in all graduate psychology programs in the department: Female–full-time 29, part-time 0; Male–full-time 21, part-time 0; African American/Black–full-time 4, part-time 0; Hispanic/Latino (a)–full-time 0, part-time 0; Asian/Pacific Islander–full-time 2, part-time 0; American Indian/Alaska Native–full-time 0, part-time 0; Multi-ethnic–full-time 0, part-time 0; students subject to the Americans with Disabilities Act–full-time 2, part-time 0.

Financial Information/Assistance:

Tuition for Full-Time Study: *Doctoral:* State residents: per academic year $3,584, $112 per credit hour; nonstate residents: per academic year $7,168, $224 per credit hour.

Financial Assistance:

First Year Students: Fellowships and scholarships available for first-year. Average amount paid per academic year: $13,000. Average number of hours worked per week: 15. Apply by January 15. Tuition remission given: full.

Advanced Students: Teaching assistantships available for advanced students. Average amount paid per academic year: $14,500. Average number of hours worked per week: 20. Tuition remission given: partial. Research assistantships available for advanced students. Average amount paid per academic year: $15,000. Average number of hours worked per week: 20. Tuition remission given: partial. Traineeships available for advanced students. Average amount paid per academic year: $15,000. Average number of hours worked per week: 20. Tuition remission given: partial. Fellowships and scholarships available for advanced students. Average amount paid per academic year: $16,500. Average number of hours worked per week: 20. Tuition remission given: partial.

Contact Information: Of all students currently enrolled full-time, 100% benefitted from one or more of the listed financial assistance programs. For information on financial assistance, contact: Program Directors. Clinical: Dr. Jesse Milby; Developmental: Dr. Jan Wallander; Behavioral Neuroscience: Dr. Alan Randich; Cognitive Science: Dr. Michael Sloane.

Internships/Practica:

For those doctoral students for whom a professional internship is required prior to graduation, 6 applied in 2000–2001. Of those who applied, 6 were placed in internships listed by the Association of Psychology Postdoctoral and Internship Programs (APPIC); 6 were placed in APA accredited internships.

Housing and Day Care:

On-campus housing and day care facilities are available.

Employment of Department Graduates:

Master's Degree Graduates: Of those who graduated in the academic year 2000–2001, the following categories and numbers represent the post-graduate activities and employment of master's

degree graduates: Enrolled in a post-doctoral residency/fellowship (n/a), employed in independent practice (n/a).

Doctoral Degree Graduates: Of those who graduated in the academic year 2000–2001, the following categories and numbers represent the post-graduate activities and employment of doctoral degree graduates: Enrolled in a psychology doctoral program (n/a), enrolled in another graduate/professional program (n/a).

Additional Information:

Orientation, Objectives, and Emphasis of Department: The Department offers four doctoral programs: Clinical/Medical Psychology, Behavioral Neuroscience, Developmental Psychology, and Cognitive Science. Each program promotes rigorous scientific training for students pursuing basic or applied research careers. The programs are designed to produce scholars who will engage in independent research, practice, and teaching. Medical Psychology is a specialty within clinical psychology that focuses on psychological factors in health care. It is cosponsored by the UAB School of Medicine. The Behavioral Neuroscience Program provides individualized, interdisciplinary training for research on the biological bases of behavior. The Developmental Program trains students to conduct research to discover and apply basic principles of developmental psychology across the lifespan in an interdisciplinary context. Students are exposed to the issues of development in its natural and social contexts, as well as in laboratories. The Cognitive Science Program explores systematic, comprehensive issues concerning mind/brain in general and about intelligence and cognition in particular. Faculty research interests include: health psychology, substance abuse, clinical neuropsychology, psychopharmacology, human psychophysiology, brain imaging, sensation and perception, spinal cord injury, control of movement, aging, mental retardation/developmental disabilities, pediatric psychology, social ecology, cognitive development, developmental psychopathology, psychosocial influences on cancer, pain, and clinical outcomes evaluation.

Special Facilities or Resources: The University of Alabama at Birmingham is a comprehensive, urban research university, recently ranked by *U.S. News and World Report* as the number one up-and-coming university in the country. The UAB Psychology Department, in the School of Social and Behavioral Sciences, ranks among the top 5 psychology departments in the U.S. in federal/research funding. The UAB campus encompasses a 65-block area on Birmingham's Southside, offering all of the advantages of a university within a highly supportive city. Resources are available from the School of Medicine, Department of Physiological Optics, School of Public Health, Civitan International Research Center, Sparks Center for Developmental and Learning Disorders, Center for Aging, Department of Pediatrics, Department of Psychiatry and Behavioral Neurobiology, Neurobiology Research Center, School of Education, School of Nursing, Department of Computer and Information Sciences, Department of Biocommunications, University Hospital, a psychiatric hospital, and Children's Hospital.

Application Information:
Send to: The Graduate School, University of Alabama at Birmingham, Birmingham, AL 35294. Students are admitted in the Fall, application deadline February 1. Medical/Clinical - December 15. *Fee:* $25.

Alabama, University of, at Huntsville
Department of Psychology
Liberal Arts
Morton Hall 335, University of Alabama in Huntsville
Huntsville, AL 35899
Telephone: (256) 824-6191
Fax: (256) 824-6949
E-mail: *carpens@email.uah.edu*
Web: *http://www.uah.edu/colleges/liberal/psychology/*

Department Established:
1968. Chairperson: Sandra Carpenter. Number of Faculty: total–full-time 7; women–full-time 4; minority–full-time 1.

Programs and Degrees Offered:
Listed in the following order: Program area, degree type (T if terminal Master's), number awarded 7/00-6/01. Experimental-general MA (T) 4.

Student Applications/Admissions:
Student Applications

Experimental-general MA—Applications 2001–2002, 8. Total applicants accepted 2001–2002, 5. New applicants enrolled 2001–2002, 4. Total enrolled 2001–2002 full-time, 6, part-time, 2. Openings 2002–2003, 10. The Median number of years required for completion of a degree are 2.

Admissions Requirements:

Scores: Entries appear in this order: required test or GPA, minimum score (if required), median score of students entering in 2001–2002. Master's Programs: GRE-V+Q 1000, 1060; GRE-V+Q+Analytical 1500, 1570. Doctoral Programs: last 2 years GPA no minimum stated; psychology GPA no minimum stated; psychology GPA no minimum stated.

Other Criteria: (importance of criteria rated low, medium, or high): GRE/MAT scores medium, research experience medium, work experience low, clinically related public service low, GPA medium, letters of recommendation medium, interview low, statement of goals and objectives medium.

Student Characteristics: The following represents characteristics of students in 2001–2002 in all graduate psychology programs in the department: Female–full-time 6, part-time 1; Male–full-time 0, part-time 2; African American/Black–full-time 1, part-time 0; Hispanic/Latino (a)–full-time 0, part-time 0; Asian/Pacific Islander–full-time 0, part-time 1; American Indian/Alaska Native–full-time 0, part-time 0.

Financial Information/Assistance:
Tuition for Full-Time Study: *Master's:* State residents per academic year $3,200, $226 per credit hour; nonstate residents: per academic year $6,564, $457 per credit hour.

Financial Assistance:

First Year Students: Fellowships and scholarships available for first-year. Apply by May 1.

Advanced Students: Teaching assistantships available for advanced students. Average amount paid per academic year: $8,000. Average number of hours worked per week: 20. Apply by May 1. Tuition remission given: full. Research assistantships available for advanced students. Average amount paid per academic year: $8,000. Average number of hours worked per week: 20. Apply by May 1.

Contact Information: Of all students currently enrolled full-time, 33% benefitted from one or more of the listed financial assistance programs. For information on financial assistance, contact: Chair.

Internships/Practica: No information provided.

Housing and Day Care: No on-campus housing and day care facilities are available.

Employment of Department Graduates:

Master's Degree Graduates: Of those who graduated in the academic year 2000–2001, the following categories and numbers represent the post-graduate activities and employment of master's degree graduates: Enrolled in a psychology doctoral program (1), enrolled in another graduate/professional program (1), enrolled in a post-doctoral residency/fellowship (n/a), employed in independent practice (n/a), employed in an academic position at a university (1), employed in business or industry (research/consulting) (1).

Doctoral Degree Graduates: Of those who graduated in the academic year 2000–2001, the following categories and numbers represent the post-graduate activities and employment of doctoral degree graduates: Enrolled in a psychology doctoral program (n/a), enrolled in another graduate/professional program (n/a).

Additional Information:

Orientation, Objectives, and Emphasis of Department: The content of our program is directed toward the study of psychology as an intellectual and scientific pursuit as contrasted with training directly applicable to counselor or psychologist licensure and practice. Specialization areas include industrial, human factors, social, cognitive, developmental and biopsychological psychology. The program is designed for a small number of students who will work in close interaction with individual faculty members and with each other. Although there are a few structured courses that are required of all students, a substantial portion of the students' program focuses on individual readings, research, and thesis.

Special Facilities or Resources: Access to research facilities at NASA's Marshall Space Flight Center is available via an existing Space Act Agreement. Students also have access to an avian behavior research laboratory.

Application Information:
Send to: Department Chair, Department of Psychology, Morton Hall 335, University of Alabama in Huntsville, Huntsville, AL 35899. Students are admitted in the Fall, application deadline June 1; Spring, application deadline January 1. *Fee:* $35.

Auburn University
Counseling and Counseling Psychology
College of Education
2084 Haley Center
Auburn University, AL 36849-5222
Telephone: (334) 844-5160
Fax: (334) 844-2860
E-mail: *pipesrb@auburn.edu*
Web: *http://www.auburn.edu/ccp*

Department Established:

1975. Professor & Head of Department: Holly A. Stadler. Number of Faculty: total–full-time 9, part-time 1; women–full-time 7, part-time 1; minority–full-time 2, part-time 1; faculty subject to the Americans with Disabilities Act 1.

Programs and Degrees Offered:

Listed in the following order: Program area, degree type (T if terminal Master's), number awarded 7/00-6/01. Counseling MA (T) 12, Counseling Psychology PhD 3, Counselor Education PhD 5, Education Specialist EdS 1, School Counseling MA (T) 5, School Psychology PhD 2, School Psychometry MA (T).

APA Accreditation: Counseling PhD: full.

Student Applications/Admissions:

Student Applications

Counseling MA—Applications 2001–2002, 24. Total applicants accepted 2001–2002, 14. New applicants enrolled 2001–2002, 11. Total enrolled 2001–2002 full-time, 29, part-time, 3. Openings 2002–2003, 12. The Median number of years required for completion of a degree are 2. The number of students enrolled full and part-time, who were dismissed or voluntarily withdrew from this program area were 0. *Counseling Psychology PhD*—Applications 2001–2002, 40. Total applicants accepted 2001–2002, 11. New applicants enrolled 2001–2002, 5. Total enrolled 2001–2002 full-time, 37. Openings 2002–2003, 6. The Median number of years required for completion of a degree are 6. The number of students enrolled full and part-time, who were dismissed or voluntarily withdrew from this program area were 1. *Counselor Education PhD*—Applications 2001–2002, 15. Total applicants accepted 2001–2002, 7. New applicants enrolled 2001–2002, 7. Total enrolled 2001–2002 full-time, 4, part-time, 21. Openings 2002–2003, 5. The Median number of years required for completion of a degree are 4. The number of students enrolled full and part-time, who were dismissed or voluntarily withdrew from this program area were 1. *Education Specialist EdS*—Applications 2001–2002, 5. Total applicants accepted 2001–2002, 2. New applicants enrolled 2001–2002, 1. Total enrolled 2001–2002 full-time, 3. Openings 2002–2003, 2. The Median number of years required for completion of a degree are 4. The number of students enrolled full and part-time, who were dismissed or voluntarily withdrew from this program area were 0. *School Counseling MA*—Applications 2001–2002, 20. Total applicants accepted 2001–2002, 10. New applicants enrolled 2001–2002, 6. Total enrolled 2001–2002 full-time, 10, part-time, 1. Openings 2002–2003, 10. The Median number of years required for completion of a degree are 2. The number of students enrolled full and part-time, who were dismissed or voluntarily withdrew from this program area were 1. *School Psychology PhD*—Applications 2001–2002, 5. Total applicants accepted 2001–2002, 3. New applicants enrolled 2001–2002, 2. Total enrolled 2001–2002 full-time, 7, part-time, 3. Openings 2002–2003, 2. The Median number of years required for completion of a degree are 5. The number of students enrolled full and part-time, who were dismissed or voluntarily withdrew from this program area were 0. *School Psychometry MA*—Applications 2001–2002, 4. Total applicants accepted 2001–2002, 2. Total enrolled 2001–2002 full-time, 1, part-time, 4. Openings 2002–2003, 4. The number of students enrolled full and part-time, who were dismissed or voluntarily withdrew from this program area were 0.

Admissions Requirements:

Scores: Entries appear in this order: required test or GPA, minimum score (if required), median score of students entering in 2001–2002. Master's Programs: GRE-V no minimum stated; GRE-Q no minimum stated. Doctoral Programs: GRE-V no minimum stated, 538; GRE-Q no minimum stated, 630; GRE-V+Q no minimum stated, 1168; overall undergraduate GPA no minimum stated, 3.4 ; last 2 years GPA no minimum stated, 3.5 ; psychology GPA no minimum stated, 3.9 ; psychology GPA no minimum stated, 3.8. This information in item 13 is for the PhD program in Counseling Psychology.

Other Criteria: (importance of criteria rated low, medium, or high): GRE/MAT scores medium, research experience medium, work experience medium, extracurricular activity low, clinically related public service low, GPA high, letters of recommendation high, interview high, statement of goals and objectives high. This pattern of criteria is generally the same across program areas.

Student Characteristics: The following represents characteristics of students in 2001–2002 in all graduate psychology programs in the department: Female–full-time 38, part-time 3; Male–full-time 9, part-time 0; African American/Black–full-time 8, part-time 1; Hispanic/Latino(a)–full-time 2, part-time 0; Asian/Pacific Islander–full-time 0, part-time 0; American Indian/Alaska Native–full-time 1, part-time 0; Multi-ethnic–full-time 0, part-time 0; students subject to the Americans with Disabilities Act–full-time 0, part-time 0.

Financial Information/Assistance:

Tuition for Full-Time Study: *Master's:* State residents per academic year $3,380, $135 per credit hour; nonstate residents: per academic year $9,900, $405 per credit hour. *Doctoral:* State residents: per academic year $3,380, $135 per credit hour; nonstate residents: per academic year $9,900, $405 per credit hour.

Financial Assistance:

First Year Students: Teaching assistantships available for first-year. Average amount paid per academic year: $5,500. Average number of hours worked per week: 10. Apply by April 1. Tuition remission given: full. Research assistantships available for first-year. Average amount paid per academic year: $5,500. Average number of hours worked per week: 10. Apply by April 1. Tuition remission given: partial. Fellowships and scholarships available for first-year. Average amount paid per academic year: $15,000. Average number of hours worked per week: 10. Apply by varies. Tuition remission given: full.

Advanced Students: Teaching assistantships available for advanced students. Average amount paid per academic year: $5,500. Average number of hours worked per week: 10. Apply by April 1. Tuition remission given: full. Research assistantships available for advanced students. Average amount paid per academic year: $5,500. Average number of hours worked per week: 10. Apply by April 1. Tuition remission given: partial. Fellowships and scholarships available for advanced students. Average amount paid per academic year: $15,000. Average number of hours worked per week: 10. Apply by varies. Tuition remission given: full.

Contact Information: Of all students currently enrolled full-time, 20% benefitted from one or more of the listed financial assistance programs. For information on financial assistance, contact: Office of financial aid or departmental administrative assistant—all doctoral students who request it are supported with assistantships.

Internships/Practica: University counseling centers; community mental health centers; community counseling agencies. For those doctoral students for whom a professional internship is required prior to graduation, 6 applied in 2000–2001. Of those who applied, 4 were placed in internships listed by the Association of Psychology Postdoctoral and Internship Programs (APPIC); 4 were placed in APA accredited internships.

Housing and Day Care: No on-campus housing and day care facilities are available.

Employment of Department Graduates:

Master's Degree Graduates: Of those who graduated in the academic year 2000–2001, the following categories and numbers represent the post-graduate activities and employment of master's degree graduates: Enrolled in a post-doctoral residency/fellowship (n/a), employed in independent practice (n/a).

Doctoral Degree Graduates: Of those who graduated in the academic year 2000–2001, the following categories and numbers represent the post-graduate activities and employment of doctoral degree graduates: Enrolled in a psychology doctoral program (n/a), enrolled in another graduate/professional program (n/a), enrolled in a post-doctoral residency/fellowship (1), employed in a professional position in a school system (2), employed in a community mental health/counseling center (2).

Additional Information:

Orientation, Objectives, and Emphasis of Department: The Department offers high quality graduate education programs for counseling psychologists, school psychologists, counselors, and counselor educators. Graduates will develop the tools to address psychological, social, and environmental barriers to educational achievement and personal development. In this process students will engage in rigorous and challenging educational experiences in order to fashion their own unique contributions to society. The department values teaching, research, and outreach that contributes to the missions of the College and University. Further, the department seeks to foster a culture in which individual creativity and scholarship is reinforced and nurtured.

Special Facilities or Resources: Interdisciplinary community. University partnership serving underserved, rural minority communities devoted to education, research, and service. We also partner with University Student Affairs, Housing, and the Athletic Department.

Information for Students With Physical Disabilities: It is our policy to provide accessible programs, services, and activities and reasonable accommodations for any student with a documented disability as defined by Section 504 of the Rehabilitation Act of 1973, as amended, and by the Americans with Disabilities Act of 1990. Program staff work to ensure that students with disabilities have an equal opportunity to pursue an education.

Application Information:

Send to: (Program Name), Counseling & Counseling Psychology, 2084 Haley Center, Auburn University, AL 36849-5222. Students are admitted in the Fall, application deadline January 15. Ph.D. in Counseling Psychology- January 15. Ph.D. in School Psychology, Counselor Education-February 1. M.A. in Community Agency Counseling, School Counseling, School Psychometry, Ed.S. in School Counseling, School Psychology-March 15. *Fee:* $25.

Auburn University

Department of Human Development and Family Studies
Human Sciences
203 Spidle Hall
Auburn, AL 36849
Telephone: (334) 844-3227
Fax: (334) 844-4515
E-mail: *mbradbard@auburn.edu*
Web: *http://www.humsci.auburn.edu/hdfs/index.html*

Department Established:

1933. Chairperson: Marilyn R. Bradbard. Number of Faculty: total–full-time 17, part-time 6; women–full-time 9, part-time 6.

Student Applications/Admissions:

Admissions Requirements:

Scores: Entries appear in this order: required test or GPA, minimum score (if required), median score of students entering in 2001–2002. Doctoral Programs: last 2 years GPA no minimum stated; psychology GPA no minimum stated; psychology GPA no minimum stated.

Other Criteria: (importance of criteria rated low, medium, or high): GRE/MAT scores medium, research experience medium, work experience medium, extracurricular activity low, clinically related public service medium, GPA high, letters of recommendation high, interview low, statement of goals and objectives high.

Student Characteristics: The following represents characteristics of students in 2001–2002 in all graduate psychology programs in the department: Female–full-time 45, part-time 2; Male–full-time 12, part-time 0; African American/Black–full-time 2, part-time 0; Hispanic/Latino (a)–full-time 0, part-time 0; Asian/Pacific Islander–full-time 2, part-time 0; American Indian/Alaska Native–full-time 0, part-time 0; students subject to the Americans with Disabilities Act–full-time 1, part-time 0.

Financial Information/Assistance:

Tuition for Full-Time Study: *Master's:* State residents per academic year $3,380; nonstate residents: per academic year $9,900, *Doctoral:* State residents: per academic year $3,380; nonstate residents: per academic year $9,900.

Financial Assistance:

First Year Students: Teaching assistantships available for first-year. Average amount paid per academic year: $8,000. Average number of hours worked per week: 13. Apply by March 1. Tuition remission given: full. Research assistantships available for first-year. Average amount paid per academic year: $8,000. Average number of hours worked per week: 13. Apply by March 1. Fellowships and scholarships available for first-year. Average amount paid per academic year: $1,000. Apply by March 1.

Advanced Students: Teaching assistantships available for advanced students. Average amount paid per academic year: $8,000. Average number of hours worked per week: 13. Tuition remission given: full. Research assistantships available for advanced students. Average amount paid per academic year: $8,000. Average number of hours worked per week: 13. Tuition remission given: partial. Fellowships and scholarships available for advanced students.

Contact Information: Of all students currently enrolled full-time, 100% benefitted from one or more of the listed financial assistance programs. For information on financial assistance, contact: Department Head.

Internships/Practica: All graduate students who are focused on the Marriage and Family Therapy Master's degree option are required to complete a year-long internship in an agency setting.

Housing and Day Care: On-campus housing and day care facilities are available.

Employment of Department Graduates:

Master's Degree Graduates: Of those who graduated in the academic year 2000–2001, the following categories and numbers represent the post-graduate activities and employment of master's degree graduates: Enrolled in a post-doctoral residency/fellowship (n/a), employed in independent practice (n/a).

Doctoral Degree Graduates: Of those who graduated in the academic year 2000–2001, the following categories and numbers represent the post-graduate activities and employment of doctoral degree graduates: Enrolled in a psychology doctoral program (n/a), enrolled in another graduate/professional program (n/a).

Additional Information:

Orientation, Objectives, and Emphasis of Department: The major focus of faculty and graduate students in the Department of Human Development and Family Studies is the study of interpersonal competence and relationship dynamics in the context of the family. We approach interpersonal competence issues by examining both functional and dysfunctional aspects of relationships.

Special Facilities or Resources: See the following Web site: http://www.humsci.auburn.edu/hdfs/index.html. Click on student resources.

Application Information:

Send to: Graduate Program Director. Students are admitted in the Fall, application deadline March 1. *Fee:* $50.

Auburn University

Department of Psychology
226 Thach Hall
Auburn , AL 36849-5214
Telephone: (334) 844-4412
Fax: (334) 844-4447
E-mail: *bryangt@auburn.edu*
Web: *http://www.auburn.edu/psychology*

Department Established:

1948. Chairperson: Lewis Barker. Number of Faculty: total–full-time 16, part-time 3; women–full-time 2, part-time 2; minority–full-time 2.

Programs and Degrees Offered:

Listed in the following order: Program area, degree type (T if terminal Master's), number awarded 7/00-6/01. Clinical PhD 7, experimental PhD 1, industrial/organizational PhD.

APA Accreditation: Clinical PhD: full.

Student Applications/Admissions:

Student Applications

Clinical PhD—Applications 2001–2002, 97. Total applicants accepted 2001–2002, 10. New applicants enrolled 2001–2002, 8. Total enrolled 2001–2002 full-time, 49. Openings 2002-2003, 5-8. The Median number of years required for completion of a degree are 8. The number of students enrolled full and part-time, who were dismissed or voluntarily withdrew from this program area were 0. *Experimental PhD*—Applications 2001–2002, 15. Total applicants accepted 2001–2002, 5. New applicants enrolled 2001–2002, 5. Total enrolled 2001–2002 full-time, 22. Openings 2002–2003, 3-6. The Median number of years required for completion of a degree are 8. The number of students enrolled full and part-time, who were dismissed or voluntarily withdrew from this program area were 0. *Industrial/organizational PhD*—Applications 2001–2002, 0. Total enrolled 2001–2002 full-time, 12. The number of students enrolled full and part-time, who were dismissed or voluntarily withdrew from this program area were 1.

Admissions Requirements:

Scores: Entries appear in this order: required test or GPA, minimum score (if required), median score of students entering in 2001–2002. Doctoral Programs: GRE-V no minimum stated, 530; GRE-Q no minimum stated, 620; GRE-V+Q no minimum stated, 1150; GRE-Analytical no minimum stated, 620; GRE-V+Q+Analytical no minimum stated, 1770; overall undergraduate GPA no minimum stated, 3.6 ; last 2 years GPA no minimum stated; psychology GPA no minimum stated, 3.8 ; psychology GPA no minimum stated, 3.9.

Other Criteria: (importance of criteria rated low, medium, or high): GRE/MAT scores medium, research experience high, work experience medium, extracurricular activity low, clinically related public service medium, GPA high, letters of recommendation high, interview high, statement of goals and objectives medium. For I/O and EXP programs, clinically related public service has less significance.

Student Characteristics: The following represents characteristics of students in 2001–2002 in all graduate psychology programs in the department: Female–full-time 53, part-time 0; Male–full-time 26, part-time 0; African American/Black–full-time 4, part-time 0; Hispanic/Latino(a)–full-time 3, part-time 0; Asian/Pacific Islander–full-time 1, part-time 0; American Indian/Alaska Native–full-time 0, part-time 0; Multi-ethnic–full-time 3, part-time 0; students subject to the Americans with Disabilities Act–full-time 0, part-time 0.

Financial Information/Assistance:

Tuition for Full-Time Study: Master's: State residents per academic year $4,575, $126 per credit hour; nonstate residents: per academic year $13,725, $378 per credit hour. *Doctoral:* State residents: per academic year $4,575, $126 per credit hour; nonstate residents: per academic year $13,725, $378 per credit hour.

Financial Assistance:

First Year Students: Teaching assistantships available for first-year. Average amount paid per academic year: $10,920. Average number of hours worked per week: 13. Apply by 1/14. Tuition remission given: full.

Advanced Students: Teaching assistantships available for advanced students. Average amount paid per academic year: $13,000. Average number of hours worked per week: 16. Tuition remission given: full. Research assistantships available for advanced students. Average amount paid per academic year: $13,000. Average number of hours worked per week: 16. Tuition remission given: partial.

Contact Information: Of all students currently enrolled full-time, 75% benefitted from one or more of the listed financial assistance programs. For information on financial assistance, contact: Web page: www.auburn.edu/psychology or e-mail bryangt@auburn.edu or call 334-844-6471.

Internships/Practica: Current practicum sites that offer assistantships for clinical graduate students are Roosevelt Warm Springs Institute of Rehabilitation (Warm Springs, GA), Personal Assessment and Counseling Center (Auburn University, AL), Mt. Meigs Adolescent Correctional Facility (Mt. Meigs, AL), Lee County Youth Development Center (Opelika, AL), Head Start Program of Lee County (Auburn and Opelika, AL), the Auburn University School of Pharmacy, the Auburn University College of Veterinary Medicine, and Circle of Care (Lannett, AL). Industrial/organizational psychology students receive paid practicum training at a number of area organizations, including Auburn University's Center for Governmental Services, Auburn University at Montgomery's Center for Business and Economic Development, and the Fort Benning Field Station of the Army Research Institute. Many I/O students participate in paid internships before completing their doctoral work. Experimental students have participated in practica at the Bancroft Center (NJ), Warm Springs Rehabilitation Center (GA), and the Army Research Institute (GA). For those doctoral students for whom a professional internship is required prior to graduation, 6 applied in 2000–2001. Of those who applied, 6 were placed in internships listed by the Association of Psychology Postdoctoral and Internship Programs (APPIC); 6 were placed in APA accredited internships.

Housing and Day Care: No on-campus housing and day care facilities are available.

Employment of Department Graduates:

Master's Degree Graduates: Of those who graduated in the academic year 2000–2001, the following categories and numbers represent the post-graduate activities and employment of master's degree graduates: Enrolled in a post-doctoral residency/fellowship (n/a), employed in independent practice (n/a).

Doctoral Degree Graduates: Of those who graduated in the academic year 2000–2001, the following categories and numbers represent the post-graduate activities and employment of doctoral degree graduates: Enrolled in a psychology doctoral program (n/a), enrolled in another graduate/professional program (n/a), enrolled in a post-doctoral residency/fellowship (1), employed in independent practice (2), employed in an academic position at a 2-year/4-year college (1), employed in a government agency (professional services) (1), employed in a community mental health/counseling center (1), employed in a hospital/medical center (1).

Additional Information:

Orientation, Objectives, and Emphasis of Department: Graduate education in Auburn's psychology programs is intended to provide a balance between the skills and understanding required to generate new knowledge and the application of existing knowledge and theory to the solution of societal problems. While the majority of the department's full-time faculty are in the applied specializations of clinical and industrial/organizational psychology, most of these are active scholars and all departmental faculty are committed to the premise that psychology is a developing discipline in which inquiry, breadth, and flexibility are to be valued. Students are provided with a considerable amount of direct experience, training, and supervision within community agencies and organizations, where the theory and techniques of clinical psychology, experimental psychology, and industrial/organizational psychology can be practiced and refined. The clinical psychology training program emphasizes an integration of classroom instruction, research, and individualized clinical-community practica under close faculty supervision within a scientist-practitioner model. The experimental program seeks to broadly inform its students about the issues and problems of psychology in general, and to provide the basic conceptual and technical skills needed to make original contributions to knowledge and theory in psychology. The industrial/organizational program focuses on understanding, predicting, and modifying behavior in organizational settings, typically but not limited to work environments.

Special Facilities or Resources: A substantial clinical psychology training grant from the State of Alabama, university teaching assistantships, a wide variety of contracts with community agencies, and faculty research contracts and grants have typically provided all psychology graduate students with financial support throughout their graduate careers. The department administers a multipurpose psychological services center. Relationships with extra-university agencies and organizations facilitate training in applied research.

Application Information:

Send to: Thane Bryant, Department of Psychology, 226 Thach Hall, Auburn University, AL 36849-5214. Students are admitted in the Fall, application deadline January 14. *Fee:* $25.

Auburn University at Montgomery

Department of Psychology
School of Sciences
210 Goodwyn Hall
Montgomery, AL 36124-4023
Telephone: (334) 244-3306
Fax: (334) 244-3947
E-mail: *lobello@strudel.aum.edu*
Web: *http://sciences.aum.edu/pg/welcome.html*

Department Established:

1969. Head: Allen K. Hess. Number of Faculty: total–full-time 10, part-time 12; women–full-time 3, part-time 6.

Programs and Degrees Offered:

Listed in the following order: Program area, degree type (T if terminal Master's), number awarded 7/00-6/01. Applied/clinical counseling MA (T) 7.

Student Applications/Admissions:

Student Applications

Applied/clinical counseling MA—Total enrolled 2001–2002 full-time, 28, part-time, 8. Openings 2002–2003, 25. The Median number of years required for completion of a degree are 2.

Admissions Requirements:

Scores: Entries appear in this order: required test or GPA, minimum score (if required), median score of students entering in 2001–2002. Master's Programs: MAT no minimum stated; overall undergraduate GPA no minimum stated. We require either the MAT or the GRE, plus undergraduate transcripts. Two letters of reference and a statement of interest are encouraged. Doctoral Programs: last 2 years GPA no minimum stated; psychology GPA no minimum stated; psychology GPA no minimum stated.

Other Criteria: (importance of criteria rated low, medium, or high): GRE/MAT scores high, research experience medium, work experience medium, extracurricular activity medium, clinically related public service medium, GPA high, letters of recommendation medium, interview low, statement of goals and objectives medium.

Student Characteristics: The following represents characteristics of students in 2001–2002 in all graduate psychology programs in the department: Female–full-time 12, part-time 0; Male–full-time 10, part-time 0; African American/Black–full-time 0, part-time 0; Hispanic/Latino(a)–full-time 0, part-time 0; Asian/Pacific Islander–full-time 1, part-time 0; American Indian/Alaska Native–full-time 0, part-time 0.

Financial Information/Assistance:

Tuition for Full-Time Study: *Master's:* State residents $120 per credit hour; nonstate residents: $360 per credit hour.

Financial Assistance:

First Year Students: No information provided.

Advanced Students: Teaching assistantships available for advanced students. Average number of hours worked per week: 15. Tuition remission given: partial.

Contact Information: Of all students currently enrolled full-time, 75% benefitted from one or more of the listed financial assistance programs. For information on financial assistance, contact: department head.

Internships/Practica: Internship and practica are available at several local agencies and organizations. Practica are often tailored to the interests and career objectives of the student.

Housing and Day Care: No on-campus housing and day care facilities are available.

Employment of Department Graduates:

Master's Degree Graduates: Of those who graduated in the academic year 2000–2001, the following categories and numbers represent the post-graduate activities and employment of master's degree graduates: Enrolled in a psychology doctoral program (5), enrolled in another graduate/professional program (1), enrolled in a post-doctoral residency/fellowship (n/a), employed in independent practice (n/a), employed in an academic position at a university (0), employed in an academic position at a 2-year/4-year college (0), employed in other positions at a higher education institution (0), employed in a professional position in a school system (0), employed in business or industry (research/consulting) (0), employed in business or industry (management) (0), employed in a government agency (research) (0), employed in a government agency (professional services) (0), employed in a community mental health/counseling center (4), employed in a hospital/medical center (0), still seeeking employment (0), other employment position (0).

Doctoral Degree Graduates: Of those who graduated in the academic year 2000–2001, the following categories and numbers represent the post-graduate activities and employment of doctoral degree graduates: Enrolled in a psychology doctoral program (n/a), enrolled in another graduate/professional program (n/a).

Additional Information:

Orientation, Objectives, and Emphasis of Department: Our MS program is designed to provide a core curriculum for those intending to pursue doctoral studies and to offer course and practicum experiences for those wishing to enter direct service positions.

Special Facilities or Resources: Computer facilities and an animal colony are available for student use.

Information for Students With Physical Disabilities: Our campus is designed for access to all. It is engineered for those with physical disabilities and has a wide variety of supporting services.

Application Information:
Send to: Office of Enrollment Services, 130 Taylor Center, Auburn University Montgomery, P.O. Box 244023, Montgomery, AL 36124-4023. Students are admitted in the Fall, Spring, Summer. *Fee:* $25.

Jacksonville State University

Department of Psychology
College of Graduate Studies
700 Pelham Road, N.
Jacksonville, AL 36265-1602
Telephone: (256) 782-5402
Fax: (256) 782-5637
E-mail: *dpatters@jsucc.jsu.edu*
Web: *http://www.jsu.edu/depart/psychology/welcome.html*

Department Established:

1971. Department Head: Donald D. Patterson. Number of Faculty: total–full-time 8, part-time 4; women–full-time 3, part-time 3; minority–full-time 2.

Programs and Degrees Offered:

Listed in the following order: Program area, degree type (T if terminal Master's), number awarded 7/00-6/01. General.

Student Applications/Admissions:

Admissions Requirements:

Scores: Entries appear in this order: required test or GPA, minimum score (if required), median score of students entering in 2001–2002. Master's Programs: GRE-V+Q+Analytical no minimum stated; MAT no minimum stated; overall undergraduate GPA no minimum stated. 450 times undergraduate GPA + GRE V + Q + Analytical = 2000 or more or 15 times undergraduate GPA + MAT = 60 or more. Doctoral Programs: last 2 years GPA no minimum stated; psychology GPA no minimum stated; psychology GPA no minimum stated.

Other Criteria: (importance of criteria rated low, medium, or high): GRE/MAT scores high, GPA high, letters of recommendation medium.

Student Characteristics: The following represents characteristics of students in 2001–2002 in all graduate psychology programs in the department: Female–full-time 7, part-time 17; Male–full-time 5, part-time 6; African American/Black–full-time 3, part-time 6; Hispanic/Latino (a)–full-time 0, part-time 1; Asian/Pacific Islander–full-time 0, part-time 0; American Indian/Alaska Native–full-time 0, part-time 0; Multi-ethnic–full-time 1, part-time 0; students subject to the Americans with Disabilities Act–full-time 0, part-time 0.

Financial Information/Assistance:

Tuition for Full-Time Study: *Master's:* State residents $147 per credit hour; nonstate residents: $294 per credit hour.

Financial Assistance:

First Year Students: Fellowships and scholarships available for first-year. Average amount paid per academic year: $5,000. Average number of hours worked per week: 20. Apply by Aug. 29.

Advanced Students: No information provided.

Contact Information: Of all students currently enrolled full-time, 0% benefitted from one or more of the listed financial assistance programs. For information on financial assistance, contact: Student financial aid office, JSU, 700 Pelham Rd. N., Jacksonville, AL 36265.

Internships/Practica: Clinical and Behavior Analysis and Instructional Practica are offered. The Clinical Practicum includes supervised clinical assessment, report writing, ethical principles, as well as the design and implementation of psychological treatment programs with a client population, in an on-campus clinic. The Behavior Analysis Practicum includes the application of psychological principles in areas such as developmental disabilities, organizational behavior management, remediation of academic behavior, and environmental psychology. The Instructional Practicum allows students to gain teaching experience in a lab course.

Housing and Day Care: On-campus housing and day care facilities are available.

Employment of Department Graduates:

Master's Degree Graduates: Of those who graduated in the academic year 2000–2001, the following categories and numbers represent the post-graduate activities and employment of master's degree graduates: Enrolled in a post-doctoral residency/fellowship (n/a), employed in independent practice (n/a), employed in an academic position at a 2-year/4-year college (1), employed in a community mental health/counseling center (1), still seeeking employment (1), other employment position (1).

Doctoral Degree Graduates: Of those who graduated in the academic year 2000–2001, the following categories and numbers represent the post-graduate activities and employment of doctoral degree graduates: Enrolled in a psychology doctoral program (n/a), enrolled in another graduate/professional program (n/a).

Additional Information:

Orientation, Objectives, and Emphasis of Department: The objective of the program is to provide students with the requisite methodological skills as well as the theoretical and ethical background necessary for practice or research. Consistent with this objective is a 15 hour core sequence of courses covering biological, quantitative, methodological, and preprofessional areas. Students can then tailor the remaining coursework, research program, and practicum/internship experiences to fit their career objectives. Overall, the courses reflect a behavioral emphasis. Training is available to prepare students for state level licensure or national certification as a behavior analyst. Student research and thesis is encouraged, especially for students preparing to pursue doctoral-level studies.

Special Facilities or Resources: The department has an on-campus clinic designed for psychological services and research in support of its teaching mission. The clinic affords opportunities for on-campus practica experiences. Practicum arrangements with a variety of agencies allow students to gain experience in a variety of applications of behavior analysis. Special facilities include an animal room, a running room with 15 chambers, student offices, and a seminar computer room. A network of control computers (which were developed at JSU and used in many other universities) with Macintoshes, PCs, and Vaxes runs experiments and provides interactive graphical analyses. Environmental Studies: There is an environmental studies center. This center is a clearinghouse for technical information on visitor behavior and publishes an international newsletter. Applied Human Learning: The Learning Skills department is affiliated with the Psychology Department and offers students opportunities to apply psychological principles in an instructional setting using computer assisted instruction.

Information for Students With Physical Disabilities: JSU is in compliance with Section 504 of the Americans With Disabilities Act of 1973, as amended. The University does not discriminate on the basis of disability and no qualified disabled person shall, on the basis of disability, be excluded from participation in, be denied the benefits of, or otherwise be subjected to discrimination under any program or activity which receives or benefits from federal assistance.

Application Information:
Send to: Jacksonville State University, College of Graduate Studies, 700 Pelham Rd. N., Jacksonville, AL 36265-1602. Students are admitted in the Fall, application deadline Aug. 29; Spring, application deadline January 3; Summer, application deadline May 1. *Fee:* $20.

South Alabama, University of

Department of Psychology
Arts and Sciences
LSCB Room 326
Mobile, AL 36688
Telephone: (334) 460-6371
Fax: (334) 460-6320
E-mail: *lchriste@usouthal.edu*
Web: *http://www.usouthal.edu/bulletin/artpsy.htm*

Department Established:
1964. Chairperson: Larry Christensen. Number of Faculty: total–full-time 14, part-time 10; women–full-time 7, part-time 5; minority–full-time 1, part-time 1.

Programs and Degrees Offered:
Listed in the following order: Program area, degree type (T if terminal Master's), number awarded 7/00-6/01. Clinical MA (T) 9, experimental MA (T).

Student Applications/Admissions:

Student Applications

Clinical MA—Applications 2001–2002, 31. Total applicants accepted 2001–2002, 12. New applicants enrolled 2001–2002, 10. Total enrolled 2001–2002 full-time, 20. Openings 2002–2003, 12. The Median number of years required for completion of a degree are 2. *Experimental* MA—Applications 2001–2002, 2. Total applicants accepted 2001–2002, 2. New applicants enrolled 2001–2002, 2. Total enrolled 2001–2002 full-time, 4. Openings 2002–2003, 3. The Median number of years required for completion of a degree are 2.

Admissions Requirements:

Scores: Entries appear in this order: required test or GPA, minimum score (if required), median score of students entering in 2001–2002. Master's Programs: GRE-V+Q 1000, 1050; overall undergraduate GPA 3.0, 3.44; psychology GPA 3.0, 3.84. Doctoral Programs: last 2 years GPA no minimum stated; psychology GPA no minimum stated; psychology GPA no minimum stated.

Other Criteria: (importance of criteria rated low, medium, or high): GRE/MAT scores high, research experience medium, work experience low, extracurricular activity low, clinically related public service medium, GPA high, letters of recommendation high, statement of goals and objectives medium.

Student Characteristics: The following represents characteristics of students in 2001–2002 in all graduate psychology programs in the department: Female–full-time 6, part-time 0; Male–full-time 6, part-time 0; African American/Black–full-time 0, part-time 0; Hispanic/Latino (a)–full-time 0, part-time 0; Asian/Pacific Islander–full-time 2, part-time 0; American Indian/Alaska Native–full-time 0, part-time 0; Multi-ethnic–full-time 0, part-time 0; students subject to the Americans with Disabilities Act–full-time 0, part-time 0.

Financial Information/Assistance:

Tuition for Full-Time Study: *Master's:* State residents per academic year $2,540, $127 per credit hour; nonstate residents: per academic year $5,080, $254 per credit hour.

Financial Assistance:

First Year Students: Research assistantships available for first-year. Average amount paid per academic year: $5,000. Average number of hours worked per week: 20. Apply by March 1. Tuition remission given: full.

Advanced Students: No information provided.

Contact Information: Of all students currently enrolled full-time, 80% benefitted from one or more of the listed financial assistance programs. For information on financial assistance, contact: Psychology Department University of South Alabama, Mobile, AL 36688.

Internships/Practica: Graduate students receive practical experience in the application of psychological assessment and treatment procedures in a variety of clinical settings. Emphasis is given to ethical and professional issues with intensive individual and group supervision. The Department of Psychology operates an outpatient teaching clinic where a variety of children and adults are seen for short-term assessment and treatment. External practicum placements are also available in a variety of community settings including a state mental hospital, a mental retardation facility, and community substance abuse programs.

Housing and Day Care: On-campus housing and day care facilities are available.

Employment of Department Graduates:

Master's Degree Graduates: Of those who graduated in the academic year 2000–2001, the following categories and numbers represent the post-graduate activities and employment of master's degree graduates: Enrolled in a psychology doctoral program (4), enrolled in a post-doctoral residency/fellowship (n/a), employed in independent practice (n/a), still seeeking employment (2), other employment position (4).

Doctoral Degree Graduates: Of those who graduated in the academic year 2000–2001, the following categories and numbers represent the post-graduate activities and employment of doctoral degree graduates: Enrolled in a psychology doctoral program (n/a), enrolled in another graduate/professional program (n/a).

Additional Information:

Orientation, Objectives, and Emphasis of Department: The University of South Alabama offers a master's program in general psychology that allows the student to choose either an applied or experimental focus. All students complete a core curriculum designed to provide them with knowledge of current theories, principles, and methods of experimental and applied psychology. This is followed by courses in either clinical or experimental areas. The clinical courses are designed to equip students with basic psychological assessment and treatment skills that will enable them to function later in an applied employment setting under supervision of a licensed psychologist. Courses for the experimental student are designed to provide more extensive information in research design and experimental methods as well as theoretical background related to the student's thesis research. Both programs, as well as the core curriculum, are designed to provide students with the necessary theoretical and research background to pursue further graduate study, if they so choose. Graduate students in both areas receive individual attention and close supervision by departmental faculty.

Special Facilities or Resources: The Comparative Hearing Laboratory maintains exceptional sound room, computer, and animal facilities. Through the comparison of human, monkey, gerbil, and computer simulations of perception, the laboratory seeks to study how the brain has become specialized for language, and what has gone wrong with particular classes of communication and learning disorders. In addition to the Psychological Clinic and the Comparative Hearing Laboratory, the Department has laboratory facilities for neuropsychological and behavioral research, and has access to both mainframe and personal computer facilities. Standard animal facilities are also available.

Application Information:

Send to: Director of Admission, Administration Bldg., Room 182, University of South Alabama, Mobile, AL 36688. Students are admitted in the Fall, application deadline March 1. *Fee:* $25.

Alaska Pacific University

Master of Science in Counseling Psychology (MSCP)
4101 University Drive
Anchorage, AK 99508
Telephone: (907) 564-8225
Fax: (907) 564-8396
E-mail: *ecole@alaskapacific.edu*
Web: *http://www.alaskapacific.edu*

Department Established:
1990. Director: Ellen Cole. Number of Faculty: total–full-time 4, part-time 6; women–full-time 2, part-time 2.

Programs and Degrees Offered:
Listed in the following order: Program area, degree type (T if terminal Master's), number awarded 7/00-6/01. Counseling MA (T) 18.

Student Applications/Admissions:

Student Applications

Counseling MA—Applications 2001–2002, 43. Total applicants accepted 2001–2002, 24. New applicants enrolled 2001–2002, 21. Total enrolled 2001–2002 full-time, 36, part-time, 4. Openings 2002–2003, 20. The Median number of years required for completion of a degree are 2. The number of students enrolled full and part-time, who were dismissed or voluntarily withdrew from this program area were 1.

Admissions Requirements:

Scores: Entries appear in this order: required test or GPA, minimum score (if required), median score of students entering in 2001–2002. Master's Programs: MAT no minimum stated; overall undergraduate GPA 3.0, 3.2; psychology GPA 3.0, 3.0. Doctoral Programs: last 2 years GPA no minimum stated; psychology GPA no minimum stated; psychology GPA no minimum stated.

Other Criteria: (importance of criteria rated low, medium, or high): GRE/MAT scores medium, work experience high, extracurricular activity medium, clinically related public service medium, GPA medium, letters of recommendation high, interview high, statement of goals and objectives high.

Student Characteristics: The following represents characteristics of students in 2001–2002 in all graduate psychology programs in the department: Female–full-time 25, part-time 3; Male–full-time 9, part-time 3; African American/Black–full-time 3, part-time 0; Hispanic/Latino (a)–full-time 0, part-time 1; Asian/Pacific Islander–full-time 0, part-time 1; American Indian/Alaska Native–full-time 1, part-time 1.

Financial Information/Assistance:
Tuition for Full-Time Study: *Master's:* State residents $450 per credit hour; nonstate residents: $450 per credit hour.

Financial Assistance:
First Year Students: No information provided.

Advanced Students: Traineeships available for advanced students. Apply by April 1. Tuition remission given: partial.

Contact Information: Of all students currently enrolled full-time, 10% benefitted from one or more of the listed financial assistance programs. For information on financial assistance, contact: Peter Miller, (907) 564-8341.

Internships/Practica: A significant part of a counselor's education occurs outside the classroom through an internship experience. This is a two-semester opportunity for students to begin to apply theories and techniques of their classroom education as well as to focus their professional development in a specialized area of counseling. Internship opportunities are diverse in clientele and therapeutic context. In collaboration with the MSCP director and faculty, students identify internship sites consistent with their interests and needs. Examples of internship sites are Southcentral Foundation (Alaska Native services), Anchorage Center for Families, Alaska Children's Services, Southcentral Counseling Center (state mental health services), Alaska Human Services, Salvation Army Clitheroe Center, Alaska Native Hospital, McLaughlin Youth Center, Catholic Social Services, and private practitioners.

Housing and Day Care: On-campus housing and day care facilities are available.

Employment of Department Graduates:
Master's Degree Graduates: Of those who graduated in the academic year 2000–2001, the following categories and numbers represent the post-graduate activities and employment of master's degree graduates: Enrolled in a post-doctoral residency/fellowship (n/a), employed in independent practice (n/a).

Doctoral Degree Graduates: Of those who graduated in the academic year 2000–2001, the following categories and numbers represent the post-graduate activities and employment of doctoral degree graduates: Enrolled in a psychology doctoral program (n/a), enrolled in another graduate/professional program (n/a).

Additional Information:
Orientation, Objectives, and Emphasis of Department: The master of science in counseling psychology (MSCP) program at Alaska Pacific University is a selective, rigorous program for the creative adult who plans to become a mental health practitioner or enter a doctoral program. Main objectives of the MSCP program are to foster the knowledge and skills needed to succeed as a professional counselor, to promote the integration of learning with practical "real life" issues in the field, and to encourage the development of leadership skills. To accomplish these educational objectives, the MSCP program is committed to providing individual attention to students, a personal and supportive atmosphere, and a mentorship approach to education. The curriculum is eclectic in theoretical orientation and celebrates diversity within the range of professional mental health approaches and techniques. A "hands on" approach to learning is emphasized along with an integration of theory and practice throughout the program. The program is committed to the centrality of multicultural awareness, ethical responsibility, and each student's personal growth and development. When students graduate from the MSCP program, they will have acquired a better understanding of themselves as human

beings, greater sensitivity for others, and professional competence in theory, research, practice, skills, and ethics.

Special Facilities or Resources: Our special resources lie in our unique blend of theoretical knowledge and practical experience that make up our counselor education program. This is enhanced by the diverse faculty and unique internship sites available in Alaska. Further, a cooperative rather than a competitive spirit is fostered. Because MSCP students progress through the program as an intact group, they develop a strong spirit of community. Class assignments and projects often are completed in a small-group format, with each member taking active responsibility for the final product of all. The MSCP curriculum includes a variety of course styles, with greatest emphasis given to seminar-style classroom interactions, experiential activities, and student-designed projects. Even in lecture-oriented courses, students engage in small-group learning activities and personal discovery. Practicing counselors and psychologists are regularly brought into the classroom as visitors and also serve on a regular basis as adjunct faculty. And faculty doors are open to students all of the time. Further, the curriculum is responsive to current factors that influence the profession, such as managed care and certification and licensure laws throughout the United States, and "cutting edge" therapies and techniques.

Application Information:
Send to: Graduate Admissions Office, Alaska Pacific University, 4101 University Drive, Anchorage, AK 99508. Students are admitted in the Fall, application deadline April 1. *Fee:* $25.

Alaska, University of, Anchorage
Psychology/MS in Clinical Psychology
Arts and Sciences
3211 Providence Drive
Anchorage, AK 99508
Telephone: (907) 786-1795
Fax: (907) 786-4898
E-mail: *aypsych@uaa.alaska.edu*
Web: *http://www.uaa.alaska.edu/psych*

Department Established:
1967. Acting Head: G. Donald Maloney. Number of Faculty: total–full-time 19, part-time 6; women–full-time 8, part-time 3; minority–full-time 1.

Programs and Degrees Offered:
Listed in the following order: Program area, degree type (T if terminal Master's), number awarded 7/00-6/01. Clinical psychology MA (T) 8.

Student Applications/Admissions:
Student Applications
Clinical psychology MA—Applications 2001–2002, 30. Total applicants accepted 2001–2002, 10. New applicants enrolled 2001–2002, 8. Total enrolled 2001–2002 full-time, 18, part-time, 10. Openings 2002–2003, 10. The Median number of years required for completion of a degree are 2. The number of students enrolled full and part-time, who were dismissed or voluntarily withdrew from this program area were 2.

Admissions Requirements:
Scores: Entries appear in this order: required test or GPA, minimum score (if required), median score of students entering in 2001–2002. Master's Programs: GRE-V no minimum stated, 510; GRE-Q no minimum stated, 540; GRE-V+Q no minimum stated, 1070; GRE-Analytical no minimum stated, 545; GRE-V+Q+Analytical no minimum stated, 1615; GRE-Subject(Psych) no minimum stated, 530; overall undergraduate GPA no minimum stated, 3.5; psychology GPA no minimum stated, 3.65. The GRE Psychology Subtest is not required if students have an undergraduate psychology major with a psychology GPA of 3.0 or greater. Doctoral Programs: last 2 years GPA no minimum stated; psychology GPA no minimum stated; psychology GPA no minimum stated.
Other Criteria: (importance of criteria rated low, medium, or high): GRE/MAT scores medium, research experience medium, work experience medium, extracurricular activity low, clinically related public service medium, GPA medium, letters of recommendation medium, statement of goals and objectives medium.

Student Characteristics: The following represents characteristics of students in 2001–2002 in all graduate psychology programs in the department: Female–full-time 7, part-time 0; Male–full-time 1, part-time 0; African American/Black–full-time 0, part-time 0; Hispanic/Latino (a)–full-time 0, part-time 0; Asian/Pacific Islander–full-time 0, part-time 0; American Indian/Alaska Native–full-time 0, part-time 0; students subject to the Americans with Disabilities Act–full-time 1.

Financial Information/Assistance:
Tuition for Full-Time Study: *Master's:* State residents $184 per credit hour; nonstate residents: $358 per credit hour.

Financial Assistance:
First Year Students: Teaching assistantships available for first-year. Average amount paid per academic year: $2,400. Average number of hours worked per week: 15. Apply by June 1. Tuition remission given: full. Research assistantships available for first-year. Average amount paid per academic year: $2,400. Average number of hours worked per week: 15. Apply by June 1. Tuition remission given: full.
Advanced Students: Teaching assistantships available for advanced students. Average amount paid per academic year: $2,400. Average number of hours worked per week: 15. Apply by April 1. Tuition remission given: partial. Research assistantships available for advanced students. Average amount paid per academic year: $2,400. Average number of hours worked per week: 15. Apply by April 1. Tuition remission given: full.
Contact Information: Of all students currently enrolled full-time, 70% benefitted from one or more of the listed financial assistance programs. For information on financial assistance, contact: Financial Aid Office: (907) 786-1586.

Internships/Practica: All students complete one semester of practicum in the Psychological Services Center, which is run by the Psychology Department. This closely supervised experience involves direct clinical contact with psychotherapy clients of all ages and backgrounds. Students spend an average of 20 hours per week on practicum and typically schedule five or six hours of face-to-face contact time with clients. All students also complete two semesters of internship at a community agency. Internship sites are selected on the basis of student preferences and their professional goals. Potential internship sites include private or public psychiatric inpatient facilities; private or public psychiatric outpatient facilities, including those that specialize in the treatment of Alaskan Natives, college students, or families; the school district; and residential homes for adolescents or the elderly. As with practicum, students typically spend 20 hours per week on internship and receive close supervision.

Housing and Day Care: On-campus housing and day care facilities are available.

Employment of Department Graduates:

Master's Degree Graduates: Of those who graduated in the academic year 2000–2001, the following categories and numbers represent the post-graduate activities and employment of master's degree graduates: Enrolled in a psychology doctoral program (15), enrolled in a post-doctoral residency/fellowship (n/a), employed in independent practice (n/a), employed in a community mental health/counseling center (60), employed in a hospital/medical center (5), other employment position (20).

Doctoral Degree Graduates: Of those who graduated in the academic year 2000–2001, the following categories and numbers represent the post-graduate activities and employment of doctoral degree graduates: Enrolled in a psychology doctoral program (n/a), enrolled in another graduate/professional program (n/a).

Additional Information:

Orientation, Objectives, and Emphasis of Department: The MS program requires two years of study (50-credit hours) and is designed to provide students with: (a) a solid foundation in skills for diagnosis, treatment planning, psychotherapy, and assessment; (b) the ability to critically evaluate research, to develop and test new treatment programs, and to conduct research in applied settings; and (c) the foundation skills necessary to pursue a doctoral-level career in psychology, should this be a goal. The program is structured in four specialty tracks, all of which build on a common core of clinical and research courses. The Research Track is designed for students wishing to pursue a doctorate in psychology and it emphasizes methodology, statistical analysis, and experience conducting research. The Clinical Track is designed for students planning on a career in clinical service and it emphasizes the development of theoretically and empirically-grounded clinical skills in diagnosis, treatment planning, psychotherapy, and assessment. The Addictive Behaviors Track is also designed for students planning a career in clinical service, though it emphasizes developing skills for intervening with a variety of addictive or substance abuse problems. The Public Service Track is designed to prepare students for work in a community agency and it emphasizes program evaluation and development.

Special Facilities or Resources: The Psychology Department runs an experimental research laboratory and a mental health clinic. Both settings have up-to-date computer terminals (with mainframe connections) and capacities for audio-visual recording or one-way observation. In addition, the department maintains close ties to the Center for Human Development: University Affiliated Program, which provides interdisciplinary training, research, and support for people with developmental disabilities by collaborating with a variety of state agencies and community providers. The Consortium Library is the major research library for Southcentral Alaska, with a collection of more than 69,400 volumes and sub-

scriptions to more than 3,600 journals, including a well-maintained selection of psychology resources. The UAA Information Technology Services provides microcomputer, mainframe, and Internet resources and it maintains four general access computer labs across the campus. The university also houses the Center for Alcohol and Addiction Studies, which addresses the problem of substance abuse in Alaska through educational, research, and public service programs; the Institute for Circumpolar Health Studies, which addresses health problems in Alaska and the Circumpolar North through instruction, information services, and basic and applied research in health and medicine; and the Institute of Social and Economic Research, which is devoted to studying economic and social conditions in Alaska.

Information for Students With Physical Disabilities: The Disability Support Services (DSS) program is responsible for coordinating services for University of Alaska Anchorage students who experience disabilities. Students who experience all types of disabilities are eligible for support services, including registration assistance, liaison to faculty, assistive technology (e.g., computer equipment, tape recorders, assistive listening devices, video magnifiers), liaison with the Alaska Division of Vocational Rehabilitation, use of a resource loan library, and use of the DSS Computer and Study Lab. Qualifying students also may receive accommodations, including testing accommodations (e.g., extended time), note-taking assistance, scribing assistance, interpreters, FM listening systems, books and other course materials in alternative formats (e.g., enlarged, Braille, audio tape), and on-campus transportation.

Application Information:
Send to: Enrollment Services, University of Alaska Anchorage, 3211 Providence Drive, Anchorage, AK 99508. Students are admitted in the Fall, application deadline March 1. *Fee:* $45.

Alaska, University of, Fairbanks

Department of Psychology/MA Program in Community
   Psychology
College of Liberal Arts
University of Alaska Fairbanks, P.O. Box 756480
Fairbanks, AK 99775-6480
Telephone: (907) 474-7007
Fax: (907) 474-5781
E-mail: *fypsych@uaf.edu*
Web: *http://www.uaf.edu/psych/grad/gradwelcome*

Department Established:
1984. Director, Community Psychology Program: Kelly L. Hazel, PhD Number of Faculty: total–full-time 6, part-time 4; women–full-time 3, part-time 2; minority–full-time 1, part-time 2.

Programs and Degrees Offered:
Listed in the following order: Program area, degree type (T if terminal Master's), number awarded 7/00-6/01. Community psychology MA (T) 2.

Student Applications/Admissions:
Student Applications
Community psychology MA—Applications 2001–2002, 18. Total applicants accepted 2001–2002, 10. New applicants en-

rolled 2001–2002, 8. Total enrolled 2001–2002 full-time, 15, part-time, 13. Openings 2002–2003, 10. The Median number of years required for completion of a degree are 4. The number of students enrolled full and part-time, who were dismissed or voluntarily withdrew from this program area were 2.

Admissions Requirements:

Scores: Entries appear in this order: required test or GPA, minimum score (if required), median score of students entering in 2001–2002. Master's Programs: overall undergraduate GPA no minimum stated, 3.6. The UAF Graduate School requires the GRE for admission to graduate studies if an applicant's undergraduate GPA is lower than 3.0. Doctoral Programs: last 2 years GPA no minimum stated; psychology GPA no minimum stated; psychology GPA no minimum stated.

Other Criteria: (importance of criteria rated low, medium, or high): GRE/MAT scores medium, research experience medium, work experience high, extracurricular activity medium, clinically related public service high, GPA medium, letters of recommendation high, statement of goals and objectives high, Cross-Cultural and/or Rural Experience high.

Student Characteristics: The following represents characteristics of students in 2001–2002 in all graduate psychology programs in the department: Female–full-time 12, part-time 8; Male–full-time 5, part-time 3; African American/Black–full-time 0, part-time 0; Hispanic/Latino (a)–full-time 0, part-time 0; Asian/Pacific Islander–full-time 0, part-time 0; American Indian/Alaska Native–full-time 6, part-time 1.

Financial Information/Assistance:

Tuition for Full-Time Study: *Master's:* State residents per academic year $178; nonstate residents: per academic year $347.

Financial Assistance:

First Year Students: Teaching assistantships available for first-year. Average amount paid per academic year: $8,740. Average number of hours worked per week: 20. Apply by Feb. 1. Tuition remission given: full. Research assistantships available for first-year. Average amount paid per academic year: $8,740. Average number of hours worked per week: 20. Apply by Feb. 1. Tuition remission given: full. Fellowships and scholarships available for first-year. Average amount paid per academic year: $10,000. Average number of hours worked per week: 20. Apply by Feb. 1. Tuition remission given: full.

Advanced Students: Teaching assistantships available for advanced students. Average amount paid per academic year: $9,120. Average number of hours worked per week: 20. Apply by Feb. 1. Tuition remission given: full. Research assistantships available for advanced students. Average amount paid per academic year: $9,120. Average number of hours worked per week: 20. Apply by Feb. 1. Tuition remission given: full. Fellowships and scholarships available for advanced students. Average amount paid per academic year: $10,000. Average number of hours worked per week: 20. Apply by Feb. 1. Tuition remission given: full.

Contact Information: Of all students currently enrolled full-time, 77% benefitted from one or more of the listed financial assistance programs. For information on financial assistance, contact: Don Schaeffer, Office of Financial Aid, Box 756360, UAF, Fairbanks, AK 99775-6360 or e-mail: fyfinaid@uaf.edu.

Internships/Practica: Several supervised internships are available to our Community Psychology graduate students. Chief Andrew

Issacs Health Center and Yukon-Tanana Counseling Center, which are part of the mental health branch of Tanana Chiefs Conference, our local Athabaskan regional corporation, offers experience with this indigenous Alaskan population. Additional internships are available at Fort Wainwright Mental Health Center and the Fairbanks Mental Health Center which offer services for adults, and the Farenkamp Youth Center, child, adolescent, family and adult services. Also available to the interested student are internships at the Fairbanks Vet Center, the University of Alaska Fairbanks Women's Center, and the Fairbanks National Alliance for the Mentally Ill. All our training sites offer exposure to work with Alaska Native populations. Students on internships engage in direct client contact as well as program development, evaluation research, and prevention work.

Housing and Day Care: On-campus housing and day care facilities are available.

Employment of Department Graduates:

Master's Degree Graduates: Of those who graduated in the academic year 2000–2001, the following categories and numbers represent the post-graduate activities and employment of master's degree graduates: Enrolled in a psychology doctoral program (1), enrolled in a post-doctoral residency/fellowship (n/a), employed in independent practice (n/a).

Doctoral Degree Graduates: Of those who graduated in the academic year 2000–2001, the following categories and numbers represent the post-graduate activities and employment of doctoral degree graduates: Enrolled in a psychology doctoral program (n/a), enrolled in another graduate/professional program (n/a).

Additional Information:

Orientation, Objectives, and Emphasis of Department: The orientation of the M.A. program in Community Psychology is cross-cultural and rural. The program objective is to train community psychologists to meet the demand for mental health professionals in rural Alaska. This requires individuals who can work sensitively and effectively in urban and rural cross-cultural community contexts. Therefore, the program embodies a commitment to training in cross-cultural psychology that we believe is unique in terms of the extent of its emphasis. A special focus of the program is work with Alaska Native people. It includes courses devoted exclusively to cross-cultural applications in community psychology, counseling, psychological assessment, and psychopathology. These courses are in addition to basic coursework in these areas. Students also receive a strong grounding in the field of substance abuse and prevention psychology. Elective courses are available in prevention, consultation, and individual, group, and family therapy. Instruction is characterized by small class size and a high faculty-to-student ratio. In keeping with the social change orientation of community psychology, students receive training in program development, evaluation, and field-based research. Thesis work directed toward social change, cross-cultural issues in psychology, Native American issues, rural community psychology, rural service delivery, disabilities in rural areas, and psychological adjustment in extreme northern climates is encouraged. Finally, an internship requirement involving supervised training indicates our commitment to a skill-based, experimental component as an essential part of graduate psychology training.

Special Facilities or Resources: Community Psychology is housed in the Gruening Building on the UAF campus, a seven-story structure completed in 1970. Facilities available to graduate students include individual therapy rooms and a family/group therapy room, all upgraded this year with state-of-the-art computer video training equipment. Other computer facilities available to graduate students include a departmental lab and several university labs with PC's and Mac's. UAF is an international center for research in the Arctic and the North.

Information for Students With Physical Disabilities: All Psychology Department facilities are physically accessible. The UAF Office of Disability Services is committed to meeting any additional access needs of all students.

Application Information:
Send to: Director, Community Psychology Program, University of Alaska Fairbanks, P.O. Box 756480, Fairbanks, AK 99775-6480. Students are admitted in the Fall, application deadline February 1. *Fee:* $50. If a student receives a teaching or research assistantship or a fellowship, he/she also receives a tuition waiver.

ARIZONA

Argosy University, Phoenix
Clinical Psychology, Sport-Exercise Psychology, Professional Counseling
2301 W. Dunlap Avenue, Ste. 211
Phoenix, AZ 85021
Telephone: (866)216-2777 (toll-free)
Fax: (602) 216-2601
E-mail: gbartkovich@argosyu.edu
Web: http://www.argosyu.edu

Department Established:
1997. Campus President: Michael J. Patton. Number of Faculty: total–full-time 13, part-time 2; women–full-time 5, part-time 1; minority–full-time 3.

Programs and Degrees Offered:
Listed in the following order: Program area, degree type (T if terminal Master's), number awarded 7/00-6/01. Clinical Psychology PsyD (T), Counseling MA (T), MA Clinical Psychology MA (T), Sport-Exercise Psychology MA (T).

Student Applications/Admissions:
Student Applications

Clinical Psychology PsyD—Applications 2001–2002, 150. Total applicants accepted 2001–2002, 70. New applicants enrolled 2001–2002, 35. Total enrolled 2001–2002 full-time, 140, part-time, 10. Openings 2002–2003, 35. The Median number of years required for completion of a degree are 5. *Counseling MA*—Applications 2001–2002, 40. Total applicants accepted 2001–2002, 30. New applicants enrolled 2001–2002, 22. Total enrolled 2001–2002 part-time, 22. Openings 2002–2003, 20. The Median number of years required for completion of a degree are 2. The number of students enrolled full and part-time, who were dismissed or voluntarily withdrew from this program area were 0. *MA Clinical Psychology MA*—Applications 2001–2002, 45. Total applicants accepted 2001–2002, 30. New applicants enrolled 2001–2002, 15. Total enrolled 2001–2002 full-time, 15, part-time, 10. Openings 2002–2003, 15. The Median number of years required for completion of a degree are 3. *Sport-Exercise Psychology MA*—Applications 2001–2002, 30. Total applicants accepted 2001–2002, 20. New applicants enrolled 2001–2002, 15. Total enrolled 2001–2002 full-time, 28. Openings 2002–2003, 15. The Median number of years required for completion of a degree are 2.

Admissions Requirements:

Scores: Entries appear in this order: required test or GPA, minimum score (if required), median score of students entering in 2001–2002. Doctoral Programs: last 2 years GPA 3.25, 3.41; psychology GPA 3.25, 3.43; psychology GPA no minimum stated.

Other Criteria: (importance of criteria rated low, medium, or high): research experience low, work experience high, extracurricular activity medium, clinically related public service high, GPA high, letters of recommendation medium, interview high, statement of goals and objectives high, resume medium.

Student Characteristics: The following represents characteristics of students in 2001–2002 in all graduate psychology programs in the department: Female–full-time 120, part-time 30; Male–full-time 40, part-time 10; African American/Black–full-time 16, part-time 0; Hispanic/Latino (a)–full-time 16, part-time 0; Asian/Pacific Islander–full-time 4, part-time 0; American Indian/Alaska Native–full-time 2, part-time 0; students subject to the Americans with Disabilities Act–full-time 7, part-time 0.

Financial Information/Assistance:
Tuition for Full-Time Study: *Master's:* State residents per academic year $16,000, $640 per credit hour; nonstate residents: per academic year $16,000, $640 per credit hour. *Doctoral:* State residents: per academic year $16,000, $640 per credit hour; nonstate residents: per academic year $16,000, $640 per credit hour.

Financial Assistance:
First Year Students: No information provided.

Advanced Students: Teaching assistantships available for advanced students. Tuition remission given: partial.

Contact Information: Of all students currently enrolled full-time, 10% benefitted from one or more of the listed financial assistance programs. For information on financial assistance, contact: Office of Admissions.

Internships/Practica: The School maintains an extensive clinical training network including public and private hospitals, community mental health agencies, private practices, substance abuse and rehabilitation agencies, and the Indian Health Service.

Housing and Day Care: No on-campus housing and day care facilities are available.

Employment of Department Graduates:
Master's Degree Graduates: Of those who graduated in the academic year 2000–2001, the following categories and numbers represent the post-graduate activities and employment of master's degree graduates: Enrolled in a post-doctoral residency/fellowship (n/a), employed in independent practice (n/a).

Doctoral Degree Graduates: Of those who graduated in the academic year 2000–2001, the following categories and numbers represent the post-graduate activities and employment of doctoral degree graduates: Enrolled in a psychology doctoral program (n/a), enrolled in another graduate/professional program (n/a).

Additional Information:
Orientation, Objectives, and Emphasis of Department: The mission of Argosy University/Phoenix is to educate and train students in the major areas of clinical psychology, sport-exercise psychology and professional counseling, and prepare students for successful practitioner careers. The curriculum integrates theory, training, research, and practice and prepares students to work with a wide range of populations in need of psychological services. Faculty are both scholars and practitioners and guide students through coursework and field experiences so that they might understand how formal knowledge and practice operate to inform and enrich each other. The School follows a generalist practitioner-scholar orientation exposing students to a broad array of clinical theories

and interventions. Sensitivity to diverse populations, populations with specific needs, and multicultural awareness are important components of the school's training model.

Special Facilities or Resources: Specialty training in Sport-Exercise Psychology within the clinical doctoral program.

Information for Students With Physical Disabilities: The School is committed to meeting the needs of physically disabled students and has policies and procedures for accommodating the needs of disabled students.

Application Information:
Send to: Gail Bartkovich, M.A., Director of Admissions, AU/Phoenix 2301 W. Dunlap Ave., Ste. 211, Phoenix, AZ 85021. Students are admitted in the Fall, application deadline May 15; Spring, application deadline October 15. Deadlines vary by program; priority deadline of January 15 for fall admission. *Fee:* $50.

Arizona State University
Department of Psychology
Box 871104
Tempe, AZ 85287-1104
Telephone: (480) 965-3326
Fax: (480) 965-8544
E-mail: *psygrad@asu.edu*
Web: *http://www.asu.edu/clas/psych*

Department Established:
1932. Chairperson: Darwyn E. Linder. Number of Faculty: total–full-time 48, part-time 2; women–full-time 14; minority–full-time 8; faculty subject to the Americans with Disabilities Act 1.

Programs and Degrees Offered:
Listed in the following order: Program area, degree type (T if terminal Master's), number awarded 7/00-6/01. Clinical PhD 5, cognitive systems, behavior PhD 3, developmental PhD 1, quantitative PhD 2, social PhD 1.

APA Accreditation: Clinical PhD: full.

Student Applications/Admissions:
Student Applications
   Clinical PhD—Applications 2001–2002, 146. Total applicants accepted 2001–2002, 6. New applicants enrolled 2001–2002, 6. Total enrolled 2001–2002 full-time, 47. Openings 2002–2003, 6. *Cognitive systems, behavior PhD*—Applications 2001–2002, 26. Total applicants accepted 2001–2002, 5. New applicants enrolled 2001–2002, 5. Total enrolled 2001–2002 full-time, 26. Openings 2002–2003, 6. *Developmental PhD*—Applications 2001–2002, 16. Total applicants accepted 2001–2002, 2. New applicants enrolled 2001–2002, 2. Total enrolled 2001–2002 full-time, 11. Openings 2002–2003, 5. *Quantitative PhD*—Applications 2001–2002, 8. Total applicants accepted 2001–2002, 3. New applicants enrolled 2001–2002, 3. Total enrolled 2001–2002 full-time, 6. Openings 2002–2003, 3. *Social PhD*—Applications 2001–2002, 50. Total applicants accepted 2001–2002, 4. New applicants enrolled 2001–2002,

4. Total enrolled 2001–2002 full-time, 32. Openings 2002–2003, 5.

Admissions Requirements:
   Scores: Entries appear in this order: required test or GPA, minimum score (if required), median score of students entering in 2001–2002. Master's Programs: GRE-V no minimum stated; GRE-Q no minimum stated; GRE-Analytical no minimum stated. GRE-Subject (Psychology) is required for clinical applicants only. Doctoral Programs: GRE-V no minimum stated, 630; GRE-Q no minimum stated, 705; GRE-Subject(Psych) no minimum stated, 715; last 2 years GPA no minimum stated; psychology GPA no minimum stated; psychology GPA no minimum stated. Subject test is required for clinical applicants only.
   Other Criteria: (importance of criteria rated low, medium, or high): GRE/MAT scores medium, research experience high, work experience low, extracurricular activity low, clinically related public service medium, GPA medium, letters of recommendation high, interview high, statement of goals and objectives high.

Student Characteristics: The following represents characteristics of students in 2001–2002 in all graduate psychology programs in the department: Female–full-time 64, part-time 0; Male–full-time 42, part-time 0; African American/Black–full-time 0, part-time 0; Hispanic/Latino (a)–full-time 2, part-time 0; Asian/Pacific Islander–full-time 2, part-time 0; American Indian/Alaska Native–full-time 1, part-time 0; Multi-ethnic–full-time 0, part-time 0; students subject to the Americans with Disabilities Act–full-time 0, part-time 0.

Financial Information/Assistance:
Tuition for Full-Time Study: *Master's:* State residents per academic year $2,188; nonstate residents: per academic year $10,278, *Doctoral:* State residents: per academic year $2,188; nonstate residents: per academic year $10,278.

Financial Assistance:
   First Year Students: No information provided.
   Advanced Students: No information provided.
   Contact Information: Of all students currently enrolled full-time, 0% benefitted from one or more of the listed financial assistance programs. For information on financial assistance, contact: Student Financial Aid Office.

Internships/Practica: No information provided.

Housing and Day Care: No on-campus housing and day care facilities are available.

Employment of Department Graduates:
Master's Degree Graduates: Of those who graduated in the academic year 2000–2001, the following categories and numbers represent the post-graduate activities and employment of master's degree graduates: Enrolled in a post-doctoral residency/fellowship (n/a), employed in independent practice (n/a).
Doctoral Degree Graduates: Of those who graduated in the academic year 2000–2001, the following categories and numbers represent the post-graduate activities and employment of doctoral degree graduates: Enrolled in a psychology doctoral program (n/a), enrolled in another graduate/professional program (n/a).

Additional Information:

Orientation, Objectives, and Emphasis of Department: The department seeks to instill in students knowledge, skills, and an appreciation of psychology as a science and as a profession. To do so, it offers undergraduate and graduate programs emphasizing theory, research, and applied practice. The department encourages a multiplicity of theoretical viewpoints and research interests. The behavioral neuroscience area emphasizes the neural bases of motor disorders, drug abuse and recovery of function following brain damage. The clinical program includes areas of emphasis in health psychology, child-clinical psychology, and community-prevention. Also offered are classes in psychopathology, prevention, assessment, and psychotherapy. The cognitive systems area includes cognitive psychology, adaptive systems, learning, sensation and perception, and cognitive development. The developmental area includes coursework and research experience in the core areas of cognitive and social development. The environmental area emphasizes the application of psychological research to environmental and population problems, including architectural design, urban planning, and human ecology. The quantitative area focuses on design, measurement, and statistical analysis issues that arise in diverse areas of psychological research. The social area emphasizes theoretical and laboratory skills combined with program evaluation and applied social psychology.

Special Facilities or Resources: The department has the Child Study Laboratory for training and research in developmental psychology, including both normal and clinical groups, particularly of preschool age; the Clinical Psychology Center, whose clients represent a wide range of psychological disorders and are not limited to the university community; and the experimental laboratories, with exceptional computer facilities for the study of speech perception, neural networks, categorization, memory, sensory processes, and learning. The clinical and social programs maintain continuing liaison with a wide range of off-campus agencies for research applications of psychological theory and research. Our NIMH-funded Preventive Intervention Research Center provides a site for training in the design, implementation, and evaluation of preventative interventions. Quantitatively oriented students receive methodological experience in large-scale research programs and in our statistical laboratory.

Application Information:

Send to: Admissions Secretary, Department of Psychology, Arizona State University, PO Box 871104, Tempe, AZ 85287-1104. Students are admitted in the Fall, application deadline December 1. *Fee:* $45.

Arizona State University

Division of Psychology in Education
B-302, Payne Hall, P.O. Box 870611
Tempe, AZ 85287-0611
Telephone: (480) 965-3384
Fax: (480) 965-0300
E-mail: *dpe@asu.edu*
Web: *http://coe.asu.edu/psyched/*

Department Established:

1968. Division Director: Elsie G.J. Moore. Number of Faculty: total–full-time 38, part-time 4; women–full-time 19, part-time 1; minority–full-time 8.

Programs and Degrees Offered:

Listed in the following order: Program area, degree type (T if terminal Master's), number awarded 7/00-6/01. Counseling Psychology PhD 10, Educational Psychology (T) 3, Educational Technology PhD 3, Educational: Learning PhD, Educational: Measurement, stat MA 2, Educational: Lifespan developme MA 2, Educational:Measurement, stat PhD, Educational: School Psychology PhD 4, Master of Counseling MA (T) 48, Master of Education in Counsel (T) 3.

APA Accreditation: Counseling PhD: full. School PhD: full.

Student Applications/Admissions:

Student Applications

Counseling Psychology PhD—Applications 2001–2002, 108. Total applicants accepted 2001–2002, 19. New applicants enrolled 2001–2002, 11. Total enrolled 2001–2002 full-time, 36, part-time, 21. Openings 2002–2003, 10. The Median number of years required for completion of a degree are 5. The number of students enrolled full and part-time, who were dismissed or voluntarily withdrew from this program area were 1. *Educational Technology PhD*—Applications 2001–2002, 41. Total applicants accepted 2001–2002, 8. New applicants enrolled 2001–2002, 6. Total enrolled 2001–2002 full-time, 10, part-time, 15. Openings 2002–2003, 7. The Median number of years required for completion of a degree are 5. The number of students enrolled full and part-time, who were dismissed or voluntarily withdrew from this program area were 2. *Educational: Learning PhD*—Applications 2001–2002, 6. Total applicants accepted 2001–2002, 2. New applicants enrolled 2001–2002, 2. Total enrolled 2001–2002 full-time, 8, part-time, 3. Openings 2002–2003, 4. The Median number of years required for completion of a degree are na. The number of students enrolled full and part-time, who were dismissed or voluntarily withdrew from this program area were 0. *Educational: Measurement, stat MA*—Applications 2001–2002, 1. Total enrolled 2001–2002 full-time, 2, part-time, 3. Openings 2002–2003, 3. The Median number of years required for completion of a degree are 2. The number of students enrolled full and part-time, who were dismissed or voluntarily withdrew from this program area were 0. *Educational: Lifespan developme MA*—Applications 2001–2002, 4. Total applicants accepted 2001–2002, 3. New applicants enrolled 2001–2002, 3. Total enrolled 2001–2002 full-time, 5, part-time, 1. Openings 2002–2003, 3. The Median number of years required for completion of a degree are 2. The number of students enrolled full and part-time, who were dismissed or voluntarily withdrew from this program area were 0. *Educational: Measurement, stat PhD*—Applications 2001–2002, 4. Total applicants accepted 2001–2002, 3. New applicants enrolled 2001–2002, 3. Total enrolled 2001–2002 full-time, 4, part-time, 11. Openings 2002–2003, 2. The number of students enrolled full and part-time, who were dismissed or voluntarily withdrew from this program area were 0. *Educational: School Psychology PhD*—Applications 2001–2002, 71. Total applicants accepted 2001–2002, 16. New applicants enrolled 2001–2002, 5. Total enrolled 2001–2002 full-time, 18, part-time, 12. Openings 2002–2003, 10. The

Median number of years required for completion of a degree are 6. The number of students enrolled full and part-time, who were dismissed or voluntarily withdrew from this program area were 0. *Master of Counseling MA*—Applications 2001–2002, 115. Total applicants accepted 2001–2002, 76. New applicants enrolled 2001–2002, 54. Total enrolled 2001–2002 full-time, 73, part-time, 53. Openings 2002–2003, 50. The Median number of years required for completion of a degree are 3. The number of students enrolled full and part-time, who were dismissed or voluntarily withdrew from this program area were 7.

Admissions Requirements:

Scores: Entries appear in this order: required test or GPA, minimum score (if required), median score of students entering in 2001–2002. Master's Programs: GRE-V no minimum stated, 516; GRE-Q no minimum stated, 552; MAT no minimum stated, 59; overall undergraduate GPA no minimum stated, 3.40; last 2 years GPA no minimum stated, 3.67. Counselor Education and Educational Technology will accept a MAT score in lieu of the GRE. Otherwise, the GRE is required by all programs. Doctoral Programs: GRE-V no minimum stated, 545; GRE-Q no minimum stated, 581; GRE-V+Q no minimum stated; overall undergraduate GPA 3.0, 3.67; last 2 years GPA no minimum stated, 3.53; psychology GPA no minimum stated; psychology GPA no minimum stated. Educational Technology requires a 3.2 or above undergraduate GPA and 1200 GRE-V+Q.

Other Criteria: (importance of criteria rated low, medium, or high): research experience high, work experience low, clinically related public service medium, letters of recommendation medium, interview low, statement of goals and objectives low. Programs use the FRK index which combines GRE-V+Q with undergraduate GPA. Minimum FRKs are set by faculty admissions committees.

Student Characteristics: The following represents characteristics of students in 2001–2002 in all graduate psychology programs in the department: Female–full-time 146, part-time 128; Male–full-time 41, part-time 46; African American/Black–full-time 11, part-time 0; Hispanic/Latino (a)–full-time 22, part-time 14; Asian/Pacific Islander–full-time 10, part-time 8; American Indian/Alaska Native–full-time 4, part-time 3; students subject to the Americans with Disabilities Act–full-time 0, part-time 1.

Financial Information/Assistance:

Tuition for Full-Time Study: *Master's:* State residents $126 per credit hour; nonstate residents: $428 per credit hour. *Doctoral:* State residents: $126 per credit hour; nonstate residents: $428 per credit hour.

Financial Assistance:

First Year Students: Teaching assistantships available for first-year. Average amount paid per academic year: $5,450. Average number of hours worked per week: 10. Apply by April 15. Tuition remission given: partial. Research assistantships available for first-year. Average amount paid per academic year: $5,450. Average number of hours worked per week: 10. Apply by April 15. Tuition remission given: partial.

Advanced Students: Teaching assistantships available for advanced students. Average amount paid per academic year: $5,450. Average number of hours worked per week: 10. Apply by

April 15. Tuition remission given: partial. Research assistantships available for advanced students. Average amount paid per academic year: $5,450. Average number of hours worked per week: 10. Apply by April 15. Tuition remission given: partial.

Contact Information: Of all students currently enrolled full-time, 24% benefitted from one or more of the listed financial assistance programs. For information on financial assistance, contact: http://www.asu.edu/graduate/financial.html.

Internships/Practica: For those doctoral students for whom a professional internship is required prior to graduation, 11 applied in 2000–2001. Of those who applied, 8 were placed in internships listed by the Association of Psychology Postdoctoral and Internship Programs (APPIC); 8 were placed in APA accredited internships.

Housing and Day Care: No on-campus housing and day care facilities are available.

Employment of Department Graduates:

Master's Degree Graduates: Of those who graduated in the academic year 2000–2001, the following categories and numbers represent the post-graduate activities and employment of master's degree graduates: Enrolled in a post-doctoral residency/fellowship (n/a), employed in independent practice (n/a).

Doctoral Degree Graduates: Of those who graduated in the academic year 2000–2001, the following categories and numbers represent the post-graduate activities and employment of doctoral degree graduates: Enrolled in a psychology doctoral program (n/a), enrolled in another graduate/professional program (n/a).

Additional Information:

Orientation, Objectives, and Emphasis of Department: The Division adheres to a scientist-practitioner model across all areas. The Counseling and School Psychology programs are APA accredited. Less than half of the Division's doctoral graduates accept positions in colleges and universities, the remainder function in applied settings.

Special Facilities or Resources: The department staffs and operates a large-scale psychological assessment laboratory, and most students are currently assigned research and study space. Strong research relations exist with local schools, agencies, and private industry. The Counseling Training Center is a training facility for Master's and PhD level counseling students. The center serves clients from both the university and the general public.

Information for Students With Physical Disabilities: Contact Disability Resources for Students, Arizona State University, P.O. Box 873202, Tempe, AZ 85287-3202; (480) 965-1234.

Application Information:

Send to: Admissions Secretary, Psychology in Education, Arizona State University, P.O. Box 870611, Tempe, AZ 85287-0611. Counseling Psychology - Dec. 1; School Psychology and Master of Counseling - Jan. 15; Educational Psychology- Feb. 15 & Oct. 15. *Fee:* $45. The application fee cannot be waived.

Arizona, University of
Department of Psychology
Social and Behavioral Sciences
PO Box 210068
Tucson, AZ 85721
Telephone: (520) 621-7447
Fax: (520) 621-9306
E-mail: *nadel@u.arizona.edu*
Web: *http://w3.arizona.edu/~psych/*

Department Established:
1914. Head: Lynn Nadel. Number of Faculty: total–full-time 28, part-time 7; women–full-time 11, part-time 2; minority–full-time 2.

Programs and Degrees Offered:
Listed in the following order: Program area, degree type (T if terminal Master's), number awarded 7/00-6/01. Clinical PhD 4, cognition and neural systems PhD, cognitive PhD, ethology and evolutionary PhD, program evaluation PhD, psychology, policy, and law, social PhD 1.

APA Accreditation: Clinical PhD: full.

Student Applications/Admissions:
Student Applications
Clinical PhD—Applications 2001–2002, 326. Total applicants accepted 2001–2002, 11. New applicants enrolled 2001–2002, 6. Total enrolled 2001–2002 full-time, 47. *Cognition and neural systems PhD*—Applications 2001–2002, 22. Total applicants accepted 2001–2002, 5. New applicants enrolled 2001–2002, 3. Total enrolled 2001–2002 full-time, 10. Openings 2002–2003, 2. The Median number of years required for completion of a degree are na. The number of students enrolled full and part-time, who were dismissed or voluntarily withdrew from this program area were 3. *Cognitive PhD*—Applications 2001–2002, 33. Total applicants accepted 2001–2002, 9. New applicants enrolled 2001–2002, 4. Total enrolled 2001–2002 full-time, 13. Openings 2002–2003, 4. The Median number of years required for completion of a degree are 0. The number of students enrolled full and part-time, who were dismissed or voluntarily withdrew from this program area were 2. *Ethology and evolutionary PhD*—Applications 2001–2002, 22. Total applicants accepted 2001–2002, 2. New applicants enrolled 2001–2002, 3. Total enrolled 2001–2002 full-time, 7. The Median number of years required for completion of a degree are na. The number of students enrolled full and part-time, who were dismissed or voluntarily withdrew from this program area were 0. *Program evaluation PhD*—Applications 2001–2002, 0. Total enrolled 2001–2002 full-time, 7. The Median number of years required for completion of a degree are na. The number of students enrolled full and part-time, who were dismissed or voluntarily withdrew from this program area were 1. *Social PhD*—Applications 2001–2002, 23. Total applicants accepted 2001–2002, 3. Total enrolled 2001–2002 full-time, 3. Openings 2002–2003, 2. The Median number of years required for completion of a degree are 4. The number of students enrolled full and part-time, who were dismissed or voluntarily withdrew from this program area were 0.

Admissions Requirements:
Scores: Entries appear in this order: required test or GPA, minimum score (if required), median score of students entering in 2001–2002. Doctoral Programs: GRE-V no minimum stated, 603; GRE-Q no minimum stated, 682; GRE-Analytical no minimum stated, 649; GRE-Subject(Psych) no minimum stated, 690; overall undergraduate GPA 3.0, 3.77; last 2 years GPA no minimum stated; psychology GPA no minimum stated; psychology GPA no minimum stated.
Other Criteria: (importance of criteria rated low, medium, or high): research experience high, work experience low, extracurricular activity low, clinically related public service low, letters of recommendation high, interview medium, statement of goals and objectives high.

Student Characteristics: The following represents characteristics of students in 2001–2002 in all graduate psychology programs in the department: Female–full-time 6, part-time 0; Male–full-time 9, part-time 0; African American/Black–full-time 1, part-time 0; Hispanic/Latino (a)–full-time 1, part-time 0; Asian/Pacific Islander–full-time 0, part-time 0; American Indian/Alaska Native–full-time 0, part-time 0.

Financial Information/Assistance:
Tuition for Full-Time Study: *Doctoral:* State residents: per academic year $1,245, $134 per credit hour; nonstate residents: per academic year $5,178, $436 per credit hour.

Financial Assistance:
First Year Students: Teaching assistantships available for first-year. Average amount paid per academic year: $12,000. Average number of hours worked per week: 14. Apply by Jan 1. Tuition remission given: partial. Traineeships available for first-year. Average amount paid per academic year: $12,000. Average number of hours worked per week: 14. Tuition remission given: partial. Fellowships and scholarships available for first-year. Average amount paid per academic year: $12,000. Average number of hours worked per week: 14. Tuition remission given: partial.
Advanced Students: Teaching assistantships available for advanced students. Average amount paid per academic year: $12,000. Average number of hours worked per week: 14. Tuition remission given: partial. Traineeships available for advanced students. Average amount paid per academic year: $12,000. Average number of hours worked per week: 14. Tuition remission given: partial. Fellowships and scholarships available for advanced students. Average amount paid per academic year: $12,000. Average number of hours worked per week: 14. Tuition remission given: partial.
Contact Information: No information provided.

Internships/Practica: No information provided.

Housing and Day Care: On-campus housing and day care facilities are available.

Employment of Department Graduates:
Master's Degree Graduates: Of those who graduated in the academic year 2000–2001, the following categories and numbers represent the post-graduate activities and employment of master's degree graduates: Enrolled in a post-doctoral residency/fellowship (n/a), employed in independent practice (n/a).

Doctoral Degree Graduates: Of those who graduated in the academic year 2000–2001, the following categories and numbers represent the post-graduate activities and employment of doctoral degree graduates: Enrolled in a psychology doctoral program (n/a), enrolled in another graduate/professional program (n/a).

Additional Information:

Orientation, Objectives, and Emphasis of Department: Our objectives as a department include contributing to the growth of knowledge about the mind and its workings, and the training of students to participate in this pursuit, as well as using this knowledge to benefit society. The department emphasizes research and training students headed toward both academic and applied careers. Required courses provide breadth of coverage, but emphasis is on research within the area of specialization, relying on independent work with individual faculty members. The interdisciplinary nature of the department fosters specialization in areas that cut across program boundaries and permits work with faculty members in various programs. The cognitive psychology area emphasizes language, perception, and memory, with a major focus on cognitive neuroscience; the clinical area emphasizes clinical neuropsychology, psychotherapy research, sleep disorders and psychophysiology; and assessment; the social area emphasizes prejudice and sterotyping, cognitive dissonance, self-esteem, and motivational factors in thought and behavior; the psychology, policy and law area emphasizes quantitative ethology, invertebrate behavior and human behavioral ecology; and the cognition and neural systems area emphasizes memory, attention, aging, ensemble, recording of neural activity, and human neuroimaging. In addition to these formal programs, the department also offers specializations in evaluation and research methods, and in environmental psychology. The department is the administrative home for the Center on Consciousness Studies, and the Cognition and Neuroimaging Laboratory.

Special Facilities or Resources: The department has modern laboratories devoted to research in various areas of cognitive, clinical, neuroscientific, social, and comparative research. The department employs 5 technicians available for assistance with computers and other equipment. There are a number of clinics within the department, bringing in patients associated with research projects on aging, sleep disorders, memory disorders, depression, and others. The department has ties with a number of other programs on campus, including the departments of Anatomy, Family and Community Medicine, Neurology, Ophthalmology, Pediatrics, Pharmacology, Physiology and Psychiatry in the College of Medicine, and the departments of Ecology and Evolutionary Biology, Family Studies, Linguistics, Management and Policy, Mathematics, Philosophy, Renewable and Natural Resources, Speech and Hearing Sciences, and Physics on the main campus. Ties also exist with various interdisciplinary programs, including Cognitive Science (many of whose laboratories are located in the Psychology Building), Applied Mathematics, and Neuroscience. Most of the department's faculty members are holders of research grants, permitting a significant proportion of the graduate students to serve as research assistants at various times during their training.

Application Information:
Send to: Department Chair. Students are admitted in the Fall, application deadline January 1. *Fee:* $45.

Northern Arizona University
Department of Psychology
Social and Behavioral Sciences
NAU Box 15106
Flagstaff, AZ 86011
Telephone: (520) 523-3063
Fax: (520) 523-6777
E-mail: *robert.till@nau.edu*
Web: *http://www.nau.edu*

Department Established:
1967. Chairperson: Robert E. Till. Number of Faculty: total–full-time 20, part-time 3; women–full-time 8, part-time 1.

Programs and Degrees Offered:
Listed in the following order: Program area, degree type (T if terminal Master's), number awarded 7/00-6/01. Applied Health MA (T) 1, General MA (T) 4.

Student Applications/Admissions:
Student Applications
Applied Health MA—Applications 2001–2002, 22. Total applicants accepted 2001–2002, 12. New applicants enrolled 2001–2002, 3. Total enrolled 2001–2002 full-time, 3. Openings 2002–2003, 10. *General MA*—Applications 2001–2002, 14. Total applicants accepted 2001–2002, 9. New applicants enrolled 2001–2002, 4. Total enrolled 2001–2002 full-time, 4. Openings 2002–2003, 10. The number of students enrolled full and part-time, who were dismissed or voluntarily withdrew from this program area were 0.

Admissions Requirements:
Scores: Entries appear in this order: required test or GPA, minimum score (if required), median score of students entering in 2001–2002. Master's Programs: GRE-V 500, 520; GRE-Q 500, 550; GRE-V+Q 1000, 1080; overall undergraduate GPA 3.0, 3.4; last 2 years GPA no minimum stated, 3.6; psychology GPA no minimum stated, 3.5. Doctoral Programs: last 2 years GPA no minimum stated; psychology GPA no minimum stated; psychology GPA no minimum stated.
Other Criteria: (importance of criteria rated low, medium, or high): GRE/MAT scores, research experience medium, clinically related public service medium, GPA, letters of recommendation high, interview high, statement of goals and objectives high. Clinically related public service used only for applied health psychology program.

Student Characteristics: The following represents characteristics of students in 2001–2002 in all graduate psychology programs in the department: Female–full-time 25, part-time 0; Male–full-time 6, part-time 0; African American/Black–full-time 0, part-time 0; Hispanic/Latino (a)–full-time 1, part-time 0; Asian/Pacific Islander–full-time 0, part-time 0; American Indian/Alaska Native–full-time 0, part-time 0.

Financial Information/Assistance:
Tuition for Full-Time Study: *Master's:* State residents per academic year $1,206, $126 per credit hour; nonstate residents: per academic year $5,139, $428 per credit hour.

Financial Assistance:

First Year Students: Teaching assistantships available for first-year. Average number of hours worked per week: 10. Apply by Feb 15. Research assistantships available for first-year. Average number of hours worked per week: 10. Apply by Feb 15.

Advanced Students: Teaching assistantships available for advanced students. Average number of hours worked per week: 10. Apply by n/a. Research assistantships available for advanced students. Average number of hours worked per week: 10. Apply by n/a.

Contact Information: Of all students currently enrolled full-time, 58% benefitted from one or more of the listed financial assistance programs. For information on financial assistance, contact: Financial Aid Office, (928) 523-4951.

Internships/Practica: Applied Health Psychology students are required to take two semesters of practicum in the department's Health Psychology Center. Our multipurpose training and service facility serves NAU students, faculty, and staff as well as community residents. In the Center, supervised graduate students in applied health psychology work to promote wellness and healthy lifestyles in adults and children through a variety of educational and treatment modalities. The Center offers programs on such topics as stress management, healthy eating and weight control, exercise, and smoking cessation, as well as group and individual interventions for these topics. The Center also provides psychological evaluation and behavioral management for health-related problems such as headaches, high blood pressure, cardiovascular disease, obesity, premenstrual syndrome, ulcers, diabetes, asthma, smoking, cancer, and chronic pain. Applied Health Psychology students also are encouraged to take one or more semesters of fieldwork placement at a variety of agencies in the surrounding communities (including ethnic and rural communities). General Psychology students also may enroll in fieldwork placement.

Housing and Day Care: No on-campus housing and day care facilities are available.

Employment of Department Graduates:

Master's Degree Graduates: Of those who graduated in the academic year 2000–2001, the following categories and numbers represent the post-graduate activities and employment of master's degree graduates: Enrolled in a psychology doctoral program (1), enrolled in a post-doctoral residency/fellowship (n/a), employed in independent practice (n/a), employed in business or industry (research/consulting) (1).

Doctoral Degree Graduates: Of those who graduated in the academic year 2000–2001, the following categories and numbers represent the post-graduate activities and employment of doctoral degree graduates: Enrolled in a psychology doctoral program (n/a), enrolled in another graduate/professional program (n/a).

Additional Information:

Orientation, Objectives, and Emphasis of Department: The psychology department is committed to excellence in education at the graduate level, emphasizing teaching, scholarship, and service to the university and to the larger community. The nature of our discipline is such that it helps students understand the biological, social, and cultural influences on human thought, emotions, and behavior. The department's approach to these issues emphasizes the theoretical foundations, empirical research, innovative curriculum, and practical hands-on applications of psychological knowledge. In addition, the department strongly supports the university's mission of promoting opportunities for multicultural experiences and encouraging ethnic diversity of students and faculty. Throughout its curriculum, the department integrates research and scholarship with teaching. This includes the use of existing research to enhance course content and structure and also includes students' participation in faculty-directed research, student-initiated research, and collaborative faculty-student research. In addition to supporting research and scholarship within the university community, the department participates in the larger discipline of psychology by encouraging faculty and student attendance at professional conferences as well as publication in professional journals.

Special Facilities or Resources: The Department of Psychology has over 1,500 square feet of clinic space dedicated to training in Applied Health Psychology and a state-of-the-art psychophysiology/biofeedback laboratory. Other well-equipped research facilities are available in an adjunct building, and are assigned to faculty members engaged in research. A computer laboratory used for teaching purposes is also available for data collection. The department is housed in a modern building at the south end of the Flagstaff Mountain Campus. All teaching rooms are equipped with up-to-date technology. NAU is located in the city of Flagstaff, a four-season community of approximately 50,000 residents at the base of the majestic, 12,670-foot-high San Francisco Peaks. Flagstaff and the surrounding area offer excellent hiking and mountain-biking trails as well as cross-country and downhill skiing. Students enjoy the nearby diversity of Arizona's climate and attractions, from Grand Canyon National Park to metropolitan Phoenix in the Sonoran desert.

Information for Students With Physical Disabilities: All facilities are accessible. The University Disabled Student Services Office, (520)523-8773, provides assistance and consultation.

Application Information:
Send to: Departmental Application: Department of Psychology, Graduate Programs, Northern Arizona University, Box 15106, Flagstaff, AZ 86011. Graduate Application: NAU Graduate College, PO Box 4125, Flagstaff, AZ 86011-4125. Students are admitted in the Fall, application deadline February 15. *Fee:* $45.

Northern Arizona University
Educational Psychology
Center for Excellence in Education
CEE 5774
Flagstaff, AZ 86011
Telephone: (928) 523-6534 or (928) 523-7103
Fax: (928) 523-1929
E-mail: *ramona.mellott@nau.edu*
Web: *http://www.nauedu/~cee/academics/eps/index.htm1*

Department Established:
1962. Chairperson: Ramona N. Mellott. Number of Faculty: total–full-time 21, part-time 6; women–full-time 11, part-time 5; minority–full-time 4.

Programs and Degrees Offered:

Listed in the following order: Program area, degree type (T if terminal Master's), number awarded 7/00-6/01. Certification in School Psycho MA (T) 12, Community Counseling MA (T) 15, Counseling Psychology EdD 1, Learning and Instructional EdD, School Counseling (T) 10, School Psychology EdD 2, Student Affairs.

Student Applications/Admissions:

Student Applications

Certification in School Psycho MA—Applications 2001–2002, 27. Total applicants accepted 2001–2002, 16. New applicants enrolled 2001–2002, 16. Total enrolled 2001–2002 full-time, 19, part-time, 6. Openings 2002–2003, 12. The Median number of years required for completion of a degree are 2. The number of students enrolled full and part-time, who were dismissed or voluntarily withdrew from this program area were 1. *Community Counseling MA*—Applications 2001–2002, 34. Total applicants accepted 2001–2002, 16. New applicants enrolled 2001–2002, 16. Total enrolled 2001–2002 full-time, 21, part-time, 9. Openings 2002–2003, 16. The Median number of years required for completion of a degree are 2. The number of students enrolled full and part-time, who were dismissed or voluntarily withdrew from this program area were 0. *Counseling Psychology EdD*—Applications 2001–2002, 8. Total applicants accepted 2001–2002, 6. New applicants enrolled 2001–2002, 6. Total enrolled 2001–2002 full-time, 15, part-time, 16. Openings 2002–2003, 7. The Median number of years required for completion of a degree are 3. The number of students enrolled full and part-time, who were dismissed or voluntarily withdrew from this program area were 1. *Learning and Instructional EdD*—Applications 2001–2002, 1. Total applicants accepted 2001–2002, 1. New applicants enrolled 2001–2002, 1. Total enrolled 2001–2002 full-time, 3. Openings 2002–2003, 5. The Median number of years required for completion of a degree are 3. The number of students enrolled full and part-time, who were dismissed or voluntarily withdrew from this program area were 1. *School Psychology EdD*—Applications 2001–2002, 8. Total applicants accepted 2001–2002, 6. New applicants enrolled 2001–2002, 6. Total enrolled 2001–2002 full-time, 15, part-time, 12. Openings 2002–2003, 7. The Median number of years required for completion of a degree are 3.

Admissions Requirements:

Scores: Entries appear in this order: required test or GPA, minimum score (if required), median score of students entering in 2001–2002. Master's Programs: GRE-V no minimum stated; GRE-Q no minimum stated; overall undergraduate GPA no minimum stated; last 2 years GPA no minimum stated. Doctoral Programs: GRE-V no minimum stated; GRE-Q no minimum stated; last 2 years GPA no minimum stated; psychology GPA no minimum stated; psychology GPA no minimum stated.

Other Criteria: (importance of criteria rated low, medium, or high): GRE/MAT scores high, research experience low, work experience medium, extracurricular activity low, clinically related public service low, GPA high, letters of recommendation low, statement of goals and objectives medium, Goodness of Fit medium.

Student Characteristics: The following represents characteristics of students in 2001–2002 in all graduate psychology programs in the department: Female–full-time 58, part-time 50; Male–full-time 24, part-time 14; African American/Black–full-time 5, part-time 2; Hispanic/Latino (a)–full-time 12, part-time 4; Asian/Pacific Islander–full-time 2, part-time 1; American Indian/Alaska Native–full-time 4, part-time 2; students subject to the Americans with Disabilities Act–full-time 1.

Financial Information/Assistance:

Tuition for Full-Time Study: *Master's:* State residents per academic year $2,488, $137 per credit hour; nonstate residents: per academic year $7,780, $439 per credit hour. *Doctoral:* State residents: per academic year $2,488, $137 per credit hour; nonstate residents: per academic year $7,780, $439 per credit hour.

Financial Assistance:

First Year Students: Teaching assistantships available for first-year. Average amount paid per academic year: $8,000. Average number of hours worked per week: 20. Apply by April 15. Tuition remission given: partial. Average amount paid per academic year: $500. Average number of hours worked per week: 0. Apply by March 15.

Advanced Students: Teaching assistantships available for advanced students. Average amount paid per academic year: $8,000. Average number of hours worked per week: 20. Apply by April 15. Tuition remission given: partial. Research assistantships available for advanced students. Average amount paid per academic year: $8,000. Average number of hours worked per week: 20. Apply by April 15. Tuition remission given: partial. Average amount paid per academic year: $500. Apply by March 15.

Contact Information: Of all students currently enrolled full-time, 50% benefitted from one or more of the listed financial assistance programs. For information on financial assistance, contact: Student Financial Aid, NAU, P.O. Box 4108, Flagstaff, AZ 86011-4108. Partial and full tuition waivers are also awarded.

Internships/Practica: Our practitioner programs are built on competency-based models and include closely supervised experiential practica and internship components. Many of these experiences are offered in NAU's Counseling and Testing Center and the Institute for Human Development; student service facilities; public-school settings; reservation schools and communities; rural settings; and community agencies. In addition, the Center for Excellence in Education houses a Skills Lab Network that includes comprehensive testing and curriculum libraries and a practicum facility that uses both videotape and direct live feedback in the supervision of students working with clients. For those doctoral students for whom a professional internship is required prior to graduation, 5 applied in 2000–2001. Of those who applied, 3 were placed in internships listed by the Association of Psychology Postdoctoral and Internship Programs (APPIC).

Housing and Day Care: On-campus housing and day care facilities are available.

Employment of Department Graduates:

Master's Degree Graduates: Of those who graduated in the academic year 2000–2001, the following categories and numbers represent the post-graduate activities and employment of master's degree graduates: Enrolled in a psychology doctoral program (8), enrolled in another graduate/professional program (2), enrolled in a post-doctoral residency/fellowship (n/a), employed in independent practice (n/a).

Doctoral Degree Graduates: Of those who graduated in the academic year 2000–2001, the following categories and numbers represent the post-graduate activities and employment of doctoral degree graduates: Enrolled in a psychology doctoral program (n/a), enrolled in another graduate/professional program (n/a), enrolled in a post-doctoral residency/fellowship (0), employed in independent practice (2), employed in an academic position at a university (0), employed in an academic position at a 2-year/4-year college (0), employed in a professional position in a school system (1).

Additional Information:

Orientation, Objectives, and Emphasis of Department: Because of the barriers to learning and living in our society, there is an increasing need for professionally trained counseling and school psychology personnel. Our graduate programs are based on a developmental, experiential training model that includes understanding theory, learning assessment and intervention skills, practicing skills in a supervised clinical setting, and performing skills in vivo.

Integrated throughout our programs is a scientist-practitioner orientation that prepares students to ascertain the efficacy of assessment and intervention techniques.

Information for Students With Physical Disabilities: NAU provides comprehensive services to persons with disabilities. Please contact Disability Support Services, NAU, P.O. Box 5663, Flagstaff, AZ 86011, (520) 523-8773.

Application Information:

Send to: Graduate College, Box 4125, NAU, Flagstaff, AZ 86011; Educational Psychology, CEE 5774, NAU, Flagstaff, AZ 86011. Students are admitted in the Fall, application deadline September 15; Spring, application deadline February 15. Ed.D - Counseling Psychology and School Psychology - January 15. Ed.D.-Learning and Instruction - No deadline. Certification in School Psychology - February 15. M.A. Community Counseling, M.Ed. School Counseling & Student Affairs - Dates above for Fall and Spring apply. *Fee:* $45.

Arkansas, University of
Department of Psychology
J.William Fulbright College of Arts and Science
216 Memorial Hall
Fayetteville, AR 72701
Telephone: (501) 575-4256
Fax: (501) 575-3219
E-mail: *psycapp@comp.uark.edu*
Web: *http://www.uark.edu/depts/psyc*

Department Established:
1926. Chairperson: David A. Schroeder. Number of Faculty: total–full-time 17; women–full-time 3.

Programs and Degrees Offered:
Listed in the following order: Program area, degree type (T if terminal Master's), number awarded 7/00-6/01. Clinical PhD 8, experimental PhD 2.

APA Accreditation: Clinical PhD: full.

Student Applications/Admissions:
Student Applications
Clinical PhD—Applications 2001–2002, 150. Total applicants accepted 2001–2002, 6. New applicants enrolled 2001–2002, 6. Total enrolled 2001–2002 full-time, 22, part-time, 6. Openings 2002–2003, 8. The Median number of years required for completion of a degree are 5. *Experimental PhD*—Applications 2001–2002, 35. Total applicants accepted 2001–2002, 3. New applicants enrolled 2001–2002, 3. Total enrolled 2001–2002 full-time, 13. Openings 2002–2003, 4. The Median number of years required for completion of a degree are 5.

Admissions Requirements:
Scores: Entries appear in this order: required test or GPA, minimum score (if required), median score of students entering in 2001–2002. Doctoral Programs: GRE-V 500, 590; GRE-Q 500, 620; GRE-Analytical 500, 660; overall undergraduate GPA 3.0, 3.65; last 2 years GPA no minimum stated; psychology GPA no minimum stated; psychology GPA no minimum stated.
Other Criteria: (importance of criteria rated low, medium, or high): GRE/MAT scores high, research experience high, work experience low, extracurricular activity low, clinically related public service medium, GPA high, letters of recommendation high, interview medium, statement of goals and objectives high, faculty research match high. Clinically relevant service only considered for clinical applicants.

Student Characteristics: The following represents characteristics of students in 2001–2002 in all graduate psychology programs in the department: Female–full-time 23, part-time 4; Male–full-time 12, part-time 2; African American/Black–full-time 1, part-time 1; Hispanic/Latino (a)–full-time 2, part-time 0; Asian/Pacific Islander–full-time 0, part-time 0; American Indian/Alaska Native–full-time 0, part-time 0; Multi-ethnic–full-time 0, part-time 0; students subject to the Americans with Disabilities Act–full-time 0, part-time 0.

Financial Information/Assistance:
Tuition for Full-Time Study: *Master's:* State residents per academic year $1,777, $197 per credit hour; nonstate residents: per academic year $4,206, $467 per credit hour. *Doctoral:* State residents: per academic year $1,777, $197 per credit hour; nonstate residents: per academic year $4,206, $467 per credit hour.

Financial Assistance:
First Year Students: Teaching assistantships available for first-year. Average amount paid per academic year: $8,300. Average number of hours worked per week: 20. Apply by January 15. Tuition remission given: full. Research assistantships available for first-year. Average amount paid per academic year: $8,300. Average number of hours worked per week: 20. Apply by January 15. Tuition remission given: full.
Advanced Students: Teaching assistantships available for advanced students. Average amount paid per academic year: $8,300. Average number of hours worked per week: 20. Tuition remission given: full. Research assistantships available for advanced students. Average amount paid per academic year: $8,300. Average number of hours worked per week: 20. Tuition remission given: full.
Contact Information: Of all students currently enrolled full-time, 100% benefitted from one or more of the listed financial assistance programs. For information on financial assistance, contact: Admissions Secretary; all admitted students are immediately considered for financial aid. Significant financial support supplements may be available to qualified students from the Graduate School.

Internships/Practica: Doctoral students in the Clinical Training Program have always been able to obtain high-quality, APA-accredited predoctoral internships. Additionally, our students have numerous mental health agency placement opportunities throughout their tenure with us. These clerkship placements include local community mental health centers, the University Health Service, inpatient psychiatric hospitals, and several facilities dealing with disabilities, neuropsychology, and other clinical specialties. For those doctoral students for whom a professional internship is required prior to graduation, 6 applied in 2000–2001. Of those who applied, 6 were placed in internships listed by the Association of Psychology Postdoctoral and Internship Programs (APPIC); 6 were placed in APA accredited internships.

Housing and Day Care: No on-campus housing and day care facilities are available.

Employment of Department Graduates:
Master's Degree Graduates: Of those who graduated in the academic year 2000–2001, the following categories and numbers represent the post-graduate activities and employment of master's degree graduates: Enrolled in a post-doctoral residency/fellowship (n/a), employed in independent practice (n/a).
Doctoral Degree Graduates: Of those who graduated in the academic year 2000–2001, the following categories and numbers

represent the post-graduate activities and employment of doctoral degree graduates: Enrolled in a psychology doctoral program (n/a), enrolled in another graduate/professional program (n/a).

Additional Information:

Orientation, Objectives, and Emphasis of Department: The PhD program in clinical psychology follows the scientist-practitioner model of training. The academic courses and clinical experiences offered to students during their years of study are designed to promote the development of broad competencies. The objective of the clinical training program is to graduate clinical psychologists capable of applying psychological theory, research methodology, and clinical skills to complex clinical problems and diverse populations. The PhD program in experimental psychology provides students with a broad knowledge of psychology via a core curriculum, with a specialized training emphasis in our Social and Cognitive Processes focus area via research team meetings, colloquia, and advanced seminars. Training in social, developmental and cognitive psychology within the focus area includes independent research experience and extensive, supervised classroom teaching experience. The program provides students with a thorough understanding of psychological principles and prepares them for careers as academicians and researchers.

Special Facilities or Resources: The Department of Psychology is housed in Memorial Hall, a multilevel building with 58,000 square feet of office and research space for faculty and students. The building contains modern facilities for both human and small animal research, including specialized space for use with individuals and small groups of children and adults. The on-site Psychological Clinic is a state-of-the-art training and research facility dedicated to providing practicum and applied research experiences for clinical students. The Clinic's treatment, testing, and research rooms are equipped with a closed-circuit videotaping system. Memorial Hall has comprehensive data analysis facilities, including personal computers and interactive terminals linked to the University's mainframe computer. The Department also houses the Center for Research on Aggression and Violence (CRAV), staffed by clinical faculty and students and dedicated to basic and applied research on interpersonal conflict and violence. Finally, the Department is the beneficiary of a generous bequest that established the Marie Wilson Howells Fund, which provides funding for all students' thesis and dissertation research, numerous research assistantships, student travel, and departmental colloquia.

Application Information:
Send to: Admissions Secretary, Department of Psychology. Students are admitted in the Fall, application deadline January 15. Experimental Program will continue to consider applications received after January 15. *Fee:* U.S. applicants should apply directly to the Department of Psychology for most efficient consideration; application materials of students accepted by the Department for admission will be submitted to the Graduate School for processing. The Department will pay the Graduate School application fees for admitted students. EXCEPTION: International applicants must apply to the Graduate School and pay a $50 application fee.

Central Arkansas, University of
Department of Psychology and Counseling
Education
201 Donaghey
Conway, AR 72035-0001
Telephone: (501) 450-3193
Fax: (501) 450-5424
E-mail: *DavidS@mail.uca.edu*
Web: *http://www.coe.uca.edu*

Department Established:
1967. Chairperson: David Skotko. Number of Faculty: total–full-time 20, part-time 5; women–full-time 8, part-time 3.

Programs and Degrees Offered:
Listed in the following order: Program area, degree type (T if terminal Master's), number awarded 7/00-6/01. Counseling Psychology MA, School Psychology PhD, School Psychology MA.

Student Applications/Admissions:
Student Applications

Counseling Psychology MA—Total applicants accepted 2001–2002, 18. New applicants enrolled 2001–2002, 18. The Median number of years required for completion of a degree are 2. The number of students enrolled full and part-time, who were dismissed or voluntarily withdrew from this program area were 1. *School Psychology PhD*—Total applicants accepted 2001–2002, 5. New applicants enrolled 2001–2002, 5. The number of students enrolled full and part-time, who were dismissed or voluntarily withdrew from this program area were 0. *School Psychology MA*—Total applicants accepted 2001–2002, 7. New applicants enrolled 2001–2002, 7. The Median number of years required for completion of a degree are 2. The number of students enrolled full and part-time, who were dismissed or voluntarily withdrew from this program area were 0.

Admissions Requirements:
Scores: Entries appear in this order: required test or GPA, minimum score (if required), median score of students entering in 2001–2002. Master's Programs: GRE-V 380, 475; GRE-Q 360, 450; GRE-V+Q 780, 940; overall undergraduate GPA 2.75, 3.4; last 2 years GPA no minimum stated; psychology GPA no minimum stated. Doctoral Programs: GRE-V 430, 500; GRE-Q 420, 500; overall undergraduate GPA 3.25, 3.50; last 2 years GPA no minimum stated; psychology GPA no minimum stated; psychology GPA no minimum stated.
Other Criteria: (importance of criteria rated low, medium, or high): GRE/MAT scores medium, research experience medium, work experience medium, extracurricular activity medium, clinically related public service medium, GPA high, letters of recommendation medium, interview high, statement of goals and objectives medium.

Student Characteristics: The following represents characteristics of students in 2001–2002 in all graduate psychology programs in the department: Female–full-time 24, part-time 0; Male–full-time 5, part-time 0; African American/Black–full-time 4, part-time 0; Hispanic/Latino (a)–full-time 1, part-time 0; Asian/Pacific Islander–full-time 2, part-time 0; American Indian/Alaska Native–

full-time 1, part-time 0; students subject to the Americans with Disabilities Act–full-time 1.

Financial Information/Assistance:

Tuition for Full-Time Study: *Master's:* State residents $183 per credit hour; nonstate residents: $329 per credit hour. *Doctoral:* State residents: $183 per credit hour; nonstate residents: $329 per credit hour.

Financial Assistance:

First Year Students: Teaching assistantships available for first-year. Average amount paid per academic year: $5,700. Average number of hours worked per week: 20. Research assistantships available for first-year. Average number of hours worked per week: 20.

Advanced Students: Teaching assistantships available for advanced students. Average number of hours worked per week: 20. Research assistantships available for advanced students. Average amount paid per academic year: $8,000. Average number of hours worked per week: 20.

Contact Information: Of all students currently enrolled full-time, 0% benefitted from one or more of the listed financial assistance programs. For information on financial assistance, contact: Graduate School, University of Central Arkansas, 201 Donaghey, Conway AR 72035.

Internships/Practica: Students are placed in a wide-range of practica and internships depending on their program of study and career aspirations. Examples of placements include schools, community agencies, hospitals, and clinics.

Housing and Day Care: On-campus housing and day care facilities are available.

Employment of Department Graduates:

Master's Degree Graduates: Of those who graduated in the academic year 2000–2001, the following categories and numbers represent the post-graduate activities and employment of master's degree graduates: Enrolled in a psychology doctoral program (5), enrolled in a post-doctoral residency/fellowship (n/a), employed in independent practice (n/a), employed in other positions at a higher education institution (1), employed in a professional position in a school system (8), employed in a community mental health/counseling center (12), employed in a hospital/medical center (1), other employment position (3).

Doctoral Degree Graduates: Of those who graduated in the academic year 2000–2001, the following categories and numbers represent the post-graduate activities and employment of doctoral degree graduates: Enrolled in a psychology doctoral program (n/a), enrolled in another graduate/professional program (n/a).

Additional Information:

Orientation, Objectives, and Emphasis of Department: The M.S. degree in Counseling Psychology and School Psychology is designed so that it may serve either as terminal degree with professional employment opportunities or as a firm foundation for prospective doctoral candidates. Broad training is offered in understanding of psychological theories, assessment, and mental health interventions to enable graduates to function successfully in a variety of mental health and educational settings. The Ph.D. in School Psychology is grounded in the scientist-practitioner model of training. Strong emphasis is placed on child mental health promotion, primary prevention, and intervention with a broad range of community related problems involving children, families, and schools. The program is responsive to on-going societal concerns facing children. It prepares its graduates to function in schools, clinics, community agencies, and hospitals.

Application Information:

Send to: Dept. Chair, Box 4915, UCA, Conway, AR 72035. Students are admitted in the Fall, application deadline 3/15; 7/15; Summer, application deadline 3/15. *Fee:* $65.

Alliant International University
PhD and PsyD Clinical Psychology
California School of Professional Psychology-Fresno Campus
5130 East Clinton Way
Fresno, CA 93727
Telephone: (559) 456-2777
Fax: (559) 253-2267
E-mail: *admissions@alliant.edu*
Web: *http://www.alliant.edu*

Department Established:
1973. Dean: Adele Rabin, Ph.D. (arabin@alliant.edu). Number of Faculty: total–full-time 15, part-time 28; women–full-time 5, part-time 12; minority–full-time 3, part-time 3.

Programs and Degrees Offered:
Listed in the following order: Program area, degree type (T if terminal Master's), number awarded 7/00-6/01. Clinical PhD 63.

APA Accreditation: Clinical PhD: full. Clinical PsyD: full.

Student Applications/Admissions:
Student Applications

Clinical PhD—Applications 2001–2002, 49. Total applicants accepted 2001–2002, 18. New applicants enrolled 2001–2002, 12. Total enrolled 2001–2002 full-time, 183, part-time, 31. Openings 2002–2003, 20. The Median number of years required for completion of a degree are 5.

Admissions Requirements:

Scores: Entries appear in this order: required test or GPA, minimum score (if required), median score of students entering in 2001–2002. Master's Programs: overall undergraduate GPA 3.0. Doctoral Programs: overall undergraduate GPA 3.00; last 2 years GPA no minimum stated; psychology GPA 3.00; psychology GPA no minimum stated.

Other Criteria: (importance of criteria rated low, medium, or high): GRE/MAT scores, research experience medium, work experience medium, extracurricular activity low, clinically related public service medium, GPA high, letters of recommendation high, interview high, statement of goals and objectives high, essay high. Research experience is more critical for the Ph.D. program.

Student Characteristics: The following represents characteristics of students in 2001–2002 in all graduate psychology programs in the department: Female–full-time 132, part-time 21; Male–full-time 51, part-time 10; African American/Black–full-time 7, part-time 0; Hispanic/Latino (a)–full-time 19, part-time 2; Asian/Pacific Islander–full-time 5, part-time 1; American Indian/Alaska Native–full-time 5, part-time 1; Multi-ethnic–full-time 0, part-time 0.

Financial Information/Assistance:
Tuition for Full-Time Study: *Doctoral:* State residents: $630 per credit hour; nonstate residents: $630 per credit hour.

Financial Assistance:
First Year Students: Teaching assistantships available for first-year. Average number of hours worked per week: 10. Research assistantships available for first-year. Average number of hours worked per week: 10.

Advanced Students: Teaching assistantships available for advanced students. Average number of hours worked per week: 10. Research assistantships available for advanced students. Average number of hours worked per week: 10.

Contact Information: Of all students currently enrolled full-time, 20% benefitted from one or more of the listed financial assistance programs. For information on financial assistance, contact: Jeannie Lewis, Director of Financial Aid (559) 456-2777, ext. 2208.

Internships/Practica: CSPP at AIU Fresno emphasizes the integration of academic coursework with clinical practice. In order to integrate appropriate skills with material learned in the classroom, students participate in a professional training placement experience beginning the first year for clinical PsyD students, and in the second year for clinical PhD students. The settings where students complete the professional training requirements include community mental health center, clinics, inpatient mental health facilities, medical settings, specialized service centers, rehabilitation programs, residential/day care programs, forensic/correctional facilities, and educational programs. Third year clinical PsyD and PhD students will spend fifteen hours per week in a practicum either at CSPP's Psychological Service Center or at some other CSPP-approved agency. During their final year, clinical students complete a full year internship (2080 hours) at an appropriate APA or Association of Psychology Postdoctoral and Internship Programs (APPIC) internship. CSPP also has formed the Central California Psychology Internship Consortium for students working to complete their internship in the region. For those doctoral students for whom a professional internship is required prior to graduation, 35 applied in 2000–2001. Of those who applied, 7 were placed in internships listed by the APPIC; 22 were placed in APA accredited internships.

Housing and Day Care: No on-campus housing and day care facilities are available.

Employment of Department Graduates:
Master's Degree Graduates: Of those who graduated in the academic year 2000–2001, the following categories and numbers represent the post-graduate activities and employment of master's degree graduates: Enrolled in a post-doctoral residency/fellowship (n/a), employed in independent practice (n/a).

Doctoral Degree Graduates: Of those who graduated in the academic year 2000–2001, the following categories and numbers represent the post-graduate activities and employment of doctoral degree graduates: Enrolled in a psychology doctoral program (n/a), enrolled in another graduate/professional program (n/a).

Additional Information:
Orientation, Objectives, and Emphasis of Department: The PsyD program emphasizes training in clinical skills and clinical application of research knowledge. The program is designed for

students who are interested in careers as practitioners. It includes a research component but with a lesser emphasis than the PhD program. The PhD program is designed for students who anticipate that teaching and/or the conduct of research will be significant components of their professional careers. Students work with faculty research mentors throughout the program. Clinical coursework is less heavily emphasized than in the PsyD program. CSPP at AIU Fresno offers proficiency areas: (1) Ecosystemic Clinical Child trains students to work with infants, children, and adolescents, as well as with the adults in these clients' lives using the contextual frame of their familial, peer, educational, medical, legal, cultural, and historical systems. (2) Cross-Cultural Psychology is designed to prepare students for professional practice in a pluralistic society in a variety of settings. The goal is to produce a clinical psychologist who is culturally competent. (3) Clinical neuropsychology is designed to prepare students for work in the highly technical field of neuropsychology. (4) Health Psychology, within the context of the clinical psychology program, provides students with exposure to the expanding field of health psychology and behavioral medicine. (5) Depth Psychology provides students the opportunity to study in-depth psychodynamic psychology. (6) Forensic clinical psychology provides students with necessary knowledge to adapt skills to the forensic environment.

Special Facilities or Resources: CSPP at AIU Fresno relocated our campus to a new facility in June 1996. The new facility has nine classrooms, including a neuropsychology classroom, office space for faculty and staff, and a large auditorium. The building is equipped with an updated phone system, giving voice mail access to staff and faculty. The building has a state-of-the-art network cabling system for voice and data lines with fiber optics installed for future expansion into new technologies or distance learning programs. The Psychological Service Center serves the dual purpose of offering high quality psychological services to the community, particularly underserved segments, and continuing the tradition of education, training, and service. The facility consists of eight therapy and two play therapy rooms, large conference room, student work room, TV/monitor, and staff offices. Services of the library are carefully planned to meet the special curricular and research needs of all academic programs. It houses over 15,000 printed volumes and has over 255 current journal subscriptions, and approximately 300 volume units of microfilm and fiche. The library houses the psychological test materials center with over 1000 testing resources for curriculum, research, and clinical use by students and faculty. Computerized searches using more than 500 databases are available through the library including network CD-ROM-databases, Internet Web browsing, and Online Public Access Computer. In 1999, a video conference facility was added.

Information for Students With Physical Disabilities: CSPP recognizes its responsibility under Title III of the Americans with Disabilities Act to provide appropriate and effective academic accommodation. CSPP's goal is non-discrimination on the basis of disability. CSPP is committed to providing equal access to its academic programs, educational or other services and facilities by students with disabilities as well as able-bodied individuals in compliance with the Americans with Disabilities Act (ADA) Section 504.

Application Information:
Send to: Alliant International University Admissions 2728 Hyde Street, Suite 100, San Francisco, CA 94109. Students are admitted in the Fall, application deadline January 2; Spring, application deadline November 15. Applicants completing all paperwork and meeting the January 2nd deadline for Ph.D. and Psy.D. Clinical Programs will be notified by April 1st. Applications may be, considered on a space-available basis following this date. *Fee:* $65. A limited number of application fee waivers are available to students with demonstrated need. Unfortunately, all fee waivers requested cannot be granted; they will be granted only to on-time applicants with the greatest financial need. A fee waiver request must be submitted in writing, with an explanation of current financial circumstances and prior Federal Income Tax Form 1040 enclosed with the Admissions application. If both the written statement of fee waiver request and documentation are not submitted, the fee waiver will not be considered.

Alliant International University, San Diego

Clinical Psy.D.
California School of Professional Psychology
10455 Pomerado Road, Daley Hall
San Diego, CA 92131
Telephone: (858) 635-4542
Fax: (858) 635-4585
E-mail: *admissions@cspp.edu*
Web: *http://www.cspp.edu*

Department Established:
1972. Dean: Adele Rabin. Number of Faculty: total–full-time 29, part-time 60; women–full-time 12, part-time 28; minority–full-time 17, part-time 32.

Programs and Degrees Offered:
Listed in the following order: Program area, degree type (T if terminal Master's), number awarded 7/00-6/01. Clinical and I/O PhD 1, Clinical PhD 36, Clinical Psychology PsyD 32, culture and human behavior PsyD, health psychology PhD 4, industrial/organizational PhD 8, organizational MA (T) 9, organizational development PsyD, psychophys/biofeed MA (T) 9.

APA Accreditation: Clinical PhD: full. Clinical PsyD: full.

Student Applications/Admissions:
Student Applications
Clinical and I/O PhD—Applications 2001–2002, 9. Total applicants accepted 2001–2002, 9. New applicants enrolled 2001–2002, 4. Total enrolled 2001–2002 full-time, 33. Openings 2002–2003, 10. *Clinical PhD*—Applications 2001–2002, 114. Total applicants accepted 2001–2002, 54. New applicants enrolled 2001–2002, 32. Total enrolled 2001–2002 full-time, 251. Openings 2002–2003, 30. *Clinical Psychology PsyD*—Applications 2001–2002, 148. Total applicants accepted 2001–2002, 84. New applicants enrolled 2001–2002, 29. Total enrolled 2001–2002 full-time, 125, part-time, 54. Openings 2002–2003, 36. The Median number of years required for completion of a degree are 5. The number of students enrolled full and part-time, who were dismissed or voluntarily withdrew from this program area were 7. *Culture and human behavior PsyD*—Applications 2001–2002, 23. Total applicants accepted 2001–2002, 20. New applicants enrolled 2001–2002, 10. Total enrolled 2001–2002 full-time, 21. Openings 2002–2003, 10. *Health psychology PhD*—Applications 2001–2002, 40. Total

applicants accepted 2001–2002, 32. New applicants enrolled 2001–2002, 23. Total enrolled 2001–2002 full-time, 53. Openings 2002–2003, 15. *Industrial/organizational PhD*—Applications 2001–2002, 29. Total applicants accepted 2001–2002, 15. New applicants enrolled 2001–2002, 13. Total enrolled 2001–2002 full-time, 61. Openings 2002–2003, 15. *Organizational MA*—Applications 2001–2002, 17. Total applicants accepted 2001–2002, 11. New applicants enrolled 2001–2002, 5. Total enrolled 2001–2002 full-time, 9. Openings 2002–2003, 15. *Organizational development PsyD*—Applications 2001–2002, 4. Total applicants accepted 2001–2002, 1. New applicants enrolled 2001–2002, 2. Total enrolled 2001–2002 full-time, 5. Openings 2002–2003, 5. *Psychophys/biofeed MA*—Applications 2001–2002, 13. Total applicants accepted 2001–2002, 11. New applicants enrolled 2001–2002, 9. Total enrolled 2001–2002 full-time, 9. Openings 2002–2003, 15.

Admissions Requirements:

Scores: Entries appear in this order: required test or GPA, minimum score (if required), median score of students entering in 2001–2002. Master's Programs: overall undergraduate GPA 3.00, 3.40. Graduate GPA's over 3.5 and GRE scores over 600 will be considered in admission determinations, as well as quality of undergraduate institution. Doctoral Programs: overall undergraduate GPA 3.00, 3.40; last 2 years GPA no minimum stated; psychology GPA no minimum stated; psychology GPA no minimum stated.

Other Criteria: (importance of criteria rated low, medium, or high): GRE/MAT scores low, research experience medium, work experience medium, clinically related public service medium, GPA high, letters of recommendation medium, interview high, statement of goals and objectives high, Graduate work high.

Student Characteristics: The following represents characteristics of students in 2001–2002 in all graduate psychology programs in the department: Female–full-time 96, part-time 11; Male–full-time 28, part-time 11; African American/Black–full-time 6, part-time 0; Hispanic/Latino (a)–full-time 5, part-time 0; Asian/Pacific Islander–full-time 12, part-time 0; American Indian/Alaska Native–full-time 1, part-time 0.

Financial Information/Assistance:

Tuition for Full-Time Study: *Doctoral:* State residents: $630 per credit hour; nonstate residents: $630 per credit hour.

Financial Assistance:

First Year Students: Research assistantships available for first-year. Average number of hours worked per week: 12. Fellowships and scholarships available for first-year.

Advanced Students: Teaching assistantships available for advanced students. Average amount paid per academic year: $600. Average amount paid per academic year: $1,500. Traineeships available for advanced students. Fellowships and scholarships available for advanced students.

Contact Information: Of all students currently enrolled full-time, 40% benefitted from one or more of the listed financial assistance programs. For information on financial assistance, contact: Financial Aid Department, Richard Comstock, Financial Aid Counselor.

Internships/Practica: Clinical doctoral students receive practicum and internship experience at more than 80 agencies which meet the requirements for licensure set by the California Board of Psychology. Assignments to these agencies result from an application process conducted by year level, with third, fourth, and fifth year students receiving priority for licensable placements. The option of doing an APA-accredited full-time internship in the fourth or fifth years (depending on the program and year level requirements) is also available and encouraged. Of the current 380 training positions available in San Diego, approximately 90 of them are paid. Organizational Psychology doctoral students are also required to participate in internships within various organizations in the San Diego area. Third and fourth year students receive a total of four units per semester (for a total of four semesters) in field placement. For those doctoral students for whom a professional internship is required prior to graduation, 33 applied in 2000–2001. Of those who applied, 3 were placed in internships listed by the Association of Psychology Postdoctoral and Internship Programs (APPIC); 4 were placed in APA accredited internships.

Housing and Day Care: No on-campus housing and day care facilities are available.

Employment of Department Graduates:

Master's Degree Graduates: Of those who graduated in the academic year 2000–2001, the following categories and numbers represent the post-graduate activities and employment of master's degree graduates: Enrolled in a post-doctoral residency/fellowship (n/a), employed in independent practice (n/a).

Doctoral Degree Graduates: Of those who graduated in the academic year 2000–2001, the following categories and numbers represent the post-graduate activities and employment of doctoral degree graduates: Enrolled in a psychology doctoral program (n/a), enrolled in another graduate/professional program (n/a), employed in independent practice (50), employed in an academic position at a university (1), employed in an academic position at a 2-year/4-year college (1), employed in a professional position in a school system (4), employed in a community mental health/counseling center (45), employed in a hospital/medical center (17).

Additional Information:

Orientation, Objectives, and Emphasis of Department: The California School of Professional Psychology (CSPP) at Alliant International University offers a comprehensive program of instruction in professional psychology with an emphasis on doctoral training in clinical, organizational, and health psychology in which academic requirements are integrated with supervised field experience. Students are evaluated by instructors and field supervisors on the basis of their performance and participation throughout the year. Evaluations are used for planning the student's program, for advising on career choices, and for determining qualifications for a higher degree level. Theory, personal growth, professional skill, humanities, investigatory skills, and field experience are combined in a semester program of instruction designed to stimulate the graduate toward a scholarly as well as a professional contribution to society. Elective areas of emphasis in health psychology, family and child psychology, psychoanalytic psychotherapy, and gender and human sexualities are available within the clinical programs.

Special Facilities or Resources: The Center for Applied Behavioral Services (CABS) is a multi-service and training center. The center incorporates the expertise of CSPP faculty in the delivery of direct services and in modeling specific techniques of treatment and service for practicum and interns. This is currently accomplished through an array of clinical and community services which are directed by faculty members. Clinics and services currently directed by CSPP faculty include: general psychological service, psychoeducational services, stress management, women's issues, hard of hearing/late deafened services, the Border Project, child and family services, treatment of children who are autistic, and continuing education. Each of these service components provides specialized opportunities for students to participate in some form of training experience with appropriate supervision.

Information for Students With Physical Disabilities: CSPP San Diego complies with all current ADA requirements for students with physical and learning challenges. Our physical facilities easily accommodate those with physical disabilities with a combination of ramps and elevators, widened doorways, and appropriate parking and restroom facilities. A range of other accommodations are made as individual physical or learning circumstances dictate, including provision of readers and note takers, extended time for or other alternative testing, computer support, and special mentoring assistance. We also have an active program for students with hearing loss through our Rehabilitation Research and Training Center for persons who are late deafened or hard of hearing.

Application Information:
Send to: CSPP, Systemwide Admissions Office, 2749 Hyde St., San Francisco, CA 94109. Students are admitted in the Fall; Winter, application deadline October 15. Deadlines vary by program. Clinical PsyD and PhD - December 1, Forensic PsyD and PhD - January 3, Culture Human Behavior PsyD - February 1. Health PhD - February 1, Dual Health/Clinical PhD - February 1, Psychophysiology and Biofeedback - April 1, Dual Clinical I/O - February 1. Students applying to more than one CSPP campus must submit application by December 1. Organizational and consulting PsyD and PhD due February 1. Dual Clinical I/O due February 1, MAOB and OPMA due April 1. *Fee:* $65. Fees vary by program. Fee waived if sufficient financial need demonstrated.

Antioch University, Santa Barbara (2001 data)
Graduate Psychology Program
801 Garden Street
Santa Barbara, CA 93101
Telephone: (805) 962-8179
Fax: (805) 962-4786
E-mail: *admissions@antiochsb.edu*
Web: *http://www.antiochsb.edu*

Department Established:
1977. Chairperson: Catherine Radecki-Bush, Ph.D. Number of Faculty: total–full-time 4, part-time 35; women–full-time 3, part-time 20.

Programs and Degrees Offered:
Listed in the following order: Program area, degree type (T if terminal Master's), number awarded 7/00-6/01. Clinical MA (T) 38, individualized concentration MA (T) 2, organizational psychology MA (T) 2, professional develop and caree MA (T).

Student Applications/Admissions:
Student Applications
   Clinical MA—Applications 2001–2002, 57. Total applicants accepted 2001–2002, 48. New applicants enrolled 2001–2002, 45. Total enrolled 2001–2002 full-time, 63, part-time, 20. Openings 2002–2003, 60. *Individualized concentration MA*— Applications 2001–2002, 7. Total applicants accepted 2001–2002, 5. New applicants enrolled 2001–2002, 4. Total enrolled 2001–2002 full-time, 6, part-time, 6. Openings 2002–2003, 10. *Organizational psychology MA*—Applications 2001–2002, 6. Total applicants accepted 2001–2002, 4. New applicants enrolled 2001–2002, 4. Total enrolled 2001–2002 full-time, 4, part-time, 2. Openings 2002–2003, 10. *Professional develop and caree MA*—Applications 2001–2002, 7. Total applicants accepted 2001–2002, 6. New applicants enrolled 2001–2002, 6. Total enrolled 2001–2002 full-time, 8, part-time, 2. Openings 2002–2003, 20.

Admissions Requirements:
   Scores: Entries appear in this order: required test or GPA, minimum score (if required), median score of students entering in 2001–2002. Master's Programs: overall undergraduate GPA no minimum stated, 3.0; last 2 years GPA no minimum stated, 3.0; psychology GPA no minimum stated, 3.0.
   Other Criteria: (importance of criteria rated low, medium, or high): GRE/MAT scores work experience high, extracurricular activity high, clinically related public service high, GPA high, letters of recommendation medium, interview high, statement of goals and objectives medium, goals in individualized high.

Student Characteristics: The following represents characteristics of students in 2001–2002 in all graduate psychology programs in the department: Female–full-time 36, part-time 8; Male–full-time 14, part-time 5; African American/Black–full-time 4, part-time 2; Hispanic/Latino (a)–full-time 4, part-time 1; Asian/Pacific Islander–full-time 3, part-time 0; American Indian/Alaska Native–full-time 1, part-time 0.

Financial Information/Assistance:
Tuition for Full-Time Study: No information provided.

Financial Assistance:
   First Year Students: No information provided.
   Advanced Students: No information provided.
   Contact Information: Of all students currently enrolled full-time, 0% benefitted from one or more of the listed financial assistance programs. For information on financial assistance, contact: Financial Aid office.

Internships/Practica: Traineeships are available in community agencies, schools, and clinics, in Santa Barbara, San Luis Obispo, and Ventura Counties. Students may find placements working with children, adolescents, and seniors; with clients in recovery from chemical dependency; with survivors of sexual abuse, domestic violence, and child abuse; with mental health clients; with court-referred clients; and with adults, couples, and families.

Housing and Day Care: No on-campus housing and day care facilities are available.

Employment of Department Graduates:

Master's Degree Graduates: Of those who graduated in the academic year 2000–2001, the following categories and numbers represent the post-graduate activities and employment of master's degree graduates: Enrolled in a post-doctoral residency/fellowship (n/a), employed in independent practice (n/a).

Doctoral Degree Graduates: Of those who graduated in the academic year 2000–2001, the following categories and numbers represent the post-graduate activities and employment of doctoral degree graduates: Enrolled in a psychology doctoral program (n/a), enrolled in another graduate/professional program (n/a).

Additional Information:

Orientation, Objectives, and Emphasis of Department: The MA Clinical Psychology program is committed to the education and training of students to develop: 1) critical thinking and reflective learning in the acquisition of psychological knowledge; 2) basic skills in clinical psychology required to become ethical, professional therapists; 3) self-awareness, particularly as it pertains to professional clinical practice; 4) awareness of self as an integral part of families, the mental health community, and local communities; 5) understanding of diversity, including culture, ethnicity, gender, sexual orientation, age, and theoretical orientation. The MA Psychology-Individualized Concentration allows students to define and develop expertise in a particular area of interest. Past students have completed concentrations in Human Development, Feminist Psychology, and Interpersonal Relationships. For some areas of concentration, such as Organizational Psychology and Professional Development and Career Counseling, a core curriculum has been developed. This nonclinical degree program is for students interested in pursuing professional careers in consulting, education, program development, business and government, as well as for students interested in applying to doctoral degree programs.

Special Facilities or Resources: Faculty are all practicing professionals in their respective areas of expertise.

Information for Students With Physical Disabilities: The office of the Dean of Academic Affairs assists students with disabilities by providing accommodations as dictated by the students' disability and the course content.

Application Information:

Send to: Admissions Office, Antioch University Santa Barbara, 801 Garden Street, Santa Barbara, CA 93101. Students are admitted in the Fall, application deadline August 17; Winter, application deadline November 16; Spring, application deadline February 15. Spring admission for non-clinical programs only. Professional Development and Career Counseling Program, Organizational Psychology, and Individualized Concentrations. Transfer students may apply for any quarter. Admissions to Professional Development and Career Counseling Program is Winter and Spring only. *Fee:* $60.

Argosy University

Psychology
School of Psychology and Behavioral Sciences
3745 W. Chapman Avenue Suite100
Orange, CA 92868 USA
Telephone: (714) 940-0025
Fax: (714) 940-0630
E-mail: *jbuechner@argosyu.edu*
Web: *http://www.argosyu.edu*

Department Established:

2001. Dean: Marc Lubin, Ph.D. Number of Faculty: total–full-time 3, part-time 5; women–full-time 1, part-time 1; faculty subject to the Americans with Disabilities Act 1.

Programs and Degrees Offered:

Listed in the following order: Program area, degree type (T if terminal Master's), number awarded 7/00-6/01. Counseling Psychology EdD, Counseling Psychology MA (T), PsyD.

Student Applications/Admissions:

Student Applications

Counseling Psychology EdD—Applications 2001–2002, 70. Total applicants accepted 2001–2002, 44. New applicants enrolled 2001–2002, 44. Total enrolled 2001–2002 full-time, 33, part-time, 11. Openings 2002–2003, 50. The Median number of years required for completion of a degree are 0. The number of students enrolled full and part-time, who were dismissed or voluntarily withdrew from this program area were 2. *Counseling Psychology MA*—Applications 2001–2002, 17. Total applicants accepted 2001–2002, 11. New applicants enrolled 2001–2002, 11. Total enrolled 2001–2002 full-time, 11. Openings 2002–2003, 30. The Median number of years required for completion of a degree are 0. The number of students enrolled full and part-time, who were dismissed or voluntarily withdrew from this program area were 0. *PsyD*—Applications 2001–2002, 38. Total applicants accepted 2001–2002, 11. New applicants enrolled 2001–2002, 11. Total enrolled 2001–2002 full-time, 11. Openings 2002–2003, 50. The Median number of years required for completion of a degree are 0. The number of students enrolled full and part-time, who were dismissed or voluntarily withdrew from this program area were 0.

Admissions Requirements:

Scores: Entries appear in this order: required test or GPA, minimum score (if required), median score of students entering in 2001–2002. Master's Programs: overall undergraduate GPA 3.0. Doctoral Programs: overall undergraduate GPA 3.00; last 2 years GPA no minimum stated; psychology GPA no minimum stated; psychology GPA 3.00. Psy.D. program requires a minimum GPA of 3.25.

Other Criteria: (importance of criteria rated low, medium, or high): GRE/MAT scores medium, research experience medium, work experience medium, extracurricular activity low, clinically related public service medium, GPA medium, letters of recommendation medium, interview medium, statement of goals and objectives medium.

Student Characteristics: The following represents characteristics of students in 2001–2002 in all graduate psychology programs in

2002 STUDENT AFFILIATE APPLICATION & JOURNAL ORDER FORM

Student Applicant Information

☎ Please provide the information requested and mark any journals to which you wish to subscribe. Return your competed application and journal order form, with payment, to the **American Psychological Association, 750 First Street, NE, Washington, DC 20002-4242, USA**. Applications accompanied by credit card payments may be faxed to **202-336-5568**. For questions regarding the *Student Affiliate Application*, please call **202-336-5580**, **800-374-2721**, E-mail: **membership@apa.org**, or TDD/TTY **202-336-6123**. Payment may be made by credit card, check, or money order (in U.S. dollars drawn on a U.S. bank) made payable to the *American Psychological Association*.

Application will not be processed without payment.

Please print clearly or type.

Name:

_____
First   Middle   Last

_____
Home Street Address

_____
City/State/ZIP Code

_____
Telephone (Area Code)

_____
Fax (Area Code)

_____
E-mail Address

_____
Name of School

Your affiliation with APA is considered part of the public record. Listings of your affiliation may be produced at any time. If you DO NOT wish to have any contact information released or made public, please check here. ☐

Have you at any time been convicted of a felony, sanctioned by any professional ethics body, licensing board, other regulatory body, or any professional scientific organization?

☐ Yes   ☐ No (If yes, please provide an explanation on a separate sheet.)

In making this application, I subscribe to and will support the objectives of the American Psychological Association as set forth in Article 1 of the Bylaws and the Ethical Principles of Psychologists and Code of Conduct, as adopted by the Association, and I affirm that the statements made in this application correctly represent my qualifications and understand that if they do not, my affiliation may be voided. The Ethical Principles of Psychologists and Code of Conduct is available at www.apa.org/ethics. The Bylaws are available at www.apa.org/governance. Copies of these documents are available to me upon request.

_____
Applicant's Signature   Date

Student Status

Please provide us with the following information so that we may better serve you:
☐ Female   ☐ Male

Please mark ONE alternative that best describes your status for the 2002 academic year.
☐ Undergraduate   ☐ Graduate Student   ☐ Intern   ☐ Post doctorate

What degree are you expecting to attain? (Mark only ONE for highest degree for which you are currently enrolled.)
☐ B.A./B.S. or other undergraduate degree
☐ M.A. (terminal – not part of work toward a doctoral degree)
☐ M.S. (terminal – not part of work toward a doctoral degree)
☐ M.Ed.
☐ Education Specialist
☐ School Specialist
☐ Ph.D.
☐ Psy.D.
☐ Ed.D.
☐ Other (please specify)_____

Major Field Code: [   ]
(See Major Field Code List on separate panel in this brochure)

I expect to receive my degree (or have received my degree) in 20____.

If you are currently a master's level student or in a terminal master's program, do you intend to pursue a doctorate?
☐ Yes   ☐ No

Answer only if the graduate degree for which you are currently enrolled is a health-service provider subfield (e.g., clinical, counseling, school, etc.). Do you intend to seek licensure/certification by a state/provincial board of psychological examiners?

☐ No, it is not necessary for my work in psychology
☐ Yes, within the next year
☐ Yes, eventually
☐ N/A, already licensed/certified in psychology

Please complete the following voluntary information.

Date of birth: ____/____/____
              MM DD YY

What is your ethnic heritage? (Mark all that apply.)
☐ American Indian or Alaskan Native
☐ Asian, Asian American, or Pacific Islander
☐ African American/Black
☐ Hispanic/Latino
☐ Caucasian/White
☐ Other
(Specify):_____

FOR OFFICE USE ONLY

[   ]

Journal Order/Fee Payment

American Psychological Asszociation Publications

Please Check	2002 Subscriptions	U.S. Domestic	Int'l Surface	Amount $
☐ ABN	Journal of Abnormal Psychology	$33.00	$43.00	_____
☐ APL	Journal of Applied Psychology	$47.00	$59.00	_____
☐ BNE	Behavioral Neuroscience	$62.00	$74.00	_____
☐ CRD	Clinician's Research Digest	$27.00	$45.00	_____
☐ COM	Journal of Comparative Psychology	$19.00	$29.00	_____
☐ CCP	Journal of Consulting and Clinical Psychology	$57.00	$69.00	_____
☐ CNT	Contemporary Psychology	$39.00	$51.00	_____
☐ COU	Journal of Counseling Psychology	$23.00	$33.00	_____
☐ DEV	Developmental Psychology	$54.00	$66.00	_____
☐ EDU	Journal of Educational Psychology	$37.00	$47.00	_____
☐ EMO	Emotion	$22.00	$32.00	_____
☐ PHA	Experimental and Clinical Psychopharmacology	$29.00	$39.00	_____
☐ FAM	Journal of Family Psychology	$29.00	$39.00	_____
☐ HEA	Health Psychology	$28.00	$40.00	_____

Journals of Experimental Psychology (JEP)

Please Check		U.S. Domestic	Int'l Surface	Amount $
☐ XAN	JEP: Animal Behavior Processes	$23.00	$33.00	_____
☐ XAP	JEP: Applied	$19.00	$29.00	_____
☐ XGE	JEP: General	$19.00	$29.00	_____
☐ XHP	JEP: Human Perception and Performance	$75.00	$87.00	_____
☐ XLM	JEP: Learning, Memory, and Cognition	$75.00	$87.00	_____
☐ NEU	Neuropsychology	$29.00	$39.00	_____
☐ PSP	Journal of Personality and Social Psychology	$105.00	$123.00	_____
☐ PRO	Professional Psychology: Research and Practice	$29.00	$41.00	_____
☐ PAS	Psychological Assessment	$29.00	$39.00	_____
☐ BUL	Psychological Bulletin	$47.00	$59.00	_____
☐ MET	Psychological Methods	$19.00	$29.00	_____
☐ REV	Psychological Review	$35.00	$45.00	_____
☐ PAG	Psychology and Aging	$33.00	$43.00	_____
☐ LAW	Psychology, Public Policy, and Law	$19.00	$29.00	_____
☐ ABS	Psychological Abstracts (issues and indexes)	$815.00	$893.00	_____
☐ PSN	Neuropsychology Abstracts*	$40.00	$50.00	_____
☐ PSY	Pyschoanalytic Abstracts*	$40.00	$50.00	_____
☐ PSA	PsycSCAN: Applied Psychology*	$30.00	$40.00	_____
☐ PSB	PsycSCAN: Behavior Analysis & Therapy*	$30.00	$40.00	_____
☐ PSC	PsycSCAN: Clinical Psychology*	$30.00	$40.00	_____
☐ PSD	PsycSCAN: Developmental Psychology*	$30.00	$40.00	_____
☐ PSL	PsycSCAN: LD/MR*	$30.00	$40.00	_____

*Includes access to online database.

1. APA Subscriptions
(DC residents add 5.75% sales tax; MD residents add 5% sales tax) $_____

2. Less $10 Journal Credit
(Journal Credit applies to APA Publications only; not applicable to EPF Publications, Online Databases, or Student Affiliate fee payment) $ 10.00

3. Subtotal APA Subscriptions
(subtract line 2 from line 1) $_____

Educational Publishing Foundation (EPF) Publications
(Note: The $10 Journal credit is not applicable to EPF orders.)

Please Check	2002 Subscriptions	U.S. Domestic	Int'l Surface	Amount $
☐ ADB	Psychology of Addictive Behaviors	$56.00	$66.00	_____
☐ CPB	Consulting Psychology Journal	$33.00	$43.00	_____
☐ CDP	Cultural Diversity and Ethnic Minority Psychology	$37.00	$47.00	_____
☐ EPP	European Psychologist	$39.00	N/A	_____
☐ GDN	Group Dynamics	$37.00	$47.00	_____
☐ HOP	History of Psychology	$35.00	$45.00	_____
☐ MEN	Psychology of Men and Masculinity	$37.00	$42.00	_____
☐ OCP	Occupational Health Psychology	$33.00	$43.00	_____
☐ ORT	American Journal of Orthopsychiatry	$70.00	$80.00	_____
☐ PAP	Psychoanalytic Psychology	$46.00	$56.00	_____
☐ INT	Journal of Psychotherapy Integration	$55.00	$65.00	_____
☐ REP	Rehabilitation Psychology	$33.00	$43.00	_____
☐ GPR	Review of General Psychology	$30.00	$40.00	_____

4. Subtotal EPF Subscriptions
(DC residents add 5.75% sales tax; MD residents add 5% sales tax) $_____

2002 Online Databases

(Note: If you have ordered at least one APA publication, you may purchase 2002 online access to one of the following database packages. The $10 Journal Credit is not applicable to Online Database orders.)

Online Database Package	Rate	Code	Amount
(For a complete description of the Silver, Gold, and Platinum Package see far left panel.)			
Silver Package			
Current and previous three years of PsycINFO® and PsycARTICLES™	$89.00	PFL	$_____
Gold Package			
Complete PsycINFO® and PsycARTICLES™ databases	$129.00	PTB	$_____
Platinum Package All!			
Premium Full-Electronic Access	$249.00	ALL	$_____

5. Subtotal Online Databases
(DC residents add 5.75% sales tax) $_____

2002 Student Affiliate Fee

6. 2002 Student Affiliate Fee
☐ Undergraduate $_____

☐ Optional Undergraduate Affiliation with APAGS ($13.00) $_____

☐ Graduate $_____

7. Subtotal Student Affiliate Fee
$_____

Grand Total Calculations

A. Enter Line 3 Amount (APA Subscriptions) $_____
B. Enter Line 4 Amount (EPF Subscriptions) $_____
C. Enter Line 5 Amount (Online Database) $_____
D. Enter Line 7 Amount (Annual Fee) $_____
E. Grand Total (Add lines A, B, C, and D) (Pay this amount to APA in U.S. Dollars) **$_____**

Application fee, journal subscriptions, and electronic product orders must be prepaid. (Payment must be drawn on a U.S. bank in U.S. dollars.) Please allow 6–8 weeks for delivery of your first publications. The affiliate fee is required whether or not you order journals.

☐ I have enclosed a check or money order in the amount of $_____

☐ I authorize APA to charge my Student Affiliate fee and subscription orders to my credit card as listed below:

Very Important! Please print clearly or type.

_____
Cardholder Name

_____
Credit Card Billing Address

_____
City/State/ZIP Code/Country

_____
Daytime Telephone (Area Code)

Amount to be charged $_____
☐ AMERICAN EXPRESS   ☐ MASTERCARD   ☐ VISA

_____
Account Number   Expiration Date

(Signature Required for all charge orders.)

the department: Female–full-time 46, part-time 4; Male–full-time 10, part-time 7; African American/Black–full-time 5, part-time 1; Hispanic/Latino (a)–full-time 10, part-time 2; Asian/Pacific Islander–full-time 7, part-time 2; American Indian/Alaska Native–full-time 0, part-time 0; Multi-ethnic–full-time 5, part-time 1; students subject to the Americans with Disabilities Act–full-time 0, part-time 0.

Financial Information/Assistance:

Tuition for Full-Time Study: *Master's:* State residents $424 per credit hour; nonstate residents: $424 per credit hour. *Doctoral:* State residents: $437 per credit hour; nonstate residents: $437 per credit hour.

Financial Assistance:

First Year Students: Average amount paid per academic year: $0. Average number of hours worked per week: 0. Average amount paid per academic year: $0. Average number of hours worked per week: 0. Average amount paid per academic year: $0. Average number of hours worked per week: 0. Fellowships and scholarships available for first-year. Average amount paid per academic year: $1,500. Average number of hours worked per week: 0.

Advanced Students: Average amount paid per academic year: $0. Average number of hours worked per week: 0. Average amount paid per academic year: $0. Average number of hours worked per week: 0. Average amount paid per academic year: $0. Average number of hours worked per week: 0. Fellowships and scholarships available for advanced students. Average amount paid per academic year: $3,000. Average number of hours worked per week: 0.

Contact Information: Of all students currently enrolled full-time, 7% benefitted from one or more of the listed financial assistance programs. For information on financial assistance, contact: Christy McAffee 3745 W. Chapman Ave. Suite 100 Orange, CA 92868.

Internships/Practica: The specific clinical focus of the practicum varies according to the student's program, training needs, interests, and the availability of practicum sites.

Housing and Day Care: No on-campus housing and day care facilities are available.

Employment of Department Graduates:

Master's Degree Graduates: Of those who graduated in the academic year 2000–2001, the following categories and numbers represent the post-graduate activities and employment of master's degree graduates: Enrolled in a psychology doctoral program (0), enrolled in another graduate/professional program (0), enrolled in a post-doctoral residency/fellowship (n/a), employed in independent practice (n/a), employed in an academic position at a university (0), employed in an academic position at a 2-year/4-year college (0), employed in other positions at a higher education institution (0), employed in a professional position in a school system (0), employed in business or industry (research/consulting) (0), employed in business or industry (management) (0), employed in a government agency (research) (0), employed in a government agency (professional services) (0), employed in a community mental health/counseling center (0), employed in a hospital/medical center (0), still seeking employment (0), other employment position (0).

Doctoral Degree Graduates: Of those who graduated in the academic year 2000–2001, the following categories and numbers represent the post-graduate activities and employment of doctoral degree graduates: Enrolled in a psychology doctoral program (n/a), enrolled in another graduate/professional program (n/a), enrolled in a post-doctoral residency/fellowship (0), employed in independent practice (0), employed in an academic position at a university (0), employed in an academic position at a 2-year/4-year college (0), employed in other positions at a higher education institution (0), employed in a professional position in a school system (0), employed in business or industry (research/consulting) (0), employed in business or industry (management) (0), employed in a government agency (research) (0), employed in a government agency (professional services) (0), employed in a community mental health/counseling center (0), employed in a hospital/medical center (0), still seeking employment (0), other employment position (0).

Additional Information:

Orientation, Objectives, and Emphasis of Department: The field of psychology has grown significantly within recent years, and as a result a larger number of settings offer opportunities in a variety of areas within the field of psychology. In order to help meet societies need for professional counselors, Argosy University offers the MACP, EdD-CP and PsyD degree programs.

Application Information:

Send to: Joe Buechner, Director of Admissions 3745 W. Chapman Ave. Suite 100 Orange, CA. 92868. Students are admitted in the Fall, application deadline May 15; Spring, application deadline Oct 15. We offer a year around rolling admissions process for both the EdD-CP and MACP programs. *Fee:* $50.

Argosy University, San Francisco Bay Area
999 A Canal Blvd.
Pt. Richmond, CA 94804
Telephone: (510) 215-0277
Fax: (510) 215-0299
E-mail: *nkobrin@argosyu.edu*
Web: *http://www.argosyu.edu*

Department Established:

1999. President: Neil Kobrin, Ph.D. Number of Faculty: total–full-time 7, part-time 2; women–full-time 4; minority–full-time 2.

Programs and Degrees Offered:

Listed in the following order: Program area, degree type (T if terminal Master's), number awarded 7/00-6/01. Clinical Psychology PsyD 4, Counseling Psychology MA (T), EdD (T), MAeD MA (T).

Student Applications/Admissions:

Student Applications

Clinical Psychology PsyD—Applications 2001–2002, 75. Total applicants accepted 2001–2002, 60. New applicants enrolled 2001–2002, 39. Total enrolled 2001–2002 full-time, 33, part-time, 6. Openings 2002–2003, 55. The Median number of years required for completion of a degree are 5. The number of students enrolled full and part-time, who were dismissed or voluntarily withdrew from this program area were 1. *Counseling Psychology MA*—Applications 2001–2002, 40. Total applicants accepted 2001–2002, 32. New applicants enrolled 2001–2002, 30. Total enrolled 2001–2002 full-time, 30. Openings 2002–2003, 40. The Median number of years required for completion of a degree are 2. The number of students enrolled full and part-time, who were dismissed or voluntarily withdrew from this program area were 2. *EdD Openings 2002–2003, 20. MAeD MA Openings 2002–2003, 20.*

Admissions Requirements:

Scores: Entries appear in this order: required test or GPA, minimum score (if required), median score of students entering in 2001–2002. Master's Programs: overall undergraduate GPA 3.0; last 2 years GPA 3.0; psychology GPA 3.0. Doctoral Programs: overall undergraduate GPA 3.25; last 2 years GPA 3.25; psychology GPA 3.25.

Other Criteria: (importance of criteria rated low, medium, or high): research experience low, work experience low, extracurricular activity medium, clinically related public service medium, GPA medium, letters of recommendation high, interview high, statement of goals and objectives high.

Student Characteristics: The following represents characteristics of students in 2001–2002 in all graduate psychology programs in the department: Female–full-time 85, part-time 15; Male–full-time 27, part-time 5; African American/Black–full-time 12, part-time 2; Hispanic/Latino (a)–full-time 6, part-time 3; Asian/Pacific Islander–full-time 8, part-time 5; American Indian/Alaska Native–full-time 2, part-time 1; Multi-ethnic–full-time 5, part-time 2; students subject to the Americans with Disabilities Act–full-time 1, part-time 2.

Financial Information/Assistance:

Tuition for Full-Time Study: *Master's:* State residents $374 per credit hour; nonstate residents: $374 per credit hour. *Doctoral:* State residents: $510 per credit hour; nonstate residents: $510 per credit hour.

Financial Assistance:

First Year Students: No information provided.

Advanced Students: Teaching assistantships available for advanced students. Average amount paid per academic year: $400. Average number of hours worked per week: 1. Research assistantships available for advanced students. Traineeships available for advanced students.

Contact Information: Of all students currently enrolled full-time, 2% benefitted from one or more of the listed financial assistance programs. For information on financial assistance, contact: Ariana Heller 510-215-0277x203, Aheller@argosyu.edu.

Internships/Practica: Argosy University SFBA's database of approved San Francisco Bay Area sites includes community mental health centers, consortiums, state, community and private psychiatric hospitals, medical and trauma centers, university counseling centers, schools, correctional facilities, residential treatment programs, independent and group practices, and corporate settings. Some sites serve the general population while others service specific populations (e.g., children, adolescents, geriatrics, particular ethnic or racial groups, criminal offenders, etc.) or clinical problems (e.g., chemical dependency, eating disorders, medical and psychiatric rehabilitation, etc.). Argosy University SFBA is a

member of the California Psychology Internship Council (CAPIC) which is a collaboration between Bay Area psychology graduate programs and internship programs in California. The Training Department works throughout the year to maintain positive relationships with existing sites and affiliate itself with new sites throughout the Bay area. Students are encouraged to review the database, CAPIC, APPIC and other site files kept in the training department and talk with the Training Director to identify placements that provide the type of experience desired. Argosy University SFBA strongly encourages students to complete their training in settings that provide opportunities to work with diverse populations. It is essential that students learn to work with people who are different from themselves (e.g., race, ethnicity, disability, sexual orientation, etc.) in a supervised setting where they can learn the skills, knowledge, and attitudes necessary to practice as a competent clinician. For those doctoral students for whom a professional internship is required prior to graduation, 2 applied in 2000–2001.

Housing and Day Care: No on-campus housing and day care facilities are available.

Employment of Department Graduates:

Master's Degree Graduates: Of those who graduated in the academic year 2000–2001, the following categories and numbers represent the post-graduate activities and employment of master's degree graduates: Enrolled in a post-doctoral residency/fellowship (n/a), employed in independent practice (n/a).

Doctoral Degree Graduates: Of those who graduated in the academic year 2000–2001, the following categories and numbers represent the post-graduate activities and employment of doctoral degree graduates: Enrolled in a psychology doctoral program (n/a), enrolled in another graduate/professional program (n/a).

Additional Information:

Orientation, Objectives, and Emphasis of Department: The clinical orientation of the program is integrative. All major theoritical orientations are presented including psychodyanmic, family systems, developmental, cognitive, and humanistic.

Special Facilities or Resources: Argosy University San Francisco Bay Area campus emphasizes specialized "hands-on" clinical training through our Intensive Clinical Training facility and our certificate program in Clinical Hypnotherapy. Through the Intensive Clinical Training series, students work directly with clients referred from the community while being observed by a team through a one-way mirror. The team consists of the instructor and/or clinical assistant and fellow students who participate in pre- and post-therapy sessions in which they provide input and feedback about the therapeutic process. Each client session is guided by the instructor/assistant who, through the use of a microphone, provides clinical guidance and interventions directly to the student therapist through an earpiece worn by the student. As the session progresses, the instructor/assistant educates the team about the dynamics of the therapist/client interaction and the treatment approach. Students may participate on three levels: 1) as a clinical observer and a member of the team; 2) as a student therapist working directly with clients, and 3) as a clinical assistant in concert with our Supervision/Consultation course. Our yearlong Clinical Hypnotherapy program is taught by a Certified Clinical Hypnotherapist, and provides students the opportunity to complete their hours for certification while providing hypnotherapy services to clients.

Application Information:

Send to: Admissions Department, 999A Canal Blvd., Point Richmond, CA 94804. Students are admitted in the Fall; Spring, application deadline Oct. 15. January 15th priority deadline for Fall. May 15th final deadlline depending on space availability. October 15th final deadline for Spring. *Fee:* $50.

Azusa Pacific University

Department of Graduate Psychology
901 E. Alosta, P.O. Box 7000
Azusa, CA 91702-7000
Telephone: (626) 815-5008
Fax: (626) 815-5015
E-mail: *mstanton@apu.edu*
Web: *http://www.apu.edu/* Then use Search: PsyD

Department Established:

1976. Chairperson: Mark Stanton. Number of Faculty: total–full-time 10, part-time 7; women–full-time 5, part-time 5; minority–full-time 2, part-time 1.

Programs and Degrees Offered:

Listed in the following order: Program area, degree type (T if terminal Master's), number awarded 7/00-6/01. Clinical Psychology - MA (T) 27, Clinical Psychology PsyD 7.

APA Accreditation: Clinical PsyD: full.

Student Applications/Admissions:

Student Applications

Clinical Psychology - MA—Applications 2001–2002, 71. Total applicants accepted 2001–2002, 66. New applicants enrolled 2001–2002, 51. Total enrolled 2001–2002 full-time, 34, part-time, 52. Openings 2002–2003, 45. The Median number of years required for completion of a degree are 3. The number of students enrolled full and part-time, who were dismissed or voluntarily withdrew from this program area were 7. *Clinical Psychology PsyD*—Applications 2001–2002, 21. Total applicants accepted 2001–2002, 15. New applicants enrolled 2001–2002, 13. Total enrolled 2001–2002 full-time, 22, part-time, 30. Openings 2002–2003, 18. The Median number of years required for completion of a degree are 5. The number of students enrolled full and part-time, who were dismissed or voluntarily withdrew from this program area were 2.

Admissions Requirements:

Scores: Entries appear in this order: required test or GPA, minimum score (if required), median score of students entering in 2001–2002. Master's Programs: overall undergraduate GPA 3.0; psychology GPA 3.0. Doctoral Programs: GRE-V+Q no minimum stated; MAT no minimum stated; overall undergraduate GPA 3.0; last 2 years GPA 3.5, 3.5 ; psychology GPA 3.0; psychology GPA 3.5, 3.5. Note: One examination is required-GRE or MAT. Scores are one consideration in the entire application. Verbal ability is important to success in the PsyD program. GRE Writing Assessment is required.

Other Criteria: (importance of criteria rated low, medium, or high): GRE/MAT scores medium, research experience medium, work experience high, extracurricular activity medium, clinically related public service medium, GPA high, letters of recommendation high, interview high, statement of goals and objectives high, GRE Writing Assessment high. No GRE/MAT scores required for MA; work experience of medium importance for MA; research experience of medium importance for MA; clinically related public service low for MA.

Student Characteristics: The following represents characteristics of students in 2001–2002 in all graduate psychology programs in the department: Female–full-time 60, part-time 57; Male–full-time 16, part-time 25; African American/Black–full-time 4, part-time 9; Hispanic/Latino (a)–full-time 9, part-time 13; Asian/Pacific Islander–full-time 11, part-time 8; American Indian/Alaska Native–full-time 1, part-time 0; Multi-ethnic–full-time 2, part-time 4; students subject to the Americans with Disabilities Act–full-time 0, part-time 0.

Financial Information/Assistance:

Tuition for Full-Time Study: *Master's:* State residents $385 per credit hour; nonstate residents: $385 per credit hour. *Doctoral:* State residents $500 per credit hour; nonstate residents: $500 per credit hour.

Financial Assistance:

First Year Students: Teaching assistantships available for first-year. Average amount paid per academic year: $2,750. Average number of hours worked per week: 8. Apply by Feb 15. Tuition remission given: partial. Research assistantships available for first-year. Average amount paid per academic year: $5,500. Average number of hours worked per week: 15. Apply by Feb 15. Tuition remission given: partial.

Advanced Students: No information provided.

Contact Information: Of all students currently enrolled full-time, 8% benefitted from one or more of the listed financial assistance programs. Assistantship positions are available to PsyD students. Positions are awarded to begin in the first year and continue for 3 years. For information on financial assistance, contact: Graduate Student Financial Services at (626) 815-5440.

Internships/Practica: PsyD students are required to complete 6 semesters of practicum experience. These experiences are gained in placements throughout Los Angeles, Orange, and San Bernardino Counties which provide diverse clinical and multicultural experiences. A Counseling Center on the Azusa Pacific University campus also serves as a practicum site for doctoral students. A sequence of clinical practicum courses is offered simultaneously with the field placement experience. All doctoral students are required to complete one full year of psychology internship. APU places interns in a variety of sites (must be APA approved or those meeting APPIC standards) across the country. Students enrolled in the M.A. Program in Clinical Psychology complete a clinical training sequence that meets all requirements for future licensure as a Marital and Family Therapist (MFT) in the state of California. Students complete 250 hours of direct client contact in diverse, multi-cultural settings, such as community counseling centers, domestic violence clinics, and schools. Students receive training in individual, marital, and group therapy and exposure to treatments that have been demonstrated to be effective with specific problems. A sequence of clinical placement courses is offered simultaneously with the field placement experience. For those doctoral students for whom a professional internship is required prior to graduation, 12 applied in 2000–2001. Of those who applied, 2 were placed in internships listed by the Association of Psychology Postdoctoral and Internship Programs (APPIC); 5 were placed in APA accredited internships.

Housing and Day Care: No on-campus housing and day care facilities are available.

Employment of Department Graduates:
   Master's Degree Graduates: Of those who graduated in the academic year 2000–2001, the following categories and numbers represent the post-graduate activities and employment of master's degree graduates: Enrolled in a post-doctoral residency/fellowship (n/a), employed in independent practice (n/a).
   Doctoral Degree Graduates: Of those who graduated in the academic year 2000–2001, the following categories and numbers represent the post-graduate activities and employment of doctoral degree graduates: Enrolled in a psychology doctoral program (n/a), enrolled in another graduate/professional program (n/a).

Additional Information:
   Orientation, Objectives, and Emphasis of Department: The Psy.D. in Clinical Psychology with an emphasis in Family Psychology (APA accredited) prepares students for the practice of professional psychology. The program adheres to a practitioner-scholar model of training and emphasizes development of the core competencies in clinical psychology adopted by the National Council of Schools and Programs of Professional Psychology. The program requires completion of a rigorous sequence of courses in the science and practice of psychology. Requirements include three years of clinical training, successful demonstration of clinical competency through examination, completion of a clinical dissertation, and a predoctoral internship. Prespecialty education in family psychology and an emphasis in interdisciplinary studies, relating psychology to ethics, theology, and philosophy, is included. The program was designed to be consistent with the requirements of the Guidelines and Principles for Accreditation of Programs in Professional Psychology (APA, 1996). The MA in Clinical Psychology with an emphasis in Marital and Family Therapy meets requirements for California MFT licensure. Concepts of individual psychology are integrated with interpersonal and ecological concepts of systems theory. Goals include cultivating the examined life, fostering theoretical mastery, developing practical clinical skills, encouraging clinically integrative strategies, and preparing psychotherapists to work in a culturally diverse world.

   Special Facilities or Resources: All students have access to the APA PsycINFO database and all APA journals full-text on-line as part of their student library privileges. The new Darling Library provides an attractive and functional set of resources for the APU PsyD and MA. The library is technology-friendly and includes the Ahmanson Information Technology Center, an area with 75 computer desks. Each computer is wired into the university system for Internet and library catalog system searches. PsycINFO, as well as over 100 additional licensed databases, are available for student literature and subject searches. Eight "scholar rooms" were designed as a part of the Darling Graduate Library to be used for conducting research and writing. Doctoral students in the dissertation phase of their program are given priority in the reservation of these rooms. There are also several conference rooms in the Darling Library that may be reserved for student study groups or research teams. The Department of Graduate Psychology runs the Child and Family Development Center (CFDC), which offers psychological services to the surrounding community as well as to faculty, staff, and university students. The CFDC also contracts to provide services to the surrounding 12 schools in the Azusa Unified School District. The CFDC currently trains 25 MA and PsyD graduate students and has provided data for two doctoral dissertations.

   Information for Students With Physical Disabilities: All facilities are wheelchair accessible, having both ramps and elevators available to all classroom locations and library facilities.

Application Information:
Send to: Azusa Pacific University, Graduate Center, 901 E. Alosta, P.O. Box 7000, Azusa, CA 91702-7000. Students are admitted in the Fall, application deadline February 15; Spring, application deadline 10/31-MA; Summer, application deadline 2/28-MA. PsyApplication deadline is February 15 (if space is available, extended case by case deadline June 15). *Fee:* $45.

Biola University
Rosemead School of Psychology
13800 Biola Avenue
La Mirada, CA 90639
Telephone: (800) 652-4652
Fax: (562) 903-4864
E-mail: *admissions@biola.edu*
Web: *http://www.rosemead.edu*

Department Established:
   1970. Dean: Patricia L. Pike. Number of Faculty: total–full-time 18, part-time 4; women–full-time 8, part-time 1; minority–full-time 3; faculty subject to the Americans with Disabilities Act 1.

Programs and Degrees Offered:
   Listed in the following order: Program area, degree type (T if terminal Master's), number awarded 7/00-6/01. PhD and PsyD in clinical 27.

APA Accreditation: Clinical PhD: full. Clinical PsyD: full.

Student Applications/Admissions:
   Student Applications
   PhD and PsyD in clinical—Applications 2001–2002, 116. Total applicants accepted 2001–2002, 35. New applicants enrolled 2001–2002, 25. Total enrolled 2001–2002 full-time, 120. Openings 2002–2003, 25. The Median number of years required for completion of a degree are 6. The number of students enrolled full and part-time, who were dismissed or voluntarily withdrew from this program area were 1.

   Admissions Requirements:
   Scores: Entries appear in this order: required test or GPA, minimum score (if required), median score of students entering in 2001–2002. Doctoral Programs: GRE-V+Q 1000, 1159; GRE-Subject(Psych) no minimum stated; overall undergradu-

ate GPA 3.00; last 2 years GPA 3.00, 3.30; psychology GPA no minimum stated, 3.50; psychology GPA no minimum stated. **Other Criteria:** (importance of criteria rated low, medium, or high): GRE/MAT scores high, research experience medium, work experience medium, extracurricular activity low, clinically related public service medium, GPA high, letters of recommendation high, interview high, statement of goals and objectives medium.

Student Characteristics: The following represents characteristics of students in 2001–2002 in all graduate psychology programs in the department: Female–full-time 69, part-time 7; Male–full-time 39, part-time 5; African American/Black–full-time 1, part-time 1; Hispanic/Latino (a)–full-time 4, part-time 1; Asian/Pacific Islander–full-time 30, part-time 0; American Indian/Alaska Native–full-time 2, part-time 0; Multi-ethnic–full-time 1, part-time 0; students subject to the Americans with Disabilities Act–full-time 1, part-time 1.

Financial Information/Assistance:

Tuition for Full-Time Study: *Doctoral:* State residents: per academic year $15,882; nonstate residents: per academic year $15,882.

Financial Assistance:

First Year Students: Fellowships and scholarships available for first-year. Average amount paid per academic year: $3,000.

Advanced Students: Teaching assistantships available for advanced students. Average amount paid per academic year: $3,000. Average number of hours worked per week: 12. Apply by March 15. Fellowships and scholarships available for advanced students. Average amount paid per academic year: $3,000. Average number of hours worked per week: 0. Apply by March 15.

Contact Information: Of all students currently enrolled full-time, 60% benefitted from one or more of the listed financial assistance programs. For information on financial assistance, contact: Admissions Office and Financial Aid by phone at (800) 652-4652, by e-mail at admissions@biola.edu, or via mail at Graduate Admissions Office, Biola University, 13800 Biola Avenue, La Mirada, CA 90639.

Internships/Practica: PhD students are required to complete 4 semesters of practicum experience; PsyD students are required to complete 6 semesters of practicum experience. Such experience is gained in placements spread across the Los Angeles basin, which provides rich opportunities for professional development. A Counseling Center on the Biola University campus also serves as a practicum site for Rosemead doctoral students. All doctoral students are required to complete one full year of psychology internship. Rosemead places interns in a variety of sites (most are APA approved) across the country. For those doctoral students for whom a professional internship is required prior to graduation, 24 applied in 2000–2001. Of those who applied, 21 were placed in internships listed by the Association of Psychology Postdoctoral and Internship Programs (APPIC); 20 were placed in APA accredited internships.

Housing and Day Care: No on-campus housing and day care facilities are available.

Employment of Department Graduates:

Master's Degree Graduates: Of those who graduated in the academic year 2000–2001, the following categories and numbers

represent the post-graduate activities and employment of master's degree graduates: Enrolled in a post-doctoral residency/fellowship (n/a), employed in independent practice (n/a).

Doctoral Degree Graduates: Of those who graduated in the academic year 2000–2001, the following categories and numbers represent the post-graduate activities and employment of doctoral degree graduates: Enrolled in a psychology doctoral program (n/a), enrolled in another graduate/professional program (n/a), enrolled in a post-doctoral residency/fellowship (1), employed in independent practice (1), employed in an academic position at a university (2), employed in an academic position at a 2-year/4-year college (1), employed in other positions at a higher education institution (1), employed in a professional position in a school system (2), employed in business or industry (research/consulting) (0), employed in business or industry (management) (0), employed in a government agency (research) (0), employed in a government agency (professional services) (5), employed in a community mental health/counseling center (13), employed in a hospital/medical center (3), still seeking employment (0), other employment position (1).

Additional Information:

Orientation, Objectives, and Emphasis of Department: The doctoral program has two special emphases. The first is on professional training following a professional-scholar model. All students complete a minimum of two years of practicum prior to internship. They also take at least four psychotherapy lab courses involving both lectures and supervised clinical experiences within the theoretical perspective of the course. These intervention courses are offered from various perspectives, including psychodynamic, family systems, and cognitive behavioral approaches to therapy. In addition to coursework, psychotherapy labs, and practicum experiences, all students complete both group and individual psychotherapy as part of their professional growth experience. The second distinctive emphasis of the doctoral program is on the relationship of psychological theory, research, and practice to Christian theology. All doctoral students take five semesters of coursework in theology and several interdisciplinary courses relating psychological and theological perspectives on human nature and adjustment.

Special Facilities or Resources: Biola has a commitment to academic computing which provides substantial computing resources for Rosemead students and faculty. Biola maintains a very fast (T1) connection to the Internet, which is available to the faculty via the staff network and to students through either a dial-up system or ethernet in the computer labs. There are several computer labs on campus, the largest is the Welch Computer Center, which has over 70 computers (Macintosh and Windows) for student use. Through agreements with university library, several large research databases are available via the Internet, some with full-text journal articles. SPSS software is available for use by our students either as a dial-in service or directly from the Welch Computer Center.

Information for Students With Physical Disabilities: Biola University has a Department for Disabilities Services.

Application Information:
Send to: Office of Graduate Admissions, Rosemead School of Psychology, 13800 Biola Ave., La Mirada, CA 90639-9987. Students are admitted in the Fall, application deadline January 15. *Fee:* $45. In

addition to the application fee, there is a fee of $75 for candidate interview.

California Institute of Integral Studies

School of Professional Psychology
1453 Mission Street
San Francisco, CA 94103
Telephone: (415) 575-6100
Fax: (415) 575-6111
E-mail: *info@ciis.edu*
Web: *http://www.ciis.edu*

Department Established:

1979. Chairperson: Harrison Voigt. Number of Faculty: total–full-time 18, part-time 35; women–full-time 10, part-time 20; minority–full-time 4, part-time 8.

Programs and Degrees Offered:

Listed in the following order: Program area, degree type (T if terminal Master's), number awarded 7/00-6/01. Clinical Psychology PsyD 15, Counseling Psychology MA (T) 41.

Student Applications/Admissions:

Student Applications

Clinical Psychology PsyD—Applications 2001–2002, 108. Total applicants accepted 2001–2002, 53. New applicants enrolled 2001–2002, 30. Total enrolled 2001–2002 full-time, 120, part-time, 60. Openings 2002–2003, 29. The number of students enrolled full and part-time, who were dismissed or voluntarily withdrew from this program area were 6. *Counseling Psychology MA*—Applications 2001–2002, 54. Total applicants accepted 2001–2002, 38. New applicants enrolled 2001–2002, 27. Total enrolled 2001–2002 full-time, 110, part-time, 30. Openings 2002–2003, 30. The Median number of years required for completion of a degree are 3. The number of students enrolled full and part-time, who were dismissed or voluntarily withdrew from this program area were 8.

Admissions Requirements:

Scores: Entries appear in this order: required test or GPA, minimum score (if required), median score of students entering in 2001–2002. Master's Programs: overall undergraduate GPA 3.0, 3.1. Doctoral Programs: overall undergraduate GPA 3.1, 3.4 ; last 2 years GPA no minimum stated; psychology GPA no minimum stated; psychology GPA no minimum stated.

Other Criteria: (importance of criteria rated low, medium, or high): research experience low, work experience medium, extracurricular activity medium, clinically related public service medium, GPA medium, letters of recommendation high, interview high, statement of goals and objectives medium, Volunteer service medium. Some variation between MA and PsyD programs in application of criteria.

Student Characteristics: The following represents characteristics of students in 2001–2002 in all graduate psychology programs in the department: Female–full-time 180, part-time 60; Male–full-time 60, part-time 20; African American/Black–full-time 17, part-time 0; Hispanic/Latino (a)–full-time 15, part-time 0; Asian/Pacific Islander–full-time 24, part-time 0; American Indian/Alaska Native–full-time 2, part-time 0; Multi-ethnic–full-time 5, students subject to the Americans with Disabilities Act–full-time 2.

Financial Information/Assistance:

Tuition for Full-Time Study: *Master's:* State residents per academic year $5,750, $605 per credit hour; nonstate residents: per academic year $5,750, $605 per credit hour. *Doctoral:* State residents: per academic year $7,410, $780 per credit hour; nonstate residents: per academic year $7,410, $780 per credit hour.

Financial Assistance:

First Year Students: Teaching assistantships available for first-year. Fellowships and scholarships available for first-year. Average amount paid per academic year: $5,000. Apply by May 1. Tuition remission given: partial.

Advanced Students: Teaching assistantships available for advanced students. Apply by varies. Fellowships and scholarships available for advanced students. Average amount paid per academic year: $5,000. Apply by May 1. Tuition remission given: partial.

Contact Information: Of all students currently enrolled full-time, 15% benefitted from one or more of the listed financial assistance programs. Federal work/study positions available. Minority scholarships available. Please contact the Financial Aid Office (finaid@ciis.edu) for information.

Internships/Practica: Internship and practicum placements are available throughout the greater San Francisco Bay Area at a broad variety of mental health service agencies. All doctoral internships are CAPIC-approved. For those doctoral students for whom a professional internship is required prior to graduation, 25 applied in 2000–2001. Of those who applied, 3 were placed in internships listed by the Association of Psychology Postdoctoral and Internship Programs (APPIC); 3 were placed in APA accredited internships.

Housing and Day Care: No on-campus housing and day care facilities are available.

Employment of Department Graduates:

Master's Degree Graduates: Of those who graduated in the academic year 2000–2001, the following categories and numbers represent the post-graduate activities and employment of master's degree graduates: Enrolled in a post-doctoral residency/fellowship (n/a), employed in independent practice (n/a).

Doctoral Degree Graduates: Of those who graduated in the academic year 2000–2001, the following categories and numbers represent the post-graduate activities and employment of doctoral degree graduates: Enrolled in a psychology doctoral program (n/a), enrolled in another graduate/professional program (n/a).

Additional Information:

Orientation, Objectives, and Emphasis of Department: The institute offers a unique program of education and training, broadening the usual conceptual framework for graduate training in psychology by including Asian philosophical, humanistic, and transpersonal approaches to understanding human experience. The educational philosophy simultaneously values scholarly knowledge, inner development, applied research, and human service. Psychology programs at CIIS flourish within a fertile and broadening climate provided by other social science graduate programs in philosophy/religion, anthropology, and women's spirituality, along with on-line degree programs. Within the practitioner-scientist training model, the psychology doctoral training program provides knowledge of the foundations of scientific and professional psychology while emphasizing the understanding of consciousness, self-knowledge, and human evolution embodied in the philosophical and psychological traditions of both East and West. The clinical specialization prepares students for work with the broad range of clientele and systems found across the range of multidisciplinary service settings and the spectrum of populations served by the clinical psychologist. Experiential growth work is required in all programs. Several clinical concentrations are available. The clinical psychology program is listed as a Designated Program by the National Register of Health Service Providers in Psychology. CIIS has a 28,000-volume library and a well-developed field placement program to support academic studies.

Special Facilities or Resources: CIIS operates four separate community-based counseling centers, including the on-campus Psychological Services Center operated by the clinical psychology doctoral program. All four counseling centers serve as primary training sites for both the MA and PsyD programs.

Application Information:
Send to: Office of Admissions. Students are admitted in the Fall, application deadline March 1; Spring, application deadline October 15. MA programs: April 15 for Fall, September 15 for Spring. *Fee:* $65. Spring: September 15 for certain programs.

California Lutheran University

Psychology Department
60 W. Olsen Road
Thousand Oaks, CA 91360
Telephone: (805) 493-3124
Fax: (805) 493-3479
E-mail: *carpente@clunet.edu*
Web: *http://www.clunet.edu*

Department Established:
1959. Director, Psychology Graduate Programs: Leanne Neilson, PsyD. Number of Faculty: total–full-time 7, part-time 12; women–full-time 4, part-time 6.

Programs and Degrees Offered:
Listed in the following order: Program area, degree type (T if terminal Master's), number awarded 7/00-6/01. Clinical MA (T) 5, Marital and Family Therapy MA (T) 11.

Student Applications/Admissions:
Student Applications
    Clinical MA—Applications 2001–2002, 17. Total applicants accepted 2001–2002, 10. New applicants enrolled 2001–2002, 8. Total enrolled 2001–2002 full-time, 9, part-time, 7. Openings 2002–2003, 15. The Median number of years required for completion of a degree are 2. The number of students enrolled full and part-time, who were dismissed or voluntarily withdrew from this program area were 0. *Marital and Family Therapy MA*—Applications 2001–2002, 30. Total applicants accepted 2001–2002, 18. New applicants enrolled 2001–2002, 12. Total enrolled 2001–2002 full-time, 16, part-time, 12. Openings 2002–2003, 20. The Median number of years required for completion of a degree are 2. The number of students enrolled full and part-time, who were dismissed or voluntarily withdrew from this program area were 0.

Admissions Requirements:
    Scores: Entries appear in this order: required test or GPA, minimum score (if required), median score of students entering in 2001–2002. Master's Programs: GRE-V+Q+Analytical no minimum stated; last 2 years GPA 3.0. GRE is required only if upper division undergraduate GPA is below 3.0. Doctoral Programs: last 2 years GPA no minimum stated; psychology GPA no minimum stated; psychology GPA no minimum stated.
    Other Criteria: (importance of criteria rated low, medium, or high): GRE/MAT scores low, research experience medium, work experience medium, extracurricular activity low, clinically related public service medium, GPA high, letters of recommendation high, interview high, statement of goals and objectives high.

Student Characteristics: The following represents characteristics of students in 2001–2002 in all graduate psychology programs in the department: Female–full-time 22, part-time 15; Male–full-time 3, part-time 4; African American/Black–full-time 1, part-time 2; Hispanic/Latino (a)–full-time 1, part-time 1; Asian/Pacific Islander–full-time 1, part-time 1; American Indian/Alaska Native–full-time 0, part-time 0; Multi-ethnic–full-time 0, part-time 0; students subject to the Americans with Disabilities Act–full-time 0, part-time 0.

Financial Information/Assistance:
    Tuition for Full-Time Study: *Master's:* State residents $370 per credit hour; nonstate residents: $370 per credit hour.

Financial Assistance:
    First Year Students: Teaching assistantships available for first-year. Average number of hours worked per week: 10. Apply by August 15. Tuition remission given: partial. Research assistantships available for first-year. Average number of hours worked per week: 10. Apply by August 15. Tuition remission given: partial.
    Advanced Students: Teaching assistantships available for advanced students. Apply by August 15. Tuition remission given: partial. Research assistantships available for advanced students. Apply by August 15. Tuition remission given: partial.
    Contact Information: Of all students currently enrolled full-time, 15% benefitted from one or more of the listed financial assistance programs. For information on financial assistance, contact: Student Financial Planning Office (805) 493-3115.

Internships/Practica: A special feature of the Marital and Family Therapy Program is a 12-month practicum placement in the University's Marriage, Family, and Child Counseling Center. The Center is a low-cost community counseling facility, which provides an intensive on-site clinical training experience. Individual supervision, group supervision, staff training, peer support and sharing of learning experiences in an atmosphere designed to facilitate growth as a therapist create exceptional opportunities. Approximately 500 hours applicable to the California licensing requirement can be obtained through the MFT practicum experience.

Housing and Day Care: No on-campus housing and day care facilities are available.

Employment of Department Graduates:

Master's Degree Graduates: Of those who graduated in the academic year 2000–2001, the following categories and numbers represent the post-graduate activities and employment of master's degree graduates: Enrolled in a post-doctoral residency/fellowship (n/a), employed in independent practice (n/a).

Doctoral Degree Graduates: Of those who graduated in the academic year 2000–2001, the following categories and numbers represent the post-graduate activities and employment of doctoral degree graduates: Enrolled in a psychology doctoral program (n/a), enrolled in another graduate/professional program (n/a).

Additional Information:

Orientation, Objectives, and Emphasis of Department: The Master of Science degree in Clinical Psychology provides both a scientific and practitioner foundation, with courses in research as well as clinical and assessment training. Students choose either a two-course sequence in Child & Adolescent Therapy or a two-course sequence in Psychiatric Rehabilitation, which focuses on clients who have serious mental illnesses. The Master of Science in Clinical Psychology provides excellent preparation for application to doctoral programs, provides skills leading toward careers in the mental health profession, and qualifies the graduate to teach in community colleges. The Master of Science Degree in Counseling Psychology prepares the student to become a professional Marital and Family Therapist. The program is designed to meet all academic requirements for the California state license in marital and family counseling. Over the years, graduates of this program have an outstanding record of successfully passing the state licensing examination. Graduates have built successful practices in both private and institutional fields. All of the Master's degree programs can be completed in two years, or three years on a part-time basis.

Application Information:

Send to: Marilyn Carpenter, Graduate Admission Counselor, 60 W Olsen Rd., Thousand Oaks, CA 91360. Students are admitted in the Fall, application deadline February 15; Spring, application deadline December 1; Summer, application deadline April 1. Master's program in Counseling Psychology (Marital & Family Therapy) only admits students in the fall semester. *Fee:* $50.

California Polytechnic State University

Psychology/Master of Science in Psychology
Liberal Arts
Cal Poly Psychology/Child Development Department
San Luis Obispo, CA 93407
Telephone: (805) 756-2456
Fax: (805) 756-1134
E-mail: *mbooker@calpoly.edu*
Web: *http://www.calpoly.edu/~psychhd*

Department Established:

1969. Chairperson: Linden L. Nelson. Number of Faculty: total–full-time 21, part-time 12; women–full-time 10, part-time 7; minority–full-time 4, part-time 2.

Programs and Degrees Offered:

Listed in the following order: Program area, degree type (T if terminal Master's), number awarded 7/00-6/01. Counseling Marriage and Family MA (T) 10.

Student Applications/Admissions:

Student Applications

Counseling Marriage and Family MA—Applications 2001–2002, 54. Total applicants accepted 2001–2002, 29. New applicants enrolled 2001–2002, 16. Total enrolled 2001–2002 full-time, 33, part-time, 5. Openings 2002–2003, 20. The Median number of years required for completion of a degree are 3. The number of students enrolled full and part-time, who were dismissed or voluntarily withdrew from this program area were 5.

Admissions Requirements:

Scores: Entries appear in this order: required test or GPA, minimum score (if required), median score of students entering in 2001–2002. Master's Programs: GRE-V+Q+Analytical no minimum stated, 1612; last 2 years GPA 3.0, 3.54. Doctoral Programs: last 2 years GPA no minimum stated; psychology GPA no minimum stated; psychology GPA no minimum stated.

Other Criteria: (importance of criteria rated low, medium, or high): GRE/MAT scores high, research experience low, work experience medium, extracurricular activity medium, clinically related public service medium, GPA high, letters of recommendation high, interview high, statement of goals and objectives high.

Student Characteristics: The following represents characteristics of students in 2001–2002 in all graduate psychology programs in the department: Female–full-time 26, part-time 4; Male–full-time 7, part-time 1; African American/Black–full-time 0, part-time 0; Hispanic/Latino (a)–full-time 2, part-time 0; Asian/Pacific Islander–full-time 0, part-time 0; American Indian/Alaska Native–full-time 0, part-time 0; Multi-ethnic–full-time 0, part-time 0; students subject to the Americans with Disabilities Act–full-time 0, part-time 0.

Financial Information/Assistance:

Tuition for Full-Time Study: *Master's:* State residents per academic year $2,243; nonstate residents per academic year $2,243, $164 per credit hour.

Financial Assistance:

First Year Students: No information provided.

Advanced Students: No information provided.

Contact Information: Of all students currently enrolled full-time, 0% benefitted from one or more of the listed financial assistance programs. For information on financial assistance, contact: Financial Aid office (805) 756-2927.

Internships/Practica: The Central Coast of California offers numerous well-supervised clinical internships in public and private non-profit agencies with a variety of client populations. Internships are selected based on their ability to provide: 1) quality supervision by a state-qualified licensed clinician; 2) clients with a wide variety of psychological disorders; 3) a variety of treatment modalities, i.e., individual, couple, family, and group therapy; 4) a wide variety of clients that represent the diversity of the community. Most internship students are placed at public agency sites which serve the country's entire range of ethnic and minority populations.

Housing and Day Care: No on-campus housing and day care facilities are available.

Employment of Department Graduates:

Master's Degree Graduates: Of those who graduated in the academic year 2000–2001, the following categories and numbers represent the post-graduate activities and employment of master's degree graduates: Enrolled in a post-doctoral residency/fellowship (n/a), employed in independent practice (n/a).

Doctoral Degree Graduates: Of those who graduated in the academic year 2000–2001, the following categories and numbers represent the post-graduate activities and employment of doctoral degree graduates: Enrolled in a psychology doctoral program (n/a), enrolled in another graduate/professional program (n/a).

Additional Information:

Orientation, Objectives, and Emphasis of Department: The M.S. in Psychology is designed for persons who desire to practice in the field of clinical/counseling psychology. The M.S. in Psychology is accredited in the area of marriage and family counseling/therapy by the Council for Accreditation of Counseling and Related Educational Programs (CACREP), a specialized accrediting body recognized by the Council on Postsecondary Accreditation (COPA). The program's mission is to provide the state of California with highly competent master-level clinicians who are academically prepared for the Marriage and Family therapist (MFT) license and counseling with individuals, couples, families, and groups in a multicultural society. The program fulfills the educational requirements for the state of California's Marriage and Family Therapist (MFT) License. Its mission is also to provide students who want to proceed on to doctoral programs in clinical or counseling psychology with sound research skills, thesis experience, and clinical intervention training. Graduates find career opportunities in public social service agencies such as Mental Health and Departments of Social Services as well as in private non-profit and private practice counseling centers. Ten to twenty percent of graduates go on to doctoral programs in clinical or counseling psychology.

Special Facilities or Resources: Closely supervised on-campus practicum experiences leading to challenging internships in community agencies are the cornerstone of Cal Poly's preparation for the future clinician. The program runs a community counseling services clinic with three counseling offices and an observation room that provides direct viewing through one-way mirrors and remotely controlled video equipment. Closely supervised experience in Cal Poly's practicum clinic serving clients from the community provides trainees with the opportunity to develop skills and confidence before undertaking an internship.

Application Information:

Send to: Admissions Office, California Polytechnic State University, San Luis Obispo, CA 93407. Students are admitted in the Fall, application deadline February 15. *Fee:* $55.

California School of Professional Psychology/AIU: Alameda

Professional School
1005 Atlantic Avenue
Alameda, CA 94501
Telephone: (510) 523-2300
Fax: (510) 521-3678
E-mail: *admissions@alliant.edu*
Web: *http://www.alliant.edu/cspp/*

Department Established:

1969. Clinical PhD & PsyD Program Directors: R. Turner; D. Adams; K. Goldman-Schuyler. Number of Faculty: total–full-time 35, part-time 95; women–full-time 14, part-time 43; minority–full-time 12, part-time 13.

Programs and Degrees Offered:

Listed in the following order: Program area, degree type (T if terminal Master's), number awarded 7/00-6/01. Clinical PsyD, clinical—child & family track PsyD, clinical-Forensic Family/Child PsyD, organizational PhD 2, organizational consultation PsyD, organizational development MA.

APA Accreditation: Clinical PhD: full. Clinical PsyD: full.

Student Applications/Admissions:

Student Applications

Clinical PsyD—Applications 2001–2002, 6. Total applicants accepted 2001–2002, 5. New applicants enrolled 2001–2002, 2. Total enrolled 2001–2002 full-time, 4. Openings 2002–2003, 10. *Clinical—child & family track PsyD*—Applications 2001–2002, 48. Total applicants accepted 2001–2002, 33. New applicants enrolled 2001–2002, 18. Total enrolled 2001–2002 full-time, 29. Openings 2002–2003, 20. *Clinical—Forensic Family/Child PsyD*—Applications 2001–2002, 8. Total applicants accepted 2001–2002, 6. New applicants enrolled 2001–2002, 3. Total enrolled 2001–2002 full-time, 4. Openings 2002–2003, 10. *Organizational PhD*—Applications 2001–2002, 17. Total applicants accepted 2001–2002, 14. New applicants enrolled 2001–2002, 11. Total enrolled 2001–2002 full-time, 48, part-time, 18. Openings 2002–2003, 15. *Organizational consultation PsyD*—Applications 2001–2002, 11. Total applicants accepted 2001–2002, 9. New applicants enrolled 2001–2002, 5. Total enrolled 2001–2002 full-time, 18, part-time, 2. Openings 2002–2003, 10. *Organizational development MA Openings 2002–2003, 20.*

Admissions Requirements:

Scores: Entries appear in this order: required test or GPA, minimum score (if required), median score of students entering in 2001–2002. Master's Programs: GRE scores are optional and not required. Doctoral Programs: overall undergraduate GPA 3.00; last 2 years GPA no minimum stated; psychology GPA 3.00; psychology GPA 3.00. Applicants with GPA below 3.00 will be considered if they submit explanation of low GPA and demonstrate ability to perform in intensive academic environment. MA not required for admission, but GPA must be above 3.00 for any graduate work.

Other Criteria: (importance of criteria rated low, medium, or high): GRE/MAT scores low, research experience high, work experience high, extracurricular activity low, clinically related public service high, GPA high, letters of recommendation high, interview high, statement of goals and objectives high, written essay high. Weight given to research experience higher for PhD programs than for PsyD programs. Weight given to work/clinical experience higher for PsyD than for PhD. Community Service/leadership potential high.

Student Characteristics: The following represents characteristics of students in 2001–2002 in all graduate psychology programs in the department: Female–full-time 11, part-time 0; Male–full-time 26, part-time 1; African American/Black–full-time 9, part-time 0; Hispanic/Latino (a)–full-time 6, part-time 0; Asian/Pacific Islander–full-time 17, part-time 0; American Indian/Alaska Native–full-time 0, part-time 0.

Financial Information/Assistance:

Tuition for Full-Time Study: No information provided.

Financial Assistance:

First Year Students: No information provided.
Advanced Students: No information provided.
Contact Information: For information on financial assistance, contact: CSPP/AIU Systemwide Office, 800-457-1273.

Internships/Practica: During the first three years of the clinical PsyD program and during the second and third years of the clinical PhD program, students are engaged in field practica 8–16 hours per week. Professional training placements are selected and approved by CSPP based on the quality of training experience and supervision provided for the students. They are found in a wide range of facilities, including community mental health clinics, hospitals and neuropsychiatric institutions, child guidance clinics, college counseling centers, residential treatment centers, forensic settings, and corporate settings. Clinical students begin the required internship in the fourth year (PsyD program) or the fifth year (PhD program). Full-time internship options include APA-accredited or APPIC-member training programs pursued through the national selection process or local internship programs approved by CSPP faculty. Students also have the option of completing the internship requirement in two years of half-time experience in local agencies. Organizational program students develop practical skills through professional training experiences during the third and fourth years of the doctoral programs. Placements are available in a variety of settings including consulting firms, major corporations, government agencies, and non-profit organizations.

Housing and Day Care: No on-campus housing and day care facilities are available.

Employment of Department Graduates:

Master's Degree Graduates: Of those who graduated in the academic year 2000–2001, the following categories and numbers represent the post-graduate activities and employment of master's degree graduates: Enrolled in a post-doctoral residency/fellowship (n/a), employed in independent practice (n/a).
Doctoral Degree Graduates: Of those who graduated in the academic year 2000–2001, the following categories and numbers represent the post-graduate activities and employment of doctoral degree graduates: Enrolled in a psychology doctoral program (n/a), enrolled in another graduate/professional program (n/a).

Additional Information:

Orientation, Objectives, and Emphasis of Department: California School of Professional Psychology (CSPP) offers clinical psychology doctoral programs which combine supervised field experiences with study of psychological theory, clinical techniques, and applied research. The PsyD program is designed for those who wish to emphasize clinical practice and make effective use of research in their work. The PhD program provides a balance of clinical training and applied research training and is intended for those who expect independent research and scholarship to be a part of their professional careers. Five emphasis areas and two tracks offer students the opportunity to develop a foundation for specialization in specific areas within the practice of psychology. The emphasis areas are Family/Child Psychology, Health Psychology, Multicultural and Community, Psychodynamic/Life Development, and Gender Studies (Psychology of Women, Men, Gender Roles, and Sexual Orientations). Tracks provide more focused training for PsyD program students planning careers in the areas of Child & Family Psychology and Forensix Family/Child Psychology. CSPP's organizational psychology PhD and organizational consultation PsyD programs blend instruction in organizational theory, organizational culture and values, professional practice, and research methods with practical professional training experiences. The PhD program prepares graduates to serve a diverse range of organizations through the generation and application of research. The PsyD program provides the training necessary for consultation in the field of organizational psychology.

Special Facilities or Resources: CSPP students may receive training and "hands on" research and service experience in professional psychology through CSPP's community mental health center, the Psychological Services Center (PSC). The PSC provides faculty the opportunity to model professional service delivery and to supervise and evaluate student clinical work. Clinical services provided at the PSC sites in Oakland and Alameda include psychodiagnostic assessment and individual, couple, family, and group psychotherapy. Indirect services provided by PSC faculty and trainees include consultation, training, and research. The PSC's special programs are the Family and Violence Institute and The Child and Family Program. Graduate psychology programs are offered through the Alameda, Fresno, Los Angeles, and San Diego campuses.

Information for Students With Physical Disabilities: All CSPP facilities are essentially barrier free and accessible to persons with disabilities. All buildings are equipped with restroom and telephone services for the disabled and assistance is available for library resources. The Faculty Advisor for Students with Disabilities provides mentoring and advising for students with physical and learning disabilities and also teaches a research cluster on physical disabilities. Unfortunately, CSPP cannot guarantee full accessibility for persons with disabilities at all field placement and internship sites.

Application Information:

Send to: CSPP/AIU Systemwide Admissions Office, 2728 Hyde Street, Suite 100, San Fransisco, CA 94109. Students are admitted in the Fall, application deadline December 1; Winter, application deadline open; Spring, application deadline open. January 3 deadline for single-campus clinical applicants; February 1 deadline for organizational applicants. Prospective students are encouraged to apply after the December 1st early notification deadline. After December 1st we will review applicants on rolling admissions basis. *Fee:* $65. Limited number of fee waivers for on-time applicants with highest financial need.

California School of Professional Psychology/AIU: Los Angeles

Professional School
1000 S. Fremont Avenue
Alhambra, CA 91803-1360
Telephone: (626) 284-2777
Fax: (626) 284-0550
E-mail: *sbyers-bell@alliant.edu*
Web: *http://www.alliant.edu/cspp/*

Department Established:

1970. Director of the Clinical Program: Ellin L. Bloch. Number of Faculty: total–full-time 36, part-time 69; women–full-time 19, part-time 41; minority–full-time 10, part-time 13.

Programs and Degrees Offered:

Listed in the following order: Program area, degree type (T if terminal Master's), number awarded 7/00-6/01. Behavioral healthcare managem MA (T) 5, clinical PhD 42.

APA Accreditation: Clinical PhD: full. Clinical PsyD: full.

Student Applications/Admissions:

Student Applications

Behavioral healthcare managem MA—Applications 2001–2002, 8. Total applicants accepted 2001–2002, 6. Total enrolled 2001–2002 full-time, 7. *Clinical PhD*—Applications 2001–2002, 104. Total applicants accepted 2001–2002, 84. New applicants enrolled 2001–2002, 40. Total enrolled 2001–2002 full-time, 229, part-time, 21. Openings 2002–2003, 26. The number of students enrolled full and part-time, who were dismissed or voluntarily withdrew from this program area were 1.

Admissions Requirements:

Scores: Entries appear in this order: required test or GPA, minimum score (if required), median score of students entering in 2001–2002. Master's Programs: overall undergraduate GPA 3.0; psychology GPA 3.0. If the GPA is below a 3.0, applicants may complete the exemption form (E) to explain their circumstances. Doctoral Programs: overall undergraduate GPA 3.0, 3.13; last 2 years GPA no minimum stated; psychology GPA 3.0; psychology GPA no minimum stated. If the GPA is below a 3.0, applicants may complete the exemption form (E) to explain their circumstances.

Other Criteria: (importance of criteria rated low, medium, or high): research experience high, work experience medium, clinically related public service medium, letters of recommendation medium, interview high, statement of goals and objectives high. Research experience is of more importance for both PhD programs; clinically related public service is of more importance to both clinical degree programs.

Student Characteristics: The following represents characteristics of students in 2001–2002 in all graduate psychology programs in the department: Female–full-time 15, part-time 0; Male–full-time 35, part-time 0; African American/Black–full-time 10, part-time 0; Hispanic/Latino (a)–full-time 13, part-time 0; Asian/Pacific Islander–full-time 10, part-time 0; American Indian/Alaska Native–full-time 0, part-time 0.

Financial Information/Assistance:

Tuition for Full-Time Study: No information provided.

Financial Assistance:

First Year Students: No information provided.
Advanced Students: No information provided.
Contact Information: For information on financial assistance, contact: Stephanie Greenstein, Director of Financial Aid.

Internships/Practica: 68 practicum sites, 75 half-time internships in the Greater Los Angeles area. These agencies serve a diverse range of clients/patients including ethnicity, religion, sexual orientation. These sites provide excellent training, offering a variety of theoretical orientations related to children, adolescents, adults, families, and the elderly. For those doctoral students for whom a professional internship is required prior to graduation, 205 applied in 2000–2001. Of those who applied, 1 was placed in internships listed by the Association of Psychology Postdoctoral and Internship Programs (APPIC); 9 were placed in APA accredited internships.

Housing and Day Care: No on-campus housing and day care facilities are available.

Employment of Department Graduates:

Master's Degree Graduates: Of those who graduated in the academic year 2000–2001, the following categories and numbers represent the post-graduate activities and employment of master's degree graduates: Enrolled in a post-doctoral residency/fellowship (n/a), employed in independent practice (n/a).
Doctoral Degree Graduates: Of those who graduated in the academic year 2000–2001, the following categories and numbers represent the post-graduate activities and employment of doctoral degree graduates: Enrolled in a psychology doctoral program (n/a), enrolled in another graduate/professional program (n/a).

Additional Information:

Orientation, Objectives, and Emphasis of Department: The California School of Professional Psychology offers comprehensive programs of instruction in professional psychology leading to the PhD and PsyD in clinical psychology, the PhD in organizational psychology, and the master's degree in behavioral healthcare management (MBHM). The clinical PsyD and PhD programs prepare students to function as multifaceted clinical psychologists through a curriculum based on an integration of psychological theory, research, and practice. Students in both programs develop competencies in seven areas: interpersonal/relationship; general assessment, appraisal, and ascertainment; multifaceted multimodal intervention; research and evaluation; consultation/teaching; management/supervision/training; and quality assurance. PsyD candidates gain relatively greater mastery in assessment, intervention, and management/supervision; PhD candidates emphasize research and evaluation. Practica and internship experiences are integrated throughout the programs. Students have the opportunity to emphasize in clinical health psychology, multicultural community clinical, or individual and family clinical psychology.

The organizational PhD program combines rigorous academic training in basic psychology and organizational theory with advanced education in organizational design and development, management consultation and decision-making, and strategic human resource management. Academic studies are integrated with the equivalent of two half-time years of field placement in business and organizations, preparing students for careers in a wide variety of business settings.

Special Facilities or Resources: The Professional Services Center (PSC) is charged with the mission of developing professional training, research, and consultation opportunities for CSPP faculty and students, while providing services to a variety of public/private agencies. It is committed to developing effective and innovative service strategies and resources that address the needs of a wide range of clients; with a particular focus on ethnically diverse, underserved populations. As a center "without walls," the PSC is the administrative umbrella for two major community-based programs: the Children, Youth, and Family Consortium and the Diversity Consultation and Training Program. These programs enable participating CSPP faculty, staff, students, alumni/ae, and external consultant associates to provide services few other institutions can offer. CSPP students also receive unique training and supervision that prepares them for critically needed roles as community and organizational psychologists, advocates, and leaders. The Center for Innovation and Change (CIC) involves faculty and students in applied research and consultation projects for organizational clients. Projects are designed to provide hands-on research and consulting experience for students and to enhance the human resource performance of the organizations. A wide range of services are offered to small businesses, non-profits, and large corporations covering the full range of traditional organizational development needs: priority-setting; organizational culture analysis, diagnosis, and training; and general problem solving.

Application Information:
Send to: CSPP/AIU - System Office, 2759 Hyde Street, San Francisco, CA 94108. Students are admitted in the Fall. Application deadlines are December 1 for single-campus applications, January 2 for multiple-campus applications. May 15 is the deadline for the master's program in behavioral healthcare management. *Fee:* $65. Fee waivers are available to students with demonstrated need.

California State University, Bakersfield
Department of Psychology
School of Humanities and Social Sciences
9001 Stockdale Highway
Bakersfield, CA 93311-1099
Telephone: (661) 664-2363
Fax: (661) 665-6955
E-mail: *kishida@csub.edu*
Web: *http://www.csubak.edu/*

Department Established:
1970. Chairperson: Jess F. Deegan II. Number of Faculty: total—full-time 16, part-time 4; women—full-time 6, part-time 3; minority—full-time 4.

Programs and Degrees Offered:
Listed in the following order: Program area, degree type (T if terminal Master's), number awarded 7/00-6/01. College teaching MA (T) 1, doctoral preparation MA (T), general MA (T) 1, marriage, family, and child.

Student Applications/Admissions:
Student Applications
College teaching MA—Applications 2001–2002, 3. Total applicants accepted 2001–2002, 2. New applicants enrolled 2001–2002, 2. Total enrolled 2001–2002 part-time, 2. Openings 2002–2003, 3. The Median number of years required for completion of a degree are 2. *Doctoral preparation* MA—Applications 2001–2002, 3. Total applicants accepted 2001–2002, 1. New applicants enrolled 2001–2002, 1. Total enrolled 2001–2002 part-time, 1. Openings 2002–2003, 3. The Median number of years required for completion of a degree are 2. The number of students enrolled full and part-time, who were dismissed or voluntarily withdrew from this program area were 0. *General* MA—Applications 2001–2002, 3. Total applicants accepted 2001–2002, 2. New applicants enrolled 2001–2002, 2. Total enrolled 2001–2002 part-time, 2. Openings 2002–2003, 3. The Median number of years required for completion of a degree are 2. The number of students enrolled full and part-time, who were dismissed or voluntarily withdrew from this program area were 0.

Admissions Requirements:
Scores: Entries appear in this order: required test or GPA, minimum score (if required), median score of students entering in 2001–2002. Master's Programs: GRE-V no minimum stated, 500; GRE-Q no minimum stated, 500; GRE-V+Q no minimum stated, 1000; last 2 years GPA 3.00; psychology GPA 3.00. Those not meeting minima may petition for exceptional admission. For the M.S. in Counseling Psychology the GRE is not required. Doctoral Programs: last 2 years GPA no minimum stated; psychology GPA no minimum stated; psychology GPA no minimum stated.
Other Criteria: (importance of criteria rated low, medium, or high): work experience high, extracurricular activity low, clinically related public service high, GPA medium, letters of recommendation high, interview low, statement of goals and objectives medium. Admission Criteria above for M.S. in Counseling Psychology. For M.A. in Psychology: GRE-Medium (High for pre-doctoral emphasis), Research Exp.-Low (High for pre-doctoral), Work exp.-Med., Extra. Act- med., Clin.Rel. Pub. Serv.-Low, GPA-Med (High for pre-doctoral), Letters-High, Intv-None, Statement of Goals and Objectives-Med.

Student Characteristics: The following represents characteristics of students in 2001–2002 in all graduate psychology programs in the department: Female–full-time 10, part-time 34; Male–full-time 4, part-time 6; African American/Black–full-time 0, part-time 0; Hispanic/Latino (a)–full-time 0, part-time 7; Asian/Pacific Islander–full-time 0, part-time 0; American Indian/Alaska Native–full-time 0, part-time 0; students subject to the Americans with Disabilities Act–full-time 0, part-time 0.

Financial Information/Assistance:
Tuition for Full-Time Study: *Master's:* State residents per academic year $1,506; nonstate residents: per academic year $8,806.

Financial Assistance:

First Year Students: Fellowships and scholarships available for first-year. Apply by ASAP.

Advanced Students: Fellowships and scholarships available for advanced students.

Contact Information: For information on financial assistance, contact: Office of Financial Aid and Scholarships at http://www.csub.edu/FinAid/requirements/index.html.

Internships/Practica: The M.S. program features practica in human communication, diagnostic interviewing, and individual, child, family, and group treatment in a university counselor training clinic. Two quarters of training in a modern, well-equipped on-campus counselor training clinic is required. Two quarters of traineeship is required in one of a wide variety of community placements including substance abuse, dual diagnosis, perinatal intervention, child guidance, domestic violence, forensics, and college counseling. For program objectives, course description, and application information visit http://www.csubak.edu/cpsy.

Housing and Day Care: On-campus housing and day care facilities are available.

Employment of Department Graduates:

Master's Degree Graduates: Of those who graduated in the academic year 2000–2001, the following categories and numbers represent the post-graduate activities and employment of master's degree graduates: Enrolled in a psychology doctoral program (1), enrolled in another graduate/professional program (0), enrolled in a post-doctoral residency/fellowship (n/a), employed in independent practice (n/a), employed in an academic position at a 2-year/4-year college (6), employed in other positions at a higher education institution (5), employed in a professional position in a school system (5), employed in business or industry (research/consulting) (1), employed in business or industry (management) (1), employed in a government agency (research) (2), employed in a community mental health/counseling center (111), still seeking employment (5).

Doctoral Degree Graduates: Of those who graduated in the academic year 2000–2001, the following categories and numbers represent the post-graduate activities and employment of doctoral degree graduates: Enrolled in a psychology doctoral program (n/a), enrolled in another graduate/professional program (n/a), enrolled in a post-doctoral residency/fellowship (0).

Additional Information:

Orientation, Objectives, and Emphasis of Department: The Department of Psychology offers a 45-unit program with the following options: (1) doctoral preparation primarily intended for those planning to go on for doctoral studies, but who wish to develop their research base; (2) teaching psychology in community college settings; (3) general psychology for those seeking a master's degree for academic or career advancement. The MS is a jointly-sponsored program of the Psychology Department in the School of Arts and Sciences and Advanced Educational Studies in the School of Education. Faculty teach principles and skills for the developing professional to work effectively and ethically with children, adolescents, adults, couples, and families from diverse populations. The curriculum emphasizes a balance between content and application, theory and practice, and science and art. It is designed to meet the academic requirements established by the Board of Behavioral Sciences (BBS), Section 4980.37 of the Business and Professions Code for the California license in Marriage and Family Therapy (MFT).

Special Facilities or Resources: For M.A. students there is an active program in vision research with extensive spatial frequency presentation and measuring equipment. There is an animal laboratory meeting stringent Federal standards. The department maintains a file of psychological tests. For M.S. students three of the 4 full-time clinical faculty are licensed in the state of California. A modern university counselor training clinic is supervised by a licensed MFT.

Information for Students With Physical Disabilities: The Services for Students with Disabilities Office coordinates programs and support for students with visual limitations, communitcation disabilities, mobility limitations, or specific learning disabilities. The Department of Psychology is committed to empowerment of students with physical disabilities.

Application Information:
Send to: For M.A.: Steve Bacon, PhD, Psychology Graduate Coordinator, Psychology Department, California State University, Bakersfield, CA 93311-1099; for M.S.: Ms. Maria Delgado, Rm. 325, School of Education, California State University, Bakersfield, CA 93311-1099. Students are admitted in the Fall, application deadline April 15; Winter, application deadline October 15; Spring, application deadline February 15. *Fee:* There is a separate application process for university admission. Contact: Admissions and Records, California State University Bakersfield, 9001 Stockdale Highway, Bakersfield, CA 93311-1099.

California State University, Chico
Psychology Department
College of Behavioral and Social Sciences
Chico, CA 95929-0234
Telephone: (530) 898-5147
Fax: (530) 898-4740
E-mail: *pspear@csuchico.edu*
Web: *http://www.csuchico.edu*

Department Established:
1961. Chairperson: Paul Spear. Number of Faculty: total–full-time 25, part-time 17; women–full-time 9, part-time 8; minority–full-time 4, part-time 1.

Programs and Degrees Offered:
Listed in the following order: Program area, degree type (T if terminal Master's), number awarded 7/00-6/01. MA/PPS, MA/Psychological Science MA (T) 18, MS/MFT.

Student Applications/Admissions:

Student Applications

MA/Psychological Science MA—Applications 2001–2002, 20. Total applicants accepted 2001–2002, 14. New applicants enrolled 2001–2002, 14. Total enrolled 2001–2002 full-time, 40. Openings 2002–2003, 14.

Admissions Requirements:

Scores: Entries appear in this order: required test or GPA, minimum score (if required), median score of students entering

in 2001–2002. Master's Programs: last 2 years GPA 2.75. Completion of either GRE V+Q+A or MAT. GRE-Subject (Psychology) not required but is considered if available. Last 60 units GPA - 2.75 minimum; last 30 units GPA - 3.00 minimum Doctoral Programs: last 2 years GPA no minimum stated; psychology GPA no minimum stated; psychology GPA no minimum stated.

Other Criteria: (importance of criteria rated low, medium, or high): GRE/MAT scores medium, research experience low, work experience low, extracurricular activity low, clinically related public service medium, GPA high, letters of recommendation high, statement of goals and objectives high.

Student Characteristics: The following represents characteristics of students in 2001–2002 in all graduate psychology programs in the department: Female–full-time 114, part-time 0; Male–full-time 34, part-time 0; African American/Black–full-time 0, part-time 0; Hispanic/Latino(a)–full-time 4, part-time 0; Asian/Pacific Islander–full-time 2, part-time 0; American Indian/Alaska Native–full-time 0, part-time 0; Multi-ethnic–full-time 2.

Financial Information/Assistance:

Tuition for Full-Time Study: *Master's:* State residents per academic year $2,030, $246 per credit hour; nonstate residents: per academic year $4,006, $246 per credit hour.

Financial Assistance:

First Year Students: No information provided.

Advanced Students: Tuition remission given: partial.

Contact Information: Of all students currently enrolled full-time, 10% benefitted from one or more of the listed financial assistance programs. For information on financial assistance, contact: For MA Option in Psychological Science: Out-of-state or international non-resident tuition waivers and a limited number of teaching assistantships are available on a competitive basis. Separate application required. Contact Department Chair [pspear@csuchico.edu; (530) 898-5147]. Application deadline April 10. Other assistance: Student Affairs Financial Aid Office (530) 898-6451.

Internships/Practica: For the MS degree: Individual and Child Counseling, Group Counseling, and Family Therapy practica are offered as well as post-practicum internships. School Psychology internships are required of all students seeking the School Psychology Credential.

Housing and Day Care: On-campus housing and day care facilities are available.

Employment of Department Graduates:

Master's Degree Graduates: Of those who graduated in the academic year 2000–2001, the following categories and numbers represent the post-graduate activities and employment of master's degree graduates: Enrolled in a post-doctoral residency/fellowship (n/a), employed in independent practice (n/a), employed in a professional position in a school system (14), employed in a community mental health/counseling center (15).

Doctoral Degree Graduates: Of those who graduated in the academic year 2000–2001, the following categories and numbers represent the post-graduate activities and employment of doctoral degree graduates: Enrolled in a psychology doctoral program (n/a), enrolled in another graduate/professional program (n/a).

Additional Information:

Orientation, Objectives, and Emphasis of Department: The Department offers three graduate programs. The Master of Science Degree prepares students to meet the educational requirements for Marriage and Family Therapy licensure in the State of California. It is designed to train competent professional counselors to work in mental health agencies and private practice. The curriculum is competency based and includes laboratory courses and practica, culminating in a family practicum and/or a post-practicum internship in a counseling agency. The Master of Arts Degree, Psychological Science Option, is designed to prepare students for doctoral work or teaching at the community college level. It offers extensive research experience, supervised teaching, and advanced coursework in experimental psychology and statistics. The Master of Arts Degree, Applied Psychology Option, is designed for students intending to enter our Pupil Personnel Services Credential program, which meets California requirements for a School Psychology Credential. The program has a prevention-oriented philosophy, is competency based, and provides practice in a variety of skills which enable school psychologists to serve all children. Trainees work in schools several days a week during 2 years of fieldwork.

Special Facilities or Resources: The Department of Psychology has modern, up-to-date laboratories, classrooms, and seminar rooms, including laboratories in biopsychology, perception, learning, statistics, and counseling.

Information for Students With Physical Disabilities: Our office of Disability Support Services actively addresses the special needs of students with disabilities.

Application Information:

Send to: Graduate Coordinator. Students are admitted in the Fall, application deadline March 1. *Fee:* $55.

California State University, Dominguez Hills

Department of Psychology/MA in Clinical Psychology Program
1000 East Victoria Street
Carson, CA 90747
Telephone: (310) 243-3435
Fax: (310) 516-3642
E-mail: *bpalmer@csudh.edu*
Web: *http://www.csudh.edu/*

Department Established:

1969. Coordinator, M.A. in Clinical Psychology Program: Beverly B. Palmer. Number of Faculty: total–full-time 5, part-time 1; women–full-time 3; minority–full-time 2.

Programs and Degrees Offered:

Listed in the following order: Program area, degree type (T if terminal Master's), number awarded 7/00-6/01. Clinical MA (T) 16.

Student Applications/Admissions:

Student Applications

Clinical MA—Applications 2001–2002, 155. Total applicants accepted 2001–2002, 20. New applicants enrolled 2001–2002,

17. Total enrolled 2001–2002 full-time, 32, part-time, 9. Openings 2002–2003, 20. The Median number of years required for completion of a degree are 2. The number of students enrolled full and part-time, who were dismissed or voluntarily withdrew from this program area were 0.

Admissions Requirements:

Scores: Entries appear in this order: required test or GPA, minimum score (if required), median score of students entering in 2001–2002. Master's Programs: GRE-V+Q+Analytical 1300, 1500; last 2 years GPA 3.00, 3.40. Doctoral Programs: last 2 years GPA no minimum stated; psychology GPA no minimum stated; psychology GPA no minimum stated.

Other Criteria: (importance of criteria rated low, medium, or high): GRE/MAT scores high, research experience medium, work experience low, clinically related public service medium, GPA high, letters of recommendation high, interview low, statement of goals and objectives high.

Student Characteristics: The following represents characteristics of students in 2001–2002 in all graduate psychology programs in the department: Female–full-time 25, part-time 8; Male–full-time 7, part-time 1; African American/Black–full-time 11, part-time 4; Hispanic/Latino (a)–full-time 5, part-time 2; Asian/Pacific Islander–full-time 1, part-time 0; American Indian/Alaska Native–full-time 0, part-time 0.

Financial Information/Assistance:

Tuition for Full-Time Study: *Master's:* State residents per academic year $1,818; nonstate residents: $246 per credit hour.

Financial Assistance:

First Year Students: Fellowships and scholarships available for first-year. Average amount paid per academic year: $500. Apply by February 1.

Advanced Students: Fellowships and scholarships available for advanced students. Average amount paid per academic year: $500. Apply by February.

Contact Information: Of all students currently enrolled full-time, 15% benefitted from one or more of the listed financial assistance programs.

Internships/Practica: The Master of Arts in Clinical Psychology offers you 550 supervised hours of practicum experience in a variety of settings.

Housing and Day Care: On-campus housing and day care facilities are available.

Employment of Department Graduates:

Master's Degree Graduates: Of those who graduated in the academic year 2000–2001, the following categories and numbers represent the post-graduate activities and employment of master's degree graduates: Enrolled in a psychology doctoral program (5), enrolled in another graduate/professional program (1), enrolled in a post-doctoral residency/fellowship (n/a), employed in independent practice (n/a), employed in an academic position at a 2-year/4-year college (3), employed in a government agency (research) (1), employed in a government agency (professional services) (2), employed in a community mental health/counseling center (5).

Doctoral Degree Graduates: Of those who graduated in the academic year 2000–2001, the following categories and numbers represent the post-graduate activities and employment of doctoral degree graduates: Enrolled in a psychology doctoral program (n/a), enrolled in another graduate/professional program (n/a).

Additional Information:

Orientation, Objectives, and Emphasis of Department: The Clinical Psychology Master of Arts Program provides you with a solid academic background in clinical psychology as it is applied within a community mental health framework. This program prepares you for a career in counseling, teaching, and research in community settings, which includes public or private agencies. Eighteen units of additional coursework prepare you for practice as a marriage and family therapist. Our graduates are successful in gaining admission to and graduating from the doctoral programs of their choice.

Special Facilities or Resources: Special resources include laboratory facilities, a course and experience in teaching psychology, computer facilities, and online PsychLIT retrieval system.

Application Information:

Send to: Department of Psychology, California State University, Dominguez Hills, 1000 E. Victoria St., Carson, CA 90747. Students are admitted in the Fall, application deadline March 1. *Fee:* $55.

California State University, Fullerton
Department of Psychology
Humanities and Social Sciences
P.O. Box 6846
Fullerton, CA 92834-6846
Telephone: (714) 278-3589
Fax: (714) 278-7134
E-mail: *kkarlson@fullerton.edu*
Web: *http//Psych.fullerton.edu/*

Department Established:

1957. Chairperson: David Perkins. Number of Faculty: total–full-time 25, part-time 35; women–full-time 13, part-time 21; minority–full-time 4, part-time 5.

Programs and Degrees Offered:

Listed in the following order: Program area, degree type (T if terminal Master's), number awarded 7/00-6/01. Clinical Psychology MA (T) 9, Psychological Research MA (T) 5.

Student Applications/Admissions:

Student Applications

Clinical Psychology MA—Applications 2001–2002, 50. Total applicants accepted 2001–2002, 19. New applicants enrolled 2001–2002, 18. Total enrolled 2001–2002 full-time, 32, part-time, 10. Openings 2002–2003, 15. The Median number of years required for completion of a degree are 2. The number of students enrolled full and part-time, who were dismissed or voluntarily withdrew from this program area were 2. *Psychological Research MA*—Applications 2001–2002, 40. Total applicants accepted 2001–2002, 18. New applicants enrolled 2001–

2002, 16. Total enrolled 2001–2002 full-time, 20, part-time, 13. Openings 2002–2003, 15. The Median number of years required for completion of a degree are 2.

Admissions Requirements:

Scores: Entries appear in this order: required test or GPA, minimum score (if required), median score of students entering in 2001–2002. Master's Programs: GRE-V 300, 506; GRE-Q 300, 616; GRE-Analytical 300; GRE-Subject(Psych) 300, 590; overall undergraduate GPA 2.5, 3.4; last 2 years GPA 2.5, 3.62; psychology GPA 3.0, 3.75. MA requires no minimum. Doctoral Programs: last 2 years GPA no minimum stated; psychology GPA no minimum stated; psychology GPA no minimum stated.

Other Criteria: (importance of criteria rated low, medium, or high): GRE/MAT scores high, research experience high, work experience, clinically related public service high, GPA high, letters of recommendation high, interview high, statement of goals and objectives high. Criteria are weighted equally.

Student Characteristics: The following represents characteristics of students in 2001–2002 in all graduate psychology programs in the department: Female–full-time 41, part-time 15; Male–full-time 11, part-time 8; African American/Black–full-time 0, part-time 0; Hispanic/Latino (a)–full-time 6, part-time 0; Asian/Pacific Islander–full-time 8, part-time 0; American Indian/Alaska Native–full-time 0, part-time 0.

Financial Information/Assistance:

Tuition for Full-Time Study: *Master's:* State residents per academic year $1,927; nonstate residents: $246 per credit hour.

Financial Assistance:

First Year Students: No information provided.
Advanced Students: No information provided.
Contact Information: Of all students currently enrolled full-time, 0% benefitted from one or more of the listed financial assistance programs. For information on financial assistance, contact: Financial Aid Office 714-278-3125. The Department of Psychology and CSU, Fullerton employ graduate students as Graduate Assistants. These positions vary in responsibility (assist with lab class or academic advisement) and time (5 hrs–20hrs per week).

Internships/Practica: A majority of the internships are done in agencies which do family therapy and substance abuse prevention and training. Most internships have live and videotape supervision. Students have done internships in policy psychology, county clinics, and inpatient settings as well. Most agencies combine clinical and community work and serve low income and minority populations.

Housing and Day Care: On-campus housing and day care facilities are available.

Employment of Department Graduates:

Master's Degree Graduates: Of those who graduated in the academic year 2000–2001, the following categories and numbers represent the post-graduate activities and employment of master's degree graduates: Enrolled in a post-doctoral residency/fellowship (n/a), employed in independent practice (n/a).

Doctoral Degree Graduates: Of those who graduated in the academic year 2000–2001, the following categories and numbers represent the post-graduate activities and employment of doctoral degree graduates: Enrolled in a psychology doctoral program (n/a), enrolled in another graduate/professional program (n/a).

Additional Information:

Orientation, Objectives, and Emphasis of Department: The MA program provides advanced coursework and research training in core areas of psychology. Completion of the MA can facilitate application to PhD programs in psychology and provides skills important to careers in education, the health professions, and industry. The MS program in clinical psychology is intended to prepare students for work in a variety of mental health settings, and the program contains coursework relevant for the MFT license in California. The program is also designed to prepare students for PhD work in both academic and professional schools of clinical psychology.

Special Facilities or Resources: The department has laboratories for research in information processing, conditioning, pharmacology, social psychology, biofeedback, psychological testing, and developmental psychology. The department has extensive computer facilities and an electronics shop.

Application Information:
Send to: Graduate Office, Department of Psychology, California State Fullerton, P.O. Box 6846, Fullerton CA 92834-6846. Students are admitted in the Fall, application deadline March 1. Department Application and University Application *Fee:* $55. Application Fee for University application.

California State University, Long Beach
Department of Psychology
1250 Bellflower Boulevard
Long Beach, CA 90840-0901
Telephone: (562) 985-5000
E-mail: *psygrad@csulb.edu*
Web: *http://www.csulb.edu/~psych/*

Department Established:
1949. Chairperson: Keith Colman. Number of Faculty: total–full-time 34, part-time 23; women–full-time 13, part-time 17; minority–full-time 6, part-time 6.

Programs and Degrees Offered:
Listed in the following order: Program area, degree type (T if terminal Master's), number awarded 7/00-6/01. Industrial/Organizational MA (T) 8, Research MA (T) 9.

Student Applications/Admissions:
Student Applications
Industrial/Organizational MA—Applications 2001–2002, 41. Total applicants accepted 2001–2002, 15. New applicants enrolled 2001–2002, 8. Total enrolled 2001–2002 full-time, 8, part-time, 12. Openings 2002–2003, 15. *Research MA*—Applications 2001–2002, 23. Total applicants accepted 2001–2002, 19. New applicants enrolled 2001–2002, 8. Total enrolled

2001–2002 full-time, 17, part-time, 19. Openings 2002–2003, 20.

Admissions Requirements:

Scores: Entries appear in this order: required test or GPA, minimum score (if required), median score of students entering in 2001–2002. Master's Programs: GRE-V no minimum stated, 505; GRE-Q no minimum stated, 590; GRE-V+Q no minimum stated, 1095; GRE-Analytical no minimum stated, 576; GRE-Subject(Psych) no minimum stated, 595; last 2 years GPA no minimum stated, 3.59; psychology GPA no minimum stated, 3.62. GRE-Subject (Psychology) no longer required for either program. Doctoral Programs: last 2 years GPA no minimum stated; psychology GPA no minimum stated; psychology GPA no minimum stated.

Other Criteria: (importance of criteria rated low, medium, or high): GRE/MAT scores high, research experience medium, work experience low, extracurricular activity low, GPA high, letters of recommendation high, statement of goals and objectives high.

Student Characteristics: The following represents characteristics of students in 2001–2002 in all graduate psychology programs in the department: Female–full-time 20, part-time 23; Male–full-time 4, part-time 9; African American/Black–full-time 0, part-time 1; Hispanic/Latino (a)–full-time 2, part-time 2; Asian/Pacific Islander–full-time 4, part-time 1; American Indian/Alaska Native–full-time 0, part-time 1.

Financial Information/Assistance:

Tuition for Full-Time Study: *Master's:* State residents per academic year $1,822; nonstate residents: per academic year $6,250, $246 per credit hour.

Financial Assistance:

First Year Students: Research assistantships available for first-year. Average amount paid per academic year: $5,000. Average number of hours worked per week: 10. Apply by April 15th. Fellowships and scholarships available for first-year. Average amount paid per academic year: $2,500. Apply by March 1st.

Advanced Students: Research assistantships available for advanced students. Average amount paid per academic year: $5,000. Average number of hours worked per week: 10. Apply by April 15th. Fellowships and scholarships available for advanced students. Average amount paid per academic year: $2,500. Apply by March 1st.

Contact Information: Of all students currently enrolled full-time, 1% benefitted from one or more of the listed financial assistance programs. For information on financial assistance, contact: Financial Aid Office (562) 985-4641, http://www.csulb.edu/depts/enrollment/html/financial_aid.html.

Internships/Practica: Graduate assistantship positions provide teaching, computer, and internship experiences to selected students in all the master's programs. Applications for graduate assistantships are available through the Graduate Office and are included in the application packet. Graduate assistantship assignments are based upon the pairing of each applicant's academic background, interests, and experience with current department needs. Specific assignments are geared toward providing educational experiences most appropriate for students in each program. Appointments are for ten hours per week. Available teaching assignments include assistance to the introductory and intermediate statistics, psychological assessment, critical thinking, program evaluation, computer applications, and research methods courses. In addition to the aforementioned paid departmental positions, volunteer and/or externally funded research positions can be arranged with individual faculty members. Such research opportunities are often available in the physiological, cognition, language, human factors, language acquisition, and social psychology laboratories. Various internships in outside industrial and organizational settings are options for second-year MAIO students.

Housing and Day Care: On-campus housing and day care facilities are available.

Employment of Department Graduates:

Master's Degree Graduates: Of those who graduated in the academic year 2000–2001, the following categories and numbers represent the post-graduate activities and employment of master's degree graduates: Enrolled in a post-doctoral residency/fellowship (n/a), employed in independent practice (n/a).

Doctoral Degree Graduates: Of those who graduated in the academic year 2000–2001, the following categories and numbers represent the post-graduate activities and employment of doctoral degree graduates: Enrolled in a psychology doctoral program (n/a), enrolled in another graduate/professional program (n/a).

Additional Information:

Orientation, Objectives, and Emphasis of Department: California State University Long Beach has two master's programs in psychology. The Master of Arts, Research Option (MA-R) prepares students for doctoral work in any psychology field or for master's-level research or teaching positions. Core seminars include cognition, learning, physiological and sensory psychology, social, personality, and developmental psychology, and quantitative methods. MA-R graduates who apply to doctoral programs have high acceptance rates with financial support. An option within the MA-R program is an emphasis in applied experimental/human factors. This option prepares students to apply knowledge of psychology to the design of jobs, information systems, consumer products, workplaces, and equipment in order to improve user performance, safety, and comfort. Students acquire a background in the core areas of experimental psychology, research design and methodology, human factors, computer applications, and applied research methods. The master of arts, industrial and organizational option (MAIO) offers preparation for careers for which a background in industrial/organizational psychology is essential. These fields include personnel, organizational development, industrial relations, employee training, and marketing research.

Special Facilities or Resources: The psychology building has extensive facilities available without charge. Computer facilities, with microcomputers and mainframe stations include many current software packages. The physiological research lab, with a staffed animal compound, is used to study conditioned analgesia and neurotransmission. For research in stress and coping, interpersonal relations, social influence, gender psychology, and the biopsychology of mood, there are many research suites and a test materials center. These facilities, located in the psychology building, are for research and training in interviewing and case studies, forensic psychology, program and treatment evaluation, assessment of social support and family systems, self-management, and intervention strategies for hard-to-reach populations. Computer facilities are central to research in decision analysis, human-computer interface, statistical theory, assessment, and computer-aided instruction. Research in child temperament and hyperactivity, language acquisition, and cognition in older adults are done in special labs. A computerized human-factors lab is used to study audition and vision. Our diversified facilities also accommodate a large AIDS-education project, research in managing diversity in the workplace, and other topics in industrial/organizational psychology. Outstanding CSULB Library facilities are available.

Application Information:

Send to: Psychology Graduate Office, 1250 Bellflower Blvd., Long Beach, CA 90840-0901. Students are admitted in the Fall, application deadline March 1. *Fee:* $55.

California State University, Northridge

Department of Psychology
Social and Behavioral Sciences
18111 Nordhoff Street
Northridge, CA 91330-8255
Telephone: (818) 677-2827
Fax: (818) 677-2829
E-mail: *paul.skolnick@csun.edu*
Web: *http://www.csun.edu/hfpsy004*

Department Established:

1958. Chair: Paul Skolnick. Number of Faculty: total–full-time 27, part-time 38; women–full-time 13, part-time 12; minority–full-time 5; faculty subject to the Americans with Disabilities Act 4.

Programs and Degrees Offered:

Listed in the following order: Program area, degree type (T if terminal Master's), number awarded 7/00-6/01. Clinical Psychology MA 8, General Psychology MA 5, Human Factors MA (T) 10.

Student Applications/Admissions:

Student Applications

Clinical Psychology MA—Applications 2001–2002, 28. Total applicants accepted 2001–2002, 15. New applicants enrolled 2001–2002, 11. Total enrolled 2001–2002 full-time, 11. Openings 2002–2003, 12. The Median number of years required for completion of a degree are 2. The number of students enrolled full and part-time, who were dismissed or voluntarily withdrew from this program area were 0. *General Psychology* MA—Applications 2001–2002, 20. Total applicants accepted 2001–2002, 17. New applicants enrolled 2001–2002, 12. Total enrolled 2001–2002 full-time, 12. Openings 2002–2003, 12. The Median number of years required for completion of a degree are 2. The number of students enrolled full and part-time, who were dismissed or voluntarily withdrew from this program area were 0. *Human Factors* MA—Applications 2001–2002, 11. Total applicants accepted 2001–2002, 8. New applicants enrolled 2001–2002, 6. Total enrolled 2001–2002 full-time, 6.

Openings 2002–2003, 12. The Median number of years required for completion of a degree are 2. The number of students enrolled full and part-time, who were dismissed or voluntarily withdrew from this program area were 0.

Admissions Requirements:

Scores: Entries appear in this order: required test or GPA, minimum score (if required), median score of students entering in 2001–2002. Master's Programs: GRE-V 500, 500; GRE-Q 540, 540; GRE-V+Q no minimum stated; GRE-Analytical no minimum stated; GRE-V+Q+Analytical no minimum stated; GRE-Subject(Psych) 540, 540; overall undergraduate GPA 3.0, 3.5; last 2 years GPA 3.0, 3.5; psychology GPA 3.0, 3.5. Doctoral Programs: last 2 years GPA no minimum stated; psychology GPA no minimum stated; psychology GPA no minimum stated.

Other Criteria: (importance of criteria rated low, medium, or high): GRE/MAT scores low, research experience high, work experience medium, extracurricular activity medium, clinically related public service high, GPA medium, letters of recommendation high, statement of goals and objectives high.

Student Characteristics: The following represents characteristics of students in 2001–2002 in all graduate psychology programs in the department: Female–full-time 39, part-time 0; Male–full-time 21, part-time 0; African American/Black–full-time 0, part-time 0; Hispanic/Latino (a)–full-time 0, part-time 0; Asian/Pacific Islander–full-time 0, part-time 0; American Indian/Alaska Native–full-time 0, part-time 0.

Financial Information/Assistance:

Tuition for Full-Time Study: *Master's:* State residents per academic year $946; nonstate residents: per academic year $946, $246 per credit hour.

Financial Assistance:

First Year Students: No information provided.
Advanced Students: No information provided.
Contact Information: For information on financial assistance, contact: Office of Financial Aid at (818) 677-3000 and/or the Office of Graduate Studies at (818) 677-2138.

Internships/Practica: Students in applied fields have available an array of internships in the area. Clinical internships are available at many sites including the University Counseling Services and local mental health care facilities. Human Factors students are connected with research and applications positions in the region. General Experimental students work both with departmental faculty as well as those at neighboring universities.

Housing and Day Care: On-campus housing and day care facilities are available.

Employment of Department Graduates:

Master's Degree Graduates: Of those who graduated in the academic year 2000–2001, the following categories and numbers represent the post-graduate activities and employment of master's degree graduates: Enrolled in a post-doctoral residency/fellowship (n/a), employed in independent practice (n/a).
Doctoral Degree Graduates: Of those who graduated in the academic year 2000–2001, the following categories and numbers represent the post-graduate activities and employment of doctoral

degree graduates: Enrolled in a psychology doctoral program (n/a), enrolled in another graduate/professional program (n/a).

Additional Information:

Orientation, Objectives, and Emphasis of Department: The Department of Psychology has, as a primary goal, the assurance that students receive a strong theoretical foundation as well as rigorous methodological and statistical coursework. In addition, all students must complete a project or a thesis in order to display their knowledge of their content area and their methodological sophistication. The applied Human Factors program emphasizes both job-related skills and general skills should students desire to continue their education at the doctoral level (and many do). The General Experimental and Clinical programs emphasize the basic research and content knowledge required to enhance students' opportunities for entry into doctoral programs.

Special Facilities or Resources: Some professors have federal or private grants that employ graduate students as research assistants. In addition, we have laboratories in Physiological Psychology (Neuro Scan), computer applications for Cognitive and Human Factors Psychology, multiple childcare sites for observation of children, and extensive research space.

Information for Students With Physical Disabilities: The campus' Office of Students with Disabilities Resources provides students with transportation, note-taking, ASL interpretation, and many other services. The campus houses the National Center on Deafness and the Center on Disabilities, both a tribute to our commitment to students with disabilities.

Application Information:

Send to: Psychology Graduate Office, California State University Northridge, 18111 Nordhoff Street, Northridge, CA 91330-8255. Students are admitted in the Fall, application deadline February 15; Spring, application deadline November 1. *Fee:* $55. Contact Admissions and Records Office for details (818) 677-3700.

California State University, Sacramento
Department of Psychology
6000 J Street
Sacramento, CA 95819-6007
Telephone: (916) 278-6254
Fax: (916) 278-6820
E-mail: *bourgt@csus.edu*
Web: *http://www.csus.edu/psyc/index.html*

Department Established:

1947. Chairperson: Tammy Bourg. Number of Faculty: total–full-time 21, part-time 12; women–full-time 11, part-time 8; minority–full-time 2.

Programs and Degrees Offered:

Listed in the following order: Program area, degree type (T if terminal Master's), number awarded 7/00-6/01. Counseling-marriage and family MA (T), doctoral preparation MA (T), industrial/organizational MA (T).

Student Applications/Admissions:
Student Applications

Counseling-marriage and family MA—Total applicants accepted 2001–2002, 10. The Median number of years required for completion of a degree are 4. *Doctoral preparation MA*—Total applicants accepted 2001–2002, 14. The Median number of years required for completion of a degree are 3. *Industrial/organizational MA*—Total applicants accepted 2001–2002, 8. The Median number of years required for completion of a degree are 3.

Admissions Requirements:

Scores: Entries appear in this order: required test or GPA, minimum score (if required), median score of students entering in 2001–2002. Master's Programs: GRE-V no minimum stated, 580; GRE-Q no minimum stated, 580; GRE-Analytical no minimum stated, 580; GRE-Subject(Psych) no minimum stated, 580. Doctoral Programs: last 2 years GPA no minimum stated; psychology GPA no minimum stated; psychology GPA no minimum stated.
Other Criteria: (importance of criteria rated low, medium, or high): GRE/MAT scores high, GPA high, letters of recommendation high.

Student Characteristics: The following represents characteristics of students in 2001–2002 in all graduate psychology programs in the department: Female–full-time 9, part-time 21; Male–full-time 1, part-time 4; African American/Black–full-time 2, part-time 0; Hispanic/Latino (a)–full-time 2, part-time 0; Asian/Pacific Islander–full-time 2, part-time 0; American Indian/Alaska Native–full-time 0, part-time 0.

Financial Information/Assistance:
Tuition for Full-Time Study: No information provided.

Financial Assistance:

First Year Students: No information provided.
Advanced Students: Teaching assistantships available for advanced students. Fellowships and scholarships available for advanced students.
Contact Information: Of all students currently enrolled full-time, 10% benefitted from one or more of the listed financial assistance programs.

Internships/Practica: Students following both the Industrial-Organizational (I/O) and the Counseling Psychology programs will gain supervised on-site experience. I/O students typically enroll for several semesters of internship supervised by one of our faculty members. Opportunities are available in both public sector organizations (e.g., state, county, and city personnel departments; public utilities) as well as private sector consulting firms, small businesses, and large corporations. Counseling Psychology students must also enroll for additional fieldwork in a community mental health setting with an on-site supervisor. Students may choose from more than a hundred sites in the Sacramento metropolitan area. These community sites must enter into a formal arrangement with the department, and the student's supervision hours must be officially logged.

Housing and Day Care: On-campus housing and day care facilities are available.

Employment of Department Graduates:

Master's Degree Graduates: Of those who graduated in the academic year 2000–2001, the following categories and numbers represent the post-graduate activities and employment of master's degree graduates: Enrolled in a psychology doctoral program (3), enrolled in a post-doctoral residency/fellowship (n/a), employed in independent practice (n/a), employed in business or industry (research/consulting) (2), employed in a government agency (research) (3), employed in a government agency (professional services) (4), employed in a community mental health/counseling center (3).

Doctoral Degree Graduates: Of those who graduated in the academic year 2000–2001, the following categories and numbers represent the post-graduate activities and employment of doctoral degree graduates: Enrolled in a psychology doctoral program (n/a), enrolled in another graduate/professional program (n/a).

Additional Information:

Orientation, Objectives, and Emphasis of Department: Our major programs are Doctoral Preparation, Industrial-Organizational (I/O), and Counseling Psychology. Doctoral preparation students take a strong research methods and quantitative course sequence in addition to content coursework in their interest area. They also engage in research during most of their program, and are encouraged to become teaching assistants. Our I/O program has been designed to meet the competencies specified by SIOP and involved both classroom and fieldwork experience. Students take both general survey and current literature I/O courses in addition to their research, statistics, and measurement/testing courses, and are also expected to gain job experience as an intern. The Counseling Psychology program meets the state licensing requirements for Marriage and Family Therapy; students are exposed to a variety of therapeutic orientations and must participate in multiple practicum courses. In addition, graduate students can supplement their program with a Teaching of Psychology mini-program in which they enroll in a formal teaching course and are then eligible to team teach an introductory psychology course in a subsequent semester. Those oriented toward a teaching career in a community college are advised to supplement their main course of study with this mini-program.

Special Facilities or Resources: The department occupies much of a relatively large building. Extensive facilities for human and animal research are available. We have a modern surgery room, animal colony, electronics and woodworking shops, a well-equipped sleep and dream laboratory, small group rooms with capabilities for audiovisual monitoring and recording, and a perception lab. A multi-room counseling suite within the building also has audiovisual capabilities; students enrolled in our practicum course provide services in this suite (under supervision) to clients from the community. One room in the building is maintained by the computer center; it contains thirty workstations.

Application Information:
Send to: Graduate Coordinator, Psychology Department, CSU, Sacramento, Sacramento, CA 95819-6007. Students are admitted in the Fall, application deadline March 1; Spring, application deadline November 1.

California State University, San Bernardino
Department of Psychology
College of Social and Behavioral Sciences
5500 University Parkway
San Bernardino, CA 92407-2397
Telephone: (909) 880-5570
Fax: (909) 880-7003
E-mail: *Ivanloon@csusb.edu*
Web: *http://www.csusb.edu*

Department Established:
1967. Chairperson: Stuart R. Ellins. Number of Faculty: total–full-time 31, part-time 32; women–full-time 15, part-time 24; minority–full-time 8, part-time 6.

Programs and Degrees Offered:
Listed in the following order: Program area, degree type (T if terminal Master's), number awarded 7/00-6/01. Child Development MA (T), clinical/counseling MA (T) 8, general experimental MA (T) 5, industrial/organization.

Student Applications/Admissions:

Student Applications

Child Development MA—Applications 2001–2002, 37. Total applicants accepted 2001–2002, 16. New applicants enrolled 2001–2002, 16. Total enrolled 2001–2002 full-time, 25, part-time, 12. Openings 2002–2003, 15. The Median number of years required for completion of a degree are 2. The number of students enrolled full and part-time, who were dismissed or voluntarily withdrew from this program area were 0. *Clinical/counseling MA*—Applications 2001–2002, 40. Total applicants accepted 2001–2002, 10. New applicants enrolled 2001–2002, 10. Total enrolled 2001–2002 full-time, 24. Openings 2002–2003, 10. The Median number of years required for completion of a degree are 2. *General experimental MA*—Applications 2001–2002, 37. Total applicants accepted 2001–2002, 7. New applicants enrolled 2001–2002, 7. Total enrolled 2001–2002 full-time, 20, part-time, 9. Openings 2002–2003, 15. The Median number of years required for completion of a degree are 3.

Admissions Requirements:

Scores: Entries appear in this order: required test or GPA, minimum score (if required), median score of students entering in 2001–2002. Master's Programs: GRE-V+Q+Analytical no minimum stated; GRE-Subject(Psych) no minimum stated; overall undergraduate GPA 3.00; psychology GPA 3.00. Only the MA/GE program requires GRE scores. Doctoral Programs: last 2 years GPA no minimum stated; psychology GPA no minimum stated; psychology GPA no minimum stated.

Other Criteria: (importance of criteria rated low, medium, or high): GRE/MAT scores, research experience high, work experience medium, extracurricular activity medium, clinically related public service medium, GPA high, letters of recommendation high, interview high, statement of goals and objectives high. Research experience is medium for clinical and I/O. Work experience and extracurricular activity is low for life-span. Clinically related public service is high for clinical and medium for GE. There are no interviews for lifespan or GE.

Student Characteristics: The following represents characteristics of students in 2001–2002 in all graduate psychology programs in the department: Female–full-time 48, part-time 22; Male–full-time 14, part-time 10; African American/Black–full-time 6, part-time 2; Hispanic/Latino (a)–full-time 15, part-time 5; Asian/Pacific Islander–full-time 8, part-time 4; American Indian/Alaska Native–full-time 1, part-time 0; Multi-ethnic–full-time 2, students subject to the Americans with Disabilities Act–full-time 1.

Financial Information/Assistance:
Tuition for Full-Time Study: *Master's:* State residents per academic year $1,425; nonstate residents: per academic year $7,329, $164 per credit hour.

Financial Assistance:
First Year Students: Research assistantships available for first-year. Average amount paid per academic year: $4,005. Average number of hours worked per week: 10. Apply by Sept. 1.
Advanced Students: Teaching assistantships available for advanced students. Average amount paid per academic year: $1,314. Average number of hours worked per week: 5. Apply by May 1.
Contact Information: Of all students currently enrolled full-time, 20% benefitted from one or more of the listed financial assistance programs. For information on financial assistance, contact: Financial Aid Office, 5500 University Parkway, San Bernardino, CA 92407. Application Process, 909-880-7800.

Internships/Practica: Off campus internships are available for Clinical students during their second year and for Industrial/Organizational students at the end of their first year.

Housing and Day Care: On-campus housing and day care facilities are available.

Employment of Department Graduates:
Master's Degree Graduates: Of those who graduated in the academic year 2000–2001, the following categories and numbers represent the post-graduate activities and employment of master's degree graduates: Enrolled in a post-doctoral residency/fellowship (n/a), employed in independent practice (n/a).
Doctoral Degree Graduates: Of those who graduated in the academic year 2000–2001, the following categories and numbers represent the post-graduate activities and employment of doctoral degree graduates: Enrolled in a psychology doctoral program (n/a), enrolled in another graduate/professional program (n/a).

Additional Information:
Orientation, Objectives, and Emphasis of Department: The objective of the master of arts in psychology is to provide a program of study with courses selected from a variety of basic areas in psychology. The general-experimental psychology concentration provides a broad background suitable for entry into doctoral programs and employment requiring a master of arts in psychology. The Child Development program provides an in-depth background in child growth and development; suitable for students planning on pursuing (or currently in) careers dealing with children or families; or for pursuing a doctoral degree. The areas of concentration for the master of science degree program are clinical/counseling psychology or industrial/organizational psychology. The principal objective of the clinical/counseling program is to provide students with practical skills in counseling, through supervised training and experience and an understanding of relevant subject matter, knowledge, and research methodology. The program is designed to meet the basic requirements of California Assembly Bill 3657 (Section 4980.37) which specifies educational qualifications for licensure as marriage, family, and child counselors. The principal objective of the industrial/organizational program is to provide students with the skills to apply the principles and methods of psychology with organizations, public and private, and to settings where people are engaged in work. Although each of these concentrations differs in emphasis, both will prepare students for doctoral programs and career objectives such as teaching in a community college.

Special Facilities or Resources: Facilities include a community counseling center, physiological research laboratory, child development research institute and lab, small animal research laboratory, and perception laboratory. The department also has its own biofeedback laboratory, computerized cognitive laboratory, a well-equipped neuropharmacology laboratory, access to on-site child care center, and numerous agreements with community agencies.

Information for Students With Physical Disabilities: Services to Students with Disabilities (SSD) provides academic support to disabled students. The services include: tape recording of course related materials, test-taking accommodations, priority registration, and mobility assistance. SSD can be reached at (909) 880-5238 or (909) 880-5242 Voice/TDD.

Application Information:
Send to: Luci Van Loon, Administrative Support Coordinator II, Department of Psychology, 5500 University Parkway, San Bernardino, CA 92407-2397. Students are admitted in the Fall, application deadline see below; Spring, application deadline 4/1. Fall deadlines: MA General/Experimental April 1, MS Clinical/Counseling February 1, MA Child Development. March 1, MS Indus/Org March 1. *Fee:* $55.

California State University, San Marcos
Psychology
San Marcos, CA 92096
Telephone: (760) 750-4102
Fax: (760) 750-3418
E-mail: *mkidd@.csusm.edu*
Web: *http://www.csusm.edu/psychology/*

Department Established:
1989. Chairperson: Marie D. Thomas. Number of Faculty: total–full-time 12, part-time 4; women–full-time 9, part-time 3; minority–full-time 2.

Programs and Degrees Offered:
Listed in the following order: Program area, degree type (T if terminal Master's), number awarded 7/00-6/01. General experimental MA (T) 2.

Student Applications/Admissions:

Student Applications

General experimental MA—Applications 2001–2002, 20. Total applicants accepted 2001–2002, 11. New applicants enrolled 2001–2002, 10. Total enrolled 2001–2002 full-time, 31. Openings 2002–2003, 12. The Median number of years required for completion of a degree are 4. The number of students enrolled full and part-time, who were dismissed or voluntarily withdrew from this program area were 1.

Admissions Requirements:

Scores: Entries appear in this order: required test or GPA, minimum score (if required), median score of students entering in 2001–2002. Master's Programs: GRE-V no minimum stated, 500; GRE-Q no minimum stated, 500; GRE-Analytical no minimum stated, 550; GRE-Subject(Psych) no minimum stated, 550*; overall undergraduate GPA 3.0; last 2 years GPA 3.0; psychology GPA 3.0. GRE-Subject (Psychology) is recommended but not required. Doctoral Programs: last 2 years GPA no minimum stated; psychology GPA no minimum stated; psychology GPA no minimum stated.

Other Criteria: (importance of criteria rated low, medium, or high): GRE/MAT scores medium, research experience high, work experience low, extracurricular activity low, clinically related public service low, GPA high, letters of recommendation high, statement of goals and objectives high.

Student Characteristics: The following represents characteristics of students in 2001–2002 in all graduate psychology programs in the department: Female–full-time 22, part-time 0; Male–full-time 9, part-time 0; African American/Black–full-time 0, part-time 0; Hispanic/Latino (a)–full-time 3, part-time 0; Asian/Pacific Islander–full-time 0, part-time 0; American Indian/Alaska Native–full-time 0, part-time 0.

Financial Information/Assistance:

Tuition for Full-Time Study: No information provided.

Financial Assistance:

First Year Students: No information provided.

Advanced Students: No information provided.

Contact Information: For information on financial assistance, contact: Department of Psychology and the Office of Financial Aid.

Internships/Practica: Our program allows for the application of advanced training in the student's choice of one of the following two courses: Teaching of Psychology or Field Placement. In Teaching of Psychology, designed for students who hope someday to teach at either a community college or a 4-year institution, students learn pedagogical techniques associated with the discipline of psychology and will become eligible for teaching assignments in the university. In Field Placement, students receive supervised experience in a community setting relevant to individual career goals (e.g., industry, counseling agencies).

Housing and Day Care: No on-campus housing and day care facilities are available.

Employment of Department Graduates:

Master's Degree Graduates: Of those who graduated in the academic year 2000–2001, the following categories and numbers represent the post-graduate activities and employment of master's degree graduates: Enrolled in a post-doctoral residency/fellowship (n/a), employed in independent practice (n/a).

Doctoral Degree Graduates: Of those who graduated in the academic year 2000–2001, the following categories and numbers represent the post-graduate activities and employment of doctoral degree graduates: Enrolled in a psychology doctoral program (n/a), enrolled in another graduate/professional program (n/a).

Additional Information:

Orientation, Objectives, and Emphasis of Department: Our program is designed to accommodate students with different goals. The active research programs of our faculty, and our recognition of psychology as a scientific enterprise, provides students with the intensive research training and coursework in primary content areas that are central to preparation for more advanced graduate work in any area of psychology. Likewise, students who have in mind careers in community college teaching, community service, mental health, or business and industry, will benefit from our program's emphasis on critical thinking, research methods, and advanced coursework. It is our belief that excellent graduate education is best accomplished in an atmosphere in which graduate students are closely mentored by the faculty.

Special Facilities or Resources: Established in 1989, CSUSM is the 20th campus of the California State University system. Our facilities are new and are growing to meet the demands of our increasing student population. In Psychology, we offer excellent computer support, a specialized classroom for instruction in research methods, and shared research space for graduate students. Our faculty provide research opportunities for graduate students in a number of off-campus settings in the San Diego area. Among these are the Veterans Affairs Medical Center, Scripps Memorial Hospital, the San Diego Zoo and Wild Animal Park, and the Escondido Boys and Girls Club.

Information for Students With Physical Disabilities: Our office of Disabled Student Services actively addresses the special needs of students with physical disabilities.

Application Information:

Send to: Margie Kidd, Department of Psychology, California State University San Marcos, San Marcos, CA 92096. Students are admitted in the Fall, application deadline March 15. *Fee:* $55. Fee may be waived for a limited number of low income applicants. Ask for a Request for Application Fee Waiver Form.

California, University of, at Berkeley

School Psychology Program, Graduate School of Education
Cognition and Development
Berkeley, CA 94720-1670
Telephone: (510) 642-7581
Fax: (510) 642-3555
E-mail: *nlambert@socrates.berkeley.edu*
Web: *http://www-gse.berkeley.edu/program/sp/sp.html*

Department Established:

1966. Chairperson: Nadine M. Lambert. Number of Faculty: total–full-time 8, part-time 4; women–full-time 3, part-time 1.

Programs and Degrees Offered:

Listed in the following order: Program area, degree type (T if terminal Master's), number awarded 7/00-6/01. School PhD 8.

APA Accreditation: Clinical PhD: probationary. School PhD: probationary.

Student Applications/Admissions:

Student Applications

School PhD—Applications 2001–2002, 70. Total applicants accepted 2001–2002, 10. New applicants enrolled 2001–2002, 3. Total enrolled 2001–2002 full-time, 34. Openings 2002–2003, 6. The Median number of years required for completion of a degree are 7. The number of students enrolled full and part-time, who were dismissed or voluntarily withdrew from this program area were 1.

Admissions Requirements:

Scores: Entries appear in this order: required test or GPA, minimum score (if required), median score of students entering in 2001–2002. Doctoral Programs: GRE-V no minimum stated, 570; GRE-Q no minimum stated, 610; GRE-V+Q no minimum stated, 1260; overall undergraduate GPA 3.00, 3.88; last 2 years GPA no minimum stated; psychology GPA no minimum stated; psychology GPA no minimum stated.

Other Criteria: (importance of criteria rated low, medium, or high): GRE/MAT scores high, research experience high, work experience medium, extracurricular activity medium, clinically related public service medium, GPA high, letters of recommendation high, interview medium, statement of goals and objectives high, Match w/ CD fac.research

Student Characteristics: The following represents characteristics of students in 2001–2002 in all graduate psychology programs in the department: Female–full-time 31, part-time 0; Male–full-time 3, part-time 0; African American/Black–full-time 4, part-time 0; Hispanic/Latino (a)–full-time 3, part-time 0; Asian/Pacific Islander–full-time 4, part-time 0; American Indian/Alaska Native–full-time 0, part-time 0; Multi-ethnic–full-time 0; students subject to the Americans with Disabilities Act–full-time 0.

Financial Information/Assistance:

Tuition for Full-Time Study: *Doctoral:* State residents: per academic year $4,348; nonstate residents: per academic year $15,243.

Financial Assistance:

First Year Students: Teaching assistantships available for first-year. Average amount paid per academic year: $7,200. Average number of hours worked per week: 20. Apply by Before F & S. Tuition remission given: partial. Research assistantships available for first-year. Average amount paid per academic year: $7,000. Average number of hours worked per week: 20. Apply by varies. Tuition remission given: partial. Tuition remission given: partial. Fellowships and scholarships available for first-year. Average amount paid per academic year: $5,000. Apply by December 14. Tuition remission given: full and partial.

Advanced Students: Teaching assistantships available for advanced students. Average amount paid per academic year: $7,200. Apply by Before F & S. Tuition remission given: partial. Research assistantships available for advanced students. Average amount paid per academic year: $7,000. Apply by varies. Tuition remission given: partial. Fellowships and scholarships available

for advanced students. Average amount paid per academic year: $5,000. Apply by March 1. Tuition remission given: full and partial.

Contact Information: Of all students currently enrolled full-time, 80% benefitted from one or more of the listed financial assistance programs. For information on financial assistance, contact: See application materials.

Internships/Practica: Students on school-based internships are usually paid on the basis of school-district schedule for half to three quarter time usually from $10,000-$16,000/ school year. For those doctoral students for whom a professional internship is required prior to graduation, 5 applied in 2000–2001.

Housing and Day Care: No on-campus housing and day care facilities are available.

Employment of Department Graduates:

Master's Degree Graduates: Of those who graduated in the academic year 2000–2001, the following categories and numbers represent the post-graduate activities and employment of master's degree graduates: Enrolled in a post-doctoral residency/fellowship (n/a), employed in independent practice (n/a).

Doctoral Degree Graduates: Of those who graduated in the academic year 2000–2001, the following categories and numbers represent the post-graduate activities and employment of doctoral degree graduates: Enrolled in a psychology doctoral program (n/a), enrolled in another graduate/professional program (n/a), enrolled in a post-doctoral residency/fellowship (1), employed in independent practice (0), employed in an academic position at a university (1), employed in an academic position at a 2-year/4-year college (0), employed in other positions at a higher education institution (0), employed in a professional position in a school system (5), employed in a hospital/medical center (1).

Additional Information:

Orientation, Objectives, and Emphasis of Department: The school psychology program is a doctoral program within the cognition and development area. The program emphasizes the scientist-professional model of school psychological services, linking strong preparation in theory and research to applications in the professional context of schools and school systems. Through the thoughtful application of knowledge and skills, school psychologists work together with teachers and other school professionals to clarify and resolve problems regarding the educational and mental health needs of children in classrooms. Working as consultants and collaborators, school psychologists help others to accommodate the social systems of schools to the individual differences of students, with the ultimate goal of promoting academic and social development. Graduate work within the program is supervised by professors from the Departments of Education and Psychology. Students fulfill all requirements for the academic PhD in human development, with additional coursework representing professional preparation for the specialty practice of school psychology. The program is accredited by APA. A program brochure is available for anyone wishing further information.

Special Facilities or Resources: The school psychology program is based at the University of California, Berkeley, which is a major research university in a large metropolitan area of the country. Students have access to faculty research and university resources in countless topics and areas of specialization. The university and department sponsor numerous colloquia, speakers, and visiting lecturers from around the world throughout the year. Both intellectual and cultural resources abound. Ongoing research programs of faculty offer students opportunities to engage in applications of psychology to educational problems during their first three years of the program and in their dissertation research.

Information for Students With Physical Disabilities: The Berkeley community as well as the campus is fully accessible for students with disabilities.

Application Information:

Send to: Admission Office, Graduate School of Education. Students are admitted in the Fall, application deadline December 15. *Fee:* $40.

California, University of, Davis

Department of Psychology
College of Letters and Science
One Shields Avenue
Davis, CA 95616-8686
Telephone: (530) 752-9362
Fax: (530) 754-5728
E-mail: *wrantaramian@ucdavis.edu*
Web: *http://psychology.ucdavis.edu*

Department Established:

1957. Chairperson: Phillip R. Shaver. Number of Faculty: total–full-time 33, part-time 1; women–full-time 10, part-time 1; minority–full-time 2.

Programs and Degrees Offered:

Listed in the following order: Program area, degree type (T if terminal Master's), number awarded 7/00-6/01. Cognitive PhD 2, comparative PhD, developmental PhD, perception PhD, personality PhD 2, physiological PhD 1, Quantitative PhD, social PhD 1.

Student Applications/Admissions:

Student Applications

Cognitive PhD—Applications 2001–2002, 23. Total applicants accepted 2001–2002, 5. New applicants enrolled 2001–2002, 2. Total enrolled 2001–2002 full-time, 7. The Median number of years required for completion of a degree are 5. *Comparative PhD*—Applications 2001–2002, 5. Total applicants accepted 2001–2002, 1. Total enrolled 2001–2002 full-time, 1. The Median number of years required for completion of a degree are na. *Developmental PhD*—Applications 2001–2002, 7. Total applicants accepted 2001–2002, 4. New applicants enrolled 2001–2002, 3. Total enrolled 2001–2002 full-time, 6. The Median number of years required for completion of a degree are na. *Perception PhD*—Applications 2001–2002, 2. Total enrolled 2001–2002 full-time, 2. The Median number of years required for completion of a degree are na. *Personality PhD*—Applications 2001–2002, 15. Total applicants accepted 2001–2002, 5. New applicants enrolled 2001–2002, 2. Total enrolled 2001–2002 full-time, 8. The Median number of years required for completion of a degree are 5. *Physiological PhD*—Applications 2001–2002, 10. Total applicants accepted 2001–2002, 3. Total enrolled 2001–2002 full-time, 3. The Median number

of years required for completion of a degree are 5. *Quantitative PhD*—Applications 2001–2002, 3. Total applicants accepted 2001–2002, 1. New applicants enrolled 2001–2002, 1. Total enrolled 2001–2002 full-time, 3. The Median number of years required for completion of a degree are na. *Social PhD*—Applications 2001–2002, 31. Total applicants accepted 2001–2002, 12. New applicants enrolled 2001–2002, 6. Total enrolled 2001–2002 full-time, 21. The Median number of years required for completion of a degree are 5.

Admissions Requirements:

Scores: Entries appear in this order: required test or GPA, minimum score (if required), median score of students entering in 2001–2002. Doctoral Programs: GRE-V no minimum stated, 630; GRE-Q no minimum stated, 660; overall undergraduate GPA 3.00, 3.60; last 2 years GPA no minimum stated; psychology GPA no minimum stated; psychology GPA no minimum stated.

Other Criteria: (importance of criteria rated low, medium, or high): GRE/MAT scores high, research experience high, clinically related public service GPA high, letters of recommendation high, interview, statement of goals and objectives high.

Student Characteristics: The following represents characteristics of students in 2001–2002 in all graduate psychology programs in the department: Female–full-time 36, part-time 0; Male–full-time 16, part-time 0; African American/Black–full-time 0, part-time 0; Hispanic/Latino(a)–full-time 2, part-time 0; Asian/Pacific Islander–full-time 10, part-time 0; American Indian/Alaska Native–full-time 1, part-time 0; students subject to the Americans with Disabilities Act–full-time 1.

Financial Information/Assistance:

Tuition for Full-Time Study: *Doctoral:* State residents: per academic year $4,716; nonstate residents: per academic year $15,420.

Financial Assistance:

First Year Students: Teaching assistantships available for first-year. Average amount paid per academic year: $14,200. Average number of hours worked per week: 20. Apply by January 15. Tuition remission given: full. Research assistantships available for first-year. Average amount paid per academic year: $10,970. Average number of hours worked per week: 20. Apply by various. Tuition remission given: full. Fellowships and scholarships available for first-year. Average amount paid per academic year: $15,000. Apply by January 15.

Advanced Students: Teaching assistantships available for advanced students. Average amount paid per academic year: $14,200. Average number of hours worked per week: 20. Apply by April 1. Tuition remission given: full. Research assistantships available for advanced students. Average amount paid per academic year: $10,970. Average number of hours worked per week: 20. Apply by various. Tuition remission given: full. Fellowships and scholarships available for advanced students. Average amount paid per academic year: $3,000. Apply by January 15.

Contact Information: Of all students currently enrolled full-time, 100% benefitted from one or more of the listed financial assistance programs. For information on financial assistance, contact: Graduate Program Coordinator (530) 752-9362.

Internships/Practica: No information provided.

Housing and Day Care: No on-campus housing and day care facilities are available.

Employment of Department Graduates:

Master's Degree Graduates: Of those who graduated in the academic year 2000–2001, the following categories and numbers represent the post-graduate activities and employment of master's degree graduates: Enrolled in a post-doctoral residency/fellowship (n/a), employed in independent practice (n/a).

Doctoral Degree Graduates: Of those who graduated in the academic year 2000–2001, the following categories and numbers represent the post-graduate activities and employment of doctoral degree graduates: Enrolled in a psychology doctoral program (n/a), enrolled in another graduate/professional program (n/a), enrolled in a post-doctoral residency/fellowship (4), employed in an academic position at a university (1), employed in an academic position at a 2-year/4-year college (1).

Additional Information:

Orientation, Objectives, and Emphasis of Department: The department places a strong emphasis on empirical research training in psychobiology, social and personality psychology, cognition, perception and cognitive neuroscience, developmental, and quantitative psychology. These areas form basic intellectual units that provide graduate students with a close peer group of fellow students and faculty. Weekly area colloquia provide students with the opportunity to hear about new research, and to present their work and ideas to an interested and supportive audience. A period of growth in the size of the faculty, its research expertise, and physical facilities provides new opportunities for doctoral students. Several new laboratories permit students to gain experience in everything from cellular recording and human brain imaging, to advanced computational methods and observational analyses in both humans and animals. Overall, the primary objective of the graduate program is to provide training of the highest quality via close interactions of students, postdoctoral fellows, and faculty. Toward this end our program is designed to be both intellectually challenging and forward-looking as we train new generations of teacher-scientist-scholars ready and able to face the exciting opportunities present in the study of mind, brain, and behavior.

Special Facilities or Resources: There are numerous research facilities located in Young Hall and the Center for Neuroscience, including laboratories in human learning, auditory behavior, neuropsychological testing, visual perception, electrophysiology, and visual neurophysiology; a functional magnetic resonance imaging (fMRI) center; a microcomputer room; observational facilities for social and developmental psychological research. Animal spaces and facilities are also located within Young Hall.

Application Information:
Send to: Bill Antaramian, Graduate Program Coordinator, Psychology Department, University of California, One Shields Ave., Davis, CA 95616-8686. Students are admitted in the Fall, application deadline December 31. *Fee:* $40.

California, University of, Davis (2001 data)
Division of Human Development: Department of Human and
  Community Development
Agricultural and Environmental Sciences
Department of Human and Community Development, One
  Shields Avenue
Davis, CA 95616-8523
Telephone: (530) 752-1926
Fax: (530) 752-5660
E-mail: *gjerwin@ucdavis.edu*
Web: *http://hcd.ucdavis.edu*

Department Established:
1971. Chair, Human Development Graduate Group: Lawrence V. Harper. Number of Faculty: total–full-time 48; women–full-time 24; minority–full-time 4.

Programs and Degrees Offered:
Listed in the following order: Program area, degree type (T if terminal Master's), number awarded 7/00-6/01. Child development MS (T) 2.

Student Applications/Admissions:
Student Applications

Child development MS—Applications 2001–2002, 25. Total applicants accepted 2001–2002, 7. New applicants enrolled 2001–2002, 5. Total enrolled 2001–2002 full-time, 12. Openings 2002–2003, 5.

Admissions Requirements:

Scores: Entries appear in this order: required test or GPA, minimum score (if required), median score of students entering in 2001–2002. Master's Programs: GRE-V no minimum stated, 526; GRE-Q no minimum stated, 632; GRE-Analytical no minimum stated, 704; overall undergraduate GPA 3.0, 3.47.

Other Criteria: (importance of criteria rated low, medium, or high): research experience medium, work experience medium, extracurricular activity low, clinically related public service low, GPA high, letters of recommendation high, interview low, statement of goals and objectives high.

Student Characteristics: The following represents characteristics of students in 2001–2002 in all graduate psychology programs in the department: Female–full-time 4, part-time 0; Male–full-time 1, part-time 0; African American/Black–full-time 1, part-time 0; Hispanic/Latino (a)–full-time 0, part-time 0; Asian/Pacific Islander–full-time 0, part-time 0; American Indian/Alaska Native–full-time 0, part-time 0.

Financial Information/Assistance:
Tuition for Full-Time Study: No information provided.

Financial Assistance:

> *First Year Students:* No information provided.
> *Advanced Students:* No information provided.
> *Contact Information:* No information provided.

Internships/Practica: Application of theories of learning and development to interaction with children six months to five years at the Center for Child and Family Studies. Field Studies with Children and Adolescents. Study of children's affective, cognitive, and social development within the context of family/school environments, hospitals, and foster group homes. Child Life internships through the University of California Davis Medical Center. Internships through the 4-H Center for Youth Development, includng 4-H and CE-sponsored out-of-school childcare, etc.

Housing and Day Care: No on-campus housing and day care facilities are available.

Employment of Department Graduates:

> *Master's Degree Graduates:* Of those who graduated in the academic year 2000–2001, the following categories and numbers represent the post-graduate activities and employment of master's degree graduates: Enrolled in a post-doctoral residency/fellowship (n/a), employed in independent practice (n/a).
> *Doctoral Degree Graduates:* Of those who graduated in the academic year 2000–2001, the following categories and numbers represent the post-graduate activities and employment of doctoral degree graduates: Enrolled in a psychology doctoral program (n/a), enrolled in another graduate/professional program (n/a).

Additional Information:

> *Orientation, Objectives, and Emphasis of Department:* The degree offered by this graduate group is interdisciplinary in nature, with a core faculty housed in the Department of Human and Community Development, and other graduate group faculty housed in education, law, medicine, psychiatry, and psychology. Student will be prepared to teach at the community college level cognitive, social-emotional, infancy, childhood, middle childhood, and adolescence with various contexts of development (family, school, heath, social-cultural, and social policy). There are extensive student research opportunities within all the departments from which faculty are drawn, as well as the Center for Child and Family Studies, the 4-H Extension Program's Center for Youth Development, and the Center for Neuroscience.

> *Special Facilities or Resources:* Center for Child and Family Studies, Infant Sleep Lab, Parent and Child Lab Center for Neuroscience, Center for Youth Development, Cooperative Research and Extension Services for Schools.

> *Information for Students With Physical Disabilities:* UC Davis has appropriate facilities/resources for students with disabilities. Physical accommodations-Disability Resource Center.

Application Information:
Send to: Judy Erwin, Graduate Assistant, Child Development Graduate Group, University of California, One Shields Ave., Davis, CA 65616-8523. Students are admitted in the Fall, application deadline January 15. January 15-fellowship deadline. *Fee:* $40.

California, University of, Irvine

Cognitive Sciences Department
School of Social Sciences, UCI
Irvine, CA 92697-5100
Telephone: (949) 824-6800
Fax: (949) 824-2307
E-mail: *bdosher@uci.edu*
Web: *http://www.socsci.uci.edu/cogsci*

Department Established:

> 1986. Chairperson: Barbara A. Dosher. Number of Faculty: total–full-time 24, part-time 15; women–full-time 4; minority–full-time 3.

Programs and Degrees Offered:

> Listed in the following order: Program area, degree type (T if terminal Master's), number awarded 7/00-6/01. Cognitive PhD 7.

Student Applications/Admissions:

> *Student Applications*
>
> *Cognitive PhD*—Applications 2001–2002, 48. Total applicants accepted 2001–2002, 23. New applicants enrolled 2001–2002, 8. Total enrolled 2001–2002 full-time, 30. Openings 2002–2003, 15. The Median number of years required for completion of a degree are 6. The number of students enrolled full and part-time, who were dismissed or voluntarily withdrew from this program area were 0.

> *Admissions Requirements:*
>
> *Scores:* Entries appear in this order: required test or GPA, minimum score (if required), median score of students entering in 2001–2002. Doctoral Programs: GRE-V no minimum stated, 570; GRE-Q no minimum stated, 723; GRE-Analytical no minimum stated, 690; overall undergraduate GPA 3.0; last 2 years GPA 3.5; psychology GPA no minimum stated; psychology GPA 3.5.
>
> *Other Criteria:* (importance of criteria rated low, medium, or high): GRE/MAT scores high, research experience high, work experience low, GPA medium, letters of recommendation high, interview high, statement of goals and objectives high, math/science courses medium.

> *Student Characteristics:* The following represents characteristics of students in 2001–2002 in all graduate psychology programs in the department: Female–full-time 15, part-time 0; Male–full-time 15, part-time 0; African American/Black–full-time 0, part-time 0; Hispanic/Latino(a)–full-time 1, part-time 0; Asian/Pacific Islander–full-time 9, part-time 0; American Indian/Alaska Native–full-time 0, part-time 0; Multi-ethnic–full-time 0; students subject to the Americans with Disabilities Act–full-time 0.

Financial Information/Assistance:

> **Tuition for Full-Time Study:** *Doctoral:* State residents: per academic year $5,294; nonstate residents: per academic year $16,188.

Financial Assistance:

> *First Year Students:* Teaching assistantships available for first-year. Average amount paid per academic year: $14,300. Average number of hours worked per week: 20. Apply by April 15. Tuition remission given: partial. Research assistantships available

for first-year. Average amount paid per academic year: $12,000. Average number of hours worked per week: 20. Apply by April 15. Tuition remission given: full. Fellowships and scholarships available for first-year. Apply by April 15. Tuition remission given: full and partial.

Advanced Students: Teaching assistantships available for advanced students. Average amount paid per academic year: $14,300. Average number of hours worked per week: 20. Apply by 3wks bef qtr. Tuition remission given: partial. Research assistantships available for advanced students. Average amount paid per academic year: $14,000. Average number of hours worked per week: 20. Tuition remission given: full. Fellowships and scholarships available for advanced students. Apply by varies. Tuition remission given: full.

Contact Information: Of all students currently enrolled full-time, 99% benefitted from one or more of the listed financial assistance programs. For information on financial assistance, contact: Office of Financial Aid and Educational Financing, University of CA, Irvine, CA 92697-2825, (949) 824-8261, 8262 or http://www.fao.uci.edu.

Internships/Practica: None.

Housing and Day Care: On-campus housing and day care facilities are available.

Employment of Department Graduates:

Master's Degree Graduates: Of those who graduated in the academic year 2000–2001, the following categories and numbers represent the post-graduate activities and employment of master's degree graduates: Enrolled in a post-doctoral residency/fellowship (n/a), employed in independent practice (n/a).

Doctoral Degree Graduates: Of those who graduated in the academic year 2000–2001, the following categories and numbers represent the post-graduate activities and employment of doctoral degree graduates: Enrolled in a psychology doctoral program (n/a), enrolled in another graduate/professional program (n/a), enrolled in a post-doctoral residency/fellowship (3), employed in an academic position at a university (1), employed in an academic position at a 2-year/4-year college (1), employed in business or industry (research/consulting) (1), other employment position (1).

Additional Information:

Orientation, Objectives, and Emphasis of Department: The graduate program in psychology is administered by the Department of Cognitive Sciences, which has faculty interested in human cognition, perception, skill learning, cognitive psychology, cognitive neuroscience, neuropsychology, and mathematical psychology. The faculty lay special stress on precise scientific approaches to issues in human cognition and view formal models as instrumental in understanding the nature of the human mind. Research interests include: mathematical psychology, perception (visual and auditory), cognitive development, problem solving, artificial intelligence, learning, memory, motor behavior, psycholinguistics, and semiotics. The graduate program does not emphasize traditional training in psychology: rather it stresses the integration of research in the areas mentioned above, and in related areas, into a discipline whose central focus is the study of human knowledge and human information processing, regardless of the medium in which it is expressed.

Special Facilities or Resources: The Virtual Reality Lab, directed by Cognitive Sciences Professor Michael D'Zmura, supports work on visual perception, visuomotor coordination, and virtual environments. Equipment in the lab includes a Silicon Graphics Onyx2 computer with two Infinite Reality graphics pipelines, each driving a high resolution monitor and a head mounted display with position tracking. A Phantom 3D device is available for research involving haptic texture perception. The University recently purchased a 4 Tesla MRI scanner that currently is being set up on the main campus in the medical school complex. This high-power, research-dedicated system will be used for a broad range of scientific investigations. Among these will be studies allowing cognitive neuroscientists to map brain function with exceptionally high sensitivity and spatial resolution.

Application Information:
Send to: Graduate Advisor, Department of Cognitive Sciences, 3151 Social Science Plaza, University of California, Irvine, CA 92697. Students are admitted in the Fall, application deadline January 15. Application must be received before fall deadline of January 15 to ensure consideration for financial aid. *Fee:* $40.

California, University of, Irvine
Department of Psychology and Social Behavior
University of California
Irvine, CA 92697-7085
Telephone: (949) 824-5917
Fax: (949) 824-3002
E-mail: *jhaynes@uci.edu*
Web: *http://www.seweb.uci.edu/psb_home.html*

Department Established:
1992. Chairperson: Chuansheng Chen. Number of Faculty: total–full-time 19, part-time 6; women–full-time 11, part-time 4; minority–full-time 3.

Programs and Degrees Offered:
Listed in the following order: Program area, degree type (T if terminal Master's), number awarded 7/00-6/01. Psychology and Social Behavior PhD N/A.

Student Applications/Admissions:
Student Applications
Psychology and Social Behavior PhD—Applications 2001–2002, N/A. Total applicants accepted 2001–2002, N/A. New applicants enrolled 2001–2002, N/A. Total enrolled 2001–2002 full-time, N/A, part-time, N/A. Openings 2002–2003, 12. The Median number of years required for completion of a degree are NA. The number of students enrolled full and part-time, who were dismissed or voluntarily withdrew from this program area were N/A.

Admissions Requirements:
Scores: Entries appear in this order: required test or GPA, minimum score (if required), median score of students entering in 2001–2002. Doctoral Programs: GRE-V no minimum stated, 620; GRE-Q no minimum stated, 660; GRE-V+Q no minimum stated; overall undergraduate GPA 3.0, 3.6 ; last 2 years

GPA no minimum stated; psychology GPA no minimum stated; psychology GPA no minimum stated.

Other Criteria: (importance of criteria rated low, medium, or high): GRE/MAT scores medium, research experience high, work experience low, extracurricular activity low, clinically related public service low, GPA high, letters of recommendation high, interview high, statement of goals and objectives high.

Student Characteristics: The following represents characteristics of students in 2001–2002 in all graduate psychology programs in the department: Female–full-time 5, part-time 0; Male–full-time 2, part-time 0; African American/Black–full-time 0, part-time 0; Hispanic/Latino (a)–full-time 0, part-time 0; Asian/Pacific Islander–full-time 1, part-time 0; American Indian/Alaska Native–full-time 0, part-time 0.

Financial Information/Assistance:

Tuition for Full-Time Study: *Doctoral:* State residents: per academic year $5,294; nonstate residents: per academic year $16,616.

Financial Assistance:

First Year Students: Teaching assistantships available for first-year. Average amount paid per academic year: $14,050. Average number of hours worked per week: 20. Apply by varies. Tuition remission given: partial. Research assistantships available for first-year. Average amount paid per academic year: $13,500. Average number of hours worked per week: 20. Apply by varies. Fellowships and scholarships available for first-year. Average amount paid per academic year: $12,000. Average number of hours worked per week: 0. Apply by varies.

Advanced Students: Teaching assistantships available for advanced students. Average amount paid per academic year: $14,050. Apply by varies. Research assistantships available for advanced students. Average amount paid per academic year: $13,500. Apply by varies. Fellowships and scholarships available for advanced students. Average amount paid per academic year: $6,500. Apply by varies.

Contact Information: Of all students currently enrolled full-time, 95% benefitted from one or more of the listed financial assistance programs. For information on financial assistance, contact: Financial Aid, 949-824-8262.

Internships/Practica: The school places a strong emphasis on field experiences as part of the education of students and maintains an extensive list of community agencies where students may seek various forms of research involvement. All students are required to take the course "Applied Psychological Research." An optional course "Applied Psychological Research in Community Settings" is available to students who would like to have field placement experience.

Housing and Day Care: On-campus housing and day care facilities are available.

Employment of Department Graduates:

Master's Degree Graduates: Of those who graduated in the academic year 2000–2001, the following categories and numbers represent the post-graduate activities and employment of master's degree graduates: Enrolled in a post-doctoral residency/fellowship (n/a), employed in independent practice (n/a).

Doctoral Degree Graduates: Of those who graduated in the academic year 2000–2001, the following categories and numbers represent the post-graduate activities and employment of doctoral degree graduates: Enrolled in a psychology doctoral program (n/a), enrolled in another graduate/professional program (n/a).

Additional Information:

Orientation, Objectives, and Emphasis of Department: The Department of Psychology and Social Behavior is united by an overarching interest in human adaptation in various sociocultural and developmental contexts. The department has emphases in four areas (Health Psychology, Developmental Psychology, Social and Personality Psychology, and Psychopathology and Behavioral Disorder). The multidisciplinary faculty, whose training is mainly in social, developmental, clinical, and community psychology, examines human health, well-being, and the ways in which individuals respond and adjust to changing circumstances over the life span. Faculty interests include stress and coping, cognitive and biobehavioral processes in health behavior, subjective well-being, cognition and emotion, social development and developmental transitions across the life span, cultural influences on cognition and behavior, psychology and law, aging and health, and societal problems such as violence and unemployment.

Special Facilities or Resources: In-house laboratories, including the Consortium for Integrative Health Studies, the Family Studies Lab, the Development in Cultural Contexts Lab, and the Health Psychology Lab, provide graduate students with direct access to state-of-the-art facilities and opportunities for research training. In addition, the department maintains strong ties with psychologists at other campuses in the area, including UC Los Angeles, UC Riverside, and UC San Diego (each approximately one hour away), and the UCI College of Medicine. For example, we participate in the Consortium on Families and Human Development, a joint undertaking of faculty members and graduate students at UCLA, UCR, UCI, and the University of Southern California. Selected students participate as predoctoral fellows in the Department's NIMH Training Program, and opportunities continually arise for all students to become involved in many ongoing faculty research projects.

Application Information:
Send to: Jeanne Haynes, 205 Social Ecology I, Graduate Counseling Office, School of Social Ecology UCI, Irvine, CA 92697-7065. Students are admitted in the Fall, application deadline January 9. *Fee:* $40.

California, University of, Los Angeles
Department of Psychology
Letters and Science
405 Hilgard Avenue
Los Angeles, CA 90095-1563
Telephone: (310) 825-2617
Fax: (310) 206-5895
E-mail: *gradadm@psych.ucla.edu*
Web: *http://www.psych.ucla.edu*

Department Established:
Chairperson: Peter Bentler. Number of Faculty: total–full-time 60, part-time 20; women–full-time 18, part-time 10; minority–full-time 9.

Programs and Degrees Offered:

Listed in the following order: Program area, degree type (T if terminal Master's), number awarded 7/00-6/01. Behavioral neuroscience PhD, clinical PhD 10, cognitive PhD 3, developmental PhD 5, learning and behavior PhD 1, psychometrics and measurement PhD, social PhD 6.

APA Accreditation: Clinical PhD: full.

Student Applications/Admissions:

Student Applications

Behavioral neuroscience PhD—Applications 2001–2002, 20. Total applicants accepted 2001–2002, 7. New applicants enrolled 2001–2002, 3. Total enrolled 2001–2002 full-time, 21. Openings 2002–2003, 5. *Clinical PhD*—Applications 2001–2002, 273. Total applicants accepted 2001–2002, 22. New applicants enrolled 2001–2002, 11. Total enrolled 2001–2002 full-time, 67. Openings 2002–2003, 12. *Cognitive PhD*—Applications 2001–2002, 33. Total applicants accepted 2001–2002, 12. New applicants enrolled 2001–2002, 7. Total enrolled 2001–2002 full-time, 24. Openings 2002–2003, 5. *Developmental PhD*—Applications 2001–2002, 26. Total applicants accepted 2001–2002, 7. New applicants enrolled 2001–2002, 4. Total enrolled 2001–2002 full-time, 13. Openings 2002–2003, 4. *Learning and behavior PhD*—Applications 2001–2002, 3. Total applicants accepted 2001–2002, 1. New applicants enrolled 2001–2002, 1. Total enrolled 2001–2002 full-time, 9. Openings 2002–2003, 2. *Psychometrics and measurement PhD*—Applications 2001–2002, 5. Total applicants accepted 2001–2002, 2. New applicants enrolled 2001–2002, 1. Total enrolled 2001–2002 full-time, 8. Openings 2002–2003, 2. *Social PhD*—Applications 2001–2002, 86. Total applicants accepted 2001–2002, 13. New applicants enrolled 2001–2002, 8. Total enrolled 2001–2002 full-time, 20. Openings 2002–2003, 5.

Admissions Requirements:

Scores: Entries appear in this order: required test or GPA, minimum score (if required), median score of students entering in 2001–2002. Doctoral Programs: GRE-V no minimum stated, 636; GRE-Q no minimum stated, 719; GRE-Analytical no minimum stated, 728; GRE-Subject(Psych) no minimum stated, 708; overall undergraduate GPA no minimum stated, 3.71; last 2 years GPA no minimum stated; psychology GPA no minimum stated; psychology GPA no minimum stated.

Other Criteria: (importance of criteria rated low, medium, or high): research experience high, work experience medium, extracurricular activity medium, clinically related public service medium, letters of recommendation high, interview high, statement of goals and objectives high.

Student Characteristics: The following represents characteristics of students in 2001–2002 in all graduate psychology programs in the department: Female–full-time 104, part-time 0; Male–full-time 59, part-time 0; African American/Black–full-time 7, part-time 0; Hispanic/Latino (a)–full-time 8, part-time 0; Asian/Pacific Islander–full-time 21, part-time 0; American Indian/Alaska Native–full-time 1, part-time 0; Multi-ethnic–full-time 0, part-time 0; students subject to the Americans with Disabilities Act–full-time 0, part-time 0.

Financial Information/Assistance:

Tuition for Full-Time Study: *Master's:* State residents per academic year $4,550; nonstate residents: per academic year $15,444. *Doctoral:* State residents: per academic year $4,550; nonstate residents: per academic year $15,444.

Financial Assistance:

First Year Students: Teaching assistantships available for first-year. Average amount paid per academic year: $14,000. Average number of hours worked per week: 20. Tuition remission given: partial. Research assistantships available for first-year. Average amount paid per academic year: $15,500. Average number of hours worked per week: 20. Tuition remission given: partial. Traineeships available for first-year. Average amount paid per academic year: $16,000. Average number of hours worked per week: 0. Fellowships and scholarships available for first-year. Average amount paid per academic year: $16,000. Average number of hours worked per week: 0.

Advanced Students: Teaching assistantships available for advanced students. Average amount paid per academic year: $16,500. Average number of hours worked per week: 20. Tuition remission given: partial. Research assistantships available for advanced students. Average amount paid per academic year: $19,500. Average number of hours worked per week: 20. Tuition remission given: partial. Traineeships available for advanced students. Average amount paid per academic year: $18,000. Average number of hours worked per week: 0. Fellowships and scholarships available for advanced students. Average amount paid per academic year: $16,000. Average number of hours worked per week: 0.

Contact Information: Of all students currently enrolled full-time, 0% benefitted from one or more of the listed financial assistance programs. For information on financial assistance, contact: Melina Dorian gradadm@psych.ucla.edu.

Internships/Practica: VA Hospitals; San Fernando Valley Child Guidance Center; St. John's Child Development Center; Neuropsychiatric Institute/UCLA; UCLA Student Psych Services.

Housing and Day Care: On-campus housing and day care facilities are available.

Employment of Department Graduates:

Master's Degree Graduates: Of those who graduated in the academic year 2000–2001, the following categories and numbers represent the post-graduate activities and employment of master's degree graduates: Enrolled in a post-doctoral residency/fellowship (n/a), employed in independent practice (n/a).

Doctoral Degree Graduates: Of those who graduated in the academic year 2000–2001, the following categories and numbers represent the post-graduate activities and employment of doctoral degree graduates: Enrolled in a psychology doctoral program (n/a), enrolled in another graduate/professional program (n/a), enrolled in a post-doctoral residency/fellowship (15), employed in independent practice (0), employed in an academic position at a university (7), employed in an academic position at a 2-year/4-year college (0), employed in other positions at a higher education institution (2), employed in a professional position in a school system (0), employed in business or industry (research/consulting) (2), employed in business or industry (management) (0), employed in a government agency (research) (1), employed in a government agency (professional services) (0), employed in a community mental health/counseling center (0), employed in a hospital/medical center (5), still seeking employment (0), other employment position (2).

Additional Information:

Orientation, Objectives, and Emphasis of Department: Rigorous scientific training is the foundation of the PhD program. The graduate curriculum focuses on the usage of systematic methods of investigation to understand and quantify general principles of human behavior, pathology, cognition, and emotion. More specifically, the department includes such research clusters as psychobiology and the brain; child-clinical and developmental psychology; adult psychopathology and family dynamics; cognition and memory; health, community, and political psychology; minority mental health; social cognition and intergroup relations; measurement; and learning and behavior. In all these areas, the department's central aim is to train researchers dedicated to expanding the scientific knowledge upon which the discipline of psychology rests. This orientation also applies to the clinical program; while it offers excellent clinical training, its emphasis is on training researchers rather than private practitioners. In sum, the graduate training is designed to prepare research psychologists for careers in academic and applied settings—as college and university instructors; for leadership roles in community, government, and business organizations; and as professional research psychologists.

Special Facilities or Resources: The department is one of the largest on campus. Our three-connected buildings (known collectively as Franz Hall) provide ample space (over 120,000 square feet) for psychological research. Laboratory facilities are of the highest quality. Precision equipment is available for electro-physiological stimulation and recording, magnetic resonance imaging (MRI), and for all major areas of sensory study. Specially designed laboratories exist for studies of group behavior and naturalistic observation. An extensive vivarium contains facilities for physiological animal studies. Computing facilities are leading-edge at all levels, from microcomputers to mainframes. The department also houses the Psychology Clinic, a training and research center for psychotherapy and diagnostics. Other resources include the Fernald Child Study Center (a research facility committed to investigating childhood behavioral disorders); the National Research Center for Asian American Mental Health; the California Self-Help Center; and the Center for Computer-Based Behavioral Studies. Departmental affiliations with the Brain Research Institute, the University Elementary School, the Neuropsychiatric Institute, and the local Veterans Administration also provide year-round research opportunities.

Application Information:
Send to: Graduate Admissions Advisor, Psychology Department, 1285 Franz Hall, Box 951563, Los Angeles, CA 90095-1563. Students are admitted in the Fall, application deadline December 15. Only clinical area has a different deadline— December 15 for clinical; December 30 for other areas. *Fee:* $40.

California, University of, Riverside
Department of Psychology
1419 Life Science Building
Riverside, CA 92521-0426
Telephone: (909) 787-6306
Fax: (909) 787-3985
E-mail: *advisor@psych.ucr.edu*
Web: *http://www.psych.ucr.edu*

Department Established:
1962. Chairperson: John H. Ashe. Number of Faculty: total–full-time 19, part-time 3; women–full-time 8, part-time 2; minority–full-time 2, part-time 2.

Programs and Degrees Offered:
Listed in the following order: Program area, degree type (T if terminal Master's), number awarded 7/00-6/01. Cognitive PhD 1, developmental PhD 6, social/personality PhD 4, systems neuroscience PhD.

APA Accreditation: Combined PhD: full.

Student Applications/Admissions:

Student Applications

Cognitive PhD—Applications 2001–2002, 26. Total applicants accepted 2001–2002, 6. New applicants enrolled 2001–2002, 3. Total enrolled 2001–2002 full-time, 11. Openings 2002–2003, 4. The Median number of years required for completion of a degree are 5. The number of students enrolled full and part-time, who were dismissed or voluntarily withdrew from this program area were 0. *Developmental PhD*—Applications 2001–2002, 39. Total applicants accepted 2001–2002, 7. New applicants enrolled 2001–2002, 3. Total enrolled 2001–2002 full-time, 14. Openings 2002–2003, 4. The Median number of years required for completion of a degree are 6. The number of students enrolled full and part-time, who were dismissed or voluntarily withdrew from this program area were 0. *Social/ personality PhD*—Applications 2001–2002, 42. Total applicants accepted 2001–2002, 12. New applicants enrolled 2001–2002, 4. Total enrolled 2001–2002 full-time, 23. Openings 2002–2003, 4. The Median number of years required for completion of a degree are 5. The number of students enrolled full and part-time, who were dismissed or voluntarily withdrew from this program area were 0. *Systems neuroscience PhD*—Applications 2001–2002, 7. Total applicants accepted 2001–2002, 3. New applicants enrolled 2001–2002, 1. Total enrolled 2001–2002 full-time, 4. Openings 2002–2003, 2. The Median number of years required for completion of a degree are na. The number of students enrolled full and part-time, who were dismissed or voluntarily withdrew from this program area were 0.

Admissions Requirements:

Scores: Entries appear in this order: required test or GPA, minimum score (if required), median score of students entering in 2001–2002. Doctoral Programs: GRE-V no minimum stated; GRE-Q no minimum stated; GRE-V+Q 1100, 1168; last 2 years GPA 3.0, 3.83; psychology GPA no minimum stated, 3.8; psychology GPA no minimum stated. A strong GPA in science courses is recommened for applicants to the Systems Neuroscience area.

Other Criteria: (importance of criteria rated low, medium, or high): GRE/MAT scores medium, research experience high, work experience low, extracurricular activity low, GPA medium, letters of recommendation high, interview high, statement of goals and objectives high.

Student Characteristics: The following represents characteristics of students in 2001–2002 in all graduate psychology programs in the department: Female–full-time 37, part-time 0; Male–full-time 15, part-time 0; African American/Black–full-time 2, part-time 0; Hispanic/Latino (a)–full-time 6, part-time 0; Asian/Pacific Islander–full-time 4, part-time 0; American Indian/Alaska Native–full-time 0, part-time 0; Multi-ethnic–full-time 2, part-time 0; students subject to the Americans with Disabilities Act–full-time 0, part-time 0.

Financial Information/Assistance:

Tuition for Full-Time Study: *Doctoral:* State residents: per academic year $5,349; nonstate residents: per academic year $17,000.

Financial Assistance:

First Year Students: Teaching assistantships available for first-year. Average amount paid per academic year: $13,000. Average number of hours worked per week: 20. Apply by Jan 3. Tuition remission given: full and partial. Research assistantships available for first-year. Average amount paid per academic year: $13,000. Average number of hours worked per week: 20. Apply by Jan 3. Tuition remission given: full and partial. Fellowships and scholarships available for first-year. Average amount paid per academic year: $13,000. Average number of hours worked per week: 0. Apply by Jan 3. Tuition remission given: full.

Advanced Students: No information provided.

Contact Information: Of all students currently enrolled full-time, 95% benefitted from one or more of the listed financial assistance programs. For information on financial assistance, contact: View Web site or contact department for information.

Internships/Practica: No information provided.

Housing and Day Care: On-campus housing and day care facilities are available.

Employment of Department Graduates:

Master's Degree Graduates: Of those who graduated in the academic year 2000–2001, the following categories and numbers represent the post-graduate activities and employment of master's degree graduates: Enrolled in a post-doctoral residency/fellowship (n/a), employed in independent practice (n/a).

Doctoral Degree Graduates: Of those who graduated in the academic year 2000–2001, the following categories and numbers represent the post-graduate activities and employment of doctoral degree graduates: Enrolled in a psychology doctoral program (n/a), enrolled in another graduate/professional program (n/a), enrolled in a post-doctoral residency/fellowship (5), employed in an academic position at a university (3), employed in an academic position at a 2-year/4-year college (1), employed in other positions at a higher education institution (2).

Additional Information:

Orientation, Objectives, and Emphasis of Department: The orientation is toward theoretical and research training. Objectives are to provide the appropriate theoretical, quantitative, and methodological background to enable graduates of the program to engage in high-quality research. Additionally, training and experience in university-level teaching are provided. We also offer a minor in quantitative which may be completed by any student in the PhD program in Psychology regardless of main area of interest. A concentration in health psychology is also offered in the social and developmental areas.

Special Facilities or Resources: The department has equipment and support systems to help students conduct research in all aspects of behavior. The neuroscience laboratories are equipped with the latest instrumentation for hormonal assays, extracellular and intracellular electrophysiology, and microscopic analysis of neuronal morphology. Research in the cognitive area incorporates computer-assisted experimental control for most any kind of reaction time experiment and has facilities for video and speech digitization, and infrared eye-tracking. SGI and multi-processor Suns are used for more graphics or data-intensive applications. The developmental faculty have laboratory facilities to study parents and children, have access to the campus day-care center for studies that involve toddlers and preschool children, and have been very successful in conducting research in a culturally diverse local school system. The developmental faculty all participate in the Center for Family Studies, an interdisciplinary center. The social/personality psychology labs support research in social perception, nonverbal communication, health psychology, emotional expression, and attribution processes using audio-visual laboratories and observation rooms. Direct, free, access is available to PsycLIT, Medline, and many other online journals and databases.

Application Information:

Send to: Graduate Admissions Psychology Department, University of California, Riverside, Riverside, CA 92521. Students are admitted in the Fall, application deadline 1/3. *Fee:* $40. Contact Graduate Admissions in the Graduate Division, 909-787-3313.

California, University of, Riverside
School Psychology Program
Graduate School of Education
Graduate School of Education -
8 University of California, Riverside
Riverside, CA 92521-0128
Telephone: (909) 8-346
Fax: (909) 787-3942
E-mail: *frank.gresham@ucr.edu*

Department Established:

1991. Program Director and Distinguished Professor: Frank Gresham. Number of Faculty: total–full-time 2, part-time 3.

Programs and Degrees Offered:

Listed in the following order: Program area, degree type (T if terminal Master's), number awarded 7/00-6/01. School Psychology PhD.

Student Applications/Admissions:

Student Applications

School Psychology PhD—Applications 2001–2002, 7. Total applicants accepted 2001–2002, 3. New applicants enrolled

2001–2002, 2. Total enrolled 2001–2002 full-time, 12. Openings 2002–2003, 12.

Admissions Requirements:

Scores: Entries appear in this order: required test or GPA, minimum score (if required), median score of students entering in 2001–2002. Doctoral Programs: GRE-V+Q 1100, 1170; GRE-Subject(Psych) 550, 610; overall undergraduate GPA 3.5, 3.8 ; last 2 years GPA 3.5, 3.85; psychology GPA 3.5, 3.8 ; psychology GPA 3.5.

Other Criteria: (importance of criteria rated low, medium, or high): research experience medium, work experience low, extracurricular activity low, clinically related public service low, letters of recommendation high, interview high, statement of goals and objectives high, writing sample high.

Student Characteristics: The following represents characteristics of students in 2001–2002 in all graduate psychology programs in the department: Female–full-time 9, part-time 0; Male–full-time 3, part-time 0; African American/Black–full-time 0, part-time 0; Hispanic/Latino (a)–full-time 0, part-time 0; Asian/Pacific Islander–full-time 1, part-time 0; American Indian/Alaska Native–full-time 0, part-time 0.

Financial Information/Assistance:

Tuition for Full-Time Study: *Doctoral:* State residents: per academic year $1,667; nonstate residents: per academic year $5,298.

Financial Assistance:

First Year Students: No information provided.

Advanced Students: No information provided.

Contact Information: For information on financial assistance, contact: Office of Financial Aid, UCR, 1156 Hinderaker Hall, Riverside, CA 92521; 909-787-3878.

Internships/Practica: The UCR School Psychology practica experiences consist of a minimum of 600 clock hours under the supervision of a licensed or credentialed school psychologist. Students begin practica during their second quarter at UCR. Practicum requirements include one day per week for 8 quarters in a school or clinical setting in addition to attending a one-hour seminar on campus per week. Students are responsible for selecting sites and supervisors, the documentation of hours, and soliciting evaluations of their practicum performance each quarter. The UCR School Psychology internship occurs during the fourth year of training and after the completion of all coursework, the successful completion of written and oral comprehensive exams, and approval of dissertation proposal. The internship is completed on a full-time basis over the period of one calendar year and requires a minimum of 1500 clock hours under the supervision of a licensed doctoral-level psychologist. Although students are responsible for securing their internships, placement help and opportunities are available.

Housing and Day Care: No on-campus housing and day care facilities are available.

Employment of Department Graduates:

Master's Degree Graduates: Of those who graduated in the academic year 2000–2001, the following categories and numbers represent the post-graduate activities and employment of master's degree graduates: Enrolled in a post-doctoral residency/fellowship (n/a), employed in independent practice (n/a).

Doctoral Degree Graduates: Of those who graduated in the academic year 2000–2001, the following categories and numbers represent the post-graduate activities and employment of doctoral degree graduates: Enrolled in a psychology doctoral program (n/a), enrolled in another graduate/professional program (n/a).

Additional Information:

Orientation, Objectives, and Emphasis of Department: The School Psychology Program at the University of California-Riverside (UCR) prepares school psychologists to work in university settings, schools, state agencies, and clinical settings. The primary goal of the program is to develop professional psychologists whose activities increase the educational and psychological well-being of children and youth. These activities include research, training, and practice. The doctoral-level school psychologist is expected to have competence in each of these roles. Within this context, the School Psychology Program embraces a decidedly behavioral philosophy with concentration of the scientist-scholar-practitioner model of training. The integration of scientist, scholar, and practitioner roles provides a basis for graduates to assume leadership roles in research and practice within the field of school psychology.

Special Facilities or Resources: Currently, the School Psychology Program houses two research grants funded through the Office of Special Education Program (OSEP). The two most recent projects, entitled the "Utility of alternative assessment models in mildly handicapped children" and "Longitudinal affective and social outcomes of special education placement options for students with mild disabilities" have involved 420 and 450 (respectively) elementary school children at risk and/or receiving special education services. The total budgets for these two projects exceed $1.5 million. To date, all School Psychology students have been employed on a funded grant. The California Educational Research Cooperative (CERC) is a unique relationship between county offices of education, local school districts, and the School of Education. It is designed to serve as a research, development, and graduate training center for members and the School by combining the theoretical interests and research talents of the UCR's School of Education faculty with the help of graduate student interaction in the conduct of research.

Information for Students With Physical Disabilities: All campus facilities are accessible to persons with disabilities. The Disabled Student Services office offers preadmission counseling to prospective students to discuss available services, financial aid, housing, mobility, or other concerns related to attending UCR. Once accepted, services available include registration assistance, counseling, mobility assistance, academic support, special testing arrangements, and adaptive equipment.

Application Information:
Send to: Graduate School of Education, UCR, Riverside, CA 92521-0128. Students are admitted in the Fall, application deadline May 1; Winter, application deadline September 1; Spring, application deadline December 1. *Fee:* $40.

California, University of, San Diego

Department of Psychology
0133
La Jolla, CA 92093
Telephone: (858) 534-3002
Fax: (858) 534-7190
E-mail: *jkulik@ucsd.edu*
Web: *http://www.psy.ucsd.edu/*

Department Established:

1965. Chairperson: James A. Kulik. Number of Faculty: total–full-time 26, part-time 7; women–full-time 8, part-time 3; minority–full-time 2, part-time 1.

Programs and Degrees Offered:

Listed in the following order: Program area, degree type (T if terminal Master's), number awarded 7/00-6/01. Experimental PhD 11.

Student Applications/Admissions:

Student Applications

Experimental PhD—Applications 2001–2002, 140. Total applicants accepted 2001–2002, 21. New applicants enrolled 2001–2002, 7. Total enrolled 2001–2002 full-time, 44. Openings 2002–2003, 15. The Median number of years required for completion of a degree are 6. The number of students enrolled full and part-time, who were dismissed or voluntarily withdrew from this program area were 0.

Admissions Requirements:

Scores: Entries appear in this order: required test or GPA, minimum score (if required), median score of students entering in 2001–2002. Doctoral Programs: GRE-V 600, 650; GRE-Q 600, 660; GRE-V+Q 1200, 1310; overall undergraduate GPA 3.0, 3.6 ; last 2 years GPA no minimum stated; psychology GPA no minimum stated; psychology GPA no minimum stated.

Other Criteria: (importance of criteria rated low, medium, or high): GRE/MAT scores high, research experience high, work experience low, extracurricular activity medium, clinically related public service low, GPA high, letters of recommendation high, interview medium, statement of goals and objectives medium.

Student Characteristics: The following represents characteristics of students in 2001–2002 in all graduate psychology programs in the department: Female–full-time 23, part-time 0; Male–full-time 21, part-time 0; African American/Black–full-time 0, part-time 0; Hispanic/Latino (a)–full-time 5, part-time 0; Asian/Pacific Islander–full-time 1, part-time 0; American Indian/Alaska Native–full-time 0, part-time 0.

Financial Information/Assistance:

Tuition for Full-Time Study: No information provided.

Financial Assistance:

First Year Students: No information provided.
Advanced Students: No information provided.
Contact Information: For information on financial assistance, contact: Graduate students receive full financial support (including annual stipend, tuition, fees, and health insurance) for their first four years.

Internships/Practica: No information provided.

Housing and Day Care: On-campus housing and day care facilities are available.

Employment of Department Graduates:

Master's Degree Graduates: Of those who graduated in the academic year 2000–2001, the following categories and numbers represent the post-graduate activities and employment of master's degree graduates: Enrolled in a post-doctoral residency/fellowship (n/a), employed in independent practice (n/a).

Doctoral Degree Graduates: Of those who graduated in the academic year 2000–2001, the following categories and numbers represent the post-graduate activities and employment of doctoral degree graduates: Enrolled in a psychology doctoral program (n/a), enrolled in another graduate/professional program (n/a), enrolled in a post-doctoral residency/fellowship (4), employed in an academic position at a 2-year/4-year college (1), employed in other positions at a higher education institution (2), employed in business or industry (research/consulting) (3), employed in a government agency (research) (1).

Additional Information:

Orientation, Objectives, and Emphasis of Department: The Department of Psychology at the University of California San Diego provides advanced training in research on most aspects of experimental psychology. Modern laboratories and an attractive physical setting combine with a distinguished faculty, both within the Department of Psychology and in supporting disciplines, to provide research opportunities and training at the frontiers of psychological science. The graduate training program emphasizes and supports individual research, starting with the first year of study. The Department offers the following emphases: behavior analysis, biopsychology, cognitive psychology, developmental psychology, sensation and perception, and social psychology.

Special Facilities or Resources: The Department shares research space and facilities with the Center for Brain and Cognition. Within the joint facilities, there are two computing facilities, a computational laboratory, visual and auditory laboratories, social psychology laboratories, cognitive laboratories, developmental laboratories, a clinic for autistic children, animal facilities, and extensive contacts with hospitals, industry, and the legal system. In addition to the numerous impressive libraries on campus, the Department also keeps a large selection of literature within our Mandler Library. Collaborative research is carried on with members of the Departments of Linguistics (who share our building), Cognitive Science, Computer Science and Engineering, Sociology, Music, Ophthalmology, Neurosciences, members of the UCSD School of Medicine, Scripps Clinic and Research Foundation, and with the Salk Institute for Biological Studies. The Scripps Institution of Oceanography, located on campus, provides facilities in neurosciences as does the School of Medicine. For a complete tour of the university and its facilities, visit: www.ucsd.edu/visit.

Application Information:

Send to: Graduate Admission, Dept. of Psychology-0133, University of California-San Diego, La Jolla, CA 92093. Students are admitted in the Fall, application deadline January 5. *Fee:* $40.

California, University of, San Francisco

Department of Psychiatry-LPPI/Health Psychology Program
3333 California Street, Suite 465
San Francisco, CA 94143-0848
Telephone: (415) 476-7407
Fax: (415) 476-7744
E-mail: *nadler@itsa.ucsf.edu*
Web: *http://www.healthpsyc.ucsf.edu*

Department Established:
Chairperson: Nancy E. Adler. Number of Faculty: total–full-time 8; women–full-time 5.

Student Applications/Admissions:
Admissions Requirements: No information provided.
Scores: Entries appear in this order: required test or GPA, minimum score (if required), median score of students entering in 2001–2002. Doctoral Programs: last 2 years GPA no minimum stated; psychology GPA no minimum stated; psychology GPA no minimum stated.

Student Characteristics: The following represents characteristics of students in 2001–2002 in all graduate psychology programs in the department: Female–full-time 0, part-time 0; Male–full-time 0, part-time 0; African American/Black–full-time 0, part-time 0; Hispanic/Latino (a)–full-time 0, part-time 0; Asian/Pacific Islander–full-time 0, part-time 0; American Indian/Alaska Native–full-time 0, part-time 0; Multi-ethnic–full-time 0, part-time 0; students subject to the Americans with Disabilities Act–full-time 0, part-time 0.

Financial Information/Assistance:
Tuition for Full-Time Study: No information provided.

Financial Assistance:
First Year Students: No information provided.
Advanced Students: No information provided.
Contact Information: No information provided.

Internships/Practica: No information provided.

Housing and Day Care: No on-campus housing and day care facilities are available.

Employment of Department Graduates:
Master's Degree Graduates: Of those who graduated in the academic year 2000–2001, the following categories and numbers represent the post-graduate activities and employment of master's degree graduates: Enrolled in a post-doctoral residency/fellowship (n/a), employed in independent practice (n/a).
Doctoral Degree Graduates: Of those who graduated in the academic year 2000–2001, the following categories and numbers represent the post-graduate activities and employment of doctoral degree graduates: Enrolled in a psychology doctoral program (n/a), enrolled in another graduate/professional program (n/a).

Additional Information:
Orientation, Objectives, and Emphasis of Department: The Health Psychology Program in the Department of Psychiatry/LPPI at the University of California, San Francisco currently has a Postdoctoral Training Program funded by NIMH. The Health Psychology Program is in the process of establishing a PhD program in collaboration with University of California, Berkeley. It is hoped to begin accepting applications for the PhD program fall of 2003.

Application Information:
Send to: Postdoctoral Training Program titled Psychology & Medicine: An Integrative Research Approach. Students are admitted in the Spring, application deadline Feb 1, 2003.

California, University of, Santa Barbara

Counseling/Clinical/School Psychology
Graduate School of Education, Phelps Hall 1110
Santa Barbara, CA 93106-9490
Telephone: (805) 893-3375
Fax: (805) 893-7264
E-mail: *cosden@education.ucsb.edu*
Web: *http://www.education.ucsb.edu*

Department Established:
1965. Director of Training: Merith Cosden, PhD. Number of Faculty: total–full-time 11; women–full-time 4; minority–full-time 3.

Programs and Degrees Offered:
Listed in the following order: Program area, degree type (T if terminal Master's), number awarded 7/00-6/01. Counseling/clinical/school PhD 11, school (T) 5.

APA Accreditation: Combined PhD: full.

Student Applications/Admissions:
Student Applications
Counseling/clinical/school PhD—Applications 2001–2002, 214. Total applicants accepted 2001–2002, 19. New applicants enrolled 2001–2002, 10. Total enrolled 2001–2002 full-time, 56. Openings 2002–2003, 12. The Median number of years required for completion of a degree are 6. The number of students enrolled full and part-time, who were dismissed or voluntarily withdrew from this program area were 3.

Admissions Requirements:
Scores: Entries appear in this order: required test or GPA, minimum score (if required), median score of students entering in 2001–2002. Master's Programs: GRE-V+Q+Analytical no minimum stated; MAT no minimum stated; last 2 years GPA 3.0. GRE is preferred and MAT is accepted. Doctoral Programs: GRE-V+Q+Analytical no minimum stated; MAT no minimum stated; last 2 years GPA 3.0; psychology GPA no minimum stated; psychology GPA no minimum stated. GRE-V+Q or V+A is preferred and 1100–1200 score is competitive. MAT is accepted and 65 score is competitive.
Other Criteria: (importance of criteria rated low, medium, or high): GRE/MAT scores medium, research experience medium, work experience medium, extracurricular activity medium, clinically related public service medium, GPA high,

letters of recommendation high, interview high, statement of goals and objectives high.

Student Characteristics: The following represents characteristics of students in 2001–2002 in all graduate psychology programs in the department: Female–full-time 55, part-time 0; Male–full-time 14, part-time 0; African American/Black–full-time 3, part-time 0; Hispanic/Latino (a)–full-time 9, part-time 0; Asian/Pacific Islander–full-time 16, part-time 0; American Indian/Alaska Native–full-time 0, part-time 0; students subject to the Americans with Disabilities Act–full-time 3.

Financial Information/Assistance:

Tuition for Full-Time Study: *Master's:* State residents per academic year $5,000; nonstate residents: per academic year $16,000. *Doctoral:* State residents: per academic year $5,000; nonstate residents: per academic year $16,000.

Financial Assistance:

First Year Students: Teaching assistantships available for first-year. Average amount paid per academic year: $12,000. Average number of hours worked per week: 20. Apply by December 10. Tuition remission given: full and partial. Research assistantships available for first-year. Average amount paid per academic year: $14,000. Average number of hours worked per week: 20. Apply by December 10. Tuition remission given: full and partial. Fellowships and scholarships available for first-year. Average amount paid per academic year: $16,000. Average number of hours worked per week: 0. Apply by December 10. Tuition remission given: full.

Advanced Students: Teaching assistantships available for advanced students. Average amount paid per academic year: $12,000. Average number of hours worked per week: 20. Tuition remission given: full and partial. Research assistantships available for advanced students. Average amount paid per academic year: $14,000. Average number of hours worked per week: 20. Tuition remission given: full and partial. Fellowships and scholarships available for advanced students. Average amount paid per academic year: $16,000. Average number of hours worked per week: 20. Tuition remission given: full.

Contact Information: Of all students currently enrolled full-time, 85% benefitted from one or more of the listed financial assistance programs. For information on financial assistance, contact: Graduate Division, University of California, Santa Barbara 93106.

Internships/Practica: We provide supervised training in our Hosford Clinic, a sliding scale agency which serves clients from the community. Students in the clinical emphasis have external practica in community based agencies, students in the counseling emphasis have external practica at our Counseling and Career Services Center, and students in the school emphasis have external practica in the schools. For those doctoral students for whom a professional internship is required prior to graduation, 4 applied in 2000–2001. Of those who applied, 4 were placed in internships listed by the Association of Psychology Postdoctoral and Internship Programs (APPIC); 4 were placed in APA accredited internships.

Housing and Day Care: On-campus housing and day care facilities are available.

Employment of Department Graduates:

Master's Degree Graduates: Of those who graduated in the academic year 2000–2001, the following categories and numbers represent the post-graduate activities and employment of master's degree graduates: Enrolled in a psychology doctoral program (1), enrolled in a post-doctoral residency/fellowship (n/a), employed in independent practice (n/a), employed in other positions at a higher education institution (1), employed in a professional position in a school system (3).

Doctoral Degree Graduates: Of those who graduated in the academic year 2000–2001, the following categories and numbers represent the post-graduate activities and employment of doctoral degree graduates: Enrolled in a psychology doctoral program (n/a), enrolled in another graduate/professional program (n/a), enrolled in a post-doctoral residency/fellowship (5), employed in an academic position at a university (2), employed in other positions at a higher education institution (1), employed in a community mental health/counseling center (2), employed in a hospital/medical center (1).

Additional Information:

Orientation, Objectives, and Emphasis of Department: The primary goal of the combined psychology program is to prepare graduates who will (a) conduct research and teach in university settings and (b) assume leadership roles in the academic community and in the helping professions. The program has a secondary goal of training students to provide psychological services in university, school, and community agency settings.

Special Facilities or Resources: The UCSB Combined Psychology Program has its own training clinic, which was completely renovated in 1987 and equipped with state-of-the-art video equipment for recording, reviewing, editing, and live monitoring of assessment and counseling sessions. Computer laboratories equipped with Macintosh and IBM personal computers are available for student use. Special computing facilities for statistical analyses are also easily accessible.

Application Information:
Send to: Student Affairs Office, Gevirtz Graduate School of Education, University of California, Santa Barbara CA 93106. Students are admitted in the Fall, application deadline December 10. *Fee:* $40.

California, University of, Santa Barbara
Department of Psychology
Santa Barbara, CA 93106-9660
Telephone: (805) 893-2793
Fax: (805) 893-4303
E-mail: *grad-info@psych.ucsb.edu*
Web: *http://www.psych.ucsb.edu*

Department Established:
1953. Chairperson: James Blascovich. Number of Faculty: total–full-time 25; women–full-time 7; minority–full-time 2.

Programs and Degrees Offered:
Listed in the following order: Program area, degree type (T if terminal Master's), number awarded 7/00-6/01. Cognitive and

perception MA 2, development and evolution MA, neuroscience and behavior MA 2, social MA 1.

Student Applications/Admissions:

Student Applications

Cognitive and perception MA—Applications 2001–2002, 0. The Median number of years required for completion of a degree are 3. The number of students enrolled full and part-time, who were dismissed or voluntarily withdrew from this program area were 0. *Development and evolution MA*—Applications 2001–2002, 0. The Median number of years required for completion of a degree are na. The number of students enrolled full and part-time, who were dismissed or voluntarily withdrew from this program area were 0. *Neuroscience and behavior MA*—Applications 2001–2002, 0. The Median number of years required for completion of a degree are 3. The number of students enrolled full and part-time, who were dismissed or voluntarily withdrew from this program area were 0. *Social MA*—Applications 2001–2002, 0. The Median number of years required for completion of a degree are 2. The number of students enrolled full and part-time, who were dismissed or voluntarily withdrew from this program area were 0.

Admissions Requirements:

Scores: Entries appear in this order: required test or GPA, minimum score (if required), median score of students entering in 2001–2002. Master's Programs: GRE-V no minimum stated; GRE-Q no minimum stated; GRE-Analytical no minimum stated; last 2 years GPA no minimum stated; psychology GPA no minimum stated. There were no MA students admitted in 2001. Doctoral Programs: GRE-V no minimum stated, 580; GRE-Q no minimum stated, 667; GRE-Analytical no minimum stated, 683; last 2 years GPA no minimum stated, 3.62; psychology GPA no minimum stated; psychology GPA no minimum stated.

Other Criteria: (importance of criteria rated low, medium, or high): GRE/MAT scores medium, research experience high, work experience low, GPA medium, letters of recommendation high, statement of goals and objectives high. If applicant is interviewed (not required), this can be very important.

Student Characteristics: The following represents characteristics of students in 2001–2002 in all graduate psychology programs in the department: Female–full-time 40, part-time 0; Male–full-time 19, part-time 0; African American/Black–full-time 3, part-time 0; Hispanic/Latino (a)–full-time 3, part-time 0; Asian/Pacific Islander–full-time 2, part-time 0; American Indian/Alaska Native–full-time 1, part-time 0.

Financial Information/Assistance:

Tuition for Full-Time Study: *Master's:* State residents per academic year $4,971; nonstate residents: per academic year $15,867. *Doctoral:* State residents: per academic year $4,970; nonstate residents: per academic year $15,867.

Financial Assistance:

First Year Students: Teaching assistantships available for first-year. Average amount paid per academic year: $14,000. Average number of hours worked per week: 20. Apply by December 15. Tuition remission given: partial. Research assistantships available for first-year. Average amount paid per academic year: $13,000. Average number of hours worked per week: 20. Apply by December 15. Tuition remission given: full. Fellowships and scholarships available for first-year. Average amount paid per academic year: $15,000. Average number of hours worked per week: 0. Apply by December 15. Tuition remission given: full.

Advanced Students: Teaching assistantships available for advanced students. Average amount paid per academic year: $14,000. Average number of hours worked per week: 20. Research assistantships available for advanced students. Average amount paid per academic year: $14,000. Average number of hours worked per week: 20. Tuition remission given: full. Fellowships and scholarships available for advanced students. Average amount paid per academic year: $15,000. Average number of hours worked per week: 0. Tuition remission given: full.

Contact Information: Of all students currently enrolled full-time, 100% benefitted from one or more of the listed financial assistance programs.

Internships/Practica: No information provided.

Housing and Day Care: No on-campus housing and day care facilities are available.

Employment of Department Graduates:

Master's Degree Graduates: Of those who graduated in the academic year 2000–2001, the following categories and numbers represent the post-graduate activities and employment of master's degree graduates: Enrolled in a psychology doctoral program (2), enrolled in a post-doctoral residency/fellowship (n/a), employed in independent practice (n/a), employed in an academic position at a 2-year/4-year college (1), employed in other positions at a higher education institution (1), employed in a professional position in a school system (1).

Doctoral Degree Graduates: Of those who graduated in the academic year 2000–2001, the following categories and numbers represent the post-graduate activities and employment of doctoral degree graduates: Enrolled in a psychology doctoral program (n/a), enrolled in another graduate/professional program (n/a), enrolled in a post-doctoral residency/fellowship (3), employed in an academic position at a university (3), employed in business or industry (research/consulting) (1).

Additional Information:

Orientation, Objectives, and Emphasis of Department: The major graduate program of the Department of Psychology consists of work leading to the PhD degree; however, the MA is also awarded. Specialized training is offered in neuroscience and behavior, cognitive and perceptual sciences, developmental and evolutionary psychology, and social psychology.

Special Facilities or Resources: Graduate students have access to 4 multi-user computer laboratories consisting of IBM computers, Apple computers, DEC computers, and on-line communications to the campus computer center, as well as access to over two dozen specialized research laboratories. Support facilities include approximately 90 computers, an electronics shop, a machine shop, and photographic facilities. Biopsychology facilities also include a fully-staffed animal vivarium, histology, and stereotoxic surgery labs.

Application Information:

Send to: Graduate Admissions. Students are admitted in the Fall, application deadline December 15. *Fee:* $40.

California, University of, Santa Cruz

Psychology Department
273 Social Sciences 2
Santa Cruz, CA 95064
Telephone: (831) 459-4932
Fax: (831) 459-3519
E-mail: *jpcrutch@cats.ucsc.edu*
Web: *http://www.psych.ucsc.edu/*

Department Established:

1965. Chairperson: Maureen Callanan. Number of Faculty: total–full-time 27, part-time 14; women–full-time 13, part-time 8; minority–full-time 6.

Programs and Degrees Offered:

Listed in the following order: Program area, degree type (T if terminal Master's), number awarded 7/00-6/01. Cognitive PhD 2, developmental PhD 3, social PhD 1.

APA Accreditation: School PhD: full.

Student Applications/Admissions:

Student Applications

Cognitive PhD—Applications 2001–2002, 13. Total applicants accepted 2001–2002, 8. New applicants enrolled 2001–2002, 3. Total enrolled 2001–2002 full-time, 16, part-time, 1. Openings 2002–2003, 3. The number of students enrolled full and part-time, who were dismissed or voluntarily withdrew from this program area were 1. *Developmental PhD*—Applications 2001–2002, 21. Total applicants accepted 2001–2002, 5. New applicants enrolled 2001–2002, 3. Total enrolled 2001–2002 full-time, 18. Openings 2002–2003, 7. The number of students enrolled full and part-time, who were dismissed or voluntarily withdrew from this program area were 0. *Social PhD*—Applications 2001–2002, 39. Total applicants accepted 2001–2002, 6. New applicants enrolled 2001–2002, 3. Total enrolled 2001–2002 full-time, 19, part-time, 1. Openings 2002–2003, 5. The number of students enrolled full and part-time, who were dismissed or voluntarily withdrew from this program area were 1.

Admissions Requirements:

Scores: Entries appear in this order: required test or GPA, minimum score (if required), median score of students entering in 2001–2002. Doctoral Programs: GRE-V 50%, 585; GRE-Q 50%, 650; GRE-Analytical 50%, 665; GRE-Subject(Psych) 50%, 640; overall undergraduate GPA 2.75, 3.5 ; last 2 years GPA 2.86, 3.6 ; psychology GPA no minimum stated; psychology GPA no minimum stated.

Other Criteria: (importance of criteria rated low, medium, or high): research experience high, work experience medium, extracurricular activity medium, GPA high, letters of recommendation high, statement of goals and objectives high.

Student Characteristics: The following represents characteristics of students in 2001–2002 in all graduate psychology programs in the department: Female–full-time 39, part-time 1; Male–full-time 14, part-time 1; African American/Black–full-time 1, part-time 0; Hispanic/Latino (a)–full-time 11, part-time 0; Asian/Pacific Islander–full-time 10, part-time 0; American Indian/Alaska Na-

tive–full-time 1, part-time 0; Multi-ethnic–full-time 0, students subject to the Americans with Disabilities Act–full-time 0.

Financial Information/Assistance:

Tuition for Full-Time Study: No information provided.

Financial Assistance:

First Year Students: Teaching assistantships available for first-year. Research assistantships available for first-year.

Advanced Students: No information provided.

Contact Information: Of all students currently enrolled full-time, 0% benefitted from one or more of the listed financial assistance programs. For information on financial assistance, contact: Division of Graduate Studies.

Internships/Practica: None.

Housing and Day Care: On-campus housing and day care facilities are available.

Employment of Department Graduates:

Master's Degree Graduates: Of those who graduated in the academic year 2000–2001, the following categories and numbers represent the post-graduate activities and employment of master's degree graduates: Enrolled in a post-doctoral residency/fellowship (n/a), employed in independent practice (n/a), employed in a professional position in a school system (1), employed in business or industry (research/consulting) (1), employed in a government agency (research) (1).

Doctoral Degree Graduates: Of those who graduated in the academic year 2000–2001, the following categories and numbers represent the post-graduate activities and employment of doctoral degree graduates: Enrolled in a psychology doctoral program (n/a), enrolled in another graduate/professional program (n/a), employed in an academic position at a university (4).

Additional Information:

Orientation, Objectives, and Emphasis of Department: The Department of Psychology at UC Santa Cruz offers a Ph.D. degree in psychology with areas of specialization in cognitive, developmental, and social psychology. (The program does not offer courses, training, or supervision in counseling or clinical psychology.) Our program prepares individuals for research, teaching, and administrative positions in colleges and universities, as well as for positions in schools, government, and other public and private organizations. The Ph.D. is a research degree. Students are required to demonstrate the ability to carry through to completion rigorous empirical research and to be active in research throughout their graduate career. The course requirements in the Ph.D,. program are directed toward establishing a foundation for critical evaluation of research literature and designing conceptually important empirical research. To aid students in carrying out their work, each student must be associated with one of the faculty who will serve as academic adviser and research sponsor. The program requires full-time enrollment as a graduate student. Cognitive psychology at UCSC focuses on training students in the traditional methods of experimental psychology and in mastering contemporary knowledge in the broad areas of cognitive science and psychobiology. The cognitive faculty have specific expertise in the study of psycholinguistics, sensation/perception, memory and cognitive psychology. Research interests of the faculty include human information processing, cognitive processes in learning and memory, language and discourse comprehension, reading, speech perception and production, computer simulation and mathematical modeling of cognitive processes, face perception, spatial vision, visual psychophysics, and physiological mechanisms of visual perception throughout the life span. Developmental psychology at UCSC is concerned with the processes of developmental change in individuals and relationships through the life span and in commnuity and cultural contexts. The developmental faculty are especially interested in issues of diversity in development, including ethnicity, gender, personality, home language, and diversity of family forms, and in the interplay between human development and the social contexts of family, peers, school, work, community, and culture. Among the topics studied by faculty are the role of family communication in the development of self, identity and relational competence in childhood and adolescence, classroom interaction, psychology of creativity and creative environments, gender-related variations in communication styles in children and adolescents, language and cognitive development, within the contexts of conversations with parents, siblings, and peers, and adult attachment and personality development using longitudinal methodologies. Graduate work in the social psychology area focuses on the study of social justice. Students receive training in the theories and methods of social psychology with the aim of applying their training to the analysis and solutions of social problems. In turn, it is expected that students' experiences in the field will be used to critically assess theories and methods. Students are encouraged to examine theoretical and empirical issues in different cultural, political and policy contexts. Students are trained to conduct research with laboratory, field and survey methodologies. The research interests of the faculty include such topics as leadership and group processes, intergroup relations, gender issues, psychology and law, the study of social class, and feminist psychology.

Special Facilities or Resources: The department provides training to prepare the student for academic and applied settings. Graduate students have the use of a variety of research facilities, including a number of computer-controlled experimental laboratories. Electronic equipment is available to allow the generation of sophisticated written and pictorial vision displays, musical sequences, and synthesized and visual speech patterns. There are observational facilities for developmental psychological research, and a discourse analysis lab. A bilingual survey unit is under development which will utilize public opinion survey technology to study significant public policy, legal, and political issues that are critical to California's emerging majority population. Research opportunities exist with diverse sample groups in both laboratory and natural settings. The department has collaborative relationships with the National Center for Research on Cultural Diversity, Second Language Learning, and the Bilingual Research Center.

Information for Students With Physical Disabilities: UCSC has an active Disability Resource Center available to all students, undergraduate and graduate.

Application Information:
Send to: Division of Graduate Studies, 1156 High Street, Social Science 2, Room 150, University of California, Santa Cruz, CA 95064-1077, phone: (831) 459-2301; email: gradadm@cats.ucsc.edu. Students are admitted in the Fall, application deadline December 15. *Fee:* $40.

Chapman University (2001 data)
Division of Psychology
333 North Glassell
Orange, CA 92866
Telephone: (714) 997-6776
Fax: (714) 997-6780
E-mail: *flowers@chapman.edu*

Department Established:
1930. Chair of the Division of Psychology: John Flowers. Number of Faculty: total–full-time 10, part-time 5; women–full-time 4, part-time 3; minority–full-time 3.

Programs and Degrees Offered:
Listed in the following order: Program area, degree type (T if terminal Master's), number awarded 7/00-6/01. Marriage, family, child couns. MA (T) 45.

Student Applications/Admissions:
Student Applications
Marriage, family, child couns. MA—Applications 2001–2002, 80. Total applicants accepted 2001–2002, 30. New applicants enrolled 2001–2002, 12. Total enrolled 2001–2002 full-time, 31, part-time, 40. Openings 2002–2003, 75. The Median number of years required for completion of a degree are 3.

Admissions Requirements:
Scores: Entries appear in this order: required test or GPA, minimum score (if required), median score of students entering in 2001–2002. Master's Programs: GRE-V+Q 900; MAT 57; last 2 years GPA 3.00. The V&Q of the GRE or the MAT is required if the applicant's incoming GPA on the last 60 semester units or last 90 quarter units is below a 3.00.
Other Criteria: (importance of criteria rated low, medium, or high): GRE/MAT scores work experience medium, extracurricular activity low, clinically related public service high, GPA letters of recommendation high, interview medium, statement of goals and objectives high, autobiography high,

Student Characteristics: The following represents characteristics of students in 2001–2002 in all graduate psychology programs in the department: Female–full-time 5, part-time 3; Male–full-time 0, part-time 0; African American/Black–full-time 0, part-time 0; Hispanic/Latino (a)–full-time 0, part-time 0; Asian/Pacific Islander–full-time 1, part-time 0; American Indian/Alaska Native–full-time 0, part-time 0.

Financial Information/Assistance:
Tuition for Full-Time Study: No information provided.

Financial Assistance:
First Year Students: No information provided.
Advanced Students: No information provided.
Contact Information: Of all students currently enrolled full-time, 0% benefitted from one or more of the listed financial assistance programs. For information on financial assistance, contact: Graduate Studies Office, Chapman University, 333 N. Glassell, Orange, CA 92866.

Internships/Practica: A three semester (nine units) internship is conducted in our university-sponsored Community Clinic. A minimum of 180 hours of client contact is required, with an additional 270 hours of supervision and clinic-related activities required as well. These hours are credited towards the California licensing requirement of 3000 internship hours. The Community Clinic is a full-service mental health counseling outpatient clinic serving ithe counseling needs of lower income people in the greater Orange County area.

Housing and Day Care: No on-campus housing and day care facilities are available.

Employment of Department Graduates:

Master's Degree Graduates: Of those who graduated in the academic year 2000–2001, the following categories and numbers represent the post-graduate activities and employment of master's degree graduates: Enrolled in a post-doctoral residency/fellowship (n/a), employed in independent practice (n/a).

Doctoral Degree Graduates: Of those who graduated in the academic year 2000–2001, the following categories and numbers represent the post-graduate activities and employment of doctoral degree graduates: Enrolled in a psychology doctoral program (n/a), enrolled in another graduate/professional program (n/a).

Additional Information:

Orientation, Objectives, and Emphasis of Department: The Division of Psychology at Chapman is eclectic with a strong cognitive-behavioral and family systems approach. Faculty is represented by a mix of experimental psychologists as well as practicing clinicians. The division takes pride in educating and training clinicians who are competent and ethical when working with clients with diverse backgrounds and clinical issues.

Information for Students With Physical Disabilities: Chapman University does not discriminate on the basis of race, gender, color, age, disability, national origin, or ethnicity in any of its policies or practices, including, but not limited to: admissions, academic requirements, financial aid, employment, housing, athletics, or any other school-administered program or service. Any individual who, because of a disability, needs special accommodations with respect to any university policy, practice, service, or benefit must notify the university of his or her need for accommodation, including the reason for the request and the specific need of the accommodation requested. The university is committed to providing reasonable accommodations to persons with disabilities, whenever an accommodation can be made without imposing undue hardship on the university. Any student or prospective student of the Orange campus who wishes to request a special accommodation because of his or her disability should contact the Equal Opportunity Officer or the Dean of Graduate Studies.

Application Information:

Send to: Office of Graduate Admission, Chapman University, 333 N. Glassell, Orange, CA 92866. Students are admitted in the Fall; Spring; Summer. *Fee:* $40.

Claremont Graduate University

Graduate Department of Psychology
School of Behavioral and Organizational Sciences
123 East Eighth Street
Claremont, CA 91711-3955
Telephone: (909) 621-8084
Fax: (909) 621-8905
E-mail: *cgupsych@cgu.edu*
Web: *http://www.cgu.edu/sbos*

Department Established:

1926. Dean: Stewart I. Donaldson. Number of Faculty: total–full-time 6, part-time 44; women–full-time 2, part-time 22; minority–full-time 2, part-time 6.

Programs and Degrees Offered:

Listed in the following order: Program area, degree type (T if terminal Master's), number awarded 7/00-6/01. Applied developmental MA (T) 6, cognitive MA (T) 2, evaluation MA (T) 15, human resources design, organizational MA (T) 7, social MA (T) 11.

Student Applications/Admissions:

Student Applications

Applied developmental MA—Applications 2001–2002, 23. Total applicants accepted 2001–2002, 13. New applicants enrolled 2001–2002, 1. Total enrolled 2001–2002 full-time, 7, part-time, 23. Openings 2002–2003, 5. The Median number of years required for completion of a degree are 2. The number of students enrolled full and part-time, who were dismissed or voluntarily withdrew from this program area were 4. *Cognitive MA*—Applications 2001–2002, 12. Total applicants accepted 2001–2002, 11. New applicants enrolled 2001–2002, 4. Total enrolled 2001–2002 full-time, 10, part-time, 11. Openings 2002–2003, 5. The Median number of years required for completion of a degree are 3. The number of students enrolled full and part-time, who were dismissed or voluntarily withdrew from this program area were 1. *Evaluation MA*—Applications 2001–2002, 47. Total applicants accepted 2001–2002, 41. New applicants enrolled 2001–2002, 12. Total enrolled 2001–2002 full-time, 19. Openings 2002–2003, 20. The Median number of years required for completion of a degree is 1. The number of students enrolled full and part-time, who were dismissed or voluntarily withdrew from this program area were 2. *Organizational MA*—Applications 2001–2002, 68. Total applicants accepted 2001–2002, 9. New applicants enrolled 2001–2002, 4. Total enrolled 2001–2002 full-time, 10, part-time, 22. Openings 2002–2003, 5. The Median number of years required for completion of a degree are 6. The number of students enrolled full and part-time, who were dismissed or voluntarily withdrew from this program area were 1. *Social MA*—Applications 2001–2002, 43. Total applicants accepted 2001–2002, 28. New applicants enrolled 2001–2002, 6. Total enrolled 2001–2002 full-time, 16, part-time, 45. Openings 2002–2003, 8. The Median number of years required for completion of a degree are 4. The number of students enrolled full and part-time, who were dismissed or voluntarily withdrew from this program area were 11.

Admissions Requirements:

Scores: Entries appear in this order: required test or GPA, minimum score (if required), median score of students entering in 2001–2002. Master's Programs: GRE-V no minimum stated, 480; GRE-Q no minimum stated, 522; GRE-V+Q no minimum stated, 1022; GRE-Analytical no minimum stated, 545; GRE-V+Q+Analytical no minimum stated, 1564; overall undergraduate GPA no minimum stated. HRD program requires either GRE or GMAT scores and weights work experience more heavily in admissions. Doctoral Programs: GRE-V no minimum stated, 535; GRE-Q no minimum stated, 582; GRE-V+Q no minimum stated, 1142; GRE-Analytical no minimum stated, 610; GRE-V+Q+Analytical no minimum stated, 1801; overall undergraduate GPA no minimum stated; last 2 years GPA no minimum stated; psychology GPA no minimum stated; psychology GPA no minimum stated.

Other Criteria: (importance of criteria rated low, medium, or high): GRE/MAT scores medium, research experience medium, work experience medium, extracurricular activity medium, clinically related public service low, GPA medium, letters of recommendation high, interview medium, statement of goals and objectives high. HRD program does not require research experience but emphasizes work experience more strongly.

Student Characteristics: The following represents characteristics of students in 2001–2002 in all graduate psychology programs in the department: Female–full-time 94, part-time 30; Male–full-time 34, part-time 11; African American/Black–full-time 8, Hispanic/Latino(a)–full-time 21, Asian/Pacific Islander–full-time 24, American Indian/Alaska Native–full-time 2.

Financial Information/Assistance:

Tuition for Full-Time Study: *Master's:* State residents per academic year $22,984, $1,000 per credit hour; nonstate residents: per academic year $22,984, $1,000 per credit hour. *Doctoral:* State residents: per academic year $22,984, $1,000 per credit hour; nonstate residents: per academic year $22,984, $1,000 per credit hour.

Financial Assistance:

First Year Students: Research assistantships available for first-year. Average amount paid per academic year: $2,600. Average number of hours worked per week: 12. Fellowships and scholarships available for first-year. Average amount paid per academic year: $5,734. Apply by February 15. Tuition remission given: partial.

Advanced Students: Teaching assistantships available for advanced students. Average amount paid per academic year: $2,600. Average number of hours worked per week: 12. Research assistantships available for advanced students. Average amount paid per academic year: $2,600. Average number of hours worked per week: 12. Fellowships and scholarships available for advanced students. Average amount paid per academic year: $5,734. Apply by February 15. Tuition remission given: partial.

Contact Information: Of all students currently enrolled full-time, 0% benefitted from one or more of the listed financial assistance programs. For information on financial assistance, contact: Admissions Office.

Internships/Practica: Research and consulting internships are available and encouraged for all students. Appropriate settings and roles are arranged according to the interests of individual students within the wide range of opportunities available in a large urban area. Typical settings include social service agencies; business and industrial organizations; hospitals, clinics, and mental health agencies; schools; governmental and regulatory agencies; and nonacademic research institutions.

Housing and Day Care: No on-campus housing and day care facilities are available.

Employment of Department Graduates:

Master's Degree Graduates: Of those who graduated in the academic year 2000–2001, the following categories and numbers represent the post-graduate activities and employment of master's degree graduates: Enrolled in a post-doctoral residency/fellowship (n/a), employed in independent practice (n/a).

Doctoral Degree Graduates: Of those who graduated in the academic year 2000–2001, the following categories and numbers represent the post-graduate activities and employment of doctoral degree graduates: Enrolled in a psychology doctoral program (n/a), enrolled in another graduate/professional program (n/a).

Additional Information:

Orientation, Objectives, and Emphasis of Department: The program emphasis is upon contemporary human problems and social issues, and the organizations and systems involved in such issues, as well as on basic substantive research in social, organizational, developmental, and cognitive psychology. Unusual specialty opportunities are available in organizational behavior, applied cognitive psychology, applied social psychology, health psychology, program evaluation research. The program offers preparation for careers in public service and business and industry as well as teaching and research. Research, theory, and practice are stressed in such policy and program areas as organizations and work; human social and physical environments; social service systems; psychological effects of television and computer technology; health and mental health systems; crime, delinquency, and law; aging and life span education. Many opportunities are available for research, consulting, and field experiences in these and related areas. Strong emphasis is given to training in a broad range of research methodologies, from naturalistic observation to experimental design, with special attention to field research methods. Seminars, tutorials, independent research, individualized student program plans, practical field experience, and close advisory and collaborative relations with the faculty are designed to foster clarifications of individual goals, intellectual and professional growth, self-pacing, and attractive career opportunities.

Special Facilities or Resources: The department is housed in a building with rooms for social, developmental, and cognitive research, supplies and equipment for field research, a student-faculty lounge, and department library. The computer facilities are excellent, conveniently located, and include a wide variety of application programs. The department cooperates in overseeing a research institute for student-faculty grant or contract research, which includes major problems of organizational research and consulting. Claremont Graduate University is a free-standing graduate school within the context of the cluster of Claremont Colleges, allowing the department to concentrate exclusively on graduate education in a relaxed, intimate context while enjoying the resources of a major university. In addition to the full-time graduate psychology faculty, there are more than 40 full-time faculty members from the five contiguous undergraduate Claremont Colleges who participate in the graduate program and who are available to students for research, advising, and instruction. Resources from other programs within the Graduate School are also available to psychology students, in such areas as public policy, education, information sciences, business administration, executive management, economics, and government. The nearby Los Angeles basin is a major urban area that offers rich and varied opportunities for interesting research, field placements and internships, part-time employment, and career development.

Information for Students With Physical Disabilities: All facilities of the department and the university are accessible to wheelchairs.

Application Information:

Send to: Admissions Office, McManus Hall 131, Claremont Graduate University, Claremont, CA 91711. Students are admitted in the Fall, application deadline February 15; Spring, application deadline November 1. HRD program accepts applications throughout the year on a space-available basis. *Fee:* $40. Fee waived or deferred if need is certified.

Fielding Graduate Institute
School of Psychology
Clinical Psychology Doctoral Program
2112 Santa Barbara Street
Santa Barbara, CA 93105
Telephone: (805) 687-1099
Fax: (805) 687-4590
E-mail: *admissions@fielding.edu*
Web: *http://www.fielding.edu*

Department Established:

1974. Dean, Psychology: Ronald A. Giannetti. Number of Faculty: total–full-time 33, part-time 3; women–full-time 16, part-time 1; minority–full-time 4.

Programs and Degrees Offered:

Listed in the following order: Program area, degree type (T if terminal Master's), number awarded 7/00-6/01. Clinical PhD 28, Respecialization in Clin Psych Respecialization Diploma.

APA Accreditation: Clinical PhD: full.

Student Applications/Admissions:

Student Applications

Clinical PhD—Applications 2001–2002, 262. Total applicants accepted 2001–2002, 116. New applicants enrolled 2001–2002, 62. Total enrolled 2001–2002 full-time, 460. Openings 2002–2003, 42. The number of students enrolled full and part-time, who were dismissed or voluntarily withdrew from this program area were 37. *Respecialization in Clin Psych Respecialization Diploma*—Applications 2001–2002, 8. Total applicants accepted 2001–2002, 5. New applicants enrolled 2001–2002, 5. Total enrolled 2001–2002 full-time, 11. The number of students enrolled full and part-time, who were dismissed or voluntarily withdrew from this program area were 1.

Admissions Requirements:

Scores: Entries appear in this order: required test or GPA, minimum score (if required), median score of students entering in 2001–2002. Doctoral Programs: overall undergraduate GPA 3.0; last 2 years GPA 3.0; psychology GPA 3.0; psychology GPA no minimum stated. A minimum GPA of 3.0 for the highest degree earned is recommended.

Other Criteria: (importance of criteria rated low, medium, or high): GRE/MAT scores research experience high, work experience high, extracurricular activity medium, clinically related public service medium, GPA letters of recommendation medium, interview high, statement of goals and objectives high, computer literacy medium.

Student Characteristics: The following represents characteristics of students in 2001–2002 in all graduate psychology programs in the department: Female–full-time 46, part-time 0; Male–full-time 16, part-time 0; African American/Black–full-time 9, part-time 0; Hispanic/Latino (a)–full-time 8, part-time 0; Asian/Pacific Islander–full-time 0, part-time 0; American Indian/Alaska Native–full-time 1, part-time 0; Multi-ethnic–full-time 0, students subject to the Americans with Disabilities Act–full-time 1.

Financial Information/Assistance:

Tuition for Full-Time Study: *Doctoral:* State residents: per academic year $14,300; nonstate residents: per academic year $14,300.

Financial Assistance:

First Year Students: Fellowships and scholarships available for first-year. Average amount paid per academic year: $1,500.

Advanced Students: Fellowships and scholarships available for advanced students. Average amount paid per academic year: $1,500.

Contact Information: Of all students currently enrolled full-time, 5% benefitted from one or more of the listed financial assistance programs. For information on financial assistance, contact: Raul Aldama and Vanessa Hayward.

Internships/Practica: Students apply to APA or APPIC approved internships or comparable sites which offer an organized training program lasting one year full-time or two consecutive years half-time. Such internships provide a planned, integrated sequence of clinical and didactic experiences with the goal of providing sufficient training and supervision so that the intern can, upon completion, function responsibly as a postdoctoral psychologist. For those doctoral students for whom a professional internship is required prior to graduation, 21 applied in 2000–2001. Of those who applied, 15 were placed in internships listed by the Association of Psychology Postdoctoral and Internship Programs (APPIC); 8 were placed in APA accredited internships.

Housing and Day Care: No on-campus housing and day care facilities are available.

Employment of Department Graduates:

Master's Degree Graduates: Of those who graduated in the academic year 2000–2001, the following categories and numbers represent the post-graduate activities and employment of master's degree graduates: Enrolled in a post-doctoral residency/fellowship (n/a), employed in independent practice (n/a).

Doctoral Degree Graduates: Of those who graduated in the academic year 2000–2001, the following categories and numbers represent the post-graduate activities and employment of doctoral degree graduates: Enrolled in a psychology doctoral program (n/a), enrolled in another graduate/professional program (n/a).

Additional Information:

Orientation, Objectives, and Emphasis of Department: The clinical psychology program of the Fielding Graduate Institute enables mid-career adults with mental health and human service experience to earn the PhD in clinical psychology. Our students bring a sense of autonomy, extensive personal and professional experience, and multiple adult responsibilities to their studies. The program's design accommodates these special characteristics of adult students. The program is based on the scholar/practitioner model. Progress is measured through explicit demonstrations of competence at a standard established by the faculty. Through seminars and guided study, the adult learner can pursue study at whatever location life circumstances permit. The program includes 3 components taken concurrently: academic, research, and clinical. The academic component consists of completing 12 core courses plus other required courses and their choice of electives courses to accumulate 84 units. Details of this process are contained in our catalog. The research component is designed to educate students in research methodology to ensure that students become critical consumers of research and scholars capable of contributing to research. It also trains students in the skills necessary to complete a theoretically based dissertation consisting of imaginative and scholarly inquiry. The clinical component consists of a practicum and internship as well as training and evaluation activities to help students learn and demonstrate their ability to function responsibly as practicing psychologists. Additionally, there is a respecialization in Clinical Psychology which is a certificate program for posdoctoral psychologists who wish to respecialize as clinical psychologists.

Special Facilities or Resources: Students become members of a "cluster" or doctoral studies seminar in their geographical area consisting of a Regional Faculty and other students. Regular meetings are held and consist of a variety of learning activities including knowledge area and seminars, clinical and research training, faculty supervision consultation, as well as peer contact and support. Associate Deans are located in Santa Barbara. Each student is assigned to an Associate Dean who oversees the student's academic program. Our learning community is tied together by the Fielding Electronic Network, a rapid, cost-effective means of communication among faculty, students, and administrative staff. The use of a personal computer enables contact with other members or groups of members. It is also used to offer electronic seminars. Two intensive week-long residential sessions are offered each year. These bring together all faculty and other scholars who offer seminars and other educational and training events. Two residential research sessions are held each year. These include research training, dissertation seminars, instruction in the use of research libraries and electronic data bases, and lectures by invited research scholars. Psychological assessment laboratories are offered to provide training in conducting comprehensive psychodiagnostic evaluations.

Application Information:
Send to: Marine Dumas, Psychology Enrollment Officer, Fielding Graduate Institute, 2112 Santa Barbara Street, Santa Barbara, CA 93105.

Students are admitted in the Fall, application deadline March 15; Spring, application deadline September 15. *Fee:* $75.

Humboldt State University (2001 data)
Department of Psychology
College of Natural Resources & Sciences
1 Harpst Street
Arcata, CA 95521
Telephone: (707) 826-3755
Fax: (707) 826-4993
E-mail: *law3@humboldt.edu*

Department Established:
1964. Professor: Lou Ann Wieand. Number of Faculty: total–full-time 14, part-time 18; women–full-time 5, part-time 11; minority–full-time 4, part-time 1.

Programs and Degrees Offered:
Listed in the following order: Program area, degree type (T if terminal Master's), number awarded 7/00-6/01. Academic research MA (T) 8, counseling MA (T) 16, school psychology MA (T) 9.

Student Applications/Admissions:
Student Applications
Academic research MA—Applications 2001–2002, 15. Total applicants accepted 2001–2002, 10. New applicants enrolled 2001–2002, 9. Total enrolled 2001–2002 full-time, 16. Openings 2002–2003, 10. The Median number of years required for completion of a degree are 2. *Counseling MA*—Applications 2001–2002, 40. Total applicants accepted 2001–2002, 12. New applicants enrolled 2001–2002, 9. Total enrolled 2001–2002 full-time, 17. Openings 2002–2003, 10. The Median number of years required for completion of a degree are 2. The number of students enrolled full and part-time, who were dismissed or voluntarily withdrew from this program area were 0. *School psychology MA*—Applications 2001–2002, 55. Total applicants accepted 2001–2002, 12. New applicants enrolled 2001–2002, 10. Total enrolled 2001–2002 full-time, 20. Openings 2002–2003, 10. The Median number of years required for completion of a degree are 2.

Admissions Requirements:
Scores: Entries appear in this order: required test or GPA, minimum score (if required), median score of students entering in 2001–2002. Master's Programs: last 2 years GPA 3.00. GRE's are required for the Academic Research; recommended but not required for PPS; not required for Counseling.
Other Criteria: (importance of criteria rated low, medium, or high): GRE/MAT scores medium, research experience high, work experience high, extracurricular activity low, clinically related public service medium, GPA high, letters of recommendation high, interview high, statement of goals and objectives high. An interview is highly important for Counseling and School Psychology; research experience is highly important for Academic Research; clinically related public service or work experience is highly important for Counseling and School Psychology; school/child related work experience highly important for School Psychology.

Student Characteristics: The following represents characteristics of students in 2001–2002 in all graduate psychology programs in the department: Female–full-time 23, part-time 0; Male–full-time 12, part-time 0; African American/Black–full-time 0, part-time 0; Hispanic/Latino (a)–full-time 2, part-time 0; Asian/Pacific Islander–full-time 2, part-time 0; American Indian/Alaska Native–full-time 1, part-time 0.

Financial Information/Assistance:

Tuition for Full-Time Study: No information provided.

Financial Assistance:

First Year Students: No information provided.
Advanced Students: No information provided.
Contact Information: Of all students currently enrolled full-time, 0% benefitted from one or more of the listed financial assistance programs. For information on financial assistance, contact: Financial Aid, Student and Business Services Bldg., 707-826-4321.

Internships/Practica: Humboldt's Future Faculty Training Program provides teaching internship opportunities (some paid) at the local community college. School Psychology internships (usually paid) are required of all students seeking the School Psychology credential. Counseling MA students are provided the opportunity to do fieldwork/practica in the department's counseling clinic as well as in several local mental heath agencies.

Housing and Day Care: No on-campus housing and day care facilities are available.

Employment of Department Graduates:

Master's Degree Graduates: Of those who graduated in the academic year 2000–2001, the following categories and numbers represent the post-graduate activities and employment of master's degree graduates: Enrolled in a post-doctoral residency/fellowship (n/a), employed in independent practice (n/a).
Doctoral Degree Graduates: Of those who graduated in the academic year 2000–2001, the following categories and numbers represent the post-graduate activities and employment of doctoral degree graduates: Enrolled in a psychology doctoral program (n/a), enrolled in another graduate/professional program (n/a).

Additional Information:

Orientation, Objectives, and Emphasis of Department: The objectives of psychology are to furnish students with an introduction to principles and theories concerning the behavior of living organisms and to the processes by which such information is obtained; to provide courses that deal with psychological principles pertaining to specialized areas like business, teaching, and engineering for students majoring in other disciplines; to provide a sound academic education for those working for degrees in psychology with a future goal of professional work in psychology; to offer a liberal arts major and minor in psychology for students primarily concerned with seeking a liberal education; to provide a group of varied courses that students in all disciplines may elect to enhance their liberal education; to provide quality professional education for students working toward pupil personnel credentials, counseling and other specialized occupational fields; and to provide a flexibility in our offerings that will enable us to respond to changing societal and student needs.

Special Facilities or Resources: The department has an on-campus clinic staffed by MA counseling students, an electronic equipment shop, a lab with biofeedback and EEG equipment, a lab equipped for research on motion sickness, observation and research access to an on-campus demonstration nursery school, a test library, and a computer laboratory.

Information for Students With Physical Disabilities: Humboldt State's Office of Disabled Student Services provides services in support of the educational experience of students with disabilities. It provides a detailed campus map indicating parking for disabled persons, accessible building entrances, elevators and restrooms, as well as inaccessible buildings. There is a wheel-chair accessible van which provides transportation to classes. The university is strongly committed to the fostering of an environment guaranteeing students with disabilities full access to all of its educational programs, activities, and facilities.

Application Information:

Send to: 1. Office of Admissions, Humboldt State University, Arcata, CA 95521 - general admissions; 2. Department of Psychology, Humboldt State University, Arcata, CA 95521 - specific admissions requirements for each of the three programs - contact department office. Students are admitted in the Fall, application deadline Feb 15. *Fee:* $55. Partial out-of-state tuition waiver available.

John F. Kennedy University
Graduate School of Professional Psychology
12 Altarinda Road
Orinda, CA 94563
Telephone: (925) 254-0110
Fax: (925) 254-4870
E-mail: *psyd@jfku.edu*
Web: *http://www.jfku.edu*

Department Established:

1965. Dean: H. Keith McConnell. Number of Faculty: total–full-time 20, part-time 200; women–full-time 7, part-time 100; minority–full-time 6, part-time 35.

Programs and Degrees Offered:

Listed in the following order: Program area, degree type (T if terminal Master's), number awarded 7/00-6/01. Addiction, Conflict Resolution 5, Counseling psychology MA (T) 71, Cross Cultural 1, Expressive Arts Therapy, Organizational psychology MA (T) 1, PsyD 20, Sport Psychology MA (T) 12, Sports Psychology PsyD (T).

Student Applications/Admissions:

Student Applications

Counseling psychology MA—Applications 2001–2002, 62. Total applicants accepted 2001–2002, 51. New applicants enrolled 2001–2002, 30. Total enrolled 2001–2002 full-time, 127, part-time, 164. Openings 2002–2003, 70. The Median number of years required for completion of a degree are 2. *Organizational psychology MA*—Applications 2001–2002, 11. Total applicants accepted 2001–2002, 10. New applicants enrolled 2001–2002, 8. Total enrolled 2001–2002 full-time, 2, part-time, 9. Openings 2002–2003, 15. The Median number of years required for completion of a degree are 2. *PsyD*—Applications 2001–2002, 100. Total applicants accepted 2001–2002, 49. New applicants enrolled 2001–2002, 24. Total enrolled 2001–2002 full-time, 89, part-time, 31. Openings 2002–2003, 25. The Median number of years required for completion of a degree are 4. *Sport Psychology MA*—Applications 2001–2002, 21. Total applicants accepted 2001–2002, 18. New applicants enrolled 2001–2002, 9. Total enrolled 2001–2002 full-time, 16. Openings 2002–2003, 20. The Median number of years required for completion of a degree are 2. *Sports Psychology PsyD*—Applications 2001–2002, 1. Total applicants accepted 2001–2002, 1. New applicants enrolled 2001–2002, 1. Total enrolled 2001–2002 full-time, 1. Openings 2002–2003, 5. The Median number of years required for completion of a degree are 5.

Admissions Requirements:

Scores: Entries appear in this order: required test or GPA, minimum score (if required), median score of students entering in 2001–2002. Master's Programs: overall undergraduate GPA 3.0, 3.0. Doctoral Programs: GRE-Subject(Psych) no minimum stated; overall undergraduate GPA 3.0; last 2 years GPA no minimum stated; psychology GPA 3.0; psychology GPA 3.0.

Other Criteria: (importance of criteria rated low, medium, or high): GRE/MAT scores, research experience low, work experience high, extracurricular activity high, clinically related public service high, GPA medium, letters of recommendation high, interview high, statement of goals and objectives high, personal readiness high.

Student Characteristics: The following represents characteristics of students in 2001–2002 in all graduate psychology programs in the department: Female–full-time 225, part-time 100; Male–full-time 75, part-time 50; African American/Black–full-time 20, part-time 6; Hispanic/Latino (a)–full-time 45, part-time 15; Asian/Pacific Islander–full-time 20, part-time 10; American Indian/Alaska Native–full-time 5, part-time 2; students subject to the Americans with Disabilities Act–full-time 4, part-time 2.

Financial Information/Assistance:

Tuition for Full-Time Study: *Master's:* State residents $348 per credit hour; nonstate residents: $348 per credit hour. *Doctoral:* State residents: $446 per credit hour; nonstate residents: $446 per credit hour.

Financial Assistance:

First Year Students: No information provided.

Advanced Students: No information provided.

Contact Information: Of all students currently enrolled full-time, 0% benefitted from one or more of the listed financial assistance programs. For information on financial assistance, contact: Office of Financial Aid - John F. Kennedy University - 12 Altarinda Rd, Orinda, CA 94563.

Internships/Practica: The Graduate School of Professional Psychology has two community counseling centers, each located near one of our two campuses, which provide state of the art supervision for students and provide thousands of hours of low-fee counseling each year. Additionally, approximately 150 external fieldwork sites, monitored by our faculty, are available in the surrounding counties. Students in the Counseling MA program and the PsyD program accumulate hours toward their respective licenses at both the community counseling centers and the external sites. The MA in Sport Psychology and Expressive Art programs offer summer camps for children which also serve as additional field placement sites for graduate students. For those doctoral students for whom a professional internship is required prior to graduation, 26 applied in 2000–2001. Of those who applied, 3 were placed in internships listed by the Association of Psychology Postdoctoral and Internship Programs (APPIC).

Housing and Day Care: No on-campus housing and day care facilities are available.

Employment of Department Graduates:

Master's Degree Graduates: Of those who graduated in the academic year 2000–2001, the following categories and numbers represent the post-graduate activities and employment of master's degree graduates: Enrolled in a post-doctoral residency/fellowship (n/a), employed in independent practice (n/a).

Doctoral Degree Graduates: Of those who graduated in the academic year 2000–2001, the following categories and numbers represent the post-graduate activities and employment of doctoral degree graduates: Enrolled in a psychology doctoral program (n/a), enrolled in another graduate/professional program (n/a).

Additional Information:

Orientation, Objectives, and Emphasis of Department: Our mission is to create a graduate school with a diverse faculty and student body and curricula which focus on training practitioner-scholars to provide comprehensive and culturally sensitive service in meeting the individual needs of today's society. The program emphasizes an awareness of social, cultural, economic, and historical conditions and how these may affect and expand the definitions of clinical work and other avenues of professional psychology practice. Students are trained to think critically and contextually about theory, practice, and research as they explore new and emerging clinical paradigms which are more inclusive of diverse populations. Graduates will be prepared to competently serve a range of communities which are diverse in such ways as: class, race, culture, ethnicity, sexual orientation, ability/disability, age, gender, religious belief, spiritual tradition, and world view. The educational and training models of the school bring together professors who work in the field with highly motivated students in diverse life experiences resulting in a rich, challenging, and student-centered learning environment. Students develop personally as well as professionally as they strive for greater self-understanding and an appreciation of human differences.

Special Facilities or Resources: As noted, the Graduate School of Professional Psychology community counseling centers serve a broad-based clientele throughout the surrounding communities. The JFKU library is linked to I.L.L. (Interlibrary Loan). The University maintains student computer labs at each campus.

Information for Students With Physical Disabilities: John F. Kennedy University meets all state and federal regulations for students with disabilities. Disability services are overseen by the Disability Services Director/Student Services.

Application Information:
Send to: Office of Admissions - John F. Kennedy University, 12 Altarinda Road - Orinda, CA 94563. Students are admitted in the Fall, application deadline rolling; Winter, application deadline rolling; Spring, application deadline rolling; Summer, application deadline rolling. January 15th for Psy.D. (only have Fall admission). *Fee:* $50.

La Verne, University of
PsyD Program in Clinical-Community Psychology
1950 Third Street
La Verne, CA 91750
Telephone: (909) 593-3511, ext. 4179
Fax: (909) 392-2745
E-mail: *jordanv@ulv.edu*
Web: *http://www.ulvedu*

Department Established:
1997. Doctoral Program Chair: Valerie B. Jordan, Ph.D. Number of Faculty: total–full-time 10, part-time 15; women–full-time 3, part-time 8; minority–full-time 4, part-time 1; faculty subject to the Americans with Disabilities Act 1.

Programs and Degrees Offered:
Listed in the following order: Program area, degree type (T if terminal Master's), number awarded 7/00-6/01. Clinical-community PsyD.

Student Applications/Admissions:
Student Applications
Clinical-community PsyD—Applications 2001–2002, 46. Total applicants accepted 2001–2002, 32. New applicants enrolled 2001–2002, 17. Total enrolled 2001–2002 full-time, 43. Openings 2002–2003, 15. The Median number of years required for completion of a degree are 5. The number of students enrolled full and part-time, who were dismissed or voluntarily withdrew from this program area were 2.

Admissions Requirements:
Scores: Entries appear in this order: required test or GPA, minimum score (if required), median score of students entering in 2001–2002. Doctoral Programs: overall undergraduate GPA 3.25, 3.05; last 2 years GPA 3.00, 3.30; psychology GPA 3.00, 3.30; psychology GPA 3.65, 3.50.

Other Criteria: (importance of criteria rated low, medium, or high): research experience medium, work experience high, extracurricular activity low, clinically related public service high, GPA high, letters of recommendation high, interview high, statement of goals and objectives high.

Student Characteristics: The following represents characteristics of students in 2001–2002 in all graduate psychology programs in the department: Female–full-time 40, part-time 0; Male–full-time 3, part-time 0; African American/Black–full-time 5, part-time 0; Hispanic/Latino (a)–full-time 15, part-time 0; Asian/Pacific Islander–full-time 4, part-time 0; American Indian/Alaska Native–full-time 0, part-time 0; Multi-ethnic–full-time 0, part-time 0; students subject to the Americans with Disabilities Act–full-time 0, part-time 0.

Financial Information/Assistance:
Tuition for Full-Time Study: *Doctoral:* State residents: per academic year $16,200, $540 per credit hour; nonstate residents: per academic year $16,200, $540 per credit hour.

Financial Assistance:
First Year Students: Teaching assistantships available for first-year. Average amount paid per academic year: $750. Average number of hours worked per week: 4. Apply by June. Tuition remission given: partial. Research assistantships available for first-year. Average amount paid per academic year: $500. Average number of hours worked per week: 4. Apply by June. Tuition remission given: partial. Fellowships and scholarships available for first-year. Average amount paid per academic year: $1,500. Average number of hours worked per week: 0. Apply by March. Tuition remission given: partial.

Advanced Students: Teaching assistantships available for advanced students. Average amount paid per academic year: $1,000. Average number of hours worked per week: 6. Apply by June. Tuition remission given: partial. Research assistantships available for advanced students. Average amount paid per academic year: $500. Average number of hours worked per week: 4. Apply by June. Tuition remission given: partial. Traineeships available for advanced students. Average amount paid per academic year: $3,500. Average number of hours worked per week: 16. Apply by March. Tuition remission given: partial.

Contact Information: Of all students currently enrolled full-time, 33% benefitted from one or more of the listed financial assistance programs. For information on financial assistance, contact: Financial aid office.

Internships/Practica: The PsyD program includes supervised practica in the second and third years of the program, and consists of 900 hours of clinical-community activities. The culminating pre-doctoral internship in the fifth and final year of the program consists of 1500 clinical hours, and can be completed in a one-year full-time, or two year, half-time internship. The Psychology department has an extensive network of practica and internship sites with mental health and educational settings throughout the San Gabriel and Pomona valleys, and the Inland Empire region. The on-campus Counseling Center is part of the Psychology department, is staffed by Psy.D. and Master's students, and is one of the largest practicum training sites. The Psy.D. program participates in a regional consortium of program and training site directors for doctoral programs, and is a graduate program member of CAPIC. For those doctoral students for whom a professional internship is required prior to graduation, 4 applied in 2000–2001. Of those who applied, 1 were placed in internships listed by the Association of Psychology Postdoctoral and Internship Programs (APPIC).

Housing and Day Care: No on-campus housing and day care facilities are available.

Employment of Department Graduates:
Master's Degree Graduates: Of those who graduated in the academic year 2000–2001, the following categories and numbers

represent the post-graduate activities and employment of master's degree graduates: Enrolled in a post-doctoral residency/fellowship (n/a), employed in independent practice (n/a).

Doctoral Degree Graduates: Of those who graduated in the academic year 2000–2001, the following categories and numbers represent the post-graduate activities and employment of doctoral degree graduates: Enrolled in a psychology doctoral program (n/a), enrolled in another graduate/professional program (n/a).

Additional Information:

Orientation, Objectives, and Emphasis of Department: The Psychology Department is part of the Behavioral Sciences Division, which also includes the Sociology/Anthropology Department. The clinical faculty consists of licensed psychologists whose theoretical orientations include psychodynamic, humanist, behavioral, family systems, and community psychology, and who are clinically active in a range of clinical settings and populations. Faculty research interests include topics such as multi-culturalism, substance abuse, psychotherapy outcome research, cancer and quality of life, racial identity and acculturation of African-American populations, professional violations of mental health professionals, to name some of the current research activities. The curriculum of the PsyD program in Clinical-Community psychology is anchored in an ecological and multi-cultural perspective, and involves a multi-disciplinary faculty who are activity involved in clinical and/or research activities. The PsyD program meets all pre-doctoral requirements for California psychology licensure, and is designed to meet the criteria for APA accreditation, which will be pursued when the program becomes eligible. An en-route MS in Psychology is awarded to students at the end of the second year in the program.

Special Facilities or Resources: Doctoral students have access to a wide network of local and regional clinical, research, and library facilities in the metropolitan Los Angeles and Southern California area. The campus University Counseling Center is directed by the Psychology department and provides counseling services to university students and staff. The Center is equipped with videotape and biofeedback equipment. ULV's Wilson Library contains 200,000 volumes and over 2,000 current journal subscriptions. Access to library resources is available through reciprocal borrowing privileges at many academic libraries in the Southern California area, as well as through online catalogs and CD-ROM databases.

Information for Students With Physical Disabilities: The Division of Student Affairs and the Learning Enhancement Center assist physically and learning disabled students in accommodating their student life and academic needs. The office of Services for Students with Disabilities is located in the Student Health Center. The small campus is completely accessible for physically disabled students, staff, and faculty.

Application Information:

Send to: Graduate Student Services. Students are admitted in the Fall, application deadline January 15. Students will be considered after the deadline on a space available basis. *Fee:* $75. The application fee is waived for ULV students.

Loma Linda University

Department of Psychology
11130 Anderson Street, CB102
Loma Linda, CA 92350
Telephone: (909) 558-8577
Fax: (909) 558-0171
E-mail: *Abradshaw@univ.llu.edu*
Web: *http://www.llu.edu*

Department Established:

1994. Chairperson: Louis Jenkins. Number of Faculty: total–full-time 8, part-time 4; women–full-time 2, part-time 2; minority–full-time 3.

Programs and Degrees Offered:

Listed in the following order: Program area, degree type (T if terminal Master's), number awarded 7/00-6/01. Clinical PhD 9, experimental PhD, Experimental Master's MA 4, psychology PsyD 4.

APA Accreditation: Clinical PhD: full. Clinical PsyD: full.

Student Applications/Admissions:

Student Applications

Clinical PhD—Applications 2001–2002, 24. Total applicants accepted 2001–2002, 19. New applicants enrolled 2001–2002, 12. Total enrolled 2001–2002 full-time, 66. Openings 2002–2003, 8. The Median number of years required for completion of a degree are 7. The number of students enrolled full and part-time, who were dismissed or voluntarily withdrew from this program area were 0. *Experimental PhD*—Applications 2001–2002, 0. Total enrolled 2001–2002 full-time, 7. Openings 2002–2003, 3. The Median number of years required for completion of a degree are 5. The number of students enrolled full and part-time, who were dismissed or voluntarily withdrew from this program area were 0. *Experimental Master's MA*—Applications 2001–2002, 6. Total applicants accepted 2001–2002, 4. New applicants enrolled 2001–2002, 4. Total enrolled 2001–2002 full-time, 13. Openings 2002–2003, 10. The Median number of years required for completion of a degree are 02. The number of students enrolled full and part-time, who were dismissed or voluntarily withdrew from this program area were 01. *Psychology PsyD*—Applications 2001–2002, 21. Total applicants accepted 2001–2002, 15. New applicants enrolled 2001–2002, 8. Total enrolled 2001–2002 full-time, 68. Openings 2002–2003, 8. The Median number of years required for completion of a degree are 2. The number of students enrolled full and part-time, who were dismissed or voluntarily withdrew from this program area were 0.

Admissions Requirements:

Scores: Entries appear in this order: required test or GPA, minimum score (if required), median score of students entering in 2001–2002. Master's Programs: GRE-V no minimum stated, 500; GRE-Q no minimum stated, 500; GRE-V+Q 1000, 1000; GRE-Analytical no minimum stated, 510; GRE-V+Q+Analytical 1270, 1450; GRE-Subject(Psych) no minimum stated, 500; overall undergraduate GPA 3.0, 3.35. Doctoral Programs: GRE-V no minimum stated, 550; GRE-Q 500, 560; GRE-V+Q 1000, 1100; GRE-Analytical no minimum stated, 610; GRE-V+Q+Analytical 1500, 1650; GRE-Subject(Psych) no minimum stated, 580; overall undergraduate GPA 3.0, 3.60; last 2 years GPA no minimum stated; psychology GPA no minimum stated; psychology GPA no minimum stated.

Other Criteria: (importance of criteria rated low, medium, or high): GRE/MAT scores high, research experience high, work experience medium, extracurricular activity medium, clinically related public service high, GPA high, letters of recommendation high, interview high, statement of goals and objectives high. For PhD applicants, research experience is highly desirable. For PsyD applicants, clinical related experience is highly desirable.

Student Characteristics: The following represents characteristics of students in 2001–2002 in all graduate psychology programs in the department: Female–full-time 102, part-time 0; Male–full-time 45, part-time 0; African American/Black–full-time 11, part-time 0; Hispanic/Latino (a)–full-time 27, part-time 0; Asian/Pacific Islander–full-time 18, part-time 0; American Indian/Alaska Native–full-time 1, part-time 0; Multi-ethnic–full-time 0, students subject to the Americans with Disabilities Act–full-time 5.

Financial Information/Assistance:

Tuition for Full-Time Study: *Master's:* State residents per academic year $10,500, $420 per credit hour; nonstate residents: per academic year $10,500, $420 per credit hour. *Doctoral:* State residents: per academic year $15,120, $420 per credit hour; nonstate residents: per academic year $15,120, $420 per credit hour.

Financial Assistance:

First Year Students: Research assistantships available for first-year. Average amount paid per academic year: $3,783. Average number of hours worked per week: 5. Fellowships and scholarships available for first-year. Average amount paid per academic year: $3,000. Apply by August 15. Tuition remission given: full.

Advanced Students: Teaching assistantships available for advanced students. Average amount paid per academic year: $2,522. Average number of hours worked per week: 7. Research assistantships available for advanced students. Average amount paid per academic year: $7,566. Average number of hours worked per week: 10. Fellowships and scholarships available for advanced students. Average amount paid per academic year: $3,000. Apply by August 15. Tuition remission given: full.

Contact Information: Of all students currently enrolled full-time, 35% benefitted from one or more of the listed financial assistance programs. For information on financial assistance, contact: Financial Aid Office, 909/558-4509.

Internships/Practica: Second-year practicum experiences are obtained in the departmental clinic and in a satellite clinic which reaches a previously underserved area of the City of San Bernardino. Other department training experiences include the LLU Craniofacial Team Clinic & Growing Fit Multidisciplinary clinic for obese children. Second-year practicum students may also receive some supervised clinical training in area public and private

school settings. The external practicum (20 hours per week, normally in the third year of the program) is entirely off the departmental campus. Students are expected to accumulate 950 to 1000 hours of supervised experience while on external practicum, with an absolute minimum of 250 hours being spent in direct service experiences with patients. External practicum students are presently placed in six settings: 1) The Rehabilitation Unit of the Loma Linda University Medical Center; 2) the California Institution for Women; 3) the California Youth Authority; 4) the Riverside County Department of Mental Health; 5) The San Bernardino County Department of Mental Health; and 6) the Casa Colina Hospital for Rehabilitative Medicine. A full-year (40 hours per week) of internship is required with sites available across the country. All acceptable internship sites must meet the criteria for membership in the Association of Psychology Postdoctoral and Internship Centers. For those doctoral students for whom a professional internship is required prior to graduation, 11 applied in 2000–2001. Of those who applied, 11 were placed in internships listed by the Association of Psychology Postdoctoral and Internship Programs (APPIC); 6 were placed in APA accredited internships.

Housing and Day Care: On-campus housing and day care facilities are available.

Employment of Department Graduates:

Master's Degree Graduates: Of those who graduated in the academic year 2000–2001, the following categories and numbers represent the post-graduate activities and employment of master's degree graduates: Enrolled in a psychology doctoral program (9), enrolled in another graduate/professional program (3), enrolled in a post-doctoral residency/fellowship (n/a), employed in independent practice (n/a), employed in an academic position at a university (0), employed in an academic position at a 2-year/4-year college (0), employed in other positions at a higher education institution (0), employed in a professional position in a school system (0), employed in business or industry (research/consulting) (0), employed in business or industry (management) (0), employed in a government agency (research) (0), employed in a government agency (professional services) (0), employed in a community mental health/counseling center (0), employed in a hospital/medical center (0), still seeking employment (0), other employment position (0).

Doctoral Degree Graduates: Of those who graduated in the academic year 2000–2001, the following categories and numbers represent the post-graduate activities and employment of doctoral degree graduates: Enrolled in a psychology doctoral program (n/a), enrolled in another graduate/professional program (n/a), enrolled in a post-doctoral residency/fellowship (0), employed in independent practice (0), employed in an academic position at a university (1), employed in an academic position at a 2-year/4-year college (1), employed in other positions at a higher education institution (2), employed in a professional position in a school system (0), employed in business or industry (research/consulting) (0), employed in business or industry (management) (0), employed in a government agency (research) (1), employed in a government agency (professional services) (0), employed in a community mental health/counseling center (3), employed in a hospital/medical center (1), still seeking employment (0), other employment position (0).

Additional Information:

Orientation, Objectives, and Emphasis of Department: Doctoral training at Loma Linda University takes place within the context of a holistic approach to human health and welfare. The university motto to make man whole takes in every aspect of being human—the physical, psychological, spiritual, and social. Building on a university tradition of health sciences research, training, and service, the doctoral programs in the department offer a combination of traditional and innovative training opportunities. The PhD in clinical psychology follows the traditional scientist-practitioner model and emphasizes research and clinical training. The PsyD is oriented toward clinical practice with emphasis on the understanding and application of the principles and research of psychological science. The PsyD/DrPH dual degree program offers an innovative combination of education in psychology and the health sciences to train practitioners who are highly qualified in the application of psychology to health promotion, preventive medicine, and health care as well as clinical practice and research. The PhD in experimental psychology is designed to train a small number of individuals for careers in research and academia. Students in the experimental PhD program work closely with a research mentor; a current list of faculty and their research interests may be obtained from the department.

Special Facilities or Resources: As a health sciences university, Loma Linda provides an ideal environment with resources for research and clinical training in such areas as health psychology/behavioral medicine and the delivery of health services. LLU Medical Center has nearly 900 beds, is staffed by more than 5000 people, and is the "flagship" of a system including hundreds of health care institutions around the world. In addition, a number of institutions in the area, such as the LLU Behavioral Medicine Center, Jerry L. Pettis VA Hospital, Patton State Hospital, and the San Bernardino County Mental Health Department represent numerous opportunities for research and clinical training in psychology. In the area of teaching and research the department has a consortial agreement with the department of psychology at California State University, San Bernardino. By this agreement, students at a post-master's level have TA opportunities to get experience teaching undergraduate courses. At the same time, a select group of graduate faculty members at CSUSB have appointments at LLU significantly enhancing advanced seminar offerings and opportunities for research training in a number of areas, strengthening and complementing those available at LLU.

Information for Students With Physical Disabilities: The University meets ADA requirements.

Application Information:
Send to: Graduate School Admissions, Loma Linda, CA 92350. Students are admitted in the Fall, application deadline December 31. Applicants to our dual-degree program, Psy.D./Dr.PH must apply to our School of Public Health concurrently with their application to our Psy.D. program in the Department of Psychology. *Fee:* $60. Waivers must be approved by the Department of Psychology. It is necessary to have information about your GPA and GRE scores to make an adequate decision on fee waiver requests.

Pacific Graduate School of Psychology
Clinical Psychology Program
940 East Meadow Drive
Palo Alto, CA 94303
Telephone: (650) 843-3419 & 800-818-6136
Fax: (650) 493-6147
E-mail: *b.bell@pgsp.edu*
Web: *http://www.pgsp.edu*

Department Established:
1975. Chairperson: Barbara Bell. Number of Faculty: total–full-time 11, part-time 2; women–full-time 5; minority–full-time 2.

Programs and Degrees Offered:
Listed in the following order: Program area, degree type (T if terminal Master's), number awarded 7/00-6/01. Clinical PhD 42, law and psychology, MBA/Ph.D., Psy.D.

APA Accreditation: Clinical PhD: full. Combined PhD: full.

Student Applications/Admissions:
Student Applications

Clinical PhD—Applications 2001–2002, 220. Total applicants accepted 2001–2002, 57. New applicants enrolled 2001–2002, 52. Total enrolled 2001–2002 full-time, 300. Openings 2002–2003, 70. *Psy.D.*—Applications 2001–2002, 0. Openings 2002–2003, 20. The Median number of years required for completion of a degree are na. The number of students enrolled full and part-time, who were dismissed or voluntarily withdrew from this program area were 0.

Admissions Requirements:

Scores: Entries appear in this order: required test or GPA, minimum score (if required), median score of students entering in 2001–2002. Doctoral Programs: GRE-V+Q no minimum stated, 1185; last 2 years GPA no minimum stated; psychology GPA no minimum stated; psychology GPA no minimum stated.

Other Criteria: (importance of criteria rated low, medium, or high): GRE/MAT scores low, research experience medium, work experience medium, extracurricular activity medium, clinically related public service medium, GPA medium, letters of recommendation high, statement of goals and objectives high, personal statement high.

Student Characteristics: The following represents characteristics of students in 2001–2002 in all graduate psychology programs in the department: Female–full-time 30, part-time 0; Male–full-time 27, part-time 0; African American/Black–full-time 9, part-time 0; Hispanic/Latino (a)–full-time 7, part-time 0; Asian/Pacific Islander–full-time 6, part-time 0; American Indian/Alaska Native–full-time 3, part-time 0.

Financial Information/Assistance:
Tuition for Full-Time Study: *Doctoral:* State residents: per academic year $21,960.

Financial Assistance:
First Year Students: Average amount paid per academic year: $20,000. Apply by 1/15.

Advanced Students: No information provided.

Contact Information: Of all students currently enrolled full-time, 25% benefitted from one or more of the listed financial assistance programs. For information on financial assistance, contact: Financial Aid Coordinator at 650-843-3411.

Internships/Practica: All students take their second year of practicum in our Kurt and Barbara Gronowski Clinic and the third and fourth years in local agencies. All students are expected to complete an APA-accredited, APPIC or CAPIC-approved internship. For those doctoral students for whom a professional internship is required prior to graduation, 46 applied in 2000–2001. Of those who applied, 29 were placed in internships listed by the Association of Psychology Postdoctoral and Internship Programs (APPIC); 24 were placed in APA accredited internships.

Housing and Day Care: No on-campus housing and day care facilities are available.

Employment of Department Graduates:

Master's Degree Graduates: Of those who graduated in the academic year 2000–2001, the following categories and numbers represent the post-graduate activities and employment of master's degree graduates: Enrolled in a post-doctoral residency/fellowship (n/a), employed in independent practice (n/a).

Doctoral Degree Graduates: Of those who graduated in the academic year 2000–2001, the following categories and numbers represent the post-graduate activities and employment of doctoral degree graduates: Enrolled in a psychology doctoral program (n/a), enrolled in another graduate/professional program (n/a), enrolled in a post-doctoral residency/fellowship (1), employed in a professional position in a school system (1), employed in a community mental health/counseling center (3), employed in a hospital/medical center (3), other employment position (2).

Additional Information:

Orientation, Objectives, and Emphasis of Department: Pacific Graduate School of Psychology is a free-standing graduate school offering the PhD degree in clinical psychology to students from diverse backgrounds. The program is designed to integrate academic work, research, and clinical experiences at every level of the student's training. All students must develop a thorough understanding of a systematic body of knowledge that comprises the current field of psychology. They are expected to carry out an independent investigation that makes an original contribution to scientific knowledge in psychology and to demonstrate excellence in the application of specific clinical skills. PGSP considers this integration of scholarship, research, and practical experience the best training model for preparing psychologists to meet the highest standards of scholarly research and community service. Graduates are expected to enter the community at large prepared to do research, practice, and teach in culturally and professionally diverse settings. The integrated program in both psychology and law leads to a PhD in Clinical Psychology and a JD from Golden Gate University School of Law (ABA accredited). Students who complete this new joint program are expected to make significant contributions in the areas of forensic psychology, the practice of law related to mental health issues, litigation consultation, university teaching, research, and advancing public policy.

Special Facilities or Resources: PGSP's setting as a free-standing graduate school of psychology is much enhanced by our Bay area location. We provide students with access to local university libraries (e.g., Stanford, UC Berkeley). Our library and computer lab have direct access to the Internet. The range of clinical experience available to students is inexhaustible. All faculty have active research programs in which students participate.

Application Information:

Send to: Office of Admissions, Pacific Graduate School of Psychology, 940 East Meadow Drive, Palo Alto, CA 94303. Students are admitted in the Fall. Rolling Admission; however application is due January 15 for those who want to be considered for a PGSP fellowship. *Fee:* $50.

Pacific, University of the
Department of Psychology
Stockton, CA 95211
Telephone: (209) 946-2133
Fax: (209) 946-2454
E-mail: *gradschool@uop.edu*
Web: *http://www.uop.edu/cop/psychology*

Department Established:

1960. Chairperson: Kenneth Beauchamp. Ph.D. Number of Faculty: total–full-time 7; women–full-time 2; minority–full-time 1.

Programs and Degrees Offered:

Listed in the following order: Program area, degree type (T if terminal Master's), number awarded 7/00-6/01. Behavioral MA (T) 10.

Student Applications/Admissions:

Student Applications

Behavioral MA—Applications 2001–2002, 13. Total applicants accepted 2001–2002, 10. New applicants enrolled 2001–2002, 6. Total enrolled 2001–2002 full-time, 14, part-time, 1. Openings 2002–2003, 12. The Median number of years required for completion of a degree are 2. The number of students enrolled full and part-time, who were dismissed or voluntarily withdrew from this program area were 1.

Admissions Requirements:

Scores: Entries appear in this order: required test or GPA, minimum score (if required), median score of students entering in 2001–2002. Master's Programs: GRE-V no minimum stated, 470; GRE-Q no minimum stated, 560; GRE-V+Q no minimum stated, 1030; GRE-Analytical no minimum stated, 590; overall undergraduate GPA no minimum stated, 3.20; last 2 years GPA no minimum stated, 3.25; psychology GPA no minimum stated, 3.40. Doctoral Programs: last 2 years GPA no minimum stated; psychology GPA no minimum stated; psychology GPA no minimum stated.

Other Criteria: (importance of criteria rated low, medium, or high): GRE/MAT scores low, research experience high, work experience medium, clinically related public service low, GPA high, letters of recommendation high, statement of goals and objectives high, applied experience high.

Student Characteristics: The following represents characteristics of students in 2001–2002 in all graduate psychology programs in

the department: Female–full-time 10, part-time 1; Male–full-time 4, part-time 0; African American/Black–full-time 0, part-time 0; Hispanic/Latino (a)–full-time 1, part-time 0; Asian/Pacific Islander–full-time 4, part-time 1; American Indian/Alaska Native–full-time 0, part-time 0.

Financial Information/Assistance:

Tuition for Full-Time Study: *Master's:* State residents per academic year $10,576, $661 per credit hour; nonstate residents: per academic year $10,576, $661 per credit hour.

Financial Assistance:

First Year Students: Teaching assistantships available for first-year. Average amount paid per academic year: $6,450. Average number of hours worked per week: 20. Apply by March 1. Tuition remission given: partial. Traineeships available for first-year. Average amount paid per academic year: $8,200. Average number of hours worked per week: 20. Apply by March 1. Tuition remission given: partial.

Advanced Students: Teaching assistantships available for advanced students. Average amount paid per academic year: $6,450. Average number of hours worked per week: 20. Apply by March 1. Tuition remission given: partial. Traineeships available for advanced students. Average amount paid per academic year: $8,200. Average number of hours worked per week: 20. Apply by March 1. Tuition remission given: partial.

Contact Information: Of all students currently enrolled full-time, 93% benefitted from one or more of the listed financial assistance programs. For information on financial assistance, contact: Dean of the Graduate School and Department of Psychology.

Internships/Practica: Contained directly within the department is the Psychology Clinic, which provides services for families and children (e.g., child custody, parent training, and attention deficit disorder). All students are required to complete two years of experience working in the Clinic during their M.A. studies, or else to complete an appropriate alternative applied experience (e.g., business settings, educational settings). The department also directs the Community Re-entry Program (contracted directly with the local county), which provides a wide range of programs to assist the mentally disabled/ill in becoming independent. This program provides half-time employment for eight graduate students per year. Students interested in developmental disabilities can work with the Behavioral Instructional Service (in cooperation with Valley Mountain Regional Center, which serves these clients), and part-time employment is available with this program.

Housing and Day Care: On-campus housing and day care facilities are available.

Employment of Department Graduates:

Master's Degree Graduates: Of those who graduated in the academic year 2000–2001, the following categories and numbers represent the post-graduate activities and employment of master's degree graduates: Enrolled in a psychology doctoral program (2), enrolled in another graduate/professional program (1), enrolled in a post-doctoral residency/fellowship (n/a), employed in independent practice (n/a), employed in a community mental health/counseling center (1), other employment position (6).

Doctoral Degree Graduates: Of those who graduated in the academic year 2000–2001, the following categories and numbers represent the post-graduate activities and employment of doctoral degree graduates: Enrolled in a psychology doctoral program (n/a), enrolled in another graduate/professional program (n/a).

Additional Information:

Orientation, Objectives, and Emphasis of Department: The M.A. program emphasizes a behavioral approach. The coursework and academic training cover behavioral theories and strategies for behavior change and behavior maintenance. The design and conduct of research are stressed throughout a student's graduate work and an emprical thesis is required. Multiple settings are available for practicum work and research, and experience in relevant applied settings is required. A coordinated program of courses, research, and applied experiences is developed for each student, and the faculty maintains an environment in which students achieve significant research accomplishments and applied interventions. Close contact between faculty and students is highly regarded and encouraged. Graduates are prepared for entrance into doctoral programs and for employment in a variety of applied settings including mental health, medicine/health care, and business. Graduates have qualified for and passed the behavior analysis certification examination of the Association for Applied Behavior Analysis.

Special Facilities or Resources: The department provides space, computing equipment, and video equipment for research projects. Applied research projects are also conducted in community settings (e.g., schools, medical settings). The Community Re-entry Program and Valley Mountain Regional Center (described above) also provide rich opportunities for research in community settings.

Application Information:

Send to: Dean of the Graduate School, University of the Pacific, Stockton, CA 95211. Students are admitted in the Fall, application deadline March 1; Spring, application deadline November 1. *Fee:* $50.

Pepperdine University
Division of Psychology
Graduate School of Education and Psychology
400 Corporate Pointe
Culver City, CA 90230
Telephone: (800) 888-4849
Fax: (310) 568-5755
E-mail: *csaunder@pepperdine.edu*
Web: *http://gsep.pepperdine.edu/gsep*

Department Established:

1951. Associate Dean: Cary L. Mitchell. Number of Faculty: total–full-time 25, part-time 45; women–full-time 10, part-time 23; minority–full-time 6, part-time 3; faculty subject to the Americans with Disabilities Act 1.

Programs and Degrees Offered:

Listed in the following order: Program area, degree type (T if terminal Master's), number awarded 7/00-6/01. Clinical MA (T) 100, Clinical PsyD 18, Clinical (Malibu campus) MA (T) 21, General MA (T) 119.

APA Accreditation: Clinical PsyD: full.

Student Applications/Admissions:

Student Applications

Clinical MA—Applications 2001–2002, 301. Total applicants accepted 2001–2002, 253. New applicants enrolled 2001–2002, 172. Total enrolled 2001–2002 full-time, 268, part-time, 77. Openings 2002–2003, 100. The Median number of years required for completion of a degree are 2. *Clinical PsyD*—Applications 2001–2002, 95. Total applicants accepted 2001–2002, 43. New applicants enrolled 2001–2002, 26. Total enrolled 2001–2002 full-time, 133. Openings 2002–2003, 26. The Median number of years required for completion of a degree are 5. The number of students enrolled full and part-time, who were dismissed or voluntarily withdrew from this program area were 2. *Clinical (Malibu campus) MA*—Applications 2001–2002, 112. Total applicants accepted 2001–2002, 59. New applicants enrolled 2001–2002, 24. Total enrolled 2001–2002 full-time, 39. Openings 2002–2003, 24. The Median number of years required for completion of a degree are 2. The number of students enrolled full and part-time, who were dismissed or voluntarily withdrew from this program area were 2. *General MA*—Applications 2001–2002, 105. Total applicants accepted 2001–2002, 82. New applicants enrolled 2001–2002, 64. Total enrolled 2001–2002 full-time, 120, part-time, 41. Openings 2002–2003, 50. The Median number of years required for completion of a degree are 2.

Admissions Requirements:

Scores: Entries appear in this order: required test or GPA, minimum score (if required), median score of students entering in 2001–2002. Master's Programs: GRE-V no minimum stated, 470; GRE-Q no minimum stated, 500; GRE-V+Q no minimum stated, 1026; MAT no minimum stated, 40; overall undergraduate GPA no minimum stated, 3.02. For the Evening Format MA programs, the GRE or MAT may be waived for applicants with seven or more years of qualified full-time work experience or a cumulative undergraduate GPA of 3.7 or higher. Doctoral Programs: GRE-V no minimum stated, 510; GRE-Q no minimum stated, 580; GRE-V+Q no minimum stated, 1100; GRE-Subject(Psych) no minimum stated, 590; overall undergraduate GPA no minimum stated, 3.16; last 2 years GPA no minimum stated; psychology GPA no minimum stated; psychology GPA 3.50, 3.89.

Other Criteria: (importance of criteria rated low, medium, or high): GRE/MAT scores medium, research experience medium, work experience low, extracurricular activity low, clinically related public service low, GPA high, letters of recommendation high, interview high, statement of goals and objectives high, Clinical Experience high. For the MA in Psychology and the MA in Clinical Psychology - work experience, letters of recommendation, and personal statements have medium importance, while previous research or clinical experience has low importance.

Student Characteristics: The following represents characteristics of students in 2001–2002 in all graduate psychology programs in the department: Female–full-time 459, part-time 90; Male–full-time 101, part-time 28; African American/Black–full-time 46, part-time 6; Hispanic/Latino (a)–full-time 50, part-time 18; Asian/Pacific Islander–full-time 36, part-time 10; American Indian/Alaska Native–full-time 5, part-time 0; Multi-ethnic–full-time 3, part-time 0; students subject to the Americans with Disabilities Act–full-time 8, part-time 0.

Financial Information/Assistance:

Tuition for Full-Time Study: Master's: State residents $620 per credit hour; nonstate residents: $620 per credit hour. *Doctoral:* State residents: $785 per credit hour; nonstate residents: $785 per credit hour.

Financial Assistance:

First Year Students: Teaching assistantships available for first-year. Average amount paid per academic year: $4,400. Average number of hours worked per week: 10. Apply by variable. Research assistantships available for first-year. Average amount paid per academic year: $4,400. Average number of hours worked per week: 10. Apply by variable. Traineeships available for first-year. Average amount paid per academic year: $4,400. Average number of hours worked per week: 10. Apply by variable. Fellowships and scholarships available for first-year. Average amount paid per academic year: $3,000. Average number of hours worked per week: 0. Apply by April 15. Tuition remission given: partial.

Advanced Students: Teaching assistantships available for advanced students. Average amount paid per academic year: $4,400. Average number of hours worked per week: 10. Apply by variable. Research assistantships available for advanced students. Average amount paid per academic year: $4,400. Average number of hours worked per week: 10. Apply by variable. Traineeships available for advanced students. Average amount paid per academic year: $4,400. Average number of hours worked per week: 10. Apply by variable. Fellowships and scholarships available for advanced students. Average amount paid per academic year: $5,300. Average number of hours worked per week: 0. Apply by April 15. Tuition remission given: partial.

Contact Information: Of all students currently enrolled full-time, 30% benefitted from one or more of the listed financial assistance programs. For information on financial assistance, contact: Graduate School of Education and Psychology, Financial Aid Office at (310) 258-2848 or http://gsep.pepperdine.edu/af/finaid. Need-based grants and scholarships are available.

Internships/Practica: Students in the PsyD and MA in Clinical Psychology programs complete practicum requirements at Pepperdine clinics or affiliated agencies in the community. PsyD students complete predoctoral internships in approved agencies. Pepperdine clinical training staff assists students in locating training positions. For those doctoral students for whom a professional internship is required prior to graduation, 25 applied in 2000–2001. Of those who applied, 24 were placed in internships listed by the Association of Psychology Postdoctoral and Internship Programs (APPIC); 19 were placed in APA accredited internships.

Housing and Day Care: No on-campus housing and day care facilities are available.

Employment of Department Graduates:

Master's Degree Graduates: Of those who graduated in the academic year 2000–2001, the following categories and numbers represent the post-graduate activities and employment of master's degree graduates: Enrolled in a post-doctoral residency/fellowship (n/a), employed in independent practice (n/a).

Doctoral Degree Graduates: Of those who graduated in the academic year 2000–2001, the following categories and numbers represent the post-graduate activities and employment of doctoral degree graduates: Enrolled in a psychology doctoral program (n/a), enrolled in another graduate/professional program (n/a), enrolled in a post-doctoral residency/fellowship (5), employed in independent practice (2), employed in other positions at a higher education institution (3), employed in a professional position in a school system (1), employed in a government agency (professional services) (4), employed in a community mental health/counseling center (7), employed in a hospital/medical center (1), still seeking employment (1).

Additional Information:

Orientation, Objectives, and Emphasis of Department: The psychology degree programs are designed to provide the student with a theoretical and practical understanding of the principles of psychology within the framework of a strong clinical emphasis. Courses present various aspects of the art and science of psychology as it is applied to the understanding of human behavior, and to the prevention, diagnosis, and treatment of mental and emotional problems. The MA in psychology serves as the prerequisite for the PsyD degree, or for students seeking human services positions in community agencies and organizations. The MA in clinical psychology provides the academic preparation for the Marriage and Family Therapist license. The PsyD program ascribes to a practitioner-scholar model of training.

Special Facilities or Resources: The Master of Arts in Psychology and Clinical Psychology programs at Pepperdine University are offered at four campuses throughout Southern California. Computer laboratories and libraries are available at all four campuses offering the psychology program. Psychology clinics are located at Culver City, Irvine, and Encino.

Information for Students With Physical Disabilities: Pepperdine University is commited to complying with all mandates set forth in Section 504 of the Rehabilitation Act and Americans with Disabilities Act.

Application Information:
Send to: Pepperdine University, Graduate School of Education and Psychology, Office of Admissions, 400 Corporate Pointe, Culver City, CA 90230. Students are admitted in the Fall, application deadline July 1; Spring, application deadline November 1; Summer, application deadline March 1. PsyD and MA Clinical (Malibu, daytime format) programs: Fall admission only; February 1st application deadline. Evening format MA Clinical and General programs: Fall admission - July 1st application deadline; Spring admission - November 1st application deadline; Summer admission - March 1st application deadline. *Fee:* $55.

San Diego State University/University of California, San Diego Joint Doctoral Program in Clinical Psychology

SDSU Department of Psychology/UCSD Department of Psychiatry
SDSU: College of Sciences   UCSD: School of Medicine
San Diego State University, 6363 Alvarado Court, Suite #103
San Diego, CA 92120-4913
Telephone: (619) 594-2246
Fax: (619) 594-6780
E-mail: *akienle@psychology.sdsu.edu*
Web: *http://www.psychology.sdsu.edu/doctoral*

Department Established:
1985. Co-Directors: Elizabeth A. Klonoff, Robert K. Heaton. Number of Faculty: total–full-time 8, part-time 92; women–full-time 5, part-time 30; minority–full-time 1, part-time 4.

Programs and Degrees Offered:
Listed in the following order: Program area, degree type (T if terminal Master's), number awarded 7/00-6/01. Clinical PhD 11.

APA Accreditation: Clinical PhD: full.

Student Applications/Admissions:

Student Applications

Clinical PhD—Applications 2001–2002, 277. Total applicants accepted 2001–2002, 13. New applicants enrolled 2001–2002, 13. Total enrolled 2001–2002 full-time, 66. Openings 2002–2003, 14. The Median number of years required for completion of a degree are 6. The number of students enrolled full and part-time, who were dismissed or voluntarily withdrew from this program area were 0.

Admissions Requirements:

Scores: Entries appear in this order: required test or GPA, minimum score (if required), median score of students entering in 2001–2002. Doctoral Programs: GRE-V 550, 650; GRE-Q 550, 700; GRE-V+Q 1100, 1350; GRE-Subject(Psych) no minimum stated, 700; overall undergraduate GPA 3.0, 3.55; last 2 years GPA 3.25; psychology GPA no minimum stated, 3.82; psychology GPA no minimum stated. Master's not required for this program. JDP usually requires much higher scores and GPAs than the Graduate Admissions minimum.

Other Criteria: (importance of criteria rated low, medium, or high): GRE/MAT scores medium, research experience high, work experience low, clinically related public service medium, GPA high, letters of recommendation high, interview high, statement of goals and objectives high.

Student Characteristics: The following represents characteristics of students in 2001–2002 in all graduate psychology programs in the department: Female–full-time 49, part-time 0; Male–full-time 17, part-time 0; African American/Black–full-time 3, part-time 0; Hispanic/Latino (a)–full-time 5, part-time 0; Asian/Pacific Islander–full-time 4, part-time 0; American Indian/Alaska Native–full-time 1, part-time 0; students subject to the Americans with Disabilities Act–full-time 0.

Financial Information/Assistance:

Tuition for Full-Time Study: *Doctoral:* State residents: per academic year $1,854; nonstate residents: per academic year $1,854, $246 per credit hour.

Financial Assistance:

First Year Students: Research assistantships available for first-year. Average amount paid per academic year: $14,000. Average number of hours worked per week: 20. Apply by N/A. Tuition remission given: full.

Advanced Students: Teaching assistantships available for advanced students. Average amount paid per academic year: $14,970. Average number of hours worked per week: 20. Apply by N/A. Tuition remission given: full. Research assistantships available for advanced students. Average amount paid per academic year: $14,000. Average number of hours worked per week: 20. Apply by N/A. Tuition remission given: full.

Contact Information: Of all students currently enrolled full-time, 100% benefitted from one or more of the listed financial assistance programs. For information on financial assistance, contact: SDSU Financial Aid Office, SDSU Scholarship Office.

Internships/Practica: For doctoral students only- SDSU: Primary placement is the Psychology Clinic in which various specialty clinics function in any given year. Stress/Anxiety, Child/Family, Depression/Cognitive Intervention, Social Deficits, Atypical Disorders, and Behavioral Medicine. Students are taught general clinical skills. Therapy sessions are routinely videotaped for review in weekly supervision session. UCSD: VA Outpatient Clinic: psychiatric outpatients—assessment and individual and group therapy. VA Medical Center: psychiatric inpatients—assessment, individual and group therapy. UCSD Outpatient Psychiatric Clinic: psychiatric outpatients—neuropsychological assessment and individual and group therapy. UCSD Medical Center: assessment and therapy of all types. Practicum placements are assigned for one full year beginning in the student's second year. For those doctoral students for whom a professional internship is required prior to graduation, 10 applied in 2000–2001. Of those who applied, 9 were placed in internships listed by the Association of Psychology Postdoctoral and Internship Programs (APPIC); 9 were placed in APA accredited internships.

Housing and Day Care: On-campus housing and day care facilities are available.

Employment of Department Graduates:

Master's Degree Graduates:

Doctoral Degree Graduates: Of those who graduated in the academic year 2000–2001, the following categories and numbers represent the post-graduate activities and employment of doctoral degree graduates: Enrolled in a psychology doctoral program (n/a), enrolled in another graduate/professional program (n/a), enrolled in a post-doctoral residency/fellowship (10), employed in an academic position at a university (1).

Additional Information:

Orientation, Objectives, and Emphasis of Department: Our PhD program is a cooperative venture of an academic Department of Psychology (SDSU) and a medical school Department of Psychiatry (UCSD). This partnership between two different departments in two universities provides unusual opportunities for interdisciplinary research. We currently offer concentrations in behavioral medicine, neuropsychology, and experimental psychopathology. The scientist-practitioner model on which the program is based involves a strong commitment to research as well as clinical training. The program aims to prepare students for leadership roles in academic and research settings. Our program is designed as a 5-year curriculum with a core of classroom instruction followed by apprenticeship training in specialty areas with appropriate seminars and tutorials. Clinical experiences are integrated with formal instruction throughout. The program as a whole is designed to satisfy the criteria for APA accreditation.

Special Facilities or Resources: The UCSD Department of Psychiatry, through the medical school and VA Medical Center, has available modern, fully equipped research laboratories with polygraphs, an acoustic chamber, and a major computing facility that includes batch processing, on-line computers, and all of the necessary support services. State-of-the-art neurochemical and biochemical laboratory facilities are also available to qualified students. At SDSU, the Center for Behavioral and Community Health Studies, jointly administered by the Department of Psychology and the College of Human Services, sponsors research, provides training, consultation, and an opportunity for interdisciplinary collaboration. Also, the Doctoral Training Facility at SDSU has a computerized physiological assessment and biofeedback laboratory, as well as a state-of-the-art video-equipped therapy training complex. Animal research is conducted on campus where small animals are housed in a modern vivarium staffed with a veterinarian. SDSU faculty also supervise research on more exotic species at Sea World and the San Diego Zoo. Experimental rooms, equipment, and supplies for graduate research are available in the department. The College of Sciences maintains a completely equipped electronics shop, a wood shop, a metal shop, and computer support facilities with several high end Unix servers, all staffed with full-time technicians. SDSU has modern computer infrastructure and support services. In addition, there are a large number of computer systems readily available within the Department of Psychology.

Information for Students With Physical Disabilities: Students should be aware that the two campuses are located in different parts of the city and that academic, research, and clinical assignments can be at both universities in any given semester/quarter. Travel between campuses is difficult to manage without the student's own personal transportation. Students may contact the SDSU Disabled Student Services Office for information on available assistance.

Application Information:

Send to: Student Selection Committee, 6363 Alvarado Ct. #103, San Diego, CA 92120-4913. Students must also apply to the SDSU Office of Admissions & Records, 5500 Campanile Dr., San Diego CA 92182. Only the application for SDSU Admissions & Records is available on line. Deadlines for both - 12/15. Students are admitted in the Fall, application deadline December 15. *Fee:* $55. Applicants must secure a waiver form from SDSU Admissions & Records. Must demonstrate financial need.

San Francisco State University

Psychology
Behavioral and Social Science
1600 Holloway Avenue
San Francisco, CA 94132
Telephone: (415) 338-1275
Fax: (415) 338-2398
E-mail: *lberry@sfsu.edu*
Web: *http://www.sfsu.edu/~psych/*

Department Established:

Chairperson: Caran Colvin. Number of Faculty: total–full-time 21, part-time 26; women–full-time 10, part-time 14; minority–full-time 6.

Programs and Degrees Offered:

Listed in the following order: Program area, degree type (T if terminal Master's), number awarded 7/00-6/01. Clinical psychology MA (T) 9, developmental psychology MA (T) 4, I/0 psychology MA (T) 6, research psychology MA (T) 6, school psychology MA (T) 3, social psychology MA (T) 7.

Student Applications/Admissions:

Student Applications

Clinical psychology MA—Applications 2001–2002, 95. Total applicants accepted 2001–2002, 14. New applicants enrolled 2001–2002, 12. Total enrolled 2001–2002 full-time, 25. Openings 2002–2003, 12. The Median number of years required for completion of a degree are 2. *Developmental psychology* MA—Applications 2001–2002, 20. Total applicants accepted 2001–2002, 15. New applicants enrolled 2001–2002, 9. Total enrolled 2001–2002 full-time, 18. Openings 2002–2003, 12. The Median number of years required for completion of a degree are 3. *I/0 psychology* MA—Applications 2001–2002, 68. Total applicants accepted 2001–2002, 20. New applicants enrolled 2001–2002, 12. Total enrolled 2001–2002 full-time, 26. Openings 2002–2003, 12. The Median number of years required for completion of a degree are 3. *Research psychology* MA—Applications 2001–2002, 20. Total applicants accepted 2001–2002, 17. New applicants enrolled 2001–2002, 10. Total enrolled 2001–2002 full-time, 10. Openings 2002–2003, 12. The Median number of years required for completion of a degree are 3. *School psychology* MA—Applications 2001–2002, 64. Total applicants accepted 2001–2002, 13. New applicants enrolled 2001–2002, 10. Total enrolled 2001–2002 full-time, 20. Openings 2002–2003, 10. *Social psychology* MA—Applications 2001–2002, 18. Total applicants accepted 2001–2002, 12. New applicants enrolled 2001–2002, 8. Total enrolled 2001–2002 full-time, 15. Openings 2002–2003, 10. The Median number of years required for completion of a degree are 3.

Admissions Requirements:

Scores: Entries appear in this order: required test or GPA, minimum score (if required), median score of students entering in 2001–2002. Master's Programs: GRE-V no minimum stated; GRE-Q no minimum stated; GRE-Analytical no minimum stated; overall undergraduate GPA no minimum stated; last 2 years GPA no minimum stated; psychology GPA no minimum stated. Research Psychology does not require the GRE-Analytical test. Social requires the GRE-Subject test. Indus/Org re-quires the GRE-Writing test. None of the programs have a required minimum GPA; median GPAs vary by program areas. Doctoral Programs: last 2 years GPA no minimum stated; psychology GPA no minimum stated; psychology GPA no minimum stated.

Other Criteria: (importance of criteria rated low, medium, or high): GRE/MAT scores medium, research experience medium, work experience medium, extracurricular activity low, clinically related public service medium, GPA medium, letters of recommendation medium, interview medium, statement of goals and objectives medium. Clinical—clinical service; interview; statement. Developmental—goals & objectives statement; I/0—GRE; GPA; statement of experience; Research—research experience; letters of recommendation. School—statement of goals and objectives; interview; GPA; clinical service.

Student Characteristics: The following represents characteristics of students in 2001–2002 in all graduate psychology programs in the department: Female–full-time 122, part-time 0; Male–full-time 22, part-time 0; African American/Black–full-time 4, part-time 0; Hispanic/Latino(a)–full-time 7, part-time 0; Asian/Pacific Islander–full-time 24, part-time 0; American Indian/Alaska Native–full-time 0, part-time 0; Multi-ethnic–full-time 1.

Financial Information/Assistance:

Tuition for Full-Time Study: *Master's:* State residents per academic year $1,904; nonstate residents: per academic year $7,808.

Financial Assistance:

First Year Students: No information provided.

Advanced Students: Teaching assistantships available for advanced students. Research assistantships available for advanced students.

Contact Information: For information on financial assistance, contact: Graduate Secretary at 415-338-2711.

Internships/Practica: For clinical students, practica in the first year is provided in the Psychology Clinic. Second year internships are located throughout the San Francisco Bay area. For I/0 students, an internship is required during the second year of study. Students are placed in various work organizations throughout the San Francisco Bay area. Students enrolled in the school Psychology program are required to complete a third year paid internship. The Social Psychology students have a year-long field placement.

Housing and Day Care: No on-campus housing and day care facilities are available.

Employment of Department Graduates:

Master's Degree Graduates: Of those who graduated in the academic year 2000–2001, the following categories and numbers represent the post-graduate activities and employment of master's degree graduates: Enrolled in a post-doctoral residency/fellowship (n/a), employed in independent practice (n/a).

Doctoral Degree Graduates: Of those who graduated in the academic year 2000–2001, the following categories and numbers represent the post-graduate activities and employment of doctoral degree graduates: Enrolled in a psychology doctoral program (n/a), enrolled in another graduate/professional program (n/a).

Additional Information:

Orientation, Objectives, and Emphasis of Department: The theoretical orientation of the clinical program is psychodynamic with emphases on family and community systems. The School Psych program emphasizes developmental and psychodynamic theories with an applied interpersonal relations and family systems approach. The Developmental program takes a life span orientation. The I/O program has a science/practice approach to workplace issues. The Social program has a research and community orientation. The Research program takes a basic scientific approach, including study of physiological issues.

Special Facilities or Resources: The Child Study Center is a research and observation facility consisting of 342 pre-schoolers and their families. The Psychology Department Training Clinic is a full service clinic offering psychotherapy to the campus and the larger community. The Clinic is staffed by graduate students under the supervision of licensed clinicians. The Psychology Department Test Library is available to qualified users including students with faculty permission and supervision. Several faculty-led research laboratories are in operation.

Application Information:

Send to: Graduate Secretary, Department of Psychology, San Francisco State University, 1600 Holloway Ave., San Francisco, CA 94132. Students are admitted in the Fall, application deadline March 1. Developmental Psy. also accepts students for the spring semester. Application deadline is October 1. *Fee:* $55.

San Jose State University

Department of Psychology
Social Sciences
One Washington Square
San Jose, CA 95192-0120
Telephone: (408) 924-5600
Fax: (408) 924-5605
E-mail: *nakamura@email.sjsu.edu*
Web: *http://www.psych.sjsu.edu*

Department Established:

Chairperson: Robert Pellegrini. Number of Faculty: total–full-time 21, part-time 11; women–full-time 12, part-time 5; minority–full-time 5, part-time 1; faculty subject to the Americans with Disabilities Act 1.

Programs and Degrees Offered:

Listed in the following order: Program area, degree type (T if terminal Master's), number awarded 7/00-6/01. Clinical/counseling MA (T) 8, general MA (T) 5, industrial/organizational MA (T) 6.

Student Applications/Admissions:

Student Applications

Clinical/counseling MA—Applications 2001–2002, 36. Total applicants accepted 2001–2002, 15. New applicants enrolled 2001–2002, 15. Total enrolled 2001–2002 full-time, 15. Openings 2002–2003, 15. The number of students enrolled full and part-time, who were dismissed or voluntarily withdrew from this program area were 1. *General MA*—Applications 2001–

2002, 33. Total applicants accepted 2001–2002, 17. New applicants enrolled 2001–2002, 7. Total enrolled 2001–2002 full-time, 7. Openings 2002–2003, 18. *Industrial/organizational MA*—Applications 2001–2002, 37. Total applicants accepted 2001–2002, 15. New applicants enrolled 2001–2002, 14. Total enrolled 2001–2002 full-time, 14. Openings 2002–2003, 15. The number of students enrolled full and part-time, who were dismissed or voluntarily withdrew from this program area were 1.

Admissions Requirements:

Scores: Entries appear in this order: required test or GPA, minimum score (if required), median score of students entering in 2001–2002. Master's Programs: GRE-V no minimum stated; GRE-Q no minimum stated; psychology GPA 3.0. GRE required for I/O & MA General ONLY - No GRE for Clinical. Doctoral Programs: last 2 years GPA no minimum stated; psychology GPA no minimum stated; psychology GPA no minimum stated.

Other Criteria: (importance of criteria rated low, medium, or high): Clinical Program has specific course requirements for admission.

Student Characteristics: The following represents characteristics of students in 2001–2002 in all graduate psychology programs in the department: Female–full-time 47, part-time 0; Male–full-time 16, part-time 0; African American/Black–full-time 1, part-time 0; Hispanic/Latino (a)–full-time 3, part-time 0; Asian/Pacific Islander–full-time 5, part-time 0; American Indian/Alaska Native–full-time 0, part-time 0; Multi-ethnic–full-time 2, students subject to the Americans with Disabilities Act–full-time 0.

Financial Information/Assistance:

Tuition for Full-Time Study: *Master's:* State residents per academic year $2,000; nonstate residents: per academic year $2,000, $246 per credit hour.

Financial Assistance:

First Year Students: No information provided.
Advanced Students: No information provided.
Contact Information: For information on financial assistance, contact: www@sjsu.edu/depts/finaid.

Internships/Practica: No information provided.

Housing and Day Care: No on-campus housing and day care facilities are available.

Employment of Department Graduates:

Master's Degree Graduates: Of those who graduated in the academic year 2000–2001, the following categories and numbers represent the post-graduate activities and employment of master's degree graduates: Enrolled in a post-doctoral residency/fellowship (n/a), employed in independent practice (n/a).

Doctoral Degree Graduates: Of those who graduated in the academic year 2000–2001, the following categories and numbers represent the post-graduate activities and employment of doctoral degree graduates: Enrolled in a psychology doctoral program (n/a), enrolled in another graduate/professional program (n/a).

Additional Information:

Special Facilities or Resources: The department maintains a variety of facilities and support staff to enhance instruction and research. For biological and cognitive research and instruction, the department has a number of laboratories and specialized laboratory equipment on campus, and lab technicians are available to construct additional equipment. For work in clinical and counseling psychology, the department has a Psychology Clinic consisting of therapy rooms and adjoining observation rooms equipped with audio and video equipment. These rooms are also available to individuals working in other areas, such as developmental, personality, and social psychology. In addition, students interested in counseling-related activities have access to a number of off-campus organizations. Three computer laboratories containing microcomputers and terminals hooked up to minicomputers and mainframes are available for students. These labs have extensive software, and computer consultants are on call to help with software and hardware problems, design and interpretation of statistical analyses, and computer exercises.

Application Information:
Send to: Program information and application are available online. Send department application to: San Jose State University, Psychology Department, One Washington Square, San Jose, CA 95192-0120. Send University application to: San Jose State University, Admissions and Records, One Washington Square, San Jose, CA 95192-0009. Students are admitted in the Fall. Deadline for clinical/counseling is January 1; for the psychology program and industrial/organizational, it is February 1. *Fee:* $55.

Saybrook Graduate School and Research Center
Graduate School
450 Pacific Avenue, Third Floor
San Francisco, CA 94133-4640
Telephone: (415) 433-9200
Fax: (415) 433-9271
E-mail: *saybrook@saybrook.edu*
Web: *http://www.saybrook.edu*

Department Established:
1971. President: Maureen O'Hara. Number of Faculty: total–full-time 10, part-time 74; women–full-time 7, part-time 15.

Programs and Degrees Offered:
Listed in the following order: Program area, degree type (T if terminal Master's), number awarded 7/00-6/01. Human science MA, human science PhD 3, Psychology Licensure MA, Organizational Systems MA 1, Organizational Systems PhD 2, psychology MA 4, psychology PhD 15.

Student Applications/Admissions:
Student Applications
Human science MA—Applications 2001–2002, 12. Total applicants accepted 2001–2002, 4. New applicants enrolled 2001–2002, 4. Total enrolled 2001–2002 full-time, 8. Openings 2002–2003, 10. The Median number of years required for completion of a degree are 2. *Human science PhD*—Applications 2001–2002, 36. Total applicants accepted 2001–2002, 6. New applicants enrolled 2001–2002, 3. Total enrolled 2001–2002 full-time, 46. Openings 2002–2003, 20. The Median number of years required for completion of a degree are 4. *Psychology Licensure* MA—Applications 2001–2002, 23. Total

applicants accepted 2001–2002, 20. New applicants enrolled 2001–2002, 19. Total enrolled 2001–2002 full-time, 19. *Organizational Systems MA*—Applications 2001–2002, 10. Total applicants accepted 2001–2002, 9. New applicants enrolled 2001–2002, 8. Total enrolled 2001–2002 full-time, 48. Openings 2002–2003, 20. The Median number of years required for completion of a degree are 2. *Organizational Systems PhD*—Total enrolled 2001–2002 full-time, 61. The Median number of years required for completion of a degree are 4. *Psychology MA*—Applications 2001–2002, 49. Total applicants accepted 2001–2002, 19. New applicants enrolled 2001–2002, 15. Total enrolled 2001–2002 full-time, 51. Openings 2002–2003, 15. The Median number of years required for completion of a degree are 2. *Psychology PhD*—Applications 2001–2002, 88. Total applicants accepted 2001–2002, 24. New applicants enrolled 2001–2002, 20. Total enrolled 2001–2002 full-time, 219. Openings 2002–2003, 45. The Median number of years required for completion of a degree are 5.

Admissions Requirements:
Scores: Entries appear in this order: required test or GPA, minimum score (if required), median score of students entering in 2001–2002. Doctoral Programs: last 2 years GPA no minimum stated; psychology GPA no minimum stated; psychology GPA 3.0.
Other Criteria: (importance of criteria rated low, medium, or high): GRE/MAT scores, research experience high, work experience high, extracurricular activity medium, clinically related public service medium, GPA letters of recommendation low, statement of goals and objectives high, writing ability high.

Student Characteristics: The following represents characteristics of students in 2001–2002 in all graduate psychology programs in the department: Female–full-time 246, part-time 0; Male–full-time 146, part-time 0; African American/Black–full-time 28, part-time 0; Hispanic/Latino(a)–full-time 14, part-time 0; Asian/Pacific Islander–full-time 16, part-time 0; American Indian/Alaska Native–full-time 5, part-time 0.

Financial Information/Assistance:
Tuition for Full-Time Study: *Master's:* State residents per academic year $14,500; nonstate residents: per academic year $14,500. *Doctoral:* State residents: per academic year $14,500; nonstate residents: per academic year $14,500.

Financial Assistance:
First Year Students: Fellowships and scholarships available for first-year. Average amount paid per academic year: $1,000.
Advanced Students: Fellowships and scholarships available for advanced students. Average amount paid per academic year: $5,000.
Contact Information: Of all students currently enrolled full-time, 5% benefitted from one or more of the listed financial assistance programs. For information on financial assistance, contact: Bruce Gordon, Director of Financial Aid. (800)825-4480 Ext. #5640 or bgordon@saybrook.edu.

Internships/Practica: No information provided.

Housing and Day Care: No on-campus housing and day care facilities are available.

Employment of Department Graduates:

Master's Degree Graduates: Of those who graduated in the academic year 2000–2001, the following categories and numbers represent the post-graduate activities and employment of master's degree graduates: Enrolled in a post-doctoral residency/fellowship (n/a), employed in independent practice (n/a).

Doctoral Degree Graduates: Of those who graduated in the academic year 2000–2001, the following categories and numbers represent the post-graduate activities and employment of doctoral degree graduates: Enrolled in a psychology doctoral program (n/a), enrolled in another graduate/professional program (n/a).

Additional Information:

Orientation, Objectives, and Emphasis of Department: The mission of Saybrook Graduate School and Research Center is to provide a unique and creative environment for graduate study, research, and communication in humanistic psychology, focused on understanding the human experience, in a distance learning format. Applying the highest standards of scholarship, Saybrook is dedicated to fostering the full expression of the human spirit and humanistic values in society.

Application Information:

Send to: Saybrook Graduate School, Admissions Department, 450 Pacific, 3rd floor, S.F., CA 94133. Students are admitted in the Fall, application deadline June 1; Spring, application deadline December 16. *Fee:* $70.

Sonoma State University
Department of Counseling
1801 East Cotati Avenue
Rohnert Park, CA 94928
Telephone: (707) 664-2544
Fax: (707) 664-2038
E-mail: *carolyn.saarni@sonoma.edu*
Web: *http://www.sonoma.edu/counseling*

Department Established:

1973. Chairperson: Carolyn Saarni. Number of Faculty: total–full-time 6, part-time 8; women–full-time 4, part-time 5.

Programs and Degrees Offered:

Listed in the following order: Program area, degree type (T if terminal Master's), number awarded 7/00-6/01. Marriage and Family Therapy MA (T) 22, School Counseling MA (T) 18.

Student Applications/Admissions:

Student Applications

Marriage and Family Therapy MA—Applications 2001–2002, 90. Total applicants accepted 2001–2002, 24. New applicants enrolled 2001–2002, 23. Total enrolled 2001–2002 full-time, 47, part-time, 15. Openings 2002–2003, 24. The Median number of years required for completion of a degree are 3. The number of students enrolled full and part-time, who were dismissed or voluntarily withdrew from this program area were 1. *School Counseling* MA—Applications 2001–2002, 40. Total applicants accepted 2001–2002, 18. New applicants enrolled 2001–2002, 16. Total enrolled 2001–2002 full-time, 30, part-time, 6. Openings 2002–2003, 16. The Median number of

years required for completion of a degree are 2. The number of students enrolled full and part-time, who were dismissed or voluntarily withdrew from this program area were 2.

Admissions Requirements:

Scores: Entries appear in this order: required test or GPA, minimum score (if required), median score of students entering in 2001–2002. Master's Programs: overall undergraduate GPA 3.0, 3.0; last 2 years GPA 3.0, 3.5. Doctoral Programs: last 2 years GPA no minimum stated; psychology GPA no minimum stated; psychology GPA no minimum stated.

Other Criteria: (importance of criteria rated low, medium, or high): research experience low, work experience medium, extracurricular activity medium, clinically related public service high, GPA medium, letters of recommendation high, interview high, statement of goals and objectives high. School counseling program looks for school-related service or clinical/social work with children or youth.

Student Characteristics: The following represents characteristics of students in 2001–2002 in all graduate psychology programs in the department: Female–full-time 61, part-time 16; Male–full-time 17, part-time 4; African American/Black–full-time 2, part-time 0; Hispanic/Latino (a)–full-time 10, part-time 3; Asian/Pacific Islander–full-time 5, part-time 0; American Indian/Alaska Native–full-time 1, part-time 0; Multi-ethnic–full-time 4.

Financial Information/Assistance:

Tuition for Full-Time Study: *Master's:* State residents per academic year $2,080; nonstate residents: $246 per credit hour.

Financial Assistance:

First Year Students: Fellowships and scholarships available for first-year. Average amount paid per academic year: $1,400. Apply by Feb. 15.

Advanced Students: Fellowships and scholarships available for advanced students. Average amount paid per academic year: $1,400. Apply by Feb. 15.

Contact Information: Of all students currently enrolled full-time, 40% benefitted from one or more of the listed financial assistance programs. For information on financial assistance, contact: Financial Aid Office, Scholarship Office, individual faculty: www.sonoma.edu/FinAid/, www.sonoma.edu/Scholarship.

Internships/Practica: Our students generally have several internship options to choose from, and they are highly sought by agencies and schools as interns. We do limit the internship sites to Sonoma State University's service area, which is the North Bay/tri-county region of the San Francisco Bay Area.

Housing and Day Care: On-campus housing and day care facilities are available.

Employment of Department Graduates:

Master's Degree Graduates: Of those who graduated in the academic year 2000–2001, the following categories and numbers represent the post-graduate activities and employment of master's degree graduates: Enrolled in a post-doctoral residency/fellowship (n/a), employed in independent practice (n/a).

Doctoral Degree Graduates: Of those who graduated in the academic year 2000–2001, the following categories and numbers represent the post-graduate activities and employment of doctoral

degree graduates: Enrolled in a psychology doctoral program (n/a), enrolled in another graduate/professional program (n/a).

Additional Information:

Orientation, Objectives, and Emphasis of Department: The 60-unit graduate program in counseling (nationally accredited through CACREP, affiliated with the American Counseling Association) prepares students for entry into the profession of counseling or student personnel services. The Marriage & Family Therapy (MFT) students prepare for licensure as MFT's in California; the School Counseling students obtain a Pupil Personnel Services Credential. The program relies heavily on interpersonal skill training and field experience, beginning during the first semester and culminating with an intensive supervised internship in some aspect of counseling, permitting the integration of theoretical constructs and research appraisal with practical application during the second year. The department is prepared to assist students in obtaining field placements relevant to their projected professional goals. These placements include, but are not limited to, marriage and family counseling agencies, mental health clinics, counseling centers, public schools, community colleges, and college-level student counseling centers. Special characteristics of the program include the following: (1) early involvement in actual counseling settings, (2) development of a core of knowledge and experience in both individual and group counseling theory and practice, (3) encouragement in the maintenance and development of individual counseling styles, and (4) commitment to self-exploration and personal growth through participation in peer counseling, individual counseling, and group experiences. This aspect of the program is seen as crucial to the development of counseling skills and is given special consideration by the faculty as part of its evaluation of student readiness to undertake internship responsibilities.

Special Facilities or Resources: Center for Community Counseling (on campus).

Information for Students With Physical Disabilities: Disability Resource Center (on campus).

Application Information:

Send to: Counseling Department, Sonoma State University, 1801 E. Cotati Ave., N220, Rohnert Park, CA 94928. Students are admitted in the Fall, application deadline Jan 31, 2003. *Fee:* $80. $25 fee for application to the Counseling Department, $55 fee for application to Sonoma State University, Total: $80.

Sonoma State University
Department of Psychology
1801 East Cotati Avenue
Rohnert Park, CA 94928
Telephone: (707) 664-2682
Fax: (707) 664-3113
E-mail: *charles.merrill@sonoma.edu*
Web: *http://www.sonoma.edu/psychology*

Department Established:
1961. Chairperson: Arthur Warmoth, Ph.D. Number of Faculty: total–full-time 14, part-time 9; women–full-time 7, part-time 9; minority–full-time 1.

Programs and Degrees Offered:
Listed in the following order: Program area, degree type (T if terminal Master's), number awarded 7/00-6/01. Art therapy MA 4, Depth Psych. MA 6, Humanistic MA 5, organization development MA 10.

Student Applications/Admissions:
Student Applications
Art therapy MA—Applications 2001–2002, 17. Total applicants accepted 2001–2002, 12. New applicants enrolled 2001–2002, 12. Total enrolled 2001–2002 full-time, 25, part-time, 5. The Median number of years required for completion of a degree are 3. The number of students enrolled full and part-time, who were dismissed or voluntarily withdrew from this program area were 0. *Depth Psych.* MA—Applications 2001–2002, 17. Total applicants accepted 2001–2002, 14. New applicants enrolled 2001–2002, 12. Total enrolled 2001–2002 full-time, 11. Openings 2002–2003, 14. The Median number of years required for completion of a degree are 2. The number of students enrolled full and part-time, who were dismissed or voluntarily withdrew from this program area were 1. *Humanistic* MA—Applications 2001–2002, 10. Total applicants accepted 2001–2002, 6. New applicants enrolled 2001–2002, 6. Total enrolled 2001–2002 full-time, 15, part-time, 10. Openings 2002–2003, 6. The Median number of years required for completion of a degree are 2. The number of students enrolled full and part-time, who were dismissed or voluntarily withdrew from this program area were 0. *Organization development MA*—Applications 2001–2002, 21. Total applicants accepted 2001–2002, 15. New applicants enrolled 2001–2002, 14. Total enrolled 2001–2002 full-time, 25. Openings 2002–2003, 15. The Median number of years required for completion of a degree are 2. The number of students enrolled full and part-time, who were dismissed or voluntarily withdrew from this program area were 1.

Admissions Requirements:
Scores: Entries appear in this order: required test or GPA, minimum score (if required), median score of students entering in 2001–2002. Master's Programs: last 2 years GPA 3.00, 3.40. Doctoral Programs: last 2 years GPA no minimum stated; psychology GPA no minimum stated; psychology GPA no minimum stated.
Other Criteria: (importance of criteria rated low, medium, or high): work experience medium, extracurricular activity low, clinically related public service medium, GPA high, letters of recommendation high, interview high, statement of goals and objectives high, Biographical information medium, Demonstrated writing ability in all programs.

Student Characteristics: The following represents characteristics of students in 2001–2002 in all graduate psychology programs in the department: Female–full-time 25, part-time 0; Male–full-time 8, part-time 0; African American/Black–full-time 0, part-time 0; Hispanic/Latino (a)–full-time 0, part-time 0; Asian/Pacific Islander–full-time 0, part-time 0; American Indian/Alaska Native–full-time 2, part-time 0.

Financial Information/Assistance:
Tuition for Full-Time Study: *Master's:* State residents per academic year $6,375, $375 per credit hour; nonstate residents: per academic year $6,375, $375 per credit hour.

Financial Assistance:

First Year Students: No information provided.

Advanced Students: No information provided.

Contact Information: Of all students currently enrolled full-time, 0% benefitted from one or more of the listed financial assistance programs. For information on financial assistance, contact: Office of Financial Aid; Office of Scholarships.

Internships/Practica: Internships are optional for Humanistic and Depth Psychology. Internships are required as part of the Art Therapy program. Field projects working in a team of two or three students in an organization are required for the Organization Development program.

Housing and Day Care: On-campus housing and day care facilities are available.

Employment of Department Graduates:

Master's Degree Graduates: Of those who graduated in the academic year 2000–2001, the following categories and numbers represent the post-graduate activities and employment of master's degree graduates: Enrolled in a psychology doctoral program (2), enrolled in another graduate/professional program (1), enrolled in a post-doctoral residency/fellowship (n/a), employed in independent practice (n/a), employed in an academic position at a university (0), employed in an academic position at a 2-year/4-year college (2), employed in other positions at a higher education institution (0), employed in a professional position in a school system (0), employed in business or industry (research/consulting) (5), employed in business or industry (management) (2), employed in a government agency (research) (0), employed in a government agency (professional services) (0), employed in a community mental health/counseling center (0), employed in a hospital/medical center (0), still seeking employment (6), other employment position (0).

Doctoral Degree Graduates: Of those who graduated in the academic year 2000–2001, the following categories and numbers represent the post-graduate activities and employment of doctoral degree graduates: Enrolled in a psychology doctoral program (n/a), enrolled in another graduate/professional program (n/a).

Additional Information:

Orientation, Objectives, and Emphasis of Department: Art Therapy: Offers 34-units of coursework that meets both the educational standards of the American Art Therapy Association and continues the humanistic tradition of the SSU Psychology Department. To become professionally registered as an A.T.R., an additional 2,000 post-master's supervised hours of work are required. Depth Psychology: An embodied 34-unit curriculum which integrates intensive personal process work in Jungian and archetypal psychology with conceptual learning and practical skills development. A small group environment enables students to develop skills in process work, group facilitation, arts expressions, dream work, personal growth facilitation and cross-cultural awareness. Humanistic/Transpersonal Psychology: A 34-unit semester program for self-directed individuals who may already be in the professional workplace and have not been able to further their educational and individualized curriculum, work closely with a graduate mentor from the SSU psychology faculty, and take a core course in psychology each semester. Organization Development: Provides professional preparation for mid-career individuals interested in learning how to develop more effective and humane

organizations. A 34-unit program of seminar discussions, skill-building activities, and extensive field projects under faculty guidance. Participants gain the practical skills, conceptual knowledge, and field-tested experience to successfully lead organization improvement efforts.

Special Facilities or Resources: Facilities include a biofeedback lab and computer lab. The faculty are open to investigations in humanistic, existential, and transpersonal areas of psychology. The department has excellent interdisciplinary cooperation with sociology, gerontology, business, and other related programs.

Application Information:

Send to: Office of Extended Education/ Special Sessions. Students are admitted in the Fall, application deadline May 1. Applications accepted on a rolling basis until number reached. *Fee:* $55.

Southern California, University of

Department of Psychology
College of Letters, Arts and Sciences
University Park - SGM 501
Los Angeles, CA 90089-1061
Telephone: (213) 740-2203
Fax: (213) 746-9082
E-mail: *itakarag@usc.edu*
Web: *http://www.usc.edu/dept/LAS/psychology*

Department Established:

1929. Chairperson: Gerald C. Davison. Number of Faculty: total–full-time 34; women–full-time 7; minority–full-time 3.

Programs and Degrees Offered:

Listed in the following order: Program area, degree type (T if terminal Master's), number awarded 7/00-6/01. Clinical science PhD 5, developmental-aging PhD, developmental-child PhD, neuroscience PhD 2, quantitative PhD, social PhD 4.

APA Accreditation: Clinical PhD: full.

Student Applications/Admissions:

Student Applications

Clinical science PhD—Applications 2001–2002, 235. Total applicants accepted 2001–2002, 17. New applicants enrolled 2001–2002, 10. Total enrolled 2001–2002 full-time, 38. Openings 2002–2003, 6. The Median number of years required for completion of a degree are 5. The number of students enrolled full and part-time, who were dismissed or voluntarily withdrew from this program area were 0. *Developmental-aging PhD*—Applications 2001–2002, 5. Total applicants accepted 2001–2002, 3. New applicants enrolled 2001–2002, 1. Total enrolled 2001–2002 full-time, 5. Openings 2002–2003, 1. The number of students enrolled full and part-time, who were dismissed or voluntarily withdrew from this program area were 0. *Developmental-child PhD*—Applications 2001–2002, 19. Total applicants accepted 2001–2002, 4. New applicants enrolled 2001–2002, 2. Total enrolled 2001–2002 full-time, 9. Openings 2002–2003, 1. The number of students enrolled full and part-time, who were dismissed or voluntarily withdrew from this program area were 0. *Neuroscience PhD*—Applications 2001–2002, 42. Total applicants accepted 2001–2002, 12. New applicants enrolled 2001–2002, 5. Total enrolled 2001–2002 full-time, 25. Openings 2002–2003, 6. The Median number of years required for completion of a degree are 6. The number of students enrolled full and part-time, who were dismissed or voluntarily withdrew from this program area were 3. *Quantitative PhD*—Applications 2001–2002, 8. Total applicants accepted 2001–2002, 3. New applicants enrolled 2001–2002, 1. Total enrolled 2001–2002 full-time, 4. Openings 2002–2003, 1. The number of students enrolled full and part-time, who were dismissed or voluntarily withdrew from this program area were 0. *Social PhD*—Applications 2001–2002, 31. Total applicants accepted 2001–2002, 4. New applicants enrolled 2001–2002, 2. Total enrolled 2001–2002 full-time, 16. Openings 2002–2003, 2. The Median number of years required for completion of a degree are 7. The number of students enrolled full and part-time, who were dismissed or voluntarily withdrew from this program area were 2.

Admissions Requirements:

Scores: Entries appear in this order: required test or GPA, minimum score (if required), median score of students entering in 2001–2002. Doctoral Programs: GRE-V no minimum stated, 596; GRE-Q 560, 671; GRE-V+Q no minimum stated, 1267; GRE-Analytical no minimum stated; GRE-V+Q+Analytical no minimum stated; overall undergraduate GPA no minimum stated, 3.35; last 2 years GPA no minimum stated; psychology GPA no minimum stated; psychology GPA no minimum stated.

Other Criteria: (importance of criteria rated low, medium, or high): GRE/MAT scores high, research experience high, work experience medium, extracurricular activity low, clinically related public service medium, GPA high, letters of recommendation high, interview, statement of goals and objectives high. Interview and clinically related public service are very important for the Clinical Science program but less so for other areas.

Student Characteristics: The following represents characteristics of students in 2001–2002 in all graduate psychology programs in the department: Female–full-time 60, part-time 0; Male–full-time 37, part-time 0; African American/Black–full-time 7, part-time 0; Hispanic/Latino (a)–full-time 13, part-time 0; Asian/Pacific Islander–full-time 10, part-time 0; American Indian/Alaska Native–full-time 2, part-time 0; Multi-ethnic–full-time 0, students subject to the Americans with Disabilities Act–full-time 0.

Financial Information/Assistance:

Tuition for Full-Time Study: *Doctoral:* State residents: per academic year $13,504, $844 per credit hour; nonstate residents: per academic year $13,504, $844 per credit hour.

Financial Assistance:

First Year Students: Teaching assistantships available for first-year. Average amount paid per academic year: $14,420. Average number of hours worked per week: 20. Tuition remission given: full. Research assistantships available for first-year. Average amount paid per academic year: $14,420. Average number of hours worked per week: 20. Tuition remission given: full. Traineeships available for first-year. Average amount paid per academic year: $15,000. Average number of hours worked per week: 0. Tuition remission given: full. Fellowships and scholarships available for first-year. Average amount paid per academic year: $15,000. Average number of hours worked per week: 0. Tuition remission given: full.

Advanced Students: Teaching assistantships available for advanced students. Average amount paid per academic year: $14,420. Average number of hours worked per week: 20. Tuition remission given: full. Research assistantships available for advanced students. Average amount paid per academic year: $14,420. Average number of hours worked per week: 20. Tuition remission given: full. Traineeships available for advanced students. Average amount paid per academic year: $15,000. Average number of hours worked per week: 0. Tuition remission given: full. Fellowships and scholarships available for advanced students. Average amount paid per academic year: $15,000. Average number of hours worked per week: 0. Tuition remission given: full.

Contact Information: Of all students currently enrolled full-time, 68% benefitted from one or more of the listed financial assistance programs. For information on financial assistance, contact: Irene Takaragawa, Graduate Advisor, Department of Psychology, University of Southern California/SGM 508, Los Angeles, CA 90089-1061.

Internships/Practica: For those doctoral students for whom a professional internship is required prior to graduation, 7 applied in 2000–2001. Of those who applied, 7 were placed in internships listed by the Association of Psychology Postdoctoral and Internship Programs (APPIC); 7 were placed in APA accredited internships.

Housing and Day Care: No on-campus housing or day care facilities are available.

Employment of Department Graduates:

Master's Degree Graduates: Of those who graduated in the academic year 2000–2001, the following categories and numbers represent the post-graduate activities and employment of master's degree graduates: Enrolled in a post-doctoral residency/fellowship (n/a), employed in independent practice (n/a).

Doctoral Degree Graduates: Of those who graduated in the academic year 2000–2001, the following categories and numbers represent the post-graduate activities and employment of doctoral degree graduates: Enrolled in a psychology doctoral program (n/a), enrolled in another graduate/professional program (n/a), enrolled in a post-doctoral residency/fellowship (3), employed in an academic position at a university (2), employed in an academic position at a 2-year/4-year college (1), employed in other positions at a higher education institution (2), employed in business or industry (research/consulting) (1), employed in a hospital/medical center (1).

Additional Information:

Orientation, Objectives, and Emphasis of Department: Though oriented toward research and teaching, graduate training in psychology also shows concern for the applications of psychology. In addition to completing the required coursework, students in all specialty areas are expected to engage in empirical research throughout graduate study. Areas of specialization include clinical psychology, child development, adult development and aging, cognitive psychology, behavioral neuroscience, quantitative, and social psychology. Within the clinical science program, there are formal tracks in clinical-aging and child and family. The APA-approved clinical program incorporates the scientist-professional model and prepares students for careers in teaching and research, as well as in empirically oriented applied settings.

Special Facilities or Resources: We are housed in the upper six floors of a 10 story building. Ample laboratory and office space are supplemented by facilities in the Hedco Neurosciences building that is adjacent to the main Psychology building.

Application Information:
Send to: Irene Takaragawa, Department of Psychology/SGM 508, University of Southern California, Los Angeles, CA 90089-1061. Students are admitted in the Fall, application deadline December 15. Extended deadline of December 31 for any unfilled slots in Brain and Cognitive Sciences, Developmental, Quantitative and Social Psychology. *Fee:* $65. Must send to the Office of Graduate Admissions, USC, Los Angeles, CA, 90089-0913, the most current financial aid statement from current/last school of enrollment.

Southern California, University of, School of Medicine
Department of Preventive Medicine, Division of Health Behavior Research
USC/IPR, 1000 S. Fremont Avenue, Box 8, Attn: Doctoral Program
Alhambra, CA 91803
Telephone: (626) 457-6648
Fax: (626) 457-4161
E-mail: *barovich@hsc.usc.edu*
Web: *http://www.usc.edu/go/ipr*

Department Established:
1984. Director: C. Anderson Johnson. Number of Faculty: total–full-time 20; women–full-time 9; minority–full-time 5.

Programs and Degrees Offered:
Listed in the following order: Program area, degree type (T if terminal Master's), number awarded 7/00-6/01. Health Behavior Research PhD.

Student Applications/Admissions:
Student Applications
Health Behavior Research PhD—Applications 2001–2002, 16. Total applicants accepted 2001–2002, 6. New applicants enrolled 2001–2002, 6. Total enrolled 2001–2002 full-time, 24. Openings 2002–2003, 3. The number of students enrolled full and part-time, who were dismissed or voluntarily withdrew from this program area were 1.

Admissions Requirements:
Scores: Entries appear in this order: required test or GPA, minimum score (if required), median score of students entering in 2001–2002. Doctoral Programs: GRE-V+Q 1000, 1215; overall undergraduate GPA 3.0, 3.72; last 2 years GPA no minimum stated; psychology GPA no minimum stated; psychology GPA no minimum stated. A master's degree is not required, but if a student has a master's degree, GPA is necessary.
Other Criteria: (importance of criteria rated low, medium, or high): GRE/MAT scores, research experience low, work experience low, GPA letters of recommendation high, interview high, statement of goals and objectives high.

Student Characteristics: The following represents characteristics of students in 2001–2002 in all graduate psychology programs in the department: Female–full-time 17, part-time 0; Male–full-time 8, part-time 0; African American/Black–full-time 0, part-time 0; Hispanic/Latino (a)–full-time 3, part-time 0; Asian/Pacific Islander–full-time 7, part-time 0; American Indian/Alaska Native–full-time 0, part-time 0; Multi-ethnic–full-time 1, part-time 0; students subject to the Americans with Disabilities Act–full-time 0, part-time 0.

Financial Information/Assistance:
Tuition for Full-Time Study: *Master's:* State residents per academic year $20,256, $844 per credit hour; nonstate residents: per academic year $20,256, $844 per credit hour. *Doctoral:* State residents: per academic year $20,256, $844 per credit hour; nonstate residents: per academic year $20,256, $844 per credit hour.

Financial Assistance:
First Year Students: Teaching assistantships available for first-year. Average amount paid per academic year: $21,200. Average number of hours worked per week: 20. Apply by Feb. 1. Tuition remission given: full. Research assistantships available for first-year. Average amount paid per academic year: $21,200. Average number of hours worked per week: 20. Apply by Feb. 1. Tuition remission given: full. Traineeships available for first-year. Average amount paid per academic year: $21,200. Average number of hours worked per week: 20. Apply by as available. Tuition remission given: full. Fellowships and scholarships available for first-year. Average amount paid per academic year: $21,200. Average number of hours worked per week: 20. Apply by Feb. 1. Tuition remission given: full.
Advanced Students: Teaching assistantships available for advanced students. Average amount paid per academic year: $21,235. Average number of hours worked per week: 20. Apply by n/a. Tuition remission given: full. Research assistantships available for advanced students. Average amount paid per academic year: $21,235. Average number of hours worked per week: 20. Apply by n/a. Tuition remission given: full. Traineeships available for advanced students. Average amount paid per academic year: $21,235. Average number of hours worked per week: 20. Apply by as available. Tuition remission given: full. Fellowships and scholarships available for advanced students. Average amount paid per academic year: $21,235. Average number of hours worked per week: 20. Apply by Feb. 1. Tuition remission given: full.
Contact Information: Of all students currently enrolled full-time, 92% benefitted from one or more of the listed financial assistance programs. For information on financial assistance, contact: For fellowships, contact: Fellowship Office, The Graduate School. For federal financial aid, contact: Office of Financial Aid at 213-740-1111.

Internships/Practica: Three practica in health behavior are available to doctoral students: a) prevention, b) compliance, and c) health behavior topics. Through the practica, students gain practical experience in a variety of field settings to gain a certain type of skill such as curriculum development, media production, and patient education.

Housing and Day Care: On-campus housing and day care facilities are available.

Employment of Department Graduates:

Master's Degree Graduates: Of those who graduated in the academic year 2000–2001, the following categories and numbers represent the post-graduate activities and employment of master's degree graduates: , enrolled in a post-doctoral residency/fellowship (n/a), employed in independent practice (n/a).

Doctoral Degree Graduates: Of those who graduated in the academic year 2000–2001, the following categories and numbers represent the post-graduate activities and employment of doctoral degree graduates: Enrolled in a psychology doctoral program (n/a), enrolled in another graduate/professional program (n/a).

Additional Information:

Orientation, Objectives, and Emphasis of Department: The University of Southern California (USC) School of Medicine, Department of Preventive Medicine, Division of Health Behavior Research, offers a doctorate in preventive medicine, health behavior research (HBR), providing academic and research training for students interested in pursuing career opportunities in the field of health promotion and disease prevention research. The specific objective of the program is to train exceptional researchers and scholars in the multidisciplinary field of health behavior research. Students receive well-rounded training that encompasses theory and methods from many allied fields, including communication, psychology, preventive medicine, statistics, public health, and epidemiology. Students receive research experience participating in projects conducted through the USC Institute for Health Promotion and Disease Prevention Research (IPR). Required core courses: foundations of health behavior, data analysis, behavioral epidemiology, biological basis of disease, basic theory and strategies in prevention, basic theories and strategies for compliance/adaptation, health behavior research methods, and research seminar in health behavior. Each student is required to develop a formal minor in a university department outside of the School of Medicine (e.g., Department of Psychology). In addition to core course requirements, the curriculum includes content courses from the Department of Preventive Medicine, Divisions of Biometry, Epidemiology, or Occupational Medicine.

Special Facilities or Resources: Essential characteristics of graduate training programs relevant to health behavior research are met at IPR. Faculty at the Institute are drawn from 13 schools, departments, and divisions at USC. More than 15 longitudinal prospective studies involving approximately 250,000 people in multiple communities are under way in several states. These and other federal, state, and private grants provided more than $8 million last year in ongoing research support. Research areas include: drug abuse prevention, drug policy research, obesity prevention, HIV/AIDS prevention in adolescents and adults, cardiovascular disease epidemiologic research, health communication, cancer control in high risk populations, ethnic/cultural issues in health promotion and disease prevention, epidemiologic research in homeless youth, and adaptation to disease. Computer facilities are outstanding at the Institute. Extensive collaboration with state and local agencies in several states is carried out by means of good working agreements with many school systems, state departments, local governmental agencies, voluntary health agencies, and television stations.

Application Information:

Send to: Graduate Admissions (doctoral), USC/IPR, 1000 S. Fremont Ave., Box 8, Alhambra, CA 91803. Students are admitted in the Fall, application deadline February 1. *Fee:* $65. $75 for international students.

Stanford University

Department of Psychology
Humanities & Sciences
Building 420
Stanford, CA 94305-2130
Telephone: (650) 725-2400
Fax: (650) 725-5699
E-mail: *admissions-info@psych.stanford.edu*
Web: *http://www-psych.stanford.edu*

Department Established:

1892. Chairperson: Mark R. Lepper. Number of Faculty: total–full-time 30; women–full-time 9; minority–full-time 3.

Programs and Degrees Offered:

Listed in the following order: Program area, degree type (T if terminal Master's), number awarded 7/00-6/01. Cognitive, perception, mathema PhD, developmental PhD, personality and psychopa. PhD, social PhD.

APA Accreditation: School PhD: full.

Student Applications/Admissions:

Student Applications

Cognitive, perception, mathema PhD—Applications 2001–2002, 54. Total applicants accepted 2001–2002, 6. New applicants enrolled 2001–2002, 4. Total enrolled 2001–2002 full-time, 20. Openings 2002–2003, 4. The Median number of years required for completion of a degree are 5. *Developmental PhD*—Applications 2001–2002, 16. Total applicants accepted 2001–2002, 4. New applicants enrolled 2001–2002, 2. Total enrolled 2001–2002 full-time, 10. Openings 2002–2003, 3. The Median number of years required for completion of a degree are 5. *Personality and psychopa. PhD*—Applications 2001–2002, 51. Total applicants accepted 2001–2002, 6. New applicants enrolled 2001–2002, 4. Total enrolled 2001–2002 full-time, 16. Openings 2002–2003, 3. The Median number of years required for completion of a degree are 5. *Social PhD*—Applications 2001–2002, 74. Total applicants accepted 2001–2002, 3. New applicants enrolled 2001–2002, 2. Total enrolled 2001–2002 full-time, 17. Openings 2002–2003, 3. The Median number of years required for completion of a degree are 5.

Admissions Requirements:

Scores: Entries appear in this order: required test or GPA, minimum score (if required), median score of students entering in 2001–2002. Doctoral Programs: GRE-V no minimum stated; GRE-Q no minimum stated; GRE-Analytical no minimum stated; GRE-Subject(Psych) no minimum stated; last 2 years GPA no minimum stated; psychology GPA no minimum stated; psychology GPA no minimum stated.

Other Criteria: (importance of criteria rated low, medium, or high): research experience high, letters of recommendation high, statement of purpose.

Student Characteristics: The following represents characteristics of students in 2001–2002 in all graduate psychology programs in the department: Female–full-time 43, part-time 0; Male–full-time 19, part-time 0; African American/Black–full-time 6, part-time 0; Hispanic/Latino (a)–full-time 5, part-time 0; Asian/Pacific Islander–full-time 6, part-time 0; American Indian/Alaska Native–full-time 1, part-time 0.

Financial Information/Assistance:

Tuition for Full-Time Study: No information provided.

Financial Assistance:

First Year Students: Research assistantships available for first-year. Traineeships available for first-year. Fellowships and scholarships available for first-year.

Advanced Students: Teaching assistantships available for advanced students. Research assistantships available for advanced students. Traineeships available for advanced students. Fellowships and scholarships available for advanced students.

Contact Information: For information on financial assistance, contact: Student Services Officer, Psychology Department.

Internships/Practica: No information provided.

Housing and Day Care: On-campus housing and day care facilities are available.

Employment of Department Graduates:

Master's Degree Graduates: Of those who graduated in the academic year 2000–2001, the following categories and numbers represent the post-graduate activities and employment of master's degree graduates: Enrolled in a post-doctoral residency/fellowship (n/a), employed in independent practice (n/a).

Doctoral Degree Graduates: Of those who graduated in the academic year 2000–2001, the following categories and numbers represent the post-graduate activities and employment of doctoral degree graduates: Enrolled in a psychology doctoral program (n/a), enrolled in another graduate/professional program (n/a).

Additional Information:

Orientation, Objectives, and Emphasis of Department: The department comprises facilities and personnel housed in Jordan Hall, where it maintains a psychology library and extensive laboratory and shop facilities, supervised by specialized technical assistants. Most of the laboratories are equipped with computer terminals linked directly to the university's computer center. Others are equipped with their own computers. In addition, the department has its own computer and a computer programmer on the psychology staff. The department maintains a nursery school close to the married students' housing area. This provides a laboratory for child observation, for training in nursery school practice, and for research.

Special Facilities or Resources: The department comprises facilities and personnel housed in Jordan Hall, where it maintains a psychology library and extensive laboratory and shop facilities, supervised by specialized technical assistants. Most of the laboratories are equipped with computer terminals linked directly to the university's computer center. Others are equipped with their own computers. In addition, the department has its own computer and a computer programmer on the psychology staff. The department maintains a nursery school close to the married students'

housing area. This provides a laboratory for child observation, for training in nursery school practice, and for research.

Information for Students With Physical Disabilities: The Disability Resource Center (DRC) coordinates a variety of services and resources for students with documented disabilities. Its mission is to provide disabled students equal access to all facets of University life: education, housing, recreation, and extracurricular activities. Services include, but are not limited to, notetaking, brailling, oral or sign language interpretation, stenocaptioning, books on tape, and extended time on examinations.

Application Information:

Send to: Follow instructions in application materials package, Dept. of Psychology, Admissions Committee. Students are admitted in the Fall, application deadline December 15. *Fee:* $75. Fee waiver from UG institution. Applications fee is $75 for US citizens and permanent residents and $90 for international applicants.

Stanford University

School of Education, Program in Psychological Studies in Education

School of Education, 485 Lasuen Mall, Stanford University
Stanford, CA 94305-3096
Telephone: (650) 723-2115
Fax: (650) 725-7412
E-mail: *suse-info@stanford.edu*
Web: *http://www.standford.edu/dept/SUSE/*

Department Established:

1917. Professor: Kenji Hakuta. Number of Faculty: total–full-time 13, part-time 9; women–full-time 2, part-time 4; minority–full-time 3, part-time 3.

Programs and Degrees Offered:

Listed in the following order: Program area, degree type (T if terminal Master's), number awarded 7/00-6/01. Child and adolescent developme PhD 2, counseling PhD 6, educational PhD 5.

APA Accreditation: Counseling PhD: full.

Student Applications/Admissions:

Student Applications

Child and adolescent developme PhD—Applications 2001–2002, 31. Total applicants accepted 2001–2002, 5. New applicants enrolled 2001–2002, 4. Total enrolled 2001–2002 full-time, 13. Openings 2002–2003, 5. *Counseling PhD*—Applications 2001–2002, 150. Total applicants accepted 2001–2002, 2. New applicants enrolled 2001–2002, 2. Total enrolled 2001–2002 full-time, 15. *Educational PhD*—Applications 2001–2002, 14. Total applicants accepted 2001–2002, 4. New applicants enrolled 2001–2002, 4. Total enrolled 2001–2002 full-time, 19. Openings 2002–2003, 5.

Admissions Requirements:

Scores: Entries appear in this order: required test or GPA, minimum score (if required), median score of students entering in 2001–2002. Doctoral Programs: GRE-V+Q+Analytical no minimum stated; overall undergraduate GPA no minimum stated; last 2 years GPA no minimum stated; psychology GPA no minimum stated; psychology GPA no minimum stated. *Other Criteria:* (importance of criteria rated low, medium, or high): GRE/MAT scores medium, research experience high, work experience high, extracurricular activity medium, clinically related public service medium, GPA medium, letters of recommendation medium, statement of goals and objectives high.

Student Characteristics: The following represents characteristics of students in 2001–2002 in all graduate psychology programs in the department: Female–full-time 7, part-time 0; Male–full-time 3, part-time 0; African American/Black–full-time 0, part-time 0; Hispanic/Latino (a)–full-time 2, part-time 0; Asian/Pacific Islander–full-time 1, part-time 0; American Indian/Alaska Native–full-time 0, part-time 0.

Financial Information/Assistance:
Tuition for Full-Time Study: *Doctoral:* State residents: per academic year $27,204; nonstate residents: per academic year $27,204.

Financial Assistance:
First Year Students: Research assistantships available for first-year. Average number of hours worked per week: 10. Apply by January 2. Tuition remission given: partial. Fellowships and scholarships available for first-year. Average number of hours worked per week: 10. Apply by January 2. Tuition remission given: partial.
Advanced Students: Teaching assistantships available for advanced students. Average number of hours worked per week: 20. Apply by January 2. Tuition remission given: partial. Research assistantships available for advanced students. Average number of hours worked per week: 20. Apply by January 2. Tuition remission given: partial.
Contact Information: Of all students currently enrolled full-time, 95% benefitted from one or more of the listed financial assistance programs. For information on financial assistance, contact: Financial Aid Coordinator, Telephone: 650-723-4794.

Internships/Practica: For Counseling Psychology only: coursework, practicum training, and research experience occur continually throughout the years of training. From the first quarter, students start counseling clients under supervision, taking courses in counseling and research methods, and engaging in research. A requirement for graduation for counseling psychology students is that they must complete a one-year internship in counseling at an APA-accredited (or equivalent) internship site.

Housing and Day Care: On-campus housing and day care facilities are available.

Employment of Department Graduates:
Master's Degree Graduates: Of those who graduated in the academic year 2000–2001, the following categories and numbers represent the post-graduate activities and employment of master's degree graduates: Enrolled in a post-doctoral residency/fellowship (n/a), employed in independent practice (n/a).

Doctoral Degree Graduates: Of those who graduated in the academic year 2000–2001, the following categories and numbers represent the post-graduate activities and employment of doctoral degree graduates: Enrolled in a psychology doctoral program (n/a), enrolled in another graduate/professional program (n/a).

Additional Information:
Orientation, Objectives, and Emphasis of Department: The orientation is toward modern cognitive, social, behavioral, and developmental psychology as these intersect with contemporary educational problems and phenomena. In the educational psychology and child and adolescent development subprogram, the approach is eclectic; the counseling psychology program is oriented toward cognitive, behavioral, and social learning. Ongoing research in educational psychology includes studies of teaching and teacher training; learning and related information processing as a function of varying instructional conditions; individual differences in aptitude for learning; cognitive processes in the development of reading, mathematics, problem-solving skills, and related intellectual skills; and measurement and research methodology. Research activities in child and adolescent development touch on processes related to the development of social and personal responsibility; self-direction, self-control, and self-regulation capabilities; the effect of family backgrounds and interaction upon cognitive ability and other school-relevant behavior; motivation; language development; and intellectual development. The counseling psychology program focuses on professional and academic training in the areas of interpersonal skills, career planning, and health psychology. Supervised practica, required for licensing as a psychologist, are offered in various settings. Current research interests include self-control regulations, chronic stress in children and adults, effects of divorce, psychosocial factors in health, career decision-making, irrational beliefs, cognitive approaches in depression, and friendship behavior.

Special Facilities or Resources: In combination with resources of the Psychology Department, the program provides special opportunities in application of mathematical techniques and models, analysis of instructional variables, reading and psycholinguistics, multicultural studies of development and socialization, and early childhood education. Affiliation of some faculty with other groups on campus provides special opportunities for interdisciplinary research. The Stanford Counseling Institute provides a setting for doctoral students in counseling psychology to obtain practical counseling experience under faculty supervision.

Information for Students With Physical Disabilities: Recent renovations have brought School of Education buildings and facilities into full compliance with the ADA.

Application Information:
Send to: Office of Admissions School of Education, 485 Lasuen Mall Stanford Univeristy, Stanford, CA 94305-3096. Students are admitted in the Fall, application deadline January 2. Apply online at: https://apply.embark.com/grad/stanford. *Fee:* $75. Request fee waiver form from Office of Graduate Admission, Stanford University, Stanford, CA 94305-3005. Only for US or permanent residents.

Vanguard University of Southern California
Graduate Program in Clinical Psychology
55 Fair Drive
Costa Mesa, CA 92626
Telephone: (714) 556-3610
Fax: (714) 662-5226
E-mail: *gradpsychinfo@vanguard.edu*
Web: *http://www.vanguard.edu/gradpsych/*

Department Established:
1998. Director: Marty Harris. Number of Faculty: total–full-time 2, part-time 5; women–full-time 1, part-time 2; minority–full-time 1.

Programs and Degrees Offered:
Listed in the following order: Program area, degree type (T if terminal Master's), number awarded 7/00-6/01. Clinical Psychology MA (T) 9.

Student Applications/Admissions:
Student Applications
Clinical Psychology MA—Applications 2001–2002, 41. Total applicants accepted 2001–2002, 40. New applicants enrolled 2001–2002, 33. Total enrolled 2001–2002 full-time, 49, part-time, 19. Openings 2002–2003, 25. The Median number of years required for completion of a degree are 2. The number of students enrolled full and part-time, who were dismissed or voluntarily withdrew from this program area were 3.

Admissions Requirements:
Scores: Entries appear in this order: required test or GPA, minimum score (if required), median score of students entering in 2001–2002. Master's Programs: overall undergraduate GPA 2.5, 3.3; psychology GPA 3.0, 3.5. Doctoral Programs: last 2 years GPA no minimum stated; psychology GPA no minimum stated; psychology GPA no minimum stated.
Other Criteria: (importance of criteria rated low, medium, or high): research experience low, work experience medium, extracurricular activity low, clinically related public service medium, GPA high, letters of recommendation high, interview low, statement of goals and objectives high.

Student Characteristics: The following represents characteristics of students in 2001–2002 in all graduate psychology programs in the department: Female–full-time 37, part-time 13; Male–full-time 12, part-time 6; African American/Black–full-time 3, part-time 1; Hispanic/Latino (a)–full-time 9, part-time 5; Asian/Pacific Islander–full-time 3, part-time 0; American Indian/Alaska Native–full-time 0, part-time 0.

Financial Information/Assistance:
Tuition for Full-Time Study: *Master's:* State residents per academic year $13,594, $566 per credit hour; nonstate residents: per academic year $13,594, $566 per credit hour.

Financial Assistance:
First Year Students: Fellowships and scholarships available for first-year. Average amount paid per academic year: $2,000.
Advanced Students: Teaching assistantships available for advanced students. Average amount paid per academic year: $2,000. Average number of hours worked per week: 8. Research assistantships available for advanced students. Average amount paid per academic year: $2,000. Average number of hours worked per week: 8. Fellowships and scholarships available for advanced students. Average amount paid per academic year: $2,000.

Contact Information: Of all students currently enrolled full-time, 90% benefitted from one or more of the listed financial assistance programs. For information on financial assistance, contact: Financial Aid Office, Vanguard University, 55 Fair Drive, Costa Mesa, CA 92626.

Internships/Practica: Each student is required to complete a minimum of 150 client contact hours at approved practicum sites. These sites currently include domestic violence shelters, county agencies, community clinics, and student counseling centers serving a variety of populations.

Housing and Day Care: No on-campus housing and day care facilities are available.

Employment of Department Graduates:
Master's Degree Graduates: Of those who graduated in the academic year 2000–2001, the following categories and numbers represent the post-graduate activities and employment of master's degree graduates: Enrolled in a psychology doctoral program (1), enrolled in another graduate/professional program (0), enrolled in a post-doctoral residency/fellowship (n/a), employed in independent practice (n/a), employed in an academic position at a university (1), employed in an academic position at a 2-year/4-year college (0), employed in other positions at a higher education institution (0), employed in a professional position in a school system (0), employed in business or industry (research/consulting) (0), employed in business or industry (management) (0), employed in a government agency (research) (0), employed in a government agency (professional services) (1), employed in a community mental health/counseling center (7), employed in a hospital/medical center (0), still seeking employment (0), other employment position (0).
Doctoral Degree Graduates: Of those who graduated in the academic year 2000–2001, the following categories and numbers represent the post-graduate activities and employment of doctoral degree graduates: Enrolled in a psychology doctoral program (n/a), enrolled in another graduate/professional program (n/a).

Additional Information:
Orientation, Objectives, and Emphasis of Department: Vanguard University of Southern California (VUSC) offers a Master of Science degree in Clinical Psychology. Special emphasis is placed on the multidisciplinary approach integrating theory, research, and practice within the areas of psychology, sociology, counseling, psychopharmacology, and theology. Class size is limited, enabling students to be mentored in their spiritual and professional development. The shape of the curriculum is front-loaded academically and rear-loaded clinically. The curriculum is designed to enable students to work in secular and/or Christian settings as a professional counselor and allows students to apply for PhD or PsyD programs in counseling and psychology. The mission of the Graduate Program in Clinical Psychology is to incorporate graduate students into a community of Christian scholars and counselors, whose purpose is to assist individuals and families toward healthy living. The program is approved by the

Board of Behavioral Sciences, Department of Consumer Affairs (California) to prepare students for MFT licensure.

Special Facilities or Resources: None applicable.

Information for Students With Physical Disabilities: None applicable.

Application Information:
Send to: Graduate Admissions, 55 Fair Drive, Costa Mesa, CA 92626. Students are admitted in the Fall, application deadline April 1. *Fee:* $30.

Wright Institute
Graduate School of Psychology
2728 Durant Avenue
Berkeley, CA 94704
Telephone: (510) 841-9230
Fax: (510) 841-0167
E-mail: *amorrison@wrightinst.edu*
Web: *http://www.wrightinst.edu*

Department Established:
1969. Dean: Andrea Morrison. Number of Faculty: total–full-time 5, part-time 50; women–full-time 3, part-time 30; minority–full-time 1, part-time 2.

Programs and Degrees Offered:
Listed in the following order: Program area, degree type (T if terminal Master's), number awarded 7/00-6/01. Clinical PhD 27.

APA Accreditation: Clinical PsyD: full.

Student Applications/Admissions:
Student Applications
Clinical PhD—Applications 2001–2002, 0. Total enrolled 2001–2002 full-time, 58.

Admissions Requirements:
Scores: Entries appear in this order: required test or GPA, minimum score (if required), median score of students entering in 2001–2002. Doctoral Programs: overall undergraduate GPA 3.0, 3.40; last 2 years GPA no minimum stated; psychology GPA no minimum stated; psychology GPA no minimum stated. Because the Wright Institute seeks applicants with significant life accomplishment rather than simply those who test well, GRE scores are not factored into our decision-making process. For research purposes, students are required to take the GRE V+ Q prior to matriculation. Students are also required to take the GRE Writing Assessment prior to matriculation.
Other Criteria: (importance of criteria rated low, medium, or high): GRE/MAT scores, research experience medium, work experience medium, extracurricular activity medium, clinically related public service high, GPA letters of recommendation medium, interview high, statement of goals and objectives high.

Student Characteristics: The following represents characteristics of students in 2001–2002 in all graduate psychology programs in the department: Female–full-time 46, part-time 0; Male–full-time 12, part-time 0; African American/Black–full-time 5, part-time 0; Hispanic/Latino(a)–full-time 3, part-time 0; Asian/Pacific Islander–full-time 8, part-time 0; American Indian/Alaska Native–full-time 1, part-time 0.

Financial Information/Assistance:
Tuition for Full-Time Study: No information provided.

Financial Assistance:
First Year Students: No information provided.
Advanced Students: No information provided.
Contact Information: Of all students currently enrolled full-time, 20% benefitted from one or more of the listed financial assistance programs. For information on financial assistance, contact: Financial Aid Officer.

Internships/Practica: The goal of the Wright Institute's field training program, which culminates with the clinical internship, is to enable students to integrate theoretical knowledge with professional clinical experience. Beginning with the first-year practicum, students learn how to work with a range of populations, treatment modalities, and professional roles with the assistance of small-group case conferences which span the 3 years of academic residency. Case conference leaders provide individualized assistance in planning each student's training sequence. The Institute's Field Placement Office furnishes information and support for students in the practicum and internship application and selection processes. Students are encouraged to conduct their internships at APA-approved agencies. They are highly valued by the Bay Area's most well-regarded internship sites, including the University of California, San Francisco Medical Center; San Francisco General Hospital; Stanford Medical Center; California Pacific Medical Center; and the University of California, Berkeley. The broad range of internship sites allows students to receive training in a variety of clinical settings serving the diverse ethnic and cultural groups of the Bay Area.

Housing and Day Care: No on-campus housing and day care facilities are available.

Employment of Department Graduates:
Master's Degree Graduates: Of those who graduated in the academic year 2000–2001, the following categories and numbers represent the post-graduate activities and employment of master's degree graduates: Enrolled in a post-doctoral residency/fellowship (n/a), employed in independent practice (n/a).
Doctoral Degree Graduates: Of those who graduated in the academic year 2000–2001, the following categories and numbers represent the post-graduate activities and employment of doctoral degree graduates: Enrolled in a psychology doctoral program (n/a), enrolled in another graduate/professional program (n/a).

Additional Information:
Orientation, Objectives, and Emphasis of Department: The Wright Institute teaches the scientific knowledge base of clinical psychology, and enriches that learning by exploring the meanings of students' experiences with clients. This unique learning method enables students to formulate and address clinical problems by examining the lenses through which they filter experience. The Institute promotes that educational endeavor by teaching students to think rigorously and critically. The program helps students

apply critical thinking skills to three fundamental areas: clinical theory and research, understanding of the self in social context, and appreciation of the interaction between clinician and client. The curriculum at the Institute solidly grounds students in science and research methods, while challenging them to explore the conscious and unconscious ways in which they and their clients influence the creation and direction of therapy. Coursework is integrated with practical experience, providing for the systematic, progressive acquisition of skills and knowledge. Case conferences provide a forum for developing and integrating theory, technique, and reflective judgment. Practica and internship experiences consolidate the applied aspects of theoretical knowledge. Education about the multiple roles of the modern psychologist—clinician, supervisor, and consultant—prepares students for working in fulfilling ways amid the changing realities of the health-care field.

Special Facilities or Resources: The Wright Institute is located in a three-story English Tudor-style building one block from the UC Berkeley campus. The Institute operates an on-site, low-fee clinic which has been providing well-respected community mental health services for 25 years. The clinic is primarily staffed by second year Wright Institute practicum students who are supervised by experienced adjunct faculty community supervisors. In addition to videotaping capabilities, the clinic maintains a database for research on the therapeutic process and related areas. The Institute's library provides free on-line access to major bibliographic databases including PsychINFO, MEDLINE, and ERIC. These on-line resources are also available to students from their home computers. The library's Scholar's Room houses the archives of Institute founder Nevitt Sanford, along with the personal library of Abraham Maslow, a founder of humanistic psychology. Wright Institute students have library privileges at a UC Berkeley, as well as access to the vast holdings of the nine-campus University of California library system. The Institute has two computer labs in addition to four public access computers in the library. All the Institute's computers are networked with full access to the Internet.

Information for Students With Physical Disabilities: During the 2000-2001 academic year, the building was renovated to fully comply with the requirements of the Americans with Disabilities Act.

Application Information:
Send to: Admissions Director, The Wright Institute, 2728 Durant Avenue, Berkeley, CA 94704. Students are admitted in the Fall, application deadline January 15. *Fee:* $50.

COLORADO

Colorado State University
Department of Psychology
Natural Sciences
200 W. Lake Street
Fort Collins, CO 80523-1876
Telephone: (970) 491-6363
Fax: (970) 491-1032
E-mail: *echavez@lamar.colostate.edu*
Web: *http://www.colostate.edu/Depts/Psychology/graduate*

Department Established:
1962. Chairperson: Ernest L. Chavez. Number of Faculty: total–full-time 31, part-time 5; women–full-time 10, part-time 3; minority–full-time 5, part-time 1.

Programs and Degrees Offered:
Listed in the following order: Program area, degree type (T if terminal Master's), number awarded 7/00-6/01. Applied Social PhD 2, Behavioral Neuroscience PhD, Cogntive PhD, Counseling PhD 6, I/O PhD 4.

APA Accreditation: Counseling PhD: full.

Student Applications/Admissions:
Student Applications
Applied Social PhD—Applications 2001–2002, 25. Total applicants accepted 2001–2002, 4. New applicants enrolled 2001–2002, 2. Total enrolled 2001–2002 full-time, 8. Openings 2002–2003, 2. The Median number of years required for completion of a degree are 6. The number of students enrolled full and part-time, who were dismissed or voluntarily withdrew from this program area were 0. *Behavioral Neuroscience PhD*—Applications 2001–2002, 10. Total applicants accepted 2001–2002, 2. New applicants enrolled 2001–2002, 2. Total enrolled 2001–2002 full-time, 5. Openings 2002–2003, 1. The Median number of years required for completion of a degree are 6. The number of students enrolled full and part-time, who were dismissed or voluntarily withdrew from this program area were 0. *Cognitve PhD*—Applications 2001–2002, 10. Total applicants accepted 2001–2002, 2. New applicants enrolled 2001–2002, 2. Total enrolled 2001–2002 full-time, 5. Openings 2002–2003, 1. The Median number of years required for completion of a degree are 6. The number of students enrolled full and part-time, who were dismissed or voluntarily withdrew from this program area were 0. *Counseling PhD*—Applications 2001–2002, 275. Total applicants accepted 2001–2002, 10. New applicants enrolled 2001–2002, 5. Total enrolled 2001–2002 full-time, 48. Openings 2002–2003, 6. The Median number of years required for completion of a degree are 5. The number of students enrolled full and part-time, who were dismissed or voluntarily withdrew from this program area were 0. *I/O PhD*—Applications 2001–2002, 150. Total applicants accepted 2001–2002, 12. New applicants enrolled 2001–2002, 6. Total enrolled 2001–2002 full-time, 32. Openings 2002–2003, 5. The Median number of years required for completion of a degree are 6. The number of students enrolled full and

part-time, who were dismissed or voluntarily withdrew from this program area were 0.

Admissions Requirements:
Scores: Entries appear in this order: required test or GPA, minimum score (if required), median score of students entering in 2001–2002. Doctoral Programs: GRE-V no minimum stated; GRE-Q no minimum stated; GRE-V+Q+Analytical no minimum stated, 650; GRE-Subject(Psych) no minimum stated, 630; overall undergraduate GPA 3.0., 3.7 ; last 2 years GPA no minimum stated; psychology GPA no minimum stated; psychology GPA no minimum stated, 3.75.

Other Criteria: (importance of criteria rated low, medium, or high): GRE/MAT scores medium, research experience high, work experience medium, extracurricular activity medium, clinically related public service medium, GPA high, letters of recommendation high, statement of goals and objectives high.

Student Characteristics: The following represents characteristics of students in 2001–2002 in all graduate psychology programs in the department: Female–full-time 53, part-time 0; Male–full-time 16, part-time 0; African American/Black–full-time 0, part-time 0; Hispanic/Latino (a)–full-time 1, part-time 0; Asian/Pacific Islander–full-time 5, part-time 0; American Indian/Alaska Native–full-time 0, part-time 0.

Financial Information/Assistance:
Tuition for Full-Time Study: *Master's:* State residents per academic year $1,708, $150 per credit hour; nonstate residents: per academic year $5,591, $581 per credit hour. *Doctoral:* State residents: per academic year $1,708, $150 per credit hour; nonstate residents: per academic year $5,591, $581 per credit hour.

Financial Assistance:
First Year Students: Teaching assistantships available for first-year. Average amount paid per academic year: $9,000. Average number of hours worked per week: 20. Apply by March 15. Tuition remission given: full. Research assistantships available for first-year. Average amount paid per academic year: $9,000. Average number of hours worked per week: 20. Apply by March 15. Tuition remission given: full. Fellowships and scholarships available for first-year. Average amount paid per academic year: $1,500. Average number of hours worked per week: 0. Apply by March 15. Tuition remission given: partial.

Advanced Students: Teaching assistantships available for advanced students. Average amount paid per academic year: $9,000. Apply by march 15. Tuition remission given: full. Research assistantships available for advanced students. Average amount paid per academic year: $9,000. Apply by March 15. Tuition remission given: full. Traineeships available for advanced students. Average amount paid per academic year: $9,000. Apply by March 15. Tuition remission given: full. Fellowships and scholarships available for advanced students. Average amount paid per academic year: $1,500. Apply by March 15. Tuition remission given: partial.

Contact Information: Of all students currently enrolled full-time, 80% benefitted from one or more of the listed financial

assistance programs. For information on financial assistance, contact: Office of Financial Aid.

Internships/Practica: A 1998 five year excellence award by the Colorado Commission on Higher Education has allowed for the development of health related practica throughout Northern Colorado; oncology program, neuropsychology, and cancer resource center. The Tri Ethnic Center for Prevention Research, a NIDA funded research center, is a part of the department. This center was designated a Center of Research and Scholarly Excellence by the University in 1991 and again in 1998. For those doctoral students for whom a professional internship is required prior to graduation, 5 applied in 2000–2001. Of those who applied, 5 were placed in internships listed by the Association of Psychology Postdoctoral and Internship Programs (APPIC); 5 were placed in APA accredited internships.

Housing and Day Care: On-campus housing and day care facilities are available.

Employment of Department Graduates:

Master's Degree Graduates: Of those who graduated in the academic year 2000–2001, the following categories and numbers represent the post-graduate activities and employment of master's degree graduates: Enrolled in a post-doctoral residency/fellowship (n/a), employed in independent practice (n/a).

Doctoral Degree Graduates: Of those who graduated in the academic year 2000–2001, the following categories and numbers represent the post-graduate activities and employment of doctoral degree graduates: Enrolled in a psychology doctoral program (n/a), enrolled in another graduate/professional program (n/a), enrolled in a post-doctoral residency/fellowship (3), employed in independent practice (2), employed in an academic position at a university (1), employed in business or industry (research/consulting) (4), employed in a community mental health/counseling center (2).

Additional Information:

Orientation, Objectives, and Emphasis of Department: Colorado State University offers graduate training: Leading to the MS and PhD degrees in applied social, behavioral neuroscience, cognitive, counseling and industrial organizational psychology. A core program of study is required of all students in the first years of graduate work to insure a broad and thorough grounding in psychology. Graduate students in applied social, cognitive and behavioral neuroscience areas take positions in academic, research, or government agencies. Industrial/Organizational has opportunities for students to have experiences in selection techniques, assessment centers, organizational climate and structure, and consultation. Counseling students are trained in academic and applied skills with opportunities in behavior therapy, group techniques, assessment, outreach, consultation, and supervision. Emphasis is on diversity and breadth. In addition to the adult speciality, a program is available that will lead to a PhD in counseling psychology with advanced courses that deal with children and adolescents.

Special Facilities or Resources: Tri Ethnic Center for Prevention research, a NIDA funded research center focusing on adolescent issues such as substance use, violence rural issues, and culturally appropriate prevention strategies.

Application Information:
Send to: Graduate Admissions Coordinator Joanne Moran, Psychology, Colorado State University, Fort Collins, CO 80526-1876. Students are admitted in the Fall, application deadline January 15. *Fee:* $30.

Colorado, University of, at Boulder
Department of Psychology
Arts and Sciences
Muenzinger D244, UCB 345
Boulder, CO 80309-0345
Telephone: (303) 492-1553
Fax: (303) 492-2967
E-mail: *jrudy@clipr.colorado.edu*
Web: *http:/www.colorado.edu*

Department Established:
1910. Chairperson: Jerry Rudy. Number of Faculty: total–full-time 59, part-time 1; women–full-time 18, part-time 1; minority–full-time 4.

Programs and Degrees Offered:
Listed in the following order: Program area, degree type (T if terminal Master's), number awarded 7/00-6/01. Behavior neuroscience PhD 2, behavioral genetics PhD 1, clinical PhD 5, cognitive PhD 3, social PhD 2.

APA Accreditation: Clinical PhD: full.

Student Applications/Admissions:

Student Applications

Behavior neuroscience PhD—Applications 2001–2002, 54. Total applicants accepted 2001–2002, 4. New applicants enrolled 2001–2002, 4. Total enrolled 2001–2002 full-time, 18. Openings 2002–2003, 4. The Median number of years required for completion of a degree are 5. The number of students enrolled full and part-time, who were dismissed or voluntarily withdrew from this program area were 0. *Behavioral genetics PhD*—Applications 2001–2002, 15. Total applicants accepted 2001–2002, 2. New applicants enrolled 2001–2002, 2. Total enrolled 2001–2002 full-time, 11. Openings 2002–2003, 3. The Median number of years required for completion of a degree are 5. *Clinical PhD*—Applications 2001–2002, 185. Total applicants accepted 2001–2002, 8. New applicants enrolled 2001–2002, 4. Total enrolled 2001–2002 full-time, 29. Openings 2002–2003, 5. The number of students enrolled full and part-time, who were dismissed or voluntarily withdrew from this program area were 1. *Cognitive PhD*—Applications 2001–2002, 48. Total applicants accepted 2001–2002, 6. New applicants enrolled 2001–2002, 5. Total enrolled 2001–2002 full-time, 27, part-time, 2. Openings 2002–2003, 6. *Social PhD*—Applications 2001–2002, 47. Total applicants accepted 2001–2002, 2. New applicants enrolled 2001–2002, 2. Total enrolled 2001–2002 full-time, 12. Openings 2002–2003, 3. The Median number of years required for completion of a degree are 5. The number of students enrolled full and part-time, who were dismissed or voluntarily withdrew from this program area were 0.

Admissions Requirements:

Scores: Entries appear in this order: required test or GPA, minimum score (if required), median score of students entering

in 2001–2002. Doctoral Programs: GRE-V no minimum stated, 615; GRE-Q no minimum stated, 695; GRE-V+Q no minimum stated, 1275; GRE-Analytical no minimum stated, 670; GRE-V+Q+Analytical no minimum stated, 1970; overall undergraduate GPA no minimum stated, 3.6 ; last 2 years GPA no minimum stated, 3.5 ; psychology GPA no minimum stated; psychology GPA no minimum stated.

Other Criteria: (importance of criteria rated low, medium, or high): GRE/MAT scores high, research experience high, work experience medium, extracurricular activity medium, clinically related public service medium, GPA high, letters of recommendation high, interview high, statement of goals and objectives high. Interview only for clinical.

Student Characteristics: The following represents characteristics of students in 2001–2002 in all graduate psychology programs in the department: Female–full-time 12, part-time 0; Male–full-time 6, part-time 0; African American/Black–full-time 0, part-time 0; Hispanic/Latino (a)–full-time 2, part-time 0; Asian/Pacific Islander–full-time 1, part-time 0; American Indian/Alaska Native–full-time 0, part-time 0.

Financial Information/Assistance:

Tuition for Full-Time Study: *Doctoral:* State residents: $582 per credit hour; nonstate residents: $2,805 per credit hour.

Financial Assistance:

First Year Students: Teaching assistantships available for first-year. Average amount paid per academic year: $11,981. Average number of hours worked per week: 20. Research assistantships available for first-year. Average amount paid per academic year: $11,981. Average number of hours worked per week: 20. Fellowships and scholarships available for first-year. Average amount paid per academic year: $3,636. Tuition remission given: partial.

Advanced Students: Teaching assistantships available for advanced students. Average amount paid per academic year: $11,981. Average number of hours worked per week: 20. Research assistantships available for advanced students. Average amount paid per academic year: $11,981. Average number of hours worked per week: 20. Fellowships and scholarships available for advanced students. Average amount paid per academic year: $3,636. Tuition remission given: partial.

Contact Information: Of all students currently enrolled full-time, 85% benefitted from one or more of the listed financial assistance programs. For information on financial assistance, contact: Financial Aid Office.

Internships/Practica: For those doctoral students for whom a professional internship is required prior to graduation, 5 applied in 2000–2001. Of those who applied, 4 were placed in internships listed by the Association of Psychology Postdoctoral and Internship Programs (APPIC); 4 were placed in APA accredited internships.

Housing and Day Care: No on-campus housing and day care facilities are available.

Employment of Department Graduates:

Master's Degree Graduates: Of those who graduated in the academic year 2000–2001, the following categories and numbers represent the post-graduate activities and employment of master's degree graduates: Enrolled in a post-doctoral residency/fellowship (n/a), employed in independent practice (n/a).

Doctoral Degree Graduates: Of those who graduated in the academic year 2000–2001, the following categories and numbers represent the post-graduate activities and employment of doctoral degree graduates: Enrolled in a psychology doctoral program (n/a), enrolled in another graduate/professional program (n/a), enrolled in a post-doctoral residency/fellowship (4), employed in an academic position at a university (2), employed in other positions at a higher education institution (1), employed in a government agency (professional services) (1), employed in a community mental health/counseling center (1).

Additional Information:

Orientation, Objectives, and Emphasis of Department: Our emphasis is on training graduate students who have the capability to advance knowledge in the field, and who are committed to applying their knowledge. We emphasize rigorous training in both the theory and methods of psychological research.

Special Facilities or Resources: The department is housed in a large and modern four-story building that contains ample space for offices, a clinic, and research laboratories. There are extensive research facilities available to students, both in individual laboratories and from the department generally. The department maintains its own network of VAX/VMS, Ultrix, Macintosh, and DOS computers used for data collection, data analysis, and manuscript preparation. There is also a departmental laboratory of Macintosh and DOS personal computers for "real-time" research. In addition, numerous laboratories in the department have their own computing capabilities. The facilities of the Institute of Behavioral Genetics, the Institute of Behavioral Science, and the Institute of Cognitive Science are available to students. Each of these institutes has its own laboratory space and specialized computer facilities. In addition, they attract a number of scholars from other disciplines on the campus.

Application Information:

Send to: Department of Psychology, Muenzinger Psychology Building, UCB 345, Boulder, CO 80309-0345. Students are admitted in the Fall, application deadline 12/15; 1/1. Clinical - December 15; others January 1. *Fee:* $50. ($60 Foreign Students).

Colorado, University of, at Colorado Springs (2001 data)

Department of Psychology
Letters, Arts, and Sciences
1420 Austin Bluffs Parkway, P.O. Box 7150
Colorado Springs, CO 80933-7150
Telephone: (719) 262-4500
Fax: (719) 262-4166
E-mail: *ddubois@uccs.edu*
Web: *http://web.uccs.edu/psychology*

Department Established:

1965. Chairperson: Dr. Robert L. Durham. Number of Faculty: total–full-time 14, part-time 5; women–full-time 6, part-time 3; minority–full-time 1.

Programs and Degrees Offered:
Listed in the following order: Program area, degree type (T if terminal Master's), number awarded 7/00-6/01. Aging MA (T), clinical MA (T) 8, general experimental MA (T) 1.

Student Applications/Admissions:
Student Applications
Aging MA—Openings 2002–2003, 5. *Clinical MA*—Applications 2001–2002, 59. Total applicants accepted 2001–2002, 22. New applicants enrolled 2001–2002, 12. Total enrolled 2001–2002 full-time, 22, part-time, 9. Openings 2002–2003, 12. *General experimental MA*—Applications 2001–2002, 19. Total applicants accepted 2001–2002, 12. New applicants enrolled 2001–2002, 1. Total enrolled 2001–2002 full-time, 2, part-time, 2. Openings 2002–2003, 5.

Admissions Requirements:
Scores: Entries appear in this order: required test or GPA, minimum score (if required), median score of students entering in 2001–2002. Master's Programs: GRE-V no minimum stated, 560; GRE-Q no minimum stated, 610; GRE-V+Q no minimum stated, 1160; GRE-Analytical no minimum stated, 640; overall undergraduate GPA no minimum stated, 3.44. Doctoral Programs: last 2 years GPA no minimum stated; psychology GPA no minimum stated; psychology GPA no minimum stated.
Other Criteria: (importance of criteria rated low, medium, or high): GRE/MAT scores medium, research experience high, work experience low, extracurricular activity medium, clinically related public service high, GPA medium, letters of recommendation high, statement of goals and objectives high. Clinically related public service is not required for experimental.

Student Characteristics: The following represents characteristics of students in 2001–2002 in all graduate psychology programs in the department: Female–full-time 11, part-time 0; Male–full-time 2, part-time 0; African American/Black–full-time 0, part-time 1; Hispanic/Latino (a)–full-time 1, part-time 0; Asian/Pacific Islander–full-time 0, part-time 0; American Indian/Alaska Native–full-time 0, part-time 0.

Financial Information/Assistance:
Tuition for Full-Time Study: Tuition for full time study; state residents $118 per credit hour; nonstate residents $425 per credit hour.

Financial Assistance:
First Year Students: No information provided.
Advanced Students: No information provided.
Contact Information: For information on financial assistance, contact: Andrea Williams or Financial Aid Office.

Internships/Practica: Practicum experiences are completed at the departmental CU Aging Center, the CU Counseling Center, or in community placements under licensed supervision (e.g., school settings, community health centers, state mental health facility, domestic violence center, impatient psychiatric hospital). The goal of these experiences is to expose students to clinical settings, to roles of clinical psychologists, and to begin the development of clinical skills.

Housing and Day Care: No on-campus housing and day care facilities are available.

Employment of Department Graduates:
Master's Degree Graduates: Of those who graduated in the academic year 2000–2001, the following categories and numbers represent the post-graduate activities and employment of master's degree graduates: Enrolled in a post-doctoral residency/fellowship (n/a), employed in independent practice (n/a).
Doctoral Degree Graduates: Of those who graduated in the academic year 2000–2001, the following categories and numbers represent the post-graduate activities and employment of doctoral degree graduates: Enrolled in a psychology doctoral program (n/a), enrolled in another graduate/professional program (n/a).

Additional Information:
Orientation, Objectives, and Emphasis of Department: The program places special emphasis in general areas of applied clinical practice and general experimental psychology. The training will enable a student to prepare for a doctoral program, teach in community colleges, work under a licensed psychologist in private and public agencies, or work in university counseling centers. A research thesis is required of all students. There is a broad range of faculty research interests including: aging (e.g., psychopathology and psychological treatment of older adults, family dynamics, self-concept development, memory, cognition, and personality), social psychology, psychology and the law, personality, program evaluation, prevention of child abuse, and psychological trauma. Please see our web site for additional information.

Special Facilities or Resources: Research facilities include clinical training laboratories with observational capabilities, laboratories for individual and small group research, a psychophysiological laboratory, and a computer laboratory. Columbine Hall houses a 50-station computer lab that is available for general use. The CU Aging Center, administered through the Psychology Department, is a community-based nonprofit mental health clinic designed to serve the mental health needs of older adults and their families. The mission of the Center is to provide state-of-the-art psychological assessment and treatment services to older persons and their families, to study psychological aging processes, and to train students in clinical psychology and related disciplines.

Information for Students With Physical Disabilities: The campus has an office of Disability Services. The purpose of Disability Services is to provide comprehensive support to meet the individual needs of students with disabilities. Some of the services offered include: readers, workshops, tutoring, note taking, counseling, interpreters, faculty liaison, taped textbooks, parking permits, alternative testing, library assistance and strategy development. To arrange for appropriate accommodations, students are encouraged to schedule an appointment with the Coordinator of Disability Services as soon as they are admitted. For more information on the Center and its events contact them at (729) 262-3065.

Application Information:
Send to: Dr. Hasker P. Davis, Director of Graduate Studies/Psychology Department. Students are admitted in the Fall, application deadline February 1. *Fee:* $60.

Colorado, University of, at Denver

Department of Psychology
P.O. Box 173364, Campus Box 173
Denver, CO 80217-3364
Telephone: (303) 556-8565
Fax: (303) 556-3520
E-mail: *mzinser@carbon.cudenver.edu*
Web: *http://www.cudenver.edu/public/psych/index.html*

Department Established:

Chairperson: Dr. Elliot Hirshman. Number of Faculty: total–full-time 13, part-time 4; women–full-time 3, part-time 3; minority–full-time 2.

Programs and Degrees Offered:

Listed in the following order: Program area, degree type (T if terminal Master's), number awarded 7/00-6/01. Clinical Psychology MA (T) 8, industrial psychology MA (T) 8.

Student Applications/Admissions:

Student Applications

Clinical Psychology MA—Applications 2001–2002, 64. Total applicants accepted 2001–2002, 8. New applicants enrolled 2001–2002, 8. Total enrolled 2001–2002 full-time, 7, part-time, 5. Openings 2002–2003, 8. The number of students enrolled full and part-time, who were dismissed or voluntarily withdrew from this program area were 0. *Industrial psychology MA*—Applications 2001–2002, 70. Total applicants accepted 2001–2002, 8. New applicants enrolled 2001–2002, 6. Total enrolled 2001–2002 full-time, 6. Openings 2002–2003, 8.

Admissions Requirements:

Scores: Entries appear in this order: required test or GPA, minimum score (if required), median score of students entering in 2001–2002. Master's Programs: GRE-V 600; GRE-Q 600; GRE-V+Q 1200; GRE-Analytical no minimum stated; GRE-V+Q+Analytical no minimum stated; GRE-Subject(Psych) no minimum stated; overall undergraduate GPA 2.75, 3.50. Doctoral Programs: last 2 years GPA no minimum stated; psychology GPA no minimum stated; psychology GPA no minimum stated.

Other Criteria: (importance of criteria rated low, medium, or high): GRE/MAT scores high, research experience high, work experience high, extracurricular activity low, clinically related public service medium, GPA high, letters of recommendation high, interview medium, statement of goals and objectives high. These are for clinical program. For I/O MA: GRE/MAT scores high, research experience high, work experience high, extracurricular activity low, GPA high, letters of recommendation high, statement of goals and objectives high.

Student Characteristics: The following represents characteristics of students in 2001–2002 in all graduate psychology programs in the department: Female–full-time 10, part-time 0; Male–full-time 3, part-time 0; African American/Black–full-time 0, part-time 0;

Hispanic/Latino (a)–full-time 0, part-time 0; Asian/Pacific Islander–full-time 0, part-time 0; American Indian/Alaska Native–full-time 0, part-time 0.

Financial Information/Assistance:

Tuition for Full-Time Study: *Master's:* State residents per academic year $1,642; nonstate residents: per academic year $6,690.

Financial Assistance:

First Year Students: Teaching assistantships available for first-year. Average amount paid per academic year: $4,500. Average number of hours worked per week: 10. Research assistantships available for first-year.

Advanced Students: Teaching assistantships available for advanced students. Average amount paid per academic year: $4,500. Average number of hours worked per week: 10. Research assistantships available for advanced students.

Contact Information: No information provided.

Internships/Practica: Internships in community agencies available for both master's programs. Students have the option of completing a thesis or pursuing an internship. Some students elect to complete both because that combination is in their best interests. Students electing the internship option may begin internships after completing the first year of courses. A total of 800 hours of supervised field experience is required for the internship. All field placements are subject to approval of the program coordinator. It is sometimes possible to build the internship into a student's existing job, provided that the work performed is consistent with the objectives and emphasis of the program.

Housing and Day Care: No on-campus housing and day care facilities are available.

Employment of Department Graduates:

Master's Degree Graduates: Of those who graduated in the academic year 2000–2001, the following categories and numbers represent the post-graduate activities and employment of master's degree graduates: Enrolled in a post-doctoral residency/fellowship (n/a), employed in independent practice (n/a).

Doctoral Degree Graduates: Of those who graduated in the academic year 2000–2001, the following categories and numbers represent the post-graduate activities and employment of doctoral degree graduates: Enrolled in a psychology doctoral program (n/a), enrolled in another graduate/professional program (n/a).

Additional Information:

Orientation, Objectives, and Emphasis of Department: The principal objective of the specialty in clinical psychology is to prepare graduates for doctoral level work. Those graduates who have applied to doctoral programs have typically been admitted to one or more programs. For individuals not interested in pursuing further graduate work, the program offers rigorous training in applied skills such as diagnostic evaluation, psychological assessment of both adults and children, and psychotherapy. Students have the option of completing a thesis, pursuing an internship, or both. The thesis is an empirical research project culminating in a product suitable for publication or presentation at a professional meeting. Internships may be started following completion of all required course work. Clinical experience with a wide variety of populations in the Denver/Boulder area is available. Our intern applicants have been competitive in obtaining these placements. The primary objective of the industrial/organizational program is to train individuals to perform psychological research, evaluation, and services in public or private sector organizations. Students also receive state-of-the-art training in theories and methods in I/O psychology, which in turn can prepare them for further graduate study. Course content is evenly distributed among three general domains: industrial psychology, organizational psychology, and quantitative methods.

Application Information:
Send to: Clinical: Dr. Mitchell Handelsman, I/O: Dr. Kurt Kraiger, Department of Psychology, University of Colorado Denver, Campus Box 173, PO Box 173364, Denver, CO 80217-3364. Students are admitted in the Fall, application deadline March 1. *Fee:* $50.

Colorado, University of, Boulder
Educational Psychology Program
School of Education
Campus Box 249
Boulder, CO 80309-0249
Telephone: (303) 492-8399
Fax: (303) 492-7090
E-mail: *Hilda.Borko@Colorado.EDU*

Department Established:
Chairperson: Hilda Borko. Number of Faculty: total–full-time 4; women–full-time 1.

Programs and Degrees Offered:
Listed in the following order: Program area, degree type (T if terminal Master's), number awarded 7/00-6/01. Educational Psychological Stud PhD, Educational Psychological Stud MA.

Student Applications/Admissions:
Student Applications
Educational Psychological Stud PhD. Educational Psychological Stud MA.

Admissions Requirements:
Scores: Entries appear in this order: required test or GPA, minimum score (if required), median score of students entering in 2001–2002. Master's Programs: GRE-V+Q+Analytical no minimum stated; overall undergraduate GPA no minimum stated; last 2 years GPA no minimum stated; psychology GPA no minimum stated. Doctoral Programs: GRE-V+Q+Analytical no minimum stated; overall undergraduate GPA no minimum stated; last 2 years GPA no minimum stated; psychology GPA no minimum stated; psychology GPA no minimum stated.
Other Criteria: (importance of criteria rated low, medium, or high): GRE/MAT scores high, research experience medium, work experience medium, extracurricular activity low, GPA high, letters of recommendation high, statement of goals and objectives high.

Financial Information/Assistance:
Tuition for Full-Time Study: *Master's:* State residents per academic year $1,737; nonstate residents: per academic year $8,312, *Doctoral:* State residents: per academic year $1,737; nonstate residents: per academic year $8,312.

Financial Assistance:
First Year Students: Teaching assistantships available for first-year. Apply by Feb 1. Research assistantships available for first-year. Apply by Feb 1. Fellowships and scholarships available for first-year. Apply by Feb 1.
Advanced Students: Teaching assistantships available for advanced students. Research assistantships available for advanced students. Fellowships and scholarships available for advanced students.
Contact Information: No information provided.

Internships/Practica: No information provided.

Housing and Day Care: On-campus housing and day care facilities are available.

Employment of Department Graduates:
Master's Degree Graduates: Of those who graduated in the academic year 2000–2001, the following categories and numbers represent the post-graduate activities and employment of master's degree graduates: Enrolled in a post-doctoral residency/fellowship (n/a), employed in independent practice (n/a).
Doctoral Degree Graduates: Of those who graduated in the academic year 2000–2001, the following categories and numbers represent the post-graduate activities and employment of doctoral degree graduates: Enrolled in a psychology doctoral program (n/a), enrolled in another graduate/professional program (n/a).

Additional Information:
Orientation, Objectives, and Emphasis of Department: The concentration in Educational Foundations, Policy, and Practice (EFPP) offers a program devoted to the critical examination of the relations among education, society, culture, and government, with special emphasis on problems of race, gender, social class, and multiculturalism. The program stresses analysis and evaluation of educational theory, practice, and policy, by drawing on philosophy and the social sciences. Its foundation is critical scholarship, which examines educational institutions within broad social, political, cultural, legal, and economic contexts in the United States. Program faculty offer courses in social, cultural, historical, and philosophical foundations; policy analysis; evaluation; curriculum theory; and international and comparative education. Additional related courses are available in other programs of the School of Education and in other departments of the university. The program is designed to train scholars, teachers, evaluators, and policy analysts for careers in academic institutions and agencies at the state and federal levels.

Special Facilities or Resources: affiliation with Collage (Children's Museum), Boulder.

Application Information:
Send to: Office of Student Services, School of Education, Campus Box 249, University of Colorado, Boulder, CO 80309-0249. Students are admitted in the Fall, application deadline February 1.

Denver, University of
Counseling Psychology
College of Education
2450 South Vine Street
Denver, CO 80208
Telephone: (303) 871-2509
Fax: (303) 871-4456
E-mail: *mriva@du.edu*
Web: *http://www.du.edu*

Department Established:
1980. Director: Maria T. Riva. Number of Faculty: total–full-time 5, part-time 2; women–full-time 3, part-time 1; minority–full-time 1.

Programs and Degrees Offered:
Listed in the following order: Program area, degree type (T if terminal Master's), number awarded 7/00-6/01. Counseling MA (T) 17, counseling psychology PhD 7, educational psychology PhD (T) 1, school psychology PhD 4.

APA Accreditation: Counseling PhD: full.

Student Applications/Admissions:
Student Applications
Counseling MA—Applications 2001–2002, 80. Total applicants accepted 2001–2002, 30. New applicants enrolled 2001–2002, 20. Total enrolled 2001–2002 full-time, 30, part-time, 4. Openings 2002–2003, 22. The Median number of years required for completion of a degree are 2. The number of students enrolled full and part-time, who were dismissed or voluntarily withdrew from this program area were 1. *Counseling psychology PhD*—Applications 2001–2002, 85. Total applicants accepted 2001–2002, 15. New applicants enrolled 2001–2002, 9. Total enrolled 2001–2002 full-time, 20, part-time, 23. Openings 2002–2003, 7. The number of students enrolled full and part-time, who were dismissed or voluntarily withdrew from this program area were 0. *Educational psychology PhD*—Applications 2001–2002, 8. Total applicants accepted 2001–2002, 3. New applicants enrolled 2001–2002, 2. Total enrolled 2001–2002 full-time, 2. Openings 2002–2003, 3. The Median number of years required for completion of a degree are 5. The number of students enrolled full and part-time, who were dismissed or voluntarily withdrew from this program area were 0. *School psychology PhD*—Applications 2001–2002, 25. Total applicants accepted 2001–2002, 4. New applicants enrolled 2001–2002, 2. Total enrolled 2001–2002 full-time, 15, part-time, 5. Openings 2002–2003, 5. The Median number of years required for completion of a degree are 5. The number of students enrolled full and part-time, who were dismissed or voluntarily withdrew from this program area were 0.

Admissions Requirements:
Scores: Entries appear in this order: required test or GPA, minimum score (if required), median score of students entering in 2001–2002. Master's Programs: GRE-V 500, 530; GRE-Q 500, 560; GRE-V+Q 1000, 1090; overall undergraduate GPA no minimum stated. Doctoral Programs: GRE-V 550, 575; GRE-Q 550, 617; GRE-V+Q 1100, 1192; overall undergraduate GPA no minimum stated; last 2 years GPA no minimum stated; psychology GPA no minimum stated; psychology GPA no minimum stated.

Other Criteria: (importance of criteria rated low, medium, or high): GRE/MAT scores medium, research experience high, work experience high, extracurricular activity medium, clinically related public service high, GPA medium, letters of recommendation high, interview high, statement of goals and objectives high.

Student Characteristics: The following represents characteristics of students in 2001–2002 in all graduate psychology programs in the department: Female–full-time 26, part-time 2; Male–full-time 7, part-time 0; African American/Black–full-time 0, part-time 0; Hispanic/Latino (a)–full-time 1, part-time 0; Asian/Pacific Islander–full-time 6, part-time 0; American Indian/Alaska Native–full-time 0, part-time 0; Multi-ethnic–full-time 2, part-time 0; students subject to the Americans with Disabilities Act–full-time 0, part-time 0.

Financial Information/Assistance:
Tuition for Full-Time Study: Master's: State residents $630 per credit hour; nonstate residents: $630 per credit hour. *Doctoral:* State residents: $630 per credit hour; nonstate residents: $630 per credit hour.

Financial Assistance:
First Year Students: Teaching assistantships available for first-year. Average number of hours worked per week: 10. Tuition remission given: partial. Research assistantships available for first-year. Average number of hours worked per week: 10. Tuition remission given: partial. Fellowships and scholarships available for first-year. Average number of hours worked per week: 0. Tuition remission given: partial.

Advanced Students: Teaching assistantships available for advanced students. Average number of hours worked per week: 10. Tuition remission given: partial. Research assistantships available for advanced students. Average number of hours worked per week: 10. Tuition remission given: partial. Fellowships and scholarships available for advanced students. Average number of hours worked per week: 0. Tuition remission given: partial.

Contact Information: Of all students currently enrolled full-time, 50% benefitted from one or more of the listed financial assistance programs. For information on financial assistance, contact: Linda McCarthy, College of Education, Ammi Hyde Building, University of Denver, Denver, CO 80208, (303) 871-2509.

Internships/Practica:
Both Doctoral and Master's student complete practica and internship as well as hours in a campus clinic. Most practica and internships are off campus. Doctoral students must complete APA approved internships (exceptions made in unusual circumstances). Doctoral students have opportunities to complete advanced practica in variety of settings including college counseling centers, hospitals and mental health agencies. MA students complete practica and internships in Denver area including adolescent treatment facilities, mental health centers, women's crisis centers, schools, etc. For those doctoral students for whom a professional internship is required prior to graduation, 3 applied in 2000–2001. Of those who applied, 3 were placed in internships listed by the Association of Psychology Postdoctoral and Internship Programs (APPIC); 3 were placed in APA accredited internships.

Housing and Day Care: On-campus housing and day care facilities are available.

Employment of Department Graduates:

Master's Degree Graduates: Of those who graduated in the academic year 2000–2001, the following categories and numbers represent the post-graduate activities and employment of master's degree graduates: Enrolled in a psychology doctoral program (1), enrolled in another graduate/professional program (3), enrolled in a post-doctoral residency/fellowship (n/a), employed in independent practice (n/a), employed in an academic position at a university (0), employed in an academic position at a 2-year/4-year college (0), employed in other positions at a higher education institution (3), employed in a professional position in a school system (5), employed in business or industry (research/consulting) (2), employed in business or industry (management) (0), employed in a government agency (research) (0), employed in a government agency (professional services) (0), employed in a community mental health/counseling center (5), employed in a hospital/medical center (1).

Doctoral Degree Graduates: Of those who graduated in the academic year 2000–2001, the following categories and numbers represent the post-graduate activities and employment of doctoral degree graduates: Enrolled in a psychology doctoral program (n/a), enrolled in another graduate/professional program (n/a), enrolled in a post-doctoral residency/fellowship (1), employed in independent practice (1), employed in an academic position at a university (2), employed in an academic position at a 2-year/4-year college (0), employed in a community mental health/counseling center (1), employed in a hospital/medical center (1).

Additional Information:

Orientation, Objectives, and Emphasis of Department: The counseling psychology program at the University of Denver is designed to train counseling psychologists to work with normal populations of adolescents or adults who may be involved in life crises or who need help in making decisions. Counseling psychologists focus on encouraging individuals to understand themselves and their behavior, to develop necessary coping skills, and to solve life problems in light of this understanding and skill development. Life crises such as those that normally occur in the aging process, that is, developing an identity, midlife reevaluation, retirement, and grief or loss, are appropriate areas of concern for the counseling psychologists. They are equally concerned with helping individuals make vocational-educational decisions and take productive action in nuclear groups such as families or couples. They may teach communication or other interpersonal skills, time and stress management, and parenting. They may work in a remedial sense with individuals or groups in crisis or in a developmental, preventative role by providing information and training to prevent crisis or more serious mental health problems. In these last two roles, they often function as educators whether with individuals or with institutions. Although a counseling psychologist may employ some of the same techniques and study some of the same academic disciplines as do clinical psychologists and social workers, the emphasis on the developmental and educational aspects of mental health makes the discipline of counseling psychology unique.

Special Facilities or Resources: PhD students are required to complete a minor in one of two APA-approved clinical psychology programs on campus. Microcomputers and video equipment are available for use in conjunction with coursework. In-house clinic is available. Students are required to spend one night a week for two quarters in clinic. Intense supervision provided.

Information for Students With Physical Disabilities: Facilities are accessible.

Application Information:

Send to: Graduate Studies, Office of Admission, 2199 South University Boulevard, Denver, CO 80208-0302. Students are admitted in the Fall, application deadline January 1. Master's Degree in Counseling applcation deadline is February 1. For the Doctorate in Counseling Psychology, the deadline is January 1. *Fee:* $50.

Denver, University of
Department of Psychology
Frontier Hall, 2155 South Race Street
Denver, CO 80208
Telephone: (303) 871-3803
Fax: (303) 871-4747
E-mail: *rroberts@du.edu*
Web: *http://www.du.edu/psychology*

Department Established:

1952. Chairperson: Ralph J. Roberts. Number of Faculty: total–full-time 18, part-time 2; women–full-time 6, part-time 1; minority–full-time 3, part-time 1.

Programs and Degrees Offered:

Listed in the following order: Program area, degree type (T if terminal Master's), number awarded 7/00-6/01. Child Clinical PhD 5, Cognitive PhD, Develop Cognitive Neuroscience PhD, Developmental PhD 3, Psychology and the Law MA (T), Quantitative PhD 1, Social PhD.

APA Accreditation: Clinical PhD: full.

Student Applications/Admissions:

Student Applications

Child Clinical PhD—Applications 2001–2002, 17. Total applicants accepted 2001–2002, 4. New applicants enrolled 2001–2002, 4. Total enrolled 2001–2002 full-time, 36. Openings 2002–2003, 6. The Median number of years required for completion of a degree are 4. *Cognitive PhD*—Applications 2001–2002, 9. Total applicants accepted 2001–2002, 4. New applicants enrolled 2001–2002, 2. Total enrolled 2001–2002 full-time, 7. Openings 2002–2003, 4. The Median number of years required for completion of a degree are 5. The number of students enrolled full and part-time, who were dismissed or voluntarily withdrew from this program area were 1. *Develop Cognitive Neuroscience PhD*—Total enrolled 2001–2002 full-time, 18. Openings 2002–2003, 6. The Median number of years required for completion of a degree are 5. The number of students enrolled full and part-time, who were dismissed or voluntarily withdrew from this program area were 1. *Developmental PhD*—Applications 2001–2002, 25. Total applicants accepted 2001–2002, 2. New applicants enrolled 2001–2002, 2. Total enrolled 2001–2002 full-time, 12. Openings 2002–

2003, 2. The Median number of years required for completion of a degree are 5. *Psychology and the Law MA*—Applications 2001–2002, 5. Total applicants accepted 2001–2002, 2. Total enrolled 2001–2002 full-time, 1. Openings 2002–2003, 2. The Median number of years required for completion of a degree are 2. *Quantitative PhD*—Applications 2001–2002, 2. Total enrolled 2001–2002 full-time, 1. Openings 2002–2003, 1. The Median number of years required for completion of a degree are 4. The number of students enrolled full and part-time, who were dismissed or voluntarily withdrew from this program area were 0. *Social PhD*—Applications 2001–2002, 6. Total applicants accepted 2001–2002, 3. New applicants enrolled 2001–2002, 1. Total enrolled 2001–2002 full-time, 3. Openings 2002–2003, 3. The Median number of years required for completion of a degree are 5. The number of students enrolled full and part-time, who were dismissed or voluntarily withdrew from this program area were 0.

Admissions Requirements:

Scores: Entries appear in this order: required test or GPA, minimum score (if required), median score of students entering in 2001–2002. Master's Programs: GRE-V 600, 630; GRE-Q 600, 650; GRE-V+Q 1200, 1290; overall undergraduate GPA 3.0, 3.39. Doctoral Programs: GRE-V 600, 630; GRE-Q 600, 650; GRE-V+Q 1200, 1290; overall undergraduate GPA 3.0, 3.39; last 2 years GPA no minimum stated; psychology GPA no minimum stated; psychology GPA no minimum stated.

Other Criteria: (importance of criteria rated low, medium, or high): GRE/MAT scores high, research experience high, work experience medium, extracurricular activity medium, clinically related public service high, GPA high, letters of recommendation high, interview high, statement of goals and objectives high.

Student Characteristics: The following represents characteristics of students in 2001–2002 in all graduate psychology programs in the department: Female–full-time 48, part-time 0; Male–full-time 12, part-time 0; African American/Black–full-time 2, part-time 0; Hispanic/Latino (a)–full-time 4, part-time 0; Asian/Pacific Islander–full-time 7, part-time 0; American Indian/Alaska Native–full-time 0, part-time 0.

Financial Information/Assistance:

Tuition for Full-Time Study: *Master's:* State residents per academic year $17,880; nonstate residents: per academic year $17,880, *Doctoral:* State residents: per academic year $17,880; nonstate residents: per academic year $17,880.

Financial Assistance:

First Year Students: Teaching assistantships available for first-year. Average amount paid per academic year: $9,705. Average number of hours worked per week: 20. Tuition remission given: full. Research assistantships available for first-year. Average amount paid per academic year: $9,705. Average number of hours worked per week: 20. Tuition remission given: full.

Advanced Students: Teaching assistantships available for advanced students. Average amount paid per academic year: $9,705. Average number of hours worked per week: 20. Tuition remission given: full. Research assistantships available for advanced students. Average amount paid per academic year: $9,705. Average number of hours worked per week: 20. Tuition remission given: full.

Contact Information: Of all students currently enrolled full-time, 100% benefitted from one or more of the listed financial assistance programs. For information on financial assistance, contact: Paula Houghtaling, Department of Psychology.

Internships/Practica: Students in the Developmental Cognitive Neuroscience program attend neuropsychology rounds at a local rehab center their first year and intern in the department's Neuropsychology Clinic. Practica in neuroimaging and research with abnormal populations are also provided. We have our own clinical facility, the Child Study Center (CSC). Our work in the CSC includes assessment and psychotherapy with children, families, and adults. Students in their third or fourth year often do clinical placements in the community. Students currently have placements at local hospitals, day treatment programs, and other community agencies. For those doctoral students for whom a professional internship is required prior to graduation, 4 applied in 2000–2001. Of those who applied, 4 were placed in internships listed by the Association of Psychology Postdoctoral and Internship Programs (APPIC); 4 were placed in APA accredited internships.

Housing and Day Care: No on-campus housing and day care facilities are available.

Employment of Department Graduates:

Master's Degree Graduates: Of those who graduated in the academic year 2000–2001, the following categories and numbers represent the post-graduate activities and employment of master's degree graduates: Enrolled in a post-doctoral residency/fellowship (n/a), employed in independent practice (n/a).

Doctoral Degree Graduates: Of those who graduated in the academic year 2000–2001, the following categories and numbers represent the post-graduate activities and employment of doctoral degree graduates: Enrolled in a psychology doctoral program (n/a), enrolled in another graduate/professional program (n/a), employed in independent practice (3), employed in an academic position at a university (3).

Additional Information:

Orientation, Objectives, and Emphasis of Department: Programs are oriented toward training students to pursue careers in research, teaching, and professional practice. They include Child Clinical, Cognitive, Developmental, Quantitative, and Social, as well as an integrative program in Developmental Cognitive Neuroscience, open to students in any of the other programs, that fosters an interdisciplinary approach to cognitive neuroscience. The department is ranked 2nd in the world in publication impact by the American Psychological Society, ranked 13th in the nation in Developmental Psychology by *U.S. News and World Report*, and one of the few APA accredited child clinical programs. The department offers close collaborative relationships between faculty and students, with an emphasis on individualized tutorial relationships. The atmosphere encourages and offers students the freedom to seek out and work with multiple faculty members as fits the student's evolving interests. Our students are successful in publishing in prestigious journals, in winning predoctoral grants, and obtaining their first choice for clinical internships. Situated at the foot of the Rocky Mountains, Denver combines urban culture with readily accessible skiing, hiking, & biking in a climate that has over 300 days of sunshine.

Special Facilities or Resources: Our recently renovated building includes labs which are custom-designed for the kinds of research conducted in our department, including the Center for Marital and Family Studies, the Relationship Center, the Developmental Neuropsychology Center, the Cognitive Psychology Lab, the Reading & Language Lab, the Center for Infant Development, the Center for the Study of Self and Others, the Perception/Action Lab and the Psychophysiology Lab including equipment to measure EDA, ECG, and EMG. We are closely partnered with the neuroimaging facilities at the University of Colorado Health Sciences Center that allow us to conduct fMRI and MEG studies. In addition to research laboratories, the department also maintains its own clinical training facility, the Child Study Center, and it houses a Neuropsychology Clinic. The department enjoys excellent computer facilities. It maintains a local area computer network (LAN) that interconnects over 100 departmental PCs. Many graduate student offices are equipped with at least one PC, and there is a graduate student computer lab with 10 PCs, printers, and scanners. Research subjects are available from undergraduate classes, and from nearby schools and the university daycare center, and local hospitals and rehab centers for patients with neuropsychological disorders. Classrooms are smart-to-the-seat, allowing internet access for students' laptops.

Information for Students With Physical Disabilities: Services and accommodations for students with disabilities are coordinated through the Disabled Persons' Resources office. Examples of accommodations include advocacy, priority registration, and coordination of readers, notetakers, test accommodations, library assistance, and sign language interpreters. Limited adaptive technology is also available. Students admitted to graduate programs who need accommodations for a disability should contact DPR at (303) 871-2585 (voice/TDD*) or (303) 871-2278 well ahead of the quarter in which enrollment is planned so appropriate arrangements can be made. Decisions regarding accommodations are made in collaboration with the individual student, and documentation of disability may be required.

Application Information:
Send to: Graduate Studies Office, University of Denver, 2199 S. University Blvd, Denver, CO 80208 (self-addressed envelope is enclosed in application materials). Students are admitted in the Fall, application deadline December 15th. *Fee:* $50.

Denver, University of
Graduate School of Professional Psychology
2450 South Vine Street
Denver, CO 80208-3626
Telephone: (303) 871-3873
Fax: (303) 871-4220
E-mail: ppsy02@denver.du.edu
Web: http://www.du.edu/gspp

Department Established:
1976. Dean: Dr. Peter Buirski. Number of Faculty: total–full-time 12, part-time 32; women–full-time 5, part-time 19; minority–full-time 4, part-time 2.

Programs and Degrees Offered:
Listed in the following order: Program area, degree type (T if terminal Master's), number awarded 7/00-6/01. Clinical forensic MA (T), clinical psychology PsyD 32.

APA Accreditation: Clinical PsyD: full.

Student Applications/Admissions:
Student Applications
Clinical forensic MA—Applications 2001–2002, 145. Total applicants accepted 2001–2002, 25. New applicants enrolled 2001–2002, 25. Total enrolled 2001–2002 full-time, 37. Openings 2002–2003, 23. The Median number of years required for completion of a degree are 2. The number of students enrolled full and part-time, who were dismissed or voluntarily withdrew from this program area were 3. *Clinical psychology PsyD*—Applications 2001–2002, 125. Total applicants accepted 2001–2002, 32. New applicants enrolled 2001–2002, 32. Total enrolled 2001–2002 full-time, 100. Openings 2002–2003, 33. The Median number of years required for completion of a degree are 4. The number of students enrolled full and part-time, who were dismissed or voluntarily withdrew from this program area were 3.

Admissions Requirements:
Scores: Entries appear in this order: required test or GPA, minimum score (if required), median score of students entering in 2001–2002. Master's Programs: GRE-V no minimum stated, 550; GRE-Q no minimum stated, 550; GRE-Analytical no minimum stated, 550; overall undergraduate GPA no minimum stated, 3.00. GRE-Subject (Psychology) is not required for MA applicants. Doctoral Programs: GRE-V no minimum stated, 550; GRE-Q no minimum stated, 570; GRE-Analytical no minimum stated, 600; GRE-Subject(Psych) no minimum stated, 600; overall undergraduate GPA no minimum stated, 3.5 ; last 2 years GPA no minimum stated; psychology GPA no minimum stated; psychology GPA no minimum stated.
Other Criteria: (importance of criteria rated low, medium, or high): GRE/MAT scores medium, research experience medium, work experience high, extracurricular activity medium, clinically related public service high, GPA high, letters of recommendation high, interview high, statement of goals and objectives high. Three reference letters, personal statement.

Student Characteristics: The following represents characteristics of students in 2001–2002 in all graduate psychology programs in the department: Female–full-time 108, part-time 0; Male–full-time 26, part-time 0; African American/Black–full-time 3, part-time 0; Hispanic/Latino (a)–full-time 7, part-time 0; Asian/Pacific Islander–full-time 10, part-time 0; American Indian/Alaska Native–full-time 1, part-time 0.

Financial Information/Assistance:
Tuition for Full-Time Study: *Master's:* State residents per academic year $25,000, $630 per credit hour; nonstate residents: per academic year $25,000, $630 per credit hour. *Doctoral:* State residents: per academic year $30,000, $630 per credit hour; nonstate residents: per academic year $30,000, $630 per credit hour.

Financial Assistance:
First Year Students: Research assistantships available for first-year. Average amount paid per academic year: $2,500. Tu-

ition remission given: partial. Fellowships and scholarships available for first-year. Average amount paid per academic year: $2,500.

Advanced Students: Research assistantships available for advanced students. Average amount paid per academic year: $2,500. Tuition remission given: partial.

Contact Information: Of all students currently enrolled full-time, 25% benefitted from one or more of the listed financial assistance programs. For information on financial assistance, contact: All students must submit a FAFSA to receive any financial assistance. No other application is required. Financial Services (303) 871-4900.

Internships/Practica: There are 2 1/2 intern slots which are reserved for doctoral students in psychology from the University of Denver in the University of Denver Counseling Center. For those doctoral students for whom a professional internship is required prior to graduation, 32 applied in 2000–2001. Of those who applied, 30 were placed in internships listed by the Association of Psychology Postdoctoral and Internship Programs (APPIC); 30 were placed in APA accredited internships.

Housing and Day Care: On-campus housing and day care facilities are available.

Employment of Department Graduates:

Master's Degree Graduates: Of those who graduated in the academic year 2000–2001, the following categories and numbers represent the post-graduate activities and employment of master's degree graduates: Enrolled in a post-doctoral residency/fellowship (n/a), employed in independent practice (n/a).

Doctoral Degree Graduates: Of those who graduated in the academic year 2000–2001, the following categories and numbers represent the post-graduate activities and employment of doctoral degree graduates: Enrolled in a psychology doctoral program (n/a), enrolled in another graduate/professional program (n/a).

Additional Information:

Orientation, Objectives, and Emphasis of Department: The PsyD degree focuses on scientifically based training for applied professional work rather than on the more traditional academic-scientific approach to clinical training. In addition to the basic clinical curriculum, special emphases are available in several areas. The PsyD student should have a probing, questioning stance toward human problems and, therefore, should be (1) knowledgeable about intra- and interpersonal theories, including assessment and intervention, (2) conversant with relevant issues and techniques in research, (3) sensitive to self and to interpersonal interactions as primary clinical tools, (4) skilled in assessing and effectively intervening in human problems, (5) able to assess effectiveness of outcomes, and (6) aware of current professional and ethical issues. To these ends the program focuses on major social and psychological theories; research training directed toward the consumer rather than the producer of research; technical knowledge of assessment; and intervention in problems involving individuals, families, groups, and institutional systems. Strong emphasis is placed on practicum training. There are no requirements for empirical research output. The Master's degree in Forensic Psychology supplements graduate-level clinical training with course work and practicum experiences in the legal, criminal justice, and law enforcement systems. Students will complete the degree in two academic years of full-time study, attending fall, winter, and spring quarters.

Special Facilities or Resources: The program offers its own in-house community psychological services center and varied opportunities are available in many community facilities for the required practicum experiences.

Information for Students With Physical Disabilities: The University of Denver's Office of Disability Services (303) 871-2455 will assist students in making accommodations.

Application Information:
Send to: Graduate Admissions Office #216, University of Denver, 2197 S. University Blvd., Denver, CO 80208. Students are admitted in the Fall, application deadline Jan. 5, 2003. (for PsyD), first week of February (for MA). *Fee:* $50.

Northern Colorado, University of
Division of Professional Psychology
College of Education
501 20th Street
Greeley, CO 80639
Telephone: (970) 351-2731
Fax: (970) 351-2625
E-mail: *david.gonzalez@unco.edu*
Web: *http://www.unco.edu/coe/ppsy*

Department Established:
1911. Division Director: David M. Gonzalez. Number of Faculty: total–full-time 14, part-time 3; women–full-time 8, part-time 2; minority–full-time 3.

Programs and Degrees Offered:
Listed in the following order: Program area, degree type (T if terminal Master's), number awarded 7/00-6/01. Community counseling MA (T) 45, community counseling marriage MA 25, counseling PsyD 6, school EdS 10, school counseling MA (T) 10.

APA Accreditation: Counseling PsyD: full. School PhD: full.

Student Applications/Admissions:
Student Applications
Community counseling MA—Applications 2001–2002, 100. Total applicants accepted 2001–2002, 75. New applicants enrolled 2001–2002, 75. Total enrolled 2001–2002 full-time, 180, part-time, 10. Openings 2002–2003, 75. *Community counseling marriage MA*—Applications 2001–2002, 35. Total applicants accepted 2001–2002, 30. New applicants enrolled 2001–2002, 30. Total enrolled 2001–2002 full-time, 40. Openings 2002–2003, 30. *Counseling PsyD*—Applications 2001–2002, 40. Total applicants accepted 2001–2002, 7. New applicants enrolled 2001–2002, 7. Total enrolled 2001–2002 full-time, 29, part-time, 5. Openings 2002–2003, 6. *School EdS*—Applications 2001–2002, 45. Total applicants accepted 2001–2002, 20. New applicants enrolled 2001–2002, 17. Total enrolled 2001–2002 full-time, 40, part-time, 5. Openings 2002–2003, 15. *School counseling MA*—Applications 2001–2002, 25. Total applicants accepted 2001–2002, 20. New applicants enrolled 2001–2002, 20. Total enrolled 2001–2002 full-time, 40. Openings 2002–2003, 25.

Admissions Requirements:

Scores: Entries appear in this order: required test or GPA, minimum score (if required), median score of students entering in 2001–2002. Master's Programs: overall undergraduate GPA 3.00. 1350 combined GRE if GPA is lower than 3.00 Doctoral Programs: GRE-V 500, 600; GRE-Q 500, 600; GRE-V+Q 1000, 1200; GRE-Analytical 500, 600; GRE-V+Q+Analytical no minimum stated, 1800; last 2 years GPA 3.5, 3.7 ; psychology GPA no minimum stated; psychology GPA 3.5, 3.7.

Other Criteria: (importance of criteria rated low, medium, or high): GRE/MAT scores high, research experience medium, work experience high, extracurricular activity low, clinically related public service medium, GPA high, letters of recommendation high, interview high, statement of goals and objectives high.

Student Characteristics: The following represents characteristics of students in 2001–2002 in all graduate psychology programs in the department: Female–full-time 323, part-time 0; Male–full-time 80, part-time 0; African American/Black–full-time 1, part-time 0; Hispanic/Latino (a)–full-time 2, part-time 0; Asian/Pacific Islander–full-time 4, part-time 0; American Indian/Alaska Native–full-time 1, part-time 0.

Financial Information/Assistance:

Tuition for Full-Time Study: *Master's:* State residents per academic year $2,450, $136 per credit hour; nonstate residents: per academic year $9,960, $553 per credit hour. *Doctoral:* State residents: per academic year $2,450, $136 per credit hour; nonstate residents: per academic year $9,960, $553 per credit hour.

Financial Assistance:

First Year Students: Research assistantships available for first-year. Average amount paid per academic year: $6,000. Average number of hours worked per week: 8. Apply by April 15. Tuition remission given: partial. Fellowships and scholarships available for first-year. Average amount paid per academic year: $1,500. Apply by April 15. Tuition remission given: partial.

Advanced Students: Teaching assistantships available for advanced students. Average amount paid per academic year: $2,000. Apply by Variable. Research assistantships available for advanced students. Average amount paid per academic year: $6,000. Average number of hours worked per week: 8. Apply by April 15. Tuition remission given: partial. Fellowships and scholarships available for advanced students. Average amount paid per academic year: $1,500. Apply by Variable. Tuition remission given: partial.

Contact Information: Of all students currently enrolled full-time, 80% benefitted from one or more of the listed financial assistance programs. For information on financial assistance, contact: Financial Aid Office.

Internships/Practica: Master's and doctoral practica are in our in house clinic. Master's internships are in mental health agencies or schools. Doctoral internships are APPIC and/or APA accredited. For those doctoral students for whom a professional internship is required prior to graduation, 5 applied in 2000–2001. Of those who applied, 4 were placed in internships listed by the Association of Psychology Postdoctoral and Internship Programs (APPIC); 3 were placed in APA accredited internships.

Housing and Day Care: On-campus housing and day care facilities are available.

Employment of Department Graduates:

Master's Degree Graduates: Of those who graduated in the academic year 2000–2001, the following categories and numbers represent the post-graduate activities and employment of master's degree graduates: Enrolled in a post-doctoral residency/fellowship (n/a), employed in independent practice (n/a).

Doctoral Degree Graduates: Of those who graduated in the academic year 2000–2001, the following categories and numbers represent the post-graduate activities and employment of doctoral degree graduates: Enrolled in a psychology doctoral program (n/a), enrolled in another graduate/professional program (n/a), enrolled in a post-doctoral residency/fellowship (3), employed in independent practice (4), employed in an academic position at a university (2), employed in a professional position in a school system (6), employed in business or industry (research/consulting) (2), employed in a community mental health/counseling center (4).

Additional Information:

Orientation, Objectives, and Emphasis of Department: The Division of Professional Psychology offers graduate programs in the fields of counseling and school psychology that prepare students for careers in schools, community agencies, industry, higher education, and private practice. The division offers professional psychological services to the university and the local community through its clinic, a research and training facility. The school psychology program is based on the scientist-practitioner model of training (called a Data-Based Ecological Interventionist) and focuses on the interaction of content knowledge, process and assessment skills, the educational and community context, and research. The counseling psychology programs are based on the practitioner model of training and focus on content knowledge, the educational and community context, therapeutic skills, and their interaction. Students can be part of a cluster of outstanding psychology training programs. All programs are nestled within the Division of Professional Psychology with training in counseling psychology, school psychology, professional counseling, community counseling, and family therapy. Students have the opportunity to pursue elective course work in any or all of these areas.

Special Facilities or Resources: The division maintains a laboratory facility for use by the counseling and school psychology programs. This facility is built around a central observation area, from which eight counseling rooms, five testing rooms, three neuropsychology labs, and two play therapy rooms can be observed and videotaped through one-way windows. All are furnished appropriately for the specific functions of each. All rooms are equipped with ceiling-mounted microphones with the observation area for each room supplied with an amplifier and earphone jacks. Several observation areas are also equipped with speakers. The main university library has provided excellent support for the professional psychology programs. Sufficient funding is provided annually for the purchase of relevant books, tapes, microforms, and microfiche. The journal collection is also updated annually, and facilities are available for several types of computer literature searches. Additionally, funding is available for purchasing tests listed in the Mental Measurements Yearbook.

Application Information:

Send to: Admissions Secretary, Division of Professional Psychology, University of Northern Colorado, Greeley, CO 80639. Students are admitted in the Spring, application deadline January 15. PsyD Jan 1,

School Psy Jan 15, Master's March 15, PhD Counselor Education January 1. *Fee:* $35.

Northern Colorado, University of
Educational Psychology
518 McKee
Greeley, CO 80639
Telephone: (970) 351-2807
Fax: (970) 351-1622
E-mail: *randy.lennon@unco.edu*

Department Established:
1982. Chairperson: Dr. Randy Lennon. Number of Faculty: total–full-time 6, part-time 4; women–full-time 3, part-time 4.

Programs and Degrees Offered:
Listed in the following order: Program area, degree type (T if terminal Master's), number awarded 7/00-6/01. Educational PhD 7.

Student Applications/Admissions:
Student Applications
Educational PhD—Applications 2001–2002, 18. Total applicants accepted 2001–2002, 3. New applicants enrolled 2001–2002, 3. Total enrolled 2001–2002 full-time, 35. Openings 2002–2003, 8. The number of students enrolled full and part-time, who were dismissed or voluntarily withdrew from this program area were 0.

Admissions Requirements:
Scores: Entries appear in this order: required test or GPA, minimum score (if required), median score of students entering in 2001–2002. Master's Programs: GRE-V 500; GRE-Q 500; GRE-Analytical 500; GRE-V+Q+Analytical 1500; overall undergraduate GPA 3.0; last 2 years GPA 3.0. Doctoral Programs: GRE-V 550; GRE-Q 550; GRE-Analytical 550; GRE-V+Q+Analytical 1650; overall undergraduate GPA 3.0; last 2 years GPA no minimum stated; psychology GPA no minimum stated; psychology GPA no minimum stated.
Other Criteria: (importance of criteria rated low, medium, or high): GRE/MAT scores medium, research experience high, work experience low, GPA medium, letters of recommendation medium, statement of goals and objectives high.

Student Characteristics: The following represents characteristics of students in 2001–2002 in all graduate psychology programs in the department: Female–full-time 8, part-time 1; Male–full-time 8, part-time 12; African American/Black–full-time 1, part-time 0; Hispanic/Latino (a)–full-time 1, part-time 0; Asian/Pacific Islander–full-time 0, part-time 0; American Indian/Alaska Native–full-time 0, part-time 0.

Financial Information/Assistance:
Tuition for Full-Time Study: *Master's:* State residents per academic year $3,180; nonstate residents: per academic year $11,080. *Doctoral:* State residents: per academic year $3,180; nonstate residents: per academic year $11,080.

Financial Assistance:
First Year Students: Teaching assistantships available for first-year. Average amount paid per academic year: $5,280. Average number of hours worked per week: 10. Tuition remission given: partial. Research assistantships available for first-year. Average amount paid per academic year: $5,280. Average number of hours worked per week: 10. Tuition remission given: partial.
Advanced Students: Teaching assistantships available for advanced students. Average amount paid per academic year: $5,280. Average number of hours worked per week: 10. Tuition remission given: partial. Research assistantships available for advanced students. Average amount paid per academic year: $5,280. Average number of hours worked per week: 10. Tuition remission given: partial.
Contact Information: Of all students currently enrolled full-time, 75% benefitted from one or more of the listed financial assistance programs. For information on financial assistance, contact: Graduate School.

Internships/Practica: Student practica are usually set up by the student in a school or related setting.

Housing and Day Care: No on-campus housing and day care facilities are available.

Employment of Department Graduates:
Master's Degree Graduates: Of those who graduated in the academic year 2000–2001, the following categories and numbers represent the post-graduate activities and employment of master's degree graduates: Enrolled in a psychology doctoral program (3), enrolled in a post-doctoral residency/fellowship (n/a), employed in independent practice (n/a).
Doctoral Degree Graduates: Of those who graduated in the academic year 2000–2001, the following categories and numbers represent the post-graduate activities and employment of doctoral degree graduates: Enrolled in a psychology doctoral program (n/a), enrolled in another graduate/professional program (n/a), employed in an academic position at a university (4).

Additional Information:
Orientation, Objectives, and Emphasis of Department: The overall goal of both the master's and doctoral programs is to train scholars to undertake original basic and applied research in psychological processes as they apply to education. At the master's level, students take a core of educational psychology courses and then concentrate in one of 4 areas: research, measurement and evaluation; human development; learning and cognitive processes; or an individually tailored domain. Master's level courses prepare students for a variety of careers depending on their area of concentration. Graduates may be prepared to design instructional materials in educational and business settings; to serve research, measurement, and evaluation functions in school districts, social agencies, or business organizations; or to serve as consultants in applied developmental settings such as day-care facilities, youth centers, or social agencies. At the doctoral level, students obtain a comprehensive general background in educational psychology and then specialize in one of two areas of emphasis: learning and cognitive processes or human development. Graduates of the doctoral program are qualified to work as university professors, school consultants, and researchers in government agencies and business settings.

Special Facilities or Resources: UNC has been designated as the primary institution for graduate teacher education in the state. The College of Education includes more than 100 faculty members, and provides an excellent institutional environment for its master's and doctoral programs in educational psychology. In addition to the 6 full time educational psychology faculty, students may draw upon the varied expertise of faculty in educational technology, psychology, elementary and secondary education, special education, and applied statistics. The main campus library contains approximately 1.2 million units of hardbound volumes, periodicals, monographs, and government documents and houses the largest collection of educational literature in the state. The Colorado Alliance of Research Libraries provides access to other libraries in the region. The University Laboratory School (K-12) is an excellent research facility available to students and faculty. The Interdisciplinary Center for Educational Technology provides media support, microcomputers, instructional design assistance, software, and consulting services for both students and faculty. Faculty and students also take advantage of the computer laboratories maintained by the university. These centers allow students and faculty the use of two different computer platforms and some centers maintain several statistical packages designed for research in the social and behavioral sciences.

Application Information:
Send to: Graduate School, UNC. Students are admitted in the Fall, application deadline October; Spring, application deadline April. Deadline for Master's Degree is March 1 and September 15. *Fee:* $35. Graduate School determines conditions for waiver or deferral of fee.

Northern Colorado, University of
Psychology
Arts & Sciences
501 20th Street
Greeley, CO 80639-0001
Telephone: (970) 351-2957
Fax: (970) 351-1103
E-mail: *dmgilli@unco.edu*
Web: *http://www.unco.edu/psychology/*

Department Established:
1982. Chairperson: Mark Alcorn. Number of Faculty: total–full-time 14, part-time 1; women–full-time 6.

Programs and Degrees Offered:
Listed in the following order: Program area, degree type (T if terminal Master's), number awarded 7/00-6/01. General Psychology MA (T) 4, Human Neuropsychology MA (T) 10.

Student Applications/Admissions:
Student Applications
General Psychology MA—Applications 2001–2002, 10. Total applicants accepted 2001–2002, 1. New applicants enrolled 2001–2002, 1. Total enrolled 2001–2002 full-time, 1. Openings 2002–2003, 5. The Median number of years required for completion of a degree are 3. The number of students enrolled full and part-time, who were dismissed or voluntarily withdrew from this program area were 0. *Human Neuropsychology MA*—Applications 2001–2002, 54. Total applicants accepted 2001–

2002, 14. New applicants enrolled 2001–2002, 8. Total enrolled 2001–2002 full-time, 15. Openings 2002–2003, 7. The Median number of years required for completion of a degree are 3. The number of students enrolled full and part-time, who were dismissed or voluntarily withdrew from this program area were 1.

Admissions Requirements:
Scores: Entries appear in this order: required test or GPA, minimum score (if required), median score of students entering in 2001–2002. Master's Programs: GRE-V 600; GRE-Q 600; GRE-Analytical 600; overall undergraduate GPA 3.2. Doctoral Programs: last 2 years GPA no minimum stated; psychology GPA no minimum stated; psychology GPA no minimum stated.
Other Criteria: (importance of criteria rated low, medium, or high): GRE/MAT scores high, research experience medium, work experience medium, extracurricular activity medium, clinically related public service low, GPA high, letters of recommendation high, statement of goals and objectives high.

Student Characteristics: The following represents characteristics of students in 2001–2002 in all graduate psychology programs in the department: Female–full-time 10, part-time 0; Male–full-time 6, part-time 0; African American/Black–full-time 0, part-time 0; Hispanic/Latino (a)–full-time 0, part-time 0; Asian/Pacific Islander–full-time 0, part-time 0; American Indian/Alaska Native–full-time 0, part-time 0; Multi-ethnic–full-time 1, part-time 0; students subject to the Americans with Disabilities Act–full-time 0, part-time 0.

Financial Information/Assistance:
Tuition for Full-Time Study: *Master's:* State residents per academic year $1,225; nonstate residents: per academic year $4,980.

Financial Assistance:
First Year Students: Teaching assistantships available for first-year. Average amount paid per academic year: $4,431. Average number of hours worked per week: 9. Apply by March 15. Tuition remission given: partial. Research assistantships available for first-year. Average amount paid per academic year: $4,431. Average number of hours worked per week: 9. Apply by March 15. Tuition remission given: partial. Average amount paid per academic year: $0. Average number of hours worked per week: 0. Fellowships and scholarships available for first-year. Average amount paid per academic year: $1,200. Average number of hours worked per week: 0. Apply by March 1.
Advanced Students: Average amount paid per academic year: $0. Average number of hours worked per week: 0. Average amount paid per academic year: $0. Average number of hours worked per week: 0. Average amount paid per academic year: $0. Average number of hours worked per week: 0. Average amount paid per academic year: $0. Average number of hours worked per week: 0.
Contact Information: Of all students currently enrolled full-time, 25% benefitted from one or more of the listed financial assistance programs. For information on financial assistance, contact: http://www.unco.edu/.

Internships/Practica: Teaching internship: Student learns how to conduct an Introductory Psychology class.

Housing and Day Care: On-campus housing and day care facilities are available.

Employment of Department Graduates:

Master's Degree Graduates: Of those who graduated in the academic year 2000–2001, the following categories and numbers represent the post-graduate activities and employment of master's degree graduates: Enrolled in a psychology doctoral program (4), enrolled in another graduate/professional program (2), enrolled in a post-doctoral residency/fellowship (n/a), employed in independent practice (n/a), employed in an academic position at a university (1), employed in an academic position at a 2-year/4-year college (0), employed in other positions at a higher education institution (0), employed in a professional position in a school system (2), employed in business or industry (research/consulting) (2), employed in business or industry (management) (0), employed in a government agency (research) (0), employed in a government agency (professional services) (1), employed in a community mental health/counseling center (0), employed in a hospital/medical center (0), still seeking employment (0), other employment position (0).

Doctoral Degree Graduates: Of those who graduated in the academic year 2000–2001, the following categories and numbers represent the post-graduate activities and employment of doctoral degree graduates: Enrolled in a psychology doctoral program (n/a), enrolled in another graduate/professional program (n/a), enrolled in a post-doctoral residency/fellowship (0), employed in independent practice (0), employed in an academic position at a university (0), employed in an academic position at a 2-year/4-year college (0), employed in other positions at a higher education institution (0), employed in a professional position in a school system (0), employed in business or industry (research/consulting) (0), employed in business or industry (management) (0), employed in a government agency (research) (0), employed in a government agency (professional services) (0), employed in a community mental health/counseling center (0), employed in a hospital/medical center (0), still seeking employment (0), other employment position (0).

Additional Information:

Orientation, Objectives, and Emphasis of Department: The goal of psychology is to understand the processes involved in thoughts, actions, feelings, and experiences. To explain these processes, psychologists develop theories which guide hypotheses that are tested scientifically through qualitative and quantitative research methods. This scientific approach is applied by psychologists to the study of humans and other animals. The results of psychological research provide the basis for clinicians and counselors to help people overcome a variety of problems and assist people in achieving their full potential.

Special Facilities or Resources: Physiological Psychology Laboratory, Animal Facility Laboratory, School, K-12.

Application Information:
Send to: Graduate School, University of Northern Colorado, Greeley, CO 80639. Students are admitted in the Fall, application deadline February 15. March 15 for statement of intent to Psychology Department: Dr. David Gilliam, Psychology Dept., McKee 14, University of Northern Colorado, Greeley, CO 80639. *Fee:* $35.

Central Connecticut State University

Department of Psychology
1615 Stanley Street
New Britain, CT 06050-4010
Telephone: (860) 832-3100
Fax: (860) 832-3123
E-mail: *donis@ccsu.edu*
Web: *http://www.psychology.ccsu.edu*

Department Established:

1967. Chairperson: Francisco Donis. Number of Faculty: total–full-time 19, part-time 20; women–full-time 7, part-time 7; minority–full-time 6, part-time 2.

Programs and Degrees Offered:

Listed in the following order: Program area, degree type (T if terminal Master's), number awarded 7/00-6/01. Community MA (T) 1, general MA (T) 7.

Student Applications/Admissions:

Student Applications

Community MA—Applications 2001–2002, 5. Total applicants accepted 2001–2002, 4. New applicants enrolled 2001–2002, 2. Total enrolled 2001–2002 full-time, 1, part-time, 1. Openings 2002–2003, 6. *General MA*—Applications 2001–2002, 36. Total applicants accepted 2001–2002, 22. New applicants enrolled 2001–2002, 11. Total enrolled 2001–2002 full-time, 3, part-time, 8. Openings 2002–2003, 10.

Admissions Requirements:

Scores: Entries appear in this order: required test or GPA, minimum score (if required), median score of students entering in 2001–2002. Master's Programs: overall undergraduate GPA 2.75. Doctoral Programs: last 2 years GPA no minimum stated; psychology GPA no minimum stated; psychology GPA no minimum stated.

Other Criteria: (importance of criteria rated low, medium, or high): GRE/MAT scores, research experience low, work experience high, extracurricular activity low, clinically related public service high, GPA high, letters of recommendation high, interview low, statement of goals and objectives high.

Student Characteristics: The following represents characteristics of students in 2001–2002 in all graduate psychology programs in the department: Female–full-time 3, part-time 20; Male–full-time 1, part-time 3; African American/Black–full-time 1, part-time 3; Hispanic/Latino (a)–full-time 0, part-time 2; Asian/Pacific Islander–full-time 0, part-time 0; American Indian/Alaska Native–full-time 0, part-time 1; part-time 3; students subject to the Americans with Disabilities Act–full-time 0, part-time 0.

Financial Information/Assistance:

Tuition for Full-Time Study: *Master's:* State residents per academic year $1,334, $195 per credit hour; nonstate residents: per academic year $3,718, $195 per credit hour.

Financial Assistance:

First Year Students: No information provided.
Advanced Students: No information provided.
Contact Information: Of all students currently enrolled full-time, 0% benefitted from one or more of the listed financial assistance programs. For information on financial assistance, contact: Chair, Psychology Department.

Internships/Practica: We offer a variety of internships. For students in the community specialization, there are internships in prevention-oriented community programs dealing with substance abuse, teen pregnancy, etc. We also offer internships in developmental and counseling areas.

Housing and Day Care: On-campus housing and day care facilities are available.

Employment of Department Graduates:

Master's Degree Graduates: Of those who graduated in the academic year 2000–2001, the following categories and numbers represent the post-graduate activities and employment of master's degree graduates: Enrolled in a psychology doctoral program (3), enrolled in a post-doctoral residency/fellowship (n/a), employed in independent practice (n/a), employed in an academic position at a 2-year/4-year college (0).

Doctoral Degree Graduates: Of those who graduated in the academic year 2000–2001, the following categories and numbers represent the post-graduate activities and employment of doctoral degree graduates: Enrolled in a psychology doctoral program (n/a), enrolled in another graduate/professional program (n/a).

Additional Information:

Orientation, Objectives, and Emphasis of Department: The psychology department contains 19 faculty members whose interests cover a wide range of psychological areas. Collectively, the orientation of the department is toward applied areas (clinical, community, health, applied, developmental), with generally little emphasis on animal learning/behavior. The specialization in community psychology focuses heavily on primary prevention, while the general program is intended to expose students to a broad range of applied areas in psychology. Both programs have a strong research emphasis.

Special Facilities or Resources: The psychology department has limited space available for human experimental research. The department has a computer laboratory, and the university has very good computer facilities available for student use. Students may also work on applied research projects with faculty through the Center for Social Research at the University.

Information for Students With Physical Disabilities: The main office bilding for psychology (faculty offices) is handicapped accessible.

Application Information:

Send to: Office of Graduate Admissions, Central CT State University, 1615 Stanley St., New Britain, CT 06050-4010. Students are admitted in the Fall, application deadline March 31; Spring, application deadline November 10. *Fee:* $40.

Connecticut College (2001 data)

Department of Psychology
Mohegan Avenue
New London, CT 06320
Telephone: (860) 439-2330
Fax: (860) 439-5300
E-mail: *nmmac@conncoll.edu*
Web: *http://www.camel.conncoll.edu/ccacad/psycholgy/ind*

Department Established:

1960. Chairperson: Jefferson A. Singer. Number of Faculty: total–full-time 7, part-time 1; women–full-time 4.

Programs and Degrees Offered:

Listed in the following order: Program area, degree type (T if terminal Master's), number awarded 7/00-6/01. General MA (T) 15.

Student Applications/Admissions:

Student Applications

General MA—Applications 2001–2002, 22. Total applicants accepted 2001–2002, 14. New applicants enrolled 2001–2002, 7. Total enrolled 2001–2002 full-time, 12, part-time, 4. Openings 2002–2003, 12. The Median number of years required for completion of a degree are 2. The number of students enrolled full and part-time, who were dismissed or voluntarily withdrew from this program area were 1.

Admissions Requirements:

Scores: Entries appear in this order: required test or GPA, minimum score (if required), median score of students entering in 2001–2002. Master's Programs: GRE-V+Q+Analytical no minimum stated, 1615; GRE-Subject(Psych) no minimum stated, 565; overall undergraduate GPA 3.00, 3.52; psychology GPA no minimum stated, 3.69.

Other Criteria: (importance of criteria rated low, medium, or high): GRE/MAT scores medium, research experience high, work experience low, extracurricular activity low, clinically related public service low, GPA high, letters of recommendation high, statement of goals and objectives medium.

Student Characteristics: The following represents characteristics of students in 2001–2002 in all graduate psychology programs in the department: Female–full-time 6, part-time 0; Male–full-time 1, part-time 0; African American/Black–full-time 0, part-time 0; Hispanic/Latino (a)–full-time 0, part-time 0; Asian/Pacific Islander–full-time 0, part-time 0; American Indian/Alaska Native–full-time 0, part-time 0.

Financial Information/Assistance:

Tuition for Full-Time Study: No information provided.

Financial Assistance:

First Year Students: No information provided.
Advanced Students: No information provided.

Contact Information: Of all students currently enrolled full-time, 0% benefitted from one or more of the listed financial assistance programs.

Internships/Practica: The Master's Program offers two types of practicum courses - a research practicum or a clinical practicum. Each of these practicum courses lasts two semesters and requires a commitment of two 8-hour days a week. The research practicum is conducted under the supervision of an experienced scientist (typically a PhD or MD) in a setting outside the Psychology Department. This research is distinct from and in addition to both the student's Master's thesis and any involvement in Connecticut College faculty research. Past examples include research work at Yale University, University of Massachusetts Medical Center, Pfizer Pharmaceuticals Inc., the United States Naval Base in Groton, and Whiting Forensic Institute. The Clinical practicum consists of clinical experience in a variety of modalities and therapeutic settings. All clinical work is conducted under the supervision of experienced clinicians (typically a PhD or licensed MSW). Students perform evaluations, facilitate groups, engage in individual and family therapy, and conduct clinical research, depending upon the type of setting. Students also participate in case conferences, in-services, and research seminars at their settings, as well as a weekly seminar conducted in the Psychology Department. Examples of clinical settings include the West Haven VA Health Psychology Program, St. Francis Hospital, Child Guidance Clinic, Lawrence and Memorial Hospital Adolescent Partial Hospitalization program, University of Massachusetts Medical Center, University of Connecticut Medical Center, Waterford Country School, Rhode Island College Counseling Center, among many others.

Housing and Day Care: No on-campus housing and day care facilities are available.

Employment of Department Graduates:

Master's Degree Graduates: Of those who graduated in the academic year 2000–2001, the following categories and numbers represent the post-graduate activities and employment of master's degree graduates: Enrolled in a post-doctoral residency/fellowship (n/a), employed in independent practice (n/a).

Doctoral Degree Graduates: Of those who graduated in the academic year 2000–2001, the following categories and numbers represent the post-graduate activities and employment of doctoral degree graduates: Enrolled in a psychology doctoral program (n/a), enrolled in another graduate/professional program (n/a).

Additional Information:

Orientation, Objectives, and Emphasis of Department: The department offers both clinical and research orientations. Concentrations are available in behavioral medicine, clinical, behavioral neuroscience, and personality-social. The faculty is diversified in their theoretical emphases. We provide training in traditional fields of experimental and clinical psychology and in special areas such as behavioral neuroscience, health psychology, environmental psychology, women and gender, behavior analysis, and personality research. The aim of most graduating students is to pursue the PhD, primarily in clinical psychology.

Special Facilities or Resources: In addition to shop and laboratory space for social, physiological, and conditioning and learning psychology, the Psychology Department has one-way observation suites and biofeedback and video equipment. The college's computer is housed in Bill Hall, the home of the Psychology Department, and graduate students have access to the building's computer terminals and microprocessors. Each graduate student is assigned desk space within Bill Hall.

Information for Students With Physical Disabilities: The building has no elevator or entrance ramp.

Application Information:

Send to: Department Chair. Students are admitted in the Fall, application deadline February 1. *Fee:* $50.

Connecticut, University of (2001 data)

Department of Educational Psychology
NEAG School of Education
249 Glenbrook Road, Unit 2064
Storrs, CT 06269-2064
Telephone: (860) 486-4031
Fax: (860) 486-0180
E-mail: *reis@uconn.edu*
Web: *http://www.ucc.uconn.edu/~wwwepsy*

Department Established:

1960. Department Head: Sally M. Reis. Number of Faculty: total–full-time 24, part-time 8; women–full-time 14, part-time 6; minority–full-time 4.

Programs and Degrees Offered:

Listed in the following order: Program area, degree type (T if terminal Master's), number awarded 7/00-6/01. Cognition and instruction PhD (T) 4, counseling psychology MA (T) 6, school psychology PhD 5.

APA Accreditation: School PhD: full.

Student Applications/Admissions:

Student Applications

Cognition and instruction PhD—Applications 2001–2002, 7. Total applicants accepted 2001–2002, 3. New applicants enrolled 2001–2002, 2. Total enrolled 2001–2002 full-time, 6, part-time, 4. Openings 2002–2003, 5. The Median number of years required for completion of a degree are 5. The number of students enrolled full and part-time, who were dismissed or voluntarily withdrew from this program area were 0. *Counseling psychology MA*—Applications 2001–2002, 30. Total applicants accepted 2001–2002, 10. New applicants enrolled 2001–2002, 10. Total enrolled 2001–2002 full-time, 10, part-time, 2. Openings 2002–2003, 12. The Median number of years required for completion of a degree are 3. The number of students enrolled full and part-time, who were dismissed or voluntarily

withdrew from this program area were 0. *School psychology PhD*—Applications 2001–2002, 42. Total applicants accepted 2001–2002, 13. New applicants enrolled 2001–2002, 5. Total enrolled 2001–2002 full-time, 17, part-time, 8. Openings 2002–2003, 12. The Median number of years required for completion of a degree are 6. The number of students enrolled full and part-time, who were dismissed or voluntarily withdrew from this program area were 0.

Admissions Requirements:

Scores: Entries appear in this order: required test or GPA, minimum score (if required), median score of students entering in 2001–2002. Master's Programs: GRE-V+Q no minimum stated, 1170; overall undergraduate GPA 2.8, 3.1. GRE-V and Q required for School Psychology and Cognition & Instruction. Counseling Psychology requires MATs not GREs. Doctoral Programs: GRE-V+Q no minimum stated, 1240; overall undergraduate GPA 2.8, 3.1 ; last 2 years GPA no minimum stated; psychology GPA no minimum stated; psychology GPA no minimum stated.

Other Criteria: (importance of criteria rated low, medium, or high): GRE/MAT scores medium, research experience medium, work experience medium, extracurricular activity medium, clinically related public service medium, GPA high, letters of recommendation high, interview medium, statement of goals and objectives high. Counseling and School Psychology require interviews—Cognition and Instruction does not.

Student Characteristics: The following represents characteristics of students in 2001–2002 in all graduate psychology programs in the department: Female–full-time 8, part-time 1; Male–full-time 2, part-time 1; African American/Black–full-time 0, part-time 0; Hispanic/Latino (a)–full-time 0, part-time 0; Asian/Pacific Islander–full-time 2, part-time 0; American Indian/Alaska Native–full-time 0, part-time 0.

Financial Information/Assistance:

Tuition for Full-Time Study: No information provided.

Financial Assistance:

First Year Students: No information provided.
Advanced Students: No information provided.
Contact Information: Of all students currently enrolled full-time, 90% benefitted from one or more of the listed financial assistance programs. For information on financial assistance, contact: Department Head, Educational Psychology Department, 249 Glenbrook Road, Unit 2064, UConn, Storrs, CT 06269-2064.

Internships/Practica: There are a number of practica opportunities for master's and doctoral students at the University of Connecticut and affiliated sites. For the past five years the department has contracted with public school systems for practica and internship sites for school psychology students. On campus, Counseling Psychology students have obtained funded practica positions in student services, residential life, and the student health center. They have also obtained funded internships in public school systems. All programs have been able to find some level of support for several students through one or more of the following centers: The National Research Center for Gifted and Talented; The Pappanikou Special Education Center; and the University Program for Students with Learning Disabilities. Each of these centers is affiliated with the Educational Psychology department.

Housing and Day Care: No on-campus housing and day care facilities are available.

Employment of Department Graduates:

Master's Degree Graduates: Of those who graduated in the academic year 2000–2001, the following categories and numbers represent the post-graduate activities and employment of master's degree graduates: Enrolled in a post-doctoral residency/fellowship (n/a), employed in independent practice (n/a).

Doctoral Degree Graduates: Of those who graduated in the academic year 2000–2001, the following categories and numbers represent the post-graduate activities and employment of doctoral degree graduates: Enrolled in a psychology doctoral program (n/a), enrolled in another graduate/professional program (n/a).

Additional Information:

Orientation, Objectives, and Emphasis of Department: The Department of Educational Psychology offers degree programs in the areas of counseling, cognition and instruction, evaluation and measurement, gifted and talented education, instructional media and technology, school psychology and special education at the graduate level and special education at the undergraduate level. The department also offers foundation or service courses for students who are pursuing majors in other disciplines. The department emphasizes the preparation of practitioners who are well grounded in theory to work in public education fields at all levels from elementary school through college and university settings. An equally important commitment has been made to advancing the science of education and expanding the body of knowledge that defines our discipline. To this end, a major portion of departmental activity is directed toward basic and applied research projects. Finally, the department is committed to the improvement of public education through participation in service activities of schools, institutions, agencies and professional organizations.

Special Facilities or Resources: Research space, equipment and/or opportunities exist in the following center/labs: The National Research Center for Gifted and Talented; The Pappanikou Special Education Center; and the University Program for Students with Learning Disabilities; The University of Connecticut Educational Microcomputing Laboratory; The Hartford Professional Development Academy.

Information for Students With Physical Disabilities: Students with physical disabilities are strongly encouraged to consider the Educational Psychology department programs because of the strong emphasis on special education and rehabilitation counseling within the department programs. Special support services are provided within The Pappanikou Special Education Center and the University Affiliated Program.

Application Information:
Send to: Graduate Admissions, Room 108, Whetten Center Box U-6A, , 438 Whitney Road Ext, Storrs, CT 06269. Students are admitted in the Winter, application deadline February 15. February 15th deadline for all admissions—Fall admits only. *Fee:* $40.

Connecticut, University of
Department of Psychology
College of Liberal Arts and Sciences
U-20, 406 Babbidge Road
Storrs, CT 06269-1020
Telephone: (860) 486-3528
Fax: (860) 486-2760
E-mail: *clowe@uconnvm.uconn.edu*
Web: *http://www.ucc.uconn.edu/~wwwpsyc*

Department Established:
1939. Head: Charles A. Lowe. Number of Faculty: total–full-time 41, part-time 2; women–full-time 11, part-time 2; minority–full-time 2; faculty subject to the Americans with Disabilities Act 1.

Programs and Degrees Offered:
Listed in the following order: Program area, degree type (T if terminal Master's), number awarded 7/00-6/01. Behavioral neuroscience PhD 1, clinical PhD 6, developmental PhD 2, experimental PhD 1, industrial/organizational PhD 2, social PhD.

APA Accreditation: Clinical PhD: full.

Student Applications/Admissions:

Student Applications

Behavioral neuroscience PhD—Applications 2001–2002, 30. Total applicants accepted 2001–2002, 6. New applicants enrolled 2001–2002, 2. Total enrolled 2001–2002 full-time, 16. Openings 2002–2003, 3. The Median number of years required for completion of a degree are 5. The number of students enrolled full and part-time, who were dismissed or voluntarily withdrew from this program area were 0. *Clinical PhD*—Applications 2001–2002, 189. Total applicants accepted 2001–2002, 17. New applicants enrolled 2001–2002, 9. Total enrolled 2001–2002 full-time, 42, part-time, 3. Openings 2002–2003, 8. The Median number of years required for completion of a degree are 6. The number of students enrolled full and part-time, who were dismissed or voluntarily withdrew from this program area were 1. *Developmental PhD*—Applications 2001–2002, 30. Total applicants accepted 2001–2002, 5. New applicants enrolled 2001–2002, 3. Total enrolled 2001–2002 full-time, 13, part-time, 3. Openings 2002–2003, 3. The Median number of years required for completion of a degree are 6. The number of students enrolled full and part-time, who were dismissed or voluntarily withdrew from this program area were 2. *Experimental PhD*—Applications 2001–2002, 10. Total applicants accepted 2001–2002, 7. New applicants enrolled 2001–2002, 3. Total enrolled 2001–2002 full-time, 25, part-time, 4. Openings 2002–2003, 4. The Median number of years required for completion of a degree are 6. *Industrial/organizational PhD*—Applications 2001–2002, 45. Total applicants accepted 2001–2002, 14. New applicants enrolled 2001–2002, 5. Total enrolled 2001–2002 full-time, 14, part-time, 3. Openings 2002–2003, 5. The Median number of years required for completion of a degree are 6. The number of students enrolled full and part-time, who were dismissed or voluntarily withdrew from this program area were 2. *Social PhD*—Applications 2001–2002, 45. Total applicants accepted 2001–2002, 14. New applicants enrolled 2001–2002, 5. Total enrolled 2001–2002 full-time, 14, part-time, 3. Openings 2002–2003, 3. The number of students enrolled full and part-time, who were dismissed or voluntarily withdrew from this program area were 2.

Admissions Requirements:

Scores: Entries appear in this order: required test or GPA, minimum score (if required), median score of students entering in 2001–2002. Master's Programs: last 2 years GPA no minimum stated; psychology GPA no minimum stated. Doctoral Programs: GRE-V no minimum stated; GRE-Q no minimum stated; GRE-Analytical no minimum stated; GRE-V+Q+Analytical 569, 640; overall undergraduate GPA 3.0, 3.6 ; last 2 years GPA no minimum stated, 3.5 ; psychology GPA 3.4, 3.7 ; psychology GPA no minimum stated. Clinical GPA range for students entering program in Fall 2002: 3.10-4.0 with 100% of new clinical students having 3.7 GPA for last two years of college. Median GRE scores for clinical students, 2001applicants: verbal 630; quantitative-690; analytic 700; psych. 690. GRE range of scores for clinical 2001 acceptances: V-420-690; Q-510-740; A-34-800; Psych 660-770. Subject test is not required, but is HIGHLY RECOMMENDED.

Other Criteria: (importance of criteria rated low, medium, or high): GRE/MAT scores medium, research experience high, work experience low, clinically related public service low, GPA medium, letters of recommendation high, interview medium, statement of goals and objectives high. Check department admissions requirements for specific program areas on the Psych. Dept. website. Three divisions (Clinical, Social, and Behavioral Neuroscience) interview applicants, by invitation only. The other three divisions (Developmental, Experimental, Industrial/Organizational) do not interview applicants.

Student Characteristics: The following represents characteristics of students in 2001–2002 in all graduate psychology programs in the department: Female–full-time 83, part-time 9; Male–full-time 51, part-time 8; African American/Black–full-time 8, part-time 1; Hispanic/Latino (a)–full-time 3, part-time 0; Asian/Pacific Islander–full-time 11, part-time 0; American Indian/Alaska Native–full-time 0, part-time 0; Multi-ethnic–full-time 0, part-time 0; students subject to the Americans with Disabilities Act–full-time 0, part-time 0.

Financial Information/Assistance:

Tuition for Full-Time Study: *Doctoral:* State residents: per academic year $3,292; nonstate residents: per academic year $7,668.

Financial Assistance:

First Year Students: Teaching assistantships available for first-year. Average amount paid per academic year: $7,959. Average number of hours worked per week: 10. Apply by Jan 1st. Tuition remission given: full. Research assistantships available for first-year. Average amount paid per academic year: $7,959. Average number of hours worked per week: 10. Apply by Jan 1st. Tuition remission given: full. Fellowships and scholarships available for first-year. Average amount paid per academic year: $2,000. Average number of hours worked per week: 0. Apply by Jan 1st.

Advanced Students: Teaching assistantships available for advanced students. Average amount paid per academic year: $8,377. Average number of hours worked per week: 10. Tuition remission given: full. Research assistantships available for advanced students. Average amount paid per academic year: $8,377. Average number of hours worked per week: 10. Tuition remission given: full. Fellowships and scholarships available for advanced students. Average amount paid per academic year: $2,000. Average number of hours worked per week: 0. Tuition remission given: full.

Contact Information: Of all students currently enrolled full-time, 90% benefitted from one or more of the listed financial assistance programs. For information on financial assistance, contact: Psychology Department website and/or UConn. Financial Aid Office at: http://vm.uconn.edu/~faid.

Internships/Practica: For those doctoral students for whom a professional internship is required prior to graduation, 9 applied in 2000–2001. Of those who applied, 6 were placed in internships listed by the Association of Psychology Postdoctoral and Internship Programs (APPIC); 6 were placed in APA accredited internships.

Housing and Day Care: On-campus housing and day care facilities are available.

Employment of Department Graduates:

Master's Degree Graduates: Of those who graduated in the academic year 2000–2001, the following categories and numbers represent the post-graduate activities and employment of master's degree graduates: Enrolled in a psychology doctoral program (26), enrolled in another graduate/professional program (0), enrolled in a post-doctoral residency/fellowship (n/a), employed in independent practice (n/a), employed in a professional position in a school system (0), employed in business or industry (research/consulting) (3), employed in a government agency (research) (0).

Doctoral Degree Graduates: Of those who graduated in the academic year 2000–2001, the following categories and numbers represent the post-graduate activities and employment of doctoral degree graduates: Enrolled in a psychology doctoral program (n/a), enrolled in another graduate/professional program (n/a), enrolled in a post-doctoral residency/fellowship (11), employed in independent practice (0), employed in an academic position at a university (0), employed in an academic position at a 2-year/4-year college (3), employed in other positions at a higher education institution (0), employed in a professional position in a school system (0), employed in business or industry (research/consulting) (3), employed in business or industry (management) (0), employed in a government agency (research) (0), employed in a government agency (professional services) (0), employed in a community mental health/counseling center (0), employed in a hospital/medical center (2), still seeking employment (1).

Additional Information:

Orientation, Objectives, and Emphasis of Department: All programs lead to the PhD in the fields of study of psychology. The areas within psychology are administered by six divisions, some of which have more than one area of concentration: (1) behavioral neuroscience (biopsychology, neuroscience); (2) developmental; (3) clinical; (4) experimental (cognition, ecological psychology, language); (5) industrial/organizational; and (6) social. Students must apply for admission to the psychology department and specify which area of concentration they want to be considered for. Areas of concentration are in close and friendly cooperation; however, they maintain semiautonomy in admission and program development. No single theoretical view dominates the department or any section thereof. While there is thorough training available in the application of psychology, the predominant orientation of the department is in the generation of new ideas through research.

Special Facilities or Resources: Resources include research rooms for individual experiments; computer-based laboratories for research in psycholinguistics, perception, and visual psychophysics. Graduate student computer laboratory; strong LAN and mainframe support with easy internet access; on-site psychological services clinic; various types of electronic recording equipment; laboratories for comparative and physiological research with avian and mammalian species; laboratories in affiliated research institutions, including Haskins Laboratory in New Haven; psychological clinics/hospitals, mental hospital affiliates; child development laboratories, nursery school, day-care center in the School of Family Studies.

Information for Students With Physical Disabilities: Building is completely accessible, with appropriate restroom facilities.

Application Information:

Send to: Graduate Admissions, U-1030, Department of Psychology, University of Connecticut, 406 Babbidge Road, Storrs, CT 06269-1030. Students are admitted in the Fall, application deadline 1/15. Clinical division ONLY: December 31. *Fee:* $40. $45 for international students.

Fairfield University
School and Applied Psychology & Special Education
Graduate School of Education and Allied Professions
Fairfield, CT 06430
Telephone: (203) 254-4000 ext. 2324
Fax: (203) 254-4047
E-mail: *dgeller@fair1.fairfield.edu*

Department Established:

1970. Professor and Chair, Programs in Psychology and Special Ed: Daniel Geller. Number of Faculty: total–full-time 5, part-time 10; women–full-time 3, part-time 5.

Programs and Degrees Offered:

Listed in the following order: Program area, degree type (T if terminal Master's), number awarded 7/00-6/01. Foundation of advanced psychol MA 24, human services MA 24, industrial/organizationa psy MA 24, personnel psychology MA 24, school psychology MA 13.

Student Applications/Admissions:

Student Applications

Foundation of advanced psychol MA—Applications 2001–2002, 51. Total applicants accepted 2001–2002, 36. New applicants enrolled 2001–2002, 14. Total enrolled 2001–2002 full-time, 17, part-time, 44. *Human services* MA—Applications 2001–2002, 51. Total applicants accepted 2001–2002, 36. New applicants enrolled 2001–2002, 14. Total enrolled 2001–2002 full-time, 17, part-time, 44. *Industrial/organizationa psy* MA—Applications 2001–2002, 51. Total applicants accepted 2001–2002, 36. New applicants enrolled 2001–2002, 14. Total enrolled 2001–2002 full-time, 17, part-time, 44. *Personnel psychology* MA—Applications 2001–2002, 51. Total applicants accepted 2001–2002, 36. New applicants enrolled 2001–2002, 14. Total enrolled 2001–2002 full-time, 17, part-time, 44. *School psychology* MA—Applications 2001–2002, 47. Total applicants accepted 2001–2002, 21. New applicants enrolled 2001–2002, 8. Total enrolled 2001–2002 full-time, 21, part-time, 19.

Admissions Requirements:

Scores: Entries appear in this order: required test or GPA, minimum score (if required), median score of students entering in 2001–2002. Master's Programs: overall undergraduate GPA 2.67. 2.67 for School Psychology; 2.90 other grad psych-minimum Doctoral Programs: last 2 years GPA no minimum stated; psychology GPA no minimum stated; psychology GPA no minimum stated.

Other Criteria: (importance of criteria rated low, medium, or high): GRE/MAT scores, research experience, work experience medium, extracurricular activity medium, clinically related public service medium, GPA high, letters of recommendation high, interview high, statement of goals and objectives high.

Student Characteristics: The following represents characteristics of students in 2001–2002 in all graduate psychology programs in the department: Female–full-time 8, part-time 44; Male–full-time 6, part-time 16; African American/Black–full-time 0, part-time 4; Hispanic/Latino (a)–full-time 0, part-time 7; Asian/Pacific Islander–full-time 0, part-time 0; American Indian/Alaska Native–full-time 0, part-time 0.

Financial Information/Assistance:

Tuition for Full-Time Study: *Master's:* State residents $390 per credit hour; nonstate residents: $390 per credit hour.

Financial Assistance:

First Year Students: No information provided.

Advanced Students: No information provided.

Contact Information: For information on financial assistance, contact: Financial Aid Office.

Internships/Practica: A full year's internship in school psychology offers supervised experience in a school or clinical setting under joint supervision of the faculty and school or agency psychologist. This internship follows the "Field Work in Child Study" requirement, which is a more time-limited experience in school, agency, or mental health clinic settings. The field work in Applied Psychology is also a time limited experience in a psychologically oriented environment. The field work for the I/O program is a time limited experience in a corporate related organization.

Housing and Day Care: No on-campus housing and day care facilities are available.

Employment of Department Graduates:

Master's Degree Graduates: Of those who graduated in the academic year 2000–2001, the following categories and numbers represent the post-graduate activities and employment of master's degree graduates: Enrolled in a psychology doctoral program (4), enrolled in another graduate/professional program (1), enrolled in a post-doctoral residency/fellowship (n/a), employed in independent practice (n/a), employed in a professional position in a school system (12), employed in business or industry (research/consulting) (15), employed in business or industry (management) (5), employed in a community mental health/counseling center (6), other employment position (6).

Doctoral Degree Graduates: Of those who graduated in the academic year 2000–2001, the following categories and numbers represent the post-graduate activities and employment of doctoral degree graduates: Enrolled in a psychology doctoral program (n/a), enrolled in another graduate/professional program (n/a).

Additional Information:

Orientation, Objectives, and Emphasis of Department: The school psychology program subscribes to the philosophy that students should be broadly educated and trained for a profession that serves people. In order to further the understanding of the complexities of human behavior, there must be an adequate grounding in concepts drawn from psychological science as well as a familiarity with the social and biological conditions that are basic to normal and deviant human development. The program covers a wide range of approaches, introduces students to them, and encourages students to evaluate their own responses from scholarly study and from an examination of themselves. Coursework encompasses the processes of healthy psychological development, interferences in such development, and interventive procedures intended to create a more favorable environment for learning and for improvement of the child's functioning. The Master of Arts program in applied psychology offers courses in psychology, combined with selected courses from other programs and schools of the university, to help prepare students to deal with a range of human problems in business, industry, and the public sector.

Special Facilities or Resources: The faculty have established close working relationships with various settings in which psychological services are provided. Included among these are schools, child guidance clinics, family agencies, and corporations having human resource development services. Research facilities, including an excellent computer center and excellent library, are available.

Application Information:
Students are admitted in the Fall, application deadline May 1; Spring, application deadline September 15; Summer, application deadline January 15. *Fee:* $50.

Hartford, University of
Department of Psychology
Arts & Sciences
200 Bloomfield Avenue
West Hartford, CT 06117
Telephone: (860) 768-4544
Fax: (860) 768-5292
E-mail: *psych@mail.hartford.edu*

Department Established:
1953. Chairperson: Jack L. Powell. Number of Faculty: total–full-time 11, part-time 25; women–full-time 5, part-time 6.

Programs and Degrees Offered:
Listed in the following order: Program area, degree type (T if terminal Master's), number awarded 7/00-6/01. Clinical Practices in psycholo MA (T) 16, general experimental MA (T) 10, school psychology.

Student Applications/Admissions:

Student Applications
Clinical Practices in psycholo MA—Applications 2001–2002, 70. Total applicants accepted 2001–2002, 42. New applicants enrolled 2001–2002, 18. Total enrolled 2001–2002 full-time, 27, part-time, 2. Openings 2002–2003, 20. *General experimental MA*—Applications 2001–2002, 19. Total applicants accepted 2001–2002, 16. New applicants enrolled 2001–2002, 5. Total enrolled 2001–2002 full-time, 5, part-time, 11. Openings 2002–2003, 20. The Median number of years required for completion of a degree are 2. The number of students enrolled full and part-time, who were dismissed or voluntarily withdrew from this program area were 1.

Admissions Requirements:
Scores: Entries appear in this order: required test or GPA, minimum score (if required), median score of students entering in 2001–2002. Master's Programs: GRE-V no minimum stated, 440; GRE-Q no minimum stated, 500; GRE-V+Q no minimum stated; GRE-Analytical no minimum stated, 520; GRE-V+Q+Analytical no minimum stated; GRE-Subject(Psych) no minimum stated, 510; overall undergraduate GPA no minimum stated, 3.3; last 2 years GPA no minimum stated; psychology GPA no minimum stated, 3.2. Doctoral Programs: last 2 years GPA no minimum stated; psychology GPA no minimum stated; psychology GPA no minimum stated.

Other Criteria: (importance of criteria rated low, medium, or high): GRE/MAT scores medium, research experience medium, work experience medium, extracurricular activity low, clinically related public service medium, GPA medium, letters of recommendation high, statement of goals and objectives high.

Student Characteristics: The following represents characteristics of students in 2001–2002 in all graduate psychology programs in the department: Female–full-time 27, part-time 1; Male–full-time 4, part-time 0; African American/Black–full-time 3, part-time 0; Hispanic/Latino (a)–full-time 2, part-time 0; Asian/Pacific Islander–full-time 1, part-time 0; American Indian/Alaska Native–full-time 0, part-time 0.

Financial Information/Assistance:

Tuition for Full-Time Study: *Master's:* state residents $300 per credit hour, nonstate residents, $385 per credit hour.

Financial Assistance:

First Year Students: No information provided.

Advanced Students: Teaching assistantships available for advanced students. Average amount paid per academic year: $2,400. Average number of hours worked per week: 15. Research assistantships available for advanced students. Average amount paid per academic year: $2,000. Average number of hours worked per week: 10.

Contact Information: Of all students currently enrolled full-time, 0% benefitted from one or more of the listed financial assistance programs. For information on financial assistance, contact: Financial Aid Office (860-768-4296).

Internships/Practica: All Clinical Practices in Psychology students are assigned a half-time practicum throughout the second year of their academic program. The assignments for practica include mental health clinics, in- and outpatient services in hospitals, community centers, schools, and correctional institutions. Students are supervised both onsite by professional psychologists and at the University by the faculty. All School Psychology students are assigned a half-time practicum throughout their second year in a school setting and a full-time internship in their third year. Students are supervised by school psychologists on site and at the university by the faculty. General Experimental students have an option of a two semester, half-time practicum at a facility in the area of human resources.

Housing and Day Care: No on-campus housing and day care facilities are available.

Employment of Department Graduates:

Master's Degree Graduates: Of those who graduated in the academic year 2000–2001, the following categories and numbers represent the post-graduate activities and employment of master's degree graduates: Enrolled in a post-doctoral residency/fellowship (n/a), employed in independent practice (n/a).

Doctoral Degree Graduates: Of those who graduated in the academic year 2000–2001, the following categories and numbers represent the post-graduate activities and employment of doctoral degree graduates: Enrolled in a psychology doctoral program (n/a), enrolled in another graduate/professional program (n/a).

Additional Information:

Orientation, Objectives, and Emphasis of Department: The primary orientation of the department in terms of undergraduate training might be best described as eclectic, and the goal is to provide a broadly based foundation in psychology for both the student who will graduate with an undergraduate major and the student who will use the major as a building block for further graduate training in the field. At the level of graduate training, the emphasis varies with the separate programs. The Clinical Practices in Psychology and School Psychology programs tend to be precisely focused in terms of professional preparation at the master's level of training while the General Experimental program is more broadly based and is viewed as being preparatory to doctoral training.

Application Information:

Send to: Center for Graduate and Adult Academic Services, Univ. of Hartford, 200 Bloomfield Ave., West Hartford, CT 06117. Students are admitted in the Fall; Spring. All Programs - Fall-Review begins February 15. Rolling admission until filled. *Fee:* $40.

Hartford, University of

Neuroscience Graduate Master's Program,
  Department of Biology
Arts & Sciences
200 Bloomfield Avenue
West Hartford, CT 06117
Telephone: (860) 768-4531
Fax: (860) 768-5002
E-mail: *harney@mail.hartford.edu*
Web: *http://uhaweb.hartford.edu/biology/MNeuroscience.h*

Department Established:

1967. Director: Jacob P. Harney, Ph.D. Number of Faculty: total–full-time 7, part-time 5; women–full-time 2, part-time 3.

Programs and Degrees Offered:

Listed in the following order: Program area, degree type (T if terminal Master's), number awarded 7/00-6/01. Neuroscience MA (T) 5.

Student Applications/Admissions:

Student Applications

Neuroscience MA—Applications 2001–2002, 16. Total applicants accepted 2001–2002, 12. New applicants enrolled 2001–2002, 6. Total enrolled 2001–2002 full-time, 9, part-time, 7. Openings 2002–2003, 10. The Median number of years required for completion of a degree are 2.

Admissions Requirements:

Scores: Entries appear in this order: required test or GPA, minimum score (if required), median score of students entering in 2001–2002. Master's Programs: GRE-V no minimum stated, 530; GRE-Q no minimum stated, 540; GRE-V+Q no minimum stated; GRE-Analytical no minimum stated, 560; GRE-V+Q+Analytical no minimum stated; overall undergraduate GPA 2.5, 3.11. Doctoral Programs: last 2 years GPA no minimum stated; psychology GPA no minimum stated; psychology GPA no minimum stated.

Other Criteria: (importance of criteria rated low, medium, or high): GRE/MAT scores medium, research experience low, work experience medium, extracurricular activity medium, clinically related public service medium, GPA medium, letters of recommendation medium, interview medium, statement of goals and objectives high, GPA in science courses high,

Student Characteristics: The following represents characteristics of students in 2001–2002 in all graduate psychology programs in the department: Female–full-time 3, part-time 0; Male–full-time 2, part-time 1; African American/Black–full-time 0, part-time 0; Hispanic/Latino (a)–full-time 0, part-time 0; Asian/Pacific Islander–full-time 0, part-time 0; American Indian/Alaska Native–full-time 0, part-time 0.

Financial Information/Assistance:

Tuition for Full-Time Study: *Master's:* State residents $300 per credit hour; nonstate residents: $300 per credit hour.

Financial Assistance:

First Year Students: No information provided.
Advanced Students: No information provided.
Contact Information: For information on financial assistance, contact: Joseph Martin Kovic, Director of Student Financial Aid, University of Hartford (860) 768-4296.

Internships/Practica: No information provided.

Housing and Day Care: No on-campus housing and day care facilities are available.

Employment of Department Graduates:

Master's Degree Graduates: Of those who graduated in the academic year 2000–2001, the following categories and numbers represent the post-graduate activities and employment of master's degree graduates: Enrolled in a post-doctoral residency/fellowship (n/a), employed in independent practice (n/a).
Doctoral Degree Graduates: Of those who graduated in the academic year 2000–2001, the following categories and numbers represent the post-graduate activities and employment of doctoral degree graduates: Enrolled in a psychology doctoral program (n/a), enrolled in another graduate/professional program (n/a).

Application Information:

Send to: Dr. Jacob P. Harney, Director, Neuroscience Graduate Program, University of Hartford, 200 Bloomfield Avenue, West Hartford, CT 06117. Students are admitted in the Fall, application deadline none; Winter, application deadline none; Spring, application deadline none; Summer, application deadline none. Rolling admission. The earlier the better. *Fee:* $40.

Southern Connecticut State University
Department of Psychology
501 Crescent Street
New Haven, CT 06515
Telephone: (203) 392-6868
Fax: (203) 392-6805
E-mail: *mazur@southernct.edu*
Web: *http://www.southernct.edu/departments/psychology/*

Department Established:

1893. Chairperson: Linda Mackey. Number of Faculty: total–full-time 20, part-time 19; women–full-time 11, part-time 11.

Programs and Degrees Offered:

Listed in the following order: Program area, degree type (T if terminal Master's), number awarded 7/00-6/01. Psychology MA (T) 17.

Student Applications/Admissions:

Student Applications
Psychology MA—Applications 2001–2002, 54. Total applicants accepted 2001–2002, 39. New applicants enrolled 2001–2002, 26. Total enrolled 2001–2002 full-time, 17, part-time, 27. Openings 2002–2003, 25. The number of students enrolled full and part-time, who were dismissed or voluntarily withdrew from this program area were 2.

Admissions Requirements:

Scores: Entries appear in this order: required test or GPA, minimum score (if required), median score of students entering in 2001–2002. Master's Programs: overall undergraduate GPA 2.5, 3.0; psychology GPA 3.0, 3.2. Doctoral Programs: last 2 years GPA no minimum stated; psychology GPA no minimum stated; psychology GPA no minimum stated.
Other Criteria: (importance of criteria rated low, medium, or high): research experience low, work experience low, GPA high, letters of recommendation low.

Student Characteristics: The following represents characteristics of students in 2001–2002 in all graduate psychology programs in the department: Female–full-time 9, part-time 8; Male–full-time 2, part-time 3.

Financial Information/Assistance:

Tuition for Full-Time Study: *Master's:* State residents per academic year $2,772, $293 per credit hour; nonstate residents: per academic year $7,726, $293 per credit hour.

Financial Assistance:

First Year Students: Teaching assistantships available for first-year. Average amount paid per academic year: $4,500. Average number of hours worked per week: 16. Apply by May 1. Tuition remission given: partial.
Advanced Students: Teaching assistantships available for advanced students. Average amount paid per academic year: $4,500. Average number of hours worked per week: 16. Apply by May 1. Tuition remission given: partial.
Contact Information: Of all students currently enrolled full-time, 20% benefitted from one or more of the listed financial assistance programs. For information on financial assistance, contact: Dr. James E. Mazur (203) 392-6876 or Financial Aid Office (203) 392-5222.

Internships/Practica: With departmental permission, M.A. students may arrange a one- or two-semester clinical internship (3 credits for one semester; 6 credits for two semesters).

Housing and Day Care: On-campus housing and day care facilities are available.

Employment of Department Graduates:

Master's Degree Graduates: Of those who graduated in the academic year 2000–2001, the following categories and numbers represent the post-graduate activities and employment of master's degree graduates: Enrolled in a post-doctoral residency/fellowship (n/a), employed in independent practice (n/a).
Doctoral Degree Graduates: Of those who graduated in the academic year 2000–2001, the following categories and numbers represent the post-graduate activities and employment of doctoral degree graduates: Enrolled in a psychology doctoral program (n/a), enrolled in another graduate/professional program (n/a).

Additional Information:

Orientation, Objectives, and Emphasis of Department: This rigorous, research-based program is designed to develop creative, problem-solving skills that graduates can apply to a variety of clinical, industrial, and educational settings. Leading to a master of arts degree, this program is flexible enough to be completed on either a full- or part-time basis, meeting the needs of a wide range of candidates. For potential doctoral candidates who can enter neither a PhD nor a PsyD program at the present time, this program provides the basis for later acceptance into a doctoral program. For those who are already working in clinical, educational, or industrial settings, it offers updating and credentials. In addition, this program provides ideal training for people who want to explore their personal interest in careers related to psychology. High school teachers may use the program to prepare themselves to teach psychology in addition to their current certification. In any case, this program emphasizes faculty advisement to help tailor the program to the needs of each individual student.

Information for Students With Physical Disabilities: SCSU has a very active Disabilities Resources office that offers assistance to individuals with a wide range of disabilities.

Application Information:
Send to: Graduate Office, Southern Connecticut State University, New Haven, CT 06515. Students are admitted in the Fall, application deadline July 31; Spring, application deadline December 31; Summer, application deadline April 30. *Fee:* $40.

Wesleyan University
Psychology
207 High Street
Middletown, CT 06459-0408
Telephone: (860) 685-2343
Fax: (860) 685-2761
E-mail: *crace@mail.wesleyan.edu*
Web: *http://www.wesleyan.edu/psyc/*

Department Established:
1913. Chairperson: Robert S. Steele. Number of Faculty: total–full-time 12, part-time 3; women–full-time 6, part-time 2; minority–full-time 1.

Programs and Degrees Offered:
Listed in the following order: Program area, degree type (T if terminal Master's), number awarded 7/00-6/01. General MA (T).

Student Applications/Admissions:
Student Applications
General MA—Applications 2001–2002, 13. Total applicants accepted 2001–2002, n/a. New applicants enrolled 2001–2002, 3. Total enrolled 2001–2002 full-time, 5. Openings 2002–2003, 3. The Median number of years required for completion of a degree are 2. The number of students enrolled full and part-time, who were dismissed or voluntarily withdrew from this program area were 1.

Admissions Requirements:
Scores: Entries appear in this order: required test or GPA, minimum score (if required), median score of students entering in 2001–2002. Master's Programs: GRE-V+Q+Analytical no minimum stated; overall undergraduate GPA no minimum stated. Doctoral Programs: last 2 years GPA no minimum stated; psychology GPA no minimum stated; psychology GPA no minimum stated.

Other Criteria: (importance of criteria rated low, medium, or high): GRE/MAT scores medium, research experience medium, GPA medium, letters of recommendation high, interview low, statement of goals and objectives high.

Student Characteristics: The following represents characteristics of students in 2001–2002 in all graduate psychology programs in the department: Female–full-time 3, part-time 0; Male–full-time 1, part-time 0; African American/Black–full-time 1, part-time 0; Hispanic/Latino (a)–full-time 0, part-time 0; Asian/Pacific Islander–full-time 0, part-time 0; American Indian/Alaska Native–full-time 0, part-time 0; Multi-ethnic–full-time 0, part-time 0; students subject to the Americans with Disabilities Act–full-time 0, part-time 0.

Financial Information/Assistance:
Tuition for Full-Time Study: No information provided.

Financial Assistance:
First Year Students: No information provided.
Advanced Students: No information provided.
Contact Information: Of all students currently enrolled full-time, 100% benefitted from one or more of the listed financial assistance programs. For information on financial assistance, contact: Office of Graduate Student Services, 860-685-2390; mailto: gradoffice@wesleyan.edu; website address: http://www.wesleyan.edu/grad/. Contact graduate office for this information.

Internships/Practica: No information provided.

Housing and Day Care: No on-campus housing and day care facilities are available.

Employment of Department Graduates:
Master's Degree Graduates: Of those who graduated in the academic year 2000–2001, the following categories and numbers represent the post-graduate activities and employment of master's degree graduates: Enrolled in a post-doctoral residency/fellowship (n/a), employed in independent practice (n/a).

Doctoral Degree Graduates: Of those who graduated in the academic year 2000–2001, the following categories and numbers represent the post-graduate activities and employment of doctoral degree graduates: Enrolled in a psychology doctoral program (n/a), enrolled in another graduate/professional program (n/a).

Additional Information:
Orientation, Objectives, and Emphasis of Department: The department of Psychology at Wesleyan University offers a two-year program of study culminating in the master of arts degree. The hallmarks of the program are its selectivity, small size, and research orientation. Most students go on to pursue doctoral studies. Toward this end, the program is designed to provide a solid foundation of training in general psychology and additional experience in the fundamentals of research in a more specialized area of interest. Areas of expertise represented in the department include behavioral neuroscience, clinical, cognitive, developmental, personality, social psychology, and women's studies.

Special Facilities or Resources: 10 laboratories. The 2050 Program is an intensive academic and career monitoring program for highly motivated students who come from underrepresented groups in psychology (e.g., ethnic and racial minorities, first-generation college students, individuals with a disability). To be eligible, Wesleyan students must be in the spring semester of their sophomore year and must meet the requirements for entry into the psychology major. Program participants are chosen on a competitive basis and are matched with a faculty member who serves as their primary mentor.

Information for Students With Physical Disabilities: Judd Hall is handicap accessible and has an elevator.

Application Information:

Send to: Graduate Coordinator Psychology Department, Wesleyan University, 207 High Street, Middletown, CT 06459-0408. Students are admitted in the Spring, application deadline February 1.

Yale University
Department of Psychology
P.O. Box 208205
New Haven, CT 06520-8205
Telephone: (203) 432-4518
Fax: (203) 432-7172
E-mail: lauretta.olivi@yale.edu
Web: http://www.yale.edu/psychology

Department Established:

1928. Chair: Peter Salovey. Number of Faculty: total–full-time 25, part-time 20; women–full-time 6, part-time 10; minority–full-time 1.

Programs and Degrees Offered:

Listed in the following order: Program area, degree type (T if terminal Master's), number awarded 7/00-6/01. Behavioral neuroscience PhD 1, clinical PhD 7, cognitive PhD 3, developmental PhD 3, social personality PhD 4.

APA Accreditation: Clinical PhD: full.

Student Applications/Admissions:

Student Applications

Behavioral neuroscience PhD—Applications 2001–2002, 26. Total applicants accepted 2001–2002, 5. New applicants enrolled 2001–2002, 5. Total enrolled 2001–2002 full-time, 13. Openings 2002–2003, 2. The Median number of years required for completion of a degree are 6. The number of students enrolled full and part-time, who were dismissed or voluntarily withdrew from this program area were 0. *Clinical PhD*—Applications 2001–2002, 284. Total applicants accepted 2001–2002, 3. New applicants enrolled 2001–2002, 3. Total enrolled 2001–2002 full-time, 18. Openings 2002–2003, 2. The Median number of years required for completion of a degree are 5. The number of students enrolled full and part-time, who were dismissed or voluntarily withdrew from this program area were 0. *Cognitive PhD*—Applications 2001–2002, 46. Total applicants accepted 2001–2002, 6. New applicants enrolled 2001–

2002, 2. Total enrolled 2001–2002 full-time, 10. Openings 2002–2003, 3. The Median number of years required for completion of a degree are 6. The number of students enrolled full and part-time, who were dismissed or voluntarily withdrew from this program area were 0. *Developmental PhD*—Applications 2001–2002, 60. Total applicants accepted 2001–2002, 3. New applicants enrolled 2001–2002, 3. Total enrolled 2001–2002 full-time, 22. Openings 2002–2003, 2. The Median number of years required for completion of a degree are 6. The number of students enrolled full and part-time, who were dismissed or voluntarily withdrew from this program area were 0. *Social personality PhD*—Applications 2001–2002, 73. Total applicants accepted 2001–2002, 4. New applicants enrolled 2001–2002, 1. Total enrolled 2001–2002 full-time, 18. Openings 2002–2003, 3. The Median number of years required for completion of a degree are 5. The number of students enrolled full and part-time, who were dismissed or voluntarily withdrew from this program area were 1.

Admissions Requirements:

Scores: Entries appear in this order: required test or GPA, minimum score (if required), median score of students entering in 2001–2002. Master's Programs: We do not offer a terminal Master's Program. Doctoral Programs: GRE-V no minimum stated, 640; GRE-Q no minimum stated, 720; GRE-V+Q no minimum stated, 1360; GRE-Analytical no minimum stated, 780; overall undergraduate GPA no minimum stated, 3.76; last 2 years GPA no minimum stated; psychology GPA no minimum stated; psychology GPA no minimum stated.

Other Criteria: (importance of criteria rated low, medium, or high): GRE/MAT scores medium, research experience high, work experience low, extracurricular activity low, clinically related public service medium, GPA medium, letters of recommendation high, statement of goals and objectives high, interests match dept. high.

Student Characteristics: The following represents characteristics of students in 2001–2002 in all graduate psychology programs in the department: Female–full-time 54, part-time 0; Male–full-time 24, part-time 0; African American/Black–full-time 0, part-time 0; Hispanic/Latino (a)–full-time 0, part-time 0; Asian/Pacific Islander–full-time 4, part-time 0; American Indian/Alaska Native–full-time 1, part-time 0; Multi-ethnic–full-time 1, part-time 0; students subject to the Americans with Disabilities Act–full-time 0, part-time 0.

Financial Information/Assistance:

Tuition for Full-Time Study: No information provided.

Financial Assistance:

First Year Students: No information provided.

Advanced Students: Teaching assistantships available for advanced students. Average amount paid per academic year: $12,000. Average number of hours worked per week: 15. Apply by 8/31. Tuition remission given: full. Research assistantships available for advanced students. Average number of hours worked per week: 10. Tuition remission given: full. Traineeships available for advanced students. Tuition remission given: full. Fellowships and scholarships available for advanced students. Tuition remission given: full.

Contact Information: Of all students currently enrolled full-time, 1% benefitted from one or more of the listed financial assistance programs. For information on financial assistance, contact: Office of Finance and Financial Aid, Graduate School of Arts and Sciences, Yale Universtiy, P.O. Box 208236, New Haven, CT 06520-8236. Website: www.yale.edu/graduateschool/financial/index.html.

Internships/Practica: Students are required to assist in teaching an average of 10-15 hours per week in their second, third, and fourth years as part of their educational program. Local facilities for predoctoral internships are the Veterans Administration Center in West Haven, Yale Psychological Services Clinic, the Yale Child Study Center, and Yale Department of Psychiatry, with placement in the Connecticut Mental Health Center, Yale-New Haven Hospital, or the Yale Psychiatric Institute. Also, internships are arranged in accredited facilities throughout the United States. For those doctoral students for whom a professional internship is required prior to graduation, 5 applied in 2000–2001. Of those who applied, 5 were placed in internships listed by the Association of Psychology Postdoctoral and Internship Programs (APPIC); 5 were placed in APA accredited internships.

Housing and Day Care: No on-campus housing and day care facilities are available.

Employment of Department Graduates:

Master's Degree Graduates: Of those who graduated in the academic year 2000–2001, the following categories and numbers represent the post-graduate activities and employment of master's degree graduates: Enrolled in a psychology doctoral program (1), enrolled in another graduate/professional program (0), enrolled in a post-doctoral residency/fellowship (n/a), employed in independent practice (n/a), employed in an academic position at a university (0), employed in an academic position at a 2-year/4-year college (0), employed in other positions at a higher education institution (0), employed in a professional position in a school system (0), employed in business or industry (research/consulting) (1), employed in business or industry (management) (1), employed in a government agency (research) (2), employed in a government agency (professional services) (0), employed in a community mental health/counseling center (0), employed in a hospital/medical center (0), still seeking employment (1), other employment position (0).

Doctoral Degree Graduates: Of those who graduated in the academic year 2000–2001, the following categories and numbers represent the post-graduate activities and employment of doctoral degree graduates: Enrolled in a psychology doctoral program (n/a), enrolled in another graduate/professional program (n/a), enrolled in a post-doctoral residency/fellowship (10), employed in independent practice (0), employed in an academic position at a university (5), employed in an academic position at a 2-year/4-year college (0), employed in other positions at a higher education institution (0), employed in a professional position in a school system (0), employed in business or industry (research/consulting) (1), employed in business or industry (management) (0), employed in a government agency (research) (0), employed in a government agency (professional services) (0), employed in a community mental health/counseling center (0), employed in a hospital/medical center (1), still seeking employment (0), other employment position (1).

Additional Information:

Orientation, Objectives, and Emphasis of Department: The chief goal of graduate education in psychology at Yale University is the training of research workers in academic and other settings who will broaden the basic scientific knowledge on which the discipline of psychology rests. Major emphasis is given to preparation for research; a definite effort is made to give students a background for teaching. The concentration of doctoral training on research and teaching is consistent with a variety of career objectives in addition to traditional academics. The department believes that rigorous and balanced exposure to basic psychology is the best preparation for research careers. The first important aspect of graduate training is advanced study of general psychology, including method and psychological theory. The second is specialized training within a subfield. Third, the student is encouraged to take advantage of opportunities for wider training emphasizing research rather than practice. For the clinical area, research and practica are strongly integrated. Training is geared to the expectation that the majority of students will have research careers.

Special Facilities or Resources: Technical facilities available as adjuncts to research and teaching include university mechanical and electronics shops with full-time instrument-makers; animal colony, animal surgery, and histology laboratory; and special rooms equipped for observation, intercommunication, and recording as required for clinical supervision or testing or for interview training and research in experimental social psychology and also in child development. The department shares the use of the Yale Computer Center (equipped with an IBM 3090, VAX and UNIX workstations). Training is available in a variety of programming languages and simulation techniques. Remote computer terminals are available, and individual microcomputers are commonly located in faculty laboratories. A networked computer laboratory for training students in research on intrapersonal and interpersonal processes is available. Computers are linked together in a local area network (LAN) and laboratory rooms share a common observation corridor equipped with one-way mirrors. The facility allows training in application of emerging research technologies to traditional and innovative research problems.

Information for Students With Physical Disabilities: The University maintains a Resource Office for Students and Employees with Disabilities that facilitates individual accommodations for students and provides access to programs and activities at the University, and there is a University Advisory Committee composed of faculty, students, and staff that makes recommendations to the Provost with respect to policies affecting persons with disabilities. This Committee works with and provides information about student organizations concerned with these issues. Sighted guides, attendants, note-takers, readers and other types of assistance are available from the Resources Office.

Application Information:
Send to: Graduate School, Yale University, Office of Admissions, P.O. Box 208323, New Haven, CT 06520-8323. Students are admitted in the Fall, application deadline January 2. *Fee:* $50. Applications received before December 1st pay $50 for the Application Fee. After December 1st, the application fee will be increased to $80.

Delaware, University of
Department of Psychology
College of Arts and Science
Newark, DE 19716
Telephone: (302) 831-2271
Fax: (302) 831-3645
E-mail: *ehavens@udel.edu*
Web: *http://www.psych.udel.edu/grad/index.html*

Department Established:
1946. Chairperson: Brian Ackerman. Number of Faculty: total–full-time 27; women–full-time 7; minority–full-time 2.

Programs and Degrees Offered:
Listed in the following order: Program area, degree type (T if terminal Master's), number awarded 7/00-6/01. Behavioral neuroscience PhD 3, clinical PhD 7, cognitive PhD, social PhD 1.

APA Accreditation: Clinical PhD: full.

Student Applications/Admissions:
Student Applications
Behavioral neuroscience PhD—Applications 2001–2002, 15. Total applicants accepted 2001–2002, 5. New applicants enrolled 2001–2002, 1. Total enrolled 2001–2002 full-time, 4. Openings 2002–2003, 1. The number of students enrolled full and part-time, who were dismissed or voluntarily withdrew from this program area were 0. *Clinical PhD*—Applications 2001–2002, 127. Total applicants accepted 2001–2002, 5. New applicants enrolled 2001–2002, 4. Total enrolled 2001–2002 full-time, 24. Openings 2002–2003, 5. The number of students enrolled full and part-time, who were dismissed or voluntarily withdrew from this program area were 0. *Cognitive PhD*—Applications 2001–2002, 10. Total applicants accepted 2001–2002, 1. Total enrolled 2001–2002 full-time, 3. Openings 2002–2003, 1. The number of students enrolled full and part-time, who were dismissed or voluntarily withdrew from this program area were 0. *Social PhD*—Applications 2001–2002, 26. Total applicants accepted 2001–2002, 6. New applicants enrolled 2001–2002, 3. Total enrolled 2001–2002 full-time, 8. Openings 2002–2003, 4. The number of students enrolled full and part-time, who were dismissed or voluntarily withdrew from this program area were 0.

Admissions Requirements:
Scores: Entries appear in this order: required test or GPA, minimum score (if required), median score of students entering in 2001–2002. Master's Programs: overall undergraduate GPA no minimum stated. Doctoral Programs: GRE-V 600, 580; GRE-Q 600, 660; GRE-V+Q 1200, 1280; GRE-Analytical no minimum stated; GRE-V+Q+Analytical no minimum stated, 1970; overall undergraduate GPA 3.50, 3.50; last 2 years GPA no minimum stated; psychology GPA no minimum stated; psychology GPA no minimum stated.
Other Criteria: (importance of criteria rated low, medium, or high): GRE/MAT scores high, research experience high, GPA high, letters of recommendation medium, interview medium, statement of goals and objectives medium.

Student Characteristics: The following represents characteristics of students in 2001–2002 in all graduate psychology programs in the department: Female–full-time 28, part-time 0; Male–full-time 17, part-time 0; African American/Black–full-time 1, part-time 0; Hispanic/Latino (a)–full-time 2, part-time 0; Asian/Pacific Islander–full-time 0, part-time 0; American Indian/Alaska Native–full-time 0, part-time 0.

Financial Information/Assistance:
Tuition for Full-Time Study: No information provided.

Financial Assistance:
First Year Students: No information provided.
Advanced Students: No information provided.
Contact Information: For information on financial assistance, contact: Brian P. Ackerman.

Internships/Practica: A wide range of practica experiences are available for clinical graduate students.

Housing and Day Care: On-campus housing and day care facilities are available.

Employment of Department Graduates:
Master's Degree Graduates: Of those who graduated in the academic year 2000–2001, the following categories and numbers represent the post-graduate activities and employment of master's degree graduates: Enrolled in a post-doctoral residency/fellowship (n/a), employed in independent practice (n/a).
Doctoral Degree Graduates: Of those who graduated in the academic year 2000–2001, the following categories and numbers represent the post-graduate activities and employment of doctoral degree graduates: Enrolled in a psychology doctoral program (n/a), enrolled in another graduate/professional program (n/a).

Additional Information:
Orientation, Objectives, and Emphasis of Department: The department fosters a scientific approach to all areas of psychology. The training is organized around clinical, cognitive, behavioral neuroscience, and social areas, as well as an integrative developmental focus that cuts across area. All first-year students are required to complete first and second year research projects as well as take seminars in their program area of study. In the third and fourth year students take additional seminars, take a comprehensive qualifying exam or prepare a comprehensive paper and prepare dissertation proposals. Clinical students also participate in the training of practice skills. Beyond the first year, students work out their own research programs with faculty advice. The goal of this training is to prepare students to function as scientists and teachers in academic, applied, and clinical settings. Major current research interests in these areas are as follows: (1) clinical: evaluation of therapy, social development of children, community mental health, theory of emotions, communication of emotions, organic brain syndromes, family therapy, sex roles, sensation seeking, and sexuality; (2) cognitive: artificial intelligence, attention,

pattern recognition, psycholinguistics, problem solving, visual information processing, memory, and cognitive development; (3) behavioral neuroscience: neuroanatomy, central activation and inhibition, neurochemistry, and neural coding; and (4) social: interpersonal conflict, racism, helping behavior, nonverbal communications, social power and influence, and decision-making. The program is flexible and encourages each student to develop his or her unique interests. The clinical program emphasizes the integration of theory, research, and practice. Special programs are available in child-clinical and in family intervention through a family systems approach.

Special Facilities or Resources: The department's mainframe computing needs are met by several VAX UNIX timesharing systems and a large IBM VM/CMS timesharing system. The VAX systems are used primarily for cognitive science model simulations. The IBM system is used for statistical analysis and word processing. In addition, the department possesses a large assortment of DEC, Apple, and IBM minicomputers and microcomputers that are used for on-line control of experiments for human and animal subjects, as well as for data analysis, cognitive science modeling and word processing. The laboratories are well equipped with videotape, acoustic, reaction time, and physiological recording systems. The department operates the Psychological Services Training Center for practicum training in clinical psychology.

Application Information:
Send to: Office of Graduate Studies, 234 Hullihen Hall, University of Delaware, Newark, DE 19716. Students are admitted in the Fall, application deadline January 7. *Fee:* $50. The fee may be waived or deferred by the Office of the Department of Psychology.

American University
Department of Psychology
CAS
321 Asbury
Washington, DC 20016-8062
Telephone: (202) 885-1710
Fax: (202) 885-1023
E-mail: *psychology@american.edu*
Web: *http://www.american.edu/cas/department_psychology.*

Department Established:
1929. Chairperson: Anthony L. Riley. Number of Faculty: total–full-time 15, part-time 1; women–full-time 4; minority–full-time 2.

Programs and Degrees Offered:
Listed in the following order: Program area, degree type (T if terminal Master's), number awarded 7/00-6/01. Behavioral neuroscience PhD 1, behavioral neuroscience MA (T), clinical PhD 5, general MA (T) 11, personality/social MA (T).

APA Accreditation: Clinical PhD: full.

Student Applications/Admissions:
Student Applications
Behavioral neuroscience PhD—Applications 2001–2002, 23. Total applicants accepted 2001–2002, 9. New applicants enrolled 2001–2002, 6. Total enrolled 2001–2002 full-time, 19, part-time, 4. Openings 2002–2003, 5. The Median number of years required for completion of a degree are 8. The number of students enrolled full and part-time, who were dismissed or voluntarily withdrew from this program area were 1. *Behavioral neuroscience MA. Clinical PhD*—Applications 2001–2002, 266. Total applicants accepted 2001–2002, 13. New applicants enrolled 2001–2002, 7. Total enrolled 2001–2002 full-time, 40, part-time, 5. Openings 2002–2003, 7. The Median number of years required for completion of a degree are 8. The number of students enrolled full and part-time, who were dismissed or voluntarily withdrew from this program area were 0. *General MA*—Applications 2001–2002, 95. Total applicants accepted 2001–2002, 59. New applicants enrolled 2001–2002, 17. Total enrolled 2001–2002 full-time, 27, part-time, 11. Openings 2002–2003, 20. The Median number of years required for completion of a degree are 2. The number of students enrolled full and part-time, who were dismissed or voluntarily withdrew from this program area were 1. *Personality/social MA.*

Admissions Requirements:
Scores: Entries appear in this order: required test or GPA, minimum score (if required), median score of students entering in 2001–2002. Master's Programs: GRE-V no minimum stated, 555; GRE-Q no minimum stated, 620; GRE-Analytical no minimum stated, 645; overall undergraduate GPA no minimum stated, 3.49. Doctoral Programs: GRE-V no minimum stated, 563; GRE-Q no minimum stated, 630; GRE-Analytical no minimum stated, 664; GRE-Subject(Psych) no minimum

stated, 648; overall undergraduate GPA no minimum stated, 3.54; last 2 years GPA no minimum stated; psychology GPA no minimum stated; psychology GPA no minimum stated.
Other Criteria: (importance of criteria rated low, medium, or high): GRE/MAT scores high, research experience high, work experience medium, clinically related public service medium, GPA high, letters of recommendation high, interview high, statement of goals and objectives high. Interview, clinically related public service not required for Behavioral Neuroscience program.

Student Characteristics: The following represents characteristics of students in 2001–2002 in all graduate psychology programs in the department: Female–full-time 72, part-time 18; Male–full-time 14, part-time 2; African American/Black–full-time 4, part-time 3; Hispanic/Latino (a)–full-time 3, part-time 1; Asian/Pacific Islander–full-time 7, part-time 3; American Indian/Alaska Native–full-time 0, part-time 0; Multi-ethnic–full-time 0, part-time 2; students subject to the Americans with Disabilities Act–full-time 0, part-time 0.

Financial Information/Assistance:
Tuition for Full-Time Study: *Master's:* State residents $827 per credit hour; nonstate residents: $827 per credit hour. *Doctoral:* State residents: $827 per credit hour; nonstate residents: $827 per credit hour.

Financial Assistance:
First Year Students: Teaching assistantships available for first-year. Average amount paid per academic year: $9,500. Average number of hours worked per week: 20. Apply by 1/1. Tuition remission given: full.

Advanced Students: Teaching assistantships available for advanced students. Average amount paid per academic year: $9,500. Average number of hours worked per week: 20. Apply by 1/1. Tuition remission given: full.

Contact Information: Of all students currently enrolled full-time, 20% benefitted from one or more of the listed financial assistance programs. For information on financial assistance, contact: Graduate Admissions.

Internships/Practica: The greater Washington, DC metropolitan area provides a wealth of applied and research resources to complement our students' work in the classroom and faculty laboratories. These include the university's Counseling Center, local hospitals (Children's, St. Elizabeth's, Walter Reed, Georgetown University, National Rehabilitation), the Kennedy Institute, Gallaudet University, the NIH (NIMH, NINDS, NIA, NCI), the National Zoo, and the national offices of many agencies (e.g., APA, APS, NAMI). Field work and short-term internships are available in many city, county, and private organizations, such as the Alexandria, VA Community Mental Health Center, the Montgomery County, MD Department of Addiction, Victim, and Mental Health Services, the DC Rape Crisis Center, and Big Brothers. MA and PhD students can also earn degree credit while obtaining practical experience working in the private sector with autistic children, teaching self-management skills, volunteering at shelters for battered women or the homeless, or assisting at a psychologist's

131

private practice. Many of these positions sometimes can provide funding. Externships offering practica in Rogerian, behavioral, and psychodynamic therapy are available for clinical PhD students either through the department or through clinical adjuncts or other local institutions. For those doctoral students for whom a professional internship is required prior to graduation, 7 applied in 2000–2001. Of those who applied, 7 were placed in internships listed by the Association of Psychology Postdoctoral and Internship Programs (APPIC); 7 were placed in APA accredited internships.

Housing and Day Care: On-campus housing and day care facilities are available.

Employment of Department Graduates:

Master's Degree Graduates: Of those who graduated in the academic year 2000–2001, the following categories and numbers represent the post-graduate activities and employment of master's degree graduates: Enrolled in a post-doctoral residency/fellowship (n/a), employed in independent practice (n/a).

Doctoral Degree Graduates: Of those who graduated in the academic year 2000–2001, the following categories and numbers represent the post-graduate activities and employment of doctoral degree graduates: Enrolled in a psychology doctoral program (n/a), enrolled in another graduate/professional program (n/a).

Additional Information:

Orientation, Objectives, and Emphasis of Department: The psychology department of American University offers two graduate programs. The PhD program has separate tracks in clinical psychology and behavioral neuroscience. The MA program has tracks in general, personality/social, and biological/experimental psychology. The doctoral program in clinical psychology trains psychologists to do therapy, assessment, research, university teaching, and consultation. The theoretical orientation is eclectic and follows the Boulder scientist-practitioner model. The doctoral program in behavioral neuroscience/experimental psychology involves intensive training in both pure and applied research settings. Students can work in laboratories exploring conditioning and learning, the experimental analysis of behavior, cognition and memory, physiological psychology, neuropsychology, and neuropharmacology. Study at the master's level provides the basis for further doctoral-level work and prepares students for immediate employment in a variety of careers including clinical-medical research, teaching, counseling and policy formulation, law enforcement, and government work. Our graduate students are expected to be professional, ethical, committed, full-time members of our psychology community. This concept of community implies an atmosphere of mutual support rather than competition, communication rather than isolation, and stimulation rather than disinterest.

Special Facilities or Resources: Nine well-equipped laboratories investigate conditioning and learning, clinical and experimental neuropsychology, human cognition and memory, neuropharmacology, physiological psychology, rodent olfaction, social behavior, psychopathology, depression, anxiety disorders, emotion, eating disorders, parent-child interaction, addictive behavior, child development, and various other issues in applied and experimental psychology. In addition, students train in the Department's cognitive behavioral training clinic. Close working relationships with laboratories at the National Institutes of Health, the Walter

Reed Army Institutes of Research, and Georgetown University's Hospital and School of Medicine allow additional training opportunities. The Washington Research Library Consortium (WRLC) provides access to six local college and university libraries in addition to AU's Bender Library, The National Library of Medicine, and the Library of Congress. AU's computing center supports IBM, Macintosh, and Unix systems, has dial-in access, and maintains fifteen computing labs. EagleNet, a campus-wide network service runs on Novell Netware 4.x and 5.0. Applications include WordPerfect, Quattro Pro, Presentations, Paradox, SAS, SPSS, Photoshop, Netscape, and e-mail as well as many Internet applications and services (Usenet newsgroups, electronic discussion lists-Listserv, file transfer, FTP, the ALADIN online catalog of the WRLC).

Application Information:
Send to: Office of Graduate Affairs and Admissions, American University, Washington, DC 20016-8111. Students are admitted in the Fall, application deadline 1/1,1/1,3/1. Fall deadlines — Clinical, January 1; Behavioral Neuroscience, January 1; MA, March 1. *Fee:* $50. The online application free is $50.00. The fee for paper mailed applications is $80.00.

Gallaudet University
Department of Psychology
College of Liberal Arts, Sciences & Technologies
800 Florida Avenue, N.E.
Washington, DC 20002
Telephone: (202) 651-5540
Fax: (202) 651-5747
E-mail: *Virginia.Gutman@gallaudet.edu*
Web: *http://www.gallaudet.edu*

Department Established:
1955. Chairperson: Virginia Gutman, Ph.D. Number of Faculty: total–full-time 16, part-time 3; women–full-time 12, part-time 1; minority–full-time 5; faculty subject to the Americans with Disabilities Act 3.

Programs and Degrees Offered:
Listed in the following order: Program area, degree type (T if terminal Master's), number awarded 7/00-6/01. Clinical PhD 9, school EdS 6.

APA Accreditation: Clinical PhD: full.

Student Applications/Admissions:
Student Applications

Clinical PhD—Applications 2001–2002, 21. Total applicants accepted 2001–2002, 8. New applicants enrolled 2001–2002, 7. Total enrolled 2001–2002 full-time, 30. Openings 2002–2003, 6. The Median number of years required for completion of a degree are 6. The number of students enrolled full and part-time, who were dismissed or voluntarily withdrew from this program area were 2. *School EdS*—Applications 2001–

2002, 21. Total applicants accepted 2001–2002, 8. New applicants enrolled 2001–2002, 7. Total enrolled 2001–2002 full-time, 18. Openings 2002–2003, 10. The Median number of years required for completion of a degree are 3. The number of students enrolled full and part-time, who were dismissed or voluntarily withdrew from this program area were 1.

Admissions Requirements:

Scores: Entries appear in this order: required test or GPA, minimum score (if required), median score of students entering in 2001–2002. Master's Programs: GRE-V no minimum stated; GRE-Q no minimum stated; GRE-Analytical no minimum stated; overall undergraduate GPA 3.0. Occasionally, applicants with a GPA lower than 3.0 may be admitted conditionally. Doctoral Programs: GRE-V no minimum stated, 450; GRE-Q no minimum stated, 540; GRE-Analytical no minimum stated, 635; overall undergraduate GPA no minimum stated, 3.3 ; last 2 years GPA no minimum stated; psychology GPA no minimum stated, 3.60; psychology GPA no minimum stated. Occasionally, students with GPA's below this level may be admitted conditionally. A summer HCOP program is available for otherwise qualified students who need to improve quantitative or writing skills prior to matriculation.

Other Criteria: (importance of criteria rated low, medium, or high): GRE/MAT scores medium, research experience medium, work experience high, extracurricular activity low, clinically related public service high, GPA high, letters of recommendation high, interview high, statement of goals and objectives high, Interest in deafness high, Varies per program. Students with little experience in deafness or sign language may be required to take a summer immersion program prior to enrolling.

Student Characteristics: The following represents characteristics of students in 2001–2002 in all graduate psychology programs in the department: Female–full-time 44, part-time 0; Male–full-time 10, part-time 0; African American/Black–full-time 3, part-time 0; Hispanic/Latino (a)–full-time 2, part-time 0; Asian/Pacific Islander–full-time 2, part-time 0; American Indian/Alaska Native–full-time 0, part-time 0; Multi-ethnic–full-time 1, students subject to the Americans with Disabilities Act–full-time 12.

Financial Information/Assistance:

Tuition for Full-Time Study: *Master's:* State residents per academic year $8,660, $433 per credit hour; nonstate residents: per academic year $8,660, $433 per credit hour. *Doctoral:* State residents: per academic year $8,660, $433 per credit hour; nonstate residents: per academic year $8,660, $433 per credit hour.

Financial Assistance:

First Year Students: Teaching assistantships available for first-year. Average number of hours worked per week: 10. Research assistantships available for first-year. Average number of hours worked per week: 10. Fellowships and scholarships available for first-year. Tuition remission given: partial.

Advanced Students: Teaching assistantships available for advanced students. Average number of hours worked per week: 10. Research assistantships available for advanced students. Average number of hours worked per week: 10. Fellowships and scholarships available for advanced students. Tuition remission given: partial.

Contact Information: Of all students currently enrolled full-time, 90% benefitted from one or more of the listed financial assistance programs. For information on financial assistance, contact: Office of Financial Aid, or the Graduate School, Gallaudet University. Assistantship amounts and time commitments vary by program.

Internships/Practica: Students in the Psy S which includes the M.A. as a non-terminal degree, begin with a practicum experience in their first semester, visiting and observing school programs as part of their Introduction to School Psychology course. During their second semester they are involved in Practicum I (3 credit course), which involves closely supervised practicum doing cognitive assessments of deaf and hearing children (if appropriate) at laboratory schools on campus and a D.C. neighborhood school. Practicum II (3 credits) is taken the third semester and requires two full days per week for a minimum of 14 weeks in which they work with a school psychologist in the Washington Metropolitan areas doing comprehensive assessments, some counseling, if opportunities are available, and observation on a limited basis during their fourth semester (an option). The third year (semesters 5 and 6) are spent in a full time internship in a school program approved by the program. These internships are typically located in both residential schools for the deaf as well as public school systems serving main streamed deaf youngsters. Internship sites are located in all parts of the United States. Students in the clinical psychology program begin practicum in their second year, conducting psychological assessments and psychotherapy at the Gallaudet University Mental Health Center. Advanced students can apply for any of the more than 80 externships available in the Washington, DC area. These externships allow students to work with a wide variety of settings and populations in assessment, psychotherapy, and other psychological interventions. Experiences with both deaf and hearing clients are available. The predoctoral internship can be taken in any program approved by the faculty. For those doctoral students for whom a professional internship is required prior to graduation, 2 applied in 2000–2001. Of those who applied, 2 were placed in internships listed by the Association of Psychology Postdoctoral and Internship Programs (APPIC); 2 were placed in APA accredited internships.

Housing and Day Care: On-campus housing and day care facilities are available.

Employment of Department Graduates:

Master's Degree Graduates: Of those who graduated in the academic year 2000–2001, the following categories and numbers represent the post-graduate activities and employment of master's degree graduates: Enrolled in a post-doctoral residency/fellowship (n/a), employed in independent practice (n/a).

Doctoral Degree Graduates: Of those who graduated in the academic year 2000–2001, the following categories and numbers represent the post-graduate activities and employment of doctoral degree graduates: Enrolled in a psychology doctoral program (n/a), enrolled in another graduate/professional program (n/a), enrolled in a post-doctoral residency/fellowship (5), employed in independent practice (1), employed in a community mental health/counseling center (3), employed in a hospital/medical center (1).

Additional Information:

Orientation, Objectives, and Emphasis of Department: The Psychology department at Gallaudet University offers graduate programs in school psychology and clinical psychology. The school psychology program awards a nonterminal Master of Arts degree in developmental psychology plus a Specialist in School Psychology degree with specialization in deafness. The clinical psychology program is a scholar-practitioner model PhD program, and trains generalist clinical psychologists to work with deaf, hard-of-hearing, and hearing populations. The school psychology program is both NCATE/NASP and NASDTEC-approved, and leads to certification as a school psychologist in the District of Columbia and approximately 24 states with reciprocity of certification. The full-time, three-year program requires completion of at least 72 graduate semester hours, including a one-year internship. The APA accredited clinical psychology program is a five-year program providing balanced training in research and clinical skills with a variety of age groups, including deaf and hard-of-hearing children, adults, and older adults. The fifth year is designed as a full-time clinical psychology internship. A research-based dissertation is required.

Special Facilities or Resources: Gallaudet University is an internationally recognized center for research and training in areas related to deafness. With a student body of approximately 2100, the university trains deaf and hearing students in a variety of fields at the bachelor, master's, and doctoral levels. Gallaudet programs are located on historic Kendall Green, in northeast Washington, DC near the US Capitol, the Library of Congress, and the Smithsonian Institute. Also located on the campus are the Gallaudet University Mental Health Center, the Kendall Demonstration Elementary School, the Model Secondary School for the Deaf, the Gallaudet Research Institute, the Kellogg Conference Center, and the Merrill Learning Center, which contains the largest collection of references on deafness in the world. Gallaudet faculty, including both deaf and hearing individuals, possess a unique combination of scholarly activity in their respective disciplines and experience with deaf clients and research on deafness. The University is committed to a working model of a bilingual (American Sign Language and English), multicultural community, where deaf, hard of hearing, and hearing people can work together without communication barriers. Gallaudet University is accredited by the Middle States Association of Colleges and Secondary Schools and is a member of the Consortium of Universities of the Washington Metropolitan Area.

Information for Students With Physical Disabilities: At Gallaudet University, accessiblity is a high priority. All faculty, staff, and students are expected to develop sign language skills. Sign language interpreting services are available as needed. Real-time captioning is used at a number of campus events, as are audio loop systems. All classroom buildings and residence halls are wheelchair accessible.

Application Information:

Send to: Office of Graduate Admissions, Gallaudet University, 800 Florida Ave. N.E., Washington, DC 20002. Students are admitted in the Fall, application deadline 2/1; 2/15. 2/1 for Clinical Psy; 2/15 for School Psy. *Fee:* $50.

George Washington University
Center for Professional Psychology, PsyD Program in Clinical Psychology
Columbian College of Arts and Sciences
2300 M Street, N.W., Suite 910
Washington, DC 20037
Telephone: (202) 496-6260
Fax: (202) 496-6263
E-mail: *psyd@gwu.edu*
Web: *http://www.gwu.edu/~psyd*

Department Established:

1996. Director: James C. Miller, PhD. Number of Faculty: total–full-time 2, part-time 11.

Programs and Degrees Offered:

Listed in the following order: Program area, degree type (T if terminal Master's), number awarded 7/00-6/01. Clinical PsyD.

APA Accreditation: Clinical PsyD: full.

medians V: 548
Q: 588
A: 592
GPA: 3.26

Student Applications/Admissions:

Student Applications

Clinical PsyD—Applications 2001–2002, 300. Total applicants accepted 2001–2002, 50. New applicants enrolled 2001–2002, 39. Total enrolled 2001–2002 full-time, 68, part-time, 2. Openings 2002–2003, 43.

Admissions Requirements:

Scores: Entries appear in this order: required test or GPA, minimum score (if required), median score of students entering in 2001–2002. Doctoral Programs: GRE-V no minimum stated, 548; GRE-Q no minimum stated, 588; GRE-V+Q no minimum stated; GRE-Analytical no minimum stated, 592; GRE-V+Q+Analytical no minimum stated; overall undergraduate GPA no minimum stated, 3.26; last 2 years GPA no minimum stated; psychology GPA no minimum stated; psychology GPA no minimum stated.

Other Criteria: (importance of criteria rated low, medium, or high): GRE/MAT scores medium, research experience medium, work experience medium, clinically related public service high, GPA medium, letters of recommendation high, interview high, statement of goals and objectives high.

Student Characteristics: The following represents characteristics of students in 2001–2002 in all graduate psychology programs in the department: Female–full-time 29, part-time 0; Male–full-time 10, part-time 0; African American/Black–full-time 3, part-time 0; Hispanic/Latino (a)–full-time 3, part-time 0; Asian/Pacific Islander–full-time 2, part-time 0; American Indian/Alaska Native–full-time 0, part-time 0.

Financial Information/Assistance:

Tuition for Full-Time Study: *Doctoral:* State residents: $742 per credit hour; nonstate residents: $742 per credit hour.

Financial Assistance:

First Year Students: Fellowships and scholarships available for first-year. Average amount paid per academic year: $6,600. Average number of hours worked per week: 0. Apply by none.

Advanced Students: Fellowships and scholarships available for advanced students. Average amount paid per academic year: $6,600. Average number of hours worked per week: 0. Apply by none.

Contact Information: Of all students currently enrolled full-time, 30% benefitted from one or more of the listed financial assistance programs. For information on financial assistance, contact: PsyD Program for fellowships, Financial Aid Office for loans.

Internships/Practica: The principal practicum setup is Center Clinic, our framing clinic run by faculty, clinical faculty, and students under supervision. We have Clinic Affiliate Settings who provide patients and clinical opportunities under our supervision. Special interests and needs as served by independent Externship settings. For those doctoral students for whom a professional internship is required prior to graduation, 44 applied in 2000–2001. Of those who applied, 34 were placed in internships listed by the Association of Psychology Postdoctoral and Internship Programs (APPIC); 16 were placed in APA accredited internships.

Housing and Day Care: No on-campus housing and day care facilities are available.

Employment of Department Graduates:
Master's Degree Graduates: Of those who graduated in the academic year 2000–2001, the following categories and numbers represent the post-graduate activities and employment of master's degree graduates: Enrolled in a post-doctoral residency/fellowship (n/a), employed in independent practice (n/a).
Doctoral Degree Graduates: Of those who graduated in the academic year 2000–2001, the following categories and numbers represent the post-graduate activities and employment of doctoral degree graduates: Enrolled in a psychology doctoral program (n/a), enrolled in another graduate/professional program (n/a).

Additional Information:
Orientation, Objectives, and Emphasis of Department: The George Washington University PsyD program in Clinical Psychology has a broadly-based psychodynamic orientation. After completing the core curriculum in the first year, students choose from among four advanced tracks: (a) psychodynamic psychotherapy, (b) group and community intervention, (c) child and family therapy, and (d) diagnostic assessment. Students choose major and minor areas of concentration, with the goal of obtaining advanced, in-depth training in their specialties. The principal emphasis from the first semester of the program is on high-quality clinical training. For all three years of class work students participate in case seminars, practica, and externships, culminating in a fourth-year internship. In the third year the student writes a major area paper on a clinical topic of interest. Additional emphases of the program include: group and organizational dynamics, psychodynamic theory, psychodynamic child development and intervention, psychology and law, and comprehensive (biopsychosocial) diagnosis.

Special Facilities or Resources: On 08-07-97 our PsyD Program moved into a special facility designed for our needs, with all faculty and program offices, classrooms, training clinics, lounges, and study areas in one location.

Information for Students With Physical Disabilities: Our building is fully disability equipped. Also, our Office of Disabled Services provides a range of services for the disabled.

Application Information:
Send to: Graduate Admissions, Columbian School of Arts and Sciences, The George Washington University, 801 22nd St. NW, Suite 107, Washington DC 20052, 202-994-6211, fax: 202-994-6213, e-mail: asgrad@acad.ccgs.gwu.edu. Students are admitted in the Winter, application deadline January 15. *Fee:* $55.

George Washington University
Department of Psychology
2125 G Street, N.W.
Washington, DC 20052
Telephone: (202) 994-6320
Fax: (202) 994-1602
E-mail: *psych@gwu.edu*
Web: *http://www.gwu.edu/~psycdept*

Department Established:
1922. Chairperson: Elliot Hirshman. Number of Faculty: total–full-time 17, part-time 3; women–full-time 8, part-time 3; minority–full-time 5.

Programs and Degrees Offered:
Listed in the following order: Program area, degree type (T if terminal Master's), number awarded 7/00-6/01. Applied Social/I/O PhD 6, clinical PhD 11, cognitive neuropsychology PhD 1.

APA Accreditation: Clinical PhD: full.

(handwritten: V: 570, Q: 650 >1220, A: 620, GPA: 3.80)

Student Applications/Admissions:
Student Applications
Applied Social/I/O PhD—Applications 2001–2002, 121. Total applicants accepted 2001–2002, 5. New applicants enrolled 2001–2002, 2. Total enrolled 2001–2002 full-time, 12. Openings 2002–2003, 3. The Median number of years required for completion of a degree are 6. *Clinical PhD*—Applications 2001–2002, 195. Total applicants accepted 2001–2002, 12. New applicants enrolled 2001–2002, 7. Total enrolled 2001–2002 full-time, 39. Openings 2002–2003, 6. The Median number of years required for completion of a degree are 6. *Cognitive neuropsychology PhD*—Applications 2001–2002, 45. Total applicants accepted 2001–2002, 4. New applicants enrolled 2001–2002, 2. Total enrolled 2001–2002 full-time, 8. Openings 2002–2003, 2. The Median number of years required for completion of a degree are 7.

Admissions Requirements:
Scores: Entries appear in this order: required test or GPA, minimum score (if required), median score of students entering in 2001–2002. Doctoral Programs: GRE-V no minimum stated, 570; GRE-Q no minimum stated, 650; GRE-Analytical no minimum stated, 620; overall undergraduate GPA no minimum stated, 3.80; last 2 years GPA no minimum stated; psychology GPA no minimum stated; psychology GPA no minimum stated.
Other Criteria: (importance of criteria rated low, medium, or high): GRE/MAT scores medium, research experience high, work experience medium, extracurricular activity medium, clinically related public service medium, GPA medium, letters of recommendation high, interview high, statement of goals

and objectives high. Criteria mainly for clinical psychology PhD.

Student Characteristics: The following represents characteristics of students in 2001–2002 in all graduate psychology programs in the department: Female–full-time 66, part-time 0; Male–full-time 14, part-time 0; African American/Black–full-time 6, part-time 0; Hispanic/Latino (a)–full-time 6, part-time 0; Asian/Pacific Islander–full-time 8, part-time 0; American Indian/Alaska Native–full-time 0, part-time 0; students subject to the Americans with Disabilities Act–full-time 1.

Financial Information/Assistance:

Tuition for Full-Time Study: *Doctoral:* State residents: $810 per credit hour; nonstate residents: $810 per credit hour.

Financial Assistance:

First Year Students: Teaching assistantships available for first-year. Tuition remission given: partial. Research assistantships available for first-year. Fellowships and scholarships available for first-year. Tuition remission given: partial.

Advanced Students: Teaching assistantships available for advanced students. Tuition remission given: partial. Research assistantships available for advanced students. Tuition remission given: partial. Fellowships and scholarships available for advanced students. Tuition remission given: partial.

Contact Information: Of all students currently enrolled full-time, 70% benefitted from one or more of the listed financial assistance programs. For information on financial assistance, contact: Graduate School and Department of Psychology.

Internships/Practica: There is a wide variety of placements available in the DC Metro area. Placements are required part of training in the clinical and applied social organization programs. For those doctoral students for whom a professional internship is required prior to graduation, 7 applied in 2000–2001. Of those who applied, 7 were placed in internships listed by the Association of Psychology Postdoctoral and Internship Programs (APPIC); 7 were placed in APA accredited internships.

Housing and Day Care: No on-campus housing and day care facilities are available.

Employment of Department Graduates:

Master's Degree Graduates: Of those who graduated in the academic year 2000–2001, the following categories and numbers represent the post-graduate activities and employment of master's degree graduates: Enrolled in a post-doctoral residency/fellowship (n/a), employed in independent practice (n/a).

Doctoral Degree Graduates: Of those who graduated in the academic year 2000–2001, the following categories and numbers represent the post-graduate activities and employment of doctoral degree graduates: Enrolled in a psychology doctoral program (n/a), enrolled in another graduate/professional program (n/a), enrolled in a post-doctoral residency/fellowship (5), employed in independent practice (0), employed in an academic position at a university (1), employed in business or industry (research/consulting) (2), employed in a government agency (research) (1).

Additional Information:

Orientation, Objectives, and Emphasis of Department: The department provides training in the basic science of psychology for each of its graduate programs. Specialized training is offered in three program areas: applied social-industrial/organizational, clinical, and cognitive neuropsychology. Three broad research areas connect the programs: health psychology, organizational effectiveness, and neuropsychology. The applied social program focuses on theory and methods of addressing current social problems such as in health care, education, and the prevention of high risk social behaviors. The clinical program is an APA-approved program emphasizing both the basic science and applied aspects of clinical psychology, via a bio/behavioral emphasis. The cognitive neuropsychology program focuses on cognition, learning, and memory with emphasis on the psychobiological determinants of these functions. The training in each program addresses both scientific and professional objectives: students are trained for careers in basic research, applied research, and professional practice.

Special Facilities or Resources: Excellent on-campus computer facilities; laboratories for child study, group studies, and small animal research. Convenient access to staff, libraries, and facilities at national health and mental health institutes (NIH, NIMH, NIAAA); close connections with national organizations concerned with personnel assessment and human resource development (US ARI, OPM); strong affiliations with organizations doing research on major social problems (private corporations and government organizations such as GAO, NIMH); Mental Health Training Centers for Clinical Students (3 on campus). See Home Page for information.

Application Information:
Send to: Graduate School, CSAS, George Washington University, Washington, DC 20052. Students are admitted in the Fall, application deadline 12/15 clin. Cognitive-Neuropsychology and Applied Social/I/O-February 1. *Fee:* $65.

Georgetown University
Department of Psychology
Arts and Sciences
306A White Gravenor Building
Washington, DC 20057
Telephone: (202) 687-4042
Fax: (202) 687-6050
E-mail: *lhr@georgetown.edu*
Web: *http://www.georgetown.edu/department/psychology*

V+Q – 1300
GRE psych – 600
GPA – 3.50

Department Established:
1962. Chairperson: Deborah Phillips. Number of Faculty: total–full-time 15, part-time 6; women–full-time 7, part-time 3; minority–full-time 1.

Programs and Degrees Offered:
Listed in the following order: Program area, degree type (T if terminal Master's), number awarded 7/00-6/01. Cognitive Neuroscience PhD, Human Development and Public Policy PhD.

Student Applications/Admissions:
Student Applications
Cognitive Neuroscience PhD Openings 2002–2003, 2. *Human Development and Public Policy PhD*—Applications 2001–2002, 0. Openings 2002–2003, 2.

Admissions Requirements:

Scores: Entries appear in this order: required test or GPA, minimum score (if required), median score of students entering in 2001–2002. Doctoral Programs: GRE-V no minimum stated; GRE-Q no minimum stated; GRE-V+Q 1300; GRE-Analytical no minimum stated; GRE-V+Q+Analytical no minimum stated; GRE-Subject(Psych) 600; overall undergraduate GPA 3.50; last 2 years GPA no minimum stated; psychology GPA no minimum stated; psychology GPA no minimum stated. Applicants should have at least scored 1300 on the GRE (Verbal and Quantitative OR Verbal and Analytic)

Other Criteria: (importance of criteria rated low, medium, or high): GRE/MAT scores high, research experience high, work experience low, extracurricular activity low, clinically related public service low, GPA high, letters of recommendation high, interview high, statement of goals and objectives high, Writing Sample high. Statement of Goals and Objectives should include a 750 word statement of academic, professional, and personal goals, and a discussion of how graduate school in Developmental Science will help you to achieve these goals. The statement should also specify your interest in one of the two areas of concentration and particular faculty with whom you would like to work. Writing sample, typically chosen from undergraduate work, which best reflects your abilities and interests.

Student Characteristics: The following represents characteristics of students in 2001–2002 in all graduate psychology programs in the department: Female–full-time 0, part-time 0; Male–full-time 0, part-time 0; African American/Black–full-time 0, part-time 0; Hispanic/Latino (a)–full-time 0, part-time 0; Asian/Pacific Islander–full-time 0, part-time 0; American Indian/Alaska Native–full-time 0, part-time 0.

Financial Information/Assistance:

Tuition for Full-Time Study: *Doctoral:* State residents: per academic year $23,832; nonstate residents: per academic year $23,832.

Financial Assistance:

First Year Students: Teaching assistantships available for first-year. Average amount paid per academic year: $14,000. Average number of hours worked per week: 15. Tuition remission given: full.

Advanced Students: Teaching assistantships available for advanced students. Average amount paid per academic year: $14,000. Average number of hours worked per week: 15. Tuition remission given: full.

Contact Information: For information on financial assistance, contact: http://www.georgetown.edu/grad/prospective/admissions.

Internships/Practica: No information provided.

Housing and Day Care: On-campus housing and day care facilities are available.

Employment of Department Graduates:

Master's Degree Graduates: Of those who graduated in the academic year 2000–2001, the following categories and numbers represent the post-graduate activities and employment of master's degree graduates: Enrolled in a post-doctoral residency/fellowship (n/a), employed in independent practice (n/a).

Doctoral Degree Graduates: Of those who graduated in the academic year 2000–2001, the following categories and numbers represent the post-graduate activities and employment of doctoral degree graduates: Enrolled in a psychology doctoral program (n/a), enrolled in another graduate/professional program (n/a).

Additional Information:

Orientation, Objectives, and Emphasis of Department: The new graduate program provides an interdisciplinary education in the sciences that concern themselves with the processes and contexts of development across the lifespan. It is explicitly designed to offer students rigorous training in the range of theories and methods that characterize the developmental sciences and enable them to place the study of development into broader contexts - biological, familial, social, cultural, economic, historical, political - from which the field draws its societal applications. Students will be prepared for a wide variety of post-degree career options ranging from traditional academic jobs to policy positions, positions in non-profit organizations, and positions in non-academic research organizations.

Special Facilities or Resources: The psychology department includes an observational laboratory facility and the medical school affords the opportunity to conduct research using MRI technology. Graduate students will have office space in a graduate student suite or faculty laboratory space.

Information for Students With Physical Disabilities: On-campus housing is provided for students with physical disabilities.

Application Information:

Send to: Deborah A. Phillips, Professor and Chair, Department of Psychology, 306A White-Gravenor, Georgetown University, 37th and O Sts., NW, Washington DC 20057. Students are admitted in the Fall, application deadline December 31. *Fee:* $65.

Howard University
Department of Psychology
The Graduate School
525 Bryant Street, N.W.
Washington, DC 20059
Telephone: (202) 806-6805
Fax: (202) 806-4873
E-mail: *aroberts@howard.edu*
Web: *http://www.howard.edu*

Department Established:

1928. Chairperson: Albert Roberts. Number of Faculty: total–full-time 21, part-time 2; women–full-time 9, part-time 2; minority–full-time 13, part-time 2.

Programs and Degrees Offered:

Listed in the following order: Program area, degree type (T if terminal Master's), number awarded 7/00-6/01. Clinical PhD 7, developmental PhD 2, neuropsychology PhD 1, personality PhD 1, social PhD.

APA Accreditation: Clinical PhD: full.

Student Applications/Admissions:

Student Applications

Clinical PhD—Applications 2001–2002, 110. Total applicants accepted 2001–2002, 6. New applicants enrolled 2001–2002, 6. Total enrolled 2001–2002 full-time, 43, part-time, 5. Openings 2002–2003, 5. The number of students enrolled full and part-time, who were dismissed or voluntarily withdrew from this program area were 1. Developmental PhD—Applications 2001–2002, 24. Total applicants accepted 2001–2002, 6. New applicants enrolled 2001–2002, 3. Total enrolled 2001–2002 full-time, 25, part-time, 6. Openings 2002–2003, 4. The Median number of years required for completion of a degree are 5. The number of students enrolled full and part-time, who were dismissed or voluntarily withdrew from this program area were 0. Neuropsychology PhD—Applications 2001–2002, 7. Total applicants accepted 2001–2002, 2. New applicants enrolled 2001–2002, 2. Total enrolled 2001–2002 full-time, 7, part-time, 2. Openings 2002–2003, 3. The Median number of years required for completion of a degree are 5. The number of students enrolled full and part-time, who were dismissed or voluntarily withdrew from this program area were 0. Personality PhD—Applications 2001–2002, 10. Total applicants accepted 2001–2002, 2. New applicants enrolled 2001–2002, 2. Total enrolled 2001–2002 full-time, 11, part-time, 2. Openings 2002–2003, 3. The Median number of years required for completion of a degree are 6. The number of students enrolled full and part-time, who were dismissed or voluntarily withdrew from this program area were 0. Social PhD—Applications 2001–2002, 16. Total applicants accepted 2001–2002, 6. New applicants enrolled 2001–2002, 4. Total enrolled 2001–2002 full-time, 15, part-time, 3. Openings 2002–2003, 4. The Median number of years required for completion of a degree are 6. The number of students enrolled full and part-time, who were dismissed or voluntarily withdrew from this program area were 1.

Admissions Requirements:

Scores: Entries appear in this order: required test or GPA, minimum score (if required), median score of students entering in 2001–2002. Master's Programs: GRE-V no minimum stated; GRE-Q no minimum stated; overall undergraduate GPA 3.0, 3.4. Doctoral Programs: GRE-V no minimum stated; GRE-Q no minimum stated; overall undergraduate GPA 3.00, 3.5 ; last 2 years GPA no minimum stated; psychology GPA no minimum stated; psychology GPA no minimum stated.

Other Criteria: (importance of criteria rated low, medium, or high): GRE/MAT scores low, research experience medium, GPA high, letters of recommendation medium, interview high, statement of goals and objectives medium. Interview is of high importance for the clinical area only.

Student Characteristics: The following represents characteristics of students in 2001–2002 in all graduate psychology programs in the department: Female–full-time 54, part-time 17; Male–full-time 16, part-time 5; African American/Black–full-time 48, part-time 21; Hispanic/Latino (a)–full-time 0, part-time 0; Asian/Pacific Islander–full-time 3, part-time 0; American Indian/Alaska Native–full-time 0, part-time 0; students subject to the Americans with Disabilities Act–full-time 0, part-time 0.

Financial Information/Assistance:

Tuition for Full-Time Study: Master's: State residents per academic year $9,800; nonstate residents: per academic year $9,800,
Doctoral: State residents: per academic year $9,800; nonstate residents: per academic year $9,800.

Financial Assistance:

First Year Students: Teaching assistantships available for first-year. Average amount paid per academic year: $10,000. Average number of hours worked per week: 20. Apply by May 1. Tuition remission given: full. Fellowships and scholarships available for first-year. Average amount paid per academic year: $13,500. Average number of hours worked per week: 0. Tuition remission given: full.

Advanced Students: Teaching assistantships available for advanced students. Average amount paid per academic year: $13,500. Apply by May 1. Fellowships and scholarships available for advanced students. Average amount paid per academic year: $15,000. Apply by May 1.

Contact Information: Of all students currently enrolled full-time, 25% benefitted from one or more of the listed financial assistance programs. For information on financial assistance, contact: Chairman, Graduate Admissions Committee, Psychology Department, Howard University.

Internships/Practica: Internships and practica are available at various clinical sites in the District of Columbia, Maryland, and Virginia for students beginning in their first year of study. For those doctoral students for whom a professional internship is required prior to graduation, 8 applied in 2000–2001. Of those who applied, 7 were placed in internships listed by the Association of Psychology Postdoctoral and Internship Programs (APPIC); 7 were placed in APA accredited internships.

Housing and Day Care: No on-campus housing and day care facilities are available.

Employment of Department Graduates:

Master's Degree Graduates: Of those who graduated in the academic year 2000–2001, the following categories and numbers represent the post-graduate activities and employment of master's degree graduates: Enrolled in a post-doctoral residency/fellowship (n/a), employed in independent practice (n/a).

Doctoral Degree Graduates: Of those who graduated in the academic year 2000–2001, the following categories and numbers represent the post-graduate activities and employment of doctoral degree graduates: Enrolled in a psychology doctoral program (n/a), enrolled in another graduate/professional program (n/a).

Additional Information:

Orientation, Objectives, and Emphasis of Department: The Graduate Program at Howard prepares students for careers in research, teaching, and the practice of psychology. Advanced study in clinical, developmental, social, personality, and neuropsychology is offered. A major emphasis of the program is research training, and students are expected to conduct research throughout their graduate study.

Information for Students With Physical Disabilities: Elevators are located at the west end of the C.B. Powell Building near the entrance to the Pyschology area.

Application Information:

Send to: Graduate Admissions, Graduate School of Arts and Sciences, Howard University, Washington, DC 20059. Students are admitted in the Fall, application deadline April 1. February 1 for Fall admissions for the Clinical Psychology Program. *Fee:* $45.

The Catholic University of America
Department of Psychology
4001 Harewood Road, N.E., O'Boyle Hall, Room 314
Washington, DC 20064
Telephone: (202) 319-5750
Fax: (202) 319-6263
E-mail: *wright@cua.edu*
Web: *http://www.cua.edu/www/psy/*

Department Established:
1891. Acting Chair: Thomas L. Wright. Number of Faculty: total–full-time 14, part-time 4; women–full-time 5, part-time 1; minority–full-time 1.

Programs and Degrees Offered:
Listed in the following order: Program area, degree type (T if terminal Master's), number awarded 7/00-6/01. Applied experimental PhD 3, clinical PhD 3, general MA (T) 10, human development PhD, human factors MA (T), psychology/law.

APA Accreditation: Clinical PhD: full.

Student Applications/Admissions:
Student Applications
Applied experimental PhD—Applications 2001–2002, 7. Total applicants accepted 2001–2002, 4. New applicants enrolled 2001–2002, 1. Total enrolled 2001–2002 full-time, 11. Openings 2002–2003, 2. The Median number of years required for completion of a degree are 6. The number of students enrolled full and part-time, who were dismissed or voluntarily withdrew from this program area were 0. *Clinical PhD*—Applications 2001–2002, 167. Total applicants accepted 2001–2002, 10. New applicants enrolled 2001–2002, 5. Total enrolled 2001–2002 full-time, 46, part-time, 10. Openings 2002–2003, 6. The Median number of years required for completion of a degree are 6. The number of students enrolled full and part-time, who were dismissed or voluntarily withdrew from this program area were 1. *General MA*—Applications 2001–2002, 79. Total applicants accepted 2001–2002, 28. New applicants enrolled 2001–2002, 10. Total enrolled 2001–2002 full-time, 23, part-time, 8. Openings 2002–2003, 16. The Median number of years required for completion of a degree are 3. *Human development PhD*—Applications 2001–2002, 12. Total applicants accepted 2001–2002, 1. New applicants enrolled 2001–2002, 1. Total enrolled 2001–2002 full-time, 5. Openings 2002–2003, 2. *Human factors MA*—Applications 2001–2002, 5. Total applicants accepted 2001–2002, 3. New applicants enrolled 2001–2002, 1. Total enrolled 2001–2002 full-time, 3. Openings 2002–2003, 2. The number of students enrolled full and part-time, who were dismissed or voluntarily withdrew from this program area were 1.

Admissions Requirements:
Scores: Entries appear in this order: required test or GPA, minimum score (if required), median score of students entering in 2001–2002. Master's Programs: GRE-V no minimum stated, 576; GRE-Q no minimum stated, 613; GRE-V+Q no minimum stated, 1189; GRE-Analytical no minimum stated, 638; GRE-V+Q+Analytical no minimum stated, 1827; overall undergraduate GPA no minimum stated, 3.6. Doctoral Programs: GRE-V no minimum stated, 610; GRE-Q no minimum stated, 680; GRE-V+Q no minimum stated, 1290; overall undergraduate GPA no minimum stated, 3.7 ; last 2 years GPA no minimum stated; psychology GPA no minimum stated; psychology GPA no minimum stated.
Other Criteria: (importance of criteria rated low, medium, or high): GRE/MAT scores medium, research experience high, work experience medium, extracurricular activity low, clinically related public service medium, GPA high, letters of recommendation high, interview high, statement of goals and objectives medium. Interview only for clinical PhD programs.

Student Characteristics: The following represents characteristics of students in 2001–2002 in all graduate psychology programs in the department: Female–full-time 68, part-time 2; Male–full-time 27, part-time 1; African American/Black–full-time 2, part-time 1; Hispanic/Latino (a)–full-time 1, part-time 0; Asian/Pacific Islander–full-time 4, part-time 0; American Indian/Alaska Native–full-time 1, part-time 0; students subject to the Americans with Disabilities Act–full-time 1.

Financial Information/Assistance:
Tuition for Full-Time Study: *Master's:* State residents per academic year $21,050, $810 per credit hour; nonstate residents: per academic year $21,050, $810 per credit hour. *Doctoral:* State residents: per academic year $21,050, $810 per credit hour; nonstate residents: per academic year $21,050, $810 per credit hour.

Financial Assistance:
First Year Students: No information provided.
Advanced Students: No information provided.
Contact Information: For information on financial assistance, contact: Director of Program.

Internships/Practica: The following applies to doctoral students in the clinical program. Students begin practicum experience in their first year as a part of their courses in assessment and psychotherapy. Advanced courses are available in neuropsychology assessment, objective personality assessment, and projective personality assessment. Each of these courses incorporates practicum experience. In their second year, clinical students do a practicum in individual psychotherapy in the university's counseling center, in which the clients are undergraduate and graduate students. The core clinical faculty supervises this yearlong practicum. Advanced psychotherapy practica, supervised by core clinical faculty, are available in family therapy, couples therapy, and group therapy. All on-campus practica are supervised very closely. For example, in the second-year psychotherapy practicum, students are given 2–5 hours of supervision a week while they are seeing 2 or 3 clients. Additionally, in their third or fourth year, clinical students can do a 16-hour-a-week externship, supervised by a licensed clinical psychologist, in one of many community settings in the area, such as a community mental health center, a clinic, or a hospital. The clinical training culminates in a yearlong internship, preferably an APA-accredited internship.

Housing and Day Care: No on-campus housing and day care facilities are available.

Employment of Department Graduates:

Master's Degree Graduates: Of those who graduated in the academic year 2000–2001, the following categories and numbers represent the post-graduate activities and employment of master's degree graduates: Enrolled in a post-doctoral residency/fellowship (n/a), employed in independent practice (n/a).

Doctoral Degree Graduates: Of those who graduated in the academic year 2000–2001, the following categories and numbers represent the post-graduate activities and employment of doctoral degree graduates: Enrolled in a psychology doctoral program (n/a), enrolled in another graduate/professional program (n/a).

Additional Information:

Orientation, Objectives, and Emphasis of Department: Three PhD programs, clinical, human development, and applied-experimental, are offered. Further specialization is offered in Children, Families, and Cultures and in the Cognitive, Affective, and Neural Sciences. The objectives of the clinical program are to train according to the science-practitioner model in clinical and applied areas. The Children, Families, and Cultures specialization provides interdisciplinary training in both normal and abnormal developmental processes in the clinical program or in the human development program. The emphasis in human development is research in Children, Families, and Cultures. The applied-experimental program emphasizes research in human cognition: current areas of interest include cognitive aging (serial pattern learning, alzheimers), visual attention (stroop, air traffic control), spatial mental models (virtual reality, information visualization and memory applied to health issues). The Cognitive, Affective, and Neural Sciences track focuses on department-wide expertise in specific areas of human cognition and human emotion. Additional Master's programs are offered in Human Factors and General Psychology. A dual degree program M.A. Psychology/JD Law is available. Admission to CUA Columbus School of Law is a prerequisite.

Special Facilities or Resources: The department maintains several well-equipped laboratories for both cognitive science and clinical research. Capabilities exist for studies on auditory and visual perception, attention and memory, simulation, human computer interaction, virtual reality, and social interaction.

Information for Students With Physical Disabilities: The building is equipped with an elevator from the ground level to the third floor. The Office of Multicultural and Special Services aids students with Physical and Learning Disabilities.

Application Information:

Send to: Office of Graduate Admissions, The Catholic University of America, 110 McMahon Hall, Washington DC 20064. Students are admitted in the Fall, application deadline January 15; Spring, application deadline October 1. *Fee:* $50. Self described ethnic minority candidates can waive the fee.

Argosy University, Tampa
Florida School of Professional Psychology
School of Psychology
410 Ware Boulevard, Suite 500
Tampa, FL 33619
Telephone: (800) 850-6488
Fax: (813) 246-4045
E-mail: *dvaldez@argosyu.edu*
Web: *http://www.argosyu.edu*

Department Established:
1995. Dean: Douglas Riedmiller. Number of Faculty: total–full-time 6, part-time 8; women–full-time 3, part-time 4; minority–full-time 1, part-time 2; faculty subject to the Americans with Disabilities Act 3.

Programs and Degrees Offered:
Listed in the following order: Program area, degree type (T if terminal Master's), number awarded 7/00-6/01. Clinical PsyD 6.

Student Applications/Admissions:
Student Applications
Clinical PsyD—New applicants enrolled 2001–2002, 26. Total enrolled 2001–2002 full-time, 87. Openings 2002–2003, 44. The Median number of years required for completion of a degree are 6. The number of students enrolled full and part-time, who were dismissed or voluntarily withdrew from this program area were 3.

Admissions Requirements:
Scores: Entries appear in this order: required test or GPA, minimum score (if required), median score of students entering in 2001–2002. Doctoral Programs: GRE-V+Q+Analytical no minimum stated, 1500; MAT no minimum stated, 47.5; overall undergraduate GPA no minimum stated, 3.53; last 2 years GPA no minimum stated; psychology GPA 3.0; psychology GPA no minimum stated.
Other Criteria: (importance of criteria rated low, medium, or high): GRE/MAT scores low, research experience low, work experience high, extracurricular activity medium, clinically related public service medium, GPA medium, letters of recommendation high, interview high, statement of goals and objectives high.

Student Characteristics: The following represents characteristics of students in 2001–2002 in all graduate psychology programs in the department: Female–full-time 64, part-time 25; Male–full-time 18, part-time 5; African American/Black–full-time 10, part-time 5; Hispanic/Latino (a)–full-time 6, part-time 1; Asian/Pacific Islander–full-time 3, part-time 0; American Indian/Alaska Native–full-time 0, part-time 1; Multi-ethnic–full-time 2.

Financial Information/Assistance:
Tuition for Full-Time Study: *Master's:* State residents $640 per credit hour; nonstate residents: $640 per credit hour. *Doctoral:*
State residents: $640 per credit hour; nonstate residents: $640 per credit hour.

Financial Assistance:
First Year Students: No information provided.
Advanced Students: No information provided.
Contact Information: No information provided.

Internships/Practica: All students are required to complete a 1000-hour diagnostic practicum and a 1000-hour therapy practicum. Opportunities for practicum experience are available at many sites throughout the community including community mental health centers, forensic, geriatric and child treatment centers, medical centers, and rehabilitation centers. Specialty practicum sites are developed based on student interest and availability. For those doctoral students for whom a professional internship is required prior to graduation, 14 applied in 2000–2001. Of those who applied, 14 were placed in internships listed by the Association of Psychology Postdoctoral and Internship Programs (APPIC); 7 were placed in APA accredited internships.

Housing and Day Care: No on-campus housing and day care facilities are available.

Employment of Department Graduates:
Master's Degree Graduates: Of those who graduated in the academic year 2000–2001, the following categories and numbers represent the post-graduate activities and employment of master's degree graduates: Enrolled in a post-doctoral residency/fellowship (n/a), employed in independent practice (n/a).
Doctoral Degree Graduates: Of those who graduated in the academic year 2000–2001, the following categories and numbers represent the post-graduate activities and employment of doctoral degree graduates: Enrolled in a psychology doctoral program (n/a), enrolled in another graduate/professional program (n/a), enrolled in a post-doctoral residency/fellowship (6), still seeking employment (0).

Additional Information:
Orientation, Objectives, and Emphasis of Department: The Florida School of Professional Psychology is a practitioner-oriented program established with the aim of training highly qualified clinical psychologists. In the belief that it is the responsibility of each clinician to determine his or her approach to therapy, the program strives to introduce students to a variety of clinical orientations. Emphasis is on clinical skills, particularly psychological assessment, diagnosis, and psychotherapy. Students have the opportunity to focus on neuropsychology, gerontological psychology, or child psychology.

Special Facilities or Resources: All faculty are experienced clinicians as well as educators. A number of general and specialized practicum sites are available to students. The departmental library houses a focused collection of monographs and journals and provides students access to electronic library resources throughout the Argosy University system. There is an observation room with one-way mirror and videotaping facilities on campus.

Application Information:
Send to: Director of Admissions/FSPP, 410 Ware Blvd., Suite 500, Tampa, FL 33619. Students are admitted in the Fall, application deadline Mar. 15; Winter, application deadline Nov. 15; Summer, application deadline Mar. 30. *Fee:* $50.

Barry University
Department of Psychology
School of Arts and Sciences
11300 N.E. 2nd Avenue
Miami Shores, FL 33161
Telephone: (305) 899-3270
Fax: (305) 899-3279
E-mail: *lpeterson@mail.barry.edu*
Web: *http://www.barry.edu*

Department Established:
1978. Chairperson: Linda M. Peterson. Number of Faculty: total–full-time 11, part-time 4; women–full-time 7, part-time 2; minority–full-time 1, part-time 1.

Programs and Degrees Offered:
Listed in the following order: Program area, degree type (T if terminal Master's), number awarded 7/00-6/01. Clinical psychology, school psychology.

Student Applications/Admissions:
Admissions Requirements:
Scores: Entries appear in this order: required test or GPA, minimum score (if required), median score of students entering in 2001–2002. Master's Programs: GRE-V no minimum stated, 470; GRE-Q no minimum stated, 450; GRE-V+Q 1000, 900; overall undergraduate GPA 3.0, 3.40; last 2 years GPA no minimum stated; psychology GPA no minimum stated. Doctoral Programs: last 2 years GPA no minimum stated; psychology GPA no minimum stated; psychology GPA no minimum stated.

Other Criteria: (importance of criteria rated low, medium, or high): GRE/MAT scores medium, research experience medium, work experience medium, extracurricular activity low, clinically related public service medium, GPA high, letters of recommendation high, statement of goals and objectives medium.

Student Characteristics: The following represents characteristics of students in 2001–2002 in all graduate psychology programs in the department: Female–full-time 49, part-time 15; Male–full-time 4, part-time 2; African American/Black–full-time 7, part-time 4; Hispanic/Latino (a)–full-time 12, part-time 3; Asian/Pacific Islander–full-time 0, part-time 0; American Indian/Alaska Native–full-time 0, part-time 0.

Financial Information/Assistance:
Tuition for Full-Time Study: *Master's:* State residents $520 per credit hour; nonstate residents: $520 per credit hour.

Financial Assistance:
First Year Students: Research assistantships available for first-year. Average amount paid per academic year: $3,000. Aver-

age number of hours worked per week: 15. Apply by May 31. Tuition remission given: partial.

Advanced Students: Research assistantships available for advanced students. Average amount paid per academic year: $3,000. Average number of hours worked per week: 15. Apply by May 31. Tuition remission given: partial.

Contact Information: Of all students currently enrolled full-time, 10% benefitted from one or more of the listed financial assistance programs. For information on financial assistance, contact: Office of Financial Aid 305/899-3673. For information on graduate assistantships contact the Department of Psychology directly.

Internships/Practica: All master's degree students must complete an internship. Because Barry University is located in a large, multi-cultural metropolitan area, the program is able to offer more than the usual number and variety of settings for the internship experience. Sites include but are not limited to community mental health centers, assessment centers (primarily for the assessment of children), psychiatric hospitals, addiction treatment programs, nursing homes, and prison settings. Supervision is provided both at the site and by a clinical supervisor on campus.

Housing and Day Care: No on-campus housing and day care facilities are available.

Employment of Department Graduates:
Master's Degree Graduates: Of those who graduated in the academic year 2000–2001, the following categories and numbers represent the post-graduate activities and employment of master's degree graduates: Enrolled in a psychology doctoral program (0), enrolled in another graduate/professional program (0), enrolled in a post-doctoral residency/fellowship (n/a), employed in independent practice (n/a), employed in a professional position in a school system (5).
Doctoral Degree Graduates: Of those who graduated in the academic year 2000–2001, the following categories and numbers represent the post-graduate activities and employment of doctoral degree graduates: Enrolled in a psychology doctoral program (n/a), enrolled in another graduate/professional program (n/a).

Additional Information:
Orientation, Objectives, and Emphasis of Department: The goal of the master's program in clinical psychology is to provide students with a thorough knowledge of the basic principles and practices of clinical psychology. Students are expected to achieve competence in the areas of theory, assessment, therapy, and research. All clinical psychology students complete a thesis and an internship. The program provides opportunities for students to apply their knowledge through practical experiences. The Specialist degree program in school psychology is designed to provide students with the knowledge and experience to perform both as scientists and practitioners of school psychology. The program integrates theoretical and practical training to prevent and remediate academic and emotional problems in the schools. Students will gain expertise in evaluation, diagnosis, prescription, interventions, psychometric applications, research, consultation, and professional ethics and standards. Students who successfully complete the school psychology program will be prepared to meet licensure requirements for the private practice of school psychology in the state of Florida. Students will also meet certification requirements set forth by the Florida State Board of Education. The School

Psychology Program has been approved by the Department of Education of the state of Florida. The program is designed to meet standards as set forth by the National Association of School Psychologists.

Special Facilities or Resources: The psychology department is composed of 10 full-time faculty members. Classes are small and the students are given individual attention and supervision.

Application Information:

Send to: Office of Enrollment Services, Barry University, 11300 NE 2nd Avenue, Miami FL 33161. Students are admitted in the Fall; Winter; Spring; Summer. Rolling admissions. Students are advised to have their appliations complete at least 30 days prior to the semester in which they would like to enroll. *Fee:* $30.

Carlos Albizu University, Miami Campus (2001 data)

Doctoral Program, Non-Terminal Master's Program, Terminal Master Progams
2173 N.W. 99th Avenue
Miami, FL 33172-2209
Telephone: (305) 593-1223
Fax: (305) 629-8052
E-mail: *jrivera@albizu.edu*
Web: *http://www.albizu.edu*

Department Established:

1980. Chancellor: Jose M. Rivera-Berg, Psy.D. Number of Faculty: total–full-time 17, part-time 39; women–full-time 8, part-time 21; minority–full-time 13, part-time 20.

Programs and Degrees Offered:

Listed in the following order: Program area, degree type (T if terminal Master's), number awarded 7/00-6/01. Industrial/Organizational MS (T), Non-Terminal Master's Program MS 78, PsyD Program 98, Terminal Master's Program MS (T) 55.

APA Accreditation: Clinical PsyD: full.

Student Applications/Admissions:

Student Applications

Industrial/Organizational MS—Applications 2001–2002, 29. Total applicants accepted 2001–2002, 16. New applicants enrolled 2001–2002, 14. Total enrolled 2001–2002 full-time, 20, part-time, 2. Openings 2002–2003, 50. The Median number of years required for completion of a degree are 0. The number of students enrolled full and part-time, who were dismissed or voluntarily withdrew from this program area were 1. *Non-Terminal Master's Program MS*—Applications 2001–2002, 172. Total applicants accepted 2001–2002, 64. New applicants enrolled 2001–2002, 49. Total enrolled 2001–2002 full-time, 112, part-time, 7. Openings 2002–2003, 75. The Median number of years required for completion of a degree are 4. The number of students enrolled full and part-time, who were dismissed or voluntarily withdrew from this program area were 15. *PsyD Program*—Applications 2001–2002, 0. New applicants enrolled 2001–2002, 16. Total enrolled 2001–2002 full-

time, 253, part-time, 4. Openings 2002–2003, 36. The Median number of years required for completion of a degree are 7. The number of students enrolled full and part-time, who were dismissed or voluntarily withdrew from this program area were 6. *Terminal Master's Program MS*—Applications 2001–2002, 121. Total applicants accepted 2001–2002, 45. New applicants enrolled 2001–2002, 39. Total enrolled 2001–2002 full-time, 78, part-time, 7. Openings 2002–2003, 75. The Median number of years required for completion of a degree are 4. The number of students enrolled full and part-time, who were dismissed or voluntarily withdrew from this program area were 8.

Admissions Requirements:

Scores: Entries appear in this order: required test or GPA, minimum score (if required), median score of students entering in 2001–2002. Master's Programs: overall undergraduate GPA 3.00, 3.04. Doctoral Programs: psychology GPA 3.00, 3.04.
Other Criteria: (importance of criteria rated low, medium, or high): GRE/MAT scores low, research experience low, work experience medium, extracurricular activity low, clinically related public service low, GPA high, letters of recommendation high, interview high, statement of goals and objectives high, Stated interest in Multic high. For Terminal MS Programs Only: Extracurricular Activity medium.

Student Characteristics: The following represents characteristics of students in 2001–2002 in all graduate psychology programs in the department: Female–full-time 77, part-time 2; Male–full-time 19, part-time 4; African American/Black–full-time 18, part-time 0; Hispanic/Latino (a)–full-time 61, part-time 8; Asian/Pacific Islander–full-time 1, part-time 0; American Indian/Alaska Native–full-time 0, part-time 0.

Financial Information/Assistance:

Tuition for Full-Time Study: No information provided.

Financial Assistance:

First Year Students: No information provided.
Advanced Students: No information provided.
Contact Information: Of all students currently enrolled full-time, 3% benefitted from one or more of the listed financial assistance programs. For information on financial assistance, contact: Ms. Kay Midkiff, Director of Financial Aid, Carlos Albizu University, 2173 N.W. 99th Avenue, Miami, FL 33172.

Internships/Practica: Carlos Albizu University, Miami Campus, operates the Goodman Psychological Services Center which provides low-cost services to the community and functions as both a Practicum and internship site for doctoral students. All non-terminal master's students begin their Practicum work in the Center and later have the option of moving on to any of about fifty (50) Practicum sites in the community. The Goodman Center is also an APPIC member and offers a pre-doctoral internship which, in some instances, utilizes rotations with other clinical providers in the community. The majority of internship candidates seek outside internships with the support and assistance of the Department of Field Placement. Terminal Master's students are placed during their senior year (8–12 months) at a variety of corporations, schools, and human services settings with diverse client populations. Sixty Practicum sites are available in the tri-county area (Miami-Dade, Broward, Palm Beach). For those doctoral students for whom a professional internship is required prior to graduation, 70 applied in 2000–2001. Of those who applied, 64 were placed in internships listed by the Association of Psychology Postdoctoral and Internship Programs (APPIC); 26 were placed in APA accredited internships.

Housing and Day Care: No on-campus housing and day care facilities are available.

Employment of Department Graduates:
Master's Degree Graduates: Of those who graduated in the academic year 2000–2001, the following categories and numbers represent the post-graduate activities and employment of master's degree graduates: Enrolled in a post-doctoral residency/fellowship (n/a), employed in independent practice (n/a).
Doctoral Degree Graduates: Of those who graduated in the academic year 2000–2001, the following categories and numbers represent the post-graduate activities and employment of doctoral degree graduates: Enrolled in a psychology doctoral program (n/a), enrolled in another graduate/professional program (n/a).

Additional Information:
Orientation, Objectives, and Emphasis of Department: Carlos Albizu University (CAU) has as its primary objective the training of psychologists, mental health counselors, marriage and family therapists, school counselors, and master's level industrial and organizational psychology practitioners at the highest level of professional competence with a special sensitivity to multicultural issues. The academic curriculum emphasizes a core of traditional courses, including training in theory and research methodology. Academic courses are sequenced to foster steady growth in conceptual mastery and technical skills within a multicultural context. Clinical training provides for the opportunity of applied practice in the areas of psychotherapy, psychodiagnostics, school counseling, and industrial and organizational services within settings serving a multicultural population. The Psy.D. Program curriculum offers three concentrations: General Practice, Neuropsychology, and Forensic Psychology, which allows for early career specialization while the student is in training.

Special Facilities or Resources: The University has its own Psychological Services Center which provides varied clinical services to the community while serving as a training site for Practicum and pre-doctoral interns. Throughout their internship and practica, students are supervised by licensed psychologists who monitor their work and evaluate their performance. Tools such as two-way mirrors and audiovisual equipment are used to provide supervision and feedback to the students. Faculty in the Doctoral Program wrote a psychologial service grant which resulted in a $100,000 award which has allowed for the funding of a program at the Goodman Center to treat victims of traumatic brain injury and their affected families. The Psy.D. program requires the completion of a dissertation as part of its academic requirements. A Dissertation Coordinator, who is a member of the core faculty, oversees the process and assists the faculty in a consulting capacity in their role as dissertation chairs and readers. This is designed to foster and facilitate the research interests and activities of the students.

Information for Students With Physical Disabilities: The physical facility, where the school is housed, is user-friendly to students who are physically challenged (e.g., designated parking spaces, entryways, restrooms, classrooms, etc.).

Application Information:
Send to: Recruitment and Admissions Department, Carlos Albizu University, Miami Campus, 2173 N.W. 99th Avenue, Miami, FL 33172-2209. Students are admitted in the Fall, application deadline 60/90 days; Spring, application deadline same; Summer, application deadline same. *Fee:* $50. Fee waived for on-site applications during select institutional events (i.e., Open House).

Central Florida, University of
Department of Psychology
Arts and Sciences
P.O. Box 161390
Orlando, FL 32816-1390
Telephone: (407) 823-1011
Fax: (407) 823-5862
E-mail: *sballard@pegasus.cc.ucf.edu*
Web: *http://pegasus.cc.ucf.edu/~psych*

Department Established:
1968. Chairperson: Jack M. McGuire. Number of Faculty: total–full-time 37, part-time 22; women–full-time 11, part-time 8; minority–full-time 4, part-time 6.

Programs and Degrees Offered:
Listed in the following order: Program area, degree type (T if terminal Master's), number awarded 7/00-6/01. Applied Experimental and HF PhD 2, clinical MA (T) 6, industrial/organizational MA (T) 2.

Student Applications/Admissions:
Student Applications
Applied Experimental and HF PhD—Applications 2001–2002, 25. Total applicants accepted 2001–2002, 12. New applicants enrolled 2001–2002, 10. Total enrolled 2001–2002 full-time, 37, part-time, 2. Openings 2002–2003, 15. The number of students enrolled full and part-time, who were dismissed or voluntarily withdrew from this program area were 0. *Clinical MA*—Applications 2001–2002, 85. Total applicants accepted 2001–2002, 16. New applicants enrolled 2001–2002, 12. Openings 2002–2003, 16. The number of students enrolled full and part-time, who were dismissed or voluntarily withdrew from this program area were 2. *Industrial/organizational MA*—Applications 2001–2002, 90. Total applicants accepted 2001–2002, 11. New applicants enrolled 2001–2002, 11. Total enrolled 2001–2002 full-time, 10. Openings 2002–2003, 12.

Admissions Requirements:
Scores: Entries appear in this order: required test or GPA, minimum score (if required), median score of students entering in 2001–2002. Master's Programs: GRE-V+Q 1000, 1105; last 2 years GPA 3.0, 3.5; psychology GPA no minimum stated. Doctoral Programs: GRE-V+Q 1000, 1197; last 2 years GPA 3.0, 3.7 ; psychology GPA no minimum stated; psychology GPA no minimum stated. GRE of 1000 and 3.0 GPA are minimum requirements to apply to Clinical Ph.D., Clinical

MA, I/O MS and I/O Ph.D. program. For AEHF the minimum GRE is 1100 and GPA 3.2.

Other Criteria: (importance of criteria rated low, medium, or high): GRE/MAT scores high, research experience high, work experience low, extracurricular activity medium, clinically related public service medium, GPA high, letters of recommendation high, interview high, statement of goals and objectives high, Research orientation high. Criteria vary by program.

Student Characteristics: The following represents characteristics of students in 2001–2002 in all graduate psychology programs in the department: Female–full-time 114, part-time 32; Male–full-time 41, part-time 22; African American/Black–full-time 11, part-time 2; Hispanic/Latino (a)–full-time 18, part-time 8; Asian/Pacific Islander–full-time 5, part-time 0; American Indian/Alaska Native–full-time 1, part-time 0; Multi-ethnic–full-time 3, part-time 0; students subject to the Americans with Disabilities Act–full-time 0, part-time 0.

Financial Information/Assistance:

Tuition for Full-Time Study: *Master's:* State residents per academic year $3,244, $162 per credit hour; nonstate residents: per academic year $11,380, $570 per credit hour. *Doctoral:* State residents: per academic year $3,244, $162 per credit hour; nonstate residents: per academic year $11,380, $570 per credit hour.

Financial Assistance:

First Year Students: Teaching assistantships available for first-year. Average amount paid per academic year: $7,000. Average number of hours worked per week: 20. Tuition remission given: full and partial. Research assistantships available for first-year. Average amount paid per academic year: $8,000. Average number of hours worked per week: 20. Tuition remission given: full and partial. Fellowships and scholarships available for first-year. Average amount paid per academic year: $6,000. Average number of hours worked per week: 10. Tuition remission given: full and partial.

Advanced Students: Teaching assistantships available for advanced students. Average amount paid per academic year: $7,000. Average number of hours worked per week: 20. Tuition remission given: full and partial. Research assistantships available for advanced students. Average amount paid per academic year: $8,000. Average number of hours worked per week: 20. Tuition remission given: full and partial. Fellowships and scholarships available for advanced students. Average amount paid per academic year: $6,000. Average number of hours worked per week: 10. Tuition remission given: full and partial.

Contact Information: Of all students currently enrolled full-time, 90% benefitted from one or more of the listed financial assistance programs. For information on financial assistance, contact: Web site: http://pegasus.cc.ucf.edu/~finaid.

Internships/Practica: Clinical: Internships for clinical master's students exist in community mental health centers and other agencies throughout Central Florida. Doctoral students complete their practica in our on-campus clinic as well as in a variety of community based clinical agencies. Human Factors: Human Factors students complete internships in a variety of government, business, and industry settings. Industrial/Organizational: I/O master's students complete practica placements in a variety of government, business, and industry settings. Doctoral students complete an internship in a variety of business, industry, and government settings. For those doctoral students for whom a professional internship is required prior to graduation, 3 applied in 2000–2001. Of those who applied, 3 were placed in internships listed by the Association of Psychology Postdoctoral and Internship Programs (APPIC); 3 were placed in APA accredited internships.

Housing and Day Care: On-campus housing and day care facilities are available.

Employment of Department Graduates:

Master's Degree Graduates: Of those who graduated in the academic year 2000–2001, the following categories and numbers represent the post-graduate activities and employment of master's degree graduates: Enrolled in a post-doctoral residency/fellowship (n/a), employed in independent practice (n/a).

Doctoral Degree Graduates: Of those who graduated in the academic year 2000–2001, the following categories and numbers represent the post-graduate activities and employment of doctoral degree graduates: Enrolled in a psychology doctoral program (n/a), enrolled in another graduate/professional program (n/a).

Additional Information:

Orientation, Objectives, and Emphasis of Department: The Ph.D. program in clinical psychology is designed for individuals seeking a research oriented career in the field of clinical psychology. The program also emphasizes training in consultation, teaching, supervision, and the design/evaluation of mental health programs. The MA program in clinical psychology has major emphases in assessment and evaluation skills; intervention, counseling, and psychotherapy skills; and an academic foundation in research methods. The program is designed to provide training and preparation for persons desiring to deliver clinical services at the master's level through community agencies. Graduates of this program meet the educational requirements for the mental health counselor state license. The MS program in industrial/organizational psychology has major emphases in selection and training of employees, applied theories of organizational behavior, job satisfaction, test theory and construction, assessment center technology, statistics and experimental design. As of Fall 2000 a Ph.D. in Industrial/Organizational was approved and admitted an initial class of 10 students. I/O students receive training in the 21 competence areas detailed by Division 14 of the APA. The PhD program in human factors is patterned on the scientist-practitioner model of the APA. It adheres to the guidelines for education and training established by the committee for Education and Training of APA's Division 21 (Applied Experimental and Engineering Psychology). The Human Factors program is accredited by the Educational Committee of the Human Factors and Ergonomics Society. Concentration areas include human-computer interaction, human performance, and human factors in simulation and training.

Special Facilities or Resources: The department's facilities and resources include extensive videotape capability, an intelligence and personality testing library, a statistics library, computer facilities within the department and in the computer center, a counseling and testing center, a creative school for children, and a communicative disorders clinic. Doctoral students have use of specialized equipment in the department-based Human Visual Performance Laboratory and Team Performance Laboratory. The clinical program has extensive ties to a number of community agencies for practica and assistantship.

Application Information:
Send to: University of Central Florida, Graduate Admissions, P.O. Box 160112, Orlando, FL 32816-0112. Students are admitted in the Fall. Clin Ph.D 1/1 Clin. MA 2/15. I/O MS 2/1. I/O Ph.D. 1/15. AEHF 2/1. *Fee:* $20.

Embry-Riddle Aeronautical University
Human Factors and Systems
600 S. Clyde Morris Boulevard
Daytona Beach, FL 32114
Telephone: (386) 226-6790
Fax: (386) 226-7050
E-mail: *greenef@db.erau.edu*
Web: *http://www.erau.edu*

Department Established:
1997. Chairperson: Fran Greene, Ph.D. Number of Faculty: total–full-time 7, part-time 3; women–full-time 3, part-time 2.

Programs and Degrees Offered:
Listed in the following order: Program area, degree type (T if terminal Master's), number awarded 7/00-6/01. Human Factors & Systems MA (T) 8.

Student Applications/Admissions:
Student Applications
Human Factors & Systems MA—Applications 2001–2002, 26. Total applicants accepted 2001–2002, 19. New applicants enrolled 2001–2002, 14. Total enrolled 2001–2002 full-time, 15, part-time, 29. Openings 2002–2003, 45. The Median number of years required for completion of a degree are 2. The number of students enrolled full and part-time, who were dismissed or voluntarily withdrew from this program area were 0.

Admissions Requirements:
Scores: Entries appear in this order: required test or GPA, minimum score (if required), median score of students entering in 2001–2002. Master's Programs: overall undergraduate GPA 2.75. Doctoral Programs: last 2 years GPA no minimum stated; psychology GPA no minimum stated; psychology GPA no minimum stated.
Other Criteria: (importance of criteria rated low, medium, or high): research experience high, work experience medium, extracurricular activity low, clinically related public service low, GPA high, letters of recommendation high, interview low, statement of goals and objectives high.

Student Characteristics: The following represents characteristics of students in 2001–2002 in all graduate psychology programs in the department: Female–full-time 8, part-time 17; Male–full-time 7, part-time 12; African American/Black–full-time 0, part-time 4; Hispanic/Latino (a)–full-time 1, part-time 2; Asian/Pacific Islander–full-time 0, part-time 0; American Indian/Alaska Native–full-time 0, part-time 0; Multi-ethnic–full-time 0, part-time 0; students subject to the Americans with Disabilities Act–full-time 0, part-time 0.

Financial Information/Assistance:
Tuition for Full-Time Study: *Master's:* State residents $790 per credit hour; nonstate residents: $790 per credit hour.

Financial Assistance:
First Year Students: Teaching assistantships available for first-year. Average amount paid per academic year: $6,500. Average number of hours worked per week: 20. Tuition remission given: partial. Research assistantships available for first-year. Average amount paid per academic year: $6,500. Average number of hours worked per week: 20. Tuition remission given: partial. Fellowships and scholarships available for first-year. Tuition remission given: partial.
Advanced Students: Teaching assistantships available for advanced students. Average amount paid per academic year: $6,500. Average number of hours worked per week: 20. Tuition remission given: partial. Research assistantships available for advanced students. Average amount paid per academic year: $6,500. Average number of hours worked per week: 20. Tuition remission given: partial. Fellowships and scholarships available for advanced students. Tuition remission given: partial.
Contact Information: Of all students currently enrolled full-time, 40% benefitted from one or more of the listed financial assistance programs. For information on financial assistance, contact: The average amount paid in fellowships and scholarships varies. For information on financial assistance, contact the Graduate Admissions Office. Note: Students offered assistantships can choose to accept paid employment or a tuition waiver or a combination of both.

Internships/Practica: The Master's Degree program at Embry-Riddle provides extensive opportunities for students to engage in paid and/or credit-based internship or co-op placements. Master's students are strongly encouraged, although not required, to take advantage of these placements. Previous placements of graduate students include premiere companies such as: Lockheed Martin, IBM, Veritas Software, Sikorsky Helicopter, the FAA, NTSB, and the United States Air Force. Placements typically range from 3–6 months and can be done at any time during the student's program.

Housing and Day Care: No on-campus housing and day care facilities are available.

Employment of Department Graduates:
Master's Degree Graduates: Of those who graduated in the academic year 2000–2001, the following categories and numbers represent the post-graduate activities and employment of master's degree graduates: Enrolled in a psychology doctoral program (2), enrolled in a post-doctoral residency/fellowship (n/a), employed in independent practice (n/a), employed in business or industry (research/consulting) (4), employed in business or industry (management) (2), employed in a government agency (professional services) (1).
Doctoral Degree Graduates: Of those who graduated in the academic year 2000–2001, the following categories and numbers represent the post-graduate activities and employment of doctoral degree graduates: Enrolled in a psychology doctoral program (n/a), enrolled in another graduate/professional program (n/a).

Additional Information:
Orientation, Objectives, and Emphasis of Department: Embry-Riddle Aeronautical University prides itself on being the largest

Aviation and Aerospace-based University in the world. As such, the focus of education is oriented to issues related to those domains and in other technologically advanced areas. The Human Factors and Systems Master's Degree program provides a fundamental, theoretical, and applied education in the fields of human factors and systems engineering. Electives in the program are then oriented toward exploring human factors and systems engineering principles within aviation domains. Faculty interests and research opportunities for students in the program are diverse. Current research interests range from personnel selection, to motivational issues, to design of cockpits. The diversity of faculty backgrounds adds to the eclectic nature of the research interests at Embry-Riddle. As such, students in the program can choose from a wide array of projects or thesis topics to pursue. Particular areas of faculty and student research currently include: development of heads-up displays, tunnel in the sky technology, pilot selection, pilot motivation, prediction of flight performance, virtual and augmented reality displays, security screening, human-computer interaction, and air traffic management systems. The University facilities include flight simulation laboratories, an air traffic management laboratory, and other computer laboratories. The overall goal of the Embry-Riddle program is to train an individual to move directly into a career as a Human Factors or Systems Engineering specialist in industry, government, or the military. In order to achieve this goal, the program provides training in research methodology and human factors applications. In addition, classes emphasize teamwork and development, as well as refinement of writing and oral communication skills.

Special Facilities or Resources: A fleet of more than 100 single- and multi-engine general aviation aircraft flying over 80.000 h/year on various levels of training missions; 20 dedicated procedures trainers and simulators ranging from FRASCA 141s through Level D Boeing 737-300 and Beechcraft 1900-C. The department has access to flight faculty/instructors with extensive background and experience and over 1500 students enrolled at various levels of flight training. The Human Performance Lab has an Applied Science Lab Series 4000 Eye Tracking System installed in a fully instrumented Frasca 141 research simulator and an eight-channel physiological data collection and analysis device, and it houses a variety of PC-based stimulus-generation tools for the study of a variety of information display issues. A simulated free light research environment includes generic two-pilot glass-cockpit twin-engine air transport aircraft (e.g., B-757, B-767, MD-90, A-320), AGATE class single-pilot cockpit, and two futuristic air traffic service stations. This lab can run human factors studies that involve person-in-the-loop, large-scale, complex air traffic problems that can operate under both current ATC and futuristic free flight environments. The traditional ATC training lab has 15 ATC workstations and access to ATC faculty/instructors with extensive background and experience in civilian and military air traffic control both in the US and internationally.

Application Information:
Send to: Graduate Programs, Embry-Riddle Aeronautical University, 600 S. Clyde Morris Blvd., Daytona Beach, FL 32114-3900. Students are admitted in the Fall, application deadline 08/01; Spring, application deadline 12/01; Summer, application deadline 04/01. *Fee:* $30. $50 for non residents.

Florida Atlantic University
Psychology
Science
777 Glades Road, P.O. Box 3091
Boca Raton, FL 33431-0991
Telephone: (561) 297-3360
Fax: (561) 297-2160
E-mail: *psychology@fau.edu*
Web: *http://www.psy.fau.edu*

Department Established:
1965. Chairperson: David L. Wolgin. Number of Faculty: total–full-time 33, part-time 1; women–full-time 11, part-time 1; minority–full-time 1.

Programs and Degrees Offered:
Listed in the following order: Program area, degree type (T if terminal Master's), number awarded 7/00-6/01. Psychology MA (T) 4, Psychology PhD (T) 4.

Student Applications/Admissions:
Student Applications
Psychology MA—Applications 2001–2002, 40. Total applicants accepted 2001–2002, 6. New applicants enrolled 2001–2002, 6. Total enrolled 2001–2002 full-time, 32. Openings 2002–2003, 8. The Median number of years required for completion of a degree are 2. The number of students enrolled full and part-time, who were dismissed or voluntarily withdrew from this program area were 1. *Psychology PhD*—Applications 2001–2002, 46. Total applicants accepted 2001–2002, 9. New applicants enrolled 2001–2002, 8. Total enrolled 2001–2002 full-time, 28. Openings 2002–2003, 6. The Median number of years required for completion of a degree are 4. The number of students enrolled full and part-time, who were dismissed or voluntarily withdrew from this program area were 1.

Admissions Requirements:
Scores: Entries appear in this order: required test or GPA, minimum score (if required), median score of students entering in 2001–2002. Master's Programs: GRE-V+Q 1100, 1085; last 2 years GPA 3.00, 3.8. GRE-Subject (Psychology) recommended but not required. Doctoral Programs: GRE-V+Q 1100, 1140; last 2 years GPA 3.00, 3.88; psychology GPA no minimum stated; psychology GPA no minimum stated. GRE-Subject (Psychology) recommended but not required.
Other Criteria: (importance of criteria rated low, medium, or high): GRE/MAT scores high, research experience high, work experience low, extracurricular activity low, clinically related public service low, GPA high, letters of recommendation high, statement of goals and objectives medium.

Student Characteristics: The following represents characteristics of students in 2001–2002 in all graduate psychology programs in the department: Female–full-time 40, part-time 0; Male–full-time 20, part-time 0; African American/Black–full-time 0, part-time 0; Hispanic/Latino (a)–full-time 1, part-time 0; Asian/Pacific Islander–full-time 0, part-time 0; American Indian/Alaska Native–full-time 1, part-time 0.

Financial Information/Assistance:

Tuition for Full-Time Study: *Master's:* State residents per academic year $3,098, $172 per credit hour; nonstate residents: per academic year $10,427, $579 per credit hour. *Doctoral:* State residents: per academic year $619, $34 per credit hour; nonstate residents: per academic year $2,085, $116 per credit hour.

Financial Assistance:

First Year Students: Teaching assistantships available for first-year. Average amount paid per academic year: $11,200. Average number of hours worked per week: 20. Apply by 08/01. Tuition remission given: partial.

Advanced Students: Teaching assistantships available for advanced students. Average amount paid per academic year: $11,950. Average number of hours worked per week: 20. Apply by 08/01. Tuition remission given: partial. Research assistantships available for advanced students. Fellowships and scholarships available for advanced students.

Contact Information: Of all students currently enrolled full-time, 30% benefitted from one or more of the listed financial assistance programs. For information on financial assistance, contact: For supplemental financial assistance apply to Office of Financial Aid by April 15.

Internships/Practica: No information provided.

Housing and Day Care: On-campus housing and day care facilities are available.

Employment of Department Graduates:

Master's Degree Graduates: Of those who graduated in the academic year 2000–2001, the following categories and numbers represent the post-graduate activities and employment of master's degree graduates: Enrolled in a post-doctoral residency/fellowship (n/a), employed in independent practice (n/a).

Doctoral Degree Graduates: Of those who graduated in the academic year 2000–2001, the following categories and numbers represent the post-graduate activities and employment of doctoral degree graduates: Enrolled in a psychology doctoral program (n/a), enrolled in another graduate/professional program (n/a).

Additional Information:

Orientation, Objectives, and Emphasis of Department: The PhD program emphasizes basic research in several areas of experimental psychology. Students may select courses and conduct research in four areas: cognitive psychology, developmental psychology, personality and social psychology, and psychobiology. Current research by faculty in these areas includes psycholinguistics, sentence processing, perception-action systems, visual perception, speech production and perception; developmental investigations into altruism, morality, aggression, sex roles, concept formation, problem solving, and memory; social cognition, the use of traits to predict behavior, gender roles and their impact on behavior, the dynamics of social influence; neural mechanisms in recovery of function from brain damage, nerve growth and regeneration, pattern generation during speech and limb coordination, drug tolerance and sensitization, developmental psychobiology of learning and memory, developmental psychopharmacology, electrophysiological functioning of the brain, developmental neuroanatomy, and nonlinear dynamics of brain and behavior. The MA program provides broad training in general-experimental psychology. It is designed to prepare students for entry into doctoral-level programs in all areas of psychology. Research in developmental psychology frequently uses a campus laboratory school for children in kindergarten through the eighth grade. Research in social psychology utilizes observation/social interaction laboratories with video and on-line computer facilities. The cognitive psychology laboratories include several testing rooms with a network of PCs for online control of experiments in perception, learning, language, and cognition. The EEG laboratory includes an acoustic isolation chamber, four microcomputers, and a variety of amplifying and recording systems.

Special Facilities or Resources: Additional information and online application forms are available at http://www.psy.fau.edu.

Information for Students With Physical Disabilities: Information available through Office for Students with Disabilities, www.fau.edu.

Application Information:
Send to: (1) FAU Admissions Office, 777 Glades Road, Boca Raton, FL 33431; (2) Graduate Coordinator, Department of Psychology, FAU; P.O. Box 3091, Boca Raton, FL 33431. Students are admitted in the Spring, application deadline January 15; Summer, application deadline June 1. PhD Application Deadline January 15. MA Application Deadline June 1. *Fee:* $20.

Florida Institute of Technology
School of Psychology
150 West University Boulevard
Melbourne, FL 32901-6988
Telephone: (321) 674-8104
Fax: (321) 674-7105
E-mail: *mkenkel@fit.edu*
Web: *http://www.fit.edu/acadres/psych*

Department Established:
1978. Dean: Mary Beth Kenkel. Number of Faculty: total–full-time 14, part-time 23; women–full-time 5, part-time 7; minority–full-time 1, part-time 1.

Programs and Degrees Offered:
Listed in the following order: Program area, degree type ('T' if terminal Master's), number awarded 7/00-6/01. ABA MA (T) 5, clinical PsyD 19, I/O MA (T) 7, I/O PhD.

APA Accreditation: Clinical PsyD: full.

Student Applications/Admissions:
Student Applications

ABA MA—Applications 2001–2002, 9. Total applicants accepted 2001–2002, 8. New applicants enrolled 2001–2002, 8. Total enrolled 2001–2002 full-time, 15, part-time, 5. Openings 2002–2003, 10. The Median number of years required for completion of a degree is 1. The number of students enrolled full and part-time, who were dismissed or voluntarily withdrew from this program area were 1. *Clinical PsyD*—Applications 2001–2002, 109. Total applicants accepted 2001–2002, 20. New applicants enrolled 2001–2002, 20. Total enrolled 2001–

2002 full-time, 85. Openings 2002–2003, 20. The Median number of years required for completion of a degree are 4. The number of students enrolled full and part-time, who were dismissed or voluntarily withdrew from this program area were 2. *I/O MA*—Applications 2001–2002, 35. Total applicants accepted 2001–2002, 8. New applicants enrolled 2001–2002, 7. Total enrolled 2001–2002 full-time, 11, part-time, 2. Openings 2002–2003, 10. The Median number of years required for completion of a degree are 5. The number of students enrolled full and part-time, who were dismissed or voluntarily withdrew from this program area were 1. *I/O PhD*—Applications 2001–2002, 19. Total applicants accepted 2001–2002, 8. New applicants enrolled 2001–2002, 8. Total enrolled 2001–2002 full-time, 6, part-time, 3. Openings 2002–2003, 5. The Median number of years required for completion of a degree are 4. The number of students enrolled full and part-time, who were dismissed or voluntarily withdrew from this program area were 1.

Admissions Requirements:

Scores: Entries appear in this order: required test or GPA, minimum score (if required), median score of students entering in 2001–2002. Master's Programs: GRE-V no minimum stated, 455; GRE-Q no minimum stated, 540; GRE-V+Q no minimum stated, 970; overall undergraduate GPA no minimum stated, 3.38; last 2 years GPA no minimum stated, 3.55; psychology GPA no minimum stated, 3.43. Doctoral Programs: GRE-V no minimum stated, 510; GRE-Q no minimum stated, 585; GRE-V+Q no minimum stated, 1095; GRE-Subject(Psych) 600, 600; overall undergraduate GPA no minimum stated, 3.57; last 2 years GPA no minimum stated, 3.79; psychology GPA no minimum stated, 3.78; psychology GPA no minimum stated, 3.93.

Other Criteria: (importance of criteria rated low, medium, or high): GRE/MAT scores, research experience low, work experience high, extracurricular activity medium, clinically related public service high, GPA letters of recommendation high, interview low, statement of goals and objectives medium.

Student Characteristics: The following represents characteristics of students in 2001–2002 in all graduate psychology programs in the department: Female–full-time 86, part-time 7; Male–full-time 30, part-time 3; African American/Black–full-time 5, part-time 1; Hispanic/Latino (a)–full-time 3, part-time 1; Asian/Pacific Islander–full-time 3, part-time 0; American Indian/Alaska Native–full-time 0, part-time 0; Multi-ethnic–full-time 0, part-time 0; students subject to the Americans with Disabilities Act–full-time 0, part-time 0.

Financial Information/Assistance:

Tuition for Full-Time Study: *Master's:* State residents per academic year $12,420, $690 per credit hour; nonstate residents: per academic year $12,420, $690 per credit hour. *Doctoral:* State residents: per academic year $1,650, $690 per credit hour; nonstate residents: per academic year $16,050, $690 per credit hour.

Financial Assistance:

First Year Students: Research assistantships available for first-year. Average amount paid per academic year: $3,600. Average number of hours worked per week: 5. Apply by Feb 1.

Advanced Students: Teaching assistantships available for advanced students. Average amount paid per academic year: $7,200. Average number of hours worked per week: 10. Apply by Feb 1. Research assistantships available for advanced students. Average amount paid per academic year: $3,600. Average number of hours worked per week: 5. Apply by Feb 1.

Contact Information: Of all students currently enrolled full-time, 40% benefitted from one or more of the listed financial assistance programs. For information on financial assistance, contact: Office of Financial Aid (for grants and loans); School Psychology (for assistantships).

Internships/Practica: Students in the PsyD program complete a sequence of three or more separate practicum placements prior to internship. These include the Florida Tech's Community Psychological Services Center, and then options at other outpatient and inpatient facilities. Ten inpatient sites are available, including adult psychiatric hospitals, rehabilitation hospitals, children and adolescent inpatient units, behavioral medicine practica within a medical hospital and a prison setting. Twenty-two outpatient sites are available, including mental health centers, private practice settings, VA outpatient clinics, and neuropsychological practices. Students gain experience in assessment and treatment of individuals, groups, couples and families, consultation and psychoeducational presentations. Treatment specialties include eating disorders, neuropsychology, aging, sexual abuse, domestic violence, PTSD, and drug and alcohol abuse. The I/O program has strong ties to local business in Brevard County. Students have been placed in a wide range of practicum sites including county and federal departments, aerospace and electronics industries, financial institutions, health care organizations, and management consulting firms. The Applied Behavior Analysis program has practicum sites with private and public agencies working with children with developmental disabilities and serious emotional and behavioral disorders. For those doctoral students for whom a professional internship is required prior to graduation, 21 applied in 2000–2001. Of those who applied, 21 were placed in internships listed by the Association of Psychology Postdoctoral and Internship Programs (APPIC); 21 were placed in APA accredited internships.

Housing and Day Care: No on-campus housing and day care facilities are available.

Employment of Department Graduates:

Master's Degree Graduates: Of those who graduated in the academic year 2000–2001, the following categories and numbers represent the post-graduate activities and employment of master's degree graduates: Enrolled in a psychology doctoral program (3), enrolled in another graduate/professional program (0), enrolled in a post-doctoral residency/fellowship (n/a), employed in independent practice (n/a), employed in an academic position at a university (0), employed in an academic position at a 2-year/4-year college (0), employed in other positions at a higher education institution (7), employed in a professional position in a school system (0), employed in business or industry (research/consulting) (3), employed in business or industry (management) (0), employed in a government agency (research) (0), employed in a government agency (professional services) (1), employed in a community mental health/counseling center (1), employed in a hospital/medical center (0), still seeking employment (1), other employment position (1).

Doctoral Degree Graduates: Of those who graduated in the academic year 2000–2001, the following categories and numbers

represent the post-graduate activities and employment of doctoral degree graduates: Enrolled in a psychology doctoral program (n/a), enrolled in another graduate/professional program (n/a), enrolled in a post-doctoral residency/fellowship (0), employed in independent practice (3), employed in an academic position at a university (0), employed in an academic position at a 2-year/4-year college (0), employed in other positions at a higher education institution (0), employed in a professional position in a school system (1), employed in business or industry (research/consulting) (0), employed in business or industry (management) (0), employed in a government agency (research) (0), employed in a government agency (professional services) (0), employed in a community mental health/counseling center (6), employed in a hospital/medical center (4), still seeking employment (0), other employment position (5).

Additional Information:

Orientation, Objectives, and Emphasis of Department: The School of Psychology at Florida Institute of Technology offers the M.S. and Ph.D. in industrial/organizational psychology, the M.S. in behavior analysis, and the Psy.D. in clinical psychology. The clinical Psy.D. program trains students based on a practitioner/scientist model focused on development of clinical skills. The program incorporates multiple theoretical orientations and has emphases in neuropsychology, child psychology, marriage and family therapy, multi-cultural issues, and forensic issues. In the Industrial/Organizational Psychology program, students are trained in advanced statistics, organizational research, industrial training and development, personnel selection, performance appraisal, group and team development, and organizational research methodology. The program prepares graduates for a wide variety of careers in academics, management, human resources, and consulting. The Florida Tech School of Psychology is one of a few institutions in the United States that offers a master's program in Applied Behavior Analysis. The program focuses primarily on providing training and consulting services for the benefit of autistic and learning delayed children and for those in health and institutional settings.

Special Facilities or Resources: The facilities of the School of Psychology include the Psychology building, the University Counseling Center, and the Community Psychological Services Center of Florida Tech. The academic building contains offices, classrooms, human research cubicles and rooms, computer facilities, observation and treatment rooms, and a graduate study room. The university's Academic Computing Services-Microcenter provides computers and software, media conversion, digital graphic assistance, and professional editing of theses and papers for publication. The counseling centers include group and individual treatment rooms. Additionally students receive training and conduct research in several community service programs operated by the School of Psychology. These include: Center for Professional Services, is a campus based consulting and research organization. East Central Florida Memory Disorder Clinic, a joint project with Holmes Regional Medical Center serves families in the community who have a member afflicted with Alzheimer's Disease by providing memory screenings, case management, education, wellness and support groups; and to participate in research designed to improve diagnosis and treatment of memory disorders. Family Learning Program offers psychological assessment and treatment to children who have suffered the trauma of sexual abuse and to all family members. Center for Traumatology Studies provides

counseling services for combat veterans, and support groups for spouses and children.

Application Information:
Send to: School of Psychology, Admissions, 150 W. University Blvd., Melbourne, FL 32901. Students are admitted in the Fall. PsyD = Jan 15; MS = March 1; PhD = March 1. *Fee:* PsyD = $60; PhD = $60; MS $50.

Florida International University (2001 data)
Department of Psychology
Arts and Sciences
University Park and North Miami Campuses
Miami, FL 33199
Telephone: (305) 348-2881
Fax: (305) 348-3879
E-mail: *avilesl@fiu.edu*
Web: *http://www.fiu.edu/orgs/psych*

Department Established:
1972. Chairperson: Marvin Dunn. Number of Faculty: total–full-time 21, part-time 25; women–full-time 8, part-time 14; minority–full-time 3, part-time 10.

Programs and Degrees Offered:
Listed in the following order: Program area, degree type (T if terminal Master's), number awarded 7/00-6/01. Behavior Analysis MS (T) 3, Developmental MS (T), Industrial and Organizational PhD 2, Industrial/Organization MS (T), Life-Span Developmental PhD 3, Mental Health MS (T) 3, Psychology and Law PhD.

Student Applications/Admissions:
Student Applications

Behavior Analysis MS—Applications 2001–2002, 17. Total applicants accepted 2001–2002, 4. New applicants enrolled 2001–2002, 4. Total enrolled 2001–2002 full-time, 11, part-time, 3. Openings 2002–2003, 6. *Developmental MS*—Total applicants accepted 2001–2002, 3. New applicants enrolled 2001–2002, 3. Total enrolled 2001–2002 full-time, 9. Openings 2002–2003, 7. *Industrial and Organizational PhD*—Applications 2001–2002, 41. Total applicants accepted 2001–2002, 5. New applicants enrolled 2001–2002, 2. Total enrolled 2001–2002 full-time, 26. Openings 2002–2003, 5. *Industrial/Organization MS*—Total applicants accepted 2001–2002, 5. New applicants enrolled 2001–2002, 5. Total enrolled 2001–2002 full-time, 16. Openings 2002–2003, 7. *Life-Span Developmental PhD*—Applications 2001–2002, 28. Total applicants accepted 2001–2002, 12. New applicants enrolled 2001–2002, 9. Total enrolled 2001–2002 full-time, 32. Openings 2002–2003, 5. *Mental Health MS*—Applications 2001–2002, 12. Total applicants accepted 2001–2002, 8. New applicants enrolled 2001–2002, 8. Total enrolled 2001–2002 full-time, 11. Openings 2002–2003, 6. *Psychology and Law PhD*—Applications 2001–2002, 48. Total applicants accepted 2001–2002, 1. New applicants enrolled 2001–2002, 1. Total enrolled 2001–2002 full-time, 9, part-time, 3. Openings 2002–2003, 3.

Admissions Requirements:
Scores: Entries appear in this order: required test or GPA, minimum score (if required), median score of students entering

in 2001–2002. Master's Programs: GRE-V no minimum stated; GRE-V+Q 1000, 1075; overall undergraduate GPA 3.0, 3.41. Doctoral Programs: overall undergraduate GPA 3.00, 3.58. *Other Criteria:* (importance of criteria rated low, medium, or high): GRE/MAT scores high, research experience high, work experience medium, extracurricular activity low, clinically related public service medium, GPA high, letters of recommendation medium, statement of goals and objectives high.

Student Characteristics: The following represents characteristics of students in 2001–2002 in all graduate psychology programs in the department: Female–full-time 10, part-time 1; Male–full-time 11, part-time 5; African American/Black–full-time 0, part-time 0; Hispanic/Latino (a)–full-time 5, part-time 1; Asian/Pacific Islander–full-time 0, part-time 0; American Indian/Alaska Native–full-time 0, part-time 0.

Financial Information/Assistance:

Tuition for Full-Time Study: No information provided.

Financial Assistance:

First Year Students: No information provided.
Advanced Students: No information provided.
Contact Information: For information on financial assistance, contact: Luz Aviles, Graduate Secretary.

Internships/Practica: Numerous internships and practica sites are available depending on the graduate track a student pursues. Contact the department for details.

Housing and Day Care: No on-campus housing and day care facilities are available.

Employment of Department Graduates:

Master's Degree Graduates: Of those who graduated in the academic year 2000–2001, the following categories and numbers represent the post-graduate activities and employment of master's degree graduates: Enrolled in a post-doctoral residency/fellowship (n/a), employed in independent practice (n/a).
Doctoral Degree Graduates: Of those who graduated in the academic year 2000–2001, the following categories and numbers represent the post-graduate activities and employment of doctoral degree graduates: Enrolled in a psychology doctoral program (n/a), enrolled in another graduate/professional program (n/a).

Additional Information:

Orientation, Objectives, and Emphasis of Department: The Psychology Department at Florida International University is accepting applications for its PhD and MS programs. The PhD program has major emphasis on life-span developmental psychology and applied psychology. Students can build developmental concentrations in infancy, child, adult development, and aging. Students can build applied concentrations in industrial/organizational and legal psychology. The MS program is in general psychology with concentrations in all of the above areas plus community, environmental, experimental, and social. In all graduate programs, students are encouraged to develop an area of specialization early in their graduate training. Students take a series of core-courses designed to facilitate a thorough grounding in theory, methodology, and content in both basic and applied research. In addition, a number of advanced seminars in key areas are offered. Students are encouraged to pursue specific areas of interest through independent study with individual faculty members and through apprenticeships with a primary advisor to acquire direct research experience. Emphasis is on academic excellence and admissions are competitive.

Special Facilities or Resources: The department has laboratories for Infant Development, Cognitive Processes, Behavior Analysis, Gerontology, Adolescent Development, and Health Psychology. In addition, there is an Anxiety and Phobia Clinic, a mock courtroom, and a team training simulation lab.

Information for Students With Physical Disabilities: The department and all labs are accessible to people with physical disabilities.

Application Information:

Send to: Luz Aviles, Graduate Secretary. Students are admitted in the Fall, application deadline January 15. *Fee:* $35. Contact Department.

Florida State University
Department of Psychology
Arts and Sciences
Tallahassee, FL 32306-1270
Telephone: (850) 644-2499
Fax: (850) 644-7739
E-mail: *grad-info@psy.fsu.edu*
Web: *http://www.psy.fsu.edu*

Department Established:

1918. Chairperson: Janet A. Kistner. Number of Faculty: total–full-time 44, part-time 1; women–full-time 13; minority–full-time 2, part-time 1.

Programs and Degrees Offered:

Listed in the following order: Program area, degree type (T if terminal Master's), number awarded 7/00-6/01. Applied Behavior Analysis MA (T) 8, Clinical PhD 6, Cognitive & Behavioral Science PhD 7, Neuroscience PhD 1.

APA Accreditation: Clinical PhD: full.

Student Applications/Admissions:

Student Applications

Applied Behavior Analysis MA—Applications 2001–2002, 27. Total applicants accepted 2001–2002, 14. New applicants enrolled 2001–2002, 9. Total enrolled 2001–2002 full-time, 15, part-time, 5. Openings 2002–2003, 15. The Median number of years required for completion of a degree are 2. The number of students enrolled full and part-time, who were dismissed or voluntarily withdrew from this program area were 1. *Clinical PhD*—Applications 2001–2002, 229. Total applicants accepted 2001–2002, 13. New applicants enrolled 2001–2002, 8. Total enrolled 2001–2002 full-time, 53. Openings 2002–2003, 10. The Median number of years required for completion of a degree are 7. The number of students enrolled full and part-time, who were dismissed or voluntarily withdrew from this program area were 1. *Cognitive & Behavioral Science PhD*—Applications 2001–2002, 49. Total applicants accepted 2001–2002, 10. New applicants enrolled 2001–2002, 2. Total enrolled 2001–2002 full-time, 26. Openings 2002–2003, 6. The Median number of years required for completion of a degree are 5. The number of students enrolled full and part-time, who were dismissed or voluntarily withdrew from this program area were 0. *Neuroscience PhD*—Applications 2001–2002, 22. Total applicants accepted 2001–2002, 6. New applicants enrolled 2001–2002, 5. Total enrolled 2001–2002 full-time, 15. Openings 2002–2003, 6. The Median number of years required for completion of a degree are 5. The number of students enrolled full and part-time, who were dismissed or voluntarily withdrew from this program area were 0.

Admissions Requirements:

Scores: Entries appear in this order: required test or GPA, minimum score (if required), median score of students entering in 2001–2002. Master's Programs: GRE-V no minimum stated, 490; GRE-V+Q 1000, 1020; last 2 years GPA 3.0, 3.5. GRE/ GPA are for the Applied Behavior Analysis master's specialty. Doctoral Programs: GRE-V no minimum stated, 640; GRE-Q no minimum stated, 640; GRE-V+Q 1100, 1240; last 2 years GPA 3.2, 3.7 ; psychology GPA no minimum stated; psychology GPA no minimum stated. The required minimum GRE & GPA vary slightly across the doctoral programs.

Other Criteria: (importance of criteria rated low, medium, or high): GRE/MAT scores high, research experience high, work experience low, extracurricular activity low, clinically related public service low, GPA high, letters of recommendation high, interview medium, statement of goals and objectives high, research area of interest high. Research experience is not relevant for the Applied Behavior Analysis master's specialty. Programs vary on the importance of interviews.

Student Characteristics: The following represents characteristics of students in 2001–2002 in all graduate psychology programs in the department: Female–full-time 63, part-time 11; Male–full-time 34, part-time 6; African American/Black–full-time 8, part-time 1; Hispanic/Latino (a)–full-time 7, part-time 0; Asian/Pacific Islander–full-time 1, part-time 0; American Indian/Alaska Native–full-time 0, part-time 1; Multi-ethnic–full-time 0, part-time 0; students subject to the Americans with Disabilities Act–full-time 0, part-time 0.

Financial Information/Assistance:

Tuition for Full-Time Study: *Master's:* State residents per academic year $2,935, $163 per credit hour; nonstate residents: per academic year $10,264, $570 per credit hour. *Doctoral:* State residents: per academic year $2,935, $163 per credit hour; nonstate residents: per academic year $10,264, $570 per credit hour.

Financial Assistance:

First Year Students: Research assistantships available for first-year. Average amount paid per academic year: $12,500. Average number of hours worked per week: 16. Tuition remission given: full. Traineeships available for first-year. Average amount paid per academic year: $12,000. Average number of hours worked per week: 16. Tuition remission given: full. Fellowships and scholarships available for first-year. Average amount paid per academic year: $15,000. Average number of hours worked per week: 0. Tuition remission given: full.

Advanced Students: Teaching assistantships available for advanced students. Average amount paid per academic year: $12,600. Tuition remission given: full. Research assistantships available for advanced students. Average amount paid per academic year: $13,000. Tuition remission given: full. Traineeships available for advanced students. Average amount paid per academic year: $13,000. Tuition remission given: full. Fellowships and scholarships available for advanced students. Average amount paid per academic year: $15,000. Tuition remission given: full.

Contact Information: Of all students currently enrolled full-time, 74% benefitted from one or more of the listed financial assistance programs. For information on financial assistance, contact: Applications are not required for departmental financial assistance. Neuroscience students receive supplementary funding beyond the stipends noted above in order for FSU to remain competitive with other Neuroscience programs across the country. All students in the doctoral programs who request funding are typically provided stipends and tuition waivers. Students in the master's speciality in Applied Behavior Analysis generally do not receive departmental stipends and waivers.

Internships/Practica: Community facilities provide a multitude of settings for practicum placements for clinical students and for master's and doctoral students interested in applied behavior analysis. Students in the doctoral programs typically receive a stipend and tuition waivers for their practicum work in the community as well as excellent supervised experience in these facilities. For the clinical psychology students, a 12-month unpaid practicum at the on-campus Psychology Clinic is required during the second year of study. The Clinic provides empirically based assessment and therapy services to adults, children, and families in the north Florida region. Psychology faculty typically provides supervision. The clinical program culminates in a required one-year internship in an APA-approved facility. Clinical students from the FSU program have, over the years, been highly successful in obtaining excellent internships throughout the country. Students in the Applied Behavior Analysis master's specialty have access to a variety of practicum settings. Faculty and certified behavior analysts closely supervise students. Some practicum and other sites provide stipends. For those doctoral students for whom a professional internship is required prior to graduation, 9 applied in 2000–2001. Of those who applied, 9 were placed in internships listed by the Association of Psychology Postdoctoral and Internship Programs (APPIC); 9 were placed in APA accredited internships.

Housing and Day Care: On-campus housing and day care facilities are available.

Employment of Department Graduates:

Master's Degree Graduates: Of those who graduated in the academic year 2000–2001, the following categories and numbers represent the post-graduate activities and employment of master's degree graduates: Enrolled in a post-doctoral residency/fellowship (n/a), employed in independent practice (n/a), employed in other positions at a higher education institution (1), other employment position (7).

Doctoral Degree Graduates: Of those who graduated in the academic year 2000–2001, the following categories and numbers represent the post-graduate activities and employment of doctoral degree graduates: Enrolled in a psychology doctoral program (n/a), enrolled in another graduate/professional program (n/a), employed in independent practice (2), employed in an academic position at a university (4), employed in an academic position at a 2-year/4-year college (1), employed in other positions at a higher education institution (1), employed in a hospital/medical center (2), other employment position (4).

Additional Information:

Orientation, Objectives, and Emphasis of Department: The Clinical Psychology program promotes a scientifically based approach to understanding, assessing, and ameliorating cognitive, emotional, behavioral, and health problems. Integrative training in clinical science and clinical service delivery are provided so that students will be prepared to apply current knowledge, theories, and techniques, and will be able and motivated to remain at the cutting edge of the field. The Cognitive and Behavioral Science program consists of three tracks, cognitive, social, and behavioral psychology. Beginning in Fall 2003, this program will be divided into three separate programs: Cognitive Psychology, Social Psychology, and Behavioral Psychology (applied behavior analysis). The Neuroscience program offers students broad training in brain and behavior research. Areas of emphasis include sensory processes, neural development and plasticity, circadian rhythms, behavioral and molecular genetics, and hormonal control of behavior. The Departments of Psychology, Biology, and Nutrition, Food and Exercise Science, as well as the College of Medicine, jointly administer the program. Opportunities for graduate students to learn teaching philosophy and techniques and to apply those skills are excellent. Students may participate in Preparing Future Faculty, a nationally based program designed to prepare students for the full range of faculty roles subsumed by the terms teaching, research, and service.

Special Facilities or Resources: The department has a wide range of resources and technical support. For example, faculty and students have available to them on-line computers, a supercomputer, and workstations offering human eyetracking and brain wave and psychophysiological recording, among others. The department has fully staffed and equipped electronic and machine shops. Highly trained staff provides assistance in graphic arts, photography, instrument and computer software design, and electronic communication services. A neurosurgical operating room, a neurohistological laboratory, and electrically or acoustically shielded rooms are available. A new molecular neuroscience laboratory provides equipment and training for studies of gene cloning and gene expression, as well as techniques to measure levels of hormones and neurotransmitters. The Clinical program administers an on-campus outpatient clinic that offers empirically based assessment and therapy services to members of the Tallahassee community and surrounding areas. Audio and videotaping equipment and therapy rooms with one-way mirrors permit direct observation of therapy cases by faculty. Active clinical training/research programs are maintained by faculty and graduate students in several community agencies.

Information for Students With Physical Disabilities: All offices, laboratories, and other facilities are accessible to physical and sensory-impaired individuals.

Application Information:
Send to: Graduate Program, Department of Psychology, Florida State University, Tallahassee, FL 32306-1270. Students are admitted in the Fall, application deadline 12/15; 1/15. Application deadline is December 15 for Clinical and for Cognitive and Behavioral Science and January 15 for Neuroscience. Applied Behavior Analysis deadline is May 15. *Fee:* $20. No waivers or deferrals of fee are available.

Florida State University
Psychological Services in Education
Education
215 Stone Building
Tallahassee, FL 32306-4458
Telephone: (850) 644-3854
Fax: (850) 644-4335
E-mail: *gpeterso@admin.fsu.edu*
Web: *http://www.fsu.edu/~coe/departments/hss/cpsp.html*

Department Established:
1988. Program Coordinator: Gary Peterson. Number of Faculty: total–full-time 3, part-time 2; women–full-time 2.

Programs and Degrees Offered:
Listed in the following order: Program area, degree type (T if terminal Master's), number awarded 7/00-6/01. Combined counseling and school PhD 6, counseling.

APA Accreditation: Combined PhD: full.

Student Applications/Admissions:
Student Applications
Combined counseling and school PhD—Applications 2001–2002, 62. Total applicants accepted 2001–2002, 10. New applicants enrolled 2001–2002, 9. Total enrolled 2001–2002 full-time, 29, part-time 15. Openings 2002–2003, 7. The Median number of years required for completion of a degree are 6. The number of students enrolled full and part-time, who were dismissed or voluntarily withdrew from this program area were 0.

Admissions Requirements:
Scores: Entries appear in this order: required test or GPA, minimum score (if required), median score of students entering in 2001–2002. Master's Programs: GRE-V+Q 1000, 950; last 2 years GPA 3.0, 3.4. Doctoral Programs: GRE-V+Q 1000, 1100; last 2 years GPA 3.0, 3.4 ; psychology GPA no minimum stated; psychology GPA no minimum stated.
Other Criteria: (importance of criteria rated low, medium, or high): GRE/MAT scores medium, research experience high, work experience medium, extracurricular activity low, clinically related public service medium, GPA letters of recommendation high, interview medium, statement of goals and objectives high.

Student Characteristics: The following represents characteristics of students in 2001–2002 in all graduate psychology programs in the department: Female–full-time 42, part-time 0; Male–full-time 5, part-time 0; African American/Black–full-time 4, part-time 0; Hispanic/Latino (a)–full-time 5, part-time 0; Asian/Pacific Islander–full-time 0, part-time 0; American Indian/Alaska Native–full-time 0, part-time 0.

Financial Information/Assistance:
Tuition for Full-Time Study: *Master's:* State residents per academic year $3,669, $153 per credit hour; nonstate residents: per academic year $12,760, $532 per credit hour. *Doctoral:* State residents: per academic year $3,669, $153 per credit hour; nonstate residents: per academic year $12,760, $532 per credit hour.

Financial Assistance:

First Year Students: Teaching assistantships available for first-year. Average amount paid per academic year: $3,000. Average number of hours worked per week: 10. Apply by open. Research assistantships available for first-year. Average amount paid per academic year: $3,000. Average number of hours worked per week: 10. Apply by open. Fellowships and scholarships available for first-year. Average amount paid per academic year: $6,000. Average number of hours worked per week: 10. Apply by March 1.

Advanced Students: Teaching assistantships available for advanced students. Average amount paid per academic year: $3,000. Average number of hours worked per week: 10. Apply by open. Research assistantships available for advanced students. Average amount paid per academic year: $3,000. Average number of hours worked per week: 10. Apply by open. Fellowships and scholarships available for advanced students. Average amount paid per academic year: $5,000. Apply by March 1.

Contact Information: Of all students currently enrolled full-time, 50% benefitted from one or more of the listed financial assistance programs. For information on financial assistance, contact: Dr. Stephen Rollin, 850-644-9440, rollin@COE.fsu.edu.

Internships/Practica: For those doctoral students for whom a professional internship is required prior to graduation, 1 applied in 2000–2001. Of those who applied, 1 were placed in internships listed by the Association of Psychology Postdoctoral and Internship Programs (APPIC); 1 were placed in APA accredited internships.

Housing and Day Care: No on-campus housing and day care facilities are available.

Employment of Department Graduates:

Master's Degree Graduates: Of those who graduated in the academic year 2000–2001, the following categories and numbers represent the post-graduate activities and employment of master's degree graduates: Enrolled in a post-doctoral residency/fellowship (n/a), employed in independent practice (n/a).

Doctoral Degree Graduates: Of those who graduated in the academic year 2000–2001, the following categories and numbers represent the post-graduate activities and employment of doctoral degree graduates: Enrolled in a psychology doctoral program (n/a), enrolled in another graduate/professional program (n/a).

Additional Information:

Orientation, Objectives, and Emphasis of Department: The Combined Doctoral Program in Counseling Psychology and School Psychology allows students to acquire knowledge and skills necessary for the practice of counseling psychology and school psychology in a variety of applied settings, as well as enabling students to contribute to the advancement of the profession through research and service. Students are expected to acquire basic competency in counseling psychology or school psychology, leading to appropriate national certification and state licensure. Within this combined program, all students share a common core of experience in research and practice in counseling psychology and school psychology, while expressing a professional focus by selecting a concentration in counseling psychology or school psychology. The Combined Program reflects a scientist-practitioner model within the context of the mission of the College of Education. The faculty members in the program have work experience and research interests in the areas of career counseling, mental health counseling throughout the life span, and in the delivery of psychological services in schools.

Special Facilities or Resources: The program uses three primary facilities for the development of counseling skills: (1) the Human Services Center and the Career Center. The Human Services Center is a service, research, and training facility that provides counseling services at a nominal cost to residents of Tallahassee and surrounding communities. This center offers individual counseling for anxiety or depression, relationship counseling, family counseling, and personal growth and development. The Human Services Center also serves as a referral source for public schools. (2) The Adult Learning and Evaluation Center is a referral source for FSU, FAMU, TCC and the community and is located in the College of Education. It serves to assist adults in identifying learning disabilities that may impede the attainment of educational and career progress. It offers students practica and assistantships in psychological assessment and consultation. (3) The Career Center is located in the Student Services Center and provides one of the most modern technologically-advanced career facilities in the nation. The Career Center provides opportunities for practica and internships as well as for student employment opportunities as career advisors. This Center serves as many as 6000 students per year with a variety of career concerns from choice of major to job placement. The overarching philosophy is one of a full-service career center that is able to treat not only the presenting career concern but related mental health issues as well.

Application Information:
Send to: Stephen A. Rollin, Professor and Chair, Admissions Committee, Florida State University, 215 Stone Building, Tallahassee, FL 32306-4458. Students are admitted in the Fall, application deadline February 1. *Fee:* $20.

Florida, University of
Department of Clinical and Health Psychology
Health Professions
Box 100165 HSC
Gainesville, FL 32610-0165
Telephone: (352) 265-0455
Fax: (352) 265-0468
E-mail: *vcarter@hp.ufl.edu*
Web: *http://www.hp.ufl.edu/chp/*

Department Established:
1959. Chairperson: Ronald Rozensky. Number of Faculty: total–full-time 28; women–full-time 9; minority–full-time 2.

Programs and Degrees Offered:
Listed in the following order: Program area, degree type (T if terminal Master's), number awarded 7/00-6/01. Clinical PhD 13.

APA Accreditation: Clinical PhD: full.

Student Applications/Admissions:

Student Applications

Clinical PhD—Applications 2001–2002, 266. Total applicants accepted 2001–2002, 25. New applicants enrolled 2001–2002,

15. Total enrolled 2001–2002 full-time, 70, part-time, 11. Openings 2002–2003, 12. The Median number of years required for completion of a degree are 5. The number of students enrolled full and part-time, who were dismissed or voluntarily withdrew from this program area were 2.

Admissions Requirements:

Scores: Entries appear in this order: required test or GPA, minimum score (if required), median score of students entering in 2001–2002. Master's Programs: We do not offer a terminal master's degree program. Doctoral Programs: GRE-V 500, 640; GRE-Q 500, 640; GRE-V+Q 1000, 1280; GRE-Analytical no minimum stated; GRE-V+Q+Analytical no minimum stated; last 2 years GPA 3.00, 3.8 ; psychology GPA no minimum stated; psychology GPA no minimum stated.

Other Criteria: (importance of criteria rated low, medium, or high): GRE/MAT scores medium, research experience high, work experience medium, extracurricular activity medium, clinically related public service high, GPA medium, letters of recommendation high, interview high, statement of goals and objectives high.

Student Characteristics: The following represents characteristics of students in 2001–2002 in all graduate psychology programs in the department: Female–full-time 49, part-time 6; Male–full-time 21, part-time 5; African American/Black–full-time 6, part-time 2; Hispanic/Latino (a)–full-time 3, part-time 0; Asian/Pacific Islander–full-time 5, part-time 0; American Indian/Alaska Native–full-time 0, part-time 0; Multi-ethnic–full-time 1, part-time 0; students subject to the Americans with Disabilities Act–full-time 1, part-time 0.

Financial Information/Assistance:

Tuition for Full-Time Study: *Doctoral:* State residents: per academic year $3,215; nonstate residents: per academic year $13,700.

Financial Assistance:

First Year Students: Research assistantships available for first-year. Average amount paid per academic year: $9,700. Average number of hours worked per week: 13. Apply by December 1. Tuition remission given: full and partial. Fellowships and scholarships available for first-year. Average amount paid per academic year: $15,000. Apply by December 1. Tuition remission given: full.

Advanced Students: Teaching assistantships available for advanced students. Average amount paid per academic year: $11,000. Average number of hours worked per week: 20. Tuition remission given: full and partial. Research assistantships available for advanced students. Average amount paid per academic year: $11,000. Average number of hours worked per week: 20. Tuition remission given: full and partial. Fellowships and scholarships available for advanced students. Average amount paid per academic year: $18,000. Tuition remission given: full.

Contact Information: Of all students currently enrolled full-time, 98% benefitted from one or more of the listed financial assistance programs. For information on financial assistance, contact: The Program Assistant regarding fellowships/assistantships at 352-395-0455.

Internships/Practica: The Department of Clinical and Health Psychology runs a Psychology Clinic which is part of the Shands Teaching Hospital of the UF academic health science center. This Clinic provides consultation, assessment, and intervention services to medical-surgical inpatients and outpatients, as well as community patients with emotional and behavioral problems. Major services include clinical health psychology, child/pediatric psychology, and clinical neuropsychology. For those doctoral students for whom a professional internship is required prior to graduation, 10 applied in 2000–2001. Of those who applied, 10 were placed in internships listed by the Association of Psychology Postdoctoral and Internship Programs (APPIC); 10 were placed in APA accredited internships.

Housing and Day Care: No on-campus housing and day care facilities are available.

Employment of Department Graduates:

Master's Degree Graduates: Of those who graduated in the academic year 2000–2001, the following categories and numbers represent the post-graduate activities and employment of master's degree graduates: Enrolled in a post-doctoral residency/fellowship (n/a), employed in independent practice (n/a), employed in an academic position at a university (2), employed in a community mental health/counseling center (1), employed in a hospital/medical center (5).

Doctoral Degree Graduates: Of those who graduated in the academic year 2000–2001, the following categories and numbers represent the post-graduate activities and employment of doctoral degree graduates: Enrolled in a psychology doctoral program (n/a), enrolled in another graduate/professional program (n/a).

Additional Information:

Orientation, Objectives, and Emphasis of Department: The program is designed to develop doctoral-level professional psychologists in the scientist-practitioner model through development of broad clinical skills and competencies, through mastery of broad areas of knowledge in psychology and clinical psychology, and through demonstrated competencies in contributing to that knowledge by research. Within these program objectives particular emphases can be identified: clinical health psychology, clinical neuropsychology, and clinical child psychology. Courses, practica, conferences, committees, supervision, and settings are designed to augment each emphasis.

Special Facilities or Resources: Department faculty currently occupy several thousand square feet of laboratory space for clinical and basic research. The Department is particularly strong in instrumentation and methodology for cognitive and psychophysiological studies. The clinical psychology program uses the extensive resources of the campus and community. The primary focus is in the Center for Clinical and Health Psychology of the University of Florida Health Science Center with its six colleges, and Shands Teaching Hospital and Clinics. Other sites utilized for clinical training include the university student health services; the university counseling center; and the VA hospital in Gainesville. Agencies and centers throughout the state and nation are also used, principally for intern training for students. The use of these varied resources is consonant with the program objectives. The trainee is directly involved with a broad scope of clinical and health problems, professionals, agencies, and settings.

Information for Students With Physical Disabilities: The University of Florida, under the guidelines of ADA and 504 federal legislation, is required to make reasonable accommodations to the known physical and mental limitations of otherwise qualified individuals with disabilities. To help provide the best possible service to students, staff, faculty, and visitors, the University of Florida has an Americans with Disabilities Act Office with a coordinator responsible for access for persons with disabilities. The ADA coordinator assists anyone with questions about access. Contact information for the ADA office is: Voice: (352) 392-7056; , TDD: (352) 846-1046; email: Osfield@ufl.edu.

Application Information:
Send to: Graduate Admissions, Department of Clinical and Health Psychology, Box 100165 HSC, University of Florida, Gainesville, FL 32610-0165. Students are admitted in the Fall, application deadline December 1. Ph.D. program only - starts Fall only. December 1 is the deadline for receipt of all application materials for entry into the following fall semester. *Fee:* $20.

Florida, University of
Department of Psychology
Liberal Arts and Sciences
P.O. Box 112250
Gainesville, FL 32611-2250
Telephone: (352) 392-0601
Fax: (352) 392-7985
E-mail: *heesack@psych.ufl.edu*
Web: *http://www.psych.ufl.edu*

Department Established:
1947. Professor and Chair: Martin Heesacker. Number of Faculty: total–full-time 52, part-time 4; women–full-time 11, part-time 1; minority–full-time 3.

Programs and Degrees Offered:
Listed in the following order: Program area, degree type (T if terminal Master's), number awarded 7/00-6/01. Behavior Analysis PhD 3, cognitive PhD 1, counseling PhD 10, developmental PhD 1, psychobiology PhD, social PhD 2.

APA Accreditation: Counseling PhD: full.

Student Applications/Admissions:
Student Applications
Behavior Analysis PhD—Applications 2001–2002, 22. Total applicants accepted 2001–2002, 8. New applicants enrolled 2001–2002, 6. Total enrolled 2001–2002 full-time, 24, part-time, 2. The Median number of years required for completion of a degree are 4. The number of students enrolled full and part-time, who were dismissed or voluntarily withdrew from this program area were 1. *Cognitive PhD*—Applications 2001–2002, 17. Total applicants accepted 2001–2002, 4. New applicants enrolled 2001–2002, 1. Total enrolled 2001–2002 full-time, 7, part-time, 3. The Median number of years required for completion of a degree are 4. The number of students enrolled full and part-time, who were dismissed or voluntarily withdrew from this program area were 0. *Counseling PhD*—Applications 2001–2002, 151. Total applicants accepted 2001–2002, 12. New applicants enrolled 2001–2002, 7. Total enrolled 2001–2002 full-time, 29, part-time, 8. The Median number of years required for completion of a degree are 4. The number of students enrolled full and part-time, who were

dismissed or voluntarily withdrew from this program area were 0. *Developmental PhD*—Applications 2001–2002, 18. Total applicants accepted 2001–2002, 5. New applicants enrolled 2001–2002, 2. Total enrolled 2001–2002 full-time, 24, part-time, 2. The Median number of years required for completion of a degree are 4. The number of students enrolled full and part-time, who were dismissed or voluntarily withdrew from this program area were 2. *Psychobiology PhD*—Applications 2001–2002, 24. Total applicants accepted 2001–2002, 7. Total enrolled 2001–2002 full-time, 8. The Median number of years required for completion of a degree are 4. The number of students enrolled full and part-time, who were dismissed or voluntarily withdrew from this program area were 1. *Social PhD*—Applications 2001–2002, 38. Total applicants accepted 2001–2002, 12. New applicants enrolled 2001–2002, 6. Total enrolled 2001–2002 full-time, 16. The Median number of years required for completion of a degree are 4. The number of students enrolled full and part-time, who were dismissed or voluntarily withdrew from this program area were 2.

Admissions Requirements:
Scores: Entries appear in this order: required test or GPA, minimum score (if required), median score of students entering in 2001–2002. Doctoral Programs: GRE-V+Q 1200, 1259; last 2 years GPA 3.3, 2 ; psychology GPA no minimum stated; psychology GPA no minimum stated.
Other Criteria: (importance of criteria rated low, medium, or high): GRE/MAT scores medium, research experience high, work experience medium, extracurricular activity medium, clinically related public service high, GPA medium, letters of recommendation high, interview medium, statement of goals and objectives high. Only the Counseling Psychology program requires clinically related experience.

Student Characteristics: The following represents characteristics of students in 2001–2002 in all graduate psychology programs in the department: Female–full-time 55, part-time 10; Male–full-time 39, part-time 7; African American/Black–full-time 7, part-time 9; Hispanic/Latino (a)–full-time 6, part-time 2; Asian/Pacific Islander–full-time 3, part-time 0; American Indian/Alaska Native–full-time 0, part-time 0.

Financial Information/Assistance:
Tuition for Full-Time Study: *Master's:* State residents $152 per credit hour; nonstate residents: $531 per credit hour. *Doctoral:* State residents: $152 per credit hour; nonstate residents: $531 per credit hour.

Financial Assistance:
First Year Students: Teaching assistantships available for first-year. Average amount paid per academic year: $10,080. Average number of hours worked per week: 15. Apply by January 15. Tuition remission given: full. Research assistantships available for first-year. Average amount paid per academic year: $7,800. Average number of hours worked per week: 13. Apply by January 15. Tuition remission given: full. Fellowships and scholarships available for first-year. Average amount paid per academic year: $15,000. Apply by January 15.
Advanced Students: Teaching assistantships available for advanced students. Average amount paid per academic year: $9,200. Average number of hours worked per week: 10. Apply by January 15. Tuition remission given: full. Research assistantships

available for advanced students. Average amount paid per academic year: $8,500. Average number of hours worked per week: 16. Apply by January 15. Tuition remission given: full.

Contact Information: Of all students currently enrolled full-time, 0% benefitted from one or more of the listed financial assistance programs. For information on financial assistance, contact: For general information, contact Graduate Studies Secretary. For specific information, contact Area Admissions Chair.

Internships/Practica: University Counseling Center, University of Florida Student Health Service, Family Practice Medical Group, Meridian Behavioral Healthcare, Alachua County Crisis Center, VA Medical Center, North Florida Treatment and Evaluation Center, and Northeast Florida State Hospital. For those doctoral students for whom a professional internship is required prior to graduation, 6 applied in 2000–2001.

Housing and Day Care: On-campus housing and day care facilities are available.

Employment of Department Graduates:

Master's Degree Graduates: Of those who graduated in the academic year 2000–2001, the following categories and numbers represent the post-graduate activities and employment of master's degree graduates: Enrolled in a post-doctoral residency/fellowship (n/a), employed in independent practice (n/a).

Doctoral Degree Graduates: Of those who graduated in the academic year 2000–2001, the following categories and numbers represent the post-graduate activities and employment of doctoral degree graduates: Enrolled in a psychology doctoral program (n/a), enrolled in another graduate/professional program (n/a).

Additional Information:

Orientation, Objectives, and Emphasis of Department: The graduate program in Psychology at the University of Florida is designed for those planning careers as researchers, teacher-scholars, and scientist-practitioners in Psychology. In addition to specialized training in one or more areas, a core program of theories, methods, and research in general psychology insures that each student will be well prepared in the basic areas of Psychology. The primary goal of the Department is educating scientists who will help advance psychology as a science through teaching, research, and professional practice. Because the University of Florida is a broad spectrum university, including almost all the major academic departments as well as professional schools on a single campus, a unique atmosphere exists for the evolution of the general program and the development of personal programs of study. Each student also receives specialized training in at least one of the areas of specialization including cognition and sensory processes, counseling psychology, developmental, experimental analysis of behavior, psychobiology (comparative-physiological), and social. One of the fundamental goals of the doctoral program is to engage the student as early as possible in the area of interest while assuring a sound background of knowledge of theory, methodology, and major content areas so that maximum integration may be achieved. All students participate in various ongoing aspects of the academic community such as teaching, research, field experience, and professional activities. Seminars are offered in techniques of teaching accompanied by supervised undergraduate teaching. Continuous research experience is required. The Department participates in a number of interdisciplinary programs including sensory studies, neurobiological sciences, and gerontological studies.

Special Facilities or Resources: Special facilities in the department include laboratories in comparative, developmental, experimental analysis of behavior, cognitive and information processing, perception, personality, psychobiology, sensory, and social; an animal colony; a statistical computation laboratory; a laboratory in neuropsychology and developmental learning disabilities; the Communication Sciences Laboratory; and the Computing Center.

Application Information:

Send to: Graduate Studies Secretary; Psychology Department; University of Florida; Gainesville, FL 32611-2250. Students are admitted in the Fall, application deadline January 15. *Fee:* $20.

Miami, University of

Department of Educational & Psychological Studies/Area of Counseling Psychology
Education
P.O. Box 248065
Coral Gables, FL 33124-2040
Telephone: (305) 284-3001
Fax: (305) 284-3003
E-mail: bfowers@miami.edu
Web: http://www.education.miami.edu/Depts/EPS/eps_home.

Department Established:

1967. Director of Training, Counseling Psychology Program: Blaine J. Fowers. Number of Faculty: total–full-time 7, part-time 4; women–full-time 2, part-time 2; minority–full-time 2, part-time 3.

Programs and Degrees Offered:

Listed in the following order: Program area, degree type (T if terminal Master's), number awarded 7/00-6/01. Counseling psychology PhD 4, marriage and family therapy, mental health counseling.

APA Accreditation: Counseling PhD: full.

Student Applications/Admissions:

Student Applications

Counseling psychology PhD—Applications 2001–2002, 75. Total applicants accepted 2001–2002, 8. New applicants enrolled 2001–2002, 6. Total enrolled 2001–2002 full-time, 25, part-time, 17. Openings 2002–2003, 6. The Median number of years required for completion of a degree are 6.

Admissions Requirements:

Scores: Entries appear in this order: required test or GPA, minimum score (if required), median score of students entering in 2001–2002. Master's Programs: GRE-V no minimum stated, 470; GRE-Q no minimum stated, 530; GRE-V+Q no minimum stated, 1000; overall undergraduate GPA no minimum stated, 3.28. Doctoral Programs: GRE-V no minimum stated, 610; GRE-Q no minimum stated, 650; GRE-V+Q no minimum stated, 1260; overall undergraduate GPA no minimum stated, 3.40; last 2 years GPA no minimum stated; psychology GPA no minimum stated; psychology GPA no minimum stated, 3.9.

Other Criteria: (importance of criteria rated low, medium, or high): GRE/MAT scores high, research experience medium, work experience medium, extracurricular activity low, clinically related public service medium, GPA high, letters of recommendation high, interview high, statement of goals and objectives high, multicultural experience high.

Student Characteristics: The following represents characteristics of students in 2001–2002 in all graduate psychology programs in the department: Female–full-time 18, part-time 7; Male–full-time 9, part-time 3; African American/Black–full-time 0, part-time 2; Hispanic/Latino (a)–full-time 5, part-time 2; Asian/Pacific Islander–full-time 1, part-time 0; American Indian/Alaska Native–full-time 0, part-time 0; Multi-ethnic–full-time 1.

Financial Information/Assistance:

Tuition for Full-Time Study: *Master's:* State residents $980 per credit hour; nonstate residents: $980 per credit hour. *Doctoral:* State residents: $980 per credit hour; nonstate residents: $980 per credit hour.

Financial Assistance:

First Year Students: Teaching assistantships available for first-year. Average amount paid per academic year: $11,000. Average number of hours worked per week: 20. Apply by Jan. 2. Tuition remission given: partial. Research assistantships available for first-year. Average amount paid per academic year: $11,000. Average number of hours worked per week: 20. Apply by Jan. 2. Tuition remission given: partial. Fellowships and scholarships available for first-year. Average amount paid per academic year: $17,000. Average number of hours worked per week: 0. Apply by Jan. 2. Tuition remission given: partial.

Advanced Students: Teaching assistantships available for advanced students. Average amount paid per academic year: $11,000. Average number of hours worked per week: 20. Apply by April 15. Tuition remission given: partial. Research assistantships available for advanced students. Average amount paid per academic year: $13,000. Average number of hours worked per week: 20. Apply by April 15. Tuition remission given: partial. Fellowships and scholarships available for advanced students. Average amount paid per academic year: $17,000. Average number of hours worked per week: 0. Apply by Feb. 1. Tuition remission given: partial.

Contact Information: Of all students currently enrolled full-time, 100% benefitted from one or more of the listed financial assistance programs. For information on financial assistance, contact: Dr. Blaine Fowers (305) 284-5261.

Internships/Practica: Students complete a one academic year practicum in our on-campus training clinic. Program faculty supervise the practicum through weekly one-to-one meetings and group supervision meetings. The practicum experience is supplemented by an off campus placement. Therapeutic modalities in these placements include individual, couple, and group therapies. The off-campus placement is tailored to the student's career goals. Many students also complete an optional advanced practicum in their third year with placements tailored to their career goals. Placements include university counseling centers, psychiatric facilities, VA hospitals, behavioral medicine settings, correctional facilities, schools, among others. For those doctoral students for whom a professional internship is required prior to graduation, 5 applied in 2000–2001. Of those who applied, 5 were placed in internships listed by the Association of Psychology Postdoctoral and Internship Programs (APPIC); 5 were placed in APA accredited internships.

Housing and Day Care: On-campus housing and day care facilities are available.

Employment of Department Graduates:

Master's Degree Graduates: Of those who graduated in the academic year 2000–2001, the following categories and numbers represent the post-graduate activities and employment of master's degree graduates: Enrolled in a post-doctoral residency/fellowship (n/a), employed in independent practice (n/a).

Doctoral Degree Graduates: Of those who graduated in the academic year 2000–2001, the following categories and numbers represent the post-graduate activities and employment of doctoral degree graduates: Enrolled in a psychology doctoral program (n/a), enrolled in another graduate/professional program (n/a), enrolled in a post-doctoral residency/fellowship (2), employed in an academic position at a university (1), employed in business or industry (management) (1).

Additional Information:

Orientation, Objectives, and Emphasis of Department: The multicultural, health psychology, and family areas are foci in the doctoral program that is designed to educate counseling psychologists following the scientist-practitioner model to prepare individuals who will contribute to knowledge in psychology and who will be exemplary practitioners of psychological science. A sequence of research experiences is required as well as at least two semesters of supervised practicum and a full-year internship. In addition to coursework in the psychological foundations, requirements include the study of human development and personality (including career development), theories of therapy and the change process, therapeutic methodologies, and psychological assessment. We have begun to offer a 5 course sequence leading to a certificate in bilingual counseling (Spanish/English). The titles of the courses are: Professional Psychological Spanish, Hispanic and Latino Psychology, Community Interventions for Latino and Hispanic Populations, and Supervised Practice in Bilingual Counseling. Two of the five courses can be taken as required electives in the program.

Special Facilities or Resources: The Institute for Individual and Family Counseling, an on-campus clinic, is used as the primary practicum site. It is equipped with facilities for audio, video, and live supervision. The multi-cultural clientele of the Institute and the other agencies and schools in the Miami area are available for practica and fieldwork. Biofeedback and computer laboratories are available to students in the department. A biofeedback laboratory is available in the Institute for Individual and Family Counseling. A microcomputer laboratory is available to all students in the department. In addition, an assessment laboratory is an integral part of assessment training in the program.

Information for Students With Physical Disabilities: All facilities are accessible to those with physical disabilities and accommodations are made for disabilities.

Application Information:

Send to: Coordinator of Graduate Studies, School of Education, (312 Merrick Building), University of Miami, P.O. Box 248065, Coral Gables, FL 33124. Students are admitted in the Fall, application deadline Jan. 2 (Doct). *Fee:* $50.

Miami, University of (Florida)

Department of Psychology
P.O. Box 248185
Coral Gables, FL 33124
Telephone: (305) 284-2814
Fax: (305) 284-3402
E-mail: *inquire@mail.psy.miami.edu*
Web: *http://www.psy.miami.edu*

Department Established:

1959. Chairperson: A. Rodney Wellens. Number of Faculty: total–full-time 38; women–full-time 17; minority–full-time 6.

Programs and Degrees Offered:

Listed in the following order: Program area, degree type (T if terminal Master's), number awarded 7/00-6/01. Applied development PhD 2, behavioral medicine PhD, behavioral neuroscience PhD, clinical (adult) PhD 3, clinical child PhD 4, health PhD 5.

APA Accreditation: Clinical PhD: full.

Student Applications/Admissions:

Student Applications

Applied development PhD—Applications 2001–2002, 11. Total applicants accepted 2001–2002, 4. New applicants enrolled 2001–2002, 2. Total enrolled 2001–2002 full-time, 7. Openings 2002–2003, 2. The Median number of years required for completion of a degree are 5. The number of students enrolled full and part-time, who were dismissed or voluntarily withdrew from this program area were 0. *Behavioral medicine PhD*—Applications 2001–2002, 1. The Median number of years required for completion of a degree are 5. The number of students enrolled full and part-time, who were dismissed or voluntarily withdrew from this program area were 0. *Behavioral neuroscience PhD*—Applications 2001–2002, 1. Total enrolled 2001–2002 full-time, 5. The Median number of years required for completion of a degree are 5. The number of students enrolled full and part-time, who were dismissed or voluntarily withdrew from this program area were 0. *Clinical (adult) PhD*—Applications 2001–2002, 40. Total applicants accepted 2001–2002, 5. New applicants enrolled 2001–2002, 2. Total enrolled 2001–2002 full-time, 13. Openings 2002–2003, 5. The Median number of years required for completion of a degree are 5. The number of students enrolled full and part-time, who were dismissed or voluntarily withdrew from this program area were 0. *Clinical child PhD*—Applications 2001–2002, 80. Total applicants accepted 2001–2002, 6. New applicants enrolled 2001–2002, 5. Total enrolled 2001–2002 full-time, 17. Openings 2002–2003, 7. The Median number of years required for completion of a degree are 5. The number of students enrolled full and part-time, who were dismissed or voluntarily withdrew from this program area were 1. *Health PhD*—Applications 2001–2002, 38. Total applicants accepted 2001–2002, 13. New applicants enrolled 2001–2002, 9. Total enrolled 2001–2002 full-time, 27. Openings 2002–2003, 7. The Median number of years required for completion of a degree are 5. The number of students enrolled full and part-time, who were dismissed or voluntarily withdrew from this program area were 1.

Admissions Requirements:

Scores: Entries appear in this order: required test or GPA, minimum score (if required), median score of students entering in 2001–2002. Doctoral Programs: GRE-V 590, 630; GRE-Q 620, 650; GRE-V+Q 1210, 1300; overall undergraduate GPA 3.5, 3.5 ; last 2 years GPA no minimum stated; psychology GPA no minimum stated; psychology GPA no minimum stated.

Other Criteria: (importance of criteria rated low, medium, or high): GRE/MAT scores high, research experience high, work experience medium, extracurricular activity medium, clinically related public service medium, GPA high, letters of recommendation high, interview high, statement of goals and objectives high. Clinically related public service not weighted for non-clinical programs.

Student Characteristics: The following represents characteristics of students in 2001–2002 in all graduate psychology programs in the department: Female–full-time 12, part-time 0; Male–full-time 5, part-time 0; African American/Black–full-time 0, part-time 0; Hispanic/Latino (a)–full-time 3, part-time 0; Asian/Pacific Islander–full-time 2, part-time 0; American Indian/Alaska Native–full-time 0, part-time 0.

Financial Information/Assistance:

Tuition for Full-Time Study: *Doctoral:* State residents: per academic year $18,180, $1,010 per credit hour; nonstate residents: per academic year $18,180, $1,010 per credit hour.

Financial Assistance:

First Year Students: Teaching assistantships available for first-year. Average amount paid per academic year: $12,700. Average number of hours worked per week: 15. Apply by 12/1. Tuition remission given: full. Research assistantships available for first-year. Average amount paid per academic year: $18,000. Average number of hours worked per week: 15. Apply by 12/1. Tuition remission given: full. Traineeships available for first-year. Average amount paid per academic year: $18,000. Average number of hours worked per week: 15. Apply by 12/1. Tuition remission given: full. Fellowships and scholarships available for first-year. Average amount paid per academic year: $17,000. Apply by 12/1. Tuition remission given: full.

Advanced Students: Teaching assistantships available for advanced students. Average amount paid per academic year: $12,700. Average number of hours worked per week: 15. Tuition remission given: full. Research assistantships available for advanced students. Average amount paid per academic year: $18,000. Average number of hours worked per week: 15. Tuition remission given: full. Traineeships available for advanced students. Average amount paid per academic year: $18,000. Average number of hours worked per week: 15. Tuition remission given: full. Fellowships and scholarships available for advanced students.

Average amount paid per academic year: $17,000. Tuition remission given: full.

Contact Information: Of all students currently enrolled full-time, 100% benefitted from one or more of the listed financial assistance programs.

Internships/Practica: For those doctoral students for whom a professional internship is required prior to graduation, 8 applied in 2000–2001. Of those who applied, 8 were placed in internships listed by the Association of Psychology Postdoctoral and Internship Programs (APPIC); 8 were placed in APA accredited internships.

Housing and Day Care: No on-campus housing and day care facilities are available.

Employment of Department Graduates:
Master's Degree Graduates: Of those who graduated in the academic year 2000–2001, the following categories and numbers represent the post-graduate activities and employment of master's degree graduates: Enrolled in a post-doctoral residency/fellowship (n/a), employed in independent practice (n/a).
Doctoral Degree Graduates: Of those who graduated in the academic year 2000–2001, the following categories and numbers represent the post-graduate activities and employment of doctoral degree graduates: Enrolled in a psychology doctoral program (n/a), enrolled in another graduate/professional program (n/a), enrolled in a post-doctoral residency/fellowship (9), employed in an academic position at a university (1).

Additional Information:
Orientation, Objectives, and Emphasis of Department: The University of Miami Department of Psychology offers courses leading to the degree of Doctor of Philosophy. Prospective degree applicants are admitted to graduate study in psychology within one of three divisions: adult, child, or health. The only area of specialization available to students admitted to the adult division is a clinical program called adult clinical. Students admitted to the child division may choose from clinical child and family, pediatric health clinical, and applied developmental. Students in the health division may choose from health clinical, behavioral neuroscience, or behavioral medicine.

Special Facilities or Resources: The Psychological Services Center serves as a training site for clinical students, and many other placements are available in the community. A Behavioral Medicine Research Building provides superb training opportunities in behavioral medicine, behavioral neuroscience, and health psychology. The department has remote access to the university computer and many small computers for research. Faculty research is supported by more than $10,000,000 external funds. Additional health psychology faculty are available through the medical campus.

Application Information:
Send to: Graduate Admissions, Department of Psychology, P.O. Box 248185, Coral Gables, FL 33124. Students are admitted in the Fall, application deadline December 1. *Fee:* $50.

North Florida, University of
Department of Psychology
4567 St. John's Bluff Road, South
Jacksonville, FL 32224-2673
Telephone: (904) 620-2807
Fax: (904) 620-3814
E-mail: *mchambli@unf.edu*
Web: *http://www.unf.edu*

Department Established:
1972. Chairperson: Minor H. Chamblin. Number of Faculty: total–full-time 18, part-time 7; women–full-time 7, part-time 1; minority–full-time 3; faculty subject to the Americans with Disabilities Act 2.

Programs and Degrees Offered:
Listed in the following order: Program area, degree type (T if terminal Master's), number awarded 7/00-6/01. Counseling Psychology, General Psychology MA (T) 8.

Student Applications/Admissions:
Student Applications
General Psychology MA—Applications 2001–2002, 30. Total applicants accepted 2001–2002, 10. New applicants enrolled 2001–2002, 8. Total enrolled 2001–2002 full-time, 8. Openings 2002–2003, 10. The Median number of years required for completion of a degree are 2.

Admissions Requirements:
Scores: Entries appear in this order: required test or GPA, minimum score (if required), median score of students entering in 2001–2002. Master's Programs: GRE-V 500, 560; GRE-Q 500, 540; last 2 years GPA 3.0, 3.4; psychology GPA 3.0, 3.4. Doctoral Programs: last 2 years GPA no minimum stated; psychology GPA no minimum stated; psychology GPA no minimum stated.
Other Criteria: (importance of criteria rated low, medium, or high): GRE/MAT scores medium, research experience high, work experience medium, clinically related public service medium, GPA medium, letters of recommendation medium, statement of goals and objectives medium. Research experience for general psychology and clinically related public service for counseling psychology.

Student Characteristics: The following represents characteristics of students in 2001–2002 in all graduate psychology programs in the department: Female–full-time 30, Male–full-time 5, African American/Black–full-time 1, Hispanic/Latino (a)–full-time 1, Asian/Pacific Islander–full-time 1, American Indian/Alaska Native–full-time 0, part-time 0; students subject to the Americans with Disabilities Act–full-time 0.

Financial Information/Assistance:
Tuition for Full-Time Study: *Master's:* State residents $157 per credit hour; nonstate residents: $536 per credit hour.

Financial Assistance:
First Year Students: No information provided.
Advanced Students: No information provided.

Contact Information: For information on financial assistance, contact: Office of Financial Aid, University of North Florida, Jacksonville, FL 32225.

Internships/Practica: No information provided.

Housing and Day Care: On-campus housing and day care facilities are available.

Employment of Department Graduates:

Master's Degree Graduates: Of those who graduated in the academic year 2000–2001, the following categories and numbers represent the post-graduate activities and employment of master's degree graduates: Enrolled in a post-doctoral residency/fellowship (n/a), employed in independent practice (n/a).

Doctoral Degree Graduates: Of those who graduated in the academic year 2000–2001, the following categories and numbers represent the post-graduate activities and employment of doctoral degree graduates: Enrolled in a psychology doctoral program (n/a), enrolled in another graduate/professional program (n/a).

Additional Information:

Orientation, Objectives, and Emphasis of Department: The Master of Arts in Counseling Psychology program is designed to prepare students for emerging professional roles as Florida licensed master's level practitioners. The program consists of 60 semester hours of course work, including a two-semester practicum in a community mental health agency. The program balances theory and practice and is designed to provide the prospective practitioner with a firm theoretical foundation for developing counseling strategies as well as the ability to apply particular goal-oriented intervention tactics. The Master of Arts in General Psychology program is a broad-based, research-oriented program intended to equip students with the critical skills and knowledge necessary for continued occupation and educational advancement in fields related to psychology. The program consists of 37 semester hours of course work designed around a core curriculum of statistics, research design, substantive areas of psychology, and a research-based thesis.

Special Facilities or Resources: Several teaching laboratories are housed within the psychology department. The counseling lab and the psychometric lab each consist of a large observation room, three small rooms for individual counseling/testing and one large seminar/classroom. The computer applications lab has 24 individual computer work stations and an instructor's server, with a local area network and connections to the university mainframe. New computers and printers were purchased during the 2001-2002 school year. The animal lab has six computerized stations for student research on rodents. In addition to these teaching laboratories, individual faculty research labs are also housed within the psychology department. These labs include a social cognition lab, social interaction lab, psychophysiology lab, community research lab, psychology and law lab, and human performance lab.

Application Information:

Send to: Maury Nation, Coordinator, Master of Arts in Counseling Psychology; John Eisler, Coordinator, Master of Arts in General Psychology. Students are admitted in the Fall, application deadline 2/1, 6/1. Application deadlines for (MACP) February 1; May 1, (MAGP) June 1. *Fee:* $20.

Nova Southeastern University

Center for Psychological Studies
3301 College Avenue
Fort Lauderdale, FL 33314
Telephone: (954) 262-5700
Fax: (954) 262-3859
E-mail: *cpsinfo@nova.edu*
Web: *http://www.cps.nova.edu*

Department Established:

1967. Dean: Ronald F. Levant. Number of Faculty: total–full-time 31, part-time 60; women–full-time 8, part-time 19; minority–full-time 4, part-time 5.

Programs and Degrees Offered:

Listed in the following order: Program area, degree type (T if terminal Master's), number awarded 7/00-6/01. Clinical psychology PhD 19, clinical psychology PsyD 55, clinical psychopharmacology MA (T) 1, mental health counseling MA (T) 109, school guidance and counseling MA (T) 21, school psychology.

APA Accreditation: Clinical PhD: full. Clinical PsyD: full.

Student Applications/Admissions:

Student Applications

Clinical psychology PhD—Applications 2001–2002, 175. Total applicants accepted 2001–2002, 41. New applicants enrolled 2001–2002, 15. Total enrolled 2001–2002 full-time, 122. Openings 2002–2003, 18. The Median number of years required for completion of a degree are 6. The number of students enrolled full and part-time, who were dismissed or voluntarily withdrew from this program area were 1. *Clinical psychology PsyD*—Applications 2001–2002, 240. Total applicants accepted 2001–2002, 106. New applicants enrolled 2001–2002, 70. Total enrolled 2001–2002 full-time, 308. Openings 2002–2003, 70. The Median number of years required for completion of a degree are 5. The number of students enrolled full and part-time, who were dismissed or voluntarily withdrew from this program area were 7. *Clinical psychopharmacology MA*—Applications 2001–2002, 18. Total applicants accepted 2001–2002, 12. New applicants enrolled 2001–2002, 12. Total enrolled 2001–2002 full-time, 23. *Mental health counseling MA*—Applications 2001–2002, 138. Total applicants accepted 2001–2002, 92. New applicants enrolled 2001–2002, 89. Total enrolled 2001–2002 full-time, 110, part-time, 250. The number of students enrolled full and part-time, who were dismissed or voluntarily withdrew from this program area were 1. *School guidance and counseling MA*—Applications 2001–2002, 104. Total applicants accepted 2001–2002, 81. New applicants enrolled 2001–2002, 70. Total enrolled 2001–2002 full-time, 150. The Median number of years required for completion of a degree are 2. The number of students enrolled full and part-time, who were dismissed or voluntarily withdrew from this program area were 0.

Admissions Requirements:

Scores: Entries appear in this order: required test or GPA, minimum score (if required), median score of students entering in 2001–2002. Doctoral Programs: GRE-V no minimum stated, 528; GRE-Q no minimum stated, 563; GRE-V+Q 1000; GRE-

Subject(Psych) no minimum stated, 593; overall undergraduate GPA 3.0, 3.45; last 2 years GPA no minimum stated; psychology GPA no minimum stated; psychology GPA no minimum stated. GRE-V + Q > 1000 is preferred. GPA requirement may be satisfied by a Master's GPA> 3.5. GRE-P is recommended, but not required.

Other Criteria: (importance of criteria rated low, medium, or high): GRE/MAT scores high, research experience, work experience medium, extracurricular activity low, clinically related public service medium, GPA high, letters of recommendation high, interview high, statement of goals and objectives high. The importance of research is high for the PhD program.

Student Characteristics: The following represents characteristics of students in 2001–2002 in all graduate psychology programs in the department: Female–full-time 330, part-time 0; Male–full-time 100, part-time 0; African American/Black–full-time 20, part-time 0; Hispanic/Latino (a)–full-time 55, part-time 0; Asian/Pacific Islander–full-time 11, part-time 0; American Indian/Alaska Native–full-time 1, part-time 0; Multi-ethnic–full-time 9, part-time 0; students subject to the Americans with Disabilities Act–full-time 8, part-time 0.

Financial Information/Assistance:

Tuition for Full-Time Study: *Master's:* State residents $460 per credit hour; nonstate residents: $460 per credit hour. *Doctoral:* State residents: $600 per credit hour; nonstate residents: $600 per credit hour.

Financial Assistance:

First Year Students: Research assistantships available for first-year. Average amount paid per academic year: $5,600. Average number of hours worked per week: 15.

Advanced Students: Teaching assistantships available for advanced students. Average amount paid per academic year: $2,000. Average number of hours worked per week: 6. Research assistantships available for advanced students. Average amount paid per academic year: $5,600. Average number of hours worked per week: 15. Traineeships available for advanced students. Average amount paid per academic year: $5,400. Average number of hours worked per week: 15.

Contact Information: Of all students currently enrolled full-time, 11% benefitted from one or more of the listed financial assistance programs. For information on financial assistance, contact: Maria Pinto, Director of Employee Services.

Internships/Practica: The Center for Psychological Studies maintains two pre-doctoral internships: an APA-approved internship program located within the Community Mental Health Center and the Consortium Internship Program (APPIC member) that provides internship experiences in hospital and other settings within the South Florida Community. The center's Community Mental Health Center provides research opportunities for students through various faculty supervised applied-research clinical programs. Areas of research include alcohol and substance abuse, child and adolescent traumatic stress, clinical biofeedback, interpersonal violence, neuropsychological assessment, the seriously emotionally disturbed, and trauma resolution integration. Additionally, the CMHC provides more than 100 practicum placements for the center's students in addition to the extensive practicum placements available in the community. For those doctoral students for whom a professional internship is required prior to

graduation, 65 applied in 2000–2001. Of those who applied, 65 were placed in internships listed by the Association of Psychology Postdoctoral and Internship Programs (APPIC); 49 were placed in APA accredited internships.

Housing and Day Care: On-campus housing and day care facilities are available.

Employment of Department Graduates:

Master's Degree Graduates: Of those who graduated in the academic year 2000–2001, the following categories and numbers represent the post-graduate activities and employment of master's degree graduates: Enrolled in a post-doctoral residency/fellowship (n/a), employed in independent practice (n/a).

Doctoral Degree Graduates: Of those who graduated in the academic year 2000–2001, the following categories and numbers represent the post-graduate activities and employment of doctoral degree graduates: Enrolled in a psychology doctoral program (n/a), enrolled in another graduate/professional program (n/a).

Additional Information:

Orientation, Objectives, and Emphasis of Department: The Center for Psychological Studies (CPS) is committed to providing the highest quality educational experiences to future psychologists and counseling professionals by maintaining its tripartite mission of education and training in psychology, service to the community, and clinical research. Through the intimate interplay between its Community Mental Health Center (CMHC) and its academic programs, learning becomes rooted in real problems, and research activities attempt to find answers to extant concerns. The center offers master's programs in mental health counseling and school guidance and counseling, two APA-accredited doctoral programs in clinical psychology, and a postdoctoral master's program in psychopharmacology. The doctor of psychology (PsyD) program provides emphasis on training professionals to do service while the doctor of philosophy (PhD) program provides greater emphasis on applied research. In response to changes in health care delivery and the profession of psychology, the center developed concentrations at the doctoral level. Concentrations based on the existing PsyD and PhD curriculum are available in the areas of Clinical Neuropsychology, Clinical Health Psychology, Forensic Psychology, Psychodynamic Psychology, and the Psychology of Long-Term Mental Illness.

Special Facilities or Resources: In 1996, CPS moved into a 65,000 square-foot building designed to advance its tripartite mission by housing together the School of Psychology and the main branch of its Community Mental Health Center. Facilities for students in the Maltz Psychology Building include classrooms with state-of-the-art computer technology, therapy rooms with audio and video monitoring, a microcomputer lab with 30 multimedia computers connected to major databases and the internet, workstations for practicum students in specialty clinics, study carrels, lounges and meeting rooms, and a fitness center. As a university-based professional school, CPS provides access to Nova Southeastern University's Schools of Law, Business, and Systemic Studies, the colleges of its Health Professions Division (Medicine, Dentistry, Pharmacy, Allied Health, and Optometry), and its Family and School Center. Also included on NSU's 232-acre campus are libraries, five residence halls, recreation facilities, and the Miami Dolphins Training Center.

Information for Students With Physical Disabilities: Nova Southeastern University complies with Section 504 of the Rehabilitation Act of 1973 and the Americans with Disabilities Act of 1990 and related Florida Statutes. No qualified individual with a disability shall be excluded from participation in, be denied the benefits of, or be subjected to discrimination in any activity, service, or program of the University solely by reasons of his or her disability. Requests for information on policies, procedures or assistance should be directed to Joyce Silverman at 954-262-5780.

Application Information:

Send to: Graduate Admissions, Center for Psychological Studies, Nova Southeastern University, 3301 College Avenue, Ft. Lauderdale, FL 33314. Students are admitted in the Fall, application deadline 1-8-03; Winter, application deadline TBA; Summer, application deadline TBA. Applications for the doctoral programs are accepted only for the fall; the deadline is January 8, 2003. Application deadlines for master's and school psychology programs vary by site. Visit website www.cps.nova. edu for specifics. *Fee:* $50.

South Florida, University of
Department of Psychological and Social Foundations
College of Education
EDU 162
Tampa, FL 33620-7750
Telephone: (813) 974-3246
Fax: (813) 974-5814
E-mail: *batsche@tempest.coedu.usf.edu*
Web: *http://www.coedu.usf.edu/schoolpsych*

Department Established:

1970. Chairperson: Harold Keller, Ph.D. Number of Faculty: total–full-time 31, part-time 3; women–full-time 16, part-time 2; minority–full-time 4, part-time 1.

Programs and Degrees Offered:

Listed in the following order: Program area, degree type (T if terminal Master's), number awarded 7/00-6/01. School PhD 4.

APA Accreditation: School PhD: full.

Student Applications/Admissions:

Student Applications

School PhD—Applications 2001–2002, 45. Total applicants accepted 2001–2002, 9. New applicants enrolled 2001–2002, 7. Total enrolled 2001–2002 full-time, 51. Openings 2002–2003, 8. The Median number of years required for completion of a degree are 5. The number of students enrolled full and part-time, who were dismissed or voluntarily withdrew from this program area were 0.

Admissions Requirements:

Scores: Entries appear in this order: required test or GPA, minimum score (if required), median score of students entering in 2001–2002. Doctoral Programs: GRE-V no minimum stated, 575; GRE-Q no minimum stated, 565; GRE-V+Q 1000, 1160; last 2 years GPA 3.00, 3.82; psychology GPA no minimum stated; psychology GPA 3.50, 3.80.

Other Criteria: (importance of criteria rated low, medium, or high): GRE/MAT scores medium, research experience high, work experience medium, extracurricular activity medium, clinically related public service medium, GPA medium, letters of recommendation high, interview high, statement of goals and objectives high, writing sample medium,

Student Characteristics: The following represents characteristics of students in 2001–2002 in all graduate psychology programs in the department: Female–full-time 37, part-time 0; Male–full-time 12, part-time 0; African American/Black–full-time 7, part-time 0; Hispanic/Latino (a)–full-time 3, part-time 0; Asian/Pacific Islander–full-time 0, part-time 0; American Indian/Alaska Native–full-time 0, part-time 0; students subject to the Americans with Disabilities Act–full-time 1.

Financial Information/Assistance:

Tuition for Full-Time Study: *Master's:* State residents $134 per credit hour; nonstate residents: $407 per credit hour. *Doctoral:* State residents: $134 per credit hour; nonstate residents: $407 per credit hour.

Financial Assistance:

First Year Students: Research assistantships available for first-year. Average amount paid per academic year: $10,000. Average number of hours worked per week: 16. Apply by May 1. Tuition remission given: partial. Fellowships and scholarships available for first-year. Average amount paid per academic year: $12,000. Average number of hours worked per week: 0. Apply by March 1. Tuition remission given: partial.

Advanced Students: Teaching assistantships available for advanced students. Average amount paid per academic year: $10,000. Average number of hours worked per week: 16. Apply by May 1. Tuition remission given: partial. Research assistantships available for advanced students. Average amount paid per academic year: $10,000. Average number of hours worked per week: 16. Apply by May 1. Tuition remission given: partial. Fellowships and scholarships available for advanced students. Average amount paid per academic year: $12,000. Average number of hours worked per week: 0. Apply by March 1. Tuition remission given: partial.

Contact Information: Of all students currently enrolled full-time, 100% benefitted from one or more of the listed financial assistance programs. For information on financial assistance, contact: Dr. George Batsche, School Psychology Program.

Internships/Practica: Our practica and internships integrate home, school, and community service programs for students at risk for educational failure and their families, including students with disabilities. We especially focus on the priorities of researching and promoting effective educational and mental health practices for all children, youth, and their families. All doctoral students participate in practica during the first three years of the program. Practica settings include schools (public, charter, alternative), hospital settings, research settings, special agencies (e.g., Tampa Children's Cancer Center), and special programs (e.g., Early Intervention Program). Doctoral students participate in approximately 1000 hours of practicum prior to internship. All doctoral students complete a 2000-hour pre-doctoral internship in an APA-accredited/APPIC site or one that meets the APA/APPIC criteria. For those doctoral students for whom a professional internship is required prior to graduation, 2 applied in 2000–2001.

Housing and Day Care: On-campus housing and day care facilities are available.

Employment of Department Graduates:

Master's Degree Graduates: Of those who graduated in the academic year 2000–2001, the following categories and numbers represent the post-graduate activities and employment of master's degree graduates: Enrolled in a post-doctoral residency/fellowship (n/a), employed in independent practice (n/a).

Doctoral Degree Graduates: Of those who graduated in the academic year 2000–2001, the following categories and numbers represent the post-graduate activities and employment of doctoral degree graduates: Enrolled in a psychology doctoral program (n/a), enrolled in another graduate/professional program (n/a), employed in an academic position at a university (2), employed in a professional position in a school system (2).

Additional Information:

Orientation, Objectives, and Emphasis of Department: Thorough admissions procedures result in the selection of outstanding students. This makes possible a faculty commitment to do everything possible to guide each student to a high level of professional competence. The curriculum is well organized and explicit such that students are always aware of program expectations and their progress in relation to these expectations. The student body is kept small, resulting in greater student-faculty contact than would otherwise be possible. Skills of practice are developed through non-threatening apprenticeship networks established with local school systems. This model encourages students to assist several professors and practicing school psychologists throughout their training. The notion here is to provide positive environments, containing rich feedback, in which competent psychological skills develop. We emphasize a scientist-practitioner model representing primarily a cognitive-behavioral orientation. Further, we support comprehensive school psychology, including consultation, prevention, intervention, and program evaluation.

Special Facilities or Resources: The University of South Florida is a comprehensive Research I (FL) and Doctoral/Research Universities-Extensive (Carnegie) university that has over 37,000 students on a 1,700 acre campus 10 miles northeast of downtown Tampa, a city of over 250,000 people. Amongst its faculty, the School Psychology Program has two APA Fellows, three past presidents of the National Association of School Psychologists, and faculty who have received over $12 million in federal and state grants over the past years. Students collaborate with professors and researchers in the program, the College of Education, Departments of Psychology and Psychiatry, the Florida Mental Health Institute, the Early Intervention Program, Shriner's Hospital, Tampa General and St. Joseph's hospitals, the Florida Department of Education and other settings. The program is housed in a new College of Education physical plant that has the latest fiber optic based technology, clinical and research observation areas, and strong technology support. Strong links exist with community schools and agencies.

Information for Students With Physical Disabilities: USF is an Equal Opportunity, Equal Access, Affirmitive Action institution.

Application Information:

Send to: Linda Raffaele, Coordinator of Admissions, School Psychology Program, EDU 162, University of South Florida, Tampa, FL 33620-

7750. Students are admitted in the Fall, application deadline January 15. All application materials and fees should be submitted directly to the Coordinator of Admissions, School Psychology Program (address above). *Fee:* $20. Contact Program Director/Admissions Coordinator, School Psychology Program.

South Florida, University of

Department of Psychology
Arts and Sciences
4202 E. Fowler Avenue, PCD 4118G
Tampa, FL 33620-7200
Telephone: (813) 974-2492
Fax: (813) 974-4617
E-mail: *donchin@chuma.cas.usf.edu*
Web: *http://www.cas.usf.edu/psychology*

Department Established:

1964. Chairperson: Emanuel Donchin. Number of Faculty: total–full-time 31; women–full-time 9; minority–full-time 3.

Programs and Degrees Offered:

Listed in the following order: Program area, degree type (T if terminal Master's), number awarded 7/00-6/01. Clinical PhD 11, cognitive and neuroscience PhD 2, industrial/organizational PhD 3.

APA Accreditation: Clinical PhD: full.

Student Applications/Admissions:

Student Applications

Clinical PhD—Applications 2001–2002, 235. Total applicants accepted 2001–2002, 9. New applicants enrolled 2001–2002, 9. Total enrolled 2001–2002 full-time, 70. Openings 2002–2003, 10. The Median number of years required for completion of a degree are 7. *Cognitive and neuroscience PhD*—Applications 2001–2002, 26. Total applicants accepted 2001–2002, 5. New applicants enrolled 2001–2002, 4. Total enrolled 2001–2002 full-time, 33. Openings 2002–2003, 6. The Median number of years required for completion of a degree are 7. The number of students enrolled full and part-time, who were dismissed or voluntarily withdrew from this program area were 1. *Industrial/organizational PhD*—Applications 2001–2002, 120. Total applicants accepted 2001–2002, 22. New applicants enrolled 2001–2002, 7. Total enrolled 2001–2002 full-time, 50. Openings 2002–2003, 8. The Median number of years required for completion of a degree are 6.

Admissions Requirements:

Scores: Entries appear in this order: required test or GPA, minimum score (if required), median score of students entering in 2001–2002. Doctoral Programs: GRE-V no minimum stated; GRE-Q no minimum stated; GRE-V+Q 1000, 1290; last 2 years GPA 3.00, 4.0 ; psychology GPA no minimum stated; psychology GPA no minimum stated. Our Clinical Program recommends that GRE-Subject (Psychology) be taken.

Other Criteria: (importance of criteria rated low, medium, or high): GRE/MAT scores high, research experience high, work experience low, clinically related public service low, GPA high, letters of recommendation high, interview medium, statement of goals and objectives medium.

Student Characteristics: The following represents characteristics of students in 2001–2002 in all graduate psychology programs in the department: Female–full-time 15, part-time 0; Male–full-time 5, part-time 0; African American/Black–full-time 2, part-time 0; Hispanic/Latino (a)–full-time 3, part-time 0; Asian/Pacific Islander–full-time 0, part-time 0; American Indian/Alaska Native–full-time 0, part-time 0; Multi-ethnic–full-time 0, part-time 0; students subject to the Americans with Disabilities Act–full-time 0, part-time 0.

Financial Information/Assistance:
Tuition for Full-Time Study: No information provided.

Financial Assistance:
First Year Students: Teaching assistantships available for first-year. Average amount paid per academic year: $12,500. Apply by NA. Tuition remission given: partial. Research assistantships available for first-year. Average amount paid per academic year: $12,500. Apply by NA. Tuition remission given: partial. Apply by NA. Fellowships and scholarships available for first-year. Average amount paid per academic year: $15,500. Apply by NA. Tuition remission given: partial.

Advanced Students: Teaching assistantships available for advanced students. Average amount paid per academic year: $13,000. Apply by NA. Tuition remission given: partial. Research assistantships available for advanced students. Average amount paid per academic year: $13,000. Apply by NA. Tuition remission given: partial. Apply by NA. Fellowships and scholarships available for advanced students. Average amount paid per academic year: $15,500. Apply by NA. Tuition remission given: partial.

Contact Information: For information on financial assistance, contact: Department of Psychology or Graduate School, University of South Florida, 4202 E Fowler Ave, FAO 126, Tampa, FL 33620.

Internships/Practica: The Clinical Program operates its own Psychology Clinic within the Psychology Department, providing opportunity for a practical training in clinical assessment and clinical psychological interventions. Students are active in the Psychology Clinic throughout their training. Clinical core-faculty provides most of the supervision of Clinic cases. The Clinical Psychology Program is fortunate to have a unique cluster of campus and community training facilities available for student placement. For example, we have student placements at or near such campus facilities as the USF Florida Mental Health Research Institute, the USF Counseling Center for Human Development, the Moffitt Cancer Center and Research Institute, and the Tampa Veterans Administration Hospital as well as carefully selected community agencies. Students in the Industrial/Organizational Program are required to complete a predoctoral internship. Placements are made in numerous governmental, corporate, and consulting firms both locally and nationally. Recent placements have included Cities of Tampa and Clearwater, GTE, Tampa Electric Company, Personnel Decisions Research Institute, Personnel Decisions, Inc., Florida Power, and USF&G.

Housing and Day Care: On-campus housing and day care facilities are available.

Employment of Department Graduates:
Master's Degree Graduates: Of those who graduated in the academic year 2000–2001, the following categories and numbers represent the post-graduate activities and employment of master's degree graduates: Enrolled in a post-doctoral residency/fellowship (n/a), employed in independent practice (n/a).

Doctoral Degree Graduates: Of those who graduated in the academic year 2000–2001, the following categories and numbers represent the post-graduate activities and employment of doctoral degree graduates: Enrolled in a psychology doctoral program (n/a), enrolled in another graduate/professional program (n/a), enrolled in a post-doctoral residency/fellowship (5), employed in independent practice (1), employed in an academic position at a university (3), employed in an academic position at a 2-year/4-year college (1), employed in other positions at a higher education institution (3), employed in business or industry (research/consulting) (6), employed in a hospital/medical center (3).

Additional Information:
Orientation, Objectives, and Emphasis of Department: The department attempts to educate graduate students to a high level of proficiency in research and in practice. The department expects its doctoral students to be of such quality as to take their place at major institutions of learning if they choose academic careers and to assume roles of responsibility and importance if they choose professional careers. The doctoral program in clinical psychology provides broad-based professional and research training to prepare students for careers in a variety of applied, research, and teaching settings. The doctoral program in cognitive and neural sciences psychology has been planned to prepare students for research careers in both applied and academic environments. The doctoral program in industrial/organizational psychology provides professional and research training to prepare students for careers in industrial, governmental, academic, and related organizational settings. An Interdisciplinary program in psycholinguistics (PhD) is being offered in conjunction with the Department of Communication Sciences and Disorders (Speech, Language, and Hearing Science).

Special Facilities or Resources: Twenty to twenty-five rooms provide research space for faculty, graduate, and advanced undergraduate students. A large room has been equipped with computer terminals that access the mainframe computer on campus. The University Computer Center is available for unsupported research. The Psychological Services Center is operated as the department's facility for clinical practicum work. A state-of-the-art video system permits supervisory capabilities for clinical practica. In Spring 2001 a new building with state of the art facilities and equipment will house the Psychology Department.

Application Information:
Send to: Psychology Dept., University of South Florida, 4202 E Fowler Ave, PCD4118G, Tampa, FL 33620-7200. Students are admitted in the Fall, application deadline January 15. *Fee:* $20. Proof of financial hardship.

West Florida, The University of
Department of Psychology
College of Arts and Sciences
11000 University Parkway
Pensacola, FL 32514-5751
Telephone: (850) 474-2363
Fax: (850) 857-6060
E-mail: *psych@uwf.edu*
Web: *http://uwf.edu/psych*

Department Established:
1967. Chairperson: Ronald W. Belter. Number of Faculty: total–full-time 11, part-time 2; women–full-time 4, part-time 1; minority–full-time 1.

Programs and Degrees Offered:
Listed in the following order: Program area, degree type (T if terminal Master's), number awarded 7/00-6/01. Counseling psychology MA (T) 8, general psychology MA (T) 4, industrial/organizational psyc MA (T) 16.

Student Applications/Admissions:
Student Applications

Counseling psychology MA—Applications 2001–2002, 67. Total applicants accepted 2001–2002, 36. New applicants enrolled 2001–2002, 18. Total enrolled 2001–2002 full-time, 27, part-time, 14. Openings 2002–2003, 18. *General psychology* MA—Applications 2001–2002, 32. Total applicants accepted 2001–2002, 20. New applicants enrolled 2001–2002, 15. Total enrolled 2001–2002 full-time, 18, part-time, 12. Openings 2002–2003, 15. *Industrial/organizational psyc* MA—Applications 2001–2002, 61. Total applicants accepted 2001–2002, 25. New applicants enrolled 2001–2002, 11. Total enrolled 2001–2002 full-time, 13, part-time, 11. Openings 2002–2003, 15.

Admissions Requirements:
Scores: Entries appear in this order: required test or GPA, minimum score (if required), median score of students entering in 2001–2002. Master's Programs: GRE-V no minimum stated, 459; GRE-Q no minimum stated, 540; GRE-V+Q 1000; last 2 years GPA 3.53, 3.77. Doctoral Programs: last 2 years GPA no minimum stated; psychology GPA no minimum stated; psychology GPA no minimum stated.
Other Criteria: (importance of criteria rated low, medium, or high): GRE/MAT scores high, research experience medium, work experience medium, extracurricular activity medium, clinically related public service medium, GPA high, letters of recommendation high, statement of goals and objectives high, Supplemental Form high. Counseling applicants may be interviewed.

Student Characteristics: The following represents characteristics of students in 2001–2002 in all graduate psychology programs in the department: Female–full-time 48, part-time 31; Male–full-time 22, part-time 14; African American/Black–full-time 3, part-time 0; Hispanic/Latino (a)–full-time 5, part-time 0; Asian/Pacific Islander–full-time 2, part-time 1; American Indian/Alaska Native–full-time 1, part-time 0.

Financial Information/Assistance:
Tuition for Full-Time Study: *Master's:* State residents $156 per credit hour; nonstate residents: $535 per credit hour.

Financial Assistance:
First Year Students: Teaching assistantships available for first-year. Average amount paid per academic year: $2,000. Average number of hours worked per week: 10. Apply by April 15th. Tuition remission given: partial. Fellowships and scholarships available for first-year. Average amount paid per academic year: $1,000. Apply by April 15th.
Advanced Students: Teaching assistantships available for advanced students. Average amount paid per academic year: $2,000. Average number of hours worked per week: 10. Apply by April 15th. Tuition remission given: partial. Fellowships and scholarships available for advanced students. Average amount paid per academic year: $750. Apply by April 15th.
Contact Information: Of all students currently enrolled full-time, 59% benefitted from one or more of the listed financial assistance programs. For information on financial assistance, contact: Susan Walch, Ph.D. swalch@uwf.edu.

Internships/Practica: Master's students may elect either thesis or 600-hour internship (850-hour for mental health counseling licensure option). Faculty assist in finding suitable placements in field settings under qualified supervision. Intern also prepares a portfolio demonstrating mastery of several specific competencies and including an integrative paper reflecting on professional development. Practica (required for counseling students, optional but common for other students) are completed earlier in the program and involve more limited applied experience and closer supervision by faculty. Counseling practica include group and individual practice experiences.

Housing and Day Care: On-campus housing and day care facilities are available.

Employment of Department Graduates:
Master's Degree Graduates: Of those who graduated in the academic year 2000–2001, the following categories and numbers represent the post-graduate activities and employment of master's degree graduates: Enrolled in a psychology doctoral program (12), enrolled in another graduate/professional program (3), enrolled in a post-doctoral residency/fellowship (n/a), employed in independent practice (n/a), employed in a professional position in a school system (5), employed in business or industry (management) (14), employed in a community mental health/counseling center (15), employed in a hospital/medical center (6), still seeking employment (15), other employment position (30).
Doctoral Degree Graduates: Of those who graduated in the academic year 2000–2001, the following categories and numbers represent the post-graduate activities and employment of doctoral degree graduates: Enrolled in a psychology doctoral program (n/a), enrolled in another graduate/professional program (n/a).

Additional Information:
Orientation, Objectives, and Emphasis of Department: The department is a member of the Council of Applied Master's Programs in Psychology and is committed to the philosophy of training with foundation in general psychology (individual, social, biological, learned bases of behavior) as basis for training in application of psychology. Applied students receive significant supervised field

experience. Departmental mission is preparation of master's level practitioners but we successfully prepare students for doctoral work as well. We are developing departmental specialties on application of psychology to the issues of health across the lifespan (health psychology/behavioral medicine) and to cognitive psychology.

Special Facilities or Resources: The department has recently moved into a new spacious building with excellent research facilities including Behavioral Medicine Lab and Neurocognition Lab. The Counseling Psychology program is also offered at the Fort Walton Beach campus. Other University resources include Institute for Business and Economic Research and the Institute for Human and Machine Cognition. We have links with CMHCs and local health/mental health professionals and organizations. Community resources include three major hospitals and large Naval training facility. Department hosts student chapters of Psi Chi, Society for Human Resource Management (SHRM), and Student Psychological Association.

Information for Students With Physical Disabilities: Our building is ADA compliant.

Application Information:
Send to: Department of Psychology-Graduate Admissions, University of West Florida, Pensacola FL 32514-5751. Students are admitted in the Fall, application deadline February 1; Spring, application deadline February 1; Summer, application deadline February 1. April 1st deadline if spaces available. *Fee:* $20.

Augusta State University

Department of Psychology
2500 Walton Way
Augusta, GA 30904-2200
Telephone: (706) 737-1694
Fax: (706) 737-1538
E-mail: *pboyd@aug.edu*
Web: *http://www.aug.edu/psychology/*

Department Established:

1963. Chairperson: Deborah S. Richardson. Number of Faculty: total–full-time 9; women–full-time 5; minority–full-time 1.

Programs and Degrees Offered:

Listed in the following order: Program area, degree type (T if terminal Master's), number awarded 7/00-6/01. Applied Psychology MA (T) 9, Experimental Psychology.

Student Applications/Admissions:

Student Applications

Applied Psychology MA—Applications 2001–2002, 28. Total applicants accepted 2001–2002, 25. New applicants enrolled 2001–2002, 16. Total enrolled 2001–2002 full-time, 25. Openings 2002–2003, 24. The Median number of years required for completion of a degree are 2. The number of students enrolled full and part-time, who were dismissed or voluntarily withdrew from this program area were 4.

Admissions Requirements:

Scores: Entries appear in this order: required test or GPA, minimum score (if required), median score of students entering in 2001–2002. Master's Programs: GRE-V 400, 450; GRE-Q 400, 500; GRE-Analytical 400, 560; overall undergraduate GPA 2.5, 3.14. For both program areas, a minimum score of 450 on each subtest (verbal, quantitative, and analytical) is targeted, with at least two of the three subtests having scores of at least 450. The GRE scores must be recent; within the last five years. Doctoral Programs: last 2 years GPA no minimum stated; psychology GPA no minimum stated; psychology GPA no minimum stated.

Other Criteria: (importance of criteria rated low, medium, or high): GRE/MAT scores medium, research experience medium, work experience medium, extracurricular activity low, clinically related public service low, GPA medium, letters of recommendation medium, statement of goals and objectives medium.

Student Characteristics: The following represents characteristics of students in 2001–2002 in all graduate psychology programs in the department: Female–full-time 21, part-time 0; Male–full-time 4, part-time 0; African American/Black–full-time 6, part-time 0; Hispanic/Latino (a)–full-time 0, part-time 0; Asian/Pacific Islander–full-time 1, part-time 0; American Indian/Alaska Native–full-time 0, part-time 0.

Financial Information/Assistance:

Tuition for Full-Time Study: Master's: State residents per academic year $3,047, $97 per credit hour; nonstate residents: per academic year $1,006, $387 per credit hour.

Financial Assistance:

First Year Students: Traineeships available for first-year. Average amount paid per academic year: $2,400. Average number of hours worked per week: 10. Tuition remission given: partial.

Advanced Students: Traineeships available for advanced students. Average amount paid per academic year: $2,400. Average number of hours worked per week: 10. Tuition remission given: partial.

Contact Information: Of all students currently enrolled full-time, 60% benefitted from one or more of the listed financial assistance programs. For information on financial assistance, contact: Contact the chair of the department for a graduate assistantship and the Office of Financial Aid for other forms of support.

Internships/Practica: Institutions that provide unique opportunities for fieldwork and internship experiences include two Veterans Administration hospitals, a regional psychiatric hospital, the Medical College of Georgia, Gracewood State School and Hospital, Dwight David Eisenhower Medical Center, and various other agencies. Internships are also available in business, education, and private practice settings.

Housing and Day Care: No on-campus housing and day care facilities are available.

Employment of Department Graduates:

Master's Degree Graduates: Of those who graduated in the academic year 2000–2001, the following categories and numbers represent the post-graduate activities and employment of master's degree graduates: Enrolled in a psychology doctoral program (0), enrolled in another graduate/professional program (0), enrolled in a post-doctoral residency/fellowship (n/a), employed in independent practice (n/a), employed in an academic position at a university (0), employed in an academic position at a 2-year/4-year college (0), employed in other positions at a higher education institution (2), employed in a professional position in a school system (0), employed in a government agency (research) (1), employed in a government agency (professional services) (1), employed in a community mental health/counseling center (1), employed in a hospital/medical center (1), still seeking employment (1), other employment position (1).

Doctoral Degree Graduates: Of those who graduated in the academic year 2000–2001, the following categories and numbers represent the post-graduate activities and employment of doctoral degree graduates: Enrolled in a psychology doctoral program (n/a), enrolled in another graduate/professional program (n/a).

Additional Information:

Orientation, Objectives, and Emphasis of Department: The graduate program in psychology at Augusta State University provides intensive training oriented toward the local and regional job markets. A secondary emphasis of the program is to provide an opportunity for graduate work in experimental psychology. The MS program is, for most students, a two-year program consisting of equal amounts of advanced experimental and theoretical coursework combined with courses relevant to professional psychology. Supervised internship experience in approved treatment or research facilities is also required.

Special Facilities or Resources: The department maintains an active human and animal research laboratory and a clinical facility with video taping and closed circuit television capabilities, and the university provides easy access to advanced computer resources. Students and faculty additionally engage in collaborative research at the Medical College of Georgia and Veterans Medical Center. Social and Developmental labs available for teaching and research.

Information for Students With Physical Disabilities: The university has a full-time ADA officer, and the program provides special consideration for students with physical disabilities.

Application Information:

Send to: Director of Graduate Studies, Department of Psychology, 2500 Walton Way, Augusta State University, Augusta, GA 30904-2200. Students are admitted in the Fall, application deadline August 1; Summer, application deadline Rolling. *Fee:* $20.

Emory University
Department of Psychology
532 North Kilgo Circle
Atlanta, GA 30322
Telephone: (404) 727-7438
Fax: (404) 727-0372
E-mail: *psych@emory.edu*
Web: *http://www.emory.edu/PSYCH/*

Department Established:
1945. Chairperson: Darryl Neill. Number of Faculty: total–full-time 36; women–full-time 14; minority–full-time 1.

Programs and Degrees Offered:
Listed in the following order: Program area, degree type (T if terminal Master's), number awarded 7/00-6/01. Clinical PhD 3, Cognition & Development PhD 4, Neuroscience & Animal Behavior PhD 1.

APA Accreditation: Clinical PhD: full.

Student Applications/Admissions:
Student Applications
Clinical PhD—Applications 2001–2002, 177. Total applicants accepted 2001–2002, 5. New applicants enrolled 2001–2002, 5. Total enrolled 2001–2002 full-time, 34. Openings 2002–2003, 6. The Median number of years required for completion of a degree are 6. The number of students enrolled full and part-time, who were dismissed or voluntarily withdrew from this program area were 0. *Cognition & Development PhD*—Applications 2001–2002, 38. Total applicants accepted 2001–2002, 7. New applicants enrolled 2001–2002, 3. Total enrolled 2001–2002 full-time, 14. Openings 2002–2003, 6. The Median number of years required for completion of a degree are 5. The number of students enrolled full and part-time, who were dismissed or voluntarily withdrew from this program area were 0. *Neuroscience & Animal Behavior PhD*—Applications 2001–2002, 38. Total applicants accepted 2001–2002, 4. New applicants enrolled 2001–2002, 3. Total enrolled 2001–2002 full-time, 28. Openings 2002–2003, 4. The Median number of years required for completion of a degree are 7. The number of students enrolled full and part-time, who were dismissed or voluntarily withdrew from this program area were 1.

Admissions Requirements:
Scores: Entries appear in this order: required test or GPA, minimum score (if required), median score of students entering in 2001–2002. Doctoral Programs: GRE-V 600, 590; GRE-Q 600, 705; GRE-V+Q 1200, 1275; GRE-Analytical 600, 670; GRE-V+Q+Analytical 1800, 1880; overall undergraduate GPA 3.0, 3.14; last 2 years GPA no minimum stated; psychology GPA no minimum stated; psychology GPA no minimum stated. The Clinical program requires the verbal and quantitative GRE scores. The Cognition and Development program and the Neuroscience and Animal Behavior program requires the verbal, quantitative, and analytical scores. For international students, the TOEFL score must be submitted as well. *Other Criteria:* (importance of criteria rated low, medium, or high): GRE/MAT scores high, research experience high, work experience low, extracurricular activity low, clinically related public service medium, GPA high, letters of recommendation high, interview medium, statement of goals and objectives high.

Student Characteristics: The following represents characteristics of students in 2001–2002 in all graduate psychology programs in the department: Female–full-time 55, part-time 0; Male–full-time 20, part-time 0; African American/Black–full-time 2, part-time 0; Hispanic/Latino (a)–full-time 1, part-time 0; Asian/Pacific Islander–full-time 5, part-time 0; American Indian/Alaska Native–full-time 0, part-time 0.

Financial Information/Assistance:
Tuition for Full-Time Study: *Doctoral:* State residents: per academic year $24,770, $1,032 per credit hour; nonstate residents: per academic year $24,770, $1,032 per credit hour.

Financial Assistance:
First Year Students: No information provided.
Advanced Students: Teaching assistantships available for advanced students. Fellowships and scholarships available for advanced students.
Contact Information: Of all students currently enrolled full-time, 100% benefitted from one or more of the listed financial assistance programs. For information on financial assistance, contact: The Department of Psychology.

Internships/Practica: No information provided.

Housing and Day Care: On-campus housing and day care facilities are available.

Employment of Department Graduates:

Master's Degree Graduates: Of those who graduated in the academic year 2000–2001, the following categories and numbers represent the post-graduate activities and employment of master's degree graduates: Enrolled in a post-doctoral residency/fellowship (n/a), employed in independent practice (n/a).

Doctoral Degree Graduates: Of those who graduated in the academic year 2000–2001, the following categories and numbers represent the post-graduate activities and employment of doctoral degree graduates: Enrolled in a psychology doctoral program (n/a), enrolled in another graduate/professional program (n/a), enrolled in a post-doctoral residency/fellowship (4), employed in an academic position at a 2-year/4-year college (1), employed in business or industry (research/consulting) (3), other employment position (2).

Additional Information:

Orientation, Objectives, and Emphasis of Department: The clinical psychology doctoral program is accredited by the American Psychological Association. Scientific and scholarly activities receive equal emphasis with professional training. Accordingly, a broad background in academic psychology is provided along with appropriate quantitative skills. Minimum independent student research includes the MA thesis and the Ph.D. dissertation. The doctoral program in cognition and development is designed to prepare individuals for careers in research and college teaching. The training is broad, encompassing cognition, memory, psycholinguistics, and cognitive neuroscience. Beginning with the first semester on campus, students are expected to work closely with faculty members in formal and informal research endeavors. Areas of current interest are memory, cognitive development, particularly mother/child relations, and self-concept. The program in neuroscience and animal behavior (NAB) approaches topics within the traditional areas of physiological psychology, acquired behavior, and ethnology as a unified entity. The emphasis is on behavior as a biological phenomenon; physiological psychology explores brain-behavior relationships; research on acquired behavior studies the on-going and evolutionary factors influencing individual adaptation; and animal behavior is concerned with understanding how animals function in their natural environment. Research is conducted mainly with animals, although the findings are applied to understanding human as well as animal behavior.

Special Facilities or Resources: The Yerkes Primate Center and Center for Behavioral Neuroscience are available to the department.

Information for Students With Physical Disabilities: The University and department attempt to be compliant with the Americans with Disabilities Act.

Application Information:
Send to: Instructions on application. Inquiries to: Graduate Coordinator, Dept. Psychology, Emory Univ., Atlanta, GA 30322. Students are admitted in the Fall, application deadline January 20. *Fee:* $50.

Georgia College & State University
Department of Psychology
College of Arts and Sciences
Campus Box 90
Milledgeville, GA 31061
Telephone: (478) 445-4574
Fax: (478) 445-0856
E-mail: *lgillis@gcsu.edu*
Web: *http://www.gcsu.edu/acad_affairs/coll_artsci/psy/ms.html*

Department Established:
Chair: Sheree Barron. Number of Faculty: total–full-time 11, part-time 3; women–full-time 3, part-time 1; minority–full-time 1, part-time 1.

Programs and Degrees Offered:
Listed in the following order: Program area, degree type (T if terminal Master's), number awarded 7/00-6/01. Experimental - general MA (T) 5.

Student Applications/Admissions:
Student Applications
Experimental - general MA—Applications 2001–2002, 8. Total applicants accepted 2001–2002, 5. New applicants enrolled 2001–2002, 4. Total enrolled 2001–2002 full-time, 8, part-time, 2. Openings 2002–2003, 12. The Median number of years required for completion of a degree are 2. The number of students enrolled full and part-time, who were dismissed or voluntarily withdrew from this program area were 0.

Admissions Requirements:
Scores: Entries appear in this order: required test or GPA, minimum score (if required), median score of students entering in 2001–2002. Master's Programs: GRE-V 450, 460; GRE-Q 450, 490; GRE-V+Q 900, 950; GRE-Analytical 450, 560; GRE-V+Q+Analytical 1350, 1500; overall undergraduate GPA 2.5, 3.08. Doctoral Programs: last 2 years GPA no minimum stated; psychology GPA no minimum stated; psychology GPA no minimum stated.

Other Criteria: (importance of criteria rated low, medium, or high): research experience medium, extracurricular activity medium, clinically related public service medium, letters of recommendation medium, statement of goals and objectives medium.

Student Characteristics: The following represents characteristics of students in 2001–2002 in all graduate psychology programs in the department: Female–full-time 3, part-time 1; Male–full-time 2, part-time 1; African American/Black–full-time 1, part-time 0; Hispanic/Latino (a)–full-time 0, part-time 0; Asian/Pacific Islander–full-time 0, part-time 0; American Indian/Alaska Native–full-time 0, part-time 0; Multi-ethnic–full-time 0, part-time 0; students subject to the Americans with Disabilities Act–full-time 0, part-time 0.

Financial Information/Assistance:
Tuition for Full-Time Study: *Master's:* State residents $127 per credit hour; nonstate residents: $506 per credit hour.

Financial Assistance:

First Year Students: Research assistantships available for first-year. Average amount paid per academic year: $1,900. Average number of hours worked per week: 20. Apply by ASAP. Tuition remission given: full.

Advanced Students: No information provided.

Contact Information: Of all students currently enrolled full-time, 100% benefitted from one or more of the listed financial assistance programs. For information on financial assistance, contact: Graduate School and Research Services, GC&SU CBX 073 Milledgeville, GA 31061 http://www.gcsu.edu/acad_affairs/grad_school/GradAsstInfo.html.

Internships/Practica: None Available.

Housing and Day Care: No on-campus housing and day care facilities are available.

Employment of Department Graduates:

Master's Degree Graduates: Of those who graduated in the academic year 2000–2001, the following categories and numbers represent the post-graduate activities and employment of master's degree graduates: Enrolled in a post-doctoral residency/fellowship (n/a), employed in independent practice (n/a).

Doctoral Degree Graduates: Of those who graduated in the academic year 2000–2001, the following categories and numbers represent the post-graduate activities and employment of doctoral degree graduates: Enrolled in a psychology doctoral program (n/a), enrolled in another graduate/professional program (n/a).

Additional Information:

Orientation, Objectives, and Emphasis of Department: The M.S. in Psychology at GC&SU is intended primarily for students with doctoral-level aspirations who seek to improve the probability of their acceptance into a doctoral program elsewhere. The program offers NO "clinical" or "counseling" courses and it is NOT designed, nor will it accept or endorse, students who wish to pursue professional licensing at the master's level. Course work and laboratory experiences are available in theoretical, experimental, and applied psychology, as well as behavioral neuroscience. Courses emphasize the basic principles and methods of psychology as an empirical science. Primary emphasis is placed on scholarly research. The degree is obtained by completing 36 hours of required course work including a thesis. The M.S. in Psychology is designed to be completed within one calendar year. The full time program accepts only 8–12 students as a "cohort" who take all of their courses together. Students will be considered for regular admissions based on their research interest expressed in a letter of intent. Regularly admitted students will begin Fall Semester having already taken 12 hours (4 courses x 3 semester hours) at the 5000 level. All requirements for the M.S. in Psychology must be completed within two years after beginning graduate study.

Special Facilities or Resources: Current research interests of faculty are located on the web at: http://www.gcsu.edu/acad_affairs/coll_artsci/psy/grad_res.html.

Application Information:
Send to: Graduate Admissions Office, GC&SU CBX 023, Milledgeville, GA 31061-0490; 478-445-6289. Students are admitted in the Fall, application deadline April 1. *Fee:* $25.

Georgia Institute of Technology
School of Psychology
274 Fifth Street, Psychology Building
Atlanta, GA 30332-0170
Telephone: (404) 894-2680
Fax: (404) 894-8905
E-mail: *jd234@prism.gatech.edu*
Web: *http://www.psychology.gatech.edu*

Department Established:

1945. Chairperson: Randall W. Engle. Number of Faculty: total–full-time 22, part-time 1; women–full-time 5, part-time 1; minority–full-time 1.

Programs and Degrees Offered:

Listed in the following order: Program area, degree type (T if terminal Master's), number awarded 7/00-6/01. Engineering PhD 5, general experimental PhD 3, human computer interaction, industrial/organization PhD 5.

APA Accreditation: School PhD: full.

Student Applications/Admissions:

Student Applications

Engineering PhD—Applications 2001–2002, 22. Total applicants accepted 2001–2002, 3. New applicants enrolled 2001–2002, 4. Total enrolled 2001–2002 full-time, 10. Openings 2002–2003, 6. *General experimental PhD*—Applications 2001–2002, 45. Total applicants accepted 2001–2002, 7. New applicants enrolled 2001–2002, 6. Total enrolled 2001–2002 full-time, 24. Openings 2002–2003, 10. *Industrial/organization PhD*—Applications 2001–2002, 89. Total applicants accepted 2001–2002, 6. New applicants enrolled 2001–2002, 5. Total enrolled 2001–2002 full-time, 15. Openings 2002–2003, 6.

Admissions Requirements:

Scores: Entries appear in this order: required test or GPA, minimum score (if required), median score of students entering in 2001–2002. Doctoral Programs: GRE-V 550, 600; GRE-Q 550, 640; GRE-V+Q 1100, 1240; GRE-V+Q+Analytical 1500, 1910; overall undergraduate GPA 3.0, 3.6 ; last 2 years GPA no minimum stated; psychology GPA no minimum stated; psychology GPA no minimum stated.

Other Criteria: (importance of criteria rated low, medium, or high): GRE/MAT scores high, research experience high, work experience low, extracurricular activity low, GPA medium, letters of recommendation medium, statement of goals and objectives high.

Student Characteristics: The following represents characteristics of students in 2001–2002 in all graduate psychology programs in the department: Female–full-time 9, part-time 0; Male–full-time 9, part-time 0; African American/Black–full-time 1, part-time 0; Hispanic/Latino (a)–full-time 0, part-time 0; Asian/Pacific Islander–full-time 2, part-time 0; American Indian/Alaska Native–full-time 0, part-time 0; Multi-ethnic–full-time 0, part-time 0; students subject to the Americans with Disabilities Act–full-time 0, part-time 0.

Financial Information/Assistance:

Tuition for Full-Time Study: No information provided.

Financial Assistance:

First Year Students: Teaching assistantships available for first-year. Average amount paid per academic year: $12,500. Apply by Jan 1. Tuition remission given: full. Research assistantships available for first-year. Average amount paid per academic year: $12,500. Apply by Jan 1. Tuition remission given: full.

Advanced Students: Teaching assistantships available for advanced students. Average amount paid per academic year: $12,500. Apply by Jan 1. Tuition remission given: full. Research assistantships available for advanced students. Average amount paid per academic year: $12,500. Apply by Jan 1. Tuition remission given: full.

Contact Information: Of all students currently enrolled full-time, 100% benefitted from one or more of the listed financial assistance programs. For information on financial assistance, contact: Graduate Coordinator.

Internships/Practica: Internships are available for Industrial/Organizational and Engineering Psychology doctoral students in local corporations.

Housing and Day Care: On-campus housing and day care facilities are available.

Employment of Department Graduates:

Master's Degree Graduates: Of those who graduated in the academic year 2000–2001, the following categories and numbers represent the post-graduate activities and employment of master's degree graduates: Enrolled in a post-doctoral residency/fellowship (n/a), employed in independent practice (n/a).

Doctoral Degree Graduates: Of those who graduated in the academic year 2000–2001, the following categories and numbers represent the post-graduate activities and employment of doctoral degree graduates: Enrolled in a psychology doctoral program (n/a), enrolled in another graduate/professional program (n/a).

Additional Information:

Orientation, Objectives, and Emphasis of Department: Programs are offered leading to the MS and PhD degrees with three areas of specialization: general-experimental (including cognitive psychology, cognitive aging, and animal behavior), industrial/organizational, and engineering psychology. Each program of study involves intensive exposure to the experimental and theoretical foundations of psychology with a strong emphasis on quantitative methods. It is the basic philosophy of the faculty that the student is trained as a psychologist first and a specialist second. Individual initiative in research and study is strongly encouraged and supported by close faculty-student contact.

Special Facilities or Resources: Special facilities or resources include affiliations with Southeast Center for Applied Cognitive Research on Aging, Georgia State Gerontology Center, Zoo Atlanta, close ties with College Computing (Graphics, Visualization and Usability Center), and the Georgia Tech Research Institute.

Application Information:

Send to: Graduate Coordinator, School of Psychology, Georgia Institute of Technology, Atlanta, GA 30332-0170. Students are admitted in the Fall, application deadline January 1. for all programs and degrees.

Fee: $50. The Institute has a pre-application form without fee to determine the student's potential for acceptance into the program.

Georgia Southern University

Department of Psychology
College of Liberal Arts and Social Sciences
P.O. Box 8041
Statesboro, GA 30460-8041
Telephone: (912) 681-5539
Fax: (912) 681-0751
E-mail: *rrogers@gasou.edu*
Web: *http://www2.gasou.edu/psychology/*

Department Established:

1967. Chairperson: Richard L. Rogers. Number of Faculty: total–full-time 16, part-time 1; women–full-time 6, part-time 1.

Programs and Degrees Offered:

Listed in the following order: Program area, degree type (T if terminal Master's), number awarded 7/00-6/01. Psychology MA (T) 8.

Student Applications/Admissions:

Student Applications

Psychology MA—Applications 2001–2002, 30. Total applicants accepted 2001–2002, 18. New applicants enrolled 2001–2002, 14. Total enrolled 2001–2002 full-time, 21, part-time, 3. Openings 2002–2003, 16. The Median number of years required for completion of a degree are 2. The number of students enrolled full and part-time, who were dismissed or voluntarily withdrew from this program area were 4.

Admissions Requirements:

Scores: Entries appear in this order: required test or GPA, minimum score (if required), median score of students entering in 2001–2002. Master's Programs: GRE-V 450, 470; GRE-Q 450, 480; overall undergraduate GPA 3.00, 3.25. Applicants failing to meet one of the two requirements (GRE or GPA) but meeting the other may be admitted provisionally upon the recommendation of the graduate admissions committee. Doctoral Programs: last 2 years GPA no minimum stated; psychology GPA no minimum stated; psychology GPA no minimum stated.

Other Criteria: (importance of criteria rated low, medium, or high): GRE/MAT scores high, research experience medium, work experience, extracurricular activity, clinically related public service, GPA high, letters of recommendation high, interview, statement of goals and objectives high.

Student Characteristics: The following represents characteristics of students in 2001–2002 in all graduate psychology programs in the department: Female–full-time 16, part-time 3; Male–full-time 2, part-time 0; African American/Black–full-time 2, part-time 2; Hispanic/Latino (a)–full-time 0, part-time 0; Asian/Pacific Islander–full-time 1, part-time 0; American Indian/Alaska Native–full-time 0, part-time 0; Multi-ethnic–full-time 1, part-time 0; students subject to the Americans with Disabilities Act–full-time 0, part-time 0.

Financial Information/Assistance:

Tuition for Full-Time Study: *Master's:* State residents per academic year $1,746, $97 per credit hour; nonstate residents: per academic year $6,966, $387 per credit hour.

Financial Assistance:

First Year Students: Research assistantships available for first-year. Average amount paid per academic year: $5,000. Average number of hours worked per week: 15. Apply by April 15. Tuition remission given: full.

Advanced Students: Research assistantships available for advanced students. Average amount paid per academic year: $5,000. Average number of hours worked per week: 15. Apply by April 15. Tuition remission given: full.

Contact Information: Of all students currently enrolled full-time, 33% benefitted from one or more of the listed financial assistance programs. For information on financial assistance, contact: Department of Financial Aid, P.O. Box 8065, Georgia Southern University, Statesboro, GA 30460-8065; (912) 681-5413.

Internships/Practica: No information provided.

Housing and Day Care: No on-campus housing and day care facilities are available.

Employment of Department Graduates:

Master's Degree Graduates: Of those who graduated in the academic year 2000–2001, the following categories and numbers represent the post-graduate activities and employment of master's degree graduates: Enrolled in a psychology doctoral program (3), enrolled in another graduate/professional program (1), enrolled in a post-doctoral residency/fellowship (n/a), employed in independent practice (n/a), employed in an academic position at a 2-year/4-year college (1), employed in a community mental health/counseling center (3).

Doctoral Degree Graduates: Of those who graduated in the academic year 2000–2001, the following categories and numbers represent the post-graduate activities and employment of doctoral degree graduates: Enrolled in a psychology doctoral program (n/a), enrolled in another graduate/professional program (n/a).

Additional Information:

Orientation, Objectives, and Emphasis of Department: This two-year degree program has two tracks: the clinical track for those seeking immediate employment in the human services delivery settings and the experimental psychology track for those preparing to pursue immediately a PhD in psychology. The clinical track consists of coursework and practica in clinical assessment and therapy and has a thesis option. The experimental track consists of coursework and supervised research in traditional areas of interest such as social, developmental, personality, learning, cognitive, physiological, and sensation/perception and has a thesis requirement.

Application Information:

Send to: The College of Graduate Studies, Georgia Southern University, P.O. Box 8113, Statesboro, GA 30460-8113. Students are admitted in the Fall, application deadline July 15.

Georgia State University (2001 data)
Counseling and Psychological Services
College of Education
University Plaza
Atlanta, GA 30303
Telephone: (404) 651-2550
Fax: (404) 651-1160
E-mail: *jwhite@gsu.edu*
Web: *http://www.gsu.edu-cps*

Department Established:

1967. Chairperson: Joanna F. White. Number of Faculty: total–full-time 25, part-time 1; women–full-time 13, part-time 1; minority–full-time 4.

Programs and Degrees Offered:

Listed in the following order: Program area, degree type (T if terminal Master's), number awarded 7/00-6/01. Counseling PhD 4, Counseling psychology PhD 16, professional counseling MSc 82, rehabilitation counseling MSc 4, school counseling MSEd 28, school psychology PhD 8, school (T) MSEd 16.

APA Accreditation: Counseling PhD: full. School PhD: full.

Student Applications/Admissions:

Student Applications

Counseling PhD—Applications 2001–2002, 18. Total applicants accepted 2001–2002, 3. New applicants enrolled 2001–2002, 3. Total enrolled 2001–2002 full-time, 11. Openings 2002–2003, 3. *Counseling psychology PhD*—Applications 2001–2002, 100. Total applicants accepted 2001–2002, 5. New applicants enrolled 2001–2002, 4. Total enrolled 2001–2002 full-time, 26. Openings 2002–2003, 4. *Professional counseling MSc*—Applications 2001–2002, 230. Total applicants accepted 2001–2002, 103. New applicants enrolled 2001–2002, 86. Total enrolled 2001–2002 full-time, 90, part-time, 130. Openings 2002–2003, 80. *Rehabilitation counseling MSc*—Applications 2001–2002, 18. Total applicants accepted 2001–2002, 10. New applicants enrolled 2001–2002, 10. Total enrolled 2001–2002 full-time, 8, part-time, 2. Openings 2002–2003, 10. *School counseling MSEd*—Applications 2001–2002, 56. Total applicants accepted 2001–2002, 24. New applicants enrolled 2001–2002, 23. Total enrolled 2001–2002 full-time, 6, part-time, 28. Openings 2002–2003, 20. *School psychology PhD*—Applications 2001–2002, 22. Total applicants accepted 2001–2002, 3. New applicants enrolled 2001–2002, 3. Total enrolled 2001–2002 full-time, 20, part-time, 12. Openings 2002–2003, 3. *School MSEd*—Applications 2001–2002, 27. Total applicants accepted 2001–2002, 20. New applicants enrolled 2001–2002, 18. Total enrolled 2001–2002 full-time, 18. Openings 2002–2003, 20.

Admissions Requirements:

Scores: Entries appear in this order: required test or GPA, minimum score (if required), median score of students entering in 2001–2002. Master's Programs: GRE-V 400, 540; GRE-Q 400, 520; overall undergraduate GPA 2.5, 3.4. Doctoral Programs: GRE-V 500, 1320; GRE-Q 500, 1210; overall undergraduate GPA 2.5, 3.35; psychology GPA 3.5, 4.0.

Other Criteria: (importance of criteria rated low, medium, or high): GRE/MAT scores medium, research experience high, work experience high, GPA high, letters of recommendation low, interview high, statement of goals and objectives medium.

Student Characteristics: The following represents characteristics of students in 2001–2002 in all graduate psychology programs in the department: Female–full-time 72, part-time 40; Male–full-time 23, part-time 12; African American/Black–full-time 6, part-time 4; Hispanic/Latino (a)–full-time 3, part-time 3; Asian/Pacific Islander–full-time 3, part-time 3; American Indian/Alaska Native–full-time 2, part-time 1.

Financial Information/Assistance:
Tuition for Full-Time Study: No information provided.

Financial Assistance:
First Year Students: No information provided.
Advanced Students: No information provided.
Contact Information: For information on financial assistance, contact: Office of Academic Assistance, College of Education/Academic Advisor, CPS.

Internships/Practica: Over 200 sites have been approved by the Department using CACREP/APA standards.

Housing and Day Care: No on-campus housing and day care facilities are available.

Employment of Department Graduates:
Master's Degree Graduates: Of those who graduated in the academic year 2000–2001, the following categories and numbers represent the post-graduate activities and employment of master's degree graduates: Enrolled in a post-doctoral residency/fellowship (n/a), employed in independent practice (n/a).
Doctoral Degree Graduates: Of those who graduated in the academic year 2000–2001, the following categories and numbers represent the post-graduate activities and employment of doctoral degree graduates: Enrolled in a psychology doctoral program (n/a), enrolled in another graduate/professional program (n/a).

Additional Information:
Orientation, Objectives, and Emphasis of Department: We conduct information sessions 8 x/yr. Orientation each semester for each degree program.

Special Facilities or Resources: All current state of the art PC/Laptops with wireless capability; Coe Research Laboratory; Department Research Lab.

Information for Students With Physical Disabilities: Buildings are designed to accommodate those with physical disabilities; other services available for special needs, i.e., homebound, blind, deaf, etc.

Application Information:
Send to: Office of Academic Assistance, College of Education, Georgia State University, Atlanta, GA 30303. Students are admitted in the Fall, application deadline January 15; Spring, application deadline October 1; Summer, application deadline March 1. *Fee:* $25.

Georgia State University
Department of Psychology
College of Arts and Sciences
University Plaza
Atlanta, GA 30303-3083
Telephone: (404) 651-2456
Fax: (404) 651-1391
E-mail: *psyadvise-g@langate.gsu.edu*
Web: *http://www.gsu.edu/psychology*

Department Established:
1955. Chairperson: Lauren B. Adamson. Number of Faculty: total–full-time 35; women–full-time 17; minority–full-time 8.

Programs and Degrees Offered:
Listed in the following order: Program area, degree type (T if terminal Master's), number awarded 7/00-6/01. Clinical PhD 7, community PhD 1, developmental PhD 1, neuropsychology and behavioral PhD 1, social/cognitive PhD 1.

APA Accreditation: Clinical PhD: full.

Student Applications/Admissions:
Student Applications
Clinical PhD—Applications 2001–2002, 253. Total applicants accepted 2001–2002, 23. New applicants enrolled 2001–2002, 11. Total enrolled 2001–2002 full-time, 64. Openings 2002–2003, 10. The Median number of years required for completion of a degree are 7. The number of students enrolled full and part-time, who were dismissed or voluntarily withdrew from this program area were 0. *Community PhD*—Applications 2001–2002, 39. Total applicants accepted 2001–2002, 10. New applicants enrolled 2001–2002, 4. Total enrolled 2001–2002 full-time, 26. Openings 2002–2003, 5. The Median number of years required for completion of a degree are 7. *Developmental PhD*—Applications 2001–2002, 15. Total applicants accepted 2001–2002, 4. New applicants enrolled 2001–2002, 4. Total enrolled 2001–2002 full-time, 7. Openings 2002–2003, 3. The Median number of years required for completion of a degree are 6. The number of students enrolled full and part-time, who were dismissed or voluntarily withdrew from this program area were 0. *Neuropsychology and behavioral PhD*—Applications 2001–2002, 23. Total applicants accepted 2001–2002, 4. New applicants enrolled 2001–2002, 3. Total enrolled 2001–2002 full-time, 10. Openings 2002–2003, 3. The Median number of years required for completion of a degree are 9. The number of students enrolled full and part-time, who were dismissed or voluntarily withdrew from this program area were 0. *Social/cognitive PhD*—Applications 2001–2002, 31. Total applicants accepted 2001–2002, 4. New applicants enrolled 2001–2002, 1. Total enrolled 2001–2002 full-time, 11. Openings 2002–2003, 1. The Median number of years required for completion of a degree are 10. The number of students enrolled full and

part-time, who were dismissed or voluntarily withdrew from this program area were 1.

Admissions Requirements:
Scores: Entries appear in this order: required test or GPA, minimum score (if required), median score of students entering in 2001–2002. Doctoral Programs: GRE-V no minimum stated, 540; GRE-Q no minimum stated, 620; GRE-V+Q no minimum stated, 1150; GRE-Analytical no minimum stated, 610; GRE-V+Q+Analytical no minimum stated, 1760; overall undergraduate GPA no minimum stated, 3.50; last 2 years GPA no minimum stated; psychology GPA no minimum stated; psychology GPA no minimum stated.
Other Criteria: (importance of criteria rated low, medium, or high): research experience high, work experience medium, extracurricular activity low, clinically related public service medium, letters of recommendation medium, interview high, statement of goals and objectives high.

Student Characteristics: The following represents characteristics of students in 2001–2002 in all graduate psychology programs in the department: Female–full-time 79, part-time 0; Male–full-time 26, part-time 0; African American/Black–full-time 13, part-time 0; Hispanic/Latino (a)–full-time 3, part-time 0; Asian/Pacific Islander–full-time 4, part-time 0; American Indian/Alaska Native–full-time 1, part-time 0; Multi-ethnic–full-time 0, students subject to the Americans with Disabilities Act–full-time 0.

Financial Information/Assistance:
Tuition for Full-Time Study: *Doctoral:* State residents: per academic year $1,578, $132 per credit hour; nonstate residents: per academic year $6,312, $526 per credit hour.

Financial Assistance:
First Year Students: Research assistantships available for first-year.
Advanced Students: Teaching assistantships available for advanced students. Research assistantships available for advanced students.
Contact Information: Of all students currently enrolled full-time, 95% benefitted from one or more of the listed financial assistance programs. For information on financial assistance, contact: Office of Financial Aid (404) 651-2227.

Internships/Practica: Practicum experiences are an important component of the clinical training program. Supervised therapy and assessment practica are available in a variety of settings. For clinical students, the main source of training is the Psychology Clinic which is located within the department. It provides services to students and members of the community in a variety of modalities, including assessment, individual therapy, group therapy, and family therapy. Another facility within the department is the Regent's Center for Learning Disorders, which offers comprehensive psychoeducational assessments to students and members of the community. Student clinicians are the primary providers of services in both of these clinics. In addition, there are numerous off-campus settings that offer supervised practicum experiences in a variety of areas including health psychology, neuropsychological assessment, personality assessment, psychiatric emergency room services, day treatment programs, etc. Many of these practica are available at Grady Memorial Hospital, a major metropolitan full-service facility located two blocks from the center of campus.

Community students likewise do practica at various community based organizations. Often this research takes the form of needs assessment, program development, and program evaluation.

Housing and Day Care: On-campus housing and day care facilities are available.

Employment of Department Graduates:
Master's Degree Graduates: Of those who graduated in the academic year 2000–2001, the following categories and numbers represent the post-graduate activities and employment of master's degree graduates: Enrolled in a post-doctoral residency/fellowship (n/a), employed in independent practice (n/a).
Doctoral Degree Graduates: Of those who graduated in the academic year 2000–2001, the following categories and numbers represent the post-graduate activities and employment of doctoral degree graduates: Enrolled in a psychology doctoral program (n/a), enrolled in another graduate/professional program (n/a).

Additional Information:
Orientation, Objectives, and Emphasis of Department: The department is eclectic, and many philosophical perspectives and research interests are represented. The policy of the department is to promote the personal and professional development of students. This includes the discovery of individual interests and goals, the growth of independent scholarship and research skills, the mastery of fundamental psychological knowledge and methodology, and the development of various professional skills (e.g., clinical skills, community intervention).

Special Facilities or Resources: The facilities of the department permit work in cognition, development, neuropsychology, learning, infant behavior, sensation and perception, motivation, aging, social psychology, assessment, individual, group and family therapy, behavior therapy, and community psychology. Students may work with both human and nonhuman populations. Human populations include all age ranges and a variety of ethnic and socioeconomic backgrounds. Nonhuman populations include several species ranging from hamsters to the great apes.

Information for Students With Physical Disabilities: Georgia State Univesity provides program accessibility and reasonable accomodations for persons with disabilities. Specifically, GSU provides evaluation of individual needs, advisement, and appropriate support for academic programs of identified persons with disabilities. All buildings on the main campus are wheelchair accessible, and special arrangements for parking can be made. Information about student support services can be obtained by calling (404) 651-1487.

Application Information:
Send to: Graduate Admissions Advisor, Department of Psychology, for inquiries. Applications must be submitted to Office of Graduate Studies, College of Arts & Sciences. Students are admitted in the Fall, application deadline January 5. Deadlines vary by programs. Beginning students will be admitted for fall only, and the department will have a uniform deadline. *Fee:* $25.

Georgia, University of

Department of Counseling and Human Development Services,
  Counseling Psychology Program
College of Education
402 Aderhold Hall
Athens, GA 30602
Telephone: (706) 542-1812
Fax: (706) 542-4130
E-mail: *bglaser@coe.uga.edu*
Web: *http://www.coe.uga.edu/echd*

Department Established:

1946. Department Head: John C. Dagley. Number of Faculty: total–full-time 15, part-time 3; women–full-time 9, part-time 2; minority–full-time 2, part-time 1.

Programs and Degrees Offered:

Listed in the following order: Program area, degree type (T if terminal Master's), number awarded 7/00-6/01. Counseling (T) 8, counseling psychology PhD (T) 8.

APA Accreditation: Counseling PhD: full.

Student Applications/Admissions:

Student Applications

Counseling psychology PhD—Applications 2001–2002, 41. Total applicants accepted 2001–2002, 13. New applicants enrolled 2001–2002, 7. Total enrolled 2001–2002 full-time, 31, part-time, 21. Openings 2002–2003, 10. The number of students enrolled full and part-time, who were dismissed or voluntarily withdrew from this program area were 1.

Admissions Requirements:

Scores: Entries appear in this order: required test or GPA, minimum score (if required), median score of students entering in 2001–2002. Master's Programs: GRE-V no minimum stated, 560; GRE-Q no minimum stated, 630; GRE-V+Q no minimum stated, 1130. Doctoral Programs: GRE-V no minimum stated, 560; GRE-Q no minimum stated, 670; GRE-V+Q no minimum stated, 1240; overall undergraduate GPA no minimum stated, 3.09; last 2 years GPA no minimum stated; psychology GPA no minimum stated; psychology GPA no minimum stated, 3.97.

Other Criteria: (importance of criteria rated low, medium, or high): GRE/MAT scores medium, research experience high, work experience high, extracurricular activity low, clinically related public service medium, GPA medium, letters of recommendation high, interview high, statement of goals and objectives high.

Student Characteristics: The following represents characteristics of students in 2001–2002 in all graduate psychology programs in the department: Female–full-time 16, part-time 0; Male–full-time 4, part-time 0; African American/Black–full-time 8, part-time 0; Hispanic/Latino (a)–full-time 0, part-time 0; Asian/Pacific Islander–full-time 0, part-time 0; American Indian/Alaska Native–full-time 0, part-time 0; Multi-ethnic–full-time 1, students subject to the Americans with Disabilities Act–full-time 0.

Financial Information/Assistance:

Tuition for Full-Time Study: Master's: State residents per academic year $3,942, $132 per credit hour; nonstate residents: per academic year $13,410, $528 per credit hour. *Doctoral:* State residents: per academic year $3,972, $132 per credit hour; nonstate residents: per academic year $13,410, $528 per credit hour.

Financial Assistance:

First Year Students: Research assistantships available for first-year. Average amount paid per academic year: $9,800. Average number of hours worked per week: 13. Apply by Dec 1. Tuition remission given: full.

Advanced Students: Research assistantships available for advanced students. Average amount paid per academic year: $9,800. Average number of hours worked per week: 13. Apply by Dec 1. Tuition remission given: full.

Contact Information: Of all students currently enrolled full-time, 70% benefitted from one or more of the listed financial assistance programs. For information on financial assistance, contact: Financial Aid Office (706)542-3476.

Internships/Practica: Practica opportunities are provided in two on-campus clinics: The Counseling and Personal Evaluation Center and the Counseling and Testing Center. For those doctoral students for whom a professional internship is required prior to graduation, 8 applied in 2000–2001. Of those who applied, 8 were placed in internships listed by the Association of Psychology Postdoctoral and Internship Programs (APPIC); 8 were placed in APA accredited internships.

Housing and Day Care: On-campus housing and day care facilities are available.

Employment of Department Graduates:

Master's Degree Graduates: Of those who graduated in the academic year 2000–2001, the following categories and numbers represent the post-graduate activities and employment of master's degree graduates: Enrolled in a psychology doctoral program (4), enrolled in another graduate/professional program (3), enrolled in a post-doctoral residency/fellowship (n/a), employed in independent practice (n/a).

Doctoral Degree Graduates: Of those who graduated in the academic year 2000–2001, the following categories and numbers represent the post-graduate activities and employment of doctoral degree graduates: Enrolled in a psychology doctoral program (n/a), enrolled in another graduate/professional program (n/a), enrolled in a post-doctoral residency/fellowship (1), employed in independent practice (2), employed in an academic position at a university (2), employed in other positions at a higher education institution (2).

Additional Information:

Orientation, Objectives, and Emphasis of Department: The goal of the program is to educate students in the scientist-practitioner model of training in professional counseling psychology. The program focuses on professional competency development in three areas: teaching, research, and clinical service. The theoretical orientations of faculty members vary widely including representatives of most major schools of thought. The broad emphases of the program include developmental perspectives, cultural diversity perspectives, cognitive-behavioral approaches, and psychodynamic therapies.

Special Facilities or Resources: The University, the College, and the Department separately and collectively offer a number of services and fully-equipped facilities to assist students in conducting academic inquiry, including special computer labs, research assistance centers, and major libraries. Several members of the university's Counseling and Testing Center are adjunct faculty members, thereby offering consultation and instructional assistance.

Application Information:

Send to: Graduate Coordinator, Department of Counseling and Human Development Services, 402 Aderhold Hall, The University of Georgia, Athens, GA 30602-7142. Students are admitted in the Fall, application deadline December 1. Master's February 1st. *Fee:* $30. Fee is for Graduate School Application, subject to change.

Georgia, University of (2001 data)
Department of Psychology
Franklin College of Arts and Sciences
Athens, GA 30602-3013
Telephone: (706) 542-2174
Fax: (706) 542-3275
E-mail: *gradadm@uga.cc.uga.edu*
Web: *http://teach.psy.uga.edu/dept/home/home.htm*

Department Established:

1921. Department Head: Garnett S. Stokes. Number of Faculty: total–full-time 39, part-time 4; women–full-time 13, part-time 2; minority–full-time 4.

Programs and Degrees Offered:

Listed in the following order: Program area, degree type (T if terminal Master's), number awarded 7/00-6/01. Applied PhD 8, biopsychology PhD 7, clinical PhD 6, cognitive experimental PhD 3, lifespan developmental PhD 2, social PhD 4.

APA Accreditation: Clinical PhD: full.

Student Applications/Admissions:

Student Applications

Applied PhD—Applications 2001–2002, 90. Total applicants accepted 2001–2002, 10. New applicants enrolled 2001–2002, 5. Total enrolled 2001–2002 full-time, 20, part-time, 18. *Biopsychology PhD*—Applications 2001–2002, 41. Total applicants accepted 2001–2002, 15. New applicants enrolled 2001–2002, 5. Total enrolled 2001–2002 full-time, 15, part-time, 4. *Clinical PhD*—Applications 2001–2002, 136. Total applicants accepted 2001–2002, 18. New applicants enrolled 2001–2002, 8. Total enrolled 2001–2002 full-time, 28, part-time, 5. *Cognitive experimental PhD*—Applications 2001–2002, 29. Total applicants accepted 2001–2002, 6. New applicants enrolled 2001–2002, 4. Total enrolled 2001–2002 full-time, 15, part-time, 2. *Lifespan developmental PhD*—Applications 2001–2002, 49. Total applicants accepted 2001–2002, 7. New applicants enrolled 2001–2002, 3. Total enrolled 2001–2002 full-time, 12, part-time, 3. *Social PhD*—Applications 2001–2002, 38. Total applicants accepted 2001–2002, 10. New applicants enrolled 2001–2002, 2. Total enrolled 2001–2002 full-time, 8, part-time, 4.

Admissions Requirements:

Scores: Entries appear in this order: required test or GPA, minimum score (if required), median score of students entering in 2001–2002. Doctoral Programs: GRE-V+Q no minimum stated, 1225; overall undergraduate GPA 3.0.

Other Criteria: (importance of criteria rated low, medium, or high): GRE/MAT scores medium, research experience high, work experience high, extracurricular activity medium, clinically related public service medium, GPA medium, letters of recommendation high, interview medium, statement of goals and objectives high. Each program weighs according to its own criteria.

Student Characteristics: The following represents characteristics of students in 2001–2002 in all graduate psychology programs in the department: Female–full-time 17, part-time 0; Male–full-time 10, part-time 0; African American/Black–full-time 1, part-time 0; Hispanic/Latino (a)–full-time 1, part-time 0; Asian/Pacific Islander–full-time 0, part-time 0; American Indian/Alaska Native–full-time 0, part-time 0.

Financial Information/Assistance:

Tuition for Full-Time Study: No information provided.

Financial Assistance:

First Year Students: No information provided.
Advanced Students: No information provided.
Contact Information: Of all students currently enrolled full-time, 90% benefitted from one or more of the listed financial assistance programs.

Internships/Practica: For those doctoral students for whom a professional internship is required prior to graduation, 3 applied in 2000–2001. Of those who applied, 1 was placed in internships listed by the Association of Psychology Postdoctoral and Internship Programs (APPIC); 1 was placed in APA accredited internships.

Housing and Day Care: No on-campus housing and day care facilities are available.

Employment of Department Graduates:

Master's Degree Graduates: Of those who graduated in the academic year 2000–2001, the following categories and numbers represent the post-graduate activities and employment of master's degree graduates: Enrolled in a post-doctoral residency/fellowship (n/a), employed in independent practice (n/a).

Doctoral Degree Graduates: Of those who graduated in the academic year 2000–2001, the following categories and numbers represent the post-graduate activities and employment of doctoral degree graduates: Enrolled in a psychology doctoral program (n/a), enrolled in another graduate/professional program (n/a).

Additional Information:

Orientation, Objectives, and Emphasis of Department: Our emphasis is on research and the basic science aspects of psychology with a focus on doctoral education. A few state and private facilities provide internships. We have a cooperative liaison with several mental health facilities in the region as well as other universities.

Special Facilities or Resources: Facilities include a research and training center for mental retardation and the Institute for Behavioral Research and Psychology Clinic.

Information for Students With Physical Disabilities: We comply with the law on Americans with Disabilities.

Application Information:
Send to: Spplemental application and reference letters to: Department of Psychology c/o Graduate Coordinator, University of Georgia, Athens, GA 30602-3013. Admission application to Graduate Admissions Boyd GSRC. Students are admitted in the Fall, application deadline 1/1 & 1/15. Application deadline for clinical, biopsychology, developmental is December 1; Janary 15 is deadline for applied, cog/exp and social. *Fee:* $30.

Georgia, University of
Program in School Psychology
Education
325 Aderhold Hall
Athens, GA 30602-7143
Telephone: (706) 542-4110
Fax: (706) 542-4240
E-mail: *rpmartin@coe.uga.edu*
Web: *http://www.coe.uga.edu/edpsych/*

Department Established:
1968. Program Coordinator: Roy P. Martin. Number of Faculty: total–full-time 5; women–full-time 2; minority–full-time 1.

Programs and Degrees Offered:
Listed in the following order: Program area, degree type (T if terminal Master's), number awarded 7/00-6/01. School PhD 5.

APA Accreditation: School PhD: full.

Student Applications/Admissions:
Student Applications
School PhD—Applications 2001–2002, 63. Total applicants accepted 2001–2002, 11. New applicants enrolled 2001–2002, 6. Total enrolled 2001–2002 full-time, 6. Openings 2002–2003, 6.

Admissions Requirements:
Scores: Entries appear in this order: required test or GPA, minimum score (if required), median score of students entering in 2001–2002. Doctoral Programs: GRE-V+Q 1000, 1235; overall undergraduate GPA 3.0, 3.3 ; last 2 years GPA no minimum stated; psychology GPA no minimum stated; psychology GPA no minimum stated.
Other Criteria: (importance of criteria rated low, medium, or high): GRE/MAT scores medium, research experience low, work experience low, extracurricular activity low, clinically related public service medium, GPA medium, letters of recommendation medium, interview low, statement of goals and objectives medium.

Student Characteristics: The following represents characteristics of students in 2001–2002 in all graduate psychology programs in the department: Female–full-time 38, part-time 0; Male–full-time 4, part-time 0; African American/Black–full-time 3, Hispanic/Latino (a)–full-time 0, part-time 0; Asian/Pacific Islander–full-time 1, part-time 0; American Indian/Alaska Native–full-time 0, part-time 0; Multi-ethnic–full-time 1.

Financial Information/Assistance:
Tuition for Full-Time Study: No information provided.

Financial Assistance:
First Year Students: Teaching assistantships available for first-year. Average amount paid per academic year: $9,719. Average number of hours worked per week: 13. Apply by Feb. 1. Research assistantships available for first-year. Average amount paid per academic year: $9,719. Average number of hours worked per week: 13. Apply by Feb. 1.
Advanced Students: Teaching assistantships available for advanced students. Average amount paid per academic year: $9,719. Average number of hours worked per week: 13. Apply by Feb. 1. Research assistantships available for advanced students. Average amount paid per academic year: $9,719. Average number of hours worked per week: 13. Apply by Feb. 1.
Contact Information: Of all students currently enrolled full-time, 74% benefitted from one or more of the listed financial assistance programs. For information on financial assistance, contact: Graduate Coordinator, Department of Educational Psychology, 329 Aderhold Hall, Athens, GA 30602.

Internships/Practica: No information provided.

Housing and Day Care: No on-campus housing and day care facilities are available.

Employment of Department Graduates:
Master's Degree Graduates: Of those who graduated in the academic year 2000–2001, the following categories and numbers represent the post-graduate activities and employment of master's degree graduates: Enrolled in a post-doctoral residency/fellowship (n/a), employed in independent practice (n/a).
Doctoral Degree Graduates: Of those who graduated in the academic year 2000–2001, the following categories and numbers represent the post-graduate activities and employment of doctoral degree graduates: Enrolled in a psychology doctoral program (n/a), enrolled in another graduate/professional program (n/a), enrolled in a post-doctoral residency/fellowship (1), employed in independent practice (0), employed in an academic position at a university (0), employed in an academic position at a 2-year/4-year college (0), employed in other positions at a higher education institution (0), employed in a professional position in a school system (4), employed in business or industry (research/consulting) (0), employed in business or industry (management) (0), employed in a government agency (research) (0), employed in a government agency (professional services) (0), employed in a community mental health/counseling center (0), employed in a hospital/medical center (0), still seeking employment (0), other employment position (0).

Additional Information:

Orientation, Objectives, and Emphasis of Department: The PhD program in school psychology supplies research-oriented school psychologists to educational settings, hospitals, clinics, and universities in which they can provide leadership in applied practice, research, and teaching. The school psychology program follows the scientist-practitioner model, and emphasizes human development and developmental psychopathology and the central core elements of training.

Special Facilities or Resources: Special facilities and resources include access to a superior computer center, decentralized computational equipment, a major research library, and faculty members who are extraordinarily accessible to students. The department is strongly committed to affirmative action and fair treatment and is very proud that the majority of our students are women. Despite the suburban setting (a small urban area of 75,000 over an hour from Atlanta), we attract increasing numbers of black, Asian, and out-of-state and out-of-region students and faculty. NASP and APA requirements and full accreditation from APA and NCATE form the foundation of our programs.

Application Information:

Send to: Graduate Admissions Office, Graduate Studies Building, The University of Georgia, Athens, GA 30602. Students are admitted in the Fall, application deadline February 1. Deadline dates are unrelated to degree; all applications are considered only for Fall admission. *Fee:* $30.

State University of West Georgia
Counseling & Educational Psychology
Education
237 Education Annex
Carrollton, GA 30118
Telephone: (770) 836-6554
Fax: (770) 836-4645
E-mail: *bsnow@westga.edu*
Web: *http://coe.westga.edu/cep/*

Department Established:

1969. Chairperson: Brent M. Snow, Ph.D. Number of Faculty: total–full-time 12; women–full-time 6; minority–full-time 2.

Programs and Degrees Offered:

Listed in the following order: Program area, degree type (T if terminal Master's), number awarded 7/00-6/01. Counseling EdS, Counseling MEd (T).

Student Applications/Admissions:

Student Applications
Counseling EdS.

Admissions Requirements:

Scores: Entries appear in this order: required test or GPA, minimum score (if required), median score of students entering in 2001–2002. Master's Programs: GRE-V 450; GRE-Q 450; GRE-V+Q 900; GRE-Analytical 450; overall undergraduate GPA 2.7. Doctoral Programs: last 2 years GPA no minimum stated; psychology GPA no minimum stated; psychology GPA no minimum stated.

Other Criteria: (importance of criteria rated low, medium, or high): GRE/MAT scores high, research experience low, work experience low, extracurricular activity low, clinically related public service low, GPA high, letters of recommendation high, interview high, statement of goals and objectives high.

Financial Information/Assistance:

Tuition for Full-Time Study: Master's: State residents per academic year $1,428, $97 per credit hour; nonstate residents: per academic year $4,908, $387 per credit hour.

Financial Assistance:

First Year Students: Research assistantships available for first-year. Average amount paid per academic year: $6,000. Average number of hours worked per week: 20. Apply by July. Tuition remission given: full.

Advanced Students: Research assistantships available for advanced students. Average amount paid per academic year: $6,000. Apply by July. Tuition remission given: full.

Contact Information: Of all students currently enrolled full-time, 5% benefitted from one or more of the listed financial assistance programs. For information on financial assistance, contact: Financial Aid Office, kjordan@westga.edu.

Internships/Practica: Practicum (100 hours) and Internship (600 hours) is required of all graduate students in school and community counseling.

Housing and Day Care: On-campus housing and day care facilities are available.

Employment of Department Graduates:

Master's Degree Graduates: Of those who graduated in the academic year 2000–2001, the following categories and numbers represent the post-graduate activities and employment of master's degree graduates: Enrolled in a post-doctoral residency/fellowship (n/a), employed in independent practice (n/a).

Doctoral Degree Graduates: Of those who graduated in the academic year 2000–2001, the following categories and numbers represent the post-graduate activities and employment of doctoral degree graduates: Enrolled in a psychology doctoral program (n/a), enrolled in another graduate/professional program (n/a).

Additional Information:

Orientation, Objectives, and Emphasis of Department: The Department's identity is in training professional counselors for schools and community agencies. Master's programs are accredited by the Council for Accreditation of Counseling and Related Educational Programs (CACREP).

Application Information:

Send to: Department Chair. Students are admitted in the Fall, application deadline July; Spring, application deadline November; Summer, application deadline April.

State University of West Georgia (2001 data)

Department of Psychology
Arts and Sciences
Maple Street
Carrollton, GA 30118
Telephone: (770) 836-6510
Fax: (770) 836-6791
E-mail: *drice@westga.edu*
Web: *http://www.westga.edu*

Department Established:

1967. Professor and Chair: Donadrian L. Rice. Number of Faculty: total–full-time 14, part-time 2; women–full-time 3, part-time 1; minority–full-time 1.

Programs and Degrees Offered:

Listed in the following order: Program area, degree type (T if terminal Master's), number awarded 7/00-6/01. Humanistic/Transpersonal MA (T) 12.

Student Applications/Admissions:

Student Applications

Humanistic/Transpersonal MA—Applications 2001–2002, 50. Total applicants accepted 2001–2002, 35. New applicants enrolled 2001–2002, 28. Total enrolled 2001–2002 full-time, 57, part-time, 30. Openings 2002–2003, 40. The Median number of years required for completion of a degree are 3. The number of students enrolled full and part-time, who were dismissed or voluntarily withdrew from this program area were 4.

Admissions Requirements:

Scores: Entries appear in this order: required test or GPA, minimum score (if required), median score of students entering in 2001–2002. Master's Programs: GRE-V+Q 800; overall undergraduate GPA 2.5.

Other Criteria: (importance of criteria rated low, medium, or high): GRE/MAT scores, research experience high, work experience high, clinically related public service medium, GPA, letters of recommendation high, interview high, statement of goals and objectives high.

Student Characteristics: The following represents characteristics of students in 2001–2002 in all graduate psychology programs in the department: Female–full-time 13, part-time 5; Male–full-time 7, part-time 3; African American/Black–full-time 5, part-time 1; Hispanic/Latino (a)–full-time 2, part-time 0; Asian/Pacific Islander–full-time 1, part-time 0; American Indian/Alaska Native–full-time 0, part-time 0.

Financial Information/Assistance:

Tuition for Full-Time Study: No information provided.

Financial Assistance:

First Year Students: No information provided.
Advanced Students: No information provided.
Contact Information: Of all students currently enrolled full-time, 25% benefitted from one or more of the listed financial assistance programs. For information on financial assistance, contact: Office of Financial Aid, State University of West Georgia, Carrollton, GA 30118.

Internships/Practica: Internships are available at local facilities.

Housing and Day Care: No on-campus housing and day care facilities are available.

Employment of Department Graduates:

Master's Degree Graduates: Of those who graduated in the academic year 2000–2001, the following categories and numbers represent the post-graduate activities and employment of master's degree graduates: Enrolled in a post-doctoral residency/fellowship (n/a), employed in independent practice (n/a).

Doctoral Degree Graduates: Of those who graduated in the academic year 2000–2001, the following categories and numbers represent the post-graduate activities and employment of doctoral degree graduates: Enrolled in a psychology doctoral program (n/a), enrolled in another graduate/professional program (n/a).

Additional Information:

Orientation, Objectives, and Emphasis of Department: The department is a pioneer of humanistic-transpersonal psychology. It differs from other programs in that it goes beyond conventional subjects and approaches a holistic and integrative understanding of human experience. Alongside demanding academic work, student growth and personal awareness are inherent to this venture since such reflection is considered an important factor in human understanding. Individual programs are designed according to personal needs and interests; the overall atmosphere is communal, encouraging personal and intellectual dialogue and encounter. Most conventional topic areas are taught. Beyond these are areas almost uniquely explorable in a program such as this: the horizons of consciousness through such vantages as Eastern and transpersonal psychologies, hermeneutics, existential and phenomenological psychologies, and critical psychology. Specific areas include women's studies; aesthetic and sacred experience; myths, dreams, and symbols; and creativity. Areas of applied interest are viewed as correlates of the learning process: skill courses related to human services, prevention and community psychology, counseling psychology, organizational development, and growth therapies. The department offers training in qualitative and traditional methodologies of research. Practicum and internship experience along with individual research and reading are highly encouraged for those who can profit from these. Interest areas include human science research; parapsychology; transpersonal and Eastern psychologies; counseling, clinical, community, and organizational development; and psychology in the classroom.

Special Facilities or Resources: Special resources include large library holdings in the areas of humanistic, parapsychology, transpersonal, philosophical, and Oriental psychology. The library holds papers of Sidney M. Jourard, Edith Weiskoff-Joelsen, and the Psychical Research Foundation Library. The department hosts major conferences, and faculty are associated with several journals and newsletters exploring orientation areas.

Information for Students With Physical Disabilities: Facilities are wheelchair accessible.

Application Information:

Send to: Graduate Coordinator, Department of Psychology, State University of West Georgia, Carrollton, GA 30118. Students are admitted in the Fall, application deadline March 1; Spring, application deadline October 1; Summer, application deadline March 1. *Fee:* $20.

Valdosta State University

Psychology and Counseling
1500 North Patterson Street
Valdosta, GA 31698-0100
Telephone: (229) 333-5930
Fax: (229) 259-5576
E-mail: *bbauer@valdosta.edu*
Web: *http://education.valdosta.edu/info/psy/*

Department Established:

1965. Head: Robert E. L. Bauer. Number of Faculty: total–full-time 18, part-time 2; women–full-time 5, part-time 1; minority–full-time 3.

Programs and Degrees Offered:

Listed in the following order: Program area, degree type (T if terminal Master's), number awarded 7/00-6/01. Clinical/counseling MA (T) 9, Industrial/Organizational MA (T) 9, School Counseling EdS 1, School Counseling EdS 1, School Psychology EdS 5.

Student Applications/Admissions:

Student Applications

Clinical/counseling MA—Applications 2001–2002, 20. Total applicants accepted 2001–2002, 11. New applicants enrolled 2001–2002, 10. Total enrolled 2001–2002 full-time, 2, part-time, 12. Openings 2002–2003, 14. *Industrial/Organizational MA*—Applications 2001–2002, 18. Total applicants accepted 2001–2002, 8. New applicants enrolled 2001–2002, 8. Total enrolled 2001–2002 full-time, 7, part-time, 5. Openings 2002–2003, 14. *School Counseling EdS*—Applications 2001–2002, 4. Total applicants accepted 2001–2002, 2. New applicants enrolled 2001–2002, 2. Total enrolled 2001–2002 part-time, 7. Openings 2002–2003, 10. *School Counseling EdS*—Applications 2001–2002, 4. Total applicants accepted 2001–2002, 2. New applicants enrolled 2001–2002, 2. Total enrolled 2001–2002 part-time, 7. Openings 2002–2003, 10. *School Psychology EdS*—Applications 2001–2002, 10. Total applicants accepted 2001–2002, 6. New applicants enrolled 2001–2002, 6. Total enrolled 2001–2002 part-time, 12. Openings 2002–2003, 10.

Admissions Requirements:

Scores: Entries appear in this order: required test or GPA, minimum score (if required), median score of students entering in 2001–2002. Master's Programs: GRE-V 400; GRE-Q 400; overall undergraduate GPA 3.00. MS in Psychology (reported here) differs from MEd and EdS in admissions criteria. Please write for details. Doctoral Programs: last 2 years GPA no minimum stated; psychology GPA no minimum stated; psychology GPA no minimum stated.

Other Criteria: (importance of criteria rated low, medium, or high): GRE/MAT scores high, research experience medium, work experience medium, extracurricular activity low, clinically related public service low, GPA high, letters of recommendation medium, interview low. Please write for details by program.

Student Characteristics: The following represents characteristics of students in 2001–2002 in all graduate psychology programs in the department: Female–full-time 6, part-time 40; Male–full-time 6, part-time 15; African American/Black–full-time 2, part-time

9; Hispanic/Latino (a)–full-time 0, part-time 2; Asian/Pacific Islander–full-time 0, part-time 0; American Indian/Alaska Native–full-time 0, part-time 0; Multi-ethnic–full-time 0, part-time 0; students subject to the Americans with Disabilities Act–full-time 0, part-time 0.

Financial Information/Assistance:

Tuition for Full-Time Study: *Master's:* State residents per academic year $2,320, $97 per credit hour; nonstate residents: per academic year $9,280, $387 per credit hour.

Financial Assistance:

First Year Students: Research assistantships available for first-year. Average amount paid per academic year: $2,452. Average number of hours worked per week: 15. Apply by July 15. Tuition remission given: full.

Advanced Students: Research assistantships available for advanced students. Average amount paid per academic year: $2,452. Average number of hours worked per week: 15. Apply by July 15. Tuition remission given: full.

Contact Information: Of all students currently enrolled full-time, 10% benefitted from one or more of the listed financial assistance programs. For information on financial assistance, contact: Graduate Assistantships may include research and teaching. Finanical Aid Office.

Internships/Practica: Master's students are assigned to appropriate practica sites, related to their programs of study. Some sites offer stipends. All School Psychology EdS students work in schools during their internships and receive a stipend.

Housing and Day Care: No on-campus housing and day care facilities are available.

Employment of Department Graduates:

Master's Degree Graduates: Of those who graduated in the academic year 2000–2001, the following categories and numbers represent the post-graduate activities and employment of master's degree graduates: Enrolled in a psychology doctoral program (2), enrolled in another graduate/professional program (3), enrolled in a post-doctoral residency/fellowship (n/a), employed in independent practice (n/a), employed in an academic position at a university (0), employed in an academic position at a 2-year/4-year college (0), employed in other positions at a higher education institution (0), employed in a professional position in a school system (11), employed in business or industry (research/consulting) (1), employed in business or industry (management) (5), employed in a government agency (research) (0), employed in a government agency (professional services) (0), employed in a community mental health/counseling center (4), employed in a hospital/medical center (0), still seeking employment (0), other employment position (0).

Doctoral Degree Graduates: Of those who graduated in the academic year 2000–2001, the following categories and numbers represent the post-graduate activities and employment of doctoral degree graduates: Enrolled in a psychology doctoral program (n/a), enrolled in another graduate/professional program (n/a).

Additional Information:

Orientation, Objectives, and Emphasis of Department: The Department of Psychology and Counseling serves the citizens of the region and state by offering instruction, research, and services designed to advance the understanding of behavioral and cognitive processes and to improve the quality of life. The principle function of the department is to prepare students at the undergraduate and graduate levels to pursue careers within the discipline and affiliated areas. A related purpose is to provide courses for programs in education, nursing, and other disciplines. At the baccalaureate level, the students develop basic skills in scientific research, knowledge of psychological nomenclature and concepts, and are introduced to the diverse applications of psychology. The graduate programs prepare students to apply skills in schools, mental health agencies, government, industry, and other settings.

Training at the graduate level is designed to prepare qualified, responsible professionals who may provide assessment, consulting, counseling, and other services to the citizenry of the region.

Information for Students With Physical Disabilities: The campus is flat and all classroom facilities are wheelchair accessible.

Application Information:
Send to: Graduate School, Valdosta State University, 1500 North Patterson Street, Valdosta, GA 31602-9966. Students are admitted in the Fall, application deadline July 15; Spring, application deadline November 15; Summer, application deadline May 1. *Fee:* $20.

Argosy University, Honolulu
Clinical Psychology
400 Pacific Tower, 1001 Bishop Street
Honolulu, HI 96813
Telephone: (808) 536-5555
Fax: (808) 536-5505
E-mail: *hawaii@argosyu.edu*
Web: *http://www.argosyu.edu*

Department Established:
1994. Head of Graduate Psychology Department: Nancy M. Sidun, Psy.D., ATR. Number of Faculty: total–full-time 7, part-time 2; women–full-time 3; minority–full-time 2, part-time 1; faculty subject to the Americans with Disabilities Act 2.

Programs and Degrees Offered:
Listed in the following order: Program area, degree type (T if terminal Master's), number awarded 7/00-6/01. Clinical PsyD 20, clinical Respecialization Diploma 12, professional counseling MA (T) 31.

APA Accreditation: Clinical PsyD: full.

Student Applications/Admissions:
Student Applications
Clinical PsyD—Applications 2001–2002, 81. Total applicants accepted 2001–2002, 41. New applicants enrolled 2001–2002, 34. Total enrolled 2001–2002 full-time, 96, part-time, 27. Openings 2002–2003, 37. The Median number of years required for completion of a degree are 5. The number of students enrolled full and part-time, who were dismissed or voluntarily withdrew from this program area were 5. *Clinical Respecialization Diploma*—Applications 2001–2002, 12. Total applicants accepted 2001–2002, 12. New applicants enrolled 2001–2002, 12. Total enrolled 2001–2002 full-time, 12. Openings 2002–2003, 15. The Median number of years required for completion of a degree are 2. The number of students enrolled full and part-time, who were dismissed or voluntarily withdrew from this program area were 0. *Professional counseling MA*—Applications 2001–2002, 60. Total applicants accepted 2001–2002, 40. New applicants enrolled 2001–2002, 38. Total enrolled 2001–2002 full-time, 80, part-time, 5. Openings 2002–2003, 60. The Median number of years required for completion of a degree are 2. The number of students enrolled full and part-time, who were dismissed or voluntarily withdrew from this program area were 1.

Admissions Requirements:
Scores: Entries appear in this order: required test or GPA, minimum score (if required), median score of students entering in 2001–2002. Master's Programs: overall undergraduate GPA 3.00; last 2 years GPA 3.00, 3.30; psychology GPA 3.00, 3.65. No set GPA requirement for professional counseling program. Doctoral Programs: overall undergraduate GPA 3.25, 3.29; last 2 years GPA 3.25, 3.24; psychology GPA 3.25, 3.45; psychology GPA 3.25, 3.65.

Other Criteria: (importance of criteria rated low, medium, or high): research experience low, work experience medium, extracurricular activity low, clinically related public service medium, letters of recommendation medium, interview high, statement of goals and objectives high.

Student Characteristics: The following represents characteristics of students in 2001–2002 in all graduate psychology programs in the department: Female–full-time 145, part-time 30; Male–full-time 43, part-time 8; African American/Black–full-time 4, part-time 0; Hispanic/Latino (a)–full-time 5, part-time 0; Asian/Pacific Islander–full-time 77, part-time 2; American Indian/Alaska Native–full-time 1, part-time 0; Multi-ethnic–full-time 5.

Financial Information/Assistance:
Tuition for Full-Time Study: Master's: State residents $530 per credit hour; nonstate residents: $530 per credit hour. *Doctoral:* State residents: $530 per credit hour; nonstate residents: $530 per credit hour.

Financial Assistance:
First Year Students: Fellowships and scholarships available for first-year. Average amount paid per academic year: $10,000. Apply by Aug 31. Tuition remission given: partial.

Advanced Students: Teaching assistantships available for advanced students. Average amount paid per academic year: $500. Average number of hours worked per week: 20. Apply by n/a. Tuition remission given: partial. Fellowships and scholarships available for advanced students. Average amount paid per academic year: $10,000. Apply by Aug 31. Tuition remission given: partial.

Contact Information: Of all students currently enrolled full-time, 10% benefitted from one or more of the listed financial assistance programs. For information on financial assistance, contact: Director of Admissions.

Internships/Practica: Programs at Argosy University/ Honolulu provide training in assessment and intervention through placement in community practica on O'ahu and throughout the Hawaiian Islands. Supervision is provided by licensed psychologists at these settings, and students are simultaneously enrolled in practicum seminars led by faculty with relevant expertise. These seminars combine teaching and case consultation to train students in specific clinical skills. Students are currently placed at settings which include university counseling centers, community mental health centers, outpatient treatment centers, residential adolescent treatment centers, day treatment and hospice programs, developmental evaluation clinics, substance abuse treatment centers, public and private schools, state courts, parole agencies, prisons, and psychiatric, medical, and veteran's hospitals. AU/ Honolulu maintains a predoctoral internship consortium for its Doctoral Program students which is listed with the Association of Psychology Postdoctoral and Internship Centers (APPIC). Both practicum and consortium internship sites serve client populations which are culturally diverse. For those doctoral students for whom a professional internship is required prior to graduation, 20 applied in 2000–2001. Of those who applied, 20 were placed in internships listed by the Association of Psychology Postdoctoral and Internship Programs (APPIC); 11 were placed in APA accredited internships.

Housing and Day Care: No on-campus housing and day care facilities are available.

Employment of Department Graduates:

Master's Degree Graduates: Of those who graduated in the academic year 2000–2001, the following categories and numbers represent the post-graduate activities and employment of master's degree graduates: Enrolled in a psychology doctoral program (57), enrolled in another graduate/professional program (57), enrolled in a post-doctoral residency/fellowship (n/a), employed in independent practice (n/a), employed in an academic position at a university (3), employed in an academic position at a 2-year/4-year college (8), employed in other positions at a higher education institution (10), employed in a professional position in a school system (10), employed in business or industry (research/consulting) (0), employed in business or industry (management) (0), employed in a government agency (research) (1), employed in a government agency (professional services) (0), employed in a community mental health/counseling center (30), employed in a hospital/medical center (25), still seeking employment (1), other employment position (2).

Doctoral Degree Graduates: Of those who graduated in the academic year 2000–2001, the following categories and numbers represent the post-graduate activities and employment of doctoral degree graduates: Enrolled in a psychology doctoral program (n/a), enrolled in another graduate/professional program (n/a), enrolled in a post-doctoral residency/fellowship (3), employed in independent practice (0), employed in an academic position at a university (3), employed in an academic position at a 2-year/4-year college (5), employed in other positions at a higher education institution (10), employed in a professional position in a school system (10), employed in business or industry (research/consulting) (0), employed in business or industry (management) (0), employed in a government agency (research) (1), employed in a government agency (professional services) (10), employed in a community mental health/counseling center (30), employed in a hospital/medical center (25), still seeking employment (1), other employment position (2).

Additional Information:

Orientation, Objectives, and Emphasis of Department: The Argosy University/ Honolulu Doctoral Program in Clinical Psychology (PsyD) prepares scholar-practitioners for both contemporary and emerging roles in professional psychology. The program supports the development of core competencies in psychological assessment, intervention, consultation/education, and management/supervision. Training emphasizes attention to human diversity and difference, self-reflexivity in clinical relationships, and critical evaluation and application of empirical literature to guide clinical decision making. Concentrations, or minors, may be selected in Diversity and Clinical Practice and in Child and Family Clinical Practice. The Master of Arts in Clinical Psychology Program is designed to meet the needs of both those students seeking a terminal degree for work in the mental health field and those students who eventually plan to pursue a doctoral degree. The Clinical Respecialization Postdoctoral Program provides doctoral level psychologists with clinical courses and experiences. The Post-Doctoral Program in Clinical Psychopharmacology integrates relevant knowledge from medicine, pharmacology, nursing,

and psychology. The Master of Arts in Professional Counseling - Marriage and Family Therapy Specialty Program is offered through weekend courses which are scheduled to allow concurrent employment; the format provides students an opportunity to continue professional development or to pursue a career change.

Application Information:

Send to: Admissions Office, Argosy University / Honolulu, 400 Pacific Tower, 1001 Bishop Street, Honolulu, HI 96813. Students are admitted in the Fall, application deadline January 15; Winter, application deadline October 15. Fall deadlines—January 15, May 15. Winter deadlines October 15. Professional Counseling: 11/01, 05/01. *Fee:* $50.

Hawaii, University of (2001 data)
Department of Educational Psychology
College of Education
1776 University Avenue
Honolulu, HI 96822
Telephone: (808) 956-7775
Fax: (808) 956-6615
E-mail: *edpsych@hawaii.edu*
Web: *http://www.hawaii.edu/edpsych/*

Department Established:
1965. Chairperson: Ann Bayer. Number of Faculty: total–full-time 7; women–full-time 3; minority–full-time 2.

Programs and Degrees Offered:
Listed in the following order: Program area, degree type (T if terminal Master's), number awarded 7/00-6/01. Educational Psychology MEd 1.

Student Applications/Admissions:
Student Applications

Educational Psychology MEd—Applications 2001–2002, 2. Total applicants accepted 2001–2002, 1. New applicants enrolled 2001–2002, 1. Total enrolled 2001–2002 part-time, 1. The Median number of years required for completion of a degree are 5. The number of students enrolled full and part-time, who were dismissed or voluntarily withdrew from this program area were 1.

Admissions Requirements:

Scores: Entries appear in this order: required test or GPA, minimum score (if required), median score of students entering in 2001–2002. Master's Programs: last 2 years GPA 3.0, 3.12. Doctoral Programs: GRE-V+Q+Analytical no minimum stated, 1830; last 2 years GPA 3.0, 3.02.

Other Criteria: (importance of criteria rated low, medium, or high): GRE/MAT scores medium, research experience medium, work experience, extracurricular activity, clinically related public service, GPA medium, letters of recommendation medium, interview, statement of goals and objectives medium. Criteria above pertain to the PhD program. The MEd program does not require the GRE or research experience.

Student Characteristics: The following represents characteristics of students in 2001–2002 in all graduate psychology programs in

the department: Female–full-time 0, part-time 12; Male–full-time 0, part-time 0; African American/Black–full-time 0, part-time 0; Hispanic/Latino (a)–full-time 0, part-time 0; Asian/Pacific Islander–full-time 0, part-time 8; American Indian/Alaska Native–full-time 0, part-time 0.

Financial Information/Assistance:

Tuition for Full-Time Study: No information provided.

Financial Assistance:

First Year Students: No information provided.
Advanced Students: No information provided.
Contact Information: Of all students currently enrolled full-time, 50% benefitted from one or more of the listed financial assistance programs. For information on financial assistance, contact: UHM Financial Aid Services, Student Services Center, 2600 Campus Rd., Honolulu, HI 96822. Phone: (808) 956-7251.

Internships/Practica: Research and teaching internships are highly recommended for doctoral students; however, financial support continues to be very limited.

Housing and Day Care: No on-campus housing and day care facilities are available.

Employment of Department Graduates:

Master's Degree Graduates: Of those who graduated in the academic year 2000–2001, the following categories and numbers represent the post-graduate activities and employment of master's degree graduates: Enrolled in a post-doctoral residency/fellowship (n/a), employed in independent practice (n/a).
Doctoral Degree Graduates: Of those who graduated in the academic year 2000–2001, the following categories and numbers represent the post-graduate activities and employment of doctoral degree graduates: Enrolled in a psychology doctoral program (n/a), enrolled in another graduate/professional program (n/a).

Additional Information:

Orientation, Objectives, and Emphasis of Department: The primary objective of graduate training is the development of competent scholars in the discipline of educational psychology. Therefore, the faculty seeks students with research interests and abilities, independence of thought, and a willingness to actively participate in both formal and informal teaching and learning experiences. The students' efforts may be directed toward the attainment of the MEd or the PhD degree. Thesis (Plan A) and nonthesis (Plan B) options are available at the MEd level. Members of the faculty share a commitment to a model of graduate education that is humanistic and inquiry oriented. An extensive core of quantitative coursework—measurement, statistics, and research methodology—underlies most programs of study, especially at the doctoral level. In addition, core courses in human learning and development give the student a contextual framework within which inquiry methodologies are applied. The small size of the department ensures a high level of interaction among students and faculty in and out of class. Working closely with the faculty, each student creates a degree plan uniquely suited to his or her academic goals. Interdisciplinary study is particularly encouraged.

Special Facilities or Resources: The college's Curriculum Research and Development Group affords opportunities for involvement in a wide variety of educational research and program evalua-tion activities, many of which are centered in the K-12 laboratory school on campus.

Application Information:

Send to: Department of Educational Psychology, College of Education, 1776 University Avenue, Honolulu, HI 96822. Students are admitted in the Fall, application deadline February 1; Spring, application deadline September 1. PhD program has Fall admission only. Applications from foreign students have deadlines of January 15 and August 1 for Fall and Spring admission, respectively. *Fee:* $25. Application fee for non-U.S. Citizens is $50.00. Separate applications materials are submitted to the department and to the Graduate Division.

Hawaii, University of
Department of Psychology
College of Social Sciences
2430 Campus Road
Honolulu, HI 96822
Telephone: (808) 956-8414
Fax: (808) 956-4700
E-mail: *psych@hawaii.edu*
Web: *http://www2.soc.hawaii.edu/psy/default.html*

Department Established:

1939. Chairperson: Karl Minke, PhD. Number of Faculty: total–full-time 12, part-time 3; women–full-time 6, part-time 1; minority–full-time 2.

Programs and Degrees Offered:

Listed in the following order: Program area, degree type (T if terminal Master's), number awarded 7/00-6/01. Behavioral neuroscience PhD 1, clinical PhD 4, community and culture PhD 2, developmental PhD, experimental psychopathology PhD, health psychology PhD, marine mammal behavior & biol PhD 1, marine mammal sensory systems PhD, social-personality PhD 1, teaching, learning & cognition PhD.

APA Accreditation: Clinical PhD: full.

Student Applications/Admissions:

Student Applications

Behavioral neuroscience PhD—Applications 2001–2002, 8. Total applicants accepted 2001–2002, 1. New applicants enrolled 2001–2002, 1. Total enrolled 2001–2002 full-time, 9. Openings 2002–2003, 6. The Median number of years required for completion of a degree are 6. The number of students enrolled full and part-time, who were dismissed or voluntarily withdrew from this program area were 0. *Clinical PhD*—Applications 2001–2002, 101. Total applicants accepted 2001–2002, 11. New applicants enrolled 2001–2002, 8. Total enrolled 2001–2002 full-time, 52. Openings 2002–2003, 8. The Median number of years required for completion of a degree are 8. The number of students enrolled full and part-time, who were dismissed or voluntarily withdrew from this program area were 2. *Community and culture PhD*—Applications 2001–2002, 11. Total applicants accepted 2001–2002, 5. New applicants enrolled 2001–2002, 4. Total enrolled 2001–2002 full-time, 11. Openings 2002–2003, 3. The Median number of years required for completion of a degree are 6. The number of students enrolled full and part-time, who were dismissed or voluntarily withdrew from this program area were 0. *Developmental PhD*—Applications 2001–2002, 4. Total enrolled 2001–2002 full-time, 1. Openings 2002–2003, 4. The number of students enrolled full and part-time, who were dismissed or voluntarily withdrew from this program area were 000. *Experimental psychopathology PhD*—Applications 2001–2002, 5. Total applicants accepted 2001–2002, 1. New applicants enrolled 2001–2002, 1. Total enrolled 2001–2002 full-time, 1. Openings 2002–2003, 2. The number of students enrolled full and part-time, who were dismissed or voluntarily withdrew from this program area were 0. *Health psychology PhD*—Applications 2001–2002, 6. The number of students enrolled full and part-time, who were dismissed or voluntarily withdrew from this program area were 0. *Marine mammal behavior & biol PhD*—Applications 2001–2002, 17. Total applicants accepted 2001–2002, 2. New applicants enrolled 2001–2002, 2. Total enrolled 2001–2002 full-time, 12. Openings 2002–2003, 4. The Median number of years required for completion of a degree are 6. The number of students enrolled full and part-time, who were dismissed or voluntarily withdrew from this program area were 0. *Marine mammal sensory systems PhD*—Applications 2001–2002, 2. The number of students enrolled full and part-time, who were dismissed or voluntarily withdrew from this program area were 0. *Social-personality PhD*—Applications 2001–2002, 15. Total applicants accepted 2001–2002, 4. New applicants enrolled 2001–2002, 3. Total enrolled 2001–2002 full-time, 12. Openings 2002–2003, 4. The Median number of years required for completion of a degree are 6. The number of students enrolled full and part-time, who were dismissed or voluntarily withdrew from this program area were 0. *Teaching, learning & cognition PhD*—Applications 2001–2002, 3. Total applicants accepted 2001–2002, 1. New applicants enrolled 2001–2002, 1. Total enrolled 2001–2002 full-time, 3. Openings 2002–2003, 3. The number of students enrolled full and part-time, who were dismissed or voluntarily withdrew from this program area were 0.

Admissions Requirements:

Scores: Entries appear in this order: required test or GPA, minimum score (if required), median score of students entering in 2001–2002. Master's Programs: GRE-V no minimum stated, 620; GRE-Q no minimum stated, 640; GRE-V+Q 1000, 1260; GRE-Analytical no minimum stated, 670; GRE-V+Q+Analytical no minimum stated; GRE-Subject(Psych) no minimum stated, 620; overall undergraduate GPA 3.0, 3.5. Doctoral Programs: GRE-V+Q+Analytical no minimum stated; GRE-Subject(Psych) no minimum stated, 620; overall undergraduate GPA 3.0, 3.5 ; last 2 years GPA no minimum stated; psychology GPA no minimum stated; psychology GPA no minimum stated. Numbers are same for MA/PhD. Students are initially admitted into MA program and proceed to doctoral candidacy.

Other Criteria: (importance of criteria rated low, medium, or high): GRE/MAT scores high, research experience high, work experience low, extracurricular activity low, clinically related public service medium, GPA high, letters of recommendation high, statement of goals and objectives high.

Student Characteristics: The following represents characteristics of students in 2001–2002 in all graduate psychology programs in the department: Female–full-time 75, part-time 0; Male–full-time 36, part-time 0; African American/Black–full-time 1, part-time 0; Hispanic/Latino (a)–full-time 1, part-time 0; Asian/Pacific Islander–full-time 33, part-time 0; American Indian/Alaska Native–full-time 0, part-time 0; students subject to the Americans with Disabilities Act–full-time 0.

Financial Information/Assistance:

Tuition for Full-Time Study: *Master's:* State residents per academic year $3,264; nonstate residents: per academic year $7,764. *Doctoral:* State residents: per academic year $3,264; nonstate residents: per academic year $7,764.

Financial Assistance:

First Year Students: Teaching assistantships available for first-year. Average amount paid per academic year: $12,786. Average number of hours worked per week: 20. Apply by January lst. Research assistantships available for first-year. Average amount paid per academic year: $14,958. Average number of hours worked per week: 20. Apply by January 1st.

Advanced Students: Teaching assistantships available for advanced students. Average amount paid per academic year: $13,830. Average number of hours worked per week: 20. Apply by January 1st. Research assistantships available for advanced students. Average amount paid per academic year: $16,176. Average number of hours worked per week: 20. Apply by January 1st.

Contact Information: Of all students currently enrolled full-time, 40% benefitted from one or more of the listed financial assistance programs. For information on financial assistance, contact: Information is sent with application materials.

Internships/Practica: A minimum of 2 years of practica experience (18 to 20 hours per week) are required for all 2nd through 4th year graduate students in the clinical studies program. A variety of practica sites are available throughout the state and most include stipend support (average $14,000 per academic year). Sites include the department's Cognitive Behavior Therapy Clinic, community mental health outpatient centers, VA (including PTSD specialty clinics), mental health hospitals, child mental health institutions, Cancer Research Center, UH counseling center, Rehab Hospital, and state supported work with the seriously mentally disabled population. Additional specialty practica are available in treating sex offenders, neuro psychology, and forensic psychology, as well as a variety of community psychology placements. For those doctoral students for whom a professional internship is required prior to graduation, 6 applied in 2000–2001. Of those who applied, 5 were placed in internships listed by the Association of Psychology Postdoctoral and Internship Programs (APPIC); 5 were placed in APA accredited internships.

Housing and Day Care: On-campus housing and day care facilities are available.

Employment of Department Graduates:

Master's Degree Graduates: Of those who graduated in the academic year 2000–2001, the following categories and numbers represent the post-graduate activities and employment of master's degree graduates: Enrolled in a post-doctoral residency/fellowship (n/a), employed in independent practice (n/a).

Doctoral Degree Graduates: Of those who graduated in the academic year 2000–2001, the following categories and numbers represent the post-graduate activities and employment of doctoral

degree graduates: Enrolled in a psychology doctoral program (n/a), enrolled in another graduate/professional program (n/a).

Additional Information:

Orientation, Objectives, and Emphasis of Department: The Department of Psychology's orientation is best characterized as a synthesis of biological, behavioral, and cognitive areas, with an overriding emphasis on empiricism (i.e., the study of psychological phenomena based on sound research findings). The graduate programs in clinical, development, community, behavioral-neuroscience, experimental psychopathology, marine mammal behavior and biology, social-personality, and community emphasize the development of research skills and knowledge that are applicable to a wide range of academic and applied settings. The clinical program adheres to the scientist-practitioner model of training, wherein research and clinical skills are equally emphasized. Research opportunities in child and adult psychopathology, health psychology, marine mammals, community psychology, behavioral neuroscience, and psychopharmacology are available. The faculty is particularly interested in admitting students who are interested in pursuing academically related careers.

Special Facilities or Resources: The Psychology Department is mainly housed in Gartley Hall, all of which is devoted to facilities for office space, research, and teaching. In addition to the department's Gartley Hall facilities, additional opportunities for study and research exist at the university and elsewhere in the community. These include the Behavioral Biology Laboratory, the Laboratory of Sensory Sciences, the Newborn Psychological Research Laboratory, the Center for Student Development, the Child Learning Laboratory, the Hawaii State Hospital at Kaneohe, the State Department of Education, the Youth Development and Research Center, the Diamond Head Health Center, Kamehameha School, the Pacific Biomedical Research Center, the Social Science Research Institute, and the Kewalo Basin Marine Mammal Laboratory Facility. In addition, the university maintains a computing center with a variety of personal computers, plotters, and scanners. Both the computing center and the Department of Information and Computer Sciences offer training and research opportunities. The Psychology Department has its own personal computers (IBMs, Macintoshes), as well as telecommunications (email, bitnet) and direct access to mainframe computer facilities. Beyond the physical facilities available to the department is the unusual opportunity for research provided by the unique social and environmental structure of Hawaii. An important dimension is also provided by the East-West Center for Cultural Interchange, which provides fellowships for Asian and U.S. students and for senior scholars from mainland and foreign universities. The surrounding ocean offers the department a unique opportunity for marine mammal research.

Information for Students With Physical Disabilities: Gartley Hall and classrooms within are accessible to students with wheelchairs. The KOLUA program at the University of Hawaii provides a wide-range of academic access services to students with disabilities. Academic access services include priority registration, academic advising/counseling, note taking, sign language interpreting, transcription, intra-campus transportation (where available), and faculty liaison. Students who may require such services are strongly encouraged to contact KOKUA at least 2 months before anticipated enrollment/need (808) 956-7511. Many of the city's buses are equipped to transport wheelchairs on a regularly scheduled basis.

Application Information:
Send to: Chair, Graduate Studies, Department of Psychology, University of Hawaii, 2430 Campus Road, Gartley Hall, Honolulu Hawaii 96822. Students are admitted in the Fall, application deadline January 1. *Fee:* $25.

Idaho State University

Department of Psychology
Arts and Sciences
Box 8112
Pocatello, ID 83209
Telephone: (208) 282-2462
Fax: (208) 282-4832
E-mail: *joevict@isu.edu*
Web: *http://www.isu.edu/departments/psych*

Department Established:

1968. Chairperson: Victor C. Joe. Number of Faculty: total–full-time 11, part-time 3; women–full-time 4; minority–full-time 1.

Programs and Degrees Offered:

Listed in the following order: Program area, degree type (T if terminal Master's), number awarded 7/00-6/01. Clinical PhD 3, experimental-general MA (T) 2.

APA Accreditation: Clinical PhD: full.

Student Applications/Admissions:

Student Applications

Clinical PhD—Applications 2001–2002, 30. Total applicants accepted 2001–2002, 9. New applicants enrolled 2001–2002, 5. Total enrolled 2001–2002 full-time, 19, part-time, 6. Openings 2002–2003, 6. The Median number of years required for completion of a degree are 6. The number of students enrolled full and part-time, who were dismissed or voluntarily withdrew from this program area were 1. *Experimental-general MA*—Applications 2001–2002, 5. Total enrolled 2001–2002 full-time, 2, part-time, 2. Openings 2002–2003, 6. The Median number of years required for completion of a degree are 3. The number of students enrolled full and part-time, who were dismissed or voluntarily withdrew from this program area were 1.

Admissions Requirements:

Scores: Entries appear in this order: required test or GPA, minimum score (if required), median score of students entering in 2001–2002. Master's Programs: GRE-V no minimum stated; GRE-Q no minimum stated; GRE-Analytical no minimum stated; GRE-Subject(Psych) no minimum stated; last 2 years GPA 3.0. GREs at the 50th percentile or higher are preferred on 2 of 3 aptitude tests and on the subject test in psychology. Since no students were admitted to the general MS program for the 2001–2002 academic year, median scores are not available. Doctoral Programs: GRE-V no minimum stated, 560; GRE-Q no minimum stated, 560; GRE-Analytical no minimum stated, 645; GRE-Subject(Psych) no minimum stated, 680; last 2 years GPA 3.0, 3.6 ; psychology GPA no minimum stated; psychology GPA no minimum stated. GREs at the 50th percentile or higher are preferred on 2 of 3 aptitude tests and on the subject test in psychology.

Other Criteria: (importance of criteria rated low, medium, or high): GRE/MAT scores medium, research experience me-

dium, work experience low, extracurricular activity low, clinically related public service medium, GPA medium, letters of recommendation medium, interview medium, statement of goals and objectives medium. For the general MS program, clinically related public service is not relevant.

Student Characteristics: The following represents characteristics of students in 2001–2002 in all graduate psychology programs in the department: Female–full-time 14, part-time 1; Male–full-time 7, part-time 5; African American/Black–full-time 0, part-time 0; Hispanic/Latino (a)–full-time 1, part-time 0; Asian/Pacific Islander–full-time 0, part-time 0; American Indian/Alaska Native–full-time 0, part-time 1; Multi-ethnic–full-time 0, part-time 0; students subject to the Americans with Disabilities Act–full-time 0, part-time 0.

Financial Information/Assistance:

Tuition for Full-Time Study: *Master's:* State residents per academic year $3,956, $172 per credit hour; nonstate residents: per academic year $10,196, $262 per credit hour. *Doctoral:* State residents: per academic year $3,956, $172 per credit hour; nonstate residents: per academic year $10,196, $262 per credit hour.

Financial Assistance:

First Year Students: Teaching assistantships available for first-year. Average amount paid per academic year: $10,594. Average number of hours worked per week: 15. Apply by March 1. Tuition remission given: full. Traineeships available for first-year. Average amount paid per academic year: $8,485. Average number of hours worked per week: 20. Apply by March 1. Fellowships and scholarships available for first-year. Average amount paid per academic year: $1,800. Average number of hours worked per week: 0. Apply by March 1.

Advanced Students: Teaching assistantships available for advanced students. Average amount paid per academic year: $10,594. Average number of hours worked per week: 15. Apply by March 1. Tuition remission given: full. Research assistantships available for advanced students. Average amount paid per academic year: $15,782. Average number of hours worked per week: 15. Apply by March 1. Tuition remission given: full. Traineeships available for advanced students. Average amount paid per academic year: $12,096. Average number of hours worked per week: 15. Apply by March 1. Fellowships and scholarships available for advanced students. Average amount paid per academic year: $1,800. Average number of hours worked per week: 0. Apply by March 1.

Contact Information: Of all students currently enrolled full-time, 100% benefitted from one or more of the listed financial assistance programs. For information on financial assistance, contact: Deparment Chair, Director of Clinical Training, Office of Financial Aid (208) 282-2756. Teaching Assistants for General MA are paid $8,117. Traineeships are 11–12 month contracts; non-resident tuition waivers are pending, but not yet approved for Traineeships; over 90% of students with traineeships are granted general university non-resident tuition waivers by their second semester at ISU.

Internships/Practica: Clinical practica are required for doctoral students admitted into the MS-PhD clinical program. First and second year students complete practica in the ISU Psychology Clinic under the supervision of clinical faculty. Third and fourth year students, however, often participate in community practica under the supervision of licensed psychologists employed by local mental health providers/agencies. One semester participation on an interdisciplinary evaluation team is also required. Six externships are also available for advanced students, providing stipends and supervised practice in applied settings. Currently, students average 1500 hours of supervised practica during the four on-campus years of the clinical doctorate, prior to departure to a predoctoral internship at an APPIC-member site. For those doctoral students for whom a professional internship is required prior to graduation, 3 applied in 2000–2001. Of those who applied, 3 were placed in internships listed by the Association of Psychology Postdoctoral and Internship Programs (APPIC); 2 were placed in APA accredited internships.

Housing and Day Care: On-campus housing and day care facilities are available.

Employment of Department Graduates:

Master's Degree Graduates: Of those who graduated in the academic year 2000–2001, the following categories and numbers represent the post-graduate activities and employment of master's degree graduates: Enrolled in a psychology doctoral program (1), enrolled in another graduate/professional program (1), enrolled in a post-doctoral residency/fellowship (n/a), employed in independent practice (n/a).

Doctoral Degree Graduates: Of those who graduated in the academic year 2000–2001, the following categories and numbers represent the post-graduate activities and employment of doctoral degree graduates: Enrolled in a psychology doctoral program (n/a), enrolled in another graduate/professional program (n/a), employed in independent practice (1), employed in a community mental health/counseling center (1), other employment position (1).

Additional Information:

Orientation, Objectives, and Emphasis of Department: The master of science program in general/experimental psychology provides students with an education in core areas of psychological science, such as personality/social, perception/cognitive, and sensory/physiological. This program of study, culminating in defense of a thesis, is designed to prepare students for doctoral work in psychology or careers in psychology or related fields that require mastery of the principles and methods of general/experimental psychology. The experimental MS in psychology is not intended to prepare students for careers in mental health. The mission of the ISU doctoral program is to train competent clinical psychologists who can apply and adapt general conceptual and technical skills in diverse regional and professional settings. An effective clinical psychologist possesses a strong professional identity that includes: (a) a firm grounding in the science of psychology, and (b) knowledge of relevant theories and technical skills that aid in the amelioration of human suffering. Most importantly, a clinical psychologist understands the interactive relationship between science and practice. As such, the educational philosophy of the clinical training program at ISU is based on the traditional Scientist-Practitioner model of clinical training.

Special Facilities or Resources: The department has a microcomputer room and the usual laboratory equipment for demonstration and research purposes. The ISU Psychology Clinic, housed in Graveley Hall, provides five individual therapy rooms, a child/family room, and a group therapy room, all equipped with observation, sound, and videotape capabilities. Office space is provided to all graduate students. Additional facilities include a university-managed animal colony, the university library, a computer center located near the department, and many personal computers within the department.

Information for Students With Physical Disabilities: The ISU Psychology Clinic meets all current standards of accessibility for students with physical disabilities.

Application Information:

Send to: Department Chair. Students are admitted in the Fall, application deadline January 15; Spring, application deadline November 1. For fall admission, the deadline for clinical students is January 15. For general MS students the fall admission deadline is March 1 (June 15 without financial aid consideration). General MS students may enter the program in Spring Semester by meeting a November 1 application deadline. *Fee:* $35.

Idaho, University of
Department of Psychology
Letters and Science
University of Idaho
Moscow, ID 83844-3043
Telephone: (208) 885-6324
Fax: (208) 885-7710
E-mail: cberreth@uidaho.edu

Department Established:

Chairperson: Richard Reardon. Number of Faculty: total–full-time 10, part-time 2; women–full-time 2, part-time 1; minority–full-time 1.

Programs and Degrees Offered:

Listed in the following order: Program area, degree type (T if terminal Master's), number awarded 7/00-6/01. General experimental, Human Factors, Industrial/Organizational.

Student Applications/Admissions:

Admissions Requirements:

Scores: Entries appear in this order: required test or GPA, minimum score (if required), median score of students entering in 2001–2002. Master's Programs: GRE-V+Q 1000, 1120; overall undergraduate GPA 3.0, 3.5. Doctoral Programs: last 2 years GPA no minimum stated; psychology GPA no minimum stated; psychology GPA no minimum stated.

Other Criteria: (importance of criteria rated low, medium, or high): GRE/MAT scores high, research experience high, work experience medium, extracurricular activity low, GPA high, letters of recommendation high, statement of goals and objectives high. Work experience more important for Human factors and I/O candidates than General Experimental candidates.

Student Characteristics: The following represents characteristics of students in 2001–2002 in all graduate psychology programs in

the department: Female–full-time 9, part-time 5; Male–full-time 7, part-time 8; African American/Black–full-time 0, part-time 0; Hispanic/Latino (a)–full-time 0, part-time 0; Asian/Pacific Islander–full-time 1, part-time 1; American Indian/Alaska Native–full-time 0, part-time 0; Multi-ethnic–full-time 0, part-time 0; students subject to the Americans with Disabilities Act–full-time 1, part-time 0.

Financial Information/Assistance:

Tuition for Full-Time Study: *Master's:* State residents per academic year $3,000, $150 per credit hour; nonstate residents: per academic year $9,000, $250 per credit hour.

Financial Assistance:

First Year Students: Teaching assistantships available for first-year. Average amount paid per academic year: $4,300. Average number of hours worked per week: 10. Apply by March 1. Tuition remission given: partial. Research assistantships available for first-year. Average amount paid per academic year: $9,000. Average number of hours worked per week: 20. Apply by March 1. Tuition remission given: partial.

Advanced Students: Teaching assistantships available for advanced students. Average amount paid per academic year: $4,500. Average number of hours worked per week: 10. Apply by March 1. Tuition remission given: partial. Research assistantships available for advanced students. Average amount paid per academic year: $9,500. Average number of hours worked per week: 20. Apply by March 1. Tuition remission given: partial.

Contact Information: Of all students currently enrolled full-time, 100% benefitted from one or more of the listed financial assistance programs. For information on financial assistance, contact: Chair of Graduate Studies.

Internships/Practica: A few internships are available locally. Course credit is available in lieu of salary.

Housing and Day Care: On-campus housing and day care facilities are available.

Employment of Department Graduates:

Master's Degree Graduates: Of those who graduated in the academic year 2000–2001, the following categories and numbers represent the post-graduate activities and employment of master's degree graduates: Enrolled in a psychology doctoral program (3), enrolled in another graduate/professional program (0), enrolled in a post-doctoral residency/fellowship (n/a), employed in independent practice (n/a), employed in an academic position at a university (0), employed in an academic position at a 2-year/4-year college (0), employed in other positions at a higher education institution (0), employed in a professional position in a school system (0), employed in business or industry (research/consulting) (0), employed in business or industry (management) (4), employed in a government agency (research) (4), employed in a government agency (professional services) (3), employed in a community mental health/counseling center (0), employed in a hospital/medical center (0), still seeking employment (0), other employment position (0).

Doctoral Degree Graduates: Of those who graduated in the academic year 2000–2001, the following categories and numbers represent the post-graduate activities and employment of doctoral degree graduates: Enrolled in a psychology doctoral program (n/a), enrolled in another graduate/professional program (n/a).

Additional Information:

Orientation, Objectives, and Emphasis of Department: In the Land Grant tradition of providing a "practical education," the Department of Psychology at the University of Idaho offers the MS degree in psychology with emphases in either Industrial/Organizational psychology (human resources, personnel, selection, organizational behavior) or Human Factors psychology (human technology interaction, ergonomics, human performance). The Department also provides off-campus and distance educational outreach by offering the MS in Psychology (human factors option only) through video and compressed video. The intent of both emphases is to develop knowledge and skills germane to a professional position. However, both programs also provide appropriate preparation for further graduate study. Thus, students are encouraged to develop analytical and problem solving skills that will serve them well in whatever they choose to do after graduation. Student placement figures show that most graduates have been very successful in obtaining positions in technical industries. The Department is small, but is able to address the broad needs of its students through working relationships with the College of Business and Economics, the College of Engineering, and the Department of Psychology at nearby (10 miles) Washington State University. Department will consider, and has occasionally admitted, students for the general experimental MS. General experimental students typically use the program to prepare for admission to doctoral programs elsewhere.

Special Facilities or Resources: The Department is in temporary quarters, but is still able to provide approximately 2500 square feet of research space. Labs are equipped with up-to-date computers, graphics displays, and other apparatus. Research opportunities are available at remote sites, such as the Motion Analysis Lab at Shriners Hospital in Spokane, WA.

Information for Students With Physical Disabilities: All research and office space is accessible to students with physical disabilities.

Application Information:

Send to: Graduate Admissions. Students are admitted in the Fall, application deadline March 1. Applications will be considered after the deadline, but availability of funding declines with passage of time. *Fee:* $30.

Adler School of Professional Psychology
(2001 data)
Professional School
65 East Wacker Place, Suite 2100
Chicago, IL 60601-7203
Telephone: (312) 201-5900
Fax: (312) 201-5917
E-mail: *information@adler.edu*
Web: *http://www.adler.edu*

Department Established:
1952. Provost: Mark Stone. Number of Faculty: total–full-time 18, part-time 8; women–full-time 8, part-time 2; minority–full-time 1, part-time 2.

Programs and Degrees Offered:
Listed in the following order: Program area, degree type (T if terminal Master's), number awarded 7/00-6/01. Art therapy/counseling MA (T) 5, clinical psychology PsyD 30, counseling psychology MA (T) 98, gerontological psychology MA (T) 1, marriage and family counseling MA (T) 3, organizational MA (T), substance abuse counseling MA (T) 1.

APA Accreditation: Clinical PsyD: full.

Student Applications/Admissions:
Student Applications
Art therapy/counseling MA—Applications 2001–2002, 15. Total applicants accepted 2001–2002, 10. New applicants enrolled 2001–2002, 7. Total enrolled 2001–2002 full-time, 7, part-time, 11. Openings 2002–2003, 30. *Clinical psychology PsyD*—Applications 2001–2002, 120. Total applicants accepted 2001–2002, 61. New applicants enrolled 2001–2002, 30. Total enrolled 2001–2002 full-time, 82, part-time, 127. Openings 2002–2003, 60. *Counseling psychology* MA—Applications 2001–2002, 125. Total applicants accepted 2001–2002, 41. New applicants enrolled 2001–2002, 25. Total enrolled 2001–2002 full-time, 14, part-time, 25. Openings 2002–2003, 50. *Gerontological psychology* MA—Applications 2001–2002, 0. Total enrolled 2001–2002 part-time, 1. Openings 2002–2003, 20. *Marriage and family counseling* MA—Applications 2001–2002, 30. Total applicants accepted 2001–2002, 14. New applicants enrolled 2001–2002, 10. Total enrolled 2001–2002 full-time, 3, part-time, 15. Openings 2002–2003, 30. *Organizational* MA—Applications 2001–2002, 11. Total applicants accepted 2001–2002, 5. New applicants enrolled 2001–2002, 5. Total enrolled 2001–2002 part-time, 23. Openings 2002–2003, 20. *Substance abuse counseling* MA—Applications 2001–2002, 5. Total enrolled 2001–2002 part-time, 4. Openings 2002–2003, 30.

Admissions Requirements:
Scores: Entries appear in this order: required test or GPA, minimum score (if required), median score of students entering in 2001–2002. Master's Programs: overall undergraduate GPA 3.00; last 2 years GPA 3.00; psychology GPA 3.00. Doctoral Programs: overall undergraduate GPA 3.25; last 2 years GPA 3.25; psychology GPA 3.25.

Other Criteria: (importance of criteria rated low, medium, or high): research experience low, work experience high, extra-curricular activity medium, clinically related public service medium, letters of recommendation high, interview high, statement of goals and objectives high, writing ability high.

Student Characteristics: The following represents characteristics of students in 2001–2002 in all graduate psychology programs in the department: Female–full-time 15, part-time 34; Male–full-time 9, part-time 20; African American/Black–full-time 2, part-time 2; Hispanic/Latino (a)–full-time 0, part-time 1; Asian/Pacific Islander–full-time 1, part-time 2; American Indian/Alaska Native–full-time 0, part-time 0.

Financial Information/Assistance:
Tuition for Full-Time Study: No information provided.

Financial Assistance:
First Year Students: No information provided.
Advanced Students: No information provided.
Contact Information: For information on financial assistance, contact: Suzann Lebda, Director of Financial Aid.

Internships/Practica: Practicum students, pre-doctoral interns, and post-doctoral interns have the opportunity to receive training at the school's licensed Psychological Services Center, which serves more than 250 clients weekly. Students under faculty supervision provide a wide range of services to the public including psychotherapy, psychological testing, art therapy, neurological assessments, forensic evaluations, support groups, and parenting classes. In addition to the counseling center on campus, students are placed in a number of satellite locations throughout the Chicago area in settings such as elementary and high schools, prisons, church counseling centers, transitional homes, and gerontological facilities.

Housing and Day Care: No on-campus housing and day care facilities are available.

Employment of Department Graduates:
Master's Degree Graduates: Of those who graduated in the academic year 2000–2001, the following categories and numbers represent the post-graduate activities and employment of master's degree graduates: Enrolled in a post-doctoral residency/fellowship (n/a), employed in independent practice (n/a).
Doctoral Degree Graduates: Of those who graduated in the academic year 2000–2001, the following categories and numbers represent the post-graduate activities and employment of doctoral degree graduates: Enrolled in a psychology doctoral program (n/a), enrolled in another graduate/professional program (n/a).

Additional Information:
Orientation, Objectives, and Emphasis of Department: The Adler School is the only accredited doctoral degree-granting institution in the world having Individual Psychology, which was originated and developed by the well-known Austrian psychiatrist,

Alfred Adler (1870-1937), as its major theoretical orientation. The school is committed to the practitioner training model in professional psychology and has been training highly qualified professionals since 1952. The reputation of the school has been built by an outstanding faculty who combine professional practice with their research, instructional, and clinical supervision responsibilities. The Adler School offers master of arts degrees in six program areas, a PsyD program in clinical psychology, and several post-graduate certificate programs. MA programs are offered in counseling, art therapy, gerontological psychology, substance abuse counseling, marriage and family therapy, clinical neuropsychology, and clinical hypnosis. Students may elect to earn a certificate in a specialized area of study in conjunction with an MA or PsyD degree. Specialized training opportunities include cognitive therapy, group psychotherapy, ethnocultural diversity, gender studies, art therapy, clinical neuropsychology, clinical hypnosis, gerontological psychology, marriage and family therapy, and substance abuse counseling. The year-round instructional format consists of four 10-week terms. A wide range of courses are offered during both day and evening hours to accommodate both full- and part-time students. In addition to the Chicago campus, courses are also offered in Vancouver, British Columbia; Toronto, Ontario; Montreal, Quebec; and Fort Wayne, Indiana.

Special Facilities or Resources: An especially valuable asset to the programs offered is the school's licensed Psychological Services Center, which serves more than 250 clients weekly. Students under faculty supervision provide a wide range of services to the public including psychotherapy, psychological testing, art therapy, neurological assessments, forensic evaluations, support groups, and parenting classes. Practicum students, pre-doctoral interns, and post-doctoral interns are involved at the counseling center on campus and at a number of satellite locations throughout the Chicago area in settings such as elementary and high schools, prisons, churches, transitional homes, and gerontological facilities. In addition to the Chicago campus, courses are also offered in Vancouver, British Columbia; Toronto, Ontario; Montreal, Quebec; and Fort Wayne, Indiana. The Adler School of Professional Psychology is located in the center of downtown Chicago on the Chicago River. The School's location provides easy access to libraries and related facilities of some of the nation's best educational institutions, some with whom the library maintains cooperative lending agreements. The building is handicap accessible, available 365 days of the year, and has 24-hour security.

Information for Students With Physical Disabilities: In addition to persons of ethnocultural minority heritage and foreign students, the student body has included a number of physically challenged students. Not all of these individuals identify themselves as subject to ADA. Nevertheless, physical, instructional, and assessment accommodations have been designed to meet their varying needs. Two doctoral students are blind. Several students who are hard of hearing have matriculated through the program, although none have required the use of sign language or interpreters. Students with various problems affecting muscle coordination or movement, such as cerebral palsy, continue their enrollment or have graduated. Accommodations are provided on an individual basis, after consultation with the student.

Application Information:
Send to: Admissions Department. Students are admitted in the Fall, application deadline March 1; Winter, application deadline June 1;

Spring, application deadline September 1; Summer, application deadline December 1. *Fee:* $50. Fee waived upon request by applicant.

Argosy University, Illinois School of Professional Psychology, Chicago Campus

Clinical Psychology Department
20 South Clark Street, Third floor
Chicago, IL 60603
Telephone: (888) 488-7537
Fax: (312) 201-1907
E-mail: *adelaney@argosyu.edu*
Web: *http://www.argosyu.edu*

Department Established:
1976. Chairperson: Annemarie Slobig. Number of Faculty: total–full-time 21, part-time 58; women–full-time 13, part-time 24; minority–full-time 5, part-time 6.

Programs and Degrees Offered:
Listed in the following order: Program area, degree type (T if terminal Master's), number awarded 7/00-6/01. Clinical MA (T) 37, clinical psychology Respecialization Diploma 1, Clinical Psychology PsyD (T) 65, professional counseling MA (T) 19.

APA Accreditation: Clinical PsyD: full.

Student Applications/Admissions:
Student Applications
Clinical MA—Applications 2001–2002, 142. Total applicants accepted 2001–2002, 87. New applicants enrolled 2001–2002, 42. Total enrolled 2001–2002 full-time, 68, part-time, 41. Openings 2002–2003, 45. The Median number of years required for completion of a degree are 2. *Clinical psychology Respecialization Diploma*—Applications 2001–2002, 0. Total enrolled 2001–2002 part-time, 2. Openings 2002–2003, 5. The Median number of years required for completion of a degree are 3. *Clinical Psychology PsyD*—Applications 2001–2002, 240. Total applicants accepted 2001–2002, 172. New applicants enrolled 2001–2002, 69. Total enrolled 2001–2002 full-time, 282, part-time, 130. Openings 2002–2003, 65. The Median number of years required for completion of a degree are 5. The number of students enrolled full and part-time, who were dismissed or voluntarily withdrew from this program area were 15. *Professional counseling MA*—Applications 2001–2002, 50. Total applicants accepted 2001–2002, 38. New applicants enrolled 2001–2002, 28. Total enrolled 2001–2002 full-time, 46, part-time, 8. Openings 2002–2003, 40. The Median number of years required for completion of a degree are 2. The number of students enrolled full and part-time, who were dismissed or voluntarily withdrew from this program area were 1.

Admissions Requirements:
Scores: Entries appear in this order: required test or GPA, minimum score (if required), median score of students entering in 2001–2002. Master's Programs: overall undergraduate GPA 3.0, 3.27; last 2 years GPA 3.0, 3.29; psychology GPA 3.0, 3.25. Doctoral Programs: overall undergraduate GPA 3.25, 3.27; last 2 years GPA 3.25, 3.43. For PsyD, require at least one of GPA categories to be 3.25 minimum.

Other Criteria: (importance of criteria rated low, medium, or high): research experience medium, work experience high, extracurricular activity medium, clinically related public service high, GPA high, letters of recommendation high, interview high, statement of goals and objectives high. MA Professional Counseling Program admits students after successful completion (including faculty review) of first four courses in program.

Student Characteristics: The following represents characteristics of students in 2001–2002 in all graduate psychology programs in the department: Female–full-time 304, part-time 30; Male–full-time 99, part-time 40; African American/Black–full-time 40, part-time 20; Hispanic/Latino (a)–full-time 10, part-time 10; Asian/Pacific Islander–full-time 11, part-time 13; American Indian/Alaska Native–full-time 0, part-time 0; Multi-ethnic–full-time 0, part-time 0; students subject to the Americans with Disabilities Act–full-time 0, part-time 0.

Financial Information/Assistance:
Tuition for Full-Time Study: *Master's:* State residents per academic year $12,096, $672 per credit hour; *Doctoral:* State residents: per academic year $12,096, $672 per credit hour.

Financial Assistance:
First Year Students: Average amount paid per academic year: $2,000. Average number of hours worked per week: 5. Apply by May 1. Tuition remission given: partial. Fellowships and scholarships available for first-year. Average amount paid per academic year: $2,000. Average number of hours worked per week: 5. Apply by May 1. Tuition remission given: partial.

Advanced Students: Teaching assistantships available for advanced students. Average amount paid per academic year: $500. Average number of hours worked per week: 5. Apply by No Deadline. Tuition remission given: partial. Research assistantships available for advanced students. Average amount paid per academic year: $2,000. Average number of hours worked per week: 5. Apply by May 1. Tuition remission given: partial. Fellowships and scholarships available for advanced students. Average amount paid per academic year: $2,000. Average number of hours worked per week: 5. Apply by May 1. Tuition remission given: partial.

Contact Information: Of all students currently enrolled full-time, 7% benefitted from one or more of the listed financial assistance programs. For information on financial assistance, contact: Raquel Brown (312-279-3909), Director of Student Finance.

Internships/Practica: The School approves and monitors over 200 practica sites and assists students in locating and applying for internships across the country and in Canada. Both practica and internship sites offer a wide range of training populations and approaches to students in the school programs. For those doctoral students for whom a professional internship is required prior to graduation, 76 applied in 2000–2001. Of those who applied, 56 were placed in internships listed by the Association of Psychology Postdoctoral and Internship Programs (APPIC); 43 were placed in APA accredited internships.

Housing and Day Care: No on-campus housing and day care facilities are available.

Employment of Department Graduates:
Master's Degree Graduates: Of those who graduated in the academic year 2000–2001, the following categories and numbers represent the post-graduate activities and employment of master's degree graduates: Enrolled in a post-doctoral residency/fellowship (n/a), employed in independent practice (n/a).

Doctoral Degree Graduates: Of those who graduated in the academic year 2000–2001, the following categories and numbers represent the post-graduate activities and employment of doctoral degree graduates: Enrolled in a psychology doctoral program (n/a), enrolled in another graduate/professional program (n/a).

Additional Information:
Orientation, Objectives, and Emphasis of Department: The ISPP/Chicago programs prepare students for contemporary practice through a clinically focused curriculum, taught by practitioner-scholar faculty, with a strong commitment to quality teaching and supervision. The current curricula have been structured to provide students with the fundamental knowledge and skills in psychological assessment and psychotherapy necessary to work with a wide range of traditional clinical populations. In addition, the required curricula include courses and perspectives designed to prepare students for emerging populations from diverse backgrounds and contemporary practice approaches now addressed by clinical psychology. PsyD students may satisfy basic requirements that address the learning of fundamental knowledge and competencies in intervention, assessment, population diversity, and professional practice areas through elective clusters that also provide choices that may conform to their individualized professional goals. As part of the commitment to providing both general and concentrated education and training for doctoral students, the PsyD program offers nine minors, or optional areas of electives choices for students wishing to focus their predoctoral studies in particular areas.

Special Facilities or Resources: The Illinois School of Professional Psychology offers pre-doctoral minors which support students' interests in the following areas: Child/Adolescent Psychology, Health Psychology, Family Psychology, Forensic Psychology, Psychoanalytic Psychology, Psychology of Maltreatment and Trauma, Client-Centered and Experiential Psychology, and Psychology and Spirituality. The School has over 200 practicum sites available for student training in agencies, schools, clinics, hospitals, and practice organizations. Several faculty at the School have ongoing research projects in the following areas, in which students are invited to participate as they engage in their Clinical Research Projects: Effects of mindfulness meditation techniques on medical residents, intergenerational patterns related to sexual abuse, psychology of women, psychology in the schools, intergenerational cultural patterns in mother-daughter relationships, client-centered therapy with the severely mentally ill, personality disorders.

Information for Students With Physical Disabilities: The School has a Disability Committee which reviews the needs of students with physical disabilities. Accommodations are available in terms of teaching and tutoring aids and physical facilities.

Application Information:
Send to: Admissions Department, Argosy University/Chicago Campus, (ISPP) 3rd Floor, 20 S. Clark Street, Chicago, IL 60603. Students are admitted in the Fall, application deadline January 15; Spring, application deadline January 30; Summer, application deadline April 30. Professional Counseling-Spring deadline, October 30; Fall deadline, June 30; Health Services-winter deadline, November 15; Fall deadline,

July 15; Spring deadline, January 30; summer deadline, April 30. *Fee:* $50.

Argosy University, Illinois School of Professional Psychology, Chicago Northwest Campus (2001 data)

Clinical Psychology/Professional Counseling
1 Continental Towers, 1701 Golf Road, Suite #101
Rolling Meadows, IL 60008
Telephone: (847) 290-7400
Fax: (847) 290-8432
E-mail: *jlmiller@argosyu.edu*
Web: *http://www.argosyu.edu*

Department Established:

1994. Department Head: Jim Wasner, Ph.D. Number of Faculty: total–full-time 11, part-time 12; women–full-time 4, part-time 6; minority–full-time 2, part-time 1.

Programs and Degrees Offered:

Listed in the following order: Program area, degree type (T if terminal Master's), number awarded 7/00-6/01. Clinical PsyD (T) 27, professional counseling MA (T) 12.

APA Accreditation: Clinical PsyD: full.

Student Applications/Admissions:

Student Applications

Clinical PsyD—Applications 2001–2002, 35. Total applicants accepted 2001–2002, 25. New applicants enrolled 2001–2002, 16. Total enrolled 2001–2002 full-time, 30, part-time, 5. Openings 2002–2003, 15. The Median number of years required for completion of a degree are 2. The number of students enrolled full and part-time, who were dismissed or voluntarily withdrew from this program area were 1. *Professional counseling MA*—Applications 2001–2002, 43. Total applicants accepted 2001–2002, 37. New applicants enrolled 2001–2002, 27. Total enrolled 2001–2002 full-time, 55, part-time, 10. Openings 2002–2003, 40.

Admissions Requirements:

Scores: Entries appear in this order: required test or GPA, minimum score (if required), median score of students entering in 2001–2002. Master's Programs: overall undergraduate GPA 3.00, 3.20; last 2 years GPA 3.00, 3.35; psychology GPA 3.00, 3.33. Above requirements for the MA Clinical Program. MA Professional Counseling - no minimum GPA required. Doctoral Programs: overall undergraduate GPA 3.25, 3.40; last 2 years GPA 3.25, 3.52; psychology GPA 3.25, 3.60; psychology GPA 3.25, 3.80. Students may be admitted into the doctoral program with only a BA/BS degree.

Other Criteria: (importance of criteria rated low, medium, or high): research experience low, work experience medium, extracurricular activity low, clinically related public service medium, letters of recommendation high, interview high, statement of goals and objectives high.

Student Characteristics: The following represents characteristics of students in 2001–2002 in all graduate psychology programs in the department: Female–full-time 41, part-time 5; Male–full-time 14, part-time 2; African American/Black–full-time 5, part-time 0; Hispanic/Latino (a)–full-time 1, part-time 1; Asian/Pacific Islander–full-time 7, part-time 0; American Indian/Alaska Native–full-time 0, part-time 0.

Financial Information/Assistance:

Tuition for Full-Time Study: No information provided.

Financial Assistance:

First Year Students: No information provided.
Advanced Students: No information provided.
Contact Information: For information on financial assistance, contact: Marlene R. Hanson, J.D., Coordinator of Student Enrollment.

Internships/Practica: Clinical field training is a required component of all programs at the Illinois School of Professional Psychology/Meadows Campus and is a direct outgrowth of the practitioner emphasis of professional psychology. The school provides advisement and assistance in placing students in a wide variety of clinical sites, including hospitals, schools, mental health facilities, treatment centers, and social service agencies. The MA in clinical psychology requires a minimum of 750 hours of practicum experience; the MA in professional counseling requires a 600-hour minimum. The PsyD program includes two years of practicum experience, with a minimum of 600 hours per year; plus an additional one-year full-time clinical internship.

Housing and Day Care: No on-campus housing and day care facilities are available.

Employment of Department Graduates:

Master's Degree Graduates: Of those who graduated in the academic year 2000–2001, the following categories and numbers represent the post-graduate activities and employment of master's degree graduates: Enrolled in a post-doctoral residency/fellowship (n/a), employed in independent practice (n/a).

Doctoral Degree Graduates: Of those who graduated in the academic year 2000–2001, the following categories and numbers represent the post-graduate activities and employment of doctoral degree graduates: Enrolled in a psychology doctoral program (n/a), enrolled in another graduate/professional program (n/a).

Additional Information:

Orientation, Objectives, and Emphasis of Department: The primary purpose of the Illinois School of Professional Psychology/Meadows Campus programs in Professional Counseling and Clinical Psychology is to educate and train students in the major aspects of clinical practice and prepare students for careers as practitioners. To ensure that students are prepared adequately, the curriculum integrates theory, training, research, and practice in preparing students to work with a wide range of populations in need of psychological services. Faculty are both scholars and practitioners and guide students through coursework and field experiences so that they might learn the work involved in professional psychology and understand how formal knowledge and practice operate to inform and enrich each other. The emphasis of the school is a scholar/practitioner orientation, with faculty skilled in all major theories of assessment and intervention. Working closely with faculty, students are provided with exposure to a variety of diagnostic and therapeutic approaches. Sensitivity to diverse populations, populations with specific needs, and multicultural issues are important components of all programs.

Special Facilities or Resources: Faculty members actively encourage student involvement in research projects as a means of fostering mentoring relationships. The Illinois School of Professional Psychology/Meadows Campus has core faculty with extensive experience, enthusiasm, and expertise in the following areas: clinical research, brief psychotherapy, cognitive-behavioral therapy, client-centered therapy, severe psychopathology, substance abuse, addictive disorders, child development and therapy, psychodiagnostics, psychology of women, sexual orientation diversity, domestic violence, forensic psychology, and psychoanalysis.

Information for Students With Physical Disabilities: Once the disability is documented, the campus will work to accommodate the student accordingly.

Application Information:

Send to: Darryl Lockett, Coordinator of Student Enrollment, One Continental Towers, 1701 Golf Rd., Suite 101, Rolling Meodows, Illinois 60008. Students are admitted in the Fall, application deadline May 15; Winter, application deadline November 15. Master's in Professional Counseling accepts applications all four quarters on a rolling basis. Deadlines may be extended dependent upon space availability. *Fee:* $55.

Benedictine University
Graduate Department of Clinical Psychology
5700 College Road
Lisle, IL 60532
Telephone: (630) 829-6230, 6485
Fax: (630) 829-6231
E-mail: *esummers@ben.edu*
Web: *http://www.ben.edu*

Department Established:

1967. Chairperson: James F. Iaccino. Number of Faculty: total–full-time 4, part-time 2; women–full-time 3, part-time 2.

Programs and Degrees Offered:

Listed in the following order: Program area, degree type (T if terminal Master's), number awarded 7/00-6/01. MS in Clinical Psychology MA (T) 22.

Student Applications/Admissions:
Student Applications

MS in Clinical Psychology MA—New applicants enrolled 2001–2002, 14. Total enrolled 2001–2002 full-time, 22, part-time, 44. Openings 2002–2003, 20. The Median number of years required for completion of a degree are 3. The number of students enrolled full and part-time, who were dismissed or voluntarily withdrew from this program area were 5.

Admissions Requirements:

Scores: Entries appear in this order: required test or GPA, minimum score (if required), median score of students entering in 2001–2002. Master's Programs: MAT no minimum stated;

overall undergraduate GPA no minimum stated; last 2 years GPA no minimum stated. Doctoral Programs: last 2 years GPA no minimum stated; psychology GPA no minimum stated; psychology GPA no minimum stated.

Other Criteria: (importance of criteria rated low, medium, or high): GRE/MAT scores medium, research experience low, work experience medium, extracurricular activity medium, clinically related public service high, GPA medium, letters of recommendation high, interview high, statement of goals and objectives high.

Student Characteristics: The following represents characteristics of students in 2001–2002 in all graduate psychology programs in the department: Female–full-time 2, part-time 11; Male–full-time 0, part-time 1; African American/Black–full-time 0, part-time 1; Hispanic/Latino (a)–full-time 0, part-time 0; Asian/Pacific Islander–full-time 0, part-time 0; American Indian/Alaska Native–full-time 0, part-time 0; Multi-ethnic–full-time 0, part-time 0; students subject to the Americans with Disabilities Act–full-time 0, part-time 0.

Financial Information/Assistance:

Tuition for Full-Time Study: *Master's:* State residents $370 per credit hour.

Financial Assistance:

First Year Students: No information provided.
Advanced Students: No information provided.
Contact Information: Of all students currently enrolled full-time, 0% benefitted from one or more of the listed financial assistance programs. For information on financial assistance, contact: Financial Aid Office, Benedictine University, 5700 College Road, Lisle, IL 60532.

Internships/Practica: The program has established relationships with over 100 mental health agencies, in-patient, out-patient, and social service agencies in the Chicago metropolitan area.

Housing and Day Care: On-campus housing and day care facilities are available.

Employment of Department Graduates:

Master's Degree Graduates: Of those who graduated in the academic year 2000–2001, the following categories and numbers represent the post-graduate activities and employment of master's degree graduates: Enrolled in a psychology doctoral program (2), enrolled in another graduate/professional program (0), enrolled in a post-doctoral residency/fellowship (n/a), employed in independent practice (n/a), employed in an academic position at a university (2), employed in other positions at a higher education institution (1), employed in a government agency (professional services) (2), employed in a community mental health/counseling center (8).

Doctoral Degree Graduates: Of those who graduated in the academic year 2000–2001, the following categories and numbers represent the post-graduate activities and employment of doctoral degree graduates: Enrolled in a psychology doctoral program (n/a), enrolled in another graduate/professional program (n/a).

Additional Information:

Orientation, Objectives, and Emphasis of Department: Our program is a rigorous one, offering two clinical internship experiences that more than meet the number of hours required for state licensure. Our program has a curriculum in place that satisfies all Licensed Clinical Professional Counselor (LCPC) licensure requirements. To date, more than 50% of our alums have successfully passed the licensure exam.

Special Facilities or Resources: The department has lab space provided for role play and audio and video taping. The university opened the state-of-art Kindlon Hall of Learning in fall 2001. The building has a beautiful new library and teaching facilities.

Application Information:

Send to: Graduate Admissions, Benedictine University, 5700 College Road, Lisle, IL 60532. Students are admitted in the Fall, application deadline August; Winter, application deadline November; Spring, application deadline February; Summer, application deadline April. *Fee:* $30. Application fee waived for Benedictine University, Illinois Benedictine College, or St. Procopius College alumni.

Chicago School of Professional Psychology
Professional School
47 West Polk Street, 2nd floor
Chicago, IL 60605
Telephone: (312) 786-9443
Fax: (312) 322-3273
E-mail: *admissions@csopp.edu*
Web: *http://www.csopp.edu*

Department Established:

1979. Program Director: Kelly Ducheny, Psy.D. Number of Faculty: total–full-time 13, part-time 7; women–full-time 8, part-time 3; minority–full-time 3, part-time 3.

Programs and Degrees Offered:

Listed in the following order: Program area, degree type (T if terminal Master's), number awarded 7/00-6/01. Clinical PsyD (T), Forensic Psychology MA (T), Organizational & Industrial MA (T).

APA Accreditation: Clinical PsyD: full.

Student Applications/Admissions:

Student Applications

Clinical PsyD—New applicants enrolled 2001–2002, 64. Openings 2002–2003, 65. *Forensic Psychology* MA Openings 2002–2003, 30. *Organizational & Industrial* MA—Total enrolled 2001–2002 full-time, 20, part-time, 2. Openings 2002–2003, 30. The number of students enrolled full and part-time, who were dismissed or voluntarily withdrew from this program area were 0.

Admissions Requirements:

Scores: Entries appear in this order: required test or GPA, minimum score (if required), median score of students entering in 2001–2002. Master's Programs: overall undergraduate GPA 3.0. Doctoral Programs: GRE-V no minimum stated; GRE-Q no minimum stated; GRE-V+Q no minimum stated; GRE-Analytical no minimum stated; overall undergraduate GPA

3.0; last 2 years GPA no minimum stated; psychology GPA no minimum stated; psychology GPA no minimum stated.
Other Criteria: (importance of criteria rated low, medium, or high): GRE/MAT scores medium, research experience low, work experience high, extracurricular activity low, clinically related public service high, GPA high, letters of recommendation high, interview high, statement of goals and objectives medium.

Student Characteristics: The following represents characteristics of students in 2001–2002 in all graduate psychology programs in the department: Female–full-time 200, part-time 62; Male–full-time 62, part-time 21; African American/Black–full-time 24, part-time 9; Hispanic/Latino (a)–full-time 16, part-time 4; Asian/Pacific Islander–full-time 10, part-time 4; American Indian/Alaska Native–full-time 0, part-time 0; Multi-ethnic–full-time 0, part-time 0; students subject to the Americans with Disabilities Act–full-time 4, part-time 0.

Financial Information/Assistance:

Tuition for Full-Time Study: Master's: State residents $550 per credit hour; nonstate residents: $550 per credit hour. *Doctoral:* State residents: $645 per credit hour; nonstate residents: $645 per credit hour.

Financial Assistance:

First Year Students: Research assistantships available for first-year. Apply by March 1. Tuition remission given: partial. Fellowships and scholarships available for first-year. Apply by March 1. Tuition remission given: partial.

Advanced Students: Teaching assistantships available for advanced students. Tuition remission given: partial. Research assistantships available for advanced students. Tuition remission given: partial.

Contact Information: Of all students currently enrolled full-time, 30% benefitted from one or more of the listed financial assistance programs. For information on financial assistance, contact: Denise McCluskey, 312.786.9443, Ext. 3016; finaid@csopp.edu.

Internships/Practica: Currently there are 135 Assessment and Therapy Practicum sites in the city and surrounding area at which our students train. For those doctoral students for whom a professional internship is required prior to graduation, 42 applied in 2000–2001. Of those who applied, 8 were placed in internships listed by the Association of Psychology Postdoctoral and Internship Programs (APPIC); 30 were placed in APA accredited internships.

Housing and Day Care: No on-campus housing and day care facilities are available.

Employment of Department Graduates:

Master's Degree Graduates: Of those who graduated in the academic year 2000–2001, the following categories and numbers represent the post-graduate activities and employment of master's degree graduates: Enrolled in a post-doctoral residency/fellowship (n/a), employed in independent practice (n/a).
Doctoral Degree Graduates: Of those who graduated in the academic year 2000–2001, the following categories and numbers represent the post-graduate activities and employment of doctoral

degree graduates: Enrolled in a psychology doctoral program (n/a), enrolled in another graduate/professional program (n/a).

Additional Information:

Orientation, Objectives, and Emphasis of Department: The Chicago School educates students to be competent practitioners by providing curricula that emphasize both a broad knowledge of the scientific and theoretical bases of psychology and the ability to apply that knowledge to specific employment situations. Small class size and personal advising and supervision provide opportunities for deepening awareness, knowledge, and skills. The programs are designed to integrate the study of cultural and individual differences and their impact in the clinical and work settings. The professional and ethical development of the student is of foremost concern throughout the educational program.

Special Facilities or Resources: The school has a Center for Intercultural Psychology that coordinates extracurricular learning activites and colloquia, sponsors a bi-annual Cultural Impact Conference, and supports research opportunities with underserved populations in the community.

Application Information:

Send to: Office of Admission, Chicago School of Professional Psychology, 47 W. Polk Street, 2nd Floor, Chicago, IL 60605, Director of Admission. Students are admitted in the Fall, application deadline March 1; Spring, application deadline November 7. Early consideration deadline: January 15. *Fee:* $50.

Chicago, University of (2001 data)
Department of Psychology
5848 South University Avenue
Chicago, IL 60637
Telephone: (312) 702-8861
Fax: (312) 702-0886
E-mail: *marj@uchicago.edu*
Web: *http://psychology.uchicago.edu/*

Department Established:

1893. Chairperson: Howard Nusbaum. Number of Faculty: total–full-time 30; women–full-time 10.

Programs and Degrees Offered:

Listed in the following order: Program area, degree type (T if terminal Master's), number awarded 7/00-6/01. Biopsychology PhD, Cognition & Neuroscience Cogni PhD 6, Developmental PhD 3, Language PhD, Perception PhD, Social PhD.

Student Applications/Admissions:

Student Applications

Biopsychology PhD Openings 2002–2003, 3. *Cognition & Neuroscience Cogni PhD*—Applications 2001–2002, 19. New applicants enrolled 2001–2002, 4. Total enrolled 2001–2002 full-time, 10. Openings 2002–2003, 15. *Developmental PhD*—Applications 2001–2002, 15. Total applicants accepted 2001–2002, 7. New applicants enrolled 2001–2002, 4. Total enrolled 2001–2002 full-time, 22. Openings 2002–2003, 5. *Language PhD*—Applications 2001–2002, 0. Openings 2002–2003, 5.

Perception PhD—Applications 2001–2002, 0. Openings 2002–2003, 5. *Social PhD*—Applications 2001–2002, 1. Total applicants accepted 2001–2002, 1. New applicants enrolled 2001–2002, 1. Total enrolled 2001–2002 full-time, 1. Openings 2002–2003, 5.

Admissions Requirements:

Scores: Entries appear in this order: required test or GPA, minimum score (if required), median score of students entering in 2001–2002. Doctoral Programs: GRE-V no minimum stated, 650; GRE-Q no minimum stated, 709; GRE-Analytical no minimum stated, 718; GRE-V+Q+Analytical no minimum stated; overall undergraduate GPA no minimum stated; last 2 years GPA no minimum stated; psychology GPA no minimum stated; psychology GPA no minimum stated.

Other Criteria: (importance of criteria rated low, medium, or high): GRE/MAT scores high, research experience high, work experience medium, extracurricular activity medium, clinically related public service low, GPA high, letters of recommendation high, interview low, statement of goals and objectives high.

Student Characteristics:

The following represents characteristics of students in 2001–2002 in all graduate psychology programs in the department: Female–full-time 31, part-time 0; Male–full-time 17, part-time 0; African American/Black–full-time 2, part-time 0; Hispanic/Latino (a)–full-time 2, part-time 0; American Indian/Alaska Native–full-time 0, part-time 0.

Financial Information/Assistance:

Tuition for Full-Time Study: No information provided.

Financial Assistance:

First Year Students: Research assistantships available for first-year. Fellowships and scholarships available for first-year.

Advanced Students: Teaching assistantships available for advanced students. Tuition remission given: partial. Research assistantships available for advanced students. Fellowships and scholarships available for advanced students.

Contact Information: Of all students currently enrolled full-time, 99% benefitted from one or more of the listed financial assistance programs. For information on financial assistance, contact: Marjorie Wash, 773-702-8861; Marj@ccp.uchicago.edu.

Internships/Practica: No information provided.

Housing and Day Care: No on-campus housing and day care facilities are available.

Employment of Department Graduates:

Master's Degree Graduates: Of those who graduated in the academic year 2000–2001, the following categories and numbers represent the post-graduate activities and employment of master's degree graduates: Enrolled in a post-doctoral residency/fellowship (n/a), employed in independent practice (n/a).

Doctoral Degree Graduates: Of those who graduated in the academic year 2000–2001, the following categories and numbers represent the post-graduate activities and employment of doctoral degree graduates: Enrolled in a psychology doctoral program (n/a), enrolled in another graduate/professional program (n/a).

Additional Information:

Orientation, Objectives, and Emphasis of Department: Our emphasis is on research. The department is made up of five different program committees. Write directly to the department for specific information on the different programs. These programs are the Language Program, the Developmental Psychology Program, the Perception Program, and the Cognition and Cognitive Neuroscience Program.

Special Facilities or Resources: Facilities include the National Opinion Research Center, the University Computation Center, a laboratory for conceptual psychology, an Audio Visual Laboratory, an Early Childhood Initiative, and an Institute for Mind and Biology, and a wide range of laboratory facilities.

Information for Students With Physical Disabilities: The University will do anything possible to assist students with physical disabilities.

Application Information:
Send to: Social Science Division, Office of Admissions, Foster Hall 105 1130 E. 59th Street, Univ. of Chicago, Chicago, IL 60637. Students are admitted in the Fall, application deadline January 5. *Fee:* $55. U.S. citizens who are currently undergrads and are currently receiving financial aid, or who are under-represented O.S. Minorities may include a petition to have fee returned to them. Fee must be initially included with application in all circumstances.

DePaul University
Department of Psychology
2219 North Kenmore - Room 420
Chicago, IL 60614
Telephone: (773) 325-7887
E-mail: *rerber@depaul.edu*
Web: *http://www.depaul.edu/~psych/*

Department Established:
1936. Chairperson: Ralph Erber. Number of Faculty: total–full-time 26, part-time 5; women–full-time 15, part-time 3; minority–full-time 7, part-time 2.

Programs and Degrees Offered:
Listed in the following order: Program area, degree type (T if terminal Master's), number awarded 7/00-6/01. Clinical child PhD 4, clinical community PhD 4, Community PhD, experimental PhD 2, industrial PhD.

APA Accreditation: Clinical PhD: full.

Student Applications/Admissions:
Student Applications
*Clinical child PhD—*Applications 2001–2002, 115. Total applicants accepted 2001–2002, 4. New applicants enrolled 2001–2002, 4. Total enrolled 2001–2002 full-time, 30. Openings 2002–2003, 5. The Median number of years required for completion of a degree are 6. The number of students enrolled full and part-time, who were dismissed or voluntarily withdrew from this program area were 1. *Clinical community PhD—*Appli-

cations 2001–2002, 43. Total applicants accepted 2001–2002, 4. New applicants enrolled 2001–2002, 4. Total enrolled 2001–2002 full-time, 31. Openings 2002–2003, 5. The Median number of years required for completion of a degree are 6. The number of students enrolled full and part-time, who were dismissed or voluntarily withdrew from this program area were 1. *Community PhD—*Applications 2001–2002, 43. Total applicants accepted 2001–2002, 3. New applicants enrolled 2001–2002, 2. Total enrolled 2001–2002 full-time, 2. Openings 2002–2003, 3. *Experimental PhD—*Applications 2001–2002, 19. Total applicants accepted 2001–2002, 5. New applicants enrolled 2001–2002, 4. Total enrolled 2001–2002 full-time, 22. Openings 2002–2003, 5. The Median number of years required for completion of a degree are 6. The number of students enrolled full and part-time, who were dismissed or voluntarily withdrew from this program area were 0. *Industrial PhD—*Applications 2001–2002, 64. Total applicants accepted 2001–2002, 4. New applicants enrolled 2001–2002, 3. Total enrolled 2001–2002 full-time, 40. Openings 2002–2003, 6.

Admissions Requirements:
Scores: Entries appear in this order: required test or GPA, minimum score (if required), median score of students entering in 2001–2002. Doctoral Programs: GRE-V 575, 520; GRE-Q 575, 591; GRE-Subject(Psych) 575, 620; overall undergraduate GPA 3.3, 3.54; last 2 years GPA no minimum stated; psychology GPA no minimum stated; psychology GPA no minimum stated.
Other Criteria: (importance of criteria rated low, medium, or high): GRE/MAT scores high, research experience high, work experience medium, extracurricular activity medium, clinically related public service medium, GPA high, letters of recommendation high, interview high, statement of goals and objectives high. Clinically related public service is not important to the experimental or I/O programs.

Student Characteristics: The following represents characteristics of students in 2001–2002 in all graduate psychology programs in the department: Female–full-time 84, part-time 0; Male–full-time 42, part-time 0; African American/Black–full-time 19, part-time 0; Hispanic/Latino (a)–full-time 16, part-time 0; Asian/Pacific Islander–full-time 12, part-time 0; American Indian/Alaska Native–full-time 3, part-time 0; Multi-ethnic–full-time 9, students subject to the Americans with Disabilities Act–full-time 0.

Financial Information/Assistance:
Tuition for Full-Time Study: *Doctoral:* State residents: per academic year $13,032, $362 per credit hour; nonstate residents: per academic year $13,032, $362 per credit hour.

Financial Assistance:
First Year Students: Teaching assistantships available for first-year. Average amount paid per academic year: $5,000. Average number of hours worked per week: 12. Apply by Jan 10. Tuition remission given: full and partial. Research assistantships available for first-year. Average amount paid per academic year: $5,000. Average number of hours worked per week: 12. Apply by Jan 10. Tuition remission given: full and partial.

Advanced Students: Teaching assistantships available for advanced students. Average amount paid per academic year: $5,000. Average number of hours worked per week: 12. Apply by Jan 10. Tuition remission given: full and partial. Research assistantships available for advanced students. Average amount paid per academic year: $5,000. Average number of hours worked per week: 12. Apply by Jan 10. Tuition remission given: full and partial. Traineeships available for advanced students. Average amount paid per academic year: $7,500. Average number of hours worked per week: 25. Apply by March 1. Tuition remission given: full.

Contact Information: Of all students currently enrolled full-time, 100% benefitted from one or more of the listed financial assistance programs. For information on financial assistance, contact: Department of Psychology, De Paul University, 2219 No. Kenmore, Chicago, IL 60614, Attn: Admissions Coordinator.

Internships/Practica: All of our clinical students are required to take a practica course every quarter for the three years of their coursework here. Though DePaul does not have an internship program, our students successfully obtain internships at top facilities in Chicago and across the nation. For those doctoral students for whom a professional internship is required prior to graduation, 4 applied in 2000–2001. Of those who applied, 4 were placed in internships listed by the Association of Psychology Postdoctoral and Internship Programs (APPIC); 4 were placed in APA accredited internships.

Housing and Day Care: No on-campus housing and day care facilities are available.

Employment of Department Graduates:
Master's Degree Graduates: Of those who graduated in the academic year 2000–2001, the following categories and numbers represent the post-graduate activities and employment of master's degree graduates: Enrolled in a post-doctoral residency/fellowship (n/a), employed in independent practice (n/a).
Doctoral Degree Graduates: Of those who graduated in the academic year 2000–2001, the following categories and numbers represent the post-graduate activities and employment of doctoral degree graduates: Enrolled in a psychology doctoral program (n/a), enrolled in another graduate/professional program (n/a).

Additional Information:
Orientation, Objectives, and Emphasis of Department: The educational philosophy of the Department of Psychology is based upon a recognition of three components of modern psychology. The first of these is academic: the accumulated body of knowledge and theory relevant to the many areas of psychological study. The second is research: the methodologies and skills whereby the science of psychology is advanced. The third is application: the use of psychology for individuals and society. A major function of the graduate curriculum in psychology is to bring to the student an awareness of the real unity of psychological study and practice despite apparent diversity. The student must come to appreciate the fact that psychology is both a pure science and an applied science, and that these aspects are not mutually exclusive. This educational philosophy underlies all programs within the department. Each seeks to incorporate the three interrelated components of psychology at the graduate and professional levels; hence each program contains an academic, a research, and an applied component. It is the emphasis given each component that is distinctive for each of our graduate programs. Students are strongly encouraged to work with faculty in research and tutorial settings. Doctoral candidates are given opportunities to gain teaching experience. Many students work in applied or research settings in the metropolitan Chicago area so that they can apply their graduate education to practical settings.

Special Facilities or Resources: The department is located in a newly renovated building with extensive laboratory facilities. We have smart classrooms and substantial research space available. The university also boasts of a new library, recreation center, athletic facility, and student center. We have state-of-the-art computer facilities with terminals located in the psychology department so that work can be done without leaving the building. A community mental health center is located in the Psychology Building. The center serves a catchment area of approximately 150,000 people. Most of our clinical students gain their practicum experiences in the mental health center. In addition, the community mental health center serves as a fertile area for community and applied research because of our active mental health program and our relationships with other service facilities. The university has prominent law and business colleges that enjoy an excellent reputation in the midwestern business community and therefore provide many work opportunities for our experimental and industrial/organizational students. The department maintains an active network of our PhD graduates to help in obtaining jobs. DePaul shares library and computer facilities with other universities in the Chicago area. There are many educational opportunities in this area, including colloquia, lectures, and regional and national organizations and conferences. We have an active graduate student organization that has contacts with graduate students from other universities, and there are opportunities to share in educational experiences and recreational activities.

Information for Students With Physical Disabilities: Our building is accessible to students with physical disabilities, as are all classroom buildings on campus.

Application Information:
Send to: Admissions Committee, Department of Psychology, 2219 No. Kenmore, Chicago, IL 60614. Students are admitted in the Fall, application deadline January 10. Experimental (including MS), February 15; industrial/organizational, January 31. *Fee:* $40. If financial need is demonstrated, waiver of fee can be requested by letter from applicant to DePaul LA&S, dean, requesting waiver, letter from financial aid officer of present school stating need, and an official transcript.

Eastern Illinois University
Department of Psychology
College of Sciences
Department of Psychology, Eastern Illinois University
Charleston, IL 61920
Telephone: (217) 581-2127
Fax: (217) 581-6764
E-mail: *cfjmh@eiu.edu*
Web: *http://www.eiu.edu/~psych/*

Department Established:
1963. Chairperson: William A. Addison. Number of Faculty: total–full-time 22; women–full-time 7; minority–full-time 4.

Programs and Degrees Offered:

Listed in the following order: Program area, degree type (T if terminal Master's), number awarded 7/00-6/01. Clinical MA (T) 10, school psychology 10.

Student Applications/Admissions:

Student Applications

Clinical MA—Applications 2001–2002, 35. Total applicants accepted 2001–2002, 15. New applicants enrolled 2001–2002, 10. Total enrolled 2001–2002 full-time, 22, part-time, 1. Openings 2002–2003, 10. The Median number of years required for completion of a degree are 2. The number of students enrolled full and part-time, who were dismissed or voluntarily withdrew from this program area were 1.

Admissions Requirements:

Scores: Entries appear in this order: required test or GPA, minimum score (if required), median score of students entering in 2001–2002. Master's Programs: GRE-V+Q+Analytical no minimum stated, 1542; overall undergraduate GPA 3.00, 3.44; last 2 years GPA no minimum stated; psychology GPA 3.25, 3.54. Doctoral Programs: last 2 years GPA no minimum stated; psychology GPA no minimum stated; psychology GPA no minimum stated.

Other Criteria: (importance of criteria rated low, medium, or high): GRE/MAT scores high, research experience medium, work experience medium, extracurricular activity medium, clinically related public service low, GPA high, letters of recommendation high, interview high, statement of goals and objectives high, field work (clinical).

Student Characteristics: The following represents characteristics of students in 2001–2002 in all graduate psychology programs in the department: Female–full-time 17, part-time 0; Male–full-time 3, part-time 0; African American/Black–full-time 0, part-time 0; Hispanic/Latino (a)–full-time 1, part-time 0; Asian/Pacific Islander–full-time 2, part-time 0; American Indian/Alaska Native–full-time 0, part-time 0.

Financial Information/Assistance:

Tuition for Full-Time Study: *Master's:* State residents per academic year $1,900, $153 per credit hour; nonstate residents: per academic year $4,430, $363 per credit hour.

Financial Assistance:

First Year Students: Research assistantships available for first-year. Average amount paid per academic year: $5,400. Average number of hours worked per week: 16. Apply by March 1. Tuition remission given: full.

Advanced Students: No information provided.

Contact Information: Of all students currently enrolled full-time, 90% benefitted from one or more of the listed financial assistance programs. For information on financial assistance, contact: William G. Kirk, Clinical; Michael Havey, School.

Internships/Practica: A two-semester clinical internship in the second year of graduate study is required for the Master of Arts degree. The 12 semester hour internship includes a weekly seminar emphasizing treatment planning, ethical practice, and case management, and requires 600 hours of supervised clinical practice in an approved community agency setting with regular on-campus clinical supervision coordinated with on-site supervision provided by an approved agency supervisor. Some internships carry a stipend and tuition waiver. During the two years of on-campus study required by the school psychology program, students participate in three practica. First-semester students complete a school-based practicum which is designed to orient them to the workings of the public education system. During the first semester of the second year students participate in an assessment practicum centered in the on-campus psychological assessment center. A field-based component of this practicum allows students to also complete assessment activities in a public school setting. During their last semester on campus students participate in a field-based practicum devoted to enhancing counseling and consultation skills.

Housing and Day Care: On-campus housing and day care facilities are available.

Employment of Department Graduates:

Master's Degree Graduates: Of those who graduated in the academic year 2000–2001, the following categories and numbers represent the post-graduate activities and employment of master's degree graduates: Enrolled in a psychology doctoral program (1), enrolled in a post-doctoral residency/fellowship (n/a), employed in independent practice (n/a), employed in a professional position in a school system (10), employed in a community mental health/counseling center (9).

Doctoral Degree Graduates: Of those who graduated in the academic year 2000–2001, the following categories and numbers represent the post-graduate activities and employment of doctoral degree graduates: Enrolled in a psychology doctoral program (n/a), enrolled in another graduate/professional program (n/a).

Additional Information:

Orientation, Objectives, and Emphasis of Department: The Master of Arts degree in Clinical Psychology at Eastern Illinois University is designed to provide graduate training with a solid foundation in the art and science of clinical psychology. The program is a terminal master's degree training experience, which is approved by the Council of Applied Master's Programs in Psychology. The emphases highlight training and instruction in psychological interventions and therapy, assessment, and research. EIU graduates in Clinical Psychology possess a combination of skills in assessment, data management, and analysis that uniquely position them amongst other master's level practitioners when it comes to assisting mental health organizations to meet the increasing demands of accurate evaluation, current, state-of-the-art programming, timely treatment protocols, and accountability. The purpose of the school psychology program is to prepare students to deliver high quality services to students, parents, and professional personnel in public school settings. The program offers a generalist curriculum designed to allow students to develop the flexibility to practice in varied settings. Particular emphasis is placed on assessment, consultation, behavior management, and counseling. The importance of applied experiences is stressed.

Special Facilities or Resources: The Department of Psychology has a computer/statistics lab, an animal research lab as well as faculty directed research labs, one currently in use as the setting for an NIH Grant. Training facilities include a three room suite used as a Psychology Assessment Center with one-way-mirror viewing for testing and interviews and video taping facilities. A further Clinical/Observation research suite, with video and one-way mirror equipment is available for clinical training and supervised community services. Both applied programs enjoy viable cooperative agreements with a number of area educational, correctional, and mental health agencies which serve as training and practica sites for graduate clinical experiences in addition to the internship sites.

Information for Students With Physical Disabilities: The campus is fully accessible with an Office for Disability Services specifically established to provide ancillary services to aid disabled students in their education. Eastern Illinois University has specific equal opportunity/non-discrimination policies and is fully compliant with the American with Disabilities Act of 1990.

Application Information:
Send to: Michael Havey, Coordinator, School Psychology Program; William G. Kirk, Coordinator, Graduate Program in Clinical Psychology, Department of Psychology, Eastern Illinois University, Charleston, IL 61920. Students are admitted in the Fall, application deadline March 1. *Fee:* $30.

Finch University of Health Sciences, The Chicago Medical School
Department of Psychology
3333 Green Bay Road
North Chicago, IL 60064
Telephone: (847) 578-3305
Fax: (847) 578-8758
E-mail: *michael.seidenberg@finchcms.edu*
Web: *http://www.finchcms.edu*

Department Established:
1977. Professor and Chairman: Michael Seidenberg. Number of Faculty: total–full-time 8, part-time 2; women–full-time 1, part-time 2.

Programs and Degrees Offered:
Listed in the following order: Program area, degree type (T if terminal Master's), number awarded 7/00-6/01. Clinical PhD 13.

APA Accreditation: Clinical PhD: full.

Student Applications/Admissions:
Student Applications
Clinical PhD—Applications 2001–2002, 82. Total applicants accepted 2001–2002, 34. New applicants enrolled 2001–2002, 10. Total enrolled 2001–2002 full-time, 81. Openings 2002–2003, 10. The Median number of years required for completion of a degree are 7.

Admissions Requirements:
Scores: Entries appear in this order: required test or GPA, minimum score (if required), median score of students entering in 2001–2002. Doctoral Programs: GRE-V 600, 545; GRE-Q 600, 615; GRE-Analytical 600, 690; GRE-Subject(Psych) 600, 620; last 2 years GPA 3.2, 3.48; psychology GPA no minimum stated; psychology GPA no minimum stated.
Other Criteria: (importance of criteria rated low, medium, or high): GRE/MAT scores medium, research experience high,

work experience low, extracurricular activity medium, clinically related public service medium, GPA high, letters of recommendation high, interview high, statement of goals and objectives high. These criteria are identical for all programs. Students are welcome to visit the Department throughout the year.

Student Characteristics: The following represents characteristics of students in 2001–2002 in all graduate psychology programs in the department: Female–full-time 5, part-time 0; Male–full-time 5, part-time 0; African American/Black–full-time 0, part-time 0; Hispanic/Latino (a)–full-time 0, part-time 0; Asian/Pacific Islander–full-time 1, part-time 0; American Indian/Alaska Native–full-time 0, part-time 0.

Financial Information/Assistance:
Tuition for Full-Time Study: *Doctoral:* State residents: per academic year $16,390; nonstate residents: per academic year $16,390.

Financial Assistance:
First Year Students: Research assistantships available for first-year. Tuition remission given: full and partial. Fellowships and scholarships available for first-year. Tuition remission given: full and partial.
Advanced Students: Teaching assistantships available for advanced students. Tuition remission given: full and partial. Research assistantships available for advanced students. Tuition remission given: full and partial. Traineeships available for advanced students. Tuition remission given: full and partial. Fellowships and scholarships available for advanced students. Tuition remission given: full and partial.
Contact Information: Of all students currently enrolled full-time, 38% benefitted from one or more of the listed financial assistance programs. For information on financial assistance, contact: Financial Aid Department, FUHS/The Chicago Medical School, 3333 Green Bay Road, North Chicago, IL 60064; (847) 578-3216.

Internships/Practica: The Department enjoys formal relationships with any of the major clinical, health, and neuropsychology facilities in the catchment area from Chicago to the south and Milwaukee to the north. These include both inpatient and outpatient facilities. Thus, students have the opportunity to obtain experience and clinical training with a diverse range of clinical populations and socio-economic strata. In addition, the FUHS and CMS operates primary care clinics that function side by side with Department-operated Psychology Clinics. The University Counseling Center is also run by the Department of Psychology and it provides a variety of assessment and intervention services to members of the University. For those doctoral students for whom a professional internship is required prior to graduation, 13 applied in 2000–2001. Of those who applied, 12 were placed in internships listed by the Association of Psychology Postdoctoral and Internship Programs (APPIC); 12 were placed in APA accredited internships.

Housing and Day Care: No on-campus housing and day care facilities are available.

Employment of Department Graduates:
Master's Degree Graduates: Of those who graduated in the academic year 2000–2001, the following categories and numbers

represent the post-graduate activities and employment of master's degree graduates: Enrolled in a post-doctoral residency/fellowship (n/a), employed in independent practice (n/a).

Doctoral Degree Graduates: Of those who graduated in the academic year 2000–2001, the following categories and numbers represent the post-graduate activities and employment of doctoral degree graduates: Enrolled in a psychology doctoral program (n/a), enrolled in another graduate/professional program (n/a), enrolled in a post-doctoral residency/fellowship (8), employed in independent practice (1), employed in an academic position at a university (1), employed in a community mental health/counseling center (1), employed in a hospital/medical center (1).

Additional Information:

Orientation, Objectives, and Emphasis of Department: The Department of Psychology offers an APA approved program leading to the Ph.D. degree in clinical psychology, with specialties in Health Psychology and Clinical Neuropsychology. In addition, substantial training emphasis in psychopathology is also available. Within the context of the general clinical training program, students select a specialty emphasis in either clinical neuropsychology or health/behavioral medicine. The program provides students with intensive training in the methods and theories of clinical practice with emphasis in these specialty areas. Research is a vital part of the program and students work closely with professors throughout their training. Research topics include biopsychosocial issues associated with various medical illnesses (e.g., cancer, diabetes, heart disease, chronic pain), aging, psychopathology (e.g., schizophrenia, OCD, psychopathy), and neuropsychological features of various clinical populations (e.g., epilepsy, head injury, multiple sclerosis, AIDS, Alzheimer's disease, dementia, stroke). Subject populations range in age from childhood through adulthood and include those with physical and psychiatric disorders. The Department subscribes to the philosophy that a clinical psychologist is knowledgeable in formulating and solving scientific problems, and skilled in formulating clinical problems and applying empirically supported interventions. To this end, core courses are organized as integrated theory-research-practice units with a problem solving orientation. Our goal is to graduate clinical psychologists who are highly trained, clinically effective, and able to contribute to the continuing development of the profession as practitioners, teachers, and researchers.

Special Facilities or Resources: The Department operates several specialty clinics at the Chicago Medical School including an Anxiety Disorders Clinic and Neuropsychological Assessment Clinic, which provide both clinical training and research opportunities. Research facilities within the Department include an Experimental Neuropsychology Lab, Clinical Health Psychophysiology Lab, Animal Neurophysiology Lab, and a Behavioral Therapy Lab. There are ongoing research programs in arthritis, oncology, diabetes, blood pressure regulation, pain and stress, epilepsy, anxiety disorders, schizophrenia, psychopathy, aging, and dementia. Collaborative research opportunities are also ongoing with a number of community and academic institutions in the area and include projects using MRI to study higher order cognitive processes.

Information for Students With Physical Disabilities: The University is committed to providing students with the resources necessary to accommodate any physical disability. For more infor-

mation, prospective students should contact the Chairman of the Department.

Application Information:
Send to: FUHS/The Chicago Medical School, Graduate Admissions Office, 3333 Green Bay Road, North Chicago, IL 60064. Students are admitted in the Fall, application deadline January 15. *Fee:* $25.

Governors State University
Division of Psychology and Counseling
College of Education
University Park, IL 60466
Telephone: (708) 534-4991
Fax: (708) 534-8451
E-mail: *gsunow@govst.edu*

Department Established:
1979. Interim Chairperson: Linda S. Buyer. Number of Faculty: total–full-time 22; women–full-time 13, part-time 1; minority–full-time 7, part-time 1.

Programs and Degrees Offered:
Listed in the following order: Program area, degree type (T if terminal Master's), number awarded 7/00-6/01. Counseling MA (T) 36, general MA (T), school MA (T).

Student Applications/Admissions:

Student Applications

Counseling MA—Applications 2001–2002, 85. Total applicants accepted 2001–2002, 73. New applicants enrolled 2001–2002, 22. Total enrolled 2001–2002 full-time, 13, part-time, 156. Openings 2002–2003, 50. *General MA*—Applications 2001–2002, 20. Total applicants accepted 2001–2002, 15. New applicants enrolled 2001–2002, 2. Total enrolled 2001–2002 full-time, 3, part-time, 18. Openings 2002–2003, 40. *School MA*—Applications 2001–2002, 60. Total applicants accepted 2001–2002, 30. New applicants enrolled 2001–2002, 10. Total enrolled 2001–2002 full-time, 5, part-time, 98. Openings 2002–2003, 50.

Admissions Requirements:

Scores: Entries appear in this order: required test or GPA, minimum score (if required), median score of students entering in 2001–2002. Master's Programs: GRE-Subject(Psych) no minimum stated; overall undergraduate GPA 3.0; last 2 years GPA 3.0. Doctoral Programs: last 2 years GPA no minimum stated; psychology GPA no minimum stated; psychology GPA no minimum stated.

Other Criteria: (importance of criteria rated low, medium, or high): GPA medium, letters of recommendation medium, interview high, statement of goals and objectives high.

Student Characteristics: The following represents characteristics of students in 2001–2002 in all graduate psychology programs in the department: Female–full-time 1, part-time 25; Male–full-time 2, part-time 6; African American/Black–full-time 0, part-time 10; Hispanic/Latino (a)–full-time 0, part-time 1; Asian/Pacific Islander–full-time 0, part-time 1; American Indian/Alaska Native–full-time 0, part-time 0.

Financial Information/Assistance:

Tuition for Full-Time Study: *Master's:* State residents $98 per credit hour; nonstate residents: $294 per credit hour.

Financial Assistance:

First Year Students: No information provided.
Advanced Students: No information provided.
Contact Information: For information on financial assistance, contact: Director of Financial Aid. http://www.govst.edu/financial/.

Internships/Practica: School Psychology internships typically are available in a wide variety of suburban school districts as well as the Chicago public schools. Counseling internships are readily available in a wide variety of community mental health and human service agencies.

Housing and Day Care: On-campus housing and day care facilities are available.

Employment of Department Graduates:

Master's Degree Graduates: Of those who graduated in the academic year 2000–2001, the following categories and numbers represent the post-graduate activities and employment of master's degree graduates: Enrolled in a post-doctoral residency/fellowship (n/a), employed in independent practice (n/a).

Doctoral Degree Graduates: Of those who graduated in the academic year 2000–2001, the following categories and numbers represent the post-graduate activities and employment of doctoral degree graduates: Enrolled in a psychology doctoral program (n/a), enrolled in another graduate/professional program (n/a).

Additional Information:

Orientation, Objectives, and Emphasis of Department: The graduate programs in the Division of Psychology and Counseling are appropriate for the returning adult student. Required classes are primarily offered during the early evening or evening hours. Most students work and are completing their program of studies on a part-time basis. Some classes are scheduled on the weekend.

Application Information:

Send to: Admissions, Governors State University, University Park, Illinois 60466. Students are admitted in the Fall, application deadline June 15; Winter, application deadline October 15; Spring, application deadline March 15. *Fee:* No application fee.

Illinois Institute of Technology
Institute of Psychology
LS252, 3101 South Dearborn
Chicago, IL 60616
Telephone: (312) 567-3500
Fax: (312) 567-3493
E-mail: *mitchelle@iit.edu*
Web: *http://www.iit.edu/~psych*

Department Established:

1929. Director: M. Ellen Mitchell. Number of Faculty: total–full-time 18, part-time 5; women–full-time 8, part-time 2; minority–full-time 1; faculty subject to the Americans with Disabilities Act 1.

Programs and Degrees Offered:

Listed in the following order: Program area, degree type (T if terminal Master's), number awarded 7/00-6/01. Clinical PhD 6, industrial/organization PhD 3, personal and human resources, rehabilitation PhD, rehabilitation counseling.

APA Accreditation: Clinical PhD: full.

Student Applications/Admissions:

Student Applications

Clinical PhD—Applications 2001–2002, 86. Total applicants accepted 2001–2002, 25. New applicants enrolled 2001–2002, 14. Total enrolled 2001–2002 full-time, 28, part-time, 42. Openings 2002–2003, 13. *Industrial/organization PhD*—Applications 2001–2002, 66. Total applicants accepted 2001–2002, 33. New applicants enrolled 2001–2002, 9. Total enrolled 2001–2002 full-time, 11, part-time, 7. Openings 2002–2003, 12. *Rehabilitation PhD*—Applications 2001–2002, 2. Total applicants accepted 2001–2002, 1. New applicants enrolled 2001–2002, 1. Total enrolled 2001–2002 full-time, 1. Openings 2002–2003, 3.

Admissions Requirements:

Scores: Entries appear in this order: required test or GPA, minimum score (if required), median score of students entering in 2001–2002. Master's Programs: GRE-V+Q 1000, 1200; overall undergraduate GPA 3.0, 3.6. The Master's in Rehabilitation does not require a GRE. The PHRD requires a minimum GPA of 3.2. Doctoral Programs: GRE-V+Q 1000, 1240; overall undergraduate GPA 3.0; last 2 years GPA no minimum stated; psychology GPA 3.5; psychology GPA no minimum stated, 3.76.

Other Criteria: (importance of criteria rated low, medium, or high): GRE/MAT scores high, research experience high, work experience high, extracurricular activity low, clinically related public service medium, GPA high, letters of recommendation high, interview high, statement of goals and objectives high. GPA and GRE are less important for MS programs; MS in rehabilitation weekend program does not require the GRE.

Student Characteristics: The following represents characteristics of students in 2001–2002 in all graduate psychology programs in the department: Female–full-time 28, part-time 4; Male–full-time 23, part-time 2; African American/Black–full-time 4, part-time 2; Hispanic/Latino (a)–full-time 2, part-time 1; Asian/Pacific Islander–full-time 4, part-time 1; American Indian/Alaska Native–full-time 1, part-time 0.

Financial Information/Assistance:

Tuition for Full-Time Study: *Master's:* State residents $610 per credit hour; nonstate residents: $610 per credit hour. *Doctoral:* State residents: $610 per credit hour; nonstate residents: $610 per credit hour.

Financial Assistance:

First Year Students: Teaching assistantships available for first-year. Average amount paid per academic year: $4,690. Average number of hours worked per week: 20. Apply by 4/1/03.

Tuition remission given: partial. Fellowships and scholarships available for first-year. Tuition remission given: partial.

Advanced Students: Teaching assistantships available for advanced students. Average amount paid per academic year: $4,690. Average number of hours worked per week: 20. Apply by 4/1/03. Tuition remission given: partial. Research assistantships available for advanced students. Average number of hours worked per week: 15. Apply by varies. Tuition remission given: partial. Fellowships and scholarships available for advanced students. Apply by varies. Tuition remission given: partial.

Contact Information: Of all students currently enrolled full-time, 50% benefitted from one or more of the listed financial assistance programs. For information on financial assistance, contact: Program Director and/or Office of Financial Aid.

Internships/Practica: All students are required to complete field-work internships and practica. Experiences vary by program. As one of the largest cities in the United States, Chicago provides access to diverse practicum and internship sites. For those doctoral students for whom a professional internship is required prior to graduation, 11 applied in 2000–2001. Of those who applied, 11 were placed in internships listed by the Association of Psychology Postdoctoral and Internship Programs (APPIC); 11 were placed in APA accredited internships.

Housing and Day Care: On-campus housing and day care facilities are available.

Employment of Department Graduates:

Master's Degree Graduates: Of those who graduated in the academic year 2000–2001, the following categories and numbers represent the post-graduate activities and employment of master's degree graduates: Enrolled in a post-doctoral residency/fellowship (n/a), employed in independent practice (n/a).

Doctoral Degree Graduates: Of those who graduated in the academic year 2000–2001, the following categories and numbers represent the post-graduate activities and employment of doctoral degree graduates: Enrolled in a psychology doctoral program (n/a), enrolled in another graduate/professional program (n/a).

Additional Information:

Orientation, Objectives, and Emphasis of Department: The primary emphasis in the department is on a scientist-practitioner model of training. Our APA-approved clinical psychology program offers intensive clinical and research training with an emphasis on a cognitive theoretical framework, community involvement, and exposure to underserved populations. The MS in rehabilitation counseling prepares students to function as rehabilitation counselors for disabled persons. The PhD program in rehabilitation psychology prepares students for careers in rehabilitation education, research, and the practice of rehabilitation psychology. Our industrial/organizational program provides a solid scientific background as well as knowledge and expertise in personnel selection, evaluation, training and development, motivation, and organizational behavior.

Special Facilities or Resources: Facilities include laboratories for human behavior studies, psychophysiological research, infant and maternal attachment, and a testing and interviewing laboratory with attached one-way viewing rooms. Equipment includes programming apparatus for learning studies, specialized computer facilities, and videotaping and other audiovisual equipment. There are graduate student offices, a testing library of assessment equipment, and a student lounge. The Disabilities Resource Center is housed within psychology.

Information for Students With Physical Disabilities: Most university facilities are accessible to students with disabilities. Students with disabilities are given priority in traineeship awards in the rehabilitation counseling program. The Center for Disability Resources is housed with Psychology. Students are encouraged to call to discuss their special needs.

Application Information:
Send to: Admissions, Institute of Psychology. Students are admitted in the Fall, application deadline January 15. Rehabilitation deadline is April 1, and I/O deadline is February 15. *Fee:* $30.

Illinois State University
Department of Psychology
College of Arts and Sciences
Campus Box 4620
Normal, IL 61790-4620
Telephone: (309) 438-8701
Fax: (309) 438-5789
E-mail: *mkammle@ilstu.edu*
Web: *http://www.cas.ilstu.edu/psychology/*

Department Established:
1966. Chair: David Patton Barone. Number of Faculty: total–full-time 35, part-time 11; women–full-time 12, part-time 5; minority–full-time 1; faculty subject to the Americans with Disabilities Act 1.

Programs and Degrees Offered:
Listed in the following order: Program area, degree type (T if terminal Master's), number awarded 7/00-6/01. Clinical-counseling psychology MA (T) 14, Cognitive & Behavioral Sciences MA (T) 3, developmental psychology, educational psychology MA (T) 1, general psychology MA (T) 5, Industrial/Org-Social MA (T) 10, quantitative MA (T) 2, School Psychology EdS (T) 4, school psychology PhD 2.

APA Accreditation: School PhD: full.

Student Applications/Admissions:
Student Applications

Clinical-counseling psychology MA—Applications 2001–2002, 68. Total applicants accepted 2001–2002, 21. New applicants enrolled 2001–2002, 16. Total enrolled 2001–2002 full-time, 31, part-time, 8. Openings 2002–2003, 15. The Median number of years required for completion of a degree are 2. The number of students enrolled full and part-time, who were dismissed or voluntarily withdrew from this program area were 1. *Cognitive & Behavioral Sciences* MA—Applications 2001–2002, 7. Total applicants accepted 2001–2002, 5. New applicants enrolled 2001–2002, 3. Total enrolled 2001–2002 full-time, 8, part-time, 3. Openings 2002–2003, 5. The Median number of years required for completion of a degree are 4. The number of students enrolled full and part-time, who were dismissed or voluntarily withdrew from this program area were 0. *Educational psychology* MA—Applications 2001–2002, 0. The Median number of years required for completion of a degree are 3. The number of students enrolled full and part-time, who were dismissed or voluntarily withdrew from this program area were 0. *General psychology* MA—Applications 2001–2002, 2. Total applicants accepted 2001–2002, 1. New applicants enrolled 2001–2002, 1. Total enrolled 2001–2002 full-time, 2, part-time, 7. The Median number of years required for completion of a degree are 3. The number of students enrolled full and part-time, who were dismissed or voluntarily withdrew from this program area were 0. *Industrial/Org-Social* MA—Applications 2001–2002, 21. Total applicants accepted 2001–2002, 13. New applicants enrolled 2001–2002, 4. Total enrolled 2001–2002 full-time, 14, part-time, 8. Openings 2002–2003, 8. The Median number of years required for completion of a degree are 3. The number of students enrolled full and part-time, who were dismissed or voluntarily withdrew from this program area were 0. *Quantitative* MA—Applications 2001–2002, 4. Total applicants accepted 2001–2002, 3. New applicants enrolled 2001–2002, 2. Total enrolled 2001–2002 full-time, 2, part-time, 2. Openings 2002–2003, 2. The Median number of years required for completion of a degree are 2. The number of students enrolled full and part-time, who were dismissed or voluntarily withdrew from this program area were 0. *School Psychology EdS*—Applications 2001–2002, 24. Total applicants accepted 2001–2002, 14. New applicants enrolled 2001–2002, 7. Total enrolled 2001–2002 full-time, 13, part-time, 7. Openings 2002–2003, 7. The Median number of years required for completion of a degree are 4. The number of students enrolled full and part-time, who were dismissed or voluntarily withdrew from this program area were 1. *School psychology PhD*—Applications 2001–2002, 17. Total applicants accepted 2001–2002, 10. New applicants enrolled 2001–2002, 7. Total enrolled 2001–2002 full-time, 21, part-time, 14. Openings 2002–2003, 7. The Median number of years required for completion of a degree are 5. The number of students enrolled full and part-time, who were dismissed or voluntarily withdrew from this program area were 0.

Admissions Requirements:

Scores: Entries appear in this order: required test or GPA, minimum score (if required), median score of students entering in 2001–2002. Master's Programs: GRE-V no minimum stated, 490; GRE-Q no minimum stated, 560; GRE-V+Q no minimum stated, 1060; GRE-Subject(Psych) no minimum stated; overall undergraduate GPA no minimum stated, 3.71; last 2 years GPA 3.0, 3.80; psychology GPA no minimum stated, 3.79. EdS/SSP degree figures have been included in the figures for the master's degree. Doctoral Programs: GRE-V no minimum stated, 430; GRE-Q no minimum stated, 530; GRE-V+Q no minimum stated, 950; GRE-Analytical no minimum stated, 540; GRE-Subject(Psych) no minimum stated; overall undergraduate GPA no minimum stated, 3.66; last 2 years GPA 3.0, 3.87; psychology GPA no minimum stated, 3.76; psychology GPA no minimum stated.

Other Criteria: (importance of criteria rated low, medium, or high): GRE/MAT scores medium, research experience medium, work experience medium, extracurricular activity low, clinically related public service medium, GPA high, letters of recommendation medium, interview medium, statement of goals and objectives medium. Interview required only for the PhD degree.

Student Characteristics: The following represents characteristics of students in 2001–2002 in all graduate psychology programs in the department: Female–full-time 77, part-time 5; Male–full-time 15, part-time 18; African American/Black–full-time 4, part-time 0; Hispanic/Latino (a)–full-time 4, part-time 0; Asian/Pacific Islander–full-time 4, part-time 2; American Indian/Alaska Native–full-time 2, part-time 0; Multi-ethnic–full-time 0, part-time 0; students subject to the Americans with Disabilities Act–full-time 0, part-time 2.

Financial Information/Assistance:

Tuition for Full-Time Study: *Master's:* State residents per academic year $2,691, $112 per credit hour; nonstate residents: per academic year $5,880, $245 per credit hour. *Doctoral:* State residents: per academic year $2,915, $112 per credit hour; nonstate residents: per academic year $6,370, $245 per credit hour.

Financial Assistance:

First Year Students: Teaching assistantships available for first-year. Average amount paid per academic year: $5,575. Average number of hours worked per week: 20. Apply by 2/15. Tuition remission given: full. Research assistantships available for first-year. Average amount paid per academic year: $9,000. Average number of hours worked per week: 20. Apply by 2/15. Tuition remission given: full. Traineeships available for first-year. Average amount paid per academic year: $6,300. Average number of hours worked per week: 20. Apply by 2/15. Tuition remission given: full. Fellowships and scholarships available for first-year. Average amount paid per academic year: $4,000. Average number of hours worked per week: 0. Apply by 3/15. Tuition remission given: full.

Advanced Students: Teaching assistantships available for advanced students. Average amount paid per academic year: $7,125. Average number of hours worked per week: 20. Apply by 2/15. Tuition remission given: full. Research assistantships available for advanced students. Average amount paid per academic year: $10,500. Average number of hours worked per week: 20. Apply by 2/15. Tuition remission given: full. Traineeships available for advanced students. Average amount paid per academic year: $7,125. Average number of hours worked per week: 20. Apply by 2/15. Tuition remission given: full. Fellowships and scholarships available for advanced students. Average amount paid per academic year: $4,000. Average number of hours worked per week: 0. Apply by 3/15. Tuition remission given: full.

Contact Information: Of all students currently enrolled full-time, 89% benefitted from one or more of the listed financial assistance programs. For information on financial assistance, contact: Financial Aid Office (www.fao.ilstu.edu/; 309/438-2231); Department of Psychology (http://www.cas.ilstu.edu/psychology/; 309/438-8701).

Internships/Practica: Students in the clinical-counseling master's program are provided with extensive supervised experience in practica in either external mental health agencies or the university's Student Counseling Services. Students in the School Psychology specialist (SSP) and doctoral (PhD) programs participate from their first semester in supervised practica in public and private schools, Head Start centers, and the on-campus Psychological Services Center. Full-time internships are required for all school psychology students. For those doctoral students for whom a professional internship is required prior to graduation, 6 applied in 2000–2001. Of those who applied, 1 were placed in internships listed by the Association of Psychology Postdoctoral and Internship Programs (APPIC).

Housing and Day Care: On-campus housing and day care facilities are available.

Employment of Department Graduates:

Master's Degree Graduates: Of those who graduated in the academic year 2000–2001, the following categories and numbers represent the post-graduate activities and employment of master's degree graduates: Enrolled in a psychology doctoral program (5), enrolled in another graduate/professional program (4), enrolled in a post-doctoral residency/fellowship (n/a), employed in independent practice (n/a), employed in an academic position at a university (0), employed in an academic position at a 2-year/4-year college (0), employed in other positions at a higher education institution (1), employed in a professional position in a school system (5), employed in business or industry (research/consulting) (0), employed in business or industry (management) (2), employed in a government agency (research) (0), employed in a government agency (professional services) (0), employed in a community mental health/counseling center (7), employed in a hospital/medical center (0), still seeking employment (0), other employment position (0).

Doctoral Degree Graduates: Of those who graduated in the academic year 2000–2001, the following categories and numbers represent the post-graduate activities and employment of doctoral degree graduates: Enrolled in a psychology doctoral program (n/a), enrolled in another graduate/professional program (n/a), enrolled in a post-doctoral residency/fellowship (0), employed in independent practice (0), employed in an academic position at a university (0), employed in an academic position at a 2-year/4-year college (0), employed in other positions at a higher education institution (0), employed in a professional position in a school system (1), employed in business or industry (research/consulting) (0), employed in business or industry (management) (0), employed in a government agency (research) (0), employed in a government agency (professional services) (0), employed in a community mental health/counseling center (0), employed in a hospital/medical center (1), still seeking employment (0), other employment position (0).

Additional Information:

Orientation, Objectives, and Emphasis of Department: The department provides training in professional areas supplemented by options in developmental, cognitive and behavioral sciences, and quantitative. Training in the professional areas takes advantage of the professional experience of the faculty in human service settings and industry so that instruction is both practical and theoretical. While comprehensive examinations provide an alternative, most programs require a master's thesis or doctoral dissertation.

Special Facilities or Resources: The department has computer facilities and human and animal laboratories. The department also has a Psychological Services Center for assessment and treatment of children and families. For the clinical-counseling and school psychology programs, a large number of community agencies participate in the one-year practicum (schools, hospitals,

mental health centers, and alcohol and drug rehabilitation centers).

Application Information:

Send to: Illinois State University, Department of Psychology, Graduate Psychology Programs, Campus Box 4620, Normal IL 61790-4620. Students are admitted in the Fall, application deadline February 15; Spring, application deadline October 30. Fall and Summer application deadline for the PhD program only is January 15. Fall application deadline for remaining programs is February 15. Spring application deadline for only Developmental, Cognitive & Behavioral Sciences (Experimental), Industrial/Organizational-Social, and Quantitative (Measurement & Statistics) is October 30. *Fee:* $30.

Illinois, University of, at Chicago

Department of Psychology (M/C 285)
Liberal Arts and Sciences
1007 West Harrison Street
Chicago, IL 60607-7137
Telephone: (312) 996-2434
Fax: (312) 413-4122
E-mail: *pschinfo@uic.edu*
Web: *http://www.uic.edu/depts/psch/*

Department Established:

1965. Chairperson: Christopher B. Keys. Number of Faculty: total–full-time 26, part-time 7; women–full-time 8, part-time 2; minority–full-time 3, part-time 2.

Programs and Degrees Offered:

Listed in the following order: Program area, degree type (T if terminal Master's), number awarded 7/00-6/01. Biopsychology PhD 1, clinical PhD 10, cognitive PhD, community and prevention resea PhD 1, social and personality PhD 1.

APA Accreditation: Clinical PhD: full.

Student Applications/Admissions:

Student Applications

Biopsychology PhD—Applications 2001–2002, 7. Total applicants accepted 2001–2002, 4. New applicants enrolled 2001–2002, 3. Total enrolled 2001–2002 full-time, 7, part-time, DNA. Openings 2002–2003, 2-3. The Median number of years required for completion of a degree are 8. *Clinical PhD*—Applications 2001–2002, 133. Total applicants accepted 2001–2002, 9. New applicants enrolled 2001–2002, 6. Total enrolled 2001–2002 full-time, 43, part-time, n/a. Openings 2002–2003, 5. The Median number of years required for completion of a degree are 7. The number of students enrolled full and part-time, who were dismissed or voluntarily withdrew from this program area were 3. *Cognitive PhD*—Applications 2001–2002, 12. Total applicants accepted 2001–2002, 10. New applicants enrolled 2001–2002, 5. Total enrolled 2001–2002 full-time, 20, part-time, n/a. Openings 2002–2003, 4. *Community and prevention resea PhD*—Applications 2001–2002, 39. Total applicants accepted 2001–2002, 10. New applicants enrolled 2001–2002, 9. Total enrolled 2001–2002 full-time, 28, part-time, n/a. Openings 2002–2003, 3-5. The Median number of years required for completion of a degree are 6. The number of students enrolled full and part-time, who were dismissed or voluntarily withdrew from this program area were 3. *Social and personality PhD*—Applications 2001–2002, 39. Total applicants accepted 2001–2002, 7. New applicants enrolled 2001–2002, 4. Total enrolled 2001–2002 full-time, 19, part-time, n/a. Openings 2002–2003, 3-5. The Median number of years required for completion of a degree are 6. The number of students enrolled full and part-time, who were dismissed or voluntarily withdrew from this program area were 2.

Admissions Requirements:

Scores: Entries appear in this order: required test or GPA, minimum score (if required), median score of students entering in 2001–2002. Doctoral Programs: GRE-V no minimum stated, 600; GRE-Q no minimum stated, 620; GRE-Analytical no minimum stated, 680; GRE-Subject(Psych) no minimum stated, 650; last 2 years GPA 4.2, 4.7 ; psychology GPA no minimum stated; psychology GPA no minimum stated.

Other Criteria: (importance of criteria rated low, medium, or high): GRE/MAT scores medium, research experience high, work experience medium, extracurricular activity medium, clinically related public service medium, GPA high, letters of recommendation high, interview medium, statement of goals and objectives high, fit with faculty research high.

Student Characteristics: The following represents characteristics of students in 2001–2002 in all graduate psychology programs in the department: Female–full-time 81, part-time 0; Male–full-time 37, part-time 0; African American/Black–full-time 12, part-time 0; Hispanic/Latino (a)–full-time 8, part-time 0; Asian/Pacific Islander–full-time 3, part-time 0; American Indian/Alaska Native–full-time 2, part-time 0.

Financial Information/Assistance:

Tuition for Full-Time Study: *Doctoral:* State residents: per academic year $6,120; nonstate residents: per academic year $13,376.

Financial Assistance:

First Year Students: Teaching assistantships available for first-year. Average amount paid per academic year: $11,125. Average number of hours worked per week: 18. Apply by January 1. Tuition remission given: full. Research assistantships available for first-year. Average amount paid per academic year: $11,125. Average number of hours worked per week: 18. Apply by January 1. Tuition remission given: full. Traineeships available for first-year. Average amount paid per academic year: $12,000. Average number of hours worked per week: 0. Apply by January 1. Tuition remission given: full. Fellowships and scholarships available for first-year. Average amount paid per academic year: $15,000. Average number of hours worked per week: 0. Apply by January 1. Tuition remission given: full.

Advanced Students: Teaching assistantships available for advanced students. Average amount paid per academic year: $12,825. Average number of hours worked per week: 18. Tuition remission given: full. Research assistantships available for advanced students. Average amount paid per academic year: $12,825. Average number of hours worked per week: 18. Tuition remission given: full. Traineeships available for advanced students. Average amount paid per academic year: $12,825. Average number of hours worked per week: 0. Tuition remission given: full. Fellowships and scholarships available for advanced students.

Average amount paid per academic year: $15,000. Average number of hours worked per week: 0. Tuition remission given: full.

Contact Information: Of all students currently enrolled full-time, 100% benefitted from one or more of the listed financial assistance programs. For information on financial assistance, contact: 312-996-3126, The Office of Financial Aid.

Internships/Practica: Access to a wide variety of practicum and research sites is available to advanced students. These include the UIC Counseling Service, Cook County Hospital, Rush-Presbyterian-St. Luke's Medical Center, the Institute for Juvenile Research, the Institute on Disabilities and Human Development, several Veterans Administration hospitals and mental health clinics, schools, and diverse community agencies throughout the Chicago area, in addition to our own Office of Applied Psychology. For those doctoral students for whom a professional internship is required prior to graduation, 2 applied in 2000–2001. Of those who applied, 2 were placed in internships listed by the Association of Psychology Postdoctoral and Internship Programs (APPIC); 2 were placed in APA accredited internships.

Housing and Day Care: On-campus housing and day care facilities are available.

Employment of Department Graduates:

Master's Degree Graduates: Of those who graduated in the academic year 2000–2001, the following categories and numbers represent the post-graduate activities and employment of master's degree graduates: Enrolled in a psychology doctoral program (7), enrolled in a post-doctoral residency/fellowship (n/a), employed in independent practice (n/a).

Doctoral Degree Graduates: Of those who graduated in the academic year 2000–2001, the following categories and numbers represent the post-graduate activities and employment of doctoral degree graduates: Enrolled in a psychology doctoral program (n/a), enrolled in another graduate/professional program (n/a), enrolled in a post-doctoral residency/fellowship (1), employed in independent practice (3), employed in an academic position at a university (1), employed in an academic position at a 2-year/4-year college (1), employed in other positions at a higher education institution (1), employed in a community mental health/counseling center (1), employed in a hospital/medical center (5).

Additional Information:

Orientation, Objectives, and Emphasis of Department: The goal of the psychology department's doctoral program is to educate scholars and researchers who will contribute to the growth of psychological knowledge whether they work in academic, applied, or policy settings. Within the framework of satisfying the requirements of a major division and a minor, the department encourages students in consultation with their advisors to construct programs individually tailored to their research interests. The psychology department has more than 30 faculty and over 100 graduate students. It has 5 major divisions: biopsychology, clinical, cognitive, community and prevention research, and social and personality. It has a psychology and law minor, a statistics, methods and measurement minor, a predoctoral and postdoctoral Prevention Research Training Program in urban children's mental health, and an interdepartmental specialization in neuroscience. We have close collaborations with the Institute for Juvenile Research, the Institute for Disabilities and Human Development, the School of Public Health, the Center for Urban Educational Research and

Development, Center for Literacy, and the Institute of Government, and Public Affairs. These partnerships provide students and faculties having interest in interdisciplinary research an opportunity to work with scholars from diverse fields.

Special Facilities or Resources: The department is located in the 4-floor Behavioral Sciences Building, a fully equipped facility designed to serve the needs of the behavioral and social sciences. Physical facilities include seminar rooms, animal laboratories, human research labs, clinical observation rooms with one-way observational windows and video-recording and biofeedback equipment, a well-equipped electronics and mechanics shop with an on-staff engineer, a department library, the Office of Applied Psychological Services which coordinates clinical and community interventions, the Office of Social Science Research which provides research support, and faculty-student lounge. The Department maintains its own computer room, in which personal computer workstations connected to a mainframe and stand alone PCs (MS-DOS based and Macintosh) are offered for student use.

Information for Students With Physical Disabilities: UIC is committed to equitable and equivalent treatment of persons with disabilities. Not only is there a legal requirement to treat disabled individuals equitably, but the campus commitment to inclusiveness requires actions that are consonant with the principles of access and equity. An important resource is the Office of Disability Services, which provides support in designing plans to accommodate the needs of persons with disabilities. UIC is the home of the first doctoral program in the nation in disability studies. Students with research interests in disabilities will find a campus environment rich with relevant coursework, intervention and research opportunities concerning disability issues.

Application Information:
Send to: Graduate Admissions, University of Illinois at Chicago, Department of Psychology, MC 285, 1007 W. Harrison Street, Chicago, IL 60607-7137. Students are admitted in the Fall, application deadline January 1. *Fee:* $40. There are no application fee waivers.

Illinois, University of, at Urbana-Champaign
Department of Educational Psychology
College of Education
226 Education Building, 1310 South Sixth Street
Champaign, IL 61820
Telephone: (217) 333-2245
Fax: (217) 244-7620
E-mail: *edpsy@uiuc.edu*
Web: *http://www.ed.uiuc.edu/EDPSY/MAIN/*

Department Established:
1962. Chairperson: Michelle Perry. Number of Faculty: total–full-time 30, part-time 12; women–full-time 14, part-time 12; minority–full-time 2, part-time 3; faculty subject to the Americans with Disabilities Act 1.

Programs and Degrees Offered:
Listed in the following order: Program area, degree type (T if terminal Master's), number awarded 7/00-6/01. CLLIC (Cognition, Learning, Language Instruction and Culture), Counseling

Psychology PhD 8, Development and Socialization PhD 1, Quantitative and Evaluation PhD 3.

APA Accreditation: Counseling PhD: full.

Student Applications/Admissions:
Student Applications
Counseling Psychology PhD—Applications 2001–2002, 47. Total applicants accepted 2001–2002, 14. New applicants enrolled 2001–2002, 6. Total enrolled 2001–2002 full-time, 28. The Median number of years required for completion of a degree are 7. *Development and Socialization PhD*—Applications 2001–2002, 14. Total applicants accepted 2001–2002, 6. New applicants enrolled 2001–2002, 1. Total enrolled 2001–2002 full-time, 10. The Median number of years required for completion of a degree are 4. *Quantitative and Evaluation PhD*—Applications 2001–2002, 13. Total applicants accepted 2001–2002, 11. New applicants enrolled 2001–2002, 4. Total enrolled 2001–2002 full-time, 18. The Median number of years required for completion of a degree are 5.

Admissions Requirements:
Scores: Entries appear in this order: required test or GPA, minimum score (if required), median score of students entering in 2001–2002. Master's Programs: GRE-V 600, 592; GRE-Q 600, 707; GRE-V+Q 1200, 1299; last 2 years GPA 3.5, 3.5. Doctoral Programs: GRE-V 600, 600; GRE-Q 600, 660; GRE-V+Q 1200, 1230; last 2 years GPA 3.5, 3.5 ; psychology GPA no minimum stated; psychology GPA no minimum stated.
Other Criteria: (importance of criteria rated low, medium, or high): GRE/MAT scores medium, research experience high, work experience medium, extracurricular activity medium, clinically related public service medium, GPA medium, letters of recommendation high, interview low, statement of goals and objectives high, compatibility of interest high.

Student Characteristics: The following represents characteristics of students in 2001–2002 in all graduate psychology programs in the department: Female–full-time 101, part-time 2; Male–full-time 55, part-time 2; African American/Black–full-time 3; Hispanic/Latino (a)–full-time 3; Asian/Pacific Islander–full-time 3; American Indian/Alaska Native–full-time 1.

Financial Information/Assistance:
Tuition for Full-Time Study: *Master's:* State residents per academic year $3,227; nonstate residents: per academic year $7,169. *Doctoral:* State residents: per academic year $3,227; nonstate residents: per academic year $7,169.

Financial Assistance:
First Year Students: Teaching assistantships available for first-year. Average amount paid per academic year: $5,550. Average number of hours worked per week: 10. Apply by Varies. Tuition remission given: full. Research assistantships available for first-year. Average amount paid per academic year: $5,550. Average number of hours worked per week: 10. Apply by Varies. Tuition remission given: full. Traineeships available for first-year. Average amount paid per academic year: $5,550. Average number of hours worked per week: 10. Apply by Varies. Tuition remission given: full. Fellowships and scholarships available for first-year. Apply by Varies. Tuition remission given: full.

Advanced Students: Teaching assistantships available for advanced students. Average amount paid per academic year: $6,186. Average number of hours worked per week: 10. Apply by Varies. Tuition remission given: full. Research assistantships available for advanced students. Average amount paid per academic year: $6,186. Average number of hours worked per week: 10. Apply by Varies. Tuition remission given: full. Traineeships available for advanced students. Average amount paid per academic year: $6,186. Average number of hours worked per week: 10. Apply by Varies. Tuition remission given: full. Fellowships and scholarships available for advanced students. Apply by Varies. Tuition remission given: full.

Contact Information: Of all students currently enrolled full-time, 90% benefitted from one or more of the listed financial assistance programs. For information on financial assistance, contact: Admissions Secretary, Department of Educational Psychology, 226 Education, 1310 S. Sixth St., Champaign, IL 61820.

Internships/Practica: The Counseling Division offers of variety of practica and students are placed for practicum work within University-affiliated agencies, such as the Counseling Center, the Career Development and Placement Center, McKinley Health Center, and the Psychological Services Center or in a variety of community agencies such as the Champaign County Mental Health Center, Carle Clinic, Veterans Administration Medical Center, Cunningham Children's Home, and the Illinois State University Counseling Center. Supervision is provided by on-site supervisors and by faculty members. Each doctoral student is required to complete a year long, formal, full-time predoctoral internship at an outside service agency that is approved by the Association of Psychology Internship Centers, or the equivalent. Sites to which students apply for internships include university counseling centers, hospitals, and community mental health agencies across the nation. For those doctoral students for whom a professional internship is required prior to graduation, 3 applied in 2000–2001. Of those who applied, 3 were placed in internships listed by the Association of Psychology Postdoctoral and Internship Programs (APPIC); 3 were placed in APA accredited internships.

Housing and Day Care: On-campus housing and day care facilities are available.

Employment of Department Graduates:
Master's Degree Graduates: Of those who graduated in the academic year 2000–2001, the following categories and numbers represent the post-graduate activities and employment of master's degree graduates: Enrolled in a post-doctoral residency/fellowship (n/a), employed in independent practice (n/a).
Doctoral Degree Graduates: Of those who graduated in the academic year 2000–2001, the following categories and numbers represent the post-graduate activities and employment of doctoral degree graduates: Enrolled in a psychology doctoral program (n/a), enrolled in another graduate/professional program (n/a), employed in an academic position at a university (4), employed in other positions at a higher education institution (3), employed in business or industry (research/consulting) (1), employed in a government agency (professional services) (1), employed in a community mental health/counseling center (2), employed in a hospital/medical center (1), still seeking employment (1).

Additional Information:
Orientation, Objectives, and Emphasis of Department: The Department of Educational Psychology is located within the College of Education. Programs in the department are all at the graduate level and come under the purview of the Graduate College. The Department is divided into four instructional divisions: Counseling Psychology; Development and Socialization Processes (DASP); Quantitative and Evaluative; Research Methodologies (QUERIES); Cognition, Learning, Language, Instruction and Culture (CLLIC). Placement of doctoral graduates from this department includes positions as university/college professors, administrators, research assistants, counselors, psychologists/therapists, and in private and government agencies, and post doctoral fellowships.

Special Facilities or Resources: The Department of Educational Psychology is under the purview of the College of Education which is rated one of the top in the nation. The University of Illinois offers a rich academic environment which includes top-ranked departments: Departments of Psychology, Computer, Science, Anthropology and Speech Communication. There are also strong programs in Cognitive Neuroscience, Artificial Intelligence, Human Development and Family Studies, Women's Studies, Afro-American Studies, and Latin American and Caribbean Studies. Other academic and research facilities available for students and faculty are the second largest university library system in the nation. Computer facilities available include the Educational Psychology Statistical Laboratory, the College of Education Computer Laboratory, and numerous computer sites across campus. Research facilities available for use: Computer-based Education Research Laboratory, Computer-based Eye Movement Laboratory, Institute for Research on Human Development, Model-based Measurement Laboratory, Survey Research Laboratory, Statistical Consulting Services, Teaching Techniques Laboratory, Interview and experimental rooms, equipped with video-and audio-taping, Classrooms for video demonstration, telecommunications, and computer-based education. Research centers on campus include Beckman Institute for Advanced Science and Technology, Bureau of Educational Research, Office of Multicultural and Bilingual Education, Office of International Mathematics Study, Center for the Study of Reading. Among academic libraries in the U.S., this university has the 3rd largest system, ranking only behind Harvard and Yale.

Information for Students With Physical Disabilities: The Division of Rehabilitation-Education Services (DRES) is the designated office of the UIUC that obtains and files disability-related documents, certifies eligibility for services, determines reasonable accommodations, and develops plans for the provision of such accommodations for students with disabilities. Reasonable accommodations are provided to ensure access to all UIUC courses, program, activities, and facilities. The Education Building is handicapped accessible.

Application Information:
Send to: Admissions Secretary, Department of Educational Psychology, 220 Education, 1310 S. Sixth St., Champaign, IL 61820. Students are admitted in the Fall, application deadline January 15; Spring, application deadline October 15; Summer, application deadline January 15. Only CLLIC accepts for Spring or Summer. CTER on-line EDM program accepts for Summer only, deadline February 15. *Fee:* $40. International fee $50.

Illinois, University of, at Urbana-Champaign

Department of Psychology
Psychology Building, 603 East Daniel Street
Champaign, IL 61820
Telephone: (217) 333-2169
Fax: (217) 244-5876
E-mail: *gradstdy@s.psych.uiuc.edu*
Web: *http://www.psych.uiuc.edu*

Department Established:

1893. Head: Edward J. Shoben. Number of Faculty: total–full-time 41, part-time 11; women–full-time 14, part-time 3; minority–full-time 4.

Programs and Degrees Offered:

Listed in the following order: Program area, degree type (T if terminal Master's), number awarded 7/00-6/01. Applied engineering MA (T) 1, applied measurement MA (T) 1, applied personnel MA (T), biological PhD, clinical PhD 7, cognitive PhD 2, developmental PhD 3, quantitative PhD 2, Social-Personality-Organizatio PhD 8, Visual Cog & Human Performance PhD 3.

APA Accreditation: Clinical PhD: full.

Student Applications/Admissions:

Student Applications

Applied engineering MA—Applications 2001–2002, 5. Total applicants accepted 2001–2002, 3. New applicants enrolled 2001–2002, 2. Total enrolled 2001–2002 full-time, 5. Openings 2002–2003, 2. The Median number of years required for completion of a degree are 2. The number of students enrolled full and part-time, who were dismissed or voluntarily withdrew from this program area were 0. *Applied measurement* MA—Applications 2001–2002, 1. Total enrolled 2001–2002 full-time, 1. Openings 2002–2003, 2. The Median number of years required for completion of a degree are 2. The number of students enrolled full and part-time, who were dismissed or voluntarily withdrew from this program area were 0. *Applied personnel* MA—Applications 2001–2002, 7. Total applicants accepted 2001–2002, 2. New applicants enrolled 2001–2002, 1. Total enrolled 2001–2002 full-time, 1. The Median number of years required for completion of a degree are 2. The number of students enrolled full and part-time, who were dismissed or voluntarily withdrew from this program area were 0. *Biological* PhD—Applications 2001–2002, 22. Total applicants accepted 2001–2002, 6. New applicants enrolled 2001–2002, 3. Total enrolled 2001–2002 full-time, 13. Openings 2002–2003, 5. The Median number of years required for completion of a degree are 6. The number of students enrolled full and part-time, who were dismissed or voluntarily withdrew from this program area were 1. *Clinical PhD*—Applications 2001–2002, 200. Total applicants accepted 2001–2002, 16. New applicants enrolled 2001–2002, 6. Total enrolled 2001–2002 full-time, 41. Openings 2002–2003, 8. The Median number of years required for completion of a degree are 6. The number of students enrolled full and part-time, who were dismissed or voluntarily withdrew from this program area were 0. *Cognitive* PhD—Applications 2001–2002, 38. Total applicants accepted 2001–2002, 3. Total enrolled 2001–2002 full-time, 15. Openings 2002–2003, 7. The Median number of years required for

completion of a degree are 6. The number of students enrolled full and part-time, who were dismissed or voluntarily withdrew from this program area were 0. *Developmental PhD*—Applications 2001–2002, 32. Total applicants accepted 2001–2002, 8. New applicants enrolled 2001–2002, 1. Total enrolled 2001–2002 full-time, 14. Openings 2002–2003, 8. The Median number of years required for completion of a degree are 6. The number of students enrolled full and part-time, who were dismissed or voluntarily withdrew from this program area were 0. *Quantitative PhD*—Applications 2001–2002, 12. Total applicants accepted 2001–2002, 5. New applicants enrolled 2001–2002, 2. Total enrolled 2001–2002 full-time, 15. Openings 2002–2003, 6. The Median number of years required for completion of a degree are 6. The number of students enrolled full and part-time, who were dismissed or voluntarily withdrew from this program area were 0. *Social-Personality-Organizatio PhD*—Applications 2001–2002, 131. Total applicants accepted 2001–2002, 27. New applicants enrolled 2001–2002, 8. Total enrolled 2001–2002 full-time, 40. Openings 2002–2003, 15. The Median number of years required for completion of a degree are 6. The number of students enrolled full and part-time, who were dismissed or voluntarily withdrew from this program area were 0. *Visual Cog & Human Performance PhD*—Applications 2001–2002, 13. Total applicants accepted 2001–2002, 7. New applicants enrolled 2001–2002, 2. Total enrolled 2001–2002 full-time, 13. Openings 2002–2003, 10. The Median number of years required for completion of a degree are 6. The number of students enrolled full and part-time, who were dismissed or voluntarily withdrew from this program area were 0.

Admissions Requirements:

Scores: Entries appear in this order: required test or GPA, minimum score (if required), median score of students entering in 2001–2002. Master's Programs: GRE-V no minimum stated, 561; GRE-Q no minimum stated, 678; GRE-Subject(Psych) no minimum stated; last 2 years GPA 3.0, 3.22. Subject test is recommended but not required. GPA above a B average. Doctoral Programs: GRE-V no minimum stated, 612; GRE-Q no minimum stated, 699; GRE-Subject(Psych) no minimum stated, 790; last 2 years GPA 3.0, 3.66; psychology GPA no minimum stated; psychology GPA no minimum stated. Subject test is recommeded but not required.

Other Criteria: (importance of criteria rated low, medium, or high): GRE/MAT scores high, research experience high, work experience medium, clinically related public service high, GPA high, letters of recommendation high, interview high, statement of goals and objectives high.

Student Characteristics: The following represents characteristics of students in 2001–2002 in all graduate psychology programs in the department: Female–full-time 91, part-time 0; Male–full-time 66, part-time 0; African American/Black–full-time 7, part-time 0; Hispanic/Latino (a)–full-time 4, part-time 0; Asian/Pacific Islander–full-time 12, part-time 0; American Indian/Alaska Native–full-time 0, part-time 0; Multi-ethnic–full-time 0, part-time 0; students subject to the Americans with Disabilities Act–full-time 0, part-time 0.

Financial Information/Assistance:

Tuition for Full-Time Study: *Master's:* State residents per academic year $8,943; nonstate residents: per academic year $19,807.

Doctoral: State residents: per academic year $8,943; nonstate residents: per academic year $19,807.

Financial Assistance:

First Year Students: Teaching assistantships available for first-year. Average amount paid per academic year: $13,585. Average number of hours worked per week: 20. Apply by January 1. Tuition remission given: full. Research assistantships available for first-year. Average amount paid per academic year: $13,585. Average number of hours worked per week: 20. Apply by January 1. Tuition remission given: full. Traineeships available for first-year. Average amount paid per academic year: $16,500. Apply by January 1. Tuition remission given: full. Fellowships and scholarships available for first-year. Average amount paid per academic year: $15,000. Apply by January 1. Tuition remission given: full.

Advanced Students: Teaching assistantships available for advanced students. Average amount paid per academic year: $13,585. Average number of hours worked per week: 20. Apply by January 1. Tuition remission given: full. Research assistantships available for advanced students. Average amount paid per academic year: $13,585. Average number of hours worked per week: 20. Apply by January 1. Tuition remission given: full. Traineeships available for advanced students. Average amount paid per academic year: $16,500. Apply by January 1. Tuition remission given: full. Fellowships and scholarships available for advanced students. Average amount paid per academic year: $15,000. Apply by January 1. Tuition remission given: full.

Contact Information: Of all students currently enrolled full-time, 100% benefitted from one or more of the listed financial assistance programs. For information on financial assistance, contact: Department of Psychology, Graduate Student Affairs Office, 603 E. Daniel St., Champaign, IL 61820.

Internships/Practica: Laboratories in Clinical Psychology—Intensive practice in techniques of clinical assessment and behavior modification with emphasis on recent innovations; small sections of the course formed according to the specialized interests of students and staff. For those doctoral students for whom a professional internship is required prior to graduation, 4 applied in 2000–2001. Of those who applied, 3 were placed in internships listed by the Association of Psychology Postdoctoral and Internship Programs (APPIC); 3 were placed in APA accredited internships.

Housing and Day Care: On-campus housing and day care facilities are available.

Employment of Department Graduates:

Master's Degree Graduates: Of those who graduated in the academic year 2000–2001, the following categories and numbers represent the post-graduate activities and employment of master's degree graduates: Enrolled in a post-doctoral residency/fellowship (n/a), employed in independent practice (n/a).

Doctoral Degree Graduates: Of those who graduated in the academic year 2000–2001, the following categories and numbers represent the post-graduate activities and employment of doctoral degree graduates: Enrolled in a psychology doctoral program (n/a), enrolled in another graduate/professional program (n/a).

Additional Information:

Orientation, Objectives, and Emphasis of Department: The department trains students at the doctoral level for basic research in all areas. Students are admitted in one of the seven divisions: biological, cognitive, clinical/community, developmental, quantitative, social-personality-organizational, visual cognition & human performance. Interactions with faculty in other divisions are quite common; interdisciplinary training is encouraged. Applied research training is offered in engineering, measurement, and personnel psychology. There is a strong emphasis on individualized training programs in an apprenticeship model. Each student's program is tailored to his or her research interests. Wide opportunities exist for students to participate in ongoing research programs. Students are encouraged to develop their own programs.

Special Facilities or Resources: The department has extensive laboratory facilities in all areas, including biological psychology. Excellent departmental and university computer facilities are readily available to graduate students. Most faculty laboratories are computerized. The department maintains a computer system that supports text processing, data management, and communication between laboratories and campus computers. There are very advanced facilities for research in all areas, including psychophysiology, cognitive psychology, neurochemistry, and neuroanatomy. A first-rate animal colony is maintained by the department. A departmental video facility allows sophisticated taping of observational data. Facilities for observing and taping group interactions are very advanced. There is an excellent machine shop and a fine electronics shop. The department's library carries most important journals in psychology. Programs are coordinated with other campus departments and institutes, including life sciences, communications, labor, education, and child study.

Information for Students With Physical Disabilities: The University of Illinois Urbana-Champaign campus as well as the housing units are accessible to persons with disabilities. Interested applicants can contact the Division of Rehabilitation Education Services at (217) 333-1970 for information about services available on campus for persons with disabilities (federal—state agency services, physical therapy and functional training, sensory accommodations, etc.).

Application Information:

Send to: Graduate Student Affairs Office, 314 Psychology Building, 603 E. Daniel St., Champaign, IL 61820. Students are admitted in the Fall, application deadline January 1. *Fee:* $40. The fee for International application is $50.

Lewis University
Department of Psychology
One University Parkway
Romeoville, IL 60446
Telephone: (815) 836-5594
Fax: (815) 836-5032
E-mail: *Kearneed@LewisU.edu*
Web: *http://www.lewisu.edu*

Department Established:

1993. Graduate Program Director: Edmund M. Kearney. Number of Faculty: total—full-time 7, part-time 6; women—full-time 3, part-time 3; minority—full-time 2, part-time 2.

Programs and Degrees Offered:
Listed in the following order: Program area, degree type (T if terminal Master's), number awarded 7/00-6/01. Counseling psychology MA (T) 16, guidance counseling MA (T) 12.

Student Applications/Admissions:
Student Applications
Counseling psychology MA—Applications 2001–2002, 25. Total applicants accepted 2001–2002, 20. New applicants enrolled 2001–2002, 15. Total enrolled 2001–2002 full-time, 10, part-time, 45. Openings 2002–2003, 20. The Median number of years required for completion of a degree are 3. *Guidance counseling MA*—Applications 2001–2002, 40. Total applicants accepted 2001–2002, 30. New applicants enrolled 2001–2002, 25. Total enrolled 2001–2002 full-time, 10, part-time, 60. Openings 2002–2003, 25. The Median number of years required for completion of a degree are 3.

Admissions Requirements:
Scores: Entries appear in this order: required test or GPA, minimum score (if required), median score of students entering in 2001–2002. Master's Programs: overall undergraduate GPA no minimum stated, 3.0; last 2 years GPA no minimum stated, 3.0; psychology GPA no minimum stated, 3.0. Doctoral Programs: last 2 years GPA no minimum stated; psychology GPA no minimum stated; psychology GPA no minimum stated.
Other Criteria: (importance of criteria rated low, medium, or high): research experience low, work experience high, extracurricular activity medium, clinically related public service high, GPA high, letters of recommendation medium, interview low, statement of goals and objectives high.

Student Characteristics: The following represents characteristics of students in 2001–2002 in all graduate psychology programs in the department: Female–full-time 5, part-time 110; Male–full-time 0, part-time 20; African American/Black–full-time 0, part-time 10; Hispanic/Latino (a)–full-time 0, part-time 2; Asian/Pacific Islander–full-time 0, part-time 1; American Indian/Alaska Native–full-time 0, part-time 0.

Financial Information/Assistance:
Tuition for Full-Time Study: *Master's:* State residents $480 per credit hour; nonstate residents: $480 per credit hour.

Financial Assistance:
First Year Students: No information provided.
Advanced Students: Research assistantships available for advanced students. Average amount paid per academic year: $0. Average number of hours worked per week: 10. Tuition remission given: partial.
Contact Information: For information on financial assistance, contact: Graduate Program Director.

Internships/Practica: Numerous practica available in community.

Housing and Day Care: No on-campus housing and day care facilities are available.

Employment of Department Graduates:
Master's Degree Graduates: Of those who graduated in the academic year 2000–2001, the following categories and numbers represent the post-graduate activities and employment of master's degree graduates: Enrolled in a post-doctoral residency/fellowship (n/a), employed in independent practice (n/a).
Doctoral Degree Graduates: Of those who graduated in the academic year 2000–2001, the following categories and numbers represent the post-graduate activities and employment of doctoral degree graduates: Enrolled in a psychology doctoral program (n/a), enrolled in another graduate/professional program (n/a).

Additional Information:
Orientation, Objectives, and Emphasis of Department: The program in counseling psychology is oriented toward individuals who have some experience in behavioral, social service, or educational interventions or assessment. It is designed primarily as part-time with courses offered in the evenings and on weekends. The Program has two subspecialty areas: 1. Mental Health counseling; 2. Child and Adolescent Counseling. There is a second program in Guidance Counseling designed for those individuals who already possess a teaching certificate.

Application Information:
Send to: Graduate Program Director, Department of Psychology, Lewis University, One University Parkway, Romeoville, IL 60446. Students are admitted in the Fall; Spring; Summer. Rolling admission. *Fee:* $35. Need based waiver.

Loyola University of Chicago
Department of Leadership, Foundations & Counseling
  Psychology
School of Education
820 N. Michigan Avenue
Chicago, IL 60611
Telephone: (312) 915-6000
E-mail: *evera@luc.edu*
Web: *http://www.luc.edu*

Department Established:
1969. Graduate Program Directors: Elizabeth M. Vera, Steven D. Brown. Number of Faculty: total–full-time 5; women–full-time 3; minority–full-time 3.

APA Accreditation: Counseling PhD: full.

Student Applications/Admissions:
Admissions Requirements:
Scores: Entries appear in this order: required test or GPA, minimum score (if required), median score of students entering in 2001–2002. Master's Programs: GRE-V no minimum stated; GRE-Q no minimum stated; overall undergraduate GPA 3.00. Doctoral Programs: GRE-V no minimum stated, 510; GRE-Q no minimum stated, 590; GRE-Analytical no minimum

stated, 570; GRE-Subject(Psych) no minimum stated, 550; overall undergraduate GPA 3.00, 3.25; last 2 years GPA no minimum stated; psychology GPA no minimum stated; psychology GPA 3.50, 3.93. These scores refer to the Ph.D. program in Counseling Psychology

Other Criteria: (importance of criteria rated low, medium, or high): GRE/MAT scores medium, research experience high, work experience medium, clinically related public service high, GPA high, letters of recommendation high, interview high, statement of goals and objectives high, master's degree required high. These are for the Ph.D. program in Counseling Psychology.

Student Characteristics: The following represents characteristics of students in 2001–2002 in all graduate psychology programs in the department: Female–full-time 24, part-time 0; Male–full-time 17, part-time 0; African American/Black–full-time 8, part-time 0; Hispanic/Latino (a)–full-time 2, part-time 0; Asian/Pacific Islander–full-time 6, part-time 0; American Indian/Alaska Native–full-time 0, part-time 0; Multi-ethnic–full-time 0, students subject to the Americans with Disabilities Act–full-time 0.

Financial Information/Assistance:

Tuition for Full-Time Study: *Master's:* State residents $529 per credit hour; nonstate residents: $529 per credit hour. *Doctoral:* State residents: $529 per credit hour; nonstate residents: $529 per credit hour.

Financial Assistance:

First Year Students: Teaching assistantships available for first-year. Average amount paid per academic year: $10,000. Average number of hours worked per week: 20. Apply by February 1. Tuition remission given: full. Research assistantships available for first-year. Average amount paid per academic year: $10,000. Average number of hours worked per week: 20. Apply by February 1. Tuition remission given: full. Traineeships available for first-year. Average amount paid per academic year: $10,000. Average number of hours worked per week: 20. Apply by February 1. Tuition remission given: full. Fellowships and scholarships available for first-year. Average amount paid per academic year: $10,000. Average number of hours worked per week: 20. Apply by Varies. Tuition remission given: full.

Advanced Students: Teaching assistantships available for advanced students. Average amount paid per academic year: $10,000. Average number of hours worked per week: 20. Apply by February 1. Tuition remission given: full. Research assistantships available for advanced students. Average amount paid per academic year: $10,000. Average number of hours worked per week: 20. Apply by February 1. Tuition remission given: full. Traineeships available for advanced students. Average amount paid per academic year: $10,000. Average number of hours worked per week: 20. Apply by February 1. Tuition remission given: full. Fellowships and scholarships available for advanced students. Average amount paid per academic year: $10,000. Average number of hours worked per week: 20. Apply by Varies. Tuition remission given: full.

Contact Information: Of all students currently enrolled full-time, 90% benefitted from one or more of the listed financial assistance programs. For information on financial assistance, contact: Dr. Elizabeth Vera, Graduate Program Director, evera@luc.edu.

Internships/Practica: Internships and practica are available at many excellent training facilities in the greater Chicago-land area, including university counseling centers, hospitals, VA Centers, and mental health clinics. There are both therapy-oriented and diagnostic/assessment-oriented practica. Most practicum sites serve a diverse clientele. For those doctoral students for whom a professional internship is required prior to graduation, 3 applied in 2000–2001. Of those who applied, 3 were placed in internships listed by the Association of Psychology Postdoctoral and Internship Programs (APPIC); 3 were placed in APA accredited internships.

Housing and Day Care: On-campus housing and day care facilities are available.

Employment of Department Graduates:

Master's Degree Graduates: Of those who graduated in the academic year 2000–2001, the following categories and numbers represent the post-graduate activities and employment of master's degree graduates: Enrolled in a post-doctoral residency/fellowship (n/a), employed in independent practice (n/a).

Doctoral Degree Graduates: Of those who graduated in the academic year 2000–2001, the following categories and numbers represent the post-graduate activities and employment of doctoral degree graduates: Enrolled in a psychology doctoral program (n/a), enrolled in another graduate/professional program (n/a), enrolled in a post-doctoral residency/fellowship (1), employed in an academic position at a university (1), employed in a professional position in a school system (1), employed in a hospital/medical center (1).

Additional Information:

Orientation, Objectives, and Emphasis of Department: The Ph.D. program, accredited by APA, is based on the scientist-practitioner model of graduate education and emphasizes the interdependence of science and practice in aspects of the program. Doctoral students are provided with opportunities to collaborate with faculty in terms of research, prevention/intervention, and teaching activites from the first year of enrollment. Additionally, the doctoral program in counseling psychology offers minors for specialized training, including: applied psychological measurement, career development, marital and family counseling, and multicultural counseling & consultation. Students are required to choose one of these areas for special concentration. Regardless of the field of interest, each student is exposed to the scientist-practitioner model. Graduates are prepared for teaching, research, and professional practice.

Special Facilities or Resources: The school has excellent library and research facilities and computer resources available to students.

Application Information:
Send to: The Graduate School, Loyola University Chicago, 450 Granada Centre, 6525 N. Sheridan Road, Chicago, IL 60626; www.luc.edu.schools/grad. Students are admitted in the Fall, application deadline January 2. The PhD program admits only in the Fall. *Fee:* $40. Contact the Dean of the Graduate School.

Loyola University of Chicago

Department of Psychology
Arts and Sciences
6525 North Sheridan Road
Chicago, IL 60626
Telephone: (773) 508-3001
Fax: (773) 508-8713
E-mail: *icrawfo@luc.edu*
Web: *http://www.luc.edu*

Department Established:

1930. Chairperson: Isiaah Crawford. Number of Faculty: total–full-time 29; women–full-time 12; minority–full-time 3.

Programs and Degrees Offered:

Listed in the following order: Program area, degree type (T if terminal Master's), number awarded 7/00-6/01. Applied social MA 7, clinical PhD 7, developmental PhD 7, perception PhD 2, social PhD 3.

APA Accreditation: Clinical PhD: full.

Student Applications/Admissions:

Student Applications

Applied social MA—Applications 2001–2002, 15. Total applicants accepted 2001–2002, 2. New applicants enrolled 2001–2002, 4. Total enrolled 2001–2002 full-time, 6. Openings 2002–2003, 4. The Median number of years required for completion of a degree are 2. The number of students enrolled full and part-time, who were dismissed or voluntarily withdrew from this program area were 0. *Clinical PhD*—Applications 2001–2002, 179. Total applicants accepted 2001–2002, 15. New applicants enrolled 2001–2002, 7. Total enrolled 2001–2002 full-time, 44. Openings 2002–2003, 8. The Median number of years required for completion of a degree are 6. The number of students enrolled full and part-time, who were dismissed or voluntarily withdrew from this program area were 0. *Developmental PhD*—Applications 2001–2002, 6. Total applicants accepted 2001–2002, 4. New applicants enrolled 2001–2002, 2. Total enrolled 2001–2002 full-time, 12. Openings 2002–2003, 1. The Median number of years required for completion of a degree are 6. The number of students enrolled full and part-time, who were dismissed or voluntarily withdrew from this program area were 0. *Perception PhD*—Applications 2001–2002, 0. Total enrolled 2001–2002 full-time, 3. Openings 2002–2003, 2. The number of students enrolled full and part-time, who were dismissed or voluntarily withdrew from this program area were 0. *Social PhD*—Applications 2001–2002, 55. Total applicants accepted 2001–2002, 15. New applicants enrolled 2001–2002, 6. Total enrolled 2001–2002 full-time, 48. Openings 2002–2003, 5. The Median number of years required for completion of a degree are 5. The number of students enrolled full and part-time, who were dismissed or voluntarily withdrew from this program area were 0.

Admissions Requirements:

Scores: Entries appear in this order: required test or GPA, minimum score (if required), median score of students entering in 2001–2002. Master's Programs: GRE-V 450; GRE-Q 450; GRE-V+Q 900; GRE-Analytical no minimum stated; GRE-

Subject(Psych) 500; overall undergraduate GPA 3.00. These are the scores for the Terminal Master's Program in applied social psychology. Doctoral Programs: GRE-V 520, 600; GRE-Q 520, 670; GRE-V+Q 1040, 1255; GRE-Subject(Psych) 550, 670; overall undergraduate GPA 3.00, 3.70; last 2 years GPA no minimum stated; psychology GPA no minimum stated; psychology GPA no minimum stated.

Other Criteria: (importance of criteria rated low, medium, or high): research experience high, work experience low, extra-curricular activity low, clinically related public service medium, letters of recommendation high, interview high, statement of goals and objectives high.

Student Characteristics: The following represents characteristics of students in 2001–2002 in all graduate psychology programs in the department: Female–full-time 77, part-time 0; Male–full-time 28, part-time 0; African American/Black–full-time 8, part-time 0; Hispanic/Latino (a)–full-time 8, part-time 0; Asian/Pacific Islander–full-time 10, part-time 0; American Indian/Alaska Native–full-time 0, part-time 0; Multi-ethnic–full-time 0, part-time 0; students subject to the Americans with Disabilities Act–full-time 0, part-time 0.

Financial Information/Assistance:

Tuition for Full-Time Study: *Master's:* State residents per academic year $1,269, $529 per credit hour; *Doctoral:* State residents: per academic year $1,269, $529 per credit hour.

Financial Assistance:

First Year Students: Research assistantships available for first-year. Average amount paid per academic year: $10,000. Average number of hours worked per week: 20. Apply by December 15. Tuition remission given: full.

Advanced Students: Teaching assistantships available for advanced students. Average amount paid per academic year: $10,000. Average number of hours worked per week: 20. Apply by March 1. Tuition remission given: full. Research assistantships available for advanced students. Average amount paid per academic year: $10,000. Average number of hours worked per week: 20. Apply by March 1. Tuition remission given: full.

Contact Information: Of all students currently enrolled full-time, 80% benefitted from one or more of the listed financial assistance programs. For information on financial assistance, contact: Graduate School.

Internships/Practica: Externship experiences are available for clinical psychology students through our in-house Training Clinic and Student Counseling Center. In addition, numerous training opportunities are available throughout the Chicago metropolitan area. Students in the doctoral applied social psychology program serve a 1000-hour planning, research, and evaluation internship during their third year, while students in the developmental program complete a 250-hour internship. These positions are usually found in health-related, governmental, and research organizations in the Chicago area. For those doctoral students for whom a professional internship is required prior to graduation, 6 applied in 2000–2001. Of those who applied, 4 were placed in internships listed by the Association of Psychology Postdoctoral and Internship Programs (APPIC); 5 were placed in APA accredited internships.

Housing and Day Care: On-campus housing and day care facilities are available.

Employment of Department Graduates:

Master's Degree Graduates: Of those who graduated in the academic year 2000–2001, the following categories and numbers represent the post-graduate activities and employment of master's degree graduates: Enrolled in a psychology doctoral program (8), enrolled in another graduate/professional program (0), enrolled in a post-doctoral residency/fellowship (n/a), employed in independent practice (n/a), employed in an academic position at a university (0), employed in an academic position at a 2-year/4-year college (0), employed in other positions at a higher education institution (0), employed in a professional position in a school system (0), employed in business or industry (research/consulting) (2), employed in business or industry (management) (0), employed in a government agency (research) (0), employed in a government agency (professional services) (0), employed in a community mental health/counseling center (0), employed in a hospital/medical center (0), still seeking employment (0).

Doctoral Degree Graduates: Of those who graduated in the academic year 2000–2001, the following categories and numbers represent the post-graduate activities and employment of doctoral degree graduates: Enrolled in a psychology doctoral program (n/a), enrolled in another graduate/professional program (n/a), enrolled in a post-doctoral residency/fellowship (5), employed in independent practice (0), employed in an academic position at a university (4), employed in an academic position at a 2-year/4-year college (0), employed in other positions at a higher education institution (0), employed in a professional position in a school system (1), employed in business or industry (research/consulting) (5), employed in business or industry (management) (1), employed in a government agency (research) (0), employed in a government agency (professional services) (0), employed in a community mental health/counseling center (3), employed in a hospital/medical center (3), still seeking employment (0).

Additional Information:

Orientation, Objectives, and Emphasis of Department: Graduate study is organized into four areas: clinical, developmental, perception, and social. All programs offer the PhD; only the social program offers a terminal MA in applied social psychology. The clinical program emphasizes the scientist-practitioner model, with students receiving extensive training in both areas. Students may specialize in work with children or adults. The developmental program provides training for students wishing to pursue the study of human development, particularly among infants, children, and adolescents. Cognition, social, gender role, and personality development are covered. The perception program fosters research on fundamental issues of cognition, perception, and sensory processes. Several faculty members have affiliations with Loyola's Parmly Hearing Institute, an internationally recognized center for basic research in sensory science. The perception program has suspended admission of new students for Academic Year 2002–2003. The social psychology program includes training in both basic and applied social psychology. The emphasis in the applied program is on developing social psychologists who are capable of conducting applied research on the planning, evaluating, and modification of social programs in the areas of law and criminal justice, educational systems, health services, and organizational psychology.

Special Facilities or Resources: Excellent libraries and computer support are available. Departmental facilities include specialized laboratories for audition, vision, and neurophysiology research; a general purpose laboratory for sensory processes; suites of research and observation rooms for clinical research; observation and videotaping rooms and equipment; an extensive psychological test library; a psychophysiology and biofeedback laboratory; and computer facilities.

Application Information:
Send to: Department of Psychology, [Name of Program,] Loyola University Chicago, 6525 N. Sheridan Road, Chicago, IL 60626. Students are admitted in the Fall, application deadline December 15. For the Fall semester the deadlines for each program are as follows: Developmental, February 1; Perception, February 1; Social, February 1; Clinical, December 15. *Fee:* $40.

Northern Illinois University
Department of Psychology
College of Liberal Arts and Sciences
DeKalb, IL 60115-2892
Telephone: (815) 753-0372
Fax: (815) 753-8088
E-mail: *lcalderone@niu.edu*
Web: *http://www.niu.edu/acad/psych.html*

Department Established:
1959. Chairperson: Charles E. Miller. Number of Faculty: total–full-time 28; women–full-time 10; minority–full-time 3.

Programs and Degrees Offered:
Listed in the following order: Program area, degree type (T if terminal Master's), number awarded 7/00-6/01. Clinical PhD 10, Cognitive-Development-School PhD 2.5, Neuroscience and Behavior PhD, Social/I-O PhD 6.

APA Accreditation: Clinical PhD: full.

Student Applications/Admissions:

Student Applications

Clinical PhD—Applications 2001–2002, 111. Total applicants accepted 2001–2002, 23. New applicants enrolled 2001–2002, 8. Total enrolled 2001–2002 full-time, 49, part-time, 2. Openings 2002–2003, 10. *Cognitive-Development-School PhD*—Applications 2001–2002, 35. Total applicants accepted 2001–2002, 10. New applicants enrolled 2001–2002, 6. Total enrolled 2001–2002 full-time, 13, part-time, 4. Openings 2002–2003, 8. *Neuroscience and Behavior PhD*—Applications 2001–2002, 7. Total applicants accepted 2001–2002, 3. New applicants enrolled 2001–2002, 2. Total enrolled 2001–2002 full-time, 6. Openings 2002–2003, 4. *Social/I-O PhD*—Applications 2001–2002, 42. Total applicants accepted 2001–2002, 14. New applicants enrolled 2001–2002, 9. Total enrolled 2001–2002 full-time, 24, part-time, 13. Openings 2002–2003, 6.

Admissions Requirements:

Scores: Entries appear in this order: required test or GPA, minimum score (if required), median score of students entering in 2001–2002. Doctoral Programs: GRE-V+Q+Analytical no minimum stated, 1840; overall undergraduate GPA no minimum stated, 3.59; last 2 years GPA no minimum stated; psychology GPA no minimum stated; psychology GPA no minimum stated, 3.82.

Other Criteria: (importance of criteria rated low, medium, or high): GRE/MAT scores medium, research experience medium, work experience low, extracurricular activity low, clinically related public service low, letters of recommendation high, interview medium, statement of goals and objectives high, grades, GRE high. Clinical and School programs interview students; other programs generally do not.

Student Characteristics: The following represents characteristics of students in 2001–2002 in all graduate psychology programs in the department: Female–full-time 81, part-time 14; Male–full-time 39, part-time 5; African American/Black–full-time 5, part-time 1; Hispanic/Latino (a)–full-time 6, part-time 1; Asian/Pacific Islander–full-time 6, part-time 1; American Indian/Alaska Native–full-time 0, part-time 0.

Financial Information/Assistance:

Tuition for Full-Time Study: *Master's:* State residents per academic year $3,258; nonstate residents: per academic year $6,516. *Doctoral:* State residents: per academic year $3,258; nonstate residents: per academic year $6,516.

Financial Assistance:

First Year Students: Teaching assistantships available for first-year. Average amount paid per academic year: $9,990. Average number of hours worked per week: 20. Tuition remission given: full. Research assistantships available for first-year. Average amount paid per academic year: $9,990. Average number of hours worked per week: 20. Tuition remission given: full. Traineeships available for first-year. Tuition remission given: full. Fellowships and scholarships available for first-year. Tuition remission given: full.

Advanced Students: Teaching assistantships available for advanced students. Average amount paid per academic year: $9,990. Average number of hours worked per week: 20. Tuition remission given: full. Research assistantships available for advanced students. Average amount paid per academic year: $9,990. Average number of hours worked per week: 20. Tuition remission given: full. Traineeships available for advanced students. Tuition remission given: full. Fellowships and scholarships available for advanced students. Tuition remission given: full.

Contact Information: Of all students currently enrolled full-time, 93% benefitted from one or more of the listed financial assistance programs. For information on financial assistance, contact: Student Financial Aid Office; also The Graduate School.

Internships/Practica: Clinical and school psychology internships are required for students in those areas. Clinical externships (equivalent to in-residence assistantships) are available and recommended.

Housing and Day Care: On-campus housing and day care facilities are available.

Employment of Department Graduates:

Master's Degree Graduates: Of those who graduated in the academic year 2000–2001, the following categories and numbers represent the post-graduate activities and employment of master's degree graduates: Enrolled in a post-doctoral residency/fellowship (n/a), employed in independent practice (n/a).

Doctoral Degree Graduates: Of those who graduated in the academic year 2000–2001, the following categories and numbers represent the post-graduate activities and employment of doctoral degree graduates: Enrolled in a psychology doctoral program (n/a), enrolled in another graduate/professional program (n/a).

Additional Information:

Orientation, Objectives, and Emphasis of Department: The PhD program in psychology is designed to prepare graduate students to function in a variety of settings such as academic institutions, which emphasize research and/or teaching, non-academic institutions, which emphasize research on mental health, human factors, or skill acquisition, and various consultative modalities, which emphasize practitioner applications and the delivery of human services. Doctorates in psychology are awarded in four specialty areas: a fully accredited APA program in clinical psychology; cognitive/instructional, developmental, and school psychology (NASP approved); neuroscience and behavior; and social and organizational psychology. Faculty in all areas endorse the value of well-trained researchers and practitioners. Students are equipped to conduct sophisticated theoretically based empirical research and to teach at the graduate or undergraduate level. In addition to academic placements, students can also find suitable employment as applied researchers or service practitioners in a variety of mental health (clinical), educational (instructional, developmental, school), physical health (neuroscience), or business (social and organizational) settings. The overall goal of the graduate program is to produce doctoral graduates who appreciate and are deeply committed to the study of psychological processes and behavior, who are familiar with fundamental knowledge in the field, and who are well-trained in methodology and modern techniques of data analysis.

Special Facilities or Resources: The department has a modern psychology building with offices for faculty, staff, and graduate students; classrooms; shops; a six-story research wing with research equipment, including minicomputers and direct access to the university computer and Internet applications; and a Psychological Services Center for practicum training in clinical, school, organizational, and other applied psychological areas.

Application Information:

Send to: The Graduate School, Northern Illinois University, DeKalb, IL 60115-2864. Students are admitted in the Fall, application deadline March 1; Spring, application deadline October 1; Summer, application deadline March 1. Spring admissions are rare. February 1 deadline for clinical applicants. *Fee:* $30. Fees waived/deferred if applicant was exempt from GRE fees, is NIU employee, or is currently enrolled in graduate program at NIU.

Northwestern University
Department of Psychology
102 Swift Hall, 2029 Sheridan Road
Evanston, IL 60208-2710
Telephone: (847) 491-5190
Fax: (847) 491-7859
E-mail: *medin@northwestern.edu*
Web: *http://www.psych.nwu.edu*

Department Established:
1909. Chairperson: Douglas L. Medin. Number of Faculty: total–full-time 21, part-time 5; women–full-time 6, part-time 3; minority–full-time 3.

Programs and Degrees Offered:
Listed in the following order: Program area, degree type (T if terminal Master's), number awarded 7/00-6/01. Clinical Psychology PhD 3, Cognitive Psychology PhD 2, Personality Psychology PhD 1, Psychobiology PhD 1, Social Psychology PhD 4.

APA Accreditation: Clinical PhD: full.

Student Applications/Admissions:
Student Applications

Clinical Psychology PhD—Applications 2001–2002, 62. Total applicants accepted 2001–2002, 4. New applicants enrolled 2001–2002, 2. Total enrolled 2001–2002 full-time, 14. Openings 2002–2003, 2. The Median number of years required for completion of a degree are 6. The number of students enrolled full and part-time, who were dismissed or voluntarily withdrew from this program area were 1. *Cognitive Psychology PhD*—Applications 2001–2002, 55. Total applicants accepted 2001–2002, 16. New applicants enrolled 2001–2002, 7. Total enrolled 2001–2002 full-time, 15. Openings 2002–2003, 3-4. The Median number of years required for completion of a degree are 5. The number of students enrolled full and part-time, who were dismissed or voluntarily withdrew from this program area were 4. *Personality Psychology PhD*—Applications 2001–2002, 15. Total applicants accepted 2001–2002, 2. Total enrolled 2001–2002 full-time, 1. The Median number of years required for completion of a degree are 5. The number of students enrolled full and part-time, who were dismissed or voluntarily withdrew from this program area were 1. *Psychobiology PhD*—Applications 2001–2002, 14. Total applicants accepted 2001–2002, 4. Total enrolled 2001–2002 full-time, 4. Openings 2002–2003, 2. The Median number of years required for completion of a degree are 5. The number of students enrolled full and part-time, who were dismissed or voluntarily withdrew from this program area were 1. *Social Psychology PhD*—Applications 2001–2002, 53. Total applicants accepted 2001–2002, 4. New applicants enrolled 2001–2002, 4. Total enrolled 2001–2002 full-time, 11. Openings 2002–2003, 1-2. The Median number of years required for completion of a degree are 5. The number of students enrolled full and part-time, who were dismissed or voluntarily withdrew from this program area were 0.

Admissions Requirements:
Scores: Entries appear in this order: required test or GPA, minimum score (if required), median score of students entering in 2001–2002. Doctoral Programs: GRE-V no minimum stated, 590; GRE-Q no minimum stated, 720; GRE-V+Q no minimum stated, 1310; GRE-Analytical no minimum stated, 750; GRE-V+Q+Analytical no minimum stated, 2060; overall undergraduate GPA no minimum stated, 3.69; last 2 years GPA no minimum stated; psychology GPA no minimum stated; psychology GPA no minimum stated.

Other Criteria: (importance of criteria rated low, medium, or high): GRE/MAT scores high, research experience high, GPA high, letters of recommendation medium, statement of goals and objectives medium.

Student Characteristics: The following represents characteristics of students in 2001–2002 in all graduate psychology programs in the department: Female–full-time 8, part-time 0; Male–full-time 5, part-time 0; African American/Black–full-time 0, part-time 0; Hispanic/Latino (a)–full-time 0, part-time 0; Asian/Pacific Islander–full-time 1, part-time 0; American Indian/Alaska Native–full-time 0, part-time 0.

Financial Information/Assistance:
Tuition for Full-Time Study: *Doctoral:* State residents: per academic year $24,840; nonstate residents: per academic year $24,840.

Financial Assistance:
First Year Students: Fellowships and scholarships available for first-year. Average amount paid per academic year: $24,840. Apply by December 31. Tuition remission given: full.

Advanced Students: Teaching assistantships available for advanced students. Average amount paid per academic year: $13,419. Average number of hours worked per week: 10. Tuition remission given: full. Research assistantships available for advanced students. Average amount paid per academic year: $14,418. Tuition remission given: partial. Fellowships and scholarships available for advanced students. Average amount paid per academic year: $12,996. Tuition remission given: full.

Contact Information: Of all students currently enrolled full-time, 100% benefitted from one or more of the listed financial assistance programs. For information on financial assistance, contact: Florence Sales: f-sales@northwestern.edu. Most tuition is remitted for students supported as research assistants. Teaching assistant support numbers are based on 9 month support.

Internships/Practica: A variety of internships in community settings is available. For those doctoral students for whom a professional internship is required prior to graduation, 3 applied in 2000–2001. Of those who applied, 3 were placed in internships listed by the Association of Psychology Postdoctoral and Internship Programs (APPIC); 3 were placed in APA accredited internships.

Housing and Day Care: On-campus housing and day care facilities are available.

Employment of Department Graduates:
Master's Degree Graduates: Of those who graduated in the academic year 2000–2001, the following categories and numbers represent the post-graduate activities and employment of master's degree graduates: Enrolled in a post-doctoral residency/fellowship (n/a), employed in independent practice (n/a).

Doctoral Degree Graduates: Of those who graduated in the academic year 2000–2001, the following categories and numbers represent the post-graduate activities and employment of doctoral degree graduates: Enrolled in a psychology doctoral program (n/a), enrolled in another graduate/professional program (n/a), employed in an academic position at a university (4), employed in other positions at a higher education institution (5), employed in a hospital/medical center (1), still seeking employment (1).

Additional Information:

Orientation, Objectives, and Emphasis of Department: The faculty in each graduate area has designed programs tailored to the needs of students in that area. Whatever a student's field of interest, the department tries to produce doctoral students with a strong research orientation. Administrative barriers between areas are permeable; most faculty members take an active part in the instruction and research programs of more than one interest area. A significant population of postdoctoral fellows enhances the informal professional education of graduate students. In addition, all graduate students are given opportunities for teaching. Teaching is independent of type of financial aid.

Application Information:

Send to: Florence Sales, Graduate Admissions Coordinator, 102 Swift Hall, Dept. of Psychology, Northwestern University, 2029 Sheridan Rd., Evanston, IL 60208-2710; email: f-sales@northwestern.edu. Students are admitted in the Fall, application deadline Dec. 31. *Fee:* $50.

Northwestern University Medical School

Department of Psychiatry and Behavioral Sciences, Division of Psychology
Abbott Hall Rm 1205, 710 N. Lake Shore Drive
Chicago, IL 60611
Telephone: (312) 908-8262
Fax: (312) 908-5070
E-mail: *m-reinecke@northwestern.edu*
Web: *http://www.clinpsych.nwu.edu*

Department Established:

1970. Director: Mark A. Reinecke, Ph.D. Number of Faculty: total–full-time 13, part-time 30; women–full-time 6, part-time 16.

Programs and Degrees Offered:

Listed in the following order: Program area, degree type (T if terminal Master's), number awarded 7/00-6/01. Clinical PhD 6.

APA Accreditation: Clinical PhD: full.

Student Applications/Admissions:

Student Applications

Clinical PhD—Applications 2001–2002, 124. Total applicants accepted 2001–2002, 9. New applicants enrolled 2001–2002, 5. Total enrolled 2001–2002 full-time, 25. Openings 2002–2003, 5. The Median number of years required for completion of a degree are 6. The number of students enrolled full and part-time, who were dismissed or voluntarily withdrew from this program area were 0.

Admissions Requirements:

Scores: Entries appear in this order: required test or GPA, minimum score (if required), median score of students entering in 2001–2002. Doctoral Programs: GRE-V no minimum stated, 600; GRE-Q no minimum stated, 695; GRE-Subject(Psych) no minimum stated, 710; overall undergraduate GPA no minimum stated, 3.5 ; last 2 years GPA no minimum stated; psychology GPA no minimum stated; psychology GPA no minimum stated.

Other Criteria: (importance of criteria rated low, medium, or high): GRE/MAT scores medium, research experience medium, work experience low, extracurricular activity medium, clinically related public service medium, GPA medium, letters of recommendation medium, interview medium, statement of goals and objectives medium.

Student Characteristics: The following represents characteristics of students in 2001–2002 in all graduate psychology programs in the department: Female–full-time 20, part-time 0; Male–full-time 5, part-time 0; African American/Black–full-time 2, part-time 0; Hispanic/Latino (a)–full-time 0, part-time 0; Asian/Pacific Islander–full-time 0, part-time 0; American Indian/Alaska Native–full-time 0, part-time 0; Multi-ethnic–full-time 0, students subject to the Americans with Disabilities Act–full-time 0.

Financial Information/Assistance:

Tuition for Full-Time Study: *Doctoral:* State residents: per academic year $26,526; nonstate residents: per academic year $26,526.

Financial Assistance:

First Year Students: Research assistantships available for first-year. Fellowships and scholarships available for first-year.

Advanced Students: Research assistantships available for advanced students. Fellowships and scholarships available for advanced students.

Contact Information: Of all students currently enrolled full-time, 75% benefitted from one or more of the listed financial assistance programs. For information on financial assistance, contact: Financial Aid Office at Graduate School (847) 491-7266.

Internships/Practica: All practica are located at clinical sites affiliated with Northwestern University Medical School or Northwestern Memorial Hospital. They include a university counseling center, an adult outpatient psychiatry clinic, several partial hospital programs, several neuropsychological sites, and programs at several child/adolescent sites. For those doctoral students for whom a professional internship is required prior to graduation, 5 applied in 2000–2001. Of those who applied, 5 were placed in internships listed by the Association of Psychology Postdoctoral and Internship Programs (APPIC); 5 were placed in APA accredited internships.

Housing and Day Care: No on-campus housing and day care facilities are available.

Employment of Department Graduates:

Master's Degree Graduates: Of those who graduated in the academic year 2000–2001, the following categories and numbers represent the post-graduate activities and employment of master's degree graduates: Enrolled in a post-doctoral residency/fellowship (n/a), employed in independent practice (n/a).

Doctoral Degree Graduates: Of those who graduated in the academic year 2000–2001, the following categories and numbers represent the post-graduate activities and employment of doctoral degree graduates: Enrolled in a psychology doctoral program (n/a), enrolled in another graduate/professional program (n/a), enrolled in a post-doctoral residency/fellowship (2), employed in independent practice (2), employed in a hospital/medical center (1).

Additional Information:

Orientation, Objectives, and Emphasis of Department: The goal of the PhD program is to develop clinical psychologists well-trained in the scientist-practitioner model of the profession. The complete graduate is skilled in both clinical practice and research. During tenure in this five-year program, a student completes a curriculum of required courses, participates in at least two years of clinical practica, apprentices as a research assistant for one year, conducts an originally conceived small research project, acts as a teaching assistant for one year, writes and defends a major paper, completes a clinical internship, and writes a doctoral dissertation. The student's contacts with clinical populations begin during the first year in the program in a variety of treatment contexts staffed by departmental faculty. The division is committed to a training model in which intensive supervision in basic diagnostic, interviewing, and treatment skills acts as a basis for competent functioning in most clinical settings and with most patient populations. The division also offers subspecialties in neuropsychology and health psychology.

Special Facilities or Resources: The PhD program in clinical psychology is an integral part of the hospital complex at Northwestern University Medical School. As a result, students are eligible for training in a wide variety of clinical and research sites including programs with the following special emphases: inpatient, outpatient, day hospital neuropsychology, eating disorders, high-risk infant development, chronic pain clinic, and psychosocial oncology.

Application Information:

Send to: Division of Psychology, Northwestern University Medical School, Abbott Hall 12-1205, 710 North Lake Shore Drive, Chicago, IL 60611. Students are admitted in the Fall, application deadline January 15. *Fee:* $50.

Roosevelt University (2001 data)
School of Psychology
Arts and Sciences
430 South Michigan Avenue
Chicago, IL 60605
Telephone: (312) 341-3750
Fax: (312) 341-6362
E-mail: *erossini@roosevelt.edu*
Web: *http://www.roosevelt.edu*

Department Established:

1945. Director: Edward D. Rossini. Number of Faculty: total–full-time 13, part-time 27; women–full-time 5, part-time 17; minority–full-time 2, part-time 5.

Programs and Degrees Offered:

Listed in the following order: Program area, degree type (T if terminal Master's), number awarded 7/00-6/01. Clinical MA (T) 33, general MA (T) 2, industrial/organizational MA (T) 12.

Student Applications/Admissions:

Student Applications

Clinical MA—Applications 2001–2002, 89. Total applicants accepted 2001–2002, 67. New applicants enrolled 2001–2002, 55. Total enrolled 2001–2002 full-time, 23, part-time, 32. Openings 2002–2003, 50. *General MA*—Applications 2001–2002, 34. Total applicants accepted 2001–2002, 26. New applicants enrolled 2001–2002, 12. Total enrolled 2001–2002 full-time, 6, part-time, 6. Openings 2002–2003, 20. *Industrial/organizational MA*—Applications 2001–2002, 37. Total applicants accepted 2001–2002, 28. New applicants enrolled 2001–2002, 28. Total enrolled 2001–2002 full-time, 12, part-time, 16. Openings 2002–2003, 40.

Admissions Requirements:

Scores: Entries appear in this order: required test or GPA, minimum score (if required), median score of students entering in 2001–2002. Master's Programs: overall undergraduate GPA 2.70, 3.10; last 2 years GPA 2.70, 3.20; psychology GPA 3.00, 3.25. Doctoral Programs: GRE-V no minimum stated; GRE-Q no minimum stated; GRE-V+Q no minimum stated; overall undergraduate GPA 3.00, 3.05; last 2 years GPA 3.00, 3.27; psychology GPA 3.00, 3.35; psychology GPA 3.50, 3.70.

Other Criteria: (importance of criteria rated low, medium, or high): GRE/MAT scores medium, research experience medium, work experience medium, extracurricular activity medium, clinically related public service low, GPA high, letters of recommendation high, interview medium, statement of goals and objectives medium. Ratings shown are for the PsyD program. All these additional criteria have low priority for the master's programs.

Student Characteristics: The following represents characteristics of students in 2001–2002 in all graduate psychology programs in the department: Female–full-time 15, part-time 60; Male–full-time 10, part-time 30; African American/Black–full-time 4, part-time 4; Hispanic/Latino (a)–full-time 2, part-time 2; Asian/Pacific Islander–full-time 2, part-time 1; American Indian/Alaska Native–full-time 0, part-time 0.

Financial Information/Assistance:

Tuition for Full-Time Study: No information provided.

Financial Assistance:

First Year Students: No information provided.
Advanced Students: No information provided.
Contact Information: Of all students currently enrolled full-time, 0% benefitted from one or more of the listed financial assistance programs. For information on financial assistance, contact: Graduate Advisor, School of Psychology.

Internships/Practica: Students in our programs have available over 130 sites in the Chicago area for internships. We have a full-time Practicum Coordinator. We have a 100% placement rate for predoctoral (full-time) internships in the PsyD program. Both I/O and Clinical MA students have ample opportunities for training; I/O students nearly always get paid practicum experience.

For those doctoral students for whom a professional internship is required prior to graduation, 4 applied in 2000–2001. Of those who applied, 1 were placed in internships listed by the Association of Psychology Postdoctoral and Internship Programs (APPIC); 1 were placed in APA accredited internships.

Housing and Day Care: No on-campus housing and day care facilities are available.

Employment of Department Graduates:

Master's Degree Graduates: Of those who graduated in the academic year 2000–2001, the following categories and numbers represent the post-graduate activities and employment of master's degree graduates: Enrolled in a post-doctoral residency/fellowship (n/a), employed in independent practice (n/a).

Doctoral Degree Graduates: Of those who graduated in the academic year 2000–2001, the following categories and numbers represent the post-graduate activities and employment of doctoral degree graduates: Enrolled in a psychology doctoral program (n/a), enrolled in another graduate/professional program (n/a).

Additional Information:

Orientation, Objectives, and Emphasis of Department: Roosevelt University was founded on the principles of social justice and equal educational access for all students. We have a long history of openness and cultural diversity. Our programmatic orientation is not homogeneous and reflects the diversity of contemporary psychology, however the majority of faculty members have a cognitive-behavioral orientation. A primary goal of the School of Psychology is to prepare students to work effectively with diverse cultures in urban/metropolitan settings. Master's degree programs in Psychology have been offered since 1952, and the PsyD program, the first university based clinical PsyD program in Chicago, was added in 1996. The PsyD program is designed to provide a broad-based general background in all facets of clinical practice, in preparation for post-doctoral specialization of the student's choice. There are several programmatic emphases, described below. Three master's degree programs are offered, serving several groups of students. We offer streamlined and personally tailored predoctoral training designed to help qualified students enter PhD and PsyD programs, including our own. Approximately 85 percent of our graduates who have applied to doctoral programs have been accepted. We prepare students for professional master's level employment in mental health and I/O careers. Many of our students are several years beyond college graduation and continue to work full- or part-time while arranging their schedules around evening, daytime, and weekend courses offered at our downtown or suburban campuses. Special attention is given to helping students develop educational and professional programs that fit their career goals.

Special Facilities or Resources: The department has a highly qualified teaching staff who are actively involved in research and clinical practice, supplemented by a large and highly trained adjunct faculty who also are involved in clinical and experimental work. In addition to the extensive Roosevelt library and other facilities, there is access to clinical, research, computer, and library facilities of major Chicago universities, hospitals, and clinics. Volunteer research assistantships are available to qualified students interested in doing publishable research, with in-house computer and audiovisual equipment available. A major resource is the urban location with varied employment, educational, and cultural opportunities. The Roosevelt University Stress Institute offers a Certificate in Stress Management which incorporates a wide range of cognitive-behavioral courses for students and health professionals interested in enhancing their clinical stress management skills. The Institute is dedicated to quality training in group treatment methods, professional applications, and the scientific study of group behavior in a culturally diverse society particularly in psychotherapy and psycho-educational settings.

Application Information:
Send to: Graduate Admissions, Roosevelt Univesity, 430 S. Michigan Avenue, Chicago, IL 60605. Students are admitted in the Fall; Spring, application deadline Dec. 30 (MA); Summer, application deadline May 1 (MA). Fall admission; February 15 PsyD, August 25 MA. *Fee:* $25.

Southern Illinois University at Carbondale
Department of Psychology
Life Science Building II, Room 281
Carbondale, IL 62901
Telephone: (618) 453-3564
Fax: (618) 453-3563
E-mail: *alanvaux@siu.edu*
Web: *http://www.siu.edu/~psyc/default.htm*

Department Established:
1948. Chairperson: Alan Vaux. Number of Faculty: total–full-time 27, part-time 4; women–full-time 10, part-time 4; minority–full-time 1, part-time 1.

Programs and Degrees Offered:
Listed in the following order: Program area, degree type (T if terminal Master's), number awarded 7/00-6/01. Clinical PhD 7, counseling PhD 6, experimental PhD 5.

APA Accreditation: Clinical PhD: full. Counseling PhD: full.

Student Applications/Admissions:
Student Applications

Clinical PhD—Applications 2001–2002, 138. Total applicants accepted 2001–2002, 19. New applicants enrolled 2001–2002, 10. Total enrolled 2001–2002 full-time, 30. Openings 2002–2003, 8. *Counseling PhD*—Applications 2001–2002, 53. Total applicants accepted 2001–2002, 12. New applicants enrolled 2001–2002, 7. Total enrolled 2001–2002 full-time, 26. Openings 2002–2003, 7. *Experimental PhD*—Applications 2001–2002, 18. Total applicants accepted 2001–2002, 11. New applicants enrolled 2001–2002, 7. Total enrolled 2001–2002 full-time, 22. Openings 2002–2003, 7.

Admissions Requirements:
Scores: Entries appear in this order: required test or GPA, minimum score (if required), median score of students entering in 2001–2002. Doctoral Programs: GRE-V no minimum stated, 610; GRE-Q no minimum stated, 690; GRE-V+Q 1200; GRE-Subject(Psych) no minimum stated, 660; overall undergraduate GPA 3.25, 3.76; last 2 years GPA no minimum stated; psychology GPA no minimum stated; psychology GPA no minimum stated.

Other Criteria: (importance of criteria rated low, medium, or high): research experience high, work experience medium, extracurricular activity medium, clinically related public service medium, letters of recommendation high, statement of goals and objectives high. Some variation across programs. Clinical/work experiences relevant to programs are important.

Student Characteristics: The following represents characteristics of students in 2001–2002 in all graduate psychology programs in the department: Female–full-time 54, part-time 26; Male–full-time 20, part-time 9; African American/Black–full-time 10, part-time 3; Hispanic/Latino (a)–full-time 4, part-time 1; Asian/Pacific Islander–full-time 6, part-time 3; American Indian/Alaska Native–full-time 0, part-time 0.

Financial Information/Assistance:

Tuition for Full-Time Study: *Master's:* State residents per academic year $5,447, $121 per credit hour; nonstate residents: per academic year $10,894, $242 per credit hour. *Doctoral:* State residents: per academic year $5,447, $121 per credit hour; nonstate residents: per academic year $10,894, $242 per credit hour.

Financial Assistance:

First Year Students: No information provided.
Advanced Students: No information provided.
Contact Information: No information provided.

Internships/Practica: A variety of practica and field experiences are available at a university Clinical Center, campus Counseling Center, campus Health Service, Applied Research Consultants, and various local mental health centers, hospitals, and human service agencies. For those doctoral students for whom a professional internship is required prior to graduation, 9 applied in 2000–2001. Of those who applied, 8 were placed in internships listed by the Association of Psychology Postdoctoral and Internship Programs (APPIC); 8 were placed in APA accredited internships.

Housing and Day Care: On-campus housing and day care facilities are available.

Employment of Department Graduates:

Master's Degree Graduates: Of those who graduated in the academic year 2000–2001, the following categories and numbers represent the post-graduate activities and employment of master's degree graduates: Enrolled in a post-doctoral residency/fellowship (n/a), employed in independent practice (n/a).

Doctoral Degree Graduates: Of those who graduated in the academic year 2000–2001, the following categories and numbers represent the post-graduate activities and employment of doctoral degree graduates: Enrolled in a psychology doctoral program (n/a), enrolled in another graduate/professional program (n/a).

Additional Information:

Orientation, Objectives, and Emphasis of Department: In all programs the student selects courses from a curriculum required for the major and from a curriculum tailored to the student's own interests. A favorable student-faculty ratio permits close supervision and training assignments committed to the training of psychologists of both depth and breadth through involvement in ongoing research, supervised teaching experience, and service activities in addition to formal coursework. A variety of research,

practica, and training assignments are required as part of the students' training and serve to expose the students to many of the activities in which they will ultimately be engaged after receiving their degrees. In addition to the PhD requirements noted above, the following are necessary for the PhD program: an M.A. and one year of statistics are required for all programs; four courses from four areas other than the major are required for all students; meeting the minimal distributive accreditation requirement of the American Psychological Association.

Special Facilities or Resources: The department is located in a building having extensive laboratory facilities for human and animal research available to all students. Additional facilities include a clinic and a counseling center for practicum and research experiences.

Application Information:

Send to: Psychology Graduate Admissions, SIU-C, Mailcode 6502, Carbondale, IL 62901-6502. Students are admitted in the Fall, application deadline February 1. It is to your advantage, both for admissions and financial support, to have a completed application on file by January 15. *Fee:* $20.

Southern Illinois University Edwardsville

Department of Psychology
Box 1121
Edwardsville, IL 62026-1121
Telephone: (618) 650-2202
Fax: (618) 650-5087
E-mail: *bsulliv@siue.edu*
Web: *http://www.siue.edu/PSYCHOLOGY/grad.htm*

Department Established:

1964. Chairperson: Bryce F. Sullivan. Number of Faculty: total–full-time 16; women–full-time 8.

Programs and Degrees Offered:

Listed in the following order: Program area, degree type (T if terminal Master's), number awarded 7/00-6/01. Clinical-Adult Psychology MA (T) 10, Community-School Psychology, General Psychology MA (T) 4, Industrial Organizational Psy MA (T) 8, School Psychology.

Student Applications/Admissions:

Student Applications

Clinical-Adult Psychology MA—Applications 2001–2002, 18. Total applicants accepted 2001–2002, 10. New applicants enrolled 2001–2002, 6. Total enrolled 2001–2002 full-time, 15. Openings 2002–2003, 10. The number of students enrolled full and part-time, who were dismissed or voluntarily withdrew from this program area were 0. *General Psychology* MA—Applications 2001–2002, 3. Total applicants accepted 2001–2002, 2. Total enrolled 2001–2002 full-time, 2. Openings 2002–2003, 10. *Industrial Organizational Psy* MA—Applications 2001–2002, 24. Total applicants accepted 2001–2002, 10. New applicants enrolled 2001–2002, 8. Total enrolled 2001–2002 full-time, 16. Openings 2002–2003, 10.

Admissions Requirements:

Scores: Entries appear in this order: required test or GPA, minimum score (if required), median score of students entering in 2001–2002. Master's Programs: GRE-V 400, 480; GRE-Q 400, 550; GRE-V+Q 800, 1030; GRE-Subject(Psych) 500, 540; overall undergraduate GPA 3.0, 3.52; last 2 years GPA no minimum stated; psychology GPA 3.0. Doctoral Programs: last 2 years GPA no minimum stated; psychology GPA no minimum stated; psychology GPA no minimum stated.

Other Criteria: (importance of criteria rated low, medium, or high): GRE/MAT scores medium, research experience high, work experience medium, extracurricular activity medium, clinically related public service medium, GPA high, letters of recommendation high, interview high, statement of goals and objectives high.

Student Characteristics: The following represents characteristics of students in 2001–2002 in all graduate psychology programs in the department: Female–full-time 52, part-time 0; Male–full-time 12, part-time 0; African American/Black–full-time 2, part-time 0; Hispanic/Latino (a)–full-time 1, part-time 0; Asian/Pacific Islander–full-time 1, part-time 0; American Indian/Alaska Native–full-time 0, part-time 0; Multi-ethnic–full-time 0, part-time 0; students subject to the Americans with Disabilities Act–full-time 0, part-time 0.

Financial Information/Assistance:

Tuition for Full-Time Study: *Master's:* State residents per academic year $2,712; nonstate residents: per academic year $5,424.

Financial Assistance:

First Year Students: Research assistantships available for first-year. Average amount paid per academic year: $3,352. Average number of hours worked per week: 10. Apply by March 1. Tuition remission given: full. Fellowships and scholarships available for first-year. Average amount paid per academic year: $6,705. Average number of hours worked per week: 0. Apply by February 4. Tuition remission given: full.

Advanced Students: Research assistantships available for advanced students. Average amount paid per academic year: $3,578. Average number of hours worked per week: 10. Apply by March 1. Tuition remission given: full.

Contact Information: Of all students currently enrolled full-time, 80% benefitted from one or more of the listed financial assistance programs. For information on financial assistance, contact: Graduate Records Secretary, Psychology Department, (618) 650-2203.

Internships/Practica: All graduate programs require at least four credit hours of supervised practicum experience in appropriate professional settings. The Specialist Degree Program also requires a 10-hour paid internship.

Housing and Day Care: On-campus housing and day care facilities are available.

Employment of Department Graduates:

Master's Degree Graduates: Of those who graduated in the academic year 2000–2001, the following categories and numbers represent the post-graduate activities and employment of master's degree graduates: Enrolled in a post-doctoral residency/fellowship (n/a), employed in independent practice (n/a).

Doctoral Degree Graduates: Of those who graduated in the academic year 2000–2001, the following categories and numbers represent the post-graduate activities and employment of doctoral degree graduates: Enrolled in a psychology doctoral program (n/a), enrolled in another graduate/professional program (n/a).

Additional Information:

Orientation, Objectives, and Emphasis of Department: The faculty comprises members whose skills span the entire field of psychology — clinical, experimental, social, organizational, school, community, and developmental. On the whole, the department is eclectic in orientation. Students in each specialization are provided with training that is balanced between experimental and applied-clinical orientations.

Special Facilities or Resources: The psychology department facilities house faculty offices, classrooms, and approximately 10,000 square feet of laboratory space. Sophisticated research and instructional equipment is available, including mini- and microcomputers, videotaping equipment, and computer terminals. Special laboratories are available for learning, motivation, physiological, information processing, developmental, clinical, and psychometric activities.

Information for Students With Physical Disabilities: The Coordinator of Disability Support Services in Student Affairs is responsible for the implementation and coordination of many of the programs, activities, and services for persons with disabilities. The Coordinator offers guidance and counseling, referrals to related offices and departments, and assistance in obtaining specialized equipment or supplies, support services, and special accommodations. All persons with disabilities should visit the Disability Support Service Office, located in Peck Building, room 1311, at their earliest convenience to meet the coordinator and discuss available services. Persons may also contact the coordinator by calling (618) 650-3782, voice or Telecommunications Device for the Deaf. Hours are 8:00 am to 4:30 pm on Monday through Friday, 8:00 am to 7:30 pm on Wednesday, or by appointment.

Application Information:
Send to: Graduate Records Secretary, Psychology Department, Box 1121. Students are admitted in the Fall, application deadline March 1. October 15 date Specialist degree only. *Fee:* $30.

Trinity International University (2001 data)
Department of Pastoral Counseling and Psychology
2065 Half Day Road
Deerfield, IL 60015
Telephone: (847) 945-8800
Fax: (847) 317-8141
E-mail: *tedsfac@tiu.edu*
Web: *http://www.tiu.edu*

Department Established:
1964. Chairperson: Stephen P. Greggo. Number of Faculty: total–full-time 4, part-time 4; women–full-time 1, part-time 1.

Programs and Degrees Offered:

Listed in the following order: Program area, degree type (T if terminal Master's), number awarded 7/00-6/01. Counseling ministries MA (T) 4, counseling psychology.

Student Applications/Admissions:

Student Applications

Counseling ministries MA—Applications 2001–2002, 14. Total applicants accepted 2001–2002, 11. New applicants enrolled 2001–2002, 9. Total enrolled 2001–2002 full-time, 5.

Admissions Requirements:

Scores: Entries appear in this order: required test or GPA, minimum score (if required), median score of students entering in 2001–2002. Master's Programs: GRE-V no minimum stated; GRE-Q no minimum stated; GRE-Analytical no minimum stated; GRE-V+Q+Analytical no minimum stated; overall undergraduate GPA 2.5.

Other Criteria: (importance of criteria rated low, medium, or high): work experience medium, extracurricular activity medium, clinically related public service low, letters of recommendation high, statement of goals and objectives high.

Student Characteristics: The following represents characteristics of students in 2001–2002 in all graduate psychology programs in the department: Female–full-time 22, part-time 0; Male–full-time 10, part-time 0; African American/Black–full-time 0, part-time 0; Hispanic/Latino (a)–full-time 0, part-time 1; Asian/Pacific Islander–full-time 2, part-time 0; American Indian/Alaska Native–full-time 0, part-time 0.

Financial Information/Assistance:

Tuition for Full-Time Study: No information provided.

Financial Assistance:

First Year Students: No information provided.
Advanced Students: No information provided.
Contact Information: No information provided.

Internships/Practica: Internship is done in the last year of the program and requires a full year. Students participate 12 to 15 hours per week in field placement. This includes direct client services. Additional time is spent in class and group supervision. Candidacy status and departmental approval are necessary before placement can be sought. Placement is generally in a counseling setting of the student's choice in the surrounding communities.

Housing and Day Care: No on-campus housing and day care facilities are available.

Employment of Department Graduates:

Master's Degree Graduates: Of those who graduated in the academic year 2000–2001, the following categories and numbers represent the post-graduate activities and employment of master's degree graduates: Enrolled in a post-doctoral residency/fellowship (n/a), employed in independent practice (n/a).

Doctoral Degree Graduates: Of those who graduated in the academic year 2000–2001, the following categories and numbers represent the post-graduate activities and employment of doctoral degree graduates: Enrolled in a psychology doctoral program (n/a), enrolled in another graduate/professional program (n/a).

Additional Information:

Orientation, Objectives, and Emphasis of Department: The department works on the assumption that all psychology, including counseling, is built on a set of implicit or clearly stated philosophical assumptions. The department is built on the conviction that Christianity provides the clearest presuppositional foundation on which to build psychology. Courses seek to (a) acquaint students with the methods, research findings, and theories of psychology, especially as they relate to counseling; (b) provide skills training counseling and interpersonal relations; (c) create a concern for the needs of others and an appreciation for the differences between people; (d) assist in the personal development of students so that they will be more competent in their service to others; (e) acquaint students with the areas of conflict between psychology and theology and suggest approaches to the resolution of such conflict; (f) prepare students for state licensure as professional counselors and mental health workers.

Application Information:

Send to: Admissions Office, Trinity International Univ., 2065 Half Day Road, Deerfield, IL 60015. Students are admitted in the Fall, application deadline July 15; Spring, application deadline November 15; Summer, application deadline April 1. *Fee:* $25.

University of Illinois (2001 data)
Community Health
1207 S. Oak Street
Champaign, IL 61820
Telephone: (217) 333-4622
Fax: (217) 244-6784
E-mail: *chrisann@ux1.cso.uiuc.edu*

Student Applications/Admissions:
Admissions Requirements:

Student Characteristics: The following represents characteristics of students in 2001–2002 in all graduate psychology programs in the department: Female–full-time 0, part-time 0; Male–full-time 0, part-time 0; African American/Black–full-time 0, part-time 0; Hispanic/Latino (a)–full-time 0, part-time 0; Asian/Pacific Islander–full-time 0, part-time 0; American Indian/Alaska Native–full-time 0, part-time 0.

Financial Information/Assistance:
Tuition for Full-Time Study: No information provided.

Financial Assistance:
First Year Students: No information provided.
Advanced Students: No information provided.
Contact Information: No information provided.

Internships/Practica: Students in the MS in Rehabilitation Counseling track must take an internship of 700 clinical hours. Students in Administration and Supported Employment tracks will take one 200 hour practicum experience with the option of extending into an internship experience. Many internships are available in the Chicago and Champaign-Urbana area and many of the internships are paid by the facilities in which they are available.

Housing and Day Care: No on-campus housing and day care facilities are available.

Employment of Department Graduates:

Master's Degree Graduates: Of those who graduated in the academic year 2000–2001, the following categories and numbers represent the post-graduate activities and employment of master's degree graduates: Enrolled in a post-doctoral residency/fellowship (n/a), employed in independent practice (n/a).

Doctoral Degree Graduates: Of those who graduated in the academic year 2000–2001, the following categories and numbers represent the post-graduate activities and employment of doctoral degree graduates: Enrolled in a psychology doctoral program (n/a), enrolled in another graduate/professional program (n/a).

Additional Information:

Orientation, Objectives, and Emphasis of Department: The orientation of the program is focused on beginning graduate level training in rehabilitation. The program articulates with an APA fully approved program in Counseling Psychology, within the College of Education, Division of Counseling Psychology. Students who successfully complete the MS in Rehabilitation are encouraged to experience working in the field of rehabilitation before moving on to the doctoral level.

Special Facilities or Resources: The Division of Rehabilitation Education Services was the first student services program established in the United States in 1947 to serve physically disabled college students. The graduate program in rehabilitation is distinguished for its academic excellence, research capabilities, and superlative facilities. Today it remains a leader in educating students with disabilities, in facilitating access through special programs and facilities, and in educating rehabilitation professionals.

Western Illinois University

Department of Psychology
Waggoner Hall
Macomb, IL 61455
Telephone: (309) 298-1593
Fax: (309) 298-2585
E-mail: *mipsy@wiu.edu*
Web: *http://www.wiu.edu/users/mipsy*

Department Established:

1960. Chairperson: James E. Ackil. Number of Faculty: total–full-time 24; women–full-time 10.

Programs and Degrees Offered:

Listed in the following order: Program area, degree type (T if terminal Master's), number awarded 7/00-6/01. Clinical/community mental health, general experimental MA (T) 6, school 5.

Student Applications/Admissions:

Student Applications

General experimental MA—Applications 2001–2002, 26. Total applicants accepted 2001–2002, 15. New applicants enrolled 2001–2002, 10. Total enrolled 2001–2002 full-time, 19, part-time, 3. Openings 2002–2003, 12. The Median number of years required for completion of a degree are 2.

Admissions Requirements:

Scores: Entries appear in this order: required test or GPA, minimum score (if required), median score of students entering in 2001–2002. Master's Programs: GRE-V no minimum stated, 530; GRE-Q no minimum stated, 552; GRE-V+Q no minimum stated, 1082; overall undergraduate GPA no minimum stated, 3.20; last 2 years GPA no minimum stated, 3.30; psychology GPA no minimum stated, 3.30. Doctoral Programs: last 2 years GPA no minimum stated; psychology GPA no minimum stated; psychology GPA no minimum stated.

Other Criteria: (importance of criteria rated low, medium, or high): GRE/MAT scores medium, research experience medium, work experience medium, extracurricular activity low, clinically related public service medium, GPA high, letters of recommendation high, interview low, statement of goals and objectives medium.

Student Characteristics: The following represents characteristics of students in 2001–2002 in all graduate psychology programs in the department: Female–full-time 35, part-time 2; Male–full-time 15, part-time 0; African American/Black–full-time 0, part-time 0; Hispanic/Latino (a)–full-time 0, part-time 0; Asian/Pacific Islander–full-time 1, part-time 1; American Indian/Alaska Native–full-time 0, part-time 0.

Financial Information/Assistance:

Tuition for Full-Time Study: *Master's:* State residents per academic year $1,297, $108 per credit hour; nonstate residents: per academic year $2,595, $216 per credit hour.

Financial Assistance:

First Year Students: Research assistantships available for first-year. Average amount paid per academic year: $5,200. Average number of hours worked per week: 15. Tuition remission given: full.

Advanced Students: Research assistantships available for advanced students. Average amount paid per academic year: $5,200. Average number of hours worked per week: 15. Tuition remission given: full.

Contact Information: Of all students currently enrolled full-time, 80% benefitted from one or more of the listed financial assistance programs. For information on financial assistance, contact: Director, School of Graduate Studies.

Internships/Practica: No information provided.

Housing and Day Care: No on-campus housing and day care facilities are available.

Employment of Department Graduates:

Master's Degree Graduates: Of those who graduated in the academic year 2000–2001, the following categories and numbers represent the post-graduate activities and employment of master's degree graduates: Enrolled in a psychology doctoral program (5), enrolled in a post-doctoral residency/fellowship (n/a), employed in independent practice (n/a), employed in an academic position at a 2-year/4-year college (1), employed in a professional position in a school system (6), employed in a community mental health/counseling center (6).

Doctoral Degree Graduates: Of those who graduated in the academic year 2000–2001, the following categories and numbers represent the post-graduate activities and employment of doctoral

degree graduates: Enrolled in a psychology doctoral program (n/a), enrolled in another graduate/professional program (n/a).

Additional Information:

Orientation, Objectives, and Emphasis of Department: The psychology department offers master's degrees in clinical/community mental health (Clin/CMH), and general experimental psychology, and a Specialist degree in school psychology. Clin/CMH-MS and School-Specialist degrees are three year programs with the third year consisting of a paid internship. The emphasis in the Clin/CMH program is to prepare students to assume professional responsibilities in outpatient mental health settings. Central to the program is the practicum experience offered through the university psychology clinic. Graduates of the Clin/CMH program have found employment in a variety of mental health agencies, with over 90 percent of all graduates currently employed in mental health positions. Students in the general psychology program engage in one to two years of course work in psychology. The opportunity to specialize in industrial/organizational, social, developmental, or experimental psychology is available within the general psychology program. Many students completing the general program have been admitted to PhD programs in psychology. Students in the school psychology program acquire an academic background in psychology and a practical awareness of public school systems. During the first year of the program, students are placed in elementary schools for practical experience, and during their second year, students work in the university psychoeducational clinic. Graduates of the program have had no difficulty finding employment as school psychologists following their internships. Many have also pursued doctoral training.

Special Facilities or Resources: The Department of Psychology is housed in a large modern structure providing facilities for teaching, clinical training, and human and animal research. The department has 55 rooms, including regular classrooms, seminar rooms, observation rooms, and small experimental cubicles. Computers are available throughout the department and campus. The department operates a psychology clinic for community referrals, which aids in clinical training, and a psychoeducational clinic for training in school psychology.

Application Information:
Send to: School of Graduate Studies, Western Illinois University, Macomb, IL 61455. Students are admitted in the Fall, application deadline none.

Wheaton College
Department of Psychology
501 College Avenue
Wheaton, IL 60187-5593
Telephone: (630) 752-5762
Fax: (630) 752-7033
E-mail: carlos.f.pozzi@wheaton.edu
Web: http://www.wheaton.edu

Department Established:
1979. Chairperson: Cynthia Neal Kimball, PhD. Number of Faculty: total–full-time 19, part-time 16; women–full-time 6, part-time 7; minority–full-time 2, part-time 5; faculty subject to the Americans with Disabilities Act 1.

Programs and Degrees Offered:
Listed in the following order: Program area, degree type (T if terminal Master's), number awarded 7/00-6/01. Clinical Psychology PsyD 28.

APA Accreditation: Clinical PsyD: full.

Student Applications/Admissions:

Student Applications

Clinical Psychology PsyD—Applications 2001–2002, 65. Total applicants accepted 2001–2002, 31. New applicants enrolled 2001–2002, 23. Total enrolled 2001–2002 full-time, 90, part-time, 4. Openings 2002–2003, 20. The Median number of years required for completion of a degree are 5. The number of students enrolled full and part-time, who were dismissed or voluntarily withdrew from this program area were 0.

Admissions Requirements:

Scores: Entries appear in this order: required test or GPA, minimum score (if required), median score of students entering in 2001–2002. Master's Programs: GRE-V+Q+Analytical no minimum stated, 1700; overall undergraduate GPA 2.8, 3.6. Doctoral Programs: GRE-V+Q+Analytical no minimum stated, 1630; overall undergraduate GPA 3.0, 3.5 ; last 2 years GPA no minimum stated; psychology GPA no minimum stated; psychology GPA no minimum stated.

Other Criteria: (importance of criteria rated low, medium, or high): GRE/MAT scores medium, research experience medium, work experience medium, extracurricular activity low, clinically related public service medium, GPA medium, letters of recommendation high, interview high, statement of goals and objectives high, Fit to Mission Statement.

Student Characteristics: The following represents characteristics of students in 2001–2002 in all graduate psychology programs in the department: Female–full-time 71, part-time 4; Male–full-time 47, part-time 4; African American/Black–full-time 6, part-time 0; Hispanic/Latino (a)–full-time 7, part-time 0; Asian/Pacific Islander–full-time 16, part-time 0; American Indian/Alaska Native–full-time 0, part-time 0; students subject to the Americans with Disabilities Act–full-time 3.

Financial Information/Assistance:

Tuition for Full-Time Study: *Master's:* State residents per academic year $9,840, $410 per credit hour; nonstate residents: per academic year $9,840, $410 per credit hour. *Doctoral:* State residents: per academic year $16,598, $530 per credit hour; nonstate residents: per academic year $16,598, $530 per credit hour.

Financial Assistance:

First Year Students: Fellowships and scholarships available for first-year. Average amount paid per academic year: $3,000. Apply by N/A.

Advanced Students: Teaching assistantships available for advanced students. Average amount paid per academic year: $5,000. Average number of hours worked per week: 10. Apply by March 15. Fellowships and scholarships available for advanced students. Average amount paid per academic year: $3,000. Apply by N/A.

Contact Information: Of all students currently enrolled full-time, 100% benefitted from one or more of the listed financial assistance programs. For information on financial assistance, contact: Financial Aid Office.

Internships/Practica: The Graduate Psychology Programs have liaisons with over 90 agencies in the Chicago and Suburban Area with facility types ranging from hospitals, clinics, community agencies, residential, and correctional facilities. The MA Program requires 500 on-site hours and the PsyD requires a minimum of 1200 hours. Faculty are involved through professional development groups while students are placed in field assignments. For those doctoral students for whom a professional internship is required prior to graduation, 20 applied in 2000–2001. Of those who applied, 19 were placed in internships listed by the Association of Psychology Postdoctoral and Internship Programs (AP-PIC); 13 were placed in APA accredited internships.

Housing and Day Care: No on-campus housing or day care facilities are available.

Employment of Department Graduates:
Master's Degree Graduates: Of those who graduated in the academic year 2000–2001, the following categories and numbers represent the post-graduate activities and employment of master's degree graduates: Enrolled in a post-doctoral residency/fellowship (n/a), employed in independent practice (n/a).
Doctoral Degree Graduates: Of those who graduated in the academic year 2000–2001, the following categories and numbers represent the post-graduate activities and employment of doctoral degree graduates: Enrolled in a psychology doctoral program (n/a), enrolled in another graduate/professional program (n/a), enrolled in a post-doctoral residency/fellowship (4), employed in independent practice (3), employed in an academic position at a university (1), employed in a government agency (professional services) (1), employed in a community mental health/counseling center (3),

employed in a hospital/medical center (3), still seeking employment (1), other employment position (1).

Additional Information:
Orientation, Objectives, and Emphasis of Department: The doctoral program aims to produce competent scholar-practitioners in clinical psychology who will understand professional practice as service. The primary emphasis of the MA program is the professional preparation of the master's level therapist for employment in clinical settings; a secondary objective is the preparation of selected students for doctoral studies. The departmental orientation is eclectic, with students exposed to the theory, research, and practical clinical skills of the major clinical models in use today. A pre-eminent concern of all faculty is the interface of psychological theory and practice with Christian faith. Thus, students also take coursework in the theory and practice of integrating psychology and Christian faith, and coursework in theology/biblical studies. All students participate in a growth-oriented group therapy experience or an individual therapy experience. The objectives of the department are to produce mature, capable master's and doctoral level clinicians who are well grounded in clinical theory and the essentials of professional practice, and who responsibly and capably relate their Christian faith and professional interests.

Special Facilities or Resources: The PsyD Program has its own computer lab/reading room for research and study. Many students work with faculty research projects. Opportunities exist for professional conference presentations and involvement in international projects.

Application Information:
Send to: Graduate Admissions Office, Wheaton College, 501 College Ave., Wheaton, IL, 60187. Students are admitted in the Fall, application deadline January 1. January deadline PsyD, March deadline MA. *Fee:* $30.

Ball State University

Department of Counseling Psychology and Guidance Services
Teachers College, Room 622
Muncie, IN 47306-0585
Telephone: (765) 285-8040
Fax: (765) 285-2067
E-mail: *sbowman@bsu.edu*
Web: *http://www.bsu.edu*

Department Established:

1967. Chairperson: Sharon L. Bowman. Number of Faculty: total–full-time 11; women–full-time 7; minority–full-time 2; faculty subject to the Americans with Disabilities Act 1.

Programs and Degrees Offered:

Listed in the following order: Program area, degree type (T if terminal Master's), number awarded 7/00-6/01. Counseling MA (T) 36, counseling psychology PhD 7, social MA (T) 3.

APA Accreditation: Counseling PhD: full.

Student Applications/Admissions:

Student Applications

Counseling MA—Applications 2001–2002, 111. Total applicants accepted 2001–2002, 75. New applicants enrolled 2001–2002, 46. Total enrolled 2001–2002 full-time, 63, part-time, 27. Openings 2002–2003, 35. The Median number of years required for completion of a degree are 2. The number of students enrolled full and part-time, who were dismissed or voluntarily withdrew from this program area were 1. *Counseling psychology PhD*—Applications 2001–2002, 44. Total applicants accepted 2001–2002, 15. New applicants enrolled 2001–2002, 9. Total enrolled 2001–2002 full-time, 40, part-time, 11. Openings 2002–2003, 10. The Median number of years required for completion of a degree are 5. *Social MA*—Applications 2001–2002, 20. Total applicants accepted 2001–2002, 11. New applicants enrolled 2001–2002, 6. Total enrolled 2001–2002 full-time, 12, part-time, 5. Openings 2002–2003, 15. The Median number of years required for completion of a degree are 2.

Admissions Requirements:

Scores: Entries appear in this order: required test or GPA, minimum score (if required), median score of students entering in 2001–2002. Master's Programs: GRE-V+Q no minimum stated, 983; overall undergraduate GPA 2.75, 3.33; psychology GPA 3.00. Doctoral Programs: GRE-V+Q 1000, 980; GRE-Subject(Psych) no minimum stated; overall undergraduate GPA 3.20, 3.89; last 2 years GPA no minimum stated; psychology GPA no minimum stated; psychology GPA 3.20, 3.92.
Other Criteria: (importance of criteria rated low, medium, or high): GRE/MAT scores high, research experience high, work experience high, extracurricular activity medium, clinically related public service medium, GPA high, letters of recommendation high, interview medium, statement of goals and objec-

tives high, multicultural experience high. Interview is a requirement of the Doctoral Program, not the Master's programs.

Student Characteristics: The following represents characteristics of students in 2001–2002 in all graduate psychology programs in the department: Female–full-time 100, part-time 10; Male–full-time 45, part-time 5; African American/Black–full-time 7, part-time 0; Hispanic/Latino (a)–full-time 3, part-time 0; Asian/Pacific Islander–full-time 5, part-time 0; American Indian/Alaska Native–full-time 1, part-time 0; students subject to the Americans with Disabilities Act–full-time 3.

Financial Information/Assistance:

Tuition for Full-Time Study: *Master's:* State residents per academic year $1,590; nonstate residents: per academic year $4,085. *Doctoral:* State residents: per academic year $1,590; nonstate residents: per academic year $4,085.

Financial Assistance:

First Year Students: Teaching assistantships available for first-year. Average amount paid per academic year: $8,700. Average number of hours worked per week: 20. Apply by February 1. Tuition remission given: full. Research assistantships available for first-year. Average amount paid per academic year: $8,700. Average number of hours worked per week: 20. Apply by February 1. Tuition remission given: full. Fellowships and scholarships available for first-year. Average amount paid per academic year: $12,000. Average number of hours worked per week: 0. Apply by February 1. Tuition remission given: full.

Advanced Students: Teaching assistantships available for advanced students. Average amount paid per academic year: $8,700. Average number of hours worked per week: 20. Apply by March 1. Tuition remission given: full. Average number of hours worked per week: 20. Tuition remission given: full. Traineeships available for advanced students. Average amount paid per academic year: $8,700. Apply by March 1. Fellowships and scholarships available for advanced students. Average amount paid per academic year: $12,000. Average number of hours worked per week: 0. Apply by March 1. Tuition remission given: full.

Contact Information: Of all students currently enrolled full-time, 85% benefitted from one or more of the listed financial assistance programs. For information on financial assistance, contact: Department of Scholarships and Financial Aid @ 765/285-5600.

Internships/Practica: The department operates a practicum clinic that serves the surrounding community on a low-cost basis. All counseling master's students and doctoral students are required to complete at least one practicum in this clinic. Other practicum opportunities are available at the university counseling center, a local elementary school, and the nearby medical hospital. Master's students also are required to complete an internship prior to graduation. The Internship Director maintains a listing of available sites and assists students in identifying and securing such a site. Most of these sites are unpaid, although a few are paying sites. Doctoral students typically seek APA-approved pre-doctoral internship sites. There is one such site on campus, in the university's counseling center. Although that site does not guarantee a slot to students from this program, usually one student a year is placed there. For those doctoral students for whom a professional internship is required prior to graduation, 13 applied in 2000–2001. Of those who applied, 11 were placed in internships listed by the Association of Psychology Postdoctoral and Internship Programs (APPIC); 11 were placed in APA accredited internships.

Housing and Day Care: On-campus housing and day care facilities are available.

Employment of Department Graduates:

Master's Degree Graduates: Of those who graduated in the academic year 2000–2001, the following categories and numbers represent the post-graduate activities and employment of master's degree graduates: Enrolled in a psychology doctoral program (20), enrolled in another graduate/professional program (5), enrolled in a post-doctoral residency/fellowship (n/a), employed in independent practice (n/a), employed in an academic position at a university (0), employed in an academic position at a 2-year/4-year college (0), employed in other positions at a higher education institution (7), employed in a professional position in a school system (10), employed in business or industry (research/consulting) (0), employed in business or industry (management) (0), employed in a government agency (research) (0), employed in a government agency (professional services) (5), employed in a community mental health/counseling center (3), employed in a hospital/medical center (3), other employment position (3).

Doctoral Degree Graduates: Of those who graduated in the academic year 2000–2001, the following categories and numbers represent the post-graduate activities and employment of doctoral degree graduates: Enrolled in a psychology doctoral program (n/a), enrolled in another graduate/professional program (n/a), enrolled in a post-doctoral residency/fellowship (2), employed in independent practice (2), employed in an academic position at a university (1), employed in an academic position at a 2-year/4-year college (0), employed in other positions at a higher education institution (2), employed in a professional position in a school system (0), employed in business or industry (research/consulting) (0), employed in business or industry (management) (0), employed in a government agency (research) (0), employed in a government agency (professional services) (0), employed in a community mental health/counseling center (1), employed in a hospital/medical center (1), still seeking employment (0), other employment position (0).

Additional Information:

Orientation, Objectives, and Emphasis of Department: The objective of the master's counseling programs is to prepare persons to be effective counselors by providing students with a common professional core of courses and experiences. The faculty is committed to keeping abreast of trends, skills, and knowledge and to modifying the program to prepare students for their profession. Students will be able to practice in a variety of settings using therapeutic, preventive, or developmental counseling approaches. The counseling programs also prepare students for doctoral study in counseling psychology. The program goals are to develop an atmosphere conducive to inquiry, creativity, and learning and to the discovery of new knowledge through research, counseling, and interactive involvement between students and faculty. The master's program in social psychology provides a conceptual background for those pursuing careers in education, counseling, crimi-

nology, personnel work, etc. and prepares students for entry into doctoral programs in social psychology. The doctoral program is designed to broaden students' knowledge beyond the master's degree. The rigorous program includes a sound theoretical basis, a substantial experiential component, a research component, and a variety of assistantship assignments. A basic core of courses stresses competence in the social, psychological, biological, cognitive, and affective bases of behavior. The counseling psychology PhD program is structured within a scientist-professional model of training.

Special Facilities or Resources: Departmental instructional and research facilities are exceptional. The facilities of the department occupy the sixth floor of the Teachers College building and include ten practicum rooms, an observation corridor, several group observation rooms, and computer access. Most of these facilities are linked to a control room for use of audio and video media. The computer terminals are connected to the university VAX computer cluster. The department operates an outpatient counseling clinic that serves as the training facility for all counseling graduate students. The clinic serves clients from Muncie and surrounding communities as well as Ball State faculty/staff. The university operates a separate state-of-the-art counseling center that serves as a training site for a select number of graduate students from the department.

Information for Students With Physical Disabilities: Ball State University and the Department of Counseling Psychology and Guidance Services are committed to providing reasonable accommodations to students with disabilities. Several counseling/observation rooms in the Practicum Clinic are adapted for wheelchair accessibility. The department presently maintains a computer with a large monitor, along with a scanner, designated for use by graduate students with visual disabilities. The Office of Disabled Student Services can assist students in identifying a note-taker or a signer, or locating other resources as deemed necessary. Several facilities on campus offer accessible computers.

Application Information:
Send to: Department of Counseling Psychology, Guidance Services, Ball State University, Muncie, IN 47306. Students are admitted in the Winter, application deadline February 1; Summer, application deadline June 15. Counseling (Rehabilitation track) has rolling admissions, so students may apply throughout the year. The summer deadline applies only to the master's programs. *Fee:* $25 for BSU alumni; $35 for those who have not received a degree from Ball State University.

Ball State University
Department of Educational Psychology
Teachers College
Muncie, IN 47306
Telephone: (765) 285-8500
Fax: (765) 285-3653
E-mail: *jhall2@bsu.edu*
Web: *http://www.bsu.edu/teachers/departments/edpsy*

Department Established:
1967. Chairperson: Dan Lapsley. Number of Faculty: total–full-time 16, part-time 15; women–full-time 8, part-time 6; minority–full-time 2.

Programs and Degrees Offered:
Listed in the following order: Program area, degree type (T if terminal Master's), number awarded 7/00-6/01. Educational psychology MA (T) 2, school PhD 10, School Psychology MA 10, School Psychology EdS 3.

APA Accreditation: School PhD: full.

Student Applications/Admissions:
Student Applications
Educational psychology MA—Applications 2001–2002, 7. Total applicants accepted 2001–2002, 3. New applicants enrolled 2001–2002, 3. Total enrolled 2001–2002 full-time, 5. *School PhD*—Applications 2001–2002, 60. Total applicants accepted 2001–2002, 15. New applicants enrolled 2001–2002, 10. Total enrolled 2001–2002 full-time, 38, part-time, 9. Openings 2002–2003, 10. The Median number of years required for completion of a degree are 5. *School Psychology 2* MA—Applications 2001–2002, 70. Total applicants accepted 2001–2002, 10. New applicants enrolled 2001–2002, 10. Total enrolled 2001–2002 full-time, 10. Openings 2002–2003, 10. The Median number of years required for completion of a degree is 1. The number of students enrolled full and part-time, who were dismissed or voluntarily withdrew from this program area were 0. *School Psychology 3 EdS*—Applications 2001–2002, 10. Total applicants accepted 2001–2002, 5. New applicants enrolled 2001–2002, 5. Total enrolled 2001–2002 full-time, 5. Openings 2002–2003, 6. The Median number of years required for completion of a degree are 3. The number of students enrolled full and part-time, who were dismissed or voluntarily withdrew from this program area were 0.

Admissions Requirements:
Scores: Entries appear in this order: required test or GPA, minimum score (if required), median score of students entering in 2001–2002. Master's Programs: GRE-V no minimum stated, 480; GRE-Q no minimum stated, 560; GRE-V+Q 1000; GRE-Analytical no minimum stated; overall undergraduate GPA 2.8, 3.4. Doctoral Programs: GRE-V no minimum stated, 555; GRE-Q no minimum stated, 600; GRE-V+Q 1000, 1150; last 2 years GPA no minimum stated; psychology GPA no minimum stated; psychology GPA 3.2.
Other Criteria: (importance of criteria rated low, medium, or high): GRE/MAT scores medium, research experience medium, work experience medium, extracurricular activity medium, clinically related public service high, GPA medium, letters of recommendation high, statement of goals and objectives medium.

Student Characteristics: The following represents characteristics of students in 2001–2002 in all graduate psychology programs in the department: Female–full-time 18, part-time 0; Male–full-time 6, part-time 0; African American/Black–full-time 0, part-time 0; Hispanic/Latino (a)–full-time 1, part-time 0; Asian/Pacific Islander–full-time 0, part-time 0; American Indian/Alaska Native–full-time 0, part-time 0.

Financial Information/Assistance:
Tuition for Full-Time Study: *Master's:* State residents per academic year $3,924; nonstate residents: per academic year $10,800, *Doctoral:* State residents: per academic year $3,924; nonstate residents: per academic year $10,800.

Financial Assistance:
First Year Students: Teaching assistantships available for first-year. Average number of hours worked per week: 20. Apply by Feb 15. Tuition remission given: full. Research assistantships available for first-year. Average number of hours worked per week: 20. Apply by Feb 15. Tuition remission given: full. Fellowships and scholarships available for first-year. Average number of hours worked per week: 0. Apply by Feb 15. Tuition remission given: full.
Advanced Students: Teaching assistantships available for advanced students. Average number of hours worked per week: 20. Apply by Feb 15. Tuition remission given: full. Research assistantships available for advanced students. Average number of hours worked per week: 20. Apply by Feb 15. Tuition remission given: full. Fellowships and scholarships available for advanced students. Average number of hours worked per week: 0. Apply by Feb 15. Tuition remission given: full.
Contact Information: Of all students currently enrolled full-time, 100% benefitted from one or more of the listed financial assistance programs.

Internships/Practica: Students are expected to be involved in practicum experiences from very early in their programs and to continue such experiences until they enroll in internships. (500 clock hours in practicum are expected.) A school-based internship of one academic year is required of MA/EdS students.

Housing and Day Care: No on-campus housing and day care facilities are available.

Employment of Department Graduates:
Master's Degree Graduates: Of those who graduated in the academic year 2000–2001, the following categories and numbers represent the post-graduate activities and employment of master's degree graduates: Enrolled in a post-doctoral residency/fellowship (n/a), employed in independent practice (n/a).
Doctoral Degree Graduates: Of those who graduated in the academic year 2000–2001, the following categories and numbers represent the post-graduate activities and employment of doctoral degree graduates: Enrolled in a psychology doctoral program (n/a), enrolled in another graduate/professional program (n/a).

Additional Information:
Orientation, Objectives, and Emphasis of Department: The mission of the PhD School Psychology Program is to train school psychologists in the scientist-practitioner model. As social scientists they participate in educational program planning and policy formation. As practitioners they render diagnostic and remedial services and educational consultation. In addition students are trained in a specialty area. Among these include neuropsychology, counseling, and developmental psychology. Doctoral students are encouraged to become involved in on-going research with faculty members. The MA/EdS program is designed to train students for the professional practice of School Psychology, and to meet licensure requirements of Indiana and most states. The MA in Educational Psychology provides specialization options in human development, gifted and talented studies, and educational technology. Other specialization options can be tailored to meet the needs and interests of individual students.

Special Facilities or Resources: The department has an on-campus school psychology clinic, a computer laboratory, videotaping facilities, and adequate research facilities. A neuropsychology laboratory is available for doctoral students pursuing a cognate in neuropsychology.

Application Information:
Send to: Educational Psychology, TC 524, Ball State University, Muncie, IN 47306. Students are admitted in the Spring, application deadline February 15. *Fee:* $25.

Ball State University
Department of Psychological Science
Muncie, IN 47306-0520
Telephone: (765) 285-1690
Fax: (765) 285-8980
E-mail: *00dvperkins@bsu.edu*
Web: *http://www.bsu.edu/provost/graduate/psysc*

Department Established:
1968. Chairperson: David Perkins. Number of Faculty: total–full-time 21, part-time 4; women–full-time 7, part-time 2.

Programs and Degrees Offered:
Listed in the following order: Program area, degree type (T if terminal Master's), number awarded 7/00-6/01. Clinical MA (T) 10, cognitive and social processes MA (T) 3.

Student Applications/Admissions:
Student Applications
Clinical MA—Applications 2001–2002, 50. Total applicants accepted 2001–2002, 12. New applicants enrolled 2001–2002, 12. Total enrolled 2001–2002 full-time, 22. Openings 2002–2003, 12. *Cognitive and social processes MA*—Applications 2001–2002, 15. Total applicants accepted 2001–2002, 5. New applicants enrolled 2001–2002, 4. Total enrolled 2001–2002 full-time, 6. Openings 2002–2003, 8.

Admissions Requirements:
Scores: Entries appear in this order: required test or GPA, minimum score (if required), median score of students entering in 2001–2002. Master's Programs: GRE-V no minimum stated, 490; GRE-Q no minimum stated, 530; GRE-Analytical no minimum stated, 610; overall undergraduate GPA no minimum stated, 3.53; last 2 years GPA no minimum stated, 3.71; psychology GPA no minimum stated, 3.85. Doctoral Programs: last 2 years GPA no minimum stated; psychology GPA no minimum stated; psychology GPA no minimum stated.
Other Criteria: (importance of criteria rated low, medium, or high): GRE/MAT scores high, research experience high, work experience medium, extracurricular activity medium, clinically related public service medium, GPA high, letters of recommendation high, statement of goals and objectives high. Clinical service not important for Cognitive and Social Processes program.

Student Characteristics: The following represents characteristics of students in 2001–2002 in all graduate psychology programs in the department: Female–full-time 19, part-time 0; Male–full-time 8, part-time 0; African American/Black–full-time 2, part-time 0; Hispanic/Latino (a)–full-time 1, part-time 0; Asian/Pacific Is-lander–full-time 1, part-time 0; American Indian/Alaska Native–full-time 0, part-time 0.

Financial Information/Assistance:
Tuition for Full-Time Study: No information provided.

Financial Assistance:
First Year Students: Teaching assistantships available for first-year. Average amount paid per academic year: $6,733. Average number of hours worked per week: 20. Apply by March 1. Tuition remission given: partial. Research assistantships available for first-year. Average amount paid per academic year: $6,733. Average number of hours worked per week: 20. Apply by March 1. Tuition remission given: partial.
Advanced Students: Teaching assistantships available for advanced students. Average amount paid per academic year: $6,733. Average number of hours worked per week: 20. Apply by March 1. Tuition remission given: partial. Research assistantships available for advanced students. Average amount paid per academic year: $6,733. Average number of hours worked per week: 20. Apply by March 1. Tuition remission given: partial.
Contact Information: No information provided.

Internships/Practica: Practica are available at the University Counseling Center, Community Mental Health Centers, Youth Opportunity Center, and a V.A. hospital.

Housing and Day Care: No on-campus housing and day care facilities are available.

Employment of Department Graduates:
Master's Degree Graduates: Of those who graduated in the academic year 2000–2001, the following categories and numbers represent the post-graduate activities and employment of master's degree graduates: Enrolled in a post-doctoral residency/fellowship (n/a), employed in independent practice (n/a).
Doctoral Degree Graduates: Of those who graduated in the academic year 2000–2001, the following categories and numbers represent the post-graduate activities and employment of doctoral degree graduates: Enrolled in a psychology doctoral program (n/a), enrolled in another graduate/professional program (n/a).

Additional Information:
Orientation, Objectives, and Emphasis of Department: The department functions as an arts and sciences psychology department and offers courses in the core content areas of the discipline along with more specialized clinical courses. The faculty are diverse in their backgrounds: approximately seven have experimental backgrounds, and the remainder for the most part have more specialized backgrounds in applied fields such as clinical, counseling, industrial, and neuropsychology. Among the clinical faculty, cognitive behavioral and traditional approaches are present. The department strives to serve both those students seeking employment upon completion of the master's degree and those seeking admission to doctoral level programs.

Special Facilities or Resources: Students have access to university and departmental computers. The department maintains space for faculty and student research. For clinical majors, various cooperative agencies are available for practicum placement.

Information for Students With Physical Disabilities: Students who need special services may contact the Office of Disabled Student Development, (765)285-5293.

Application Information:
Send to: Kerri Pickel, PhD, Director of Graduate Studies, Department of Psychological Science, Ball State University, Muncie, IN 47306-0520. Students are admitted in the Fall, application deadline March 1. For cognitive and social processes program, 6 weeks prior to semester. *Fee:* $35.

Indiana State University
Department of Counseling, Counseling Psychology Program
School of Education 1518
Terre Haute, IN 47809
Telephone: (812) 237-2832
Fax: (812) 237-2729
E-mail: *eglande@befac.indstate.edu*
Web: *http://counseling.indstate.edu/dcp*

Department Established:
1968. Chairperson: Michele C. Boyer. Number of Faculty: total–full-time 8; women–full-time 2; minority–full-time 1.

Programs and Degrees Offered:
Listed in the following order: Program area, degree type (T if terminal Master's), number awarded 7/00-6/01. Counseling PhD 8.

APA Accreditation: Counseling PhD: full.

Student Applications/Admissions:
Student Applications
Counseling PhD—Applications 2001–2002, 23. Total applicants accepted 2001–2002, 12. New applicants enrolled 2001–2002, 7. Total enrolled 2001–2002 full-time, 27, part-time, 5. Openings 2002–2003, 8. The Median number of years required for completion of a degree are 4. The number of students enrolled full and part-time, who were dismissed or voluntarily withdrew from this program area were 0.

Admissions Requirements:
Scores: Entries appear in this order: required test or GPA, minimum score (if required), median score of students entering in 2001–2002. Master's Programs: GRE-Analytical no minimum stated; overall undergraduate GPA 2.75. Doctoral Programs: GRE-V no minimum stated, 490; GRE-Q no minimum stated, 510; GRE-V+Q no minimum stated, 1000; GRE-Analytical no minimum stated, 510; GRE-V+Q+Analytical no minimum stated, 1510; overall undergraduate GPA no minimum stated, 3.75; last 2 years GPA no minimum stated; psychology GPA no minimum stated; psychology GPA no minimum stated, 3.85.
Other Criteria: (importance of criteria rated low, medium, or high): GRE/MAT scores high, research experience medium, work experience high, extracurricular activity medium, clinically related public service medium, GPA high, letters of recommendation high, interview high, statement of goals and objectives high.

Student Characteristics: The following represents characteristics of students in 2001–2002 in all graduate psychology programs in the department: Female–full-time 18, part-time 4; Male–full-time 9, part-time 11; African American/Black–full-time 1, part-time 2; Hispanic/Latino (a)–full-time 1, part-time 0; Asian/Pacific Islander–full-time 0, part-time 0; American Indian/Alaska Native–full-time 0, part-time 0.

Financial Information/Assistance:
Tuition for Full-Time Study: *Master's:* State residents per academic year $2,142, $102 per credit hour; nonstate residents: per academic year $6,489, $309 per credit hour. *Doctoral:* State residents: per academic year $2,448, $102 per credit hour; nonstate residents: per academic year $7,416, $309 per credit hour.

Financial Assistance:
First Year Students: Teaching assistantships available for first-year. Average amount paid per academic year: $5,000. Average number of hours worked per week: 15. Apply by March 1. Tuition remission given: partial. Research assistantships available for first-year. Average amount paid per academic year: $5,000. Average number of hours worked per week: 15. Apply by March 1. Tuition remission given: partial. Fellowships and scholarships available for first-year. Average amount paid per academic year: $5,000. Average number of hours worked per week: 15. Apply by March 1. Tuition remission given: partial.
Advanced Students: Teaching assistantships available for advanced students. Average amount paid per academic year: $5,000. Average number of hours worked per week: 15. Apply by March 1. Tuition remission given: partial. Research assistantships available for advanced students. Average amount paid per academic year: $5,000. Average number of hours worked per week: 15. Apply by March 1. Tuition remission given: partial. Fellowships and scholarships available for advanced students. Average amount paid per academic year: $5,000. Average number of hours worked per week: 15. Apply by March 1. Tuition remission given: partial.
Contact Information: Of all students currently enrolled full-time, 80% benefitted from one or more of the listed financial assistance programs. For information on financial assistance, contact: Student Financial Aid, Indiana State University, Terre Haute, IN 47809.

Internships/Practica: Doctoral practica are available on campus (Student Counseling Center) and in a variety of community settings (CMHC, Schools, Hospitals, Prisons, VAMC, Primary Care Medical Settings), Residential Treatment facilities, and community college counseling centers. For those doctoral students for whom a professional internship is required prior to graduation, 8 applied in 2000–2001. Of those who applied, 8 were placed in internships listed by the Association of Psychology Postdoctoral and Internship Programs (APPIC); 8 were placed in APA accredited internships.

Housing and Day Care: On-campus housing and day care facilities are available.

Employment of Department Graduates:
Master's Degree Graduates: Of those who graduated in the academic year 2000–2001, the following categories and numbers represent the post-graduate activities and employment of master's

degree graduates: Enrolled in a post-doctoral residency/fellowship (n/a), employed in independent practice (n/a).

Doctoral Degree Graduates: Of those who graduated in the academic year 2000–2001, the following categories and numbers represent the post-graduate activities and employment of doctoral degree graduates: Enrolled in a psychology doctoral program (n/a), enrolled in another graduate/professional program (n/a), enrolled in a post-doctoral residency/fellowship (3), employed in independent practice (1), employed in an academic position at a university (1), employed in a government agency (professional services) (2), employed in a community mental health/counseling center (1).

Additional Information:

Orientation, Objectives, and Emphasis of Department: The Department of Counseling is concerned with the application of principles, methods, and procedures for facilitating effective psychological functioning during the entire life-span. The focus is a developmental orientation on positive aspects of growth and preventable and remediable conditions and situations. Activities include the preparation of entry and advanced level practitioners, the conduct of research and scholarly activities, and consultation and leadership services to schools, agencies, and settings where counselors provide professional services. Such services include assessment, evaluation, and diagnosis; counseling interventions with individuals, couples, families, and groups; consultation; program development; and evaluation. These services are intended to help persons acquire or alter personal-social skills, improve adaptability to changing life demands, enhance environmental coping skills, and develop a variety of problem solving and decision making capabilities. Such services are intended to help individuals, groups, organization, couples, or families at all age levels to cope more successfully with problems connected with education, career choice and development, work, sex, marriage, family, health, social relations, aging, and handicaps of a social or physical nature. Educative in nature, the orientation is upon avoiding or remediating problems and situations. Departmental activities and services can occur in University classrooms and laboratories, social services, mental and physical health institutions, rehabilitation and correctional institutions, and in a variety of other public and private agencies committed to service in one or more of the problem areas cited above.

Special Facilities or Resources: The counseling psychology training area is housed in the School of Education, a 15-story modern structure. This area provides faculty and student offices, and a departmental clinic (individual and group therapy rooms, videotaping equipment with observation rooms, a biofeedback center, and a career and testing laboratory). Also available in the building are research stations, computer terminal and microcomputer labs, a statistics laboratory, a psychological evaluation library, testing rooms, and an instructional resource center.

Information for Students With Physical Disabilities: The Student Academic Services Center provides Student Support Services/Disabled Student Services for students who are differently-abled. Student Support Services also provides consultation to faculty and staff members in programs enrolling students with special educational needs.

Application Information:

Send to: (PhD)—Director of Training, ATTN: E. Landes, SE 1518, Counseling Psychology, Indiana State University, Terre Haute, IN

47809. MS in Counseling Psychology, ATTN: N. Hall, SE 1517, Department of Counseling, Indiana State University, Terre Haute, IN 47809. Students are admitted in the Fall, application deadline February 1. MS in Counseling Psychology deadline March 1. *Fee:* $35.

Indiana State University
Department of Educational and School Psychology
School of Education
Terre Haute, IN 47809
Telephone: (812) 237-3588
Fax: (812) 237-7613
E-mail: *epbisch@befac.indstate.edu*
Web: *http://soe.indstate.edu/espy/*

Department Established:

1981. Chairperson: Michael W. Bahr. Number of Faculty: total–full-time 9; women–full-time 4.

Programs and Degrees Offered:

Listed in the following order: Program area, degree type (T if terminal Master's), number awarded 7/00-6/01. School PhD 5.

APA Accreditation: School PhD: full.

Student Applications/Admissions:

Student Applications

School PhD—Applications 2001–2002, 10. Total applicants accepted 2001–2002, 6. New applicants enrolled 2001–2002, 2. Total enrolled 2001–2002 full-time, 14, part-time, 15. Openings 2002–2003, 5.

Admissions Requirements:

Scores: Entries appear in this order: required test or GPA, minimum score (if required), median score of students entering in 2001–2002. Master's Programs: GRE-V 450, 500; GRE-Q 450, 590; GRE-Analytical 450, 600; overall undergraduate GPA 2.5, 3.52. Doctoral Programs: GRE-V 500, 500; GRE-Q 500, 505; GRE-Analytical 500, 590; overall undergraduate GPA 2.5, 3.25; last 2 years GPA no minimum stated; psychology GPA no minimum stated; psychology GPA 3.5, 3.87.

Other Criteria: (importance of criteria rated low, medium, or high): GRE/MAT scores medium, research experience medium, work experience medium, extracurricular activity high, clinically related public service high, GPA high, letters of recommendation high, interview medium, statement of goals and objectives high.

Student Characteristics: The following represents characteristics of students in 2001–2002 in all graduate psychology programs in the department: Female–full-time 20, part-time 7; Male–full-time 4, part-time 3; African American/Black–full-time 1, part-time 0; Hispanic/Latino (a)–full-time 3, part-time 0; Asian/Pacific Islander–full-time 1, part-time 0; American Indian/Alaska Native–full-time 0, part-time 0; Multi-ethnic–full-time 1, part-time 0; students subject to the Americans with Disabilities Act–full-time 0, part-time 0.

Financial Information/Assistance:

Tuition for Full-Time Study: *Master's:* State residents per academic year $3,888, $162 per credit hour; nonstate residents: per academic year $8,856, $369 per credit hour. *Doctoral:* State residents: per academic year $3,888, $162 per credit hour; nonstate residents: per academic year $8,856, $369 per credit hour.

Financial Assistance:

First Year Students: Teaching assistantships available for first-year. Average amount paid per academic year: $5,000. Average number of hours worked per week: 20. Tuition remission given: partial. Research assistantships available for first-year. Average amount paid per academic year: $5,000. Average number of hours worked per week: 20. Tuition remission given: partial. Fellowships and scholarships available for first-year. Average amount paid per academic year: $6,000. Average number of hours worked per week: 15. Tuition remission given: partial.

Advanced Students: Teaching assistantships available for advanced students. Average amount paid per academic year: $5,000. Tuition remission given: partial. Research assistantships available for advanced students. Average amount paid per academic year: $5,000. Tuition remission given: partial. Fellowships and scholarships available for advanced students. Average amount paid per academic year: $6,000. Tuition remission given: partial.

Contact Information: Of all students currently enrolled full-time, 100% benefitted from one or more of the listed financial assistance programs. For information on financial assistance, contact: Student Financial Aid, etc.

Internships/Practica: The School Psychology Program operates the Porter School Psychology Center, a clinic serving the university and local community. In addition, the School Psychology Program is a participant in Indiana State University's Professional Development Schools Partnership. Students complete practica in both the clinic and public schools, internships in the public schools, and predoctoral internships in clinic and school settings. For those doctoral students for whom a professional internship is required prior to graduation, 6 applied in 2000–2001. Of those who applied, 6 were placed in internships listed by the Association of Psychology Postdoctoral and Internship Programs (APPIC); 6 were placed in APA accredited internships.

Housing and Day Care: No on-campus housing and day care facilities are available.

Employment of Department Graduates:

Master's Degree Graduates: Of those who graduated in the academic year 2000–2001, the following categories and numbers represent the post-graduate activities and employment of master's degree graduates: Enrolled in another graduate/professional program (3), enrolled in a post-doctoral residency/fellowship (n/a), employed in independent practice (n/a).

Doctoral Degree Graduates: Of those who graduated in the academic year 2000–2001, the following categories and numbers represent the post-graduate activities and employment of doctoral degree graduates: Enrolled in a psychology doctoral program (n/a), enrolled in another graduate/professional program (n/a), employed in independent practice (5), employed in an academic position at a 2-year/4-year college (1), employed in a professional position in a school system (4), still seeking employment (0).

Additional Information:

Orientation, Objectives, and Emphasis of Department: The Ph.D. program in guidance and psychological services specialization in school psychology follows a scientist-practitioner model which serves as a foundation upon which program goals and objectives are based. The mission states "The School Psychology Program is designed to prepare School Psychologists as scientist-practitioners with a broad cognitive-behavioral orientation through a program that is research-based and theory-driven, school-focused, and experiential in nature. The program is committed to addressing issues of diversity, technology, research, theoretical orientation, professional values, and human development through preparation in the areas of educational and psychological foundations, research methodology, assessment, interventions, consultation, and school psychology."

Special Facilities or Resources: The School Psychology Program has two school-based programs that provide clinical training and research opportunities to students. These are the Cognitive, Academic, and Social Skills Training Program (CAST) and the Reading Enhancement for Academic Development Program (READ). In addition to these programs, faculty and students engage in research through the Office of Educational Research and Evaluation and the Blumberg Center for Interdisciplinary Studies, both of which are located in the School of Education. Students may also complete practica in the ADHD Clinic which is housed in the Department of Psychology.

Information for Students With Physical Disabilities: The School of Education is accessible to all persons.

Application Information:
Send to: Lisa G. Bischoff, Director of School Psychology Training Program, School of Education, Room 606, Indiana State University, Terrre Haute, IN 47809. Students are admitted in the Fall, application deadline January 15; Spring, application deadline October 15. *Fee:* $35.

Indiana State University
Department of Psychology
Root Hall
Terre Haute, IN 47809
Telephone: (812) 237-4314
Fax: (812) 237-4378
E-mail: *pyjudy@scifac.indstate.edu*
Web: *http://www.web.indstate.edu/psych*

Department Established:
1968. Chairperson: Douglas J. Herrmann. Number of Faculty: total–full-time 13; women–full-time 6.

Programs and Degrees Offered:
Listed in the following order: Program area, degree type (T if terminal Master's), number awarded 7/00-6/01. Clinical PsyD 8, general MA (T) 2.

APA Accreditation: Clinical PsyD: full.

Student Applications/Admissions:
Student Applications
Clinical PsyD—Applications 2001–2002, 80. Total applicants accepted 2001–2002, 14. New applicants enrolled 2001–2002, 10. Total enrolled 2001–2002 full-time, 36. Openings 2002–

2003, 10. The Median number of years required for completion of a degree are 5. The number of students enrolled full and part-time, who were dismissed or voluntarily withdrew from this program area were 2. *General MA*—Applications 2001–2002, 42. Total applicants accepted 2001–2002, 8. New applicants enrolled 2001–2002, 4. Total enrolled 2001–2002 full-time, 5. Openings 2002–2003, 4. The Median number of years required for completion of a degree are 2. The number of students enrolled full and part-time, who were dismissed or voluntarily withdrew from this program area were 0.

Admissions Requirements:

Scores: Entries appear in this order: required test or GPA, minimum score (if required), median score of students entering in 2001–2002. Master's Programs: GRE-V 450, 478; GRE-Q 450, 550; GRE-Analytical 450, 603; overall undergraduate GPA 2.75, 3.35. GRE test criteria are not rigidly applied in all cases. Doctoral Programs: GRE-V 575, 564; GRE-Q 575, 639; GRE-Analytical 575, 640; overall undergraduate GPA 3.00, 3.58; last 2 years GPA no minimum stated; psychology GPA no minimum stated; psychology GPA 3.50, 3.55. Either the GRE or GPA criteria may be waived if other qualifications are strong. A master's degree is not required for admission, but a 3.50 GPA or above is needed if graduate work has been done.

Other Criteria: (importance of criteria rated low, medium, or high): GRE/MAT scores high, research experience high, work experience medium, extracurricular activity low, clinically related public service high, GPA medium, letters of recommendation high, interview high, statement of goals and objectives high. An interview is not required for the Master's Program.

Student Characteristics: The following represents characteristics of students in 2001–2002 in all graduate psychology programs in the department: Female–full-time 27, part-time 0; Male–full-time 14, part-time 0; African American/Black–full-time 1, part-time 0; Hispanic/Latino (a)–full-time 3, part-time 0; Asian/Pacific Islander–full-time 1, part-time 0; American Indian/Alaska Native–full-time 0, part-time 0; Multi-ethnic–full-time 0, part-time 0; students subject to the Americans with Disabilities Act–full-time 0, part-time 0.

Financial Information/Assistance:

Tuition for Full-Time Study: *Master's:* State residents per academic year $3,888, $162 per credit hour; nonstate residents: per academic year $8,856, $369 per credit hour. *Doctoral:* State residents: per academic year $3,888, $162 per credit hour; nonstate residents: per academic year $8,856, $369 per credit hour.

Financial Assistance:

First Year Students: Teaching assistantships available for first-year. Average amount paid per academic year: $5,000. Average number of hours worked per week: 20. Apply by March 15. Tuition remission given: full. Research assistantships available for first-year. Average amount paid per academic year: $5,000. Average number of hours worked per week: 20. Apply by March 15. Tuition remission given: full. Fellowships and scholarships available for first-year. Average amount paid per academic year: $5,000. Average number of hours worked per week: 15. Apply by March 15. Tuition remission given: full.

Advanced Students: Teaching assistantships available for advanced students. Average amount paid per academic year:

$5,000. Average number of hours worked per week: 20. Apply by March 15. Tuition remission given: full. Research assistantships available for advanced students. Average amount paid per academic year: $5,000. Average number of hours worked per week: 20. Apply by March 15. Tuition remission given: full. Fellowships and scholarships available for advanced students. Average amount paid per academic year: $5,000. Average number of hours worked per week: 15. Apply by March 15. Tuition remission given: full.

Contact Information: Of all students currently enrolled full-time, 100% benefitted from one or more of the listed financial assistance programs. For information on financial assistance, contact: Psychology Department, c/o Graduate Admissions, Root Hall, Indiana State University, Terre Haute, IN 47809 or 812-237-4314 or pyjudy@scifac.indstate.edu.

Internships/Practica: Psy.D. students are expected to participate in practicum experiences from the beginning of the program, with clinical responsibilities gradually increasing throughout enrollment. Second year and third year Psy.D. students see clients in the Psychology Clinic and are supervised by clinical faculty. Fourth year students are placed in community mental health facilities under the supervision of a licensed psychologist. For those doctoral students for whom a professional internship is required prior to graduation, 9 applied in 2000–2001. Of those who applied, 9 were placed in internships listed by the Association of Psychology Postdoctoral and Internship Programs (APPIC); 9 were placed in APA accredited internships.

Housing and Day Care: On-campus housing and day care facilities are available.

Employment of Department Graduates:

Master's Degree Graduates: Of those who graduated in the academic year 2000–2001, the following categories and numbers represent the post-graduate activities and employment of master's degree graduates: Enrolled in a post-doctoral residency/fellowship (n/a), employed in independent practice (n/a), employed in other positions at a higher education institution (1), employed in a government agency (research) (1).

Doctoral Degree Graduates: Of those who graduated in the academic year 2000–2001, the following categories and numbers represent the post-graduate activities and employment of doctoral degree graduates: Enrolled in a psychology doctoral program (n/a), enrolled in another graduate/professional program (n/a), enrolled in a post-doctoral residency/fellowship (3), employed in independent practice (3), employed in an academic position at a university (1), employed in a community mental health/counseling center (1).

Additional Information:

Orientation, Objectives, and Emphasis of Department: The Doctor of Psychology program at Indiana State University follows a practitioner-scientist model of training in clinical psychology to guide the preparation and evaluation of its students. The primary goal is the training of skilled clinical psychologists in the assessment and treatment of psychological problems. The program seeks to develop a professional identity which values and pursues: excellence in clinical practice; a spirit of active inquiry and critical thought; a commitment to the development and application of new knowledge in the field; an active sense of social responsibility combined with an appreciation and respect for cultural and individual differences; and an enduring commitment to personal and professional development. The program philosophy is to prepare all students as broad-based general clinicians, with encouragement to specialize through electives, research area, internship selection, and postdoctoral training. The Master's program, with an emphasis on basic psychology and research, is intended to serve as preparatory to entrance into doctoral level study. Students are encouraged to become involved in research beginning with their first term in the program. Although the degree is in general psychology, some concentration is often possible. A main goal of the program is to have students leave with a sense of what it means to be a research psychologist.

Special Facilities or Resources: The department has a psychology clinic, mini- and micro-computers, and good laboratory facilities.

Information for Students With Physical Disabilities: All department facilities are handicapped accessible.

Application Information:

Send to: Department of Psychology, c/o Graduate Admissions, Root Hall, Indiana State University, Terre Haute, IN 47809. Students are admitted in the Fall, application deadline January 1 (PsyD); March 15 (Master's) *Fee:* $35.

Indiana University
Cognitive Science Program
Psychology 343
Bloomington, IN 47405
Telephone: (812) 855-2722
Fax: (812) 855-1086
E-mail: *shiffrin@indiana.edu*
Web: *http://www.psych.indiana.edu*

Programs and Degrees Offered:

Listed in the following order: Program area, degree type (T if terminal Master's), number awarded 7/00-6/01. Cognitive science PhD 5.

Student Applications/Admissions:

Student Applications

Cognitive science PhD—Applications 2001–2002, INA. Total applicants accepted 2001–2002, INA. New applicants enrolled 2001–2002, INA. Total enrolled 2001–2002 full-time, 93. Openings 2002–2003, INA.

Admissions Requirements:

Scores: Entries appear in this order: required test or GPA, minimum score (if required), median score of students entering in 2001–2002. Doctoral Programs: GRE-V+Q+Analytical no minimum stated; last 2 years GPA no minimum stated; psychology GPA no minimum stated; psychology GPA no minimum stated. Doctoral students are admitted by their originating department as part of a joint (multi-department) program.

Student Characteristics: The following represents characteristics of students in 2001–2002 in all graduate psychology programs in the department: Female–full-time 0, part-time 0; Male–full-time 0, part-time 0; African American/Black–full-time 0, part-time 0;

Hispanic/Latino (a)–full-time 0, part-time 0; Asian/Pacific Islander–full-time 0, part-time 0; American Indian/Alaska Native–full-time 0, part-time 0.

Financial Information/Assistance:

Tuition for Full-Time Study: *Doctoral:* State residents: per academic year $4,797, $180 per credit hour; nonstate residents: per academic year $15,151, $525 per credit hour.

Financial Assistance:

First Year Students: Teaching assistantships available for first-year. Average amount paid per academic year: $12,000. Average number of hours worked per week: 20. Apply by January 1. Tuition remission given: full. Research assistantships available for first-year. Average amount paid per academic year: $18,000. Average number of hours worked per week: 20. Apply by January 1. Tuition remission given: full. Traineeships available for first-year. Average amount paid per academic year: $16,000. Average number of hours worked per week: 20. Apply by January 1. Tuition remission given: full. Fellowships and scholarships available for first-year. Average amount paid per academic year: $18,000. Apply by January 1. Tuition remission given: full.

Advanced Students: No information provided.

Contact Information: For information on financial assistance, contact: Cognitive Science Program Office at 812-855-2722.

Internships/Practica: No information provided.

Housing and Day Care: On-campus housing and day care facilities are available.

Employment of Department Graduates:

Master's Degree Graduates: Of those who graduated in the academic year 2000–2001, the following categories and numbers represent the post-graduate activities and employment of master's degree graduates: Enrolled in a post-doctoral residency/fellowship (n/a), employed in independent practice (n/a).

Doctoral Degree Graduates: Of those who graduated in the academic year 2000–2001, the following categories and numbers represent the post-graduate activities and employment of doctoral degree graduates: Enrolled in a psychology doctoral program (n/a), enrolled in another graduate/professional program (n/a).

Additional Information:

Orientation, Objectives, and Emphasis of Department: The Program in Cognitive Science comprises an interdisciplinary research program and a doctoral degree program. Students carry out intensive research projects in state-of-the-art computer-based laboratories. The PhD degree in Cognitive Science may be a major or a minor; it must also be associated with another departmental major. The program is designed to train students in theory development and model building (mathematical, formal, and computer simulation models), in empirical research, and in the development of the conceptual framework and technical skills for successful careers in research, teaching, business, and government. Broad areas of research concentration include: neural networks; connectionist models; parallel and serial models; machine intelligence; non-linear dynamic stochastic models; learning, memory and retrieval; classification and categorization; attention, automatism, and capacity; perception; reasoning and problem solving; decision making and heuristics; language development; second language acquisition; syntax and semantics; speech perception and production; communication; development and use of motor skills; neural basis of cognition; nature of intelligent communication; music production and perception; human factors and capabilities; teaching; and reading.

Special Facilities or Resources: The computer facilities are extensive and are growing almost daily. All students in our program have access to the university computing facilities, including connection to university-wide and world-wide computer networks. The Bloomington facilities include a number of VAX machines (one 8820, two 8560s, and 6440, and one 6420) using both VMS and ULTRIX operating systems, a DEC 5840, and an IBM 3090/300s. There are a variety of computer clusters scattered about campus in convenient locations, some staffed and some unstaffed, containing approximately 500 PCs and workstations with a variety of software, hundreds of terminals connected to the university system, and peripherals such as printers and plotters. In addition, the Center for Innovative Computer Applications has a Titan, a Silicon Graphics 4D/25 Personal IRIS, and a number of workstations (NeXt, SUN, DEC, etc.). A campus-wide fiber optics communications network interconnects all university systems, and most departmental research computers as well.

Application Information:
Send to: As we are a joint degree program, students are admitted through these other departments on campus. Students are admitted in the Fall, application deadline January 1. *Fee:* $40.

Indiana University
Department of Counseling and Educational Psychology
School of Education
201 North Rose Avenue
Bloomington, IN 47405-1006
Telephone: (812) 856-8300
Fax: (812) 856-8333
E-mail: *mueller@indiana.edu*
Web: *http://education.indiana.edu/cep*

Department Established:
Chairperson: Daniel J. Mueller. Number of Faculty: total–full-time 25, part-time 8; women–full-time 10, part-time 3; minority–full-time 4.

Programs and Degrees Offered:
Listed in the following order: Program area, degree type (T if terminal Master's), number awarded 7/00-6/01. Counseling PhD 5, counseling and counselor edu MA 42, counseling and counselor educ EdS 4, educational PhD 4, school PhD 3.

APA Accreditation: Counseling PhD: full. School PhD: full.

Student Applications/Admissions:
Student Applications

Counseling PhD—Applications 2001–2002, 86. Total applicants accepted 2001–2002, 9. New applicants enrolled 2001–2002, 6. Total enrolled 2001–2002 full-time, 38. Openings 2002–2003, 9. The number of students enrolled full and part-time, who were dismissed or voluntarily withdrew from this program area were 2. *Counseling and counselor edu MA*—Applications 2001–2002, 110. Total applicants accepted 2001–2002, 80. New applicants enrolled 2001–2002, 38. Total enrolled 2001–2002 full-time, 85. Openings 2002–2003, 45. *Counseling and counselor educ EdS*—Applications 2001–2002, 12. Total applicants accepted 2001–2002, 11. New applicants enrolled 2001–2002, 11. Total enrolled 2001–2002 full-time, 18. Openings 2002–2003, 15. *Educational PhD*—Applications 2001–2002, 18. Total applicants accepted 2001–2002, 14. New applicants enrolled 2001–2002, 6. Total enrolled 2001–2002 full-time, 24. Openings 2002–2003, 8. *School PhD*—Applications 2001–2002, 21. Total applicants accepted 2001–2002, 6. New applicants enrolled 2001–2002, 4. Total enrolled 2001–2002 full-time, 16. Openings 2002–2003, 5.

Admissions Requirements:
Scores: Entries appear in this order: required test or GPA, minimum score (if required), median score of students entering in 2001–2002. Master's Programs: GRE-V no minimum stated, 480; GRE-Q no minimum stated, 580; GRE-V+Q+Analytical 1300, 1635; overall undergraduate GPA 2.75, 3.3; last 2 years GPA 3.0. Doctoral Programs: GRE-V no minimum stated, 530; GRE-Q no minimum stated, 600; GRE-V+Q 1000, 1130; GRE-V+Q+Analytical 1500, 1815; overall undergraduate GPA 3.0, 3.32; last 2 years GPA no minimum stated; psychology GPA no minimum stated; psychology GPA 3.5, 3.85.

Other Criteria: (importance of criteria rated low, medium, or high): GRE/MAT scores high, research experience medium, work experience medium, extracurricular activity medium, clinically related public service medium, GPA high, letters of recommendation medium, interview high, statement of goals and objectives medium. In both the PhD in Counseling Psychology and PhD in School Psychology programs personal interviews are required. GRE scores are interpreted differently for domestic and international applicants.

Student Characteristics: The following represents characteristics of students in 2001–2002 in all graduate psychology programs in the department: Female–full-time 53, part-time 0; Male–full-time 25, part-time 0; African American/Black–full-time 10, part-time 0; Hispanic/Latino (a)–full-time 5, part-time 0; Asian/Pacific Islander–full-time 5, part-time 0; American Indian/Alaska Native–full-time 0, part-time 0; students subject to the Americans with Disabilities Act–full-time 1.

Financial Information/Assistance:
Tuition for Full-Time Study: *Master's:* State residents $180 per credit hour; nonstate residents: $180 per credit hour. *Doctoral:* State residents: $180 per credit hour; nonstate residents: $526 per credit hour.

Financial Assistance:
First Year Students: Teaching assistantships available for first-year. Average amount paid per academic year: $12,000. Average number of hours worked per week: 20. Tuition remission given: partial. Research assistantships available for first-year. Average amount paid per academic year: $10,000. Average number of hours worked per week: 20. Tuition remission given: partial. Fellowships and scholarships available for first-year. Average amount paid per academic year: $17,000. Tuition remission given: full.

Advanced Students: Teaching assistantships available for advanced students. Average amount paid per academic year: $12,000. Tuition remission given: partial. Research assistantships available for advanced students. Average amount paid per academic year: $10,000. Tuition remission given: partial. Fellowships and scholarships available for advanced students. Average amount paid per academic year: $17,000. Tuition remission given: full.

Contact Information: Of all students currently enrolled full-time, 30% benefitted from one or more of the listed financial assistance programs. For information on financial assistance, contact: Most doctoral students receive some financial support; master students usually do not receive financial support. Teaching Assistantships-Dept. Assistantships-contact Dept. Chair; for Project Assistantships-contact Project Director; for Fellowship/Scholarships contact Director of Graduate Studies, Wright Educ. 1000, Bloomington, IN 47405.

Internships/Practica: Internships for master's and doctoral level students are available by contacting the department chair. All counseling and school psychology students must take both practica and internships. For those doctoral students for whom a professional internship is required prior to graduation, 11 applied in 2000–2001. Of those who applied, 9 were placed in internships listed by the Association of Psychology Postdoctoral and Internship Programs (APPIC); 9 were placed in APA accredited internships.

Housing and Day Care: On-campus housing and day care facilities are available.

Employment of Department Graduates:

Master's Degree Graduates: Of those who graduated in the academic year 2000–2001, the following categories and numbers represent the post-graduate activities and employment of master's degree graduates: Enrolled in a post-doctoral residency/fellowship (n/a), employed in independent practice (n/a).

Doctoral Degree Graduates: Of those who graduated in the academic year 2000–2001, the following categories and numbers represent the post-graduate activities and employment of doctoral degree graduates: Enrolled in a psychology doctoral program (n/a), enrolled in another graduate/professional program (n/a).

Additional Information:

Orientation, Objectives, and Emphasis of Department: The Department has multiple missions, but at the heart of our enterprise is a community of scholars working to contribute solutions to the problems faced by children, adolescents, and adults in the context of contemporary education. Additionally, the counseling psychology program promotes a broad range of interventions designed to facilitate the maximal adjustment of individuals. Faculty, staff, and students share a commitment to open-mindedness and to social justice. We recognize the complex and dynamic nature of the social fabric and welcome qualified students of all ethnic, racial, national, religious, gender, social class, sexual, political, and philosophic orientations. Faculty and students collaboratively investigate numerous facets of child and adolescent development, creativity, learning, metacognition, aging, semiotics, and inquiry methodologies. Our programs require an understanding of both quantitative and qualitative research paradigms. We ascribe to the scientist-practitioner model for preparing professional psychologists. Our graduates work in various research and practice settings; universities, public schools, state departments of education, mental health centers, hospitals, and corporations.

Special Facilities or Resources: Special facilities include the Institute for Child Study, Center for Human Growth, and the Indiana Institute on Disability and Community.

Information for Students With Physical Disabilities: Students with any type of disability should contact: Disabled Student Services, Franklin Hall 327 (812-855-3508) to discuss their needs.

Application Information:

Send to: Applications are accepted via the web at: www.indiana.edu/~educate/admiss.html. Students are admitted in the Fall, application deadline January 15. *Fee:* $45.

Indiana University

Department of Psychology
Arts and Sciences
Psychology Building, 1101 E. 10th Street
Bloomington, IN 47405
Telephone: (812) 855-2012
Fax: (812) 855-4691
E-mail: *psychgrd@indiana.edu*
Web: *http://www.indiana.edu/~psych*

Department Established:

1919. Chairperson: Joseph E. Steinmetz. Number of Faculty: total–full-time 39; women–full-time 10.

Programs and Degrees Offered:

Listed in the following order: Program area, degree type (T if terminal Master's), number awarded 7/00-6/01. Biology and behavior PhD 5, clinical science PhD 5, cognitive PhD 2, developmental PhD 2, social PhD 1.

APA Accreditation: Clinical PhD: full.

Student Applications/Admissions:

Student Applications

Biology and behavior PhD—Applications 2001–2002, 26. Total applicants accepted 2001–2002, 5. New applicants enrolled 2001–2002, 5. Total enrolled 2001–2002 full-time, 10. Openings 2002–2003, 4. The Median number of years required for completion of a degree are 7. *Clinical science PhD*—Applications 2001–2002, 64. Total applicants accepted 2001–2002, 6. New applicants enrolled 2001–2002, 5. Total enrolled 2001–2002 full-time, 26. Openings 2002–2003, 3. *Cognitive PhD*—Applications 2001–2002, 54. Total applicants accepted 2001–2002, 15. New applicants enrolled 2001–2002, 8. Total enrolled 2001–2002 full-time, 22. Openings 2002–2003, 5. *Developmental PhD*—Applications 2001–2002, 13. Total applicants accepted 2001–2002, 8. New applicants enrolled 2001–2002, 2. Total enrolled 2001–2002 full-time, 15. Openings 2002–2003, 4. *Social PhD*—Applications 2001–2002, 26. Total applicants accepted 2001–2002, 9. New applicants enrolled 2001–2002, 2. Total enrolled 2001–2002 full-time, 12. Openings 2002–2003, 1.

Admissions Requirements:

Scores: Entries appear in this order: required test or GPA, minimum score (if required), median score of students entering in 2001–2002. Doctoral Programs: GRE-V 543; GRE-Q 650; GRE-Analytical 659; GRE-Subject(Psych) 650; overall undergraduate GPA 3.0, 3.53; last 2 years GPA no minimum stated; psychology GPA no minimum stated; psychology GPA no minimum stated.

Other Criteria: (importance of criteria rated low, medium, or high): GRE/MAT scores high, research experience high, work experience low, extracurricular activity low, clinically related public service high, GPA high, letters of recommendation medium, interview high, statement of goals and objectives medium.

Student Characteristics: The following represents characteristics of students in 2001–2002 in all graduate psychology programs in the department: Female–full-time 16, part-time 0; Male–full-time 17, part-time 0; African American/Black–full-time 0, part-time 0; Hispanic/Latino (a)–full-time 1, part-time 0; Asian/Pacific Islander–full-time 4, part-time 0; American Indian/Alaska Native–full-time 0, part-time 0; Multi-ethnic–full-time 0, students subject to the Americans with Disabilities Act–full-time 0.

Financial Information/Assistance:

Tuition for Full-Time Study: *Doctoral:* State residents: per academic year $2,000, $180 per credit hour; nonstate residents: per academic year $15,500, $525 per credit hour.

Financial Assistance:

First Year Students: No information provided.
Advanced Students: No information provided.
Contact Information: No information provided.

Internships/Practica: Internships are required for a clinical psychology major.

Housing and Day Care: On-campus housing and day care facilities are available.

Employment of Department Graduates:

Master's Degree Graduates: Of those who graduated in the academic year 2000–2001, the following categories and numbers represent the post-graduate activities and employment of master's degree graduates: Enrolled in a post-doctoral residency/fellowship (n/a), employed in independent practice (n/a).

Doctoral Degree Graduates: Of those who graduated in the academic year 2000–2001, the following categories and numbers represent the post-graduate activities and employment of doctoral degree graduates: Enrolled in a psychology doctoral program (n/a), enrolled in another graduate/professional program (n/a), enrolled in a post-doctoral residency/fellowship (15), employed in other positions at a higher education institution (11), employed in business or industry (research/consulting) (1), employed in business or industry (management) (1), employed in a government agency (research) (1), employed in a community mental health/counseling center (1), employed in a hospital/medical center (1), still seeking employment (1).

Additional Information:

Orientation, Objectives, and Emphasis of Department: Students acquire fundamental knowledge and are offered specialized training so that they may develop competence in research, teaching (college and university levels), and service. Close contact between faculty and students is made possible by a low ratio of graduate students to faculty. Extensive laboratory facilities are available for research in the major areas. A psychological clinic is maintained as a specialized unit of the department. The primary emphasis of the clinical training program is on the theoretical and scientific aspects of clinical psychology. However, in view of the diverse and changing nature of the field, the program's goal is to produce clinical psychologists who are well trained scientifically and clinically and who are capable of achieving excellence in their careers in either a clinical or an academic and research setting.

Application Information:
Send to: Indiana University, Department of Psychology Graduate Admissions, 1101 East 10th Street, Bloomington, IN 47405. Students are admitted in the Fall, application deadline December 15. December 15 is the application deadline for international graduate student candidates. *Fee:* $45. The department does not give application fee waivers or deferrals. However, certain fellowship programs that our applicants can apply for do.

Indiana University South Bend
Department of Psychology/Master of Arts in Applied
  Psychology
College of Liberal Arts & Science
P.O. Box 7111
South Bend, IN 46634-7111
Telephone: (219) 237-4334
Fax: (219) 237-4538
E-mail: *jmcintos@iusb.edu*
Web: *http://www.iusb.edu/~psy/MAAppliedPsych.html*

Department Established:
1967. Chairperson: John McIntosh. Number of Faculty: total–full-time 11, part-time 8; women–full-time 4, part-time 4; minority–full-time 2.

Programs and Degrees Offered:
Listed in the following order: Program area, degree type (T if terminal Master's), number awarded 7/00-6/01. Applied developmental MA (T) 2, Applied social/community MA (T).

Student Applications/Admissions:
Student Applications
Applied developmental MA—Applications 2001–2002, 3. Openings 2002–2003, 15. The Median number of years required for completion of a degree are 4. *Applied social/community MA*—Applications 2001–2002, 4. Openings 2002–2003, 15.

Admissions Requirements:
Scores: Entries appear in this order: required test or GPA, minimum score (if required), median score of students entering in 2001–2002. Master's Programs: overall undergraduate GPA 3.0, 3.8. Doctoral Programs: last 2 years GPA no minimum

stated; psychology GPA no minimum stated; psychology GPA no minimum stated.

Other Criteria: (importance of criteria rated low, medium, or high): research experience high, GPA medium, letters of recommendation high, statement of goals and objectives high.

Student Characteristics: The following represents characteristics of students in 2001–2002 in all graduate psychology programs in the department: Female–full-time 0, part-time 2; Male–full-time 0, part-time 0; African American/Black–full-time 0, part-time 0; Hispanic/Latino (a)–full-time 0, part-time 0; Asian/Pacific Islander–full-time 0, part-time 0; American Indian/Alaska Native–full-time 0, part-time 0.

Financial Information/Assistance:

Tuition for Full-Time Study: *Master's:* State residents $142 per credit hour; nonstate residents: $345 per credit hour.

Financial Assistance:

First Year Students: No information provided.

Advanced Students: No information provided.

Contact Information: Of all students currently enrolled full-time, 0% benefitted from one or more of the listed financial assistance programs. For information on financial assistance, contact: Financial Aid Office, IUSB (219) 237-4357.

Internships/Practica: To earn the MA degree in Applied Psychology requires that among students' total of 42 graduate credit hours, they will complete two semesters of community based practicum. The practicum provides students with the opportunity to develop their skills in a professional setting. This experience is supervised by an on-site supervisor and is also supervised and monitored by the department's Graduate Practicum Coordinator. Students are required to perform two consecutive semesters in the same placement setting to fulfill their practicum requirement. Practicum placements are arranged individually for students through the Graduate Practicum Coordinator to complement the student's concentration area. Among possible sites for practicum placement are health and mental health agencies and facilities, business, law enforcement settings, community agencies and groups, as well as agencies and organizations focused on issues of youth, families, or the elderly.

Housing and Day Care: No on-campus housing and day care facilities are available.

Employment of Department Graduates:

Master's Degree Graduates: Of those who graduated in the academic year 2000–2001, the following categories and numbers represent the post-graduate activities and employment of master's degree graduates: Enrolled in a psychology doctoral program (0), enrolled in another graduate/professional program (0), enrolled in a post-doctoral residency/fellowship (n/a), employed in independent practice (n/a), employed in an academic position at a university (1), employed in an academic position at a 2-year/4-year college (0), employed in other positions at a higher education institution (1), employed in a professional position in a school system (0), employed in business or industry (research/consulting) (0), employed in business or industry (management) (0), employed in a government agency (research) (0), employed in a government agency (professional services) (0), employed in a community mental health/counseling center (0), employed in a hospital/medical center (0), still seeking employment (0), other employment position (0).

Doctoral Degree Graduates: Of those who graduated in the academic year 2000–2001, the following categories and numbers represent the post-graduate activities and employment of doctoral degree graduates: Enrolled in a psychology doctoral program (n/a), enrolled in another graduate/professional program (n/a).

Additional Information:

Orientation, Objectives, and Emphasis of Department: The Master of Arts in Applied Psychology is a graduate degree designed to provide students with a general background in the science of psychology and to educate and train students to function competently, in one of two major areas of applied behavioral science. Graduates will gain employment in business settings, health and mental health agencies, and a variety of other organizations that serve the developmental needs of the individual and the community. Examples of the types of training graduates will receive are: research design, implementation, analyses, interpretation, and application; program development projects; program evaluation and efficacy studies; needs assessments; client satisfaction studies. Concentrations: The Social/Community concentration is intended for students who wish to use psychological knowledge about social relationships, community dynamics and social structure, attitude and behaviors change, and human cognitive abilities to design environments, tasks, and organizations in order to bring about change or to achieve specific community goals. The Life-Span Developmental concentration provides a comprehensive background in normal social and cognitive development with a focus either on children or elders. It prepares professionals to deal with the many problems encountered during the life-span as well as identifying and developing community resources to deal with the individual's needs.

Special Facilities or Resources: The Department of Psychology maintains laboratory space in which basic psychological research may be performed. Included in these facilities are individual as well as group rooms for research. A number of these rooms are equipped with observation capabilities and an intercom system. The laboratory space exists in a building less than three years old.

Information for Students With Physical Disabilities: Provide any information that might be useful to students with physical disabilities. IUSB is committed to providing equal access to higher education for academically qualified students with disabilities. For example, the physical setting of the campus and the building in which the Psychology Department is housed are fully wheelchair accessible. In addition, a variety of services are provided and may be arranged through the campus Office of Disabled Students (219-237-4479).

Application Information:

Send to: Graduate Program Director, Dept. of Psychology, Indiana University, South Bend, P.O. Box 7111, South Bend, IN 46634-7111. Students are admitted in the Fall, application deadline April 15. *Fee:* $40.

Indiana University—Purdue University Indianapolis

Department of Psychology
Science
402 North Blackford Street, Room LD 124
Indianapolis, IN 46202-3275
Telephone: (317) 274-6945
Fax: (317) 274-6756
E-mail: *gradpsy.iupui.edu*
Web: *http://www.psynt.iupui.edu*

Department Established:

1969. Chairperson: J. Gregor Fetterman, Ph.D. Number of Faculty: total–full-time 23, part-time 13; women–full-time 6, part-time 4; minority–full-time 3.

Programs and Degrees Offered:

Listed in the following order: Program area, degree type (T if terminal Master's), number awarded 7/00-6/01. Clinical rehabilitation PhD 4, industrial/organization MA (T) 2, psychobiology PhD.

APA Accreditation: Clinical PhD: full.

Student Applications/Admissions:

Student Applications

Clinical rehabilitation PhD—Applications 2001–2002, 32. Total applicants accepted 2001–2002, 6. New applicants enrolled 2001–2002, 3. Total enrolled 2001–2002 full-time, 21. Openings 2002–2003, 3-6. The Median number of years required for completion of a degree are 6. The number of students enrolled full and part-time, who were dismissed or voluntarily withdrew from this program area were 1. *Industrial/organization MA*—Applications 2001–2002, 49. Total applicants accepted 2001–2002, 6. New applicants enrolled 2001–2002, 6. Total enrolled 2001–2002 full-time, 9, part-time, 1. Openings 2002–2003, 5. The Median number of years required for completion of a degree are 2. The number of students enrolled full and part-time, who were dismissed or voluntarily withdrew from this program area were 0. *Psychobiology PhD*—Applications 2001–2002, 12. Total applicants accepted 2001–2002, 5. New applicants enrolled 2001–2002, 3. Total enrolled 2001–2002 full-time, 11. Openings 2002–2003, 3. The Median number of years required for completion of a degree are 6. The number of students enrolled full and part-time, who were dismissed or voluntarily withdrew from this program area were 0.

Admissions Requirements:

Scores: Entries appear in this order: required test or GPA, minimum score (if required), median score of students entering in 2001–2002. Master's Programs: GRE-V 550, 490; GRE-Q 550, 670; GRE-V+Q 1100, 1210; GRE-Analytical no minimum stated, 620; overall undergraduate GPA 3.0, 3.42. Note: Minimum GRE scores are neither necessary nor sufficient for admission. Doctoral Programs: GRE-V 600; GRE-Q 600; GRE-

V+Q 1200; GRE-Analytical no minimum stated; GRE-Subject(Psych) 600; overall undergraduate GPA 3.2, 3.68; last 2 years GPA no minimum stated; psychology GPA no minimum stated; psychology GPA no minimum stated. Median scores for Clinical Rehabilitation Psychology PhD:V-620; Q-610; V+Q-1230; A-700. Median scores for Psychobiology of Addictions PhD:V-540; Q-670; V+Q-1210; A-620. Note: Minimum GRE scores are neither necessary nor sufficient for admission. *Other Criteria:* (importance of criteria rated low, medium, or high): GRE/MAT scores high, research experience high, GPA high, letters of recommendation high, interview medium, statement of goals and objectives high.

Student Characteristics: The following represents characteristics of students in 2001–2002 in all graduate psychology programs in the department: Female–full-time 33, part-time 1; Male–full-time 13, part-time 1; African American/Black–full-time 1, part-time 0; Hispanic/Latino (a)–full-time 2, part-time 0; Asian/Pacific Islander–full-time 2, part-time 0; American Indian/Alaska Native–full-time 0, part-time 0; students subject to the Americans with Disabilities Act–full-time 0, part-time 0.

Financial Information/Assistance:

Tuition for Full-Time Study: *Master's:* State residents per academic year $2,055, $171 per credit hour; nonstate residents: per academic year $5,930, $494 per credit hour. *Doctoral:* State residents: per academic year $2,055, $171 per credit hour; nonstate residents: per academic year $5,930, $494 per credit hour.

Financial Assistance:

First Year Students: Tuition remission given: partial. Research assistantships available for first-year. Average amount paid per academic year: $9,000. Average number of hours worked per week: 20. Apply by February 1. Tuition remission given: partial. Fellowships and scholarships available for first-year. Average number of hours worked per week: 0. Apply by February 1. Tuition remission given: partial.

Advanced Students: Teaching assistantships available for advanced students. Average amount paid per academic year: $9,000. Average number of hours worked per week: 20. Apply by February 1. Tuition remission given: partial. Research assistantships available for advanced students. Average amount paid per academic year: $9,000. Average number of hours worked per week: 20. Apply by February 1. Tuition remission given: partial. Tuition remission given: partial. Fellowships and scholarships available for advanced students. Average amount paid per academic year: $12,000. Average number of hours worked per week: 0. Apply by February 1. Tuition remission given: partial.

Contact Information: Of all students currently enrolled full-time, 100% benefitted from one or more of the listed financial assistance programs. For information on financial assistance, contact: 317-274-4162. Note: Fellowships and Scholarships are available in two amounts: $12,000 and $18,000.

Internships/Practica: Clinical practica sites are located at IUPUI and within the Indianapolis area, and involve supervised clinical training individually tailored for each student. A practicum coordinator, the site supervisor, and the student develop specific contracts that emphasize education and the acquisition of clinical skills and knowledge, rather than experience per se. These contractual activities and goals are monitored and evaluated at the end of each placement. Practicum opportunities are varied and numerous and include many different types of clinical settings with different clinical populations. On-site supervisors are usually psychologists but also include psychiatrists, physiatrists, and other health professionals. Many sites in different settings are available. General practicum sties include a university counseling center and several psychiatric clinics. More advanced settings can be categorized as 1) Neuropsychology; 2) Behavioral Medicine or Health Psychology; 3) Severe Mental Illness/Psychiatric Rehabilitation. The I/O Master's Program offers opportunities to achieve applied experience in business settings. Students have the opportunity to sign up for practicum in the spring of their second year. Students are typically placed in an organization for one 8-hour day each week of the semester. Paid summer internships (15–20 hours per week) in the community are also available. For those doctoral students for whom a professional internship is required prior to graduation, 3 applied in 2000–2001. Of those who applied, 3 were placed in internships listed by the Association of Psychology Postdoctoral and Internship Programs (APPIC); 3 were placed in APA accredited internships.

Housing and Day Care: On-campus housing and day care facilities are available.

Employment of Department Graduates:

Master's Degree Graduates: Of those who graduated in the academic year 2000–2001, the following categories and numbers represent the post-graduate activities and employment of master's degree graduates: Enrolled in a psychology doctoral program (1), enrolled in a post-doctoral residency/fellowship (n/a), employed in independent practice (n/a), still seeking employment (1).

Doctoral Degree Graduates: Of those who graduated in the academic year 2000–2001, the following categories and numbers represent the post-graduate activities and employment of doctoral degree graduates: Enrolled in a psychology doctoral program (n/a), enrolled in another graduate/professional program (n/a), enrolled in a post-doctoral residency/fellowship (1), employed in an academic position at a 2-year/4-year college (1), employed in a hospital/medical center (2).

Additional Information:

Orientation, Objectives, and Emphasis of Department: Graduate education is offered at the PhD level in Clinical Rehabilitation Psychology and the Psychobiology of Addictions. The APA-Accredited Clinical program follows the scientist-practitioner model. A rigorous academic and research education is combined with supervised practical training. The clinical program provides specialization in behavioral medicine/health psychology, neuropsychology, and severe mental illness/psychiatric rehabilitation. The PhD program in the psychobiological bases of addictions emphasizes the core content areas of psychology along with specialization in psychobiology and animal models of addiction. Research, scholarship, and close faculty-student mentor relationships are viewed as integral training elements within both programs. Graduate training at the MS level is designed to provide students with theory and practice that will enable them to apply psychological techniques and findings to subsequent jobs. All students are required to take departmental methods courses and then specific area core courses and electives. The MS degree areas are applied in focus and science-based, and this reflects the interests and orientation of the faculty.

Special Facilities or Resources: IUPUI is a unique urban university campus with 27,000 students enrolled in 235 degree programs at the undergraduate and graduate level. The campus includes schools of law, dentistry, and medicine, among others, along with undergraduate programs in the arts, humanities, and science. In addition, there are over 75 research institutes, centers, laboratories, and specialized programs. The Department of Psychology at IUPUI occupies teaching and research facilities in a modern science building in the heart of campus. Facilities include a 4000-square foot space and self-contained area devoted to faculty and graduate student basic animal research in experimental psychology and psychobiology. Many of the research rooms are equipped for on-line computer recording to one of the faculty offices. Laboratories for human research, research rooms, and teaching laboratories are separately located on the first floor of the building. The Psychology Department maintains ties with the faculty and programs in other schools within IUPUI, including the School of Nursing, and the Departments of Psychiatry, Adolescent Medicine, and Neurology. The clinical program provides an unusually rich array of practicum opportunities in behavioral medicine, neuropsychology, and psychiatric rehabilitation.

Application Information:
Send to: Susie Wiesinger, IUPUI, Department of Psychology, LD124, 422 N. Blackford Street, Indianapolis, IN 46202-3275. Students are admitted in the Fall, application deadline February 1. *Fee:* $35. International - $55.

Indianapolis, University of
Psychology
Arts and Sciences
1400 East Hanna Avenue
Indianapolis, IN 46227
Telephone: (317) 788-3353
Fax: (317) 788-2120
E-mail: *jmcilvried@uindy.edu*
Web: *http://www.uindy.edu/academics/psychology/index.ht*

Department Established:
1994. Dean: John McIlvried. Number of Faculty: total–full-time 11, part-time 8; women–full-time 6, part-time 3; minority–full-time 2, part-time 1.

Programs and Degrees Offered:
Listed in the following order: Program area, degree type (T if terminal Master's), number awarded 7/00-6/01. Clinical MA 18, Clinical PsyD 14.

APA Accreditation: Clinical PsyD: full.

Student Applications/Admissions:
Student Applications
Clinical MA—Applications 2001–2002, 20. Total applicants accepted 2001–2002, 17. New applicants enrolled 2001–2002,

15. Total enrolled 2001–2002 full-time, 18, part-time, 2. Openings 2002–2003, 18. The Median number of years required for completion of a degree are 2. The number of students enrolled full and part-time, who were dismissed or voluntarily withdrew from this program area were 1. *Clinical PsyD*—Applications 2001–2002, 48. Total applicants accepted 2001–2002, 32. New applicants enrolled 2001–2002, 11. Total enrolled 2001–2002 full-time, 54, part-time, 17. Openings 2002–2003, 24. The Median number of years required for completion of a degree are 4. The number of students enrolled full and part-time, who were dismissed or voluntarily withdrew from this program area were 4.

Admissions Requirements:

Scores: Entries appear in this order: required test or GPA, minimum score (if required), median score of students entering in 2001–2002. Master's Programs: GRE-V no minimum stated, 455; GRE-Q no minimum stated, 520; GRE-V+Q no minimum stated, 990; GRE-Analytical no minimum stated, 520; GRE-V+Q+Analytical no minimum stated, 1500; GRE-Subject(Psych) no minimum stated, 505; overall undergraduate GPA no minimum stated, 3.22; last 2 years GPA no minimum stated, 3.32; psychology GPA no minimum stated, 3.71. GRE and GRE subject (Psych). Doctoral Programs: GRE-V no minimum stated, 480; GRE-Q no minimum stated, 520; GRE-V+Q no minimum stated, 1020; GRE-Analytical no minimum stated, 610; GRE-V+Q+Analytical no minimum stated, 1650; GRE-Subject(Psych) no minimum stated, 590; overall undergraduate GPA 3.0, 3.69; last 2 years GPA no minimum stated, 3.75; psychology GPA 3.0, 3.72; psychology GPA no minimum stated, 3.61.

Other Criteria: (importance of criteria rated low, medium, or high): GRE/MAT scores high, research experience low, work experience medium, extracurricular activity low, clinically related public service medium, GPA high, letters of recommendation medium, interview high, statement of goals and objectives high.

Student Characteristics: The following represents characteristics of students in 2001–2002 in all graduate psychology programs in the department: Female–full-time 63, part-time 15; Male–full-time 9, part-time 4; African American/Black–full-time 1, part-time 2; Hispanic/Latino (a)–full-time 1, part-time 0; Asian/Pacific Islander–full-time 3, part-time 0; American Indian/Alaska Native–full-time 0, part-time 0; Multi-ethnic–full-time 0, part-time 0; students subject to the Americans with Disabilities Act–full-time 2, part-time 0.

Financial Information/Assistance:

Tuition for Full-Time Study: *Master's:* State residents $511 per credit hour; nonstate residents: $511 per credit hour. *Doctoral:* State residents: $511 per credit hour; nonstate residents: $511 per credit hour.

Financial Assistance:

First Year Students: Teaching assistantships available for first-year. Average amount paid per academic year: $5,100. Average number of hours worked per week: 12. Apply by 1/15. Research assistantships available for first-year. Average amount paid per academic year: $5,100. Average number of hours worked per week: 12. Apply by 1/15. Fellowships and scholarships available for first-year. Average number of hours worked per week: 0. Apply by 1/15. Tuition remission given: full.

Advanced Students: Teaching assistantships available for advanced students. Average amount paid per academic year: $5,400. Average number of hours worked per week: 12. Research assistantships available for advanced students. Average amount paid per academic year: $5,400. Average number of hours worked per week: 12.

Contact Information: Of all students currently enrolled full-time, 25% benefitted from one or more of the listed financial assistance programs. For information on financial assistance, contact: Blas Davila, Coordinator of Graduate Student Admissions, Department of Psychology, University of Indianapolis, 1400 East Hanna Avenue, Indianapolis, IN 46227.

Internships/Practica: There are numerous clinical practica experiences available for both master's and doctoral students. Master's students obtain a minimum of 225 hours of supervised clinical practica experience, and doctoral students receive a minimum of 1200 hours of supervised clinical practica experience. Practica are available at numerous settings, including major training medical center, local community hospitals, forensic settings, private practice placements, elementary schools, social service agencies, and mental health centers. At these placements, students gain supervised experience in clinical assessment and testing, therapy, collaboration and consultation with interdisciplinary teams, program development and evaluation, treatment planning and case management, and participation in development and delivery of inservices to professional staff. In addition to mainstream psychological services, practicum students have opportunities to obtain specific training in Christian counseling, forensics, neuropsychology, health psychology, pain, substance abuse/dependence, developmental disabilities, and HIV/AIDS. All practica are supervised by mental health professionals on-site. In conjunction with practicum, students enroll in a professional practice seminar that addresses a wide variety of issues that confront mental health professionals and students. This professional practice seminar is taught by full time University faculty. Doctoral students also must complete a 2000 hour internship. The Director of Clinical Training provides assistance in locating training placements. For those doctoral students for whom a professional internship is required prior to graduation, 7 applied in 2000–2001. Of those who applied, 7 were placed in internships listed by the Association of Psychology Postdoctoral and Internship Programs (APPIC); 5 were placed in APA accredited internships.

Housing and Day Care: On-campus housing and day care facilities are available.

Employment of Department Graduates:

Master's Degree Graduates: Of those who graduated in the academic year 2000–2001, the following categories and numbers represent the post-graduate activities and employment of master's degree graduates: Enrolled in a post-doctoral residency/fellowship (n/a), employed in independent practice (n/a).

Doctoral Degree Graduates: Of those who graduated in the academic year 2000–2001, the following categories and numbers represent the post-graduate activities and employment of doctoral degree graduates: Enrolled in a psychology doctoral program (n/a), enrolled in another graduate/professional program (n/a), enrolled in a post-doctoral residency/fellowship (3), employed in independent practice (4), employed in an academic position at a university

(0), employed in an academic position at a 2-year/4-year college (0), employed in other positions at a higher education institution (2), employed in a professional position in a school system (0), employed in business or industry (research/consulting) (0), employed in business or industry (management) (0), employed in a government agency (research) (1), employed in a government agency (professional services) (1), employed in a community mental health/counseling center (2), employed in a hospital/medical center (2), still seeking employment (0), other employment position (0).

Additional Information:

Orientation, Objectives, and Emphasis of Department: The graduate program in clinical psychology at the University of Indianapolis is based on a practitioner-scholar model of training. As such, the program is committed to developing highly competent and qualified professionals. The focus of the program is on preparing individuals to aid in the prevention and treatment of human problems, as well as the enhancement of human functioning and potential. The program trains students in the general, integrative practice of professional psychology through a broad-based exposure to a variety of psychological approaches and modalities. In addition, the program offers specialized training in three clinical emphasis areas: health psychology/behavioral medicine, childhood and adolescent psychology, and adult development and geropsychology. The faculty believe that education is most effective when the relationship between students and faculty is characterized by mutual respect, responsibility, and dedication to excellence. The program is founded on a deep and abiding respect for diversity in individuals, the ethical practice of psychology, and a commitment to service to others. These foundation themes are reflected in the selection of students, the coursework and training experiences offered, and the faculty who serve as role models and mentors.

Special Facilities or Resources: Specialized training facilities include several clinical therapy labs designed for supervised assessment, testing, and therapy, and for videotaping of clinical sessions utilized in feedback and instruction. The Large Groups Lab includes interconnected classrooms used for videotaping and monitoring of experiential group or class exercises, psychoeducational programs, and other large group activities. Individualized Study and Research Labs equipped with Pentium computers are available for research projects, classroom assignments, and personal study. Computer facilities in the School of Psychology and throughout the university allow access to word processing, spreadsheets, database operations, statistical packages, e-mail, Internet connection, and on-line searching of library holdings. In addition, they offer the capability of conducting direct, on-line literature searches using a variety of different databases (e.g., PsychINFO, MedLine). The library subscribes to the major psychology journals and contains the latest publications in the field of clinical psychology. The department has a graduate student lounge in which students meet to confer about class assignments, have group study sessions, practice presentations, or just relax between classes. The department also has an on-site Psychological Services Center, which offers treatment services to community residents on a sliding fee scale. Students receive applied training experience at the Center while conducting intake assessments or providing therapeutic services.

Application Information:

Send to: Blas Davila, Coordinator of Graduate Student Admissions. Students are admitted in the Fall, application deadline 1/15 (PsyD); 3/1 (MA). *Fee:* $50.

Notre Dame, University of
Department of Psychology
Arts & Letters
118 Haggar Hall
Notre Dame, IN 46556
Telephone: (219) 631-6650
Fax: (219) 631-8883
E-mail: *LCarlson@nd.edu*
Web: *http://www.nd.edu*

Department Established:

1965. Chairperson: Jeanne D. Day. Number of Faculty: total–full-time 29, part-time 9; women–full-time 10, part-time 6; minority–full-time 2.

Programs and Degrees Offered:

Listed in the following order: Program area, degree type (T if terminal Master's), number awarded 7/00-6/01. Cognitive psychology PhD 1, counseling psychology PhD 4, developmental psychology PhD 1, quantitative psychology PhD 2.

APA Accreditation: Counseling PhD: full.

Student Applications/Admissions:

Student Applications

Cognitive psychology PhD—Applications 2001–2002, 16. Total applicants accepted 2001–2002, 2. New applicants enrolled 2001–2002, 1. Total enrolled 2001–2002 full-time, 7. Openings 2002–2003, 2. The Median number of years required for completion of a degree are 7. The number of students enrolled full and part-time, who were dismissed or voluntarily withdrew from this program area were 1. *Counseling psychology PhD*—Applications 2001–2002, 128. Total applicants accepted 2001–2002, 5. New applicants enrolled 2001–2002, 4. Total enrolled 2001–2002 full-time, 19. Openings 2002–2003, 3. The Median number of years required for completion of a degree are 6. *Developmental psychology PhD*—Applications 2001–2002, 37. Total applicants accepted 2001–2002, 11. New applicants enrolled 2001–2002, 7. Total enrolled 2001–2002 full-time, 30. Openings 2002–2003, 8. The Median number of years required for completion of a degree are 6. *Quantitative psychology PhD*—Applications 2001–2002, 8. Total applicants accepted 2001–2002, 4. New applicants enrolled 2001–2002, 3. Total enrolled 2001–2002 full-time, 6. Openings 2002–2003, 3. The Median number of years required for completion of a degree are 5.

Admissions Requirements:

Scores: Entries appear in this order: required test or GPA, minimum score (if required), median score of students entering in 2001–2002. Doctoral Programs: GRE-V no minimum stated, 590; GRE-Q no minimum stated, 665; GRE-Analytical no minimum stated, 725; overall undergraduate GPA no minimum stated, 3.71; last 2 years GPA no minimum stated; psychology GPA no minimum stated; psychology GPA no minimum stated.

Other Criteria: (importance of criteria rated low, medium, or high): GRE/MAT scores high, research experience high, extracurricular activity low, clinically related public service low, GPA high, letters of recommendation high, interview medium, statement of goals and objectives high.

Student Characteristics: The following represents characteristics of students in 2001–2002 in all graduate psychology programs in the department: Female–full-time 12, part-time 0; Male–full-time 2, part-time 0; African American/Black–full-time 1, part-time 0; Hispanic/Latino (a)–full-time 1, part-time 0; Asian/Pacific Islander–full-time 1, part-time 0; American Indian/Alaska Native–full-time 0, part-time 0.

Financial Information/Assistance:

Tuition for Full-Time Study: *Doctoral:* State residents: per academic year $24,200; nonstate residents: per academic year $24,200.

Financial Assistance:

First Year Students: Teaching assistantships available for first-year. Average amount paid per academic year: $12,000. Tuition remission given: full. Research assistantships available for first-year. Average amount paid per academic year: $12,000. Tuition remission given: full. Fellowships and scholarships available for first-year. Average amount paid per academic year: $15,000. Tuition remission given: full.

Advanced Students: Teaching assistantships available for advanced students. Average amount paid per academic year: $12,000. Research assistantships available for advanced students. Average amount paid per academic year: $12,000. Fellowships and scholarships available for advanced students. Average amount paid per academic year: $15,000.

Contact Information: Of all students currently enrolled full-time, 100% benefitted from one or more of the listed financial assistance programs. For information on financial assistance, contact: Graduate Director, Department of Psychology.

Internships/Practica: All students in the APA-accredited counseling program have an initial practicum 13–17 hours per week at the University Counseling Center. These same students have opportunities for additional practicum placements in agencies in the community. The University Counseling Center also houses an APA-accredited internship. Advanced students in the accredited program are eligible to apply. For those doctoral students for whom a professional internship is required prior to graduation, 3 applied in 2000–2001. Of those who applied, 3 were placed in internships listed by the Association of Psychology Postdoctoral and Internship Programs (APPIC); 3 were placed in APA accredited internships.

Housing and Day Care: On-campus housing and day care facilities are available.

Employment of Department Graduates:

Master's Degree Graduates: Of those who graduated in the academic year 2000–2001, the following categories and numbers represent the post-graduate activities and employment of master's degree graduates: Enrolled in a post-doctoral residency/fellowship (n/a), employed in independent practice (n/a).

Doctoral Degree Graduates: Of those who graduated in the academic year 2000–2001, the following categories and numbers represent the post-graduate activities and employment of doctoral degree graduates: Enrolled in a psychology doctoral program (n/a), enrolled in another graduate/professional program (n/a), employed in an academic position at a 2-year/4-year college (3), employed in other positions at a higher education institution (2), employed in business or industry (research/consulting) (1), employed in a government agency (professional services) (1), employed in a community mental health/counseling center (1).

Additional Information:

Orientation, Objectives, and Emphasis of Department: The Department of Psychology at the University of Notre Dame is committed to excellence in psychological science and its applications. To realize this commitment a major focus is upon developing knowledge and expertise in the increasingly sophisticated methodology of the discipline. With this methodological core as its major emphasis and integrating link, the department has emphasized four content areas: cognitive, counseling, developmental, and quantitative psychology. In the context of the mores of the academy, the faculty of each content area organize and coordinate work in the three domains of research, graduate education, and undergraduate education. Using our methodological understandings as a base, we strive to find intellectual common ground among the content areas within our department and other disciplines throughout the social sciences and the academy.

Special Facilities or Resources: We are involved in the development of innovative science and practice experiences for undergraduate and graduate students in the local community. Currently, many faculty have excellent relationships with community groups (e.g., the local schools, hospitals, Logan center, Center for the Homeless, Head Start). Many faculty conduct research with undergraduate and graduate students in these settings. Over and above these research activities, many students volunteer in these agencies. Finally, a few counseling psychology graduate students receive supervision to work in the Center for the Homeless and, in a new initiative, postdoctoral positions exist in the Multicultural Research Institute.

Information for Students With Physical Disabilities: The Office for Students with Disabilities (OSD) provides a variety of services to ensure that students with disabilities have access to the programs and facilities of the University. Services do not lower course standards or alter essential degree requirements, but instead give students the opportunity to demonstrate their academic abilities. A student can initiate a request for services by registering with the OSD, and providing information that documents his or her disability. While the services or accommodations provided depend on the student's disability and course or program, some of the services that have been used include: extended time on exams and/or separate testing rooms; textbooks on cassette tape, large-print, Braille, or on computer disk; readers, note takers, and academic aids; screening and referral for diagnostic testing for a learning disability or attention deficit disorder; housing modifications; and hearing amplification equipment. For more information on services or to receive a copy of the University of Notre Dame Policies and Procedures for Students and Applicants with Disabilities, please contact: Coordinator, Office for Students with Disabilities; 109 Badin Hall, (219) 631-7141 (voice) or (219) 631-7173 (TTY).

Application Information:

Send to: Graduate Admissions, The Graduate School, University of Notre Dame, Notre Dame, IN 46556. Students are admitted in the Fall, application deadline January 2. *Fee:* $50. In certain circumstances the Graduate School (at the address above) can approve the waiver of fees. Fee is $35.00 for applications received before December 1st.

Purdue University

Department of Psychological Sciences
School of Liberal Arts
1364 Psychological Sciences Building
West Lafayette, IN 47907
Telephone: (765) 494-6067
Fax: (765) 496-1264
E-mail: *mann@psych.purdue.edu*
Web: *http://www.psych.purdue.edu*

Department Established:

1954. Professor and Head: Thomas J. Berndt. Number of Faculty: total–full-time 44, part-time 4; women–full-time 12, part-time 3; minority–full-time 3.

Programs and Degrees Offered:

Listed in the following order: Program area, degree type (T if terminal Master's), number awarded 7/00-6/01. Clinical PhD 4, cognitive PhD 4, developmental PhD 1, industrial/organizational PhD, learning and memory PhD, psychobiology PhD 1, quantitative PhD 1, social PhD.

APA Accreditation: Clinical PhD: full.

Student Applications/Admissions:

Student Applications

Clinical PhD—Applications 2001–2002, 167. Total applicants accepted 2001–2002, 9. New applicants enrolled 2001–2002, 8. Total enrolled 2001–2002 full-time, 33. Openings 2002–2003, 6. *Cognitive PhD*—Applications 2001–2002, 17. Total applicants accepted 2001–2002, 6. New applicants enrolled 2001–2002, 4. Total enrolled 2001–2002 full-time, 11. Openings 2002–2003, 4. The number of students enrolled full and part-time, who were dismissed or voluntarily withdrew from this program area were 0. *Developmental PhD*—Applications 2001–2002, 16. Total enrolled 2001–2002 full-time, 18. Openings 2002–2003, 4. *Industrial/organizational PhD*—Applications 2001–2002, 80. Total applicants accepted 2001–2002, 6. New applicants enrolled 2001–2002, 2. Total enrolled 2001–2002 full-time, 12. Openings 2002–2003, 5. *Learning and memory PhD*—Applications 2001–2002, 4. Total applicants accepted 2001–2002, 2. Total enrolled 2001–2002 full-time, 3. Openings 2002–2003, 2. *Psychobiology PhD*—Applications 2001–2002, 4. Total applicants accepted 2001–2002, 2. New applicants enrolled 2001–2002, 2. Total enrolled 2001–2002 full-time, 4. Openings 2002–2003, 3. *Quantitative PhD*—Applications 2001–2002, 11. Total applicants accepted 2001–2002, 4. New applicants enrolled 2001–2002, 1. Total enrolled 2001–2002 full-time, 6. Openings 2002–2003, 3. *Social PhD*—Applications 2001–2002, 36. Total applicants accepted 2001–2002, 5. New applicants enrolled 2001–2002, 1. Total enrolled 2001–2002 full-time, 18. Openings 2002–2003, 7.

Admissions Requirements:

Scores: Entries appear in this order: required test or GPA, minimum score (if required), median score of students entering in 2001–2002. Master's Programs: Doctoral Programs: GRE-V no minimum stated, 593; GRE-Q no minimum stated, 700; GRE-Analytical no minimum stated, 660; overall undergraduate GPA no minimum stated, 3.60; last 2 years GPA no minimum stated; psychology GPA no minimum stated; psychology GPA no minimum stated. Master's GPA is only required of those who have worked toward a Master's degree.
Other Criteria: (importance of criteria rated low, medium, or high): GRE/MAT scores medium, research experience medium, work experience medium, extracurricular activity low, clinically related public service high, GPA high, letters of recommendation medium, interview high, statement of goals and objectives medium. Not all areas hold formal interviews. Clinically related public service is important if you are applying to the clinical program.

Student Characteristics: The following represents characteristics of students in 2001–2002 in all graduate psychology programs in the department: Female–full-time 69, part-time 0; Male–full-time 27, part-time 0; African American/Black–full-time 2, part-time 0; Hispanic/Latino (a)–full-time 3, part-time 0; Asian/Pacific Islander–full-time 5, part-time 0; American Indian/Alaska Native–full-time 0, part-time 0; Multi-ethnic–full-time 0, students subject to the Americans with Disabilities Act–full-time 0.

Financial Information/Assistance:

Tuition for Full-Time Study: *Master's:* State residents per academic year $4,162, $149 per credit hour; nonstate residents: per academic year $13,872, $458 per credit hour. *Doctoral:* State residents: per academic year $4,162, $149 per credit hour; nonstate residents: per academic year $13,872, $458 per credit hour.

Financial Assistance:

First Year Students: Teaching assistantships available for first-year. Average amount paid per academic year: $10,920. Average number of hours worked per week: 20. Apply by January 1. Tuition remission given: partial. Research assistantships available for first-year. Average amount paid per academic year: $10,920. Average number of hours worked per week: 20. Apply by January 1. Tuition remission given: partial. Fellowships and scholarships available for first-year. Average amount paid per academic year: $13,500. Average number of hours worked per week: 20. Apply by January 1. Tuition remission given: partial.

Advanced Students: Teaching assistantships available for advanced students. Average amount paid per academic year: $11,220. Average number of hours worked per week: 20. Apply by January 1. Tuition remission given: partial. Research assistantships available for advanced students. Average amount paid per academic year: $11,220. Average number of hours worked per week: 20. Apply by January 1. Tuition remission given: partial. Fellowships and scholarships available for advanced students. Average amount paid per academic year: $13,500. Average number of hours worked per week: 20. Apply by January 1. Tuition remission given: partial.

Contact Information: Of all students currently enrolled full-time, 100% benefitted from one or more of the listed financial assistance programs. For information on financial assistance, contact: (765) 494-5050.

Internships/Practica: For those doctoral students for whom a professional internship is required prior to graduation, 4 applied in 2000–2001. Of those who applied, 4 were placed in internships listed by the Association of Psychology Postdoctoral and Internship Programs (APPIC); 4 were placed in APA accredited internships.

Housing and Day Care: No on-campus housing and day care facilities are available.

Employment of Department Graduates:
Master's Degree Graduates: Of those who graduated in the academic year 2000–2001, the following categories and numbers represent the post-graduate activities and employment of master's degree graduates: Enrolled in a post-doctoral residency/fellowship (n/a), employed in independent practice (n/a).
Doctoral Degree Graduates: Of those who graduated in the academic year 2000–2001, the following categories and numbers represent the post-graduate activities and employment of doctoral degree graduates: Enrolled in a psychology doctoral program (n/a), enrolled in another graduate/professional program (n/a).

Additional Information:
Orientation, Objectives, and Emphasis of Department: The dominant emphasis of the department is a commitment to research and scholarship as the major core of graduate education. All programs are structured so that students become involved in research activities almost immediately upon beginning their graduate education, and this involvement is expected to continue throughout an individual's entire graduate career.

Special Facilities or Resources: The department moved into the psychological sciences building in 1980. Excellent research facilities are available in many areas, including more than 35 computer-controlled laboratories.

Information for Students With Physical Disabilities: The Psychological Sciences building and all of its classrooms are handicapped accessible.

Application Information:
Send to: Marlene Mann, Administrative Assistant, Psychological Sciences, 1364 Psychological Sciences Bldg., Purdue University, West Lafayette, IN 47907-1364 USA. Students are admitted in the Fall, application deadline January 1. *Fee:* $30.

Saint Francis, University of
Psychology and Counseling
2701 Spring Street
Fort Wayne, IN 46808
Telephone: (260) 434-7443
Fax: (260) 434-7562
E-mail: rdaniel@sf.edu
Web: http://www.sf.edu

Department Established:
1971. Chairperson: Rolf Daniel, Ph.D. Number of Faculty: total–full-time 4, part-time 5; women–full-time 2, part-time 3; minority–full-time 1.

Programs and Degrees Offered:
Listed in the following order: Program area, degree type (T if terminal Master's), number awarded 7/00-6/01. General psychology MA (T) 6, mental health counseling MA (T) 10.

Student Applications/Admissions:
Student Applications
General psychology MA—Applications 2001–2002, 6. Total applicants accepted 2001–2002, 6. New applicants enrolled 2001–2002, 6. Total enrolled 2001–2002 full-time, 11, part-time, 4. Openings 2002–2003, 5. The Median number of years required for completion of a degree are 2. The number of students enrolled full and part-time, who were dismissed or voluntarily withdrew from this program area were 0. *Mental health counseling* MA—Applications 2001–2002, 8. Total applicants accepted 2001–2002, 5. New applicants enrolled 2001–2002, 5. Total enrolled 2001–2002 full-time, 12, part-time, 13. Openings 2002–2003, 7. The Median number of years required for completion of a degree are 3. The number of students enrolled full and part-time, who were dismissed or voluntarily withdrew from this program area were 0.

Admissions Requirements:
Scores: Entries appear in this order: required test or GPA, minimum score (if required), median score of students entering in 2001–2002. Master's Programs: overall undergraduate GPA 3.0, 3.0. Doctoral Programs: last 2 years GPA no minimum stated; psychology GPA no minimum stated; psychology GPA no minimum stated.
Other Criteria: (importance of criteria rated low, medium, or high): research experience medium, work experience medium, extracurricular activity low, clinically related public service medium, GPA high, letters of recommendation high, interview high, statement of goals and objectives high.

Student Characteristics: The following represents characteristics of students in 2001–2002 in all graduate psychology programs in the department: Female–full-time 12, part-time 23; Male–full-time 6, part-time 3; African American/Black–full-time 3, part-time 0; Hispanic/Latino (a)–full-time 0, part-time 0; Asian/Pacific Islander–full-time 1, part-time 0; American Indian/Alaska Native–full-time 0, part-time 0; Multi-ethnic–full-time 0, part-time 0; students subject to the Americans with Disabilities Act–full-time 1, part-time 0.

Financial Information/Assistance:
Tuition for Full-Time Study: *Master's:* State residents $430 per credit hour.

Financial Assistance:
First Year Students: Teaching assistantships available for first-year. Average amount paid per academic year: $3,870. Average number of hours worked per week: 10. Apply by June 30.
Advanced Students: Teaching assistantships available for advanced students. Average amount paid per academic year: $3,870. Average number of hours worked per week: 10. Apply by June 30.
Contact Information: Of all students currently enrolled full-time, 30% benefitted from one or more of the listed financial assistance programs. For information on financial assistance, contact: Office of Financial Aid, (219) 434-3283.

Internships/Practica: Students can elect to do a practicum experience. This experience would be 150 clock hours (10 hours/week) of supervised practical field experience tailored to the individual needs/interests of the students. Students choosing to have a practicum experience have an "on-site" supervisor who helps define, mentor, and direct the student's activities. Students also have 15 hours of supervision on campus. This experience is designed to give students an opportunity to integrate formal education with work experience. Mental Health Counseling (M.S.) — Practicum- 1 semester-100 hours/60 face-to-face client contact hours. Internship- 1 or 2 semesters - 600 hours/240 face-to-face client contact hours. Advanced Internship- 1 semester-300 hours/120 face-to-face client contact hours.

Housing and Day Care: No on-campus housing and day care facilities are available.

Employment of Department Graduates:

Master's Degree Graduates: Of those who graduated in the academic year 2000–2001, the following categories and numbers represent the post-graduate activities and employment of master's degree graduates: Enrolled in a psychology doctoral program (1), enrolled in another graduate/professional program (0), enrolled in a post-doctoral residency/fellowship (n/a), employed in independent practice (n/a), employed in an academic position at a university (0), employed in an academic position at a 2-year/4-year college (0), employed in other positions at a higher education institution (0), employed in a professional position in a school system (4), employed in business or industry (research/consulting) (0), employed in business or industry (management) (0), employed in a government agency (research) (0), employed in a government agency (professional services) (0), employed in a community mental health/counseling center (5), employed in a hospital/medical center (2), still seeking employment (0), other employment position (0).

Doctoral Degree Graduates: Of those who graduated in the academic year 2000–2001, the following categories and numbers represent the post-graduate activities and employment of doctoral degree graduates: Enrolled in a psychology doctoral program (n/a), enrolled in another graduate/professional program (n/a).

Additional Information:

Orientation, Objectives, and Emphasis of Department: The M.S. in Psychology Program is designed for people who are either interested in preparation for doctoral work, or furthering their professional careers through a greater understanding of basic psychological principles. The primary goal of the program is to give students a solid, graduate-level grounding in psychology. This program emphasizes a mastery of psychological fundamentals, i.e., theories and research methods, areas of specialization (development, social, abnormal behavior, physiological data, personality development, and behavior management techniques. Mental Health Counseling (M.S.) —The program of study leading to the M.S. Degree in Mental Health Counseling is designed to prepare persons to function as Licensed Mental Health Counselors (LMHC) in health care residential, private practice, community agency, governmental, business, and industrial settings. The scope of practice for mental health counseling is defined in Section 24. IC 25-23.6-1-7.5 of the Indiana Code, which is available from the Psychology & Counseling Department. To successfully complete the M.S. in Mental Health Counseling, students will: 1. Demonstrate ability to analyze, synthesize, and critique in a schol-

arly manner academic subject matter, professional journal articles, and other professional resources. Students will demonstrate ability to write coherently and professionally according to the Publication Manual of the American Psychological Association (4th edition) standards. 2. Promote and adhere to the standards/guidelines for ethical and professional conduct in all classroom and field experiences (i.e., American Counseling Association's Ethical Standards for Mental Health Professionals, and the American Psychological Association's Ethical Principles), as well as legal mandates regarding the practice of their profession. 3. Demonstrate an ability to synthesize, evaluate, and articulate broad knowledge of counseling theories and approaches. This will include ability to apply scientific and measurement principles to the study of psychology. 4. Develop a capacity to communicate respect, empathy, and unconditional positive regard toward others, including demonstration of a tolerant, non-judgmental attitude toward different ethnic/cultural heritage, value orientations, and lifestyles. 5. Recognize and effectively conceptualize the special needs of persons with varying mental, adjustment, developmental and/or chemical dependence disorders. Students will recognize the need for, request, and benefit from consultation and supervision when practicing in areas of insufficient competence. 6. Demonstrate competence to counsel/interview using basic listening and influencing skills in one-to-one, marital, family, and group counseling modalities. 7. Be prepared to seek employment as a Licensed Mental Health Counselor, enter a program of additional education/training, and/or seek other appropriate certifications.

Special Facilities or Resources: None.

Information for Students With Physical Disabilities: We have accommodations for students with physical mobility problems. We also have a program to provide academic assistance to students with physical and learning disabilities.

Application Information:
Send to: Office of Admissions, Trinity Hall, Room 110A, University of Saint Francis, Fort Wayne, IN 46808. Students are admitted in the Fall, application deadline 6/30; Spring, application deadline 10/15; Summer, application deadline 5/1. *Fee:* $20.

Valparaiso University
Department of Psychology
Dickmeyer Hall
Valparaiso, IN 46383
Telephone: (219) 464-5440
Fax: (219) 464-6878
E-mail: *daniel.arkkelin@valpo.edu*
Web: *http://www.valpo.edu/psych*

Department Established:
1958. Chairperson: Daniel Arkkelin. Number of Faculty: total–full-time 8, part-time 6; women–full-time 3, part-time 4.

Programs and Degrees Offered:
Listed in the following order: Program area, degree type (T if terminal Master's), number awarded 7/00-6/01. Counseling MA (T) 2, mental health counseling MA (T) 10, psychology/law, school psychology.

Student Applications/Admissions:

Student Applications

Counseling MA—Applications 2001–2002, 10. Total applicants accepted 2001–2002, 8. New applicants enrolled 2001–2002, 3. Total enrolled 2001–2002 full-time, 5, part-time, 5. Openings 2002–2003, 5. The Median number of years required for completion of a degree are 3. The number of students enrolled full and part-time, who were dismissed or voluntarily withdrew from this program area were 1. *Mental health counseling MA*—Applications 2001–2002, 20. Total applicants accepted 2001–2002, 16. New applicants enrolled 2001–2002, 5. Total enrolled 2001–2002 full-time, 10, part-time, 10. Openings 2002–2003, 10. The Median number of years required for completion of a degree are 3. The number of students enrolled full and part-time, who were dismissed or voluntarily withdrew from this program area were 0.

Admissions Requirements:

Scores: Entries appear in this order: required test or GPA, minimum score (if required), median score of students entering in 2001–2002. Master's Programs: overall undergraduate GPA 3.0, 3.29; last 2 years GPA 3.2, 3.35. Doctoral Programs: last 2 years GPA no minimum stated; psychology GPA no minimum stated; psychology GPA no minimum stated.

Other Criteria: (importance of criteria rated low, medium, or high): research experience medium, work experience medium, extracurricular activity low, clinically related public service medium, GPA high, letters of recommendation high, interview medium, statement of goals and objectives high.

Student Characteristics: The following represents characteristics of students in 2001–2002 in all graduate psychology programs in the department: Female–full-time 20, part-time 20; Male–full-time 5, part-time 5; African American/Black–full-time 1, part-time 0; Hispanic/Latino (a)–full-time 1, part-time 0; Asian/Pacific Islander–full-time 1, part-time 0; American Indian/Alaska Native–full-time 1, part-time 0; students subject to the Americans with Disabilities Act–full-time 1, part-time 0.

Financial Information/Assistance:

Tuition for Full-Time Study: *Master's:* State residents $300 per credit hour; nonstate residents: $300 per credit hour.

Financial Assistance:

First Year Students: Teaching assistantships available for first-year. Average amount paid per academic year: $1,000. Apply by March 1. Research assistantships available for first-year. Average amount paid per academic year: $2,000. Apply by March 1. Traineeships available for first-year. Average amount paid per academic year: $8,000. Apply by March 1. Tuition remission given: partial.

Advanced Students: Teaching assistantships available for advanced students. Average amount paid per academic year: $1,000. Apply by March 1. Research assistantships available for advanced students. Average amount paid per academic year: $2,000. Apply by March 1. Traineeships available for advanced students. Average amount paid per academic year: $8,000. Apply by March 1. Tuition remission given: partial.

Contact Information: Of all students currently enrolled full-time, 35% benefitted from one or more of the listed financial assistance programs. For information on financial assistance, contact: Dave Fevig, Director, Financial Aid Office, Valparaiso University, Valparaiso, IN 46383.

Internships/Practica: Counseling and clinical mental health counseling students obtain practical training (practica and internships) in a variety of mental health settings in Northwest Indiana. School psychology students obtain practica training (practical and internships) in school systems and special education cooperatives in Northwest Indiana.

Housing and Day Care: On-campus housing and day care facilities are available.

Employment of Department Graduates:

Master's Degree Graduates: Of those who graduated in the academic year 2000–2001, the following categories and numbers represent the post-graduate activities and employment of master's degree graduates: Enrolled in a psychology doctoral program (1), enrolled in another graduate/professional program (0), enrolled in a post-doctoral residency/fellowship (n/a), employed in independent practice (n/a), employed in an academic position at a university (0), employed in an academic position at a 2-year/4-year college (0), employed in other positions at a higher education institution (0), employed in a professional position in a school system (5), employed in business or industry (research/consulting) (0), employed in business or industry (management) (0), employed in a government agency (research) (0), employed in a government agency (professional services) (3), employed in a community mental health/counseling center (6), employed in a hospital/medical center (1), still seeking employment (0), other employment position (0).

Doctoral Degree Graduates: Of those who graduated in the academic year 2000–2001, the following categories and numbers represent the post-graduate activities and employment of doctoral degree graduates: Enrolled in a psychology doctoral program (n/a), enrolled in another graduate/professional program (n/a).

Additional Information:

Orientation, Objectives, and Emphasis of Department: The counseling program is designed to provide advanced training to persons planning or continuing in a counseling career. The program combines a strong theoretical background in counseling with applied work through both coursework and supervised practica. A thesis option is available. The clinical mental health counseling program is designed to lead toward licensure or certification in most of the 50 states. It involves additional coursework and experiential requirements. The school psychology program is designed to provide advanced training to persons seeking certification in Indiana as school psychologists. The program is offered jointly by the psychology and education departments. The UD/MA program provides traditional legal training, exposure to psychological theory and methods and integrator training, in the application of psychological foundations to the practice of law. The program is offered jointly by the law school and psychology department.

Special Facilities or Resources: The Department maintains strong contacts with community and regional agencies involved in mental health and counseling as well as with the campus counseling center. In addition, an in-house clinical training lab utilizing audio-video taping may be used in student training of clinical skills. Both micro- and mainframe computer facilities are available in the department and throughout campus.

Application Information:
Send to: Office of Graduate Studies, Kretzmann Hall, Valparaiso University, Valparaiso, IN 46383. Students are admitted in the Fall, application deadline March 1. *Fee:* $30. Hardship.

Iowa State University

Department of Psychology
Liberal Arts & Sciences
Lagomarcino Hall
Ames, IA 50011-3180
Telephone: (515) 294-1742
Fax: (515) 294-6424
E-mail: *psychadm@iastate.edu*
Web: *http://psychology.iastate.edu/*

Department Established:
1924. Chair: Craig A. Anderson. Number of Faculty: total–full-time 22, part-time 9; women–full-time 8, part-time 4; minority–full-time 1.

Programs and Degrees Offered:
Listed in the following order: Program area, degree type (T if terminal Master's), number awarded 7/00-6/01. Counseling PhD 3, experimental PhD, general, social PhD 3.

APA Accreditation: Counseling PhD: full.

Student Applications/Admissions:
Student Applications
Counseling PhD—Applications 2001–2002, 51. Total applicants accepted 2001–2002, 12. New applicants enrolled 2001–2002, 4. Total enrolled 2001–2002 full-time, 17, part-time, 10. Openings 2002–2003, 5. The Median number of years required for completion of a degree are 6. The number of students enrolled full and part-time, who were dismissed or voluntarily withdrew from this program area were 0. *Experimental PhD*—Applications 2001–2002, 8. Total applicants accepted 2001–2002, 2. New applicants enrolled 2001–2002, 1. Total enrolled 2001–2002 full-time, 2, part-time, 1. Openings 2002–2003, 4. The Median number of years required for completion of a degree are NA. The number of students enrolled full and part-time, who were dismissed or voluntarily withdrew from this program area were 0. *Social PhD*—Applications 2001–2002, 30. Total applicants accepted 2001–2002, 10. New applicants enrolled 2001–2002, 5. Total enrolled 2001–2002 full-time, 13. Openings 2002–2003, 4. The Median number of years required for completion of a degree are 5. The number of students enrolled full and part-time, who were dismissed or voluntarily withdrew from this program area were 0.

Admissions Requirements:
Scores: Entries appear in this order: required test or GPA, minimum score (if required), median score of students entering in 2001–2002. Master's Programs: GRE-V no minimum stated, 500; GRE-Q no minimum stated, 600; GRE-Analytical no minimum stated, 715; GRE-Subject(Psych) no minimum stated, 590; overall undergraduate GPA no minimum stated, 3.57; last 2 years GPA no minimum stated, 3.57; psychology GPA no minimum stated, 3.61. TOEFL required for international applicants. Doctoral Programs: GRE-V no minimum stated, 575; GRE-Q no minimum stated, 670; GRE-Analytical

no minimum stated, 675; GRE-V+Q+Analytical no minimum stated; GRE-Subject(Psych) no minimum stated, 640; overall undergraduate GPA no minimum stated, 3.71; last 2 years GPA no minimum stated, 3.80; psychology GPA no minimum stated, 3.88; psychology GPA no minimum stated. TOEFL required for international applicants.
Other Criteria: (importance of criteria rated low, medium, or high): GRE/MAT scores high, research experience high, work experience low, extracurricular activity low, clinically related public service low, GPA, letters of recommendation high, interview medium, statement of goals and objectives high. Our applied/professional programs place greater weight on the interview and relevant work/service experience.

Student Characteristics: The following represents characteristics of students in 2001–2002 in all graduate psychology programs in the department: Female–full-time 28, part-time 9; Male–full-time 17, part-time 3; African American/Black–full-time 2, part-time 0; Hispanic/Latino (a)–full-time 2, part-time 0; Asian/Pacific Islander–full-time 1, part-time 0; American Indian/Alaska Native–full-time 0, part-time 0; Multi-ethnic–full-time 0, part-time 0; students subject to the Americans with Disabilities Act–full-time 0, part-time 0.

Financial Information/Assistance:
Tuition for Full-Time Study: *Master's:* State residents per academic year $3,702, $206 per credit hour; nonstate residents: per academic year $10,898, $606 per credit hour. *Doctoral:* State residents: per academic year $3,702, $206 per credit hour; nonstate residents: per academic year $10,898, $606 per credit hour.

Financial Assistance:
First Year Students: Teaching assistantships available for first-year. Average amount paid per academic year: $9,640. Average number of hours worked per week: 20. Apply by 1/3/03. Tuition remission given: full. Research assistantships available for first-year. Average amount paid per academic year: $9,640. Average number of hours worked per week: 20. Apply by 1/3/03. Tuition remission given: full. Fellowships and scholarships available for first-year. Average amount paid per academic year: $10,400. Average number of hours worked per week: 20. Apply by 1/3/03. Tuition remission given: full.
Advanced Students: Teaching assistantships available for advanced students. Average amount paid per academic year: $10,400. Average number of hours worked per week: 20. Apply by NA. Tuition remission given: partial. Research assistantships available for advanced students. Average amount paid per academic year: $10,400. Average number of hours worked per week: 20. Apply by NA. Tuition remission given: partial.
Contact Information: Of all students currently enrolled full-time, 100% benefitted from one or more of the listed financial assistance programs. For information on financial assistance, contact: Graduate Admissions (psychadm@iastate.edu or 512-294-1743).

Internships/Practica: Sequential, progressive practica provide students in our professional programs with individually supervised applied training in their specialty area. All supervision is provided by appropriately certified/licensed faculty and adjuncts in a range of settings, including university counseling centers, major hospitals, outpatient clinics, child and adolescent treatment centers, correctional facilities, and the public school system. Based on such practica experience and their academic training, ISU students compete successfully for select predoctoral internships across the country. For those doctoral students for whom a professional internship is required prior to graduation, 6 applied in 2000–2001. Of those who applied, 6 were placed in internships listed by the Association of Psychology Postdoctoral and Internship Programs (APPIC); 6 were placed in APA accredited internships.

Housing and Day Care: On-campus housing and day care facilities are available.

Employment of Department Graduates:

Master's Degree Graduates: Of those who graduated in the academic year 2000–2001, the following categories and numbers represent the post-graduate activities and employment of master's degree graduates: Enrolled in a psychology doctoral program (3), enrolled in another graduate/professional program (3), enrolled in a post-doctoral residency/fellowship (n/a), employed in independent practice (n/a), employed in business or industry (management) (1), other employment position (3).

Doctoral Degree Graduates: Of those who graduated in the academic year 2000–2001, the following categories and numbers represent the post-graduate activities and employment of doctoral degree graduates: Enrolled in a psychology doctoral program (n/a), enrolled in another graduate/professional program (n/a), employed in an academic position at a university (1), employed in an academic position at a 2-year/4-year college (1), employed in other positions at a higher education institution (1), employed in a professional position in a school system (2), employed in business or industry (research/consulting) (1), employed in a government agency (professional services) (1), other employment position (1).

Additional Information:

Orientation, Objectives, and Emphasis of Department: Graduate programs emphasize the acquisition of a broad base of knowledge in psychology as well as concentration on the content and methodological skills requisite to performance in teaching, research, and applied activities. A strong research orientation is evident in all areas of the department, with involvement in research being required of all doctoral students throughout their graduate studies. Curriculum requirements for the degrees are based on a core course system, which is designed to enable students to tailor a program best suited to their particular objectives. Subsequent courses, seminars, research, and applied experiences are determined by the student and his or her graduate advisory committee. Additionally, teaching experience is available to all doctoral students, and extensive supervised practica experience is required of students in the applied programs.

Special Facilities or Resources: The department maintains the full array of physical facilities and equipment required for behavioral research. Observational and videotaping facilities are available for research and applied training. The department maintains a microcomputer lab, and the university maintains a superior computation center.

Application Information:

Send to: Graduate Admissions. Students are admitted in the Fall, application deadline January 3. MS deadline is March 15 for fall admission. *Fee:* $20. $50 fee for international application.

Iowa, University of
Department of Psychology
Liberal Arts and Sciences
11 Seashore Hall East
Iowa City, IA 52242-1407
Telephone: (319) 335-2406
Fax: (319) 335-0191
E-mail: *psychology@uiowa.edu*
Web: *http://www.psychology.uiowa.edu.*

Department Established:

1887. Chairperson: Gregg C. Oden. Number of Faculty: total–full-time 30, part-time 6; women–full-time 9, part-time 4.

Programs and Degrees Offered:

Listed in the following order: Program area, degree type (T if terminal Master's), number awarded 7/00-6/01. Behavioral and cognitive neuro PhD 1, clinical PhD 5, cognition and perception PhD 1, developmental PhD 2, personality and social PhD 3.

APA Accreditation: Clinical PhD: full.

Student Applications/Admissions:

Student Applications

Behavioral and cognitive neuro PhD—Applications 2001–2002, 17. Total applicants accepted 2001–2002, 1. New applicants enrolled 2001–2002, 1. Total enrolled 2001–2002 full-time, 11. Openings 2002–2003, 4. The Median number of years required for completion of a degree are 5. The number of students enrolled full and part-time, who were dismissed or voluntarily withdrew from this program area were 1. *Clinical PhD*—Applications 2001–2002, 135. Total applicants accepted 2001–2002, 11. New applicants enrolled 2001–2002, 5. Total enrolled 2001–2002 full-time, 20. Openings 2002–2003, 5. The Median number of years required for completion of a degree are 7. The number of students enrolled full and part-time, who were dismissed or voluntarily withdrew from this program area were 1. *Cognition and perception PhD*—Applications 2001–2002, 22. Total applicants accepted 2001–2002, 11. New applicants enrolled 2001–2002, 1. Total enrolled 2001–2002 full-time, 6. Openings 2002–2003, 4. The Median number of years required for completion of a degree are 5. The number of students enrolled full and part-time, who were dismissed or voluntarily withdrew from this program area were 1. *Developmental PhD*—Applications 2001–2002, 13. Total applicants accepted 2001–2002, 4. New applicants enrolled 2001–2002, 2. Total enrolled 2001–2002 full-time, 8. Openings 2002–2003, 4. The Median number of years required for completion of a degree are 6. The number of students enrolled full and part-time, who were dismissed or voluntarily withdrew from this program area were 0. *Personality and social PhD*—Applications 2001–2002, 40. Total applicants accepted 2001–2002, 9. New applicants enrolled 2001–2002, 4. Total enrolled 2001–2002 full-time, 19. Openings 2002–2003, 4. The Median number of years required for completion of a degree are 8. The number of students enrolled full and part-time, who were dismissed or voluntarily withdrew from this program area were 0.

Admissions Requirements:
Scores: Entries appear in this order: required test or GPA, minimum score (if required), median score of students entering in 2001–2002. Doctoral Programs: GRE-V no minimum stated; GRE-Q no minimum stated; GRE-V+Q no minimum stated, 1270; GRE-Analytical no minimum stated; overall undergraduate GPA no minimum stated; last 2 years GPA no minimum stated; psychology GPA no minimum stated; psychology GPA no minimum stated.
Other Criteria: (importance of criteria rated low, medium, or high): GRE/MAT scores high, research experience high, work experience medium, extracurricular activity low, clinically related public service medium, GPA high, letters of recommendation high, interview medium, statement of goals and objectives high, commitment to research high. Interview of high importance for behavioral and cognitive neuroscience and clinical areas.

Student Characteristics: The following represents characteristics of students in 2001–2002 in all graduate psychology programs in the department: Female–full-time 6, part-time 0; Male–full-time 8, part-time 0; African American/Black–full-time 0, part-time 0; Hispanic/Latino (a)–full-time 0, part-time 0; Asian/Pacific Islander–full-time 0, part-time 0; American Indian/Alaska Native–full-time 0, part-time 0.

Financial Information/Assistance:
Tuition for Full-Time Study: *Doctoral:* State residents: per academic year $3,702; nonstate residents: per academic year $11,924.

Financial Assistance:
First Year Students: Teaching assistantships available for first-year. Average amount paid per academic year: $14,718. Average number of hours worked per week: 20. Research assistantships available for first-year. Average amount paid per academic year: $14,718. Average number of hours worked per week: 20. Fellowships and scholarships available for first-year. Average amount paid per academic year: $13,000. Average number of hours worked per week: 0. Tuition remission given: full.
Advanced Students: Teaching assistantships available for advanced students. Average amount paid per academic year: $15,316. Average number of hours worked per week: 20. Research assistantships available for advanced students. Average amount paid per academic year: $15,316. Average number of hours worked per week: 20. Fellowships and scholarships available for advanced students. Average amount paid per academic year: $15,500. Average number of hours worked per week: 0. Tuition remission given: full.
Contact Information: Of all students currently enrolled full-time, 100% benefitted from one or more of the listed financial assistance programs.

Internships/Practica: For those doctoral students for whom a professional internship is required prior to graduation, 4 applied in 2000–2001. Of those who applied, 4 were placed in internships listed by the Association of Psychology Postdoctoral and Intern-

ship Programs (APPIC); 4 were placed in APA accredited internships.

Housing and Day Care: On-campus housing and day care facilities are available.

Employment of Department Graduates:
Master's Degree Graduates: Of those who graduated in the academic year 2000–2001, the following categories and numbers represent the post-graduate activities and employment of master's degree graduates: Enrolled in a post-doctoral residency/fellowship (n/a), employed in independent practice (n/a).
Doctoral Degree Graduates: Of those who graduated in the academic year 2000–2001, the following categories and numbers represent the post-graduate activities and employment of doctoral degree graduates: Enrolled in a psychology doctoral program (n/a), enrolled in another graduate/professional program (n/a), enrolled in a post-doctoral residency/fellowship (4), employed in an academic position at a university (2), employed in other positions at a higher education institution (1), employed in business or industry (research/consulting) (1).

Additional Information:
Orientation, Objectives, and Emphasis of Department: The mission of the PhD program is to produce professional scholars whose preparation will enable them to contribute significantly to the advancement of scientific psychological knowledge as well as effectively teach undergraduate and graduate students about the science of psychology. Some of these scholars may, in addition, be prepared to deliver psychological services. The value of well-trained researchers and practitioners (Boulder Model) is endorsed by faculty in all areas. The overall goal of the graduate program is to produce PhD's who appreciate and are deeply committed to the study of psychological processes and behavior, who are familiar with fundamental knowledge in the field, and who are well-trained in methodology and modern techniques of data analysis. Graduate training is organized into five broad training areas: clinical psychology, developmental psychology, cognition and perception, behavioral and cognitive neuroscience, and personality and social psychology. The training programs are flexible, and there is considerable overlap in study, research, and interaction among students and faculty in all areas. For example, there is an emphasis on health psychology that cuts across several training areas. Students typically graduate in five years and students in good standing receive full support during the five years of study. Because the department is committed to a "full funding approach," the student-faculty ratio remains quite low, usually less than 2 to 1. The department has been successful in establishing strong ties with other campus units such as counseling psychology, law, the business school, and the medical school. Through these associations, one may study such topics as the law and psychology, aging, organizational and consumer behavior, communications, and neurobehavioral science.

Special Facilities or Resources: The Kenneth W. Spence Laboratories of Psychology and adjoining space in Seashore Hall include automated data acquisition and analysis systems, extensive computing facilities, observation suites with remote audiovisual control and recording equipment, multiple animal facilities, several surgeries, a histology laboratory, soundproof chambers, closed-circuit TV systems, electrophysiological recording rooms, conditioning laboratories, the Carl E. Seashore Psychology Training

Clinic, and well-equipped electronic, mechanical, and woodworking shops. We are currently undergoing a multi-million dollar laboratory expansion and renovation project to keep our laboratories at the cutting edge of science. In addition, many resources are available through collaboration with colleagues at the university hospital, the Iowa Veterans Administration Hospital, community service centers, and the Colleges of Medicine, Nursing, Dentistry, Engineering, Business, Education, and Law.

Information for Students With Physical Disabilities: Psychology teaching and research facilities are handicap accessible.

Application Information:
Send to: Graduate Admissions Office, 11 Seashore Hall E. Students are admitted in the Fall, application deadline January 1. *Fee:* $30.

Iowa, University of
Division of Psychological and Quantitative Foundations
College of Education
361 Lindquist Center
Iowa City, IA 52242
Telephone: (319) 335-5577
Fax: (319) 335-6145
E-mail: *janet-ervin@uiowa.edu*
Web: *http://www.uiowa.edu*

Department Established:
Chairperson: Tom Rocklin. Number of Faculty: total–full-time 13, part-time 12; women–full-time 5, part-time 3; minority–full-time 1, part-time 1.

Programs and Degrees Offered:
Listed in the following order: Program area, degree type (T if terminal Master's), number awarded 7/00-6/01. Counseling PhD 8, educational PhD (T) 1, educational measurement & stat MA 3, educational measurement and st PhD 5, school PhD 5.

APA Accreditation: Counseling PhD: full. School PhD: full.

Student Applications/Admissions:
Student Applications

Counseling PhD—Applications 2001–2002, 65. Total applicants accepted 2001–2002, 11. New applicants enrolled 2001–2002, 6. Total enrolled 2001–2002 full-time, 35. Openings 2002–2003, 6. *Educational PhD*—Applications 2001–2002, 13. Total applicants accepted 2001–2002, 7. New applicants enrolled 2001–2002, 4. Total enrolled 2001–2002 full-time, 18. *Educational measurement & stat MA*—Applications 2001–2002, 10. Total applicants accepted 2001–2002, 10. New applicants enrolled 2001–2002, 9. Total enrolled 2001–2002 full-time, 24. *Educational measurement and st PhD*—Applications 2001–2002, 14. Total applicants accepted 2001–2002, 7. New applicants enrolled 2001–2002, 6. Total enrolled 2001–2002 full-time, 39. *School PhD*—Applications 2001–2002, 26. Total applicants accepted 2001–2002, 7. New applicants enrolled 2001–2002, 4. Total enrolled 2001–2002 full-time, 38.

Admissions Requirements:
Scores: Entries appear in this order: required test or GPA, minimum score (if required), median score of students entering

in 2001–2002. Master's Programs: GRE-V+Q 1100. Doctoral Programs: GRE-V+Q 1200; overall undergraduate GPA 3.00; last 2 years GPA no minimum stated; psychology GPA no minimum stated; psychology GPA no minimum stated.
Other Criteria: (importance of criteria rated low, medium, or high): GRE/MAT scores high, research experience high, work experience medium, extracurricular activity low, clinically related public service high, GPA high, letters of recommendation high, interview medium, statement of goals and objectives high. School psychology PhD/education specialist in school psychology: GRE/MAT scores high, work experience high, clinically related public service high, GPA high, letters of recommendation high, interview high, statement of goals and objectives high, research experience medium, extracurricular activity low. For the counseling psychology program: GPA high, letters of recommendation high, statement of goals and objectives high, GRE/MAT scores medium, research experience medium, work experience medium, clinically related public service medium, interview none.

Student Characteristics: The following represents characteristics of students in 2001–2002 in all graduate psychology programs in the department: Female–full-time 66, part-time 0; Male–full-time 23, part-time 0; African American/Black–full-time 13, part-time 0; Hispanic/Latino (a)–full-time 11, part-time 0; Asian/Pacific Islander–full-time 5, part-time 0; American Indian/Alaska Native–full-time 2, part-time 0.

Financial Information/Assistance:
Tuition for Full-Time Study: *Master's:* State residents $206 per credit hour; nonstate residents: $206 per credit hour. *Doctoral:* State residents: $206 per credit hour; nonstate residents: $206 per credit hour.

Financial Assistance:
First Year Students: Research assistantships available for first-year. Average amount paid per academic year: $14,718. Average number of hours worked per week: 20. Apply by April 1.
Advanced Students: Research assistantships available for advanced students. Average amount paid per academic year: $14,718. Average number of hours worked per week: 20. Apply by April 1. Fellowships and scholarships available for advanced students. Average amount paid per academic year: $14,718. Average number of hours worked per week: 20. Tuition remission given: partial.
Contact Information: Of all students currently enrolled full-time, 5% benefitted from one or more of the listed financial assistance programs. For information on financial assistance, contact: Financial Aid Office.

Internships/Practica: There are multiple practicum sites at a variety of agencies, (e.g., university counseling centers, VA medical centers, community mental health centers). Educational Psychology Program: Formal internship and practica experiences are not available for MA students, although some students do find paid positions as teaching or research assistants in fields in which they have prior experience. At the PhD level, most students are supported by half-time fellowships or assistantships. In a research-oriented program, these paid positions serve the purpose of an internship or fellowship. School Psychology Program—Practica: Available in the public schools, The University of Iowa Hospitals and Clinics (Department of Pediatrics, Psychiatry and Neurology), the Berlin-Blank National Center for Gifted, located in the College of Education, The Wendell Johnson Speech and Hearing Clinic at the University of Iowa, and in local mental health agencies.

Housing and Day Care: On-campus housing and day care facilities are available.

Employment of Department Graduates:

Master's Degree Graduates: Of those who graduated in the academic year 2000–2001, the following categories and numbers represent the post-graduate activities and employment of master's degree graduates: Enrolled in a psychology doctoral program (4), enrolled in another graduate/professional program (1), enrolled in a post-doctoral residency/fellowship (n/a), employed in independent practice (n/a), employed in an academic position at a university (3), employed in other positions at a higher education institution (3), employed in a professional position in a school system (4), employed in business or industry (research/consulting) (7), employed in a community mental health/counseling center (1), employed in a hospital/medical center (2).

Doctoral Degree Graduates: Of those who graduated in the academic year 2000–2001, the following categories and numbers represent the post-graduate activities and employment of doctoral degree graduates: Enrolled in a psychology doctoral program (n/a), enrolled in another graduate/professional program (n/a), enrolled in a post-doctoral residency/fellowship (1), employed in independent practice (3).

Additional Information:

Orientation, Objectives, and Emphasis of Department: The counseling psychology program endorses a scientist-practitioner model and expects students to be competent researchers and practitioners at the completion of their program. At the PhD level, the educational psychology program at the University of Iowa is designed to provide students with strong grounding in the psychology of learning and instruction. Students are encouraged to become proficient in both quantitative and qualitative research methods with an emphasis on the former. The study of individual differences is one program emphasis. At the MA level, the program provides a broad introduction to educational psychology and flexible accommodation of individual students' interest in diverse areas such as instructional technology, reading acquisition, and program evaluation. The doctoral program in school psychology is committed to training professional psychologists who are knowledgeable about providing services to children in school, medical and mental health settings. The students will possess expertise in addressing children's social/emotional needs and learning processes. The program's curriculum has been developed to reflect consideration of multicultural issues within psychological theory, research, and professional development. The program strives to produce psychologists who are competent in working in a variety of settings with children/adolescents with a wide array of problems and be able to provide a wide range of psychological services to children and the adults in their lives.

Special Facilities or Resources: The University of Iowa Hospitals and Clinics provide multiple research opportunities. Outstanding computer facilities exist on the campus. Educational Psychology Program—Students in the educational psychology program frequently make use of two important resources of the University of Iowa College of Education. The Iowa Testing Programs, creator of the Iowa Tests of Basic Skills and the Iowa Tests of Educational Development, are housed here. Students have access to test databases for research and may work with faculty or research assistantships supported by the Iowa Measurement Research Foundation. The Berlin/Blank International Center for Gifted Education also provides opportunities for research, teaching, and counseling experiences as well as assistantship support. School Psychology Program—All of the above settings are open to applied research and have existing data available to students as do American College Testing and National Computer Systems, located in Iowa City, IA.

Information for Students With Physical Disabilities: There is a well-staffed office for students with disabilities housed in the University Division of Student Affairs. Educational Psychology Program—The College of Education is well-equipped with computer-based assistive technology that is available to students with disabilities. The campus is adjacent to the center of town, and both public and campus transportation services are available to people with disabilities, including those who use wheelchairs. School Psychology Program—Several offices within the University of Iowa provide services or assist in arranging accommodations for students, staff, and faculty with physical disabilities.

Application Information:
Send to: Susan Cline, Student Services Admissions, College of Education, N310 Lindquist Center, Iowa City, IA 52242. For students admitted in the Fall, application deadlines are: MA: May 1-MS, January 1-EP; PhD: January 1-EP, March 1-MS, January 15-CP, January 1-SP. For students admitted in the Spring, deadlines are: MA November 1-MS; PhD September 1-MS. *Fee:* $30.

Northern Iowa, University of
Department of Psychology
Social and Behavioral Sciences
334 Baker Hall
Cedar Falls, IA 50614-0505
Telephone: (319) 273-2303
Fax: (319) 273-6188
E-mail: *helen.harton@uni.edu*
Web: *http://www.uni.edu/psych*

Department Established:
1968. Head: Frank Barrios. Number of Faculty: total–full-time 14, part-time 6; women–full-time 6, part-time 5; minority–full-time 3, part-time 1.

Programs and Degrees Offered:
Listed in the following order: Program area, degree type (T if terminal Master's), number awarded 7/00-6/01. Applied clinical MA (T) 7, experimental social MA (T), industrial/organizational MA (T) 3.

Student Applications/Admissions:
Student Applications

Applied clinical MA—Applications 2001–2002, 19. Total applicants accepted 2001–2002, 17. New applicants enrolled 2001–2002, 9. Total enrolled 2001–2002 full-time, 14. Openings 2002–2003, 9. The Median number of years required for completion of a degree are 2. The number of students enrolled full and part-time, who were dismissed or voluntarily withdrew from this program area were 1. *Experimental social* MA—Applications 2001–2002, 6. Total applicants accepted 2001–2002, 4. New applicants enrolled 2001–2002, 2. Total enrolled 2001–2002 full-time, 2. Openings 2002–2003, 4. The Median number of years required for completion of a degree are 2. The number of students enrolled full and part-time, who were dismissed or voluntarily withdrew from this program area were 0. *Industrial/organizational* MA—Applications 2001–2002, 13. Total applicants accepted 2001–2002, 8. New applicants enrolled 2001–2002, 3. Total enrolled 2001–2002 full-time, 7. Openings 2002–2003, 5. The Median number of years required for completion of a degree are 2. The number of students enrolled full and part-time, who were dismissed or voluntarily withdrew from this program area were 0.

Admissions Requirements:

Scores: Entries appear in this order: required test or GPA, minimum score (if required), median score of students entering in 2001–2002. Master's Programs: GRE-V 450, 450; GRE-Q 450, 500; GRE-V+Q 900, 950; GRE-Analytical 500, 580; GRE-V+Q+Analytical 1400, 1530; overall undergraduate GPA 3.00, 3.40. If the student does not have an undergraduate major in psychology, the GRE-Subject test in Psychology is required as part of the application. Minimum score is 450. Doctoral Programs: last 2 years GPA no minimum stated; psychology GPA no minimum stated; psychology GPA no minimum stated.

Other Criteria: (importance of criteria rated low, medium, or high): GRE/MAT scores high, research experience high, work experience medium, extracurricular activity low, clinically related public service medium, GPA high, letters of recommendation high, interview medium, statement of goals and objectives high.

Student Characteristics: The following represents characteristics of students in 2001–2002 in all graduate psychology programs in the department: Female–full-time 13, part-time 0; Male–full-time 9, part-time 0; African American/Black–full-time 3, part-time 0; Hispanic/Latino (a)–full-time 1, part-time 0; Asian/Pacific Islander–full-time 2, part-time 0; American Indian/Alaska Native–full-time 0, part-time 0; students subject to the Americans with Disabilities Act–full-time 1.

Financial Information/Assistance:

Tuition for Full-Time Study: *Master's:* State residents per academic year $3,702; nonstate residents: per academic year $8,438.

Financial Assistance:

First Year Students: Teaching assistantships available for first-year. Average amount paid per academic year: $3,200. Average number of hours worked per week: 10. Apply by March 1. Research assistantships available for first-year. Average amount paid per academic year: $3,200. Average number of hours worked per week: 10. Apply by March 1. Fellowships and scholarships available for first-year. Average amount paid per academic year: $1,851. Average number of hours worked per week: 0. Apply by March 1.

Advanced Students: Teaching assistantships available for advanced students. Average amount paid per academic year: $3,200. Average number of hours worked per week: 10. Apply by March 1. Research assistantships available for advanced students. Average amount paid per academic year: $3,200. Average number of hours worked per week: 10. Apply by March 1. Fellowships and scholarships available for advanced students. Average amount paid per academic year: $1,851. Average number of hours worked per week: 0. Apply by March 1.

Contact Information: Of all students currently enrolled full-time, 81% benefitted from one or more of the listed financial assistance programs. For information on financial assistance, contact: Graduate Coordinator, Department of Psychology, University of Northern Iowa, Cedar Falls, IA 50614-0505.

Internships/Practica: A variety of practicum sites are available for second year students in the applied-clinical and industrial-organizational tracks. Clinical practicum sites have included the University Counseling Center, the State Psychiatric Hospital, and community-based agencies. I/O practicum sites have included the University's Human Resources Office, local businesses, and some nationally known out-of-state businesses (during the summer terms). Students in the experimental social track conduct independent research projects during their first year under faculty supervision and present these research projects during the second year at regional and national professional conferences.

Housing and Day Care: On-campus housing and day care facilities are available.

Employment of Department Graduates:

Master's Degree Graduates: Of those who graduated in the academic year 2000–2001, the following categories and numbers represent the post-graduate activities and employment of master's degree graduates: Enrolled in a psychology doctoral program (40), enrolled in a post-doctoral residency/fellowship (n/a), employed in independent practice (n/a), employed in other positions at a higher education institution (10), employed in business or industry (research/consulting) (10), employed in business or industry (management) (10), employed in a government agency (professional services) (10), employed in a community mental health/counseling center (10), other employment position (10).

Doctoral Degree Graduates: Of those who graduated in the academic year 2000–2001, the following categories and numbers represent the post-graduate activities and employment of doctoral degree graduates: Enrolled in a psychology doctoral program (n/a), enrolled in another graduate/professional program (n/a).

Additional Information:

Orientation, Objectives, and Emphasis of Department: The M.A. program in general psychology provides a strong empirical, research-based approach to the study of human behavior. Students select one of three tracks: a) applied clinical; b) experimental social; or c) industrial-organizational. The objectives of the program are: a) to provide students with opportunities to develop skills in research methodology; b) to gain knowledge of basic areas of scientific psychology; and c) to obtain competence in research, consulting, and/or clinical skills. The experimental social emphasis is designed for students who wish to pursue doctoral degrees in social psychology. The applied-clinical emphasis is designed for those who wish to either obtain doctoral degrees in clinical or counseling psychology or become master's level providers of services operating in clinical settings under appropriate supervision. The industrial/organizational emphasis is designed for those planning doctoral study in I/O psychology or a position in Human Resources.

Special Facilities or Resources: The department provides laboratory space for research with human subjects; access to community facilities and populations for applied research; good access to computers for graduate students; and adequate office space for graduate students.

Application Information:
Send to: Graduate Coordinator, Department of Psychology, University of Northern Iowa, Cedar Falls, IA 50614-0505. Students are admitted in the Fall, application deadline April 30. For full consideration, applications should be completed by March 1, although applications will continued to be considered if they are received by April 30. *Fee:* $20.

Emporia State University
Department of Psychology and Special Education
The Teachers College
1200 Commercial Street
Emporia, KS 66801-5087
Telephone: (620) 341-5317
Fax: (620) 341-5801
E-mail: *weaverke@emporia.edu*
Web: *http://psychspe.emporia.edu*

Department Established:

1932. Chairperson: Kenneth A. Weaver. Number of Faculty: to-tal–full-time 16, part-time 3; women–full-time 7, part-time 3; minority–full-time 1; faculty subject to the Americans with Disabilities Act 1.

Programs and Degrees Offered:

Listed in the following order: Program area, degree type (T if terminal Master's), number awarded 7/00-6/01. Art therapy MA (T) 5, general MA (T) 19, school EdS 6, special education MA (T) 29.

Student Applications/Admissions:

Student Applications

Art therapy MA—Applications 2001–2002, 9. Total applicants accepted 2001–2002, 9. New applicants enrolled 2001–2002, 9. Total enrolled 2001–2002 full-time, 15, part-time, 4. Openings 2002–2003, 20. The Median number of years required for completion of a degree are 2. The number of students enrolled full and part-time, who were dismissed or voluntarily withdrew from this program area were 1. *General MA*—Applications 2001–2002, 33. Total applicants accepted 2001–2002, 30. New applicants enrolled 2001–2002, 21. Total enrolled 2001–2002 full-time, 38, part-time, 9. Openings 2002–2003, 45. The Median number of years required for completion of a degree are 3. The number of students enrolled full and part-time, who were dismissed or voluntarily withdrew from this program area were 1. *School EdS*—Applications 2001–2002, 10. Total applicants accepted 2001–2002, 12. New applicants enrolled 2001–2002, 5. Total enrolled 2001–2002 full-time, 13, part-time, 2. Openings 2002–2003, 10. The Median number of years required for completion of a degree are 3. The number of students enrolled full and part-time, who were dismissed or voluntarily withdrew from this program area were 0. *Special education MA*—Applications 2001–2002, 40. Total applicants accepted 2001–2002, 38. New applicants enrolled 2001–2002, 38. Total enrolled 2001–2002 part-time, 47. Openings 2002–2003, 45. The Median number of years required for completion of a degree are 4. The number of students enrolled full and part-time, who were dismissed or voluntarily withdrew from this program area were 0.

Admissions Requirements:

Scores: Entries appear in this order: required test or GPA, minimum score (if required), median score of students entering in 2001–2002. Master's Programs: GRE-V no minimum stated; GRE-Q no minimum stated; GRE-V+Q no minimum stated; MAT no minimum stated; overall undergraduate GPA 3.00; last 2 years GPA 3.25. 2.75 for Special Education. Doctoral Programs: last 2 years GPA no minimum stated; psychology GPA no minimum stated; psychology GPA no minimum stated.

Other Criteria: (importance of criteria rated low, medium, or high): GRE/MAT scores low, research experience medium, work experience low, extracurricular activity low, GPA high, letters of recommendation medium, statement of goals and objectives medium. Special Education does not require GRE/MAT scores

Student Characteristics: The following represents characteristics of students in 2001–2002 in all graduate psychology programs in the department: Female–full-time 34, part-time 8; Male–full-time 16, part-time 4; African American/Black–full-time 10, part-time 0; Hispanic/Latino (a)–full-time 2, part-time 0; Asian/Pacific Islander–full-time 1, part-time 1; American Indian/Alaska Native–full-time 0, part-time 0.

Financial Information/Assistance:

Tuition for Full-Time Study: *Master's:* State residents per academic year $2,632, $119 per credit hour; nonstate residents: per academic year $6,734, $290 per credit hour.

Financial Assistance:

First Year Students: Teaching assistantships available for first-year. Average amount paid per academic year: $5,273. Average number of hours worked per week: 20. Apply by March 15. Tuition remission given: full. Research assistantships available for first-year. Average amount paid per academic year: $5,632. Average number of hours worked per week: 20. Apply by March 15. Tuition remission given: partial.

Advanced Students: Teaching assistantships available for advanced students. Average amount paid per academic year: $5,273. Average number of hours worked per week: 20. Apply by March 15. Tuition remission given: full. Research assistantships available for advanced students. Average amount paid per academic year: $5,632. Average number of hours worked per week: 20. Apply by March 15. Tuition remission given: partial.

Contact Information: Of all students currently enrolled full-time, 95% benefitted from one or more of the listed financial assistance programs. For information on financial assistance, contact: Office of Financial Aid, (620) 341-5457.

Internships/Practica: MS Psychology students must do internships. For Clinical students, it is 750 clock hours in a mental health setting supervised by a PhD psychologist. For I/O students it is 350 clock hours in a business setting. For Experimental students, it is a semester working in a laboratory setting.

Housing and Day Care: On-campus housing and day care facilities are available.

Employment of Department Graduates:

Master's Degree Graduates: Of those who graduated in the academic year 2000–2001, the following categories and numbers represent the post-graduate activities and employment of master's degree graduates: Enrolled in a psychology doctoral program (6), enrolled in another graduate/professional program (0), enrolled in a post-doctoral residency/fellowship (n/a), employed in independent practice (n/a), employed in an academic position at a university (0), employed in an academic position at a 2-year/4-year college (0), employed in other positions at a higher education institution (0), employed in a professional position in a school system (0), employed in business or industry (research/consulting) (3), employed in business or industry (management) (0), employed in a community mental health/counseling center (4), still seeking employment (0).

Doctoral Degree Graduates: Of those who graduated in the academic year 2000–2001, the following categories and numbers represent the post-graduate activities and employment of doctoral degree graduates: Enrolled in a psychology doctoral program (n/a), enrolled in another graduate/professional program (n/a).

Additional Information:

Orientation, Objectives, and Emphasis of Department: Emporia State offers the Master of Science degree in psychology, school psychology, art therapy, and special education. Emporia State also offers a Specialist in Education degree in school psychology. The MS degree in psychology is offered with specialization in the following areas: clinical, industrial/organizational, and general experimental. The MS degree in special education is offered with specialization in the following areas: mentally retarded, learning disabled, behavior disorders, gifted, and interrelated. Additionally, students may opt to pursue the MS and EdS degrees in school psychology, or the MS degree in art therapy.

Special Facilities or Resources: The Department of Psychology is housed in the $3.5 million Teachers College Building, which was completed in 1979. In 1999, all classrooms were upgraded with multimedia technology. Facilities include human, cognition, animal behavior, and physiological psychology laboratories; a complete animal vivarium; suites of rooms for administration of psychological tests and observation of testing or clinical and counseling sessions; and microprocessors and mainframe computer facilities.

Information for Students With Physical Disabilities: The Emporia State University is completely wheelchair accessible.

Application Information:

Send to: Dean of Graduate Studies and Research. Students are admitted in the Fall, application deadline October 1; Spring, application deadline March 1; Summer, application deadline June 1. School Psychology Program, No deadline. *Fee:* $30.

Fort Hays State University

Department of Psychology
600 Park Street
Hays, KS 67601-4099
Telephone: (785) 628-4405
Fax: (785) 628-5861
E-mail: *rmarkley@fhsu.edu*
Web: *http://www.fhsu.edu/psych/index.html*

Department Established:

1929. Chair: Robert P. Markley. Number of Faculty: total–full-time 8, part-time 5; women–full-time 2, part-time 2.

Programs and Degrees Offered:

Listed in the following order: Program area, degree type (T if terminal Master's), number awarded 7/00-6/01. Applied clinical MA (T) 5, general MA (T) 1, school EdS (T) 3.

Student Applications/Admissions:

Student Applications

Applied clinical MA—Applications 2001–2002, 16. Total applicants accepted 2001–2002, 11. New applicants enrolled 2001–2002, 8. Total enrolled 2001–2002 full-time, 11, part-time, 2. Openings 2002–2003, 10. The Median number of years required for completion of a degree are 2. The number of students enrolled full and part-time, who were dismissed or voluntarily withdrew from this program area were 0. *General* MA—Applications 2001–2002, 2. Total applicants accepted 2001–2002, 2. Total enrolled 2001–2002 part-time, 1. Openings 2002–2003, 5. The Median number of years required for completion of a degree are 2. The number of students enrolled full and part-time, who were dismissed or voluntarily withdrew from this program area were 0. *School EdS*—Applications 2001–2002, 9. Total applicants accepted 2001–2002, 7. New applicants enrolled 2001–2002, 4. Total enrolled 2001–2002 full-time, 12, part-time, 1. Openings 2002–2003, 10. The Median number of years required for completion of a degree are 2. The number of students enrolled full and part-time, who were dismissed or voluntarily withdrew from this program area were 1.

Admissions Requirements:

Scores: Entries appear in this order: required test or GPA, minimum score (if required), median score of students entering in 2001–2002. Master's Programs: GRE-V no minimum stated, 444; GRE-Q no minimum stated, 522; GRE-V+Q no minimum stated, 944; overall undergraduate GPA 2.5, 3.39; psychology GPA 2.5, 3.43. Doctoral Programs: last 2 years GPA no minimum stated; psychology GPA no minimum stated; psychology GPA no minimum stated.

Other Criteria: (importance of criteria rated low, medium, or high): GRE/MAT scores medium, research experience high, work experience low, extracurricular activity low, clinically related public service medium, GPA high, letters of recommendation medium, interview medium, statement of goals and objectives medium.

Student Characteristics: The following represents characteristics of students in 2001–2002 in all graduate psychology programs in the department: Female–full-time 21, part-time 3; Male–full-time

5, part-time 1; African American/Black–full-time 0, part-time 0; Hispanic/Latino (a)–full-time 0, part-time 0; Asian/Pacific Islander–full-time 0, part-time 0; American Indian/Alaska Native–full-time 0, part-time 0.

Financial Information/Assistance:
Tuition for Full-Time Study: *Master's:* State residents $103 per credit hour; nonstate residents: $274 per credit hour.

Financial Assistance:
First Year Students: Teaching assistantships available for first-year. Average amount paid per academic year: $2,500. Average number of hours worked per week: 10. Apply by March 1st. Tuition remission given: partial.
Advanced Students: Teaching assistantships available for advanced students. Average amount paid per academic year: $2,500. Average number of hours worked per week: 10. Apply by March 1st. Tuition remission given: partial.
Contact Information: Of all students currently enrolled full-time, 70% benefitted from one or more of the listed financial assistance programs. For information on financial assistance, contact: Graduate School, Fort Hays State University, Hays, KS 67601.

Internships/Practica: All students in the applied psychology programs (clinical, school) are required to take a practicum in their specialty area. Students in the clinical psychology program receive initial practicum experience in the Kelly Center (an on-campus psychological services center), and then are required to complete an internship off-campus at a regional mental health agency or other approved agency. Students in the school psychology program receive initial practicum experience in the local school district, and then are required to complete additional practicum training at the same or another school district. School psychology graduates are also required to complete one year of paid, supervised post-EdS internship before being recommended for full certification. Students in the general psychology program have the opportunity to take apprenticeships concentrating on the teaching of psychology.

Housing and Day Care: On-campus housing and day care facilities are available.

Employment of Department Graduates:
Master's Degree Graduates: Of those who graduated in the academic year 2000–2001, the following categories and numbers represent the post-graduate activities and employment of master's degree graduates: Enrolled in a post-doctoral residency/fellowship (n/a), employed in independent practice (n/a), employed in a professional position in a school system (4), employed in a government agency (research) (1), employed in a community mental health/counseling center (5).
Doctoral Degree Graduates: Of those who graduated in the academic year 2000–2001, the following categories and numbers represent the post-graduate activities and employment of doctoral degree graduates: Enrolled in a psychology doctoral program (n/a), enrolled in another graduate/professional program (n/a).

Additional Information:
Orientation, Objectives, and Emphasis of Department: The department emphasizes a research approach to the understanding of behavior. We strive to provide basic empirical and theoretical foundations of psychology to prepare the student for doctoral study, for teaching, or for employment in a service or professional agency. The school program offers broad preparation for students in both psychology and education and includes training as a consultant to work with educators and parents as well as with children. The clinical program emphasizes the preparation of rural mental health workers, although many graduates go on to doctoral programs. The general program is intended to prepare the student for doctoral study.

Special Facilities or Resources: The department of psychology now occupies a newly remodeled building in the center of campus. Some of the new facilities in this building include: a 25-machine computer facility with separate spaces for individualized research and full Internet connections; testing and observation rooms for children, adults, and small groups; separate research and teaching labs for the major areas of psychology; an isolated small animal facility; and several seminar rooms. We are located adjacent to the student psychological services center. There is an active social organization for psychology graduate students. All students at the university have free remote Internet access.

Information for Students With Physical Disabilities: All classrooms, offices, and other facilities usually used by psychology graduate students will be accessible.

Application Information:
Send to: Dean of the Graduate School, Fort Hays State University, 600 Park Street, Hays, KS 67601-4099. Students are admitted in the Fall; Summer. Rolling admissions. Deadline for financial aid is March 1st. *Fee:* $25.

Kansas State University
Department of Psychology
College of Arts and Sciences
Bluemont Hall - 1100 Mid-Campus Drive
Manhattan, KS 66506-5302
Telephone: (785) 532-6850
Fax: (785) 532-5401
E-mail: *psych@ksu.edu*
Web: *http://www.ksu.edu/psych*

Department Established:
1951. Head; Director of Graduate Studies: Stephen W. Kiefer; John Uhlarik. Number of Faculty: total–full-time 15, part-time 2; women–full-time 3, part-time 1.

Programs and Degrees Offered:
Listed in the following order: Program area, degree type (T if terminal Master's), number awarded 7/00-6/01. Animal learning PhD 1, applied experimental PhD, behavioral neuroscience PhD, general experimental, human factors PhD, human judgment PhD 1, human learning/memory PhD 3, industrial/organizational PhD, perception-sensation PhD, psycholinguistics PhD, social-personality PhD 1.

Student Applications/Admissions:
Student Applications
Animal learning PhD—Applications 2001–2002, 6. Total applicants accepted 2001–2002, 3. New applicants enrolled 2001–

2002, 2. Total enrolled 2001–2002 full-time, 3. Openings 2002–2003, 1. The Median number of years required for completion of a degree are 5. The number of students enrolled full and part-time, who were dismissed or voluntarily withdrew from this program area were 0. *Applied experimental PhD*—Applications 2001–2002, 11. Total enrolled 2001–2002 full-time, 1. Openings 2002–2003, 2. *Behavioral neuroscience PhD*—Applications 2001–2002, 11. Total applicants accepted 2001–2002, 3. Total enrolled 2001–2002 full-time, 2. Openings 2002–2003, 2. The Median number of years required for completion of a degree are 5. The number of students enrolled full and part-time, who were dismissed or voluntarily withdrew from this program area were 0. *Human factors PhD*—Applications 2001–2002, 20. Total applicants accepted 2001–2002, 5. New applicants enrolled 2001–2002, 3. Total enrolled 2001–2002 full-time, 8, part-time, 3. Openings 2002–2003, 4. *Human judgment PhD*—Applications 2001–2002, 5. Total enrolled 2001–2002 full-time, 2, part-time, 2. Openings 2002–2003, 2. The Median number of years required for completion of a degree are 5. *Human learning/memory PhD*—Applications 2001–2002, 5. Total applicants accepted 2001–2002, 1. New applicants enrolled 2001–2002, 1. Total enrolled 2001–2002 full-time, 3. Openings 2002–2003, 1. *Industrial/organizational PhD*—Applications 2001–2002, 19. Total enrolled 2001–2002 full-time, 10, part-time, 12. Openings 2002–2003, 3. The Median number of years required for completion of a degree are 6. *Perception-sensation PhD*—Applications 2001–2002, 3. Total enrolled 2001–2002 full-time, 1. Openings 2002–2003, 1. *Psycholinguistics PhD*—Applications 2001–2002, 4. Total applicants accepted 2001–2002, 2. New applicants enrolled 2001–2002, 2. Total enrolled 2001–2002 full-time, 5. Openings 2002–2003, 2. *Social-personality PhD*—Applications 2001–2002, 28. Total applicants accepted 2001–2002, 5. New applicants enrolled 2001–2002, 3. Total enrolled 2001–2002 full-time, 11. Openings 2002–2003, 3. The Median number of years required for completion of a degree are 5.

Admissions Requirements:

Scores: Entries appear in this order: required test or GPA, minimum score (if required), median score of students entering in 2001–2002. Master's Programs: GRE-V no minimum stated; GRE-Q no minimum stated; GRE-V+Q no minimum stated; GRE-Analytical no minimum stated; overall undergraduate GPA no minimum stated. Doctoral Programs: GRE-V no minimum stated, 461; GRE-Q no minimum stated, 590; GRE-V+Q no minimum stated, 460; GRE-Analytical no minimum stated, 527; overall undergraduate GPA no minimum stated, 3.67; last 2 years GPA no minimum stated; psychology GPA no minimum stated; psychology GPA no minimum stated.

Other Criteria: (importance of criteria rated low, medium, or high): GRE/MAT scores medium, research experience high, work experience low, extracurricular activity low, clinically related public service low, GPA medium, letters of recommendation high, interview medium, statement of goals and objectives high.

Student Characteristics: The following represents characteristics of students in 2001–2002 in all graduate psychology programs in the department: Female–full-time 21, part-time 4; Male–full-time 22, part-time 11; African American/Black–full-time 0, part-time 1; Hispanic/Latino (a)–full-time 0, part-time 0; Asian/Pacific Islander–full-time 2, part-time 0; American Indian/Alaska Native–full-time 0, part-time 0.

Financial Information/Assistance:

Tuition for Full-Time Study: *Master's:* State residents $113 per credit hour; nonstate residents: $358 per credit hour. *Doctoral:* State residents: $113 per credit hour; nonstate residents: $358 per credit hour.

Financial Assistance:

First Year Students: Teaching assistantships available for first-year. Average amount paid per academic year: $8,495. Average number of hours worked per week: 20. Tuition remission given: full. Research assistantships available for first-year. Average amount paid per academic year: $9,000. Average number of hours worked per week: 20. Tuition remission given: partial.

Advanced Students: Teaching assistantships available for advanced students. Average amount paid per academic year: $9,301. Average number of hours worked per week: 20. Tuition remission given: full. Research assistantships available for advanced students. Average amount paid per academic year: $10,000. Average number of hours worked per week: 20. Tuition remission given: partial.

Contact Information: Of all students currently enrolled full-time, 95% benefitted from one or more of the listed financial assistance programs. For information on financial assistance, contact: Director of Graduate Admissions.

Internships/Practica: Arrangements for internships in human factors/applied experimental and industrial/organizational psychology vary widely and are made on an individual basis.

Housing and Day Care: On-campus housing and day care facilities are available.

Employment of Department Graduates:

Master's Degree Graduates: Of those who graduated in the academic year 2000–2001, the following categories and numbers represent the post-graduate activities and employment of master's degree graduates: Enrolled in a psychology doctoral program (9), enrolled in a post-doctoral residency/fellowship (n/a), employed in independent practice (n/a).

Doctoral Degree Graduates: Of those who graduated in the academic year 2000–2001, the following categories and numbers represent the post-graduate activities and employment of doctoral degree graduates: Enrolled in a psychology doctoral program (n/a), enrolled in another graduate/professional program (n/a), enrolled in a post-doctoral residency/fellowship (1), employed in business or industry (research/consulting) (2).

Additional Information:

Orientation, Objectives, and Emphasis of Department: Both teaching and research are heavily emphasized. Training prepares students for a variety of positions, including teaching and research positions in colleges and universities. Students have also assumed research and evaluative positions in hospitals, clinics, governmental agencies, and industry.

Special Facilities or Resources: The department has rooms for individual and group research; several computer laboratories and remote terminal access to mainframe computers; a photographic darkroom; one-way observation facilities; an electrically shielded, light-tight, sound-deadened room for auditory and visual research; laboratories for behavioral research with animals; surgical and histological facilities; and colony rooms.

Application Information:

Send to: Graduate Admissions Department of Psychology, 492 Bluemont Hall, 1100 Midcampus Drive, Kansas State University, Manhattan, KS 66506-5302. Students are admitted in the Fall, application deadline Feburary 15. *Fee:* No fee for US citizens or permanent residents. International applicants must pay a $25.00 application fee.

Kansas State University

Family Studies and Human Services
Human Ecology
303 Justin Hall
Manhattan, KS 66506-1403
Telephone: (785) 532-5510
Fax: (785) 532-5505
E-mail: *fshs@ksu.edu*
Web: *http://www.ksu.edu/humec/fshs/fshs.htm*

Department Established:

1928. Director: William H. Meredith. Number of Faculty: total–full-time 42, part-time 2; women–full-time 27, part-time 1; minority–full-time 2.

Programs and Degrees Offered:

Listed in the following order: Program area, degree type (T if terminal Master's), number awarded 7/00-6/01. Comm. Science and Disorders MA 11, Early Childhood Education MA 4, Early Childhood Special Ed. MA 6, Family Financial Planning MA 0, Family Life Ed. and Consult. PhD 2, Family Life Ed. and Consult. MA 2, Life Span Human Dev. MA 3, Life Span Human Dev. PhD, Marriage and Family Therapy MA 5, Marriage and Family Therapy PhD 3.

Student Applications/Admissions:

Student Applications

Comm. Science and Disorders MA—Total enrolled 2001–2002 full-time, 10, part-time, 9. The Median number of years required for completion of a degree are 2. *Early Childhood Education* MA—Total enrolled 2001–2002 full-time, 2, part-time, 7. The Median number of years required for completion of a degree are 2. *Early Childhood Special Ed.* MA—Total enrolled 2001–2002 full-time, 5, part-time, 7. The Median number of years required for completion of a degree are 2. *Family Financial Planning* MA—Total enrolled 2001–2002 full-time, 20, part-time, 13. The Median number of years required for completion of a degree are 2. *Family Life Ed. and Consult.* PhD—Total enrolled 2001–2002 full-time, 12, part-time, 13. The Median number of years required for completion of a degree are 3. *Family Life Ed. and Consult.* MA—Total enrolled 2001–2002 full-time, 7, part-time, 8. The Median number of years required for completion of a degree are 2. *Life Span Human Dev.* MA—Total enrolled 2001–2002 full-time, 3, part-time, 3. The Median number of years required for completion of a degree are 2. *Life Span Human Dev.* PhD—Total enrolled 2001–2002 full-time, 4, part-time, 8. The Median number of years required for completion of a degree are 3. *Marriage and Family Therapy*

MA—Total enrolled 2001–2002 full-time, 21, part-time, 2. The Median number of years required for completion of a degree are 2. *Marriage and Family Therapy PhD*—Total enrolled 2001–2002 full-time, 6, part-time, 8. The Median number of years required for completion of a degree are 3.

Admissions Requirements:

Scores: Entries appear in this order: required test or GPA, minimum score (if required), median score of students entering in 2001–2002. Master's Programs: overall undergraduate GPA 3.0, 3.3. Doctoral Programs: GRE-V no minimum stated, 550; GRE-Q no minimum stated, 550; GRE-Analytical no minimum stated, 530; GRE-V+Q+Analytical no minimum stated; overall undergraduate GPA 3.0, 3.4 ; last 2 years GPA no minimum stated; psychology GPA no minimum stated; psychology GPA 3.5, 3.8.

Other Criteria: (importance of criteria rated low, medium, or high): GRE/MAT scores low, research experience low, work experience low, clinically related public service low, GPA medium, letters of recommendation high, interview medium, statement of goals and objectives high.

Student Characteristics: The following represents characteristics of students in 2001–2002 in all graduate psychology programs in the department: Female–full-time 19, part-time 8; Male–full-time 8, part-time 0; African American/Black–full-time 1, part-time 1; Hispanic/Latino (a)–full-time 1, part-time 0; Asian/Pacific Islander–full-time 0, part-time 0; American Indian/Alaska Native–full-time 0, part-time 0; Multi-ethnic–full-time 1, part-time 0.

Financial Information/Assistance:

Tuition for Full-Time Study: *Master's:* State residents $113 per credit hour; nonstate residents: $358 per credit hour. *Doctoral:* State residents: $113 per credit hour; nonstate residents: $358 per credit hour.

Financial Assistance:

First Year Students: Teaching assistantships available for first-year. Average amount paid per academic year: $10,800. Average number of hours worked per week: 20. Apply by Variable. Tuition remission given: full. Research assistantships available for first-year. Average amount paid per academic year: $10,800. Average number of hours worked per week: 20. Apply by Variable. Tuition remission given: partial. Fellowships and scholarships available for first-year. Average amount paid per academic year: $5,000. Apply by Variable.

Advanced Students: Teaching assistantships available for advanced students. Average amount paid per academic year: $10,800. Average number of hours worked per week: 20. Apply by Variable. Tuition remission given: full. Research assistantships available for advanced students. Average amount paid per academic year: $10,800. Average number of hours worked per week: 20. Apply by Variable. Tuition remission given: partial. Fellowships and scholarships available for advanced students. Average amount paid per academic year: $5,000. Apply by Variable.

Contact Information: Of all students currently enrolled full-time, 75% benefitted from one or more of the listed financial assistance programs. For information on financial assistance, contact: School of Family Studies and Human Services, 303 Justin Hall, Kansas State University, Manhattan, KS 66506; 785-532-5510.

Internships/Practica: No information provided.

Housing and Day Care: On-campus housing and day care facilities are available.

Employment of Department Graduates:

Master's Degree Graduates: Of those who graduated in the academic year 2000–2001, the following categories and numbers represent the post-graduate activities and employment of master's degree graduates: Enrolled in a post-doctoral residency/fellowship (n/a), employed in independent practice (n/a).

Doctoral Degree Graduates: Of those who graduated in the academic year 2000–2001, the following categories and numbers represent the post-graduate activities and employment of doctoral degree graduates: Enrolled in a psychology doctoral program (n/a), enrolled in another graduate/professional program (n/a).

Additional Information:

Orientation, Objectives, and Emphasis of Department: The School of Family Studies and Human Services is a multidisciplinary unit that includes study in communication sciences and disorders, early childhood education, family financial planning, family life education and consultation, life span human development, and marriage and family therapy. The goal of the marriage and family therapy master's program is to provide the academic, clinical, and professional training necessary for graduates to be successful clinicians in a variety of mental health settings. The goal of the marriage and family therapy doctoral program is to provide a training experience utilizing a scientist-practitioner model that balances continued development as a family therapist, training in clinical supervision, and the acquisition of strong research skills.

Application Information:

Send to: Graduate Admissions Coordinator, School of Family Studies and Human Services, 304 Justin Hall, Kansas State University, Manhattan, KS 66506-1403. Students are admitted in the Fall, application deadline Jan. 15(MFT); Spring, application deadline Jan. 15(MFT); Summer, application deadline Jan. 15(MFT). CSD: Feb. 20 for Fall, Oct. 1 for Spring. FLEC & LSHD: Feb. 1 for Summer and Fall, Oct. 1 for Spring.

Kansas, University of
Department of Human Development & Family Life
College of Arts and Sciences
1000 Sunnyside Avenue
Lawrence, KS 66045-7555
Telephone: (785) 864-4840
Fax: (785) 864-5202
E-mail: hdfl@ku.edu
Web: http://www.ku.edu/~hdfl

Department Established:

1968. Chairperson: Edward K. Morris. Number of Faculty: total–full-time 21; women–full-time 6; minority–full-time 2; faculty subject to the Americans with Disabilities Act 1.

Programs and Degrees Offered:

Listed in the following order: Program area, degree type (T if terminal Master's), number awarded 7/00-6/01. Developmental and Child Psych PhD 10, Human Development MA 8.

Student Applications/Admissions:
Student Applications

Developmental and Child Psych PhD—Applications 2001–2002, 40. Total applicants accepted 2001–2002, 10. New applicants enrolled 2001–2002, 10. Total enrolled 2001–2002 full-time, 85, part-time, 10. Openings 2002–2003, 15. The Median number of years required for completion of a degree are 6. The number of students enrolled full and part-time, who were dismissed or voluntarily withdrew from this program area were 5. *Human Development MA*—Applications 2001–2002, 20. Total applicants accepted 2001–2002, 4. New applicants enrolled 2001–2002, 4. Total enrolled 2001–2002 full-time, 12. Openings 2002–2003, 10. The Median number of years required for completion of a degree are 2. The number of students enrolled full and part-time, who were dismissed or voluntarily withdrew from this program area were 0.

Admissions Requirements:

Scores: Entries appear in this order: required test or GPA, minimum score (if required), median score of students entering in 2001–2002. Master's Programs: overall undergraduate GPA 3.0, 3.4. Doctoral Programs: overall undergraduate GPA 3.0, 3.7 ; last 2 years GPA no minimum stated; psychology GPA no minimum stated; psychology GPA no minimum stated. GRE scores are not required for admission, however, several very competitive fellowship programs are available through the University which do require the GRE (median V+Q+Analytic = 2,100).

Other Criteria: (importance of criteria rated low, medium, or high): GRE/MAT scores low, research experience high, work experience medium, extracurricular activity low, clinically related public service high, GPA medium, letters of recommendation high, interview high, statement of goals and objectives medium. All admission decisions are made by individual faculty members, thus admission criteria vary.

Student Characteristics: The following represents characteristics of students in 2001–2002 in all graduate psychology programs in the department: Female–full-time 73, part-time 7; Male–full-time 24, part-time 3; African American/Black–full-time 6, part-time 1; Hispanic/Latino (a)–full-time 3, Asian/Pacific Islander–full-time 3, part-time 1; Multi-ethnic–full-time 2, students subject to the Americans with Disabilities Act–full-time 5.

Financial Information/Assistance:

Tuition for Full-Time Study: *Master's:* State residents per academic year $2,034, $113 per credit hour; nonstate residents: per academic year $6,444, $358 per credit hour. *Doctoral:* State residents: per academic year $2,034, $113 per credit hour; nonstate residents: per academic year $6,444, $358 per credit hour.

Financial Assistance:

First Year Students: Teaching assistantships available for first-year. Apply by Feb. 1. Tuition remission given: full. Research assistantships available for first-year. Apply by Feb. 1. Tuition remission given: partial. Traineeships available for first-year. Apply by Feb. 1. Tuition remission given: full. Fellowships and scholarships available for first-year. Apply by Feb. 1. Tuition remission given: full and partial.

Advanced Students: Teaching assistantships available for advanced students. Apply by vary. Tuition remission given: full. Research assistantships available for advanced students. Apply by vary. Tuition remission given: partial. Traineeships available for advanced students. Apply by vary. Tuition remission given: full. Fellowships and scholarships available for advanced students. Apply by vary. Tuition remission given: full and partial.

Contact Information: Of all students currently enrolled full-time, 80% benefitted from one or more of the listed financial assistance programs. Graduate students holding a research assistantship of 40% time or greater pay in-state tuition rates. Faculty affiliated with the Department of Human Development had 64 externally-funded research projects in 2001, funded at over $6,000,000.

Internships/Practica: A wide variety of research settings and practica sites are available to graduate students. They include: Behavioral pediatrics; Center for Independent Living; Center for the Study of Mental Retardation and Related Problems; Child and Family Research Center; Community Programs for Adults with Mental Retardation; Edna A. Hill Child Development Center; Experimental Analysis of Behavior Laboratories; Family Enhancement Project; Gerontology Center; Juniper Gardens Project; Research on Children with Retardation; Schiefelbusch Institute for Life Span Studies; Work Group on Health Promotion and Community Development.

Housing and Day Care: On-campus housing and day care facilities are available.

Employment of Department Graduates:

Master's Degree Graduates: Of those who graduated in the academic year 2000–2001, the following categories and numbers represent the post-graduate activities and employment of master's degree graduates: Enrolled in a psychology doctoral program (5), enrolled in another graduate/professional program (1), enrolled in a post-doctoral residency/fellowship (n/a), employed in independent practice (n/a), employed in a professional position in a school system (1), employed in a government agency (professional services) (1).

Doctoral Degree Graduates: Of those who graduated in the academic year 2000–2001, the following categories and numbers represent the post-graduate activities and employment of doctoral degree graduates: Enrolled in a psychology doctoral program (n/a), enrolled in another graduate/professional program (n/a), enrolled in a post-doctoral residency/fellowship (2), employed in an academic position at a university (2), employed in a professional position in a school system (3), employed in a community mental health/counseling center (2).

Additional Information:

Orientation, Objectives, and Emphasis of Department: The primary purpose of the program is to train students in basic and applied research on typical and atypical development. It features emphases in applied behavior analysis, infant and child development and learning, cognitive development, community psychology and development, the experimental and conceptual analysis of behavior, behavioral pharmacology, independent living, and rehabilitation. Junior Colleague Model. Throughout the Ph.D. training sequence, students work closely as junior colleagues with

a faculty adviser and a research group. Although students typically work with one faculty adviser, they are free to select a different adviser if their interests change during the course of their training. Continuous Research Involvement. Students participate in research throughout their graduate careers in an individualized, intensive program. As a result, most students complete more research projects than those required for the degree.

Special Facilities or Resources: A wide range of research settings are available to graduate students. Populations and settings include both typically developing and disabled infants, toddlers, preschool children, elementary school settings, adolescents, adults, and elders.

Application Information:
Send to: Department of Human Development 1000 Sunnyside Ave., University of Kansas, Lawrence, KS 66045-7555. Students are admitted in the Fall, application deadline Feb. 1. All admissions are based on selections by individual faculty members (no centralized admissions committee) willing to serve as a mentor to the student. Thus, there is no set number of students admitted in any year and some admissions occur throughout the year. *Fee:* $35.

Kansas, University of
Department of Psychology
426 Fraser Hall 1415 Jayhawk Boulevard
Lawrence, KS 66045-2160
Telephone: (785) 864-4131
Fax: (785) 864-5696
E-mail: *psycgrad@ku.edu*
Web: *http://www.psych.ukans.edu*

Department Established:
1916. Chairperson: Greg B. Simpson. Number of Faculty: total–full-time 34; women–full-time 11; minority–full-time 2.

Programs and Degrees Offered:
Listed in the following order: Program area, degree type (T if terminal Master's), number awarded 7/00-6/01. Clinical Child PhD 3, Clinical PhD 7, Cognitive PhD, Quantitative PhD, Social PhD 1.

APA Accreditation: Clinical PhD: full.

Student Applications/Admissions:
Student Applications

Clinical Child PhD—Applications 2001–2002, 92. Total applicants accepted 2001–2002, 7. New applicants enrolled 2001–2002, 6. Total enrolled 2001–2002 full-time, 36. Openings 2002–2003, 6. The Median number of years required for completion of a degree are 6. The number of students enrolled full and part-time, who were dismissed or voluntarily withdrew from this program area were 1. *Clinical PhD*—Applications 2001–2002, 113. Total applicants accepted 2001–2002, 16. New applicants enrolled 2001–2002, 10. Total enrolled 2001–2002 full-time, 67. Openings 2002–2003, 8. The Median number of years required for completion of a degree are 6. The number of students enrolled full and part-time, who were dismissed or voluntarily withdrew from this program area were 1. *Cognitive PhD*—Applications 2001–2002, 14. Total applicants accepted 2001–2002, 8. New applicants enrolled 2001–2002, 3. Total enrolled 2001–2002 full-time, 23. Openings 2002–2003, 3. The Median number of years required for completion of a degree are 5. The number of students enrolled full and part-time, who were dismissed or voluntarily withdrew from this program area were 0. *Quantitative PhD*—Applications 2001–2002, 3. Total applicants accepted 2001–2002, 3. Total enrolled 2001–2002 full-time, 8. Openings 2002–2003, 4. The Median number of years required for completion of a degree are 5. The number of students enrolled full and part-time, who were dismissed or voluntarily withdrew from this program area were 0. *Social PhD*—Applications 2001–2002, 49. Total applicants accepted 2001–2002, 11. New applicants enrolled 2001–2002, 4. Total enrolled 2001–2002 full-time, 26. Openings 2002–2003, 4. The Median number of years required for completion of a degree are 6. The number of students enrolled full and part-time, who were dismissed or voluntarily withdrew from this program area were 1.

Admissions Requirements:

Scores: Entries appear in this order: required test or GPA, minimum score (if required), median score of students entering in 2001–2002. Doctoral Programs: GRE-V no minimum stated, 567; GRE-Q no minimum stated, 585; GRE-Analytical no minimum stated, 601; overall undergraduate GPA no minimum stated, 3.63; last 2 years GPA no minimum stated; psychology GPA no minimum stated; psychology GPA no minimum stated.

Other Criteria: (importance of criteria rated low, medium, or high): GRE/MAT scores high, research experience high, work experience low, extracurricular activity low, clinically related public service medium, GPA high, letters of recommendation high, statement of goals and objectives high, writing sample high. Writing sample for Clinical programs only. Interview in Clinical Child only at this time.

Student Characteristics: The following represents characteristics of students in 2001–2002 in all graduate psychology programs in the department: Female–full-time 115, part-time 0; Male–full-time 47, part-time 0; African American/Black–full-time 2, part-time 0; Hispanic/Latino (a)–full-time 8, part-time 0; Asian/Pacific Islander–full-time 10, part-time 0; American Indian/Alaska Native–full-time 3, part-time 0; Multi-ethnic–full-time 2, students subject to the Americans with Disabilities Act–full-time 0.

Financial Information/Assistance:

Tuition for Full-Time Study: *Master's:* State residents $113 per credit hour; nonstate residents: $357 per credit hour. *Doctoral:* State residents: $113 per credit hour; nonstate residents: $357 per credit hour.

Financial Assistance:

First Year Students: Teaching assistantships available for first-year. Average amount paid per academic year: $9,082. Average number of hours worked per week: 20. Apply by 1/15. Tuition remission given: full. Research assistantships available for first-year. Average amount paid per academic year: $10,100. Average number of hours worked per week: 20. Apply by 1/15. Fellowships and scholarships available for first-year. Average amount paid per

academic year: $9,082. Average number of hours worked per week: 0. Apply by 1/15.

Advanced Students: Teaching assistantships available for advanced students. Average amount paid per academic year: $9,082. Average number of hours worked per week: 20. Apply by 1/15. Tuition remission given: full. Research assistantships available for advanced students. Average amount paid per academic year: $10,100. Average number of hours worked per week: 20. Apply by 1/15. Fellowships and scholarships available for advanced students. Average amount paid per academic year: $9,082. Average number of hours worked per week: 0. Apply by 1/15.

Contact Information: Of all students currently enrolled full-time, 48% benefitted from one or more of the listed financial assistance programs. For information on financial assistance, contact: Financial Aid Dept: 785-864-4700.

Internships/Practica: For those doctoral students for whom a professional internship is required prior to graduation, 15 applied in 2000–2001. Of those who applied, 15 were placed in internships listed by the Association of Psychology Postdoctoral and Internship Programs (APPIC); 15 were placed in APA accredited internships.

Housing and Day Care: On-campus housing and day care facilities are available.

Employment of Department Graduates:

Master's Degree Graduates: Of those who graduated in the academic year 2000–2001, the following categories and numbers represent the post-graduate activities and employment of master's degree graduates: Enrolled in a post-doctoral residency/fellowship (n/a), employed in independent practice (n/a).

Doctoral Degree Graduates: Of those who graduated in the academic year 2000–2001, the following categories and numbers represent the post-graduate activities and employment of doctoral degree graduates: Enrolled in a psychology doctoral program (n/a), enrolled in another graduate/professional program (n/a), employed in other positions at a higher education institution (2), employed in a government agency (professional services) (3), employed in a community mental health/counseling center (2).

Additional Information:

Orientation, Objectives, and Emphasis of Department: With 34 full-time faculty, the department offers a wide range of opportunities for the study and treatment of human psychological and behavioral functioning. Students develop skills in statistics, research methods, and specific content areas with basic and applied emphases, with the flexibility to tailor programs to individual students' needs. Students in all programs (Clinical Child, Quantitative, Cognitive or Social) may also complete coursework toward a minor in quantitative psychology.

Special Facilities or Resources: The department has well-equipped computer labs, and access to university mainframe computers. The department maintains a computer and electronics shop, for the construction of specialized equipment. Clinical and research support facilities include an on-site clinic with a test resource library, individual and group therapy rooms, and play and psychodrama rooms. Specialized research facilities include interview rooms with audio and video capacities, psychophysiological and stress laboratories, an ERP laboratory, and an anechoir chamber.

Application Information:
Send to: Committee on Admissions, Department of Pyschology, 1415 Jayhawk Blvd, 426 Fraser Hall, University of Kansas, Lawrence, KS 66045-7556. Students are admitted in the Fall, application deadline January 15. *Fee:* $35.

Kansas, University of
Psychology and Research in Education
School of Education
Joseph R. Pearson Hall, 1122 West Campus Road, Room 621
Lawrence, KS 66045
Telephone: (785) 864-3931
Fax: (785) 864-3820
E-mail: *preadmit@ku.edu*
Web: *http://www.soe.ku.edu/pre/*

Department Established:
1955. Chairperson: Thomas S. Krieshok. Number of Faculty: total–full-time 15, part-time 2; women–full-time 5, part-time 1; minority–full-time 1.

Programs and Degrees Offered:
Listed in the following order: Program area, degree type (T if terminal Master's), number awarded 7/00-6/01. Counseling Psychology MA (T) 24, Counseling Psychology PhD 11, Educational Psych and Research PhD 2, Educational Psych and Research 2, School Psychology PhD 1, School Psychology EdS 8.

APA Accreditation: Counseling PhD: full. School PhD: full.

Student Applications/Admissions:
Student Applications
Counseling Psychology MA—Applications 2001–2002, 64. Total applicants accepted 2001–2002, 41. New applicants enrolled 2001–2002, 25. Total enrolled 2001–2002 full-time, 25, part-time, 40. Openings 2002–2003, 25. The Median number of years required for completion of a degree are 3. The number of students enrolled full and part-time, who were dismissed or voluntarily withdrew from this program area were 0. *Counseling Psychology PhD*—Applications 2001–2002, 55. Total applicants accepted 2001–2002, 14. New applicants enrolled 2001–2002, 7. Total enrolled 2001–2002 full-time, 22, part-time, 15. Openings 2002–2003, 6. The Median number of years required for completion of a degree are 5. The number of students enrolled full and part-time, who were dismissed or voluntarily withdrew from this program area were 0. *Educational Psych and Research PhD*—Applications 2001–2002, 5. Total applicants accepted 2001–2002, 3. New applicants enrolled 2001–2002, 3. Total enrolled 2001–2002 full-time, 3, part-time, 5. Openings 2002–2003, 5. The Median number of years required for completion of a degree are 4. The number of students enrolled full and part-time, who were dismissed or voluntarily withdrew from this program area were 0. *School Psychology PhD*—Applications 2001–2002, 4. Total applicants accepted 2001–2002, 4. New applicants enrolled 2001–2002, 4. Total enrolled 2001–2002 full-time, 6, part-time, 5. Open-

ings 2002–2003, 4. The Median number of years required for completion of a degree are 5. The number of students enrolled full and part-time, who were dismissed or voluntarily withdrew from this program area were 1. *School Psychology EdS*—Applications 2001–2002, 14. Total applicants accepted 2001–2002, 11. New applicants enrolled 2001–2002, 10. Total enrolled 2001–2002 full-time, 15, part-time, 9. Openings 2002–2003, 10. The Median number of years required for completion of a degree are 3. The number of students enrolled full and part-time, who were dismissed or voluntarily withdrew from this program area were 1.

Admissions Requirements:
Scores: Entries appear in this order: required test or GPA, minimum score (if required), median score of students entering in 2001–2002. Master's Programs: GRE-V no minimum stated, 505; GRE-Q no minimum stated, 535; GRE-Analytical no minimum stated, 590; overall undergraduate GPA no minimum stated, 3.55. Ed.S.—School Psychology: GRE Medians: V-500; Q-575; A-615; Overall undergraduate GPA 3.56. Doctoral Programs: GRE-V no minimum stated, 575; GRE-Q no minimum stated, 605; GRE-Analytical no minimum stated, 640; overall undergraduate GPA no minimum stated, 3.56; last 2 years GPA no minimum stated; psychology GPA no minimum stated; psychology GPA no minimum stated, 3.82. The scores above are for students who entered the program in Counseling Psychology. Listed below are scores for the School Psychology Ph.D. program: GRE-V, 555; GRE-Q, 560; GRE-A, 605; Undergraduate GPA, 3.40. And for the Ph.D. program in Educational Psychology & Research: GRE-V, 540; GRE-Q, 605; GRE-A, 585; Undergraduate GPA, 3.15.
Other Criteria: (importance of criteria rated low, medium, or high): GRE/MAT scores high, research experience medium, work experience medium, extracurricular activity low, clinically related public service low, GPA high, letters of recommendation high, interview high, statement of goals and objectives high. The admission criteria above are for applicants to the Counseling Psychology Ph.D. program. For School Psychology Ph.D. program: GRE/MAT Scores high, research experience high, work experience medium, extracurricular activity low, clinically related public service high, GPA high, letters of recommendation high, statement of goals and objectives high.

Student Characteristics: The following represents characteristics of students in 2001–2002 in all graduate psychology programs in the department: Female–full-time 68, part-time 74; Male–full-time 12, part-time 17; African American/Black–full-time 1, part-time 2; Hispanic/Latino (a)–full-time 5, part-time 2; Asian/Pacific Islander–full-time 3, part-time 1; American Indian/Alaska Native–full-time 2, part-time 1; part-time 1.

Financial Information/Assistance:
Tuition for Full-Time Study: *Master's:* State residents per academic year $2,712, $113 per credit hour; nonstate residents: per academic year $8,592, $358 per credit hour. *Doctoral:* State residents: per academic year $2,712, $113 per credit hour; nonstate residents: per academic year $8,592, $358 per credit hour.

Financial Assistance:
First Year Students: Teaching assistantships available for first-year. Average amount paid per academic year: $5,000. Aver-

age number of hours worked per week: 12. Apply by Feb 15. Tuition remission given: full and partial. Research assistantships available for first-year. Average amount paid per academic year: $5,000. Average number of hours worked per week: 12. Apply by Varies. Fellowships and scholarships available for first-year. Apply by Jan 15. Tuition remission given: full and partial.

Advanced Students: Teaching assistantships available for advanced students. Average amount paid per academic year: $5,000. Average number of hours worked per week: 12. Apply by Feb 15. Tuition remission given: full and partial. Research assistantships available for advanced students. Average amount paid per academic year: $5,000. Average number of hours worked per week: 12. Apply by Varies. Traineeships available for advanced students. Apply by Varies. Fellowships and scholarships available for advanced students. Apply by Varies. Tuition remission given: full and partial.

Contact Information: Of all students currently enrolled full-time, 70% benefitted from one or more of the listed financial assistance programs. For information on financial assistance, contact: Student Financial Office, 50 Strong Hall (785) 864-4700, email: osfa@ukans.edu, (www.ku.edu/~osfa); Department for Graduate Teaching Assistantships (with application for admission); Graduate School for some forms of aid (www.ku.edu/~graduate).

Internships/Practica: Both master's and doctoral students in the School Psychology and Counseling Psychology programs complete their practica in a variety of local applied settings. Our doctoral students in Counseling Psychology have been successful in obtaining APA accredited internships in University counseling centers, veterans administration medical centers, community mental health centers, and other human service agencies. Students in the School Psychology program have received practica and internships in a variety of elementary, secondary, and special needs school settings throughout the country. In addition, all students have access to the recently developed Center for Psychoeducational Services on the first floor of our building. The Center is an interdisciplinary School of Education facility serving the needs of local schools and community members. For those doctoral students for whom a professional internship is required prior to graduation, 10 applied in 2000–2001. Of those who applied, 10 were placed in internships listed by the Association of Psychology Postdoctoral and Internship Programs (APPIC); 10 were placed in APA accredited internships.

Housing and Day Care: On-campus housing and day care facilities are available.

Employment of Department Graduates:
Master's Degree Graduates: Of those who graduated in the academic year 2000–2001, the following categories and numbers represent the post-graduate activities and employment of master's degree graduates: Enrolled in a post-doctoral residency/fellowship (n/a), employed in independent practice (n/a).
Doctoral Degree Graduates: Of those who graduated in the academic year 2000–2001, the following categories and numbers represent the post-graduate activities and employment of doctoral degree graduates: Enrolled in a psychology doctoral program (n/a), enrolled in another graduate/professional program (n/a), employed in an academic position at a university (1), employed in an academic position at a 2-year/4-year college (1), employed in other positions at a higher education institution (3), employed in a community mental health/counseling center (4), employed in a hospital/medical center (2).

Additional Information:
Orientation, Objectives, and Emphasis of Department: The department offers graduate training in three programs. The Counseling Psychology Program is strongly committed to the training of scientist-practitioners focused on facilitating the personal, social, educational, and vocational development of individuals, and on enhancing the environments in which they function. Our goal is to train competent professionals who possess the generalist skills necessary to function in the wide array of work settings available to counseling psychologists. The School Psychology Program endorses the training model of the psychoeducational consultant with multifaceted skills drawn from psychology and education, who has as a main function the assistance of children toward greater realization of their potential. The psychoeducational consultant is vitally concerned with enhancing teacher effectiveness, creating a positive classroom environment for children, and influencing educational thought within that school system. The Educational Psychology and Research Program offers instruction in the following areas: cognition and learning; applied human development; instructional psychology as related to educational practice; applied statistics, measurement, program evaluation, and research methods. Graduate study includes experiences in designing, conducting, and evaluating research and field experiences in a variety of settings. The objectives of the program are to prepare students to become faculty members, researchers, and measurement specialists.

Special Facilities or Resources: Students have access to an instructional materials library, extensive audio visual resources, computer labs, an assessment resource library, and the University's law and medical libraries. The School of Education is located in Pearson Hall, a state-of-the-art facility with extensive media and Internet technology, a complete instructional and assessment materials library, and mediated classrooms and laboratories. The Center for Psychoeducational Services offers an excellent training opportunity for School Psychology and Counseling Psychology students to work with school-age children from the local community area. Students in the School Psychology program also have access to special preschool programs. Students have opportunities to conduct research in a variety of settings including public and private schools, the Center for Educational Testing and Evaluation (CETE), and the Life Span Institute. In the Center for Educational Testing and Evaluation, students in the Educational Psychology and Research degree program may help design assessment instruments, analyze test results, and evaluate tests and programs. The Life Span Institute supports a wide variety of social science research (e.g., mental retardation, human development, aging, and speech development).

Information for Students With Physical Disabilities: Special services for students with disabilities are available.

Application Information:
Send to: Admissions Coordinator, Psychology and Research in Education, Joseph R. Pearson Hall, Room 621, 1122 West Campus Road Lawrence, KS 66045-3101. Students are admitted in the Fall; Spring; Summer. Jan 15: Counseling Psychology, Ph.D. program, Summer or Fall Admission. Feb 15: School Psychology Ph.D. & Ed.S. programs, Summer or Fall Admission. Feb 15: Counseling Psychology, M.S. pro-

gram, Summer or Fall Admission. Feb 15: Educational Psychology & Research Programs, Summer or Fall Admission. Nov 15: Educational Psychology & Research programs, Spring Admission. *Fee:* $35. Application for fee waiver must be made directly to the University of Kansas Graduate School rather than the department.

Pittsburg State University
Department of Psychology and Counseling
College of Education
112 Hughes Hall, 1701 S. Broadway
Pittsburg, KS 66762-7551
Telephone: (620) 235-4522
Fax: (620) 235-4520
E-mail: *psych@pittstate.edu*
Web: *http://www.pittstate.edu/psych/*

Department Established:
1929. Chairperson: David P. Hurford. Number of Faculty: total–full-time 14, part-time 6; women–full-time 6, part-time 4.

Programs and Degrees Offered:
Listed in the following order: Program area, degree type (T if terminal Master's), number awarded 7/00-6/01. Clinical MA (T) 9, community counseling MA (T) 21, counseling EdS 8, general MA (T) 12, school counseling MA (T) 12, school psychology EdS 9.

Student Applications/Admissions:
Student Applications

Clinical MA—Applications 2001–2002, 31. Total applicants accepted 2001–2002, 12. New applicants enrolled 2001–2002, 10. Total enrolled 2001–2002 full-time, 9, part-time, 1. Openings 2002–2003, 10. *Community counseling MA*—Applications 2001–2002, 38. Total applicants accepted 2001–2002, 20. New applicants enrolled 2001–2002, 19. Total enrolled 2001–2002 full-time, 12, part-time, 7. Openings 2002–2003, 15. *Counseling EdS*—Applications 2001–2002, 10. Total applicants accepted 2001–2002, 8. New applicants enrolled 2001–2002, 7. Total enrolled 2001–2002 part-time, 7. Openings 2002–2003, 5. *General MA*—Applications 2001–2002, 16. Total applicants accepted 2001–2002, 12. New applicants enrolled 2001–2002, 12. Total enrolled 2001–2002 full-time, 7, part-time, 5. Openings 2002–2003, 12. *School counseling MA*—Applications 2001–2002, 23. Total applicants accepted 2001–2002, 16. New applicants enrolled 2001–2002, 15. Total enrolled 2001–2002 full-time, 1, part-time, 14. Openings 2002–2003, 10. *School psychology EdS*—Applications 2001–2002, 15. Total applicants accepted 2001–2002, 10. New applicants enrolled 2001–2002, 10. Total enrolled 2001–2002 full-time, 8, part-time, 2. Openings 2002–2003, 10.

Admissions Requirements:
Scores: Entries appear in this order: required test or GPA, minimum score (if required), median score of students entering in 2001–2002. Master's Programs: GRE-V 400, 470; GRE-Q 400, 530; GRE-Analytical 400, 540; GRE-V+Q+Analytical 1200, 1540; overall undergraduate GPA 3.00, 3.43; last 2 years GPA 3.00, 3.56; psychology GPA 3.00, 3.65. Same for all programs, but medians differ by program area. Doctoral Pro-

grams: last 2 years GPA no minimum stated; psychology GPA no minimum stated; psychology GPA no minimum stated.
Other Criteria: (importance of criteria rated low, medium, or high): GRE/MAT scores high, research experience medium, work experience high, extracurricular activity low, clinically related public service medium, GPA high, letters of recommendation high, interview medium, statement of goals and objectives high.

Student Characteristics: The following represents characteristics of students in 2001–2002 in all graduate psychology programs in the department: Female–full-time 22, part-time 24; Male–full-time 15, part-time 12; African American/Black–full-time 3, part-time 1; Hispanic/Latino (a)–full-time 2, part-time 0; Asian/Pacific Islander–full-time 6, part-time 0; American Indian/Alaska Native–full-time 2, part-time 1.

Financial Information/Assistance:
Tuition for Full-Time Study: Master's: State residents per academic year $2,686, $114 per credit hour; nonstate residents: per academic year $6,788, $285 per credit hour.

Financial Assistance:
First Year Students: Teaching assistantships available for first-year. Average amount paid per academic year: $4,520. Average number of hours worked per week: 20. Apply by March 1. Tuition remission given: full.

Advanced Students: Teaching assistantships available for advanced students. Average amount paid per academic year: $4,520. Average number of hours worked per week: 20. Apply by March 1. Tuition remission given: full.

Contact Information: Of all students currently enrolled full-time, 5% benefitted from one or more of the listed financial assistance programs. For information on financial assistance, contact: Office of Student Financial Assistance, 1701 S. Broadway, Pittsburg State Univ., Pittsburg, KS 66762-7534; (620) 235-4240.

Internships/Practica: All M.S. and EdS practitioner programs include a 3–8 semester hour (150–400 clock hour) practicum sequence and a 4–32 semester hour (600–1200 clock hour) internship at a site appropriate to the specialty, and under the supervision of faculty and site supervisors. The internship in school psychology is post-degree, and is typically a paid internship. Some internships in other programs are also paid. All internships meet guidelines of the professional association or accrediting body of the specialty (i.e., CACREP, MPAC, NASP).

Housing and Day Care: On-campus housing and day care facilities are available.

Employment of Department Graduates:
Master's Degree Graduates: Of those who graduated in the academic year 2000–2001, the following categories and numbers represent the post-graduate activities and employment of master's degree graduates: Enrolled in a psychology doctoral program (2), enrolled in another graduate/professional program (3), enrolled in a post-doctoral residency/fellowship (n/a), employed in independent practice (n/a), employed in an academic position at a university (1), employed in an academic position at a 2-year/4-year college (2), employed in other positions at a higher education institution (0), employed in a professional position in a school system (20), employed in business or industry (research/con-

sulting) (0), employed in business or industry (management) (5), employed in a government agency (research) (0), employed in a government agency (professional services) (3), employed in a community mental health/counseling center (16), employed in a hospital/medical center (2), still seeking employment (2), other employment position (3).

Doctoral Degree Graduates: Of those who graduated in the academic year 2000–2001, the following categories and numbers represent the post-graduate activities and employment of doctoral degree graduates: Enrolled in a psychology doctoral program (n/a), enrolled in another graduate/professional program (n/a).

Additional Information:

Orientation, Objectives, and Emphasis of Department: The Department of Psychology and Counseling uses an interdiscplinary model to provide broad-based training, understanding and appreciation of the specialties that we represent. The major objective of the department is to prepare graduates with knowledge in scientific foundations and practical applied skills to function as mental health service providers or to pursue study at the doctoral level. Faculty in the department represent a diverse collection of theoretical backgrounds in scientific and applied psychology. All faculty teach coursework in each program area, providing students with the opportunity to learn multidisciplinary approaches and models. The emphasis in the department is on integrated, cross-disciplinary studies within a close faculty-student colleague model that promotes frequent contact and close supervision, aimed at developing practitioner skills. The department is pleased to have the first accredited master's degree program in clinical psychology in the nation (MPAC accreditation received in May 1997), and enjoys CACREP accreditation of the master's degree program in community counseling. The department also enjoys NCATE accreditation of the M.S. Degree program in school counseling and the EdS Degree program in school psychology.

Special Facilities or Resources: The department has counseling and psychotherapy training facilities equipped with one-way mirrors and audio and video taping equipment. Microcomputer laboratories with network capacity, word processing, and SAS and SPSS software are available in the department. The university library, in addition to a large book collection, currently maintains over 150 periodical subscriptions in psychology. The department operates the Center for Human Services, an on-campus training, research, and service facility, which includes University Testing Services, a family counseling center, an adult assessment center, the Center for Assessment and Remediation of Reading Difficulties, the Attention Deficit/Hyperactivity Disorder Neurofeedback Diagnostic and Treatment Center, and the Welfare to Work Assessment Center. The department has a close working relationship with local hospitals and mental health facilities, and is a constituent member of the regional community service coalition.

Information for Students With Physical Disabilities: Hughes Hall, which houses the Department of Psychology and Counseling, has undergone major renovation, meets ADA standards in all psychology and counseling classrooms and offices, and is fully handicapped-accessible. Curbside parking for individuals with disabilities is available just outside the north entrance to the building. All classrooms are fully mediated.

Application Information:

Send to: Chairperson, Department of Psychology and Counseling, Pittsburg State University, 1701 S. Broadway, Pittsburg, KS 66762-

7551. Students are admitted in the Fall, application deadline March 1; Spring, application deadline October 1; Summer, application deadline March 1. Clinical Psychology admitted only for Fall Semester. *Fee:* $30.

Washburn University
Department of Psychology
1700 College
Topeka, KS 66621
Telephone: (785) 231-1010
Fax: (785) 231-1004
E-mail: *zzdppy@washburn.edu*
Web: *http://www.washburn.edu/cas/psychology/grad/*

Department Established:

1940. Chairperson: Laura A. Stephenson. Number of Faculty: total–full-time 8; women–full-time 4.

Programs and Degrees Offered:

Listed in the following order: Program area, degree type (T if terminal Master's), number awarded 7/00-6/01. Clinical MA (T) 3.

Student Applications/Admissions:

Student Applications

Clinical MA—Applications 2001–2002, 24. Total applicants accepted 2001–2002, 19. New applicants enrolled 2001–2002, 7. Total enrolled 2001–2002 full-time, 16, part-time, 3. Openings 2002–2003, 15. The Median number of years required for completion of a degree are 2. The number of students enrolled full and part-time, who were dismissed or voluntarily withdrew from this program area were 1.

Admissions Requirements:

Scores: Entries appear in this order: required test or GPA, minimum score (if required), median score of students entering in 2001–2002. Master's Programs: GRE-V no minimum stated, 420; GRE-Q no minimum stated, 510; GRE-Analytical no minimum stated, 540; overall undergraduate GPA no minimum stated, 3.37; last 2 years GPA no minimum stated, 3.60; psychology GPA no minimum stated, 3.20. Doctoral Programs: last 2 years GPA no minimum stated; psychology GPA no minimum stated; psychology GPA no minimum stated.

Other Criteria: (importance of criteria rated low, medium, or high): GRE/MAT scores medium, research experience medium, work experience medium, extracurricular activity low, clinically related public service medium, GPA medium, letters of recommendation high, statement of goals and objectives high.

Student Characteristics: The following represents characteristics of students in 2001–2002 in all graduate psychology programs in the department: Female–full-time 8, part-time 1; Male–full-time 1, part-time 1; African American/Black–full-time 0, part-time 0; Hispanic/Latino (a)–full-time 1, part-time 0; Asian/Pacific Islander–full-time 0, part-time 0; American Indian/Alaska Native–full-time 0, part-time 0.

Financial Information/Assistance:

Tuition for Full-Time Study: *Master's:* State residents per academic year $4,500, $150 per credit hour; nonstate residents: per academic year $9,210, $307 per credit hour.

Financial Assistance:

First Year Students: Average amount paid per academic year: $4,000. Average number of hours worked per week: 10. Apply by March 15.

Advanced Students: Average amount paid per academic year: $5,000. Average number of hours worked per week: 10. Apply by May 15.

Contact Information: Of all students currently enrolled full-time, 72% benefitted from one or more of the listed financial assistance programs. For information on financial assistance, contact: Psychology Department or Financial Aid Office.

Internships/Practica: Psychological Services are offered to the community through a clinic staffed by first year graduate students enrolled in PY 590 and 591 (practica). Services focus on anxiety and depression. Student therapists practice skills of diagnostic interviewing, and integrating interview information with personality and intelligence testing into the formulation of a DSM-IV diagnosis. Under the close supervision of a faculty clinical psychologist, they use this information to conceptualize etiologies and develop therapeutic treatment options. The therapy processes implemented reflect several theoretical orientations, including Interpersonal Process, Cognitive, Behavioral and Brief approaches. Issues of suicide, cultural sensitivity, and individual therapist development are also addressed. An internship consisting of 750 supervised hours over an academic year is required of each second year graduate student. This requirement is met by working twenty hours per week at an assigned site and meeting three hours weekly in a classroom setting. Both on-site and academic supervisors are available to the student during this experience. The type of experience provided for these student interns include therapy, assessment, team approaches, individual clients, group therapy opportunities, and opportunities for case presentations.

Housing and Day Care: No on-campus housing and day care facilities are available.

Employment of Department Graduates:

Master's Degree Graduates: Of those who graduated in the academic year 2000–2001, the following categories and numbers represent the post-graduate activities and employment of master's degree graduates: Enrolled in a psychology doctoral program (2), enrolled in a post-doctoral residency/fellowship (n/a), employed in independent practice (n/a), other employment position (1).

Doctoral Degree Graduates: Of those who graduated in the academic year 2000–2001, the following categories and numbers represent the post-graduate activities and employment of doctoral degree graduates: Enrolled in a psychology doctoral program (n/a), enrolled in another graduate/professional program (n/a).

Additional Information:

Orientation, Objectives, and Emphasis of Department: The faculty are of diverse theoretical orientations. The MA program is designed to prepare students for future employment as providers of psychological services in clinics, community centers, and social service programs that now require a master's degree in psychology, as well as to prepare those students who are prospective candidates for the pursuit of a doctoral degree in clinical psychology. The department emphasizes the necessity that students acquire a foundation in the content and methods of psychology.

Special Facilities or Resources: The psychology department, housed with other departments in a modern building, has well-equipped laboratories available for human experimentation. These facilities also include observation areas designed for the supervision of psychotherapy and psychological testing. The psychology department provides access to the University Academic Computer Center for computer hardware and software resources.

Information for Students With Physical Disabilities: Students with physical disabilities requiring wheelchair access will find the facility which houses the department resources easily accessible. Accommodations for visual or hearing impaired students may be arranged.

Application Information:

Send to: Department of Psychology, Washburn University, Topeka, KS 66621. Students are admitted in the Fall, application deadline March 15; Spring, application deadline December 1.

Wichita State University
Department of Psychology
1845 Fairmount
Wichita, KS 67260-0034
Telephone: (316) 689-3170
Fax: (316) 689-3086
E-mail: *charles.burdsal@wichita.edu*
Web: *http://psychology.wichita.edu*

Department Established:

1948. Chairperson: Charles A. Burdsal. Number of Faculty: total–full-time 16; women–full-time 5; minority–full-time 2.

Programs and Degrees Offered:

Listed in the following order: Program area, degree type (T if terminal Master's), number awarded 7/00-6/01. Community-Clinical Psychology PhD 3, Human Factors PhD 4.

Student Applications/Admissions:

Student Applications

Community-Clinical Psychology PhD—Applications 2001–2002, 35. Total applicants accepted 2001–2002, 11. New applicants enrolled 2001–2002, 8. Total enrolled 2001–2002 full-time, 27. Openings 2002–2003, 6. *Human Factors PhD*—Applications 2001–2002, 12. Total applicants accepted 2001–2002, 9. New applicants enrolled 2001–2002, 3. Total enrolled 2001–2002 full-time, 31. Openings 2002–2003, 6.

Admissions Requirements:

Scores: Entries appear in this order: required test or GPA, minimum score (if required), median score of students entering in 2001–2002. Doctoral Programs: GRE-V no minimum stated, 510; GRE-Q no minimum stated, 515; GRE-V+Q no minimum stated, 1015; overall undergraduate GPA 3.00, 3.5 ; last

2 years GPA no minimum stated, 3.5 ; psychology GPA no minimum stated, 3.5 ; psychology GPA no minimum stated. *Other Criteria:* (importance of criteria rated low, medium, or high): GRE/MAT scores medium, research experience medium, work experience medium, clinically related public service low, GPA high, letters of recommendation medium, interview low, statement of goals and objectives high.

Student Characteristics: The following represents characteristics of students in 2001–2002 in all graduate psychology programs in the department: Female–full-time 41, part-time 0; Male–full-time 13, part-time 0; African American/Black–full-time 3, part-time 0; Hispanic/Latino (a)–full-time 0, part-time 0; Asian/Pacific Islander–full-time 2, part-time 0; American Indian/Alaska Native–full-time 2, part-time 0.

Financial Information/Assistance:
Tuition for Full-Time Study: *Doctoral:* State residents: per academic year $2,800, $139 per credit hour; nonstate residents: per academic year $8,300, $400 per credit hour.

Financial Assistance:
First Year Students: Teaching assistantships available for first-year. Average amount paid per academic year: $6,500. Average number of hours worked per week: 20. Tuition remission given: full and partial. Research assistantships available for first-year. Average amount paid per academic year: $6,500. Average number of hours worked per week: 20.

Advanced Students: Teaching assistantships available for advanced students. Average amount paid per academic year: $6,500. Average number of hours worked per week: 20. Tuition remission given: full and partial. Research assistantships available for advanced students. Average amount paid per academic year: $6,500. Average number of hours worked per week: 20.

Contact Information: Of all students currently enrolled full-time, 95% benefitted from one or more of the listed financial assistance programs. Out of state students receiving a 16 hour or more assistantship (either GTA or GRA) automatically pay instate tuition. Depending on the duties assigned, graduate teaching assistants receive an additional tuition reduction ranging from 50% to 100%, typically 75%.

Internships/Practica: An important aspect of the human factors program is its requirement that all students complete a minimum six month internship. The internship is designed to provide students with practical experience in integrating their education in real-world situations. Internships have included positions with FAA National Cash Register, Pizza Hut, Bell Laboratories, IBM, Microsoft, and other similar settings. It is expected that these experiences will lead to post-PhD employment opportunities. In the community-clinical program, practicum opportunities, most of them funded, are available in on-campus training facilities and community agencies. Settings include the Psychology Clinic and the Counseling and Testing Center, both at Wichita State University; the Sedgwick County Department of Mental Health; Head Start, and various community-based projects. Students in the clinical track are also required to complete one year of internship experience towards the end of their graduate studies. For those doctoral students for whom a professional internship is required prior to graduation, 4 applied in 2000–2001. Of those who applied, 4 were placed in internships listed by the Association of Psychol-

ogy Postdoctoral and Internship Programs (APPIC); 4 were placed in APA accredited internships.

Housing and Day Care: On-campus housing and day care facilities are available.

Employment of Department Graduates:
Master's Degree Graduates: Of those who graduated in the academic year 2000–2001, the following categories and numbers represent the post-graduate activities and employment of master's degree graduates: Enrolled in a post-doctoral residency/fellowship (n/a), employed in independent practice (n/a).
Doctoral Degree Graduates: Of those who graduated in the academic year 2000–2001, the following categories and numbers represent the post-graduate activities and employment of doctoral degree graduates: Enrolled in a psychology doctoral program (n/a), enrolled in another graduate/professional program (n/a), enrolled in a post-doctoral residency/fellowship (2), employed in other positions at a higher education institution (3), employed in business or industry (research/consulting) (2), employed in a government agency (research) (1).

Additional Information:
Orientation, Objectives, and Emphasis of Department: The Psychology Department, open to various theoretical orientations, emphasizes research in all of its programs. The empirical focus of the human factors area seeks to provide students wide exposure to research training, practice, and literature, as well as to theory in the wider context of issues in basic and applied experimental psychology. Current human factors research involves cognitive functioning, aging, development, human-computer interactions, aerospace issues, and human-animal relationship. The community-clinical doctoral program seeks to integrate community and clinical psychology. The goal of the program is to train psychologists competent to conceptualize, research, intervene, and treat problems at the individual, group, organizational, and societal levels. The Community-Clinical Program has two tracks, a community track and a clinical track which requires a clinical internship. The applied research focus includes training in the development, delivery, and evaluation of psychosocial interventions, as well as the dissemination of research in the community. Special areas of research and practice include: parent-child interaction, treatment and prevention of depression, animal welfare, self-help groups, and other voluntary helping relationships, close relationships and health issues, treatment and prevention of delinquency, adolescent health and development, and assessment of personality and psychopathology.

Special Facilities or Resources: The department is located in Jabara Hall and maintains fully equipped laboratories. The facilities include the Human Information Processes Lab, Motor Skills Performance Lab, Micro-Experimental Lab, Cognitive Research Lab. Our computer facilities are state-of-the-art and are available to students for coursework and research. The department also has research access to the National Aviation Research Institute, and the University Computing Center. The Psychology Clinic, which is part of the psychology department, provides outpatient services via individual, group, and family modalities. The clinic has facilities for individual and group research. A state-wide Self-Help Network, with a computerized database and an 800 number, also operates out of the psychology department. Faculty maintain working relationships with a number of governmental and community agencies which facilitate student involvement in community practice and research. The agencies include the public school system, the Sedgwick County Department of Mental Health, and Kansas Mental Health and Retardation Services.

Information for Students With Physical Disabilities: The Office of Disability Services provides supportive services for students who experience physical or mental disabilities. Students qualified for this service can receive a handbook of services by contacting the office: Disabilities Services, Wichita State University, 1845 N. Fairmount, Wichita, Kansas, 67260-0132, (316) 978-3170.

Services are designed on an individual basis and may include the following: note taking, assistance to class, library assistance, test proctors, study partners, assistance in typing papers, and brailling notes. Some auxiliary aids are available for student's use. Textbooks also can be recorded on tape when requested. Disability Services encourage students to be as independent as possible on campus and to use those services which help maximize learning.

Application Information:
Send to: Graduate Coordinator, Psychology Department. Students are admitted in the Fall. Community-Clinical Psychology, February 1. Human Factors March 15. *Fee:* $25.

Eastern Kentucky University

Department of Psychology
Arts and Sciences
Cammack 127
Richmond, KY 40475
Telephone: (859) 622-1105
Fax: (859) 622-5871
E-mail: robert.adams@eku.edu
Web: http://www.psychology.eku.edu

Department Established:
1967. Chairperson: Robert M. Adams. Number of Faculty: total–full-time 21, part-time 8; women–full-time 11, part-time 8; minority–full-time 1.

Programs and Degrees Offered:
Listed in the following order: Program area, degree type (T if terminal Master's), number awarded 7/00-6/01. Clinical psychology MA (T) 10, Industrial/organizational, school psychology EdS (T) 8.

Student Applications/Admissions:
Student Applications
Clinical psychology MA—Applications 2001–2002, 57. Total applicants accepted 2001–2002, 22. New applicants enrolled 2001–2002, 10. Total enrolled 2001–2002 full-time, 8, part-time, 2. Openings 2002–2003, 12. The Median number of years required for completion of a degree are 2. The number of students enrolled full and part-time, who were dismissed or voluntarily withdrew from this program area were 1. *School psychology EdS*—Applications 2001–2002, 25. Total applicants accepted 2001–2002, 13. New applicants enrolled 2001–2002, 11. Total enrolled 2001–2002 full-time, 25. Openings 2002–2003, 8. The Median number of years required for completion of a degree are 3. The number of students enrolled full and part-time, who were dismissed or voluntarily withdrew from this program area were 0.

Admissions Requirements:
Scores: Entries appear in this order: required test or GPA, minimum score (if required), median score of students entering in 2001–2002. Master's Programs: GRE-V+Q+Analytical 1200, 1500; overall undergraduate GPA 2.5, 3.5. Doctoral Programs: last 2 years GPA no minimum stated; psychology GPA no minimum stated; psychology GPA no minimum stated.
Other Criteria: (importance of criteria rated low, medium, or high): GRE/MAT scores medium, research experience medium, work experience medium, extracurricular activity low, clinically related public service medium, GPA medium, letters of recommendation high, interview low, statement of goals and objectives medium.

Student Characteristics: The following represents characteristics of students in 2001–2002 in all graduate psychology programs in the department: Female–full-time 60, part-time 1; Male–full-time 4, part-time 0; African American/Black–full-time 2, part-time 0; Hispanic/Latino (a)–full-time 0, part-time 0; Asian/Pacific Islander–full-time 1, part-time 0; American Indian/Alaska Native–full-time 0, part-time 0.

Financial Information/Assistance:
Tuition for Full-Time Study: Master's: State residents per academic year $1,193; nonstate residents: per academic year $2,906.

Financial Assistance:
First Year Students: Average amount paid per academic year: $3,000. Average number of hours worked per week: 8. Apply by March 15. Tuition remission given: partial. Average amount paid per academic year: $3,000. Average number of hours worked per week: 8. Apply by March 15. Tuition remission given: partial.
Advanced Students: Average amount paid per academic year: $3,000. Average number of hours worked per week: 8. Apply by May 1. Tuition remission given: partial. Average amount paid per academic year: $3,000. Average number of hours worked per week: 8. Apply by May 1. Tuition remission given: partial.
Contact Information: Of all students currently enrolled full-time, 80% benefitted from one or more of the listed financial assistance programs. For information on financial assistance, contact: Department Chair.

Internships/Practica: A variety of field placements are available within easy commuting distance from Richmond. Practicum sites have included private psychiatric and V.A. hospitals, the University counseling center, a residential treatment facility for children, alcohol and drug abuse treatment programs, and several adult and child outpatient mental health centers. School psychology students can choose from a variety of public and private elementary and secondary schools. Students have completed internships in Kentucky as well as many other states. Students in the I-O program work on practicum projects with various for-profit and non-profit organizations in the region.

Housing and Day Care: On-campus housing and day care facilities are available.

Employment of Department Graduates:
Master's Degree Graduates: Of those who graduated in the academic year 2000–2001, the following categories and numbers represent the post-graduate activities and employment of master's degree graduates: Enrolled in a psychology doctoral program (3), enrolled in a post-doctoral residency/fellowship (n/a), employed in independent practice (n/a), employed in a community mental health/counseling center (4).
Doctoral Degree Graduates: Of those who graduated in the academic year 2000–2001, the following categories and numbers represent the post-graduate activities and employment of doctoral degree graduates: Enrolled in a psychology doctoral program (n/a), enrolled in another graduate/professional program (n/a).

Additional Information:
Orientation, Objectives, and Emphasis of Department: The MS program in clinical psychology is designed to train professional psychologists to work in clinics, hospitals, or other agencies. In

the clinical program, approximately one-third of the course hours are devoted to theory and research, one-third to clinical skills training, and one-third to practicum and internship placements in the community. The clinical program also offers a certification in mental health services to deaf and hard of hearing individuals. The PsyS program in school psychology is designed to train professional psychologists to work in schools and school-related agencies. The program involves 71 graduate hours including internship, is NASP approved, and meets Kentucky certification requirements. The certification program in school psychology is designed individually for the student with a degree in a related area who wishes to meet school psychology certification standards. Both programs meet the curriculum standards required for membership in the Council of Applied Master's Programs in Psychology and the North American Association for Master's Psychology, in which the department is an active participant. The clinical program is one of seven approved nationally by the Master's Program Accreditation Council. The I-O program is designed to meet the education and training guidelines established by the Society for Industrial and Organizational Psychology. The scientist-practitioner I-O program prepares students to work in organizations and/or pursue a doctoral degree. Degree requirements include intensive required courses and electives, and practicum. Research opportunities are available in all programs, and all programs prepare students for doctoral study.

Special Facilities or Resources: Laboratories include several multipurpose rooms. The clinical training facility includes a group therapy room, individual therapy rooms, a testing room, and a play therapy room. All rooms have two-way mirror viewing and videotape facilities. The department operates a child and family clinic providing services to the community, with its primary mission the training of students.

Information for Students With Physical Disabilities: Department is fully accessible to students with disabilities.

Application Information:
Send to: Graduate School Eastern Kentucky University, 521 Lancaster Ave., Richmond, KY 40475, letters of recommendation to Department Chair. Students are admitted in the Fall, application deadline March 15. March 15th is the deadline for all programs. Applications after this date are considered on a space-available basis.

Kentucky, University of
Department of Educational and Counseling Psychology
Counseling, School, and Educational Psychology
Dickey Hall, Room 245
Lexington, KY 40506-0017
Telephone: (606) 257-7881
Fax: (606) 257-5662
E-mail: eande1@uky.edu
Web: http://www.uky.edu/education/edphead.html

Department Established:
1968. Chairperson: Thomas Prout. Number of Faculty: total–full-time 16, part-time 2; women–full-time 8, part-time 2; minority–full-time 1.

Programs and Degrees Offered:
Listed in the following order: Program area, degree type (T if terminal Master's), number awarded 7/00-6/01. Counseling MA 21, educational MA, school MA 8.

APA Accreditation: Counseling PhD: full. School PhD: full.

Student Applications/Admissions:
Student Applications

Counseling MA—Applications 2001–2002, 42. Total applicants accepted 2001–2002, 34. New applicants enrolled 2001–2002, 15. Total enrolled 2001–2002 full-time, 15. Openings 2002–2003, 24. The Median number of years required for completion of a degree are 2. The number of students enrolled full and part-time, who were dismissed or voluntarily withdrew from this program area were 0. *Educational MA*—Applications 2001–2002, 3. Total applicants accepted 2001–2002, 3. Total enrolled 2001–2002 part-time, 4. Openings 2002–2003, 4. The Median number of years required for completion of a degree are 2. The number of students enrolled full and part-time, who were dismissed or voluntarily withdrew from this program area were 0. *School MA*—Applications 2001–2002, 35. Total applicants accepted 2001–2002, 14. New applicants enrolled 2001–2002, 9. Total enrolled 2001–2002 full-time, 9. Openings 2002–2003, 10. The Median number of years required for completion of a degree is 1. The number of students enrolled full and part-time, who were dismissed or voluntarily withdrew from this program area were 0.

Admissions Requirements:
Scores: Entries appear in this order: required test or GPA, minimum score (if required), median score of students entering in 2001–2002. Master's Programs: GRE-V no minimum stated; GRE-Q no minimum stated; GRE-V+Q no minimum stated. Doctoral Programs: GRE-V no minimum stated; GRE-Q no minimum stated; GRE-V+Q no minimum stated; overall undergraduate GPA 3.00, 3.37; last 2 years GPA no minimum stated; psychology GPA no minimum stated; psychology GPA 3.50, 3.86.

Other Criteria: (importance of criteria rated low, medium, or high): GRE/MAT scores medium, research experience high, work experience high, extracurricular activity medium, clinically related public service high, GPA medium, letters of recommendation high, interview high, statement of goals and objectives high.

Student Characteristics: The following represents characteristics of students in 2001–2002 in all graduate psychology programs in the department: Female–full-time 178, part-time 0; Male–full-time 44, part-time 0; African American/Black–full-time 24, part-time 0; Hispanic/Latino (a)–full-time 0, part-time 0; Asian/Pacific Islander–full-time 8, part-time 0; American Indian/Alaska Native–full-time 2, part-time 0; Multi-ethnic–full-time 0, students subject to the Americans with Disabilities Act–full-time 2.

Financial Information/Assistance:
Tuition for Full-Time Study: *Master's:* State residents per academic year $2,037, $212 per credit hour; nonstate residents: per academic year $5,647, $613 per credit hour. *Doctoral:* State residents: per academic year $2,037, $212 per credit hour; nonstate residents: per academic year $5,647, $613 per credit hour.

Financial Assistance:

First Year Students: Average amount paid per academic year: $9,652. Average number of hours worked per week: 20. Tuition remission given: full. Average amount paid per academic year: $5,250. Average number of hours worked per week: 20. Tuition remission given: partial.

Advanced Students: Average amount paid per academic year: $9,652. Average number of hours worked per week: 20. Tuition remission given: full. Average amount paid per academic year: $6,748. Average number of hours worked per week: 20. Tuition remission given: partial.

Contact Information: Of all students currently enrolled full-time, 16% benefitted from one or more of the listed financial assistance programs. For information on financial assistance, contact: Dr. Eric Anderman.

Internships/Practica: No information provided.

Housing and Day Care: No on-campus housing and day care facilities are available.

Employment of Department Graduates:

Master's Degree Graduates: Of those who graduated in the academic year 2000–2001, the following categories and numbers represent the post-graduate activities and employment of master's degree graduates: Enrolled in a psychology doctoral program (5), enrolled in another graduate/professional program (1), enrolled in a post-doctoral residency/fellowship (n/a), employed in independent practice (n/a), employed in other positions at a higher education institution (2), employed in a professional position in a school system (1), employed in business or industry (research/consulting) (1), employed in a government agency (professional services) (1), employed in a hospital/medical center (1).

Doctoral Degree Graduates: Of those who graduated in the academic year 2000–2001, the following categories and numbers represent the post-graduate activities and employment of doctoral degree graduates: Enrolled in a psychology doctoral program (n/a), enrolled in another graduate/professional program (n/a), enrolled in a post-doctoral residency/fellowship (2).

Additional Information:

Orientation, Objectives, and Emphasis of Department: Three programs are housed within the department: counseling psychology, educational psychology, and school psychology. The program faculties in counseling psychology and in school psychology are committed to the scientist-practitioner model for professional training, while educational psychology faculty emphasize the researcher-teacher model. A strong emphasis has been placed upon the psychology core for all professional training. Counseling faculty research interests focus upon cognitive social learning theory, consultation models, experiential therapies, and humanistic psychology. The school psychology faculty research interests focus upon consultation strategies, evaluation and assessment, training, and direct interventions. The educational psychology faculty research interests include motivation, cardiovascular stress in minority children, engagement in risky behaviors, forgiveness, and sleep deprivation. Students in each program are encouraged to establish mentoring relationships with their major professor by the beginning of their second semester. The counseling faculty intends to prepare professionals for diverse settings, e.g., colleges and universities, research facilities, hospitals, regional mental health centers, and private practice. The school psychology faculty aims to prepare scientist-practitioners who will function in school and university settings, in mental health consortia, and in private practice. The educational psychology faculty prepare graduates for research and teaching careers within higher education and applied research settings.

Special Facilities or Resources: The University of Kentucky is located on the western edge of Appalachia, which provides students with the opportunity to interact with a rich and varied American culture. The uniqueness of this potential client and research pool allows our students to examine attributes of the bridge between old, rural America and the future, more technological America. Microcomputer facilities are available within the department and within the college for student use in word processing, model development, simulation and evaluation, and data analysis. The university provides all the facilities and resources expected of a major research institution (e.g., extensive libraries, computer facilities, research environment, and medical center).

Application Information:
Send to: Dr. Eric Anderman, Director of Graduate Study, Department of Educational and Counseling Psychology, College of Education, University of Kentucky, 245 Dickey Hall, Lexington, KY 40506-0017. Students are admitted in the Fall, application deadline January 1. Jan. 1 deadline for Ph.D., March 1 deadline for Master's. *Fee:* $30. $35 International.

Kentucky, University of
Department of Psychology
Arts and Sciences
Kastle Hall
Lexington, KY 40506-0044
Telephone: (859) 257-6839
Fax: (859) 323-1979
E-mail: *jldard0@uky.edu*
Web: *http://www.uky.edu/ArtsSciences/Psychology*

Department Established:

1917. Chairperson: Rick Hoyle. Number of Faculty: total–full-time 29; women–full-time 10; minority–full-time 4.

Programs and Degrees Offered:

Listed in the following order: Program area, degree type (T if terminal Master's), number awarded 7/00-6/01. Clinical PhD 11, Experimental PhD 5.

APA Accreditation: Clinical PhD: full.

Student Applications/Admissions:

Student Applications

Clinical PhD—Applications 2001–2002, 145. Total applicants accepted 2001–2002, 7. New applicants enrolled 2001–2002, 7. Total enrolled 2001–2002 full-time, 39. Openings 2002–2003, 8. The Median number of years required for completion of a degree are 5. The number of students enrolled full and part-time, who were dismissed or voluntarily withdrew from this program area were 0. *Experimental PhD*—Applications 2001–2002, 47. Total applicants accepted 2001–2002, 8. New applicants enrolled 2001–2002, 8. Total enrolled 2001–2002 full-time, 39. Openings 2002–2003, 8. The Median number of years required for completion of a degree are 5. The number of students enrolled full and part-time, who were dismissed or voluntarily withdrew from this program area were 0.

Admissions Requirements:

Scores: Entries appear in this order: required test or GPA, minimum score (if required), median score of students entering in 2001–2002. Master's Programs: GRE-V no minimum stated; GRE-Q no minimum stated; GRE-Analytical no minimum stated; overall undergraduate GPA 2.75. Doctoral Programs: GRE-V+Q+Analytical 1200; overall undergraduate GPA 2.75; last 2 years GPA no minimum stated; psychology GPA no minimum stated; psychology GPA no minimum stated.

Other Criteria: (importance of criteria rated low, medium, or high): GRE/MAT scores high, research experience high, clinically related public service medium, GPA high, letters of recommendation high, interview high, statement of goals and objectives high.

Student Characteristics: The following represents characteristics of students in 2001–2002 in all graduate psychology programs in the department: Female–full-time 48, part-time 0; Male–full-time 27, part-time 0; African American/Black–full-time 7, part-time 0; Hispanic/Latino (a)–full-time 3, part-time 0; Asian/Pacific Islander–full-time 2, part-time 0; American Indian/Alaska Native–full-time 1, part-time 0; Multi-ethnic–full-time 0, students subject to the Americans with Disabilities Act–full-time 0.

Financial Information/Assistance:

Tuition for Full-Time Study: *Master's:* State residents per academic year $2,158, $225 per credit hour; nonstate residents: per academic year $5,767, $626 per credit hour. *Doctoral:* State residents: per academic year $2,158, $225 per credit hour; nonstate residents: per academic year $5,767, $626 per credit hour.

Financial Assistance:

First Year Students: Teaching assistantships available for first-year. Average amount paid per academic year: $10,750. Average number of hours worked per week: 20. Apply by January 15. Tuition remission given: full. Research assistantships available for first-year. Average amount paid per academic year: $10,750. Average number of hours worked per week: 20. Apply by January 15. Tuition remission given: full. Fellowships and scholarships available for first-year. Average amount paid per academic year: $15,000. Average number of hours worked per week: 20. Apply by January 15. Tuition remission given: full.

Advanced Students: Teaching assistantships available for advanced students. Average amount paid per academic year: $10,750. Average number of hours worked per week: 20. Apply by January 15. Tuition remission given: full. Research assistantships available for advanced students. Average amount paid per academic year: $10,750. Average number of hours worked per week: 20. Apply by January 15. Tuition remission given: full. Fellowships and scholarships available for advanced students. Average amount paid per academic year: $15,000. Average number of hours worked per week: 20. Apply by January 15. Tuition remission given: full.

Contact Information: Of all students currently enrolled full-time, 100% benefitted from one or more of the listed financial assistance programs. For information on financial assistance, contact: Jennifer Darden.

Internships/Practica: For those doctoral students for whom a professional internship is required prior to graduation, 10 applied in 2000–2001. Of those who applied, 10 were placed in internships listed by the Association of Psychology Postdoctoral and Internship Programs (APPIC); 10 were placed in APA accredited internships.

Housing and Day Care: No on-campus housing and day care facilities are available.

Employment of Department Graduates:

Master's Degree Graduates: Of those who graduated in the academic year 2000–2001, the following categories and numbers represent the post-graduate activities and employment of master's degree graduates: Enrolled in a psychology doctoral program (0), enrolled in another graduate/professional program (0), enrolled in a post-doctoral residency/fellowship (n/a), employed in independent practice (n/a).

Doctoral Degree Graduates: Of those who graduated in the academic year 2000–2001, the following categories and numbers represent the post-graduate activities and employment of doctoral degree graduates: Enrolled in a psychology doctoral program (n/a), enrolled in another graduate/professional program (n/a), enrolled in a post-doctoral residency/fellowship (4), employed in independent practice (1), employed in an academic position at a university (0), employed in an academic position at a 2-year/4-year college (4), employed in other positions at a higher education institution (0), employed in a professional position in a school system (0), employed in business or industry (research/consulting) (1), employed in business or industry (management) (0), employed in a government agency (research) (0), employed in a government agency (professional services) (1), employed in a community mental health/counseling center (0), employed in a hospital/medical center (0), still seeking employment (0), other employment position (0).

Additional Information:

Orientation, Objectives, and Emphasis of Department: The goals of the doctoral program depend partly upon the specific program area in which a student enrolls. The program in Clinical Psychology follows the Boulder scientist-practitioner model. Students in the program receive broad exposure to the major theoretical perspectives influencing clinical psychology. All students are actively engaged in research throughout their graduate training. Beginning in the second year of study, each student also receives extensive clinical experience via placements in mental health setting. Graduates of the program are prepared to pursue an academic career or to be a practitioner. Students in the program in Experimental Psychology, Cognitive, Developmental, Social, Animal Learning and Behavioral Neuroscience are trained as research scientists. They are exposed to the important theoretical perspectives and research paradigms of their respective areas. There is a good deal of latitude for individuals to define their specific programs of study. Graduates are prepared to pursue an academic career or a research position in an applied setting. Graduate study is based on a core curriculum model with no set number of hours required for the PhD degree. All students complete a Master's thesis, written and oral doctoral qualifying examinations, and a dissertation demonstrating accomplishment in independent research.

Special Facilities or Resources: The psychology department occupies its own three-story building located by the computer center and main campus library. Kastle Hall houses faculty and student offices, classrooms, and research space. Research facilities in the building include: animal laboratories for behavioral and physiological research; observation rooms with one-way mirrors; extensive video equipment; and microcomputer equipped rooms for cognitive research. Two additional buildings on campus are available for behavioral research. Current faculty have collaborative arrangements with several facilities on campus, including: the neuropsychology laboratories in the Department of Neurology; the Oral-Facial Pain Clinic in the College of Dentistry; the Central Animal Research Facility; and the Sanders-Brown Center on Aging. The department maintains a large undergraduate subject pool. Clinical training facilities are excellent and include a departmental clinic housed in a separate building and clinical placement arrangements with a variety of mental health facilities in Lexington.

Application Information:
Send to: Jennifer Darden, Graduate Secretary, 116 Kastle Hall, Department of Psychology, University of Kentucky, Lexington, KY 40506-0044. Students are admitted in the Fall, application deadline January 15. *Fee:* $35.

Louisville, University of
Psychological and Brain Sciences
Arts and Sciences
317 Life Sciences Building
Louisville, KY 40292
Telephone: (502) 852-6775
Fax: (502) 852-8904
E-mail: *dmolfese@louisville.edu*
Web: *http://www.louisville.edu/a-s/psychology/*

Department Established:
1963. Chairperson: Dennis L. Molfese. Number of Faculty: total–full-time 21; women–full-time 7; minority–full-time 2.

Programs and Degrees Offered:
Listed in the following order: Program area, degree type (T if terminal Master's), number awarded 7/00-6/01. Clinical PhD 8, Experimental PhD 6.

APA Accreditation: Clinical PhD: full.

Student Applications/Admissions:
Student Applications
Clinical PhD—Applications 2001–2002, 80. Total applicants accepted 2001–2002, 8. New applicants enrolled 2001–2002, 8. Total enrolled 2001–2002 full-time, 45. Openings 2002–2003, 8. Experimental PhD—Applications 2001–2002, 19. Total applicants accepted 2001–2002, 7. New applicants enrolled 2001–2002, 7. Total enrolled 2001–2002 full-time, 22. Openings 2002–2003, 8.

Admissions Requirements:
Scores: Entries appear in this order: required test or GPA, minimum score (if required), median score of students entering in 2001–2002. Doctoral Programs: GRE-V 550, 590; GRE-Q

550, 655; GRE-V+Q 1100; overall undergraduate GPA 3.0, 3.65; last 2 years GPA 3.0, 3.33; psychology GPA 3.0, 3.86; psychology GPA no minimum stated.
Other Criteria: (importance of criteria rated low, medium, or high): GRE/MAT scores high, research experience high, work experience medium, extracurricular activity medium, clinically related public service medium, GPA high, letters of recommendation high, interview high, statement of goals and objectives medium. Experimental PhD does not require clinically-related public service or interview.

Student Characteristics: The following represents characteristics of students in 2001–2002 in all graduate psychology programs in the department: Female–full-time 46, part-time 0; Male–full-time 25, part-time 0; African American/Black–full-time 3, part-time 0; Hispanic/Latino (a)–full-time 2, part-time 0; Asian/Pacific Islander–full-time 2, part-time 0; American Indian/Alaska Native–full-time 0, part-time 0; students subject to the Americans with Disabilities Act–full-time 1.

Financial Information/Assistance:
Tuition for Full-Time Study: *Doctoral:* State residents: per academic year $4,134, $235 per credit hour; nonstate residents: per academic year $11,486, $642 per credit hour.

Financial Assistance:
First Year Students: Teaching assistantships available for first-year. Average amount paid per academic year: $12,500. Average number of hours worked per week: 20. Apply by July 1. Tuition remission given: full. Research assistantships available for first-year. Average amount paid per academic year: $12,500. Average number of hours worked per week: 20. Apply by July 1. Tuition remission given: full. Fellowships and scholarships available for first-year. Average amount paid per academic year: $18,000. Average number of hours worked per week: 0. Apply by Feb 1. Tuition remission given: full.

Advanced Students: Teaching assistantships available for advanced students. Average amount paid per academic year: $12,500. Average number of hours worked per week: 20. Apply by July 1. Tuition remission given: full. Research assistantships available for advanced students. Average amount paid per academic year: $12,500. Average number of hours worked per week: 20. Apply by July 1. Tuition remission given: full. Traineeships available for advanced students. Average amount paid per academic year: $0. Average number of hours worked per week: 0. Apply by varies. Fellowships and scholarships available for advanced students. Average amount paid per academic year: $18,000. Average number of hours worked per week: 0. Apply by Feb 1. Tuition remission given: full.

Contact Information: Of all students currently enrolled full-time, 65% benefitted from one or more of the listed financial assistance programs. For information on financial assistance, contact: Financial Aid Office at 502-852-5511.

Internships/Practica: Internship and practica are available in a number of community and government agencies. These include the Department of Psychiatry and Behavioral Sciences, The Child Evaluation Center, Central State Hospital, Veterans Administration Medical Center, Seven Counties Services, and numerous other agencies. For those doctoral students for whom a professional internship is required prior to graduation, 7 applied in 2000–2001. Of those who applied, 7 were placed in internships listed by the Association of Psychology Postdoctoral and Internship Programs (APPIC); 7 were placed in APA accredited internships.

Housing and Day Care: No on-campus housing and day care facilities are available.

Employment of Department Graduates:

Master's Degree Graduates: Of those who graduated in the academic year 2000–2001, the following categories and numbers represent the post-graduate activities and employment of master's degree graduates: Enrolled in a post-doctoral residency/fellowship (n/a), employed in independent practice (n/a).

Doctoral Degree Graduates: Of those who graduated in the academic year 2000–2001, the following categories and numbers represent the post-graduate activities and employment of doctoral degree graduates: Enrolled in a psychology doctoral program (n/a), enrolled in another graduate/professional program (n/a), employed in an academic position at a university (1), employed in an academic position at a 2-year/4-year college (1), employed in a professional position in a school system (1).

Additional Information:

Orientation, Objectives, and Emphasis of Department: The experimental program offers two areas of specialization: 1) Cognitive: which focuses on memory, conceptual behavior, problem solving, language, judgment, decision making, attention, cognitive development, and mathematical models; and 2) Perception and Sensory Physiology: which focuses on visual perception, visual neurosciences, and the physiology of the visual system. The Clinical Program adheres to a scientist-practitioner model and is designed to provide training in research, psychological assessment, psychological intervention, and legal and professional issues. The program covers basic theories, current state of knowledge, and skill training in clinical psychology. Faculty expertise is strongest in the areas of anxiety disorders in children and adults, mental health and adjustments of older adults, stress management and behavioral medicine, ethnic mental health, interpersonal relations, social influence, social cognition, aggression, group behavior, and health psychology. Clinical emphasis includes interpersonal and cognitive-behavioral approaches.

Special Facilities or Resources: Departmental facilities include several computerized laboratories, an electronic shop, physiological laboratories, and a Psychological Services Center. The University also has a Computer Center that is available from departmental stations via a campus-wide network. Additional training opportunities are available through such facilities as the Department of Psychiatry and Behavioral Sciences, the Child Evaluation Center, Central State Hospital, and numerous other community agencies.

Information for Students With Physical Disabilities: The Disability Resource Center at the University of Louisville provides services and advocacy for prospective and currently enrolled students with disabilities. Their goal is to assure equal educational opportunity by providing services and advocacy which mainstream the student with a disability into the University community.

Application Information:

Send to: Admissions Office, Department O/A, University of Louisville, Louisville, KY 40292-0001. Students are admitted in the Fall, application deadline January 10. *Fee:* $25.

Morehead State University (Kentucky)
Department of Psychology
Science & Technology
601 Ginger Hall
Morehead, KY 40351
Telephone: (606) 783-2981
Fax: (606) 783-5077
E-mail: *b.mattin@morehead-st.edu*
Web: *http://www.morehead-st.edu/education/psychology/index.htm*

Department Established:

1968. Chairperson: Bruce A. Mattingly. Number of Faculty: total–full-time 11, part-time 4; women–full-time 4, part-time 2.

Programs and Degrees Offered:

Listed in the following order: Program area, degree type (T if terminal Master's), number awarded 7/00-6/01. Clinical MA (T) 13, counseling psychology MA (T) 5, experimental-general MA (T) 3.

Student Applications/Admissions:

Student Applications

Clinical MA—Applications 2001–2002, 35. Total applicants accepted 2001–2002, 18. New applicants enrolled 2001–2002, 14. Total enrolled 2001–2002 full-time, 28. Openings 2002–2003, 15. The Median number of years required for completion of a degree are 2. The number of students enrolled full and part-time, who were dismissed or voluntarily withdrew from this program area were 1. *Counseling psychology* MA—Applications 2001–2002, 19. Total applicants accepted 2001–2002, 10. New applicants enrolled 2001–2002, 7. Total enrolled 2001–2002 full-time, 14. Openings 2002–2003, 10. The Median number of years required for completion of a degree are 2. The number of students enrolled full and part-time, who were dismissed or voluntarily withdrew from this program area were 0. *Experimental-general MA*—Applications 2001–2002, 8. Total applicants accepted 2001–2002, 4. New applicants enrolled 2001–2002, 3. Total enrolled 2001–2002 full-time, 8. Openings 2002–2003, 7. The Median number of years required for completion of a degree are 2.

Admissions Requirements:

Scores: Entries appear in this order: required test or GPA, minimum score (if required), median score of students entering in 2001–2002. Master's Programs: GRE-V+Q 800, 1050; overall undergraduate GPA 3.0. Doctoral Programs: last 2 years GPA no minimum stated; psychology GPA no minimum stated; psychology GPA no minimum stated.

Other Criteria: (importance of criteria rated low, medium, or high): GRE/MAT scores medium, research experience low, work experience low, extracurricular activity low, clinically related public service low, GPA high, letters of recommendation high, interview medium, statement of goals and objectives medium.

Student Characteristics: The following represents characteristics of students in 2001–2002 in all graduate psychology programs in the department: Female–full-time 20, part-time 0; Male–full-time 15, part-time 0; African American/Black–full-time 0, part-time

0; Hispanic/Latino (a)–full-time 0, part-time 0; Asian/Pacific Islander–full-time 1, part-time 0; American Indian/Alaska Native–full-time 0, part-time 0.

Financial Information/Assistance:

Tuition for Full-Time Study: *Master's:* State residents per academic year $1,584, $176 per credit hour; nonstate residents: per academic year $4,247, $472 per credit hour.

Financial Assistance:

First Year Students: Teaching assistantships available for first-year. Average amount paid per academic year: $5,000. Average number of hours worked per week: 20. Tuition remission given: partial. Research assistantships available for first-year. Average amount paid per academic year: $5,000. Average number of hours worked per week: 20. Tuition remission given: partial.

Advanced Students: Teaching assistantships available for advanced students. Average amount paid per academic year: $5,000. Average number of hours worked per week: 20. Tuition remission given: partial. Research assistantships available for advanced students. Average amount paid per academic year: $5,000. Average number of hours worked per week: 20. Tuition remission given: partial.

Contact Information: Of all students currently enrolled full-time, 100% benefitted from one or more of the listed financial assistance programs. For information on financial assistance, contact: department chair.

Internships/Practica: Internships and practica placement sites are available in several different states.

Housing and Day Care: On-campus housing and day care facilities are available.

Employment of Department Graduates:

Master's Degree Graduates: Of those who graduated in the academic year 2000–2001, the following categories and numbers represent the post-graduate activities and employment of master's degree graduates: Enrolled in a post-doctoral residency/fellowship (n/a), employed in independent practice (n/a).

Doctoral Degree Graduates: Of those who graduated in the academic year 2000–2001, the following categories and numbers represent the post-graduate activities and employment of doctoral degree graduates: Enrolled in a psychology doctoral program (n/a), enrolled in another graduate/professional program (n/a).

Additional Information:

Orientation, Objectives, and Emphasis of Department: The clinical and counseling programs are designed primarily to train MA level psychologists to practice in a variety of settings, and lead to certification in states that provide for certification of master's level psychologists. However, approximately 25% of our students enter doctoral level programs upon graduation. The practitioner model is emphasized in the program, with primary emphases on acquisition of applied clinical skills and knowledge of the general field of psychology. Consequently, competencies in critical analysis of theories, experimental design, and quantitative data analysis are expected. Clinical and counseling students are encouraged to participate in or conduct research ongoing in the department. Students interested in pursuing doctoral level training are encouraged to complete a thesis. The purpose of the experimental program is primarily to prepare students for entry into doctoral programs. Students and faculty are involved in research in several areas including cognitive, perception, animal learning and motivation, psychopharmacology, neurophysiology, developmental, social, and personality.

Special Facilities or Resources: The psychology program provides excellent laboratory facilities for the study of animal and human behavior. Faculty/student research programs are funded through both intra- and extramural grants. The department maintains two microcomputer laboratories, and offers training in statistical packages such as SAS and SPSS. All accepted students are supported by graduate assistantships. Financial assistance for paper presentations at professional conferences is normally available.

Application Information:
Send to: Graduate Office, Morehead State Unviersity, Ginger Hall, room 701, Morehead, KY 40351. Students are admitted in the Fall, application deadline June 15. Rolling admission procedure for fall semester beginning March 1.

Murray State University
Department of Psychology
Humanities and Fine Arts
212 Wells Hall
Murray, KY 42071-3318
Telephone: (270) 762-2851
Fax: (270) 762-2991
E-mail: *sherry.fortner@murraystate.edu*
Web: *http://www.mursuky.edu/qacd/chs/psychology/psyhom.*

Department Established:
1966. Chairperson: Dr. Renae D. Duncan. Number of Faculty: total–full-time 10; women–full-time 5.

Programs and Degrees Offered:
Listed in the following order: Program area, degree type (T if terminal Master's), number awarded 7/00-6/01. Clinical MA (T) 6, general MA (T).

Student Applications/Admissions:
Student Applications

Clinical MA—Applications 2001–2002, 35. Total applicants accepted 2001–2002, 14. New applicants enrolled 2001–2002, 7. Total enrolled 2001–2002 full-time, 17, part-time, 4. Openings 2002–2003, 12. The Median number of years required for completion of a degree are 3. The number of students enrolled full and part-time, who were dismissed or voluntarily withdrew from this program area were 1. *General MA*—Applications 2001–2002, 3. Total applicants accepted 2001–2002, 2. New applicants enrolled 2001–2002, 2. Total enrolled 2001–2002 full-time, 2. Openings 2002–2003, 3. The Median number of years required for completion of a degree are 2. The number of students enrolled full and part-time, who were dismissed or voluntarily withdrew from this program area were 0.

Admissions Requirements:

Scores: Entries appear in this order: required test or GPA, minimum score (if required), median score of students entering in 2001–2002. Master's Programs: GRE-V+Q 800, 981; overall undergraduate GPA 3.00, 3.33; psychology GPA 3.00, 3.41. Doctoral Programs: last 2 years GPA no minimum stated; psychology GPA no minimum stated; psychology GPA no minimum stated.

Other Criteria: (importance of criteria rated low, medium, or high): GRE/MAT scores medium, research experience medium, work experience low, clinically related public service low, GPA high, letters of recommendation high, statement of goals and objectives high.

Student Characteristics: The following represents characteristics of students in 2001–2002 in all graduate psychology programs in the department: Female–full-time 11, part-time 4; Male–full-time 6, part-time 1; African American/Black–full-time 0, part-time 0; Hispanic/Latino (a)–full-time 2, part-time 1; Asian/Pacific Islander–full-time 1, part-time 0; American Indian/Alaska Native–full-time 0, part-time 0; Multi-ethnic–full-time 0, part-time 0; students subject to the Americans with Disabilities Act–full-time 1, part-time 1.

Financial Information/Assistance:

Tuition for Full-Time Study: *Master's:* State residents per academic year $1,439, $168 per credit hour; nonstate residents: per academic year $4,003, $449 per credit hour.

Financial Assistance:

First Year Students: Research assistantships available for first-year. Average amount paid per academic year: $3,940. Average number of hours worked per week: 10. Apply by March 1. Tuition remission given: full and partial.

Advanced Students: Research assistantships available for advanced students. Average amount paid per academic year: $3,940. Average number of hours worked per week: 10. Apply by March 1. Tuition remission given: full and partial.

Contact Information: Of all students currently enrolled full-time, 40% benefitted from one or more of the listed financial assistance programs. For information on financial assistance, contact: Department Chair.

Internships/Practica: To gain experience conducting therapy and psychological evaluations, a supervised two-semester, 20 hour per week clinical practicum is required. Clinical psychology students serve their practica at the MSU Psychological Center, an on-campus treatment center, which provides therapy and assessments for children, adults, and families from the community as well as for university students and staff. In addition to gaining experience conducting therapy and assessments, our clinical graduate students receive 2 hours per week of supervision with our Ph.D. level licensed clinical psychologists. This allows for a fine-tuning of clinical skills as well as an added assurance that the clinician is providing the best and most ethical services to the Center's clients.

Housing and Day Care: On-campus housing and day care facilities are available.

Employment of Department Graduates:

Master's Degree Graduates: Of those who graduated in the academic year 2000–2001, the following categories and numbers represent the post-graduate activities and employment of master's degree graduates: Enrolled in a psychology doctoral program (2), enrolled in another graduate/professional program (0), enrolled in a post-doctoral residency/fellowship (n/a), employed in independent practice (n/a), employed in an academic position at a university (0), employed in an academic position at a 2-year/4-year college (0), employed in other positions at a higher education institution (1), employed in a professional position in a school system (2), employed in business or industry (research/consulting) (0), employed in business or industry (management) (0), employed in a government agency (research) (0), employed in a government agency (professional services) (0), employed in a community mental health/counseling center (2), employed in a hospital/medical center (0), still seeking employment (0), other employment position (0).

Doctoral Degree Graduates: Of those who graduated in the academic year 2000–2001, the following categories and numbers represent the post-graduate activities and employment of doctoral degree graduates: Enrolled in a psychology doctoral program (n/a), enrolled in another graduate/professional program (n/a).

Additional Information:

Orientation, Objectives, and Emphasis of Department: The clinical program is based on the philosophy that the master's degree is first and foremost a degree in psychology and that students should achieve a broad base of knowledge in the field. Thus, students are required to take 5 psychological foundations courses which prepare the graduate to enter the field of psychology and also provide the general psychology courses required by state licensing boards. Clinical students also receive intensive instruction in psychodiagnostics, which emphasizes the administration, scoring, and interpretation of a variety of intelligence and personality tests. The psychotherapy curriculum is primarily cognitive-behavioral in nature though a variety of techniques and orientations are presented which teach the student how best to conduct psychotherapy with adults, children, families, and couples. Students are expected to participate in research, and a master's thesis is required. The general program emphasizes psychological foundations and research methodology as preparation for doctoral studies, community college teaching, or applied research.

Special Facilities or Resources: The department has research laboratories, an on-site psychological clinic with testing and observation rooms, and complete facilities for practica in diagnostics and therapy.

Application Information:

Send to: Department Chair. Students are admitted in the Fall, application deadline March 15; Spring, application deadline rolling adm. Applications will be accepted after the deadline. However, late applications will be considered only if openings remain after review of applications received before the due date. *Fee:* $25.

Spalding University

School of Professional Psychology
851 South Fourth Street
Louisville, KY 40203
Telephone: (502) 585-7127
Fax: (502) 585-7159
E-mail: *gradadmissions@spalding.edu*
Web: *http://www.spalding.edu*

Department Established:

1952. Dean, School of Professional Psychology: Barbara Williams, Ph.D., ABPP. Number of Faculty: total–full-time 9, part-time 19; women–full-time 3, part-time 10; minority–full-time 1.

Programs and Degrees Offered:

Listed in the following order: Program area, degree type (T if terminal Master's), number awarded 7/00-6/01. Clinical Psychology PsyD 20, Master of Arts in Clinical Psy MA (T) 8.

APA Accreditation: Clinical PsyD: full.

Student Applications/Admissions:

Student Applications

Clinical Psychology PsyD—Applications 2001–2002, 84. Total applicants accepted 2001–2002, 47. New applicants enrolled 2001–2002, 25. Total enrolled 2001–2002 full-time, 73, part-time, 45. Openings 2002–2003, 40. The Median number of years required for completion of a degree are 5. The number of students enrolled full and part-time, who were dismissed or voluntarily withdrew from this program area were 1. *Master of Arts in Clinical Psy* MA—Applications 2001–2002, 13. Total applicants accepted 2001–2002, 6. New applicants enrolled 2001–2002, 7. Total enrolled 2001–2002 full-time, 14. Openings 2002–2003, 10. The Median number of years required for completion of a degree are 3. The number of students enrolled full and part-time, who were dismissed or voluntarily withdrew from this program area were 2.

Admissions Requirements:

Scores: Entries appear in this order: required test or GPA, minimum score (if required), median score of students entering in 2001–2002. Master's Programs: GRE-V no minimum stated, 430; GRE-Q no minimum stated, 410; GRE-V+Q no minimum stated, 840; GRE-Analytical no minimum stated, 460; GRE-V+Q+Analytical no minimum stated, 1300; overall undergraduate GPA 3.4. Doctoral Programs: GRE-V no minimum stated, 480; GRE-Q no minimum stated, 540; GRE-V+Q no minimum stated, 1020; GRE-Analytical no minimum stated, 640; GRE-V+Q+Analytical no minimum stated, 1660; overall undergraduate GPA 3.5; last 2 years GPA no minimum stated; psychology GPA no minimum stated; psychology GPA no minimum stated.

Other Criteria: (importance of criteria rated low, medium, or high): GRE/MAT scores medium, research experience low, work experience medium, extracurricular activity medium, clinically related public service high, GPA medium, letters of recommendation high, interview high, statement of goals and objectives high.

Student Characteristics: The following represents characteristics of students in 2001–2002 in all graduate psychology programs in the department: Female–full-time 63, part-time 33; Male–full-time 13, part-time 23; African American/Black–full-time 4, part-time 3; Hispanic/Latino (a)–full-time 0, part-time 1; Asian/Pacific Islander–full-time 2, part-time 1; American Indian/Alaska Native–full-time 0, part-time 1.

Financial Information/Assistance:

Tuition for Full-Time Study: *Master's:* State residents $425 per credit hour; nonstate residents: $425 per credit hour. *Doctoral:* State residents: $515 per credit hour; nonstate residents: $515 per credit hour.

Financial Assistance:

First Year Students: Research assistantships available for first-year. Average amount paid per academic year: $5,000. Apply by March 15. Tuition remission given: partial. Fellowships and scholarships available for first-year. Average amount paid per academic year: $6,000. Apply by March 15. Tuition remission given: partial.

Advanced Students: No information provided.

Contact Information: Of all students currently enrolled full-time, 25% benefitted from one or more of the listed financial assistance programs. For information on financial assistance, contact: Jeanne Mullins, Financial Aid Office.

Internships/Practica: In the School of Professional Psychology at Spalding University, we pride ourselves on our extensive network of practica experiences. While we have a University Counseling Center with practica available, we are more broadly known for the extensive practica available through community contacts. These include various community agencies (i.e., Seven Counties Services,), hospitals (i.e., CARITAS Peace Center), health centers (Portland Family Health Center), the Kentucky Correctional System, and children and family service centers (i.e., contracts with the Archdiocese and public school system). Students experience this diversity of settings beginning in their second year with assessment and intervention practica, and continuing through their Practica IV, during which they supervise a beginning level psychotherapy student under the university supervision of a skilled practitioner. A select list of specific clinical sites available include the following: Archdiocese of Louisville (Family Counseling), Ireland Army Community Hospital, Bellarmine University Counseling Center, Bellewood Presbyterian Home for Children, Brooklawn Psychiatric Residential Treatment Facilities, CARITAS Peace Center, Central State Hospital, Jefferson County Division of Family Services, Department of Juvenile Justice Center, Department of Corrections (Division of Mental Health), Lifespring Mental Health Services, Solutions Center for Brief Therapy, University of Louisville Counseling Center, and the VA Medical Center. These diverse practica placements prepare our students well for an equally diverse number of internship placements. For those doctoral students for whom a professional internship is required prior to graduation, 27 applied in 2000–2001. Of those who applied, 1 were placed in internships listed by the Association of Psychology Postdoctoral and Internship Programs (APPIC); 25 were placed in APA accredited internships.

Housing and Day Care: No on-campus housing and day care facilities are available.

Employment of Department Graduates:

Master's Degree Graduates: Of those who graduated in the academic year 2000–2001, the following categories and numbers represent the post-graduate activities and employment of master's degree graduates: Enrolled in a post-doctoral residency/fellowship (n/a), employed in independent practice (n/a).

Doctoral Degree Graduates: Of those who graduated in the academic year 2000–2001, the following categories and numbers represent the post-graduate activities and employment of doctoral degree graduates: Enrolled in a psychology doctoral program (n/a), enrolled in another graduate/professional program (n/a).

Additional Information:

Orientation, Objectives, and Emphasis of Department: The training model of the Spalding School of Professional Psychology is a competency-based disciplined inquiry model. This model integrates professional activity as disciplined inquiry with the goal of professional activities as achieving professional competencies as identified by NCSPP. These competencies are relationship, assessment, intervention, research, supervision, and consultation. In the Spalding Model, professional activities start with issues the client brings to the situation. The professional brings all the relevant knowledge available to address the presenting situation. Relevant knowledge includes scientific knowledge, training in the various competencies identified by NCSPP, and personal knowledge from professional experience. Thus, we educate and train students simultaneously in scientifically based knowledge relevant to the local situations encountered and in the professional competencies needed to address the specific issues raised by clients. The academic scientific core content specified by APA includes: biological basis of behavior, cognitive-affective bases (learning), social bases of behavior, individual differences, history and systems of psychology, and research methods and statistics. These areas cover the theoretical and research basis for guiding conceptions relevant to situations that the professional encounters. The Spalding Program is organizing within an emphasis area structure. Existing emphasis areas are a General Emphasis Area, a Health Psychology Emphasis Area, and a Child, Adolescent, Family Emphasis Area. The degree is a PsyD in clinical psychology, with an emphasis.

Special Facilities or Resources: The faculty have various areas of expertise and interest and form research groups around these areas of interest. For example, Ken Linfield has an interest group around issues of religion/spirituality and how this integrates with the practice of professional psychology. Tom Bergandi has an interest group around sports psychology, which has led to at least ten dissertations over the past fifteen years and Catherine Aponte has a group research project underway teaching undergraduates relationship skills. Barbara Williams has been conducting empirical research on the effects of intercessory prayer and has five students finishing dissertations on the project. Those interested in child and family research usually contact DeDe Wohlfarth who works with them to design and implement professionally relevant research. Darlene Shelton has assisted students to design and conduct research in the areas of diversity issues and several dissertations are currently in process in this area. Because we are a professional training model, research is conducted in action settings. Andy Meyer has health psychology students conducting research and program evaluations in clinics, hospitals, and community agencies. Students are encouraged to select dissertation and other research projects based on their own desires as well as the interests of the faculty.

Information for Students With Physical Disabilities: We make every effort to work with students with disabilities. All major facilities are wheelchair accessible.

Application Information:
Send to: Graduate Admissions Office. Students are admitted in the Fall, application deadline January 15. *Fee:* $30.

Louisiana State University
Department of Psychology
Audubon Hall
Baton Rouge, LA 70803
Telephone: (225) 578-8745
Fax: (225) 578-4125
E-mail: *irvlane@lsu.edu*
Web: *http://www.artsci.lsu.edu/psych*

Department Established:
1916. Chairperson: Irving M. Lane. Number of Faculty: total–full-time 25; women–full-time 7.

Programs and Degrees Offered:
Listed in the following order: Program area, degree type (T if terminal Master's), number awarded 7/00-6/01. Biological PhD, clinical PhD 12, cognitive PhD 3, developmental PhD 1, industrial/organizational PhD, school PhD 3.

APA Accreditation: Clinical PhD: full. School PhD: full.

Student Applications/Admissions:
Student Applications
Biological PhD—Applications 2001–2002, 1. Total enrolled 2001–2002 full-time, 4. Openings 2002–2003, 1. The Median number of years required for completion of a degree are na. The number of students enrolled full and part-time, who were dismissed or voluntarily withdrew from this program area were 1. *Clinical PhD*—Applications 2001–2002, 114. Total applicants accepted 2001–2002, 12. New applicants enrolled 2001–2002, 12. Total enrolled 2001–2002 full-time, 69. Openings 2002–2003, 10. The Median number of years required for completion of a degree are 6. The number of students enrolled full and part-time, who were dismissed or voluntarily withdrew from this program area were 0. *Cognitive PhD*—Applications 2001–2002, 8. Total applicants accepted 2001–2002, 1. New applicants enrolled 2001–2002, 1. Total enrolled 2001–2002 full-time, 5. Openings 2002–2003, 2. The Median number of years required for completion of a degree are 5. The number of students enrolled full and part-time, who were dismissed or voluntarily withdrew from this program area were 1. *Developmental PhD*—Applications 2001–2002, 13. Total enrolled 2001–2002 full-time, 4. Openings 2002–2003, 2. The Median number of years required for completion of a degree are 4. The number of students enrolled full and part-time, who were dismissed or voluntarily withdrew from this program area were 0. *Industrial/organizational PhD*—Applications 2001–2002, 33. Total applicants accepted 2001–2002, 3. New applicants enrolled 2001–2002, 3. Total enrolled 2001–2002 full-time, 13. Openings 2002–2003, 2. The Median number of years required for completion of a degree are na. The number of students enrolled full and part-time, who were dismissed or voluntarily withdrew from this program area were 0. *School PhD*—Applications 2001–2002, 10. Total applicants accepted 2001–2002, 5. New applicants enrolled 2001–2002, 5. Total enrolled 2001–2002 full-time, 17. Openings 2002–2003, 6. The Median num-ber of years required for completion of a degree are 6. The number of students enrolled full and part-time, who were dismissed or voluntarily withdrew from this program area were 0.

Admissions Requirements:
Scores: Entries appear in this order: required test or GPA, minimum score (if required), median score of students entering in 2001–2002. Doctoral Programs: GRE-V 500, 530; GRE-Q 500, 610; GRE-V+Q 1000, 1140; overall undergraduate GPA 3.0, 3.3 ; last 2 years GPA no minimum stated; psychology GPA no minimum stated; psychology GPA no minimum stated.
Other Criteria: (importance of criteria rated low, medium, or high): GRE/MAT scores high, research experience high, work experience medium, extracurricular activity medium, clinically related public service medium, GPA high, letters of recommendation high, interview medium, statement of goals and objectives high. Interview-clinical and school only.

Student Characteristics: The following represents characteristics of students in 2001–2002 in all graduate psychology programs in the department: Female–full-time 77, part-time 0; Male–full-time 36, part-time 0; African American/Black–full-time 3, part-time 0; Hispanic/Latino (a)–full-time 2, part-time 0; Asian/Pacific Islander–full-time 1, part-time 0; American Indian/Alaska Native–full-time 0, part-time 0; Multi-ethnic–full-time 0, part-time 0; students subject to the Americans with Disabilities Act–full-time 1, part-time 0.

Financial Information/Assistance:
Tuition for Full-Time Study: *Doctoral:* State residents: per academic year $1,708; nonstate residents: per academic year $4,358.

Financial Assistance:
First Year Students: Teaching assistantships available for first-year. Average amount paid per academic year: $9,500. Average number of hours worked per week: 20. Apply by January 15. Research assistantships available for first-year. Average amount paid per academic year: $9,500. Average number of hours worked per week: 20. Apply by January 15. Fellowships and scholarships available for first-year. Average amount paid per academic year: $15,000. Apply by January 15. Tuition remission given: full.
Advanced Students: Teaching assistantships available for advanced students. Average amount paid per academic year: $9,500. Average number of hours worked per week: 20. Research assistantships available for advanced students. Average amount paid per academic year: $9,500. Average number of hours worked per week: 20. Traineeships available for advanced students. Average amount paid per academic year: $12,000. Average number of hours worked per week: 20. Fellowships and scholarships available for advanced students. Average amount paid per academic year: $15,000. Tuition remission given: full.
Contact Information: Of all students currently enrolled full-time, 80% benefitted from one or more of the listed financial assistance programs. For information on financial assistance, contact: Sally Allen, Department Secretary.

Internships/Practica: For those doctoral students for whom a professional internship is required prior to graduation, 16 applied in 2000–2001. Of those who applied, 15 were placed in internships listed by the Association of Psychology Postdoctoral and Internship Programs (APPIC); 15 were placed in APA accredited internships.

Housing and Day Care: On-campus housing and day care facilities are available.

Employment of Department Graduates:

Master's Degree Graduates: Of those who graduated in the academic year 2000–2001, the following categories and numbers represent the post-graduate activities and employment of master's degree graduates: Enrolled in a post-doctoral residency/fellowship (n/a), employed in independent practice (n/a).

Doctoral Degree Graduates: Of those who graduated in the academic year 2000–2001, the following categories and numbers represent the post-graduate activities and employment of doctoral degree graduates: Enrolled in a psychology doctoral program (n/a), enrolled in another graduate/professional program (n/a).

Additional Information:

Orientation, Objectives, and Emphasis of Department: The Department of Psychology at Louisiana State University is committed to the view that psychology is both a science and a profession, and it regards all areas of specialization as interdependent. All graduate students, regardless of intended areas of specialization, receive broad training to develop the research skills needed to make scholarly contributions to the discipline of psychology throughout their subsequent careers. A student interested only in professional application of psychology without regard for research will not be comfortable in the graduate training program in this department. Both faculty and students in psychology recognize, however, that the model of the psychologist as a practitioner is a legitimate one. Those students whose main interest is in research are encouraged to develop familiarity with clinical, industrial, or developmental and educational settings as potential research environments. The sequence of graduate education reflects these emphases on research and on professional aspects of psychology.

Special Facilities or Resources: The department occupies a centrally located building, designed specifically to accommodate our program. Audubon Hall houses faculty offices, instructional space, desk space for graduate assistants, and research facilities for a wide array of human studies. Animal laboratories are separately housed. A training clinic is located in the Louisiana State University Student Health Services Building and has been recently renovated and enlarged. Additional research and clinical training facilities are located at the Earl K. Long Memorial Hospital, Louisiana State University Medical School Unit.

Information for Students With Physical Disabilities: Facilities are designed to accommodate students with handicaps.

Application Information:

Send to: Admissions Committee, 236 Audubon Hall, Department of Psychology, Louisiana State University, Baton Rouge, LA 70803-5501. Students are admitted in the Fall, application deadline January 15. *Fee:* There is no fee for the Department of Psychology application. There is a $25 fee for the Graduate School application.

Louisiana State University in Shreveport

Psychology Department
College of Education
One University Place
Shreveport, LA 71115
Telephone: (318) 797-5044
Fax: (318) 798-4171
E-mail: *mringer@pilot.lsus.edu*
Web: *http://www.lsus.edu*

Department Established:

1967. Director, Specialist in School Psychology Program: Merikay M. Ringer, Ph.D. Number of Faculty: total–full-time 10, part-time 13; women–full-time 7, part-time 8; minority–full-time 2.

Programs and Degrees Offered:

Listed in the following order: Program area, degree type (T if terminal Master's), number awarded 7/00-6/01. School psychology 6.

Student Applications/Admissions:

Admissions Requirements:

Scores: Entries appear in this order: required test or GPA, minimum score (if required), median score of students entering in 2001–2002. Master's Programs: GRE-V 400; GRE-Q 400; overall undergraduate GPA 2.75. These requirements are for the psychology specialist degree. Those not meeting these requirements may be admitted on a provisional basis. Doctoral Programs: last 2 years GPA no minimum stated; psychology GPA no minimum stated; psychology GPA no minimum stated.

Other Criteria: (importance of criteria rated low, medium, or high): GRE/MAT scores medium, clinically related public service low, GPA medium, letters of recommendation high, interview medium, statement of goals and objectives high.

Student Characteristics: The following represents characteristics of students in 2001–2002 in all graduate psychology programs in the department: Female–full-time 7, part-time 12; Male–full-time 1, part-time 2; African American/Black–full-time 0, part-time 2; Hispanic/Latino (a)–full-time 0, part-time 1; Asian/Pacific Islander–full-time 0, part-time 0; American Indian/Alaska Native–full-time 0, part-time 0.

Financial Information/Assistance:

Tuition for Full-Time Study: *Master's:* State residents per academic year $2,846, $162 per credit hour; nonstate residents: per academic year $7,806, $387 per credit hour.

Financial Assistance:

First Year Students: Research assistantships available for first-year. Average amount paid per academic year: $750. Average number of hours worked per week: 10. Apply by Aug. 1. Tuition remission given: partial.

Advanced Students: Teaching assistantships available for advanced students. Average amount paid per academic year: $1,500. Average number of hours worked per week: 20. Apply by Aug. 1.

Contact Information: Of all students currently enrolled full-time, 15% benefitted from one or more of the listed financial

assistance programs. For information on financial assistance, contact: Chair of Department, Dr. Jean Hollenshead or Ed Chase, Director Financial Aid.

Internships/Practica: Practica for our Specialist degree students are carried out in surrounding parishes which have cooperative agreements with the university for training purposes. There are two distinct practica experiences for our students. The first involves an observational practica required during the Introductory to School Psychology course. The second occurs during Psych 754-a formal 200-plus-hour practica that is carried out in cooperating training parishes with supervisory field school psychologists. Internships are available within the state or students may pursue internships in other states.

Housing and Day Care: No on-campus housing and day care facilities are available.

Employment of Department Graduates:

Master's Degree Graduates: Of those who graduated in the academic year 2000–2001, the following categories and numbers represent the post-graduate activities and employment of master's degree graduates: Enrolled in a psychology doctoral program (0), enrolled in another graduate/professional program (0), enrolled in a post-doctoral residency/fellowship (n/a), employed in independent practice (n/a), employed in an academic position at a university (0), employed in an academic position at a 2-year/4-year college (0), employed in a professional position in a school system (6), employed in business or industry (research/consulting) (0), employed in business or industry (management) (0), employed in a government agency (research) (0), employed in a government agency (professional services) (0), employed in a community mental health/counseling center (2), employed in a hospital/medical center (0), still seeking employment (0), other employment position (0).

Doctoral Degree Graduates: Of those who graduated in the academic year 2000–2001, the following categories and numbers represent the post-graduate activities and employment of doctoral degree graduates: Enrolled in a psychology doctoral program (n/a), enrolled in another graduate/professional program (n/a).

Additional Information:

Orientation, Objectives, and Emphasis of Department: The curriculum model upon which the program rests is based on the National Association of School Psychologists Training Standards outlined in School Psychology: A Blueprint for Training and Practice II. The model to which the program adheres is the data-based problem solver. It is important for school psychologists to establish accountability within the system by providing data that demonstrates their effectiveness. The School Psychology Training committee advocates a practitioner approach to fulfilling this goal. As a result, students are required to participate in two practica in the school system as well as a minimum 1200-hour internship.

Information for Students With Physical Disabilities: Students with disabilities must be able to provide all services of a school psychologist. Our University is Handicap Accessible. Information concerning other possible services can be obtained through Student Affairs.

Application Information:

Send to: Merikay M. Ringer, Psychology Department, Lousiana State University Shreveport, One University Place, Shreveport, LA 71115.

Students are admitted in the Fall, application deadline June 1; Spring, application deadline November 1; Summer, application deadline April 1. *Fee:* $15.

Louisiana, University of, Lafayette

Department of Psychology
P.O. Box 43131 UL-Lafayette Station
Lafayette, LA 70504-3131
Telephone: (337) 482-6597
Fax: (337) 482-6587
E-mail: *psychology@louisiana.edu*
Web: *http://www.louisiana.edu/Academic/LiberalArts/PSYC*

Department Established:

1970. Department Head: Aline M. Garrett. Number of Faculty: total–full-time 13, part-time 2; women–full-time 5; minority–full-time 2.

Programs and Degrees Offered:

Listed in the following order: Program area, degree type (T if terminal Master's), number awarded 7/00-6/01. Experimental, applied MA (T) 5.

Student Applications/Admissions:

Student Applications

Experimental, applied MA—Applications 2001–2002, 24. Total applicants accepted 2001–2002, 19. New applicants enrolled 2001–2002, 12. Total enrolled 2001–2002 full-time, 10, part-time, 17. Openings 2002–2003, 12. The Median number of years required for completion of a degree are 3. The number of students enrolled full and part-time, who were dismissed or voluntarily withdrew from this program area were 3.

Admissions Requirements:

Scores: Entries appear in this order: required test or GPA, minimum score (if required), median score of students entering in 2001–2002. Master's Programs: GRE-V+Q+Analytical 1500, 1570; last 2 years GPA 3.0, 3.0. Exceptions to the minimum scores will be considered on a case-by-case basis if there is high strength/promise through another indicator. Doctoral Programs: last 2 years GPA no minimum stated; psychology GPA no minimum stated; psychology GPA no minimum stated.

Other Criteria: (importance of criteria rated low, medium, or high): GRE/MAT scores, research experience medium, work experience medium, extracurricular activity low, clinically related public service medium, GPA, letters of recommendation high, statement of goals and objectives medium.

Student Characteristics: The following represents characteristics of students in 2001–2002 in all graduate psychology programs in the department: Female–full-time 6, part-time 12; Male–full-time 4, part-time 5; African American/Black–full-time 1, part-time 0; Hispanic/Latino (a)–full-time 0, part-time 0; Asian/Pacific Islander–full-time 0, part-time 0; American Indian/Alaska Native–full-time 0, part-time 0.

Financial Information/Assistance:

Tuition for Full-Time Study: *Master's:* State residents per academic year $2,277; nonstate residents: per academic year $8,457.

Financial Assistance:

First Year Students: Teaching assistantships available for first-year. Average amount paid per academic year: $5,500. Average number of hours worked per week: 15. Apply by April 12. Tuition remission given: full.

Advanced Students: Teaching assistantships available for advanced students. Average amount paid per academic year: $5,500. Average number of hours worked per week: 15. Apply by April 12. Tuition remission given: full.

Contact Information: Of all students currently enrolled full-time, 60% benefitted from one or more of the listed financial assistance programs. For information on financial assistance, contact: Graduate School Office.

Internships/Practica: Internships for master's students in the applied option are available at the Community Mental Health Center, local psychiatric hospitals, and at the University Counseling and Testing Center.

Housing and Day Care: No on-campus housing and day care facilities are available.

Employment of Department Graduates:

Master's Degree Graduates: Of those who graduated in the academic year 2000–2001, the following categories and numbers represent the post-graduate activities and employment of master's degree graduates: Enrolled in a psychology doctoral program (2), enrolled in a post-doctoral residency/fellowship (n/a), employed in independent practice (n/a), employed in a community mental health/counseling center (1), other employment position (2).

Doctoral Degree Graduates: Of those who graduated in the academic year 2000–2001, the following categories and numbers represent the post-graduate activities and employment of doctoral degree graduates: Enrolled in a psychology doctoral program (n/a), enrolled in another graduate/professional program (n/a).

Additional Information:

Orientation, Objectives, and Emphasis of Department: The Department of Psychology at the University of Louisiana at Lafayette strives to promote the study of psychology as a science, as a profession, and as a means of promoting human welfare. A master's program is offered with options in general experimental or applied psychology. After obtaining their degree, general experimental students pursue the doctorate at other universities. Applied program students have found employment in the locality or have returned to work in their original home settings.

Special Facilities or Resources: The Psychology Department houses a computer laboratory for cognitive and social research. Computer assisted instruction is available for several courses. Major physiological research is conducted at the nearby primate center, The New Iberia Research Center. An additional smaller physiological laboratory is housed in the Psychology Department. The University of Louisiana at Lafayette has excellent computer facilities. Many members of the department are also affiliated with the university's Institute for Cognitive Science, providing additional opportunities for research. There is also the possibility that students may be simultaneously enrolled in the Psychology MS program and the Cognitive Science PhD program.

Information for Students With Physical Disabilities: A wheelevator and an elevator are located in the psychology building to provide access. Students can make use of the Department of Services for Students with Disabilities for special needs regarding test-taking, registration, etc.

Application Information:

Send to: Graduate School Director, Martin Hall, University of Louisiana, Lafayette, 70504. Students are admitted in the Fall, application deadline 30 days; Spring, application deadline 30 days; Summer, application deadline 30 days. US students' applications are due 30 days prior to start of semester. For international students, the deadline is 90 days prior to the semester. *Fee:* $20.

Louisiana, University of, Monroe
Department of Psychology
700 University Avenue
Monroe, LA 71209
Telephone: (318) 342-1330
Fax: (318) 342-1240
E-mail: *pswilliamson@ulm.edu*

Department Established:
1965. Head: David Williamson. Number of Faculty: total–full-time 16, part-time 15; women–full-time 8, part-time 11; minority–full-time 1, part-time 2.

Programs and Degrees Offered:
Listed in the following order: Program area, degree type (T if terminal Master's), number awarded 7/00-6/01. General, specialist in school psycholog EdS 6.

Student Applications/Admissions:
Student Applications

Specialist in school psycholog EdS—Applications 2001–2002, 10. Total applicants accepted 2001–2002, 8. New applicants enrolled 2001–2002, 7. Total enrolled 2001–2002 full-time, 20. Openings 2002–2003, 10. The number of students enrolled full and part-time, who were dismissed or voluntarily withdrew from this program area were 1.

Admissions Requirements:

Scores: Entries appear in this order: required test or GPA, minimum score (if required), median score of students entering in 2001–2002. Master's Programs: GRE-V+Q 900; overall undergraduate GPA 2.75. For MS Program two of the three following are required: 900 Verbal/Quant GRE, 2.75 GPA, and 1900 when GPA 400 + GRE. For SSP Program two of the three following are required: 1000 Verbal/Quant GRE, 3.00 GPA, and 2000 on combined. Doctoral Programs: last 2 years GPA no minimum stated; psychology GPA no minimum stated; psychology GPA no minimum stated.

Other Criteria: (importance of criteria rated low, medium, or high): GRE/MAT scores high, research experience medium, work experience medium, extracurricular activity low, clinically related public service medium, GPA high, letters of recommendation high.

Student Characteristics: The following represents characteristics of students in 2001–2002 in all graduate psychology programs in

the department: Female–full-time 37, part-time 0; Male–full-time 14, part-time 0; African American/Black–full-time 9, part-time 0; Hispanic/Latino (a)–full-time 0, part-time 0; Asian/Pacific Islander–full-time 2, part-time 0; American Indian/Alaska Native–full-time 0, part-time 0.

Financial Information/Assistance:

Tuition for Full-Time Study: *Master's:* State residents per academic year $1,142, $106 per credit hour; nonstate residents: per academic year $4,120.

Financial Assistance:

First Year Students: Research assistantships available for first-year. Average amount paid per academic year: $4,000. Average number of hours worked per week: 20. Tuition remission given: full.

Advanced Students: No information provided.

Contact Information: Of all students currently enrolled full-time, 75% benefitted from one or more of the listed financial assistance programs. For information on financial assistance, contact: Dr. David Williamson, Department Head.

Internships/Practica: Practica and internships are required for the MS program. Field, practica, and internships are included as an integral part of the specialist in school psychology program.

Housing and Day Care: On-campus housing and day care facilities are available.

Employment of Department Graduates:

Master's Degree Graduates: Of those who graduated in the academic year 2000–2001, the following categories and numbers represent the post-graduate activities and employment of master's degree graduates: Enrolled in a psychology doctoral program (3), enrolled in another graduate/professional program (34), enrolled in a post-doctoral residency/fellowship (n/a), employed in independent practice (n/a), employed in a professional position in a school system (30), employed in business or industry (management) (3).

Doctoral Degree Graduates: Of those who graduated in the academic year 2000–2001, the following categories and numbers represent the post-graduate activities and employment of doctoral degree graduates: Enrolled in a psychology doctoral program (n/a), enrolled in another graduate/professional program (n/a).

Additional Information:

Orientation, Objectives, and Emphasis of Department: Two areas of concentration are available in the MS program. The general-experimental option focuses upon the basic science areas of psychology. The psychometric (preclinical) option is structured for those whose primary interest is employment in mental health or related settings. The specialist in school psychology program is designed so that a MS degree is awarded upon completion of the first phase of the program. All programs require a comprehensive examination and a thesis.

Special Facilities or Resources: The department facilities include laboratories in sensation-perception and learning and motivation, as well as a small animal colony. A psychological services center includes a test library and special rooms. The department also has several on-line terminals and a printer connected with the university's IBM/4341 computer system.

Application Information:

Send to: Department Chair, Graduate School. Students are admitted in the Fall, application deadline rolling; Winter, application deadline rolling; Spring, application deadline rolling; Summer, application deadline rolling. *Fee:* $20.

Lousiana Tech University
Department of Psychology and Behavioral Sciences
Box 10048, T.S.
Ruston, LA 71272
Telephone: (318) 257-4315
Fax: (318) 5-344
E-mail: *psychology@latech.edu*
Web: *http://www.latech.edu*

Department Established:

1972. Department Head: Tony R. Young. Number of Faculty: total–full-time 13, part-time 2; women–full-time 4, part-time 2; minority–full-time 1, part-time 1.

Programs and Degrees Offered:

Listed in the following order: Program area, degree type (T if terminal Master's), number awarded 7/00-6/01. Counseling and guidance MA (T) 69, counseling psychology PhD 3, educational psychology MA (T) 7, industrial/organizational MA (T) 59.

Student Applications/Admissions:

Student Applications

Counseling and guidance MA—Total enrolled 2001–2002 full-time, 173. Openings 2002–2003, 80. The Median number of years required for completion of a degree are 2. *Counseling psychology PhD*—Applications 2001–2002, 28. Total applicants accepted 2001–2002, 6. New applicants enrolled 2001–2002, 6. Total enrolled 2001–2002 full-time, 29. Openings 2002–2003, 6. *Educational psychology MA*—Applications 2001–2002, 13. Total applicants accepted 2001–2002, 6. New applicants enrolled 2001–2002, 6. Total enrolled 2001–2002 full-time, 6. Openings 2002–2003, 10. *Industrial/organizational MA*—Total enrolled 2001–2002 full-time, 109. Openings 2002–2003, 60.

Admissions Requirements:

Scores: Entries appear in this order: required test or GPA, minimum score (if required), median score of students entering in 2001–2002. Master's Programs: GRE-V no minimum stated; GRE-Q no minimum stated; GRE-V+Q no minimum stated; overall undergraduate GPA no minimum stated; last 2 years GPA no minimum stated; psychology GPA no minimum stated. Doctoral Programs: GRE-V no minimum stated, 560; GRE-Q no minimum stated, 612; GRE-V+Q 1000, 1172; GRE-Subject(Psych) no minimum stated; overall undergraduate GPA no minimum stated, 3.50; last 2 years GPA no minimum stated; psychology GPA no minimum stated; psychology GPA no minimum stated. Comment: Minimal composite GRE (V + Q) score for admission consideration is normally 1000.

Other Criteria: (importance of criteria rated low, medium, or high): GRE/MAT scores high, research experience medium, work experience medium, extracurricular activity low, clinically related public service medium, GPA high, letters of recommendation high, interview low, statement of goals and objectives medium. These criteria apply to the PhD program.

Student Characteristics: The following represents characteristics of students in 2001–2002 in all graduate psychology programs in the department: Female–full-time 0, part-time 0; Male–full-time 0, part-time 0; African American/Black–full-time 0, part-time 0; Hispanic/Latino (a)–full-time 0, part-time 0; Asian/Pacific Islander–full-time 0, part-time 0; American Indian/Alaska Native–full-time 0, part-time 0.

Financial Information/Assistance:
Tuition for Full-Time Study: No information provided.

Financial Assistance:
First Year Students: No information provided.
Advanced Students: No information provided.
Contact Information: Of all students currently enrolled full-time, 40% benefitted from one or more of the listed financial assistance programs. For information on financial assistance, contact: psychology@latech.edu.

Internships/Practica: PhD counseling psychology students must complete a year-long internship. Practica are available throughout the region for PhD and MA students in their respective areas. For those doctoral students for whom a professional internship is required prior to graduation, 5 applied in 2000–2001. Of those who applied, 5 were placed in internships listed by the Association of Psychology Postdoctoral and Internship Programs (APPIC); 5 were placed in APA accredited internships.

Housing and Day Care: No on-campus housing and day care facilities are available.

Employment of Department Graduates:
Master's Degree Graduates: Of those who graduated in the academic year 2000–2001, the following categories and numbers represent the post-graduate activities and employment of master's degree graduates: Enrolled in a post-doctoral residency/fellowship (n/a), employed in independent practice (n/a).
Doctoral Degree Graduates: Of those who graduated in the academic year 2000–2001, the following categories and numbers represent the post-graduate activities and employment of doctoral degree graduates: Enrolled in a psychology doctoral program (n/a), enrolled in another graduate/professional program (n/a).

Additional Information:
Orientation, Objectives, and Emphasis of Department: The Department of Psychology and Behavioral Sciences offers master's degree programs in counseling and guidance, educational psychology, and industrial/organizational psychology, in addition to the PhD in counseling psychology. The department features excellent faculty who strive to provide an eclectic and integrated approach to theory, research, and practice. The scientist-practitioner model provides the framework for most graduate programs. Successful degree candidates are provided knowledge and skills necessary for appropriate level positions in their respective fields in settings such as education, business, mental health, and government. The counseling psychology PhD explores assessment, career/vocational, and psychotherapy.

Information for Students With Physical Disabilities: The library building housing the psychology and behavioral sciences department is accessible to wheelchairs. A number of persons with physical disabilities attend the university.

Application Information:
Send to: Department of Psychology and Behavioral Sciences. Students are admitted in the Fall, application deadline September 1; Winter, application deadline November 30; Spring, application deadline March 2; Summer, application deadline May 31. PhD: full admissions in the Fall only, deadline February 15. Application deadline dates may vary slightly from year to year. *Fee:* $20.

New Orleans, University of
Department of Psychology
2001 Geology and Psychology Building
New Orleans, LA 70148
Telephone: (504) 280-6291
Fax: (504) 280-6049
E-mail: *pfrick@uno.edu*
Web: *http://www.uno.edu/~psyc/*

Department Established:
1982. Chairperson: Matthew Stanford. Number of Faculty: total–full-time 18, part-time 4; women–full-time 6, part-time 1; minority–full-time 1.

Programs and Degrees Offered:
Listed in the following order: Program area, degree type (T if terminal Master's), number awarded 7/00-6/01. Applied biopsychology PhD 1, applied developmental psych. PhD 4.

Student Applications/Admissions:
Student Applications
Applied biopsychology PhD—Applications 2001–2002, 20. Total applicants accepted 2001–2002, 6. New applicants enrolled 2001–2002, 4. Total enrolled 2001–2002 full-time, 14. Openings 2002–2003, 4. The number of students enrolled full and part-time, who were dismissed or voluntarily withdrew from this program area were 0. *Applied developmental psych. PhD*—Applications 2001–2002, 40. Total applicants accepted 2001–2002, 7. New applicants enrolled 2001–2002, 4. Total enrolled 2001–2002 full-time, 10. Openings 2002–2003, 4. The number of students enrolled full and part-time, who were dismissed or voluntarily withdrew from this program area were 0.

Admissions Requirements:
Scores: Entries appear in this order: required test or GPA, minimum score (if required), median score of students entering in 2001–2002. Doctoral Programs: GRE-V+Q 1000; overall undergraduate GPA 3.0; last 2 years GPA no minimum stated; psychology GPA no minimum stated; psychology GPA no minimum stated. Minimum criterion for admission: (GRE V+Q/400) plus undergraduate GPA equals 6.1.
Other Criteria: (importance of criteria rated low, medium, or high): GRE/MAT scores high, research experience high, work experience low, extracurricular activity low, clinically related public service medium, GPA high, letters of recommendation high, statement of goals and objectives high.

Student Characteristics: The following represents characteristics of students in 2001–2002 in all graduate psychology programs in the department: Female–full-time 17, part-time 0; Male–full-time 8, part-time 0; African American/Black–full-time 1, part-time 0; Hispanic/Latino (a)–full-time 1, part-time 0; Asian/Pacific Islander–full-time 1, part-time 0; American Indian/Alaska Native–full-time 0, part-time 0.

Financial Information/Assistance:

Tuition for Full-Time Study: *Doctoral:* State residents: $115 per credit hour; nonstate residents: $407 per credit hour.

Financial Assistance:

First Year Students: Teaching assistantships available for first-year. Average amount paid per academic year: $12,040. Average number of hours worked per week: 20. Tuition remission given: partial. Research assistantships available for first-year. Average amount paid per academic year: $12,040. Average number of hours worked per week: 20. Tuition remission given: full. Fellowships and scholarships available for first-year. Average amount paid per academic year: $14,000. Tuition remission given: full.

Advanced Students: Teaching assistantships available for advanced students. Average amount paid per academic year: $12,040. Average number of hours worked per week: 20. Tuition remission given: partial. Research assistantships available for advanced students. Average amount paid per academic year: $12,040. Average number of hours worked per week: 20. Tuition remission given: full. Fellowships and scholarships available for advanced students. Average amount paid per academic year: $14,000. Tuition remission given: full.

Contact Information: Of all students currently enrolled full-time, 100% benefitted from one or more of the listed financial assistance programs. For information on financial assistance, contact: Graduate Coordinator (504-348-6012).

Internships/Practica: Students in both applied specialties are required to complete 12 semester hours of practicum for the doctoral degree. There are a wide array of practicum experiences available and student's choice of practicum is based on his or her specific career objectives.

Housing and Day Care: On-campus housing and day care facilities are available.

Employment of Department Graduates:

Master's Degree Graduates: Of those who graduated in the academic year 2000–2001, the following categories and numbers represent the post-graduate activities and employment of master's degree graduates: Enrolled in a post-doctoral residency/fellowship (n/a), employed in independent practice (n/a).

Doctoral Degree Graduates: Of those who graduated in the academic year 2000–2001, the following categories and numbers represent the post-graduate activities and employment of doctoral degree graduates: Enrolled in a psychology doctoral program (n/a), enrolled in another graduate/professional program (n/a), enrolled in a post-doctoral residency/fellowship (1).

Additional Information:

Orientation, Objectives, and Emphasis of Department: The University of New Orleans, Department of Psychology offers a PhD program with specializations in applied biopsychology and applied developmental psychology. The program was established in 1980 in response to a growing need for persons who are thoroughly trained in the basic content areas of human development or biopsychology, and who are able to translate that knowledge into practical applications. Both specialties emphasize research and service delivery in applied contexts. Graduates will be able to conduct original research as well as provide consulting and services to agencies concerned with problems of human health and development. Applied biopsychologists, for example, might be involved in research and service concerning the neuropsychological evaluation and rehabilitation of stroke patients, or in the behavioral or electrophysiological testing of sensory disturbances caused by diseases like multiple sclerosis. Others might research the psychological aspects of drug addiction or hormone disturbances with anatomists, physiologists, or pharmacologists. The applied developmental program has chosen to focus its training in the area of developmental psychopathology. Graduates are trained to work in a variety of settings where they can advance programmatic research focused on understanding psychopathological conditions from a developmental perspective and where they can make practical applications from this research (e.g., design and implement innovative prevention programs, or develop assessments for at risk children).

Special Facilities or Resources: Special resources of the department include laboratory computers, computer terminal room, specialized surgical equipment, videotape equipment, psychophysiological recording equipment, and a psychology department clinic.

Application Information:
Send to: Graduate Coordinator, Department of Psychology, 2001 Geology & Psychology Bldg., New Orleans, LA 70148. Students are admitted in the Fall, application deadline February 15. *Fee:* $20.

Northwestern State University of Louisiana

Department of Psychology
Liberal Arts
Natchitoches, LA 71497
Telephone: (318) 357-6594
Fax: (318) 357-6802
E-mail: *moultonp@nsula.edu*

Department Established:
1957. Chairperson: Patrice Moulton. Number of Faculty: total–full-time 8, part-time 1; women–full-time 6, part-time 1.

Programs and Degrees Offered:
Listed in the following order: Program area, degree type (T if terminal Master's), number awarded 7/00-6/01. Clinical Psychology MA (T) 10.

Student Applications/Admissions:
Student Applications
Clinical Psychology MA—Applications 2001–2002, 51. Total applicants accepted 2001–2002, 17. New applicants enrolled 2001–2002, 15. Total enrolled 2001–2002 full-time, 19. Openings 2002–2003, 18. The Median number of years required for completion of a degree are 3. The number of students enrolled full and part-time, who were dismissed or voluntarily withdrew from this program area were 1.

Admissions Requirements:

Scores: Entries appear in this order: required test or GPA, minimum score (if required), median score of students entering in 2001–2002. Master's Programs: GRE-V+Q 900, 990; overall undergraduate GPA 2.5, 3.2. Doctoral Programs: last 2 years GPA no minimum stated; psychology GPA no minimum stated; psychology GPA no minimum stated.

Other Criteria: (importance of criteria rated low, medium, or high): GRE/MAT scores high, research experience medium, work experience low, extracurricular activity low, clinically related public service low, GPA high, letters of recommendation high, statement of goals and objectives medium.

Student Characteristics: The following represents characteristics of students in 2001–2002 in all graduate psychology programs in the department: Female–full-time 16, part-time 0; Male–full-time 3, part-time 0; African American/Black–full-time 0, part-time 0; Hispanic/Latino (a)–full-time 1, part-time 0; Asian/Pacific Islander–full-time 1, part-time 0; American Indian/Alaska Native–full-time 0, part-time 0.

Financial Information/Assistance:

Tuition for Full-Time Study: *Master's:* State residents per academic year $2,600; nonstate residents: per academic year $6,000.

Financial Assistance:

First Year Students: Teaching assistantships available for first-year. Average amount paid per academic year: $6,000. Average number of hours worked per week: 20. Apply by April 1.

Advanced Students: Teaching assistantships available for advanced students. Average amount paid per academic year: $6,000. Average number of hours worked per week: 20. Apply by April 1.

Contact Information: Of all students currently enrolled full-time, 79% benefitted from one or more of the listed financial assistance programs. For information on financial assistance, contact: Graduate Office.

Internships/Practica: During the second year, a practicum worth 6 credit hours is required. We require a 640-hour externship after completion of all coursework. Both paid and non-paid placements are available at VA hospitals, public and private clinics, community mental health centers, and state inpatient facilities. At each site, a licensed, PhD level clinical psychologist supervises the structured externship experience.

Housing and Day Care: No on-campus housing and day care facilities are available.

Employment of Department Graduates:

Master's Degree Graduates: Of those who graduated in the academic year 2000–2001, the following categories and numbers represent the post-graduate activities and employment of master's degree graduates: Enrolled in a post-doctoral residency/fellowship (n/a), employed in independent practice (n/a).

Doctoral Degree Graduates: Of those who graduated in the academic year 2000–2001, the following categories and numbers represent the post-graduate activities and employment of doctoral degree graduates: Enrolled in a psychology doctoral program (n/a), enrolled in another graduate/professional program (n/a).

Additional Information:

Orientation, Objectives, and Emphasis of Department: The department is oriented toward providing students with a solid foundation in the theory, research, and clinical practice of psychology. By equally emphasizing these elements, the program prepares the student for both immediate employment in the field and/or additional training at the doctoral level. After graduation, 65% of our students gain immediate employment while 35% are accepted into doctoral level education. The basic goals of the program are to provide general knowledge of the discipline of psychology and to insure depth of understanding in assessing and treating clinical populations. Because the department participates in the Louisiana Consortium for Graduate Training in Professional Psychology, the student can compete for admission to doctoral study directly following master's degree training. Successful completion of qualifying exams results in admission to the consortium program administered by Louisiana State University.

Special Facilities or Resources: Special facilities include clinical observation and testing rooms, videotaping capability, and a new departmental computer facility.

Application Information:

Send to: Graduate School, Northwestern State University Louisiana, Natchitoches, LA 71450. Students are admitted in the Fall, application deadline April 1. *Fee:* $20.

Southeastern Louisiana University
Department of Psychology
Arts and Sciences
SLU 10831
Hammond, LA 70402
Telephone: (985) 549-2154
Fax: (985) 549-3892
E-mail: *aburstein@selu.edu*
Web: *http://www.selu.edu/Academic/Dept/Psyc*

Department Established:

Chairperson: Alvin G. Burstein. Number of Faculty: total–full-time 12, part-time 3; women–full-time 4, part-time 1; minority–full-time 2.

Programs and Degrees Offered:

Listed in the following order: Program area, degree type (T if terminal Master's), number awarded 7/00-6/01. General psychology MA (T) 9.

Student Applications/Admissions:

Student Applications

General psychology MA—Total applicants accepted 2001–2002, 10. New applicants enrolled 2001–2002, 8. Total enrolled 2001–2002 full-time, 23, part-time, 7. Openings 2002–2003, 12.

Admissions Requirements:

Scores: Entries appear in this order: required test or GPA, minimum score (if required), median score of students entering in 2001–2002. Master's Programs: GRE-V no minimum stated;

GRE-Q no minimum stated; GRE-V+Q 950; overall undergraduate GPA 3.0; psychology GPA 3.0. Minimum GPA of 2.5 and Minimum GRE (V+Q) of 850 required for conditional admittance. Doctoral Programs: last 2 years GPA no minimum stated; psychology GPA no minimum stated; psychology GPA no minimum stated.

Other Criteria: (importance of criteria rated low, medium, or high): GRE/MAT scores high, research experience high, work experience low, extracurricular activity low, clinically related public service low, letters of recommendation high, statement of goals and objectives medium.

Student Characteristics: The following represents characteristics of students in 2001–2002 in all graduate psychology programs in the department: Female–full-time 18, part-time 1; Male–full-time 11, part-time 0; African American/Black–full-time 5, part-time 0; Hispanic/Latino (a)–full-time 1, part-time 0; Asian/Pacific Islander–full-time 0, part-time 0; American Indian/Alaska Native–full-time 0, part-time 0.

Financial Information/Assistance:

Tuition for Full-Time Study: *Master's:* State residents per academic year $2,318; nonstate residents: per academic year $6,314.

Financial Assistance:

First Year Students: Research assistantships available for first-year. Average amount paid per academic year: $4,400. Average number of hours worked per week: 20. Tuition remission given: full.

Advanced Students: Research assistantships available for advanced students. Average amount paid per academic year: $4,400. Average number of hours worked per week: 20. Tuition remission given: full.

Contact Information: Of all students currently enrolled full-time, 50% benefitted from one or more of the listed financial assistance programs. For information on financial assistance, contact: Southeastern Louisiana University, Office of Admissions and Financial Aid, SLU, 10768 W. Tornado Drive, North Campus Building A, Hammond, LA 70402; Phone: 1-800-222-7358 or (985) 549-2245; FAX: (985) 549-5077.

Internships/Practica: Practica are available in counseling, testing, and industrial psychology.

Housing and Day Care: On-campus housing and day care facilities are available.

Employment of Department Graduates:

Master's Degree Graduates: Of those who graduated in the academic year 2000–2001, the following categories and numbers represent the post-graduate activities and employment of master's degree graduates: Enrolled in a psychology doctoral program (8), enrolled in another graduate/professional program (0), enrolled in a post-doctoral residency/fellowship (n/a), employed in independent practice (n/a), employed in an academic position at a university (0), employed in an academic position at a 2-year/4-year college (0), employed in other positions at a higher education institution (0), employed in a professional position in a school system (0), employed in business or industry (research/consulting) (1), employed in business or industry (management) (0), employed in a government agency (research) (0), employed in a government agency (professional services) (0), employed in a community mental health/counseling center (0), employed in a hospital/medical center (0), still seeking employment (0), other employment position (0).

Doctoral Degree Graduates: Of those who graduated in the academic year 2000–2001, the following categories and numbers represent the post-graduate activities and employment of doctoral degree graduates: Enrolled in a psychology doctoral program (n/a), enrolled in another graduate/professional program (n/a).

Additional Information:

Orientation, Objectives, and Emphasis of Department: The primary purpose of the M.A. in general psychology is to prepare the student for doctoral study. This goal is achieved by providing extensive research experience and advanced knowledge in several basic areas within psychology. The department participates in the Louisiana Consortium of Graduate Training in Psychology. After successfully completing the M.A. at Southeastern and passing several qualifying examinations within a 2-year period, the student is permitted to enroll at Louisiana State University to pursue the doctoral degree.

Special Facilities or Resources: The department has three 5-room laboratory suites for conducting research with humans and one 5-room suite for research with small animals. There are about 40 microcomputers and 7 printers in the department, about half of which are in a microcomputer laboratory. Statistical packages, such as SPSS, are available on the microcomputers and (via departmental terminal) on the university's mainframe computers.

Application Information:

Send to: Official transcripts, GRE scores, Application for Admission form, immunization form, and application fee should be sent to the following address: Enrollment Services, Graduate Admissions, SLU, 10752 Hammond, Louisiana 70402-0752 Your letter of application and the letters from your three references should be sent directly to the Graduate Coordinator. In addition, send copies of everything sent to Enrollment Services (unofficial copies are acceptable). Send these to the following address: James B. Worthen, Ph.D., SLU, Box 10831, Hammond, LA 70402. Students are admitted in the Fall, application deadline April 1; Spring, application deadline December 1. *Fee:* $20.

Tulane University
Department of Psychology
2007 Stern Hall
New Orleans, LA 70118
Telephone: (504) 865-5331
Fax: (504) 862-8744
E-mail: *lockman@tulane.edu*
Web: *http://www.tulane.edu/~psych/psychome.html*

Department Established:

1911. Chairperson: Jeffrey Lockman. Number of Faculty: total–full-time 16, part-time 3; women–full-time 4, part-time 1; minority–full-time 2.

Programs and Degrees Offered:

Listed in the following order: Program area, degree type (T if terminal Master's), number awarded 7/00-6/01. Animal behavior

PhD, developmental PhD, industrial/organizational PhD 6, psychobiology PhD 2, quantitative PhD 1, school PhD 3, social PhD 1.

APA Accreditation: School PhD: full.

Student Applications/Admissions:

Student Applications

Animal behavior PhD—Applications 2001–2002, 3. Total enrolled 2001–2002 full-time, 1. *Developmental PhD*—Applications 2001–2002, 7. Total enrolled 2001–2002 full-time, 1. Openings 2002–2003, 1. *Industrial/organizational PhD*—Applications 2001–2002, 40. Total applicants accepted 2001–2002, 7. New applicants enrolled 2001–2002, 4. Total enrolled 2001–2002 full-time, 12. Openings 2002–2003, 4. The Median number of years required for completion of a degree are 3. *Psychobiology PhD*—Applications 2001–2002, 12. Total applicants accepted 2001–2002, 4. New applicants enrolled 2001–2002, 2. Total enrolled 2001–2002 full-time, 4, part-time, 1. Openings 2002–2003, 2. The Median number of years required for completion of a degree are 2. *Quantitative PhD*—Applications 2001–2002, 2. Total enrolled 2001–2002 full-time, 1. The Median number of years required for completion of a degree are 4. *School PhD*—Applications 2001–2002, 28. Total applicants accepted 2001–2002, 9. New applicants enrolled 2001–2002, 5. Total enrolled 2001–2002 full-time, 20. Openings 2002–2003, 4. The Median number of years required for completion of a degree are 3. The number of students enrolled full and part-time, who were dismissed or voluntarily withdrew from this program area were 0. *Social PhD*—Applications 2001–2002, 13. Total applicants accepted 2001–2002, 2. New applicants enrolled 2001–2002, 1. Total enrolled 2001–2002 full-time, 4. Openings 2002–2003, 2. The Median number of years required for completion of a degree are 3. The number of students enrolled full and part-time, who were dismissed or voluntarily withdrew from this program area were 1.

Admissions Requirements:

Scores: Entries appear in this order: required test or GPA, minimum score (if required), median score of students entering in 2001–2002. Doctoral Programs: GRE-V no minimum stated, 600; GRE-Q no minimum stated, 600; GRE-V+Q no minimum stated, 1220; overall undergraduate GPA no minimum stated, 3.58; last 2 years GPA no minimum stated; psychology GPA no minimum stated; psychology GPA no minimum stated. Subject test is required for I/O and recommended for other programs.

Other Criteria: (importance of criteria rated low, medium, or high): GRE/MAT scores high, research experience high, work experience medium, extracurricular activity low, clinically related public service medium, GPA high, letters of recommendation high, interview medium, statement of goals and objectives medium. Clinical experience and interview important for school psychology. Relevant work experience can be looked upon favorably in other programs (e.g., statistical consulting; market research).

Student Characteristics: The following represents characteristics of students in 2001–2002 in all graduate psychology programs in the department: Female–full-time 28, part-time 1; Male–full-time 10, part-time 0; African American/Black–full-time 4, part-time 0; Hispanic/Latino (a)–full-time 1, part-time 0; Asian/Pacific Is-

lander–full-time 1, part-time 0; American Indian/Alaska Native–full-time 0, part-time 0; students subject to the Americans with Disabilities Act–full-time 1.

Financial Information/Assistance:

Tuition for Full-Time Study: *Doctoral:* State residents: $1,400 per credit hour.

Financial Assistance:

First Year Students: Teaching assistantships available for first-year. Average amount paid per academic year: $11,796. Average number of hours worked per week: 15. Apply by February 1. Tuition remission given: full. Research assistantships available for first-year. Average amount paid per academic year: $11,796. Average number of hours worked per week: 15. Apply by February 1. Tuition remission given: full. Fellowships and scholarships available for first-year. Average amount paid per academic year: $15,000. Average number of hours worked per week: 15. Apply by February 1. Tuition remission given: full.

Advanced Students: Teaching assistantships available for advanced students. Average amount paid per academic year: $11,796. Average number of hours worked per week: 15. Tuition remission given: full. Research assistantships available for advanced students. Average amount paid per academic year: $16,000. Average number of hours worked per week: 15. Tuition remission given: full. Fellowships and scholarships available for advanced students. Average amount paid per academic year: $15,000. Average number of hours worked per week: 15. Tuition remission given: full.

Contact Information: Of all students currently enrolled full-time, 95% benefitted from one or more of the listed financial assistance programs. For information on financial assistance, contact: Graduate School, Tulane University.

Internships/Practica: Practice in Psychoeducational Assessment, School Consultation, Family-School Intervention, Cognitive-Behavioral Assessment/Intervention, Industrial/Organizational Psychology. For those doctoral students for whom a professional internship is required prior to graduation, 4 applied in 2000–2001. Of those who applied, 3 were placed in APA accredited internships.

Housing and Day Care: No on-campus housing and day care facilities are available.

Employment of Department Graduates:

Master's Degree Graduates: Of those who graduated in the academic year 2000–2001, the following categories and numbers represent the post-graduate activities and employment of master's degree graduates: Enrolled in a post-doctoral residency/fellowship (n/a), employed in independent practice (n/a), employed in business or industry (research/consulting) (1).

Doctoral Degree Graduates: Of those who graduated in the academic year 2000–2001, the following categories and numbers represent the post-graduate activities and employment of doctoral degree graduates: Enrolled in a psychology doctoral program (n/a), enrolled in another graduate/professional program (n/a), enrolled in a post-doctoral residency/fellowship (1), employed in an academic position at a university (1), employed in an academic position at a 2-year/4-year college (1), employed in a professional position in a school system (4), employed in business or industry (research/consulting) (1).

Additional Information:

Orientation, Objectives, and Emphasis of Department: Tulane's department of psychology offers the PhD in the research areas listed above, as well as in applied areas of school and industrial/organizational psychology. The department does not offer programs in clinical or counseling psychology. All students are expected to articulate an individualized plan of study by the end of the first year of training, a plan developed in consultation with an advisor and a committee of faculty members. This plan will guide students' coursework and form the basis for the preliminary examinations for the PhD. Students are required to complete empirical studies for the master's thesis and the dissertation, and are expected to carry out additional research while in training. The program in school psychology, which emphasizes normal developmental processes, will take a minimum of four years to complete, including a year's internship. The industrial/organizational program provides the student with a strong theoretical background in industrial/organizational psychology, with an emphasis on personnel psychology. Applied skills in industrial/organizational are developed through a series of practicum experiences.

Applicants for admission should be adequately prepared in basic principles and theories of psychology and in the commonly used quantitative and experimental techniques.

Special Facilities or Resources: The department has research laboratories and computer resources to facilitate research efforts requiring special equipment or space, including physiological, social, sensory, comparative, cognitive, and developmental psychology and human and animal learning. The Newcomb Children's Center, the Hebert facilities at Riverside for natural observation of animals, the laboratories of the Delta Primate Center, and the Audubon Zoological Gardens are available as research sites. There are also opportunities for research in the New Orleans area in organizations and industries, in public and private schools, and in hospitals and other settings serving children.

Application Information:

Send to: Dean of the Graduate School, Tulane University, New Orleans 70118. Students are admitted in the Fall, application deadline February 1. *Fee:* $45.

MAINE

Maine, University of
Department of Psychology
301 Little Hall
Orono, ME 04469
Telephone: (207) 581-2030
E-mail: *joel.gold@umit.maineedu*

Department Established:
1926. Chairperson: Joel A. Gold. Number of Faculty: total–full-time 18; women–full-time 5, part-time 1.

Programs and Degrees Offered:
Listed in the following order: Program area, degree type (T if terminal Master's), number awarded 7/00-6/01. Clinical PhD 1, development MA, developmental-clinical PhD, general MA 1, social-personality MA.

APA Accreditation: Clinical PhD: full.

Student Applications/Admissions:
Student Applications
Clinical PhD—Applications 2001–2002, 57. Total applicants accepted 2001–2002, 3. New applicants enrolled 2001–2002, 3. Total enrolled 2001–2002 full-time, 16. Openings 2002–2003, 4. The Median number of years required for completion of a degree are 5. The number of students enrolled full and part-time, who were dismissed or voluntarily withdrew from this program area were 1. *Development MA*—Applications 2001–2002, 5. Total applicants accepted 2001–2002, 1. Total enrolled 2001–2002 full-time, 2. Openings 2002–2003, 2. The number of students enrolled full and part-time, who were dismissed or voluntarily withdrew from this program area were 0. *Developmental-clinical PhD*—Applications 2001–2002, 19. Total applicants accepted 2001–2002, 3. New applicants enrolled 2001–2002, 2. Total enrolled 2001–2002 full-time, 15. Openings 2002–2003, 4. The number of students enrolled full and part-time, who were dismissed or voluntarily withdrew from this program area were 0. *General MA*—Applications 2001–2002, 3. Total applicants accepted 2001–2002, 1. New applicants enrolled 2001–2002, 1. Total enrolled 2001–2002 full-time, 3. Openings 2002–2003, 2. The Median number of years required for completion of a degree are 6. The number of students enrolled full and part-time, who were dismissed or voluntarily withdrew from this program area were 0. *Social-personality MA*—Applications 2001–2002, 12. Total enrolled 2001–2002 full-time, 2. Openings 2002–2003, 1. The number of students enrolled full and part-time, who were dismissed or voluntarily withdrew from this program area were 0.

Admissions Requirements:
Scores: Entries appear in this order: required test or GPA, minimum score (if required), median score of students entering in 2001–2002. Master's Programs: GRE-V no minimum stated, 485; GRE-Q no minimum stated, 540; GRE-Analytical no minimum stated, 565; GRE-Subject(Psych) no minimum stated, 620; overall undergraduate GPA no minimum stated,

3.40. Doctoral Programs: GRE-V no minimum stated, 610; GRE-Q no minimum stated, 615; GRE-Analytical no minimum stated, 700; GRE-Subject(Psych) no minimum stated, 620; overall undergraduate GPA no minimum stated, 3.59; last 2 years GPA no minimum stated; psychology GPA no minimum stated; psychology GPA no minimum stated.

Other Criteria: (importance of criteria rated low, medium, or high): GRE/MAT scores high, research experience high, work experience low, extracurricular activity low, clinically related public service medium, GPA high, letters of recommendation high, interview high, statement of goals and objectives high.

Student Characteristics: The following represents characteristics of students in 2001–2002 in all graduate psychology programs in the department: Female–full-time 26, part-time 0; Male–full-time 10, part-time 0; African American/Black–full-time 0, part-time 0; Hispanic/Latino (a)–full-time 0, part-time 0; Asian/Pacific Islander–full-time 0, part-time 0; American Indian/Alaska Native–full-time 3, part-time 0; students subject to the Americans with Disabilities Act–full-time 3.

Financial Information/Assistance:
Tuition for Full-Time Study: *Master's:* State residents $210 per credit hour; nonstate residents: $599 per credit hour. *Doctoral:* State residents: $210 per credit hour; nonstate residents: $599 per credit hour.

Financial Assistance:
First Year Students: Teaching assistantships available for first-year. Average number of hours worked per week: 20. Apply by No deadline. Tuition remission given: full.

Advanced Students: Teaching assistantships available for advanced students. Average number of hours worked per week: 20. Apply by No deadline. Tuition remission given: full. Research assistantships available for advanced students. Average number of hours worked per week: 20. Apply by March 1. Tuition remission given: full. Traineeships available for advanced students. Average number of hours worked per week: 20. Apply by No deadline. Tuition remission given: full. Fellowships and scholarships available for advanced students. Average number of hours worked per week: 0. Apply by March 1. Tuition remission given: full.

Contact Information: Of all students currently enrolled full-time, 92% benefitted from one or more of the listed financial assistance programs. For information on financial assistance, contact: Department Chair.

Internships/Practica: Several settings are used for practicum training: The Psychological Services Center housed within the department, Penobscot Job Corps, Kennebec Valley Mental Health Center, Behavioral and Developmental Pediatrics program at Eastern Maine Medical Center, Bangor Mental Health Institute, Penqis CAPS Head Start, School Administrative District #4, Kids Peace. For those doctoral students for whom a professional internship is required prior to graduation, 5 applied in 2000–2001. Of those who applied, 5 were placed in internships listed by the Association of Psychology Postdoctoral and Internship Programs (APPIC); 5 were placed in APA accredited internships.

Housing and Day Care: No on-campus housing and day care facilities are available.

Employment of Department Graduates:

Master's Degree Graduates: Of those who graduated in the academic year 2000–2001, the following categories and numbers represent the post-graduate activities and employment of master's degree graduates: Enrolled in a post-doctoral residency/fellowship (n/a), employed in independent practice (n/a).

Doctoral Degree Graduates: Of those who graduated in the academic year 2000–2001, the following categories and numbers represent the post-graduate activities and employment of doctoral degree graduates: Enrolled in a psychology doctoral program (n/a), enrolled in another graduate/professional program (n/a), enrolled in a post-doctoral residency/fellowship (2).

Additional Information:

Orientation, Objectives, and Emphasis of Department: The department believes that the best graduate education involves close working relationships between the faculty and the student. Thus, a high faculty-to-student ratio and small class sizes characterize the department. In addition, every incoming student is expected to work with a faculty member as a means of gaining valuable teaching, research, and professional experience. There are also opportunities for individualized study and experience in directed readings, research, and teaching. A faculty committee, selected to represent the student's interests, will assist the student in planning an appropriate graduate program.

Special Facilities or Resources: An equipped physiological laboratory, perception and EEG laboratories, a community psychological services center, and a child study center are among the department's resources and facilities.

Information for Students With Physical Disabilities: Both Little Hall and Stevens Hall are handicapped accessible.

Application Information:
Send to: Graduate School, Winslow Hall, University of Maine, Orono, ME 04469. Students are admitted in the Spring, application deadline December 31. No deadlines for nonclinical programs. *Fee:* $50. $40 for on-line application.

Baltimore, University of
Division of Applied Psychology and Quantitative Methods
Yale Gordon College of Liberal Arts
1420 North Charles Street
Baltimore, MD 21201-5779
Telephone: (410) 837-5310
Fax: (410) 837-4059
E-mail: pmastrangelo@ubmail.ubalt.edu
Web: http://www.ubalt.edu/dapqm

Department Established:
1970. Graduate Program Director: Paul M. Mastrangelo, Ph.D. Number of Faculty: total–full-time 7, part-time 2; women–full-time 3; minority–full-time 1, part-time 1.

Programs and Degrees Offered:
Listed in the following order: Program area, degree type (T if terminal Master's), number awarded 7/00-6/01. Appl. Assessment & Consulting PsyD n/a, Counseling MA (T) 25, Industrial/Organizational MA (T) 32, Psychological Applications MA (T) n/a.

Student Applications/Admissions:
Student Applications
Appl. Assessment & Consulting PsyD—Applications 2001–2002, n/a. Total applicants accepted 2001–2002, n/a. New applicants enrolled 2001–2002, n/a. Openings 2002–2003, 6. *Counseling MA*—Applications 2001–2002, 30. Total applicants accepted 2001–2002, 18. New applicants enrolled 2001–2002, 10. Total enrolled 2001–2002 full-time, 9, part-time, 18. Openings 2002–2003, 20. The Median number of years required for completion of a degree are 4. *Industrial/Organizational MA*—Applications 2001–2002, 70. Total applicants accepted 2001–2002, 47. New applicants enrolled 2001–2002, 24. Total enrolled 2001–2002 full-time, 35, part-time, 17. Openings 2002–2003, 30. The Median number of years required for completion of a degree are 3. *Psychological Applications MA*—Applications 2001–2002, 3. Total applicants accepted 2001–2002, 3. New applicants enrolled 2001–2002, 3. Total enrolled 2001–2002 full-time, 3, part-time, 5. Openings 2002–2003, 10.

Admissions Requirements:
Scores: Entries appear in this order: required test or GPA, minimum score (if required), median score of students entering in 2001–2002. Master's Programs: GRE-V no minimum stated, 460; GRE-Q no minimum stated, 550; GRE-Analytical no minimum stated; overall undergraduate GPA 3.0, 3.43. Doctoral Programs: GRE-V no minimum stated; GRE-Q no minimum stated; GRE-Analytical no minimum stated; GRE-Subject(Psych) no minimum stated; overall undergraduate GPA no minimum stated; last 2 years GPA no minimum stated; psychology GPA no minimum stated; psychology GPA no minimum stated.
Other Criteria: (importance of criteria rated low, medium, or high): GRE/MAT scores medium, research experience me-

dium, work experience medium, clinically related public service low, GPA high, letters of recommendation low, statement of goals and objectives low, grades: Stats, Res. Meth. high.

Student Characteristics: The following represents characteristics of students in 2001–2002 in all graduate psychology programs in the department: Female–full-time 9, part-time 9; Male–full-time 4, part-time 2; African American/Black–full-time 2, part-time 4; Hispanic/Latino (a)–full-time 0, part-time 1; Asian/Pacific Islander–full-time 1, part-time 0; American Indian/Alaska Native–full-time 0, part-time 0.

Financial Information/Assistance:
Tuition for Full-Time Study: *Master's:* State residents $324 per credit hour; nonstate residents: $468 per credit hour. *Doctoral:* State residents: $324 per credit hour; nonstate residents: $468 per credit hour.

Financial Assistance:
First Year Students: Research assistantships available for first-year. Average amount paid per academic year: $1,200. Average number of hours worked per week: 20. Apply by March 1. Tuition remission given: full.
Advanced Students: Research assistantships available for advanced students. Average amount paid per academic year: $1,200. Average number of hours worked per week: 20. Tuition remission given: full.
Contact Information: Of all students currently enrolled full-time, 6% benefitted from one or more of the listed financial assistance programs. For information on financial assistance, contact: 1-877-APPLY-UB or admissions@ubmail.ubalt.edu.

Internships/Practica: The Baltimore/Washington Metropolitan area provides a wide range of settings for paid practicum and internships. The coordinator and student work together to arrange a suitable site.

Housing and Day Care: No on-campus housing and day care facilities are available.

Employment of Department Graduates:
Master's Degree Graduates: Of those who graduated in the academic year 2000–2001, the following categories and numbers represent the post-graduate activities and employment of master's degree graduates: Enrolled in a post-doctoral residency/fellowship (n/a), employed in independent practice (n/a).
Doctoral Degree Graduates: Of those who graduated in the academic year 2000–2001, the following categories and numbers represent the post-graduate activities and employment of doctoral degree graduates: Enrolled in a psychology doctoral program (n/a), enrolled in another graduate/professional program (n/a).

Additional Information:
Orientation, Objectives, and Emphasis of Department: The Division of Applied Psychology and Quantitative Methods is an empirically oriented faculty of applied psychologists and researchers. For more information contact www.ubalt.edu/dapqm on the Web.

Special Facilities or Resources: We are developing an Organizational Assessment and Development Laboratory to house current and future grants/contracts. Four different university labs and over 90% of our classrooms, which provide Internet access, MS Office, and SPSS for students and faculty members.

Information for Students With Physical Disabilities: An on-campus Director of Disability Support Services is available to coordinate disability services for students who provide documentation that they require these services.

Application Information:

Send to: Office of Graduate Admissions, University of Baltimore, 1420 N. Charles Street, Baltimore, MD 21201-5779. Students are admitted in the Fall, application deadline Mar 1 (PsyD)/July 1 (M.S.); Spring, application deadline December 1 (M.S. only). *Fee:* $30.

Frostburg State University
MS in Counseling Psychology Program
Department of Psychology
Frostburg, MD 21532
Telephone: (301) 687-4446
Fax: (301) 687-7418
E-mail: *abristow@frostburg.edu*
Web: *http://www.frostburg.edu*

Department Established:
1977. Ann R. Bristow, Graduate Program Coordinator: Cindy Herzog. Number of Faculty: total–full-time 12; women–full-time 7; minority–full-time 1.

Programs and Degrees Offered:
Listed in the following order: Program area, degree type (T if terminal Master's), number awarded 7/00-6/01. Counseling MA (T) 11.

Student Applications/Admissions:
Student Applications
Counseling MA—Applications 2001–2002, 35. Total applicants accepted 2001–2002, 17. New applicants enrolled 2001–2002, 11. Total enrolled 2001–2002 full-time, 26, part-time, 9. Openings 2002–2003, 17. The Median number of years required for completion of a degree are 3. The number of students enrolled full and part-time, who were dismissed or voluntarily withdrew from this program area were 5.

Admissions Requirements:
Scores: Entries appear in this order: required test or GPA, minimum score (if required), median score of students entering in 2001–2002. Master's Programs: overall undergraduate GPA 3.0. Minimum score on GRE (V + Q = 1000) or MAT (50) required only if the GPA is less than 3.0. Otherwise, scores do not need to be submitted. Doctoral Programs: last 2 years GPA no minimum stated; psychology GPA no minimum stated; psychology GPA no minimum stated.
Other Criteria: (importance of criteria rated low, medium, or high): GRE/MAT scores low, research experience low, work experience high, extracurricular activity low, clinically related

public service medium, GPA high, letters of recommendation high, interview high, statement of goals and objectives high, undergrad. internship medium.

Student Characteristics: The following represents characteristics of students in 2001–2002 in all graduate psychology programs in the department: Female–full-time 14, part-time 6; Male–full-time 3, part-time 3; African American/Black–full-time 0, part-time 0; Hispanic/Latino (a)–full-time 1, part-time 0; Asian/Pacific Islander–full-time 0, part-time 0; American Indian/Alaska Native–full-time 0, part-time 0.

Financial Information/Assistance:
Tuition for Full-Time Study: *Master's:* State residents $187 per credit hour; nonstate residents: $217 per credit hour.

Financial Assistance:
First Year Students: Teaching assistantships available for first-year. Average amount paid per academic year: $5,000. Average number of hours worked per week: 20. Apply by Feb. 1. Tuition remission given: full. Research assistantships available for first-year. Average amount paid per academic year: $5,000. Average number of hours worked per week: 20. Apply by Feb. 1. Tuition remission given: full.

Advanced Students: Average amount paid per academic year: $5,000. Average number of hours worked per week: 20. Apply by Feb. 1. Tuition remission given: full. Average amount paid per academic year: $5,000. Average number of hours worked per week: 20. Apply by Feb. 1. Tuition remission given: full.

Contact Information: Of all students currently enrolled full-time, 35% benefitted from one or more of the listed financial assistance programs. For information on financial assistance, contact: Ms. Patty Spiker, Director, Office of Graduate Services, pspiker@frostburg.edu.

Internships/Practica: An extensive, two semester internship experience is required which facilitates students' receptivity to supervisory feedback, enhances self-awareness, and provides a setting in which the transition from student to professional is accomplished. In addition to on-site supervision, students participate in individual and group supervision with FSU faculty. Past graduate internship sites for the M.S. Counseling Psychology program have included: outpatient community mental health (the most frequent internship setting); college counseling; inpatient psychiatric; inpatient and outpatient addictions; family services; K-12 psychological assessment and alternative classroom and after school care programs; community health advocacy and counseling; criminal justice system; nursing homes; hospital-based crisis services; hospice; domestic violence programs. Students construct their internship experiences in order to meet training goals they formulate. Students electing to complete graduate certificate programs in Addictions Counseling Psychology and Child and Family Counseling Psychology must complete at least one of their two semesters of internship providing services in settings consistent with the certificate program's focus. Internship experiences, in addition to at least four academic semesters of study, prepare graduates for positions as mental health counselors, marriage and family counselors, crisis counselors, drug and alcohol counselors, community health specialists, and in supervisory positions in a variety of settings.

Housing and Day Care: On-campus housing and day care facilities are available.

Employment of Department Graduates:

Master's Degree Graduates: Of those who graduated in the academic year 2000–2001, the following categories and numbers represent the post-graduate activities and employment of master's degree graduates: Enrolled in a psychology doctoral program (1), enrolled in another graduate/professional program (0), enrolled in a post-doctoral residency/fellowship (n/a), employed in independent practice (n/a), employed in an academic position at a university (0), employed in an academic position at a 2-year/4-year college (0), employed in other positions at a higher education institution (1), employed in a professional position in a school system (0), employed in business or industry (research/consulting) (0), employed in business or industry (management) (0), employed in a government agency (research) (0), employed in a government agency (professional services) (0), employed in a community mental health/counseling center (8), employed in a hospital/medical center (1), still seeking employment (0).

Doctoral Degree Graduates: Of those who graduated in the academic year 2000–2001, the following categories and numbers represent the post-graduate activities and employment of doctoral degree graduates: Enrolled in a psychology doctoral program (n/a), enrolled in another graduate/professional program (n/a).

Additional Information:

Orientation, Objectives, and Emphasis of Department: Providing training in professional psychology at the Master's level, FSU's program is designed for those pursuing further study in science-based counseling psychology. Our theoretical perspective is integrative, including cognitive-behavioral, family systems, developmental, feminist, multicultural, humanistic, and brief therapies. We emphasize training in empirically-supported treatments for children, adolescents, families, and adults. Students develop counseling skills through learning about self, client, counselor-client relationships, and the importance of cultural contexts. Considerable attention is given not only to development of professional skills but also to personal development and multicultural awareness. These emphases reflect our belief that an effective counselor is one who is self-aware and receptive to consultation. For continuing study at the doctoral level, experience and knowledge gained in this program provide a firm foundation. Optional research opportunities prepare students for advanced graduate study in psychology. The Center for Children and Families offers unique research and service experiences. Two certificate programs provide specialized training in Addictions Counseling Psychology and Child and Family Counseling Psychology. These can be completed within the three-year program of study, as well as courses required for licensure. All National Counselor Exam course areas are offered, and FSU offers this exam. The Master's in Psychology Accreditation Council accredits this program.

Special Facilities or Resources: Resources include specially designed counseling practice rooms for individual and group counseling. Two-way mirrors with adjacent observation rooms are available for supervision. Audiotaping and videotaping resources are available for faculty and student use. There is a separate library and reading room available, as well as a number of audio, video, and film media demonstrating various counseling techniques or explaining theory. The program's library includes a variety of journals and books for reference, including microfiche of various articles. The faculty have made several of their personal library book holdings available on loan to the graduate students in our program library. In addition, students' audiotapes, videotapes, and case conceptualization write-ups; all previous internship papers; and several thousand journal abstracts are available for restricted use by students.

Information for Students With Physical Disabilities: Frostburg State University is an Affirmative Action/Equal Opportunity Institution. Admission shall be determined without regard to race, color, religion, sex, national origin, age, or handicap. FSU is committed to making all of its programs, services, and activities accessible to persons with disabilities. You may request accommodations through the ADA Compliance Office, FSU Library Room 228, 301-687-4102, TDD 301-687-7955.

Application Information:
Send to: Ms. Patty Spiker, Director, Office of Graduate Services, Frostburg State University, Frostburg, MD 21532. Students are admitted in the Fall, application deadline February 1. March 15 for Graduate Assistantship applications. *Fee:* $30.

Johns Hopkins University
Department of Psychological and Brain Sciences
3400 North Charles Street
Baltimore, MD 21218
Telephone: (410) 516-6175
Fax: (410) 516-4478
E-mail: *krach@jhu.edu*
Web: *http://www.psy.jhu.edu*

Department Established:
1881. Chairperson: Michela Gallagher. Number of Faculty: total–full-time 9, part-time 15; women–full-time 3, part-time 8.

Programs and Degrees Offered:
Listed in the following order: Program area, degree type (T if terminal Master's), number awarded 7/00-6/01. Biopsychology PhD 2, cognitive PhD 1, cognitive neuroscience PhD, developmental PhD, quantitative PhD.

Student Applications/Admissions:
Student Applications
Biopsychology PhD—Total enrolled 2001–2002 full-time, 2. Openings 2002–2003, 4. *Cognitive PhD*—Total enrolled 2001–2002 full-time, 3. Openings 2002–2003, 2. *Cognitive neuroscience PhD*—Total applicants accepted 2001–2002, 1. New applicants enrolled 2001–2002, 1. Total enrolled 2001–2002 full-time, 6. Openings 2002–2003, 2. *Developmental PhD*—New applicants enrolled 2001–2002, 1. Total enrolled 2001–2002 full-time, 3. *Quantitative PhD*.

Admissions Requirements:
Scores: Entries appear in this order: required test or GPA, minimum score (if required), median score of students entering in 2001–2002. Doctoral Programs: GRE-V no minimum stated, 650; GRE-Q no minimum stated, 693; GRE-V+Q no minimum stated, 670; GRE-Analytical no minimum stated, 620; GRE-V+Q+Analytical no minimum stated, 671; GRE-Subject(Psych) no minimum stated, 620; overall undergraduate GPA no minimum stated; last 2 years GPA no minimum

stated; psychology GPA no minimum stated; psychology GPA no minimum stated.

Other Criteria: (importance of criteria rated low, medium, or high): GRE/MAT scores high, research experience high, work experience medium, extracurricular activity low, clinically related public service low, GPA medium, letters of recommendation high, interview high, statement of goals and objectives high.

Student Characteristics: The following represents characteristics of students in 2001–2002 in all graduate psychology programs in the department: Female–full-time 10, part-time 0; Male–full-time 6, part-time 0; African American/Black–full-time 0, part-time 0; Hispanic/Latino (a)–full-time 1, part-time 0; Asian/Pacific Islander–full-time 1, part-time 0; American Indian/Alaska Native–full-time 0, part-time 0.

Financial Information/Assistance:

Tuition for Full-Time Study: No information provided.

Financial Assistance:

First Year Students: Teaching assistantships available for first-year. Tuition remission given: full.

Advanced Students: Teaching assistantships available for advanced students. Tuition remission given: full.

Contact Information: Of all students currently enrolled full-time, 100% benefitted from one or more of the listed financial assistance programs. For information on financial assistance, contact: Joan Krach, Department Psychological and Brain Sciences, krach@jhu.edu. Read Web pages http://www.psy.jhu.edu.

Internships/Practica: No information provided.

Housing and Day Care: No on-campus housing and day care facilities are available.

Employment of Department Graduates:

Master's Degree Graduates: Of those who graduated in the academic year 2000–2001, the following categories and numbers represent the post-graduate activities and employment of master's degree graduates: Enrolled in a post-doctoral residency/fellowship (n/a), employed in independent practice (n/a).

Doctoral Degree Graduates: Of those who graduated in the academic year 2000–2001, the following categories and numbers represent the post-graduate activities and employment of doctoral degree graduates: Enrolled in a psychology doctoral program (n/a), enrolled in another graduate/professional program (n/a), enrolled in a post-doctoral residency/fellowship (3), employed in an academic position at a 2-year/4-year college (1).

Additional Information:

Orientation, Objectives, and Emphasis of Department: The graduate program in psychology at The Johns Hopkins University emphasizes research training, stressing the application of basic research methodology to theoretical problems in psychology. Students are actively engaged in research projects within the first semester. There is a low student/faculty ratio; students work closely with their advisors. Courses, seminars, and research activities provide training so that students will emerge as independent investigators who can embark on successful research careers in psychology. Courses cover fundamental issues in experimental design and analysis, and provide a broad background in all the major areas of psychology. Advanced seminars deal with topics of current interest in various specific areas. The department has programs in cognitive psychology (including perceptual and cognitive development), cognitive neuroscience, quantitative psychology, and biopsychology. The evaluation of applications to our graduate program is based on many factors. They include both objective indicators, such as required GRE scores and undergraduate GPA, and more subjective information, such as a statement of purpose, a description of applicant's background and experience, and letters of recommendation. To select among the top candidates, we rely on letters of recommendation to provide a personal assessment of applicant's potential for graduate work by faculty mentors and advisors who know the applicant well. Students in good standing can expect to receive both tuition remission and salary.

Special Facilities or Resources: Each faculty member in the Department of Psychology maintains a laboratory for conducting research. The psychology building was recently renovated, and the research space is both excellent and plentiful. Every lab contains multiple microcomputer systems for experimentation, analysis, and word processing; most machines are connected via a local-area network to one another and to the Internet. In addition, individual laboratories contain special-purpose equipment designed for the research carried out there. Laboratories in cognition, for example, include high-resolution display devices for experiments in visual. Quantitative psychology laboratories include UNIX work stations for computational analysis and simulation studies. Biopsychology laboratories have facilities for animal surgery, histology, electrophysiological recording of single units and evoked potentials, analysis of neurotransmitters through assays and high-pressure liquid chromatography, bioacoustics, and for general behavioral testing.

Information for Students With Physical Disabilities: The campus is wheelchair accessible.

Application Information:
Send to: Joan Krach, Administrative Assistant, JHU, Department of Psychological and Brain Sciences, 222 Ames Hall, Charles & 34th Streets, Baltimore, MD 21218 Applications on line at http://www.psy.jhu.edu. Students are admitted in the Fall, application deadline January 15. *Fee:* $55.

Loyola College
Department of Psychology
4501 North Charles Street
Baltimore, MD 21210
Telephone: (410) 617-2696
Fax: (410) 617-5341
E-mail: *Sobelman@Loyola.edu*
Web: *http://www.Loyola.edu/Psychology*

Department Established:
1968. Chairperson: Dr. Amanda M. Thomas. Number of Faculty: total–full-time 14, part-time 10; women–full-time 5, part-time 4.

Programs and Degrees Offered:
Listed in the following order: Program area, degree type (T if terminal Master's), number awarded 7/00-6/01. Clinical MA (T) 43, Clinical PsyD 10, Counseling MA (T) 14.

APA Accreditation: Clinical PsyD: full.

Student Applications/Admissions:
Student Applications
Clinical MA—Applications 2001–2002, 82. Total applicants accepted 2001–2002, 59. New applicants enrolled 2001–2002, 32. Total enrolled 2001–2002 full-time, 65, part-time, 35. Openings 2002–2003, 45. The Median number of years required for completion of a degree are NA. The number of students enrolled full and part-time, who were dismissed or voluntarily withdrew from this program area were 0. *Clinical PsyD*—Applications 2001–2002, 140. Total applicants accepted 2001–2002, 15. New applicants enrolled 2001–2002, 15. Total enrolled 2001–2002 full-time, 48. Openings 2002–2003, 15. The Median number of years required for completion of a degree are 4. The number of students enrolled full and part-time, who were dismissed or voluntarily withdrew from this program area were 1. *Counseling MA*—Applications 2001–2002, 56. Total applicants accepted 2001–2002, 31. New applicants enrolled 2001–2002, 11. Total enrolled 2001–2002 full-time, 21, part-time, 16. Openings 2002–2003, 45. The Median number of years required for completion of a degree are NA. The number of students enrolled full and part-time, who were dismissed or voluntarily withdrew from this program area were 0.

Admissions Requirements:
Scores: Entries appear in this order: required test or GPA, minimum score (if required), median score of students entering in 2001–2002. Master's Programs: GRE-V no minimum stated, 480; GRE-Q no minimum stated, 540; GRE-V+Q no minimum stated, 1000; overall undergraduate GPA 3.0, 3.38; psychology GPA 3.0. Doctoral Programs: GRE-V no minimum stated, 510; GRE-Q no minimum stated, 695; GRE-V+Q no minimum stated, 1205; overall undergraduate GPA 3.0, 3.54; last 2 years GPA no minimum stated; psychology GPA no minimum stated; psychology GPA no minimum stated.
Other Criteria: (importance of criteria rated low, medium, or high): GRE/MAT scores high, research experience high, work experience high, extracurricular activity medium, clinically related public service high, GPA high, letters of recommendation high, interview high, statement of goals and objectives medium. Interviews by invitation only for PsyD program. Interviews for Master's Program not applicable.

Student Characteristics: The following represents characteristics of students in 2001–2002 in all graduate psychology programs in the department: Female–full-time 90, part-time 50; Male–full-time 25, part-time 13; African American/Black–full-time 5, part-time 5; Hispanic/Latino (a)–full-time 2, part-time 2; Asian/Pacific Islander–full-time 3, part-time 1; American Indian/Alaska Native–full-time 0, part-time 0; Multi-ethnic–full-time 0, part-time 0; students subject to the Americans with Disabilities Act–full-time 0, part-time 2.

Financial Information/Assistance:
Tuition for Full-Time Study: *Master's:* State residents $312 per credit hour; nonstate residents: $312 per credit hour. *Doctoral:* State residents: per academic year $16,799; nonstate residents: per academic year $16,799.

Financial Assistance:
First Year Students: No information provided.
Advanced Students: Teaching assistantships available for advanced students. Average amount paid per academic year: $1,200. Average number of hours worked per week: 7. Apply by May 15/Nov 15. Research assistantships available for advanced students. Average amount paid per academic year: $1,200. Average number of hours worked per week: 7. Apply by May 15/Nov 15. Fellowships and scholarships available for advanced students. Apply by varies. Tuition remission given: partial.
Contact Information: Of all students currently enrolled full-time, 30% benefitted from one or more of the listed financial assistance programs. For information on financial assistance, contact: Financial Aid Office.

Internships/Practica: The MS program requires 300 hours of externship experience. Students are able to choose from a wide variety of sites approved by the Department. The PsyD program incorporates field placement training throughout the curriculum; a minimum total of 1,260 hours of field training is required. The Final (fifth) year of the PsyD program is a full-time internship. For those doctoral students for whom a professional internship is required prior to graduation, 10 applied in 2000–2001. Of those who applied, 10 were placed in internships listed by the Association of Psychology Postdoctoral and Internship Programs (APPIC); 8 were placed in APA accredited internships.

Housing and Day Care: No on-campus housing and day care facilities are available.

Employment of Department Graduates:
Master's Degree Graduates: Of those who graduated in the academic year 2000–2001, the following categories and numbers represent the post-graduate activities and employment of master's degree graduates: Enrolled in a psychology doctoral program (14), enrolled in another graduate/professional program (12), enrolled in a post-doctoral residency/fellowship (n/a), employed in independent practice (n/a).
Doctoral Degree Graduates: Of those who graduated in the academic year 2000–2001, the following categories and numbers represent the post-graduate activities and employment of doctoral degree graduates: Enrolled in a psychology doctoral program (n/a), enrolled in another graduate/professional program (n/a), enrolled in a post-doctoral residency/fellowship (10), employed in independent practice (0).

Additional Information:
Orientation, Objectives, and Emphasis of Department: The Master's programs in Clinical and Counseling Psychology at Loyola College provide training to individuals who wish to promote mental health in individuals, families, organizations, and communities though careers in direct service, leadership, research, and education. We strive to provide a learning environment that facilitates the development of skills in critical thinking, scholarship, assessment and intervention, and that is grounded in an appreciation for both psychological science and human diversity. The goals of the PsyD program in Clinical Psychology are based on the "scholar-professional" model of training, designed to train autonomous practitioners of professional psychology who will de-

liver mental health services and lead others in service to the general public in diverse settings.

Special Facilities or Resources: Departmental facilities include a health psychology/behavioral medicine laboratory, audiovisual recording facilities, assessment and therapy training rooms, and a student lounge. Students have access to a campus-wide computer system, including SPSS and SASS software. All graduate students have telephone voicemail and e-mail addresses. Advanced doctoral students are provided with individual workstations with computers.

Information for Students With Physical Disabilities: Loyola College complies with the Americans with Disabilities Act, Section 504 of the Rehabilitation Act, and state and local requirements regarding students with disabilities. Questions about services or accommodations should be directed to the Office of Disability Support Services at 410-617-2062 or 410-617-2141 (TTD).

Application Information:
Send to: Office of Graduate Admissions, Loyola College in Maryland, 4501 N. Charles Street, Baltimore, MD 21210. Students are admitted in the Fall, application deadline Jan 1/Apr 15; Spring, application deadline November 15; Summer, application deadline April 15. For Fall, deadlines are as follows: PsyD—January 1; MA—March 15; MS—April 15. For both Spring and Summer, applications are accepted for MS only. *Fee:* $35.

Maryland, University of
Department of Psychology
Biology-Psychology Building
College Park, MD 20742-4411
Telephone: (301) 405-5865
Fax: (301) 314-9566
E-mail: *psycgrad@deans.umd.edu*
Web: *http://www.bsos.umd.edu/psyc/*

Department Established:
1937. Chairperson: Professor William S. Hall. Number of Faculty: total–full-time 42; women–full-time 9; minority–full-time 4.

Programs and Degrees Offered:
Listed in the following order: Program area, degree type (T if terminal Master's), number awarded 7/00-6/01. Clinical PhD 5, Cognitive PhD 2, counseling PhD 8, developmental PhD 2, industrial and organizational PhD 9, Integrative Neuroscience PhD 1, Sensorineural and Perceptual PhD, social PhD 2.

APA Accreditation: Clinical PhD: full. Counseling PhD: full.

Student Applications/Admissions:
Student Applications
Clinical PhD—Applications 2001–2002, 196. Total applicants accepted 2001–2002, 14. New applicants enrolled 2001–2002, 6. Total enrolled 2001–2002 full-time, 32. Openings 2002–

2003, 6. The Median number of years required for completion of a degree are 7. The number of students enrolled full and part-time, who were dismissed or voluntarily withdrew from this program area were 0. *Cognitive PhD*—Applications 2001–2002, 20. Total applicants accepted 2001–2002, 5. New applicants enrolled 2001–2002, 1. Total enrolled 2001–2002 full-time, 6. Openings 2002–2003, 4. The number of students enrolled full and part-time, who were dismissed or voluntarily withdrew from this program area were 1. *Counseling PhD*—Applications 2001–2002, 200. Total applicants accepted 2001–2002, 5. New applicants enrolled 2001–2002, 4. Total enrolled 2001–2002 full-time, 24. Openings 2002–2003, 4. The number of students enrolled full and part-time, who were dismissed or voluntarily withdrew from this program area were 0. *Developmental PhD*—Applications 2001–2002, 18. Total applicants accepted 2001–2002, 3. New applicants enrolled 2001–2002, 1. Total enrolled 2001–2002 full-time, 6. Openings 2002–2003, 2. The number of students enrolled full and part-time, who were dismissed or voluntarily withdrew from this program area were 0. *Industrial and organizational PhD*—Applications 2001–2002, 99. Total applicants accepted 2001–2002, 5. New applicants enrolled 2001–2002, 4. Total enrolled 2001–2002 full-time, 22. Openings 2002–2003, 2. The number of students enrolled full and part-time, who were dismissed or voluntarily withdrew from this program area were 2. *Integrative Neuroscience PhD*—Applications 2001–2002, 9. Total applicants accepted 2001–2002, 1. Total enrolled 2001–2002 full-time, 7. Openings 2002–2003, 2. The number of students enrolled full and part-time, who were dismissed or voluntarily withdrew from this program area were 0. *Sensorineural and Perceptual PhD*—Applications 2001–2002, 5. Total enrolled 2001–2002 full-time, 3. Openings 2002–2003, 2. The number of students enrolled full and part-time, who were dismissed or voluntarily withdrew from this program area were 0. *Social PhD*—Applications 2001–2002, 29. Total applicants accepted 2001–2002, 12. New applicants enrolled 2001–2002, 3. Total enrolled 2001–2002 full-time, 13. Openings 2002–2003, 2. The Median number of years required for completion of a degree are 5. The number of students enrolled full and part-time, who were dismissed or voluntarily withdrew from this program area were 0.

Admissions Requirements:
Scores: Entries appear in this order: required test or GPA, minimum score (if required), median score of students entering in 2001–2002. Doctoral Programs: GRE-V no minimum stated, 610; GRE-Q no minimum stated, 660; GRE-V+Q no minimum stated, 1270; GRE-Analytical no minimum stated, 670; GRE-V+Q+Analytical no minimum stated, 1940; overall undergraduate GPA no minimum stated, 3.74; last 2 years GPA no minimum stated, 3.80; psychology GPA no minimum stated, 3.70; psychology GPA no minimum stated. Each area sets its own specific requirements.
Other Criteria: (importance of criteria rated low, medium, or high): GRE/MAT scores high, research experience high, work experience low, extracurricular activity low, clinically related public service low, GPA high, letters of recommendation high, interview high, statement of goals and objectives high. The specific criteria vary across our 8 programs. Some require extra-curricular activity, service, and interview—whereas others do not. Currently clinical holds a formal interview for applicants who rank in their top group.

Student Characteristics: The following represents characteristics of students in 2001–2002 in all graduate psychology programs in the department: Female–full-time 82, part-time 0; Male–full-time 39, part-time 0; African American/Black–full-time 17, part-time 0; Hispanic/Latino (a)–full-time 5, part-time 0; Asian/Pacific Islander–full-time 16, part-time 0; American Indian/Alaska Native–full-time 0, part-time 0; Multi-ethnic–full-time 2, part-time 0; students subject to the Americans with Disabilities Act–full-time 0, part-time 0.

Financial Information/Assistance:

Tuition for Full-Time Study: *Doctoral:* State residents: $289 per credit hour; nonstate residents: $448 per credit hour.

Financial Assistance:

First Year Students: Teaching assistantships available for first-year. Average amount paid per academic year: $12,044. Average number of hours worked per week: 20. Apply by January 1. Tuition remission given: full. Research assistantships available for first-year. Average amount paid per academic year: $12,044. Average number of hours worked per week: 20. Apply by January 1. Tuition remission given: full. Fellowships and scholarships available for first-year. Average amount paid per academic year: $12,131. Apply by January 1. Tuition remission given: full.

Advanced Students: Teaching assistantships available for advanced students. Average amount paid per academic year: $12,494. Average number of hours worked per week: 20. Tuition remission given: full. Research assistantships available for advanced students. Average amount paid per academic year: $12,494. Average number of hours worked per week: 20. Tuition remission given: full. Fellowships and scholarships available for advanced students. Average amount paid per academic year: $12,653. Average number of hours worked per week: 20. Tuition remission given: full.

Contact Information: Of all students currently enrolled full-time, 75% benefitted from one or more of the listed financial assistance programs.

Internships/Practica: The metropolitan area also has many psychologists who can provide students with excellent opportunities for collaboration and/or consultation. The specialty areas have established collaborative relationships with several federal and community agencies and hospitals as well as with businesses and consulting firms, where it is possible for students to arrange for research, practicum, and internship placement. These opportunities are available for Clinical and Counseling students at the National Institutes of Health, Veteran's Administration clinics, and hospitals in Washington, DC, Baltimore Perry Point, Coatesville, Martinsburg, Kecoughton, and a number of others within a hundred mile radius of the University. Experiences include a wide range of research activities, as well as psychodiagnostic work, psychotherapy, and work within drug and alcohol abuse clinics. Various other hospitals, clinics, and research facilities in the Washington, DC and Baltimore metropolitan area are also available. Industrial/Organizational students also have opportunities for practitioner experiences in organizations such as The US Office of Personnel Management, GEICO, Bell Atlantic, and various consulting firms. For those doctoral students for whom a professional internship is required prior to graduation, 7 applied

in 2000–2001. Of those who applied, 7 were placed in APA accredited internships.

Housing and Day Care: On-campus housing and day care facilities are available.

Employment of Department Graduates:

Master's Degree Graduates: Of those who graduated in the academic year 2000–2001, the following categories and numbers represent the post-graduate activities and employment of master's degree graduates: Enrolled in a post-doctoral residency/fellowship (n/a), employed in independent practice (n/a).

Doctoral Degree Graduates: Of those who graduated in the academic year 2000–2001, the following categories and numbers represent the post-graduate activities and employment of doctoral degree graduates: Enrolled in a psychology doctoral program (n/a), enrolled in another graduate/professional program (n/a).

Additional Information:

Orientation, Objectives, and Emphasis of Department: The department offers a full-time graduate program with an emphasis on intensive individual training made possible by a 4-to-1 student/faculty ratio. All students are expected to participate in a variety of relevant experiences that, in addition to coursework and research training, can include practicum experiences, field training, and teaching. The department offers a variety of programs described in the admissions brochure as well as other emphases that cut across the various specialties. All programs have a strong research emphasis with programs in clinical, counseling, and industrial advocating the scientist-practitioner model. Please note that the Department of Psychology receives a large number of applications. As required by the Graduate School, we will consider any applicant who has all materials in by December 15.

Special Facilities or Resources: The Department of Psychology has all of the advantages of a large state university, and also has advantages offered by the many resources available in the metropolitan Washington-Baltimore area. The University is approximately 15 miles from the center of Washington, DC and is in close proximity to a number of libraries and state and federal agencies. Students are able to benefit from the excellent additional library resources of the community, such as the Library of Congress, National Library of Medicine, and the National Archives (which is located on the UMCP campus). The building in which the Department is housed was designed by the faculty to incorporate research and educational facilities for all specialty areas. The building contains special centers for research, with acoustical centers, observational units, video equipment, computer facilities, surgical facilities, and radio frequency shielding. Departmental laboratories are well equipped for research in animal behavior, audition, biopsychology, cognition, coordinated motor control, counseling, industrial/organizational psychology, learning, life-span development, psycholinguistics, psychotherapy, social psychology, and vision.

Application Information:

Send to: Ms. Betty Padgett, Graduate Program Specialist, Department of Psychology, University of Maryland, College Park, MD, 20742-4411. Students are admitted in the Fall, application deadline January 1. *Fee:* $50.

Maryland, University of (2001 data)
Institute for Child Study/Department of Human Development
College of Education
College Park, MD 20742
Telephone: (301) 405-2827
Fax: (301) 405-2891
E-mail: cf9@umail.umd.edu
Web: http://www.inform.umd.edu/educ/depts/edhd

Department Established:
1947. Acting Chair: Charles H. Flatter. Number of Faculty: total–full-time 22, part-time 4; women–full-time 10, part-time 2; minority–full-time 2.

Programs and Degrees Offered:
Listed in the following order: Program area, degree type (T if terminal Master's), number awarded 7/00-6/01. Developmental MA 8, educational psychology PhD 2.

Student Applications/Admissions:
Student Applications
Developmental MA—Applications 2001–2002, 26. Total applicants accepted 2001–2002, 11. New applicants enrolled 2001–2002, 3. Total enrolled 2001–2002 full-time, 6, part-time, 4. Openings 2002–2003, 20. *Educational psychology PhD*—Applications 2001–2002, 14. Total applicants accepted 2001–2002, 9. New applicants enrolled 2001–2002, 3. Total enrolled 2001–2002 full-time, 15, part-time, 5. Openings 2002–2003, 10.

Admissions Requirements:
Scores: Entries appear in this order: required test or GPA, minimum score (if required), median score of students entering in 2001–2002. Master's Programs: GRE-V 450, 560; GRE-Q 485, 600; overall undergraduate GPA 3.0, 3.25. Doctoral Programs: GRE-V 450, 580; GRE-Q 485, 620; overall undergraduate GPA 3.0, 3.32.

Other Criteria: (importance of criteria rated low, medium, or high): GRE/MAT scores, research experience high, work experience medium, clinically related public service medium, GPA, letters of recommendation high, interview medium, statement of goals and objectives high.

Student Characteristics:
Student Characteristics: The following represents characteristics of students in 2001–2002 in all graduate psychology programs in the department: Female–full-time 9, part-time 2; Male–full-time 4, part-time 0; African American/Black–full-time 0, part-time 0; Hispanic/Latino (a)–full-time 0, part-time 0; Asian/Pacific Islander–full-time 1, part-time 1; American Indian/Alaska Native–full-time 0, part-time 0.

Financial Information/Assistance:
Tuition for Full-Time Study: No information provided.

Financial Assistance:
First Year Students: No information provided.
Advanced Students: No information provided.
Contact Information: Of all students currently enrolled full-time, 0% benefitted from one or more of the listed financial assistance programs. For information on financial assistance, contact: Chair, Department of Human Development; Dawn Kriebel, Graduate Secretary (301) 405-8432.

Internships/Practica: No information provided.

Housing and Day Care: No on-campus housing and day care facilities are available.

Employment of Department Graduates:
Master's Degree Graduates: Of those who graduated in the academic year 2000–2001, the following categories and numbers represent the post-graduate activities and employment of master's degree graduates: Enrolled in a post-doctoral residency/fellowship (n/a), employed in independent practice (n/a).
Doctoral Degree Graduates: Of those who graduated in the academic year 2000–2001, the following categories and numbers represent the post-graduate activities and employment of doctoral degree graduates: Enrolled in a psychology doctoral program (n/a), enrolled in another graduate/professional program (n/a).

Additional Information:
Orientation, Objectives, and Emphasis of Department: Human development courses are psychological in nature and are intended to increase the student's understanding of human behavior, including development, learning, and adjustment. Areas of concentration that relate to the institute's goals and interests include, but are not limited to, infancy and early childhood, adolescence, adult development and aging, development over the life span, cultural processes, neuropsychology, cognitive processes, personality, and learning. Information is drawn primarily from the major fields of psychology, sociology, and physiology. The graduate specialization in educational psychology program is intended to prepare educational psychologists for service in schools and other community agencies dealing with individuals of all ages, to prepare teachers of human development and educational psychology in higher education, and to prepare research-oriented individuals for service in public (state or federal) or private organizations. A graduate joint specialization in development science with the psychology department is also available. The research thrust of this specialization is primarily concerned with social and cognitive aspects of development. The developmental science specialization is designed to prepare researchers and teachers in higher eduation.

Special Facilities or Resources: Special facilities or resources include extensive research and computer facilities. Videotaping studios and observation rooms are located in the building. The Child Development Assessment Laboratory is associated with the department and is heavily used for neuropsychological assessments on children. Testing and observation rooms are available in the Center for Family Relationships and Culture. In addition, the Center for Young Children, a child care center for preschool children, is under the auspices of the unit and is a resource for students studying and researching this age group.

Application Information:
Send to: department chair. Students are admitted in the Fall, application deadline June 1; Spring, application deadline October 1; Summer, application deadline February 1. Deadline for financial aid consideration is January 2. *Fee:* $50.

Maryland, University of (2001 data)

School and Counseling Psychology Programs, Department of
  Counseling and Personnel Services
College of Education
College Park, MD 20742
Telephone: (301) 405-2858
Fax: (301) 405-9995
E-mail: kg12@umail.umd.edu
Web: http://www.umd.edu

Department Established:

1967. Chairperson: Kenneth Greenberg. Number of Faculty: total–full-time 15, part-time 4; women–full-time 8, part-time 3; minority–full-time 2, part-time 1.

Programs and Degrees Offered:

Listed in the following order: Program area, degree type (T if terminal Master's), number awarded 7/00-6/01. Counseling psychology PhD (T) 7, school PhD 1.

APA Accreditation: Counseling PhD: full. School PhD: full.

Student Applications/Admissions:

Student Applications

Counseling psychology PhD—Applications 2001–2002, 223. Total applicants accepted 2001–2002, 12. New applicants enrolled 2001–2002, 5. Total enrolled 2001–2002 full-time, 21. Openings 2002–2003, 8. *School PhD*—Applications 2001–2002, 37. Total applicants accepted 2001–2002, 10. New applicants enrolled 2001–2002, 5. Total enrolled 2001–2002 full-time, 26, part-time, 14. Openings 2002–2003, 6.

Admissions Requirements:

Scores: Entries appear in this order: required test or GPA, minimum score (if required), median score of students entering in 2001–2002. Master's Programs: GRE-V+Q no minimum stated; overall undergraduate GPA no minimum stated; last 2 years GPA no minimum stated. Doctoral Programs: GRE-V no minimum stated, 630; GRE-Q no minimum stated, 590; GRE-V+Q no minimum stated, 1200; GRE-Analytical no minimum stated; overall undergraduate GPA no minimum stated, 3.6; last 2 years GPA no minimum stated, 3.6; psychology GPA no minimum stated, 3.9.

Other Criteria: (importance of criteria rated low, medium, or high): research experience medium, work experience medium, letters of recommendation high, interview medium, statement of goals and objectives high, counseling experiences medium. Criteria vary by program. Applicants should contact specific programs for detailed information.

Student Characteristics: The following represents characteristics of students in 2001–2002 in all graduate psychology programs in the department: Female–full-time 11, part-time 0; Male–full-time 0, part-time 0; African American/Black–full-time 0, part-time 0; Hispanic/Latino (a)–full-time 0, part-time 0; Asian/Pacific Islander–full-time 1, part-time 0; American Indian/Alaska Native–full-time 0, part-time 0.

Financial Information/Assistance:

Tuition for Full-Time Study: No information provided.

Financial Assistance:

First Year Students: No information provided.
Advanced Students: No information provided.
Contact Information: For information on financial assistance, contact: Program Directors after admission to program.

Internships/Practica: The Washington DC area offers an abundance of training settings which supplement our on-campus training facilities. A number of practica are offered at the University of Maryland Counseling Center. In addition, other practica and externships are offered at schools, community agencies, hospitals, and other counseling centers.

Housing and Day Care: No on-campus housing and day care facilities are available.

Employment of Department Graduates:

Master's Degree Graduates: Of those who graduated in the academic year 2000–2001, the following categories and numbers represent the post-graduate activities and employment of master's degree graduates: Enrolled in a post-doctoral residency/fellowship (n/a), employed in independent practice (n/a).

Doctoral Degree Graduates: Of those who graduated in the academic year 2000–2001, the following categories and numbers represent the post-graduate activities and employment of doctoral degree graduates: Enrolled in a psychology doctoral program (n/a), enrolled in another graduate/professional program (n/a).

Additional Information:

Orientation, Objectives, and Emphasis of Department: Both the Counseling Psychology and School Psychology programs espouse the scientist practitioner model of training. These programs enable students to become psychologists who are trained in general psychology, competent in providing effective assessment and intervention from a variety of theoretical perspectives, and in conducting research on a wide range of psychological topics. Note: The Counseling Psychology program is administered collaboratively by the departments of Counseling and Personnel Services and Psychology.

Special Facilities or Resources: Observation/training facilities and access to extensive library facilities both on and off campus (e.g., NIH Library of Medicine, Library of Congress).

Information for Students With Physical Disabilities: The university has an office of Disabled Student Services. The university has made a concerted effort to make the campus accessible to persons with physical disabilities. The buildings housing the activities associated with these programs are wheel-chair accessible.

Application Information:

Send to: Graduate Admission, College of Education, 1210 Benjamin Building, University of Maryland, College Park, MD 20742. Students are admitted in the Fall, application deadline January 2nd. *Fee:* $50.

Maryland, University of, Baltimore County

Department of Psychology
Arts and Sciences
1000 Hilltop Circle
Baltimore, MD 21250
Telephone: (410) 455-2567
Fax: (410) 455-1055
E-mail: *psycdept@umbc.edu*
Web: *http://www.psych.umbc.edu*

Department Established:

1966. Chairperson: Carlo C. DiClemente, Ph.D. Number of Faculty: total–full-time 27, part-time 11; women–full-time 9, part-time 6; minority–full-time 2, part-time 1; faculty subject to the Americans with Disabilities Act 1.

Programs and Degrees Offered:

Listed in the following order: Program area, degree type (T if terminal Master's), number awarded 7/00-6/01. Applied behavior analysis MA (T) 6, applied developmental 4, human services PhD 9.

APA Accreditation: Clinical PhD: full.

Student Applications/Admissions:

Student Applications

Applied behavior analysis MA—Total enrolled 2001–2002 full-time, 6, part-time, 3. Openings 2002–2003, 12. The Median number of years required for completion of a degree are 2. The number of students enrolled full and part-time, who were dismissed or voluntarily withdrew from this program area were 0. *Human services PhD*—Applications 2001–2002, 104. Total enrolled 2001–2002 full-time, 75, part-time, 1. Openings 2002–2003, 12. The Median number of years required for completion of a degree are 6. The number of students enrolled full and part-time, who were dismissed or voluntarily withdrew from this program area were 1.

Admissions Requirements:

Scores: Entries appear in this order: required test or GPA, minimum score (if required), median score of students entering in 2001–2002. Master's Programs: GRE-V no minimum stated; GRE-Q no minimum stated; GRE-V+Q no minimum stated; GRE-Analytical no minimum stated; GRE-V+Q+Analytical no minimum stated; overall undergraduate GPA 3.0. Doctoral Programs: GRE-V no minimum stated; GRE-Q no minimum stated; GRE-V+Q no minimum stated; GRE-Analytical no minimum stated; GRE-V+Q+Analytical no minimum stated; GRE-Subject(Psych) 550; overall undergraduate GPA 3.0; last 2 years GPA no minimum stated; psychology GPA no minimum stated; psychology GPA no minimum stated.

Other Criteria: (importance of criteria rated low, medium, or high): GRE/MAT scores high, research experience high, work experience medium, extracurricular activity medium, clinically related public service medium, GPA high, letters of recommendation high, interview high, statement of goals and objectives high.

Student Characteristics: The following represents characteristics of students in 2001–2002 in all graduate psychology programs in the department: Female–full-time 55, part-time 35; Male–full-time 14, part-time 11; African American/Black–full-time 10, part-time 6; Hispanic/Latino (a)–full-time 3, part-time 0; Asian/Pacific Islander–full-time 4, part-time 0; American Indian/Alaska Native–full-time 0, part-time 0.

Financial Information/Assistance:

Tuition for Full-Time Study: *Master's:* State residents $292 per credit hour; nonstate residents: $480 per credit hour. *Doctoral:* State residents: $292 per credit hour; nonstate residents: $480 per credit hour.

Financial Assistance:

First Year Students: Teaching assistantships available for first-year. Average amount paid per academic year: $13,198. Average number of hours worked per week: 20. Tuition remission given: full. Research assistantships available for first-year. Average amount paid per academic year: $13,198. Average number of hours worked per week: 20. Tuition remission given: full. Fellowships and scholarships available for first-year. Average amount paid per academic year: $13,198. Tuition remission given: full.

Advanced Students: Teaching assistantships available for advanced students. Average amount paid per academic year: $14,212. Average number of hours worked per week: 20. Tuition remission given: full. Research assistantships available for advanced students. Average amount paid per academic year: $14,212. Average number of hours worked per week: 20. Tuition remission given: full. Fellowships and scholarships available for advanced students. Average amount paid per academic year: $14,212. Tuition remission given: full.

Contact Information: Of all students currently enrolled full-time, 48% benefitted from one or more of the listed financial assistance programs. For information on financial assistance, contact: The department.

Internships/Practica: Many of the clinical courses, and Applied Developmental Psychology courses in infant and child assessment, have a one-credit linked practicum. These practica provide students with a focused experience in the application of the skills and knowledge presented in the associated course. The course instructor is responsible for arranging these practica. Beyond the course-linked practica, students in the HSP and ADP programs are required to take a minimum of six additional credits of practicum, usually in their second and third years. These practica, in various clinical, research, and human services settings, are intended to give students a broader and more integrative experience in the application of the skills and knowledge that they have acquired in the various courses they have taken. For those doctoral students for whom a professional internship is required prior to graduation, 10 applied in 2000–2001. Of those who applied, 9 were placed in internships listed by the Association of Psychology Postdoctoral and Internship Programs (APPIC); 9 were placed in APA accredited internships.

Housing and Day Care: On-campus housing and day care facilities are available.

Employment of Department Graduates:

Master's Degree Graduates: Of those who graduated in the academic year 2000–2001, the following categories and numbers represent the post-graduate activities and employment of master's degree graduates: Enrolled in a post-doctoral residency/fellowship (n/a), employed in independent practice (n/a), employed in a hospital/medical center (1), other employment position (5).

Doctoral Degree Graduates: Of those who graduated in the academic year 2000–2001, the following categories and numbers represent the post-graduate activities and employment of doctoral degree graduates: Enrolled in a psychology doctoral program (n/a), enrolled in another graduate/professional program (n/a).

Additional Information:

Orientation, Objectives, and Emphasis of Department: UMBC Psychology is committed to a scientist-practitioner model and emphasizes science with an applied psychological research focus. The department uses a biopsychosocial interactive framework as the foundation for exploring various problems and issues in psychology. Two graduate programs are housed in the department: Applied Developmental Psychology (ADP) and Human Services Psychology (HSP). The ADP program has two concentrations: Early Development/Early Intervention, and Educational Contexts of Development, and students can affiliate flexibly with either or both. The ADP program is accredited by the ASPPB/National Register of Health Service Providers in Psychology. The HSP program consists of three subprograms - community/social, behavioral medicine, and an APA approved clinical subprogram. Many HSP students take cross-area training in clinical/behavioral medicine or clinical/community - social areas. Faculty represent a broad range of theoretical perspectives and maintain active research programs. The psychology department has many collaborative relationships for research and clinical and practical training opportunities with institutions in the Baltimore-Washington Corridor.

Special Facilities or Resources: The Psychology Department at UMBC has numerous faculty research laboratories on campus in close proximity to faculty offices. Laboratories include equipment for psychological assessments, videotaping and coding, observation as well as an animal laboratory. The department has access to several large computer laboratories on campus and has a small computer laboratory for graduate students. Through collaborative arrangements with the medical school and other University of Maryland System facilities, graduate students have access to different patient populations and opportunities for community based projects.

Information for Students With Physical Disabilities: University of Maryland Baltimore County is handicap accessible. A department on campus, Student Support Services, is available to assist students who have physical disabilities with academic support, such as note taking and special testing.

Application Information:

Send to: Dean of Graduate School, 1000 Hilltop Circle, Baltimore, MD 21250. Students are admitted in the Fall, application deadline January 5. Applied Behavior Analysis Master's program deadline is May 1. Doctoral Program in Applied Developmental Psychology is January 23. *Fee:* $45.

Towson University
Department of Psychology
8000 York Road
Towson, MD 21252
Telephone: (410) 704-3080
Fax: (410) 704-3800
E-mail: *mfracasso@towson.edu*
Web: *http://www.towson.edu*

Department Established:

1965. Chairperson: Maria P. Fracasso, Ph.D. Number of Faculty: total–full-time 33, part-time 63; women–full-time 16, part-time 25; minority–full-time 6, part-time 5.

Programs and Degrees Offered:

Listed in the following order: Program area, degree type (T if terminal Master's), number awarded 7/00-6/01. Clinical MA (T) 12, counseling MA 21, experimental MA (T) 9, school MA 10.

Student Applications/Admissions:

Student Applications

Clinical MA—Applications 2001–2002, 60. Total applicants accepted 2001–2002, 16. New applicants enrolled 2001–2002, 12. Total enrolled 2001–2002 full-time, 25, part-time, 3. Openings 2002–2003, 16. The number of students enrolled full and part-time, who were dismissed or voluntarily withdrew from this program area were 0. *Counseling MA*—Applications 2001–2002, 95. Total applicants accepted 2001–2002, 50. New applicants enrolled 2001–2002, 42. Total enrolled 2001–2002 full-time, 90, part-time, 80. Openings 2002–2003, 40. *Experimental MA*—Applications 2001–2002, 31. Total applicants accepted 2001–2002, 15. New applicants enrolled 2001–2002, 14. Total enrolled 2001–2002 full-time, 20, part-time, 20. Openings 2002–2003, 20. *School MA*—Applications 2001–2002, 65. Total applicants accepted 2001–2002, 16. New applicants enrolled 2001–2002, 14. Total enrolled 2001–2002 full-time, 34, part-time, 8. Openings 2002–2003, 16. The Median number of years required for completion of a degree are 3. The number of students enrolled full and part-time, who were dismissed or voluntarily withdrew from this program area were 2.

Admissions Requirements:

Scores: Entries appear in this order: required test or GPA, minimum score (if required), median score of students entering in 2001–2002. Master's Programs: GRE-V no minimum stated, 510; GRE-Q no minimum stated, 520; GRE-V+Q no minimum stated, 1000; GRE-Analytical no minimum stated, 550; GRE-V+Q+Analytical no minimum stated, 1550; last 2 years GPA 3.0, 3.25. GRE for Clinical and School - no minimum required Doctoral Programs: last 2 years GPA no minimum stated; psychology GPA no minimum stated; psychology GPA no minimum stated.

Other Criteria: (importance of criteria rated low, medium, or high): GRE/MAT scores medium, research experience low, work experience medium, clinically related public service medium, GPA high, letters of recommendation high, interview high, statement of goals and objectives medium. Clinically related public service, letters of recommendation, and interview are all used by the clinical psychology and school psychology programs only. School psychology also uses letter of intent and considers it very important.

Student Characteristics: The following represents characteristics of students in 2001–2002 in all graduate psychology programs in the department: Female–full-time 70, part-time 25; Male–full-time 12, part-time 7; African American/Black–full-time 3, part-time 1; Hispanic/Latino (a)–full-time 1, part-time 0; Asian/Pacific Islander–full-time 1, part-time 0; American Indian/Alaska Native–full-time 0, part-time 0.

Financial Information/Assistance:

Tuition for Full-Time Study: *Master's:* State residents $211 per credit hour; nonstate residents: $435 per credit hour.

Financial Assistance:

First Year Students: Teaching assistantships available for first-year. Average amount paid per academic year: $4,000. Average number of hours worked per week: 20. Apply by Feb 1. Tuition remission given: full.

Advanced Students: Teaching assistantships available for advanced students. Average amount paid per academic year: $4,000. Average number of hours worked per week: 20. Apply by Feb 1. Tuition remission given: full.

Contact Information: Of all students currently enrolled full-time, 25% benefitted from one or more of the listed financial assistance programs. For information on financial assistance, contact: Financial Aid Office, Towson University, Towson, MD 21252.

Internships/Practica: School Psychology students are required to complete two 100-hour practica over two semesters in a local school system. The program culminates in a 1200-hour internship that is to be completed full-time over one year or part-time over two consecutive years. Students in clinical psychology can specialize by working in either an inpatient or outpatient facility. Among the internship placement sites for students in the clinical psychology program are community mental health centers and clinics, state psychiatric hospitals, and government agencies including the Department of Veteran Affairs and other specialized psychological service centers. A limited number of nonteaching graduate assistantships are available for students in the experimental psychology program. Counseling students complete practicum and internship experiences.

Housing and Day Care: On-campus housing and day care facilities are available.

Employment of Department Graduates:

Master's Degree Graduates: Of those who graduated in the academic year 2000–2001, the following categories and numbers represent the post-graduate activities and employment of master's degree graduates: Enrolled in a post-doctoral residency/fellowship (n/a), employed in independent practice (n/a).

Doctoral Degree Graduates: Of those who graduated in the academic year 2000–2001, the following categories and numbers represent the post-graduate activities and employment of doctoral degree graduates: Enrolled in a psychology doctoral program (n/a), enrolled in another graduate/professional program (n/a).

Additional Information:

Orientation, Objectives, and Emphasis of Department: The Experimental Psychology MA Program is designed to prepare students for enrollment in PhD programs or for conducting research in industrial, government, private consulting, or hospital settings. Students receive comprehensive instruction in research design, statistical methods (both univariate and multivariate), computer applications (both for data collection and analysis), professional writing, and specialized areas of psychology. Areas of specialization include cognitive, ethnology/comparative, industrial, social/personality, sensation/perception, and physiological psychology and human neuropsychology. A meaningful individualized program of electives may be pursued by taking courses in a number of different areas. The Master of Arts in Clinical Psychology is designed for students seeking training and experience in the applied professional aspects of clinical psychology. Although a significant number of graduates go on to further graduate study in psychology, the primary focus of the program is the preparation of master's-level psychologists for employment in state and other non-profit organizations. Because of the applied professional emphasis the majority of required clinical courses address the theoretical and practical issues involved in providing direct clinical services. Students take courses in psychotherapy and behavior change, preparing them to practice individual, family, and group intervention techniques. Other courses in assessment prepare students to administer and interpret psychometric instruments used to conduct intellectual, neurological, and personality assessments. Advanced seminars in cognitive-behavior therapy are offered regularly. Practical supervised clinical experiences constitute a major portion of the program. Students complete a nine-month half-time internship during which they provide supervised psychological services to clients in an off-campus mental health setting. The Counseling Psychology Program trains individuals who will be capable of facilitating a counselee's personal growth and development. Students are trained to help clients explore educational, vocational, and personal goals. The Towson University School Psychology Program is fully accredited by the National Association of School Psychologists (NASP) and trains graduate students to become school psychologists. The program emphasizes consultation and early intervention. It is unique in its close relationship with its surrounding urban and suburban communities, which welcomes Towson's school psychology students in both practicum and internship settings. The Program offers a single 63-credit degree: the Master of Arts in Psychology with a concentration in School Psychology and the Certificate of Advanced Study (CAS) in School Psychology.

Special Facilities or Resources: The Psychology Building houses laboratories for histology and computer analysis as well as for the conduct of research in learning/motivation, physiological, comparative, and general experimental psychology. Additionally, because of the popularity of the undergraduate Psychology major, there are many students willing to participate in research studies.

Information for Students With Physical Disabilities: Towson University provides services to students with disabilities. These services include extended time on tests, interpreters, note takers, use of tape recorders, large print hand-outs and exams, readers/scribes for tests and alternate test formats.

Application Information:

Send to: Graduate School, Towson University, Towson, MD 21252. Students are admitted in the Fall, application deadline February 1; Spring, application deadline October 1. School and clinical—fall admissions only. Feb 1 and March 1 for experimental and counseling. *Fee:* $44.

Washington College
Department of Psychology
Washington Avenue
Chestertown, MD 21620-1197
Telephone: (410) 778-2800
Fax: (410) 778-7275
E-mail: *george.spilich@washcoll.edu*
Web: *http://www.psychology.washcoll.edu*

Department Established:
1953. Chairperson: George Spilich. Number of Faculty: total–full-time 6, part-time 5; women–full-time 2.

Programs and Degrees Offered:
Listed in the following order: Program area, degree type (T if terminal Master's), number awarded 7/00-6/01. General Experimental MA (T) 12.

Student Applications/Admissions:
Student Applications
General Experimental MA—Applications 2001–2002, 30. Total applicants accepted 2001–2002, 25. New applicants enrolled 2001–2002, 12. Total enrolled 2001–2002 part-time, 60. Openings 2002–2003, 20. The number of students enrolled full and part-time, who were dismissed or voluntarily withdrew from this program area were 1.

Admissions Requirements:
Scores: Entries appear in this order: required test or GPA, minimum score (if required), median score of students entering in 2001–2002. Master's Programs: GRE-V no minimum stated, 520; GRE-Q no minimum stated, 520; GRE-V+Q 1000. Doctoral Programs: last 2 years GPA no minimum stated; psychology GPA no minimum stated; psychology GPA no minimum stated.
Other Criteria: (importance of criteria rated low, medium, or high): GRE/MAT scores low, research experience medium, work experience medium, clinically related public service medium, GPA medium, letters of recommendation medium, statement of goals and objectives low, undergrad degree in psych high. If an applicant does not have an undergraduate degree in psychology, they must take an entry course (proseminar) or score above the 50% median on the psychology GRE test.

Student Characteristics: The following represents characteristics of students in 2001–2002 in all graduate psychology programs in the department: Female–full-time 0, part-time 15; Male–full-time 0, part-time 10; African American/Black–full-time 0, part-time 3; Hispanic/Latino (a)–full-time 0, part-time 0; Asian/Pacific Islander–full-time 0, part-time 0; American Indian/Alaska Native–full-time 0, part-time 0.

Financial Information/Assistance:
Tuition for Full-Time Study: *Master's:* State residents $243 per credit hour; nonstate residents: $243 per credit hour.

Financial Assistance:
First Year Students: No information provided.
Advanced Students: No information provided.
Contact Information: No information provided.

Internships/Practica: The department enjoys excellent ties to local agencies such as the Upper Shore Community Mental Health Center (the regional residential facility located in Chestertown), Upper Shore Aging, both Kent and Queen Anne's counties school systems, residential facilities for developmentally disadvantaged individuals, troubled adolescents, etc. A variety of internships are available through the cooperation of these agencies.

Housing and Day Care: No on-campus housing and day care facilities are available.

Employment of Department Graduates:
Master's Degree Graduates: Of those who graduated in the academic year 2000–2001, the following categories and numbers represent the post-graduate activities and employment of master's degree graduates: Enrolled in a post-doctoral residency/fellowship (n/a), employed in independent practice (n/a).
Doctoral Degree Graduates: Of those who graduated in the academic year 2000–2001, the following categories and numbers represent the post-graduate activities and employment of doctoral degree graduates: Enrolled in a psychology doctoral program (n/a), enrolled in another graduate/professional program (n/a).

Additional Information:
Orientation, Objectives, and Emphasis of Department: The goal of this program is to prepare graduate students for entry into a doctoral program of their choice and to generate master's level professionals. The emphasis of the curriculum is on psychology as a scientific endeavor and the applications of that scientific discipline to real-world problems.

Special Facilities or Resources: The department enjoys a computerized learning lab, video and audio taping facilities, biofeedback, equipment, both 16 and a 64 channel EEG/ERP labs, an eye movement lab, acoustic startle lab, small mammal surgery suite, a computerized psychological testing laboratory, and a social psychology lab.

Application Information:
Send to: Director of The Graduate Programs, 300 Washington Avenue, Chestertown, MD 21620-1197. Rolling admission. *Fee:* none.

American International College
Department of Graduate Psychology
1000 State Street
Springfield, MA 01109
Telephone: (413) 737-7000
Fax: (413) 737-2803
E-mail: *inquiry@www.aic.edu*
Web: *http://www.aic.edu/web*

Department Established:
1979. Chairperson: Richard C. Sprinthall. Number of Faculty: total–full-time 17, part-time 8; women–full-time 8, part-time 4.

Programs and Degrees Offered:
Listed in the following order: Program area, degree type (T if terminal Master's), number awarded 7/00-6/01. Clinical MA (T) 4, educational MA 11, Forensic Psychology MA, school.

Student Applications/Admissions:
Student Applications
Clinical MA—Applications 2001–2002, 23. Total applicants accepted 2001–2002, 15. New applicants enrolled 2001–2002, 11. Total enrolled 2001–2002 full-time, 18, part-time, 11. Openings 2002–2003, 15. The Median number of years required for completion of a degree are 3. The number of students enrolled full and part-time, who were dismissed or voluntarily withdrew from this program area were 4. *Educational MA—* Applications 2001–2002, 17. Total applicants accepted 2001–2002, 12. New applicants enrolled 2001–2002, 12. Total enrolled 2001–2002 full-time, 6, part-time, 12. Openings 2002–2003, 15. *Forensic Psychology MA—*Applications 2001–2002, 32. Total applicants accepted 2001–2002, 10. New applicants enrolled 2001–2002, 10. Total enrolled 2001–2002 full-time, 7, part-time, 3. Openings 2002–2003, 10. The Median number of years required for completion of a degree are na. The number of students enrolled full and part-time, who were dismissed or voluntarily withdrew from this program area were 0.

Admissions Requirements:
Scores: Entries appear in this order: required test or GPA, minimum score (if required), median score of students entering in 2001–2002. Master's Programs: overall undergraduate GPA no minimum stated, 3.00; last 2 years GPA no minimum stated, 3.20; psychology GPA no minimum stated, 3.30. Doctoral Programs: GRE-V no minimum stated, 550; GRE-Q no minimum stated, 480; GRE-V+Q no minimum stated, 1030; overall undergraduate GPA no minimum stated, 3.10; last 2 years GPA no minimum stated, 3.2 ; psychology GPA no minimum stated, 3.3 ; psychology GPA no minimum stated, 3.5.
Other Criteria: (importance of criteria rated low, medium, or high): GRE/MAT scores high, research experience high, work experience high, extracurricular activity medium, clinically related public service medium, GPA high, letters of recommendation high, interview high, statement of goals and objectives high. GRE only for EdD.

Student Characteristics: The following represents characteristics of students in 2001–2002 in all graduate psychology programs in the department: Female–full-time 14, part-time 23; Male–full-time 11, part-time 14; African American/Black–full-time 4, part-time 4; Hispanic/Latino (a)–full-time 3, part-time 4; Asian/Pacific Islander–full-time 0, part-time 0; American Indian/Alaska Native–full-time 0, part-time 0; Multi-ethnic–full-time 0, part-time 0; students subject to the Americans with Disabilities Act–full-time 0, part-time 0.

Financial Information/Assistance:
Tuition for Full-Time Study: *Master's:* State residents per academic year $8,082, $449 per credit hour; nonstate residents: per academic year $8,082, $449 per credit hour. *Doctoral:* State residents: per academic year $8,082, $449 per credit hour; nonstate residents: per academic year $8,082, $449 per credit hour.

Financial Assistance:
First Year Students: Teaching assistantships available for first-year. Average number of hours worked per week: 10. Apply by Apr 15. Tuition remission given: full. Research assistantships available for first-year. Average number of hours worked per week: 10. Apply by Apr 15. Tuition remission given: full. Fellowships and scholarships available for first-year. Average number of hours worked per week: 10. Apply by Apr 15. Tuition remission given: full.
Advanced Students: Teaching assistantships available for advanced students. Apply by Apr 15. Tuition remission given: full. Research assistantships available for advanced students. Apply by Apr 15. Tuition remission given: full. Fellowships and scholarships available for advanced students. Apply by Apr 15. Tuition remission given: full.
Contact Information: Of all students currently enrolled full-time, 25% benefitted from one or more of the listed financial assistance programs. For information on financial assistance, contact: Lee Sirois, Director of Financial Aid.

Internships/Practica: Internships for doctoral candidates are available at the Curtis Blake Center for Learning Disabilities and at the college-operated Curtis Blake Day School for learning-disabled children.

Housing and Day Care: No on-campus housing and day care facilities are available.

Employment of Department Graduates:
Master's Degree Graduates: Of those who graduated in the academic year 2000–2001, the following categories and numbers represent the post-graduate activities and employment of master's degree graduates: Enrolled in a post-doctoral residency/fellowship (n/a), employed in independent practice (n/a).
Doctoral Degree Graduates: Of those who graduated in the academic year 2000–2001, the following categories and numbers represent the post-graduate activities and employment of doctoral degree graduates: Enrolled in a psychology doctoral program (n/a), enrolled in another graduate/professional program (n/a).

Additional Information:

Orientation, Objectives, and Emphasis of Department: All graduate programs are based on an integrated curriculum designed to produce psychologists trained in both theory and clinical skills. Solid courses in history, systems, learning theory, and research are included. Heavy emphasis is placed on experience in the context of a broad academic and research-oriented curriculum. The program includes an extensive practicum experience, affording opportunity for the student to gain familiarity with the field and to apply and sharpen skills developed previously. The school psychology program (60 hours) leads to certification by the Commonwealth of Massachusetts. The EdD program in educational psychology is focused primarily on the area of learning disabilities. Supervision is provided both on campus and at the practicum site.

Special Facilities or Resources: A wide range of supervised internship sites is available to MA and Ed.D. candidates in mental health centers, the college counseling center, and professional agencies.

Application Information:

Send to: Department Chair. Students are admitted in the Fall, application deadline Mar 15. *Fee:* $25.

Assumption College
Division of Counseling Psychology
500 Salisbury Street
Worcester, MA 01609-1296
Telephone: (508) 767-7390
Fax: (508) 767-7382
E-mail: *doerfler@.assumption.edu*
Web: *http://www.assumption.edu*

Department Established:

1962. Program Director: Leonard A. Doerfler. Number of Faculty: total–full-time 8, part-time 14; women–full-time 4, part-time 2.

Programs and Degrees Offered:

Listed in the following order: Program area, degree type (T if terminal Master's), number awarded 7/00-6/01. Counseling MA (T) 14.

Student Applications/Admissions:

Student Applications

Counseling MA—Applications 2001–2002, 50. Total applicants accepted 2001–2002, 37. New applicants enrolled 2001–2002, 30. Total enrolled 2001–2002 full-time, 30, part-time, 20. Openings 2002–2003, 35.

Admissions Requirements:

Scores: Entries appear in this order: required test or GPA, minimum score (if required), median score of students entering in 2001–2002. Master's Programs: overall undergraduate GPA 3.0, 3.25; psychology GPA 3.0, 3.25. Doctoral Programs: last 2 years GPA no minimum stated; psychology GPA no minimum stated; psychology GPA no minimum stated.

Other Criteria: (importance of criteria rated low, medium, or high): research experience low, work experience medium,

extracurricular activity low, clinically related public service low, GPA high, letters of recommendation high, statement of goals and objectives medium.

Student Characteristics: The following represents characteristics of students in 2001–2002 in all graduate psychology programs in the department: Female–full-time 20, part-time 8; Male–full-time 2, part-time 0; African American/Black–full-time 0, part-time 0; Hispanic/Latino (a)–full-time 0, part-time 0; Asian/Pacific Islander–full-time 0, part-time 0; American Indian/Alaska Native–full-time 0, part-time 0.

Financial Information/Assistance:

Tuition for Full-Time Study: *Master's:* State residents $335 per credit hour; nonstate residents: $335 per credit hour.

Financial Assistance:

First Year Students: Fellowships and scholarships available for first-year. Apply by March 1. Tuition remission given: partial.

Advanced Students: Fellowships and scholarships available for advanced students. Apply by March 1. Tuition remission given: partial.

Contact Information: Of all students currently enrolled full-time, 25% benefitted from one or more of the listed financial assistance programs.

Internships/Practica: Practicum and internship placements are available in a wide range of community settings. Students can elect to work in outpatient/community, college counseling centers, substance abuse, inpatient, residential, and correctional settings. Opportunities to work with children, adolescents, adults, and families are available. The department maintains a close working relationship with the University of Massachusetts Medical Center, McLean Hospital/Harvard Medical School, and other mental health training agencies; students attend clinical case conferences, workshops, and lectures at these agencies. Students often receive training in innovative treatment models like home-based, brief problem-focused, or cognitive-behavioral treatments.

Housing and Day Care: No on-campus housing and day care facilities are available.

Employment of Department Graduates:

Master's Degree Graduates: Of those who graduated in the academic year 2000–2001, the following categories and numbers represent the post-graduate activities and employment of master's degree graduates: Enrolled in a psychology doctoral program (5), enrolled in a post-doctoral residency/fellowship (n/a), employed in independent practice (n/a), employed in a professional position in a school system (15), employed in a government agency (research) (5), employed in a community mental health/counseling center (75).

Doctoral Degree Graduates: Of those who graduated in the academic year 2000–2001, the following categories and numbers represent the post-graduate activities and employment of doctoral degree graduates: Enrolled in a psychology doctoral program (n/a), enrolled in another graduate/professional program (n/a).

Additional Information:

Orientation, Objectives, and Emphasis of Department: The program is organized to prepare students for entrance into doctoral programs in clinical and counseling psychology and for master's degree entry-level positions in a variety of mental health and related social service settings. Students are given conceptual preparation in a variety of theoretical positions in clinical and counseling psychology. A number of skill courses in counseling, testing, and research are an integral part of the program at both the entry and advanced levels. The goal of the program is to produce master's level psychologists who show conceptual versatility in theory and practice and depth of preparation in one of several special areas of counseling work. The student takes classwork in areas such as personality theory, abnormal psychology, child development, counseling, advanced therapeutic procedure, measurement and research. Outside of class the student gains applied experience in clinical practice in the one-semester practicum and two-semester internship.

Special Facilities or Resources: Special facilities on campus include a well-equipped media center and an observation laboratory. Students also have access to in-service training at a local medical school, agencies, and hospitals. The college is located within commuting distance of Boston training facilities. College libraries in Worcester operate on a consortium basis. Programs of study are available on campus in the summer.

Application Information:
Send to: Dean of Graduate Studies, Graduate Office, Assumption College, 500 Salisbury Street, Worcester, MA 01609-1296. Students are admitted in the Fall, application deadline rolling; Spring, application deadline rolling; Summer, application deadline rolling. *Fee:* $30. Application fee waived for Assumption College alumni.

Boston College
Department of Counseling, Developmental, and Educational
  Psychology
309 Campion Hall, School of Education
Chestnut Hill, MA 02467
Telephone: (617) 552-4710
Fax: (617) 552-1981
E-mail: *lernerj@bc.edu*
Web: *http://www.bc.edu/bc_org/avp/soe/counselpsy/*

Department Established:
1950. Chairperson: Jacqueline Lerner, Ph.D. Number of Faculty: total–full-time 18, part-time 6; women–full-time 13, part-time 3; minority–full-time 4.

Programs and Degrees Offered:
Listed in the following order: Program area, degree type (T if terminal Master's), number awarded 7/00-6/01. Counseling psychology PhD 3, counseling-mental health MA (T) 64, counseling-school MA (T) 20, developmental educational psyc MA (T) 25, Developmental/Educational Psyc PhD 6.

APA Accreditation: Counseling PhD: full.

Student Applications/Admissions:
Student Applications
  Counseling psychology PhD—Applications 2001–2002, 104. Total applicants accepted 2001–2002, 7. New applicants enrolled

2001–2002, 6. Total enrolled 2001–2002 full-time, 51. Openings 2002–2003, 6-8. The Median number of years required for completion of a degree are 6. The number of students enrolled full and part-time, who were dismissed or voluntarily withdrew from this program area were 0. *Counseling-mental health MA*—Applications 2001–2002, 242. Total applicants accepted 2001–2002, 142. New applicants enrolled 2001–2002, 51. Total enrolled 2001–2002 full-time, 134. Openings 2002–2003, 50. The Median number of years required for completion of a degree are 2. The number of students enrolled full and part-time, who were dismissed or voluntarily withdrew from this program area were 2. *Counseling-school MA*—Applications 2001–2002, 70. Total applicants accepted 2001–2002, 41. New applicants enrolled 2001–2002, 13. Total enrolled 2001–2002 full-time, 26. Openings 2002–2003, 15. The Median number of years required for completion of a degree are 2. The number of students enrolled full and part-time, who were dismissed or voluntarily withdrew from this program area were 2. *Developmental educational psyc MA*—Applications 2001–2002, 66. Total applicants accepted 2001–2002, 38. New applicants enrolled 2001–2002, 10. Total enrolled 2001–2002 full-time, 36. Openings 2002–2003, 25. The Median number of years required for completion of a degree is 1. The number of students enrolled full and part-time, who were dismissed or voluntarily withdrew from this program area were 2. *Developmental/Educational Psyc PhD*—Applications 2001–2002, 25. Total applicants accepted 2001–2002, 8. New applicants enrolled 2001–2002, 4. Total enrolled 2001–2002 full-time, 34. Openings 2002–2003, 4-5. The Median number of years required for completion of a degree are 6. The number of students enrolled full and part-time, who were dismissed or voluntarily withdrew from this program area were 0.

Admissions Requirements:
  Scores: Entries appear in this order: required test or GPA, minimum score (if required), median score of students entering in 2001–2002. Master's Programs: GRE-V no minimum stated, 510; GRE-Q no minimum stated, 570; GRE-V+Q no minimum stated, 1080; GRE-Analytical no minimum stated, 600; GRE-V+Q+Analytical no minimum stated, 1680; overall undergraduate GPA no minimum stated, 3.4. Doctoral Programs: GRE-V no minimum stated, 550; GRE-Q no minimum stated, 600; GRE-V+Q no minimum stated, 1150; GRE-Analytical no minimum stated, 670; GRE-V+Q+Analytical no minimum stated, 1820; overall undergraduate GPA no minimum stated, 3.51; last 2 years GPA no minimum stated; psychology GPA no minimum stated; psychology GPA no minimum stated.
  Other Criteria: (importance of criteria rated low, medium, or high): GRE/MAT scores medium, research experience high, work experience medium, extracurricular activity low, clinically related public service high, GPA high, letters of recommendation high, interview medium, statement of goals and objectives high. For developmental programs, clinically related public service is low.

Student Characteristics: The following represents characteristics of students in 2001–2002 in all graduate psychology programs in the department: Female–full-time 225, part-time 0; Male–full-time 55, part-time 0; African American/Black–full-time 15, part-time 0; Hispanic/Latino (a)–full-time 18, part-time 0; Asian/Pacific Islander–full-time 15, part-time 0; American Indian/Alaska Native–full-time 1, part-time 0.

Financial Information/Assistance:

Tuition for Full-Time Study: *Master's:* State residents $722 per credit hour; nonstate residents: $722 per credit hour. *Doctoral:* State residents: $722 per credit hour; nonstate residents: $722 per credit hour.

Financial Assistance:

First Year Students: Research assistantships available for first-year. Average amount paid per academic year: $11,000. Average number of hours worked per week: 20. Apply by variable. Tuition remission given: partial.

Advanced Students: Teaching assistantships available for advanced students. Average amount paid per academic year: $11,000. Average number of hours worked per week: 20. Apply by variable. Tuition remission given: partial. Research assistantships available for advanced students. Average amount paid per academic year: $13,000. Apply by variable. Tuition remission given: partial.

Contact Information: Of all students currently enrolled full-time, 50% benefitted from one or more of the listed financial assistance programs. For information on financial assistance, contact: Financial Aid, Lyons Hall, (617) 552-3320 and Graduate Admission, School of Education, Champion Hall (617) 522-4204.

Internships/Practica: Doctoral students in Counseling Psychology complete an Advanced Practicum in community mental health agencies, schools, clinics, hospitals, and college counseling centers. They also complete a one year pre-doctoral internship. Master's students in mental health and school counseling work with the Master's Program Coordinator to identify internships that meet requirements for mental health licensure or school counselor certification. For those doctoral students for whom a professional internship is required prior to graduation, 11 applied in 2000–2001. Of those who applied, 9 were placed in internships listed by the Association of Psychology Postdoctoral and Internship Programs (APPIC); 9 were placed in APA accredited internships.

Housing and Day Care: No on-campus housing and day care facilities are available.

Employment of Department Graduates:

Master's Degree Graduates: Of those who graduated in the academic year 2000–2001, the following categories and numbers represent the post-graduate activities and employment of master's degree graduates: Enrolled in a post-doctoral residency/fellowship (n/a), employed in independent practice (n/a).

Doctoral Degree Graduates: Of those who graduated in the academic year 2000–2001, the following categories and numbers represent the post-graduate activities and employment of doctoral degree graduates: Enrolled in a psychology doctoral program (n/a), enrolled in another graduate/professional program (n/a).

Additional Information:

Orientation, Objectives, and Emphasis of Department: The Programs in Counseling, Developmental and Educational Psychology emphasize a foundation in developmental theory, research skills, and a commitment to preparing professionals to work in public practice, public service, academic or research institutions. The counseling psychology doctoral program espouses a scientist-practitioner model and provides broad-based training with special attention to group and individual counseling processes, theory and skill in research and assessment, and understanding individual development within a social context. Master's counseling students specialize in mental health counseling or school counseling. The program in Applied Developmental and Educational Psychology focuses on application and draws on psychology, educational, and community programs, and engages public policies to enhance the development of individuals and their key institutional contexts — schools, families, and work settings — across the life span. Faculty research interests include psychotherapy, process and outcome, career and moral development, individual differences in cognitive and affective development including developmental disabilities, influence of gender role strain on the well-being of men, Asian-American and Latino mental health, racial identity, marital and community violence, marital satisfaction, and prevention and intervention for promoting positive development among youth.

Special Facilities or Resources: Boston College offers ample student access to computing facilities (Alpha mainframe, Macintosh and PC's) at no charge to students. The Educational Resource Center houses current psychological assessment kits and computerized instructional software. The Thomas P. O'Neill Library is fully automated with all major computerized databases. Through the consortium, students may cross-register in courses in other greater Boston universities (Boston University, Brandeis, and Tufts). The career center provides comprehensive resources and information regarding career planning and placement.

Application Information:

Send to: Graduate Admissions, Boston College, School of Education, Champion Hall 103, Chestnut Hill, MA 02467. Students are admitted in the Fall, application deadline PhD 1/1; MA 2/1. All MA programs 2/01; all PhD 1/01. *Fee:* $40.

Boston College
Department of Psychology
College of Arts and Sciences
140 Commonwealth Avenue, McGuinn 301
Chestnut Hill, MA 02467
Telephone: (617) 552-4100
Fax: (617) 552-0523
E-mail: *ellen.winner@bc.edu*
Web: *http://www.bc.edu/bc_org/avp/cas/psych/psych.html*

Department Established:

1894. Chairperson: Hiram Brownell. Number of Faculty: total–full-time 20, part-time 4; women–full-time 9, part-time 3; minority–full-time 3.

Programs and Degrees Offered:

Listed in the following order: Program area, degree type (T if terminal Master's), number awarded 7/00-6/01. Biopsychology PhD, cognition and perception PhD 1, cultural PhD, developmental PhD 1, social PhD.

Student Applications/Admissions:

Student Applications

Biopsychology PhD—Applications 2001–2002, 10. Total enrolled 2001–2002 full-time, 1. Openings 2002–2003, 1. The Median number of years required for completion of a degree are 4. The number of students enrolled full and part-time, who were dismissed or voluntarily withdrew from this program area were 0. *Cognition and perception PhD*—Applications 2001–2002, 13. Total enrolled 2001–2002 full-time, 2. Openings 2002–2003, 1. The Median number of years required for completion of a degree are 4. *Cultural PhD*—Applications 2001–2002, 17. Total enrolled 2001–2002 full-time, 4. Openings 2002–2003, 1. The Median number of years required for completion of a degree are 4. *Developmental PhD*—Applications 2001–2002, 23. Total applicants accepted 2001–2002, 2. New applicants enrolled 2001–2002, 2. Total enrolled 2001–2002 full-time, 8. Openings 2002–2003, 2. The Median number of years required for completion of a degree are 4. *Social PhD*—Applications 2001–2002, 34. Total applicants accepted 2001–2002, 1. New applicants enrolled 2001–2002, 1. Total enrolled 2001–2002 full-time, 3. Openings 2002–2003, 1. The Median number of years required for completion of a degree are 4. The number of students enrolled full and part-time, who were dismissed or voluntarily withdrew from this program area were 1.

Admissions Requirements:

Scores: Entries appear in this order: required test or GPA, minimum score (if required), median score of students entering in 2001–2002. Master's Programs: overall undergraduate GPA no minimum stated; psychology GPA no minimum stated. Doctoral Programs: GRE-V+Q+Analytical no minimum stated; GRE-Subject(Psych) no minimum stated; last 2 years GPA no minimum stated; psychology GPA no minimum stated; psychology GPA no minimum stated.

Other Criteria: (importance of criteria rated low, medium, or high): GRE/MAT scores high, research experience high, work experience low, extracurricular activity low, clinically related public service low, GPA high, letters of recommendation high, interview high, statement of goals and objectives high, Match Faculty Research high.

Student Characteristics: The following represents characteristics of students in 2001–2002 in all graduate psychology programs in the department: Female–full-time 17, Male–full-time 1, African American/Black–full-time 0, Hispanic/Latino (a)–full-time 0, Asian/Pacific Islander–full-time 3, American Indian/Alaska Native–full-time 1, Multi-ethnic–full-time 0, students subject to the Americans with Disabilities Act–full-time 0.

Financial Information/Assistance:

Tuition for Full-Time Study: No information provided.

Financial Assistance:

First Year Students: Research assistantships available for first-year. Average amount paid per academic year: $13,750. Average number of hours worked per week: 20. Apply by Jan. 2nd. Tuition remission given: full.

Advanced Students: Teaching assistantships available for advanced students. Average amount paid per academic year: $13,750. Average number of hours worked per week: 20. Apply by Jan. 2nd. Tuition remission given: full.

Contact Information: Of all students currently enrolled full-time, 100% benefitted from one or more of the listed financial assistance programs. For information on financial assistance, contact: Boston College Graduate School of Arts and Sciences, McGuinn Hall, 140 Commonwealth Avenue, Chestnut Hill, MA 02467; 617-552-3268 info request line; 617-552-2244; gsasinfo@bc.edu.

Internships/Practica: No information provided.

Housing and Day Care: No on-campus housing and day care facilities are available.

Employment of Department Graduates:

Master's Degree Graduates: Of those who graduated in the academic year 2000–2001, the following categories and numbers represent the post-graduate activities and employment of master's degree graduates: Enrolled in a post-doctoral residency/fellowship (n/a), employed in independent practice (n/a).

Doctoral Degree Graduates: Of those who graduated in the academic year 2000–2001, the following categories and numbers represent the post-graduate activities and employment of doctoral degree graduates: Enrolled in a psychology doctoral program (n/a), enrolled in another graduate/professional program (n/a), enrolled in a post-doctoral residency/fellowship (1), employed in an academic position at a university (1).

Additional Information:

Special Facilities or Resources: The Psychology Department has a computer lab with 13 workstations. Individual faculty maintain research laboratories. The Biopsychology concentration has fully equipped new research laboratories. The new lab facility contains two components: An animal facility and research laboratory space. The animal facility includes state of the art small animal housing and behavioral testing rooms, a surgery suite, and special procedure rooms that are equipped with hoods. The research laboratories consist of (1) Microscopy suite; (2) Dark room; (3) Data analysis room; (4) 3 Research labs/wet labs equipped with hoods, sinks, and workspace.

Application Information:

Send to: Boston College Graduate School of Arts and Sciences, 140 Commonwealth Avenue, McGuinn 221, Chestnut Hill, MA 02467. Students are admitted in the Fall, application deadline January 2nd. *Fee:* $50.

Boston University
Department of Psychology
64 Cummington Street
Boston, MA 02215
Telephone: (617) 353-2580
Fax: (617) 353-6933
E-mail: *hm@bu.edu*
Web: *http://www.bu.edu/PSYCH*

Department Established:

1935. Chairperson: Henry Marcucella. Number of Faculty: total–full-time 31, part-time 15; women–full-time 16, part-time 8; minority–full-time 1, part-time 3.

Programs and Degrees Offered:

Listed in the following order: Program area, degree type (T if terminal Master's), number awarded 7/00-6/01. Brain, behavior, and cognition PhD 2, clinical PhD 10, general MA (T) 35, Human Development PhD 3.

APA Accreditation: Clinical PhD: full.

Student Applications/Admissions:
Student Applications
Brain, behavior, and cognition PhD—Applications 2001–2002, 78. Total applicants accepted 2001–2002, 13. New applicants enrolled 2001–2002, 3. Total enrolled 2001–2002 full-time, 3. Openings 2002–2003, 3. *Clinical PhD*—Applications 2001–2002, 443. Total applicants accepted 2001–2002, 17. New applicants enrolled 2001–2002, 14. Total enrolled 2001–2002 full-time, 14. Openings 2002–2003, 11. *General MA*—Applications 2001–2002, 147. Total applicants accepted 2001–2002, 110. New applicants enrolled 2001–2002, 32. Total enrolled 2001–2002 full-time, 23, part-time, 20. Openings 2002–2003, 35. *Human Development PhD*—Applications 2001–2002, 64. Total applicants accepted 2001–2002, 7. New applicants enrolled 2001–2002, 3. Total enrolled 2001–2002 full-time, 3. Openings 2002–2003, 2.

Admissions Requirements:
Scores: Entries appear in this order: required test or GPA, minimum score (if required), median score of students entering in 2001–2002. Master's Programs: GRE-V+Q+Analytical no minimum stated, 1740; overall undergraduate GPA no minimum stated; last 2 years GPA no minimum stated; psychology GPA no minimum stated. Doctoral Programs: GRE-V+Q+Analytical no minimum stated, 2020; overall undergraduate GPA no minimum stated; last 2 years GPA no minimum stated; psychology GPA no minimum stated; psychology GPA no minimum stated.
Other Criteria: (importance of criteria rated low, medium, or high): research experience high, work experience low, extracurricular activity low, clinically related public service high, letters of recommendation high, interview high.

Student Characteristics: The following represents characteristics of students in 2001–2002 in all graduate psychology programs in the department: Female–full-time 119, part-time 12; Male–full-time 20, part-time 8; African American/Black–full-time 0, part-time 0; Hispanic/Latino (a)–full-time 0, part-time 0; Asian/Pacific Islander–full-time 0, part-time 0; American Indian/Alaska Native–full-time 0, part-time 0.

Financial Information/Assistance:
Tuition for Full-Time Study: *Master's:* State residents per academic year $27,200, $924 per credit hour; *Doctoral:* State residents: per academic year $27,200, $924 per credit hour.

Financial Assistance:
First Year Students: Tuition remission given: full.
Advanced Students: No information provided.
Contact Information: For information on financial assistance, contact: Graduate School of Arts and Sciences, 705 Commonwealth Ave., Boston, MA 02215.

Internships/Practica: Students in the clinical doctoral program are involved in internships and practica as part of their degree requirements.

Housing and Day Care: No on-campus housing and day care facilities are available.

Employment of Department Graduates:
Master's Degree Graduates: Of those who graduated in the academic year 2000–2001, the following categories and numbers represent the post-graduate activities and employment of master's degree graduates: Enrolled in a post-doctoral residency/fellowship (n/a), employed in independent practice (n/a).
Doctoral Degree Graduates: Of those who graduated in the academic year 2000–2001, the following categories and numbers represent the post-graduate activities and employment of doctoral degree graduates: Enrolled in a psychology doctoral program (n/a), enrolled in another graduate/professional program (n/a).

Additional Information:
Orientation, Objectives, and Emphasis of Department: The department offers specialized training leading to the PhD degree in three areas of concentration: clinical; brain, behavior, and cognition; and the program in human development with specializations in developmental, personality, social, and family. The PhD degree in psychology is awarded to students of scholarly competence as reflected by course achievement and by performance on written and oral examinations and by research competence as reflected by student's skillful application and communication of knowledge in the area of specialization. Breadth is encouraged within psychology and in related social, behavioral, and biological sciences, but it is also expected that the student will engage in intensive and penetrating study of a specialized area of the field.

Special Facilities or Resources: Laboratories for research pursuits in animal behavior, behavior disorders, child development, cognition, neurophysiology, molecular biology and psychopharmacology add to the department's facilities. The Center for Anxiety and Related Disorders (CARD), a nationally recognized clinical research and treatment center, is a recent addition to the department and allows students to engage in a variety of ongoing research projects and receive training in focused clinical interventions. In addition, the Boston area is fortunate to have a number of nationally known hospitals, counseling centers, and community mental health centers directly affiliated with our clinical program where students have opportunities to gain experience in a variety of clinical settings with different client populations. The New England Regional Primate Center, which is supported by the National Institutes of Health, is also available to Boston University faculty and students.

Information for Students With Physical Disabilities: Disabled Student Services provides optional support for more than 700 students with disabilities, faculty, and staff, including people with ambulatory, sight, hearing, and speech impairments, learning disabilities, and medical conditions such as diabetes and hypoglycemia. A booklet outlining services is available in print and in alternative formats.

Application Information:
Send to: Graduate School of Arts and Sciences, 705 Commonwealth Ave., Boston, MA 02215. Students are admitted in the Fall, application deadline 12/15; 1/15. Applicants for the MA-only program are reviewed in two rounds. The first deadline for completed applications is March 1st. The second deadline for completed applications is June 1. *Fee:* $60.

Boston University (2001 data)
Division of Religious and Theological Studies
745 Commonwealth Avenue
Boston, MA 02215
Telephone: (617) 353-3047
Fax: (617) 353-5539
E-mail: *crschlau@bu.edu*
Web: *http://www.bu.edu/religion/grad.html*

Department Established:
Chairperson: Chris Schlauch. Number of Faculty: total–full-time 2, part-time 4; women–full-time 1, part-time 2.

Programs and Degrees Offered:
Listed in the following order: Program area, degree type (T if terminal Master's), number awarded 7/00-6/01. Counseling pscyh & religion PhD 1.

Student Applications/Admissions:
Student Applications

Counseling pscyh & religion PhD—Applications 2001–2002, 6. Total applicants accepted 2001–2002, 2. Total enrolled 2001–2002 full-time, 5, part-time, 2. Openings 2002–2003, 3. The Median number of years required for completion of a degree are 6. The number of students enrolled full and part-time, who were dismissed or voluntarily withdrew from this program area were 0.

Admissions Requirements:

Scores: Entries appear in this order: required test or GPA, minimum score (if required), median score of students entering in 2001–2002. Doctoral Programs: GRE-V+Q+Analytical 1850; MAT 55.

Other Criteria: (importance of criteria rated low, medium, or high): GRE/MAT scores high, work experience medium, GPA high, letters of recommendation high, interview high, statement of goals and objectives high, M.A. in psych or rel stud high.

Student Characteristics: The following represents characteristics of students in 2001–2002 in all graduate psychology programs in the department: Female–full-time 2, part-time 0; Male–full-time 0, part-time 0; African American/Black–full-time 0, part-time 0; Hispanic/Latino (a)–full-time 0, part-time 0; Asian/Pacific Islander–full-time 1, part-time 0; American Indian/Alaska Native–full-time 0, part-time 0.

Financial Information/Assistance:
Tuition for Full-Time Study: No information provided.

Financial Assistance:

First Year Students: No information provided.
Advanced Students: No information provided.
Contact Information: Of all students currently enrolled full-time, 80% benefitted from one or more of the listed financial assistance programs. For information on financial assistance, contact: Dr. Chris Schlauch, Chair (crschlau@bu.edu).

Internships/Practica: A 2-year, 20-hour per week, 11-month clinical internship at the Danielsen Institute with a $6000 stipend is available and tuition remission for two courses. In the second year, fellows spend eight hours at CARD (the Center for Anxiety and Related Disorders) at Boston University. For those doctoral students for whom a professional internship is required prior to graduation, 1 applied in 2000–2001. Of those who applied, 1 were placed in internships listed by the Association of Psychology Postdoctoral and Internship Programs (APPIC); 1 were placed in APA accredited internships.

Housing and Day Care: No on-campus housing and day care facilities are available.

Employment of Department Graduates:
Master's Degree Graduates: Of those who graduated in the academic year 2000–2001, the following categories and numbers represent the post-graduate activities and employment of master's degree graduates: Enrolled in a post-doctoral residency/fellowship (n/a), employed in independent practice (n/a).

Doctoral Degree Graduates: Of those who graduated in the academic year 2000–2001, the following categories and numbers represent the post-graduate activities and employment of doctoral degree graduates: Enrolled in a psychology doctoral program (n/a), enrolled in another graduate/professional program (n/a).

Additional Information:
Orientation, Objectives, and Emphasis of Department: Counseling Psychology and Religion (CPAR) is a multidisciplinary doctoral program committed to training professional psychologists. What makes CPAR unique is our requirement that students complete prior graduate study in religious and/or theological studies. Graduates of our program are equipped to practice professional psychology with sensitivity to systems of meaning, value, and belief. Following a scholar-practitioner model of training, we prepare students for positions as professors as well as clinicians. Students take courses in counseling psychology, religious and theological studies, and in ways of coordinating research and scholarship across these disciplines. We also require a two-year part-time clinical practicum and a full-time (or equivalent) internship. Dissertation research draws from multidisciplinary contributions and is carried out according to empirical methods and designs.

Special Facilities or Resources: A CPAR research seminar with guest adjunct faculty member Dr. Kenneth Pargament, a distinguished researcher in the psychology of religion, is required for all students.

Information for Students With Physical Disabilities: The department will accommodate for physical disabilities as deemed necessary. Classes are held in buildings accessible to those with disabilities; the practicum site (the Danielsen Institute) has handicapped access as well.

Application Information:
Send to: Division of Religious and Theological Studies, 745 Commonwealth Ave., Boston, MA 02215. Students are admitted in the Fall, application deadline February 1. *Fee:* $50.

Brandeis University

Department of Psychology
415 South Street, Mail Stop 62
Waltham, MA 02454-9110
Telephone: (781) 736-3300
Fax: (781) 736-3291
E-mail: mcdonough@brandeis.edu
Web: http://www.brandeis.edu/departments/psych

Department Established:

1948. Chairperson: Joseph Cunningham. Number of Faculty: total–full-time 19, part-time 3; women–full-time 4, part-time 2.

Programs and Degrees Offered:

Listed in the following order: Program area, degree type (T if terminal Master's), number awarded 7/00-6/01. Cognitive neuroscience PhD 1, general MA (T) 4, social/developmental PhD 1.

Student Applications/Admissions:

Student Applications

Cognitive neuroscience PhD—Applications 2001–2002, 16. Total applicants accepted 2001–2002, 6. New applicants enrolled 2001–2002, 2. Total enrolled 2001–2002 full-time, 7. Openings 2002–2003, 3. The Median number of years required for completion of a degree are 5. The number of students enrolled full and part-time, who were dismissed or voluntarily withdrew from this program area were 0. *General MA*—Applications 2001–2002, 25. Total applicants accepted 2001–2002, 9. New applicants enrolled 2001–2002, 4. Total enrolled 2001–2002 full-time, 4, part-time. Openings 2002–2003, 8. The Median number of years required for completion of a degree is 1. *Social/developmental PhD*—Applications 2001–2002, 28. Total applicants accepted 2001–2002, 9. New applicants enrolled 2001–2002, 3. Total enrolled 2001–2002 full-time, 14. Openings 2002–2003, 3. The Median number of years required for completion of a degree are 6.

Admissions Requirements:

Scores: Entries appear in this order: required test or GPA, minimum score (if required), median score of students entering in 2001–2002. Master's Programs: GRE-V no minimum stated, 630; GRE-Q no minimum stated, 690; GRE-Analytical no minimum stated, 700; overall undergraduate GPA no minimum stated, 3.5. Doctoral Programs: GRE-V no minimum stated, 530; GRE-Q no minimum stated, 770; GRE-Analytical no minimum stated, 570; GRE-Subject(Psych) no minimum stated, 660; overall undergraduate GPA no minimum stated, 3.5 ; last 2 years GPA no minimum stated; psychology GPA no minimum stated; psychology GPA no minimum stated.

Other Criteria: (importance of criteria rated low, medium, or high): GRE/MAT scores high, research experience high, work experience medium, extracurricular activity low, clinically related public service low, GPA high, letters of recommendation high, interview high, statement of goals and objectives high.

Student Characteristics: The following represents characteristics of students in 2001–2002 in all graduate psychology programs in the department: Female–full-time 18, part-time 0; Male–full-time 7, part-time 0; African American/Black–full-time 1, part-time 0; Hispanic/Latino (a)–full-time 2, part-time 0; Asian/Pacific Is-

lander–full-time 5, part-time 0; American Indian/Alaska Native–full-time 0, part-time 0.

Financial Information/Assistance:

Tuition for Full-Time Study: *Master's:* State residents per academic year $26,281; nonstate residents: per academic year $26,281. *Doctoral:* State residents: per academic year $26,281; nonstate residents: per academic year $26,281.

Financial Assistance:

First Year Students: Research assistantships available for first-year. Fellowships and scholarships available for first-year. Average amount paid per academic year: $16,000. Average number of hours worked per week: 15. Apply by January 15. Tuition remission given: full.

Advanced Students: Fellowships and scholarships available for advanced students. Average amount paid per academic year: $16,000. Average number of hours worked per week: 15. Tuition remission given: full.

Contact Information: Of all students currently enrolled full-time, 80% benefitted from one or more of the listed financial assistance programs. For information on financial assistance, contact: Peggy Higgins, Graduate School, MS 31, Brandeis University, Waltham, MA 02454-9110; email phiggins@brandeis.edu.

Internships/Practica: No information provided.

Housing and Day Care: On-campus housing and day care facilities are available.

Employment of Department Graduates:

Master's Degree Graduates: Of those who graduated in the academic year 2000–2001, the following categories and numbers represent the post-graduate activities and employment of master's degree graduates: Enrolled in a post-doctoral residency/fellowship (n/a), employed in independent practice (n/a), employed in other positions at a higher education institution (1), employed in a community mental health/counseling center (1), other employment position (2).

Doctoral Degree Graduates: Of those who graduated in the academic year 2000–2001, the following categories and numbers represent the post-graduate activities and employment of doctoral degree graduates: Enrolled in a psychology doctoral program (n/a), enrolled in another graduate/professional program (n/a), employed in an academic position at a 2-year/4-year college (1), employed in other positions at a higher education institution (2).

Additional Information:

Orientation, Objectives, and Emphasis of Department: The goal of the Ph.D. Program is to develop excellent researchers and teachers who will become leaders in psychological science. From the start of graduate study, research activity is emphasized. The program helps students develop an area of research specialization, and gives them opportunities to work in one of two general areas: social/developmental psychology or cognitive neuroscience. In both areas, dissertation supervisors are leaders in the following areas: motor control, visual perception, taste physiology and psychophysics, memory, learning, aggression, emotion, personality and cognition in adulthood and old age, social relations and health, stereotypes, and nonverbal communication.

Special Facilities or Resources: Extensive experimental psychology laboratories are equipped for research on language, cognition, visual psychophysics, visual perception, motor control, and spatial orientation, including a NASA-sponsored laboratory for research on space-motion sickness and human spatial orientation in unusual environments. New social and developmental psychology laboratories include one-way observation rooms and videorecording apparatus. Child development research is facilitated by cooperative relations with the Lemberg Children's Center on the Brandeis campus; applied social research is facilitated by cooperative relations with the Brandeis University Florence Heller Graduate School for Advanced Studies in Social Welfare. Training and research in aging is carried out under a training grant on "Cognitive Aging in a Social Context." The psychology department also participates in an interdisciplinary neuroscience program at the Volen Center for the study of complex systems.

Application Information:
Send to: Graduate School of Arts & Sciences, MS 31, Brandeis University, Waltham, MA 02454-9110. Students are admitted in the Fall, application deadline January 15. Ph.D. Fall Deadline is January 15. Master Fall Deadline is June 1st. Brandeis offers 3 ways to obtain an application: 1. Request a hard copy application be sent to you by mail, 2. Download & print out an application from our website, 3. Fill out our on-line application & submit electronically. Website address: http://www.brandeis.edu/gsas/apply/index.html. *Fee:* $60. The Application Fee for applications submitted by mail is $60.00. The application fee for applications completed on-line and submitted electronically is $50.00.

Clark University

Frances L. Hiatt School of Psychology
950 Main Street
Worcester, MA 01610
Telephone: (508) 793-7274
Fax: (508) 793-7265
E-mail: *jvalsiner@clarku.edu*
Web: *http://www.clarku.edu/~psydept/*

Department Established:
1889. Chairperson: Jaan Valsiner, Ph.D. Number of Faculty: total–full-time 15, part-time 10; women–full-time 6, part-time 3.

Programs and Degrees Offered:
Listed in the following order: Program area, degree type (T if terminal Master's), number awarded 7/00-6/01. Clinical PhD 7, developmental PhD 3, social PhD 3.

APA Accreditation: Clinical PhD: full.

Student Applications/Admissions:
Student Applications
Clinical PhD—Applications 2001–2002, 127. Total applicants accepted 2001–2002, 19. New applicants enrolled 2001–2002, 4. Total enrolled 2001–2002 full-time, 33. Openings 2002–2003, 6. The Median number of years required for completion of a degree are 7. The number of students enrolled full and part-time, who were dismissed or voluntarily withdrew from this program area were 0. *Developmental PhD*—Applications 2001–2002, 15. Total applicants accepted 2001–2002, 5. New applicants enrolled 2001–2002, 1. Total enrolled 2001–2002

full-time, 12. Openings 2002–2003, 6. The Median number of years required for completion of a degree are 6. The number of students enrolled full and part-time, who were dismissed or voluntarily withdrew from this program area were 0. *Social PhD*—Applications 2001–2002, 19. Total applicants accepted 2001–2002, 3. Total enrolled 2001–2002 full-time, 2. Openings 2002–2003, 6. The Median number of years required for completion of a degree are 8.

Admissions Requirements:
Scores: Entries appear in this order: required test or GPA, minimum score (if required), median score of students entering in 2001–2002. Doctoral Programs: GRE-V no minimum stated, 574; GRE-Q no minimum stated, 602; GRE-V+Q no minimum stated, 1176; overall undergraduate GPA no minimum stated, 3.64; last 2 years GPA no minimum stated; psychology GPA no minimum stated; psychology GPA no minimum stated.

Other Criteria: (importance of criteria rated low, medium, or high): GRE/MAT scores medium, research experience high, work experience medium, extracurricular activity medium, clinically related public service medium, GPA medium, letters of recommendation high, statement of goals and objectives high.

Student Characteristics: The following represents characteristics of students in 2001–2002 in all graduate psychology programs in the department: Female–full-time 39, part-time 0; Male–full-time 9, part-time 0; African American/Black–full-time 0, part-time 0; Hispanic/Latino (a)–full-time 1, part-time 0; Asian/Pacific Islander–full-time 2, part-time 0; American Indian/Alaska Native–full-time 0, part-time 0; Multi-ethnic–full-time 1.

Financial Information/Assistance:
Tuition for Full-Time Study: *Doctoral:* State residents: per academic year $24,400; nonstate residents: per academic year $24,400.

Financial Assistance:
First Year Students: Teaching assistantships available for first-year. Average amount paid per academic year: $10,900. Average number of hours worked per week: 17. Tuition remission given: full. Research assistantships available for first-year. Average amount paid per academic year: $10,900. Average number of hours worked per week: 17. Tuition remission given: full. Fellowships and scholarships available for first-year. Average amount paid per academic year: $12,500. Average number of hours worked per week: 0. Tuition remission given: full.

Advanced Students: Teaching assistantships available for advanced students. Average amount paid per academic year: $12,900. Average number of hours worked per week: 17. Tuition remission given: full. Research assistantships available for advanced students. Average amount paid per academic year: $12,900. Average number of hours worked per week: 17. Tuition remission given: full. Fellowships and scholarships available for advanced students. Average amount paid per academic year: $12,900. Average number of hours worked per week: 0. Tuition remission given: full.

Contact Information: Of all students currently enrolled full-time, 100% benefitted from one or more of the listed financial assistance programs.

Internships/Practica: Doctoral students in clinical psychology enroll in a supervised practicum each year. These practica involve college students, children, couples, and families. In the 3rd year, practicum sites are individually arranged to provide experience in the student's special area of interest. These sites have included state mental institutions, VA neuropsychological units, residential child treatment facilities, etc. Doctoral clinical students also take one full-time year of internship training in APA accredited agencies around the country. For those doctoral students for whom a professional internship is required prior to graduation, 3 applied in 2000–2001. Of those who applied, 3 were placed in internships listed by the Association of Psychology Postdoctoral and Internship Programs (APPIC); 3 were placed in APA accredited internships.

Housing and Day Care: On-campus housing and day care facilities are available.

Employment of Department Graduates:

Master's Degree Graduates: Of those who graduated in the academic year 2000–2001, the following categories and numbers represent the post-graduate activities and employment of master's degree graduates: Enrolled in a post-doctoral residency/fellowship (n/a), employed in independent practice (n/a).

Doctoral Degree Graduates: Of those who graduated in the academic year 2000–2001, the following categories and numbers represent the post-graduate activities and employment of doctoral degree graduates: Enrolled in a psychology doctoral program (n/a), enrolled in another graduate/professional program (n/a), enrolled in a post-doctoral residency/fellowship (2), employed in an academic position at a university (1), employed in an academic position at a 2-year/4-year college (1), employed in other positions at a higher education institution (1), employed in business or industry (research/consulting) (1), employed in a community mental health/counseling center (1), still seeking employment (1).

Additional Information:

Orientation, Objectives, and Emphasis of Department: The Department's philosophy affirms the unity of psychology as a subject matter and discourages rigid distinctions among kinds of psychologists and kinds of department programs. Nonetheless, the Department provides in-depth training in the student's area of specialization with a primary concern for theory development, conceptual analysis, and empirical investigation. A diversity of theoretical viewpoints is represented, including various developmental viewpoints. Students become acquainted with a variety of methods of investigation, not only with traditional experimental and naturalistic methods, but also with phenomenological, structural, hermeneutic, and other qualitative methodologies. Each student's program is individualized to some degree, and education takes place through small seminars, one-to-one research, practicum training, individualized papers, and MA thesis and PhD dissertation work. Research and other scholarly work are strongly encouraged throughout the graduate experience.

Special Facilities or Resources: The Psychology Department possesses ample space, two entire floors and substantial parts of two others, most of it recently renovated, for offices, classes, laboratories, and clinical training. These include a child study area, facilities for studying family interactions, a human physiology laboratory, a personality-social research area, and dyadic and group

clinical training facilities, all with one-way vision and recording facilities, as well as a chemosensory laboratory. The Heinz Werner Institute for Developmental Analysis functions in close connection with the Department. Additional opportunities for research exist in connection with the University of Massachusetts Medical School, the Worcester Foundation for Experimental Biology, schools, and other community settings. Clinical practicum settings include various area agencies.

Information for Students With Physical Disabilities: The Tamara Dembo Scholarship, which pays a stipend of $9,600 and offers tuition remission, is available selectively to accepted students with physical disabilities.

Application Information:
Send to: Graduate Admissions Secretary Frances L. Hiatt, School of Psychology, Clark University, 950 Main Street, Worcester, MA 01610. Students are admitted in the Fall, application deadline January 15. *Fee:* $40. Fees waived in cases of financial need.

Harvard University
Department of Psychology
33 Kirkland Street
Cambridge, MA 02138
Telephone: (617) 495-3800
E-mail: *psyinfo@wjh.harvard.edu*
Web: *http://www.wjh.harvard.edu/psych/grad_main.html*

Department Established:
1936. Chairperson: Daniel Schacter. Number of Faculty: total–full-time 24, part-time 12; women–full-time 10, part-time 2; minority–full-time 1.

Programs and Degrees Offered:
Listed in the following order: Program area, degree type (T if terminal Master's), number awarded 7/00-6/01. Clinical psychology PhD, cognition, brain, and behavior PhD 3, developmental PhD 4, experimental psychopathology PhD 4, organizational behavior PhD 3, social PhD 3.

Student Applications/Admissions:
Student Applications

Clinical psychology PhD—Applications 2001–2002, 70. Total applicants accepted 2001–2002, 6. New applicants enrolled 2001–2002, 3. Total enrolled 2001–2002 full-time, 5. Openings 2002–2003, 3. The number of students enrolled full and part-time, who were dismissed or voluntarily withdrew from this program area were 0. *Cognition, brain, and behavior PhD*—Applications 2001–2002, 76. Total applicants accepted 2001–2002, 7. New applicants enrolled 2001–2002, 4. Total enrolled 2001–2002 full-time, 26. Openings 2002–2003, 4. The Median number of years required for completion of a degree are 6. The number of students enrolled full and part-time, who were dismissed or voluntarily withdrew from this program area were 0. *Developmental PhD*—Applications 2001–2002, 35. Total applicants accepted 2001–2002, 8. New applicants enrolled 2001–2002, 5. Total enrolled 2001–2002 full-time, 9. Openings 2002–2003, 4. The Median number of years required for completion of a degree are 6. *Experimental psychopathology*

PhD—Applications 2001–2002, 70. Total applicants accepted 2001–2002, 6. New applicants enrolled 2001–2002, 5. Total enrolled 2001–2002 full-time, 12. Openings 2002–2003, 4. The Median number of years required for completion of a degree are 8. The number of students enrolled full and part-time, who were dismissed or voluntarily withdrew from this program area were 1. *Organizational behavior PhD*—New applicants enrolled 2001–2002, 1. Total enrolled 2001–2002 full-time, 10. Openings 2002–2003, 1. The number of students enrolled full and part-time, who were dismissed or voluntarily withdrew from this program area were 0. *Social PhD*—Applications 2001–2002, 64. Total applicants accepted 2001–2002, 5. New applicants enrolled 2001–2002, 3. Total enrolled 2001–2002 full-time, 19. Openings 2002–2003, 4. The Median number of years required for completion of a degree are 6. The number of students enrolled full and part-time, who were dismissed or voluntarily withdrew from this program area were 0.

Admissions Requirements:

Scores: Entries appear in this order: required test or GPA, minimum score (if required), median score of students entering in 2001–2002. Doctoral Programs: GRE-V no minimum stated; GRE-Q no minimum stated; GRE-V+Q no minimum stated, 1390; GRE-Analytical no minimum stated; last 2 years GPA no minimum stated; psychology GPA no minimum stated; psychology GPA no minimum stated. TOEFL exam with minimum score of 550 required for foreign applicants.

Other Criteria: (importance of criteria rated low, medium, or high): GRE/MAT scores high, research experience high, work experience medium, extracurricular activity low, clinically related public service medium, GPA high, letters of recommendation high, interview medium, statement of goals and objectives high, fit high.

Student Characteristics: The following represents characteristics of students in 2001–2002 in all graduate psychology programs in the department: Female–full-time 57, part-time 0; Male–full-time 26, part-time 0; African American/Black–full-time 3, part-time 0; Hispanic/Latino (a)–full-time 4, part-time 0; Asian/Pacific Islander–full-time 3, part-time 0; American Indian/Alaska Native–full-time 10, part-time 0.

Financial Information/Assistance:

Tuition for Full-Time Study: *Doctoral:* State residents: per academic year $24,854; nonstate residents: per academic year $24,854.

Financial Assistance:

First Year Students: Research assistantships available for first-year. Fellowships and scholarships available for first-year. Average amount paid per academic year: $16,200. Apply by Dec. 30. Tuition remission given: full.

Advanced Students: Teaching assistantships available for advanced students. Average amount paid per academic year: $15,720. Average number of hours worked per week: 20. Apply by May 30. Research assistantships available for advanced students.

Contact Information: Of all students currently enrolled full-time, 90% benefitted from one or more of the listed financial assistance programs. For information on financial assistance, contact: Admissions and Financial Aid Office, Graduate School of Arts and Sciences, 8 Garden St., Cambridge, MA 02138; (617) 495-5396.

Internships/Practica: Students in the clinical track will have pre-doctoral practicum placements in a local Harvard-affiliated hospital. Clinical track students are expected to complete their thesis projects before taking on a clinical internship.

Housing and Day Care: On-campus housing and day care facilities are available.

Employment of Department Graduates:

Master's Degree Graduates: Of those who graduated in the academic year 2000–2001, the following categories and numbers represent the post-graduate activities and employment of master's degree graduates: Enrolled in a post-doctoral residency/fellowship (n/a), employed in independent practice (n/a).

Doctoral Degree Graduates: Of those who graduated in the academic year 2000–2001, the following categories and numbers represent the post-graduate activities and employment of doctoral degree graduates: Enrolled in a psychology doctoral program (n/a), enrolled in another graduate/professional program (n/a), enrolled in a post-doctoral residency/fellowship (9), employed in independent practice (0), employed in an academic position at a university (2), employed in other positions at a higher education institution (1), employed in business or industry (research/consulting) (1), employed in a hospital/medical center (1).

Additional Information:

Orientation, Objectives, and Emphasis of Department: The psychology department offers PhDs in psychology and social psychology. In conjunction with the Harvard Business School, there is also a PhD program in organizational behavior. The psychology department is divided into a social psychology program, a cognition, brain, and behavior program, and research and training groups in developmental psychology, experimental psychopathology, including a clinical track. The aim of the program is to train students for careers in psychological research and teaching. These careers are mainly in academia. The emphasis of the program is heavily on research training; in addition to a small number of required courses, students do a first-year research project, a second-year research project, and the doctoral dissertation. Students take a major examination or intense seminar(s) in their major specialty fields. Since most students prepare for academic careers, there is ample opportunity to serve as teaching fellows.

Special Facilities or Resources: The department is well equipped with facilities for conducting research. Faculty are the recipients of many grants in various areas of psychology, and graduate students play an essential role in the conduct of most of this research. William James Hall houses a well-staffed computer lab to serve faculty and students. The building also houses a psychology research library. Students are given offices, the use of laboratory space, and a sum of money for research support. The department encourages interdisciplinary study, and students have the benefit of taking courses and working with the faculty at other Harvard graduate schools (Education, Medical School, Public Health, etc.), and at MIT. The Cambridge and Boston areas are well endowed with research facilities and hospitals that offer resources, such as MRI equipment, to students.

Information for Students With Physical Disabilities: Most campus buildings, including William James Hall, are handicapped accessible. The university maintains an adaptive technology lab with specialized computer equipment, and there is an office for disabled students.

Application Information:
Send to: Admissions Office, Graduate School of Arts and Sciences, Byerly Hall, 8 Garden Street, Cambridge, MA 02138. Students are admitted in the Fall, application deadline December 30. Dec. 14 deadline for Organizational Behavior. *Fee:* $70.

Lesley University
Division of Counseling and Psychology
29 Everett Street
Cambridge, MA 02138-2790
Telephone: (617) 349-8370
Fax: (617) 349-8333
E-mail: *lhoshman@mail.lesley.edu*
Web: *http://www.lesley.edu/gsass/30cpp.html*

Department Established:
1975. Division Director: Lisa Hoshmand, Ph.D. Number of Faculty: total–full-time 8, part-time 40; women–full-time 5, part-time 26; minority–full-time 3, part-time 5.

Programs and Degrees Offered:
Listed in the following order: Program area, degree type (T if terminal Master's), number awarded 7/00-6/01. Clinical mental health counsel MA (T) 45, couns psych-prof counseling MA (T) 20, counseling and psychology MA 20, counseling psychology-school MA (T) 8.

Student Applications/Admissions:
Student Applications
Clinical mental health counsel MA—Openings 2002–2003, 50. The Median number of years required for completion of a degree are 4. Couns psych-prof counseling MA—Openings 2002–2003, 30. The Median number of years required for completion of a degree are 4. Counseling and psychology MA—Openings 2002–2003, 30. The Median number of years required for completion of a degree are 3. Counseling psychology-school MA—Openings 2002–2003, 15. The Median number of years required for completion of a degree are 3.

Admissions Requirements:
Scores: Entries appear in this order: required test or GPA, minimum score (if required), median score of students entering in 2001–2002. Master's Programs: MAT 40, 47; overall undergraduate GPA 3.0, 3.2. Doctoral Programs: last 2 years GPA no minimum stated; psychology GPA no minimum stated; psychology GPA no minimum stated.
Other Criteria: (importance of criteria rated low, medium, or high): GRE/MAT scores medium, research experience low, work experience medium, extracurricular activity medium, clinically related public service high, GPA high, letters of recommendation high, interview high, statement of goals and objectives high, writing ability medium. Admissions review is holistically based. All elements are given full consideration.

Student Characteristics: The following represents characteristics of students in 2001–2002 in all graduate psychology programs in the department: Female–full-time 0, part-time 0; Male–full-time 0, part-time 0; African American/Black–full-time 0, part-time 0; Hispanic/Latino (a)–full-time 0, part-time 0; Asian/Pacific Islander–full-time 0, part-time 0; American Indian/Alaska Native–full-time 0, part-time 0.

Financial Information/Assistance:
Tuition for Full-Time Study: *Master's:* State residents $495 per credit hour; nonstate residents: $495 per credit hour.

Financial Assistance:
First Year Students: Research assistantships available for first-year. Average amount paid per academic year: $3,000. Average number of hours worked per week: 10. Apply by 6/30.
Advanced Students: Research assistantships available for advanced students. Average amount paid per academic year: $3,000. Average number of hours worked per week: 10. Apply by 6/30.
Contact Information: For information on financial assistance, contact: Financial Aid Office, Lesley University, 29 Everett Street, Cambridge, MA 02138-2790.

Internships/Practica: Field-based training is a vital component of the Counseling and Psychology programs. These experiences offer a way for students to verify, clarify, and challenge the theory acquired in the classroom as well as examine their own role as a clinician. The Field Training Office works closely with several hundred placement sites nationwide to ensure students diverse and personalized learning experiences that provide closely supervised opportunities to do counseling and consultative work with individuals, groups, and families. Students choose sites that fit their professional interests, and their own schedules and locations. Students are required to complete 100 hours of practicum and 600 hours of internship. Some programs require additional 600 hours of internship. Students receive group supervision in the year-long seminar Clinical Practice and Supervision. Most placements are contracted with schools and agencies on a volunteer basis.

Housing and Day Care: No on-campus housing and day care facilities are available.

Employment of Department Graduates:
Master's Degree Graduates: Of those who graduated in the academic year 2000–2001, the following categories and numbers represent the post-graduate activities and employment of master's degree graduates: Enrolled in a post-doctoral residency/fellowship (n/a), employed in independent practice (n/a).
Doctoral Degree Graduates: Of those who graduated in the academic year 2000–2001, the following categories and numbers represent the post-graduate activities and employment of doctoral degree graduates: Enrolled in a psychology doctoral program (n/a), enrolled in another graduate/professional program (n/a).

Additional Information:
Orientation, Objectives, and Emphasis of Department: The counseling and psychology degree programs prepare professionals in the fields of counseling and psychology at the master's and CAGS levels. The Master of Arts in Clinical Mental Health Counseling program is a 60-credit option for those wishing the

319

most comprehensive clinical training available at the master's level to support clinical mental health counseling practice and to pursue professional licensure in most states. Within the clinical mental health counseling program, a student has the option of specializing in holistic studies, expressive therapies, and school and community counseling (licensure options in either school guidance or school adjustment counseling). The Master of Arts in Counseling Psychology degree program is a 48-credit option. Within this program a school counseling specialization leads to guidance counselor licensure. The Master of Arts in Counseling Psychology, Professional Counseling Specialization program is a 60-credit option for those who have some clinical experience and wish to gain comprehensive clinical training at the master's level to support clinical mental health counseling practice and to pursue professional licensure in most states. All programs integrate theory and practice through course-based learning and field training. The self of the clinician as an instrument of change is a primary focus as is the understanding of the impact of power, privilege, and oppression in all our lives. Graduates are prepared for clinical positions in mental health and school settings. Graduates are prepared for clinical positions, or may elect to use the program to support further graduate work at the doctoral level.

Special Facilities or Resources: Counseling Psychology students have available to them all of the general resource facilities of Lesley University, such as the university library (including a testing center), computer facilities, the Kresge Student Center, and the Career Resource Center. In addition, the department has its own resource center, where bulletins announce area resources and opportunities for further professional study both locally and nationally. Additionally, audio- and videotape equipment is available to degree students for special projects.

Information for Students With Physical Disabilities: Lesley University is committed to ensuring the full participation of all students in its program. Students with documented disabilities are urged to request reasonable accommodation by consulting the Office of Disability Services.

Application Information:
Send to: Office of Graduate Admissions, Lesley University, 29 Everett Street, Cambridge, MA 02138-2790. Students are admitted in the Fall, application deadline revolving; Spring, application deadline revolving. *Fee:* $50.

Massachusetts School of Professional Psychology
Professional School
221 Rivermoor Street
Boston, MA 02132
Telephone: (617) 327-6777
Fax: (617) 327-4447
E-mail: *admissions@mspp.edu*
Web: *http://www.mspp.edu*

Department Established:
1974. President: Bruce J. Weiss. Number of Faculty: total–part-time 34.

Programs and Degrees Offered:
Listed in the following order: Program area, degree type (T if terminal Master's), number awarded 7/00-6/01. Clinical PsyD 36, Respecialization Diploma 1.

APA Accreditation: Clinical PsyD: full.

Student Applications/Admissions:
Student Applications
Clinical PsyD—Applications 2001–2002, 182. Total applicants accepted 2001–2002, 78. New applicants enrolled 2001–2002, 40. Total enrolled 2001–2002 full-time, 119, part-time, 36. Openings 2002–2003, 35. The Median number of years required for completion of a degree are 4. The number of students enrolled full and part-time, who were dismissed or voluntarily withdrew from this program area were 1. *Respecialization Diploma*—Applications 2001–2002, 3. Total applicants accepted 2001–2002, 3. New applicants enrolled 2001–2002, 1. Total enrolled 2001–2002 full-time, 1. The Median number of years required for completion of a degree are 3. The number of students enrolled full and part-time, who were dismissed or voluntarily withdrew from this program area were 0.

Admissions Requirements:
Scores: Entries appear in this order: required test or GPA, minimum score (if required), median score of students entering in 2001–2002. Doctoral Programs: GRE-V no minimum stated, 550; GRE-Q no minimum stated, 600; GRE-V+Q 1150; overall undergraduate GPA 3.00; last 2 years GPA 3.00; psychology GPA 3.00.
Other Criteria: (importance of criteria rated low, medium, or high): GRE/MAT scores medium, research experience low, work experience medium, extracurricular activity high, clinically related public service high, GPA high, letters of recommendation high, interview high, statement of goals and objectives high, autobiography high.

Student Characteristics: The following represents characteristics of students in 2001–2002 in all graduate psychology programs in the department: Female–full-time 22, part-time 1; Male–full-time 7, part-time 0; African American/Black–full-time 1, part-time 0; Hispanic/Latino (a)–full-time 0, part-time 0; Asian/Pacific Islander–full-time 2, part-time 0; American Indian/Alaska Native–full-time 1, part-time 0.

Financial Information/Assistance:
Tuition for Full-Time Study: *Doctoral:* State residents: per academic year $20,256, $633 per credit hour; nonstate residents: per academic year $20,256, $633 per credit hour.

Financial Assistance:
First Year Students: No information provided.
Advanced Students: No information provided.
Contact Information: Of all students currently enrolled full-time, 0% benefitted from one or more of the listed financial assistance programs. For information on financial assistance, contact: Eileen Healy, Financial Aid Office.

Internships/Practica: Field placements are an integral part of the program throughout the four years. The practica and internship experiences are integrated with the curriculum and individual's educational needs at each level of the program. Over 150 training sites are available in the greater Boston area including hospitals, mental health centers, court clinics, and other agencies offering mental health services. They provide students the opportunity to work with varied populations, life span issues, theoretical orientations, and treatment modalities in the context of supervised training. The large number of qualified agencies included in our training network enable students the option of applying for full or half-time APA-approved internships or securing suitable, high quality, local internships.

Housing and Day Care: No on-campus housing and day care facilities are available.

Employment of Department Graduates:

Master's Degree Graduates: Of those who graduated in the academic year 2000–2001, the following categories and numbers represent the post-graduate activities and employment of master's degree graduates: Enrolled in a post-doctoral residency/fellowship (n/a), employed in independent practice (n/a).

Doctoral Degree Graduates: Of those who graduated in the academic year 2000–2001, the following categories and numbers represent the post-graduate activities and employment of doctoral degree graduates: Enrolled in a psychology doctoral program (n/a), enrolled in another graduate/professional program (n/a).

Additional Information:

Orientation, Objectives, and Emphasis of Department: The mission is to improve the quality of life by educating psychology practitioners to be capable of providing high quality human services. Graduates should be able to help evaluate, ameliorate, and prevent psychosocial problems; help individuals, families, groups, organizations, and communities function effectively; exhibit competence in the practical application of existing psychosocial knowledge and an awareness of the possibility of extending this knowledge; and develop new professional roles, service models, and delivery systems capable of meeting the changing needs of society. The educational philosophy is evident in several characteristics that distinguish it from the traditional PhD program. Course content is presented as a foundation for professional practice rather than as scientific inquiry. This entails more of a difference in course objectives and emphasis than in content. Curriculum stresses seminars integrated with field placements, focusing on helping students to coordinate theory with skills and the development of insights useful in the practice of psychology. Courses are taught by psychologists experienced in the application of knowledge in their teaching areas. The first two years of the program provide students with a solid generic foundation for psychological practice; third and fourth years allow for concentration in areas of individual interest.

Application Information:
Send to: Admissions Office. Students are admitted in the Fall, application deadline January 10. Respecialization Diploma-Rolling Admissions. *Fee:* $50.

Massachusetts, University of
Department of Psychology
Tobin Hall
Amherst, MA 01003
Telephone: (413) 545-2383
Fax: (413) 545-0996
E-mail: *daehler@psych.umass.edu*
Web: *http://www.umass.edu/psychology*

Department Established:

1947. Chairperson: Melinda Novak. Number of Faculty: total–full-time 45, part-time 5; women–full-time 16, part-time 4.

Programs and Degrees Offered:

Listed in the following order: Program area, degree type (T if terminal Master's), number awarded 7/00-6/01. Clinical PhD 3, cognitive PhD 2, developmental PhD, educational PhD 2, learning-animal PhD 1, neuroscience and behavior MA (T), personality social PhD 2.

APA Accreditation: Clinical PhD: full.

Student Applications/Admissions:

Student Applications

Clinical PhD—Applications 2001–2002, 290. Total applicants accepted 2001–2002, 15. New applicants enrolled 2001–2002, 7. Total enrolled 2001–2002 full-time, 37. Openings 2002–2003, 8. The Median number of years required for completion of a degree are 5. *Cognitive PhD*—Applications 2001–2002, 29. Total applicants accepted 2001–2002, 8. New applicants enrolled 2001–2002, 3. Total enrolled 2001–2002 full-time, 11. Openings 2002–2003, 3. *Developmental PhD*—Applications 2001–2002, 21. Total applicants accepted 2001–2002, 4. New applicants enrolled 2001–2002, 1. Total enrolled 2001–2002 full-time, 12. Openings 2002–2003, 3. *Educational PhD*—Applications 2001–2002, 6. Total applicants accepted 2001–2002, 2. New applicants enrolled 2001–2002, 1. Total enrolled 2001–2002 full-time, 4. Openings 2002–2003, 1. *Learning-animal PhD*—Applications 2001–2002, 4. Total enrolled 2001–2002 full-time, 1. *Neuroscience and behavior MA*—Applications 2001–2002, 12. Total applicants accepted 2001–2002, 1. New applicants enrolled 2001–2002, 1. Total enrolled 2001–2002 full-time, 2. Openings 2002–2003, 2. *Personality social PhD*—Applications 2001–2002, 59. Total applicants accepted 2001–2002, 7. New applicants enrolled 2001–2002, 2. Total enrolled 2001–2002 full-time, 14. Openings 2002–2003, 3.

Admissions Requirements:

Scores: Entries appear in this order: required test or GPA, minimum score (if required), median score of students entering in 2001–2002. Doctoral Programs: GRE-V no minimum stated, 596; GRE-Q no minimum stated, 662; GRE-V+Q no minimum stated, 1258; GRE-Analytical no minimum stated, 640; overall undergraduate GPA no minimum stated, 3.79; last 2 years GPA no minimum stated; psychology GPA no minimum stated; psychology GPA no minimum stated.

Other Criteria: (importance of criteria rated low, medium, or high): GRE/MAT scores high, research experience high, work experience low, GPA high, letters of recommendation high, interview medium, statement of goals and objectives medium. Only clinical requires an interview. Clinically related public service also is a criteria (low) in admission to clinical.

Student Characteristics: The following represents characteristics of students in 2001–2002 in all graduate psychology programs in the department: Female–full-time 53, part-time 0; Male–full-time 25, part-time 0; African American/Black–full-time 2, part-time 0; Hispanic/Latino (a)–full-time 4, part-time 0; Asian/Pacific Islander–full-time 2, part-time 0; American Indian/Alaska Native–full-time 0, part-time 0; Multi-ethnic–full-time 0, part-time 0; students subject to the Americans with Disabilities Act–full-time 0, part-time 0.

Financial Information/Assistance:

Tuition for Full-Time Study: *Doctoral:* State residents: $110 per credit hour; nonstate residents: $415 per credit hour.

Financial Assistance:

First Year Students: Teaching assistantships available for first-year. Average amount paid per academic year: $10,700. Average number of hours worked per week: 20. Tuition remission given: full. Research assistantships available for first-year. Average amount paid per academic year: $12,000. Average number of hours worked per week: 20. Tuition remission given: full. Traineeships available for first-year. Average amount paid per academic year: $12,000. Average number of hours worked per week: 20. Tuition remission given: full. Fellowships and scholarships available for first-year. Average amount paid per academic year: $10,500. Average number of hours worked per week: 0. Tuition remission given: full.

Advanced Students: Teaching assistantships available for advanced students. Average amount paid per academic year: $10,951. Average number of hours worked per week: 20. Tuition remission given: full. Research assistantships available for advanced students. Average amount paid per academic year: $12,000. Average number of hours worked per week: 20. Tuition remission given: full. Traineeships available for advanced students. Average amount paid per academic year: $12,000. Average number of hours worked per week: 20. Tuition remission given: full. Fellowships and scholarships available for advanced students. Average amount paid per academic year: $10,500. Average number of hours worked per week: 0. Tuition remission given: full.

Contact Information: Of all students currently enrolled full-time, 100% benefitted from one or more of the listed financial assistance programs. For information on financial assistance, contact: Financial Aid Home Page: www.umass.edu/umfa.

Internships/Practica: Clinical students must complete an APA-approved clinical internship. None of these required internships are offered by our program. For those doctoral students for whom a professional internship is required prior to graduation, 6 applied in 2000–2001. Of those who applied, 6 were placed in APA accredited internships.

Housing and Day Care: No on-campus housing and day care facilities are available.

Employment of Department Graduates:

Master's Degree Graduates: Of those who graduated in the academic year 2000–2001, the following categories and numbers represent the post-graduate activities and employment of master's degree graduates: Enrolled in a post-doctoral residency/fellowship (n/a), employed in independent practice (n/a).

Doctoral Degree Graduates: Of those who graduated in the academic year 2000–2001, the following categories and numbers represent the post-graduate activities and employment of doctoral degree graduates: Enrolled in a psychology doctoral program (n/a), enrolled in another graduate/professional program (n/a).

Additional Information:

Orientation, Objectives, and Emphasis of Department: The psychology program is designed to develop research scholars, college teachers, and scientific/professional psychologists in the seven areas listed. Individual student programs combine basic courses and seminars in a variety of specialized areas, research experience, and practica in both on- and off-campus settings. Students may elect to minor in certain areas as well, including clinical, personality-social, quantitative methods, applied social research, neuroscience, and behavior. Students with applied interests, such as clinical, educational, developmental, and evaluation, have ample opportunity for in-depth practical experience.

Special Facilities or Resources: The Department has specialized laboratory facilities, including biochemistry, eyetracking, video data analysis, and other laboratories. It maintains its own clinic for research, clinical training, and service to the community. It provides students with access to microcomputers and to the VAX mainframes at University Computing Services. Departmental facilities and faculty are supplemented by the University's participation in Five-College programs (with Amherst, Hampshire, Mount Holyoke, and Smith Colleges) and by cooperation with other University departments including Computer and Information Science, Industrial Engineering, Education, Linguistics, Sociology, and Biology. The University of Massachusetts also offers a separate PhD degree-granting program in neuroscience and behavior. Many of the students in this program receive the bulk of their training in the Psychology Department and work primarily with Psychology faculty. Students interested in training in neuroscience and behavior should apply for admission directly to that program.

Application Information:

Send to: Graduate Admissions Office, Goodell Building, University of Massachusetts, Amherst, MA 01003. Students are admitted in the Fall, application deadline see below. January 2nd for Clinical; January 15th for Neuroscience & Behavior; February 1st for all others. *Fee:* $40. Application Fee can be waived if GRE fees were waived.

Massachusetts, University of, at Boston
Department of Psychology
College of Arts and Sciences
Harbor Campus
Boston, MA 02125-3393
Telephone: (617) 287-6000
Fax: (617) 287-6336
E-mail: *clinical.psych@umb.edu*
Web: *http://psych.umb.edu*

Department Established:
1967. Department Chair: Steven Schwartz. Number of Faculty: total–full-time 25, part-time 14; women–full-time 16, part-time 8; minority–full-time 5, part-time 1.

Programs and Degrees Offered:
Listed in the following order: Program area, degree type (T if terminal Master's), number awarded 7/00-6/01. Clinical PhD (T) 6.

APA Accreditation: Clinical PhD: full.

Student Applications/Admissions:
Student Applications
Clinical PhD—Applications 2001–2002, 274. Total applicants accepted 2001–2002, 13. New applicants enrolled 2001–2002, 8. Total enrolled 2001–2002 full-time, 56. Openings 2002–2003, 8.

Admissions Requirements:
Scores: Entries appear in this order: required test or GPA, minimum score (if required), median score of students entering in 2001–2002. Doctoral Programs: GRE-V no minimum stated, 645; GRE-Q no minimum stated, 710; GRE-V+Q no minimum stated, 1355; GRE-Analytical no minimum stated, 730; GRE-V+Q+Analytical no minimum stated, 2085; GRE-Subject(Psych) no minimum stated, 675; overall undergraduate GPA no minimum stated, 3.62; last 2 years GPA no minimum stated, 3.69; psychology GPA no minimum stated, 3.73; psychology GPA no minimum stated.

Other Criteria: (importance of criteria rated low, medium, or high): GRE/MAT scores medium, research experience high, work experience high, extracurricular activity medium, clinically related public service high, GPA high, letters of recommendation high, interview high, statement of goals and objectives high.

Student Characteristics: The following represents characteristics of students in 2001–2002 in all graduate psychology programs in the department: Female–full-time 44, part-time 0; Male–full-time 12, part-time 0; African American/Black–full-time 6, part-time 0; Hispanic/Latino (a)–full-time 6, part-time 0; Asian/Pacific Islander–full-time 8, part-time 0; American Indian/Alaska Native–full-time 0, part-time 0.

Financial Information/Assistance:
Tuition for Full-Time Study: No information provided.

Financial Assistance:
First Year Students: Teaching assistantships available for first-year. Average amount paid per academic year: $11,000. Average number of hours worked per week: 20. Tuition remission given: full. Research assistantships available for first-year. Average amount paid per academic year: $11,000. Average number of hours worked per week: 20. Tuition remission given: full. Fellowships and scholarships available for first-year. Tuition remission given: full.

Advanced Students: Teaching assistantships available for advanced students. Average amount paid per academic year: $12,000. Average number of hours worked per week: 20. Tuition remission given: full. Research assistantships available for advanced students. Average amount paid per academic year: $12,000. Average number of hours worked per week: 20. Tuition remission given: full. Fellowships and scholarships available for advanced students. Tuition remission given: full.

Contact Information: Of all students currently enrolled full-time, 77% benefitted from one or more of the listed financial assistance programs. For information on financial assistance, contact: Financial Aid Office.

Internships/Practica: Students do a 15 hour per week clinical practicum in the University Counseling Center in their second year. They obtain supervised clinical experience doing intake evaluations, short-term dynamic and cognitive behavioral therapy, and some group and couples treatment. Students also do a 24 hour per week clinical practica in a training hospital or community health center in their third year. Examples of external practica include: Cambridge Hospital, Children's Hospital, McLean Hospital, Southern Jamaica Plain Health Center, The Boston Evening Clinic, Chelsea Memorial Health Center, and Roxbury Comprehensive Health Center. These agencies all serve a significant number of low income and ethnic minority clients. Students get supervised clinical training in testing and assessment and a range of psychotherapeutic interventions with children, adolescents, and adults at their external practica. Students do a full-time APA approved clinical internship in their fifth year. For those doctoral students for whom a professional internship is required prior to graduation, 9 applied in 2000–2001. Of those who applied, 9 were placed in internships listed by the Association of Psychology Postdoctoral and Internship Programs (APPIC); 9 were placed in APA accredited internships.

Housing and Day Care: No on-campus housing and day care facilities are available.

Employment of Department Graduates:
Master's Degree Graduates: Of those who graduated in the academic year 2000–2001, the following categories and numbers represent the post-graduate activities and employment of master's degree graduates: Enrolled in a post-doctoral residency/fellowship (n/a), employed in independent practice (n/a).
Doctoral Degree Graduates: Of those who graduated in the academic year 2000–2001, the following categories and numbers represent the post-graduate activities and employment of doctoral degree graduates: Enrolled in a psychology doctoral program (n/a),

enrolled in another graduate/professional program (n/a), enrolled in a post-doctoral residency/fellowship (1), employed in other positions at a higher education institution (1), employed in business or industry (research/consulting) (2), employed in a hospital/medical center (3).

Additional Information:

Orientation, Objectives, and Emphasis of Department: The Clinical Psychology Ph.D. Program follows the scientist-practitioner model of clinical training. It provides a strong theoretical background in psychology and related social science disciplines as well as training in essential clinical skills and in conducting research. Its graduates function as professional psychologists who can translate their basic knowledge into practical applications and who can advance understanding of key problems through research or other scholarly activities. The program's primary goals and objects are to provide students with (a) a strong theoretical and empirical foundation in normal and abnormal development from early childhood through adolescence and adulthood; (b) a strong theoretical and empirical foundation in social and cultural perspectives on development especially as they affect students' understanding of ethnic minority and low income groups; (c) to provide students with solid grounding in the bio-psycho-social approach to explaining and treating problems in living, symptomatic behavior, and mental illness, and with learning opportunities that foster interdisciplinary thinking; (d) a broad range of assessment and intervention skills that will help them treat problem behavior, promote healthy adaptation, and prevent individual and social problems from developing; (e) opportunities to develop competence in the basic research methodologies and data analytic techniques of psychology and their application to clinical issues. The program was one of three recipients of the 2001 APA Suinn Minority Achievement Award in recognition or our program's success in recruiting, educating, supporting, retaining, and graduating significant numbers of ethnic minority doctoral students.

Special Facilities or Resources: The Psychology Department's research laboratories support a wide range of research and teaching functions. There are several interaction rooms with one-way mirrors that can be used for clinical, social, and developmental research. These rooms are equipped with state-of-the-art audio and video recording equipment. The animal laboratories are fully equipped to conduct research in animal behavior, learning, and physiology. Other laboratories in the department support ongoing research in cognition, perception, and human electrophysiology. The department maintains a network of microcomputers that can be used for research, data analysis, and other related functions. For larger projects, the University Computing Center operates a VAX cluster and a CDC Cyber 175 computer (housed at the University of Massachusetts at Amherst). The department's laboratory facilities also include woodworking and electronic shops, which are staffed by full-time experienced technicians. The technical staff provides programming, electronic, and other related support to the faculty and students in the department. Students in the clinical psychology program may also gain experience and have access to the facilities of other research centers and the university, including the Center for Survey Research, the Center for the Study of Social Acceptance, the William Monroe Trotter Institute for the Study of Black Culture, and the William Joiner Center for the Study of War and Social Consequences.

Application Information:

Send to: Graduate Admissions, University of Massachusetts at Boston, 100 Morrissey Blvd, Boston, MA 02125. Students are admitted in the Fall, application deadline January 2. *Fee:* $50. Need basis waivers.

Massachusetts, University of, at Dartmouth

Psychology Department
North Dartmouth, MA 02747
Telephone: (508) 999-8380
Fax: (508) 999-9169
E-mail: *dcorriveau@umassd.edu*
Web: *http://www.umassd.edu*

Department Established:

1962. Chairperson: Donald P. Corriveau. Number of Faculty: total–full-time 16, part-time 10; women–full-time 8, part-time 4; faculty subject to the Americans with Disabilities Act 1.

Programs and Degrees Offered:

Listed in the following order: Program area, degree type (T if terminal Master's), number awarded 7/00-6/01. Clinical MA (T) 7, general/research MA (T) 3.

Student Applications/Admissions:

Student Applications

Clinical MA—Applications 2001–2002, 50. Total applicants accepted 2001–2002, 14. New applicants enrolled 2001–2002, 13. Total enrolled 2001–2002 full-time, 30. Openings 2002–2003, 12. The Median number of years required for completion of a degree are 3. *General/research MA*—Applications 2001–2002, 10. Total applicants accepted 2001–2002, 5. New applicants enrolled 2001–2002, 4. Total enrolled 2001–2002 full-time, 8. Openings 2002–2003, 5. The Median number of years required for completion of a degree are 2.

Admissions Requirements:

Scores: Entries appear in this order: required test or GPA, minimum score (if required), median score of students entering in 2001–2002. Master's Programs: overall undergraduate GPA no minimum stated; last 2 years GPA no minimum stated; psychology GPA no minimum stated. Minimums are applied differently across programs. Doctoral Programs: last 2 years GPA no minimum stated; psychology GPA no minimum stated; psychology GPA no minimum stated.
Other Criteria: (importance of criteria rated low, medium, or high): work experience high, clinically related public service high. These criteria vary across programs and apply on an individual basis.

Student Characteristics: The following represents characteristics of students in 2001–2002 in all graduate psychology programs in the department: Female–full-time 28, part-time 0; Male–full-time 10, part-time 0; African American/Black–full-time 1, part-time 0; Hispanic/Latino (a)–full-time 5, part-time 0; Asian/Pacific Islander–full-time 0, part-time 0; American Indian/Alaska Native–full-time 0, part-time 0; Multi-ethnic–full-time 2.

Financial Information/Assistance:

Tuition for Full-Time Study: *Master's:* State residents per academic year $4,044; nonstate residents: per academic year $8,799.

Financial Assistance:

First Year Students: Teaching assistantships available for first-year. Average amount paid per academic year: $3,500. Average number of hours worked per week: 10. Tuition remission given: full. Research assistantships available for first-year. Average amount paid per academic year: $7,000. Average number of hours worked per week: 20. Tuition remission given: full.

Advanced Students: Research assistantships available for advanced students. Average amount paid per academic year: $7,000. Average number of hours worked per week: 20. Traineeships available for advanced students. Tuition remission given: full.

Contact Information: Of all students currently enrolled full-time, 50% benefitted from one or more of the listed financial assistance programs. For information on financial assistance, contact: Dr. Paul Donnelly, Department of Psychology.

Internships/Practica: We have a wide variety of internship and practica experiences available. Field experiences are tailored to specific student needs.

Housing and Day Care: No on-campus housing and day care facilities are available.

Employment of Department Graduates:

Master's Degree Graduates: Of those who graduated in the academic year 2000–2001, the following categories and numbers represent the post-graduate activities and employment of master's degree graduates: Enrolled in a post-doctoral residency/fellowship (n/a), employed in independent practice (n/a).

Doctoral Degree Graduates: Of those who graduated in the academic year 2000–2001, the following categories and numbers represent the post-graduate activities and employment of doctoral degree graduates: Enrolled in a psychology doctoral program (n/a), enrolled in another graduate/professional program (n/a).

Additional Information:

Orientation, Objectives, and Emphasis of Department: The general psychology option of the MA program in psychology is designed to prepare students for doctoral work in psychology and related fields, including cognitive science. The program combines coursework in basic areas of psychology with the opportunity to do collaborative research with faculty members. Students have considerable flexibility to tailor their programs to their individual needs. The outstanding feature of this program is the opportunity for close interaction between faculty and students, both in the classroom and in the laboratory, because of the low student/faculty ratio. The objectives of the Clinical/Behavioral Analysis option are: to provide students with specific and applied research and problem-solving skills; to provide all clinical students with a broad exposure to a variety of therapy modalities; to provide students with extensive experiential learning opportunities, practica, internships and intensive supervision; and to prepare students for licensure as Certified Mental Health Counselors.

Application Information:
Send to: Office of Graduate Studies (508) 999-8604. Students are admitted in the Fall, application deadline March 31. No set deadline for general option. *Fee:* $40. $20 in state.

Massachusetts, University of, Lowell
Community Social Psychology Master's Program
Arts and Sciences
870 Broadway Street, Suite 1
Lowell, MA 01854-3043
Telephone: (978) 934-3952; (978)934-3950
Fax: (978) 934-3074
E-mail: *Richard_Siegel@uml.edu*
Web: *http://www.uml.edu/Dept/Psychology/csp*

Department Established:
1980. Graduate Program Co-Coordinator: Richard Siegel. Number of Faculty: total–full-time 11; women–full-time 7; minority–full-time 1.

Programs and Degrees Offered:
Listed in the following order: Program area, degree type (T if terminal Master's), number awarded 7/00-6/01. Community Social MA (T) 12.

Student Applications/Admissions:
Student Applications

Community Social MA—Applications 2001–2002, 39. Total applicants accepted 2001–2002, 33. New applicants enrolled 2001–2002, 27. Total enrolled 2001–2002 full-time, 16, part-time, 20. Openings 2002–2003, 25. The Median number of years required for completion of a degree are 3. The number of students enrolled full and part-time, who were dismissed or voluntarily withdrew from this program area were 2.

Admissions Requirements:

Scores: Entries appear in this order: required test or GPA, minimum score (if required), median score of students entering in 2001–2002. Master's Programs: overall undergraduate GPA 3.0. Either the GRE V+Q+Analytical or the MAT is required. Doctoral Programs: last 2 years GPA no minimum stated; psychology GPA no minimum stated; psychology GPA no minimum stated.

Other Criteria: (importance of criteria rated low, medium, or high): GRE/MAT scores medium, research experience medium, work experience high, extracurricular activity low, clinically related public service low, GPA high, letters of recommendation high, interview low, statement of goals and objectives high.

Student Characteristics: The following represents characteristics of students in 2001–2002 in all graduate psychology programs in the department: Female–full-time 14, part-time 18; Male–full-time 4, part-time 0; African American/Black–full-time 2, part-time 0; Hispanic/Latino (a)–full-time 2, part-time 0; Asian/Pacific Islander–full-time 0, part-time 0; American Indian/Alaska Native–full-time 0, part-time 0; Multi-ethnic–full-time 0, part-time 0; students subject to the Americans with Disabilities Act–full-time 0, part-time 0.

Financial Information/Assistance:
Tuition for Full-Time Study: *Master's:* State residents per academic year $4,593, $255 per credit hour; nonstate residents: per academic year $9,624, $535 per credit hour.

Financial Assistance:

First Year Students: Teaching assistantships available for first-year. Average amount paid per academic year: $5,690. Average number of hours worked per week: 9. Apply by 6/1. Tuition remission given: full. Research assistantships available for first-year. Average amount paid per academic year: $5,690. Average number of hours worked per week: 9. Apply by 6/1. Tuition remission given: full.

Advanced Students: Teaching assistantships available for advanced students. Average amount paid per academic year: $5,690. Average number of hours worked per week: 9. Apply by 6/1. Tuition remission given: full. Research assistantships available for advanced students. Average amount paid per academic year: $5,690. Average number of hours worked per week: 9. Apply by 6/1. Tuition remission given: full.

Contact Information: Of all students currently enrolled full-time, 25% benefitted from one or more of the listed financial assistance programs. For information on financial assistance, contact: Richard Siegel, Department of Psychology, University of Massachusetts Lowell, Lowell, MA 01854.

Internships/Practica: There is a one-year practicum requirement of 10 to 12 hours a week. Settings vary but have a community emphasis.

Housing and Day Care: On-campus housing and day care facilities are available.

Employment of Department Graduates:

Master's Degree Graduates: Of those who graduated in the academic year 2000–2001, the following categories and numbers represent the post-graduate activities and employment of master's degree graduates: Enrolled in a psychology doctoral program (1), enrolled in another graduate/professional program (0), enrolled in a post-doctoral residency/fellowship (n/a), employed in independent practice (n/a), employed in an academic position at a university (0), employed in an academic position at a 2-year/4-year college (0), employed in other positions at a higher education institution (3), employed in a professional position in a school system (1), employed in business or industry (research/consulting) (0), employed in business or industry (management) (0), employed in a government agency (research) (0), employed in a government agency (professional services) (6), employed in a community mental health/counseling center (0), still seeking employment (1).

Doctoral Degree Graduates: Of those who graduated in the academic year 2000–2001, the following categories and numbers represent the post-graduate activities and employment of doctoral degree graduates: Enrolled in a psychology doctoral program (n/a), enrolled in another graduate/professional program (n/a).

Additional Information:

Orientation, Objectives, and Emphasis of Department: The program is designed to benefit recent college graduates interested in community service careers as well as older and nontraditional students with experience in community settings. The goal of the program is to provide both kinds of students with an understanding of how urban environments affect people; the research skills necessary for program development and evaluation; the opportunity to apply their learning in community settings in the greater Merrimack Valley and to gain skills through direct experience and supervision in those settings; and the ability to apply psychological

principles to community problem-solving in such areas as discrimination, inadequate housing, and organizational change.

Special Facilities or Resources: Special facilities and resources consist of computer facilities, a campus-based elementary magnet school, grant-related technical services from the University Research Foundation, numerous research centers such as the Center for Family, Work and Community, and a unique multi-ethnic urban setting in a middle-sized city accessible to Boston.

Information for Students With Physical Disabilities: Main classroom building is handicapped assessible.

Application Information:
Send to: Graduate School Admissions, 1 University Avenue, Lowell, MA 01854. Students are admitted in the Fall, application deadline November 1; Winter, application deadline January 15; Spring, application deadline April 1; Summer, application deadline July 1. Rolling admission. *Fee:* $20.

Northeastern University
Department of Counseling & Applied Educational Psychology
Bouve College of Health Sciences
203 Lake Hall
Boston, MA 02115
Telephone: (617) 373-2485
Fax: (617) 373-8892
E-mail: *emason@neu.edu*
Web: *http://www.bouve.neu.edu/department/crs/caep.html*

Department Established:
1983. Chairperson: Emanuel J. Mason. Number of Faculty: total–full-time 16, part-time 27; women–full-time 10, part-time 14; minority–full-time 6, part-time 1.

Programs and Degrees Offered:
Listed in the following order: Program area, degree type (T if terminal Master's), number awarded 7/00-6/01. Applied behavioral analysis MA (T) 11, College Student Development MA (T) 9, combined PhD 6, counseling psychology MA (T) 18, rehabilitation counseling MA (T) 3, school counseling MA (T) 15, School Psychology MS/CAGS MA 24, special education MA (T) 1.

APA Accreditation: Combined PhD: full.

Student Applications/Admissions:
Student Applications

Applied behavioral analysis MA—Applications 2001–2002, 20. Total applicants accepted 2001–2002, 18. New applicants enrolled 2001–2002, 13. Total enrolled 2001–2002 full-time, 22, part-time, 52. Openings 2002–2003, 10. The Median number of years required for completion of a degree are 2. The number of students enrolled full and part-time, who were dismissed or voluntarily withdrew from this program area were 2. *College Student Development MA*—Applications 2001–2002, 29. Total applicants accepted 2001–2002, 27. New applicants enrolled 2001–2002, 10. Total enrolled 2001–2002 full-time, 18, part-time, 10. Openings 2002–2003, 14. The Median number of years required for completion of a degree are 2. The number of students enrolled full and part-time, who were dismissed or voluntarily withdrew from this program area were 1. *Combined PhD*—Applications 2001–2002, 50. Total applicants accepted 2001–2002, 12. New applicants enrolled 2001–2002, 8. Total enrolled 2001–2002 full-time, 30, part-time, 2. Openings 2002–2003, 8. The Median number of years required for completion of a degree are 6. The number of students enrolled full and part-time, who were dismissed or voluntarily withdrew from this program area were 0. *Counseling psychology MA*—Applications 2001–2002, 110. Total applicants accepted 2001–2002, 57. New applicants enrolled 2001–2002, 24. Total enrolled 2001–2002 full-time, 51, part-time, 4. Openings 2002–2003, 24. The Median number of years required for completion of a degree are 2. The number of students enrolled full and part-time, who were dismissed or voluntarily withdrew from this program area were 0. *Rehabilitation counseling MA*—Applications 2001–2002, 7. Total applicants accepted 2001–2002, 6. New applicants enrolled 2001–2002, 2. Total enrolled 2001–2002 full-time, 2, part-time, 1. Openings 2002–2003, 10. The Median number of years required for completion of a degree are 2. The number of students enrolled full and part-time, who were dismissed or voluntarily withdrew from this program area were 0. *School counseling MA*—Applications 2001–2002, 31. Total applicants accepted 2001–2002, 29. New applicants enrolled 2001–2002, 10. Total enrolled 2001–2002 full-time, 18, part-time, 7. Openings 2002–2003, 16. The Median number of years required for completion of a degree are 2. The number of students enrolled full and part-time, who were dismissed or voluntarily withdrew from this program area were 0. *School Psychology MS/CAGS MA*—Applications 2001–2002, 80. Total applicants accepted 2001–2002, 53. New applicants enrolled 2001–2002, 25. Total enrolled 2001–2002 full-time, 49, part-time, 1. Openings 2002–2003, 20. The Median number of years required for completion of a degree are 3. The number of students enrolled full and part-time, who were dismissed or voluntarily withdrew from this program area were 1. *Special education MA*—Applications 2001–2002, 26. Total applicants accepted 2001–2002, 19. New applicants enrolled 2001–2002, 4. Total enrolled 2001–2002 full-time, 4. Openings 2002–2003, 9.

Admissions Requirements:

Scores: Entries appear in this order: required test or GPA, minimum score (if required), median score of students entering in 2001–2002. Master's Programs: GRE-V no minimum stated, 470; GRE-Q no minimum stated, 540; GRE-V+Q no minimum stated; overall undergraduate GPA 3.0, 3.28; psychology GPA no minimum stated. Programs scores are competitive. Department prefers 500 minimum in GRE Q and V. TOEFL scores for international applicants who do not hold undergraduate or graduate degrees from US institutions, and whose native language is not English. Doctoral Programs: GRE-V 500, 560; GRE-Q 500, 560; GRE-V+Q no minimum stated; overall undergraduate GPA 3.00, 3.47; last 2 years GPA no minimum stated; psychology GPA no minimum stated; psychology GPA 3.50, 3.82.

Other Criteria: (importance of criteria rated low, medium, or high): GRE/MAT scores medium, research experience medium, work experience high, extracurricular activity medium, clinically related public service high, GPA medium, letters of recommendation high, interview high, statement of goals and objectives high.

Student Characteristics: The following represents characteristics of students in 2001–2002 in all graduate psychology programs in the department: Female–full-time 189, part-time 50; Male–full-time 35, part-time 8; African American/Black–full-time 11, part-time 3; Hispanic/Latino (a)–full-time 9, part-time 5; Asian/Pacific Islander–full-time 6, part-time 2; American Indian/Alaska Native–full-time 0, part-time 0; part-time 2.

Financial Information/Assistance:

Tuition for Full-Time Study: *Master's:* State residents $505 per credit hour; nonstate residents: $505 per credit hour. *Doctoral:* State residents: $505 per credit hour; nonstate residents: $505 per credit hour.

Financial Assistance:

First Year Students: Teaching assistantships available for first-year. Average number of hours worked per week: 10. Tuition remission given: partial. Tuition remission given: partial. Fellowships and scholarships available for first-year. Average number of hours worked per week: 0. Tuition remission given: partial.

Advanced Students: Teaching assistantships available for advanced students. Average number of hours worked per week: 10. Tuition remission given: full and partial. Research assistantships available for advanced students. Average amount paid per academic year: $11,000. Average number of hours worked per week: 20. Tuition remission given: full and partial. Fellowships and scholarships available for advanced students. Average number of hours worked per week: 0. Tuition remission given: full and partial.

Contact Information: Of all students currently enrolled full-time, 10% benefitted from one or more of the listed financial assistance programs. For information on financial assistance, contact: Associate Dean, Graduate School.

Internships/Practica: Internship and field placement sites are varied depending on the program and specialization. Sites are in the Boston metropolitan area and include some of the most desirable and prestigious settings in the field. For those doctoral students for whom a professional internship is required prior to graduation, 11 applied in 2000–2001. Of those who applied, 1 were placed in internships listed by the Association of Psychology Postdoctoral and Internship Programs (APPIC); 9 were placed in APA accredited internships.

Housing and Day Care: On-campus housing and day care facilities are available.

Employment of Department Graduates:

Master's Degree Graduates: Of those who graduated in the academic year 2000–2001, the following categories and numbers represent the post-graduate activities and employment of master's degree graduates: Enrolled in a post-doctoral residency/fellowship (n/a), employed in independent practice (n/a).

Doctoral Degree Graduates: Of those who graduated in the academic year 2000–2001, the following categories and numbers

represent the post-graduate activities and employment of doctoral degree graduates: Enrolled in a psychology doctoral program (n/a), enrolled in another graduate/professional program (n/a).

Additional Information:

Orientation, Objectives, and Emphasis of Department: Philosophically, the combined school and counseling doctoral program is based on an ecological model. This model focuses on the contexts in which people and their environments intersect, including individuals' families, groups, cultures, and social, political, and economic institutions. Thus, the ecological model includes individual and interpersonal relationships along with their interactive physical and sociocultural environments. It employs a general systems perspective to understand the mutually reciprocal interactions of all of these elements. Central to this theoretical stance are assumptions of interdependence, circular and multilevel influence and causality, and interactive identities. Issues of gender, status, and culture are given special emphasis as well as the developmental stages of the individual, family, or group. The ecological model is large enough and sufficiently comprehensive to allow for teaching and using other models such as psychodynamic, behaviorist, and humanistic, as they help to explain behavior and phenomena in individuals, families, and groups. This allows faculty and students to teach, understand, and use many explanations of human activities. This ecological orientation provides the lenses through which students study psychological and counseling theory and research. In their varied fieldwork settings, students have the opportunity to translate this orientation into practice.

Special Facilities or Resources: Northeastern University, one of the largest private universities in the country, is located in Boston, a center of academic excellence and psychological research. There are numerous opportunities for diverse experiences, such as placements specializing in neuropsychology, early intervention, and sexual abuse. The campus is in the Back Bay, an area with a large student population and rich cultural opportunities. The Snell Library, one of the most advanced college libraries in the Boston area, provides access for students not only to its large psychology and education collections, but also to media and microcomputer centers and an extensive global academic computer networking system. Northeastern students also have privileges at the other Boston area research libraries.

Information for Students With Physical Disabilities: The Disability Resource Center provides a variety of disability-related services and accommodations to Northeastern University students and employees with disabilities. Northeastern University's compliance with Section 504 of the Rehabilitation Act of 1973 and the Americans with Disabilities Act of 1990 is coordinated by the Dean and Director of the Disability Resource Center.

Application Information:

Send to: Graduate Dean, Bouve College of Health Sciences, 103 Mugar, Northeastern University, Boston, MA 02169. Students are admitted in the Fall, application deadline see below. Combined School and Counseling Psychology Ph.D.- January 15 for admission following fall. MS Counseling Psychology - Feb 1 for admission following fall. MS/CAGS School Psychology - Suggested Feb 1 for admission following fall. All other program have a suggested May 1 deadline. *Fee:* $50.

Northeastern University
Department of Psychology
Arts and Sciences
125 Nightingale Hall
Boston, MA 02115
Telephone: (617) 373-3076
Fax: (617) 373-8714
E-mail: *psychology@neu.edu*
Web: *http://www.psych.neu.edu*

Department Established:

1966. Chairperson: Stephen G. Harkins. Number of Faculty: total–full-time 18, part-time 3; women–full-time 4, part-time 2; minority–full-time 2, part-time 1.

Programs and Degrees Offered:

Listed in the following order: Program area, degree type (T if terminal Master's), number awarded 7/00-6/01. Cognitive PhD, psychobiology PhD 2, sensation PhD 1, social/personality PhD 1.

Student Applications/Admissions:

Student Applications

Cognitive PhD—Applications 2001–2002, 14. Total applicants accepted 2001–2002, 2. Total enrolled 2001–2002 full-time, 8. Openings 2002–2003, 3. *Psychobiology PhD*—Applications 2001–2002, 12. Total applicants accepted 2001–2002, 2. New applicants enrolled 2001–2002, 2. Total enrolled 2001–2002 full-time, 4. Openings 2002–2003, 2. The Median number of years required for completion of a degree are 5. The number of students enrolled full and part-time, who were dismissed or voluntarily withdrew from this program area were 1. *Sensation PhD*—Applications 2001–2002, 7. Total applicants accepted 2001–2002, 2. New applicants enrolled 2001–2002, 1. Total enrolled 2001–2002 full-time, 2. Openings 2002–2003, 2. The Median number of years required for completion of a degree are 5. *Social/personality PhD*—Applications 2001–2002, 34. Total applicants accepted 2001–2002, 2. New applicants enrolled 2001–2002, 2. Total enrolled 2001–2002 full-time, 7. Openings 2002–2003, 2. The Median number of years required for completion of a degree are 5.

Admissions Requirements:

Scores: Entries appear in this order: required test or GPA, minimum score (if required), median score of students entering in 2001–2002. Master's Programs: GRE-V+Q is recommended strongly. Doctoral Programs: GRE-V no minimum stated, 590; GRE-Q no minimum stated, 610; GRE-V+Q no minimum stated, 1200; last 2 years GPA no minimum stated; psychology GPA no minimum stated; psychology GPA no minimum stated.

Other Criteria: (importance of criteria rated low, medium, or high): GRE/MAT scores high, research experience high, work experience low, extracurricular activity low, clinically related public service low, GPA high, letters of recommendation high, interview high, statement of goals and objectives high.

Student Characteristics: The following represents characteristics of students in 2001–2002 in all graduate psychology programs in the department: Female–full-time 23, part-time 0; Male–full-time 7, part-time 0; African American/Black–full-time 2, part-time 0;

Hispanic/Latino (a)–full-time 0, part-time 0; Asian/Pacific Islander–full-time 1, part-time 0; American Indian/Alaska Native–full-time 1, part-time 0.

Financial Information/Assistance:

Tuition for Full-Time Study: *Doctoral:* State residents: $505 per credit hour; nonstate residents: $505 per credit hour.

Financial Assistance:

First Year Students: Teaching assistantships available for first-year. Average amount paid per academic year: $19,100. Average number of hours worked per week: 20. Apply by Jan 15. Tuition remission given: full. Research assistantships available for first-year. Average amount paid per academic year: $19,100. Average number of hours worked per week: 20. Apply by Jan 15. Tuition remission given: full. Traineeships available for first-year. Average amount paid per academic year: $19,100. Average number of hours worked per week: 20. Apply by Jan 15. Tuition remission given: full.

Advanced Students: Teaching assistantships available for advanced students. Average amount paid per academic year: $19,100. Average number of hours worked per week: 20. Apply by Jan 15. Tuition remission given: full. Research assistantships available for advanced students. Average amount paid per academic year: $19,100. Average number of hours worked per week: 20. Apply by Jan 15. Tuition remission given: full. Traineeships available for advanced students. Average amount paid per academic year: $19,100. Average number of hours worked per week: 20. Apply by Jan 15. Tuition remission given: full.

Contact Information: Of all students currently enrolled full-time, 100% benefitted from one or more of the listed financial assistance programs. For information on financial assistance, contact: Department at same address.

Internships/Practica: No information provided.

Housing and Day Care: No on-campus housing and day care facilities are available.

Employment of Department Graduates:

Master's Degree Graduates: Of those who graduated in the academic year 2000–2001, the following categories and numbers represent the post-graduate activities and employment of master's degree graduates: Enrolled in a post-doctoral residency/fellowship (n/a), employed in independent practice (n/a).

Doctoral Degree Graduates: Of those who graduated in the academic year 2000–2001, the following categories and numbers represent the post-graduate activities and employment of doctoral degree graduates: Enrolled in a psychology doctoral program (n/a), enrolled in another graduate/professional program (n/a), enrolled in a post-doctoral residency/fellowship (4).

Additional Information:

Orientation, Objectives, and Emphasis of Department: The PhD program aims to train students to undertake basic research in the following areas: neuropsychology and psychobiology; sensation and perception; language and cognition; and experimental-social and personality. Students may expect to collaborate with faculty in conducting research in these areas, using technically sophisticated research laboratories. The doctoral program also provides opportunities to gain teaching experience. It does not, however, provide clinical training.

Special Facilities or Resources: The department has a wide range of research laboratories containing state-of-the-art facilities in the following areas: neuropsychology and psychobiology; sensation and perception; language and cognition; and experimental-social and personality. These facilities include an array of mini- and microcomputers used for subject testing, data acquisition and analysis, graphics, and word processing. The facilities also house numerous special-purpose systems (e.g., eye-tracker, histology facilities, and speech processing system). In addition, laboratory resources outside the department are available to students through the collaborative network the department maintains with other institutions in the Boston/Cambridge area.

Application Information:
Send to: Department of Psychology, 125 NI, Northeastern University, Boston, MA 02115. Students are admitted in the Fall, application deadline January 15. *Fee:* $50. Waived for financial need.

Springfield College (2001 data)
Department of Psychology
263 Alden Street
Springfield, MA 01109
Telephone: (413) 748-3328
Fax: (413) 748-3854
E-mail: *barbara_mandell@spfldcol.edu*
Web: *http://www.spfldcol.edu*

Department Established:
1946. Chairperson: Barbara Mandell. Number of Faculty: total–full-time 12, part-time 21; women–full-time 7, part-time 11.

Programs and Degrees Offered:
Listed in the following order: Program area, degree type (T if terminal Master's), number awarded 7/00-6/01. Athletic counseling MS (T) 10, general counseling MS (T) 3, industrial/organizational MS (T) 15, marriage and family therapy MS (T) 8, mental health counseling MS (T) 12, school guidance and counseling MS (T) 4, students personnel admin MS (T) 12.

Student Applications/Admissions:
Student Applications
*Athletic counseling MS—*Applications 2001–2002, 32. Total applicants accepted 2001–2002, 21. New applicants enrolled 2001–2002, 9. Total enrolled 2001–2002 full-time, 19. Openings 2002–2003, 18. *General counseling MS—*Applications 2001–2002, 12. Total applicants accepted 2001–2002, 10. New applicants enrolled 2001–2002, 4. Total enrolled 2001–2002 full-time, 7, part-time, 1. Openings 2002–2003, 7. *Industrial/organizational MS—*Applications 2001–2002, 38. Total applicants accepted 2001–2002, 28. New applicants enrolled 2001–2002, 16. Total enrolled 2001–2002 full-time, 30, part-time, 5. Openings 2002–2003, 17. *Marriage and family therapy MS—*Applications 2001–2002, 22. Total applicants accepted 2001–2002, 16. New applicants enrolled 2001–2002, 8. Total enrolled 2001–2002 full-time, 15, part-time, 1. Openings 2002–2003, 14. *Mental health counseling MS—*Applications 2001–2002, 17. Total applicants accepted 2001–2002, 16. New applicants enrolled 2001–2002, 15. Total enrolled 2001–2002 full-time, 25, part-time, 2. Openings 2002–2003, 15. *School guid-*

ance and counseling MS—Applications 2001–2002, 12. Total applicants accepted 2001–2002, 10. New applicants enrolled 2001–2002, 10. Total enrolled 2001–2002 full-time, 21, part-time, 2. Openings 2002–2003, 15. *Students personnel admin MS*—Applications 2001–2002, 24. Total applicants accepted 2001–2002, 17. New applicants enrolled 2001–2002, 13. Total enrolled 2001–2002 full-time, 24, part-time, 3. Openings 2002–2003, 14.

Admissions Requirements:

Scores: Entries appear in this order: required test or GPA, minimum score (if required), median score of students entering in 2001–2002. Master's Programs: overall undergraduate GPA 2.6, 3.0; last 2 years GPA no minimum stated; psychology GPA no minimum stated. Different GPAs are required for different programs.

Other Criteria: (importance of criteria rated low, medium, or high): GRE/MAT scores low, research experience medium, work experience high, extracurricular activity medium, clinically related public service high, GPA medium, letters of recommendation high, interview medium, statement of goals and objectives high. These criteria vary for different program areas.

Student Characteristics: The following represents characteristics of students in 2001–2002 in all graduate psychology programs in the department: Female–full-time 70, part-time 15; Male–full-time 47, part-time 8; African American/Black–full-time 8, part-time 0; Hispanic/Latino (a)–full-time 5, part-time 0; Asian/Pacific Islander–full-time 1, part-time 0; American Indian/Alaska Native–full-time 0, part-time 0.

Financial Information/Assistance:

Tuition for Full-Time Study: No information provided.

Financial Assistance:

First Year Students: No information provided.
Advanced Students: No information provided.
Contact Information: Of all students currently enrolled full-time, 75% benefitted from one or more of the listed financial assistance programs. For information on financial assistance, contact: (413) 748-3108.

Internships/Practica: Numerous internships, paid and unpaid, exist for students in their field of study. Established affiliation agreements are in place with regional corporate, clinical, and counseling settings. A Cooperative Education Program provides students with opportunities for credited, paid internships.

Housing and Day Care: No on-campus housing and day care facilities are available.

Employment of Department Graduates:

Master's Degree Graduates: Of those who graduated in the academic year 2000–2001, the following categories and numbers represent the post-graduate activities and employment of master's degree graduates: Enrolled in a post-doctoral residency/fellowship (n/a), employed in independent practice (n/a).

Doctoral Degree Graduates: Of those who graduated in the academic year 2000–2001, the following categories and numbers represent the post-graduate activities and employment of doctoral degree graduates: Enrolled in a psychology doctoral program (n/a), enrolled in another graduate/professional program (n/a).

Additional Information:

Orientation, Objectives, and Emphasis of Department: Understanding of personal values, attitudes, and needs is a primary characteristic of effective facilitators. The psychology and counseling programs, therefore, design many experiences to help students increase their awareness of self and the ways in which personal behavior affects others. While mastery of content areas is expected, continual reference to personal relevance of that content is encouraged. Frequent opportunities are afforded for students to understand themselves better through participation in group and individual experiences. As a reflection of the value placed upon individual program development, the comprehensive examination requirement is not the traditional written and oral exercise. Some of the Psychology and Counseling programs use the portfolio system, which is an ongoing, active evaluation process. A more traditional thesis or research project is also offered and supported when chosen, and individual attention is readily available for both options.

Special Facilities or Resources: The department offers fully equipped counseling and research laboratories and audiovisual facility. Access to computers, a well-equipped behavior modification laboratory, and an excellent physiological and fitness laboratories is available. The Department also sponsors the Center for Performance Enhancement and Applied Research (CPEAR), which serves as a clearinghouse for information about grants and research opportunities.

Information for Students With Physical Disabilities: The Springfield College campus is accessible to students with physical disabilities through elevators, ramps, and other accommodations.

Application Information:

Send to: Graduate Admissions, 263 Alden St., Springfield, MA 01109. Students are admitted in the Fall, application deadline rolling; Winter; Spring; Summer. *Fee:* $40.

Suffolk University
Department of Psychology
41 Temple Street
Boston, MA 02114
Telephone: (617) 573-8293
Fax: (617) 367-2924
E-mail: *phd@acad.suffolk.edu*
Web: *http://www.cas.suffolk.edu/psych/ndonovan/psych.htm*

Department Established:

1968. Chairperson: Robert Webb. Number of Faculty: total–full-time 12, part-time 3; women–full-time 9, part-time 2; minority–full-time 2.

Programs and Degrees Offered:

Listed in the following order: Program area, degree type (T if terminal Master's), number awarded 7/00-6/01. Clin Psych Respecialization Diploma, Clinical Psychology PhD 5.

APA Accreditation: Clinical PhD: full.

Student Applications/Admissions:

Student Applications

Clin Psych Respecialization Diploma—Applications 2001–2002, 0. Total enrolled 2001–2002 full-time, 1. Openings 2002–2003, 2. The Median number of years required for completion of a degree are 2. The number of students enrolled full and part-time, who were dismissed or voluntarily withdrew from this program area were 0. Clinical Psychology PhD—Applications 2001–2002, 70. Total applicants accepted 2001–2002, 16. New applicants enrolled 2001–2002, 15. Total enrolled 2001–2002 full-time, 51, part-time, 14. Openings 2002–2003, 12. The Median number of years required for completion of a degree are 6. The number of students enrolled full and part-time, who were dismissed or voluntarily withdrew from this program area were 3.

Admissions Requirements:

Scores: Entries appear in this order: required test or GPA, minimum score (if required), median score of students entering in 2001–2002. Doctoral Programs: GRE-V no minimum stated, 505; GRE-Q no minimum stated, 605; GRE-V+Q no minimum stated, 1110; GRE-Analytical no minimum stated, 630; GRE-V+Q+Analytical no minimum stated, 1740; overall undergraduate GPA no minimum stated, 3.45; last 2 years GPA no minimum stated; psychology GPA no minimum stated; psychology GPA no minimum stated.

Other Criteria: (importance of criteria rated low, medium, or high): GRE/MAT scores high, research experience high, work experience medium, extracurricular activity medium, clinically related public service medium, GPA high, letters of recommendation medium, interview high, statement of goals and objectives high.

Student Characteristics: The following represents characteristics of students in 2001–2002 in all graduate psychology programs in the department: Female–full-time 51, part-time 11; Male–full-time 14, part-time 3; African American/Black–full-time 2, part-time 0; Hispanic/Latino (a)–full-time 4, part-time 0; Asian/Pacific Islander–full-time 6, part-time 0; American Indian/Alaska Native–full-time 0, part-time 0; Multi-ethnic–full-time 0, students subject to the Americans with Disabilities Act–full-time 0.

Financial Information/Assistance:

Tuition for Full-Time Study: Doctoral: State residents: per academic year $22,920, $2,292 per credit hour; nonstate residents: per academic year $22,920, $2,292 per credit hour.

Financial Assistance:

First Year Students: Teaching assistantships available for first-year. Tuition remission given: partial. Research assistantships available for first-year. Tuition remission given: partial. Fellowships and scholarships available for first-year. Tuition remission given: partial.

Advanced Students: Teaching assistantships available for advanced students. Tuition remission given: partial. Research assistantships available for advanced students. Tuition remission given: partial. Fellowships and scholarships available for advanced students. Tuition remission given: partial.

Contact Information: Of all students currently enrolled full-time, 100% benefitted from one or more of the listed financial assistance programs. For information on financial assistance, contact: Office of Financial Aid, 617-573-8470.

Internships/Practica: Suffolk University's psychology doctoral program is committed to providing the highest quality program experiences available. Practicum sites have been chosen that are committed to training and provide students with supervision by appropriate professionals as well as offer training that is holistic and integrated in nature. Each practicum is designed to be consistent with the goal of the doctoral program, which emphasizes using clinical-developmental frameworks to address psychological problems in the context of direct client service, consultation, and applied research. Three years of practicum experience, beginning in the second year, are required of our doctoral students. Students receive weekly supervision by professionals at their practicum sites and attend a weekly practicum seminar at Suffolk University where they are able to integrate their practical experiences and educational training within the program. Students receive a total of 4 hours per week, on average, of individual and group supervision during each of their 3 years of practicum training. Students' first practicum experience occurs on-site at Suffolk University's Learning Center working with a population of college-age students. The second practicum experience occurs at the Intensive Psychiatric Community Care program at the Edith Nourse Rogers Memorial Veterans Hospital in Bedford, MA. Students' third practicum experience includes more advanced training and preparation for internships at one of a selected set of approved sites during their fourth year of academic training. Students can choose among inpatient, outpatient, school-based, children, adolescents, adults, and/or neuropsychology based sites. After students have completed 3 years of practica and have submitted a dissertation prospectus, students must complete a 1600-hour predoctoral internship in their chosen area. For those doctoral students for whom a professional internship is required prior to graduation, 11 applied in 2000–2001. Of those who applied, 9 were placed in internships listed by the Association of Psychology Postdoctoral and Internship Programs (APPIC); 2 were placed in APA accredited internships.

Housing and Day Care: No on-campus housing and day care facilities are available.

Employment of Department Graduates:

Master's Degree Graduates: Of those who graduated in the academic year 2000–2001, the following categories and numbers represent the post-graduate activities and employment of master's degree graduates: Enrolled in a post-doctoral residency/fellowship (n/a), employed in independent practice (n/a).

Doctoral Degree Graduates: Of those who graduated in the academic year 2000–2001, the following categories and numbers represent the post-graduate activities and employment of doctoral degree graduates: Enrolled in a psychology doctoral program (n/a), enrolled in another graduate/professional program (n/a), enrolled in a post-doctoral residency/fellowship (4), still seeking employment (2).

Additional Information:

Orientation, Objectives, and Emphasis of Department: Suffolk University's PhD program in clinical psychology is unique in several respects: (a) It emphasizes that clinical problems are best understood in the context of knowledge about normal and optimal development over the life span; (b) conceptualizing clinical and developmental psychology in broad terms, it prepares students to work as creative problem solvers in a wide range of research, clinical, educational, organizational, and public policy settings;

and (c) in the tradition of the scientist-practitioner model, it emphasizes a rigorous understanding of the interrelations between basic and applied research and between qualitative and quantitative methodologies in contributing to theoretical and practical knowledge. The program combines a strong theoretical/research background in a wide range of subfields of psychology with preparation to deliver high-quality psychological services to children, adolescents, and adults. Training emphasizes students' ability to think critically about knowledge, to conduct original research, and to design and carry out effective interventions at individual, family, community, and societal levels.

Special Facilities or Resources: The department has a variety of laboratory spaces available for general use by faculty and doctoral students. Special equipment includes one-way mirrors and video cameras. A great deal of research occurs off-site in the clinical, medical, and scholastic institutions of the Boston area. Every graduate student is assigned office space. There is a computer lab for graduate student use within the department in addition to larger computer labs throughout the university. All computers provide access to SPSS, the Internet, and major academic search systems. Graduate students receive inter-library loan and on-line document delivery privileges and have access to most of the academic libraries in the Boston area.

Application Information:

Send to: Office of Graduate Admissions, 8 Ashburton Place, Boston, MA 02108. Students are admitted in the Fall, application deadline January15. Same deadline for all. *Fee:* $50.

Tufts University
Department of Education; School Psychology Program
Graduate School of Arts and Sciences
Paige Hall
Medford, MA 02155
Telephone: (617) 627-3244
Fax: (617) 627-3901
E-mail: *cwandle@tufts.edu*
Web: *http://www.tufts.edu/as/ed*

Department Established:

1910. Program Director-School Psychology: Caroline Wandle. Number of Faculty: total–full-time 12, part-time 17; women–full-time 9, part-time 8; minority–full-time 2, part-time 4.

Programs and Degrees Offered:

Listed in the following order: Program area, degree type (T if terminal Master's), number awarded 7/00-6/01. School MA 15.

Student Applications/Admissions:
Student Applications

School MA—Applications 2001–2002, 60. Total applicants accepted 2001–2002, 28. New applicants enrolled 2001–2002,

16. Total enrolled 2001–2002 full-time, 45. Openings 2002–2003, 15. The Median number of years required for completion of a degree are 3. The number of students enrolled full and part-time, who were dismissed or voluntarily withdrew from this program area were 1.

Admissions Requirements:

Scores: Entries appear in this order: required test or GPA, minimum score (if required), median score of students entering in 2001–2002. Master's Programs: GRE-V no minimum stated, 550; GRE-Q no minimum stated, 550; GRE-V+Q no minimum stated, 1100; GRE-Analytical no minimum stated, 550; GRE-V+Q+Analytical no minimum stated, 1650; overall undergraduate GPA 3.0, 3.4. Doctoral Programs: last 2 years GPA no minimum stated; psychology GPA no minimum stated; psychology GPA no minimum stated.
Other Criteria: (importance of criteria rated low, medium, or high): GRE/MAT scores medium, research experience medium, work experience high, extracurricular activity medium, clinically related public service high, GPA high, letters of recommendation high, interview high, statement of goals and objectives high.

Student Characteristics: The following represents characteristics of students in 2001–2002 in all graduate psychology programs in the department: Female–full-time 42, part-time 0; Male–full-time 3, part-time 0; African American/Black–full-time 2, part-time 0; Hispanic/Latino (a)–full-time 0, part-time 0; Asian/Pacific Islander–full-time 2, part-time 0; American Indian/Alaska Native–full-time 0, part-time 0; students subject to the Americans with Disabilities Act–full-time 0.

Financial Information/Assistance:

Tuition for Full-Time Study: *Master's:* State residents per academic year $2,350; nonstate residents: per academic year $2,350.

Financial Assistance:

First Year Students: Teaching assistantships available for first-year. Average amount paid per academic year: $1,300. Average number of hours worked per week: 4. Apply by 9/1. Research assistantships available for first-year. Average amount paid per academic year: $1,300. Average number of hours worked per week: 4. Apply by 9/1. Fellowships and scholarships available for first-year. Average amount paid per academic year: $5,000. Apply by 2/15. Tuition remission given: partial.

Advanced Students: Teaching assistantships available for advanced students. Average amount paid per academic year: $1,300. Average number of hours worked per week: 4. Apply by 9/1. Research assistantships available for advanced students. Average amount paid per academic year: $1,300. Average number of hours worked per week: 4. Apply by 9/1. Fellowships and scholarships available for advanced students. Average amount paid per academic year: $5,000. Apply by 2/15. Tuition remission given: partial.

Contact Information: Of all students currently enrolled full-time, 80% benefitted from one or more of the listed financial assistance programs. For information on financial assistance, contact: The Graduate School of Arts and Sciences at 617-627-3395.

Internships/Practica: Students complete a school-based practicum of 600 hours during their second year. Students complete a 1200-hour internship during their third year. This may be completed through 600 hours in a school setting and 600 hours in a clinical setting, or all 1200 hours in a school setting.

Housing and Day Care: On-campus housing and day care facilities are available.

Employment of Department Graduates:

Master's Degree Graduates: Of those who graduated in the academic year 2000–2001, the following categories and numbers represent the post-graduate activities and employment of master's degree graduates: Enrolled in a psychology doctoral program (0), enrolled in another graduate/professional program (0), enrolled in a post-doctoral residency/fellowship (n/a), employed in independent practice (n/a), employed in an academic position at a university (0), employed in an academic position at a 2-year/4-year college (0), employed in other positions at a higher education institution (0), employed in a professional position in a school system (15), employed in business or industry (research/consulting) (0), employed in business or industry (management) (0), employed in a government agency (research) (0), employed in a government agency (professional services) (0), employed in a community mental health/counseling center (0), employed in a hospital/medical center (0), still seeking employment (0), other employment position (0).

Doctoral Degree Graduates: Of those who graduated in the academic year 2000–2001, the following categories and numbers represent the post-graduate activities and employment of doctoral degree graduates: Enrolled in a psychology doctoral program (n/a), enrolled in another graduate/professional program (n/a).

Additional Information:

Orientation, Objectives, and Emphasis of Department: Students are exposed to a broad spectrum of assessment and intervention techniques from various theoretical perspectives including psychodynamic, humanistic, cognitive-behavioral, and family systems. Assessment and intervention strategies are anchored in a developmental perspective which stresses the social, intellectual, and emotional growth of the individual from childhood through the early adult years. The school psychology program is approved by the Massachusetts Department of Education. Graduates who complete program requirements will be eligible for state licensure as a school psychologist.

Special Facilities or Resources: Several required courses are offered through the Eliot-Pearson Department of Child Study. These include evaluation of the young child, emotional problems of young children, and applied aspects of physiological development. Thus, the school psychology program is partially interdepartmental. Tufts students may also cross-register for courses at other Boston universities.

Application Information:

Send to: Graduate School of Arts and Sciences. Students are admitted in the Fall, application deadline February 15. *Fee:* $50.

Tufts University
Department of Psychology
Psychology Building
Medford, MA 02155
Telephone: (617) 627-3523
Fax: (617) 627-3181
E-mail: *rcook1@tufts.edu*
Web: *http://ase.tufts.edu/psychology/*

Department Established:
Chair: Joseph DeBold. Number of Faculty: total–full-time 16, part-time 16; women–full-time 6, part-time 3; minority–full-time 2, part-time 1.

Programs and Degrees Offered:
Listed in the following order: Program area, degree type (T if terminal Master's), number awarded 7/00-6/01. General experimental PhD.

Student Applications/Admissions:
Student Applications

General experimental PhD—Applications 2001–2002, 79. Total applicants accepted 2001–2002, 6. New applicants enrolled 2001–2002, 5. Total enrolled 2001–2002 full-time, 5. Openings 2002–2003, 9. The Median number of years required for completion of a degree are 5.

Admissions Requirements:

Scores: Entries appear in this order: required test or GPA, minimum score (if required), median score of students entering in 2001–2002. Master's Programs: GRE-V+Q+Analytical no minimum stated. GRE-Subject is not required, but it is strongly recommended. Doctoral Programs: GRE-V+Q+Analytical no minimum stated; last 2 years GPA no minimum stated; psychology GPA no minimum stated; psychology GPA no minimum stated. GRE-Subject is not required but is strongly recommended.

Other Criteria: (importance of criteria rated low, medium, or high): GRE/MAT scores medium, research experience high, work experience medium, extracurricular activity low, GPA low, letters of recommendation high, interview medium, statement of goals and objectives high.

Student Characteristics: The following represents characteristics of students in 2001–2002 in all graduate psychology programs in the department: Female–full-time 22, part-time 0; Male–full-time 5, part-time 0; African American/Black–full-time 0, part-time 0; Hispanic/Latino (a)–full-time 1, part-time 0; Asian/Pacific Islander–full-time 3, part-time 0; American Indian/Alaska Native–full-time 0, part-time 0.

Financial Information/Assistance:
Tuition for Full-Time Study: *Doctoral:* State residents: per academic year $26,944.

Financial Assistance:
First Year Students: Teaching assistantships available for first-year. Average amount paid per academic year: $12,000. Average number of hours worked per week: 20. Research assistantships

available for first-year. Average amount paid per academic year: $12,000.

Advanced Students: Teaching assistantships available for advanced students. Average amount paid per academic year: $12,125. Research assistantships available for advanced students. Average amount paid per academic year: $12,125.

Contact Information: Of all students currently enrolled full-time, 100% benefitted from one or more of the listed financial assistance programs.

Internships/Practica: No information provided.

Housing and Day Care: No on-campus housing and day care facilities are available.

Employment of Department Graduates:

Master's Degree Graduates: Of those who graduated in the academic year 2000–2001, the following categories and numbers represent the post-graduate activities and employment of master's degree graduates: Enrolled in a post-doctoral residency/fellowship (n/a), employed in independent practice (n/a).

Doctoral Degree Graduates: Of those who graduated in the academic year 2000–2001, the following categories and numbers represent the post-graduate activities and employment of doctoral degree graduates: Enrolled in a psychology doctoral program (n/a), enrolled in another graduate/professional program (n/a).

Additional Information:

Orientation, Objectives, and Emphasis of Department: The Department of Psychology offers a graduate program in experimental psychology, with specializations in cognition, neuroscience, psychopathology, and developmental, social, and engineer psychology. The program is designed to produce broadly trained graduates who are prepared for careers in teaching, research, or applied psychology. The department does not offer clinical training. Accepted applicants generally possess a substantial college background in psychology, including familiarity with fundamental statistical concepts and research design. The university is a PhD track program although completion of an MS is required as an integral part of the program. Students who already possess a master's degree may be admitted to the PhD program if a sufficient number of credits are acceptable for transfer and a thesis has been done. Areas of faculty research include infant perception, memory processes, animal cognition and learning, neural and hormonal control of animal sexual behavior, psychopharmacology, shame and guilt proneness and narcissism, event-related brain potentials, neuropsychology of language processes, nutrition and behavior, semantic models of information processing, sex/gender development, human factors, decision making, and the social psychology of prejudicial attitudes. All graduate students participate in supervised research and/or teaching activities each semester. The department provides laboratory space and equipment for many kinds of research, and facilities are available for the behavioral and physiological study of humans and experimental animals.

Special Facilities or Resources: Department has brand new research facilities for both human and animal research in areas of cognition, biopsychology, neuroscience, human factors, developmental and social psychology.

Application Information:
Send to: Graduate School, Tufts University, Ballou Hall, Medford, MA 02155. Students are admitted in the Fall, application deadline February 15. *Fee:* $50.

Tufts University
Eliot-Pearson Department of Child Development
Graduate School of Arts and Sciences
105 College Avenue
Medford, MA 02155
Telephone: (617) 627-3355
Fax: (617) 627-3503
E-mail: *marguerite.phillips@tufts.edu*
Web: *http://ase.tufts.edu/epcd*

Department Established:
1964. Chairperson: Ann Easterbrooks. Number of Faculty: total–full-time 17, part-time 13; women–full-time 8, part-time 10; minority–full-time 2, part-time 3.

Programs and Degrees Offered:
Listed in the following order: Program area, degree type (T if terminal Master's), number awarded 7/00-6/01. CAGS (T) 1, MA (T) 35, MAT, PhD 1.

Student Applications/Admissions:
Student Applications

MA—Applications 2001–2002, 58. Total applicants accepted 2001–2002, 63. New applicants enrolled 2001–2002, 33. Total enrolled 2001–2002 full-time, 76, part-time, 5. Openings 2002–2003, 60. *PhD*—Applications 2001–2002, 44. Total applicants accepted 2001–2002, 3. New applicants enrolled 2001–2002, 3. Total enrolled 2001–2002 full-time, 9, part-time, 15. Openings 2002–2003, 4.

Admissions Requirements:

Scores: Entries appear in this order: required test or GPA, minimum score (if required), median score of students entering in 2001–2002. Master's Programs: GRE-V no minimum stated; GRE-Q no minimum stated; GRE-V+Q no minimum stated; GRE-Analytical no minimum stated; GRE-V+Q+Analytical no minimum stated; overall undergraduate GPA no minimum stated; last 2 years GPA no minimum stated. Doctoral Programs: GRE-V no minimum stated; GRE-Q no minimum stated; GRE-V+Q no minimum stated; GRE-Analytical no minimum stated; GRE-V+Q+Analytical no minimum stated; overall undergraduate GPA no minimum stated; last 2 years GPA no minimum stated; psychology GPA no minimum stated; psychology GPA no minimum stated.

Other Criteria: (importance of criteria rated low, medium, or high): GRE/MAT scores medium, research experience medium, work experience medium, extracurricular activity low, clinically related public service medium, GPA medium, letters of recommendation high, statement of goals and objectives high.

Student Characteristics: The following represents characteristics of students in 2001–2002 in all graduate psychology programs in the department: Female–full-time 42, part-time 2; Male–full-time

5, part-time 0; African American/Black–full-time 2, part-time 0; Hispanic/Latino (a)–full-time 5, part-time 0; Asian/Pacific Islander–full-time 5, part-time 0; American Indian/Alaska Native–full-time 0, part-time 0.

Financial Information/Assistance:

Tuition for Full-Time Study: *Master's:* State residents per academic year $26,944, $2,694 per credit hour; nonstate residents: per academic year $26,944, $2,694 per credit hour. *Doctoral:* State residents: per academic year $26,944, $2,694 per credit hour; nonstate residents: per academic year $26,944, $2,694 per credit hour.

Financial Assistance:

First Year Students: Teaching assistantships available for first-year. Average number of hours worked per week: 20. Apply by Jan. 15. Tuition remission given: partial. Research assistantships available for first-year. Apply by Varies. Fellowships and scholarships available for first-year. Average amount paid per academic year: $500. Apply by Jan. 15. Tuition remission given: full and partial.

Advanced Students: Teaching assistantships available for advanced students. Average number of hours worked per week: 20. Apply by Jan. 15. Tuition remission given: partial. Research assistantships available for advanced students. Apply by Varies. Fellowships and scholarships available for advanced students. Average amount paid per academic year: $500. Apply by Jan. 15. Tuition remission given: full and partial.

Contact Information: Of all students currently enrolled full-time, 40% benefitted from one or more of the listed financial assistance programs. For information on financial assistance, contact: Graduate and Professional Studies department for departmental financial aid at (617) 627-3395. Contact Tufts Financial Aid office for Federal Aid at (617) 627-2000.

Internships/Practica: M.A. students engage in a semester-long internship in applied settings such as hospitals, mental health clinics, policy centers, museums. PhD students engage in full-time 1-semester or half-time full-year applied internships in varied settings.

Housing and Day Care: On-campus housing and day care facilities are available.

Employment of Department Graduates:

Master's Degree Graduates: Of those who graduated in the academic year 2000–2001, the following categories and numbers represent the post-graduate activities and employment of master's degree graduates: Enrolled in a post-doctoral residency/fellowship (n/a), employed in independent practice (n/a).

Doctoral Degree Graduates: Of those who graduated in the academic year 2000–2001, the following categories and numbers represent the post-graduate activities and employment of doctoral degree graduates: Enrolled in a psychology doctoral program (n/a), enrolled in another graduate/professional program (n/a).

Additional Information:

Orientation, Objectives, and Emphasis of Department: The department prepares students for a variety of careers that have, as their common prerequisite, a comprehensive understanding of children and their development. Students receive a foundation in psychological theory and research concerning the social, emotional, intellectual, linguistic, and physiological growth of children. Course material is complemented with progressively more involved practica encompassing observations and works with children in a wide variety of applied and research settings. The major aim of the program is to train people who can translate their knowledge about development into effective strategies for working with and on behalf of children. We believe that a background in child development is the best possible preparation for teaching and administrative careers in schools, children's advocacy and mental health agencies, hospitals, the media, government agencies concerned with the rights and welfare of children, and related fields. There is considerable room for flexibility in the program. For example, students with proficiency in one area, such as field experience, may concentrate on others, such as clinical theory and research. Also, students may choose from a rich variety of elective courses that touch upon such diverse topics as child advocacy, divorce and the family, and children's literature. The largest number of courses are in the area of developmental psychology, but there are also several courses in clinical and educational psychology and in the study of children and family policy.

Special Facilities or Resources: The department is housed in a complex of buildings on the Medford campus. The main building contains faculty and staff offices, class meeting rooms, and a library. This building includes the Eliot-Pearson Children's School, which serves normal and special-needs children aged 2 to 6. The school has observation booths for student use. Another building houses several faculty research projects, classrooms, and meeting rooms. The department is also associated with the Tufts Educational Day Care Center. Students may work, as well as observe, in all of these settings. Both facilities are integrated into faculty research and research training for graduate students.

Information for Students With Physical Disabilities: The department buildings are accessible.

Application Information:

Send to: Tufts University, Graduate and Professional Studies, Ballou Hall, Medford, MA 02155. Students are admitted in the Fall, application deadline January 15. *Fee:* $50.

Andrews University (2001 data)
Department of Educational and Counseling Psychology
Bell Hall Room 151
Berrien Springs, MI 49104-0104
Telephone: (616) 471-3113
Fax: (616) 471-6374
E-mail: *ecp@andrews.edu*
Web: *http://www.educ.andrews.edu*

Department Established:
Chairperson: Jerome D. Thayer. Number of Faculty: total–full-time 10, part-time 1; women–full-time 5; minority–full-time 5.

Programs and Degrees Offered:
Listed in the following order: Program area, degree type (T if terminal Master's), number awarded 7/00-6/01. Community counseling MA (T) 11, counseling psychology PhD 3, educational psychology MA 8, school counseling MA (T) 5, school psychology EdS (T) 2.

Student Applications/Admissions:
Student Applications

Community counseling MA—Applications 2001–2002, 30. Total applicants accepted 2001–2002, 16. New applicants enrolled 2001–2002, 14. Total enrolled 2001–2002 full-time, 32. Openings 2002–2003, 25. *Counseling psychology PhD*—Applications 2001–2002, 10. Total applicants accepted 2001–2002, 6. New applicants enrolled 2001–2002, 4. Total enrolled 2001–2002 full-time, 29. *Educational psychology* MA—Applications 2001–2002, 16. Total applicants accepted 2001–2002, 9. New applicants enrolled 2001–2002, 7. Total enrolled 2001–2002 full-time, 28. Openings 2002–2003, 12. *School counseling* MA—Applications 2001–2002, 10. Total applicants accepted 2001–2002, 7. New applicants enrolled 2001–2002, 5. Total enrolled 2001–2002 full-time, 13. Openings 2002–2003, 5. *School psychology EdS*—Applications 2001–2002, 6. Total applicants accepted 2001–2002, 4. New applicants enrolled 2001–2002, 3. Total enrolled 2001–2002 full-time, 7. Openings 2002–2003, 5.

Admissions Requirements:

Scores: Entries appear in this order: required test or GPA, minimum score (if required), median score of students entering in 2001–2002. Master's Programs: GRE-V+Q+Analytical no minimum stated; overall undergraduate GPA 2.6. Doctoral Programs: GRE-V+Q+Analytical no minimum stated; overall undergraduate GPA 3.0; psychology GPA 3.5.

Other Criteria: (importance of criteria rated low, medium, or high): GRE/MAT scores medium, research experience low, work experience low, extracurricular activity low, clinically related public service low, GPA high, letters of recommendation high, interview high, statement of goals and objectives high.

Student Characteristics: The following represents characteristics of students in 2001–2002 in all graduate psychology programs in the department: Female–full-time 19, part-time 0; Male–full-time 14, part-time 0; African American/Black–full-time 12, part-time 0; Hispanic/Latino (a)–full-time 6, part-time 0; Asian/Pacific Islander–full-time 2, part-time 0; American Indian/Alaska Native–full-time 4, part-time 0.

Financial Information/Assistance:
Tuition for Full-Time Study: No information provided.

Financial Assistance:
First Year Students: No information provided.
Advanced Students: No information provided.
Contact Information: Of all students currently enrolled full-time, 0% benefitted from one or more of the listed financial assistance programs. For information on financial assistance, contact: Dr. J. Thayer, School of Education, Graduate Program.

Internships/Practica: The professional training programs in counseling and counseling psychology are designed to produce professionals who have well developed skills in assesssment, diagnosis, and counseling. All trainees in the counseling and counseling psychology programs work in the department's Counseling and Psychological Services Center, where they see clients from the surrounding community who present a wide range of concerns, in order to prepare them for their internship experience. Master's students in the school counseling or community counseling programs must complete a 600-clock-hour internship in a school or community agency setting. These agencies include community mental health centers, youth/adolescent treatment centers, drug-alcohol treatment programs, private counseling centers, schools, and other human service agencies. Counseling psychology doctoral students must complete a 2,000-clock-hour internship in an approved health care setting under the direct supervision of a psychologist licensed to practice independently. Students are strongly encouraged to seek APA-approved or APPIC internships. Students in the master's and doctoral programs in educational psychology are provided with opportunities to do field work in educational psychology. Students in school psychology must complete a 1,200-clock-hour internship under the supervision of a certified or licensed school psychologist in a local school district.

Housing and Day Care: No on-campus housing and day care facilities are available.

Employment of Department Graduates:
Master's Degree Graduates: Of those who graduated in the academic year 2000–2001, the following categories and numbers represent the post-graduate activities and employment of master's degree graduates: Enrolled in a post-doctoral residency/fellowship (n/a), employed in independent practice (n/a).
Doctoral Degree Graduates: Of those who graduated in the academic year 2000–2001, the following categories and numbers represent the post-graduate activities and employment of doctoral degree graduates: Enrolled in a psychology doctoral program (n/a), enrolled in another graduate/professional program (n/a).

Additional Information:
Orientation, Objectives, and Emphasis of Department: The objective of the master's programs is to prepare students for profes-

sional employment in educational and mental health settings as counselors and learning specialists. Students obtaining an EdS in school psychology are prepared for a professional career as certified or licensed school psychologists to work in public or private schools, preschools, and child development centers. Doctoral students are prepared for teaching, research, and professional practice. Students are exposed to a variety of theoretical orientations and are expected to develop an eclectic model for delivering counseling and psychological services. The university is sponsored by the Seventh-Day Adventist Church. However, students from all religious persuasions are welcome and considered without bias. While there is an emphasis in the department on the relationship between psychological theory, research, and practice and Christian theology and religious experience, respect is maintained for individual differences. PhD students in counseling psychology are trained using the scientist-practitioner model. They are given instruction in scientific and professional ethics and standards, research design and methodology, statistics and psychometrics. In addition, coursework in the following areas is required: biological bases of behavior, cognitive-affective bases of behavior, social bases of behavior, and individual differences. Special emphases are available in marital and family therapy, substance abuse counseling, adult or child mental health services.

Special Facilities or Resources: The department operates a Counseling and Psychological Services Center that provides mental health services to children, adolescents, and adults who reside in the surrounding area. The Center includes space for individual, family, group, and child therapy. Video monitors and videotape are used in the supervision of all trainees. The department also has access to a statistical research center with mainframe accessibility and a number of microcomputers. A separate microcomputer lab is also available.

Information for Students With Physical Disabilities: Buildings, including classrooms and bathrooms, are equipped for wheelchair accessibility.

Application Information:
Send to: Eileen Lesher/Graduate Admissions, Andrews University, Berrien Springs, MI 49104-0740. Students are admitted in the Fall. Rolling deadline, ask for details. *Fee:* $40.

Center for Humanistic Studies Graduate School
40 E. Ferry Avenue
Detroit, MI 48202
Telephone: (313) 875-7440
Fax: (313) 875-2610
E-mail: *chs@humanpsych.edu*
Web: *http://www.humanpsych.edu*

Department Established:
1980. President: Kerry Moustakas, Ph.D. Number of Faculty: total–full-time 4, part-time 10; women–full-time 2, part-time 4; minority–full-time 1.

Programs and Degrees Offered:
Listed in the following order: Program area, degree type (T if terminal Master's), number awarded 7/00-6/01. MA (T) 30, PsyD.

Student Applications/Admissions:
Student Applications
MA—Applications 2001–2002, 92. Total applicants accepted 2001–2002, 34. New applicants enrolled 2001–2002, 30. Total enrolled 2001–2002 full-time, 30. Openings 2002–2003, 36. The Median number of years required for completion of a degree is 1. The number of students enrolled full and part-time, who were dismissed or voluntarily withdrew from this program area were 0. *PsyD*—Applications 2001–2002, 23. Total applicants accepted 2001–2002, 16. New applicants enrolled 2001–2002, 16. Total enrolled 2001–2002 full-time, 54. Openings 2002–2003, 16. The number of students enrolled full and part-time, who were dismissed or voluntarily withdrew from this program area were 2.

Admissions Requirements:
Scores: Entries appear in this order: required test or GPA, minimum score (if required), median score of students entering in 2001–2002. Master's Programs: overall undergraduate GPA 3.00, 3.30. Doctoral Programs: overall undergraduate GPA 3.0, 3.3 ; last 2 years GPA no minimum stated; psychology GPA no minimum stated; psychology GPA 3.0, 3.3.
Other Criteria: (importance of criteria rated low, medium, or high): research experience low, work experience high, clinically related public service high, GPA high, letters of recommendation high, interview high, statement of goals and objectives high.

Student Characteristics: The following represents characteristics of students in 2001–2002 in all graduate psychology programs in the department: Female–full-time 60, part-time 0; Male–full-time 23, part-time 0; African American/Black–full-time 13, part-time 0; Hispanic/Latino (a)–full-time 0, part-time 0; Asian/Pacific Islander–full-time 1, part-time 0; American Indian/Alaska Native–full-time 0, part-time 0; Multi-ethnic–full-time 0, part-time 0; students subject to the Americans with Disabilities Act–full-time 0, part-time 0.

Financial Information/Assistance:
Tuition for Full-Time Study: *Master's:* State residents per academic year $14,070; nonstate residents: per academic year $14,070. *Doctoral:* State residents: per academic year $14,070; nonstate residents: per academic year $14,070.

Financial Assistance:
First Year Students: No information provided.
Advanced Students: No information provided.
Contact Information: Of all students currently enrolled full-time, 0% benefitted from one or more of the listed financial assistance programs. For information on financial assistance, contact: Financial Aid Dept., Vange Puszcz Center for Humanistic Studies Graduate School, 40 E. Ferry Ave., Detroit, MI 48202-3802.

Internships/Practica: There is a mandatory 500 hour practicum for master's students, a 500 hour practicum for doctoral students and a two-thousand hour internship for doctoral students in order to receive their degree and satisfy the state licensing board's requirements. For those doctoral students for whom a professional internship is required prior to graduation, 9 applied in 2000–2001.

Housing and Day Care: No on-campus housing and day care facilities are available.

Employment of Department Graduates:

Master's Degree Graduates: Of those who graduated in the academic year 2000–2001, the following categories and numbers represent the post-graduate activities and employment of master's degree graduates: Enrolled in a post-doctoral residency/fellowship (n/a), employed in independent practice (n/a).

Doctoral Degree Graduates: Of those who graduated in the academic year 2000–2001, the following categories and numbers represent the post-graduate activities and employment of doctoral degree graduates: Enrolled in a psychology doctoral program (n/a), enrolled in another graduate/professional program (n/a).

Additional Information:

Orientation, Objectives, and Emphasis of Department: The mission of CHS is to offer education and training programs that enable students to obtain the knowledge and competencies needed to grow as persons, psychologists, and as educators in order to serve the mental health needs of individuals, families, schools, and communities. The programs emphasize theoretical and practical knowledge of humanistic and clinical psychology and education, qualitative investigations of human experience, and training in psychotherapy and psychological assessments.

Special Facilities or Resources: n/a.

Application Information:

Send to: Admissions Department CHS, 40 E. Ferry Ave., Detroit, MI 48202-3802. Students are admitted in the Fall, application deadline March 1st. We accept on a rolling admissions policy-Our deadline is March 1 but will still accept applications if there are openings. Student may have to be wait-listed. *Fee:* $75.

Central Michigan University
Department of Psychology
Humanities and Social and Behavioral Sciences
Sloan Hall
Mt. Pleasant, MI 48859
Telephone: (989) 774-3001
Fax: (989) 774-2553
E-mail: *psy@cmich.edu*
Web: *http://www.chsbs.cmich.edu/psychology*

Department Established:

1965. Chairperson: Gary Dunbar. Number of Faculty: total–full-time 30, part-time 7; women–full-time 11, part-time 3; minority–full-time 4, part-time 1.

Programs and Degrees Offered:

Listed in the following order: Program area, degree type (T if terminal Master's), number awarded 7/00-6/01. Clinical PhD 9, experimental PhD 2, general MA (T) 13, industrial/organizational PhD (T) 3, school PhD 2, School EdS 9.

APA Accreditation: Clinical PhD: full.

Student Applications/Admissions:

Student Applications

Clinical PhD—Applications 2001–2002, 69. Total applicants accepted 2001–2002, 8. New applicants enrolled 2001–2002, 8. Total enrolled 2001–2002 full-time, 39. Openings 2002–2003, 10. The Median number of years required for completion of a degree are 6. The number of students enrolled full and part-time, who were dismissed or voluntarily withdrew from this program area were 2. *Experimental PhD*—Applications 2001–2002, 16. Total applicants accepted 2001–2002, 2. New applicants enrolled 2001–2002, 2. Total enrolled 2001–2002 full-time, 8. Openings 2002–2003, 2. The Median number of years required for completion of a degree are 5. The number of students enrolled full and part-time, who were dismissed or voluntarily withdrew from this program area were 1. *General MA*—Applications 2001–2002, 24. Total applicants accepted 2001–2002, 12. New applicants enrolled 2001–2002, 4. Total enrolled 2001–2002 full-time, 26. Openings 2002–2003, 15. The Median number of years required for completion of a degree are 3. The number of students enrolled full and part-time, who were dismissed or voluntarily withdrew from this program area were 2. *Industrial/organizational PhD*—Applications 2001–2002, 99. Total applicants accepted 2001–2002, 8. New applicants enrolled 2001–2002, 8. Total enrolled 2001–2002 full-time, 20. Openings 2002–2003, 10. The Median number of years required for completion of a degree are 4. The number of students enrolled full and part-time, who were dismissed or voluntarily withdrew from this program area were 1. *School PhD*—Applications 2001–2002, 14. Total applicants accepted 2001–2002, 6. New applicants enrolled 2001–2002, 3. Total enrolled 2001–2002 full-time, 12. Openings 2002–2003, 4. The Median number of years required for completion of a degree are 5. The number of students enrolled full and part-time, who were dismissed or voluntarily withdrew from this program area were 0. *School EdS*—Applications 2001–2002, 28. Total applicants accepted 2001–2002, 8. New applicants enrolled 2001–2002, 8. Total enrolled 2001–2002 full-time, 34. Openings 2002–2003, 8. The Median number of years required for completion of a degree are 5. The number of students enrolled full and part-time, who were dismissed or voluntarily withdrew from this program area were 1.

Admissions Requirements:

Scores: Entries appear in this order: required test or GPA, minimum score (if required), median score of students entering in 2001–2002. Master's Programs: GRE-V no minimum stated; GRE-Q no minimum stated; overall undergraduate GPA 3.00; psychology GPA 3.00. GRE-V and GRE-Q score requirements vary with each application pool. Doctoral Programs: GRE-V no minimum stated; GRE-Q no minimum stated; overall undergraduate GPA 3.00; last 2 years GPA no minimum stated; psychology GPA 3.00; psychology GPA no minimum stated. GRE-V & GRE-Q requirements vary with each application pool.

Other Criteria: (importance of criteria rated low, medium, or high): GRE/MAT scores medium, research experience high, work experience medium, extracurricular activity low, clinically related public service medium, GPA high, letters of recommendation high, statement of goals and objectives high.

Student Characteristics: The following represents characteristics of students in 2001–2002 in all graduate psychology programs in

the department: Female–full-time 85, part-time 0; Male–full-time 36, part-time 0; African American/Black–full-time 3, part-time 0; Hispanic/Latino (a)–full-time 2, part-time 0; Asian/Pacific Islander–full-time 4, part-time 0; American Indian/Alaska Native–full-time 0, part-time 0.

Financial Information/Assistance:

Tuition for Full-Time Study: *Master's:* State residents $162 per credit hour; nonstate residents: $323 per credit hour. *Doctoral:* State residents: $175 per credit hour; nonstate residents: $348 per credit hour.

Financial Assistance:

First Year Students: Teaching assistantships available for first-year. Average amount paid per academic year: $9,600. Average number of hours worked per week: 20. Apply by February 6. Tuition remission given: partial. Research assistantships available for first-year. Average amount paid per academic year: $8,600. Average number of hours worked per week: 20. Apply by February 6. Tuition remission given: partial. Fellowships and scholarships available for first-year. Average amount paid per academic year: $8,000. Average number of hours worked per week: 20. Apply by February 6. Tuition remission given: partial.

Advanced Students: Teaching assistantships available for advanced students. Average amount paid per academic year: $10,650. Average number of hours worked per week: 20. Apply by February 6. Tuition remission given: partial. Research assistantships available for advanced students. Average amount paid per academic year: $9,650. Average number of hours worked per week: 20. Apply by February 6. Tuition remission given: partial. Fellowships and scholarships available for advanced students. Average amount paid per academic year: $9,300. Average number of hours worked per week: 20. Apply by February 6. Tuition remission given: partial.

Contact Information: Of all students currently enrolled full-time, 88% benefitted from one or more of the listed financial assistance programs. For information on financial assistance, contact: Department of Psychology. Note: Some students receive a half time assistantship instead of the full time listed above, and are included in the %.

Internships/Practica:
Most practica and internships are arranged through agencies and schools outside the University. However, practica experiences are available through the Department's Psychological Training and Consultation Center. Second-year clinical students routinely have their first practicum at the Center. For those doctoral students for whom a professional internship is required prior to graduation, 5 applied in 2000–2001. Of those who applied, 5 were placed in internships listed by the Association of Psychology Postdoctoral and Internship Programs (APPIC); 5 were placed in APA accredited internships.

Housing and Day Care:
On-campus housing and day care facilities are available.

Employment of Department Graduates:

Master's Degree Graduates: Of those who graduated in the academic year 2000–2001, the following categories and numbers represent the post-graduate activities and employment of master's degree graduates: Enrolled in a psychology doctoral program (13), enrolled in a post-doctoral residency/fellowship (n/a), employed in independent practice (n/a), employed in other positions at a higher education institution (1), employed in a professional position in a school system (8), employed in business or industry (research/consulting) (2).

Doctoral Degree Graduates: Of those who graduated in the academic year 2000–2001, the following categories and numbers represent the post-graduate activities and employment of doctoral degree graduates: Enrolled in a psychology doctoral program (n/a), enrolled in another graduate/professional program (n/a), enrolled in a post-doctoral residency/fellowship (1), employed in an academic position at a university (2), employed in an academic position at a 2-year/4-year college (1), employed in business or industry (research/consulting) (2), employed in a community mental health/counseling center (7).

Additional Information:

Orientation, Objectives, and Emphasis of Department: Specialization is possible in the areas of clinical, applied experimental, industrial/organizational, and school psychology. There is also a general/experimental MS program with emphasis on foundations, statistics, methodology, and research, which is designed to prepare students for doctoral training or research positions in the public or private sectors. The clinical program follows a practitioner-scientist model focusing on training for applied settings. The industrial/organizational program is oriented toward training students for careers in research, university, or business settings. The school program prepares school psychologists to provide consultation, intervention, and diagnositc services to schools and school children. The program meets Michigan requirements for certification.

Special Facilities or Resources: Space is reserved for student research with human subjects. Special equipment permits studies in learning, cognition, human factors, psychophysiology, neuropsychology, and perception. Computer laboratories are available, one specifically designated for clinical and school students. All computer labs have direct email, and Internet access, as well as statistical and research software. The Psychology Training and Consultation Center provides training, research, and service functions. In a separate building space is devoted to animal research and teaching of behavioral neuroscience and experimental behavior analysis. The behavioral neuroscience laboratory contains a fully equipped surgical/historological suite, behavioral testing area and equipment, and a data analysis room including microscopes and an image analysis system. The experimental analysis laboratory is equipped with automated operant chambers for both birds and rodents. A Life-Span Development Research Center has been established in the Department.

Information for Students With Physical Disabilities: A barrier-free computer laboratory exists in the department's main building.

Application Information:
Send to: Psychology Department, Sloan Hall, Central Michigan University, Mt. Pleasant, MI 48859. Students are admitted in the Fall. Clinical deadline is January 15, all others are February 1. *Fee:* $30.

Detroit-Mercy, University of

Department of Psychology
College of Liberal Arts
P.O. Box 19900
Detroit, MI 48219-0900
Telephone: (313) 993-6192
Fax: (313) 993-6397
E-mail: *abellsc@udmercy.edu*
Web: *http://www.udmercy.edu/psychology*

Department Established:

1946. Chairperson: Christine M. Paryard, Ph.D. Number of Faculty: total–full-time 13; women–full-time 10; minority–full-time 2.

Programs and Degrees Offered:

Listed in the following order: Program area, degree type (T if terminal Master's), number awarded 7/00-6/01. Clinical MA (T) 25, industrial/organizational MA (T) 7, school.

APA Accreditation: Clinical PhD: full.

Student Applications/Admissions:

Student Applications

Clinical MA—Applications 2001–2002, 40. Total applicants accepted 2001–2002, 24. New applicants enrolled 2001–2002, 14. Total enrolled 2001–2002 full-time, 25, part-time, 11. Openings 2002–2003, 15. *Industrial/organizational* MA—Applications 2001–2002, 20. Total applicants accepted 2001–2002, 16. New applicants enrolled 2001–2002, 7. Total enrolled 2001–2002 full-time, 12, part-time, 10. Openings 2002–2003, 14.

Admissions Requirements:

Scores: Entries appear in this order: required test or GPA, minimum score (if required), median score of students entering in 2001–2002. Master's Programs: GRE-V 450, 550; GRE-Q 450, 500; GRE-V+Q 900, 1050; GRE-V+Q+Analytical 1200, 1550; overall undergraduate GPA 3.0, 3.3; last 2 years GPA 3.0, 3.4; psychology GPA 3.0, 3.5. Doctoral Programs: GRE-V 500, 550; GRE-Q 500, 550; GRE-V+Q 1000, 1100; GRE-V+Q+Analytical 1500, 1550; overall undergraduate GPA 3.0, 3.4 ; last 2 years GPA 3.4, 3.5; psychology GPA 3.5, 3.6.
Other Criteria: (importance of criteria rated low, medium, or high): research experience medium, work experience medium, extracurricular activity medium, clinically related public service medium, letters of recommendation high, interview high, statement of goals and objectives high.

Student Characteristics:

The following represents characteristics of students in 2001–2002 in all graduate psychology programs in the department: Female–full-time 20, part-time 8; Male–full-time 7, part-time 5; African American/Black–full-time 5, part-time 0; Hispanic/Latino (a)–full-time 1, part-time 0; Asian/Pacific Islander–full-time 2, part-time 3; American Indian/Alaska Native–full-time 0, part-time 0.

Financial Information/Assistance:

Tuition for Full-Time Study: No information provided.

Financial Assistance:

First Year Students: No information provided.
Advanced Students: No information provided.
Contact Information: No information provided.

Internships/Practica: Students have available for practicum and internship experiences a wide range of settings ranging from hospitals, inpatient and outpatient units, schools, community agencies, and businesses. Populations served can range from children, adolescents, and adults to prisoners and those requiring rehabilitation services. Assessments and interventions of various kinds are performed under the supervision of licensed or appropriately credentialed psychologists.

Housing and Day Care: On-campus housing and day care facilities are available.

Employment of Department Graduates:

Master's Degree Graduates: Of those who graduated in the academic year 2000–2001, the following categories and numbers represent the post-graduate activities and employment of master's degree graduates: Enrolled in a post-doctoral residency/fellowship (n/a), employed in independent practice (n/a).
Doctoral Degree Graduates: Of those who graduated in the academic year 2000–2001, the following categories and numbers represent the post-graduate activities and employment of doctoral degree graduates: Enrolled in a psychology doctoral program (n/a), enrolled in another graduate/professional program (n/a).

Additional Information:

Orientation, Objectives, and Emphasis of Department: The overall goal of graduate education in the Psychology Department is to train psychologists who are well-grounded in theory and research and who can function in a variety of settings. The theoretical emphasis of the doctoral program in clinical psychology is psychodynamic, while the orientations of the other programs are more eclectic. Regardless of orientation, however, students are exposed to different kinds of intervention techniques, each with its own theoretical rationale. The master's program in clinical psychology allows students to specialize in working with substance abusers or children. The specialist program in school psychology prepares students to function as psychologists in school settings, dealing with children and families. The master's program in industrial psychology focuses on human resource development and personnel management.

Special Facilities or Resources: The University of Detroit-Mercy runs the University Psychology Clinic, which serves the metropolitan area as a community mental health clinic. The clinic work is directed or supervised by faculty members and psychologists from the community. Students in the doctoral programs in clinical and students in the specialist program in school psychology begin their clinical work in their second year and continue with increasingly responsible supervised experiences.

Application Information:

Send to: Patricia Hall-Thomas, College of Liberal Arts. Students are admitted in the Fall. The application deadline for the fall semester varies by program: January 1 to March 15. *Fee:* The amount of fee is $30 for the MA or Specialist program and $50 for the PhD program.

Eastern Michigan University
Department of Psychology
College of Arts and Sciences
537 Mark Jefferson Hall
Ypsilanti, MI 48197
Telephone: (313) 487-1155
Fax: (313) 487-6553
E-mail: *ken.rusiniak@emich.edu*
Web: *http://www.emich.edu*

Department Established:

1962. Department Head: Kenneth W. Rusiniak. Number of Faculty: total–full-time 22, part-time 13; women–full-time 9, part-time 5; minority–full-time 1, part-time 1.

Programs and Degrees Offered:

Listed in the following order: Program area, degree type (T if terminal Master's), number awarded 7/00-6/01. Clinical Behavioral Psychology MA (T) 9, Clinical Psychology PhD, General Clinical Psychology MA (T) 14, General Experimental Psych. MA (T) 1.

Student Applications/Admissions:

Student Applications

Clinical Behavioral Psychology MA—Applications 2001–2002, 25. Total applicants accepted 2001–2002, 16. New applicants enrolled 2001–2002, 12. Total enrolled 2001–2002 full-time, 20, part-time, 5. Openings 2002–2003, 15. The Median number of years required for completion of a degree are 2. *Clinical Psychology PhD*—Applications 2001–2002, 37. Total applicants accepted 2001–2002, 10. New applicants enrolled 2001–2002, 10. Total enrolled 2001–2002 full-time, 10. Openings 2002–2003, 10. The number of students enrolled full and part-time, who were dismissed or voluntarily withdrew from this program area were 0. *General Clinical Psychology MA*—Applications 2001–2002, 36. Total applicants accepted 2001–2002, 16. New applicants enrolled 2001–2002, 14. Total enrolled 2001–2002 full-time, 22, part-time, 8. Openings 2002–2003, 15. The Median number of years required for completion of a degree are 2. *General Clinical Psychology MA*—Applications 2001–2002, 36. Total applicants accepted 2001–2002, 16. New applicants enrolled 2001–2002, 14. Total enrolled 2001–2002 full-time, 22, part-time, 8. Openings 2002–2003, 15. The Median number of years required for completion of a degree are 2. *General Experimental Psych. MA*—Applications 2001–2002, 8. Total applicants accepted 2001–2002, 4. New applicants enrolled 2001–2002, 4. Total enrolled 2001–2002 full-time, 2, part-time, 8. Openings 2002–2003, 4. The Median number of years required for completion of a degree are 3.

Admissions Requirements:

Scores: Entries appear in this order: required test or GPA, minimum score (if required), median score of students entering in 2001–2002. Master's Programs: GRE-V+Q 1000; overall undergraduate GPA 3.0. The GRE scores of 500 and 500 (or 1000 combined) are our suggested scores, however this is not an absolute cut off point. There is also a minimum GPA of 3.0 that is advised. At least two letters of recommendation are necessary and a personal statement/writing sample are required for some programs. Doctoral Programs: GRE-V+Q 1000; overall undergraduate GPA 3.0; last 2 years GPA no minimum stated; psychology GPA no minimum stated; psychology GPA no minimum stated.

Other Criteria: (importance of criteria rated low, medium, or high): GRE/MAT scores medium, research experience medium, work experience medium, extracurricular activity medium, clinically related public service medium, GPA medium, letters of recommendation medium, interview medium, statement of goals and objectives medium. Weight given to criteria vary among each of three programs.

Student Characteristics: The following represents characteristics of students in 2001–2002 in all graduate psychology programs in the department: Female–full-time 28, part-time 7; Male–full-time 5, part-time 2; African American/Black–full-time 3, part-time 0; Hispanic/Latino (a)–full-time 1, part-time 0; Asian/Pacific Islander–full-time 2, part-time 0; American Indian/Alaska Native–full-time 0, part-time 0; Multi-ethnic–full-time 0, part-time 1; students subject to the Americans with Disabilities Act–full-time 0, part-time 0.

Financial Information/Assistance:

Tuition for Full-Time Study: *Master's:* State residents $160 per credit hour; nonstate residents: $360 per credit hour. *Doctoral:* State residents: $196 per credit hour; nonstate residents: $410 per credit hour.

Financial Assistance:

First Year Students: Teaching assistantships available for first-year. Average amount paid per academic year: $6,315. Average number of hours worked per week: 20. Apply by Feb 15. Tuition remission given: partial. Fellowships and scholarships available for first-year. Average amount paid per academic year: $4,000. Average number of hours worked per week: 20. Apply by Feb 15. Tuition remission given: full and partial.

Advanced Students: Teaching assistantships available for advanced students. Average amount paid per academic year: $6,580. Average number of hours worked per week: 20. Apply by Feb 15. Tuition remission given: partial. Fellowships and scholarships available for advanced students. Average amount paid per academic year: $4,000. Average number of hours worked per week: 20. Apply by Feb 15. Tuition remission given: full and partial.

Contact Information: Of all students currently enrolled full-time, 22% benefitted from one or more of the listed financial assistance programs. For information on financial assistance, contact: Office of Financial Aid, 403 Pierce Hall, Eastern Michigan University, Ypsilanti, MI 48197; Graduate School, Starkweather Hall, Eastern Michigan University, Ypsilanti, MI 48197.

Internships/Practica: Practicum settings (unpaid) are available in the surrounding community for clinical and clinical behavioral students. In addition, the university offers mental health services involving practicum experiences at both the campus Snow Health Center and the EMU Psychology Clinic. Both terminal MS and PhD programs require sufficient practicum hours to meet the State of Michigan requirements for the Limited License in Psychology (LLP).

Housing and Day Care: On-campus housing and day care facilities are available.

Employment of Department Graduates:

Master's Degree Graduates: Of those who graduated in the academic year 2000–2001, the following categories and numbers represent the post-graduate activities and employment of master's degree graduates: Enrolled in a psychology doctoral program (3), enrolled in a post-doctoral residency/fellowship (n/a), employed in independent practice (n/a), employed in business or industry (research/consulting) (3), employed in a community mental health/counseling center (15), employed in a hospital/medical center (2).

Doctoral Degree Graduates: Of those who graduated in the academic year 2000–2001, the following categories and numbers represent the post-graduate activities and employment of doctoral degree graduates: Enrolled in a psychology doctoral program (n/a), enrolled in another graduate/professional program (n/a).

Additional Information:

Orientation, Objectives, and Emphasis of Department: The Psychology Department offers three terminal Master's Degree programs and courses in several orientations, including behavioral, social, insight, developmental, and physiological. Within the two Master's clinical programs, the major emphases are on psychological assessment (Clinical Program) and behavioral treatment (Clinical Behavioral Program). Within each program there are a wide variety of theoretical, applied, and research interests. The goal of the Clinical and Clinical Behavioral programs is on giving students the background to immediately begin work in clinical treatment settings or to prepare them for entry into doctoral programs, as matches the student's educational objectives. The emphasis of the Master's in General Experimental Psychology is to prepare students for entry into higher level study in psychology or as researchers in applied/research settings. Because Psychology is considered a natural science at Eastern Michigan University, there is also an emphasis on basing clinical practice on research findings. Theses, although optional in the clinical programs, are expected to be research based. A new five-year Ph.D. program in Clinical Psychology, designed to give advanced training in the supervision of mental health professionals in mental health care settings, accepted the first class in the Fall 2001. The entry requirements for this program are somewhat more stringent than those of our Master's Program with a more competitive applicant pool. The Ph.D. offers specializations in either general clinical or behavioral psychology, a terminal Master's Degree en route, a Full four-year doctoral fellowship which covers tuition and fees plus a stipend. For more information on this program, please contact: Graduate Secretary, 537 Mark Jefferson, Psychology Department, Eastern Michigan University, Ypsilanti, MI; 734-487-1155. Information is also available at on the EMU-Psychology Department website: http://164.76.13.213/EMUPsych/index.html.

Special Facilities or Resources: The faculty, which consists of approximately 23 full-time members with PhDs and varying number of part-time lecturers, is eclectic in orientation with a wide variety of interests and professional backgrounds. Research interests and publication record of the faculty include psychological test construction and validation, basic behavioral research with humans and non-humans, the history of psychology, consumer fraud, applied behavior analysis, physiological psychology, forensic psychology, personality, social psychology, and many more. Student enrollment is intentionally kept low in order to provide the students with ample opportunities to develop close working relationships with the faculty. Students regularly present at regional, national, and international conventions, as well as co-author published papers with faculty. The facilities of the Psychology Department are located in the Mark Jefferson Science building and in the newly renovated Psychology Clinic at 611 West Cross. The department features a state-of-the-art computer laboratory, IEEE 802.11 (AirPort) wireless networking capabilities, human and animal research facilities, seminar rooms, a clinic with one-way observation capabilities, a new university library less than three-minutes away on foot, and other equipment and supplies needed for advanced study.

Information for Students With Physical Disabilities: Students with physical disabilities are encouraged to apply. Applicable rules and laws regarding accommodations and access will be observed.

Application Information:
Send to: Graduate Admissions, 401 Pierce Hall, Eastern Michigan University, Ypsilanti, MI 48197. Students are admitted in the Fall, application deadline Mar 15. March 15 is a "priority deadline." Applications received after that date may be considered if places remain open. A January 15 deadline applies to our Ph.D. psychology program. Submit duplicate application directly to: Graduate Secretary, 537 Mark Jefferson, Department of Psychology, Eastern Michigan University, Ypsilanti, MI 48197. *Fee:* $30.

Michigan State University
Counseling Psychology Program
College of Education
435 Erickson Hall, Michigan State University
East Lansing, MI 48824
Telephone: (517) 355-8502
Fax: (517) 353-6393
E-mail: *gsmith@msu.edu*
Web: *http://www.ed-web3.educ.msu.edu/cepse/cp/*

Department Established:
1977. Program Director: Gloria S. Smith. Number of Faculty: total–full-time 3, part-time 7; women–full-time 1, part-time 3; minority–full-time 1, part-time 2; faculty subject to the Americans with Disabilities Act 1.

Programs and Degrees Offered:
Listed in the following order: Program area, degree type (T if terminal Master's), number awarded 7/00-6/01. Counseling psychology PhD 3.

APA Accreditation: Counseling PhD: full.

Student Applications/Admissions:

Student Applications

Counseling psychology PhD—Applications 2001–2002, 56. Total applicants accepted 2001–2002, 8. New applicants enrolled 2001–2002, 5. Total enrolled 2001–2002 full-time, 34. Openings 2002–2003, 8. The Median number of years required for completion of a degree are 5. The number of students enrolled full and part-time, who were dismissed or voluntarily withdrew from this program area were 0.

Admissions Requirements:

Scores: Entries appear in this order: required test or GPA, minimum score (if required), median score of students entering in 2001–2002. Doctoral Programs: GRE-V no minimum stated, 580; GRE-Q no minimum stated, 670; GRE-V+Q no minimum stated, 1250; GRE-Analytical no minimum stated, 660; overall undergraduate GPA no minimum stated, 3.39; last 2 years GPA no minimum stated, 3.75; psychology GPA no minimum stated; psychology GPA no minimum stated, 3.70.

Other Criteria: (importance of criteria rated low, medium, or high): GRE/MAT scores medium, research experience high, work experience medium, extracurricular activity medium, clinically related public service medium, GPA medium, letters of recommendation high, interview high, statement of goals and objectives high.

Student Characteristics: The following represents characteristics of students in 2001–2002 in all graduate psychology programs in the department: Female–full-time 21, part-time 0; Male–full-time 13, part-time 0; African American/Black–full-time 5, part-time 0; Hispanic/Latino (a)–full-time 1, part-time 0; Asian/Pacific Islander–full-time 4, part-time 0; American Indian/Alaska Native–full-time 0, part-time 0; Multi-ethnic–full-time 0, students subject to the Americans with Disabilities Act–full-time 1.

Financial Information/Assistance:

Tuition for Full-Time Study: *Doctoral:* State residents: $244 per credit hour; nonstate residents: $494 per credit hour.

Financial Assistance:

First Year Students: Teaching assistantships available for first-year. Average amount paid per academic year: $6,057. Average number of hours worked per week: 10. Tuition remission given: full.

Advanced Students: Teaching assistantships available for advanced students. Average amount paid per academic year: $6,057. Average number of hours worked per week: 10. Tuition remission given: full.

Contact Information: Of all students currently enrolled full-time, 96% benefitted from one or more of the listed financial assistance programs. For information on financial assistance, contact: Richard S. Prawat, 449 Erickson Hall, MSU, East Lansing, MI 48824.

Internships/Practica: All students complete a 500-hour practicum at the MSU Counseling Center and a 225-hour advanced practicum in a community or university setting. For those doctoral students for whom a professional internship is required prior to graduation, 3 applied in 2000–2001. Of those who applied, 3 were placed in internships listed by the Association of Psychology Postdoctoral and Internship Programs (APPIC); 3 were placed in APA accredited internships.

Housing and Day Care: No on-campus housing and day care facilities are available.

Employment of Department Graduates:

Master's Degree Graduates: Of those who graduated in the academic year 2000–2001, the following categories and numbers represent the post-graduate activities and employment of master's degree graduates: Enrolled in a post-doctoral residency/fellowship (n/a), employed in independent practice (n/a).

Doctoral Degree Graduates: Of those who graduated in the academic year 2000–2001, the following categories and numbers represent the post-graduate activities and employment of doctoral degree graduates: Enrolled in a psychology doctoral program (n/a), enrolled in another graduate/professional program (n/a), employed in an academic position at a university (1), employed in other positions at a higher education institution (1), employed in a hospital/medical center (1).

Additional Information:

Orientation, Objectives, and Emphasis of Department: A fundamental goal of the program is to train highly skilled professionals who are proficient in applying counseling and research skills toward the advancement of human welfare in a variety of settings. The major emphasis, however, of the MSU Counseling Psychology program is on preparing students to work in university settings as a counseling psychologist, teacher, and scholar. Given this focus, the program's curriculum is based on the scientist-practitioner model of doctoral training, which emphasizes the thoughtful integration of theory, research, and practice in professional psychology. The theoretical foundations component of the program emphasizes theories of counseling and personality, career development, and cultural diversity; the research component is aimed at promoting understanding of psychological inquiry, and at developing competencies in research methodology and design, measurement, and evaluation; finally, the practice component seeks to develop diagnostic, assessment, intervention, supervision, and consultation skills to provide and support preventive, developmental, and remedial counseling.

Special Facilities or Resources: The College of Education, which houses the counseling psychology program, has a number of technology support resources for graduate students, including several microcomputing labs and a technology exploration center. At the time of their initial registration, all graduate students receive an electronic mailing address which enables them to access local information networks (e.g., MSU Library holdings, campus listings of graduate employment opportunities, etc.) as well as the Internet and World Wide Web. The MSU Library system is extensive, with holdings numbering approximately 3,300,000 volumes. The Counseling Psychology program also provides organized training services for its students who are assigned undergraduate teaching (graduate assistantships) responsibilities within the College. These services are designed to help students develop their teaching, presentational, and classroom management skills.

Application Information:

Send to: Kathy Dimoff, Admissions Secretary, 447 Erickson Hall, MSU, East Lansing, MI 48824-1034. Students are admitted in the Fall, application deadline January 5. *Fee:* $30. In extreme cases of financial need, the university will sometimes waive the application fee.

Michigan State University

Department of Psychology
Social Science
149 Snyder Hall
East Lansing, MI 48824-1117
Telephone: (517) 353-5258
Fax: (517) 432-2476
E-mail: *detwiler@msu.edu*
Web: *http://psychology.msu.edu*

Department Established:

1946. Chairperson: Neal Schmitt. Number of Faculty: total–full-time 52, part-time 2; women–full-time 16, part-time 3; minority–full-time 5.

Programs and Degrees Offered:

Listed in the following order: Program area, degree type (T if terminal Master's), number awarded 7/00-6/01. Behvavorial neuroscience PhD 1, clinical PhD 7, Cognitive PhD, developmental PhD 1, ecological-community PhD, industrial/organizational PhD 6, social/personality PhD.

APA Accreditation: Clinical PhD: full.

Student Applications/Admissions:

Student Applications

Behvavorial neuroscience PhD—Applications 2001–2002, 17. Total applicants accepted 2001–2002, 5. New applicants enrolled 2001–2002, 3. Total enrolled 2001–2002 full-time, 18. Openings 2002–2003, 6. The Median number of years required for completion of a degree are 6. The number of students enrolled full and part-time, who were dismissed or voluntarily withdrew from this program area were 3. *Clinical PhD*—Applications 2001–2002, 148. Total applicants accepted 2001–2002, 14. New applicants enrolled 2001–2002, 5. Total enrolled 2001–2002 full-time, 55. Openings 2002–2003, 6. The Median number of years required for completion of a degree are 6. The number of students enrolled full and part-time, who were dismissed or voluntarily withdrew from this program area were 4. *Cognitive PhD. Developmental PhD*—Applications 2001–2002, 0. Total enrolled 2001–2002 full-time, 11. The Median number of years required for completion of a degree are 9. The number of students enrolled full and part-time, who were dismissed or voluntarily withdrew from this program area were 0. *Ecological-community PhD*—Applications 2001–2002, 22. Total applicants accepted 2001–2002, 5. New applicants enrolled 2001–2002, 5. Total enrolled 2001–2002 full-time, 27. Openings 2002–2003, 5. The number of students enrolled full and part-time, who were dismissed or voluntarily withdrew from this program area were 5. *Industrial/organizational PhD*—Applications 2001–2002, 69. Total applicants accepted 2001–2002, 6. New applicants enrolled 2001–2002, 4. Total enrolled 2001–2002 full-time, 27. The Median number of years required for completion of a degree are 5. The number of students enrolled full and part-time, who were dismissed or voluntarily withdrew from this program area were 0. *Social/personality PhD*—Applications 2001–2002, 25. Total applicants accepted 2001–2002, 11. New applicants enrolled 2001–2002, 5. Total enrolled 2001–2002 full-time, 11. Openings 2002–2003, 2. The number of students enrolled full and part-time, who were dismissed or voluntarily withdrew from this program area were 1.

Admissions Requirements:

Scores: Entries appear in this order: required test or GPA, minimum score (if required), median score of students entering in 2001–2002. Doctoral Programs: GRE-V no minimum stated, 538; GRE-Q no minimum stated, 618; GRE-Analytical no minimum stated, 641; GRE-Subject(Psych) no minimum stated, 515; overall undergraduate GPA no minimum stated, 3.79; last 2 years GPA no minimum stated; psychology GPA no minimum stated; psychology GPA no minimum stated.

Other Criteria: (importance of criteria rated low, medium, or high): GRE/MAT scores medium, research experience high, work experience low, extracurricular activity low, clinically related public service low, GPA medium, letters of recommendation high, interview statement of goals and objectives high. Extracurricular, public service, and clinical activities are important for applicants to the clinical and ecological/community programs.

Student Characteristics: The following represents characteristics of students in 2001–2002 in all graduate psychology programs in the department: Female–full-time 16, part-time 0; Male–full-time 6, part-time 0; African American/Black–full-time 2, part-time 0; Hispanic/Latino (a)–full-time 0, part-time 0; Asian/Pacific Islander–full-time 3, part-time 0; American Indian/Alaska Native–full-time 0, part-time 0.

Financial Information/Assistance:

Tuition for Full-Time Study: No information provided.

Financial Assistance:

First Year Students: No information provided.
Advanced Students: No information provided.
Contact Information: Of all students currently enrolled full-time, 0% benefitted from one or more of the listed financial assistance programs.

Internships/Practica: Clinical practica provided by the clinical program at the department's Psychological Clinic and the MSU Counseling Center.

Housing and Day Care: No on-campus housing and day care facilities are available.

Employment of Department Graduates:

Master's Degree Graduates: Of those who graduated in the academic year 2000–2001, the following categories and numbers represent the post-graduate activities and employment of master's degree graduates: Enrolled in a post-doctoral residency/fellowship (n/a), employed in independent practice (n/a).

Doctoral Degree Graduates: Of those who graduated in the academic year 2000–2001, the following categories and numbers represent the post-graduate activities and employment of doctoral degree graduates: Enrolled in a psychology doctoral program (n/a), enrolled in another graduate/professional program (n/a).

Additional Information:

Orientation, Objectives, and Emphasis of Department: The main objective of our programs is to train researchers who will engage in the generation and application of knowledge in a wide range of areas in psychology.

Special Facilities or Resources: Facilities include the Psychological Clinic for the clinical program, which includes playrooms equipped for audio and video recording, testing equipment, computer-based record keeping system, and neuropsychological assessment lab. The Neuroscience-Biological Psychology Laboratories include research animal facilities, computers, light and electron-microscopy, histology and endocrinology labs. The Vision Research Laboratory, Cognitive Processes Laboratories, Eye-Movement Lab, and Speech Processing Lab provide automated facilities for conducting research in cognitive science. Additional observational labs equipped with video remote control equipment, one-way windows, and automated data recording equipment are available. The department also supports a photo lab and shop for mechanical, electrical, and electronic equipment. Computer labs are available within the department and across campus.

Application Information:

Send to: Graduate Secretary, Department of Psychology, 149 Snyder Hall, Michigan State University, East Lansing, MI 48824-1117. Students are admitted in the Fall, application deadline January 5. Department application, as well as university application, is required by January 5. *Fee:* $30. Department application, as well as university application, is required by January 5.

Michigan, University of
Combined Program in Education and Psychology
1406 School of Education, 610 E. University
Ann Arbor, MI 48109-1259
Telephone: (734) 647-0626
Fax: (734) 615-2164
E-mail: *CPEP@umich.edu*
Web: *http://www.soe.umich.edu/programs/comb.html*

Department Established:

1956. Chairperson: Paul R. Pintrich. Number of Faculty: total–full-time 3, part-time 12; women–full-time 1, part-time 5.

Programs and Degrees Offered:

Listed in the following order: Program area, degree type (T if terminal Master's), number awarded 7/00-6/01. Education and psychology PhD 2.

Student Applications/Admissions:
Student Applications

Education and psychology PhD—Applications 2001–2002, 76. Total applicants accepted 2001–2002, 9. New applicants enrolled 2001–2002, 5. Total enrolled 2001–2002 full-time, 27. Openings 2002–2003, 5. The Median number of years required for completion of a degree are 5. The number of students enrolled full and part-time, who were dismissed or voluntarily withdrew from this program area were 1.

Admissions Requirements:

Scores: Entries appear in this order: required test or GPA, minimum score (if required), median score of students entering in 2001–2002. Doctoral Programs: GRE-V no minimum stated, 560; GRE-Q no minimum stated, 644; GRE-V+Q no minimum stated, 1204; GRE-Analytical no minimum stated, 666; GRE-V+Q+Analytical no minimum stated, 1870; overall undergraduate GPA 3.0, 3.75; last 2 years GPA 3.5, 3.5; psychology GPA 3.5, 3.79.

Other Criteria: (importance of criteria rated low, medium, or high): GRE/MAT scores medium, research experience high, work experience high, extracurricular activity low, clinically related public service low, GPA medium, letters of recommendation high, interview medium, statement of goals and objectives high.

Student Characteristics: The following represents characteristics of students in 2001–2002 in all graduate psychology programs in the department: Female–full-time 3, part-time 0; Male–full-time 2, part-time 0; African American/Black–full-time 5, part-time 0; Hispanic/Latino (a)–full-time 2, part-time 0; Asian/Pacific Islander–full-time 2, part-time 0; American Indian/Alaska Native–full-time 0, part-time 0.

Financial Information/Assistance:

Tuition for Full-Time Study: *Doctoral:* State residents: per academic year $11,338, $630 per credit hour; nonstate residents: per academic year $22,978, $1,277 per credit hour.

Financial Assistance:

First Year Students: Research assistantships available for first-year. Average amount paid per academic year: $19,200. Average number of hours worked per week: 22. Apply by Jan. 1. Tuition remission given: full. Fellowships and scholarships available for first-year. Average amount paid per academic year: $18,000. Average number of hours worked per week: 22. Apply by Jan. 1. Tuition remission given: full.

Advanced Students: Teaching assistantships available for advanced students. Average amount paid per academic year: $19,281. Average number of hours worked per week: 22. Apply by Jan. 1. Tuition remission given: full. Research assistantships available for advanced students. Average amount paid per academic year: $19,200. Average number of hours worked per week: 22. Apply by Jan. 1. Tuition remission given: full. Fellowships and scholarships available for advanced students. Average amount paid per academic year: $18,000. Average number of hours worked per week: 22. Apply by Jan. 1.

Contact Information: Of all students currently enrolled full-time, 96% benefitted from one or more of the listed financial assistance programs. For information on financial assistance, contact: the department chair.

Internships/Practica: No information provided.

Housing and Day Care: On-campus housing and day care facilities are available.

Employment of Department Graduates:

Master's Degree Graduates: Of those who graduated in the academic year 2000–2001, the following categories and numbers represent the post-graduate activities and employment of master's degree graduates: Enrolled in a post-doctoral residency/fellowship (n/a), employed in independent practice (n/a).

Doctoral Degree Graduates: Of those who graduated in the academic year 2000–2001, the following categories and numbers

represent the post-graduate activities and employment of doctoral degree graduates: Enrolled in a psychology doctoral program (n/a), enrolled in another graduate/professional program (n/a), employed in an academic position at a university (2).

Additional Information:

Orientation, Objectives, and Emphasis of Department: The Combined Program in Education and Psychology focuses on research training in instructional psychology, broadly defined. Students are trained to study educational issues and do research in school settings, on significant educational problems related to learning. Faculty affiliated with the program have ongoing research programs on various important issues. These include projects on children's cognitive development and reading skills, children's achievement motivation, socialization in the schools, how computers are changing the ways in which children learn, and learning and achievement of ethnically diverse students. Students in the Combined Program work with faculty on these projects, and learn to design projects in their own areas of interest. They take courses taught by faculty members in the program, and also courses taught by faculty in the Psychology Department and the School of Education. Because the department is an independent interdepartmental unit, students have the unique opportunity to work with faculty in both the Psychology Department and the School of Education, in addition to the faculty directly affiliated with the program. Graduates are well-prepared for teaching and research careers in academic and non-academic settings.

Special Facilities or Resources: The University of Michigan provides a rich environment for graduate studies. The faculty in both education and psychology are internationally known for their scholarly productivity, and so students receive excellent training in how to conduct educational research. Faculty in the Combined Program have ties to school officials in Ann Arbor and the greater Detroit area, which means students receive ample opportunities for working on many different kinds of educational projects. Students can take advantage of the university's excellent library and computer facilities, both of which are among the best in the country. A distinct advantage of the program is that it is interdepartmental in the graduate school with full resources and faculty available from both the Psychology Department and the School of Education. The department has close collaborative relationships with the Center for Human Growth and Development, the Center for Research on Learning and Teaching, the Human Performance Center, the Institute of Gerontology, the Institute for Social Research, the Cognitive Science and Machine Intelligence Laboratory, the Evolution and Human Behavior Program, and the Children's Center.

Information for Students With Physical Disabilities: Contact the following University Office: Services for Students with Disabilities, G-625 Haven Hall, Ann Arbor, MI 48109-1045, Voice/TDD (734) 763-3000, www.umich.edu/~plantext/accguide.

Application Information:
Send to: Department chair. Students are admitted in the Fall, application deadline January 1. May apply to up to 3 separate graduate programs within the Rackham School of Graduate Studies with one fee payment. However, duplicate transcripts, test scores, references, and other application materials must be provided to each program. Read all application materials. *Fee:* $55.

Michigan, University of (2001 data)
Department of Psychology
College of Literature, Science, and the Arts
525 E. University
Ann Arbor, MI 48109-1109
Telephone: (734) 764-6316
Fax: (734) 764-3520
E-mail: *berlykim@umich.edu*
Web: *http://www.umich.edu/~psycdept*

Department Established:
1928. Graduate Program Chair: Jill Becker. Number of Faculty: total–full-time 52, part-time 32; women–full-time 22, part-time 14; minority–full-time 14, part-time 8.

Programs and Degrees Offered:
Listed in the following order: Program area, degree type (T if terminal Master's), number awarded 7/00-6/01. Biopsychology PhD 6, clinical PhD 9, cognition/perception PhD 3, developmental PhD 5, general PhD, organizational PhD 3, personality PhD 3, social PhD 6.

APA Accreditation: Clinical PhD: full.

Student Applications/Admissions:
Student Applications
Biopsychology PhD—Applications 2001–2002, 35. Total applicants accepted 2001–2002, 9. New applicants enrolled 2001–2002, 5. Total enrolled 2001–2002 full-time, 18. Openings 2002–2003, 3. *Clinical PhD*—Applications 2001–2002, 289. Total applicants accepted 2001–2002, 6. New applicants enrolled 2001–2002, 6. Total enrolled 2001–2002 full-time, 57. Openings 2002–2003, 4. *Cognition/perception PhD*—Applications 2001–2002, 51. Total applicants accepted 2001–2002, 8. New applicants enrolled 2001–2002, 2. Total enrolled 2001–2002 full-time, 27. Openings 2002–2003, 3. *Developmental PhD*—Applications 2001–2002, 62. Total applicants accepted 2001–2002, 13. New applicants enrolled 2001–2002, 6. Total enrolled 2001–2002 full-time, 28. Openings 2002–2003, 5. *General PhD*—Applications 2001–2002, 0. Total enrolled 2001–2002 full-time, 2. *Organizational PhD*—Applications 2001–2002, 47. Total applicants accepted 2001–2002, 4. New applicants enrolled 2001–2002, 2. Total enrolled 2001–2002 full-time, 5. Openings 2002–2003, 2. *Personality PhD*—Applications 2001–2002, 9. Total applicants accepted 2001–2002, 6. New applicants enrolled 2001–2002, 2. Total enrolled 2001–2002 full-time, 14. Openings 2002–2003, 2. *Social PhD*—Applications 2001–2002, 89. Total applicants accepted 2001–2002, 10. New applicants enrolled 2001–2002, 6. Total enrolled 2001–2002 full-time, 33. Openings 2002–2003, 5.

Admissions Requirements:
Scores: Entries appear in this order: required test or GPA, minimum score (if required), median score of students entering in 2001–2002. Doctoral Programs: GRE-V no minimum stated, 610; GRE-Q no minimum stated, 690; GRE-V+Q no minimum stated, 1270; GRE-Analytical no minimum stated, 680; GRE-V+Q+Analytical no minimum stated, 1950; GRE-Subject(Psych) no minimum stated, 690; overall undergraduate GPA no minimum stated, 3.86.

Other Criteria: (importance of criteria rated low, medium, or high): GRE/MAT scores, research experience high, work experience medium, extracurricular activity medium, clinically related public service medium, GPA, letters of recommendation high, interview high, statement of goals and objectives high. Clinical has a two-stage interview process.

Student Characteristics: The following represents characteristics of students in 2001–2002 in all graduate psychology programs in the department: Female–full-time 18, part-time 0; Male–full-time 11, part-time 0; African American/Black–full-time 4, part-time 0; Hispanic/Latino (a)–full-time 3, part-time 0; Asian/Pacific Islander–full-time 4, part-time 0; American Indian/Alaska Native–full-time 0, part-time 0.

Financial Information/Assistance:

Tuition for Full-Time Study: No information provided.

Financial Assistance:
First Year Students: No information provided.
Advanced Students: No information provided.
Contact Information: Of all students currently enrolled full-time, 0% benefitted from one or more of the listed financial assistance programs. For information on financial assistance, contact: berlykim@umich.edu.

Internships/Practica: No information provided.

Housing and Day Care: No on-campus housing and day care facilities are available.

Employment of Department Graduates:
Master's Degree Graduates: Of those who graduated in the academic year 2000–2001, the following categories and numbers represent the post-graduate activities and employment of master's degree graduates: Enrolled in a post-doctoral residency/fellowship (n/a), employed in independent practice (n/a).
Doctoral Degree Graduates: Of those who graduated in the academic year 2000–2001, the following categories and numbers represent the post-graduate activities and employment of doctoral degree graduates: Enrolled in a psychology doctoral program (n/a), enrolled in another graduate/professional program (n/a).

Additional Information:
Orientation, Objectives, and Emphasis of Department: In addition to eight specialized areas of doctoral study, the department also has subspecialties and joint programs. Hence, faculty and students pursue professional and scientific goals over a broad range. Applied programs are closely related to the scientist-practitioner model of training, and all areas regard experience and formal instruction in teaching to be essential for the student seeking an academic career. Within the standards of training set by all departments, the student is given wide latitude in pursuing individual interests and educational goals.

Special Facilities or Resources: The University of Michigan is blessed with an extensive scientific-scholarly community of psychologists that is virtually unique in breadth, diversity, and quality. Because of the close collaborative relationships that have evolved over the years, graduate and postgraduate students have the opportunity to learn and work in a wide variety of well-developed specialty centers. These include: the Center for Human Growth and Development, the Center for Research on Learning and Teaching, the Department of Psychiatry's Mental Health Research Institute, Neuropsychiatric Institute and Children's Psychiatric Hospital, the Human Performance Center, the Institute of Gerontology, the Institute for Human Adjustment (i.e., Psychological Clinic, Counseling Center, Reading and Learning Skills Center), the Institute for Social Research (i.e., Survey Research Center, Research Center for Group Dynamics, Center for Political Studies), the NASA Center of Excellence in Man-Systems Research, the Cognitive Science and Machine Intelligence Laboratory, the Human Factors Division of the University of Michigan Transportation Research Institute, the Kresge Hearing Research Institute, the Neuroscience Laboratory, the Evolution and Human Behavior Program, the Children's Center, the Vision Research Laboratory, and the Women's Studies Program. In addition to these resources, the Michigan campus also offers an unusually diverse series of stimulating colloquium and seminar presentations, involving both local and visiting speakers, that contributes significantly to the available opportunities for professional growth and development.

Application Information:
Send to: Jill Becker, Graduate Program Chair, Department of Psychology, 525 E. University, University of Michigan, Ann Arbor, MI 48109-1109, (734) 764-6316. Students are admitted in the Fall, application deadline December 15. *Fee:* $55.

Northern Michigan University
Department of Psychology
2401 Presque Isle
Marquette, MI 49855
Telephone: (906) 227-1409
E-mail: *bolson@nmu.edu*
Web: *http://www.nmu.edu*

Department Established:
1950. Head and Professor: Harry Whittaker. Number of Faculty: total–full-time 10; women–full-time 4.

Programs and Degrees Offered:
Listed in the following order: Program area, degree type (T if terminal Master's), number awarded 7/00-6/01. Psychology MA 1.

Student Applications/Admissions:
Student Applications
Psychology MA—Applications 2001–2002, 9. Total applicants accepted 2001–2002, 6. New applicants enrolled 2001–2002, 10. Total enrolled 2001–2002 full-time, 10. Openings 2002–2003, 8. The Median number of years required for completion of a degree are 2.

Admissions Requirements:
Scores: Entries appear in this order: required test or GPA, minimum score (if required), median score of students entering in 2001–2002. Master's Programs: GRE-V no minimum stated; GRE-Q no minimum stated; GRE-V+Q 1000; GRE-Subject(Psych) no minimum stated; overall undergraduate GPA 3.00. Doctoral Programs: last 2 years GPA no minimum stated;

psychology GPA no minimum stated; psychology GPA no minimum stated.

Other Criteria: (importance of criteria rated low, medium, or high): GRE/MAT scores high, research experience medium, extracurricular activity low, GPA high, letters of recommendation high, statement of goals and objectives high.

Student Characteristics: The following represents characteristics of students in 2001–2002 in all graduate psychology programs in the department: Female–full-time 5, Male–full-time 0, African American/Black–full-time 0, Hispanic/Latino (a)–full-time 0, Asian/Pacific Islander–full-time 0, American Indian/Alaska Native–full-time 0, Multi-ethnic–full-time 0, students subject to the Americans with Disabilities Act–full-time 0.

Financial Information/Assistance:

Tuition for Full-Time Study: *Master's:* State residents $135 per credit hour; nonstate residents: $135 per credit hour.

Financial Assistance:

First Year Students: Teaching assistantships available for first-year. Average amount paid per academic year: $4,000. Average number of hours worked per week: 8. Apply by May. Tuition remission given: full.

Advanced Students: No information provided.

Contact Information: No information provided.

Internships/Practica: No information provided.

Housing and Day Care: No on-campus housing and day care facilities are available.

Employment of Department Graduates:

Master's Degree Graduates: Of those who graduated in the academic year 2000–2001, the following categories and numbers represent the post-graduate activities and employment of master's degree graduates: Enrolled in a psychology doctoral program (4), enrolled in another graduate/professional program (0), enrolled in a post-doctoral residency/fellowship (n/a), employed in independent practice (n/a), employed in an academic position at a university (0), employed in an academic position at a 2-year/4-year college (0), employed in other positions at a higher education institution (0), employed in a professional position in a school system (0), employed in business or industry (research/consulting) (0), employed in business or industry (management) (0), employed in a government agency (research) (0), employed in a government agency (professional services) (0), employed in a community mental health/counseling center (0), employed in a hospital/medical center (0), still seeking employment (0), other employment position (0).

Doctoral Degree Graduates: Of those who graduated in the academic year 2000–2001, the following categories and numbers represent the post-graduate activities and employment of doctoral degree graduates: Enrolled in a psychology doctoral program (n/a), enrolled in another graduate/professional program (n/a), enrolled

in a post-doctoral residency/fellowship (0), employed in independent practice (0), employed in an academic position at a university (0), employed in an academic position at a 2-year/4-year college (0), employed in other positions at a higher education institution (0), employed in a professional position in a school system (0), employed in business or industry (research/consulting) (0), employed in business or industry (management) (0), employed in a government agency (research) (0), employed in a government agency (professional services) (0), employed in a community mental health/counseling center (0), employed in a hospital/medical center (0), still seeking employment (0), other employment position (0).

Additional Information:

Orientation, Objectives, and Emphasis of Department: The program is a general experimental program. Students may develop their own program of study.

Special Facilities or Resources: Graduate students are provided with office and research space.

Application Information:
Send to: Bradley C. Olson, Ph.D., Director of Graduate Studies, Department of Psychology, Northern Michigan University, Marquette, MI 49855. Students are admitted in the Fall; Winter; Spring; Summer. *Fee:* $35.

Wayne State University
Department of Psychology
Science
71 West Warren
Detroit, MI 48202
Telephone: (313) 577-2800
Fax: (313) 577-7636
E-mail: *aallen@sun.science.wayne.edu*
Web: *http://www.science.wayne.edu/~psych*

Department Established:
1923. Chairperson: Joseph L. Jacobson. Number of Faculty: total–full-time 38; women–full-time 16; minority–full-time 2; faculty subject to the Americans with Disabilities Act 1.

Programs and Degrees Offered:
Listed in the following order: Program area, degree type (T if terminal Master's), number awarded 7/00-6/01. Biopsychology PhD 2, clinical PhD 11, cognitive PhD, developmental PhD, human development MA (T) 4, industrial/orgranizational PhD 4, social PhD 1.

APA Accreditation: Clinical PhD: full.

Student Applications/Admissions:
Student Applications
Biopsychology PhD—Applications 2001–2002, 8. Total applicants accepted 2001–2002, 3. New applicants enrolled 2001–2002, 1. Total enrolled 2001–2002 full-time, 8. Openings 2002–2003, 2. *Clinical PhD*—Applications 2001–2002, 165. Total applicants accepted 2001–2002, 24. New applicants en-

rolled 2001–2002, 10. Total enrolled 2001–2002 full-time, 84. Openings 2002–2003, 12. *Cognitive PhD*—Applications 2001–2002, 2. Total applicants accepted 2001–2002, 1. New applicants enrolled 2001–2002, 1. Total enrolled 2001–2002 full-time, 13. Openings 2002–2003, 2. *Developmental PhD*—Applications 2001–2002, 13. Total applicants accepted 2001–2002, 3. New applicants enrolled 2001–2002, 1. Total enrolled 2001–2002 full-time, 26. Openings 2002–2003, 5. *Human development MA*—Applications 2001–2002, 10. Total applicants accepted 2001–2002, 7. New applicants enrolled 2001–2002, 5. Total enrolled 2001–2002 full-time, 20. Openings 2002–2003, 6. *Industrial/organizational PhD*—Applications 2001–2002, 40. Total applicants accepted 2001–2002, 10. New applicants enrolled 2001–2002, 4. Total enrolled 2001–2002 full-time, 43. Openings 2002–2003, 5. *Social PhD*—Applications 2001–2002, 14. Total applicants accepted 2001–2002, 4. New applicants enrolled 2001–2002, 2. Total enrolled 2001–2002 full-time, 34. Openings 2002–2003, 4.

Admissions Requirements:

Scores: Entries appear in this order: required test or GPA, minimum score (if required), median score of students entering in 2001–2002. Master's Programs: GRE-V no minimum stated, 500; GRE-Q no minimum stated, 480; GRE-Analytical no minimum stated, 500; overall undergraduate GPA 2.80, 3.00; last 2 years GPA 3.00. Doctoral Programs: GRE-V no minimum stated, 610; GRE-Q no minimum stated, 620; GRE-Analytical no minimum stated, 600; GRE-Subject(Psych) no minimum stated, 550; overall undergraduate GPA 3.00, 3.50; last 2 years GPA 3.00; psychology GPA no minimum stated; psychology GPA no minimum stated.

Other Criteria: (importance of criteria rated low, medium, or high): GRE/MAT scores high, research experience high, work experience low, extracurricular activity low, clinically related public service low, GPA high, letters of recommendation medium, interview low, statement of goals and objectives high.

Student Characteristics: The following represents characteristics of students in 2001–2002 in all graduate psychology programs in the department: Female–full-time 103, part-time 0; Male–full-time 40, part-time 0; African American/Black–full-time 16, part-time 0; Hispanic/Latino (a)–full-time 4, part-time 0; Asian/Pacific Islander–full-time 3, part-time 0; American Indian/Alaska Native–full-time 0, part-time 0; Multi-ethnic–full-time 3, students subject to the Americans with Disabilities Act–full-time 0.

Financial Information/Assistance:

Tuition for Full-Time Study: *Master's:* State residents $305 per credit hour; nonstate residents: $556 per credit hour. *Doctoral:* State residents: $305 per credit hour; nonstate residents: $556 per credit hour.

Financial Assistance:

First Year Students: Teaching assistantships available for first-year. Average amount paid per academic year: $11,500. Tuition remission given: full. Research assistantships available for first-year. Average amount paid per academic year: $11,500. Tuition remission given: full. Fellowships and scholarships available for first-year. Average amount paid per academic year: $11,500. Tuition remission given: full.

Advanced Students: Teaching assistantships available for advanced students. Average amount paid per academic year:

$11,500. Tuition remission given: full. Research assistantships available for advanced students. Average amount paid per academic year: $11,500. Tuition remission given: full. Fellowships and scholarships available for advanced students. Average amount paid per academic year: $11,500. Tuition remission given: full.

Contact Information: For information on financial assistance, contact: Teaching and Research at (313) 577-2823 or aallen@sun.science.wayne.edu.

Internships/Practica: No information provided.

Housing and Day Care: On-campus housing and day care facilities are available.

Employment of Department Graduates:

Master's Degree Graduates: Of those who graduated in the academic year 2000–2001, the following categories and numbers represent the post-graduate activities and employment of master's degree graduates: Enrolled in a post-doctoral residency/fellowship (n/a), employed in independent practice (n/a).

Doctoral Degree Graduates: Of those who graduated in the academic year 2000–2001, the following categories and numbers represent the post-graduate activities and employment of doctoral degree graduates: Enrolled in a psychology doctoral program (n/a), enrolled in another graduate/professional program (n/a).

Additional Information:

Orientation, Objectives, and Emphasis of Department: This department strives to select graduate students with a strong educational background and outstanding potential and to train them to be knowledgeable, ethical practitioners and research scholars in their chosen areas. Program admission is limited to persons planning to obtain the doctoral degree. Initial broad training is followed by specialized training.

Special Facilities or Resources: The biopsychology area participates in the university neuroscience program. Excellent laboratory facilities are available in neurobiology, neuropharmacology, psychopharmacology, neuropsychology, and ethology. Several faculty in biopsychology and other areas in the department work in the area of substance abuse. The clinical program emphasizes psychotherapy, community mental health, diagnostics, alcohol abuse issues, neuropsychology, and child and geropsychology. Clinical practice and research experience are obtained in a variety of clinical placements and in our own clinic. The cognitive program emphasizes cognition theory and its application to applied problems. The developmental area emphasizes life-span studies and is affiliated with the Institute of Gerontology. The social psychology program has both basic and applied research emphases. Well-equipped laboratories in the department and at the Merrill-Palmer Institute, which is affiliated with the department, are available for cognitive, social, and developmental research. In addition, social psychology uses its urban setting to carry out field studies. The industrial/organizational area emphasizes organizational psychology, personnel research, and field placements. Excellent computer facilities and libraries support research in all areas.

Application Information:

Send to: Graduate Office, Psychology Department, WSU, 71 W. Warren, Detroit, MI 48202. Students are admitted in the Fall, application deadline January 15. MA Human Development Fall application deadline- July 1; Winter application deadline-October 1. *Fee:* $20.

Wayne State University
Division of Theoretical and Behavioral Foundations-
  Educational Psychology
College of Education
Detroit, MI 48202
Telephone: (313) 557-1614
Fax: (313) 577-5235
E-mail: *s.b.hillman@wayne.edu*

Department Established:
1957. Chairperson: Stephen B. Hillman. Number of Faculty: total–full-time 5, part-time 12; women–full-time 2, part-time 5.

Programs and Degrees Offered:
Listed in the following order: Program area, degree type (T if terminal Master's), number awarded 7/00-6/01. Educational PhD 8, school MA 30.

Student Applications/Admissions:
Student Applications

Educational PhD—Applications 2001–2002, 20. Total applicants accepted 2001–2002, 10. New applicants enrolled 2001–2002, 10. Total enrolled 2001–2002 part-time, 10. Openings 2002–2003, 15. The Median number of years required for completion of a degree are 7. The number of students enrolled full and part-time, who were dismissed or voluntarily withdrew from this program area were 3. *School MA*—Applications 2001–2002, 60. Total applicants accepted 2001–2002, 29. New applicants enrolled 2001–2002, 28. Total enrolled 2001–2002 part-time, 28. Openings 2002–2003, 32. The Median number of years required for completion of a degree are 2. The number of students enrolled full and part-time, who were dismissed or voluntarily withdrew from this program area were 3.

Admissions Requirements:

Scores: Entries appear in this order: required test or GPA, minimum score (if required), median score of students entering in 2001–2002. Master's Programs: GRE-V no minimum stated; GRE-Q no minimum stated; GRE-V+Q no minimum stated; overall undergraduate GPA no minimum stated. GRE for MA Program (School Psychology) only. Doctoral Programs: overall undergraduate GPA no minimum stated; last 2 years GPA no minimum stated; psychology GPA no minimum stated; psychology GPA no minimum stated.

Other Criteria: (importance of criteria rated low, medium, or high): research experience medium, work experience medium, extracurricular activity medium, clinically related public service medium, GPA high, letters of recommendation high, interview high, statement of goals and objectives high.

Student Characteristics: The following represents characteristics of students in 2001–2002 in all graduate psychology programs in the department: Female–full-time 7, part-time 42; Male–full-time 3, part-time 9; African American/Black–full-time 0, part-time 5; Hispanic/Latino (a)–full-time 0, part-time 0; Asian/Pacific Is-

lander–full-time 0, part-time 1; American Indian/Alaska Native–full-time 0, part-time 0.

Financial Information/Assistance:
Tuition for Full-Time Study: *Master's:* State residents per academic year $3,800, $186 per credit hour; nonstate residents: per academic year $7,600, $186 per credit hour. *Doctoral:* State residents: per academic year $3,800, $186 per credit hour; nonstate residents: per academic year $7,600, $186 per credit hour.

Financial Assistance:
First Year Students: Fellowships and scholarships available for first-year. Apply by March 1. Tuition remission given: full.

Advanced Students: Fellowships and scholarships available for advanced students. Apply by March 1. Tuition remission given: full.

Contact Information: Of all students currently enrolled full-time, 15% benefitted from one or more of the listed financial assistance programs.

Internships/Practica: No information provided.

Housing and Day Care: On-campus housing and day care facilities are available.

Employment of Department Graduates:
Master's Degree Graduates: Of those who graduated in the academic year 2000–2001, the following categories and numbers represent the post-graduate activities and employment of master's degree graduates: Enrolled in a post-doctoral residency/fellowship (n/a), employed in independent practice (n/a), employed in a professional position in a school system (15).

Doctoral Degree Graduates: Of those who graduated in the academic year 2000–2001, the following categories and numbers represent the post-graduate activities and employment of doctoral degree graduates: Enrolled in a psychology doctoral program (n/a), enrolled in another graduate/professional program (n/a), employed in independent practice (2), employed in a professional position in a school system (4), employed in a hospital/medical center (1).

Additional Information:
Orientation, Objectives, and Emphasis of Department: The department offers MA programs in school and community psychology and MEd and PhD programs in educational psychology. The program orientations are eclectic, using the scientific-practitioner model, with emphasis on application of theory at the master's degree level and on theoretical issues at the PhD level.

Application Information:
Send to: Department Chair. Students are admitted in the Spring, application deadline February 15. MEd Program rolling admissions throughout the year. *Fee:* $20.

Western Michigan University
Department of Psychology
Room 3740, Wood Hall
Kalamazoo, MI 49008
Telephone: (616) 387-4474
Fax: (616) 387-4550
E-mail: *r.wayne.fuqua@wmich.edu*
Web: *http://www.wmich.edu/psychology*

Department Established:

1952. Chairperson: R. Wayne Fuqua. Number of Faculty: total–full-time 19, part-time 5; women–full-time 6, part-time 3; minority–full-time 1.

Programs and Degrees Offered:

Listed in the following order: Program area, degree type (T if terminal Master's), number awarded 7/00-6/01. Applied behavior analysis PhD 5, behavior analysis MA (T) 14, clinical PhD 10, experimental PhD 2, industrial/organizational MA (T) 4, school psychology EdS 20.

APA Accreditation: Clinical PhD: full.

Student Applications/Admissions:

Student Applications

Applied behavior analysis PhD—Applications 2001–2002, 24. Total applicants accepted 2001–2002, 8. New applicants enrolled 2001–2002, 7. Total enrolled 2001–2002 full-time, 25. Openings 2002–2003, 6. The Median number of years required for completion of a degree are 5. The number of students enrolled full and part-time, who were dismissed or voluntarily withdrew from this program area were 0. *Behavior analysis MA*—Applications 2001–2002, 57. Total applicants accepted 2001–2002, 22. New applicants enrolled 2001–2002, 16. Total enrolled 2001–2002 full-time, 42. Openings 2002–2003, 20. The Median number of years required for completion of a degree are 2. The number of students enrolled full and part-time, who were dismissed or voluntarily withdrew from this program area were 0. *Clinical PhD*—Applications 2001–2002, 65. Total applicants accepted 2001–2002, 10. New applicants enrolled 2001–2002, 7. Total enrolled 2001–2002 full-time, 29. Openings 2002–2003, 6. The Median number of years required for completion of a degree are 5. The number of students enrolled full and part-time, who were dismissed or voluntarily withdrew from this program area were 0. *Experimental PhD*—Applications 2001–2002, 3. Total applicants accepted 2001–2002, 1. New applicants enrolled 2001–2002, 1. Total enrolled 2001–2002 full-time, 5. Openings 2002–2003, 3. The Median number of years required for completion of a degree are 6. *Industrial/organizational MA*—Applications 2001–2002, 32. Total applicants accepted 2001–2002, 5. New applicants enrolled 2001–2002, 4. Total enrolled 2001–2002 full-time, 14. Openings 2002–2003, 4. *School psychology EdS*—Applications 2001–2002, 48. Total applicants accepted 2001–2002, 15. New applicants enrolled 2001–2002, 11. Total enrolled 2001–2002 full-time, 21. Openings 2002–2003, 8.

Admissions Requirements:

Scores: Entries appear in this order: required test or GPA, minimum score (if required), median score of students entering in 2001–2002. Master's Programs: GRE-V 500, 556; GRE-Q 500, 569; overall undergraduate GPA 3.00, 3.69. Behavior Analysis Master's Minimum Score: No subscore below 400 and a minimum combined score of 900. Doctoral Programs: GRE-V 500, 579; GRE-Q 500, 572; overall undergraduate GPA 3.0, 3.72; last 2 years GPA no minimum stated; psychology GPA no minimum stated; psychology GPA no minimum stated. Behavior Analysis GRE: no subscore below 400 and combined total minimum of 900. Clinical and School: No subscore below 500 and combined total minimum of 1000.

Other Criteria: (importance of criteria rated low, medium, or high): GRE/MAT scores medium, research experience high, work experience low, extracurricular activity low, clinically related public service medium, GPA medium, letters of recommendation high, interview high, statement of goals and objectives high, training in beh. analysi high. High importance placed on interpersonal skills.

Student Characteristics: The following represents characteristics of students in 2001–2002 in all graduate psychology programs in the department: Female–full-time 32, part-time 0; Male–full-time 18, part-time 0; African American/Black–full-time 1, part-time 0; Hispanic/Latino (a)–full-time 1, part-time 0; Asian/Pacific Islander–full-time 1, part-time 0; American Indian/Alaska Native–full-time 0, part-time 0.

Financial Information/Assistance:

Tuition for Full-Time Study: *Master's:* State residents $185 per credit hour; nonstate residents: $441 per credit hour. *Doctoral:* State residents: $185 per credit hour; nonstate residents: $441 per credit hour.

Financial Assistance:

First Year Students: Teaching assistantships available for first-year. Average amount paid per academic year: $8,672. Average number of hours worked per week: 20. Tuition remission given: full and partial. Research assistantships available for first-year. Average amount paid per academic year: $8,672. Average number of hours worked per week: 20. Tuition remission given: full and partial. Traineeships available for first-year. Average amount paid per academic year: $8,672. Average number of hours worked per week: 20. Tuition remission given: full. Fellowships and scholarships available for first-year. Average amount paid per academic year: $8,672. Average number of hours worked per week: 0. Tuition remission given: full.

Advanced Students: Teaching assistantships available for advanced students. Average amount paid per academic year: $8,950. Average number of hours worked per week: 20. Tuition remission given: full and partial. Average amount paid per academic year: $8,950. Average number of hours worked per week: 20. Tuition remission given: full and partial. Average amount paid per academic year: $8,950. Average number of hours worked per week: 20. Tuition remission given: full and partial. Average amount paid per academic year: $11,500. Average number of hours worked per week: 20. Tuition remission given: full and partial.

Contact Information: Of all students currently enrolled full-time, 70% benefitted from one or more of the listed financial

assistance programs. For information on financial assistance, contact: Graduate Secretary, Department of Psychology.

Internships/Practica: No information provided.

Housing and Day Care: On-campus housing and day care facilities are available.

Employment of Department Graduates:

Master's Degree Graduates: Of those who graduated in the academic year 2000–2001, the following categories and numbers represent the post-graduate activities and employment of master's degree graduates: Enrolled in a post-doctoral residency/fellowship (n/a), employed in independent practice (n/a).

Doctoral Degree Graduates: Of those who graduated in the academic year 2000–2001, the following categories and numbers represent the post-graduate activities and employment of doctoral degree graduates: Enrolled in a psychology doctoral program (n/a), enrolled in another graduate/professional program (n/a).

Additional Information:

Orientation, Objectives, and Emphasis of Department: The Department of Psychology has a pervasive behavior analytic orientation which is reflected in all of its graduate programs. Although the student may design a program of study to meet specific career goals, all programs require courses in behavior analysis. Applicants accepted into the program receive a personal appointment to an advisor and two faculty sponsors who serve as the thesis-dissertation committee and provide both academic and professional advising throughout the student's tenure at the University. The emphasis of the program is upon cooperation between student and faculty, and students are expected to assume positions of responsibility in teaching, research, and service within the department and in community-based programs. The faculty are involved in professional organizations and publish in a variety of scholarly journals. Students are also expected to become involved in these activities and contribute to research projects as co-investigators, and to publications as co-authors.

Special Facilities or Resources: Western Michigan University emphasizes computer usage and maintains several microcomputer laboratories for student use as well as a state-of-the-art mainframe computer system. The department research laboratories include microcomputer control systems and other support equipment for research with birds and small mammals. The clinical research laboratories include equipment for electrophysiological recording, fitness testing, and human operant research. The department also maintains an in-house clinic for training in therapeutic techniques under faculty supervision; the clinic includes facilities for adult, child, and family therapy.

Application Information:
Send to: Psychology Graduate Training, Department of Psychology, Western Michigan University, Kalamazoo, MI 49008. Students are admitted in the Fall, application deadline January 20. *Fee:* $25.

Western Michigan University (WMU)
Counselor Education & Counseling Psychology
College of Education
3102 Sangren Hall, WMU, 1201 Oliver Street
Kalamazoo, MI 49008-5226
Telephone: (616) 387-5100
Fax: (616) 387-5090
E-mail: *joseph.morris@wmich.edu*
Web: *http://www.wmich.edu/cecp*

Department Established:
1970. Professor & Chair: Joseph R. Morris. Number of Faculty: total–full-time 19, part-time 8; women–full-time 4, part-time 5; minority–full-time 4, part-time 4.

Programs and Degrees Offered:
Listed in the following order: Program area, degree type (T if terminal Master's), number awarded 7/00-6/01. Counseling Psycholgy PhD (T) 7, Counseling Psychology MA (T) 47.

APA Accreditation: Counseling PhD: full.

Student Applications/Admissions:

Student Applications

Counseling Psycholgy PhD—Applications 2001–2002, 50. Total applicants accepted 2001–2002, 8. New applicants enrolled 2001–2002, 8. Total enrolled 2001–2002 full-time, 44. Openings 2002–2003, 8. The Median number of years required for completion of a degree are 6. The number of students enrolled full and part-time, who were dismissed or voluntarily withdrew from this program area were 1. *Counseling Psychology MA*—Applications 2001–2002, 74. Total applicants accepted 2001–2002, 61. New applicants enrolled 2001–2002, 41. Total enrolled 2001–2002 full-time, 96, part-time, 64. Openings 2002–2003, 60. The Median number of years required for completion of a degree are 4.

Admissions Requirements:

Scores: Entries appear in this order: required test or GPA, minimum score (if required), median score of students entering in 2001–2002. Master's Programs: overall undergraduate GPA 3.0; last 2 years GPA 3.0. Doctoral Programs: GRE-V 500; GRE-Q 500; GRE-V+Q 1000; overall undergraduate GPA 3.00; last 2 years GPA no minimum stated; psychology GPA no minimum stated; psychology GPA 3.25.

Other Criteria: (importance of criteria rated low, medium, or high): GRE/MAT scores high, research experience high, work experience medium, extracurricular activity low, clinically related public service low, GPA high, letters of recommendation high, interview high, statement of goals and objectives high, quality of submitted writ high.

Student Characteristics: The following represents characteristics of students in 2001–2002 in all graduate psychology programs in the department: Female–full-time 104, part-time 54; Male–full-time 32, part-time 11; African American/Black–full-time 23, part-time 0; Hispanic/Latino (a)–full-time 4, part-time 0; Asian/Pacific Islander–full-time 4, part-time 0; American Indian/Alaska Native–full-time 1, part-time 0; Multi-ethnic–full-time 0, part-time

0; students subject to the Americans with Disabilities Act–full-time 0, part-time 0.

Financial Information/Assistance:

Tuition for Full-Time Study: *Master's:* State residents $166 per credit hour; nonstate residents: $399 per credit hour. *Doctoral:* State residents: $166 per credit hour; nonstate residents: $399 per credit hour.

Financial Assistance:

First Year Students: Teaching assistantships available for first-year. Average amount paid per academic year: $13,884. Average number of hours worked per week: 20. Apply by February 15. Tuition remission given: full. Research assistantships available for first-year. Average amount paid per academic year: $13,884. Average number of hours worked per week: 20. Apply by February 15. Tuition remission given: full. Fellowships and scholarships available for first-year. Average amount paid per academic year: $13,884. Average number of hours worked per week: 20. Apply by February 15. Tuition remission given: full.

Advanced Students: Teaching assistantships available for advanced students. Average amount paid per academic year: $14,368. Average number of hours worked per week: 20. Apply by February 15. Tuition remission given: full. Research assistantships available for advanced students. Average amount paid per academic year: $14,368. Average number of hours worked per week: 20. Apply by February 15. Tuition remission given: full. Traineeships available for advanced students. Fellowships and scholarships available for advanced students. Average amount paid per academic year: $14,368. Average number of hours worked per week: 20. Apply by February 15. Tuition remission given: full.

Contact Information: Of all students currently enrolled full-time, 87% benefitted from one or more of the listed financial assistance programs. For information on financial assistance, contact: Student Financial Assistance 616-387-6000; http://www.wmich.edu/finaid/splash3.html http://www.wmich.edu/grad/financial/finance_graduate.html.

Internships/Practica: Master's level practica are available in a wide range of settings. Doctoral practica are also available in hospitals, clinics, university counseling centers, etc. For those doctoral students for whom a professional internship is required prior to graduation, 7 applied in 2000–2001. Of those who applied, 7 were placed in internships listed by the Association of Psychology Postdoctoral and Internship Programs (APPIC); 7 were placed in APA accredited internships.

Housing and Day Care: On-campus housing and day care facilities are available.

Employment of Department Graduates:

Master's Degree Graduates: Of those who graduated in the academic year 2000–2001, the following categories and numbers represent the post-graduate activities and employment of master's degree graduates: Enrolled in a post-doctoral residency/fellowship (n/a), employed in independent practice (n/a).

Doctoral Degree Graduates: Of those who graduated in the academic year 2000–2001, the following categories and numbers represent the post-graduate activities and employment of doctoral degree graduates: Enrolled in a psychology doctoral program (n/a), enrolled in another graduate/professional program (n/a), employed in independent practice (1), employed in an academic position at a university (1), employed in other positions at a higher education institution (5).

Additional Information:

Orientation, Objectives, and Emphasis of Department: The department prepares professional counseling psychologists at the master's and doctoral levels. The philosophy of the counseling psychology doctoral program is that theory, research, and practice are interdependent and complementary dimensions of a professional education within a scientist-practitioner training model. The curriculum and the practical experiences of the program are designed to ensure competency in all three dimensions and to facilitate their integration into the development of a professional identity as a counseling psychologist. Counseling psychologists are employed in a variety of professional settings including academic departments, college and university counseling and student development centers, private practices, mental health systems and agencies, and in business, government, and industry. Consistent with the philosophy of training, the development of professional identity, and the employment objectives of counseling psychology students, the program consists of courses and related experiences in (1) the science of psychology, (2) counseling psychology specialization, (3) counseling and psychotherapy, and (4) research. Persons considering admission to the Counseling Psychology Doctoral Program need to know that the program recognizes the importance of increasing the educational opportunities of minority students, as well as ensuring a diversity of role models in the counseling psychology program. Therefore, the department of counselor education and counseling psychology in which the counseling psychology program is housed, strives to create an atmosphere conducive to the concerns of diverse populations, to integrate these concerns into programs and courses, and to fulfill its commitment to recruit, admit, and graduate minority students prepared for their chosen careers. To this end, the department, the College of Education and the Graduate College provide financial support for eligible minority students. Additional information: The department uses an affirmative recruitment program.

Special Facilities or Resources: The department's primary training facility is the Center for Counseling and Psychological Services, which includes interview rooms, two group/family therapy rooms, and a seminar room; it is equipped with audio and video recording systems and provides for observation and telephone supervision. The department also maintains a comparable training clinic at the Graduate Center in Grand Rapids, Michigan. A wide variety of regional resources, including community clinics, schools, hospitals, and private clinics, are available to students.

Information for Students With Physical Disabilities: Disabled Student Resources and Services (DSRS) assists Western Michigan University students who have disabilities as they seek to find effective accommodations, maximize their abilities, and gain independence. DSRS offers advocacy, registration assistance, readers/scribes and other test accommodations, textbook taping, accessibility information, handi-van transportation, adaptive equipment, and referral to other campus and community agencies.

Application Information:

Send to: Department of Counselor Ed. & Counseling Psych., 3102 Sangren Hall, WMU, Kalamazoo, MI 49008-5195. Students are admitted in the Fall, application deadline January 10. Application deadline for MA Admission is January 15. *Fee:* $25.

Argosy University, Twin Cities

Clinical Psychology
Minnesota School of Professional Psychology
5503 Green Valley Drive, Suite 150
Minneapolis, MN 55437
Telephone: (952) 921-9500
Fax: (952) 921-9574
E-mail: *tcadmissions@argosyu.edu*
Web: *http://www.argosyu.edu*

Department Established:
1987. Department Head: Kenneth B. Solberg. Number of Faculty: total–full-time 12, part-time 17; women–full-time 6, part-time 6; minority–full-time 1, part-time 1.

Programs and Degrees Offered:
Listed in the following order: Program area, degree type (T if terminal Master's), number awarded 7/00-6/01. Clinical MA (T) 16, Clinical PsyD 51, Counseling MA MA 15.

APA Accreditation: Clinical PsyD: full.

Student Applications/Admissions:

Student Applications

Clinical MA—Applications 2001–2002, 22. Total applicants accepted 2001–2002, 15. New applicants enrolled 2001–2002, 14. Total enrolled 2001–2002 full-time, 21, part-time, 1. Openings 2002–2003, 15. The Median number of years required for completion of a degree are 2. The number of students enrolled full and part-time, who were dismissed or voluntarily withdrew from this program area were 0. *Clinical PsyD*—Applications 2001–2002, 173. Total applicants accepted 2001–2002, 102. New applicants enrolled 2001–2002, 50. Total enrolled 2001–2002 full-time, 233, part-time, 122. Openings 2002–2003, 45. The Median number of years required for completion of a degree are 5. The number of students enrolled full and part-time, who were dismissed or voluntarily withdrew from this program area were 7. *Counseling MA*—Applications 2001–2002, 61. Total applicants accepted 2001–2002, 44. New applicants enrolled 2001–2002, 36. Total enrolled 2001–2002 full-time, 70, part-time, 13. Openings 2002–2003, 50. The Median number of years required for completion of a degree are 2.

Admissions Requirements:

Scores: Entries appear in this order: required test or GPA, minimum score (if required), median score of students entering in 2001–2002. Master's Programs: GRE-V no minimum stated, 473; GRE-Q no minimum stated, 522; GRE-V+Q no minimum stated, 995; GRE-Analytical no minimum stated, 630; GRE-V+Q+Analytical no minimum stated, 1625; MAT no minimum stated, 49; overall undergraduate GPA no minimum stated, 3.3; last 2 years GPA no minimum stated, 3.5; psychology GPA no minimum stated, 3.5. Doctoral Programs: GRE-V no minimum stated, 536; GRE-Q no minimum stated, 565; GRE-V+Q no minimum stated, 1101; GRE-Analytical no

minimum stated, 577; GRE-V+Q+Analytical no minimum stated, 1678; MAT no minimum stated, 57; overall undergraduate GPA no minimum stated, 3.6 ; last 2 years GPA no minimum stated, 3.7 ; psychology GPA no minimum stated, 3.7 ; psychology GPA no minimum stated, 3.7.

Other Criteria: (importance of criteria rated low, medium, or high): GRE/MAT scores medium, research experience low, work experience medium, extracurricular activity low, clinically related public service medium, GPA medium, letters of recommendation high, interview high, statement of goals and objectives high.

Student Characteristics: The following represents characteristics of students in 2001–2002 in all graduate psychology programs in the department: Female–full-time 192, part-time 83; Male–full-time 41, part-time 39; African American/Black–full-time 3, part-time 2; Hispanic/Latino (a)–full-time 6, part-time 1; Asian/Pacific Islander–full-time 8, part-time 0; American Indian/Alaska Native–full-time 1, part-time 0; students subject to the Americans with Disabilities Act–full-time 1, part-time 1.

Financial Information/Assistance:

Tuition for Full-Time Study: *Master's:* State residents $424 per credit hour; nonstate residents: $424 per credit hour. *Doctoral:* State residents: $640 per credit hour; nonstate residents: $640 per credit hour.

Financial Assistance:

First Year Students: Fellowships and scholarships available for first-year. Average amount paid per academic year: $3,000. Average number of hours worked per week: 3. Apply by April. Tuition remission given: full and partial.

Advanced Students: Teaching assistantships available for advanced students. Average amount paid per academic year: $1,920. Average number of hours worked per week: 6. Apply by Per Term. Tuition remission given: full and partial. Fellowships and scholarships available for advanced students. Average amount paid per academic year: $3,000. Average number of hours worked per week: 3. Apply by April. Tuition remission given: full and partial.

Contact Information: For information on financial assistance, contact: Student Services Department.

Internships/Practica: AU/TC places students in over 50 practicum sites. These training sites cover the full range of training interests that students may have, including medical centers, clinics, counseling centers, prisons, state hospitals, schools, private practice, chemical dependency treatment centers, neuropsychological/rehabilitation centers, pain treatment centers, and managed care facilities. Students are placed in these sites based on their interests and training needs. Each practicum lasts nine months and 500 to 600 hours. Students in the PsyD program focus on assessment skills during their first practicum and intervention skills during their second practicum, and are supervised by a licensed, doctoral-level psychologist. For those doctoral students for whom a professional internship is required prior to graduation, 32 applied in 2000–2001. Of those who applied, 13 were placed in internships listed by the Association of Psychology Postdoctoral and Internship Programs (APPIC); 12 were placed in APA accredited internships.

Housing and Day Care: No on-campus housing and day care facilities are available.

Employment of Department Graduates:

Master's Degree Graduates: Of those who graduated in the academic year 2000–2001, the following categories and numbers represent the post-graduate activities and employment of master's degree graduates: Enrolled in a psychology doctoral program (10), enrolled in a post-doctoral residency/fellowship (n/a), employed in independent practice (n/a).

Doctoral Degree Graduates: Of those who graduated in the academic year 2000–2001, the following categories and numbers represent the post-graduate activities and employment of doctoral degree graduates: Enrolled in a psychology doctoral program (n/a), enrolled in another graduate/professional program (n/a), enrolled in a post-doctoral residency/fellowship (4), employed in independent practice (7), employed in an academic position at a 2-year/4-year college (1), employed in other positions at a higher education institution (2), employed in business or industry (research/consulting) (1), employed in a government agency (professional services) (2), employed in a community mental health/counseling center (15), still seeking employment (3), other employment position (2).

Additional Information:

Orientation, Objectives, and Emphasis of Department: The PsyD Program at AU/TC (formerly MSPP) requires 90 semester hours and is eclectic, experiential, and competency-based. Faculty represent a range of orientations including psychodynamic, cognitive behavioral, systemic, interpersonal, narrative, and experiential. The program is committed to fostering the growth and development of each student's identity as a professional psychologist. The MA in Professional Counseling/Marriage & Family Therapy emphasizes development of a working theory and practice in interactional, systemic, and contextual therapy across interpersonal, intrapersonal, and social-cultural relationships. This MA program requires 45 semester credits, and includes a required portfolio process.

Special Facilities or Resources: Predoctoral concentrations are available in Marriage & Family Therapy (qualifies for MN licensure as a Marriage & Family therapist), Clinical Health Psychology, Forensic Psychology, and Clinical Child Psychology.

Information for Students With Physical Disabilities: MSPP can accommodate students with a variety of disabilities and has a history of reasonably accommodating students.

Application Information:

Send to: Admissions Department, Argosy University/Twin Cities, 5503 Green Valley Drive, Suite 150, Minneapolis, MN 55437. Students are admitted in the Fall, application deadline May 15; Winter, application deadline October 15. Early application deadline is January 15. *Fee:* $50.

Minnesota State University Moorhead
School Psychology Program
Social and Natural Sciences
1104 7th Avenue South
Moorhead, MN 56563
Telephone: (218) 236-2802
Fax: (218) 236-2168
E-mail: *potter@mnstate.edu*
Web: *http://www.mnstate.edu/gradpsyc*

Department Established:

1970. Program Director: Margaret L. Potter. Number of Faculty: total–full-time 11; women–full-time 6; minority–full-time 1.

Programs and Degrees Offered:

Listed in the following order: Program area, degree type (T if terminal Master's), number awarded 7/00-6/01. School Psychology EdS 9.

Student Applications/Admissions:

Student Applications

School Psychology EdS—Applications 2001–2002, 20. Total applicants accepted 2001–2002, 12. New applicants enrolled 2001–2002, 5. Total enrolled 2001–2002 full-time, 11. Openings 2002–2003, 10. The Median number of years required for completion of a degree are 3. The number of students enrolled full and part-time, who were dismissed or voluntarily withdrew from this program area were 0.

Admissions Requirements:

Scores: Entries appear in this order: required test or GPA, minimum score (if required), median score of students entering in 2001–2002. Master's Programs: GRE-V+Q 1000, 1050; overall undergraduate GPA 3.00, 3.4; last 2 years GPA 3.25. Doctoral Programs: last 2 years GPA no minimum stated; psychology GPA no minimum stated; psychology GPA no minimum stated.

Other Criteria: (importance of criteria rated low, medium, or high): GRE/MAT scores high, research experience medium, work experience medium, extracurricular activity medium, clinically related public service low, GPA high, letters of recommendation high, interview medium, statement of goals and objectives high.

Student Characteristics: The following represents characteristics of students in 2001–2002 in all graduate psychology programs in the department: Female–full-time 11; Male–full-time 6, part-time 0; African American/Black–full-time 0, part-time 0; Hispanic/Latino (a)–full-time 0, part-time 0; Asian/Pacific Islander–full-time 0, part-time 0; American Indian/Alaska Native–full-time 0, part-time 0; Multi-ethnic–full-time 0, part-time 0; students subject to the Americans with Disabilities Act–full-time 0, part-time 0.

Financial Information/Assistance:

Tuition for Full-Time Study: *Master's:* State residents per academic year $3,360, $168 per credit hour; nonstate residents: per academic year $3,360, $168 per credit hour.

Financial Assistance:

First Year Students: Research assistantships available for first-year. Average amount paid per academic year: $1,800. Average number of hours worked per week: 6. Apply by May 15.

Advanced Students: Research assistantships available for advanced students. Average amount paid per academic year: $2,000. Average number of hours worked per week: 6. Apply by May 15.

Contact Information: Of all students currently enrolled full-time, 100% benefitted from one or more of the listed financial assistance programs. For information on financial assistance, contact: Director of Financial Aid, 218-236-2085.

Internships/Practica: Field-based practica in both first and second years of study provide actual experience to students. Practica are supervised by local educators and school psychologists and are coordinated with on-campus coursework so students can apply concepts and techniques learned in class. A 1200-hour internship during the third year of study serves as the capstone experience for student's training. Internships are usually positions within school districts or special education cooperatives in the tri-state area.

Housing and Day Care: On-campus housing and day care facilities are available.

Employment of Department Graduates:

Master's Degree Graduates: Of those who graduated in the academic year 2000–2001, the following categories and numbers represent the post-graduate activities and employment of master's degree graduates: Enrolled in a psychology doctoral program (1), enrolled in another graduate/professional program (0), enrolled in a post-doctoral residency/fellowship (n/a), employed in independent practice (n/a), employed in an academic position at a university (0), employed in an academic position at a 2-year/4-year college (0), employed in other positions at a higher education institution (0), employed in a professional position in a school system (6).

Doctoral Degree Graduates: Of those who graduated in the academic year 2000–2001, the following categories and numbers represent the post-graduate activities and employment of doctoral degree graduates: Enrolled in a psychology doctoral program (n/a), enrolled in another graduate/professional program (n/a).

Additional Information:

Orientation, Objectives, and Emphasis of Department: Our goal is to provide the training necessary for our graduates to be skilled problem solvers in dealing with the needs of children, families, and others involved in the learning enterprise. Within a scientist-practitioner model and integrative perspective, the program's primary focus is on educating Specialist-level professionals capable of working effectively in educational agencies and in collaboration with other human services providers. Our graduates are highly regarded by the schools and agencies within which they work because of their knowledge of current best practices in the field and because of their skills as team members.

Information for Students With Physical Disabilities: Minnesota State Moorhead University has a committment to ensure that all students with physical, sensory, psychological or learning disabilities have equal access to programs and services. The Office of Disability Services addresses the needs of students who have disabilities or other health impairments which may interfere with a succcessful college experience.

Application Information:
Send to: Graduate Admissions Office, Minnesota State University Moorhead, 1104 7th Avenue S., Moorhead, Minnesota 56563. Students are admitted in the Fall, application deadline February 15. applications will be accepted after February 15 if space is available *Fee:* $20.

Minnesota, University of (2001 data)
Department of Educational Psychology: Counseling and
   Student Personnel and School Psychology
Education and Human Development
178 Pillsbury Drive S.E., 204 Burton Hall
Minneapolis, MN 55455
Telephone: (612) 624-1698
Fax: (612) 624-8241
E-mail: *mmcevoy@tc.umn.edu*
Web: *http://www.education.umn.edu/edpsych*

Department Established:
1947. Chairperson: Mary McEvoy, Chair. Number of Faculty: total–full-time 11, part-time 2; women–full-time 5, part-time 2; minority–full-time 2.

Programs and Degrees Offered:
Listed in the following order: Program area, degree type (T if terminal Master's), number awarded 7/00–6/01. Counseling & student personnel MA (T) 30, school PhD 4.

APA Accreditation: Counseling PhD: full. School PhD: full.

Student Applications/Admissions:
Student Applications
Counseling & student personnel MA—Applications 2001–2002, 65. Total applicants accepted 2001–2002, 26. New applicants enrolled 2001–2002, 21. Total enrolled 2001–2002 full-time, 21. Openings 2002–2003, 25. *School PhD*—Applications 2001–2002, 28. Total applicants accepted 2001–2002, 6. New applicants enrolled 2001–2002, 6. Total enrolled 2001–2002 full-time, 6. Openings 2002–2003, 6.

Admissions Requirements:
Scores: Entries appear in this order: required test or GPA, minimum score (if required), median score of students entering in 2001–2002. Master's Programs: GRE-V no minimum stated, 490; GRE-Q no minimum stated, 600; GRE-V+Q no minimum stated, 1090; GRE-Analytical no minimum stated, 560; overall undergraduate GPA no minimum stated, 3.45; last 2 years GPA 3.1, 3.7. Doctoral Programs: GRE-V+Q no minimum stated, 1185; overall undergraduate GPA 3.00, 3.73; psychology GPA no minimum stated, 3.83.
Other Criteria: (importance of criteria rated low, medium, or high): research experience medium, work experience medium, extracurricular activity medium, clinically related public service low, letters of recommendation high, interview high, statement of goals and objectives high. CSPP/PhD: research - high, work - high, extracurricular - high, public service - high,

letters of recommendation - high, statement of goals - high, interview - none.

Student Characteristics: The following represents characteristics of students in 2001–2002 in all graduate psychology programs in the department: Female–full-time 28, part-time 0; Male–full-time 11, part-time 0; African American/Black–full-time 4, part-time 0; Hispanic/Latino (a)–full-time 1, part-time 0; Asian/Pacific Islander–full-time 0, part-time 0; American Indian/Alaska Native–full-time 0, part-time 0.

Financial Information/Assistance:

Tuition for Full-Time Study: No information provided.

Financial Assistance:

First Year Students: No information provided.

Advanced Students: No information provided.

Contact Information: For information on financial assistance, contact: Individual Program offices or U's Scholarship and Financial Aid Office, 210 Fraser Hall, 106 Pleasant St SE, Mpls., MN 55455.

Internships/Practica: Doctoral students have three tiers of applied training. Tier 1 - Year-long practica tied to assessment coursework followed by a second year of practica tied to intervention coursework. All of these experiences occur in metro area schools. Tier 2 - Formal school practicum under the supervision of a school psychologist in Twin Cities area schools. In addition, doctoral students complete a community/clinical practica. These practica occur in a wide variety of settings including mental health and community agencies such as Indian Health Board, Washburn Child Guidance Center, Community University Health Care Center, Fraser Family and Children services. Tier 3 - Internship. The majority completes their year-long internships in public schools settings, although some have found internships in settings that are a collaboration of community and educational settings. In one setting, interns work as part of a mental health and educational team providing school based services to identified students with emotional and behavioral disorders.

Housing and Day Care: No on-campus housing and day care facilities are available.

Employment of Department Graduates:

Master's Degree Graduates: Of those who graduated in the academic year 2000–2001, the following categories and numbers represent the post-graduate activities and employment of master's degree graduates: Enrolled in a post-doctoral residency/fellowship (n/a), employed in independent practice (n/a).

Doctoral Degree Graduates: Of those who graduated in the academic year 2000–2001, the following categories and numbers represent the post-graduate activities and employment of doctoral degree graduates: Enrolled in a psychology doctoral program (n/a), enrolled in another graduate/professional program (n/a).

Additional Information:

Orientation, Objectives, and Emphasis of Department: Counseling and Student Personnel Psychology is intended to provide a fundamental body of knowledge and skills to prepare counselors and counseling psychologists for work in a variety of settings— counseling and human development, career development, staff development, and student personnel work. While the focus is primarily on facilitating human development in educational settings, it is possible for individuals to prepare for community and agency settings as well. The faculty is committed to addressing current social issues such as diversity concerns and adolescent well-being gender roles. The CSPP program is designed for a select group of individuals with a demonstrated capacity for leadership and a commitment in the human services. School Psychology: The range of the school psychologist's impact includes, but is not limited to, the application of theory and research in the psychosocial development and learning of children and youth, social interaction processes, prevention and competence enhancement strategies, instructional intervention and program development, and delivery of mental health services. Our major training goal is to prepare school psychologists for roles within the educational enterprise. Competencies needed include knowledge in developmental psychology, personality and learning theory, and social psychology; assessing individual and systems needs; generating and implementing prevention programs and intervention strategies; collaborative consultation; diversity; and evaluating and redesigning programs. Training modalities include a variety of seminars and independent study projects. A wide range of community resources is available to facilitate goals of the program.

Special Facilities or Resources: CSPP: The department has some flexibility in the design of student programs. Excellent facilities for research opportunities exist throughout the university. There is a time-shared instructional computing laboratory with batch and online computer facilities available for student use; and free access to the central university computer. Students may borrow audiorecorders, overheads, and VCRs. CSPP has a career development library; two job files (academic and professional service positions) exist within the school psychology program. School Psychology Resources houses journals, books, and intervention and assessment materials. This collection supplements the Psychology Department Journal Seminar Room (for psychology majors) and the Florence Goodenough Reading Room (for child psychology majors), the University Psychology and Educational Library with its specialized computer search facilities, and the extensive University libraries system with holdings numbering approximately 3.5 million volumes. School psychology also maintains a collection of standardized, individual, and group psychometric tests, measures, and protocols which can be borrowed for coursework use.

Information for Students With Physical Disabilities: The mission of the Disabled Student Cultural Center is to foster and develop disability community and pride. It sponsors regular programs and events. Disability Services at the U of MN is a component of the Office of the Associate Vice President for Academic Affairs. The mission of Disability Services is to be a catalyst for ensuring equal learning and working opportunities for disabled students, faculty, staff, and guests by increasing the capacity of communities to eliminate physical, programmatic, policy, informational, and attitudinal barriers. DS also seeks to develop, evaluate, and disseminate innovative models and exemplary practices that promote disability leadership, community, culture, and pride.

Application Information:

Send to: School Psych Program, 344 Elliott Hall, U. Of MN, Mpls, MN 55455; Counseling and Student Personnel Psych, 129 Burton Hall, U of MN, Mpls MN 55455. Students are admitted in the Fall, application deadline 12/1; 12/15. January 15 deadline is for School Psych. CSPP deadline January 1. *Fee:* $50.

Minnesota, University of
Department of Psychology
N218 Elliott Hall, 75 East River Road
Minneapolis, MN 55455
Telephone: (612) 625-4042
Fax: (612) 626-2079
E-mail: *psyapply@tc.umn.edu*
Web: *http://www.psych.umn.edu*

Department Established:
1919. Chairperson: John Campbell. Number of Faculty: total–full-time 37, part-time 34; women–full-time 8, part-time 11; minority–full-time 3, part-time 2.

Programs and Degrees Offered:
Listed in the following order: Program area, degree type (T if terminal Master's), number awarded 7/00–6/01. Biological psychopathology PhD, clinical PhD 3, cognitive and biological PhD 3, counseling PhD 2, differential/behavioral geneti PhD, industrial/organizational PhD 1, personality research PhD, psychometric methods PsyD (T), school PhD, social PhD 3.

APA Accreditation: Clinical PhD: full. Counseling PhD: full. School PhD: full.

Student Applications/Admissions:
Student Applications
Biological psychopathology PhD—Applications 2001–2002, 8. Total applicants accepted 2001–2002, 1. New applicants enrolled 2001–2002, 1. Total enrolled 2001–2002 full-time, 3. Openings 2002–2003, 2. The number of students enrolled full and part-time, who were dismissed or voluntarily withdrew from this program area were 1. *Clinical PhD*—Applications 2001–2002, 89. Total applicants accepted 2001–2002, 8. New applicants enrolled 2001–2002, 4. Total enrolled 2001–2002 full-time, 21. Openings 2002–2003, 4. The number of students enrolled full and part-time, who were dismissed or voluntarily withdrew from this program area were 0. *Cognitive and biological PhD*—Applications 2001–2002, 27. Total applicants accepted 2001–2002, 9. New applicants enrolled 2001–2002, 5. Total enrolled 2001–2002 full-time, 27. Openings 2002–2003, 8. The number of students enrolled full and part-time, who were dismissed or voluntarily withdrew from this program area were 0. *Counseling PhD*—Applications 2001–2002, 58. Total applicants accepted 2001–2002, 6. New applicants enrolled 2001–2002, 4. Total enrolled 2001–2002 full-time, 29. Openings 2002–2003, 4. The number of students enrolled full and part-time, who were dismissed or voluntarily withdrew from this program area were 0. *Differential/behavioral geneti PhD*—Applications 2001–2002, 10. Total applicants accepted 2001–2002, 3. New applicants enrolled 2001–2002, 2. Total enrolled 2001–2002 full-time, 5. Openings 2002–2003, 2. The number of students enrolled full and part-time, who were dismissed or voluntarily withdrew from this program area were 0. *Industrial/organizational PhD*—Applications 2001–2002, 72. Total applicants accepted 2001–2002, 8. New applicants enrolled 2001–

2002, 2. Total enrolled 2001–2002 full-time, 18. Openings 2002–2003, 4. The number of students enrolled full and part-time, who were dismissed or voluntarily withdrew from this program area were 0. *Personality research PhD*—Applications 2001–2002, 11. Total applicants accepted 2001–2002, 3. Total enrolled 2001–2002 full-time, 7. Openings 2002–2003, 3. The number of students enrolled full and part-time, who were dismissed or voluntarily withdrew from this program area were 0. *Psychometric methods PsyD*—Applications 2001–2002, 10. Total applicants accepted 2001–2002, 4. New applicants enrolled 2001–2002, 4. Total enrolled 2001–2002 full-time, 12. Openings 2002–2003, 4. The number of students enrolled full and part-time, who were dismissed or voluntarily withdrew from this program area were 0. *School PhD*—Applications 2001–2002, 1. Total enrolled 2001–2002 full-time, 2. Openings 2002–2003, 2. *Social PhD*—Applications 2001–2002, 50. Total applicants accepted 2001–2002, 9. New applicants enrolled 2001–2002, 2. Total enrolled 2001–2002 full-time, 17. Openings 2002–2003, 6. The number of students enrolled full and part-time, who were dismissed or voluntarily withdrew from this program area were 0.

Admissions Requirements:
Scores: Entries appear in this order: required test or GPA, minimum score (if required), median score of students entering in 2001–2002. Master's Programs: GRE-V no minimum stated; GRE-Q no minimum stated; overall undergraduate GPA no minimum stated. Doctoral Programs: GRE-V no minimum stated, 608; GRE-Q no minimum stated, 692; overall undergraduate GPA no minimum stated, 3.73; last 2 years GPA no minimum stated; psychology GPA no minimum stated; psychology GPA no minimum stated. While we have no fixed requirements and admission decisions are based on an individual's complete record, it is desirable that applicants have either a GPA of 3.0 and GRE scores of at least 600 on both the verbal and quantitative sections or a GPA of 3.3 and scores of 500 or greater on the GRE verbal and quantitative sections. For the clinical program and the personality research program, it is desirable that applicants have at least a 3.5 GPA and scores of at least 600 on the verbal and quantitative sections of the GRE. The following programs also recommend that you submit GRE Subject Test in Psychology scores: Clinical, Counseling, Differential/Behavioral Genetics, and Personality Research.
Other Criteria: (importance of criteria rated low, medium, or high): GRE/MAT scores high, research experience high, work experience medium, extracurricular activity medium, clinically related public service medium, GPA high, letters of recommendation high, statement of goals and objectives high.

Student Characteristics: The following represents characteristics of students in 2001–2002 in all graduate psychology programs in the department: Female–full-time 15, part-time 0; Male–full-time 9, part-time 0; African American/Black–full-time 0, part-time 0; Hispanic/Latino (a)–full-time 0, part-time 0; Asian/Pacific Islander–full-time 3, part-time 0; American Indian/Alaska Native–full-time 0, part-time 0; Multi-ethnic–full-time 0, part-time 0; students subject to the Americans with Disabilities Act–full-time 0, part-time 0.

Financial Information/Assistance:
Tuition for Full-Time Study: *Master's:* State residents per academic year $5,863, $489 per credit hour; nonstate residents: per

academic year $11,516, $960 per credit hour. *Doctoral:* State residents: per academic year $5,863, $489 per credit hour; nonstate residents: per academic year $11,516, $960 per credit hour.

Financial Assistance:

First Year Students: Teaching assistantships available for first-year. Average amount paid per academic year: $10,234. Average number of hours worked per week: 20. Apply by January 5. Tuition remission given: full. Research assistantships available for first-year. Average amount paid per academic year: $10,234. Average number of hours worked per week: 20. Apply by January 5. Tuition remission given: full. Traineeships available for first-year. Average amount paid per academic year: $16,500. Average number of hours worked per week: 0. Apply by January 5. Tuition remission given: full. Fellowships and scholarships available for first-year. Average amount paid per academic year: $13,500. Average number of hours worked per week: 0. Apply by January 5. Tuition remission given: full.

Advanced Students: Teaching assistantships available for advanced students. Average amount paid per academic year: $10,234. Average number of hours worked per week: 20. Tuition remission given: full. Research assistantships available for advanced students. Average amount paid per academic year: $10,234. Average number of hours worked per week: 20. Tuition remission given: full. Traineeships available for advanced students. Average amount paid per academic year: $16,500. Average number of hours worked per week: 0. Tuition remission given: full. Fellowships and scholarships available for advanced students. Average amount paid per academic year: $13,000. Average number of hours worked per week: 0. Tuition remission given: full.

Contact Information: Of all students currently enrolled full-time, 78% benefited from one or more of the listed financial assistance programs. For information on financial assistance, contact: Coordinator of Graduate Admissions.

Internships/Practica: Internships are available at the university hospitals, the department's Vocational Assessment Clinic, the University Counseling and Consulting Services, the Veterans Administration, and several other governmental and private agencies throughout the area. Full listings are included in the departmental brochure. For those doctoral students for whom a professional internship is required prior to graduation, 3 applied in 2000–2001. Of those who applied, 3 were placed in internships listed by the Association of Psychology Postdoctoral and Internship Programs (APPIC); 3 were placed in APA accredited internships.

Housing and Day Care: On-campus housing and day care facilities are available.

Employment of Department Graduates:

Master's Degree Graduates: Of those who graduated in the academic year 2000–2001, the following categories and numbers represent the post-graduate activities and employment of master's degree graduates: Enrolled in a post-doctoral residency/fellowship (n/a), employed in independent practice (n/a).

Doctoral Degree Graduates: Of those who graduated in the academic year 2000–2001, the following categories and numbers represent the post-graduate activities and employment of doctoral degree graduates: Enrolled in a psychology doctoral program (n/a), enrolled in another graduate/professional program (n/a), enrolled in a post-doctoral residency/fellowship (1), employed in independent practice (2), employed in an academic position at a university (2), employed in an academic position at a 2-year/4-year college (2), employed in business or industry (research/consulting) (3), employed in a hospital/medical center (1), other employment position (1).

Additional Information:

Orientation, Objectives, and Emphasis of Department: Minnesota has a broad range of areas of specialization in the department, which cannot be described in detail here. The departmental application materials and brochures contain detailed relevant information on each program area. In general, the overall goal is to train the people who will become leaders in their chosen area of specialization. Consequently, the graduate training programs in the department are oriented first to the training of skilled researchers and teachers in psychology, and then to the training of specialists and practitioners. The PhD programs in Clinical, Counseling, and School Psychology are accredited by APA. Department faculty also participate in independent degree programs in neuroscience and cognitive science. The Department of Psychology and the Institute of Child Development offer a joint training program in child clinical psychology focused on the study of psychopathology in the context of development. The child clinical psychology/developmental psychopathology program is APA-accredited as part of the clinical psychology program. Admission to the joint program is coordinated by the Institute of Child Development, 51 East River Road, University of Minnesota, Minneapolis, MN 55455. The school psychology PhD is offered jointly with the School Psychology Program. For information about this program, please write directly to the School Psychology Program, 344 Elliott Hall, 75 East River Road, University of Minnesota, Minneapolis, MN 55455.

Special Facilities or Resources: The department offers extensive laboratory and computer facilities, a wide variety of resources and collaborative relationships both on and off campus, and several federally funded research projects.

Information for Students With Physical Disabilities: The Disability Services Office promotes program and physical access, which means ensuring the rights of students with disabilities and assisting the University in meeting its obligations under federal and state statutes. Disability Services provides direct assistance such as information, referral, support, and academic accommodations for enrolled and prospective students, as well as consultation to faculty and staff to ensure access to their programs and facilities. Campus accessibility maps also are available.

Application Information:

Send to: Coordinator of Graduate Admissions, Department of Psychology, 249 Elliott Hall, 75 East River Road, Minneapolis, MN 55455. Students are admitted in the Fall, application deadline January 5. If you wish to be considered for financial support, we recommend that you send the Graduate School application form, transcripts, and fee to the Graduate School by December 1. The departmental application form and supporting materials should be sent to the Department of Psychology by January 5. *Fee:* $50. $55 for international applicants. The application fee cannot be waived or deferred and is not refundable.

Minnesota, University of

Institute of Child Development
College of Education and Human Development
51 East River Road
Minneapolis, MN 55455
Telephone: (612) 624-2576
Fax: (612) 624-6373
E-mail: *amasten@umn.edu*
Web: *http://icd.coled.umn.edu*

Department Established:
1925. Director: Ann Masten. Number of Faculty: total–full-time 15, part-time 2; women–full-time 7; minority–full-time 1.

Programs and Degrees Offered:
Listed in the following order: Program area, degree type (T if terminal Master's), number awarded 7/00–6/01. Child PhD 16.

APA Accreditation: Clinical PhD: full. School PhD: full.

Student Applications/Admissions:

Student Applications
Child PhD—Applications 2001–2002, 67. Total applicants accepted 2001–2002, 18. New applicants enrolled 2001–2002, 11. Total enrolled 2001–2002 full-time, 63. Openings 2002–2003, 10. The Median number of years required for completion of a degree are 7.

Admissions Requirements:
Scores: Entries appear in this order: required test or GPA, minimum score (if required), median score of students entering in 2001–2002. Doctoral Programs: GRE-V no minimum stated, 615; GRE-Q no minimum stated, 730; GRE-V+Q no minimum stated, 1345; GRE-Analytical no minimum stated, 705; overall undergraduate GPA no minimum stated, 3.71; last 2 years GPA no minimum stated; psychology GPA no minimum stated; psychology GPA no minimum stated.
Other Criteria: (importance of criteria rated low, medium, or high): GRE/MAT scores medium, research experience high, work experience low, extracurricular activity low, clinically related public service low, GPA high, letters of recommendation high, statement of goals and objectives high, K–12 experience medium. Clinically related public service rated low for joint child/clinical program. K-12 experience applies only to joint school psychology program.

Student Characteristics: The following represents characteristics of students in 2001–2002 in all graduate psychology programs in the department: Female–full-time 50, part-time 3; Male–full-time 7, part-time 0; African American/Black–full-time 1, part-time 0; Hispanic/Latino (a)–full-time 2, part-time 0; Asian/Pacific Islander–full-time 2, part-time 0; American Indian/Alaska Native–full-time 0, part-time 0; students subject to the Americans with Disabilities Act–full-time 2.

Financial Information/Assistance:
Tuition for Full-Time Study: *Doctoral:* State residents: per academic year $5,864, $489 per credit hour; nonstate residents: per academic year $11,516, $960 per credit hour.

Financial Assistance:
First Year Students: Teaching assistantships available for first-year. Average amount paid per academic year: $10,350. Average number of hours worked per week: 20. Tuition remission given: full. Research assistantships available for first-year. Average amount paid per academic year: $10,350. Average number of hours worked per week: 20. Tuition remission given: full. Traineeships available for first-year. Average amount paid per academic year: $11,633. Average number of hours worked per week: 20. Tuition remission given: full. Fellowships and scholarships available for first-year. Average amount paid per academic year: $13,500. Tuition remission given: full.
Advanced Students: Teaching assistantships available for advanced students. Average amount paid per academic year: $10,350. Average number of hours worked per week: 20. Tuition remission given: full. Research assistantships available for advanced students. Average amount paid per academic year: $10,350. Average number of hours worked per week: 20. Tuition remission given: full. Traineeships available for advanced students. Average amount paid per academic year: $11,633. Average number of hours worked per week: 20. Tuition remission given: full. Fellowships and scholarships available for advanced students. Average amount paid per academic year: $13,500. Tuition remission given: full.
Contact Information: Of all students currently enrolled full-time, 100% benefited from one or more of the listed financial assistance programs. For information on financial assistance, contact: Graduate Admissions.

Internships/Practica: Internships and practica are available within the community to joint program students and are offered through our departmental affiliates. Field experiences are also offered to students in our Applied Developmental Psychology Certificate program. For those doctoral students for whom a professional internship is required prior to graduation, 3 applied in 2000–2001. Of those who applied, 3 were placed in APA accredited internships.

Housing and Day Care: No on-campus housing and day care facilities are available.

Employment of Department Graduates:
Master's Degree Graduates: Of those who graduated in the academic year 2000–2001, the following categories and numbers represent the post-graduate activities and employment of master's degree graduates: Enrolled in a post-doctoral residency/fellowship (n/a), employed in independent practice (n/a).
Doctoral Degree Graduates: Of those who graduated in the academic year 2000–2001, the following categories and numbers represent the post-graduate activities and employment of doctoral degree graduates: Enrolled in a psychology doctoral program (n/a), enrolled in another graduate/professional program (n/a), enrolled in a post-doctoral residency/fellowship (6), employed in an academic position at a university (3), employed in other positions at a higher education institution (2), employed in a professional position in a school system (1), employed in business or industry (research/consulting) (1), employed in business or industry (management) (1), employed in a community mental health/counseling center (2).

Additional Information:
Orientation, Objectives, and Emphasis of Department: The Institute program emphasizes training for research and academic

careers and provides supplementary opportunities in areas of applied developmental psychology. The program offers a diversity of substantive and methodological approaches. In the core program, special strengths are in infancy, personality and social development, perception, cognitive processes, language development, biological bases of development, and neuropsychology. Applied training is available in Developmental Psychopathology and Clinical Science (DPCS), School Psychology, developmental neuropsychology, educational programs and research, public policy, and policy-relevant research. Special training is also available through affiliations with the Center for Cognitive Sciences, the Harris Center, the Center for Neurobehavioral Development, the Center for Early Education and Development, and the Consortium on Children, Youth, and Families.

Special Facilities or Resources: Physical and research facilities include an office for every student each equipped with an Ethernet connected computer and printer; a reference room with more than 4,500 volumes and 64 journal subscriptions; twenty-five experiment rooms; a computer laboratory; a shop for construction of apparatus; and a laboratory nursery school.

Application Information:

Send to: Chair of Admissions, University of Minnesota, Institute of Child Development, 51 E River Rd., Minneapolis, MN 55422. Students are admitted in the Fall, application deadline December. *Fee:* $50. $55 for international applicants. Visa, Mastercard, Discover accepted. Waivers for extreme financial hardship upon written request to the director of graduate studies.

Saint Mary's University of Minnesota
Counseling and Psychological Services
School of Graduate Studies
2500 Park Avenue
Minneapolis, MN 55404
Telephone: (612) 728-5113
Fax: (612) 728-5121
E-mail: *chuck@smumn.edu*
Web: *http://www.smumn.edu*

Department Established:

1983. Program Director: Christina Huck, PhD, LP. Number of Faculty: total–full-time 2, part-time 71; women–full-time 2, part-time 36.

Programs and Degrees Offered:

Listed in the following order: Program area, degree type (T if terminal Master's), number awarded 7/00–6/01. Counseling and psychological MA (T) 121, marriage and family therapy.

Student Applications/Admissions:

Student Applications

Counseling and psychological MA—New applicants enrolled 2001–2002, 98. Total enrolled 2001–2002 full-time, 130, part-time, 111.

Admissions Requirements:

Scores: Entries appear in this order: required test or GPA, minimum score (if required), median score of students entering

in 2001–2002. Master's Programs: overall undergraduate GPA 2.75. Doctoral Programs: last 2 years GPA no minimum stated; psychology GPA no minimum stated; psychology GPA no minimum stated.

Other Criteria: (importance of criteria rated low, medium, or high): GRE/MAT scores, research experience medium, work experience high, extracurricular activity medium, clinically related public service high, GPA medium, letters of recommendation high, interview high, statement of goals and objectives high.

Student Characteristics: The following represents characteristics of students in 2001–2002 in all graduate psychology programs in the department: Female–full-time 0, part-time 0; Male–full-time 0, part-time 0; African American/Black–full-time 0, part-time 0; Hispanic/Latino (a)–full-time 0, part-time 0; Asian/Pacific Islander–full-time 0, part-time 0; American Indian/Alaska Native–full-time 0, part-time 0.

Financial Information/Assistance:

Tuition for Full-Time Study: *Master's:* State residents $245 per credit hour; nonstate residents: $245 per credit hour.

Financial Assistance:

First Year Students: No information provided.
Advanced Students: No information provided.
Contact Information: Of all students currently enrolled full-time, 0% benefited from one or more of the listed financial assistance programs.

Internships/Practica: A wide variety of practicum sites are available for students.

Housing and Day Care: No on-campus housing and day care facilities are available.

Employment of Department Graduates:

Master's Degree Graduates: Of those who graduated in the academic year 2000–2001, the following categories and numbers represent the post-graduate activities and employment of master's degree graduates: Enrolled in a post-doctoral residency/fellowship (n/a), employed in independent practice (n/a).
Doctoral Degree Graduates: Of those who graduated in the academic year 2000–2001, the following categories and numbers represent the post-graduate activities and employment of doctoral degree graduates: Enrolled in a psychology doctoral program (n/a), enrolled in another graduate/professional program (n/a).

Additional Information:

Orientation, Objectives, and Emphasis of Department: The Master of Arts Program in Counseling and Psychological Services prepares graduates for professional work in counseling, psychotherapy, and other psychological services. It is designed to enhance the student's understanding of the complex nature of human behavior and social interaction, and to develop tools for assessing human problems and assisting individuals in developing greater understanding and acceptance of themselves and their relationships with others. The program is designed to meet the educational requirements for Minnesota licensure for Psychological Practitioners. This program is offered in Rochester, MN, as well as in Minneapolis.

Special Facilities or Resources: The majority of our faculty are adjunct (part-time) instructors who are practicing in the field. They bring a wealth of real-world experience to their teaching and possess strong academic credentials. Since our emphasis is on applied psychological competence, we consider the backgrounds of these practitioner-scholars to be a major strength of the program.

Application Information:

Send to: Admissions, Saint Mary's University of MN, 2500 Park Ave., Minneapolis, MN 55404. Students are admitted in the Fall; Winter; Summer. No deadline dates, recommended applying 3 months before semester. *Fee:* $20.

St. Cloud State University
Counseling and Educational Psychology
College of Education
Education Building, 720 South 4th Avenue
St. Cloud, MN 56301
Telephone: (612) 255-3131
Fax: (612) 255-4082
E-mail: *jpreble@stcloudstate.edu*
Web: *http://www.saintcloudstate.edu*

Department Established:

2001. Chairperson: Jana Preble. Number of Faculty: total–full-time 13, part-time 5; women–full-time 4, part-time 3; minority–full-time 3, part-time 1.

Programs and Degrees Offered:

Listed in the following order: Program area, degree type (T if terminal Master's), number awarded 7/00–6/01. College Student Development MA (T) N/A.

Student Applications/Admissions:

Student Applications

College Student Development MA—Applications 2001–2002, 4. Total applicants accepted 2001–2002, 4. New applicants enrolled 2001–2002, 4. Total enrolled 2001–2002 full-time, 4, part-time, 3. The Median number of years required for completion of a degree are NA.

Admissions Requirements:

Scores: Entries appear in this order: required test or GPA, minimum score (if required), median score of students entering in 2001–2002. Master's Programs: GRE-V no minimum stated; GRE-Q no minimum stated; GRE-V+Q no minimum stated; GRE-Analytical no minimum stated; GRE-V+Q+Analytical no minimum stated; overall undergraduate GPA no minimum stated; last 2 years GPA no minimum stated. Doctoral Programs: last 2 years GPA no minimum stated; psychology GPA no minimum stated; psychology GPA no minimum stated.

Other Criteria: (importance of criteria rated low, medium, or high): GRE/MAT scores medium, research experience medium, work experience high, extracurricular activity medium, clinically related public service medium, GPA high, letters of recommendation high, interview high, statement of goals and objectives high.

Student Characteristics: The following represents characteristics of students in 2001–2002 in all graduate psychology programs in the department: Female–full-time 25, part-time 15; Male–full-time 5, part-time 5; African American/Black–full-time 0, part-time 0; Hispanic/Latino (a)–full-time 2, part-time 0; Asian/Pacific Islander–full-time 2, part-time 0; American Indian/Alaska Native–full-time 2, part-time 0; students subject to the Americans with Disabilities Act–full-time 7, part-time 3.

Financial Information/Assistance:

Tuition for Full-Time Study: *Master's:* State residents $170 per credit hour; nonstate residents: $300 per credit hour.

Financial Assistance:

First Year Students: Teaching assistantships available for first-year. Average amount paid per academic year: $5,000. Average number of hours worked per week: 10. Tuition remission given: partial. Research assistantships available for first-year. Average amount paid per academic year: $5,000. Average number of hours worked per week: 10. Tuition remission given: partial.

Advanced Students: No information provided.

Contact Information: Of all students currently enrolled full-time, 50% benefited from one or more of the listed financial assistance programs. For information on financial assistance, contact: Office of Graduate Studies, 121 Administrative Services Bldg.

Internships/Practica: Internship opportunities exist in mental health centers, university counseling centers, Veterans Administration hospitals, general hospitals, social service and welfare agencies, state rehabilitation offices, private rehabilitation companies, rehabilitation workshops and facilities, medical rehabilitation centers, and a number of human services agencies and school settings.

Housing and Day Care: On-campus housing and day care facilities are available.

Employment of Department Graduates:

Master's Degree Graduates: Of those who graduated in the academic year 2000–2001, the following categories and numbers represent the post-graduate activities and employment of master's degree graduates: Enrolled in a psychology doctoral program (5), enrolled in another graduate/professional program (3), enrolled in a post-doctoral residency/fellowship (n/a), employed in independent practice (n/a), employed in other positions at a higher education institution (4), employed in a professional position in a school system (35), employed in business or industry (research/consulting) (13), employed in a government agency (professional services) (3), employed in a community mental health/counseling center (2).

Doctoral Degree Graduates: Of those who graduated in the academic year 2000–2001, the following categories and numbers represent the post-graduate activities and employment of doctoral degree graduates: Enrolled in a psychology doctoral program (n/a), enrolled in another graduate/professional program (n/a).

Additional Information:

Orientation, Objectives, and Emphasis of Department: The college student development program prepares students to work in college counseling centers, career centers, and other student affairs positions in higher education. The Rehabilitation Counseling

Program is accredited by the Council on Rehabilitation Education and prepares students to work in a variety of public and private rehabilitation settings. The School Counseling Program prepares students for licensure as elementary or secondary school counselors and is accredited by the Council for the Accreditation of Counseling and Related Educational Programs (CACREP).

Special Facilities or Resources: A counseling classroom surrounded by 10 counseling and observation suites allows for both individual and group counseling experiences. Audio and video equipment is available for taping and reviewing counseling sessions. A separate group room is also available for training and observation experiences. There is an animal laboratory containing pigeon and rat boxes with events controlled via a PDP-8.

Application Information:
Send to: Department of Counselor and Educational Psychology. Students are admitted in the Spring, application deadline April 1. *Fee:* $20. Subject to change with revision of university graduate bulletin.

St. Thomas, University of (2001 data)
Graduate School of Professional Psychology
TMH451, 1000 La Salle Avenue
Minneapolis, MN 55403
Telephone: (651) 962-4650
Fax: (651) 962-4651
E-mail: *gradadmissions@stthomas.edu*
Web: *http://www.stthomas.edu*

Department Established:
1960. Dean: Burton F. Nolan. Number of Faculty: total–full-time 8, part-time 10; women–full-time 4, part-time 4; minority–full-time 1, part-time 1.

Programs and Degrees Offered:
Listed in the following order: Program area, degree type (T if terminal Master's), number awarded 7/00–6/01. Counseling MA (T) 33.

APA Accreditation: Counseling PsyD: full.

Student Applications/Admissions:
Student Applications
Counseling MA—Applications 2001–2002, 81. Total applicants accepted 2001–2002, 41. New applicants enrolled 2001–2002, 39. Total enrolled 2001–2002 full-time, 17, part-time, 94. Openings 2002–2003, 40. The Median number of years required for completion of a degree are 4. The number of students enrolled full and part-time, who were dismissed or voluntarily withdrew from this program area were 0.

Admissions Requirements:
Scores: Entries appear in this order: required test or GPA, minimum score (if required), median score of students entering in 2001–2002. Master's Programs: MAT no minimum stated, 54; overall undergraduate GPA 2.75, 3.0. Doctoral Programs: MAT no minimum stated, 58; psychology GPA 3.00, 3.68.
Other Criteria: (importance of criteria rated low, medium, or high): GRE/MAT scores medium, work experience medium,

clinically related public service medium, GPA high, letters of recommendation medium, interview high, statement of goals and objectives high.

Student Characteristics: The following represents characteristics of students in 2001–2002 in all graduate psychology programs in the department: Female–full-time 26, part-time 18; Male–full-time 8, part-time 7; African American/Black–full-time 2, part-time 2; Hispanic/Latino (a)–full-time 1, part-time 1; Asian/Pacific Islander–full-time 2, part-time 0; American Indian/Alaska Native–full-time 0, part-time 0.

Financial Information/Assistance:
Tuition for Full-Time Study: No information provided.

Financial Assistance:
First Year Students: No information provided.
Advanced Students: No information provided.
Contact Information: For information on financial assistance, contact: Admissions Chair, Department of Professional Psychology, U. of St. Thomas, 1000 La Salle Avenue, Minneapolis, MN 55403.

Internships/Practica: No information provided.

Housing and Day Care: No on-campus housing and day care facilities are available.

Employment of Department Graduates:
Master's Degree Graduates: Of those who graduated in the academic year 2000–2001, the following categories and numbers represent the post-graduate activities and employment of master's degree graduates: Enrolled in a post-doctoral residency/fellowship (n/a), employed in independent practice (n/a).
Doctoral Degree Graduates: Of those who graduated in the academic year 2000–2001, the following categories and numbers represent the post-graduate activities and employment of doctoral degree graduates: Enrolled in a psychology doctoral program (n/a), enrolled in another graduate/professional program (n/a).

Additional Information:
Orientation, Objectives, and Emphasis of Department: The Graduate Programs in Professional Psychology are dedicated to the development of general practitioners who will make ethical, professional, creative contributions to their communities and their profession. The programs strive toward leadership in emphasizing a practitioner focus with adult learners. Teaching, scholarship, and service are responsive to diverse perspectives, a blend of practical and reflective inquiry, and social needs. The recently developed PsyD program meets designation criteria of the ASPPB/National Register Joint Designation Project.

Information for Students With Physical Disabilities: The Office of Specialized Services provides reasonable and appropriate accommodations to qualified students with physical disabilities. To be eligible for these services, documentation from a licensed professional is required.

Application Information:
Send to: Admissions Chair, Department of Professional Psychology, University of St. Thomas, 1000 La Salle Avenue, Minneapolis, MN 55403. Students are admitted in the Fall, application deadline October

1; Winter, application deadline February 1; Summer, application deadline April 1. Application deadlines for the Fall - October 1 MA. Summer deadline April 1 for MA; February 1 for PsyD. *Fee*: $50.

Walden University
Professional Psychology Program
155 Fifth Avenue South
Minneapolis, MN 55401
Telephone: (800) WALDENU
Fax: (612) 338-5092
E-mail: *hglazer@waldenu.edu*
Web: *http://www.waldnu.edu*

Department Established:
1996. Chairperson: Hilda Glazer. Number of Faculty: total–full-time 3, part-time 40; women–full-time 1, part-time 14; faculty subject to the Americans with Disabilities Act 2.

Programs and Degrees Offered:
Listed in the following order: Program area, degree type (T if terminal Master's), number awarded 7/00–6/01. Academic Psychology PhD, Clinical or Coun - Hlth PhD, Clinical or Coun-Org PhD, Clinical Psychology PhD 16, Counseling Psychology PhD 5, General Psychology MA 10, Health Psycholog PhD, Organizational Psychology.

Student Applications/Admissions:
Student Applications
Academic Psychology PhD. Clinical or Coun - Hlth PhD—Total enrolled 2001–2002 full-time, 9. *Clinical or Coun-Org PhD*—Total enrolled 2001–2002 full-time, 8. *Clinical Psychology PhD*—Total enrolled 2001–2002 full-time, 170. The Median number of years required for completion of a degree are 5. *Counseling Psychology PhD*—Total enrolled 2001–2002 full-time, 117. The Median number of years required for completion of a degree are 5. *General Psychology MA*—Total enrolled 2001–2002 full-time, 101. The Median number of years required for completion of a degree is 1. *Health Psycholog PhD*—Total enrolled 2001–2002 full-time, 56.

Admissions Requirements:
Scores: Entries appear in this order: required test or GPA, minimum score (if required), median score of students entering in 2001–2002. Master's Programs: overall undergraduate GPA 3.0, 3.5; last 2 years GPA 3.0, 3.5; psychology GPA 3.0, 3.5. Doctoral Programs: last 2 years GPA 3.0.
Other Criteria: (importance of criteria rated low, medium, or high): research experience low, work experience high, extra-curricular activity high, clinically related public service high,
GPA high, letters of recommendation high, interview high, statement of goals and objectives high.

Student Characteristics: The following represents characteristics of students in 2001–2002 in all graduate psychology programs in the department: Female–full-time 409, Male–full-time 216, African American/Black–full-time 122, Hispanic/Latino (a)–full-time 26, Asian/Pacific Islander–full-time 10, American Indian/Alaska Native–full-time 9, Multi-ethnic–full-time 13, students subject to the Americans with Disabilities Act–full-time 9.

Financial Information/Assistance:
Tuition for full-time study: Nonstate residents: $320 per credit hour.

Financial Assistance:
First Year Students: No information provided.
Advanced Students: No information provided.
Contact Information: Of all students currently enrolled full-time, 70% benefited from one or more of the listed financial assistance programs. For information on financial assistance, contact: an enrollment counselor at 866-4Walden; www.ealdenu.edu/financial.

Internships/Practica: No information provided.

Housing and Day Care: No on-campus housing and day care facilities are available.

Employment of Department Graduates:
Master's Degree Graduates: Of those who graduated in the academic year 2000–2001, the following categories and numbers represent the post-graduate activities and employment of master's degree graduates: Enrolled in a psychology doctoral program (50), enrolled in a post-doctoral residency/fellowship (n/a), employed in independent practice (n/a).
Doctoral Degree Graduates: Of those who graduated in the academic year 2000–2001, the following categories and numbers represent the post-graduate activities and employment of doctoral degree graduates: Enrolled in a psychology doctoral program (n/a), enrolled in another graduate/professional program (n/a).

Additional Information:
Orientation, Objectives, and Emphasis of Department: We pride ourselves on providing students opportunities to work with faculty from different theoretical orientations who are practicing psychologists.

Application Information:
Send to: Office of Student Enrollment Walden University 24311 Walden Center Drive, Suite 300, Bonita Springs, FL 34134. Students are admitted in the Fall, application deadline July 1; Winter, application deadline October 1; Spring, application deadline January 1; Summer, application deadline April 1. *Fee*: $50.

Jackson State University
Department of Psychology
Liberal Arts
P.O. Box 17550
Jackson, MS 39217-0350
Telephone: (601) 979-3385
Fax: (601) 979-2393
E-mail: *cassisi@worldnet.att.net*
Web: *http://www.jsums.edu/liberalarts/psych/phdpsych.ht*

Department Established:
1971. Professor and Chair: Shih-Sung Wen. Number of Faculty: total–full-time 13, part-time 1; women–full-time 5; minority–full-time 6.

Programs and Degrees Offered:
Listed in the following order: Program area, degree type (T if terminal Master's), number awarded 7/00–6/01. Clinical psychology PhD.

Student Applications/Admissions:
Student Applications

Clinical psychology PhD—Applications 2001–2002, 35. Total applicants accepted 2001–2002, 10. New applicants enrolled 2001–2002, 7. Total enrolled 2001–2002 full-time, 29, part-time, 1. Openings 2002–2003, 8. The number of students enrolled full and part-time, who were dismissed or voluntarily withdrew from this program area were 1.

Admissions Requirements:
Scores: Entries appear in this order: required test or GPA, minimum score (if required), median score of students entering in 2001–2002. Doctoral Programs: GRE-V no minimum stated, 460; GRE-Q no minimum stated, 470; GRE-V+Q no minimum stated, 930; overall undergraduate GPA no minimum stated, 3.7 ; last 2 years GPA no minimum stated, 3.9 ; psychology GPA no minimum stated; psychology GPA no minimum stated, 3.9.
Other Criteria: (importance of criteria rated low, medium, or high): GRE/MAT scores low, research experience high, work experience high, extracurricular activity low, clinically related public service medium, GPA high, letters of recommendation high, interview high, statement of goals and objectives medium.

Student Characteristics: The following represents characteristics of students in 2001–2002 in all graduate psychology programs in the department: Female–full-time 22, part-time 1; Male–full-time 8, part-time 0; African American/Black–full-time 11, part-time 0; Hispanic/Latino (a)–full-time 0, part-time 0; Asian/Pacific Islander–full-time 1, part-time 0; American Indian/Alaska Native–full-time 0, part-time 0.

Financial Information/Assistance:
Tuition for Full-Time Study: *Doctoral:* State residents: per academic year $2,788, $155 per credit hour; nonstate residents: per academic year $6,414.

Financial Assistance:
First Year Students: Research assistantships available for first-year. Average amount paid per academic year: $8,000. Average number of hours worked per week: 14. Fellowships and scholarships available for first-year. Average amount paid per academic year: $8,000. Average number of hours worked per week: 14. Tuition remission given: partial.
Advanced Students: Teaching assistantships available for advanced students. Average amount paid per academic year: $8,000. Average number of hours worked per week: 14. Research assistantships available for advanced students. Average amount paid per academic year: $8,000. Average number of hours worked per week: 14. Fellowships and scholarships available for advanced students. Average amount paid per academic year: $8,000. Average number of hours worked per week: 14.
Contact Information: Of all students currently enrolled full-time, 90% benefited from one or more of the listed financial assistance programs. For information on financial assistance, contact: Jeffery E. Cassisi (601) 979-3385.

Internships/Practica: Extensive Practicum and Externship experiences are required. Students have recently been placed at the Mississippi State Hospital at Whitfield, Baptist Medical Center, and the Jackson Veteran's Administration Medical Center. For those doctoral students for whom a professional internship is required prior to graduation, 4 applied in 2000–2001. Of those who applied, 4 were placed in internships listed by the Association of Psychology Postdoctoral and Internship Programs (APPIC); 4 were placed in APA accredited internships.

Housing and Day Care: No on-campus housing and day care facilities are available.

Employment of Department Graduates:
Master's Degree Graduates: Of those who graduated in the academic year 2000–2001, the following categories and numbers represent the post-graduate activities and employment of master's degree graduates: Enrolled in a post-doctoral residency/fellowship (n/a), employed in independent practice (n/a).
Doctoral Degree Graduates: Of those who graduated in the academic year 2000–2001, the following categories and numbers represent the post-graduate activities and employment of doctoral degree graduates: Enrolled in a psychology doctoral program (n/a), enrolled in another graduate/professional program (n/a).

Additional Information:
Orientation, Objectives, and Emphasis of Department: The Mississippi Board of Trustees of Institutions of Higher Learning authorized a PhD program in clinical psychology for the Department of Psychology in 1994. The first class began in the fall of 1995.

The program follows the scientist-practitioner model and is in the process of applying for APA Accreditation. We had our accreditation site visit Oct 2001 and we are awaiting notice of the outcome. A distinctive and vital feature of the program is its multi-cultural emphasis. Cross-cultural psychology and psychology in the urban environment are core requirements. Cross-cultural perspectives are integrated into the content of most courses. Additional concentrations in health psychology or quantitative methods are available. Jackson State University is located in Jackson, Mississippi, the capital and largest city of the state. The metropolitan area consists of a growing population estimated to be 400,000. The campus is located on a scenic 106-acre tract situated one mile west of the main business district of the city. Jackson is also the hub for health-care in the state. A Veterans Administration medical center, the University of Mississippi Medical School, Whitfield State Hospital, Baptist Medical Center, Methodist Medical Center, and St. Dominic's Medical Center are all within a 20-minute radius of the campus. These sites and others offer many potential research and practicum opportunities.

Special Facilities or Resources: The Department of Psychology relocated to a new $16-million Liberal Arts Building in 2000; it contains faculty offices, computing facilities, and a Psychology Clinic. A $12-million expansion of the H.T. Sampson Library has just been completed. The Community Health Program is administered by the Department of Psychology and is an important resource for graduate student research. This program has been awarded several multiyear grants from the National Institutes of Health and the Centers for Disease Control. Several students have chosen to conduct their dissertations at this facility. The Community Health Program is located at the Jackson Medical Mall.

Application Information:

Send to: Clinical Program Admissions, Department of Psychology, Jackson State University, P.O. Box 17550, Jackson, MS 39217-0350. Students are admitted in the Fall, application deadline March 1. *Fee:* $20.

Mississippi State University
Department of Counselor Education and Educational
  Psychology
College of Education
P.O. Box 9727
Mississippi State, MS 39762-5670
Telephone: (662) 325-3426
Fax: (662) 325-3263
E-mail: *hosie@ra.msstate.edu*

Department Established:

1954. Department Head: Thomas W. Hosie. Number of Faculty: total–full-time 18, part-time 1; women–full-time 5, part-time 1; minority–full-time 3.

Programs and Degrees Offered:

Listed in the following order: Program area, degree type (T if terminal Master's), number awarded 7/00–6/01. Educational PhD 1, school PhD 5.

APA Accreditation: School PhD: full.

Student Applications/Admissions:

Student Applications

Educational PhD—Applications 2001–2002, 7. Total applicants accepted 2001–2002, 6. New applicants enrolled 2001–2002, 5. Total enrolled 2001–2002 full-time, 5. Openings 2002–2003, 6. The Median number of years required for completion of a degree are 4. *School PhD*—Applications 2001–2002, 14. Total applicants accepted 2001–2002, 8. New applicants enrolled 2001–2002, 5. Total enrolled 2001–2002 full-time, 25. Openings 2002–2003, 6-8. The Median number of years required for completion of a degree are 5. The number of students enrolled full and part-time, who were dismissed or voluntarily withdrew from this program area were 2.

Admissions Requirements:

Scores: Entries appear in this order: required test or GPA, minimum score (if required), median score of students entering in 2001–2002. Master's Programs: GRE-V+Q+Analytical no minimum stated, 1540; overall undergraduate GPA 3.0, 3.3; last 2 years GPA 3.0, 3.7. Doctoral Programs: GRE-V+Q+Analytical no minimum stated, 1500; overall undergraduate GPA no minimum stated, 3.3 ; last 2 years GPA 3.0, 3.7 ; psychology GPA no minimum stated; psychology GPA no minimum stated.

Other Criteria: (importance of criteria rated low, medium, or high): GRE/MAT scores medium, research experience medium, work experience medium, extracurricular activity low, clinically related public service low, GPA high, letters of recommendation high, interview high, statement of goals and objectives high.

Student Characteristics: The following represents characteristics of students in 2001–2002 in all graduate psychology programs in the department: Female–full-time 18, part-time 6; Male–full-time 4, part-time 3; African American/Black–full-time 4, part-time 0; Hispanic/Latino (a)–full-time 1, part-time 0; Asian/Pacific Islander–full-time 1, part-time 0; American Indian/Alaska Native–full-time 0, part-time 0; Multi-ethnic–full-time 0, part-time 0; students subject to the Americans with Disabilities Act–full-time 0.

Financial Information/Assistance:

Tuition for Full-Time Study: *Master's:* State residents $168 per credit hour; nonstate residents: $340 per credit hour. *Doctoral:* State residents: $168 per credit hour; nonstate residents: $340 per credit hour.

Financial Assistance:

First Year Students: Teaching assistantships available for first-year. Average amount paid per academic year: $6,000. Average number of hours worked per week: 20. Tuition remission given: full. Research assistantships available for first-year. Average amount paid per academic year: $9,000. Average number of hours worked per week: 20. Tuition remission given: full.

Advanced Students: Teaching assistantships available for advanced students. Average amount paid per academic year: $6,000. Average number of hours worked per week: 20. Tuition remission given: full. Research assistantships available for advanced students. Average amount paid per academic year: $9,000.

Average number of hours worked per week: 20. Tuition remission given: full.

Contact Information: Of all students currently enrolled full-time, 50% benefited from one or more of the listed financial assistance programs. For information on financial assistance, contact: Dr. Tom Hosie at department address.

Internships/Practica: The school psychology program offers students numerous practica and internship opportunities. Most are coordinated with school districts, medical centers/hospitals, community counseling centers, and the like. Internship and practica opportunities are tailored to meet the individual needs of students and a variety of options can be arranged. In general, students are encouraged to seek APA-approved internships.

Housing and Day Care: On-campus housing and day care facilities are available.

Employment of Department Graduates:

Master's Degree Graduates: Of those who graduated in the academic year 2000–2001, the following categories and numbers represent the post-graduate activities and employment of master's degree graduates: Enrolled in a psychology doctoral program (2), enrolled in a post-doctoral residency/fellowship (n/a), employed in independent practice (n/a).

Doctoral Degree Graduates: Of those who graduated in the academic year 2000–2001, the following categories and numbers represent the post-graduate activities and employment of doctoral degree graduates: Enrolled in a psychology doctoral program (n/a), enrolled in another graduate/professional program (n/a).

Additional Information:

Orientation, Objectives, and Emphasis of Department: Our graduate programs are designed primarily to help develop and train competent and ethical psychologists in several areas: school psychometry, school psychology, generalist, and educational psychology. The programs are based on a scientist-practitioner model. The flexibility of these offerings gives the student the option of functioning as an educational psychologist in a variety of settings, thereby enhancing employment opportunities.

Special Facilities or Resources: The Educational Psychology faculty maintain close working relationships with the Department of Psychology, Special Education Division, Department of Counselor Education, and others. Such relationships afford students the opportunity to work closely with diverse faculty members with various human services backgrounds. Moreover, students are encouraged to work closely with faculty on various creative projects and research. Additional opportunities exist at the Rehabilitation Research and Training Center on Blindness and Low Vision, the Bureau of Educational Research and Evaluation, and the Research and Curriculum Unit for Vocational-Technical Education, all of which are connected with Mississippi State University.

Application Information:
Send to: Department Chair. Students are admitted in the Fall, application deadline February 15. MS for Fall due March 15; same for CAS Educational psychology programs offer spring, summer admission as well. Fee: $25 Admission fee for out of state applicants.

Mississippi State University
Department of Psychology
Arts and Sciences
P.O. Drawer 6161
Mississippi State, MS 39762
Telephone: (662) 325-3202
Fax: (662) 325-7212
E-mail: sbk1@ra.msstate.edu
Web: http://www.msstate.edu/Dept/Psychology/psych.html

Department Established:
1966. Department Head: Stephen B. Klein. Number of Faculty: total–full-time 17, part-time 7; women–full-time 7, part-time 2; minority–full-time 1.

Programs and Degrees Offered:
Listed in the following order: Program area, degree type (T if terminal Master's), number awarded 7/00–6/01. Clinical psychology MA (T) 8, cognitive science PhD, experimental psychology MA (T) 2.

Student Applications/Admissions:
Student Applications
Clinical psychology MA—Applications 2001–2002, 39. Total applicants accepted 2001–2002, 21. New applicants enrolled 2001–2002, 8. Total enrolled 2001–2002 full-time, 30. Openings 2002–2003, 10. Cognitive science PhD—Applications 2001–2002, 8. Total applicants accepted 2001–2002, 7. New applicants enrolled 2001–2002, 3. Total enrolled 2001–2002 full-time, 6. Openings 2002–2003, 3. The number of students enrolled full and part-time, who were dismissed or voluntarily withdrew from this program area were 1. Experimental psychology MA—Applications 2001–2002, 3. Total applicants accepted 2001–2002, 2. New applicants enrolled 2001–2002, 1. Total enrolled 2001–2002 full-time, 2. Openings 2002–2003, 3.

Admissions Requirements:
Scores: Entries appear in this order: required test or GPA, minimum score (if required), median score of students entering in 2001–2002. Master's Programs: last 2 years GPA 2.75, 3.78. The GPA of 2.75 is the minimum our Office of Graduate Admissions will accept for entry into the Graduate School. We look for a minimum GRE of 1000 (quantitative and verbal), but it's not an absolute requirement. The median numbers median are the figures for the latest group of applicants we accepted and are actually enrolled in the clinical program. Doctoral Programs: GRE-Q 500, 640; GRE-V+Q 1000, 1270; last 2 years GPA 3.00, 3.48; psychology GPA no minimum stated; psychology GPA no minimum stated. The median scores are the actual figures for the latest group of applicants we accepted into the program.

Other Criteria: (importance of criteria rated low, medium, or high): GRE/MAT scores medium, research experience medium, work experience medium, extracurricular activity low, clinically related public service medium, GPA medium, letters of recommendation medium, interview low, statement of goals and objectives medium, computer experience medium. The clinically related public service would be relevant for applicants to the master's program, clinical concentration. Computer-related experience is relevant to the cognitive PhD program.

Student Characteristics: The following represents characteristics of students in 2001–2002 in all graduate psychology programs in the department: Female–full-time 8, part-time 0; Male–full-time 6, part-time 0; African American/Black–full-time 2, part-time 0; Hispanic/Latino (a)–full-time 0, part-time 0; Asian/Pacific Islander–full-time 0, part-time 0; American Indian/Alaska Native–full-time 0, part-time 0.

Financial Information/Assistance:

Tuition for Full-Time Study: *Master's:* State residents per academic year $1,793, $199 per credit hour; nonstate residents: per academic year $4,050, $450 per credit hour. *Doctoral:* State residents: per academic year $1,793, $199 per credit hour; nonstate residents: per academic year $4,050, $450 per credit hour.

Financial Assistance:

First Year Students: Teaching assistantships available for first-year. Average amount paid per academic year: $5,940. Average number of hours worked per week: 20. Apply by May 1. Tuition remission given: full.

Advanced Students: Teaching assistantships available for advanced students. Average amount paid per academic year: $10,000. Average number of hours worked per week: 20. Apply by May 1. Tuition remission given: full. Research assistantships available for advanced students. Average amount paid per academic year: $10,000. Average number of hours worked per week: 20. Apply by May 1. Tuition remission given: full.

Contact Information: Of all students currently enrolled full-time, 50% benefited from one or more of the listed financial assistance programs. For information on financial assistance, contact: Dr. Steve Klein at sbk1@ra.msstate.edu.

Internships/Practica: Students in the clinical-emphasis program complete two 300 clock-hour practicum courses. These practica occur in a variety of settings, including public and private psychiatric hospitals and mental retardation facilities, community mental health centers, etc. Students are exposed to diverse client populations (e.g., in- and outpatient, children and adults with varied diagnoses and ethnic backgrounds).

Housing and Day Care: No on-campus housing and day care facilities are available.

Employment of Department Graduates:

Master's Degree Graduates: Of those who graduated in the academic year 2000–2001, the following categories and numbers represent the post-graduate activities and employment of master's degree graduates: Enrolled in a post-doctoral residency/fellowship (n/a), employed in independent practice (n/a).

Doctoral Degree Graduates: Of those who graduated in the academic year 2000–2001, the following categories and numbers represent the post-graduate activities and employment of doctoral degree graduates: Enrolled in a psychology doctoral program (n/a), enrolled in another graduate/professional program (n/a).

Additional Information:

Orientation, Objectives, and Emphasis of Department: The department offers a terminal MS degree with two concentrations: clinical and experimental. We recognize that the functional de-

gree in psychology·is the doctorate, so we perceive our major role as twofold: (1) to give the student an opportunity to successfully complete graduate-level courses and to acquire the credentials for entering doctoral-level programs, and (2) to provide the student with skills attractive to potential employers in the broad human relations areas. In addition, the department has recently acquired a multidisciplinary PhD degree in applied cognitive science.

Special Facilities or Resources: State-of-the-art computer lab; individual faculty have research facilities and ties to other research facilities either on-campus or off.

Application Information:

Send to: Graduate Admissions, Drawer 6305, Miss. State, MS 39762. Students are admitted in the Fall, application deadline May 1; Spring, application deadline November 1. The application deadlines are the same for each of our programs. *Fee:* None for in-state applicants; $25 for out-of-state and foreign applicants.

Mississippi, University of (2001 data)
Department of Psychology
205 Peabody
University, MS 38677
Telephone: (662) 915-7383
Fax: (662) 915-5398
E-mail: *psych@olemiss.edu*
Web: *http://www.olemiss.edu/depts/psychology*

Department Established:

Chairperson: David S. Hargrove. Number of Faculty: total–full-time 15, part-time 1; women–full-time 5, part-time 1; minority–full-time 1.

Programs and Degrees Offered:

Listed in the following order: Program area, degree type (T if terminal Master's), number awarded 7/00–6/01. Clinical PhD 9, experimental PhD 1.

APA Accreditation: Clinical PhD: full.

Student Applications/Admissions:

Student Applications

Clinical PhD—Applications 2001–2002, 94. Total applicants accepted 2001–2002, 17. New applicants enrolled 2001–2002, 7. Total enrolled 2001–2002 full-time, 48. Openings 2002–2003, 8. *Experimental PhD*—Applications 2001–2002, 12. Total applicants accepted 2001–2002, 6. New applicants enrolled 2001–2002, 4. Total enrolled 2001–2002 full-time, 14. Openings 2002–2003, 5.

Admissions Requirements:

Scores: Entries appear in this order: required test or GPA, minimum score (if required), median score of students entering in 2001–2002. Master's Programs: psychology GPA no minimum stated. Doctoral Programs: GRE-V no minimum stated, 530; GRE-Q no minimum stated, 640; GRE-V+Q 1000, 1190; GRE-Analytical no minimum stated, 630; GRE-Subject(Psych) no minimum stated, 580; overall undergraduate

GPA no minimum stated. Master's GPA only applies to students entering with Master's degrees.

Other Criteria: (importance of criteria rated low, medium, or high): GRE/MAT scores research experience high, work experience medium, extracurricular activity medium, clinically related public service medium, GPA letters of recommendation high, interview high, statement of goals and objectives high.

Student Characteristics: The following represents characteristics of students in 2001–2002 in all graduate psychology programs in the department: Female–full-time 3, part-time 0; Male–full-time 8, part-time 0; African American/Black–full-time 0, part-time 0; Hispanic/Latino (a)–full-time 0, part-time 0; Asian/Pacific Islander–full-time 1, part-time 0; American Indian/Alaska Native–full-time 0, part-time 0.

Financial Information/Assistance:

Tuition for Full-Time Study: No information provided.

Financial Assistance:

First Year Students: No information provided.
Advanced Students: No information provided.
Contact Information: No information provided.

Internships/Practica: Practica or Field Placements are available for clinical students beginning in the second year of the program. Students serve as therapists on practicum teams in our in house clinic for a minimum of three years under the direct supervision of the members of our clinical faculty, all of whom are licensed psychologists. After students have demonstrated a minimum level of competence in the clinic, they are allowed to apply for practicum positions at field placement agencies in the community where they are supervised by licensed practitioners who are employed by the field placement agency. In recent years, students have completed field placements at the University Counseling Center; Community Mental Health Centers in Oxford, Greenwood, and Tupelo; State Mental Hospitals in Meridian, Whitfield, and Bolivar, TN; North Mississippi Regional Center in Oxford; North Mississippi Medical Center in Tupelo; the VAMC in Memphis, and the Mantachie Clinic in Mantachie, MS. Students are assisted and advised by faculty in choosing field placements most appropriate to their individual career goals.

Housing and Day Care: No on-campus housing and day care facilities are available.

Employment of Department Graduates:

Master's Degree Graduates: Of those who graduated in the academic year 2000–2001, the following categories and numbers represent the post-graduate activities and employment of master's degree graduates: Enrolled in a post-doctoral residency/fellowship (n/a), employed in independent practice (n/a).

Doctoral Degree Graduates: Of those who graduated in the academic year 2000–2001, the following categories and numbers represent the post-graduate activities and employment of doctoral degree graduates: Enrolled in a psychology doctoral program (n/a), enrolled in another graduate/professional program (n/a).

Additional Information:

Orientation, Objectives, and Emphasis of Department: The Department of Psychology offers programs of study in clinical and

general-experimental psychology leading to the Doctor of Philosophy degree. The clinical program, which is fully accredited by the American Psychological Association, ordinarily requires five years beyond the bachelor's level to complete. Four of the five years are devoted to coursework and research, and the remaining year entails a clinical internship at an APA-approved training site. Requirements for the master's degree are also fulfilled during this period; however, the MA is considered to be a step in the doctoral training. The clinical program adheres to the scientist-practitioner model and emphasizes an empirical approach to clinical practice. A social learning or behavioral approach characterizes the clinical training offered. The experimental program is designed to prepare psychologists for careers in teaching and research. Specific programs include Behavioral Neuroscience, Cognitive Psychology, Experimental Analysis of Behavior, and Social Psychology. Students entering the experimental program are assigned a faculty mentor (major professor) whose research interests match their training goals. All students are required to engage in significant research projects.

Special Facilities or Resources: The department's offices, classrooms, laboratories, and psychology clinic are housed in the George Peabody Building. The six rooms of the psychology clinic include four multipurpose rooms for evaluation, consultation, and therapy and two observation rooms equipped with one-way mirrors and videotape equipment. Having a total of 17 micro- or minicomputers, the department offers computer-based laboratories for psychopharmacology, psychophysiology, operant conditioning, and behavioral toxicology. For conducting the psychophysiological research, the department has a 6-channel Grass Model 7 polygraph and an 8-channel scanning electromyograph. Autogen biofeedback instrumentation is also available for the measurement and feedback of skin temperature, muscle tension, heart rate, and skin conductance. The department has close ties with the pharmacy and law schools (located on the Oxford campus) and with the medical school in Jackson.

Application Information:
Send to: Admissions Chairperson for desired program. Students are admitted in the Fall, application deadline February 1. *Fee:* $25. The application fee is for out-of-state students only.

Southern Mississippi, University of
Department of Psychology
College of Education and Psychology
Box 5025
Hattiesburg, MS 39401
Telephone: (601) 266-4177
Fax: (601) 266-5580
E-mail: *s.kuczaj@usm.edu*
Web: *http://www-dept.usm.edu/~psy/dept/home.htm*

Department Established:
1960. Chairperson: Stan Kuczaj. Number of Faculty: total–full-time 26, part-time 4; women–full-time 6; minority–full-time 2, part-time 1.

Programs and Degrees Offered:
Listed in the following order: Program area, degree type (T if terminal Master's), number awarded 7/00–6/01. Clinical Psychol-

ogy PhD 4, Coun MS/MA (T) 13, Counseling PhD 4, Experimental PhD 2, Industrial/Organizational PhD, School Psychology PhD 3.

APA Accreditation: Clinical PhD: full. Counseling PhD: full. School PhD: full.

Student Applications/Admissions:

Student Applications

Clinical Psychology PhD—Applications 2001–2002, 79. Total applicants accepted 2001–2002, 7. New applicants enrolled 2001–2002, 7. Total enrolled 2001–2002 full-time, 30, part-time, 10. Openings 2002–2003, 7. The Median number of years required for completion of a degree are 5. The number of students enrolled full and part-time, who were dismissed or voluntarily withdrew from this program area were 0. *Coun MS/MA*—Applications 2001–2002, 40. Total applicants accepted 2001–2002, 14. New applicants enrolled 2001–2002, 13. Total enrolled 2001–2002 full-time, 22. Openings 2002–2003, 14. The Median number of years required for completion of a degree are 2. The number of students enrolled full and part-time, who were dismissed or voluntarily withdrew from this program area were 2. *Counseling PhD*—Applications 2001–2002, 40. Total applicants accepted 2001–2002, 8. New applicants enrolled 2001–2002, 6. Total enrolled 2001–2002 full-time, 24, part-time, 12. Openings 2002–2003, 5. The Median number of years required for completion of a degree are 4. The number of students enrolled full and part-time, who were dismissed or voluntarily withdrew from this program area were 0. *Experimental PhD*—Applications 2001–2002, 22. Total applicants accepted 2001–2002, 8. New applicants enrolled 2001–2002, 6. Total enrolled 2001–2002 full-time, 12, part-time, 1. Openings 2002–2003, 4-6. The Median number of years required for completion of a degree are 6. The number of students enrolled full and part-time, who were dismissed or voluntarily withdrew from this program area were 0. *Industrial/Organizational PhD*—Applications 2001–2002, 34. Total applicants accepted 2001–2002, 7. New applicants enrolled 2001–2002, 4. Total enrolled 2001–2002 full-time, 9, part-time, 12. Openings 2002–2003, 3-4. The Median number of years required for completion of a degree are n/a. The number of students enrolled full and part-time, who were dismissed or voluntarily withdrew from this program area were 1. *School Psychology PhD*—Applications 2001–2002, 18. Total applicants accepted 2001–2002, 8. New applicants enrolled 2001–2002, 6. Total enrolled 2001–2002 full-time, 21, part-time, 8. Openings 2002–2003, 6. The Median number of years required for completion of a degree are 4. The number of students enrolled full and part-time, who were dismissed or voluntarily withdrew from this program area were 1.

Admissions Requirements:

Scores: Entries appear in this order: required test or GPA, minimum score (if required), median score of students entering in 2001–2002. Master's Programs: GRE-V no minimum stated, 485; GRE-Q no minimum stated, 530; GRE-V+Q no minimum stated, 1060. Doctoral Programs: GRE-V no minimum stated, 510; GRE-Q no minimum stated, 600; GRE-V+Q no minimum stated, 1110; overall undergraduate GPA no minimum stated, 3.58; last 2 years GPA no minimum stated; psychology GPA no minimum stated; psychology GPA no minimum stated. Check with program directors.

Other Criteria: (importance of criteria rated low, medium, or high): GRE/MAT scores high, research experience high, work experience medium, extracurricular activity low, clinically related public service low, GPA high, letters of recommendation high, interview high, statement of goals and objectives high. Criteria vary by program. Check with program directors.

Student Characteristics: The following represents characteristics of students in 2001–2002 in all graduate psychology programs in the department: Female–full-time 78, part-time 29; Male–full-time 40, part-time 13; African American/Black–full-time 8, part-time 2; Hispanic/Latino (a)–full-time 1, part-time 0; Asian/Pacific Islander–full-time 3, part-time 0; American Indian/Alaska Native–full-time 0, part-time 0; Multi-ethnic–full-time 0, part-time 0; students subject to the Americans with Disabilities Act–full-time 0, part-time 0.

Financial Information/Assistance:

Tuition for Full-Time Study: *Master's:* State residents per academic year $2,970, $165 per credit hour; nonstate residents: per academic year $6,898, $383 per credit hour. *Doctoral:* State residents: per academic year $2,970, $165 per credit hour; nonstate residents: per academic year $6,898, $383 per credit hour.

Financial Assistance:

First Year Students: Research assistantships available for first-year. Average amount paid per academic year: $4,400. Average number of hours worked per week: 20. Apply by 2/15. Tuition remission given: full.

Advanced Students: Teaching assistantships available for advanced students. Average amount paid per academic year: $5,190. Average number of hours worked per week: 20. Apply by 2/15. Tuition remission given: full. Research assistantships available for advanced students. Average amount paid per academic year: $5,190. Average number of hours worked per week: 20. Apply by 2/15. Tuition remission given: full.

Contact Information: Of all students currently enrolled full-time, 99% benefited from one or more of the listed financial assistance programs. For information on financial assistance, contact: Financial Aid Office, Box 5101, USM, Hattiesburg, MS 39406-5101.

Internships/Practica: Doctoral students from our three APA-approved programs (Clinical, Counseling, and School) begin practicum experiences in the on-campus clinics and progress to community externship placements, as they gain experience and training. A student's final year is a full-time internship in an APA-accredited internship. Students have been placed throughout the United States, with the majority in health service settings, such as Veterans Administration Medical Centers, medical schools, and comprehensive community mental health centers. For those doctoral students for whom a professional internship is required prior to graduation, 16 applied in 2000–2001. Of those who applied, 16 were placed in internships listed by the Association of Psychology Postdoctoral and Internship Programs (APPIC); 16 were placed in APA accredited internships.

Housing and Day Care: On-campus housing and day care facilities are available.

Employment of Department Graduates:

Master's Degree Graduates: Of those who graduated in the academic year 2000–2001, the following categories and numbers

represent the post-graduate activities and employment of master's degree graduates: Enrolled in a psychology doctoral program (5), enrolled in a post-doctoral residency/fellowship (n/a), employed in independent practice (n/a), employed in a community mental health/counseling center (7).

Doctoral Degree Graduates: Of those who graduated in the academic year 2000–2001, the following categories and numbers represent the post-graduate activities and employment of doctoral degree graduates: Enrolled in a psychology doctoral program (n/a), enrolled in another graduate/professional program (n/a), enrolled in a post-doctoral residency/fellowship (2), employed in an academic position at a university (1), employed in a community mental health/counseling center (4), employed in a hospital/medical center (4), still seeking employment (1), other employment position (1).

Additional Information:

Orientation, Objectives, and Emphasis of Department: The department has five psychology doctoral programs (Clinical, Counseling, Experimental, Industrial/Organizational, and School), each with different emphases and orientations. Specific information about each program can be obtained from our Website (http://www~dept.usm.edu/~psy/psy.htm). The departmental philosophy is built on the assumption that psychology is first and foremost a scientific discipline. Therefore, a common element of all the programs is a commitment to science and research, with exposure to the breadth and depth of the field of psychology. Students are challenged to develop critical thinking skills, and are taught to respect discovery and inquiry. The applied programs espouse the scientist-practitioner model of training and emphasize training in research as well as delivery of psychological services. The department offers opportunities for research and clinical training in several subareas, such as health psychology/behavioral medicine, multicultural issues, neuropsychology, and child/family interventions.

Special Facilities or Resources: The department houses three psychology service training clinics. Research laboratories provide training in various areas such as sleep, psychophysiology, neuropsychology, behavioral neuroscience, and personality and experimental psychopathology. Off-campus facilities provide opportunities for research with marine mammals. Opportunities for research are also available at community facilities such as local hospitals and schools.

Information for Students With Physical Disabilities: The University complies with Section 504 of the Rehabilitation Act of 1973 and the Americans with Disabilities Act. No otherwise qualified handicapped person, solely on the basis of handicap, will be excluded from participation in, be denied the benefits of, or be subjected to discrimination in the administration of any educational program or activity including admission or access thereto or in treatment or employment therein by the University. The Office of Support Services for Students with Disabilities can be contacted at (601) 266-5024.

Application Information:

Send to: Admissions Coordinator _____ Program. Students are admitted in the Fall, application deadline February 15. *Fee:* $25. Legal residents of Mississippi are exempt from the application fee.

Avila College
Master of Science in Counseling Psychology
11901 Wornall Road
Kansas City, MO 64145-1698
Telephone: (816) 501-3792
Fax: (816) 501-2455
E-mail: bogartcj@mail.avila.edu
Web: http://www.avila.edu/departments/psychology/MSCPW

Department Established:
1977. Director: Cathy J. Bogart. Number of Faculty: total–full-time 4, part-time 1; women–full-time 3, part-time 1.

Programs and Degrees Offered:
Listed in the following order: Program area, degree type (T if terminal Master's), number awarded 7/00–6/01. Counseling psychology MA (T) 12.

Student Applications/Admissions:
Student Applications
Counseling psychology MA—Applications 2001–2002, 12. Total applicants accepted 2001–2002, 10. New applicants enrolled 2001–2002, 8. Total enrolled 2001–2002 full-time, 20, part-time, 25. Openings 2002–2003, 12. The Median number of years required for completion of a degree are 3. The number of students enrolled full and part-time, who were dismissed or voluntarily withdrew from this program area were 4.

Admissions Requirements:
Scores: Entries appear in this order: required test or GPA, minimum score (if required), median score of students entering in 2001–2002. Master's Programs: GRE-V no minimum stated, 500; GRE-Q no minimum stated, 465; GRE-Analytical no minimum stated, 535; last 2 years GPA 3.0. Doctoral Programs: last 2 years GPA no minimum stated; psychology GPA no minimum stated; psychology GPA no minimum stated.
Other Criteria: (importance of criteria rated low, medium, or high): research experience medium, work experience medium, extracurricular activity medium, clinically related public service medium, letters of recommendation high, statement of goals and objectives medium.

Student Characteristics: The following represents characteristics of students in 2001–2002 in all graduate psychology programs in the department: part-time 37; Male–full-time 0, part-time 8; African American/Black–full-time 0, Hispanic/Latino (a)–full-time 0, part-time 0; Asian/Pacific Islander–full-time 0, part-time 0; American Indian/Alaska Native–full-time 0, part-time 0.

Financial Information/Assistance:
Tuition for Full-Time Study: *Master's:* State residents $350 per credit hour; nonstate residents: $350 per credit hour.

Financial Assistance:
First Year Students: Fellowships and scholarships available for first-year. Average amount paid per academic year: $500. Apply by August 15.

Advanced Students: No information provided.
Contact Information: For information on financial assistance, contact: Financial Aid Office.

Internships/Practica: There is a 750 contact hour internship (6 credit hours) at a site chosen by the student. There are a wide variety of internship sites—mental health agencies, psychiatric hospitals, and residential treatment programs, for example. Some students choose to work with specific populations, such as children and adolescents, the chronically mentally ill, in substance abuse treatment, to name a few. All interns have an approved on-site supervisor, and also meet once a week with the faculty internship advisor.

Housing and Day Care: No on-campus housing and day care facilities are available.

Employment of Department Graduates:
Master's Degree Graduates: Of those who graduated in the academic year 2000–2001, the following categories and numbers represent the post-graduate activities and employment of master's degree graduates: Enrolled in a post-doctoral residency/fellowship (n/a), employed in independent practice (n/a).
Doctoral Degree Graduates: Of those who graduated in the academic year 2000–2001, the following categories and numbers represent the post-graduate activities and employment of doctoral degree graduates: Enrolled in a psychology doctoral program (n/a), enrolled in another graduate/professional program (n/a).

Additional Information:
Orientation, Objectives, and Emphasis of Department: The Master of Science in Counseling Psychology (MSCP) program of Avila College is a part of a values-based community of learning which respects the worth and dignity of all persons. Within this context, we are committed to the scientist-practitioner model to (1) train master's-level counseling psychologists for the delivery of mental health services in a variety of settings, such as mental health clinics, counseling centers, and human service agencies, and (2) prepare graduates for further study at the doctoral level. These purposes are accomplished through a rigorous course of study that focuses on the integration of psychological theory and counseling skills. The curriculum is designed around a set of educational outcomes that specifies the knowledge and skills students are expected to demonstrate upon graduation. Successful graduates will demonstrate an understanding of people and situations they can expect to encounter in their professional life, and will be able to develop a course of action with regard to these people and situations. The MSCP program meets the Missouri state educational requirements for licensure as a counselor (Licensed Professional Counselor-LPC), and Kansas state educational requirements for licensure as a master's-level psychologist (Licensed Master's-level Psychologist-LMLP). The program is a member of the Council of Applied Master's Programs in Psychology (CAMPP), and is accredited by the Master's in Psychology Accreditation Council (MPAC).

Application Information:
Send to: Director of Graduate Studies in Psychology, Avila College, 11901 Wornall Road, Kansas City, MO 64145. Students are admitted

in the Fall, application deadline August 20; Spring, application deadline January 15; Summer, application deadline May 25. *Fee:* no application fee.

Forest Institute of Professional Psychology
Programs in Clinical Psychology
2885 W. Battlefield Road
Springfield, MO 65807
Telephone: (417) 823-3477
Fax: (417) 823-3442
E-mail: *praleigh@forest.edu*
Web: *http://www.forest.edu*

Department Established:
1979. President: Mark E. Skrade, Psy.D. Number of Faculty: total–full-time 21, part-time 18; women–full-time 9, part-time 9; minority–full-time 3; faculty subject to the Americans with Disabilities Act 2.

Programs and Degrees Offered:
Listed in the following order: Program area, degree type (T if terminal Master's), number awarded 7/00-6/01. Clinical Psychology MA (T) 29, Clinical Psychology PsyD 48.

APA Accreditation: Clinical PsyD: full.

Student Applications/Admissions:
Student Applications
Clinical Psychology MA—Applications 2001–2002, 13. Total applicants accepted 2001–2002, 8. New applicants enrolled 2001–2002, 8. Total enrolled 2001–2002 full-time, 6, part-time, 2. Openings 2002–2003, 20. The Median number of years required for completion of a degree are 2. The number of students enrolled full and part-time, who were dismissed or voluntarily withdrew from this program area were 2. *Clinical Psychology PsyD*—Applications 2001–2002, 229. Total applicants accepted 2001–2002, 102. New applicants enrolled 2001–2002, 66. Total enrolled 2001–2002 full-time, 229, part-time, 14. Openings 2002–2003, 75. The Median number of years required for completion of a degree are 4. The number of students enrolled full and part-time, who were dismissed or voluntarily withdrew from this program area were 5.

Admissions Requirements:
Scores: Entries appear in this order: required test or GPA, minimum score (if required), median score of students entering in 2001–2002. Master's Programs: GRE-V+Q+Analytical no minimum stated; overall undergraduate GPA 3.0; last 2 years GPA 3.0; psychology GPA 3.0. Doctoral Programs: GRE-V+Q+Analytical no minimum stated; overall undergraduate GPA 3.00; last 2 years GPA 3.00; psychology GPA 3.25.
Other Criteria: (importance of criteria rated low, medium, or high): GRE/MAT scores medium, research experience medium, work experience medium, extracurricular activity, clinically related public service medium, GPA high, letters of recommendation high, interview high, statement of goals and objectives high.

Student Characteristics: The following represents characteristics of students in 2001–2002 in all graduate psychology programs in the department: Female–full-time 138, part-time 5; Male–full-time 91, part-time 9; African American/Black–full-time 11, part-time 0; Hispanic/Latino (a)–full-time 2, part-time 0; Asian/Pacific Islander–full-time 4, part-time 0; American Indian/Alaska Native–full-time 3, part-time 0; Multi-ethnic–full-time 2, students subject to the Americans with Disabilities Act–full-time 12.

Financial Information/Assistance:
Tuition for Full-Time Study: *Master's:* State residents $395 per credit hour; nonstate residents: $395 per credit hour. *Doctoral:* State residents: $395 per credit hour; nonstate residents: $395 per credit hour.

Financial Assistance:
First Year Students: Fellowships and scholarships available for first-year.
Advanced Students: Teaching assistantships available for advanced students.
Contact Information: For information on financial assistance, contact: Carolyn Burros, Financial Aid Director, Forest Institute of Professional Psychology, 2885 W Battlefield Road, Springfield, MO 65807, Tel: 800-424-7793; E-mail: cburros@forest.edu.

Internships/Practica: Forest Institute of Professional Psychology enjoys a close relationship with the major state and city mental health facilities in the metropolitan and rural areas. Currently, there are 50 practicum experiences available to students. These opportunities provide a vast array of clinical experiences for a total of 1,200 practicum hours accumulated by the end of your required course work. During the fourth year of study, all students are required to complete a 2,000 hour internship. Forest institute has several on-site internship opportunities ranging in a number of clinical experiences. For those doctoral students for whom a professional internship is required prior to graduation, 48 applied in 2000–2001. Of those who applied, 48 were placed in internships listed by the Association of Psychology Postdoctoral and Internship Programs (APPIC); 25 were placed in APA accredited internships.

Housing and Day Care: On-campus housing and day care facilities are available.

Employment of Department Graduates:
Master's Degree Graduates: Of those who graduated in the academic year 2000–2001, the following categories and numbers represent the post-graduate activities and employment of master's degree graduates: Enrolled in a post-doctoral residency/fellowship (n/a), employed in independent practice (n/a).
Doctoral Degree Graduates: Of those who graduated in the academic year 2000–2001, the following categories and numbers represent the post-graduate activities and employment of doctoral degree graduates: Enrolled in a psychology doctoral program (n/a), enrolled in another graduate/professional program (n/a), enrolled in a post-doctoral residency/fellowship (46), employed in independent practice (6), employed in an academic position at a university (1), employed in a government agency (professional services) (3), employed in a community mental health/counseling center (12), employed in a hospital/medical center (6).

Additional Information:

Orientation, Objectives, and Emphasis of Department: The design of the clinical psychology PsyD program is based on the belief that a thorough understanding of the comprehensive body of psychological knowledge, skills, and attitudes is essential for professional practitioners. The acquisition of this broad-based understanding and these abilities requires that the curriculum cover a combination of didactic knowledge, skill training, and supervised clinical experience with faculty and supervisors who provide appropriate role models. The PsyD degree is designed for individuals seeking an educational and training program geared toward professional application. Students are prepared to offer professional services in diagnostic, therapeutic, consultative, and administrative settings. Research and investigation skills are complemented by an increased focus on the use of research findings and theoretical formulations. The field practicum and internship are supervised clinical experiences that are integrated with the academic coursework. The faculty represents a variety of theoretical orientations and is committed to the rigorous preparation of students to become competent providers of service as well as ethical contributing members of the professional community. The MA in psychology program is intended to provide a comprehensive exposure to the scientific foundations of psychology, including theories, concepts, and empirical knowledge of human development and behavior. The master's program is valuable to those who wish to increase their understanding of human behavior. These would include teachers, clergy, and training and personnel officers. The program also provides a solid foundation for eventual pursuit of a doctoral program. The MA program provides the necessary course work to obtain a counseling licensure at the master's level in most, if not all states.

Special Facilities or Resources: Forest Institute is located in the heart of the Ozarks. The academic/administrative center sits on 58 acres of land and provides students with a modern facility and state of the art equipment. Forest has both an on-site outpatient community mental health clinic and a rehabilitation-health psychology-neuropsychology clinic. Practicum involves a high degree of community services and resources. Students provide services in the rural Ozarks, are actively involved with the homeless organizations of the Ozarks, correctional facilities, and many other community based opportunities.

Information for Students With Physical Disabilities: Notification to the school of any and all types of personal needs involving physical, emotional, and learning difficulties and/or needs related to the Americans with Disabilities Act is the sole responsibility of the student. While all reasonable efforts will be made to accommodate individual needs, it is conceivable that some conditions and circumstances may exist which cannot be reasonably accommodated. Inquiries and requests for reasonable accommodations regarding an individual's needs should be addressed to Equal Opportunities Officer, 2885 West Battlefield Road, Springfield, MO 65807; (417) 823-3477; or by email equalopportunitiesofficer@forestinstitute.org.

Application Information:
Send to: Forest Institute of Professional Psychology, Office of Admissions, 2885 W Battlefield Road, Springfield, MO 65807. Students are admitted in the Fall; Winter; Spring; Summer. Applications for admission are accepted on a rolling basis. *Fee:* $50.

Missouri, University of, Columbia (2001 data)
Department of Educational and Counseling Psychology
College of Education
16 Hill Hall
Columbia, MO 65211
Telephone: (573) 882-7731
Fax: (573) 884-5989
E-mail: *CallisonC@missouri.edu*
Web: *http://www.coe.missouri.edu/~ecp/index.html*

Department Established:
1953. Chairperson: P. Paul Heppner. Number of Faculty: total–full-time 11, part-time 7; women–full-time 4, part-time 3; minority–full-time 3, part-time 1; faculty subject to the Americans with Disabilities Act 1.

Programs and Degrees Offered:
Listed in the following order: Program area, degree type (T if terminal Master's), number awarded 7/00–6/01. Counseling EdS 1, educational MA (T), school MA (T) 1.

APA Accreditation: Counseling PhD: full. School PhD: full.

Student Applications/Admissions:
Student Applications
Counseling EdS—Applications 2001–2002, 1. Total enrolled 2001–2002 full-time, 2. *Educational MA*—Applications 2001–2002, 4. Total applicants accepted 2001–2002, 3. New applicants enrolled 2001–2002, 3. Total enrolled 2001–2002 full-time, 3. Openings 2002–2003, 2. *School MA*—Applications 2001–2002, 11. Total applicants accepted 2001–2002, 4. New applicants enrolled 2001–2002, 3. Total enrolled 2001–2002 full-time, 3. Openings 2002–2003, 2.

Admissions Requirements:
Scores: Entries appear in this order: required test or GPA, minimum score (if required), median score of students entering in 2001–2002. Master's Programs: GRE-V no minimum stated, 485; GRE-Q no minimum stated, 535; GRE-V+Q no minimum stated; GRE-Analytical no minimum stated, 563; GRE-V+Q+Analytical no minimum stated. School Psychology Educational Specialist Degree students included in MA/MEd totals. Do not accept MAT, only GRE. Doctoral Programs: GRE-V no minimum stated, 512; GRE-Q no minimum stated, 602; GRE-V+Q no minimum stated; GRE-Analytical no minimum stated, 602; GRE-V+Q+Analytical no minimum stated; overall undergraduate GPA 3.0, 3.45; psychology GPA 3.0, 3.71. Do not accept MAT for admission.
Other Criteria: (importance of criteria rated low, medium, or high): GRE/MAT scores medium, research experience high, work experience medium, clinically related public service medium, GPA medium, letters of recommendation medium, interview low, statement of goals and objectives high, multicultural experience medium. Research experience is not a criterion for MEd and EdS options.

Student Characteristics: The following represents characteristics of students in 2001–2002 in all graduate psychology programs in the department: Female–full-time 38, part-time 0; Male–full-time 13, part-time 0; African American/Black–full-time 3, part-time

0; Hispanic/Latino (a)–full-time 1, part-time 0; Asian/Pacific Islander–full-time 5, part-time 0; American Indian/Alaska Native–full-time 1, part-time 0.

Financial Information/Assistance:

Tuition for Full-Time Study: No information provided.

Financial Assistance:

First Year Students: No information provided.
Advanced Students: No information provided.
Contact Information: For information on financial assistance, contact: Financial Aid, Jesse Hall. For departmental assistantship applications, contact the admissions secretary.

Internships/Practica: Internships are available in counseling psychology: VA hospitals, rehabilitation centers, mental health centers, university student counseling services; in school psychology: public schools, schools of medicine; in school counseling: public schools; in rehabilitation counseling: rehabilitation centers, mental health centers, and drug and alcohol centers.

Housing and Day Care: No on-campus housing and day care facilities are available.

Employment of Department Graduates:

Master's Degree Graduates: Of those who graduated in the academic year 2000–2001, the following categories and numbers represent the post-graduate activities and employment of master's degree graduates: Enrolled in a post-doctoral residency/fellowship (n/a), employed in independent practice (n/a).

Doctoral Degree Graduates: Of those who graduated in the academic year 2000–2001, the following categories and numbers represent the post-graduate activities and employment of doctoral degree graduates: Enrolled in a psychology doctoral program (n/a), enrolled in another graduate/professional program (n/a).

Additional Information:

Orientation, Objectives, and Emphasis of Department: The goals of the department include the preparation of students in the professional specialties of counseling, school and educational psychology, rehabilitation counseling, school counseling and student personnel work, and the conduct of research on the applications of psychological knowledge to counseling and educational settings. The department emphasizes general psychological foundations, assessment, career development, counselor training and supervision, group processes, and research on counseling processes and psychological measurement and assessment. The theoretical orientation of the faculty is eclectic.

Special Facilities or Resources: Individual and group counseling and psychological assessment training facilities are available in the department, the College of Education and the department's assessment and consultation clinic, and on campus in the Student Counseling Services. Supervised training opportunities also occur in the Career Planning and Placement Center and with the Vocational Assessment Program. A well-stocked library of references in the specialty areas is located in the department. Access to computer services is available across the campus.

Information for Students With Physical Disabilities: Campus is handicapped accessible, and physically challenged students have resources available to them from the Access Office for Students with Disabilities.

Application Information:

Send to: Admissions Secretary, 16 Hill Hall, University of Missouri-Columbia, Educational and Counseling Psychology, Columbia, MO 65211. Students are admitted in the Fall. Deadline is January 8 for PhD. March 1 for MA/EDS. *Fee:* $25. International applicants pay a $50 admissions fee, paid directly to International Admissions, 230 Jesse Hall.

Missouri, University of, Columbia
The Department of Psychological Sciences
210 McAlester Hall
Columbia, MO 65211
Telephone: (573) 882-6860
Fax: (573) 882-7710
E-mail: *SkylesB@missouri.edu*
Web: *http://www.missouri.edu/~psywww*

Department Established:

1900. Chairperson: David Geary. Number of Faculty: total–full-time 38, part-time 4; women–full-time 13, part-time 2; minority–full-time 2.

Programs and Degrees Offered:

Listed in the following order: Program area, degree type (T if terminal Master's), number awarded 7/00–6/01. Clinical PhD 8, cognition and neuroscience PhD 2, developmental PhD, quantitative PhD, social PhD 1.

APA Accreditation: Clinical PhD: full.

Student Applications/Admissions:

Student Applications

Clinical PhD—Applications 2001–2002, 83. Total applicants accepted 2001–2002, 10. New applicants enrolled 2001–2002, 6. Total enrolled 2001–2002 full-time, 34. Openings 2002–2003, 12. The number of students enrolled full and part-time, who were dismissed or voluntarily withdrew from this program area were 3. *Cognition and neuroscience PhD*—Applications 2001–2002, 23. Total applicants accepted 2001–2002, 7. New applicants enrolled 2001–2002, 3. Total enrolled 2001–2002 full-time, 12. Openings 2002–2003, 3. The number of students enrolled full and part-time, who were dismissed or voluntarily withdrew from this program area were 2. *Developmental PhD*—Applications 2001–2002, 5. Total applicants accepted 2001–2002, 2. New applicants enrolled 2001–2002, 2. Total enrolled 2001–2002 full-time, 6. Openings 2002–2003, 2. The number of students enrolled full and part-time, who were dismissed or voluntarily withdrew from this program area were 1. *Quantitative PhD*—Applications 2001–2002, 5. Total applicants accepted 2001–2002, 2. Total enrolled 2001–2002 full-time, 2. Openings 2002–2003, 1. The number of students enrolled full and part-time, who were dismissed or voluntarily withdrew from this program area were 0. *Social PhD*—Applications 2001–2002, 27. Total applicants accepted 2001–2002, 6. New applicants enrolled 2001–2002, 4. Total enrolled 2001–2002 full-time, 11. Openings 2002–2003, 3. The number of students enrolled full and part-time, who were dismissed or voluntarily withdrew from this program area were 0.

Admissions Requirements:

Scores: Entries appear in this order: required test or GPA, minimum score (if required), median score of students entering in 2001–2002. Doctoral Programs: GRE-V no minimum stated, 620; GRE-Q no minimum stated, 700; GRE-V+Q 1000, 1320; GRE-Analytical no minimum stated, 730; overall undergraduate GPA 3.0, 3.62; last 2 years GPA no minimum stated, 3.79; psychology GPA no minimum stated, 3.92; psychology GPA no minimum stated.

Other Criteria: (importance of criteria rated low, medium, or high): GRE/MAT scores high, research experience high, work experience low, extracurricular activity low, clinically related public service low, GPA high, letters of recommendation high, statement of goals and objectives medium. The clinical program requires an interview.

Student Characteristics: The following represents characteristics of students in 2001–2002 in all graduate psychology programs in the department: Female–full-time 51, part-time 0; Male–full-time 17, part-time 0; African American/Black–full-time 3, part-time 0; Hispanic/Latino (a)–full-time 3, part-time 0; Asian/Pacific Islander–full-time 0, part-time 0; American Indian/Alaska Native–full-time 0, part-time 0; Multi-ethnic–full-time 0, part-time 0; students subject to the Americans with Disabilities Act–full-time 0, part-time 0.

Financial Information/Assistance:

Tuition for Full-Time Study: *Master's:* State residents $180 per credit hour; nonstate residents: $539 per credit hour. *Doctoral:* State residents: $180 per credit hour; nonstate residents: $539 per credit hour.

Financial Assistance:

First Year Students: Teaching assistantships available for first-year. Average amount paid per academic year: $10,800. Average number of hours worked per week: 20. Tuition remission given: full. Research assistantships available for first-year. Average amount paid per academic year: $10,800. Average number of hours worked per week: 20. Tuition remission given: full.

Advanced Students: Teaching assistantships available for advanced students. Average amount paid per academic year: $11,300. Average number of hours worked per week: 20. Tuition remission given: full. Research assistantships available for advanced students. Average amount paid per academic year: $11,300. Average number of hours worked per week: 20. Tuition remission given: full. Traineeships available for advanced students. Average amount paid per academic year: $11,300. Average number of hours worked per week: 20. Tuition remission given: partial.

Contact Information: Of all students currently enrolled full-time, 100% benefited from one or more of the listed financial assistance programs. The department is committed to providing financial support for students in good standing through at least the first four years of their graduate career. Support is in the form of graduate teaching or research assistantships, campus fellowships, or part-time work in training placements and carries with it an exemption from tuition. Departmental assistantships will pay $10,800 during the 2002–2003 academic year for 9 months of half-time work. All graduate students who have a master's degree approved by MU faculty will receive an additional $1000 stipend in the year following receipt of the degree.

Internships/Practica: In clinical psychology, an APA-approved internship is required for the PhD degree. For those doctoral students for whom a professional internship is required prior to graduation, 5 applied in 2000–2001. Of those who applied, 5 were placed in APA accredited internships.

Housing and Day Care: On-campus housing and day care facilities are available.

Employment of Department Graduates:

Master's Degree Graduates: Of those who graduated in the academic year 2000–2001, the following categories and numbers represent the post-graduate activities and employment of master's degree graduates: Enrolled in a post-doctoral residency/fellowship (n/a), employed in independent practice (n/a).

Doctoral Degree Graduates: Of those who graduated in the academic year 2000–2001, the following categories and numbers represent the post-graduate activities and employment of doctoral degree graduates: Enrolled in a psychology doctoral program (n/a), enrolled in another graduate/professional program (n/a).

Additional Information:

Orientation, Objectives, and Emphasis of Department: The clinical program is fully accredited by the American Psychological Association and is a charter member of the Academy of Psychological Clinical Science. All programs offer broad empirical and theoretical training with a research emphasis.

Special Facilities or Resources: The department has the following special facilities or resources: a psychology research facility, a psychological clinic, a medical school, a VA hospital, Mid-Missouri Mental Health Center, a counseling center, human experimental laboratories, a central computer system with extensive program library and remote terminal support, and departmental computers with terminals.

Application Information:

Send to: Director of Graduate Admissions, Department of Psychology, 210 McAlester Hall, University of Missouri-Columbia, Columbia, MO 65211. Students are admitted in the Fall, application deadline January 8.

Missouri, University of, Kansas City
Department of Psychology
5319 Holmes
Kansas City, MO 64110
Telephone: (816) 235-1321
Fax: (816) 235-1062
E-mail: *psychology@umkc.edu*

Department Established:

1940. Chairperson: James F. Collins. Number of Faculty: total–full-time 14; women–full-time 5; minority–full-time 1.

Programs and Degrees Offered:

Listed in the following order: Program area, degree type (T if terminal Master's), number awarded 7/00–6/01. Community psychology PhD, general psychology MA 4, interdisciplinary clinical health PhD, interdisciplinary health pysch PhD, interdisciplinary psychology MA.

Student Applications/Admissions:

Student Applications

Community psychology PhD—Applications 2001–2002, 12. Total applicants accepted 2001–2002, 9. New applicants enrolled 2001–2002, 3. Total enrolled 2001–2002 full-time, 14, part-time, 5. *General psychology MA*—Applications 2001–2002, 15. Total applicants accepted 2001–2002, 5. New applicants enrolled 2001–2002, 4. Total enrolled 2001–2002 full-time, 12, part-time, 15. *Interdisciplinary clinical health PhD*—Applications 2001–2002, 12. Total applicants accepted 2001–2002, 6. New applicants enrolled 2001–2002, 5. Total enrolled 2001–2002 full-time, 8. The number of students enrolled full and part-time, who were dismissed or voluntarily withdrew from this program area were 1. *Interdisciplinary health pysch PhD*—Applications 2001–2002, 4. Total applicants accepted 2001–2002, 2. New applicants enrolled 2001–2002, 2. Total enrolled 2001–2002 full-time, 4. *Interdisciplinary psychology MA*—Applications 2001–2002, 6. Total applicants accepted 2001–2002, 1. New applicants enrolled 2001–2002, 1. Total enrolled 2001–2002 full-time, 4. The number of students enrolled full and part-time, who were dismissed or voluntarily withdrew from this program area were 2.

Admissions Requirements:

Scores: Entries appear in this order: required test or GPA, minimum score (if required), median score of students entering in 2001–2002. Master's Programs: overall undergraduate GPA 3.0; psychology GPA 3.5. Doctoral Programs: GRE-V no minimum stated; GRE-Q no minimum stated; GRE-Analytical no minimum stated; GRE-Subject(Psych) no minimum stated; overall undergraduate GPA no minimum stated; last 2 years GPA no minimum stated; psychology GPA no minimum stated; psychology GPA no minimum stated. Be sure to check with appropriate Program Director for program-specific requirements.

Other Criteria: (importance of criteria rated low, medium, or high): SEE BELOW. As these criteria vary for different program areas, be sure to contact the appropriate Program Director for program-specific requirements/criteria/information.

Student Characteristics: The following represents characteristics of students in 2001–2002 in all graduate psychology programs in the department: Female–full-time 32, part-time 15; Male–full-time 10, part-time 5; African American/Black–full-time 2, part-time 0; Hispanic/Latino (a)–full-time 1, part-time 0; Asian/Pacific Islander–full-time 1, part-time 0; American Indian/Alaska Native–full-time 1, part-time 0.

Financial Information/Assistance:

Tuition for Full-Time Study: *Master's:* State residents $202 per credit hour; nonstate residents: $562 per credit hour. *Doctoral:* State residents: $202 per credit hour; nonstate residents: $562 per credit hour.

Financial Assistance:

First Year Students: Teaching assistantships available for first-year. Average amount paid per academic year: $9,000. Average number of hours worked per week: 20. Apply by March 15. Tuition remission given: partial. Research assistantships available for first-year. Average amount paid per academic year: $9,000. Average number of hours worked per week: 20. Apply by March 15. Tuition remission given: partial. Fellowships and scholarships available for first-year. Apply by March 1. Tuition remission given: partial.

Advanced Students: Teaching assistantships available for advanced students. Average amount paid per academic year: $9,000. Average number of hours worked per week: 20. Apply by March 15. Tuition remission given: partial. Research assistantships available for advanced students. Average amount paid per academic year: $9,000. Average number of hours worked per week: 20. Apply by March 15. Tuition remission given: partial. Fellowships and scholarships available for advanced students. Apply by March 1. Tuition remission given: partial.

Contact Information: Of all students currently enrolled full-time, 70% benefited from one or more of the listed financial assistance programs. For teaching assistantships, contact Department Chair and for research assistantships, contact principal investigators.

Internships/Practica: With a population of over 1.5 million, Kansas City offers numerous opportunities for community involvement and research addressing social problems inherent in urban communities. There are numerous agencies, organizations, businesses, schools and so forth that offer students practicum sites and research settings. Formal community practicum opportunities are offered to both Master's and Community Psychology PhD students. The practicum is designed to provide experience working in community agencies that address social and community problems. Students gain experience in methods such as: advocacy, community organizing, community consultation, institution or system level analyses, program assessment, development and evaluation, and applied research. Practicum is optional for MA students. Community Psychology PhD students are required to take practicum for four semesters. Interdisciplinary Psychology PhD Program: Internships/practica are not required for this program. Interdisciplinary Clinical Health Psychology PhD Program: Kansas City offers numerous practicum opportunities for clinical psychology doctoral students. A variety of community agencies, medical centers, and other applied settings are available for clinical practica. Clinical health psychology students are required to enroll in six semesters of practicum during which they are involved in many different types of clinical experiences, ranging from supervised work in specialized health care programs to more general outpatient settings for psychotherapy and psychological assessment. For example, UMKC has an affiliation with the Mid-America Heart Institute (MAHI) at St. Luke's Hospital, the largest volume interventional cardiology, open-heart surgery, and cardiovascular program in the Midwest. Clinical health psychology students can receive both basic and advanced practicum training from a multidisciplinary staff at MAHI and the St. Luke's Hospital Behavioral Health Center. Basic clinical practica include training in general mental health assessment and treatment areas such as crisis intervention, depression screening, personnel and disability evaluations, and treatment of adjustment problems, depression, and anxiety disorders. Advanced training opportunities in the assessment and treatment of obesity and eating disorders, smoking and other substance abuse, managed care, and mental health administration also are available. In the fifth year of study, students are required to complete a one-year, clinical internship. Interdisciplinary Health Psychology (Non-Clinical) PhD Program: Practica can be tailored to individual student needs through the many available agencies in the Kansas City metropolitan area. To cite specific examples, the Health Psychology discipline has strong ties to the Mid-America Heart Institute and to UMKC's Bloch Cancer Center, which is administered through the Department of Psychology, and to the Center for Aging Studies, which is on our campus. Both Clinical and non-clinical practica can be arranged in these agencies.

Housing and Day Care: On-campus housing and day care facilities are available.

Employment of Department Graduates:

Master's Degree Graduates: Of those who graduated in the academic year 2000–2001, the following categories and numbers represent the post-graduate activities and employment of master's degree graduates: Enrolled in a post-doctoral residency/fellowship (n/a), employed in independent practice (n/a).

Doctoral Degree Graduates: Of those who graduated in the academic year 2000–2001, the following categories and numbers represent the post-graduate activities and employment of doctoral degree graduates: Enrolled in a psychology doctoral program (n/a), enrolled in another graduate/professional program (n/a).

Additional Information:

Orientation, Objectives, and Emphasis of Department: The orientation of the Department of Psychology is broadly eclectic with an empirical emphasis. A broad range of points of view are represented by faculty and by research in the department. The major educational goal within the department is to convey methodological and problem-solving techniques to the students. Also, we attempt to provide students with tools to evaluate the research of others and to produce research.

Special Facilities or Resources: For all graduate Psychology programs at UMKC: The Psychology Department is well equipped for research and training. Student computer labs are available in the department and across campus. Interdisciplinary Psychology PhD Program: The School of Graduate Studies, which administers this program, makes numerous resources available to Interdisciplinary PhD students. Interdisciplinary Clinical Health Psychology PhD Program: Several UMKC Clinical Health Psychology faculty have appointments at the Mid-America Heart Institute (MAHI) at St. Luke's Hospital and direct the Behavioral Cardiology Research Program. Under the auspices of this program, research opportunities are available in many areas including cardiovascular and cardiothoracic surgery, health outcomes research (psychosocial outcomes, quality of life, cost-effectiveness), and basic research in lipid metabolism and diabetes. Clinical health psychology students gain multidisciplinary research experience in any of the above areas and can develop individual projects for conference, thesis, or dissertation research. Interdisciplinary Health Psychology (Non-Clinical) PhD Program: The Department has a strong linkage to the Mid-America Heart Institute, the leading cardiology service in our area, and the UMKC Center for Aging Studies.

Information for Students With Physical Disabilities: The University of Missouri-Kansas City is committed to providing equality of access to its programs and activities for students with disabilities. The Office of Services for Students with Disabilities (OSSD) is tasked with carrying out the mission of academic accommodations for students with disabilities. While all the efforts of the University are designed to be in compliance with the Americans with Disabilities Act and Section 504 of the Rehabilitation Act, as well as applicable state and local laws, it is not enough to simply comply. UMKC is committed to cultivating a campus climate where individuals with disabilities are welcomed and invited. We are committed to viewing the accommodation process, not merely as satisfying a legal obligation, but rather as the hallmark of a quality education. Our goal is to create an atmosphere where students with disabilities, not only can learn, but are motivated to become life-long learners and leaders in their fields.

Application Information:
Send to: For MA Degree and Community Psychology PhD: University of Missouri-Kansas City, Office of Admissions, Administrative Center, 5115 Oak, Kansas City, MO 64110, For any Interdisciplinary PhD: Ms. Quincy Bennett, School of Graduate Studies, University of Missouri-Kansas City, 5115 Oak, Kansas City, MO 64110. Students are admitted in the Fall; Winter; Summer. Fall-(MA) March 15, Fall-(Community Psychology) February 1, Fall-(Interdisciplinary Psychology) March 1, Fall-(Interdisciplinary Health Psychology) March 1, Fall-(Interdisciplinary Clinical Health Psychology) February 15; Winter-(MA) October 1, Winter-(Interdisciplinary Psychology) October 15, Winter-(Interdisciplinary Health Psychology) October 15. *Fee:* $25.

Missouri, University of, Kansas City
Division of Counseling, Educational Psychology, and Exercise Science
College: School of Education
5100 Rockhill Road, 215, School of Education
Kansas City, MO 64110
Telephone: (816) 235-2722
Fax: (816) 235-5270
E-mail: *MurdockN@umkc.edu*
Web: *http://umkc.edu/education/divs/cpce/*

Department Established:
Interim Chair: John Jacobson. Number of Faculty: total–full-time 16; women–full-time 7; minority–full-time 3.

Programs and Degrees Offered:
Listed in the following order: Program area, degree type (T if terminal Master's), number awarded 7/00–6/01. Counseling and guidance MA (T), Counseling and Guidance EdS, Counseling Psychology PhD 5.

APA Accreditation: Counseling PhD: full.

Student Applications/Admissions:
Student Applications
Counseling and guidance MA—Applications 2001–2002, 94. Total applicants accepted 2001–2002, 67. New applicants enrolled 2001–2002, 35. Openings 2002–2003, 50. *Counseling and Guidance EdS*—Applications 2001–2002, 4. Total applicants accepted 2001–2002, 4. New applicants enrolled 2001–2002, 4. Total enrolled 2001–2002 full-time, 1. Openings

2002–2003, 6. *Counseling Psychology PhD*—Applications 2001–2002, 54. Total applicants accepted 2001–2002, 10. New applicants enrolled 2001–2002, 10. Total enrolled 2001–2002 full-time, 45. Openings 2002–2003, 8. The Median number of years required for completion of a degree are 6. The number of students enrolled full and part-time, who were dismissed or voluntarily withdrew from this program area were 0.

Admissions Requirements:

Scores: Entries appear in this order: required test or GPA, minimum score (if required), median score of students entering in 2001–2002. Master's Programs: overall undergraduate GPA 2.75. Applicants may choose between the GRE or MAT. Doctoral Programs: GRE-V+Q 1000, 1030; overall undergraduate GPA 3.0, 3.7 ; last 2 years GPA no minimum stated; psychology GPA no minimum stated; psychology GPA 3.5, 3.7.

Other Criteria: (importance of criteria rated low, medium, or high): GRE/MAT scores medium, research experience high, work experience medium, extracurricular activity medium, clinically related public service medium, GPA medium, letters of recommendation high, interview high, statement of goals and objectives high, professional identity high.

Student Characteristics: The following represents characteristics of students in 2001–2002 in all graduate psychology programs in the department: Female–full-time 7, part-time 0; Male–full-time 3, part-time 0; African American/Black–full-time 0, part-time 0; Hispanic/Latino (a)–full-time 0, part-time 0; Asian/Pacific Islander–full-time 0, part-time 0; American Indian/Alaska Native–full-time 0, part-time 0.

Financial Information/Assistance:

Tuition for Full-Time Study: *Master's:* State residents $179 per credit hour; nonstate residents: $538 per credit hour. *Doctoral:* State residents: $179 per credit hour; nonstate residents: $538 per credit hour.

Financial Assistance:

First Year Students: Teaching assistantships available for first-year. Average amount paid per academic year: $10,920. Average number of hours worked per week: 20. Apply by varies. Tuition remission given: partial. Research assistantships available for first-year. Average amount paid per academic year: $10,920. Average number of hours worked per week: 20. Apply by varies. Tuition remission given: partial. Fellowships and scholarships available for first-year. Apply by March 1. Tuition remission given: partial.

Advanced Students: Average amount paid per academic year: $10,920. Average number of hours worked per week: 20. Apply by varies. Tuition remission given: partial. Average amount paid per academic year: $10,920. Average number of hours worked per week: 20. Apply by varies. Tuition remission given: partial. Tuition remission given: partial. Apply by varies. Tuition remission given: partial.

Contact Information: Of all students currently enrolled full-time, 50% benefited from one or more of the listed financial assistance programs. For information on financial assistance, contact: Counseling Psychology and Counselor Education at 816-235-2722 or www.umkc.edu/sgs/financial.

Internships/Practica: All programs offer a wide range of practicum and internship placements. The Division of Counseling Psychology and Counselor Education operates the Community Counseling Services, an in-house training facility serving individuals, couples, and families in the surrounding community. Advanced practica are also available in a variety of agencies including local community mental health centers, Veterans Affairs Hospitals, and other local service provision agencies. For those doctoral students for whom a professional internship is required prior to graduation, 6 applied in 2000–2001. Of those who applied, 5 were placed in internships listed by the Association of Psychology Postdoctoral and Internship Programs (APPIC); 5 were placed in APA accredited internships.

Housing and Day Care: On-campus housing and day care facilities are available.

Employment of Department Graduates:

Master's Degree Graduates: Of those who graduated in the academic year 2000–2001, the following categories and numbers represent the post-graduate activities and employment of master's degree graduates: Enrolled in a post-doctoral residency/fellowship (n/a), employed in independent practice (n/a).

Doctoral Degree Graduates: Of those who graduated in the academic year 2000–2001, the following categories and numbers represent the post-graduate activities and employment of doctoral degree graduates: Enrolled in a psychology doctoral program (n/a), enrolled in another graduate/professional program (n/a), enrolled in a post-doctoral residency/fellowship (1), employed in a community mental health/counseling center (5), employed in a hospital/medical center (1).

Additional Information:

Orientation, Objectives, and Emphasis of Department: The program is designed to educate professional counseling psychologists within the following model, with special attention to the location of the program, in an urban setting: scientist-practitioners understand the relationship between theory, research, and practice. The program requires educational experiences in a) core areas of psychology, including research design and statistics, and b) the core of professional counseling psychology, including history and philosophy of counseling psychology. The program faculty recognizes guiding themes of counseling psychology and incorporates these themes in both program content and philosophy; a) work with a wide range of psychological dysfunction; b) focus on assets, strengths, and positive mental health; c) an emphasis on relatively brief interventions; d) an emphasis on person-environment interactions; and e) an emphasis on educational and career development. Education in the scientist-practitioner model follows a developmental model in which integration of scientific and practice components of counseling psychology is emphasized throughout the program. Counseling psychologists recognize the value of human diversity. Counseling psychologists are skilled in educative, preventive, and remedial interventions, and, as scientist-practitioners, their practice is based in research and approached with a scientific attitude. Counseling psychologists abide by the American Psychological Association code of ethics.

Application Information:

Send to: Applications go to two places: Office of Admissions University of Missouri-Kansas City, Kansas City, Missouri 64110; and Counseling Psychology Program, University of Missouri-Kansas City, ED 215, 5100 Rockhill Road, Kansas City, Missouri 64110. Students are admitted in the Fall, application deadline January 15. Please see program website for more details on application requirements and process (www.um-kc.edu/education/divs/cpce). *Fee:* $25.

Missouri, University of, St. Louis
Department of Psychology
8001 Natural Bridge Road
St. Louis, MO 63121
Telephone: (314) 516-5391
Fax: (314) 516-5392
E-mail: *gillespieg@msx.umsl.edu*
Web: *http://www.umsl.edu/divisions/artscience/psychology*

Department Established:
1967. Chairperson: Miles Patterson. Number of Faculty: total–full-time 17; women–full-time 6; minority–full-time 1.

Programs and Degrees Offered:
Listed in the following order: Program area, degree type (T if terminal Master's), number awarded 7/00–6/01. Clinical PhD 6, experimental MA 2, industrial/organizational PhD (T) 3.

APA Accreditation: Clinical PhD: full.

Student Applications/Admissions:
Student Applications
Clinical PhD—Applications 2001–2002, 75. Total applicants accepted 2001–2002, 6. New applicants enrolled 2001–2002, 6. Total enrolled 2001–2002 full-time, 37. Openings 2002–2003, 6. The Median number of years required for completion of a degree are 6. The number of students enrolled full and part-time, who were dismissed or voluntarily withdrew from this program area were 1. *Experimental MA*—Applications 2001–2002, 6. Total applicants accepted 2001–2002, 1. New applicants enrolled 2001–2002, 1. Total enrolled 2001–2002 full-time, 1, part-time, 1. Openings 2002–2003, 2. The Median number of years required for completion of a degree are 6. *Industrial/organizational PhD*—Applications 2001–2002, 45. Total applicants accepted 2001–2002, 9. New applicants enrolled 2001–2002, 4. Total enrolled 2001–2002 full-time, 26, part-time, 1. Openings 2002–2003, 4. The Median number of years required for completion of a degree are 7. The number of students enrolled full and part-time, who were dismissed or voluntarily withdrew from this program area were 1.

Admissions Requirements:
Scores: Entries appear in this order: required test or GPA, minimum score (if required), median score of students entering in 2001–2002. Master's Programs: GRE-V no minimum stated; GRE-Q no minimum stated; GRE-V+Q no minimum stated; GRE-Analytical no minimum stated; GRE-V+Q+Analytical no minimum stated; GRE-Subject(Psych) no minimum stated; overall undergraduate GPA no minimum stated; last 2 years GPA no minimum stated; psychology GPA no minimum stated. There are no minimum requirements. Median values vary by program. Doctoral Programs: GRE-V no minimum stated, 620; GRE-Q no minimum stated, 640; GRE-Analytical no minimum stated, 660; GRE-V+Q+Analytical no minimum stated, 1920; GRE-Subject(Psych) no minimum stated, 630; overall undergraduate GPA no minimum stated, 3.55; last 2

years GPA no minimum stated; psychology GPA no minimum stated, 3.70; psychology GPA no minimum stated. Information above applies primarily to clinical program.
Other Criteria: (importance of criteria rated low, medium, or high): GRE/MAT scores high, research experience high, work experience medium, extracurricular activity medium, clinically related public service medium, GPA high, letters of recommendation high, interview high, statement of goals and objectives high. Only the clinical program has a formal interview procedure. Importance of criteria varies by program.

Student Characteristics: The following represents characteristics of students in 2001–2002 in all graduate psychology programs in the department: Female–full-time 20, part-time 34; Male–full-time 9, part-time 14; African American/Black–full-time 5, part-time 1; Hispanic/Latino (a)–full-time 0, part-time 1; Asian/Pacific Islander–full-time 1, part-time 1; American Indian/Alaska Native–full-time 0, part-time 0.

Financial Information/Assistance:
Tuition for Full-Time Study: *Master's:* State residents $179 per credit hour; nonstate residents: $539 per credit hour. *Doctoral:* State residents: $179 per credit hour; nonstate residents: $539 per credit hour.

Financial Assistance:
First Year Students: Teaching assistantships available for first-year. Average amount paid per academic year: $9,500. Average number of hours worked per week: 20. Apply by January 15. Tuition remission given: full. Research assistantships available for first-year. Average amount paid per academic year: $9,500. Average number of hours worked per week: 20. Apply by January 15. Tuition remission given: full.
Advanced Students: Teaching assistantships available for advanced students. Average amount paid per academic year: $9,500. Average number of hours worked per week: 15. Apply by January 15. Tuition remission given: full and partial. Research assistantships available for advanced students. Average amount paid per academic year: $9,500. Average number of hours worked per week: 15. Apply by January 15. Tuition remission given: full and partial.
Contact Information: Of all students currently enrolled full-time, 50% benefited from one or more of the listed financial assistance programs. For information on financial assistance, contact: Graduate Admissions.

Internships/Practica: Students (clinical) participate in practica in our Community Psychological Service (the psychology clinic), and a paid clinical clerkship, which may be in a community or university-based program. For those doctoral students for whom a professional internship is required prior to graduation, 6 applied in 2000–2001. Of those who applied, 6 were placed in internships listed by the Association of Psychology Postdoctoral and Internship Programs (APPIC); 6 were placed in APA accredited internships.

Housing and Day Care: On-campus housing and day care facilities are available.

Employment of Department Graduates:
Master's Degree Graduates: Of those who graduated in the academic year 2000–2001, the following categories and numbers

represent the post-graduate activities and employment of master's degree graduates: Enrolled in a post-doctoral residency/fellowship (n/a), employed in independent practice (n/a).

Doctoral Degree Graduates: Of those who graduated in the academic year 2000–2001, the following categories and numbers represent the post-graduate activities and employment of doctoral degree graduates: Enrolled in a psychology doctoral program (n/a), enrolled in another graduate/professional program (n/a).

Additional Information:

Orientation, Objectives, and Emphasis of Department: The orientation of the department emphasizes psychology as science yet also recognizes the important social responsibilities of psychology, especially in the clinical and applied areas. Emphasis of experimental is in behavioral neuropharmacology/endocrinology or in developmental with a secondary interest in neuroscience. The department offers a broad spectrum of high-quality programs at the bachelors, master's, and doctoral levels.

Special Facilities or Resources: The Department of Psychology is housed in Stadler Hall, and research laboratories and computers are conveniently located in the building. The psychological clinic (Community Psychological Service) is also contained within Stadler Hall. The Center for Trauma Recovery and Child Advocacy Center each have community clinics, which are housed on campus. Physical facilities include workshops and comparative, social, and human experimental laboratories. A wide range of research equipment is available, including videotaping facilities, computer terminals, and personal computers.

Information for Students With Physical Disabilities: The buildings in which all facilities and clinics are housed are accessible to those with physical disabilities.

Application Information:

Send to: Graduate Admissions, University of Missouri-St. Louis, 358 Millennium Student Center, 8001 Natural Bridge, St. Louis, MO 63121. Clinical deadline is January 15, I/O deadline is February 1, Experimental is February 1. *Fee:* $25. Fee for McNair Scholars is waived.

Northwest Missouri State University
Department of Psychology/Sociology/Counseling
Colden Hall 2440
Maryville, MO 64468
Telephone: (660) 562-1260
Fax: (660) 562-1731
E-mail: *teaneyc@mail.nwmissouri.edu*
Web: *http://www.nwmissouri.edu/~0500605/psychomepage.htm*

Department Established:

1968. Chairperson: John K. Bowers. Number of Faculty: total–full-time 13, part-time 2; women–full-time 6, part-time 4; minority–full-time 1.

Programs and Degrees Offered:

Listed in the following order: Program area, degree type (T if terminal Master's), number awarded 7/00–6/01. Counseling psychology, school counseling.

Student Applications/Admissions:
Admissions Requirements:

Scores: Entries appear in this order: required test or GPA, minimum score (if required), median score of students entering in 2001–2002. Master's Programs: GRE-V+Q+Analytical 1450, 1633; GRE-Subject(Psych) 500, 504; overall undergraduate GPA 2.75, 3.5; psychology GPA 3.0, 3.6. MSEd: minimum GPA of 2.5 in declared major; submission of GRE scores. Doctoral Programs: last 2 years GPA no minimum stated; psychology GPA no minimum stated; psychology GPA no minimum stated.

Other Criteria: (importance of criteria rated low, medium, or high): GRE/MAT scores medium, research experience medium, work experience medium, extracurricular activity low, clinically related public service medium, GPA high, letters of recommendation high, statement of goals and objectives high.

Student Characteristics: The following represents characteristics of students in 2001–2002 in all graduate psychology programs in the department: Female–full-time 20, part-time 0; Male–full-time 2, part-time 0; African American/Black–full-time 0, part-time 0; Hispanic/Latino (a)–full-time 0, part-time 0; Asian/Pacific Islander–full-time 0, part-time 0; American Indian/Alaska Native–full-time 0, part-time 0.

Financial Information/Assistance:
Tuition for Full-Time Study: No information provided.

Financial Assistance:

First Year Students: Teaching assistantships available for first-year. Average amount paid per academic year: $5,250. Average number of hours worked per week: 20. Apply by open. Tuition remission given: full.

Advanced Students: Teaching assistantships available for advanced students. Average amount paid per academic year: $5,250. Average number of hours worked per week: 20. Apply by open. Tuition remission given: full.

Contact Information: Of all students currently enrolled full-time, 20% benefited from one or more of the listed financial assistance programs. For information on financial assistance, contact: Graduate School Dean.

Internships/Practica: No information provided.

Housing and Day Care: No on-campus housing or day care facilities are available.

Employment of Department Graduates:

Master's Degree Graduates: Of those who graduated in the academic year 2000–2001, the following categories and numbers represent the post-graduate activities and employment of master's degree graduates: Enrolled in a post-doctoral residency/fellowship (n/a), employed in independent practice (n/a), employed in a community mental health/counseling center (3).

Doctoral Degree Graduates: Of those who graduated in the academic year 2000–2001, the following categories and numbers represent the post-graduate activities and employment of doctoral degree graduates: Enrolled in a psychology doctoral program (n/a), enrolled in another graduate/professional program (n/a).

Additional Information:

Orientation, Objectives, and Emphasis of Department: Professional counselors provide services to assist people in coping with the stresses and strains engendered by the changing and complex world in which they live. This program is designed to prepare students to provide counseling services in a variety of settings ranging from mental health clinics and psychiatric hospitals to private practice clinics and social service agencies. Particular emphasis is given to assessment, both in terms of theory and practice. The MSEd program prepares professional counselors for careers in elementary and secondary schools.

Special Facilities or Resources: Training rooms for individual and group therapy; association with the university counseling center; association with laboratory school.

Application Information:
Send to: Dean, Graduate School. Students are admitted in the Fall, application deadline March 1. *Fee:* $50.

Southwest Missouri State University
Psychology Department
Health and Human Services
901 South National Avenue
Springfield, MO 65804-0095
Telephone: (417) 836-5797
Fax: (417) 836-8330
E-mail: *fredmaxwell@smsu.edu*
Web: *http://www.smsu.edu/chhs/chhs.html*

Department Established:
1967. Head: Fred Maxwell. Number of Faculty: total–full-time 30, part-time 11; women–full-time 9, part-time 6; minority–full-time 2.

Programs and Degrees Offered:
Listed in the following order: Program area, degree type (T if terminal Master's), number awarded 7/00–6/01. Clinical, experimental, industrial/organizational.

Student Applications/Admissions:
Admissions Requirements:
Scores: Entries appear in this order: required test or GPA, minimum score (if required), median score of students entering in 2001–2002. Master's Programs: GRE-V 475, 542; GRE-Q 475, 550; GRE-V+Q 1000, 1092; GRE-Subject(Psych) 550, 615; overall undergraduate GPA 3.00, 3.72; psychology GPA 3.25, 3.88. Doctoral Programs: last 2 years GPA no minimum stated; psychology GPA no minimum stated; psychology GPA no minimum stated.
Other Criteria: (importance of criteria rated low, medium, or high): GRE/MAT scores medium, research experience high, work experience medium, extracurricular activity medium, clinically related public service high, GPA high, letters of recommendation high, statement of goals and objectives high.

Student Characteristics: The following represents characteristics of students in 2001–2002 in all graduate psychology programs in the department: Female–full-time 30, part-time 0; Male–full-time 14, part-time 0; African American/Black–full-time 2, part-time 0; Hispanic/Latino (a)–full-time 3, part-time 0; Asian/Pacific Islander–full-time 2, part-time 0; American Indian/Alaska Native–full-time 0, part-time 0; Multi-ethnic–full-time 0, part-time 0; students subject to the Americans with Disabilities Act–full-time 0, part-time 0.

Financial Information/Assistance:
Tuition for Full-Time Study: *Master's:* State residents per academic year $3,048, $127 per credit hour; nonstate residents: per academic year $6,096, $254 per credit hour.

Financial Assistance:
First Year Students: Research assistantships available for first-year. Average amount paid per academic year: $6,150. Average number of hours worked per week: 20. Apply by July. Tuition remission given: full.
Advanced Students: Teaching assistantships available for advanced students. Average amount paid per academic year: $8,200. Average number of hours worked per week: 20. Apply by March. Tuition remission given: full. Research assistantships available for advanced students. Average amount paid per academic year: $6,150. Average number of hours worked per week: 20. Apply by July. Tuition remission given: full.
Contact Information: Of all students currently enrolled full-time, 75% benefited from one or more of the listed financial assistance programs. For information on financial assistance, contact: Graduate College, 417-836-5335.

Internships/Practica: No information provided.

Housing and Day Care: No on-campus housing and day care facilities are available.

Employment of Department Graduates:
Master's Degree Graduates: Of those who graduated in the academic year 2000–2001, the following categories and numbers represent the post-graduate activities and employment of master's degree graduates: Enrolled in a psychology doctoral program (3), enrolled in a post-doctoral residency/fellowship (n/a), employed in independent practice (n/a), employed in other positions at a higher education institution (1), employed in business or industry (research/consulting) (2), employed in business or industry (management) (5), employed in a government agency (professional services) (1), employed in a community mental health/counseling center (1), employed in a hospital/medical center (1), still seeking employment (1).
Doctoral Degree Graduates: Of those who graduated in the academic year 2000–2001, the following categories and numbers represent the post-graduate activities and employment of doctoral degree graduates: Enrolled in a psychology doctoral program (n/a), enrolled in another graduate/professional program (n/a).

Additional Information:

Orientation, Objectives, and Emphasis of Department: We are an eclectic department of 30 full-time faculty serving over 500 undergraduate majors. The faculty have diverse research interests including clinical, I/O, stress management, sport psychology, human learning, perception, motivation, animal learning, human skills, and memory. The department operates the Learning Diagnostic Clinic for diagnosis and remediation of special populations.

Application Information:

Send to: Admissions Secretary. Students are admitted in the Fall, application deadline March 1. Will accept applications up to June 1 if all 8 openings in each track aren't filled.

St. Louis University

Department of Psychology
Arts and Sciences
221 North Grand Boulevard
St. Louis, MO 63103
Telephone: (314) 977-2300
Fax: (314) 977-3679
E-mail: *kelloggr@slu.edu*
Web: *http://www.slu.edu/colleges/AS/PSY/whatnew.html*

Department Established:

1926. Chairperson: Ronald Kellogg. Number of Faculty: total–full-time 23, part-time 6; women–full-time 8, part-time 2; minority–full-time 3.

Programs and Degrees Offered:

Listed in the following order: Program area, degree type (T if terminal Master's), number awarded 7/00–6/01. Clinical PhD 4, developmental PhD 2, experimental PhD 2, organizational PhD 3, social PhD 1.

APA Accreditation: Clinical PhD: full.

Student Applications/Admissions:

Student Applications

Clinical PhD—Applications 2001–2002, 129. Total applicants accepted 2001–2002, 10. New applicants enrolled 2001–2002, 8. Total enrolled 2001–2002 full-time, 40. Openings 2002–2003, 8. *Developmental PhD*—Applications 2001–2002, 3. Total enrolled 2001–2002 full-time, 11. Openings 2002–2003, 2. *Experimental PhD*—Applications 2001–2002, 6. Total applicants accepted 2001–2002, 4. New applicants enrolled 2001–2002, 1. Total enrolled 2001–2002 full-time, 14. Openings 2002–2003, 3. *Organizational PhD*—Applications 2001–2002, 28. Total applicants accepted 2001–2002, 13. New applicants enrolled 2001–2002, 5. Total enrolled 2001–2002 full-time, 21. Openings 2002–2003, 4. *Social PhD*—Applications 2001–2002, 19. Total applicants accepted 2001–2002, 10. New applicants enrolled 2001–2002, 2. Total enrolled 2001–2002 full-time, 12. Openings 2002–2003, 3.

Admissions Requirements:

Scores: Entries appear in this order: required test or GPA, minimum score (if required), median score of students entering in 2001–2002. Doctoral Programs: GRE-V no minimum stated, 590; GRE-Q no minimum stated, 610; GRE-Analytical no minimum stated, 710; overall undergraduate GPA 3.0; last 2 years GPA no minimum stated; psychology GPA no minimum stated; psychology GPA no minimum stated. Clinical prefers verbal (550), quantitative (550). Others prefer verbal + quantitative= 1000.

Other Criteria: (importance of criteria rated low, medium, or high): GRE/MAT scores high, research experience high, work experience medium, extracurricular activity medium, clinically related public service high, GPA high, letters of recommendation high, interview high, statement of goals and objectives high. For nonclinical specialties clinically related public service is "low," and interview is "medium."

Student Characteristics: The following represents characteristics of students in 2001–2002 in all graduate psychology programs in the department: Female–full-time 47, part-time 0; Male–full-time 34, part-time 0; African American/Black–full-time 7, part-time 0; Hispanic/Latino (a)–full-time 1, part-time 0; Asian/Pacific Islander–full-time 1, part-time 0; American Indian/Alaska Native–full-time 0, part-time 0.

Financial Information/Assistance:

Tuition for Full-Time Study: No information provided.

Financial Assistance:

First Year Students: Teaching assistantships available for first-year. Average number of hours worked per week: 20. Tuition remission given: full and partial. Research assistantships available for first-year. Tuition remission given: full and partial. Fellowships and scholarships available for first-year. Average number of hours worked per week: 20. Tuition remission given: full.

Advanced Students: Teaching assistantships available for advanced students. Average number of hours worked per week: 20. Tuition remission given: partial. Research assistantships available for advanced students. Average number of hours worked per week: 20. Tuition remission given: partial. Traineeships available for advanced students. Average number of hours worked per week: 20. Tuition remission given: partial. Fellowships and scholarships available for advanced students. Average number of hours worked per week: 20. Tuition remission given: full.

Contact Information: Of all students currently enrolled full-time, 65% benefited from one or more of the listed financial assistance programs.

Internships/Practica: No information provided.

Housing and Day Care: No on-campus housing and day care facilities are available.

Employment of Department Graduates:

Master's Degree Graduates: Of those who graduated in the academic year 2000–2001, the following categories and numbers represent the post-graduate activities and employment of master's degree graduates: Enrolled in a post-doctoral residency/fellowship (n/a), employed in independent practice (n/a).

Doctoral Degree Graduates: Of those who graduated in the academic year 2000–2001, the following categories and numbers

represent the post-graduate activities and employment of doctoral degree graduates: Enrolled in a psychology doctoral program (n/a), enrolled in another graduate/professional program (n/a).

Additional Information:

Orientation, Objectives, and Emphasis of Department: The graduate programs in the Department of Psychology work collaboratively to educate and train psychologists for careers in academia, research, consultation, and professional practice through an integrated curriculum of coursework, research training, and supervised practica. The Clinical psychology program offers broad-based education and training in both the science and practice of psychology to prepare its graduates to function as competent, ethical scientist-practitioners across a wide range of settings with diverse populations, problems, and approaches. The Experimental, Developmental, Social, and Organizational specialties within the department are organized under the title of Applied-Experimental Psychology. The major training goals within the Applied-Experimental Program are directed at preparing students for careers in academic or applied settings, providing both breadth of training across areas, and specialized training within specialty areas. The Experimental specialty reflects faculty research interests in neuroscience, psychopharmacology, sleep, memory/language, and cognitive aging. The Developmental specialty reflects faculty research interests concerning the cognitive, emotional, and cultural aspects of social development during childhood and adolescence. The Social specialty examines basic and applied research questions on attitudes, close relationships, health, psychology of oppression, prejudice and stigma, and self-change. The Organizational specialty applies research, assessment, and intervention skills to organizations, groups, and individuals at work.

Special Facilities or Resources: The clinical program operates an on-campus Psychological Services Center which serves as a primary site for supervised clinical experiences with children, adolescents, adults, couples, and families. The Clinical program also has established collaborative relationships with Saint Louis University Health Sciences Center and with various hospitals, agencies, institutions, and private practitioners throughout the community to provide advanced training and experience in the science and practice of psychology. Resources available to the Applied-Experimental program include animal housing shared with biology; a research suite of five rooms for behavioral, physiological, psychopharmacological, and sleep research; an undergraduate laboratory room; and several laboratory suites for social, cognitive, and organizational research. A number of laboratory rooms are equipped with computer and video capacities. Comparative relationships are maintained with the Public Policy program and the School of Law. The Center for the Application of the Behavioral Science located within the department provides opportunities for training in organizational consulting and program evaluation. The Developmental specialty has contacts with several local school systems to provide students with opportunities for research and service.

Application Information:
Send to: The Graduate School, Saint Louis University, 3663 Lindell Blvd., St. Louis, MO 63108, (314) 977-2240. Students are admitted in the Fall. For the Fall semester, the application deadline for the clinical program is January 1 and February 1 for all other programs. *Fee:* $40.

Washington University (St. Louis) (2001 data)
Department of Psychology
One Brookings Drive, Box 1125
St. Louis, MO 63130
Telephone: (314) 935-6565
Fax: (314) 935-7588
E-mail: *psych@artsci.wustl.edu*
Web: *http://www.artsci.wustl.edu/~psych/index.html*

Department Established:
1924. Chairperson: Henry L. Roediger, III. Number of Faculty: total–full-time 28, part-time 6; women–full-time 7, part-time 2; minority–full-time 1.

Programs and Degrees Offered:
Listed in the following order: Program area, degree type (T if terminal Master's), number awarded 7/00–6/01. Clinical PhD 5, developmental and aging PhD 1, experimental PhD 1, social PhD 2.

APA Accreditation: Clinical PhD: full.

Student Applications/Admissions:
Student Applications

Clinical PhD—Applications 2001–2002, 112. Total applicants accepted 2001–2002, 5. New applicants enrolled 2001–2002, 2. Total enrolled 2001–2002 full-time, 29. Openings 2002–2003, 6. The Median number of years required for completion of a degree are 6. The number of students enrolled full and part-time, who were dismissed or voluntarily withdrew from this program area were 0. *Developmental and aging PhD*—Applications 2001–2002, 9. Total enrolled 2001–2002 full-time, 3. Openings 2002–2003, 4. The Median number of years required for completion of a degree are 6. The number of students enrolled full and part-time, who were dismissed or voluntarily withdrew from this program area were 0. *Experimental PhD*—Applications 2001–2002, 49. Total applicants accepted 2001–2002, 13. New applicants enrolled 2001–2002, 4. Total enrolled 2001–2002 full-time, 23, part-time, 2. Openings 2002–2003, 10. The Median number of years required for completion of a degree are 5. The number of students enrolled full and part-time, who were dismissed or voluntarily withdrew from this program area were 1. *Social PhD*—Applications 2001–2002, 20. Total applicants accepted 2001–2002, 5. New applicants enrolled 2001–2002, 1. Total enrolled 2001–2002 full-time, 9. Openings 2002–2003, 3. The Median number of years required for completion of a degree are 6. The number of students enrolled full and part-time, who were dismissed or voluntarily withdrew from this program area were 0.

Admissions Requirements:

Scores: Entries appear in this order: required test or GPA, minimum score (if required), median score of students entering in 2001–2002. Doctoral Programs: GRE-V no minimum stated, 594; GRE-Q no minimum stated, 720; GRE-Analytical no minimum stated, 753; psychology GPA no minimum stated, 3.83.

Other Criteria: (importance of criteria rated low, medium, or high): GRE/MAT scores high, research experience high, work experience medium, clinically related public service low, GPA medium, letters of recommendation high, interview high, statement of goals and objectives high. Interview is only required for clinical applicants.

Student Characteristics: The following represents characteristics of students in 2001–2002 in all graduate psychology programs in the department: Female–full-time 4, part-time 0; Male–full-time 3, part-time 0; African American/Black–full-time 0, part-time 0; Hispanic/Latino (a)–full-time 0, part-time 0; Asian/Pacific Islander–full-time 0, part-time 0; American Indian/Alaska Native–full-time 0, part-time 0.

Financial Information/Assistance:
Tuition for Full-Time Study: No information provided.

Financial Assistance:
First Year Students: No information provided.
Advanced Students: No information provided.
Contact Information: Of all students currently enrolled full-time, 77% benefited from one or more of the listed financial assistance programs. For information on financial assistance, contact: Barbara Bequette.

Internships/Practica: For those doctoral students for whom a professional internship is required prior to graduation, 5 applied in 2000–2001. Of those who applied, 5 were placed in internships listed by the Association of Psychology Postdoctoral and Internship Programs (APPIC); 5 were placed in APA accredited internships.

Housing and Day Care: No on-campus housing and day care facilities are available.

Employment of Department Graduates:
Master's Degree Graduates: Of those who graduated in the academic year 2000–2001, the following categories and numbers represent the post-graduate activities and employment of master's degree graduates: Enrolled in a post-doctoral residency/fellowship (n/a), employed in independent practice (n/a).
Doctoral Degree Graduates: Of those who graduated in the academic year 2000–2001, the following categories and numbers represent the post-graduate activities and employment of doctoral degree graduates: Enrolled in a psychology doctoral program (n/a), enrolled in another graduate/professional program (n/a).

Additional Information:
Orientation, Objectives, and Emphasis of Department: The emphasis within the clinical program is on the scientist-practitioner model, and the program has special opportunities for students interested in behavioral medicine, aging, and neuropsychology. In the experimental programs, the development of generalists with one or more areas of specialization is the department's orientation.

Special Facilities or Resources: The department's extensive facilities include animal, human psychophysiological, psychoacoustic, and clinical training laboratories; digital computers; closed circuit TV; and physiological and psychophysical stimulus and recording equipment.

Information for Students With Physical Disabilities: The Psychology Department is housed in a four-story completely handicapped accessible building.

Application Information:
Send to: Barbara Bequette, Graduate Program Coordinator. Students are admitted in the Fall, application deadline January 15. *Fee:* $35.

Montana State University

Psychology
Letters and Science
Department of Psychology, 304 Taphagen Hall
Bozeman, MT 59717-3440
Telephone: (406) 994-3801
Fax: (406) 994-3804
E-mail: *capierce@montana.edu*
Web: *http://www.montana.edu/wwwpy*

Department Established:
1950. Chairperson: A. Michael Babcock, PhD. Number of Faculty: total–full-time 9, part-time 4; women–full-time 2, part-time 3.

Programs and Degrees Offered:
Listed in the following order: Program area, degree type (T if terminal Master's), number awarded 7/00–6/01. Applied Psychology MA (T) 3.

Student Applications/Admissions:
Student Applications
Applied Psychology MA—Applications 2001–2002, 20. Total applicants accepted 2001–2002, 8. New applicants enrolled 2001–2002, 5. Total enrolled 2001–2002 full-time, 14. Openings 2002–2003, 6.

Admissions Requirements:
Scores: Entries appear in this order: required test or GPA, minimum score (if required), median score of students entering in 2001–2002. Master's Programs: GRE-V 500, 530; GRE-Q 500, 584; GRE-V+Q 1000; GRE-Analytical 500, 668; GRE-V+Q+Analytical 1500; GRE-Subject(Psych) 550, 600; overall undergraduate GPA 3.00, 3.51; last 2 years GPA 3.00; psychology GPA 3.00, 3.77. GRE subject required if not an undergrad psychology major. Doctoral Programs: last 2 years GPA no minimum stated; psychology GPA no minimum stated; psychology GPA no minimum stated.
Other Criteria: (importance of criteria rated low, medium, or high): GRE/MAT scores high, research experience high, work experience low, extracurricular activity low, GPA high, letters of recommendation high, interview low, statement of goals and objectives high.

Student Characteristics: The following represents characteristics of students in 2001–2002 in all graduate psychology programs in the department: Female–full-time 8, part-time 0; Male–full-time 6, part-time 0; African American/Black–full-time 0, part-time 0; Hispanic/Latino (a)–full-time 0, part-time 0; Asian/Pacific Islander–full-time 0, part-time 0; American Indian/Alaska Native–full-time 0, part-time 0.

Financial Information/Assistance:
Tuition for Full-Time Study: *Master's:* State residents $190 per credit hour; nonstate residents: $440 per credit hour.

Financial Assistance:
First Year Students: Teaching assistantships available for first-year. Average amount paid per academic year: $5,500. Apply by Feb. 1. Tuition remission given: full. Fellowships and scholarships available for first-year. Average amount paid per academic year: $1,000. Apply by Feb. 1.
Advanced Students: Teaching assistantships available for advanced students. Average amount paid per academic year: $5,500. Apply by Feb. 1. Tuition remission given: partial.
Contact Information: For information on financial assistance, contact: Financial Aid Office at (406) 994-2845.

Internships/Practica: No information provided.

Housing and Day Care: On-campus housing and day care facilities are available.

Employment of Department Graduates:
Master's Degree Graduates: Of those who graduated in the academic year 2000–2001, the following categories and numbers represent the post-graduate activities and employment of master's degree graduates: Enrolled in a psychology doctoral program (0), enrolled in another graduate/professional program (0), enrolled in a post-doctoral residency/fellowship (n/a), employed in independent practice (n/a), employed in an academic position at a university (0), employed in an academic position at a 2-year/4-year college (1), employed in other positions at a higher education institution (0), employed in a professional position in a school system (0), employed in business or industry (research/consulting) (2), employed in business or industry (management) (0), employed in a government agency (research) (0), employed in a government agency (professional services) (0), employed in a community mental health/counseling center (0), employed in a hospital/medical center (0), still seeking employment (0), other employment position (0).
Doctoral Degree Graduates: Of those who graduated in the academic year 2000–2001, the following categories and numbers represent the post-graduate activities and employment of doctoral degree graduates: Enrolled in a psychology doctoral program (n/a), enrolled in another graduate/professional program (n/a).

Additional Information:
Orientation, Objectives, and Emphasis of Department: Our MS program in applied psychology is designed for students who are interested in social psychology, cognitive psychology, industrial/organizational psychology, physiological psychology, and related areas. The program has thesis and non-thesis options. The thesis option is aimed at full-time traditional students who want a research-oriented degree and plan to pursue a PhD at a later date. A non-thesis track is aimed at students interested in organizational behavior and human resource management. Areas of faculty interest include cognitive psychology, social psychology, industrial/organizational psychology, physiological psychology, learning, research methods, & applied statistics.

Special Facilities or Resources: Laboratory space for human and animal research is available for faculty-sponsored research.

Application Information:
Send to: Graduate Program Admissions Committee, Department of Psychology, 304 Traphagen Hall, Montana State University, Bozeman, MT 59717-3440. Students are admitted in the Fall, application deadline February 1. *Fee:* $50.

Montana State University-Billings
Psychology/Master's Degree in Psychology
Arts and Sciences
1500 N. 30th Street
Billings, MT 59101
Telephone: (406) 657-2242
Fax: (406) 657-2187
E-mail: *SCarlisle@msubillings.edu*

Department Established:
1927. Chairperson: Michael D. Havens. Number of Faculty: total–full-time 3, part-time 5.

Programs and Degrees Offered:
Listed in the following order: Program area, degree type (T if terminal Master's), number awarded 7/00–6/01. Psychology MA (T).

Student Applications/Admissions:
Student Applications
Psychology MA—Applications 2001–2002, 6. Total applicants accepted 2001–2002, 6. New applicants enrolled 2001–2002, 6. Total enrolled 2001–2002 full-time, 16. Openings 2002–2003, 12. The Median number of years required for completion of a degree are 2. The number of students enrolled full and part-time, who were dismissed or voluntarily withdrew from this program area were 2.

Admissions Requirements:
Scores: Entries appear in this order: required test or GPA, minimum score (if required), median score of students entering in 2001–2002. Master's Programs: GRE-V no minimum stated; GRE-Q no minimum stated; GRE-Analytical no minimum stated; overall undergraduate GPA no minimum stated; last 2 years GPA no minimum stated; psychology GPA no minimum stated. Doctoral Programs: last 2 years GPA no minimum stated; psychology GPA no minimum stated; psychology GPA no minimum stated.
Other Criteria: (importance of criteria rated low, medium, or high): GRE/MAT scores high, research experience medium, work experience low, extracurricular activity low, clinically related public service low, GPA high, letters of recommendation high, statement of goals and objectives high.

Student Characteristics: The following represents characteristics of students in 2001–2002 in all graduate psychology programs in the department: Female–full-time 14, part-time 0; Male–full-time 2, part-time 0; African American/Black–full-time 0, part-time 0; Hispanic/Latino (a)–full-time 0, part-time 0; Asian/Pacific Islander–full-time 0, part-time 0; American Indian/Alaska Native–full-time 0, part-time 0; students subject to the Americans with Disabilities Act–full-time 1.

Financial Information/Assistance:
Tuition for Full-Time Study: *Master's:* State residents $257 per credit hour; nonstate residents: $472 per credit hour.

Financial Assistance:
First Year Students: Teaching assistantships available for first-year. Tuition remission given: partial.
Advanced Students: Teaching assistantships available for advanced students. Tuition remission given: partial.
Contact Information: Of all students currently enrolled full-time, 75% benefited from one or more of the listed financial assistance programs. For information on financial assistance, contact: Office of Graduate Studies.

Internships/Practica: Numerous internships are available throughout the Billings area. These internships, established through a long history of cooperation between the Department of Psychology and local agencies, provide students with professionally-supervised training opportunities, off campus research associations, and practical experience in assessment. Potential internship sites include an inpatient psychiatric center, a community mental health center, a prison pre-release center, and residential and day-treatment centers for children and adolescents. These internships can be designed to accommodate the interests and career goals of students.

Housing and Day Care: On-campus housing and day care facilities are available.

Employment of Department Graduates:
Master's Degree Graduates: Of those who graduated in the academic year 2000–2001, the following categories and numbers represent the post-graduate activities and employment of master's degree graduates: Enrolled in a post-doctoral residency/fellowship (n/a), employed in independent practice (n/a).
Doctoral Degree Graduates: Of those who graduated in the academic year 2000–2001, the following categories and numbers represent the post-graduate activities and employment of doctoral degree graduates: Enrolled in a psychology doctoral program (n/a), enrolled in another graduate/professional program (n/a).

Additional Information:
Orientation, Objectives, and Emphasis of Department: The objective of the Department of Psychology at Montana State University Billings is to promote the professional, scholarly, and personal development of students. The master's program seeks out and prepares students who are interested either in pursuing further graduate study at the doctoral level or in a broad-based clinical education leading to careers as psychotherapists. Degree candidates are given the opportunity to design plans of study uniquely suited to their career goals and educational interests. Opportunities exist to participate in ongoing research, community-oriented internships, and service to a diverse population of clients in our region.

Special Facilities or Resources: Excellent university computer facilities are available for graduate student use as well as departmental facilities for word and data processing, Internet communications, psychophysiology, neurophysiology, and social psychology. Department facilities exist for research in many traditional areas of psychology.

Information for Students With Physical Disabilities: Montana State University Billings provides access to all buildings and residential units for people with disabilities. Special services for travel to and from campus and within the city of Billings are readily available from Met Transit Authority. Applicants can contact the office of Disability Support Services at (406) 657-2283 for more information.

Application Information:
Send to: Department of Psychology: Attention Admissions Committee. Students are admitted in the Fall, application deadline March 15. *Fee:* $30.

Montana, The University of
Department of Psychology
Arts and Sciences
143 Skaggs Building
Missoula, MT 59812-1584
Telephone: (406) 243-4521
Fax: (406) 243-6366
E-mail: *psycgrad@selway.umt.edu*
Web: *http://www.cas.umt.edu/psych/*

Department Established:
1920. Chairperson: Nabil Haddad. Number of Faculty: total–full-time 20; women–full-time 11; minority–full-time 1.

Programs and Degrees Offered:
Listed in the following order: Program area, degree type (T if terminal Master's), number awarded 7/00–6/01. Clinical PhD 4, developmental PhD 2, learning/comparative PhD 2, school MA (T) 7.

APA Accreditation: Clinical PhD: full.

Student Applications/Admissions:
Student Applications
Clinical PhD—Applications 2001–2002, 84. Total applicants accepted 2001–2002, 20. New applicants enrolled 2001–2002, 7. Total enrolled 2001–2002 full-time, 26, part-time, 12. Openings 2002–2003, 8. The Median number of years required for completion of a degree are 7. The number of students enrolled full and part-time, who were dismissed or voluntarily withdrew from this program area were 0. *Developmental PhD*—Applications 2001–2002, 2. Total applicants accepted 2001–2002, 2. New applicants enrolled 2001–2002, 1. Total enrolled 2001–2002 full-time, 2, part-time, 2. Openings 2002–2003, 2. The Median number of years required for completion of a degree are 6. The number of students enrolled full and part-time, who were dismissed or voluntarily withdrew from this program area were 1. *Learning/comparative PhD*—Applications 2001–2002, 6. Total applicants accepted 2001–2002, 4. New applicants enrolled 2001–2002, 2. Total enrolled 2001–2002 full-time, 4. Openings 2002–2003, 4. The Median number of years required for completion of a degree are 5. The number of students enrolled full and part-time, who were dismissed or voluntarily withdrew from this program area were 0. *School MA*—Applications 2001–2002, 11. Total applicants accepted 2001–2002, 8. New applicants enrolled 2001–2002, 5. Total

enrolled 2001–2002 full-time, 6, part-time, 10. Openings 2002–2003, 5. The Median number of years required for completion of a degree are 3. The number of students enrolled full and part-time, who were dismissed or voluntarily withdrew from this program area were 0.

Admissions Requirements:
Scores: Entries appear in this order: required test or GPA, minimum score (if required), median score of students entering in 2001–2002. Master's Programs: GRE-V 500, 570; GRE-Q 500, 600; last 2 years GPA 3.25, 3.85. Above for school psychology. Doctoral Programs: GRE-V 525, 620; GRE-Q 525, 620; GRE-V+Q no minimum stated; GRE-Subject(Psych) no minimum stated; overall undergraduate GPA 3.25, 3.6 ; last 2 years GPA no minimum stated; psychology GPA no minimum stated; psychology GPA no minimum stated.
Other Criteria: (importance of criteria rated low, medium, or high): GRE/MAT scores high, research experience medium, work experience medium, extracurricular activity low, clinically related public service medium, GPA high, letters of recommendation high, interview medium, statement of goals and objectives medium. Clinical service is a criterion for clinical program only.

Student Characteristics: The following represents characteristics of students in 2001–2002 in all graduate psychology programs in the department: Female–full-time 30, part-time 19; Male–full-time 8, part-time 5; African American/Black–full-time 0, part-time 0; Hispanic/Latino (a)–full-time 0, part-time 0; Asian/Pacific Islander–full-time 0, part-time 0; American Indian/Alaska Native–full-time 7, part-time 2; students subject to the Americans with Disabilities Act–full-time 1.

Financial Information/Assistance:
Tuition for Full-Time Study: *Master's:* State residents per academic year $1,583, $193 per credit hour; nonstate residents: per academic year $4,055, $468 per credit hour. *Doctoral:* State residents: per academic year $1,722, $208 per credit hour; nonstate residents: per academic year $4,195, $483 per credit hour.

Financial Assistance:
First Year Students: Teaching assistantships available for first-year. Average amount paid per academic year: $14,000. Average number of hours worked per week: 15. Apply by January 15. Tuition remission given: full. Research assistantships available for first-year. Average amount paid per academic year: $12,000. Average number of hours worked per week: 15. Apply by Open.
Advanced Students: Teaching assistantships available for advanced students. Average amount paid per academic year: $14,000. Average number of hours worked per week: 15. Apply by January 15. Tuition remission given: full. Research assistantships available for advanced students. Average amount paid per academic year: $12,000. Average number of hours worked per week: 15. Apply by Open.
Contact Information: Of all students currently enrolled full-time, 82% benefited from one or more of the listed financial assistance programs. For information on financial assistance, contact: Department.

Internships/Practica: For those doctoral students for whom a professional internship is required prior to graduation, 5 applied in 2000–2001. Of those who applied, 4 were placed in internships listed by the Association of Psychology Postdoctoral and Internship Programs (APPIC); 4 were placed in APA accredited internships.

Housing and Day Care: On-campus housing and day care facilities are available.

Employment of Department Graduates:

Master's Degree Graduates: Of those who graduated in the academic year 2000–2001, the following categories and numbers represent the post-graduate activities and employment of master's degree graduates: Enrolled in a post-doctoral residency/fellowship (n/a), employed in independent practice (n/a), employed in a professional position in a school system (7).

Doctoral Degree Graduates: Of those who graduated in the academic year 2000–2001, the following categories and numbers represent the post-graduate activities and employment of doctoral degree graduates: Enrolled in a psychology doctoral program (n/a), enrolled in another graduate/professional program (n/a), enrolled in a post-doctoral residency/fellowship (1), employed in independent practice (1), employed in other positions at a higher education institution (1), employed in a government agency (professional services) (1), employed in a community mental health/counseling center (2), still seeking employment (2).

Additional Information:

Orientation, Objectives, and Emphasis of Department: The clinical psychology PhD program trains students in basic psychological science and clinical skills including assessment, diagnosis, and therapeutic interventions. The program is based on the scientist-practitioner model and is eclectically oriented. The training is a balanced combination of coursework, practicum, and research. Upon completion of coursework, research practicum, and internship experiences, the graduates are well prepared for professional careers as clinical psychologists in institutional, academic, and private settings. The experimental psychology PhD program offers major emphases in the fields of learning-comparative and developmental psychology. Minor areas are offered in quantitative, program evaluation, and special areas of psychology, as well as those fields in which majors are offered. Graduates have found placement in both academic and business settings. The EdS program is offered in conjunction with the School of Education. Coursework in the Psychology Department and the School of Education provides an integrated foundation upon which practicum and internship experiences build such that a graduate has the knowledge and the experience to become an effective school psychologist.

Special Facilities or Resources: The Department of Psychology is housed in a modern building. It has classrooms; offices; research laboratories for social, developmental, and learning experimentation; a shop; and colony rooms for small animals and primates. A clinical psychology center, opened in the fall of 1983, serves as a meeting place for clinical classes, seminars, research groups, and clinical services.

Application Information:

Send to: Graduate Admissions, Department of Psychology, The University of Montana, Skaggs Building 143, Missoula, MT 59812-1584. Students are admitted in the Fall, application deadline January 15. For developmental and learning/comparative, October 15 is also acceptable. Fall application deadline for School Psychology is February 15. *Fee:* $45.

Nebraska, University of, Lincoln
Department of Educational Psychology
Teachers College
114 Teachers College Hall
Lincoln, NE 68588-0345
Telephone: (402) 472-2223
Fax: (402) 472-8319
E-mail: *rdeayala@unlserve.unl.edu*
Web: *http://tc.unl.edu/edpsych/*

Department Established:
1920. Chairperson: R.J. De Ayala. Number of Faculty: total–full-time 20, part-time 1; women–full-time 9, part-time 2; minority–full-time 3.

Programs and Degrees Offered:
Listed in the following order: Program area, degree type (T if terminal Master's), number awarded 7/00–6/01. Cognition, learning, development MA, counseling MA 16, quantitative & qual methods MA 1, school EdS 5.

APA Accreditation: Counseling PhD: full. School PhD: full.

Student Applications/Admissions:
Student Applications

Cognition, learning, development MA—Applications 2001–2002, 7. Total applicants accepted 2001–2002, 7. New applicants enrolled 2001–2002, 2. Total enrolled 2001–2002 full-time, 5. Openings 2002–2003, 3. *Counseling MA*—Applications 2001– 2002, 34. Total applicants accepted 2001–2002, 19. New applicants enrolled 2001–2002, 11. Total enrolled 2001–2002 full-time, 16. Openings 2002–2003, 12. *Quantitative & qual methods MA*—Applications 2001–2002, 6. Total applicants accepted 2001–2002, 4. New applicants enrolled 2001–2002, 3. Total enrolled 2001–2002 full-time, 4. Openings 2002–2003, 4. *School EdS*—Applications 2001–2002, 16. Total applicants accepted 2001–2002, 13. New applicants enrolled 2001–2002, 8. Total enrolled 2001–2002 full-time, 24. Openings 2002– 2003, 6.

Admissions Requirements:

Scores: Entries appear in this order: required test or GPA, minimum score (if required), median score of students entering in 2001–2002. Master's Programs: GRE-V no minimum stated, 500; GRE-Q no minimum stated, 575; GRE-V+Q no minimum stated, 1075; GRE-Analytical no minimum stated, 575; GRE-V+Q+Analytical no minimum stated, 1650; GRE-Subject(Psych) no minimum stated, 520; overall undergraduate GPA no minimum stated, 3.50; psychology GPA no minimum stated, 3.90. Doctoral Programs: GRE-V no minimum stated, 505; GRE-Q no minimum stated, 606; GRE-V+Q no minimum stated, 1111; GRE-Analytical no minimum stated, 626;

GRE-V+Q+Analytical no minimum stated, 1737; GRE-Subject(Psych) no minimum stated, 630; overall undergraduate GPA no minimum stated, 3.41; last 2 years GPA no minimum stated; psychology GPA no minimum stated, 4.0 ; psychology GPA no minimum stated, 3.45.

Other Criteria: (importance of criteria rated low, medium, or high): GRE/MAT scores high, research experience high, work experience high, extracurricular activity medium, clinically related public service high, GPA high, letters of recommendation high, statement of goals and objectives high.

Student Characteristics: The following represents characteristics of students in 2001–2002 in all graduate psychology programs in the department: Female–full-time 107, part-time 0; Male–full-time 32, part-time 0; African American/Black–full-time 5, part-time 0; Hispanic/Latino (a)–full-time 2, part-time 0; Asian/Pacific Islander–full-time 3, part-time 0; American Indian/Alaska Native–full-time 0, part-time 0; Multi-ethnic–full-time 1.

Financial Information/Assistance:
Tuition for Full-Time Study: *Master's:* State residents $134 per credit hour; nonstate residents: $346 per credit hour. *Doctoral:* State residents: $134 per credit hour; nonstate residents: $346 per credit hour.

Financial Assistance:
First Year Students: Teaching assistantships available for first-year. Average amount paid per academic year: $11,700. Average number of hours worked per week: 20. Tuition remission given: full. Research assistantships available for first-year. Average amount paid per academic year: $11,700. Average number of hours worked per week: 20. Tuition remission given: full. Fellowships and scholarships available for first-year. Average amount paid per academic year: $7,500. Average number of hours worked per week: 20. Tuition remission given: full.

Advanced Students: Teaching assistantships available for advanced students. Average amount paid per academic year: $11,700. Average number of hours worked per week: 20. Tuition remission given: full. Research assistantships available for advanced students. Average amount paid per academic year: $11,700. Average number of hours worked per week: 20. Tuition remission given: full. Fellowships and scholarships available for advanced students. Average amount paid per academic year: $7,500. Average number of hours worked per week: 20. Tuition remission given: full.

Contact Information: For information on financial assistance, contact: Admissions Secretary or Program Director.

Internships/Practica: The Counseling Psychology and School Psychology Programs both have sets of practicum courses wherein students provide direct and consultation services to students, staff, and families in urban school settings. The Nebraska Internship Consortium in Professional Psychology is affiliated with the School Psychology Programs.

Housing and Day Care: No on-campus housing and day care facilities are available.

Employment of Department Graduates:

Master's Degree Graduates: Of those who graduated in the academic year 2000–2001, the following categories and numbers represent the post-graduate activities and employment of master's degree graduates: Enrolled in a post-doctoral residency/fellowship (n/a), employed in independent practice (n/a).

Doctoral Degree Graduates: Of those who graduated in the academic year 2000–2001, the following categories and numbers represent the post-graduate activities and employment of doctoral degree graduates: Enrolled in a psychology doctoral program (n/a), enrolled in another graduate/professional program (n/a).

Additional Information:

Orientation, Objectives, and Emphasis of Department: The objective of the program is to develop applied behavioral scientists able to function in a variety of settings and roles ranging from educational settings to private practice. The broad base of the department offers a diversity of orientations and role models for students.

Special Facilities or Resources: The department operates the Counseling and School Psychology Clinic, which serves as a practicum site for School Psychology and Counseling Psychology programs. In addition, the department maintains excellent contact with the community, which promotes access to practical experiences and research subject pools. The department contains the Buros Institute of Mental Measurements and its comprehensive reference library of assessment devices. The department also is home to the Center for Instructional Innovation, which conducts research on teaching and learning.

Application Information:
Send to: Tania Aguilar, Admissions Coordinator, Graduate Student Services, Univ. of Nebraska-Lincoln, 116 Henzlik Hall, Lincoln, NE 68588-0355. Students are admitted in the Fall, application deadline January 15; Spring, application deadline October 1. Counseling and School Psychology programs only consider applications for admission annually-January 15; Cognition & Learning, Developmental, Quantitative and Qualitative Methods in Education (QQME) consider applications for admissions at October 1 and January 15 deadline. *Fee:* $35. Written request for waiver of fee indicating need/justification for waiver or deferral of application fee.

Nebraska, University of, Lincoln

Department of Psychology
Arts & Sciences
238 Burnett Hall
Lincoln, NE 68588-0308
Telephone: (402) 472-3721
Fax: (402) 472-4637
E-mail: *rbarnes1@unl.edu*
Web: *http://www.unl.edu/psypage*

Department Established:
1889. Chairperson: David J. Hansen. Number of Faculty: total–full-time 28, part-time 3; women–full-time 9, part-time 1; minority–full-time 6.

Programs and Degrees Offered:
Listed in the following order: Program area, degree type (T if terminal Master's), number awarded 7/00–6/01. Clinical PhD 7, cognitive PhD 2, comparative/biopsychology PhD, developmental PhD 1, law and psychology, MLS PhD 1, social-personality PhD 2.

APA Accreditation: Clinical PhD: full.

Student Applications/Admissions:

Student Applications

Clinical PhD—Applications 2001–2002, 157. Total applicants accepted 2001–2002, 10. New applicants enrolled 2001–2002, 8. Total enrolled 2001–2002 full-time, 41, part-time, 8. Openings 2002–2003, 9. The Median number of years required for completion of a degree are 6. *Cognitive PhD*—Applications 2001–2002, 6. Total applicants accepted 2001–2002, 2. New applicants enrolled 2001–2002, 1. Total enrolled 2001–2002 full-time, 6. Openings 2002–2003, 2. The Median number of years required for completion of a degree are 5. *Comparative/biopsychology PhD*—Applications 2001–2002, 4. Total applicants accepted 2001–2002, 1. New applicants enrolled 2001–2002, 1. Total enrolled 2001–2002 full-time, 3. Openings 2002–2003, 2. The Median number of years required for completion of a degree are 5. *Developmental PhD*—Applications 2001–2002, 12. Total applicants accepted 2001–2002, 5. New applicants enrolled 2001–2002, 2. Total enrolled 2001–2002 full-time, 14. Openings 2002–2003, 3. The Median number of years required for completion of a degree are 5. *Law and psychology, MLS PhD*—Applications 2001–2002, 6. Total applicants accepted 2001–2002, 1. New applicants enrolled 2001–2002, 1. Total enrolled 2001–2002 full-time, 3. Openings 2002–2003, 2. The Median number of years required for completion of a degree are 5. *Social-personality PhD*—Applications 2001–2002, 20. Total applicants accepted 2001–2002, 5. New applicants enrolled 2001–2002, 2. Total enrolled 2001–2002 full-time, 12. Openings 2002–2003, 3. The Median number of years required for completion of a degree are 5.

Admissions Requirements:

Scores: Entries appear in this order: required test or GPA, minimum score (if required), median score of students entering in 2001–2002. Master's Programs: GRE-V no minimum stated, 610; GRE-Q no minimum stated, 630; GRE-Analytical no minimum stated, 640; GRE-Subject(Psych) no minimum stated, 630; overall undergraduate GPA 3.0, 3.50. Doctoral Programs: GRE-V no minimum stated, 610; GRE-Q no minimum stated, 630; GRE-Analytical no minimum stated, 640; GRE-Subject(Psych) no minimum stated, 630; overall undergraduate GPA 3.0, 3.5 ; last 2 years GPA no minimum stated; psychology GPA no minimum stated; psychology GPA no minimum stated.

Other Criteria: (importance of criteria rated low, medium, or high): GRE/MAT scores medium, research experience medium, work experience medium, extracurricular activity low, clinically related public service medium, GPA medium, letters of recommendation high, interview medium, statement of goals and objectives medium.

Student Characteristics: The following represents characteristics of students in 2001–2002 in all graduate psychology programs in the department: Female–full-time 72, part-time 0; Male–full-time 37, part-time 0; African American/Black–full-time 2, part-time

0; Hispanic/Latino (a)–full-time 5, part-time 0; Asian/Pacific Islander–full-time 9, part-time 0; American Indian/Alaska Native–full-time 3, part-time 0; Multi-ethnic–full-time 5.

Financial Information/Assistance:
Tuition for Full-Time Study: No information provided.

Financial Assistance:
First Year Students: No information provided.
Advanced Students: No information provided.
Contact Information: Of all students currently enrolled full-time, 0% benefited from one or more of the listed financial assistance programs.

Internships/Practica: For those doctoral students for whom a professional internship is required prior to graduation, 9 applied in 2000–2001. Of those who applied, 9 were placed in internships listed by the Association of Psychology Postdoctoral and Internship Programs (APPIC); 9 were placed in APA accredited internships.

Housing and Day Care: On-campus housing and day care facilities are available.

Employment of Department Graduates:
Master's Degree Graduates: Of those who graduated in the academic year 2000–2001, the following categories and numbers represent the post-graduate activities and employment of master's degree graduates: Enrolled in a post-doctoral residency/fellowship (n/a), employed in independent practice (n/a).
Doctoral Degree Graduates: Of those who graduated in the academic year 2000–2001, the following categories and numbers represent the post-graduate activities and employment of doctoral degree graduates: Enrolled in a psychology doctoral program (n/a), enrolled in another graduate/professional program (n/a).

Additional Information:
Orientation, Objectives, and Emphasis of Department: The goal of the clinical program is to produce broadly trained, scientifically oriented psychologists who have skills in both research and professional activities. The emphasis of the program is on community-clinical. The cognitive, comparative, developmental, and social-personality programs all emphasize research training but also place equal importance upon training for college or university teaching and policy/applied careers. Students in the PhD/JD program take their first year in the Law College, and then concentrate on psychology plus law to graduate with the double doctorate.

Special Facilities or Resources: The department has a number of resources including the Ruth Staples Child Development Laboratory, the Center for Children, Families and the Law, the BUROS Mental Measurement Institute, the NEAR Center, and the Lincoln Regional Mental Health Center.

Application Information:
Send to: Admissions Coordinator, Dept. of Psychology, UNL, 238 Burnett, Lincoln, NE 68588-0308. Students are admitted in the Fall, application deadline January 3. The deadlines are January 3rd for clinical, January 15 for all others. *Fee:* $35.

Nebraska, University of, Omaha

Department of Psychology
Omaha, NE 68182-0274
Telephone: (402) 554-2592; 2313 Joseph Brown
Fax: (402) 554-2556
E-mail: *kdeffenbacher@mail.unomaha.edu*
Web: *http://www.unomaha.edu/~psychweb/*

Department Established:
Chairperson: Kenneth A. Deffenbacher. Number of Faculty: total–full-time 18, part-time 1; women–full-time 9, part-time 1; minority–full-time 2; faculty subject to the Americans with Disabilities Act 1.

Programs and Degrees Offered:
Listed in the following order: Program area, degree type (T if terminal Master's), number awarded 7/00–6/01. Developmental-MA 4, Developmental-PhD 3, Experimental MA (T), Industrial/Organizational-MA 7, Industrial/Organizational-MS, MA (T) 6, Industrial/Organizational-PhD PhD 3, Psychobiology PhD 1, School-EdS 5, School-MS, MA (T) 6.

Student Applications/Admissions:
Student Applications
Developmental-MA—Applications 2001–2002, 8. Total applicants accepted 2001–2002, 4. New applicants enrolled 2001–2002, 2. Total enrolled 2001–2002 full-time, 10. Openings 2002–2003, 3. The Median number of years required for completion of a degree are 3. *Developmental-PhD*—Applications 2001–2002, 2. Total applicants accepted 2001–2002, 2. New applicants enrolled 2001–2002, 1. Total enrolled 2001–2002 full-time, 3. Openings 2002–2003, 2. The Median number of years required for completion of a degree are 6. The number of students enrolled full and part-time, who were dismissed or voluntarily withdrew from this program area were 1. *Experimental MA*—Applications 2001–2002, 6. Total applicants accepted 2001–2002, 3. New applicants enrolled 2001–2002, 1. Total enrolled 2001–2002 full-time, 2. Openings 2002–2003, 3. *Industrial/Organizational-MA*—Applications 2001–2002, 18. Total applicants accepted 2001–2002, 8. New applicants enrolled 2001–2002, 5. Total enrolled 2001–2002 full-time, 13. Openings 2002–2003, 5. The Median number of years required for completion of a degree are 3. *Industrial/Organizational-MS, MA*—Applications 2001–2002, 18. Total applicants accepted 2001–2002, 6. New applicants enrolled 2001–2002, 6. Total enrolled 2001–2002 full-time, 12. Openings 2002–2003, 6. The Median number of years required for completion of a degree are 2. *Industrial/Organizational-PhD*—Applications 2001–2002, 6. Total applicants accepted 2001–2002, 2. New applicants enrolled 2001–2002, 1. Total enrolled 2001–2002 full-time, 12. Openings 2002–2003, 3. The Median number of years required for completion of a degree are 6. *Psychobiology PhD*—Applications 2001–2002, 4. Total applicants accepted 2001–2002, 2. New applicants enrolled 2001–2002, 1. Total enrolled 2001–2002 full-time, 3. Openings 2002–2003, 3. *School-EdS*—Applications 2001–2002, 6. Total applicants accepted 2001–2002, 6. New applicants enrolled 2001–2002, 5. Total enrolled 2001–2002 full-time, 10. Openings 2002–2003, 5. The Median number of years required for completion of a degree are 4. The number of students enrolled

full and part-time, who were dismissed or voluntarily withdrew from this program area were 1. *School-MS MA*—Applications 2001–2002, 26. Total applicants accepted 2001–2002, 9. New applicants enrolled 2001–2002, 6. Total enrolled 2001–2002 full-time, 12. Openings 2002–2003, 6. The Median number of years required for completion of a degree are 2.

Admissions Requirements:

Scores: Entries appear in this order: required test or GPA, minimum score (if required), median score of students entering in 2001–2002. Master's Programs: GRE-V no minimum stated, 500; GRE-Q no minimum stated, 610; GRE-V+Q no minimum stated, 1110; GRE-Analytical no minimum stated, 620; GRE-V+Q+Analytical no minimum stated, 1730; overall undergraduate GPA no minimum stated, 3.68. Doctoral Programs: GRE-V no minimum stated, 530; GRE-Q no minimum stated, 640; GRE-V+Q no minimum stated, 1200; GRE-Analytical no minimum stated, 610; GRE-V+Q+Analytical no minimum stated, 1800; GRE-Subject(Psych) no minimum stated, 610; overall undergraduate GPA no minimum stated, 3.70; last 2 years GPA no minimum stated; psychology GPA no minimum stated; psychology GPA no minimum stated.

Other Criteria: (importance of criteria rated low, medium, or high): GRE/MAT scores high, research experience high, work experience medium, extracurricular activity medium, clinically related public service low, GPA high, letters of recommendation high, interview medium, statement of goals and objectives high.

Student Characteristics: The following represents characteristics of students in 2001–2002 in all graduate psychology programs in the department: Female–full-time 49, part-time 0; Male–full-time 22, part-time 0; African American/Black–full-time 1, part-time 0; Hispanic/Latino (a)–full-time 1, part-time 0; Asian/Pacific Islander–full-time 1, part-time 0; American Indian/Alaska Native–full-time 0, part-time 0.

Financial Information/Assistance:

Tuition for Full-Time Study: *Master's:* State residents $105 per credit hour; nonstate residents: $252 per credit hour. *Doctoral:* State residents: $105 per credit hour; nonstate residents: $252 per credit hour.

Financial Assistance:

First Year Students: Teaching assistantships available for first-year. Average amount paid per academic year: $9,300. Average number of hours worked per week: 20. Apply by Feb 1. Tuition remission given: full. Research assistantships available for first-year. Average amount paid per academic year: $9,300. Average number of hours worked per week: 20. Apply by Feb 1. Tuition remission given: full. Fellowships and scholarships available for first-year. Average amount paid per academic year: $9,300. Average number of hours worked per week: 20. Apply by Feb 1. Tuition remission given: full.

Advanced Students: Teaching assistantships available for advanced students. Average amount paid per academic year: $9,300. Average number of hours worked per week: 20. Apply by Feb 1. Tuition remission given: full. Research assistantships available for advanced students. Average amount paid per academic year: $9,300. Average number of hours worked per week: 20. Apply by Feb 1. Tuition remission given: full. Traineeships available for advanced students. Average number of hours worked per week: 20. Tuition remission given: full and partial. Fellowships and scholarships available for advanced students. Average amount paid per academic year: $9,300. Average number of hours worked per week: 20. Apply by Feb 1. Tuition remission given: full and partial.

Contact Information: Of all students currently enrolled full-time, 50% benefited from one or more of the listed financial assistance programs. For information on financial assistance, contact: Department Secretary.

Internships/Practica: An internship in school psychology is available and required within the EdS program leading to certification in the field of school psychology.

Housing and Day Care: No on-campus housing and day care facilities are available.

Employment of Department Graduates:

Master's Degree Graduates: Of those who graduated in the academic year 2000–2001, the following categories and numbers represent the post-graduate activities and employment of master's degree graduates: Enrolled in a post-doctoral residency/fellowship (n/a), employed in independent practice (n/a).

Doctoral Degree Graduates: Of those who graduated in the academic year 2000–2001, the following categories and numbers represent the post-graduate activities and employment of doctoral degree graduates: Enrolled in a psychology doctoral program (n/a), enrolled in another graduate/professional program (n/a).

Additional Information:

Orientation, Objectives, and Emphasis of Department: The department is broadly eclectic, placing emphasis on theory, research, and application. The MA program is primarily for students who anticipate continuing their education at the PhD level. The MA degree may be completed in eight areas of psychology. The MS program is primarily for students who view the master's degree as terminal and who wish to emphasize application in the fields of educational-school or industrial/organizational psychology. These two areas may be emphasized within the MA program as well.

Special Facilities or Resources: The department maintains extensive laboratory facilities in a variety of experimental areas, both human and animal. The animal colony consists of rats, gerbils, mice, and golden-lion tamarins. Up-to-date interactive computer facilities are readily available. The Center for Applied Psychological Services is a departmentally controlled, faculty-student consulting service that provides an opportunity to gain practical experience in industrial psychology and school psychology. The department maintains working relations with the Children's Rehabilitation Institute, the Department of Pediatrics, the Department of Physiology, and the University of Nebraska Medical Center. In addition, contact exists with the Boys Town Institute, Boys Town Home, Henry Doorly Zoo, Union Pacific Railroad, and Mutual of Omaha.

Application Information:
Send to: Department Chair. Students are admitted in the Fall, application deadline February 1. *Fee:* $35.

Nevada, University of, Las Vegas
Department of Psychology
Liberal Arts
4505 Maryland Parkway
Las Vegas, NV 89154-5030
Telephone: (702) 895-3305
Fax: (702) 895-0195
E-mail: *crasmusse@ccmail.nevada.edu*
Web: *http://psychology.unlv.edu*

Department Established:
1960. Chairperson: Charles T. Rasmussen. Number of Faculty: total–full-time 21, part-time 11; women–full-time 7, part-time 4; minority–full-time 2.

Programs and Degrees Offered:
Listed in the following order: Program area, degree type (T if terminal Master's), number awarded 7/00–6/01. Clinical PhD, Experimental PhD.

Student Applications/Admissions:
Student Applications
Clinical PhD—Applications 2001–2002, 48. Total applicants accepted 2001–2002, 12. New applicants enrolled 2001–2002, 10. Total enrolled 2001–2002 full-time, 25. Openings 2002–2003, 9. The number of students enrolled full and part-time, who were dismissed or voluntarily withdrew from this program area were 0. *Experimental PhD*—Applications 2001–2002, 6. Total applicants accepted 2001–2002, 1. New applicants enrolled 2001–2002, 1. Total enrolled 2001–2002 full-time, 1. Openings 2002–2003, 5.

Admissions Requirements:
Scores: Entries appear in this order: required test or GPA, minimum score (if required), median score of students entering in 2001–2002. Doctoral Programs: GRE-V 500, 565; GRE-Q 500, 630; GRE-Analytical 500, 700; GRE-Subject(Psych) 500, 625; overall undergraduate GPA 3.2, 3.5 ; last 2 years GPA no minimum stated; psychology GPA 3.2, 3.82; psychology GPA no minimum stated.
Other Criteria: (importance of criteria rated low, medium, or high): GRE/MAT scores high, research experience high, work experience low, clinically related public service medium, GPA high, letters of recommendation high, interview high, statement of goals and objectives high.

Student Characteristics: The following represents characteristics of students in 2001–2002 in all graduate psychology programs in the department: Female–full-time 25, part-time 0; Male–full-time 8, part-time 0; African American/Black–full-time 0, part-time 0; Hispanic/Latino (a)–full-time 4, part-time 0; Asian/Pacific Islander–full-time 1, part-time 0; American Indian/Alaska Native–full-time 0, part-time 0; Multi-ethnic–full-time 0, part-time 0; students subject to the Americans with Disabilities Act–full-time 0, part-time 0.

Financial Information/Assistance:
Tuition for Full-Time Study: *Doctoral:* State residents: $103 per credit hour; nonstate residents: per academic year $7,215, $103 per credit hour.

Financial Assistance:
First Year Students: Teaching assistantships available for first-year. Average amount paid per academic year: $12,000. Average number of hours worked per week: 20. Apply by January 15. Tuition remission given: full. Research assistantships available for first-year. Average amount paid per academic year: $12,000. Average number of hours worked per week: 20. Apply by January 15. Tuition remission given: full.
Advanced Students: Teaching assistantships available for advanced students. Average amount paid per academic year: $12,000. Average number of hours worked per week: 20. Apply by March 1. Tuition remission given: full. Fellowships and scholarships available for advanced students. Average amount paid per academic year: $15,000. Average number of hours worked per week: 0. Apply by March 1. Tuition remission given: full.
Contact Information: Of all students currently enrolled full-time, 96% benefited from one or more of the listed financial assistance programs. For information on financial assistance, contact: the graduate dean.

Internships/Practica: Both clinical and experimental students work in various community settings as part of their training experience. Additional information is available on the program website: www.psychology.unlv.edu.

Housing and Day Care: No on-campus housing and day care facilities are available.

Employment of Department Graduates:
Master's Degree Graduates: Of those who graduated in the academic year 2000–2001, the following categories and numbers represent the post-graduate activities and employment of master's degree graduates: Enrolled in a post-doctoral residency/fellowship (n/a), employed in independent practice (n/a).
Doctoral Degree Graduates: Of those who graduated in the academic year 2000–2001, the following categories and numbers represent the post-graduate activities and employment of doctoral degree graduates: Enrolled in a psychology doctoral program (n/a), enrolled in another graduate/professional program (n/a).

Additional Information:
Orientation, Objectives, and Emphasis of Department: UNLV's Experimental Psychology program is designed to prepare experimental psychologists for the rich opportunities that are presented by a changing employment picture. This program addresses the training needs of new psychologists in ways that traditional programs do not. Specifically, the program combines a strong focus on the major content areas of Experimental Psychology and methodology/statistics, while also providing opportunities to learn skills and conduct research that can be applied to real-world problems. In short, graduate training will produce experimental psychologists who can be employed in both academic and non-academic settings. The UNLV Clinical Psychology Doctoral Program trains

students to address human concerns through both scholarly research and the application of psychological knowledge and skills. We train students as generalist scientist-practitioners prepared to conduct scientific research and clinical interventions with children and adults. Our program began in 1999. We will seek accreditation from the American Psychological Association at the earliest date of eligibility for new programs, which we anticipate to be the 2003/2004 academic year.

Special Facilities or Resources: The strongest resource of the psychology department is the many talents of its diverse faculty. Our graduate program is small enough to provide close personal interaction experiences for training, and yet we encourage students to demonstrate initiative and to undertake the major responsibility for their graduate learning experiences. Within the financial constraints of the department budget, student research is encouraged within the department and throughout the university.

Application Information:

Send to: UNLV, Graduate College, 4505 Maryland Parkway, Las Vegas, NV 89154-1017. Students are admitted in the Fall. Deadline for Clinical PhD program is January 15. Deadline for Experimental PhD program is February 1. *Fee:* $40. Waivers are obtained through the Graduate College office.

Nevada, University of, Reno
Department of Psychology/296
Arts and Science
1664 N. Virginia
Reno, NV 89557
Telephone: (775) 784-6828
Fax: (775) 784-1126
E-mail: *hayes@scs.unr.edu*
Web: *http://www.unr.edu/psych/*

Department Established:

1920. Chair: Steven Hayes. Number of Faculty: total–full-time 22, part-time 5; women–full-time 7, part-time 1; minority–full-time 1, part-time 1.

Programs and Degrees Offered:

Listed in the following order: Program area, degree type (T if terminal Master's), number awarded 7/00–6/01. Behavior analysis PhD 3, clinical PhD 5, experimental PhD 2.

Student Applications/Admissions:

Student Applications

Behavior analysis PhD—Applications 2001–2002, 30. Total applicants accepted 2001–2002, 12. New applicants enrolled 2001–2002, 10. Total enrolled 2001–2002 full-time, 32, part-time, 3. Openings 2002–2003, 10. The Median number of years required for completion of a degree are 3. The number of students enrolled full and part-time, who were dismissed or voluntarily withdrew from this program area were 8. *Clinical PhD*—Applications 2001–2002, 69. Total applicants accepted 2001–2002, 8. New applicants enrolled 2001–2002, 8. Total enrolled 2001–2002 full-time, 47. Openings 2002–2003, 10. The Median number of years required for completion of a degree are 10. The number of students enrolled full and part-

time, who were dismissed or voluntarily withdrew from this program area were 2. *Experimental PhD*—Applications 2001–2002, 4. Total applicants accepted 2001–2002, 3. New applicants enrolled 2001–2002, 2. Total enrolled 2001–2002 full-time, 25.

Admissions Requirements:

Scores: Entries appear in this order: required test or GPA, minimum score (if required), median score of students entering in 2001–2002. Master's Programs: GRE-V no minimum stated, 470; GRE-Q no minimum stated, 510; GRE-Analytical no minimum stated, 600; GRE-Subject(Psych) 550; overall undergraduate GPA 3.0. For the GRE-V+Q, the minimum score is 1200 for clinical. For the Undergraduate GPA, 3.5 is suggested for Clinical. Doctoral Programs: GRE-V no minimum stated, 550; GRE-Q no minimum stated, 545; GRE-Analytical no minimum stated, 505; GRE-Subject(Psych) 550, 550; overall undergraduate GPA 3.0; last 2 years GPA no minimum stated; psychology GPA no minimum stated; psychology GPA no minimum stated. 1200 for clinical for the GRE-V+Q. For the Undergraduate GPA, 3.5 suggested for clinical.

Other Criteria: (importance of criteria rated low, medium, or high): GRE/MAT scores high, research experience high, work experience high, extracurricular activity high, clinically related public service high, GPA high, letters of recommendation high, interview high, statement of goals and objectives high. Interviews for admission into behavior analysis and clinical is required.

Student Characteristics: The following represents characteristics of students in 2001–2002 in all graduate psychology programs in the department: Female–full-time 9, part-time 0; Male–full-time 10, part-time 0; African American/Black–full-time 2, part-time 0; Hispanic/Latino (a)–full-time 3, part-time 0; Asian/Pacific Islander–full-time 0, part-time 0; American Indian/Alaska Native–full-time 0, part-time 0.

Financial Information/Assistance:

Tuition for Full-Time Study: *Master's:* State residents per academic year $1,935, $107 per credit hour; nonstate residents: per academic year $8,445. *Doctoral:* State residents: per academic year $1,935, $107 per credit hour; nonstate residents: per academic year $8,445.

Financial Assistance:

First Year Students: Teaching assistantships available for first-year. Average amount paid per academic year: $10,000. Average number of hours worked per week: 20. Apply by n/a. Tuition remission given: full. Research assistantships available for first-year. Average amount paid per academic year: $10,000. Average number of hours worked per week: 20. Apply by n/a. Tuition remission given: full.

Advanced Students: Teaching assistantships available for advanced students. Average amount paid per academic year: $10,000. Average number of hours worked per week: 20. Apply by n/a. Tuition remission given: full. Research assistantships available for advanced students. Average amount paid per academic year: $10,000. Average number of hours worked per week: 20. Apply by n/a. Tuition remission given: full.

Contact Information: Of all students currently enrolled full-time, 100% benefited from one or more of the listed financial

assistance programs. For information on financial assistance, contact: Financial Aid at 774-784-4666.

Internships/Practica: The department offers several teaching/research assistantships. Experimental—Some students receive support as research assistants through individual faculty grants. Behavior Analysis—All doctoral students and most master's students receive full support from assistantships or consultation services. Clinical—Participation in clinical practica is required for students. From the last half of the first year through the third year students see clients at the Psychological Service Center, an in-house clinic. During the fourth year, students are required to complete a 1000 hour practicum (externship) on campus or at agencies in the area. Finally, students are required to complete a 2000 hour, APA-approved internship during their final year.

Housing and Day Care: On-campus housing and day care facilities are available.

Employment of Department Graduates:

Master's Degree Graduates: Of those who graduated in the academic year 2000–2001, the following categories and numbers represent the post-graduate activities and employment of master's degree graduates: Enrolled in a post-doctoral residency/fellowship (n/a), employed in independent practice (n/a).

Doctoral Degree Graduates: Of those who graduated in the academic year 2000–2001, the following categories and numbers represent the post-graduate activities and employment of doctoral degree graduates: Enrolled in a psychology doctoral program (n/a), enrolled in another graduate/professional program (n/a).

Additional Information:

Orientation, Objectives, and Emphasis of Department: The experimental program in psychology is research-oriented. The experimental division offers specialized work in human cognition and learning, perception and psychophysics, behaviorism, and animal communication. The clinical program has a scientist-practitioner emphasis and offers skills in psychotherapy, assessment, evaluation, and community psychology. The behavior analysis program emphasizes applied behavior analysis, especially in institutional settings, and examines both the theoretical and applied ramifications of the behavioral programs.

Special Facilities or Resources: Experimental— the program has active labs with facilities for research in visual perception, spoken word recognition, cognition, and animal behavior and communication (including opportunities for research at the primate center at Washington Central University). Behavior Analysis—the program has a lab at the Nelson Clinic where they work with autistic children and developmentally disabled clients. Clinical—the primary academic/research facility of the program is the Psychological Service Center, an in-house training clinic that serves the community by offering services on a sliding fee basis.

Information for Students With Physical Disabilities: All classroom buildings on campus are accessible to the handicapped.

Application Information:
Send to: Admission Information, Psychology Department/296, University of Nevada, Reno, NV 89557. Students are admitted in the Fall. For the Fall semester, the deadline for Clinical is January 1; and February 1st for behavior analysis, and April 1st for experimental. For the Spring semester, the deadline is November 2 for experimental only. *Fee:* $40. $20 if previously enrolled in UNR.

Antioch New England Graduate School (2001 data)
Clinical Psychology
40 Avon Street
Keene, NH 03431
Telephone: (603) 357-3122
Fax: (603) 357-0718
E-mail: *admissions@antiochne.edu*
Web: *http://www.antiochne.edu*

Department Established:
1982. Chairperson: Roger L. Peterson. Number of Faculty: total–full-time 10, part-time 17; women–full-time 5, part-time 6.

Programs and Degrees Offered:
Listed in the following order: Program area, degree type (T if terminal Master's), number awarded 7/00–6/01. Clinical PsyD 27.

APA Accreditation: Clinical PsyD: full.

Student Applications/Admissions:
Student Applications
Clinical PsyD—Applications 2001–2002, 126. Total applicants accepted 2001–2002, 60. New applicants enrolled 2001–2002, 27. Total enrolled 2001–2002 full-time, 103. Openings 2002–2003, 26.

Admissions Requirements:
Scores: Entries appear in this order: required test or GPA, minimum score (if required), median score of students entering in 2001–2002. Doctoral Programs: GRE-V no minimum stated, 500; GRE-Q no minimum stated, 520; GRE-V+Q no minimum stated, 1010; GRE-Subject(Psych) no minimum stated, 535; overall undergraduate GPA no minimum stated, 3.38.
Other Criteria: (importance of criteria rated low, medium, or high): GRE/MAT scores medium, research experience medium, work experience medium, extracurricular activity low, clinically related public service medium, GPA high, letters of recommendation high, interview high, statement of goals and objectives high. Requires evidence of academic promise, personal and interpersonal competence, and clinical and professional promise.

Student Characteristics: The following represents characteristics of students in 2001–2002 in all graduate psychology programs in the department: Female–full-time 18, part-time 0; Male–full-time 9, part-time 0; African American/Black–full-time 1, part-time 0; Hispanic/Latino (a)–full-time 0, part-time 0; Asian/ Pacific Islander–full-time 0, part-time 0; American Indian/Alaska Native– full-time 0, part-time 0.

Financial Information/Assistance:
Tuition for Full-Time Study: No information provided.

Financial Assistance:
First Year Students: No information provided.
Advanced Students: No information provided.
Contact Information: For information on financial assistance, contact: Office of Financial Aid.

Internships/Practica: Students complete practica at agencies within driving distance around New England. About 15 students per year do practicum at the Antioch Psychological Services Center (PSC), within the Department of Clinical Psychology. It functions as a mental health clinic providing a range of psychological services to residents from Keene and surrounding communities, and to Antioch New England students in departments other than Clinical Psychology. These services include individual psychotherapy, couple and family therapy, individual and family assessment, and various problem-specific psychoeducational groups and seminars. In addition, the PSC is actively involved in community outreach services; clinicians are encouraged to develop public psychoeducation and consultation activities, and to work in collaboration with other social service agencies for the purpose of ongoing community needs assessment and program development. A practicum at the PSC offers the student a unique opportunity for more concentrated interaction with core faculty—through supervision, training, and involvement in applied clinical and research projects of mutual interest. Specialized training opportunities exist for students interested in health psychology, family therapy, and assessment. In 1998–99, 13 of 19 internship applicants went to APA approved slots, 1 went to APPIC slot, 4 went to non-accredited slots, and 1 was unplaced.

Housing and Day Care: No on-campus housing and day care facilities are available.

Employment of Department Graduates:
Master's Degree Graduates: Of those who graduated in the academic year 2000–2001, the following categories and numbers represent the post-graduate activities and employment of master's degree graduates: Enrolled in a post-doctoral residency/fellowship (n/a), employed in independent practice (n/a).
Doctoral Degree Graduates: Of those who graduated in the academic year 2000–2001, the following categories and numbers represent the post-graduate activities and employment of doctoral degree graduates: Enrolled in a psychology doctoral program (n/a), enrolled in another graduate/professional program (n/a).

Additional Information:

Orientation, Objectives, and Emphasis of Department: Our scholar-practitioner program prepares professional psychologists for multiple roles for the expanded world of 21st century clinical psychology, including not only intervention, assessment, and research but also supervision, management, administration, consultation, and public policy. With a commitment to social responsibility, social justice, and diversity, we emphasize a social vision of clinical psychology, responsive to the needs of the larger society. The program includes broad training with a range of theoretical perspectives, a sound psychological knowledge base, and supervised practice. It follows the educational model developed by the National Council of Schools and Programs of Professional Psychology (NCSPP). This model specifies six core professional competency areas: relationship, assessment, intervention, research and evaluation, consultation and education, and management and supervision (we have required courses in each) and, of course, includes basic psychological science. Research for clinical psychology is rooted in solving professional and social problems, where science and practice are integrated and complementary in the required dissertation. Preparation as "local clinical scientists" includes opportunities for training in program evaluation, as well as a range of other psychological topics and methodologies. Our pedagogy brings together theory, practice, and research through integrative, reflective learning experiences which help students develop their professional "voice."

Special Facilities or Resources: The Center for Research on Psychological Practice (CROPP) in the Department of Clinical Psychology serves both the department and the community. This center is designed to address particular emerging educational aspects of doctoral training in clinical psychology that are not regularly included within the usual professional psychology curriculum—those relevant to applied clinical research skills and the associated administrative, consultative, and policy-creation roles of doctoral level psychologists. Several specific areas of research are priorities for CROPP. These include program evaluation and quality assurance issues, such as needs assessment, outcome and satisfaction research, cost-benefit analysis, policy analysis, and other topics relevant to mental health service management: public welfare issues such as treatment access, utilization, and outcome for underserved, rural, low socioeconomic, and minority populations; development of novel treatment and delivery systems; and methodological issues including the assessment and development of methods and measures appropriate for practice research. The research is done primarily in community service settings and entails collaboration with agencies and caregivers throughout the region. The development of this kind of research center, particularly within the context of a doctoral program in clinical psychology, has not, to our knowledge, been done elsewhere in the country.

Information for Students With Physical Disabilities: In accordance with Section 504 of the Rehabilitation Act of 1973 and the Americans with Disabilities Act, Antioch New England does not exclude or discriminate against otherwise qualified students with disabilities. Please write us for the booklet Enhancing Accessibility for Antioch New England Students with Disabilities: "A Handbook for Faculty, Staff, and Students."

Application Information:
Send to: Office of Doctoral Admissions, Antioch New England Graduate School, 40 Avon Street, Keene, NH, 03431-3516. Students are admitted in the Fall, application deadline January 12. *Fee:* $75.

Dartmouth College
Psychological and Brain Sciences
6207 Moore Hall
Hanover, NH 03755-3578
Telephone: (603) 646-3181
Fax: (603) 646-1419
E-mail: *psychological.and.brain.sciences@dartmouth.edu*
Web: *http://www.dartmouth.edu/artsci/psych/grad.html*

Department Established:
1894. Chairperson: Howard C. Hughes. Number of Faculty: total–full-time 22, part-time 10; women–full-time 5, part-time 4; minority–full-time 3.

Programs and Degrees Offered:
Listed in the following order: Program area, degree type (T if terminal Master's), number awarded 7/00–6/01. General experimental PhD.

Student Applications/Admissions:
Student Applications

General experimental PhD—Applications 2001–2002, 96. Total applicants accepted 2001–2002, 12. New applicants enrolled 2001–2002, 8. Total enrolled 2001–2002 full-time, 23. Openings 2002–2003, 10. The Median number of years required for completion of a degree are 4. The number of students enrolled full and part-time, who were dismissed or voluntarily withdrew from this program area were 0.

Admissions Requirements:

Scores: Entries appear in this order: required test or GPA, minimum score (if required), median score of students entering in 2001–2002. Doctoral Programs: GRE-V 600, 614; GRE-Q 600, 740; GRE-Analytical 600, 770; overall undergraduate GPA 3.3; last 2 years GPA no minimum stated; psychology GPA no minimum stated; psychology GPA no minimum stated.

Other Criteria: (importance of criteria rated low, medium, or high): GRE/MAT scores high, research experience high, work experience medium, extracurricular activity low, GPA high, letters of recommendation high, interview medium, statement of goals and objectives high.

Student Characteristics: The following represents characteristics of students in 2001–2002 in all graduate psychology programs in the department: Female–full-time 16, part-time 0; Male–full-time 7, part-time 0; African American/Black–full-time 0, part-time 0; Hispanic/Latino (a)–full-time 0, part-time 0; Asian/Pacific Islander–full-time 0, part-time 0; American Indian/Alaska Native–full-time 1, part-time 0.

Financial Information/Assistance:

Tuition for Full-Time Study: No information provided.

Financial Assistance:

First Year Students: Fellowships and scholarships available for first-year. Average amount paid per academic year: $17,386. Apply by none. Tuition remission given: full.

Advanced Students: Fellowships and scholarships available for advanced students. Average amount paid per academic year: $17,386. Tuition remission given: full.

Contact Information: Of all students currently enrolled full-time, 100% benefited from one or more of the listed financial assistance programs. For information on financial assistance, contact: Chair, Graduate Committee.

Internships/Practica: No information provided.

Housing and Day Care: On-campus housing and day care facilities are available.

Employment of Department Graduates:

Master's Degree Graduates: Of those who graduated in the academic year 2000–2001, the following categories and numbers represent the post-graduate activities and employment of master's degree graduates: Enrolled in a post-doctoral residency/fellowship (n/a), employed in independent practice (n/a).

Doctoral Degree Graduates: Of those who graduated in the academic year 2000–2001, the following categories and numbers represent the post-graduate activities and employment of doctoral degree graduates: Enrolled in a psychology doctoral program (n/a), enrolled in another graduate/professional program (n/a).

Additional Information:

Orientation, Objectives, and Emphasis of Department: The graduate program offers training in social psychology, cognition/perception, cognitive neuroscience, and behavioral neuroscience. Many of our students pursue research that bridges these areas. Because of its moderate size, the program emphasizes a close working relationship between faculty and students. The program has a strong experimental orientation in which students serve research and teaching apprenticeships with faculty. The emphasis is on professional development for academic careers.

Special Facilities or Resources: The department has excellent laboratories with ample equipment and superior computer facilities.

Information for Students With Physical Disabilities: Moore Hall is wheelchair accessible as are most of the buildings at Dartmouth.

Application Information:

Send to: Chair, Graduate Committee, 6207 Moore Hall, Hanover, NH 03755-3578. Students are admitted in the Fall, application deadline January 15. *Fee:* $40.

New Hampshire, University of
Department of Psychology
Conant Hall
Durham, NH 03824
Telephone: (603) 862-2360
Fax: (603) 862-4986
E-mail: *dlhardy@hopper.unh.edu*
Web: *http://www.unh.edu/psychology/*

Department Established:

1923. Chairperson: Kenneth Fuld. Number of Faculty: total–full-time 24, part-time 1; women–full-time 11.

Programs and Degrees Offered:

Listed in the following order: Program area, degree type (T if terminal Master's), number awarded 7/00–6/01. Behavior Analysis PhD, Cognition/Psycholinguistics PhD, Developmental PhD, History and Theory PhD, Physiological PhD, Sensation/Perception PhD, Social/Personality PhD.

Student Applications/Admissions:

Student Applications

Behavior Analysis PhD. Cognition/Psycholinguistics PhD. Developmental PhD. History and Theory PhD. Physiological PhD. Sensation/Perception PhD. Social/Personality PhD.

Admissions Requirements:

Scores: Entries appear in this order: required test or GPA, minimum score (if required), median score of students entering in 2001–2002. Doctoral Programs: GRE-V no minimum stated; GRE-Q no minimum stated; GRE-V+Q no minimum stated; GRE-Analytical no minimum stated; GRE-Subject(Psych) no minimum stated; overall undergraduate GPA no minimum stated; last 2 years GPA no minimum stated; psychology GPA no minimum stated; psychology GPA no minimum stated.

Other Criteria: (importance of criteria rated low, medium, or high): GRE/MAT scores high, research experience high, work experience low, extracurricular activity low, GPA high, letters of recommendation high, interview low, statement of goals and objectives high.

Student Characteristics: The following represents characteristics of students in 2001–2002 in all graduate psychology programs in the department: Female–full-time 14, part-time 0; Male–full-time 17, part-time 0; African American/Black–full-time 1, part-time 0; Hispanic/Latino (a)–full-time 0, part-time 0; Asian/Pacific Islander–full-time 1, part-time 0; American Indian/Alaska Native–full-time 0, part-time 0.

Financial Information/Assistance:

Tuition for Full-Time Study: No information provided.

Financial Assistance:

First Year Students: Teaching assistantships available for first-year. Average amount paid per academic year: $11,450. Average number of hours worked per week: 20. Apply by February 15. Tuition remission given: full.

Advanced Students: Teaching assistantships available for advanced students. Average amount paid per academic year: $11,750. Average number of hours worked per week: 20. Apply by

N/A. Tuition remission given: full. Fellowships and scholarships available for advanced students. Average amount paid per academic year: $12,000. Average number of hours worked per week: 0. Apply by N/A. Tuition remission given: full.

Contact Information: Of all students currently enrolled full-time, 100% benefited from one or more of the listed financial assistance programs.

Internships/Practica: No information provided.

Housing and Day Care: On-campus housing and day care facilities are available.

Employment of Department Graduates:

Master's Degree Graduates: Of those who graduated in the academic year 2000–2001, the following categories and numbers represent the post-graduate activities and employment of master's degree graduates: Enrolled in a post-doctoral residency/fellowship (n/a), employed in independent practice (n/a).

Doctoral Degree Graduates: Of those who graduated in the academic year 2000–2001, the following categories and numbers represent the post-graduate activities and employment of doctoral degree graduates: Enrolled in a psychology doctoral program (n/a), enrolled in another graduate/professional program (n/a), enrolled in a post-doctoral residency/fellowship (2), employed in business or industry (research/consulting) (1), employed in a government agency (research) (1).

Additional Information:

Orientation, Objectives, and Emphasis of Department: The program's basic goal is the development of psychologists who have a broad knowledge of psychology, who can teach and communicate effectively, and who can carry out sound research in one of the following areas of specialization: cognition-psycholinguistics, developmental psychology, history and theory of psychology, behavior analysis, physiological psychology, sensation-perception, or social/personality psychology. Besides the usual academic courses, our program places a distinctive emphasis on preparing graduate students for future roles as faculty members in college or university settings. Students complete a year-long seminar and practicum in the teaching of psychology, which introduces them to the theory and practice of teaching, while they concurrently teach under the supervision of master-teachers. Students also gain experience in other faculty roles such as sponsoring undergraduate students' research and serving on committees. After graduation, most students secure academic positions. All students receive tuition waivers and stipends for at least 4 years, in exchange for serving as teaching or research assistants in their early years and as teachers in their later years. Students can apply for research funds.

Special Facilities or Resources: The department occupies several buildings and offers research facilities, equipment, and resources in all of its areas of specialization. In addition, the department has many microcomputers and terminals that may be used to access the university's mainframe computer.

Application Information:
Send to: Dean of the Graduate School, University of New Hampshire, Thompson Hall, Durham, NH 03824. Students are admitted in the Fall, application deadline February 15. *Fee:* $50. Financial aid application.

Fairleigh Dickinson University, Madison (2001 data)
Department of Psychology M-AB1-01
Becton
285 Madison Avenue
Madison, NJ 07940
Telephone: (973) 443-8547
Fax: (973) 443-8562
E-mail: *Daniel@fdu.edu*
Web: *http://alpha.fdu.edu/psychweb*

Department Established:
1962. Daniel J. Calcagnetti, Graduate Coordin. Number of Faculty: total–full-time 10, part-time 12; women–full-time 4, part-time 8; minority–full-time 1.

Programs and Degrees Offered:
Listed in the following order: Program area, degree type (T if terminal Master's), number awarded 7/00–6/01. Applied social and community MA (T), Clinical counseling MA (T) 55, industrial MA (T) 28, Organizational Behavior MA (T) 15.

Student Applications/Admissions:
Student Applications
Applied social and community MA—Applications 2001–2002, 8. Total applicants accepted 2001–2002, 2. New applicants enrolled 2001–2002, 1. Total enrolled 2001–2002 full-time, 1. Openings 2002–2003, 3. The Median number of years required for completion of a degree are 2. The number of students enrolled full and part-time, who were dismissed or voluntarily withdrew from this program area were 0. *Clinical counseling MA*—Applications 2001–2002, 60. Total applicants accepted 2001–2002, 45. New applicants enrolled 2001–2002, 35. Total enrolled 2001–2002 full-time, 39, part-time, 15. Openings 2002–2003, 40. The Median number of years required for completion of a degree are 3. The number of students enrolled full and part-time, who were dismissed or voluntarily withdrew from this program area were 2. *Industrial MA*—Applications 2001–2002, 32. Total applicants accepted 2001–2002, 26. New applicants enrolled 2001–2002, 10. Total enrolled 2001–2002 full-time, 32, part-time, 15. Openings 2002–2003, 40. The Median number of years required for completion of a degree are 2. *Organizational Behavior MA*—Applications 2001–2002, 20. Total applicants accepted 2001–2002, 12. New applicants enrolled 2001–2002, 25. Total enrolled 2001–2002 full-time, 12. Openings 2002–2003, 15. The Median number of years required for completion of a degree are 3.

Admissions Requirements:
Scores: Entries appear in this order: required test or GPA, minimum score (if required), median score of students entering in 2001–2002. Master's Programs: GRE-V 450, 550; GRE-Q 450, 550; GRE-V+Q no minimum stated; GRE-Subject(Psych) 500, 550; overall undergraduate GPA 2.8, 3.4. Doctoral Programs: last 2 years GPA no minimum stated; psychology GPA no minimum stated; psychology GPA no minimum stated.

Other Criteria: (importance of criteria rated low, medium, or high): GRE/MAT scores low, research experience high, work experience medium, extracurricular activity medium, clinically related public service high, GPA high, letters of recommendation medium, interview high, statement of goals and objectives medium.

Student Characteristics: The following represents characteristics of students in 2001–2002 in all graduate psychology programs in the department: Female–full-time 43, part-time 26; Male–full-time 8, part-time 7; African American/Black–full-time 4, part-time 4; Hispanic/Latino (a)–full-time 3, part-time 2; Asian/Pacific Islander–full-time 2, part-time 2; American Indian/Alaska Native–full-time 0, part-time 0; Multi-ethnic–full-time 0, part-time 0; students subject to the Americans with Disabilities Act–full-time 1, part-time 0.

Financial Information/Assistance:
Tuition for Full-Time Study: *Master's:* State residents $635 per credit hour.

Financial Assistance:
First Year Students: No information provided.
Advanced Students: No information provided.
Contact Information: Of all students currently enrolled full-time, 8% benefited from one or more of the listed financial assistance programs. For information on financial assistance, contact: Daniel J. Calcagnetti, Graduate Coordinator, Department of Psychology, Fairleigh Dickinson University, 285 Madison Ave, Madison, NJ 07940, robinc@enter.net.

Internships/Practica: Both the Master's in Counseling Psychology and Industrial Psychology have practica in both in-patient, out-patient settings, and job placements.

Housing and Day Care: No on-campus housing and day care facilities are available.

Employment of Department Graduates:
Master's Degree Graduates: Of those who graduated in the academic year 2000–2001, the following categories and numbers represent the post-graduate activities and employment of master's degree graduates: Enrolled in a post-doctoral residency/fellowship (n/a), employed in independent practice (n/a).
Doctoral Degree Graduates: Of those who graduated in the academic year 2000–2001, the following categories and numbers represent the post-graduate activities and employment of doctoral degree graduates: Enrolled in a psychology doctoral program (n/a), enrolled in another graduate/professional program (n/a).

Additional Information:
Orientation, Objectives, and Emphasis of Department: The programs and courses offered by the psychology department are designed to meet the needs of students who wish to prepare for service in various scientific and professional areas of psychology such as research, teaching, and practice in different organizational settings. In addition, programs and courses also may be taken by

those students who wish to develop a background for subsequent work leading to a doctoral degree.

Special Facilities or Resources: The department is able to provide equipment and facilities for research in small group behavior, counseling, and industrial/organizational behavior. Many faculty members are practicing psychologists and provide intern-type experiences for students.

Information for Students With Physical Disabilities: Our building is up-to-code access friendly.

Application Information:

Send to: Office of Admissions, Fairleigh Dickinson University, 285 Madison Ave., Madison, NJ 07940. See the FDU web site to apply,www.fdu.edu. Rolling admission policy. *Fee:* $35.

Fairleigh Dickinson University, Teaneck-Hackensack

School of Psychology
University College: Arts-Sciences-Professional Studies
1000 River Road
Teaneck, NJ 07666
Telephone: (201) 692-2300
Fax: (201) 692-2304
E-mail: *capuano@fdu.edu*
Web: *http://www.fdu.edu*

Department Established:

1960. Director: Christopher A. Capuano, PhD. Number of Faculty: total–full-time 17, part-time 10; women–full-time 8, part-time 5; minority–full-time 1, part-time 1.

Programs and Degrees Offered:

Listed in the following order: Program area, degree type (T if terminal Master's), number awarded 7/00–6/01. Clinical PhD 9, general/theoretical MA (T) 10, school PsyD 7.

APA Accreditation: Clinical PhD: full.

Student Applications/Admissions:

Student Applications

Clinical PhD—Applications 2001–2002, 140. Total applicants accepted 2001–2002, 24. New applicants enrolled 2001–2002, 13. Total enrolled 2001–2002 full-time, 40. Openings 2002–2003, 12. The Median number of years required for completion of a degree are 5. The number of students enrolled full and part-time, who were dismissed or voluntarily withdrew from this program area were 0. *General/theoretical* MA—Applications 2001–2002, 25. Total applicants accepted 2001–2002, 18. New applicants enrolled 2001–2002, 12. Total enrolled 2001–2002 full-time, 12, part-time, 25. Openings 2002–2003, 15. The Median number of years required for completion of a degree are 3. The number of students enrolled full and part-time, who were dismissed or voluntarily withdrew from this program area were 0. *School PsyD*—Applications 2001–2002, 56. Total applicants accepted 2001–2002, 15. New applicants enrolled 2001–2002, 12. Total enrolled 2001–2002 full-time,

23. Openings 2002–2003, 13. The Median number of years required for completion of a degree are 4.

Admissions Requirements:

Scores: Entries appear in this order: required test or GPA, minimum score (if required), median score of students entering in 2001–2002. Master's Programs: GRE-V 500, 560; GRE-Q 500, 580; GRE-V+Q 1000, 1140; GRE-Subject(Psych) 500, 570; overall undergraduate GPA 3.00, 3.20; psychology GPA 3.25, 3.40. Minimum scores/GPAs indicated are preferred, not required. Doctoral Programs: GRE-V 550, 590; GRE-Q 550, 610; GRE-V+Q 1100, 1200; GRE-Subject(Psych) 600, 640; overall undergraduate GPA 3.25, 3.50; last 2 years GPA no minimum stated; psychology GPA 3.50, 3.60; psychology GPA 3.50, 3.90. Minimum scores/GPAs indicated are preferred, not required.

Other Criteria: (importance of criteria rated low, medium, or high): research experience high, work experience medium, extracurricular activity medium, clinically related public service high, letters of recommendation high, interview high, statement of goals and objectives high, work sample high. These criteria are used for admission to PhD and PsyD programs. For PsyD program, research experience would be low and work experience would be medium-high.

Student Characteristics: The following represents characteristics of students in 2001–2002 in all graduate psychology programs in the department: Female–full-time 26, part-time 12; Male–full-time 9, part-time 1; African American/Black–full-time 2, part-time 2; Hispanic/Latino (a)–full-time 4, part-time 2; Asian/Pacific Islander–full-time 2, part-time 0; American Indian/Alaska Native–full-time 0, part-time 0.

Financial Information/Assistance:

Tuition for Full-Time Study: *Master's:* State residents $638 per credit hour; nonstate residents: $638 per credit hour. *Doctoral:* State residents: per academic year $18,956; nonstate residents: per academic year $18,956.

Financial Assistance:

First Year Students: Research assistantships available for first-year. Average amount paid per academic year: $9,478. Average number of hours worked per week: 20.

Advanced Students: Research assistantships available for advanced students. Average amount paid per academic year: $7,478. Average number of hours worked per week: 20.

Contact Information: Of all students currently enrolled full-time, 33% benefited from one or more of the listed financial assistance programs. For information on financial assistance, contact: School of Psychology, Fairleigh Dickinson University, 1000 River Road, Teaneck, NJ 07666.

Internships/Practica: All PhD students are required to complete research and clinical practica during their first three years. Clinical practica may be completed on-campus at the University's Center for Psychological Services. For those doctoral students for whom a professional internship is required prior to graduation, 10 applied in 2000–2001. Of those who applied, 10 were placed in internships listed by the Association of Psychology Postdoctoral and Internship Programs (APPIC); 10 were placed in APA accredited internships.

Housing and Day Care: No on-campus housing and day care facilities are available.

Employment of Department Graduates:

Master's Degree Graduates: Of those who graduated in the academic year 2000–2001, the following categories and numbers represent the post-graduate activities and employment of master's degree graduates: Enrolled in a post-doctoral residency/fellowship (n/a), employed in independent practice (n/a).

Doctoral Degree Graduates: Of those who graduated in the academic year 2000–2001, the following categories and numbers represent the post-graduate activities and employment of doctoral degree graduates: Enrolled in a psychology doctoral program (n/a), enrolled in another graduate/professional program (n/a).

Additional Information:

Orientation, Objectives, and Emphasis of Department: The orientation of the department is essentially based on the scientist-practitioner model. In terms of theoretical orientations, some faculty are dynamicists, some behaviorists, and some humanists, though there is a sense of eclecticism that pervades those who are practitioners. There is a considerable emphasis on empirical research as the preferred basis for developing a theoretical orientation.

Special Facilities or Resources: The department operates the Center for Psychological Services which provides students in the PhD and PsyD programs opportunities in therapy and assessment with adults, children, families, and couples. The department has research laboratories equipped for experiments with humans as well as with small animals. Equipment includes computer facilities, both micro- and mainframe, a four-channel physiograph, electrophysiological stimulating and recording equipment, operant equipment for programming and recording behavior, two- and four-channel tachistoscopes, various other sensory apparatus, standard and computer-based EEG recorders, and equipment and supplies for psychopharmacological studies.

Information for Students With Physical Disabilities: Williams Hall, home of the School of Psychology, is wheel-chair accessible.

Application Information:
Send to: School of Psychology (T-WH1-01), Fairleigh Dickinson University, 1000 River Road, Teaneck, NJ 07666. Students are admitted in the Fall; Spring. Application deadline for Fall: February 1, PhD; March 1, PsyD; March 15, MA-School. Spring admission is only for applicants to the BA/MA and MA programs in general/theoretical psychology. *Fee:* $40. The application fee is waived or deferred for Fairleigh Dickinson graduates. $40 for doctoral programs and $35 for MA programs.

Georgian Court College
Psychology Department/Counseling Psychology
900 Lakewood Avenue
Lakewood, NJ 08701-2697
Telephone: (732) 364-2200, Extension 636
Fax: (732) 376-7301
E-mail: *james@georgian.edu*
Web: *http://www.georgian.edu/psychgy/ps-wwd.htm*

Department Established:
1972. Chairperson: Linda James. Number of Faculty: total–full-time 9, part-time 8; women–full-time 6, part-time 5; minority–full-time 1, part-time 3.

Programs and Degrees Offered:
Listed in the following order: Program area, degree type (T if terminal Master's), number awarded 7/00–6/01. Counseling MA (T) 11, school.

Student Applications/Admissions:

Student Applications

Counseling MA—Applications 2001–2002, 28. Total applicants accepted 2001–2002, 19. New applicants enrolled 2001–2002, 17. Total enrolled 2001–2002 full-time, 21, part-time, 67. Openings 2002–2003, 20. The Median number of years required for completion of a degree are 3. The number of students enrolled full and part-time, who were dismissed or voluntarily withdrew from this program area were 1.

Admissions Requirements:

Scores: Entries appear in this order: required test or GPA, minimum score (if required), median score of students entering in 2001–2002. Master's Programs: GRE-V no minimum stated, 450; GRE-Q no minimum stated, 510; GRE-Analytical no minimum stated, 490; GRE-Subject(Psych) no minimum stated, 500; overall undergraduate GPA 3.00. Doctoral Programs: last 2 years GPA no minimum stated; psychology GPA no minimum stated; psychology GPA no minimum stated.

Other Criteria: (importance of criteria rated low, medium, or high): GRE/MAT scores, research experience medium, work experience medium, extracurricular activity medium, clinically related public service medium, GPA, letters of recommendation high, statement of goals and objectives high.

Student Characteristics: The following represents characteristics of students in 2001–2002 in all graduate psychology programs in the department: Female–full-time 21, part-time 67; Male–full-time 1, part-time 4; African American/Black–full-time 0, part-time 2; Hispanic/Latino (a)–full-time 0, part-time 4; Asian/Pacific Islander–full-time 0, part-time 1; American Indian/Alaska Native–full-time 0, part-time 0; students subject to the Americans with Disabilities Act–full-time 1, part-time 3.

Financial Information/Assistance:
Tuition for Full-Time Study: *Master's:* State residents $406 per credit hour; nonstate residents: $406 per credit hour.

Financial Assistance:

First Year Students: Fellowships and scholarships available for first-year. Average number of hours worked per week: 35. Tuition remission given: full.

Advanced Students: Research assistantships available for advanced students. Average number of hours worked per week: 9. Apply by April 30. Tuition remission given: partial.

Contact Information: Of all students currently enrolled full-time, 8% benefited from one or more of the listed financial assistance programs. For information on financial assistance, contact: Financial Aid Office, extension 258.

Internships/Practica: Practicum experiences take place in college counseling centers, mental health outpatient facilities, inpatient state and private hospitals and schools.

Housing and Day Care: No on-campus housing and day care facilities are available.

Employment of Department Graduates:

Master's Degree Graduates: Of those who graduated in the academic year 2000–2001, the following categories and numbers represent the post-graduate activities and employment of master's degree graduates: Enrolled in a post-doctoral residency/fellowship (n/a), employed in independent practice (n/a).

Doctoral Degree Graduates: Of those who graduated in the academic year 2000–2001, the following categories and numbers represent the post-graduate activities and employment of doctoral degree graduates: Enrolled in a psychology doctoral program (n/a), enrolled in another graduate/professional program (n/a).

Additional Information:

Orientation, Objectives, and Emphasis of Department: Course work for both the Master's and School Psychology Certificate program is designed to provide sound clinical training based in theory. The majority of the faculty is full-time with experience in clinical and school settings. Four full-time faculty and three adjuncts are licensed to practice psychology in NJ and bring a wealth of diverse clinical experience. Four of the full-time faculty and one adjunct are certified school psychologists with many years of experience in the public and parochial schools. Coursework will prepare the students to work in diverse settings, to make assessments of children and adults, to develop clinical skills with strong theoretical underpinnings, to become competent professionals. Practica experiences are provided in a variety of settings in the surrounding community, with supervision provided on-site and within the classroom. School psychology externships meet NJ state requirements. Courses meet in the late afternoon and evening. Students may attend either part-time or full-time. Georgian Court College is a private Catholic college.

Special Facilities or Resources: There are 4 computer labs available on campus and an interactive television lab.

Information for Students With Physical Disabilities: The psychology department is housed in handicapped accessible facilities.

Application Information:
Send to: Department Chair. Students are admitted in the Fall; Spring. Rolling admissions. *Fee:* $40.

Kean University
Department of Psychology
Morris Avenue
Union, NJ 07083
Telephone: (201) 527-2170
Fax: (908) 629-7044
E-mail: *grad-adm@cougar.kean.edu*
Web: *http://www.kean.edu*

Department Established:
1969. Number of Faculty: total–full-time 20, part-time 1; women–full-time 12, part-time 1; minority–full-time 3; faculty subject to the Americans with Disabilities Act 1.

Programs and Degrees Offered:
Listed in the following order: Program area, degree type (T if terminal Master's), number awarded 7/00–6/01. Business & industry counseling MA (T) 1, human behavior & organizationa MA (T) 8, marriage & family therapy, psychological services MA (T) 8, school psychology.

Student Applications/Admissions:

Student Applications

Business & industry counseling MA—Applications 2001–2002, 10. Total applicants accepted 2001–2002, 5. New applicants enrolled 2001–2002, 3. Total enrolled 2001–2002 full-time, 5, part-time, 15. Openings 2002–2003, 5. The number of students enrolled full and part-time, who were dismissed or voluntarily withdrew from this program area were 0. *Human behavior & organizationa MA*—Applications 2001–2002, 26. Total applicants accepted 2001–2002, 20. New applicants enrolled 2001–2002, 19. Total enrolled 2001–2002 full-time, 8, part-time, 44. Openings 2002–2003, 20. The number of students enrolled full and part-time, who were dismissed or voluntarily withdrew from this program area were 0. *Psychological services MA*—Applications 2001–2002, 18. Total applicants accepted 2001–2002, 13. New applicants enrolled 2001–2002, 12. Total enrolled 2001–2002 full-time, 9, part-time, 30. Openings 2002–2003, 15. The number of students enrolled full and part-time, who were dismissed or voluntarily withdrew from this program area were 0.

Admissions Requirements:

Scores: Entries appear in this order: required test or GPA, minimum score (if required), median score of students entering in 2001–2002. Master's Programs: GRE-V no minimum stated, 520; GRE-Q no minimum stated, 540; GRE-V+Q no minimum stated, 1060; GRE-Analytical no minimum stated; GRE-V+Q+Analytical no minimum stated; overall undergraduate GPA 3.0; last 2 years GPA 3.0; psychology GPA 3.0. Doctoral Programs: last 2 years GPA no minimum stated; psychology GPA no minimum stated; psychology GPA no minimum stated.

Other Criteria: (importance of criteria rated low, medium, or high): GRE/MAT scores high, research experience medium, work experience medium, extracurricular activity low, clinically related public service high, GPA high, letters of recommendation high, interview medium, statement of goals and objectives medium.

Student Characteristics: The following represents characteristics of students in 2001–2002 in all graduate psychology programs in the department: Female–full-time 29, part-time 98; Male–full-time 10, part-time 32; African American/Black–full-time 0, part-time 0; Hispanic/Latino (a)–full-time 0, part-time 0; Asian/Pacific Islander–full-time 0, part-time 0; American Indian/Alaska Native–full-time 0, part-time 0.

Financial Information/Assistance:

Tuition for Full-Time Study: *Master's:* State residents per academic year $2,980, $248 per credit hour; nonstate residents: per academic year $3,743, $312 per credit hour.

Financial Assistance:

First Year Students: Teaching assistantships available for first-year. Average amount paid per academic year: $3,060. Average number of hours worked per week: 17. Apply by June 1. Tuition remission given: full.

Advanced Students: Teaching assistantships available for advanced students. Average amount paid per academic year: $3,060. Average number of hours worked per week: 17. Apply by June 1. Tuition remission given: full.

Contact Information: Of all students currently enrolled full-time, 25% benefited from one or more of the listed financial assistance programs. Graduate Assistantships — Full Tuition Remission. 15–20 hours per week at $6.00 per hour. Assistantships available in offices throughout campus. Contact Financial Aid Office.

Internships/Practica: Internships are available for school psychology, marriage and family therapy, and behavioral science students in a variety of settings.

Housing and Day Care: No on-campus housing and day care facilities are available.

Employment of Department Graduates:

Master's Degree Graduates: Of those who graduated in the academic year 2000–2001, the following categories and numbers represent the post-graduate activities and employment of master's degree graduates: Enrolled in a post-doctoral residency/fellowship (n/a), employed in independent practice (n/a).

Doctoral Degree Graduates: Of those who graduated in the academic year 2000–2001, the following categories and numbers represent the post-graduate activities and employment of doctoral degree graduates: Enrolled in a psychology doctoral program (n/a), enrolled in another graduate/professional program (n/a).

Additional Information:

Orientation, Objectives, and Emphasis of Department: Our academic emphasis is eclectic. All classes are small, which facilitates the opportunity for personal growth.

Special Facilities or Resources: Special resources include two complete computer facilities. One is integrated with statistics, tests and measurement, and experimental psychology courses; the other is used in conjunction with professional psychology testing courses and general instruction.

Application Information:

Send to: Office of Graduate Admissions, Joanne Morris, Director, Kean University, Union, NJ 07083. Students are admitted in the Fall, application deadline June 1; Spring, application deadline November 1. For School Psychology, deadline is March 15. No spring admits for all programs except School Psychology. *Fee:* $35. Fee is waived if student holds an MA from Kean and seeks admission to a nondegree program.

Princeton University
Psychology Department
Green Hall
Princeton, NJ 08544-1010
Telephone: (609) 258-5289
Fax: (609) 258-1113
E-mail: *arlener@princeton.edu*
Web: *http://www.princeton.edu/~psych/*

Department Established:

1901. Chairperson: Joan Girgus. Number of Faculty: total–full-time 20, part-time 4; women–full-time 8; minority–full-time 1.

Programs and Degrees Offered:

Listed in the following order: Program area, degree type (T if terminal Master's), number awarded 7/00–6/01. Cognitive PhD 2, neuroscience PhD 3, social/personality PhD 1.

Student Applications/Admissions:

Student Applications

Cognitive PhD—Applications 2001–2002, 26. Total applicants accepted 2001–2002, 6. New applicants enrolled 2001–2002, 4. Total enrolled 2001–2002 full-time, 9. Openings 2002–2003, 2. The Median number of years required for completion of a degree are 5. The number of students enrolled full and part-time, who were dismissed or voluntarily withdrew from this program area were 1. *Neuroscience PhD*—Applications 2001–2002, 81. Total applicants accepted 2001–2002, 6. New applicants enrolled 2001–2002, 13. Total enrolled 2001–2002 full-time, 10. Openings 2002–2003, 3. The Median number of years required for completion of a degree are 5. The number of students enrolled full and part-time, who were dismissed or voluntarily withdrew from this program area were 1. *Social/personality PhD*—Applications 2001–2002, 56. Total applicants accepted 2001–2002, 4. New applicants enrolled 2001–2002, 1. Total enrolled 2001–2002 full-time, 12. Openings 2002–2003, 2. The Median number of years required for completion of a degree are 5. The number of students enrolled full and part-time, who were dismissed or voluntarily withdrew from this program area were 0.

Admissions Requirements:

Scores: Entries appear in this order: required test or GPA, minimum score (if required), median score of students entering in 2001–2002. Doctoral Programs: GRE-V no minimum stated, 612; GRE-Q no minimum stated, 648; GRE-V+Q no minimum stated, 1260; overall undergraduate GPA no minimum stated, 3.66; last 2 years GPA no minimum stated; psychology GPA no minimum stated, 3.78; psychology GPA no minimum stated.

Other Criteria: (importance of criteria rated low, medium, or high): GRE/MAT scores high, research experience high, work experience high, extracurricular activity low, GPA high, letters of recommendation high, interview medium, statement of goals and objectives high.

Student Characteristics: The following represents characteristics of students in 2001–2002 in all graduate psychology programs in the department: Female–full-time 15, part-time 0; Male–full-time 19, part-time 0; African American/Black–full-time 0, part-time 0; Hispanic/Latino (a)–full-time 2, part-time 0; Asian/Pacific Islander–full-time 2, part-time 0; American Indian/Alaska Native–full-time 0, part-time 0; Multi-ethnic–full-time 0, part-time 0; students subject to the Americans with Disabilities Act–full-time 0, part-time 0.

Financial Information/Assistance:

Tuition for Full-Time Study: *Doctoral:* State residents: per academic year $26,530; nonstate residents: per academic year $26,530.

Financial Assistance:

First Year Students: Fellowships and scholarships available for first-year. Tuition remission given: full.

Advanced Students: Teaching assistantships available for advanced students. Average amount paid per academic year: $17,500. Average number of hours worked per week: 18. Tuition remission given: full. Research assistantships available for advanced students. Average amount paid per academic year: $19,000. Average number of hours worked per week: 20. Tuition remission given: full. Fellowships and scholarships available for advanced students. Tuition remission given: full.

Contact Information: Of all students currently enrolled full-time, 100% benefited from one or more of the listed financial assistance programs. For information on financial assistance, contact: Princeton University, The Graduate School, 201 Nassau Hall, Princeton, NJ 08544. Applications for Fellowships and Scholarships vary, as does the amount awarded to each student.

Internships/Practica: No information provided.

Housing and Day Care: On-campus housing and day care facilities are available.

Employment of Department Graduates:

Master's Degree Graduates: Of those who graduated in the academic year 2000–2001, the following categories and numbers represent the post-graduate activities and employment of master's degree graduates: Enrolled in a post-doctoral residency/fellowship (n/a), employed in independent practice (n/a).

Doctoral Degree Graduates: Of those who graduated in the academic year 2000–2001, the following categories and numbers represent the post-graduate activities and employment of doctoral degree graduates: Enrolled in a psychology doctoral program (n/a), enrolled in another graduate/professional program (n/a), enrolled in a post-doctoral residency/fellowship (3), employed in an academic position at a university (1), employed in business or industry (research/consulting) (1).

Additional Information:

Orientation, Objectives, and Emphasis of Department: The program of graduate work in psychology emphasizes preparation for teaching and research in psychology, with specialization in the following broad areas: perception and cognition, reasoning and decision-making, personality and social psychology, behavioral neuroscience and cognitive neuroscience, with developmental emphasis available in each specialization. All students are required to assist in teaching as a significant part of their graduate education as determined by the department (at least three class hours, during their graduate career). The program is designed to prepare students for attaining the degree of doctor of philosophy and a career of productive scholarship in psychology. The department requires that candidates for admission take the Graduate Record Examination (GRE). Instruction is based on the assumption that first-year students have had the equivalent of an undergraduate major in psychology or related fields. Basic undergraduate training in science and mathematics is also considered desirable. A program leading to the degree of doctor of philosophy in psychology and neuroscience is also offered. The program is oriented toward the study of the role of the central nervous system in behavior.

Special Facilities or Resources: Facilities and specialized equipment needed for thorough training in modern psychology are available in the departmental laboratories in John C. Green Hall. Laboratory units are organized around the research programs of the faculty, ranging from animal motivation and conditioning processes to decision-making in human social groups, from neurophysiological mechanisms controlling basic drives to attributional process in judging other individuals, from the sensory and perceptual roots of human cognition to concept formation and problem-solving behavior in the child and adult, from the mathematical and computer techniques employed in research to the mechanisms of attitude formation and change. The Psychology Library is also located in Green Hall. It comprises an extensive collection of more than 21,000 volumes, including about 450 of the principal journals in the various areas of psychology, as well as standard reference works, texts, and monographs. A computer terminal in the Psychology Library provides on-line access to psychological and related bibliographic databases.

Application Information:
Send to: Princeton University, Office of Graduate Admissions, P.O. Box 270, Princeton, NJ 08544-0270. Students are admitted in the Fall, application deadline Jan. 2. Contact the Office of Graduate Admssions for the exact deadline date. *Fee:* $50. $50 before Dec. 1st, and $75 after Dec. 1st until the deadline date.

Rowan University
Department of Psychology
College of Liberal Arts and Sciences
201 Mullica Hill Road
Glassboro, NJ 08028-1701
Telephone: (856) 256-4500 ext 3520
Fax: (856) 256-4892
E-mail: *cahillj@rowan.edu*
Web: *http://www.rowan.edu/mars/depts/psychology/ appliedgd.htm*

Department Established:
1969. Chairperson: Monica Greco. Number of Faculty: total–full-time 19, part-time 15; women–full-time 14, part-time 10; minority–full-time 2, part-time 3.

Programs and Degrees Offered:

Listed in the following order: Program area, degree type (T if terminal Master's), number awarded 7/00–6/01. Mental Health Counseling MA (T) 3.

Student Applications/Admissions:

Student Applications

Mental Health Counseling MA—Applications 2001–2002, 24. Total applicants accepted 2001–2002, 15. New applicants enrolled 2001–2002, 15. Total enrolled 2001–2002 full-time, 15, part-time, 22. Openings 2002–2003, 20. The Median number of years required for completion of a degree are 3. The number of students enrolled full and part-time, who were dismissed or voluntarily withdrew from this program area were 3.

Admissions Requirements:

Scores: Entries appear in this order: required test or GPA, minimum score (if required), median score of students entering in 2001–2002. Master's Programs: GRE-V+Q no minimum stated; overall undergraduate GPA 3.0. Doctoral Programs: last 2 years GPA no minimum stated; psychology GPA no minimum stated; psychology GPA no minimum stated.

Other Criteria: (importance of criteria rated low, medium, or high): GRE/MAT scores low, research experience low, work experience medium, extracurricular activity medium, clinically related public service high, GPA high, letters of recommendation high, interview high, statement of goals and objectives high.

Student Characteristics: The following represents characteristics of students in 2001–2002 in all graduate psychology programs in the department: Female–full-time 10, part-time 20; Male–full-time 2, part-time 5; African American/Black–full-time 0, part-time 1; Hispanic/Latino (a)–full-time 1, part-time 0; Asian/Pacific Islander–full-time 0, part-time 0; American Indian/Alaska Native–full-time 0, part-time 0.

Financial Information/Assistance:

Tuition for Full-Time Study: Master's: State residents per academic year $3,540, $295 per credit hour; nonstate residents: per academic year $5,664, $472 per credit hour.

Financial Assistance:

First Year Students: No information provided.

Advanced Students: No information provided.

Contact Information: Of all students currently enrolled full-time, 5% benefited from one or more of the listed financial assistance programs. For information on financial assistance, contact: 1. Graduate Assistantships: Graduate School (856-256-4250), 2. Loans: Financial Aid Office (856-256-4051).

Internships/Practica: Practica are available in a wide range of mental health settings.

Housing and Day Care: On-campus housing and day care facilities are available.

Employment of Department Graduates:

Master's Degree Graduates: Of those who graduated in the academic year 2000–2001, the following categories and numbers represent the post-graduate activities and employment of master's degree graduates: Enrolled in a post-doctoral residency/fellowship (n/a), employed in independent practice (n/a), employed in a government agency (professional services) (2), employed in a community mental health/counseling center (3).

Doctoral Degree Graduates: Of those who graduated in the academic year 2000–2001, the following categories and numbers represent the post-graduate activities and employment of doctoral degree graduates: Enrolled in a psychology doctoral program (n/a), enrolled in another graduate/professional program (n/a).

Additional Information:

Orientation, Objectives, and Emphasis of Department: This 48 credit Master's program prepares students to become mental health counselors and is designed to meet the coursework and practicum requirements of the National Board of Certified Counselors. Students completing a 12 credit hour post-master's course sequence and additional supervised hours will be eligible to apply for the New Jersey Licensed Professional Counseling Certification. The program uses a competency based approach. Emphasis is placed upon good differential diagnosis, the use of empirically validated treatment approaches, and outcome measures.

Application Information:

Send to: The Graduate School, Rowan University, 201 Mullica Hill Road, Glassboro, NJ, 08028-1701. Students are admitted in the Fall, application deadline March 15. Fee: $50.

Rutgers—The State University of New Jersey (2001 data)

Department of Clinical Psychology
Graduate School of Applied and Professional Psychology, 152 Frelinghuysen Road
Piscataway, NJ 08854-8085
Telephone: (732) 445-2004
Fax: (732) 445-4888
E-mail: zatkow@gsapp.rutgers.edu
Web: http://www.rci.rutgers.edu/~gsapp

Department Established:

1974. Acting Chair: Louis A. Sass. Number of Faculty: total–full-time 11, part-time 2; women–full-time 5, part-time 2; minority–full-time 2.

Programs and Degrees Offered:

Listed in the following order: Program area, degree type (T if terminal Master's), number awarded 7/00–6/01. Clinical PsyD 10.

APA Accreditation: Clinical PsyD: full.

Student Applications/Admissions:

Student Applications

Clinical PsyD—Applications 2001–2002, 288. Total applicants accepted 2001–2002, 25. New applicants enrolled 2001–2002, 20. Total enrolled 2001–2002 full-time, 49, part-time, 47. Openings 2002–2003, 15.

Admissions Requirements:

Scores: Entries appear in this order: required test or GPA, minimum score (if required), median score of students entering in 2001–2002. Doctoral Programs: GRE-Q no minimum stated; GRE-V+Q+Analytical N/A; GRE-Subject(Psych) N/A; overall undergraduate GPA N/A; last 2 years GPA no minimum stated; psychology GPA no minimum stated; psychology GPA no minimum stated.

Other Criteria: (importance of criteria rated low, medium, or high): GRE/MAT scores medium, research experience medium, work experience high, extracurricular activity, clinically related public service high, GPA high, letters of recommendation high, interview high, statement of goals and objectives high, essay high,

Student Characteristics: The following represents characteristics of students in 2001–2002 in all graduate psychology programs in the department: Female–full-time 15, part-time 0; Male–full-time 5, part-time 0; African American/Black–full-time 1, part-time 0; Hispanic/Latino (a)–full-time 2, part-time 0; Asian/Pacific Islander–full-time 1, part-time 0; American Indian/Alaska Native–full-time 1, part-time 0.

Financial Information/Assistance:

Tuition for Full-Time Study: No information provided.

Financial Assistance:

First Year Students: No information provided.
Advanced Students: No information provided.
Contact Information: Of all students currently enrolled full-time, 0% benefited from one or more of the listed financial assistance programs. For information on financial assistance, contact: Department Secretary at 732-445-2004.

Internships/Practica: The PsyD program provides a broadly based practicum program which is structured around the needs and interests of our students. Students can choose placements in hospitals which include a hospice program, neuropsych testing, long and short term inpatient treatment programs for both adolescents and adults. They can choose to be placed in traditional community mental health centers, college counseling centers, specialized schools for children (autism, learning disabled, emotionally disturbed). Students can be placed in public school based mental health clinics, in programs which provide service to homeless people and in programs for battered women and programs for addictive disorders. Our programs are selected for their attention to supervision but also for their balance regarding gender, race and socio-economic levels. For those doctoral students for whom a professional internship is required prior to graduation, 11 applied in 2000–2001. Of those who applied, 11 were placed in internships listed by the Association of Psychology Postdoctoral and Internship Programs (APPIC); 11 were placed in APA accredited internships.

Housing and Day Care: No on-campus housing and day care facilities are available.

Employment of Department Graduates:

Master's Degree Graduates: Of those who graduated in the academic year 2000–2001, the following categories and numbers represent the post-graduate activities and employment of master's degree graduates: Enrolled in a post-doctoral residency/fellowship (n/a), employed in independent practice (n/a).
Doctoral Degree Graduates: Of those who graduated in the academic year 2000–2001, the following categories and numbers represent the post-graduate activities and employment of doctoral degree graduates: Enrolled in a psychology doctoral program (n/a), enrolled in another graduate/professional program (n/a).

Additional Information:

Orientation, Objectives, and Emphasis of Department: The PsyD program emphasizes pragmatic training in problem solving and planned change techniques. Didactic training in basic psychological principles is coupled with practical, graduate instruction in a range of assessment and intervention modes. The level of involvement becomes progressively more intense during the student's course of training. Most courses include (1) a seminar component oriented around case discussions and substantive theoretical issues of clinical import, (2) a practicum component during which students see clients in the intervention mode or problem area under study, and (3) a supervision component by which the student receives guidance from an experienced clinical instructor in a wide range of applied clinical settings. All three components are coordinated around a central conceptual issue, such as a mode of intervention or a clinical problem area. Instruction and supervision are offered by full-time faculty and senior psychologists whose primary professional involvement is in applied clinical settings throughout the state. In addition to required general core courses, students may emphasize training within any of three perspectives: psychodynamic, behavioral, or systems approaches. This last perspective focuses on family, organizational, and community services.

Special Facilities or Resources: The Center for Applied Psychology at GSAPP is the focal point for the field experiences that are critical in the development of professional psychologists. The projects overseen by the Center are cornerstones of training for our students; the GSAPP Pyschological Clinic, the Foster Care Counseling project, the Natural Setting Therapeutic Management program, the Family Business Forum, and our extensive network of practicum placements are all available to our students. Students are placed in community-based organizations where the recipients of the services we provide are often underserved. These placements include community mental health centers, hospitals, special schools, shelters, and other programs. All students are placed in a practicum setting for at least one full day per week during their years at GSAPP. All students see clients through our Clinic and receive one-hour of individual supervision for each hour of therapy. The Clinic is developing specialty sub-clinics which will allow students to gain experience and supervision in specific treatment approaches working with Faculty experts.

Information for Students With Physical Disabilities: Rutgers' services include special assistance in academic advising, scheduling or rescheduling classes in barrier-free buildings, on-campus transportation for students with permanent or temporary mobility disabilities, assistive devices and equipment, learning assistance, and communications with faculty regarding students' general or specific needs. GSAPP has a designated coordinator of services to students with disabilities to assist our students.

Application Information:

Send to: Graduate and Professional Admissions, Rutgers, The State University of New Jersey, 18 Bishop Place, New Brunswick, NJ 08901-8530. Students are admitted in the Fall, application deadline January 5. *Fee:* $50.

Rutgers—The State University of New Jersey, Graduate School of Applied and Professional Psychology

Department of Applied Professional Psychology
152 Frelinghuysen Road, Busch Campus, Psychology
  Building, New Addition
Piscataway, NJ 08854-8085
Telephone: (732) 445-2008 or (732) 445-2000
Fax: (732) 445-4888
E-mail: *kirchner@gsapp.rutgers.edu*
Web: *http://gsappweb.rutgers.edu*

Department Established:

1974. Chairperson: Kenneth Schneider, PhD. Number of Faculty: total–full-time 6, part-time 6; women–full-time 1, part-time 6.

Programs and Degrees Offered:

Listed in the following order: Program area, degree type (T if terminal Master's), number awarded 7/00–6/01. Organizational PsyD 2, school PsyD 7.

APA Accreditation: Clinical PsyD: full. School PsyD: full.

Student Applications/Admissions:

Student Applications

Organizational PsyD—Applications 2001–2002, 31. Total applicants accepted 2001–2002, 10. New applicants enrolled 2001–2002, 6. Total enrolled 2001–2002 full-time, 6. Openings 2002–2003, 7. The Median number of years required for completion of a degree are 5. The number of students enrolled full and part-time, who were dismissed or voluntarily withdrew from this program area were 1. *School PsyD*—Applications 2001–2002, 57. Total applicants accepted 2001–2002, 17. New applicants enrolled 2001–2002, 9. Total enrolled 2001–2002 full-time, 5, part-time, 4. Openings 2002–2003, 12. The Median number of years required for completion of a degree are 5. The number of students enrolled full and part-time, who were dismissed or voluntarily withdrew from this program area were 0.

Admissions Requirements:

Scores: Entries appear in this order: required test or GPA, minimum score (if required), median score of students entering in 2001–2002. Doctoral Programs: GRE-V+Q+Analytical no minimum stated; GRE-Subject(Psych) no minimum stated; overall undergraduate GPA no minimum stated; last 2 years GPA no minimum stated; psychology GPA no minimum stated; psychology GPA no minimum stated.

Other Criteria: (importance of criteria rated low, medium, or high): GRE/MAT scores high, research experience high, work experience high, extracurricular activity medium, clinically related public service high, GPA high, letters of recommendation high, interview high, statement of goals and objectives high. MAT not required for admission into the PsyD programs.

Student Characteristics: The following represents characteristics of students in 2001–2002 in all graduate psychology programs in the department: Female–full-time 74, part-time 4; Male–full-time 19, part-time 2; African American/Black–full-time 9, part-time 0; Hispanic/Latino (a)–full-time 4, part-time 0; Asian/Pacific Is-

lander–full-time 3, part-time 0; American Indian/Alaska Native–full-time 0, part-time 0; Multi-ethnic–full-time 0, part-time 0; students subject to the Americans with Disabilities Act–full-time 0, part-time 0.

Financial Information/Assistance:

Tuition for Full-Time Study: *Doctoral:* State residents: per academic year $4,130, $348 per credit hour; nonstate residents: per academic year $6,053, $502 per credit hour.

Financial Assistance:

First Year Students: Teaching assistantships available for first-year. Average amount paid per academic year: $14,300. Research assistantships available for first-year. Average amount paid per academic year: $14,300. Traineeships available for first-year. Fellowships and scholarships available for first-year. Average amount paid per academic year: $2,000. Tuition remission given: partial.

Advanced Students: Teaching assistantships available for advanced students. Average amount paid per academic year: $14,300. Research assistantships available for advanced students. Average amount paid per academic year: $14,300. Traineeships available for advanced students. Fellowships and scholarships available for advanced students. Average amount paid per academic year: $2,000.

Contact Information: Of all students currently enrolled full-time, 56% benefited from one or more of the listed financial assistance programs. For information on financial assistance, contact: Rutgers University, Financial Aid Office, Recored Hall, College Avenue, Campus, New Brunswick, NJ 08901 (732-932-8811). Please note: Fellowships and Scholarships range from $2,000–$13.000. $13,000 scholarships may include tuition remission.

Internships/Practica: A special component of the student's training is the integration of practica experiences with didactic courses from the second semester of the first year throughout the remaining semesters of training. These experiences begin by introducing the student to the roles and functions of a school psychologist, the functioning of child study teams, and a variety of schooling issues. For three consecutive semesters, students spend a minimum of one day per week in a public school with a doctoral level school psychologist supervisor/mentor. During the fifth and sixth semester, students may elect a different practicum experience from their first based upon their interests. These practica experiences are supervised by on-site doctoral school psychologists and by on-campus faculty. The courses, the practica, and the supervision comprise the planned scaffold for educating the students. In addition, there are numerous opportunities for learning and practice through colloquia, symposia, informal discussions, faculty projects, the psychological clinic, and the Center for Applied Psychology. The total training is based upon the science of psychology and is intensive, rigorous, systematic, developmental, and it is continuously monitored for quality. For those doctoral students for whom a professional internship is required prior to graduation, 5 applied in 2000–2001. Of those who applied, 3 were placed in APA accredited internships.

Housing and Day Care: On-campus housing and day care facilities are available.

Employment of Department Graduates:

Master's Degree Graduates: Of those who graduated in the academic year 2000–2001, the following categories and numbers represent the post-graduate activities and employment of master's degree graduates: Enrolled in a post-doctoral residency/fellowship (n/a), employed in independent practice (n/a).

Doctoral Degree Graduates: Of those who graduated in the academic year 2000–2001, the following categories and numbers represent the post-graduate activities and employment of doctoral degree graduates: Enrolled in a psychology doctoral program (n/a), enrolled in another graduate/professional program (n/a), enrolled in a post-doctoral residency/fellowship (0), employed in independent practice (0), employed in an academic position at a university (0), employed in an academic position at a 2-year/4-year college (0), employed in other positions at a higher education institution (0), employed in a professional position in a school system (7), employed in business or industry (research/consulting) (2), employed in business or industry (management) (0), employed in a government agency (research) (0), employed in a government agency (professional services) (0), employed in a community mental health/counseling center (0), employed in a hospital/medical center (0), still seeking employment (0), other employment position (0).

Additional Information:

Orientation, Objectives, and Emphasis of Department: The department of applied psychology is a multi-dimensional organizational unit dedicated (1) to enhancement of instruction and learning of children, adolescents, and adults in school and related educational settings, and (2) to development of organizations that allow schooling to occur in effective and efficient ways. Three interrelated dimensions serve to structure the department. An applied research dimension signifies the important weight placed on generating new knowledge; an education and training dimension reflects concern for development of high-level practitioners and leaders of school psychology; an organizational and community services dimension is targeted at providing schools and related educational settings with consultation and technical assistance in areas of instruction and learning. A new specialization in organizational psychology is available in the department of applied psychology. A continuum of instruction ranges from observation and assessment through intervention models that include supervised experience as an essential component of didactic instruction. Core faculty are augmented by senior psychologists whose major professional involvement is in the schools or organizational and community settings.

Special Facilities or Resources: All students are placed in a practicum setting for at least one full day per week during their three years at GSAPP. There are two special facilities that are an integrated part of the training program. One is an on-site psychological clinic which serves the university and state communities. Assessment and intervention programs are offered as well as an enrichment program for young gifted children. The other is the Center for Applied Psychology, a division of GSAPP, that develops, implements, and evaluates projects involving faculty, students, and others from the community. Included in these projects are the Eating Disorders Clinic, Foster Care Counseling, a home-based intervention program for developmentally disabled individuals, and a family business consultation program.

Information for Students With Physical Disabilities: All facilities at GSAPP are wheelchair accessible.

Application Information:

Send to: Rutgers University, Graduate Admissions, 18 Bishop Place, New Brunswick, NJ 08901 or request application and catalog on-line at http://www.gradstudy.rutgers.edu. Students are admitted in the Fall, application deadline January 5. *Fee:* $50.

Rutgers—The State University of New Jersey, New Brunswick

Department of Educational Psychology
Graduate School of Education
10 Seminary Place
New Brunswick, NJ 08901-1183
Telephone: (732) 932-7496 x8327
Fax: (732) 932-6829
E-mail: *takash@rci.rutgers.edu*
Web: *http://www.rutgers.edu*

Department Established:

1923. Chairperson: Richard De Lisi. Number of Faculty: total–full-time 16; women–full-time 8; minority–full-time 2.

Programs and Degrees Offered:

Listed in the following order: Program area, degree type (T if terminal Master's), number awarded 7/00–6/01. Counseling EdD 5, counseling 8, educational psychology PhD, educational statisitcs and mea (T) 2, educational statistics and mea EdD 2, learning, cognition, and deve (T) 7, learning, cognition, and deve EdD 1, special education 31, special education EdD 1.

Student Applications/Admissions:

Student Applications

Counseling EdD—Applications 2001–2002, 0. Total enrolled 2001–2002 full-time, 8, part-time, 17. *Educational psychology PhD*—Applications 2001–2002, 25. Total applicants accepted 2001–2002, 15. New applicants enrolled 2001–2002, 12. Total enrolled 2001–2002 full-time, 11, part-time, 17. Openings 2002–2003, 15. *Educational statistics and mea EdD*—Applications 2001–2002, 0. Total enrolled 2001–2002 full-time, 2, part-time, 3. *Learning, cognition, and deve EdD*—Applications 2001–2002, 0. Total enrolled 2001–2002 full-time, 1, part-time, 15. *Special education EdD*—Applications 2001–2002, 0. Total enrolled 2001–2002 part-time, 18. Openings 2002–2003, 5.

Admissions Requirements:

Scores: Entries appear in this order: required test or GPA, minimum score (if required), median score of students entering in 2001–2002. Master's Programs: GRE-V+Q 1000; overall undergraduate GPA 3.00. Doctoral Programs: GRE-V+Q 1100; overall undergraduate GPA 3.00; last 2 years GPA no minimum stated; psychology GPA no minimum stated; psychology GPA 3.50.

Other Criteria: (importance of criteria rated low, medium, or high): GRE/MAT scores high, research experience high, work experience medium, extracurricular activity, GPA high, letters of recommendation high, interview, statement of goals and objectives high.

Student Characteristics: The following represents characteristics of students in 2001–2002 in all graduate psychology programs in the department: Female–full-time 57, part-time 145; Male–full-time 13, part-time 33; African American/Black–full-time 7, part-time 22; Hispanic/Latino (a)–full-time 1, part-time 12; Asian/ Pacific Islander–full-time 10, part-time 12; American Indian/ Alaska Native–full-time 0, part-time 2.

Financial Information/Assistance:

Tuition for Full-Time Study: *Master's:* State residents per academic year $7,472, $308 per credit hour; nonstate residents: per academic year $10,956, $455 per credit hour.

Financial Assistance:

First Year Students: Teaching assistantships available for first-year. Average amount paid per academic year: $14,000. Average number of hours worked per week: 15. Apply by March 1. Tuition remission given: full. Research assistantships available for first-year. Average amount paid per academic year: $14,000. Average number of hours worked per week: 15. Apply by March 1. Tuition remission given: full. Fellowships and scholarships available for first-year. Average number of hours worked per week: 0. Apply by April/Nov 1.

Advanced Students: Teaching assistantships available for advanced students. Average amount paid per academic year: $14,220. Average number of hours worked per week: 15. Apply by March 1. Tuition remission given: full. Research assistantships available for advanced students. Average amount paid per academic year: $14,220. Average number of hours worked per week: 15. Apply by March 1. Tuition remission given: full. Fellowships and scholarships available for advanced students. Apply by April/ Nov 1.

Contact Information: Of all students currently enrolled full-time, 70% benefited from one or more of the listed financial assistance programs. For information on financial assistance, contact: Financial Aid Office.

Internships/Practica: Supervised counseling at the doctoral level provides opportunities for students to engage in actual counseling under close supervision by faculty members. Students complete a minimum of four terms of supervised counseling in the program. First-year experience is typically provided in the department's counseling center. Second year practicum sites are outside the department.

Housing and Day Care: On-campus housing and day care facilities are available.

Employment of Department Graduates:

Master's Degree Graduates: Of those who graduated in the academic year 2000–2001, the following categories and numbers represent the post-graduate activities and employment of master's degree graduates: Enrolled in a post-doctoral residency/fellowship (n/a), employed in independent practice (n/a).

Doctoral Degree Graduates: Of those who graduated in the academic year 2000–2001, the following categories and numbers represent the post-graduate activities and employment of doctoral degree graduates: Enrolled in a psychology doctoral program (n/a), enrolled in another graduate/professional program (n/a).

Additional Information:

Orientation, Objectives, and Emphasis of Department: The Department of Educational Psychology offers graduate Master's in Education (Ed.M.) degree programs of study in (a) counseling psychology, (b) educational statistics and measurement, (c) learning, cognition, & development, and (d) special education. Completion of these master's degree programs can also result in various professional credentials including certification as Teacher of the Handicapped, Learning Disabilities Teacher Consultant, and School Counselor. The Department also offers a certificate program in Interdisciplinary Infant Studies. At the doctorate level, the Department offers a PhD in Educational Psychology that seeks to prepare scholarly researchers in areas that include theory and methods of statistical analysis, evaluation, and measurement as applied to educational issues; and the psychology of human learning, cognition and development in schools, families, and communities. An Ed.D. in Special Education, which prepares individuals seeking professional positions in the field, is also offered. All programs in the Department include research training and pertain to the description, explanation, and optimization of human development in various contexts.

Special Facilities or Resources: We have all the resources normally associated with a major research university.

Information for Students With Physical Disabilities: Appropriate services for students with physical disabilities are available upon recommendation by the unit's disability coordinator.

Application Information:
Send to: Office of Graduate and Professional Admissions, 18 Bishop Place, New Brunswick, NJ 08901-1183. Students are admitted in the Fall, application deadline November 1; Spring, application deadline March 1. Ed.D. admissions is temporarily suspended in Counseling Psychology; March 1 PhD program-Fall admission only. *Fee:* $50.

Seton Hall University
Professional Psychology and Family Therapy
Education and Human Services
400 South Orange Ave
South Orange, NJ 07079
Telephone: (973) 761 9451
Fax: (973) 275 2188
E-mail: *Masseyro@shu.edu*
Web: *http://www.shu.edu*

Department Established:
1965. Chairperson: John Smith. Number of Faculty: total–full-time 12, part-time 12; women–full-time 6, part-time 6; minority–full-time 5.

Programs and Degrees Offered:
Listed in the following order: Program area, degree type (T if terminal Master's), number awarded 7/00–6/01. Counseling MA (T) 30, Counseling Psychology PhD 6, Marriage and Family PhD, Marriage and Family Therapy MA (T) 4, Marriage and Family Therapy EdS 3, Psychological Studies MA (T) 4, School and Community EdS 6.

APA Accreditation: Counseling PhD: full.

Student Applications/Admissions:

Student Applications

Counseling MA—Applications 2001–2002, 20. Total applicants accepted 2001–2002, 18. New applicants enrolled 2001–2002, 18. Total enrolled 2001–2002 part-time, 18. Openings 2002–2003, 25. The Median number of years required for completion of a degree are 2. The number of students enrolled full and part-time, who were dismissed or voluntarily withdrew from this program area were 1. *Counseling Psychology PhD*—Applications 2001–2002, 46. Total applicants accepted 2001–2002, 5. New applicants enrolled 2001–2002, 5. Total enrolled 2001–2002 full-time, 5. Openings 2002–2003, 6. The Median number of years required for completion of a degree are 5. The number of students enrolled full and part-time, who were dismissed or voluntarily withdrew from this program area were 0. *Marriage and Family PhD*—New applicants enrolled 2001–2002, 4. Total enrolled 2001–2002 full-time, 27. Openings 2002–2003, 6. The Median number of years required for completion of a degree are 5. *Marriage and Family Therapy MA*—Applications 2001–2002, 15. Total applicants accepted 2001–2002, 11. New applicants enrolled 2001–2002, 6. Total enrolled 2001–2002 full-time, 5, part-time, 1. Openings 2002–2003, 12. The Median number of years required for completion of a degree are 3. *Marriage and Family Therapy EdS*—Applications 2001–2002, 6. Total applicants accepted 2001–2002, 5. New applicants enrolled 2001–2002, 5. Total enrolled 2001–2002 full-time, 1, part-time, 4. Openings 2002–2003, 6. The Median number of years required for completion of a degree are 3. *Psychological Studies MA*—Applications 2001–2002, 12. Total applicants accepted 2001–2002, 12. New applicants enrolled 2001–2002, 12. Total enrolled 2001–2002 part-time, 12. Openings 2002–2003, 8. The Median number of years required for completion of a degree are 3. *School and Community EdS*—Applications 2001–2002, 12. Total applicants accepted 2001–2002, 8. New applicants enrolled 2001–2002, 6. Total enrolled 2001–2002 full-time, 6. Openings 2002–2003, 12. The Median number of years required for completion of a degree are 4. The number of students enrolled full and part-time, who were dismissed or voluntarily withdrew from this program area were 0.

Admissions Requirements:

Scores: Entries appear in this order: required test or GPA, minimum score (if required), median score of students entering in 2001–2002. Master's Programs: GRE-V+Q+Analytical no minimum stated; overall undergraduate GPA no minimum stated. EdS programs (MAT or GRE), all other programs (GRE) Doctoral Programs: GRE-V+Q+Analytical no minimum stated; overall undergraduate GPA no minimum stated; last 2 years GPA no minimum stated; psychology GPA no minimum stated; psychology GPA no minimum stated.

Other Criteria: (importance of criteria rated low, medium, or high): work experience high, extracurricular activity high, clinically related public service high, GPA high, letters of recommendation high, interview high, statement of goals and objectives high. PhD programs research and clinically oreinted; master's and EdS programs clinically focused.

Student Characteristics: The following represents characteristics of students in 2001–2002 in all graduate psychology programs in the department: Multi-ethnic–full-time 0, part-time 0; students subject to the Americans with Disabilities Act–full-time 0, part-time 0.

Financial Information/Assistance:

Tuition for Full-Time Study: *Master's:* State residents $601 per credit hour; nonstate residents: $601 per credit hour. *Doctoral:* State residents: $601 per credit hour; nonstate residents: $601 per credit hour.

Financial Assistance:

First Year Students: Average amount paid per academic year: $0. Average number of hours worked per week: 0. Research assistantships available for first-year. Average amount paid per academic year: $5,000. Average number of hours worked per week: 20. Apply by early spring. Tuition remission given: full. Average amount paid per academic year: $0. Average number of hours worked per week: 0. Average amount paid per academic year: $0. Average number of hours worked per week: 0.

Advanced Students: Research assistantships available for advanced students. Average amount paid per academic year: $5,000. Average number of hours worked per week: 20. Apply by spring. Tuition remission given: full.

Contact Information: Of all students currently enrolled full-time, 50% benefited from one or more of the listed financial assistance programs. For information on financial assistance, contact: Office of Provost; Graduate Admissions (College of Education and Human Services), Program Directors.

Internships/Practica: The Counseling and Marriage and Family students are placed at off-campus sites under approved supervision. The Marriage and Family students follow the standards of the Commission on Accreditation for Marriage and Family Therapy Education. The doctoral students adhere to Psychology guidelines. For those doctoral students for whom a professional internship is required prior to graduation, 5 applied in 2000–2001. Of those who applied, 4 were placed in internships listed by the Association of Psychology Postdoctoral and Internship Programs (APPIC); 1 were placed in APA accredited internships.

Housing and Day Care: No on-campus housing and day care facilities are available.

Employment of Department Graduates:

Master's Degree Graduates: Of those who graduated in the academic year 2000–2001, the following categories and numbers represent the post-graduate activities and employment of master's degree graduates: Enrolled in a psychology doctoral program (0), enrolled in another graduate/professional program (0), enrolled in a post-doctoral residency/fellowship (n/a), employed in independent practice (n/a), employed in an academic position at a university (0), employed in an academic position at a 2-year/4-year college (0), employed in other positions at a higher education institution (0), employed in a professional position in a school system (0), employed in business or industry (research/consulting) (0), employed in business or industry (management) (0), employed in a government agency (research) (0), employed in a government agency (professional services) (0), employed in a community mental health/counseling center (0), employed in a hospital/medical center (0), still seeking employment (0), other employment position (0).

Doctoral Degree Graduates: Of those who graduated in the academic year 2000–2001, the following categories and numbers

represent the post-graduate activities and employment of doctoral degree graduates: Enrolled in a psychology doctoral program (n/a), enrolled in another graduate/professional program (n/a), enrolled in a post-doctoral residency/fellowship (0), employed in independent practice (0), employed in an academic position at a university (0), employed in an academic position at a 2-year/4-year college (0), employed in other positions at a higher education institution (0), employed in a professional position in a school system (0), employed in business or industry (research/consulting) (0), employed in business or industry (management) (0), employed in a government agency (research) (0), employed in a government agency (professional services) (0), employed in a community mental health/counseling center (0), employed in a hospital/medical center (0), still seeking employment (0), other employment position (0).

Additional Information:

Orientation, Objectives, and Emphasis of Department: The doctoral programs combine research, clinical work under supervision, and classes throughout the courses of study. The Marriage and Family programs are based on a systemic orientation to family psychology and family therapy. The goals of Counseling Psychology encompass knowledge of the science of psychology and counseling psychology as a specialty, integration of research and practice, and commitment to ongoing professional development. Professional counselors are mental health practitioners trained to help individual clients and groups address common developmental challenges and transitions as well as more severe emotional difficulties. School psychology students learn to specialize in assessment and evaluations in schools.

Special Facilities or Resources: The department has individual counseling/assessment rooms, family and couple laboratories, and group therapy rooms, all of which are wired with state-of-the-art audiovisual equipment with centralized viewing in a control room. There are rooms for data analyses.

Application Information:

Send to: Graduate Admissions, College of Education and Human Services, Seton Hall University, South Orange, NJ 07079. Counseling Psychology PhD (Jan. 15), Marriage and Family PhD (Feb. 15), all other programs rolling admissions. *Fee:* $50.

William Paterson University

Psychology/MA in Applied Clinical Psychology
Humanities & Social Sciences
300 Pompton Road
Wayne, NJ 07470
Telephone: (973) 720-2643 (Dir.); (973) 720-3629 (Asst)
Fax: (973) 720-3392
E-mail: *PAKIZEGIB@WPUNJ.EDU*
Web: *http://www.wpunj.edu/cohss/psychology/Masters.htm*

Department Established:

1999. Graduate Director: Behnaz Pakizegi, PhD. Number of Faculty: total–full-time 6, part-time 2; women–full-time 3.

Programs and Degrees Offered:

Listed in the following order: Program area, degree type (T if terminal Master's), number awarded 7/00–6/01. Applied Clinical Psychology MA (T) 7.

Student Applications/Admissions:

Student Applications

Applied Clinical Psychology MA—Applications 2001–2002, 50. Total applicants accepted 2001–2002, 28. New applicants enrolled 2001–2002, 16. Total enrolled 2001–2002 full-time, 14, part-time, 10. Openings 2002–2003, 15. The Median number of years required for completion of a degree are 2. The number of students enrolled full and part-time, who were dismissed or voluntarily withdrew from this program area were 3.

Admissions Requirements:

Scores: Entries appear in this order: required test or GPA, minimum score (if required), median score of students entering in 2001–2002. Master's Programs: GRE-V 425; GRE-Analytical 425; overall undergraduate GPA 3.0. Our requirement is a score of 850 combined in the verbal and analytic sections of the GRE. Doctoral Programs: last 2 years GPA no minimum stated; psychology GPA no minimum stated; psychology GPA no minimum stated.

Other Criteria: (importance of criteria rated low, medium, or high): GRE/MAT scores high, research experience medium, work experience medium, extracurricular activity medium, clinically related public service high, GPA high, letters of recommendation high, interview medium, statement of goals and objectives high, Courses listed below high. Also Required: Undergraduate background including (1)General Psychology, (2)Abnormal Psychology, (3)Statistics or Experimental Design, and (4)Developmental or Child Psychology.

Student Characteristics: The following represents characteristics of students in 2001–2002 in all graduate psychology programs in the department: Female–full-time 10, part-time 8; Male–full-time 3, part-time 3; African American/Black–full-time 0, part-time 0; Hispanic/Latino (a)–full-time 1, part-time 2; Asian/Pacific Islander–full-time 2, part-time 1; American Indian/Alaska Native–full-time 0, part-time 0; Multi-ethnic–full-time 0, part-time 0; students subject to the Americans with Disabilities Act–full-time 0, part-time 0.

Financial Information/Assistance:

Tuition for Full-Time Study: *Master's:* State residents per academic year $9,000, $278 per credit hour; nonstate residents: per academic year $12,000, $394 per credit hour.

Financial Assistance:

First Year Students: Traineeships available for first-year. Average amount paid per academic year: $6,000. Average number of hours worked per week: 20. Apply by 3/1. Tuition remission given: full.

Advanced Students: Traineeships available for advanced students. Average amount paid per academic year: $6,000. Average number of hours worked per week: 20. Apply by 3/1. Tuition remission given: full.

Contact Information: Of all students currently enrolled full-time, 8% benefited from one or more of the listed financial assistance programs. For information on financial assistance, contact: Bursars Office: (973) 720-2235.

Internships/Practica: Our program trains master's level practitioners for work in a wide variety of inpatient and outpatient clinical settings including hospitals, community mental health clinics, group homes, drug treatment facilities, physical rehabilitation centers, correctional facilities, gerontology programs, and, after licensure, private practice. Under supervision, graduates of our program are able to conduct diagnostic and psychological assessments; counsel individuals, groups, and families using appropriate interview and intervention techniques; participate in institutional and organizational research projects involving study design, data collection, and analysis; and work on an elective basis with such populations as children, adolescents, the aged, the severely mentally ill, the neurologically impaired, substance abusers, and others.

Housing and Day Care: On-campus housing and day care facilities are available.

Employment of Department Graduates:

Master's Degree Graduates: Of those who graduated in the academic year 2000–2001, the following categories and numbers represent the post-graduate activities and employment of master's degree graduates: Enrolled in a psychology doctoral program (1), enrolled in another graduate/professional program (0), enrolled in a post-doctoral residency/fellowship (n/a), employed in independent practice (n/a), employed in an academic position at a university (2), employed in an academic position at a 2-year/4-year college (0), employed in other positions at a higher education institution (0), employed in a professional position in a school system (0), employed in business or industry (research/consulting) (1), employed in business or industry (management) (0), employed in a government agency (research) (1), employed in a government agency (professional services) (0), employed in a community mental health/counseling center (2), employed in a hospital/medical center (1), still seeking employment (1), other employment position (1).

Doctoral Degree Graduates: Of those who graduated in the academic year 2000–2001, the following categories and numbers represent the post-graduate activities and employment of doctoral degree graduates: Enrolled in a psychology doctoral program (n/a), enrolled in another graduate/professional program (n/a).

Additional Information:

Orientation, Objectives, and Emphasis of Department: The Master's Program in Applied Clinical Psychology prepares students for psychological counseling, assessment, and mental health research in non-school settings. Graduates meet the academic requirements for eligibility to take the National Counselor Examination, currently required for licensure as a Licensed Professional Counselor in New Jersey and in the majority of the states in the country. Graduates must successfully complete 60 credit hours of coursework and supervised fieldwork. The curriculum emphasizes intervention and consists of required and elective courses in the theoretical, empirical, and ethical foundations of clinical psychology. Supervised fieldwork in clinical settings enables students to apply the theories and empirical findings discussed in the classroom to develop the competency needed for practice with clients. Students may opt to complete this program on either a full-time (two years including summers) or part-time basis (three to five years including summers). Full-time students may not be employed for more than 20 hours per week. As much as possible, courses will be offered in consecutive time slots 2 to 3 days per week, in the late afternoon and evening slots, as well as during the summer.

Special Facilities or Resources: William Paterson University is equipped with several computer and research labs, a large library, and access to several on-line databases. The Psych Dept. and graduate program own a wide array of assessment kits and dozens of relevant videos which are available to faculty and students. The graduate program faculty currently have ongoing research in the areas of body image, traumatic brain injury (TBI), narrative therapy, secondary traumatic stress, wakefulness, and depression. The university is close to urban settings and 30 minutes from NYC.

Information for Students With Physical Disabilities: Buildings are accessible and some resources are available.

Application Information:
Send to: Office of Graduate Studies, Raubinger Hall, Rm. 139, William Paterson University, 300 Pompton Rd., Wayne, NJ 07470. Students are admitted in the Fall, application deadline 3-1/rolling; Winter, application deadline rolling; Spring, application deadline rolling; Summer, application deadline rolling. *Fee:* $35.

New Mexico Highlands University
Division of Psychology
Department of Behavioral Sciences
Hewett Hall
Las Vegas, NM 87701-4073
Telephone: (505) 454-3343
Fax: (505) 454-3331
E-mail: *carltoncann@nmhu.edu*
Web: *http://www.nmhu.edu/departments/behavsci/psycholog*

Department Established:
1946. Chairperson: Carlton H. Cann. Number of Faculty: total–full-time 6, part-time 2; women–full-time 4, part-time 1.

Programs and Degrees Offered:
Listed in the following order: Program area, degree type (T if terminal Master's), number awarded 7/00–6/01. General/clinical/counseling MA (T) 2.

Student Applications/Admissions:
Student Applications
General/clinical/counseling MA—Applications 2001–2002, 16. Total applicants accepted 2001–2002, 14. New applicants enrolled 2001–2002, 8. Total enrolled 2001–2002 full-time, 16, part-time, 6. Openings 2002–2003, 15. The number of students enrolled full and part-time, who were dismissed or voluntarily withdrew from this program area were 2.

Admissions Requirements:
Scores: Entries appear in this order: required test or GPA, minimum score (if required), median score of students entering in 2001–2002. Master's Programs: psychology GPA 3.00, 3.45. Doctoral Programs: last 2 years GPA no minimum stated; psychology GPA no minimum stated; psychology GPA no minimum stated.
Other Criteria: (importance of criteria rated low, medium, or high): GRE/MAT scores, research experience medium, work experience medium, extracurricular activity low, clinically related public service medium, GPA, letters of recommendation medium, statement of goals and objectives high.

Student Characteristics: The following represents characteristics of students in 2001–2002 in all graduate psychology programs in the department: Female–full-time 11, part-time 5; Male–full-time 5, part-time 1; African American/Black–full-time 1, part-time 0; Hispanic/Latino (a)–full-time 2, part-time 1; Asian/Pacific Islander–full-time 1, part-time 0; American Indian/Alaska Native–full-time 0, part-time 0.

Financial Information/Assistance:
Tuition for Full-Time Study: *Master's:* State residents per academic year $2,238, $93 per credit hour; nonstate residents: per academic year $8,776.

Financial Assistance:
First Year Students: Teaching assistantships available for first-year. Average amount paid per academic year: $6,500. Average number of hours worked per week: 20. Tuition remission given: full and partial. Research assistantships available for first-year. Average amount paid per academic year: $6,500. Average number of hours worked per week: 20. Tuition remission given: full and partial. Fellowships and scholarships available for first-year. Average amount paid per academic year: $6,500. Average number of hours worked per week: 20. Tuition remission given: full and partial.

Advanced Students: Teaching assistantships available for advanced students. Average amount paid per academic year: $6,500. Average number of hours worked per week: 20. Tuition remission given: full and partial. Research assistantships available for advanced students. Average amount paid per academic year: $6,500. Average number of hours worked per week: 20. Tuition remission given: full and partial. Fellowships and scholarships available for advanced students. Average amount paid per academic year: $6,500. Average number of hours worked per week: 20. Tuition remission given: full and partial.

Contact Information: Of all students currently enrolled full-time, 100% benefited from one or more of the listed financial assistance programs. For information on financial assistance, contact: Office of Financial Assistance, 800-379-4038.

Internships/Practica: Students in the Clinical Psychology/Counseling track must complete 12 credit hours of Field Experience. Completion of the 12 credits hours ensures that each student in this track gains 720 hours of direct clinical experience while completing the program. Field Experience placements are arranged through cooperative planning by the student, the program, and the agency. Students from our program have been placed with the following agencies: the forensic, adolescent, and adult units of the state psychiatric hospital; the local community mental health center; the state juvenile correctional facility; local schools; an equine therapy program; and many others.

Housing and Day Care: On-campus housing and day care facilities are available.

Employment of Department Graduates:
Master's Degree Graduates: Of those who graduated in the academic year 2000–2001, the following categories and numbers represent the post-graduate activities and employment of master's degree graduates: Enrolled in a post-doctoral residency/fellowship (n/a), employed in independent practice (n/a).
Doctoral Degree Graduates: Of those who graduated in the academic year 2000–2001, the following categories and numbers represent the post-graduate activities and employment of doctoral degree graduates: Enrolled in a psychology doctoral program (n/a), enrolled in another graduate/professional program (n/a).

Additional Information:
Orientation, Objectives, and Emphasis of Department: The department offers two tracks that lead to a Master of Science degree in psychology. The General Psychology track requires 36 credit hours and is intended to provide a background similar to that given in many PhD programs. This track is organized around a general core of courses designed to educate the student in all areas of psychology with the opportunity to further pursue an area

of interest such as physiological experimental, neuropsychological, or social psychology. This track is especially useful for those students whose goals include either entering a doctoral program or working in a non-clinical position (research, etc.) upon completing the master's degree. The Clinical Psychology/Counseling track is a 63-credit hour emphasis area that is unique because it is one of the only programs in the U.S. that provides comprehensive training in psychological training and assessment in four areas: neuropsychological, behavioral, intelligence, and personality. This track is designed to prepare students to continue their education at the doctoral level or to work as a master's level clinician. The student successfully completing this track will qualify for licensure as a master's level clinician in approximately 40 states.

Special Facilities or Resources: The department offers excellent animal laboratory facilities for experimental-physiological research, as well as laboratories for human subjects research. In addition, the department has an extensive computer laboratory. We also have a close relationship with the state psychiatric hospital, which is located in the community.

Application Information:
Send to: Psychology Program Coordinator. Students are admitted in the Fall, application deadline June 1. Earlier applications receive preferential treatment for financial aid. *Fee:* $15.

New Mexico State University (2001 data)
Counseling and Educational Psychology
College of Education
Box 30001 Department 3 CEP
Las Cruces, NM 88003-8001
Telephone: (505) 646-2121
Fax: (505) 646-8035
E-mail: *lramirez@nmsu.edu*
Web: *http://education.nmsu.edu (pick CEP icon)*

Department Established:
1905. Dept Head: Michael Waldo. Number of Faculty: total–full-time 8, part-time 1; women–full-time 2, part-time 1; minority–full-time 2.

Programs and Degrees Offered:
Listed in the following order: Program area, degree type (T if terminal Master's), number awarded 7/00–6/01. Counseling and Guidance MA (T) 21, Counseling Psychology PhD 7, School Psychology EdS.

APA Accreditation: Counseling PhD: full.

Student Applications/Admissions:
Student Applications
Counseling and Guidance MA—Applications 2001–2002, 22. Total applicants accepted 2001–2002, 12. New applicants enrolled 2001–2002, 12. Total enrolled 2001–2002 full-time, 9,

part-time, 1. Openings 2002–2003, 12. *Counseling Psychology PhD*—Applications 2001–2002, 27. Total applicants accepted 2001–2002, 5. New applicants enrolled 2001–2002, 6. Total enrolled 2001–2002 full-time, 5. Openings 2002–2003, 6. *School Psychology EdS*—Applications 2001–2002, 3. Total applicants accepted 2001–2002, 3. New applicants enrolled 2001–2002, 6. Total enrolled 2001–2002 full-time, 2, part-time, 1. Openings 2002–2003, 3.

Admissions Requirements:
Scores: Entries appear in this order: required test or GPA, minimum score (if required), median score of students entering in 2001–2002. Master's Programs: GRE-V no minimum stated, 410; GRE-Q no minimum stated, 490; overall undergraduate GPA no minimum stated, 3.43; last 2 years GPA no minimum stated. Doctoral Programs: GRE-V no minimum stated, 440; GRE-Q no minimum stated, 450; psychology GPA no minimum stated, 3.87.
Other Criteria: (importance of criteria rated low, medium, or high): GRE/MAT scores medium, research experience high, work experience medium, extracurricular activity medium, clinically related public service medium, GPA high, letters of recommendation high, interview high, statement of goals and objectives high. Criteria do vary for different programs. A student's file is sent to the department when the Graduate School receives an application, all required transcripts, $15 fee, and a GPA of at least a 2.5 for Master' and a 3.0 for Doctorate. We do NOT require anything else.

Student Characteristics: The following represents characteristics of students in 2001–2002 in all graduate psychology programs in the department: Female–full-time 11, part-time 6; Male–full-time 7, part-time 0; African American/Black–full-time 0, part-time 0; Hispanic/Latino (a)–full-time 6, part-time 1; Asian/Pacific Islander–full-time 0, part-time 0; American Indian/Alaska Native–full-time 1, part-time 0.

Financial Information/Assistance:
Tuition for Full-Time Study: No information provided.

Financial Assistance:
First Year Students: No information provided.
Advanced Students: No information provided.
Contact Information: For information on financial assistance, contact: Financial Aid Office, MSC 5100, P.O. Box 30001, New Mexico State University, Las Cruces, NM 88003, email: finaid@nmsu.edu.

Internships/Practica: Placements available for doctoral students include the NMSU Counseling Center, the Las Cruces Public Schools, and Community Mental Health Centers. Placements available for master's students include schools, hospitals, adolescent residential centers, the Department of Vocational Rehabilitation, military bases, and nursing homes.

Housing and Day Care: No on-campus housing and day care facilities are available.

Employment of Department Graduates:
Master's Degree Graduates: Of those who graduated in the academic year 2000–2001, the following categories and numbers represent the post-graduate activities and employment of master's

degree graduates: Enrolled in a post-doctoral residency/fellowship (n/a), employed in independent practice (n/a).

Doctoral Degree Graduates: Of those who graduated in the academic year 2000–2001, the following categories and numbers represent the post-graduate activities and employment of doctoral degree graduates: Enrolled in a psychology doctoral program (n/a), enrolled in another graduate/professional program (n/a).

Additional Information:

Orientation, Objectives, and Emphasis of Department: The major thrust of the department is the preparation of professionals for licensure and positions in mental health and school counseling; school psychology, counseling psychology, and related areas. Three graduate degrees are available: (1) Master of Arts, (2) Specialist in Education, and (3) Doctor of Philosophy. The Master of Arts in Counseling and Guidance prepares professional counselors to offer individual, family, and group counseling in schools, agencies, hospitals, and private practice. The curriculum covers human development; appraisal; diagnosis; treatment planning; individual, professional issues. The School Psychology Program (EdS) prepares professionals for positions in public schools and other organizations which require advanced assessment, counseling, consultation, and supervision skills. A major research project (thesis) is a degree requirement. The PhD in Counseling Psychology, which is accredited by the American Psychological Association, is based on the scientist-practitioner model through which both research and service delivery skills are acquired. Graduates of the program are prepared to conduct research, provide service, teach, and supervise. Emphases in the Counseling Psychology program include cultural diversity, group and family counseling, and counselor training, supervision and consultation.

Special Facilities or Resources: The Counseling and School Psychology Training and Research Clinic is a training/service facility sponsored by the Department of Counseling and Educational Psychology which provides excellent opportunities for supervised counseling and supervision-of-supervision. Eleven rooms (one of which is a play therapy room) are available. Three of the rooms are set up for videotaping. A portable video camera is available for use in other rooms. Three of the rooms have one-way mirrors, telephones, and microphone-speakers for live supervision of counseling and live supervision of supervision. A fourth room is connected to seminar room 208 via a closed circuit camera and a telephone for supervision. Three other rooms have one-way mirrors and microphone-speakers for observation. Seminar room 208 has a one-way mirror which can be used to observe various group processes. The facility has a "state-of-the-art" bug in the ear system which helps facilitate live supervision for immediate feedback to the counselor in training.

Application Information:
Send to: NMSU, The Graduate School, PO Box 30001, Dept. 3G, Las Cruces, NM 88003-0001; Dept. of Coun. & Ed. Psy., MSC 3 CEP, NMSU, P.O. Box 30001, Las Cruces, NM 88003. Students are admitted in the Fall; Summer, application deadline January 7. The MA Program deadline is April 1.The Graduate School does NOT have any deadlines. Students must check with the department for their deadlines, if any. We accept applications year round. *Fee:* $15.

New Mexico State University
Department of Psychology
Department 3452, P.O. Box 30001
Las Cruces, NM 88003
Telephone: (505) 646-2502
Fax: (505) 646-6212
E-mail: *kenp@nmsu.edu*
Web: *http://www.psych.nmsu.edu*

Department Established:
1950. Head: Douglas J. Gillan. Number of Faculty: total–full-time 14, part-time 2; women–full-time 6, part-time 1; minority–full-time 1.

Programs and Degrees Offered:
Listed in the following order: Program area, degree type (T if terminal Master's), number awarded 7/00–6/01. Cognitive PhD, cognitive MA (T) 2, engineering MA (T) 3, Engineering PhD, experimental-general MA (T), social MA (T), social PhD.

Student Applications/Admissions:
Student Applications

Cognitive PhD—Applications 2001–2002, 3. Total applicants accepted 2001–2002, 1. New applicants enrolled 2001–2002, 1. Total enrolled 2001–2002 full-time, 6, part-time, 4. Openings 2002–2003, 2. *Cognitive MA*—Applications 2001–2002, 5. Total applicants accepted 2001–2002, 2. Total enrolled 2001–2002 full-time, 5. Openings 2002–2003, 3. The Median number of years required for completion of a degree are 3. *Engineering MA*—Applications 2001–2002, 13. Total applicants accepted 2001–2002, 11. New applicants enrolled 2001–2002, 6. Total enrolled 2001–2002 full-time, 19, part-time, 8. Openings 2002–2003, 4. *Engineering PhD*—Applications 2001–2002, 2. Total enrolled 2001–2002 full-time, 2, part-time, 1. Openings 2002–2003, 2. The number of students enrolled full and part-time, who were dismissed or voluntarily withdrew from this program area were 0. *Experimental-general MA*—Applications 2001–2002, 3. Total applicants accepted 2001–2002, 1. New applicants enrolled 2001–2002, 1. Total enrolled 2001–2002 full-time, 2. Openings 2002–2003, 1. The number of students enrolled full and part-time, who were dismissed or voluntarily withdrew from this program area were 0. *Social MA*—Applications 2001–2002, 8. Total applicants accepted 2001–2002, 4. New applicants enrolled 2001–2002, 2. Total enrolled 2001–2002 full-time, 4, part-time, 1. Openings 2002–2003, 3. The number of students enrolled full and part-time, who were dismissed or voluntarily withdrew from this program area were 0. *Social PhD*—Applications 2001–2002, 3. Total applicants accepted 2001–2002, 1. Total enrolled 2001–2002 full-time, 4, part-time, 1. Openings 2002–2003, 2. The number of students enrolled full and part-time, who were dismissed or voluntarily withdrew from this program area were 0.

Admissions Requirements:
Scores: Entries appear in this order: required test or GPA, minimum score (if required), median score of students entering in 2001–2002. Master's Programs: GRE-V no minimum stated, 520; GRE-Q no minimum stated, 610; GRE-Analytical no minimum stated, 567; overall undergraduate GPA no mini-

mum stated, 3.66. Doctoral Programs: GRE-V no minimum stated, 580; GRE-Q no minimum stated, 610; GRE-Analytical no minimum stated, 600; overall undergraduate GPA no minimum stated, 3.70; last 2 years GPA no minimum stated; psychology GPA no minimum stated; psychology GPA no minimum stated, 3.90.

Other Criteria: (importance of criteria rated low, medium, or high): GRE/MAT scores high, research experience medium, work experience low, GPA high, letters of recommendation high, statement of goals and objectives medium.

Student Characteristics: The following represents characteristics of students in 2001–2002 in all graduate psychology programs in the department: Female–full-time 25, part-time 3; Male–full-time 16, part-time 5; African American/Black–full-time 3, part-time 0; Hispanic/Latino (a)–full-time 4, part-time 0; Asian/Pacific Islander–full-time 0, part-time 0; American Indian/Alaska Native–full-time 1, part-time 0; Multi-ethnic–full-time 0, part-time 0; students subject to the Americans with Disabilities Act–full-time 0, part-time 0.

Financial Information/Assistance:

Tuition for Full-Time Study: *Master's:* State residents per academic year $1,210, $135 per credit hour; nonstate residents: per academic year $3,854, $428 per credit hour. *Doctoral:* State residents: per academic year $1,210, $135 per credit hour; nonstate residents: per academic year $3,854, $428 per credit hour.

Financial Assistance:

First Year Students: Teaching assistantships available for first-year. Average amount paid per academic year: $12,200. Average number of hours worked per week: 20. Apply by 2/15. Tuition remission given: partial. Research assistantships available for first-year. Average amount paid per academic year: $12,200. Average number of hours worked per week: 20. Apply by 2/15. Tuition remission given: partial.

Advanced Students: Teaching assistantships available for advanced students. Average amount paid per academic year: $12,600. Average number of hours worked per week: 20. Apply by 2/15. Tuition remission given: partial. Research assistantships available for advanced students. Average amount paid per academic year: $12,600. Average number of hours worked per week: 20. Apply by 2/15. Tuition remission given: partial.

Contact Information: Of all students currently enrolled full-time, 100% benefited from one or more of the listed financial assistance programs. For student loans contact the Financial Aid Office (505) 646-4105, finaid@nmsu.edu.

Internships/Practica: For the PhD degree in Engineering Psychology, students must complete an internship in an industrial, government, or other laboratory setting of at least three months in duration. Many master's students in Engineering Psychology and Cognitive Psychology spend a summer or half-year as an intern in industry, but it is not required for the MA degree.

Housing and Day Care: On-campus housing and day care facilities are available.

Employment of Department Graduates:

Master's Degree Graduates: Of those who graduated in the academic year 2000–2001, the following categories and numbers represent the post-graduate activities and employment of master's

degree graduates: Enrolled in a post-doctoral residency/fellowship (n/a), employed in independent practice (n/a).

Doctoral Degree Graduates: Of those who graduated in the academic year 2000–2001, the following categories and numbers represent the post-graduate activities and employment of doctoral degree graduates: Enrolled in a psychology doctoral program (n/a), enrolled in another graduate/professional program (n/a).

Additional Information:

Orientation, Objectives, and Emphasis of Department: The department offers an MA degree in general experimental psychology that allows an emphasis in cognitive, engineering, or social psychology. The PhD is offered in the major areas of cognitive, engineering, and social psychology. Within these areas there is special emphasis on language processing, human-computer interaction, and cross-cultural psychology, respectively. Students must earn an MA degree before being admitted to the doctoral program. All programs are experimentally oriented and have the distinctive characteristic of pursuing and extending basic research questions in applied settings.

Special Facilities or Resources: All faculty members have specialized laboratories with a wide variety of computer hardware and software. These include the CERTT lab that is used to conduct research on team cognition in complex task environments, a biopsychology lab equipped to measure ERPs, and a developmental laboratory equipped with sophisticated equipment for recording, analyzing, and editing mother-infant interactions, etc. Many members of the department have joint appointments in the Computing Research Laboratory, a nonacademic research center that specializes in computational linguistics, machine translation, and intelligent tutoring.

Information for Students With Physical Disabilities: Faculty of the Psychology and Computer Science Department hold NSF grants for research on assistive technologies. Current projects focus particularly on the design of computer interfaces for the visually impaired.

Application Information:

Send to: Chair of Graduate Committee. Students are admitted in the Fall, application deadline February 15; Spring, application deadline November 1. *Fee:* $15.

New Mexico, The University of
Department of Psychology
Arts and Science
Logan Hall
Albuquerque, NM 87131-1161
Telephone: (505) 277-5009
Fax: (505) 277-1394
E-mail: *psych@unm.edu*
Web: *http://psych.unm.edu*

V: 560
Q: 650
A: 670
psych: 630

Department Established:

1960. Chairperson: Michael J. Dougher. Number of Faculty: total–full-time 34, part-time 5; women–full-time 15, part-time 2; minority–full-time 10.

Programs and Degrees Offered:

Listed in the following order: Program area, degree type (T if terminal Master's), number awarded 7/00–6/01. Behavioral neuroscience PhD, clinical PhD 9, cognitive/learning PhD 2, developmental PhD, Evolutionary PhD, quantitative/methodology PhD, Social PhD.

APA Accreditation: Clinical PhD: full.

Student Applications/Admissions:

Student Applications

Behavioral neuroscience PhD—Applications 2001–2002, 11. Total applicants accepted 2001–2002, 2. New applicants enrolled 2001–2002, 2. Total enrolled 2001–2002 full-time, 14. Openings 2002–2003, 1. The Median number of years required for completion of a degree are 5. *Clinical PhD*—Applications 2001–2002, 81. Total applicants accepted 2001–2002, 3. New applicants enrolled 2001–2002, 3. Total enrolled 2001–2002 full-time, 42. Openings 2002–2003, 10. The Median number of years required for completion of a degree are 6. The number of students enrolled full and part-time, who were dismissed or voluntarily withdrew from this program area were 2. *Cognitive/learning PhD*—Applications 2001–2002, 4. Total applicants accepted 2001–2002, 3. New applicants enrolled 2001–2002, 1. Total enrolled 2001–2002 full-time, 15. Openings 2002–2003, 6. The Median number of years required for completion of a degree are 5. The number of students enrolled full and part-time, who were dismissed or voluntarily withdrew from this program area were 1. *Developmental PhD*—Applications 2001–2002, 0. Total enrolled 2001–2002 full-time, 1. Openings 2002–2003, 4. The Median number of years required for completion of a degree are 5. *Evolutionary PhD*—Applications 2001–2002, 18. Total enrolled 2001–2002 full-time, 4. Openings 2002–2003, 4. The Median number of years required for completion of a degree are 5. The number of students enrolled full and part-time, who were dismissed or voluntarily withdrew from this program area were 0. *Quantitative/methodology PhD*—Applications 2001–2002, 1. Total enrolled 2001–2002 full-time, 3. Openings 2002–2003, 1. The Median number of years required for completion of a degree are n/a. The number of students enrolled full and part-time, who were dismissed or voluntarily withdrew from this program area were 0. *Social PhD*—Applications 2001–2002, 2. Total enrolled 2001–2002 full-time, 1. Openings 2002–2003, 1. The Median number of years required for completion of a degree are 5. The number of students enrolled full and part-time, who were dismissed or voluntarily withdrew from this program area were 0.

Admissions Requirements:

Scores: Entries appear in this order: required test or GPA, minimum score (if required), median score of students entering in 2001–2002. Doctoral Programs: GRE-V no minimum stated, 560; GRE-Q no minimum stated, 650; GRE-Analytical no minimum stated, 670; GRE-Subject(Psych) no minimum stated, 630; last 2 years GPA no minimum stated; psychology GPA no minimum stated; psychology GPA no minimum stated.

Other Criteria: (importance of criteria rated low, medium, or high): GRE/MAT scores high, research experience high, work experience medium, extracurricular activity medium, clinically related public service medium, GPA medium, letters of recommendation high, interview medium, statement of goals and objectives high, special skills, medium. The importance for the interview and special skills varies.

Student Characteristics: The following represents characteristics of students in 2001–2002 in all graduate psychology programs in the department: Female–full-time 50, part-time 0; Male–full-time 36, part-time 0; African American/Black–full-time 1, part-time 0; Hispanic/Latino (a)–full-time 6, part-time 0; Asian/Pacific Islander–full-time 1, part-time 0; American Indian/Alaska Native–full-time 0, part-time 0; Multi-ethnic–full-time 1.

Financial Information/Assistance:

Tuition for Full-Time Study: *Master's:* State residents per academic year $3,280; nonstate residents: per academic year $11,736, *Doctoral:* State residents: per academic year $3,280; nonstate residents: per academic year $11,736.

Financial Assistance:

First Year Students: Teaching assistantships available for first-year. Average number of hours worked per week: 20. Apply by January 15. Tuition remission given: full. Research assistantships available for first-year. Average number of hours worked per week: 20. Apply by January 15. Tuition remission given: full.

Advanced Students: Teaching assistantships available for advanced students. Average number of hours worked per week: 20. Apply by January 15. Tuition remission given: full. Research assistantships available for advanced students. Average number of hours worked per week: 20. Apply by January 15. Tuition remission given: full.

Contact Information: Of all students currently enrolled full-time, 0% benefited from one or more of the listed financial assistance programs. For information on financial assistance, contact: The University of New Mexico, The Office of Graduate Studies, Albuquerque, NM 87131.

Internships/Practica: For those doctoral students for whom a professional internship is required prior to graduation, 8 applied in 2000–2001. Of those who applied, 7 were placed in internships listed by the Association of Psychology Postdoctoral and Internship Programs (APPIC); 7 were placed in APA accredited internships.

Housing and Day Care: On-campus housing and day care facilities are available.

Employment of Department Graduates:

Master's Degree Graduates: Of those who graduated in the academic year 2000–2001, the following categories and numbers represent the post-graduate activities and employment of master's degree graduates: Enrolled in a post-doctoral residency/fellowship (n/a), employed in independent practice (n/a).

Doctoral Degree Graduates: Of those who graduated in the academic year 2000–2001, the following categories and numbers represent the post-graduate activities and employment of doctoral degree graduates: Enrolled in a psychology doctoral program (n/a), enrolled in another graduate/professional program (n/a).

Additional Information:

Orientation, Objectives, and Emphasis of Department: Founded in 1960, the doctoral training program in psychology is based on the premise that psychology, in all of its areas, is fundamentally an experimental discipline. For all students, the PhD degree is awarded in general experimental psychology and students acquire a solid foundation in both scientific methodology and general psychology. Within this framework, students specialize in any of several competency areas. The well-trained psychologist, within this perspective, is one who combines competence in the general discipline of psychology with excellence in his or her chosen specialization.

Special Facilities or Resources: The department is housed in a building on the central campus. In addition to faculty and administrative offices and seminar rooms, the building is equipped for sophisticated research. There are soundproof chambers for conducting experiments, a variety of timing devices, computer terminals, and electromechanical measuring equipment. Laboratory facilities exist for research in human memory, learning, cognitive psychology, perception, information processing, attention, decision making, developmental, social, personality, neuropsychology, psychophysiology, and clinical psychology. The building also has a large animal research facility with primates and rodents. The campus animal research facility is equipped for surgery and for delicate measurements of brain activities as well as for tests of physical, cognitive, and emotional responses. Microcomputers are widely used in individual faculty laboratories and in a graduate student computer room. The Department of Psychology Clinic opened in 1982 and offers diagnostic and therapeutic services to the Albuquerque community while providing an excellent training facility for clinical students.

Application Information:
Send to: The University of New Mexico, Office of Graduate Studies, 107 Humanities Building, Albuquerque, NM 87131. Students are admitted in the Fall, application deadline January 15. Although the deadline for full financial consideration is January 15, we will continue to review applications until May 1st. *Fee:* $40.

NEW YORK

Adelphi University

The Derner Institute of Advanced Psychological Studies,
  School of Professional Psychology
Adelphi University
Garden City, NY 11530
Telephone: (516) 877-4800
Fax: (516) 877-4805
E-mail: *primaver@adelphi.edu*
Web: *http://www.adelphi.edu*

Department Established:
1960. Dean: Louis Primavera. Number of Faculty: total–full-time 22, part-time 25; women–full-time 9, part-time 17; minority–full-time 2, part-time 4.

Programs and Degrees Offered:
Listed in the following order: Program area, degree type (T if terminal Master's), number awarded 7/00–6/01. Clinical PhD 21, general psychology MA (T) 49, psychoanalysis 15, Respecialization Diploma 1.

APA Accreditation: Clinical PhD: full.

Student Applications/Admissions:
Student Applications

Clinical PhD—Applications 2001–2002, 200. Total applicants accepted 2001–2002, 25. New applicants enrolled 2001–2002, 23. Total enrolled 2001–2002 full-time, 130. Openings 2002–2003, 22. The Median number of years required for completion of a degree are 6. The number of students enrolled full and part-time, who were dismissed or voluntarily withdrew from this program area were 3. *General psychology* MA—Applications 2001–2002, 60. Total applicants accepted 2001–2002, 48. New applicants enrolled 2001–2002, 42. Total enrolled 2001–2002 part-time, 96. Openings 2002–2003, 45. The Median number of years required for completion of a degree are 3. The number of students enrolled full and part-time, who were dismissed or voluntarily withdrew from this program area were 8. *Respecialization Diploma*—Applications 2001–2002, 1. Total enrolled 2001–2002 full-time, 1. Openings 2002–2003, 1. The Median number of years required for completion of a degree are 3. The number of students enrolled full and part-time, who were dismissed or voluntarily withdrew from this program area were 0.

Admissions Requirements:
Scores: Entries appear in this order: required test or GPA, minimum score (if required), median score of students entering in 2001–2002. Master's Programs: overall undergraduate GPA 2.00, 2.90; last 2 years GPA no minimum stated, 3.00; psychology GPA no minimum stated, 3.10. Doctoral Programs: GRE-V 550, 610; GRE-Q 550, 620; GRE-V+Q no minimum stated; GRE-Subject(Psych) 550, 625; overall undergraduate GPA 3.00, 3.40; last 2 years GPA 3.00, 3.50; psychology GPA 3.00, 3.50; psychology GPA no minimum stated. We consider all applications, and will admit students below 550 GRE's if there

are compensatory situations. But, applicants with scores below the listed minima are infrequently accepted.
Other Criteria: (importance of criteria rated low, medium, or high): research experience high, work experience high, extracurricular activity low, clinically related public service high, letters of recommendation high, interview high, statement of goals and objectives high.

Student Characteristics: The following represents characteristics of students in 2001–2002 in all graduate psychology programs in the department: Female–full-time 80, part-time 105; Male–full-time 25, part-time 29; African American/Black–full-time 6, part-time 24; Hispanic/Latino (a)–full-time 5, part-time 5; Asian/Pacific Islander–full-time 11, part-time 4; American Indian/Alaska Native–full-time 0, part-time 0.

Financial Information/Assistance:
Tuition for Full-Time Study: *Master's:* State residents $540 per credit hour; nonstate residents: $540 per credit hour. *Doctoral:* State residents: per academic year $22,000; nonstate residents: per academic year $22,000.

Financial Assistance:
First Year Students: Teaching assistantships available for first-year. Average amount paid per academic year: $4,000. Average number of hours worked per week: 5. Apply by 4/15. Tuition remission given: partial. Research assistantships available for first-year. Average amount paid per academic year: $4,000. Average number of hours worked per week: 5. Apply by 4/15. Tuition remission given: partial.
Advanced Students: Teaching assistantships available for advanced students. Average amount paid per academic year: $6,000. Average number of hours worked per week: 7. Apply by 4/15. Tuition remission given: partial. Research assistantships available for advanced students. Average amount paid per academic year: $6,000. Average number of hours worked per week: 7. Apply by 4/15. Tuition remission given: partial.
Contact Information: Of all students currently enrolled full-time, 60% benefited from one or more of the listed financial assistance programs. For information on financial assistance, contact: Patrick L. Ross, PhD Chair, Financial Aid Committee.

Internships/Practica: For the doctoral program, students are assigned to the Psychological Services Clinic, the training facility of the PhD Program. Beginning in the first year of the doctoral program, students are trained to perform intake evaluations. In the following years, students are to perform psychodiagnostic evaluations and psychotherapy. Students are also assigned to externships at fall service mental health centers during their second year of training. During their fifth year, students complete a one-year internship in clinical psychology. For the Postdoctoral Program, students are assigned to the Postdoctoral Psychotherapy Center, the training facility of the Postdoctoral Program. For those doctoral students for whom a professional internship is required prior to graduation, 30 applied in 2000–2001. Of those who applied, 29 were placed in internships listed by the Association of Psychology Postdoctoral and Internship Programs (APPIC); 29 were placed in APA accredited internships.

Housing and Day Care: No on-campus housing and day care facilities are available.

Employment of Department Graduates:

Master's Degree Graduates: Of those who graduated in the academic year 2000–2001, the following categories and numbers represent the post-graduate activities and employment of master's degree graduates: Enrolled in a psychology doctoral program (40), enrolled in another graduate/professional program (15), enrolled in a post-doctoral residency/fellowship (n/a), employed in independent practice (n/a).

Doctoral Degree Graduates: Of those who graduated in the academic year 2000–2001, the following categories and numbers represent the post-graduate activities and employment of doctoral degree graduates: Enrolled in a psychology doctoral program (n/a), enrolled in another graduate/professional program (n/a), enrolled in a post-doctoral residency/fellowship (30), employed in independent practice (30), employed in an academic position at a university (5), employed in other positions at a higher education institution (10), employed in a professional position in a school system (5), employed in a community mental health/counseling center (35), employed in a hospital/medical center (50).

Additional Information:

Orientation, Objectives, and Emphasis of Department: The Derner Institute of Advanced Psychological Studies is the first university-based professional school of psychology. The orientation is psychodynamic and scholar-professional. The doctoral program in clinical and the respecialization program are oriented toward community service and prepare the students for careers in clinical service; the postdoctoral programs prepare graduates for the practice of psychoanalysis and psychotherapy. All doctoral programs offer supervised experience in research and theory. The clinical program consists of four years of coursework, which includes at least one day a week of supervised practice each year and a fifth-year full-time internship; the respecialization program consists of two years of coursework, including at least one day a week of supervised practice each year and a third-year full-time internship; the postdoctoral programs consist of four years of seminars, case conferences, personal therapy, and supervised practice, the masters program consists of two years of coursework, which includes a thesis or project.

Special Facilities or Resources: Facilities include a videotape recording studio and perception, learning, developmental, cognition, and applied research laboratories. The institute has close interaction with two health-related professional schools, the Adelphi School of Nursing and the Adelphi School of Social Work, and with affiliated community school and clinical facilities. The institute maintains two major clinical facilities, the Adelphi University Psychological Services Center and the Postdoctoral Psychotherapy Center. An APA-accredited continuing education program brings a series of distinguished workshops to the campus.

Information for Students With Physical Disabilities: The Institute's facilities are equipped with ramps and an elevator. We have enrolled students with severe (wheelchair-bound) disabilities, blindness with severe hearing impairment. Each student has completed their programs with only a few modifications, and with distinction.

Application Information:

Send to: Graduate Admissions. Students are admitted in the Winter, application deadline January 15. Applicants for the PhD program have a January 15 deadline. MA applicants may begin in either Fall or Spring semester. Postdoctoral applicants begin in Fall only, but no application deadline. *Fee:* $40. Graduate admissions will waive application fee if a request for waiver is completed.

Alfred University
Division of School Psychology
College of Engineering & Professional Studies
Saxon Drive
Alfred, NY 14802-1205
Telephone: (607) 871-2212
Fax: (607) 871-3422
E-mail: *Fgaughan@alfred.edu*
Web: *http://www.alfred.edu*

Department Established:

1993. Chairperson: John D. Cerio. Number of Faculty: total–full-time 6, part-time 2; women–full-time 2, part-time 2.

Programs and Degrees Offered:

Listed in the following order: Program area, degree type (T if terminal Master's), number awarded 7/00–6/01. School EdS 17, School PsyD 7.

APA Accreditation: School PsyD: full.

Student Applications/Admissions:

Student Applications

School EdS—Applications 2001–2002, 47. Total applicants accepted 2001–2002, 28. New applicants enrolled 2001–2002, 13. Total enrolled 2001–2002 full-time, 28, part-time, 4. Openings 2002–2003, 18. The number of students enrolled full and part-time, who were dismissed or voluntarily withdrew from this program area were 1. *School PsyD*—Applications 2001–2002, 23. Total applicants accepted 2001–2002, 14. New applicants enrolled 2001–2002, 12. Total enrolled 2001–2002 full-time, 16, part-time, 20. Openings 2002–2003, 13. The Median number of years required for completion of a degree are 5. The number of students enrolled full and part-time, who were dismissed or voluntarily withdrew from this program area were 0.

Admissions Requirements:

Scores: Entries appear in this order: required test or GPA, minimum score (if required), median score of students entering in 2001–2002. Master's Programs: GRE-V no minimum stated, 466; GRE-Q no minimum stated, 503; GRE-V+Q no minimum stated, 969; overall undergraduate GPA no minimum stated, 3.37. Doctoral Programs: GRE-V no minimum stated, 515; GRE-Q no minimum stated, 559; GRE-V+Q no minimum stated, 1074; GRE-Analytical no minimum stated; overall undergraduate GPA no minimum stated, 3.57; last 2 years GPA no minimum stated; psychology GPA no minimum stated; psychology GPA no minimum stated.

Other Criteria: (importance of criteria rated low, medium, or high): GRE/MAT scores medium, research experience low, work experience medium, extracurricular activity medium, clinically related public service low, GPA high, letters of recommendation medium, interview high, statement of goals and objectives high. The PsyD program places a higher emphasis on research experience.

Student Characteristics: The following represents characteristics of students in 2001–2002 in all graduate psychology programs in the department: Female–full-time 57, part-time 3; Male–full-time 9, part-time 0; African American/Black–full-time 1, part-time 0; Hispanic/Latino (a)–full-time 2, part-time 0; Asian/Pacific Islander–full-time 1, part-time 0; American Indian/Alaska Native–full-time 0, part-time 0; part-time 0; students subject to the Americans with Disabilities Act–full-time 1, part-time 0.

Financial Information/Assistance:

Tuition for Full-Time Study: *Master's:* State residents per academic year $24,720; nonstate residents: per academic year $24,720. *Doctoral:* State residents: per academic year $24,720; nonstate residents: per academic year $24,720.

Financial Assistance:

First Year Students: No information provided.
Advanced Students: No information provided.
Contact Information: For information on financial assistance, contact: The Division of School Psychology, The Graduate Office of Admissions, or The Student Financial Aid Office.

Internships/Practica: Requests for our internships annually exceed the number of internships available by approximately 20%.

Housing and Day Care: No on-campus housing and day care facilities are available.

Employment of Department Graduates:

Master's Degree Graduates: Of those who graduated in the academic year 2000–2001, the following categories and numbers represent the post-graduate activities and employment of master's degree graduates: Enrolled in a post-doctoral residency/fellowship (n/a), employed in independent practice (n/a), employed in a professional position in a school system (14), employed in a community mental health/counseling center (1).

Doctoral Degree Graduates: Of those who graduated in the academic year 2000–2001, the following categories and numbers represent the post-graduate activities and employment of doctoral degree graduates: Enrolled in a psychology doctoral program (n/a), enrolled in another graduate/professional program (n/a), employed in a professional position in a school system (6), employed in a community mental health/counseling center (1).

Additional Information:

Orientation, Objectives, and Emphasis of Department: The Alfred School Psychology program emphasizes a field-centered, systems-oriented, Practitioner-Scientist approach. The primary goal of the program is the preparation of problem-solving psychologists with special concern for the application of psychological knowledge in a variety of child and family related settings. Students acquire knowledge in a wide variety of psychological theories and practices; skills are learned and then demonstrated in a number of different applied settings. They develop the personal characteristics and academic competencies necessary to work effectively with others in the identification, prevention, and remediation of psychological and educational problems with children and adults. Training in school psychology at Alfred University offers extensive one-to-one contact between students and faculty members to encourage the personalized learning process. Students are involved in field experience and research orientation (PsyD) from the first semester on. Training in the following areas is provided: knowledge base in psychology and education, assessment, intervention and remediation including counseling, play therapy, and family work, consulting/training with teachers, administrators, and parents, research methodology, program evaluation, and professional identification and functioning. Training at the doctoral level emphasizes applied research and the development of an area of specialization.

Special Facilities or Resources: Departmental resources include 6 one-way mirror observation rooms, counseling cubicles, an audio-video tape library, and an extensive library of psychological and educational assessment materials. In addition, all students gain practicum experience in the on-campus Child and Family Services Center, operated by the Division of School Psychology. The Center provides consultation, assessment, and counseling services to children and families of the region. The Center is a state of the art facility with all consultation rooms equipped with observation mirrors and remote audio-video recording equipment. The Center serves training, service, and research functions for faculty and students. Graduate students have a work/computer room and a spacious lounge. Additionally, all graduate students have access to the mainframe computer and numerous PCs at no cost.

Application Information:

Send to: Graduate Admissions, Alfred University, Saxon Drive, Alfred, NY 14802. Students are admitted in the Fall. Deadline for fall admission to the MA/CAS program is February 15; for the PsyD program, January 15. Late applications may be considered if places in the class still exist for qualified applicants. *Fee:* $50. Waiver of fee available for on-line application submission only.

Binghamton University
Psychology
P.O. Box 6000
Binghamton, NY 13902-6000
Telephone: (607) 777-2449
Fax: (607) 777-4890
E-mail: *lspear@binghamton.edu*
Web: *http://psychology.binghamton.edu*

Department Established:

1965. Chairperson: Linda P. Spear. Number of Faculty: total–full-time 25, part-time 5; women–full-time 11, part-time 2; minority–full-time 2.

Programs and Degrees Offered:

Listed in the following order: Program area, degree type (T if terminal Master's), number awarded 7/00–6/01. Behavioral Neuroscience PhD 9, Clinical PhD 5, Cognitive PhD 5.

APA Accreditation: Clinical PhD: full.

Student Applications/Admissions:

Student Applications

Behavioral Neuroscience PhD—Applications 2001–2002, 35. Total applicants accepted 2001–2002, 14. New applicants enrolled 2001–2002, 7. Total enrolled 2001–2002 full-time, 7. Openings 2002–2003, 5-8. The Median number of years required for completion of a degree are 5. *Clinical PhD*—Applications 2001–2002, 140. Total applicants accepted 2001–2002, 16. New applicants enrolled 2001–2002, 8. Total enrolled 2001–2002 full-time, 8. Openings 2002–2003, 6. The Median number of years required for completion of a degree are 6. *Cognitive PhD*—Applications 2001–2002, 26. Total applicants accepted 2001–2002, 14. New applicants enrolled 2001–2002, 5. Total enrolled 2001–2002 full-time, 5. Openings 2002–2003, 5-8. The Median number of years required for completion of a degree are 5.

Admissions Requirements:

Scores: Entries appear in this order: required test or GPA, minimum score (if required), median score of students entering in 2001–2002. Master's Programs: GRE-V no minimum stated, 550; GRE-Q no minimum stated, 620; GRE-V+Q no minimum stated, 1170; GRE-Analytical no minimum stated, 665; GRE-V+Q+Analytical no minimum stated, 1835; GRE-Subject(Psych) no minimum stated, 675; overall undergraduate GPA no minimum stated, 3.57; psychology GPA no minimum stated. Doctoral Programs: GRE-V no minimum stated, 550; GRE-Q no minimum stated, 620; GRE-V+Q no minimum stated, 1170; GRE-Analytical no minimum stated, 665; GRE-V+Q+Analytical no minimum stated, 1835; GRE-Subject(Psych) no minimum stated; overall undergraduate GPA no minimum stated; last 2 years GPA no minimum stated; psychology GPA no minimum stated; psychology GPA no minimum stated. Although we don't require a minimum GRE in all areas we look at each applicant on an individual basis. **Other Criteria:** (importance of criteria rated low, medium, or high): GRE/MAT scores high, research experience high, work experience medium, extracurricular activity low, clinically related public service low, GPA letters of recommendation high, interview high, statement of goals and objectives high.

Student Characteristics: The following represents characteristics of students in 2001–2002 in all graduate psychology programs in the department: Female–full-time 16, part-time 0; Male–full-time 7, part-time 0; African American/Black–full-time 0, part-time 0; Hispanic/Latino (a)–full-time 0, part-time 0; Asian/Pacific Islander–full-time 0, part-time 0; American Indian/Alaska Native–full-time 0, part-time 0.

Financial Information/Assistance:

Tuition for Full-Time Study: *Doctoral:* State residents: per academic year $5,100; nonstate residents: per academic year $8,416.

Financial Assistance:

First Year Students: Teaching assistantships available for first-year. Average amount paid per academic year: $12,000. Tuition remission given: full. Research assistantships available for first-year. Average amount paid per academic year: $12,000. Tuition remission given: full. Fellowships and scholarships available for first-year. Average amount paid per academic year: $12,000. Tuition remission given: full.

Advanced Students: Teaching assistantships available for advanced students. Average amount paid per academic year: $12,000. Tuition remission given: full. Research assistantships available for advanced students. Average amount paid per academic year: $12,000. Tuition remission given: full. Fellowships and scholarships available for advanced students. Average amount paid per academic year: $12,000. Tuition remission given: full.

Contact Information: Of all students currently enrolled full-time, 99% benefited from one or more of the listed financial assistance programs. For information on financial assistance, contact: Director of Graduate Studies.

Internships/Practica: Students in the clinical area are required to complete two practica, a psychotherapy practicum and a community practicum. The psychotherapy practicum is conducted in the department clinic under the supervision of a faculty member and generally involves the joint treatment of a variety of problems across a broad range of ages and diagnoses. The community practicum consists of supervised clinical activity and/or research at one of a wide range of local agencies, hospitals, or clinics. Students in cognitive psychology are invited—but not required—to complete a research-related practicum in industry. Past internships included training at GE, IBM, Microsoft, Lockheed Martin, and others.

Housing and Day Care: On-campus housing and day care facilities are available.

Employment of Department Graduates:

Master's Degree Graduates: Of those who graduated in the academic year 2000–2001, the following categories and numbers represent the post-graduate activities and employment of master's degree graduates: Enrolled in a post-doctoral residency/fellowship (n/a), employed in independent practice (n/a).

Doctoral Degree Graduates: Of those who graduated in the academic year 2000–2001, the following categories and numbers represent the post-graduate activities and employment of doctoral degree graduates: Enrolled in a psychology doctoral program (n/a), enrolled in another graduate/professional program (n/a), enrolled in a post-doctoral residency/fellowship (6), employed in independent practice (0), employed in an academic position at a university (1), employed in an academic position at a 2-year/4-year college (0), employed in other positions at a higher education institution (0), employed in a professional position in a school system (0), employed in business or industry (research/consulting) (2), employed in business or industry (management) (0), employed in a government agency (research) (0), employed in a government agency (professional services) (0), employed in a community mental health/counseling center (1), employed in a hospital/medical center (0), still seeking employment (0), other employment position (0).

Additional Information:

Orientation, Objectives, and Emphasis of Department: The psychology department emphasizes basic and applied research in its three areas of specialization, clinical psychology, cognitive psychology, and behavioral neuroscience. The goal of our APA-accredited Clinical program is to develop knowledgeable and caring health professionals who are also scientists. By virtue of ongoing research involvement, students are expected to contribute to knowledge about psychopathology, assessment, and treatment. Our cognitive program has two major research emphases, one on perception and language (both in the visual and auditory domains) and one on learning and memory. Researchers in this area also work in industrial settings and collaborate with local industry. Our behavioral neuroscience program emphasizes the study of neural and hormonal bases of normal and abnormal behavior and their developmental antecedents.

Special Facilities or Resources: All faculty have state-of-the-art, spacious laboratories. The clinical program supports an active in-house mental-health clinic. Members of the cognitive area have access to sophisticated systems for the manipulation of auditory and visual stimuli and the on-line measurement of cognitive processes, and members of the behavioral neurosciences area share multi-user histology and neurochemistry laboratories.

Information for Students With Physical Disabilities: The department is wheel chair accessible. The libraries have aids for students with visual disabilities.

Application Information:
Send to: Graduate Admissions Office. Clinical application deadline is February 1; Behavioral Neuroscience deadline is February 1; Cognitive deadline is February 15. *Fee:* $50.

City University of New York, Graduate School and University Center
PhD Program in Educational Psychology
365 Fifth Avenue
New York, NY 10016-4309
Telephone: (212) 817-8285
Fax: (212) 817-1516
E-mail: *agross@gc.cuny.edu*
Web: *http://www.gc.cuny.edu*

Department Established:
1969. Executive Officer: Alan L. Gross. Number of Faculty: total–full-time 16; women–full-time 9; minority–full-time 2.

Programs and Degrees Offered:
Listed in the following order: Program area, degree type (T if terminal Master's), number awarded 7/00–6/01. Educational Psychology PhD.

APA Accreditation: School PhD: full.

Student Applications/Admissions:
Student Applications
Educational Psychology PhD—Applications 2001–2002, 5. Total applicants accepted 2001–2002, 2. New applicants enrolled 2001–2002, 1. Total enrolled 2001–2002 full-time, 6, part-time, 2.

Admissions Requirements:
Scores: Entries appear in this order: required test or GPA, minimum score (if required), median score of students entering in 2001–2002. Doctoral Programs: GRE-V no minimum stated; GRE-Q no minimum stated; GRE-Analytical no minimum stated; overall undergraduate GPA no minimum stated; last 2 years GPA no minimum stated; psychology GPA no minimum stated; psychology GPA no minimum stated.
Other Criteria: (importance of criteria rated low, medium, or high): GRE/MAT scores high, research experience medium, work experience medium, extracurricular activity low, clinically related public service low, GPA medium, letters of recommendation high, interview high, statement of goals and objectives high.

Student Characteristics: The following represents characteristics of students in 2001–2002 in all graduate psychology programs in the department: Female–full-time 57, part-time 12; Male–full-time 18, part-time 3; African American/Black–full-time 4, part-time 0; Hispanic/Latino (a)–full-time 4, Asian/Pacific Islander–full-time 5, part-time 0; American Indian/Alaska Native–full-time 0, part-time 0.

Financial Information/Assistance:
Tuition for Full-Time Study: *Doctoral:* State residents: per academic year $4,350; nonstate residents: per academic year $7,600.

Financial Assistance:
First Year Students: Teaching assistantships available for first-year. Average amount paid per academic year: $12,000. Average number of hours worked per week: 10. Apply by 4/15. Research assistantships available for first-year. Average amount paid per academic year: $5,000. Average number of hours worked per week: 5. Apply by 4/15. Fellowships and scholarships available for first-year. Average amount paid per academic year: $14,000. Average number of hours worked per week: 5. Apply by 4/15.
Advanced Students: Teaching assistantships available for advanced students. Average amount paid per academic year: $12,000. Average number of hours worked per week: 10. Apply by 4/15. Research assistantships available for advanced students. Average amount paid per academic year: $5,000. Average number of hours worked per week: 5. Apply by 4/15. Fellowships and scholarships available for advanced students. Average amount paid per academic year: $14,000. Average number of hours worked per week: 5. Apply by 4/15.
Contact Information: For information on financial assistance, contact: Janet Finello, Financial Aid, 212-817-7460.

Internships/Practica: Internship in School Psychology: Students will have a one-year full-time internship in an approved setting. This training for competent professional functioning will include but not be limited to experiences in psycho-educational assessment and intervention. It may encompass direct and indirect service delivery as well as research and evaluation. Students will be expected to accept responsibility for major professional functions in the context of appropriate supervisory support both on-site and at the university. This experience is essential preparation for functioning as independent professional. The internship will be supervised by a member of the doctoral faculty in the area of School Psychology. Advanced Practica in School Psychology: The one-year practicum provides students with experience in pre-school settings. The practicum will cover assessment, consultation, and intervention. Students will be placed in a preschool setting, one day per week, serving the children who are developmentally delayed. In addition, students are required to visit and observe one other selected preschool. Supervision will be provided on site by field supervisors for a minimum of one hour per week. Students will also meet at the University every other week for two hours of supervision and instruction.

Housing and Day Care: On-campus housing and day care facilities are available.

Employment of Department Graduates:

Master's Degree Graduates: Of those who graduated in the academic year 2000–2001, the following categories and numbers represent the post-graduate activities and employment of master's degree graduates: Enrolled in a post-doctoral residency/fellowship (n/a), employed in independent practice (n/a).

Doctoral Degree Graduates: Of those who graduated in the academic year 2000–2001, the following categories and numbers represent the post-graduate activities and employment of doctoral degree graduates: Enrolled in a psychology doctoral program (n/a), enrolled in another graduate/professional program (n/a), employed in an academic position at a university (1), employed in a professional position in a school system (8).

Additional Information:

Orientation, Objectives, and Emphasis of Department: The PhD program in Educational Psychology is research oriented, preparing students for teaching, research, and program development in various educational settings such as universities, school systems, research institutions, community agencies, as well as in educational publishing, television, and in other agencies with training programs. Four areas of concentration are offered: quantitative methods in educational and psychological research, learning development and instruction, school psychology, and educational policy analysis.

Special Facilities or Resources: The Educational Psychology program is affiliated with a university based research institute, CASE (Center for Advanced Study in Education). CASE is heavily involved in the evaluation and implementation of various applied educational programs. Our faculty and students have worked as principle investigators and research assistants on CASE projects.

Information for Students With Physical Disabilities: The Graduate Center is a barrier-free building. The Office of the Vice President for Finance and Administration will facilitate physical access and provide additional services to students with disabilities where needed.

Application Information:
Send to: Admissions Office, CUNY Graduate Center, 365 Fifth Avenue, New York City, New York 10016-4309. Students are admitted in the Fall. February 15 for School Psychology. April 15 for all others. *Fee:* $40.

City University of New York, Graduate School and University Center
PhD Program in Psychology
365 Fifth Avenue
New York, NY 10016-4309
Telephone: (212) 817-8705/8753
Fax: (212) 817-1533
E-mail: *psychology@gc.cuny.edu*
Web: *http://www.gc.cuny.edu*

Department Established:
1961. Executive Officer: Joseph Glick. Number of Faculty: total–full-time 121, part-time 47; women–full-time 46, part-time 18; minority–full-time 8, part-time 1.

Programs and Degrees Offered:
Listed in the following order: Program area, degree type (T if terminal Master's), number awarded 7/00–6/01. Biopsychology PhD 1, clinical PhD 17, developmental PhD 1, environmental PhD 6, experimental PhD 2, experimental cognition PhD 1, industrial/organizational PhD 5, learning processes PhD, neuropsychology PhD 6, social/personality PhD 4.

APA Accreditation: Clinical PhD: full.

Student Applications/Admissions:
Student Applications

Biopsychology PhD—Applications 2001–2002, 12. Total applicants accepted 2001–2002, 8. New applicants enrolled 2001–2002, 3. Total enrolled 2001–2002 full-time, 35. Openings 2002–2003, 12. *Clinical PhD*—Applications 2001–2002, 276. Total applicants accepted 2001–2002, 12. New applicants enrolled 2001–2002, 11. Total enrolled 2001–2002 full-time, 88. Openings 2002–2003, 12. *Developmental PhD*—Applications 2001–2002, 45. Total applicants accepted 2001–2002, 15. New applicants enrolled 2001–2002, 8. Total enrolled 2001–2002 full-time, 50. Openings 2002–2003, 10. *Environmental PhD*—Applications 2001–2002, 15. Total applicants accepted 2001–2002, 10. New applicants enrolled 2001–2002, 7. Total enrolled 2001–2002 full-time, 48. Openings 2002–2003, 10. *Experimental PhD*—Applications 2001–2002, 17. Total applicants accepted 2001–2002, 8. New applicants enrolled 2001–2002, 6. Total enrolled 2001–2002 full-time, 32. Openings 2002–2003, 8. *Experimental cognition PhD*—Applications 2001–2002, 12. Total applicants accepted 2001–2002, 7. New applicants enrolled 2001–2002, 7. Total enrolled 2001–2002 full-time, 32. Openings 2002–2003, 5. *Industrial/organizational PhD*—Applications 2001–2002, 61. Total applicants accepted 2001–2002, 7. New applicants enrolled 2001–2002, 5. Total enrolled 2001–2002 full-time, 43. Openings 2002–2003, 7. *Learning processes PhD*—Applications 2001–2002, 19. Total applicants accepted 2001–2002, 11. New applicants enrolled 2001–2002, 7. Total enrolled 2001–2002 full-time, 33. Openings 2002–2003, 10. *Neuropsychology PhD*—Applications 2001–2002, 40. Total applicants accepted 2001–2002, 9. New applicants enrolled 2001–2002, 6. Total enrolled 2001–2002 full-time, 53. Openings 2002–2003, 8. *Social/personality PhD*—Applications 2001–2002, 53. Total applicants accepted 2001–2002, 10. New applicants enrolled 2001–2002, 8. Total enrolled 2001–2002 full-time, 54. Openings 2002–2003, 7.

Admissions Requirements:

Scores: Entries appear in this order: required test or GPA, minimum score (if required), median score of students entering in 2001–2002. Doctoral Programs: GRE-V 550; GRE-Q 550; GRE-Analytical 550; GRE-Subject(Psych) 550; overall undergraduate GPA 3.0; last 2 years GPA no minimum stated; psychology GPA 3.0; psychology GPA no minimum stated.

Other Criteria: (importance of criteria rated low, medium, or high): GRE/MAT scores medium, research experience medium, work experience low, extracurricular activity low, clinically related public service medium, GPA medium, letters of recommendation high, interview high, statement of goals and objectives high.

Student Characteristics: The following represents characteristics of students in 2001–2002 in all graduate psychology programs in the department: Female–full-time 335, part-time 2; Male–full-time 128, part-time 2; African American/Black–full-time 39, part-time 0; Hispanic/Latino (a)–full-time 72, part-time 0; Asian/Pacific Islander–full-time 20, part-time 0; American Indian/Alaska Native–full-time 1, part-time 0.

Financial Information/Assistance:

Tuition for Full-Time Study: No information provided.

Financial Assistance:

First Year Students: Research assistantships available for first-year. Average amount paid per academic year: $7,552. Fellowships and scholarships available for first-year. Average amount paid per academic year: $12,000. Average number of hours worked per week: 20.

Advanced Students: Teaching assistantships available for advanced students. Average amount paid per academic year: $3,000. Research assistantships available for advanced students. Fellowships and scholarships available for advanced students.

Contact Information: Of all students currently enrolled full-time, 90% benefited from one or more of the listed financial assistance programs. For information on financial assistance, contact: Financial Aid Office, City University of NY, Graduate School and University Center, 365 Fifth Ave, New York, NY 10016-4309, (212) 817-7460.

Internships/Practica: No information provided.

Housing and Day Care: No on-campus housing and day care facilities are available.

Employment of Department Graduates:

Master's Degree Graduates: Of those who graduated in the academic year 2000–2001, the following categories and numbers represent the post-graduate activities and employment of master's degree graduates: Enrolled in a post-doctoral residency/fellowship (n/a), employed in independent practice (n/a).

Doctoral Degree Graduates: Of those who graduated in the academic year 2000–2001, the following categories and numbers represent the post-graduate activities and employment of doctoral degree graduates: Enrolled in a psychology doctoral program (n/a), enrolled in another graduate/professional program (n/a).

Additional Information:

Orientation, Objectives, and Emphasis of Department: The developmental subprogram offers training in all areas of developmental research, with emphasis on social, cognitive, and language development. The Environmental subprogram provides interdisciplinary training with relationships between the physical environment and behavior. Concepts and approaches of fields such as urban planning, psychology, architecture, geography, anthropology, landscape architecture, and sociology are learned in a context that emphasizes the integration of systematic research and applied work with the development of theory. The social-personality subprogram trains students in the theory and research methods of both social and personality psychology. A health psychology concentration is available to students in all subprograms. Through courses, research projects, and practica, the concentration seeks to train psychologists to be able to work in a variety of health-related settings. Industrial/Organizational psychology trains people to do research in organizations and in personnel issues. Neuropsychology trains students in both basic and clinical neuroscience. Learning processes offers training in Applied Behavior Analysis. Clinical offers training in psychodynamic approaches to mental health with particular attention paid to minority populations. Experimental psychology and Experimental Cognition focus on the experimental approach to a wide variety of phenomena.

Special Facilities or Resources: Computers for student use are available in the library; computer hubs, on most academic floors; and student carrel spaces, in the academic program offices. An assortment of programming languages and statistical, graphical, wordprocessing, and specialty software applications are provided. Also available are laser printers, file format translation, image scanning, and optical character recognition facilities. Adaptive technology for students with disabilities is available and includes screen-access software and such peripheral devices as reading machines, a computer-linked closed-circuit TV, and a Braille printer. Most computers designated for students are 400Mhz Celeron processor systems with 6GB hard drives, 64 MB Ram, and 15-inch flat-screen monitors. Five special-purpose classrooms, with a total of more than 100 computers, are furnished with 450 Mhz Pentium III computers and 15-inch flat-screen monitors. Students may access UNIX-based academic software from home or via a telnet session upon request. The UNIX accounts provide access to statistical or other academic software but not e-mail support. Information Resources maintains an ongoing program of equipment, computer hardware, and software modernization and provides such client services as documentation, training, and lab consulting. Workshops are held throughout the year on a wide range of topics and include many hands-on training programs.

Information for Students With Physical Disabilities: Questions regarding access to these resources for students with disabilities should be directed to the Office of the Vice President for Student Affairs.

Application Information:

Send to: Admissions Office, City University Graduate Center, 365 Fifth Ave., New York, NY 10016-4309; 212-817-7470, admissions@gc.cuny.edu. Students are admitted in the Fall. Deadline is January 1st for clinical and neuropsychology; February 1st for experimental cognition, industrial/organizational, social/personality; March 1st for biopsychology, developmental, environmental; March 15 for learning process. *Fee:* $40.

City University of New York: Brooklyn College

Graduate Program in School Psychology, School of Education
Brooklyn College
2900 Bedford Avenue, Room 1105 James
Brooklyn, NY 11210
Telephone: (718) 951-5876
Fax: (718) 951-4232
E-mail: *barbanel@brooklyn.cuny.edu*
Web: *http://depthome.brooklyn.cuny.edu/schooled*

Department Established:
1968. Program Head: Laura Barbanel. Number of Faculty: total–full-time 5, part-time 4; women–full-time 4, part-time 2; minority–full-time 1.

Programs and Degrees Offered:
Listed in the following order: Program area, degree type (T if terminal Master's), number awarded 7/00–6/01. School.

Student Applications/Admissions:
Admissions Requirements:
Scores: Entries appear in this order: required test or GPA, minimum score (if required), median score of students entering in 2001–2002. Master's Programs: overall undergraduate GPA 3.0, 3.5. Doctoral Programs: last 2 years GPA no minimum stated; psychology GPA no minimum stated; psychology GPA no minimum stated.
Other Criteria: (importance of criteria rated low, medium, or high): research experience low, work experience high, extra-curricular activity medium, clinically related public service high, GPA high, letters of recommendation high, interview high, statement of goals and objectives high.

Student Characteristics: The following represents characteristics of students in 2001–2002 in all graduate psychology programs in the department: Female–full-time 13, part-time 14; Male–full-time 2, part-time 6; African American/Black–full-time 2, part-time 5; Hispanic/Latino (a)–full-time 3, part-time 2; Asian/Pacific Islander–full-time 0, part-time 0; American Indian/Alaska Native–full-time 0, part-time 0.

Financial Information/Assistance:
Tuition for Full-Time Study: Master's: State residents $185 per credit hour; nonstate residents: $320 per credit hour.

Financial Assistance:
First Year Students: Fellowships and scholarships available for first-year. Apply by March 15.
Advanced Students: Fellowships and scholarships available for advanced students. Apply by March 15.
Contact Information: Of all students currently enrolled full-time, 10% benefited from one or more of the listed financial assistance programs. For information on financial assistance, contact: Financial Aid Office at (718) 951-5051.

Internships/Practica: Internships: Internships are available and coordinated through our program with various schools, both public and private, working with both the mainstream population, as well as special populations. In addition, internships are available in mental health clinics, agencies, and hospitals. Practica: Practica are designed to be part of the students' coursework. Practicum is an intensive five-hour, four-credit course the students take during their internship year that represents an opportunity to incorporate and share with their classmates experiences from their internship sites in the academic setting.

Housing and Day Care: No on-campus housing and day care facilities are available.

Employment of Department Graduates:
Master's Degree Graduates: Of those who graduated in the academic year 2000–2001, the following categories and numbers represent the post-graduate activities and employment of master's degree graduates: Enrolled in a post-doctoral residency/fellowship (n/a), employed in independent practice (n/a).
Doctoral Degree Graduates: Of those who graduated in the academic year 2000–2001, the following categories and numbers represent the post-graduate activities and employment of doctoral degree graduates: Enrolled in a psychology doctoral program (n/a), enrolled in another graduate/professional program (n/a).

Additional Information:
Orientation, Objectives, and Emphasis of Department: The aim of the school psychologists' training program is to meet the community needs for professionally competent personnel to function in the schools as consultants on psychological aspects of learning and mental health. They will be prepared to make assessments of situations involving children, parents, and school personnel to achieve the more optimal functioning of children in the school setting. Coursework will prepare students in the areas of measurement and evaluation, personality understanding, educational objectives and procedures, curriculum development, and research. They will also be trained to achieve greater integration between school and community. Elements of the program will provide students with opportunities for self-exploration and understanding. Completion of this program will train students to work in public or private schools, as well as mental health centers, clinics, hospitals, and other community agencies.

Special Facilities or Resources: In addition to the use of the Brooklyn College library, students are welcome to use all the libraries at other colleges within the CUNY system. The School Psychology Program also has a small library of texts and journals for the students' use.

Information for Students With Physical Disabilities: Our campus is now fully accessible to students with physical disabilities. In addition, through the Office For Students With Disabilities, many services and support programs are available for this population.

Application Information:
Send to: Department Chair. Students are admitted in the Fall, application deadline March 1. We need 2 applications for the Department and Graduate Admissions. *Fee:* $40.

City University of New York: Hunter College

Department of Psychology/Biopsychology PhD Program
695 Park Avenue, Room 611 North Building
New York, NY 10021
Telephone: (212) 772-5550 Psych; (212) 772-5621 Biops
Fax: (212) 772-5620
E-mail: *biopsych@hunter.cuny.edu*
Web: *http://maxweber.hunter.cuny.edu/psych/biopsych.htm*

Department Established:

1962. Program Head for Biopsychology: Darlene DeFour; Peter Moller, Program Head. Number of Faculty: total–full-time 11, part-time 21; women–full-time 8, part-time 6; minority–full-time 6.

Programs and Degrees Offered:

Listed in the following order: Program area, degree type (T if terminal Master's), number awarded 7/00–6/01. Biopsychology PhD 6.

Student Applications/Admissions:

Student Applications

Biopsychology PhD—Applications 2001–2002, 18. Total applicants accepted 2001–2002, 12. New applicants enrolled 2001–2002, 7. Total enrolled 2001–2002 full-time, 35. Openings 2002–2003, 5. The Median number of years required for completion of a degree are 7. The number of students enrolled full and part-time, who were dismissed or voluntarily withdrew from this program area were 1.

Admissions Requirements:

Scores: Entries appear in this order: required test or GPA, minimum score (if required), median score of students entering in 2001–2002. Master's Programs: GRE-V no minimum stated; GRE-Q no minimum stated; GRE-Analytical no minimum stated; overall undergraduate GPA no minimum stated; psychology GPA no minimum stated. Doctoral Programs: GRE-V 600; GRE-Q 600; GRE-V+Q 1200; GRE-Analytical 600; GRE-V+Q+Analytical 1800; GRE-Subject(Psych) 75%; overall undergraduate GPA 3.00; last 2 years GPA 3.00; psychology GPA 3.00; psychology GPA no minimum stated. GRE in Subject area by end of first year of program.

Other Criteria: (importance of criteria rated low, medium, or high): GRE/MAT scores medium, research experience high, extracurricular activity low, GPA, letters of recommendation high, interview medium, statement of goals and objectives high.

Student Characteristics: The following represents characteristics of students in 2001–2002 in all graduate psychology programs in the department: Female–full-time 25, part-time 1; Male–full-time 10, part-time 0; African American/Black–full-time 2, Hispanic/Latino (a)–full-time 3, part-time 1; Asian/Pacific Islander–full-time 3, part-time 0; American Indian/Alaska Native–full-time 0, part-time 0.

Financial Information/Assistance:

Tuition for Full-Time Study: *Doctoral:* State residents: per academic year $4,350; nonstate residents: per academic year $7,600.

Financial Assistance:

First Year Students: Teaching assistantships available for first-year. Average amount paid per academic year: $15,000. Tuition remission given: partial. Fellowships and scholarships available for first-year. Average amount paid per academic year: $18,000. Tuition remission given: full.

Advanced Students: Teaching assistantships available for advanced students. Average amount paid per academic year: $17,000. Tuition remission given: partial. Fellowships and scholarships available for advanced students. Average amount paid per academic year: $18,000. Tuition remission given: full.

Contact Information: Of all students currently enrolled full-time, 50% benefited from one or more of the listed financial assistance programs. For information on financial assistance, contact: Office of Financial Aid, Hunter College, 695 Park Ave., NY, NY 10021 for the Master's Program; Office of Financial Aid, Graduate School-CUNY 365 Fifth Avenue, NY, NY 10016-4309 for Psychology PhD Program.

Internships/Practica: No information provided.

Housing and Day Care: No on-campus housing and day care facilities are available.

Employment of Department Graduates:

Master's Degree Graduates: Of those who graduated in the academic year 2000–2001, the following categories and numbers represent the post-graduate activities and employment of master's degree graduates: Enrolled in a post-doctoral residency/fellowship (n/a), employed in independent practice (n/a).

Doctoral Degree Graduates: Of those who graduated in the academic year 2000–2001, the following categories and numbers represent the post-graduate activities and employment of doctoral degree graduates: Enrolled in a psychology doctoral program (n/a), enrolled in another graduate/professional program (n/a), enrolled in a post-doctoral residency/fellowship (6).

Additional Information:

Orientation, Objectives, and Emphasis of Department: The doctoral program in biopsychology interrelates the concepts and methods of neuroscience, cognitive science, the biological disciplines, and behavior analysis to offer a comparative and ontogenetic perspective on species-typical behavior and behavior acquired and modified during the individual's life-cycle. Basis psychological processes are studied in conjunction with contributions from neurobiology, ethology, ecology, evolutionary biology, genetics, endocrinology, pharmacology, and other sciences to illuminate the many ways in which all species adapt, survive, reproduce, and evolve. Through diversified laboratory experiences plus core courses, electives, seminars, colloquia, and field studies, students develop an interdisciplinary perspective. Neuroscience and animal behavior are taught jointly with the biology faculty. Electives address a wide range of topics in basic and applied areas of traditional psychology, neuroscience, and cognitive science. The biopsychology program provides unique training for basic research and teaching in the field of animal and human behavior, and in the application of biobehavioral knowledge to problems in industrial, business, institutional, health, and environmental settings. Students in the MA program may take courses in social, developmental, cognitive, and other areas of psychology as well as in biopsychology. We try to arrange individualized programs for two populations of students: those oriented toward the PhD for whom research training is a prime concern, and those with diverse career aspirations who are oriented toward a general graduate background in psychology.

Special Facilities or Resources: Laboratories for research with human subjects and with a variety of animal species are located at Hunter College. The College has a modern animal-care facility. Facilities for field research in animal behavior are available at the Southwest Field Station of the American Museum of Natural History in the Chiricahua Mountains of Arizona. Research with human infants is carried out at the Albert Einstein College of Medicine and at the Institute for Basic Research in Developmental Disabilities. Additional research opportunities are available through faculty affiliations with many other academic and research institutes in New York City. Hunter College lab facilities include equipment for electrophysiology, phase-fluorescence, and transmission microscopy, electron- and scanning-electron microscopy, radio immunoassay, high-performance liquid chromatography, autoradiography and other radioreceptor techniques, human and animal psychophysiology, histology, operant and classical conditioning, and video/cinematographic analysis. Computer facilities include a variety of micro- and minicomputers as well as access to the University computer center. Doctoral students may register for specialized courses at any CUNY campus and have privileges at all CUNY libraries.

Application Information:
Send to: Graduate Admissions, 695 Park Ave., Hunter College, CUNY, New York, NY 10021 for the Master's Program, Office of Admissions, Graduate School-CUNY, 365 Fifth Avenue, NY, NY 10016-4309 for the Psychology PhD Program; a copy should be sent to the Biopsychology Program here at Hunter College-Rm. 611 North Building as well. Students are admitted in the Fall, application deadline 2/1 (PhD). Fall deadline; November 7-MA, February 1-PhD. Applications for Biospsychology PhD are: Admissions Office, City University Graduate Center, 365 Fifth Avenue, NY, NY 10016-4309, (212) 817-7000. *Fee:* $40.

City University of New York: John Jay College of Criminal Justice

Department of Psychology, MA Program in Forensic Psychology
John Jay College of Criminal Justice, CUNY
445 West 59th Street
New York, NY 10019
Telephone: (212) 237-8782
Fax: (212) 237-8742
E-mail: *jwulach@jjay.cuny.edu*
Web: *http://www.jjay.cuny.edu*

Department Established:
1976. Director, MA Program in Forensic Psychology: James S. Wulach. Number of Faculty: total–full-time 20, part-time 15; women–full-time 3, part-time 9; minority–full-time 3; faculty subject to the Americans with Disabilities Act 4.

Programs and Degrees Offered:
Listed in the following order: Program area, degree type (T if terminal Master's), number awarded 7/00–6/01. Forensic psychology MA (T) 148.

Student Applications/Admissions:
Student Applications
Forensic psychology MA—Applications 2001–2002, 249. Total applicants accepted 2001–2002, 166. New applicants enrolled 2001–2002, 93. Total enrolled 2001–2002 full-time, 196, part-time, 209. Openings 2002–2003, 175. The Median number of years required for completion of a degree are 2. The number of students enrolled full and part-time, who were dismissed or voluntarily withdrew from this program area were 26.

Admissions Requirements:
Scores: Entries appear in this order: required test or GPA, minimum score (if required), median score of students entering in 2001–2002. Master's Programs: GRE-V+Q 950, 1050; overall undergraduate GPA 3.0, 3.2. Doctoral Programs: last 2 years GPA no minimum stated; psychology GPA no minimum stated; psychology GPA no minimum stated.
Other Criteria: (importance of criteria rated low, medium, or high): GRE/MAT scores high, research experience low, work experience low, GPA high, letters of recommendation low, statement of goals and objectives low.

Student Characteristics: The following represents characteristics of students in 2001–2002 in all graduate psychology programs in the department: Female–full-time 140, part-time 143; Male–full-time 64, part-time 62; African American/Black–full-time 6, part-time 8; Hispanic/Latino (a)–full-time 8, part-time 8; Asian/Pacific Islander–full-time 5, part-time 1; American Indian/Alaska Native–full-time 0, part-time 0.

Financial Information/Assistance:
Tuition for Full-Time Study: *Master's:* State residents per academic year $4,350, $185 per credit hour; nonstate residents: per academic year $7,600, $320 per credit hour.

Financial Assistance:
First Year Students: No information provided.
Advanced Students: No information provided.
Contact Information: Of all students currently enrolled full-time, 0% benefited from one or more of the listed financial assistance programs.

Internships/Practica: Most students complete a 400-hour externship in local forensic psychology settings, such as hospitals or prisons.

Housing and Day Care: No on-campus housing and day care facilities are available.

Employment of Department Graduates:
Master's Degree Graduates: Of those who graduated in the academic year 2000–2001, the following categories and numbers represent the post-graduate activities and employment of master's degree graduates: Enrolled in a post-doctoral residency/fellowship (n/a), employed in independent practice (n/a).
Doctoral Degree Graduates: Of those who graduated in the academic year 2000–2001, the following categories and numbers represent the post-graduate activities and employment of doctoral degree graduates: Enrolled in a psychology doctoral program (n/a), enrolled in another graduate/professional program (n/a).

Additional Information:

Orientation, Objectives, and Emphasis of Department: Our program is designed to train students to provide professional psychological services to, and within, the legal system—especially the criminal justice system. Thus, in addition to offering (and requiring) traditional master's level clinical psychology courses, we offer specialized courses in psychology and the law; the psychology and treatment of juvenile and adult offenders and the victims of crime; forensic evaluation and testimony; jury research; psychological profiles of homicidal offenders; psychology of terrorism; and forensic psychological research. All courses are offered in the afternoon and evening. Many of our 22 full-time faculty members have postdoctoral psychological certifications; 4 are lawyers as well as psychologists; and many have extensive forensic experience as practitioners and/or researchers. In addition, the full educational resources of the John Jay College of Criminal Justice are available to our students. Some of our graduates become psychological counselors and psychologists within the criminal justice system, working with offenders, delinquents, and victims. Other graduates enhance their present careers in law enforcement, probation, or parole by completing the program. Many of our graduates continue their education in psychology doctoral programs, in John Jay's doctoral program in criminal justice, or in law.

Special Facilities or Resources: The department maintains affiliations with the major forensic psychology institutions in the New York metropolitan area. The Program is endowed for student-psychology research, in the Forensic Psychology Research Institute. In addition, the full academic resources and educational milieu of John Jay College of Criminal Justice, CUNY, are available to our students.

Application Information:

Send to: Graduate Admissions, John Jay College of Criminal Justice, CUNY, Room 4205N, 445 West 59th Street, New York, NY 10019, Phone number: 212-237-8863. Students are admitted in the Fall, application deadline June 30; Spring, application deadline December 1; Summer, application deadline December 1. *Fee:* $40.

City University of New York: Graduate Center
Neuropsychology Doctoral Program
Queens College
65-30 Kissena Boulevard
Flushing, NY 11367
Telephone: (718) 997-3630
Fax: (718) 997-3257
E-mail: *mschimat@qc1.qc.edu*
Web: *http://www.qc.edu/Psychology/neuro/homepage.htm*

Department Established:

1968. Program head: Jeffrey M. Halperin, PhD. Number of Faculty: total–full-time 16; women–full-time 7.

Programs and Degrees Offered:

Listed in the following order: Program area, degree type (T if terminal Master's), number awarded 7/00–6/01. Neuropsychology PhD 9.

Student Applications/Admissions:

Student Applications

Neuropsychology PhD—Applications 2001–2002, 43. Total applicants accepted 2001–2002, 19. New applicants enrolled 2001–2002, 10. Total enrolled 2001–2002 full-time, 55. Openings 2002–2003, 10. The Median number of years required for completion of a degree are 7. The number of students enrolled full and part-time, who were dismissed or voluntarily withdrew from this program area were 1.

Admissions Requirements:

Scores: Entries appear in this order: required test or GPA, minimum score (if required), median score of students entering in 2001–2002. Doctoral Programs: GRE-V no minimum stated; GRE-Q no minimum stated; GRE-V+Q no minimum stated; GRE-Analytical no minimum stated; GRE-V+Q+Analytical no minimum stated; GRE-Subject(Psych) no minimum stated; overall undergraduate GPA no minimum stated; last 2 years GPA no minimum stated; psychology GPA no minimum stated; psychology GPA no minimum stated.

Other Criteria: (importance of criteria rated low, medium, or high): GRE/MAT scores medium, research experience high, work experience low, extracurricular activity low, clinically related public service low, GPA high, letters of recommendation high, statement of goals and objectives high.

Student Characteristics: The following represents characteristics of students in 2001–2002 in all graduate psychology programs in the department: Female–full-time 42, part-time 0; Male–full-time 13, part-time 0; African American/Black–full-time 2, part-time 0; Hispanic/Latino (a)–full-time 2, part-time 0; Asian/Pacific Islander–full-time 1, part-time 0; American Indian/Alaska Native–full-time 0, part-time 0; Multi-ethnic–full-time 0, part-time 0; students subject to the Americans with Disabilities Act–full-time 0, part-time 0.

Financial Information/Assistance:

Tuition for Full-Time Study: *Doctoral:* State residents: per academic year $2,175, $245 per credit hour; nonstate residents: per academic year $3,800, $425 per credit hour.

Financial Assistance:

First Year Students: Fellowships and scholarships available for first-year. Average amount paid per academic year: $18,000. Average number of hours worked per week: 15.

Advanced Students: Teaching assistantships available for advanced students. Average amount paid per academic year: $7,000. Average number of hours worked per week: 4. Research assistantships available for advanced students. Average amount paid per academic year: $7,552. Average number of hours worked per week: 15. Average amount paid per academic year: $0. Average number of hours worked per week: 0. Fellowships and scholarships available for advanced students. Average amount paid per academic year: $11,214. Average number of hours worked per week: 9.

Contact Information: Of all students currently enrolled full-time, 40% benefited from one or more of the listed financial assistance programs.

Internships/Practica: For those doctoral students for whom a professional internship is required prior to graduation, 4 applied in 2000–2001. Of those who applied, 3 were placed in internships listed by the Association of Psychology Postdoctoral and Internship Programs (APPIC); 3 were placed in APA accredited internships.

Housing and Day Care: No on-campus housing and day care facilities are available.

Employment of Department Graduates:

Master's Degree Graduates: Of those who graduated in the academic year 2000–2001, the following categories and numbers represent the post-graduate activities and employment of master's degree graduates: Enrolled in a psychology doctoral program (0), enrolled in another graduate/professional program (0), enrolled in a post-doctoral residency/fellowship (n/a), employed in independent practice (n/a), employed in an academic position at a university (0), employed in an academic position at a 2-year/4-year college (0), employed in other positions at a higher education institution (0), employed in a professional position in a school system (0), employed in business or industry (research/consulting) (0), employed in business or industry (management) (0), employed in a government agency (research) (0), employed in a government agency (professional services) (0), employed in a community mental health/counseling center (0), employed in a hospital/medical center (0), still seeking employment (0), other employment position (0).

Doctoral Degree Graduates: Of those who graduated in the academic year 2000–2001, the following categories and numbers represent the post-graduate activities and employment of doctoral degree graduates: Enrolled in a psychology doctoral program (n/a), enrolled in another graduate/professional program (n/a), enrolled in a post-doctoral residency/fellowship (5), employed in independent practice (0), employed in an academic position at a university (0), employed in an academic position at a 2-year/4-year college (0), employed in other positions at a higher education institution (0), employed in a professional position in a school system (0), employed in business or industry (research/consulting) (0), employed in business or industry (management) (0), employed in a government agency (research) (0), employed in a government agency (professional services) (0), employed in a community mental health/counseling center (0), employed in a hospital/medical center (2), still seeking employment (0), other employment position (0).

Additional Information:

Orientation, Objectives, and Emphasis of Department: The Neuropsychology Subprogram is an academically-oriented PhD program. Its core philosophy is based on two premises. The first of these is that productive research, effective teaching, and responsible clinical practice are integrally interdependent. That is, effective teaching must include critical analysis of current research data, and clinical assessment and treatment procedures must be empirically validated. The second premise is that the understanding of impaired or disordered brain function in humans requires rigorous training in the neurosciences as well as in the traditional clinical topics. The Subprogram was designed to train professionals with competence in research and teaching in the area of brain-behavior relationships, and in the application of these competencies in clinical settings. It has a rigorous 72-credit curriculum that focuses heavily on neuroscience topics, and provides intensive experience in human and animal experimentation, and also offers students the opportunity to acquire and apply the skills appropriate to the practice of clinical neuropsychology. These include training in the evaluation of psychological and neuropsychological func-

tion in children and adults in neurological, neurosurgical, rehabilitation medicine, and psychiatric populations; as well as in the use of rehabilitation, psychotherapeutic, and remediation techniques.

Special Facilities or Resources: http://www.qc.edu/Psychology/neuro/homepage.htm.

Application Information:

Send to: Office of Admissions, The Graduate School & University Center of the City University of New York, 365 Fifth Avenue, New York, NY 10016-4309. Students are admitted in the Fall, application deadline January 1. *Fee:* $40.

City University of New York: Graduate Center
Learning Processes Doctoral Subprogram
Queens College
65-30 Kissena Boulevard
Flushing, NY 11367
Telephone: (718) 997-3630
Fax: (718) 997-3257
E-mail: *BBrown@qc1.qc.edu*
Web: *http://www.qc.edu/Psychology/lph.htm*

Department Established:

1967. Program Head: Bruce L. Brown. Number of Faculty: total–full-time 7; women–full-time 2.

Programs and Degrees Offered:

Listed in the following order: Program area, degree type (T if terminal Master's), number awarded 7/00–6/01. Learning Processes PhD 2.

Student Applications/Admissions:

Student Applications

Learning Processes PhD—Applications 2001–2002, 11. Total applicants accepted 2001–2002, 8. New applicants enrolled 2001–2002, 4. Total enrolled 2001–2002 full-time, 34. Openings 2002–2003, 5. The Median number of years required for completion of a degree are 8. The number of students enrolled full and part-time, who were dismissed or voluntarily withdrew from this program area were 0.

Admissions Requirements:

Scores: Entries appear in this order: required test or GPA, minimum score (if required), median score of students entering in 2001–2002. Master's Programs: GRE-V+Q+Analytical no minimum stated. Doctoral Programs: GRE-V no minimum stated; GRE-Q no minimum stated; GRE-Analytical no minimum stated; last 2 years GPA no minimum stated; psychology GPA no minimum stated; psychology GPA no minimum stated.

Other Criteria: (importance of criteria rated low, medium, or high): GRE/MAT scores medium, research experience medium, work experience low, extracurricular activity low, clinically related public service low, GPA high, letters of recommendation high, interview low, statement of goals and objectives medium.

Student Characteristics: The following represents characteristics of students in 2001–2002 in all graduate psychology programs in the department: Female–full-time 25, part-time 0; Male–full-time 9, part-time 0; African American/Black–full-time 0, part-time 0; Hispanic/Latino (a)–full-time 1, part-time 0; Asian/Pacific Islander–full-time 3, part-time 0; American Indian/Alaska Native–full-time 0, part-time 0; Multi-ethnic–full-time 0, part-time 0; students subject to the Americans with Disabilities Act–full-time 0, part-time 0.

Financial Information/Assistance:

Tuition for Full-Time Study: *Doctoral:* State residents: per academic year $2,175, $245 per credit hour; nonstate residents: per academic year $3,800, $425 per credit hour.

Financial Assistance:

First Year Students: Average amount paid per academic year: $18,000. Average number of hours worked per week: 20. Apply by 3/1.

Advanced Students: Average amount paid per academic year: $10,000. Average number of hours worked per week: 4. Average amount paid per academic year: $7,000. Average number of hours worked per week: 20. Average amount paid per academic year: $0. Average number of hours worked per week: 0.

Contact Information: No information provided.

Internships/Practica: No information provided.

Housing and Day Care: No on-campus housing and day care facilities are available.

Employment of Department Graduates:

Master's Degree Graduates: Of those who graduated in the academic year 2000–2001, the following categories and numbers represent the post-graduate activities and employment of master's degree graduates: Enrolled in a psychology doctoral program (0), enrolled in another graduate/professional program (0), enrolled in a post-doctoral residency/fellowship (n/a), employed in independent practice (n/a), employed in an academic position at a university (0), employed in an academic position at a 2-year/4-year college (0), employed in other positions at a higher education institution (0), employed in a professional position in a school system (0), employed in business or industry (research/consulting) (0), employed in business or industry (management) (0), employed in a government agency (research) (0), employed in a government agency (professional services) (0), employed in a community mental health/counseling center (0), employed in a hospital/medical center (0), still seeking employment (0), other employment position (0).

Doctoral Degree Graduates: Of those who graduated in the academic year 2000–2001, the following categories and numbers represent the post-graduate activities and employment of doctoral degree graduates: Enrolled in a psychology doctoral program (n/a), enrolled in another graduate/professional program (n/a), enrolled in a post-doctoral residency/fellowship (0), employed in independent practice (0), employed in an academic position at a university (0), employed in an academic position at a 2-year/4-year college (0), employed in other positions at a higher education institution (0), employed in a professional position in a school system (2), employed in business or industry (research/consulting) (0), employed in business or industry (management) (0), employed in a government agency (research) (0), employed in a government agency (professional services) (1), employed in a community mental health/counseling center (0), employed in a hospital/medical center (0), still seeking employment (0), other employment position (0).

Additional Information:

Special Facilities or Resources: http://www.qc.edu/Psychology/lph.htm.

Application Information:

Send to: Office of Admissions, The Graduate School & University Center of the City University of New York, 365 Fifth Avenue, New York, NY 10016-4309. Students are admitted in the Fall, application deadline March 1. *Fee:* $40.

Columbia University
Health and Behavior Studies/School Psychology
Teachers College
525 West 120th Street, Box 120
New York, NY 10027
Telephone: (212) 678-3942
Fax: (212) 678-4034
E-mail: *stp4@columbia.edu*
Web: *http://www.tc.columbia.edu/academic/health*

Department Established:

1986. Chairperson: Charles Basch. Number of Faculty: total–full-time 2, part-time 3; women–full-time 1, part-time 2.

Programs and Degrees Offered:

Listed in the following order: Program area, degree type (T if terminal Master's), number awarded 7/00–6/01. School psychology EdD (T) 6.

APA Accreditation: School EdD: full.

Student Applications/Admissions:

Student Applications

School psychology EdD—Applications 2001–2002, 35. Total applicants accepted 2001–2002, 6. New applicants enrolled 2001–2002, 4. Total enrolled 2001–2002 full-time, 18, part-time, 21. Openings 2002–2003, 4. The Median number of years required for completion of a degree are 7. The number of students enrolled full and part-time, who were dismissed or voluntarily withdrew from this program area were 0.

Admissions Requirements:

Scores: Entries appear in this order: required test or GPA, minimum score (if required), median score of students entering in 2001–2002. Master's Programs: GRE-V no minimum stated, 500; GRE-Q no minimum stated, 570; GRE-V+Q no minimum stated, 1070; GRE-Analytical no minimum stated, 640; GRE-V+Q+Analytical no minimum stated, 1710; overall undergraduate GPA no minimum stated, 3.52. Doctoral Programs: GRE-V no minimum stated, 650; GRE-Q no minimum stated, 660; GRE-V+Q no minimum stated, 1300; GRE-Analytical no minimum stated, 690; GRE-V+Q+Analytical no minimum stated, 1990; overall undergraduate GPA no minimum stated, 3.51; last 2 years GPA no minimum stated; psychology GPA no minimum stated; psychology GPA no minimum stated.

Other Criteria: (importance of criteria rated low, medium, or high): research experience high, work experience medium, extracurricular activity low, clinically related public service low, GPA high, letters of recommendation high, interview high, statement of goals and objectives high, writing skills high.

Student Characteristics: The following represents characteristics of students in 2001–2002 in all graduate psychology programs in the department: Female–full-time 17, part-time 18; Male–full-time 1, part-time 3; African American/Black–full-time 0, part-time 4; Hispanic/Latino (a)–full-time 1, part-time 0; Asian/Pacific Islander–full-time 3, part-time 4; American Indian/Alaska Native–full-time 0, part-time 0; Multi-ethnic–full-time 0, part-time 0; students subject to the Americans with Disabilities Act–full-time 0, part-time 0.

Financial Information/Assistance:

Tuition for Full-Time Study: *Master's:* State residents $770 per credit hour; nonstate residents: $770 per credit hour. *Doctoral:* State residents $770 per credit hour; nonstate residents: $770 per credit hour.

Financial Assistance:

First Year Students: No information provided.
Advanced Students: No information provided.
Contact Information: For information on financial assistance, contact: Office of Student Aid, Box 309.

Internships/Practica: First year—Two practica in our Center for Educational and Psychological Services: (1) Practicum in Assessment of Reading and School Subject Difficulties (Fall); (2) Practicum in Psychoeducational Assessment with Culturally Diverse Students (Spring); Second year—Students engage in (1) Fieldwork (2 days/week over the academic year in one of our cooperating inner-city schools); (2) a practicum in psychoeducational groups (the groups are run within students' fieldwork sites); Third year—Externship (2 days/week over an academic year; most students are required to do 2 externships: one is a school and one in a hospital or clinic); Fourth or Fifth year—Internship (full calendar year; we encourage students to do the internship after completing most or all of their dissertation). For those doctoral students for whom a professional internship is required prior to graduation, 4 applied in 2000–2001. Of those who applied, 1 were placed in internships listed by the Association of Psychology Postdoctoral and Internship Programs (APPIC); 1 were placed in APA accredited internships.

Housing and Day Care: On-campus housing and day care facilities are available.

Employment of Department Graduates:

Master's Degree Graduates: Of those who graduated in the academic year 2000–2001, the following categories and numbers represent the post-graduate activities and employment of master's degree graduates: Enrolled in a psychology doctoral program (2), enrolled in another graduate/professional program (0), enrolled in a post-doctoral residency/fellowship (n/a), employed in independent practice (n/a), employed in a professional position in a school system (8).

Doctoral Degree Graduates: Of those who graduated in the academic year 2000–2001, the following categories and numbers represent the post-graduate activities and employment of doctoral degree graduates: Enrolled in a psychology doctoral program (n/a), enrolled in another graduate/professional program (n/a), enrolled in a post-doctoral residency/fellowship (2), employed in independent practice (0), employed in an academic position at a university (0), employed in an academic position at a 2-year/4-year college (0), employed in other positions at a higher education institution (0), employed in a professional position in a school system (1), employed in business or industry (research/consulting) (1), employed in business or industry (management) (1), employed in a government agency (research) (0), employed in a government agency (professional services) (0), employed in a community mental health/counseling center (0), employed in a hospital/medical center (1).

Additional Information:

Orientation, Objectives, and Emphasis of Department: The primary theoretical orientation of our program is cognitive with strong applications to instruction and mental health. We place a particularly strong emphasis on prevention and intervention in these areas. Throughout the curriculum, there is a balance between science and practice and we ensure that all students are well grounded in the theory and methods of psychological science. Most students opt to go through the general curriculum. Some adopt a specialization in one of the following areas: neuropsychological assessment, or the deaf and hearing impaired.

Special Facilities or Resources: The School Psychology program has strong collaborative relationships with 3 inner-city schools that serve as fieldwork and sites for our master's and doctoral students.

Information for Students With Physical Disabilities: College facilities are accessible to students with physical disabilities and the Office of Services for Students with Disabilities is available to counsel students, arrange accommodations, and advocate on behalf of students with disabilities. Limited parking also is available.

Application Information:
Send to: Office of Admissions. Students are admitted in the Fall, application deadline January 15; Spring, application deadline November 30. *Fee:* $50.

Columbia University
Psychology
1190 Amsterdam Avenue
New York, NY 10027
Telephone: (212) 854-3010
Fax: (212) 854-3609
E-mail: *winnie@psych.columbia.edu*

Department Established:
1867. Number of Faculty: total–full-time 19; women–full-time 8.

Student Applications/Admissions:

Admissions Requirements:

Scores: Entries appear in this order: required test or GPA, minimum score (if required), median score of students entering in 2001–2002. Doctoral Programs: GRE-V+Q 1200; last 2 years GPA no minimum stated; psychology GPA no minimum stated; psychology GPA no minimum stated.

Other Criteria: (importance of criteria rated low, medium, or high): GRE/MAT scores high, research experience high, work experience medium, extracurricular activity medium, clinically related public service medium, GPA high, letters of recommendation high, interview high, statement of goals and objectives high.

Student Characteristics: The following represents characteristics of students in 2001–2002 in all graduate psychology programs in the department: Female–full-time 18, part-time 0; Male–full-time 15, part-time 0; African American/Black–full-time 1, part-time 0; Hispanic/Latino (a)–full-time 2, part-time 0; Asian/Pacific Islander–full-time 2, part-time 0; American Indian/Alaska Native–full-time 0, part-time 0.

Financial Information/Assistance:

Tuition for Full-Time Study: *Doctoral:* State residents: per academic year $20,000.

Financial Assistance:

First Year Students: Fellowships and scholarships available for first-year. Tuition remission given: full.

Advanced Students: No information provided.

Contact Information: For information on financial assistance, contact: Thomas Tarduogno, Director Graduate School of Arts & Sciences.

Internships/Practica: No information provided.

Housing and Day Care: On-campus housing and day care facilities are available.

Employment of Department Graduates:

Master's Degree Graduates: Of those who graduated in the academic year 2000–2001, the following categories and numbers represent the post-graduate activities and employment of master's degree graduates: Enrolled in a post-doctoral residency/fellowship (n/a), employed in independent practice (n/a).

Doctoral Degree Graduates: Of those who graduated in the academic year 2000–2001, the following categories and numbers represent the post-graduate activities and employment of doctoral degree graduates: Enrolled in a psychology doctoral program (n/a), enrolled in another graduate/professional program (n/a).

Additional Information:

Orientation, Objectives, and Emphasis of Department: The program has a research-apprenticeship orientation, and trains students for careers in basic and applied research and teaching.

Special Facilities or Resources: All admitted students are guaranteed up to five years of support (tuition plus stipend). All are required to serve as teaching assistants for one semester per year.

Application Information:

Send to: Graduate School of Arts and Sciences, Columbia University, 107 Low Library, MC 4304 535 West 116th Street, New York, NY 10027-7004. Students are admitted in the Fall, application deadline Dec. 31st. *Fee:* $65. Must be enrolled at another University and be on financial aid at the university. Financial hardship.

Cornell University (2001 data)
Department of Psychology
The New York State College of Human Ecology
211 Uris Hall
Ithaca, NY 14853-4401
Telephone: (607) 255-6364
Fax: (607) 255-8433
E-mail: *dad6@cornell.edu*
Web: *http://www.gradschool.cornell.edu/grad/fields_2/ht*

Department Established:

1925. Chairperson: Elizabeth Adkins Regan. Number of Faculty: total–full-time 22; women–full-time 10; minority–full-time 2.

Programs and Degrees Offered:

Listed in the following order: Program area, degree type (T if terminal Master's), number awarded 7/00–6/01. Developmental PhD 7, human development family PhD.

Student Applications/Admissions:

Student Applications

Developmental PhD—Applications 2001–2002, 44. Total applicants accepted 2001–2002, 16. New applicants enrolled 2001–2002, 7. Total enrolled 2001–2002 full-time, 21. Openings 2002–2003, 7. *Human development family PhD*—Applications 2001–2002, 27. Total applicants accepted 2001–2002, 7. New applicants enrolled 2001–2002, 6. Total enrolled 2001–2002 full-time, 11. Openings 2002–2003, 3.

Admissions Requirements:

Scores: Entries appear in this order: required test or GPA, minimum score (if required), median score of students entering in 2001–2002. Doctoral Programs: GRE-V+Q+Analytical 1800, 1990.

Other Criteria: (importance of criteria rated low, medium, or high): GRE/MAT scores high, research experience high, work experience medium, extracurricular activity low, clinically related public service low, GPA high, letters of recommendation high, statement of goals and objectives high, match between interests high.

Student Characteristics: The following represents characteristics of students in 2001–2002 in all graduate psychology programs in the department: Female–full-time 10, part-time 0; Male–full-time 3, part-time 0; African American/Black–full-time 1, part-time 0; Hispanic/Latino (a)–full-time 0, part-time 0; Asian/Pacific Islander–full-time 0, part-time 0; American Indian/Alaska Native–full-time 0, part-time 0.

Financial Information/Assistance:

Tuition for Full-Time Study: No information provided.

Financial Assistance:

First Year Students: No information provided.

Advanced Students: No information provided.

Contact Information: For information on financial assistance, contact: The Graduate School.

Internships/Practica: No information provided.

Housing and Day Care: No on-campus housing and day care facilities are available.

Employment of Department Graduates:

Master's Degree Graduates: Of those who graduated in the academic year 2000–2001, the following categories and numbers represent the post-graduate activities and employment of master's degree graduates: Enrolled in a post-doctoral residency/fellowship (n/a), employed in independent practice (n/a).

Doctoral Degree Graduates: Of those who graduated in the academic year 2000–2001, the following categories and numbers represent the post-graduate activities and employment of doctoral degree graduates: Enrolled in a psychology doctoral program (n/a), enrolled in another graduate/professional program (n/a).

Additional Information:

Orientation, Objectives, and Emphasis of Department: The field offers two general majors. The major in Developmental Psychology focuses on individual development and the effects on it of various intrinsic and extrinsic factors. The major in Life Course Development focuses on the interrelationships among the individual, the family, and the larger society. The PhD in developmental psychology is intended to provide students with strong training in the general discipline of developmental psychology as well as more focused training within one or more of its sub-areas (cognitive, social-personality, biological, infancy, childhood, adolescence, and adulthood). The Life Course Development major is designed to meet the needs of students seeking advanced training that bridges basic and applied research in human development from a life course perspective. The program places heavy emphasis on research training. Students are prepared for careers in academic life in departments of psychology, sociology, or human development, in government agencies concerned with research or social policy, and in a range of programs involving community agencies or private enterprise. Training is not offered in clinical or counseling psychology, marriage counseling, or family therapy, nor is teacher certification offered.

Special Facilities or Resources: The department houses a number of laboratories directed by individual faculty conducting observational and experimental studies of basic processes in development. In addition, the Cornell Early Childhood Program operates a day care program that provides numerous opportunities for research. Students may become involved in research or demonstration projects in the College's Family Life Development Center (child maltreatment and families under stress) and Bronfenbrenner Life Course Institute (adulthood and aging). The department also maintains close relationships with many public schools, nursery schools, day care centers, and youth service agencies, and much research is conducted in those settings. Additionally, there are several experimental labs as well as graduate student computer facilities and data decoding rooms.

Application Information:
Send to: The Graduate School, Caldwell Hall, Cornell University, Ithaca, NY 14853; also available at: http://cuinfo.cornell.edu/cgi-bin/ gradask.fx. Students are admitted in the Fall, application deadline January 15. *Fee:* $65. In cases of extreme financial need, a fee waiver will be considered. A letter of request for a waiver and documentation of need such as a letter from the college financial aid office needs to be submitted.

Cornell University
Graduate Field of Psychology
212 Uris Hall
Ithaca, NY 14853-7601
Telephone: (607) 255-6364
Fax: (607) 255-8433
E-mail: *lap5@cornell.edu*
Web: *http://comp9.psych.cornell.edu*

Department Established:
1885. Director of Graduate Studies: Robert Johnston. Number of Faculty: total–full-time 23, part-time 1; women–full-time 6.

Programs and Degrees Offered:
Listed in the following order: Program area, degree type (T if terminal Master's), number awarded 7/00–6/01. Biopsychology & neuroscience PhD 2, cognition & perception PhD 2, personality and social PhD 1.

Student Applications/Admissions:

Student Applications

Biopsychology & neuroscience PhD—Applications 2001–2002, 26. Total applicants accepted 2001–2002, 3. New applicants enrolled 2001–2002, 3. Total enrolled 2001–2002 full-time, 13. Openings 2002–2003, 4. *Cognition & perception PhD*—Applications 2001–2002, 33. Total applicants accepted 2001–2002, 3. New applicants enrolled 2001–2002, 1. Total enrolled 2001–2002 full-time, 8. Openings 2002–2003, 4. *Personality and social PhD*—Applications 2001–2002, 73. Total applicants accepted 2001–2002, 1. New applicants enrolled 2001–2002, 1. Total enrolled 2001–2002 full-time, 8. Openings 2002–2003, 3.

Admissions Requirements:

Scores: Entries appear in this order: required test or GPA, minimum score (if required), median score of students entering in 2001–2002. Doctoral Programs: GRE-V no minimum stated, 562; GRE-Q no minimum stated, 685; GRE-V+Q no minimum stated, 1247; GRE-Analytical no minimum stated, 707; GRE-V+Q+Analytical no minimum stated, 1954; GRE-Subject(Psych) no minimum stated, 720; overall undergraduate GPA no minimum stated; last 2 years GPA no minimum stated; psychology GPA no minimum stated; psychology GPA no minimum stated.

Other Criteria: (importance of criteria rated low, medium, or high): GRE/MAT scores high, research experience high, work experience low, extracurricular activity low, GPA high, letters of recommendation high, statement of goals and objectives high, research interests high.

Student Characteristics: The following represents characteristics of students in 2001–2002 in all graduate psychology programs in the department: Female–full-time 6, part-time 0; Male–full-time

2, part-time 0; African American/Black–full-time 0, part-time 0; Hispanic/Latino (a)–full-time 0, part-time 0; Asian/Pacific Islander–full-time 0, part-time 0; American Indian/Alaska Native–full-time 0, part-time 0.

Financial Information/Assistance:

Tuition for Full-Time Study: No information provided.

Financial Assistance:

First Year Students: No information provided.
Advanced Students: No information provided.
Contact Information: Of all students currently enrolled full-time, 0% benefited from one or more of the listed financial assistance programs.

Internships/Practica: No information provided.

Housing and Day Care: No on-campus housing and day care facilities are available.

Employment of Department Graduates:

Master's Degree Graduates: Of those who graduated in the academic year 2000–2001, the following categories and numbers represent the post-graduate activities and employment of master's degree graduates: Enrolled in a post-doctoral residency/fellowship (n/a), employed in independent practice (n/a).
Doctoral Degree Graduates: Of those who graduated in the academic year 2000–2001, the following categories and numbers represent the post-graduate activities and employment of doctoral degree graduates: Enrolled in a psychology doctoral program (n/a), enrolled in another graduate/professional program (n/a).

Additional Information:

Orientation, Objectives, and Emphasis of Department: The Psychology Department of the College of Arts and Sciences at Cornell has a faculty of 24 psychologists and is divided into three areas—cognition & perception (encompassing cognition, language, perception, and its developmental perspectives), biopsychology & neuroscience (focusing on hormones and behavior, neural development, and sensory systems), and social/personality (social cognition, judgment, and decision making). We do not have clinical, community, or counseling programs. We have a strong research orientation, training our students to become professional academics or researchers. Our 28 students design their graduate programs under the supervision of their special committees. These committees consist of at least four members of the graduate faculty at Cornell; at least three are from within the department. The chair of the committee is a member of the Graduate Field of Psychology, which consists of the 24 members of our department plus 20 researchers in allied fields (human development and family studies, education, industrial and labor relations, and neurobiology and behavior). Two other committee members serve as minor members, one of whom can be outside the Graduate Field of Psychology, and the fourth member oversees breadth requirements.

Special Facilities or Resources: The three areas of our program each have laboratories associated with them. Each of the members of the cognition & perception program has a separate laboratory, fully equipped with state-of-the-art computer equipment. In addition, the program has several computer-based teaching laboratories. The biopsychologists each have separate labs and computers, and animal housing facilities where relevant, but they share much equipment and lab space. There is also a teaching lab associated with the biopsychology group labs. The social-personality psychologists share a large lab space with the sociology department. The department also has a small research library, machine, wood, and electronic shops.

Application Information:

Send to: Graduate School, Caldwell Hall, Cornell University, Ithaca, NY 14853. Students are admitted in the Fall, application deadline January 15. *Fee:* $65.

Fordham University (2001 data)
Department of Psychology
Fordham Road and Southern Boulevard
Bronx, NY 10458
Telephone: (718) 817-3775
Fax: (718) 817-3785
E-mail: *wertz@fordham.edu*
Web: *http://www.fordham.edu*

Department Established:

Chairperson: Frederick J. Wertz. Number of Faculty: total–full-time 27, part-time 3; women–full-time 7, part-time 2; minority–full-time 2.

Programs and Degrees Offered:

Listed in the following order: Program area, degree type (T if terminal Master's), number awarded 7/00–6/01. Applied developmental psycho PhD 5, clinical PhD 24, psychometric PhD 1.

APA Accreditation: Clinical PhD: full.

Student Applications/Admissions:
Student Applications

Applied developmental psycho PhD—Applications 2001–2002, 47. Total applicants accepted 2001–2002, 14. New applicants enrolled 2001–2002, 10. Total enrolled 2001–2002 full-time, 51. Openings 2002–2003, 15. *Clinical PhD*—Applications 2001–2002, 325. Total applicants accepted 2001–2002, 26. New applicants enrolled 2001–2002, 13. Total enrolled 2001–2002 full-time, 70. Openings 2002–2003, 15. *Psychometric PhD*—Applications 2001–2002, 9. Total applicants accepted 2001–2002, 5. New applicants enrolled 2001–2002, 2. Total enrolled 2001–2002 full-time, 12. Openings 2002–2003, 5.

Admissions Requirements:

Scores: Entries appear in this order: required test or GPA, minimum score (if required), median score of students entering in 2001–2002. Master's Programs: overall undergraduate GPA no minimum stated. Doctoral Programs: GRE-Analytical 650; GRE-V+Q+Analytical 650; overall undergraduate GPA 3.5. Clinical average GRE and V+Q is 650.
Other Criteria: (importance of criteria rated low, medium, or high): GRE/MAT scores high, research experience high, work experience high, extracurricular activity high, clinically related public service high, GPA high, letters of recommendation high, interview high, statement of goals and objectives high.

Student Characteristics: The following represents characteristics of students in 2001–2002 in all graduate psychology programs in the department: Female–full-time 18, part-time 0; Male–full-time 7, part-time 0; African American/Black–full-time 3, part-time 0; Hispanic/Latino (a)–full-time 2, part-time 0; Asian/Pacific Islander–full-time 3, part-time 0; American Indian/Alaska Native–full-time 0, part-time 0.

Financial Information/Assistance:

Tuition for Full-Time Study: No information provided.

Financial Assistance:

First Year Students: Teaching assistantships available for first-year. Average amount paid per academic year: $10,500. Average number of hours worked per week: 15. Apply by Jan 8. Tuition remission given: full. Research assistantships available for first-year. Average amount paid per academic year: $10,500. Average number of hours worked per week: 15. Apply by Jan 8. Tuition remission given: full. Fellowships and scholarships available for first-year. Average amount paid per academic year: $15,000. Average number of hours worked per week: 8. Apply by Jan 8. Tuition remission given: full.

Advanced Students: Teaching assistantships available for advanced students. Average amount paid per academic year: $10,500. Average number of hours worked per week: 15. Apply by Feb 15. Tuition remission given: full. Research assistantships available for advanced students. Average amount paid per academic year: $10,500. Average number of hours worked per week: 15. Apply by Feb 15. Tuition remission given: full. Fellowships and scholarships available for advanced students. Average amount paid per academic year: $15,000. Average number of hours worked per week: 15. Apply by Feb 15. Tuition remission given: full.

Contact Information: Of all students currently enrolled full-time, 85% benefited from one or more of the listed financial assistance programs. For information on financial assistance, contact: Graduate Admissions for Financial Aid application.

Internships/Practica: Internships in a variety of public and private facilities are available for students after they have completed their coursework in the program.

Housing and Day Care: No on-campus housing and day care facilities are available.

Employment of Department Graduates:

Master's Degree Graduates: Of those who graduated in the academic year 2000–2001, the following categories and numbers represent the post-graduate activities and employment of master's degree graduates: Enrolled in a post-doctoral residency/fellowship (n/a), employed in independent practice (n/a).

Doctoral Degree Graduates: Of those who graduated in the academic year 2000–2001, the following categories and numbers represent the post-graduate activities and employment of doctoral degree graduates: Enrolled in a psychology doctoral program (n/a), enrolled in another graduate/professional program (n/a).

Additional Information:

Orientation, Objectives, and Emphasis of Department: The clinical psychology program prepares students for practice, research, and teaching in the clinical field, emphasizing that they are both professionals and scientists. The courses in the clinical program can be grouped under four major areas: clinical theory and meth-odology, research topics and methods, behavioral classification and assessment, and treatment approaches, and includes a full-time, one-year internship. The developmental psychology program is designed to train professionals who can conduct both basic and applied research in developmental processes across the life-span and who can share their knowledge in academic and community-based setting. A subspecialty in applied developmental psychology (ADP) focuses on the interplay between developmental processes and social contexts including design and evaluation of programs; consultation to courts, lawyers, and public policy makers; development and evaluation of programs and materials directed at children and families; and parent and family education. The psychometrics program focuses on the quantitative and research-oriented communalities relevant to most of the behavioral sciences, and their applications in industry, education, and the health services. Students in the psychometrics program become familiar with statistics, psychological testing, use of computer systems, and other research techniques, as well as with the psychology of individual differences.

Special Facilities or Resources: Clinical psychology uses three large rooms with one-way vision screens and sound recording equipment for testing, interviewing, and psychotherapy. The Human Development Laboratory, which consists of observation rooms and smaller testing rooms, is available for a wide range of psychological projects. Practicum training in both applied developmental and clinical psychology is conducted at various agencies in the metropolitan area. The department has microcomputers for student use as well as terminals connected with the university's central computer.

Application Information:
Send to: Graduate Admissions Office, Keating 216. Students are admitted in the Fall, application deadline January 8. *Fee:* $50. Paper Application fee is $60; electronic application fee is $50.

Fordham University
Pastoral Counseling and Spiritual Care (Pastoral Psychology)
Graduate School of Religion and Religious Education
441 E. Fordham Road
Bronx, NY 10458-9993
Telephone: (718) 817-4800
Fax: (718) 817-3352
E-mail: *vnovak@fordham.edu*
Web: *http://www.fordham.edu/gsre/grrb_main.html*

Department Established:
1999. Dean and Chair: Vincent M. Novak, S. J. Number of Faculty: total–full-time 3, part-time 5; women–full-time 2, part-time 3.

Programs and Degrees Offered:
Listed in the following order: Program area, degree type (T if terminal Master's), number awarded 7/00–6/01. Pastoral counseling and spirit MA (T) N/A.

APA Accreditation: School PhD: full.

Student Applications/Admissions:

Student Applications

Pastoral counseling and spirit MA—Applications 2001–2002, 8. Total applicants accepted 2001–2002, 8. New applicants enrolled 2001–2002, 8. Total enrolled 2001–2002 full-time, 8. Openings 2002–2003, 12. The Median number of years required for completion of a degree are 2. The number of students enrolled full and part-time, who were dismissed or voluntarily withdrew from this program area were 0.

Admissions Requirements:

Scores: Entries appear in this order: required test or GPA, minimum score (if required), median score of students entering in 2001–2002. Master's Programs: MAT no minimum stated; overall undergraduate GPA no minimum stated; last 2 years GPA no minimum stated. Doctoral Programs: MAT no minimum stated; last 2 years GPA no minimum stated; psychology GPA no minimum stated; psychology GPA no minimum stated. N/A

Other Criteria: (importance of criteria rated low, medium, or high): GRE/MAT scores medium, work experience low, extracurricular activity low, GPA high, letters of recommendation high, interview high, statement of goals and objectives high, perceived motivation high.

Student Characteristics: The following represents characteristics of students in 2001–2002 in all graduate psychology programs in the department: Female–full-time 4, part-time 0; Male–full-time 4, part-time 0; African American/Black–full-time 1, part-time 0; Hispanic/Latino (a)–full-time 2, part-time 0; Asian/Pacific Islander–full-time 0, part-time 0; American Indian/Alaska Native–full-time 0, part-time 0.

Financial Information/Assistance:

Tuition for Full-Time Study: *Master's:* State residents $535 per credit hour; nonstate residents: $535 per credit hour. *Doctoral:* State residents: $535 per credit hour; nonstate residents: $535 per credit hour.

Financial Assistance:

First Year Students: No information provided.
Advanced Students: No information provided.
Contact Information: Of all students currently enrolled full-time, 0% benefited from one or more of the listed financial assistance programs. For information on financial assistance, contact: Dean Vincent Novak, S. J. at same address.

Internships/Practica: In conjunction with the MA program, Clinical Pastoral Education (CPE) is available in neighboring hospitals in New York City. One unit of CPE can account for the equivalent of 6 graduate credits in the degree program. Field Placement will be an essential part of the core curriculum, along with Pastoral Interviewing and Diagnosis.

Housing and Day Care: No on-campus housing and day care facilities are available.

Employment of Department Graduates:

Master's Degree Graduates: Of those who graduated in the academic year 2000–2001, the following categories and numbers represent the post-graduate activities and employment of master's degree graduates: Enrolled in a post-doctoral residency/fellowship (n/a), employed in independent practice (n/a).

Doctoral Degree Graduates: Of those who graduated in the academic year 2000–2001, the following categories and numbers represent the post-graduate activities and employment of doctoral degree graduates: Enrolled in a psychology doctoral program (n/a), enrolled in another graduate/professional program (n/a).

Additional Information:

Orientation, Objectives, and Emphasis of Department: The Master of Arts in Pastoral Counseling and Spiritual Care is a professional degree registered in 1999 with the Office of Higher Education for the State of New York. It accepted the first cohort of 8 degree candidates in this graduate school for the Fall semester 2000, commencing August 28 at Fordham University's Rose Hill campus. Its overarching goal is to integrate the human sciences and counseling skills with the spiritual insights degree candidates seek to derive from their religious faiths. It aims to train pastoral counselors for all institutional environments of church and state: Practitioners in health care and care of the elderly, nursing and medical personnel, parish personnel, clergy and lay, who minister to persons, in need emotionally and spiritually. The body-mind-spirit model operates here in serving the needs of complete human beings in all facets of their personhood. With problematic HMOs, short-term hospital care, and increasing necessity for long-term home care, the program seeks to turn out knowledgeable and highly motivated leaders for the different institutions of society. Partners in Healing is the program's theme, providing a rich association with a New York ecumenical organization with that name, founded by one of our present full-time faculty.

Special Facilities or Resources: This graduate school enjoys its own professional library. The University library, it should be noted, is state-of-the-art on the Rose Hill campus. Computer facilities are available to students.

Information for Students With Physical Disabilities: Since this graduate school is part of Fordham University, special effort is made university-wide to accommodate students with physical disabilities.

Application Information:

Send to: Dean, Graduate School of Religion and Religious Education, 441. E. Fordham Road, Bronx, NY 10458-9993. Students are admitted in the Fall, application deadline April 15. *Fee:* $55.

Hofstra University
Department of Psychology
Hofstra College of Liberal Arts and Sciences
Hauser Hall
Hempstead, NY 11549
Telephone: (516) 463-5624
Fax: (516) 463-6052
E-mail: *psymls@Mail1.Hofstra.edu*
Web: *http://www.hofstra.edu/Academics/HCLAS/Psychology/*

Department Established:

1948. Chairperson: Howard Kassinove. Number of Faculty: total–full-time 26, part-time 32; women–full-time 5, part-time 16; minority–full-time 2, part-time 2.

Programs and Degrees Offered:

Listed in the following order: Program area, degree type (T if terminal Master's), number awarded 7/00–6/01. Clinical-school PhD 21, industrial/organization MA (T) 30, school-community PsyD 12.

APA Accreditation: Combined PhD: full.

Student Applications/Admissions:

Student Applications

Clinical-school PhD—Applications 2001–2002, 137. Total applicants accepted 2001–2002, 41. New applicants enrolled 2001–2002, 21. Total enrolled 2001–2002 full-time, 129. Openings 2002–2003, 24. Industrial/organization MA—Applications 2001–2002, 85. Total applicants accepted 2001–2002, 40. New applicants enrolled 2001–2002, 26. Total enrolled 2001–2002 full-time, 17, part-time, 8. Openings 2002–2003, 30. School-community PsyD—Applications 2001–2002, 80. Total applicants accepted 2001–2002, 31. New applicants enrolled 2001–2002, 19. Total enrolled 2001–2002 full-time, 50, part-time, 25. Openings 2002–2003, 20.

Admissions Requirements:

Scores: Entries appear in this order: required test or GPA, minimum score (if required), median score of students entering in 2001–2002. Master's Programs: GRE-V 500, 530; GRE-Q 500, 560; overall undergraduate GPA 3.0, 3.30. Doctoral Programs: GRE-V 500, 547; GRE-Q 500, 566; GRE-V+Q 1000, 1114; GRE-Subject(Psych) no minimum stated, 610; overall undergraduate GPA 3.0, 3.3; last 2 years GPA no minimum stated; psychology GPA no minimum stated; psychology GPA no minimum stated.

Other Criteria: (importance of criteria rated low, medium, or high): GRE/MAT scores high, research experience medium, work experience medium, extracurricular activity low, clinically related public service medium, GPA high, letters of recommendation medium, interview high, statement of goals and objectives low. For PsyD program: research experience low, clinically related public service medium, statement of goals and objectives medium. For PhD program: research experience high, especially professional presentations and publications, clinically related public service high, statement of goals and objectives high.

Student Characteristics: The following represents characteristics of students in 2001–2002 in all graduate psychology programs in the department: Female–full-time 46, part-time 11; Male–full-time 15, part-time 1; African American/Black–full-time 4, part-time 0; Hispanic/Latino (a)–full-time 2, part-time 0; Asian/Pacific Islander–full-time 1, part-time 0; American Indian/Alaska Native–full-time 0, part-time 0.

Financial Information/Assistance:

Tuition for Full-Time Study: No information provided.

Financial Assistance:

First Year Students: Teaching assistantships available for first-year. Research assistantships available for first-year. Fellowships and scholarships available for first-year. Tuition remission given: full and partial.

Advanced Students: Teaching assistantships available for advanced students. Research assistantships available for advanced students. Fellowships and scholarships available for advanced students. Tuition remission given: full and partial.

Contact Information: No information provided.

Internships/Practica: In the PhD program in Combined Clinical and School Psychology, from the first year onward, students begin a series of practica experiences in which assessment, testing, and interviewing skills are developed by working with patients in hospital, school, and clinic settings. As students become more familiar with the concepts of psychopathology, they are exposed to serious disorders through a diversified and extended internship experience over a two year period. Students are placed in community mental health centers, psychiatric hospitals, special educational facilities, general medical centers, public schools, etc.

Housing and Day Care: No on-campus housing or day care facilities are available.

Employment of Department Graduates:

Master's Degree Graduates: Of those who graduated in the academic year 2000–2001, the following categories and numbers represent the post-graduate activities and employment of master's degree graduates: Enrolled in a post-doctoral residency/fellowship (n/a), employed in independent practice (n/a).

Doctoral Degree Graduates: Of those who graduated in the academic year 2000–2001, the following categories and numbers represent the post-graduate activities and employment of doctoral degree graduates: Enrolled in a psychology doctoral program (n/a), enrolled in another graduate/professional program (n/a).

Additional Information:

Orientation, Objectives, and Emphasis of Department: The PhD program in Combined Clinical and School Psychology provides a full-time, comprehensive educational experience which prepares students for independent and institutional practice, and academic careers. Established in 1967, and fully APA accredited, it immerses students into the theory, history, research and practice of professional Psychology in clinical and school settings. From the first year onward, students begin a series of practica experiences in which assessment, testing, and interviewing skills are developed by working with patients in hospital, school, and clinic settings. In addition to classes on assessment and the practice of psychotherapy, coursework focuses upon the basic findings of psychological science. The combined clinical and school psychology PhD program develops psychologists with a strong background in psychological theory, skill and competence in working with individuals and groups, and the ability to initiate and assume responsibility for meaningful research. The program provides a sound foundation so that the student may grow to think scientifically and to develop the professional competence necessary for working with individuals in educational, clinical, and other community settings. The primary theoretical orientation of the program is based upon behavioral theory, with the spectrum from applied behavior analysis to cognitive behavioral approaches being represented. Recent graduates of our program have readily found employment in schools, mental health clinics, and hospitals. Others have chosen less traveled paths by becoming college and university faculty members, research scientists, or editors for psychological publishers. Additionally, many engage in private practice. The school-community PsyD program trains practitioners who are skilled in providing psychological services to schools and other community mental health settings. In addition to being trained in a traditional model of helping families and individuals, special emphasis is placed upon training the psychologist to work as a consultant whose subject of study is the system in which health services are provided. Thus, school-community PsyD students will be trained as consultants who are involved in mental health program implementation and evaluation in setting such as the judicial system, the schools, personnel agencies, police departments, immigration centers, etc. The theoretical orientation of the program is based upon a social learning perspective. The MA Program in Industrial/Organizational Psychology prepares students for careers in human resources, training, management, and organizational development. It provides a background in statistics, research design, social psychology, cognition and perception, and learning. The courses in I/O Psychology include selection, training, performance appraisal, worker motivation, and organization development. The curriculum is strengthened by an internship sequence which provides on-site supervised experience working on applied projects in business. The types of work that graduates perform include employee selection, management development, survey research, training, organizational development, performance appraisal, career development, and program evaluation.

Special Facilities or Resources: A psychological clinic where students have their practica is run by the department. A laboratory, which is instrumented for videotaping, is equipped to handle research in areas of interviewing, communication, problem solving, and team building. An outstanding library and a computer center are available, as well as several department terminals, microcomputers, and videotape equipment.

Application Information:
Send to: Graduate Admissions, Bernon Hall, Hofstra University, Hempstead, NY 11549. Students are admitted in the Fall, application deadline January 15. *Fee:* $40.

Iona College
Department of Psychology/Master of Arts in Psychology
715 North Avenue
New Rochelle, NY 10801
Telephone: (914) 633-2048
Fax: (914) 633-2528
E-mail: *pgreene@iona.edu*
Web: *http://www.iona.edu/academic/arts_sci/departments/*

Department Established:
1963. Chairperson: Paul Greene. Number of Faculty: total–full-time 9, part-time 20; women–full-time 7, part-time 15; minority–full-time 2.

Programs and Degrees Offered:
Listed in the following order: Program area, degree type (T if terminal Master's), number awarded 7/00–6/01. General MA (T) 4, Guidance and Counseling MA (T), school.

Student Applications/Admissions:
Student Applications
General MA—Applications 2001–2002, 8. Total applicants accepted 2001–2002, 6. New applicants enrolled 2001–2002, 6. Total enrolled 2001–2002 full-time, 8, part-time, 4. Open-ings 2002–2003, 15. The Median number of years required for completion of a degree are 3. The number of students enrolled full and part-time, who were dismissed or voluntarily withdrew from this program area were 2. *Guidance and Counseling MA*—Applications 2001–2002, 2. Total applicants accepted 2001–2002, 1. New applicants enrolled 2001–2002, 1. Total enrolled 2001–2002 full-time, 1. Openings 2002–2003, 5. The Median number of years required for completion of a degree are 2. The number of students enrolled full and part-time, who were dismissed or voluntarily withdrew from this program area were 0.

Admissions Requirements:
Scores: Entries appear in this order: required test or GPA, minimum score (if required), median score of students entering in 2001–2002. Master's Programs: overall undergraduate GPA 3.0. The Chair may grant exceptions to the minimum requirements for admission as a non-matriculated student. Doctoral Programs: last 2 years GPA no minimum stated; psychology GPA no minimum stated; psychology GPA no minimum stated.
Other Criteria: (importance of criteria rated low, medium, or high): research experience high, work experience medium, extracurricular activity medium, clinically related public service medium, GPA high, letters of recommendation high, interview medium.

Student Characteristics: The following represents characteristics of students in 2001–2002 in all graduate psychology programs in the department: Female–full-time 19, part-time 22; Male–full-time 1, part-time 2; African American/Black–full-time 1, part-time 4; Hispanic/Latino (a)–full-time 1, part-time 4; Asian/Pacific Islander–full-time 0, part-time 0; American Indian/Alaska Native–full-time 0, part-time 0.

Financial Information/Assistance:
Tuition for Full-Time Study: No information provided.

Financial Assistance:
First Year Students: Fellowships and scholarships available for first-year. Average number of hours worked per week: 20. Tuition remission given: partial.
Advanced Students: Fellowships and scholarships available for advanced students. Average number of hours worked per week: 20. Tuition remission given: partial.
Contact Information: Of all students currently enrolled full-time, 15% benefited from one or more of the listed financial assistance programs. For information on financial assistance, contact: Office of Financial Aid.

Internships/Practica: Students specializing in applied psychology who intend to go on to meet New York State requirements to be employed as a School Psychologist or School Counselor are required to take appropriate internship courses. While there is no guarantee that the student will get accepted by a site, the Department fully assists its students providing a written manual of instructions and personal guidance.

Housing and Day Care: No on-campus housing and day care facilities are available.

Employment of Department Graduates:

Master's Degree Graduates: Of those who graduated in the academic year 2000–2001, the following categories and numbers represent the post-graduate activities and employment of master's degree graduates: Enrolled in a psychology doctoral program (1), enrolled in another graduate/professional program (1), enrolled in a post-doctoral residency/fellowship (n/a), employed in independent practice (n/a), employed in an academic position at a 2-year/4-year college (3), employed in a professional position in a school system (3), employed in business or industry (research/consulting) (2), employed in a hospital/medical center (1), other employment position (1).

Doctoral Degree Graduates: Of those who graduated in the academic year 2000–2001, the following categories and numbers represent the post-graduate activities and employment of doctoral degree graduates: Enrolled in a psychology doctoral program (n/a), enrolled in another graduate/professional program (n/a).

Additional Information:

Orientation, Objectives, and Emphasis of Department: The MA in Psychology degree, with areas of specialization in Experimental Psychology, School Psychology, Counseling and Guidance, and Applied Psychology, has been designed for persons who are considering a career in psychology or who are en route to doctoral study in psychology, or are already employed in the field. The program provides a balance of theoretical, methodological, and practical expertise, as well as extensive training in written and oral expression. It is designed to provide pertinent new experiences, to enhance knowledge in substantive areas, and to facilitate maximum development of essential professional competencies and attitudes. The master's program in Psychology has several goals. Students gain an understanding of the scientific method and training in how to frame, test, and evaluate hypotheses; an appreciation of how human problems can be resolved through the application of psychological knowledge, scientific skills, and problem solving strategies; expertise in utilizing the scientific database of psychology to advance the welfare of their fellow citizens; an opportunity to address quality of life issues and complex social problems with techniques of cooperation, social facilitation, listening, and self-improvement.

Special Facilities or Resources: The Department contains 2000 square feet of research space and supports research projects in specialties of psychology including social, perception, developmental, clinical, sports physiological, learning, and cognition. Extensive computer and software capabilities are available.

Information for Students With Physical Disabilities: Per Section 504 of the Rehabilitation Act of 1973 and the Americans with Disabilities Act of 1990, Iona College does not discriminate on the basis of handicap against otherwise qualified persons by excluding them from participating in, denying them the benefit of, or otherwise subjecting them to discrimination under any college program or activity. In addition, the college provides reasonable auxiliary aids and academic adjustments without charge.

Application Information:
Send to: Office of Graduate Admissions, School of Arts and Sciences. Students are admitted in the Fall; Winter; Spring; Summer. *Fee:* $25.

Long Island University
Department of Psychology
C.W. Post
720 Northern Boulevard
Brookville, NY 11548
Telephone: (516) 299-2377
Fax: (516) 299-3105
E-mail: *gerald.lachter@liu.edu*
Web: *http://www.cwpost.liunet.edu/cwis/cwp/psych/psych.htm*

Department Established:
1954. Chairperson: Gerald D. Lachter. Number of Faculty: total–full-time 17, part-time 7; women–full-time 6, part-time 5; minority–full-time 1.

Programs and Degrees Offered:
Listed in the following order: Program area, degree type (T if terminal Master's), number awarded 7/00–6/01. Clinical PsyD 12, experimental MA (T) 2.

APA Accreditation: Clinical PsyD: full.

Student Applications/Admissions:
Student Applications

Clinical PsyD—Applications 2001–2002, 177. Total applicants accepted 2001–2002, 49. New applicants enrolled 2001–2002, 14. Total enrolled 2001–2002 full-time, 72. Openings 2002–2003, 14. The Median number of years required for completion of a degree are 4. *Experimental MA*—Applications 2001–2002, 35. Total applicants accepted 2001–2002, 13. New applicants enrolled 2001–2002, 3. Total enrolled 2001–2002 full-time, 3, part-time, 2. Openings 2002–2003, 10. The Median number of years required for completion of a degree are 2. The number of students enrolled full and part-time, who were dismissed or voluntarily withdrew from this program area were 1.

Admissions Requirements:
Scores: Entries appear in this order: required test or GPA, minimum score (if required), median score of students entering in 2001–2002. Master's Programs: GRE-V 500, 573; GRE-Q 500, 573; overall undergraduate GPA 3.0, 3.33. Doctoral Programs: GRE-V 550; GRE-Q 550; GRE-Subject(Psych) 610; overall undergraduate GPA 3.6; last 2 years GPA no minimum stated; psychology GPA no minimum stated; psychology GPA no minimum stated.

Other Criteria: (importance of criteria rated low, medium, or high): GRE/MAT scores medium, research experience high, work experience high, extracurricular activity low, clinically related public service high, GPA high, letters of recommendation high, interview high, statement of goals and objectives medium.

Student Characteristics: The following represents characteristics of students in 2001–2002 in all graduate psychology programs in the department: Female–full-time 58, part-time 3; Male–full-time 17, part-time 0; African American/Black–full-time 3, part-time 0; Hispanic/Latino (a)–full-time 7, part-time 0; Asian/Pacific Islander–full-time 7, part-time 0; American Indian/Alaska Native–full-time 1, part-time 0; students subject to the Americans with Disabilities Act–full-time 1.

Financial Information/Assistance:

Tuition for Full-Time Study: *Master's:* State residents per academic year $10,296, $573 per credit hour; nonstate residents: per academic year $10,296, $573 per credit hour.

Financial Assistance:

First Year Students: Teaching assistantships available for first-year. Tuition remission given: partial. Research assistantships available for first-year.

Advanced Students: No information provided.

Contact Information: Of all students currently enrolled full-time, 75% benefited from one or more of the listed financial assistance programs. For information on financial assistance, contact: Director, Graduate Program.

Internships/Practica: A wide range of internship and practicum placements are available. For those doctoral students for whom a professional internship is required prior to graduation, 12 applied in 2000–2001. Of those who applied, 12 were placed in internships listed by the Association of Psychology Postdoctoral and Internship Programs (APPIC); 12 were placed in APA accredited internships.

Housing and Day Care: On-campus housing and day care facilities are available.

Employment of Department Graduates:

Master's Degree Graduates: Of those who graduated in the academic year 2000–2001, the following categories and numbers represent the post-graduate activities and employment of master's degree graduates: Enrolled in a post-doctoral residency/fellowship (n/a), employed in independent practice (n/a).

Doctoral Degree Graduates: Of those who graduated in the academic year 2000–2001, the following categories and numbers represent the post-graduate activities and employment of doctoral degree graduates: Enrolled in a psychology doctoral program (n/a), enrolled in another graduate/professional program (n/a).

Additional Information:

Orientation, Objectives, and Emphasis of Department: The clinical psychology doctoral program is distinctive in three ways. First, the mission of the program is to teach scholar-practitioners to provide clinical psychology services in the public sector. Second, in addition to developing clinical psychologists with the basic knowledge, skills, and values necessary for competent and ethical practice, students receive advanced training in one of three areas of concentration: family violence, developmental disabilities, or serious and persistent mental illness. These concentrations represent an attempt to provide underserved populations with highly trained clinical psychologists motivated and able to offer helpful services. Third, the program offers students a focus on two theoretical orientations; psychodynamic and cognitive-behavioral. Each year students receive supervised training in clinical practice at various area mental health facilities. Students also receive considerable individual attention throughout the educational experience. The Master's degree program gives students a broad background in Experimental Psychology. Faculty interests include Behavior Analysis, Cognition and Perception, and Neuroscience. The program is designed to prepare students for admission to doctoral programs, or to give them the skills necessary to obtain employment.

Special Facilities or Resources: Laboratories exist for the study of animal and human learning, cognition and perception, and neuroscience.

Application Information:

Send to: Graduate Admissions, C.W. Post, Brookville, NY 11548. Students are admitted in the Fall. Fall deadlines — February 1, PsyD; June 1, MA. *Fee:* $30.

Long Island University (2001 data)

Psychology/Clinical Psychology
Richard L. Conolly College
1 University Plaza
Brooklyn, NY 11201
Telephone: (718) 488-1164
Fax: (718) 488-1179
E-mail: *nicholas.papouchis@liu.edu*

Department Established:

1967. Director, PhD Program in Clinical Psychology: Nicholas Papouchis. Number of Faculty: total–full-time 14, part-time 6; women–full-time 6, part-time 2; minority–full-time 3, part-time 2.

Programs and Degrees Offered:

Listed in the following order: Program area, degree type (T if terminal Master's), number awarded 7/00–6/01. Clinical PhD 18, general MA (T) 27.

APA Accreditation: Clinical PhD: full.

Student Applications/Admissions:

Student Applications

Clinical PhD—Applications 2001–2002, 175. Total applicants accepted 2001–2002, 26. New applicants enrolled 2001–2002, 16. Total enrolled 2001–2002 full-time, 90, part-time, 23. Openings 2002–2003, 16. The Median number of years required for completion of a degree are 6. *General MA*—Applications 2001–2002, 30. Total applicants accepted 2001–2002, 27. New applicants enrolled 2001–2002, 54. Total enrolled 2001–2002 full-time, 28, part-time, 20. Openings 2002–2003, 28.

Admissions Requirements:

Scores: Entries appear in this order: required test or GPA, minimum score (if required), median score of students entering in 2001–2002. Master's Programs: overall undergraduate GPA 2.75, 3.0; psychology GPA 3.0, 3.2. Doctoral Programs: GRE-V 550, 650; GRE-Q 550, 625; GRE-V+Q 1100, 1275; GRE-Analytical 600, 625; GRE-V+Q+Analytical 1700, 1850; GRE-Subject(Psych) 550, 625; overall undergraduate GPA 3.2, 3.6; psychology GPA 3.50, 3.50.

Other Criteria: (importance of criteria rated low, medium, or high): GRE/MAT scores high, research experience medium, work experience medium, extracurricular activity low, clinically related public service medium, GPA high, letters of recommendation high, interview high, statement of goals and objectives medium.

Student Characteristics: The following represents characteristics of students in 2001–2002 in all graduate psychology programs in the department: Female–full-time 28, part-time 26; Male–full-time 9, part-time 7; African American/Black–full-time 7, part-time 13; Hispanic/Latino (a)–full-time 5, part-time 5; Asian/Pacific Islander–full-time 2, part-time 3; American Indian/Alaska Native–full-time 2, part-time 1.

Financial Information/Assistance:

Tuition for Full-Time Study: No information provided.

Financial Assistance:

First Year Students: No information provided.
Advanced Students: No information provided.
Contact Information: Of all students currently enrolled full-time, 100% benefited from one or more of the listed financial assistance programs. For information on financial assistance, contact: Dr. Nicholas Papouchis, Director, PhD program in clinical psychology.

Internships/Practica: Students in the master's program have a variety of practica available to them. Practicum settings and internships in the New York City Metropolitan area are among the best in the country and offer training with a wide range of clinical patients and a number of specializations. Among these are child training, family training, neuropsychology, and forensic training. For those doctoral students for whom a professional internship is required prior to graduation, 10 applied in 2000–2001. Of those who applied, 10 were placed in internships listed by the Association of Psychology Postdoctoral and Internship Programs (APPIC); 10 were placed in APA accredited internships.

Housing and Day Care: No on-campus housing and day care facilities are available.

Employment of Department Graduates:

Master's Degree Graduates: Of those who graduated in the academic year 2000–2001, the following categories and numbers represent the post-graduate activities and employment of master's degree graduates: Enrolled in a post-doctoral residency/fellowship (n/a), employed in independent practice (n/a).

Doctoral Degree Graduates: Of those who graduated in the academic year 2000–2001, the following categories and numbers represent the post-graduate activities and employment of doctoral degree graduates: Enrolled in a psychology doctoral program (n/a), enrolled in another graduate/professional program (n/a).

Additional Information:

Orientation, Objectives, and Emphasis of Department: The PhD and master's programs are housed in an urban institution with a multicultural undergraduate student body. This diversity enriches the students' appreciation of the complexity of the clinical and theoretical issues relevant to work in psychology. The theoretical orientation of the clinical training sequence reflects the spectrum of psychodynamic approaches to treatment as well as cognitive-behavioral and family systems approaches. Clinical students are exposed, in a graded series of practicum experiences, to both short-term and longer term approaches to psychotherapy with the New York area's culturally diverse clinical populations. Students are also trained in a range of psychological assessment procedures including cognitive, projective, and neuropsychological testing. The program also seeks to train clinical psychologists who are competent in research and carefully grounded in the science of psychology. To this end doctoral students receive extensive training in research design and statistics early in their coursework and complete a second-year research project preparatory to beginning their dissertation. The final goal and emphasis of the department and the PhD program is to enable students to develop a broad base of knowledge in clinical psychology. To this end doctoral students are provided with opportunities for clinical training with adults, children, and adolescents; training in family therapy; and research training in a range of topics relevant to psychology.

Special Facilities or Resources: The Department of Psychology and the PhD Program in Clinical Psychology have the following special facilities and resources: An on-site Psychological Services Center where second-year clinical students receive an opportunity to have their clinical work carefully supervised by the doctoral faculty; opportunity for training in child and adolescent clinical work in conjunction with a number of New York area clinical training facilities; opportunity for specialized electives in neuropsychology; free access to computer training and computer facilities; full-tuition research fellowships for selected minority doctoral candidates; half-tuition scholarships for master's applicants who have an undergraduate GPA of at least 3.50. Finally, students in the PhD program at Long Island University's Brooklyn campus have the spectrum of New York City's clinical and educational facilities available for them to learn from. The program has also developed the Center for Ethnic and Minority under the leadership of Dr. Carol Magai. This center will be devoted to research with diverse ethnic groups and minorities.

Application Information:
Send to: Admissions Office, Long Island University, Brooklyn Campus, 1 University Plaza, Brooklyn, NY 11201. Students are admitted in the Fall, application deadline February 1. For MA program, deadline is one month before. *Fee:* $30.

Marist College
Department of Psychology
Poughkeepsie, NY 12601
Telephone: (845) 575-3000
Fax: (845) 575-3965
E-mail: *john.scileppi@marist.edu*
Web: *http://www.marist.edu/graduate*

Department Established:
1972. Director: John Scileppi. Number of Faculty: total–full-time 14, part-time 21; women–full-time 5, part-time 8; minority–full-time 2, part-time 1.

Programs and Degrees Offered:
Listed in the following order: Program area, degree type (T if terminal Master's), number awarded 7/00–6/01. Counseling/community MA (T) 25, educational MA (T) 14, school MA (T) 14.

Student Applications/Admissions:
Student Applications
Counseling/community MA—Applications 2001–2002, 70. Total applicants accepted 2001–2002, 60. New applicants enrolled 2001–2002, 32. Total enrolled 2001–2002 full-time, 32,

part-time, 35. Openings 2002–2003, 30. The Median number of years required for completion of a degree are 2. The number of students enrolled full and part-time, who were dismissed or voluntarily withdrew from this program area were 3. *Educational MA*—Applications 2001–2002, 23. Total applicants accepted 2001–2002, 20. New applicants enrolled 2001–2002, 15. Total enrolled 2001–2002 full-time, 5, part-time, 20. Openings 2002–2003, 20. The Median number of years required for completion of a degree is 1. *School MA*—Applications 2001–2002, 96. Total applicants accepted 2001–2002, 77. New applicants enrolled 2001–2002, 28. Total enrolled 2001–2002 full-time, 26, part-time, 39. Openings 2002–2003, 30. The Median number of years required for completion of a degree are 3.

Admissions Requirements:

Scores: Entries appear in this order: required test or GPA, minimum score (if required), median score of students entering in 2001–2002. Master's Programs: GRE-V no minimum stated; GRE-Q no minimum stated; GRE-V+Q no minimum stated, 1000; GRE-Analytical no minimum stated; GRE-V+Q+Analytical no minimum stated, 1500; overall undergraduate GPA 3.00, 3.30; psychology GPA 3.00, 3.40. Doctoral Programs: last 2 years GPA no minimum stated; psychology GPA no minimum stated; psychology GPA no minimum stated.

Other Criteria: (importance of criteria rated low, medium, or high): GRE/MAT scores medium, research experience medium, work experience medium, extracurricular activity low, clinically related public service medium, GPA high, letters of recommendation medium, interview medium, statement of goals and objectives medium.

Student Characteristics: The following represents characteristics of students in 2001–2002 in all graduate psychology programs in the department: Female–full-time 50, part-time 72; Male–full-time 13, part-time 22; African American/Black–full-time 5, part-time 4; Hispanic/Latino (a)–full-time 4, part-time 9; Asian/Pacific Islander–full-time 1, part-time 3; American Indian/Alaska Native–full-time 0, part-time 3; students subject to the Americans with Disabilities Act–full-time 1, part-time 2.

Financial Information/Assistance:

Tuition for Full-Time Study: *Master's:* State residents per academic year $11,520, $480 per credit hour; nonstate residents: per academic year $11,520, $480 per credit hour.

Financial Assistance:

First Year Students: Research assistantships available for first-year. Average amount paid per academic year: $3,000. Average number of hours worked per week: 10. Apply by July 15. Tuition remission given: partial. Fellowships and scholarships available for first-year. Average amount paid per academic year: $2,000. Apply by July 15.

Advanced Students: Research assistantships available for advanced students. Average amount paid per academic year: $3,000. Average number of hours worked per week: 10. Apply by July 15. Tuition remission given: partial. Average amount paid per academic year: $2,000. Apply by July 15.

Contact Information: Of all students currently enrolled full-time, 80% benefited from one or more of the listed financial assistance programs. For information on financial assistance, contact: Director of Graduate Admissions.

Internships/Practica: The mid-Hudson area has many public and private agencies dealing with mental health, developmental disabilities, criminal justice, and social services. Students choose their own placement site in consultation with faculty supervisor.

Housing and Day Care: No on-campus housing and day care facilities are available.

Employment of Department Graduates:

Master's Degree Graduates: Of those who graduated in the academic year 2000–2001, the following categories and numbers represent the post-graduate activities and employment of master's degree graduates: Enrolled in a psychology doctoral program (3), enrolled in another graduate/professional program (5), enrolled in a post-doctoral residency/fellowship (n/a), employed in independent practice (n/a), employed in other positions at a higher education institution (3), employed in a professional position in a school system (22), employed in business or industry (research/consulting) (2), employed in business or industry (management) (3), employed in a government agency (research) (2), employed in a government agency (professional services) (1), employed in a community mental health/counseling center (8), employed in a hospital/medical center (2), still seeking employment (2).

Doctoral Degree Graduates: Of those who graduated in the academic year 2000–2001, the following categories and numbers represent the post-graduate activities and employment of doctoral degree graduates: Enrolled in a psychology doctoral program (n/a), enrolled in another graduate/professional program (n/a).

Additional Information:

Orientation, Objectives, and Emphasis of Department: The department is located in completely refurbished and modern quarters that include a psychology clinic, two undergraduate teaching laboratories, and ample space for both faculty and student research. A full range of computer services is available at no charge to students. Located in a large metropolitan area, Marquette University is within easy commuting distance to a variety of hospitals and agencies in which training and research opportunities may be available.

Special Facilities or Resources: Interested students can assist in research at facilities such as the Nathan Kline Research Institute, The Center for Advanced Brain Imaging, The Marist Institute for Community Research, Hudson River Psychiatric Center, Dutchess Country Department of Mental Hygiene and Public Health, and the Montrose and Castlepoint Veterans Hospitals.

Information for Students With Physical Disabilities: The college has an office of special services available to students needing physical assistance. All buildings are wheelchair accessible.

Application Information:

Send to: Director of Graduate Admissions, Marist College, Poughkeepsie, NY 12601. Students are admitted in the Fall, application deadline August 15; Spring, application deadline January 2; Summer, application deadline May 7. Rolling deadline until classes are full. *Fee:* $30.

New School University

Graduate Faculty, Department of Psychology
65 Fifth Avenue
New York, NY 10003
Telephone: (212) 229-5727
Fax: (212) 989-0846
E-mail: *gfadmit@newschool.edu*
Web: *http://www.newschool.edu*

Department Established:

1936. Chairperson: Michael Schober. Number of Faculty: total–full-time 16, part-time 8; women–full-time 4, part-time 2; minority–full-time 3.

Programs and Degrees Offered:

Listed in the following order: Program area, degree type (T if terminal Master's), number awarded 7/00–6/01. Clinical PhD 21, general MA (T) 33, mental health substance abuse MA (T).

APA Accreditation: Clinical PhD: full.

Student Applications/Admissions:

Student Applications

Clinical PhD—Applications 2001–2002, 22. Total applicants accepted 2001–2002, 14. New applicants enrolled 2001–2002, 11. Total enrolled 2001–2002 full-time, 75, part-time, 14. Openings 2002–2003, 15. *General MA*—Applications 2001–2002, 198. Total applicants accepted 2001–2002, 152. New applicants enrolled 2001–2002, 14. Total enrolled 2001–2002 full-time, 93, part-time, 40. *Mental health substance abuse MA*.

Admissions Requirements:

Scores: Entries appear in this order: required test or GPA, minimum score (if required), median score of students entering in 2001–2002. Master's Programs: GRE-V no minimum stated, 510; GRE-Q no minimum stated, 550; GRE-Analytical no minimum stated, 570; overall undergraduate GPA no minimum stated, 3.17. Doctoral Programs: GRE-V no minimum stated, 554; GRE-Q no minimum stated, 615; GRE-Analytical no minimum stated, 629; overall undergraduate GPA no minimum stated, 3.25; last 2 years GPA no minimum stated; psychology GPA no minimum stated; psychology GPA 3.30, 3.69. Scores reported above are for Clinical PhD students only. Median scores for the General PhD students (3) in 1997–98 are as follows: Undergraduate GPA: 3.69/Graduate GPA: 3.92 *Other Criteria:* (importance of criteria rated low, medium, or high): research experience high, work experience high, extracurricular activity medium, clinically related public service high, GPA high, letters of recommendation low, interview high, statement of goals and objectives high. The criteria above are applicable to Clinical PhD applicants. General PhD applicants must carry a 3.30 GPA and must successfully complete the MA comprehensive examinations.

Student Characteristics: The following represents characteristics of students in 2001–2002 in all graduate psychology programs in the department: Female–full-time 18, part-time 5; Male–full-time 4, part-time 1; African American/Black–full-time 1, part-time 0; Hispanic/Latino (a)–full-time 1, part-time 1; Asian/Pacific Is-lander–full-time 1, part-time 0; American Indian/Alaska Native–full-time 4, part-time 2.

Financial Information/Assistance:

Tuition for Full-Time Study: *Master's:* State residents $1,040 per credit hour; nonstate residents: $1,040 per credit hour. *Doctoral:* State residents: $1,040 per credit hour; nonstate residents: $1,040 per credit hour.

Financial Assistance:

First Year Students: No information provided.

Advanced Students: Teaching assistantships available for advanced students. Average amount paid per academic year: $3,360. Average number of hours worked per week: 14. Apply by May 15th. Research assistantships available for advanced students. Average amount paid per academic year: $6,000. Average number of hours worked per week: 16. Apply by May 15th. Fellowships and scholarships available for advanced students. Apply by March 15.

Contact Information: Of all students currently enrolled full-time, 0% benefited from one or more of the listed financial assistance programs. For information on financial assistance, contact: Robert Kostrzewa, Director; Graduate Faculty, Academic Affairs and Scholarships: (212) 229-5805, 65 Fifth Ave, NY, NY 10003.

Internships/Practica: Master's level psychology students who are interested in pursuing a Clinical PhD are strongly encouraged to pursue volunteer clinical positions that may become available at local hospitals or institutes. The Clinical Coordinator is available to assist these students in placement at appropriate sites. First year doctoral students in the Clinical program participate in an assessment and diagnosis practicum in which they conduct supervised psychological intake evaluations on Beth Israel Medical Center's outpatient psychiatry service. These students will also spend 4 hours per week on a selected inpatient rotation co-leading groups and attending relevant unit meetings. This experience provides a strong foundation upon which they are required to then complete a 16–20 hour per week externship in their second year of study at an approved, affiliated site. Third year students may elect to complete another full-time externship or spend 8 hours per week at Beth Israel conducting intake evaluations and providing psychotherapy for two individual cases. Interested students may also carry cases in Beth Israel's Family Therapy Program or the Brief Psychotherapy Research Program. All clinical PhD students are required to complete an APA-accredited internship and receive administrative and academic support services during the application process through the Assistant Director of Clinical Training and the Clinical Coordinator.

Housing and Day Care: No on-campus housing and day care facilities are available.

Employment of Department Graduates:

Master's Degree Graduates: Of those who graduated in the academic year 2000–2001, the following categories and numbers represent the post-graduate activities and employment of master's degree graduates: Enrolled in a post-doctoral residency/fellowship (n/a), employed in independent practice (n/a).

Doctoral Degree Graduates: Of those who graduated in the academic year 2000–2001, the following categories and numbers represent the post-graduate activities and employment of doctoral degree graduates: Enrolled in a psychology doctoral program (n/a), enrolled in another graduate/professional program (n/a), enrolled in a post-doctoral residency/fellowship (4), employed in independent practice (2), employed in an academic position at a university (2), employed in other positions at a higher education institution (2), employed in a professional position in a school system (0), employed in business or industry (research/consulting) (1), employed in business or industry (management) (0), employed in a government agency (research) (3), employed in a government agency (professional services) (0), employed in a community mental health/counseling center (2), employed in a hospital/medical center (4), still seeking employment (0), other employment position (1).

Additional Information:

Orientation, Objectives, and Emphasis of Department: The department's objective is to provide a broad theoretical background emphasizing the scientific study of psychology and representing the several academic approaches to the study of human experience and behavior. The master's program is designed to meet the needs of both full- and part-time students, with courses in cognitive, personality, developmental, social, and clinical psychology. At the PhD level, students specialize in general psychology (cognitive, social-personality, developmental) or clinical psychology. Admission to doctoral candidacy is based on performance in our program—a 3.3 GPA in residence and passing the psychology comprehensive examination. Broadly speaking, the objective of the Clinical PhD program is the training of students as scientist-practitioners who are equally at home in clinical service, research, and teaching settings.

Special Facilities or Resources: Several experimental laboratories are available for students. All currently registered students are permitted to use the University computer facility, which provides all major software programs as well as e-mail and Internet access. The establishment of the New School-Beth Israel Center for Clinical Training and Research in 1996 has broadened significantly the training opportunities for the clinical PhD students. This collaborative program affords clinical PhD students practicum experience in a variety of settings at Beth Israel Medical Center. First year students are required to complete a year-long practicum of supervised training in psychological intakes and assessment on the outpatient psychiatric unit. The students will also participate as group co-leaders on assigned inpatient units (general, geriatric, dual diagnosis) and at Beth Israel's Day Treatment facility. Attendance at hospital grand rounds and case conferences highlights this first year practicum. Clinical students are permitted and encouraged to pursue more focused training following the first year practicum with opportunities to participate in the Brief Psychotherapy Research Program and to conduct child assessments in the outpatient service. In the third year of the clinical program, students may return to Beth Israel to hone their psychotherapy training with two individual cases. The opportunity to take on family therapy cases is also available. Psychotherapy sessions are videotaped and students review these sessions in weekly supervision at Beth Israel and in a required seminar at the New School.

Information for Students With Physical Disabilities: The university seeks to foster an environment that encourages all students to reach their highest level of personal achievement. Through various student programs and services, the importance of recognizing and embracing individual differences is emphasized. Through designated administrators in each of its seven divisions, the university will consider reasonable accommodations for students who have presented adequate medical documentation of their disability and limitations. Information for Students with Disabilities, a pamphlet available through the division student life offices, provides students with disabilities a list of the designated administrators.

Application Information:
Send to: Emanual Lomax, Director of Admissions, Graduate Faculty—New School University, 65 Fifth Ave., NY, NY 10003. Students are admitted in the Fall, application deadline January 15; Spring, application deadline November 15. Deadline is January 15 for financial aid consideration. For master's level students who will be applying for admission without financial aid, admission will be made up to the beginning date of fall classes. *Fee:* $30.

New York University
Department of Applied Psychology
School of Education
239 Greene Street, Room 400 and Room 500
New York, NY 10003
Telephone: (212) 998-5555
Fax: (212) 995-4358
E-mail: *applied.psychology@nyu.edu*
Web: *http://www.nyu.edu/education/appsych*

Department Established:
1991. Chairperson: Dr. Theresa Jordan. Number of Faculty: total–full-time 25; women–full-time 15; minority–full-time 6.

Programs and Degrees Offered:
Listed in the following order: Program area, degree type (T if terminal Master's), number awarded 7/00–6/01. Applied MA (T) 36, counseling PhD 4, counseling and guidance MA (T) 56, psychological development PhD 4, psychological foun. of reading PhD 1, Rehabilitation Counseling MA, school PsyD 15, school psychologist PhD.

APA Accreditation: Counseling PhD: full. School PhD: full. School PsyD: full.

Student Applications/Admissions:
Student Applications
Applied MA—Applications 2001–2002, 53. Total applicants accepted 2001–2002, 34. New applicants enrolled 2001–2002, 18. Total enrolled 2001–2002 full-time, 15, part-time, 37. Openings 2002–2003, 25. *Counseling PhD*—Applications 2001–2002, 129. Total applicants accepted 2001–2002, 9. New applicants enrolled 2001–2002, 9. Total enrolled 2001–2002 full-time, 32, part-time, 32. Openings 2002–2003, 6. *Counseling and guidance MA*—Applications 2001–2002, 149. Total applicants accepted 2001–2002, 83. New applicants enrolled 2001–2002, 50. Total enrolled 2001–2002 full-time, 70, part-time, 63. Openings 2002–2003, 60. *Psychological development PhD*—Applications 2001–2002, 35. Total applicants accepted 2001–2002, 3. New applicants enrolled 2001–2002, 3. Total enrolled 2001–2002 full-time, 15. Openings 2002–2003, 3. The number of students enrolled full and part-time, who were dismissed or voluntarily withdrew from this program area were 0. *Psychological foun. of reading PhD*—Applications 2001–2002,

7. Total enrolled 2001–2002 full-time, 1, part-time, 4. The Median number of years required for completion of a degree are 7. *Rehabilitation Counseling MA. School PsyD*—Applications 2001–2002, 64. Total applicants accepted 2001–2002, 8. New applicants enrolled 2001–2002, 5. Total enrolled 2001–2002 full-time, 25, part-time, 25. Openings 2002–2003, 8. *School psychologist PhD*—Applications 2001–2002, 28. Total applicants accepted 2001–2002, 2. New applicants enrolled 2001–2002, 2. Total enrolled 2001–2002 full-time, 5, part-time, 2. Openings 2002–2003, 4.

Admissions Requirements:

Scores: Entries appear in this order: required test or GPA, minimum score (if required), median score of students entering in 2001–2002. Master's Programs: overall undergraduate GPA no minimum stated, 3.20. Master's programs do not require GRE scores. Doctoral Programs: GRE-V 500, 520; GRE-Q 500, 600; GRE-V+Q 1000, 1100; overall undergraduate GPA no minimum stated, 3.20; last 2 years GPA no minimum stated; psychology GPA no minimum stated; psychology GPA no minimum stated, 3.50.

Other Criteria: (importance of criteria rated low, medium, or high): research experience high, work experience medium, extracurricular activity medium, clinically related public service high, letters of recommendation medium, interview high, statement of goals and objectives medium. The above criteria range from "medium" to "high" for admission into the doctoral programs. Master's programs primarily consider GPA, statement of goals and objectives, and letters of recommendation; interviews sometimes required for master's applicants.

Student Characteristics: The following represents characteristics of students in 2001–2002 in all graduate psychology programs in the department: Female–full-time 54, part-time 32; Male–full-time 0, part-time 0; African American/Black–full-time 12, part-time 12; Hispanic/Latino (a)–full-time 7, part-time 0; Asian/Pacific Islander–full-time 11, part-time 5; American Indian/Alaska Native–full-time 0, part-time 0.

Financial Information/Assistance:
Tuition for Full-Time Study: No information provided.

Financial Assistance:
First Year Students: Teaching assistantships available for first-year. Research assistantships available for first-year. Traineeships available for first-year. Fellowships and scholarships available for first-year.

Advanced Students: Teaching assistantships available for advanced students. Research assistantships available for advanced students. Traineeships available for advanced students. Fellowships and scholarships available for advanced students.

Contact Information: For information on financial assistance, contact: Office of Graduate Admissions, 212-998-5030.

Internships/Practica: Available in the following areas: school and university counseling; counseling in community agencies, hospitals, and business; school psychology; psychological development; measurement and evaluation.

Housing and Day Care: On-campus housing and day care facilities are available.

Employment of Department Graduates:
Master's Degree Graduates: Of those who graduated in the academic year 2000–2001, the following categories and numbers represent the post-graduate activities and employment of master's degree graduates: Enrolled in a post-doctoral residency/fellowship (n/a), employed in independent practice (n/a).

Doctoral Degree Graduates: Of those who graduated in the academic year 2000–2001, the following categories and numbers represent the post-graduate activities and employment of doctoral degree graduates: Enrolled in a psychology doctoral program (n/a), enrolled in another graduate/professional program (n/a).

Additional Information:
Orientation, Objectives, and Emphasis of Department: It is the philosophy of the department that the applied fields must rest on a solid base of psychology. To this end, core courses are offered in all the major areas of psychology and requirements for all the advanced programs include core areas. Emphasis and specific core requirements differ somewhat from program to program, but each program is characterized by this central approach. Departmental faculty have research projects in several areas, and students have the opportunity to participate in laboratory-based data collection in infant development, perceptual processes in adults and the elderly, early childhood and adolescent development. Students can also observe and collect data in settlement houses and other community facilities, as well as in the school settings that have been traditional for the department.

Special Facilities or Resources: The Infancy Studies Laboratory is a resource for students conducting research in infant temperament, perceptual development, learning and attention, and parenting views and child rearing styles. The Measurement Laboratory houses a collection of educational and psychological tests and reference books. PC and Macintosh computers are available for data analysis and word processing. The Psychoeducational Center is the training unit of the school psychology programs, assigning school psychologists-in-training to schools, settlement houses, clinics, and day care centers. It is also a clearinghouse of scholarly papers resulting from collaborative activities of doctoral students and faculty. Center for Reading Studies provides service to the local community through its outreach to parents and schools, offering tutoring for children and adolescents, a library of children's literature, parent newsletters, and telephone consultation with regard to reading and related learning problems.

Information for Students With Physical Disabilities: The Moses Center for Students with Disabilities assists students with mobility, hearing, and visual impairments as well as those with chronic conditions.

Application Information:
Send to: Office of Graduate Admissions, School of Education, New York University, 82 Washington Sq. East, Floor 2, New York, NY 10003. Students are admitted in the Fall, application deadline MA-March 1; Spring, application deadline MA-Dec 1. Fall deadline: doctoral-January 15, Master's-March 1. *Fee:* $40. $60 for international students.

New York University, Graduate School of Arts and Science

Department of Psychology
6 Washington Place, Room 550
New York, NY 10003
Telephone: (212) 998-7900
Fax: (212) 995-4018
E-mail: *psychq@psych.nyu.edu*
Web: *http://www.psych.nyu.edu*

Department Established:

1950. Chairperson: Marisa Carrasco. Number of Faculty: total–full-time 37; women–full-time 12; minority–full-time 5.

Programs and Degrees Offered:

Listed in the following order: Program area, degree type (T if terminal Master's), number awarded 7/00–6/01. Cognition and Perception PhD 1, Community PhD, General Psychology MA (T) 11, Industrial/Organizational MA (T) 12, Social PhD.

Student Applications/Admissions:

Student Applications

Cognition and Perception PhD—Applications 2001–2002, 58. Total applicants accepted 2001–2002, 12. New applicants enrolled 2001–2002, 6. Total enrolled 2001–2002 full-time, 18. Openings 2002–2003, 7. *Community PhD*—Applications 2001–2002, 47. Total applicants accepted 2001–2002, 6. New applicants enrolled 2001–2002, 5. Total enrolled 2001–2002 full-time, 20. Openings 2002–2003, 2. *General Psychology MA*—Applications 2001–2002, 140. Total applicants accepted 2001–2002, 69. New applicants enrolled 2001–2002, 37. Total enrolled 2001–2002 part-time, 111. Openings 2002–2003, 40. The Median number of years required for completion of a degree are 3. *Industrial/Organizational MA*—Applications 2001–2002, 148. Total applicants accepted 2001– 2002, 67. New applicants enrolled 2001–2002, 34. Total enrolled 2001–2002 part-time, 104. Openings 2002–2003, 40. The Median number of years required for completion of a degree are 2. *Social PhD.*

Admissions Requirements:

Scores: Entries appear in this order: required test or GPA, minimum score (if required), median score of students entering in 2001–2002. Master's Programs: GRE-V 530, 550; GRE-Q 530, 630; GRE-Analytical 530, 650; overall undergraduate GPA 3.0. Doctoral Programs: GRE-V no minimum stated, 660; GRE-Q no minimum stated, 710; GRE-Analytical no minimum stated, 720; GRE-V+Q+Analytical no minimum stated; GRE-Subject(Psych) no minimum stated, 700; last 2 years GPA no minimum stated; psychology GPA no minimum stated; psychology GPA no minimum stated.

Other Criteria: (importance of criteria rated low, medium, or high): GRE/MAT scores medium, research experience high, work experience low, extracurricular activity low, clinically related public service low, GPA medium, letters of recommendation high, statement of goals and objectives high. These rankings are for the PhD only. For master's program, letters of recommendation and statement of goals and objectives have high importance; other criteria are low; no interviews are given. GRE/GPA varies by program.

Student Characteristics: The following represents characteristics of students in 2001–2002 in all graduate psychology programs in the department: Female–full-time 76, part-time 166; Male–full-time 28, part-time 48; African American/Black–full-time 6, part-time 8; Hispanic/Latino (a)–full-time 8, part-time 9; Asian/Pacific Islander–full-time 9, part-time 30; Multi-ethnic–full-time 2, part-time 4.

Financial Information/Assistance:

Tuition for Full-Time Study: *Master's:* State residents $814 per credit hour; *Doctoral:* State residents: $814 per credit hour.

Financial Assistance:

First Year Students: Teaching assistantships available for first-year. Average amount paid per academic year: $16,000. Average number of hours worked per week: 20. Apply by January 4. Tuition remission given: full. Research assistantships available for first-year. Average amount paid per academic year: $16,000. Average number of hours worked per week: 20. Apply by January 4. Tuition remission given: full. Traineeships available for first-year. Tuition remission given: full. Fellowships and scholarships available for first-year. Apply by January 4. Tuition remission given: full.

Advanced Students: Teaching assistantships available for advanced students. Average amount paid per academic year: $16,000. Average number of hours worked per week: 20. Apply by January 4. Tuition remission given: full. Research assistantships available for advanced students. Average amount paid per academic year: $16,000. Average number of hours worked per week: 20. Apply by January 4. Tuition remission given: full. Traineeships available for advanced students. Tuition remission given: full. Fellowships and scholarships available for advanced students. Apply by January 4. Tuition remission given: full.

Contact Information: Financial Aid applies to PhD students only. For more information contact Graduate Enrollment Services at (212) 998-8050.

Internships/Practica: Master's students may opt to take Fieldwork, which would enable them to obtain supervised experience in selected agencies, clinics, and industrial and non-profit organizations relevant to the career or academic objectives of the student.

Housing and Day Care: On-campus housing and day care facilities are available.

Employment of Department Graduates:

Master's Degree Graduates: Of those who graduated in the academic year 2000–2001, the following categories and numbers represent the post-graduate activities and employment of master's degree graduates: Enrolled in a post-doctoral residency/fellowship (n/a), employed in independent practice (n/a).

Doctoral Degree Graduates: Of those who graduated in the academic year 2000–2001, the following categories and numbers represent the post-graduate activities and employment of doctoral degree graduates: Enrolled in a psychology doctoral program (n/a), enrolled in another graduate/professional program (n/a).

Additional Information:

Orientation, Objectives, and Emphasis of Department: The doctoral programs all emphasize research. The community psychology program addresses critical social problems in context through action, research, and theory. It trains students for direct roles in academia, action-research, and policy analysis. The cognition-perception program has faculty whose research focuses on memory, emotion, psycholinguistics, categorization, visual perception, and attention. Some of the faculty have expertise in cognitive neuroscience, and we are currently hiring faculty in this area. The social program trains researchers in theory and methods for understanding individuals and groups in social and organizational contexts. Training is provided in subareas ranging from social cognition to motivation, personality, close relationships, groups, and organizations. A doctoral concentration in developmental psychology emphasizes research training cutting across the traditional areas of psychology. Students may minor in quantitative psychology or in any of the above programs. The Master's Program in General Psychology has the flexibility to suit students who wish to explore several areas of psychology to find the area that interests them most, as well as students who wish to shape their course of study to fit special interests and needs, including preparation for admission to a doctoral program. The Master's Program in Industrial/Organizational Psychology is designed to prepare graduates to apply research and principles of human behavior to a variety of organizational settings, such as human resources departments, and management consulting firms. The program can also be modified for students who are preparing for admission to doctoral programs in Industrial/Organizational and related fields. Students in the master's programs may opt for either full- or part-time status.

Special Facilities or Resources: The Department of Psychology maintains laboratories, classrooms, project rooms, and a magnetic resonance (MR) neuroimaging facility in an 11-story building near Washington Square Park. Modern laboratories are continually improved through grants from foundations and federal agencies. The Center for Brain Imaging houses a research-dedicated 3 Tesla Seimens MR system for the use of faculty and students interested in research using function brain imaging. The center includes faculty members from both the Department of Psychology and the Center for Neural Science, as well as individuals whose expertise is in MR physics and statistical methods for analysis. The department maintains several computer classrooms and laboratories, and the University offers technical courses on emerging computational tools. Faculty laboratories are equipped with specialized computer equipment within each of the graduate programs. The department collaborates closely with the Center for Neural Science in maintaining a technical shop.

Application Information:
Send to: New York University, Graduate School of Arts & Sciences, Graduate Enrollment Services, P.O. Box 907, New York, NY 10276-0907. Students are admitted in the Fall, application deadline March 15; Spring, application deadline October 15; Summer, application deadline March 15. These deadlines are for the MA programs only. Please note that applications to the General Psychology MA program may be accepted after the deadline as space allows. PhD students admitted only in the Fall (application deadline January 4). *Fee:* $60. The Graduate School of Arts & Sciences does not waive application fees.

Pace University
Department of Psychology
Dyson College of Arts and Sciences
One Pace Plaza
New York, NY 10038
Telephone: (212) 346-1506
Fax: (212) 346-1618
E-mail: *HKrauss@pace.edu*
Web: *http://www.pace.edu/dyson/psychology*

Department Established:
1961. Chairperson: Herbert H. Krauss. Number of Faculty: total–full-time 15, part-time 12; women–full-time 7, part-time 6; minority–full-time 3, part-time 2.

Programs and Degrees Offered:
Listed in the following order: Program area, degree type (T if terminal Master's), number awarded 7/00–6/01. General MA (T) 5, school-clinical child psycholo PsyD 21.

APA Accreditation: Clinical PsyD: full. School PsyD: full. Combined PsyD: full.

Student Applications/Admissions:
Student Applications
General MA—Applications 2001–2002, 20. Total applicants accepted 2001–2002, 15. New applicants enrolled 2001–2002, 7. Total enrolled 2001–2002 full-time, 4, part-time, 20. Openings 2002–2003, 25. The Median number of years required for completion of a degree are NA. The number of students enrolled full and part-time, who were dismissed or voluntarily withdrew from this program area were NA. *School-clinical child psycholo PsyD*—Applications 2001–2002, 167. Total applicants accepted 2001–2002, 58. New applicants enrolled 2001–2002, 23. Total enrolled 2001–2002 full-time, 21, part-time, 2. Openings 2002–2003, 20. The Median number of years required for completion of a degree are 7. The number of students enrolled full and part-time, who were dismissed or voluntarily withdrew from this program area were 1.

Admissions Requirements:
Scores: Entries appear in this order: required test or GPA, minimum score (if required), median score of students entering in 2001–2002. Master's Programs: GRE-V NA; GRE-Q NA; GRE-V+Q NA; GRE-Subject(Psych) NA; overall undergraduate GPA NA. Doctoral Programs: GRE-V no minimum stated, 525; GRE-Q no minimum stated, 515; GRE-V+Q no minimum stated, 1040; GRE-Analytical no minimum stated, 595; GRE-V+Q+Analytical no minimum stated, 1635; GRE-Subject(Psych) no minimum stated, 565; overall undergraduate GPA no minimum stated, 3.50; last 2 years GPA no minimum stated; psychology GPA no minimum stated; psychology GPA no minimum stated.
Other Criteria: (importance of criteria rated low, medium, or high): GRE/MAT scores high, research experience low, work experience medium, extracurricular activity low, clinically related public service medium, GPA high, letters of recommendation high, interview high, statement of goals and objectives high. These criteria are used for the MSEd and PsyD programs only.

Student Characteristics: The following represents characteristics of students in 2001–2002 in all graduate psychology programs in the department: Female–full-time 124, part-time 23; Male–full-time 19, part-time 3; African American/Black–full-time 6, part-time 1; Hispanic/Latino (a)–full-time 9, part-time 0; Asian/Pacific Islander–full-time 5, part-time 0; American Indian/Alaska Native–full-time 0, part-time 0.

Financial Information/Assistance:
Tuition for Full-Time Study: No information provided.

Financial Assistance:
First Year Students: Research assistantships available for first-year. Average amount paid per academic year: $2,500. Average number of hours worked per week: 10. Apply by Feb. 1, 2003. Tuition remission given: partial. Fellowships and scholarships available for first-year. Average amount paid per academic year: $4,000. Apply by Feb. 1, 2003.

Advanced Students: Teaching assistantships available for advanced students. Apply by Feb. 1, 2003. Research assistantships available for advanced students. Average amount paid per academic year: $2,500. Average number of hours worked per week: 10. Apply by Feb. 1, 2003. Tuition remission given: partial. Fellowships and scholarships available for advanced students. Average amount paid per academic year: $4,000. Apply by Feb. 1, 2003.

Contact Information: Of all students currently enrolled full-time, 50% benefited from one or more of the listed financial assistance programs. For information on financial assistance, contact: Financial Aid Office.

Internships/Practica: A wide array of fieldwork experiences and internships are available for graduate students in the PsyD program. The doctoral program offers students the opportunity to obtain training in hospital, community mental health, and educational facilities. All field training is under the coordination of the Director of Field Training. For those doctoral students for whom a professional internship is required prior to graduation, 21 applied in 2000–2001. Of those who applied, 5 were placed in internships listed by the Association of Psychology Postdoctoral and Internship Programs (APPIC); 15 were placed in APA accredited internships.

Housing and Day Care: On-campus housing and day care facilities are available.

Employment of Department Graduates:
Master's Degree Graduates: Of those who graduated in the academic year 2000–2001, the following categories and numbers represent the post-graduate activities and employment of master's degree graduates: Enrolled in a post-doctoral residency/fellowship (n/a), employed in independent practice (n/a).
Doctoral Degree Graduates: Of those who graduated in the academic year 2000–2001, the following categories and numbers represent the post-graduate activities and employment of doctoral degree graduates: Enrolled in a psychology doctoral program (n/a), enrolled in another graduate/professional program (n/a).

Additional Information:
Orientation, Objectives, and Emphasis of Department: The PsyD program in School-Clinical Child Psychology at Pace University is a professional practice training program that is dedicated to the training model of school psychologists as scholar-practitioners. The focus is on developing individuals whose theoretical and research knowledge, and professional skills enable them to deliver a broad array of direct and indirect psychological services to infants, children, adolescents, and families, and the personnel, organizations, and institutions that serve them. The purpose of the program is to train school psychology practitioners to possess broad knowledge about general psychological theoretical foundations, as well as more specific knowledge pertaining to the scientific foundations of psychological practice and professional School-Clinical Child Psychology practice competencies. School psychologists-in-training receive instruction and supervision related to following ethical guidelines and being sensitive to diversity and multicultural issues. The program coordinates placement in University-based and Field-based supervised training experiences, which are carefully integrated with theoretical coursework and a seminar, enabling practitioners in training to compare key aspects of professional functioning across a wide variety of settings. There are sixteen specific training goals of the School-Clinical Child Psychology Program, which are detailed in materials available from the program. Note: This description is only for the doctoral program. A description of the master's degree programs (MA, MSEd and MSEd Bilingual) is available by contacting the Psychology Department.

Special Facilities or Resources: The Psychology Department facilities include a laboratory equipped for applied and basic research, the McShane Center for Psychological Services, which provides for training and treatment in a variety of intervention techniques, and liaison with the facilities and staff of the speech and hearing clinic and the university computer center. The psychological test library includes the major individual and group aptitude, achievement, personality, and neuropsychological tests and batteries. The resources include biofeedback equipment. Two-way mirrors in the Center for Psychological Services allow observation of groups and individuals. There are also research and treatment rooms.

Application Information:
Send to: Graduate Admissions, Pace University, 1 Pace Plaza, NY, NY 10038. Students are admitted in the Fall, application deadline February 1; Winter, application deadline August 1; Spring, application deadline December 1; Summer, application deadline May 1. February 1 deadline for MSEd and PsyD programs. Fall deadline for MA-August 1. Winter and Spring admission for MA. *Fee:* $65. Check with graduate admissions for current application fee.

Rensselaer Polytechnic Institute
Philosophy, Psychology and Cognitive Science
110 8th Street, Carnegie Building, Room #305
Troy, NY 12180-3590
Telephone: (518) 276-6472
Fax: (518) 276-8268
E-mail: *bestlj@rpi.edu*
Web: *http://www.rpi.edu/~brings/dept/ppcs.htm*

Department Established:
1959. Chairperson: Michael J. Kalsher. Number of Faculty: total–full-time 10, part-time 6; women–full-time 1.

Programs and Degrees Offered:

Listed in the following order: Program area, degree type (T if terminal Master's), number awarded 7/00–6/01. Human Factors MA (T) 2, Industrial/Organ. Psyc.

Student Applications/Admissions:

Student Applications

Human Factors MA—Applications 2001–2002, 7. Total applicants accepted 2001–2002, 2. New applicants enrolled 2001–2002, 3. Total enrolled 2001–2002 full-time, 3. Openings 2002–2003, 5. The Median number of years required for completion of a degree are 2. The number of students enrolled full and part-time, who were dismissed or voluntarily withdrew from this program area were 0.

Admissions Requirements:

Scores: Entries appear in this order: required test or GPA, minimum score (if required), median score of students entering in 2001–2002. Master's Programs: GRE-V no minimum stated, 550; GRE-Q no minimum stated, 600; GRE-Analytical no minimum stated, 600; GRE-Subject(Psych) no minimum stated, 550. GRE Subject not required for Human Factors Program. Doctoral Programs: last 2 years GPA no minimum stated; psychology GPA no minimum stated; psychology GPA no minimum stated.

Other Criteria: (importance of criteria rated low, medium, or high): GRE/MAT scores high, research experience, work experience, extracurricular activity, clinically related public service, GPA medium, letters of recommendation, interview, statement of goals and objectives medium.

Student Characteristics: The following represents characteristics of students in 2001–2002 in all graduate psychology programs in the department: Female–full-time 7, part-time 2; Male–full-time 8, part-time 0; African American/Black–full-time 1, part-time 0; Hispanic/Latino (a)–full-time 0, part-time 0; Asian/Pacific Islander–full-time 0, part-time 0; American Indian/Alaska Native–full-time 0, part-time 0.

Financial Information/Assistance:

Tuition for Full-Time Study: *Master's:* State residents per academic year $2,640; nonstate residents: per academic year $2,640.

Financial Assistance:

First Year Students: Teaching assistantships available for first-year. Average amount paid per academic year: $12,000. Average number of hours worked per week: 20. Apply by Feb. 15. Tuition remission given: full. Fellowships and scholarships available for first-year. Apply by Feb 1. Tuition remission given: full.

Advanced Students: Teaching assistantships available for advanced students. Average amount paid per academic year: $1,200. Average number of hours worked per week: 20.

Contact Information: Of all students currently enrolled full-time, 2% benefited from one or more of the listed financial assistance programs. For information on financial assistance, contact: Jean S. Bestle, Dept. of PP&CS, email: bestlj@rpi.edu.

Internships/Practica: Cooperative internships are available, as well as course-related externships. These are limited to advanced students. Interested students apply directly to the organization with permission of their advisor.

Housing and Day Care: On-campus housing and day care facilities are available.

Employment of Department Graduates:

Master's Degree Graduates: Of those who graduated in the academic year 2000–2001, the following categories and numbers represent the post-graduate activities and employment of master's degree graduates: Enrolled in a psychology doctoral program (3), enrolled in a post-doctoral residency/fellowship (n/a), employed in independent practice (n/a).

Doctoral Degree Graduates: Of those who graduated in the academic year 2000–2001, the following categories and numbers represent the post-graduate activities and employment of doctoral degree graduates: Enrolled in a psychology doctoral program (n/a), enrolled in another graduate/professional program (n/a).

Additional Information:

Orientation, Objectives, and Emphasis of Department: The department is research oriented. All students are required to do research throughout their graduate training. The program is designed to train students who are interested in either industry/government positions or in pursuing a doctoral degree.

Application Information:

Send to: Admissions, Rensselaer Polytechnic Inst., Troy, NY 12180. Students are admitted in the Fall, application deadline Feb. 15. *Fee:* $45.

Rochester, University of
Department of Clinical and Social Sciences in Psychology
Arts, Sciences and Engineering
Meliora Hall 355-RC Box 270266
Rochester, NY 14627-0266
Telephone: (585) 275-8649
Fax: (585) 273-1100
E-mail: *loretta@psych.rochester.edu*
Web: *http://www.psych.rochester.edu/scp/*

Department Established:

1935. Chairperson: Miron Zuckerman. Number of Faculty: total–full-time 15, part-time 11; women–full-time 5, part-time 5; minority–full-time 1, part-time 1.

Programs and Degrees Offered:

Listed in the following order: Program area, degree type (T if terminal Master's), number awarded 7/00–6/01. Clinical PhD 5, developmental PhD, social-personality PhD 2.

APA Accreditation: Clinical PhD: full.

Student Applications/Admissions:

Student Applications

Clinical PhD—Applications 2001–2002, 111. Total applicants accepted 2001–2002, 3. New applicants enrolled 2001–2002, 3. Total enrolled 2001–2002 full-time, 29. Openings 2002–2003, 4. The number of students enrolled full and part-time, who were dismissed or voluntarily withdrew from this program area were 1. *Developmental PhD*—Applications 2001–2002,

22. Total applicants accepted 2001–2002, 2. New applicants enrolled 2001–2002, 2. Total enrolled 2001–2002 full-time, 6. Openings 2002–2003, 3. *Social-personality PhD*—Applications 2001–2002, 33. Total applicants accepted 2001–2002, 7. New applicants enrolled 2001–2002, 3. Total enrolled 2001–2002 full-time, 9. Openings 2002–2003, 4.

Admissions Requirements:

Scores: Entries appear in this order: required test or GPA, minimum score (if required), median score of students entering in 2001–2002. Doctoral Programs: GRE-V no minimum stated, 613; GRE-Q no minimum stated, 637; GRE-V+Q no minimum stated, 1250; GRE-Analytical no minimum stated, 680; GRE-V+Q+Analytical no minimum stated, 1930; overall undergraduate GPA no minimum stated, 3.6; last 2 years GPA no minimum stated; psychology GPA no minimum stated; psychology GPA no minimum stated. Scores reflected above are only for clinical program.

Other Criteria: (importance of criteria rated low, medium, or high): GRE/MAT scores medium, research experience high, work experience high, extracurricular activity medium, clinically related public service medium, GPA high, letters of recommendation high, interview high, statement of goals and objectives high.

Student Characteristics: The following represents characteristics of students in 2001–2002 in all graduate psychology programs in the department: Female–full-time 32, part-time 0; Male–full-time 13, part-time 0; African American/Black–full-time 2, part-time 0; Hispanic/Latino (a)–full-time 1, part-time 0; Asian/Pacific Islander–full-time 1, part-time 0; American Indian/Alaska Native–full-time 0, part-time 0; Multi-ethnic–full-time 0, part-time 0; students subject to the Americans with Disabilities Act–full-time 0, part-time 0.

Financial Information/Assistance:
Tuition for Full-Time Study: No information provided.

Financial Assistance:
First Year Students: No information provided.
Advanced Students: No information provided.
Contact Information: Of all students currently enrolled full-time, 75% benefited from one or more of the listed financial assistance programs.

Internships/Practica: Some students are supported via teaching and research assistantships as well as part-time assignments at several local agencies including: Mt. Hope Family Center, Center for Community Study, University of Rochester Medical Center, and the University of Rochester Counseling and Mental Health Services. Suitable clinical practica and a one-year clinical internship ensure continuity of clinical training throughout the student's stay in the program. For those doctoral students for whom a professional internship is required prior to graduation, 3 applied in 2000–2001. Of those who applied, 2 were placed in APA accredited internships.

Housing and Day Care: On-campus housing and day care facilities are available.

Employment of Department Graduates:
Master's Degree Graduates: Of those who graduated in the academic year 2000–2001, the following categories and numbers represent the post-graduate activities and employment of master's degree graduates: Enrolled in a post-doctoral residency/fellowship (n/a), employed in independent practice (n/a).

Doctoral Degree Graduates: Of those who graduated in the academic year 2000–2001, the following categories and numbers represent the post-graduate activities and employment of doctoral degree graduates: Enrolled in a psychology doctoral program (n/a), enrolled in another graduate/professional program (n/a), enrolled in a post-doctoral residency/fellowship (2), employed in an academic position at a university (1), employed in a community mental health/counseling center (2).

Additional Information:
Orientation, Objectives, and Emphasis of Department: The Department of Clinical and Social Sciences in Psychology offers PhD training in three areas of Psychology: Clinical, Developmental, and Social-Personality. The department also includes a research program in Human Motivation that includes faculty and students from all three areas. Two additional research units are affiliated with the department - the Mt. Hope Family Center and the Center for Community Study. The Mt. Hope Family Center provides opportunities for training and research in developmental psychopathology. The Center for Community Study provides similar opportunities for work on the detection and prevention of young children's adjustment problems. Graduate training emphasizes the development of research skills. To excel in any discipline, students need outstanding facilities, distinguished faculty, and an environment promoting their full integration in the research endeavor. We feel that our Department combines all of these characteristics.

Special Facilities or Resources: The Mt. Hope Family Center offers a unique combination of service, training, and research. The service component focuses on the assessment and treatment of families experiencing severe familial dysfunction and of children at risk of foster care placement and/or emotional difficulties. Treatment programs include: a) a full-time preschool program with psycho-educational treatment for families and a parent-child attachment intervention for children ages 3 to 5 and their caregivers, and b) an after school program for at-risk school-aged children. The Center for Community Study aims to: 1) develop, implement, and evaluate programs to maximize adjustment of individuals (particularly young children) to their environments; and 2) apply psychological methods and knowledge to the solution of community problems in mental health. The Center develops programs to address longstanding mental health problems from a preventive standpoint: a) by analyzing and modifying social environments (such as schools); b) by training young children in age-appropriate, adaptive social competencies; c) by identifying ways to reduce stress and training children to cope with it; and d) by developing programs for early identification and prevention of school adjustment problems and enhancing wellness.

Information for Students With Physical Disabilities: Meliora Hall is equipped with ramps, elevators, and handicapped-accessible doors.

Application Information:
Send to: Maryann Gilbert, Academic Coordinator, Department of Clinical and Social Sciences in Psychology, University of Rochester, Meliora Hall 355, RC Box 270266, Rochester, NY 14627-0266. Stu-

dents are admitted in the Fall, application deadline January 20. *Fee:* $25.

Saint Bonaventure University
Department of Counselor Education
P.O. Box AV
St. Bonaventure, NY 14778
Telephone: (716) 375-2368
Fax: (716) 375-2360
E-mail: *silliker@sbu.edu*
Web: *http://schoolofed.sbu.edu/*

Department Established:
1950. Chairperson: S. Alan Silliker. Number of Faculty: total–full-time 6, part-time 1; women–full-time 2; minority–full-time 1.

Programs and Degrees Offered:
Listed in the following order: Program area, degree type (T if terminal Master's), number awarded 7/00–6/01. Advanced Certificate in Agency 5, Advanced Certificate in School 15, Agency Counseling (T) 10, School Counseling (T) 40.

Student Applications/Admissions:
Admissions Requirements:
Scores: Entries appear in this order: required test or GPA, minimum score (if required), median score of students entering in 2001–2002. Master's Programs: GRE-V+Q+Analytical no minimum stated; MAT no minimum stated; overall undergraduate GPA no minimum stated. Students may submit either the GRE or MAT Doctoral Programs: last 2 years GPA no minimum stated; psychology GPA no minimum stated; psychology GPA no minimum stated.
Other Criteria: (importance of criteria rated low, medium, or high): GRE/MAT scores medium, extracurricular activity low, GPA high, letters of recommendation medium, interview high, statement of goals and objectives medium.

Student Characteristics: The following represents characteristics of students in 2001–2002 in all graduate psychology programs in the department: Female–full-time 90, part-time 55; Male–full-time 15, part-time 10; African American/Black–full-time 3, part-time 2; Hispanic/Latino (a)–full-time 2, part-time 1; Asian/Pacific Islander–full-time 0, part-time 0; American Indian/Alaska Native–full-time 1, part-time 1; Multi-ethnic–full-time 0, part-time 0; students subject to the Americans with Disabilities Act–full-time 2, part-time 1.

Financial Information/Assistance:
Tuition for Full-Time Study: *Master's:* State residents $530 per credit hour; nonstate residents: $530 per credit hour.

Financial Assistance:
First Year Students: No information provided.
Advanced Students: No information provided.
Contact Information: No information provided.

Internships/Practica: Many local opportunities exist for internships in both school counseling programs and at agency counseling sites.

Housing and Day Care: No on-campus housing and day care facilities are available.

Employment of Department Graduates:
Master's Degree Graduates: Of those who graduated in the academic year 2000–2001, the following categories and numbers represent the post-graduate activities and employment of master's degree graduates: Enrolled in a post-doctoral residency/fellowship (n/a), employed in independent practice (n/a).
Doctoral Degree Graduates: Of those who graduated in the academic year 2000–2001, the following categories and numbers represent the post-graduate activities and employment of doctoral degree graduates: Enrolled in a psychology doctoral program (n/a), enrolled in another graduate/professional program (n/a).

Additional Information:
Orientation, Objectives, and Emphasis of Department: The mission of the Department of Counselor Education is to prepare students for the professional practice of counseling in a multicultural and diverse society. Specific program goals are: (a) support for the mission of St. Bonaventure University; and (b) adherence to the highest standards of counselor education.

Application Information:
Send to: School of Graduate Studies. Students are admitted in the Fall, application deadline July 15; Spring, application deadline Dec 15; Summer, application deadline April 15. *Fee:* $35.

Saint Bonaventure University (2001 data)
Department of Psychology
St. Bonaventure, NY 14778
Telephone: (716) 375-2504
Fax: (716) 375-7618
E-mail: *rvaleri@sbu.edu*
Web: *http://www.sbu.edu*

Department Established:
1943. Chairperson: Harold Gelfand. Number of Faculty: total–full-time 6, part-time 2; women–full-time 2.

Programs and Degrees Offered:
Listed in the following order: Program area, degree type (T if terminal Master's), number awarded 7/00–6/01. General experimental MA (T) 4.

Student Applications/Admissions:
Student Applications
General experimental MA—Applications 2001–2002, 5. Total applicants accepted 2001–2002, 12. New applicants enrolled 2001–2002, 5. Total enrolled 2001–2002 full-time, 11, part-time, 1. Openings 2002–2003, 8.

Admissions Requirements:
Scores: Entries appear in this order: required test or GPA, minimum score (if required), median score of students entering in 2001–2002. Master's Programs: GRE-V 500, 521; GRE-Q 500, 537; GRE-V+Q 1000, 1050; overall undergraduate GPA 2.75, 3.13.

Other Criteria: (importance of criteria rated low, medium, or high): GRE/MAT scores medium, research experience medium, work experience medium, extracurricular activity low, clinically related public service low, GPA medium, letters of recommendation high, interview high, statement of goals and objectives medium.

Student Characteristics: The following represents characteristics of students in 2001–2002 in all graduate psychology programs in the department: Female–full-time 1, part-time 0; Male–full-time 1, part-time 0; African American/Black–full-time 0, part-time 0; Hispanic/Latino (a)–full-time 0, part-time 0; Asian/Pacific Islander–full-time 0, part-time 0; American Indian/Alaska Native–full-time 0, part-time 0.

Financial Information/Assistance:
Tuition for Full-Time Study: No information provided.

Financial Assistance:
First Year Students: No information provided.
Advanced Students: No information provided.
Contact Information: Of all students currently enrolled full-time, 100% benefited from one or more of the listed financial assistance programs. For more information contact: Director of Financial Aid, St. Bonaventure University, St. Bonaventure, NY 14778, (716) 375-2528.

Internships/Practica: No information provided.

Housing and Day Care: No on-campus housing and day care facilities are available.

Employment of Department Graduates:
Master's Degree Graduates: Of those who graduated in the academic year 2000–2001, the following categories and numbers represent the post-graduate activities and employment of master's degree graduates: Enrolled in a post-doctoral residency/fellowship (n/a), employed in independent practice (n/a).
Doctoral Degree Graduates: Of those who graduated in the academic year 2000–2001, the following categories and numbers represent the post-graduate activities and employment of doctoral degree graduates: Enrolled in a psychology doctoral program (n/a), enrolled in another graduate/professional program (n/a).

Additional Information:
Orientation, Objectives, and Emphasis of Department: The core program focuses on psychology as a behavioral science; electives permit focus on sociobiology, learning, social, memory and cognition, organizational development, and media effects. Also, we wish to prepare students for doctoral work or for a terminal master's for teaching or applied careers. Research skills are strongly emphasized in order to develop professional and skilled psychologists.

Special Facilities or Resources: The department has two computer terminals, a social laboratory, a media-television laboratory, a memory-cognition laboratory, statistics-quantitative measurement, an animal laboratory, and a learning measurement center. Upgraded computer facilities to include: 3 (386 SX) and 3 (486 SX) computers, color laserjet printer, a scanner, and 2 laptop computers. In addition, the department now has 7 Pentium Gateway 2000 computers.

Application Information:
Send to: Robin Valeri, PhD, Department of Psychology, St. Bonaventure University, St. Bonaventure, NY 14778. Students are admitted in the Fall, application deadline April 15. *Fee:* $30.

St. John's University
Department of Psychology
St. John's College of Arts & Sciences
8000 Utopia Parkway
Jamaica, NY 11439
Telephone: (718) 990-6368
Fax: (718) 990-6705
E-mail: *digiuser@stjohns.edu*
Web: *http://www.stjohns.edu*

Department Established:
1958. Acting Chairperson: Raymond DiGiuseppe. Number of Faculty: total–full-time 28, part-time 32; women–full-time 8, part-time 10; minority–full-time 4.

Programs and Degrees Offered:
Listed in the following order: Program area, degree type (T if terminal Master's), number awarded 7/00–6/01. Clinical PhD 20, general-experiment MA (T) 2, school MA (T) 31, School Psychology PsyD 1.

APA Accreditation: Clinical PhD: full.

Student Applications/Admissions:
Student Applications
Clinical PhD—Applications 2001–2002, 187. Total applicants accepted 2001–2002, 38. New applicants enrolled 2001–2002, 12. Total enrolled 2001–2002 full-time, 95, part-time, 6. Openings 2002–2003, 12. The Median number of years required for completion of a degree are 7. *General-experiment MA*—Applications 2001–2002, 15. Total applicants accepted 2001–2002, 5. New applicants enrolled 2001–2002, 5. Total enrolled 2001–2002 full-time, 13, part-time, 5. The number of students enrolled full and part-time, who were dismissed or voluntarily withdrew from this program area were 0. *School MA*—Applications 2001–2002, 75. Total applicants accepted 2001–2002, 16. New applicants enrolled 2001–2002, 216. Total enrolled 2001–2002 full-time, 20, part-time, 21. Openings 2002–2003, 16. The Median number of years required for completion of a degree are 3. *School Psychology PsyD*—Applications 2001–2002, 100. Total applicants accepted 2001–2002, 16. New applicants enrolled 2001–2002, 18. Total enrolled 2001–2002 full-time, 45, part-time, 46. Openings 2002–2003, 16. The Median number of years required for completion of a degree are 5. The number of students enrolled full and part-time, who were dismissed or voluntarily withdrew from this program area were 1.

Admissions Requirements:
Scores: Entries appear in this order: required test or GPA, minimum score (if required), median score of students entering in 2001–2002. Master's Programs: GRE-V no minimum stated, 450; GRE-Q no minimum stated, 500; GRE-V+Q no minimum stated, 920; GRE-Subject(Psych) no minimum stated,

520; overall undergraduate GPA no minimum stated, 3.3; psychology GPA no minimum stated. GRE not required for MA in General Experimental Psychology. Doctoral Programs: GRE-V no minimum stated, 600; GRE-Q no minimum stated, 610; GRE-V+Q no minimum stated, 1210; GRE-Subject(Psych) no minimum stated, 640; overall undergraduate GPA no minimum stated, 3.61; last 2 years GPA no minimum stated; psychology GPA no minimum stated, 3.82; psychology GPA no minimum stated, 3.87.

Other Criteria: (importance of criteria rated low, medium, or high): GRE/MAT scores high, research experience high, work experience medium, extracurricular activity low, clinically related public service medium, GPA high, letters of recommendation high, interview high, statement of goals and objectives high, writing sample medium. Interview for PhD and PsyD programs only. Clinically related public service not applicable to MA program.

Student Characteristics: The following represents characteristics of students in 2001–2002 in all graduate psychology programs in the department: Female–full-time 59, part-time 14; Male–full-time 9, part-time 7; African American/Black–full-time 4, part-time 4; Hispanic/Latino (a)–full-time 5, part-time 2; Asian/Pacific Islander–full-time 0, part-time 0; American Indian/Alaska Native–full-time 0, part-time 1.

Financial Information/Assistance:

Tuition for Full-Time Study: *Master's:* State residents $580 per credit hour; nonstate residents: $655 per credit hour.

Financial Assistance:

First Year Students: Average amount paid per academic year: $5,000. Tuition remission given: full. Average amount paid per academic year: $7,000. Tuition remission given: full. Average amount paid per academic year: $8,000. Tuition remission given: full.

Advanced Students: Average amount paid per academic year: $5,000. Tuition remission given: full. Average amount paid per academic year: $7,000. Tuition remission given: full. Average amount paid per academic year: $8,000. Tuition remission given: full.

Contact Information: Of all students currently enrolled full-time, 25% benefited from one or more of the listed financial assistance programs. For information on financial assistance, contact: Office of Financial Aid, Newman Hall, B28, St. John's University, 8000 Utopia Pkwy, Jamaica, NY 11439.

Internships/Practica: Students in the PhD program in clinical psychology see clients in our Center for Psychological Services and Clinical Studies during all four full-time years of study. They also compete a 1–2 day per week externship in a clinical facility during their third and fourth years. A full-time internship is required in the fifth year. Students in the MS program in school psychology complete a one year practicum at the Center for Psychological Services and Clinical Studies which includes work at one or more area schools. They also complete a five day per week internship during their final year either in a public school setting or at an agency serving children or adolescents. Students in the PsyD program in school psychology complete two years of practice at the Center for Psychological Services and Clinical Studies which includes work at one or more area schools. They also complete a 3-day per week internship in a public school and

a 3-day per week externship in a school for exceptional children. A full-time internship is required in the fifth year. For those doctoral students for whom a professional internship is required prior to graduation, 17 applied in 2000–2001. Of those who applied, 15 were placed in internships listed by the Association of Psychology Postdoctoral and Internship Programs (APPIC); 15 were placed in APA accredited internships.

Housing and Day Care: No on-campus housing and day care facilities are available.

Employment of Department Graduates:

Master's Degree Graduates: Of those who graduated in the academic year 2000–2001, the following categories and numbers represent the post-graduate activities and employment of master's degree graduates: Enrolled in a post-doctoral residency/fellowship (n/a), employed in independent practice (n/a).

Doctoral Degree Graduates: Of those who graduated in the academic year 2000–2001, the following categories and numbers represent the post-graduate activities and employment of doctoral degree graduates: Enrolled in a psychology doctoral program (n/a), enrolled in another graduate/professional program (n/a).

Additional Information:

Orientation, Objectives, and Emphasis of Department: The department emphasizes advanced preparation in the science of psychology by integrating theory and practice. Training at the master's degree level is provided in school psychology (MS) and general-experimental psychology (MA). The MA program offers a thesis and non-thesis track. Training at the doctoral level is provided in clinical psychology (PhD) and school psychology (PsyD). The doctoral program in clinical psychology is anchored within the scientist-practitioner model. Students are exposed to diverse theoretical approaches in contemporary clinical practice, particularly psychoanalytic and cognitive-behavioral. Students follow either a general track of study in clinical psychology or subspeciality training in clinical child psychology. The doctoral program in school psychology is anchored within the scholar-practitioner model. Students receive a firm foundation in the basic science of psychology upon which training in the practice of psychology is built. The MS and PsyD programs in school psychology lead to certification as a school psychologist. Students who are bilingual may select a track of study leading to certification as a bilingual school psychologist. Both doctoral programs allow students to obtain advanced training in group or marital/family therapy, or neuropsychology, on an elective basis.

Special Facilities or Resources: The Center for Psychological Services and Clinical Studies is an on-campus training site for students in clinical and school psychology. The Center provides comprehensive psychological services to community residents at a modest cost. The Center also serves as a site for student and faculty research.

Application Information:

Send to: Graduate Admissions, Newman Hall Room 106, St. John's University, 8000 Utopia Pkwy, Jamaica, NY 11439. Students are admitted in the Fall, application deadline 2/1;3/15; Spring, application deadline rolling; Summer, application deadline rolling. Doctoral Programs, Fall only, deadline February 1; MS in School Psychology, Fall only, deadline is March 15. *Fee:* $40.

State University of New York at Buffalo (2001 data)
Department of Counseling, School and Educational
  Psychology
409 Baldy Hall
Buffalo, NY 14260-1000
Telephone: (716) 645-2485
Fax: (716) 645-6616
E-mail: *shuell@buffalo.edu*
Web: *http://www.gse.buffalo.edu*

Department Established:
1949. Chairperson: Timothy Janikowski. Number of Faculty: total–full-time 14, part-time 10; women–full-time 5, part-time 6; minority–full-time 1, part-time 1.

Programs and Degrees Offered:
Listed in the following order: Program area, degree type (T if terminal Master's), number awarded 7/00–6/01. Counseling psychology PhD 8, counselor education PhD 1, educational psychology PhD 3, rehabilitation counseling MS (T) 9, school counseling MEd 19, school psychology MA 9.

APA Accreditation: Combined PhD: full.

Student Applications/Admissions:
Student Applications
Counseling psychology PhD—Applications 2001–2002, 84. Total applicants accepted 2001–2002, 8. New applicants enrolled 2001–2002, 8. Total enrolled 2001–2002 full-time, 44. Openings 2002–2003, 6. *Counselor education PhD*—Applications 2001–2002, 12. Total applicants accepted 2001–2002, 5. New applicants enrolled 2001–2002, 5. Total enrolled 2001–2002 full-time, 20. Openings 2002–2003, 4. *Educational psychology PhD*—Applications 2001–2002, 24. Total applicants accepted 2001–2002, 5. New applicants enrolled 2001–2002, 4. Total enrolled 2001–2002 full-time, 27. Openings 2002–2003, 5. *Rehabilitation counseling MS*—Applications 2001–2002, 25. Total applicants accepted 2001–2002, 10. New applicants enrolled 2001–2002, 9. Total enrolled 2001–2002 full-time, 24. Openings 2002–2003, 10. *School counseling MEd*—Applications 2001–2002, 60. Total applicants accepted 2001–2002, 24. New applicants enrolled 2001–2002, 24. Total enrolled 2001–2002 full-time, 74. Openings 2002–2003, 15. *School psychology MA*—Applications 2001–2002, 50. Total applicants accepted 2001–2002, 12. New applicants enrolled 2001–2002, 12. Total enrolled 2001–2002 full-time, 40. Openings 2002–2003, 12.

Admissions Requirements:
Scores: Entries appear in this order: required test or GPA, minimum score (if required), median score of students entering in 2001–2002. Master's Programs: GRE-V no minimum stated, 505; GRE-Q no minimum stated, 565; GRE-V+Q no minimum stated, 1070; overall undergraduate GPA no minimum stated, 3.3. Doctoral Programs: GRE-V no minimum stated, 545; GRE-Q no minimum stated, 612; GRE-V+Q no minimum stated, 1157; overall undergraduate GPA no minimum stated, 3.3; last 2 years GPA no minimum stated; psychology GPA no minimum stated; psychology GPA no minimum stated, 3.6.

Other Criteria: (importance of criteria rated low, medium, or high): GRE/MAT scores high, research experience medium, work experience medium, extracurricular activity low, clinically related public service medium, GPA medium, letters of recommendation medium, interview high, statement of goals and objectives medium. Not all programs conduct personal interviews

Student Characteristics: The following represents characteristics of students in 2001–2002 in all graduate psychology programs in the department: Female–full-time 46, part-time 0; Male–full-time 16, part-time 0; African American/Black–full-time 0, part-time 0; Hispanic/Latino (a)–full-time 2, part-time 0; Asian/Pacific Islander–full-time 1, part-time 0; American Indian/Alaska Native–full-time 0, part-time 0.

Financial Information/Assistance:
Tuition for Full-Time Study: No information provided.

Financial Assistance:
First Year Students: No information provided.
Advanced Students: No information provided.
Contact Information: Of all students currently enrolled full-time, 0% benefited from one or more of the listed financial assistance programs. For information on financial assistance, contact: The Department.

Internships/Practica: No information provided.

Housing and Day Care: No on-campus housing and day care facilities are available.

Employment of Department Graduates:
Master's Degree Graduates: Of those who graduated in the academic year 2000–2001, the following categories and numbers represent the post-graduate activities and employment of master's degree graduates: Enrolled in a post-doctoral residency/fellowship (n/a), employed in independent practice (n/a).
Doctoral Degree Graduates: Of those who graduated in the academic year 2000–2001, the following categories and numbers represent the post-graduate activities and employment of doctoral degree graduates: Enrolled in a psychology doctoral program (n/a), enrolled in another graduate/professional program (n/a).

Additional Information:
Orientation, Objectives, and Emphasis of Department: Departmental foci are children and youth, families, college students, and school processes. Doctoral programs follow the practitioner-scientist model. Increased integration of counseling, school, and educational psychology programs is developing. Field experience and research experience are continuous through the programs.

Special Facilities or Resources: Department offers training experiences in a wide variety of schools, agencies, and colleges in both urban and suburban settings.

Application Information:
Send to: 409 Baldy Hall, University at Buffalo, The State University of New York; Amherst, NY 14260-1000. Students are admitted in the Fall, application deadline February 1; Summer, application deadline May 24. Counselor Education fall application deadline March 1. Educa-

tional Psychology, applications considered for fall and spring admission. *Fee:* $50.

State University of New York at New Paltz
Department of Psychology
Jacobson Faculty Tower 302, 75 South Manheim Blvd.,
 Suite 9
New Paltz, NY 12561-2440
Telephone: (845) 257-3467
Fax: (845) 257-3474
E-mail: *halpernj@newpaltz.edu*
Web: *http://www.newpaltz.edu*

Department Established:
 1969. Chairperson: Michael Gayle. Number of Faculty: total–full-time 14; women–full-time 6; minority–full-time 3; faculty subject to the Americans with Disabilities Act 1.

Programs and Degrees Offered:
 Listed in the following order: Program area, degree type (T if terminal Master's), number awarded 7/00–6/01. (Unknown Program) MA (T), general MA (T) 7.

Student Applications/Admissions:
 Student Applications
 (Unknown Program) MA. General MA—Applications 2001–2002, 27. Total applicants accepted 2001–2002, 16. New applicants enrolled 2001–2002, 13. Total enrolled 2001–2002 full-time, 11, part-time, 2. Openings 2002–2003, 12. The number of students enrolled full and part-time, who were dismissed or voluntarily withdrew from this program area were 1.

 Admissions Requirements:
 Scores: Entries appear in this order: required test or GPA, minimum score (if required), median score of students entering in 2001–2002. Master's Programs: GRE-V no minimum stated, 500; GRE-Q no minimum stated, 550; GRE-V+Q no minimum stated, 1050; GRE-Analytical no minimum stated, 610; GRE-V+Q+Analytical no minimum stated, 1660; GRE-Subject(Psych) no minimum stated, 550; overall undergraduate GPA 3.0, 3.3; psychology GPA 3.00, 3.5. Doctoral Programs: last 2 years GPA no minimum stated; psychology GPA no minimum stated; psychology GPA no minimum stated.
 Other Criteria: (importance of criteria rated low, medium, or high): GRE/MAT scores medium, research experience medium, work experience, extracurricular activity medium, clinically related public service medium, GPA high, letters of recommendation high, interview low, statement of goals and objectives high.

Student Characteristics: The following represents characteristics of students in 2001–2002 in all graduate psychology programs in the department: Female–full-time 14, part-time 1; Male–full-time 3, part-time 1; African American/Black–full-time 1, part-time 0; Hispanic/Latino (a)–full-time 1, part-time 0; Asian/Pacific Islander–full-time 1, part-time 0; American Indian/Alaska Native–full-time 0, part-time 0.

Financial Information/Assistance:
 Tuition for Full-Time Study: *Master's:* State residents per academic year $5,100; nonstate residents: per academic year $8,416.

Financial Assistance:
 First Year Students: Teaching assistantships available for first-year. Average amount paid per academic year: $4,500. Average number of hours worked per week: 20. Tuition remission given: partial. Fellowships and scholarships available for first-year. Average number of hours worked per week: 10. Tuition remission given: partial.
 Advanced Students: Teaching assistantships available for advanced students. Average amount paid per academic year: $4,500. Average number of hours worked per week: 20. Tuition remission given: partial. Fellowships and scholarships available for advanced students. Average number of hours worked per week: 10. Tuition remission given: partial.
 Contact Information: Of all students currently enrolled full-time, 15% benefited from one or more of the listed financial assistance programs. For information on financial assistance, contact: Coordinator, Graduate Psychology Program, FT 302, Suny New Paltz, 75 S. Manheim Blvd. Suite 9, New Paltz, NY 12562-2440.

Internships/Practica: All students in the counseling concentration complete a practicum at the college counseling center and the career advising center. Additional internship opportunities are available with regional public and private mental health agencies.

Housing and Day Care: On-campus housing and day care facilities are available.

Employment of Department Graduates:
 Master's Degree Graduates: Of those who graduated in the academic year 2000–2001, the following categories and numbers represent the post-graduate activities and employment of master's degree graduates: Enrolled in a post-doctoral residency/fellowship (n/a), employed in independent practice (n/a).
 Doctoral Degree Graduates: Of those who graduated in the academic year 2000–2001, the following categories and numbers represent the post-graduate activities and employment of doctoral degree graduates: Enrolled in a psychology doctoral program (n/a), enrolled in another graduate/professional program (n/a).

Additional Information:
 Orientation, Objectives, and Emphasis of Department: The objective of the MA program is to provide students with a broad-based education in psychology. The program offers students exposure to a variety of fields including: developmental, cognitive, social, counseling, physiological, and industrial/organizational psychology. The program prepares students for entry into doctoral programs or employment in a variety of settings (human services, industry, education, government) where psychology can be applied. In addition, students may pursue a concentration in counseling psychology. The purpose of the counseling concentration is to provide students an opportunity to develop academic and applied skills in counseling and psychotherapy.

Special Facilities or Resources: Laboratory facilities and equipment (computers, videotaping equipment) are available to support student and faculty research in a variety of research areas such as: cognition, constructivisim, human development, social/organizational interaction, and autism. The department also maintains links to local and community organizations for research opportunities. In addition the department has a computer lab for research and instruction with Internet access. All graduate students have access to word processing, SPSS, and the World-Wide Web through the campus computer network.

Application Information:

Send to: James Halpern, Coordinator, Psychology Graduate Program, Jacobson Faculty Tower, Room 302, 75 S. Manheim Blvd. Suite 9, New Paltz, New York 12561-2440. Students are admitted in the Fall, application deadline February 15; Spring, application deadline November 1. Applications considered for summer admission if space in the incoming class is available. *Fee:* $50.

State University of New York at Stony Brook
Department of Psychology
Stony Brook, NY 11794-2500
Telephone: (631) 632-7814
Fax: (631) 632-632-7876
E-mail: *dcampani@notes.cc.sunysb.edu*
Web: *http://www.psy.sunysb.edu*

Department Established:

1961. Chair: Nancy Squires. Number of Faculty: total–full-time 29; women–full-time 12; minority–full-time 1.

Programs and Degrees Offered:

Listed in the following order: Program area, degree type (T if terminal Master's), number awarded 7/00–6/01. Biopsychology PhD 3, clinical PhD 4, experimental PhD 1, social/health PhD 2.

APA Accreditation: Clinical PhD: full.

Student Applications/Admissions:

Student Applications

Biopsychology PhD—Applications 2001–2002, 30. Total applicants accepted 2001–2002, 6. New applicants enrolled 2001–2002, 2. Total enrolled 2001–2002 full-time, 17. Openings 2002–2003. *Clinical PhD*—Applications 2001–2002, 220. Total applicants accepted 2001–2002, 13. New applicants enrolled 2001–2002, 9. Total enrolled 2001–2002 full-time, 44. Openings 2002–2003. *Experimental PhD*—Applications 2001–2002, 21. Total applicants accepted 2001–2002, 9. New applicants enrolled 2001–2002, 3. Total enrolled 2001–2002 full-time, 17. Openings 2002–2003. *Social/health PhD*—Applications 2001–2002, 56. Total applicants accepted 2001–2002, 7. New applicants enrolled 2001–2002, 3. Total enrolled 2001–2002 full-time, 21. Openings 2002–2003.

Admissions Requirements:

Scores: Entries appear in this order: required test or GPA, minimum score (if required), median score of students entering in 2001–2002. Master's Programs: GRE-V no minimum stated; GRE-Q no minimum stated; GRE-Analytical no minimum stated; overall undergraduate GPA 3.50. Doctoral Programs: GRE-V+Q 1250; overall undergraduate GPA 3.5; last 2 years GPA no minimum stated; psychology GPA no minimum stated; psychology GPA no minimum stated.

Other Criteria: (importance of criteria rated low, medium, or high): GRE/MAT scores medium, research experience high, work experience low, extracurricular activity low, clinically related public service low, GPA medium, letters of recommendation high, statement of goals and objectives high.

Student Characteristics: The following represents characteristics of students in 2001–2002 in all graduate psychology programs in the department: Female–full-time 58, part-time 0; Male–full-time 41, part-time 0; African American/Black–full-time 6, part-time 0; Hispanic/Latino (a)–full-time 9, part-time 0; Asian/Pacific Islander–full-time 3, part-time 0; American Indian/Alaska Native–full-time 0, part-time 0.

Financial Information/Assistance:

Tuition for Full-Time Study: Doctoral: State residents: per academic year $5,100, $213 per credit hour; nonstate residents: per academic year $8,416, $351 per credit hour.

Financial Assistance:

First Year Students: Average amount paid per academic year: $11,260. Average number of hours worked per week: 20. Apply by Jan 15. Tuition remission given: full. Average amount paid per academic year: $11,260. Average number of hours worked per week: 20. Apply by Jan 15. Tuition remission given: full. Average amount paid per academic year: $10,000. Average number of hours worked per week: 0. Apply by Jan 15. Tuition remission given: full.

Advanced Students: Average amount paid per academic year: $11,260. Average number of hours worked per week: 20. Tuition remission given: full. Average amount paid per academic year: $11,260. Average number of hours worked per week: 20. Tuition remission given: full. Average amount paid per academic year: $10,000. Average number of hours worked per week: 0. Tuition remission given: full.

Contact Information: Of all students currently enrolled full-time, 65% benefited from one or more of the listed financial assistance programs. For information on financial assistance, contact: Office of Financial Aid and Student Employment, 516-632-6840.

Internships/Practica: No information provided.

Housing and Day Care: On-campus housing and day care facilities are available.

Employment of Department Graduates:

Master's Degree Graduates: Of those who graduated in the academic year 2000–2001, the following categories and numbers represent the post-graduate activities and employment of master's degree graduates: Enrolled in a post-doctoral residency/fellowship (n/a), employed in independent practice (n/a).

Doctoral Degree Graduates: Of those who graduated in the academic year 2000–2001, the following categories and numbers represent the post-graduate activities and employment of doctoral degree graduates: Enrolled in a psychology doctoral program (n/a), enrolled in another graduate/professional program (n/a).

Additional Information:

Orientation, Objectives, and Emphasis of Department: In all areas, the primary emphasis is on research training through research advisement and apprenticeship. Students are encouraged to become involved in ongoing research immediately and to engage in independent research when sufficient skills and knowledge permit, with the goal of becoming active and original contributors. As the first behavioral clinical curriculum in the country, Stony Brook has served as a model for a number of other behaviorally oriented clinical programs and continues to be a leader in that field. Research in the experimental area has always included both human and animal learning and now includes spatial cognition, psycholinguistics, cognitive development, memory, attention, judgement and choice, sensation and perception, and psychophysics. Biopsychology offers three areas of concentration: psychophysiology, neuropsychology, and behavioral neuroscience. Social psychology offers a general education and research in social and health psychology. Health psychology and psychophysiology are interarea concentrations.

Special Facilities or Resources: Besides faculty laboratories for human, animal, and physiological research, and electronics and machine shops, other campus facilities for research and graduate training include: Psychological Center, the training, research, and service unit for clinical psychology; Point of Woods Laboratory School with a special education class for elementary students; University Preschool with children from 18 months to 5 years of age; University Marital Therapy Clinic; and Suffolk Child Development Center, a private school for autistic, retarded, aphasic, and developmentally delayed children. Clinical neuropsychology uses affiliations with the University Health Sciences Center, local schools, an agency for the mentally retarded, and a Veterans Administration hospital. Departmental CRT terminals and 12 additional terminals and two printers in the division's Social Science Data Laboratory are used with campus computers.

Application Information:

Send to: Graduate Office-Department of Psychology, SUNY at Stony Brook, Stony Brook, NY 11794-2500. Students are admitted in the Fall, application deadline January 15. *Fee:* $50.

State University of New York, College at Brockport
Psychology Department
350 New Campus Drive
Brockport, NY 14420
Telephone: (585) 395-2488
Fax: (585) 395-2116
E-mail: *psychdpt@brockport.edu*
Web: *http://www.brockport.edu*

Department Established:
1965. Chairperson: Robert J. Miller. Number of Faculty: total–full-time 14, part-time 4; women–full-time 6, part-time 2; minority–full-time 2.

Programs and Degrees Offered:
Listed in the following order: Program area, degree type (T if terminal Master's), number awarded 7/00–6/01. Clinical MA (T) 7.

Student Applications/Admissions:
Student Applications
Clinical MA—Applications 2001–2002, 24. Total applicants accepted 2001–2002, 5. New applicants enrolled 2001–2002, 5. Total enrolled 2001–2002 full-time, 8, part-time, 14. Openings 2002–2003, 15. The Median number of years required for completion of a degree are 2. The number of students enrolled full and part-time, who were dismissed or voluntarily withdrew from this program area were 0.

Admissions Requirements:
Scores: Entries appear in this order: required test or GPA, minimum score (if required), median score of students entering in 2001–2002. Master's Programs: GRE-V 500; GRE-Q 500; GRE-Analytical 500; GRE-V+Q+Analytical 1500, 1670; overall undergraduate GPA 3.00, 3.63; last 2 years GPA 3.25, 3.63. Doctoral Programs: last 2 years GPA no minimum stated; psychology GPA no minimum stated; psychology GPA no minimum stated.

Other Criteria: (importance of criteria rated low, medium, or high): GRE/MAT scores medium, research experience high, work experience low, clinically related public service medium, GPA high, letters of recommendation high, interview high, statement of goals and objectives high. TOEFL if appropriate 550.

Student Characteristics: The following represents characteristics of students in 2001–2002 in all graduate psychology programs in the department: Female–full-time 6, part-time 12; Male–full-time 2, part-time 1; African American/Black–full-time 0, part-time 0; Hispanic/Latino (a)–full-time 0, part-time 0; Asian/Pacific Islander–full-time 0, part-time 0; American Indian/Alaska Native–full-time 0, part-time 0; Multi-ethnic–full-time 0, part-time 0; students subject to the Americans with Disabilities Act–full-time 0, part-time 0.

Financial Information/Assistance:
Tuition for Full-Time Study: *Master's:* State residents per academic year $2,556, $213 per credit hour; nonstate residents: per academic year $4,212, $351 per credit hour.

Financial Assistance:
First Year Students: Teaching assistantships available for first-year. Average amount paid per academic year: $6,000. Average number of hours worked per week: 20. Apply by April 15. Tuition remission given: partial.

Advanced Students: Teaching assistantships available for advanced students. Average amount paid per academic year: $6,000. Average number of hours worked per week: 20. Apply by April 15. Tuition remission given: partial.

Contact Information: Of all students currently enrolled full-time, 25% benefited from one or more of the listed financial assistance programs. For information on financial assistance, contact: Financial Aid Office.

Internships/Practica: Practical experience is in one of over 40 human service agencies in western New York, including the college counseling center, VA and academic medical centers, and state and local mental health and community service agencies. Each practicum placement is developed individually, based on the specific student and agency involved. Each practicum is supervised by an agency staff member as well as a faculty member from the Department of Psychology. Students must successfully complete all required coursework before beginning the practicum.

Housing and Day Care: No on-campus housing and day care facilities are available.

Employment of Department Graduates:

Master's Degree Graduates: Of those who graduated in the academic year 2000–2001, the following categories and numbers represent the post-graduate activities and employment of master's degree graduates: Enrolled in a psychology doctoral program (2), enrolled in another graduate/professional program (0), enrolled in a post-doctoral residency/fellowship (n/a), employed in independent practice (n/a), employed in an academic position at a university (0), employed in an academic position at a 2-year/4-year college (0), employed in other positions at a higher education institution (0), employed in a professional position in a school system (1), employed in business or industry (research/consulting) (0), employed in business or industry (management) (0), employed in a government agency (research) (0), employed in a government agency (professional services) (0), employed in a community mental health/counseling center (2), employed in a hospital/medical center (2), still seeking employment (0), other employment position (4).

Doctoral Degree Graduates: Of those who graduated in the academic year 2000–2001, the following categories and numbers represent the post-graduate activities and employment of doctoral degree graduates: Enrolled in a psychology doctoral program (n/a), enrolled in another graduate/professional program (n/a).

Additional Information:

Orientation, Objectives, and Emphasis of Department: The MA in psychology program is designed to prepare students for both doctoral work and also careers in applied psychology and the helping professions. Students are trained as scientists and practitioners, concerned with the application of psychological principles to the treatment and prevention of behavior disorders. Courses provide theoretical and practical training in contemporary methods of assessment, behavioral and cognitive-behavioral clinical intervention, and program evaluation.

Special Facilities or Resources: The department has facilities for research in the biobehavioral sciences, as well as sensory-perceptual, clinical, developmental, and personality psychology topics; and assessment/intervention training. Laboratory space, computer equipment, and an extensive file of psychological assessment instruments are also available.

Information for Students With Physical Disabilities: Campus buildings are all accessible.

Application Information:

Send to: Office of Graduate Studies, SUNY College at Brockport, 350 New Campus Dr., Brockport, NY 14420-2914. Students are admitted in the Fall, application deadline April 15. *Fee:* $50.

State University of New York, College at Plattsburgh

Psychology Department
Beaumont Hall, 101 Broad Street
Plattsburgh, NY 12901
Telephone: (518) 564-3076
Fax: (518) 564-3397
E-mail: *William.Gaeddert@plattsburgh.edu*
Web: *http://www.plattsburgh.edu/psy*

Department Established:

Chairperson: William Gaeddert. Number of Faculty: total–full-time 13, part-time 7; women–full-time 4, part-time 4; minority–full-time 1.

Programs and Degrees Offered:

Listed in the following order: Program area, degree type (T if terminal Master's), number awarded 7/00–6/01. School Psychology MA (T).

Student Applications/Admissions:

Student Applications

School Psychology MA—Applications 2001–2002, 25. Total applicants accepted 2001–2002, 8. New applicants enrolled 2001–2002, 4. Total enrolled 2001–2002 full-time, 14. Openings 2002–2003, 10. The Median number of years required for completion of a degree are 4.

Admissions Requirements:

Scores: Entries appear in this order: required test or GPA, minimum score (if required), median score of students entering in 2001–2002. Master's Programs: GRE-V no minimum stated; GRE-Q no minimum stated; GRE-V+Q 1000, 1100; overall undergraduate GPA 3.00, 3.20. Doctoral Programs: last 2 years GPA no minimum stated; psychology GPA no minimum stated; psychology GPA no minimum stated.

Other Criteria: (importance of criteria rated low, medium, or high): GRE/MAT scores medium, research experience medium, work experience medium, extracurricular activity medium, clinically related public service, GPA medium, letters of recommendation high, interview high, statement of goals and objectives high.

Student Characteristics: The following represents characteristics of students in 2001–2002 in all graduate psychology programs in the department: Female–full-time 12, part-time 0; Male–full-time 4, part-time 0; African American/Black–full-time 0, part-time 0; Hispanic/Latino (a)–full-time 0, part-time 0; Asian/Pacific Islander–full-time 0, part-time 0; American Indian/Alaska Native–full-time 0, part-time 0; Multi-ethnic–full-time 0, part-time 0; students subject to the Americans with Disabilities Act–full-time 0, part-time 0.

Financial Information/Assistance:

Tuition for Full-Time Study: *Master's:* State residents per academic year $2,550, $213 per credit hour; nonstate residents: per academic year $4,208, $351 per credit hour.

Financial Assistance:

First Year Students: Research assistantships available for first-year. Average amount paid per academic year: $4,600. Aver-

461

age number of hours worked per week: 10. Apply by March 1. Tuition remission given: partial.

Advanced Students: Research assistantships available for advanced students. Average amount paid per academic year: $4,600. Average number of hours worked per week: 10. Apply by March 1. Tuition remission given: partial. Traineeships available for advanced students. Average amount paid per academic year: $5,000. Average number of hours worked per week: 10. Apply by March 1. Tuition remission given: partial.

Contact Information: Of all students currently enrolled full-time, 25% benefited from one or more of the listed financial assistance programs. For information on financial assistance, contact: Financial Aid Office, Kehoe Bldg., SUNY-Plattsburgh, 101 Broad St., Plattsburgh NY 12901.

Internships/Practica: No information provided.

Housing and Day Care: On-campus housing and day care facilities are available.

Employment of Department Graduates:

Master's Degree Graduates: Of those who graduated in the academic year 2000–2001, the following categories and numbers represent the post-graduate activities and employment of master's degree graduates: Enrolled in a post-doctoral residency/fellowship (n/a), employed in independent practice (n/a).

Doctoral Degree Graduates: Of those who graduated in the academic year 2000–2001, the following categories and numbers represent the post-graduate activities and employment of doctoral degree graduates: Enrolled in a psychology doctoral program (n/a), enrolled in another graduate/professional program (n/a).

Additional Information:

Orientation, Objectives, and Emphasis of Department: The curriculum is a three-year, 69-hour MA program in psychology. The program offers coursework in psychological theories and skill development and applied experiences in area schools and community agencies. The goal of the program is to enable students to work effectively with individuals and groups and to act as psychological resources in schools and the community. A unique feature of the program is that many courses, beginning in the first semester, combine theory and research with practicum experiences in school and clinical work. Students develop competencies in personality, research methods, psychological assessment, behavior modification, individual and group psychotherapy, and community mental health. An important aspect of graduate training is the internship served the third year of graduate study at area schools. The Psychology Department and the agencies involved provide extensive supervision of students' work.

Special Facilities or Resources: The Neuropsychology Clinic and Psychoeducational Services center provide graduate students with on site practicum experiences. As part of course assignments, all students are required to provide supervised practicum work in the clinic to clients from the community and college.

Application Information:
Send to: Graduate Admissions, Kehoe Hall, SUNY-Plattsburgh, 101 Broad St., Plattsburgh, NY 12901. Students are admitted in the Fall, application deadline March 1. *Fee:* $50.

State University of New York, University at Albany
Department of Psychology
College of Arts and Sciences
1400 Washington Avenue
Albany, NY 12222
Telephone: (518) 442-4820
Fax: (518) 442-4867
E-mail: *cm949@cas.albany.edu*
Web: *http://www.albany.edu/psy/*

Department Established:
1950. Chairperson: Robert A. Rosellini. Number of Faculty: total–full-time 30; women–full-time 12; minority–full-time 5.

Programs and Degrees Offered:
Listed in the following order: Program area, degree type (T if terminal Master's), number awarded 7/00–6/01. Biopsychology PhD, clinical PhD 3, cognitive PhD, industrial/organizational PhD, social/personality PhD 1.

APA Accreditation: Clinical PhD: full.

Student Applications/Admissions:

Student Applications

Biopsychology PhD—Applications 2001–2002, 9. Total applicants accepted 2001–2002, 5. New applicants enrolled 2001–2002, 2. Total enrolled 2001–2002 full-time, 14. Openings 2002–2003, 3. The Median number of years required for completion of a degree are n/a. The number of students enrolled full and part-time, who were dismissed or voluntarily withdrew from this program area were 0. *Clinical PhD*—Applications 2001–2002, 158. Total applicants accepted 2001–2002, 20. New applicants enrolled 2001–2002, 10. Total enrolled 2001–2002 full-time, 49, part-time, 6. Openings 2002–2003, 6. The Median number of years required for completion of a degree are 7. The number of students enrolled full and part-time, who were dismissed or voluntarily withdrew from this program area were 0. *Cognitive PhD*—Applications 2001–2002, 13. Total applicants accepted 2001–2002, 7. New applicants enrolled 2001–2002, 2. Total enrolled 2001–2002 full-time, 8, part-time, 3. Openings 2002–2003, 2. The number of students enrolled full and part-time, who were dismissed or voluntarily withdrew from this program area were 0. *Industrial/organizational PhD*—Applications 2001–2002, 32. Total applicants accepted 2001–2002, 13. New applicants enrolled 2001–2002, 4. Total enrolled 2001–2002 full-time, 9, part-time, 12. Openings 2002–2003, 4. The number of students enrolled full and part-time, who were dismissed or voluntarily withdrew from this program area were 0. *Social/personality PhD*—Applications 2001–2002, 23. Total applicants accepted 2001–2002, 6. New applicants enrolled 2001–2002, 5. Total enrolled 2001–2002 full-time, 17, part-time, 11. Openings 2002–2003, 2. The Median number of years required for completion of a degree are 6. The number of students enrolled full and part-time, who were dismissed or voluntarily withdrew from this program area were 0.

Admissions Requirements:

Scores: Entries appear in this order: required test or GPA, minimum score (if required), median score of students entering in 2001–2002. Doctoral Programs: GRE-V 500, 570; GRE-Q 600, 640; GRE-V+Q 1000, 1200; GRE-Subject(Psych) 600, 640; overall undergraduate GPA 3.0, 3.66; last 2 years GPA no minimum stated; psychology GPA 3.25, 3.74; psychology GPA no minimum stated.

Other Criteria: (importance of criteria rated low, medium, or high): GRE/MAT scores high, research experience high, work experience medium, extracurricular activity low, clinically related public service medium, GPA high, letters of recommendation high, interview high, statement of goals and objectives high. The interview process is only done in clinical psychology program.

Student Characteristics: The following represents characteristics of students in 2001–2002 in all graduate psychology programs in the department: Female–full-time 66, part-time 18; Male–full-time 33, part-time 11; African American/Black–full-time 1, part-time 0; Hispanic/Latino (a)–full-time 2, part-time 0; Asian/Pacific Islander–full-time 4, part-time 0; American Indian/Alaska Native–full-time 1, part-time 0.

Financial Information/Assistance:

Tuition for Full-Time Study: *Doctoral:* State residents: per academic year $2,550, $213 per credit hour; nonstate residents: per academic year $4,208, $351 per credit hour.

Financial Assistance:

First Year Students: Teaching assistantships available for first-year. Average amount paid per academic year: $8,600. Average number of hours worked per week: 20. Apply by January 1. Tuition remission given: full. Research assistantships available for first-year. Average amount paid per academic year: $8,600. Average number of hours worked per week: 20. Apply by January 1. Tuition remission given: full.

Advanced Students: Teaching assistantships available for advanced students. Average amount paid per academic year: $8,600. Average number of hours worked per week: 20. Tuition remission given: full and partial. Research assistantships available for advanced students. Average amount paid per academic year: $8,600. Average number of hours worked per week: 20. Tuition remission given: full and partial. Fellowships and scholarships available for advanced students. Average amount paid per academic year: $8,600. Average number of hours worked per week: 20. Tuition remission given: full and partial.

Contact Information: Of all students currently enrolled full-time, 82% benefited from one or more of the listed financial assistance programs.

Internships/Practica: For those doctoral students for whom a professional internship is required prior to graduation, 6 applied in 2000–2001. Of those who applied, 6 were placed in internships listed by the Association of Psychology Postdoctoral and Internship Programs (APPIC); 6 were placed in APA accredited internships.

Housing and Day Care: On-campus housing and day care facilities are available.

Employment of Department Graduates:

Master's Degree Graduates: Of those who graduated in the academic year 2000–2001, the following categories and numbers represent the post-graduate activities and employment of master's degree graduates: Enrolled in a post-doctoral residency/fellowship (n/a), employed in independent practice (n/a).

Doctoral Degree Graduates: Of those who graduated in the academic year 2000–2001, the following categories and numbers represent the post-graduate activities and employment of doctoral degree graduates: Enrolled in a psychology doctoral program (n/a), enrolled in another graduate/professional program (n/a), enrolled in a post-doctoral residency/fellowship (0), employed in independent practice (0), employed in an academic position at a university (4), employed in an academic position at a 2-year/4-year college (0), employed in other positions at a higher education institution (0), employed in a professional position in a school system (0), employed in business or industry (research/consulting) (0), employed in business or industry (management) (0), employed in a government agency (research) (0), employed in a government agency (professional services) (0), employed in a community mental health/counseling center (0), employed in a hospital/medical center (0), still seeking employment (0), other employment position (0).

Additional Information:

Orientation, Objectives, and Emphasis of Department: All facets of the graduate program reflect a commitment to the empirical tradition in psychology. Thus, involvement in research is stressed in all areas of study. Students enter into an apprentice relationship with faculty members upon entry into the department and are expected to remain actively involved in research throughout their graduate careers. A major goal of the department is to train individuals who will make research contributions to the field. All areas of concentration train students for careers as teachers and research scientists. In addition, the social, clinical, and industrial/organizational areas prepare students for careers in applied settings. The orientation of the clinical program emphasizes cognitive and behavioral approaches. Admission is offered in five areas: biopsychology, clinical, cognitive, industrial/organizational, and social-personality.

Special Facilities or Resources: Resources and facilities include university- and grant-funded student stipends, plus stipends from other campus sources; an animal research facility and colony; several human research laboratories; grant-supported research and treatment clinics; the Psychological Services Center for practicum training; a technical shop and specialist; and a variety of research equipment.

Application Information:

Send to: The Office of Graduate Admissions, University Administration Building 121, 1400 Washington Avenue, Albany, NY 12222. Students are admitted in the Fall, application deadline January 1. *Fee:* $50.

State University of New York, University at Buffalo

Department of Psychology
College of Arts and Sciences
Park Hall
Buffalo, NY 14260-4110
Telephone: (716) 645-3650
Fax: (716) 645-3801
E-mail: *psych@acsu.buffalo.edu*
Web: *http://www.wings.buffalo.edu/psychology/*

Department Established:
1921. Chair: Jack A. Meacham. Number of Faculty: total–full-time 26; women–full-time 9; minority–full-time 1.

Programs and Degrees Offered:
Listed in the following order: Program area, degree type (T if terminal Master's), number awarded 7/00–6/01. Behavioral neuroscience PhD 2, clinical PhD 4, cognitive PhD 1, general MA (T) 5, social-personality PhD 1.

APA Accreditation: Clinical PhD: full.

Student Applications/Admissions:

Student Applications

Behavioral neuroscience PhD—Applications 2001–2002, 6. Total applicants accepted 2001–2002, 4. New applicants enrolled 2001–2002, 3. Total enrolled 2001–2002 full-time, 13. Openings 2002–2003, 4. The Median number of years required for completion of a degree are 5. The number of students enrolled full and part-time, who were dismissed or voluntarily withdrew from this program area were 1. *Clinical PhD*—Applications 2001–2002, 83. Total applicants accepted 2001–2002, 21. New applicants enrolled 2001–2002, 9. Total enrolled 2001–2002 full-time, 33. Openings 2002–2003, 6. The Median number of years required for completion of a degree are 7. *Cognitive PhD*—Applications 2001–2002, 10. Total applicants accepted 2001–2002, 8. New applicants enrolled 2001–2002, 2. Total enrolled 2001–2002 full-time, 9. Openings 2002–2003, 5. The Median number of years required for completion of a degree are 6. The number of students enrolled full and part-time, who were dismissed or voluntarily withdrew from this program area were 1. *General MA*—Applications 2001–2002, 52. Total applicants accepted 2001–2002, 40. New applicants enrolled 2001–2002, 21. Total enrolled 2001–2002 full-time, 36. Openings 2002–2003, 10. The Median number of years required for completion of a degree are 2. The number of students enrolled full and part-time, who were dismissed or voluntarily withdrew from this program area were 6. *Social-personality PhD*—Applications 2001–2002, 22. Total applicants accepted 2001–2002, 5. New applicants enrolled 2001–2002, 1. Total enrolled 2001–2002 full-time, 10. Openings 2002–2003, 5. The Median number of years required for completion of a degree are 10. The number of students enrolled full and part-time, who were dismissed or voluntarily withdrew from this program area were 1.

Admissions Requirements:

Scores: Entries appear in this order: required test or GPA, minimum score (if required), median score of students entering in 2001–2002. Master's Programs: GRE-V 480; GRE-Q 590;

GRE-Analytical 575. Doctoral Programs: GRE-V 570; GRE-Q 620; GRE-Analytical 575; last 2 years GPA no minimum stated; psychology GPA no minimum stated; psychology GPA no minimum stated.

Other Criteria: (importance of criteria rated low, medium, or high): GRE/MAT scores medium, research experience high, work experience low, extracurricular activity low, clinically related public service medium, GPA medium, letters of recommendation high, interview medium, statement of goals and objectives high, transcripts medium. Interview for clinical only.

Student Characteristics: The following represents characteristics of students in 2001–2002 in all graduate psychology programs in the department: Female–full-time 61, part-time 0; Male–full-time 41, part-time 0; African American/Black–full-time 5, part-time 0; Hispanic/Latino (a)–full-time 4, part-time 0; Asian/Pacific Islander–full-time 0, part-time 0; American Indian/Alaska Native–full-time 0, part-time 0; Multi-ethnic–full-time 0, part-time 0; students subject to the Americans with Disabilities Act–full-time 0, part-time 0.

Financial Information/Assistance:
Tuition for Full-Time Study: *Master's:* State residents per academic year $3,059, $291 per credit hour; nonstate residents: per academic year $4,717, $429 per credit hour. *Doctoral:* State residents: per academic year $3,059, $291 per credit hour; nonstate residents: per academic year $4,717, $429 per credit hour.

Financial Assistance:
First Year Students: Teaching assistantships available for first-year. Average amount paid per academic year: $8,400. Average number of hours worked per week: 20. Tuition remission given: full. Research assistantships available for first-year. Average amount paid per academic year: $8,400. Average number of hours worked per week: 20. Tuition remission given: full. Fellowships and scholarships available for first-year. Average amount paid per academic year: $10,400. Tuition remission given: full.

Advanced Students: Teaching assistantships available for advanced students. Average amount paid per academic year: $8,900. Average number of hours worked per week: 20. Tuition remission given: full. Research assistantships available for advanced students. Average amount paid per academic year: $8,900. Average number of hours worked per week: 20. Tuition remission given: full. Fellowships and scholarships available for advanced students. Average amount paid per academic year: $16,400. Tuition remission given: full.

Contact Information: Of all students currently enrolled full-time, 60% benefited from one or more of the listed financial assistance programs. For information on financial assistance, contact: http://www.grad.buffalo.edu.

Internships/Practica: Several clinical practica are offered each year for students in the doctoral program in Clinical Psychology and for other doctoral students with permission of the instructor. In addition, there is a summer practicum focused on treatment of children with attention deficit/hyperactivity disorder. For those doctoral students for whom a professional internship is required prior to graduation, 2 applied in 2000–2001. Of those who applied, 2 were placed in internships listed by the Association of Psychology Postdoctoral and Internship Programs (APPIC); 2 were placed in APA accredited internships.

Housing and Day Care: No on-campus housing and day care facilities are available.

Employment of Department Graduates:

Master's Degree Graduates: Of those who graduated in the academic year 2000–2001, the following categories and numbers represent the post-graduate activities and employment of master's degree graduates: Enrolled in a post-doctoral residency/fellowship (n/a), employed in independent practice (n/a).

Doctoral Degree Graduates: Of those who graduated in the academic year 2000–2001, the following categories and numbers represent the post-graduate activities and employment of doctoral degree graduates: Enrolled in a psychology doctoral program (n/a), enrolled in another graduate/professional program (n/a).

Additional Information:

Orientation, Objectives, and Emphasis of Department: The Department of Psychology offers doctoral degrees in Behavioral Neuroscience, Clinical Psychology, Cognitive Psychology, and Social-Personality Psychology and a Master's degree in psychology with several specializations. The department has as its defining characteristic and distinguishing mission, the conduct and communication of research and scholarship that contributes to the scientific understanding of psychology and the provision of high-quality graduate education and training. The department is dedicated to offering state-of-the-art education and training to its graduate students to prepare them to become leading researchers and to assume important positions in academic institutions or professional practice. We offer students a learning environment that is exciting and challenging, one that will allow them to follow their interests and fully develop their research skills. The research emphasis in the doctoral program in Behavorial Neuroscience is on the neural, endocrine, and molecular bases of behavior. Areas of specialization in Clinical Psychology include adult mood and anxiety disorders, relationship dysfunction, behavioral medicine, attention deficit/hyperactivity disorder, and child and adolescent aggression and substance abuse. The program in Cognitive Psychology focuses on the processes underlying perception, attention, memory, spoken and written language comprehension, language acquisition, categorization, problem solving, and thinking. Faculty research interests in the Social-Personality Program include close relationships, social cognition, self-concept, and self-esteem. Complete information is available on the department's web site, http://wings.buffalo.edu/psychology.

Special Facilities or Resources: The Department of Psychology has specialized research facilities for the study of language comprehension, auditory and speech perception, memory, categorization, animal cognition, visual perception, attention, social interaction, small group processes, animal surgery research, behavior therapy, human psychophysiology and biofeedback, and neurochemical and electrophysiological investigations into the physiological bases of behavior. Many of these laboratories are computer-based. The department also has ample facilities for individual and group therapy, marriage counseling, and therapeutic work with children. One-way vision screens and videotape equipment are available for observation and supervision. Internships are available through the department's Psychological Services Center. Excellent facilities are available for working with animals. Students have liberal access to the University's computing services on the North Campus.

Information for Students With Physical Disabilities: Students with a disability who would like reasonable accommodations to enable them to participate in a course, such as note takers, readers, or extended time on exams and assignments, should contact the Office of Disability Services, 716-645-2608.

Application Information:
Send to: Director of Graduate Admissions, Department of Psychology, University at Buffalo—The State University of New York, Park Hall Room 210, Buffalo, NY 14260-4110. Students are admitted in the Fall, application deadline January 5. MA Application Period for fall enrollment is January 5 to May 1. PhD deadline for fall enrollment is January 5. *Fee:* $35.

Syracuse University
Department of Psychology
Arts & Sciences
430 Huntington Hall, 150 Marshall Street
Syracuse, NY 13244-2340
Telephone: (315) 443-2354
Fax: (315) 443-4085
E-mail: *mlcripps@syr.edu*
Web: *http://psychweb.syr.edu*

Department Established:
1952. Chairperson: Barbara H. Fiese. Number of Faculty: total–full-time 22, part-time 24; women–full-time 4, part-time 9; minority–full-time 1.

Programs and Degrees Offered:
Listed in the following order: Program area, degree type (T if terminal Master's), number awarded 7/00–6/01. Clinical PhD 4, experimental PhD 1, school PhD 3, social PhD 1.

APA Accreditation: Clinical PhD: full. School PhD: full.

Student Applications/Admissions:

Student Applications

Clinical PhD—Applications 2001–2002, 58. Total applicants accepted 2001–2002, 13. New applicants enrolled 2001–2002, 3. Total enrolled 2001–2002 full-time, 26. Openings 2002–2003, 4. The number of students enrolled full and part-time, who were dismissed or voluntarily withdrew from this program area were 0. *Experimental PhD*—Applications 2001–2002, 18. Total applicants accepted 2001–2002, 3. New applicants enrolled 2001–2002, 2. Total enrolled 2001–2002 full-time, 10. Openings 2002–2003, 4. The number of students enrolled full and part-time, who were dismissed or voluntarily withdrew from this program area were 1. *School PhD*—Applications 2001–2002, 35. Total applicants accepted 2001–2002, 7. New applicants enrolled 2001–2002, 4. Total enrolled 2001–2002 full-time, 22. Openings 2002–2003, 4. The number of students enrolled full and part-time, who were dismissed or voluntarily withdrew from this program area were 0. *Social PhD*—Applications 2001–2002, 21. Total applicants accepted 2001–2002, 1. New applicants enrolled 2001–2002, 1. Total enrolled 2001–2002 full-time, 13. Openings 2002–2003, 2. The number of students enrolled full and part-time, who were dismissed or voluntarily withdrew from this program area were 1.

Admissions Requirements:

Scores: Entries appear in this order: required test or GPA, minimum score (if required), median score of students entering in 2001–2002. Doctoral Programs: GRE-V 550; GRE-Q 630; GRE-V+Q 1100, 0; overall undergraduate GPA 3.0, 0; last 2 years GPA no minimum stated; psychology GPA no minimum stated; psychology GPA 3.0. GRE+ Subject required for Clinical Psychology Program only. Subject minimum score is 500.

Other Criteria: (importance of criteria rated low, medium, or high): GRE/MAT scores high, research experience high, work experience medium, extracurricular activity low, clinically related public service medium, GPA high, letters of recommendation high, interview high, statement of goals and objectives high. Interview requirements vary from program to program.

Student Characteristics: The following represents characteristics of students in 2001–2002 in all graduate psychology programs in the department: Female–full-time 41, part-time 0; Male–full-time 30, part-time 0; African American/Black–full-time 1, part-time 0; Hispanic/Latino (a)–full-time 0, part-time 0; Asian/Pacific Islander–full-time 0, part-time 0; American Indian/Alaska Native–full-time 0, part-time 0.

Financial Information/Assistance:

Tuition for Full-Time Study: *Doctoral:* State residents: per academic year $7,764, $647 per credit hour; nonstate residents: per academic year $7,764, $647 per credit hour.

Financial Assistance:

First Year Students: Teaching assistantships available for first-year. Average amount paid per academic year: $9,980. Average number of hours worked per week: 10. Apply by February 1. Tuition remission given: full. Research assistantships available for first-year. Average amount paid per academic year: $9,980. Average number of hours worked per week: 20. Apply by February 1. Tuition remission given: full and partial. Fellowships and scholarships available for first-year. Average amount paid per academic year: $12,313. Average number of hours worked per week: 0. Apply by January 10. Tuition remission given: full.

Advanced Students: Teaching assistantships available for advanced students. Average amount paid per academic year: $9,980. Average number of hours worked per week: 20. Apply by NA. Tuition remission given: full. Research assistantships available for advanced students. Average amount paid per academic year: $9,980. Average number of hours worked per week: 20. Apply by NA. Tuition remission given: full and partial. Fellowships and scholarships available for advanced students. Average amount paid per academic year: $12,313. Average number of hours worked per week: 0. Apply by NA. Tuition remission given: full.

Contact Information: Of all students currently enrolled full-time, 65% benefited from one or more of the listed financial assistance programs. For information on financial assistance, contact: Department of Psychology, 430 Huntington Hall, Syracuse, NY 13244.

Internships/Practica: Students in the clinical and school psychology training programs have appropriate internship and practica experiences available in hospitals, schools, and other community and University settings. Following completion of their coursework, students complete APA approved internships as part of their required program of study. For those doctoral students for whom a professional internship is required prior to graduation, 5 applied in 2000–2001. Of those who applied, 5 were placed in internships listed by the Association of Psychology Postdoctoral and Internship Programs (APPIC).

Housing and Day Care: On-campus housing and day care facilities are available.

Employment of Department Graduates:

Master's Degree Graduates: Of those who graduated in the academic year 2000–2001, the following categories and numbers represent the post-graduate activities and employment of master's degree graduates: Enrolled in a post-doctoral residency/fellowship (n/a), employed in independent practice (n/a).

Doctoral Degree Graduates: Of those who graduated in the academic year 2000–2001, the following categories and numbers represent the post-graduate activities and employment of doctoral degree graduates: Enrolled in a psychology doctoral program (n/a), enrolled in another graduate/professional program (n/a).

Additional Information:

Orientation, Objectives, and Emphasis of Department: Our goal is to train research scientists in psychology. This is best accomplished by having students work closely with a faculty advisor whose research interests are similar to the student's (one can change to a new advisor, however, if one's research interests change). Clinical and school programs provide practicum experiences on the Boulder, scientist-practitioner model. A new Center for Health and Behavior in the Department provides cross-program training in health psychology/behavioral medicine, which are a major shared focus of faculty research. Students in different subfields thus can gain exposure to topics such as cognition and aging, sexual health/HIV, personality and disease, family coping processes in chronic illness, and alcohol/substance abuse. A second major emphasis is teaching. Students typically engage in several semesters of teaching, beginning with sections of introductory psychology and moving on to teach more specialized courses. Entering students participate in the University's "Future Professoriate Program," a teaching practicum nationally known for helping new graduate students enter the profession. Other teaching opportunities are available in the Department's Allport Project, which involves undergraduates in faculty research activities. As part of this program, graduate students may offer supervised but essentially independent seminars for undergraduates in their specialty area.

Special Facilities or Resources: The Department of Psychology is housed in Huntington Hall, an historic building that has been remodeled to provide offices and seminar rooms, as well as laboratories for the study of cognition, social psychosociology, behavioral medicine, family interaction, and group processes. Labs and offices are equipped with microcomputers for data collection and analysis. A separate wing houses the Department's Psychological Services Center, which offers facilities for clinical and school psychology practicum training, and research. In addition, the Department has two other facilities on campus that provide extra lab space for social psychology and animal behavior research. The Department and its Center for Health and Behavior support two full-time computer technicians. Other facilities are available through faculty collaborations with researchers at the Upstate Health Sciences Center, which is adjacent to Huntington Hall.

Information for Students With Physical Disabilities: Syracuse University campus facilities, the Department of Psychology offices, laboratories, and other facilities are entirely accessible to the physically challenged.

Application Information:

Send to: Graduate School, Suite 303 Bowne Hall, Syracuse University, Syracuse, NY 13244-1200. Students are admitted in the Fall, application deadline February 1. To be considered for a University Fellowship, completed applications must be received by January 10. *Fee:* $50.

Teachers College, Columbia University
Department of Counseling and Clinical Psychology
Box 102 525 West 120th Street
New York, NY 10027-6696
Telephone: (212) 678-3257
Fax: (212) 678-3275
E-mail: *mc816@columbia.edu*
Web: *http://www.tc.columbia.edu*

Department Established:

1996. Chairperson: Madonna G. Constantine. Number of Faculty: total–full-time 11, part-time 11; women–full-time 6, part-time 6; minority–full-time 4, part-time 4.

Programs and Degrees Offered:

Listed in the following order: Program area, degree type (T if terminal Master's), number awarded 7/00–6/01. Clinical psychology PhD 10, counseling psychology PhD 4, Postdoctoral Respecialization Diploma 3, psychological counseling, psychology in education:applie MA (T) 13.

APA Accreditation: Clinical PhD: full. Counseling PhD: full.

Student Applications/Admissions:

Student Applications

Clinical psychology PhD—Applications 2001–2002, 182. Total applicants accepted 2001–2002, 8. New applicants enrolled 2001–2002, 8. Total enrolled 2001–2002 full-time, 55, part-time, 12. Openings 2002–2003, 9. *Counseling psychology PhD*—Applications 2001–2002, 140. Total applicants accepted 2001–2002, 7. New applicants enrolled 2001–2002, 1. Total enrolled 2001–2002 full-time, 59, part-time, 30. Openings 2002–2003, 8. The Median number of years required for completion of a degree are 6. *Postdoctoral Respecialization Diploma*—Applications 2001–2002, 10. Total applicants accepted 2001–2002, 3. New applicants enrolled 2001–2002, 1. Total enrolled 2001–2002 full-time, 3, part-time, 1. Openings 2002–2003, 3. *Psychology in education:applie MA*—Applications 2001–2002, 98. Total applicants accepted 2001–2002, 98. New applicants enrolled 2001–2002, 66. Total enrolled 2001–2002 full-time, 84, part-time, 34. Openings 2002–2003, 80.

Admissions Requirements:

Scores: Entries appear in this order: required test or GPA, minimum score (if required), median score of students entering in 2001–2002. Master's Programs: overall undergraduate GPA no minimum stated, 3.65; last 2 years GPA no minimum stated; psychology GPA no minimum stated. GRE scores are not required for MEd. For MA, GRE scores are strongly recommended but not required. Doctoral Programs: GRE-V+Q 1300, 1340; GRE-V+Q+Analytical 1900, 1940; last 2 years GPA no minimum stated; psychology GPA no minimum stated; psychology GPA no minimum stated. MAT recommended for Clinical Psychology PhD applicants only.

Other Criteria: (importance of criteria rated low, medium, or high): GRE/MAT scores high, research experience high, work experience medium, extracurricular activity low, clinically related public service medium, GPA medium, letters of recommendation high, interview high, statement of goals and objectives high, writing sample high.

Student Characteristics: The following represents characteristics of students in 2001–2002 in all graduate psychology programs in the department: Female–full-time 65, part-time 26; Male–full-time 14, part-time 9; African American/Black–full-time 6, part-time 3; Hispanic/Latino (a)–full-time 9, part-time 3; Asian/Pacific Islander–full-time 8, part-time 2; American Indian/Alaska Native–full-time 0, part-time 0.

Financial Information/Assistance:

Tuition for Full-Time Study: No information provided.

Financial Assistance:

First Year Students: No information provided.
Advanced Students: No information provided.
Contact Information: For information on financial assistance, contact: Office of Student Aid at (212) 678-3714. Teachers College, Columbia University, 525 West 120th St., New York, NY 10027-6696.

Internships/Practica: Master's students in the Department of Counseling and Clinical Psychology complete fieldwork appropriate to their track or area of interest in a variety of settings including schools, hospitals, diverse mental health clinics, and rehabilitation centers. Doctoral students do externships in settings similar to the ones indicated above, in preparation for their required APA-approved internships. In addition, all PhD students as well as the MEd students engage in practicum experiences at the Center for Educational and Psychological Services at the College. The Center is a community resource that provides low-cost services for the public utilizing graduate students from several departments within the College. All students receive supervision provided by full-time and adjunct faculty.

Housing and Day Care: No on-campus housing and day care facilities are available.

Employment of Department Graduates:

Master's Degree Graduates: Of those who graduated in the academic year 2000–2001, the following categories and numbers represent the post-graduate activities and employment of master's degree graduates: Enrolled in a post-doctoral residency/fellowship (n/a), employed in independent practice (n/a).

Doctoral Degree Graduates: Of those who graduated in the academic year 2000–2001, the following categories and numbers represent the post-graduate activities and employment of doctoral

degree graduates: Enrolled in a psychology doctoral program (n/a), enrolled in another graduate/professional program (n/a).

Additional Information:

Orientation, Objectives, and Emphasis of Department: This department prepares students to investigate and address the psychological needs of individuals, families, groups, organizations/institutions, and communities. Counseling psychology focuses on normal and optimal development across the lifespan, with particular attention to expanding knowledge and skills in occupational choice and transitions, and multicultural and group counseling. Clinical Psychology primarily uses a broad-based psychodynamic perspective to study and treat a variety of psychological and psychoeducational problems. In addition to sharing an interest and appreciation for the critical role of culture in development and adaptation, both programs highly value the teaching of clinical and research skills. Thus, students in this department are trained to become knowledgeable and proficient researchers, to provide psychological and educational leadership, and to be effective practitioners. Specifically, graduates from these programs seek positions in teaching, research, policy, administration, psychotherapy, and counseling.

Special Facilities or Resources: The College provides academic/research support in several ways. Students of the College have access to all the libraries of Columbia University. Of particular interest in addition to the Milbank Memorial Library here at Teachers College, are the Psychology Library on the main Columbia campus and the library at the School of Social Work. Technology has transformed most libraries to computer-oriented environments with immediate access to information. The Library not only provides the access but instruction to students so they may avail themselves of the new technology. The ERIC system as well as Inter-Library Loan are also available. The Microcomputer Center provides students with access to PC and Mac computers, which allow for sharing disk, file, and printer resources as well as email services to Columbia University and to the Internet. Other hardware includes CD-ROMs, zip drives, a color scanner, and a sound and video digitizer.

Information for Students With Physical Disabilities: Programs and services have been developed to ensure that the higher education environments at Teachers College are physically, programmatically, and attitudinally accessible to students with such disabilities as vision, hearing, or mobility impairments, medical condition such as diabetes, cancer, or heart disease, or a learning disability that affects one or more academic services. Limited parking is available for students with disabilities. A full-time Director of Services for Students with Disabilities and assistants are available to counsel students, arrange accommodations, and advocate on behalf of students with disabilities.

Application Information:
Send to: Admissions Office, Box 302, Teachers College, Columbia University, 525 West 120th Street, New York, NY 10027-6696. Students are admitted in the Fall; Spring. Fall application deadline for PhD December 15th. Spring application deadline for EdM November 1st. Fall Edm application deadline-April 15th. *Fee:* $50. Waiver is available. Hardship verification is done via a letter from Financial Aid Officer at the applicant's previous academic institution.

The Sage Colleges
Division of Psychology
Troy, NY 12180
Telephone: (518) 244-2221
E-mail: *hills@sage.edu*

Department Established:
Division Chair: Dr. Samuel Hill. Number of Faculty: total–full-time 11, part-time 1; women–full-time 9, part-time 1.

Programs and Degrees Offered:
Listed in the following order: Program area, degree type (T if terminal Master's), number awarded 7/00–6/01. Community MA (T) 15, Forensic MA (T).

Student Applications/Admissions:
Student Applications
Community MA—Applications 2001–2002, 35. Total applicants accepted 2001–2002, 30. New applicants enrolled 2001–2002, 15. Total enrolled 2001–2002 full-time, 5, part-time, 40. Openings 2002–2003, 25. The Median number of years required for completion of a degree are 4. The number of students enrolled full and part-time, who were dismissed or voluntarily withdrew from this program area were 0. *Forensic MA*—Applications 2001–2002, 75. Total applicants accepted 2001–2002, 30. New applicants enrolled 2001–2002, 22. Total enrolled 2001–2002 full-time, 11, part-time, 35. Openings 2002–2003, 25. The Median number of years required for completion of a degree are 4. The number of students enrolled full and part-time, who were dismissed or voluntarily withdrew from this program area were 2.

Admissions Requirements:
Scores: Entries appear in this order: required test or GPA, minimum score (if required), median score of students entering in 2001–2002. Master's Programs: overall undergraduate GPA no minimum stated. Community Psychology: 2.75. Forensic Psychology: 3.00 Doctoral Programs: last 2 years GPA no minimum stated; psychology GPA no minimum stated; psychology GPA no minimum stated.
Other Criteria: (importance of criteria rated low, medium, or high): research experience low, work experience low, clinically related public service low, GPA high, letters of recommendation high, interview medium, statement of goals and objectives high. Forensic psychology: competitive assessment because enrollments are limited per academic year.

Student Characteristics: The following represents characteristics of students in 2001–2002 in all graduate psychology programs in the department: Female–full-time 4, part-time 63; Male–full-time 0, part-time 20; African American/Black–full-time 0, part-time 7; Hispanic/Latino (a)–full-time 0, part-time 4; Asian/Pacific Islander–full-time 0, part-time 1; American Indian/Alaska Native–full-time 0, part-time 0; part-time 3.

Financial Information/Assistance:
Tuition for Full-Time Study: *Master's:* State residents $415 per credit hour; nonstate residents $415 per credit hour.

Financial Assistance:

First Year Students: Research assistantships available for first-year. Average number of hours worked per week: 8. Apply by June 1. Tuition remission given: full.

Advanced Students: Research assistantships available for advanced students. Average number of hours worked per week: 8. Tuition remission given: full.

Contact Information: Of all students currently enrolled full-time, 10% benefited from one or more of the listed financial assistance programs. For information on financial assistance, contact: Graduate Dean, The Sage Colleges, 45 Ferry Street, Troy, New York 12180, 518-244-2264.

Internships/Practica: As part of each degree, all students are required to complete an internship (direct services) and/or externship (not direct services) placement, depending upon the selected area of concentration. Internships comprise one year placements in a setting appropriate to the student's interests; externships are one semester projects in a setting of the student's choice.

Housing and Day Care: On-campus housing and day care facilities are available.

Employment of Department Graduates:

Master's Degree Graduates: Of those who graduated in the academic year 2000–2001, the following categories and numbers represent the post-graduate activities and employment of master's degree graduates: Enrolled in a psychology doctoral program (2), enrolled in a post-doctoral residency/fellowship (n/a), employed in independent practice (n/a), employed in business or industry (research/consulting) (2), employed in a community mental health/counseling center (3), other employment position (8).

Doctoral Degree Graduates: Of those who graduated in the academic year 2000–2001, the following categories and numbers represent the post-graduate activities and employment of doctoral degree graduates: Enrolled in a psychology doctoral program (n/a), enrolled in another graduate/professional program (n/a).

Additional Information:

Orientation, Objectives, and Emphasis of Department: Our two degrees (MA in Community Psychology, and MA in Forensic Psychology) provide students with the academic and skills training to become practitioners at the master's level. The programs range in credits from 39 to 48, depending on degree and, for Community Psychology, track. The emphasis is on developing and strengthening student skills for application (whether individual or systems level) in the context of strong theoretical foundations.

Special Facilities or Resources: In addition to the faculty resources one would assume at the master's level, a particular advantage for psychology programs at Sage Graduate School is our prime location in the Capital District area of New York State. The geographic size, population density, and availability of widely varied populations make possible a wide variety of experiences.

Application Information:
Send to: Graduate Admissions, The Sage Colleges, 45 Ferry Street, Troy, New York 12180. Students are admitted in the Fall; Winter; Spring; Summer. Community Psychology: rolling admissions. Forensic Psychology: November 1st for Spring; April 1st for Summer and Fall *Fee:* $40. Fee waived for graduates of The Sage Colleges.

Yeshiva University
Ferkauf Graduate School of Psychology
1300 Morris Park Avenue
Bronx, NY 10461-1602
Telephone: (718) 430-3850
Fax: (718) 430-3960
E-mail: *gill@aecom.yu.edu*
Web: *http://www.yu.edu/fgs/*

Department Established:
1957. Dean: Lawrence J. Siegel, PhD, ABPP. Number of Faculty: total–full-time 28, part-time 19; women–full-time 15, part-time 13; minority–full-time 3, part-time 2.

Programs and Degrees Offered:
Listed in the following order: Program area, degree type (T if terminal Master's), number awarded 7/00–6/01. Applied MA (T) 7, Clinical PsyD 22, Clinical Health PhD 15, Developmental PhD 2, School/Clinical Child PsyD 27.

APA Accreditation: Clinical PsyD: full. School PsyD: full.

Student Applications/Admissions:
Student Applications

Applied MA—Applications 2001–2002, 25. Total applicants accepted 2001–2002, 15. New applicants enrolled 2001–2002, 13. Total enrolled 2001–2002 full-time, 17, part-time, 4. Openings 2002–2003, 15. The Median number of years required for completion of a degree are 2. The number of students enrolled full and part-time, who were dismissed or voluntarily withdrew from this program area were 3. *Clinical PsyD*—Applications 2001–2002, 275. Total applicants accepted 2001–2002, 75. New applicants enrolled 2001–2002, 25. Total enrolled 2001–2002 full-time, 125, part-time, 19. Openings 2002–2003, 25. The Median number of years required for completion of a degree are 5. The number of students enrolled full and part-time, who were dismissed or voluntarily withdrew from this program area were 2. *Clinical Health PhD*—Applications 2001–2002, 90. Total applicants accepted 2001–2002, 45. New applicants enrolled 2001–2002, 15. Total enrolled 2001–2002 full-time, 82, part-time, 5. Openings 2002–2003, 17. The Median number of years required for completion of a degree are 5. The number of students enrolled full and part-time, who were dismissed or voluntarily withdrew from this program area were 1. *Developmental PhD*—Applications 2001–2002, 30. Total applicants accepted 2001–2002, 7. New applicants enrolled 2001–2002, 2. Total enrolled 2001–2002 full-time, 12, part-time, 3. Openings 2002–2003, 4. The Median number of years required for completion of a degree are 5. *School/Clinical Child PsyD*—Applications 2001–2002, 150. Total applicants accepted 2001–2002, 63. New applicants enrolled 2001–2002, 27. Total enrolled 2001–2002 full-time, 117, part-time, 14. Openings 2002–2003, 27. The Median number of years required for completion of a degree are 5. The number of students enrolled full and part-time, who were dismissed or voluntarily withdrew from this program area were 1.

Admissions Requirements:
Scores: Entries appear in this order: required test or GPA, minimum score (if required), median score of students entering

in 2001–2002. Master's Programs: GRE-V no minimum stated; GRE-Q no minimum stated; GRE-V+Q 1100, 1200; GRE-Analytical no minimum stated; overall undergraduate GPA 3.0, 3.5; psychology GPA 3.0, 3.5. Doctoral Programs: GRE-V no minimum stated; GRE-Q no minimum stated; GRE-V+Q 1100, 1200; GRE-Analytical no minimum stated; overall undergraduate GPA 3.0, 3.5; last 2 years GPA no minimum stated; psychology GPA no minimum stated; psychology GPA no minimum stated.

Other Criteria: (importance of criteria rated low, medium, or high): GRE/MAT scores high, research experience high, work experience high, extracurricular activity medium, clinically related public service high, GPA high, letters of recommendation high, interview high, statement of goals and objectives high.

Student Characteristics: The following represents characteristics of students in 2001–2002 in all graduate psychology programs in the department: Female–full-time 257, part-time 23; Male–full-time 96, part-time 12; African American/Black–full-time 8, part-time 0; Hispanic/Latino (a)–full-time 19, part-time 1; Asian/Pacific Islander–full-time 9, part-time 0; American Indian/Alaska Native–full-time 0, part-time 1; Multi-ethnic–full-time 3, part-time 1; students subject to the Americans with Disabilities Act–full-time 2, part-time 1.

Financial Information/Assistance:

Tuition for Full-Time Study: *Master's:* State residents $910 per credit hour; nonstate residents: $910 per credit hour. *Doctoral:* State residents: $940 per credit hour; nonstate residents: $940 per credit hour.

Financial Assistance:

First Year Students: Teaching assistantships available for first-year. Average amount paid per academic year: $2,000. Average number of hours worked per week: 12. Research assistantships available for first-year. Average amount paid per academic year: $5,000. Average number of hours worked per week: 20. Fellowships and scholarships available for first-year. Average amount paid per academic year: $5,000. Average number of hours worked per week: 0.

Advanced Students: Teaching assistantships available for advanced students. Average amount paid per academic year: $2,000. Average number of hours worked per week: 12. Research assistantships available for advanced students. Average amount paid per academic year: $5,000. Average number of hours worked per week: 20. Fellowships and scholarships available for advanced students. Average amount paid per academic year: $5,000. Average number of hours worked per week: 0.

Contact Information: Of all students currently enrolled full-time, 75% benefited from one or more of the listed financial assistance programs. For information on financial assistance, contact: Office of Student Finances, 500 W. 185 M. Street, New York, NY 10033; email: yufinaid@ymail.yu.edu, www.yu.edu.

Internships/Practica: Examples listed in catalog. For those doctoral students for whom a professional internship is required prior to graduation, 40 applied in 2000–2001. Of those who applied, 37 were placed in internships listed by the Association of Psychology Postdoctoral and Internship Programs (APPIC); 35 were placed in APA accredited internships.

Housing and Day Care: No on-campus housing and day care facilities are available.

Employment of Department Graduates:

Master's Degree Graduates: Of those who graduated in the academic year 2000–2001, the following categories and numbers represent the post-graduate activities and employment of master's degree graduates: Enrolled in a psychology doctoral program (7), enrolled in another graduate/professional program (3), enrolled in a post-doctoral residency/fellowship (n/a), employed in independent practice (n/a).

Doctoral Degree Graduates: Of those who graduated in the academic year 2000–2001, the following categories and numbers represent the post-graduate activities and employment of doctoral degree graduates: Enrolled in a psychology doctoral program (n/a), enrolled in another graduate/professional program (n/a), enrolled in a post-doctoral residency/fellowship (3), employed in independent practice (10).

Additional Information:

Orientation, Objectives, and Emphasis of Department: The objective of the Ferkauf Graduate School of Psychology is to promote a balance between the scientific-research orientation and the practitioner model. Developmental and Health psychology place greater emphasis upon applied and basic research, whereas the school and clinical psychology programs focus on the scientist-practitioner model with integrated clinical research and supervised practicum experiences. Further, Ferkauf offers PhD and PsyD degrees placing emphasis on research in the former and on application in the latter. A comprehensive theoretical orientation is offered with a psychodynamic focus and an applied behavioral emphasis. In all specialty areas, and at all levels of training, there is a strong commitment to the foundations of psychology, and a core of basic courses is required in all programs. Collaborations with the major NYC health and hospital institutions are well established for all programs, and a joint program with Albert Einstein College of Medicine (AECOM) offers health psychology doctoral research opportunities. Ferkauf has affiliations with the AECOM Department of Pediatrics and the Rose Kennedy Center for Research in Mental Retardation and Human Development that provide interdisciplinary training for students.

Special Facilities or Resources: The clinical and school psychology programs offer practicum experience through Ferkauf's Center for Psychological and Psychoeducational Services. The Center provides a wide range of evaluation, remediation, and therapeutic services for children, adolescents, and adults in the neighboring communities, in addition to consultation services directly to the local schools. Ferkauf is located on Yeshiva University's campus of the Albert Einstein College of Medicine which has led to the development of cooperative programs and activities with various disciplines in medicine as well as added training opportunities for students at the various service delivery agencies affiliated with the medical college. A Behavioral Medicine/Psychophysiological laboratory and Anxiety Disorders Clinic has been established to provide a research service for phobic individuals. The Leonard and Murial Marcus Family Project for the Study of the Disturbed Adolescent and the Robert M. Beren Center for Psychological Intervention support research and services for family intervention.

Information for Students With Physical Disabilities: University complies with all ADA stipulations.

Application Information:
Send to: Director of Admissions, Ferkauf Graduate School of Psychology, 1300 Morris Park Avenue, Bronx, NY 10461. Students are admitted in the Fall, application deadline January 15. *Fee:* $50.

Appalachian State University (2001 data)
Department of Psychology
Arts and Science
Smith-Wright Hall
Boone, NC 28608
Telephone: (828) 262-2272
Fax: (828) 262-2974
E-mail: *psychology@appstate.edu*
Web: *http://www.als.appstate.edu/dept/psych*

Department Established:
1966. Chairperson: Stan Aeschleman. Number of Faculty: total–full-time 28, part-time 4; women–full-time 10, part-time 3.

Programs and Degrees Offered:
Listed in the following order: Program area, degree type (T if terminal Master's), number awarded 7/00–6/01. Clinical MA (T) 8, General MA (T) 4, Health MA (T) 7, Industrial/Organizational MA (T) 5, School CAGS 10.

Student Applications/Admissions:
Student Applications
Clinical MA—Applications 2001–2002, 90. Total applicants accepted 2001–2002, 18. New applicants enrolled 2001–2002, 7. Total enrolled 2001–2002 full-time, 23. Openings 2002–2003, 10. *General MA*—Applications 2001–2002, 14. Total applicants accepted 2001–2002, 6. New applicants enrolled 2001–2002, 1. Total enrolled 2001–2002 full-time, 12. Openings 2002–2003, 5. *Health MA*—Applications 2001–2002, 24. Total applicants accepted 2001–2002, 14. New applicants enrolled 2001–2002, 8. Total enrolled 2001–2002 full-time, 12. Openings 2002–2003, 10. *Industrial/Organizational MA*—Applications 2001–2002, 72. Total applicants accepted 2001–2002, 20. New applicants enrolled 2001–2002, 7. Total enrolled 2001–2002 full-time, 18. Openings 2002–2003, 10. *School CAGS*—Applications 2001–2002, 42. Total applicants accepted 2001–2002, 16. New applicants enrolled 2001–2002, 9. Total enrolled 2001–2002 full-time, 29. Openings 2002–2003, 10.

Admissions Requirements:
Scores: Entries appear in this order: required test or GPA, minimum score (if required), median score of students entering in 2001–2002. Master's Programs: GRE-V no minimum stated, 510; GRE-Q no minimum stated, 570; GRE-V+Q no minimum stated, 1080; overall undergraduate GPA 3.0, 3.4.
Other Criteria: (importance of criteria rated low, medium, or high): GRE/MAT scores research experience medium, work experience low, extracurricular activity low, clinically related public service low, GPA, letters of recommendation medium, interview high, statement of goals and objectives high. An interview is not required for Industrial/Organizational, General-Theoretical, or Rehabilitation Psychology.

Student Characteristics: The following represents characteristics of students in 2001–2002 in all graduate psychology programs in the department: Female–full-time 25, part-time 0; Male–full-time 7, part-time 0; African American/Black–full-time 0, part-time 0; Hispanic/Latino (a)–full-time 1, part-time 0; Asian/Pacific Islander–full-time 0, part-time 0; American Indian/Alaska Native–full-time 0, part-time 0.

Financial Information/Assistance:
Tuition for Full-Time Study: No information provided.

Financial Assistance:
First Year Students: No information provided.
Advanced Students: No information provided.
Contact Information: Of all students currently enrolled full-time, 90% benefited from one or more of the listed financial assistance programs. For information on financial assistance, contact: Stan Aeschleman, Chair, Department of Psychology, Appalachian State University, Boone, NC 28608.

Internships/Practica: Clinical—Students complete a practicum at the University Counseling Center and two other practica at regional mental health institutes. Students complete a 1,000-hour internship at a mental health center. School—Students complete a practicum at a regional public school and a 1200-hour internship at a regional public school. Health—Students complete a practicum and a 600-hour internship at a rehabilitation or health psychology center. Industrial/Organizational—Students have the option of completing a 600-hour internship at a local business.

Housing and Day Care: No on-campus housing or day care facilities are available.

Employment of Department Graduates:
Master's Degree Graduates: Of those who graduated in the academic year 2000–2001, the following categories and numbers represent the post-graduate activities and employment of master's degree graduates: Enrolled in a post-doctoral residency/fellowship (n/a), employed in independent practice (n/a).
Doctoral Degree Graduates: Of those who graduated in the academic year 2000–2001, the following categories and numbers represent the post-graduate activities and employment of doctoral degree graduates: Enrolled in a psychology doctoral program (n/a), enrolled in another graduate/professional program (n/a).

Additional Information:
Orientation, Objectives, and Emphasis of Department: The department is student oriented, with a director for each graduate program. The general-experimental program is primarily predoctoral, but one can structure an applied orientation. The clinical, school, and health programs stress professional training, and the majority of graduates obtain positions in the area of preparation after finishing their master's degree. The industrial/organizational and human resource management program is a cooperative program with the Department of Management in the College of Business.

Special Facilities or Resources: Biofeedback facilities, student computer laboratory, neuroscience laboratory, and an animal operant conditioning laboratory are available.

Information for Students With Physical Disabilities: The Department does whatever is required to accommodate students with disabilities.

Application Information:
Send to: The Dean, Cratis D. Williams Graduate School, Dougherty Administration Building, Appalachian State University, Boone, NC 28608. Students are admitted in the Fall, application deadline March 1. *Fee:* $35.

Duke University
Department of Psychology: Social and Health Sciences
229 Psychology/Sociology Building, P.O. Box 90085
Flowers Drive
Durham, NC 27708
Telephone: (919) 660-5711
Fax: (919) 660-5648
E-mail: *bseymore@duke.edu*
Web: *http://www.psych.duke.edu*

Department Established:
1948. Chairperson: Dr. Susan Roth. Number of Faculty: total–full-time 11, part-time 43; women–full-time 7, part-time 15; minority–full-time 2, part-time 4.

APA Accreditation: Clinical PhD: full.

Student Applications/Admissions:
Admissions Requirements:
Scores: Entries appear in this order: required test or GPA, minimum score (if required), median score of students entering in 2001–2002. Doctoral Programs: GRE-V no minimum stated; GRE-Q no minimum stated; GRE-V+Q no minimum stated; GRE-Analytical no minimum stated; GRE-V+Q+Analytical no minimum stated; overall undergraduate GPA no minimum stated; last 2 years GPA no minimum stated; psychology GPA no minimum stated; psychology GPA no minimum stated.
Other Criteria: (importance of criteria rated low, medium, or high): GRE/MAT scores high, research experience high, work experience medium, extracurricular activity low, clinically related public service medium, GPA high, letters of recommendation high, interview high, statement of goals and objectives high.

Student Characteristics: The following represents characteristics of students in 2001–2002 in all graduate psychology programs in the department: Female–full-time 29, part-time 0; Male–full-time 6, part-time 0; African American/Black–full-time 4, part-time 0; Hispanic/Latino (a)–full-time 1, part-time 0; Asian/Pacific Islander–full-time 1, part-time 0; American Indian/Alaska Native–full-time 0, part-time 0; Multi-ethnic–full-time 1, students subject to the Americans with Disabilities Act–full-time 0.

Financial Information/Assistance:
Tuition for Full-Time Study: No information provided.

Financial Assistance:
First Year Students: No information provided.

Advanced Students: No information provided.
Contact Information: Of all students currently enrolled full-time, 100% benefited from one or more of the listed financial assistance programs. For information on financial assistance, contact: bseymore@duke.edu.

Internships/Practica: Doctoral students in our program receive experience in our own departmental clinic as well as a great number of local institutions and medical center facilities. For those doctoral students for whom a professional internship is required prior to graduation, 4 applied in 2000–2001. Of those who applied, 4 were placed in internships listed by the Association of Psychology Postdoctoral and Internship Programs (APPIC); 4 were placed in APA accredited internships.

Housing and Day Care: No on-campus housing or day care facilities are available.

Employment of Department Graduates:
Master's Degree Graduates: Of those who graduated in the academic year 2000–2001, the following categories and numbers represent the post-graduate activities and employment of master's degree graduates: Enrolled in a post-doctoral residency/fellowship (n/a), employed in independent practice (n/a).
Doctoral Degree Graduates: Of those who graduated in the academic year 2000–2001, the following categories and numbers represent the post-graduate activities and employment of doctoral degree graduates: Enrolled in a psychology doctoral program (n/a), enrolled in another graduate/professional program (n/a).

Additional Information:
Orientation, Objectives, and Emphasis of Department: The department features a strong mentor-oriented training program with areas of specialization in cognitive, developmental, clinical, and health psychology. Emphasis is placed on informal interaction among faculty and students; seminars and small groups of faculty and graduate students meet regularly.

Special Facilities or Resources: The department features a strong mentor-oriented training program with areas of specialization in cognitive, developmental, clinical, and health psychology. Emphasis is placed on informal interaction among faculty and students; seminars and small groups of faculty and graduate students meet regularly. Training in cognitive psychology is currently being reconfigured; collaborations are available with faculty in the Center for Cognitive Neuroscience, the Center for the Study of Aging and Human Development, Computer Science, and the Fuqua School of Business. Training in developmental psychology focuses on cognitive, linguistic, personality, and social development. Additional collaborations are available with faculty in Medical Psychology, the Center for Aging and Human Development, the Center for Child and Family Policy, and the Carolina Consortium on Human Development. Recent approval from the Graduate School Executive Committee has been given for the UNC-Duke Collaborative Graduate Certificate Program in Developmental Psychology. This is a joint effort between Duke's Psychology, Social and Health Sciences and Psychology, Experimental, and the University of North Carolina at Chapel Hill Developmental Program. The Clinical Training Program is conducted jointly with the Division of Medical Psychology at Duke University Medical Center. This program has three major foci: child psychopathology and intervention, adult disorders and treatment, and health psychology. State-of-the-art facilities including specially equipped laboratories and clinics are available for student use. These include computational facilities for word processing, data analysis, and experimental programming. Collaborative ties also exist with the Center for Child and Family Policy.

Information for Students With Physical Disabilities: The goals of support services for students with disabilities are in keeping with the goals of all services provided through the Academic Resource Center and the Office of Services for Students with Disabilities: to help students achieve their academic potential within the context of a competitive university setting; to promote a disciplined approach to study; and to foster active, independent learning. Section 504 of the Rehabilitation Act of 1973 and the Americans with Disabilities Act of 1990 prohibit discrimination on the basis of disability. In a postsecondary educational setting, federal regulations mandate reasonable accommodation for all students with documented disabilities. What constitutes reasonable accommodation for a particular student is determined on a case-by-case basis after a careful review of the documentation that student has provided. Examples of academic adjustments which might be warranted in certain instances and at given times include: Extended time to complete quizzes, tests, and examinations, separate administration of tests and examinations in a quiet room with minimal distractions, provision of books on tape or enlarged print texts, provision of an American Sign Language interpreter, permission to use a four-function calculator during tests and examinations, provision of a notetaker to supplement student notes. Graduate School Disabilities contact person: Lyndee Champion, Program Coordinator, Graduate Student Affairs, 919-681-1551.

Application Information:
Send to: The Graduate School, 127 Allen Building, Box 90066, Durham, NC 27708. Students are admitted in the Fall, application deadline 12/1. Due to the high volume of clinical applications we received we ask that clinical applications be submitted by December 1. *Fee:* $75. There is a discount of $10 for applications received by the December 1 deadline.

East Carolina University
Department of Psychology
Arts & Sciences
104 Rawl
Greenville, NC 27858-4353
Telephone: (252) 328-6800
Fax: (252) 328-6283
E-mail: *nowaczykr@mail.ecu.edu*
Web: *http://www.ecu.edu/psyc*

Department Established:
1959. Chairperson: Ronald Nowaczyk. Number of Faculty: total–full-time 34, part-time 13; women–full-time 14, part-time 6; minority–full-time 3; faculty subject to the Americans with Disabilities Act 1.

Programs and Degrees Offered:
Listed in the following order: Program area, degree type (T if terminal Master's), number awarded 7/00–6/01. Clinical Psychology MA (T) 12, General MA (T) 8, School Psychology MA (T) 7.

Student Applications/Admissions:
Student Applications
Clinical Psychology MA—Applications 2001–2002, 48. Total applicants accepted 2001–2002, 10. New applicants enrolled 2001–2002, 8. Total enrolled 2001–2002 full-time, 16. Openings 2002–2003, 12. The Median number of years required for completion of a degree are 2. *General MA*—Applications 2001–2002, 39. Total applicants accepted 2001–2002, 21. New applicants enrolled 2001–2002, 17. Total enrolled 2001–2002 full-time, 19. Openings 2002–2003, 14. The Median number of years required for completion of a degree are 2. The number of students enrolled full and part-time, who were dismissed or voluntarily withdrew from this program area were 4. *School Psychology MA*—Applications 2001–2002, 32. Total applicants accepted 2001–2002, 15. New applicants enrolled 2001–2002, 8. Total enrolled 2001–2002 full-time, 21. Openings 2002–2003, 8. The Median number of years required for completion of a degree are 3.

Admissions Requirements:
Scores: Entries appear in this order: required test or GPA, minimum score (if required), median score of students entering in 2001–2002. Master's Programs: GRE-V 450, 510; GRE-Q 450, 600; GRE-Analytical 450, 600; GRE-V+Q+Analytical 1500, 1670; overall undergraduate GPA 2.80, 3.40; last 2 years GPA 3.00, 3.60. Doctoral Programs: last 2 years GPA no minimum stated; psychology GPA no minimum stated; psychology GPA no minimum stated.
Other Criteria: (importance of criteria rated low, medium, or high): GRE/MAT scores high, research experience medium, work experience medium, extracurricular activity low, clinically related public service medium, GPA high, letters of recommendation high, statement of goals and objectives medium. Clinical requires interview.

Student Characteristics: The following represents characteristics of students in 2001–2002 in all graduate psychology programs in the department: Female–full-time 56, part-time 0; Male–full-time 5, part-time 0; African American/Black–full-time 2, part-time 0; Hispanic/Latino (a)–full-time 1, part-time 0; Asian/Pacific Islander–full-time 1, part-time 0; American Indian/Alaska Native–full-time 0, part-time 0; Multi-ethnic–full-time 0, part-time 0; students subject to the Americans with Disabilities Act–full-time 0, part-time 0.

Financial Information/Assistance:
Tuition for Full-Time Study: *Master's:* State residents per academic year $1,393, $174 per credit hour; nonstate residents: per academic year $9,256, $1,157 per credit hour.

Financial Assistance:
First Year Students: Teaching assistantships available for first-year. Average amount paid per academic year: $3,750. Average number of hours worked per week: 10. Apply by Mar 1. Tuition remission given: partial. Research assistantships available for first-year. Average amount paid per academic year: $3,750. Average number of hours worked per week: 10. Apply by Mar 1. Tuition remission given: partial. Fellowships and scholarships available for first-year. Average amount paid per academic year: $10,500. Average number of hours worked per week: 20. Apply by Mar 1. Tuition remission given: partial.

Advanced Students: Teaching assistantships available for advanced students. Average amount paid per academic year: $3,750. Average number of hours worked per week: 10. Apply by Mar 1. Research assistantships available for advanced students. Average amount paid per academic year: $3,750. Average number of hours worked per week: 10. Apply by Mar 1. Fellowships and scholarships available for advanced students. Average amount paid per academic year: $10,500. Average number of hours worked per week: 20. Apply by Mar 1. Tuition remission given: partial.

Contact Information: Of all students currently enrolled full-time, 80% benefited from one or more of the listed financial assistance programs. For information on financial assistance, contact: Graduate Program Director, Department of Psychology, East Carolina University, Greenville, NC 27858.

Internships/Practica: Clinical internships in mental health clinics offer stipends between $600 and $800 per month for six months; School internships in area school systems offer stipends of up to $2,450 per month for 10 months. Paid I/O internships are usually available during the summer.

Housing and Day Care: No on-campus housing and day care facilities are available.

Employment of Department Graduates:

Master's Degree Graduates: Of those who graduated in the academic year 2000–2001, the following categories and numbers represent the post-graduate activities and employment of master's degree graduates: Enrolled in a psychology doctoral program (4), enrolled in another graduate/professional program (0), enrolled in a post-doctoral residency/fellowship (n/a), employed in independent practice (n/a), employed in an academic position at a university (0), employed in an academic position at a 2-year/4-year college (0), employed in other positions at a higher education institution (0), employed in a professional position in a school system (6), employed in business or industry (research/consulting) (0), employed in business or industry (management) (3), employed in a government agency (research) (0), employed in a government agency (professional services) (2), employed in a community mental health/counseling center (4), employed in a hospital/medical center (0), still seeking employment (0), other employment position (0).

Doctoral Degree Graduates: Of those who graduated in the academic year 2000–2001, the following categories and numbers represent the post-graduate activities and employment of doctoral degree graduates: Enrolled in a psychology doctoral program (n/a), enrolled in another graduate/professional program (n/a).

Additional Information:

Orientation, Objectives, and Emphasis of Department: The primary objective of the Clinical Psychology program is to prepare students for licensure in NC as a Licensed Psychological Associate. Training is applied with a focus on psychological assessment and psychotherapy skills development. The program offers tracks in child clinical, adult, and MR/DD. The School Psychology MA/CAS program is approved by the National Association of School Psychologists and the NC Department of Public Instruction. The program provides training and experience in assessment, consultation, and intervention. Most graduates of the Clinical and School programs are employed in mental health and school settings. The General Psychology program offers students the opportunity to specialize in one of three concentrations. The Academic concen-

tration prepares students to teach psychology at the Community/Junior College level. The Research concentration focuses on preparing the student for research and doctoral training. The Industrial/Organizational concentration prepares students for careers involving the application of psychology and human resources in organizations.

Special Facilities or Resources: The department has student computer facilities, interview and testing facilities, and animal laboratory. The Clinical and School programs work closely with community schools and mental health agencies.

Information for Students With Physical Disabilities: The Psychology Department Building is fully accessible to those with physical disabilities. The University Department for Disability Support Services integrates individuals with disabilities into the life of the university and assists them in benefiting from the programs, services, and activities that are enjoyed by all individuals.

Application Information:
Send to: East Carolina University Graduate School, Greenville, NC 27858-4353. Students are admitted in the Fall, application deadline March 1. *Fee:* $40.

North Carolina State University
Department of Psychology
College of Humanities and Social Sciences
640 Poe Hall, Box 7801
Raleigh, NC 27695-7801
Telephone: (919) 515-2251
Fax: (919) 515-1716
E-mail: *psych@ncsu.edu*
Web: *http://www.ncsu.edu/psychology*

[handwritten: V: 610 612 / Q: 610 590 / A: 620 / GRE GPA: 3.2 / Psych GPA: 3.5]

Department Established:
1938. Department Head: David W. Martin. Number of Faculty: total–full-time 28, part-time 5; women–full-time 8, part-time 2.

Programs and Degrees Offered:
Listed in the following order: Program area, degree type (T if terminal Master's), number awarded 7/00–6/01. Developmental PhD 7, Ergonomics & Experimental PhD 4, Industrial/Organizational PhD 6, Public Interest PhD 6, School Psychology PhD 2. *[handwritten: ~ not APA accred.]*

APA Accreditation: School PhD: full.

Student Applications/Admissions:

Student Applications
Developmental PhD—Applications 2001–2002, 17. New applicants enrolled 2001–2002, 4. Total enrolled 2001–2002 full-time, 12. Openings 2002–2003, 4. The Median number of years required for completion of a degree are 8. The number of students enrolled full and part-time, who were dismissed or voluntarily withdrew from this program area were 0. *Ergonomics & Experimental PhD*—Applications 2001–2002, 9. New applicants enrolled 2001–2002, 1. Total enrolled 2001–2002 full-time, 21. Openings 2002–2003, 6. The Median number

of years required for completion of a degree are 8. The number of students enrolled full and part-time, who were dismissed or voluntarily withdrew from this program area were 1. *Industrial/ Organizational PhD*—Applications 2001–2002, 46. New applicants enrolled 2001–2002, 2. Total enrolled 2001–2002 full-time, 27. Openings 2002–2003, 4. The Median number of years required for completion of a degree are 8. The number of students enrolled full and part-time, who were dismissed or voluntarily withdrew from this program area were 0. *Public Interest PhD*—Applications 2001–2002, 8. New applicants enrolled 2001–2002, 2. Total enrolled 2001–2002 full-time, 21. Openings 2002–2003, 4. The Median number of years required for completion of a degree are 8. The number of students enrolled full and part-time, who were dismissed or voluntarily withdrew from this program area were 1. *School Psychology PhD*—Applications 2001–2002, 34. New applicants enrolled 2001–2002, 5. Total enrolled 2001–2002 full-time, 22. Openings 2002–2003, 4. The Median number of years required for completion of a degree are 8. The number of students enrolled full and part-time, who were dismissed or voluntarily withdrew from this program area were 0.

Admissions Requirements:

Scores: Entries appear in this order: required test or GPA, minimum score (if required), median score of students entering in 2001–2002. Master's Programs: GRE-V no minimum stated, 510; GRE-Q no minimum stated, 610; GRE-Analytical no minimum stated, 628; overall undergraduate GPA no minimum stated, 3.5. GRE Subject Test Required for program in I/O Psychology; recommended for others. Doctoral Programs: GRE-V no minimum stated, 612; GRE-Q no minimum stated, 590; GRE-Analytical no minimum stated, 620; overall undergraduate GPA no minimum stated, 3.2; last 2 years GPA no minimum stated; psychology GPA no minimum stated, 3.4; psychology GPA no minimum stated, 3.5. GRE Subject Test Required for program in I/O Psychology; recommended for others.

Other Criteria: (importance of criteria rated low, medium, or high): GRE/MAT scores high, research experience high, work experience medium, extracurricular activity low, clinically related public service low, GPA high, letters of recommendation high, interview medium, statement of goals and objectives high, fit with program high. Psychology in the Public Interest gives greater weight to work experience and public service than do other program areas.

Student Characteristics: The following represents characteristics of students in 2001–2002 in all graduate psychology programs in the department: Female–full-time 71, part-time 0; Male–full-time 34, part-time 0; African American/Black–full-time 8, part-time 0; Hispanic/Latino (a)–full-time 2, part-time 0; Asian/Pacific Islander–full-time 6, part-time 0; American Indian/Alaska Native–full-time 0, part-time 0; Multi-ethnic–full-time 1, students subject to the Americans with Disabilities Act–full-time 1.

Financial Information/Assistance:

Tuition for Full-Time Study: *Master's:* State residents per academic year $2,512; nonstate residents: per academic year $12,822, *Doctoral:* State residents: per academic year $2,512; nonstate residents: per academic year $12,822.

Financial Assistance:

First Year Students: Teaching assistantships available for first-year. Average amount paid per academic year: $10,000. Average number of hours worked per week: 20. Apply by Jan 15. Tuition remission given: full. Research assistantships available for first-year. Average amount paid per academic year: $10,000. Average number of hours worked per week: 20. Apply by Jan 15. Tuition remission given: full. Traineeships available for first-year. Average amount paid per academic year: $11,000. Apply by Jan 15. Tuition remission given: full.

Advanced Students: Teaching assistantships available for advanced students. Average amount paid per academic year: $10,000. Average number of hours worked per week: 20. Tuition remission given: full. Research assistantships available for advanced students. Average amount paid per academic year: $10,000. Average number of hours worked per week: 20. Tuition remission given: full.

Contact Information: Of all students currently enrolled full-time, 40% benefited from one or more of the listed financial assistance programs. For information on financial assistance, contact: Office of Financial Aid, NCSU Box 7302, Raleigh, NC 27695-7302.

Internships/Practica: Practica and internships are required for both master's and doctoral students in the School Psychology program. These include supervised experiences in assessment, consultation, intervention, research, and professional school psychology in a wide variety of school-related settings. Students in Ergonomics also usually obtain employment for at least one summer/ semester in one of the many suitable companies located in the Research Triangle area. For those doctoral students for whom a professional internship is required prior to graduation, 3 applied in 2000–2001. Of those who applied, 1 were placed in internships listed by the Association of Psychology Postdoctoral and Internship Programs (APPIC).

Housing and Day Care: On-campus housing and day care facilities are available.

Employment of Department Graduates:

Master's Degree Graduates: Of those who graduated in the academic year 2000–2001, the following categories and numbers represent the post-graduate activities and employment of master's degree graduates: Enrolled in a psychology doctoral program (7), enrolled in a post-doctoral residency/fellowship (n/a), employed in independent practice (n/a).

Doctoral Degree Graduates: Of those who graduated in the academic year 2000–2001, the following categories and numbers represent the post-graduate activities and employment of doctoral degree graduates: Enrolled in a psychology doctoral program (n/a), enrolled in another graduate/professional program (n/a), enrolled in a post-doctoral residency/fellowship (1), employed in independent practice (1), employed in other positions at a higher education institution (4), employed in a professional position in a school system (1), employed in business or industry (research/ consulting) (5), employed in a hospital/medical center (1).

Additional Information:

Orientation, Objectives, and Emphasis of Department: The department trains in the scientist-practitioner model. Students are expected to become knowledgeable about both research and application within their area of study. There are five specialty areas with different emphases. Developmental Psychology stresses a balance of conceptual, research-analytical, and application skills and encompasses social and cognitive development from infancy to old age. Ergonomics and Experimental Psychology includes two tracks. The ergonomics track emphasizes the cognitive/perceptual aspects of human factors, including research on visual displays, visual/auditory spatial judgments, and effective information transfer for complex systems. This track has a cooperative relationship with the Biomechanics Program in IE. The experimental psychology track provides extensive research training with concentrations in biopsychology, cognition, learning, motivation, and perception. The Psychology in the Public Interest program (formerly known as Human Resource Development/Community) is a problem-oriented program dealing with research and professional issues in communities and social systems. Industrial/Organizational (I/O) students may concentrate in such areas as performance appraisal, selection, training, job analysis, work motivation, organizational theory, and development. Other students study vocational behavior and adjustment. School Psychology develops behavioral scientists who apply psychological knowledge and techniques in school and family settings to help students, parents, and teachers.

Special Facilities or Resources: The department is housed on two floors of a modern building. Students with assistantships share offices. All programs have appropriate laboratory space and facilities. These include specialized lab facilities: Audition Laboratory, Cognitive-Development Laboratory, Ergonomics Laboratory, Neuropsychology Laboratory, Social Development Laboratory, and Visual Perception Laboratory. Ergonomics, Human Resource Development, I/O and vocational, and School students may have opportunities to work in state government, industry, schools, and community agencies to gain practical and research experience. As this area is developing rapidly, more opportunities appear each year. Students are, however, required to maintain continuous registration and carry an adequate course load each semester. Students are permitted to enroll in courses at the University of North Carolina-Chapel Hill and at Duke University, as if the courses were offered on this campus. Once basic research, statistics, and area course requirements are satisfied, students have considerable flexibility in developing tailored programs of study.

Information for Students With Physical Disabilities: NCSU is committed to providing as complete access as possible to all students, regardless of physical disability. Great strides have been made in recent years to remove various campus barriers, although work is continuing.

Application Information:
Send to: Application, Fees & Transcripts: The Graduate School, Box 7102, NCSU, Raleigh, NC 27695-7102. Letters & Questionnaires: Director of Graduate Programs, Psychology Department, Box 7801, NCSU, Raleigh, NC 27695-7801. Students are admitted in the Fall, application deadline January 15. *Fee:* $55. $65 for International Applications.

North Carolina, University of, at Chapel Hill
Department of Psychology
CB #3270
Chapel Hill, NC 27599-3270
Telephone: (919) 962-4155
Fax: (919) 962-2537
E-mail: *psychwww@unc.edu*
Web: *http://www.psych.unc.edu*

Department Established:
1921. Chairperson: Peter A. Ornstein. Number of Faculty: total–full-time 34, part-time 5; women–full-time 15, part-time 1; minority–full-time 1, part-time 3.

Programs and Degrees Offered:
Listed in the following order: Program area, degree type (T if terminal Master's), number awarded 7/00–6/01. Clinical PhD 12, cognitive PhD 2, developmental PhD 1, experimental/biological PhD 3, experimental/biological PhD 3, quantitative PhD 2, social PhD 8.

APA Accreditation: Clinical PhD: full.

Student Applications/Admissions:
Student Applications
Clinical PhD—Applications 2001–2002, 352. Total applicants accepted 2001–2002, 10. New applicants enrolled 2001–2002, 9. Total enrolled 2001–2002 full-time, 53. Openings 2002–2003, 8. The Median number of years required for completion of a degree are 5. *Cognitive PhD*—Applications 2001–2002, 26. Total applicants accepted 2001–2002, 8. New applicants enrolled 2001–2002, 3. Total enrolled 2001–2002 full-time, 9. Openings 2002–2003, 3. The Median number of years required for completion of a degree are 5. *Developmental PhD*—Applications 2001–2002, 51. Total applicants accepted 2001–2002, 4. New applicants enrolled 2001–2002, 3. Total enrolled 2001–2002 full-time, 19. Openings 2002–2003, 3. The Median number of years required for completion of a degree are 5. *Experimental/biological PhD*—Applications 2001–2002, 27. Total applicants accepted 2001–2002, 8. New applicants enrolled 2001–2002, 4. Total enrolled 2001–2002 full-time, 9. Openings 2002–2003, 4. The Median number of years required for completion of a degree are 5. *Experimental/biological PhD*—Applications 2001–2002, 27. Total applicants accepted 2001–2002, 8. New applicants enrolled 2001–2002, 4. Total enrolled 2001–2002 full-time, 9. Openings 2002–2003, 4. The Median number of years required for completion of a degree are 5. *Quantitative PhD*—Applications 2001–2002, 15. Total applicants accepted 2001–2002, 3. New applicants enrolled 2001–2002, 2. Total enrolled 2001–2002 full-time, 10. Openings 2002–2003, 3. The Median number of years required for completion of a degree are 5. *Social PhD*—Applications 2001–2002, 37. Total applicants accepted 2001–2002, 7. New applicants enrolled 2001–2002, 5. Total enrolled 2001–2002 full-time, 21. Openings 2002–2003, 4. The Median number of years required for completion of a degree are 5.

Admissions Requirements:
Scores: Entries appear in this order: required test or GPA, minimum score (if required), median score of students entering

in 2001–2002. Doctoral Programs: GRE-V 50%, 627; GRE-Q 50%, 701; last 2 years GPA 3.0, 3.68; psychology GPA no minimum stated; psychology GPA no minimum stated.

Other Criteria: (importance of criteria rated low, medium, or high): GRE/MAT scores high, research experience high, work experience medium, clinically related public service medium, GPA high, letters of recommendation high, interview medium, statement of goals and objectives high, research interest high.

Student Characteristics: The following represents characteristics of students in 2001–2002 in all graduate psychology programs in the department: Female–full-time 14, part-time 0; Male–full-time 12, part-time 0; African American/Black–full-time 4, part-time 0; Hispanic/Latino (a)–full-time 1, part-time 0; Asian/Pacific Islander–full-time 0, part-time 0; American Indian/Alaska Native–full-time 0, part-time 0.

Financial Information/Assistance:

Tuition for Full-Time Study: *Doctoral:* State residents: per academic year $3,448; nonstate residents: per academic year $13,758.

Financial Assistance:

First Year Students: Research assistantships available for first-year. Average amount paid per academic year: $12,000. Average number of hours worked per week: 15. Tuition remission given: full and partial. Traineeships available for first-year. Average amount paid per academic year: $15,000. Tuition remission given: full and partial. Fellowships and scholarships available for first-year. Average amount paid per academic year: $15,000. Tuition remission given: full and partial.

Advanced Students: Teaching assistantships available for advanced students. Average amount paid per academic year: $11,800. Average number of hours worked per week: 15. Tuition remission given: full and partial. Research assistantships available for advanced students. Average amount paid per academic year: $12,000. Average number of hours worked per week: 15. Tuition remission given: full and partial. Traineeships available for advanced students. Average amount paid per academic year: $15,000. Tuition remission given: full. Fellowships and scholarships available for advanced students. Average amount paid per academic year: $15,000. Tuition remission given: full.

Contact Information: Of all students currently enrolled full-time, 74% benefited from one or more of the listed financial assistance programs. For information on financial assistance, contact: Psychology Department. All admitted students are automatically considered for financial aid. Does not require a separate application.

Internships/Practica: Students within the doctoral program in clinical psychology engage in a wide range of clinical practica activities beginning in the first year of doctoral study. A variety of sites are included in our practicum arrangements. One of these sites is the University of North Carolina Medical School, which includes opportunities in a number of areas including child, family, adolescent, and adults. There are also specialized opportunities at that site to work with children with developmental disabilities and college students in a university counseling setting. Students also receive training at John Umstead Hospital, a state psychiatric hospital; opportunities there range from child, adolescent, adult, and geriatric patients. Overall Umstead Hospital emphasizes treatment of more disturbed individuals, but opportunities are available as well for outpatient treatment. Third, students are involved in

our Psychology Department Psychological Services Center, our in-house outpatient treatment facility. Students work with a wide variety of clients within that context, with specialized opportunities in the anxiety disorders and marital therapy. Among other sites, students provide consultation to the local school system, to the Orange-Person-Chatham Mental Health Center, and a variety of other sites that are arranged on an as needed basis. For those doctoral students for whom a professional internship is required prior to graduation, 9 applied in 2000–2001. Of those who applied, 9 were placed in internships listed by the Association of Psychology Postdoctoral and Internship Programs (APPIC); 9 were placed in APA accredited internships.

Housing and Day Care: No on-campus housing and day care facilities are available.

Employment of Department Graduates:

Master's Degree Graduates: Of those who graduated in the academic year 2000–2001, the following categories and numbers represent the post-graduate activities and employment of master's degree graduates: Enrolled in a post-doctoral residency/fellowship (n/a), employed in independent practice (n/a).

Doctoral Degree Graduates: Of those who graduated in the academic year 2000–2001, the following categories and numbers represent the post-graduate activities and employment of doctoral degree graduates: Enrolled in a psychology doctoral program (n/a), enrolled in another graduate/professional program (n/a).

Additional Information:

Orientation, Objectives, and Emphasis of Department: Each graduate training program is designed to acquaint students with the theoretical and research content of their specialty and to train them in the research and teaching skills needed to make contributions to science and society. In addition, certain programs (for example, the clinical program) include an emphasis on the development of competence in appropriate professional skills. Faculty members maintain a balance of commitments to research, teaching, and service.

Special Facilities or Resources: Affiliated clinical and research facilities are: the Psychological Services Center, Psychology Department; John Umstead State Hospital, Butner, NC; North Carolina Memorial Hospital, Chapel Hill; Murdoch Center for the Retarded, Butner; Division for Disorders of Development and Learning, Chapel Hill; VA Hospital, Durham; Frank Porter Graham Child Development Center, Chapel Hill; Carolina Population Center, Chapel Hill; Alcoholic Rehabilitation Center, Butner; North Carolina Highway Safety Research Center, Chapel Hill; L.L. Thurstone Psychometric Laboratory, Chapel Hill; Human Psychophysiology Laboratory, Chapel Hill; Institute for Research in Social Sciences, Chapel Hill; Laboratory for Computing and Cognition, Chapel Hill; Neurobiology Curriculum, University of North Carolina; Research Laboratories of the U.S. Environmental Protection Agency, Research Triangle Park; and TEACCH Division, North Carolina Memorial Hospital, specializing in the treatment and education of victims of autism and related disorders of communication.

Information for Students With Physical Disabilities: The University of North Carolina is committed to providing equal access for persons with disabilities by providing reasonable accommodations to meet their needs. The Department of Disability Services works with individuals and with the Department of Psychology to achieve this objective.

Application Information:

Send to: Graduate Admissions, CB#3270, 203 Davie Hall, Department of Psychology, UNC-Chapel Hill, NC 27599-3270. Students are admitted in the Fall, application deadline December 1. *Fee:* $60.

North Carolina, University of, at Charlotte

Department of Psychology
Arts and Sciences
9201 University City Boulevard
Charlotte, NC 28223-0001
Telephone: (704) 687-4731
Fax: (704) 687-3096
E-mail: *wsterry@email.uncc.edu*
Web: *http://www.uncc.edu/index3.htm*

Department Established:

1960. Graduate Coordinator: Dr. Scott Terry. Number of Faculty: total–full-time 28, part-time 8; women–full-time 8, part-time 4; minority–full-time 2, part-time 1.

Programs and Degrees Offered:

Listed in the following order: Program area, degree type (T if terminal Master's), number awarded 7/00–6/01. Clinical/community MA (T) 6, industrial/organizational MA (T) 11.

Student Applications/Admissions:

Student Applications

Clinical/community MA—Applications 2001–2002, 70. Total applicants accepted 2001–2002, 15. New applicants enrolled 2001–2002, 10. Total enrolled 2001–2002 full-time, 18, part-time, 6. Openings 2002–2003, 10. The Median number of years required for completion of a degree are 2. The number of students enrolled full and part-time, who were dismissed or voluntarily withdrew from this program area were 1. *Industrial/organizational* MA—Applications 2001–2002, 70. Total applicants accepted 2001–2002, 30. New applicants enrolled 2001–2002, 11. Total enrolled 2001–2002 full-time, 25, part-time, 10. Openings 2002–2003, 12. The Median number of years required for completion of a degree are 2. The number of students enrolled full and part-time, who were dismissed or voluntarily withdrew from this program area were 1.

Admissions Requirements:

Scores: Entries appear in this order: required test or GPA, minimum score (if required), median score of students entering in 2001–2002. Master's Programs: GRE-V no minimum stated, 554; GRE-Q no minimum stated, 600; GRE-V+Q no minimum stated, 1150; GRE-Subject(Psych) no minimum stated, 570; overall undergraduate GPA no minimum stated, 3.4. Doctoral Programs: last 2 years GPA no minimum stated; psychology GPA no minimum stated; psychology GPA no minimum stated.

Other Criteria: (importance of criteria rated low, medium, or high): GRE/MAT scores high, research experience high, work experience high, extracurricular activity low, clinically related public service medium, GPA high, letters of recommendation high, interview low, statement of goals and objectives high, community work high, for clinical/community only.

Student Characteristics: The following represents characteristics of students in 2001–2002 in all graduate psychology programs in the department: Female–full-time 20, part-time 3; Male–full-time 7, part-time 4; African American/Black–full-time 3, part-time 1.

Financial Information/Assistance:

Tuition for Full-Time Study: *Master's:* State residents per academic year $2,526, $324 per credit hour; nonstate residents: per academic year $10,890, $1,370 per credit hour.

Financial Assistance:

First Year Students: Teaching assistantships available for first-year. Average amount paid per academic year: $9,000. Average number of hours worked per week: 20. Apply by March 1. Research assistantships available for first-year. Average amount paid per academic year: $8,500. Average number of hours worked per week: 20. Apply by March 1. Fellowships and scholarships available for first-year. Average amount paid per academic year: $2,150. Apply by March 1.

Advanced Students: Teaching assistantships available for advanced students. Average amount paid per academic year: $9,000. Average number of hours worked per week: 20. Research assistantships available for advanced students. Average amount paid per academic year: $8,500. Average number of hours worked per week: 20.

Contact Information: Of all students currently enrolled full-time, 60% benefited from one or more of the listed financial assistance programs. For information on financial assistance, contact: Financial Aid Office, UNCC at (704) 647-2461, or www.uncc.edu/finaid.

Internships/Practica: Clinical/Community: Students are required to enroll in 2 semesters of practicum, working 22 hrs/week in community agencies such as mental health centers, prisons, hospitals, and non-profit organizations. Industrial/Organizational: An extensive practicum component utilizes the Charlotte area as setting for applied experience. All students must complete 3 hours of Projects in I/O Psychology and they are strongly encouraged to take 6 hours.

Housing and Day Care: No on-campus housing and day care facilities are available.

Employment of Department Graduates:

Master's Degree Graduates: Of those who graduated in the academic year 2000–2001, the following categories and numbers represent the post-graduate activities and employment of master's degree graduates: Enrolled in a psychology doctoral program (2), enrolled in a post-doctoral residency/fellowship (n/a), employed in independent practice (n/a), employed in business or industry (research/consulting) (7), employed in a community mental health/counseling center (4), other employment position (2).

Doctoral Degree Graduates: Of those who graduated in the academic year 2000–2001, the following categories and numbers represent the post-graduate activities and employment of doctoral degree graduates: Enrolled in a psychology doctoral program (n/a), enrolled in another graduate/professional program (n/a).

Additional Information:

Orientation, Objectives, and Emphasis of Department: The objective of the master's degree program is to train psychologists in the knowledge and skills necessary to address problems encountered in industry, organizations, and the community. The program has an applied emphasis. Graduates of the program are eligible to apply for licensing in North Carolina as psychological associates. Although our goals emphasize application of psychological principles in organizational, clinical, and community settings, the rigorous program allows students to prepare themselves well for further education in psychology.

Special Facilities or Resources: The psychology department is housed in a modern classroom office building that provides offices, demonstration rooms, a workshop, and specialty laboratories for research. Facilities include a computerized laboratory with 37 microcomputers; many small testing, training, and interview rooms with one-way mirrors for direct observation; audio intercommunications; and closed circuit television. There is extensive audio and video equipment available as well as a research trailer, tachistoscopes, programming and timing equipment, and microcomputers. The psychometric laboratory contains an extensive inventory of current tests of intelligence, personality, and interest, as well as calculators and microcomputers for testing, test score evaluation, and data analysis. A well-equipped physiological laboratory is available for work including human electrophysiology.

Information for Students With Physical Disabilities: The campus office of disability services provides help for students with disabilities.

Application Information:

Send to: Graduate Admissions, UNC-Charlotte, 9201 University City Blvd., Charlotte, NC 28223. Students are admitted in the Fall, application deadline 3/1; 2/1. February 1st is the deadline for Industrial/Organizational program. March 1st - clinical/community MA. *Fee:* $35.

North Carolina, University of, at Greensboro

Department of Psychology
College of Arts and Sciences
296 Eberhart Building, P.O. Box 26164
Greensboro, NC 27402-6164
Telephone: (336) 334-5013
Fax: (336) 334-5066
E-mail: *johnston@uncg.edu*
Web: *http://www.uncg.edu/psy/*

V: 590 ⟩ 1290
Q: 640
GPA: 3.4
last 2 yrs GPA: 3.64

Department Established:

1925. Department Head: Timothy D. Johnston. Number of Faculty: total–full-time 25, part-time 2; women–full-time 9.

Programs and Degrees Offered:

Listed in the following order: Program area, degree type (T if terminal Master's), number awarded 7/00–6/01. Clinical PhD 10, cognitive PhD, developmental PhD, social PhD 1.

APA Accreditation: Clinical PhD: full.

Student Applications/Admissions:

Student Applications

Clinical PhD—Applications 2001–2002, 168. Total applicants accepted 2001–2002, 7. New applicants enrolled 2001–2002, 7. Total enrolled 2001–2002 full-time, 42. Openings 2002–2003, 6. *Cognitive PhD*—Applications 2001–2002, 10. Total applicants accepted 2001–2002, 2. New applicants enrolled 2001–2002, 2. Total enrolled 2001–2002 full-time, 5. Openings 2002–2003, 3. The number of students enrolled full and part-time, who were dismissed or voluntarily withdrew from this program area were 0. *Developmental PhD*—Applications 2001–2002, 10. Total applicants accepted 2001–2002, 2. New applicants enrolled 2001–2002, 2. Total enrolled 2001–2002 full-time, 5. Openings 2002–2003, 3. The number of students enrolled full and part-time, who were dismissed or voluntarily withdrew from this program area were 1. *Social PhD*—Applications 2001–2002, 24. Total applicants accepted 2001–2002, 1. New applicants enrolled 2001–2002, 1. Total enrolled 2001–2002 full-time, 8. Openings 2002–2003, 2. The Median number of years required for completion of a degree are 6. The number of students enrolled full and part-time, who were dismissed or voluntarily withdrew from this program area were 0.

Admissions Requirements:

Scores: Entries appear in this order: required test or GPA, minimum score (if required), median score of students entering in 2001–2002. Master's Programs: GRE-V 590, 680; GRE-Q 640, 780; GRE-V+Q 1230, 1370; GRE-Subject(Psych) 660, 700; overall undergraduate GPA 3.4, 3.8. Doctoral Programs: GRE-V no minimum stated, 590; GRE-Q no minimum stated, 640; GRE-V+Q no minimum stated, 1290; GRE-Subject(Psych) no minimum stated; overall undergraduate GPA no minimum stated, 3.4; last 2 years GPA no minimum stated, 3.64; psychology GPA no minimum stated; psychology GPA no minimum stated.

Other Criteria: (importance of criteria rated low, medium, or high): GRE/MAT scores high, research experience high, work experience low, extracurricular activity low, clinically related public service medium, GPA high, letters of recommendation high, interview high, statement of goals and objectives low.

Student Characteristics: The following represents characteristics of students in 2001–2002 in all graduate psychology programs in the department: Female–full-time 45, part-time 0; Male–full-time 11, part-time 0; African American/Black–full-time 1, part-time 0; Hispanic/Latino (a)–full-time 1, part-time 0; Asian/Pacific Islander–full-time 1, part-time 0; American Indian/Alaska Native–full-time 0, part-time 0; students subject to the Americans with Disabilities Act–full-time 1.

Financial Information/Assistance:

Tuition for Full-Time Study: *Master's:* State residents per academic year $687, $172 per credit hour.

Financial Assistance:

First Year Students: Research assistantships available for first-year. Average amount paid per academic year: $8,500. Average number of hours worked per week: 12. Apply by 1/15. Tuition remission given: partial.

Advanced Students: Teaching assistantships available for advanced students. Average amount paid per academic year:

$3,500. Apply by 1/15. Research assistantships available for advanced students. Average amount paid per academic year: $8,500. Apply by 1/15.

Contact Information: For information on financial assistance, contact: Office of Financial Aid, UNCG, Greensboro, NC 27412-5001, 336-334-5702.

Internships/Practica: No information provided.

Housing and Day Care: On-campus housing and day care facilities are available.

Employment of Department Graduates:

Master's Degree Graduates: Of those who graduated in the academic year 2000–2001, the following categories and numbers represent the post-graduate activities and employment of master's degree graduates: Enrolled in a post-doctoral residency/fellowship (n/a), employed in independent practice (n/a).

Doctoral Degree Graduates: Of those who graduated in the academic year 2000–2001, the following categories and numbers represent the post-graduate activities and employment of doctoral degree graduates: Enrolled in a psychology doctoral program (n/a), enrolled in another graduate/professional program (n/a), employed in an academic position at a 2-year/4-year college (3), employed in other positions at a higher education institution (4), employed in business or industry (research/consulting) (2), employed in a community mental health/counseling center (2), employed in a hospital/medical center (2).

Additional Information:

Orientation, Objectives, and Emphasis of Department: The objective is to provide scholarship and methodological and practical skills to enable the student to function in a variety of academic, research, and service settings. The program has an experimental orientation, with four major areas of concentration: clinical, which includes applied training and clinical research training in a variety of service settings; developmental, which includes basic research in behavioral, cognitive, language, and social development in infant, child, adolescent, and adult humans and in animals; cognitive, which includes basic research in human memory, cognition, and language; social, designed to introduce students to theoretical issues and to applied, biological, and developmental perspectives in social psychology. Although the program is oriented toward the PhD as the terminal degree, an applicant with a bachelor's degree is admitted into the master's program. Upon successful completion of the requirements for the master's degree, the student's work is reviewed for admission into the PhD program.

Special Facilities or Resources: The Department of Psychology is located in the Life Sciences Building. Space is devoted to classrooms; research laboratories; vivaria; the Psychology Clinic; faculty, student, and secretarial offices; a computer terminal room; a library; and a lounge. Graduate students share offices with one or two other students. Active research laboratories in each of the specialty areas contain an assortment of items: animal test chambers with supporting apparatus for research in perception, learning, and the development of social behavior; automated equipment for studying concept formation and problem-solving behavior in humans; signal-averaging computers with XY plotters for analyses of electrophysical correlates of behavior; soundproof chambers; electronic psychoacoustic equipment for stimulus control in auditory research with humans and animals; videotape studio; polygraphs for psychological recording; and observation rooms with one-way mirrors. The university computer center is available to faculty members and graduate students involved in research. Facilities include interactive and batch access to the large-sized computer on campus. Virtually all computer languages and standard software packages are available. The university library has an exceptional collection of journals and books. The department also has its own library located in the Life Sciences Building.

Application Information:
Send to: Dean of Graduate School, PO Box 26176, UNCG, Greensboro, NC 27402-6176. Students are admitted in the Fall, application deadline 1/15 & 2/1. January 15 for clinical; February 1 for all others. *Fee:* $35.

North Carolina, University of, at Wilmington
Psychology
601 South College Road
Wilmington, NC 28403-5612
Telephone: (910) 962-3370
Fax: (910) 962-7010
E-mail: *noeln@uncwil.edu*
Web: *http://www2.uncwil.edu/psy*

Department Established:
1972. Chairperson: Lee A. Jackson, Jr. Number of Faculty: total–full-time 28; women–full-time 10; minority–full-time 4; faculty subject to the Americans with Disabilities Act 2.

Programs and Degrees Offered:
Listed in the following order: Program area, degree type (T if terminal Master's), number awarded 7/00–6/01. General Psychology MA (T) 4, Substance Abuse Treatment Psyc MA (T) 7.

Student Applications/Admissions:

Student Applications

General Psychology MA—Applications 2001–2002, 50. Total applicants accepted 2001–2002, 20. New applicants enrolled 2001–2002, 8. Total enrolled 2001–2002 full-time, 18, part-time, 2. Openings 2002–2003, 8. The Median number of years required for completion of a degree are 2. The number of students enrolled full and part-time, who were dismissed or voluntarily withdrew from this program area were 1. *Substance Abuse Treatment Psyc MA*—Applications 2001–2002, 20. Total applicants accepted 2001–2002, 10. New applicants enrolled 2001–2002, 7. Total enrolled 2001–2002 full-time, 13, part-time, 1. Openings 2002–2003, 7. The Median number of years required for completion of a degree are 3. The number of students enrolled full and part-time, who were dismissed or voluntarily withdrew from this program area were 1.

Admissions Requirements:

Scores: Entries appear in this order: required test or GPA, minimum score (if required), median score of students entering in 2001–2002. Master's Programs: GRE-V no minimum stated, 530; GRE-Q no minimum stated, 530; GRE-V+Q no minimum stated, 1060; GRE-Analytical no minimum stated, 580; overall undergraduate GPA no minimum stated, 3.2; last 2 years GPA no minimum stated, 3.5. Doctoral Programs: last 2 years GPA no minimum stated; psychology GPA no minimum stated; psychology GPA no minimum stated.

Other Criteria: (importance of criteria rated low, medium, or high): GRE/MAT scores high, research experience high, work experience low, extracurricular activity low, clinically related public service medium, GPA high, letters of recommendation high, interview high, statement of goals and objectives high. In the Substance Abuse Treatment Psychology concentration, clinically related public service may be given more weight, since this concentration emphasizes the development of clinical as well as research skills.

Student Characteristics: The following represents characteristics of students in 2001–2002 in all graduate psychology programs in the department: Female–full-time 21, part-time 3; Male–full-time 10, part-time 0; African American/Black–full-time 1, part-time 0; Hispanic/Latino (a)–full-time 1, part-time 0; Asian/Pacific Islander–full-time 0, part-time 0; American Indian/Alaska Native–full-time 0, part-time 0; Multi-ethnic–full-time 0, students subject to the Americans with Disabilities Act–full-time 0.

Financial Information/Assistance:

Tuition for Full-Time Study: *Master's:* State residents per academic year $2,713; nonstate residents: per academic year $10,936.

Financial Assistance:

First Year Students: Teaching assistantships available for first-year. Average amount paid per academic year: $9,000. Average number of hours worked per week: 20. Apply by Feb 1. Research assistantships available for first-year. Average amount paid per academic year: $9,000. Average number of hours worked per week: 20. Apply by Varied. Tuition remission given: partial. Traineeships available for first-year. Average amount paid per academic year: $9,000. Average number of hours worked per week: 20. Apply by Varied. Fellowships and scholarships available for first-year. Average amount paid per academic year: $7,000. Average number of hours worked per week: 0. Apply by Varied.

Advanced Students: Teaching assistantships available for advanced students. Average amount paid per academic year: $9,000. Average number of hours worked per week: 20. Apply by Feb 1. Research assistantships available for advanced students. Average amount paid per academic year: $9,000. Average number of hours worked per week: 20. Apply by Varied. Tuition remission given: partial. Traineeships available for advanced students. Average amount paid per academic year: $9,000. Average number of hours worked per week: 20. Apply by Varied. Fellowships and scholarships available for advanced students. Average amount paid per academic year: $7,000. Average number of hours worked per week: 0. Apply by Varied.

Contact Information: Of all students currently enrolled full-time, 76% benefited from one or more of the listed financial assistance programs. In regard to Teaching Assistantships and Research Assistantships, contact Graduate Coordinator, Psychology Department. In regard to all other financial assistance, contact The Graduate School.

Internships/Practica: In the Substance Abuse Treatment Psychology Concentration, students are prepared for work with dual diagnosis clients through the completion of a required practicum and internship. The required internship and practicum consist of 1500 hours total of supervised experience working with substance abuse and other psychological and behavioral problems. Training sites include: Community Mental Health Centers, Correctional Institutions, University Counseling Centers, Inpatient and Outpatient Substance Abuse Treatment Centers.

Housing and Day Care: No on-campus housing and day care facilities are available.

Employment of Department Graduates:

Master's Degree Graduates: Of those who graduated in the academic year 2000–2001, the following categories and numbers represent the post-graduate activities and employment of master's degree graduates: Enrolled in a psychology doctoral program (3), enrolled in another graduate/professional program (1), enrolled in a post-doctoral residency/fellowship (n/a), employed in independent practice (n/a), employed in an academic position at a university (2), employed in an academic position at a 2-year/4-year college (3), employed in other positions at a higher education institution (0), employed in a professional position in a school system (0), employed in business or industry (research/consulting) (2), employed in business or industry (management) (1), employed in a government agency (research) (0), employed in a government agency (professional services) (3), employed in a community mental health/counseling center (3), employed in a hospital/medical center (0), still seeking employment (0).

Doctoral Degree Graduates: Of those who graduated in the academic year 2000–2001, the following categories and numbers represent the post-graduate activities and employment of doctoral degree graduates: Enrolled in a psychology doctoral program (n/a), enrolled in another graduate/professional program (n/a).

Additional Information:

Orientation, Objectives, and Emphasis of Department: The department is committed to fostering an understanding of psychological research and it stresses the relationship between students and professors in this process. Research methodology and application are emphasized for all students. Students in the General Psychology concentration are prepared to continue to the PhD in a variety of content areas. Students completing the Substance Abuse Treatment Psychology concentration are prepared for work with dual diagnosis clients in mental health clinics and other public service agencies. The SATP graduates have met all academic requirements to apply for North Carolina state licensure as a Psychological Associate and North Carolina state certification as a Certified Clinical Addictions Specialist.

Special Facilities or Resources: Special facilities or resources include state-of-the-art microcomputers with CD-ROM, research laboratories (including behavioral pharmacology laboratories), an animal laboratory, and videotape equipment. All students have access to word processing, SAS, and SPSS on the university computer system.

Information for Students With Physical Disabilities: All buildings and facilities at the University are fully accessible to wheelchairs.

Application Information:

Send to: Graduate School, University of North Carolina Wilmington, 601 South College Road, Wilmington, NC 28403-5955. Students are admitted in the Fall, application deadline February 1. Applications will be accepted until June 20, but complete applications received by

February 1 will be given first consideration. Generally, all spaces are taken early (i.e., by people with complete applications by early February). *Fee:* $45.

Wake Forest University
Department of Psychology
Arts & Sciences
P.O. Box 7778
Winston-Salem, NC 27109
Telephone: (336) 758-5424
Fax: (336) 758-4733
E-mail: *teehill@wfu.edu*
Web: *http://www.psych.wfu.edu/psychology/*

Department Established:
1958. Chairperson: Deborah L. Best. Number of Faculty: total—full-time 16, part-time 7; women—full-time 8, part-time 4.

Programs and Degrees Offered:
Listed in the following order: Program area, degree type (T if terminal Master's), number awarded 7/00–6/01. General MA (T) 15.

Student Applications/Admissions:
Student Applications
General MA—Applications 2001–2002, 87. Total applicants accepted 2001–2002, 19. New applicants enrolled 2001–2002, 13. Total enrolled 2001–2002 full-time, 13. Openings 2002–2003, 12. The Median number of years required for completion of a degree are 2. The number of students enrolled full and part-time, who were dismissed or voluntarily withdrew from this program area were 0.

Admissions Requirements:
Scores: Entries appear in this order: required test or GPA, minimum score (if required), median score of students entering in 2001–2002. Master's Programs: GRE-V no minimum stated, 555; GRE-Q no minimum stated, 625; GRE-V+Q no minimum stated, 1180; overall undergraduate GPA 3.00, 3.59; psychology GPA 3.00, 3.80. Doctoral Programs: last 2 years GPA no minimum stated; psychology GPA no minimum stated; psychology GPA no minimum stated.
Other Criteria: (importance of criteria rated low, medium, or high): GRE/MAT scores medium, research experience high, GPA medium, letters of recommendation high, interview medium, statement of goals and objectives high.

Student Characteristics: The following represents characteristics of students in 2001–2002 in all graduate psychology programs in the department: Female—full-time 16, part-time 0; Male—full-time 10, part-time 0; African American/Black—full-time 3, part-time 0; Hispanic/Latino (a)—full-time 0, part-time 0; Asian/Pacific Islander—full-time 1, part-time 0; American Indian/Alaska Native—full-time 0, part-time 0; Multi-ethnic—full-time 0, part-time 0; students subject to the Americans with Disabilities Act—full-time 0, part-time 0.

Financial Information/Assistance:
Tuition for Full-Time Study: *Master's:* State residents per academic year $20,790.

Financial Assistance:
First Year Students: Teaching assistantships available for first-year. Average amount paid per academic year: $8,500. Average number of hours worked per week: 12. Apply by February 1.
Advanced Students: Teaching assistantships available for advanced students. Average amount paid per academic year: $8,500. Average number of hours worked per week: 12. Apply by February 1.
Contact Information: Of all students currently enrolled full-time, 100% benefited from one or more of the listed financial assistance programs. For information on financial assistance, contact: Office of the Graduate School, Wake Forest University, Winston-Salem, NC 27109.

Internships/Practica: No information provided.

Housing and Day Care: No on-campus housing and day care facilities are available.

Employment of Department Graduates:
Master's Degree Graduates: Of those who graduated in the academic year 2000–2001, the following categories and numbers represent the post-graduate activities and employment of master's degree graduates: Enrolled in a psychology doctoral program (58), enrolled in a post-doctoral residency/fellowship (n/a), employed in independent practice (n/a).
Doctoral Degree Graduates: Of those who graduated in the academic year 2000–2001, the following categories and numbers represent the post-graduate activities and employment of doctoral degree graduates: Enrolled in a psychology doctoral program (n/a), enrolled in another graduate/professional program (n/a).

Additional Information:
Orientation, Objectives, and Emphasis of Department: The department aims to provide rigorous master's level training, with an emphasis on mastery of theory, research methodology, and content in the basic areas of psychology. This is a general, research-oriented MA program for capable students, most of whom will continue to the PhD.

Special Facilities or Resources: The department of psychology occupies a beautiful and spacious new building that is equipped with state-of-the art teaching and laboratory facilities. Learning resources include in-class multimedia instruction equipment, departmental mini- and microcomputers, departmental and university libraries, and information technology centers. Ample research space is available, including social, developmental, cognitive, perception, physiological, and animal behavior laboratories. Office space is available for graduate students. The department has links with the Wake Forest University School of Medicine (e.g., Neuroscience) which can provide opportunities for students. All students work closely with individual faculty on research during both years (2:1 student/faculty ratio). Wake Forest University offers the academic and technological resources, facilities, and Division I athletic programs music, theater, and art associated with a larger university, with the individual attention that a smaller university can provide.

Information for Students With Physical Disabilities: A system of ramps and elevators makes all of the buildings accessible to those in wheelchairs or with limited mobility.

Application Information:
Send to: Dean of Graduate School, Wake Forest University, PO 7487, Winston-Salem, NC 27109. Students are admitted in the Spring, application deadline February 1. *Fee: $25.*

Western Carolina University
Department of Psychology
College of Education & Allied Professions
Killian Building
Cullowhee, NC 28723
Telephone: (828) 227-7361
Fax: (828) 227-7388
E-mail: *jgoodwin@wcu.edu*
Web: *http://www.wcu.edu/ceap/psychology/psyhome.htm*

Department Established:
1919. Department Head: C. James Goodwin. Number of Faculty: total–full-time 13, part-time 6; women–full-time 6, part-time 3.

Programs and Degrees Offered:
Listed in the following order: Program area, degree type (T if terminal Master's), number awarded 7/00–6/01. Clinical MA (T) 8, school MA (T) 6.

Student Applications/Admissions:
Student Applications

Clinical MA—Applications 2001–2002, 30. Total applicants accepted 2001–2002, 8. New applicants enrolled 2001–2002, 7. Total enrolled 2001–2002 full-time, 16. Openings 2002–2003, 10. The Median number of years required for completion of a degree are 2. The number of students enrolled full and part-time, who were dismissed or voluntarily withdrew from this program area were 0. *School MA*—Applications 2001–2002, 25. Total applicants accepted 2001–2002, 11. New applicants enrolled 2001–2002, 7. Total enrolled 2001–2002 full-time, 11. Openings 2002–2003, 9. The Median number of years required for completion of a degree are 3. The number of students enrolled full and part-time, who were dismissed or voluntarily withdrew from this program area were 1.

Admissions Requirements:
Scores: Entries appear in this order: required test or GPA, minimum score (if required), median score of students entering in 2001–2002. Master's Programs: GRE-V 500; GRE-Q 500; GRE-V+Q 1000, 1000; last 2 years GPA 3.00, 3.20; psychology GPA 3.00, 3.40. Doctoral Programs: GRE-V no minimum stated; GRE-Q no minimum stated; overall undergraduate GPA no minimum stated; last 2 years GPA no minimum stated; psychology GPA no minimum stated; psychology GPA no minimum stated.
Other Criteria: (importance of criteria rated low, medium, or high): GRE/MAT scores high, research experience high, work experience medium, extracurricular activity medium, clinically related public service medium, GPA high, letters of recommendation high, interview high, statement of goals and objectives high.

Student Characteristics: The following represents characteristics of students in 2001–2002 in all graduate psychology programs in

the department: Female–full-time 26, part-time 0; Male–full-time 7, part-time 0; African American/Black–full-time 0, part-time 0; Hispanic/Latino (a)–full-time 0, part-time 0; Asian/Pacific Islander–full-time 0, part-time 0; American Indian/Alaska Native–full-time 0, part-time 0; Multi-ethnic–full-time 2, part-time 0.

Financial Information/Assistance:
Tuition for Full-Time Study: *Master's:* State residents per academic year $1,127, $174 per credit hour; nonstate residents: per academic year $4,762, $1,082 per credit hour.

Financial Assistance:
First Year Students: Teaching assistantships available for first-year. Average amount paid per academic year: $6,000. Average number of hours worked per week: 20. Apply by Feb 1. Average amount paid per academic year: $6,000. Average number of hours worked per week: 20. Apply by Feb 1.
Advanced Students: Teaching assistantships available for advanced students. Average amount paid per academic year: $6,000. Average number of hours worked per week: 20. Apply by Feb 1. Research assistantships available for advanced students. Average amount paid per academic year: $6,000. Average number of hours worked per week: 20. Apply by Feb 1.
Contact Information: For information on financial assistance, contact: Graduate School.

Internships/Practica: Public schools, mental health centers, private hospitals, psychological services center, private schools, alternative schools.

Housing and Day Care: No on-campus housing and day care facilities are available.

Employment of Department Graduates:
Master's Degree Graduates: Of those who graduated in the academic year 2000–2001, the following categories and numbers represent the post-graduate activities and employment of master's degree graduates: Enrolled in a post-doctoral residency/fellowship (n/a), employed in independent practice (n/a).
Doctoral Degree Graduates: Of those who graduated in the academic year 2000–2001, the following categories and numbers represent the post-graduate activities and employment of doctoral degree graduates: Enrolled in a psychology doctoral program (n/a), enrolled in another graduate/professional program (n/a).

Additional Information:
Orientation, Objectives, and Emphasis of Department: Both the Clinical Psychology and School Psychology programs emphasize a scientist-practitioner model. Master of Arts in Psychology-Clinical (2 years). Purpose: 1. To provide students with professional training in the practice of clinical psychology including skills in diagnosis, assessment, therapy, and research. 2. To prepare the student for doctoral training in clinical psychology. Master of Arts in Psychology - School (3 years). Purpose: The school psychology curriculum is organized to accomplish several goals: to gain an understanding of psychological theories, concepts, and research regarding human behavior, and apply that knowledge to promote human welfare in the school setting. 1. They will have a basic background in both psychology and education designed to provide a general theoretical applied orientation in order to function effectively as a psychologist in an educational setting. 2. They will have sufficient academic training to interpret and apply edu-

cational and psychological research in a critical manner. 3. They will develop at least one area of expertise to make a distinct contribution as a school psychologist in a school system. 4. They will gain an understanding of the educational system. 5. They will have an understanding of professional problems and issues as well as how to follow approved ethical practices. Purpose and general description of General-Experimental track. This track is a part of a master's program in psychology that was established in 1970. The purpose of the track is to prepare students for entry into doctoral programs in areas of experimental psychology, such as cognitive, developmental, social, and neuropsychology. To achieve this objective, advanced coursework is offered in research methodology and content areas of experimental psychology, and students engage in research through a thesis requirement, as well as through elective directed study courses that provide opportunities for involvement in faculty research.

Special Facilities or Resources: Special departmental facilities include space and equipment for human subjects research, and testing and observation rooms with videotape equipment. Provide graduate and undergraduate with research facilities, testing and observation rooms, and videotaping equipment. We also have several student oriented research sources.

Application Information:
Send to: School of Research and Graduate Studies: WCU, Cullowhee, NC 28723. Students are admitted in the Fall, application deadline February 1. *Fee:* $35.

Minot State University

Psychology
Education & Human Services
500 University Avenue West
Minot, ND 58707
Telephone: (701) 858-4262
Fax: (701) 858-4260
E-mail: *fordalis@minotstateu.edu*
Web: *http://www.misu.nodak.edu/*

Department Established:
1991. Director: Donald Burke. Number of Faculty: total–full-time 9, part-time 4; women–full-time 4, part-time 2; minority–full-time 1.

Programs and Degrees Offered:
Listed in the following order: Program area, degree type (T if terminal Master's), number awarded 7/00–6/01. Education specialist EdS (T) 4.

Student Applications/Admissions:

Student Applications
Education specialist EdS—Applications 2001–2002, 12. Total applicants accepted 2001–2002, 7. New applicants enrolled 2001–2002, 7. Total enrolled 2001–2002 full-time, 20, part-time, 2. Openings 2002–2003, 6. The Median number of years required for completion of a degree are 3. The number of students enrolled full and part-time, who were dismissed or voluntarily withdrew from this program area were 1.

Admissions Requirements:
Scores: Entries appear in this order: required test or GPA, minimum score (if required), median score of students entering in 2001–2002. Master's Programs: GRE-V no minimum stated, 550; GRE-Q no minimum stated, 500; GRE-Analytical no minimum stated, 650; GRE-V+Q+Analytical 1400, 1700; overall undergraduate GPA 2.75, 3.25. Students without the overall GPA must appeal to the chairperson and receive special written permission to be considered for admission. Doctoral Programs: last 2 years GPA no minimum stated; psychology GPA no minimum stated; psychology GPA no minimum stated.
Other Criteria: (importance of criteria rated low, medium, or high): GRE/MAT scores high, research experience low, work experience high, extracurricular activity medium, clinically related public service medium, GPA medium, letters of recommendation low, interview medium, statement of goals and objectives medium.

Student Characteristics: The following represents characteristics of students in 2001–2002 in all graduate psychology programs in the department: Female–full-time 15, part-time 1; Male–full-time 5, part-time 1; African American/Black–full-time 0, part-time 0; Hispanic/Latino (a)–full-time 0, part-time 0; Asian/Pacific Islander–full-time 0, part-time 0; American Indian/Alaska Native–full-time 3, part-time 0; Multi-ethnic–full-time 0, part-time 0;

students subject to the Americans with Disabilities Act–full-time 0, part-time 0.

Financial Information/Assistance:
Tuition for Full-Time Study: *Master's:* State residents $137 per credit hour; nonstate residents: $343 per credit hour.

Financial Assistance:
First Year Students: Research assistantships available for first-year. Tuition remission given: partial.
Advanced Students: Research assistantships available for advanced students. Tuition remission given: partial.
Contact Information: Of all students currently enrolled full-time, 10% benefited from one or more of the listed financial assistance programs. For information on financial assistance, contact: Dale Gehring, Financial Aid Director.

Internships/Practica: School Psychology Practicum I: This practicum provides students an opportunity to apply their learning from content courses to elementary and secondary students who are failing to find success in school. The assessment of processing problems that sometimes underlie learning disabilities will be examined. School Psychology Practicum II: This is a cap-stone course wherein the students apply information learned and skills acquired in previous courses in diagnosis and remediation planning of actual school-based cases. Theory and techniques are applied to assisting school children with challenging learning and behavior problems. Emphasis will be placed on deciding whether a diagnostic or consultative role will best meet a particular child's needs. Internship: The internship will involve spending 1200 hours in schools or a similar setting. It will also involve an integrative experience where the individual will demonstrate competencies in assessment, programming, consultation, and counseling.

Housing and Day Care: No on-campus housing and day care facilities are available.

Employment of Department Graduates:
Master's Degree Graduates: Of those who graduated in the academic year 2000–2001, the following categories and numbers represent the post-graduate activities and employment of master's degree graduates: Enrolled in a psychology doctoral program (0), enrolled in another graduate/professional program (0), enrolled in a post-doctoral residency/fellowship (n/a), employed in independent practice (n/a), employed in an academic position at a university (0), employed in an academic position at a 2-year/4-year college (0), employed in other positions at a higher education institution (0), employed in a professional position in a school system (4), employed in business or industry (research/consulting) (0), employed in business or industry (management) (0), employed in a government agency (research) (0), employed in a government agency (professional services) (0), employed in a community mental health/counseling center (0), employed in a hospital/medical center (0), still seeking employment (0), other employment position (0).
Doctoral Degree Graduates: Of those who graduated in the academic year 2000–2001, the following categories and numbers represent the post-graduate activities and employment of doctoral

degree graduates: Enrolled in a psychology doctoral program (n/a), enrolled in another graduate/professional program (n/a).

Additional Information:

Orientation, Objectives, and Emphasis of Department: The Education Specialist degree in school psychology is designed to prepare students for certification by the National Association of School Psychology (NASP) and as a School Psychologist in the State of North Dakota. Graduate students participate in a rigorous three-year program. The program emphasizes hands-on experience culminating in a one-year, 1,200-hour internship. The emphasis of the program is to provide the student with the theoretical and practical skills to be an effective school psychologist. The curriculum stresses teaching assessment skills, intervention techniques, and consultative strategies through numerous practicum opportunities. The program trains practitioners who are culturally competent service providers. The school psychology program at Minot State University trains practitioners who are prepared to work as problem solvers in rurally based schools that typify a state like North Dakota. The ideal practitioner in a rural setting is a generalist who combines appropriate educational and behavioral assessments with a knowledge of educational curriculum and instruction to develop appropriate interventions for a broad range of student concerns.

Information for Students With Physical Disabilities: The primary responsibility of the Student Development Center is to assist students in the areas of educational planning, vocational planning, and personal counseling.

Application Information:

Send to: Graduate School, Minot State University, 500 University Avenue West, Minot, ND 58707. Students are admitted in the Fall, application deadline March 1. *Fee:* $35.

North Dakota State University

Department of Psychology
Science and Mathematics
115 Minard Hall
Fargo, ND 58105
Telephone: (701) 231-8622
Fax: (701) 231-8426
E-mail: *NDSU.psych@ndsu.nodak.edu*
Web: *http://www.ndsu.nodak.edu/ndsu/psychology*

Department Established:

1965. Chairperson: James R. Council. Number of Faculty: total–full-time 15, part-time 6; women–full-time 2, part-time 5.

Programs and Degrees Offered:

Listed in the following order: Program area, degree type (T if terminal Master's), number awarded 7/00–6/01. Clinical MA (T) 7, Experimental PhD.

Student Applications/Admissions:

Student Applications

Clinical MA—Applications 2001–2002, 35. Total applicants accepted 2001–2002, 8. New applicants enrolled 2001–2002,

7. Total enrolled 2001–2002 full-time, 15. Openings 2002–2003, 8. The Median number of years required for completion of a degree are 2. The number of students enrolled full and part-time, who were dismissed or voluntarily withdrew from this program area were 1. *Experimental PhD*—Applications 2001–2002, 4. Total applicants accepted 2001–2002, 3. New applicants enrolled 2001–2002, 2. Total enrolled 2001–2002 full-time, 2. Openings 2002–2003, 4. The Median number of years required for completion of a degree are 5. The number of students enrolled full and part-time, who were dismissed or voluntarily withdrew from this program area were 0.

Admissions Requirements:

Scores: Entries appear in this order: required test or GPA, minimum score (if required), median score of students entering in 2001–2002. Master's Programs: GRE-V no minimum stated, 560; GRE-Q no minimum stated, 580; GRE-V+Q no minimum stated, 1155; GRE-Analytical no minimum stated, 620; GRE-V+Q+Analytical no minimum stated, 1730; GRE-Subject(Psych) no minimum stated, 580; overall undergraduate GPA no minimum stated, 3.72. Doctoral Programs: GRE-V no minimum stated, 580; GRE-Q no minimum stated, 630; GRE-V+Q no minimum stated, 1240; GRE-Analytical no minimum stated, 620; GRE-V+Q+Analytical no minimum stated, 1860; GRE-Subject(Psych) no minimum stated, 690; overall undergraduate GPA no minimum stated, 3.72; last 2 years GPA no minimum stated, 3.84; psychology GPA no minimum stated, 3.84; psychology GPA no minimum stated. *Other Criteria:* (importance of criteria rated low, medium, or high): GRE/MAT scores high, research experience high, work experience low, extracurricular activity low, clinically related public service low, GPA high, letters of recommendation medium, statement of goals and objectives medium. Interview for PhD prog. For students applying to the clinical master's program, clinically related experience is more important than for students in the experimental doctoral program.

Student Characteristics: The following represents characteristics of students in 2001–2002 in all graduate psychology programs in the department: Female–full-time 4, part-time 0; Male–full-time 5, part-time 0; African American/Black–full-time 0, part-time 0; Hispanic/Latino (a)–full-time 0, part-time 0; Asian/Pacific Islander–full-time 0, part-time 0; American Indian/Alaska Native–full-time 0, part-time 0.

Financial Information/Assistance:

Tuition for Full-Time Study: *Master's:* State residents per academic year $2,612, $148 per credit hour; nonstate residents: per academic year $6,324, $351 per credit hour. *Doctoral:* State residents: per academic year $2,612, $148 per credit hour; nonstate residents: per academic year $6,324, $351 per credit hour.

Financial Assistance:

First Year Students: Teaching assistantships available for first-year. Average amount paid per academic year: $5,218. Average number of hours worked per week: 20. Apply by 3/1. Tuition remission given: full. Research assistantships available for first-year. Average amount paid per academic year: $5,400. Average number of hours worked per week: 20. Apply by 3/1. Tuition remission given: full. Traineeships available for first-year. Apply by 3/1. Tuition remission given: full. Fellowships and scholarships available for first-year. Apply by 3/1. Tuition remission given: full.

Advanced Students: Teaching assistantships available for advanced students. Average amount paid per academic year: $10,000. Average number of hours worked per week: 20. Apply by 3/1. Tuition remission given: full. Research assistantships available for advanced students. Average amount paid per academic year: $10,000. Average number of hours worked per week: 20. Apply by 3/1. Tuition remission given: full. Traineeships available for advanced students. Apply by 3/1. Tuition remission given: full. Fellowships and scholarships available for advanced students. Average amount paid per academic year: $16,000. Average number of hours worked per week: 20. Apply by 3/1. Tuition remission given: full.

Contact Information: Of all students currently enrolled full-time, 100% benefited from one or more of the listed financial assistance programs. For information on financial assistance, contact: Graduate School, (701) 231-7346; www.ndsu.edu/ gradschool, Financial Aid Office, (701) 231-7533; www.ndsu.edu/finaid.

Internships/Practica: Our master's program in clinical psychology has a number of clinical practica that provide a variety of experiences. These include work with traditional one-on-one counseling, chronic pain, eating disorders, behavior analysis, developmental disabilities, child and adolescent psychotherapy, community mental health, and clinical neuropsychology. Research practica are available for doctoral students who wish to develop applied research skills and experiences. Sites include a private foundation for research on addictions and eating disorders, a nationally prominent organization for clinical drug trials, a chronic pain treatment program, a community mental health center, and several sites devoted to survey research.

Housing and Day Care: On-campus housing and day care facilities are available.

Employment of Department Graduates:

Master's Degree Graduates: Of those who graduated in the academic year 2000–2001, the following categories and numbers represent the post-graduate activities and employment of master's degree graduates: Enrolled in a psychology doctoral program (4), enrolled in a post-doctoral residency/fellowship (n/a), employed in independent practice (n/a), employed in other positions at a higher education institution (1), employed in a government agency (professional services) (1), still seeking employment (1).

Doctoral Degree Graduates: Of those who graduated in the academic year 2000–2001, the following categories and numbers represent the post-graduate activities and employment of doctoral degree graduates: Enrolled in a psychology doctoral program (n/a), enrolled in another graduate/professional program (n/a).

Additional Information:

Orientation, Objectives, and Emphasis of Department: Our strong research tradition has earned us a reputation as one of the best small psychology departments in the nation. Our clinical master's program is over 30 years old, and many of our alumni have gone on to earn PhD's at top institutions. Our doctoral program emphasizes our strengths in health psychology and neuroscience. PhD training is designed to produce graduates with records in research and teaching, which will make them highly competitive for employment in both traditional academic and nontraditional government and private sector settings. Our programs are based on a mentoring model in which students work closely with specific faculty members who match their research interests. Potential applicants should visit our website (www.ndsu .nodak.edu/ndsu/psychology) to learn about specific faculty interests and accomplishments.

Special Facilities or Resources: The department has state-of-the-art facilities for research in electrophysiology (including ERP), vision, and cognition, as well as ample space for other research projects. A center for research on multisensory integration is under development. As the largest population center in the region, Fargo-Moorhead serves as a center for medical services for a large geographic area. There are 4 major hospitals (including a VA), a medical school Department of Neuroscience, a neuroscience research institute, and a private pharmaceutical research institute, which offers opportunities for collaboration. NDSU has recently established a Research and Technology Park that will offer a variety of research experiences involving advanced technology. Many opportunities are likely to exist for psychology students.

Information for Students With Physical Disabilities: NDSU is fully committed to equal opportunity in educational programs and is in compliance with all applicable federal and state laws.

Application Information:
Send to: Office of Graduate Studies, PO Box 5790, NDSU, Fargo, ND 58105-5790. Materials available online at: http:// www.ndsu.nodak.edu/ gradschool/. Students are admitted in the Fall, application deadline March 1. For detailed information on programs, application, forms, and fellowships see our website: www.ndsu.no-dak.edu/ndsu/psychology. *Fee:* $30.

North Dakota, University of
Department of Psychology
P.O. Box 8380
Grand Forks, ND 58202-8380
Telephone: (701) 777-3451
Fax: (701) 777-3454
E-mail: *pam_bethke@und.nodak.edu*
Web: *http://www.und.nodak.edu/dept/psychol*

Department Established:
1921. Chairperson: Mark Grabe. Number of Faculty: total–full-time 16; women–full-time 3; minority–full-time 1.

Programs and Degrees Offered:
Listed in the following order: Program area, degree type (T if terminal Master's), number awarded 7/00–6/01. Clinical, general/ experimental.

APA Accreditation: Clinical PhD: full.

Student Applications/Admissions:
Admissions Requirements:
Scores: Entries appear in this order: required test or GPA, minimum score (if required), median score of students entering in 2001–2002. Master's Programs: GRE-V no minimum stated, 530; GRE-Q no minimum stated, 620; GRE-Analytical no minimum stated, 650; GRE-Subject(Psych) no minimum

stated, 590; overall undergraduate GPA no minimum stated, 3.77; last 2 years GPA no minimum stated, 3.87. Doctoral Programs: GRE-V no minimum stated; GRE-Q no minimum stated; GRE-Analytical no minimum stated; GRE-Subject(Psych) no minimum stated; last 2 years GPA no minimum stated; psychology GPA no minimum stated; psychology GPA no minimum stated. Not calculated separately

Other Criteria: (importance of criteria rated low, medium, or high): GRE/MAT scores medium, research experience high, work experience low, extracurricular activity, clinically related public service low, GPA medium, letters of recommendation medium, interview medium, statement of goals and objectives medium, Match faculty interests high.

Student Characteristics: The following represents characteristics of students in 2001–2002 in all graduate psychology programs in the department: Female–full-time 20, part-time 0; Male–full-time 15, part-time 0; African American/Black–full-time 0, part-time 0; Hispanic/Latino (a)–full-time 0, part-time 0; Asian/Pacific Islander–full-time 0, part-time 0; American Indian/Alaska Native–full-time 8, part-time 0.

Financial Information/Assistance:

Tuition for Full-Time Study: *Master's:* State residents per academic year $3,298; nonstate residents: per academic year $8,000. *Doctoral:* State residents: per academic year $3,298; nonstate residents: per academic year $8,000.

Financial Assistance:

First Year Students: Teaching assistantships available for first-year. Average amount paid per academic year: $9,000. Average number of hours worked per week: 15. Apply by 2/1. Tuition remission given: full.

Advanced Students: Traineeships available for advanced students. Tuition remission given: full.

Contact Information: Of all students currently enrolled full-time, 100% benefited from one or more of the listed financial assistance programs.

Internships/Practica: No information provided.

Housing and Day Care: On-campus housing and day care facilities are available.

Employment of Department Graduates:

Master's Degree Graduates: Of those who graduated in the academic year 2000–2001, the following categories and numbers represent the post-graduate activities and employment of master's degree graduates: Enrolled in a post-doctoral residency/fellowship (n/a), employed in independent practice (n/a).

Doctoral Degree Graduates: Of those who graduated in the academic year 2000–2001, the following categories and numbers represent the post-graduate activities and employment of doctoral degree graduates: Enrolled in a psychology doctoral program (n/a), enrolled in another graduate/professional program (n/a).

Additional Information:

Orientation, Objectives, and Emphasis of Department: The Psychology Department at the University of North Dakota offers doctoral programs in experimental and clinical psychology. Experimental students work out individualized programs of study and research with their advisory committees and are encouraged to develop research productivity early in the program. Coursework and research opportunities are strongest in the cognitive, social, and behavioral areas. Because the clinical program leads to a PhD rather than a professional PsyD degree, the emphasis is on the understanding of general psychological theory and the application of the scientific method to research issues. Clinical students work on developing interpersonal skills, and applying both analytic thought and intuitive judgment to problems of individuals, families, and communities. A variety of ongoing research programs help train students in the scientist-practitioner model. The clinical program works closely with the Indians in Psychology Doctoral Education (INPSYDE) program to facilitate entry of Native Americans into clinical psychology and to improve services available to rural, Native American communities. Finally, all students, with specific encouragement for the experimental students, have opportunities to develop expertise in teaching.

Special Facilities or Resources: The department has practicum placements for training in rural community mental health, a low faculty-student ratio, a campus-based psychological services center, and a faculty with active research programs. The Department also has dedicated laboratories capable of computer-assisted monitoring and recording of various physiological and psychological measures in humans (e.g., eye movements, reaction time, sexual response, autonomic nervous system function) as well as in animals (e.g., operant behavior). The University's library has a wide range of holdings in psychology and is tied into an interlibrary loan network. The Department's computers are available for research and provide access to UND's main computer system. Medline, PSYCLIT, and ERIC computer literature searches are available to students. Additional research facilities have been developed in conjunction with the adjacent USDA Grand Forks Human Nutrition Research Center and include a computerized neuropsychological laboratory, sleep EEG rooms, and animal behavior laboratories.

Information for Students With Physical Disabilities: The Department is housed in its own four-story building with an elevator and wheelchair accessibility.

Application Information:

Send to: Graduate School. Students are admitted in the Fall, application deadline February 1. *Fee:* $30.

Akron, University of

Department of Psychology
Buchtel College of Arts and Sciences
Arts & Sciences Building
Akron, OH 44325-4301
Telephone: (330) 972-7280
Fax: (330) 972-5174
E-mail: lsubich@uakron.edu
Web: http://www.uakron.edu/psychology

Department Established:

1921. Chairperson: Linda Mezydlo Subich. Number of Faculty: total–full-time 21; women–full-time 7.

Programs and Degrees Offered:

Listed in the following order: Program area, degree type (T if terminal Master's), number awarded 7/00–6/01. Applied cognitive aging PhD 2, applied cognitive aging (thes) MA (T) 3, counseling PhD 1, industrial/gerontological PhD, industrial/organizational PhD 11, industrial/organl (thesis) MA (T), industrial/organl (non thesis) MA (T) 5.

APA Accreditation: Counseling PhD: full.

Student Applications/Admissions:

Student Applications

Applied cognitive aging PhD—Applications 2001–2002, 7. Total applicants accepted 2001–2002, 5. New applicants enrolled 2001–2002, 3. Total enrolled 2001–2002 full-time, 10. The Median number of years required for completion of a degree are 4. The number of students enrolled full and part-time, who were dismissed or voluntarily withdrew from this program area were 2. *Applied cognitive aging (thes) MA*—Applications 2001–2002, 1. Total applicants accepted 2001–2002, 1. New applicants enrolled 2001–2002, 1. Total enrolled 2001–2002 full-time, 1. The Median number of years required for completion of a degree are 2. The number of students enrolled full and part-time, who were dismissed or voluntarily withdrew from this program area were 1. *Counseling PhD*—Applications 2001–2002, 105. Total applicants accepted 2001–2002, 7. New applicants enrolled 2001–2002, 5. Total enrolled 2001–2002 full-time, 19, part-time, 7. Openings 2002–2003, 5. The Median number of years required for completion of a degree are 7. The number of students enrolled full and part-time, who were dismissed or voluntarily withdrew from this program area were 1. *Industrial/gerontological PhD*—Applications 2001–2002, 1. Total enrolled 2001–2002 part-time, 1. Openings 2002–2003, 1. The Median number of years required for completion of a degree are n/a. The number of students enrolled full and part-time, who were dismissed or voluntarily withdrew from this program area were 0. *Industrial/organizational PhD*—Applications 2001–2002, 72. Total applicants accepted 2001–2002, 16. New applicants enrolled 2001–2002, 8. Total enrolled 2001–2002 full-time, 33, part-time, 24. Openings 2002–2003, 7. The Median number of years required for completion of a degree are 7. The number of students enrolled full and part-time, who were dismissed or voluntarily withdrew from this program area were 0. *Industrial/organl (thesis) MA*—Applications 2001–2002, 5. Total enrolled 2001–2002 part-time, 1. Openings 2002–2003, 1. The Median number of years required for completion of a degree are n/a. The number of students enrolled full and part-time, who were dismissed or voluntarily withdrew from this program area were 0. *Industrial/organl (non thesis) MA*—Applications 2001–2002, 28. Total applicants accepted 2001–2002, 10. New applicants enrolled 2001–2002, 6. Total enrolled 2001–2002 full-time, 9, part-time, 2. Openings 2002–2003, 4. The Median number of years required for completion of a degree are 2. The number of students enrolled full and part-time, who were dismissed or voluntarily withdrew from this program area were 0.

Admissions Requirements:

Scores: Entries appear in this order: required test or GPA, minimum score (if required), median score of students entering in 2001–2002. Master's Programs: GRE-V 500, 550; GRE-Q 500, 630; GRE-V+Q 1000, 1180; GRE-Subject(Psych) 500, 640; overall undergraduate GPA 3.00, 3.67; psychology GPA 3.00, 3.87. Doctoral Programs: GRE-V 550, 580; GRE-Q 550, 620; GRE-V+Q 1100, 1200; GRE-Subject(Psych) 550, 660; overall undergraduate GPA 3.25, 3.68; last 2 years GPA no minimum stated; psychology GPA 3.25, 3.85; psychology GPA 3.25, 3.90.

Other Criteria: (importance of criteria rated low, medium, or high): GRE/MAT scores high, research experience high, work experience low, extracurricular activity low, clinically related public service low, GPA high, letters of recommendation medium, interview medium, statement of goals and objectives high. Telephone interviews are used as a selection criterion only in the Counseling Psychology program.

Student Characteristics:

The following represents characteristics of students in 2001–2002 in all graduate psychology programs in the department: Female–full-time 46, part-time 7; Male–full-time 25, part-time 7; African American/Black–full-time 0, part-time 1; Hispanic/Latino (a)–full-time 0, part-time 1; Asian/Pacific Islander–full-time 0, part-time 0; American Indian/Alaska Native–full-time 0, part-time 0; Multi-ethnic–full-time 0, part-time 0; students subject to the Americans with Disabilities Act–full-time 0, part-time 0.

Financial Information/Assistance:

Tuition for Full-Time Study: *Master's:* State residents per academic year $7,290, $243 per credit hour; nonstate residents: per academic year $12,210, $407 per credit hour. *Doctoral:* State residents: per academic year $7,290, $243 per credit hour; nonstate residents: per academic year $12,210, $407 per credit hour.

Financial Assistance:

First Year Students: Teaching assistantships available for first-year. Average amount paid per academic year: $11,300. Average number of hours worked per week: 20. Apply by February 1st. Tuition remission given: full.

Advanced Students: Teaching assistantships available for advanced students. Average amount paid per academic year:

$10,500. Average number of hours worked per week: 20. Apply by April 15th. Tuition remission given: full. Research assistantships available for advanced students. Average amount paid per academic year: $10,500. Average number of hours worked per week: 20. Apply by April 15th. Tuition remission given: full.

Contact Information: Of all students currently enrolled full-time, 85% benefited from one or more of the listed financial assistance programs. For information on financial assistance, contact: Financial Aid and Employment, The University of Akron, Akron, OH 44325-6211 for loans, grants, and workstudy.

Internships/Practica: Practica are offered in the department's own Counseling Clinic and Center for Organizational Research. The department also offers a wide variety of community-based practica in industrial and public settings, hospitals, the University Counseling Center, and community mental health centers. For those doctoral students for whom a professional internship is required prior to graduation, 4 applied in 2000–2001. Of those who applied, 4 were placed in internships listed by the Association of Psychology Postdoctoral and Internship Programs (APPIC); 4 were placed in APA accredited internships.

Housing and Day Care: On-campus housing and day care facilities are available.

Employment of Department Graduates:

Master's Degree Graduates: Of those who graduated in the academic year 2000–2001, the following categories and numbers represent the post-graduate activities and employment of master's degree graduates: Enrolled in a psychology doctoral program (0), enrolled in another graduate/professional program (1), enrolled in a post-doctoral residency/fellowship (n/a), employed in independent practice (n/a), employed in an academic position at a university (0), employed in an academic position at a 2-year/4-year college (0), employed in other positions at a higher education institution (0), employed in a professional position in a school system (0), employed in business or industry (research/consulting) (1), employed in business or industry (management) (4), employed in a government agency (research) (0), employed in a government agency (professional services) (0), employed in a community mental health/counseling center (0), employed in a hospital/medical center (1), still seeking employment (0), other employment position (0).

Doctoral Degree Graduates: Of those who graduated in the academic year 2000–2001, the following categories and numbers represent the post-graduate activities and employment of doctoral degree graduates: Enrolled in a psychology doctoral program (n/a), enrolled in another graduate/professional program (n/a), enrolled in a post-doctoral residency/fellowship (0), employed in independent practice (0), employed in an academic position at a university (6), employed in an academic position at a 2-year/4-year college (0), employed in other positions at a higher education institution (1), employed in a professional position in a school system (0), employed in business or industry (research/consulting) (7), employed in business or industry (management) (0), employed in a government agency (research) (0), employed in a government agency (professional services) (0), employed in a community mental health/counseling center (0), employed in a hospital/medical center (0), still seeking employment (0), other employment position (0).

Additional Information:

Orientation, Objectives, and Emphasis of Department: The department subscribes to a scientist-practitioner model of training. Its objective is to provide a core of courses in general psychology with the student beginning study in the specialty area early in graduate training. The emphasis is on preparation for teaching as well as for research, industrial, or professional career paths. Industrial/organizational, industrial gerontological, and counseling psychology are the emphases at the MA and PhD level.

Special Facilities or Resources: The department has available to it several human performance laboratories with on-line computer control for research and instruction, an institute for life-span development and gerontology, small group laboratories, a counseling clinic, and the archives of the history of American psychology.

Application Information:
Send to: Admissions Committee, Department of Psychology, The University of Akron, Akron, OH 44325-4301. Students are admitted in the Fall, application deadline February 1st. We request a full application package be submitted at one time. *Fee:* $25. Minority applicants should apply to Dr. Lathardus Goggins, The Graduate School, The University of Akron, Akron, OH 44325-2101.

Bowling Green State University
Department of Psychology
Bowling Green, OH 43403
Telephone: (419) 372-2301
Fax: (419) 372-6013
E-mail: *khelm@bgnet.bgsu.edu*
Web: *http://www.bgsu.edu/departments/psych/*

Department Established:
1947. Chairperson: Dale S. Klopfer. Number of Faculty: total–full-time 30, part-time 10; women–full-time 10, part-time 3; minority–full-time 4.

Programs and Degrees Offered:
Listed in the following order: Program area, degree type (T if terminal Master's), number awarded 7/00–6/01. Clinical PhD 9, developmental PhD 1, experimental PhD 4, industrial/organizational PhD 3, quantitative PhD.

APA Accreditation: Clinical PhD: full.

Student Applications/Admissions:
Student Applications

Clinical PhD—Applications 2001–2002, 129. Total applicants accepted 2001–2002, 17. New applicants enrolled 2001–2002, 10. Total enrolled 2001–2002 full-time, 53. Openings 2002–2003, 10. The Median number of years required for completion of a degree are 6. The number of students enrolled full and part-time, who were dismissed or voluntarily withdrew from this program area were 0. *Developmental PhD*—Applications 2001–2002, 7. Total applicants accepted 2001–2002, 4. New applicants enrolled 2001–2002, 2. Total enrolled 2001–2002 full-time, 6. Openings 2002–2003, 3. The Median number of years required for completion of a degree are 5. The number of students enrolled full and part-time, who were dismissed or voluntarily withdrew from this program area were 0. *Experimental PhD*—Applications 2001–2002, 15. Total applicants accepted 2001–2002, 11. New applicants enrolled 2001–2002, 6. Total enrolled 2001–2002 full-time, 18. Openings 2002–2003, 6. The Median number of years required for completion of a degree are 6. The number of students enrolled full and part-time, who were dismissed or voluntarily withdrew from this program area were 0. *Industrial/organizational PhD*—Applications 2001–2002, 88. Total applicants accepted 2001–2002, 7. New applicants enrolled 2001–2002, 5. Total enrolled 2001–2002 full-time, 18. Openings 2002–2003, 6. The Median number of years required for completion of a degree are 5. The number of students enrolled full and part-time, who were dismissed or voluntarily withdrew from this program area were 2. *Quantitative PhD*—Applications 2001–2002, 3. Total applicants accepted 2001–2002, 1. New applicants enrolled 2001–2002, 1. Total enrolled 2001–2002 full-time, 3. Openings 2002–2003, 1. The number of students enrolled full and part-time, who were dismissed or voluntarily withdrew from this program area were 0.

Admissions Requirements:

Scores: Entries appear in this order: required test or GPA, minimum score (if required), median score of students entering in 2001–2002. Doctoral Programs: GRE-V no minimum stated, 560; GRE-Q no minimum stated, 680; GRE-Subject(Psych) no minimum stated, 660; overall undergraduate GPA no minimum stated, 3.79; last 2 years GPA no minimum stated; psychology GPA no minimum stated, 3.89; psychology GPA no minimum stated.

Other Criteria: (importance of criteria rated low, medium, or high): GRE/MAT scores high, research experience high, work experience medium, extracurricular activity medium, clinically related public service high, GPA high, letters of recommendation high, interview high, statement of goals and objectives high, research interest matches high. Clinically related public service and interview are high for Clinical program only.

Student Characteristics: The following represents characteristics of students in 2001–2002 in all graduate psychology programs in the department: Female–full-time 65, part-time 0; Male–full-time 33, part-time 0; African American/Black–full-time 2, part-time 0; Hispanic/Latino (a)–full-time 4, part-time 0; Asian/Pacific Islander–full-time 6, part-time 0; American Indian/Alaska Native–full-time 0, part-time 0; Multi-ethnic–full-time 0, part-time 0; students subject to the Americans with Disabilities Act–full-time 0, part-time 0.

Financial Information/Assistance:

Tuition for Full-Time Study: *Doctoral:* State residents: per academic year $7,312, $350 per credit hour; nonstate residents: per academic year $13,564, $648 per credit hour.

Financial Assistance:

First Year Students: Teaching assistantships available for first-year. Average amount paid per academic year: $9,300. Average number of hours worked per week: 20. Apply by Jan 1. Tuition remission given: full. Research assistantships available for first-year. Average amount paid per academic year: $9,300. Average number of hours worked per week: 20. Apply by Jan 1. Tuition remission given: full.

Advanced Students: Teaching assistantships available for advanced students. Average amount paid per academic year: $11,100. Average number of hours worked per week: 20. Apply by Jan 1. Tuition remission given: full. Research assistantships available for advanced students. Average amount paid per academic year: $11,100. Average number of hours worked per week: 20. Apply by Jan 1. Tuition remission given: full. Traineeships available for advanced students. Average amount paid per academic year: $11,100. Average number of hours worked per week: 20. Apply by Jan 1. Tuition remission given: full. Fellowships and scholarships available for advanced students. Average amount paid per academic year: $13,875. Average number of hours worked per week: 0. Apply by March. Tuition remission given: full.

Contact Information: Of all students currently enrolled full-time, 100% benefited from one or more of the listed financial assistance programs.

Internships/Practica: In their beginning years, clinical students are placed on Basic Clinical Skills practicum teams through the Department's Psychological Services Center (PSC) that provide experience with a broad range of clients and clinical problems. Students focus on the application of such basic clinical skills as psychological assessment and interventions, the integration of science and practice, case conceptualization, clinical judgement, and decision-making report writing. In their second year students begin receiving in-house training in psychotherapy through the PSC. As clinical students progress through the program they are placed on Advanced Clinical Skills teams that involve them in current projects providing "hands-on" experience with the integration of research and practice as it applies to individuals, health/ behavioral medicine, the community, or special populations (e.g., children; problem drinkers). More advanced clinical students are provided practicum opportunities consistent with their interest through a number of outside placements, such as community mental health centers, a nearby medical college, the university counseling center and health service, an inpatient child and adolescent facility, hospital-based rehabilitation centers, treatment centers for children and families, and programs for individuals with severe mental disabilities and emotional disorders. Industrial/ Organizational students are strongly encouraged to apply for a formal internship after completion of their Master's project. Although such experiences are encouraged and typically followed, internships are not required of I/O students for completion of the doctoral degree. Other experiences through coursework activities and Institute for Psychological Research and Application (IPRA) projects can collectively serve the same function as an internship. For those doctoral students for whom a professional internship is required prior to graduation, 9 applied in 2000–2001. Of those who applied, 9 were placed in internships listed by the Association of Psychology Postdoctoral and Internship Programs (APPIC); 9 were placed in APA accredited internships.

Housing and Day Care: No on-campus housing and day care facilities are available.

Employment of Department Graduates:

Master's Degree Graduates: Of those who graduated in the academic year 2000–2001, the following categories and numbers represent the post-graduate activities and employment of master's degree graduates: Enrolled in a post-doctoral residency/fellowship (n/a), employed in independent practice (n/a).

Doctoral Degree Graduates: Of those who graduated in the academic year 2000–2001, the following categories and numbers represent the post-graduate activities and employment of doctoral degree graduates: Enrolled in a psychology doctoral program (n/a), enrolled in another graduate/professional program (n/a), employed in an academic position at a university (2), employed in an academic position at a 2-year/4-year college (3), employed in business or industry (research/consulting) (3), employed in a government agency (professional services) (1), employed in a community mental health/counseling center (4), employed in a hospital/medical center (4).

Additional Information:

Orientation, Objectives, and Emphasis of Department: The primary goal of the PhD program is the development of scientists capable of advancing psychological knowledge. The program is characterized by both an emphasis on extensive academic training in general psychology and an early and continuing commitment to research. Although each graduate student will seek an area in which to develop his or her own expertise, students will be expected to be knowledgeable about many areas and will be encouraged to pursue interests that cross conventional specialty lines. The program is research oriented. Each student normally works in close association with a sponsor or chairperson whose special competence matches the student's interest but students are free to pursue research interests with any faculty member and in any area(s) they choose. Both basic and applied research are well represented within the department. The clinical program has concentrations in: clinical child, behavioral medicine, and community, as well as general clinical.

Special Facilities or Resources: The department is located in the psychology building with excellent facilities for all forms of research. The building houses all faculty and graduate students. The department operates a community-oriented Psychological Services Center and the Institute for Psychological Research and Application. The department operates its own computer facility with terminals to the mainframe computer available in the building, as well as a microcomputer facility.

Application Information:

Send to: Graduate Secretary. Students are admitted in the Fall, application deadline January 1. *Fee:* $30. Application fee may be deferred for members of minority groups.

Case Western Reserve University

Department of Psychology
Mather Memorial Building, 11220 Bellflower Road
Cleveland, OH 44106-7123
Telephone: (216) 368-2686
Fax: (216) 368-4891
E-mail: *rlg2@po.cwru.edu*
Web: *http://www.cwru.edu/artsci/pscl/pscl.html*

Department Established:

1928. Chairperson: Robert L. Greene. Number of Faculty: total–full-time 15, part-time 1; women–full-time 5; minority–full-time 2.

Programs and Degrees Offered:

Listed in the following order: Program area, degree type (T if terminal Master's), number awarded 7/00–6/01. Clinical PhD 8, experimental PhD 1, mental retardation PhD 1.

APA Accreditation: Clinical PhD: full.

Student Applications/Admissions:

Student Applications

Clinical PhD—Applications 2001–2002, 109. Total applicants accepted 2001–2002, 11. New applicants enrolled 2001–2002, 6. Total enrolled 2001–2002 full-time, 26. Openings 2002–2003, 5. *Experimental PhD*—Applications 2001–2002, 25. Total applicants accepted 2001–2002, 2. New applicants enrolled 2001–2002, 2. Total enrolled 2001–2002 full-time, 6. Openings 2002–2003, 3. The Median number of years required for completion of a degree are 5. *Mental retardation PhD*—Applications 2001–2002, 5. Total applicants accepted 2001–2002, 2. Total enrolled 2001–2002 full-time, 5. Openings 2002–2003, 2. The Median number of years required for completion of a degree are 4.

Admissions Requirements:

Scores: Entries appear in this order: required test or GPA, minimum score (if required), median score of students entering in 2001–2002. Doctoral Programs: GRE-V 600, 620; GRE-Q 600, 620; GRE-V+Q 1200, 1240; GRE-Subject(Psych) 600, 715; overall undergraduate GPA 3.00, 3.64; last 2 years GPA no minimum stated; psychology GPA no minimum stated; psychology GPA no minimum stated.

Other Criteria: (importance of criteria rated low, medium, or high): GRE/MAT scores high, research experience high, work experience medium, extracurricular activity low, clinically related public service medium, GPA high, letters of recommendation medium, interview high, statement of goals and objectives medium.

Student Characteristics: The following represents characteristics of students in 2001–2002 in all graduate psychology programs in the department: Female–full-time 30, part-time 0; Male–full-time 12, part-time 0; African American/Black–full-time 1, part-time 0; Hispanic/Latino (a)–full-time 0, part-time 0; Asian/Pacific Islander–full-time 3, part-time 0; American Indian/Alaska Native–full-time 0, part-time 0.

Financial Information/Assistance:

Tuition for Full-Time Study: *Doctoral:* State residents: $938 per credit hour; nonstate residents: $938 per credit hour.

Financial Assistance:

First Year Students: Research assistantships available for first-year. Average amount paid per academic year: $15,000. Tuition remission given: full. Traineeships available for first-year. Average amount paid per academic year: $15,000. Tuition remission given: full. Fellowships and scholarships available for first-year. Average amount paid per academic year: $15,000. Tuition remission given: full.

Advanced Students: Teaching assistantships available for advanced students. Average amount paid per academic year: $3,000. Research assistantships available for advanced students. Average amount paid per academic year: $15,000. Tuition remission given: full. Traineeships available for advanced students.

Average amount paid per academic year: $15,000. Tuition remission given: full. Fellowships and scholarships available for advanced students. Average amount paid per academic year: $15,000. Tuition remission given: full.

Contact Information: Of all students currently enrolled full-time, 100% benefited from one or more of the listed financial assistance programs. For information on financial assistance, contact: Office of Graduate Studies.

Internships/Practica: The clinical psychology graduate program has a number of practica placements in the Cleveland area. Students spend time in different settings during their second, third, and fourth years. In addition, the department requires two in-house practica in different types of psychotherapy.

Housing and Day Care: No on-campus housing and day care facilities are available.

Employment of Department Graduates:

Master's Degree Graduates: Of those who graduated in the academic year 2000–2001, the following categories and numbers represent the post-graduate activities and employment of master's degree graduates: Enrolled in a post-doctoral residency/fellowship (n/a), employed in independent practice (n/a).

Doctoral Degree Graduates: Of those who graduated in the academic year 2000–2001, the following categories and numbers represent the post-graduate activities and employment of doctoral degree graduates: Enrolled in a psychology doctoral program (n/a), enrolled in another graduate/professional program (n/a), enrolled in a post-doctoral residency/fellowship (4), employed in independent practice (1), employed in an academic position at a university (1).

Additional Information:

Orientation, Objectives, and Emphasis of Department: The graduate program seeks to give students a thorough grounding in basic areas of fact and theory in psychology, to train them in research methods by which knowledge in the behavioral sciences is advanced, and to prepare them for careers as teachers and researchers. During the first year, students begin a research clerkship under the tutelage of a faculty member. A variety of facilities and subject populations are available for the study of developmental processes, and a number of well-equipped laboratories are used for research in perception, memory, cognition, learning, physiological psychology, and individual differences. The department offers programs in experimental and clinical psychology. Within each of these major areas of concentration, a number of subspecializations are available. For clinical psychology, these include adult, child, and pediatric psychology. For experimental psychology, the areas of specialization are determined by the faculty member with whom the student works. These include, but are not limited to, developmental, human intelligence, aging, cognition, social, and physiological psychology.

Special Facilities or Resources: A number of excellent facilities for clinical training and research are available on campus and in the surrounding community, such as the Student Counseling Center of Case Western Reserve, University Hospitals, the Cleveland Veterans Administration Hospital, and MetroHealth Medical Center. The department also maintains an extensive perceptual development laboratory to study the developmental aspects of learning, cognition, and language acquisition, and several ex-perimental laboratories for the study of learning, perception, cognition, and physiological psychology, and social psychology.

Information for Students With Physical Disabilities: The university follows all federal guidelines covering accommodations for students with physical disabilities.

Application Information:
Send to: Department of Psychology, 10900 Euclid Ave., Cleveland, OH 44106-7123. Students are admitted in the Fall. Deadline is January 10 for Clinical and Respecialization, February 15 for Experimental and Mental Retardation. *Fee:* $25.

Cincinnati, University of (2001 data)
Department of Psychology
Arts and Sciences
429 Dyer Hall
Cincinnati, OH 45221-0376
Telephone: (513) 556-5580
Fax: (513) 556-1904
E-mail: *psych@uc.edu*
Web: *http://www.ucaswww.mcm.uc.edu/psychology*

Department Established:
1901. Chairperson: Kevin J. Corcoran. Number of Faculty: total–full-time 26, part-time 5; women–full-time 7, part-time 1; minority–full-time 4, part-time 1.

Programs and Degrees Offered:
Listed in the following order: Program area, degree type (T if terminal Master's), number awarded 7/00–6/01. Clinical-child PhD, clinical-general PhD, clinical-health PhD, clinical-neuropsychology PhD, experimental neuropsychology PhD, health PhD, human factors PhD.

APA Accreditation: Clinical PhD: full.

Student Applications/Admissions:
Student Applications
Clinical-child PhD—Applications 2001–2002, 20. Total applicants accepted 2001–2002, 3. New applicants enrolled 2001–2002, 3. Total enrolled 2001–2002 full-time, 13. Openings 2002–2003, 4. *Clinical-general PhD*—Applications 2001–2002, 60. Total applicants accepted 2001–2002, 3. New applicants enrolled 2001–2002, 2. Total enrolled 2001–2002 full-time, 15. Openings 2002–2003, 3. *Clinical-health PhD*—Applications 2001–2002, 110. Total applicants accepted 2001–2002, 4. New applicants enrolled 2001–2002, 4. Total enrolled 2001–2002 full-time, 11. Openings 2002–2003, 2. *Clinical-neuropsychology PhD*—Applications 2001–2002, 69. Total applicants accepted 2001–2002, 4. New applicants enrolled 2001–2002, 3. Total enrolled 2001–2002 full-time, 13. Openings 2002–2003, 2. *Experimental neuropsychology PhD*—Applications 2001–2002, 2. Total enrolled 2001–2002 full-time, 5. Openings 2002–2003, 1. *Health PhD*—Applications 2001–2002, 15. Total applicants accepted 2001–2002, 4. New applicants enrolled 2001–2002, 3. Total enrolled 2001–2002 full-time, 9. Openings 2002–2003, 2. *Human factors PhD*—Applications 2001–

2002, 18. Total applicants accepted 2001–2002, 4. New applicants enrolled 2001–2002, 4. Total enrolled 2001–2002 full-time, 15. Openings 2002–2003, 4.

Admissions Requirements:

Scores: Entries appear in this order: required test or GPA, minimum score (if required), median score of students entering in 2001–2002. Doctoral Programs: GRE-V no minimum stated, 580; GRE-Q no minimum stated, 625; GRE-Analytical no minimum stated, 645; GRE-Subject(Psych) no minimum stated, 620; overall undergraduate GPA no minimum stated. *Other Criteria:* (importance of criteria rated low, medium, or high): GRE/MAT scores medium, research experience high, work experience low, extracurricular activity low, clinically related public service medium, GPA medium, letters of recommendation high, interview high, statement of goals and objectives high, compatability w/ faculty high. Clinically related public service is only relevent to students applying to clinical.

Student Characteristics: The following represents characteristics of students in 2001–2002 in all graduate psychology programs in the department: Female–full-time 10, part-time 0; Male–full-time 7, part-time 0; African American/Black–full-time 1, part-time 0; Hispanic/Latino (a)–full-time 0, part-time 0; Asian/Pacific Islander–full-time 0, part-time 0; American Indian/Alaska Native–full-time 0, part-time 0.

Financial Information/Assistance:

Tuition for Full-Time Study: No information provided.

Financial Assistance:

First Year Students: No information provided.
Advanced Students: No information provided.
Contact Information: Of all students currently enrolled full-time, 100% benefited from one or more of the listed financial assistance programs. For information on financial assistance, contact: Our web site.

Internships/Practica: All clinical students in years three and four typically perform a paid, 20 hour/week clinical (or clinical research) training placement at an external site in the Greater Cincinnati area. Often these placements are at the University of Cincinnati Medical Center, the Children's Hospital Medical Center, or agencies affiliated with one of these centers. If students need a fifth year of support prior to going off on an APA-accredited clinical internship, the contacts that they make and the skills they gain during years three and four are often decisive in helping them land positions. While most of our non-clinical students do most of their paid training assignments within the department, there are also paid external training slots available for some of our students in private industry or with the federal government. For those doctoral students for whom a professional internship is required prior to graduation, 11 applied in 2000–2001. Of those who applied, 11 were placed in internships listed by the Association of Psychology Postdoctoral and Internship Programs (APPIC); 11 were placed in APA accredited internships.

Housing and Day Care: No on-campus housing and day care facilities are available.

Employment of Department Graduates:

Master's Degree Graduates: Of those who graduated in the academic year 2000–2001, the following categories and numbers represent the post-graduate activities and employment of master's degree graduates: Enrolled in a post-doctoral residency/fellowship (n/a), employed in independent practice (n/a).
Doctoral Degree Graduates: Of those who graduated in the academic year 2000–2001, the following categories and numbers represent the post-graduate activities and employment of doctoral degree graduates: Enrolled in a psychology doctoral program (n/a), enrolled in another graduate/professional program (n/a).

Additional Information:

Orientation, Objectives, and Emphasis of Department: The University of Cincinnati offers the PhD in psychology, including an APA-accredited training program in clinical psychology. Clinical students must specify a specialty training area, which might include child, health, neuropsychology or mental health policy and program evaluation. For students who do not want clinical training we offer training in human factors (we are part of the Southwest Ohio Human Factors/Ergonomics Consortium), applied social psychology, and experimental neuroscience. The doctoral program is limited to full-time students who show outstanding promise. It is VERY important that applicants identify one or more faculty members with whom they might wish to work. Students are admitted to the doctoral program to work with a faculty research mentor. Faculty mentors are responsible for ensuring that students are actively engaged in doing research from the very start of their graduate school career, and that this work leads successfully to a Master's thesis and a dissertation within the prescribed period.

Special Facilities or Resources: The department's clinical program has close ties to the medical centers and the UC School of Medicine (a site for fMRI research for our students) and a whole range of community agencies. The human factors faculty at UC are involved in the Southwest Ohio Human Factors/Ergonomics Consortium. Through this consortium, students have access to courses offered at nearby universities and to training sites at the Wright Patterson Air Force Base.

Application Information:

Send to: Admissions Secretary, Department of Psychology, University of Cincinnati, P.O. Box 210376, Cincinnati, OH 45221-0376. Students are admitted in the Fall, application deadline January 7th. *Fee:* $35.

Cincinnati, University of
Human Services/School Psychology
Education
P.O. Box 210002
Cincinnati, OH 45221-0002
Telephone: (513) 556-3335
Fax: (513) 556-3898
E-mail: *janet.graden@uc.edu*
Web: *http://www.uc.edu/schoolpsychology/*

Department Established:

1992. Head: Janet Graden. Number of Faculty: total–full-time 5, part-time 3; women–full-time 2, part-time 2.

Programs and Degrees Offered:
Listed in the following order: Program area, degree type (T if terminal Master's), number awarded 7/00–6/01. School psychology PhD (T) 4.

APA Accreditation: School PhD: probationary.

Student Applications/Admissions:
Student Applications
School psychology PhD—Applications 2001–2002, 14. Total applicants accepted 2001–2002, 5. New applicants enrolled 2001–2002, 5. Total enrolled 2001–2002 full-time, 15, part-time, 18. Openings 2002–2003, 6-8. The Median number of years required for completion of a degree are 6. The number of students enrolled full and part-time, who were dismissed or voluntarily withdrew from this program area were 2.

Admissions Requirements:
Scores: Entries appear in this order: required test or GPA, minimum score (if required), median score of students entering in 2001–2002. Master's Programs: GRE-V no minimum stated, 500; GRE-Q no minimum stated, 550; GRE-V+Q no minimum stated, 1050; GRE-Analytical no minimum stated; GRE-V+Q+Analytical no minimum stated; overall undergraduate GPA no minimum stated, 3.6; last 2 years GPA no minimum stated, 3.8; psychology GPA no minimum stated, 3.8. Doctoral Programs: GRE-V no minimum stated, 510; GRE-Q no minimum stated, 570; GRE-V+Q no minimum stated, 1080; GRE-Analytical no minimum stated, 650; GRE-V+Q+Analytical no minimum stated, 1730; GRE-Subject(Psych) no minimum stated, 600; overall undergraduate GPA no minimum stated, 3.94; last 2 years GPA no minimum stated, 4.00; psychology GPA no minimum stated, 3.9; psychology GPA no minimum stated.
Other Criteria: (importance of criteria rated low, medium, or high): GRE/MAT scores high, research experience medium, work experience medium, extracurricular activity medium, clinically related public service high, GPA high, letters of recommendation medium, interview high, statement of goals and objectives high. Specific, focused goals reflected for doctoral study.

Student Characteristics: The following represents characteristics of students in 2001–2002 in all graduate psychology programs in the department: Female–full-time 12, part-time 13; Male–full-time 1, part-time 2; African American/Black–full-time 0, part-time 2; Hispanic/Latino (a)–full-time 1, part-time 0; Asian/Pacific Islander–full-time 0, part-time 0; American Indian/Alaska Native–full-time 0, part-time 0; Multi-ethnic–full-time 1, part-time 0; students subject to the Americans with Disabilities Act–full-time 0, part-time 0.

Financial Information/Assistance:
Tuition for Full-Time Study: *Master's:* State residents per academic year $6,622; nonstate residents: per academic year $12,705, *Doctoral:* State residents: per academic year $6,622; nonstate residents: per academic year $12,705.

Financial Assistance:
First Year Students: Research assistantships available for first-year. Average amount paid per academic year: $10,000. Average number of hours worked per week: 20. Tuition remission given: full. Fellowships and scholarships available for first-year. Average amount paid per academic year: $15,000. Average number of hours worked per week: 20. Tuition remission given: full.
Advanced Students: Teaching assistantships available for advanced students. Average amount paid per academic year: $10,000. Average number of hours worked per week: 20. Tuition remission given: full. Research assistantships available for advanced students. Average amount paid per academic year: $10,000. Average number of hours worked per week: 20. Tuition remission given: full. Traineeships available for advanced students. Average amount paid per academic year: $25,000. Average number of hours worked per week: 40. Tuition remission given: partial. Fellowships and scholarships available for advanced students. Average amount paid per academic year: $15,000. Average number of hours worked per week: 20. Tuition remission given: full and partial.
Contact Information: Of all students currently enrolled full-time, 100% benefited from one or more of the listed financial assistance programs. For information on financial assistance, contact: Admission Coordinator.

Internships/Practica: All students, specialist and doctoral level, complete extensive practica experiences prior to internship. In the first year, students are enrolled in Externship, in which they are placed in schools (urban settings, K–12) to learn about schooling, educational issues, effective instruction, and roles and responsibilities of various personnel. Field experiences also occur to support foundation skills in applied behavior analysis and academic intervention. Throughout the second year, students are enrolled each quarter in an integrated Practicum experience, in which students obtain extensive supervised experience in delivery of services from a consultative, intervention-based model. Students collaborate to design, implement, and evaluate intervention plans for referred students in the practicum, incorporating elements of their learning from across coursework. In addition, they complete field experiences in counseling, functional assessment, and facilitation of group problem solving. All students, specialist and doctoral level, complete a 10-month, 1500 hour foundation school-based internship. These internships are arranged through the program and are paid. In the internship, students provide a full range of comprehensive school psychological services, with supervision from a licensed school psychologist and from university faculty. In addition, doctoral students complete a 500 hour internship related to their doctoral specialty area. For those doctoral students for whom a professional internship is required prior to graduation, 2 applied in 2000–2001.

Housing and Day Care: No on-campus housing and day care facilities are available.

Employment of Department Graduates:
Master's Degree Graduates: Of those who graduated in the academic year 2000–2001, the following categories and numbers represent the post-graduate activities and employment of master's degree graduates: Enrolled in a psychology doctoral program (3), enrolled in a post-doctoral residency/fellowship (n/a), employed in independent practice (n/a), employed in a professional position in a school system (4).

Doctoral Degree Graduates: Of those who graduated in the academic year 2000–2001, the following categories and numbers represent the post-graduate activities and employment of doctoral degree graduates: Enrolled in a psychology doctoral program (n/a), enrolled in another graduate/professional program (n/a), employed in an academic position at a university (1), employed in a professional position in a school system (4), employed in a government agency (professional services) (2).

Additional Information:

Orientation, Objectives, and Emphasis of Department: The School Psychology Program at the University of Cincinnati is dedicated to preparing highly competent professional school psychologists, at the specialist and doctoral level, according to the scientist practitioner model. The Program builds on foundations in psychology and education and fosters a special sensitivity to cultural diversity of all people and respect for the uniqueness and human dignity of each person. The major emphasis of the Program is the preparation of the school psychologist as a highly competent problem solver within a scientist practitioner framework. Students are prepared from an eco-behavioral model to develop, implement, and evaluate the effectiveness of strategies for preventing and resolving problem situations. The Program emphasizes the delivery of school psychological services from a collaborative consultation framework to prevent and remediate learning and adjustment problems of children and adolescents. Students learn to view problems from a systems/ecological perspective focusing on the child, family, school, and community. A child advocacy perspective, along with the scientist practitioner foundation, provides a framework for guiding decisions and practices to support positive outcomes for all children. Both theoretical and empirical bases of professional practice are emphasized and a diverse range of practical experiences are provided throughout all preparation (preschool to high school, in urban, suburban, and rural settings). In addition to these program themes, training at the doctoral level emphasizes advanced research and evaluation training, leadership, and systems-level change facilitation.

Special Facilities or Resources: The Program has access to excellent field-based training experiences through collaborative relationships with several local school districts and Head Start programs. The Program is linked to teacher preparation through professional development schools and collaboration with teacher interns in their training. Research facilities include statistical consultation for students, a college evaluation services center, and support for student research through college-sponsored mentoring grants.

Information for Students With Physical Disabilities: The University Office for Disability Services provides support to students with disabilities.

Application Information:
Send to: Admission Coordinator, School Psychology Program, University of Cincinnati, P.O. Box 210002, Cincinnati, OH 45221-0002. Students are admitted in the Fall, application deadline February 1. *Fee:* $35.

Cleveland State University
Department of Psychology
Arts & Sciences
East 24th Street at Euclid Avenue
Cleveland, OH 44115
Telephone: (216) 687-2544
Fax: (216) 687-9294
E-mail: *m.ashcraft@popmail.csuohio.edu*
Web: *http://www.csuohio.edu/psy/*

Department Established:
1964. Chairperson: Mark H. Ashcraft. Number of Faculty: total–full-time 20, part-time 12; women–full-time 8, part-time 7; minority–full-time 3, part-time 1; faculty subject to the Americans with Disabilities Act 3.

Programs and Degrees Offered:
Listed in the following order: Program area, degree type (T if terminal Master's), number awarded 7/00–6/01. Clinical/counseling MA (T) 18, consumer-industrial MA (T) 5, diversity management program MA (T) 17, experimental research MA (T) 4, school psychology 9.

Student Applications/Admissions:
Student Applications

Clinical/counseling MA—Applications 2001–2002, 91. Total applicants accepted 2001–2002, 18. New applicants enrolled 2001–2002, 12. Total enrolled 2001–2002 full-time, 38. Openings 2002–2003, 18. The Median number of years required for completion of a degree are 2. The number of students enrolled full and part-time, who were dismissed or voluntarily withdrew from this program area were 2. *Consumer-industrial MA*—Applications 2001–2002, 28. Total applicants accepted 2001–2002, 12. New applicants enrolled 2001–2002, 12. Total enrolled 2001–2002 full-time, 22, part-time, 1. Openings 2002–2003, 10. The Median number of years required for completion of a degree are 2. The number of students enrolled full and part-time, who were dismissed or voluntarily withdrew from this program area were 1. *Diversity management program MA*—Applications 2001–2002, 30. Total applicants accepted 2001–2002, 24. New applicants enrolled 2001–2002, 18. Total enrolled 2001–2002 part-time, 38. Openings 2002–2003, 25. The Median number of years required for completion of a degree are 2. *Experimental research MA*—Applications 2001–2002, 15. Total applicants accepted 2001–2002, 8. New applicants enrolled 2001–2002, 2. Total enrolled 2001–2002 full-time, 7, part-time, 3. Openings 2002–2003, 10. The Median number of years required for completion of a degree are 3. The number of students enrolled full and part-time, who were dismissed or voluntarily withdrew from this program area were 0.

Admissions Requirements:

Scores: Entries appear in this order: required test or GPA, minimum score (if required), median score of students entering in 2001–2002. Master's Programs: GRE-V no minimum stated, 445; GRE-Q no minimum stated, 530; GRE-Analytical no minimum stated, 520; GRE-Subject(Psych) no minimum stated, 3.72. Requirements vary per program. All programs look for GREs at about the 500 level; the Diversity program does not require GRE. Doctoral Programs: last 2 years GPA no minimum stated; psychology GPA no minimum stated; psychology GPA no minimum stated.

Other Criteria: (importance of criteria rated low, medium, or high): GRE/MAT scores medium, research experience medium, work experience low, clinically related public service low, GPA medium, letters of recommendation high, interview high, statement of goals and objectives high. Only the clinical/counseling requires an interview.

Student Characteristics: The following represents characteristics of students in 2001–2002 in all graduate psychology programs in the department: Female–full-time 61, part-time 21; Male–full-time 24, part-time 5; African American/Black–full-time 3, part-time 13; Hispanic/Latino (a)–full-time 1, part-time 0; Asian/Pacific Islander–full-time 1, part-time 1; American Indian/Alaska Native–full-time 0, part-time 0.

Financial Information/Assistance:

Tuition for Full-Time Study: *Master's:* State residents per academic year $6,649, $207 per credit hour; nonstate residents: per academic year $12,139, $414 per credit hour.

Financial Assistance:

First Year Students: Teaching assistantships available for first-year. Average number of hours worked per week: 10. Apply by Feb 15. Tuition remission given: full.

Advanced Students: Teaching assistantships available for advanced students. Average number of hours worked per week: 10. Apply by Mar 15. Tuition remission given: full.

Contact Information: Of all students currently enrolled full-time, 40% benefited from one or more of the listed financial assistance programs. Tuition grants only; does not carry a stipend. Traditionally, all first-year students receive a Teaching Assistantship in the form of full tuition remission; a limited number of advanced students also receive a TA award.

Internships/Practica: Master's students and 3rd year School Psychology students complete a 20 hour/40 hour per week internship, respectively, as part of the degree requirements. Practica during the two year curriculum are integrated into coursework.

Housing and Day Care: No on-campus housing and day care facilities are available.

Employment of Department Graduates:

Master's Degree Graduates: Of those who graduated in the academic year 2000–2001, the following categories and numbers represent the post-graduate activities and employment of master's degree graduates: Enrolled in a psychology doctoral program (8), enrolled in another graduate/professional program (5), enrolled in a post-doctoral residency/fellowship (n/a), employed in independent practice (n/a), employed in a professional position in a school system (8).

Doctoral Degree Graduates: Of those who graduated in the academic year 2000–2001, the following categories and numbers represent the post-graduate activities and employment of doctoral degree graduates: Enrolled in a psychology doctoral program (n/a), enrolled in another graduate/professional program (n/a).

Additional Information:

Orientation, Objectives, and Emphasis of Department: The clinical/counseling program is a CAMPP approved program. Departmental faculty provide significant breadth across the entire discipline as well as considerable depth in professional and applied areas. Substantive areas include social, developmental, cognitive-affective, clinical, industrial, and experimental psychology. The clinical-counseling program emphasizes theory, principles and application, and preparing general practitioners to provide psychological service in clinical, community, and educational settings. Orientations include psychodynamic, cognitive, and behavioral viewpoints in assessment and individual, group, family, and community intervention. A post-MA year fulfills requirements for certification as a school psychologist in Ohio. The primary goals of the experimental research program are to train students to conduct scientific research in a chosen area of psychology, and to prepare students for further graduate work in psychology or for employment in research settings and institutions. The three main components of the program are coursework in several core areas of psychology, an apprenticeship or tutorial relationship between the student and faculty adviser, and continual involvement in research activity that culminates in a master's thesis project. The program in consumer-industrial research prepares students to apply psychological concepts and research techniques in business and in institutional settings. It combines advanced quantitative research with hands-on experience involving problems and issues encountered in industrial and service organizations.

Special Facilities or Resources: Many students in the clinical-community program will apply to doctoral programs after obtaining their MA degree. To better prepare these students for doctoral study, we offer a formal thesis option, in which a student is permitted to drop two required courses and to complete a research thesis instead.

Application Information:
Send to: Graduate Secretary, Dept. of Psychology, Cleveland State University, 1983 East 24 St., Cleveland, OH 44115-2440. Students are admitted in the Fall, application deadline February 15. March 1 for research, consumer, no deadline for diversity. Applications received after February 15 may be considered. Rolling deadline for diversity. *Fee:* $25.

Dayton, University of
Department of Psychology
300 College Park Avenue
Dayton, OH 45469-1430
Telephone: (937) 229-2713
Fax: (937) 229-3900
E-mail: *biers@udayton.edu*
Web: *http://www.udayton.edu/~psych*

Department Established:
1937. Chairperson: David W. Biers. Number of Faculty: total–full-time 19, part-time 14; women–full-time 5, part-time 7; minority–full-time 1.

Programs and Degrees Offered:
Listed in the following order: Program area, degree type (T if terminal Master's), number awarded 7/00–6/01. Clinical MA (T) 4, experimental human factors MA (T) 1, general MA (T) 1.

Student Applications/Admissions:

Student Applications

Clinical MA—Applications 2001–2002, 43. Total applicants accepted 2001–2002, 24. New applicants enrolled 2001–2002, 12. Total enrolled 2001–2002 full-time, 23, part-time, 1. Openings 2002–2003, 12. Experimental human factors MA—Applications 2001–2002, 10. Total applicants accepted 2001–2002, 8. New applicants enrolled 2001–2002, 2. Total enrolled 2001–2002 full-time, 2, part-time, 9. Openings 2002–2003, 6. General MA—Applications 2001–2002, 10. Total applicants accepted 2001–2002, 7. New applicants enrolled 2001–2002, 3. Total enrolled 2001–2002 full-time, 4, part-time, 4. Openings 2002–2003, 5.

Admissions Requirements:

Scores: Entries appear in this order: required test or GPA, minimum score (if required), median score of students entering in 2001–2002. Master's Programs: GRE-V 450; GRE-Q 450; GRE-V+Q 1000; GRE-Subject(Psych) 450; overall undergraduate GPA 3.0; last 2 years GPA 3.0; psychology GPA 3.0. Doctoral Programs: last 2 years GPA no minimum stated; psychology GPA no minimum stated; psychology GPA no minimum stated.

Other Criteria: (importance of criteria rated low, medium, or high): GRE/MAT scores medium, research experience high, work experience medium, extracurricular activity low, clinically related public service medium, GPA high, letters of recommendation high, interview low, statement of goals and objectives medium.

Student Characteristics: The following represents characteristics of students in 2001–2002 in all graduate psychology programs in the department: Female–full-time 26, part-time 6; Male–full-time 3, part-time 8; African American/Black–full-time 3, part-time 0; Hispanic/Latino (a)–full-time 0, part-time 0; Asian/Pacific Islander–full-time 1, part-time 0; American Indian/Alaska Native–full-time 0, part-time 0.

Financial Information/Assistance:

Tuition for Full-Time Study: Master's: State residents $453 per credit hour; nonstate residents: $453 per credit hour.

Financial Assistance:

First Year Students: Teaching assistantships available for first-year. Average amount paid per academic year: $8,400. Average number of hours worked per week: 20. Apply by Mar 1. Tuition remission given: full. Research assistantships available for first-year. Average amount paid per academic year: $8,400. Average number of hours worked per week: 20. Apply by Mar 1. Tuition remission given: full. Traineeships available for first-year. Average amount paid per academic year: $6,000. Average number of hours worked per week: 17. Apply by Mar 1. Tuition remission given: partial.

Advanced Students: Teaching assistantships available for advanced students. Average amount paid per academic year: $8,400. Average number of hours worked per week: 20. Apply by Mar 1. Tuition remission given: full. Research assistantships available for advanced students. Average amount paid per academic year: $8,400. Average number of hours worked per week: 20. Apply by Mar 1. Tuition remission given: full.

Contact Information: Of all students currently enrolled full-time, 79% benefited from one or more of the listed financial assistance programs. For information on financial assistance, contact: Student Aid Office for Work Study or Loan Information.

Internships/Practica: A limited number of paid traineeship placements at local mental health agencies are available for both first and second year clinical students. These traineeships satisfy the programs's practica requirements and include partial tuition remission. The human factors practicum is required of all program students and enables the student to gain practical experience working for governmental agencies or industrial firms during the summer between their first and second years.

Housing and Day Care: No on-campus housing and day care facilities are available.

Employment of Department Graduates:

Master's Degree Graduates: Of those who graduated in the academic year 2000–2001, the following categories and numbers represent the post-graduate activities and employment of master's degree graduates: Enrolled in a psychology doctoral program (1), enrolled in a post-doctoral residency/fellowship (n/a), employed in independent practice (n/a), employed in business or industry (research/consulting) (1), employed in a government agency (professional services) (1), employed in a community mental health/counseling center (3).

Doctoral Degree Graduates: Of those who graduated in the academic year 2000–2001, the following categories and numbers represent the post-graduate activities and employment of doctoral degree graduates: Enrolled in a psychology doctoral program (n/a), enrolled in another graduate/professional program (n/a).

Additional Information:

Orientation, Objectives, and Emphasis of Department: The Department of Psychology offers graduate programs leading to the MA degree in clinical, experimental-human factors, and general psychology. Emphasis is placed on integrating theory and literature with appropriate applied experience and on competence in the development of relevant research. This is the product of individual supervision and a low student-to-faculty ratio. The aim of the department is to prepare the student for doctoral training or employment at the MA level in an applied/community setting, in research, or in teaching. A recent survey has shown that over 90% of our MA graduates who applied for doctoral programs in the last 23 years were accepted. Also, 93% of Human Factors students seeking employment at the MA level have found jobs in human factors or a closely related field.

Special Facilities or Resources: Laboratory and computer facilities are available to support student and faculty research. These include microlaboratory facilities for research in cognitive science, human factors, social psychology, and clinical psychology as well as a state-of-the-art Information Science Research Laboratory for multidisciplinary research in human-computer interaction. In addition, research opportunities are available through the university's Research Institute, the Center for Family and Community Research, and local community agencies.

Application Information:

Send to: Office of Graduate Applications and Records, University of Dayton, Dayton, OH 45469-1619. Apply on-line at www.udayton.edu/~gradsch/app.htm. Students are admitted in the Fall, application deadline March 1. Fee: $30. Fee waived if apply on-line.

Kent State University

Department of Psychology
Kent, OH 44242
Telephone: (330) 672-2166
Fax: (330) 672-3786
E-mail: ksupsych@kent.edu
Web: http://www.kent.edu/psychology/

Department Established:

1936. Chairperson: Maria S. Zaragoza. Number of Faculty: total–full-time 28, part-time 10; women–full-time 13, part-time 4; minority–full-time 5, part-time 1; faculty subject to the Americans with Disabilities Act 2.

Programs and Degrees Offered:

Listed in the following order: Program area, degree type (T if terminal Master's), number awarded 7/00–6/01. Clinical PhD 6, experimental PhD 7.

APA Accreditation: Clinical PhD: full.

Student Applications/Admissions:

Student Applications

Clinical PhD—Applications 2001–2002, 124. Total applicants accepted 2001–2002, 21. New applicants enrolled 2001–2002, 11. Total enrolled 2001–2002 full-time, 75. Openings 2002–2003, 10. The Median number of years required for completion of a degree are 8. The number of students enrolled full and part-time, who were dismissed or voluntarily withdrew from this program area were 0. Experimental PhD—Applications 2001–2002, 39. Total applicants accepted 2001–2002, 20. New applicants enrolled 2001–2002, 8. Total enrolled 2001–2002 full-time, 46. Openings 2002–2003, 10. The Median number of years required for completion of a degree are 5. The number of students enrolled full and part-time, who were dismissed or voluntarily withdrew from this program area were 1.

Admissions Requirements:

Scores: Entries appear in this order: required test or GPA, minimum score (if required), median score of students entering in 2001–2002. Doctoral Programs: GRE-V no minimum stated, 540; GRE-Q no minimum stated, 610; GRE-Analytical no minimum stated; GRE-Subject(Psych) no minimum stated; overall undergraduate GPA 3.00, 3.65; last 2 years GPA no minimum stated; psychology GPA no minimum stated; psychology GPA 3.50.

Other Criteria: (importance of criteria rated low, medium, or high): GRE/MAT scores high, research experience high, work experience low, extracurricular activity low, clinically related public service low, GPA high, letters of recommendation high, interview high, statement of goals and objectives high.

Student Characteristics: The following represents characteristics of students in 2001–2002 in all graduate psychology programs in the department: Female–full-time 85, part-time 0; Male–full-time 36, part-time 0; African American/Black–full-time 6, part-time 0; Hispanic/Latino (a)–full-time 5, part-time 0; Asian/Pacific Islander–full-time 1, part-time 0; American Indian/Alaska Native–full-time 0, part-time 0.

Financial Information/Assistance:

Tuition for Full-Time Study: *Master's:* State residents per academic year $6,248, $280 per credit hour; nonstate residents: per academic year $10,710, $530 per credit hour. *Doctoral:* State residents: per academic year $6,248, $280 per credit hour; nonstate residents: per academic year $10,710, $530 per credit hour.

Financial Assistance:

First Year Students: Teaching assistantships available for first-year. Average amount paid per academic year: $10,500. Average number of hours worked per week: 20. Apply by January 1. Tuition remission given: full. Research assistantships available for first-year. Average amount paid per academic year: $10,500. Average number of hours worked per week: 20. Apply by January 1. Tuition remission given: full.

Advanced Students: Teaching assistantships available for advanced students. Average amount paid per academic year: $10,500. Average number of hours worked per week: 20. Apply by January 1. Tuition remission given: full. Research assistantships available for advanced students. Average amount paid per academic year: $10,500. Average number of hours worked per week: 20. Apply by January 1. Tuition remission given: full. Traineeships available for advanced students. Average amount paid per academic year: $10,000. Average number of hours worked per week: 20. Apply by January 1. Tuition remission given: full. Fellowships and scholarships available for advanced students. Average amount paid per academic year: $6,000. Average number of hours worked per week: 20. Apply by January 1. Tuition remission given: full.

Contact Information: Of all students currently enrolled full-time, 100% benefited from one or more of the listed financial assistance programs.

Internships/Practica: Seven semesters of clinical practica are required through the department's Psychological Clinic; 1,000 hours of supervised clinical experience at local field placement sites are provided with additional hours sometimes available; 2,000 hours of supervised internship experience in a program accredited by the American Psychological Association (these are competitive internships) are required. For those doctoral students for whom a professional internship is required prior to graduation, 10 applied in 2000–2001. Of those who applied, 9 were placed in internships listed by the Association of Psychology Postdoctoral and Internship Programs (APPIC); 9 were placed in APA accredited internships.

Housing and Day Care: No on-campus housing and day care facilities are available.

Employment of Department Graduates:

Master's Degree Graduates: Of those who graduated in the academic year 2000–2001, the following categories and numbers represent the post-graduate activities and employment of master's degree graduates: Enrolled in a psychology doctoral program (22), enrolled in a post-doctoral residency/fellowship (n/a), employed in independent practice (n/a).

Doctoral Degree Graduates: Of those who graduated in the academic year 2000–2001, the following categories and numbers represent the post-graduate activities and employment of doctoral degree graduates: Enrolled in a psychology doctoral program (n/a), enrolled in another graduate/professional program (n/a), enrolled in a post-doctoral residency/fellowship (4), employed in an academic position at a university (2), employed in an academic position at a 2-year/4-year college (2), employed in a professional position in a school system (2), employed in business or industry (research/consulting) (1), employed in a government agency (professional services) (2).

Additional Information:

Orientation, Objectives, and Emphasis of Department: Doctoral training is provided in clinical and in various experimental areas. Students in clinical or experimental may major in health psychology. There is also an opportunity for subspecialization in child/developmental psychology. A common program of basic core courses is required of all students. Training facilities and laboratories are freely available to graduate students. The doctoral program requires full-time, continuous enrollment and is strongly research oriented. Students are encouraged to become involved in a variety of research projects before they begin dissertation work. The program's objective is to train those who can contribute through teaching, research, service, innovation, and administration.

Special Facilities or Resources: The department has well-equipped laboratories available for human and animal experimentation. Research opportunities are also available in various mental health settings in the area. Clinical training opportunities are available in the Psychological Clinic, which is staffed by clinical faculty and graduate students. The Applied Psychology Center supports research focused on psychological problems of social significance.

Information for Students With Physical Disabilities: The Office of Disabled Student Services exists to ensure that students with disabilities have the technical, academic, and emotional support necessary to achieve academic success at Kent State University.

Application Information:

Send to: Chair, Graduate Admissions, Department of Psychology, Kent State University, Kent, OH 44242. Students are admitted in the Fall, application deadline January 1. *Fee:* $30.

Kent State University
Educational Foundations and Special Services/ Graduate Program in School Psychology
Education
405 White Hall
Kent, OH 44242
Telephone: (330) 672-2294
Fax: (330) 672-2512
E-mail: *ctelzrow@kent.edu*
Web: *http://spsy.educ.kent.edu*

Department Established:

1969. Department Chair: Paul Zionts. Number of Faculty: total–full-time 3, part-time 2; women–full-time 2, part-time 2.

Programs and Degrees Offered:

Listed in the following order: Program area, degree type (T if terminal Master's), number awarded 7/00–6/01. School Psychology PhD 3.

APA Accreditation: School PhD: full.

Student Applications/Admissions:
Student Applications

School Psychology PhD—Applications 2001–2002, 12. Total applicants accepted 2001–2002, 3. New applicants enrolled 2001–2002, 3. Total enrolled 2001–2002 full-time, 13, part-time, 3. Openings 2002–2003, 4. The Median number of years required for completion of a degree are 0. The number of students enrolled full and part-time, who were dismissed or voluntarily withdrew from this program area were 0.

Admissions Requirements:

Scores: Entries appear in this order: required test or GPA, minimum score (if required), median score of students entering in 2001–2002. Doctoral Programs: GRE-V 550, 615; overall undergraduate GPA 3.5, 2.99; last 2 years GPA no minimum stated; psychology GPA no minimum stated; psychology GPA no minimum stated.

Other Criteria: (importance of criteria rated low, medium, or high): GRE/MAT scores high, research experience medium, work experience medium, extracurricular activity medium, clinically related public service medium, GPA medium, letters of recommendation high, interview high, statement of goals and objectives high, written exam high.

Student Characteristics: The following represents characteristics of students in 2001–2002 in all graduate psychology programs in the department: Female–full-time 5, part-time 8; Male–full-time 1, part-time 2; African American/Black–full-time 0, part-time 0; Hispanic/Latino (a)–full-time 0, part-time 1; Asian/Pacific Islander–full-time 0, part-time 0; American Indian/Alaska Native–full-time 0, part-time 0.

Financial Information/Assistance:

Tuition for Full-Time Study: *Doctoral:* State residents: per academic year $2,977, $266 per credit hour; nonstate residents: per academic year $5,721, $516 per credit hour.

Financial Assistance:

First Year Students: No information provided.

Advanced Students: Teaching assistantships available for advanced students. Average amount paid per academic year: $9,000. Average number of hours worked per week: 20. Research assistantships available for advanced students. Average amount paid per academic year: $9,000. Average number of hours worked per week: 20. Traineeships available for advanced students. Average amount paid per academic year: $9,000. Average number of hours worked per week: 20. Fellowships and scholarships available for advanced students. Average amount paid per academic year: $9,000. Average number of hours worked per week: 20.

Contact Information: Of all students currently enrolled full-time, 29% benefited from one or more of the listed financial assistance programs. For information on financial assistance, contact: Office of Student Financial Aid, 103 Michael Schwartz Center, Kent State University, Kent, OH 44242.

Internships/Practica: EdS Program: Students enroll in a full year (two semesters) of practica, and work 300 hours in a wide variety of educational and on-campus clinic settings. For students who enter the program without a teaching certificate, additional field experiences in educationally-related settings are acquired. All students participate in a full academic year internship (9–10 months) in educational settings. To the degree funding is available, state-funded, paid internships are provided. PhD program: Students enroll in one full year of practica, and work a minimum of 600 hours in a wide variety of educational and on-campus clinic settings. For students who enter the program without a teaching certificate, additional field experiences in educationally-related settings are acquired. All students participate in a full academic year internship (9–10 months) in educational settings. To the degree funding is available, state-funded, paid internships are provided. Additional supervised hours (approximately 400) are obtained in a personally-designed internship experience to develop research/teaching/leadership skills. For those doctoral students for whom a professional internship is required prior to graduation, 1 applied in 2000–2001.

Housing and Day Care: No on-campus housing and day care facilities are available.

Employment of Department Graduates:

Master's Degree Graduates: Of those who graduated in the academic year 2000–2001, the following categories and numbers represent the post-graduate activities and employment of master's degree graduates: Enrolled in a post-doctoral residency/fellowship (n/a), employed in independent practice (n/a).

Doctoral Degree Graduates: Of those who graduated in the academic year 2000–2001, the following categories and numbers represent the post-graduate activities and employment of doctoral degree graduates: Enrolled in a psychology doctoral program (n/a), enrolled in another graduate/professional program (n/a), employed in other positions at a higher education institution (1), employed in a professional position in a school system (2).

Additional Information:

Orientation, Objectives, and Emphasis of Department: Kent State University's 95 semester hour program in school psychology—while continuing to teach traditional tools and methodologies—has increased its emphasis on consultation, collaboration with teachers/co-professionals/parents, instructional consultation, and those intervention-based multifactored evaluations which incorporate direct, authentic assessments. The KSU program is based on the assumption that individuals cannot be understood apart from the contexts in which they live and grow, and reflects a practitioner-scientist model. We prepare students to think and act as both social scientists and applied psychologists. As social scientists we expect them to become involved in research, educational program planning, and policy formation. In turn, they learn to serve as a resource to school personnel and parents—with the goal of promoting children's positive psychological development through prevention and intervention. As practitioners they must have preparation in rendering direct intervention-focused assessment services which incorporate multifactored evaluations. The objectives of the doctoral program in school psychology are to ensure, through the scientist-practitioner model of training, that each student exhibits the personal characteristics, academic knowledge, and practitioner-competencies that fully qualify him or her as a professional psychologist dedicated to the practice of school psychology.

Special Facilities or Resources: The Center for Training and Research within the Graduate College of Education is available to assist in research activities and to provide research-focused outreach support to educational partners in the community. The Center for Counseling and Human Development, a clinic setting within the College of Education that provides multiple rooms for group and individual counseling and assessment, is available for supervised practica experiences. The Family Child Learning Center provides model services to infants and toddlers with disabilities and their families, as well as providing interdisciplinary training experiences and research opportunities in the areas of early intervention environments and parent-child interactions. The Child Development Center is a state-of-the-art on-campus early childhood facility for typically-developing children ages birth–five, which provides applied and research-based experiences for students and faculty.

Information for Students With Physical Disabilities: Special transportation services and an extensive program of facilities modification have resulted in opening all areas of the campus to students with physical disabilities. The KSU Student Disability Services provides such services as referrals for attendant care, notetaking, reading, and interpreters; preferred registration, test proctoring; tape material arrangements; academic and personal counseling; and special parking arrangements.

Application Information:

Send to: Dr. Cathy Telzrow, Program Coordinator, 405 White Hall, Kent State University, Kent, OH 44242. Students are admitted in the Fall, application deadline November 1; Spring, application deadline March 1; Summer, application deadline July 1. *Fee:* $30.

Miami University (Ohio)
Department of Psychology
Oxford, OH 45056
Telephone: (513) 529-2400
Fax: (513) 529-2420
E-mail: *howardcm@muohio.edu*
Web: *http://www.muohio.edu/~psycwis/*

Department Established:

1888. Chairperson: Karen Maitland Schilling. Number of Faculty: total–full-time 28, part-time 3; women–full-time 10, part-time 1; minority–full-time 2.

Programs and Degrees Offered:

Listed in the following order: Program area, degree type (T if terminal Master's), number awarded 7/00–6/01. Brain & Cognitive Science PhD, clinical PhD 5, developmental PhD, social PhD 1.

APA Accreditation: Clinical PhD: full.

Student Applications/Admissions:

Student Applications

Brain & Cognitive Science PhD—Applications 2001–2002, 14. Total applicants accepted 2001–2002, 8. New applicants enrolled 2001–2002, 8. Total enrolled 2001–2002 full-time, 15, part-time, 4. Openings 2002–2003, 2. *Clinical PhD*—Applications 2001–2002, 79. Total applicants accepted 2001–2002, 6. New applicants enrolled 2001–2002, 6. Total enrolled 2001–2002 full-time, 30, part-time, 10. Openings 2002–2003, 7. The Median number of years required for completion of a degree are 5. *Developmental PhD*—Applications 2001–2002, 2. Total enrolled 2001–2002 full-time, 2. Openings 2002–2003, 1. The Median number of years required for completion of a degree are na. The number of students enrolled full and part-time, who were dismissed or voluntarily withdrew from this program area were 0. *Social PhD*—Applications 2001–2002, 24. Total applicants accepted 2001–2002, 3. New applicants enrolled 2001–2002, 3. Total enrolled 2001–2002 full-time, 17. Openings 2002–2003, 3. The Median number of years required for completion of a degree are 5. The number of students enrolled full and part-time, who were dismissed or voluntarily withdrew from this program area were 0.

Admissions Requirements:

Scores: Entries appear in this order: required test or GPA, minimum score (if required), median score of students entering in 2001–2002. Doctoral Programs: GRE-V no minimum stated, 580; GRE-Q no minimum stated, 640; GRE-Analytical no minimum stated, 640; GRE-Subject(Psych) no minimum stated, 610; overall undergraduate GPA no minimum stated, 3.7; last 2 years GPA no minimum stated; psychology GPA no minimum stated; psychology GPA no minimum stated.

Other Criteria: (importance of criteria rated low, medium, or high): GRE/MAT scores, research experience high, work experience medium, extracurricular activity medium, clinically related public service medium, GPA medium, letters of recommendation high, interview medium, statement of goals and objectives high.

Student Characteristics: The following represents characteristics of students in 2001–2002 in all graduate psychology programs in the department: Female–full-time 42, part-time 11; Male–full-time 21, part-time 6; African American/Black–full-time 9, part-time 0; Hispanic/Latino (a)–full-time 1, part-time 1; Asian/Pacific Islander–full-time 1, part-time 2; American Indian/Alaska Native–full-time 0, part-time 0; Multi-ethnic–full-time 0, part-time 0; students subject to the Americans with Disabilities Act–full-time 0, part-time 0.

Financial Information/Assistance:

Tuition for Full-Time Study: *Doctoral:* State residents: per academic year $3,305, $276 per credit hour; nonstate residents: per academic year $6,824, $570 per credit hour.

Financial Assistance:

First Year Students: Teaching assistantships available for first-year. Average amount paid per academic year: $10,734. Average number of hours worked per week: 20. Apply by January. Tuition remission given: full. Research assistantships available for first-year. Average amount paid per academic year: $10,734. Average number of hours worked per week: 20. Apply by January. Tuition remission given: full.

Advanced Students: Teaching assistantships available for advanced students. Average amount paid per academic year: $12,937. Average number of hours worked per week: 20. Apply by January. Tuition remission given: full. Research assistantships available for advanced students. Average amount paid per academic year: $10,734. Average number of hours worked per week: 20. Apply by January. Tuition remission given: full. Traineeships available for advanced students. Average amount paid per academic year: $10,734. Average number of hours worked per week: 20. Apply by January. Tuition remission given: full. Fellowships and scholarships available for advanced students. Average amount paid per academic year: $12,996. Average number of hours worked per week: 0. Apply by January. Tuition remission given: full.

Contact Information: Of all students currently enrolled full-time, 100% benefited from one or more of the listed financial assistance programs. For information on financial assistance, contact: The Graduate School, 102 Roudebush, Miami University, Oxford, Ohio 45056.

Internships/Practica: There are opportunities for students to engage in practica and internships as well as conduct applied research. Traineeships for advanced clinical students are available in a wide range of settings including community mental health centers, hospitals, and school systems. For those doctoral students for whom a professional internship is required prior to graduation, 5 applied in 2000–2001. Of those who applied, 5 were placed in internships listed by the Association of Psychology Postdoctoral and Internship Programs (APPIC); 5 were placed in APA accredited internships.

Housing and Day Care: On-campus housing and day care facilities are available.

Employment of Department Graduates:

Master's Degree Graduates: Of those who graduated in the academic year 2000–2001, the following categories and numbers represent the post-graduate activities and employment of master's degree graduates: Enrolled in a post-doctoral residency/fellowship (n/a), employed in independent practice (n/a).

Doctoral Degree Graduates: Of those who graduated in the academic year 2000–2001, the following categories and numbers represent the post-graduate activities and employment of doctoral degree graduates: Enrolled in a psychology doctoral program (n/a), enrolled in another graduate/professional program (n/a), enrolled in a post-doctoral residency/fellowship (6), employed in independent practice (0), employed in other positions at a higher education institution (1).

Additional Information:

Orientation, Objectives, and Emphasis of Department: The goal of the department is to provide an environment in which students thrive intellectually. We strive for a balance between enough structure to gauge student progress and provide grounding in the breadth of psychology and enough freedom for students to design programs optimal to their own professional goals. The department provides training and experience in research, teaching, and application of psychology. The department offers basic and applied research orientations in all programs. The clinical program emphasizes a theory-research-practicum combination, so that graduates will be able to function in a variety of academic and service settings. The objective of the department is to produce skilled, informed, and enthusiastic psychologists, capable of contributing to their field in a variety of ways.

Special Facilities or Resources: The department has two social interaction laboratories with remote-controlled audio-visual equipment that are specially equipped for research on group processes and observing parent-child interactions. Four psychobiology laboratories offer advanced facilities for neurological recording, drug delivery, and pharmacological and histological analyses. The Center of Ergonomic Research provides a variety of ergonomic equipment used in studying human-computer interactions. The Psychology Clinic includes group and child therapy rooms, individual assessment and therapy rooms, a test library, conference room, and offices for the clinic director and a full-time secretary. Clinical services are offered in a training or research context to university students and the Oxford community. Research with children is facilitated by a good relationship with the Oxford public schools. Access to clinical populations is available through the Psychology Clinic and through cooperative arrangements with mental health centers in nearby communities.

Information for Students With Physical Disabilities: Benton Hall, housing the Department of Psychology, is fully accessible for individuals with physical disabilities. Through the Office of Disability Resources, accommodations and support services are made available to any qualified student.

Application Information:
Send to: The Graduate School, 102 Roudebush, Miami University, Oxford, Ohio 45056. Students are admitted in the Fall, application deadline January 1. *Fee:* $35.

Ohio State University
Department of Psychology
Social and Behavioral Sciences
238 Townshend Hall, 1885 Neil Avenue Mall
Columbus, OH 43210-1222
Telephone: (614) 292-4112
Fax: (614) 292-4537
E-mail: *psygrad@osu.edu*
Web: *http://www.psy.ohio-state.edu*

Department Established:
1907. Chairperson: Gifford Weary. Number of Faculty: total–full-time 53, part-time 7; women–full-time 13, part-time 4; minority–full-time 3.

Programs and Degrees Offered:
Listed in the following order: Program area, degree type (T if terminal Master's), number awarded 7/00–6/01. Clinical PhD 8, cognitive/experimental PhD 2, counseling psychology PhD 7, developmental PhD 5, industrial/organizational PhD 2, mental retardation/developmen PhD 2, psychobio & behav. neuroscience PhD 1, quantitative PhD 3, social PhD 2.

APA Accreditation: Clinical PhD: full. Counseling PhD: full.

Student Applications/Admissions:
Student Applications
Clinical PhD—Applications 2001–2002, 118. Total applicants accepted 2001–2002, 11. New applicants enrolled 2001–2002, 7. Total enrolled 2001–2002 full-time, 45. Openings 2002–2003, 5. The Median number of years required for completion of a degree are 6. The number of students enrolled full and part-time, who were dismissed or voluntarily withdrew from this program area were 1. *Cognitive/experimental PhD*—Applications 2001–2002, 36. Total applicants accepted 2001–2002, 15. New applicants enrolled 2001–2002, 6. Total enrolled 2001–2002 full-time, 14. Openings 2002–2003, 5. The Median

number of years required for completion of a degree are 6. The number of students enrolled full and part-time, who were dismissed or voluntarily withdrew from this program area were 0. *Counseling psychology PhD*—Applications 2001–2002, 129. Total applicants accepted 2001–2002, 15. New applicants enrolled 2001–2002, 8. Total enrolled 2001–2002 full-time, 40, part-time, 3. Openings 2002–2003, 5. The Median number of years required for completion of a degree are 6. The number of students enrolled full and part-time, who were dismissed or voluntarily withdrew from this program area were 0. *Developmental PhD*—Applications 2001–2002, 26. Total applicants accepted 2001–2002, 10. New applicants enrolled 2001–2002, 3. Total enrolled 2001–2002 full-time, 6. Openings 2002–2003, 3. The Median number of years required for completion of a degree are 6. The number of students enrolled full and part-time, who were dismissed or voluntarily withdrew from this program area were 4. *Industrial/organizational PhD*—Applications 2001–2002, 0. Total enrolled 2001–2002 full-time, 9, part-time, 1. The Median number of years required for completion of a degree are 4. The number of students enrolled full and part-time, who were dismissed or voluntarily withdrew from this program area were 0. *Mental retardation/developmen PhD*—Applications 2001–2002, 12. Total applicants accepted 2001–2002, 3. New applicants enrolled 2001–2002, 2. Total enrolled 2001–2002 full-time, 7. The Median number of years required for completion of a degree are 10. The number of students enrolled full and part-time, who were dismissed or voluntarily withdrew from this program area were 0. *Psychobio & behav. neuroscience PhD*—Applications 2001–2002, 26. Total applicants accepted 2001–2002, 9. New applicants enrolled 2001–2002, 7. Total enrolled 2001–2002 full-time, 9. Openings 2002–2003, 5. The Median number of years required for completion of a degree are 6. The number of students enrolled full and part-time, who were dismissed or voluntarily withdrew from this program area were 3. *Quantitative PhD*—Applications 2001–2002, 14. Total applicants accepted 2001–2002, 12. New applicants enrolled 2001–2002, 5. Total enrolled 2001–2002 full-time, 10. Openings 2002–2003, 3. The Median number of years required for completion of a degree are 5. The number of students enrolled full and part-time, who were dismissed or voluntarily withdrew from this program area were 2. *Social PhD*—Applications 2001–2002, 76. Total applicants accepted 2001–2002, 21. New applicants enrolled 2001–2002, 9. Total enrolled 2001–2002 full-time, 29, part-time, 1. Openings 2002–2003, 7. The Median number of years required for completion of a degree are 6. The number of students enrolled full and part-time, who were dismissed or voluntarily withdrew from this program area were 2.

Admissions Requirements:
Scores: Entries appear in this order: required test or GPA, minimum score (if required), median score of students entering in 2001–2002. Doctoral Programs: GRE-V 600, 625; GRE-Q 600, 700; GRE-V+Q 1200, 1325; GRE-Analytical 600, 705; overall undergraduate GPA 3.2, 3.73; last 2 years GPA no minimum stated; psychology GPA no minimum stated; psychology GPA no minimum stated. GRE exceptions can be made when there is other evidence of high potential. Please note that to qualify for University Fellowships, the above required scores must be met.
Other Criteria: (importance of criteria rated low, medium, or high): GRE/MAT scores research experience high, work

experience low, extracurricular activity low, clinically related public service low, GPA letters of recommendation high, statement of goals and objectives high, GRE scores & overall GPA high. Clinical and Counseling areas rank Interview as High.

Student Characteristics: The following represents characteristics of students in 2001–2002 in all graduate psychology programs in the department: Female–full-time 114, part-time 2; Male–full-time 55, part-time 3; African American/Black–full-time 11, part-time 2; Hispanic/Latino (a)–full-time 4, part-time 1; Asian/Pacific Islander–full-time 9, part-time 0; American Indian/Alaska Native–full-time 0, part-time 0; students subject to the Americans with Disabilities Act–full-time 1.

Financial Information/Assistance:

Tuition for Full-Time Study: *Doctoral:* State residents: per academic year $8,444, $272 per credit hour; nonstate residents: per academic year $21,872, $608 per credit hour.

Financial Assistance:

First Year Students: Teaching assistantships available for first-year. Average amount paid per academic year: $9,450. Average number of hours worked per week: 20. Apply by Dec. 31. Tuition remission given: full. Research assistantships available for first-year. Average amount paid per academic year: $9,450. Average number of hours worked per week: 20. Apply by Dec. 31. Tuition remission given: full. Fellowships and scholarships available for first-year. Average amount paid per academic year: $12,000. Average number of hours worked per week: 0. Apply by Dec. 31. Tuition remission given: full.

Advanced Students: Teaching assistantships available for advanced students. Average amount paid per academic year: $10,800. Average number of hours worked per week: 20. Apply by Dec. 31. Tuition remission given: full. Research assistantships available for advanced students. Average amount paid per academic year: $10,800. Average number of hours worked per week: 20. Apply by Dec. 31. Tuition remission given: full. Traineeships available for advanced students. Average amount paid per academic year: $10,800. Average number of hours worked per week: 20. Apply by Dec. 31. Tuition remission given: full.

Contact Information: Of all students currently enrolled full-time, 99% benefited from one or more of the listed financial assistance programs. No specific information available. Every applicant is considered for financial assistance.

Internships/Practica: For those doctoral students for whom a professional internship is required prior to graduation, 16 applied in 2000–2001. Of those who applied, 9 were placed in internships listed by the Association of Psychology Postdoctoral and Internship Programs (APPIC); 7 were placed in APA accredited internships.

Housing and Day Care: On-campus housing and day care facilities are available.

Employment of Department Graduates:

Master's Degree Graduates: Of those who graduated in the academic year 2000–2001, the following categories and numbers represent the post-graduate activities and employment of master's degree graduates: Enrolled in a psychology doctoral program (28), enrolled in another graduate/professional program (0), enrolled in a post-doctoral residency/fellowship (n/a), employed in independent practice (n/a).

Doctoral Degree Graduates: Of those who graduated in the academic year 2000–2001, the following categories and numbers represent the post-graduate activities and employment of doctoral degree graduates: Enrolled in a psychology doctoral program (n/a), enrolled in another graduate/professional program (n/a), enrolled in a post-doctoral residency/fellowship (10), employed in independent practice (2), employed in an academic position at a university (6), employed in other positions at a higher education institution (1), employed in a professional position in a school system (1), employed in business or industry (research/consulting) (6), employed in business or industry (management) (1), employed in a hospital/medical center (1), still seeking employment (2), other employment position (2).

Additional Information:

Orientation, Objectives, and Emphasis of Department: The department is comprehensive in nature, with PhD programs in nearly all the major fields of study in psychology. The programs all strive to educate psychological scientists, and there is consequently a strong emphasis on research training in the doctoral programs, even in the applied areas. Our objective is to prepare theoretically sophisticated psychologists who leave us with effective skills to build upon in their later careers and with the ability to grow as psychology develops as a science and profession.

Special Facilities or Resources: There are several research labs specializing in the various programs of the OSU psychology department. Please visit www.psy.ohio-state.edu and click on Labs in the header for more detailed information. In addition, since The Ohio State University is a well-known and well-established research institution, there are several non-department labs located throughout the campus that would be of possible interest to Psychology Graduate Students.

Application Information:
Send to: Students are strongly encouraged to apply on-line. The on-line application is available at www.psy.ohio-state.edu then click on Graduate for further instructions. Otherwise, applications may be mailed to: Graduate Studies Coordinator, 123 Townshend Hall, 1885 Neil Avenue, Columbus, OH 43210-1222. Students are admitted in the Fall, application deadline December 31. Our clinical program has an earlier deadline of December 15. *Fee:* $30.

Ohio State University
School of Physical Activity and Educational Services
Education
1760 Neil Avenue
Columbus, OH 43210
Telephone: (614) 292-0956
Fax: (614) 688-4613
E-mail: *sherman.4@osu.edu*
Web: *http://www.coe.ohio-state.edu-paes*

Department Established:
1996. director: Michael Sherman. Number of Faculty: total–full-time 3; women–full-time 3; minority–full-time 1.

Programs and Degrees Offered:
Listed in the following order: Program area, degree type (T if terminal Master's), number awarded 7/00–6/01. School MA (T) 7.

Student Applications/Admissions:
Student Applications
School MA—Applications 2001–2002, 50. Total applicants accepted 2001–2002, 16. New applicants enrolled 2001–2002, 12. Total enrolled 2001–2002 full-time, 20. Openings 2002–2003, 15.

Admissions Requirements:
Scores: Entries appear in this order: required test or GPA, minimum score (if required), median score of students entering in 2001–2002. Master's Programs: GRE-V 500, 643; GRE-Q 500, 607; GRE-V+Q 1000; overall undergraduate GPA 3.0, 3.6. Doctoral Programs: GRE-V 500, 687; GRE-Q 500, 653; GRE-V+Q 1000; overall undergraduate GPA 3.0, 3.7; last 2 years GPA no minimum stated; psychology GPA no minimum stated; psychology GPA 3.2, 3.8.
Other Criteria: (importance of criteria rated low, medium, or high): GRE/MAT scores medium, research experience medium, work experience medium, extracurricular activity low, clinically related public service medium, GPA high, letters of recommendation high, interview high, statement of goals and objectives high, congruence with program high.

Student Characteristics: The following represents characteristics of students in 2001–2002 in all graduate psychology programs in the department: Female–full-time 20, part-time 2; Male–full-time 2, part-time 1; African American/Black–full-time 1, part-time 0; Hispanic/Latino (a)–full-time 2, part-time 0; Asian/Pacific Islander–full-time 0, part-time 0; American Indian/Alaska Native–full-time 0, part-time 0.

Financial Information/Assistance:
Tuition for Full-Time Study: *Master's:* State residents per academic year $6,306; nonstate residents: per academic year $16,377. *Doctoral:* State residents: per academic year $6,306; nonstate residents: per academic year $16,377.

Financial Assistance:
First Year Students: Fellowships and scholarships available for first-year. Average amount paid per academic year: $10,000. Apply by January 1. Tuition remission given: full.
Advanced Students: Fellowships and scholarships available for advanced students. Average amount paid per academic year: $10,000. Apply by January 1. Tuition remission given: full.
Contact Information: Of all students currently enrolled full-time, 40% benefited from one or more of the listed financial assistance programs. For information on financial assistance, contact: Office of Student Services at (614) 292-6787.

Internships/Practica: Master's students are engaged in practica during their two years of study. All students gain experience in an urban school district as well as either a rural or suburban setting. Students are involved in a 9-month school-based internship in the Central Ohio area. Internships are paid. For those doctoral students for whom a professional internship is required prior to graduation, 1 applied in 2000–2001. Of those who applied, 1 were placed in APA accredited internships.

Housing and Day Care: On-campus housing and day care facilities are available.

Employment of Department Graduates:
Master's Degree Graduates: Of those who graduated in the academic year 2000–2001, the following categories and numbers represent the post-graduate activities and employment of master's degree graduates: Enrolled in a post-doctoral residency/fellowship (n/a), employed in independent practice (n/a), employed in a professional position in a school system (7).
Doctoral Degree Graduates: Of those who graduated in the academic year 2000–2001, the following categories and numbers represent the post-graduate activities and employment of doctoral degree graduates: Enrolled in a psychology doctoral program (n/a), enrolled in another graduate/professional program (n/a).

Additional Information:
Orientation, Objectives, and Emphasis of Department: The Counselor Education, Rehabilitation Services, and School Psychology Section in the School of Physical Activity and Educational Services emphasizes the preparation of individuals who can function in human services settings such as public and private schools and universities, social agencies, state and federal government agencies, business and industry, hospitals and health care facilities, and rehabilitation agencies. Emphasizing primary prevention, the program will help students, learners, and clients achieve optimal levels of human functioning and advocate for organizations and systems that promote optimal levels of human functioning. Students in the program may undertake coursework to emphasize one or more of the three areas: (a) counselor education; (b) rehabilitation services; (c) school psychology.

Information for Students With Physical Disabilities: The Ohio State University has a very active Office of Disabilities Services.

Application Information:
Send to: School of Physical Activity and Educational Services, Student Services and Academic Programs, 215 Pomerene Hall, 1760 Neil Avenue, Columbus, OH 43210. Students are admitted in the Fall, application deadline January 15. *Fee:* $30.

Ohio University
Department of Psychology
Porter Hall
Athens, OH 45701-2979
Telephone: (740) 593-1707
Fax: (740) 593-0579
E-mail: *psychology@ohiou.edu*
Web: *http://www.psych.ohiou.edu*

Department Established:
1922. Chairperson: Ben Ogles. Number of Faculty: total–full-time 29, part-time 12; women–full-time 11, part-time 3; minority–full-time 1.

Programs and Degrees Offered:
Listed in the following order: Program area, degree type (T if terminal Master's), number awarded 7/00–6/01. Clinical PhD 11, experimental PhD 2, organizational PhD 2.

APA Accreditation: Clinical PhD: full.

Student Applications/Admissions:

Student Applications

Clinical PhD—Applications 2001–2002, 142. Total applicants accepted 2001–2002, 29. New applicants enrolled 2001–2002, 10. Total enrolled 2001–2002 full-time, 46. Openings 2002–2003, 10. Experimental PhD—Applications 2001–2002, 21. Total applicants accepted 2001–2002, 13. New applicants enrolled 2001–2002, 6. Total enrolled 2001–2002 full-time, 17. Openings 2002–2003, 7. Organizational PhD—Applications 2001–2002, 22. Total applicants accepted 2001–2002, 6. New applicants enrolled 2001–2002, 1. Total enrolled 2001–2002 full-time, 6. Openings 2002–2003, 3.

Admissions Requirements:

Scores: Entries appear in this order: required test or GPA, minimum score (if required), median score of students entering in 2001–2002. Doctoral Programs: GRE-V no minimum stated, 550; GRE-Q no minimum stated, 630; GRE-V+Q no minimum stated; GRE-Analytical no minimum stated, 670; GRE-V+Q+Analytical no minimum stated; GRE-Subject(Psych) no minimum stated, 650; overall undergraduate GPA no minimum stated, 3.69; last 2 years GPA no minimum stated; psychology GPA no minimum stated; psychology GPA no minimum stated.

Other Criteria: (importance of criteria rated low, medium, or high): GRE/MAT scores medium, research experience high, work experience low, extracurricular activity low, clinically related public service medium, GPA high, letters of recommendation high, interview low, statement of goals and objectives high.

Student Characteristics: The following represents characteristics of students in 2001–2002 in all graduate psychology programs in the department: Female–full-time 41, part-time 0; Male–full-time 28, part-time 0; African American/Black–full-time 0, part-time 0; Hispanic/Latino (a)–full-time 1, part-time 0; Asian/Pacific Islander–full-time 8, part-time 0; American Indian/Alaska Native–full-time 1, part-time 0; Multi-ethnic–full-time 0, part-time 0; students subject to the Americans with Disabilities Act–full-time 0, part-time 0.

Financial Information/Assistance:

Tuition for Full-Time Study: No information provided.

Financial Assistance:

First Year Students: Teaching assistantships available for first-year. Average amount paid per academic year: $12,000. Average number of hours worked per week: 15. Tuition remission given: full. Research assistantships available for first-year. Average amount paid per academic year: $12,000. Average number of hours worked per week: 15. Tuition remission given: full. Tuition remission given: full. Fellowships and scholarships available for first-year. Average amount paid per academic year: $15,000. Average number of hours worked per week: 15. Tuition remission given: full.

Advanced Students: Teaching assistantships available for advanced students. Average amount paid per academic year: $12,000. Average number of hours worked per week: 15. Tuition remission given: full. Research assistantships available for advanced students. Average amount paid per academic year: $12,000. Average number of hours worked per week: 15. Tuition remission given: full. Traineeships available for advanced students. Average amount paid per academic year: $12,000. Average number of hours worked per week: 15. Tuition remission given: full. Fellowships and scholarships available for advanced students. Average amount paid per academic year: $15,000. Average number of hours worked per week: 15. Tuition remission given: full.

Contact Information: Of all students currently enrolled full-time, 100% benefited from one or more of the listed financial assistance programs. For information on financial assistance, contact: Assistant Chair for Graduate Studies.

Internships/Practica: Clinical doctoral interns are placed in APA-approved, one-year internships throughout the country. Supervised training in clinical skills is provided for all clinical students in area mental health agencies. Such training is in addition to traineeships and internships. Supervised practicum experience is provided for organizational students in area industries and organizations. For those doctoral students for whom a professional internship is required prior to graduation, 11 applied in 2000–2001. Of those who applied, 10 were placed in internships listed by the Association of Psychology Postdoctoral and Internship Programs (APPIC); 10 were placed in APA accredited internships.

Housing and Day Care: On-campus housing and day care facilities are available.

Employment of Department Graduates:

Master's Degree Graduates: Of those who graduated in the academic year 2000–2001, the following categories and numbers represent the post-graduate activities and employment of master's degree graduates: Enrolled in a post-doctoral residency/fellowship (n/a), employed in independent practice (n/a).

Doctoral Degree Graduates: Of those who graduated in the academic year 2000–2001, the following categories and numbers represent the post-graduate activities and employment of doctoral degree graduates: Enrolled in a psychology doctoral program (n/a), enrolled in another graduate/professional program (n/a).

Additional Information:

Orientation, Objectives, and Emphasis of Department: The clinical doctoral program is a scientist/practitioner program, offering balanced training in research and clinical skills. Practicum training is offered in intellectual and personality assessment. Therapy sequences are offered in health psychology, individual and group psychotherapy, behavior modification, and child psychology. Traineeships are available at the university counseling center and area mental health agencies. The doctoral program in experimental psychology provides intensive training in scholarly and research activities, preparing the student for positions in academic and research settings.

Special Facilities or Resources: Anderson Laboratories, adjacent to the psychology building, are equipped for a wide variety of human research activities, including psychophysiology, cognitive, social, and health. The department has its own clinic, which is used to train clinical doctoral students. Two computer laboratories in the Psychology Department, one with 30 microcomputers and one with 8 microcomputers, are also available for student research. All computer services are free of charge. Ohio University recently awarded the Psychology Department selective-investment funds, which represent a major increase in funding for the department.

Information for Students With Physical Disabilities: Porter Hall, the site for nearly all our training, is handicapped accessible. The university also has a coordinator for disability services.

Application Information:

Send to: Office of Graduate Student Services, Ohio University, Wilson Hall, 304 Athens, OH 45701-2979. Students are admitted in the Fall, application deadline January 15. *Fee:* $30. The fee is waived or deferred with a statement of need from the financial aid office of the applicant's college.

Toledo, University of
Department of Psychology
Mail Stop 948
Toledo, OH 43606
Telephone: (419) 530-2717
Fax: (419) 530-8479
E-mail: *robert.haaf@utoledo.edu*
Web: *http://www.utoledo.edu/psychology/*

Department Established:

Chairperson: Robert A. Haaf. Number of Faculty: total–full-time 21, part-time 3; women–full-time 9, part-time 2; minority–full-time 3.

Programs and Degrees Offered:

Listed in the following order: Program area, degree type (T if terminal Master's), number awarded 7/00–6/01. Behavioral science PhD 4, clinical PhD 6, general MA (T) 2.

APA Accreditation: Clinical PhD: full.

Student Applications/Admissions:

Student Applications

Behavioral science PhD—Applications 2001–2002, 32. New applicants enrolled 2001–2002, 5. Total enrolled 2001– 2002 full-time, 21, part-time, 5. Openings 2002–2003, 8. The Median number of years required for completion of a degree are 7. *Clinical PhD*—Applications 2001–2002, 108. New applicants enrolled 2001–2002, 6. Total enrolled 2001–2002 full-time, 26. Openings 2002–2003, 5. The Median number of years required for completion of a degree are 6. The number of students enrolled full and part-time, who were dismissed or voluntarily withdrew from this program area were 1. *General MA*—Applications 2001–2002, 8. Total enrolled 2001–2002 full-time, 2. Openings 2002–2003, 4. The Median number of years required for completion of a degree are 2.

Admissions Requirements:

Scores: Entries appear in this order: required test or GPA, minimum score (if required), median score of students entering in 2001–2002. Master's Programs: GRE-V+Q+Analytical no minimum stated; GRE-Subject(Psych) no minimum stated. Doctoral Programs: GRE-V+Q+Analytical no minimum stated; GRE-Subject(Psych) no minimum stated; last 2 years GPA no minimum stated; psychology GPA no minimum stated; psychology GPA no minimum stated.
Other Criteria: (importance of criteria rated low, medium, or high): GRE/MAT scores medium, research experience me-

dium, work experience low, clinically related public service medium, GPA high, letters of recommendation high, interview high, statement of goals and objectives high.

Student Characteristics: The following represents characteristics of students in 2001–2002 in all graduate psychology programs in the department: Female–full-time 7, part-time 0; Male–full-time 1, part-time 0; African American/Black–full-time 0, part-time 0; Hispanic/Latino (a)–full-time 0, part-time 0; Asian/Pacific Islander–full-time 0, part-time 0; American Indian/Alaska Native–full-time 0, part-time 0.

Financial Information/Assistance:

Tuition for Full-Time Study: *Master's:* State residents per academic year $6,335, $264 per credit hour; nonstate residents: $570 per credit hour. *Doctoral:* State residents: per academic year $6,335, $264 per credit hour; nonstate residents: $570 per credit hour.

Financial Assistance:

First Year Students: Research assistantships available for first-year. Average amount paid per academic year: $8,000. Average number of hours worked per week: 20. Tuition remission given: full. Fellowships and scholarships available for first-year. Tuition remission given: full.

Advanced Students: Teaching assistantships available for advanced students. Average amount paid per academic year: $9,100. Average number of hours worked per week: 20. Tuition remission given: full. Research assistantships available for advanced students. Average amount paid per academic year: $9,100. Average number of hours worked per week: 20. Tuition remission given: full. Traineeships available for advanced students. Average amount paid per academic year: $9,100. Average number of hours worked per week: 20. Tuition remission given: full. Fellowships and scholarships available for advanced students. Tuition remission given: full.

Contact Information: Of all students currently enrolled full-time, 100% benefited from one or more of the listed financial assistance programs. For information on financial assistance, contact: Department of Psychology.

Internships/Practica: No information provided.

Housing and Day Care: On-campus housing and day care facilities are available.

Employment of Department Graduates:

Master's Degree Graduates: Of those who graduated in the academic year 2000–2001, the following categories and numbers represent the post-graduate activities and employment of master's degree graduates: Enrolled in a post-doctoral residency/fellowship (n/a), employed in independent practice (n/a).

Doctoral Degree Graduates: Of those who graduated in the academic year 2000–2001, the following categories and numbers represent the post-graduate activities and employment of doctoral degree graduates: Enrolled in a psychology doctoral program (n/a), enrolled in another graduate/professional program (n/a).

Additional Information:

Orientation, Objectives, and Emphasis of Department: The clinical psychology program's main goal is to train scholar-practitioners. A second goal of the program is to generate research that can contribute to the fund of general knowledge. The third goal of the program is to provide public service. The program in behavioral science is founded on the assumption that we are charged with the training of students who will become researchers in one of several branches of psychology. Most of these students will also become college or university teachers. For these reasons, the program places major emphasis on the student's development as a researcher and a teacher. The department requires that students have a thorough grounding in research methods, possess a high level of knowledge in their chosen specialty, have a broad knowledge of general psychology, and show competence as a teacher. Areas of student emphasis in the behavioral science program: cognitive, developmental, psychobiology/animal learning, social psychology.

Application Information:

Send to: Graduate School, University of Toledo, Toledo, OH 43606. Students are admitted in the Fall. Application deadline January 15 for Clinical, March 15 for Behavioral Science stipend, May 15 for Behavioral Science admission. *Fee:* $35.

Wright State University
Department of Psychology
College of Science and Mathematics
335 Fawcett Hall, 3640 Colonel Glenn Highway
Dayton, OH 45435-0001
Telephone: (937) 775-3348
Fax: (937) 775-3347
E-mail: *psych@wright.edu*
Web: *http://www.psych.wright.edu*

Department Established:

1964. Chairperson: Wayne L. Shebilske. Number of Faculty: total–full-time 21, part-time 18; women–full-time 7, part-time 9; minority–full-time 1, part-time 2.

Programs and Degrees Offered:

Listed in the following order: Program area, degree type (T if terminal Master's), number awarded 7/00–6/01. Human factors PhD (T) 6, industrial/organizational PhD.

Student Applications/Admissions:

Student Applications

Human factors PhD—Applications 2001–2002, 19. Total applicants accepted 2001–2002, 9. New applicants enrolled 2001–2002, 9. Total enrolled 2001–2002 full-time, 19, part-time, 10. Openings 2002–2003, 2. *Industrial/organizational PhD*—Applications 2001–2002, 30. Total applicants accepted 2001–2002, 2. New applicants enrolled 2001–2002, 1. Total enrolled 2001–2002 full-time, 11. Openings 2002–2003, 3.

Admissions Requirements:

Scores: Entries appear in this order: required test or GPA, minimum score (if required), median score of students entering in 2001–2002. Master's Programs: GRE-V+Q 1100, 1116; overall undergraduate GPA 3.15, 3.18. Doctoral Programs: GRE-V+Q 1100, 1185; overall undergraduate GPA 3.15, 3.75; last 2 years GPA no minimum stated; psychology GPA no minimum stated; psychology GPA no minimum stated.

Other Criteria: (importance of criteria rated low, medium, or high): GRE/MAT scores high, research experience high, work experience medium, extracurricular activity low, GPA high, letters of recommendation high, interview medium, statement of goals and objectives medium.

Student Characteristics: The following represents characteristics of students in 2001–2002 in all graduate psychology programs in the department: Female–full-time 11, part-time 0; Male–full-time 2, part-time 1; African American/Black–full-time 0, part-time 0; Hispanic/Latino (a)–full-time 2, part-time 0; Asian/Pacific Islander–full-time 5, part-time 0; American Indian/Alaska Native–full-time 0, part-time 0; Multi-ethnic–full-time 0, part-time 0; students subject to the Americans with Disabilities Act–full-time 0, part-time 0.

Financial Information/Assistance:

Tuition for Full-Time Study: *Master's:* State residents per academic year $2,066, $195 per credit hour; nonstate residents: per academic year $3,598, $337 per credit hour. *Doctoral:* State residents: per academic year $2,066, $195 per credit hour; nonstate residents: per academic year $3,598, $337 per credit hour.

Financial Assistance:

First Year Students: Teaching assistantships available for first-year. Average amount paid per academic year: $10,208. Average number of hours worked per week: 20. Apply by January 1. Tuition remission given: full. Research assistantships available for first-year. Average amount paid per academic year: $10. Average number of hours worked per week: 20. Apply by January 1. Tuition remission given: full. Fellowships and scholarships available for first-year. Apply by January 1. Tuition remission given: full.

Advanced Students: Teaching assistantships available for advanced students. Average amount paid per academic year: $10,208. Average number of hours worked per week: 20. Apply by January 1. Tuition remission given: full. Research assistantships available for advanced students. Average amount paid per academic year: $10,208. Apply by January 1. Tuition remission given: full.

Contact Information: Of all students currently enrolled full-time, 100% benefited from one or more of the listed financial assistance programs. For assistance above and beyond the assistantship, contact Financial Aid (937) 775-5721.

Internships/Practica: No information provided.

Housing and Day Care: No on-campus housing and day care facilities are available.

Employment of Department Graduates:

Master's Degree Graduates: Of those who graduated in the academic year 2000–2001, the following categories and numbers represent the post-graduate activities and employment of master's degree graduates: Enrolled in a psychology doctoral program (1), enrolled in another graduate/professional program (0), enrolled in a post-doctoral residency/fellowship (n/a), employed in independent practice (n/a), employed in an academic position at a university (0), employed in an academic position at a 2-year/4-year college (0), employed in other positions at a higher education institution (0), employed in a professional position in a school system (0), employed in business or industry (research/consulting) (0), employed in business or industry (management) (8), employed in a government agency (research) (1), employed in a government agency (professional services) (0), employed in a community mental health/counseling center (0), employed in a hospital/medical center (0), still seeking employment (0), other employment position (0).

Doctoral Degree Graduates: Of those who graduated in the academic year 2000–2001, the following categories and numbers represent the post-graduate activities and employment of doctoral degree graduates: Enrolled in a psychology doctoral program (n/a), enrolled in another graduate/professional program (n/a), enrolled in a post-doctoral residency/fellowship (0), employed in independent practice (0), employed in an academic position at a university (0), employed in an academic position at a 2-year/4-year college (0), employed in other positions at a higher education institution (0), employed in a professional position in a school system (0), employed in business or industry (research/consulting) (0), employed in business or industry (management) (2), employed in a government agency (research) (0), employed in a government agency (professional services) (0), employed in a community mental health/counseling center (0), employed in a hospital/medical center (0), still seeking employment (0), other employment position (0).

Additional Information:

Orientation, Objectives, and Emphasis of Department: The Department offers MS and PhD degrees in Human Factors and Industrial/Organizational Psychology. Students specialize in one of these areas, but the program is designed to foster an understanding of both areas and the importance of considering both aspects in the design of industrial, aerospace, or other systems. The program prepares students for careers in research, teaching, design and practice in government, consulting, business, or industry. It includes coursework, research training, and experience with system design and applications. Students work closely with faculty beginning early in the program. Human factors, also called ergonomics or engineering psychology, deals with human-machine interactions (microsystem variables) while industrial/organizational deals with individual or group behaviors in work settings (macrosystem variables). The department has a critical mass of students and faculty in these areas and is unique because its focus on applied psychology does not include students in clinical psychology or other health-related areas. Both programs are strengthened by being located in the Dayton, Ohio metropolitan region, which is a rapidly developing high technology sector, a major human factors research and development center, and a region of considerable industrial and corporate strength.

Special Facilities or Resources: The Department of Psychology has recently moved to newly renovated space, which includes modern state-of-the-art research laboratories, well equipped teaching laboratories, and office space for faculty and graduate assistants. Specialized equipment in dedicated research laboratories supports research on sensory processes, motor control, spatial orientation, human computer interaction and display design, flight simulation, memory, aging, expertise, teamwork, assessment, training, and stress in the workplace. Computer facilities include numerous UNIX workstations, PCs, and Macintoshes. The De-

partment is particularly proud of its facilities for virtual environment generation, including 3-D visual displays, 3-D auditory displays, and tactile/haptic displays. The Virtual Environment Research, Interactive Technology, and Simulation (VERITAS) facility, which is owned and operated by Wright State University but housed at Wright Patterson Air Force Base, is unique in the world. The facility includes a room-size display that surrounds the user with interactive 3-D auditory and visual images. The Department of Psychology has a Memorandum of Agreement with the US Air Force Research Laboratory, which facilitates utilization of its sophisticated behavioral laboratories such as flight simulators and the Auditory Localization Facility.

Application Information:

Send to: School of Graduate Studies, Wright State University, E344 Student Union, 3640 Colonel Glenn Highway, Dayton, OH 45435-0001. Students are admitted in the Fall, application deadline January 1. Send letters of recommendation on letterhead (no form required) to the School of Graduate Studies at the address listed above. *Fee:* $25.

Wright State University (2001 data)

School of Professional Psychology
3640 Colonel Glenn Highway
Dayton, OH 45435
Telephone: (937) 775-3490
Fax: (937) 775-3434
E-mail: *Kathleen.glaus@wright.edu*
Web: *http://www.wright.edu/sopp/*

Department Established:

1979. Dean: Kathleen Glaus, PhD. Number of Faculty: total–full-time 13, part-time 9; women–full-time 8, part-time 5; minority–full-time 4, part-time 2.

Programs and Degrees Offered:

Listed in the following order: Program area, degree type (T if terminal Master's), number awarded 7/00–6/01. Clinical PsyD 24.

APA Accreditation: Clinical PsyD: full.

Student Applications/Admissions:

Student Applications

Clinical PsyD—Applications 2001–2002, 174. Total applicants accepted 2001–2002, 32. New applicants enrolled 2001–2002, 26. Total enrolled 2001–2002 full-time, 110, part-time, 1. Openings 2002–2003, 27.

Admissions Requirements:

Scores: Entries appear in this order: required test or GPA, minimum score (if required), median score of students entering in 2001–2002. Doctoral Programs: GRE-V no minimum stated, 508; GRE-Q no minimum stated, 542; GRE-V+Q no minimum stated, 1050; GRE-Analytical no minimum stated, 1618; GRE-V+Q+Analytical no minimum stated, 1618; GRE-Subject(Psych) no minimum stated, 558; overall undergraduate GPA no minimum stated, 3.4; psychology GPA no minimum stated, 3.6; psychology GPA no minimum stated, 3.7.

Other Criteria: (importance of criteria rated low, medium, or high): GRE/MAT scores, research experience low, work experience medium, extracurricular activity medium, clinically related public service high, GPA letters of recommendation high, interview high, statement of goals and objectives high.

Student Characteristics: The following represents characteristics of students in 2001–2002 in all graduate psychology programs in the department: Female–full-time 18, part-time 0; Male–full-time 8, part-time 0; African American/Black–full-time 5, part-time 0; Hispanic/Latino (a)–full-time 2, part-time 0; Asian/Pacific Islander–full-time 2, part-time 0; American Indian/Alaska Native–full-time 0, part-time 0.

Financial Information/Assistance:
Tuition for Full-Time Study: No information provided.

Financial Assistance:
First Year Students: No information provided.
Advanced Students: No information provided.
Contact Information: Of all students currently enrolled full-time, 100% benefited from one or more of the listed financial assistance programs. For information on financial assistance, contact: Office of Admissions/Alumni Relations.

Internships/Practica: During years two, three, and four of the doctoral program, students are assigned to year long practicum placements for 2 days (16–20 hours) per week. Most practicum placements are paid positions, at an average rate of $6,000 per year. Approximately half the practicum placements are in the two clinical/teaching facilities operated by the school. These include the Center for Psychological Services on WSU's campus, which provides psychological services for the university's student body, and the Ellis Institute, which is located in an urban, predominately African American section of the city and which provides a broad range of psychological services and special treatment programs developed in response to the needs of the Dayton community. The remaining practicum placements are located in a broad array of service settings located primarily in the Dayton and Cincinnati areas. These practicum settings include: public agencies, correctional settings, hospitals, health and mental health clinics, and a number of private practices of area psychologists. For those doctoral students for whom a professional internship is required prior to graduation, 11 applied in 2000–2001. Of those who applied, 11 were placed in internships listed by the Association of Psychology Postdoctoral and Internship Programs (APPIC); 11 were placed in APA accredited internships.

Housing and Day Care: No on-campus housing and day care facilities are available.

Employment of Department Graduates:
Master's Degree Graduates: Of those who graduated in the academic year 2000–2001, the following categories and numbers represent the post-graduate activities and employment of master's degree graduates: Enrolled in a post-doctoral residency/fellowship (n/a), employed in independent practice (n/a).
Doctoral Degree Graduates: Of those who graduated in the academic year 2000–2001, the following categories and numbers represent the post-graduate activities and employment of doctoral degree graduates: Enrolled in a psychology doctoral program (n/a), enrolled in another graduate/professional program (n/a).

Additional Information:
Orientation, Objectives, and Emphasis of Department: The School of Professional Psychology is committed to a practitioner model of professional education that educates students at the doctoral level for the eclectic, general practice of psychology. As a part of its educational mission, the school emphasizes cultural and other aspects of diversity in the composition of its student body, faculty, and curriculum. The curriculum is organized around six core competency areas that are fundamental to the practice of psychology currently and in the future, including research and evaluation, assessment, intervention, management and supervision, and consultation and education. In years 1 and 2 the curriculum is designed around foundation coursework and the development of basic competencies. Years 3 and 4 are devoted to the development of advanced competency levels.

Special Facilities or Resources: The program operates two large clinical service centers that are designed to accommodate academic teaching, clinical training, clinical program development, and research. The Psychology Service Center is located in an outpatient health care facility on the university's campus. This service center provides assessment and group and individual therapy services to the university student body which numbers approximately 15,000. Opportunities are available for trainees to participate in crisis intervention, prevention programs, outreach to residence halls, and multidisciplinary training with medical and nursing students. The second service center, the Ellis Institute, is located in an urban, primarily African-American section of Dayton. The Ellis Institute provides assessment and group and individual therapy to children, adolescents, and adults from the Dayton community. Several special treatment programs provide unique opportunities for trainees. These include violence prevention programs for minority adolescents, treatment programs addressing perpetrators and victims of domestic violence, anxiety and depression in children, mental health needs of deaf individuals, and the needs of clients and families of people with HIV/AIDS and herpes. Both service centers house classrooms, trainee and faculty offices, and computers for student use in research and training activities, and both facilities are equipped with state of the art equipment for videotaped and live clinical supervision.

Information for Students With Physical Disabilities: Wright State University was designed to be a model for higher education institutions providing accessibility for students with physical disabilities. All campus facilities are highly accessible and buildings are connected by an underground tunnel system that allows students with disabilities to move easily around campus in inclement weather. WSU's Office of Disability Services offers a number of physical and academic support services and the university provides adapted computer equipment and adapted exercise, athletic, and recreational facilities. The School of Professional Psychology has graduated a number of doctoral students with significant physical disabilities.

Application Information:
Send to: Office of Admissions/Alumni Relations, 110 Health Sciences Building, Wright State University, Dayton, OH 45435. Students are admitted in the Fall, application deadline January 15. *Fee:* $50.

Xavier University
Department of Psychology
College of Social Sciences
Elet Hall
Cincinnati, OH 45207-6511
Telephone: (513) 745-3533
Fax: (513) 745-3327
E-mail: *dacey@xu.edu*
Web: *http://www.xu.edu*

Department Established:
1964. Chairperson: Christine M. Dacey, PhD. Number of Faculty: total–full-time 14, part-time 22; women–full-time 7, part-time 13.

Programs and Degrees Offered:
Listed in the following order: Program area, degree type (T if terminal Master's), number awarded 7/00–6/01. Clinical PsyD, experimental MA (T), industrial/organizational MA (T).

APA Accreditation: Clinical PsyD: full.

Student Applications/Admissions:
Student Applications
Clinical PsyD—Applications 2001–2002, 79. Total applicants accepted 2001–2002, 36. New applicants enrolled 2001–2002, 17. Total enrolled 2001–2002 full-time, 79, part-time, 6. Openings 2002–2003, 16. The number of students enrolled full and part-time, who were dismissed or voluntarily withdrew from this program area were 0. *Experimental MA*—Applications 2001–2002, 3. Total enrolled 2001–2002 full-time, 1. Openings 2002–2003, 1. The number of students enrolled full and part-time, who were dismissed or voluntarily withdrew from this program area were 0. *Industrial/organizational MA*—Applications 2001–2002, 40. Total applicants accepted 2001–2002, 21. New applicants enrolled 2001–2002, 10. Total enrolled 2001–2002 full-time, 21. Openings 2002–2003, 10. The number of students enrolled full and part-time, who were dismissed or voluntarily withdrew from this program area were 0.

Admissions Requirements:
Scores: Entries appear in this order: required test or GPA, minimum score (if required), median score of students entering in 2001–2002. Master's Programs: GRE-V no minimum stated; GRE-Q no minimum stated; GRE-V+Q no minimum stated; overall undergraduate GPA 3.0; psychology GPA 3.0. GRE-Subject (Psychology) is required of those without psychology as their major or minor. Doctoral Programs: GRE-V no minimum stated; GRE-Q no minimum stated; GRE-V+Q no minimum stated; overall undergraduate GPA 3.0; last 2 years GPA no minimum stated; psychology GPA 3.0; psychology GPA 3.5. The GRE-Subject is required of those without psychology as their major or minor.
Other Criteria: (importance of criteria rated low, medium, or high): GRE/MAT scores high, research experience medium, work experience medium, extracurricular activity low, clinically related public service medium, GPA high, letters of recommendation high, interview low, statement of goals and objectives medium.

Student Characteristics: The following represents characteristics of students in 2001–2002 in all graduate psychology programs in the department: Female–full-time 76, part-time 2; Male–full-time 24, part-time 4; African American/Black–full-time 2, part-time 1; Hispanic/Latino (a)–full-time 1, part-time 0; Asian/Pacific Islander–full-time 1, part-time 0; American Indian/Alaska Native–full-time 1, part-time 0.

Financial Information/Assistance:
Tuition for Full-Time Study: *Master's:* State residents $450 per credit hour; *Doctoral:* State residents: $610 per credit hour.

Financial Assistance:
First Year Students: Research assistantships available for first-year. Average number of hours worked per week: 10. Apply by March 1. Tuition remission given: partial.
Advanced Students: Teaching assistantships available for advanced students. Average number of hours worked per week: 10. Apply by March 1. Tuition remission given: partial. Traineeships available for advanced students. Apply by March 1. Tuition remission given: partial.
Contact Information: Of all students currently enrolled full-time, 65% benefited from one or more of the listed financial assistance programs. For information on financial assistance, contact: Program Coordinator, Department of Psychology.

Internships/Practica: In an urban setting, the university has established relationships with a number of private and public agencies, hospitals, and mental health care centers. Also, in conjunction with the three areas of interest in our PsyD, program (child, the elderly, and the severely mentally disabled), training sites will be matched. Students are given the opportunity to work with these populations in a number of settings. For those doctoral students for whom a professional internship is required prior to graduation, 7 applied in 2000–2001. Of those who applied, 5 were placed in internships listed by the Association of Psychology Postdoctoral and Internship Programs (APPIC); 5 were placed in APA accredited internships.

Housing and Day Care: No on-campus housing and day care facilities are available.

Employment of Department Graduates:
Master's Degree Graduates: Of those who graduated in the academic year 2000–2001, the following categories and numbers represent the post-graduate activities and employment of master's degree graduates: Enrolled in a post-doctoral residency/fellowship (n/a), employed in independent practice (n/a).
Doctoral Degree Graduates: Of those who graduated in the academic year 2000–2001, the following categories and numbers represent the post-graduate activities and employment of doctoral degree graduates: Enrolled in a psychology doctoral program (n/a), enrolled in another graduate/professional program (n/a).

Additional Information:
Orientation, Objectives, and Emphasis of Department: Both the master's and doctoral programs provide students with the knowledge and range of skills necessary to provide psychological services in today's changing professional climate. Our objective for the master's students is to prepare them for entry into a doctoral program in their field or for immediate employment. The basic philosophy of the PsyD program is to educate skilled practitioners

who have a solid appreciation of the role of science in all aspects of professional activity. It is based on a practitioner-scientist model of training.

Special Facilities or Resources: The department has affiliation with the Psychological Services Center on campus, which provides psychological services to both the university population and the Greater Cincinnati community. The center provides the opportunity for training, service, and research. There are opportunities to work in various areas (e.g., student development) in the university. The department also has established contact with care providers in the community, which provides the opportunity to learn the delivery of service and research that occurs in such organizations.

Information for Students With Physical Disabilities: The university will make every effort to accommodate students with physical disabilities.

Application Information:
Send to: Margaret Maybury, Program Coordinator, Psychology, Department, Xavier University, 3800 Victory Parkway, Cincinnati, OH 45207-6511. Students are admitted in the Fall, application deadline 1/15 (PsyD). Master-March 1. There is a rolling deadline for the master's program if the open slots are not filled. *Fee:* $35.

Central Oklahoma, University of

Department of Psychology
100 North University Drive
Edmond, OK 73034
Telephone: (405) 974-5455
Fax: (405) 974-3822
E-mail: *mknight@ucok.edu*

Department Established:

1968. Chairperson: Mike Knight. Number of Faculty: total–full-time 13; women–full-time 7; minority–full-time 1.

Programs and Degrees Offered:

Listed in the following order: Program area, degree type (T if terminal Master's), number awarded 7/00–6/01. Counseling Psychology MA (T) 32, general MA (T) 15.

Student Applications/Admissions:

Student Applications

Counseling Psychology MA—Applications 2001–2002, 98. Total applicants accepted 2001–2002, 87. New applicants enrolled 2001–2002, 25. Total enrolled 2001–2002 full-time, 121, part-time, 41. Openings 2002–2003, 25. The Median number of years required for completion of a degree are 2. The number of students enrolled full and part-time, who were dismissed or voluntarily withdrew from this program area were 23. *General* MA—Applications 2001–2002, 45. Total applicants accepted 2001–2002, 40. New applicants enrolled 2001–2002, 15. Total enrolled 2001–2002 full-time, 35, part-time, 5. Openings 2002–2003, 15. The Median number of years required for completion of a degree are 2. The number of students enrolled full and part-time, who were dismissed or voluntarily withdrew from this program area were 6.

Admissions Requirements:

Scores: Entries appear in this order: required test or GPA, minimum score (if required), median score of students entering in 2001–2002. Master's Programs: GRE-V no minimum stated; GRE-Q no minimum stated; GRE-Analytical no minimum stated; overall undergraduate GPA 2.5; last 2 years GPA 2.75. Attain a combined score of 900 on Verbal+ Quantitative, or a 3.5 on the GRE Written Test. Doctoral Programs: last 2 years GPA no minimum stated; psychology GPA no minimum stated; psychology GPA no minimum stated.

Other Criteria: (importance of criteria rated low, medium, or high): GRE/MAT scores, research experience high, work experience medium, extracurricular activity medium, clinically related public service high, GPA letters of recommendation high, interview statement of goals and objectives.

Student Characteristics: The following represents characteristics of students in 2001–2002 in all graduate psychology programs in the department: Female–full-time 54, part-time 14; Male–full-time 30, part-time 12; African American/Black–full-time 9, part-time 4; Hispanic/Latino (a)–full-time 5, part-time 1; Asian/Pacific Islander–full-time 7, part-time 0; American Indian/Alaska Native–full-time 4, part-time 0.

Financial Information/Assistance:

Tuition for Full-Time Study: *Master's:* State residents $88 per credit hour; nonstate residents: $207 per credit hour.

Financial Assistance:

First Year Students: No information provided.
Advanced Students: No information provided.
Contact Information: Of all students currently enrolled full-time, 0% benefited from one or more of the listed financial assistance programs. For information on financial assistance, contact: Graduate Dean, UCO.

Internships/Practica: Practicum and internships are available through our program in Counseling Psychology. Students initially work in our departmental clinic and then are placed off-campus in community mental health clinics in our area.

Housing and Day Care: No on-campus housing and day care facilities are available.

Employment of Department Graduates:

Master's Degree Graduates: Of those who graduated in the academic year 2000–2001, the following categories and numbers represent the post-graduate activities and employment of master's degree graduates: Enrolled in a post-doctoral residency/fellowship (n/a), employed in independent practice (n/a).

Doctoral Degree Graduates: Of those who graduated in the academic year 2000–2001, the following categories and numbers represent the post-graduate activities and employment of doctoral degree graduates: Enrolled in a psychology doctoral program (n/a), enrolled in another graduate/professional program (n/a).

Additional Information:

Orientation, Objectives, and Emphasis of Department: Excellent training to pursue doctoral work. General experimental option - or Licensed Professional Counselor (LPC), or Licensed Behavioral Practitioner (LPB) - Counseling Psychology Option.

Special Facilities or Resources: The department has excellent computer facilities. It also has excellent clinic facilities with audio/visual equipment to train students in community counseling.

Information for Students With Physical Disabilities: Facilities are accessible.

Application Information:

Send to: Dean of the Graduate College, 100 North University Drive, University of Central OK, Edmund, OK 73034. Students are admitted in the Fall, application deadline open; Spring, application deadline open; Summer, application deadline open.

Oklahoma State University (2001 data)
Department of Psychology
Arts & Sciences
215 North Murray Hall
Stillwater, OK 74078-3064
Telephone: (405) 744-6027
Fax: (405) 744-8067
E-mail: *maureen@okstate.edu*
Web: *http://psychology.okstate.edu*

Department Established:
1929. Head: Maureen A. Sullivan. Number of Faculty: total–full-time 18, part-time 3; women–full-time 6, part-time 1; minority–full-time 1.

Programs and Degrees Offered:
Listed in the following order: Program area, degree type (T if terminal Master's), number awarded 7/00–6/01. Clinical PhD 6, experimental PhD 1.

APA Accreditation: Clinical PhD: full.

Student Applications/Admissions:
Student Applications
Clinical PhD—Applications 2001–2002, 66. Total applicants accepted 2001–2002, 10. New applicants enrolled 2001–2002, 10. Total enrolled 2001–2002 full-time, 43. Openings 2002–2003, 10. The Median number of years required for completion of a degree are 6. The number of students enrolled full and part-time, who were dismissed or voluntarily withdrew from this program area were 0. *Experimental PhD*—Applications 2001–2002, 11. Total applicants accepted 2001–2002, 2. New applicants enrolled 2001–2002, 2. Total enrolled 2001–2002 full-time, 8, part-time, 2. Openings 2002–2003, 3.

Admissions Requirements:
Scores: Entries appear in this order: required test or GPA, minimum score (if required), median score of students entering in 2001–2002. Doctoral Programs: GRE-V no minimum stated, 500; GRE-Q no minimum stated, 590; GRE-V+Q no minimum stated, 1070; GRE-Subject(Psych) no minimum stated, 610; last 2 years GPA no minimum stated, 3.86; psychology GPA no minimum stated, 4.00.

Student Characteristics: The following represents characteristics of students in 2001–2002 in all graduate psychology programs in the department: Female–full-time 5, part-time 0; Male–full-time 2, part-time 0; African American/Black–full-time 0, part-time 0; Hispanic/Latino (a)–full-time 0, part-time 0; Asian/Pacific Islander–full-time 0, part-time 0; American Indian/Alaska Native–full-time 1, part-time 0.

Financial Information/Assistance:
Tuition for Full-Time Study: No information provided.

Financial Assistance:
First Year Students: No information provided.
Advanced Students: No information provided.

Contact Information: For information on financial assistance, contact: Department of Psychology, Oklahoma State University, 215 N Murray, Stillwater, OK 74078.

Internships/Practica: No information provided.

Housing and Day Care: No on-campus housing and day care facilities are available.

Employment of Department Graduates:
Master's Degree Graduates: Of those who graduated in the academic year 2000–2001, the following categories and numbers represent the post-graduate activities and employment of master's degree graduates: Enrolled in a post-doctoral residency/fellowship (n/a), employed in independent practice (n/a).
Doctoral Degree Graduates: Of those who graduated in the academic year 2000–2001, the following categories and numbers represent the post-graduate activities and employment of doctoral degree graduates: Enrolled in a psychology doctoral program (n/a), enrolled in another graduate/professional program (n/a).

Additional Information:
Orientation, Objectives, and Emphasis of Department: The doctoral program in clinical psychology is based on the scientist-practitioner model. The program emphasizes the development of knowledge and skills in basic psychology, clinical theory, assessment and treatment procedures, and research. Practica, coursework, and internships are selected to enhance the student's interests. Students are expected, through additional coursework, specialized practica, and research, to develop a subspecialty in general clinical, clinical child, or health psychology. The experimental psychology program emphasizes cognitive psychology (including memory, attention, imagery, perception, and motivation), developmental psychology, biopsychology, and social psychology. Students with a primary interest in quantitative methods are also encouraged to enter the program.

Special Facilities or Resources: The department offers a variety of support services through the Psychology Diversified Students Program and the Psychology Graduate Students Association. Students are provided preadmission and postadmission assistance. The Department of Psychology is located in North Murray near the center of the OSU campus. All students are provided office space. Appropriate research space is available for clinical and experimental research; a wide variety of equipment for research and instructional purposes is also available. The department has remote computer terminal facilities which access the university's IBM 3081D and VAX 11/780 computer. These are available for student use. In addition, faculty have microcomputers that interface with the mainframe computers. Word processor systems and e-mail are also available to students. The department operates the Psychological Services center, an on-campus facility for clinical work and research. The center has equipment and facilities to accommodate a number of specialized services and functions, including biofeedback, play therapy, videotaping, direct observation of clinical work using one-way mirrors, and direct supervision through telephones placed in therapy rooms. The department maintains liaison with many off-campus organizations and agencies which provide the student with access to special populations for research as well as clinical activities.

Application Information:
Send to: Maureen A. Sullivan, Department of Psychology, OSU, 215 N Murray Hall, Stillwater, OK 74078. Students are admitted in the Fall, application deadline January 1 clinical, February 1 experimental. *Fee:* $25.

Oklahoma State University
Family Relations & Child Development
Human Environmental Sciences
Oklahoma State University
Stillwater, OK 74078
Telephone: (405) 744-2057
Fax: (405) 744-2800
E-mail: *awhitne@okstate.edu*
Web: *http://ches.okstate.edu/frcd*

Department Established:
Interim Department Head: Kathleen Briggs, PhD. Number of Faculty: total–full-time 21; women–full-time 18.

Programs and Degrees Offered:
Listed in the following order: Program area, degree type (T if terminal Master's), number awarded 7/00–6/01. PhD and Master's Program 11.

Student Applications/Admissions:
Student Applications

PhD and Masters Program—Applications 2001–2002, 113. Total applicants accepted 2001–2002, 64. New applicants enrolled 2001–2002, 60. Total enrolled 2001–2002 full-time, 95. Openings 2002–2003, 15. The number of students enrolled full and part-time, who were dismissed or voluntarily withdrew from this program area were 0.

Admissions Requirements:
Scores: Entries appear in this order: required test or GPA, minimum score (if required), median score of students entering in 2001–2002. Master's Programs: GRE-V no minimum stated; GRE-Q no minimum stated; GRE-Analytical no minimum stated. Doctoral Programs: GRE-V no minimum stated; GRE-V+Q no minimum stated; GRE-Analytical no minimum stated; last 2 years GPA no minimum stated; psychology GPA no minimum stated; psychology GPA no minimum stated.
Other Criteria: (importance of criteria rated low, medium, or high): GRE/MAT scores high, research experience high, work experience high, extracurricular activity high, clinically related public service high, GPA high, letters of recommendation high, interview high, statement of goals and objectives high.

Student Characteristics: The following represents characteristics of students in 2001–2002 in all graduate psychology programs in the department: Female–full-time 78, Male–full-time 17, African American/Black–full-time 6, Asian/Pacific Islander–full-time 2, American Indian/Alaska Native–full-time 4.

Financial Information/Assistance:
Tuition for Full-Time Study: *Master's:* State residents $112 per credit hour; nonstate residents: $318 per credit hour. *Doctoral:* State residents: $112 per credit hour; nonstate residents: $318 per credit hour.

Financial Assistance:
First Year Students: Teaching assistantships available for first-year. Average number of hours worked per week: 15. Apply by February 15. Research assistantships available for first-year. Average number of hours worked per week: 15. Apply by February 15. Fellowships and scholarships available for first-year. Apply by February 15.
Advanced Students: Teaching assistantships available for advanced students. Average number of hours worked per week: 15. Apply by February 15. Research assistantships available for advanced students. Average number of hours worked per week: 15. Apply by February 15. Fellowships and scholarships available for advanced students. Apply by February 15.
Contact Information: For information on financial assistance, contact: www.okstate.edu/finaid.

Internships/Practica: No information provided.

Housing and Day Care: On-campus housing and day care facilities are available.

Employment of Department Graduates:
Master's Degree Graduates: Of those who graduated in the academic year 2000–2001, the following categories and numbers represent the post-graduate activities and employment of master's degree graduates: Enrolled in a post-doctoral residency/fellowship (n/a), employed in independent practice (n/a).
Doctoral Degree Graduates: Of those who graduated in the academic year 2000–2001, the following categories and numbers represent the post-graduate activities and employment of doctoral degree graduates: Enrolled in a psychology doctoral program (n/a), enrolled in another graduate/professional program (n/a).

Application Information:
Send to: Graduate Coordinator, 243 HES, Oklahoma State University, Stillwater, OK 74078-6122. Students are admitted in the Fall, application deadline February 15; Spring, application deadline November 1. *Fee:* $25.

Oklahoma State University
School of Applied Health and Educational Psychology
College of Education
434 Willard
Stillwater, OK 74078
Telephone: (405) 744-6040
Fax: (405) 744-6756
E-mail: *sjacobs@okstate.edu*
Web: *http://www.okstate.edu/education/sahep/html*

Department Established:
1997. School Head: Sue C. Jacobs, PhD. Number of Faculty: total–full-time 24, part-time 4; women–full-time 11, part-time 2; minority–full-time 3.

Programs and Degrees Offered:

Listed in the following order: Program area, degree type (T if terminal Master's), number awarded 7/00–6/01. Counseling PhD 8, educational PhD 3, school PhD 5.

APA Accreditation: Counseling PhD: full. School PhD: full.

Student Applications/Admissions:

Student Applications

Counseling PhD—Applications 2001–2002, 35. Total applicants accepted 2001–2002, 11. New applicants enrolled 2001–2002, 11. Total enrolled 2001–2002 full-time, 29, part-time, 11. The Median number of years required for completion of a degree are 5. The number of students enrolled full and part-time, who were dismissed or voluntarily withdrew from this program area were 0. *Educational PhD*—Applications 2001–2002, 17. Total applicants accepted 2001–2002, 6. New applicants enrolled 2001–2002, 17. Total enrolled 2001–2002 full-time, 10, part-time, 16. The Median number of years required for completion of a degree are 9. The number of students enrolled full and part-time, who were dismissed or voluntarily withdrew from this program area were 0. *School PhD*—Applications 2001–2002, 17. Total applicants accepted 2001–2002, 6. New applicants enrolled 2001–2002, 11. Total enrolled 2001–2002 full-time, 27, part-time, 9. The Median number of years required for completion of a degree are 4. The number of students enrolled full and part-time, who were dismissed or voluntarily withdrew from this program area were 0.

Admissions Requirements:

Scores: Entries appear in this order: required test or GPA, minimum score (if required), median score of students entering in 2001–2002. Master's Programs: GRE-V+Q no minimum stated, 950; overall undergraduate GPA no minimum stated, 3.0. Doctoral Programs: GRE-V no minimum stated, 550; GRE-Q no minimum stated, 500; overall undergraduate GPA no minimum stated, 3.5; last 2 years GPA no minimum stated, 3.8; psychology GPA no minimum stated, 3.6; psychology GPA no minimum stated, 3.75.

Other Criteria: (importance of criteria rated low, medium, or high): research experience medium, work experience medium, extracurricular activity low, clinically related public service medium, letters of recommendation medium, interview medium, statement of goals and objectives high. School Psychology: work experience and clinically related public service low, letters and interview are high.

Student Characteristics: The following represents characteristics of students in 2001–2002 in all graduate psychology programs in the department: Female–full-time 45, part-time 24; Male–full-time 20, part-time 12; African American/Black–full-time 3, part-time 1; Hispanic/Latino (a)–full-time 2, part-time 0; Asian/Pacific Islander–full-time 2, part-time 3; American Indian/Alaska Native–full-time 11, part-time 2; Multi-ethnic–full-time 0, part-time 1.

Financial Information/Assistance:

Tuition for Full-Time Study: *Master's:* State residents per academic year $1,932, $92 per credit hour; nonstate residents: per academic year $4,314, $205 per credit hour. *Doctoral:* State residents: per academic year $1,931, $92 per credit hour; nonstate residents: per academic year $4,314, $205 per credit hour.

Financial Assistance:

First Year Students: Teaching assistantships available for first-year. Average amount paid per academic year: $3,812. Average number of hours worked per week: 15. Apply by April 15. Tuition remission given: partial. Research assistantships available for first-year. Average amount paid per academic year: $7,623. Average number of hours worked per week: 20. Apply by April 15. Tuition remission given: partial. Traineeships available for first-year. Apply by N/A. Tuition remission given: partial.

Advanced Students: Teaching assistantships available for advanced students. Average amount paid per academic year: $6,165. Average number of hours worked per week: 15. Apply by April 15. Tuition remission given: partial. Research assistantships available for advanced students. Average amount paid per academic year: $4,419. Average number of hours worked per week: 10. Apply by April 15. Tuition remission given: partial. Traineeships available for advanced students. Average amount paid per academic year: $8,838. Average number of hours worked per week: 20. Apply by N/A. Tuition remission given: partial.

Contact Information: Of all students currently enrolled full-time, 83% benefited from one or more of the listed financial assistance programs. For information on financial assistance, contact: Stephanie Sosbee at (405) 744-6040. Financial Aid Application required for partial departmental tuition fee waiver.

Internships/Practica: Practica are available at an on-campus training facility, as well as several locations in the surrounding community. Several off-campus sites include a stipend.

Housing and Day Care: On-campus housing and day care facilities are available.

Employment of Department Graduates:

Master's Degree Graduates: Of those who graduated in the academic year 2000–2001, the following categories and numbers represent the post-graduate activities and employment of master's degree graduates: Enrolled in a psychology doctoral program (10), enrolled in a post-doctoral residency/fellowship (n/a), employed in independent practice (n/a).

Doctoral Degree Graduates: Of those who graduated in the academic year 2000–2001, the following categories and numbers represent the post-graduate activities and employment of doctoral degree graduates: Enrolled in a psychology doctoral program (n/a), enrolled in another graduate/professional program (n/a).

Additional Information:

Orientation, Objectives, and Emphasis of Department: Counseling Psychology—The orientation of the Counseling Psychology program is consistent both with the historical development of counseling psychology and with the current roles and functions of counseling psychology. We give major emphasis to prevention/developmental/educational interventions, and to remediation of problems that arise in the normal development of relatively well functioning people. School Psychology—The School Psychology program is based on the scientist-practitioner model, which emphasizes the application of the scientific knowledge base and methodological rigor in the delivery of school psychology services and in conducting research. Training in the scientist-practitioner model at OSU is for the purpose of developing a Science-Based Learner Success (SBLS) orientation in our students. Our philosophy is that all children and youth have the right to be successful and school psychologists are important agents who assist children, families, and others to be successful. Success refers not only to accomplishment of immediate goals but also to long range goals of adulthood such as contributing to society, social integration, meaningful work, and maximizing personal potentials. The SBLS orientation focuses on prevention and intervention services related to children's psychoeducational and mental health and wellness. School Specialist and Doctoral programs are also approved by the National Association of School Psychologists.

Special Facilities or Resources: Community/School Services, Counseling Psychology Clinic, and the Reading and Math Clinic Training Facility.

Information for Students With Physical Disabilities: Student Disability Services is committed to providing support services to students with physical and learning disabilities. The underlying philosophy of the program is to provide support services that will facilitate the academic progress of each individual student. A plan for services is developed on an individual basis and may include specialized testing, recorded textbooks, academic accommodations, technological assistance, and other services as requested.

Application Information:
Send to: Graduate College Application Form: The Graduate College, Oklahoma State University, 202 Whitehurst Stillwater, OK 74078-1019. Program Admission Criteria: College of Education, Graduate Studies Records, Oklahoma State University, 327 Willard, Stillwater, OK 74078. For the Fall semester, the deadline for the Counseling PhD program is January 15, School PhD is February 1, and March 1 for the MS and EdS. *Fee:* $25.

Oklahoma, University of
Department of Psychology
Arts and Sciences
455 West Lindsey
Norman, OK 73019-2007
Telephone: (405) 325-4511, (800) 522-0772, ext 4512
Fax: (405) 325-4737
E-mail: *KPaine@ou.edu*
Web: *http://www.ou.edu/cas/psychology/*

Department Established:
1928. Chairperson: Kirby Gilliland. Number of Faculty: total—full-time 18, part-time 10; women—full-time 8, part-time 6; minority—full-time 1, part-time 1.

Programs and Degrees Offered:
Listed in the following order: Program area, degree type (T if terminal Master's), number awarded 7/00–6/01. Animal cognition PhD, cognitive PhD 1, developmental PhD, experimental personality PhD 1, industrial/organizational MA (T) 2, industrial/organizational PhD, quantitative/measurement PhD 1, social PhD 1.

Student Applications/Admissions:
Student Applications
Animal cognition PhD—Applications 2001–2002, 3. Total enrolled 2001–2002 full-time, 2. Openings 2002–2003, 1. *Cogni-*

tive PhD—Applications 2001–2002, 5. Total applicants accepted 2001–2002, 2. Total enrolled 2001–2002 full-time, 2. Openings 2002–2003, 5. The Median number of years required for completion of a degree are 5. *Developmental PhD*—Applications 2001–2002, 5. Total enrolled 2001–2002 full-time, 3. Openings 2002–2003, 1. *Experimental personality PhD*—Applications 2001–2002, 2. Openings 2002–2003, 3. The Median number of years required for completion of a degree are 5. *Industrial/organizational MA*—Applications 2001–2002, 10. Total applicants accepted 2001–2002, 5. New applicants enrolled 2001–2002, 2. Total enrolled 2001–2002 full-time, 5. Openings 2002–2003, 6. *Industrial/organizational PhD*—Applications 2001–2002, 23. Total applicants accepted 2001–2002, 4. New applicants enrolled 2001–2002, 2. Total enrolled 2001–2002 full-time, 14. Openings 2002–2003, 6. *Quantitative/measurement PhD*—Applications 2001–2002, 5. Total applicants accepted 2001–2002, 4. New applicants enrolled 2001–2002, 3. Total enrolled 2001–2002 full-time, 7. Openings 2002–2003, 2. The Median number of years required for completion of a degree are 5. *Social PhD*—Applications 2001–2002, 23. Total applicants accepted 2001–2002, 1. Total enrolled 2001–2002 full-time, 6. Openings 2002–2003, 6. The Median number of years required for completion of a degree are 5.

Admissions Requirements:
Scores: Entries appear in this order: required test or GPA, minimum score (if required), median score of students entering in 2001–2002. Master's Programs: GRE-V no minimum stated, 595; GRE-Q no minimum stated, 585; GRE-V+Q no minimum stated, 1180; GRE-V+Q+Analytical no minimum stated, 1890; overall undergraduate GPA no minimum stated, 3.79; last 2 years GPA no minimum stated; psychology GPA no minimum stated. Doctoral Programs: GRE-V no minimum stated, 555; GRE-Q no minimum stated, 683; GRE-V+Q no minimum stated, 1238; GRE-Analytical no minimum stated, 733; GRE-V+Q+Analytical no minimum stated, 1971; GRE-Subject(Psych) no minimum stated; overall undergraduate GPA no minimum stated, 3.89; last 2 years GPA no minimum stated; psychology GPA no minimum stated; psychology GPA no minimum stated.
Other Criteria: (importance of criteria rated low, medium, or high): GRE/MAT scores high, research experience high, extracurricular activity low, GPA high, letters of recommendation high, statement of goals and objectives high, area's need for students high.

Student Characteristics: The following represents characteristics of students in 2001–2002 in all graduate psychology programs in the department: Female—full-time 23, part-time 0; Male—full-time 16, part-time 0; African American/Black—full-time 0, part-time 0; Hispanic/Latino (a)—full-time 3, part-time 0; Asian/Pacific Islander—full-time 3, part-time 0; American Indian/Alaska Native—full-time 0, part-time 0; students subject to the Americans with Disabilities Act—full-time 2.

Financial Information/Assistance:
Tuition for Full-Time Study: *Master's:* State residents $92 per credit hour; nonstate residents: $297 per credit hour. *Doctoral:* State residents $92 per credit hour; nonstate residents: $297 per credit hour.

Financial Assistance:

First Year Students: Teaching assistantships available for first-year. Tuition remission given: partial. Research assistantships available for first-year. Tuition remission given: partial. Fellowships and scholarships available for first-year. Tuition remission given: full.

Advanced Students: Teaching assistantships available for advanced students. Tuition remission given: partial. Research assistantships available for advanced students. Tuition remission given: partial.

Contact Information: Of all students currently enrolled full-time, 85% benefited from one or more of the listed financial assistance programs. For information on financial assistance, contact: Financial Aid at 405-325-4521.

Internships/Practica: No information provided.

Housing and Day Care: No on-campus housing and day care facilities are available.

Employment of Department Graduates:

Master's Degree Graduates: Of those who graduated in the academic year 2000–2001, the following categories and numbers represent the post-graduate activities and employment of master's degree graduates: Enrolled in a post-doctoral residency/fellowship (n/a), employed in independent practice (n/a), employed in an academic position at a 2-year/4-year college (1), employed in business or industry (management) (1), employed in a government agency (professional services) (1), other employment position (3).

Doctoral Degree Graduates: Of those who graduated in the academic year 2000–2001, the following categories and numbers represent the post-graduate activities and employment of doctoral degree graduates: Enrolled in a psychology doctoral program (n/a), enrolled in another graduate/professional program (n/a), employed in business or industry (research/consulting) (1).

Additional Information:

Orientation, Objectives, and Emphasis of Department: All programs are highly research oriented within the broad framework of experimental psychology. The department aims to produce creative and productive psychologists to function in academic and research settings, and toward this end emphasizes early and continuing involvement in research. Achievement of orientation and objectives is demonstrated by the excellent placement record of doctoral graduates, and by the department's recent rating as ninth in the nation in percent of publishing faculty. An excellent program in Quantitative Methods in Psychology is an especially attractive feature of the quality graduate training offered.

Special Facilities or Resources: The department offers modern research facilities with microprocessor-controlled laboratories, instrumentation shops with a full-time engineer, a small animal colony, a university computing center, and graduate offices located near faculty and departmental offices.

Information for Students With Physical Disabilities: The University of Oklahoma and the Department of Psychology make every effort to provide accessibility to all facilities. The Department of Psychology works closely with the Center for Student Life to provide necessary accommodations to insure quality education for students with disabilities.

Application Information:

Send to: Graduate Admissions Committee, Department of Psychology, University of Oklahoma, 455 W. Lindsey, Room 705, Norman, OK 73019-2007. Students are admitted in the Fall, application deadline February 1. *Fee:* $25.

Oklahoma, University of, College of Education
Department of Educational Psychology
820 Van Vleet Oval
Norman, OK 73019-0260
Telephone: (405) 325-5974
Fax: (405) 325-6655
E-mail: *edpsych@ou.edu*
Web: *http://www.ou.edu/education/edpsy/epsy.htm*

Department Established:

1986. Chairperson: Terry M. Pace. Number of Faculty: total–full-time 20; women–full-time 11; minority–full-time 2; faculty subject to the Americans with Disabilities Act 1.

Programs and Degrees Offered:

Listed in the following order: Program area, degree type (T if terminal Master's), number awarded 7/00–6/01. Community counseling (T) 17, counseling psychology PhD 2.

APA Accreditation: Counseling PhD: full.

Student Applications/Admissions:

Student Applications

Counseling psychology PhD—Applications 2001–2002, 67. Total applicants accepted 2001–2002, 11. New applicants enrolled 2001–2002, 8. Total enrolled 2001–2002 full-time, 36. Openings 2002–2003, 8.

Admissions Requirements:

Scores: Entries appear in this order: required test or GPA, minimum score (if required), median score of students entering in 2001–2002. Master's Programs: GRE-V no minimum stated, 510; GRE-Q no minimum stated, 490; GRE-Analytical no minimum stated, 500; overall undergraduate GPA 3.00, 3.25; last 2 years GPA no minimum stated, 3.35. The GRE-Q or the GRE-Analytical is required. Doctoral Programs: GRE-V no minimum stated, 600; GRE-Q no minimum stated, 550; GRE-Analytical no minimum stated, 560; GRE-V+Q+Analytical no minimum stated, 1150; overall undergraduate GPA 3.00, 3.50; last 2 years GPA no minimum stated, 3.70; psychology GPA no minimum stated, 3.75; psychology GPA no minimum stated, 3.70. The GRE-Q or the GRE-Analytical is required.

Other Criteria: (importance of criteria rated low, medium, or high): research experience medium, work experience medium, extracurricular activity low, clinically related public service medium, letters of recommendation medium, interview high, statement of goals and objectives medium.

Student Characteristics: The following represents characteristics of students in 2001–2002 in all graduate psychology programs in the department: Female–full-time 15, part-time 0; Male–full-time

9, part-time 0; African American/Black–full-time 2, part-time 0; Hispanic/Latino (a)–full-time 0, part-time 0; Asian/Pacific Islander–full-time 1, part-time 0; American Indian/Alaska Native–full-time 1, part-time 0.

Financial Information/Assistance:

Tuition for Full-Time Study: *Master's:* State residents $92 per credit hour; nonstate residents: $297 per credit hour. *Doctoral:* State residents: $92 per credit hour; nonstate residents: $297 per credit hour.

Financial Assistance:

First Year Students: No information provided.
Advanced Students: No information provided.
Contact Information: No information provided.

Internships/Practica: Master's: Numerous hospitals and clinics in the local area. Doctoral: Students choose from APA-accredited sites (two in the local area, and others in the region).

Housing and Day Care: No on-campus housing and day care facilities are available.

Employment of Department Graduates:

Master's Degree Graduates: Of those who graduated in the academic year 2000–2001, the following categories and numbers represent the post-graduate activities and employment of master's degree graduates: Enrolled in a post-doctoral residency/fellowship (n/a), employed in independent practice (n/a).

Doctoral Degree Graduates: Of those who graduated in the academic year 2000–2001, the following categories and numbers represent the post-graduate activities and employment of doctoral degree graduates: Enrolled in a psychology doctoral program (n/a), enrolled in another graduate/professional program (n/a).

Additional Information:

Orientation, Objectives, and Emphasis of Department: The Counseling Psychology program emphasizes training in working with families and with children of single parents. The program has a scientist-professional orientation designed to encourage the professional development of the students. Minority applications are encouraged.

Special Facilities or Resources: The Counseling Psychology Clinic is a community-based training site for our students. The clientele reflects diverse diagnostic classifications with some cultural diversity. Couples, children, and families make up a large proportion of the population served by the clinic.

Information for Students With Physical Disabilities: OU and the department adhere to ADA guidelines. All classrooms and the clinic are handicapped accessible.

Application Information:
Send to: Graduate Programs Officer, Department of Educational Psychology. Students are admitted in the Spring, application deadline January 10. Deadline for community counseling MEd is January 31.

Oklahoma, University of, Health Sciences Center
Biological Psychology PhD Program
Graduate
P.O. Box 26901, Research Building, Room 302-R
Oklahoma City, OK 73190-3000
Telephone: (405) 271-2011, ext. 47717
Fax: (405) 271-2356
E-mail: *frank-holloway@ouhsc.edu*
Web: *http://w3.ouhsc.edu/biopsych*

Department Established:
1966. Director, Biological Psychology Program: Frank A. Holloway. Number of Faculty: total–full-time 18, part-time 14; women–full-time 8, part-time 5.

Programs and Degrees Offered:
Listed in the following order: Program area, degree type (T if terminal Master's), number awarded 7/00–6/01. Biological Psychology PhD 1.

Student Applications/Admissions:
Student Applications

Biological Psychology PhD—Applications 2001–2002, 11. Total applicants accepted 2001–2002, 3. New applicants enrolled 2001–2002, 3. Total enrolled 2001–2002 full-time, 15. Openings 2002–2003, 4. The Median number of years required for completion of a degree are 5. The number of students enrolled full and part-time, who were dismissed or voluntarily withdrew from this program area were 0.

Admissions Requirements:

Scores: Entries appear in this order: required test or GPA, minimum score (if required), median score of students entering in 2001–2002. Doctoral Programs: overall undergraduate GPA 3.0, 3.25; last 2 years GPA no minimum stated; psychology GPA no minimum stated; psychology GPA no minimum stated.

Other Criteria: (importance of criteria rated low, medium, or high): GRE/MAT scores medium, research experience high, work experience high, extracurricular activity low, GPA high, letters of recommendation high, interview medium, statement of goals and objectives high, research goals compatible high.

Student Characteristics: The following represents characteristics of students in 2001–2002 in all graduate psychology programs in the department: Female–full-time 7, part-time 0; Male–full-time 8, part-time 0; African American/Black–full-time 0, part-time 0; Hispanic/Latino (a)–full-time 0, part-time 0; Asian/Pacific Islander–full-time 0, part-time 0; American Indian/Alaska Native–full-time 0, part-time 0; Multi-ethnic–full-time 0, students subject to the Americans with Disabilities Act–full-time 0.

Financial Information/Assistance:
Tuition for Full-Time Study: *Doctoral:* State residents: $92 per credit hour; nonstate residents: $205 per credit hour.

Financial Assistance:
First Year Students: Research assistantships available for first-year. Average amount paid per academic year: $18,156. Average number of hours worked per week: 20. Apply by March 1.

Tuition remission given: partial. Traineeships available for first-year. Average amount paid per academic year: $18,156. Average number of hours worked per week: 20. Apply by March 1. Tuition remission given: full.

Advanced Students: Research assistantships available for advanced students. Average amount paid per academic year: $18,156. Average number of hours worked per week: 20. Apply by March 1. Tuition remission given: partial. Traineeships available for advanced students. Average amount paid per academic year: $18,156. Average number of hours worked per week: 20. Apply by March 1. Tuition remission given: full.

Contact Information: Of all students currently enrolled full-time, 100% benefited from one or more of the listed financial assistance programs. For information on financial assistance, contact: Chair, Admissions Committee.

Internships/Practica: No information provided.

Housing and Day Care: No on-campus housing and day care facilities are available.

Employment of Department Graduates:
Master's Degree Graduates: Of those who graduated in the academic year 2000–2001, the following categories and numbers represent the post-graduate activities and employment of master's degree graduates: Enrolled in a post-doctoral residency/fellowship (n/a), employed in independent practice (n/a).
Doctoral Degree Graduates: Of those who graduated in the academic year 2000–2001, the following categories and numbers represent the post-graduate activities and employment of doctoral degree graduates: Enrolled in a psychology doctoral program (n/a), enrolled in another graduate/professional program (n/a), employed in business or industry (research/consulting) (1).

Additional Information:
Orientation, Objectives, and Emphasis of Department: The overall objective of the program is to educate and train doctoral level candidates capable of conducting basic or applied research in biological psychology. Given the program's location in a health sciences center and the apparent need for clinical researchers, emphasis will be placed on health-related problems. Specialization beyond the core curriculum generally will be in one of three areas: (a) human neuropsychology and behavioral neuroscience, (b) behavioral medicine and health psychology-psychophysiology, and (c) substance abuse and psychopharmacology. Finally, we recruit applicants at the baccalaureate level with strong psychology and natural science backgrounds who are aiming for science careers.

Special Facilities or Resources: Biological psychology faculty and students are located in these various research and teaching areas. The University of Oklahoma Health Sciences Center is located in a large complex that includes Oklahoma Memorial Hospital, Oklahoma Children's Memorial Hospital, the Veterans Administration Hospital, and Presbyterian Hospital. Located nearby is the Federal Aviation Administration Center.

Application Information:
Send to: Chair, Admissions Committee, Biological Psychology Program, University of Oklahoma HSC, P.O. Box 26901, Research 302-R, Oklahoma City, OK 73190-3000. Students are admitted in the Fall, application deadline March 1.

Tulsa, University of
Department of Psychology
600 South College Avenue
Tulsa, OK 74104-3189
Telephone: (918) 631-2248
Fax: (918) 631-2833
E-mail: *abby-hallford@utulsa.edu*
Web: *http://www.utulsa.edu*

Department Established:
1926. Chairperson: Allan R. Harkness. Number of Faculty: total–full-time 14, part-time 5; women–full-time 5, part-time 2.

Programs and Degrees Offered:
Listed in the following order: Program area, degree type (T if terminal Master's), number awarded 7/00–6/01. Clinical Psychology MA (T) 4, Clinical Psychology PhD 2, Industrial/Organizational MA (T) 8, Industrial/Organizational PhD.

APA Accreditation: Clinical PhD: full.

Student Applications/Admissions:
Student Applications
Clinical Psychology MA—Applications 2001–2002, 12. Total applicants accepted 2001–2002, 9. New applicants enrolled 2001–2002, 5. Total enrolled 2001–2002 full-time, 11. Openings 2002–2003, 6. The Median number of years required for completion of a degree are 2. The number of students enrolled full and part-time, who were dismissed or voluntarily withdrew from this program area were 1. *Clinical Psychology PhD*—Applications 2001–2002, 36. Total applicants accepted 2001–2002, 13. New applicants enrolled 2001–2002, 7. Total enrolled 2001–2002 full-time, 25, part-time, 3. Openings 2002–2003, 4. The Median number of years required for completion of a degree are 6. The number of students enrolled full and part-time, who were dismissed or voluntarily withdrew from this program area were 1. *Industrial/Organizational MA*—Applications 2001–2002, 22. Total applicants accepted 2001–2002, 18. New applicants enrolled 2001–2002, 10. Total enrolled 2001–2002 full-time, 17. Openings 2002–2003, 10. The Median number of years required for completion of a degree are 2. The number of students enrolled full and part-time, who were dismissed or voluntarily withdrew from this program area were 0. *Industrial/Organizational PhD*—Applications 2001–2002, 33. Total applicants accepted 2001–2002, 4. New applicants enrolled 2001–2002, 3. Total enrolled 2001–2002 full-time, 23, part-time, 4. Openings 2002–2003, 4. The Median number of years required for completion of a degree are 6. The number of students enrolled full and part-time, who were dismissed or voluntarily withdrew from this program area were 0.

Admissions Requirements:
Scores: Entries appear in this order: required test or GPA, minimum score (if required), median score of students entering in 2001–2002. Master's Programs: GRE-V 500, 500; GRE-Q 500, 570; GRE-V+Q 1000; overall undergraduate GPA 3.00, 3.50. Required for clinical, strongly recommended for I/O. Medians are reported for clinical. Doctoral Programs: GRE-V 550, 585; GRE-Q 550, 630; overall undergraduate GPA 3.00,

3.56; last 2 years GPA no minimum stated; psychology GPA no minimum stated; psychology GPA no minimum stated. Minimums required for clinical, strongly recommended for I/O. Medians are reported for clinical. Admissions are based on total scores and other factors.

Other Criteria: (importance of criteria rated low, medium, or high): GRE/MAT scores high, research experience high, work experience low, extracurricular activity medium, clinically related public service medium, GPA high, letters of recommendation medium, interview medium, statement of goals and objectives high, quality of undergrad inst medium, Interview for clinical only.

Student Characteristics: The following represents characteristics of students in 2001–2002 in all graduate psychology programs in the department: Female–full-time 42, part-time 0; Male–full-time 36, part-time 0; African American/Black–full-time 0, part-time 0; Hispanic/Latino (a)–full-time 3, part-time 0; Asian/Pacific Islander–full-time 3, part-time 0; American Indian/Alaska Native–full-time 2, part-time 0.

Financial Information/Assistance:
Tuition for Full-Time Study: *Master's:* State residents $512 per credit hour; nonstate residents: $512 per credit hour. *Doctoral:* State residents: $512 per credit hour; nonstate residents: $512 per credit hour.

Financial Assistance:
First Year Students: Teaching assistantships available for first-year. Average amount paid per academic year: $6,500. Average number of hours worked per week: 20. Apply by Feb 1. Tuition remission given: full. Research assistantships available for first-year. Average amount paid per academic year: $6,500. Average number of hours worked per week: 20. Apply by Feb 1. Tuition remission given: full. Fellowships and scholarships available for first-year. Apply by varies.

Advanced Students: Teaching assistantships available for advanced students. Average amount paid per academic year: $7,800. Average number of hours worked per week: 20. Apply by Feb 1. Tuition remission given: full. Research assistantships available for advanced students. Average amount paid per academic year: $7,800. Average number of hours worked per week: 20. Apply by Feb 1. Tuition remission given: full. Fellowships and scholarships available for advanced students. Apply by varies.

Contact Information: Of all students currently enrolled full-time, 50% benefited from one or more of the listed financial assistance programs. For information on financial assistance, contact: Financial Aid Office, University of Tulsa, 600 S. College, Tulsa, OK 74104. http://www.utulsa.edu/Financial/Aid.html.

Internships/Practica: I/O master's students are required to complete 3 credit hours of I/O fieldwork. This usually takes place in local corporations although students may pursue positions elsewhere. Clinical practica are community based, offering exposure to diverse patient demographics and presenting problems. Students in both programs may also develop consulting skills relevant to the non-profit sector in our new Center for Community Research and Development. For those doctoral students for whom a professional internship is required prior to graduation, 7 applied in 2000–2001. Of those who applied, 7 were placed in APA accredited internships.

Housing and Day Care: On-campus housing and day care facilities are available.

Employment of Department Graduates:
Master's Degree Graduates: Of those who graduated in the academic year 2000–2001, the following categories and numbers represent the post-graduate activities and employment of master's degree graduates: Enrolled in a post-doctoral residency/fellowship (n/a), employed in independent practice (n/a).
Doctoral Degree Graduates: Of those who graduated in the academic year 2000–2001, the following categories and numbers represent the post-graduate activities and employment of doctoral degree graduates: Enrolled in a psychology doctoral program (n/a), enrolled in another graduate/professional program (n/a).

Additional Information:
Orientation, Objectives, and Emphasis of Department: Our graduate programs in applied psychology are central to the departmental mission, which is: To generate new psychological knowledge to help individuals, organizations, and communities make decisions and solve problems; to offer a future-oriented, intellectually challenging, and socially relevant curriculum; and to equip students to make a difference through their work by providing them with an extensive knowledge base as well as the analytical and practical skills needed to apply knowledge wisely. Our programs train students to do what applied psychologists actually do in today's society. The programs in I/O psychology emphasize personnel psychology and organizational development, theory, and behavior, with a special focus on individual assessment. The doctoral program in clinical psychology develops scientist-practitioners using five training components. First, coursework is distributed across clinical core, general psychology, methodology core, and elective offerings. Second, research mentoring is experienced in the precandidacy and dissertation projects. Third, procedural knowledge is developed in clinical practicum and internship training. Fourth, declarative knowledge is developed in the comprehensive examination with a written portion covering general psychological knowledge and methods, and an oral examination on clinical psychology modeled on state board examinations. A fifth component is annual written evaluation of the student's progress in the program.

Special Facilities or Resources: Certain features of our program deserve special mention. Our faculty is usually active in research and, due to our small size, students have ample opportunities for collaboration in faculty research and informal discussions of research projects. Our graduate programs have developed over the last decade in such a way that they complement and support each other. As a result, students are exposed to a wide variety of viewpoints and research methods. The department has splendid relations with the Tulsa business, school, and mental health communities. Students can thus apply knowledge and gain experience in a wide variety of settings.

Application Information:
Send to: Graduate School, University of Tulsa, 600 S. College, Tulsa, OK 74104. Students are admitted in the Fall, application deadline Jan 15-Clinical Programs; February 1-I/O Programs Applications are reviewed once a year for a Fall entering semester. *Fee:* $30.

George Fox University

Graduate School of Clinical Psychology
414 North Meridian Street
Newberg, OR 97132-2697
Telephone: (503) 554-2761
Fax: (503) 537-3898
E-mail: *wadams@georgefox.edu*
Web: *http://georgefox.edu/academics/grad/psyd/*

Department Established:
1990. Chairperson: Wayne Adams. Number of Faculty: total–full-time 8, part-time 7; women–full-time 3, part-time 4.

Programs and Degrees Offered:
Listed in the following order: Program area, degree type (T if terminal Master's), number awarded 7/00–6/01. Clinical PsyD 17.

APA Accreditation: Clinical PsyD: full.

Student Applications/Admissions:
Student Applications
Clinical PsyD—Applications 2001–2002, 49. Total applicants accepted 2001–2002, 28. New applicants enrolled 2001–2002, 20. Total enrolled 2001–2002 full-time, 87, part-time, 6. Openings 2002–2003, 20. The Median number of years required for completion of a degree are 6. The number of students enrolled full and part-time, who were dismissed or voluntarily withdrew from this program area were 1.

Admissions Requirements:
Scores: Entries appear in this order: required test or GPA, minimum score (if required), median score of students entering in 2001–2002. Master's Programs: GRE-V+Q 1050, 1100; overall undergraduate GPA 3.0, 3.4; psychology GPA 3.0, 3.5. No set formula is used for judging any given applicant. Each is judged on his/her own merit and exceptions are made for one or more of the above cut-offs for special circumstances or unique strengths. The scores listed are those for entrance into the master's aspect of the doctoral program. Doctoral Programs: GRE-Subject(Psych) 610, 660; last 2 years GPA no minimum stated; psychology GPA no minimum stated; psychology GPA no minimum stated. The above requirement is necessary in addition to earning a master's degree in our program, or the equivalent.
Other Criteria: (importance of criteria rated low, medium, or high): GRE/MAT scores medium, research experience low, work experience medium, extracurricular activity low, clinically related public service medium, GPA high, letters of recommendation high, interview high, statement of goals and objectives high, Faith-based perspective high.

Student Characteristics: The following represents characteristics of students in 2001–2002 in all graduate psychology programs in the department: Female–full-time 46, part-time 3; Male–full-time 41, part-time 3; African American/Black–full-time 2, part-time 0; Hispanic/Latino (a)–full-time 3, part-time 0; Asian/Pacific Is-lander–full-time 4, part-time 0; American Indian/Alaska Native–full-time 2, part-time 0; Multi-ethnic–full-time 3, students subject to the Americans with Disabilities Act–full-time 0.

Financial Information/Assistance:
Tuition for Full-Time Study: *Doctoral:* State residents: $525 per credit hour; nonstate residents: $525 per credit hour.

Financial Assistance:
First Year Students: Fellowships and scholarships available for first-year. Average amount paid per academic year: $10,000. Average number of hours worked per week: 0. Apply by February 15.
Advanced Students: Teaching assistantships available for advanced students. Average amount paid per academic year: $4,200. Average number of hours worked per week: 10. Apply by variable. Research assistantships available for advanced students. Average amount paid per academic year: $2,500. Average number of hours worked per week: 7. Apply by variable. Fellowships and scholarships available for advanced students. Average amount paid per academic year: $10,000. Average number of hours worked per week: 0. Apply by n/a.
Contact Information: Of all students currently enrolled full-time, 50% benefited from one or more of the listed financial assistance programs. For information on financial assistance, contact: Financial Aid and GSCP Graduate Admissions Offices.

Internships/Practica: Students are required to complete four years of practicum (1,500 hours) in a variety of settings in the greater Portland metropolitan area. Practicum settings include hospitals, community mental health agencies, drug and alcohol programs, behavioral medicine clinics, schools, and prisons. All practicum experience is gained under the careful supervision of licensed psychologists at the practicum sites. Additionally, students receive weekly oversight on campus by core faculty. Students apply for internships within the system developed by the Association of Psychology Postdoctoral and Internship Centers (APPIC). Students complete a one-year full-time internship (2000 hours) at an approved internship site during their fifth year in the program. For those doctoral students for whom a professional internship is required prior to graduation, 16 applied in 2000–2001. Of those who applied, 15 were placed in internships listed by the Association of Psychology Postdoctoral and Internship Programs (AP-PIC); 14 were placed in APA accredited internships.

Housing and Day Care: No on-campus housing and day care facilities are available.

Employment of Department Graduates:
Master's Degree Graduates: Of those who graduated in the academic year 2000–2001, the following categories and numbers represent the post-graduate activities and employment of master's degree graduates: Enrolled in a psychology doctoral program (17), enrolled in another graduate/professional program (0), enrolled in a post-doctoral residency/fellowship (n/a), employed in independent practice (n/a), still seeking employment (1).
Doctoral Degree Graduates: Of those who graduated in the academic year 2000–2001, the following categories and numbers

represent the post-graduate activities and employment of doctoral degree graduates: Enrolled in a psychology doctoral program (n/a), enrolled in another graduate/professional program (n/a), enrolled in a post-doctoral residency/fellowship (3), employed in independent practice (1), employed in an academic position at a university (2), employed in an academic position at a 2-year/4-year college (3), employed in other positions at a higher education institution (1), employed in a professional position in a school system (1), employed in business or industry (research/consulting) (0), employed in business or industry (management) (0), employed in a government agency (research) (0), employed in a government agency (professional services) (1), employed in a community mental health/counseling center (9), employed in a hospital/medical center (3), still seeking employment (1), other employment position (3).

Additional Information:

Orientation, Objectives, and Emphasis of Department: The goal of the Graduate School of Clinical Psychology (GSCP) is to prepare professional psychologists who are competent to provide psychological services in a wide variety of clinical settings, who are knowledgeable in critical evaluation and application of psychological research, and who are committed to the highest standards of professional ethics. The central distinctive feature the program is the integration of Christian principles and the science of psychology at philosophical, practical, and personal levels. Graduates are also trained as specialists in meeting the unique psychological needs of the Christian community within the context of a Christian worldview. Graduates are prepared for licensure as clinical psychologists. Alumni of the GSCP are licensed psychologists in numerous states throughout the U.S. They engage in practice in a variety of settings, including independent and group practice, hospital, community and public health agencies, church and para-church organizations, and mission agencies. Graduates also teach in a variety of settings, including colleges and seminaries.

Special Facilities or Resources: The psychology research lab is located in the Murdock Learning Resource Center. High-speed microcomputers, laser printers, and complete statistical (SPSS PC+) and graphics software are provided. In addition to its use for instructional purposes, the lab supports student research projects and dissertations, plus faculty research. The Murdock Learning Resource Center provides library support for the psychology program. The library has an excellent access to materials important to contemporary clinical and empirical work in most areas of clinical psychology. In addition, the library receives more than 150 periodicals in psychology and related disciplines. Students also have on-line access to major computerized databases through library services, including PsycInfo, DIALOG, ERIC, and many others. In addition to full-text access to many psychology journals, George Fox University maintains cooperative arrangements with other local educational institutions providing psychology students with a full range of user services, including interlibrary loans and direct borrowing privileges.

Information for Students With Physical Disabilities: The University accommodates the special needs of students according to the Americans with Disabilities Act.

Application Information:
Send to: Graduate Admissions Office. Students are admitted in the Winter, application deadline February 15. Special circumstances for delay or late application will be considered. *Fee:* $40.

Lewis & Clark College
Counseling Psychology Department
Graduate School of Education
615 S.W. Palatine Hill Road, Box 86
Portland, OR 97219-7899
Telephone: (503) 768-6060
Fax: (503) 768-6065
E-mail: *cpsy@lclark.edu*
Web: *http://www.lclark.edu/dept/cpsy*

Department Established:
1972. Department Chair: Dr. Carol Doyle. Number of Faculty: total–full-time 8, part-time 27; women–full-time 5, part-time 16; minority–full-time 1, part-time 3.

Programs and Degrees Offered:
Listed in the following order: Program area, degree type (T if terminal Master's), number awarded 7/00–6/01. Counseling psychology MA (T) 53, school psychology MA (T) 9.

Student Applications/Admissions:
Student Applications
Counseling psychology MA—Applications 2001–2002, 113. Total applicants accepted 2001–2002, 106. New applicants enrolled 2001–2002, 71. Total enrolled 2001–2002 full-time, 45, part-time, 26. Openings 2002–2003, 100. The Median number of years required for completion of a degree are 2. The number of students enrolled full and part-time, who were dismissed or voluntarily withdrew from this program area were 20. *School psychology* MA—Applications 2001–2002, 27. Total applicants accepted 2001–2002, 17. New applicants enrolled 2001–2002, 12. Total enrolled 2001–2002 full-time, 30, part-time, 10. Openings 2002–2003, 15. The Median number of years required for completion of a degree are 3. The number of students enrolled full and part-time, who were dismissed or voluntarily withdrew from this program area were 2.

Admissions Requirements:
Scores: Entries appear in this order: required test or GPA, minimum score (if required), median score of students entering in 2001–2002. Master's Programs: GRE-V+Q+Analytical no minimum stated; overall undergraduate GPA 2.75, 3.3. No minimum is required for GRE V+ Q+ Analytical. Doctoral Programs: last 2 years GPA no minimum stated; psychology GPA no minimum stated; psychology GPA no minimum stated.

Other Criteria: (importance of criteria rated low, medium, or high): research experience low, work experience low, extracurricular activity low, clinically related public service low, letters of recommendation high, interview medium, statement of goals and objectives high.

Student Characteristics: The following represents characteristics of students in 2001–2002 in all graduate psychology programs in

the department: Female–full-time 140, part-time 34; Male–full-time 30, part-time 15; African American/Black–full-time 0, part-time 0; Hispanic/Latino (a)–full-time 3, part-time 2; Asian/Pacific Islander–full-time 5, part-time 3; American Indian/Alaska Native–full-time 1, part-time 0; Multi-ethnic–full-time 2, part-time 2; students subject to the Americans with Disabilities Act–full-time 2, part-time 1.

Financial Information/Assistance:

Tuition for Full-Time Study: *Master's:* State residents $500 per credit hour; nonstate residents: $500 per credit hour.

Financial Assistance:
> *First Year Students:* No information provided.
> *Advanced Students:* No information provided.
> *Contact Information:* For information on financial assistance, contact: Student Financial Services, Lewis & Clark College, 0615 SW Palatine Hill Road, Box 56, Portland, OR 97219-7899.

Internships/Practica: Internship and practicum placements in community agencies and schools provide students with opportunities for supervised professional practice. As part of each placement, students receive supervision from qualified professionals in their community or school setting. Students also receive weekly instruction and supervision from on-campus instructors throughout their internship and practicum placements. Required hours, supervision, and activities meet standards set by licensing bodies for students in their respective specialty areas. This ensures that students will be qualified to pursue licensing after completing their degree program. Internships in community counseling and addictions counseling involve part-time placements. Internships in school psychology are full-time for one academic year and usually involve a stipend to the student.

Housing and Day Care: No on-campus housing and day care facilities are available.

Employment of Department Graduates:

Master's Degree Graduates: Of those who graduated in the academic year 2000–2001, the following categories and numbers represent the post-graduate activities and employment of master's degree graduates: Enrolled in a post-doctoral residency/fellowship (n/a), employed in independent practice (n/a).

Doctoral Degree Graduates: Of those who graduated in the academic year 2000–2001, the following categories and numbers represent the post-graduate activities and employment of doctoral degree graduates: Enrolled in a psychology doctoral program (n/a), enrolled in another graduate/professional program (n/a).

Additional Information:

Orientation, Objectives, and Emphasis of Department: Lewis & Clark's Department of Counseling Psychology prepares well-educated, dedicated professional counselors and psychologists to lead and serve in community and school settings. Faculty and students are committed to disseminating and expanding the knowledge base relevant to this mission, promoting the use of effective treatment and prevention procedures, and adhering to the highest ethical standards as practitioners and researchers. The programs in counseling psychology prepare highly qualified mental health professionals in counseling and school psychology for employment in public agencies, community-based programs, and schools. Curricular options also exist for those who would like to concentrate

on research and establish a foundation in pursuit of doctoral training.

Special Facilities or Resources: The program has established collaborative relationships with community schools and agencies which provide students opportunities to participate in ongoing research and program evaluation. These opportunities are open to students planning to complete a thesis and also to students who wish to secure increased training and experience without doing a full thesis.

Information for Students With Physical Disabilities: The campus has been made accessible to students with disabilities. The Office of Student Support Services provides assistance to students with disabilities. Several students with disabilities have completed degrees in this department in recent years.

Application Information:

Send to: Counseling Psychology Department, Lewis & Clark College, 0615 SW Palatine Hill Road, Box 86; Portland, OR 97219-7899. Students are admitted in the Fall, application deadline 4/1, 7/1; Spring, application deadline 11/1; Summer, application deadline 2/1, 4/1. Special Students (not fully admitted to a program who may take 9 semester hours within one year) must submit completed applications at least 3 weeks prior to the above application deadlines. *Fee:* $50.

Oregon, University of
Department of Psychology
College of Arts and Sciences
1227 University of Oregon
Eugene, OR 97403-1227
Telephone: (541) 346-5060
Fax: (541) 346-4911
E-mail: *gradsec@psych.uoregon.edu*
Web: *http://psychweb.uoregon.edu*

Department Established:

1895. Department Head: Marjorie Taylor, PhD. Number of Faculty: total–full-time 27, part-time 3; women–full-time 12; minority–full-time 3.

Programs and Degrees Offered:

Listed in the following order: Program area, degree type (T if terminal Master's), number awarded 7/00–6/01. Clinical PhD, cognitive PhD, developmental PhD, individualized masters' (T) 10, neuroscience PhD, social/personality PhD.

APA Accreditation: Clinical PhD: full.

Student Applications/Admissions:

Student Applications
> *Clinical PhD*—Applications 2001–2002, 169. Total applicants accepted 2001–2002, 5. New applicants enrolled 2001–2002, 5. Total enrolled 2001–2002 full-time, 19. Openings 2002–2003, 3. *Cognitive PhD*—Total enrolled 2001–2002 full-time, 9. Openings 2002–2003, 3. *Developmental PhD*—Total applicants accepted 2001–2002, 2. New applicants enrolled 2001–2002, 2. Openings 2002–2003, 2. *Individualized masters'*—Ap-

plications 2001–2002, 19. Total applicants accepted 2001–2002, 9. New applicants enrolled 2001–2002, 9. Openings 2002–2003, 10. *Neuroscience PhD Openings 2002–2003, 2. Social/personality PhD*—Total applicants accepted 2001–2002, 1. New applicants enrolled 2001–2002, 1. Openings 2002–2003, 2.

Admissions Requirements:

Scores: Entries appear in this order: required test or GPA, minimum score (if required), median score of students entering in 2001–2002. Master's Programs: overall undergraduate GPA no minimum stated, 3.44. The GRE is recommended (not required) for admission to the Individualized Master's Program. Doctoral Programs: GRE-V no minimum stated, 650; GRE-Q no minimum stated, 650; GRE-Analytical no minimum stated, 745; overall undergraduate GPA no minimum stated, 3.68; last 2 years GPA no minimum stated; psychology GPA no minimum stated; psychology GPA no minimum stated.

Other Criteria: (importance of criteria rated low, medium, or high): GRE/MAT scores high, research experience high, work experience low, extracurricular activity low, clinically related public service medium, GPA high, letters of recommendation high, interview medium, statement of goals and objectives high. Please check with department regarding Interviews.

Student Characteristics: The following represents characteristics of students in 2001–2002 in all graduate psychology programs in the department: Female–full-time 40, part-time 0; Male–full-time 26, part-time 0; African American/Black–full-time 1, part-time 0; Hispanic/Latino (a)–full-time 1, part-time 0; Asian/Pacific Islander–full-time 3, part-time 0; American Indian/Alaska Native–full-time 2, part-time 0; students subject to the Americans with Disabilities Act–full-time 1.

Financial Information/Assistance:

Tuition for Full-Time Study: No information provided.

Financial Assistance:

First Year Students: Teaching assistantships available for first-year. Tuition remission given: full. Research assistantships available for first-year. Tuition remission given: full.

Advanced Students: Teaching assistantships available for advanced students. Tuition remission given: full. Research assistantships available for advanced students. Tuition remission given: full.

Contact Information: Of all students currently enrolled full-time, 95% benefited from one or more of the listed financial assistance programs. For information on financial assistance, contact: Rebecca Goodrich.

Internships/Practica: No information provided.

Housing and Day Care: No on-campus housing and day care facilities are available.

Employment of Department Graduates:

Master's Degree Graduates: Of those who graduated in the academic year 2000–2001, the following categories and numbers represent the post-graduate activities and employment of master's degree graduates: Enrolled in a post-doctoral residency/fellowship (n/a), employed in independent practice (n/a).

Doctoral Degree Graduates: Of those who graduated in the academic year 2000–2001, the following categories and numbers represent the post-graduate activities and employment of doctoral degree graduates: Enrolled in a psychology doctoral program (n/a), enrolled in another graduate/professional program (n/a).

Additional Information:

Orientation, Objectives, and Emphasis of Department: The course of study is tailored largely to the student's particular needs. There are minimal formal requirements for the doctorate, which include three course sequences (contemporary issues in psychology, statistics, and a first-year research practicum); a supporting area requirement, consisting of at least two graduate-level, graded courses, and a major project, such as a paper or teaching an original course; a major preliminary examination; and, of course, the doctoral dissertation. Clinical students engage in several practica beginning in the first year. All programs require and are organized to facilitate student research from the first year.

Special Facilities or Resources: Straub Hall houses the psychology clinic, equipment for psychophysiological research, specialized facilities for research in child and social psychology, and experimental laboratories for human research. Numerous microcomputers are available for research and teaching. A short distance from the main psychology building are well-equipped animal labs for research in physiological psychology. Graduate students and faculty participate in interdisciplinary programs in cognitive science, neuroscience, and emotions research. Local nonprofit research groups including Oregon Research Institute, Oregon Social Learning Center, and Decision Research provide unusual auspices and opportunities for students.

Application Information:

Send to: Graduate Admissions, Department of Psychology, 1227 University of Oregon, Eugene, OR 97403-1227. Students are admitted in the Fall, application deadline December 15. Individualized master's deadline is May 15 for fall. *Fee:* $50.

Oregon, University of (2001 data)
Special Education Area
College of Education
5261 University of Oregon
Eugene, OR 97403-5261
Telephone: (541) 346-5521
Fax: (541) 346-2897
E-mail: *boudreau@oregon.uoregon.edu*
Web: *http://interact.uoregon.edu/dsecr/index.html*

Department Established:

1970. Director of Training: Roland H. Good III. Number of Faculty: total–full-time 5; women–full-time 3.

Programs and Degrees Offered:

Listed in the following order: Program area, degree type (T if terminal Master's), number awarded 7/00–6/01. School MA 1.

APA Accreditation: School PhD: full.

Student Applications/Admissions:

Student Applications

School MA—Applications 2001–2002, 24. Total applicants accepted 2001–2002, 3. New applicants enrolled 2001–2002, 3. Total enrolled 2001–2002 full-time, 5, part-time, 3. Openings 2002–2003, 3.

Admissions Requirements:

Scores: Entries appear in this order: required test or GPA, minimum score (if required), median score of students entering in 2001–2002. Master's Programs: GRE-V no minimum stated; GRE-Q no minimum stated; GRE-V+Q no minimum stated; GRE-Analytical no minimum stated. Doctoral Programs: GRE-V no minimum stated; GRE-Q no minimum stated; GRE-V+Q no minimum stated; GRE-Analytical no minimum stated; GRE-V+Q+Analytical no minimum stated.

Other Criteria: (importance of criteria rated low, medium, or high): research experience medium, work experience medium, extracurricular activity medium, clinically related public service medium, letters of recommendation high, interview high, statement of goals and objectives high.

Student Characteristics: The following represents characteristics of students in 2001–2002 in all graduate psychology programs in the department: Female–full-time 21, part-time 0; Male–full-time 5, part-time 0; African American/Black–full-time 0, part-time 0; Hispanic/Latino (a)–full-time 1, part-time 0; Asian/Pacific Islander–full-time 0, part-time 0; American Indian/Alaska Native–full-time 0, part-time 0.

Financial Information/Assistance:

Tuition for Full-Time Study: No information provided.

Financial Assistance:

First Year Students: No information provided.

Advanced Students: No information provided.

Contact Information: For information on financial assistance, contact: Admissions Secretary, School Psychology Program.

Internships/Practica: The sequence of coursework in the school psychology program is designed to accomplish the aim of integrating theory and practice early on in the program. There is heavy emphasis on field-based courses, with a practicum component beginning in each student's first quarter. Students complete a 360-hour supervised practicum experience during their second year in the program, with half of the experience occurring in local public schools and half in a university-based clinic. Student programs are designed to culminate in a full year, 1,500-hour internship in a school system or other applied setting. School Psychology students apply for internship positions annually.

Housing and Day Care: No on-campus housing and day care facilities are available.

Employment of Department Graduates:

Master's Degree Graduates: Of those who graduated in the academic year 2000–2001, the following categories and numbers represent the post-graduate activities and employment of master's degree graduates: Enrolled in a post-doctoral residency/fellowship (n/a), employed in independent practice (n/a).

Doctoral Degree Graduates: Of those who graduated in the academic year 2000–2001, the following categories and numbers represent the post-graduate activities and employment of doctoral degree graduates: Enrolled in a psychology doctoral program (n/a), enrolled in another graduate/professional program (n/a).

Additional Information:

Orientation, Objectives, and Emphasis of Department: The main objective of the graduate programs in School Psychology is the preparation of problem solving psychologists who work effectively with others in the identification and remediation of social and educational problems of children and adults. The aim of professional preparation is to develop school psychologists who are grounded thoroughly in the principles of human behavior and educational psychology. Attention is directed toward the mastery of skills in assessing the academic and social development of children and adults within specific environments and ecological confines; planning, implementing, and evaluating academic and behavioral interventions; and consulting and training with parents, teachers, and related school personnel. Emphasis is placed on analyzing problems at the idiographic level. That is, each problem situation is considered unique with respect to its background information, the personal characteristics of the parties involved (e.g., gender, cultural heritage), and the expectations for problem solution. School psychology students are trained to be scientists/practitioners. This approach means that students master and employ valid scientific methods and valid assessment intervention strategies to prevent and resolve problems. Interventions are treated as plausible hypotheses that must be evaluated continuously as part of service provision.

Special Facilities or Resources: The School Psychology program generated approximately $1.6 million for research and training during 1997–98. Projects of potential interest to School Psychology students include preparing young adults with severe disabilities to succeed in employment settings, preventing substance abuse through interventions with families, early intervention programs for infants and young children who have special needs or are at-risk and their families. School Psychology faculty and students have research opportunities through the College of Education's Center on Human Development, the Institute on Violent and Destructive Behavior, and the Institute for Development of Educational Achievement. Additional research opportunities exist at the Oregon Research Institute (ORI) and the Oregon Social Learning Center (OSLC), both private research organizations with the Eugene community. Several adjunct and affiliated faculty members contribute research and service capabilities to enrich the program environment. Local schools also cooperate with program training.

Information for Students With Physical Disabilities: The University of Oregon is committed to responding to the needs of students with disabilities as outlined in both the Rehabilitation Act of 1973 and the Americans With Disabilities Act of 1990. The university does not discriminate on the basis of disability in admission or access to, treatment of, or employment in its programs or activities.

Application Information:

Send to: Admissions Secretary, School Psychology Program, 5261 University of Oregon, Eugene, OR 97403-5261. Students are admitted in the Fall, application deadline January 15. *Fee:* $50. Contact main university admissions office.

Pacific University

School of Professional Psychology
2004 Pacific Avenue
Forest Grove, OR 97116
Telephone: (503) 352-2240,1-877-722-8648 ext.2240
Fax: (503) 352-2134
E-mail: *spp@pacificu.edu*
Web: *http://www.pacificu.edu*

Department Established:

1979. Dean: Michel Hersen. Number of Faculty: total–full-time 13, part-time 19; women–full-time 7, part-time 11; minority–full-time 1, part-time 2.

Programs and Degrees Offered:

Listed in the following order: Program area, degree type (T if terminal Master's), number awarded 7/00–6/01. Clinical PsyD 22, counseling psychology MA (T) 14.

APA Accreditation: Clinical PsyD: full.

Student Applications/Admissions:

Student Applications

Clinical PsyD—Applications 2001–2002, 122. Total applicants accepted 2001–2002, 75. New applicants enrolled 2001–2002, 36. Total enrolled 2001–2002 full-time, 123, part-time, 30. Openings 2002–2003, 35. The Median number of years required for completion of a degree are 6. The number of students enrolled full and part-time, who were dismissed or voluntarily withdrew from this program area were 1. *Counseling psychology MA*—Applications 2001–2002, 53. Total applicants accepted 2001–2002, 41. New applicants enrolled 2001–2002, 29. Total enrolled 2001–2002 full-time, 43, part-time, 3. Openings 2002–2003, 25. The Median number of years required for completion of a degree are 2. The number of students enrolled full and part-time, who were dismissed or voluntarily withdrew from this program area were 3.

Admissions Requirements:

Scores: Entries appear in this order: required test or GPA, minimum score (if required), median score of students entering in 2001–2002. Master's Programs: overall undergraduate GPA no minimum stated, 3.0. Doctoral Programs: GRE-V no minimum stated; GRE-Q no minimum stated; GRE-V+Q no minimum stated, 1100; GRE-Analytical no minimum stated; last 2 years GPA no minimum stated, 3.0; psychology GPA no minimum stated; psychology GPA no minimum stated, 3.8. Master's GPA is required for advanced standing applicants.

Other Criteria: (importance of criteria rated low, medium, or high): GRE/MAT scores research experience high, work experience medium, extracurricular activity low, clinically related public service low, GPA letters of recommendation high, interview high, statement of goals and objectives medium.

Student Characteristics: The following represents characteristics of students in 2001–2002 in all graduate psychology programs in the department: Female–full-time 125, part-time 24; Male–full-time 41, part-time 9; African American/Black–full-time 1, part-time 0; Hispanic/Latino (a)–full-time 5, part-time 4; Asian/Pacific Islander–full-time 13, part-time 0; American Indian/Alaska Na-tive–full-time 0, part-time 1; Multi-ethnic–full-time 2, part-time 1; students subject to the Americans with Disabilities Act–full-time 2.

Financial Information/Assistance:

Tuition for Full-Time Study: *Master's:* State residents per academic year $13,600, $520 per credit hour; nonstate residents: per academic year $13,600, $520 per credit hour. *Doctoral:* State residents: per academic year $18,250, $520 per credit hour; nonstate residents: per academic year $18,250, $520 per credit hour.

Financial Assistance:

First Year Students: Research assistantships available for first-year. Average amount paid per academic year: $3,000. Average number of hours worked per week: 7. Fellowships and scholarships available for first-year. Apply by 1/10.

Advanced Students: Teaching assistantships available for advanced students. Average amount paid per academic year: $3,600. Average number of hours worked per week: 7. Apply by 4/15. Research assistantships available for advanced students. Average amount paid per academic year: $3,000. Average number of hours worked per week: 7. Apply by 4/15. Fellowships and scholarships available for advanced students. Average amount paid per academic year: $3,000. Apply by 4/15.

Contact Information: Of all students currently enrolled full-time, 25% benefited from one or more of the listed financial assistance programs. For information on financial assistance, contact: Apply along with application by January 10. Service scholarships based on academic potential, commitment to providing service to an identified underserved population, level of understanding of the mental health needs of the identified, and financial need as ascertained on the standardized financial aid form.

Internships/Practica: Each PsyD student is required to complete 6 terms (24 credits, two years) of practica. The practicum experience includes a minimum of 550 training hours per year, approximately one third to one half of which are in direct service, one fourth in supervisory and training activities, and the remainder in administrative/clerical duties related to the above. Training entails the integration of theoretical knowledge through its application in clinical practice. The experience shall include supervised practice in the application of professional psychological competencies with a range of client populations, age groups, problems, and service settings. The initial three practica are typically served at the Psychological Service Center. Later experiences are usually taken at community placements. Upon successful completion of practicum training, required coursework, and Candidacy Examination, the student is ready to begin an internship. Internship requires one calendar year of full-time experience, or two years half time, at an approved site. Internships are available at the school's Psychological Service Center. MA Counseling Psychology students complete 15 credits (3 terms) of practicum in their second year. For those doctoral students for whom a professional internship is required prior to graduation, 17 applied in 2000–2001. Of those who applied, 9 were placed in internships listed by the Association of Psychology Postdoctoral and Internship Programs (APPIC); 5 were placed in APA accredited internships.

Housing and Day Care: No on-campus housing and day care facilities are available.

Employment of Department Graduates:

Master's Degree Graduates: Of those who graduated in the academic year 2000–2001, the following categories and numbers represent the post-graduate activities and employment of master's degree graduates: Enrolled in a post-doctoral residency/fellowship (n/a), employed in independent practice (n/a).

Doctoral Degree Graduates: Of those who graduated in the academic year 2000–2001, the following categories and numbers represent the post-graduate activities and employment of doctoral degree graduates: Enrolled in a psychology doctoral program (n/a), enrolled in another graduate/professional program (n/a), enrolled in a post-doctoral residency/fellowship (5), employed in independent practice (4), employed in a professional position in a school system (1), employed in a government agency (professional services) (1), employed in a community mental health/counseling center (13), employed in a hospital/medical center (3).

Additional Information:

Orientation, Objectives, and Emphasis of Department: The Pacific University School of Professional Psychology follows a practitioner-scholar model of professional education, with coursework reflecting the latest empirical findings in the field. We emphasize the integration of a broad range of theoretical perspectives and foster development of the full range of professional psychological competencies in assessment, intervention, research/evaluation, consultation/education, and management supervision. We promote provision of services to diverse populations at the individual, family, group, and community levels. We strive to create a facilitative academic community based in collaborative inquiry. Faculty and students work together in multiple roles in program development and governance. We affirm the principles of promoting humanity, integrity, and self-awareness and of honoring diversity.

Special Facilities or Resources: The Psychological Service Center of the Pacific University School of Professional Psychology provides a full range of quality outpatient psychological services to residents of the Portland Metropolitan area while providing intensive training for doctoral level clinical psychology students and providing a setting for on-going clinical research. The full range of psychodiagnostic and treatment services is provided to a variety of client populations, including intellectual, personality, and neuropsychological assessment, individual therapy, family therapy, group therapy, and consultation.

Information for Students With Physical Disabilities: Pacific University complies with the Americans with Disabilities Act of 1990 (ADA). Disability Support Services: This service is provided to arrange for specialized academic support or modifications to the learning environment. The university requires appropriate documentation of a disability.

Application Information:

Send to: Office of Admissions, Pacific University, 2043 College Way, Forest Grove, OR 97116, email: admissions@pacificu.edu, Tel: 503-359-2900; 1-800-933-9308. Students are admitted in the Fall, application deadline January 10. MA Counseling Psychology - March 15. *Fee:* $40.

Portland State University
Psychology Department
College of Liberal Arts & Sciences
P.O. Box 751
Portland, OR 97207-0751
Telephone: (503) 725-3923
Fax: (503) 725-3904
E-mail: *mankowskie@pdx.edu*
Web: *http://www.psy.pdx.edu/*

Department Established:

1955. Chairperson: Keith L. Kaufman. Number of Faculty: total–full-time 16; women–full-time 9, part-time 1; minority–full-time 2.

Programs and Degrees Offered:

Listed in the following order: Program area, degree type (T if terminal Master's), number awarded 7/00–6/01. Applied developmental MA, applied social & community MA, industrial/organizational MA, systems science/developmental PhD, systems science/industrial/org PhD, systems science/social & comm PhD.

Student Applications/Admissions:

Student Applications

Applied developmental MA—Applications 2001–2002, 13. Total applicants accepted 2001–2002, 6. New applicants enrolled 2001–2002, 6. Total enrolled 2001–2002 full-time, 19. Openings 2002–2003, 3. *Applied social & community MA*—Applications 2001–2002, 18. Total applicants accepted 2001–2002, 4. New applicants enrolled 2001–2002, 4. Total enrolled 2001–2002 full-time, 18. Openings 2002–2003, 3. *Industrial/organizational MA*—Applications 2001–2002, 74. Total applicants accepted 2001–2002, 8. New applicants enrolled 2001–2002, 8. Total enrolled 2001–2002 full-time, 26. Openings 2002–2003, 5. *Systems science/developmental PhD. Systems science/industrial/org PhD. Systems science/social & comm PhD.*

Admissions Requirements:

Scores: Entries appear in this order: required test or GPA, minimum score (if required), median score of students entering in 2001–2002. Master's Programs: GRE-V no minimum stated; GRE-Q no minimum stated; GRE-V+Q no minimum stated; GRE-Analytical no minimum stated; GRE-V+Q+Analytical no minimum stated; overall undergraduate GPA 3.00; last 2 years GPA no minimum stated; psychology GPA no minimum stated. Doctoral Programs: GRE-V no minimum stated; GRE-Q no minimum stated; GRE-V+Q 1100; GRE-Analytical no minimum stated; GRE-V+Q+Analytical no minimum stated; overall undergraduate GPA 3.00; last 2 years GPA no minimum stated; psychology GPA no minimum stated; psychology GPA no minimum stated. Verbal+ (quantitative or analytic) score must be at least 1100.

Other Criteria: (importance of criteria rated low, medium, or high): GRE/MAT scores high, research experience high, work experience medium, extracurricular activity medium, clinically related public service low, GPA high, letters of recommendation high, statement of goals and objectives high.

Student Characteristics: The following represents characteristics of students in 2001–2002 in all graduate psychology programs in

the department: Female–full-time 47, part-time 0; Male–full-time 19, part-time 0.

Financial Information/Assistance:
Tuition for Full-Time Study: *Master's:* State residents per academic year $2,173; nonstate residents: per academic year $3,709. *Doctoral:* State residents: per academic year $2,173; nonstate residents: per academic year $3,709.

Financial Assistance:
First Year Students: Teaching assistantships available for first-year. Average amount paid per academic year: $5,100. Average number of hours worked per week: 12. Tuition remission given: full. Research assistantships available for first-year. Average amount paid per academic year: $5,100. Average number of hours worked per week: 12. Tuition remission given: full. Fellowships and scholarships available for first-year. Average amount paid per academic year: $5,100. Average number of hours worked per week: 12. Tuition remission given: full.

Advanced Students: Teaching assistantships available for advanced students. Average amount paid per academic year: $5,100. Average number of hours worked per week: 12. Tuition remission given: full. Research assistantships available for advanced students. Average amount paid per academic year: $5,100. Average number of hours worked per week: 12. Tuition remission given: full. Fellowships and scholarships available for advanced students. Average amount paid per academic year: $5,100. Average number of hours worked per week: 12. Tuition remission given: full.

Contact Information: Of all students currently enrolled full-time, 100% benefited from one or more of the listed financial assistance programs. For information on financial assistance, contact: Financial Aid (503) 725-3461.

Internships/Practica: The university is located in downtown Portland, the major metropolitan area in the state of Oregon. Consequently internships are readily available in a variety of applied settings. Placements are also available through the ongoing research activities of the faculty. The program is structured to provide everyone with (1) training in the basics of applied psychology and research methods, and (2) expertise in the psychological theories and research methods in their area of specialty. The basic training is provided by three advanced applied courses in the three areas we consider central to the understanding of social issues: social and group processes (referred to as Applied Social); organizational and institutional processes (referred to as Industrial-Organizational); and process of change (referred to as Applied Developmental). Training in research methods is provided via a sequence of Quantitative methods courses, two of which are required. The Department offers a number of additional quantitative offerings which include: Factor Analysis, Structural Equation Modeling, and Psychometrics and Scale Construction. Since the program emphasizes applied psychology, students receive training in their area of specialty not only through close work with faculty but also through structured participation in community organizations. Graduate students work in close collaboration with their faculty advisors and other members of the faculty who serve in a mentor role. Student experiences include seminars on special topics, individual reading and conference arrangements, research practica, and collaboration on joint projects. The primary vehicles for interactions with community organizations are practica and internships. To ensure relevant learning, these are supervised by departmental faculty. The program culminates for students in their own independent research (i.e., thesis and/or dissertation).

Housing and Day Care: On-campus housing and day care facilities are available.

Employment of Department Graduates:
Master's Degree Graduates: Of those who graduated in the academic year 2000–2001, the following categories and numbers represent the post-graduate activities and employment of master's degree graduates: Enrolled in a post-doctoral residency/fellowship (n/a), employed in independent practice (n/a).
Doctoral Degree Graduates: Of those who graduated in the academic year 2000–2001, the following categories and numbers represent the post-graduate activities and employment of doctoral degree graduates: Enrolled in a psychology doctoral program (n/a), enrolled in another graduate/professional program (n/a).

Additional Information:
Orientation, Objectives, and Emphasis of Department: The department accepts applicants to both the MA/MS (initiated fall 1969) and PhD (initiated fall 1986) programs. The master's program is fully integrated into the doctoral program. Those who are admitted to the master's program may later apply for admission to the doctoral program, conditional upon demonstrated competence at the master's level. The PhD, but not the master's, program requires coursework and preliminary examinations in systems science. The aim of the program is to prepare graduates for a university career and/or a research/service career in a variety of settings, such as governmental agencies, manufacturing and service industries, health organizations, and labor organizations. Students are given a broad background in applied psychology. Doctoral students major in one of the following three specialty areas and select a minor in a second. Applied Developmental focuses on family studies, providing training in two areas: a) family development, i.e., the processes of change that families as systems of member relationships experience, and b) family and work, i.e., the interactive relationships between the two domains of family and work life. Industrial-Organizational covers areas of theory, research methods, and social issues relevant to organizational and occupational life. Areas of study include leadership, work motivation, job stress, organizational development, etc. Applied Social deals with how social-psychological research methods, findings, and theories are applied to: a) social issues (e.g., prejudice, violence, AIDS, and energy conservation); b) professions and institutions (e.g., health and law); and c) the design and evaluation of social interventions.

Special Facilities or Resources: The Department of Psychology's location in the heart of downtown Portland offers unique academic and research opportunities in the service of the Department's applied mission. Strong collaborative relationships with local industry, organizations, and community agencies offer venues for course related projects, faculty research initiatives, practicum placements, and required student research. A number of University-based resources also enhance our students' skills and experiences. For example, the University's writing center allows faculty and students to hone technical writing skills. The Instructional Development Center provides training in computer and media-based applications to foster improved teaching and more sophisticated research approaches.

OREGON

Information for Students With Physical Disabilities: Disability Services for Students is a University resource promoting barrier-free environments (physical, program, information, attitude), which means ensuring the rights of students with disabilities and assisting the University with meeting its obligations under federal and state statutes. Disability Services for Students works to ensure access to University courses, programs, facilities, services, and activities by documenting disabilities and providing or arranging reasonable accommodations, academic adjustments, auxiliary aids and services, training, consultation, and technical assistance.

Application Information:
Send to: Portland State University, Department of Psychology, P.O. Box 751, Portland, OR 97207. Students are admitted in the Fall, application deadline January 15. Application deadline previously February 1. *Fee:* $50.

531

Arcadia University

Department of Psychology
450 South Easton Road
Glenside, PA 19038-3295
Telephone: (215) 572-2988
Fax: (215) 881-8758
E-mail: *nodine@arcadia.edu*
Web: *http://www.arcadia.edu*

Department Established:
1986. Chairperson: Barbara Nodine. Number of Faculty: total–full-time 6, part-time 14; women–full-time 3, part-time 10; minority–full-time 1, part-time 1.

Programs and Degrees Offered:
Listed in the following order: Program area, degree type (T if terminal Master's), number awarded 7/00–6/01. Community Counseling MA (T) 13, elementary school counseling MA (T), secondary school counseling MA (T) 1.

Student Applications/Admissions:
Student Applications
Community Counseling MA—Applications 2001–2002, 13. Total applicants accepted 2001–2002, 14. New applicants enrolled 2001–2002, 8. Total enrolled 2001–2002 full-time, 22, part-time, 11. Openings 2002–2003, N/A. The Median number of years required for completion of a degree are 3. The number of students enrolled full and part-time, who were dismissed or voluntarily withdrew from this program area were 0. *Elementary school counseling* MA—Applications 2001–2002, 10. Total applicants accepted 2001–2002, 9. New applicants enrolled 2001–2002, 5. Total enrolled 2001–2002 full-time, 2, part-time, 17. Openings 2002–2003, N/A. The Median number of years required for completion of a degree are n/a. The number of students enrolled full and part-time, who were dismissed or voluntarily withdrew from this program area were 1. *Secondary school counseling* MA—Applications 2001–2002, 9. Total applicants accepted 2001–2002, 8. New applicants enrolled 2001–2002, 4. Total enrolled 2001–2002 full-time, 3, part-time, 18. Openings 2002–2003, N/A. The Median number of years required for completion of a degree are 3. The number of students enrolled full and part-time, who were dismissed or voluntarily withdrew from this program area were 2.

Admissions Requirements:
Scores: Entries appear in this order: required test or GPA, minimum score (if required), median score of students entering in 2001–2002. Master's Programs: GRE-V no minimum stated, 501; GRE-Q no minimum stated, 504; GRE-V+Q no minimum stated, N/A; MAT no minimum stated, 45; overall undergraduate GPA 3.0, 3.17; psychology GPA 3.0, 3.39. Either GRE or MAT is required. Doctoral Programs: last 2 years GPA no minimum stated; psychology GPA no minimum stated; psychology GPA no minimum stated.

Other Criteria: (importance of criteria rated low, medium, or high): GRE/MAT scores medium, research experience medium, work experience high, extracurricular activity medium, clinically related public service medium, GPA high, letters of recommendation medium, interview high, statement of goals and objectives high.

Student Characteristics: The following represents characteristics of students in 2001–2002 in all graduate psychology programs in the department: Female–full-time 15, part-time 43; Male–full-time 0, part-time 8; African American/Black–full-time 0, part-time 3; Hispanic/Latino (a)–full-time 0, part-time 1; Asian/Pacific Islander–full-time 1, part-time 0; American Indian/Alaska Native–full-time 0, part-time 1.

Financial Information/Assistance:
Tuition for Full-Time Study: *Master's:* State residents $420 per credit hour; nonstate residents: $420 per credit hour.

Financial Assistance:
First Year Students: No information provided.
Advanced Students: No information provided.
Contact Information: Graduate Assistantship positions are available in the Psychology department and in other campus departments. Contact the Office of Graduate and Professional Studies.

Internships/Practica: Pre-practicum and practicum required. Practica are arranged in the local community.

Housing and Day Care: No on-campus housing and day care facilities are available.

Employment of Department Graduates:
Master's Degree Graduates: Of those who graduated in the academic year 2000–2001, the following categories and numbers represent the post-graduate activities and employment of master's degree graduates: Enrolled in a psychology doctoral program (1), enrolled in a post-doctoral residency/fellowship (n/a), employed in independent practice (n/a), employed in a professional position in a school system (1), employed in a community mental health/counseling center (4), employed in a hospital/medical center (1).
Doctoral Degree Graduates: Of those who graduated in the academic year 2000–2001, the following categories and numbers represent the post-graduate activities and employment of doctoral degree graduates: Enrolled in a psychology doctoral program (n/a), enrolled in another graduate/professional program (n/a).

Additional Information:
Orientation, Objectives, and Emphasis of Department: The MA in counseling prepares master's level psychologists for professional positions in schools, social service, rehabilitation, industrial, health, and mental health settings. Graduates will be able to work as community mental health specialists, mental health counselors, crisis counselors, drug and alcohol counselors, illness and wellness counselors, geriatric counselors, employee-assistance counselors, school counselors, and staff developers or trainers. The program is designed on a part-time basis for the working professional. The

orientation of the program is eclectic although an emphasis is put upon behavioral-cognitive approaches.

Application Information:
Send to: Office of Graduate and Professional Studies, Arcadia University, Glenside, PA 19038-3295. Students are admitted in the Fall, application deadline Rolling; Winter, Spring, application deadline Rolling; Summer, application deadline Rolling. *Fee:* $35. The application fee is waived for applications submitted during Graduate Open Houses organized by the Office of Graduate and Professional Studies.

Bryn Mawr College
Department of Psychology
West House, 101 North Merion Avenue
Bryn Mawr, PA 19010-2899
Telephone: (610) 527-5190
Fax: (610) 527-2879
E-mail: *lrescorl@brynmawr.edu*
Web: *http://www.brynmawr.edu*

Department Established:
1890. Chairperson: Leslie Rescorla. Number of Faculty: total–full-time 7, part-time 6; women–full-time 3, part-time 5; minority–full-time 1.

Programs and Degrees Offered:
Listed in the following order: Program area, degree type (T if terminal Master's), number awarded 7/00–6/01. Clinical developmental PhD 9.

Student Applications/Admissions:
Student Applications
Clinical developmental PhD—Applications 2001–2002, 45. Total applicants accepted 2001–2002, 11. New applicants enrolled 2001–2002, 4. Total enrolled 2001–2002 full-time, 17, part-time, 20. Openings 2002–2003, 5. The Median number of years required for completion of a degree are 8. The number of students enrolled full and part-time, who were dismissed or voluntarily withdrew from this program area were 1.

Admissions Requirements:
Scores: Entries appear in this order: required test or GPA, minimum score (if required), median score of students entering in 2001–2002. Doctoral Programs: GRE-V 600, 662; GRE-Q 600, 630; GRE-Analytical 600, 710; overall undergraduate GPA 3.5, 3.70; last 2 years GPA no minimum stated; psychology GPA no minimum stated; psychology GPA no minimum stated.
Other Criteria: (importance of criteria rated low, medium, or high): GRE/MAT scores medium, research experience high, work experience high, extracurricular activity low, clinically related public service medium, GPA high, letters of recommendation high, interview high, statement of goals and objectives high, quality of undergraduate institution, high.

Student Characteristics: The following represents characteristics of students in 2001–2002 in all graduate psychology programs in the department: Female–full-time 20, part-time 15; Male–full-time 2, part-time 0; African American/Black–full-time 0, part-time 0; Hispanic/Latino (a)–full-time 0, part-time 0; Asian/Pacific Islander–full-time 0, part-time 1; American Indian/Alaska Native–full-time 0, part-time 0.

Financial Information/Assistance:
Tuition for Full-Time Study: No information provided.

Financial Assistance:
First Year Students: Teaching assistantships available for first-year.
Advanced Students: Teaching assistantships available for advanced students. Average amount paid per academic year: $12,000. Average number of hours worked per week: 17. Research assistantships available for advanced students. Average amount paid per academic year: $12,000. Average number of hours worked per week: 17.
Contact Information: Of all students currently enrolled full-time, 20% benefited from one or more of the listed financial assistance programs. For information on financial assistance, contact: Graduate School of Arts and Sciences. Students pay 1/3 of all tuition, receive 2/3 in remission.

Internships/Practica: one-half time assessment practicum (3rd year); one-half time therapy practicum (4th year); full-time internship (6th year; required). For those doctoral students for whom a professional internship is required prior to graduation, 5 applied in 2000–2001. Of those who applied, 2 were placed in internships listed by the Association of Psychology Postdoctoral and Internship Programs (APPIC); 2 were placed in APA accredited internships.

Housing and Day Care: No on-campus housing and day care facilities are available.

Employment of Department Graduates:
Master's Degree Graduates: Of those who graduated in the academic year 2000–2001, the following categories and numbers represent the post-graduate activities and employment of master's degree graduates: Enrolled in a post-doctoral residency/fellowship (n/a), employed in independent practice (n/a).
Doctoral Degree Graduates: Of those who graduated in the academic year 2000–2001, the following categories and numbers represent the post-graduate activities and employment of doctoral degree graduates: Enrolled in a psychology doctoral program (n/a), enrolled in another graduate/professional program (n/a), enrolled in a post-doctoral residency/fellowship (1).

Additional Information:
Orientation, Objectives, and Emphasis of Department: The department offers a broad program of graduate coursework integrated around a conception of the developing individual in changing family, school, and societal contexts. Students enrolled in the clinical developmental and school psychology doctoral program obtain an understanding of basic human psychological processes in their development across the life-span and acquire the requisite skills to conduct effective research on these processes. The clinical developmental and school psychology program adheres to the scientist-practitioner model and offers a life-span developmental context. The focus of the program is on children and families within the larger social contexts of school and community. Stu-

dents also obtain certification in school psychology by their fourth year in the program.

Special Facilities or Resources: The greater Philadelphia area features a very large and diverse community of psychologists, as well as many medical schools, teaching hospitals, mental health facilities, and research settings. The Child Study Institute (CSI) is the clinical training facility of the Department of Psychology. Staffed by licensed psychologists (including members of the department faculty), reading and math specialists, and pre-doctoral trainees in the clinical developmental program, CSI offers diagnostic assessment, school admission testing, individual, family, group psychotherapy, and reading, math, and study skills tutoring. Each year, two or three doctoral students have placements at CSI. All students in the program receive some family therapy training with live supervision at CSI. The Phebe Anna Thorne School is a nursery school and preschool research laboratory for the Department of Psychology and includes programs for both normally developing children and language-delayed preschoolers. Two first-year doctoral students in the Department of Psychology serve as teaching assistants in the Thorne School each year.

Application Information:
Send to: Department of Psychology/West House, Bryn Mawr College, 101 N. Merion Ave., Bryn Mawr, PA 19010. Students are admitted in the Fall, application deadline January 15. *Fee:* $40.

Bucknell University
Department of Psychology
Lewisburg, PA 17837
Telephone: (570) 577-1200
Fax: (570) 577-7007
E-mail: *dwevans@bucknell.edu*

Department Established:
1927. Chairperson: Joel Wade. Number of Faculty: total–full-time 11; women–full-time 2; minority–full-time 1.

Programs and Degrees Offered:
Listed in the following order: Program area, degree type (T if terminal Master's), number awarded 7/00–6/01. General, exp-general.

Student Applications/Admissions:
Admissions Requirements:
Scores: Entries appear in this order: required test or GPA, minimum score (if required), median score of students entering in 2001–2002. Master's Programs: GRE-V 500, 535; GRE-Q 500, 580; GRE-V+Q 1000, 1115; GRE-Analytical no minimum stated; GRE-V+Q+Analytical no minimum stated; GRE-Subject(Psych) no minimum stated. Doctoral Programs: last 2 years GPA no minimum stated; psychology GPA no minimum stated; psychology GPA no minimum stated.
Other Criteria: (importance of criteria rated low, medium, or high): GRE/MAT scores medium, research experience high, work experience low, extracurricular activity low, clinically related public service low, GPA medium, letters of recommendation high, statement of goals and objectives medium, fit w/ faculty interest high.

Student Characteristics: The following represents characteristics of students in 2001–2002 in all graduate psychology programs in the department: Female–full-time 3, part-time 0; Male–full-time 2, part-time 0; African American/Black–full-time 0, part-time 0; Hispanic/Latino (a)–full-time 0, part-time 0; Asian/Pacific Islander–full-time 0, part-time 0; American Indian/Alaska Native–full-time 0, part-time 0.

Financial Information/Assistance:
Tuition for Full-Time Study: *Master's:* State residents $3,125 per credit hour; nonstate residents: $3,125 per credit hour.

Financial Assistance:
First Year Students: Teaching assistantships available for first-year. Average amount paid per academic year: $7,600. Average number of hours worked per week: 20. Apply by March 1.
Advanced Students: Teaching assistantships available for advanced students. Average amount paid per academic year: $7,600. Average number of hours worked per week: 20. Apply by April 1.
Contact Information: Of all students currently enrolled full-time, 100% benefited from one or more of the listed financial assistance programs. For information on financial assistance, contact: Susan Conway at (570) 577-3655.

Internships/Practica: While we offer no formal internship placements, there is ample opportunity for students to gain practical experience during their graduate studies. Bucknell University is located near Geisinger Medical Center and Danville State Psychiatric Hospital. Students interested in animal behavior and comparative psychology have opportunities to engage in field work experience as well. Recently, students have conducted field work in Madagascar and Uganda.

Housing and Day Care: On-campus housing and day care facilities are available.

Employment of Department Graduates:
Master's Degree Graduates: Of those who graduated in the academic year 2000–2001, the following categories and numbers represent the post-graduate activities and employment of master's degree graduates: Enrolled in a post-doctoral residency/fellowship (n/a), employed in independent practice (n/a).
Doctoral Degree Graduates: Of those who graduated in the academic year 2000–2001, the following categories and numbers represent the post-graduate activities and employment of doctoral degree graduates: Enrolled in a psychology doctoral program (n/a), enrolled in another graduate/professional program (n/a).

Additional Information:
Orientation, Objectives, and Emphasis of Department: The department is committed to providing rigorous training in general experimental psychology. The great majority of our students intend to continue on to PhD programs, and thus we attempt to provide the kind of background and experience that will prepare the students for more advanced study. All of our graduate students become heavily involved in research in one of several well-equipped laboratories in comparative, physiological, learning, social, abnormal, developmental psychopathology, personality, or developmental. Whereas we have no program in clinical, our program provides an excellent background for students who hope to continue in doctoral programs in clinical psychology. We have

had great success in recent years in placing students in PhD programs in psychology.

Special Facilities or Resources: The department's primate facility includes three species of semi-naturally housed monkeys: hamadryads baboons, capuchins, and squirrel monkeys. We have equipment and/or space for research in all major subareas of psychology. In the fall of 2002 the psychology faculty and students will occupy a new building, currently under construction. Our new building will have state-of-the-art computer facilities, and excellent laboratory, office, and classroom space.

Application Information:

Send to: Graduate Admissions Office, Bucknell University, Lewisburg, PA 17837. Students are admitted in the Fall, application deadline March 1. Fall admission only, deadline for admission and financial aid applications, March 1. *Fee:* $25.

Carnegie Mellon University

Department of Psychology
Baker Hall 342E
Pittsburgh, PA 15213
Telephone: (412) 268-5690
Fax: (412) 268-2798
E-mail: *Queenie Kravitz<sk5u @andrew.cmu.edu>*
Web: *http://www.psy.cmu.edu/*

Department Established:

1948. Head: Roberta Klatzky. Number of Faculty: total–full-time 23; women–full-time 11.

Programs and Degrees Offered:

Listed in the following order: Program area, degree type (T if terminal Master's), number awarded 7/00–6/01. Cognitive PhD 1, cognitive neuroscience PhD 2, developmental PhD, social PhD.

Student Applications/Admissions:

Student Applications

Cognitive PhD—New applicants enrolled 2001–2002, 3. Total enrolled 2001–2002 full-time, 3. Openings 2002–2003, 3. *Cognitive neuroscience PhD*—New applicants enrolled 2001–2002, 1. Total enrolled 2001–2002 full-time, 11. Openings 2002–2003, 3. *Developmental PhD*—New applicants enrolled 2001–2002, 1. Total enrolled 2001–2002 full-time, 3. Openings 2002–2003, 1. *Social PhD*—New applicants enrolled 2001–2002, 1. Total enrolled 2001–2002 full-time, 5. Openings 2002–2003, 2.

Admissions Requirements:

Scores: Entries appear in this order: required test or GPA, minimum score (if required), median score of students entering in 2001–2002. Doctoral Programs: GRE-V no minimum stated; GRE-Q no minimum stated; GRE-Analytical no minimum stated; GRE-V+Q+Analytical no minimum stated; overall undergraduate GPA no minimum stated; last 2 years GPA no minimum stated; psychology GPA no minimum stated; psychology GPA no minimum stated. No specific scores—nothing weighted more than other requirements.

Other Criteria: (importance of criteria rated low, medium, or high): GRE/MAT scores high, research experience high, work experience low, GPA high, letters of recommendation high, statement of goals and objectives high.

Student Characteristics: The following represents characteristics of students in 2001–2002 in all graduate psychology programs in the department: Female–full-time 11, part-time 0; Male–full-time 14, part-time 0; African American/Black–full-time 0, part-time 0; Hispanic/Latino (a)–full-time 0, part-time 0; Asian/Pacific Islander–full-time 2, part-time 0; American Indian/Alaska Native–full-time 0, part-time 0.

Financial Information/Assistance:

Tuition for Full-Time Study: No information provided.

Financial Assistance:

First Year Students: No information provided.
Advanced Students: No information provided.
Contact Information: Of all students currently enrolled full-time, 100% benefited from one or more of the listed financial assistance programs.

Internships/Practica: No information provided.

Housing and Day Care: No on-campus housing and day care facilities are available.

Employment of Department Graduates:

Master's Degree Graduates: Of those who graduated in the academic year 2000–2001, the following categories and numbers represent the post-graduate activities and employment of master's degree graduates: Enrolled in a post-doctoral residency/fellowship (n/a), employed in independent practice (n/a).

Doctoral Degree Graduates: Of those who graduated in the academic year 2000–2001, the following categories and numbers represent the post-graduate activities and employment of doctoral degree graduates: Enrolled in a psychology doctoral program (n/a), enrolled in another graduate/professional program (n/a).

Additional Information:

Orientation, Objectives, and Emphasis of Department: The department offers doctoral programs in the areas of cognitive psychology, cognitive neuroscience, social-personality psychology, and developmental psychology. Because the graduate program is small, the student's course of study can be tailored to meet individual needs and interests. Further, students have many opportunities to work closely with faculty members on research projects of mutual interest. Carnegie Mellon University has a strong tradition of interdisciplinary research, and it is easy for students to interact with faculty and students from other graduate programs on campus. Many of our students take courses or engage in research with people from the Departments of Computer Science, Statistics, Social Science, English, Philosophy, and the Graduate School of Industrial Administration.

Special Facilities or Resources: The department maintains a wide variety of computer controlled laboratories utilizing computing systems with UNIX, VAX/VMS, IBM, and Macintosh platforms. Specialized equipment includes an automated eye-tracking system used for research in visual perception, reading, problem solving, and cognitive development, and a Silicon Graphics Computer

Server for connectionist modeling. In addition, the department maintains several laboratories at the Carnegie Mellon Children's School, a preschool and kindergarten facility for about 100 children. The laboratories have on-site videotape facilities and microcomputers for running experiments and observing group and individual behavior. Carnegie Mellon provides one of the richest computing environments in the United States. All graduate students in the department have access to ample computational facilities to support their research. Researchers at Carnegie Mellon have access to a wide variety of subject populations through local public and private systems, the Western Psychiatric Institute, the Veterans Administration Hospital, and local hospitals and clinics. The department also maintains an undergraduate subject pool that serves the needs of many experimenters.

Application Information:
Send to: Graduate Program Coordinator, Department of Psychology, Carnegie Mellon University, Pittsburgh, PA 15213. Students are admitted in the Fall, application deadline January 2. *Fee:* $45.

Carnegie Mellon University
Graduate School of Industrial Administration
Schenley Park
Pittsburgh, PA 15213
Telephone: (412) 268-2301
Fax: (412) 268-7064
E-mail: *pg14+@andrew.cmu.edu*
Web: *http://littlehurt.gsia.cmu.edu/gsiadoc.obt.asp*

Department Established:
PhD Coordinator: Paul S. Goodman. Number of Faculty: total–full-time 8; women–full-time 3; minority–full-time 1.

Programs and Degrees Offered:
Listed in the following order: Program area, degree type (T if terminal Master's), number awarded 7/00–6/01. Organizational PhD 2.

Student Applications/Admissions:
Student Applications
Organizational PhD—Total applicants accepted 2001–2002, 4. New applicants enrolled 2001–2002, 2. Total enrolled 2001–2002 full-time, 9. Openings 2002–2003, 3.

Admissions Requirements:
Scores: Entries appear in this order: required test or GPA, minimum score (if required), median score of students entering in 2001–2002. Doctoral Programs: GRE-V no minimum stated; GRE-Q no minimum stated; GRE-V+Q no minimum stated; GRE-Analytical no minimum stated; last 2 years GPA no minimum stated; psychology GPA no minimum stated; psychology GPA no minimum stated.
Other Criteria: (importance of criteria rated low, medium, or high): GRE/MAT scores high, GPA high, letters of recommendation high, statement of goals and objectives high.

Student Characteristics: The following represents characteristics of students in 2001–2002 in all graduate psychology programs in the department: Female–full-time 2, part-time 0; Male–full-time 0, part-time 0; African American/Black–full-time 0, part-time 0; Hispanic/Latino (a)–full-time 0, part-time 0; Asian/Pacific Islander–full-time 1, part-time 0; American Indian/Alaska Native–full-time 0, part-time 0.

Financial Information/Assistance:
Tuition for Full-Time Study: No information provided.

Financial Assistance:
First Year Students: No information provided.
Advanced Students: No information provided.
Contact Information: No information provided.

Internships/Practica: No information provided.

Housing and Day Care: No on-campus housing and day care facilities are available.

Employment of Department Graduates:
Master's Degree Graduates: Of those who graduated in the academic year 2000–2001, the following categories and numbers represent the post-graduate activities and employment of master's degree graduates: Enrolled in a post-doctoral residency/fellowship (n/a), employed in independent practice (n/a).
Doctoral Degree Graduates: Of those who graduated in the academic year 2000–2001, the following categories and numbers represent the post-graduate activities and employment of doctoral degree graduates: Enrolled in a psychology doctoral program (n/a), enrolled in another graduate/professional program (n/a).

Additional Information:
Orientation, Objectives, and Emphasis of Department: The goal of the doctoral program in organizational psychology and theory at the Graduate School of Industrial Administration is to produce scientists who will make significant research contributions to our understanding of the structure and functioning of organizations. To achieve this goal the student is placed in a learning environment where a unique set of quantitative and discipline-based skills can be acquired. The opportunities for interdisciplinary work at GSIA provide new avenues for approaching organizational problems. The program attempts to combine structure and flexibility. Structure is achieved by identifying a set of core areas in which the student should become competent. These are quantitative methods, design and measurement, organization theory, and a selected specialty area. Flexibility in the program is achieved by having students and their advisers work out a combination of learning activities consistent with the students' interests and needs. Courses, participation in research projects, summer papers, and special tutorials with individual faculty are some of these learning activities. We have new multiple-year NSF Traineeship Program in Groups and Technology. It draws on the CMU faculty on groups and CMU expertise in technology.

Application Information:
Students are admitted in the Fall, application deadline February 1. *Fee:* $40.

Chatham College
Counseling Psychology
Woodland Road
Pittsburgh, PA 15232
Telephone: (412) 365-1704
Fax: (412) 365-1505
E-mail: *gnouel@chatham.edu*

Department Established:
1998. Director: Gloria E. Nouel PhD. Number of Faculty: total–full-time 7, part-time 9; women–full-time 4, part-time 5; minority–full-time 1.

Programs and Degrees Offered:
Listed in the following order: Program area, degree type (T if terminal Master's), number awarded 7/00–6/01. Counseling psychology MA (T) 13.

Student Applications/Admissions:
Student Applications
Counseling psychology MA—Applications 2001–2002, 25. Total applicants accepted 2001–2002, 25. New applicants enrolled 2001–2002, 22. Total enrolled 2001–2002 full-time, 10, part-time, 55. Openings 2002–2003, 30. The Median number of years required for completion of a degree are 2. The number of students enrolled full and part-time, who were dismissed or voluntarily withdrew from this program area were 4.

Admissions Requirements:
Scores: Entries appear in this order: required test or GPA, minimum score (if required), median score of students entering in 2001–2002. Master's Programs: overall undergraduate GPA 3.0. Students with undergraduate GPAs less than 3.0 may gain admission to the program with approval from the Program Director. Doctoral Programs: last 2 years GPA no minimum stated; psychology GPA no minimum stated; psychology GPA no minimum stated.
Other Criteria: (importance of criteria rated low, medium, or high): research experience low, work experience medium, extracurricular activity medium, clinically related public service medium, GPA medium, letters of recommendation high, interview high, statement of goals and objectives medium.

Student Characteristics: The following represents characteristics of students in 2001–2002 in all graduate psychology programs in the department: Female–full-time 9, part-time 51; Male–full-time 1, part-time 4; African American/Black–full-time 1, part-time 4; Hispanic/Latino (a)–full-time 1, part-time 0; Asian/Pacific Islander–full-time 1, part-time 0; American Indian/Alaska Native–full-time 0, part-time 0.

Financial Information/Assistance:
Tuition for Full-Time Study: No information provided.

Financial Assistance:
First Year Students: No information provided.
Advanced Students: No information provided.
Contact Information: No information provided.

Internships/Practica: The program requires the completion of 48 credit hours. In addition to 14 courses (41 credit hours) of classroom instruction, students complete two field experiences: a 100 hour supervised practicum and a 600 hour supervised internship. Through these field experiences, students have the opportunity to apply the skills learned in the classroom directly to work with clients and within organizations, all under the supervision of appropriately trained professionals. Students completing the practicum and internship receive at least one (1) hour of individual supervision and $1\frac{1}{2}$ hours of group supervision per week. Individual supervision focuses on acquisition of skills, addressing issues related to the site or client, and provision of ideas to promote the growth of the client and student. Group supervision addresses a variety of topics related to the professional practice of counseling skills, including case conceptualization, ethical issues, and counselor self-care. Field placements are available at local hospitals, outpatient clinics, schools, and counseling centers. Specific experiences are available with children and adults with a variety of problems including substance abuse, mental health issues of all kinds, everyday adjustment problems, children's difficulties with school or peers, and medical problems. Paid field placement opportunities are available.

Housing and Day Care: No on-campus housing and day care facilities are available.

Employment of Department Graduates:
Master's Degree Graduates: Of those who graduated in the academic year 2000–2001, the following categories and numbers represent the post-graduate activities and employment of master's degree graduates: Enrolled in a post-doctoral residency/fellowship (n/a), employed in independent practice (n/a).
Doctoral Degree Graduates: Of those who graduated in the academic year 2000–2001, the following categories and numbers represent the post-graduate activities and employment of doctoral degree graduates: Enrolled in a psychology doctoral program (n/a), enrolled in another graduate/professional program (n/a).

Additional Information:
Orientation, Objectives, and Emphasis of Department: The Master of Counseling Psychology Program prepares students for master-level positions in professions promoting optimal development of individuals, families, groups, organizations, and environmental systems. Master level trained psychology practitioners are employed in agencies and organizations providing mental health, health, and social services. Both full-time and part-time students may attend day, evening, or weekend classes. Students are able to complete the program in four (4) consecutive semesters. They also have the opportunity to participate in one of the ongoing research projects. The curriculum integrates theory, research, and experiential approaches with practice. The program provides a strong theoretical foundation from a variety of perspectives as well as individual and group therapeutic and assessment skills. Through academic study and extensive supervised internships, students develop an understanding of issues concerning individual and socio-cultural diversity and learn to assess persons with psychological difficulties, design strategies for change, and evaluate the effectiveness of those interventions. Faculty span a range of theoretical ideologies, including Humanistic, Existential-Phenomenological, Family Systems, and Cognitive Behavioral. The department encourages the student to explore which theoretical orientation most closely relates to her/his own goal, interests, and

philosophy. In addition, a diverse range of clinical and research interests amongst the faculty enables students to participate in a wide variety of experiences.

Special Facilities or Resources: Chatham College is located in a park-like setting in Pittsburgh with ready access to dynamic research and educational opportunities throughout the city. There are nine other local colleges and universities in close proximity to Chatham College. This creates a vibrant academic atmosphere in which to learn, live, and conduct quality research. The city of Pittsburgh is home to 25,000 scientists and 170 research facilities. These include some of the best hospitals in the nation, often ranked among the top research hospitals in the country. Chatham College and the department of psychology have arrangements with many of these top quality facilities for students to engage in collaborative research and grant writing. In this manner, students can integrate their classroom experiences with clinical field work and research studies. Faculty support students' participation in ongoing research studies and in development of their own research ideas. Students receive encouragement to present their research at local and national conventions and to publish their research in professional journals. Faculty serve as mentors in these research endeavors and assist in development of community contacts. Supervisors at community agencies often offer ideas for research as well. Current grant funding enables students to engage in paid research activities.

Application Information:
Send to: Dr. Gloria E. Nouel. Students are admitted in the Fall; Spring; Summer. Students can enter the program full-time in the fall, summer or spring. There is a rolling admission process; students are encouraged to submit their applications early. *Fee:* $35.

Chestnut Hill College
Department of Professional Psychology
9601 Germantown Avenue
Philadelphia, PA 19118-2693
Telephone: (215) 248-7077
Fax: (215) 248-7155
E-mail: *profpsyc@chc.edu*
Web: *http://www.chc.edu*

Department Established:
1987. Chairperson: Judith Marsh, PhD. Number of Faculty: total–full-time 7, part-time 30; women–full-time 3, part-time 13; minority–full-time 1, part-time 2; faculty subject to the Americans with Disabilities Act 4.

Programs and Degrees Offered:
Listed in the following order: Program area, degree type (T if terminal Master's), number awarded 7/00–6/01. Counseling psy & human service MA (T) 56, professional PsyD.

Student Applications/Admissions:
Student Applications
Counseling psy & human service MA—Total enrolled 2001–2002 part-time, 281. Openings 2002–2003, 100. *Professional PsyD*—Total enrolled 2001–2002 part-time, 66. Openings

2002–2003, 20. The Median number of years required for completion of a degree are 6.

Admissions Requirements:
Scores: Entries appear in this order: required test or GPA, minimum score (if required), median score of students entering in 2001–2002. Doctoral Programs: last 2 years GPA no minimum stated; psychology GPA no minimum stated; psychology GPA no minimum stated.
Other Criteria: (importance of criteria rated low, medium, or high): GRE/MAT scores high, research experience low, work experience medium, extracurricular activity low, clinically related public service low, GPA high, letters of recommendation high, interview high, statement of goals and objectives high, other writing sample high. Master's and doctoral programs require personal interviews prior to acceptance. The only program that uses cutoff scores is the MS/PsyD.

Student Characteristics: The following represents characteristics of students in 2001–2002 in all graduate psychology programs in the department: Female–full-time 0, part-time 277; Male–full-time 0, part-time 70; African American/Black–full-time 0, part-time 26; Hispanic/Latino (a)–full-time 0, part-time 3; Asian/Pacific Islander–full-time 0, part-time 9; American Indian/Alaska Native–full-time 0, part-time 0.

Financial Information/Assistance:
Tuition for Full-Time Study: *Master's:* State residents $425 per credit hour; nonstate residents: $425 per credit hour. *Doctoral:* State residents: $615 per credit hour; nonstate residents: $615 per credit hour.

Financial Assistance:
First Year Students: No information provided.
Advanced Students: No information provided.
Contact Information: Of all students currently enrolled full-time, 0% benefited from one or more of the listed financial assistance programs. For information on financial assistance, contact: Graduate Office, Chestnut Hill College.

Internships/Practica: Every student who attends either the master's program or the doctoral program at Chestnut Hill College in the Department of Professional Psychology must complete a practicum (and internship for doctoral students). We have a faculty member dedicated to assisting students in securing the most appropriate site for their experiential training. At the present time the College has 130 mental health facilities which have been approved as sites for practica or internships. Doctoral students complete an assessment practicum as well as a clinical practicum. Students have the option of completing an APA, APPIC or non-APA/APPIC Internship. Students are encouraged to apply for APA/APPIC internships. For those doctoral students for whom a professional internship is required prior to graduation, 9 applied in 2000–2001. Of those who applied, 1 were placed in internships listed by the Association of Psychology Postdoctoral and Internship Programs (APPIC); 1 were placed in APA accredited internships.

Housing and Day Care: No on-campus housing and day care facilities are available.

Employment of Department Graduates:

Master's Degree Graduates: Of those who graduated in the academic year 2000–2001, the following categories and numbers represent the post-graduate activities and employment of master's degree graduates: Enrolled in a post-doctoral residency/fellowship (n/a), employed in independent practice (n/a).

Doctoral Degree Graduates: Of those who graduated in the academic year 2000–2001, the following categories and numbers represent the post-graduate activities and employment of doctoral degree graduates: Enrolled in a psychology doctoral program (n/a), enrolled in another graduate/professional program (n/a).

Additional Information:

Orientation, Objectives, and Emphasis of Department: The theoretical base of the Department of Professional Psychology at Chestnut Hill College is a complementary blend of psychodynamic and systems theories. The insights of psychodynamic theory, including modern object relations theory, serve as a method for understanding the personality formation and inner psychological world of the individual. Likewise, the perspective of systems theory brings individuals, families, and communities to mutually influence one another. This synergistic blend of psychodynamic and systems theories is also heuristic in that it stimulates discussion, research, and learning among faculty and students as we all move to an increasingly holistic understanding of humanness within the family and social contexts that help define us.

Special Facilities or Resources: Chestnut Hill College is located in Philadelphia, Pennsylvania. Due to our location we have numerous contacts with local academic and research facilities. Firstly, we are part of a library consortium that increases the available lending privileges offered to each student. Secondly, the research projects which are run through local hospitals have included our students as both researchers and subjects. Finally, the four PsyD programs based in Philadelphia have begun to meet together in order to establish a network to reduce replication and better serve the doctoral students who choose to study in this region.

Information for Students With Physical Disabilities: Chestnut Hill College is committed to working with students with various physical disabilities. Due to the training model used, it must be understood that a student needs to be capable of communicating with others in a role-play setting.

Application Information:
Send to: Director of Graduate Admissions (Master's) or Director of PsyD Admissions (PsyD), Chestnut Hill College, 9601 Germantown Avenue, Philadelphia, PA 19118-2693. Students are admitted in the Fall, application deadline July 17; Spring, application deadline December 1; Summer, application deadline April 16. The above deadlines are for master's applicants only. PsyD and combined MS/PsyD programs admit students beginning only in the fall semester. Early application to PsyD encouraged. *Fee:* $35. PsyD and combined MS/PsyD application fee is $50.

Drexel University
Department of Psychology
College of Arts and Sciences
3141 Chestnut Street
Philadelphia, PA 19104
Telephone: (215) 895-2453
Fax: (215) 895-1333
E-mail: *lpb22@drexel.edu*
Web: *http://www.psa.drexel.edu*

Department Established:
1970. Program Director: Lamia P. Barakat. Number of Faculty: total–full-time 8, part-time 19; women–full-time 3, part-time 9.

Programs and Degrees Offered:
Listed in the following order: Program area, degree type (T if terminal Master's), number awarded 7/00–6/01. Clinical PhD 6.

APA Accreditation: Clinical PhD: full.

Student Applications/Admissions:

Student Applications

Clinical PhD—Applications 2001–2002, 120. Total applicants accepted 2001–2002, 7. New applicants enrolled 2001–2002, 5. Total enrolled 2001–2002 full-time, 21. Openings 2002–2003, 11. The Median number of years required for completion of a degree are 5. The number of students enrolled full and part-time, who were dismissed or voluntarily withdrew from this program area were 0.

[handwritten: V - 600   A - 600   Q - 600]

Admissions Requirements:

Scores: Entries appear in this order: required test or GPA, minimum score (if required), median score of students entering in 2001–2002. Doctoral Programs: GRE-V 500, 600; GRE-Q 500, 600; GRE-V+Q 1000, 1200; GRE-Analytical 500, 600; last 2 years GPA no minimum stated; psychology GPA no minimum stated; psychology GPA no minimum stated.

Other Criteria: (importance of criteria rated low, medium, or high): GRE/MAT scores medium, research experience high, work experience high, extracurricular activity high, clinically related public service high, GPA medium, letters of recommendation high, interview high, statement of goals and objectives high, Program fit high.

Student Characteristics: The following represents characteristics of students in 2001–2002 in all graduate psychology programs in the department: Female–full-time 18, part-time 0; Male–full-time 3, part-time 0; African American/Black–full-time 1, part-time 0; Hispanic/Latino (a)–full-time 1, part-time 0; Asian/Pacific Islander–full-time 0, part-time 0; American Indian/Alaska Native–full-time 0, part-time 0; Multi-ethnic–full-time 0, part-time 0; students subject to the Americans with Disabilities Act–full-time 0, part-time 0.

Financial Information/Assistance:
Tuition for Full-Time Study: Doctoral: State residents: $534 per credit hour; nonstate residents: $534 per credit hour.

Financial Assistance:
First Year Students: Teaching assistantships available for first-year. Average amount paid per academic year: $7,000. Aver-

age number of hours worked per week: 24. Tuition remission given: full. Research assistantships available for first-year. Average amount paid per academic year: $7,000. Average number of hours worked per week: 24. Tuition remission given: full.

Advanced Students: Teaching assistantships available for advanced students. Average amount paid per academic year: $7,000. Average number of hours worked per week: 24. Tuition remission given: full. Research assistantships available for advanced students. Average amount paid per academic year: $7,000. Average number of hours worked per week: 24. Tuition remission given: full. Traineeships available for advanced students. Average amount paid per academic year: $7,000. Average number of hours worked per week: 24. Tuition remission given: full.

Contact Information: Of all students currently enrolled full-time, 100% benefited from one or more of the listed financial assistance programs. For information on financial assistance, contact: Graduate Admissions Office or Dr. Lamia P. Barakat, Program Director.

Internships/Practica: The clinical practicum or clerkship (our term) is an integral part of the Clinical Psychology Graduate program developed to provide breadth of training as well as the development of specific skills in clinical psychology with an emphasis or specialty in clinical neuropsychology. Clinical clerkships are a means of training professional psychologists. Graduate students, typically in their second and third years of the program, are placed throughout the greater Philadelphia area and Delaware Valley in medical centers, general hospitals, geriatric centers, psychiatric facilities, private practices, and rehabilitation hospitals. These are 12 month placements for 24 hours per week. In these clinical settings, students work directly under the supervision of some of the most well-known clinical psychologists and clinical neuropsychologists in the United States in both direct patient care and research endeavors within a scientist-practitioner model. For those doctoral students for whom a professional internship is required prior to graduation, 4 applied in 2000–2001. Of those who applied, 4 were placed in internships listed by the Association of Psychology Postdoctoral and Internship Programs (APPIC); 4 were placed in APA accredited internships.

Housing and Day Care: No on-campus housing and day care facilities are available.

Employment of Department Graduates:
Master's Degree Graduates: Of those who graduated in the academic year 2000–2001, the following categories and numbers represent the post-graduate activities and employment of master's degree graduates: Enrolled in a post-doctoral residency/fellowship (n/a), employed in independent practice (n/a).
Doctoral Degree Graduates: Of those who graduated in the academic year 2000–2001, the following categories and numbers represent the post-graduate activities and employment of doctoral degree graduates: Enrolled in a psychology doctoral program (n/a), enrolled in another graduate/professional program (n/a), enrolled in a post-doctoral residency/fellowship (6).

Additional Information:
Orientation, Objectives, and Emphasis of Department: Drexel University awards the MS and PhD degrees in clinical psychol-

ogy with specialization in clinical neuropsychology. The doctoral program is grounded in the scientist/practitioner model, which emphasizes clinical research as well as the application of scientific principles. Accordingly, students are required to complete a thesis, a dissertation, a teaching rotation, and applied clinical training. The curriculum integrates clinical neuropsychological training with every aspect of traditional clinical psychology training, including therapeutic intervention and personality assessment. It provides particularly strong grounding in psychological and neuropsychological assessment, neuropsychological theory, models of memory, and neuropsychological technologies. Geriatrics, pediatrics, and traumatic brain injury and rehabilitation comprise the specific clinical training and research specialties of the program. Through cross-disciplinary collaboration with sociologists and anthropologists, our graduate students gain greater sensitivity to methodological and theoretical differences in assessing and intervening with clinical populations. Graduates of the program are prepared to work in a variety of settings, including academia, medical centers, rehabilitation hospitals, health industry, and private practice. The department is currently in the process of merging with MCP/Hahnemann University, an event which will greatly expand the resources of the academic community. It is anticipated that the new combined program will continue to offer the PhD in Clinical Psychology while allowing students to pursue concentrations in neuropsychology, health psychology, or forensic psychology; a combined JD-PhD will also be available through collaboration with Villanova University.

Special Facilities or Resources: The Department of Psychology is housed along with the Department of Culture and Communications in the Neuropsychology Laboratory Building. In addition to faculty offices and research space, the building also contains office space and psychological testing facilities for graduate students. Students have access to Drexel's Hagerty Library which provides on-line search services, interlibrary loan, CD-ROM database workstations, and the extensive resources of other libraries, including the library of the University of Pennsylvania. A leader in educational computing, Drexel has made history of integrating the personal computer into curricula. Psychology graduate students are encouraged to use educational software in teaching and develop custom software for research and clinical purposes. The University supports more than 10,000 Apple Macintosh computers on campus as well as an IBM 9121/320 mainframe for data management and analysis (SPSSX or SAS). Users on campus are connected with each other through a digital voice/data system and a high-speed fiber optic backbone. This also provides access to PREPnet, a state-wide, high-speed research network. Drexel is located in the University City neighborhood of Philadelphia and enrolls students from across the U.S. and more than 90 foreign countries. Graduate students enjoy regular access to the University's physical education center, student center, and other facilities.

Application Information:
Send to: Office of Graduate Admissions, Drexel University, 3141 Chestnut Street, Philadelphia, PA 19104-2875. Students are admitted in the Fall, application deadline January 1. *Fee:* $35.

Duquesne University
Department of Psychology
McAnlty College/Graduate School of Liberal Arts
600 Forbes Avenue
Pittsburgh, PA 15282
Telephone: (412) 396-6520
Fax: (412) 396-5197
E-mail: *coleman@duq.edu*
Web: *http://www.duq.edu/liberalarts/gradpsych/psycholog*

Department Established:

1959. Chairperson: Russell Walsh, PhD. Number of Faculty: total–full-time 15, part-time 8; women–full-time 5, part-time 3; minority–full-time 3.

Programs and Degrees Offered:

Listed in the following order: Program area, degree type (T if terminal Master's), number awarded 7/00–6/01. Clinical PhD 7, developmental PhD.

Student Applications/Admissions:

Student Applications

Clinical PhD—Applications 2001–2002, 33. Total applicants accepted 2001–2002, 5. New applicants enrolled 2001–2002, 5. Total enrolled 2001–2002 full-time, 85. Openings 2002–2003, 10. The Median number of years required for completion of a degree are 11. The number of students enrolled full and part-time, who were dismissed or voluntarily withdrew from this program area were 0. *Developmental PhD*—Applications 2001–2002, 4. Total applicants accepted 2001–2002, 2. New applicants enrolled 2001–2002, 2. Total enrolled 2001–2002 full-time, 4. Openings 2002–2003, 4. The Median number of years required for completion of a degree are n/a. The number of students enrolled full and part-time, who were dismissed or voluntarily withdrew from this program area were 1.

Admissions Requirements:

Scores: Entries appear in this order: required test or GPA, minimum score (if required), median score of students entering in 2001–2002. Master's Programs: MA no longer offered. Doctoral Programs: GRE-V no minimum stated; GRE-Q no minimum stated; GRE-Analytical no minimum stated; GRE-V+Q+Analytical no minimum stated; overall undergraduate GPA no minimum stated; last 2 years GPA no minimum stated; psychology GPA no minimum stated; psychology GPA no minimum stated.

Other Criteria: (importance of criteria rated low, medium, or high): GRE/MAT scores medium, research experience medium, work experience medium, extracurricular activity medium, clinically related public service medium, GPA medium, letters of recommendation high, interview high, statement of goals and objectives high, essay, writing sample high.

Student Characteristics: The following represents characteristics of students in 2001–2002 in all graduate psychology programs in the department: Female–full-time 48, part-time 0; Male–full-time 41, part-time 1; African American/Black–full-time 3, part-time 0; Hispanic/Latino (a)–full-time 0, part-time 0; Asian/Pacific Islander–full-time 2, part-time 0; American Indian/Alaska Native–full-time 0, part-time 0.

Financial Information/Assistance:

Tuition for Full-Time Study: No information provided.

Financial Assistance:

First Year Students: Research assistantships available for first-year. Average amount paid per academic year: $11,000. Average number of hours worked per week: 15. Apply by Jan. 15. Tuition remission given: full.

Advanced Students: Teaching assistantships available for advanced students. Average amount paid per academic year: $11,000. Average number of hours worked per week: 15. Apply by Jan. 15. Tuition remission given: full. Research assistantships available for advanced students. Average amount paid per academic year: $11,000. Average number of hours worked per week: 15. Apply by Jan. 15. Tuition remission given: full.

Contact Information: Of all students currently enrolled full-time, 100% benefited from one or more of the listed financial assistance programs. For information on financial assistance, contact: The Psychology Department at 412-396-6520.

Internships/Practica: For those doctoral students for whom a professional internship is required prior to graduation, 11 applied in 2000–2001. Of those who applied, 6 were placed in internships listed by the Association of Psychology Postdoctoral and Internship Programs (APPIC); 5 were placed in APA accredited internships.

Housing and Day Care: On-campus housing and day care facilities are available.

Employment of Department Graduates:

Master's Degree Graduates: Of those who graduated in the academic year 2000–2001, the following categories and numbers represent the post-graduate activities and employment of master's degree graduates: Enrolled in a post-doctoral residency/fellowship (n/a), employed in independent practice (n/a).

Doctoral Degree Graduates: Of those who graduated in the academic year 2000–2001, the following categories and numbers represent the post-graduate activities and employment of doctoral degree graduates: Enrolled in a psychology doctoral program (n/a), enrolled in another graduate/professional program (n/a).

Additional Information:

Orientation, Objectives, and Emphasis of Department: Internationally recognized for over three decades, the Psychology Department at Duquesne University engages in the systematic and rigorous articulation of psychology as a human science. The department understands psychology as a positive response to the challenges of the 21st century—one which includes existentialism, phenomenology, hermeneutics, psychoanalysis and depth psychology, feminism, critical theory, post-structuralism, and a sensitivity to the diverse cultural contexts within which this response may find expression. Psychology as a human science pursues collaborative, qualitative research methods that pay special attention to what is particular to human beings and their worlds. Accordingly, the department educates psychologists who are sensitive to the multiple meanings of human life and who work toward the liberation and well being of persons individually as well as in community.

Special Facilities or Resources: The psychology clinic provides the opportunity for supervised training in personal counseling and for research in the field of counseling and psychotherapy. Field placements are available in clinical. The Silverman Center is a research center containing a comprehensive collection of world literature in phenomenology.

Application Information:
Send to: Department Chair. Students are admitted in the Fall, application deadline December 15. January 15 is absolute deadline for all supporting materials *Fee:* $50.

Edinboro University of Pennsylvania
Department of Psychology
Edinboro, PA 16444
Telephone: (814) 732-2774; (814) 732-2000 switchboard
Fax: 814-732-2005
E-mail: *SLABINE@Edinboro.edu*
Web: *http://www.edinboro.edu*

Department Established:
1963. Chairperson: Jack Culbertson. Number of Faculty: total–full-time 15; women–full-time 4.

Programs and Degrees Offered:
Listed in the following order: Program area, degree type (T if terminal Master's), number awarded 7/00–6/01. Clinical psychology MA (T) 11.

Student Applications/Admissions:
Student Applications
Clinical psychology MA—Applications 2001–2002, 50. Total applicants accepted 2001–2002, 28. New applicants enrolled 2001–2002, 11. Total enrolled 2001–2002 full-time, 11, part-time, 12. Openings 2002–2003, 15. The Median number of years required for completion of a degree are 2. The number of students enrolled full and part-time, who were dismissed or voluntarily withdrew from this program area were 03.

Admissions Requirements:
Scores: Entries appear in this order: required test or GPA, minimum score (if required), median score of students entering in 2001–2002. Master's Programs: GRE-V no minimum stated, 410; GRE-Q no minimum stated, 450; GRE-V+Q no minimum stated, 860; MAT no minimum stated, 48; overall undergraduate GPA 3.0, 3.73. Either GRE or MAT scores are required; both are not Doctoral Programs: last 2 years GPA no minimum stated; psychology GPA no minimum stated; psychology GPA no minimum stated.
Other Criteria: (importance of criteria rated low, medium, or high): GRE/MAT scores low, research experience low, work experience low, extracurricular activity low, clinically related public service low, GPA medium, letters of recommendation medium, statement of goals and objectives medium, specific psychology grade medium.

Student Characteristics: The following represents characteristics of students in 2001–2002 in all graduate psychology programs in the department: Female–full-time 10, part-time 9; Male–full-time 1, part-time 3; African American/Black–full-time 0, part-time 0;

Hispanic/Latino (a)–full-time 0, part-time 0; Asian/Pacific Islander–full-time 0, part-time 1; American Indian/Alaska Native–full-time 0, part-time 0; Multi-ethnic–full-time 0, part-time 0; students subject to the Americans with Disabilities Act–full-time 0, part-time 0.

Financial Information/Assistance:
Tuition for Full-Time Study: *Master's:* State residents per academic year $4,138, $230 per credit hour; nonstate residents: per academic year $7,008, $389 per credit hour.

Financial Assistance:
First Year Students: Research assistantships available for first-year. Average amount paid per academic year: $4,200. Average number of hours worked per week: 20. Apply by February 15. Tuition remission given: full.
Advanced Students: Research assistantships available for advanced students. Average amount paid per academic year: $4,200. Average number of hours worked per week: 20. Apply by February 15. Tuition remission given: full.
Contact Information: Of all students currently enrolled full-time, 36% benefited from one or more of the listed financial assistance programs. For information on financial assistance, contact: Office of Financial Aid (814-732-2821). For graduate assistantships, contact the Graduate Studies Office (814-732-2856).

Internships/Practica: All students are required to take a semester-long, full-time clinical internship. During the internship, students are expected to receive the following: (1) experience in individual and group psychotherapy; (2) assessment experience; and (3) supervision by a licensed psychologist. Internship sites may provide ongoing didactic instruction as well. Students have performed internships in a variety of sites, including the following: community mental health centers, state psychiatric hospitals, residential facilities for children and adolescents, VA outpatient facilities, local hospitals, correctional institutions, and counseling centers. Efforts are made to help each student to find an internship site which closely matches his/her interests. There is an optional summer practicum experience available for those seeking the professional counselor license in PA.

Housing and Day Care: On-campus housing and day care facilities are available.

Employment of Department Graduates:
Master's Degree Graduates: Of those who graduated in the academic year 2000–2001, the following categories and numbers represent the post-graduate activities and employment of master's degree graduates: Enrolled in a psychology doctoral program (0), enrolled in another graduate/professional program (0), enrolled in a post-doctoral residency/fellowship (n/a), employed in independent practice (n/a), employed in an academic position at a university (0), employed in an academic position at a 2-year/4-year college (0), employed in other positions at a higher education institution (1), employed in a professional position in a school system (0), employed in business or industry (research/consulting) (0), employed in business or industry (management) (0), employed in a government agency (research) (0), employed in a government agency (professional services) (2), employed in a community mental health/counseling center (6), employed in a hospital/medical center (2), still seeking employment (0), other employment position (0).

Doctoral Degree Graduates: Of those who graduated in the academic year 2000–2001, the following categories and numbers represent the post-graduate activities and employment of doctoral degree graduates: Enrolled in a psychology doctoral program (n/a), enrolled in another graduate/professional program (n/a).

Additional Information:

Orientation, Objectives, and Emphasis of Department: The purpose of the master of arts degree program in clinical psychology is to provide training for qualified college graduates in the findings and principles of the science of psychology, and the knowledge which will enable them to function on a professional level in a variety of settings where psychological principles and skills are used to aid in the solution of specific human problems and in the general promotion of human welfare. The graduate training of this program is in the area of "clinical psychology" and is designed to prepare the graduates of the program to perform clinical services in accordance with the ethical principles of psychologists at the professional level in a wide variety of human service organizations and agencies. The orientation of the faculty is eclectic, and students get a well-rounded education in psychological assessment, therapy, psychopathology, neuropsychology, psychopharmacology, ethics, and research.

Special Facilities or Resources: Part-time study is available. All courses (except the internship) can be taken in the evening for part-time study.

Information for Students With Physical Disabilities: The Office for Students with Disabilities provides services essential for the student with a disability who matriculates at Edinboro University. Services provided are based on each student's request for accommodation and corresponding documentation of need provided by the student. Services include the following: personal attendant care, van transportation, meal assistance, alternative test arrangements, readers, computer laboratory, and wheelchair maintenance.

Application Information:

Send to: Graduate Studies Office, Edinboro University, Edinboro, PA 16444. Students are admitted in the Fall, application deadline February 15. Application deadline recommended; will consider late applications. *Fee:* $25.

Edinboro University of Pennsylvania
Department of Special Education and School Psychology
Education
Butterfield Hall
Edinboro, PA 16444
Telephone: (814) 732-2200
E-mail: JFAIETA@edinboro.edu
Web: http://www.edinboro.edu

Department Established:

Chairperson: Jeanne Faieta. Number of Faculty: total–full-time 9, part-time 3; women–full-time 8, part-time 3; minority–full-time 1.

Student Applications/Admissions:

Admissions Requirements:

Scores: Entries appear in this order: required test or GPA, minimum score (if required), median score of students entering in 2001–2002. Master's Programs: GRE-V 30th; GRE-Q 30th; GRE-V+Q 30th; MAT 30th; last 2 years GPA 3.0. Applicants are required to earn a score at the 30th percentile or higher on either the GRE or the MAT. Doctoral Programs: last 2 years GPA no minimum stated; psychology GPA no minimum stated; psychology GPA no minimum stated.

Other Criteria: (importance of criteria rated low, medium, or high): GRE/MAT scores medium, work experience medium, extracurricular activity medium, clinically related public service medium, GPA medium, letters of recommendation medium, interview medium, statement of goals and objectives medium.

Student Characteristics: The following represents characteristics of students in 2001–2002 in all graduate psychology programs in the department: Female–full-time 26, part-time 16; Male–full-time 4, part-time 4; African American/Black–full-time 1, part-time 1; Hispanic/Latino (a)–full-time 0, part-time 0; Asian/Pacific Islander–full-time 3, part-time 0; American Indian/Alaska Native–full-time 0, part-time 0; Multi-ethnic–full-time 0, part-time 0; students subject to the Americans with Disabilities Act–full-time 0, part-time 0.

Financial Information/Assistance:

Tuition for Full-Time Study: *Master's:* State residents per academic year $4,138; nonstate residents: per academic year $7,008.

Financial Assistance:

First Year Students: Research assistantships available for first-year. Average amount paid per academic year: $3,150. Average number of hours worked per week: 20. Apply by 3/15. Tuition remission given: full.

Advanced Students: Research assistantships available for advanced students. Average amount paid per academic year: $3,150. Average number of hours worked per week: 20. Apply by 3/15. Tuition remission given: full.

Contact Information: For information on financial assistance, contact: 888-611-2680 or 814-732-2821, Office of Financial Aid.

Internships/Practica: Regional paid and unpaid internships available.

Housing and Day Care: On-campus housing and day care facilities are available.

Employment of Department Graduates:

Master's Degree Graduates: Of those who graduated in the academic year 2000–2001, the following categories and numbers represent the post-graduate activities and employment of master's degree graduates: Enrolled in a post-doctoral residency/fellowship (n/a), employed in independent practice (n/a).

Doctoral Degree Graduates: Of those who graduated in the academic year 2000–2001, the following categories and numbers represent the post-graduate activities and employment of doctoral degree graduates: Enrolled in a psychology doctoral program (n/a), enrolled in another graduate/professional program (n/a).

Application Information:
Send to: Dr. Margaret Bevevino, Dean of Graduate Studies, Graduate Office, Edinboro University of Pennsylvania, Edinboro, PA 16444. Students are admitted in the Spring, application deadline 3/15. Late Admission may be Considered. *Fee:* $25.

Gannon University
Counseling Psychology
College of Humanities, Business and Education
109 University Square
Erie, PA 16541-0001
Telephone: (814) 871-7538
Fax: (814) 871-5511
E-mail: *nelsen001@gannon.edu*
Web: *http://www.gannon.edu*

Department Established:
1998. Direct of Training: Robert J. Nelsen. Number of Faculty: total–full-time 5, part-time 2; women–full-time 3, part-time 1.

Programs and Degrees Offered:
Listed in the following order: Program area, degree type (T if terminal Master's), number awarded 7/00–6/01. Counseling Psych. PhD.

Student Applications/Admissions:
Student Applications
Counseling Psych. PhD—Applications 2001–2002, 15. Total applicants accepted 2001–2002, 5. New applicants enrolled 2001–2002, 4. Total enrolled 2001–2002 full-time, 4. Openings 2002–2003, 6-8.

Admissions Requirements:
Scores: Entries appear in this order: required test or GPA, minimum score (if required), median score of students entering in 2001–2002. Doctoral Programs: GRE-V+Q+Analytical 1400, 1600; last 2 years GPA no minimum stated; psychology GPA no minimum stated; psychology GPA 3.5, 3.75.
Other Criteria: (importance of criteria rated low, medium, or high): GRE/MAT scores medium, research experience low, work experience high, extracurricular activity medium, clinically related public service high, GPA high, letters of recommendation high, interview high, statement of goals and objectives high, completed Master's degree high.

Student Characteristics: The following represents characteristics of students in 2001–2002 in all graduate psychology programs in the department: Female–full-time 4, part-time 0; African American/Black–full-time 0, part-time 0; Hispanic/Latino (a)–full-time 0, part-time 0; American Indian/ Alaska Native–full-time 0, part-time 0.

Financial Information/Assistance:
Tuition for Full-Time Study: *Doctoral:* State residents: per academic year $13,000, $580 per credit hour; nonstate residents: per academic year $13,000, $580 per credit hour.

Financial Assistance:
First Year Students: No information provided.

Advanced Students: No information provided.

Contact Information: For information on financial assistance, contact: Robert J. Nelsen, EdD, Counseling Psychology, Gannon University, 109 University Square, Erie, PA, 814-871-7723 or nelsen@gannon.edu.

Internships/Practica: Four practica are offered in the curriculum plus a year-long, 2000 hour internship—Introductory Individual Practicum; Advanced Individual Practicum—Marriage and Family Practicum; Group Facilitation Practicum—Internship in Counseling Psychology (year-long, 2000 hours).

Housing and Day Care: No on-campus housing and day care facilities are available.

Employment of Department Graduates:
Master's Degree Graduates: Of those who graduated in the academic year 2000–2001, the following categories and numbers represent the post-graduate activities and employment of master's degree graduates: Enrolled in a post-doctoral residency/fellowship (n/a), employed in independent practice (n/a).
Doctoral Degree Graduates: Of those who graduated in the academic year 2000–2001, the following categories and numbers represent the post-graduate activities and employment of doctoral degree graduates: Enrolled in a psychology doctoral program (n/a), enrolled in another graduate/professional program (n/a).

Additional Information:
Orientation, Objectives, and Emphasis of Department: The PhD degree in Counseling Psychology at Gannon University seeks to contribute to and improve quality of life by educating and training psychology practitioners who deliver high quality human services. The program seeks to prepare practitioners who are sensitive to and provide psychological services to diverse populations. The PhD degree is committed to education and training which prepares practitioners within a framework which acknowledges and respects diversity in culture, gender, and life-style.

Special Facilities or Resources: The department provides a counseling laboratory in which clients may be seen. This laboratory includes 3 individual counseling rooms, two marriage and family and group rooms equipped with video cameras, sound recording, VCRs, and Monitors in a secure observation area. Observation is direct and feedback is provided following each session. Videotapes are reviewed between sessions. Testing rooms are provided with video/audio capability and observation. Clients are referred from several community agencies with which the program maintains agreements.

Information for Students With Physical Disabilities: The department classrooms, counseling rooms, and observation areas are all accessible by elevator. Other services are available through the office of the Director of Student Services.

Application Information:
Send to: Center for Adult Learning, Office of Graduate Studies, Gannon University, 109 University Sq., Erie, PA 16541-0001. Students are admitted in the Fall, application deadline March 1. *Fee:* $50.

Geneva College

Counseling
Graduate Studies in Counseling, 3200 College Avenue
Beaver Falls, PA 15010
Telephone: (724) 847-6697
Fax: (724) 847-6101
E-mail: *counseling@geneva.edu*
Web: *http://www.geneva.edu*

Department Established:

1987. Chairperson: Carol Luce, PhD. Number of Faculty: total–full-time 7, part-time 1; women–full-time 3; minority–full-time 2.

Programs and Degrees Offered:

Listed in the following order: Program area, degree type (T if terminal Master's), number awarded 7/00–6/01. Counseling MA (T) 8.

Student Applications/Admissions:

Student Applications

Counseling MA—Applications 2001–2002, 22. Total applicants accepted 2001–2002, 10. New applicants enrolled 2001–2002, 10. Total enrolled 2001–2002 full-time, 16, part-time, 31. Openings 2002–2003, 20. The Median number of years required for completion of a degree are 3.

Admissions Requirements:

Scores: Entries appear in this order: required test or GPA, minimum score (if required), median score of students entering in 2001–2002. Master's Programs: GRE-V no minimum stated; GRE-Q no minimum stated; GRE-V+Q no minimum stated; GRE-Analytical no minimum stated; GRE-V+Q+Analytical no minimum stated; MAT no minimum stated; overall undergraduate GPA 3.00. GRE General Test OR MAT required but not both. Scores need to be in the fiftieth percentile for acceptance. Doctoral Programs: last 2 years GPA no minimum stated; psychology GPA no minimum stated; psychology GPA no minimum stated.

Other Criteria: (importance of criteria rated low, medium, or high): GRE/MAT scores high, research experience low, work experience medium, extracurricular activity low, clinically related public service medium, GPA high, letters of recommendation high, interview high, statement of goals and objectives high, Christian faith statement high.

Student Characteristics: The following represents characteristics of students in 2001–2002 in all graduate psychology programs in the department: Female–full-time 14, part-time 23; Male–full-time 2, part-time 8; African American/Black–full-time 0, part-time 4; Hispanic/Latino (a)–full-time 0, part-time 0; Asian/Pacific Islander–full-time 0, part-time 0; American Indian/Alaska Native–full-time 0, part-time 0.

Financial Information/Assistance:

Tuition for Full-Time Study: *Master's:* State residents $445 per credit hour; nonstate residents: $445 per credit hour.

Financial Assistance:

First Year Students: Teaching assistantships available for first-year. Average amount paid per academic year: $2,500. Average number of hours worked per week: 8. Apply by March 1.

Advanced Students: Teaching assistantships available for advanced students. Average amount paid per academic year: $2,500. Average number of hours worked per week: 8. Apply by March 1.

Contact Information: Of all students currently enrolled full-time, 37% benefited from one or more of the listed financial assistance programs. For information on financial assistance, contact: Dr. Robin Ware, Director of Graduate Student Services.

Internships/Practica: A practicum and internship program is in place. This practicum and internship experience is in line with the CACREP standards for master's level counseling programs. Details are as follows: practica are 100 hours in length with individual and group supervision and direct client contact; marriage and family internships are 600 hours in length with 300 hours being direct client contact hours; mental health internships are 900 hours in length with 450 hours being direct client contact hours; all internships will involve site placements typically in the Beaver County and Pittsburgh area, supervision via qualified master's and/or doctoral prepared practitioners, and onsite as well as college supervision.

Housing and Day Care: No on-campus housing and day care facilities are available.

Employment of Department Graduates:

Master's Degree Graduates: Of those who graduated in the academic year 2000–2001, the following categories and numbers represent the post-graduate activities and employment of master's degree graduates: Enrolled in a post-doctoral residency/fellowship (n/a), employed in independent practice (n/a).

Doctoral Degree Graduates: Of those who graduated in the academic year 2000–2001, the following categories and numbers represent the post-graduate activities and employment of doctoral degree graduates: Enrolled in a psychology doctoral program (n/a), enrolled in another graduate/professional program (n/a).

Additional Information:

Orientation, Objectives, and Emphasis of Department: The philosophies of counseling in the MA in Counseling Program at Geneva College are embedded in a Christian view of human nature and God's created world. A growing body of research literature affirms that Christian faith establishes a basis for healthy personality development, interpersonal relations, and mental health. A multidimensional holistic view of persons examines the interweaving of physical, emotional, social, cognitive, behavioral, and spiritual aspects of life. Integrative psychotherapeutic conceptualizations based on this multidimensionality promote healing and change. Counseling students and faculty engage in Christian spiritual growth thus modeling adherence to the faith and values they profess and facilitating academic learning, counseling, effectiveness, and ability to consult in the larger church community and beyond. The MA in Counseling Program at Geneva College provides academic training in the development of knowledge, skills, and personal awareness pertinent to the counseling profession, and encourages students to integrate Christian faith and Biblical knowledge with the training and practice of counseling. The program is designed so that post-baccalaureate students who complete this degree and acquire the required postgraduate supervised experience in the practice of counseling will be eligible to become Licensed Professional Counselors.

Special Facilities or Resources: Department facilities include an animal lab, a computer lab, and a modern clinical counseling facility. The computer lab is equipped with WordPerfect for Windows, SPSS for Windows, and various experimental and clinical software resources. The lab is also connected to Internet and Netscape on the World Wide Web.

Application Information:

Send to: Dr. Robin Ware, Director of Graduate Student Services, Geneva College, 3200 College Ave., Beaver Falls, PA 15010. Students are admitted in the Fall, application deadline open; Spring, application deadline November 1; Summer, application deadline May 1. *Fee:* $50.

Immaculata College

Department of Graduate Psychology
Immaculata College
College of Graduate Studies, Loyola Hall
Immaculata, PA 19345-0500
Telephone: (215) 647-4400 Exts. 3211, 3212, 3213
Fax: (610) 993-8550
E-mail: *srollison@immaculata.edu*

Department Established:

1983. Chairperson: Jed Yalof. Number of Faculty: total–full-time 8, part-time 18; women–full-time 5, part-time 11; minority–full-time 1, part-time 2.

Programs and Degrees Offered:

Listed in the following order: Program area, degree type (T if terminal Master's), number awarded 7/00–6/01. Clinical PsyD 9, counseling MA (T) 36, elementary school, school, School Psychology PsyD, school secondary counseling.

APA Accreditation: Clinical PsyD: full.

Student Applications/Admissions:

Student Applications

Clinical PsyD—Total enrolled 2001–2002 full-time, 23, part-time, 65. Openings 2002–2003, 20. *Counseling MA*—Applications 2001–2002, 87. Total applicants accepted 2001–2002, 73. New applicants enrolled 2001–2002, 48. Total enrolled 2001–2002 full-time, 26, part-time, 133. *School Psychology PsyD*—Total enrolled 2001–2002 full-time, 3, part-time, 7.

Admissions Requirements:

Scores: Entries appear in this order: required test or GPA, minimum score (if required), median score of students entering in 2001–2002. Master's Programs: GRE-V+Q+Analytical no minimum stated; MAT no minimum stated; overall undergraduate GPA 3.0. Doctoral Programs: GRE-V+Q+Analytical no minimum stated; MAT no minimum stated; overall undergraduate GPA no minimum stated; last 2 years GPA no minimum stated; psychology GPA no minimum stated; psychology GPA no minimum stated.

Other Criteria: (importance of criteria rated low, medium, or high): GRE/MAT scores medium, research experience medium, work experience high, extracurricular activity medium, clinically related public service medium, letters of recommen-

dation high, interview high, statement of goals and objectives high. PsyD program requires MA degree or equivalency in psychology or MA in another field; admission criteria weighed differently for PhD vs MA program.

Student Characteristics: The following represents characteristics of students in 2001–2002 in all graduate psychology programs in the department: Female–full-time 45, part-time 188; Male–full-time 12, part-time 32; African American/Black–full-time 0, part-time 13; Hispanic/Latino (a)–full-time 0, part-time 1; Asian/Pacific Islander–full-time 0, part-time 2; American Indian/Alaska Native–full-time 0, part-time 0.

Financial Information/Assistance:

Tuition for Full-Time Study: *Master's:* State residents $390 per credit hour; *Doctoral:* State residents: $620 per credit hour.

Financial Assistance:

First Year Students: No information provided.
Advanced Students: No information provided.
Contact Information: For information on financial assistance, contact: Peter Lysionek, Director of Financial Aid, Immaculata College, Immacula, PA 19345.

Internships/Practica: Students work with either the master's field site coordinator or doctoral field site and pre-doctoral internship coordinator to identify prospective field placements for their different programs of study. The Graduate Psychology Department places counseling psychology, school psychology, and clinical psychology students at sites throughout the Chester and Montgomery County areas and with supervisors with qualifications specific to student and program requirements.

Housing and Day Care: No on-campus housing and day care facilities are available.

Employment of Department Graduates:

Master's Degree Graduates: Of those who graduated in the academic year 2000–2001, the following categories and numbers represent the post-graduate activities and employment of master's degree graduates: Enrolled in a post-doctoral residency/fellowship (n/a), employed in independent practice (n/a).

Doctoral Degree Graduates: Of those who graduated in the academic year 2000–2001, the following categories and numbers represent the post-graduate activities and employment of doctoral degree graduates: Enrolled in a psychology doctoral program (n/a), enrolled in another graduate/professional program (n/a).

Additional Information:

Orientation, Objectives, and Emphasis of Department: The department's orientation is the professional preparation of the master's counselor. The department also prepares students for elementary school counseling, secondary school counseling, and school psychology certification. In all cases, training emphasizes knowledge, skill, and competency through classroom, practicum, and internship. The department's orientation is the preparation of doctoral-level clinical-psychologists within the practitioner model of professional psychology. This preparation entails a generalist curriculum emphasizing theory, therapy, diagnostics, and clinical training, with doctoral dissertation research aligned with a practitioner model. The department's preparation of doctoral-level school psychologists is practitioner-oriented, focusing on advanced assessment and intervention, human diversity, biological bases, school-neuropsychological application, research, and consultation within the context of school settings.

Special Facilities or Resources: The college has a comprehensive center for academic computing and modern technology available for student computer needs and utilization. The Gabrielle Library was opened in 1993 and houses journals and texts and has on-line search available to students.

Application Information:

Send to: Director of Graduate Admission, Immaculata College, King Road, Box 500, Immaculata, PA 19345. Students are admitted in the Fall, application deadline MA rolling; Winter, application deadline MA rolling; Spring, application deadline MA rolling; Summer, application deadline MA rolling. PsyD: November 1 deadline for January classes, March 1 for May classes. June 15 deadline for Fall classes. *Fee:* $25. Application fee is $25 for master's, $50 for doctoral programs.

Indiana University of Pennsylvania
Department of Psychology
Natural Sciences and Mathematics
201 Uhler Hall
Indiana, PA 15705
Telephone: (724) 357-4519
Fax: (724) 357-4087
E-mail: *durobert@iup.edu*
Web: *http://www.iup.edu*

Department Established:

1984. Chairperson: Mary Lou Zanich, PhD. Number of Faculty: total–full-time 23, part-time 4; women–full-time 11, part-time 4; minority–full-time 2.

Programs and Degrees Offered:

Listed in the following order: Program area, degree type (T if terminal Master's), number awarded 7/00–6/01. Clinical Psychology PsyD 19.

APA Accreditation: Clinical PsyD: full.

Student Applications/Admissions:

Student Applications

Clinical Psychology PsyD—Applications 2001–2002, 95. Total applicants accepted 2001–2002, 12. New applicants enrolled 2001–2002, 11. Total enrolled 2001–2002 full-time, 56. Openings 2002–2003, 12. The Median number of years required for completion of a degree are 5. The number of students enrolled full and part-time, who were dismissed or voluntarily withdrew from this program area were 2.

Admissions Requirements:

Scores: Entries appear in this order: required test or GPA, minimum score (if required), median score of students entering in 2001–2002. Doctoral Programs: GRE-V 500, 550; GRE-Q 500, 610; GRE-Analytical 500, 690; GRE-Subject(Psych) 500, 610; overall undergraduate GPA 3.0; last 2 years GPA no minimum stated; psychology GPA 3.0, 3.6; psychology GPA 3.0, 3.9.

Other Criteria: (importance of criteria rated low, medium, or high): GRE/MAT scores high, research experience medium, work experience medium, extracurricular activity clinically related public service high, GPA high, letters of recommendation medium, interview high, statement of goals and objectives medium.

Student Characteristics: The following represents characteristics of students in 2001–2002 in all graduate psychology programs in the department: Female–full-time 9, part-time 0; Male–full-time 2, part-time 0; African American/Black–full-time 2, part-time 0; Hispanic/Latino (a)–full-time 1, part-time 0; Asian/Pacific Islander–full-time 3, part-time 0; American Indian/Alaska Native–full-time 1, part-time 0; Multi-ethnic–full-time 0, students subject to the Americans with Disabilities Act–full-time 2.

Financial Information/Assistance:

Tuition for Full-Time Study: *Doctoral:* State residents: per academic year $5,112, $256 per credit hour; nonstate residents: per academic year $8,400, $420 per credit hour.

Financial Assistance:

First Year Students: Research assistantships available for first-year. Average amount paid per academic year: $2,915. Average number of hours worked per week: 10. Apply by March 15. Tuition remission given: partial. Fellowships and scholarships available for first-year. Average amount paid per academic year: $5,000. Average number of hours worked per week: 0. Apply by March 15.

Advanced Students: Teaching assistantships available for advanced students. Average amount paid per academic year: $11,558. Average number of hours worked per week: 12. Apply by March 15. Research assistantships available for advanced students. Average amount paid per academic year: $2,915. Average number of hours worked per week: 10. Apply by March 15. Tuition remission given: partial.

Contact Information: Of all students currently enrolled full-time, 100% benefited from one or more of the listed financial assistance programs. For information on financial assistance, contact: Financial Aid Office, IUP, Clark Hall, Indiana, PA 15705, 724-357-2218.

Internships/Practica: Students begin clinical experiences in the first year through course-based practica. During the second and later years, students enroll in the department sponsored Center for Applied Psychology (CAP) training clinics. These clinics employ a live supervision model. Training in the CAP clinics is supplemented with required external practica, currently available in approximately 17 different sites. For those doctoral students for whom a professional internship is required prior to graduation, 7 applied in 2000–2001. Of those who applied, 7 were placed in internships listed by the Association of Psychology Postdoctoral and Internship Programs (APPIC); 7 were placed in APA accredited internships.

Housing and Day Care: No on-campus housing and day care facilities are available.

Employment of Department Graduates:

Master's Degree Graduates: Of those who graduated in the academic year 2000–2001, the following categories and numbers represent the post-graduate activities and employment of master's

degree graduates: Enrolled in a post-doctoral residency/fellowship (n/a), employed in independent practice (n/a).

Doctoral Degree Graduates: Of those who graduated in the academic year 2000–2001, the following categories and numbers represent the post-graduate activities and employment of doctoral degree graduates: Enrolled in a psychology doctoral program (n/a), enrolled in another graduate/professional program (n/a), employed in independent practice (2), employed in other positions at a higher education institution (4), employed in a community mental health/counseling center (8), employed in a hospital/medical center (4), other employment position (1).

Additional Information:

Orientation, Objectives, and Emphasis of Department: The Psychology Department offers a Doctor of Psychology degree in Clinical Psychology (PsyD) that places emphasis upon professional applications of psychology based on a solid grounding in the scientific knowledge base of psychology. Training follows a generalist model with opportunities to develop advanced competencies during the last two years through courses and special practica. The core curriculum consists of eight areas including behavioral and history. Heavy emphasis is placed on integrating psychological knowledge with treatment, evaluation, consultation, and service delivery program design. The program is designed to meet the academic requirements of licensure and provide the background to assume responsibilities in appropriate professional settings.

Special Facilities or Resources: The Department of Psychology has recently moved to a new building on campus. This facility includes two 16-computer laboratories, individual research space with audio/video capabilities, seminar rooms, and a graduate student lounge. Each graduate student office is provided with computer access to the department server and the internet. The facilities for the CAP include 12 treatment rooms as well as two seminar rooms, all connected with a master video system. The CAP also houses computer facilities for test administration and scoring.

Information for Students With Physical Disabilities: All department facilities are accessible to people with physical disabilities.

Application Information:
Send to: Graduate School Admissions, Indiana University of Pennsylvania, Stright Hall, Indiana, PA 15705. Students are admitted in the Fall, application deadline January 10; Summer, application deadline January 10. *Fee:* $30.

Lehigh University
Department of Education and Human Services
Education
Mountain Top Campus, 111 Research Drive
Bethlehem, PA 18015
Telephone: (610) 758-3241
Fax: (610) 758-6223
E-mail: *Ed.shapiro@lehigh.edu*
Web: *http://lehigh.edu/~ineduc/CollEd.html*

Department Established:
1995. Chairperson: Edward S. Shapiro. Number of Faculty: total–full-time 28, part-time 12; women–full-time 10, part-time 7; mi-

nority–full-time 3; faculty subject to the Americans with Disabilities Act 5.

Programs and Degrees Offered:
Listed in the following order: Program area, degree type (T if terminal Master's), number awarded 7/00–6/01. Counseling PhD 6, counseling and human services (T) 10, elementary school counseling (T) 1, school PhD 4, secondary school counseling (T) 4.

APA Accreditation: Counseling PhD: full. School PhD: full.

Student Applications/Admissions:
Student Applications

Counseling PhD—Applications 2001–2002, 58. Total applicants accepted 2001–2002, 7. New applicants enrolled 2001–2002, 5. Total enrolled 2001–2002 full-time, 20, part-time, 11. Openings 2002–2003, 5. *School PhD*—Applications 2001–2002, 54. Total applicants accepted 2001–2002, 13. New applicants enrolled 2001–2002, 7. Total enrolled 2001–2002 full-time, 37, part-time, 5. Openings 2002–2003, 7. The number of students enrolled full and part-time, who were dismissed or voluntarily withdrew from this program area were 2.

Admissions Requirements:

Scores: Entries appear in this order: required test or GPA, minimum score (if required), median score of students entering in 2001–2002. Master's Programs: GRE-V no minimum stated; GRE-Q no minimum stated; GRE-V+Q no minimum stated; GRE-Analytical no minimum stated; GRE-V+Q+Analytical no minimum stated; overall undergraduate GPA 3.00; last 2 years GPA no minimum stated; psychology GPA no minimum stated. No minimums are set by the programs. Doctoral Programs: GRE-V no minimum stated; GRE-Q no minimum stated; GRE-V+Q no minimum stated; GRE-Analytical no minimum stated; GRE-V+Q+Analytical no minimum stated; overall undergraduate GPA 3.00; last 2 years GPA no minimum stated; psychology GPA no minimum stated; psychology GPA 3.50. Varies per program.

Other Criteria: (importance of criteria rated low, medium, or high): GRE/MAT scores medium, research experience high, work experience medium, extracurricular activity medium, clinically related public service high, GPA high, letters of recommendation medium, interview high, statement of goals and objectives high. Criteria vary by program. Clinical experience somewhat higher for counseling psychology doctoral program.

Student Characteristics: The following represents characteristics of students in 2001–2002 in all graduate psychology programs in the department: Female–full-time 71, part-time 42; Male–full-time 17, part-time 12; African American/Black–full-time 6, part-time 2; Hispanic/Latino (a)–full-time 1, part-time 3; Asian/Pacific Islander–full-time 3, part-time 1; American Indian/Alaska Native–full-time 1, part-time 0; Multi-ethnic–full-time 3, part-time 1; students subject to the Americans with Disabilities Act–full-time 3, part-time 0.

Financial Information/Assistance:
Tuition for Full-Time Study: *Master's:* State residents $480 per credit hour; nonstate residents: $480 per credit hour. *Doctoral:*

State residents: $480 per credit hour; nonstate residents: $480 per credit hour.

Financial Assistance:

First Year Students: Research assistantships available for first-year. Average amount paid per academic year: $10,000. Average number of hours worked per week: 20. Apply by January 1. Tuition remission given: full and partial. Fellowships and scholarships available for first-year. Average amount paid per academic year: $12,000. Average number of hours worked per week: 20. Apply by January 1. Tuition remission given: full and partial.

Advanced Students: Research assistantships available for advanced students. Average amount paid per academic year: $10,000. Average number of hours worked per week: 20. Tuition remission given: full and partial. Traineeships available for advanced students. Average amount paid per academic year: $10,000. Average number of hours worked per week: 20. Tuition remission given: full and partial. Fellowships and scholarships available for advanced students. Average amount paid per academic year: $12,000. Average number of hours worked per week: 20. Tuition remission given: full and partial.

Contact Information: Of all students currently enrolled full-time, 50% benefited from one or more of the listed financial assistance programs. For information on financial assistance, contact: Financial Aid Office, (610) 758-3181.

Internships/Practica: The Counseling Psychology Program maintains contracts with a variety of practicum settings. Training individual, group, couples, and family counseling are readily available. Students receive at least two hours of individual and two hours group supervision per week. Many sites provide additional training on specific issues in counseling. The School Psychology and Counseling Psychology programs have established a partnership with a local urban school district to provide enhanced in-school psychological services in elementary and middle schools. For those doctoral students for whom a professional internship is required prior to graduation, 10 applied in 2000–2001. Of those who applied, 2 were placed in internships listed by the Association of Psychology Postdoctoral and Internship Programs (APPIC); 7 were placed in APA accredited internships.

Housing and Day Care: On-campus housing and day care facilities are available.

Employment of Department Graduates:

Master's Degree Graduates: Of those who graduated in the academic year 2000–2001, the following categories and numbers represent the post-graduate activities and employment of master's degree graduates: Enrolled in a post-doctoral residency/fellowship (n/a), employed in independent practice (n/a).

Doctoral Degree Graduates: Of those who graduated in the academic year 2000–2001, the following categories and numbers represent the post-graduate activities and employment of doctoral degree graduates: Enrolled in a psychology doctoral program (n/a), enrolled in another graduate/professional program (n/a).

Additional Information:

Orientation, Objectives, and Emphasis of Department: The College of Education offers degree programs in counseling and school psychology. The program in school psychology offers training at both educational specialist and doctoral (PhD) levels. Within the PhD program, subspecializations in Health/Pediatric School Psychology and in Counseling Psychology/Special Education are offered. The program at all levels is behaviorally oriented, emphasizing research, consultation, and behavioral assessment in the implementation of school psychology services. The program in counseling psychology emphasizes a scientist-practitioner model and trains professional psychologists for employment in educational, industrial, and community settings. The counseling psychology program also offers training at the master's level.

Special Facilities or Resources: The department has university-affiliated training and research programs that provide living arrangements and day treatment programs for adults with developmental disabilities. The department also operates a laboratory school for children and adolescents with emotional disturbance. All facilities are integrated into the training of students primarily in the school psychology programs. The counseling psychology program has a lab for video taping and editing. Both programs have established partnerships with an urban school district. School psychology has recently established a national internship in the University laboratory school for students with emotional/behavior disorders.

Application Information:
Send to: Ms. Betty Shook, College of Education, Lehigh University, 111 Research Dr., Bethlehem, PA 18015. Students are admitted in the Fall, application deadline January 1; Winter, application deadline January 1. Counseling Psychology Master's–March 1. Fall admission for school psychology; winter for counseling psychology. *Fee:* $50.

Lehigh University
Department of Psychology
Arts and Sciences
17 Memorial Drive East
Bethlehem, PA 18015
Telephone: (610) 758-3630
Fax: (610) 758-6277
E-mail: *hcd.gprog@lehigh.edu*
Web: *http://www.lehigh.edu/~inpsy/gradprogram.html*

Department Established:
1931. Chairperson: Barbara C. Malt. Number of Faculty: total–full-time 11, part-time 2; women–full-time 4.

Programs and Degrees Offered:
Listed in the following order: Program area, degree type (T if terminal Master's), number awarded 7/00–6/01. General PhD.

Student Applications/Admissions:
Student Applications
General PhD—Applications 2001–2002, 21. Total applicants accepted 2001–2002, 5. New applicants enrolled 2001–2002, 1. Total enrolled 2001–2002 full-time, 14. Openings 2002–2003, 5. The Median number of years required for completion of a degree are n/a. The number of students enrolled full and part-time, who were dismissed or voluntarily withdrew from this program area were 1.

Admissions Requirements:
Scores: Entries appear in this order: required test or GPA, minimum score (if required), median score of students entering

in 2001–2002. Doctoral Programs: GRE-V no minimum stated, 600; GRE-Q no minimum stated, 625; GRE-Analytical no minimum stated; overall undergraduate GPA no minimum stated, 3.75; last 2 years GPA no minimum stated; psychology GPA no minimum stated; psychology GPA no minimum stated.

Other Criteria: (importance of criteria rated low, medium, or high): GRE/MAT scores medium, research experience high, work experience low, GPA medium, letters of recommendation high, interview medium, statement of goals and objectives high.

Student Characteristics: The following represents characteristics of students in 2001–2002 in all graduate psychology programs in the department: Female–full-time 1, part-time 0; Male–full-time 0, part-time 0; African American/Black–full-time 0, part-time 0; Hispanic/Latino (a)–full-time 0, part-time 0; Asian/Pacific Islander–full-time 1, part-time 0; American Indian/Alaska Native–full-time 0, part-time 0.

Financial Information/Assistance:

Tuition for Full-Time Study: *Doctoral:* State residents: $920 per credit hour; nonstate residents: $920 per credit hour.

Financial Assistance:

First Year Students: Teaching assistantships available for first-year. Average amount paid per academic year: $12,250. Average number of hours worked per week: 18. Apply by February 1. Tuition remission given: full. Research assistantships available for first-year. Average amount paid per academic year: $12,250. Average number of hours worked per week: 18. Apply by February 1. Tuition remission given: full. Fellowships and scholarships available for first-year. Average amount paid per academic year: $12,000. Average number of hours worked per week: 0. Apply by January 15. Tuition remission given: full.

Advanced Students: Teaching assistantships available for advanced students. Average amount paid per academic year: $12,250. Average number of hours worked per week: 18. Tuition remission given: full. Research assistantships available for advanced students. Average amount paid per academic year: $12,250. Average number of hours worked per week: 18. Tuition remission given: full. Fellowships and scholarships available for advanced students. Average amount paid per academic year: $12,000. Average number of hours worked per week: 0. Tuition remission given: full.

Contact Information: Of all students currently enrolled full-time, 100% benefited from one or more of the listed financial assistance programs. For information on financial assistance, contact: Padraig G. O'Seaghdha, Graduate Program Director, hcd.gprog@lehigh.edu.

Internships/Practica: No information provided.

Housing and Day Care: On-campus housing and day care facilities are available.

Employment of Department Graduates:

Master's Degree Graduates: Of those who graduated in the academic year 2000–2001, the following categories and numbers represent the post-graduate activities and employment of master's degree graduates: Enrolled in a post-doctoral residency/fellowship (n/a), employed in independent practice (n/a).

Doctoral Degree Graduates: Of those who graduated in the academic year 2000–2001, the following categories and numbers represent the post-graduate activities and employment of doctoral degree graduates: Enrolled in a psychology doctoral program (n/a), enrolled in another graduate/professional program (n/a).

Additional Information:

Orientation, Objectives, and Emphasis of Department: The Doctoral Program in Psychology is a research intensive program that combines focus with flexibility. Focus is provided by the program emphasis on Human Cognition and Development and by a core curriculum. Flexibility is provided by the ability to tailor a research specialization in an area of Cognition and Language, Developmental Psychology, or Social Cognition. Graduate students define an area of specialization through their selection of graduate seminars and through their research experiences. All students are actively engaged in research throughout their residence in the program, and they work in collaboration with faculty members and student colleagues. Departmental faculty conduct research on basic cognitive, linguistic, and social-cognitive processes, and the development of these processes across the life-span. See web pages to obtain a more detailed sense of the range of our current research activity. In addition to research within the psychology department, the psychology faculty and students partake in interdisciplinary endeavors with researchers from other university departments and programs, including the Cognitive Science Program.

Special Facilities or Resources: The department's well-equipped laboratories provide an excellent setting for research. The department has extensive facilities available for graduate student research, including a child study center, and cognitive, developmental, and social laboratories. Lehigh has a sophisticated network system that connects all campus computers and servers together and provides easy access to the Internet and the World Wide Web. The department has its own Local Area Network providing statistical, word processing, and other software.

Information for Students With Physical Disabilities: The university has made possible handicapped access to most facilities on the campus, including the Psychology Department building.

Application Information:
Send to: Graduate Programs Office, Lehigh University, 9 West Packer Ave., Bethlehem, PA 18015-3075. Students are admitted in the Fall, application deadline February 1. *Fee:* $62.

Marywood University
Department of Psychology and Counseling
McGowan Center for Graduate and Professional Studies
Scranton, PA 18509
Telephone: (570) 348-6226
Fax: (570) 340-6040
E-mail: *OBrien@AC.Marywood.Edu*
Web: *http://www.Marywood.Edu*

Department Established:
1940. Chairperson: Edward J. O'Brien. Number of Faculty: total–full-time 14, part-time 16; women–full-time 6, part-time 6.

Programs and Degrees Offered:

Listed in the following order: Program area, degree type (T if terminal Master's), number awarded 7/00–6/01. Child clinical/school MA (T) 3, Clinical Psychology PsyD, clinical services MA (T) 7, counseling - elementary school, counseling - Mental Health MA (T) 7, counseling - secondary school, general theoretical MA (T) 12, school psychology certificate.

Student Applications/Admissions:

Student Applications

Child clinical/school MA—Applications 2001–2002, 3. Total applicants accepted 2001–2002, 2. New applicants enrolled 2001–2002, 2. Total enrolled 2001–2002 full-time, 4, part-time, 4. Openings 2002–2003, 6. The Median number of years required for completion of a degree are 3. The number of students enrolled full and part-time, who were dismissed or voluntarily withdrew from this program area were 0. *Clinical Psychology PsyD*—Applications 2001–2002, 25. Total applicants accepted 2001–2002, 6. New applicants enrolled 2001–2002, 6. Total enrolled 2001–2002 full-time, 6. Openings 2002–2003, 6. The Median number of years required for completion of a degree are 5. The number of students enrolled full and part-time, who were dismissed or voluntarily withdrew from this program area were 0. *Clinical services* MA—Applications 2001–2002, 10. Total applicants accepted 2001–2002, 5. New applicants enrolled 2001–2002, 5. Total enrolled 2001–2002 full-time, 7, part-time, 9. Openings 2002–2003, 10. The Median number of years required for completion of a degree are 3. The number of students enrolled full and part-time, who were dismissed or voluntarily withdrew from this program area were 0. *Counseling - Mental Health* MA—Applications 2001–2002, 10. Total applicants accepted 2001–2002, 6. New applicants enrolled 2001–2002, 6. Total enrolled 2001–2002 full-time, 5, part-time, 9. Openings 2002–2003, 10. The Median number of years required for completion of a degree are 3. The number of students enrolled full and part-time, who were dismissed or voluntarily withdrew from this program area were 0. *General theoretical* MA—Applications 2001–2002, 46. Total applicants accepted 2001–2002, 29. New applicants enrolled 2001–2002, 16. Total enrolled 2001–2002 full-time, 16, part-time, 17. Openings 2002–2003, 20. The Median number of years required for completion of a degree are 3. The number of students enrolled full and part-time, who were dismissed or voluntarily withdrew from this program area were 0.

Admissions Requirements:

Scores: Entries appear in this order: required test or GPA, minimum score (if required), median score of students entering in 2001–2002. Master's Programs: GRE-V 500; GRE-Q 500; GRE-V+Q 1000; MAT 50; overall undergraduate GPA 3.0, 3.20; psychology GPA 3.0, 3.20. Students applying for master' programs may take either the GRE or the MAT. Scores listed above are preferred. Individuals with scores lower than preferred will be considered. Doctoral Programs: GRE-V 500; GRE-Q 500; GRE-V+Q 1000; GRE-Analytical 520; GRE-Subject(Psych) 500; overall undergraduate GPA 3.3; last 2 years GPA no minimum stated; psychology GPA 3.3; psychology GPA no minimum stated.

Other Criteria: (importance of criteria rated low, medium, or high): GRE/MAT scores medium, research experience medium, work experience medium, extracurricular activity low, clinically related public service medium, GPA high, letters of recommendation high, interview medium, statement of goals and objectives medium.

Student Characteristics: The following represents characteristics of students in 2001–2002 in all graduate psychology programs in the department: Female–full-time 51, part-time 53; Male–full-time 12, part-time 13; African American/Black–full-time 0, part-time 0; Hispanic/Latino (a)–full-time 1, part-time 1; Asian/Pacific Islander–full-time 1, part-time 0; American Indian/Alaska Native–full-time 0, part-time 1; Multi-ethnic–full-time 0, part-time 0; students subject to the Americans with Disabilities Act–full-time 0, part-time 1.

Financial Information/Assistance:

Tuition for Full-Time Study: *Master's:* State residents $554 per credit hour; nonstate residents: $554 per credit hour. *Doctoral:* State residents: $590 per credit hour; nonstate residents: $590 per credit hour.

Financial Assistance:

First Year Students: Research assistantships available for first-year. Average amount paid per academic year: $14,472. Average number of hours worked per week: 20. Apply by February 15. Average amount paid per academic year: $4,000. Average number of hours worked per week: 0. Apply by February 15.

Advanced Students: Research assistantships available for advanced students. Average amount paid per academic year: $14,472. Average number of hours worked per week: 20. Apply by February 15. Fellowships and scholarships available for advanced students. Average amount paid per academic year: $4,000. Average number of hours worked per week: 0. Apply by February 15.

Contact Information: Of all students currently enrolled full-time, 40% benefited from one or more of the listed financial assistance programs. For information on financial assistance, contact: Admissions Office, Graduate School of Arts and Sciences.

Internships/Practica: Students in recent years have had access to many schools, psychiatric hospitals, rehabilitation programs, community mental health programs, and prisons in the region of Northeastern Pennsylvania. The long history and size of our programs has provided us with the opportunity to develop close working relationships with most schools, social service, and mental health agencies in the region. The new PsyD program (initiated in 2001) is planning for both internal and external practicum sites and regional/national placements in internship sites. For those doctoral students for whom a professional internship is required prior to graduation, 2 applied in 2000–2001. Of those who applied, 1 were placed in internships listed by the Association of Psychology Postdoctoral and Internship Programs (APPIC).

Housing and Day Care: On-campus housing and day care facilities are available.

Employment of Department Graduates:

Master's Degree Graduates: Of those who graduated in the academic year 2000–2001, the following categories and numbers represent the post-graduate activities and employment of master's degree graduates: Enrolled in a post-doctoral residency/fellowship (n/a), employed in independent practice (n/a).

Doctoral Degree Graduates: Of those who graduated in the academic year 2000–2001, the following categories and numbers represent the post-graduate activities and employment of doctoral

degree graduates: Enrolled in a psychology doctoral program (n/a), enrolled in another graduate/professional program (n/a).

Additional Information:

Orientation, Objectives, and Emphasis of Department: The department provides students with a variety of coherent training experiences that lead to diverse career paths in school counseling, agency mental health work, school psychology, and doctoral-level training in clinical psychology. The psychology and counseling programs in the department work collaboratively to optimize student training. Master's students can take electives in either the psychology or counseling programs. While the two program tracks collaborate, there are significant differences in the training approaches of these programs. The psychology programs emphasize scientific core knowledge in psychology, theory, and professional skill development, while the counseling programs emphasize theory, professional practice, and experiential aspects of training. Collaboration between psychology and counseling programs allows for more effective development of training resources. Faculty routinely teach in both programs. Effective collaboration between psychology and counseling faculty helps students appreciate interdisciplinary issues in the field. Ethical and professional practice issues are considered extensively. Professional guidelines are emphasized that increase students' awareness of their developing expertise and the limits of this expertise. Professional standards for practice, certification, and licensing guidelines are integrated into courses and advisement. Licensing of master's graduates in Counseling and Psychology in Pennsylvania is a new possibility with the implementation of the Professional Counseling Act. The PsyD program follows the Vail model, training students to be scholar-practitioners. The PsyD program includes both foundation courses in psychology and applied training. The use of empirically-supported assessments and intervention techniques is emphasized along with a focus on outcome assessment. There are opportunities for work with children, adolescents, and adults. The PsyD program primarily is cognitive-behavioral in focus, with additional training provided in interpersonal and other approaches to psychotherapy.

Special Facilities or Resources: The department moved into a new building, the McGowen Center for Graduate and Professional Studies, in the Fall, 1998 semester. The new building more than doubled the research and clinical training facilities available to students and faculty in the department. Research facilities include two new state-of-the-art computer laboratories that provide for group and individual instruction, computer-equipped research cubicles that provide for on-line data collection, psychophysiological monitoring equipment, video taping and editing facilities, digital video and CD-ROM creation capabilities, and an extensive testing laboratory. The department operates a clinic, the Psychological Services Center, that provides treatment and observation rooms for practicum training, individual therapy, play therapy, family, and group therapy.

Information for Students With Physical Disabilities: Prospective students may contact the Coordinator for Special Services, Graduate School of Arts and Sciences, for information about any needed services. All facilities in the McGowan Center are accessible to individuals with physical disabilities.

Application Information:
Send to: Admissions Office, Graduate School of Arts and Sciences. Students are admitted in the Fall, application deadline April 15; Spring,

application deadline November 15; Summer, application deadline April 15. Applications for the PsyD program are due January 15. *Fee:* $25.

MCP Hahnemman University, formerly Allegheny University of the Health Sciences
Department of Clinical and Health Psychology
School of Health Professions
MS 66, 45 N. 15th Street
Philadelphia, PA 19102
Telephone: (215) 762-7249
Fax: (215) 762-8625
E-mail: *kirk.heilbrun@drexel.edu*
Web: *http://www.mcphu.edu*

Department Established:

0. Chairperson: Kirk Heilbrun. Number of Faculty: total–full-time 12, part-time 21; women–full-time 5, part-time 7; minority–full-time 1.

Programs and Degrees Offered:

Listed in the following order: Program area, degree type (T if terminal Master's), number awarded 7/00–6/01. Clinical MA (T) 5, law and psychology.

APA Accreditation: Clinical PhD: full.

Student Applications/Admissions:

Student Applications

Clinical MA—Applications 2001–2002, 27. Total applicants accepted 2001–2002, 19. New applicants enrolled 2001–2002, 14. Total enrolled 2001–2002 full-time, 22. Openings 2002–2003, 10. The Median number of years required for completion of a degree are 3.

Admissions Requirements:

Scores: Entries appear in this order: required test or GPA, minimum score (if required), median score of students entering in 2001–2002. Master's Programs: GRE-V no minimum stated, 510; GRE-Q no minimum stated, 540; GRE-V+Q no minimum stated, 1050; GRE-Analytical no minimum stated, 540; GRE-V+Q+Analytical 1500, 1590; overall undergraduate GPA 3.0, 3.3. Doctoral Programs: GRE-V no minimum stated, 560; GRE-Q no minimum stated, 600; GRE-V+Q no minimum stated, 1160; GRE-Subject(Psych) no minimum stated, 610; overall undergraduate GPA no minimum stated, 3.6; last 2 years GPA no minimum stated; psychology GPA no minimum stated; psychology GPA no minimum stated.

Other Criteria: (importance of criteria rated low, medium, or high): GRE/MAT scores medium, research experience high, work experience medium, extracurricular activity low, clinically related public service medium, GPA medium, letters of recommendation medium, interview high, statement of goals and objectives high, research interest high.

Student Characteristics: The following represents characteristics of students in 2001–2002 in all graduate psychology programs in the department: Female–full-time 28, part-time 0; Male–full-time

8, part-time 0; African American/Black–full-time 3, part-time 0; Hispanic/Latino (a)–full-time 2, part-time 0; Asian/Pacific Islander–full-time 1, part-time 0; American Indian/Alaska Native–full-time 0, part-time 0.

Financial Information/Assistance:

Tuition for Full-Time Study: *Master's:* State residents per academic year $15,000; nonstate residents: per academic year $15,000., *Doctoral:* State residents: per academic year $15,000; nonstate residents: per academic year $15,000.

Financial Assistance:

First Year Students: Average amount paid per academic year: $6,000. Average number of hours worked per week: 10. Average amount paid per academic year: $3,000.

Advanced Students: Average amount paid per academic year: $3,000. Average number of hours worked per week: 10. Average amount paid per academic year: $6,000. Average number of hours worked per week: 10.

Contact Information: Of all students currently enrolled full-time, 50% benefited from one or more of the listed financial assistance programs. For information on financial assistance, contact: Financial Aid.

Internships/Practica: On-campus practicum sites include the Student Counseling and Development Center, the Forensic Clinic, Projects Social Fear, STOP and Challenge, and the Heart Failure/Cardiac Transplant Center. Off-campus practicum sites include a variety of in-/outpatient psychiatric units, Children's Hospital of Philadelphia, and approximately sixty other practicum sites. For those doctoral students for whom a professional internship is required prior to graduation, 18 applied in 2000–2001. Of those who applied, 18 were placed in internships listed by the Association of Psychology Postdoctoral and Internship Programs (APPIC); 18 were placed in APA accredited internships.

Housing and Day Care: No on-campus housing and day care facilities are available.

Employment of Department Graduates:

Master's Degree Graduates: Of those who graduated in the academic year 2000–2001, the following categories and numbers represent the post-graduate activities and employment of master's degree graduates: Enrolled in a psychology doctoral program (4), enrolled in another graduate/professional program (1), enrolled in a post-doctoral residency/fellowship (n/a), employed in independent practice (n/a), employed in a government agency (research) (1), employed in a community mental health/counseling center (1), employed in a hospital/medical center (1).

Doctoral Degree Graduates: Of those who graduated in the academic year 2000–2001, the following categories and numbers represent the post-graduate activities and employment of doctoral degree graduates: Enrolled in a psychology doctoral program (n/a), enrolled in another graduate/professional program (n/a), enrolled in a post-doctoral residency/fellowship (3), employed in an academic position at a university (2), employed in an academic position at a 2-year/4-year college (1), employed in other positions at a higher education institution (2), employed in a government agency (research) (3), employed in a government agency (professional services) (1), employed in a community mental health/counseling center (3), employed in a hospital/medical center (4), other employment position (1).

Additional Information:

Orientation, Objectives, and Emphasis of Department: The PhD program is based heavily upon a scientist-practitioner model of training in clinical psychology and has been designed to place equal emphasis on both components. The theoretical orientation is based largely on Social Learning Theory, in which students gain proficiency in the theory and practice of broad-spectrum behavioral approaches to assessment and intervention. Because we are housed within a health sciences university with an affiliated medical school and hospital, emphasis is also placed on the areas of health psychology and behavioral medicine. The PhD program also offers a neuropsychology subspecialty track. The Law-Psychology program has three major goals: (a) to develop scientist practitioners who will produce legally-sophisticated social science research to help the legal system make better empirically-based decisions, (b) to educate highly trained clinicians who can contribute to the advancement of forensic psychology, and (c) to produce lawyer-psychologists who can participate in the development of more data-based mental health policy in the legislature and the courts. Students can earn the PhD in clinical psychology from MCP Hahnemann University and the JD degree from Villanova Law School.

Special Facilities or Resources: The PhD program at MCP Hahnemann University is located in the central downtown of a major eastern metropolitan area, with easy access from urban and suburban locations via an excellent rapid transit system. From a substantive perspective, the PhD program is housed in a department in a major tertiary care medical center that provides exceptional opportunities in health related areas for psychology. In addition, a Division of Behavioral Neurobiology and the University Neurobiology program, as well as the University Neurosciences program, provide opportunities for learning and collaboration on research at neuropharmacologic and neurophysiologic levels to complement our neuropsychological training. In addition, in conjunction with the Villanova University School of Law, we offer the only formal JD/PhD program in the country in which the academic psychological component represents a degree in clinical psychology.

Information for Students With Physical Disabilities: MCP Hahnemann University is an organization sensitive to the needs of our disabled population. Our facility has ramps, elevators, parking, wheelchair accessible sidewalks, and many other features to accommodate our handicapped students, patients, and visitors. The seeing impaired can also take advantage of these facilities, as well as other special features made especially for them. In addition, there are residential units on campus equipped for the disabled student.

Application Information:

Send to: Office of Enrollment Management, MCP Hahnemann University, Mail Stop 4, 45 N. 15th Street, Philadelphia, PA 19102. Students are admitted in the Fall, application deadline January 15. JD/PhD February 1. *Fee:* $50.

Millersville University

Department of Psychology
Byerly Hall
Millersville, PA 17551
Telephone: (717) 872-3093
Fax: (717) 871-2480
E-mail: htuleya@marauder.millersv.edu
Web: http://www.millersville.edu

Department Established:

1967. Chairperson: Helena Tuleya-Payne. Number of Faculty: total–full-time 20, part-time 12; women–full-time 14, part-time 7; minority–full-time 4.

Programs and Degrees Offered:

Listed in the following order: Program area, degree type (T if terminal Master's), number awarded 7/00–6/01. Clinical psychology, school counseling, school psychology, supervision of school guidance, supervision of school psych se.

Student Applications/Admissions:

Admissions Requirements:

Scores: Entries appear in this order: required test or GPA, minimum score (if required), median score of students entering in 2001–2002. Master's Programs: GRE-V 475; GRE-Q 475; GRE-Analytical 475; overall undergraduate GPA 2.75. Doctoral Programs: last 2 years GPA no minimum stated; psychology GPA no minimum stated; psychology GPA no minimum stated.

Other Criteria: (importance of criteria rated low, medium, or high): GRE/MAT scores medium, research experience low, work experience medium, extracurricular activity low, clinically related public service high, GPA medium, letters of recommendation high, interview high, statement of goals and objectives medium.

Student Characteristics: The following represents characteristics of students in 2001–2002 in all graduate psychology programs in the department: Female–full-time 33, part-time 117; Male–full-time 7, part-time 34; African American/Black–full-time 1, part-time 0; Hispanic/Latino (a)–full-time 1, part-time 0; Asian/Pacific Islander–full-time 0, part-time 0; American Indian/Alaska Native–full-time 0, part-time 0.

Financial Information/Assistance:

Tuition for Full-Time Study: *Master's:* State residents per academic year $2,069; nonstate residents: per academic year $3,504.

Financial Assistance:

First Year Students: No information provided.

Advanced Students: No information provided.

Contact Information: For information on financial assistance, contact: Graduate Studies Office at (717) 872-3030 for graduate assistantships and Office of Financial Aid at (717) 872-3026 for Federal subsidized Stafford Loan programs.

Internships/Practica: Practica are required of all students in the clinical, school counseling, and school psychology programs. In addition, students in the Certification Program in School Psychology are required to engage in an internship experience that occurs on a full-time basis over a period of one academic year (minimum of 1200 hours) or on a half-time basis over a period of two consecutive academic years.

Housing and Day Care: No on-campus housing and day care facilities are available.

Employment of Department Graduates:

Master's Degree Graduates: Of those who graduated in the academic year 2000–2001, the following categories and numbers represent the post-graduate activities and employment of master's degree graduates: Enrolled in a post-doctoral residency/fellowship (n/a), employed in independent practice (n/a).

Doctoral Degree Graduates: Of those who graduated in the academic year 2000–2001, the following categories and numbers represent the post-graduate activities and employment of doctoral degree graduates: Enrolled in a psychology doctoral program (n/a), enrolled in another graduate/professional program (n/a).

Additional Information:

Orientation, Objectives, and Emphasis of Department: All programs emphasize four components: academic training in relevant theory and knowledge, research skills and an ability to evaluate research critically, practical experience that can be directly useful in subsequent professional employment, and an attempt to foster in each student a high degree of self-awareness and interpersonal relationship skills. The MS program in Clinical Psychology prepares clinicians with strong skills in psychological assessment and diagnosis, and an eclectic/cognitive-behavioral repertoire of skills in individual, group, and family therapies. Graduates may work in a wide range of inpatient and outpatient mental health and human service settings with children and adults. The Certification Program in School Psychology is approved by the National Association of Psychologists and prepares students for entry level positions as school psychologists who work with students in school settings. Knowledge about the educational process, psychological and emotional growth, and data-based decision-making are central to the training program and enable students as problem-solvers to promote effective learning in children. The program also emphasizes the various systems in which the child functions, i.e., the interface between the personal, interpersonal, family, school, culture, and community systems. The MEd and Certification in School Counseling programs prepare students for the profession of school counseling for grades K–12. Operating under a prevention/intervention model students develop into professionals who are responsive to the needs of the school setting.

Special Facilities or Resources: A microcomputer lab and terminal access to the university's mainframe computer are available in the department. There is a psychoeducational clinic with one-way observation capability and videotape facilities. The Library houses approximately a half million books and provides access to nearly 3500 periodical titles. Electronic resources available via the world wide web, as well as the Millersville University library catalog, are accessible from the University home page. The research and information needs of faculty, staff, and students, are met by subject specialists who provide extensive reference service within the library, at off-site locations, and electronically. Scholarly research is further supported by a comprehensive and well-developed library collection that is continuously being augmented by the most current and up-to-date resources available, both in print and electronic format. The Library belongs to several state-wide and regional library consortia. These consortia allow for resource sharing, reciprocal borrowing, and collaborative purchasing of resources.

Application Information:
Send to: Graduate Studies Office, Millersville University, P.O. Box 1002, Millersville, PA 17551-0302. Students are admitted in the Fall, application deadline October 1; Winter, application deadline October 1; Spring, application deadline March 1; Summer, application deadline March 1. *Fee:* $25.

Penn State Harrisburg
Psychology Program
777 W. Harrisburg Pike
Middletown, PA 17057-4898
Telephone: (717) 948-6059
Fax: (717) 948-6519
E-mail: *dzx@psu.edu*
Web: *http://www.hbg.psu.edu*

Department Established:
1992. Coordinator: Michael A. Becker. Number of Faculty: total–full-time 11, part-time 5; women–full-time 8, part-time 1; minority–full-time 1.

Programs and Degrees Offered:
Listed in the following order: Program area, degree type (T if terminal Master's), number awarded 7/00–6/01. Applied clinical psychology MA (T) 5, applied psychological research MA (T).

Student Applications/Admissions:
Student Applications
Applied clinical psychology MA—Applications 2001–2002, 18. Total applicants accepted 2001–2002, 11. New applicants enrolled 2001–2002, 7. Total enrolled 2001–2002 full-time, 6, part-time, 36. Openings 2002–2003, 15. The Median number of years required for completion of a degree are 3. The number of students enrolled full and part-time, who were dismissed or voluntarily withdrew from this program area were 2. *Applied psychological research MA*—Applications 2001–2002, 0. Openings 2002–2003, 15. The number of students enrolled full and part-time, who were dismissed or voluntarily withdrew from this program area were 0.

Admissions Requirements:
Scores: Entries appear in this order: required test or GPA, minimum score (if required), median score of students entering in 2001–2002. Master's Programs: GRE-V no minimum stated; GRE-Q no minimum stated; GRE-Analytical no minimum stated; last 2 years GPA 3.0. Doctoral Programs: last 2 years GPA no minimum stated; psychology GPA no minimum stated; psychology GPA no minimum stated.
Other Criteria: (importance of criteria rated low, medium, or high): GRE/MAT scores medium, research experience medium, work experience medium, extracurricular activity low, clinically related public service medium, GPA medium, letters of recommendation medium, interview medium, statement of goals and objectives medium.

Student Characteristics: The following represents characteristics of students in 2001–2002 in all graduate psychology programs in the department: Female–full-time 4, part-time 11; Male–full-time 2, part-time 24; African American/Black–full-time 0, part-time 2; Hispanic/Latino (a)–full-time 0, part-time 1; Asian/Pacific Islander–full-time 0, part-time 0; American Indian/Alaska Native–full-time 0, part-time 0.

Financial Information/Assistance:
Tuition for Full-Time Study: *Master's:* State residents per academic year $7,314, $309 per credit hour; nonstate residents: per academic year $13,348, $557 per credit hour.

Financial Assistance:
First Year Students: No information provided.
Advanced Students: No information provided.
Contact Information: Of all students currently enrolled full-time, 10% benefited from one or more of the listed financial assistance programs. For information on financial assistance, contact: Penn State Harrisburg Financial Aid Office, (717) 948-6307. Also see www.gradsch.psu.edu/gs_overview/gs_fellowship.html. Some students are able to assist faculty members with research, and receive a stipend for research assistance.

Internships/Practica: Students in the Applied Clinical Psychology program are required to complete 9 credits of supervised clinical internships. Students in the Applied Psychological Research program are required to complete 6 credits of research in collaboration with the program faculty.

Housing and Day Care: On-campus housing and day care facilities are available.

Employment of Department Graduates:
Master's Degree Graduates: Of those who graduated in the academic year 2000–2001, the following categories and numbers represent the post-graduate activities and employment of master's degree graduates: Enrolled in a psychology doctoral program (3), enrolled in a post-doctoral residency/fellowship (n/a), employed in independent practice (n/a), employed in an academic position at a 2-year/4-year college (2), employed in a community mental health/counseling center (2).
Doctoral Degree Graduates: Of those who graduated in the academic year 2000–2001, the following categories and numbers represent the post-graduate activities and employment of doctoral degree graduates: Enrolled in a psychology doctoral program (n/a), enrolled in another graduate/professional program (n/a).

Additional Information:
Orientation, Objectives, and Emphasis of Department: The Applied Clinical Psychology program prepares students to function in community settings as mental health professionals and provides the academic training necessary for graduates to apply for master's level licensing for mental health professionals in the Commonwealth of Pennsylvania. The overall model emphasizes the core areas of psychology, including the scientific bases of behavior and biological, social, and individual difference factors. The training model is health-oriented rather than pathology-oriented and emphasizes the development of helping skills, including both assessment and intervention. Students can choose a concentration in general clinical, forensic, or health psychology for their elective credits. The Applied Psychological Research program focuses on

the development of research skills within the context of scientific training in psychology. The program is designed to meet the needs of students who plan careers in research or administration within human services or similar organizations (rather than being direct service providers within those agencies), who plan to conduct research in other settings, or who plan to pursue doctoral study. Students can select electives and research experiences to reflect their individual interests in consultation with their advisor.

Special Facilities or Resources: The Psychology program has an on-site clinic for the assessment of specific learning disorders in college students. The clinic provides second year Applied Clinical Psychology students the opportunity to assist with psychological testing, report writing, diagnosis, and treatment recommendations under the supervision of the program faculty. In addition, the Psychology program is affiliated with the Pennsylvania Child and Adolescent Service System Program (CASSP) Training and Technical Assistance Institute. CASSP is a comprehensive mental health system of care for children, adolescents, and their families that operates throughout Pennsylvania. The mission of the Institute is to improve the clinical practice of children's mental health workers in the public sector and to build capacity in the workforce. To accomplish this, the Institute sponsors day-long trainings in clinical best practice and an annual statewide conference; provides technical assistance to individuals and provider agencies; publishes and distributes training curricula, a Publication Series, and other resources; facilitates research to evaluate the impact of training and to determine state and national trends in children's public mental health policy and clinical best practice; and works with colleges and universities to improve the training for future human service workers.

Information for Students With Physical Disabilities: Contact: Donna Howard, Assistant Coordinator Non-Traditional Student Affairs, Penn State Harrisburg, 777 W. Harrisburg Pike, Middletown, PA 17057-4898, (717) 948-6025.

Application Information:
Send to: Graduate Admissions, Penn State Harrisburg, 777 W. Harrisburg Pike, Middletown, PA 17057-4898. Students are admitted in the Fall, application deadline May 1; Spring, application deadline November 1. January 10 for consideration for University fellowships and assistantships *Fee:* $45.

Pennsylvania State University
Counseling Psychology Program
Education
327 Cedar Building
University Park, PA 16802
Telephone: (814) 865-8304
Fax: (814) 863-7750
E-mail: *trx@psu.edu*
Web: *http://www.ed.psu.edu/cnpsy/index.asp*

Department Established:
Head of Department: Robert B. Slaney. Number of Faculty: total–full-time 4, part-time 2; women–full-time 2; minority–full-time 1.

Programs and Degrees Offered:
Listed in the following order: Program area, degree type (T if terminal Master's), number awarded 7/00–6/01. Counseling psychology PhD 6.

APA Accreditation: Counseling PhD: full.

Student Applications/Admissions:
Student Applications
Counseling psychology PhD—Applications 2001–2002, 58. Total applicants accepted 2001–2002, 6. New applicants enrolled 2001–2002, 6. Total enrolled 2001–2002 full-time, 42. Openings 2002–2003, 6. The Median number of years required for completion of a degree are 5. The number of students enrolled full and part-time, who were dismissed or voluntarily withdrew from this program area were 0.

Admissions Requirements:
Scores: Entries appear in this order: required test or GPA, minimum score (if required), median score of students entering in 2001–2002. Doctoral Programs: GRE-V+Q+Analytical 1100; last 2 years GPA no minimum stated; psychology GPA no minimum stated; psychology GPA no minimum stated.
Other Criteria: (importance of criteria rated low, medium, or high): GRE/MAT scores high, research experience high, work experience medium, extracurricular activity low, clinically related public service medium, GPA medium, letters of recommendation high, interview high, statement of goals and objectives high, Vita high.

Student Characteristics: The following represents characteristics of students in 2001–2002 in all graduate psychology programs in the department: Female–full-time 28, part-time 0; Male–full-time 14, part-time 0; African American/Black–full-time 13, part-time 0; Hispanic/Latino (a)–full-time 2, part-time 0; Asian/Pacific Islander–full-time 1, part-time 0; American Indian/Alaska Native–full-time 0, part-time 0; students subject to the Americans with Disabilities Act–full-time 1.

Financial Information/Assistance:
Tuition for Full-Time Study: *Doctoral:* State residents: per academic year $6,336; nonstate residents: per academic year $12,456.

Financial Assistance:
First Year Students: Teaching assistantships available for first-year. Average amount paid per academic year: $11,025. Average number of hours worked per week: 20. Tuition remission given: full.
Advanced Students: Teaching assistantships available for advanced students. Average amount paid per academic year: $11,025. Average number of hours worked per week: 20. Tuition remission given: full.
Contact Information: Of all students currently enrolled full-time, 100% benefited from one or more of the listed financial assistance programs. For information on financial assistance, contact: 314 Shields Bldg., University Park, PA 16802, 814-865-6301.

Internships/Practica: Students are placed in practicum in the College of Education Counseling Service in their first semester. Supervision consists of 1 and 1/2 hours of individual supervision and a two-hour seminar. The same supervision and seminar arrangements are provided for the second practicum at Penn State's

Career Services. A counseling psychology faculty member conducts the seminar and coordinates the interaction of students with the staff at Career Services. Although the program does not require students to be on campus during the summer, most students continue their practicum work at Penn State's Counseling and Psychological Services (CAPS) during the summer of their first year and for all of their second year. At CAPS, in addition to a two-hour seminar for case discussion and presentation, individual supervision is provided by the members of the CAPS staff and interns from their APA-approved Internship Program. Students may also take an additional practicum in their third year at either an on-campus agency or an agency in the community. Students typically apply for internships in their third year and go on internship in their fourth year. The program specifies that students apply to and accept only APA-approved internship positions. For those doctoral students for whom a professional internship is required prior to graduation, 8 applied in 2000–2001. Of those who applied, 8 were placed in internships listed by the Association of Psychology Postdoctoral and Internship Programs (APPIC); 8 were placed in APA accredited internships.

Housing and Day Care: On-campus housing and day care facilities are available.

Employment of Department Graduates:

Master's Degree Graduates: Of those who graduated in the academic year 2000–2001, the following categories and numbers represent the post-graduate activities and employment of master's degree graduates: Enrolled in a post-doctoral residency/fellowship (n/a), employed in independent practice (n/a).

Doctoral Degree Graduates: Of those who graduated in the academic year 2000–2001, the following categories and numbers represent the post-graduate activities and employment of doctoral degree graduates: Enrolled in a psychology doctoral program (n/a), enrolled in another graduate/professional program (n/a), enrolled in a post-doctoral residency/fellowship (1), employed in an academic position at a 2-year/4-year college (2), employed in other positions at a higher education institution (3).

Additional Information:

Orientation, Objectives, and Emphasis of Department: The Counseling Psychology Program at The Pennsylvania State University endorses the scientist-practitioner model of training. Psychological training is provided within this model with equal emphasis and value placed on both scholarly and clinical work as well as their integration. A primary goal of the program is the preparation of counseling psychologists for professional roles as academics, researchers, or practitioners who are concerned with interventions involving individual behavior and institutional settings which are focused on relational, multicultural, career, and psychosocial issues. More specifically, the primary objective of Penn State's Counseling Psychology Program is to train carefully selected and promising graduate students to function as thoughtful, ethical, caring, and competent professional psychologists. Whereas the Counseling Psychology Program is fully accredited by the American Psychological Association, our faculty and students strive to exceed the standards required for accreditation. One particular area in which we attempt to do so is in engendering a multicultural perspective in our students. At Penn State, we do not merely recognize the diversity represented in our faculty, students, and clients, we actively affirm the richness of our cultures

and we embrace the continual challenge of examining ourselves to determine how to more effectively serve a pluralistic society.

Special Facilities or Resources: The department maintains a Resource Center that includes many of the professional journals, reference, and testing materials pertinent to the curriculum. Doctoral students are provided offices, when available, with access to personal computers. The university provides each student with an e-mail account. The College of Education Counseling Service is located in the building and provides practicum experiences for graduate students. The Service is coordinated by a licensed psychologist and serves clients from the campus, providing personal, academic, and vocational counseling. The Service has individual counseling rooms equipped for video recording and live observation through one-way mirrors.

Application Information:
Send to: Counseling Psychology, 327 Cedar Bldg., Penn State, University Park, PA 16802. Students are admitted in the Fall, application deadline January 12. *Fee:* $60. Other Comments: Application fee is $60 if using the paper application form. If application is submitted electronically the fee is $45.

Pennsylvania State University
Department of Human Development and Family Studies, Graduate Program in Human Development and Family Studies
College of Health and Human Development
S-110 Henderson Building
University Park, PA 16802
Telephone: (814) 863-8000
Fax: (814) 863-7963
E-mail: *x2u@psu.edu*
Web: *http://www.hhdev.psu.edu/hdfs/grad/grad.htm*

Department Established:
1969. Professors in Charge of Graduate Program: Susan McHale and Craig Edelbrock. Number of Faculty: total–full-time 33; women–full-time 17; minority–full-time 2.

Programs and Degrees Offered:
Listed in the following order: Program area, degree type (T if terminal Master's), number awarded 7/00–6/01. Human development and family studies PhD 15.

Student Applications/Admissions:
Student Applications
Human development and family studies PhD—Applications 2001– 2002, 83. Total applicants accepted 2001–2002, 29. New applicants enrolled 2001–2002, 10. Total enrolled 2001–2002 full-time, 62. Openings 2002–2003, 20. The Median number of years required for completion of a degree are 5. The number of students enrolled full and part-time, who were dismissed or voluntarily withdrew from this program area were 0.

Admissions Requirements:
Scores: Entries appear in this order: required test or GPA, minimum score (if required), median score of students entering

in 2001–2002. Doctoral Programs: 1860, 3.79; last 2 years GPA no minimum stated; psychology GPA no minimum stated; psychology GPA no minimum stated.

Other Criteria: (importance of criteria rated low, medium, or high): GRE/MAT scores high, research experience high, work experience low, extracurricular activity low, GPA high, letters of recommendation high, interview low, statement of goals and objectives high, Writing Sample medium.

Student Characteristics: The following represents characteristics of students in 2001–2002 in all graduate psychology programs in the department: Female–full-time 50, part-time 0; Male–full-time 12, part-time 0; African American/Black–full-time 3, part-time 0; Hispanic/Latino (a)–full-time 3, part-time 0; Asian/Pacific Islander–full-time 6, part-time 0; American Indian/Alaska Native–full-time 0, part-time 0; Multi-ethnic–full-time 0, part-time 0; students subject to the Americans with Disabilities Act–full-time 0, part-time 0.

Financial Information/Assistance:

Tuition for Full-Time Study: *Doctoral:* State residents: per academic year $8,224; nonstate residents: per academic year $16,484.

Financial Assistance:

First Year Students: Teaching assistantships available for first-year. Average amount paid per academic year: $12,285. Average number of hours worked per week: 20. Apply by January 15. Tuition remission given: full. Research assistantships available for first-year. Average amount paid per academic year: $12,285. Average number of hours worked per week: 20. Apply by January 15. Tuition remission given: full. Fellowships and scholarships available for first-year. Average amount paid per academic year: $14,300. Average number of hours worked per week: 10. Apply by January 15. Tuition remission given: full.

Advanced Students: Teaching assistantships available for advanced students. Average amount paid per academic year: $12,285. Average number of hours worked per week: 20. Apply by Sept & April. Tuition remission given: full. Research assistantships available for advanced students. Average amount paid per academic year: $12,285. Average number of hours worked per week: 20. Apply by Sept & April. Tuition remission given: full.

Contact Information: Of all students currently enrolled full-time, 100% benefited from one or more of the listed financial assistance programs.

Internships/Practica: No information provided.

Housing and Day Care: On-campus housing and day care facilities are available.

Employment of Department Graduates:

Master's Degree Graduates: Of those who graduated in the academic year 2000–2001, the following categories and numbers represent the post-graduate activities and employment of master's degree graduates: Enrolled in a post-doctoral residency/fellowship (n/a), employed in independent practice (n/a).

Doctoral Degree Graduates: Of those who graduated in the academic year 2000–2001, the following categories and numbers represent the post-graduate activities and employment of doctoral degree graduates: Enrolled in a psychology doctoral program (n/a), enrolled in another graduate/professional program (n/a), enrolled in a post-doctoral residency/fellowship (4), employed in independent practice (0), employed in an academic position at a university (5), employed in business or industry (research/consulting) (2).

Additional Information:

Orientation, Objectives, and Emphasis of Department: The basic objectives of the human development and family studies (HDFS) program are the following: to expand knowledge about the development and functioning of individuals, small groups, and families; to improve methods for studying processes of human development and change; and to create and disseminate improved techniques and strategies for enhancing individual and family functioning, helping people learn to cope more effectively with problems of living, and preventing normal life problems from becoming serious difficulties. The program takes a life-span perspective, recognizing that the most important aspects of development and types of life tasks and situations vary from infancy and childhood through maturity and old age, as well as through the life cycle of the family, and that each phase of development is a precursor to the next. There is a firm commitment to an interdisciplinary and multiprofessional approach to these objectives and to the development of competence in applying rigorous methods of empirical inquiry. All students are expected to acquire a broad interdisciplinary base of knowledge and to develop competence in depth in one of four primary program areas: family development, individual development, human development intervention, or methodology.

Special Facilities or Resources: Several additional facilities are associated with the College of Health and Human Development: Child development-child services laboratories are operated by the department as part of the teaching and research program. Current programs include nursery school classes and infant and preschool day care. Each unit has observational facilities, and there are adjoining rooms for study of individual and group behavior of children and adults. The "Working Collection" sponsored by the department and the Gerontology Center provides resource material for students and faculty. The collection, serving as an in-house library, includes a selection of journals, books, and conference proceedings pertinent to the study of individuals and families, particularly those focusing on adulthood and aging. The collection also includes a copy of all theses and dissertations submitted by HDFS graduates. The Individual and Family Consultation Center provides facilities for the development and operation of programs that enhance individual and family functioning through competency-building programs and the use of paraprofessionals in community mental health. The Human Development Data Laboratory provides 10 public-use terminals for accessing the IBM 370-3088 processor, the main computer on campus. In addition, the laboratory has standard statistical packages available, such as SAS and SPSS, and the laboratory staff provides consulting and programming support to students. The laboratory also provides microcomputer training and consulting.

Application Information:
Send to: Graduate Admissions c/o Mary Jo Spicer, Penn State University, Department of Human Development and Family Studies, S110 Henderson Building, University Park, PA 16802. Students are admitted in the Winter, application deadline January 15. *Fee:* $45. $45 online application fee and $60 printed application fee.

Pennsylvania State University (2001 data)

Department of Psychology
417 Bruce V. Moore Building
University Park, PA 16802-3104
Telephone: (814) 863-1721
Fax: (814) 865-9516
E-mail: *bjc2@psu.edu*
Web: *http://psych.la.psu.edu*

Department Established:
1933. Head, Department of Psychology: Keith A. Crnic. Number of Faculty: total–full-time 45; women–full-time 17; minority–full-time 4.

Programs and Degrees Offered:
Listed in the following order: Program area, degree type (T if terminal Master's), number awarded 7/00–6/01. Clinical PhD 9, clinical-child PhD 5, cognitive PhD 1, developmental PhD 1, industrial/organizational PhD 4, social PhD 1.

APA Accreditation: Clinical PhD: full.

Student Applications/Admissions:
Student Applications
Clinical PhD—Applications 2001–2002, 107. Total applicants accepted 2001–2002, 13. New applicants enrolled 2001–2002, 8. Total enrolled 2001–2002 full-time, 50, part-time, 5. Openings 2002–2003, 7. The number of students enrolled full and part-time, who were dismissed or voluntarily withdrew from this program area were 1. *Clinical-child PhD*—Applications 2001–2002, 108. Total applicants accepted 2001–2002, 8. New applicants enrolled 2001–2002, 5. Total enrolled 2001–2002 full-time, 21, part-time, 1. Openings 2002–2003, 4. The number of students enrolled full and part-time, who were dismissed or voluntarily withdrew from this program area were 1. *Cognitive PhD*—Applications 2001–2002, 16. Total applicants accepted 2001–2002, 4. New applicants enrolled 2001–2002, 1. Total enrolled 2001–2002 full-time, 14, part-time, 1. Openings 2002–2003, 3. *Developmental PhD*—Applications 2001–2002, 23. Total applicants accepted 2001–2002, 9. New applicants enrolled 2001–2002, 2. Total enrolled 2001–2002 full-time, 9, part-time, 2. Openings 2002–2003, 2. The number of students enrolled full and part-time, who were dismissed or voluntarily withdrew from this program area were 2. *Industrial/organizational PhD*—Applications 2001–2002, 71. Total applicants accepted 2001–2002, 9. New applicants enrolled 2001–2002, 5. Total enrolled 2001–2002 full-time, 19, part-time, 3. Openings 2002–2003, 4. The number of students enrolled full and part-time, who were dismissed or voluntarily withdrew from this program area were 1. *Social PhD*—Applications 2001–2002, 32. Total applicants accepted 2001–2002, 7. New applicants enrolled 2001–2002, 5. Total enrolled 2001–2002 full-time, 9. Openings 2002–2003, 2. The number of students enrolled full and part-time, who were dismissed or voluntarily withdrew from this program area were 1.

Admissions Requirements:
Scores: Entries appear in this order: required test or GPA, minimum score (if required), median score of students entering in 2001–2002. Master's Programs: last 2 years GPA no minimum stated. Doctoral Programs: GRE-V no minimum stated; GRE-Q no minimum stated; GRE-V+Q no minimum stated, 1272; GRE-Analytical no minimum stated, 683; GRE-V+Q+Analytical no minimum stated, 1938; overall undergraduate GPA no minimum stated; last 2 years GPA no minimum stated, 3.84; psychology GPA no minimum stated; psychology GPA no minimum stated. We do not have a formal cut-off score. GRE Subject exam not required.

Other Criteria: (importance of criteria rated low, medium, or high): GRE/MAT scores high, research experience high, work experience medium, extracurricular activity low, clinically related public service medium, GPA high, letters of recommendation high, interview medium, statement of goals and objectives high. Clinical weighs work, clinical experience, and interviews heavily; other areas do not weight these factors strongly.

Student Characteristics: The following represents characteristics of students in 2001–2002 in all graduate psychology programs in the department: Female–full-time 22, part-time 0; Male–full-time 4, part-time 0; African American/Black–full-time 0, part-time 0; Hispanic/Latino (a)–full-time 0, part-time 0; Asian/Pacific Islander–full-time 0, part-time 0; American Indian/Alaska Native–full-time 0, part-time 0.

Financial Information/Assistance:
Tuition for Full-Time Study: No information provided.

Financial Assistance:
First Year Students: No information provided.
Advanced Students: No information provided.
Contact Information: Of all students currently enrolled full-time, 0% benefited from one or more of the listed financial assistance programs. For information on financial assistance, contact: Director of Graduate Training, 130 Moore Bldg., Department of Psychology, Penn State University, University Park, PA 16802.

Internships/Practica: Students in the clinical area take a clinical practicum each semester of residence, selecting from practica focused on individual adult interventions, child interventions, group psychotherapy, school/community consultation, psychological/neuropsychological assessments, forensic assessment, family therapy, and agency based consultation. Practica are offered within the Department's state-licensed Psychological Clinic which, as one of the nation's largest and most comprehensive university-based training clinics, serves as a comprehensive community mental health facility. Students in the I/O program participate in the "practicum" experience as one of the program requirements. The practicum is a formal course designed to provide a learning experience by applying psychological principles. Together with I/O faculty, graduate students work on problems provided by outside industrial and educational organizations, including, for example, problems related to job analysis, performance evaluation, attitude assessment, and test validation. In addition, other kinds of practica are established on an individual basis and may include practica related to human factors, applied developmental psychology, applied social psychology, and the like. As noted earlier, the program at Penn State is highly individualized, and internship opportunities and practica fall within the scope of individualized programs.

Housing and Day Care: No on-campus housing and day care facilities are available.

Employment of Department Graduates:

Master's Degree Graduates: Of those who graduated in the academic year 2000–2001, the following categories and numbers represent the post-graduate activities and employment of master's degree graduates: Enrolled in a post-doctoral residency/fellowship (n/a), employed in independent practice (n/a).

Doctoral Degree Graduates: Of those who graduated in the academic year 2000–2001, the following categories and numbers represent the post-graduate activities and employment of doctoral degree graduates: Enrolled in a psychology doctoral program (n/a), enrolled in another graduate/professional program (n/a).

Additional Information:

Orientation, Objectives, and Emphasis of Department: Graduate study in psychology at Penn State is characterized by highly flexible, individualized programs leading to the PhD in Psychology. Each student is associated with one of the five program areas offered in the department: clinical (including child clinical); cognitive; developmental; industrial/organizational; and social. (Specialization in behavioral neuroscience is possible in any program area. Students in any program area may combine their program of study with a specialization in behavioral neuroscience by choosing appropriate courses and seminars. Students choosing this specialization may pursue the integration of neuroscience methods and theories by applying these approaches to research topics within their program areas. Within each area, certain courses are usually suggested for all students. The details of a student's program, however, are worked out on an individual basis with a faculty advisor. A major specialization and breadth outside the major are required. The major is selected from among the six specialty areas of the department listed above; breadth requirements are flexible and individualized to career goals. Depending upon the individual student's particular program of study, graduates may be employed in academic departments, research institutes, industry, governmental agencies, or various service delivery settings.

Special Facilities or Resources: The department has clinical, learning-cognition, perception, physiological, psychophysiology, developmental, and social laboratories; microcomputer laboratories; access to the University's mainframe and electronic communication system (e-mail and Internet) and computer laboratories; clinical practica in local mental health centers and hospitals in addition to the department's Psychological Clinic, which functions as a mental health center for the catchment area of central Pennsylvania; industrial/organizational practica in industrial and government organizations; developmental practica and research opportunities in day care and preschool settings. A number of centers or institutes are housed within, or affiliated with, the department, including a new Child Study Center.

Information for Students With Physical Disabilities: Penn State is committed to the policy that all persons shall have equal access to programs, facilities, admission, and employment without regard to personal characteristics not related to ability, performance, or qualifications as determined by University policy or by state or federal authorities. Information may be obtained directly from the Office for Disability Services, located at 105 Boucke Bldg., 814-863-1807. Alternatively, prospective students are invited to contact the Department directly for further information on accommodations.

Application Information:

Send to: Graduate Admissions, Department of Psychology, Penn State University, 130 Moore Building, University Park, PA 16802. Students are admitted in the Fall, application deadline December 15. December 15 is the deadline for all areas except Cognitive and Developmental Areas, which is January 15. *Fee:* $60.

Pennsylvania State University

Educational Psychology
227 Cedar Building
University Park, PA 16802
Telephone: (814) 863-2286
Fax: (814) 863-1002
E-mail: *rjs15@psu.edu*
Web: *http://roberts.ed.psu.edu/users/edpsy/edpsy.htm*

Department Established:

1968. Professor-in-Charge: Robert J. Stevens. Number of Faculty: total–full-time 8, part-time 1; women–full-time 4; minority–full-time 2.

Programs and Degrees Offered:

Listed in the following order: Program area, degree type (T if terminal Master's), number awarded 7/00–6/01. Educational PhD 6.

Student Applications/Admissions:

Student Applications

Educational PhD—Applications 2001–2002, 45. Total applicants accepted 2001–2002, 6. New applicants enrolled 2001–2002, 4. Total enrolled 2001–2002 full-time, 32, part-time, 2. Openings 2002–2003, 5. The number of students enrolled full and part-time, who were dismissed or voluntarily withdrew from this program area were 1.

Admissions Requirements:

Scores: Entries appear in this order: required test or GPA, minimum score (if required), median score of students entering in 2001–2002. Master's Programs: GRE-V no minimum stated, 550; GRE-Q no minimum stated, 600; GRE-Analytical no minimum stated, 550; last 2 years GPA no minimum stated, 3.50. Doctoral Programs: GRE-V no minimum stated, 550; GRE-Q no minimum stated, 600; GRE-Analytical no minimum stated, 550; last 2 years GPA no minimum stated, 3.50; psychology GPA no minimum stated; psychology GPA no minimum stated.

Other Criteria: (importance of criteria rated low, medium, or high): GRE/MAT scores medium, research experience medium, work experience medium, extracurricular activity low, GPA medium, letters of recommendation high, statement of goals and objectives high. Interview optional.

Student Characteristics: The following represents characteristics of students in 2001–2002 in all graduate psychology programs in the department: Female–full-time 18, part-time 0; Male–full-time 14, part-time 0; African American/Black–full-time 1, part-time 0; Hispanic/Latino (a)–full-time 1, part-time 0; Asian/Pacific Islander–full-time 6, part-time 0; American Indian/Alaska Native–full-time 0, part-time 0.

Financial Information/Assistance:
Tuition for Full-Time Study: No information provided.

Financial Assistance:
First Year Students: No information provided.
Advanced Students: No information provided.
Contact Information: Of all students currently enrolled full-time, 0% benefited from one or more of the listed financial assistance programs. For information on financial assistance, contact: Admissions Committee.

Internships/Practica: No information provided.

Housing and Day Care: No on-campus housing and day care facilities are available.

Employment of Department Graduates:
Master's Degree Graduates: Of those who graduated in the academic year 2000–2001, the following categories and numbers represent the post-graduate activities and employment of master's degree graduates: Enrolled in a psychology doctoral program (4), enrolled in another graduate/professional program (1), enrolled in a post-doctoral residency/fellowship (n/a), employed in independent practice (n/a).
Doctoral Degree Graduates: Of those who graduated in the academic year 2000–2001, the following categories and numbers represent the post-graduate activities and employment of doctoral degree graduates: Enrolled in a psychology doctoral program (n/a), enrolled in another graduate/professional program (n/a), employed in an academic position at a university (2), employed in business or industry (research/consulting) (1).

Additional Information:
Orientation, Objectives, and Emphasis of Department: Students may specialize and do research in one of the following areas: human learning and memory as applied to instruction, or education and educational and psychological measurement as applied to the evaluation of educational programs. There are two options in the master's program. A thesis option is available in either of the two areas. The MS without thesis may be taken in learning or evaluation by teachers, counselors, administrators, parents, and others concerned with intervention strategies or evaluation of educational programs. The MS with thesis is required for the PhD candidates. Doctoral degree requirements include a major emphasis in one of the two areas of educational psychology, with minor emphasis in one other related area. The doctoral program and master's program of study includes at least one course in cognitive, social, individual differences, and biological bases of behavior and at least one course in educational or philosophical foundations.

Special Facilities or Resources: Facilities include a research design laboratory, rooms for conducting research projects, a closed-circuit television studio for research and instruction, computer system facilities, access to the University mainframe computer, and a division resource center. The program has excellent computer resources with computers in labs and in most student offices. Many of these computers are hard-wired to the University mainframe. Students have ready access to statistical packages and the Internet.

Application Information:
Send to: Admissions Committee, Educational Psychology Program, 227 Cedar Bldg., Penn State University, University Park, PA 16802. Students are admitted in the Fall; Spring. Fall admission open but prefer application prior to January 15. Fee: $40.

Pennsylvania State University
Program in School Psychology
College of Education
227 Cedar Building
University Park, PA 16802
Telephone: (814) 865-1881
Fax: (814) 863-1002
E-mail: s_psy@psu.edu
Web: http://espse.ed.psu.edu/spsy/SPSY.ssi

Department Established:
1965. Professor-in-Charge: Marley W. Watkins. Number of Faculty: total–full-time 4, part-time 6; women–full-time 1, part-time 4; minority–full-time 1.

Programs and Degrees Offered:
Listed in the following order: Program area, degree type (T if terminal Master's), number awarded 7/00–6/01. School PhD 8.

APA Accreditation: School PhD: full.

Student Applications/Admissions:
Student Applications
School PhD—Applications 2001–2002, 71. Total applicants accepted 2001–2002, 7. New applicants enrolled 2001–2002, 7. Total enrolled 2001–2002 full-time, 30. Openings 2002–2003, 7. The Median number of years required for completion of a degree are 6.

Admissions Requirements:
Scores: Entries appear in this order: required test or GPA, minimum score (if required), median score of students entering in 2001–2002. Doctoral Programs: GRE-V no minimum stated, 561; GRE-Q no minimum stated, 599; GRE-Analytical no minimum stated, 639; overall undergraduate GPA no minimum stated, 3.70; last 2 years GPA no minimum stated; psychology GPA no minimum stated; psychology GPA no minimum stated.
Other Criteria: (importance of criteria rated low, medium, or high): GRE/MAT scores medium, research experience medium, work experience medium, clinically related public service low, GPA medium, letters of recommendation high, interview high, statement of goals and objectives high.

Student Characteristics: The following represents characteristics of students in 2001–2002 in all graduate psychology programs in the department: Female–full-time 7, part-time 0; Male–full-time 0, part-time 0; African American/Black–full-time 0, part-time 0; Hispanic/Latino (a)–full-time 0, part-time 0; Asian/Pacific Islander–full-time 1, part-time 0; American Indian/Alaska Native–full-time 0, part-time 0.

Financial Information/Assistance:

Tuition for Full-Time Study: *Doctoral:* State residents: per academic year $7,882; nonstate residents: per academic year $16,142.

Financial Assistance:

First Year Students: Teaching assistantships available for first-year. Average amount paid per academic year: $11,025. Average number of hours worked per week: 20. Tuition remission given: full. Research assistantships available for first-year. Average amount paid per academic year: $11,025. Average number of hours worked per week: 20. Tuition remission given: full. Fellowships and scholarships available for first-year. Average amount paid per academic year: $14,000. Average number of hours worked per week: 0. Tuition remission given: full.

Advanced Students: Teaching assistantships available for advanced students. Average amount paid per academic year: $11,025. Average number of hours worked per week: 20. Tuition remission given: full. Research assistantships available for advanced students. Average amount paid per academic year: $11,025. Average number of hours worked per week: 20. Tuition remission given: full.

Contact Information: Of all students currently enrolled full-time, 90% benefited from one or more of the listed financial assistance programs. For information on financial assistance, contact: Professor-in-Charge.

Internships/Practica:

Students complete the equivalent of more than one year of supervised training. This experience is distributed over several terms. A practicum component is built into certain courses. Other practicum experiences follow coursework in which the scientific and theoretical perspectives that inform practice and the methods and techniques that are employed in practice are studied. Participation in practicum is at various levels with initial observation and development of school psychological skills taking place on the University campus. Later, after the demonstration of basic skills, students are assigned to public schools, under the supervision of practicing school psychologists. Near the end of the training period, students return to the campus for close observation by University supervisors in the CEDAR Clinic. Students obtain experience in working with a diversity of individuals and systems. Paid doctoral internships are available in schools following completion of doctoral coursework and practica experiences. For those doctoral students for whom a professional internship is required prior to graduation, 6 applied in 2000–2001.

Housing and Day Care:

On-campus housing and day care facilities are available.

Employment of Department Graduates:

Master's Degree Graduates: Of those who graduated in the academic year 2000–2001, the following categories and numbers represent the post-graduate activities and employment of master's degree graduates: Enrolled in a post-doctoral residency/fellowship (n/a), employed in independent practice (n/a).

Doctoral Degree Graduates: Of those who graduated in the academic year 2000–2001, the following categories and numbers represent the post-graduate activities and employment of doctoral degree graduates: Enrolled in a psychology doctoral program (n/a), enrolled in another graduate/professional program (n/a), employed in other positions at a higher education institution (1), employed in a professional position in a school system (4).

Additional Information:

Orientation, Objectives, and Emphasis of Department: School psychologists from Penn State are exemplary scientist/practitioners, firmly grounded in both psychology and education. Our graduates are professional school psychologists who provide solutions for the many problems facing our children. They contribute to the practice and knowledge base of psychology as it relates to education. Penn State school psychologists become leaders in the field as well as in academia. In conjunction with providing psychological services, school psychologists will be life-long learners who sustain an interest in maintaining and developing sound practices, which derive from up-to-date, research-based information. Psychologists will thoughtfully and critically evaluate their practices and remain informed consumers of available literature, assessment tools, and intervention strategies. School psychologists will help to provide a bridge to integrate research with professional practice along with other educators, systems, and institutions.

Special Facilities or Resources: The School Psychology Program operates the CEDAR School Psychology Clinic. The CEDAR Clinic contains well appointed clinic rooms with direct observation facilities and a closed-circuit video system, which facilitate practicum supervision. Microcomputers are available to students within the program, department, and university. Access to e-mail and the Internet are provided to all students and use of technology is encouraged by faculty. The Pattee and Paterno Libraries house an impressive array of scholarly resources. As a major research university, Penn State sponsors a number of research institutes and centers in education, psychology, and human development.

Application Information:

Send to: Graduate Programs in School Psychology, Admissions Committee, 227 Cedar Bldg., Pennsylvania State University, University Park, PA 16802. Students are admitted in the Fall, application deadline February 1. *Fee:* $60.

Pennsylvania, University of (2001 data)
Department of Psychology
3815 Walnut Street
Philadelphia, PA 19104-6196
Telephone: (215) 898-7300
Fax: (215) 898-7301
E-mail: *chair@psych.upenn.edu*
Web: *http://www.psych.upenn.edu*

Department Established:

1887. Chairperson: Robert J. DeRubeis. Number of Faculty: total–full-time 28; women–full-time 9; minority–full-time 1.

Programs and Degrees Offered:
Listed in the following order: Program area, degree type (T if terminal Master's), number awarded 7/00–6/01. Clinical Psychology PhD 3, Psychology PhD 7.

APA Accreditation: Clinical PhD: full.

Student Applications/Admissions:
Student Applications
Clinical Psychology PhD—Applications 2001–2002, 228. Total applicants accepted 2001–2002, 5. New applicants enrolled 2001–2002, 4. Total enrolled 2001–2002 full-time, 14. Openings 2002–2003, 4. The Median number of years required for completion of a degree are 6. The number of students enrolled full and part-time, who were dismissed or voluntarily withdrew from this program area were 1. *Psychology PhD*—Applications 2001–2002, 363. Total applicants accepted 2001–2002, 20. New applicants enrolled 2001–2002, 9. Total enrolled 2001–2002 full-time, 38. Openings 2002–2003, 10. The Median number of years required for completion of a degree are 5. The number of students enrolled full and part-time, who were dismissed or voluntarily withdrew from this program area were 1. V-680 Q-740 A-700

Admissions Requirements:
Scores: Entries appear in this order: required test or GPA, minimum score (if required), median score of students entering in 2001–2002. Doctoral Programs: GRE-V no minimum stated, 680; GRE-Q no minimum stated, 740; GRE-Analytical no minimum stated, 700; overall undergraduate GPA no minimum stated, 3.8; last 2 years GPA no minimum stated; psychology GPA no minimum stated; psychology GPA no minimum stated.

Other Criteria: (importance of criteria rated low, medium, or high): GRE/MAT scores medium, research experience high, work experience low, clinically related public service low, GPA medium, letters of recommendation medium, interview low, statement of goals and objectives high, science background medium.

Student Characteristics: The following represents characteristics of students in 2001–2002 in all graduate psychology programs in the department: Female–full-time 25, part-time 0; Male–full-time 13, part-time 0; African American/Black–full-time 1, part-time 0; Hispanic/Latino (a)–full-time 1, part-time 0; Asian/Pacific Islander–full-time 5, part-time 0; American Indian/Alaska Native–full-time 0, part-time 0.

Financial Information/Assistance:
Tuition for Full-Time Study: No information provided.

Financial Assistance:
First Year Students: Teaching assistantships available for first-year. Average amount paid per academic year: $14,000. Average number of hours worked per week: 10. Apply by January 7. Tuition remission given: full.

Advanced Students: Teaching assistantships available for advanced students. Average amount paid per academic year: $14,000. Average number of hours worked per week: 10. Apply by January 7. Tuition remission given: full.

Contact Information: Of all students currently enrolled full-time, 100% benefited from one or more of the listed financial assistance programs.

Internships/Practica: No information provided.

Housing and Day Care: No on-campus housing and day care facilities are available.

Employment of Department Graduates:
Master's Degree Graduates: Of those who graduated in the academic year 2000–2001, the following categories and numbers represent the post-graduate activities and employment of master's degree graduates: Enrolled in a post-doctoral residency/fellowship (n/a), employed in independent practice (n/a).
Doctoral Degree Graduates: Of those who graduated in the academic year 2000–2001, the following categories and numbers represent the post-graduate activities and employment of doctoral degree graduates: Enrolled in a psychology doctoral program (n/a), enrolled in another graduate/professional program (n/a).

Additional Information:
Orientation, Objectives, and Emphasis of Department: The Department of Psychology at the University of Pennsylvania offers curricular and research opportunities for the study of sensation, perception, cognition, cognitive neuroscience, decision-making, language, learning, motivation, emotion, motor control, psychopathology, and social processes. Biological, cultural, developmental, comparative, experimental, and mathematical approaches to these areas are used in ongoing teaching and research. The department has an APA-accredited clinical program that is designed to prepare students for research careers in psychopathology and personality. The interests of the faculty and students in the department cover the entire field of research-oriented psychology. Still, the Department of Psychology at Pennsylvania functions as a single unit whose guiding principle is scientific excellence. Students are admitted to the department. The primary determinant of acceptance is academic promise rather than specific area of interest. Faculty join together from different subdisciplines for teaching and research purposes so that students become conversant with issues in a number of different areas. Most graduate students and faculty attend the weekly departmental colloquia. A high level of interaction among department members (students and faculty), within and across disciplines, helps generate both a shared set of interests in the theoretical, historical, and philosophical foundations of psychology and active collaboration in research projects. This level of intellectual interaction is made possible, in part, by the small size of the department; there are 23 full-time faculty members and approximately 40 graduate students in residence. The first-year program is divided between courses that introduce various areas of psychology and a focused research experience. A deep involvement in research continues throughout the graduate program, and is supplemented by participation in seminars, the weekly departmental colloquium, teaching, and general intellectual give and take.

Special Facilities or Resources: The department has a fully equipped wood, metal, and electronics shop. In addition, the department has a well-equipped laboratory building, a microvax connected to Internet (used extensively), and many accessible microcomputers. Also readily available for research in the near environs of the department are 4 major University-affiliated hospitals, urban public and private schools, and the Philadelphia Zoo, ten minutes from campus.

Application Information:
Send to: Graduate School of Arts and Sciences, 16 College Hall, Philadelphia, PA 19104. Students are admitted in the Fall, application deadline January 7. *Fee: $50.*

Pennsylvania, University of
Psychology in Education Division
Graduate School of Education
3700 Walnut Street
Philadelphia, PA 19104-6216
Telephone: (215) 898-4176
Fax: (215) 573-2115
E-mail: *johnp@gse.upenn.edu*
Web: *http://www.upenn.edu/gse/*

Department Established:
1975. Chair, Psychology in Education Division: John L. Puckett. Number of Faculty: total–full-time 9, part-time 6; women–full-time 1, part-time 6; minority–full-time 2, part-time 1; faculty subject to the Americans with Disabilities Act 1.

Programs and Degrees Offered:
Listed in the following order: Program area, degree type (T if terminal Master's), number awarded 7/00–6/01. Inderdisciplinary studies HD (T) 4, interdisciplinary studies in HD PhD 1, policy research, evaluation PhD 2, psychological services (T) 37, school, community, clinical child PhD 3.

APA Accreditation: Combined PhD: full.

Student Applications/Admissions:
Student Applications
Inderdisiplinary studies in HD PhD—Applications 2001–2002, 36. Total applicants accepted 2001–2002, 5. New applicants enrolled 2001–2002, 2. Total enrolled 2001–2002 full-time, 12, part-time, 2. Openings 2002–2003, 3. The Median number of years required for completion of a degree are 5. *Policy research, evaluation PhD*—Applications 2001–2002, 17. Total applicants accepted 2001–2002, 4. New applicants enrolled 2001–2002, 1. Total enrolled 2001–2002 full-time, 14, part-time, 3. Openings 2002–2003, 6. The Median number of years required for completion of a degree is 1. *School, community, clinical child PhD*—Applications 2001–2002, 48. Total applicants accepted 2001–2002, 4. New applicants enrolled 2001–2002, 4. Total enrolled 2001–2002 full-time, 15. Openings 2002– 2003, 4. The Median number of years required for completion of a degree are 4.

Admissions Requirements:
Scores: Entries appear in this order: required test or GPA, minimum score (if required), median score of students entering in 2001–2002. Master's Programs: GRE-V no minimum stated; GRE-Q no minimum stated; GRE-V+Q 1100; overall undergraduate GPA 2.70. Doctoral Programs: GRE-V no minimum stated; GRE-Q no minimum stated; GRE-V+Q 1200, 1255; GRE-Analytical no minimum stated; GRE-Subject(Psych) 600, 620; overall undergraduate GPA 3.25, 3.41; last 2 years GPA no minimum stated; psychology GPA no minimum stated; psychology GPA 3.50, 3.70. For the APA-accredited program in School, Community and Clinical Child Psychology, a master's degree in Psychological Services or a closely related area is required, along with the Advanced Psychology Test GRE scores; the other PhD programs in ISHD and PREM do not require the Advanced Psychology test.
Other Criteria: (importance of criteria rated low, medium, or high): GRE/MAT scores high, research experience medium, work experience medium, extracurricular activity low, clinically related public service medium, GPA high, letters of recommendation high, interview high, statement of goals and objectives high, maturity, positive att. high.

Student Characteristics: The following represents characteristics of students in 2001–2002 in all graduate psychology programs in the department: Female–full-time 67, part-time 7; Male–full-time 13, part-time 7; African American/Black–full-time 8, part-time 0; Hispanic/Latino (a)–full-time 3, part-time 0; Asian/Pacific Islander–full-time 13, part-time 7; American Indian/Alaska Native–full-time 0, part-time 0; Multi-ethnic–full-time 1.

Financial Information/Assistance:
Tuition for Full-Time Study: No information provided.

Financial Assistance:
First Year Students: Teaching assistantships available for first-year. Average number of hours worked per week: 20. Apply by 12/15. Tuition remission given: full. Research assistantships available for first-year. Average number of hours worked per week: 20. Apply by 12/15. Tuition remission given: full. Fellowships and scholarships available for first-year. Average number of hours worked per week: 20. Apply by 12/15. Tuition remission given: full.
Advanced Students: Teaching assistantships available for advanced students. Average number of hours worked per week: 20. Apply by ongoing. Research assistantships available for advanced students. Average number of hours worked per week: 20. Apply by ongoing. Fellowships and scholarships available for advanced students. Average number of hours worked per week: 20. Apply by ongoing.
Contact Information: Of all students currently enrolled full-time, 60% benefited from one or more of the listed financial assistance programs. For information on financial assistance, contact: Administrative Coordinator, Psychology in Education Division, (215) 898-4176.

Internships/Practica: MSEd students engage in supervised practica one day per week. Placements include hospitals, schools, community colleges, clinics, and community agencies. Supervised PhD practica are one day per week and internships are half-time (20–25 hours per week), with experiences partitioned across schools, community agencies, and clinical settings.

Housing and Day Care: On-campus housing and day care facilities are available.

Employment of Department Graduates:
Master's Degree Graduates: Of those who graduated in the academic year 2000–2001, the following categories and numbers

represent the post-graduate activities and employment of master's degree graduates: Enrolled in a post-doctoral residency/fellowship (n/a), employed in independent practice (n/a).

Doctoral Degree Graduates: Of those who graduated in the academic year 2000–2001, the following categories and numbers represent the post-graduate activities and employment of doctoral degree graduates: Enrolled in a psychology doctoral program (n/a), enrolled in another graduate/professional program (n/a).

Additional Information:

Orientation, Objectives, and Emphasis of Department: The Psychology in Education Division provides students with a foundation in the core concepts of psychology: assessment, intervention, learning and development, and field research. Students engage in the challenge of framing major psychological, educational, and social questions, of identifying and developing evidence bearing on those questions, and of working productively at the level of the individual, the community, the nation, and the world. Our orientation in psychological practice and research is toward discovery of what works best, and why, advancing our understanding of ways to characterize and resolve psychological and social problems, and promoting the use of that knowledge in professional practice and in educational and public policy contexts. Students are prepared for careers in teaching, research, and practice in schools and universities, in clinical settings and mental health agencies, in government and the corporate world. Our objectives are to provide students with the richest possible opportunities to develop productive careers. The MSEd in Psychological Services prepares students for practice in diverse community agencies; graduates may obtain certification in guidance counseling. The PhD in School, Community, and Clinical Child Psychology prepares students for certification in school psychology, state psychology licensure, and careers in applied research, clinical practice, and university teaching.

Special Facilities or Resources: The Psychology in Education Division houses the Center for Research and Evaluation in Social Policy (CRESP) and the Center for Health Achievement, Neighborhood Growth and Ethnic Studies (CHANGES), providing students with research mentorship and opportunities. We also house the Morris Viteles Computer Research Center, and maintain on-going research programs centering on domestic violence, child maltreatment, AIDS education among youth, child psychopathology, and learning styles.

Information for Students With Physical Disabilities: The University has offices which coordinate, provide, and monitor services and supports for students with disabilities.

Application Information:

Send to: Admissions Office, Graduate School of Education, Univ. of Pennsylvania, 3700 Walnut St., Philadelphia, PA 19104-6216. Students are admitted in the Fall, application deadline Jan. 4-PhD. Application may be accepted the next business day. Rolling admissions for all MSEd programs, with deadline of May 15. *Fee:* $65. Fee is usually waived upon request.

Philadelphia College of Osteopathic Medicine (2001 data)

Psychology Department
4190 City Avenue
Philadelphia, PA 19131-1693
Telephone: (215) 871-6442
Fax: (215) 871-6458
E-mail: *psych@pcom.edu*
Web: *http://www.pcom.edu*

Department Established:
1995. Chairperson: Arthur Freeman. Number of Faculty: total–full-time 7, part-time 34; women–full-time 3, part-time 15; minority–full-time 1, part-time 3.

Programs and Degrees Offered:
Listed in the following order: Program area, degree type (T if terminal Master's), number awarded 7/00–6/01. Certificate advanced grad. stu CAGS, clinical health MS (T), clinical psychology Respecialization Diploma 2, doctor of psychology PsyD 5, organizational development and MS (T).

Student Applications/Admissions:
Student Applications
Certificate advanced grad. stu CAGS—Applications 2001–2002, 5. Total applicants accepted 2001–2002, 1. Openings 2002–2003, 30. The Median number of years required for completion of a degree is 1. The number of students enrolled full and part-time, who were dismissed or voluntarily withdrew from this program area were 0. Clinical health MS—Applications 2001–2002, 30. Total applicants accepted 2001–2002, 15. New applicants enrolled 2001–2002, 12. Total enrolled 2001–2002 full-time, 20, part-time, 5. Openings 2002–2003, 25. The Median number of years required for completion of a degree are 2. The number of students enrolled full and part-time, who were dismissed or voluntarily withdrew from this program area were 1. Clinical psychology Respecialization Diploma—Applications 2001–2002, 0. Total enrolled 2001–2002 part-time, 3. Openings 2002–2003, 5. The number of students enrolled full and part-time, who were dismissed or voluntarily withdrew from this program area were 0. Doctor of psychology PsyD—Applications 2001–2002, 86. Total applicants accepted 2001–2002, 49. New applicants enrolled 2001–2002, 37. Total enrolled 2001–2002 full-time, 200. Openings 2002–2003, 50. The Median number of years required for completion of a degree are 5. The number of students enrolled full and part-time, who were dismissed or voluntarily withdrew from this program area were 1. Organizational development and MS—Applications 2001–2002, 0. Openings 2002–2003, 25. The Median number of years required for completion of a degree are 2. The number of students enrolled full and part-time, who were dismissed or voluntarily withdrew from this program area were 0.

Admissions Requirements:
Scores: Entries appear in this order: required test or GPA, minimum score (if required), median score of students entering in 2001–2002. Master's Programs: GRE-V+Q+Analytical no minimum stated; MAT no minimum stated; overall undergraduate GPA 3.0, 3.2. Doctoral Programs: MAT no minimum

stated, 59%; overall undergraduate GPA 3.0, 3.49; psychology GPA no minimum stated, 3.5; psychology GPA no minimum stated, 3.7.

Other Criteria: (importance of criteria rated low, medium, or high): GRE/MAT scores medium, research experience low, work experience high, extracurricular activity medium, clinically related public service high, GPA high, letters of recommendation high, interview high, statement of goals and objectives medium, professional affiliation medium. Work experience is weighted medium as admission criteria for the MS and CAGS programs. Work experience is weighted high as admission criteria for the PsyD program.

Student Characteristics: The following represents characteristics of students in 2001–2002 in all graduate psychology programs in the department: Female–full-time 49, part-time 3; Male–full-time 11, part-time 0; African American/Black–full-time 5, part-time 0; Hispanic/Latino (a)–full-time 3, part-time 0; Asian/Pacific Islander–full-time 4, part-time 0; American Indian/Alaska Native– full-time 0, part-time 0.

Financial Information/Assistance:
Tuition for Full-Time Study: No information provided.

Financial Assistance:
First Year Students: No information provided.
Advanced Students: No information provided.
Contact Information: Of all students currently enrolled full-time, 0% benefited from one or more of the listed financial assistance programs. For information on financial assistance, contact: PCOM Office of Financial Aid, 4190 City Avenue, Philadelphia, PA 19131-1693; (215) 871-6509; Website: www.pcom.edu.

Internships/Practica: Practica are nine-month fieldwork experiences completed by master's level and doctoral students that require a minimum of 8 hours per week at a PCOM approved clinical training site. The internship is a 1- to 2-year, 2000-hour supervised clinical work experience at a PCOM approved site. Practicum and internship sites are committed to excellence in the training of professionals, provide extensive supervision, and permit students to be active clinical team members. They offer a wide range of training and educational experiences, including the use of empirically supported interventions, brief treatment models, cognitive behavioral therapy, and treatment of psychological/medical problems. Students engage in evaluation, psychological testing (PsyD only), psychotherapy, and professional clinical work. Practica and internships include seminars taught by faculty that provide a place for students to discuss their experiences and help students integrate coursework with on-site training. Students participate in practica and internships at the Psychology Department's Center for Brief Therapy, a multi-faceted clinical training center, as well as sites including community agencies, hospitals, university counseling centers, prisons, and specialized treatment centers. The department has a broad network of practicum and internship sites in Pennsylvania, New Jersey, and Delaware. Students may also apply for APA- or APPIC-approved internships.

Housing and Day Care: No on-campus housing and day care facilities are available.

Employment of Department Graduates:
Master's Degree Graduates: Of those who graduated in the academic year 2000–2001, the following categories and numbers represent the post-graduate activities and employment of master's degree graduates: Enrolled in a post-doctoral residency/fellowship (n/a), employed in independent practice (n/a).

Doctoral Degree Graduates: Of those who graduated in the academic year 2000–2001, the following categories and numbers represent the post-graduate activities and employment of doctoral degree graduates: Enrolled in a psychology doctoral program (n/a), enrolled in another graduate/professional program (n/a).

Additional Information:
Orientation, Objectives, and Emphasis of Department: The mission of the PCOM psychology department is to prepare highly skilled, compassionate psychologists and master's level clinicians to provide empirically-based, active-focused, and collaborative treatment. The department seeks to: 1) train students under the Vail model to become general practitioner-scholars; 2) train students to provide clinical services based upon empirically-supported strategies; and 3) train practitioner-scholars who are capable of interfacing with primary care physicians as an integral part of an interdisciplinary health care team. Grounded in the cognitive behavioral tradition, the graduate programs in psychology train students to offer assessment, therapeutic interventions, consultation, and follow-up services. Students also have the opportunity to gain expertise in brief treatment models, cognitive behavior therapy, and in the treatment of health problems using a biopsychosocial model. To address the needs of diverse racial/ethnic groups, the department seeks to recognize differences in values, history, and relationship between the dominant culture and subcultures, and to train culturally competent psychologists. The department encourages students to work in the mental health field while attending a graduate psychology program to facilitate the integration of practical experience with scholarly pursuits for a richer learning experience. All graduate psychology courses are held on weekday evenings and weekends to accommodate working students.

Special Facilities or Resources: The academic facilities in Philadelphia include state-of-the-art amphitheaters and classroom facilities, a computer laboratory with extensive software including PsycLIT and SPSS, a recently renovated library that includes sophisticated on-line resources, and the HealthNet teleconferencing system. The Center for Brief Therapy, a mental health clinic housed in the Department of Psychology, provides multi-faceted clinical training and research opportunities for students. PCOM also has three neighborhood health centers in Philadelphia and one in LaPorte Pennsylvania. The Doctor of Psychology Program has 3 program sites: Philadelphia, Harrisburg, and East Stroudsburg.

Information for Students With Physical Disabilities: Philadelphia College of Osteopathic Medicine subscribes to the principles and laws of the Commonwealth of Pennsylvania and the federal government pertaining to civil rights and equal opportunity, including Title IX of the 1972 Education Amendments and Section 504 of the Rehabilitation Act of 1973. PCOM policy prohibits discrimination on the basis of age, race, color, national or ethnic origin, sex, sexual preference, religion, disability, or marital status. This policy applies in recruitment and admission of students, employment of faculty and staff, and eligibility for scholarship and loan programs. This policy is also followed in the operation of all other programs, activities, and services of the college. Any requests for special accommodations must be submitted in writing and arrangements finalized for the duration of the academic program before beginning the academic program. Evidence of practices inconsistent with this policy should be reported to the Director of Human Resources, who is the designated coordinator of PCOM's nondiscrimination program. Inquiries regarding compliance with the discrimination provisions of Title IX may also be directed to the Assistant for Civil Rights, Department of Education, Washington, D.C. or the State Human Relations Commission, Harrisburg, PA.

Application Information:

Send to: Department Chair. Students are admitted in the Fall, application deadline February 15. Other deadlines for specific programs: The PsyD program requires all application materials to be submitted to PCOM by February 15 prior to the Fall semester for which student applies. The MS and CAGS program have a rolling admissions policy in which complete applications are reviewed as they are received. *Fee:* $50.

Pittsburgh, University of (2001 data)
Department of Psychology in Education
School of Education
5C Posvar Hall
Pittsburgh, PA 15260
Telephone: (412) 624-7230
Fax: (412) 624-7231
E-mail: *lchandlr@pitt.edu*
Web: *http://www.pitt.edu/~soeforum/new/dept_pie.html*

Department Established:

1986. Chairperson: Louis A. Chandler. Number of Faculty: total–full-time 19, part-time 3; women–full-time 8, part-time 3; minority–full-time 2.

Programs and Degrees Offered:

Listed in the following order: Program area, degree type (T if terminal Master's), number awarded 7/00–6/01. Developmental and educational PhD 6, research methodology PhD 8.

APA Accreditation: Counseling PhD: full.

Student Applications/Admissions:

Student Applications

Developmental and educational PhD—Applications 2001–2002, 21. Total applicants accepted 2001–2002, 11. New applicants enrolled 2001–2002, 10. Total enrolled 2001–2002 full-time, 6, part-time, 30. Openings 2002–2003, 12. *Research methodology PhD*—Applications 2001–2002, 15. Total applicants accepted 2001–2002, 10. New applicants enrolled 2001–2002, 9. Total enrolled 2001–2002 full-time, 5, part-time, 9. Openings 2002–2003, 10.

Admissions Requirements:

Scores: Entries appear in this order: required test or GPA, minimum score (if required), median score of students entering in 2001–2002. Master's Programs: GRE-V+Q+Analytical no minimum stated; GRE-Subject(Psych) no minimum stated; overall undergraduate GPA no minimum stated, 3.00. GRE

is not required for any of the master's programs. International students are not required to take GRE, but must take TOEFL. Doctoral Programs: GRE-V no minimum stated; GRE-Q no minimum stated; GRE-V+Q no minimum stated; GRE-Analytical no minimum stated; GRE-V+Q+Analytical no minimum stated; GRE-Subject(Psych) no minimum stated; MAT no minimum stated; overall undergraduate GPA 3.00; last 2 years GPA no minimum stated; psychology GPA no minimum stated; psychology GPA 3.30. Subject GRE is not required for Research Methodology doctoral program. International students are not required to take GRE, but must take TOEFL. Research methodology students are not required to take the MAT. Developmental and Educational psychology students are not required to take the MAT.

Other Criteria: (importance of criteria rated low, medium, or high): GRE/MAT scores high, research experience medium, work experience medium, extracurricular activity low, clinically related public service medium, GPA high, letters of recommendation low, statement of goals and objectives high, writing sample high.

Student Characteristics: The following represents characteristics of students in 2001–2002 in all graduate psychology programs in the department: Female–full-time 65, part-time 0; Male–full-time 26, part-time 0; African American/Black–full-time 0, part-time 0; Hispanic/Latino (a)–full-time 0, part-time 0; Asian/Pacific Islander–full-time 0, part-time 0; American Indian/Alaska Native–full-time 0, part-time 0.

Financial Information/Assistance:

Tuition for Full-Time Study: No information provided.

Financial Assistance:

First Year Students: No information provided.
Advanced Students: No information provided.
Contact Information: For information on financial assistance, contact: Financial Assistance Coordinator, c/o Department Administrator, Department of Psychology in Education, 5C01 Forbes Quadrangle, University of Pittsburgh, Pittsburgh, PA 15260.

Internships/Practica: Field placements are available working with research and service projects through such agencies as the University's Learning Research and Development Center, Western Psychiatric Institute and Clinic, and The Children's Hospital of Pittsburgh.

Housing and Day Care: No on-campus housing and day care facilities are available.

Employment of Department Graduates:

Master's Degree Graduates: Of those who graduated in the academic year 2000–2001, the following categories and numbers represent the post-graduate activities and employment of master's degree graduates: Enrolled in a post-doctoral residency/fellowship (n/a), employed in independent practice (n/a).
Doctoral Degree Graduates: Of those who graduated in the academic year 2000–2001, the following categories and numbers represent the post-graduate activities and employment of doctoral degree graduates: Enrolled in a psychology doctoral program (n/a), enrolled in another graduate/professional program (n/a).

Additional Information:

Orientation, Objectives, and Emphasis of Department: The department offers graduate programs in two areas: developmental and educational psychology (PhD only), and research methodology (master's and PhD).

Special Facilities or Resources: Research facilities are available at various locations including the Learning, Research, and Development Center (LRDC); the Pittsburgh Board of Education; and the Western Psychiatric Institute and Clinic. These facilities are located on the university campus. Faculty in the Department have research projects on which students work.

Information for Students With Physical Disabilities: The University of Pittsburgh provides excellent services to students with disabilities through its Office of Disabled Resources and Services. Services include adoptive test administration, interpreters for the deaf, braille copy texts, and on-campus transportation service. Call (412) 648-7890 for more details or write to 216 William Pitt Union, University of Pittsburgh, Pittsburgh, PA 15260.

Application Information:

Send to: Admissions Coordinator (state the program name), Department of Psychology in Education, 5C Posvar Hall, University of Pittsburgh, Pittsburgh, PA 15260. Students are admitted in the Fall, application deadline February 1; Spring, application deadline November 15; Summer, application deadline February 1. Applications after the deadlines are seriously considered if all the places are not filled. *Fee:* $40. For tuition waiver, write and explain need.

Pittsburgh, University of
Psychology
Faculty of Arts and Sciences
MPAC - 210 S. Bouquet Street
Pittsburgh, PA 15260
Telephone: (412) 624-4502
Fax: (412) 624-4428
E-mail: *psygrad@pitt.edu*
Web: *http://www.pitt.edu/~psych/*

Department Established:

1904. Chairperson: Anthony R. Caggiula. Number of Faculty: total–full-time 33, part-time 6; women–full-time 10, part-time 3; minority–full-time 2.

Programs and Degrees Offered:

Listed in the following order: Program area, degree type (T if terminal Master's), number awarded 7/00–6/01. Clinical PhD 6, Cognitive PhD 5, Developmental PhD 2, Health PhD 1, Individualized PhD, Social PhD 1.

APA Accreditation: Clinical PhD: full.

Student Applications/Admissions:

Student Applications

Clinical PhD—Applications 2001–2002, 191. Total applicants accepted 2001–2002, 11. New applicants enrolled 2001–2002, 8. Total enrolled 2001–2002 full-time, 40. Openings 2002–

2003, 6. *Cognitive PhD*—Applications 2001–2002, 73. Total applicants accepted 2001–2002, 8. New applicants enrolled 2001–2002, 6. Total enrolled 2001–2002 full-time, 29. Openings 2002–2003, 4. *Developmental PhD*—Applications 2001–2002, 97. Total applicants accepted 2001–2002, 2. New applicants enrolled 2001–2002, 2. Total enrolled 2001–2002 full-time, 12. Openings 2002–2003, 4. *Health PhD*—Applications 2001–2002, 62. Total applicants accepted 2001–2002, 1. New applicants enrolled 2001–2002, 1. Total enrolled 2001–2002 full-time, 7. Openings 2002–2003, 6. *Individualized PhD*—Applications 2001–2002, 5. Total enrolled 2001–2002 full-time, 2. *Social PhD*—Applications 2001–2002, 24. Total applicants accepted 2001–2002, 3. New applicants enrolled 2001–2002, 1. Total enrolled 2001–2002 full-time, 6. Openings 2002–2003, 3. The number of students enrolled full and part-time, who were dismissed or voluntarily withdrew from this program area were 1. *V-548 Q-625 A-653*

Admissions Requirements:

Scores: Entries appear in this order: required test or GPA, minimum score (if required), median score of students entering in 2001–2002. Doctoral Programs: GRE-V no minimum stated, 548; GRE-Q no minimum stated, 625; GRE-V+Q no minimum stated; GRE-Analytical no minimum stated, 653; GRE-V+Q+Analytical no minimum stated; overall undergraduate GPA no minimum stated, 3.54; last 2 years GPA no minimum stated; psychology GPA no minimum stated; psychology GPA no minimum stated. GRE Psychology subject test is required for applicants to Clinical programs

Other Criteria: (importance of criteria rated low, medium, or high): GRE/MAT scores high, research experience high, work experience medium, extracurricular activity low, clinically related public service low, GPA high, letters of recommendation high, interview high, statement of goals and objectives medium.

Student Characteristics: The following represents characteristics of students in 2001–2002 in all graduate psychology programs in the department: Female–full-time 71, part-time 0; Male–full-time 28, part-time 0; African American/Black–full-time 8, part-time 0; Hispanic/Latino (a)–full-time 2, part-time 0; Asian/Pacific Islander–full-time 3, part-time 0; American Indian/Alaska Native–full-time 0, part-time 0.

Financial Information/Assistance:

Tuition for Full-Time Study: No information provided.

Financial Assistance:

First Year Students: Teaching assistantships available for first-year. Average amount paid per academic year: $11,980. Tuition remission given: full. Research assistantships available for first-year. Average amount paid per academic year: $11,190. Tuition remission given: full. Average amount paid per academic year: $13,728. Tuition remission given: full.

Advanced Students: No information provided.

Contact Information: Of all students currently enrolled full-time, 100% benefited from one or more of the listed financial assistance programs. For information on financial assistance, contact: Graduate Secretary, Department of Psychology, 455 Langley Hall, University of Pittsburgh, Pittsburgh, PA 15260.

Internships/Practica: For those doctoral students for whom a professional internship is required prior to graduation, 5 applied in 2000–2001. Of those who applied, 4 were placed in internships listed by the Association of Psychology Postdoctoral and Internship Programs (APPIC); 5 were placed in APA accredited internships.

Housing and Day Care: No on-campus housing and day care facilities are available.

Employment of Department Graduates:

Master's Degree Graduates: Of those who graduated in the academic year 2000–2001, the following categories and numbers represent the post-graduate activities and employment of master's degree graduates: Enrolled in a post-doctoral residency/fellowship (n/a), employed in independent practice (n/a), employed in an academic position at a university (6), employed in other positions at a higher education institution (8), employed in business or industry (research/consulting) (4), still seeking employment (6).
Doctoral Degree Graduates: Of those who graduated in the academic year 2000–2001, the following categories and numbers represent the post-graduate activities and employment of doctoral degree graduates: Enrolled in a psychology doctoral program (n/a), enrolled in another graduate/professional program (n/a).

Additional Information:

Orientation, Objectives, and Emphasis of Department: Basic research training is emphasized, and most projects carry out research with important practical implications. The graduate programs include Clinical Psychology, Cognitive Psychology and Cognitive Neuroscience, Developmental Psychology, Health Psychology, Social Psychology, and joint programs in Clinical-Developmental and Clinical-Health Psychology. Some examples of training opportunities are projects on infant socialization, cognitive, language and social development of children, psychological stress on the cardiovascular and immune systems, nicotine and alcohol use, decision making in groups, stereotyping, reading processes, school and non-school learning, and brain models of attention and reading. Seminars are small (5–12 students), and close working relationships are encouraged with faculty, especially the student's advisor. Excellent relationships with other departments and schools offer unusually flexible opportunities to carry out interdisciplinary work and gain access to scholars in the Pittsburgh community. All students are expected to teach at least one course, and carry out an original research dissertation. Financial support is available for most students through teaching and research.

Special Facilities or Resources: The facilities of the department include experimental laboratories, extensive computer facilities, a small-groups laboratory, the Clinical Psychology Center, and the laboratories of the Learning Research and Development Center. These services offer the advanced graduate student opportunities for supervised practicum and research experiences. The departmental facilities also include cooperative arrangements with many organizations in Pittsburgh engaged in various kinds of psychological work. These include Children's Hospital, Pittsburgh Cancer Institute, the Western Psychiatric Institute and Clinic, St. Francis Hospital, and several local agencies of the Veterans Administration Medical Centers. Collaboration with these organizations consists of part-time instruction by the staffs of these agencies, the sharing of laboratory and clinical facilities, and the appointment in those organizations of graduate students in psychology as clinical assistants, research assistants, or as part-time employees.

Application Information:
Send to: Graduate Secretary, Department of Psychology, University of Pittsburgh, MPAC - 210 S. Bouquet Street, Pittsburgh, PA 15260. Students are admitted in the Fall, application deadline January 1. This deadline will probably change for admission for Fall, 2003. Please check our Website to confirm the application deadline date: http://www.pitt.edu/~psych. *Fee:* $40. McNair Scholars, Minority Students.

Saint Joseph's University
Department of Psychology
5600 City Avenue
Philadelphia, PA 19131-1395
Telephone: (610) 660-1800
Fax: (610) 660-1819
E-mail: *jmindell@sju.edu*
Web: *http://psychology.sju.edu*

Department Established:
1960. Director, Graduate Psychology Program: Jodi A. Mindell, PhD. Number of Faculty: total–full-time 8, part-time 4; women–full-time 5, part-time 3.

Programs and Degrees Offered:
Listed in the following order: Program area, degree type (T if terminal Master's), number awarded 7/00–6/01. Experimental MA (T) 19.

Student Applications/Admissions:
Student Applications

Experimental MA—Applications 2001–2002, 40. Total applicants accepted 2001–2002, 21. New applicants enrolled 2001–2002, 14. Total enrolled 2001–2002 full-time, 14. Openings 2002–2003, 21. The Median number of years required for completion of a degree are 2. The number of students enrolled full and part-time, who were dismissed or voluntarily withdrew from this program area were 2.

Admissions Requirements:

Scores: Entries appear in this order: required test or GPA, minimum score (if required), median score of students entering in 2001–2002. Master's Programs: GRE-V 500, 520; GRE-Q 500, 560; GRE-Subject(Psych) 500, 560; overall undergraduate GPA 3.0, 3.35; last 2 years GPA 3.2, 3.3; psychology GPA 3.2, 3.2. Doctoral Programs: last 2 years GPA no minimum stated; psychology GPA no minimum stated; psychology GPA no minimum stated.
Other Criteria: (importance of criteria rated low, medium, or high): GRE/MAT scores medium, research experience high, work experience low, extracurricular activity medium, clinically related public service low, GPA high, letters of recommendation high, interview medium, statement of goals and objectives medium.

Student Characteristics: The following represents characteristics of students in 2001–2002 in all graduate psychology programs in the department: Female–full-time 16, part-time 1; Male–full-time 9, part-time 0; African American/Black–full-time 0, part-time 1; Hispanic/Latino (a)–full-time 0, part-time 0; Asian/Pacific Islander–full-time 0, part-time 0; American Indian/Alaska Native–full-time 0, part-time 0.

Financial Information/Assistance:
  Tuition for Full-Time Study: *Master's:* State residents $560 per credit hour; nonstate residents: $560 per credit hour.

  Financial Assistance:
    First Year Students: No information provided.
    Advanced Students: Teaching assistantships available for advanced students. Average amount paid per academic year: $7,100. Average number of hours worked per week: 20. Tuition remission given: full. Research assistantships available for advanced students. Average amount paid per academic year: $7,100. Average number of hours worked per week: 20. Tuition remission given: full.
    Contact Information: Of all students currently enrolled full-time, 40% benefited from one or more of the listed financial assistance programs. For information on financial assistance, contact: Paul DeVito, chairperson; Jodi Mindell, Director, Graduate Psychology Program.

  Internships/Practica: No information provided.

  Housing and Day Care: On-campus housing and day care facilities are available.

Employment of Department Graduates:
  Master's Degree Graduates: Of those who graduated in the academic year 2000–2001, the following categories and numbers represent the post-graduate activities and employment of master's degree graduates: Enrolled in a post-doctoral residency/fellowship (n/a), employed in independent practice (n/a).
  Doctoral Degree Graduates: Of those who graduated in the academic year 2000–2001, the following categories and numbers represent the post-graduate activities and employment of doctoral degree graduates: Enrolled in a psychology doctoral program (n/a), enrolled in another graduate/professional program (n/a).

Additional Information:
  Orientation, Objectives, and Emphasis of Department: The Saint Joseph's University graduate program in Experimental Psychology is designed to provide students with a solid grounding in the scientific study of psychology. Students may concentrate studies in the fields of behavioral neuroscience, conditioning and learning, developmental psychology, health psychology, human memory, neuropsychology, or social psychology. Regardless of the particular concentration chosen, graduates of the program will have a firm foundation in the scientific method and the skills with which to pursue the scientific study of psychological questions. The program offers a traditional and academically oriented 36-credit curriculum, which requires a qualifying comprehensive examination and an empirical thesis project. The program is designed for successful completion over two academic years. Additionally, a five-year combined Bachelor/Master of Science degree in psychology is offered. The Saint Joseph's University psychology graduate program has been constructed to complement the strengths and interests of the present psychology faculty and facilities and to reflect the current state of the discipline of psychology. The curriculum is composed of three major components: a 12-credit common core required of all students; 20 credits of content based courses; and a 16-credit research component in which stu-

dents complete the comprehensive examination and research thesis.

Special Facilities or Resources: All psychology faculty have equipped and active research laboratories in which graduate students pursue independent research projects for completion of their thesis requirement. Support facilities for graduate-level research and education are impressive. A vivarium, certifiable by the United States Public Health Service, for the housing of animal subjects is in operation and is fully staffed. For research involving human subjects, the department coordinates a subject pool consisting of approximately 300 subjects per semester. Additionally, the Psychology Department at Saint Joseph's operates PsyNet, a state-of-the-art Macintosh-AppleShare local area network which is attached to a campus-wide computer network through an EtherNet connection. PsyNet consists of 35 Macintosh computers and peripherals for all faculty and staff plus fileservers and laser printers. Two student computer classrooms/laboratories which include an additional 20 computers are also available within the department. PsyNet software includes various word processing, statistical, spreadsheet, database, graphics, and simulation packages.

Application Information:
Send to: Graduate Admissions Office, Saint Joseph's University, 5600 City Avenue, Philadelphia, PA 19131-1395. Students are admitted in the Fall, application deadline February 1st. *Fee:* $35.

Shippensburg University
Department of Psychology
Arts and Sciences
Gilbert Hall
Shippensburg, PA 17257
Telephone: (717) 477-1657
Fax: (717) 477-4057
E-mail: *gradsch@ship.edu*
Web: *http://www.ship.edu/gradschool/deptpsy.html*

Department Established:
  1970. Chairperson: Ronald Mehiel. Number of Faculty: total–full-time 13, part-time 3; women–full-time 4, part-time 2; minority–full-time 1.

Programs and Degrees Offered:
  Listed in the following order: Program area, degree type (T if terminal Master's), number awarded 7/00–6/01. General MA (T) 20.

Student Applications/Admissions:
  Student Applications
    General MA—Applications 2001–2002, 39. Total applicants accepted 2001–2002, 21. New applicants enrolled 2001–2002, 11. Total enrolled 2001–2002 full-time, 14, part-time, 16. Openings 2002–2003, 20. The Median number of years required for completion of a degree are 2. The number of students enrolled full and part-time, who were dismissed or voluntarily withdrew from this program area were 1.

Admissions Requirements:

Scores: Entries appear in this order: required test or GPA, minimum score (if required), median score of students entering in 2001–2002. Master's Programs: overall undergraduate GPA 2.75, 3.10. Doctoral Programs: last 2 years GPA no minimum stated; psychology GPA no minimum stated; psychology GPA no minimum stated.

Other Criteria: (importance of criteria rated low, medium, or high): research experience medium, work experience low, extracurricular activity low, GPA high, letters of recommendation medium, statement of goals and objectives high.

Student Characteristics: The following represents characteristics of students in 2001–2002 in all graduate psychology programs in the department: Female–full-time 7, part-time 10; Male–full-time 4, part-time 4; African American/Black–full-time 0, part-time 0; Hispanic/Latino (a)–full-time 1, part-time 0; Asian/Pacific Islander–full-time 1, part-time 0; American Indian/Alaska Native–full-time 0, part-time 0; Multi-ethnic–full-time 0, students subject to the Americans with Disabilities Act–full-time 0.

Financial Information/Assistance:

Tuition for Full-Time Study: *Master's:* State residents per academic year $2,069, $230 per credit hour; nonstate residents: per academic year $3,504, $389 per credit hour.

Financial Assistance:

First Year Students: Research assistantships available for first-year. Average amount paid per academic year: $2,163. Average number of hours worked per week: 14. Apply by April 1. Tuition remission given: full.

Advanced Students: Research assistantships available for advanced students. Average amount paid per academic year: $2,163. Average number of hours worked per week: 14. Apply by April 1. Tuition remission given: full.

Contact Information: Of all students currently enrolled full-time, 20% benefited from one or more of the listed financial assistance programs. For information on financial assistance, contact: Financial Aid Office, Old Main (for loans), Psychology Department or www.ship.edu (for graduate assistantships).

Internships/Practica: No internships are available at the MS. level.

Housing and Day Care: No on-campus housing and day care facilities are available.

Employment of Department Graduates:

Master's Degree Graduates: Of those who graduated in the academic year 2000–2001, the following categories and numbers represent the post-graduate activities and employment of master's degree graduates: Enrolled in a post-doctoral residency/fellowship (n/a), employed in independent practice (n/a).

Doctoral Degree Graduates: Of those who graduated in the academic year 2000–2001, the following categories and numbers represent the post-graduate activities and employment of doctoral degree graduates: Enrolled in a psychology doctoral program (n/a), enrolled in another graduate/professional program (n/a).

Additional Information:

Orientation, Objectives, and Emphasis of Department: The MS program in psychology is designed to provide advanced general knowledge of the field and the opportunity to develop more specific research skills. In conference with faculty advisors, each candidate develops a personal program designed to meet his or her own specific needs and interests. This program serves as an effective stepping stone program for those desiring further graduate training at the doctoral level.

Special Facilities or Resources: The psychology department at Shippensburg University is currently housed in Gilbert Hall. Faculty research laboratories are located in Gilbert Hall and Franklin Science Center. Animal colonies are maintained in both facilities. Animal research facilities (wet labs and testing rooms) are also located in both buildings. Human research facilities are located in Gilbert and Franklin Halls, and include a computer terminal room, microcomputer laboratory, research cubicles, videotaping equipment, and two-way mirrored rooms.

Application Information:
Send to: Graduate Admissions, Shippensburg University. Students are admitted in the Fall, application deadline April 1; Spring, application deadline November 1; Summer, application deadline April 1. *Fee:* $25.

Temple University
Department of Psychological Studies in Education
Education
Ritter Hall Annex, 2nd Floor, Broad and Montgomery Streets
Philadelphia, PA 19122
Telephone: (215) 204-6009
Fax: (215) 204-6013
E-mail: *jrosenfe@unix.Temple.edu*
Web: *http://www.temple.edu*

Department Established:
1984. Chairperson, Psychological studies in Ed.: Joseph G. Rosenfeld. Number of Faculty: total–full-time 22, part-time 30; women–full-time 10, part-time 12; minority–full-time 2, part-time 5.

Programs and Degrees Offered:
Listed in the following order: Program area, degree type (T if terminal Master's), number awarded 7/00–6/01. Adult & Organizational Develop MA (T) 14, Counseling Psychology PhD 9, Counseling Psychology MA (T) 30, Educational Psychology PhD (T) 8, Schl Psych M Ed+Certification 8, School Psychology PhD 8.

APA Accreditation: Counseling PhD: full. School PhD: full.

Student Applications/Admissions:

Student Applications

Adult & Organizational Develop MA—Applications 2001–2002, 35. Total applicants accepted 2001–2002, 28. New applicants enrolled 2001–2002, 22. Total enrolled 2001–2002 part-time, 35. Openings 2002–2003, 20. The Median number of years required for completion of a degree are 2. The number of students enrolled full and part-time, who were dismissed or voluntarily withdrew from this program area were 2. *Counseling Psychology PhD*—Applications 2001–2002, 90. Total applicants accepted 2001–2002, 15. New applicants enrolled 2001–

2002, 11. Total enrolled 2001–2002 full-time, 25, part-time, 25. Openings 2002–2003, 13. The Median number of years required for completion of a degree are 2. The number of students enrolled full and part-time, who were dismissed or voluntarily withdrew from this program area were 2. *Counseling Psychology MA*—Applications 2001–2002, 100. Total applicants accepted 2001–2002, 32. New applicants enrolled 2001–2002, 30. Total enrolled 2001–2002 full-time, 35, part-time, 30. Openings 2002–2003, 30. The Median number of years required for completion of a degree are 2. The number of students enrolled full and part-time, who were dismissed or voluntarily withdrew from this program area were 3. *Educational Psychology PhD*—Applications 2001–2002, 15. Total applicants accepted 2001–2002, 10. New applicants enrolled 2001–2002, 10. Total enrolled 2001–2002 full-time, 20, part-time, 50. Openings 2002–2003, 15. The Median number of years required for completion of a degree are 6. The number of students enrolled full and part-time, who were dismissed or voluntarily withdrew from this program area were 2. *School Psychology PhD*—Applications 2001–2002, 60. Total applicants accepted 2001–2002, 18. New applicants enrolled 2001–2002, 13. Total enrolled 2001–2002 full-time, 39, part-time, 50. Openings 2002–2003, 15. The Median number of years required for completion of a degree are 5. The number of students enrolled full and part-time, who were dismissed or voluntarily withdrew from this program area were 2.

Admissions Requirements:

Scores: Entries appear in this order: required test or GPA, minimum score (if required), median score of students entering in 2001–2002. Master's Programs: Different GPAs and Examinations are required by different programs. Contact the program. Doctoral Programs: last 2 years GPA no minimum stated; psychology GPA no minimum stated; psychology GPA no minimum stated. Different Scores and GPAs are required for different programs. Contact the program.

Other Criteria: (importance of criteria rated low, medium, or high): GRE/MAT scores medium, research experience medium, work experience medium, extracurricular activity medium, clinically related public service low, GPA high, letters of recommendation high, interview high, statement of goals and objectives high.

Student Characteristics:

Student Characteristics: The following represents characteristics of students in 2001–2002 in all graduate psychology programs in the department: Female–full-time 100, part-time 75; Male–full-time 49, part-time 75; African American/Black–full-time 20, part-time 20; Hispanic/Latino (a)–full-time 4, part-time 4; Asian/Pacific Islander–full-time 3, part-time 3; American Indian/Alaska Native–full-time 0, part-time 0.

Financial Information/Assistance:

Tuition for Full-Time Study: *Master's:* State residents $369 per credit hour; nonstate residents: $534 per credit hour. *Doctoral:* State residents: $369 per credit hour; nonstate residents: $534 per credit hour.

Financial Assistance:

First Year Students: No information provided.
Advanced Students: No information provided.
Contact Information: Of all students currently enrolled full-time, 30% benefited from one or more of the listed financial assistance programs. For information on financial assistance, contact: Student Financial Services, Temple University, 1801 North Broad Street, Philadelphia, PA 19122, and the Office of the Dean, College of Education. A limited number of assistantships and competitive fellowships are available and vary by program. Most pay approximately $14,000 plus tuition.

Internships/Practica: For a master's degree and certification as a school psychologist, students are placed in an internship for one academic year. The average renumeration is $12,000. Practicum sites include public, private, and parochial schools and community mental health centers. Internships are supervised by department faculty and doctoral level school psychologists. For the doctoral program, one-year internships are available. Renumeration is highly variable for $8,750 to $22,000. Counseling Internships are also paid. Practica experiences are part of coursework and are not paid. For those doctoral students for whom a professional internship is required prior to graduation, 14 applied in 2000–2001. Of those who applied, 4 were placed in internships listed by the Association of Psychology Postdoctoral and Internship Programs (APPIC); 6 were placed in APA accredited internships.

Housing and Day Care: On-campus housing and day care facilities are available.

Employment of Department Graduates:

Master's Degree Graduates: Of those who graduated in the academic year 2000–2001, the following categories and numbers represent the post-graduate activities and employment of master's degree graduates: Enrolled in a post-doctoral residency/fellowship (n/a), employed in independent practice (n/a), employed in a professional position in a school system (25), employed in business or industry (research/consulting) (10), employed in a community mental health/counseling center (20), employed in a hospital/medical center (5), other employment position (5).

Doctoral Degree Graduates: Of those who graduated in the academic year 2000–2001, the following categories and numbers represent the post-graduate activities and employment of doctoral degree graduates: Enrolled in a psychology doctoral program (n/a), enrolled in another graduate/professional program (n/a), employed in an academic position at a university (5), employed in an academic position at a 2-year/4-year college (3), employed in a professional position in a school system (20), employed in business or industry (research/consulting) (10), employed in a government agency (research) (3), employed in a community mental health/counseling center (5), other employment position (5).

Additional Information:

Orientation, Objectives, and Emphasis of Department: PSE is a graduate level department offering master's and doctoral programs in four areas: Adult and Organizational Development, Counseling Psychology, Educational Psychology, and School Psychology. Certification is also offered in School Psychology and Counseling Psychology. Both have APA accredited doctoral programs. The AOD program offers only the Master's Degree at this time.

Special Facilities or Resources: The department conducts a psychoeducational clinic with observation and recording facilities. The National Center for the Study of Corporal Punishment and Alternatives in the Schools is an integral part of the department.

Counseling Psychology runs clinics in Family and Community Counseling and Vocational and Educational Guidance.

Application Information:

Send to: Office of Student Services (R-A 238), 1301 Cecil B. Moore, Philadelphia, PA 19122. Students are admitted in the Fall, application deadline Jan 2. Counseling Psychology and School Psychology: January 2. AOD and Educational Psychology have rolling admissions and will admit for each session. *Fee:* $40.

Temple University
Department of Psychological Studies in Education,
 Counseling Psychology Program
College of Education
Weiss Hall, 2nd Floor, 1701 N. 13th Street
Philadelphia, PA 19122-6085
Telephone: (215) 204-7331
Fax: (215) 204-1597
E-mail: *phunt@unix.temple.edu*
Web: *http://www.temple.edu/counspsych*

Department Established:

1972. Program Coordinator: Portia Hunt. Number of Faculty: total–full-time 8, part-time 13; women–full-time 4, part-time 7; minority–full-time 1, part-time 2.

Programs and Degrees Offered:

Listed in the following order: Program area, degree type (T if terminal Master's), number awarded 7/00–6/01. Counseling Psychology PhD 13.

APA Accreditation: Counseling PhD: full.

Student Applications/Admissions:

Student Applications

Counseling Psychology PhD—Applications 2001–2002, 130. Total applicants accepted 2001–2002, 16. New applicants enrolled 2001–2002, 10. Total enrolled 2001–2002 full-time, 10. Openings 2002–2003, 10. The Median number of years required for completion of a degree are 6. The number of students enrolled full and part-time, who were dismissed or voluntarily withdrew from this program area were 01.

Admissions Requirements:

Scores: Entries appear in this order: required test or GPA, minimum score (if required), median score of students entering in 2001–2002. Master's Programs: GRE-V 500, 550; GRE-Q 450, 500; GRE-V+Q 950, 1050; GRE-Analytical 500; MAT 40, 50; overall undergraduate GPA 2.17, 3.00; last 2 years GPA 3.00, 3.00; psychology GPA 3.00, 3.00. Either the GRE or the MAT is required. Psychology GRE may be required if student's background is not in helping professions. Doctoral Programs: GRE-V 500, 600; GRE-Q 450, 550; GRE-V+Q 950, 1150; GRE-Analytical 500, 600; GRE-V+Q+Analytical 1450, 1750; GRE-Subject(Psych) no minimum stated; overall undergraduate GPA 2.50, 3.00; last 2 years GPA 3.00, 3.00; psychology GPA 3.00, 3.50; psychology GPA 3.00, 3.50. Students without graduate and undergraduate training in the helping profession will be required to take the specialty exam in Psychology (GRE).

Other Criteria: (importance of criteria rated low, medium, or high): research experience medium, work experience high, extracurricular activity medium, clinically related public service medium, GPA medium, letters of recommendation high, interview high, statement of goals and objectives high. Student criteria may be weighted differently depending on faculty interview results.

Student Characteristics: The following represents characteristics of students in 2001–2002 in all graduate psychology programs in the department: Female–full-time 74, part-time 36; Male–full-time 38, part-time 15; African American/Black–full-time 21, part-time 10; Hispanic/Latino (a)–full-time 6, part-time 3; Asian/Pacific Islander–full-time 7, part-time 0; American Indian/Alaska Native–full-time 0, part-time 0; Multi-ethnic–full-time 3, students subject to the Americans with Disabilities Act–full-time 2.

Financial Information/Assistance:

Tuition for Full-Time Study: *Master's:* State residents per academic year $13,284, $369 per credit hour; nonstate residents: per academic year $19,224, $534 per credit hour. *Doctoral:* State residents: per academic year $13,284, $369 per credit hour; nonstate residents: per academic year $19,224, $534 per credit hour.

Financial Assistance:

First Year Students: Research assistantships available for first-year. Average amount paid per academic year: $14,000. Average number of hours worked per week: 20. Apply by Jan. 15. Tuition remission given: full. Fellowships and scholarships available for first-year. Average amount paid per academic year: $16,000. Average number of hours worked per week: 20. Apply by Jan. 15. Tuition remission given: full.

Advanced Students: Teaching assistantships available for advanced students. Average amount paid per academic year: $14,000. Apply by Jan. 15. Tuition remission given: full. Research assistantships available for advanced students. Average amount paid per academic year: $14,000. Average number of hours worked per week: 20. Apply by Jan. 15. Tuition remission given: full. Fellowships and scholarships available for advanced students. Average amount paid per academic year: $16,000. Average number of hours worked per week: 20. Apply by Jan. 15. Tuition remission given: full.

Contact Information: Of all students currently enrolled full-time, 40% benefited from one or more of the listed financial assistance programs. For information on financial assistance, contact: Dept. of Student Financial Services at 215-204-2244. Presidential Fellowships are competitive and pay $20,000 per year.

Internships/Practica: No information provided.

Housing and Day Care: On-campus housing and day care facilities are available.

Employment of Department Graduates:

Master's Degree Graduates: Of those who graduated in the academic year 2000–2001, the following categories and numbers represent the post-graduate activities and employment of master's degree graduates: Enrolled in a post-doctoral residency/fellowship (n/a), employed in independent practice (n/a).

Doctoral Degree Graduates: Of those who graduated in the academic year 2000–2001, the following categories and numbers represent the post-graduate activities and employment of doctoral degree graduates: Enrolled in a psychology doctoral program (n/a), enrolled in another graduate/professional program (n/a), enrolled in a post-doctoral residency/fellowship (3), employed in independent practice (15), employed in an academic position at a university (5), employed in an academic position at a 2-year/4-year college (3), employed in other positions at a higher education institution (2), employed in business or industry (research/consulting) (4), employed in business or industry (management) (8), employed in a government agency (research) (2), employed in a government agency (professional services) (3), employed in a community mental health/counseling center (8), employed in a hospital/medical center (2).

Additional Information:

Orientation, Objectives, and Emphasis of Department: The program of counseling psychology is committed to training counseling psychologists and counselors as helping professionals in twenty-first century America. Students are provided with a didactic and experiential program that enables them to become effective counselors or counseling psychologists. Early and continuous opportunities for students to integrate theory, knowledge, and practice are required. The counselor or counseling psychologist has a threefold function: prevention, development, and rehabilitation. The professional role is neither uniform with respect to varying client problems, nor statically defined with respect to changing social conditions; therefore, flexibility in program allows for individual student needs and expertise.

Special Facilities or Resources: Students, in meeting their educational objectives, may draw on the resources of the department, the university, and the urban area of greater Philadelphia. The university is composed of 12 schools and colleges and 125 academic departments, offering extensive research, computer, and library facilities. The university is located in one of the largest metropolitan areas in the country, providing great variation in training institutes and helping resources. The counseling psychology program community clinic, established in 1948, serves individuals, couples, families, and groups, presenting a wide range of personal and interpersonal concerns, work related difficulties, and career decision-making issues. The clients represent a broad spectrum of socioeconomic classes and ethnic and cultural groups. The clinic has an extensive video system for monitoring and playing back a number of counseling sessions simultaneously. The program is also affiliated with the national Center for Research on Adolescent Drug Abuse. This multisite research center studies family treatment approaches for adolescent substance abuse in high risk families.

Application Information:

Send to: Dr. Emil Soucar, Director of Doctoral Admissions, Counseling Psychology Program, 1701 N. 13th Street, Temple University (265-63), Philadelphia, PA 19122-6085. Students are admitted in the Spring, application deadline January 15. Students are admitted to the Master's Program in the spring semester. Deadline date is February 1st. *Fee:* $40.

Temple University
Department of Psychology
College of Liberal Arts
1701 North 13th Street, Room 668
Philadelphia, PA 19122-6085
Telephone: (215) 204-7321
Fax: (215) 204-5539
E-mail: *overton@temple.edu*
Web: *http://www.temple.edu/psychology*

Department Established:
1938. Chairperson: Willis F. Overton. Number of Faculty: total–full-time 34, part-time 6; women–full-time 8, part-time 3; minority–full-time 1.

Programs and Degrees Offered:
Listed in the following order: Program area, degree type (T if terminal Master's), number awarded 7/00–6/01. Brain, behavior & cognition PhD 5, clinical PhD, developmental PhD 3, developmental psychopathology PhD, social/organizational PhD.

APA Accreditation: Clinical PhD: full.

Student Applications/Admissions:

Student Applications

Brain, behavior & cognition PhD—Applications 2001–2002, 55. Total applicants accepted 2001–2002, 5. New applicants enrolled 2001–2002, 4. Total enrolled 2001–2002 full-time, 27. Openings 2002–2003, 5. The Median number of years required for completion of a degree are 5. *Clinical PhD*—Applications 2001–2002, 222. Total applicants accepted 2001–2002, 10. New applicants enrolled 2001–2002, 8. Total enrolled 2001–2002 full-time, 57. Openings 2002–2003, 8. *Developmental PhD*—Applications 2001–2002, 32. Total applicants accepted 2001–2002, 5. New applicants enrolled 2001–2002, 3. Total enrolled 2001–2002 full-time, 12. Openings 2002–2003, 3. The Median number of years required for completion of a degree are 5. *Developmental psychopathology PhD. Social/organizational PhD*—Applications 2001–2002, 47. Total applicants accepted 2001–2002, 5. New applicants enrolled 2001–2002, 4. Total enrolled 2001–2002 full-time, 18. Openings 2002–2003, 3.

Admissions Requirements:

Scores: Entries appear in this order: required test or GPA, minimum score (if required), median score of students entering in 2001–2002. Doctoral Programs: GRE-V 550, 630; GRE-Q 550, 670; GRE-V+Q no minimum stated, 1300; GRE-Analytical no minimum stated; overall undergraduate GPA no minimum stated, 3.5; last 2 years GPA no minimum stated, 3.7; psychology GPA no minimum stated; psychology GPA no minimum stated.

Other Criteria: (importance of criteria rated low, medium, or high): GRE/MAT scores high, research experience high, work experience low, extracurricular activity low, clinically related public service low, GPA high, letters of recommendation high, interview high, statement of goals and objectives high.

Student Characteristics: The following represents characteristics of students in 2001–2002 in all graduate psychology programs in

the department: Female–full-time 11, part-time 0; Male–full-time 10, part-time 0; African American/Black–full-time 3, part-time 0; Hispanic/Latino (a)–full-time 0, part-time 0; Asian/Pacific Islander–full-time 5, part-time 0; American Indian/Alaska Native–full-time 0, part-time 0.

Financial Information/Assistance:
Tuition for Full-Time Study: No information provided.

Financial Assistance:
First Year Students: Teaching assistantships available for first-year. Average amount paid per academic year: $11,000. Average number of hours worked per week: 20. Tuition remission given: full. Research assistantships available for first-year. Average amount paid per academic year: $11,000. Average number of hours worked per week: 20. Tuition remission given: full. Fellowships and scholarships available for first-year. Average amount paid per academic year: $18,000. Average number of hours worked per week: 0. Tuition remission given: full.

Advanced Students: No information provided.

Contact Information: Of all students currently enrolled full-time, 100% benefited from one or more of the listed financial assistance programs. For information on financial assistance, contact: Graduate Secretary.

Internships/Practica: Clinical students complete a 2,000-hour predoctoral internship at an agency or hospital typically in the Philadelphia metropolitan area. For those doctoral students for whom a professional internship is required prior to graduation, 8 applied in 2000–2001. Of those who applied, 8 were placed in APA accredited internships.

Housing and Day Care: No on-campus housing and day care facilities are available.

Employment of Department Graduates:
Master's Degree Graduates: Of those who graduated in the academic year 2000–2001, the following categories and numbers represent the post-graduate activities and employment of master's degree graduates: Enrolled in a post-doctoral residency/fellowship (n/a), employed in independent practice (n/a).

Doctoral Degree Graduates: Of those who graduated in the academic year 2000–2001, the following categories and numbers represent the post-graduate activities and employment of doctoral degree graduates: Enrolled in a psychology doctoral program (n/a), enrolled in another graduate/professional program (n/a).

Additional Information:
Orientation, Objectives, and Emphasis of Department: The psychology department offers graduate training in: brain, behavior & cognition, clinical, developmental, developmental psychopathology, and social & organizational. All doctoral programs are designed to prepare students for teaching in universities and colleges, conducting research in field and laboratory settings, and providing consultation in applied settings. The clinical program trains scientist-practitioners and provides students with research and clinical experience.

Special Facilities or Resources: The psychology department occupies eight floors of a high-rise building. The physical resources housed in the building include the Psychological Services Center (an in-house mental health facility where clinical students obtain practicum experience in psychotherapy), extensive laboratory space for human and animal research, a human electrophysiology lab, an infant behavior lab, numerous observation rooms with one-way mirrors, audiovisual equipment (including mobile video equipment), and excellent computer facilities, including numerous micro- and minicomputers.

Application Information:
Send to: Department Secretary. Students are admitted in the Fall, application deadline December 15. *Fee:* $40.

Villanova University
Department of Psychology
800 Lancaster Avenue
Villanova, PA 19085
Telephone: (610) 519-4720
Fax: (610) 519-4269
E-mail: *psychologyinformation@villanova.edu*
Web: *http://www.psychology.villanova.edu*

Department Established:
1962. Chairperson: Douglas M. Klieger. Number of Faculty: total–full-time 15, part-time 12; women–full-time 3, part-time 6.

Programs and Degrees Offered:
Listed in the following order: Program area, degree type (T if terminal Master's), number awarded 7/00–6/01. General.

Student Applications/Admissions:
Admissions Requirements:
Scores: Entries appear in this order: required test or GPA, minimum score (if required), median score of students entering in 2001–2002. Master's Programs: GRE-V no minimum stated, 520; GRE-Q no minimum stated, 603; GRE-Analytical no minimum stated, 615; overall undergraduate GPA no minimum stated, 3.5; psychology GPA no minimum stated, 3.6. Medians are for students ENTERING the program during the most recent admissions cycle. Doctoral Programs: last 2 years GPA no minimum stated; psychology GPA no minimum stated; psychology GPA no minimum stated.

Other Criteria: (importance of criteria rated low, medium, or high): GRE/MAT scores high, research experience medium, work experience low, extracurricular activity low, clinically related public service low, GPA high, letters of recommendation high, interview medium, statement of goals and objectives medium.

Student Characteristics: The following represents characteristics of students in 2001–2002 in all graduate psychology programs in the department: Female–full-time 25, part-time 0; Male–full-time 7, part-time 0; African American/Black–full-time 1, part-time 0; Hispanic/Latino (a)–full-time 2, part-time 0; Asian/Pacific Islander–full-time 1, part-time 0; American Indian/Alaska Native–full-time 0, part-time 0; Multi-ethnic–full-time 0, part-time 0; students subject to the Americans with Disabilities Act–full-time 0, part-time 0.

Financial Information/Assistance:
Tuition for Full-Time Study: *Master's:* State residents $445 per credit hour; nonstate residents: $445 per credit hour.

Financial Assistance:

First Year Students: Research assistantships available for first-year. Average amount paid per academic year: $10,265. Average number of hours worked per week: 20. Apply by March 15. Tuition remission given: full. Traineeships available for first-year. Average amount paid per academic year: $5,132. Average number of hours worked per week: 14. Apply by March 15. Tuition remission given: full. Fellowships and scholarships available for first-year. Average amount paid per academic year: $0. Average number of hours worked per week: 7. Apply by March 15. Tuition remission given: full.

Advanced Students: Research assistantships available for advanced students. Average amount paid per academic year: $10,265. Average number of hours worked per week: 20. Apply by March 15. Tuition remission given: full. Traineeships available for advanced students. Average amount paid per academic year: $5,132. Average number of hours worked per week: 14. Apply by March 15. Tuition remission given: full. Fellowships and scholarships available for advanced students. Average amount paid per academic year: $0. Average number of hours worked per week: 7. Apply by March 15. Tuition remission given: full.

Contact Information: Of all students currently enrolled full-time, 60% benefited from one or more of the listed financial assistance programs. For information on financial assistance, contact: Dean, Graduate School.

Internships/Practica: No information provided.

Housing and Day Care: No on-campus housing and day care facilities are available.

Employment of Department Graduates:

Master's Degree Graduates: Of those who graduated in the academic year 2000–2001, the following categories and numbers represent the post-graduate activities and employment of master's degree graduates: Enrolled in a psychology doctoral program (3), enrolled in another graduate/professional program (1), enrolled in a post-doctoral residency/fellowship (n/a), employed in independent practice (n/a), employed in an academic position at a 2-year/4-year college (1), employed in business or industry (research/consulting) (4), employed in a community mental health/counseling center (3).

Doctoral Degree Graduates: Of those who graduated in the academic year 2000–2001, the following categories and numbers represent the post-graduate activities and employment of doctoral degree graduates: Enrolled in a psychology doctoral program (n/a), enrolled in another graduate/professional program (n/a).

Additional Information:

Orientation, Objectives, and Emphasis of Department: The department offers a program of study leading to the Master of Science in psychology. Individually tailored to meet each student's career interests and needs, the program provides a solid foundation in psychology with special emphasis on preparation for doctoral work. All incoming students are required to take a seminar in the foundations of research and a statistics course. All students also take laboratory courses in Learning & Cognition and Physiological Psychology. Depending upon the student's interest, he or she selects four elective courses from a reasonably broad range of course offerings such as psychopathology, psychological testing, developmental psychology, social psychology, personality, theories of psychotherapy, behavior modification, special topics, and individual research. During the second year, student efforts are concentrated on the thesis project, which is an intensive empirically-based project, done under the supervision of a faculty mentor. Student/faculty ratio is approximately 3:1, allowing close interaction, careful advisement, and individual attention. The department has an active, research-oriented faculty.

Special Facilities or Resources: In addition to office space for faculty and all graduate assistants, the department has approximately 5800-square feet available for research. Equipment of particular interest to the graduate student includes: electronic and computer-controlled tachistoscopes; Skinner boxes and fear-conditioning units with supporting programming equipment; cognitive/computer labs; complete facilities for surgery and histology, including stereotaxic equipment for brain implantation; a polygraph and shielded room for EEG recording; environmental chambers and rooms equipped for observation and automated recording of activity, reproductive, and maternal behaviors in non-primates; radial mazes; well-equipped vision labs; one-way vision rooms; audio/video recording and playback facilities; wood and electronics shops; and a statistics lab with programmable calculators and computer terminals. University computing facilities are all networked, with hundreds of remote terminals available.

Application Information:
Send to: Dean, Graduate School, Villanova University, 800 Lancaster Ave., Villanova, PA 19085. Students are admitted in the Fall, application deadline none. Earlier strong applications have a greater chance of acceptance and receiving financial aid. Submit application by March 15 to ensure full consideration for financial aid. *Fee:* $40.

West Chester University of Pennsylvania
Department of Psychology
West Chester, PA 19383
Telephone: (610) 436-2945
Fax: (610) 436-2846
E-mail: *psych@wcupa.edu*
Web: *http://www.wcupa.edu/_academics/sch_cas.psy/*

Department Established:
1967. Chairperson: Phillip K. Duncan. Number of Faculty: total–full-time 21, part-time 9; women–full-time 11, part-time 6; minority–full-time 2, part-time 1.

Programs and Degrees Offered:
Listed in the following order: Program area, degree type (T if terminal Master's), number awarded 7/00–6/01. Clinical MA (T) 20, general MA (T) 2, industrial/organizational MA (T) 12.

Student Applications/Admissions:

Student Applications

Clinical MA—Applications 2001–2002, 60. Total applicants accepted 2001–2002, 40. New applicants enrolled 2001–2002, 20. Total enrolled 2001–2002 full-time, 20, part-time, 20. Openings 2002–2003, 20. *General MA*—Applications 2001–2002, 7. Total applicants accepted 2001–2002, 4. New applicants enrolled 2001–2002, 2. Total enrolled 2001–2002 full-time, 3, part-time, 2. Openings 2002–2003, 4. *Industrial/organizational MA*—Applications 2001–2002, 45. Total applicants accepted 2001–2002, 30. New applicants enrolled 2001–2002, 12. Total enrolled 2001–2002 full-time, 20, part-time, 10. Openings 2002–2003, 12.

Admissions Requirements:

Scores: Entries appear in this order: required test or GPA, minimum score (if required), median score of students entering in 2001–2002. Master's Programs: GRE-V 500, 500; GRE-Q 500, 555; GRE-V+Q 1000, 1060; GRE-Analytical no minimum stated; overall undergraduate GPA 3.00, 3.3; psychology GPA 3.20, 3.4. Doctoral Programs: last 2 years GPA no minimum stated; psychology GPA no minimum stated; psychology GPA no minimum stated.

Other Criteria: (importance of criteria rated low, medium, or high): GRE/MAT scores medium, research experience medium, work experience medium, extracurricular activity low, clinically related public service medium, GPA high, letters of recommendation high, statement of goals and objectives high.

Student Characteristics: The following represents characteristics of students in 2001–2002 in all graduate psychology programs in the department: Female–full-time 30, part-time 20; Male–full-time 10, part-time 10; African American/Black–full-time 2, part-time 3; Hispanic/Latino (a)–full-time 0, part-time 0; Asian/Pacific Islander–full-time 0, part-time 0; American Indian/Alaska Native–full-time 0, part-time 0; part-time 2.

Financial Information/Assistance:

Tuition for Full-Time Study: *Master's:* State residents per academic year $2,069, $230 per credit hour; nonstate residents: per academic year $3,504, $389 per credit hour.

Financial Assistance:

First Year Students: Research assistantships available for first-year. Average amount paid per academic year: $2,500. Average number of hours worked per week: 10. Apply by March 1. Tuition remission given: partial.

Advanced Students: Research assistantships available for advanced students. Average amount paid per academic year: $2,500. Average number of hours worked per week: 10. Apply by March 1. Tuition remission given: partial.

Contact Information: Of all students currently enrolled full-time, 15% benefited from one or more of the listed financial assistance programs. For information on financial assistance, contact: gradstudy@wcupa.edu.

Internships/Practica: Clinical students are required to complete a 6 credit hour practicum in a mental health setting. I/O students are required to complete a 3 credit hour internship in business or industry.

Housing and Day Care: No on-campus housing and day care facilities are available.

Employment of Department Graduates:

Master's Degree Graduates: Of those who graduated in the academic year 2000–2001, the following categories and numbers represent the post-graduate activities and employment of master's degree graduates: Enrolled in a post-doctoral residency/fellowship (n/a), employed in independent practice (n/a).

Doctoral Degree Graduates: Of those who graduated in the academic year 2000–2001, the following categories and numbers represent the post-graduate activities and employment of doctoral degree graduates: Enrolled in a psychology doctoral program (n/a), enrolled in another graduate/professional program (n/a).

Additional Information:

Orientation, Objectives, and Emphasis of Department: The concentration in clinical psychology is designed for students who wish to work in applied settings such as community mental health facilities, hospitals, counseling centers, and other social and rehabilitation agencies, or who wish to continue their education at the doctoral level. Students with the latter goal in mind are strongly encouraged to engage in research in the course of their master's degree training by participating in faculty members' ongoing research programs or conducting their own research under faculty supervision for research report or thesis credit. The industrial/organizational concentration is appropriate for students interested in employment in business or industry, or for those who wish to continue their education at the doctoral level in a related area. A 3-credit internship and 3- to 6-credit research report or thesis are required. With careful selection of electives, internship placement, and research focus, students are able to develop specialization in human factors, personnel evaluation and placement, or group and organizational processes. The concentration in general psychology, in addition to exposing students to the major traditional subject matter of psychology, also provides the opportunity to explore particular areas of psychology in depth through the appropriate selection of elective coursework and research. The general concentration is appropriate for students interested in continuing their education at the doctoral level, as well as those interested in employment, particularly in research positions, upon the receipt of their master's degree.

Special Facilities or Resources: The department has laboratory space and equipment to support a variety of animal and human research. The university has an IBM 9221, a variety of graphics and plotting devices, and microcomputers to support student research.

Information for Students With Physical Disabilities: The University is committed to making university facilities accessible to individuals with disabilities and has established procedures to provide reasonable accommodations to allow individuals with disabilities to participate in university programs. More information can be obtained from the Office of Services for Students with Disabilities, U/TDD 610-436-3217.

Application Information:

Send to: Office of Graduate Studies and Sponsored Research, West Chester University, West Chester, PA 19383. Students are admitted in the Fall, application deadline March 1. Late applications will be reviewed if space remains in the program. *Fee:* $25.

Widener University

Institute for Graduate Clinical Psychology
One University Place
Chester, PA 19013
Telephone: (610) 499-1206
Fax: (610) 499-4625
E-mail: *Maureen.A.Brennan@widener.edu*
Web: *http://www.widener@edu*

Department Established:

1970. Associate Dean and Director: Virginia Brabender. Number of Faculty: total–full-time 14; women–full-time 6; minority–full-time 1.

Programs and Degrees Offered:

Listed in the following order: Program area, degree type (T if terminal Master's), number awarded 7/00–6/01. Clinical PsyD 27, law and psychology.

APA Accreditation: Clinical PsyD: full.

Student Applications/Admissions:

Student Applications

Clinical PsyD—Applications 2001–2002, 228. Total applicants accepted 2001–2002, 75. New applicants enrolled 2001–2002, 33. Total enrolled 2001–2002 full-time, 151. Openings 2002–2003, 32.

Admissions Requirements:

Scores: Entries appear in this order: required test or GPA, minimum score (if required), median score of students entering in 2001–2002. Doctoral Programs: GRE-V 600, 604; GRE-Q 600, 626; GRE-V+Q 1200; MAT 70, 82; overall undergraduate GPA 3.20, 3.43; last 2 years GPA no minimum stated; psychology GPA no minimum stated; psychology GPA no minimum stated.

Other Criteria: (importance of criteria rated low, medium, or high): GRE/MAT scores, work experience medium, extracurricular activity medium, clinically related public service medium, GPA, letters of recommendation high, interview high, statement of goals and objectives high.

Student Characteristics: The following represents characteristics of students in 2001–2002 in all graduate psychology programs in the department: Female–full-time 27, part-time 0; Male–full-time 9, part-time 0; African American/Black–full-time 1, part-time 0; Hispanic/Latino (a)–full-time 1, part-time 0; Asian/Pacific Islander–full-time 1, part-time 0; American Indian/Alaska Native–full-time 1, part-time 0.

Financial Information/Assistance:

Tuition for Full-Time Study: *Doctoral:* State residents: per academic year $16,000; nonstate residents: per academic year $16,000.

Financial Assistance:

First Year Students: No information provided.

Advanced Students: No information provided.

Contact Information: Of all students currently enrolled full-time, 0% benefited from one or more of the listed financial assistance programs. For information on financial assistance, contact: Financial Aid Office, Director, Ethel Desmarqis at (610) 449-4194.

Internships/Practica: The program has a captive internship that is half-time over a two-year period. All fourth and fifth year students are placed in internships.

Housing and Day Care: No on-campus housing and day care facilities are available.

Employment of Department Graduates:

Master's Degree Graduates: Of those who graduated in the academic year 2000–2001, the following categories and numbers represent the post-graduate activities and employment of master's degree graduates: Enrolled in a post-doctoral residency/fellowship (n/a), employed in independent practice (n/a).

Doctoral Degree Graduates: Of those who graduated in the academic year 2000–2001, the following categories and numbers represent the post-graduate activities and employment of doctoral degree graduates: Enrolled in a psychology doctoral program (n/a), enrolled in another graduate/professional program (n/a).

Additional Information:

Orientation, Objectives, and Emphasis of Department: The PsyD program retains the basic skills and knowledge traditional to clinical psychology, such as psychodiagnostic testing and psychotherapy, while simultaneously exposing the individual to new ideas and practices in the field. The law-psychology (JD/PsyD) program presumes that every law and court decision is in part based upon psychological assumptions about how people act and how their actions can be controlled. It is designed to train lawyer-clinical psychologists to identify and evaluate these assumptions and apply their psychological knowledge to improve the law, legal process, and legal system. Students earn a law degree from the Widener University School of Law, and a doctorate in psychology from Widener's Institute for Graduate Clinical Psychology. The PsyD/MBA program is based on the premise that health care organizations as well as the mental health and health care fields at large are in need of well-trained leaders and advocates who integrate psychological and business-organizational knowledge.

Special Facilities or Resources: The PsyD program is located in a major metropolitan area that is rich in resources for the health sciences. The wide variety of internship and practica rotations available to this program is perhaps one of the most important and special features of the program. A corollary resource is the availability of practicing clinicians to teach in the program, a factor that provides breadth, relevance, and enrichment to the curriculum.

Application Information:

Send to: Widener University, The Institute for Graduate Clinical Psychology, Admissions, One University Place, Chester, PA 19013. Students are admitted in the Fall, application deadline December 31. *Fee:* $75.

Carlos Albizu University (2001 data)
PsyD/PhD (clinical)
San Juan Campus
Box 9023711
Old San Juan, PR 00902-3711
Telephone: (787) 725-6500
Fax: (787) 721-7187
E-mail: *lgarcia@prip.edu*
Web: *http://www.albizu.edu*

Department Established:
1972. Chancellor: Lourdes R. Garcia. Number of Faculty: total–full-time 13, part-time 31; women–full-time 6, part-time 16; minority–full-time 13, part-time 30.

Programs and Degrees Offered:
Listed in the following order: Program area, degree type (T if terminal Master's), number awarded 7/00–6/01. Clinical PhD 6.

APA Accreditation: Clinical PhD: full. Clinical PsyD: full.

Student Applications/Admissions:
Student Applications
Clinical PhD—Applications 2001–2002, 30. Total applicants accepted 2001–2002, 28. New applicants enrolled 2001–2002, 28. Total enrolled 2001–2002 full-time, 137. Openings 2002–2003, 20. The Median number of years required for completion of a degree are 6. The number of students enrolled full and part-time, who were dismissed or voluntarily withdrew from this program area were 8.

Admissions Requirements:
Scores: Entries appear in this order: required test or GPA, minimum score (if required), median score of students entering in 2001–2002. Master's Programs: overall undergraduate GPA no minimum stated. P.A.E.G. - Prueba de Admisión para Estudios Graduados. Doctoral Programs: overall undergraduate GPA no minimum stated. P.A.E.G.-Prueba de Admisión para Estudios Guaduados.
Other Criteria: (importance of criteria rated low, medium, or high): GRE/MAT scores research experience medium, work experience medium, extracurricular activity medium, clinically related public service medium, GPA high, letters of recommendation high, interview high, statement of goals and objectives high, P.A.E.G. Scores high. Clinically related service, professional license, and a minimum of three years of experience in their concentration are requirements for admission to PhD in General Psychology.

Student Characteristics: The following represents characteristics of students in 2001–2002 in all graduate psychology programs in the department: Female–full-time 91, part-time 0; Male–full-time 15, part-time 0; African American/Black–full-time 0, part-time 0; Hispanic/Latino (a)–full-time 99, part-time 0; Asian/Pacific Islander–full-time 0, part-time 0; American Indian/Alaska Native–full-time 0, part-time 0.

Financial Information/Assistance:
Tuition for Full-Time Study: No information provided.

Financial Assistance:
First Year Students: No information provided.
Advanced Students: No information provided.
Contact Information: Of all students currently enrolled full-time, 66% benefited from one or more of the listed financial assistance programs. For information on financial assistance, contact: Carmen Rivera, Financial Aid Director.

Internships/Practica: For master's students: Residency requirements: Full-time residency of two years. Clinical Practicums: Complete 780 hours at the Community Mental Clinic and/or designated agency. For doctoral students: Residency requirement: Full-time residency of three years is required of all doctoral students. Clinical Practicums: All students in a clinical degree program are required to complete the clinical practicum at the Mental Health Services Clinic and/or designated agency. Industrial/Organizational Practicum: Students are required to enroll in the industrial/organizational practicum. General Psychology Practicum: PhD students are required to enroll in the PSG6801 and 6802 General Psychology Practice and RP674-675 Research Practicums for a total of four hundred (400) hours consisting of 80 hours of teaching, 256 hours of research, and 64 hours of consultation. For those doctoral students for whom a professional internship is required prior to graduation, 39 applied in 2000–2001. Of those who applied, 2 were placed in internships listed by the Association of Psychology Postdoctoral and Internship Programs (APPIC); 2 were placed in APA accredited internships.

Housing and Day Care: No on-campus housing and day care facilities are available.

Employment of Department Graduates:
Master's Degree Graduates: Of those who graduated in the academic year 2000–2001, the following categories and numbers represent the post-graduate activities and employment of master's degree graduates: Enrolled in a post-doctoral residency/fellowship (n/a), employed in independent practice (n/a).
Doctoral Degree Graduates: Of those who graduated in the academic year 2000–2001, the following categories and numbers represent the post-graduate activities and employment of doctoral degree graduates: Enrolled in a psychology doctoral program (n/a), enrolled in another graduate/professional program (n/a).

Additional Information:
Orientation, Objectives, and Emphasis of Department: The educational objective of Carlos Albizu University is to train health, mental health, occupational health, and other related fields professionals who can provide services in a manner that is sensitive and responsive to cultural and ethnic issues. Academic programs are directed towards five target areas of professional formation: 1. Development of clinical and/or organizational intervention skills with due regard for the behavioral norms, values, and belief system of the client. 2. Development of appropriate assessment skills, taking into consideration multi-cultural variables, the special needs and qualities of groups, and the integration of research

findings in the assessment process. 3. Awareness and understanding of the psychological and health needs and behaviors of different ethnic groups with their sociocultural context. 4. Development of clinical and/or organizational skills through supervised experiences. 5. Development of research skills through supervised research experiences.

Special Facilities or Resources: Community Mental Health Clinic-The purpose of the Community Mental Health Clinic (CMHC) of the San Juan Campus is to offer mental health services to the Puerto Rican community. Service offerings are designed for the specific needs of target populations and address the psychological needs that can be attended in a community clinic center. The Community Mental Health Clinic offers students a unique opportunity to receive high quality multicultural-multilingual professional training in the areas of psychotherapy, clinical assessment, community consultation, and preventive mental health. The Carlos Albizu University is able to offer a sliding fee scale to those clients that qualify. The Carlos Albizu University serves the mental health needs of children, adolescents, adults, elderly, families and offers specialized services to victims of sexual abuse under the Sexual Abuse Program. Continuing Education Program—The Continuing Education Program of the PRIP is a significant resource for the fulfillment of Continuing Education requirements for psychologists and other mental health professionals and health service providers. The program is accredited by the American Psychological Association since 1984. The Continuing Education Program is a qualified provider of Continu-

ing Education Program is a qualified provider of Continuing Education Credits as recognized by the Puerto Rico Licensing Boards for Psychologists, Occupational and Physical Therapists, Physicians, Nurses, and Mental Health Educators. Scientific Research Institute-The Scientific Research Institute (SRI) is a specialized research center established for the purpose of advancing the role of science in the understanding of human behavior and society. SRI is designed to provide training experiences for students, foment faculty involvement in research, develop data banks for present and future projects, and provide specialized services to the academic community and community at large. Depending upon availability of funds, scholarships are offered for students to work in research projects sponsored by SRI. SRI is committed to multidisciplinary studies and to collaborative efforts with Puerto Rican, United States, and International research centers.

Information for Students With Physical Disabilities: Handicapped Students—The physical facilities of the institution are designed to facilitate access for those students with restricted mobility. In accordance with the Americans with Disabilities Act, CCAS does not discriminate against any student with special needs and/or conditions.

Application Information:
Send to: Student Affairs Office, Box 9023711, Old San Juan, San Juan, PR 00902-3711. Students are admitted in the Fall, application deadline July 30; Spring, application deadline November 30; Summer, application deadline April 30. *Fee:* $75.

Student Characteristics: The following represents characteristics of students in 2001–2002 in all graduate psychology programs in the department: Female–full-time 80, Male–full-time 34, Hispanic/Latino (a)–full-time 114.

Financial Information/Assistance:
Tuition for Full-Time Study: *Doctoral:* State residents: per academic year $7,500, $245 per credit hour.

Financial Assistance:
First Year Students: No information provided.
Advanced Students: Traineeships available for advanced students. Average amount paid per academic year: $12,000. Average number of hours worked per week: 20. Apply by July 30.
Contact Information: Of all students currently enrolled full-time, 15% benefited from one or more of the listed financial assistance programs. For information on financial assistance, contact: Financial Aid Office. Different types of commercial loans are available to qualified students.

Ponce School of Medicine
Clinical Psychology Doctoral Program
Urban Industrial Reparada, Dr. Maria Perez Marchand Street
Ponce, PR 00732
Telephone: (787) 840-2575
Fax: (787) 844-5209
E-mail: *psydpsm@yahoo.com*
Web: *psm.edu*

Department Established:
1999. Chairperson: Dr. Jose Pons. Number of Faculty: total–full-time 5, part-time 18; women–full-time 2, part-time 12; minority–full-time 5, part-time 17.

Student Applications/Admissions:
Admissions Requirements:
Scores: Entries appear in this order: required test or GPA, minimum score (if required), median score of students entering in 2001–2002. Doctoral Programs: GRE-V 550, 600; GRE-Q 550, 600; GRE-V+Q 1100, 1200; overall undergraduate GPA 2.75, 3.2 ; last 2 years GPA no minimum stated; psychology GPA 3.00, 3.3 ; psychology GPA 3.00, 3.6. For Spanish Speaking candidates the PAEG is accepted instead of the GRE.
Other Criteria: (importance of criteria rated low, medium, or high): GRE/MAT scores medium, research experience medium, work experience high, extracurricular activity medium, clinically related public service high, GPA high, letters of recommendation medium, interview high, statement of goals and objectives high.

Internships/Practica: The development of clinical skills begins with the utilization of diverse techniques, which include the use of Standardized Patients to practice interviewing and crisis intervention competencies. For their second and third years at the program, students may select from various settings to develop clinical skills with different populations. We start our internship program August of 2002. For those doctoral students for whom a professional internship is required prior to graduation, 22 applied in 2000–2001. Of those who applied, 3 were placed in internships listed by the Association of Psychology Postdoctoral and Internship Programs (APPIC).

Housing and Day Care: No on-campus housing and day care facilities are available.

Employment of Department Graduates:

Master's Degree Graduates: Of those who graduated in the academic year 2000–2001, the following categories and numbers represent the post-graduate activities and employment of master's degree graduates: Enrolled in a post-doctoral residency/fellowship (n/a), employed in independent practice (n/a).

Doctoral Degree Graduates: Of those who graduated in the academic year 2000–2001, the following categories and numbers represent the post-graduate activities and employment of doctoral degree graduates: Enrolled in a psychology doctoral program (n/a), enrolled in another graduate/professional program (n/a).

Additional Information:

Orientation, Objectives, and Emphasis of Department: Consonant with the concept that Clinical Psychology is an integral component of the Health Sciences, the Clinical Psychology Program at Ponce School of Medicine aims to develop a new generation of Professional Psychologists with a strong foundation in the biological bases of behavior, a broad understanding of the psychological processes and of the socio-cultural dimension of normal and abnormal behavior. The student is immersed into a rich scientifically-based curriculum harmonized by a multidisciplinary faculty from the fields of Psychology, Biomedical Sciences, Clinical Medicine, and other disciplines of the health and social sciences, in order to provide a broad understanding of human behavior and to develop clinical skills applicable in multiple socio-cultural contexts.

Special Facilities or Resources: Some students may do research in the School's neurophysiology and genetics laboratory. Our School runs various mental health clinics, some of which provide opportunities for practica and internship. Our Program runs three service programs, which allow students to work with substance abusing adolescents, with HIV infected children and their mothers, and with pre-schoolers within an Early Head Start program.

Application Information:

Send to: Ponce School of Medicine, Admissions Office, P.O. Box 7004, Ponce, PR 00731. Students are admitted in the Spring, application deadline March 30. *Fee:* $100.

RHODE ISLAND

Rhode Island, University of, Chafee Social Sciences Center
Department of Psychology
Arts and Sciences
10 Chafee Road, Suite 8
Kingston, RI 02881
Telephone: (401) 874-2193
Fax: (401) 874-2157
E-mail: *psyadmin@etal.uri.edu*
Web: *http://www.uri.edu/artsci/psy*

Department Established:
1961. Acting chair: Kathryn Quina. Number of Faculty: total–full-time 29, part-time 1; women–full-time 11; minority–full-time 4, part-time 1.

Programs and Degrees Offered:
Listed in the following order: Program area, degree type (T if terminal Master's), number awarded 7/00–6/01. Clinical PhD 5, Experimental PhD 3, School Psychology PhD (T) 3, School Psychology MS/MA (T) 3.

APA Accreditation: Clinical PhD: full. School PhD: full.

Student Applications/Admissions:
Student Applications
Clinical PhD—Applications 2001–2002, 229. Total applicants accepted 2001–2002, 10. New applicants enrolled 2001–2002, 7. Total enrolled 2001–2002 full-time, 50, part-time, 8. Openings 2002–2003, 6. The Median number of years required for completion of a degree are 4. *Experimental PhD*—Applications 2001–2002, 27. Total applicants accepted 2001–2002, 6. New applicants enrolled 2001–2002, 6. Total enrolled 2001–2002 full-time, 40, part-time, 6. Openings 2002–2003, 7. The Median number of years required for completion of a degree are 4. *School Psychology PhD*—Applications 2001–2002, 25. Total applicants accepted 2001–2002, 15. New applicants enrolled 2001–2002, 5. Total enrolled 2001–2002 full-time, 28. Openings 2002–2003, 5. The Median number of years required for completion of a degree are 4. The number of students enrolled full and part-time, who were dismissed or voluntarily withdrew from this program area were 3. *School Psychology MS MA*—Applications 2001–2002, 33. Total applicants accepted 2001–2002, 9. New applicants enrolled 2001–2002, 6. Total enrolled 2001–2002 full-time, 12. Openings 2002–2003, 5. The Median number of years required for completion of a degree are 3. The number of students enrolled full and part-time, who were dismissed or voluntarily withdrew from this program area were 0.

Admissions Requirements:
Scores: Entries appear in this order: required test or GPA, minimum score (if required), median score of students entering in 2001–2002. Master's Programs: GRE-V+Q 1000; overall undergraduate GPA 3.00; psychology GPA 3.5. Doctoral Programs: GRE-V+Q 1200; overall undergraduate GPA 3.0; last 2

years GPA no minimum stated; psychology GPA no minimum stated; psychology GPA no minimum stated.

Other Criteria: (importance of criteria rated low, medium, or high): GRE/MAT scores high, research experience medium, work experience medium, extracurricular activity low, clinically related public service medium, GPA high, letters of recommendation high, interview high, statement of goals and objectives high, Cultural Diversity medium. Importance of criteria varies per program.

Student Characteristics: The following represents characteristics of students in 2001–2002 in all graduate psychology programs in the department: Female–full-time 114, part-time 0; Male–full-time 34, part-time 0; African American/Black–full-time 7, part-time 0; Hispanic/Latino (a)–full-time 11, part-time 0; Asian/Pacific Islander–full-time 7, part-time 0; American Indian/Alaska Native–full-time 0, part-time 0; Multi-ethnic–full-time 2.

Financial Information/Assistance:
Tuition for Full-Time Study: *Master's:* State residents per academic year $3,796, $209 per credit hour; nonstate residents: per academic year $10,814, $599 per credit hour. *Doctoral:* State residents: per academic year $3,796, $209 per credit hour; nonstate residents: per academic year $10,814, $599 per credit hour.

Financial Assistance:
First Year Students: Teaching assistantships available for first-year. Average amount paid per academic year: $10,500. Average number of hours worked per week: 20. Apply by April 1. Tuition remission given: full. Research assistantships available for first-year. Average amount paid per academic year: $10,500. Average number of hours worked per week: 20. Apply by April 1. Tuition remission given: full. Fellowships and scholarships available for first-year. Average amount paid per academic year: $10,500. Average number of hours worked per week: 0. Apply by Feb 1. Tuition remission given: full.

Advanced Students: Teaching assistantships available for advanced students. Average amount paid per academic year: $10,500. Average number of hours worked per week: 20. Tuition remission given: full. Research assistantships available for advanced students. Average amount paid per academic year: $10,500. Average number of hours worked per week: 20. Tuition remission given: full. Fellowships and scholarships available for advanced students. Average amount paid per academic year: $10,500. Average number of hours worked per week: 0. Apply by Feb 1. Tuition remission given: full.

Contact Information: Of all students currently enrolled full-time, 50% benefited from one or more of the listed financial assistance programs. For information on financial assistance, contact: Student Financial Aid, Roosevelt Hall, Kingston, RI 02881, (401) 874-2314.

Internships/Practica: The Department has an excellent record of placing Clinical and School students in high quality approved internships for the later stages of doctoral training. Many graduates are invited to postdoctoral positions. Its rich network of contacts in southern New England also provides placement opportunities for relevant practicum experience and service earlier in a student's program. For those doctoral students for whom a professional internship is required prior to graduation, 9 applied in 2000–2001. Of those who applied, 9 were placed in internships listed by the Association of Psychology Postdoctoral and Internship Programs (APPIC); 7 were placed in APA accredited internships.

Housing and Day Care: On-campus housing and day care facilities are available.

Employment of Department Graduates:

Master's Degree Graduates: Of those who graduated in the academic year 2000–2001, the following categories and numbers represent the post-graduate activities and employment of master's degree graduates: Enrolled in a post-doctoral residency/fellowship (n/a), employed in independent practice (n/a), employed in a professional position in a school system (3).

Doctoral Degree Graduates: Of those who graduated in the academic year 2000–2001, the following categories and numbers represent the post-graduate activities and employment of doctoral degree graduates: Enrolled in a psychology doctoral program (n/a), enrolled in another graduate/professional program (n/a), enrolled in a post-doctoral residency/fellowship (4), employed in other positions at a higher education institution (1), employed in a professional position in a school system (3), employed in business or industry (research/consulting) (1), employed in a government agency (research) (1), employed in a community mental health/counseling center (1), employed in a hospital/medical center (1).

Additional Information:

Orientation, Objectives, and Emphasis of Department: The URI Psychology Department has a strong scientist-practitioner orientation in its Clinical and School Psychology programs, and an applied quantitative emphasis in its Experimental Psychology program. There is a lively interaction among the programs, which is an especially attractive feature of the department. The research and professional interests of the faculty fall into these seven interest areas: (1) health psychology; (2) gender, diversity, and multicultural research; (3) neuropsychology; (4) methodology and statistics; (5) family and community research; (6) clinical psychology practice; and (7) child and school psychology practice. Graduates of our programs have developed diverse careers in academia, government service, private industry, the nonprofit sector, and private consulting and practice.

Special Facilities or Resources: The Department operates an on-campus training facility, the Psychological Consultation Center, where students train under direct faculty supervision for professional practice service roles with clients, families, and children. The department is closely allied with the Cancer Prevention Research Center, one of the nation's leading centers for behavioral health promotion and disease prevention. Students also participate in research and training activities with the URI Family Resource Partnership, as well as with several training partnerships with medical centers and community mental health service agencies.

Information for Students With Physical Disabilities: The University's ADA officer works closely with our Department's task force on diversity and multiculturalism. The Department has successfully served the needs of students with visual and other disabilities, and is prepared to address the needs of present and future students.

Application Information:

Send to: Admissions/Clinical, Admissions/School, or Admissions/Experimental Department of Psychology, 10 Chafee Rd., Suite 8, Kingston, RI 02881. Students are admitted in the Fall, application deadline February 1. Deadlines: Clinical - January 20, School - February 1, Experimental - February 1. *Fee:* $30 instate, $45 out-of-state.

Clemson University

Department of Psychology
Brackett Hall
Clemson, SC 29634-1355
Telephone: (864) 656-3210
Fax: (864) 656-0358
E-mail: *cpagano@clemson.edu*
Web: *http://hubcap.clemson.edu/psych/psych.html*

Department Established:

1976. Graduate Program Coordinator: Chris Pagano. Number of Faculty: total–full-time 21, part-time 4; women–full-time 6, part-time 2; minority–full-time 1.

Programs and Degrees Offered:

Listed in the following order: Program area, degree type (T if terminal Master's), number awarded 7/00–6/01. Human Factors MA (T) 4, Industrial Organizational PhD (T) 7.

Student Applications/Admissions:

Student Applications

Human Factors MA—Applications 2001–2002, 16. Total applicants accepted 2001–2002, 5. New applicants enrolled 2001–2002, 5. Total enrolled 2001–2002 full-time, 8, part-time, 1. Openings 2002–2003, 6. The Median number of years required for completion of a degree are 2. The number of students enrolled full and part-time, who were dismissed or voluntarily withdrew from this program area were 1. *Industrial Organizational PhD*—Applications 2001–2002, 130. Total applicants accepted 2001–2002, 5. New applicants enrolled 2001–2002, 5. Total enrolled 2001–2002 full-time, 18, part-time, 3. Openings 2002–2003, 6. The Median number of years required for completion of a degree are 5. The number of students enrolled full and part-time, who were dismissed or voluntarily withdrew from this program area were 1.

Admissions Requirements:

Scores: Entries appear in this order: required test or GPA, minimum score (if required), median score of students entering in 2001–2002. Master's Programs: GRE-V no minimum stated, 560; GRE-Q no minimum stated, 630; GRE-Analytical no minimum stated, 665; overall undergraduate GPA no minimum stated, 3.47. Doctoral Programs: GRE-V no minimum stated, 599; GRE-Q no minimum stated, 656; GRE-Analytical no minimum stated, 676; last 2 years GPA no minimum stated, 3.72; psychology GPA no minimum stated; psychology GPA no minimum stated.

Other Criteria: (importance of criteria rated low, medium, or high): GRE/MAT scores medium, research experience high, work experience medium, extracurricular activity low, GPA medium, letters of recommendation high, interview low, statement of goals and objectives high.

Student Characteristics: The following represents characteristics of students in 2001–2002 in all graduate psychology programs in the department: Female–full-time 15, part-time 3; Male–full-time 11, part-time 1; African American/Black–full-time 1, part-time 0; Hispanic/Latino (a)–full-time 0, part-time 0; Asian/Pacific Islander–full-time 1, part-time 0; American Indian/Alaska Native–full-time 0, part-time 0; Multi-ethnic–full-time 0, part-time 0; students subject to the Americans with Disabilities Act–full-time 0, part-time 0.

Financial Information/Assistance:

Tuition for Full-Time Study: *Master's:* State residents per academic year $1,462; nonstate residents: per academic year $1,462. *Doctoral:* State residents: per academic year $1,462; nonstate residents: per academic year $1,462.

Financial Assistance:

First Year Students: Teaching assistantships available for first-year. Average amount paid per academic year: $7,500. Average number of hours worked per week: 20. Apply by February 15. Tuition remission given: full. Research assistantships available for first-year. Average amount paid per academic year: $8,500. Average number of hours worked per week: 20. Apply by February 15. Tuition remission given: full. Fellowships and scholarships available for first-year. Average number of hours worked per week: 0. Apply by February 15.

Advanced Students: Teaching assistantships available for advanced students. Average amount paid per academic year: $8,500. Average number of hours worked per week: 20. Apply by February 15. Tuition remission given: full. Research assistantships available for advanced students. Average amount paid per academic year: $9,500. Average number of hours worked per week: 20. Apply by February 15. Tuition remission given: full. Fellowships and scholarships available for advanced students. Average number of hours worked per week: 0. Apply by February 15.

Contact Information: Of all students currently enrolled full-time, 90% benefited from one or more of the listed financial assistance programs. For information on financial assistance, contact: Graduate School.

Internships/Practica: No information provided.

Housing and Day Care: On-campus housing and day care facilities are available.

Employment of Department Graduates:

Master's Degree Graduates: Of those who graduated in the academic year 2000–2001, the following categories and numbers represent the post-graduate activities and employment of master's degree graduates: Enrolled in a post-doctoral residency/fellowship (n/a), employed in independent practice (n/a).

Doctoral Degree Graduates: Of those who graduated in the academic year 2000–2001, the following categories and numbers represent the post-graduate activities and employment of doctoral degree graduates: Enrolled in a psychology doctoral program (n/a), enrolled in another graduate/professional program (n/a).

Additional Information:

Orientation, Objectives, and Emphasis of Department: The faculty of the Psychology Department are committed to excellence in teaching and research. The primary goals of the master of science degree program are to provide students with an essential core of knowledge in applied psychology and to develop applied research skills. Although students could progress to a more advanced degree elsewhere, the program is specifically designed to provide the student with the requisite theoretical foundations, skills in quantitative techniques and experimental design, and the practical problem-solving skills necessary to address real world problems in industry, business, and government. The emphasis is on the direct application of acquired training upon completion of the program. The PhD program prepares the student to generate and use knowledge in accordance with the scientist-practitioner model. In addition to the traditional areas of study in Industrial/Organizational psychology, a new emphasis area in Occupational Health has been added to both the MS and PhD degree programs.

Special Facilities or Resources: The Psychology Department is housed on 3 floors of Brackett Hall. Our students have access to several laboratories, including a Process Control Simulator Lab, Psychophysiology Research Lab, Perception & Action Lab, Vision & Ergonomics Lab, Human Memory & Perception Lab, Driving Simulator Lab, Usability Testing Lab, Motion Sciences Lab, Information Processing Lab, Personnel Selection & Performance Appraisal Lab, I/O Research Lab, Social Psychology Lab, Sleep Research Lab, Occupational Stress Simulation lab, Cognitive Aging Lab, and a Virtual Reality Facility.

Information for Students With Physical Disabilities: All classrooms, offices, and laboratories are accessible for wheelchair students.

Application Information:
Send to: Graduate School, E-108 Martin Hall, Box 345713, Clemson, South Carolina, 29634-5713. On-line application: http://www.grad.clemson.edu/. Students are admitted in the Fall, application deadline February 15. *Fee:* $40.

Francis Marion University
Masters of Science in Applied Psychology
P.O. Box 100547
Florence, SC 29501-0547
Telephone: (843) 661-1378
Fax: (843) 661-1628
E-mail: *jhester@fmarion.edu*
Web: *http://www.fmarion.edu/psych*

Department Established:
1970. Chair: John R. Hester. Number of Faculty: total–full-time 10, part-time 4; women–full-time 2, part-time 2.

Programs and Degrees Offered:
Listed in the following order: Program area, degree type (T if terminal Master's), number awarded 7/00–6/01. Clinical/community MA (T) 5, school MA (T) 5.

Student Applications/Admissions:
Student Applications
Clinical/community MA—Applications 2001–2002, 35. Total applicants accepted 2001–2002, 15. New applicants enrolled

2001–2002, 7. Total enrolled 2001–2002 full-time, 3, part-time, 21. Openings 2002–2003, 10. The Median number of years required for completion of a degree are 2. The number of students enrolled full and part-time, who were dismissed or voluntarily withdrew from this program area were 3. *School MA*—Applications 2001–2002, 17. Total applicants accepted 2001–2002, 8. New applicants enrolled 2001–2002, 6. Total enrolled 2001–2002 full-time, 4, part-time, 24. Openings 2002–2003, 10. The Median number of years required for completion of a degree are 3. The number of students enrolled full and part-time, who were dismissed or voluntarily withdrew from this program area were 1.

Admissions Requirements:
Scores: Entries appear in this order: required test or GPA, minimum score (if required), median score of students entering in 2001–2002. Master's Programs: GRE-V 400, 467; GRE-Q 400, 506; GRE-V+Q 800, 974; GRE-Analytical 400, 542; GRE-V+Q+Analytical 1200, 1515; overall undergraduate GPA 3.00, 3.13; psychology GPA 3.00, 3.32. Doctoral Programs: last 2 years GPA no minimum stated; psychology GPA no minimum stated; psychology GPA no minimum stated.
Other Criteria: (importance of criteria rated low, medium, or high): GRE/MAT scores high, research experience medium, work experience medium, extracurricular activity low, clinically related public service medium, GPA high, letters of recommendation high, interview statement of goals and objectives medium.

Student Characteristics: The following represents characteristics of students in 2001–2002 in all graduate psychology programs in the department: Female–full-time 3, part-time 9; Male–full-time 1, part-time 1; African American/Black–full-time 1, part-time 0; Hispanic/Latino (a)–full-time 0, part-time 0; Asian/Pacific Islander–full-time 0, part-time 0; American Indian/Alaska Native–full-time 0, part-time 0.

Financial Information/Assistance:
Tuition for Full-Time Study: *Master's:* State residents per academic year $3,410, $180 per credit hour; nonstate residents: per academic year $6,820, $361 per credit hour.

Financial Assistance:
First Year Students: No information provided.
Advanced Students: No information provided.
Contact Information: For information on financial assistance, contact: Ginger Ridgill, Psychology Department.

Internships/Practica: No information provided.

Housing and Day Care: No on-campus housing and day care facilities are available.

Employment of Department Graduates:
Master's Degree Graduates: Of those who graduated in the academic year 2000–2001, the following categories and numbers represent the post-graduate activities and employment of master's degree graduates: Enrolled in a psychology doctoral program (1), enrolled in a post-doctoral residency/fellowship (n/a), employed in independent practice (n/a), employed in a professional position in a school system (4), employed in a community mental health/counseling center (4), other employment position (1).

Doctoral Degree Graduates: Of those who graduated in the academic year 2000–2001, the following categories and numbers represent the post-graduate activities and employment of doctoral degree graduates: Enrolled in a psychology doctoral program (n/a), enrolled in another graduate/professional program (n/a).

Additional Information:

Orientation, Objectives, and Emphasis of Department: The primary purpose of the program is to prepare professionals for employment in human services agencies or similar settings. The program also provides for the continuing education of those individuals currently employed in the helping professions and prepares students for further graduate study. Students are primarily part-time, with courses taken mainly at night.

Special Facilities or Resources: The department has excellent laboratory facilities, an animal colony, and observation rooms on campus. Regional human services facilities, community agencies, and school districts are accessible off campus.

Application Information:

Send to: Ginger Ridgill, Sr. Administrative Assistant, FMU, P.O. Box 100547, Florence, SC 29501-0547. Students are admitted in the Fall, application deadline April 15; Spring, application deadline October 15. *Fee:* $30.

South Carolina, University of

Department of Psychology
Columbia, SC 29208
Telephone: (803) 777-2312
Fax: (803) 777-9558
E-mail: *linney@sc.edu*

Department Established:

1912. Professor and Department Chair: Jean Ann Linney. Number of Faculty: total–full-time 30, part-time 1; women–full-time 8; minority–full-time 3.

Programs and Degrees Offered:

Listed in the following order: Program area, degree type (T if terminal Master's), number awarded 7/00–6/01. Clinical-community PhD 9, experimental PhD 2, school psychology PhD 5.

APA Accreditation: Clinical PhD: full. School PhD: full.

Student Applications/Admissions:

Student Applications

Clinical-community PhD—Applications 2001–2002, 178. Total applicants accepted 2001–2002, 13. New applicants enrolled 2001–2002, 10. Total enrolled 2001–2002 full-time, 63. Openings 2002–2003, 10. The Median number of years required for completion of a degree are 5. The number of students enrolled full and part-time, who were dismissed or voluntarily withdrew from this program area were 1. *Experimental PhD*—Applications 2001–2002, 21. Total applicants accepted 2001–2002, 5. New applicants enrolled 2001–2002, 3. Total enrolled 2001–2002 full-time, 17. Openings 2002–2003, 5. The Median number of years required for completion of a degree are 4. *School*

psychology PhD—Applications 2001–2002, 46. Total applicants accepted 2001–2002, 11. New applicants enrolled 2001–2002, 6. Total enrolled 2001–2002 full-time, 38. Openings 2002–2003, 6. The Median number of years required for completion of a degree are 5.

Admissions Requirements:

Scores: Entries appear in this order: required test or GPA, minimum score (if required), median score of students entering in 2001–2002. Master's Programs: GRE-V no minimum stated; GRE-Q no minimum stated; GRE-Analytical no minimum stated; GRE-Subject(Psych) no minimum stated; overall undergraduate GPA no minimum stated. Doctoral Programs: GRE-V no minimum stated, 550; GRE-Q no minimum stated, 630; GRE-Analytical no minimum stated, 620; GRE-Subject(Psych) no minimum stated, 600; last 2 years GPA no minimum stated; psychology GPA no minimum stated; psychology GPA no minimum stated. Median scores vary for different programs.

Other Criteria: (importance of criteria rated low, medium, or high): GRE/MAT scores medium, research experience high, work experience medium, extracurricular activity medium, clinically related public service medium, GPA high, letters of recommendation high, interview medium, statement of goals and objectives high. Criteria vary for different programs.

Student Characteristics: The following represents characteristics of students in 2001–2002 in all graduate psychology programs in the department: Female–full-time 80, part-time 0; Male–full-time 31, part-time 0; African American/Black–full-time 14, part-time 0; Hispanic/Latino (a)–full-time 3, part-time 0; Asian/Pacific Islander–full-time 3, part-time 0; American Indian/Alaska Native–full-time 0, part-time 0; students subject to the Americans with Disabilities Act–full-time 0.

Financial Information/Assistance:

Tuition for Full-Time Study: *Doctoral:* State residents: per academic year $2,107; nonstate residents: per academic year $4,541.

Financial Assistance:

First Year Students: Teaching assistantships available for first-year. Average amount paid per academic year: $9,000. Average number of hours worked per week: 15. Tuition remission given: full. Research assistantships available for first-year. Average amount paid per academic year: $9,000. Average number of hours worked per week: 15. Tuition remission given: full.

Advanced Students: Teaching assistantships available for advanced students. Average amount paid per academic year: $9,000. Average number of hours worked per week: 15. Tuition remission given: full. Research assistantships available for advanced students. Average amount paid per academic year: $10,000. Average number of hours worked per week: 15. Tuition remission given: full.

Contact Information: Of all students currently enrolled full-time, 100% benefited from one or more of the listed financial assistance programs. For information on financial assistance, contact: Chair, Admissions Committee for program applying to.

Internships/Practica: Students in school psychology and clinical-community psychology complete at least one year of half-time placement in a community service agency expanding their experience with a diverse client population and multidisciplinary service providers. For those doctoral students for whom a professional internship is required prior to graduation, 11 applied in 2000–2001. Of those who applied, 11 were placed in internships listed by the Association of Psychology Postdoctoral and Internship Programs (APPIC); 11 were placed in APA accredited internships.

Housing and Day Care: On-campus housing and day care facilities are available.

Employment of Department Graduates:

Master's Degree Graduates: Of those who graduated in the academic year 2000–2001, the following categories and numbers represent the post-graduate activities and employment of master's degree graduates: Enrolled in a post-doctoral residency/fellowship (n/a), employed in independent practice (n/a).

Doctoral Degree Graduates: Of those who graduated in the academic year 2000–2001, the following categories and numbers represent the post-graduate activities and employment of doctoral degree graduates: Enrolled in a psychology doctoral program (n/a), enrolled in another graduate/professional program (n/a).

Additional Information:

Orientation, Objectives, and Emphasis of Department: The department has interdisciplinary research emphases in neuroscience, prevention science, reading and language, and ethnic minority health and mental health. The experimental program offers concentrations in cognitive, developmental, and behavioral neuroscience, built on broad scientific training in experimental psychology. The school psychology program includes emphasis in child assessment, individual and group consultation, educational research, and professional roles. In clinical-community, there is a wide latitude of choices: assessment, psychotherapy and behavioral interventions, community psychology, and consultation. Regular clinical-community training includes both adults and children, with an option of special emphasis on children or community settings.

Special Facilities or Resources: The special facilities and resources of the department include the university-directed psychological service center, the medical school, the VA hospital, the department-directed outpatient psychological services center, mental health centers, and other educational and mental health service settings. Other laboratories include Behavioral Pharmacology Lab; Behavioral Neuroscience Lab with high density EEG and MRI; Developmental Sensory Neuroscience Lab; Experimental and Cognitive Processes Lab; Infant Attention Lab; Judgement and Decision Making Lab; and Attention and Perception Lab. We are actively involved in community agencies, the psychiatric training institution, and the psychopharmacology laboratory.

Application Information:
Send to: Graduate Records Secretary, Department of Psychology, University of South Carolina, Columbia, SC 29208. Students are admitted in the Fall, application deadline January 1. Application deadline for fall admission in clinical-community psychology is January 1, experimental psychology and school psychology, February 1. Applications for admissions should be submitted electronically. These materials are available at http://www.gradschool.sc.edu/login. *Fee:* $40.

The Citadel
Department of Psychology
171 Moultrie Street
Charleston, SC 29409
Telephone: (843) 953-5320
Fax: (843) 953-6797
E-mail: *cgps@citadel.edu*
Web: *http://www.citadel.edu*

Department Established:
1978. Department Head: Steve Nida. Number of Faculty: total–full-time 11, part-time 10; women–full-time 5, part-time 4; minority–full-time 1.

Programs and Degrees Offered:
Listed in the following order: Program area, degree type (T if terminal Master's), number awarded 7/00–6/01. Clinical Counseling MA (T) 10, School Psychology EdS 7.

Student Applications/Admissions:
Student Applications

Clinical Counseling MA—Applications 2001–2002, 52. Total applicants accepted 2001–2002, 43. New applicants enrolled 2001–2002, 30. Total enrolled 2001–2002 full-time, 15, part-time, 62. Openings 2002–2003, 40. The Median number of years required for completion of a degree are 3. The number of students enrolled full and part-time, who were dismissed or voluntarily withdrew from this program area were 11. *School Psychology EdS*—Applications 2001–2002, 29. Total applicants accepted 2001–2002, 27. New applicants enrolled 2001–2002, 19. Total enrolled 2001–2002 full-time, 30, part-time, 17. Openings 2002–2003, 25. The Median number of years required for completion of a degree are 3. The number of students enrolled full and part-time, who were dismissed or voluntarily withdrew from this program area were 2.

Admissions Requirements:

Scores: Entries appear in this order: required test or GPA, minimum score (if required), median score of students entering in 2001–2002. Master's Programs: Applicants must submit a score for either the GRE or the MAT. The GRE/MAT requirement is waived for applicants who have earned a master's degree with a minimum overall graduate GPA of 3.0. Doctoral Programs: last 2 years GPA no minimum stated; psychology GPA no minimum stated; psychology GPA no minimum stated.

Other Criteria: (importance of criteria rated low, medium, or high): GRE/MAT scores high, research experience medium, work experience medium, extracurricular activity low, clinically related public service medium, GPA high, letters of recommendation medium, statement of goals and objectives high.

Student Characteristics: The following represents characteristics of students in 2001–2002 in all graduate psychology programs in the department: Female–full-time 44, part-time 77; Male–full-time 5, part-time 13; African American/Black–full-time 8, part-time 6; Hispanic/Latino (a)–full-time 0, part-time 0; Asian/Pacific Islander–full-time 2, part-time 3; American Indian/Alaska Native–full-time 0, part-time 0; Multi-ethnic–full-time 0, part-time

0; students subject to the Americans with Disabilities Act–full-time 3, part-time 1.

Financial Information/Assistance:

Tuition for Full-Time Study: *Master's:* State residents $146 per credit hour; nonstate residents: $291 per credit hour.

Financial Assistance:

First Year Students: Teaching assistantships available for first-year. Average amount paid per academic year: $7,000. Average number of hours worked per week: 20. Research assistantships available for first-year. Average amount paid per academic year: $7,000. Average number of hours worked per week: 20.

Advanced Students: Teaching assistantships available for advanced students. Average amount paid per academic year: $7,000. Average number of hours worked per week: 20. Research assistantships available for advanced students. Average amount paid per academic year: $7,000. Average number of hours worked per week: 20.

Contact Information: Of all students currently enrolled full-time, 49% benefited from one or more of the listed financial assistance programs. For information on financial assistance, contact: College of Graduate and Professional Studies: 843-953-5089.

Internships/Practica: EdS in School Psychology: two practica courses where students provide services in the public school systems (40 and 125 hours, respectively); 1200-hour internship (most paid), at least 600 of which involve direct services within the public school system. MA in Psychology: Clinical Counseling: one practicum (150 hours) and one internship (600 hours) where students provide clinical/counseling services in public mental health/substance abuse treatment facilities. These are unpaid field experiences.

Housing and Day Care: No on-campus housing and day care facilities are available.

Employment of Department Graduates:

Master's Degree Graduates: Of those who graduated in the academic year 2000–2001, the following categories and numbers represent the post-graduate activities and employment of master's degree graduates: Enrolled in a psychology doctoral program (0), enrolled in another graduate/professional program (0), enrolled in a post-doctoral residency/fellowship (n/a), employed in independent practice (n/a), employed in an academic position at a university (0), employed in an academic position at a 2-year/4-year college (0), employed in other positions at a higher education institution (0), employed in a professional position in a school system (7), employed in business or industry (research/consulting) (0), employed in business or industry (management) (0), employed in a government agency (research) (0), employed in a government agency (professional services) (0), employed in a community mental health/counseling center (6), employed in a hospital/medical center (0), still seeking employment (3), other employment position (1).

Doctoral Degree Graduates: Of those who graduated in the academic year 2000–2001, the following categories and numbers represent the post-graduate activities and employment of doctoral degree graduates: Enrolled in a psychology doctoral program (n/a), enrolled in another graduate/professional program (n/a).

Additional Information:

Orientation, Objectives, and Emphasis of Department: The School Psychology program is based on the scientist-practitioner model and emphasizes the school psychologist as a data-based problem-solver who applies psychological principles, knowledge, and skill to processes and problems of education and schooling. Students are trained to provide a range of psychological assessment, consultation, intervention, prevention, program development, and evaluation services with the goal of maximizing student learning and development. Students in the Master of Arts in Psychology: Clinical Counseling Program are prepared to become scholarly practitioners of psychosocial counseling in community agencies, including college counseling centers, hospitals, mental health centers, and social services agencies. The program's model blends didactic and experience-based training to facilitate students' ability to utilize an empirical approach to assessment, goal development, intervention, and evaluation of services for a wide range of individuals and families experiencing a variety of psychosocial difficulties. The program is a member of The Council of Applied Master's Programs in Psychology.

Special Facilities or Resources: The Citadel's Department of Psychology enjoys a strong working relationship with the area school districts and agencies which provide mental health/substance abuse services. In addition, the nearby Medical University of South Carolina provides internship opportunities.

Application Information:

Send to: College of Graduate and Professional Studies, The Citadel, 171 Moultrie Street, Charleston, SC 29409. Students are admitted in the Fall, application deadline March 15; Spring, application deadline October 15. The October 15 deadline for Spring admission is only applicable to students applying to the EdS Program in School Psychology. Both the Master of Arts in Psychology: Clinical Counseling and EdS: School Psychology Programs admit students to begin their studies in the Fall (application deadline is March 15). *Fee:* $25.

Winthrop University
Department of Psychology
Arts and Sciences
135 Kinard
Rock Hill, SC 29733
Telephone: (803) 323-2117
Fax: (803) 323-2371
E-mail: *prusj@winthrop.edu*
Web: *http://www.winthrop.edu*

Department Established:

1923. Chairperson: Dr. Mel Goldstein. Number of Faculty: total–full-time 13, part-time 5; women–full-time 7, part-time 3; minority–full-time 2.

Programs and Degrees Offered:

Listed in the following order: Program area, degree type (T if terminal Master's), number awarded 7/00–6/01. School psychology 9.

Student Applications/Admissions:

Admissions Requirements:

Scores: Entries appear in this order: required test or GPA, minimum score (if required), median score of students entering in 2001–2002. Master's Programs: GRE-V no minimum stated; GRE-Q no minimum stated; GRE-V+Q no minimum stated, 990; overall undergraduate GPA no minimum stated, 3.50; last 2 years GPA no minimum stated, 3.60; psychology GPA no minimum stated, 3.60. Doctoral Programs: last 2 years GPA no minimum stated; psychology GPA no minimum stated; psychology GPA no minimum stated.

Other Criteria: (importance of criteria rated low, medium, or high): GRE/MAT scores low, research experience low, work experience medium, extracurricular activity low, clinically related public service medium, GPA high, letters of recommendation high, interview high, statement of goals and objectives medium, experience with children high.

Student Characteristics: The following represents characteristics of students in 2001–2002 in all graduate psychology programs in the department: Female–full-time 21, part-time 0; Male–full-time 4, part-time 0; African American/Black–full-time 3, part-time 0; Hispanic/Latino (a)–full-time 0, part-time 0; Asian/Pacific Islander–full-time 0, part-time 0; American Indian/Alaska Native–full-time 0, part-time 0.

Financial Information/Assistance:

Tuition for Full-Time Study: *Master's:* State residents per academic year $4,740, $198 per credit hour; nonstate residents: per academic year $6,836, $285 per credit hour.

Financial Assistance:

First Year Students: Teaching assistantships available for first-year. Average amount paid per academic year: $3,000. Average number of hours worked per week: 20. Apply by April 15. Tuition remission given: partial. Research assistantships available for first-year. Average amount paid per academic year: $3,000. Average number of hours worked per week: 20. Apply by April 15. Tuition remission given: partial. Fellowships and scholarships available for first-year. Average amount paid per academic year: $2,000. Apply by April 15. Tuition remission given: partial.

Advanced Students: Traineeships available for advanced students. Average amount paid per academic year: $6,750. Average number of hours worked per week: 30. Apply by NA. Tuition remission given: full and partial.

Contact Information: Of all students currently enrolled full-time, 90% benefited from one or more of the listed financial assistance programs. For information on financial assistance, contact: Director, School Psychology Program.

Internships/Practica: The program provides paid traineeships and internships in area school districts and agencies. Rural, suburban, and urban field settings include diverse student/client populations. Some non-school internship placements are available for up to 600 clock hours of the 1,200 hour internship. The internship includes a full range of school psychological services. Interns receive weekly supervision by both a faculty and field-based credentialed supervisors.

Housing and Day Care: On-campus housing and day care facilities are available.

Employment of Department Graduates:

Master's Degree Graduates: Of those who graduated in the academic year 2000–2001, the following categories and numbers represent the post-graduate activities and employment of master's degree graduates: Enrolled in a post-doctoral residency/fellowship (n/a), employed in independent practice (n/a), employed in a professional position in a school system (9).

Doctoral Degree Graduates: Of those who graduated in the academic year 2000–2001, the following categories and numbers represent the post-graduate activities and employment of doctoral degree graduates: Enrolled in a psychology doctoral program (n/a), enrolled in another graduate/professional program (n/a).

Additional Information:

Orientation, Objectives, and Emphasis of Department: The Winthrop School Psychology Program is designed to prepare practitioners to be competent to provide a full range of school psychological services, including consultation, behavioral intervention, psychoeducational assessment, research and evaluation, and counseling. The three-year, full-time program leading to both MS and Specialist in School Psychology degrees qualifies graduates for state and national certification as a school psychologist pending attainment of a passing score on the NTE specialty exam in school psychology. Program emphasis is placed on psychological and psychoeducational methods whose effectiveness has been demonstrated through behavioral research. Students are trained to work with diverse clients from birth to adulthood, including those with low-incidence disabilities, and with families, teachers, and others in the schools and community. The program provides an applied, competency-based approach to training that progresses sequentially from foundations courses to methods/practica courses to a 1200-hour internship and affords maximum individualized supervision. Comprehensive assessment of student learning and development, from entry into the program to acquisition of professional positions or admissions into doctoral programs, is conducted through multiple methods. Program faculty represent considerable ethnic and experiential diversity. All have advanced degrees in school psychology, are active in the profession at local, state, and national levels, and view teaching and supervision as their primary roles. A collaborative approach to learning and cooperation among students are emphasized in the program.

Special Facilities or Resources: Winthrop University is a state-supported institution of about 6,000 students which provides students with access to an academic computer center, health center, university library with nearly 500,000 volumes and 4,000 periodicals and serials, and a variety of other resources. Access to such department resources as a computer workroom and school psychology mini-library and assessment resource center are available. Winthrop's 418-acre campus is located in the greater Charlotte, NC area, which includes a great variety of school districts, human service agencies, libraries, and other resources which may be of personal or professional interest to graduate students in school psychology.

Application Information:

Send to: Office of Graduate Studies, Winthrop University, Rock Hill, SC 29733. Students are admitted in the Fall, application deadline February 15. *Fee:* $35. Application fee may be waived by program director in cases of financial hardship.

SOUTH DAKOTA

South Dakota, University of
Department of Psychology
414 E. Clark Street
Vermillion, SD 57069
Telephone: (605) 677-5351
Fax: (605) 677-6604
E-mail: *rquevill@usd.edu*
Web: *http://www.usd.edu/psyc*

Department Established:
1926. Chairperson: Randal Quevillon. Number of Faculty: total–full-time 16, part-time 1; women–full-time 6, part-time 1; minority–full-time 5.

Programs and Degrees Offered:
Listed in the following order: Program area, degree type (T if terminal Master's), number awarded 7/00–6/01. Clinical PhD 1, human factors PhD 3.

APA Accreditation: Clinical PhD: full.

Student Applications/Admissions:
Student Applications
Clinical PhD—Applications 2001–2002, 67. Total applicants accepted 2001–2002, 15. New applicants enrolled 2001–2002, 9. Total enrolled 2001–2002 full-time, 42. Openings 2002–2003, 9. The Median number of years required for completion of a degree are 5. The number of students enrolled full and part-time, who were dismissed or voluntarily withdrew from this program area were 0. *Human factors PhD*—Applications 2001–2002, 10. Total applicants accepted 2001–2002, 4. New applicants enrolled 2001–2002, 3. Total enrolled 2001–2002 full-time, 10. Openings 2002–2003, 4. The Median number of years required for completion of a degree are 5. The number of students enrolled full and part-time, who were dismissed or voluntarily withdrew from this program area were 1.

Admissions Requirements:
Scores: Entries appear in this order: required test or GPA, minimum score (if required), median score of students entering in 2001–2002. Doctoral Programs: GRE-V no minimum stated; GRE-Q no minimum stated; GRE-V+Q 1000, 1120; GRE-Analytical no minimum stated; GRE-V+Q+Analytical no minimum stated; GRE-Subject(Psych) no minimum stated; overall undergraduate GPA 3.00, 3.73; last 2 years GPA no minimum stated; psychology GPA no minimum stated; psychology GPA no minimum stated.
Other Criteria: (importance of criteria rated low, medium, or high): research experience high, work experience medium, extracurricular activity medium, clinically related public service medium, letters of recommendation high, statement of goals and objectives high. GRE and GPA weightings vary by program.

Student Characteristics: The following represents characteristics of students in 2001–2002 in all graduate psychology programs in the department: Female–full-time 6, part-time 0; Male–full-time 5, part-time 0; African American/Black–full-time 0, part-time 0; Hispanic/Latino (a)–full-time 1, part-time 0; Asian/Pacific Islander–full-time 1, part-time 0; American Indian/Alaska Native–full-time 1, part-time 0.

Financial Information/Assistance:
Tuition for Full-Time Study: *Doctoral:* State residents: $94 per credit hour; nonstate residents: $279 per credit hour.

Financial Assistance:
First Year Students: Teaching assistantships available for first-year. Average amount paid per academic year: $4,070. Average number of hours worked per week: 10. Tuition remission given: partial. Research assistantships available for first-year. Average amount paid per academic year: $4,070. Average number of hours worked per week: 10. Tuition remission given: partial. Fellowships and scholarships available for first-year. Average amount paid per academic year: $9,000. Average number of hours worked per week: 16. Tuition remission given: partial.

Advanced Students: Teaching assistantships available for advanced students. Average amount paid per academic year: $6,000. Average number of hours worked per week: 16. Tuition remission given: partial. Research assistantships available for advanced students. Average amount paid per academic year: $10,000. Average number of hours worked per week: 16. Tuition remission given: partial. Traineeships available for advanced students. Average amount paid per academic year: $10,000. Average number of hours worked per week: 16. Tuition remission given: partial. Fellowships and scholarships available for advanced students. Average amount paid per academic year: $10,000. Average number of hours worked per week: 16. Tuition remission given: partial.

Contact Information: Of all students currently enrolled full-time, 100% benefited from one or more of the listed financial assistance programs. For information on financial assistance, contact: Department of Psychology, (605) 677-5351; Financial Aid, (605) 677-5302.

Internships/Practica: Several internships are available in Human Factors: placements with IBM, Lockheed, Hewlett-Packard, and Intel have been recent examples. In Clinical, a twelve month internship is required in the final year, and we are proud of the record our students have achieved in obtaining top placements. We also have available a series of paid clinical placements (see community resources). In addition, many graduate courses include practicum components and clinical students are placed on practicum teams through the Psychological Services Center each semester. For those doctoral students for whom a professional internship is required prior to graduation, 11 applied in 2000–2001. Of those who applied, 11 were placed in internships listed by the Association of Psychology Postdoctoral and Internship Programs (APPIC); 11 were placed in APA accredited internships.

Housing and Day Care: On-campus housing and day care facilities are available.

Employment of Department Graduates:

Master's Degree Graduates: Of those who graduated in the academic year 2000–2001, the following categories and numbers represent the post-graduate activities and employment of master's degree graduates: Enrolled in a psychology doctoral program (8), enrolled in a post-doctoral residency/fellowship (n/a), employed in independent practice (n/a).

Doctoral Degree Graduates: Of those who graduated in the academic year 2000–2001, the following categories and numbers represent the post-graduate activities and employment of doctoral degree graduates: Enrolled in a psychology doctoral program (n/a), enrolled in another graduate/professional program (n/a), employed in independent practice (1), employed in business or industry (research/consulting) (2), employed in a government agency (research) (1).

Additional Information:

Orientation, Objectives, and Emphasis of Department: The department seeks to develop scholars who can contribute to the expansion of psychological information. The major goals of the theoretically eclectic program in clinical psychology are to increase students' knowledge of and identification with psychology as a method of inquiry about human behavior and to provide students with the theory, skills, and experience to function in a professional, research, or academic capacity. Training is provided in traditional areas as well as rural community psychology, cross-cultural issues (particularly work with American Indian populations), program evaluation, neuropsychology, family therapy, and women's issues. The experience thus provided serves to broaden professional competencies and increase the versatility of the program's graduates. The overall mission of Human Factors psychology is to improve living and working through knowledge of the abilities and limitations of the person part of human-machine or socio-technical systems. The program's goal is to train doctoral-level professionals qualified to do research in industry, government, and universities. As an element of their training, all graduate students conduct empirical investigations. In recent years, the Human Factors Laboratory has supported studies of information processing, human-computer interfaces, motor performance, program evaluation and testing, traffic safety, transportation systems, and the effects of chemical agents and stress on human efficiency.

Special Facilities or Resources: Available to all psychology graduate students are computer lab facilities including word processing and statistical analysis software. Microcomputers are also easily accessible within the department for personal computing and research purposes. Much general purpose, highly adaptable research equipment is available to both Clinical and Human Factors students. The Human Factors Laboratory is particularly well-equipped for experimentation within the specialty areas of current interest to associated faculty. The Disaster Mental Health Institute, newly proclaimed a Center of Excellence by the South Dakota Board of Regents, provides unique research and service opportunities for graduate students as well as specialized coursework and assistantships. The Psychological Services Center, which supplies clinical services for both University students and the general public, accepts referrals from physicians, schools, and other community and state agencies. The center has offices equipped for a variety of diagnostic and therapeutic activities, including neuropsychological work. Next door to the department, the University Affiliated Program affords our students opportunities to collaborate with members of other professions. The department's students take full advantage of training and experience available at local, state, and regional mental health centers for treatment of chemical dependency and control of pain.

Information for Students With Physical Disabilities: The University has available a special computer system for visually impaired students. We have also recently upgraded the building in which the department is housed to improve lighting and accessability (a new elevator and other improvements).

Application Information:

Send to: Dean, Graduate School, University of South Dakota, 414 E Clark St., Vermilion, SD 57069-2390. Students are admitted in the Fall, application deadline February 1. *Fee:* $15.

Austin Peay State University

Department of Psychology
College Street
Clarksville, TN 37044
Telephone: (931) 221-7233
Fax: (931) 221-6267
E-mail: grahc@apsu.edu
Web: http://www.apsu.edu/psychology

Department Established:

1968. Chairperson: Charles R. Grah. Number of Faculty: total–full-time 15, part-time 7; women–full-time 9, part-time 6; minority–full-time 1, part-time 2; faculty subject to the Americans with Disabilities Act 1.

Programs and Degrees Offered:

Listed in the following order: Program area, degree type (T if terminal Master's), number awarded 7/00–6/01. Agency counseling MA (T) 2, clinical psychology MA (T) 4, I/O psychology MA (T) 4, psychological science MA (T), school counseling, school psychology MA (T) 1, school psychology EdS 1.

Student Applications/Admissions:

Student Applications

Agency counseling MA—Applications 2001–2002, 5. Total applicants accepted 2001–2002, 4. New applicants enrolled 2001–2002, 3. Total enrolled 2001–2002 full-time, 6. Openings 2002–2003, 4. The Median number of years required for completion of a degree are 2. *Clinical psychology MA*—Applications 2001–2002, 17. Total applicants accepted 2001–2002, 8. New applicants enrolled 2001–2002, 6. Total enrolled 2001–2002 full-time, 14. Openings 2002–2003, 10. The Median number of years required for completion of a degree are 2. *I/O psychology MA*—Applications 2001–2002, 14. Total applicants accepted 2001–2002, 8. New applicants enrolled 2001–2002, 2. Total enrolled 2001–2002 full-time, 2. Openings 2002–2003, 7. The Median number of years required for completion of a degree are 2. *Psychological science MA*—Applications 2001–2002, 3. Total applicants accepted 2001–2002, 1. New applicants enrolled 2001–2002, 1. Total enrolled 2001–2002 full-time, 1. Openings 2002–2003, 5. *School psychology MA*—Applications 2001–2002, 8. Total applicants accepted 2001–2002, 6. New applicants enrolled 2001–2002, 6. Total enrolled 2001–2002 full-time, 8. Openings 2002–2003, 10. The Median number of years required for completion of a degree are 2. *School psychology EdS*—Applications 2001–2002, 1. Total applicants accepted 2001–2002, 1. New applicants enrolled 2001–2002, 1. Total enrolled 2001–2002 full-time, 1. Openings 2002–2003, 5. The Median number of years required for completion of a degree are 2.

Admissions Requirements:

Scores: Entries appear in this order: required test or GPA, minimum score (if required), median score of students entering in 2001–2002. Master's Programs: GRE-V 400, 455; GRE-Q 400, 470; overall undergraduate GPA 3.0, 3.22. Doctoral

Programs: last 2 years GPA no minimum stated; psychology GPA no minimum stated; psychology GPA no minimum stated.

Other Criteria: (importance of criteria rated low, medium, or high): GRE/MAT scores high, research experience, work experience, extracurricular activity, clinically related public service, GPA high, letters of recommendation high, interview statement of goals and objectives.

Student Characteristics: The following represents characteristics of students in 2001–2002 in all graduate psychology programs in the department: Female–full-time 38, part-time 0; Male–full-time 9, part-time 0; African American/Black–full-time 4, part-time 0; Hispanic/Latino (a)–full-time 0, part-time 0; Asian/Pacific Islander–full-time 0, part-time 0; American Indian/Alaska Native–full-time 0, part-time 0.

Financial Information/Assistance:

Tuition for Full-Time Study: *Master's:* State residents per academic year $2,984, $157 per credit hour; nonstate residents: per academic year $8,612, $400 per credit hour.

Financial Assistance:

First Year Students: Teaching assistantships available for first-year. Average amount paid per academic year: $6,900. Average number of hours worked per week: 20.

Advanced Students: Teaching assistantships available for advanced students. Average amount paid per academic year: $6,900. Average number of hours worked per week: 20.

Contact Information: Of all students currently enrolled full-time, 15% benefited from one or more of the listed financial assistance programs. For information on financial assistance, contact: Student Financial Aid Office, Austin Peay State University, Clarksville, TN 37044.

Internships/Practica: There are some paid internships available at the present. A variety of unpaid internships are available in mental health agencies, schools, or community agencies.

Housing and Day Care: On-campus housing and day care facilities are available.

Employment of Department Graduates:

Master's Degree Graduates: Of those who graduated in the academic year 2000–2001, the following categories and numbers represent the post-graduate activities and employment of master's degree graduates: Enrolled in a post-doctoral residency/fellowship (n/a), employed in independent practice (n/a).

Doctoral Degree Graduates: Of those who graduated in the academic year 2000–2001, the following categories and numbers represent the post-graduate activities and employment of doctoral degree graduates: Enrolled in a psychology doctoral program (n/a), enrolled in another graduate/professional program (n/a).

Additional Information:

Orientation, Objectives, and Emphasis of Department: The programs in the department are based on the concept that both a strong foundation in theoretical principles and the development of skills in the application of these principles and techniques is necessary in the training of psychologists or counselors. The Master of Arts with a major in psychology offers four options. Psychological Science is designed to give students, particularly those interested in pursuing the doctoral degree, a strong foundation in basic psychology. The training program in school psychology is oriented toward the development of the school psychologist as a psycho-educational specialist. The clinical program is designed to prepare competent professionals to function in outpatient clinics and mental hospitals. The industrial/organizational program educates students to design, develop, implement, and evaluate psychologically-based human resources, interventions in organizations. The Master of Science with a major in guidance and counseling also offers two options. The school counseling options are designed to meet the competencies required by the state of Tennessee and to provide students with the necessary knowledge and skills to perform efficiently in the elementary and secondary school settings. The objective of the agency counseling program is to meet the needs of employment, human services, or other agency counselors requiring a master's degree related to their particular vocational needs.

Special Facilities or Resources: The department of psychology has a variety of facilities to provide learning and research opportunities. Rooms equipped with one-way observation windows, video and other monitoring equipment are available for counseling, testing, and human research. The department has arranged for intern and practicum experiences with a variety of community agencies. Laboratories for vision, infant development, animal learning, and behavioral physiology are available for faculty and student research. The department has numerous microcomputers connected to the University's high-speed fiber-optic network for data collection, analysis, and the preparation of manuscripts.

Application Information:
Send to: Office of Graduate Studies, Austin Peay State University, Clarksville, TN 37044. Students are admitted in the Fall, application deadline March 1; Spring, application deadline November 1. *Fee:* $25.

East Tennessee State University (2001 data)
Department of Psychology
College of Arts & Sciences
Box 70649 (Psychology)
Johnson City, TN 37614-0649
Telephone: (423) 439-4424
Fax: (423) 439-5695
E-mail: *marx@etsu.edu*
Web: *http://www.etsu.edu/psychology/*

Department Established:
1966. Chairperson: David J. Marx. Number of Faculty: total–full-time 8, part-time 6; women–full-time 1.

Programs and Degrees Offered:
Listed in the following order: Program area, degree type (T if terminal Master's), number awarded 7/00–6/01. Clinical Psyc MA (T) 5, General Psyc MA (T) 3.

Student Applications/Admissions:
Student Applications
Clinical Psyc MA—Applications 2001–2002, 40. Total applicants accepted 2001–2002, 11. New applicants enrolled 2001–2002, 8. Total enrolled 2001–2002 full-time, 8. Openings 2002–2003, 8. The Median number of years required for completion of a degree are 2. The number of students enrolled full and part-time, who were dismissed or voluntarily withdrew from this program area were 0. *General Psyc MA*—Applications 2001–2002, 20. Total applicants accepted 2001–2002, 8. New applicants enrolled 2001–2002, 7. Total enrolled 2001–2002 full-time, 5. Openings 2002–2003, 6. The Median number of years required for completion of a degree are 2. The number of students enrolled full and part-time, who were dismissed or voluntarily withdrew from this program area were 0.

Admissions Requirements:
Scores: Entries appear in this order: required test or GPA, minimum score (if required), median score of students entering in 2001–2002. Master's Programs: GRE-V 400; GRE-Q 400; GRE-V+Q 1000, 1000; GRE-Analytical 400; GRE-V+Q+Analytical 1500, 1500; GRE-Subject(Psych) 500; overall undergraduate GPA 3.00, 3.40; last 2 years GPA 3.50; psychology GPA 3.3, 3.4.
Other Criteria: (importance of criteria rated low, medium, or high): GRE/MAT scores high, research experience high, work experience high, extracurricular activity medium, clinically related public service high, GPA high, letters of recommendation high, interview medium, statement of goals and objectives high. Clinically Related Public Service - Medium and Extracurricular Activities - High for General Psychology. Letters of Recommendation Medium and Interview None for Clinical Psychology.

Student Characteristics: The following represents characteristics of students in 2001–2002 in all graduate psychology programs in the department: Female–full-time 6, part-time 0; Male–full-time 7, part-time 0; African American/Black–full-time 0, part-time 0; Hispanic/Latino (a)–full-time 0, part-time 0; Asian/Pacific Islander–full-time 0, part-time 0; American Indian/Alaska Native–full-time 0, part-time 0.

Financial Information/Assistance:
Tuition for Full-Time Study: No information provided.

Financial Assistance:
First Year Students: No information provided.
Advanced Students: No information provided.
Contact Information: Of all students currently enrolled full-time, 90% benefited from one or more of the listed financial assistance programs. For information on financial assistance, contact: Dr. Marx, Dr. Zinser, Dr. Ellis, and/or the School of Graduate Studies. All graduate students admitted are funded, with the exception of those who choose other funding options.

Internships/Practica: Internships and practica in assessment and therapy are available to students enrolled in the clinical psychology option. They are conducted in the area mental health facilities under the joint supervision of departmental faculty and adjunct faculty located in the mental health facilities.

Housing and Day Care: No on-campus housing and day care facilities are available.

Employment of Department Graduates:

Master's Degree Graduates: Of those who graduated in the academic year 2000–2001, the following categories and numbers represent the post-graduate activities and employment of master's degree graduates: Enrolled in a post-doctoral residency/fellowship (n/a), employed in independent practice (n/a).

Doctoral Degree Graduates: Of those who graduated in the academic year 2000–2001, the following categories and numbers represent the post-graduate activities and employment of doctoral degree graduates: Enrolled in a psychology doctoral program (n/a), enrolled in another graduate/professional program (n/a).

Additional Information:

Orientation, Objectives, and Emphasis of Department: The Department of Psychology, College of Arts and Sciences, offers a Master of Arts Degree with options in general psychology and clinical psychology. The general psychology option prepares students for various endeavors, such as teaching at the community college level and doctoral study in psychology. The clinical psychology option provides students with training in clinical psychology leading to careers in mental health centers and other human services agencies.

Special Facilities or Resources: The psychology department maintains general experimental psychology, physiological psychology, and clinical psychology laboratory facilities. All laboratories are used for undergraduate and graduate instructional research and for student and faculty research. Assistantships/employment are available outside of the department, including the medical school.

Information for Students With Physical Disabilities: The Disability Services Office mediates in the needs of students with disabilities.

Application Information:

Send to: School of Graduate Studies. Students are admitted in the Fall, application deadline March 1. Review of applications begins March 1. Applications are normally reviewed and accepted also after March 1, but no later than July 1. *Fee:* $25.

Memphis, University of
Department of Psychology
College of Arts and Sciences
202 Psychology Building
Memphis, TN 38152-6400
Telephone: (901) 678-2145
Fax: (901) 678-2579
E-mail: *a.meyers@mail.psyc.memphis.edu*
Web: *http://www.psyc.memphis.edu/psych.htm*

Department Established:

1957. Chairman: Andrew W. Meyers. Number of Faculty: total–full-time 33, part-time 6; women–full-time 2, part-time 3; minority–full-time 1, part-time 2.

Programs and Degrees Offered:

Listed in the following order: Program area, degree type (T if terminal Master's), number awarded 7/00–6/01. Clinical Psychol-

ogy PhD 8, Experimental Psychology PhD 7, General Psychology MA (T) 28, School MA/EdS MA (T) 3, School Psychology PhD 4.

APA Accreditation: Clinical PhD: full.

Student Applications/Admissions:

Student Applications

Clinical Psychology PhD The Median number of years required for completion of a degree are 3. Experimental Psychology PhD The Median number of years required for completion of a degree are 4. General Psychology MA The Median number of years required for completion of a degree are 3. School MA/EdS MA The Median number of years required for completion of a degree are 3. School Psychology PhD The Median number of years required for completion of a degree are 3.

Admissions Requirements:

Scores: Entries appear in this order: required test or GPA, minimum score (if required), median score of students entering in 2001–2002. Master's Programs: GRE-V 400, 535; GRE-Q 400, 575; GRE-V+Q 900, 1105; overall undergraduate GPA 2.5, 2.6. The minimum undergraduate GPA required for the MA school is 3.0/4.0. There is not a minimum verbal or quantitative GRE-score required for the MSGP program, only a combined score of 900 is required. Doctoral Programs: GRE-V no minimum stated, 562; GRE-Q no minimum stated, 614; GRE-V+Q 1100, 1176; overall undergraduate GPA 2.75, 3.0; last 2 years GPA no minimum stated; psychology GPA no minimum stated; psychology GPA no minimum stated.

Other Criteria: (importance of criteria rated low, medium, or high): GRE/MAT scores high, research experience high, work experience medium, extracurricular activity low, clinically related public service low, GPA high, letters of recommendation high, interview medium, statement of goals and objectives high.

Student Characteristics: The following represents characteristics of students in 2001–2002 in all graduate psychology programs in the department: Female–full-time 67, part-time 12; Male–full-time 29, part-time 7; African American/Black–full-time 10, part-time 1; Hispanic/Latino (a)–full-time 0, part-time 0; Asian/Pacific Islander–full-time 3, part-time 1; American Indian/Alaska Native–full-time 1, part-time 0; Multi-ethnic–full-time 0, part-time 0; students subject to the Americans with Disabilities Act–full-time 0, part-time 0.

Financial Information/Assistance:

Tuition for Full-Time Study: *Master's:* State residents per academic year $3,948, $213 per credit hour; nonstate residents: per academic year $5,099, $213 per credit hour. *Doctoral:* State residents: per academic year $3,948, $213 per credit hour; nonstate residents: per academic year $5,099, $213 per credit hour.

Financial Assistance:

First Year Students: Teaching assistantships available for first-year. Average amount paid per academic year: $9,000. Average number of hours worked per week: 20. Apply by Feb 1. Tuition remission given: full. Research assistantships available for first-year. Average amount paid per academic year: $9,000. Average number of hours worked per week: 20. Apply by Feb 1. Tuition remission given: full.

Advanced Students: Teaching assistantships available for advanced students. Average amount paid per academic year: $10,000. Average number of hours worked per week: 20. Apply by Feb 1. Tuition remission given: full. Research assistantships available for advanced students. Average amount paid per academic year: $10,000. Average number of hours worked per week: 20. Apply by Feb 1. Tuition remission given: full.

Contact Information: Of all students currently enrolled full-time, 62% benefited from one or more of the listed financial assistance programs. For information on financial assistance, contact: www.psyc.memphis.edu/psych.htm.

Internships/Practica: The department has no internships. Students complete internships during the fourth or fifth year at sites nationwide. The department has an extensive network of relationships with local agencies for providing practicum experiences for students. PhD clinical students work 20 hours per week at several of these practicum sites for a minimum of one year. All students can use these sites for other forms of practicum experience and research as the need arises. For those doctoral students for whom a professional internship is required prior to graduation, 7 applied in 2000–2001. Of those who applied, 7 were placed in internships listed by the Association of Psychology Postdoctoral and Internship Programs (APPIC); 7 were placed in APA accredited internships.

Housing and Day Care: On-campus housing and day care facilities are available.

Employment of Department Graduates:

Master's Degree Graduates: Of those who graduated in the academic year 2000–2001, the following categories and numbers represent the post-graduate activities and employment of master's degree graduates: Enrolled in a psychology doctoral program (16), enrolled in another graduate/professional program (4), enrolled in a post-doctoral residency/fellowship (n/a), employed in independent practice (n/a), employed in an academic position at a university (0), employed in an academic position at a 2-year/4-year college (0), employed in other positions at a higher education institution (1), employed in a professional position in a school system (0), employed in business or industry (research/consulting) (0), employed in business or industry (management) (0), employed in a government agency (research) (0), employed in a government agency (professional services) (0), employed in a community mental health/counseling center (0), employed in a hospital/medical center (0), still seeking employment (0), other employment position (3).

Doctoral Degree Graduates: Of those who graduated in the academic year 2000–2001, the following categories and numbers represent the post-graduate activities and employment of doctoral degree graduates: Enrolled in a psychology doctoral program (n/a), enrolled in another graduate/professional program (n/a), enrolled in a post-doctoral residency/fellowship (5), employed in independent practice (3), employed in an academic position at a university (3), employed in an academic position at a 2-year/4-year college (1), employed in other positions at a higher education institution (0), employed in a professional position in a school system (2), employed in business or industry (research/consulting) (2), employed in business or industry (management) (0), employed in a government agency (research) (1), employed in a government agency (professional services) (0), employed in a community mental health/counseling center (1), employed in a hospital/medical center (2), still seeking employment (0), other employment position (0).

Additional Information:

Orientation, Objectives, and Emphasis of Department: The department philosophy emphasizes the training of experimentally sophisticated research scientists and practitioners. All programs have a strong research emphasis. Professional training is based upon a research foundation and students are exposed to a broad range of theoretical perspectives. Diversity of professional training activities and collaborative research activities is emphasized. Students are afforded maximum freedom to pursue their own interests and tailor programs to their needs. All PhD and master's programs are serviced by six research areas within the department. The Experimental PhD program offers the following areas of emphasis: Child & Family Studies, Research Design & Statistics, Behavioral Medicine & Community Psychology, Cognitive & Social Processes, and Neuropsychology & Behavioral Neuroscience. The Clinical PhD program offers these areas of emphasis: Psychopathology & Psychotherapy, Child & Family Studies, Research & Statistics, Behavioral Medicine & Community Psychology, and Neuropsychology & Behavioral Neuroscience. School Psychology students typically participate in the Child & Family research area. PhD students must apply both to one of the PhD programs and one of the research areas.

Special Facilities or Resources: The department is housed in a modern well equipped barrier-free building, providing offices and laboratory space for all students. The department also houses the Universities Prevention Center and the Psychological Services Center. The Prevention Center is a joint venture of The University of Memphis and the University of Tennessee, Memphis. Researchers and staff are dedicated to developing ways of preventing cancer and cardiovascular diseases. The Center's research is sponsored by the National Institutes of Health, and strives to alter lifestyles that contribute to premature death and to improve the health of future generations. The department and the Prevention Center have close working relationships with the University of Tennessee Center for Health Sciences. The department maintains a fee-for-service outpatient mental health clinic, the Psychological Services Center. In this clinic doctoral students receive intensive supervision as they learn to provide a wide range of assessment and intervention services. The clients are referred from the greater Memphis area. This clinic is also the context for all department research where psychological services are being provided.

Information for Students With Physical Disabilities: The entire campus including all of psychology's facilities is 100 percent accessible to students with disabilities.

Application Information:
Send to: Admissions Secretary, The University of Memphis, Department of Psychology, 202 Psychology Building, Memphis, TN 38152. Students are admitted in the Fall, application deadline February 1. The deadline for applying to master's programs is June 15. *Fee:* $35. The application fee for the graduate school is $25 for domestic students and $35 for international students. The application fee for the Department of Psychology is $10.

Middle Tennessee State University

Department of Psychology
Education and Behavioral Science
Box 87
Murfreesboro, TN 37132
Telephone: (615) 898-2706
Fax: (615) 898-5027
E-mail: *alittlep@mtsu.edu*
Web: *http://www.mtsu.edu/*

Department Established:

1967. Chairperson: Larry W. Morris. Number of Faculty: total–full-time 45, part-time 13; women–full-time 16, part-time 9; minority–full-time 3, part-time 1.

Programs and Degrees Offered:

Listed in the following order: Program area, degree type (T if terminal Master's), number awarded 7/00–6/01. Clinical MA (T) 37, experimental MA (T) 1, industrial/organizational MA (T) 12, quantitative MA (T) 2, school counseling EdD (T) 28, school psychology MA 22, school psychology EdS 18.

Student Applications/Admissions:

Student Applications

Clinical MA—Applications 2001–2002, 35. Total applicants accepted 2001–2002, 28. New applicants enrolled 2001–2002, 14. Total enrolled 2001–2002 full-time, 48. Openings 2002–2003, 28. *Experimental MA*—Applications 2001–2002, 12. Total applicants accepted 2001–2002, 10. New applicants enrolled 2001–2002, 4. Total enrolled 2001–2002 full-time, 9. Openings 2002–2003, 20. *Industrial/organizational MA*—Applications 2001–2002, 42. Total applicants accepted 2001–2002, 26. New applicants enrolled 2001–2002, 9. Total enrolled 2001–2002 full-time, 31. Openings 2002–2003, 14. *Quantitative MA*—Applications 2001–2002, 4. Total applicants accepted 2001–2002, 4. New applicants enrolled 2001–2002, 1. Total enrolled 2001–2002 full-time, 4. Openings 2002–2003, 6. *School counseling EdD*—Applications 2001–2002, 29. Total applicants accepted 2001–2002, 20. New applicants enrolled 2001–2002, 10. Total enrolled 2001–2002 full-time, 65. Openings 2002–2003, 20. *School psychology MA*—Applications 2001–2002, 20. Total applicants accepted 2001–2002, 20. New applicants enrolled 2001–2002, 7. Total enrolled 2001–2002 full-time, 27. Openings 2002–2003, 11. *School psychology EdS*—Applications 2001–2002, 2. Total applicants accepted 2001–2002, 2. New applicants enrolled 2001–2002, 2. Total enrolled 2001–2002 full-time, 8. Openings 2002–2003, 2.

Admissions Requirements:

Scores: Entries appear in this order: required test or GPA, minimum score (if required), median score of students entering in 2001–2002. Master's Programs: GRE-V no minimum stated; GRE-Q 450; GRE-V+Q 900; GRE-Analytical 450; GRE-V+Q+Analytical no minimum stated; GRE-Subject(Psych) no minimum stated; overall undergraduate GPA 3.00. I/O only: GRE-Q or GRE-A=450; Clinical only: GRE-Subject= no minimum; School Counseling V+Q=900 or V+A=900. Doctoral Programs: last 2 years GPA no minimum stated; psychology GPA no minimum stated; psychology GPA no minimum stated.

Other Criteria: (importance of criteria rated low, medium, or high): GRE/MAT scores high, research experience high, GPA high, letters of recommendation high, interview high, statement of goals and objectives high. Interview: School Counseling only.

Student Characteristics: The following represents characteristics of students in 2001–2002 in all graduate psychology programs in the department: Female–full-time 38, part-time 0; Male–full-time 5, part-time 0; African American/Black–full-time 6, part-time 0; Hispanic/Latino (a)–full-time 1, part-time 0; Asian/Pacific Islander–full-time 2, part-time 0; American Indian/Alaska Native–full-time 0, part-time 0.

Financial Information/Assistance:

Tuition for Full-Time Study: *Master's:* State residents per academic year $1,716, $181 per credit hour; nonstate residents: per academic year $4,952, $461 per credit hour.

Financial Assistance:

First Year Students: Research assistantships available for first-year. Average amount paid per academic year: $4,550. Average number of hours worked per week: 20. Apply by March/Oct 1. Tuition remission given: full and partial.

Advanced Students: No information provided.

Contact Information: Of all students currently enrolled full-time, 10% benefited from one or more of the listed financial assistance programs. For information on financial assistance, contact: alittlep@mtsu.edu.

Internships/Practica: Field placements are available in a variety of mental health facilities, inpatient facilities, the VA hospital, drug abuse facilities, K–12 school settings, and industrial sites.

Housing and Day Care: On-campus housing and day care facilities are available.

Employment of Department Graduates:

Master's Degree Graduates: Of those who graduated in the academic year 2000–2001, the following categories and numbers represent the post-graduate activities and employment of master's degree graduates: Enrolled in a post-doctoral residency/fellowship (n/a), employed in independent practice (n/a).

Doctoral Degree Graduates: Of those who graduated in the academic year 2000–2001, the following categories and numbers represent the post-graduate activities and employment of doctoral degree graduates: Enrolled in a psychology doctoral program (n/a), enrolled in another graduate/professional program (n/a).

Additional Information:

Orientation, Objectives, and Emphasis of Department: We have an applied department with research and service priorities. The clinical program is designed for students seeking licensure as psychological examiners in Tennessee. A strong academic program is available for students seeking to improve their backgrounds in core areas of psychology for admission to doctoral programs. Applied programs lead to certification and licensure in school psychology, school counseling, and industrial/organizational.

Special Facilities or Resources: On-campus facilities include a counseling laboratory for practica, an animal learning laboratory and a physiology laboratory.

Application Information:

Send to: Office of Graduate Studies, Cope Administration Building, 114 Middle, Tennessee State University, Murfreesboro, TN 37132. Students are admitted in the Fall, application deadline October 1; Spring, application deadline March 1. *Fee:* $30.

Peabody College of Vanderbilt University

Department of Psychology and Human Development
Peabody
Box 512
Nashville, TN 37203
Telephone: (615) 322-8141
Fax: (615) 343-9494
E-mail: *sharone.k.hall@vanderbilt.edu*
Web: *http://peabody.vanderbilt.edu/psychology*

Department Established:

1915. Chairperson: Kathleen V. Hoover-Dempsey. Number of Faculty: total–full-time 21, part-time 8; women–full-time 10, part-time 5.

Programs and Degrees Offered:

Listed in the following order: Program area, degree type (T if terminal Master's), number awarded 7/00–6/01. Clinical PhD 8, cognitive PhD, Community PhD, developmental PhD, Other (MS/Exchg) PhD, quantitative methods PhD.

APA Accreditation: Clinical PhD: full.

Student Applications/Admissions:

Student Applications

Clinical PhD—Applications 2001–2002, 97. Total applicants accepted 2001–2002, 5. New applicants enrolled 2001–2002, 2. Total enrolled 2001–2002 full-time, 32. Openings 2002–2003, 12. The Median number of years required for completion of a degree are 8. The number of students enrolled full and part-time, who were dismissed or voluntarily withdrew from this program area were 0. *Cognitive PhD*—Applications 2001–2002, 13. Total applicants accepted 2001–2002, 2. Total enrolled 2001–2002 full-time, 9. Openings 2002–2003, 2. The number of students enrolled full and part-time, who were dismissed or voluntarily withdrew from this program area were 0. *Community PhD*—Applications 2001–2002, 17. Total applicants accepted 2001–2002, 2. New applicants enrolled 2001–2002, 2. Total enrolled 2001–2002 full-time, 6. *Developmental PhD*—Applications 2001–2002, 21. Total enrolled 2001–2002 full-time, 11. Openings 2002–2003, 2. The number of students enrolled full and part-time, who were dismissed or voluntarily withdrew from this program area were 0. *Other (MS/Exchg) PhD*—Applications 2001–2002, 1. Total applicants accepted 2001–2002, 1. New applicants enrolled 2001–2002, 1. Total enrolled 2001–2002 full-time, 1. The number of students enrolled full and part-time, who were dismissed or voluntarily withdrew from this program area were 0. *Quantitative methods PhD*—Applications 2001–2002, 5. Total applicants accepted 2001–2002, 3. New applicants enrolled 2001–2002, 1. Total enrolled 2001–2002 full-time, 4. Openings 2002–2003, 2. The number of students enrolled full and part-time, who were

dismissed or voluntarily withdrew from this program area were 0.

Admissions Requirements:

Scores: Entries appear in this order: required test or GPA, minimum score (if required), median score of students entering in 2001–2002. Doctoral Programs: GRE-V no minimum stated, 600; GRE-Q no minimum stated, 680; GRE-V+Q no minimum stated, 1280; overall undergraduate GPA no minimum stated, 3.6; last 2 years GPA no minimum stated; psychology GPA no minimum stated; psychology GPA no minimum stated.

Other Criteria: (importance of criteria rated low, medium, or high): GRE/MAT, scores research experience high, work experience low, extracurricular activity low, clinically related public service low, GPA, letters of recommendation high, interview medium, statement of goals and objectives high. Interview is required by clinical only.

Student Characteristics: The following represents characteristics of students in 2001–2002 in all graduate psychology programs in the department: Female–full-time 32, part-time 0; Male–full-time 13, part-time 0; African American/Black–full-time 4, part-time 0; Hispanic/Latino (a)–full-time 0, part-time 0; Asian/Pacific Islander–full-time 2, part-time 0; American Indian/Alaska Native–full-time 0, part-time 0; Multi-ethnic–full-time 0, students subject to the Americans with Disabilities Act–full-time 0.

Financial Information/Assistance:

Tuition for Full-Time Study: No information provided.

Financial Assistance:

First Year Students: No information provided.
Advanced Students: No information provided.
Contact Information: Of all students currently enrolled full-time, 85% benefited from one or more of the listed financial assistance programs. For information on financial assistance, contact: James Hogge 615-322-8407.

Internships/Practica: For those doctoral students for whom a professional internship is required prior to graduation, 3 applied in 2000–2001. Of those who applied, 3 were placed in internships listed by the Association of Psychology Postdoctoral and Internship Programs (APPIC); 3 were placed in APA accredited internships.

Housing and Day Care: No on-campus housing and day care facilities are available.

Employment of Department Graduates:

Master's Degree Graduates: Of those who graduated in the academic year 2000–2001, the following categories and numbers represent the post-graduate activities and employment of master's degree graduates: Enrolled in a psychology doctoral program (6), enrolled in another graduate/professional program (1), enrolled in a post-doctoral residency/fellowship (n/a), employed in independent practice (n/a), employed in other positions at a higher education institution (1), employed in a government agency (professional services) (1), other employment position (1).

Doctoral Degree Graduates: Of those who graduated in the academic year 2000–2001, the following categories and numbers represent the post-graduate activities and employment of doctoral

degree graduates: Enrolled in a psychology doctoral program (n/a), enrolled in another graduate/professional program (n/a), enrolled in a post-doctoral residency/fellowship (1), employed in an academic position at a university (1), employed in other positions at a higher education institution (2), employed in a government agency (professional services) (1), employed in a community mental health/counseling center (3), employed in a hospital/medical center (2).

Additional Information:

Orientation, Objectives, and Emphasis of Department: The Department of Psychology and Human Development offers a rigorous program of academic and research training. Students become involved immediately in scholarly inquiry under the mentorship of a faculty advisor. The department has a clear focus on child and adolescent development, and on the persons and social systems (particularly families and schools) that influence this development. Major areas of inquiry concentrate in the following: cognitive and social development, including information processing, language development, problem solving, motivation, memory development, social referencing, motor skill development, and perceptual and spatial development in both mentally retarded and non-retarded children; developmental psychopathology, including such issues as social-cognitive factors in childhood depression and antisocial behavior in children and adolescents; and behavioral pediatrics, one major focus of which is on coping with chronic childhood illness. Another major research focus is in basic and applied social psychology, including program evaluation, victimization, health psychology, and the relationships between individuals and organizations. Other areas of interest include the philosophical foundations of psychology and mental health policy, with particular interest on the ethical dimensions of intervention. Clearly, all of these research areas are integrated among clinical, developmental, cognitive, and social domains, and we attempt to recruit students who will take advantage of the unique resources available here. There is extensive scholarly collaboration between the Peabody program and the program in Vanderbilt's College of Arts and Science. Students may work with faculty and take courses in both departments.

Special Facilities or Resources: There are exceptional resources available in the Peabody/Vanderbilt community. Members of the faculty are housed in two modern buildings with laboratory and computer facilities. The University has a state-of-the-art VAX 8800 mainframe, available to students. The library system contains over 1.7 million volumes, with particular strength in education- and psychology-related publications. In addition, most members of the department's faculty are also research scholars in the John F. Kennedy Center for Research on Education and Human Development, a major national behavioral research center located on the Peabody campus. Facilities within the Kennedy Center include the Family and Child Study Center and the Susan Gray School, which serves developmentally delayed and at-risk children. There are opportunities for research collaboration with the Vanderbilt Institute for Public Policy Studies (particularly its Center for the Study of Children and Families and its Health Policy Center), as well as with such Medical Center departments as adolescent medicine, child and adolescent psychiatry, and the comprehensive developmental evaluation center. There is a university counseling center and an ample array of community agencies available for practicum experiences.

Application Information:
Send to: Psychology and Human Development, c/o The Graduate School, 411 Kirkland Hall, Vanderbilt University, Nashville, TN 37240. Students are admitted in the Fall, application deadline January 15. *Fee:* $40.

Tennessee State University
Department of Psychology
Education
3500 John Merritt Boulevard
Nashville, TN 37209
Telephone: (615) 963-5141
Fax: (615) 963-5140
E-mail: *pmillet@tnstate.edu*

Department Established:
1940. Chairperson: Peter E. Millet, PhD. Number of Faculty: total–full-time 22, part-time 17; women–full-time 10, part-time 13; minority–full-time 8, part-time 7; faculty subject to the Americans with Disabilities Act 1.

Programs and Degrees Offered:
Listed in the following order: Program area, degree type (T if terminal Master's), number awarded 7/00–6/01. Counseling Psychology PhD 1, Guidance and Counseling MA (T) 18, School Psychology PhD, School Psychology EdS.

APA Accreditation: Counseling PhD: full.

Student Applications/Admissions:
Student Applications

Counseling Psychology PhD—Applications 2001–2002, 22. Total applicants accepted 2001–2002, 8. New applicants enrolled 2001–2002, 8. Total enrolled 2001–2002 full-time, 48, part-time, 72. Openings 2002–2003, 8. The Median number of years required for completion of a degree are 5. The number of students enrolled full and part-time, who were dismissed or voluntarily withdrew from this program area were 3. *Guidance and Counseling MA*—New applicants enrolled 2001–2002, 29. Total enrolled 2001–2002 full-time, 18, part-time, 84. Openings 2002–2003, 30. *School Psychology PhD*—Total enrolled 2001–2002 full-time, 3. Openings 2002–2003, 5. The Median number of years required for completion of a degree are 5. The number of students enrolled full and part-time, who were dismissed or voluntarily withdrew from this program area were 0. *School Psychology EdS*—Total enrolled 2001–2002 full-time, 3. Openings 2002–2003, 3. The Median number of years required for completion of a degree are 3.

Admissions Requirements:
Scores: Entries appear in this order: required test or GPA, minimum score (if required), median score of students entering in 2001–2002. Master's Programs: GRE-V no minimum stated; GRE-Q no minimum stated; GRE-V+Q no minimum stated;

GRE-Subject(Psych) no minimum stated; MAT no minimum stated; overall undergraduate GPA 2.5. Doctoral Programs: GRE-V+Q 900; last 2 years GPA no minimum stated; psychology GPA no minimum stated; psychology GPA 3.25.

Other Criteria: (importance of criteria rated low, medium, or high): GRE/MAT scores medium, research experience medium, work experience low, clinically related public service medium, GPA medium, letters of recommendation high, interview high, statement of goals and objectives high. These criteria are used for admission to PhD program; Master's program criteria are scores, GPA, and undergraduate prerequisites only.

Student Characteristics: The following represents characteristics of students in 2001–2002 in all graduate psychology programs in the department: Female–full-time 46, part-time 101; Male–full-time 17, part-time 29; African American/Black–full-time 41, part-time 6; Hispanic/Latino (a)–full-time 1, part-time 0; Asian/Pacific Islander–full-time 1, part-time 1; American Indian/Alaska Native–full-time 0, part-time 0.

Financial Information/Assistance:

Tuition for Full-Time Study: *Master's:* State residents per academic year $3,884, $209 per credit hour; nonstate residents: per academic year $10,356, $479 per credit hour. *Doctoral:* State residents: per academic year $3,884, $209 per credit hour; nonstate residents: per academic year $10,356, $479 per credit hour.

Financial Assistance:

First Year Students: No information provided.
Advanced Students: No information provided.
Contact Information: For information on financial assistance, contact: Director of Student Financial Aid or Dean of the Graduate School, Tennessee State University, 3500 John A. Merritt Blvd., Nashville, TN 37207.

Internships/Practica: Internships are available in School Psychological Services in metropolitan Nashville public schools. Internships in clinical and counseling psychology are available for master's and doctoral students in local community mental health centers in middle Tennessee and southern Kentucky; in community agencies; in family counseling services; in correctional facilities; in state hospital settings; and in school systems throughout middle Tennessee.

Housing and Day Care: No on-campus housing and day care facilities are available.

Employment of Department Graduates:

Master's Degree Graduates: Of those who graduated in the academic year 2000–2001, the following categories and numbers represent the post-graduate activities and employment of master's degree graduates: Enrolled in a post-doctoral residency/fellowship (n/a), employed in independent practice (n/a).
Doctoral Degree Graduates: Of those who graduated in the academic year 2000–2001, the following categories and numbers represent the post-graduate activities and employment of doctoral degree graduates: Enrolled in a psychology doctoral program (n/a), enrolled in another graduate/professional program (n/a).

Additional Information:

Orientation, Objectives, and Emphasis of Department: The philosophy of the Department of Psychology at Tennessee State University is embodied in the concept that psychology is a discipline that contributes to the understanding of human behavior and experience. A graduate of the Department of Psychology is expected to be both a professional person with a code of ethics and one who is committed to a scientific orientation. The doctoral program in counseling and school psychology is a designated doctoral program in psychology by the national designation system sponsored by the American Association of State Psychology Boards and Register for Health Services Providers in Psychology. The Master's Degree in Psychology is designed for students seeking preparation for a professional career in psychology, either for a doctoral program or for professional training at the master's level. The Guidance and Counseling master's program is designed for students preparing for careers in mental health agencies, juvenile and adult rehabilitation centers, personnel or management work, or school counseling.

Special Facilities or Resources: Specialized Facilities are available in department laboratories: 1) Counseling Laboratory consisting of videotaping equipment, observation room, and a two-way communication system; 2) computer laboratory- PC's and associated software for word-processing, statistics, and tutorials; 3) Testing Equipment- psychological test kit and assessment files for intelligence, personality, and psychoeducational assessment. In addition, faculty have specialized research laboratories providing opportunities for student research involvement (e.g., biofeedback/psychophysiology laboratory, group counseling laboratory).

Information for Students With Physical Disabilities: Contact the office of Disabled Students Services at 615-963-7400.

Application Information:
Send to: Dean of Graduate School, Tennessee State University, 3500 John A. Merritt Blvd. Nashville, TN 37209. Students are admitted in the Fall, application deadline July 1; Spring, application deadline November 1; Summer, application deadline April 1. Above applies to Masters Programs; deadline for admission to PhD program is February 15 *Fee:* $25.

Tennessee, University of, Chattanooga
Department of Psychology
350 Holt Hall
Chattanooga, TN 37403
Telephone: (423) 755-4262
Fax: (423) 755-4284
E-mail: *michael-biderman@utc.edu*
Web: *http://www.utc.edu/psychology*

Department Established:
Head: David J. Pittenger. Number of Faculty: total–full-time 13, part-time 5; women–full-time 3, part-time 3.

Programs and Degrees Offered:
Listed in the following order: Program area, degree type (T if terminal Master's), number awarded 7/00–6/01. Industrial/organizational, research.

Student Applications/Admissions:

Admissions Requirements:

Scores: Entries appear in this order: required test or GPA, minimum score (if required), median score of students entering in 2001–2002. Master's Programs: GRE-V no minimum stated, 460; GRE-Q no minimum stated, 550; GRE-Analytical no minimum stated, 630; overall undergraduate GPA no minimum stated, 3.40. We use a formula: $200 \times UGPA + .5 \times GREQ + .5 \times (Max(GREV,GREA))$. Generally admit those whose formula score exceeds 1200. Doctoral Programs: last 2 years GPA no minimum stated; psychology GPA no minimum stated; psychology GPA no minimum stated.

Other Criteria: (importance of criteria rated low, medium, or high): GRE/MAT scores high, research experience medium, extracurricular activity low, clinically related public service low, GPA high, letters of recommendation medium, statement of goals and objectives low.

Student Characteristics: The following represents characteristics of students in 2001–2002 in all graduate psychology programs in the department: Female–full-time 26, part-time 3; Male–full-time 8, part-time 2; African American/Black–full-time 3, part-time 1; Hispanic/Latino (a)–full-time 0, part-time 0; Asian/Pacific Islander–full-time 0, part-time 0; American Indian/Alaska Native–full-time 0, part-time 0; Multi-ethnic–full-time 1.

Financial Information/Assistance:

Tuition for Full-Time Study: *Master's:* State residents per academic year $2,620, $260 per credit hour; nonstate residents: per academic year $3,265, $340 per credit hour.

Financial Assistance:

First Year Students: Teaching assistantships available for first-year. Average amount paid per academic year: $1,000. Average number of hours worked per week: 5. Apply by August 20. Research assistantships available for first-year. Average amount paid per academic year: $2,500. Average number of hours worked per week: 10. Apply by April 15. Tuition remission given: partial.

Advanced Students: Teaching assistantships available for advanced students. Average amount paid per academic year: $1,000. Average number of hours worked per week: 5. Apply by August 20. Research assistantships available for advanced students. Average amount paid per academic year: $2,500. Average number of hours worked per week: 10. Apply by July 1. Tuition remission given: partial.

Contact Information: Of all students currently enrolled full-time, 60% benefited from one or more of the listed financial assistance programs. For information on financial assistance, contact: Graduate School and Program Coordinator.

Internships/Practica: The integration of coursework and practice throughout the students' graduate academic program makes possible the most effective learning to prepare them for applied professional careers in I/O psychology. To achieve this end, I/O students become involved in a variety of real life work organization activities through completion of an extensive practicum program. They are encouraged to start this practicum in their second semester of academic work. Six semester hours of practicum credit are required (involving at least 300 hours of actual work time), and an additional three semester hours may be taken as a part of the elective portion of the program. The practicum is carried out in private and public work organizations in which the students engage in a wide variety of projects under the guidance of field supervisors, coordinated by the I/O faculty.

Housing and Day Care: No on-campus housing and day care facilities are available.

Employment of Department Graduates:

Master's Degree Graduates: Of those who graduated in the academic year 2000–2001, the following categories and numbers represent the post-graduate activities and employment of master's degree graduates: Enrolled in a psychology doctoral program (4), enrolled in another graduate/professional program (2), enrolled in a post-doctoral residency/fellowship (n/a), employed in independent practice (n/a), employed in an academic position at a university (0), employed in an academic position at a 2-year/4-year college (0), employed in other positions at a higher education institution (1), employed in a professional position in a school system (0), employed in business or industry (management) (4), other employment position (1).

Doctoral Degree Graduates: Of those who graduated in the academic year 2000–2001, the following categories and numbers represent the post-graduate activities and employment of doctoral degree graduates: Enrolled in a psychology doctoral program (n/a), enrolled in another graduate/professional program (n/a).

Additional Information:

Orientation, Objectives, and Emphasis of Department: The goal of the I/O program is to provide students with the training necessary to pursue a variety of I/O related fields. These include, but are not limited to, positions in human resources departments in work organizations and human resource management consulting. In addition, the I/O program can be used as a preparation for the pursuit of doctoral training in I/O related fields of study. The curriculum is organized around specific core knowledge domains particular to I/O psychology. The industrial domain includes content such as job analysis, selection, statistics, and training. The organizational domain includes content such as work motivation, attitudes, leadership, organizational development, culture, group processes, and conflict management. The third domain, research methodology, includes content such as experimental design, surveying, correlation and regression, and factor analysis. The research program is designed primarily to prepare students to pursue doctoral level training. Students work in an apprenticeship model with faculty to develop strong design and communication skills.

Special Facilities or Resources: Center for Applied Social Research conducts surveys and other applied research in the community. We have a close relationship with SHRM Chattanooga, the local SHRM branch.

Application Information:

Send to: Graduate School, UTC, Chattanooga, TN 37403. Students are admitted in the Fall, application deadline March 15; Winter, application deadline March 15. Most admissions for fall, other admissions on a case-by-case basis. *Fee:* $25.

Tennessee, University of, Knoxville

Counseling Psychology
College of Education
102 Claxton Addition
Knoxville, TN 37996-3400
Telephone: (865) 974-2321
Fax: (865) 974-8674
E-mail: *pklukken@utk.edu*
Web: *http://web.utk.edu/%7Ecdhs/counsel/cephd.htm*

Department Established:
1995. Program Coordinator: P. Gary Klukken. Number of Faculty: total–full-time 3, part-time 3; women–full-time 2, part-time 1.

Programs and Degrees Offered:
Listed in the following order: Program area, degree type (T if terminal Master's), number awarded 7/00–6/01. Counseling psychology PhD 2.

APA Accreditation: Counseling PhD: full.

Student Applications/Admissions:
Student Applications
Counseling psychology PhD—Applications 2001–2002, 41. Total applicants accepted 2001–2002, 12. New applicants enrolled 2001–2002, 5. Total enrolled 2001–2002 full-time, 31. Openings 2002–2003, 5. The Median number of years required for completion of a degree are 6. The number of students enrolled full and part-time, who were dismissed or voluntarily withdrew from this program area were 1.

Admissions Requirements:
Scores: Entries appear in this order: required test or GPA, minimum score (if required), median score of students entering in 2001–2002. Doctoral Programs: GRE-V no minimum stated; GRE-Q no minimum stated; GRE-V+Q 1000, 1200; GRE-V+Q+Analytical no minimum stated; overall undergraduate GPA 3.0, 3.4; last 2 years GPA no minimum stated; psychology GPA no minimum stated; psychology GPA no minimum stated.
Other Criteria: (importance of criteria rated low, medium, or high): GRE/MAT scores medium, research experience medium, work experience medium, extracurricular activity medium, clinically related public service medium, GPA medium, letters of recommendation high, statement of goals and objectives high. The above criteria are for the PhD program.

Student Characteristics: The following represents characteristics of students in 2001–2002 in all graduate psychology programs in the department: Female–full-time 4, part-time 0; Male–full-time 1, part-time 0; African American/Black–full-time 1, part-time 0; Hispanic/Latino (a)–full-time 0, part-time 0; Asian/Pacific Islander–full-time 1, part-time 0; American Indian/Alaska Native–full-time 0, part-time 0.

Financial Information/Assistance:
Tuition for Full-Time Study: *Doctoral:* State residents: per academic year $3,452; nonstate residents: per academic year $10,596.

Financial Assistance:
First Year Students: Teaching assistantships available for first-year. Average amount paid per academic year: $4,000. Average number of hours worked per week: 10. Apply by Apr 1. Tuition remission given: full. Research assistantships available for first-year. Average amount paid per academic year: $4,000. Average number of hours worked per week: 10. Apply by Apr 1. Tuition remission given: full.
Advanced Students: Research assistantships available for advanced students. Average amount paid per academic year: $8,000. Average number of hours worked per week: 20. Apply by Apr 1. Tuition remission given: full. Traineeships available for advanced students. Average amount paid per academic year: $8,000. Average number of hours worked per week: 20. Apply by Apr 1. Tuition remission given: full.
Contact Information: Of all students currently enrolled full-time, 33% benefited from one or more of the listed financial assistance programs. For information on financial assistance, contact: Program Coordinator, Counseling Psychology Program.

Internships/Practica: Students begin their practitioner training on campus at the Career Services Center and at the Student Counseling Center. After several semesters of intensely supervised therapy training and experience, they are encouraged to pursue advanced practica in community agencies where they work in a variety of settings with diverse populations. During this time they also have a practicum in group work and another one in providing supervision. As the capstone experience of their practitioner training, students must complete a year-long internship at a qualified location. It is strongly recommended that this be at an APA-accredited Predoctoral Internship. The Student Counseling Center has such an internship and students from the Counseling Psychology Program have often been successful in securing one of four positions out of 100 applicants. For those doctoral students for whom a professional internship is required prior to graduation, 9 applied in 2000–2001. Of those who applied, 9 were placed in internships listed by the Association of Psychology Postdoctoral and Internship Programs (APPIC); 8 were placed in APA accredited internships.

Housing and Day Care: No on-campus housing and day care facilities are available.

Employment of Department Graduates:
Master's Degree Graduates: Of those who graduated in the academic year 2000–2001, the following categories and numbers represent the post-graduate activities and employment of master's degree graduates: Enrolled in a post-doctoral residency/fellowship (n/a), employed in independent practice (n/a).
Doctoral Degree Graduates: Of those who graduated in the academic year 2000–2001, the following categories and numbers represent the post-graduate activities and employment of doctoral degree graduates: Enrolled in a psychology doctoral program (n/a), enrolled in another graduate/professional program (n/a), employed in independent practice (1), employed in a hospital/medical center (1).

Additional Information:
Orientation, Objectives, and Emphasis of Department: The Counseling Psychology Program is based on the scientist-practitioner model, with a strong developmental emphasis on guiding the students through the process of becoming counseling psychol-

ogists. It is designed to develop students who are knowledgeable behavioral scientists, excellent researchers, and highly skilled practitioners.

Special Facilities or Resources: The Program has an Assessment Center which serves both as a training site in assessment and as a service to the University and the community. Students who have an interest in the assessment of learning disabilities, cognitive dysfunctions, attention deficits, and personality find this to be an excellent training and practice facility.

Information for Students With Physical Disabilities: The University of Tennessee has an Office of Disability Services (865-974-6087-V/TTY), which addresses campus-wide disability issues and is available to answer any questions.

Application Information:

Send to: College of Education Graduate Center, 211 Claxton Addition, Knoxville, TN 37996-3400. (865) 974-0906. Students are admitted in the Fall, application deadline January 1. PhD program has fall admission only. *Fee:* $35.

Tennessee, University of, Knoxville
Department of Educational Psychology
Education
434 Claxton Addition
Knoxville, TN 37996-3400
Telephone: (865) 974-8145
Fax: (865) 974-0135
E-mail: *mccallum@utk.edu*
Web: *http://www.coe.utk.edu/programs/graduate.html*

Department Established:
1956. Head: R. Steve McCallum. Number of Faculty: total–full-time 10, part-time 3; women–full-time 3, part-time 2; minority–full-time 1.

Programs and Degrees Offered:
Listed in the following order: Program area, degree type (T if terminal Master's), number awarded 7/00–6/01. Educational psychology PhD (T) 5, school psychology PhD 5.

APA Accreditation: School PhD: full.

Student Applications/Admissions:
Student Applications
Educational psychology PhD—Applications 2001–2002, 10. Total applicants accepted 2001–2002, 6. New applicants enrolled 2001–2002, 6. Total enrolled 2001–2002 full-time, 33, part-time, 3. Openings 2002–2003, 5. The Median number of years required for completion of a degree are 4. The number of students enrolled full and part-time, who were dismissed or voluntarily withdrew from this program area were 1. *School psychology PhD*—Applications 2001–2002, 15. Total applicants accepted 2001–2002, 10. New applicants enrolled 2001–2002, 6. Total enrolled 2001–2002 full-time, 35. Openings 2002–2003, 6. The Median number of years required for completion of a degree are 5.

Admissions Requirements:
Scores: Entries appear in this order: required test or GPA, minimum score (if required), median score of students entering in 2001–2002. Master's Programs: GRE-V no minimum stated; GRE-Q no minimum stated; GRE-V+Q no minimum stated; GRE-Analytical no minimum stated; GRE-V+Q+Analytical 1000, 1075; overall undergraduate GPA 2.75, 3.5. 1000 combined on at least two of three scales. Doctoral Programs: GRE-V no minimum stated; GRE-Q no minimum stated; GRE-V+Q no minimum stated; GRE-Analytical no minimum stated; GRE-V+Q+Analytical 50%, 1120; overall undergraduate GPA 2.75, 3.65; last 2 years GPA no minimum stated; psychology GPA no minimum stated; psychology GPA no minimum stated. At least 50%ile on V and 50%ile on other scale.
Other Criteria: (importance of criteria rated low, medium, or high): research experience low, work experience low, extracurricular activity medium, clinically related public service medium, letters of recommendation high, interview low, statement of goals and objectives high, work sample low.

Student Characteristics: The following represents characteristics of students in 2001–2002 in all graduate psychology programs in the department: Female–full-time 30, part-time 0; Male–full-time 15, part-time 0; African American/Black–full-time 4, part-time 0; Hispanic/Latino (a)–full-time 0, part-time 0; Asian/Pacific Islander–full-time 1, part-time 0; American Indian/Alaska Native–full-time 0, part-time 0.

Financial Information/Assistance:
Tuition for Full-Time Study: *Master's:* State residents $184 per credit hour; nonstate residents: $338 per credit hour. *Doctoral:* State residents: $184 per credit hour; nonstate residents: $338 per credit hour.

Financial Assistance:
First Year Students: Teaching assistantships available for first-year. Average amount paid per academic year: $4,200. Average number of hours worked per week: 10. Apply by January 31. Tuition remission given: full. Research assistantships available for first-year. Average amount paid per academic year: $4,000. Average number of hours worked per week: 10. Apply by January 31. Tuition remission given: full.
Advanced Students: Teaching assistantships available for advanced students. Average amount paid per academic year: $4,200. Average number of hours worked per week: 10. Apply by January 31. Tuition remission given: full. Research assistantships available for advanced students. Average amount paid per academic year: $4,000. Average number of hours worked per week: 10. Apply by January 31. Tuition remission given: full.
Contact Information: Of all students currently enrolled full-time, 25% benefited from one or more of the listed financial assistance programs.

Internships/Practica: Assessment and consultation practica are required of all school psychology students. In addition, a 1,500-hour internship is required for EdS students and a 2000-hour internship is required for PhD students. The Department is a member of an APPIC-listed internship consortium. For those doctoral students for whom a professional internship is required prior to graduation, 7 applied in 2000–2001. Of those who applied, 4 were placed in internships listed by the Association of Psychology Postdoctoral and Internship Programs (APPIC); 3 were placed in APA accredited internships.

Housing and Day Care: No on-campus housing and day care facilities are available.

Employment of Department Graduates:

Master's Degree Graduates: Of those who graduated in the academic year 2000–2001, the following categories and numbers represent the post-graduate activities and employment of master's degree graduates: Enrolled in a psychology doctoral program (5), enrolled in another graduate/professional program (5), enrolled in a post-doctoral residency/fellowship (n/a), employed in independent practice (n/a), employed in an academic position at a university (3), employed in an academic position at a 2-year/4-year college (3), employed in a professional position in a school system (10), employed in business or industry (research/consulting) (5).

Doctoral Degree Graduates: Of those who graduated in the academic year 2000–2001, the following categories and numbers represent the post-graduate activities and employment of doctoral degree graduates: Enrolled in a psychology doctoral program (n/a), enrolled in another graduate/professional program (n/a), enrolled in a post-doctoral residency/fellowship (0), employed in independent practice (4).

Additional Information:

Orientation, Objectives, and Emphasis of Department: Members of the Educational Psychology Department envision playing an instrumental role in the creation of contextually linked learning environments that promote and enhance success for all learners. We expect these environments to exemplify a spirit of collaboration and cooperation, respect for diversity, concern for mental and physical health, positive attitudes toward constructive and meaningful change, and a commitment to lifelong learning. Faculty and students in the Psychoeducational Studies Unit are expected to model the behaviors and reflect the values that are necessary to achieve this vision. The Psychoeducational Studies Unit will provide national leadership in creating learning environments that (1) foster psychological health, (2) address authentic educational needs, and (3) promote lifelong learning. Unit faculty and students will draw upon a growing body of knowledge about the psychology, biology, and social/cultural contexts of learning in promoting systematic change that leads to the enhancement of the learner. Specifically, the Unit will seek opportunities in a diversity of contexts for learners to apply information-based problem solving, engage in critical thinking, and implement the structures and processes necessary for effective collaboration.

Application Information:

Send to: Graduate Admissions, College of Education, 214 Claxton Education Building Addition, The University of Tennessee, Knoxville, TN 37996-3400. Students are admitted in the Winter. January 15 deadline for PhD and EdS in School Psychology and for EdD in Educational Psychology. No deadlines for MS in Educational Psychology. *Fee:* $35.

Tennessee, University of, Knoxville (2001 data)
Department of Psychology
Arts & Sciences
312 Austin Peay Building
Knoxville, TN 37996-0900
Telephone: (865) 974-3328
Fax: (865) 974-3330
E-mail: *cjogle@utk.edu*
Web: *http://web.utk.edu/~jlawler/newpage/admissions*

Department Established:

1957. Department Head: James E. Lawler. Number of Faculty: total–full-time 23, part-time 10; women–full-time 8, part-time 4; minority–full-time 2, part-time 1.

Programs and Degrees Offered:

Listed in the following order: Program area, degree type (T if terminal Master's), number awarded 7/00–6/01. Clinical PhD 8, experimental MA (T) 5.

APA Accreditation: Clinical PhD: full.

Student Applications/Admissions:

Student Applications

Clinical PhD—Applications 2001–2002, 124. Total applicants accepted 2001–2002, 10. New applicants enrolled 2001–2002, 7. Total enrolled 2001–2002 full-time, 37. Openings 2002–2003, 7. *Experimental MA*—Applications 2001–2002, 14. Total applicants accepted 2001–2002, 10. New applicants enrolled 2001–2002, 7. Total enrolled 2001–2002 full-time, 13. Openings 2002–2003, 6.

Admissions Requirements:

Scores: Entries appear in this order: required test or GPA, minimum score (if required), median score of students entering in 2001–2002. Master's Programs: GRE-V+Q no minimum stated, 1197; GRE-Subject(Psych) no minimum stated; overall undergraduate GPA no minimum stated, 3.49. Doctoral Programs: GRE-V+Q no minimum stated, 1200; GRE-Subject(Psych) no minimum stated; overall undergraduate GPA 3.0, 3.84.

Other Criteria: (importance of criteria rated low, medium, or high): GRE/MAT scores high, research experience high, work experience low, extracurricular activity low, clinically related public service low, GPA high, letters of recommendation high, interview high, statement of goals and objectives high. Interview rating is different for Clinical (high) and Experimental (medium) doctoral programs.

Student Characteristics: The following represents characteristics of students in 2001–2002 in all graduate psychology programs in the department: Female–full-time 9, part-time 0; Male–full-time 8, part-time 0; African American/Black–full-time 0, part-time 0; Hispanic/Latino (a)–full-time 0, part-time 0; Asian/Pacific Islander–full-time 2, part-time 0; American Indian/Alaska Native–full-time 0, part-time 0.

Financial Information/Assistance:

Tuition for Full-Time Study: No information provided.

Financial Assistance:

First Year Students: No information provided.

Advanced Students: No information provided.

Contact Information: Of all students currently enrolled full-time, 0% benefited from one or more of the listed financial assistance programs. For information on financial assistance, contact: Financial Aid Office, 115 Student Services Bldg., UTK, Knoxville, TN 37996-0210, (423) 974-3131, finaid@utk.edu.

Internships/Practica: All Clinical students are required to participate in two 12-month practica, one in our Departmental Psychological Clinic and the other in a community mental health facility. Both practica are supervised by doctoral degreed clinical psychologists, and the clientele are children, adolescents, and adults who seek help for their emotional and behavioral problems.

Housing and Day Care: No on-campus housing and day care facilities are available.

Employment of Department Graduates:

Master's Degree Graduates: Of those who graduated in the academic year 2000–2001, the following categories and numbers represent the post-graduate activities and employment of master's degree graduates: Enrolled in a post-doctoral residency/fellowship (n/a), employed in independent practice (n/a).

Doctoral Degree Graduates: Of those who graduated in the academic year 2000–2001, the following categories and numbers represent the post-graduate activities and employment of doctoral degree graduates: Enrolled in a psychology doctoral program (n/a), enrolled in another graduate/professional program (n/a).

Additional Information:

Orientation, Objectives, and Emphasis of Department: The graduate faculty maintain active research programs in cognition, developmental, ethology, gender, health, organizational, personality, phenomenology, psychobiology, psychometrics, sensation/perception, and social psychology. The department has three graduate programs. The MA program in experimental psychology is appropriate for students who desire a master's degree as part of their program toward a doctorate or for those who wish to complement a degree in a different field. The doctoral program in experimental psychology prepares students for academic/research careers and for careers involving the application of psychological principles as practitioners in industrial, forensic, organizational, and community settings. The experimental psychology program offers areas of concentration in applied psychology, child development, cognition, consciousness, health psychology, phenemenology, and social/personality. The clinical program has a strong psychodynamic component, but requires exposure to a wide range of theoretical views and technical practices. Minors in child development, health psychology, and social psychology are available to students in the doctoral clinical program, but are not required. In order to foster appropriate breadth and interdisciplinary training, some cognate work outside the department of psychology is required of all doctoral students.

Special Facilities or Resources: Facilities include computer support in equipment and staff, human and animal laboratories, a psychology clinic for training and research, and a new university library with expanded serials holdings.

Information for Students With Physical Disabilities: The Austin Peay Psychology Building is wheelchair accessible and has an elevator for easy access to all floors, including the Psychological Clinic.

Application Information:
Send to: Ms. Connie J. Ogle, 312D Austin Peay Bldg., University of Tennessee, Knoxville, TN 37996-0900. Students are admitted in the Fall, application deadline February 15. *Fee:* $35.

Tennessee, University of, Knoxville
Industrial and Organizational Psychology Program
Business Administration
408 Stokely Management Center
Knoxville, TN 37996-0545
Telephone: (865) 974-4843
Fax: (865) 974-3163
E-mail: *tladd@utk.edu*
Web: *http://bus.utk.edu/iopsyc/*

Department Established:

1964. Director: Robert T. Ladd. Number of Faculty: total–full-time 5; women–full-time 1.

Programs and Degrees Offered:

Listed in the following order: Program area, degree type (T if terminal Master's), number awarded 7/00–6/01. Industrial/organizational PhD 6.

Student Applications/Admissions:

Student Applications

Industrial/organizational PhD—Applications 2001–2002, 50. Total applicants accepted 2001–2002, 4. New applicants enrolled 2001–2002, 4. Total enrolled 2001–2002 full-time, 24, part-time, 8. Openings 2002–2003, 6. The number of students enrolled full and part-time, who were dismissed or voluntarily withdrew from this program area were 3.

Admissions Requirements:

Scores: Entries appear in this order: required test or GPA, minimum score (if required), median score of students entering in 2001–2002. Doctoral Programs: GRE-V no minimum stated, 540; GRE-Q no minimum stated, 603; GRE-V+Q 1100, 1232; overall undergraduate GPA 3.5, 3.57; last 2 years GPA no minimum stated, 3.73; psychology GPA no minimum stated; psychology GPA no minimum stated.

Other Criteria: (importance of criteria rated low, medium, or high): GRE/MAT scores high, research experience medium, work experience low, extracurricular activity low, clinically related public service low, GPA high, letters of recommendation high, statement of goals and objectives high.

Student Characteristics: The following represents characteristics of students in 2001–2002 in all graduate psychology programs in the department: Female–full-time 15, part-time 2; Male–full-time 8, part-time 0; African American/Black–full-time 1, part-time 0; Hispanic/Latino (a)–full-time 0, part-time 0; Asian/Pacific Islander–full-time 1, part-time 0; American Indian/Alaska Native–full-time 0, part-time 0; Multi-ethnic–full-time 0, part-time 0; students subject to the Americans with Disabilities Act–full-time 0, part-time 0.

Financial Information/Assistance:

Tuition for Full-Time Study: *Doctoral:* State residents: per academic year $4,280, $233 per credit hour; nonstate residents: per academic year $12,066, $666 per credit hour.

Financial Assistance:

First Year Students: Research assistantships available for first-year. Average amount paid per academic year: $11,900. Average number of hours worked per week: 20. Tuition remission given: full. Fellowships and scholarships available for first-year.

Advanced Students: Teaching assistantships available for advanced students. Average amount paid per academic year: $11,900. Average number of hours worked per week: 20. Tuition remission given: full. Research assistantships available for advanced students. Average amount paid per academic year: $11,900. Average number of hours worked per week: 20. Tuition remission given: full. Traineeships available for advanced students. Average amount paid per academic year: $11,900. Average number of hours worked per week: 20. Tuition remission given: full. Fellowships and scholarships available for advanced students.

Contact Information: Of all students currently enrolled full-time, 100% benefited from one or more of the listed financial assistance programs. For information on financial assistance, contact: The I-O Program Office or UT Financial Aid Office, (865) 974-3131, or Office of Graduate Admissions and Records, (423) 974-3251.

Internships/Practica: An internship or practicum is required but these vary considerably.

Housing and Day Care: No on-campus housing and day care facilities are available.

Employment of Department Graduates:

Master's Degree Graduates: Of those who graduated in the academic year 2000–2001, the following categories and numbers represent the post-graduate activities and employment of master's degree graduates: Enrolled in a post-doctoral residency/fellowship (n/a), employed in independent practice (n/a).

Doctoral Degree Graduates: Of those who graduated in the academic year 2000–2001, the following categories and numbers represent the post-graduate activities and employment of doctoral degree graduates: Enrolled in a psychology doctoral program (n/a), enrolled in another graduate/professional program (n/a), employed in an academic position at a university (2), employed in business or industry (research/consulting) (2), employed in business or industry (management) (2).

Additional Information:

Orientation, Objectives, and Emphasis of Department: The industrial/organizational program is designed to prepare students for personnel, managerial, and organizational research; for university teaching; and for consulting relationships with industry. The program emphasizes a scientist-practitioner model in applying and conducting research based on accepted theory found in classical and modern organization theory, organizational behavior, psychology, management, and statistics.

Special Facilities or Resources: Computing and Academic Services (CAS) provides computing facilities, services, and support for the university's teaching, research, public service, and administrative activities. Individual UNIX and Lotus Notes accounts are provided for students, faculty and staff for the duration of their affiliation with UTK at no charge. CAS maintains six staffed computing labs, 15 unstaffed labs, and supports computing installations in all residence halls. Training and documentation are also available through CAS. Statistical and mathematical consulting is available to all students, faculty, and staff. CAS operates the core mainframe and large-scale servers; equipment includes multiple systems from SUN, SGI, and IBM systems. In addition to university computing services and facilities, the Department of Management and the College of Business Administration provide students with microcomputers in student offices, which are networked to departmental printers and the Internet. The University Libraries own approximately 2 million volumes and subscribe to more than 11,000 periodicals and other serial titles. The Libraries' membership in the Association of Research Libraries reflects the University's emphasis on graduate instruction and research and the support of comprehensive collections of library materials on a permanent basis.

Information for Students With Physical Disabilities: Prospective students are encouraged to contact Disability Services (DS) to assure that campus facilities and services are adequate to meet their needs for interpreters, readers, accessible facilities, etc. Van service is provided to individuals with mobility limitations. Documentation of disability from an attending physician or the Student Health Center is required.

Application Information:

Send to: Department chair. Students are admitted in the Fall, application deadline February 1. *Fee:* $35.

The University of Memphis
Department of Counseling, Educational Psychology and
  Research, Program in Counseling Psychology
Education
100 Ball Building
Memphis, TN 38152
Telephone: (901) 678-2841
Fax: (901) 678-5114
E-mail: *slease@memphis.edu*
Web: *http://www.people.memphis.edu/~coe_cepr/*

Department Established:

1972. Chairperson: Ronnie Priest. Number of Faculty: total–full-time 25, part-time 3; women–full-time 14, part-time 1; minority–full-time 6, part-time 1.

Programs and Degrees Offered:

Listed in the following order: Program area, degree type (T if terminal Master's), number awarded 7/00–6/01. Counseling psychology PhD 8.

APA Accreditation: Counseling PhD: full.

Student Applications/Admissions:

Student Applications

Counseling psychology PhD—Applications 2001–2002, 30. Total applicants accepted 2001–2002, 12. New applicants enrolled 2001–2002, 8. Total enrolled 2001–2002 full-time, 33, part-time, 8. Openings 2002–2003, 8. The Median number of years required for completion of a degree are 4. The number of students enrolled full and part-time, who were dismissed or voluntarily withdrew from this program area were 0.

Admissions Requirements:

Scores: Entries appear in this order: required test or GPA, minimum score (if required), median score of students entering in 2001–2002. Doctoral Programs: GRE-V no minimum stated, 570; GRE-Q no minimum stated, 560; GRE-V+Q 1000, 1130; last 2 years GPA no minimum stated; psychology GPA no minimum stated; psychology GPA 3.5, 3.87. GRE score information is for PhD in Counseling Psychology only.

Other Criteria: (importance of criteria rated low, medium, or high): GRE/MAT scores high, research experience medium, work experience medium, clinically related public service low, GPA high, letters of recommendation high, interview high, statement of goals and objectives high.

Student Characteristics: The following represents characteristics of students in 2001–2002 in all graduate psychology programs in the department: Female–full-time 21, part-time 7; Male–full-time 12, part-time 1; African American/Black–full-time 1, part-time 1; Hispanic/Latino (a)–full-time 1, part-time 0; Asian/Pacific Islander–full-time 2, part-time 2; American Indian/Alaska Native–full-time 0, part-time 0; students subject to the Americans with Disabilities Act–full-time 2.

Financial Information/Assistance:

Tuition for Full-Time Study: *Master's:* State residents per academic year $6,282, $234 per credit hour; nonstate residents: per academic year $15,398, $512 per credit hour. *Doctoral:* State residents: per academic year $6,282, $234 per credit hour; nonstate residents: per academic year $15,398, $512 per credit hour.

Financial Assistance:

First Year Students: Teaching assistantships available for first-year. Average amount paid per academic year: $3,300. Average number of hours worked per week: 10. Apply by 4/1/03. Tuition remission given: full. Research assistantships available for first-year. Average amount paid per academic year: $3,300. Average number of hours worked per week: 10. Apply by 4/1/03. Tuition remission given: full.

Advanced Students: Teaching assistantships available for advanced students. Average amount paid per academic year: $3,300. Average number of hours worked per week: 10. Apply by 4/1/03. Tuition remission given: full. Research assistantships available for advanced students. Average amount paid per academic year: $3,300. Average number of hours worked per week: 10. Apply by 4/1/03. Tuition remission given: full. Traineeships available for advanced students. Average amount paid per academic year: $14,000. Average number of hours worked per week: 20. Apply by Ranges.

Contact Information: Of all students currently enrolled full-time, 100% benefited from one or more of the listed financial assistance programs. For information on financial assistance, contact: Ronnie Priest, Department Chair, 100 Ball Building, The University of Memphis, Memphis, TN 38152.

Internships/Practica: Internships. The department has no doctoral internships. Students are expected to complete a 2000 hour predoctoral APA-accredited internship upon completion of their doctoral coursework. Doctoral students complete a minimum of two practica during their three years of coursework; many students complete up to four practica. The department has an extensive network of relationships with community agencies for providing practicum placements for students. These placements include: university and college counseling centers, hospitals, community mental health centers, private practice, and correctional services. For those doctoral students for whom a professional internship is required prior to graduation, 9 applied in 2000–2001. Of those who applied, 9 were placed in internships listed by the Association of Psychology Postdoctoral and Internship Programs (APPIC); 9 were placed in APA accredited internships.

Housing and Day Care: On-campus housing and day care facilities are available.

Employment of Department Graduates:

Master's Degree Graduates: Of those who graduated in the academic year 2000–2001, the following categories and numbers represent the post-graduate activities and employment of master's degree graduates: Enrolled in a post-doctoral residency/fellowship (n/a), employed in independent practice (n/a).

Doctoral Degree Graduates: Of those who graduated in the academic year 2000–2001, the following categories and numbers represent the post-graduate activities and employment of doctoral degree graduates: Enrolled in a psychology doctoral program (n/a), enrolled in another graduate/professional program (n/a), enrolled in a post-doctoral residency/fellowship (2), employed in independent practice (1), employed in business or industry (research/consulting) (2), employed in a hospital/medical center (1).

Additional Information:

Orientation, Objectives, and Emphasis of Department: The PhD in Counseling Psychology at The University of Memphis is designed to train psychologists who promote human development in the areas of mental health, career development, emotional and social learning, and decision-making in a rapidly changing environment. Training is organized around the scientist-practitioner model of critical thinking and emphasizes responsibility and commitment to human welfare. Didactic and experiential activities are designed to anchor persons firmly within the discipline of psychology. The program emphasizes research, development, prevention, and remediation as vehicles for helping individuals, families, and groups achieve competence and a sense of well-being. The department has a strong commitment to training professionals to work with diverse populations in urban settings. Within the context of the University mission, students are expected to develop the critical thinking skills necessary for lifelong learning and to contribute to the global community. Students are expected to acquire: (1) an identity as a counseling psychologist; (2) a knowledge foundation in psychology, research, counseling, psychological evaluation, and professional standards; and (3) skills in research, practice, and teaching. The program is individualized to meet the student's goals. Graduates are prepared for positions in various settings including counseling centers, mental health centers, hospitals, private practice, or teaching and research.

Special Facilities or Resources: Department faculty have research teams that provide opportunities for faculty and students to collaborate on research and consultation products. Faculty also work closely with both the Vocational Evaluation Lab in the Rehabilitation Counseling program and the Center for Research on Educational Policy. These centers provide opportunities for faculty and students to collaborate with educational and community leaders. Students are frequently involved in grant-funded research through assistantships at The University of Memphis Prevention Center.

Information for Students With Physical Disabilities: The Student Disability Services Office provides, arranges, and coordinates academic accommodations and support services to qualified students with disabilities to enable them to fully access the educational opportunities at The University of Memphis.

Application Information:
Send to: Suzanne Lease/Thomas Sayger, Counseling Psychology Admissions, 100 Ball Building, The University of Memphis, Memphis, TN 38152. Students are admitted in the Fall, application deadline January 15. The application for the Counseling Psychology program can be obtained on-line from the program Web page. Applications for programs other than Counseling Psychology go to the Admissions Secretary, department office address. *Fee:* $25.

Vanderbilt University
Department of Psychology
111 21st Avenue South
Nashville, TN 37240-0009
Telephone: (615) 322-2874
Fax: (615) 343-8449
E-mail: *patricia.m.burns@vanderbilt.edu*
Web: *http://www.vanderbilt.edu*

Department Established:
1925. Chairperson: Timothy P. McNamara. Number of Faculty: total—full-time 27, part-time 2; women—full-time 6, part-time 1; minority—full-time 3.

Programs and Degrees Offered:
Listed in the following order: Program area, degree type (T if terminal Master's), number awarded 7/00–6/01. Clinical science PhD 3, cognitive science PhD 1, neuroscience PhD.

APA Accreditation: Clinical PhD: full.

Student Applications/Admissions:
Student Applications
Clinical science PhD—Applications 2001–2002, 91. Total applicants accepted 2001–2002, 3. New applicants enrolled 2001–2002, 2. Total enrolled 2001–2002 full-time, 19. Openings 2002–2003, 3. The Median number of years required for completion of a degree are 6. The number of students enrolled full and part-time, who were dismissed or voluntarily withdrew from this program area were 0. Cognitive science PhD—Applications 2001–2002, 22. Total applicants accepted 2001–2002, 6. New applicants enrolled 2001–2002, 3. Total enrolled 2001–2002 full-time, 11. Openings 2002–2003, 3. The Median number of years required for completion of a degree are 8. The number of students enrolled full and part-time, who were dismissed or voluntarily withdrew from this program area were 0. Neuroscience PhD—Applications 2001–2002, 17. Total ap-

plicants accepted 2001–2002, 3. New applicants enrolled 2001–2002, 2. Total enrolled 2001–2002 full-time, 13. Openings 2002–2003, 3. The number of students enrolled full and part-time, who were dismissed or voluntarily withdrew from this program area were 1.

Admissions Requirements:
Scores: Entries appear in this order: required test or GPA, minimum score (if required), median score of students entering in 2001–2002. Doctoral Programs: GRE-V 550, 595; GRE-Q 550, 750; GRE-V+Q 1100, 1315; GRE-Analytical 650, 715; GRE-V+Q+Analytical 1750, 2939; GRE-Subject(Psych) 650, 680; last 2 years GPA 3.00, 3.86; psychology GPA 3.50, 3.90; psychology GPA no minimum stated.
Other Criteria: (importance of criteria rated low, medium, or high): GRE/MAT scores medium, research experience high, work experience low, extracurricular activity low, clinically related public service low, GPA medium, letters of recommendation high, interview high, statement of goals and objectives high.

Student Characteristics: The following represents characteristics of students in 2001–2002 in all graduate psychology programs in the department: Female–full-time 21, part-time 0; Male–full-time 22, part-time 0; African American/Black–full-time 3, part-time 0; Hispanic/Latino (a)–full-time 0, part-time 0; Asian/Pacific Islander–full-time 8, part-time 0; American Indian/Alaska Native–full-time 0, part-time 0; Multi-ethnic–full-time 0, students subject to the Americans with Disabilities Act–full-time 0.

Financial Information/Assistance:
Tuition for Full-Time Study: *Doctoral:* State residents: per academic year $25,200, $1,050 per credit hour; nonstate residents: per academic year $25,200, $1,050 per credit hour.

Financial Assistance:
First Year Students: Teaching assistantships available for first-year. Average amount paid per academic year: $11,700. Average number of hours worked per week: 15. Apply by January 15. Research assistantships available for first-year. Average amount paid per academic year: $11,700. Average number of hours worked per week: 15. Apply by January 15. Traineeships available for first-year. Average amount paid per academic year: $16,500. Average number of hours worked per week: 15. Apply by January 15. Fellowships and scholarships available for first-year. Average amount paid per academic year: $11,700. Average number of hours worked per week: 15. Apply by January 15.
Advanced Students: Teaching assistantships available for advanced students. Average amount paid per academic year: $11,700. Average number of hours worked per week: 15. Apply by January 15. Research assistantships available for advanced students. Average amount paid per academic year: $11,700. Average number of hours worked per week: 15. Apply by January 15. Traineeships available for advanced students. Average amount paid per academic year: $16,500. Average number of hours worked per week: 15. Apply by January 15. Fellowships and scholarships available for advanced students. Average amount paid per academic year: $11,700. Average number of hours worked per week: 15. Apply by January 15.
Contact Information: Of all students currently enrolled full-time, 88% benefited from one or more of the listed financial

assistance programs. On the application form there is a question asking if student is applying for financial assistance.

Internships/Practica: We offer 18 different placements for students to do their practica. These include two VA Medical Centers; VU Child and Adolescent Psychiatric Hospital; VU Diabetes Center, VU Psychological and Counseling Center; Mobile Crisis Response Service; Public School System; State Prison; and Mental Health facilities for both children and adults.

Housing and Day Care: On-campus housing and day care facilities are available.

Employment of Department Graduates:

Master's Degree Graduates: Of those who graduated in the academic year 2000–2001, the following categories and numbers represent the post-graduate activities and employment of master's degree graduates: Enrolled in a post-doctoral residency/fellowship (n/a), employed in independent practice (n/a).

Doctoral Degree Graduates: Of those who graduated in the academic year 2000–2001, the following categories and numbers represent the post-graduate activities and employment of doctoral degree graduates: Enrolled in a psychology doctoral program (n/a), enrolled in another graduate/professional program (n/a), employed in an academic position at a university (1), employed in other positions at a higher education institution (1), employed in a hospital/medical center (2).

Additional Information:

Orientation, Objectives, and Emphasis of Department: The department emphasizes the basic science of psychology. The faculty are particularly concerned with research on cognitive abilities, the lifetime development of cognitive and neural function pathologies (especially depression and emotional disorders), and the development, organization, and function of the nervous system as it relates to these abilities and maladies. A major goal of the department is the placement of its graduates in academic settings. The program leads to the PhD in the three general areas of clinical science, cognitive science, and neuroscience. In addition to formal training, students receive extensive research experience by working intensively with individual faculty members. This experience is felt to be one of the more vital aspects of the student's training. Vanderbilt offers doctoral training designed to familiarize students with current problems in psychology and to prepare them for a variety of careers in psychological science.

Special Facilities or Resources: The psychology building includes facilities for computer-based research and teaching, as well as extensive space and equipment for modern neuroscience research. Collaborative research programs are operative with the Vanderbilt School of Medicine, the School of Engineering, the Department of Electrical and Biomedical Engineering, and the Department of Psychology and Human Development (Peabody). The general library provides a large collection of books and journals in all areas of psychology.

Information for Students With Physical Disabilities: The Opportunity Development Center coordinates services for persons with disabilities as part of a continuing effort to make the campus accessible.

Application Information:
Send to: Graduate School Office, Vanderbilt University, 411 Kirkland Hall, Nashville, TN 37240. Students are admitted in the Fall, application deadline January 15. *Fee:* $40. Waiver of application fee is rarely granted.

Vanderbilt University
Human & Org. Dev./Community Research & Action
Peabody College of Ed. & Human Development
Box 90
Nashville, TN 37203
Telephone: (615) 322-8484
Fax: (615) 343-2661
E-mail: *douglas.d.perkins@vanderbilt.edu*
Web: *http://peabody.vanderbilt.edu/depts/hod/*

Department Established:
1999. Chairperson: Joseph Cunningham, EdD. Number of Faculty: total–full-time 17, part-time 17; women–full-time 8, part-time 3; minority–full-time 1, part-time 2.

Programs and Degrees Offered:
Listed in the following order: Program area, degree type (T if terminal Master's), number awarded 7/00–6/01. Community Research & Action PhD 1, Human Development Counseling MA (T) 17, Human, Org., & Community Devel MA (T).

Student Applications/Admissions:
Student Applications

Community Research & Action PhD—Applications 2001–2002, 13. Total applicants accepted 2001–2002, 6. New applicants enrolled 2001–2002, 4. Total enrolled 2001–2002 full-time, 12, part-time, 1. Openings 2002–2003, 5. The Median number of years required for completion of a degree are 8. The number of students enrolled full and part-time, who were dismissed or voluntarily withdrew from this program area were 0. *Human Development Counseling MA*—Applications 2001–2002, 50. Total applicants accepted 2001–2002, 24. New applicants enrolled 2001–2002, 22. Total enrolled 2001–2002 full-time, 45, part-time, 2. Openings 2002–2003, 24. The Median number of years required for completion of a degree is 1. The number of students enrolled full and part-time, who were dismissed or voluntarily withdrew from this program area were 2. *Human, Org., & Community Devel MA*—Applications 2001–2002, 6. Total applicants accepted 2001–2002, 2. New applicants enrolled 2001–2002, 2. Total enrolled 2001–2002 full-time, 1, part-time, 1. Openings 2002–2003, 8. The Median number of years required for completion of a degree is 1. The number of students enrolled full and part-time, who were dismissed or voluntarily withdrew from this program area were 0.

Admissions Requirements:
Scores: Entries appear in this order: required test or GPA, minimum score (if required), median score of students entering in 2001–2002. Master's Programs: GRE-V 480, 550; GRE-Q 480, 560; GRE-V+Q 1000, 1100; MAT 50, 50; overall undergraduate GPA 2.9, 3.5. The MEd in HDC and HOCD will take either the MAT or GRE scores. A GPA of 3.0 is essential. Doctoral Programs: GRE-V 500, 600; GRE-Q 530,

630; GRE-V+Q 1100, 1200; overall undergraduate GPA 3.0, 3.6; last 2 years GPA 3.3, 3.7; psychology GPA 3.4, 3.8; psychology GPA 3.3, 3.7.

Other Criteria: (importance of criteria rated low, medium, or high): GRE/MAT scores high, research experience medium, work experience low, clinically related public service low, GPA high, letters of recommendation high, interview low, statement of goals and objectives high, fit with program high. Research experience and GRE less important for Master's programs than for PhD. Clinically related service helpful for counseling program; not relevant to community master's and PhD.

Student Characteristics: The following represents characteristics of students in 2001–2002 in all graduate psychology programs in the department: Female–full-time 40, part-time 2; Male–full-time 7; African American/Black–full-time 6, part-time 1; Hispanic/Latino (a)–full-time 0; Asian/Pacific Islander–full-time 0; American Indian/Alaska Native–full-time 0; Multi-ethnic–full-time 0; students subject to the Americans with Disabilities Act–full-time 1.

Financial Information/Assistance:

Tuition for Full-Time Study: *Master's:* State residents per academic year $13,446, $747 per credit hour; nonstate residents: per academic year $13,446, $747 per credit hour. *Doctoral:* State residents: per academic year $18,900, $1,050 per credit hour; nonstate residents: per academic year $18,900, $1,050 per credit hour.

Financial Assistance:

First Year Students: Teaching assistantships available for first-year. Average amount paid per academic year: $10,000. Average number of hours worked per week: 20. Apply by 1/15-2/15. Tuition remission given: full. Research assistantships available for first-year. Average amount paid per academic year: $10,000. Average number of hours worked per week: 20. Apply by 1/15-2/15. Tuition remission given: full. Traineeships available for first-year. Average amount paid per academic year: $18,156. Average number of hours worked per week: 20. Apply by 1/15-2/15. Tuition remission given: full. Fellowships and scholarships available for first-year. Average amount paid per academic year: $20,000. Average number of hours worked per week: 20. Apply by 1/15-2/15. Tuition remission given: full.

Advanced Students: Teaching assistantships available for advanced students. Average amount paid per academic year: $11,000. Average number of hours worked per week: 20. Tuition remission given: full. Research assistantships available for advanced students. Average amount paid per academic year: $11,000. Average number of hours worked per week: 20. Tuition remission given: full. Traineeships available for advanced students. Average amount paid per academic year: $18,156. Average number of hours worked per week: 20. Tuition remission given: full. Fellowships and scholarships available for advanced students. Average amount paid per academic year: $20,000. Average number of hours worked per week: 20. Tuition remission given: full.

Contact Information: Of all students currently enrolled full-time, 100% benefited from one or more of the listed financial assistance programs. Above information is for PhD program only. Some support available for Master's. Contact department.

Internships/Practica: The HOCD and CRA programs require an 8-to-15-week internship. Possible sites: Mayor's Office/Metro Council/Planning Commission, Local or international community development organization, Regional planning or civic design center, Youth development center, Healthcare corporation, Neighborhood health clinic, Alcohol and drug treatment center, Welfare or housing agency, State health and human service agencies, Vanderbilt Institute for Public Policy Studies (Centers for Mental Health Policy, Evaluation Research and Methodology, Child and Family Policy, Crime and Justice Policy, Environmental Management Studies, Health Policy, Psychotherapy Research and Policy, State and Local Policy). The HDC Program requires a one-year internship that provides opportunities to apply knowledge and skills primarily in the areas of: Social Service Agencies, Mental Health Centers, Schools (K–12), Employee Assistance Programs, Other Human Services Delivery Programs.

Housing and Day Care: On-campus housing and day care facilities are available.

Employment of Department Graduates:

Master's Degree Graduates: Of those who graduated in the academic year 2000–2001, the following categories and numbers represent the post-graduate activities and employment of master's degree graduates: Enrolled in a psychology doctoral program (2), enrolled in another graduate/professional program (0), enrolled in a post-doctoral residency/fellowship (n/a), employed in independent practice (n/a), employed in an academic position at a university (0), employed in an academic position at a 2-year/4-year college (0), employed in other positions at a higher education institution (0), employed in a professional position in a school system (10), employed in business or industry (research/consulting) (2), employed in business or industry (management) (4), employed in a government agency (research) (0), employed in a government agency (professional services) (0), employed in a community mental health/counseling center (6), employed in a hospital/medical center (0), still seeking employment (3), other employment position (0).

Doctoral Degree Graduates: Of those who graduated in the academic year 2000–2001, the following categories and numbers represent the post-graduate activities and employment of doctoral degree graduates: Enrolled in a psychology doctoral program (n/a), enrolled in another graduate/professional program (n/a).

Additional Information:

Orientation, Objectives, and Emphasis of Department: Although the vast majority of faculty in the department are psychologists, our orientation is interdisciplinary. There are three graduate programs, all oriented to helping diverse communities and individuals identify and develop their strengths: a long-standing Master's in Human Development Counseling (HDC), a Master's in Human, Organizational, and Community Development (HOCD), and a PhD in Community Research and Action (CRA). The latter two started in 2001. The HDC Program prepares students to meet the psychological needs of the normally developing population, who sometimes require professional help. Through a humanistic training model and a two-year curriculum, students develop a strong theoretical grounding in life-span human development, and school or community counseling. The HOCD program is for those who desire training for program administration/evaluation work in either public or private, international or domestic, community service, planning, or development organizations. The Doctoral Degree in Community Research and Action is designed to train action-researchers for academic or program/

policy-related careers in applied community studies: i.e., community psychology, community development, prevention, community health/mental health, organizational change, and ethics. Coursework in qualitative and quantitative methods and evaluation research is required. The program builds on the one in Community Psychology previously in the Department of Psychology and Human Development and reflects the move in the field to become interdisciplinary.

Special Facilities or Resources: Peabody College has its own library, several computer centers, and nationally known research centers, including the Learning Sciences Institute and the Kennedy Center for Research on Human Development, mental retardation and other disabilities. Also on the beautiful and historic Peabody campus is the Vanderbilt Institute for Public Policy Studies (Centers for Mental Health Policy, Evaluation Research and Methodology, Child and Family Policy, Crime and Justice Policy, Environmental Management Studies, Health Policy, Psychotherapy Research and Policy, State and Local Policy). Located in Nashville, the Tennessee state capital, opportunities abound for research and internships in state and local health and human service agencies and schools.

Application Information:
Send to: For PhD program: The Graduate School, Vanderbilt University, 411 Kirkland Hall, Nashville, Tennessee 37240, http://peabody.vanderbilt.edu/depts/hod/hodweb/grad/gradapp.html. For Master's programs: Peabody College of Vanderbilt University, Office of Administration and Records, P.O. Box 327, Nashville, TN 37203, (615) 322-8400, Email: peabody.admissions@vanderbilt.edu http://peabody.vanderbilt.edu/admin/studentsvc/forprosp.html. For further information on application procedures, write, call or email: Graduate Secretary, Department of Human and Organizational Development, Vanderbilt University, Box 90, Peabody College Nashville, Tennessee 37203, (615) 322-8484, FAX (615) 322-1141, sherrie.a.lane@vanderbilt.edu. Students are admitted in the Fall, application deadline January 15. Rolling admissions for MEd in Human Development Counseling. *Fee:* $40.

Abilene Christian University

Department of Psychology
College of Arts & Sciences
ACU Box 28011
Abilene, TX 79699
Telephone: (915) 674-2310
Fax: (915) 674-6968
E-mail: *robert.mckelvain@psyc.acu.edu*
Web: *http://www.acu.edu/psychology*

Department Established:
1968. Chair: Robert McKelvain. Number of Faculty: total–full-time 8, part-time 5; women–full-time 2, part-time 1; minority–full-time 2.

Programs and Degrees Offered:
Listed in the following order: Program area, degree type (T if terminal Master's), number awarded 7/00–6/01. Clinical psychology MA (T) 9, Counseling Psychology, School Psychology.

Student Applications/Admissions:
Student Applications
Clinical psychology MA—Applications 2001–2002, 24. Total applicants accepted 2001–2002, 21. New applicants enrolled 2001–2002, 11. Total enrolled 2001–2002 full-time, 11. Openings 2002–2003, 15. The Median number of years required for completion of a degree are 2. The number of students enrolled full and part-time, who were dismissed or voluntarily withdrew from this program area were 0.

Admissions Requirements:
Scores: Entries appear in this order: required test or GPA, minimum score (if required), median score of students entering in 2001–2002. Master's Programs: GRE-V+Q 1000; overall undergraduate GPA 3.00. Doctoral Programs: last 2 years GPA no minimum stated; psychology GPA no minimum stated; psychology GPA no minimum stated.
Other Criteria: (importance of criteria rated low, medium, or high): GRE/MAT scores high, research experience high, work experience medium, extracurricular activity medium, clinically related public service medium, GPA high, letters of recommendation high, statement of goals and objectives high.

Student Characteristics: The following represents characteristics of students in 2001–2002 in all graduate psychology programs in the department: Female–full-time 9, part-time 0; Male–full-time 6, part-time 0; African American/Black–full-time 0, part-time 0; Hispanic/Latino (a)–full-time 2, part-time 0; part-time 0; American Indian/Alaska Native–full-time 0, part-time 0.

Financial Information/Assistance:
Tuition for Full-Time Study: *Master's:* State residents $397 per credit hour; nonstate residents: $397 per credit hour.

Financial Assistance:
First Year Students: Teaching assistantships available for first-year. Average amount paid per academic year: $2,500. Aver-

age number of hours worked per week: 10. Apply by April 15. Tuition remission given: partial. Research assistantships available for first-year. Average amount paid per academic year: $2,500. Average number of hours worked per week: 10. Apply by April 15. Tuition remission given: partial. Fellowships and scholarships available for first-year. Average amount paid per academic year: $1,000. Average number of hours worked per week: 0.
Advanced Students: Teaching assistantships available for advanced students. Average amount paid per academic year: $2,500. Average number of hours worked per week: 10. Apply by April 15. Tuition remission given: partial. Research assistantships available for advanced students. Average amount paid per academic year: $2,500. Average number of hours worked per week: 10. Apply by April 15. Tuition remission given: partial.
Contact Information: Of all students currently enrolled full-time, 60% benefited from one or more of the listed financial assistance programs. For information on financial assistance, contact: Contact department chair for information on assistantships/traineeships/psychology scholarships.

Internships/Practica: Full-time paid internships are available for students in the MS in School Psychology.

Housing and Day Care: No on-campus housing and day care facilities are available.

Employment of Department Graduates:
Master's Degree Graduates: Of those who graduated in the academic year 2000–2001, the following categories and numbers represent the post-graduate activities and employment of master's degree graduates: Enrolled in a post-doctoral residency/fellowship (n/a), employed in independent practice (n/a).
Doctoral Degree Graduates: Of those who graduated in the academic year 2000–2001, the following categories and numbers represent the post-graduate activities and employment of doctoral degree graduates: Enrolled in a psychology doctoral program (n/a), enrolled in another graduate/professional program (n/a).

Additional Information:
Orientation, Objectives, and Emphasis of Department: The department has two objectives for its graduate programs: 1) prepare capable students for doctoral study in psychology; 2) prepare students to be effective in psychological assessment and intervention. Programs emphasize short-term cognitive-behavioral strategies with sound empirical support and thorough training in both cognitive and personality assessment. Students may concentrate elective courses in one of three areas: 1) child and adolescent; 2) assessment; 3) health psychology. Within the master's degree students may also pursue a "Graduate Certificate in Conflict Resolution." Faculty share and challenge students to explore the implications and application of a Christian world view.

Application Information:
Send to: ACU Graduate School, ACU Box 29140, Abilene, TX 79699.
Students are admitted in the Fall, application deadline April 15; Spring, application deadline November 1; Summer, application deadline March 1. *Fee:* $25.

Angelo State University

Department of Psychology and Sociology
2601 West Avenue North
San Angelo, TX 76909
Telephone: (915) 942-2068
Fax: (915) 942-2290
E-mail: *Bill.Davidson@angelo.edu*
Web: *http://www.angelo.edu/dept/psysoc*

Department Established:

1983. Department Head: William B. Davidson. Number of Faculty: total–full-time 11, part-time 3; women–full-time 2, part-time 1; minority–full-time 2, part-time 1.

Programs and Degrees Offered:

Listed in the following order: Program area, degree type (T if terminal Master's), number awarded 7/00–6/01. Counseling, general MA (T) 1, industrial/organizational MA (T) 1.

Student Applications/Admissions:

Student Applications

General MA—Applications 2001–2002, 4. Total applicants accepted 2001–2002, 3. New applicants enrolled 2001–2002, 1. Total enrolled 2001–2002 full-time, 1. Openings 2002–2003, 15. The Median number of years required for completion of a degree are 2. *Industrial/organizational MA*—Applications 2001–2002, 10. Total applicants accepted 2001–2002, 8. New applicants enrolled 2001–2002, 6. Total enrolled 2001–2002 full-time, 5, part-time, 1. Openings 2002–2003, 10. The Median number of years required for completion of a degree are 2.

Admissions Requirements:

Scores: Entries appear in this order: required test or GPA, minimum score (if required), median score of students entering in 2001–2002. Master's Programs: GRE-V 440; GRE-Analytical 440; overall undergraduate GPA 2.75. Doctoral Programs: last 2 years GPA no minimum stated; psychology GPA no minimum stated; psychology GPA no minimum stated.
Other Criteria: (importance of criteria rated low, medium, or high): GRE/MAT scores high, GPA high, statement of goals and objectives high.

Student Characteristics: The following represents characteristics of students in 2001–2002 in all graduate psychology programs in the department: Female–full-time 30, part-time 9; Male–full-time 6, part-time 2; African American/Black–full-time 2, part-time 0; Hispanic/Latino (a)–full-time 5, part-time 1; Asian/Pacific Islander–full-time 1, part-time 0; American Indian/Alaska Native–full-time 0, part-time 0.

Financial Information/Assistance:

Tuition for Full-Time Study: *Master's:* State residents per academic year $2,266, $95 per credit hour; nonstate residents: per academic year $7,330, $306 per credit hour.

Financial Assistance:

First Year Students: Teaching assistantships available for first-year. Average amount paid per academic year: $5,255. Average number of hours worked per week: 17. Apply by April 15.

Advanced Students: Teaching assistantships available for advanced students. Average amount paid per academic year: $9,381. Average number of hours worked per week: 20. Apply by April 15.

Contact Information: Of all students currently enrolled full-time, 50% benefited from one or more of the listed financial assistance programs. For information on financial assistance, contact: Office of Financial Aid, P.O. Box 11015, ASU.

Internships/Practica: Practicum opportunities are available in many local public and private mental health facilities and also in local corporate entities.

Housing and Day Care: No on-campus housing and day care facilities are available.

Employment of Department Graduates:

Master's Degree Graduates: Of those who graduated in the academic year 2000–2001, the following categories and numbers represent the post-graduate activities and employment of master's degree graduates: Enrolled in a post-doctoral residency/fellowship (n/a), employed in independent practice (n/a).
Doctoral Degree Graduates: Of those who graduated in the academic year 2000–2001, the following categories and numbers represent the post-graduate activities and employment of doctoral degree graduates: Enrolled in a psychology doctoral program (n/a), enrolled in another graduate/professional program (n/a).

Additional Information:

Orientation, Objectives, and Emphasis of Department: The department emphasizes personalized training, small class sizes, and a balance between research skills and practitioner skills.

Special Facilities or Resources: The department is equipped with a state-of-the-art psychology laboratory and a microcomputer laboratory.

Application Information:

Send to: Office of the Graduate Dean, P.O. Box 11025, ASU. Students are admitted in the Fall, application deadline July 15; Spring, application deadline November 15; Summer, application deadline April 15. *Fee:* $25.

Baylor University

Department of Psychology and Neuroscience,
  PhD Program in Neuroscience
Arts and Sciences
P.O. Box 97334
Waco, TX 76798-7334
Telephone: (254) 710-2961
Fax: (254) 710-3033
E-mail: *Jim_Patton@baylor.edu*
Web: *http://www.baylor.edu/~Psychology*

Department Established:

1950. Chairperson: Jim H. Patton. Number of Faculty: total–full-time 15, part-time 9; women–full-time 3, part-time 8; minority–full-time 2, part-time 1.

Programs and Degrees Offered:

Listed in the following order: Program area, degree type (T if terminal Master's), number awarded 7/00–6/01. Clinical Psychology PsyD 10.

Student Applications/Admissions:

Student Applications

Clinical Psychology PsyD—Applications 2001–2002, 129. Total applicants accepted 2001–2002, 11. New applicants enrolled 2001–2002, 11. Total enrolled 2001–2002 full-time, 43. Openings 2002–2003, 11. The Median number of years required for completion of a degree are 4. The number of students enrolled full and part-time, who were dismissed or voluntarily withdrew from this program area were 1.

Admissions Requirements:

Scores: Entries appear in this order: required test or GPA, minimum score (if required), median score of students entering in 2001–2002. Doctoral Programs: GRE-V no minimum stated; GRE-Q no minimum stated; GRE-V+Q no minimum stated; GRE-Analytical no minimum stated; GRE-V+Q+Analytical no minimum stated; overall undergraduate GPA 2.80; last 2 years GPA no minimum stated; psychology GPA 3.00; psychology GPA no minimum stated.

Other Criteria: (importance of criteria rated low, medium, or high): GRE/MAT scores high, research experience high, work experience medium, extracurricular activity medium, clinically related public service low, GPA high, letters of recommendation high, statement of goals and objectives medium, autobiography medium.

Student Characteristics: The following represents characteristics of students in 2001–2002 in all graduate psychology programs in the department: Female–full-time 36, part-time 0; Male–full-time 16, part-time 0; African American/Black–full-time 2, part-time 0; Hispanic/Latino (a)–full-time 4, part-time 0; Asian/Pacific Islander–full-time 1, part-time 0; American Indian/Alaska Native–full-time 0, part-time 0; students subject to the Americans with Disabilities Act–full-time 0.

Financial Information/Assistance:

Tuition for Full-Time Study: *Doctoral:* State residents: $654 per credit hour; nonstate residents: $654 per credit hour.

Financial Assistance:

First Year Students: Teaching assistantships available for first-year. Average amount paid per academic year: $15,000. Average number of hours worked per week: 20. Apply by Jan 15. Research assistantships available for first-year. Average amount paid per academic year: $15,000. Average number of hours worked per week: 20. Apply by Jan 15. Traineeships available for first-year. Average amount paid per academic year: $15,000. Average number of hours worked per week: 20. Apply by Jan 15.

Advanced Students: Teaching assistantships available for advanced students. Average amount paid per academic year: $15,000. Average number of hours worked per week: 20. Apply by Jan 15. Research assistantships available for advanced students. Average amount paid per academic year: $15,000. Average number of hours worked per week: 20. Apply by Jan 15. Traineeships

available for advanced students. Average amount paid per academic year: $15,000. Average number of hours worked per week: 20. Apply by Jan 15.

Contact Information: Of all students currently enrolled full-time, 100% benefited from one or more of the listed financial assistance programs. For information on financial assistance, contact: Graduate Coordinator (254) 710-2811 or P.O. Box 97334, Baylor University, Waco, TX 76798-7334.

Internships/Practica: No information provided.

Housing and Day Care: No on-campus housing and day care facilities are available.

Employment of Department Graduates:

Master's Degree Graduates: Of those who graduated in the academic year 2000–2001, the following categories and numbers represent the post-graduate activities and employment of master's degree graduates: Enrolled in a post-doctoral residency/fellowship (n/a), employed in independent practice (n/a).

Doctoral Degree Graduates: Of those who graduated in the academic year 2000–2001, the following categories and numbers represent the post-graduate activities and employment of doctoral degree graduates: Enrolled in a psychology doctoral program (n/a), enrolled in another graduate/professional program (n/a), enrolled in a post-doctoral residency/fellowship (2), employed in independent practice (11), employed in an academic position at a university (0), still seeking employment (0).

Additional Information:

Orientation, Objectives, and Emphasis of Department: The department offers a broad range of courses in the areas of behavioral and molecular clinical neuroscience. Extensive training is provided in laboratory research and design. PhD students are expected to acquire sufficient knowledge and expertise to permit them to work as independent scholars at the frontier of their field upon graduation, with most graduates pursuing academically oriented careers. The Doctor of Philosophy degree is ultimately awarded to those individuals who have attained a high level of scholarship in a selected field through independent study, research, and creative thought.

Special Facilities or Resources: The department has a number of well-equipped research laboratories. PhD program: Computer-controlled programmable laboratory in memory and cognition; complete facilities for research on animal learning and behavior (including animal colony); developmental psychobiology laboratory, with facilities for behavioral and pharmacological research, including teratological studies; inhalation chambers for administration of ethanol (and other substances). Single-subject brain-recording (EEG) and electron microscopy facilities available.

Information for Students With Physical Disabilities: Fully accessible classrooms.

Application Information:

Send to: Graduate Coordinator, Department of Psychology, Baylor University, P.O. Box 97334, Waco, TX 76798-7334. Students are admitted in the Fall. Neuroscience January 15. Clinical Psychology January 15. *Fee:* $25.

Houston Baptist University (2001 data)
Psychology Department
7502 Fondren Road
Houston, TX 77074
Telephone: (713) 774-7661
Fax: (281) 649 3361
E-mail: *aowen@hbu.edu*

Department Established:
1985. Director of Graduate Studies in Behavioral Sciences: Ann Owen, PhD. Number of Faculty: total–full-time 6, part-time 4; women–full-time 4, part-time 2; minority–full-time 1.

Programs and Degrees Offered:
Listed in the following order: Program area, degree type (T if terminal Master's), number awarded 7/00–6/01. Master of Arts in Psychology MA (T) 10.

Student Applications/Admissions:
Student Applications

Master of Arts in Psychology MA The Median number of years required for completion of a degree are 2.

Admissions Requirements:

Scores: Entries appear in this order: required test or GPA, minimum score (if required), median score of students entering in 2001–2002. Master's Programs: GRE-V 400; GRE-Q no minimum stated; GRE-V+Q 850; overall undergraduate GPA 3.2.

Other Criteria: (importance of criteria rated low, medium, or high): GRE/MAT scores high, GPA high, letters of recommendation medium, statement of goals and objectives medium.

Student Characteristics: The following represents characteristics of students in 2001–2002 in all graduate psychology programs in the department: Female–full-time 0, part-time 0; Male–full-time 0, part-time 0; African American/Black–full-time 0, part-time 0; Hispanic/Latino (a)–full-time 0, part-time 0; Asian/Pacific Islander–full-time 0, part-time 0; American Indian/Alaska Native–full-time 0, part-time 0.

Financial Information/Assistance:
Tuition for Full-Time Study: No information provided.

Financial Assistance:
First Year Students: No information provided.
Advanced Students: No information provided.
Contact Information: Of all students currently enrolled full-time, 0% benefited from one or more of the listed financial assistance programs. For information on financial assistance, contact: Office of Financial Aid.

Internships/Practica: Students complete their practicum requirements (450 clock hours supervised by a licensed psychologist) in area hospitals, social service agencies, schools, and counseling centers.

Housing and Day Care: No on-campus housing and day care facilities are available.

Employment of Department Graduates:
Master's Degree Graduates: Of those who graduated in the academic year 2000–2001, the following categories and numbers represent the post-graduate activities and employment of master's degree graduates: Enrolled in a post-doctoral residency/fellowship (n/a), employed in independent practice (n/a).

Doctoral Degree Graduates: Of those who graduated in the academic year 2000–2001, the following categories and numbers represent the post-graduate activities and employment of doctoral degree graduates: Enrolled in a psychology doctoral program (n/a), enrolled in another graduate/professional program (n/a).

Additional Information:
Orientation, Objectives, and Emphasis of Department: The master's program follows the scientist-practitioner model of training. Some students become psychological associates, some seek doctoral training, and some pursue licensure as professional counselors.

Special Facilities or Resources: The department has a faculty of dedicated, teaching professionals. All graduate faculty hold terminal degrees. Computer facilities are available for use in research and statistics.

Application Information:
Send to: Master of Arts in Psychology, Houston Baptist University, 7502 Fondren, Houston, TX 77074. Students are admitted in the Fall, application deadline August 1; Winter, application deadline November 1; Spring, application deadline February 1; Summer, application deadline May 1. Deadlines are flexible. *Fee:* $25.

Houston, University of
Department of Psychology
College of Liberal Arts and Social Sciences
126 Heyne
Houston, TX 77204-5022
Telephone: (713) 743-8508
Fax: (713) 743-8588
E-mail: *jvincent@uh.edu*
Web: *http://www.psychology.uh.edu*

Department Established:
1939. Chairperson: John P. Vincent. Number of Faculty: total–full-time 24, part-time 3; women–full-time 8.

Programs and Degrees Offered:
Listed in the following order: Program area, degree type (T if terminal Master's), number awarded 7/00–6/01. Clinical PhD 13, clinical neuropsychology PhD 1, developmental PhD 8, industrial-organizational PhD 5, social PhD 3.

APA Accreditation: Clinical PhD: full.

Student Applications/Admissions:
Student Applications

Clinical PhD—Applications 2001–2002, 73. Total applicants accepted 2001–2002, 12. New applicants enrolled 2001–2002, 5. Total enrolled 2001–2002 full-time, 64. Openings 2002–

2003, 8. The Median number of years required for completion of a degree are 5. The number of students enrolled full and part-time, who were dismissed or voluntarily withdrew from this program area were 2. *Clinical neuropsychology PhD*—Applications 2001–2002, 0. Total enrolled 2001–2002 full-time, 2. The Median number of years required for completion of a degree are 5. The number of students enrolled full and part-time, who were dismissed or voluntarily withdrew from this program area were 0. *Developmental PhD*—Applications 2001–2002, 0. Total enrolled 2001–2002 full-time, 7. The Median number of years required for completion of a degree are 4. The number of students enrolled full and part-time, who were dismissed or voluntarily withdrew from this program area were 3. *Industrial-organizational PhD*—Applications 2001–2002, 45. Total applicants accepted 2001–2002, 7. New applicants enrolled 2001–2002, 5. Total enrolled 2001–2002 full-time, 28. Openings 2002–2003, 6. The Median number of years required for completion of a degree are 4. The number of students enrolled full and part-time, who were dismissed or voluntarily withdrew from this program area were 1. *Social PhD*—Applications 2001–2002, 20. Total applicants accepted 2001–2002, 7. New applicants enrolled 2001–2002, 5. Total enrolled 2001–2002 full-time, 15. Openings 2002–2003, 4. The Median number of years required for completion of a degree are 4. The number of students enrolled full and part-time, who were dismissed or voluntarily withdrew from this program area were 0.

Admissions Requirements:

Scores: Entries appear in this order: required test or GPA, minimum score (if required), median score of students entering in 2001–2002. Doctoral Programs: GRE-V+Q+Analytical no minimum stated; overall undergraduate GPA no minimum stated; last 2 years GPA no minimum stated; psychology GPA no minimum stated; psychology GPA no minimum stated. Clinical median: GRE-V 640, GRE-Q 670, Analytical 660. Social median: GRE-V 580, GRE-Q 600, Analytical 620. Industrial/Organizational median: GRE-V 675, GRE-Q 645, Analytical 560.

Other Criteria: (importance of criteria rated low, medium, or high): GRE/MAT scores medium, research experience high, work experience medium, extracurricular activity medium, clinically related public service medium, GPA medium, letters of recommendation high, interview high, statement of goals and objectives high. The clinical program requires an interview.

Student Characteristics: The following represents characteristics of students in 2001–2002 in all graduate psychology programs in the department: Female–full-time 11, part-time 0; Male–full-time 3, part-time 0; African American/Black–full-time 0, part-time 0; Hispanic/Latino (a)–full-time 0, part-time 0; Asian/Pacific Islander–full-time 0, part-time 0; American Indian/Alaska Native–full-time 0, part-time 0.

Financial Information/Assistance:

Tuition for Full-Time Study: *Doctoral:* State residents: per academic year $4,632, $258 per credit hour; nonstate residents: per academic year $10,962, $469 per credit hour.

Financial Assistance:

First Year Students: Teaching assistantships available for first-year. Average amount paid per academic year: $11,220. Average number of hours worked per week: 20. Apply by w/app. Tuition remission given: partial. Research assistantships available for first-year. Average amount paid per academic year: $11,220. Average number of hours worked per week: 20. Apply by w/app. Tuition remission given: partial. Fellowships and scholarships available for first-year. Average amount paid per academic year: $2,000. Apply by w/app. Tuition remission given: partial.

Advanced Students: Teaching assistantships available for advanced students. Average amount paid per academic year: $12,780. Average number of hours worked per week: 20. Apply by w/app. Tuition remission given: full. Research assistantships available for advanced students. Average amount paid per academic year: $12,780. Average number of hours worked per week: 20. Apply by w/app. Tuition remission given: full. Fellowships and scholarships available for advanced students. Average amount paid per academic year: $2,000. Apply by w/app.

Contact Information: Of all students currently enrolled full-time, 85% benefited from one or more of the listed financial assistance programs. For information on financial assistance, contact: Dr. Suzanne Kieffer, Director of Administrative and Academic Affairs, Department of Psychology, 126 Heyne Building, University of Houston, Houston, TX 77204-5022, (713) 743-8500.

Internships/Practica: Internships are available for both advanced master's and doctoral students at a number of sites that include private industry, medical centers, state hospitals, and private practices. For those doctoral students for whom a professional internship is required prior to graduation, 10 applied in 2000–2001. Of those who applied, 10 were placed in internships listed by the Association of Psychology Postdoctoral and Internship Programs (APPIC); 10 were placed in APA accredited internships.

Housing and Day Care: On-campus housing and day care facilities are available.

Employment of Department Graduates:

Master's Degree Graduates: Of those who graduated in the academic year 2000–2001, the following categories and numbers represent the post-graduate activities and employment of master's degree graduates: Enrolled in a post-doctoral residency/fellowship (n/a), employed in independent practice (n/a).

Doctoral Degree Graduates: Of those who graduated in the academic year 2000–2001, the following categories and numbers represent the post-graduate activities and employment of doctoral degree graduates: Enrolled in a psychology doctoral program (n/a), enrolled in another graduate/professional program (n/a).

Additional Information:

Orientation, Objectives, and Emphasis of Department: Clinical offers APA-approved training in research, assessment, intervention, and consultation related to complex human problems, including behavioral problems having a neurological basis. Industrial/organizational offers broad training in industrial/organizational psychology with options for specialization in either the personnel or organizational subfields. Social emphasizes research careers in behavioral and preventive medicine, and interpersonal interaction processes, with an emphasis on close relationships.

Special Facilities or Resources: The facilities of the department are comparable to those of any major department in any large university. A variety of community settings are available for applied research in all areas of specialization. Specialized laboratories have modern equipment for research in small group process, family and couple interaction, biofeedback, personnel interviewing, and electrophysiology. We have complete closed-circuit TV, recording, transcribing, and duplication equipment. A laboratory preschool and its population are available on campus. Research and clinical practica are available at Houston Child Guidance Center, Texas Department of Corrections, the Neurosensory Center, and several hospitals (the Texas Medical Center is one of the largest in the world). The department has over 150 Microsoft Windows NT computer work stations. Statistical and word processing labs are also available.

Application Information:

Send to: Academic Affairs Office, Department of Psychology, University of Houston, Houston, TX 77204-5022. Students are admitted in the Fall, application deadline see below. Deadline for clinical is December 1, for I/O and Social is January 15. We are not accepting applications for developmental at this time. *Fee:* $40. In cases of financial hardship, a waiver of the application fee may be requested by writing to: Dr. Roy Lachman, Director of Graduate Education, University of Houston, Department of Psychology, 126 Heyne, Houston, TX 77204-5022.

Houston, University of, College of Education
Department of Educational Psychology
College of Education
491 Farish Hall
Houston, TX 77204-5029
Telephone: (713) 743-5019
Fax: (713) 743-4996
E-mail: *bmcph@uh.edu*
Web: *http://www.coe.uh.edu*

Department Established:

Chairperson: Robert McPherson. Number of Faculty: total–full-time 18, part-time 8; women–full-time 6, part-time 3; minority–full-time 1.

Programs and Degrees Offered:

Listed in the following order: Program area, degree type (T if terminal Master's), number awarded 7/00–6/01. Counseling Psychology PhD 4, educational psychology PhD 6.

APA Accreditation: Counseling PhD: full.

Student Applications/Admissions:

Student Applications

Counseling Psychology PhD—Applications 2001–2002, 45. Total applicants accepted 2001–2002, 9. New applicants enrolled 2001–2002, 9. Total enrolled 2001–2002 full-time, 67. Openings 2002–2003, 10. The Median number of years required for completion of a degree are 5. The number of students enrolled full and part-time, who were dismissed or voluntarily withdrew from this program area were 1. *Educational psychology PhD*—Applications 2001–2002, 15. Total applicants accepted 2001–2002, 7. New applicants enrolled 2001–2002, 7. Total enrolled 2001–2002 full-time, 25, part-time, 18. Openings 2002–2003,

10. The Median number of years required for completion of a degree are 5. The number of students enrolled full and part-time, who were dismissed or voluntarily withdrew from this program area were 0.

Admissions Requirements:

Scores: Entries appear in this order: required test or GPA, minimum score (if required), median score of students entering in 2001–2002. Master's Programs: GRE-V no minimum stated; GRE-Q no minimum stated; GRE-V+Q no minimum stated; GRE-Analytical no minimum stated; GRE-V+Q+Analytical no minimum stated; last 2 years GPA no minimum stated. Doctoral Programs: GRE-V no minimum stated; GRE-Q no minimum stated; GRE-V+Q no minimum stated; GRE-Analytical no minimum stated; GRE-V+Q+Analytical no minimum stated; last 2 years GPA no minimum stated; psychology GPA no minimum stated; psychology GPA no minimum stated. The State of Texas does not allow GRE scores to be the sole reason for denial into the program.

Other Criteria: (importance of criteria rated low, medium, or high): GRE/MAT scores high, research experience high, work experience high, extracurricular activity high, clinically related public service high, GPA high, letters of recommendation high, interview high, statement of goals and objectives high. Each applicant's admission file is reviewed in a wholistic fashion. Fit with the program's goals and faculty, research interests, and expertise are the overriding criteria for admissions.

Student Characteristics: The following represents characteristics of students in 2001–2002 in all graduate psychology programs in the department: Female–full-time 88, part-time 0; Male–full-time 31, part-time 0; African American/Black–full-time 13, part-time 0; Hispanic/Latino (a)–full-time 14, part-time 0; Asian/Pacific Islander–full-time 7, part-time 0; American Indian/Alaska Native–full-time 0, part-time 0; students subject to the Americans with Disabilities Act–full-time 5.

Financial Information/Assistance:

Tuition for Full-Time Study: *Master's:* State residents $132 per credit hour; nonstate residents: $350 per credit hour. *Doctoral:* State residents: $132 per credit hour; nonstate residents: $350 per credit hour.

Financial Assistance:

First Year Students: Teaching assistantships available for first-year. Average amount paid per academic year: $12,360. Tuition remission given: full and partial. Research assistantships available for first-year. Average amount paid per academic year: $12,360. Tuition remission given: full and partial. Fellowships and scholarships available for first-year. Tuition remission given: full and partial.

Advanced Students: Teaching assistantships available for advanced students. Average amount paid per academic year: $12,360. Tuition remission given: full and partial. Research assistantships available for advanced students. Average amount paid per academic year: $12,360. Tuition remission given: full and partial. Fellowships and scholarships available for advanced students. Tuition remission given: full and partial.

Contact Information: Of all students currently enrolled full-time, 20% benefited from one or more of the listed financial

assistance programs. For information on financial assistance, contact: (713) 743-9090.

Internships/Practica: Doctoral students in Educational Psychology do not participate in a practica or internship.

Housing and Day Care: No on-campus housing and day care facilities are available.

Employment of Department Graduates:
Master's Degree Graduates: Of those who graduated in the academic year 2000–2001, the following categories and numbers represent the post-graduate activities and employment of master's degree graduates: Enrolled in a post-doctoral residency/fellowship (n/a), employed in independent practice (n/a).
Doctoral Degree Graduates: Of those who graduated in the academic year 2000–2001, the following categories and numbers represent the post-graduate activities and employment of doctoral degree graduates: Enrolled in a psychology doctoral program (n/a), enrolled in another graduate/professional program (n/a).

Additional Information:
Orientation, Objectives, and Emphasis of Department: Students working in the program ordinarily will prepare for faculty positions in colleges or universities, or for academic leadership and research positions in school systems and other educational settings. Thus, the program has as its objectives: (a) Acquisition of knowledge related to the differences among individuals that impact educational outcomes including individual differences in intellectual and affective development, cognition, personality, motivation, and behavior in both normal and exceptional populations. (b) Acquisition of quantitative and qualitative research strategies used to assess individual differences and to investigate the environmental, social, and psychological factors related to them. (c) Development of the ability to conduct original research within one or more areas of educational psychology and individual differences.

Special Facilities or Resources: The facilities of the department are comparable to those of any major department in any large university. An extensive array of resources for data analysis and computer applications is available within the college. The Micro-Computing Center contains computer terminals that are linked to the University's mainframe running the Conversational Monitoring System (CMS). The center also includes 20 DOS machines, 20 Macintosh, and multimedia laboratory which includes modern instructional media (Laser Disc Technology, etc.). Assistance is provided to students wishing to use the computers by a staff of three graduate assistants. The laboratory functions as a teaching laboratory for courses in statistics, methodology, and data management.

Information for Students With Physical Disabilities: It is the policy of the Educational Psychology Department to encourage applications from students with disabilities and members of minority groups at both the Master's and Doctoral levels. The Department desires to educate professionals whose backgrounds reflect the multicultural environment of Houston. Students with disabilities and members of minority groups will be given the fullest consideration, including performance on non-standardized measures of scholastic potential such as a history of achievement, experience in the field, and/or a personal interview. Students

with disabilities and members of minority groups may provide a statement describing their unique circumstances and are encouraged to include additional evidence of their potential for graduate study.

Application Information:
Send to: Ms. Mary Bess Kelley, University of Houston, Room 160, Farish Hall, Houston, TX 77204-5871. Students are admitted in the Fall. January 1st for Counseling Psychology; April 1st for Educational Psychology. *Fee:* $50.

Houston, University of, College of Education
Department of Educational Psychology/Counseling Psychology
College of Education
4800 Calhoun Boulevard
Houston, TX 77204-5029
Telephone: (713) 743-5019
Fax: (713) 743-4996
E-mail: *epsy@uh.edu*
Web: *http://www.coe.uh.edu*

Department Established:
1980. Chairperson: Robert McPherson. Number of Faculty: total–full-time 18; women–full-time 5; minority–full-time 3.

Programs and Degrees Offered:
Listed in the following order: Program area, degree type (T if terminal Master's), number awarded 7/00–6/01. Counseling psychology PhD 10, Educational Psychology PhD (T) 5.

APA Accreditation: Counseling PhD: full.

Student Applications/Admissions:
Student Applications
*Counseling psychology PhD—*Applications 2001–2002, 75. Total applicants accepted 2001–2002, 9. New applicants enrolled 2001–2002, 9. Total enrolled 2001–2002 full-time, 9. Openings 2002–2003, 8. The Median number of years required for completion of a degree are 5. The number of students enrolled full and part-time, who were dismissed or voluntarily withdrew from this program area were 0. *Educational Psychology PhD—*Applications 2001–2002, 5. Total applicants accepted 2001–2002, 5. New applicants enrolled 2001–2002, 5. Total enrolled 2001–2002 full-time, 5. Openings 2002–2003, 10. The Median number of years required for completion of a degree are 5. The number of students enrolled full and part-time, who were dismissed or voluntarily withdrew from this program area were 0.

Admissions Requirements:
Scores: Entries appear in this order: required test or GPA, minimum score (if required), median score of students entering in 2001–2002. Master's Programs: GRE-V 30%; GRE-Q 30%; GRE-Analytical 30%; MAT 30%; overall undergraduate GPA 2.6, 3.0. Doctoral Programs: GRE-V 35%; GRE-Q 35%; GRE-Analytical 35%; last 2 years GPA no minimum stated; psychology GPA no minimum stated; psychology GPA 3.5.
Other Criteria: (importance of criteria rated low, medium, or high): GRE/MAT scores high, research experience high, work

experience high, extracurricular activity high, clinically related public service high, GPA high, letters of recommendation high, interview high, statement of goals and objectives high. Each applicant's admission file is reviewed in a wholistic fashion. Fit with the program's goals and faculty, research interests and expertise are the overriding criteria for admissions.

Student Characteristics: The following represents characteristics of students in 2001–2002 in all graduate psychology programs in the department: Female–full-time 50, part-time 200; Male–full-time 25, part-time 75; African American/Black–full-time 10, part-time 20; Hispanic/Latino (a)–full-time 20, part-time 15; Asian/Pacific Islander–full-time 5, part-time 10; American Indian/Alaska Native–full-time 5, part-time 10; Multi-ethnic–full-time 15, part-time 5; students subject to the Americans with Disabilities Act–full-time 0, part-time 15.

Financial Information/Assistance:
Tuition for Full-Time Study: *Master's:* State residents per academic year $1,812, $258 per credit hour; nonstate residents: per academic year $4,344, $469 per credit hour. *Doctoral:* State residents: per academic year $1,812, $258 per credit hour; nonstate residents: per academic year $4,344, $469 per credit hour.

Financial Assistance:
First Year Students: Teaching assistantships available for first-year. Average amount paid per academic year: $800. Average number of hours worked per week: 20. Tuition remission given: partial. Research assistantships available for first-year. Average amount paid per academic year: $800. Average number of hours worked per week: 20. Tuition remission given: partial.
Advanced Students: Teaching assistantships available for advanced students. Average amount paid per academic year: $850. Average number of hours worked per week: 20. Tuition remission given: partial. Research assistantships available for advanced students. Average amount paid per academic year: $850. Average number of hours worked per week: 20. Tuition remission given: partial.
Contact Information: Of all students currently enrolled full-time, 85% benefited from one or more of the listed financial assistance programs. For information on financial assistance, contact: (713) 743-9090.

Internships/Practica: All doctoral students participate in a supervised practica for a time period of one to two years. These practica take place at numerous sites throughout the Houston area. Students may choose to work at a site that follows along with their particular interest including: school systems, Veterans Hospitals, and Counseling Centers. In addition, students are required to complete a one year full time APA accredited internship approved by the faculty. These sites also range in orientation, focus, and geographic location throughout the United States. For those doctoral students for whom a professional internship is required prior to graduation, 10 applied in 2000–2001. Of those who applied, 10 were placed in internships listed by the Association of Psychology Postdoctoral and Internship Programs (APPIC); 10 were placed in APA accredited internships.

Housing and Day Care: On-campus housing and day care facilities are available.

Employment of Department Graduates:
Master's Degree Graduates: Of those who graduated in the academic year 2000–2001, the following categories and numbers represent the post-graduate activities and employment of master's degree graduates: Enrolled in a post-doctoral residency/fellowship (n/a), employed in independent practice (n/a).
Doctoral Degree Graduates: Of those who graduated in the academic year 2000–2001, the following categories and numbers represent the post-graduate activities and employment of doctoral degree graduates: Enrolled in a psychology doctoral program (n/a), enrolled in another graduate/professional program (n/a).

Additional Information:
Orientation, Objectives, and Emphasis of Department: The primary intent of the doctoral program in counseling psychology is to prepare highly skilled psychologists in the scientist-practitioner model of counseling. Several unifying themes distinguish counseling psychology from other psychological specialties. Included are its focus on: (a) working with relatively well-functioning or "healthy" people; (b) developmental and relatively short-term, situational difficulties faced at "choice points" in people's lives or during periods of stress; (c) educational and developmental theory and interventions; and (d) prevention. From this vantage point, counseling psychologists may assume several roles in a variety of settings in the professional community. These may include supervision and training of counselors and other "helping" personnel; providing personal, educational, and career counseling services; college and university teaching; research; and consultation to public systems, schools, and other community organizations concerned with psychological and interpersonal development.

Special Facilities or Resources: The facilities of the department are comparable to those of any major department in any large university. An extensive array of resources for data analysis and computer applications is available within the college. The Micro-Computing Center contains computer terminals that are linked to the University's mainframe running the Conversational Monitoring System (CMS). The center also includes 20 DOS machines, 20 Macintosh, and multimedia laboratory which includes modern instructional media (Laser Disc Technology, etc.). Assistance is provided to students wishing to use the computers by a staff of three graduate assistants. The laboratory functions as a teaching laboratory for courses in statistics, methodology, and data management.

Information for Students With Physical Disabilities: It is the policy of the Educational Psychology Department to encourage applications from students with disabilities and members of minority groups at both the Master's and Doctoral levels. The Department desires to educate professionals whose backgrounds reflect the multicultural environment of Houston. Students with disabilities and members of minority groups will be given the fullest consideration, including performance on non-standardized measures of scholastic potential such as a history of achievement, experience in the field, and/or a personal interview. Students with disabilities and members of minority groups may provide a statement describing their unique circumstances and are encouraged to include additional evidence of their potential for graduate study.

Application Information:
Send to: Ms. Mary Bess Kelley, University of Houston, Room 160, Farish Hall, Houston, TX 77204-5871. Students are admitted in the Fall, application deadline Jan. 15, Mar 1; Spring, application deadline. January 15 is for counseling psych doctoral fall admission. March 1 is for counseling master's fall admission. April 1 is for Educational Psychology doctoral for fall. *Fee:* $50. $50 is for doctoral applicants. $35 is for the master's application.

Lamar University-Beaumont
Department of Psychology
Arts & Sciences
P.O. Box 10036
Beaumont, TX 77710
Telephone: (409) 880-8285
Fax: (409) 880-1779
E-mail: *fitzpatrod@hal.lamar.edu*
Web: *http://www.Lamar.edu*

Department Established:
1964. Chairperson: Oney D. Fitzpatrick, Jr. Number of Faculty: total–full-time 9, part-time 4; women–full-time 5; minority–full-time 1.

Programs and Degrees Offered:
Listed in the following order: Program area, degree type (T if terminal Master's), number awarded 7/00–6/01. Community-clinical MA (T) 2, industrial-organizational MA (T) 5.

Student Applications/Admissions:
Student Applications
Community-clinical MA—Applications 2001–2002, 8. Total applicants accepted 2001–2002, 6. New applicants enrolled 2001–2002, 4. Total enrolled 2001–2002 full-time, 7, part-time, 3. Openings 2002–2003, 5. The Median number of years required for completion of a degree are 2. The number of students enrolled full and part-time, who were dismissed or voluntarily withdrew from this program area were 0. *Industrial-organizational MA*—Applications 2001–2002, 6. Total applicants accepted 2001–2002, 5. New applicants enrolled 2001–2002, 4. Total enrolled 2001–2002 full-time, 9, part-time, 2. Openings 2002–2003, 5. The Median number of years required for completion of a degree are 2. The number of students enrolled full and part-time, who were dismissed or voluntarily withdrew from this program area were 0.

Admissions Requirements:
Scores: Entries appear in this order: required test or GPA, minimum score (if required), median score of students entering in 2001–2002. Master's Programs: GRE-V 450, 520; GRE-Q 450, 510; GRE-V+Q 900, 1020; overall undergraduate GPA 2.75; last 2 years GPA 2.75. Doctoral Programs: last 2 years GPA no minimum stated; psychology GPA no minimum stated; psychology GPA no minimum stated.
Other Criteria: (importance of criteria rated low, medium, or high): GRE/MAT scores medium, research experience medium, work experience medium, extracurricular activity low, clinically related public service low, GPA medium, letters of recommendation medium, statement of goals and objectives low.

Student Characteristics: The following represents characteristics of students in 2001–2002 in all graduate psychology programs in the department: Female–full-time 9, part-time 2; Male–full-time 7, part-time 3; African American/Black–full-time 1, part-time 0; Hispanic/Latino (a)–full-time 1, part-time 0; Asian/Pacific Islander–full-time 0, part-time 0; American Indian/Alaska Native–full-time 0, part-time 0.

Financial Information/Assistance:
Tuition for Full-Time Study: *Master's:* State residents per academic year $2,024, $156 per credit hour; nonstate residents: per academic year $7,208, $283 per credit hour.

Financial Assistance:
First Year Students: Teaching assistantships available for first-year. Average amount paid per academic year: $4,800. Average number of hours worked per week: 20. Fellowships and scholarships available for first-year. Average amount paid per academic year: $1,000.
Advanced Students: Teaching assistantships available for advanced students. Average amount paid per academic year: $4,800. Average number of hours worked per week: 20. Fellowships and scholarships available for advanced students. Average amount paid per academic year: $1,000.
Contact Information: Of all students currently enrolled full-time, 85% benefited from one or more of the listed financial assistance programs. For information on financial assistance, contact: Department Chair.

Internships/Practica: A variety of community health settings provide useful practicum experiences for Community-Clinical students in child, adolescent, and adult counseling and assessment. Practicum experiences for the Industrial/Organizational students places them in a variety of organizational and industrial work environment.

Housing and Day Care: On-campus housing and day care facilities are available.

Employment of Department Graduates:
Master's Degree Graduates: Of those who graduated in the academic year 2000–2001, the following categories and numbers represent the post-graduate activities and employment of master's degree graduates: Enrolled in a psychology doctoral program (2), enrolled in a post-doctoral residency/fellowship (n/a), employed in independent practice (n/a), employed in business or industry (research/consulting) (2), employed in a community mental health/counseling center (1).
Doctoral Degree Graduates: Of those who graduated in the academic year 2000–2001, the following categories and numbers represent the post-graduate activities and employment of doctoral degree graduates: Enrolled in a psychology doctoral program (n/a), enrolled in another graduate/professional program (n/a).

Additional Information:
Orientation, Objectives, and Emphasis of Department: The Department of Psychology offers a program of study leading to the Master of Science degree in applied psychology. It is designed to prepare professional personnel for employment in business,

industry, or community mental health agencies. The MS in Community-Clinical Psychology includes training in therapy techniques for individuals, groups, and families. The MS in Industrial/Organizational Psychology integrates the traditional areas of industrial psychology with the more contemporary areas of organizational development and analysis.

Application Information:

Send to: Graduate Admissions, Lamar University, Box 10078, Beaumont, Texas 77710. Students are admitted in the Fall, application deadline March 15.

Midwestern State University

Department of Psychology
College of Liberal Arts
3410 Taft Boulevard
Wichita Falls, TX 76308
Telephone: (940) 397-4340
Fax: (940) 397-4682
E-mail: *george.diekhoff@mwsu.edu*
Web: *http://www.mwsu.edu*

Department Established:

1975. Chairperson: George M. Diekhoff. Number of Faculty: total–full-time 5, part-time 2; women–full-time 1; minority–full-time 1.

Programs and Degrees Offered:

Listed in the following order: Program area, degree type (T if terminal Master's), number awarded 7/00–6/01. Clinical MA (T) 5, counseling MA (T) 5, school MA (T).

Student Applications/Admissions:

Student Applications

Clinical MA—Applications 2001–2002, 11. Total applicants accepted 2001–2002, 9. New applicants enrolled 2001–2002, 7. Total enrolled 2001–2002 full-time, 16, part-time, 2. Openings 2002–2003, 15. The Median number of years required for completion of a degree are 2. The number of students enrolled full and part-time, who were dismissed or voluntarily withdrew from this program area were 0. *Counseling* MA—Applications 2001–2002, 11. Total applicants accepted 2001–2002, 9. New applicants enrolled 2001–2002, 7. Total enrolled 2001–2002 full-time, 16, part-time, 2. Openings 2002–2003, 15. The Median number of years required for completion of a degree are 2. The number of students enrolled full and part-time, who were dismissed or voluntarily withdrew from this program area were 0. *School* MA—Applications 2001–2002, 2. Total applicants accepted 2001–2002, 2. New applicants enrolled 2001–2002, 2. Total enrolled 2001–2002 full-time, 2. Openings 2002–2003, 15. The Median number of years required for completion of a degree are 3. The number of students enrolled full and part-time, who were dismissed or voluntarily withdrew from this program area were 0.

Admissions Requirements:

Scores: Entries appear in this order: required test or GPA, minimum score (if required), median score of students entering in 2001–2002. Master's Programs: GRE-V no minimum stated,

460; GRE-Q no minimum stated, 490; GRE-Analytical no minimum stated, 530; overall undergraduate GPA no minimum stated, 3.20. Doctoral Programs: last 2 years GPA no minimum stated; psychology GPA no minimum stated; psychology GPA no minimum stated.

Other Criteria: (importance of criteria rated low, medium, or high): GRE/MAT scores high, research experience low, work experience low, extracurricular activity low, clinically related public service low, GPA high, letters of recommendation medium, interview medium, statement of goals and objectives medium.

Student Characteristics: The following represents characteristics of students in 2001–2002 in all graduate psychology programs in the department: Female–full-time 14, part-time 2; Male–full-time 2, part-time 0; African American/Black–full-time 3, part-time 0; Hispanic/Latino (a)–full-time 1, part-time 0; Asian/Pacific Islander–full-time 0, part-time 0; American Indian/Alaska Native–full-time 0, part-time 0.

Financial Information/Assistance:

Tuition for Full-Time Study: *Master's:* State residents per academic year $2,200, $92 per credit hour; nonstate residents: per academic year $7,210, $300 per credit hour.

Financial Assistance:

First Year Students: Research assistantships available for first-year. Average amount paid per academic year: $3,400. Average number of hours worked per week: 5. Apply by July 1/Nov 15. Fellowships and scholarships available for first-year. Average amount paid per academic year: $1,000. Average number of hours worked per week: 0. Apply by July 1/Nov 15. Tuition remission given: partial.

Advanced Students: Teaching assistantships available for advanced students. Average amount paid per academic year: $3,400. Average number of hours worked per week: 5. Apply by July 1/Nov 15. Research assistantships available for advanced students. Average amount paid per academic year: $3,400. Average number of hours worked per week: 5. Apply by July 1/Nov 1. Fellowships and scholarships available for advanced students. Average amount paid per academic year: $1,000. Average number of hours worked per week: 0. Apply by July 1/Nov 1. Tuition remission given: partial.

Contact Information: Of all students currently enrolled full-time, 100% benefited from one or more of the listed financial assistance programs. For information on financial assistance, contact: Psychology Program Chair. Also contact Midwestern State University Financial Aid Office.

Internships/Practica: Students completing the clinical/counseling specialty option complete between 6 and 9 credit hours of practicum for a total of between 300 and 450 clock-hours of work and study in an applied clinical/counseling setting. Students pursuing the school psychology specialty option complete a 3-hour practicum consisting of 150-clock hours of work and study in an applied setting and a 3-hour internship consisting of 1200 hours of on-site supervision in a school setting.

Housing and Day Care: No on-campus housing and day care facilities are available.

Employment of Department Graduates:

> *Master's Degree Graduates:* Of those who graduated in the academic year 2000–2001, the following categories and numbers represent the post-graduate activities and employment of master's degree graduates: Enrolled in a post-doctoral residency/fellowship (n/a), employed in independent practice (n/a).

> *Doctoral Degree Graduates:* Of those who graduated in the academic year 2000–2001, the following categories and numbers represent the post-graduate activities and employment of doctoral degree graduates: Enrolled in a psychology doctoral program (n/a), enrolled in another graduate/professional program (n/a).

Additional Information:

> *Orientation, Objectives, and Emphasis of Department:* We provide two specialty options for the Master of Arts degree in psychology. The first specialty option, clinical/counseling psychology, is available in either a 50-hour or 60-hour curriculum and is designed to lead to certification as a Licensed Professional Counselor (LPC) or Licensed Psychological Associate (LPA). The second specialty option, school psychology, is a 60-hour program designed to lead to certification as a Licensed Specialist in School Psychology (LSSP). Though our emphasis is on training the master's level practitioner, we actively encourage our students to pursue doctoral training, and we see the training we provide as a first step toward that goal.

> *Special Facilities or Resources:* Midwestern State University is located near two state hospitals, a regional community mental health and mental retardation center, and two private psychiatric hospitals. A newly remodeled clinic and computer lab are available for student use, and Graduate Research and Teaching Assistants are provided with office space.

Application Information:

Send to: Program Chair, Psychology Program, Midwestern State University, 3410 Taft, Wichita Falls, TX 76308. Students are admitted in the Fall, application deadline July 1; Spring, application deadline November 15.

Our Lady of the Lake University
Psychology
School of Education and Clinical Studies
411 S.W. 24th Street
San Antonio, TX 78207
Telephone: (210) 431-3914
Fax: (210) 436-0824
E-mail: *gardg@lake.ollusa.edu*
Web: *http://www.ollusa.edu*

Department Established:

> 1983. Chairperson: Joan Biever. Number of Faculty: total–full-time 12; women–full-time 7; minority–full-time 4.

Programs and Degrees Offered:

> Listed in the following order: Program area, degree type (T if terminal Master's), number awarded 7/00–6/01. Counseling psychology PsyD 4, counseling pyschology, marriage and family therapy MA (T) 11, school MA (T) 4.

APA Accreditation: Counseling PsyD: full.

Student Applications/Admissions:

> *Student Applications*

> *Counseling psychology PsyD*—Applications 2001–2002, 45. Total applicants accepted 2001–2002, 5. New applicants enrolled 2001–2002, 5. Total enrolled 2001–2002 full-time, 23, part-time, 12. Openings 2002–2003, 10. The Median number of years required for completion of a degree are 6. The number of students enrolled full and part-time, who were dismissed or voluntarily withdrew from this program area were 2. *Marriage and family therapy MA*—Applications 2001–2002, 15. Total applicants accepted 2001–2002, 10. New applicants enrolled 2001–2002, 10. Total enrolled 2001–2002 full-time, 22, part-time, 9. Openings 2002–2003, 10. The Median number of years required for completion of a degree are 2. The number of students enrolled full and part-time, who were dismissed or voluntarily withdrew from this program area were 1. *School MA*—Applications 2001–2002, 12. Total applicants accepted 2001–2002, 10. New applicants enrolled 2001–2002, 10. Total enrolled 2001–2002 full-time, 18, part-time, 10. Openings 2002–2003, 10. The Median number of years required for completion of a degree are 2+. The number of students enrolled full and part-time, who were dismissed or voluntarily withdrew from this program area were 1.

Admissions Requirements:

> *Scores:* Entries appear in this order: required test or GPA, minimum score (if required), median score of students entering in 2001–2002. Master's Programs: GRE-V none; GRE-Q none; GRE-V+Q none; MAT none; overall undergraduate GPA 2.5; last 2 years GPA 3.0, 3.22. May take either the GRE or the MAT with no minimum score required. Doctoral Programs: GRE-V none, 500; GRE-Q none, 520; GRE-Subject(Psych) none; last 2 years GPA no minimum stated; psychology GPA no minimum stated; psychology GPA 3.5, 3.96. Doctoral applicants must take the GRE subject exam in addition to the standard GRE. There is no minimum score on the GRE subject exam that is required but the student must score a minimum of 600 on the subject exam before they graduate.

> *Other Criteria:* (importance of criteria rated low, medium, or high): GRE/MAT scores medium, research experience low, work experience high, extracurricular activity low, clinically related public service medium, GPA high, letters of recommendation high, interview high, statement of goals and objectives high, fit with program goals high.

Student Characteristics: The following represents characteristics of students in 2001–2002 in all graduate psychology programs in the department: Female–full-time 68, part-time 23; Male–full-time 19, part-time 11; African American/Black–full-time 3, part-time 2; Hispanic/Latino (a)–full-time 38, part-time 12; Asian/Pacific Islander–full-time 2, part-time 0; American Indian/Alaska Native–full-time 1, part-time 0; Multi-ethnic–full-time 0, part-time 0; students subject to the Americans with Disabilities Act–full-time 2, part-time 1.

Financial Information/Assistance:

> **Tuition for Full-Time Study:** *Master's:* State residents $439 per credit hour; nonstate residents: $439 per credit hour. *Doctoral:* State residents: $499 per credit hour; nonstate residents: $499 per credit hour.

Financial Assistance:

First Year Students: Teaching assistantships available for first-year. Average amount paid per academic year: $6,000. Average number of hours worked per week: 12. Apply by not specified. Research assistantships available for first-year. Average amount paid per academic year: $6,000. Average number of hours worked per week: 12. Apply by not specified. Fellowships and scholarships available for first-year. Average amount paid per academic year: $9,000. Average number of hours worked per week: 0. Apply by after admiss.

Advanced Students: Teaching assistantships available for advanced students. Average amount paid per academic year: $6,000. Average number of hours worked per week: 12. Apply by after admiss. Research assistantships available for advanced students. Average amount paid per academic year: $6,000. Average number of hours worked per week: 12. Apply by after admiss. Fellowships and scholarships available for advanced students. Average amount paid per academic year: $9,000. Apply by after admiss.

Contact Information: Of all students currently enrolled full-time, 20% benefited from one or more of the listed financial assistance programs. For information on financial assistance, contact: Department Chair.

Internships/Practica: The psychology department operates a training clinic, the Community Counseling Service (CCS), which serves as the initial practical site for all master's and doctoral students. At the CCS, practica students work in teams of up to six students under the live supervision of psychology faculty. The CCS is located in and serves a low-income, predominantly Mexican-American community. Supervision of Spanish-language psychotherapy is available. A variety of off-campus sites are available to students in their second and subsequent semesters of practica. Students are placed at off-campus sites according to their career interests and training needs. Available practica sites include public and private schools, hospitals, and community agencies.

Housing and Day Care: On-campus housing and day care facilities are available.

Employment of Department Graduates:

Master's Degree Graduates: Of those who graduated in the academic year 2000–2001, the following categories and numbers represent the post-graduate activities and employment of master's degree graduates: Enrolled in a post-doctoral residency/fellowship (n/a), employed in independent practice (n/a).

Doctoral Degree Graduates: Of those who graduated in the academic year 2000–2001, the following categories and numbers represent the post-graduate activities and employment of doctoral degree graduates: Enrolled in a psychology doctoral program (n/a), enrolled in another graduate/professional program (n/a).

Additional Information:

Orientation, Objectives, and Emphasis of Department: Graduate psychology programs at OLLU adhere to the practitioner-scholar model of training and emphasize brief, systemic approaches to psychotherapy. Postmodern and multicultural perspectives are infused throughout the curriculum, including practica. A subspecialty in psychological services for Spanish-speaking populations is available.

Special Facilities or Resources: The department's training clinic serves as both a training and research facility. Research facilities are also available in the building which houses the psychology department.

Information for Students With Physical Disabilities: The university complies with all provisions of the Americans With Disabilities Act. All facilities are fully accessible and support services are available as needed.

Application Information:
Send to: Graduate Admissions Office, Our Lady of the Lake University, 411 SW 24th St., San Antonio, TX 78207. Students are admitted in the Fall, application deadline February 15. February 15 for PsyD program, Fall Admission. March 1 for MS programs, Fall Admission. March 1 and July 1 for MS, School Psychology program, Fall Admission. *Fee:* $100. If accepted, the fee is applied to the first semester's tuition.

Rice University
Department of Psychology
6100 Main Street
Houston, TX 77005-1892
Telephone: (713) 348-4856
Fax: (713) 348-5221
E-mail: *dipboye@rice.edu*
Web: *http://ruf.rice.edu/~psyc/*

Department Established:

1966. Chairperson: Randi C. Martin. Number of Faculty: total–full-time 21; women–full-time 5; minority–full-time 1.

Programs and Degrees Offered:

Listed in the following order: Program area, degree type (T if terminal Master's), number awarded 7/00–6/01. Cognitive PhD 8, human-computer interaction PhD 3, industrial/organizational PhD 7.

Student Applications/Admissions:

Student Applications

Cognitive PhD—Applications 2001–2002, 28. Total applicants accepted 2001–2002, 17. New applicants enrolled 2001–2002, 13. Total enrolled 2001–2002 full-time, 23. Openings 2002–2003, 5. The Median number of years required for completion of a degree are 5. The number of students enrolled full and part-time, who were dismissed or voluntarily withdrew from this program area were 0. *Human-computer interaction PhD*—Applications 2001–2002, 10. Total applicants accepted 2001–2002, 4. New applicants enrolled 2001–2002, 3. Total enrolled 2001–2002 full-time, 7. Openings 2002–2003, 2. The Median number of years required for completion of a degree are 5. *Industrial/organizational PhD*—Applications 2001–2002, 61. Total applicants accepted 2001–2002, 3. New applicants enrolled 2001–2002, 1. Total enrolled 2001–2002 full-time, 12. Openings 2002–2003, 4. The Median number of years required for completion of a degree are 5.

Admissions Requirements:

Scores: Entries appear in this order: required test or GPA, minimum score (if required), median score of students entering

in 2001–2002. Master's Programs: GRE-V no minimum stated; GRE-Q no minimum stated; GRE-V+Q no minimum stated; GRE-Analytical no minimum stated; GRE-V+Q+Analytical no minimum stated; overall undergraduate GPA 3.0; last 2 years GPA no minimum stated; psychology GPA no minimum stated. There is no specific score requirement for test scores. Doctoral Programs: GRE-V no minimum stated, 605; GRE-Q no minimum stated, 694; GRE-V+Q no minimum stated, 1299; GRE-Analytical no minimum stated, 685; GRE-V+Q+Analytical no minimum stated, 1984; overall undergraduate GPA no minimum stated, 3.57; last 2 years GPA no minimum stated, 3.5; psychology GPA no minimum stated, 3.5; psychology GPA no minimum stated, 3.8.

Other Criteria: (importance of criteria rated low, medium, or high): GRE/MAT scores high, research experience high, work experience low, extracurricular activity low, clinically related public service low, GPA high, letters of recommendation high, statement of goals and objectives high.

Student Characteristics: The following represents characteristics of students in 2001–2002 in all graduate psychology programs in the department: Female–full-time 27, part-time 0; Male–full-time 8, part-time 0; African American/Black–full-time 1, part-time 0; Hispanic/Latino (a)–full-time 2, part-time 0; Asian/Pacific Islander–full-time 2, part-time 0; American Indian/Alaska Native–full-time 0, part-time 0.

Financial Information/Assistance:

Tuition for Full-Time Study: *Doctoral:* State residents: per academic year $17,300; nonstate residents: per academic year $17,300.

Financial Assistance:

First Year Students: Fellowships and scholarships available for first-year. Average amount paid per academic year: $12,500. Apply by January 15. Tuition remission given: full.

Advanced Students: Teaching assistantships available for advanced students. Average amount paid per academic year: $12,500. Tuition remission given: full. Research assistantships available for advanced students. Average amount paid per academic year: $12,500. Tuition remission given: full. Fellowships and scholarships available for advanced students. Average amount paid per academic year: $12,500. Apply by January 15. Tuition remission given: full.

Contact Information: Of all students currently enrolled full-time, 77% benefited from one or more of the listed financial assistance programs. For information on financial assistance, contact: Department Chair, Psychology.

Internships/Practica: Graduate students beyond their third year have the opportunity to work in internships in the Houston area. Although not required, many of our students work part-time in local organizations including NASA, the Texas Medical Center, Compaq, and a variety of consulting firms.

Housing and Day Care: No on-campus housing and day care facilities are available.

Employment of Department Graduates:

Master's Degree Graduates: Of those who graduated in the academic year 2000–2001, the following categories and numbers represent the post-graduate activities and employment of master's degree graduates: Enrolled in a psychology doctoral program (3), enrolled in a post-doctoral residency/fellowship (n/a), employed in independent practice (n/a), employed in an academic position at a university (5), employed in business or industry (research/consulting) (4).

Doctoral Degree Graduates: Of those who graduated in the academic year 2000–2001, the following categories and numbers represent the post-graduate activities and employment of doctoral degree graduates: Enrolled in a psychology doctoral program (n/a), enrolled in another graduate/professional program (n/a).

Additional Information:

Orientation, Objectives, and Emphasis of Department: The Rice program emphasizes training in basic and applied research and in the skills necessary to conduct research. The content areas to which this emphasis is applied are cognitive-experimental, neuropsychology, engineering (human factors), human-computer interaction, and industrial/organizational. We believe that training in research and research skills generalizes very broadly to the kinds of tasks that professional psychologists will be asked to perform both in the university laboratory and in addressing such diverse applied questions as organizational management, system design, or program evaluation. A unique feature of the program is that students are encouraged to develop research interests that combine these content areas. Industrial/organizational and human factors psychologists, for example, might collaborate on research dealing with organizational communication via electronic mail. Cognitive and industrial/organizational psychologists might, for instance, investigate cognitive processes underlying performance appraisal; and human factors and cognitive psychologists might collaborate on studies of risk perception and the perceptual and attentional properties of computer displays. Although some of our students prefer to devote their energies to laboratory research in preparation for academic positions in basic areas, many students take advantage of the opportunities we provide for "real world" experience. The department arranges internships or practica in a wide variety of settings for interested advanced students.

Special Facilities or Resources: Graduate students in the Rice Psychology programs benefit from their access to a large and vital Houston business community, NASA, and over 40 teaching and research centers in the Texas Medical Center. Within the department, graduate students in all programs have ready access to a variety of powerful Macintosh (G-4 and iMac) and Windows-based computers that more than meet the needs of students for data collection, simulation, instruction, word processing, and computation. The department contains facilities for the study of dyadic and small group interaction, social judgment, decision making, and computer-interface design. The neuropsychology area has benefited from the recent acquisition of a transcranial magnetic stimulation (TMS) device for investigating brain function, two eye tracking devices, a Silicon Graphics workstation for neuroimaging data analysis and 3D rendering of brains from MRI scans, and a dense-sensor array (128 channel) event-related potential (ERP) recording system that allows the detailed description of neural systems. A proposal is pending that would fund the purchase and operation of a state-of-the art MRI research facility. In addition to the facilities physically located in the Psychology Department, Rice University is constructing a state-of-the-art computer laboratory for research in the social sciences with the support of the National Science Foundation.

Application Information:
Send to: Chairperson. Students are admitted in the Fall, application deadline January 15. *Fee:* $25. Conditions for waiver of fee: Hardship.

Sam Houston State University
Department of Psychology and Philosophy
Education and Applied Science
P.O. Box 2447
Huntsville, TX 77341-2447
Telephone: (936) 294-1210
Fax: (936) 294-3798
E-mail: *psy_dkm@shsu.edu*
Web: *http://www.shsu.edu/cjcenter/forensic/forensic.htm*

Department Established:
1972. Director of Clinical Training: David K. Marcus. Number of Faculty: total–full-time 14, part-time 1; women–full-time 4, part-time 1.

Programs and Degrees Offered:
Listed in the following order: Program area, degree type (T if terminal Master's), number awarded 7/00–6/01. Clinical MA (T) 13, forensic clinical PhD, general MA (T) 2, school MA (T) 5.

Student Applications/Admissions:
Student Applications
Clinical MA—Applications 2001–2002, 41. Total applicants accepted 2001–2002, 29. New applicants enrolled 2001–2002, 19. Total enrolled 2001–2002 full-time, 33, part-time, 1. Openings 2002–2003, 15. The Median number of years required for completion of a degree are 2. The number of students enrolled full and part-time, who were dismissed or voluntarily withdrew from this program area were 2. *Forensic clinical PhD*—Applications 2001–2002, 98. Total applicants accepted 2001–2002, 11. New applicants enrolled 2001–2002, 9. Total enrolled 2001–2002 full-time, 32. Openings 2002–2003, 6. The Median number of years required for completion of a degree are NA. The number of students enrolled full and part-time, who were dismissed or voluntarily withdrew from this program area were 0. *General MA*—Applications 2001–2002, 2. Total applicants accepted 2001–2002, 2. New applicants enrolled 2001–2002, 1. Total enrolled 2001–2002 full-time, 2. Openings 2002–2003, 5. The Median number of years required for completion of a degree are 2. *School MA*—Applications 2001–2002, 6. Total applicants accepted 2001–2002, 5. New applicants enrolled 2001–2002, 4. Total enrolled 2001–2002 full-time, 8. Openings 2002–2003, 10. The Median number of years required for completion of a degree are 3. The number of students enrolled full and part-time, who were dismissed or voluntarily withdrew from this program area were 2.

Admissions Requirements:
Scores: Entries appear in this order: required test or GPA, minimum score (if required), median score of students entering in 2001–2002. Master's Programs: GRE-V no minimum stated; GRE-Q no minimum stated; GRE-V+Q no minimum stated, 1080; overall undergraduate GPA no minimum stated, 3.5. Doctoral Programs: GRE-V no minimum stated; GRE-Q no minimum stated; GRE-V+Q no minimum stated, 1245; GRE-

Subject(Psych) no minimum stated; overall undergraduate GPA no minimum stated, 3.65; last 2 years GPA no minimum stated; psychology GPA no minimum stated; psychology GPA no minimum stated.
Other Criteria: (importance of criteria rated low, medium, or high): GRE/MAT scores high, research experience high, work experience low, extracurricular activity low, clinically related public service medium, GPA high, letters of recommendation high, interview high, statement of goals and objectives high. No interview or statement of goals is required for admission to a master's program.

Student Characteristics: The following represents characteristics of students in 2001–2002 in all graduate psychology programs in the department: Female–full-time 59, part-time 0; Male–full-time 17, part-time 0; African American/Black–full-time 2, part-time 0; Hispanic/Latino (a)–full-time 5, part-time 0; Asian/Pacific Islander–full-time 1, part-time 0; American Indian/Alaska Native–full-time 1, part-time 0.

Financial Information/Assistance:
Tuition for Full-Time Study: *Master's:* State residents per academic year $2,187, $104 per credit hour; nonstate residents: per academic year $6,667, $317 per credit hour. *Doctoral:* State residents: per academic year $2,427, $104 per credit hour; nonstate residents: per academic year $7,552, $317 per credit hour.

Financial Assistance:
First Year Students: Research assistantships available for first-year. Average amount paid per academic year: $10,000. Average number of hours worked per week: 20. Fellowships and scholarships available for first-year. Average amount paid per academic year: $10,000.
Advanced Students: Teaching assistantships available for advanced students. Average amount paid per academic year: $10,000. Average number of hours worked per week: 20. Research assistantships available for advanced students. Average amount paid per academic year: $10,000. Average number of hours worked per week: 20. Traineeships available for advanced students. Average amount paid per academic year: $10,000. Average number of hours worked per week: 20. Fellowships and scholarships available for advanced students. Average amount paid per academic year: $10,000. Average number of hours worked per week: 20.
Contact Information: Of all students currently enrolled full-time, 100% benefited from one or more of the listed financial assistance programs. All of the doctoral students are fully funded with either scholarships, research, teaching, or clinical assistantships. There is no separate application deadline for this funding—admission into the doctoral program automatically comes with financial assistance. A limited number of teaching assistantships are available to students in the terminal master's programs. For information contact the Director of Clinical Training.

Internships/Practica: We offer a variety of internships and practica for each of the applied tracks. Students in the school psychology program complete a one-year internship at various Texas school systems. There are a variety of placements for students in the clinical psychology master's program, including the University Counseling Center, area community mental health centers, and the psychological services centers of the Texas Department of Criminal Justice (TDCJ). Students in the doctoral program in forensic clinical psychology may be assigned to any of the aforementioned clinical sites, as well as to a variety of other practica, including the Harris County Psychiatric Center, the Houston Child Assessment Center, the Sex Offender Treatment Unit of the TDCJ, state schools for delinquent children, and prison programs designed for dual diagnosis inmates. These students also work at our on-campus Psychological Services Center, which provides both general mental health services (e.g., individual psychotherapy, couples counseling, psychological assessment), and forensic services (e.g., risk assessments, competency and sanity evaluations). For those doctoral students for whom a professional internship is required prior to graduation, 4 applied in 2000–2001. Of those who applied, 4 were placed in internships listed by the Association of Psychology Postdoctoral and Internship Programs (APPIC); 4 were placed in APA accredited internships.

Housing and Day Care: On-campus housing and day care facilities are available.

Employment of Department Graduates:

Master's Degree Graduates: Of those who graduated in the academic year 2000–2001, the following categories and numbers represent the post-graduate activities and employment of master's degree graduates: Enrolled in a post-doctoral residency/fellowship (n/a), employed in independent practice (n/a).

Doctoral Degree Graduates: Of those who graduated in the academic year 2000–2001, the following categories and numbers represent the post-graduate activities and employment of doctoral degree graduates: Enrolled in a psychology doctoral program (n/a), enrolled in another graduate/professional program (n/a).

Additional Information:

Orientation, Objectives, and Emphasis of Department: The clinical and school tracks are applied training programs that develop effective Master's-level practitioners. Students in those programs receive extensive and eclectic training in both psychotherapy and psychometrics—including projective techniques—and conclude their training with 450 clock-hours of supervised practicum experience. Graduates can seek certification as psychological associates or licensure as licensed professional counselors in Texas, and graduates of the school program can seek national certification from NASP. The general track involves broader exposure to psychology's core disciplines and allows the student more elective flexibility to craft an individual specialty. Graduates of all three programs often go on to doctoral training elsewhere. Our forensic clinical doctoral program trains scientist-practitioners in applications of clinical psychology to the criminal justice system. Students receive training in such areas as forensic assessment and offender therapy as well as in basic clinical skills. The program is a cooperative venture between the Department of Psychology and the College of Criminal Justice at SHSU. The town of Huntsville is the home of the Texas Department of Criminal Justice—one of the largest penal systems in the world—and provides a prime location for forensic research and practice.

Special Facilities or Resources: The department enjoys ample testing and observation space, including a live animal facility. The university's computing facilities are superb, offering extensive access to personal computers loaded with the latest software. Sam Houston State is one of the country's most active Internet sites. The University's College of Criminal Justice is a prestigious center of inquiry into criminology and corrections. In addition, the state headquarters of the Texas Department of Criminal Justice is down-

town, and six prison units are located in the surrounding area. SHSU thus offers our doctoral students unparalleled resources to complement their clinical training. Nevertheless, the town of Huntsville (population 32,000) is a lovely environment surrounded on three sides by national forest, with the Houston metropolis one hour away.

Application Information:
Send to: Master's applications: Rowland Miller; Applications to PhD program: David Marcus. Department of Psychology Sam Houston State University Huntsville, TX 77341-2447. Students are admitted in the Fall, application deadline July 1; Spring, application deadline November 1; Summer, application deadline April 1. These deadlines are for master's programs. January 15 is the deadline for the forensic PhD program (Fall admission only). *Fee:* $20.

Southern Methodist University
Department of Psychology
Dallas, TX 75275-0442
Telephone: (214) 768-7792
Fax: (214) 768-3910
E-mail: *awassel@mail.smu.edu*
Web: *http://www2.smu.edu/psychology*

Department Established:

1925. Chairperson: Alan Brown. Number of Faculty: total–full-time 13, part-time 4; women–full-time 3, part-time 3; minority–full-time 1.

Programs and Degrees Offered:

Listed in the following order: Program area, degree type (T if terminal Master's), number awarded 7/00–6/01. Clinical Psychology PhD, clinical/counseling MA (T) 12, Developmental PhD.

Student Applications/Admissions:

Student Applications

Clinical Psychology PhD—Applications 2001–2002, 0. Openings 2002–2003, 5. The Median number of years required for completion of a degree are NA. *Clinical/counseling MA*—Applications 2001–2002, 60. Total applicants accepted 2001–2002, 10. New applicants enrolled 2001–2002, 10. Total enrolled 2001–2002 full-time, 20, part-time, 5. Openings 2002–2003, 10. *Developmental PhD*—Applications 2001–2002, 0. Openings 2002–2003, 2.

Admissions Requirements:

Scores: Entries appear in this order: required test or GPA, minimum score (if required), median score of students entering in 2001–2002. Master's Programs: GRE-V 500; GRE-Q 500; GRE-V+Q no minimum stated; overall undergraduate GPA 3.0. Doctoral Programs: GRE-V 500; GRE-Q 500; GRE-V+Q no minimum stated; GRE-Subject(Psych) 500; overall undergraduate GPA 3.0; last 2 years GPA no minimum stated; psychology GPA no minimum stated; psychology GPA no minimum stated.

Other Criteria: (importance of criteria rated low, medium, or high): GRE/MAT scores high, research experience high, work experience low, extracurricular activity low, clinically related public service low, GPA high, letters of recommendation high, statement of goals and objectives high, research interests high. Match of research interests with those of faculty important for graduate programs.

Student Characteristics: The following represents characteristics of students in 2001–2002 in all graduate psychology programs in the department: Female–full-time 18, part-time 0; Male–full-time 3, part-time 0; African American/Black–full-time 2, part-time 0; Hispanic/Latino (a)–full-time 2, part-time 0; Asian/Pacific Islander–full-time 0, part-time 0; American Indian/Alaska Native–full-time 0, part-time 0.

Financial Information/Assistance:

Tuition for Full-Time Study: *Master's:* State residents per academic year $13,878, $771 per credit hour; nonstate residents: per academic year $13,878, $771 per credit hour. *Doctoral:* State residents: per academic year $13,878, $771 per credit hour; nonstate residents: per academic year $13,878, $771 per credit hour.

Financial Assistance:

First Year Students: Teaching assistantships available for first-year. Average amount paid per academic year: $10,000. Average number of hours worked per week: 20. Tuition remission given: full and partial. Research assistantships available for first-year. Average amount paid per academic year: $10,000. Average number of hours worked per week: 20. Tuition remission given: full and partial.

Advanced Students: Teaching assistantships available for advanced students. Average amount paid per academic year: $10,000. Average number of hours worked per week: 20. Tuition remission given: full and partial. Research assistantships available for advanced students. Average amount paid per academic year: $10,000. Average number of hours worked per week: 20. Tuition remission given: full and partial.

Contact Information: Of all students currently enrolled full-time, 75% benefited from one or more of the listed financial assistance programs. For information on financial assistance, contact: Department Chair.

Internships/Practica: Practicum placements are available for students in both the MA program and the clinical PhD program.

Housing and Day Care: No on-campus housing and day care facilities are available.

Employment of Department Graduates:

Master's Degree Graduates: Of those who graduated in the academic year 2000–2001, the following categories and numbers represent the post-graduate activities and employment of master's degree graduates: Enrolled in a post-doctoral residency/fellowship (n/a), employed in independent practice (n/a).

Doctoral Degree Graduates: Of those who graduated in the academic year 2000–2001, the following categories and numbers represent the post-graduate activities and employment of doctoral degree graduates: Enrolled in a psychology doctoral program (n/a), enrolled in another graduate/professional program (n/a).

Additional Information:

Orientation, Objectives, and Emphasis of Department: The department currently offers PhD training in developmental psychology and clinical psychology. The emphasis of both PhD programs is on the development of conceptual and research skills. The clinical PhD program is based on the assumption that clinical psychology is a specialization within the broader area of general psychological science. Accordingly, the goal of this program is to train professionals who will be employed in all types of settings where research is conducted. The goal of the program in Developmental Psychology is to develop competent researchers who will become contributors to the state of knowledge in developmental psychology in either academic or applied research settings. For both PhD programs, students work closely with a research mentor from the time they enter the program, and are actively engaged in research throughout their enrollment. The clinical program requires 60 units of coursework that includes courses in the foundations of psychological science, clinical research methodology, quantitative methods, behavioral medicine, adult psychopathology, developmental psychopathology, ethics, and psychological assessment. The department also offers a separate MA program in clinical and counseling psychology. In this program, students take courses that help prepare them for practice as Licensed Professional Counsel in the state of Texas.

Special Facilities or Resources: The department has a number of well-equipped laboratories for research in positive psychology, developmental psychology, health psychology, experimental psychopathology, developmental psychopathology, cognition, and family and marital dysfunction.

Application Information:
Send to: The Office of Graduate Studies, Southern Methodist University, PO Box 750240, Dallas, Texas 75275-0240. Students are admitted in the Fall, application deadline February 1. *Fee:* $50.

Southwest Texas State University
Psychology Department/Health Psychology Master's Program
College of Liberal Arts
601 University Drive
San Marcos, TX 78666-4616
Telephone: (512) 245-2526
Fax: (512) 245-3153
E-mail: *gradinfo@www.psych.swt.edu*
Web: *http://www.psych.swt.edu*

Department Established:
0. Chairperson: Randall E. Osborne, PhD. Number of Faculty: total–full-time 16, part-time 4; women–full-time 4, part-time 1; minority–full-time 2.

Programs and Degrees Offered:
Listed in the following order: Program area, degree type (T if terminal Master's), number awarded 7/00–6/01. Health Psychology MA (T).

Student Applications/Admissions:
Student Applications
Health Psychology MA—Applications 2001–2002, 10. Total applicants accepted 2001–2002, 5. New applicants enrolled 2001–2002, 11. Total enrolled 2001–2002 full-time, 16. Openings 2002–2003, 15.

Admissions Requirements:

Scores: Entries appear in this order: required test or GPA, minimum score (if required), median score of students entering in 2001–2002. Master's Programs: GRE-V no minimum stated; GRE-Q no minimum stated; GRE-V+Q no minimum stated, 1000; last 2 years GPA 3.0, 3.0; psychology GPA 3.0, 3.25. Doctoral Programs: last 2 years GPA no minimum stated; psychology GPA no minimum stated; psychology GPA no minimum stated.

Other Criteria: (importance of criteria rated low, medium, or high): GRE/MAT scores high, research experience medium, work experience low, extracurricular activity low, clinically related public service low, GPA high, letters of recommendation medium, interview medium, statement of goals and objectives medium.

Student Characteristics: The following represents characteristics of students in 2001–2002 in all graduate psychology programs in the department: Female–full-time 15, part-time 0; Male–full-time 4, part-time 0; African American/Black–full-time 0, part-time 0; Hispanic/Latino (a)–full-time 3, part-time 0; Asian/Pacific Islander–full-time 0, part-time 0; American Indian/Alaska Native–full-time 0, part-time 0.

Financial Information/Assistance:

Tuition for Full-Time Study: No information provided.

Financial Assistance:

First Year Students: Teaching assistantships available for first-year. Average amount paid per academic year: $4,400. Average number of hours worked per week: 10. Apply by March 15. Research assistantships available for first-year. Average amount paid per academic year: $4,400. Average number of hours worked per week: 10. Apply by March 15. Fellowships and scholarships available for first-year. Average amount paid per academic year: $5,000. Average number of hours worked per week: 0. Apply by variable.

Advanced Students: No information provided.

Contact Information: Of all students currently enrolled full-time, 45% benefited from one or more of the listed financial assistance programs. For information on financial assistance, contact: Psychology Department, 601 Campus Dr., San Marcos, TX 78666-4616; 512-245-2526.

Internships/Practica: At Southwest Texas State University, internships have been developed for Master's students in Health Psychology. Practica include rehabilitation centers, the Veteran's Administration hospital, other hospital settings, and corporate wellness programs. Such practica will give students the opportunity to observe multidisciplinary treatment of individuals with illness/injury, who may have psychological difficulties as a result of or in conjunction with physical difficulties. Students should also be able to participate in treatment interventions for patients, including but not limited to pain management, stress management, and motivational enhancement regarding compliance with treatment. For those doctoral students for whom a professional internship is required prior to graduation, 4 applied in 2000–2001.

Housing and Day Care: No on-campus housing and day care facilities are available.

Employment of Department Graduates:

Master's Degree Graduates: Of those who graduated in the academic year 2000–2001, the following categories and numbers represent the post-graduate activities and employment of master's degree graduates: Enrolled in a post-doctoral residency/fellowship (n/a), employed in independent practice (n/a), employed in a hospital/medical center (1), other employment position (2).

Doctoral Degree Graduates: Of those who graduated in the academic year 2000–2001, the following categories and numbers represent the post-graduate activities and employment of doctoral degree graduates: Enrolled in a psychology doctoral program (n/a), enrolled in another graduate/professional program (n/a).

Additional Information:

Orientation, Objectives, and Emphasis of Department: The orientation of the psychology department at Southwest Texas State University is generally geared toward developmental, personality, and social psychology, due in large part to the majority of the faculty's interests and background. There are a number of experimentally oriented as well as clinically oriented faculty as well. The main objective of the department is to provide students with a strong background in psychology for successful entry into graduate school and many areas of employment (business, government, health) immediately upon college graduation. Recently, the department has begun a Master's program in applied Health Psychology, and has made a concerted effort to hire appropriate faculty and develop a focused curriculum. The Master's program is intended to provide Master's level counselors with specific clinical skills and cognitive behavioral intervention techniques for entry into a variety of medical and health care settings.

Special Facilities or Resources: The psychology department at Southwest Texas State University is currently developing relationships with the surrounding area's medical communities such as San Antonio's and Austin's major medical centers. We are also in the process of developing relationships with the Texas Department of Health.

Information for Students With Physical Disabilities: Southwest Texas State University does not discriminate on the basis of disability in the recruitment and admission of students to the university. Students with disabilities must meet the same admission requirements as other students. A student whose educational and/or personal goals for success have been negatively impacted due to disability-based reasons may wish to submit a supplemental essay with their admission application. This information may be considered by the admission office during the application review process.

Application Information:

Send to: The Graduate College, Southwest Texas State University, 601 University Drive, San Marcos, Texas 78666-4605. Students are admitted in the Fall, application deadline March 15. No application fee. *Fee:* $25.

Southwest Texas State University (2001 data)
School Psychology Program
College of Education
601 University
San Marcos, TX 78666
Telephone: 512-245-2575
Fax: 5122458872
E-mail: *CM15@swt.edu*
Web: *http://www.eaps.swt.edu*

Department Established:
1974. Chairperson: C. Sue McCullough. Number of Faculty: total–full-time 4, part-time 1; women–full-time 3, part-time 1; minority–full-time 1; faculty subject to the Americans with Disabilities Act 1.

Financial Information/Assistance:
Tuition for Full-Time Study: No information provided.

Financial Assistance:
First Year Students: No information provided.
Advanced Students: No information provided.
Contact Information: No information provided.

Internships/Practica: No information provided.

Housing and Day Care: No on-campus housing and day care facilities are available.

Employment of Department Graduates:
Master's Degree Graduates: Of those who graduated in the academic year 2000–2001, the following categories and numbers represent the post-graduate activities and employment of master's degree graduates: Enrolled in a post-doctoral residency/fellowship (n/a), employed in independent practice (n/a).
Doctoral Degree Graduates: Of those who graduated in the academic year 2000–2001, the following categories and numbers represent the post-graduate activities and employment of doctoral degree graduates: Enrolled in a psychology doctoral program (n/a), enrolled in another graduate/professional program (n/a).

St. Mary's University (Texas)
Department of Psychology
One Camino Santa Maria
San Antonio, TX 78228-8573
Telephone: (210) 431-4301
Fax: (210) 436-3500
E-mail: *psycwilly@stmarytx.edu*
Web: *http://www.stmarytx.edu*

Department Established:
1965. Chairperson: Patricia Owen. Number of Faculty: total–full-time 5, part-time 6; women–full-time 4, part-time 1; minority–full-time 1, part-time 2.

Programs and Degrees Offered:
Listed in the following order: Program area, degree type (T if terminal Master's), number awarded 7/00–6/01. Clinical MA (T) 10, industrial/organizational MA (T) 11, school MA (T).

Student Applications/Admissions:
Student Applications
Clinical MA—Applications 2001–2002, 48. Total applicants accepted 2001–2002, 35. New applicants enrolled 2001–2002, 22. Total enrolled 2001–2002 full-time, 20, part-time, 9. Openings 2002–2003, 20. The Median number of years required for completion of a degree are 2. *Industrial/organizational MA*—Applications 2001–2002, 18. Total applicants accepted 2001–2002, 12. New applicants enrolled 2001–2002, 7. Total enrolled 2001–2002 full-time, 15, part-time, 16. Openings 2002–2003, 20. The Median number of years required for completion of a degree are 2. *School MA*—Applications 2001–2002, 10. Total applicants accepted 2001–2002, 7. New applicants enrolled 2001–2002, 5. Total enrolled 2001–2002 full-time, 4, part-time, 1. Openings 2002–2003, 10. The number of students enrolled full and part-time, who were dismissed or voluntarily withdrew from this program area were 1.

Admissions Requirements:
Scores: Entries appear in this order: required test or GPA, minimum score (if required), median score of students entering in 2001–2002. Master's Programs: GRE-V+Q no minimum stated, 1000; overall undergraduate GPA no minimum stated. Minimum Academic Index: GPA x (verbal+quantitative GRE)=3159; Conditional Status if index is 2527. Doctoral Programs: last 2 years GPA no minimum stated; psychology GPA no minimum stated; psychology GPA no minimum stated.
Other Criteria: (importance of criteria rated low, medium, or high): GRE/MAT scores medium, research experience medium, work experience medium, extracurricular activity low, clinically related public service low, GPA medium, letters of recommendation medium, interview low, statement of goals and objectives medium.

Student Characteristics: The following represents characteristics of students in 2001–2002 in all graduate psychology programs in the department: Female–full-time 23, part-time 8; Male–full-time 5, part-time 3; African American/Black–full-time 0, part-time 0; Hispanic/Latino (a)–full-time 8, part-time 5; Asian/Pacific Islander–full-time 2, part-time 0; American Indian/Alaska Native–full-time 0, part-time 0; Multi-ethnic–full-time 4, part-time 1; students subject to the Americans with Disabilities Act–full-time 2.

Financial Information/Assistance:
Tuition for Full-Time Study: *Master's:* State residents per academic year $8,200, $455 per credit hour; nonstate residents: per academic year $8,200, $455 per credit hour.

Financial Assistance:
First Year Students: Fellowships and scholarships available for first-year. Average amount paid per academic year: $4,000. Average number of hours worked per week: 15. Apply by March 15.
Advanced Students: No information provided.

Contact Information: Of all students currently enrolled full-time, 1% benefited from one or more of the listed financial assistance programs. For information on financial assistance, contact: Office of Financial Assistance, St. Mary's University.

Internships/Practica: Clinical students are required to complete two practica. Industrial/Organizational students are required to complete one practicum. School Psychology students must complete one practicum and a one-year internship.

Housing and Day Care: On-campus housing and day care facilities are available.

Employment of Department Graduates:

Master's Degree Graduates: Of those who graduated in the academic year 2000–2001, the following categories and numbers represent the post-graduate activities and employment of master's degree graduates: Enrolled in a psychology doctoral program (1), enrolled in a post-doctoral residency/fellowship (n/a), employed in independent practice (n/a), employed in an academic position at a 2-year/4-year college (2), employed in other positions at a higher education institution (1), employed in business or industry (research/consulting) (2), employed in business or industry (management) (1), employed in a community mental health/counseling center (2).

Doctoral Degree Graduates: Of those who graduated in the academic year 2000–2001, the following categories and numbers represent the post-graduate activities and employment of doctoral degree graduates: Enrolled in a psychology doctoral program (n/a), enrolled in another graduate/professional program (n/a).

Additional Information:

Orientation, Objectives, and Emphasis of Department: Clinical Psychology graduates are prepared for entry to a PhD or PsyD program in Clinical Psychology and positions in a variety of clinical settings ranging from school district to psychiatric hospitals to university counseling centers. The focus of these positions is usually on assessment and intervention. Industrial Psychology graduates are prepared for entry to a PhD program in Industrial psychology or a career in business and industry. Those interested in a career in business and industry may expect job opportunities in positions emphasizing the quantification of human behavior. Students are prepared for positions involving personnel selection and testing, job analysis and evaluation, performance appraisal, organizational behavior, training systems, survey technology, and human factors engineering. School Psychology graduates are eligible to apply for the state and national licensing examinations for Specialist in School Psychology.

Application Information:

Send to: Graduate Admissions, St. Mary's University, One Camino Santa Maria, San Antonio, TX 78228. Students are admitted in the Fall, application deadline July 1; Spring, application deadline December 1. *Fee:* $15.

Texas A&M International University

Department of Psychology and Sociology
College of Arts and Humanities
5201 University Boulevard
Laredo, TX 78041-1900
Telephone: (956) 326-2475
Fax: (956) 326-2474
E-mail: *brudolph@tamiu.edu*
Web: *http://www.tamiu.edu/coah/psy*

Department Established:

1994. Director of Master's Program in Counseling Psy.: Bonnie A. Rudolph. Number of Faculty: total–full-time 13; women–full-time 10; minority–full-time 5.

Programs and Degrees Offered:

Listed in the following order: Program area, degree type (T if terminal Master's), number awarded 7/00–6/01. Counseling Psychology (New Program) MA (T) 5, General Psychology MA (T).

Student Applications/Admissions:

Student Applications

Counseling Psy(New Program) MA—Applications 2001–2002, 7. Total applicants accepted 2001–2002, 5. New applicants enrolled 2001–2002, 5. Total enrolled 2001–2002 full-time, 2, part-time, 18. Openings 2002–2003, 6. The Median number of years required for completion of a degree are 5. The number of students enrolled full and part-time, who were dismissed or voluntarily withdrew from this program area were 1. *General Psychology* MA—Applications 2001–2002, 0. Openings 2002–2003, 5. The Median number of years required for completion of a degree are NA. The number of students enrolled full and part-time, who were dismissed or voluntarily withdrew from this program area were 0.

Admissions Requirements:

Scores: Entries appear in this order: required test or GPA, minimum score (if required), median score of students entering in 2001–2002. Master's Programs: GRE-V+Q no minimum stated; last 2 years GPA no minimum stated. Doctoral Programs: last 2 years GPA no minimum stated; psychology GPA no minimum stated; psychology GPA no minimum stated.

Other Criteria: (importance of criteria rated low, medium, or high): GRE/MAT scores medium, research experience low, work experience medium, extracurricular activity low, clinically related public service medium, GPA medium, letters of recommendation medium, interview medium, statement of goals and objectives medium.

Student Characteristics: The following represents characteristics of students in 2001–2002 in all graduate psychology programs in the department: Female–part-time 11; Male–full-time 1, part-time 8; African American/Black–full-time 1, part-time 0; Hispanic/Latino (a)–full-time 0, part-time 18; Asian/Pacific Islander–full-time 0, part-time 0; American Indian/Alaska Native–full-time 0, part-time 1.

Financial Information/Assistance:

Tuition for Full-Time Study: *Master's:* State residents per academic year $1,637, $207 per credit hour; nonstate residents: per academic year $2,717, $340 per credit hour.

Financial Assistance:

First Year Students: No information provided.

Advanced Students: No information provided.

Contact Information: Of all students currently enrolled full-time, 0% benefited from one or more of the listed financial assistance programs. For information on financial assistance, contact: Office of Student Financial Aid, (956) 326-2225.

Internships/Practica: 150 hours in one semester at a local agency such as a college counseling center, drug and alcohol counseling/prevention agency, domestic violence/battered women shelter, children's advocacy center, among other placements. Weekly 30-minute supervision sessions are provided by an on-site supervisor who is an experienced counselor or licensed psychologist. An additional 45 minutes of supervision is provided by a licensed psychologist on campus. A minimum of 50 hours must be direct contact counseling. Practicum students also receive supervision from more advanced internship students who review audio-visual cassettes of the practicum students' counseling sessions. Internship students complete a similar process after their practicum with additional responsibilities of supervising practicum students. All graduates complete Practicum and Counseling Internship I. Students who choose the non-thesis (clinical) track must also complete Internship II. The non-thesis track provides a total of 3 semesters of practical experience in counseling (450 hours), a minimum of which is 150 hours of face-to-face counseling.

Housing and Day Care: On-campus housing and day care facilities are available.

Employment of Department Graduates:

Master's Degree Graduates: Of those who graduated in the academic year 2000–2001, the following categories and numbers represent the post-graduate activities and employment of master's degree graduates: Enrolled in a post-doctoral residency/fellowship (n/a), employed in independent practice (n/a), employed in a community mental health/counseling center (3), other employment position (1).

Doctoral Degree Graduates: Of those who graduated in the academic year 2000–2001, the following categories and numbers represent the post-graduate activities and employment of doctoral degree graduates: Enrolled in a psychology doctoral program (n/a), enrolled in another graduate/professional program (n/a).

Additional Information:

Orientation, Objectives, and Emphasis of Department: The Master of Arts in Counseling Psychology provides training as a counselor with a strong foundation in Cognitive-Behavioral and Psychodynamic perspectives. Given the ethnic composition of the campus and community, one of our major foci is Multicultural Counseling, and in Marriage and Family Therapy, a systems approach is used. Faculty are also strong in the areas of Psycholinguistics, Learning and Memory, Brief Psychotherapy, Multicultural Counseling, Person Centered Psychotherapy, Adolescent Identity Development, Psychopathology, Eating Disorders and Community Psychology. Objectives include preparation of professional counselors who would be eligible to sit for the Licensed Professional Counselor (LPC-Texas) Examination. Students can be prepared to become counselors and/or select a thesis track for students interested in research and further study at the doctoral level. Students complete courses in counseling theories and techniques; human development; psychopathology; ethical, legal, professional issues; group counseling; career development; statistics; and research design. Electives include coursework in psychological assessment, crisis counseling, psychological services for children, adolescents, adults and the elderly, alcohol and drug counseling, and the psychology of bilingualism.

Special Facilities or Resources: The Department of Psychology and Sociology is equipped with a computer lab that is currently used for research in the area of cognitive psychology. It is equipped for detailed analysis of research in memory, cognition, psycholinguistics, bilingualism, cross-linguistics, as well as other research. Audio-visual equipment is also available to students for recording of their counseling sessions. Faculty of the Master's of Arts in Counseling Psychology (MACP) Program work closely with the Department of Career Services in education and training, student-counselors. The Student Counseling Services Office also works closely with MACP faculty to facilitate training and education of MACP students.

Information for Students With Physical Disabilities: The Office of Disabled Student Services will assist students in coordinating needed support services, physical or academic, for any student who has a need due to an appropriately documented disability. Such students may request reasonable accommodation which will afford them equal access to all educational programs and activities that Texas A&M International University (TAMIU) provides or sanctions. Students with disabilities are encouraged to contact the Director of Student Counseling Services at least 3 months before entering TAMIU.

Application Information:
Send to: Texas A&M International University, College of Arts & Humanities, Department of Psychology & Sociology, 5201 University Blvd., Laredo, TX 78041-1900. Students are admitted in the Fall, application deadline April 15; Winter, application deadline Dec. 15; Spring, application deadline October 1st. *Fee:* Canadian Dollars: 10,664.88, approximately, based on a rate of 1.48 Canadian dollar= $US 1.00.

Texas A&M University
Department of Educational Psychology, Programs in
 Counseling and School Psychology
Education
4225 Texas A&M University
College Station, TX 77843-4225
Telephone: (979) 845-1831
Fax: (979) 862-1256
E-mail: *ogs@tamu.edu*
Web: *http://www.tamu.edu/epsy/*

Department Established:

Chairperson: Douglas J. Palmer. Number of Faculty: total–full-time 35, part-time 4; women–full-time 16, part-time 4; minority–full-time 4.

Programs and Degrees Offered:

Listed in the following order: Program area, degree type (T if terminal Master's), number awarded 7/00–6/01. Counseling PhD 8, gifted and talented PhD (T) 3, human learning and development MA (T) 3, Licensed Specialist in SPSY MA (T) 1, pre-doctoral training MA (T) 2, school PhD (T) 4, school counseling (T) 3, special education MA (T) 15.

APA Accreditation: Counseling PhD: full. School PhD: full.

Student Applications/Admissions:

Student Applications

Counseling PhD—Applications 2001–2002, 56. Total applicants accepted 2001–2002, 17. New applicants enrolled 2001–2002, 9. Total enrolled 2001–2002 full-time, 9. Openings 2002–2003, 10. The Median number of years required for completion of a degree are 5. *Gifted and talented PhD*—Applications 2001–2002, 7. Total applicants accepted 2001–2002, 5. New applicants enrolled 2001–2002, 3. Total enrolled 2001–2002 full-time, 7, part-time, 10. Openings 2002–2003, 3. The Median number of years required for completion of a degree are 4. *Human learning and development MA*—Applications 2001–2002, 3. Total applicants accepted 2001–2002, 3. New applicants enrolled 2001–2002, 2. Total enrolled 2001–2002 full-time, 4, part-time, 2. Openings 2002–2003, 3. The Median number of years required for completion of a degree are 2. *Licensed Specialist in SPSY MA*—Applications 2001–2002, 5. Total applicants accepted 2001–2002, 5. New applicants enrolled 2001–2002, 4. Total enrolled 2001–2002 full-time, 7, part-time, 2. Openings 2002–2003, 5. The Median number of years required for completion of a degree are 3. *Pre-doctoral training MA*—Total applicants accepted 2001–2002, 1. New applicants enrolled 2001–2002, 1. Total enrolled 2001–2002 full-time, 2. The Median number of years required for completion of a degree are 2. The number of students enrolled full and part-time, who were dismissed or voluntarily withdrew from this program area were 0. *School PhD*—Applications 2001–2002, 26. Total applicants accepted 2001–2002, 14. New applicants enrolled 2001–2002, 9. Total enrolled 2001–2002 full-time, 30, part-time, 29. Openings 2002–2003, 10. The Median number of years required for completion of a degree are 5. *Special education MA*—Applications 2001–2002, 39. Total applicants accepted 2001–2002, 27. New applicants enrolled 2001–2002, 24. Total enrolled 2001–2002 full-time, 44, part-time, 15. Openings 2002–2003, 30. The Median number of years required for completion of a degree are 3.

Admissions Requirements:

Scores: Entries appear in this order: required test or GPA, minimum score (if required), median score of students entering in 2001–2002. Master's Programs: GRE-V+Q+Analytical no minimum stated; last 2 years GPA no minimum stated. GRE scores are required; no minimum for GRE or GPA. Doctoral Programs: GRE-V+Q no minimum stated; last 2 years GPA no minimum stated; psychology GPA no minimum stated; psychology GPA no minimum stated. GRE/GPA required - no minimum; GRE-psychology required for Counseling Psychology by end of 2nd year of study.

Other Criteria: (importance of criteria rated low, medium, or high): research experience high, work experience high, extracurricular activity high, clinically related public service high, letters of recommendation high, interview high, statement of goals and objectives high. Entire application package considered in admissions process with attention to academic potential, relevant background, and similar areas. Interview required for Counseling Psychology.

Student Characteristics: The following represents characteristics of students in 2001–2002 in all graduate psychology programs in the department: Female–full-time 113, part-time 133; Male–full-time 33, part-time 32; African American/Black–full-time 3, part-time 7; Hispanic/Latino (a)–full-time 20, part-time 17; Asian/Pacific Islander–full-time 4, part-time 1; American Indian/Alaska Native–full-time 0, part-time 0.

Financial Information/Assistance:

Tuition for Full-Time Study: *Master's:* State residents $126 per credit hour; nonstate residents: $337 per credit hour. *Doctoral:* State residents: $126 per credit hour; nonstate residents: $337 per credit hour.

Financial Assistance:

First Year Students: Teaching assistantships available for first-year. Average amount paid per academic year: $10,800. Average number of hours worked per week: 20. Apply by February 1. Research assistantships available for first-year. Average amount paid per academic year: $10,200. Average number of hours worked per week: 20. Apply by February 1. Fellowships and scholarships available for first-year. Average amount paid per academic year: $20,000. Apply by n/a.

Advanced Students: Teaching assistantships available for advanced students. Average amount paid per academic year: $11,400. Average number of hours worked per week: 20. Apply by February 1. Research assistantships available for advanced students. Average amount paid per academic year: $10,800. Average number of hours worked per week: 20. Apply by February 1.

Contact Information: Of all students currently enrolled full-time, 63% benefited from one or more of the listed financial assistance programs. For information on financial assistance, contact: Department of Educational Psychology.

Internships/Practica: Practicum opportunities exist on campus, in public schools and community colleges, and in mental health agencies in the surrounding area. Facilities are available both on and off campus for many types of counseling and research activities. Professional internships at an APA-approved site are required by both the Counseling and School Psychology PhD programs. Students in other programs may include an internship as part of their degree program. For those doctoral students for whom a professional internship is required prior to graduation, 12 applied in 2000–2001. Of those who applied, 12 were placed in internships listed by the Association of Psychology Postdoctoral and Internship Programs (APPIC); 12 were placed in APA accredited internships.

Housing and Day Care: On-campus housing and day care facilities are available.

Employment of Department Graduates:

Master's Degree Graduates: Of those who graduated in the academic year 2000–2001, the following categories and numbers represent the post-graduate activities and employment of master's degree graduates: Enrolled in a psychology doctoral program (6), enrolled in a post-doctoral residency/fellowship (n/a), employed in independent practice (n/a), employed in an academic position at a university (1), employed in other positions at a higher education institution (2), employed in a professional position in a school system (27), other employment position (5).

Doctoral Degree Graduates: Of those who graduated in the academic year 2000–2001, the following categories and numbers represent the post-graduate activities and employment of doctoral degree graduates: Enrolled in a psychology doctoral program (n/a), enrolled in another graduate/professional program (n/a), enrolled in a post-doctoral residency/fellowship (4), employed in an academic position at a university (3), employed in other positions at a higher education institution (3), employed in a professional position in a school system (3), employed in a community mental health/counseling center (8), employed in a hospital/medical center (1), still seeking employment (2), other employment position (4).

Additional Information:

Orientation, Objectives, and Emphasis of Department: Graduate programs in this department provide individuals with a sound scientific background in those areas of research and application that are particularly related to psychology and education. Preparation in this department has a strong general emphasis on learning, development, measurement, and research procedures. All programs require continuous practice aimed at developing intervention skills required by the professional practitioner.

Special Facilities or Resources: Special facilities include a university computer with multiple mainframes, the Automated Information Retrieval Service (AIRS) available at the university library; a computer center in the department that includes terminals and microcomputers; the Vocational Special Needs Population Library; the Institute for Gifted and Talented Students; and the Counseling and Assessment Clinic. The Counseling and Assessment Clinic includes a site on campus, as well as a site at the Family Health Clinic in Bryan, TX.

Information for Students With Physical Disabilities: Texas A&M University does not discriminate on the basis of disabilities in admission or access to its programs. The University has a strong commitment to its students with disabilities and provides a variety of services and resources through Services For Students With Disabilities in the Department of Student Life. Students with documented disabilities such as mobility, hearing or visual impairments, learning, and/or psychological disorders are eligible for services. Services for Students With Disabilities coordinates such services as registration assistance, tape recorded texts, adapted technology, testing accommodation, attendant referrals, and academic advice. The Adaptive Technology Services lab contains specially adapted computer equipment and other adaptive technology for students with disabilities. The office also works closely with the Texas Rehabilitation Commission to assist students with disabilities.

Application Information:
Send to: Carol A. Wagner, Senior Academic Advisor, Department of Educational Psychology, 4225 Texas A&M University, College Station, TX 77843-4225. Students are admitted in the Fall, application deadline varies; Spring, application deadline varies; Summer, application deadline varies. Counseling and School Psychology - Fall only, December 15 deadline: check with department for specific deadlines for specific programs. *Fee:* $50.

Texas A&M University
Department of Psychology
Liberal Arts
Psychology Department
College Station, TX 77843-4235
Telephone: 979-458-1710
Fax: 979-845-4727
E-mail: *gradadv@psyc.tamu.edu*
Web: *psychweb.tamu.edu*

Department Established:
1968. Department Head: Paul Wellman. Number of Faculty: total–full-time 37, part-time 4; women–full-time 14, part-time 2; minority–full-time 5.

Programs and Degrees Offered:
Listed in the following order: Program area, degree type (T if terminal Master's), number awarded 7/00–6/01. Behavioral/Neurorogical PhD, clinical PhD 4, Cognitive PhD 1, Developmental PhD, Industrial/organizational PhD 5, Social PhD 1.

APA Accreditation: Clinical PhD: full.

Student Applications/Admissions:
Student Applications

Behavioral/Neurological PhD—Applications 2001–2002, 9. Total applicants accepted 2001–2002, 6. New applicants enrolled 2001–2002, 4. Total enrolled 2001–2002 full-time, 9. Openings 2002–2003, 3. The number of students enrolled full and part-time, who were dismissed or voluntarily withdrew from this program area were 0. *Clinical PhD*—Applications 2001–2002, 98. Total applicants accepted 2001–2002, 11. New applicants enrolled 2001–2002, 5. Total enrolled 2001–2002 full-time, 28, part-time, 10. Openings 2002–2003, 5. The number of students enrolled full and part-time, who were dismissed or voluntarily withdrew from this program area were 0. *Cognitive PhD*—Applications 2001–2002, 3. Total applicants accepted 2001–2002, 2. Total enrolled 2001–2002 full-time, 5. Openings 2002–2003, 2. The number of students enrolled full and part-time, who were dismissed or voluntarily withdrew from this program area were 0. *Developmental PhD*—Applications 2001–2002, 3. Total applicants accepted 2001–2002, 2. New applicants enrolled 2001–2002, 1. Total enrolled 2001–2002 full-time, 4, part-time, 2. Openings 2002–2003, 2. The number of students enrolled full and part-time, who were dismissed or voluntarily withdrew from this program area were 0. *Industrial/organizational PhD*—Applications 2001–2002, 33. Total applicants accepted 2001–2002, 9. New applicants enrolled 2001–2002, 3. Total enrolled 2001–2002 full-time, 16, part-time, 6. Openings 2002–2003, 3. The number of students enrolled full and part-time, who were dismissed or voluntarily withdrew from this program area were 0. *Social PhD*—Applications 2001–2002, 22. Total applicants accepted 2001–2002, 5. New applicants enrolled 2001–2002, 3. Total enrolled 2001–2002 full-time, 9. Openings 2002–2003, 3. The number of students enrolled full and part-time, who were dismissed or voluntarily withdrew from this program area were 0.

Admissions Requirements:
Scores: Entries appear in this order: required test or GPA, minimum score (if required), median score of students entering

in 2001–2002. Doctoral Programs: 1212; overall undergraduate GPA no minimum stated; last 2 years GPA 3.0, 3.73; psychology GPA no minimum stated; psychology GPA no minimum stated.

Other Criteria: (importance of criteria rated low, medium, or high): GRE/MAT scores high, research experience high, work experience medium, extracurricular activity medium, clinically related public service medium, GPA high, letters of recommendation high, interview medium, statement of goals and objectives medium.

Student Characteristics: The following represents characteristics of students in 2001–2002 in all graduate psychology programs in the department: Female–full-time 39, part-time 13; Male–full-time 34, part-time 5; African American/Black–full-time 0, part-time 0; Hispanic/Latino (a)–full-time 0, part-time 0; Asian/Pacific Islander–full-time 0, part-time 0; American Indian/Alaska Native–full-time 0, part-time 0; Multi-ethnic–full-time 0, part-time 0; students subject to the Americans with Disabilities Act–full-time 0, part-time 0.

Financial Information/Assistance:

Tuition for Full-Time Study: *Doctoral:* State residents: $126 per credit hour; nonstate residents: $337 per credit hour.

Financial Assistance:

First Year Students: Teaching assistantships available for first-year. Average amount paid per academic year: $8,470. Average number of hours worked per week: 20. Apply by January 5. Tuition remission given: partial. Research assistantships available for first-year. Average amount paid per academic year: $8,470. Average number of hours worked per week: 20. Apply by January 5. Tuition remission given: partial. Fellowships and scholarships available for first-year. Average amount paid per academic year: $17,000. Apply by January 5.

Advanced Students: Teaching assistantships available for advanced students. Tuition remission given: partial. Research assistantships available for advanced students. Tuition remission given: partial.

Contact Information: Of all students currently enrolled full-time, 99% benefited from one or more of the listed financial assistance programs. For information on financial assistance, contact: Texas A&M University, College Station, TX 77843-1252.

Internships/Practica: No information provided.

Housing and Day Care: On-campus housing and day care facilities are available.

Employment of Department Graduates:

Master's Degree Graduates: Of those who graduated in the academic year 2000–2001, the following categories and numbers represent the post-graduate activities and employment of master's degree graduates: Enrolled in a post-doctoral residency/fellowship (n/a), employed in independent practice (n/a).

Doctoral Degree Graduates: Of those who graduated in the academic year 2000–2001, the following categories and numbers represent the post-graduate activities and employment of doctoral degree graduates: Enrolled in a psychology doctoral program (n/a), enrolled in another graduate/professional program (n/a), enrolled in a post-doctoral residency/fellowship (2), employed in an academic position at a university (5), employed in an academic position at a 2-year/4-year college (1), employed in business or industry (research/consulting) (2), employed in a government agency (professional services) (1), employed in a community mental health/counseling center (1).

Additional Information:

Orientation, Objectives, and Emphasis of Department: The Psychology Department at Texas A&M University offers a PhD degree that provides for specialization in six areas: Behavioral Neuroscience, Clinical, Cognitive, Developmental, Industrial/Organizational, and Social. The objectives of the PhD program are: a. To prepare students to conduct high quality research, to direct research by others, and to communicate research findings through teaching and writing. b. To prepare students for the varied responsibilities and opportunities of careers in teaching/research or for careers in public or private organizations, which involve the assistance in the practical solution of personal, occupational, or social problems. All of the fields of study within the Psychology Department are intended to be sufficiently flexible to permit students to pursue courses of study that meet their individual goals. Our graduate students receive multiple offers for positions. Since inception, all graduates of our program have been placed in full-time positions.

Application Information:
Send to: Texas A&M University, Graduate Adm. Supv. Dept. of Psyc, College Station, TX 77843-4235. Students are admitted in the Fall, application deadline January 5. *Fee:* $50.

Texas A&M University - Commerce
Department of Psychology and Special Education
College of Education
Henderson Hall
Commerce, TX 75429
Telephone: (903) 886-5594
Fax: (903) 886-5510
E-mail: *dean_ginther@tamu-commerce.edu*
Web: *http://www7.tamu-commerce.edu/psychology/*

Department Established:
1962. Head: Paul F. Zelhart. Number of Faculty: total–full-time 17, part-time 6; women–full-time 5, part-time 6; minority–full-time 3.

Programs and Degrees Offered:
Listed in the following order: Program area, degree type (T if terminal Master's), number awarded 7/00–6/01. Applied MA (T) 6, Educational Psychology PhD (T) 3, School MA (T) 3.

Student Applications/Admissions:
Student Applications

Applied MA—Applications 2001–2002, 15. Total applicants accepted 2001–2002, 8. New applicants enrolled 2001–2002, 7. Total enrolled 2001–2002 full-time, 3, part-time, 4. Openings 2002–2003, 10. The Median number of years required for completion of a degree are 2. The number of students enrolled full and part-time, who were dismissed or voluntarily withdrew from this program area were 0. *Educational Psychology PhD*—Applications 2001–2002, 20. Total applicants accepted 2001–

2002, 10. New applicants enrolled 2001–2002, 10. Total enrolled 2001–2002 full-time, 2, part-time, 8. Openings 2002–2003, 10. The Median number of years required for completion of a degree are 5. The number of students enrolled full and part-time, who were dismissed or voluntarily withdrew from this program area were 1. *School MA*—Applications 2001–2002, 10. Total applicants accepted 2001–2002, 5. New applicants enrolled 2001–2002, 5. Total enrolled 2001–2002 full-time, 2, part-time, 3. Openings 2002–2003, 10. The Median number of years required for completion of a degree are 2. The number of students enrolled full and part-time, who were dismissed or voluntarily withdrew from this program area were 0.

Admissions Requirements:

Scores: Entries appear in this order: required test or GPA, minimum score (if required), median score of students entering in 2001–2002. Master's Programs: GRE-V no minimum stated, 450; GRE-Q no minimum stated, 450; GRE-V+Q no minimum stated, 900; overall undergraduate GPA 2.75, 2.9; last 2 years GPA 3.0, 3.0. Doctoral Programs: GRE-V no minimum stated, 500; GRE-Q no minimum stated, 500; GRE-V+Q no minimum stated, 1000; GRE-Analytical no minimum stated, 500; overall undergraduate GPA 3.0, 3.0; last 2 years GPA 3.00, 3.1; psychology GPA 3.00, 3.1; psychology GPA 3.5, 3.5. *Other Criteria:* (importance of criteria rated low, medium, or high): GRE/MAT scores medium, research experience low, work experience medium, extracurricular activity low, GPA high, letters of recommendation medium, interview statement of goals and objectives high.

Student Characteristics: The following represents characteristics of students in 2001–2002 in all graduate psychology programs in the department: Female–full-time 4, part-time 15; Male–full-time 1, part-time 7; African American/Black–full-time 0, part-time 2; Hispanic/Latino (a)–full-time 0, part-time 2; Asian/Pacific Islander–full-time 1, part-time 2; American Indian/Alaska Native–full-time 0, part-time 0.

Financial Information/Assistance:

Tuition for Full-Time Study: *Master's:* State residents $120 per credit hour; nonstate residents: $330 per credit hour. *Doctoral:* State residents: $120 per credit hour; nonstate residents: $330 per credit hour.

Financial Assistance:

First Year Students: Teaching assistantships available for first-year. Average amount paid per academic year: $9,000. Average number of hours worked per week: 20. Apply by fall/spring. Tuition remission given: partial. Research assistantships available for first-year. Average amount paid per academic year: $9,000. Average number of hours worked per week: 20. Apply by fall/spring. Tuition remission given: partial. Fellowships and scholarships available for first-year. Average amount paid per academic year: $1,000. Apply by fall. Tuition remission given: partial.

Advanced Students: Teaching assistantships available for advanced students. Average amount paid per academic year: $9,000. Average number of hours worked per week: 20. Apply by fall/spring. Tuition remission given: partial. Research assistantships available for advanced students. Average amount paid per academic year: $9,000. Average number of hours worked per week: 20. Apply by fall/spring. Tuition remission given: partial.

Fellowships and scholarships available for advanced students. Average amount paid per academic year: $1,000. Apply by fall. Tuition remission given: partial.

Contact Information: Of all students currently enrolled full-time, 0% benefited from one or more of the listed financial assistance programs. For information on financial assistance, contact: For assistantships: contact Dr. Zelhart at (903) 886-5594.

Internships/Practica: There are on-site university clinic practica for school and applied programs. The school psychology program requires a 1200-hour internship.

Housing and Day Care: On-campus housing and day care facilities are available.

Employment of Department Graduates:

Master's Degree Graduates: Of those who graduated in the academic year 2000–2001, the following categories and numbers represent the post-graduate activities and employment of master's degree graduates: Enrolled in a psychology doctoral program (2), enrolled in another graduate/professional program (0), enrolled in a post-doctoral residency/fellowship (n/a), employed in independent practice (n/a), employed in an academic position at a university (3), employed in an academic position at a 2-year/4-year college (1), employed in other positions at a higher education institution (0), employed in a professional position in a school system (2), employed in business or industry (research/consulting) (1), employed in business or industry (management) (0), employed in a government agency (research) (0), employed in a government agency (professional services) (0), employed in a community mental health/counseling center (0), employed in a hospital/medical center (0), still seeking employment (0), other employment position (0).

Doctoral Degree Graduates: Of those who graduated in the academic year 2000–2001, the following categories and numbers represent the post-graduate activities and employment of doctoral degree graduates: Enrolled in a psychology doctoral program (n/a), enrolled in another graduate/professional program (n/a), enrolled in a post-doctoral residency/fellowship (0), employed in independent practice (0), employed in an academic position at a university (2), employed in an academic position at a 2-year/4-year college (0), employed in other positions at a higher education institution (0), employed in a professional position in a school system (0), employed in business or industry (research/consulting) (1), employed in business or industry (management) (0), employed in a government agency (research) (0), employed in a government agency (professional services) (0), employed in a community mental health/counseling center (0), employed in a hospital/medical center (0), still seeking employment (0), other employment position (0).

Additional Information:

Orientation, Objectives, and Emphasis of Department: The vision of the Department of Psychology and Special Education (see http://www7.tamu-commerce.edu/psychology/) is to offer premier PhD and Master's degree programs in Educational Psychology, School Psychology, and Applied Psychology by providing an optimal combination of on-line instruction and face-to-face interaction, instruction, and mentoring. Currently, much of the coursework for the Educational Psychology degrees is available on-line and more courses are being added in the on-line format each semester. The School and Applied programs are not available via the distance education format due to the required practicums and internships. The Educational Psychology program has an interdisciplinary perspective, with a strong foundation in the science and methodology of psychology. The focus of the educational psychology program is human cognition and instruction. Students will acquire an in-depth knowledge of human learning and cognition, instructional strategies, and research and evaluation. This emphasis will prepare students to integrate knowledge of human cognition and instructional practice across a variety of occupational, educational, and content matter domains, with emphasis on applications of learning technologies. The applied master's program is fully accredited by the Inter-organizational Board of Accreditation for Master's in Psychology Programs (IBAMPP). The applied master's program is designed to prepare students to meet the requirements for certification as an associate psychologist in the State of Texas. Associate psychologists are employed in a variety of governmental and private organizations, such as mental health centers, clinics, and hospitals. The school psychology program is structured on the basis on the NASP requirements for an extended Master's degree which includes coursework in psychological foundations, educational foundations, assessment, interventions (direct and indirect), statistics and research design, professional school psychology, practica and internship.

Special Facilities or Resources: Multimedia Instructional Lab, Multimedia Classrooms, On-site University Clinic, Research partnerships with business industry, Center for excellence-learning technologies, support for on-line learning.

Information for Students With Physical Disabilities: Students with special needs are provided a wide range of services through Student Support Services. These services include, but not limited to, tutoring, mobility assistance, readers, transcription, etc. Texas A&M University-Commerce is an equal opportunity university. Admission to the university is based upon stated academic requirements regardless of race, color, national origin, gender, disability, age, or religion.

Application Information:
Send to: Graduate School, Texas A&M-Commerce, Commerce, TX 75429. Students are admitted in the Fall, application deadline month review; Winter, application deadline month review; Spring, application deadline month review; Summer, application deadline month review. Applications are accepted year-round and reviewed monthly by the Department.

Texas Christian University
Department of Psychology
College of Science and Engineering
TCU Box 298920
Fort Worth, TX 76129
Telephone: (817) 257-7410
Fax: (817) 257-7681
E-mail: *m.eudaly@tcu.edu*
Web: *http://www.psy.tcu.edu/psy/gradpro.html*

Department Established:
1959. Director of Graduate Studies, Department of Psychology: Steven G. Cole. Number of Faculty: total–full-time 13, part-time 2; women–full-time 2, part-time 1; minority–full-time 3.

Programs and Degrees Offered:
Listed in the following order: Program area, degree type (T if terminal Master's), number awarded 7/00–6/01. Experimental PhD (T) 8.

Student Applications/Admissions:
Student Applications
Experimental PhD—Applications 2001–2002, 17. Total applicants accepted 2001–2002, 11. New applicants enrolled 2001–2002, 8. Total enrolled 2001–2002 full-time, 37. Openings 2002–2003, 5. The Median number of years required for completion of a degree are 4. The number of students enrolled full and part-time, who were dismissed or voluntarily withdrew from this program area were 1.

Admissions Requirements:
Scores: Entries appear in this order: required test or GPA, minimum score (if required), median score of students entering in 2001–2002. Doctoral Programs: GRE-V no minimum stated, 540; GRE-Q no minimum stated, 580; GRE-V+Q 1000, 1120; overall undergraduate GPA 3.2, 3.42; last 2 years GPA 3.2, 3.45; psychology GPA 3.2, 3.72; psychology GPA no minimum stated, 3.97.
Other Criteria: (importance of criteria rated low, medium, or high): GRE/MAT scores medium, research experience high, GPA medium, letters of recommendation high, statement of goals and objectives high.

Student Characteristics: The following represents characteristics of students in 2001–2002 in all graduate psychology programs in the department: Female–full-time 21, part-time 0; Male–full-time 16, part-time 0; African American/Black–full-time 1, part-time 0; Hispanic/Latino (a)–full-time 0, part-time 0; Asian/Pacific Islander–full-time 1, part-time 0; American Indian/Alaska Native–full-time 0, part-time 0; Multi-ethnic–full-time 0, part-time 0; students subject to the Americans with Disabilities Act–full-time 0, part-time 0.

Financial Information/Assistance:
Tuition for Full-Time Study: *Master's:* State residents $455 per credit hour; nonstate residents: $455 per credit hour. *Doctoral:* State residents: $455 per credit hour; nonstate residents: $455 per credit hour.

Financial Assistance:
First Year Students: Fellowships and scholarships available for first-year. Average amount paid per academic year: $15,000. Average number of hours worked per week: 0. Apply by None. Tuition remission given: full.
Advanced Students: Teaching assistantships available for advanced students. Average amount paid per academic year: $13,000. Average number of hours worked per week: 10. Apply by None. Tuition remission given: full. Research assistantships available for advanced students. Average amount paid per academic year: $13,000. Average number of hours worked per week: 10. Apply by None. Tuition remission given: full.
Contact Information: Of all students currently enrolled full-time, 97% benefited from one or more of the listed financial assistance programs. For information on financial assistance, contact: Steven G. Cole, Director of Graduate Studies in Psychology, TCU, Box 298920, Ft. Worth, TX 76126.

Internships/Practica: No information provided.

Housing and Day Care: No on-campus housing and day care facilities are available.

Employment of Department Graduates:

Master's Degree Graduates: Of those who graduated in the academic year 2000–2001, the following categories and numbers represent the post-graduate activities and employment of master's degree graduates: Enrolled in a psychology doctoral program (2), enrolled in another graduate/professional program (0), enrolled in a post-doctoral residency/fellowship (n/a), employed in independent practice (n/a), employed in an academic position at a university (0), employed in an academic position at a 2-year/4-year college (0), employed in other positions at a higher education institution (0), employed in a professional position in a school system (0), employed in business or industry (research/consulting) (0), employed in business or industry (management) (0), employed in a government agency (research) (0), employed in a government agency (professional services) (0), employed in a community mental health/counseling center (0), employed in a hospital/medical center (0), still seeking employment (0), other employment position (0).

Doctoral Degree Graduates: Of those who graduated in the academic year 2000–2001, the following categories and numbers represent the post-graduate activities and employment of doctoral degree graduates: Enrolled in a psychology doctoral program (n/a), enrolled in another graduate/professional program (n/a), enrolled in a post-doctoral residency/fellowship (2), employed in independent practice (0), employed in an academic position at a university (2), employed in an academic position at a 2-year/4-year college (1), employed in other positions at a higher education institution (0), employed in a professional position in a school system (0), employed in business or industry (research/consulting) (2), employed in business or industry (management) (0), employed in a government agency (research) (0), employed in a government agency (professional services) (0), employed in a community mental health/counseling center (0), employed in a hospital/medical center (0), still seeking employment (0), other employment position (0).

Additional Information:

Orientation, Objectives, and Emphasis of Department: The psychology graduate program at Texas Christian University leads to a predoctoral master's in experimental psychology and a PhD in general experimental psychology. The PhD is awarded in general experimental psychology only. The program is not limited to traditional experimental psychology, nor is it committed solely to laboratory-based methods. The department has long held that a measure of specialized knowledge—built upon a firm but broad base of psychological principles and methods—constitutes the best plan for most of its students. Within this plan the student may study diverse areas of interest with emphasis possible in the following: learning-comparative, perception-cognition, social, applied quantitative methods, and physiological. All graduate students receive training in both teaching and research. The environment is stimulating, informal, and conducive to close student-faculty relations.

Special Facilities or Resources: Assuming that physical proximity is conducive to more interdisciplinary work of substance, TCU has located all its science-related activities in or near the Science Research Center, dedicated in 1971. The Department of Psychology occupies two floors of the center's Winton-Scott Hall. The university library, containing over one million volumes, is located next to the science facilities. About 140 periodicals of psychological interest are available. Full-time personnel skilled in electronics, glass blowing, woodworking, and metal working aid in construction and maintenance of special equipment or instruments. TCU has 10 open computer labs equipped with Windows-based PCs and Macintosh computers (over 100 Windows-based machines and 39 Mac-based machines). All of the labs provide full Internet access and laser printing. Additionally, some of the labs have scanners, zip drives, CD burners, and web cams. The Psychology department also has a computer lab with 6 Windows-based PCs, all of which are connected to the Internet, and a networked laser printer. Additionally, all of the research laboratories in the department have networked computers. From the various labs, students have access to a variety of software including SPSS, SAS, SYSTAT, and Microsoft office. Also, the University provides e-mail accounts and storage space on the University server.

Application Information:

Send to: Director of Graduate Studies, TCU Box 298920, Fort Worth, TX 76129. Students are admitted in the Fall, application deadline None. No deadline for admission; however, February 5 is recommended. *Fee:* $50.

Texas of the Permian Basin, The University of
Department of Behavioral Science
College of Arts and Sciences
4901 East University Boulevard
Odessa, TX 79762
Telephone: (915) 552-2325
Fax: (915) 552-3325
E-mail: *thompson_s@utpb.edu*
Web: *http://www.utpb.edu*

Department Established:

1973. Coordinator: Spencer Thompson. Number of Faculty: total–full-time 5, part-time 2; women–full-time 2, part-time 2.

Programs and Degrees Offered:

Listed in the following order: Program area, degree type (T if terminal Master's), number awarded 7/00–6/01. Applied MA (T) 1, clinical MA (T) 7.

Student Applications/Admissions:

Student Applications

Applied MA—Applications 2001–2002, 5. Total applicants accepted 2001–2002, 1. Total enrolled 2001–2002 full-time, 4, part-time, 24. Openings 2002–2003, 10. The Median number of years required for completion of a degree are 3. The number of students enrolled full and part-time, who were dismissed or voluntarily withdrew from this program area were 0. Clinical MA—Applications 2001–2002, 15. Total applicants accepted 2001–2002, 15. New applicants enrolled 2001–2002, 8. Total enrolled 2001–2002 full-time, 25. Openings 2002–2003, 15. The Median number of years required for completion of a degree are 4. The number of students enrolled full and part-time, who were dismissed or voluntarily withdrew from this program area were 1.

Admissions Requirements:

Scores: Entries appear in this order: required test or GPA, minimum score (if required), median score of students entering in 2001–2002. Master's Programs: GRE-V 500; GRE-Q 500; GRE-V+Q 1000; GRE-Analytical 500; GRE-V+Q+Analytical 1500; overall undergraduate GPA 3.0; last 2 years GPA 3.0; psychology GPA 3.0. Students are evaluated on a case by case basis and may be admitted at a provisional status. Doctoral Programs: last 2 years GPA no minimum stated; psychology GPA no minimum stated; psychology GPA no minimum stated.

Other Criteria: (importance of criteria rated low, medium, or high): GRE/MAT scores high, GPA high, letters of recommendation high, statement of goals and objectives high.

Student Characteristics: The following represents characteristics of students in 2001–2002 in all graduate psychology programs in the department: Female–full-time 20, part-time 0; Male–full-time 15, part-time 0; African American/Black–full-time 0, part-time 0; Hispanic/Latino (a)–full-time 10, Asian/Pacific Islander–full-time 0, part-time 0; American Indian/Alaska Native–full-time 0, part-time 0.

Financial Information/Assistance:

Tuition for Full-Time Study: *Master's:* State residents per academic year $1,164, $97 per credit hour; nonstate residents: per academic year $3,132, $261 per credit hour.

Financial Assistance:

First Year Students: No information provided.

Advanced Students: No information provided.

Contact Information: For information on financial assistance, contact: Spencer Thompson, PhD, Department of Behavioral Science, UTPB, 4901 E. University, Odessa, TX 79762.

Internships/Practica: No information provided.

Housing and Day Care: No on-campus housing and day care facilities are available.

Employment of Department Graduates:

Master's Degree Graduates: Of those who graduated in the academic year 2000–2001, the following categories and numbers represent the post-graduate activities and employment of master's degree graduates: Enrolled in a post-doctoral residency/fellowship (n/a), employed in independent practice (n/a).

Doctoral Degree Graduates: Of those who graduated in the academic year 2000–2001, the following categories and numbers represent the post-graduate activities and employment of doctoral degree graduates: Enrolled in a psychology doctoral program (n/a), enrolled in another graduate/professional program (n/a).

Additional Information:

Orientation, Objectives, and Emphasis of Department: The Master of Arts program in Psychology offers concentrations in both Clinical and Applied Research. The program offers students the opportunity to prepare themselves to work in mental health centers, juvenile detention centers, child service agencies, specialized school services, residential treatment facilities, family counseling agencies; teach in community colleges; or study at the doctoral level (PhD). The Clinical Psychology concentration is aimed at training students in the assessment and treatment of mental disorders, through individual, family, and group therapies. The program offers instruction in child, adolescent, and adult disorders. Successful completion of the Clinical Psychology concentration is designed to provide students with the opportunity to become eligible to take the state examinations for certification as a Psychological Associate (45 hours) or Licensed Professional Counselor (51 hours). The Licensed Professional Counselor certification requires an additional 2,000 supervised hours after the MA degree. The Applied Research concentration focuses on advanced psychological theory (i.e., developmental, personality, social, etc.), research methods, statistics, and manuscript preparation. The Applied Research concentration offers students the opportunity to prepare themselves to serve in governmental and community college or to pursue additional graduate study at the doctoral level. All students in the Applied Research concentration are expected to be involved in research activities throughout their graduate program.

Special Facilities or Resources: We have a newly remodeled on-campus center that has a counseling area for clinical practicums and research space for applied research and thesis projects. In addition cooperative arrangements are made with community health centers, schools, governmental agencies, and mental health practitioners for research and practicum opportunities.

Information for Students With Physical Disabilities: We are compliant with federal standards regarding students with disabilities.

Application Information:

Send to: Graduate Studies, The University of Texas of the Permian Basin, 4901 E. University, Odessa, TX 79762. Students are admitted in the Fall, application deadline July 15; Spring, application deadline November 15; Summer, application deadline April 15.

Texas Southwestern Medical Center at Dallas, University of

Division of Psychology, Graduate Program in Clinical Psychology
5323 Harry Hines Boulevard
Dallas, TX 75390-9044
Telephone: (214) 648-5277
Fax: (214) 648-5297
E-mail: *alyce.cadena@utsouthwestern.edu*
Web: *http://www.utsouthwestern.edu/home_pages/clpsych/*

Department Established:

1956. Chairperson: Maurice Korman. Number of Faculty: total–full-time 20, part-time 31; women–full-time 9, part-time 17; minority–full-time 1, part-time 9; faculty subject to the Americans with Disabilities Act 3.

Programs and Degrees Offered:

Listed in the following order: Program area, degree type (T if terminal Master's), number awarded 7/00–6/01. Clinical PhD 13.

APA Accreditation: Clinical PhD: full.

Student Applications/Admissions:

Student Applications

Clinical PhD—Applications 2001–2002, 122. Total applicants accepted 2001–2002, 18. New applicants enrolled 2001–2002, 12. Total enrolled 2001–2002 full-time, 49. Openings 2002–2003, 10. The Median number of years required for completion of a degree are 5. The number of students enrolled full and part-time, who were dismissed or voluntarily withdrew from this program area were 0.

Admissions Requirements:

Scores: Entries appear in this order: required test or GPA, minimum score (if required), median score of students entering in 2001–2002. Doctoral Programs: GRE-V+Q no minimum stated, 1240; overall undergraduate GPA no minimum stated, 3.70; last 2 years GPA no minimum stated; psychology GPA no minimum stated; psychology GPA no minimum stated.

Other Criteria: (importance of criteria rated low, medium, or high): GRE/MAT scores high, research experience high, work experience high, extracurricular activity medium, clinically related public service high, GPA high, letters of recommendation high, interview high, statement of goals and objectives high.

Student Characteristics: The following represents characteristics of students in 2001–2002 in all graduate psychology programs in the department: Female–full-time 37, part-time 0; Male–full-time 11, part-time 0; African American/Black–full-time 0, part-time 0; Hispanic/Latino (a)–full-time 3, part-time 0; Asian/Pacific Islander–full-time 2, part-time 0; American Indian/Alaska Native–full-time 0, part-time 0; Multi-ethnic–full-time 0, part-time 0; students subject to the Americans with Disabilities Act–full-time 2, part-time 0.

Financial Information/Assistance:

Tuition for Full-Time Study: Doctoral: State residents: $40 per credit hour; nonstate residents: $255 per credit hour.

Financial Assistance:

First Year Students: No information provided.

Advanced Students: Teaching assistantships available for advanced students. Average amount paid per academic year: $13,872. Average number of hours worked per week: 20.

Contact Information: Of all students currently enrolled full-time, 72% benefited from one or more of the listed financial assistance programs. For information on financial assistance, contact: http://www3.utsouthwestern.edu/education/finanaid.htm; call 214-648-3611; or write Office of Student Financial Aid, UT Southwestern Medical Center at Dallas, 5323 Harry Hines Blvd., Dallas, Texas 75235-9064.

Internships/Practica: The program provides the equivalent of a year's full-time internship following more than 1000 hours of practica. These clinical experiences are closely supervised. In order to achieve the goal of broad professional preparation, students will have a number of different clinical placements over the course of their practicum and internship assignments. These assignments are carried out at UT Southwestern facilities, community agencies, regional facilities, specialized agencies, and area schools. These clinical training sites include the following: Parkland Memorial Hospital; UT Southwestern Neuropsychology Service; Children's Medical Center, Cystic Fibrosis Center of Children's; UT South-western McDermott Pain Management Center; UT Dallas Callier Center for Communication Disorders; Public School Districts special education departments; Federal Medical Center (a facility of the Federal Bureau of prisons); the student mental health services of Southern Methodist University and the University of Texas at Arlington; Parkland Community Oriented Care Clinic, and Terrell State Hospital; Dallas County Juvenile Department; University Rehabilitation Center at UT Southwestern.

Housing and Day Care: On-campus housing and day care facilities are available.

Employment of Department Graduates:

Master's Degree Graduates: Of those who graduated in the academic year 2000–2001, the following categories and numbers represent the post-graduate activities and employment of master's degree graduates: Enrolled in a post-doctoral residency/fellowship (n/a), employed in independent practice (n/a).

Doctoral Degree Graduates: Of those who graduated in the academic year 2000–2001, the following categories and numbers represent the post-graduate activities and employment of doctoral degree graduates: Enrolled in a psychology doctoral program (n/a), enrolled in another graduate/professional program (n/a), enrolled in a post-doctoral residency/fellowship (5), employed in a professional position in a school system (3), employed in a government agency (professional services) (2), employed in a community mental health/counseling center (2), employed in a hospital/medical center (1).

Additional Information:

Orientation, Objectives, and Emphasis of Department: The Graduate Program in Clinical Psychology is a four-year doctoral program with an affiliated predoctoral internship program in clinical psychology, which is separately accredited by the APA. The program provides a combination of experience in both clinical and research settings reflecting our basic training philosophy, which is a clinician-researcher model. Our specific objectives include offering the student the opportunity to acquire, experience, or develop the following: 1. A closely knit integration between basic psychological knowledge (both theoretical and empirical) and responsible professional services; 2. A wide variety of supervised and broadly conceived clinical and consulting experiences; 3. A sensitivity to professional responsibilities in the context of significant social needs; 4. An understanding of research principles, methodology, and skill in formulating, designing, and implementing psychological research; 5. A competence and confidence in the role of psychology in multidisciplinary settings.

Special Facilities or Resources: UT Southwestern has a number of laboratories and clinical settings investigating brain/behavior relationship, as well as many projects focusing on the psychosocial aspects of various medical and psychiatric disorders. Disorders studied include affective illness, anxiety, schizophrenia, sleep-wake dysfunctions, and medical conditions such as Alzheimer's Disease, epilepsy, temporomandibular disorder, cystic fibrosis, and organ transplantation. Notable examples of comprehensive clinical research programs at UT Southwestern include the following: an affective disorders research program: a sleep disorders research laboratory; an Alzheimer's Disease Center; a neuropsychology laboratory; a pain management program; and research programs in basic neuroscience.

Information for Students With Physical Disabilities: Disabilities are reviewed and reasonably accommodated on an individual basis.

Application Information:
Send to: Office of the Registrar, Graduate Admissions, UT Southwestern Medical Center at Dallas, 5323 Harry Hines Blvd., Dallas, TX 75390-9096; preferred address is via Internet at www.utsouthwestern.edu/gradapp. Students are admitted in the Fall, application deadline January 1. Prefer application via Internet address above.

Texas Tech University
Department of Psychology
Box 42051
Lubbock, TX 79409-2051
Telephone: (806) 742-3711
Fax: (806) 742-0818
E-mail: *psygradapp@ttu.edu*
Web: *http://www.psychology.ttu.edu*

Department Established:
1950. Chairperson: Ruth H. Maki. Number of Faculty: total–full-time 28; women–full-time 12; minority–full-time 1; faculty subject to the Americans with Disabilities Act 1.

Programs and Degrees Offered:
Listed in the following order: Program area, degree type (T if terminal Master's), number awarded 7/00–6/01. Clinical Psychology PhD 11, Cognitive Psychology/Applied C PhD 1, Counseling Psychology PhD 7, General Experimental MA, Human Factors PhD, Social Psychology PhD 3.

APA Accreditation: Clinical PhD: full. Counseling PhD: full.

Student Applications/Admissions:
Student Applications
   Clinical Psychology PhD—Applications 2001–2002, 72. Total applicants accepted 2001–2002, 12. New applicants enrolled 2001–2002, 8. Total enrolled 2001–2002 full-time, 34. Openings 2002–2003, 7. *Cognitive Psychology/Applied C PhD*—Applications 2001–2002, 26. Total applicants accepted 2001–2002, 2. New applicants enrolled 2001–2002, 1. Total enrolled 2001–2002 full-time, 4. Openings 2002–2003, 4. *Counseling Psychology PhD*—Applications 2001–2002, 71. Total applicants accepted 2001–2002, 12. New applicants enrolled 2001–2002, 7. Total enrolled 2001–2002 full-time, 32. Openings 2002–2003, 7. *General Experimental MA*—Applications 2001–2002, 0. Openings 2002–2003, 4. *Human Factors PhD*—Applications 2001–2002, 13. Total applicants accepted 2001–2002, 6. New applicants enrolled 2001–2002, 3. Total enrolled 2001–2002 full-time, 7. Openings 2002–2003, 4. *Social Psychology PhD*—Applications 2001–2002, 7. Total applicants accepted 2001–2002, 2. New applicants enrolled 2001–2002, 2. Total enrolled 2001–2002 full-time, 4. Openings 2002–2003, 4.

Admissions Requirements:
   Scores: Entries appear in this order: required test or GPA, minimum score (if required), median score of students entering

in 2001–2002. Master's Programs: GRE-V 500, 515; GRE-Q 410, 490; GRE-V+Q 910, 1005; GRE-Analytical 390, 495; overall undergraduate GPA no minimum stated; last 2 years GPA 2.10, 2.97; psychology GPA no minimum stated. Doctoral Programs: GRE-V 420, 542; GRE-Q 530, 635; GRE-V+Q 950, 1177; GRE-Analytical 430, 630; GRE-V+Q+Analytical 1380, 1807; overall undergraduate GPA no minimum stated; last 2 years GPA 3.65, 3.85; psychology GPA no minimum stated; psychology GPA no minimum stated.
   Other Criteria: (importance of criteria rated low, medium, or high): GRE/MAT scores medium, research experience high, work experience medium, extracurricular activity low, clinically related public service medium, GPA medium, letters of recommendation high, statement of goals and objectives high, high. Work experience for experimental-low, counseling-medium, clinical-high; extracurricular activity for experimental-low, counseling-low, clinical-medium; clinically related public service for counseling-medium, clinical-medium; interview for clinical-low, experimental-low.

Student Characteristics: The following represents characteristics of students in 2001–2002 in all graduate psychology programs in the department: Female–full-time 57, part-time 0; Male–full-time 25, part-time 0; African American/Black–full-time 1, part-time 0; Hispanic/Latino (a)–full-time 12, part-time 0; Asian/Pacific Islander–full-time 2, part-time 0; American Indian/Alaska Native–full-time 0, part-time 0; students subject to the Americans with Disabilities Act–full-time 1.

Financial Information/Assistance:
   Tuition for Full-Time Study: *Master's:* State residents per academic year $1,340, $67 per credit hour; nonstate residents: per academic year $6,360, $318 per credit hour. *Doctoral:* State residents: per academic year $1,340, $67 per credit hour; nonstate residents: per academic year $6,360, $318 per credit hour.

Financial Assistance:
   First Year Students: Teaching assistantships available for first-year. Average amount paid per academic year: $9,200. Average number of hours worked per week: 20. Apply by Same as appl. Tuition remission given: partial. Research assistantships available for first-year. Average amount paid per academic year: $9,200. Average number of hours worked per week: 20. Apply by Same as appl. Tuition remission given: partial. Fellowships and scholarships available for first-year. Average amount paid per academic year: $1,000. Average number of hours worked per week: 0. Apply by Same as appl. Tuition remission given: partial.
   Advanced Students: Teaching assistantships available for advanced students. Average amount paid per academic year: $9,600. Average number of hours worked per week: 20. Apply by Same as appl. Tuition remission given: partial. Research assistantships available for advanced students. Average amount paid per academic year: $9,800. Average number of hours worked per week: 20. Apply by Same as appl. Tuition remission given: partial. Fellowships and scholarships available for advanced students. Average amount paid per academic year: $1,000. Average number of hours worked per week: 0. Apply by Same as appl. Tuition remission given: partial.
   Contact Information: Of all students currently enrolled full-time, 90% benefited from one or more of the listed financial assistance programs. For information on financial assistance, contact: Apply to Psychology Department Admissions. Most students

receive both a $1,000 scholarship (which waives out-of-state tuition) and an assistantship. Half-time assistantships waive out-of-state tuition and most University fees.

Internships/Practica: Practica in our Psychology Clinic and Texas Tech University Counseling Center. Paid practica are available in the community. Such placements include a psychiatric prison, the pain clinic and Neuropsychiatry Department in the TTU Health Sciences Center, the local school district, a juvenile justice center, and conducting assessments at the state school and with local psychologists. For those doctoral students for whom a professional internship is required prior to graduation, 10 applied in 2000–2001. Of those who applied, 10 were placed in internships listed by the Association of Psychology Postdoctoral and Internship Programs (APPIC); 10 were placed in APA accredited internships.

Housing and Day Care: On-campus housing and day care facilities are available.

Employment of Department Graduates:

Master's Degree Graduates: Of those who graduated in the academic year 2000–2001, the following categories and numbers represent the post-graduate activities and employment of master's degree graduates: Enrolled in a psychology doctoral program (1), enrolled in another graduate/professional program (0), enrolled in a post-doctoral residency/fellowship (n/a), employed in independent practice (n/a).

Doctoral Degree Graduates: Of those who graduated in the academic year 2000–2001, the following categories and numbers represent the post-graduate activities and employment of doctoral degree graduates: Enrolled in a psychology doctoral program (n/a), enrolled in another graduate/professional program (n/a), enrolled in a post-doctoral residency/fellowship (1), employed in independent practice (1), employed in an academic position at a university (1), employed in other positions at a higher education institution (3), employed in business or industry (research/consulting) (2), employed in a community mental health/counseling center (4), employed in a hospital/medical center (1), other employment position (4).

Additional Information:

Orientation, Objectives, and Emphasis of Department: The clinical program adheres to a basic scientist-practitioner model with equal emphasis given to these components of clinical training. The program strives to develop student competencies in the following areas: psychotherapy and other major patterns of psychological treatment, clinical research, psychodiagnostic assessment, psychopathology, personality, and general psychology. The doctoral specialization in counseling psychology is also firmly committed to a concept of balanced scientist-practitioner training and is designed to foster the development of competence in basic psychology, counseling and psychotherapy, psychological assessment, psychological research, and professional ethics. Programs in experimental psychology (cognitive, applied cognitive, social, human factors) encompass a variety of research interests, both basic and applied. Students in these programs are exposed to the data, methods, and theories and a wide variety of basic areas of psychology while at the same time developing a commitment to an area of special interest through research with a faculty mentor. Collaborative work across departmental programs is encouraged, and the department also collaborates with colleagues in management, industrial engineering, neuroscience, and the Health Sciences Center.

Special Facilities or Resources: The department is housed in its own four-story building, which includes a large, well-equipped psychology clinic for practicum training, numerous laboratories equipped for human research activities, and sufficient student workspace and offices. The university maintains constantly expanding computing support systems that can be accessed from computers in the psychology building. The Psychology Department has a number of microcomputers and software available for student use. The university enjoys an unusually good relationship with the local metropolitan community of over 200,000 residents. Major medical facilities, a private psychiatric hospital, a psychiatric prison, and a state school for the developmentally disabled are located within the city, and APA-accredited internship training is available in the University Counseling Center. The cost of living is quite low and the climate is excellent.

Information for Students With Physical Disabilities: We work continually to maintain and improve access to all aspects of our training programs for those with physical disabilities.

Application Information:
Send to: Texas Tech University Admissions, Psychology Department, Box 42051, Lubbock, TX 79409-2051. Students are admitted in the Fall. Deadlines for application: Counseling: January 15, Clinical: January 15, Experimental: March 15. (Materials must be received by February 15 for consideration for the University's prestigious Chancellor's Fellowships, which are presently an additional $3,000/year for 3 years.) *Fee:* $25. There is one application fee required to apply to all Texas state universities, using the Texas Common Application.

Texas Tech University
Educational Psychology and Leadership/Educational Psychology
College of Education
Box 41071
Lubbock, TX 79409-1071
Telephone: (806) 742-2393
Fax: (806) 742-2179
E-mail: *psygradapp@ttu.edu*
Web: *http://www.educ.ttu.edu*

Department Established:
Program Coordinator: Arturo Olivarez, Jr. Number of Faculty: total–full-time 4, part-time 1; minority–full-time 3.

Programs and Degrees Offered:
Listed in the following order: Program area, degree type (T if terminal Master's), number awarded 7/00–6/01. Educational Psychology EdD (T) 2.

APA Accreditation: Counseling EdD: full. Combined EdD: full.

Student Applications/Admissions:
Student Applications
Educational Psychology EdD—Applications 2001–2002, 17. Total applicants accepted 2001–2002, 7. New applicants enrolled

2001–2002, 5. Total enrolled 2001–2002 full-time, 15, part-time, 2. Openings 2002–2003, 6. The Median number of years required for completion of a degree are 4. The number of students enrolled full and part-time, who were dismissed or voluntarily withdrew from this program area were 1.

Admissions Requirements:

Scores: Entries appear in this order: required test or GPA, minimum score (if required), median score of students entering in 2001–2002. Master's Programs: GRE-V 500, 500; GRE-Q 500, 500; GRE-V+Q 1000, 1000; overall undergraduate GPA 3.00, 3.00; last 2 years GPA 3.00, 3.00. Doctoral Programs: GRE-V 550, 550; GRE-Q 550, 550; GRE-V+Q 1100, 1100; overall undergraduate GPA 3.25, 3.25; last 2 years GPA 3.25, 3.25; psychology GPA no minimum stated; psychology GPA no minimum stated. Our admissions system allow us to include information from these standardized tests, but no weights are assigned since our decision is made based on a wholistic method which includes a variety of other material (letters of recommendation, interviews, etc) that the student is required to submit.

Other Criteria: (importance of criteria rated low, medium, or high): research experience medium, work experience high, extracurricular activity medium, clinically related public service low, GPA medium, letters of recommendation high, interview medium, statement of goals and objectives high.

Student Characteristics: The following represents characteristics of students in 2001–2002 in all graduate psychology programs in the department: Female–full-time 7, part-time 0; Male–full-time 1, part-time 0; African American/Black–full-time 0, part-time 0; Hispanic/Latino (a)–full-time 0, part-time 0; Asian/Pacific Islander–full-time 2, part-time 0; American Indian/Alaska Native–full-time 0, part-time 0; Multi-ethnic–full-time 0, part-time 0; students subject to the Americans with Disabilities Act–full-time 0, part-time 0.

Financial Information/Assistance:

Tuition for Full-Time Study: *Master's:* State residents per academic year $2,200, $88 per credit hour; nonstate residents: per academic year $7,080, $295 per credit hour. *Doctoral:* State residents: per academic year $2,200, $88 per credit hour; nonstate residents: per academic year $7,080, $295 per credit hour.

Financial Assistance:

First Year Students: Teaching assistantships available for first-year. Average amount paid per academic year: $9,450. Average number of hours worked per week: 20. Apply by March 15. Tuition remission given: partial. Research assistantships available for first-year. Average amount paid per academic year: $9,450. Average number of hours worked per week: 20. Apply by March 15. Tuition remission given: partial. Fellowships and scholarships available for first-year.

Advanced Students: Teaching assistantships available for advanced students. Average amount paid per academic year: $9,450. Average number of hours worked per week: 20. Apply by March 15. Tuition remission given: partial. Research assistantships available for advanced students. Average amount paid per academic year: $9,450. Average number of hours worked per week: 20. Apply by March 15. Tuition remission given: partial.

Contact Information: Of all students currently enrolled full-time, 8% benefited from one or more of the listed financial assistance programs. For information on financial assistance, contact: Dr. Fred Hartmeister, College of Education, Box 41071, Lubbock, TX 79409-1071.

Internships/Practica: Our doctoral students typically will be allowed to team teach with faculty who have graduate status. They may also teach an undergraduate course in educational psychology.

Housing and Day Care: No on-campus housing and day care facilities are available.

Employment of Department Graduates:

Master's Degree Graduates: Of those who graduated in the academic year 2000–2001, the following categories and numbers represent the post-graduate activities and employment of master's degree graduates: Enrolled in a post-doctoral residency/fellowship (n/a), employed in independent practice (n/a), employed in an academic position at a university (0).

Doctoral Degree Graduates: Of those who graduated in the academic year 2000–2001, the following categories and numbers represent the post-graduate activities and employment of doctoral degree graduates: Enrolled in a psychology doctoral program (n/a), enrolled in another graduate/professional program (n/a), employed in an academic position at a university (2).

Additional Information:

Orientation, Objectives, and Emphasis of Department: The objectives of the Educational Psychology program are to impart the following: (a) understanding of philosophical, historical, cultural, and psychological influences on educational theory; (b) understanding of measurement processes and their relationship to educational theory and practice; (c) understanding of research processes, including the component parts of methodology and statistics and their relationship to educational theory and practice; (d) appreciation for the importance of research in graduate study and professional life; (e) ability to conduct rigorous independent research; (f) ability to add knowledge to instructional programs; and (g) ability to be a critical and reflective thinker. The doctoral program emphasizes a broad concept of professional development that focuses on knowledge of the foundations of education (history, philosophy, cultural); research (research methodology, statistics, measurement); essential areas of knowledge in educational psychology (human development, motivation and learning, etc.); and practice (internships in college teaching, research and program development in schools, etc., individual and collaborative research). Graduates of the doctoral program are prepared to assume roles as college teachers of educational psychology, research and development specialists in schools, service centers, measurement agencies (i.e., ACT and ETS), and other agencies and organizations where the knowledge and skills of educational psychology are required.

Special Facilities or Resources: Our college has a computer lab reserved for graduate students and faculty with laser printers, VAX terminals, MacIntosh and IBM computers, and an array of graphing, word processing, and statistical software. In addition, travel money is available for students with accepted proposals to professional meetings. All students have free access to their own computer accounts for access to library services, many other databases for research, and the Internet.

Information for Students With Physical Disabilities: Designated parking spaces near building entrances are available. The university provides assistance to those students who require readers for taking notes and tests.

Application Information:
Send to: Office of Graduate Admissions, Texas Tech University, P.O. Box 41030, Lubbock, TX 79409-1070, (806) 742-2787. Students are admitted in the Fall, application deadline May 15; Spring, application deadline September 15. Application must be in at least three months prior to the date of intended enrollment. *Fee:* $25. Fee waived or deferred for full-time Texas Tech employees, spouses, and dependents less than 25 years.

Texas Woman's University (2001 data)
Department of Psychology and Philosophy
Arts & Sciences
P.O. Box 425470
Denton, TX 76204
Telephone: (940) 898-2303
Fax: (940) 898-2301
E-mail: *DMiller@twu.edu*
Web: *http://www.twu.edu/as/psyphil/*

Department Established:
1942. Chairperson: Basil Hamilton, PhD. Number of Faculty: total–full-time 12, part-time 2; women–full-time 8.

Programs and Degrees Offered:
Listed in the following order: Program area, degree type (T if terminal Master's), number awarded 7/00–6/01. Counseling PhD (T) 7, school PhD (T) 3.

APA Accreditation: Counseling PhD: full.

Student Applications/Admissions:
Student Applications
Counseling PhD—Applications 2001–2002, 60. Total applicants accepted 2001–2002, 10. New applicants enrolled 2001–2002, 8. Total enrolled 2001–2002 full-time, 59. Openings 2002–2003, 9. The Median number of years required for completion of a degree are 6. The number of students enrolled full and part-time, who were dismissed or voluntarily withdrew from this program area were 1. *School PhD*—Applications 2001–2002, 8. Total applicants accepted 2001–2002, 8. New applicants enrolled 2001–2002, 8. Total enrolled 2001–2002 full-time, 30, part-time, 5. Openings 2002–2003, 5. The Median number of years required for completion of a degree are 5. The number of students enrolled full and part-time, who were dismissed or voluntarily withdrew from this program area were 1.

Admissions Requirements:
Scores: Entries appear in this order: required test or GPA, minimum score (if required), median score of students entering in 2001–2002. Master's Programs: GRE-V 500, 580; GRE-Q 500, 570; GRE-V+Q 1000, 1150; overall undergraduate GPA 3.00, 3.50; last 2 years GPA 3.00, 3.60; psychology GPA 3.50,

3.75. Doctoral Programs: GRE-V 500, 585; GRE-Q 500, 585; GRE-V+Q 1000, 1170; overall undergraduate GPA 3.0, 3.60; last 2 years GPA 3.0, 3.65; psychology GPA 3.5, 3.70; psychology GPA 3.5, 3.85.
Other Criteria: (importance of criteria rated low, medium, or high): GRE/MAT scores medium, research experience medium, work experience high, extracurricular activity low, clinically related public service medium, GPA high, letters of recommendation high, interview high, statement of goals and objectives high.

Student Characteristics: The following represents characteristics of students in 2001–2002 in all graduate psychology programs in the department: Female–full-time 18, part-time 10; Male–full-time 6, part-time 2; African American/Black–full-time 1, part-time 1; Hispanic/Latino (a)–full-time 3, part-time 1; Asian/Pacific Islander–full-time 0, part-time 0; American Indian/Alaska Native–full-time 0, part-time 0.

Financial Information/Assistance:
Tuition for Full-Time Study: No information provided.

Financial Assistance:
First Year Students: No information provided.
Advanced Students: No information provided.
Contact Information: Of all students currently enrolled full-time, 25% benefited from one or more of the listed financial assistance programs. For information on financial assistance, contact: Admissions Coordinator.

Internships/Practica: For those doctoral students for whom a professional internship is required prior to graduation, 10 applied in 2000–2001. Of those who applied, 2 were placed in internships listed by the Association of Psychology Postdoctoral and Internship Programs (APPIC); 8 were placed in APA accredited internships.

Housing and Day Care: No on-campus housing and day care facilities are available.

Employment of Department Graduates:
Master's Degree Graduates: Of those who graduated in the academic year 2000–2001, the following categories and numbers represent the post-graduate activities and employment of master's degree graduates: Enrolled in a post-doctoral residency/fellowship (n/a), employed in independent practice (n/a).
Doctoral Degree Graduates: Of those who graduated in the academic year 2000–2001, the following categories and numbers represent the post-graduate activities and employment of doctoral degree graduates: Enrolled in a psychology doctoral program (n/a), enrolled in another graduate/professional program (n/a).

Additional Information:
Orientation, Objectives, and Emphasis of Department: Both the APA-accredited Counseling Psychology doctoral program and the Counseling Psychology master's program prepare students in the practitioner-scientist model for counseling practice with particular emphasis on family systems, gender issues, assessment, and psychotherapeutic work with individuals and families in their contextual systems. The model provides clear training in both practice and science, but emphasizes practice, practice that is informed by science. The programs' philosophy, curricula, faculty,

and students, situated within the unique context of the TWU mission, attempt to create an atmosphere that is supportive, open, and flexible. Graduate training in school psychology at the master's level provides a program emphasizing direct service to school settings. Specific competencies and areas of specialization stressed in coursework and field-based training include child development, psychopathology, theories and principles of learning, behavioral intervention and prevention strategies, diagnostic assessment, and evaluation techniques. Doctoral level training in school psychology focuses on applied preparation and training experiences in professional school psychology. This program prepares students in skills required in direct-to-client services (for example, diagnostic assessment and evaluation skills, therapeutic and intervention techniques, and competencies in the application of learning principles). This program also provides training and supervised experiences in the consultation model, emphasizing such competencies as systems and organizational analysis, supervision of programs and services, diagnostic team leadership, grant proposal writing, in-service education, and general coordination of school-based services in a consultative capacity.

Special Facilities or Resources: The University Counseling Center is an APA-approved internship site.

Information for Students With Physical Disabilities: Campus meets ADA requirements.

Application Information:

Send to: Admissions Coordinator, Department of Psychology and Philosophy, Texas Woman's University, P.O. Box 425470, Denton, TX 76204-5420. Students are admitted in the Fall, application deadline February 1. March 1 and October 15 deadlines for Fall and Spring admission to MA school psychology and March 1 for MA counseling psychology program. *Fee:* $30.

Texas, University of, Arlington
Department of Psychology
College of Science
UTA Box 19528
Arlington, TX 76019-0528
Telephone: (817) 272-2281
Fax: (817) 272-2364
E-mail: *gorfein@uta.edu*
Web: *http://www.uta.edu/psychology/psych.html*

Department Established:

1959. Chairperson: Paul B. Paulus. Number of Faculty: total–full-time 15, part-time 6; women–full-time 4, part-time 2; minority–full-time 1, part-time 1.

Programs and Degrees Offered:

Listed in the following order: Program area, degree type (T if terminal Master's), number awarded 7/00–6/01. BA-MS Industrial-Organizational MA (T), Experimental-general PhD 3, general MA 4, Industrial-Organizational MA (T).

Student Applications/Admissions:
Student Applications

BA-MS *Industrial-Organizational* MA—Applications 2001–2002, 0. Total enrolled 2001-2002 part-time, 1. Openings 2002–2003, 8. The Median number of years required for completion of a degree are NA. The number of students enrolled full and part-time, who were dismissed or voluntarily withdrew from this program area were 0. *Experimental-general PhD*—Applications 2001–2002, 7. Total applicants accepted 2001–2002, 6. New applicants enrolled 2001–2002, 3. Total enrolled 2001-2002 full-time, 17, part-time, 1. Openings 2002–2003, 8. The Median number of years required for completion of a degree are 6. The number of students enrolled full and part-time, who were dismissed or voluntarily withdrew from this program area were 1. *General MA*—Applications 2001–2002, 38. Total applicants accepted 2001–2002, 18. New applicants enrolled 2001–2002, 8. Total enrolled 2001-2002 full-time, 17, part-time, 2. Openings 2002–2003, 10. The Median number of years required for completion of a degree are 2. The number of students enrolled full and part-time, who were dismissed or voluntarily withdrew from this program area were 0. *Industrial-Organizational MA*—Applications 2001–2002, 4. Total applicants accepted 2001–2002, 4. New applicants enrolled 2001–2002, 3. Total enrolled 2001-2002 full-time, 1, part-time, 2. Openings 2002–2003, 10. The Median number of years required for completion of a degree are NA. The number of students enrolled full and part-time, who were dismissed or voluntarily withdrew from this program area were 0.

Admissions Requirements:

Scores: Entries appear in this order: required test or GPA, minimum score (if required), median score of students entering in 2001–2002. Master's Programs: GRE-V n/a, 536; GRE-Q n/a, 636; GRE-V+Q n/a, 1171; last 2 years GPA 3.0, 3.40. Doctoral Programs: GRE-V n/a, 534; GRE-Q n/a, 602; GRE-V+Q n/a, 1136; last 2 years GPA 3.0, 3.75; psychology GPA no minimum stated; psychology GPA no minimum stated.
Other Criteria: (importance of criteria rated low, medium, or high): GRE/MAT scores medium, research experience high, extracurricular activity low, GPA medium, letters of recommendation medium, statement of goals and objectives medium.

Student Characteristics: The following represents characteristics of students in 2001–2002 in all graduate psychology programs in the department: Female–full-time 28, part-time 3; Male–full-time 7, part-time 2; African American/Black–full-time 1, part-time 0; Hispanic/Latino (a)–full-time 1, part-time 0; Asian/Pacific Islander–full-time 4, part-time 1; American Indian/Alaska Native–full-time 0, part-time 0; Multi-ethnic–full-time 0, part-time 0; students subject to the Americans with Disabilities Act–full-time 0, part-time 1.

Financial Information/Assistance:

Tuition for Full-Time Study: *Master's:* State residents per academic year $4,370, $282 per credit hour; nonstate residents: per academic year $10,500, $518 per credit hour. *Doctoral:* State residents: per academic year $4,370, $282 per credit hour; nonstate residents: per academic year $10,500, $518 per credit hour.

Financial Assistance:

First Year Students: Teaching assistantships available for first-year. Average amount paid per academic year: $12,000. Average number of hours worked per week: 20. Research assistantships available for first-year. Average amount paid per academic year: $12,000. Average number of hours worked per week: 20.

Advanced Students: Teaching assistantships available for advanced students. Average amount paid per academic year: $12,900. Average number of hours worked per week: 20. Research assistantships available for advanced students. Average amount paid per academic year: $12,900. Average number of hours worked per week: 20.

Contact Information: Of all students currently enrolled full-time, 85% benefited from one or more of the listed financial assistance programs. For information on financial assistance, contact: Dr. David Gorfein, Graduate Advisor, UTA Dept. of Psychology, Box 19528. gorfein@uta.edu.

Internships/Practica: The Arlington-Dallas-Fort Worth area is a major center of business and industrial growth in Texas and offers diverse practica opportunities in consulting firms, corporations, and government and private agencies.

Housing and Day Care: No on-campus housing and day care facilities are available.

Employment of Department Graduates:

Master's Degree Graduates: Of those who graduated in the academic year 2000–2001, the following categories and numbers represent the post-graduate activities and employment of master's degree graduates: Enrolled in a psychology doctoral program (2), enrolled in another graduate/professional program (1), enrolled in a post-doctoral residency/fellowship (n/a), employed in independent practice (n/a), employed in business or industry (research/consulting) (1).

Doctoral Degree Graduates: Of those who graduated in the academic year 2000–2001, the following categories and numbers represent the post-graduate activities and employment of doctoral degree graduates: Enrolled in a psychology doctoral program (n/a), enrolled in another graduate/professional program (n/a), enrolled in a post-doctoral residency/fellowship (1), employed in business or industry (research/consulting) (2).

Additional Information:

Orientation, Objectives, and Emphasis of Department: The graduate program provides comprehensive interdisciplinary training in experimental psychology and allied fields. The general experimental program trains students to be research scientists in specialty areas that include animal behavior, animal learning, neuroscience, sensation, perception, and cognitive, developmental, personality, social, mathematical or quantitative psychology. A terminal master's program emphasizing industrial-organizational psychology is also available. All students in the graduate program are broadly trained in statistics and experimental design. The objective of graduate work in the experimental psychology program is to educate the student in the methods and basic content of the discipline and to provide an apprenticeship in the execution of creative research in laboratory and/or field settings. The Master's of Science in General Experimental Psychology is designed to form a basis for the doctoral program but is open to those seeking a terminal master's degree. The terminal Master's of Science degree program emphasizing industrial-organizational psychology combines rigorous coursework in experimental design, quantitative methods, psychology, and management with practicum experience enabling students to perform effectively in the workplace. The PhD program in general experimental psychology is intended to provide students with deep knowledge of a specialty area and broad knowledge of experimental psychology.

Special Facilities or Resources: Each faculty member who is active in research has his or her own research space. The Department of Psychology is fortunate to have ample space for research, avoiding conflicts that can arise when space is tight. The department has approximately 18,000 total square feet of research space; 7,000 square feet for human subject research and 11,000 square feet for animal research. Graduate students work in faculty labs and use their research facilities. The department is able to utilize modern audiovisual technology in the classroom and is equipped with computer facilities for graduate research. Graduate students have in-office network connections as well as computer access in research laboratories and departmental computer labs. In addition to the departmental computer labs, the university academic computing services operates seven on-campus computing facilities and serves the academic and research needs of the university. The University Libraries include the Central Library, the Architecture and Fine Arts Library, and the Science and Engineering Library. Library resources include a full array of modern technological access to print and electronic information, Internet access, and an extensive interlibrary loan network in addition to the 2,430,000 books, periodicals, documents, technical reports, etc. on hand.

Information for Students With Physical Disabilities: The Office for Students with Disabilities is charged with the responsibility of ensuring full inclusion of all disabled students in all programs and activities offered at U.T. Arlington. In compliance with the Americans with Disabilities Act, all disabled students who require accommodations at U.T. Arlington should contact the director at 817-272-3364 or visit the office, located in the lower level of the E.H. Hereford University Center.

Application Information:
Send to: Graduate Advisor, Department of Psychology, Box 19528, The University of Texas at Arlington, Arlington, TX 76019-0528. Students are admitted in the Fall, application deadline June 14; Spring, application deadline Oct 25; Summer, application deadline Mar 28. These deadlines are for U.S. student applications. International student application deadlines are in April, September, and January. *Fee:* $25.

Texas, University of, at Austin (2001 data)
Department of Human Ecology, Division of Child Development and Family Relationships
Austin, TX 78712
Telephone: (512) 471-0337
Fax: (512) 471-5630
E-mail: *hegrad@uts.cc.utexas.edu*

Student Applications/Admissions:
Admissions Requirements: No information provided.
Student Characteristics: No information provided.
Financial Information/Assistance:
Tuition for Full-Time Study: No information provided.

Financial Assistance:
First Year Students: No information provided.
Advanced Students: No information provided.
Contact Information: No information provided.

Internships/Practica: A variety of practicum experiences may be arranged to meet students' individual needs.

Housing and Day Care: No on-campus housing and day care facilities are available.

Employment of Department Graduates:

Master's Degree Graduates: Of those who graduated in the academic year 2000–2001, the following categories and numbers represent the post-graduate activities and employment of master's degree graduates: Enrolled in a post-doctoral residency/fellowship (n/a), employed in independent practice (n/a).

Doctoral Degree Graduates: Of those who graduated in the academic year 2000–2001, the following categories and numbers represent the post-graduate activities and employment of doctoral degree graduates: Enrolled in a psychology doctoral program (n/a), enrolled in another graduate/professional program (n/a).

Additional Information:

Orientation, Objectives, and Emphasis of Department: The program leading to the PhD in child development and family relationships is designed to prepare individuals for research, teaching, and administrative positions in colleges and universities and for positions in research, government, and other public and private settings. The focus of the program is research concerning the interplay between individual development and family relationships. Development of the individual is considered within the context of the family, peer group, community, and culture. The family is studied as a system of relationships, with attention given to roles, communication, conflict resolution and negotiation, socialization, and family members' perceptions and emotions during interactions with one another. The program emphasizes the investigation of the family and other social processes that contribute to competence and optimal development in individuals from birth to maturity and on how such competencies, once developed, are reflected in interpersonal relationships and family interactions. The MA program in child development and family relationships is designed to deepen the student's knowledge of normal development within the context of the family, peer group, community, and culture, and to develop the student's skill in generating new knowledge in the field through basic or applied research.

Special Facilities or Resources: Students in the child development program may become involved in the university child and family laboratory, a laboratory preschool with about 80 three- to five-year-old children and infants enrolled each semester. The school contains research rooms and observation facilities. Students in the program also get extensive experience using state of the art micro- and mainframe computers. Research space and equipment (such as event recorders, videotape cameras, and multi-channel audiotape recorders) for audiotaping and videotaping of interviews and interactions are readily available. In addition to the departmental resources, the multi-cultural population of Austin constitutes a rich resource for both research and practicum experiences. The library, computation center, and support services of the University of Texas at Austin are among the best in the nation. Free services available to students include the Learning Skills Center, Career Choice Information Center, and Counseling Center.

Texas, University of, Austin
Department of Educational Psychology
College of Education
George I. Sanchez Building 504
Austin, TX 78712-1296
Telephone: (512) 471-4155
Fax: (512) 471-1288
E-mail: *edpsych@teachnet.edb.utexas.edu*
Web: *http://edpsych.edb.utexas.edu*

Department Established:

1923. Chairperson: Edmund T. Emmer. Number of Faculty: total–full-time 30, part-time 17; women–full-time 16, part-time 8; minority–full-time 4, part-time 1.

Programs and Degrees Offered:

Listed in the following order: Program area, degree type (T if terminal Master's), number awarded 7/00–6/01. Academic educational MA (T) 1, academic educational-MEd (T) 3, counseling psychology PhD 19, counselor education-MEd (T) 16, human development in education PhD 5, learning, cognition and instru PhD 2, quantitative methods PhD 2, school psychology PhD 10.

APA Accreditation: Counseling PhD: full. School PhD: full.

Student Applications/Admissions:

Student Applications

Academic educational MA—Applications 2001–2002, 23. Total applicants accepted 2001–2002, 19. New applicants enrolled 2001–2002, 10. Total enrolled 2001–2002 full-time, 13, part-time, 3. Openings 2002–2003, 10. The Median number of years required for completion of a degree are 2. The number of students enrolled full and part-time, who were dismissed or voluntarily withdrew from this program area were 7. *Counseling psychology PhD*—Applications 2001–2002, 97. Total applicants accepted 2001–2002, 20. New applicants enrolled 2001–2002, 10. Total enrolled 2001–2002 full-time, 47, part-time, 18. Openings 2002–2003, 12. The Median number of years required for completion of a degree are 6. The number of students enrolled full and part-time, who were dismissed or voluntarily withdrew from this program area were 3. *Human development in education PhD*—Applications 2001–2002, 11. Total applicants accepted 2001–2002, 8. New applicants enrolled 2001–2002, 6. Total enrolled 2001–2002 full-time, 21, part-time, 9. Openings 2002–2003, 6. The Median number of years required for completion of a degree are 7. The number of students enrolled full and part-time, who were dismissed or voluntarily withdrew from this program area were 0. *Learning, cognition and instru PhD*—Applications 2001–2002, 14. Total applicants accepted 2001–2002, 12. New applicants enrolled 2001–2002, 8. Total enrolled 2001–2002 full-time, 27, part-time, 4. Openings 2002–2003, 6. The Median number of years required for completion of a degree are 6. The number of students enrolled full and part-time, who were dismissed or voluntarily withdrew from this program area were 1. *Quantitative methods PhD*—Applications 2001–2002, 28. Total applicants accepted 2001–2002, 14. New applicants enrolled 2001–2002, 7. Total enrolled 2001–2002 full-time, 21, part-time, 9. Openings 2002–2003, 6. The Median number of years required for completion of a degree are 3. The number of students enrolled full and part-time, who were dismissed or voluntarily withdrew from this program area were 0. *School psychology PhD*—Applications 2001–2002, 54. Total applicants accepted 2001–2002, 29. New applicants enrolled 2001–2002, 12. Total enrolled 2001–2002 full-time, 56, part-time, 19. Openings 2002–2003, 12. The Median number of years required for completion of a degree are 8. The number of students enrolled full and part-time, who were dismissed or voluntarily withdrew from this program area were 5.

Admissions Requirements:

Scores: Entries appear in this order: required test or GPA, minimum score (if required), median score of students entering in 2001–2002. Master's Programs: The median upper-division and graduate coursework GPA was 3.4. Doctoral Programs: last 2 years GPA no minimum stated; psychology GPA no minimum stated; psychology GPA no minimum stated. The median upper-division and graduate coursework GPA was 3.7. *Other Criteria:* (importance of criteria rated low, medium, or high): GRE/MAT scores medium, research experience medium, work experience medium, extracurricular activity medium, clinically related public service medium, GPA medium, letters of recommendation high, interview statement of goals and objectives high.

Student Characteristics: The following represents characteristics of students in 2001–2002 in all graduate psychology programs in the department: Female–full-time 191, part-time 42; Male–full-time 44, part-time 11; African American/Black–full-time 10, part-time 3; Hispanic/Latino (a)–full-time 24, part-time 5; Asian/Pacific Islander–full-time 5, part-time 3; American Indian/Alaska Native–full-time 1, part-time 1; Multi-ethnic–full-time 0, part-time 0; students subject to the Americans with Disabilities Act–full-time 2, part-time 0.

Financial Information/Assistance:

Tuition for Full-Time Study: *Master's:* State residents per academic year $3,160, $126 per credit hour; nonstate residents: per academic year $6,958, $337 per credit hour. *Doctoral:* State residents: per academic year $3,160, $126 per credit hour; nonstate residents: per academic year $6,958, $337 per credit hour.

Financial Assistance:

First Year Students: Teaching assistantships available for first-year. Average amount paid per academic year: $4,250. Average number of hours worked per week: 10. Apply by April 1. Tuition remission given: partial. Fellowships and scholarships available for first-year. Average amount paid per academic year: $1,700. Average number of hours worked per week: 0. Apply by Jan 15.

Advanced Students: Teaching assistantships available for advanced students. Average amount paid per academic year: $4,250. Average number of hours worked per week: 10. Apply by April 1. Tuition remission given: partial. Research assistantships available for advanced students. Average amount paid per academic year: $4,500. Average number of hours worked per week: 10. Apply by April 1. Fellowships and scholarships available for advanced students. Average amount paid per academic year: $1,700. Average number of hours worked per week: 0. Apply by Feb 1.

Contact Information: Of all students currently enrolled full-time, 40% benefited from one or more of the listed financial assistance programs. For information on financial assistance, contact: http://edpsych.edb.utexas.edu.

Internships/Practica: In the Counseling Psychology Program, internships are generally available in APA-approved counseling and mental health centers, other university counseling centers, and community/hospital settings that provide in-depth supervision. In the School Psychology Program, internship sites are often in APA-approved school systems and hospital/community settings that have an educational component. Other programs coordinate a variety of practicum settings to provide both research and applied experiences. For those doctoral students for whom a professional internship is required prior to graduation, 24 applied in 2000–2001. Of those who applied, 24 were placed in internships listed by the Association of Psychology Postdoctoral and Internship Programs (APPIC); 24 were placed in APA accredited internships.

Housing and Day Care: On-campus housing and day care facilities are available.

Employment of Department Graduates:

Master's Degree Graduates: Of those who graduated in the academic year 2000–2001, the following categories and numbers represent the post-graduate activities and employment of master's degree graduates: Enrolled in a post-doctoral residency/fellowship (n/a), employed in independent practice (n/a).

Doctoral Degree Graduates: Of those who graduated in the academic year 2000–2001, the following categories and numbers represent the post-graduate activities and employment of doctoral degree graduates: Enrolled in a psychology doctoral program (n/a), enrolled in another graduate/professional program (n/a).

Additional Information:

Orientation, Objectives, and Emphasis of Department: Training in educational psychology relates human behavior to the educational process as it occurs in the home, in peer groups, in nursery school through graduate school, in business and industry, in the military, in institutions for persons with physical or mental disabilities, and in a myriad of other settings. In so doing, it includes study in the following areas: the biological bases of behavior; history and systems of psychology and of education; the psychology of learning, motivation, cognition, and instruction; developmental, social, and personality psychology; psychological and educational measurement, statistics, evaluation, and research methodology; the professional areas of school psychology and counseling psychology; and general academic educational psychology. Special interests include computer applications to learning and instruction, psychometrics, and the processing and analysis of data in psychological and educational research.

Special Facilities or Resources: The University of Texas at Austin has the fifth largest academic library in the United States and also provides online access to hundreds of electronic databases. Our department also has access, through our college's Learning Technology Center, to several microcomputer and multimedia laboratories, technical assistance, resource materials, and audiovisual equipment and services. Academic computing facilities are extensive, ranging from mainframes to microcomputers. Additional resources include several university-wide centers with which our faculty are associated, including a counseling and mental health center and the Measurement and Evaluation Center.

Information for Students With Physical Disabilities: www.utexas.edu/depts/dos/ssd, Services for Students with Disabilities, Office of the Dean of Students, SSB 4.100, The University of Texas at Austin, 512-471-6259.

Application Information:
Send to: Graduate Adviser, Educational Psychology, SZB 504, The University of Texas at Austin, Austin, TX 78712-1296. Students are admitted in the Fall, application deadline see below; Spring, application deadline October 1; Summer, application deadline March 1. These are priority deadlines. PhD applicants are admitted in the fall semester only. The priority deadline for Counseling Psychology and School Psychology is January 15. The priority deadline for other PhD areas is February 1. The priority deadlines for the master's areas are October 1 for spring, March 1 for summer, and May 1 for fall. *Fee:* $50. Fee may be waived, at the discretion of Graduate Admissions, in cases of demonstrated financial need.

Texas, University of, Austin
Department of Psychology
Austin, TX 78712
Telephone: (512) 471-3785
Fax: (512) 471-6175
E-mail: *gradoffice@psy.utexas.edu*
Web: *http://www.psy.utexas.edu*

Department Established:
1910. Chairperson: Michael P. Domjan. Number of Faculty: total–full-time 45, part-time 11; women–full-time 9, part-time 3; minority–full-time 5.

Programs and Degrees Offered:
Listed in the following order: Program area, degree type (T if terminal Master's), number awarded 7/00–6/01. Behavioral neuroscience PhD, clinical PhD 3, cognition and perception PhD 2, developmental PhD, individual differences PhD 2, sensory neuroscience PhD, social and personality PhD 4.

APA Accreditation: Clinical PhD: full.

Student Applications/Admissions:
Student Applications
Behavioral neuroscience PhD—Applications 2001–2002, 27. Total applicants accepted 2001–2002, 4. New applicants enrolled 2001–2002, 3. Total enrolled 2001–2002 full-time, 22. Openings 2002–2003, 4. *Clinical PhD*—Applications 2001–2002, 246. Total applicants accepted 2001–2002, 11. New applicants enrolled 2001–2002, 6. Total enrolled 2001–2002 full-time, 45. Openings 2002–2003, 6. *Cognition and perception PhD*—Applications 2001–2002, 31. Total applicants accepted 2001–2002, 11. New applicants enrolled 2001–2002, 4. Total enrolled 2001–2002 full-time, 20. Openings 2002–2003, 5. *Developmental PhD*—Applications 2001–2002, 33. Total applicants accepted 2001–2002, 7. New applicants enrolled 2001–2002, 4. Total enrolled 2001–2002 full-time, 19. Openings

2002–2003, 4. *Individual differences PhD*—Applications 2001–2002, 33. Total applicants accepted 2001–2002, 7. New applicants enrolled 2001–2002, 5. Total enrolled 2001–2002 full-time, 13. Openings 2002–2003, 4. *Sensory neuroscience PhD*—Applications 2001–2002, 1. Total applicants accepted 2001–2002, 1. Total enrolled 2001–2002 full-time, 3. Openings 2002–2003, 2. *Social and personality PhD*—Applications 2001–2002, 70. Total applicants accepted 2001–2002, 6. New applicants enrolled 2001–2002, 2. Total enrolled 2001–2002 full-time, 11. Openings 2002–2003, 4.

Admissions Requirements:
Scores: Entries appear in this order: required test or GPA, minimum score (if required), median score of students entering in 2001–2002. Doctoral Programs: GRE-V no minimum stated, 660; GRE-Q no minimum stated, 680; GRE-V+Q 1000, 1320; last 2 years GPA 3.00, 3.76; psychology GPA no minimum stated; psychology GPA no minimum stated.

Other Criteria: (importance of criteria rated low, medium, or high): GRE/MAT scores, research experience high, work experience low, clinically related public service low, GPA, letters of recommendation high, interview medium, statement of goals and objectives high.

Student Characteristics: The following represents characteristics of students in 2001–2002 in all graduate psychology programs in the department: Female–full-time 9, part-time 0; Male–full-time 6, part-time 0; African American/Black–full-time 0, part-time 0; Hispanic/Latino (a)–full-time 1, part-time 0; Asian/Pacific Islander–full-time 0, part-time 0; American Indian/Alaska Native–full-time 1, part-time 0.

Financial Information/Assistance:
Tuition for Full-Time Study: *Doctoral:* State residents: $310 per credit hour; nonstate residents: $521 per credit hour.

Financial Assistance:
First Year Students: Teaching assistantships available for first-year. Average amount paid per academic year: $20,300. Average number of hours worked per week: 20. Tuition remission given: full. Research assistantships available for first-year.

Advanced Students: Teaching assistantships available for advanced students. Average amount paid per academic year: $22,900. Average number of hours worked per week: 20. Tuition remission given: full. Research assistantships available for advanced students.

Contact Information: Of all students currently enrolled full-time, 83% benefited from one or more of the listed financial assistance programs. For information on financial assistance, contact: Department of Psychology, Graduate Office.

Internships/Practica: Clinical students participate in practica at agencies in the Austin area, including the Austin State Hospital, Austin Child Guidance Center, Brown Schools, and the UT Counseling-Psychological Services Center. Most students select an internship at nationally recognized clinical settings such as the Langley Porter Neuropsychiatric Institute, or the University of California at San Diego Psychological Internship Consortium. Local settings are also available. For those doctoral students for whom a professional internship is required prior to graduation, 6 applied in 2000–2001. Of those who applied, 6 were placed in APA accredited internships.

Housing and Day Care: No on-campus housing and day care facilities are available.

Employment of Department Graduates:

Master's Degree Graduates: Of those who graduated in the academic year 2000–2001, the following categories and numbers represent the post-graduate activities and employment of master's degree graduates: Enrolled in a post-doctoral residency/fellowship (n/a), employed in independent practice (n/a).

Doctoral Degree Graduates: Of those who graduated in the academic year 2000–2001, the following categories and numbers represent the post-graduate activities and employment of doctoral degree graduates: Enrolled in a psychology doctoral program (n/a), enrolled in another graduate/professional program (n/a), enrolled in a post-doctoral residency/fellowship (7), employed in an academic position at a university (3), employed in other positions at a higher education institution (1), employed in business or industry (research/consulting) (3), employed in a government agency (research) (1), other employment position (3).

Additional Information:

Orientation, Objectives, and Emphasis of Department: The major goal of graduate training in the Department of Psychology is to aid in developing the competence and professional commitment that are essential to scholarly contributions in the field of psychology. All students, upon completing the program, are expected to be well informed about general psychology, well qualified to conduct independent research, and prepared to teach in their area of interest. Within certain specialized areas, they will be prepared for professional practice. The program culminates in the PhD degree, and it is designed for the person committed to psychological research and an academic career. All of the graduate study areas have a strong academic research emphasis. All of the areas also recognize the necessity of developing knowledge and skills for applied research positions and, in the clinical area, for professional competence. Specific information about the emphases of the graduate program areas may be obtained from the department. If you request this information, please indicate the program areas in which you are interested.

Special Facilities or Resources: The buildings occupied by the Department of Psychology are centrally located and contain lecture and seminar rooms, offices, and research laboratories. The research space includes small rooms for individual testing and larger rooms for group experiments. Some rooms have adjacent observation rooms. An anechoic testing chamber is available for auditory research. All of the departmental laboratories have computers associated with them. Departmental computers are available for student use. Facilities for research with children include the Children's Research Laboratory with numerous experimental suites. The facilities of the Animal Resource Center support research with animals. The support resources of the department include two well-equipped shops with full-time technicians and staff for computer assistance. The support resources of the university include the Computation Center, one of the finest academic computation facilities in the United States, and the Perry-Castaneda Library, one of the largest academic libraries in the country. Faculty members in the department of Psychology

are affiliated with the center for Vision and Image Sciences, the Institute for Cognitive Science, and the Institute for Neuroscience.

Application Information:
Send to: University of Texas, Department of Psychology, Graduate Office, Austin, TX 78713. Students are admitted in the Fall, application deadline January 15. *Fee:* $50.

Texas, University of, El Paso

Department of Psychology
El Paso, TX 79968-0553
Telephone: (915) 747-5551
Fax: (915) 747-6553
E-mail: *jgoggin@utep.edu*
Web: *http://www.utep.edu/psych*

Department Established:
1965. Chairperson: Judith P. Goggin. Number of Faculty: total–full-time 15, part-time 1; women–full-time 3; minority–full-time 4, part-time 1.

Programs and Degrees Offered:
Listed in the following order: Program area, degree type (T if terminal Master's), number awarded 7/00–6/01. General MA (T) 2, human behavior in organization PhD, Legal Psychology PhD, psychology and health PhD 3.

Student Applications/Admissions:

Student Applications

General MA—Applications 2001–2002, 16. Total applicants accepted 2001–2002, 7. New applicants enrolled 2001–2002, 6. Total enrolled 2001–2002 full-time, 18. Openings 2002–2003, 8. The Median number of years required for completion of a degree are 2. The number of students enrolled full and part-time, who were dismissed or voluntarily withdrew from this program area were 3. *Human behavior in organization PhD*—Applications 2001–2002, 10. Total applicants accepted 2001–2002, 6. New applicants enrolled 2001–2002, 3. Total enrolled 2001–2002 full-time, 13. Openings 2002–2003, 5. The number of students enrolled full and part-time, who were dismissed or voluntarily withdrew from this program area were 0. *Legal Psychology PhD*—Openings 2002–2003, 8. *Psychology and health PhD*—Applications 2001–2002, 8. Total applicants accepted 2001–2002, 5. New applicants enrolled 2001–2002, 2. Total enrolled 2001–2002 full-time, 11. Openings 2002–2003, 8. The Median number of years required for completion of a degree are 6. The number of students enrolled full and part-time, who were dismissed or voluntarily withdrew from this program area were 0.

Admissions Requirements:

Scores: Entries appear in this order: required test or GPA, minimum score (if required), median score of students entering in 2001–2002. Master's Programs: GRE-V no minimum stated, 500; GRE-Q no minimum stated, 500; overall undergraduate GPA no minimum stated, 3.68. Doctoral Programs: GRE-V no minimum stated, 500; GRE-Q no minimum stated, 600; overall undergraduate GPA no minimum stated, 3.43; last 2 years GPA no minimum stated; psychology GPA no minimum stated; psychology GPA no minimum stated.

Other Criteria: (importance of criteria rated low, medium, or high): GRE/MAT scores high, research experience high, work experience low, extracurricular activity low, clinically related public service low, GPA high, letters of recommendation medium, statement of goals and objectives medium.

Student Characteristics: The following represents characteristics of students in 2001–2002 in all graduate psychology programs in the department: Female–full-time 30, part-time 0; Male–full-time 12, part-time 0; African American/Black–full-time 0, part-time 0; Hispanic/Latino (a)–full-time 22, part-time 0; Asian/Pacific Islander–full-time 1, part-time 0; American Indian/Alaska Native–full-time 1, part-time 0; Multi-ethnic–full-time 0, part-time 0; students subject to the Americans with Disabilities Act–full-time 0, part-time 0.

Financial Information/Assistance:

Tuition for Full-Time Study: *Master's:* State residents per academic year $1,966, $161 per credit hour; nonstate residents: per academic year $5,745, $372 per credit hour. *Doctoral:* State residents: per academic year $1,966, $161 per credit hour; nonstate residents: per academic year $5,745, $372 per credit hour.

Financial Assistance:

First Year Students: Teaching assistantships available for first-year. Average amount paid per academic year: $9,450. Average number of hours worked per week: 20. Apply by Feb. 15. Tuition remission given: partial. Research assistantships available for first-year. Average amount paid per academic year: $9,450. Average number of hours worked per week: 20. Apply by Feb. 15. Tuition remission given: partial.

Advanced Students: Teaching assistantships available for advanced students. Average amount paid per academic year: $10,200. Average number of hours worked per week: 20. Apply by Feb. 15. Tuition remission given: partial. Research assistantships available for advanced students. Average amount paid per academic year: $10,200. Average number of hours worked per week: 20. Apply by Feb. 15. Tuition remission given: partial.

Contact Information: Of all students currently enrolled full-time, 74% benefited from one or more of the listed financial assistance programs. For information on financial assistance, contact: Graduate Program Director, Department of Psychology.

Internships/Practica: Six hours of internship are required for the clinical MA program, and 6 hours of field placement are required for the PhD program. For both internships and field placements, students may work in a variety of settings, such as business and industry, educational facilities, hospitals, mental health and social service agencies, and legal settings. Because of U.T. El Paso's location on the U.S./Mexico border, some internships and field placements may involve multicultural issues.

Housing and Day Care: On-campus housing and day care facilities are available.

Employment of Department Graduates:

Master's Degree Graduates: Of those who graduated in the academic year 2000–2001, the following categories and numbers represent the post-graduate activities and employment of master's degree graduates: Enrolled in a psychology doctoral program (2),

enrolled in another graduate/professional program (0), enrolled in a post-doctoral residency/fellowship (n/a), employed in independent practice (n/a), employed in an academic position at a university (0), employed in an academic position at a 2-year/4-year college (0), employed in other positions at a higher education institution (0), employed in a professional position in a school system (0), employed in business or industry (research/consulting) (0), employed in business or industry (management) (0), employed in a government agency (research) (0), employed in a government agency (professional services) (0), employed in a community mental health/counseling center (0), employed in a hospital/medical center (0), still seeking employment (0), other employment position (0).

Doctoral Degree Graduates: Of those who graduated in the academic year 2000–2001, the following categories and numbers represent the post-graduate activities and employment of doctoral degree graduates: Enrolled in a psychology doctoral program (n/a), enrolled in another graduate/professional program (n/a), enrolled in a post-doctoral residency/fellowship (1), employed in independent practice (0), employed in an academic position at a university (0), employed in an academic position at a 2-year/4-year college (0), employed in other positions at a higher education institution (1), employed in a professional position in a school system (0), employed in business or industry (research/consulting) (0), employed in business or industry (management) (0), employed in a government agency (research) (0), employed in a government agency (professional services) (0), employed in a community mental health/counseling center (1), employed in a hospital/medical center (0), still seeking employment (0), other employment position (0).

Additional Information:

Orientation, Objectives, and Emphasis of Department: The general experimental MA program, intended for students who will pursue a PhD degree, emphasizes research methodology and experimental design, and focuses on a variety of substantive areas in psychology. The clinical MA program is designed as a terminal master's degree and emphasizes all applied skills in psychological assessment. The PhD program offers three areas of concentration—health psychology, legal psychology, and human behavior in organizations—and is designed to train research psychologists to work in applied psychology. A special focus is directed toward bilingual, bicultural research issues.

Special Facilities or Resources: The department offers opportunities for students to conduct research in a variety of areas, both experimental and applied. The department maintains laboratories for research in the following areas: neuropsychology, psychobiology, psycholinguistics, behavior technology, cross-cultural testing and measurement, psychology and law, cognitive, comparative, social, clinical decision-making, developmental, and industrial-organizational psychology.

Information for Students With Physical Disabilities: The university offers a full range of services to students with disabilities.

Application Information:
Send to: Graduate School; Administration Bldg., Room 201; University of Texas at El Paso; El Paso, TX 79968. Students are admitted in the Fall, application deadline February 1. Also November 1 for MA applicants if space is available. *Fee:* $15.

Texas, University of, Pan American

Department of Psychology and Anthropology,
  MA in Psychology
1201 West University Drive
Edinburg, TX 78539
Telephone: (956) 381-3329
Fax: (956) 381-3333
E-mail: *ecardena@panam.edu*
Web: *http://www.panam.edu/dept/gsprog*

Department Established:

1930. Chairperson: Etzel Cardeña, PhD. Number of Faculty: total–full-time 18, part-time 4; women–full-time 2, part-time 2; minority–full-time 3.

Programs and Degrees Offered:

Listed in the following order: Program area, degree type (T if terminal Master's), number awarded 7/00–6/01. Clinical MA (T) 5, Experimental MA (T) 1.

Student Applications/Admissions:

Student Applications

Clinical MA—Applications 2001–2002, 20. Total applicants accepted 2001–2002, 12. New applicants enrolled 2001–2002, 12. Total enrolled 2001–2002 full-time, 15, part-time, 15. Openings 2002–2003, 15. The Median number of years required for completion of a degree are 3. The number of students enrolled full and part-time, who were dismissed or voluntarily withdrew from this program area were 0. *Experimental MA*—Applications 2001–2002, 2. Total applicants accepted 2001–2002, 1. New applicants enrolled 2001–2002, 1. Total enrolled 2001–2002 full-time, 2. Openings 2002–2003, 5. The Median number of years required for completion of a degree are 3. The number of students enrolled full and part-time, who were dismissed or voluntarily withdrew from this program area were 0.

Admissions Requirements:

Scores: Entries appear in this order: required test or GPA, minimum score (if required), median score of students entering in 2001–2002. Master's Programs: GRE-V 400, 500; GRE-Q 400, 500; GRE-V+Q 1000; overall undergraduate GPA 2.9, 3.1; psychology GPA 3.0, 3.3. Doctoral Programs: last 2 years GPA no minimum stated; psychology GPA no minimum stated; psychology GPA no minimum stated.

Other Criteria: (importance of criteria rated low, medium, or high): GRE/MAT scores medium, research experience low, work experience low, extracurricular activity low, clinically related public service low, GPA high, letters of recommendation high, statement of goals and objectives high.

Student Characteristics: The following represents characteristics of students in 2001–2002 in all graduate psychology programs in the department: Female–full-time 10, part-time 10; Male–full-time 5, part-time 5; African American/Black–full-time 0, part-time 0; Hispanic/Latino (a)–full-time 10, part-time 10; Asian/Pacific Islander–full-time 0, part-time 0; American Indian/Alaska Native–full-time 0, part-time 0.

Financial Information/Assistance:

Tuition for Full-Time Study: Master's: State residents per academic year $1,870, $104 per credit hour; nonstate residents: per academic year $5,750, $320 per credit hour.

Financial Assistance:

First Year Students: Teaching assistantships available for first-year. Tuition remission given: partial. Research assistantships available for first-year. Tuition remission given: partial. Fellowships and scholarships available for first-year. Tuition remission given: partial.

Advanced Students: Teaching assistantships available for advanced students. Tuition remission given: partial. Research assistantships available for advanced students. Tuition remission given: partial. Fellowships and scholarships available for advanced students. Tuition remission given: partial.

Contact Information: Of all students currently enrolled full-time, 20% benefited from one or more of the listed financial assistance programs. For information on financial assistance, contact: Student Financial Services, Student Services Building, Rm. 186, 1201 West University Drive, Edinburg, TX, 78539-2999, 956-381-2501, finaid@panam.edu.

Internships/Practica: Practica are available through the graduate psychology clinic (total of 6 Semester hours). Internships are for 480 clock hours and students are placed under licensed psychologists in private practice or through public and private mental health clinics and hospitals.

Housing and Day Care: On-campus housing and day care facilities are available.

Employment of Department Graduates:

Master's Degree Graduates: Of those who graduated in the academic year 2000–2001, the following categories and numbers represent the post-graduate activities and employment of master's degree graduates: Enrolled in a post-doctoral residency/fellowship (n/a), employed in independent practice (n/a).

Doctoral Degree Graduates: Of those who graduated in the academic year 2000–2001, the following categories and numbers represent the post-graduate activities and employment of doctoral degree graduates: Enrolled in a psychology doctoral program (n/a), enrolled in another graduate/professional program (n/a).

Additional Information:

Orientation, Objectives, and Emphasis of Department: The Master's in Clinical Psychology is designed to provide theory, research-based assessment and intervention strategies, skills training, practical knowledge, DSM based diagnostic assessment skills, clinical experience, and supervision of professional practices in the field of applied psychology. Multicultural professional practices are emphasized as the community service-base is largely bilingual (English/Spanish) and of Hispanic origin. The program is designed to fulfill prerequisite and academic requirements for taking the Texas State Board of Examiners of Psychologist Exam as a Psychological Associate. Two additional graduate courses through the Educational Psychology Department fulfill the academic requirements for license as a Licensed Professional Counselor (LPC).

Special Facilities or Resources: Graduate psychology clinic has 7 consultation rooms, including monitoring equipment (A/V) for individual and group sessions and supervision. The Department also has equipment and computers to conduct research on perception, cognition, psychophysiology EEG, biofeedback, hypnosis, and other areas of faculty interest. There are also facilities through the Center on Aging and the Minority Biomedical Program for conducting research activities. There is also the possibility of conducting observational primate research through the Gladys Porter Zoo.

Information for Students With Physical Disabilities: The building meets the standards for students with disabilities. Students with some disabilities (e.g., blindness, learning disabilities) are assisted through the Student Services Office.

Application Information:
Send to: Director of MA Program, Dept. of Psychology and Anthropology, U. of Texas, Pan American, 1201 West University Drive, Edinburg, TX 78539. Students are admitted in the Fall, application deadline Mar 1; Winter, application deadline July 1; Spring, application deadline Oct. 1.

Texas, University of, Tyler
Department of Psychology
3900 University Boulevard
Tyler, TX 75799
Telephone: (903) 566-7130
Fax: (903) 565-5656
E-mail: *CStrawn@mail.uttyl.edu*
Web: *http://www.uttyler.edu*

Department Established:
1973. Chairperson: Henry Schreiber. Number of Faculty: total–full-time 9, part-time 3; women–full-time 4.

Programs and Degrees Offered:
Listed in the following order: Program area, degree type (T if terminal Master's), number awarded 7/00–6/01. Clinical MA (T) 9, counseling MA (T) 3, school counseling MA (T) 9.

Student Applications/Admissions:
Student Applications
Clinical MA—Applications 2001–2002, 25. Total applicants accepted 2001–2002, 20. New applicants enrolled 2001–2002, 17. Total enrolled 2001–2002 full-time, 20, part-time, 18. Openings 2002–2003, 20. The Median number of years required for completion of a degree are 2. *Counseling MA*—Applications 2001–2002, 10. Total applicants accepted 2001–2002, 8. New applicants enrolled 2001–2002, 6. Total enrolled 2001–2002 full-time, 12, part-time, 10. Openings 2002–2003, 8. The Median number of years required for completion of a degree are 2. *School counseling MA*—Applications 2001–2002, 12. Total applicants accepted 2001–2002, 10. New applicants enrolled 2001–2002, 7. Total enrolled 2001–2002 full-time, 4, part-time, 10. Openings 2002–2003, 8. The Median number of years required for completion of a degree are 2.

Admissions Requirements:
Scores: Entries appear in this order: required test or GPA, minimum score (if required), median score of students entering in 2001–2002. Master's Programs: GRE-V 400, 550; GRE-Q 400, 540; GRE-Analytical 400, 540; GRE-V+Q+Analytical 1400, 1630; overall undergraduate GPA 3.0, 3.3; last 2 years GPA 3.0, 3.4. Doctoral Programs: last 2 years GPA no minimum stated; psychology GPA no minimum stated; psychology GPA no minimum stated.

Other Criteria: (importance of criteria rated low, medium, or high): GRE/MAT scores high, research experience low, work experience low, extracurricular activity low, clinically related public service low, GPA high, letters of recommendation high, interview low, statement of goals and objectives medium.

Student Characteristics: The following represents characteristics of students in 2001–2002 in all graduate psychology programs in the department: Female–full-time 30, part-time 22; Male–full-time 8, part-time 5; African American/Black–full-time 3, part-time 0; Hispanic/Latino (a)–full-time 3, part-time 1; Asian/Pacific Islander–full-time 2, part-time 0; American Indian/Alaska Native–full-time 0, part-time 0.

Financial Information/Assistance:
Tuition for Full-Time Study: *Master's:* State residents per academic year $2,336, $40 per credit hour; nonstate residents: per academic year $7,520, $254 per credit hour.

Financial Assistance:
First Year Students: Fellowships and scholarships available for first-year. Average amount paid per academic year: $500. Apply by Feb 1, Oct 1. Tuition remission given: partial.

Advanced Students: Research assistantships available for advanced students. Average amount paid per academic year: $5,000. Average number of hours worked per week: 20. Apply by Feb 1, Oct 1. Tuition remission given: partial. Fellowships and scholarships available for advanced students. Average amount paid per academic year: $500. Apply by Feb 1, Oct 1. Tuition remission given: partial.

Contact Information: Of all students currently enrolled full-time, 25% benefited from one or more of the listed financial assistance programs. For information on financial assistance, contact: Office of Financial Aid.

Internships/Practica: Practicums available include nearby private psychiatric hospitals, MHMR facilities, children's therapy facilities, crisis centers and safe houses for abused women, neuropsychology rehabilitation hospitals, prisons, and schools.

Housing and Day Care: On-campus housing and day care facilities are available.

Employment of Department Graduates:
Master's Degree Graduates: Of those who graduated in the academic year 2000–2001, the following categories and numbers represent the post-graduate activities and employment of master's degree graduates: Enrolled in a psychology doctoral program (2), enrolled in a post-doctoral residency/fellowship (n/a), employed in independent practice (n/a), employed in an academic position at a 2-year/4-year college (1), employed in a professional position in a school system (3), employed in a community mental health/counseling center (4), employed in a hospital/medical center (1), still seeking employment (1).

Doctoral Degree Graduates: Of those who graduated in the academic year 2000–2001, the following categories and numbers

represent the post-graduate activities and employment of doctoral degree graduates: Enrolled in a psychology doctoral program (n/a), enrolled in another graduate/professional program (n/a).

Additional Information:
Orientation, Objectives, and Emphasis of Department: The purpose of our program is to prepare competent, applied practitioners at the master's level. The curriculum is very practical, stressing clinical assessment and intervention, and hands-on experience in relevant areas. Our students have been very successful in finding employment in mental health settings and in gaining admission to clinical and counseling doctoral programs. Special opportunities are provided for training in clinical neuropsychological assessment and psychopharmacology, for training in marital and family counseling, or for training to become a licensed specialist in school psychology. Also, a program in school counseling has been added.

Information for Students With Physical Disabilities: We have several disabled students, and facilities are wheelchair accessible.

Application Information:
Send to: Robert F. McClure, PhD, Psychology Graduate Coordinator, Dept of Psychology, Univ. of Texas at Tyler, Tyler, TX 75799. Students are admitted in the Fall, application deadline February 1; Spring, application deadline October 1.

Trinity University
Department of Education
715 Stadium Drive
San Antonio, TX 78212
Telephone: (210) 736-7501
Fax: (210) 736-7592
E-mail: *Terry.Migliore@trinity.edu*

Department Established:
1976. Director of School Psychology: Terry Migliore. Number of Faculty: total–full-time 2, part-time 10; women–full-time 1, part-time 5.

Student Applications/Admissions:
Admissions Requirements:
Scores: Entries appear in this order: required test or GPA, minimum score (if required), median score of students entering in 2001–2002. Master's Programs: GRE-V 500; GRE-Q 500; GRE-V+Q no minimum stated; GRE-Analytical no minimum stated; overall undergraduate GPA 3.0; last 2 years GPA 3.0; psychology GPA 3.0. Doctoral Programs: last 2 years GPA no minimum stated; psychology GPA no minimum stated; psychology GPA no minimum stated.
Other Criteria: (importance of criteria rated low, medium, or high): GRE/MAT scores medium, research experience medium, work experience medium, extracurricular activity medium, clinically related public service medium, GPA medium, letters of recommendation medium, interview medium, statement of goals and objectives medium, experience with children medium.

Student Characteristics: The following represents characteristics of students in 2001–2002 in all graduate psychology programs in

the department: Female–full-time 37, part-time 1; Male–full-time 6, part-time 0; African American/Black–full-time 0, part-time 0; Hispanic/Latino (a)–full-time 11, part-time 0; Asian/Pacific Islander–full-time 1, part-time 0; American Indian/Alaska Native–full-time 0, part-time 0.

Financial Information/Assistance:
Tuition for Full-Time Study: No information provided.

Financial Assistance:
First Year Students: No information provided.
Advanced Students: No information provided.
Contact Information: For information on financial assistance, contact: Office of Financial Aid, Trinity University.

Internships/Practica: All students have graduate assistantships in career-related work. The average award per student is $14,000 per year for the 2 years of academic work ($28,000). The required 3rd year internship is funded at $25,000 for each student or students may apply directly to school districts, which may offer a higher salary.

Housing and Day Care: No on-campus housing and day care facilities are available.

Employment of Department Graduates:
Master's Degree Graduates: Of those who graduated in the academic year 2000–2001, the following categories and numbers represent the post-graduate activities and employment of master's degree graduates: Enrolled in a post-doctoral residency/fellowship (n/a), employed in independent practice (n/a).
Doctoral Degree Graduates: Of those who graduated in the academic year 2000–2001, the following categories and numbers represent the post-graduate activities and employment of doctoral degree graduates: Enrolled in a psychology doctoral program (n/a), enrolled in another graduate/professional program (n/a).

Additional Information:
Orientation, Objectives, and Emphasis of Department: The Trinity University Department of Education offers the 60 semester-hour master of arts in school psychology. The purpose of this program is to prepare graduates to provide psychological services in school settings. The courses and practicum experiences offer the theory and skills necessary for assessment, consultation, and counseling functions. Specific application of assessment and consultation skills to classroom instruction is stressed in Trinity's program. All graduates will be eligible to take the examination for Licensed Specialist in School Psychology and to apply for Nationally Certified School Psychologist. The program has full approval by the National Association of School Psychologists.

Special Facilities or Resources: Part-time faculty are either psychologists or consultants with local school districts, or work at the Psychological Corporation, a major developer of assessment instruments used in schools and clinics.

Application Information:
Send to: Dr. Terry Migliore, Trinity University, Education Department, 715 Stadium Drive, San Antonio, TX 78212. Students are admitted in the Fall, application deadline April 1. *Fee:* $30.

West Texas A&M University

Department of Behavioral Sciences
P.O. Box 60296
Canyon, TX 79016
Telephone: (806) 651-2590
Fax: (806) 651-2728
E-mail: *gbyrd@mail.wtamu.edu*
Web: *http://www.wtamu.edu*

Department Established:

1971. Chairperson: Gary R. Byrd. Number of Faculty: total–full-time 5, part-time 5; women–full-time 1, part-time 3.

Programs and Degrees Offered:

Listed in the following order: Program area, degree type (T if terminal Master's), number awarded 7/00–6/01. Psychology MA (T) 5.

Student Applications/Admissions:

Student Applications

Psychology MA—Applications 2001–2002, 10. Total applicants accepted 2001–2002, 6. New applicants enrolled 2001–2002, 6. Total enrolled 2001–2002 full-time, 6. Openings 2002–2003, 10. The Median number of years required for completion of a degree are 3. The number of students enrolled full and part-time, who were dismissed or voluntarily withdrew from this program area were 1.

Admissions Requirements:

Scores: Entries appear in this order: required test or GPA, minimum score (if required), median score of students entering in 2001–2002. Master's Programs: GRE-V 300, 455; GRE-Q 300, 600; GRE-V+Q 920, 1040; overall undergraduate GPA 3.0, 3.41; psychology GPA 3.25, 3.63. Doctoral Programs: last 2 years GPA no minimum stated; psychology GPA no minimum stated; psychology GPA no minimum stated.

Other Criteria: (importance of criteria rated low, medium, or high): GRE/MAT scores high, research experience medium, work experience low, extracurricular activity low, clinically related public service low, GPA high, letters of recommendation high, statement of goals and objectives low.

Student Characteristics: The following represents characteristics of students in 2001–2002 in all graduate psychology programs in the department: Female–full-time 5, part-time 0; Male–full-time 1, part-time 0; African American/Black–full-time 0, part-time 0; Hispanic/Latino (a)–full-time 0, part-time 0; Asian/Pacific Islander–full-time 1, part-time 0; American Indian/Alaska Native–full-time 0, part-time 0; Multi-ethnic–full-time 0, students subject to the Americans with Disabilities Act–full-time 0.

Financial Information/Assistance:

Tuition for Full-Time Study: *Master's:* State residents per academic year $1,790, $99 per credit hour; nonstate residents: per academic year $5,588, $310 per credit hour.

Financial Assistance:

First Year Students: Fellowships and scholarships available for first-year. Average amount paid per academic year: $500. Apply by Aug. 1. Tuition remission given: partial.

Advanced Students: Teaching assistantships available for advanced students. Average amount paid per academic year: $3,350. Average number of hours worked per week: 15. Apply by May 1. Tuition remission given: partial. Research assistantships available for advanced students. Average amount paid per academic year: $3,300. Average number of hours worked per week: 15. Apply by May 1. Fellowships and scholarships available for advanced students. Average amount paid per academic year: $500. Apply by Aug. 1. Tuition remission given: partial.

Contact Information: Of all students currently enrolled full-time, 50% benefited from one or more of the listed financial assistance programs. For information on financial assistance, contact: Virginia Maples vmaples@mail.wtamu.edu, or Richard Harland, rharland@mail.wtamu.edu.

Internships/Practica: In addition to clinical/counseling practica, the program offers internships in program evaluation with a large public foundation.

Housing and Day Care: On-campus housing and day care facilities are available.

Employment of Department Graduates:

Master's Degree Graduates: Of those who graduated in the academic year 2000–2001, the following categories and numbers represent the post-graduate activities and employment of master's degree graduates: Enrolled in a psychology doctoral program (0), enrolled in another graduate/professional program (0), enrolled in a post-doctoral residency/fellowship (n/a), employed in independent practice (n/a), employed in an academic position at a university (0), employed in an academic position at a 2-year/4-year college (1), employed in other positions at a higher education institution (0), employed in a professional position in a school system (1), employed in business or industry (research/consulting) (0), employed in business or industry (management) (0), employed in a government agency (research) (0), employed in a government agency (professional services) (0), employed in a community mental health/counseling center (1), employed in a hospital/medical center (0), still seeking employment (0), other employment position (2).

Doctoral Degree Graduates: Of those who graduated in the academic year 2000–2001, the following categories and numbers represent the post-graduate activities and employment of doctoral degree graduates: Enrolled in a psychology doctoral program (n/a), enrolled in another graduate/professional program (n/a).

Additional Information:

Orientation, Objectives, and Emphasis of Department: The primary purpose of the program is to create opportunities for students that: have strong qualifications for graduate work and have a bachelor's degree in psychology but need clarification as to which specialization they should seek in their doctoral studies, have a weak dimension in their application qualifications for graduate studies and wish to enhance their potential for admission to a doctoral program, do NOT have a bachelor's degree in psychology but are promising students who now wish to become competitive for psychology doctoral programs, seek employment at the master's level of professional psychology.

Special Facilities or Resources: The department has a variety of facilities that can be viewed in five functional subdivisions. First, there are several large experimental research laboratories that contain equipment for electrophysiological measures (EEG, EMG, EOG, & hemisphereric electronic equipment) that is highly versatile and can be controlled by lab computers. Second, there are facilities to record data for field studies such as the behavior of children in their home setting or animals in their natural settings. Third, a psychometric lab provides storage and space for administering psychological tests. Fourth, a large community foundation has a partnership with the department to provide a setting for training a limited number of students in program evaluation for community grants and projects. And, finally, there are eight community mental health facilities (two are residential) that provide practicum settings for students interested in clinical or counseling training.

Application Information:
Send to: Dr. Richard Harland Psychology Graduate Coordinator, P.O. Box 60296, WTAMU, Canyon, TX 79016. Students are admitted in the Fall, application deadline Aug. 10; Spring, application deadline Dec. 15; Summer, application deadline May 15.

Brigham Young University

Department of Counseling Psychology and Special Education
David O. McKay School of Education
328 MCKB
Provo, UT 84602
Telephone: (801) 378-3857
Fax: (801) 378-3961
E-mail: *Richard_Heaps@byu.edu*
Web: *http://www.byu.edu/cse*

Department Established:

1969. Department Chair: Ronald D. Bingham. Number of Faculty: total–full-time 7, part-time 5; women–full-time 3, part-time 1.

Programs and Degrees Offered:

Listed in the following order: Program area, degree type (T if terminal Master's), number awarded 7/00–6/01. Counseling psychology PhD 1, school counseling psychology MA (T) 16.

APA Accreditation: Counseling PhD: full.

Student Applications/Admissions:

Student Applications

Counseling psychology PhD—Applications 2001–2002, 17. Total applicants accepted 2001–2002, 6. New applicants enrolled 2001–2002, 6. Total enrolled 2001–2002 full-time, 17, part-time, 7. Openings 2002–2003, 6. The Median number of years required for completion of a degree are 5. The number of students enrolled full and part-time, who were dismissed or voluntarily withdrew from this program area were 0. *School counseling psychology* MA—Applications 2001–2002, 54. Total applicants accepted 2001–2002, 16. New applicants enrolled 2001–2002, 16. Total enrolled 2001–2002 full-time, 32. Openings 2002–2003, 16. The Median number of years required for completion of a degree are 2. The number of students enrolled full and part-time, who were dismissed or voluntarily withdrew from this program area were 1.

Admissions Requirements:

Scores: Entries appear in this order: required test or GPA, minimum score (if required), median score of students entering in 2001–2002. Master's Programs: GRE-V 500, 510; GRE-Q 500, 580; last 2 years GPA 3.00, 3.76. Doctoral Programs: GRE-V 500, 500; GRE-Q 500, 480; last 2 years GPA 3.0, 3.76; psychology GPA no minimum stated; psychology GPA no minimum stated.

Other Criteria: (importance of criteria rated low, medium, or high): GRE/MAT scores high, research experience medium, work experience medium, extracurricular activity low, clinically related public service medium, GPA medium, letters of recommendation high, interview high, statement of goals and objectives high, overall impression medium.

Student Characteristics: The following represents characteristics of students in 2001–2002 in all graduate psychology programs in the department: Female–full-time 24, part-time 5; Male–full-time 16, part-time 3; African American/Black–full-time 0, part-time 1; Hispanic/Latino (a)–full-time 2, part-time 0; Asian/Pacific Islander–full-time 1, part-time 0; American Indian/Alaska Native–full-time 1, part-time 0.

Financial Information/Assistance:

Tuition for Full-Time Study: *Master's:* State residents per academic year $4,825, $214 per credit hour; nonstate residents: per academic year $7,238, $322 per credit hour. *Doctoral:* State residents: per academic year $4,825, $214 per credit hour; nonstate residents: per academic year $7,238, $322 per credit hour.

Financial Assistance:

First Year Students: Teaching assistantships available for first-year. Average amount paid per academic year: $5,180. Average number of hours worked per week: 10. Apply by varies. Tuition remission given: partial. Research assistantships available for first-year. Average amount paid per academic year: $5,180. Average number of hours worked per week: 10. Apply by varies. Tuition remission given: partial.

Advanced Students: Teaching assistantships available for advanced students. Average amount paid per academic year: $5,720. Average number of hours worked per week: 10. Apply by varies. Tuition remission given: partial. Research assistantships available for advanced students. Average amount paid per academic year: $5,720. Average number of hours worked per week: 10. Apply by varies. Tuition remission given: partial.

Contact Information: Of all students currently enrolled full-time, 87% benefited from one or more of the listed financial assistance programs. For information on financial assistance, contact: Financial Aid Office, A-41 ASB, BYU, Provo, UT 84602, 801/378-4104, Counseling Psychology and Special Education Department, 801/378-3859.

Internships/Practica: Master's students complete practica for 10 hours per week during the first year of study and a full-time internship (5/8 of teacher pay) the second year. Doctoral students complete 4 practica in the counseling center, 1 teaching practica, and 2 community-based practica. A full-year internship is required. Assistance is given for placements. For those doctoral students for whom a professional internship is required prior to graduation, 2 applied in 2000–2001. Of those who applied, 2 were placed in internships listed by the Association of Psychology Postdoctoral and Internship Programs (APPIC); 1 were placed in APA accredited internships.

Housing and Day Care: No on-campus housing and day care facilities are available.

Employment of Department Graduates:

Master's Degree Graduates: Of those who graduated in the academic year 2000–2001, the following categories and numbers represent the post-graduate activities and employment of master's

degree graduates: Enrolled in a psychology doctoral program (2), enrolled in another graduate/professional program (0), enrolled in a post-doctoral residency/fellowship (n/a), employed in independent practice (n/a), employed in a professional position in a school system (11).

Doctoral Degree Graduates: Of those who graduated in the academic year 2000–2001, the following categories and numbers represent the post-graduate activities and employment of doctoral degree graduates: Enrolled in a psychology doctoral program (n/a), enrolled in another graduate/professional program (n/a), enrolled in a post-doctoral residency/fellowship (1), employed in other positions at a higher education institution (1), employed in a community mental health/counseling center (1).

Additional Information:

Orientation, Objectives, and Emphasis of Department: The Department of Counseling Psychology and Special Education offers master's programs in School Counseling Psychology, and in Special Education, and a PhD program in Counseling Psychology. The MS combines School Psychology and Counseling to prepare a professional with both counseling and assessment skills. The graduate will be eligible for dual certification as a school counselor and school psychologist. With 2 additional courses and 4000 hours of supervised mental health counseling, the graduate will be eligible to apply for licensure as a Licensed Professional Counselor. The Counseling Psychology program is primarily psychological in nature and is the only graduate program in the Department leading qualified individuals to licensure as psychologists. The program is both broad-based and specific in nature; that is, one is expected to take certain courses that could be required for licensure or for certification and graduation, but the program encourages students to take coursework in varied disciplines such as marriage and family therapy, organizational behavior, and other fields allied with psychology and education. The focus of the master's program in Counseling and School Psychology is to prepare graduates for K–12 school settings. The doctoral program prepares college and university counseling psychologists for counseling centers or for academic positions.

Special Facilities or Resources: The department has a School Counseling Psychology Center (clinic) with five individual counseling rooms and one large group room available for the observation and videotaping of students in counseling and assessment. These are assigned specifically to the department while an abundance of other media-related facilities for the teaching and learning experience are available on campus as well as off campus. The department also provides spacious study and work carrels.

Information for Students With Physical Disabilities: The campus is well-suited for students with disabilities.

Application Information:

Send to: Office of Graduate Studies, B-356 ASB, BYU, Provo, UT 84602; On-line applications are preferred. See www.byu.edu/gradstudies. Students are admitted in the Fall, application deadline February 1; Summer, application deadline February 1. Counseling Psychology admits fall only. School Counseling Psychology admits summer only. Both program deadlines are February 1. *Fee:* $50.

Brigham Young University (2001 data)
Department of Psychology
Family Home & Social Science
1001 SWKT
Provo, UT 84602-5543
Telephone: (801) 378-4287
Fax: (801) 378-7862
E-mail: *erin_bigler@byu.edu*
Web: *http://www.byu.edu/psychweb/*

Department Established:
1921. Chairperson: Erin D. Bigler. Number of Faculty: total–full-time 32, part-time 5; women–full-time 4, part-time 1.

Programs and Degrees Offered:
Listed in the following order: Program area, degree type (T if terminal Master's), number awarded 7/00–6/01. Clinical and general PhD 11, general MS (T) 7.

APA Accreditation: Clinical PhD: full.

Student Applications/Admissions:
Student Applications

Clinical and general PhD—Applications 2001–2002, 61. Total applicants accepted 2001–2002, 13. New applicants enrolled 2001–2002, 12. Total enrolled 2001–2002 full-time, 88. Openings 2002–2003, 12. *General MS*—Applications 2001–2002, 35. Total applicants accepted 2001–2002, 8. New applicants enrolled 2001–2002, 5. Total enrolled 2001–2002 full-time, 46. Openings 2002–2003, 15.

Admissions Requirements:

Scores: Entries appear in this order: required test or GPA, minimum score (if required), median score of students entering in 2001–2002. Master's Programs: GRE-V 500, 545; GRE-Q 550, 615; GRE-V+Q 600, 675; last 2 years GPA 3.0, 3.7. Doctoral Programs: GRE-V 500, 545; GRE-Q 550, 615; GRE-V+Q 600, 675; last 2 years GPA 3.0, 3.8.

Other Criteria: (importance of criteria rated low, medium, or high): GRE/MAT scores medium, research experience low, work experience medium, extracurricular activity low, clinically related public service high, GPA high, letters of recommendation high, interview high, statement of goals and objectives high, reason for studying at BY medium. The clinically related public service refers to clinical graduate applicants only.

Student Characteristics: The following represents characteristics of students in 2001–2002 in all graduate psychology programs in the department: Female–full-time 10, part-time 0; Male–full-time 7, part-time 0; African American/Black–full-time 0, part-time 0; Hispanic/Latino (a)–full-time 0, part-time 0; Asian/Pacific Islander–full-time 0, part-time 0; American Indian/Alaska Native–full-time 0, part-time 0.

Financial Information/Assistance:
Tuition for Full-Time Study: No information provided.

Financial Assistance:
First Year Students: No information provided.

Advanced Students: No information provided.

Contact Information: For information on financial assistance, contact: Financial Aid Office, D 367 ASB.

Internships/Practica: One-year internship in a setting approved by the Clinical Director is required. Before going on the internship the student must complete all other requirements.

Housing and Day Care: No on-campus housing and day care facilities are available.

Employment of Department Graduates:

Master's Degree Graduates: Of those who graduated in the academic year 2000–2001, the following categories and numbers represent the post-graduate activities and employment of master's degree graduates: Enrolled in a post-doctoral residency/fellowship (n/a), employed in independent practice (n/a).

Doctoral Degree Graduates: Of those who graduated in the academic year 2000–2001, the following categories and numbers represent the post-graduate activities and employment of doctoral degree graduates: Enrolled in a psychology doctoral program (n/a), enrolled in another graduate/professional program (n/a).

Additional Information:

Orientation, Objectives, and Emphasis of Department: Graduate training in psychology at Brigham Young University emphasizes a sound general background in psychology and a broad knowledge of systematic concepts and research methods, both of which will prepare the student for constructive participation in a dynamic and growing profession. All graduate students are expected to be continuously involved in research-related activities in addition to gaining a knowledge of substantive and theoretical topics. While the university is sponsored by the LDS (Mormon) Church, non-LDS students are welcome and considered without bias. The university does expect that all students, regardless of religion, maintain the behavioral standards of the university. These include high standards of honor, integrity, and morality; graciousness in personal behavior; and abstinence from tobacco, alcohol, and the nonmedical use of drugs.

Special Facilities or Resources: In addition to the university library, the Department of Psychology maintains a small library for the exclusive use of its graduate students and faculty. This library includes selected current journals as well as important reference works in the field. The department maintains and operates a number of different laboratory facilities and equipment for clinical, experimental, and social psychology research that occupy a total space of approximately 6,000 square feet. Several microcomputers and on-line capability with the university's computer facilities are also available to assist the students in research. Cooperative arrangements exist with the Utah State Employment Service, the Utah State Hospital, the Utah State Training School, the Utah State Prison, and the BYU Counseling Center for research and training.

Application Information:

Send to: Brigham Young University, Graduate Studies Office, B-350 ASB, Provo, UT 84602. Students are admitted in the Fall, application deadline January 31. *Fee:* $50.

Utah State University
Department of Psychology
Education
2810 Old Main Hill
Logan, UT 84322-2810
Telephone: (435) 797-1460
Fax: (435) 797-1448
E-mail: *cathrynp@coe.usu.edu*
Web: *http://www.coe.usu.edu/psyc/*

Department Established:

1938. Chairperson: David M. Stein. Number of Faculty: total–full-time 18, part-time 36; women–full-time 8, part-time 13; minority–full-time 5.

Programs and Degrees Offered:

Listed in the following order: Program area, degree type (T if terminal Master's), number awarded 7/00–6/01. Professional-scientific PhD 4, research and evaluation PhD 4, school counseling, school psychology.

APA Accreditation: Combined PhD: full.

Student Applications/Admissions:

Student Applications

Professional-scientific PhD—Applications 2001–2002, 55. Total applicants accepted 2001–2002, 9. New applicants enrolled 2001–2002, 9. Total enrolled 2001–2002 full-time, 40, part-time, 2. Openings 2002–2003, 8. The number of students enrolled full and part-time, who were dismissed or voluntarily withdrew from this program area were 0. *Research and evaluation PhD*—Applications 2001–2002, 6. Total applicants accepted 2001–2002, 4. New applicants enrolled 2001–2002, 2. Total enrolled 2001–2002 full-time, 9, part-time, 4. Openings 2002–2003, 5.

Admissions Requirements:

Scores: Entries appear in this order: required test or GPA, minimum score (if required), median score of students entering in 2001–2002. Master's Programs: GRE-V 550, 504; GRE-Q 550, 556; GRE-V+Q 1100, 1059; last 2 years GPA 3.20, 3.47; psychology GPA 3.50. MAT is accepted in lieu of GRE for School Counseling. Doctoral Programs: GRE-V 550, 587; GRE-Q 550, 612; GRE-V+Q 1100, 1199; last 2 years GPA 3.20, 3.71; psychology GPA 3.50; psychology GPA no minimum stated.

Other Criteria: (importance of criteria rated low, medium, or high): GRE/MAT scores high, research experience medium, work experience medium, extracurricular activity low, clinically related public service medium, GPA high, letters of recommendation high, interview high, statement of goals and objectives medium. Some programs (Clinical/Counseling/School PhD) use the above criteria in a formula, while others (REM) rely on GPA, GRE, and letters. Also students interested in the American Indian Support Project must document prior community involvement with Indian people (e.g., evidence of being bilingual).

Student Characteristics: The following represents characteristics of students in 2001–2002 in all graduate psychology programs in

the department: Female–full-time 35, part-time 44; Male–full-time 24, part-time 35; African American/Black–full-time 1, part-time 0; Hispanic/Latino (a)–full-time 2, part-time 0; Asian/Pacific Islander–full-time 1, part-time 1; American Indian/Alaska Native–full-time 4, part-time 1; students subject to the Americans with Disabilities Act–full-time 2.

Financial Information/Assistance:

Tuition for Full-Time Study: *Master's:* State residents per academic year $2,642, $110 per credit hour; nonstate residents: per academic year $8,078, $336 per credit hour. *Doctoral:* State residents: per academic year $2,642, $110 per credit hour; nonstate residents: per academic year $8,078, $336 per credit hour.

Financial Assistance:

First Year Students: Teaching assistantships available for first-year. Average amount paid per academic year: $8,000. Average number of hours worked per week: 20. Apply by January 15. Research assistantships available for first-year. Average amount paid per academic year: $11,000. Average number of hours worked per week: 20. Apply by Varies. Fellowships and scholarships available for first-year. Average amount paid per academic year: $12,000. Apply by January 15.

Advanced Students: Teaching assistantships available for advanced students. Average amount paid per academic year: $9,000. Average number of hours worked per week: 20. Apply by January 15. Research assistantships available for advanced students. Average amount paid per academic year: $11,000. Average number of hours worked per week: 20. Apply by Varies.

Contact Information: Of all students currently enrolled full-time, 100% benefited from one or more of the listed financial assistance programs.

Internships/Practica: Practica are available for master's and doctorate degrees. USU Counseling Center Internship Site. For those doctoral students for whom a professional internship is required prior to graduation, 5 applied in 2000–2001. Of those who applied, 5 were placed in internships listed by the Association of Psychology Postdoctoral and Internship Programs (APPIC); 5 were placed in APA accredited internships.

Housing and Day Care: On-campus housing and day care facilities are available.

Employment of Department Graduates:

Master's Degree Graduates: Of those who graduated in the academic year 2000–2001, the following categories and numbers represent the post-graduate activities and employment of master's degree graduates: Enrolled in a psychology doctoral program (2), enrolled in another graduate/professional program (0), enrolled in a post-doctoral residency/fellowship (n/a), employed in independent practice (n/a), employed in an academic position at a university (0), employed in an academic position at a 2-year/4-year college (0), employed in other positions at a higher education institution (0), employed in a professional position in a school system (0), employed in business or industry (research/consulting) (2), employed in business or industry (management) (0), employed in a government agency (research) (1), employed in a government agency (professional services) (0), employed in a community mental health/counseling center (0), employed in a hospital/medical center (0), still seeking employment (0), other employment position (0).

Doctoral Degree Graduates: Of those who graduated in the academic year 2000–2001, the following categories and numbers represent the post-graduate activities and employment of doctoral degree graduates: Enrolled in a psychology doctoral program (n/a), enrolled in another graduate/professional program (n/a), enrolled in a post-doctoral residency/fellowship (1), employed in independent practice (1), employed in an academic position at a university (1), employed in an academic position at a 2-year/4-year college (0), employed in other positions at a higher education institution (0), employed in a professional position in a school system (1), employed in business or industry (research/consulting) (3), employed in business or industry (management) (0), employed in a government agency (research) (2), employed in a government agency (professional services) (1), employed in a community mental health/counseling center (1), employed in a hospital/medical center (1), still seeking employment (0), other employment position (0).

Additional Information:

Orientation, Objectives, and Emphasis of Department: The Utah State University Department of Psychology offers two graduate PhD programs. Research and evaluation methodology offers training emphasizing methods and techniques for conducting research and evaluation studies in psychology or education settings. Professional-scientific psychology offers professional or scientific training in a combination of clinical, counseling, or school psychology (accredited by the American Psychological Association) and two master's degrees in school psychology and school counseling. The two graduate PhD programs share a common core of doctoral courses intended to provide an advanced overview of several major areas of psychology. All doctoral programs offer extensive training within their specific areas; however, the common core is designed to ensure that no student will complete the PhD without being exposed to the diverse theoretical and methodological perspectives in the field of psychology. The common core also provides students the opportunity to become aware of the scholarly interests of faculty members in all programs, thus broadening students' choices of faculty advisors and dissertation chairpersons. Full tuition waivers are available to PhD students for 70 semester hours of academic credit.

Special Facilities or Resources: Students in all graduate programs benefit from the following departmental facilities: the Basic Behavior Laboratory for nonhuman research, the Human Behavior Laboratory for analysis of human behavior, the Counseling Laboratory for research and training in counseling and clinical practice, and the Community Clinic for supervised experience in actual therapy. In addition, the department has cooperative relations with other campus and off-campus facilities that provide excellent settings for student assistantships, research, and training, including the Bear River Mental Health Center, the USU Center for Persons with Disabilities, the USU Counseling Center, and the Logan Regional Hospital Behavioral Medicine Unit.

Information for Students With Physical Disabilities: We are housed in a newly designed building with easy access for those with disabilities. Also, the university has a Disability Resource Center.

Application Information:

Send to: Utah State University, School of Graduate Studies, Logan, UT 84322-0900. Students are admitted in the Fall, application deadline

January 15; Spring, application deadline February 1; Summer, application deadline June 1. Research and Evaluation Methodology PhD will accept applications if the allotted openings are not filled as of February 1. Professional-Scientific deadline is January 15 and School Psychology is June 1. *Fee:* $40. The fee for international students is $40.

Utah, University of (2001 data)

Department of Educational Psychology, Counseling
  Psychology and School Psychology Programs
College of Education
1705 E. Campus Center, Drive, Room 327
Salt Lake City, UT 84112-9255
Telephone: (801) 581-7148
Fax: (801) 581-5566
E-mail: *bhill@ed.utah.edu*
Web: *http://www.ed.utah.edu/psych*

Department Established:

1949. Chairperson: Robert D. Hill. Number of Faculty: total–full-time 17, part-time 3; women–full-time 8, part-time 2; minority–full-time 3.

Programs and Degrees Offered:

Listed in the following order: Program area, degree type (T if terminal Master's), number awarded 7/00–6/01. Counseling Psychology PhD, foundations PhD, school PhD 3.

APA Accreditation: Counseling PhD: full. School PhD: full.

Student Applications/Admissions:

Student Applications

Counseling Psychology PhD—Openings 2002–2003, 6. *Foundations PhD*—Applications 2001–2002, 6. Total applicants accepted 2001–2002, 2. New applicants enrolled 2001–2002, 1. Total enrolled 2001–2002 full-time, 2, part-time, 2. *School PhD*—Applications 2001–2002, 17. Total applicants accepted 2001–2002, 4. New applicants enrolled 2001–2002, 3. Total enrolled 2001–2002 full-time, 21, part-time, 11. Openings 2002–2003, 6.

Admissions Requirements:

Scores: Entries appear in this order: required test or GPA, minimum score (if required), median score of students entering in 2001–2002. Master's Programs: GRE-V no minimum stated, 530; GRE-Q no minimum stated, 615; GRE-V+Q no minimum stated, 1150; overall undergraduate GPA 3.00, 3.47. Doctoral Programs: GRE-V no minimum stated, 545; GRE-Q no minimum stated, 600; GRE-V+Q no minimum stated, 1115; overall undergraduate GPA no minimum stated, 3.56; last 2 years GPA no minimum stated; psychology GPA no minimum stated; psychology GPA no minimum stated.

Other Criteria: (importance of criteria rated low, medium, or high): research experience high, work experience high, extracurricular activity medium, clinically related public service medium, GPA high, letters of recommendation high, statement of goals and objectives high, vita medium. Each program reviews and rates its own applicants.

Student Characteristics: The following represents characteristics of students in 2001–2002 in all graduate psychology programs in the department: Female–full-time 18, part-time 0; Male–full-time 13, part-time 0; African American/Black–full-time 1, part-time 0; Hispanic/Latino (a)–full-time 2, part-time 0; Asian/Pacific Islander–full-time 3, part-time 0; American Indian/Alaska Native–full-time 0, part-time 0.

Financial Information/Assistance:

Tuition for Full-Time Study: *Master's:* State residents per academic year $3,000; nonstate residents: per academic year $9,000, *Doctoral:* State residents: per academic year $3,000; nonstate residents: per academic year $9,000.

Financial Assistance:

First Year Students: Teaching assistantships available for first-year. Average amount paid per academic year: $4,250. Average number of hours worked per week: 10. Apply by April. Tuition remission given: partial. Research assistantships available for first-year. Average amount paid per academic year: $4,250. Average number of hours worked per week: 10. Apply by Flexible. Tuition remission given: partial.

Advanced Students: Teaching assistantships available for advanced students. Average amount paid per academic year: $4,250. Average number of hours worked per week: 10. Apply by April. Tuition remission given: partial. Research assistantships available for advanced students. Average amount paid per academic year: $4,250. Average number of hours worked per week: 10. Apply by Flexible. Tuition remission given: partial. Traineeships available for advanced students. Apply by Variable. Fellowships and scholarships available for advanced students. Average number of hours worked per week: 0. Apply by Variable.

Contact Information: For information on financial assistance, contact: Sue Morrow, PhD, Counseling Psychology Program Director, morrow@ed.utah.edu, 801-581-3400.

Internships/Practica: Practica for counseling psychology doctoral students vary and include such settings as U of U counseling center and other campus services, community mental health settings, hospital settings, and private practice. Predoctoral internships are typically taken nationally in university counseling centers, community mental health settings, veterans hospitals, and specialty settings.

Housing and Day Care: On-campus housing and day care facilities are available.

Employment of Department Graduates:

Master's Degree Graduates: Of those who graduated in the academic year 2000–2001, the following categories and numbers represent the post-graduate activities and employment of master's degree graduates: Enrolled in a post-doctoral residency/fellowship (n/a), employed in independent practice (n/a).

Doctoral Degree Graduates: Of those who graduated in the academic year 2000–2001, the following categories and numbers represent the post-graduate activities and employment of doctoral degree graduates: Enrolled in a psychology doctoral program (n/a), enrolled in another graduate/professional program (n/a).

Additional Information:

Orientation, Objectives, and Emphasis of Department: The department of educational psychology at the University of Utah is characterized by an emphasis on the application of behavioral sciences to educational and psychological processes. The department is organized into 4 program areas: counseling psychology (PhD), school psychology (PhD), foundations (PhD), and master's level counseling programs (MEd). The basic school psychology program includes two years of academic work and one additional year of full-time internship. Doctoral programs include counseling psychology (APA accredited), school psychology (APA accredited), and foundations. The basic emphasis of the department is on the application of psychological principles in educational and human service settings. In addition, doctoral programs represent a scientist-practitioner model with considerable emphasis on the development of research as well as professional skills. Information describing the objectives and emphases of specific program areas within the department is available on request.

Special Facilities or Resources: A variety of research and training opportunities are available to students through relationships the department has developed with various university and community facilities. Included are the university counseling center, medical center, computer center, and the adjacent regional Veterans Administration Medical Center. Community facilities include local school districts, community mental health centers, children's hospital, general hospitals, child guidance clinics, and various state social service agencies. The department maintains its own statistics laboratory. Students have access to computer stations and use of college computer network.

Application Information:
Send to: Admission, University of Utah, Department of Educational Psychology, 1705 E Campus Ctr Dr., Rm 327, Salt Lake City, Utah 84112-9255. Students are admitted in the Fall, application deadline January 15. *Fee:* $40.

Utah, University of
Department of Psychology
380 S. 1530 E., Room 502
Salt Lake City, UT 84112
Telephone: (801) 581-6124
Fax: (801) 581-5841
E-mail: *nancy.seegmiller@psych.utah.edu*
Web: *http://www.psych.utah.edu*

Department Established:
1925. Chairperson: Timothy W. Smith. Number of Faculty: total–full-time 32; women–full-time 12; minority–full-time 3.

Programs and Degrees Offered:
Listed in the following order: Program area, degree type (T if terminal Master's), number awarded 7/00–6/01. Clinical Psychology PhD 3, Cognition and Neuroscience PhD 1, Developmental Psychology PhD 1, Social Psychology PhD.

APA Accreditation: Clinical PhD: full.

Student Applications/Admissions:
Student Applications
Clinical Psychology PhD—Applications 2001–2002, 66. Total applicants accepted 2001–2002, 4. New applicants enrolled

2001–2002, 4. Total enrolled 2001–2002 full-time, 25. Openings 2002–2003, 7. The Median number of years required for completion of a degree are 8. The number of students enrolled full and part-time, who were dismissed or voluntarily withdrew from this program area were 1. *Cognition and Neuroscience PhD*—Applications 2001–2002, 10. Total applicants accepted 2001–2002, 1. New applicants enrolled 2001–2002, 1. Total enrolled 2001–2002 full-time, 5. Openings 2002–2003, 5. The Median number of years required for completion of a degree are 0. The number of students enrolled full and part-time, who were dismissed or voluntarily withdrew from this program area were 0. *Developmental Psychology PhD*—Applications 2001–2002, 12. Total applicants accepted 2001–2002, 3. New applicants enrolled 2001–2002, 3. Total enrolled 2001–2002 full-time, 12. Openings 2002–2003, 2. The number of students enrolled full and part-time, who were dismissed or voluntarily withdrew from this program area were 0. *Social Psychology PhD*—Applications 2001–2002, 18. Total applicants accepted 2001–2002, 2. New applicants enrolled 2001–2002, 2. Total enrolled 2001–2002 full-time, 11. Openings 2002–2003, 4. The number of students enrolled full and part-time, who were dismissed or voluntarily withdrew from this program area were 0.

Admissions Requirements:
Scores: Entries appear in this order: required test or GPA, minimum score (if required), median score of students entering in 2001–2002. Doctoral Programs: GRE-V no minimum stated, 510; GRE-Q no minimum stated, 643; GRE-V+Q no minimum stated, 1153; GRE-Analytical no minimum stated, 709; GRE-V+Q+Analytical no minimum stated, 1862; GRE-Subject(Psych) no minimum stated, 663; overall undergraduate GPA 3.0, 3.68; last 2 years GPA no minimum stated; psychology GPA no minimum stated; psychology GPA no minimum stated.
Other Criteria: (importance of criteria rated low, medium, or high): GRE/MAT scores medium, research experience high, work experience medium, extracurricular activity medium, clinically related public service medium, GPA medium, letters of recommendation high, interview high, statement of goals and objectives high.

Student Characteristics: The following represents characteristics of students in 2001–2002 in all graduate psychology programs in the department: Female–full-time 37, part-time 0; Male–full-time 17, part-time 0; African American/Black–full-time 1, part-time 0; Hispanic/Latino (a)–full-time 1, part-time 0; Asian/Pacific Islander–full-time 2, part-time 0; American Indian/Alaska Native–full-time 0, part-time 0.

Financial Information/Assistance:
Tuition for Full-Time Study: Master's: State residents per academic year $2,314, $129 per credit hour; nonstate residents: per academic year $6,988, $388 per credit hour. *Doctoral:* State residents: per academic year $2,314, $129 per credit hour; nonstate residents: per academic year $6,988, $388 per credit hour.

Financial Assistance:
First Year Students: Teaching assistantships available for first-year. Average amount paid per academic year: $8,700. Average number of hours worked per week: 20. Apply by TBA. Tuition remission given: full. Research assistantships available for first-

year. Average amount paid per academic year: $8,700. Average number of hours worked per week: 20. Apply by TBA. Tuition remission given: full. Fellowships and scholarships available for first-year. Average amount paid per academic year: $10,000. Apply by TBA. Tuition remission given: full.

Advanced Students: Teaching assistantships available for advanced students. Average amount paid per academic year: $10,500. Average number of hours worked per week: 20. Apply by TBA. Tuition remission given: full. Research assistantships available for advanced students. Average amount paid per academic year: $10,500. Average number of hours worked per week: 20. Apply by TBA. Tuition remission given: full. Fellowships and scholarships available for advanced students. Average amount paid per academic year: $10,000. Apply by TBA. Tuition remission given: full.

Contact Information: Of all students currently enrolled full-time, 95% benefited from one or more of the listed financial assistance programs. For information on financial assistance, contact: University of Utah, Financial Aid Office, 201 S 1460 East, Rm 105, Salt Lake City, UT 84112-9055.

Internships/Practica: Extensive clinical training experiences are available through close ties with facilities in the community. A sample of these include the Veteran's Administration Hospital, The University Medical Center, Primary Children's Hospital, the Children's Behavioral Therapy Unit, the Juvenile Detention Center, The University Neuropsychiatric Institute, the University Counseling Center, and local community health centers. There are four APA approved internships in the local community. For those doctoral students for whom a professional internship is required prior to graduation, 6 applied in 2000–2001. Of those who applied, 6 were placed in internships listed by the Association of Psychology Postdoctoral and Internship Programs (APPIC); 6 were placed in APA accredited internships.

Housing and Day Care: On-campus housing and day care facilities are available.

Employment of Department Graduates:

Master's Degree Graduates: Of those who graduated in the academic year 2000–2001, the following categories and numbers represent the post-graduate activities and employment of master's degree graduates: Enrolled in a post-doctoral residency/fellowship (n/a), employed in independent practice (n/a).

Doctoral Degree Graduates: Of those who graduated in the academic year 2000–2001, the following categories and numbers represent the post-graduate activities and employment of doctoral degree graduates: Enrolled in a psychology doctoral program (n/a), enrolled in another graduate/professional program (n/a), enrolled in a post-doctoral residency/fellowship (0), employed in independent practice (0), employed in an academic position at a university (1), employed in an academic position at a 2-year/4-year college (1), employed in other positions at a higher education institution (1), employed in a hospital/medical center (2).

Additional Information:

Orientation, Objectives, and Emphasis of Department: We offer comprehensive training in psychology, including clinical (general, child-family, health emphases), developmental, experimental-physiological, and social. Students generally receive support throughout their training. Students are selected for area programs with individual faculty advisers. They do research in their areas and clinical students also receive applied training. Graduates accept jobs in academic departments, research centers, and applied settings.

Special Facilities or Resources: Special facilities include the Early Childhood Education Center and 3 on-campus hospitals.

Information for Students With Physical Disabilities: The University provides reasonable accommodation to the known disabilities of students. Physical plant facilities for the physically disabled have been incorporated into the building. In addition, the University provides services through the Center for Disabled Students Services.

Application Information:
Send to: Graduate Admissions Secretary, Psychology Department, 380 S. 1530 East, Room 502, Salt Lake City, UT 84112. Students are admitted in the Fall, application deadline January 15. *Fee:* $40.

Castleton State College

Psychology
Psychology Building
Castleton, VT 05735
Telephone: (802) 468-1405 or (802) 468-1281
Fax: (802) 468-1480 or 3020
E-mail: *Brenda.Russell@castleton.edu*
Web: *http://www.castleton.edu*

Department Established:

1967. Director of Forensic Graduate Program: Brenda L. Russell. Number of Faculty: total–full-time 7, part-time 1; women–full-time 1, part-time 1.

Programs and Degrees Offered:

Listed in the following order: Program area, degree type (T if terminal Master's), number awarded 7/00–6/01. Forensic Psychology MA (T) 12.

Student Applications/Admissions:

Student Applications

Forensic Psychology MA—Applications 2001–2002, 62. Total applicants accepted 2001–2002, 17. New applicants enrolled 2001–2002, 12. Total enrolled 2001–2002 full-time, 32. Openings 2002–2003, 17. The Median number of years required for completion of a degree are 2. The number of students enrolled full and part-time, who were dismissed or voluntarily withdrew from this program area were 0.

Admissions Requirements:

Scores: Entries appear in this order: required test or GPA, minimum score (if required), median score of students entering in 2001–2002. Master's Programs: GRE-V+Q no minimum stated, 1080; overall undergraduate GPA no minimum stated, 3.66. Doctoral Programs: last 2 years GPA no minimum stated; psychology GPA no minimum stated; psychology GPA no minimum stated.

Other Criteria: (importance of criteria rated low, medium, or high): GRE/MAT scores low, research experience high, work experience medium, extracurricular activity medium, GPA high, letters of recommendation high, statement of goals and objectives high.

Student Characteristics: The following represents characteristics of students in 2001–2002 in all graduate psychology programs in the department: Female–full-time 12, part-time 0; Male–full-time 0, part-time 0; African American/Black–full-time 1, part-time 0; Hispanic/Latino (a)–full-time 0, part-time 0; Asian/Pacific Islander–full-time 2, part-time 0; American Indian/Alaska Native–full-time 0, part-time 0.

Financial Information/Assistance:

Tuition for Full-Time Study: No information provided.

Financial Assistance:

First Year Students: Teaching assistantships available for first-year. Research assistantships available for first-year. Fellowships and scholarships available for first-year.

Advanced Students: No information provided.

Contact Information: Of all students currently enrolled full-time, 96% benefited from one or more of the listed financial assistance programs. For information on financial assistance, contact: Office of Financial Aid, Woodruff Hall, Castleton State College, Castleton, VT 05735.

Internships/Practica: The forensic program provides research internships and practica in various local, state, and federal agencies and institutions. Practicum and internship placements are available in a wide range of forensic settings. The placements are designed to provide students with practical experience that integrates classroom research skills with real-world situations. Students are encouraged to enroll in at least one practicum or internship experience during their Master's.

Housing and Day Care: No on-campus housing and day care facilities are available.

Employment of Department Graduates:

Master's Degree Graduates: Of those who graduated in the academic year 2000–2001, the following categories and numbers represent the post-graduate activities and employment of master's degree graduates: Enrolled in a psychology doctoral program (1), enrolled in another graduate/professional program (1), enrolled in a post-doctoral residency/fellowship (n/a), employed in independent practice (n/a), employed in business or industry (research/ consulting) (4), employed in a government agency (research) (4), employed in a community mental health/counseling center (2).

Doctoral Degree Graduates: Of those who graduated in the academic year 2000–2001, the following categories and numbers represent the post-graduate activities and employment of doctoral degree graduates: Enrolled in a psychology doctoral program (n/a), enrolled in another graduate/professional program (n/a).

Additional Information:

Orientation, Objectives, and Emphasis of Department: The Master's Program in Forensic Psychology at Castleton focuses on four major areas: (1) police psychology; (2) correctional psychology; (3) psychology of crime and delinquency; and (4) psychology and law. The program is designed to provide students with: (1) a comprehensive knowledge of psychology as it applies to the criminal justice and civil justice systems; (2) the research skills to evaluate competently various issues and programs within these systems; and (3) the communication skills necessary to express their findings effectively to diverse groups within the systems. The program is a research-based Master of Arts created to prepare students for: (1) careers in the various organizations and agencies of the criminal and civil justice systems; or (2) acceptance into doctoral programs in psychology, criminal justice, political science, or other social science disciplines. Graduates will be trained to analyze, interpret, organize, apply, and transmit existing knowledge in the field of forensic psychology. The overall mission of the program is to educate students to be highly knowledgeable about the various methodologies and statistical analyses critical to conducting well-designed research. Prospective students should realize that the program will not provide training in counseling, psychotherapy, or clinical practice.

Special Facilities or Resources: The department maintains ongoing professional contacts with over 70 state and federal law enforcement agencies, including a close working relationship with the Vermont Police Academy and the Vermont Department of Corrections. Opportunities for doing research at these agencies and facilities are considerable. The department has excellent computing facilities for the support of forensic research. The college and department libraries receive virtually every major recent periodical in criminal justice and forensic psychology written in the English language. The department is also the home of the scholarly journal Criminal Justice and Behavior, an international journal that publishes cutting edge research in Forensic Psychology. Graduate students will have considerable opportunity to participate in the scholarly and editorial process of the journal.

Application Information:

Send to: Admission Office, Wright House, Castleton State College, Castleton, VT 05735. Students are admitted in the Fall, application deadline February 15. *Fee:* $30.

Goddard College
MA Psychology & Counseling Program
123 Pitkin Road
Plainfield, VT 05667
Telephone: (802) 454-8311, (800) 468-4888
Fax: (802) 454-1029
E-mail: *admissions@goddard.edu*
Web: *http://www.goddard.edu*

Department Established:

1988. Director: Steven E. James, PhD. Number of Faculty: total–full-time 1, part-time 6; minority–full-time 1, part-time 2.

Programs and Degrees Offered:

Listed in the following order: Program area, degree type (T if terminal Master's), number awarded 7/00–6/01. Counseling MA (T) 18, Organizational Development MA (T) 1, Psychology MA (T) 2, Sexual Orientation MA (T).

Student Applications/Admissions:
Student Applications

Counseling MA—Applications 2001–2002, 30. Total applicants accepted 2001–2002, 18. New applicants enrolled 2001–2002, 17. Total enrolled 2001–2002 full-time, 55. Openings

2002–2003, 25. The Median number of years required for completion of a degree are 2. The number of students enrolled full and part-time, who were dismissed or voluntarily withdrew from this program area were 1. *Organizational Development MA*—Applications 2001–2002, 2. Total applicants accepted 2001–2002, 2. New applicants enrolled 2001–2002, 2. Total enrolled 2001–2002 full-time, 2. Openings 2002–2003, 10. The Median number of years required for completion of a degree are 2. The number of students enrolled full and part-time, who were dismissed or voluntarily withdrew from this program area were 0. *Psychology MA*—Applications 2001–2002, 1. Total applicants accepted 2001–2002, 1. New applicants enrolled 2001–2002, 1. Total enrolled 2001–2002 full-time, 2. Openings 2002–2003, 5. *Sexual Orientation MA*—Applications 2001–2002, 4. Total applicants accepted 2001–2002, 4. New applicants enrolled 2001–2002, 3. Total enrolled 2001–2002 full-time, 3. Openings 2002–2003, 10. The Median number of years required for completion of a degree are 2. The number of students enrolled full and part-time, who were dismissed or voluntarily withdrew from this program area were 1.

Admissions Requirements:

Scores: Entries appear in this order: required test or GPA, minimum score (if required), median score of students entering in 2001–2002. Doctoral Programs: last 2 years GPA no minimum stated; psychology GPA no minimum stated; psychology GPA no minimum stated.

Other Criteria: (importance of criteria rated low, medium, or high): research experience low, work experience high, extracurricular activity medium, clinically related public service high, letters of recommendation medium, interview low, statement of goals and objectives high, Bibliography & Study Plan medium.

Student Characteristics: The following represents characteristics of students in 2001–2002 in all graduate psychology programs in the department: Female–full-time 38, part-time 0; Male–full-time 17, part-time 0; African American/Black–full-time 5, part-time 0; Hispanic/Latino (a)–full-time 1, part-time 0; Asian/Pacific Islander–full-time 2, part-time 0; American Indian/Alaska Native–full-time 2, part-time 0; Multi-ethnic–full-time 2, students subject to the Americans with Disabilities Act–full-time 3.

Financial Information/Assistance:

Tuition for Full-Time Study: *Master's:* State residents per academic year $11,054; nonstate residents: per academic year $11,054.

Financial Assistance:

First Year Students: No information provided.
Advanced Students: No information provided.
Contact Information: For information on financial assistance, contact: Financial Aid Office.

Internships/Practica: Students are required to complete a minimum of 300 hours of supervised practicum during the program. This practicum takes place at a location convenient to the student that has been reviewed and evaluated by the program faculty as appropriate to the student's plan of study, providing appropriated licensed supervision and offering direct counseling experience. Students propose sites at which they would like to work to the faculty for review and approval.

Housing and Day Care: On-campus housing and day care facilities are available.

Employment of Department Graduates:

Master's Degree Graduates: Of those who graduated in the academic year 2000–2001, the following categories and numbers represent the post-graduate activities and employment of master's degree graduates: Enrolled in a psychology doctoral program (5), enrolled in another graduate/professional program (1), enrolled in a post-doctoral residency/fellowship (n/a), employed in independent practice (n/a), employed in an academic position at a university (1), employed in an academic position at a 2-year/4-year college (0), employed in other positions at a higher education institution (1), employed in a professional position in a school system (0), employed in business or industry (research/consulting) (3), employed in business or industry (management) (0), employed in a government agency (research) (0), employed in a government agency (professional services) (0), employed in a community mental health/counseling center (13), employed in a hospital/medical center (1), still seeking employment (1), other employment position (2).

Doctoral Degree Graduates: Of those who graduated in the academic year 2000–2001, the following categories and numbers represent the post-graduate activities and employment of doctoral degree graduates: Enrolled in a psychology doctoral program (n/a), enrolled in another graduate/professional program (n/a).

Additional Information:

Orientation, Objectives, and Emphasis of Department: Graduate study in Psychology & Counseling consists of a unique combination of intensive campus residencies and directed, independent study off campus. Students design their own emphasis of study or enter into the defined concentrations in organizational development or sexual orientation studies. The primary goal of the program is to develop skills in individual, family, and/or community psychology, grounded in theory and research, personal experience, and self-knowledge, and relevant to current social complexities. While pursuing their own specialized interests, students gain mastery in the broad range of subjects necessary for the effective and ethical practice of counseling. Study begins each semester with a week-long residency at the college, a time of planning for the ensuing semester and attending seminars. Returning home, the student begins implementation of the detailed study plan based upon the student's particular interests and needs and mastery of relevant theory and research and completion of a supervised practicum with a minimum 300 hours. Through appropriate design of their study plan, students may meet the educational requirements for master's level licensure or certification in their state. The program is approved by the Council of Applied Master's Programs in Psychology.

Application Information:

Send to: Admissions Office. Students are admitted in the Fall, application deadline 6/1; Spring, application deadline 12/1. *Fee:* $40. Waiver by written petition.

Saint Michael's College

Psychology Department/Graduate Program
in Clinical Psychology
Saint Michael's College
One Winooski Park
Colchester, VT 05439
Telephone: (802) 654-2206
Fax: (802) 654-2610
E-mail: *rmiller@smcvt.edu*
Web: *http://www.smcvt.edu/gradprograms*

Department Established:

1984. Director: Ronald B. Miller. Number of Faculty: total–full-time 5, part-time 8; women–full-time 1, part-time 6.

Programs and Degrees Offered:

Listed in the following order: Program area, degree type (T if terminal Master's), number awarded 7/00–6/01. Graduate Clinical Psychology MA (T) 16.

Student Applications/Admissions:

Student Applications

Graduate Clinical Psychology MA—Applications 2001–2002, 18. Total applicants accepted 2001–2002, 13. New applicants enrolled 2001–2002, 9. Total enrolled 2001–2002 full-time, 10, part-time, 35. Openings 2002–2003, 16. The Median number of years required for completion of a degree are 3. The number of students enrolled full and part-time, who were dismissed or voluntarily withdrew from this program area were 2.

Admissions Requirements:

Scores: Entries appear in this order: required test or GPA, minimum score (if required), median score of students entering in 2001–2002. Master's Programs: GRE-V 450, 505; GRE-Q 450, 495; GRE-V+Q 950, 1000; GRE-Analytical 550, 575; GRE-Subject(Psych) 550, 560; overall undergraduate GPA 3.00, 3.25; last 2 years GPA 3.25, 3.40; psychology GPA 3.25, 3.50. Doctoral Programs: last 2 years GPA no minimum stated; psychology GPA no minimum stated; psychology GPA no minimum stated.

Other Criteria: (importance of criteria rated low, medium, or high): GRE/MAT scores low, research experience low, work experience high, extracurricular activity medium, clinically related public service high, GPA high, letters of recommendation medium, interview high, statement of goals and objectives medium, interest in orientation high.

Student Characteristics: The following represents characteristics of students in 2001–2002 in all graduate psychology programs in the department: Female–full-time 1, part-time 50; Male–full-time 2, part-time 15; African American/Black–full-time 0, part-time 0; Hispanic/Latino (a)–full-time 0, part-time 0; Asian/Pacific Islander–full-time 1, part-time 2; American Indian/Alaska Native–full-time 0, part-time 0; part-time 2.

Financial Information/Assistance:

Tuition for Full-Time Study: *Master's:* State residents $345 per credit hour; nonstate residents: $345 per credit hour.

Financial Assistance:

First Year Students: Teaching assistantships available for first-year. Average number of hours worked per week: 20. Apply by June 1. Tuition remission given: full and partial.

Advanced Students: No information provided.

Contact Information: Of all students currently enrolled full-time, 40% benefited from one or more of the listed financial assistance programs. For information on financial assistance, contact: Financial Aid Office for Loans, 802-654-3243 or www.smcvt.edu, Director of Graduate Clinical Psychology Program for Teacher Assistantship, 802-654-2206 or tarcury@smc-vt.edu.

Internships/Practica: We have practice and internship sites in the following settings: schools, college counseling centers, teaching hospitals, correctional centers, Visiting Nurses Association, community mental health outpatient and residential offices, drug and alcohol treatment center, adolescent day treatment program.

Housing and Day Care: No on-campus housing and day care facilities are available.

Employment of Department Graduates:

Master's Degree Graduates: Of those who graduated in the academic year 2000–2001, the following categories and numbers represent the post-graduate activities and employment of master's degree graduates: Enrolled in a psychology doctoral program (1), enrolled in another graduate/professional program (0), enrolled in a post-doctoral residency/fellowship (n/a), employed in independent practice (n/a), employed in an academic position at a university (0), employed in an academic position at a 2-year/4-year college (0), employed in other positions at a higher education institution (0), employed in a professional position in a school system (4), employed in business or industry (research/consulting) (0), employed in business or industry (management) (0), employed in a government agency (research) (0), employed in a government agency (professional services) (1), employed in a community mental health/counseling center (9), employed in a hospital/medical center (1), still seeking employment (0), other employment position (0).

Doctoral Degree Graduates: Of those who graduated in the academic year 2000–2001, the following categories and numbers represent the post-graduate activities and employment of doctoral degree graduates: Enrolled in a psychology doctoral program (n/a), enrolled in another graduate/professional program (n/a).

Additional Information:

Orientation, Objectives, and Emphasis of Department: The focus of the MA program in clinical psychology is on the integration of theory, research, and practice in the preparation of professional psychologists. Our goal is to provide an educational milieu that respects the individual educational goals of the student, and fosters intellectual, personal, and professional development. The program is eclectic in orientation and the faculty offer a diversity of interests, orientations, and experiences within the framework of our curriculum. We see ourselves as preparing students for professional practice in community agencies, schools, hospitals, and public and private clinics. Cross-registration in the courses offered by the college's other master's degree programs in education, administration, and theology is available for those wishing an interdisciplinary emphasis. The curriculum is also designed with two further objectives in mind: (1) the preparation of students for state licensing examinations, and (2) further doctoral study in professional psychology at another institution. All classes are held in the evening, permitting full- or part-time study. The program seeks to integrate a psychodynamic understanding of the therapeutic relationship with humanistic values, and a social systems perspective.

Special Facilities or Resources: St. Michael's College offers the graduate student a faculty committed to teaching and professional training in a non-bureaucratic learning environment. All clinical courses are taught by highly experienced clinical practitioners who serve as part-time faculty. The full-time faculty teach core courses in general, developmental, and social psychology, as well as research methods. The college has excellent computing facilities for the support of social science research.

Information for Students With Physical Disabilities: We currently have one visually impaired adult student for whom we are making curricular accommodations.

Application Information:
Send to: Department Chair (Director). Students are admitted in the Fall, application deadline August 1; Spring, application deadline December 1; Summer, application deadline May 1. Fall enrollment is recommended, and applications for Fall are encouraged by June 1, in order to be eligible for TA positions. *Fee:* $35.

Argosy University, Washington, DC
Clinical Psychology
American School of Professional Psychology
1550 Wilson Boulevard, Suite 600
Arlington, VA 22209
Telephone: (703) 243-5300
Fax: (703) 243-8973
E-mail: *dcadmissions@argosyu.edu*
Web: *http://www.argosyu.edu*

Department Established:
1994. Program Head: Edward R. Shearin. Number of Faculty: total–full-time 12, part-time 2; women–full-time 8, part-time 2; minority–full-time 5.

Programs and Degrees Offered:
Listed in the following order: Program area, degree type (T if terminal Master's), number awarded 7/00–6/01. Clinical MA (T), Clinical Psychology PsyD (T) 20, professional counseling MA (T) 8.

APA Accreditation: Clinical PsyD: full.

Student Applications/Admissions:
Student Applications

Clinical MA—Applications 2001–2002, 34. Total applicants accepted 2001–2002, 23. New applicants enrolled 2001–2002, 19. Total enrolled 2001–2002 full-time, 34. Openings 2002–2003, 21. The Median number of years required for completion of a degree are 2. The number of students enrolled full and part-time, who were dismissed or voluntarily withdrew from this program area were 0. *Clinical Psychology PsyD*—Applications 2001–2002, 213. Total applicants accepted 2001–2002, 122. New applicants enrolled 2001–2002, 74. Total enrolled 2001–2002 full-time, 196, part-time, 61. Openings 2002–2003, 80. The Median number of years required for completion of a degree are 5. The number of students enrolled full and part-time, who were dismissed or voluntarily withdrew from this program area were 8. *Professional counseling MA*—Applications 2001–2002, 109. Total applicants accepted 2001–2002, 60. New applicants enrolled 2001–2002, 44. Total enrolled 2001–2002 full-time, 109. Openings 2002–2003, 55. The Median number of years required for completion of a degree are 2. The number of students enrolled full and part-time, who were dismissed or voluntarily withdrew from this program area were 0.

Admissions Requirements:
Scores: Entries appear in this order: required test or GPA, minimum score (if required), median score of students entering in 2001–2002. Master's Programs: overall undergraduate GPA 3.0, 3.0; last 2 years GPA 3.0, 3.1; psychology GPA 3.0, 3.3. MA applicants should have minimum of 3.0 in highest degree earned. GRE scores are optional. Doctoral Programs: overall undergraduate GPA 3.25, 3.20; last 2 years GPA 3.25, 3.50; psychology GPA 3.25, 3.50; psychology GPA 3.25, 3.67. Ap-

plicants should have a minimum of 3.25 for highest degree earned; Program will review overall GPA, last two years GPA and psychology GPA for 3.25 GPA. GRE scores are optional.
Other Criteria: (importance of criteria rated low, medium, or high): GRE/MAT scores low, research experience low, work experience high, extracurricular activity low, clinically related public service high, GPA high, letters of recommendation high, interview high, statement of goals and objectives high. Clinical experience is less important for applicants to MA program.

Student Characteristics: The following represents characteristics of students in 2001–2002 in all graduate psychology programs in the department: Female–full-time 179, part-time 56; Male–full-time 43, part-time 12; African American/Black–full-time 41, part-time 9; Hispanic/Latino (a)–full-time 8, part-time 1; Asian/Pacific Islander–full-time 7, part-time 6; American Indian/Alaska Native–full-time 2, part-time 0; Multi-ethnic–full-time 3, part-time 0; students subject to the Americans with Disabilities Act–full-time 3, part-time 2.

Financial Information/Assistance:
Tuition for Full-Time Study: *Master's:* State residents per academic year $14,280, $510 per credit hour; nonstate residents: per academic year $14,280, $510 per credit hour. *Doctoral:* State residents: per academic year $14,280, $510 per credit hour; nonstate residents: per academic year $14,280, $510 per credit hour.

Financial Assistance:
First Year Students: Fellowships and scholarships available for first-year. Average amount paid per academic year: $3,600. Average number of hours worked per week: 6. Apply by 9/03/02. Tuition remission given: full and partial.
Advanced Students: Teaching assistantships available for advanced students. Average amount paid per academic year: $1,530. Average number of hours worked per week: 8. Apply by variable. Tuition remission given: full and partial. Fellowships and scholarships available for advanced students. Average amount paid per academic year: $3,600. Average number of hours worked per week: 6. Apply by 9/03/02. Tuition remission given: full and partial.
Contact Information: Of all students currently enrolled full-time, 6% benefited from one or more of the listed financial assistance programs. For information on financial assistance, contact: Liza D. Ziegler, Director of Student Finance.

Internships/Practica: Practicum: Practicum training is designed to give students the opportunity to work under supervision with a clinical population within a mental health delivery system. Students learn to apply their theoretical knowledge implement, develop, and assess the efficacy of clinical techniques, and develop the professional attitudes important for the identity of a professional psychologist. Doctoral students complete two training practica sequences (600 hours each) focusing on assessment or psychotherapy skills or integrating the two. Master's students are required to complete one practicum (600 hours). (Clinical and Counseling) Internship: All doctoral students are required to complete a one year (12 month) internship as a condition for graduation.

This intensive and supervised contact with clients is essential for giving greater breadth and depth to the student's overall academic experience. Typically, students will begin the internship during their fourth or fifth year, depending on the student's progress through the curriculum. For those doctoral students for whom a professional internship is required prior to graduation, 42 applied in 2000–2001. Of those who applied, 42 were placed in internships listed by the Association of Psychology Postdoctoral and Internship Programs (APPIC); 30 were placed in APA accredited internships.

Housing and Day Care: No on-campus housing and day care facilities are available.

Employment of Department Graduates:

Master's Degree Graduates: Of those who graduated in the academic year 2000–2001, the following categories and numbers represent the post-graduate activities and employment of master's degree graduates: Enrolled in a psychology doctoral program (5), enrolled in a post-doctoral residency/fellowship (n/a), employed in independent practice (n/a).

Doctoral Degree Graduates: Of those who graduated in the academic year 2000–2001, the following categories and numbers represent the post-graduate activities and employment of doctoral degree graduates: Enrolled in a psychology doctoral program (n/a), enrolled in another graduate/professional program (n/a), enrolled in a post-doctoral residency/fellowship (1), employed in independent practice (2), employed in an academic position at a university (0), employed in an academic position at a 2-year/4-year college (0), employed in other positions at a higher education institution (2), employed in a professional position in a school system (2), employed in business or industry (research/consulting) (0), employed in business or industry (management) (0), employed in a government agency (research) (0), employed in a government agency (professional services) (3), employed in a community mental health/counseling center (4), employed in a hospital/medical center (1), still seeking employment (4), other employment position (1).

Additional Information:

Orientation, Objectives, and Emphasis of Department: The Doctoral Program in clinical psychology is designed to educate and train students to function effectively in diverse professional roles. The Doctoral Program emphasizes the development of attitudes, knowledge, and skills essential in the formation of professional psychologists who are committed to the ethical provision of quality services. The School offers a broad-based curriculum, providing a meaningful integration of diverse theoretical perspectives, scholarship, and practice. Opportunities are available for students to develop expertise in a number of specialized areas including the provision of services to specific populations such as children and families; theoretical perspectives such as cognitive-behavioral, family systems, psychodynamic, and Jungian theory/analysis; and areas of application such as forensics and health psychology. The MA degree in clinical psychology is designed to meet the needs of both those students seeking a terminal degree for work in the mental health field, and those who eventually plan to pursue a doctoral degree. The Master's degree provides a solid core of basic psychology, as well as a strong clinical orientation, with an emphasis in psychological assessment. Professional Counseling Program: The MA degree in professional counseling is intended for the continued professional development of persons who are currently functioning, or who wish to function, in a variety of counseling roles. This program includes theoretical and practical elements in a weekend format with a practitioner faculty. The Doctor of Psychology (PsyD) program in clinical psychology is designed to educate and train students to function effectively in a number of professional roles. The program emphasizes the development of attitudes, knowledge, and skills essential to the formation of professional psychologists who are committed to the ethical provision of quality services. The school offers a broad-based program, providing a meaningful integration of diverse theoretical perspectives, scholarship, and practice. Opportunities are available for students to develop expertise in a number of specialized areas including the provision of services to specific populations such as children and families; theoretical perspectives such as cognitive-behavioral, family systems, psychodynamic, and experiential; and areas of application such as forensic and health psychology. The Master of Arts Degree in Clinical Psychology is designed to meet the needs of those students seeking a terminal degree for work in the mental health field, those seeking licensure as professional counselors and those who eventually plan to pursue a doctoral degree. The Master's degree provides students with a solid core of basic psychology as well as strong clinical orientation with an emphasis in psychological assessment.

Special Facilities or Resources: Argosy University is conveniently located minutes from downtown Washington, DC. Students and faculty have full borrowing privileges at Georgetown University's Medical School Library. The ASPP on-site library is developing a focused psychology collection consisting of reference titles and books, journals, diagnostic assessment instruments, and audiovisual equipment. Computerized literature searches and inter-campus loans are available on site. In addition, students have access to the rich library resources of the Washington, DC area including the National Library of Medicine and the Library of Congress.

Application Information:

Send to: Admissions Department, Argosy University, Washington, DC Campus, 1550 Wilson Boulevard, Ste. 600, Arlington, VA 22209. Students are admitted in the Fall, application deadline January 15; Spring, application deadline October 15. Fall application deadline - application must be complete to qualify for the April 1st decision; Second Fall deadline is May 15, dependent on available space. *Fee:* $50.

George Mason University
Department of Psychology
Arts and Sciences
4400 University Drive, MSN 3F5
Fairfax, VA 22030-4444
Telephone: (703) 993-1342
Fax: (703) 993-1359
E-mail: *psycgrad@gmu.edu*
Web: *http://www.gmu.edu/departments/psychology*

Department Established:

1966. Chairperson: Robert F. Smith. Number of Faculty: total—full-time 48, part-time 24; women—full-time 14, part-time 14; minority—full-time 1.

Programs and Degrees Offered:
Listed in the following order: Program area, degree type (T if terminal Master's), number awarded 7/00–6/01. Applied Developmental PhD, Applied Developmental MA (T) 6, Biopsychology PhD, Biopsychology MA (T) 1, Clinical PhD 3, Human Factors/Applied Cognitio PhD, Human Factors/Applied Cognitio MA (T) 2, Industrial/Organizational PhD 9, Industrial/Organizational MA (T) 20, School/Certificate MA (T) 3.

APA Accreditation: Clinical PhD: full.

Student Applications/Admissions:
Student Applications
Applied Developmental PhD—Applications 2001–2002, 17. Total applicants accepted 2001–2002, 7. New applicants enrolled 2001–2002, 4. Total enrolled 2001–2002 full-time, 24, part-time, 4. Openings 2002–2003, 4. The Median number of years required for completion of a degree are n/a. The number of students enrolled full and part-time, who were dismissed or voluntarily withdrew from this program area were 1. *Applied Developmental MA*—Applications 2001–2002, 30. Total applicants accepted 2001–2002, 14. New applicants enrolled 2001–2002, 4. Total enrolled 2001–2002 full-time, 5, part-time, 4. Openings 2002–2003, 10. The Median number of years required for completion of a degree are 3. The number of students enrolled full and part-time, who were dismissed or voluntarily withdrew from this program area were 0. *Biopsychology PhD*—Applications 2001–2002, 5. Total applicants accepted 2001–2002, 5. New applicants enrolled 2001–2002, 2. Total enrolled 2001–2002 full-time, 4. Openings 2002–2003, 2. The Median number of years required for completion of a degree are n/a. The number of students enrolled full and part-time, who were dismissed or voluntarily withdrew from this program area were 0. *Biopsychology MA*—Applications 2001–2002, 18. Total applicants accepted 2001–2002, 13. New applicants enrolled 2001–2002, 3. Total enrolled 2001–2002 full-time, 5, part-time, 5. Openings 2002–2003, 10. The Median number of years required for completion of a degree are 2. The number of students enrolled full and part-time, who were dismissed or voluntarily withdrew from this program area were 0. *Clinical PhD*—Applications 2001–2002, 137. Total applicants accepted 2001–2002, 21. New applicants enrolled 2001–2002, 9. Total enrolled 2001–2002 full-time, 62. Openings 2002–2003, 10. The Median number of years required for completion of a degree are 8. The number of students enrolled full and part-time, who were dismissed or voluntarily withdrew from this program area were 1. *Human Factors/Applied Cognitio PhD*—Applications 2001–2002, 8. Total applicants accepted 2001–2002, 4. New applicants enrolled 2001–2002, 1. Total enrolled 2001–2002 full-time, 6, part-time, 2. Openings 2002–2003, 4. The Median number of years required for completion of a degree are n/a. The number of students enrolled full and part-time, who were dismissed or voluntarily withdrew from this program area were 1. *Human Factors/Applied Cognitio MA*—Applications 2001–2002, 27. Total applicants accepted 2001–2002, 20. New applicants enrolled 2001–2002, 10. Total enrolled 2001–2002 full-time, 5, part-time, 11. Openings 2002–2003, 15. The Median number of years required for completion of a degree are 2. The number of students enrolled full and part-time, who were dismissed or voluntarily withdrew from this program area were 0. *Industrial/Organizational PhD*—Applications 2001–2002, 57. Total applicants accepted 2001–

2002, 13. New applicants enrolled 2001–2002, 6. Total enrolled 2001–2002 full-time, 30, part-time, 33. Openings 2002–2003, 5. The Median number of years required for completion of a degree are 6. The number of students enrolled full and part-time, who were dismissed or voluntarily withdrew from this program area were 0. *Industrial/Organizational MA*—Applications 2001–2002, 86. Total applicants accepted 2001–2002, 29. New applicants enrolled 2001–2002, 15. Total enrolled 2001–2002 full-time, 12, part-time, 14. Openings 2002–2003, 15. The Median number of years required for completion of a degree are 2. The number of students enrolled full and part-time, who were dismissed or voluntarily withdrew from this program area were 0. *School/Certificate MA*—Applications 2001–2002, 49. Total applicants accepted 2001–2002, 16. New applicants enrolled 2001–2002, 7. Total enrolled 2001–2002 full-time, 25. Openings 2002–2003, 15. The Median number of years required for completion of a degree are 3. The number of students enrolled full and part-time, who were dismissed or voluntarily withdrew from this program area were 0.

Admissions Requirements:
Scores: Entries appear in this order: required test or GPA, minimum score (if required), median score of students entering in 2001–2002. Master's Programs: GRE-V no minimum stated; GRE-Q no minimum stated; GRE-V+Q 1000, 1126; overall undergraduate GPA no minimum stated, 3.4; last 2 years GPA 3.0, 3.3; psychology GPA 3.25. Doctoral Programs: GRE-V no minimum stated; GRE-Q no minimum stated; GRE-V+Q no minimum stated, 1252; overall undergraduate GPA no minimum stated; last 2 years GPA 3.0, 3.68; psychology GPA 3.25; psychology GPA no minimum stated, n/a. Clinical program has minimum V+G GRE of 1100. Other programs prefer at least 1100 combined but will consider other applicants.
Other Criteria: (importance of criteria rated low, medium, or high): GRE/MAT scores high, research experience high, work experience high, extracurricular activity low, clinically related public service low, GPA high, letters of recommendation high, interview high, statement of goals and objectives high. Industrial/Organizational and Human Factors/Applied Cognition does not require an interview.

Student Characteristics: The following represents characteristics of students in 2001–2002 in all graduate psychology programs in the department: Female–full-time 128, part-time 28; Male–full-time 44, part-time 21; African American/Black–full-time 3, part-time 3; Hispanic/Latino (a)–full-time 7, part-time 0; Asian/Pacific Islander–full-time 11, part-time 0; American Indian/Alaska Native–full-time 0, part-time 0; Multi-ethnic–full-time 0, part-time 0; students subject to the Americans with Disabilities Act–full-time 0, part-time 0.

Financial Information/Assistance:
Tuition for Full-Time Study: *Master's:* State residents per academic year $4,584, $191 per credit hour; nonstate residents: per academic year $12,696, $529 per credit hour. *Doctoral:* State residents: per academic year $4,584, $191 per credit hour; nonstate residents: per academic year $12,696, $529 per credit hour.

Financial Assistance:
First Year Students: Teaching assistantships available for first-year. Average amount paid per academic year: $3,998. Average number of hours worked per week: 13. Apply by 1/1. Tuition

remission given: partial. Research assistantships available for first-year. Average amount paid per academic year: $4,738. Average number of hours worked per week: 11. Apply by 1/1. Tuition remission given: partial. Traineeships available for first-year. Average amount paid per academic year: $4,497. Average number of hours worked per week: 10. Apply by 1/1. Tuition remission given: partial. Fellowships and scholarships available for first-year. Average amount paid per academic year: $3,500. Average number of hours worked per week: 0. Apply by 1/1. Tuition remission given: partial.

Advanced Students: Teaching assistantships available for advanced students. Average amount paid per academic year: $5,905. Average number of hours worked per week: 10. Apply by 2/15. Tuition remission given: partial. Research assistantships available for advanced students. Average amount paid per academic year: $4,484. Average number of hours worked per week: 11. Apply by 2/15. Tuition remission given: partial. Traineeships available for advanced students. Average amount paid per academic year: $4,565. Average number of hours worked per week: 10. Apply by 2/15. Tuition remission given: partial. Fellowships and scholarships available for advanced students. Average amount paid per academic year: $0. Average number of hours worked per week: 0. Apply by 0.

Contact Information: Of all students currently enrolled full-time, 100% benefited from one or more of the listed financial assistance programs. For information on financial assistance, contact: See www.gmu.edu/departments/psychology and/or contact the Financial Aid Office at 703-993-2353.

Internships/Practica: All programs either require or offer practicum placements in a wide variety of settings, including mental health treatment facilities, medical facilities, schools, government agencies, the military, and businesses and organizations. (Please see our Web site for more information.). For those doctoral students for whom a professional internship is required prior to graduation, 13 applied in 2000–2001. Of those who applied, 12 were placed in internships listed by the Association of Psychology Postdoctoral and Internship Programs (APPIC); 12 were placed in APA accredited internships.

Housing and Day Care: On-campus housing and day care facilities are available.

Employment of Department Graduates:

Master's Degree Graduates: Of those who graduated in the academic year 2000–2001, the following categories and numbers represent the post-graduate activities and employment of master's degree graduates: Enrolled in a post-doctoral residency/fellowship (n/a), employed in independent practice (n/a).

Doctoral Degree Graduates: Of those who graduated in the academic year 2000–2001, the following categories and numbers represent the post-graduate activities and employment of doctoral degree graduates: Enrolled in a psychology doctoral program (n/a), enrolled in another graduate/professional program (n/a).

Additional Information:

Orientation, Objectives, and Emphasis of Department: All graduate programs emphasize both basic research and the application of research to solving problems in families, schools, industry, government, and health care settings.

Special Facilities or Resources: The Applied Research in Cognition and Human Factors Laboratory operates as the research arm of the HF/AC Program and encourages collaborative research amount faculty and students. The Center for Cognitive and Behavioral Studies (CBCS) facilitates basic and applied research, teaching, and service activities related to the determinants of human behavior, functioning, or performance in family, work, and nonwork settings. The Psychological Clinic is the main training facility for students in the Clinical and School Psychology programs. The Krasnow Institute for Advanced Study is an independently funded institute that supports empirical and theoretical work in the neurosciences to advance the understanding of neural function and human cognition. Inova Fairfax Hospital is the site for a new joint program in Clinical Neuropsychology. The Center for Cognitive Development (CCD) provides support to school personnel, children, and families in the areas of assessment and remediation of learning problems such as attention deficit disorders (ADHD), learning disabilities (LD), and behavior disorders.

Information for Students With Physical Disabilities: The George Mason University campus is a relatively new and modern facility that is fully accessible to persons with physical disabilities.

Application Information:
Send to: Graduate Admissions, George Mason University, 4400 University Drive, Fairfax, VA 22030-4444. Students are admitted in the Fall, application deadline 1/1, 2/1, 4/15. 1/1 for all PhD programs, 2/1 for Applied Developmental MA, Biopsychology MA, and School MA, 4/15 for Industrial/Organizational MA and Human Factors/ Applied Cognition. *Fee:* $50.

James Madison University
School of Psychology
MSC 7401
Harrisonburg, VA 22807
Telephone: (540) 568-6439
Fax: (540) 568-3322
E-mail: rippysr@jmu.edu
Web: http://cep.jmu.edu/psychology

Department Established:
1967. Director: Jane S. Halonen, PhD. Number of Faculty: total–full-time 38, part-time 14; women–full-time 16, part-time 7; minority–full-time 4.

Programs and Degrees Offered:
Listed in the following order: Program area, degree type (T if terminal Master's), number awarded 7/00–6/01. Assessment and Measurement PsyD, College Student Personnel Admi MA (T) 14, Combined-Clin., Coun., School PsyD 8, Community Counseling EdS 6, Psychological Sciences MA (T) 7, School Counseling EdS (T) 7, School Psychology EdS 10.

APA Accreditation: Clinical PsyD: full.

Student Applications/Admissions:
Student Applications
Assessment and Measurement PsyD—Applications 2001–2002, 4. Total applicants accepted 2001–2002, 4. New applicants enrolled 2001–2002, 4. Total enrolled 2001–2002 full-time,

9. Openings 2002–2003, 5. *College Student Personnel Admi MA*—Applications 2001–2002, 42. Total applicants accepted 2001–2002, 14. New applicants enrolled 2001–2002, 11. Total enrolled 2001–2002 full-time, 24, part-time, 5. Openings 2002–2003, 14. *Combined-Clin., Coun., School PsyD*—Applications 2001–2002, *. Total applicants accepted 2001–2002, 6. New applicants enrolled 2001–2002, 6. Total enrolled 2001–2002 full-time, 25. Openings 2002–2003, 6. The Median number of years required for completion of a degree are 5. The number of students enrolled full and part-time, who were dismissed or voluntarily withdrew from this program area were 1. *Community Counseling EdS*—Applications 2001–2002, 55. Total applicants accepted 2001–2002, 12. New applicants enrolled 2001–2002, 10. Total enrolled 2001–2002 full-time, 27, part-time, 9. Openings 2002–2003, 10. *Psychological Sciences MA*—Applications 2001–2002, 29. Total applicants accepted 2001–2002, 11. New applicants enrolled 2001–2002, 5. Total enrolled 2001–2002 full-time, 17, part-time, 4. Openings 2002–2003, 10. *School Counseling EdS*—Applications 2001–2002, 21. Total applicants accepted 2001–2002, 13. New applicants enrolled 2001–2002, 6. Total enrolled 2001–2002 full-time, 16, part-time, 2. Openings 2002–2003, 10. *School Psychology EdS*—Applications 2001–2002, 65. Total applicants accepted 2001–2002, 13. New applicants enrolled 2001–2002, 7. Total enrolled 2001–2002 full-time, 26. Openings 2002–2003, 10.

Admissions Requirements:

Scores: Entries appear in this order: required test or GPA, minimum score (if required), median score of students entering in 2001–2002. Master's Programs: GRE-V+Q+Analytical no minimum stated; overall undergraduate GPA no minimum stated; last 2 years GPA no minimum stated; psychology GPA no minimum stated. Psychological Sciences—GRE-V 544; GRE-Q 614; GRE-A 624; GRE-S 650; Overall GPA 3.47; Jr/Sr GPA 3.70; Psych GPA 3.84. Community Counseling—GRE-V 525; GRE-Q 473; GRE-A 546; Overall GPA 328; Jr/Sr GPA 3.53; Psych GPA 3.58. School Counseling—GRE-V 525; GRE-Q 587; GRE-A 620; Overall GPA 3.08; Jr/Sr GPA 3.22; Psych GPA 3.23. School Psychology—GRE-V 471; GRE-Q 570; GRE-A 607; Overall GPA 3.24; Jr/Sr GPA 3.59; Psych GPA 3.44. College Student Personnel Administration—GRE-V 459; GRE-Q 520; GRE-A 567; Overall GPA 3.17. GRE Subject exam recommended for Psychological Sciences Program only. Doctoral Programs: last 2 years GPA no minimum stated; psychology GPA no minimum stated; psychology GPA no minimum stated. Assessment and Measurement (PsyD)—GRE-V 540; GRE-Q 570; GRE+Analytical 630. Although the Combined Doctoral Program in Clinical, Counseling, and School Psychology does require GRE V, Q, A, and Subject scores, applicants are reviewed on the basis of a wide range of admission criteria (please see http://cep.jmu.edu/clinicalpsyd for additional information).

Other Criteria: (importance of criteria rated low, medium, or high): Psychological Sciences—GRE/MAT Scores high, Research experience medium, work experience low, Clinically related public service medium, letters of recommendation high. CSPA—Research experience medium, work experience high, Clinically related public service medium, GPA high, letters of recommendation high. School Psychology—GRE/ MAT Scores low, Research experience medium, work experience medium, extracurricular activity medium, Clinically related

public service high, GPA high, letters of recommendation high. Community Counseling—GRE/MAT Scores low, Research experience high, work experience low, extracurricular activity high, Clinically related public service medium, GPA high, letters of recommendation medium. School Counseling—GRE/MAT Scores low, Research experience high, work experience low, extracurricular activity high, Clinically related public service medium, GPA high, letters of recommendation medium. PsyD Assessment and Management— GRE/MAT Scores medium, Research experience medium, work experience low, Clinically related public service high, GPA high, letters of recommendation high. PsyD Clinical, Counseling, School—GRE/MAT Scores medium, Research experience high, work experience high, extracurricular activity high, Clinically related public service high, GPA high, letters of recommendation high.

Student Characteristics: The following represents characteristics of students in 2001–2002 in all graduate psychology programs in the department: Female–full-time 120, Male–full-time 44, African American/Black–full-time 11, part-time 0; Hispanic/Latino (a)–full-time 2, part-time 0; Asian/Pacific Islander–full-time 1, part-time 0; American Indian/Alaska Native–full-time 0, part-time 0; Multi-ethnic–full-time 4.

Financial Information/Assistance:

Tuition for Full-Time Study: *Master's:* State residents $138 per credit hour; nonstate residents: $426 per credit hour.

Financial Assistance:

First Year Students: Teaching assistantships available for first-year. Tuition remission given: full. Research assistantships available for first-year. Tuition remission given: full. Traineeships available for first-year. Tuition remission given: partial. Fellowships and scholarships available for first-year. Tuition remission given: partial.

Advanced Students: Teaching assistantships available for advanced students. Tuition remission given: full. Research assistantships available for advanced students. Tuition remission given: full. Traineeships available for advanced students. Tuition remission given: partial. Fellowships and scholarships available for advanced students. Tuition remission given: partial.

Contact Information: Of all students currently enrolled full-time, 90% benefited from one or more of the listed financial assistance programs. For information on financial assistance, contact: Office of Financial Aid and Scholarships, (540) 568-7820. Email: fin_aid@jmu.edu. The Combined Doctoral Program in Clinical, Counseling, and School Psychology offers full tuition remission for all program students and an annual fellowship of $12,000.

Internships/Practica: The department maintains a large network of internship sites for specialists for EdS and PsyD students. These sites are housed in public school settings, community mental health agencies, hospitals, and other human service facilities. In addition, the department maintains two doctoral level internships in Human Development Center (an on-campus comprehensive mental health clinic for children and families). The department provides practicum training through the University's Human Development Center and the Counseling and Student Development Center.

Housing and Day Care: No on-campus housing and day care facilities are available.

Employment of Department Graduates:

Master's Degree Graduates: Of those who graduated in the academic year 2000–2001, the following categories and numbers represent the post-graduate activities and employment of master's degree graduates: Enrolled in a post-doctoral residency/fellowship (n/a), employed in independent practice (n/a).

Doctoral Degree Graduates: Of those who graduated in the academic year 2000–2001, the following categories and numbers represent the post-graduate activities and employment of doctoral degree graduates: Enrolled in a psychology doctoral program (n/a), enrolled in another graduate/professional program (n/a).

Additional Information:

Orientation, Objectives, and Emphasis of Department: All specialist and doctoral programs provide the necessary academic requirements in training for certification by the State Department of Education and licensure by the State Board of Psychology in Virginia. The counseling program meets the requirements for licensure as a professional counselor (LPC) in the Commonwealth of Virginia. The General MA program prepares students for further study at the doctoral level or for employment. The program (MA) is research based; in addition to coursework a research apprenticeship, comprehensive examination, and thesis is required. The Combined Doctoral Program in Clinical, Counseling, and School Psychology prepares students for licensure as clinical psychologists. Our program is fully accredited by the American Psychological Association, and is designed for students possessing advanced graduate degrees and professional experience in applied mental health fields. Depending upon their background, students are able to complete the coursework portion of the program in either two or three years. We have an excellent track record of placing students in APA-accredited internships; our graduates assume professional positions in a range of context including, but not limited to, mental health clinics, child and family agencies, public schools, administrative and leadership positions, training and supervisory roles, and private practice. Please see http://cep.j-mu.edu/clinicalpsyd for additional information about our innovative program.

Special Facilities or Resources: Students have access to a state-of-the-art university computer network, microcomputers, animal laboratory, test library, and videotape equipment.

Application Information:

Send to: School of Psychology, Graduate Admissions, MSC 7401, James Madison University, Harrisonburg, VA 22807. Students are admitted in the Fall, application deadline 2/15, 3/1. For Fall, Psychological Sciences, PsyD in Assessment and Measurement, and College Student Personnel Administration deadlines are March 1; Community Counseling, School Counseling, and School Psychology are February 15; Combined Doctoral Program in Clinical, Counseling, and School Psychology deadline is Feb. 1. *Fee:* $55.

Marymount University
Department of Psychology
2807 North Glebe Road
Arlington, VA 22207
Telephone: (703) 284-1620
Fax: (703) 284-1631
E-mail: *carolyn.oxenford@marymount.edu*
Web: *http://www.marymount.edu/academic/sehs/ps/index.html*

Department Established:

1987. Chairperson: Carolyn B. Oxenford. Number of Faculty: total–full-time 12, part-time 31; women–full-time 9, part-time 21; minority–full-time 2; faculty subject to the Americans with Disabilities Act 1.

Programs and Degrees Offered:

Listed in the following order: Program area, degree type (T if terminal Master's), number awarded 7/00–6/01. Counseling MA (T) 25, Forensic Psychology MA (T), School Counseling MA (T) 16.

Student Applications/Admissions:

Student Applications

Counseling MA—Applications 2001–2002, 64. Total applicants accepted 2001–2002, 36. New applicants enrolled 2001–2002, 21. Total enrolled 2001–2002 full-time, 26, part-time, 49. The Median number of years required for completion of a degree are 3. The number of students enrolled full and part-time, who were dismissed or voluntarily withdrew from this program area were 1. *Forensic Psychology MA*—Applications 2001–2002, 56. Total applicants accepted 2001–2002, 41. New applicants enrolled 2001–2002, 32. Total enrolled 2001–2002 full-time, 39, part-time, 27. The Median number of years required for completion of a degree are n/a. The number of students enrolled full and part-time, who were dismissed or voluntarily withdrew from this program area were 3. *School Counseling MA*—Applications 2001–2002, 27. Total applicants accepted 2001–2002, 9. New applicants enrolled 2001–2002, 6. Total enrolled 2001–2002 full-time, 15, part-time, 17. The Median number of years required for completion of a degree are 3. The number of students enrolled full and part-time, who were dismissed or voluntarily withdrew from this program area were 0.

Admissions Requirements:

Scores: Entries appear in this order: required test or GPA, minimum score (if required), median score of students entering in 2001–2002. Master's Programs: overall undergraduate GPA no minimum stated. GRE-Writing Assessment is required of all students. Doctoral Programs: last 2 years GPA no minimum stated; psychology GPA no minimum stated; psychology GPA no minimum stated.

Other Criteria: (importance of criteria rated low, medium, or high): research experience low, work experience medium, extracurricular activity medium, clinically related public service medium, GPA high, letters of recommendation medium, interview high, statement of goals and objectives medium, GRE-Writing high.

Student Characteristics: The following represents characteristics of students in 2001–2002 in all graduate psychology programs in the department: Female–full-time 71, part-time 80; Male–full-time 9, part-time 13; African American/Black–full-time 10, part-time 10; Hispanic/Latino (a)–full-time 3, part-time 4; Asian/Pacific Islander–full-time 0, part-time 1; American Indian/Alaska Native–full-time 0, part-time 1; Multi-ethnic–full-time 1.

Financial Information/Assistance:

Tuition for Full-Time Study: *Master's:* State residents $523 per credit hour; nonstate residents: $523 per credit hour.

Financial Assistance:

First Year Students: Research assistantships available for first-year. Average amount paid per academic year: $2,500. Average number of hours worked per week: 20. Apply by Rolling. Tuition remission given: full. Fellowships and scholarships available for first-year. Average amount paid per academic year: $3,000. Apply by July 1.

Advanced Students: No information provided.

Contact Information: Of all students currently enrolled full-time, 40% benefited from one or more of the listed financial assistance programs. For information on financial assistance, contact: Office of Financial Aid, (703) 284-1530.

Internships/Practica: MA in Counseling: Students complete a one-semester pre-internship practicum in a community agency. The capstone of Marymount University's clinical training is the internship. The graduate internship is an eight-month, 600-hour experience in providing direct services under supervision. It provides students with an opportunity to apply the principles and tenets learned in class in a supervised work setting. Internships are available at a variety of counseling settings where students are provided with a clinical case-load and expected to practice the full range of skills required of entry-level community agency counselors. The internship experience is supervised by a university faculty member and a clinical supervisor within the participating agency. The goal of the internship is to provide a transitional professional experience that assists the intern in making the transition from student to professional by engaging in practical, day-to-day work as a counselor under supervision. MA School Counseling: Students complete a pre-internship practicum in a school system to prepare them for the internship experience. The School Counseling Internship at Marymount University is a 600-hour culminating field experience in which prospective school counselors demonstrate their knowledge of subject matter, counseling skills, and child/adolescent growth and development. This important experience occurs in an existing instructional setting of a local public or accredited private school and is supervised by qualified university faculty members and cooperating counselors/on-site supervisors. The school counseling internship experience is guided by principles and strategies prescribed by current research and theory in school counselor preparation. Forensic psychology students may choose an internship in a wide variety of settings, including local and state correctional facilities, local community mental health treatment center, victim witness programs, domestic violence programs and shelters, national and local mental health advocacy organizations, child welfare agencies, child welfare advocacy organizations, adult services agencies (serving incapacitated and incompetent adult), juvenile court services, state and local law enforcement, federal law enforcement and justice agencies, and any and all areas in which psychological expertise

and psychological services (including counseling) would be applied in a legal setting (civil proceeding, criminal justice, and juvenile justice).

Housing and Day Care: No on-campus housing and day care facilities are available.

Employment of Department Graduates:

Master's Degree Graduates: Of those who graduated in the academic year 2000–2001, the following categories and numbers represent the post-graduate activities and employment of master's degree graduates: Enrolled in a post-doctoral residency/fellowship (n/a), employed in independent practice (n/a).

Doctoral Degree Graduates: Of those who graduated in the academic year 2000–2001, the following categories and numbers represent the post-graduate activities and employment of doctoral degree graduates: Enrolled in a psychology doctoral program (n/a), enrolled in another graduate/professional program (n/a).

Additional Information:

Orientation, Objectives, and Emphasis of Department: The department offers the MA in Counseling, School Counseling, and Forensic Psychology. The Counseling and School Counseling programs provide the knowledge and skills in counseling theory, principles, and practice that will allow the graduate to work in applied settings where master's level training is utilized. The programs are designed to accommodate the needs of individuals already working in the field who are seeking advancement or enhanced skills, recent undergraduates wishing to further their marketability, and individuals from other fields who wish to change careers. The general goals of the program are to provide a solid background in counseling psychology theory and research methodology, integrated with practical and supervised learning experiences; a background in professional ethics and standards; knowledge of issues related to the application of counseling services to ethnically and racially diverse populations; and specific skills in specialty areas. The focus of these programs is firmly applied and culminates in an internship placement. Both programs are CACREP accredited. The Master of Arts in Forensic Psychology provides graduates with the skills and knowledge they need to provide effective, high quality services in a variety of forensic settings. These include probation and parole, victim assistance, policing, law enforcement, evaluation, and testimony in civil and criminal matters. To accomplish this goal, the program balances traditional psychological knowledge and skills with a specialized understanding of the criminal justice and legal system.

Special Facilities or Resources: The location of Marymount in suburban Washington provides our students with a large number of opportunities for internships and employment in the area. Additionally, the university is a member of the Washington Consortium of College and Universities, which gives the students access to the library facilities and classes of most of the major universities in the area. Marymount's geographic location also enables us to employ high quality adjunct faculty, many of whom are experts in their fields.

Application Information:

Send to: Ms. Cheryl Nichols, Office of Admissions, Marymount University, 2807 N. Glebe Rd., Arlington, VA 22207. Students are admitted in the Fall, application deadline rolling; Spring, application deadline rolling; Summer, application deadline rolling. Group admissions interview required for counseling and school counseling. Rolling admissions. Admissions interviews usually are scheduled on the first Saturday in April, June, and November. In order to participate in group interviews, applicant's paperwork must be complete at least one week prior to the interview. *Fee:* $35.

Old Dominion University

Department of Psychology
Mills Godwin Building—Room 250
Norfolk, VA 23529-0267
Telephone: (757) 683-4439 or (757) 683-4440
Fax: (757) 683-5087
E-mail: *bwinstea@odu.edu*
Web: *http://www.psychology.odu.edu/psych.htm*

Department Established:
1954. Chairperson: Barbara A. Winstead. Number of Faculty: total–full-time 25, part-time 6; women–full-time 11, part-time 4; minority–full-time 2.

Programs and Degrees Offered:
Listed in the following order: Program area, degree type (T if terminal Master's), number awarded 7/00–6/01. Clinical PsyD 12, general MA (T) 12, industrial/organizational PhD 3.

APA Accreditation: Clinical PsyD: full.

Student Applications/Admissions:
Student Applications
Clinical PsyD—Applications 2001–2002, 128. Total applicants accepted 2001–2002, 20. New applicants enrolled 2001–2002, 10. Total enrolled 2001–2002 full-time, 47. Openings 2002–2003, 10. The Median number of years required for completion of a degree are 5. The number of students enrolled full and part-time, who were dismissed or voluntarily withdrew from this program area were 0. *General MA*—Applications 2001–2002, 39. Total applicants accepted 2001–2002, 21. New applicants enrolled 2001–2002, 11. Total enrolled 2001–2002 full-time, 10. Openings 2002–2003, 15. *Industrial/organizational PhD*—Applications 2001–2002, 40. Total applicants accepted 2001–2002, 8. New applicants enrolled 2001–2002, 5. Total enrolled 2001–2002 full-time, 18. Openings 2002–2003, 4. The number of students enrolled full and part-time, who were dismissed or voluntarily withdrew from this program area were 1.

Admissions Requirements:
Scores: Entries appear in this order: required test or GPA, minimum score (if required), median score of students entering in 2001–2002. Master's Programs: GRE-V no minimum stated, 539; GRE-Q no minimum stated, 584; GRE-Analytical no minimum stated, 636; overall undergraduate GPA no minimum stated, 3.45. Doctoral Programs: GRE-V no minimum stated, 561; GRE-Q no minimum stated, 639; GRE-V+Q no minimum stated, 1216; GRE-Analytical no minimum stated, 645; GRE-Subject(Psych) no minimum stated, 620; overall undergraduate GPA no minimum stated, 3.35; last 2 years GPA no minimum stated; psychology GPA no minimum stated; psychology GPA no minimum stated.

Other Criteria: (importance of criteria rated low, medium, or high): GRE/MAT scores high, research experience medium, work experience low, extracurricular activity low, GPA high, letters of recommendation high, statement of goals and objectives high.

Student Characteristics: The following represents characteristics of students in 2001–2002 in all graduate psychology programs in the department: Female–full-time 25, part-time 12; Male–full-time 7, part-time 5; African American/Black–full-time 1, part-time 2; Hispanic/Latino (a)–full-time 0, part-time 0; Asian/Pacific Islander–full-time 3, part-time 1; American Indian/Alaska Native–full-time 0, part-time 0; students subject to the Americans with Disabilities Act–full-time 1.

Financial Information/Assistance:
Tuition for Full-Time Study: No information provided.

Financial Assistance:
First Year Students: No information provided.
Advanced Students: No information provided.
Contact Information: For information on financial assistance, contact: Financial Aid Office.

Internships/Practica: Internships are required for the PhD program and are available at local businesses, hospitals, and military and government agencies, as well as out-of-state.

Housing and Day Care: No on-campus housing and day care facilities are available.

Employment of Department Graduates:
Master's Degree Graduates: Of those who graduated in the academic year 2000–2001, the following categories and numbers represent the post-graduate activities and employment of master's degree graduates: Enrolled in a psychology doctoral program (4), enrolled in another graduate/professional program (1), enrolled in a post-doctoral residency/fellowship (n/a), employed in independent practice (n/a), employed in an academic position at a university (2), employed in other positions at a higher education institution (1), still seeking employment (1).
Doctoral Degree Graduates: Of those who graduated in the academic year 2000–2001, the following categories and numbers represent the post-graduate activities and employment of doctoral degree graduates: Enrolled in a psychology doctoral program (n/a), enrolled in another graduate/professional program (n/a).

Additional Information:
Orientation, Objectives, and Emphasis of Department: The department offers a program of graduate study leading to the degree of doctor of philosophy with a concentration in industrial/organizational psychology. The concentration includes emphases in three areas: engineering and systems psychology, personnel and training psychology, and organizational and managerial psychology. The program is designed to provide broad, general training in all fields of psychology, in-depth training in all areas of industrial/organizational psychology, and specialized training in one of the three areas of major concentration. A program of graduate study leading to the degree of Master of Science with a concentration in general psychology is also offered by the department.

Special Facilities or Resources: Computer facilities are available.

Application Information:

Send to: Old Dominion University, Office of Graduate Admissions, 105 Rollins Hall, Norfolk, VA 23529-0050. Students are admitted in the Spring. February 1 for PhD, May 15 for MS. *Fee:* $30. The fee is waived or deferred if the applicant is an ODU graduate.

Radford University

Department of Psychology
Radford, VA 24142-6946
Telephone: (540) 831-5361
Fax: (540) 831-6113
E-mail: *fclemens@radford.edu*
Web: *http://www.runet.edu/psyc-web*

Department Established:

1937. Chairperson: Alastair V. Harris. Number of Faculty: total–full-time 22; women–full-time 7.

Programs and Degrees Offered:

Listed in the following order: Program area, degree type (T if terminal Master's), number awarded 7/00–6/01. Clinical MA (T) 7, counseling MA (T) 15, experimental MA (T) 3, industrial/organizational MA (T) 15, school EdS 8.

Student Applications/Admissions:

Student Applications

Clinical MA—Applications 2001–2002, 35. Total applicants accepted 2001–2002, 25. New applicants enrolled 2001–2002, 6. Total enrolled 2001–2002 full-time, 12, part-time, 1. Openings 2002–2003, 10. The Median number of years required for completion of a degree are 2. The number of students enrolled full and part-time, who were dismissed or voluntarily withdrew from this program area were 0. *Counseling MA*—Applications 2001–2002, 35. Total applicants accepted 2001–2002, 20. New applicants enrolled 2001–2002, 10. Total enrolled 2001–2002 full-time, 24, part-time, 2. Openings 2002–2003, 15. The Median number of years required for completion of a degree are 2. The number of students enrolled full and part-time, who were dismissed or voluntarily withdrew from this program area were 1. *Experimental MA*—Applications 2001–2002, 5. Total applicants accepted 2001–2002, 5. New applicants enrolled 2001–2002, 2. Total enrolled 2001–2002 full-time, 7, part-time, 4. Openings 2002–2003, 10. *Industrial/organizational MA*—Applications 2001–2002, 65. Total applicants accepted 2001–2002, 26. New applicants enrolled 2001–2002, 14. Total enrolled 2001–2002 full-time, 27. Openings 2002–2003, 15. The Median number of years required for completion of a degree are 2. The number of students enrolled full and part-time, who were dismissed or voluntarily withdrew from this program area were 0. *School EdS*—Applications 2001–2002, 25. Total applicants accepted 2001–2002, 15. New applicants enrolled 2001–2002, 6. Total enrolled 2001–2002 full-time, 22, part-time, 2. Openings 2002–2003, 10. The Median number of years required for completion of a degree are 3. The number of students enrolled full and part-time, who were dismissed or voluntarily withdrew from this program area were 0.

Admissions Requirements:

Scores: Entries appear in this order: required test or GPA, minimum score (if required), median score of students entering in 2001–2002. Master's Programs: GRE-V 430, 491; GRE-Q 430, 556; GRE-V+Q 1000, 1047; GRE-Subject(Psych) 500, 569; overall undergraduate GPA 2.7, 3.53; last 2 years GPA 3.00, 3.70; psychology GPA 3.0, 3.73. The numbers above are for the I/O psychology program only. For some programs only an acceptable score is required on subject test. Doctoral Programs: last 2 years GPA no minimum stated; psychology GPA no minimum stated; psychology GPA no minimum stated.

Other Criteria: (importance of criteria rated low, medium, or high): GRE/MAT scores medium, research experience high, work experience high, extracurricular activity medium, clinically related public service high, GPA high, letters of recommendation high, statement of goals and objectives medium. Interview recommended but not required.

Student Characteristics: The following represents characteristics of students in 2001–2002 in all graduate psychology programs in the department: Female–full-time 36, part-time 12; Male–full-time 24, part-time 5; African American/Black–full-time 12, part-time 10; Hispanic/Latino (a)–full-time 0, part-time 0; Asian/Pacific Islander–full-time 0, part-time 0; American Indian/Alaska Native–full-time 0, part-time 0.

Financial Information/Assistance:

Tuition for Full-Time Study: *Master's:* State residents per academic year $4,008, $167 per credit hour; nonstate residents: per academic year $7,754, $323 per credit hour.

Financial Assistance:

First Year Students: Teaching assistantships available for first-year. Average amount paid per academic year: $8,060. Average number of hours worked per week: 20. Tuition remission given: partial. Research assistantships available for first-year. Average amount paid per academic year: $3,720. Average number of hours worked per week: 10.

Advanced Students: Teaching assistantships available for advanced students. Average amount paid per academic year: $8,680. Average number of hours worked per week: 20. Tuition remission given: partial. Research assistantships available for advanced students. Average amount paid per academic year: $3,720. Average number of hours worked per week: 10.

Contact Information: Of all students currently enrolled full-time, 90% benefited from one or more of the listed financial assistance programs. For information on financial assistance, contact: Gen Kirouac, Coordinator for Graduate Financial Aid, College of Graduate and Extended Education.

Internships/Practica: Internships in a variety of settings are readily available for all programs.

Housing and Day Care: No on-campus housing and day care facilities are available.

Employment of Department Graduates:

Master's Degree Graduates: Of those who graduated in the academic year 2000–2001, the following categories and numbers represent the post-graduate activities and employment of master's degree graduates: Enrolled in a post-doctoral residency/fellowship (n/a), employed in independent practice (n/a).

Doctoral Degree Graduates: Of those who graduated in the academic year 2000–2001, the following categories and numbers represent the post-graduate activities and employment of doctoral degree graduates: Enrolled in a psychology doctoral program (n/a), enrolled in another graduate/professional program (n/a).

Additional Information:

Orientation, Objectives, and Emphasis of Department: The department aims to train psychologists who are well versed in both the theoretical and applied aspects of the discipline. The emphasis of the department is eclectic; school, clinical, general, industrial/organizational, and counseling options are available. The school program is an EdS program that also provides preparation for certification and licensing as a school psychologist in Virginia.

Special Facilities or Resources: Our renovated facility contains computer laboratories and research space for use by graduate students. The department has established a center for gender studies and center for brain research and informational sciences.

Information for Students With Physical Disabilities: All classrooms and labs accessible to wheelchairs.

Application Information:
Send to: College of Graduate and Extended Education, P.O. Box 6928, Radford University, Radford, VA 24142. Students are admitted in the Fall, application deadline March 1. *Fee:* $25.

Regent University
Doctoral Program in Clinical Psychology
School of Psychology & Counseling
1000 Regent University Drive
Virginia Beach, VA 23464
Telephone: (757) 226-4366
Fax: (757) 226-4304
E-mail: *willhat@regent.edu*
Web: *http://www.regent.edu*

Department Established:
1996. Chairperson: William L. Hathaway, PhD. Number of Faculty: total–full-time 7, part-time 10; women–full-time 4, part-time 3; minority–full-time 1, part-time 4.

Programs and Degrees Offered:
Listed in the following order: Program area, degree type (T if terminal Master's), number awarded 7/00–6/01. Clinical Psychology PsyD 3.

Student Applications/Admissions:
Student Applications
Clinical Psychology PsyD—Applications 2001–2002, 45. Total applicants accepted 2001–2002, 28. New applicants enrolled 2001–2002, 19. Total enrolled 2001–2002 full-time, 69, part-time, 19. Openings 2002–2003, 25. The Median number of years required for completion of a degree are 4. The number of students enrolled full and part-time, who were dismissed or voluntarily withdrew from this program area were 2.

Admissions Requirements:
Scores: Entries appear in this order: required test or GPA, minimum score (if required), median score of students entering in 2001–2002. Doctoral Programs: GRE-V+Q 1000; overall undergraduate GPA 3.0; last 2 years GPA no minimum stated; psychology GPA no minimum stated; psychology GPA no minimum stated.

Other Criteria: (importance of criteria rated low, medium, or high): GRE/MAT scores medium, research experience medium, work experience low, extracurricular activity medium, clinically related public service low, GPA medium, letters of recommendation medium, interview medium, statement of goals and objectives medium, Writing Sample medium.

Student Characteristics: The following represents characteristics of students in 2001–2002 in all graduate psychology programs in the department: Female–full-time 47, part-time 13; Male–full-time 21, part-time 5; African American/Black–full-time 8, part-time 5; Hispanic/Latino (a)–full-time 4, part-time 0; Asian/Pacific Islander–full-time 3, part-time 1; American Indian/Alaska Native–full-time 1, part-time 0; Multi-ethnic–full-time 1, part-time 0; students subject to the Americans with Disabilities Act–full-time 1, part-time 0.

Financial Information/Assistance:
Tuition for Full-Time Study: *Doctoral:* State residents: $500 per credit hour; nonstate residents: $500 per credit hour.

Financial Assistance:
First Year Students: Fellowships and scholarships available for first-year. Average amount paid per academic year: $2,000. Apply by Aug. 1. Tuition remission given: partial.

Advanced Students: Teaching assistantships available for advanced students. Average amount paid per academic year: $5,000. Average number of hours worked per week: 10. Apply by April 1. Research assistantships available for advanced students. Average amount paid per academic year: $5,000. Average number of hours worked per week: 10. Apply by April 1. Fellowships and scholarships available for advanced students. Average amount paid per academic year: $2,000. Apply by April 1. Tuition remission given: partial.

Contact Information: Of all students currently enrolled full-time, 98% benefited from one or more of the listed financial assistance programs. For information on financial assistance, contact: Office of Admissions, School of Psychology & Counseling-CRB 221, Regent University, 1000 Regent University Drive, Virginia Beach, Virginia 23464, Email: psycoun@regent.edu.

Internships/Practica: For those doctoral students for whom a professional internship is required prior to graduation, 13 applied in 2000–2001. Of those who applied, 11 were placed in internships listed by the Association of Psychology Postdoctoral and Internship Programs (APPIC); 3 were placed in APA accredited internships.

Housing and Day Care: On-campus housing and day care facilities are available.

Employment of Department Graduates:
Master's Degree Graduates: Of those who graduated in the academic year 2000–2001, the following categories and numbers represent the post-graduate activities and employment of master's

degree graduates: Enrolled in a post-doctoral residency/fellowship (n/a), employed in independent practice (n/a).

Doctoral Degree Graduates: Of those who graduated in the academic year 2000–2001, the following categories and numbers represent the post-graduate activities and employment of doctoral degree graduates: Enrolled in a psychology doctoral program (n/a), enrolled in another graduate/professional program (n/a), enrolled in a post-doctoral residency/fellowship (0), employed in independent practice (3), employed in an academic position at a university (2), employed in a hospital/medical center (1).

Additional Information:

Orientation, Objectives, and Emphasis of Department: The Doctoral Program in Clinical Psychology adopts a practitioner-scholar model of clinical training within an educational context committed to the integration of scientific psychology and a Christian worldview. The clinical training is broad and general, however marital and family therapy, health psychology, and clinical child psychology are emphases among the faculty and in the curriculum.

Special Facilities or Resources: Regent is located in Tidewater, the largest urban area in Virginia. There are numerous community resources for practica. The campus also houses the Psychological Services Center, our doctoral training clinic that provides services to the campus and surrounding community. The PSC includes state of the art technology for videotaping and observation of clinical activities.

Application Information:

Send to: Office of Admissions, School of Psychology & Counseling, CRB 221, Regent University, 1000 Regent University Drive, Virginia Beach, Virginia 23464, E-mail: psycoun@regent.edu. Students are admitted in the Fall, application deadline February 15. *Fee:* $50.

Richmond, University of
Department of Psychology
Arts and Sciences
Richmond Hall
Richmond, VA 23173
Telephone: (804) 289-8123
Fax: (804) 287-1905
E-mail: *ckinsley@richmond.edu*
Web: *http://www.richmond.edu/~psych*

Department Established:

1913. Chairperson: Craig H. Kinsley, Associate Prof. of Neuroscience. Number of Faculty: total–full-time 9, part-time 3; women–full-time 3, part-time 2; minority–full-time 1, part-time 1.

Programs and Degrees Offered:

Listed in the following order: Program area, degree type (T if terminal Master's), number awarded 7/00–6/01. General MA (T) 4.

Student Applications/Admissions:

Student Applications

General MA—Applications 2001–2002, 77. Total applicants accepted 2001–2002, 4. New applicants enrolled 2001–2002,

5. Total enrolled 2001–2002 full-time, 8. Openings 2002–2003, 5. The Median number of years required for completion of a degree are 2. The number of students enrolled full and part-time, who were dismissed or voluntarily withdrew from this program area were 0.

Admissions Requirements:

Scores: Entries appear in this order: required test or GPA, minimum score (if required), median score of students entering in 2001–2002. Master's Programs: GRE-V 600, 610; GRE-Q 600, 620; GRE-V+Q 1200, 1230; overall undergraduate GPA 3.3, 3.3; last 2 years GPA 3.0; psychology GPA 3.5, 3.5. Doctoral Programs: last 2 years GPA no minimum stated; psychology GPA no minimum stated; psychology GPA no minimum stated.

Other Criteria: (importance of criteria rated low, medium, or high): GRE/MAT scores high, research experience high, work experience medium, extracurricular activity medium, clinically related public service medium, GPA high, letters of recommendation high, interview medium, statement of goals and objectives high.

Student Characteristics: The following represents characteristics of students in 2001–2002 in all graduate psychology programs in the department: Female–full-time 4, part-time 0; Male–full-time 1, part-time 0; African American/Black–full-time 1, part-time 0; Hispanic/Latino (a)–full-time 0, part-time 0; Asian/Pacific Islander–full-time 0, part-time 0; American Indian/Alaska Native–full-time 0, part-time 0.

Financial Information/Assistance:

Tuition for Full-Time Study: No information provided.

Financial Assistance:

First Year Students: Teaching assistantships available for first-year. Average amount paid per academic year: $24,000. Tuition remission given: full. Research assistantships available for first-year. Average amount paid per academic year: $24,000. Tuition remission given: full. Fellowships and scholarships available for first-year. Average amount paid per academic year: $2,000. Tuition remission given: partial.

Advanced Students: Teaching assistantships available for advanced students. Average amount paid per academic year: $24,000. Tuition remission given: full. Research assistantships available for advanced students. Average amount paid per academic year: $24,000. Tuition remission given: full. Fellowships and scholarships available for advanced students. Average amount paid per academic year: $2,000. Tuition remission given: partial.

Contact Information: Of all students currently enrolled full-time, 100% benefited from one or more of the listed financial assistance programs. For information on financial assistance, contact: Suzanne Blyer, Graduate School, Boatwright Administrative Wing, University of Richmond, Virginia 23173.

Internships/Practica: Our department has many solid relationships with placement sites around Richmond. For example, we regularly place students in the Medical College of Virginia; Psychological Consultants; Virginia Treatment Center; and social services center.

Housing and Day Care: No on-campus housing and day care facilities are available.

Employment of Department Graduates:

Master's Degree Graduates: Of those who graduated in the academic year 2000–2001, the following categories and numbers represent the post-graduate activities and employment of master's degree graduates: Enrolled in a psychology doctoral program (2), enrolled in a post-doctoral residency/fellowship (n/a), employed in independent practice (n/a), employed in a government agency (research) (1).

Doctoral Degree Graduates: Of those who graduated in the academic year 2000–2001, the following categories and numbers represent the post-graduate activities and employment of doctoral degree graduates: Enrolled in a psychology doctoral program (n/a), enrolled in another graduate/professional program (n/a).

Additional Information:

Orientation, Objectives, and Emphasis of Department: The General MA program at the University of Richmond is comprised of a rigorous, research-oriented course of study. It sets out to produce students who are both discriminating consumers and producers of research in many different areas of psychology. The program is designed to prepare students to go on for the PhD in a variety of specialties. As soon as they arrive, students work closely with mentors in fashioning a research program and then following a course of study that will complete academic and scientific pursuits, adding new strengths and shoring-up old ones. In addition to elective courses, students choose from among courses in Biological, Cognitive/Affective, and Social Basis of Behavior. Throughout, the emphasis is on research and research skills, and how to critically evaluate their own and others' scholarship. The first year is a composition of rigorous coursework in the aforementioned areas, culminating in a comprehensive examination, and coupled with original research project(s). The second year focuses on the thesis and associated coursework. Altogether, students complete the program with a focus and the tools to equip them for advanced training in the PhD.

Special Facilities or Resources: The Department of Psychology occupies three floors of Richmond Hall on the beautiful University of Richmond campus. The hall was renovated in 1979, and again in 1990. Currently it houses state-of-the-art laboratory facilities for neuroscience research, including image analysis and computerized microscopy; excellent laboratory facilities for performing cognitive and child development; exceptional laboratory space and equipment for performing cognitive and aging-related research in psychology; and outstanding computer resources in general, in the form of laboratories and work-stations available to students. Moreover, there is ample money available for graduate student research and research related travel to scientific conferences, and a supportive environment for hardworking students in the area of psychology.

Information for Students With Physical Disabilities: The University of Richmond is committed to providing an outstanding educational experience to all students, regardless of physical disabilities, race, color, or creed. Provisions are available for students with special needs. Inquiries can be directed to the Graduate School.

Application Information:

Send to: Graduate School, Boatwright Administrative Wing, University of Richmond, Richmond, Virginia, 23173. Students are admitted in the Fall, application deadline March 1. *Fee:* $30. Financial need must be documented.

Virginia Commonwealth University
Department of Psychology
Humanities and Sciences
808 West Franklin Street - Box 842018
Richmond, VA 23284-2018
Telephone: (804) 828-1193
Fax: (804) 828-2237
E-mail: *bmyers@vcu.edu*
Web: *http://www.has.vcu.edu/psy/*

Department Established:

1969. Chairperson: Everett L. Worthington, Jr. Number of Faculty: total–full-time 30, part-time 1; women–full-time 14, part-time 1; minority–full-time 4.

Programs and Degrees Offered:

Listed in the following order: Program area, degree type (T if terminal Master's), number awarded 7/00–6/01. Clinical psychology PhD 12, counseling psychology PhD 6, experimental psychology PhD 5.

APA Accreditation: Clinical PhD: full. Counseling PhD: full.

Student Applications/Admissions:

Student Applications

Clinical psychology PhD—Applications 2001–2002, 325. Total applicants accepted 2001–2002, 7. New applicants enrolled 2001–2002, 7. Total enrolled 2001–2002 full-time, 54. Openings 2002–2003, 7-8. *Counseling psychology PhD*—Applications 2001–2002, 210. Total applicants accepted 2001–2002, 8. New applicants enrolled 2001–2002, 7. Total enrolled 2001–2002 full-time, 42. Openings 2002–2003, 6-7. *Experimental psychology PhD*—Applications 2001–2002, 65. Total applicants accepted 2001–2002, 8. New applicants enrolled 2001–2002, 7. Total enrolled 2001–2002 full-time, 43. Openings 2002–2003, 6-7.

Admissions Requirements:

Scores: Entries appear in this order: required test or GPA, minimum score (if required), median score of students entering in 2001–2002. Doctoral Programs: GRE-V no minimum stated; GRE-Q no minimum stated; GRE-Analytical no minimum stated; overall undergraduate GPA no minimum stated; last 2 years GPA no minimum stated; psychology GPA no minimum stated; psychology GPA no minimum stated.

Other Criteria: (importance of criteria rated low, medium, or high): GRE/MAT scores high, research experience high, work experience high, GPA high, letters of recommendation high, interview high, statement of goals and objectives high, Indivl match to faculty.

Student Characteristics: The following represents characteristics of students in 2001–2002 in all graduate psychology programs in the department: Female–full-time 14, part-time 0; Male–full-time 7, part-time 0; African American/Black–full-time 3, part-time 0;

Hispanic/Latino (a)–full-time 1, part-time 0; Asian/Pacific Islander–full-time 0, part-time 0; American Indian/Alaska Native–full-time 0, part-time 0.

Financial Information/Assistance:

Tuition for Full-Time Study: *Master's:* State residents $2,138 per credit hour; nonstate residents: $6,336 per credit hour. *Doctoral:* State residents: $2,138 per credit hour; nonstate residents: $6,336 per credit hour.

Financial Assistance:

First Year Students: Teaching assistantships available for first-year. Average amount paid per academic year: $9,714. Average number of hours worked per week: 20. Tuition remission given: full. Research assistantships available for first-year. Average amount paid per academic year: $9,714. Average number of hours worked per week: 20. Tuition remission given: full and partial. Fellowships and scholarships available for first-year. Average amount paid per academic year: $11,000. Tuition remission given: full.

Advanced Students: Teaching assistantships available for advanced students. Average amount paid per academic year: $9,714. Average number of hours worked per week: 20. Tuition remission given: full and partial. Research assistantships available for advanced students. Average amount paid per academic year: $9,714. Average number of hours worked per week: 20. Tuition remission given: full and partial. Fellowships and scholarships available for advanced students. Average amount paid per academic year: $11,000. Tuition remission given: full.

Contact Information: Of all students currently enrolled full-time, 80% benefited from one or more of the listed financial assistance programs.

Internships/Practica: Practicum (external) and internship required for clinical and counseling programs. Sites range from the following: VA hospitals, federal prisons, counseling centers, medical campus opportunities, Children's Hospitals, and juvenile facilities.

Housing and Day Care: No on-campus housing and day care facilities are available.

Employment of Department Graduates:

Master's Degree Graduates: Of those who graduated in the academic year 2000–2001, the following categories and numbers represent the post-graduate activities and employment of master's degree graduates: Enrolled in a post-doctoral residency/fellowship (n/a), employed in independent practice (n/a).

Doctoral Degree Graduates: Of those who graduated in the academic year 2000–2001, the following categories and numbers represent the post-graduate activities and employment of doctoral degree graduates: Enrolled in a psychology doctoral program (n/a), enrolled in another graduate/professional program (n/a).

Additional Information:

Orientation, Objectives, and Emphasis of Department: The graduate programs in psychology are designed to provide a core education in the basic science of psychology and to enable students to develop skills specific to their area of interest. Students are educated first as psychologists, and are then helped to develop competence in a more specialized area relevant to their scholarly and professional objectives. In addition to formal research require-ments for the thesis and dissertation, students in the graduate programs are encouraged to conduct independent research, participate in research teams, or collaborate with faculty conducting research on an ongoing basis. The clinical and counseling psychology programs strongly emphasize the scientist-practitioner model. Students in the clinical program may elect to develop specialized competency in one of several different tracks, including behavior therapy/cognitive behavior therapy, behavioral medicine, clinical child, and adult psychotherapy process. The counseling psychology program prepares students to function in a variety of research and applied settings and to work with people experiencing a broad range of emotional, social, or behavioral problems. The experimental program stresses the acquisition of experimental skills as well as advanced training in one of three specialty areas: biopsychology, developmental psychology, and social psychology.

Special Facilities or Resources: The department maintains laboratories for research in the areas of biopsychology, developmental, social, psychophysiology, behavioral assessment, and psychotherapy process. The department also operates the Center for Psychological Services and Development, which provides mental health services for clients referred from throughout the Richmond metropolitan area. Students in the clinical and counseling programs complete practica in the Center and in a variety of off-campus practicum facilities located in the community. Cooperation with a variety of programs and departments on the University's medical campus, the Medical College of Virginia, is extensive for both research and training.

Information for Students With Physical Disabilities: Virginia Commonwealth University is comitted to all federal disability policies.

Application Information:

Send to: School of Graduate Studies - VCU Box 843051, Richmond, VA 23284. Students are admitted in the Fall, application deadline 1/ 15; 2/15. Deadlines are January 15 for Clinical and Counseling Psychology, February 15 for Experimental Psychology. *Fee:* $30.

Virginia Consortium Program in Clinical Psychology
Program in Clinical Psychology
College of William & Mary, Eastern Virginia Medical School
Pembroke Two/Suite 301, 287 Independence Boulevard
Virginia Beach, VA 23462
Telephone: (757) 518-2550
Fax: (757) 518-2553
E-mail: *exoneill@odu.edu*
Web: *http://www.vcpcp.odu.edu/vcpcp/*

Department Established:

1978. Chairperson: Neill Watson. Number of Faculty: total–full-time 45; women–full-time 18; minority–full-time 10.

Programs and Degrees Offered:

Listed in the following order: Program area, degree type (T if terminal Master's), number awarded 7/00–6/01. Clinical psychology PsyD 12.

APA Accreditation: Clinical PsyD: full.

Student Applications/Admissions:

Student Applications

Clinical psychology PsyD—Applications 2001–2002, 128. Total applicants accepted 2001–2002, 20. New applicants enrolled 2001–2002, 10. Total enrolled 2001–2002 full-time, 47. Openings 2002–2003, 10. The Median number of years required for completion of a degree are 5. The number of students enrolled full and part-time, who were dismissed or voluntarily withdrew from this program area were 0.

Admissions Requirements:

Scores: Entries appear in this order: required test or GPA, minimum score (if required), median score of students entering in 2001–2002. Doctoral Programs: GRE-V no minimum stated, 550; GRE-Q no minimum stated, 620; GRE-Analytical no minimum stated, 660; GRE-Subject(Psych) no minimum stated, 640; overall undergraduate GPA 2.5, 3.55; last 2 years GPA 3.0; psychology GPA 3.0.

Other Criteria: (importance of criteria rated low, medium, or high): GRE/MAT scores medium, research experience medium, work experience medium, clinically related public service medium, GPA medium, letters of recommendation medium, interview high, statement of goals and objectives medium, Fit w/Program's goals high.

Student Characteristics: The following represents characteristics of students in 2001–2002 in all graduate psychology programs in the department: Female–full-time 38, part-time 0; Male–full-time 9, part-time 0; African American/Black–full-time 10, part-time 0; Hispanic/Latino (a)–full-time 0, part-time 0; Asian/Pacific Islander–full-time 2, part-time 0; American Indian/Alaska Native–full-time 0, part-time 0; Multi-ethnic–full-time 0, part-time 0; students subject to the Americans with Disabilities Act–full-time 0, part-time 0.

Financial Information/Assistance:

Tuition for Full-Time Study: *Doctoral:* State residents: per academic year $6,876; nonstate residents: per academic year $6,876.

Financial Assistance:

First Year Students: Teaching assistantships available for first-year. Average amount paid per academic year: $5,500. Average number of hours worked per week: 6. Apply by Feb 15. Tuition remission given: partial. Research assistantships available for first-year. Average amount paid per academic year: $5,000. Average number of hours worked per week: 8. Apply by Feb 15. Tuition remission given: partial.

Advanced Students: Teaching assistantships available for advanced students. Average amount paid per academic year: $6,000. Average number of hours worked per week: 6. Apply by Feb 15. Tuition remission given: partial. Research assistantships available for advanced students. Average amount paid per academic year: $5,000. Average number of hours worked per week: 8. Apply by Feb 15. Tuition remission given: partial.

Contact Information: Of all students currently enrolled full-time, 96% benefited from one or more of the listed financial assistance programs. For information on financial assistance, contact: See Web site: www.vcpcp.odu.edu/vcpcp/, or, Virginia Consortium Program Office, Pembroke Two/Suite 301, 287 Independence Blvd., Va. Beach, VA 23462.

Internships/Practica: Practicum training is offered in a variety of diverse settings, such as mental health centers, medical hospitals, children's residential treatment facilities, public school systems, university counseling centers, social services clinics, private practices and specialty services (neuropsychology-rehabilitation and family therapy). Settings include inpatient, partial hospitalization, residential, and outpatient. Populations include infants, children, adolescents, adults, and elderly from most socioeconomic levels and ethnic groups. Services include most forms of assessment; individual, group, and family intervention modalities; and consultative and other indirect services. Placements are arranged to assure that each student is exposed to several settings and populations. For those doctoral students for whom a professional internship is required prior to graduation, 11 applied in 2000–2001. Of those who applied, 11 were placed in internships listed by the Association of Psychology Postdoctoral and Internship Programs (APPIC); 10 were placed in APA accredited internships.

Housing and Day Care: No on-campus housing and day care facilities are available.

Employment of Department Graduates:

Master's Degree Graduates: Of those who graduated in the academic year 2000–2001, the following categories and numbers represent the post-graduate activities and employment of master's degree graduates: Enrolled in a post-doctoral residency/fellowship (n/a), employed in independent practice (n/a).

Doctoral Degree Graduates: Of those who graduated in the academic year 2000–2001, the following categories and numbers represent the post-graduate activities and employment of doctoral degree graduates: Enrolled in a psychology doctoral program (n/a), enrolled in another graduate/professional program (n/a).

Additional Information:

Orientation, Objectives, and Emphasis of Department: The Virginia Consortium is a single, unified program co-sponsored by four institutions: The College of William and Mary, Eastern Virginia Medical School, Norfolk State University, and Old Dominion University. Its mission is to produce practicing clinical psychologists who are educated in the basic subjects and methods of psychological science, capable of critically assimilating new knowledge, proficient in the delivery and evaluation of clinical services in the public and private sectors, and able to assume leadership positions in service delivery organizations. The curriculum is generalist in content and in theoretical orientation. It includes education in the major theoretical and technical models: psychodynamic, behavioral, phenomenological, and family systems. Training is provided in intervention at the individual, group, family, and community/organizational levels. Knowledge acquired in the classroom is applied in an orderly sequence of supervised practica providing exposure to multiple settings, populations, and intervention modalities. Practicum objectives are integrated with the goals of classroom education to facilitate systematic and cumulative acquisition of clinical skills. In the third year, the student pursues individual interests by integrating individualized coursework with advanced practica and a clinical dissertation. In the fourth year, the student receives intensive training in a full-time clinical internship.

Special Facilities or Resources: Students are considered full-time in all four sponsoring schools. This permits access to: four libraries with several computerized literature search databases and 400 periodicals in psychology; four computing centers; multiple health services; and a variety of athletic events. Research includes a social psychology laboratory with observational capabilities and facilities: 54 laboratory rooms; and 10 research rooms with various specialized capabilities. Research may also be conducted at practicum placement facilities.

Information for Students With Physical Disabilities: See catalog for ADA policies; see Web site for information about our four schools.

Application Information:

Send to: Department Chair, Virginia Consortium Program in Clinical Psychology, Pembroke Two/Suite 301, 287 Independence Blvd., Va. Beach, VA 23462. Students are admitted in the Fall, application deadline January 5. *Fee:* $30. No fee waiver available.

Virginia Polytechnic Institute and State University

Department of Psychology 0436
Arts and Sciences
5088 Derring Hall
Blacksburg, VA 24061
Telephone: (540) 231-6581
Fax: (540) 231-3652
E-mail: *stephens@vt.edu*
Web: *http://www.psyc.vt.edu/*

Department Established:

1965. Chairperson: Jack W. Finney. Number of Faculty: total–full-time 23; women–full-time 5; minority–full-time 1.

Programs and Degrees Offered:

Listed in the following order: Program area, degree type (T if terminal Master's), number awarded 7/00–6/01. Clinical PhD 5, industrial/organizational PhD 3, psychological sciences PhD 2.

APA Accreditation: Clinical PhD: full.

Student Applications/Admissions:

Student Applications

Clinical PhD—Applications 2001–2002, 105. Total applicants accepted 2001–2002, 14. New applicants enrolled 2001–2002, 9. Total enrolled 2001–2002 full-time, 37. Openings 2002–2003, 9. The number of students enrolled full and part-time, who were dismissed or voluntarily withdrew from this program area were 0. *Industrial/organizational PhD*—Applications 2001–2002, 46. Total applicants accepted 2001–2002, 14. New applicants enrolled 2001–2002, 6. Total enrolled 2001–2002 full-time, 21. Openings 2002–2003, 6. The number of students enrolled full and part-time, who were dismissed or voluntarily withdrew from this program area were 0. *Psychological sciences PhD*—Applications 2001–2002, 18. Total applicants accepted 2001–2002, 6. Total enrolled 2001–2002 full-time, 15. Openings 2002–2003, 4. The number of students enrolled full and part-time, who were dismissed or voluntarily withdrew from this program area were 0.

Admissions Requirements:

Scores: Entries appear in this order: required test or GPA, minimum score (if required), median score of students entering

in 2001–2002. Doctoral Programs: GRE-V no minimum stated, 587; GRE-Q no minimum stated, 650; GRE-V+Q no minimum stated, 1237; last 2 years GPA no minimum stated, 3.77; psychology GPA no minimum stated; psychology GPA no minimum stated.

Other Criteria: (importance of criteria rated low, medium, or high): GRE/MAT scores high, research experience high, work experience low, clinically related public service medium, GPA high, letters of recommendation high, interview medium, statement of goals and objectives medium. Congruence of applicant's goals with program objectives high.

Student Characteristics: The following represents characteristics of students in 2001–2002 in all graduate psychology programs in the department: Female–full-time 45, part-time 6; Male–full-time 23, part-time 2; African American/Black–full-time 5, part-time 0; Hispanic/Latino (a)–full-time 4, part-time 0; Asian/Pacific Islander–full-time 0, part-time 0; American Indian/Alaska Native–full-time 0, part-time 0; Multi-ethnic–full-time 0, students subject to the Americans with Disabilities Act–full-time 0.

Financial Information/Assistance:

Tuition for Full-Time Study: *Master's:* State residents per academic year $4,347, $241 per credit hour; nonstate residents: per academic year $7,317, $406 per credit hour. *Doctoral:* State residents: per academic year $4,347, $241 per credit hour; nonstate residents: per academic year $7,317, $406 per credit hour.

Financial Assistance:

First Year Students: Teaching assistantships available for first-year. Average amount paid per academic year: $7,074. Average number of hours worked per week: 15. Tuition remission given: full and partial. Research assistantships available for first-year. Average amount paid per academic year: $11,790. Average number of hours worked per week: 20. Tuition remission given: full and partial. Fellowships and scholarships available for first-year. Average amount paid per academic year: $12,500. Average number of hours worked per week: 20. Tuition remission given: full.

Advanced Students: Teaching assistantships available for advanced students. Average amount paid per academic year: $7,074. Average number of hours worked per week: 15. Tuition remission given: full and partial. Research assistantships available for advanced students. Average amount paid per academic year: $11,790. Average number of hours worked per week: 20. Tuition remission given: full and partial. Fellowships and scholarships available for advanced students. Average amount paid per academic year: $12,500. Average number of hours worked per week: 20. Tuition remission given: full.

Contact Information: Of all students currently enrolled full-time, 90% benefited from one or more of the listed financial assistance programs. For information on financial assistance, contact: Office of the Graduate School.

Internships/Practica: Students in clinical psychology complete practica in a variety of local agency and hospital settings and are required to complete a predoctoral internship as part of the PhD. Students in Industrial/Organizational psychology are encouraged to pursue summer internships. For those doctoral students for whom a professional internship is required prior to graduation, 9 applied in 2000–2001. Of those who applied, 9 were placed in internships listed by the Association of Psychology Postdoctoral and Internship Programs (APPIC); 9 were placed in APA accredited internships.

Housing and Day Care: No on-campus housing and day care facilities are available.

Employment of Department Graduates:
Master's Degree Graduates: Of those who graduated in the academic year 2000–2001, the following categories and numbers represent the post-graduate activities and employment of master's degree graduates: Enrolled in a post-doctoral residency/fellowship (n/a), employed in independent practice (n/a).
Doctoral Degree Graduates: Of those who graduated in the academic year 2000–2001, the following categories and numbers represent the post-graduate activities and employment of doctoral degree graduates: Enrolled in a psychology doctoral program (n/a), enrolled in another graduate/professional program (n/a), enrolled in a post-doctoral residency/fellowship (4), employed in an academic position at a university (1), employed in an academic position at a 2-year/4-year college (1), employed in other positions at a higher education institution (1), employed in business or industry (research/consulting) (3).

Additional Information:
Orientation, Objectives, and Emphasis of Department: The graduate programs are research oriented and designed to ensure that students receive a strong preparation in research methods and psychological theory and to provide the students with skills necessary to be successful in either academic or applied settings. The clinical psychology program is based on the scientist-professional model and emphasizes research methods and theory. Clinical specializations include child, adult, and health psychology. The industrial/organizational psychology program prepares students both for university teaching and research and for the solution of individual, group, and organizational problems in work settings. Psychometrics, research design, and statistics are emphasized. The Psychological Sciences program trains students in experimental psychology with a focus on preparing psychologists for teaching and research settings. Students in the Psychological Sciences program choose from a biobehavioral/psychophysiology or developmental psychology specialty. All doctoral programs also offer training and experience in the teaching of psychology.

Special Facilities or Resources: The Psychological Services Center and Child Study Center are located off-campus and provide the foundation for practicum and research training in Clinical Psychology. The Center for Research in Health Behavior is also located off-campus and is primarily involved in prevention research supported by the National Institutes of Health. Faculty, students, and staff benefit from Virginia Tech's state-of-the-art communications system that links every dormitory room, laboratory, office, and classroom to computing capabilities, audio and video data, and the World Wide Web. The entire campus has easy access to supercomputers across the country, worldwide libraries, and data systems. Department resources also include two state-of-the-art laboratories that are dedicated to undergraduate and graduate teaching and research. The psychophysiological laboratory includes eight computer workstations, five EEG/Evoked Potential work stations (32 channel Neuroscan; Neurosearch-24), eye tracker equipment, Coulbourn physiological units, and extensive perception equipment. The other computer laboratory includes 25 computer workstations with cognitive and neurophysio-

logical experiments, SAS and SPSS statistical packages, Bilog and Multilog programs. Graduate students also have ready access to PC and Macintosh computers for word processing and Internet access.

Information for Students With Physical Disabilities: The University's Office of Disabilities is committed to providing resources and services to students in order to best facilitate their learning and professional experiences at Virginia Tech.

Application Information:
Send to: Office of Graduate Programs, 100 Sandy Hall, Virginia Polytechnic Institute and State University, Blacksburg, VA 24061. Students are admitted in the Fall. Application Deadline for Clinical is December 15. Application Deadline for I/O and Psychological Sciences is January 15. *Fee:* $45.

Virginia, University of
Curry Programs in Clinical and School Psychology
Curry School of Education
P.O. Box 400270
Charlottesville, VA 22904-4270
Telephone: (804) 924-7472
Fax: (804) 924-1433
E-mail: *clin-psych@virginia.edu*
Web: *http://curry.edschool.virginia.edu/go/clinpsych*

Department Established:
1976. Director: Ann Loper. Number of Faculty: total–full-time 8, part-time 2; women–full-time 3, part-time 2; minority–full-time 1.

Programs and Degrees Offered:
Listed in the following order: Program area, degree type (T if terminal Master's), number awarded 7/00–6/01. Clinical PhD 10.

APA Accreditation: Clinical PhD: full.

Student Applications/Admissions:
Student Applications
Clinical PhD—Applications 2001–2002, 166. Total applicants accepted 2001–2002, 13. New applicants enrolled 2001–2002, 8. Total enrolled 2001–2002 full-time, 39. Openings 2002–2003, 8. The Median number of years required for completion of a degree are 5. The number of students enrolled full and part-time, who were dismissed or voluntarily withdrew from this program area were 0.

Admissions Requirements:
Scores: Entries appear in this order: required test or GPA, minimum score (if required), median score of students entering in 2001–2002. Doctoral Programs: GRE-V none, 600; GRE-Q none, 665; GRE-V+Q none, 1265; GRE-Subject(Psych) none, 645; overall undergraduate GPA none, 3.6 ; last 2 years GPA no minimum stated; psychology GPA no minimum stated; psychology GPA none, 3.8.
Other Criteria: (importance of criteria rated low, medium, or high): GRE/MAT scores medium, research experience me-

dium, work experience medium, extracurricular activity low, clinically related public service medium, GPA high, letters of recommendation high, interview high, statement of goals and objectives high.

Student Characteristics: The following represents characteristics of students in 2001–2002 in all graduate psychology programs in the department: Female–full-time 35, part-time 0; Male–full-time 8, part-time 0; African American/Black–full-time 7, part-time 0; Hispanic/Latino (a)–full-time 2, part-time 0; Asian/Pacific Islander–full-time 2, part-time 0; American Indian/Alaska Native–full-time 0, part-time 0; Multi-ethnic–full-time 3, students subject to the Americans with Disabilities Act–full-time 0.

Financial Information/Assistance:

Tuition for Full-Time Study: *Doctoral:* State residents: per academic year $18,278; nonstate residents: per academic year $5,188.

Financial Assistance:

First Year Students: Teaching assistantships available for first-year. Average amount paid per academic year: $4,000. Average number of hours worked per week: 10. Apply by March 1. Tuition remission given: partial. Research assistantships available for first-year. Average amount paid per academic year: $4,000. Average number of hours worked per week: 10. Apply by March 1. Fellowships and scholarships available for first-year. Average amount paid per academic year: $15,000. Average number of hours worked per week: 10. Apply by March 1.

Advanced Students: Teaching assistantships available for advanced students. Average amount paid per academic year: $4,000. Average number of hours worked per week: 10. Apply by March 1. Tuition remission given: partial. Research assistantships available for advanced students. Average amount paid per academic year: $4,000. Average number of hours worked per week: 10. Apply by March 1. Fellowships and scholarships available for advanced students. Average amount paid per academic year: $16,000. Average number of hours worked per week: 10. Apply by March 1.

Contact Information: Of all students currently enrolled full-time, 100% benefited from one or more of the listed financial assistance programs. For information on financial assistance, contact: Mary Beth Bellah, Curry Programs in Clinical and School Psychology. Note, figures reflect out-of-state funding levels. Funding is directed toward covering tuition costs plus providing a stipend.

Internships/Practica: Students may select external practica in area public and private schools, state mental hospitals/residential treatment centers for children or adults, a regional medically affiliated children's rehabilitation center, a family stress clinic, and other mental health settings in the university and community. For those doctoral students for whom a professional internship is required prior to graduation, 4 applied in 2000–2001. Of those who applied, 4 were placed in internships listed by the Association of Psychology Postdoctoral and Internship Programs (APPIC); 4 were placed in APA accredited internships.

Housing and Day Care: On-campus housing and day care facilities are available.

Employment of Department Graduates:

Master's Degree Graduates: Of those who graduated in the academic year 2000–2001, the following categories and numbers

represent the post-graduate activities and employment of master's degree graduates: Enrolled in a post-doctoral residency/fellowship (n/a), employed in independent practice (n/a).

Doctoral Degree Graduates: Of those who graduated in the academic year 2000–2001, the following categories and numbers represent the post-graduate activities and employment of doctoral degree graduates: Enrolled in a psychology doctoral program (n/a), enrolled in another graduate/professional program (n/a), enrolled in a post-doctoral residency/fellowship (8), employed in a professional position in a school system (1), employed in a hospital/medical center (1).

Additional Information:

Orientation, Objectives, and Emphasis of Department: The primary goal of the training program in the Curry School of Education is to produce clinical psychologists with potential to make outstanding contributions to the profession in a variety of roles. The majority of graduates seek careers in settings such as hospitals, mental health centers, schools, etc. A smaller percentage choose purely academic and research careers. All students complete a common core of coursework and practica in both basic science and professional skills. The students' interests and the courses they elect determine the nature of the students' programs beyond the common core. The predominant theoretical and practice orientations of the faculty are cognitive behavioral, psychodynamic, and family systems. All students are expected to develop strong clinical and research skills. Efforts are made to integrate students' clinical and research experience. The EdD program in school psychology admits experienced school psychologists who are trained for leadership in the profession, at school district or state levels, or as trainers of school psychologists.

Special Facilities or Resources: The Curry Program operates its own comprehensive psychological clinic, the Center for Clinical Psychology Services, serving families, couples, and individuals of all ages and diverse backgrounds. The Center is well equipped for live and videotaped supervision and conveniently located in Ruffner Hall along with student and faculty offices. Program students have training opportunities with the Adjustment of Incarcerated Women Project, Adolescent Parenting Stress Project, Family Assessment Project, NICHD Study of Early Child Care, National Center for Early Development and Learning, School Crisis Network, Teaching Stress Project, Virginia Youth Violence Project, Young Women Leaders Program, and others. In addition, the Program has close working relationships with numerous community agencies, schools, clinics, and hospitals that permit training and research in many different mental health and educational fields. The Curry School of Education is a national leader in instructional technology, with outstanding computing facilities and technology support, smart classrooms, and its own library. Students enjoy easy access to the extensive University of Virginia Library system, which includes a collection of nearly 5 million volumes and has state of the art electronic library resources.

Application Information:

Send to: Admissions Office, Curry School of Education, P.O. Box 400261, University of Virginia, Charlottesville, VA 22904-4261. Students are admitted in the Fall, application deadline January 15. *Fee:* $40. If fee imposes economic hardship, it may be waived. Request information from Curry School Admissions office at address above.

Virginia, University of

Department of Psychology
102 Gilmer Hall, P.O. Box 400400
Charlottesville, VA 22904-4400
Telephone: (434) 982-4750
Fax: (434) 982-4766
E-mail: *psychology@virginia.edu*
Web: *http://www.virginia.edu/~psych*

Department Established:

1929. Chairperson: Timothy D. Wilson. Number of Faculty: total–full-time 36; women–full-time 12; minority–full-time 5.

Programs and Degrees Offered:

Listed in the following order: Program area, degree type (T if terminal Master's), number awarded 7/00–6/01. Clinical PhD 4, cognitive PhD 3, community PhD 1, developmental PhD 5, psychobiology PhD 2, quantitative PhD 1, social PhD 3.

APA Accreditation: Clinical PhD: full.

Student Applications/Admissions:

Student Applications

Clinical PhD—Applications 2001–2002, 290. Total applicants accepted 2001–2002, 7. New applicants enrolled 2001–2002, 6. Total enrolled 2001–2002 full-time, 30. Openings 2002–2003, 5. The number of students enrolled full and part-time, who were dismissed or voluntarily withdrew from this program area were 0. *Cognitive PhD*—Applications 2001–2002, 24. Total applicants accepted 2001–2002, 5. New applicants enrolled 2001–2002, 3. Total enrolled 2001–2002 full-time, 12. Openings 2002–2003, 3. The number of students enrolled full and part-time, who were dismissed or voluntarily withdrew from this program area were 0. *Community PhD*—Applications 2001–2002, 44. Total applicants accepted 2001–2002, 3. New applicants enrolled 2001–2002, 2. Total enrolled 2001–2002 full-time, 9. Openings 2002–2003, 2. *Developmental PhD*—Applications 2001–2002, 49. Total applicants accepted 2001–2002, 6. New applicants enrolled 2001–2002, 3. Total enrolled 2001–2002 full-time, 11. Openings 2002–2003, 4. *Psychobiology PhD*—Applications 2001–2002, 23. Total applicants accepted 2001–2002, 2. New applicants enrolled 2001–2002, 2. Total enrolled 2001–2002 full-time, 7. Openings 2002–2003, 4. *Quantitative PhD*—Applications 2001–2002, 6. Total applicants accepted 2001–2002, 3. New applicants enrolled 2001–2002, 2. Total enrolled 2001–2002 full-time, 8. Openings 2002–2003, 2. *Social PhD*—Applications 2001–2002, 50. Total applicants accepted 2001–2002, 6. New applicants enrolled 2001–2002, 3. Total enrolled 2001–2002 full-time, 16. Openings 2002–2003, 3.

Admissions Requirements:

Scores: Entries appear in this order: required test or GPA, minimum score (if required), median score of students entering in 2001–2002. Doctoral Programs: GRE-V no minimum stated; GRE-Q no minimum stated; GRE-V+Q no minimum stated; GRE-Analytical no minimum stated; GRE-V+Q+Analytical no minimum stated; overall undergraduate GPA no minimum stated; last 2 years GPA no minimum stated; psychology GPA no minimum stated; psychology GPA no minimum stated.

Other Criteria: (importance of criteria rated low, medium, or high): GRE/MAT scores medium, research experience high, work experience medium, extracurricular activity low, clinically related public service low, GPA medium, letters of recommendation high, interview medium, statement of goals and objectives high. Publications and presentations at conferences are valued as actual work experience in an area related to the degree sought.

Student Characteristics: The following represents characteristics of students in 2001–2002 in all graduate psychology programs in the department: Female–full-time 12, part-time 0; Male–full-time 7, part-time 0; African American/Black–full-time 2, part-time 0; Hispanic/Latino (a)–full-time 2, part-time 0; Asian/Pacific Islander–full-time 1, part-time 0; American Indian/Alaska Native–full-time 1, part-time 0.

Financial Information/Assistance:

Tuition for Full-Time Study: No information provided.

Financial Assistance:

First Year Students: Teaching assistantships available for first-year. Apply by N/A. Tuition remission given: full. Research assistantships available for first-year. Apply by N/A. Tuition remission given: full. Fellowships and scholarships available for first-year. Apply by N/A.

Advanced Students: Teaching assistantships available for advanced students. Apply by N/A. Tuition remission given: full. Research assistantships available for advanced students. Apply by N/A. Tuition remission given: full. Fellowships and scholarships available for advanced students. Apply by N/A.

Contact Information: Of all students currently enrolled full-time, 100% benefited from one or more of the listed financial assistance programs. For information on financial assistance, contact: Debbie Snow, dsnow@virginia.edu.

Internships/Practica: For clinical program: Multiple practica at University Hospital, State Mental Hospital for children and adults, Kluge Children's Center; Community Mental Health Center; Law and Psychiatry Unit; Department Clinic; and other places as connections and student interest suggest.

Housing and Day Care: No on-campus housing and day care facilities are available.

Employment of Department Graduates:

Master's Degree Graduates: Of those who graduated in the academic year 2000–2001, the following categories and numbers represent the post-graduate activities and employment of master's degree graduates: Enrolled in a post-doctoral residency/fellowship (n/a), employed in independent practice (n/a).

Doctoral Degree Graduates: Of those who graduated in the academic year 2000–2001, the following categories and numbers represent the post-graduate activities and employment of doctoral degree graduates: Enrolled in a psychology doctoral program (n/a), enrolled in another graduate/professional program (n/a).

Additional Information:

Orientation, Objectives, and Emphasis of Department: The department emphasizes research in a broad spectrum of psychology with clinical, developmental, social, cognitive, psychobiology, quantitative, and community specialties. In addition, new tracks are being developed, such as social ecology and development, law and psychology, family, and minority issues.

Special Facilities or Resources: The department has in excess of 50,000 square feet for offices, laboratories, seminar rooms, and classrooms. Special facilities include rooms for psychophysical investigations, a suite of rooms devoted to developmental and clinical, social laboratories, and specialized research facilities for the study of animal behavior and psychobiology. Sound-attenuated rooms, electrically shielded rooms, numerous one-way vision rooms, surgery and vivarium rooms, and a darkroom are all available. There is also a library for psychology and biology housed in the same building. There are 3 computer labs available to students. One lab has 9 Macintosh LCIII computers. One lab contains 15 Macintosh SI computers. The third lab contains 40 microcomputers. All labs are connected to a local area network and serviced by 3 Norell servers. The microcomputer lab is mostly used for teaching and is shared with the university. All computers can connect to a University-wide local area network. This allows the labs to connect to other available University machines such as IBM RS/6000 Unix machines.

Application Information:

Send to: Dean of the Graduate School, The University of Virginia, 437 Cabell Hall, Charlottesville, VA 22903. Students are admitted in the Fall, application deadline December 1. *Fee:* $40.

William and Mary, College of
Department of Psychology/Predoctoral MA Program
P.O. Box 8795
Williamsburg, VA 23187
Telephone: (757) 221-3872
E-mail: *wlvent@wm.edu*
Web: *http://www.um.edu/psyc/*

Department Established:
1946. Chairperson: W. Larry Ventis. Number of Faculty: total–full-time 18, part-time 6; women–full-time 3, part-time 2.

Programs and Degrees Offered:
Listed in the following order: Program area, degree type (T if terminal Master's), number awarded 7/00–6/01. General MA (T) 8.

Student Applications/Admissions:
Student Applications
General MA—Applications 2001–2002, 62. Total applicants accepted 2001–2002, 26. New applicants enrolled 2001–2002, 10. Total enrolled 2001–2002 full-time, 15. Openings 2002–2003, 8. The Median number of years required for completion of a degree are 2.

Admissions Requirements:
Scores: Entries appear in this order: required test or GPA, minimum score (if required), median score of students entering in 2001–2002. Master's Programs: GRE-V no minimum stated, 568; GRE-Q no minimum stated, 619; GRE-Analytical no minimum stated, 632; GRE-V+Q+Analytical no minimum

stated, 1819; overall undergraduate GPA no minimum stated, 3.44; psychology GPA no minimum stated, 3.63. Note: No minimums required for the above. Doctoral Programs: last 2 years GPA no minimum stated; psychology GPA no minimum stated; psychology GPA no minimum stated.
Other Criteria: (importance of criteria rated low, medium, or high): GRE/MAT scores medium, research experience high, work experience medium, extracurricular activity low, clinically related public service low, GPA medium, letters of recommendation high, statement of goals and objectives high.

Student Characteristics: The following represents characteristics of students in 2001–2002 in all graduate psychology programs in the department: Female–full-time 11, part-time 0; Male–full-time 4, part-time 0; African American/Black–full-time 0, part-time 0; Hispanic/Latino (a)–full-time 0, part-time 0; Asian/Pacific Islander–full-time 0, part-time 0; American Indian/Alaska Native–full-time 0, part-time 0.

Financial Information/Assistance:
Tuition for Full-Time Study: *Master's:* State residents per academic year $5,282, $175 per credit hour.

Financial Assistance:
First Year Students: Teaching assistantships available for first-year. Average amount paid per academic year: $9,000. Average number of hours worked per week: 20. Apply by February 15. Tuition remission given: full. Research assistantships available for first-year. Average amount paid per academic year: $9,000. Average number of hours worked per week: 20. Apply by February 15. Tuition remission given: full. Fellowships and scholarships available for first-year. Average amount paid per academic year: $9,000. Average number of hours worked per week: 20. Apply by February 15. Tuition remission given: full.

Advanced Students: Teaching assistantships available for advanced students. Average amount paid per academic year: $9,000. Average number of hours worked per week: 20. Apply by February 15. Tuition remission given: full. Research assistantships available for advanced students. Average amount paid per academic year: $9,000. Average number of hours worked per week: 20. Apply by February 15. Tuition remission given: full. Fellowships and scholarships available for advanced students. Average amount paid per academic year: $9,000. Average number of hours worked per week: 20. Apply by February 15. Tuition remission given: full.

Contact Information: Of all students currently enrolled full-time, 100% benefited from one or more of the listed financial assistance programs. For information on financial assistance, contact: Edward P. Irish, Director Financial Aid, email epirish@facstaff.wm.edu.

Internships/Practica: No information provided.

Housing and Day Care: On-campus housing and day care facilities are available.

Employment of Department Graduates:
Master's Degree Graduates: Of those who graduated in the academic year 2000–2001, the following categories and numbers represent the post-graduate activities and employment of master's degree graduates: Enrolled in a psychology doctoral program (7), enrolled in a post-doctoral residency/fellowship (n/a), employed

in independent practice (n/a), employed in business or industry (research/consulting) (1).

Doctoral Degree Graduates: Of those who graduated in the academic year 2000–2001, the following categories and numbers represent the post-graduate activities and employment of doctoral degree graduates: Enrolled in a psychology doctoral program (n/a), enrolled in another graduate/professional program (n/a).

Additional Information:

Orientation, Objectives, and Emphasis of Department: The general psychology MA program is designed to prepare students for admission to PhD programs. Students are not admitted if they are not planning to further their education. There is a heavy research emphasis throughout both years of the program.

Special Facilities or Resources: There are a limited number of assistantships available to MA students at Eastern State Hospital adjacent to the campus. Computer facilities are available in the department for students. Subjects accessible for research include rats, college sophomores, institutionalized geriatric and brain-injured patients, and mental hospital inpatients.

Application Information:

Send to: Dean of Research and Graduate Studies, Arts and Sciences, The College of William and Mary, P.O. Box 8795, Williamsburg, VA 23187-8795. Students are admitted in the Fall, application deadline February 15. *Fee:* $30.

Antioch University, Seattle (2001 data)

Antioch Center for Creative Change
2326 Sixth Avenue
Seattle, WA 98121-1814
Telephone: (206) 268-4816
Fax: (206) 441-3307
E-mail: *bspraker@antiochsea.edu*

Department Established:

1990. Chairperson: Spraker, Barbara J. Number of Faculty: total–full-time 10, part-time 4; women–full-time 4, part-time 4; minority–full-time 2, part-time 2.

Programs and Degrees Offered:

Listed in the following order: Program area, degree type (T if terminal Master's), number awarded 7/00–6/01. Art therapy post master's CT, art therapy/mental health MA (T), couple and family therapy MA (T) 24, human resource development MA (T) 13, individualized study MA (T) 5, mental health counseling MA (T) 48, Organizational Psychology MA 7.

Student Applications/Admissions:

Student Applications

Art therapy post master's CT—Applications 2001–2002, 20. Total applicants accepted 2001–2002, 2. New applicants enrolled 2001–2002, 2. Openings 2002–2003, 10. *Art therapy/mental health MA*—Applications 2001–2002, 25. Total applicants accepted 2001–2002, 10. New applicants enrolled 2001–2002, 10. Total enrolled 2001–2002 part-time, 19. Openings 2002–2003, 10. *Couple and family therapy MA*—Applications 2001–2002, 125. Total applicants accepted 2001–2002, 35. New applicants enrolled 2001–2002, 31. Total enrolled 2001–2002 full-time, 40, part-time, 38. Openings 2002–2003, 30. *Human resource development MA*—Applications 2001–2002, 35. Total applicants accepted 2001–2002, 15. New applicants enrolled 2001–2002, 13. Total enrolled 2001–2002 full-time, 21, part-time, 24. Openings 2002–2003, 20. *Individualized study MA*—Applications 2001–2002, 21. Total applicants accepted 2001–2002, 10. New applicants enrolled 2001–2002, 9. Total enrolled 2001–2002 full-time, 5, part-time, 22. Openings 2002–2003, 15. *Mental health counseling MA*—Applications 2001–2002, 360. Total applicants accepted 2001–2002, 49. New applicants enrolled 2001–2002, 48. Total enrolled 2001–2002 full-time, 65, part-time, 31. Openings 2002–2003, 50. *Organizational Psychology MA*—Total applicants accepted 2001–2002, 16. New applicants enrolled 2001–2002, 16. Total enrolled 2001–2002 full-time, 6, part-time, 33. Openings 2002–2003, 25. The Median number of years required for completion of a degree are 3. The number of students enrolled full and part-time, who were dismissed or voluntarily withdrew from this program area were 1.

Admissions Requirements:

Scores: Entries appear in this order: required test or GPA, minimum score (if required), median score of students entering in 2001–2002. Doctoral Programs: last 2 years GPA no mini-

mum stated; psychology GPA no minimum stated; psychology GPA no minimum stated.

Other Criteria: (importance of criteria rated low, medium, or high): work experience high, extracurricular activity high, GPA medium, letters of recommendation high, interview high, statement of goals and objectives high.

Student Characteristics: The following represents characteristics of students in 2001–2002 in all graduate psychology programs in the department: Female–full-time 3, part-time 30; Male–full-time 0, part-time 6; African American/Black–full-time 0, part-time 0; Hispanic/Latino (a)–full-time 0, part-time 1; Asian/Pacific Islander–full-time 0, part-time 5; American Indian/Alaska Native–full-time 0, part-time 1.

Financial Information/Assistance:

Tuition for Full-Time Study: *Master's:* State residents $380 per credit hour; nonstate residents: $380 per credit hour.

Financial Assistance:

First Year Students: No information provided.
Advanced Students: No information provided.
Contact Information: For information on financial assistance, contact: Financial Aid Office.

Internships/Practica: No information provided.

Housing and Day Care: No on-campus housing and day care facilities are available.

Employment of Department Graduates:

Master's Degree Graduates: Of those who graduated in the academic year 2000–2001, the following categories and numbers represent the post-graduate activities and employment of master's degree graduates: Enrolled in a post-doctoral residency/fellowship (n/a), employed in independent practice (n/a).

Doctoral Degree Graduates: Of those who graduated in the academic year 2000–2001, the following categories and numbers represent the post-graduate activities and employment of doctoral degree graduates: Enrolled in a psychology doctoral program (n/a), enrolled in another graduate/professional program (n/a).

Additional Information:

Orientation, Objectives, and Emphasis of Department: The Organizational Psychology Master of Arts Program at Antioch University Seattle prepares graduates to effectively contribute to creating and maintaining sustainable and effective organizations. Students develop psychological and systemic perspectives for working with individuals, teams, and organizations. The Program is for those who believe their personal development is central to supporting the development of others and to achieving organizational goals. Students gain the knowledge, skills, and confidence to assist organizations in managing the continual change required in a complex, rapidly changing world.

Special Facilities or Resources: The Organizational Psychology Program at Antioch University Seattle is part of The Antioch Center for Creative Change. This interdisciplinary center also includes Master's Degree Programs in Environment and Community, Management, and Whole Systems Design. Students have a unique opportunity for greater curricular offerings and participate in a capstone Reflective Practicum with students from each of the four programs. The richness of this diversity provides an enhanced educational experience of achieving the depth of an individual degree and the breadth of interdisciplinary context.

Application Information:
Send to: Admissions Department, 2326 6th Avenue, Seattle, WA 98121-1214. Students are admitted in the Fall, application deadline 6/12; Spring, application deadline 2/12. *Fee:* $150.

Argosy University, Washington School of Professional Psychology, Seattle
Clinical Psychology (MA & PsyD), Counseling (MA),
1019 8th Avenue, North
Seattle, WA 98109
Telephone: (206) 283-4500
Fax: (206) 283-5777
E-mail: *hsimpson@argosyu.edu*
Web: *http://www.argosyu.edu*

Department Established:
1995. Interum Program Director: F. Jeri Cater, PhD. Number of Faculty: total–full-time 6, part-time 9; women–full-time 4.

Programs and Degrees Offered:
Listed in the following order: Program area, degree type (T if terminal Master's), number awarded 7/00–6/01. Clinical Psychology PsyD 2, clinical psychology MA 6, Mental Health Counseling MA (T).

Student Applications/Admissions:
Student Applications
Clinical Psychology PsyD—Applications 2001–2002, 60. Total applicants accepted 2001–2002, 45. New applicants enrolled 2001–2002, 28. The Median number of years required for completion of a degree are 5. The number of students enrolled full and part-time, who were dismissed or voluntarily withdrew from this program area were 3. *Clinical psychology MA*—Applications 2001–2002, 21. Total applicants accepted 2001–2002, 14. New applicants enrolled 2001–2002, 7. Total enrolled 2001–2002 full-time, 7. The Median number of years required for completion of a degree are 2. *Mental Health Counseling MA*—Applications 2001–2002, 20. Total applicants accepted 2001–2002, 18. New applicants enrolled 2001–2002, 18. Total enrolled 2001–2002 full-time, 18. The Median number of years required for completion of a degree are 2. The number of students enrolled full and part-time, who were dismissed or voluntarily withdrew from this program area were 2.

Admissions Requirements:
Scores: Entries appear in this order: required test or GPA, minimum score (if required), median score of students entering in 2001–2002. Master's Programs: overall undergraduate GPA 3.0; last 2 years GPA 3.0. Minimum GPA for MA clinical psychology program is 3.00 from an accredited undergraduate/graduate program. Doctoral Programs: overall undergraduate GPA 3.25; last 2 years GPA 3.25; psychology GPA no minimum stated; psychology GPA no minimum stated. Minimum GPA for PsyD Psychology program is 3.25 from an accredited undergraduate/graduate program.

Other Criteria: (importance of criteria rated low, medium, or high): GRE/MAT scores low, research experience medium, work experience medium, extracurricular activity medium, clinically related public service high, GPA high, letters of recommendation high, interview high, statement of goals and objectives high. For the Master of Arts in Mental Health Counseling, work experience is not expected.

Student Characteristics: The following represents characteristics of students in 2001–2002 in all graduate psychology programs in the department: Female–full-time 85, Male–full-time 50, African American/Black–full-time 9, Hispanic/Latino (a)–full-time 6, Asian/Pacific Islander–full-time 6, American Indian/Alaska Native–full-time 2, Multi-ethnic–full-time 2.

Financial Information/Assistance:
Tuition for Full-Time Study: No information provided.

Financial Assistance:
First Year Students: No information provided.
Advanced Students: Teaching assistantships available for advanced students. Research assistantships available for advanced students.
Contact Information: For information on financial assistance, contact: Cindy Hsieh, Director of Student Services.

Internships/Practica: WSPP's current list of approved practicum sites for master's and doctoral level students includes state and community mental health facilities, state correctional facilities from minimum to maximum security, juvenile detention centers, outpatient clinics, private psychiatric hospitals, psychiatric units and community hospitals, treatment centers for developmentally disabled and behavior disordered, and chemical dependence treatment programs. We also have practicum placements in multicultural or diverse practicum settings, including mental health agencies serving Native Americans, Asian-Americans, and African-Americans. Local internships may involve the above sites. We are in the process of developing local internship consortia.

Housing and Day Care: No on-campus housing and day care facilities are available.

Employment of Department Graduates:
Master's Degree Graduates: Of those who graduated in the academic year 2000–2001, the following categories and numbers represent the post-graduate activities and employment of master's degree graduates: Enrolled in a psychology doctoral program (5), enrolled in another graduate/professional program (1), enrolled in a post-doctoral residency/fellowship (n/a), employed in independent practice (n/a).
Doctoral Degree Graduates: Of those who graduated in the academic year 2000–2001, the following categories and numbers represent the post-graduate activities and employment of doctoral degree graduates: Enrolled in a psychology doctoral program (n/a), enrolled in another graduate/professional program (n/a).

Additional Information:
Orientation, Objectives, and Emphasis of Department: The primary purpose of the program is to educate and train students in

the major aspects of clinical practice. To ensure that students are prepared adequately, the curriculum integrates theory, training, research, and practice, preparing students to work with a wide range of populations in need of psychological services and in a broad range of roles.

Information for Students With Physical Disabilities: WSPP has handicap access.

Application Information:

Send to: Admissions Department. Students are admitted in the Fall, application deadline April 15; Spring, application deadline November 1; Summer, application deadline March 1. Rolling Admissions. The above deadline dates are recommended dates. *Fee:* $50.

Central Washington University

Department of Psychology
College of the Sciences
400 E. 8th Avenue
Ellensburg, WA 98926-7575
Telephone: (509) 963-2381
Fax: (509) 963-2307
E-mail: *tolin@cwu.edu*
Web: *http://www.cwu.edu*

Department Established:

1965. Chairperson: Philip Tolin. Number of Faculty: total–full-time 22, part-time 1; women–full-time 7, part-time 1; minority–full-time 2.

Programs and Degrees Offered:

Listed in the following order: Program area, degree type (T if terminal Master's), number awarded 7/00–6/01. Counseling, experimental MA (T) 6, organizational development MA (T) 16, school counseling (T) 3, school psychology (T) 7.

Student Applications/Admissions:

Student Applications

Experimental MA—Applications 2001–2002, 12. Total applicants accepted 2001–2002, 6. New applicants enrolled 2001–2002, 6. Total enrolled 2001–2002 full-time, 16, part-time, 3. Openings 2002–2003, 10. The Median number of years required for completion of a degree are 2. *Organizational development MA*—Applications 2001–2002, 15. Total applicants accepted 2001–2002, 10. New applicants enrolled 2001–2002, 10. Total enrolled 2001–2002 full-time, 20, part-time, 2. Openings 2002–2003, 12. The Median number of years required for completion of a degree are 2.

Admissions Requirements:

Scores: Entries appear in this order: required test or GPA, minimum score (if required), median score of students entering in 2001–2002. Master's Programs: GRE-V 450; GRE-Q 450; GRE-V+Q 950; last 2 years GPA 3.00. Students applying to the Organizational Development program may submit either GRE or GMAT scores. Doctoral Programs: last 2 years GPA no minimum stated; psychology GPA no minimum stated; psychology GPA no minimum stated.

Other Criteria: (importance of criteria rated low, medium, or high): GRE/MAT scores medium, research experience medium, work experience medium, extracurricular activity low, clinically related public service medium, GPA high, letters of recommendation high, interview medium, statement of goals and objectives high. Interview for Organizational Development program only. No interviews required for other programs.

Student Characteristics: The following represents characteristics of students in 2001–2002 in all graduate psychology programs in the department: Female–full-time 46, part-time 6; Male–full-time 25, part-time 4; African American/Black–full-time 3, part-time 0; Hispanic/Latino (a)–full-time 4, part-time 0; Asian/Pacific Islander–full-time 1, part-time 0; American Indian/Alaska Native–full-time 1, part-time 0; Multi-ethnic–full-time 0, part-time 0; students subject to the Americans with Disabilities Act–full-time 0, part-time 0.

Financial Information/Assistance:

Tuition for Full-Time Study: *Master's:* State residents per academic year $4,848; nonstate residents: per academic year $14,772.

Financial Assistance:

First Year Students: Teaching assistantships available for first-year. Average amount paid per academic year: $7,120. Average number of hours worked per week: 20. Apply by Feb 1. Tuition remission given: full and partial. Research assistantships available for first-year. Average amount paid per academic year: $7,120. Average number of hours worked per week: 20. Apply by Feb 1. Tuition remission given: full and partial.

Advanced Students: Teaching assistantships available for advanced students. Average amount paid per academic year: $7,120. Average number of hours worked per week: 20. Apply by Feb 1. Tuition remission given: full and partial. Research assistantships available for advanced students. Average amount paid per academic year: $7,120. Average number of hours worked per week: 20. Apply by Feb 1. Tuition remission given: full and partial.

Contact Information: Of all students currently enrolled full-time, 30% benefited from one or more of the listed financial assistance programs. For information on financial assistance, contact: Office of Graduate Studies and Research; Financial Aid Office.

Internships/Practica: Counseling Psychology and School Counseling Psychology Program required practica/internship: Introductory Practicum in Counseling, Practicum in Counseling: Treatment Goals and Planning, Advanced Practicum in Counseling I and II, Group Counseling, Counseling Internship. School Psychology Program required practica/internship: Introductory Practicum in Counseling, Practicum in Counseling: Treatment Goals and Planning.

Housing and Day Care: On-campus housing and day care facilities are available.

Employment of Department Graduates:

Master's Degree Graduates: Of those who graduated in the academic year 2000–2001, the following categories and numbers represent the post-graduate activities and employment of master's degree graduates: Enrolled in a psychology doctoral program (4), enrolled in a post-doctoral residency/fellowship (n/a), employed in independent practice (n/a), employed in a professional position in a school system (8), employed in business or industry (management) (15), employed in a government agency (professional services) (5), employed in a community mental health/counseling center (6).

Doctoral Degree Graduates: Of those who graduated in the academic year 2000–2001, the following categories and numbers represent the post-graduate activities and employment of doctoral degree graduates: Enrolled in a psychology doctoral program (n/a), enrolled in another graduate/professional program (n/a).

Additional Information:

Orientation, Objectives, and Emphasis of Department: The objectives of the degree programs include one or both of the following: to prepare students for professional employment in a variety of settings including mental health agencies, public schools, community colleges, business, or industry and to prepare students for university study leading to a doctorate. The programs feature intense supervision in the practica and internships and in research activities.

Special Facilities or Resources: Special facilities or resources are a counseling and testing community services center; animal research laboratories, including a laboratory for the study of language learning in chimpanzees; a human behavior laboratory; a computer lab; and a complete mechanical and electrical instrumentation services center.

Application Information:
Send to: Office of Graduate Studies and Research, Central Washington University, Ellensburg, WA 98926. Students are admitted in the Fall, application deadline June 1; Winter, application deadline June 1. Winter and spring admission possible for Experimental Psychology program. Admissions may close earlier depending on available space. Winter admission is rare and is contingent upon openings. *Fee:* $35. Application fee may be waived by demonstration of financial need.

Eastern Washington University
Department of Psychology-MS94
College Social and Behavioral Sciences
526 5th Street
Cheney, WA 99004
Telephone: (509) 359-2478
Fax: (509) 359-6325
E-mail: *tmartin@mail.ewu.edu*
Web: *http://www.class.ewu.edu/class/PSYCH/programs.html*

Department Established:
1934. Chairperson: Mahlon B. Dalley. Number of Faculty: total–full-time 12, part-time 2; women–full-time 3.

Programs and Degrees Offered:
Listed in the following order: Program area, degree type (T if terminal Master's), number awarded 7/00–6/01. Clinical MA (T) 12, Experimental/general MA (T) 1, P-Masters Sch Psy Cert 8, School Psychology MA (T) 1.

Student Applications/Admissions:
Student Applications
Clinical MA—Applications 2001–2002, 30. Total applicants accepted 2001–2002, 12. New applicants enrolled 2001–2002, 12. Total enrolled 2001–2002 full-time, 28. Openings 2002–2003, 12. The Median number of years required for completion of a degree are 2. The number of students enrolled full and part-time, who were dismissed or voluntarily withdrew from this program area were 0. *Experimental/general MA*—Applications 2001–2002, 5. Total applicants accepted 2001–2002, 2. New applicants enrolled 2001–2002, 2. Total enrolled 2001–2002 full-time, 3. Openings 2002–2003, 3. The Median number of years required for completion of a degree are 2. The number of students enrolled full and part-time, who were dismissed or voluntarily withdrew from this program area were 0. *School Psychology MA*—Applications 2001–2002, 30. Total applicants accepted 2001–2002, 14. New applicants enrolled 2001–2002, 14. Total enrolled 2001–2002 full-time, 27. Openings 2002–2003, 12. The Median number of years required for completion of a degree are 3. The number of students enrolled full and part-time, who were dismissed or voluntarily withdrew from this program area were 1.

Admissions Requirements:
Scores: Entries appear in this order: required test or GPA, minimum score (if required), median score of students entering in 2001–2002. Master's Programs: GRE-V+Q+Analytical no minimum stated, 1590; last 2 years GPA 3.0, 3.59; psychology GPA 3.0, 3.59. Doctoral Programs: last 2 years GPA no minimum stated; psychology GPA no minimum stated; psychology GPA no minimum stated.

Other Criteria: (importance of criteria rated low, medium, or high): GRE/MAT scores high, research experience high, work experience medium, extracurricular activity low, clinically related public service medium, GPA high, letters of recommendation medium, statement of goals and objectives high.

Student Characteristics: The following represents characteristics of students in 2001–2002 in all graduate psychology programs in the department: Female–full-time 16, part-time 0; Male–full-time 10, part-time 0; African American/Black–full-time 1, part-time 0; Hispanic/Latino (a)–full-time 0, part-time 0; Asian/Pacific Islander–full-time 1, part-time 0; American Indian/Alaska Native–full-time 0, part-time 0.

Financial Information/Assistance:
Tuition for Full-Time Study: *Master's:* State residents per academic year $5,277, $168 per credit hour; nonstate residents: per academic year $15,135, $497 per credit hour.

Financial Assistance:
First Year Students: Research assistantships available for first-year. Average number of hours worked per week: 20. Apply by Feb. 15. Tuition remission given: partial. Fellowships and scholarships available for first-year. Apply by Feb. 15. Tuition remission given: full and partial.

Advanced Students: No information provided.

Contact Information: Of all students currently enrolled full-time, 20% benefited from one or more of the listed financial assistance programs. For information on financial assistance, contact: Financial Aid Office, MS 142, Eastern WA University, 526-5th Street, Cheney, WA 99004-2431.

Internships/Practica: Students pursuing the clinical and school psychology options have training opportunities at both on- and off-campus facilities which include the Psychological Counseling Services, the Spokane Community Mental Health Center, Sacred Heart Hospital, and Eastern State Hospital.

Housing and Day Care: On-campus housing and day care facilities are available.

Employment of Department Graduates:

Master's Degree Graduates: Of those who graduated in the academic year 2000–2001, the following categories and numbers represent the post-graduate activities and employment of master's degree graduates: Enrolled in a post-doctoral residency/fellowship (n/a), employed in independent practice (n/a).

Doctoral Degree Graduates: Of those who graduated in the academic year 2000–2001, the following categories and numbers represent the post-graduate activities and employment of doctoral degree graduates: Enrolled in a psychology doctoral program (n/a), enrolled in another graduate/professional program (n/a).

Additional Information:

Orientation, Objectives, and Emphasis of Department: Three areas of specialization in the Department of Psychology are general-experimental, clinical, and school psychology. About one-third of those receiving the master of science degree pursue doctoral work. The remainder seek careers as school psychologists, college teachers, psychological examiners, research workers, and institutional and community mental health therapists.

Special Facilities or Resources: Students pursuing the experimental psychology option receive training and research experience, in one of several well-equipped laboratories on campus. Additional facilities are available for laboratory work in memory and cognition, and human psychophysiology research.

Information for Students With Physical Disabilities: Facilities are equipped to be accessible for people with disabilities.

Application Information:

Send to: Admissions Chairperson, Eastern WA University, 151 Martin, 526 5th St., Cheney, WA 99004-2431. Students are admitted in the Fall, application deadline February 15. Application deadlines for the School Psychology programs are March 1. *Fee:* $35.

Gonzaga University
Department of Counselor Education
School of Education
East 501 Boone Avenue
Spokane, WA 99258-0001
Telephone: (509) 323-3512
Fax: (509) 323-5964
E-mail: *ebennett@soe.gonzaga.edu*
Web: *http://www.gonzaga.edu*

Department Established:

1960. Chairperson: Lisa Bennett. Number of Faculty: total–full-time 4, part-time 12; women–full-time 2, part-time 6.

Programs and Degrees Offered:

Listed in the following order: Program area, degree type (T if terminal Master's), number awarded 7/00–6/01. Counseling psychology, communi MA (T) 15, school counseling.

Student Applications/Admissions:
Student Applications

Counseling psychology, communi MA—Applications 2001–2002, 45. Total applicants accepted 2001–2002, 20. New applicants enrolled 2001–2002, 20. Total enrolled 2001–2002 full-time, 20, part-time, 5. Openings 2002–2003, 15. The number of students enrolled full and part-time, who were dismissed or voluntarily withdrew from this program area were 1.

Admissions Requirements:

Scores: Entries appear in this order: required test or GPA, minimum score (if required), median score of students entering in 2001–2002. Master's Programs: GRE-V+Q+Analytical no minimum stated; MAT no minimum stated; overall undergraduate GPA 3.0. Either MAT or GRE is required. Doctoral Programs: last 2 years GPA no minimum stated; psychology GPA no minimum stated; psychology GPA no minimum stated.

Other Criteria: (importance of criteria rated low, medium, or high): GRE/MAT scores medium, work experience medium, extracurricular activity medium, clinically related public service medium, GPA medium, letters of recommendation high, interview high, statement of goals and objectives high, Fit to the mission of GU high.

Student Characteristics: The following represents characteristics of students in 2001–2002 in all graduate psychology programs in the department: Female–full-time 28, part-time 3; Male–full-time 8, part-time 2; African American/Black–full-time 1, part-time 0; Hispanic/Latino (a)–full-time 1, part-time 0; Asian/Pacific Islander–full-time 1, part-time 0; American Indian/Alaska Native–full-time 0, part-time 0; students subject to the Americans with Disabilities Act–full-time 1.

Financial Information/Assistance:

Tuition for Full-Time Study: *Master's:* State residents $495 per credit hour; nonstate residents: $495 per credit hour.

Financial Assistance:

First Year Students: Teaching assistantships available for first-year. Average number of hours worked per week: 4. Tuition remission given: partial. Research assistantships available for first-year. Average number of hours worked per week: 4. Tuition remission given: partial.

Advanced Students: Teaching assistantships available for advanced students. Average number of hours worked per week: 4. Tuition remission given: partial. Research assistantships available for advanced students. Average number of hours worked per week: 4. Tuition remission given: partial.

Contact Information: Of all students currently enrolled full-time, 37% benefited from one or more of the listed financial

assistance programs. For information on financial assistance, contact: Campus Financial Aid.

Internships/Practica: Students complete a 100 hour practicum and a 600 hour internship at a site chosen by the student to meet his or her professional interests. School track students currently are placed in schools at elementary, junior high, high school, and alternative settings. Agency track students are placed at sites including but not limited to geriatric, hospital, community mental health, adolescent, marriage and family, child, community college, career, and life-skills settings. A strong reputation within our community has afforded students to select quality placements.

Housing and Day Care: No on-campus housing and day care facilities are available.

Employment of Department Graduates:

Master's Degree Graduates: Of those who graduated in the academic year 2000–2001, the following categories and numbers represent the post-graduate activities and employment of master's degree graduates: Enrolled in a psychology doctoral program (3), enrolled in a post-doctoral residency/fellowship (n/a), employed in independent practice (n/a), employed in other positions at a higher education institution (1), employed in a professional position in a school system (6), employed in a community mental health/counseling center (5), employed in a hospital/medical center (1), other employment position (1).

Doctoral Degree Graduates: Of those who graduated in the academic year 2000–2001, the following categories and numbers represent the post-graduate activities and employment of doctoral degree graduates: Enrolled in a psychology doctoral program (n/a), enrolled in another graduate/professional program (n/a).

Additional Information:

Orientation, Objectives, and Emphasis of Department: The philosophical theme running throughout the university is humanism. A realistic, balanced attitude is a necessary prerequisite for assisting others professionally. Careful selection of students helps to insure the inclusion of healthy individuals with the highest potential for success, as does faculty modeling, encouragement of trust, and communication of clear expectations. Indicators of counselor success are demonstration of skills and conflict resolution, consistent interpersonal behaviors, recognition of strengths and weaknesses, a clear grasp of goals, and self-knowledge of one's impact on others, as well as a strong academic performance. Acquisition of counseling competence comes through both personal and professional growth. Immersion in an intensive course of study with a closely linked group of peers encourages open and honest processing, which, in turn, contributes to personal growth. The department believes that students must possess insight and awareness, and clarity about the boundaries between their personal issues and those of the client. Students training to become professionals must be treated as professionals. Faculty practice collegiality with students, maintain high standards of performance, and furnish an atmosphere of professionalism. Students share cases, exchanging professional advice and input. In addition to the presentation of major theories of counseling, students must develop a personal theory of counseling and demonstrate competence in its use. Faculty are humanistic, but eclectic, disseminating information about effective techniques without imposing any one approach on the students. Students are closely observed in the classroom, practicum, and internship and receive critical monitoring and evaluation from faculty, field supervisor, and peers.

Special Facilities or Resources: The Department of Counselor Education is proud to offer a modern and complete clinic training center, with two group rooms and two individual rooms. The clinic has two-way glass, and is equipped with audio-video technological equipment which can be operated in the clinic room by either the student (for taping and reviewing personal work) or by any department faculty member from faculty offices (for viewing and/or taping).

Information for Students With Physical Disabilities: Gonzaga makes every effort to accommodate students with physical difficulties. All courses are scheduled in accessible buildings. Classrooms are arranged to accommodate the student needs.

Application Information:

Send to: Graduate School, Ad Box 29, Gonzaga University, 502 East Boone, Spokane, WA 99258. Students are admitted in the Fall, application deadline March 1. Other enrollments accepted temporarily as non-matriculation (until fall deadline). Students may also seek admission on a part-time bases. *Fee:* $40.

Puget Sound, University of
School of Education
1500 North Warner
Tacoma, WA 98416
Telephone: (253) 879-3375
Fax: (253) 879-3926
E-mail: *kirchner@ups.edu*
Web: *http://www.ups.edu*

Department Established:

Director: Grace L. Kirchner. Number of Faculty: total–full-time 2, part-time 3; women–full-time 2, part-time 1.

Programs and Degrees Offered:

Listed in the following order: Program area, degree type (T if terminal Master's), number awarded 7/00–6/01. Agency counseling (T) 6, pastoral counseling (T) 3, school counseling (T) 6.

Student Applications/Admissions:

Admissions Requirements:

Scores: Entries appear in this order: required test or GPA, minimum score (if required), median score of students entering in 2001–2002. Master's Programs: GRE-V no minimum stated; GRE-Q no minimum stated; GRE-Analytical no minimum stated; overall undergraduate GPA no minimum stated. Doctoral Programs: last 2 years GPA no minimum stated; psychology GPA no minimum stated; psychology GPA no minimum stated.

Other Criteria: (importance of criteria rated low, medium, or high): GRE/MAT scores medium, work experience medium, extracurricular activity low, clinically related public service medium, GPA medium, letters of recommendation medium, interview high, statement of goals and objectives medium.

Student Characteristics: The following represents characteristics of students in 2001–2002 in all graduate psychology programs in the department: part-time 25; part-time 5; part-time 2.

Financial Information/Assistance:

Tuition for Full-Time Study: *Master's:* State residents $325 per credit hour; nonstate residents: $325 per credit hour.

Financial Assistance:

First Year Students: No information provided.

Advanced Students: No information provided.

Contact Information: For information on financial assistance, contact: Office of Financial Aid.

Internships/Practica: No information provided.

Housing and Day Care: No on-campus housing and day care facilities are available.

Employment of Department Graduates:

Master's Degree Graduates: Of those who graduated in the academic year 2000–2001, the following categories and numbers represent the post-graduate activities and employment of master's degree graduates: Enrolled in a psychology doctoral program (0), enrolled in another graduate/professional program (0), enrolled in a post-doctoral residency/fellowship (n/a), employed in independent practice (n/a), employed in an academic position at a university (0), employed in an academic position at a 2-year/4-year college (0), employed in other positions at a higher education institution (0), employed in a professional position in a school system (10), employed in business or industry (research/consulting) (0), employed in business or industry (management) (0), employed in a government agency (research) (0), employed in a government agency (professional services) (0), employed in a community mental health/counseling center (3), employed in a hospital/medical center (0), still seeking employment (2), other employment position (0).

Doctoral Degree Graduates: Of those who graduated in the academic year 2000–2001, the following categories and numbers represent the post-graduate activities and employment of doctoral degree graduates: Enrolled in a psychology doctoral program (n/a), enrolled in another graduate/professional program (n/a).

Additional Information:

Orientation, Objectives, and Emphasis of Department: We are housed in the School of Education and our primary mission is to train school counselors; however, many of our graduates find employment in social service settings. We also have a small pastoral counseling program.

Application Information:
Send to: Office of Admission. Students are admitted in the Spring, application deadline March 1. *Fee:* $65. $25 if previously admitted to university.

Seattle Pacific University

Department of Graduate Psychology
School of Psychology, Family and Community
3307 Third Avenue, West
Seattle, WA 98119
Telephone: (206) 281-2987
Fax: (206) 281-2695
E-mail: *marmol@spu.edu*
Web: *http://www.spu.ed/depts/grad~psych*

Department Established:
1995. Chairperson: Leonardo Marmol, PhD. Number of Faculty: total–full-time 10, part-time 8; women–full-time 3, part-time 3; minority–full-time 1, part-time 1.

Programs and Degrees Offered:
Listed in the following order: Program area, degree type (T if terminal Master's), number awarded 7/00–6/01. Clinical family psych PsyD 1, Clinical psychology PhD 15.

Student Applications/Admissions:

Student Applications

Clinical family psych PsyD—Applications 2001–2002, 0. Total enrolled 2001–2002 full-time, 2. *Clinical psychology PhD*—Applications 2001–2002, 56. Total applicants accepted 2001–2002, 46. New applicants enrolled 2001–2002, 22. Total enrolled 2001–2002 full-time, 82, part-time, 23. Openings 2002–2003, 22. The Median number of years required for completion of a degree are 5.

Admissions Requirements:

Scores: Entries appear in this order: required test or GPA, minimum score (if required), median score of students entering in 2001–2002. Doctoral Programs: GRE-V+Q 1100, 1070; MAT 50, 54; overall undergraduate GPA 3.25, 3.25; last 2 years GPA no minimum stated; psychology GPA no minimum stated; psychology GPA 3.25, 3.68. Require either MAT or GRE V&Q, not both.

Other Criteria: (importance of criteria rated low, medium, or high): GRE/MAT scores high, research experience medium, work experience medium, extracurricular activity low, clinically related public service medium, GPA high, letters of recommendation high, interview high, statement of goals and objectives high.

Student Characteristics: The following represents characteristics of students in 2001–2002 in all graduate psychology programs in the department: Female–full-time 67, part-time 19; Male–full-time 17, part-time 14; African American/Black–full-time 5, part-time 1; Hispanic/Latino (a)–full-time 5, part-time 1; Asian/Pacific Islander–full-time 3, part-time 1; American Indian/Alaska Native–full-time 2, part-time 0; Multi-ethnic–full-time 0, part-time 0; students subject to the Americans with Disabilities Act–full-time 0, part-time 0.

Financial Information/Assistance:

Tuition for Full-Time Study: *Doctoral:* State residents: $437 per credit hour; nonstate residents: $437 per credit hour.

Financial Assistance:

First Year Students: No information provided.

Advanced Students: Average amount paid per academic year: $2,920. Average number of hours worked per week: 10. Average amount paid per academic year: $2,920. Average number of hours worked per week: 10.

Contact Information: Of all students currently enrolled full-time, 12% benefited from one or more of the listed financial assistance programs. For information on financial assistance, contact: Financial Aid, 206-281-2061. For assistantships, contact Marie Van Norman Baleat, 206-281-2839.

Internships/Practica: Students complete a practicum experience of six to eight academic quarters, consisting of a minimum of 1000 hours of direct experience and 100 hours of supervision. The first year of pre-practicum is a lab experience offered in the University Counseling Center. All practica focus on intake, assessment, diagnostic skills, crisis intervention, and supervision. The second, third, and fourth years of practica could be at the University Counseling Center or one of SPU's off campus sites. Students can expect to spend 10–12 hours per week after the first year of the program at an agency. Pre-doctoral internships with stipend are available at the University Counseling Center Consortium, but most students utilize outside APA/APPIC approved sites for their internships. Appropriate internships generally are found in mental health agencies and institutions, hospitals, or other not-for-profit organizations which serve a broad constituency, and utilize psychologists in a variety of professional roles. The program requires a 2000-hour internship to be completed in 12 to 24 months. At least fifty per cent of the intern's time shall be spent in direct client contact, providing assessment and intervention services. For those doctoral students for whom a professional internship is required prior to graduation, 8 applied in 2000–2001. Of those who applied, 1 were placed in internships listed by the Association of Psychology Postdoctoral and Internship Programs (APPIC).

Housing and Day Care: No on-campus housing and day care facilities are available.

Employment of Department Graduates:

Master's Degree Graduates: Of those who graduated in the academic year 2000–2001, the following categories and numbers represent the post-graduate activities and employment of master's degree graduates: Enrolled in a post-doctoral residency/fellowship (n/a), employed in independent practice (n/a).

Doctoral Degree Graduates: Of those who graduated in the academic year 2000–2001, the following categories and numbers represent the post-graduate activities and employment of doctoral degree graduates: Enrolled in a psychology doctoral program (n/a), enrolled in another graduate/professional program (n/a), enrolled in a post-doctoral residency/fellowship (2), employed in independent practice (10), employed in a community mental health/counseling center (3).

Additional Information:

Orientation, Objectives, and Emphasis of Department: The doctorate of philosophy (PhD) in clinical psychology at SPU is designed to train psychologists whose clinical emphasis is the biopsychosocial assessment and treatment of persons. The goal of the program is to prepare doctoral students in the core knowledge and skills of an ecologically informed clinical psychology. The curriculum is based on the foundational scientific bases of the science of psychology. The training model is that of the local clinical-scientist. This model honors research and practice in equal proportions. After a basic foundation on the biological, cognitive, social, and historical bases of the discipline, the student is able to select a concentration area of study during the last two years on campus. These areas reflect a biopsychosocial orientation, such as health psychology, family and child psychology, and advanced clinical emphasis. All areas of the curriculum are consistent with the program's Christian and ecological foundations and are practical and relevant to the contemporary practice of clinical psychology. Multiculturalism and issues of diversity are infused throughout all courses in the curriculum. The program is a full-time, 5-year integrated and organized sequence of studies and practice experiences following the local clinical-scientist model. The capstone of the program is a full-time (2000 hours) clinical internship and the completion of an original research based dissertation. Our graduates will be capable of engaging the culture and changing the world. They will be able to function competently as researchers, psychotherapists, academics, and supervisors.

Special Facilities or Resources: In addition to the SPU library, our students have access to the Orbis system of interlibrary loans and the University of Washington libraries. We also have a lab dedicated to research with state-of-the-art computer and SPSS software. There are three functioning labs. One lab is dedicated to research in the area of child/adolescent behavior and is equipped with audio/visual equipment, computers, play therapy, and other materials used in observing, tracking, and coding children's behavior. There is also a social psychology lab and a neurophysiology lab with proper equipment for each.

Information for Students With Physical Disabilities: The University offers a variety of services for students with disabilities. Our Academic Support center coordinates services for students with learning and physical disabilities to promote academic and co-curricular program accommodations. Specifically, the department of Graduate Psychology at SPU is located in a building that is fully accessible to individuals with physical disabilities. All of our courses are also held in buildings with easy access to those with physical disabilities.

Application Information:
Send to: Program Coordinator, Graduate Psychology Department. Students are admitted in the Fall, application deadline 2/1/2003. *Fee:* $75.

Seattle University (2001 data)
Graduate Psychology Program
Arts and Sciences
900 Broadway
Seattle, WA 98122-4460
Telephone: (206) 296-5400
Fax: (206) 296-2141
E-mail: *gradpsyc@seattleu.edu*
Web: *http://www.seattleu.edu*

Department Established:

1981. Chairperson: Lane Gerber, PhD. Number of Faculty: total–full-time 6, part-time 2; women–full-time 2, part-time 1.

Programs and Degrees Offered:
Listed in the following order: Program area, degree type (T if terminal Master's), number awarded 7/00–6/01. Existential-phenomenological MA (T) 14.

Student Applications/Admissions:
Student Applications
Existential-phenomenological MA—Applications 2001–2002, 60. Total applicants accepted 2001–2002, 22. New applicants enrolled 2001–2002, 17. Total enrolled 2001–2002 full-time, 32, part-time, 1. Openings 2002–2003, 19. The Median number of years required for completion of a degree are 2. The number of students enrolled full and part-time, who were dismissed or voluntarily withdrew from this program area were 0.

Admissions Requirements:
Scores: Entries appear in this order: required test or GPA, minimum score (if required), median score of students entering in 2001–2002. Master's Programs: overall undergraduate GPA no minimum stated. Overall Undergraduate GPA 3.0
Other Criteria: (importance of criteria rated low, medium, or high): research experience medium, work experience high, extracurricular activity medium, clinically related public service high, GPA medium, letters of recommendation medium, interview high, Autobiographical Statemen high. Other: Some awareness of existential-phenomenological perspective.

Student Characteristics: The following represents characteristics of students in 2001–2002 in all graduate psychology programs in the department: Female–full-time 11, part-time 1; Male–full-time 7, part-time 0; African American/Black–full-time 0, part-time 0; Hispanic/Latino (a)–full-time 2, part-time 0; Asian/Pacific Islander–full-time 2, part-time 0; American Indian/Alaska Native–full-time 0, part-time 0.

Financial Information/Assistance:
Tuition for Full-Time Study: No information provided.

Financial Assistance:
First Year Students: No information provided.
Advanced Students: No information provided.
Contact Information: Of all students currently enrolled full-time, 0% benefited from one or more of the listed financial assistance programs. For information on financial assistance, contact: Financial Aid, (206) 296-5840.

Internships/Practica: A variety of supervised internships (typically about 20 hrs/week during second year) in a wide variety of community agencies, hospitals, shelters, and clinics.

Housing and Day Care: No on-campus housing and day care facilities are available.

Employment of Department Graduates:
Master's Degree Graduates: Of those who graduated in the academic year 2000–2001, the following categories and numbers represent the post-graduate activities and employment of master's degree graduates: Enrolled in a post-doctoral residency/fellowship (n/a), employed in independent practice (n/a).
Doctoral Degree Graduates: Of those who graduated in the academic year 2000–2001, the following categories and numbers

represent the post-graduate activities and employment of doctoral degree graduates: Enrolled in a psychology doctoral program (n/a), enrolled in another graduate/professional program (n/a).

Additional Information:
Orientation, Objectives, and Emphasis of Department: With an emphasis on existential-phenomenological psychology, this master's degree is designed to offer an interdisciplinary program focusing on the qualitative, experiential study of psychological events in the context of life. By laying the foundations for a therapeutic attitude, the program will prepare for entrance into the helping professions or for further study of the psychological world. It is humanistic in that it intends to deepen the appreciation for the human condition by rigorous reflection on immediate psychological experiences and on the wisdom accumulated by the long tradition of the humanities. It is phenomenological in that it develops an attitude of openness and wonder toward psychological reality without holding theoretical prejudgments. It is therapeutic in that it focuses on the psychological conditions that help people deal with the difficulties of life.

Information for Students With Physical Disabilities: Our campus is wheelchair accessible.

Application Information:
Send to: (1) Graduate Admissions Office, Seattle University, 900 Broadway, Seattle, WA 98122, and some material goes to, (2) Graduate Psychology, Seattle University, 900 Broadway, Seattle, WA 98122. Students are admitted in the Fall, application deadline February 1. *Fee:* $55.

Washington State University (2001 data)
Department of Psychology
P.O. Box 644820
Pullman, WA 99164-4820
Telephone: (509) 335-2631
Fax: (509) 335-5043
E-mail: *psych@wsu.edu*

Department Established:
Chairperson: Paul Whitney. Number of Faculty: total–full-time 29, part-time 6; women–full-time 10, part-time 4; minority–full-time 2, part-time 2.

Programs and Degrees Offered:
Listed in the following order: Program area, degree type (T if terminal Master's), number awarded 7/00–6/01. Clinical PhD 6, experimental PhD 5.

APA Accreditation: Clinical PhD: full.

Student Applications/Admissions:
Student Applications
Clinical PhD—Applications 2001–2002, 138. Total applicants accepted 2001–2002, 5. New applicants enrolled 2001–2002, 5. Total enrolled 2001–2002 full-time, 22, part-time, 5. Openings 2002–2003, 6. The Median number of years required for completion of a degree are 4. The number of students enrolled

full and part-time, who were dismissed or voluntarily withdrew from this program area were 1. *Experimental PhD*—Applications 2001–2002, 16. Total applicants accepted 2001–2002, 5. New applicants enrolled 2001–2002, 4. Total enrolled 2001–2002 full-time, 23. Openings 2002–2003, 5. The Median number of years required for completion of a degree are 5. The number of students enrolled full and part-time, who were dismissed or voluntarily withdrew from this program area were 1.

Admissions Requirements:

Scores: Entries appear in this order: required test or GPA, minimum score (if required), median score of students entering in 2001–2002. Doctoral Programs: GRE-V no minimum stated, 540; GRE-Q no minimum stated, 655; GRE-V+Q no minimum stated, 1195; overall undergraduate GPA no minimum stated, 3.52.

Other Criteria: (importance of criteria rated low, medium, or high): GRE/MAT scores medium, research experience high, work experience low, extracurricular activity low, clinically related public service high, GPA high, letters of recommendation high, statement of goals and objectives high, Psychology GPA medium.

Student Characteristics: The following represents characteristics of students in 2001–2002 in all graduate psychology programs in the department: Female–full-time 6, part-time 0; Male–full-time 3, part-time 0; African American/Black–full-time 0, part-time 0; Hispanic/Latino (a)–full-time 0, part-time 0; Asian/Pacific Islander–full-time 0, part-time 0; American Indian/Alaska Native–full-time 0, part-time 0.

Financial Information/Assistance:

Tuition for Full-Time Study: No information provided.

Financial Assistance:

First Year Students: No information provided.
Advanced Students: No information provided.
Contact Information: Of all students currently enrolled full-time, 96% benefited from one or more of the listed financial assistance programs. For information on financial assistance, contact: Financial Aid Office, Graduate School.

Internships/Practica: Psychology Clinic Practicum; Counseling Services Practicum; Medical Psychology Practicum at University Hospital. For those doctoral students for whom a professional internship is required prior to graduation, 7 applied in 2000–2001. Of those who applied, 5 were placed in APA accredited internships.

Housing and Day Care: No on-campus housing and day care facilities are available.

Employment of Department Graduates:

Master's Degree Graduates: Of those who graduated in the academic year 2000–2001, the following categories and numbers represent the post-graduate activities and employment of master's degree graduates: Enrolled in a post-doctoral residency/fellowship (n/a), employed in independent practice (n/a).

Doctoral Degree Graduates: Of those who graduated in the academic year 2000–2001, the following categories and numbers represent the post-graduate activities and employment of doctoral degree graduates: Enrolled in a psychology doctoral program (n/a), enrolled in another graduate/professional program (n/a).

Additional Information:

Orientation, Objectives, and Emphasis of Department: The objectives of the graduate programs are to prepare individuals to make contributions and hold leadership positions in basic and applied research, teaching, clinical psychology, public service, or some combination of these areas. The clinical program is a broad, general one requiring student commitment to both research and clinical work. The emphases within the experimental program are cognitive, behavior analysis, physiological psychology, sensation and perception, and applied psychology.

Special Facilities or Resources: The Department of Psychology is located in Johnson Tower, near the center of campus. Fully equipped laboratories and shop facilities are available for research in cognition, perception, human and animal learning, the experimental and applied analysis of behavior, and physiological and sensory psychology. The Psychology Clinic is operated as a training facility within the department.

Application Information:

Send to: Graduate Admissions, Attn: Chair, Graduate Admissions Committee, Psychology Department, Washington State University, P.O. Box 644820, Pullman, WA 99164-4820. Students are admitted in the Fall, application deadline January 1. *Fee:* $35.

Washington State University (2001 data)
Educational Leadership and Counseling Psychology
College of Education
P.O. Box 642136
Pullman, WA 99164-2136
Telephone: (509) 335-7016
Fax: (509) 335-7977
E-mail: *counseling_psychology@wsu.edu*
Web: *http://www.educ.wsu.edu/elcp/counseling_Psych/inde*

Department Established:

1985. Associate Chairperson: Brian McNeill. Number of Faculty: total–full-time 9, part-time 2; women–full-time 3, part-time 2; minority–full-time 2.

Programs and Degrees Offered:

Listed in the following order: Program area, degree type (T if terminal Master's), number awarded 7/00–6/01. Counseling MA (T) 8, counseling psychology PhD 5, educational psychology PhD 3.

APA Accreditation: Counseling PhD: full.

Student Applications/Admissions:

Student Applications

Counseling MA—Applications 2001–2002, 40. Total applicants accepted 2001–2002, 20. New applicants enrolled 2001–2002, 9. Total enrolled 2001–2002 full-time, 32, part-time, 20. Openings 2002–2003, 4. *Counseling psychology PhD*—Applications 2001–2002, 125. Total applicants accepted 2001–

2002, 12. New applicants enrolled 2001–2002, 6. Total enrolled 2001–2002 full-time, 34. Openings 2002–2003, 6. *Educational psychology PhD*—Applications 2001–2002, 7. Total applicants accepted 2001–2002, 7. New applicants enrolled 2001–2002, 5. Total enrolled 2001–2002 full-time, 12. Openings 2002–2003, 5.

Admissions Requirements:
Scores: Entries appear in this order: required test or GPA, minimum score (if required), median score of students entering in 2001–2002. Master's Programs: GRE-V no minimum stated; GRE-Q no minimum stated; GRE-V+Q no minimum stated; GRE-Analytical no minimum stated; GRE-V+Q+Analytical no minimum stated; overall undergraduate GPA 3.0; last 2 years GPA 3.0; psychology GPA 3.0. Different scores/GPAs required for different program areas. Doctoral Programs: GRE-V no minimum stated, 520; GRE-Q no minimum stated, 530; GRE-V+Q no minimum stated; GRE-Analytical no minimum stated; GRE-V+Q+Analytical no minimum stated; overall undergraduate GPA 3.0, 3.35; last 2 years GPA 3.0; psychology GPA 3.0, 3.84.
Other Criteria: (importance of criteria rated low, medium, or high): GRE/MAT scores medium, research experience high, work experience high, extracurricular activity medium, clinically related public service medium, GPA high, letters of recommendation high, statement of goals and objectives high.

Student Characteristics: The following represents characteristics of students in 2001–2002 in all graduate psychology programs in the department: Female–full-time 17, part-time 0; Male–full-time 8, part-time 0; African American/Black–full-time 2, part-time 0; Hispanic/Latino (a)–full-time 2, part-time 0; Asian/Pacific Islander–full-time 2, part-time 0; American Indian/Alaska Native–full-time 2, part-time 0.

Financial Information/Assistance:
Tuition for Full-Time Study: No information provided.

Financial Assistance:
First Year Students: No information provided.
Advanced Students: No information provided.
Contact Information: Of all students currently enrolled full-time, 0% benefited from one or more of the listed financial assistance programs.

Internships/Practica: Students obtain internships and practica in a variety of on campus placements (e.g., University Counseling Service) and off campus (e.g., Community Mental Health Center). For those doctoral students for whom a professional internship is required prior to graduation, 7 applied in 2000–2001. Of those who applied, 7 were placed in internships listed by the Association of Psychology Postdoctoral and Internship Programs (APPIC); 6 were placed in APA accredited internships.

Housing and Day Care: No on-campus housing and day care facilities are available.

Employment of Department Graduates:
Master's Degree Graduates: Of those who graduated in the academic year 2000–2001, the following categories and numbers represent the post-graduate activities and employment of master's degree graduates: Enrolled in a post-doctoral residency/fellowship (n/a), employed in independent practice (n/a).
Doctoral Degree Graduates: Of those who graduated in the academic year 2000–2001, the following categories and numbers represent the post-graduate activities and employment of doctoral degree graduates: Enrolled in a psychology doctoral program (n/a), enrolled in another graduate/professional program (n/a).

Additional Information:
Orientation, Objectives, and Emphasis of Department: The PhD program in counseling psychology at Washington State University subscribes to the scientist-practitioner model of training and prepares graduates to function as counseling psychologists in diverse academic and service delivery settings. The program is accredited by the American Psychological Association and graduates are able to obtain licensure as psychologists in Washington as well as most other states. The emphasis of the program is on the facilitation of psychological growth and development, stressing the interaction of individual, environmental, and socio-cultural factors in the treatment of psychological problems, as well as the promotion of health through better self-management and self-renewal. The emphasis of the educational psychology program is applied measurement and statistics, and program evaluation. Examples of faculty expertise and interests include multi-cultural issues, hypnosis, vocational psychology, counselor supervision, eating and habit disorders, and American Indian mental health.

Special Facilities or Resources: Excellent computer facilities; Attentional Processes Laboratory; Counseling Training Laboratory; Program Evaluation and Assessment Center.

Information for Students With Physical Disabilities: The state of Washington administers several programs of assistance to disabled students.

Application Information:
Send to: Department of Educational Leadership and Counseling Psychology, Attn: Program Coordinator. Students are admitted in the Fall, application deadline February 1. *Fee:* $35.

Washington, University of
Department of Psychology
Arts & Sciences
Box 351525
Seattle, WA 98195-1525
Telephone: (206) 543-2640
Fax: (206) 685-3157
E-mail: *psygrad@u.washington.edu*
Web: *http://depts.washington.edu/psych*

Department Established:
1917. Chairperson: Michael D. Beecher. Number of Faculty: total–full-time 46, part-time 5; women–full-time 18, part-time 4; minority–full-time 7.

Programs and Degrees Offered:
Listed in the following order: Program area, degree type (T if terminal Master's), number awarded 7/00–6/01. Animal behavior PhD, behavioral neuroscience PhD 1, child clinical PhD 3, clinical PhD 8, cognition and perception PhD 2, developmental PhD 2, social and personality PhD 1.

APA Accreditation: Clinical PhD: full.

Student Applications/Admissions:

Student Applications

Animal behavior PhD—Applications 2001–2002, 19. Total applicants accepted 2001–2002, 5. New applicants enrolled 2001–2002, 3. Total enrolled 2001–2002 full-time, 10. Openings 2002–2003, 2. The number of students enrolled full and part-time, who were dismissed or voluntarily withdrew from this program area were 1. *Behavioral neuroscience PhD*—Applications 2001–2002, 19. Total applicants accepted 2001–2002, 9. New applicants enrolled 2001–2002, 7. Total enrolled 2001–2002 full-time, 17, part-time, 1. Openings 2002–2003, 2. The Median number of years required for completion of a degree are 7. The number of students enrolled full and part-time, who were dismissed or voluntarily withdrew from this program area were 0. *Child clinical PhD*—Applications 2001–2002, 129. Total applicants accepted 2001–2002, 6. New applicants enrolled 2001–2002, 4. Total enrolled 2001–2002 full-time, 20, part-time, 4. Openings 2002–2003, 3. The Median number of years required for completion of a degree are 9. The number of students enrolled full and part-time, who were dismissed or voluntarily withdrew from this program area were 1. *Clinical PhD*—Applications 2001–2002, 142. Total applicants accepted 2001–2002, 10. New applicants enrolled 2001–2002, 8. Total enrolled 2001–2002 full-time, 36, part-time, 4. Openings 2002–2003, 6. The Median number of years required for completion of a degree are 7. The number of students enrolled full and part-time, who were dismissed or voluntarily withdrew from this program area were 0. *Cognition and perception PhD*—Applications 2001–2002, 30. Total applicants accepted 2001–2002, 9. New applicants enrolled 2001–2002, 4. Total enrolled 2001–2002 full-time, 23, part-time, 2. Openings 2002–2003, 6. The Median number of years required for completion of a degree are 8. The number of students enrolled full and part-time, who were dismissed or voluntarily withdrew from this program area were 1. *Developmental PhD*—Applications 2001–2002, 29. Total applicants accepted 2001–2002, 6. New applicants enrolled 2001–2002, 2. Total enrolled 2001–2002 full-time, 11, part-time, 1. Openings 2002–2003, 4. The Median number of years required for completion of a degree are 8. The number of students enrolled full and part-time, who were dismissed or voluntarily withdrew from this program area were 0. *Social and personality PhD*—Applications 2001–2002, 50. Total applicants accepted 2001–2002, 3. New applicants enrolled 2001–2002, 2. Total enrolled 2001–2002 full-time, 12. Openings 2002–2003, 5. The Median number of years required for completion of a degree are 6. The number of students enrolled full and part-time, who were dismissed or voluntarily withdrew from this program area were 0.

Admissions Requirements:

Scores: Entries appear in this order: required test or GPA, minimum score (if required), median score of students entering in 2001–2002. Master's Programs: GRE-V+Q+Analytical no minimum stated; last 2 years GPA no minimum stated. Doctoral Programs: GRE-V no minimum stated, 630; GRE-Q no minimum stated, 690; GRE-V+Q 1200, 1320; last 2 years GPA no minimum stated, 3.82; psychology GPA no minimum stated; psychology GPA no minimum stated. Clinical Area GPAs are generally higher. Please refer to chart on Web page for figures for most recent admissions by individual area (http://depts.washington.edu/psych) (graduate programs/onlineapplication/admissionstatistics).

Other Criteria: (importance of criteria rated low, medium, or high): GRE/MAT scores high, research experience high, work experience medium, extracurricular activity low, clinically related public service low, GPA medium, letters of recommendation high, interview high, statement of goals and objectives high, stats background medium. Individual areas evaluate applications differently, but all require a strong background in research experience and/or statistics.

Student Characteristics: The following represents characteristics of students in 2001–2002 in all graduate psychology programs in the department: Female–full-time 95, part-time 10; Male–full-time 39, part-time 2; African American/Black–full-time 2, part-time 1; Hispanic/Latino (a)–full-time 6, part-time 0; Asian/Pacific Islander–full-time 14, part-time 1; American Indian/Alaska Native–full-time 3, part-time 2; Multi-ethnic–full-time 2, part-time 0.

Financial Information/Assistance:

Tuition for Full-Time Study: *Doctoral:* State residents: per academic year $5,931; nonstate residents: per academic year $14,766.

Financial Assistance:

First Year Students: Teaching assistantships available for first-year. Average amount paid per academic year: $13,050. Average number of hours worked per week: 20. Tuition remission given: full. Research assistantships available for first-year. Average amount paid per academic year: $13,050. Average number of hours worked per week: 20. Tuition remission given: full. Traineeships available for first-year. Average amount paid per academic year: $13,050. Average number of hours worked per week: 20. Tuition remission given: full.

Advanced Students: Teaching assistantships available for advanced students. Average amount paid per academic year: $13,950. Average number of hours worked per week: 20. Tuition remission given: full. Research assistantships available for advanced students. Average amount paid per academic year: $13,950. Average number of hours worked per week: 20. Tuition remission given: full. Traineeships available for advanced students. Average amount paid per academic year: $13,950. Average number of hours worked per week: 20. Tuition remission given: full.

Contact Information: Of all students currently enrolled full-time, 95% benefited from one or more of the listed financial assistance programs. For information on financial assistance, contact: Office of Financial Aid, 105 Schmitz Hall, Box 355880. A few fellowships or scholarships may also be available.

Internships/Practica: A variety of local and national predoctoral internships are available in clinical psychology. For those doctoral students for whom a professional internship is required prior to graduation, 9 applied in 2000–2001. Of those who applied, 9 were placed in internships listed by the Association of Psychology Postdoctoral and Internship Programs (APPIC); 9 were placed in APA accredited internships.

Housing and Day Care: On-campus housing and day care facilities are available.

Employment of Department Graduates:

Master's Degree Graduates: Of those who graduated in the academic year 2000–2001, the following categories and numbers represent the post-graduate activities and employment of master's degree graduates: Enrolled in a post-doctoral residency/fellowship (n/a), employed in independent practice (n/a).

Doctoral Degree Graduates: Of those who graduated in the academic year 2000–2001, the following categories and numbers represent the post-graduate activities and employment of doctoral degree graduates: Enrolled in a psychology doctoral program (n/a), enrolled in another graduate/professional program (n/a), enrolled in a post-doctoral residency/fellowship (4), employed in independent practice (1), employed in an academic position at a university (1), employed in an academic position at a 2-year/4-year college (1), employed in other positions at a higher education institution (1), employed in business or industry (research/consulting) (1), employed in a government agency (research) (1), employed in a government agency (professional services) (2), employed in a hospital/medical center (1).

Additional Information:

Orientation, Objectives, and Emphasis of Department: The program is committed to research-oriented scientific psychology. No degree programs are available in counseling or humanistic psychology. The clinical program emphasizes both clinical and research competencies and has areas of specialization in child, clinical, behavioral medicine and health psychology, and community-minority psychology.

Special Facilities or Resources: University and urban settings provide many resources, including the university's hospital, child development and mental retardation center, counseling center, psychological services and training center, computer center, and regional primate center; Harborview Medical Center's alcohol and drug abuse center; Children's Hospital and Medical Center; nearby Veterans Administration facilities; and Seattle Mental Health Institute.

Application Information:
Send to: Graduate Selections Committee, Department of Psychology, Box 351525, University of Washington, Seattle, WA 98195-1525, USA. Students are admitted in the Fall, application deadline December 15. November 1 for international applicants to UW Graduate School (available on-line). December 15 for international applicants to Psychology Department (downloadable application forms on-line). *Fee:* $50. $45 for on-line application paid by credit or debit card. Fee waived or deferred if U.S. citizen or permanent resident and financial need is approved by the Gradate School.

Washington, University of
Educational Psychology Area in College of Education
312 Miller Hall, Box 353600
Seattle, WA 98195-3600
Telephone: (206) 543-1846 or (206) 543-1139
Fax: (206) 543-8439
E-mail: *abbottr@u.washington.edu*
Web: *http://depts.washington.edu/edpsych/*

Department Established:
1965. Chairperson: Robert D. Abbott. Number of Faculty: total–full-time 20, part-time 5; women–full-time 11, part-time 5; minority–full-time 3.

Programs and Degrees Offered:
Listed in the following order: Program area, degree type (T if terminal Master's), number awarded 7/00–6/01. Human development and cognitio 5, measurement, statistics and re 1, school counseling 15, school counseling PhD 2, school psychology 7.

APA Accreditation: School PhD: full.

Student Applications/Admissions:

Student Applications

School counseling PhD—Applications 2001–2002, 0. Total enrolled 2001–2002 part-time, 5. The number of students enrolled full and part-time, who were dismissed or voluntarily withdrew from this program area were 0.

Admissions Requirements:

Scores: Entries appear in this order: required test or GPA, minimum score (if required), median score of students entering in 2001–2002. Master's Programs: GRE-V 500, 520; GRE-Q 500, 590; GRE-V+Q 1000; last 2 years GPA 3.0, 3.5. School Counseling: GRE V+Q= 1000; School Psychology: GRE V+Q=1000, minimum of 500 each in V+Q. Doctoral Programs: GRE-V 500, 600; GRE-Q 500, 590; last 2 years GPA no minimum stated, 3.8 ; psychology GPA no minimum stated; psychology GPA no minimum stated.

Other Criteria: (importance of criteria rated low, medium, or high): GRE/MAT scores high, research experience medium, work experience high, clinically related public service medium, GPA high, letters of recommendation high, interview medium, statement of goals and objectives high.

Student Characteristics: The following represents characteristics of students in 2001–2002 in all graduate psychology programs in the department: Female–full-time 21, part-time 7; Male–full-time 3, part-time 0; African American/Black–full-time 1, part-time 0; Hispanic/Latino (a)–full-time 2, part-time 0; Asian/Pacific Islander–full-time 3, part-time 0; American Indian/Alaska Native–full-time 0, part-time 0; Multi-ethnic–full-time 0, part-time 0; students subject to the Americans with Disabilities Act–full-time 0, part-time 0.

Financial Information/Assistance:

Tuition for Full-Time Study: *Master's:* State residents per academic year $5,929; nonstate residents: per academic year $14,766. *Doctoral:* State residents: per academic year $5,929; nonstate residents: per academic year $14,766.

Financial Assistance:

First Year Students: Teaching assistantships available for first-year. Average amount paid per academic year: $9,000. Average number of hours worked per week: 20. Apply by April/filled. Tuition remission given: full. Research assistantships available for first-year. Average amount paid per academic year: $9,000. Average number of hours worked per week: 20. Apply by Open. Tuition remission given: full.

Advanced Students: Teaching assistantships available for advanced students. Average amount paid per academic year: $9,000. Average number of hours worked per week: 20. Apply by April/filled. Tuition remission given: full. Research assistantships available for advanced students. Average amount paid per academic year: $9,000. Average number of hours worked per week: 20. Apply by Open. Tuition remission given: full.

Contact Information: For information on financial assistance, contact: Office of Financial Aid; Office of Student Services.

Internships/Practica: No information provided.

Housing and Day Care: On-campus housing and day care facilities are available.

Employment of Department Graduates:

Master's Degree Graduates: Of those who graduated in the academic year 2000–2001, the following categories and numbers represent the post-graduate activities and employment of master's degree graduates: Enrolled in a post-doctoral residency/fellowship (n/a), employed in independent practice (n/a), employed in a professional position in a school system (9).

Doctoral Degree Graduates: Of those who graduated in the academic year 2000–2001, the following categories and numbers represent the post-graduate activities and employment of doctoral degree graduates: Enrolled in a psychology doctoral program (n/a), enrolled in another graduate/professional program (n/a), employed in other positions at a higher education institution (1), employed in a professional position in a school system (1).

Additional Information:

Orientation, Objectives, and Emphasis of Department: The emphasis is on the application of psychology to educational processes. The doctoral programs require extensive research preparation and involvement in research projects during a doctoral student's entire program. The master's degree program in School Psychology leads to national Certification as a School Psychologist (NASP). The doctoral program in School Psychology also includes internship experience and coursework necessary for licensure as a Psychologist.

Special Facilities or Resources: Library and computer facilities are of high quality and accessibility. A well-staffed Clinical Training Laboratory, located in the same building as classrooms and faculty offices, provides psychological services supervised by program faculty to infants, toddlers, school-aged children, and their parents. This clinic has video and audio recording, observation rooms, and microcomputers to support clinical services and research efforts, as well as an extensive library of psychological tests. There are within the University of Washington several other departments and programs with behavioral science emphases, including a health sciences complex that offers resources for coursework, clinical experience, and supervision.

Application Information:

Send to: Office of Admissions and Academic Program Support, College of Education, Box 353600, University of Washington, Seattle, WA 98195-3600. Students are admitted in the Fall, application deadline December 15; Winter, application deadline November 1; Summer, application deadline December 15. Deadlines vary by programs. School Psychology MEd and PhD programs have December 15th deadline only (for entry in Summer or Autumn Quarters). *Fee:* $45.

Western Washington University
Department of Psychology
516 High Street
Bellingham, WA 98225-9089
Telephone: (360) 650-3184
Fax: (360) 650-7305
E-mail: *Robert.Thorndike@wwu.edu*
Web: *http://www.wwu.edu/~psych/*

Department Established:

1962. Chairperson: Robert M. Thorndike. Number of Faculty: total–full-time 26, part-time 6; women–full-time 9, part-time 4; minority–full-time 4.

Programs and Degrees Offered:

Listed in the following order: Program area, degree type (T if terminal Master's), number awarded 7/00–6/01. General MA (T) 7, mental health counseling MA (T) 6, school counseling (T) 5.

Student Applications/Admissions:

Student Applications

General MA—Applications 2001–2002, 21. Total applicants accepted 2001–2002, 15. New applicants enrolled 2001–2002, 9. Total enrolled 2001–2002 full-time, 11, part-time, 2. Openings 2002–2003, 15. The Median number of years required for completion of a degree are 2. The number of students enrolled full and part-time, who were dismissed or voluntarily withdrew from this program area were 1. *Mental health counseling MA*—Applications 2001–2002, 26. Total applicants accepted 2001–2002, 9. New applicants enrolled 2001–2002, 7. Total enrolled 2001–2002 full-time, 10, part-time, 5. Openings 2002–2003, 6. The Median number of years required for completion of a degree are 2. The number of students enrolled full and part-time, who were dismissed or voluntarily withdrew from this program area were 1.

Admissions Requirements:

Scores: Entries appear in this order: required test or GPA, minimum score (if required), median score of students entering in 2001–2002. Master's Programs: GRE-V no minimum stated, 520; GRE-Q no minimum stated, 610; GRE-Analytical no minimum stated, 630; last 2 years GPA 3.0, 3.62. Doctoral Programs: last 2 years GPA no minimum stated; psychology GPA no minimum stated; psychology GPA no minimum stated.

Other Criteria: (importance of criteria rated low, medium, or high): research experience medium, work experience medium, clinically related public service medium, letters of recommendation medium, interview medium, statement of goals and objectives medium. Research experience is the most critical for the General Psychology program but not important for School Counseling. Interviews and work experience are less important for General Psychology.

Student Characteristics: The following represents characteristics of students in 2001–2002 in all graduate psychology programs in the department: Female–full-time 29, part-time 5; Male–full-time 3, part-time 3; African American/Black–full-time 0, part-time 0; Hispanic/Latino (a)–full-time 0, part-time 0; Asian/Pacific Islander–full-time 1, part-time 0; American Indian/Alaska Native– full-time 1, part-time 0; Multi-ethnic–full-time 1, part-time 0; students subject to the Americans with Disabilities Act–full-time 0, part-time 0.

Financial Information/Assistance:

Tuition for Full-Time Study: *Master's:* State residents per academic year $5,114, $161 per credit hour; nonstate residents: per academic year $15,035, $492 per credit hour.

Financial Assistance:

First Year Students: Teaching assistantships available for first-year. Average number of hours worked per week: 20. Apply by Feb 1. Tuition remission given: partial.

Advanced Students: Teaching assistantships available for advanced students. Average number of hours worked per week: 20. Apply by Feb 1. Tuition remission given: partial.

Contact Information: For information on financial assistance, contact: Kirsti Charlton, Graduate School, (360) 650-3569 and http://www.finaid.wwu.edu/.

Internships/Practica: Our Mental Health Counseling & School Counseling programs each have a two-quarter supervised practicum with families and individual clients and a three-quarter supervised internship in a school setting, a university counseling center, or mental health agency.

Housing and Day Care: On-campus housing and day care facilities are available.

Employment of Department Graduates:

Master's Degree Graduates: Of those who graduated in the academic year 2000–2001, the following categories and numbers represent the post-graduate activities and employment of master's degree graduates: Enrolled in a post-doctoral residency/fellowship (n/a), employed in independent practice (n/a).

Doctoral Degree Graduates: Of those who graduated in the academic year 2000–2001, the following categories and numbers represent the post-graduate activities and employment of doctoral degree graduates: Enrolled in a psychology doctoral program (n/a), enrolled in another graduate/professional program (n/a).

Additional Information:

Orientation, Objectives, and Emphasis of Department: We are oriented to the scientist-practitioner model; all students are given basic background in general psychology with emphasis on its empirical basis, research, and research design. The mental health counseling and school counseling curricula are applied extensions built upon this common base. Involvement in research is a strong emphasis and goal of the program. The basic orientation of the School Counseling and Mental Health Counseling program is cognitive/behavioral. Both the School Counseling and Mental Health Counseling Program are accredited by the Council for the Accreditation of Counseling and Related Educational Programs (CACREP). These programs have a two-quarter supervised practicum with families and individual clients and a three-quarter supervised internship in a school setting, a university counseling center, or mental health agency. The Mental Health Program follows the practitioner-scientist model, mixing applied courses with empirically-based courses. The General Program has its strength in research tools and experiences. The Measurement, Evaluation, and Statistical Analysis concentration provides an extensive set of research tools with coursework in ANOVAs, multiple regression, factor analysis, multivariate analysis, and structural equation modeling. Involvement in research is a strong emphasis in the General Program.

Special Facilities or Resources: Well-equipped laboratories for human and animal research are available. Counselor training facilities include modern videotaping equipment. There is virtually unrestricted access to a variety of micro- and mainframe computers. The location of the university within easy reach of major urban areas in both the United States and Canada provides a unique opportunity for diverse cultural and academic experiences.

Application Information:

Send to: Graduate School, OM 430, Western Washington University, MS 9037, 516 High St., Bellingham, WA 98225-9037. Students are admitted in the Fall, application deadline February 1. *Fee:* $35.

Marshall University

Department of Psychology
Liberal Arts
18th Street and 3rd Avenue
Huntington, WV 25755-2672
Telephone: (304) 696-6446
Fax: (304) 696-2784
E-mail: *psych@marshall.edu*
Web: *http://www.marshall.edu/psych*

Department Established:

Chairperson: Martin Amerikaner. Number of Faculty: total–full-time 19, part-time 16; women–full-time 6, part-time 10; minority–full-time 1; faculty subject to the Americans with Disabilities Act 1.

Programs and Degrees Offered:

Listed in the following order: Program area, degree type (T if terminal Master's), number awarded 7/00–6/01. Clinical MA (T) 18, Clinical Psychology PsyD new, general MA (T) 8, industrial/organizational MA (T) 3.

Student Applications/Admissions:

Student Applications

Clinical MA—Applications 2001–2002, 30. Total applicants accepted 2001–2002, 20. New applicants enrolled 2001–2002, 15. Total enrolled 2001–2002 full-time, 13, part-time, 30. Openings 2002–2003, 15. The Median number of years required for completion of a degree are 2. *Clinical Psychology PsyD*—Applications 2001–2002, new. Total applicants accepted 2001–2002, new. New applicants enrolled 2001–2002, new. Openings 2002–2003, 12. *General MA*—Applications 2001–2002, 35. Total applicants accepted 2001–2002, 20. New applicants enrolled 2001–2002, 17. Total enrolled 2001–2002 full-time, 10, part-time, 25. Openings 2002–2003, 20. The Median number of years required for completion of a degree are 3. *Industrial/organizational MA*—Applications 2001–2002, 12. Total applicants accepted 2001–2002, 7. New applicants enrolled 2001–2002, 5. Total enrolled 2001–2002 full-time, 3, part-time, 5. Openings 2002–2003, 7. The Median number of years required for completion of a degree are 3.

Admissions Requirements:

Scores: Entries appear in this order: required test or GPA, minimum score (if required), median score of students entering in 2001–2002. Master's Programs: GRE-V no minimum stated, 475; GRE-Q no minimum stated, 490; GRE-Analytical no minimum stated, 565; overall undergraduate GPA no minimum stated, 3.5; psychology GPA no minimum stated, 3.5. MAT is acceptable as an alternative to the GRE Doctoral Programs: GRE-V no minimum stated; GRE-Q no minimum stated; GRE-V+Q no minimum stated; last 2 years GPA no

minimum stated; psychology GPA no minimum stated; psychology GPA no minimum stated. PsyD program requires V and Q GRE, as well as transcripts showing all previous academic grades/GPAs. The PsyD is accepting its first class for Fall 2002; no data are yet available regarding their GREs or GPAs.

Other Criteria: (importance of criteria rated low, medium, or high): GRE/MAT scores medium, research experience medium, work experience medium, extracurricular activity low, clinically related public service medium, GPA high, letters of recommendation medium, interview low, statement of goals and objectives medium. MA program admission is based primarily on GPA and GRE scores; PsyD program considers statement of professional goals, clinical and research experience, commitment to rural psychological service delivery, and letters of recommendation. An interview may be required of PsyD applicants.

Student Characteristics: The following represents characteristics of students in 2001–2002 in all graduate psychology programs in the department: Female–full-time 20, part-time 9; Male–full-time 6, part-time 10; African American/Black–full-time 1, part-time 2; Hispanic/Latino (a)–full-time 0, part-time 0; Asian/Pacific Islander–full-time 0, part-time 0; American Indian/Alaska Native–full-time 0, part-time 0.

Financial Information/Assistance:

Tuition for Full-Time Study: *Master's:* State residents per academic year $2,396, $133 per credit hour; nonstate residents: per academic year $7,668, $426 per credit hour. *Doctoral:* State residents: per academic year $2,396, $133 per credit hour; nonstate residents: per academic year $7,668, $426 per credit hour.

Financial Assistance:

First Year Students: Traineeships available for first-year. Average amount paid per academic year: $5,000. Average number of hours worked per week: 20. Apply by ongoing. Tuition remission given: full.

Advanced Students: Teaching assistantships available for advanced students. Average amount paid per academic year: $6,000. Average number of hours worked per week: 20. Apply by April 15. Tuition remission given: full.

Contact Information: Of all students currently enrolled full-time, 50% benefited from one or more of the listed financial assistance programs. For information on financial assistance, contact: Financial Aid Office, (304) 696-3162. Psychology Department, (304) 696-6446. Most Psychology Department GA positions are dedicated to Teaching Assistantships. Several new, non-teaching assistantships will be available for students in our new doctoral (PsyD) program. Other graduate assistantships are available from departments on campus; most full time students on the Huntington campus who seek an assistantship on campus successfully find one.

Internships/Practica: Clinical MA: on campus, department clinic, as well as area mental health agencies. I/O: a range of area businesses and organizations. PsyD program: additional practicum placements at rural sites, some in collaboration with primary medical area programs.

Housing and Day Care: On-campus housing and day care facilities are available.

Employment of Department Graduates:

Master's Degree Graduates: Of those who graduated in the academic year 2000–2001, the following categories and numbers represent the post-graduate activities and employment of master's degree graduates: Enrolled in a post-doctoral residency/fellowship (n/a), employed in independent practice (n/a).

Doctoral Degree Graduates: Of those who graduated in the academic year 2000–2001, the following categories and numbers represent the post-graduate activities and employment of doctoral degree graduates: Enrolled in a psychology doctoral program (n/a), enrolled in another graduate/professional program (n/a).

Additional Information:

Orientation, Objectives, and Emphasis of Department: Our PsyD program in Clinical Psychology (offered on our Huntington WV campus) accepted its first students for Fall 2002. The program emphasis is on preparing scholar-practitioners for rural/underserved populations in Appalachia and other rural areas. A wide range of theoretical perspectives is represented on our faculty. A particular focus of the doctoral program is on understanding the needs and challenges of working in rural communities. The terminal clinical MA program (based in our S. Charleston, WV campus) focus is on producing clinicians with a strong academic background coupled with an emphasis on application. The approach is basically eclectic; clinical faculty interests include cognitive, behavioral, and psychodynamic models. The I/O program has an applied focus; students complete an internship and an applied research project. The General MA program can be individualized to address a variety of academic and professional objectives for students. It is a popular foundation program for students enrolled in Marshall's EdS program in School Psychology (contact the School Psychology Program in the Graduate College of Education and Human Services for more information).

Special Facilities or Resources: The department has computer facilities for clinical students to write reports and progress notes about clients seen in the department clinics. Departmental and university computer facilities are also available to students for research projects in all programs. Through the departmental clinic, students are afforded the opportunity to work, under supervision, with clients from the community and university. Placements available at nearby community mental health centers, state hospital, VA, medical school.

Information for Students With Physical Disabilities: All buildings are accessible.

Application Information:

Send to: Admissions Office, Marshall University Graduate College, 100 Angus Peyton Dr., S. Charleston, WV 25303-1600. Students are admitted in the Fall; Spring; Summer. January 15 deadline for PsyD program (all new PsyD students start in subsequent Fall semester); MA programs have ongoing review of applicants—new MA students can begin in any semester. *Fee:* $20. $ 30 for non-residents of WV.

West Virginia University

Department of Counseling, Rehabilitation Counseling and Counseling Psychology, Counseling Psychology Program
Human Resources and Education
502 Allen Hall, P.O. Box 6122
Morgantown, WV 26506-6122
Telephone: (304) 293-3807
Fax: (304) 293-4082
E-mail: *anita.debiase@mail.wvu.edu*
Web: *http://www.wvu.edu/~crc/*

Department Established:
1948. Chairperson: Jeffrey K. Messing. Number of Faculty: total–full-time 10, part-time 1; women–full-time 3, part-time 1; minority–full-time 1.

Programs and Degrees Offered:
Listed in the following order: Program area, degree type (T if terminal Master's), number awarded 7/00–6/01. Counseling MA (T) 46, counseling psychology PhD 6, rehabilitation counseling MA (T) 22.

APA Accreditation: Counseling PhD: full.

Student Applications/Admissions:

Student Applications

Counseling MA—Applications 2001–2002, 75. Total applicants accepted 2001–2002, 38. New applicants enrolled 2001–2002, 32. Total enrolled 2001–2002 full-time, 81, part-time, 55. Openings 2002–2003, 24. The Median number of years required for completion of a degree are 2. The number of students enrolled full and part-time, who were dismissed or voluntarily withdrew from this program area were 0. *Counseling psychology PhD*—Applications 2001–2002, 50. Total applicants accepted 2001–2002, 8. New applicants enrolled 2001–2002, 3. Total enrolled 2001–2002 full-time, 22, part-time, 14. Openings 2002–2003, 8. The Median number of years required for completion of a degree are 5. The number of students enrolled full and part-time, who were dismissed or voluntarily withdrew from this program area were 0. *Rehabilitation counseling MA*—Applications 2001–2002, 22. Total applicants accepted 2001–2002, 19. New applicants enrolled 2001–2002, 17. Total enrolled 2001–2002 full-time, 27, part-time, 12. Openings 2002–2003, 18. The Median number of years required for completion of a degree are 2. The number of students enrolled full and part-time, who were dismissed or voluntarily withdrew from this program area were 0.

Admissions Requirements:

Scores: Entries appear in this order: required test or GPA, minimum score (if required), median score of students entering in 2001–2002. Master's Programs: GRE-V no minimum stated, 465; GRE-Q no minimum stated, 521; GRE-V+Q 900, 986;

overall undergraduate GPA 2.8, 3.3. Doctoral Programs: GRE-V no minimum stated, 523; GRE-Q no minimum stated, 506; GRE-V+Q 1000, 1029; GRE-Analytical no minimum stated, 576; overall undergraduate GPA no minimum stated, 3.5 ; last 2 years GPA no minimum stated; psychology GPA no minimum stated; psychology GPA 3.5, 3.9.

Other Criteria: (importance of criteria rated low, medium, or high): GRE/MAT scores medium, research experience medium, work experience high, extracurricular activity medium, clinically related public service medium, GPA medium, letters of recommendation high, interview high, statement of goals and objectives high, goodness of fit high.

Student Characteristics: The following represents characteristics of students in 2001–2002 in all graduate psychology programs in the department: Female–full-time 31, part-time 7; Male–full-time 13, part-time 1; African American/Black–full-time 2, part-time 0; Hispanic/Latino (a)–full-time 1, part-time 0; Asian/Pacific Islander–full-time 2, part-time 0; American Indian/Alaska Native–full-time 0, part-time 0; Multi-ethnic–full-time 0, part-time 0; students subject to the Americans with Disabilities Act–full-time 0, part-time 0.

Financial Information/Assistance:

Tuition for Full-Time Study: *Master's:* State residents per academic year $3,242, $185 per credit hour; nonstate residents: per academic year $9,110, $510 per credit hour. *Doctoral:* State residents: per academic year $3,242, $185 per credit hour; nonstate residents: per academic year $9,110, $510 per credit hour.

Financial Assistance:

First Year Students: Teaching assistantships available for first-year. Average amount paid per academic year: $6,669. Average number of hours worked per week: 20. Tuition remission given: full. Research assistantships available for first-year. Average amount paid per academic year: $6,669. Average number of hours worked per week: 20. Tuition remission given: full. Fellowships and scholarships available for first-year. Average amount paid per academic year: $10,000. Average number of hours worked per week: 0. Tuition remission given: full.

Advanced Students: Teaching assistantships available for advanced students. Average amount paid per academic year: $6,669. Average number of hours worked per week: 20. Tuition remission given: full. Research assistantships available for advanced students. Average amount paid per academic year: $6,669. Average number of hours worked per week: 20. Tuition remission given: full. Fellowships and scholarships available for advanced students. Average amount paid per academic year: $10,000. Average number of hours worked per week: 0. Tuition remission given: full.

Contact Information: Of all students currently enrolled full-time, 19% benefited from one or more of the listed financial assistance programs. For information on financial assistance, contact: W.V.U. Financial Aid Office, P.O. Box 6004, Morgantown, W.V. 26505-6004, 304-293-5242, finaid@wvnum.wvnet.edu. Application deadlines vary for each position and department.

Internships/Practica: The master's and doctoral programs offer a variety of opportunities for internship and practica experience. Some of the placement sites include: The federal prison system, mental health agencies, employee assistant programs, private practices, VA hospitals, local school systems, university counseling center, and others. For those doctoral students for whom a professional internship is required prior to graduation, 5 applied in 2000–2001. Of those who applied, 5 were placed in internships listed by the Association of Psychology Postdoctoral and Internship Programs (APPIC); 5 were placed in APA accredited internships.

Housing and Day Care: On-campus housing and day care facilities are available.

Employment of Department Graduates:

Master's Degree Graduates: Of those who graduated in the academic year 2000–2001, the following categories and numbers represent the post-graduate activities and employment of master's degree graduates: Enrolled in a post-doctoral residency/fellowship (n/a), employed in independent practice (n/a).

Doctoral Degree Graduates: Of those who graduated in the academic year 2000–2001, the following categories and numbers represent the post-graduate activities and employment of doctoral degree graduates: Enrolled in a psychology doctoral program (n/a), enrolled in another graduate/professional program (n/a).

Additional Information:

Orientation, Objectives, and Emphasis of Department: The department represents a variety of theoretical orientations. The objective of the department is to train professionals to serve primarily clients who are relatively normal but who are experiencing difficulties related to personal adjustment, interpersonal relationships, developmental problems, crises, academic or career stress, or decisions. The employment settings for our graduates typically include college and university counseling and testing services, community mental health agencies, clinics, hospitals, schools, rehabilitation centers, correctional centers, the United States Armed Services, and private practice.

Special Facilities or Resources: Facilities include an extensive medical center, including video equipment and computer terminals; training and observation rooms; and practicum and internship sites in a variety of settings for master's and doctoral students.

Information for Students With Physical Disabilities: All departmental and university services are accessible to those with physical disabilities. Our program currently has three students with physical disabilities including visual, auditory, and motor disabilities. Our Rehabilitation Counseling Program prides itself in educating and assisting all people with disabilities and it works closely with the other programs to assure all necessary arrangements are met.

Application Information:

Send to: Admissions Coordinator, Department of Counseling, Rehabilitation Counseling and Counseling Psychology, West Virginia University, P.O. Box 6122, Morgantown, WV 25605-6122. Students are admitted in the Fall, application deadline January 15. Counseling Psychology Doctoral program admits for Fall only. Application deadline is January 15. Rehabilitation Counseling MS: deadline for Fall semester is April 1 (prefer to receive applications earlier). Counseling programs - deadline for enrollment in Fall semester is March 1. Deadline for part-time admission in Spring semester is October 15. *Fee:* $50.

West Virginia University

Department of Psychology
Eberly College of Arts and Sciences
P.O. Box 6040
Morgantown, WV 26506-6040
Telephone: (304) 293-2001, ext. 628
Fax: (304) 293-6606
E-mail: *Debra.Swinney@mail.wvu.edu*
Web: *http://www.as.wvu.edu/psyc*

Department Established:

1929. Chairperson: Michael Perone. Number of Faculty: total–full-time 22, part-time 2; women–full-time 9, part-time 2.

Programs and Degrees Offered:

Listed in the following order: Program area, degree type (T if terminal Master's), number awarded 7/00–6/01. Adult Clinical PhD 3, Adult Clinical Professional MA (T) 1, Behavior Analysis PhD 2, Child Clinical PhD 4, Child Clinical Professional MA (T) 1, Life-span Developmental PhD 1.

APA Accreditation: Clinical PhD: full.

Student Applications/Admissions:

Student Applications

Adult Clinical PhD—Applications 2001–2002, 87. Total applicants accepted 2001–2002, 4. New applicants enrolled 2001–2002, 4. Total enrolled 2001–2002 full-time, 18. Openings 2002–2003, 4. The Median number of years required for completion of a degree are 5. The number of students enrolled full and part-time, who were dismissed or voluntarily withdrew from this program area were 0. *Adult Clinical Professional MA*—Applications 2001–2002, 8. Total applicants accepted 2001–2002, 1. New applicants enrolled 2001–2002, 1. Total enrolled 2001–2002 full-time, 1. Openings 2002–2003, 1. The Median number of years required for completion of a degree are 2. The number of students enrolled full and part-time, who were dismissed or voluntarily withdrew from this program area were 0. *Behavior Analysis PhD*—Applications 2001–2002, 25. Total applicants accepted 2001–2002, 8. New applicants enrolled 2001–2002, 5. Total enrolled 2001–2002 full-time, 16. Openings 2002–2003, 5. The Median number of years required for completion of a degree are 4. The number of students enrolled full and part-time, who were dismissed or voluntarily withdrew from this program area were 0. *Child Clinical PhD*—Applications 2001–2002, 70. Total applicants accepted 2001–2002, 7. New applicants enrolled 2001–2002, 4. Total enrolled 2001–2002 full-time, 15. Openings 2002– 2003, 4. The Median number of years required for completion of a degree are 6. The number of students enrolled full and part-time, who were dismissed or voluntarily withdrew from this program area were 0. *Child Clinical Professional MA*—Applications 2001–2002, 10. Total applicants accepted 2001– 2002, 1. New applicants enrolled 2001–2002, 1. Total enrolled 2001–2002 full-time, 2. Openings 2002–2003, 1. The Median number of years required for completion of a degree are 2. The number of students enrolled full and part-time, who were dismissed or voluntarily withdrew from this program area were 0. *Life-span Developmental PhD*—Applications 2001–2002, 14. Total applicants accepted 2001–2002, 8. New applicants enrolled 2001–2002,

4. Total enrolled 2001–2002 full-time, 13. Openings 2002–2003, 5. The Median number of years required for completion of a degree are 7. The number of students enrolled full and part-time, who were dismissed or voluntarily withdrew from this program area were 0.

Admissions Requirements:

Scores: Entries appear in this order: required test or GPA, minimum score (if required), median score of students entering in 2001–2002. Master's Programs: GRE-V no minimum stated; GRE-Q no minimum stated; GRE-V+Q 1000, 1050; GRE-Analytical no minimum stated; GRE-V+Q+Analytical no minimum stated; overall undergraduate GPA 3.00, 3.33; last 2 years GPA no minimum stated; psychology GPA no minimum stated. Doctoral Programs: GRE-V no minimum stated; GRE-Q no minimum stated; GRE-V+Q 1000, 1220; GRE-Analytical no minimum stated; GRE-V+Q+Analytical no minimum stated; GRE-Subject(Psych) no minimum stated; overall undergraduate GPA 3.00, 3.66; last 2 years GPA no minimum stated; psychology GPA no minimum stated; psychology GPA no minimum stated. The GRE Subject Test in Psychology is required for students applying to the Adult Clinical or Child Clinical Psychology doctoral programs. The Subject Test is not required for students applying to the Behavior Analysis or Life-Span Developmental Psychology doctoral programs.

Other Criteria: (importance of criteria rated low, medium, or high): GRE/MAT scores high, research experience high, work experience medium, extracurricular activity medium, clinically related public service medium, GPA high, letters of recommendation high, interview high, statement of goals and objectives high. Match between faculty and student interests is of high importance. Only clinical programs give high value to clinically related public service.

Student Characteristics: The following represents characteristics of students in 2001–2002 in all graduate psychology programs in the department: Female–full-time 51, part-time 0; Male–full-time 14, part-time 0; African American/Black–full-time 0, part-time 0; Hispanic/Latino (a)–full-time 4, part-time 0; Asian/Pacific Islander–full-time 4, part-time 0; American Indian/Alaska Native–full-time 0, part-time 0.

Financial Information/Assistance:

Tuition for Full-Time Study: *Master's:* State residents per academic year $3,242, $185 per credit hour; nonstate residents: per academic year $9,110, $510 per credit hour. *Doctoral:* State residents: per academic year $3,242, $185 per credit hour; nonstate residents: per academic year $9,110, $510 per credit hour.

Financial Assistance:

First Year Students: Teaching assistantships available for first-year. Average amount paid per academic year: $7,690. Average number of hours worked per week: 20. Apply by January 1. Tuition remission given: full. Research assistantships available for first-year. Average amount paid per academic year: $7,690. Average number of hours worked per week: 20. Apply by January 1. Tuition remission given: full. Traineeships available for first-year. Average amount paid per academic year: $7,690. Average number of hours worked per week: 20. Apply by January 1. Tuition remission given: full. Fellowships and scholarships available for first-year. Average amount paid per academic year: $13,125. Average number of hours worked per week: 0. Apply by January 1. Tuition remission given: full.

Advanced Students: Teaching assistantships available for advanced students. Average amount paid per academic year: $8,239. Average number of hours worked per week: 20. Apply by January 1. Tuition remission given: full. Research assistantships available for advanced students. Average amount paid per academic year: $8,239. Average number of hours worked per week: 20. Apply by January 1. Tuition remission given: full. Traineeships available for advanced students. Average amount paid per academic year: $8,239. Average number of hours worked per week: 20. Apply by January 1. Tuition remission given: full. Fellowships and scholarships available for advanced students. Average amount paid per academic year: $13,125. Average number of hours worked per week: 0. Apply by January 1. Tuition remission given: full.

Contact Information: Of all students currently enrolled full-time, 100% benefited from one or more of the listed financial assistance programs.

Internships/Practica: Paid clinical placements at out-of-department sites are available for doctoral clinical students in their second year and beyond, or in their first year and beyond if entering with a master's degree and having clinical experience. Such opportunities are also available for professional master's clinical students in both years of their training. These out-of-department practicum sites include WVU School of Medicine's Chestnut Ridge Hospital, WVU Center for Excellence in Developmental Disabilities, WVU Carruth Counseling Center, "Kennedy" Federal Correctional Institution, Hopemont Hospital, Mountainview Rehabilitation Hospital, Pendleton Community Care Center, Sharpe Hospital, University of Maryland at Baltimore School of Medicine, a private practice, various behavioral/community mental health agencies, and facilities for individuals with developmental disabilities. These sites are located in Morgantown, and across the state and region. Stipends for practicum range from $7,000 to $12,000, require 16 to 20 hours of work per week, and last 9 to 12 months. During their six-month internship, professional master's students are paid more, commensurate with their full-time status. For those doctoral students for whom a professional internship is required prior to graduation, 3 applied in 2000–2001. Of those who applied, 3 were placed in APA accredited internships.

Housing and Day Care: No on-campus housing and day care facilities are available.

Employment of Department Graduates:
Master's Degree Graduates: Of those who graduated in the academic year 2000–2001, the following categories and numbers represent the post-graduate activities and employment of master's degree graduates: Enrolled in a post-doctoral residency/fellowship (n/a), employed in independent practice (n/a), employed in a community mental health/counseling center (1), still seeking employment (1).

Doctoral Degree Graduates: Of those who graduated in the academic year 2000–2001, the following categories and numbers represent the post-graduate activities and employment of doctoral degree graduates: Enrolled in a psychology doctoral program (n/a), enrolled in another graduate/professional program (n/a), enrolled in a post-doctoral residency/fellowship (4), employed in an academic position at a university (2), employed in an academic position at a 2-year/4-year college (1), employed in business or industry (research/consulting) (2).

Additional Information:
Orientation, Objectives, and Emphasis of Department: The Psychology Department offers the Doctor of Philosophy degree in Behavior Analysis and Developmental, Child Clinical, and Adult Clinical Psychology, and a terminal Professional Master's degree in Adult Clinical and Child Clinical Psychology. The Department employs a junior colleague model of training, in which graduate students participate fully in research, teaching, and clinical service activities. The Behavior Analysis Program trains students in basic research, theory, and applications of behavioral psychology. These three areas of study are integrated in the Behavior Analysis curriculum; however, a student may emphasize either basic or applied research. The Life-span Developmental Program emphasizes cognitive and social/personality development across the life span. It combines breadth of exposure across a variety of perspectives on the life span with depth and rigor in research training and the opportunity to specialize in an age period such as infancy, childhood, adolescence, or adulthood and old age. The Master's and PhD Clinical Programs have a behavioral orientation. The Clinical Doctoral Programs (Adult and Child) train scientist-practitioners who function effectively in academic, medical center, or clinical applied settings. Specializations in developmental psychology, behavior analysis, and health psychology are available. The Clinical Professional Master's Program is designed to train practitioners with a terminal Master's degree to work in rural areas.

Special Facilities or Resources: The Department will move into the new Life Sciences Building in June 2002. This building has modern animal research quarters for work with rats, pigeons, and other species. There are several computer-based laboratories and other laboratories for studies of learning in humans and animals, behavioral pharmacology, and neuropsychology. There are additional facilities for human research in learning, cognition, small group processes, developmental psychology, social behavior, and psychophysiology. Clinical practicum opportunities are available through the Department's Quin Curtis Center for Psychological Service, Training, and Research, as well as in numerous mental health agencies throughout the state. Videotaping and direct observation equipment and facilities are available. The West Virginia University Medical Center provides facilities for research and training in such departments and areas as behavioral medicine and psychiatry, pediatrics, neurology, cardiology, obstetrics and gynecology, ophthalmology, pharmacology, physiology, anatomy, and dentistry. Local preschools and public schools have been cooperative in providing access to children and facilities for child development research, local businesses and agencies offer sites for practice and research in applied behavior analysis, local senior centers and homes provide access to elderly populations, and the University's Center on Aging-Education Unit and Center for Women's Studies facilitate research related to their purviews. The University maintains an extensive network of computer facilities and the Department has a microcomputer lab available to graduate students.

Application Information:
Send to: Departmental Admissions Committee, Department of Psychology, West Virginia University, P.O. Box 6040, Morgantown, WV 26506-6040. Students are admitted in the Fall, application deadline January 1. *Fee:* $50.

Marquette University

Department of Counseling and Educational Psychology
School of Education
146 Schroeder Complex
Milwaukee, WI 53201-1881
Telephone: (414) 288-5790
Fax: (414) 288-3945
E-mail: *sallie.captain@marquette.edu*
Web: *http://www.marquette.edu/edu/education/coep*

Department Established:
1996. Chairperson: Timothy P. Melchert. Number of Faculty: total–full-time 7, part-time 5; women–full-time 3, part-time 2.

Programs and Degrees Offered:
Listed in the following order: Program area, degree type (T if terminal Master's), number awarded 7/00–6/01. Counseling MA (T) 18, counseling psychology PhD 7, educational psychology MA (T) 1.

Student Applications/Admissions:

Student Applications

Counseling MA—Applications 2001–2002, 49. Total applicants accepted 2001–2002, 29. New applicants enrolled 2001–2002, 20. Total enrolled 2001–2002 full-time, 19, part-time, 19. Openings 2002–2003, 22. The Median number of years required for completion of a degree are 2. The number of students enrolled full and part-time, who were dismissed or voluntarily withdrew from this program area were 2. *Counseling psychology PhD*—Applications 2001–2002, 19. Total applicants accepted 2001–2002, 11. New applicants enrolled 2001–2002, 7. Total enrolled 2001–2002 full-time, 21, part-time, 16. Openings 2002–2003, 6. The Median number of years required for completion of a degree are 5. The number of students enrolled full and part-time, who were dismissed or voluntarily withdrew from this program area were 1. *Educational psychology MA*—Applications 2001–2002, 2. Total applicants accepted 2001–2002, 2. New applicants enrolled 2001–2002, 2. Total enrolled 2001–2002 part-time, 4. Openings 2002–2003, 3. The Median number of years required for completion of a degree are 4. The number of students enrolled full and part-time, who were dismissed or voluntarily withdrew from this program area were 0.

Admissions Requirements:

Scores: Entries appear in this order: required test or GPA, minimum score (if required), median score of students entering in 2001–2002. Master's Programs: GRE-V+Q 810, 1030; overall undergraduate GPA no minimum stated, 3.4. Doctoral Programs: GRE-V+Q 760, 1160; overall undergraduate GPA no minimum stated, 3.7 ; last 2 years GPA no minimum stated; psychology GPA no minimum stated; psychology GPA no minimum stated.

Other Criteria: (importance of criteria rated low, medium, or high): GRE/MAT scores medium, research experience low, work experience medium, extracurricular activity low, clini-

cally related public service medium, GPA medium, letters of recommendation medium, interview medium, statement of goals and objectives medium, scholarly writing sample medium. Research experience and a sample of scholarly writing are important for admissions to our PhD program but not our Master's programs.

Student Characteristics: The following represents characteristics of students in 2001–2002 in all graduate psychology programs in the department: Female–full-time 38, part-time 29; Male–full-time 6, part-time 10; African American/Black–full-time 4, part-time 2; Hispanic/Latino (a)–full-time 3, part-time 0; Asian/Pacific Islander–full-time 2, part-time 0; American Indian/Alaska Native–full-time 0, part-time 1; Multi-ethnic–full-time 0, part-time 0; students subject to the Americans with Disabilities Act–full-time 1, part-time 1.

Financial Information/Assistance:
Tuition for Full-Time Study: *Master's:* State residents $420 per credit hour; nonstate residents: $420 per credit hour. *Doctoral:* State residents: $420 per credit hour; nonstate residents: $420 per credit hour.

Financial Assistance:

First Year Students: Teaching assistantships available for first-year. Average amount paid per academic year: $5,418. Average number of hours worked per week: 10. Apply by Jan. 15. Tuition remission given: partial. Research assistantships available for first-year. Average amount paid per academic year: $5,418. Average number of hours worked per week: 10. Apply by Jan. 15. Tuition remission given: partial. Fellowships and scholarships available for first-year. Average amount paid per academic year: $11,860. Average number of hours worked per week: 0. Apply by Jan. 15. Tuition remission given: full.

Advanced Students: Teaching assistantships available for advanced students. Average amount paid per academic year: $5,418. Average number of hours worked per week: 10. Apply by Feb. 15. Tuition remission given: partial. Research assistantships available for advanced students. Average amount paid per academic year: $5,418. Average number of hours worked per week: 10. Apply by Feb. 15. Tuition remission given: partial. Fellowships and scholarships available for advanced students. Average amount paid per academic year: $11,860. Average number of hours worked per week: 0. Apply by Varies. Tuition remission given: full.

Contact Information: Of all students currently enrolled full-time, 47% benefited from one or more of the listed financial assistance programs. For information on financial assistance, contact: Graduate School.

Internships/Practica: No information provided.

Housing and Day Care: On-campus housing and day care facilities are available.

Employment of Department Graduates:
Master's Degree Graduates: Of those who graduated in the academic year 2000–2001, the following categories and numbers represent the post-graduate activities and employment of master's

degree graduates: Enrolled in a post-doctoral residency/fellowship (n/a), employed in independent practice (n/a).

Doctoral Degree Graduates: Of those who graduated in the academic year 2000–2001, the following categories and numbers represent the post-graduate activities and employment of doctoral degree graduates: Enrolled in a psychology doctoral program (n/a), enrolled in another graduate/professional program (n/a).

Additional Information:

Orientation, Objectives, and Emphasis of Department: Our Master's in Counseling and PhD in Counseling Psychology programs are based on a comprehensive biopsychosocial approach to understanding human behavior, and we believe that a sensitivity to biological, psychological, social, multicultural, and developmental influences on behavior increases students' effectiveness both as practitioners and as researchers. We use a generalist approach that includes broad preparation in the diverse areas needed to practice competently as psychological scientists and practitioners in today's health care systems. The objectives of the Educational Psychology program are to provide knowledge and skills in the principal content areas of basic and applied psychology as required for the preparation of researchers for work in universities, research and evaluation facilities, business and industry, and schools.

Special Facilities or Resources: Our faculty, and Marquette University as a whole, are committed to offering high quality education. Our coursework, practica, research activities, and other training opportunities are all designed to provide very current and comprehensive preparation. Our student body is small, so students receive substantial individual attention. We are also committed to developing students' competencies to work with diverse multicultural groups, and we welcome applications from individuals with diverse backgrounds.

Application Information:

Send to: Graduate School, P.O. Box 1881, Milwaukee, WI 53201. Students are admitted in the Fall. For the Fall, the deadline for the PhD program is January 15 and February 15 for the Master's program. *Fee:* $40. Fee waived for Marquette Alumni.

Marquette University
Department of Psychology
Arts and Sciences
P.O. Box 1881
Milwaukee, WI 53201-1881
Telephone: (414) 288-7218
Fax: (414) 288-5333
E-mail: *psyc.dept@mu.edu*
Web: *http://www.marquette.edu/psyc*

Department Established:

1952. Chairperson: Robert J. Lueger. Number of Faculty: total–full-time 14, part-time 4; women–full-time 3, part-time 3; minority–full-time 2, part-time 1.

Programs and Degrees Offered:

Listed in the following order: Program area, degree type (T if terminal Master's), number awarded 7/00–6/01. Clinical Psychology MS/MA (T), clinical psychology PhD 2.

APA Accreditation: Clinical PhD: full.

Student Applications/Admissions:
Student Applications

Clinical Psychology MS/MA—Applications 2001–2002, 9. Total applicants accepted 2001–2002, 5. New applicants enrolled 2001–2002, 1. Total enrolled 2001–2002 full-time, 1. Openings 2002–2003, 6. The Median number of years required for completion of a degree are 2. The number of students enrolled full and part-time, who were dismissed or voluntarily withdrew from this program area were 0. *Clinical psychology PhD*—Applications 2001–2002, 23. Total applicants accepted 2001–2002, 11. New applicants enrolled 2001–2002, 7. Total enrolled 2001–2002 full-time, 36, part-time, 6. Openings 2002–2003, 8. The Median number of years required for completion of a degree are 5. The number of students enrolled full and part-time, who were dismissed or voluntarily withdrew from this program area were 0.

Admissions Requirements:

Scores: Entries appear in this order: required test or GPA, minimum score (if required), median score of students entering in 2001–2002. Master's Programs: GRE-V 550, 500; GRE-Q 500, 570; GRE-V+Q 1050, 1060; GRE-Analytical 500, 620; GRE-V+Q+Analytical 1550, 1630; GRE-Subject(Psych) 550, 550; overall undergraduate GPA 3.2, 3.58. Doctoral Programs: GRE-V 600, 580; GRE-Q 600, 620; GRE-V+Q 1200, 1200; GRE-Analytical 600, 710; GRE-V+Q+Analytical 1800, 1910; GRE-Subject(Psych) 600, 580; overall undergraduate GPA 3.40, 3.8 ; last 2 years GPA no minimum stated; psychology GPA no minimum stated; psychology GPA no minimum stated.

Other Criteria: (importance of criteria rated low, medium, or high): GRE/MAT scores medium, research experience high, work experience medium, extracurricular activity medium, clinically related public service medium, GPA medium, letters of recommendation high, interview medium, statement of goals and objectives high.

Student Characteristics: The following represents characteristics of students in 2001–2002 in all graduate psychology programs in the department: Female–full-time 27, part-time 5; Male–full-time 9, part-time 1; African American/Black–full-time 3, part-time 0; Hispanic/Latino (a)–full-time 1, part-time 0; Asian/Pacific Islander–full-time 1, part-time 0; American Indian/Alaska Native–full-time 0, part-time 0; Multi-ethnic–full-time 0, part-time 0; students subject to the Americans with Disabilities Act–full-time 0, part-time 0.

Financial Information/Assistance:

Tuition for Full-Time Study: *Master's:* State residents $600 per credit hour; nonstate residents: $600 per credit hour. *Doctoral:* State residents: $600 per credit hour; nonstate residents: $600 per credit hour.

Financial Assistance:

First Year Students: Teaching assistantships available for first-year. Average amount paid per academic year: $10,835. Aver-

age number of hours worked per week: 20. Apply by January 15. Tuition remission given: full. Research assistantships available for first-year. Average amount paid per academic year: $10,835. Average number of hours worked per week: 20. Apply by January 15. Tuition remission given: full. Fellowships and scholarships available for first-year. Average amount paid per academic year: $1,800. Average number of hours worked per week: 0. Apply by Janaury 15. Tuition remission given: full and partial.

Advanced Students: Teaching assistantships available for advanced students. Average amount paid per academic year: $10,835. Average number of hours worked per week: 20. Apply by January 15. Tuition remission given: full. Research assistantships available for advanced students. Average amount paid per academic year: $10,835. Average number of hours worked per week: 20. Apply by January 15. Tuition remission given: full. Fellowships and scholarships available for advanced students. Average amount paid per academic year: $1,800. Average number of hours worked per week: 0. Apply by January 15. Tuition remission given: full and partial.

Contact Information: Of all students currently enrolled full-time, 50% benefited from one or more of the listed financial assistance programs. For information on financial assistance, contact: Graduate School, Marquette University; www.grad.mu.edu.

Internships/Practica: Doctoral and terminal master's students obtain supervised clinical experience throughout their training. Practica are offered both in the Department's training clinic, the Center for Psychological Services, and in community agencies. The Department's training clinic provides assessment and intervention services to members of the general community under the supervision of licensed clinical faculty members. Students have averaged over 750 hours in the clinic, and over 2,000 hours in pre-internship practicum experiences. Marquette University's urban location provides a wealth of training opportunities in the community. Recent practicum experiences have included placements in agencies that provided training in neuropsychological assessment, geropsychology, behavioral medicine, pediatric health, and family therapy. Doctoral students are required to complete a 2,000 hour internship. To date, students have completed APA-approved internships in settings located in the Milwaukee area as well as eight different states. For those doctoral students for whom a professional internship is required prior to graduation, 4 applied in 2000–2001. Of those who applied, 3 were placed in internships listed by the Association of Psychology Postdoctoral and Internship Programs (APPIC); 2 were placed in APA accredited internships.

Housing and Day Care: On-campus housing and day care facilities are available.

Employment of Department Graduates:
Master's Degree Graduates: Of those who graduated in the academic year 2000–2001, the following categories and numbers represent the post-graduate activities and employment of master's degree graduates: Enrolled in a post-doctoral residency/fellowship (n/a), employed in independent practice (n/a).
Doctoral Degree Graduates: Of those who graduated in the academic year 2000–2001, the following categories and numbers represent the post-graduate activities and employment of doctoral degree graduates: Enrolled in a psychology doctoral program (n/a), enrolled in another graduate/professional program (n/a), enrolled in a post-doctoral residency/fellowship (1), employed in independent practice (1).

Additional Information:
Orientation, Objectives, and Emphasis of Department: The Clinical Psychology Program offers courses and training leading to the degrees of Doctor of Philosophy (PhD) and Master of Science (MS) in Clinical Psychology. All doctoral students acquire a Master of Science degree as they progress toward the doctoral degree. Students in the terminal master's program typically accept employment after completion of the program, but some go on to doctoral study. The doctoral program is approved by the American Psychological Association to train scientist-professionals. Students receive a solid foundation in scientific areas of psychology and in the historical foundations of psychology. Training in research skills such as statistics, measurement, and research methods ensures competence in conducting empirical research and in critically evaluating one's own and others' clinical and empirical work. Students become competent in professional practice skills such as assessment, interventions, and consultation. Supervised clinical experiences are planned throughout the curriculum. Graduates of the doctoral program are prepared to practice as clinical psychologists, consultants, teachers, researchers, and administrators.

Special Facilities or Resources: The department is located in completely refurbished and modern quarters that include a psychology clinic, two undergraduate teaching laboratories, and ample space for both faculty and student research. A full range of computer services is available at no charge to students. Located in a large metropolitan area, Marquette University is within easy commuting distance to a variety of hospitals and agencies in which training and research opportunities may be available.

Information for Students With Physical Disabilities: The department's offices, clinic, and laboratories are located in a building that is wheelchair-accessible. The university's Office of Disability Services assists qualifying students on a case-by-case basis.

Application Information:
Send to: Graduate School, 305 Holthusen Hall, Marquette University, 1324 W. Wisconsin Ave., Milwaukee, WI 53201-1881. Students are admitted in the Fall, application deadline January 15. *Fee:* $40. Waived for Marquette University alumni.

Wisconsin School of Professional Psychology
Professional School
9120 West Hampton Avenue, Suite 212
Milwaukee, WI 53225
Telephone: (414) 464-9777
Fax: (414) 358-5590
E-mail: *karen-wspp@msn.com*
Web: *http://www.execpc.com/~wspp*

Department Established:
1980. President: Kathleen M. Rusch, PhD. Number of Faculty: total–full-time 3, part-time 33; women–full-time 3, part-time 12.

Programs and Degrees Offered:

Listed in the following order: Program area, degree type (T if terminal Master's), number awarded 7/00–6/01. Clinical PsyD 14.

Student Applications/Admissions:

Student Applications

Clinical PsyD—Applications 2001–2002, 21. Total applicants accepted 2001–2002, 18. New applicants enrolled 2001–2002, 15. Total enrolled 2001–2002 full-time, 17, part-time, 31. Openings 2002–2003, 15. The Median number of years required for completion of a degree are 5. The number of students enrolled full and part-time, who were dismissed or voluntarily withdrew from this program area were 3.

Admissions Requirements:

Scores: Entries appear in this order: required test or GPA, minimum score (if required), median score of students entering in 2001–2002. Master's Programs: GRE-V+Q 1000, 1200; GRE-V+Q+Analytical no minimum stated; GRE-Subject(Psych) 500, 520; overall undergraduate GPA 3.0, 3.5; last 2 years GPA 3.2, 3.6; psychology GPA 3.2, 3.6. Doctoral Programs: GRE-V+Q 1000, 1200; GRE-V+Q+Analytical no minimum stated; GRE-Subject(Psych) 500, 550; overall undergraduate GPA 3.0, 3.5 ; last 2 years GPA no minimum stated; psychology GPA 3.2, 3.6 ; psychology GPA 3.2, 3.6.
Other Criteria: (importance of criteria rated low, medium, or high): GRE/MAT scores medium, research experience low, work experience high, extracurricular activity medium, clinically related public service high, GPA medium, letters of recommendation high, interview medium, statement of goals and objectives high, maturity high.

Student Characteristics: The following represents characteristics of students in 2001–2002 in all graduate psychology programs in the department: Female–full-time 14, part-time 26; Male–full-time 3, part-time 5; African American/Black–full-time 0, part-time 3; Hispanic/Latino (a)–full-time 0, part-time 0; Asian/Pacific Islander–full-time 0, part-time 1; American Indian/Alaska Native–full-time 0, part-time 0; Multi-ethnic–full-time 0, part-time 0; students subject to the Americans with Disabilities Act–full-time 0, part-time 0.

Financial Information/Assistance:

Tuition for Full-Time Study: *Master's:* State residents per academic year $19,000, $500 per credit hour; nonstate residents: per academic year $19,000, $500 per credit hour. *Doctoral:* State residents: per academic year $14,500, $500 per credit hour; nonstate residents: per academic year $14,500, $500 per credit hour.

Financial Assistance:

First Year Students: Fellowships and scholarships available for first-year. Average amount paid per academic year: $3,000. Average number of hours worked per week: 0. Apply by February 15. Tuition remission given: partial.

Advanced Students: Fellowships and scholarships available for advanced students. Average amount paid per academic year: $1,000. Average number of hours worked per week: 0. Apply by February 15. Tuition remission given: partial.

Contact Information: Of all students currently enrolled full-time, 4% benefited from one or more of the listed financial assistance programs. For information on financial assistance, contact: Karen Kilman, Assistant to the President.

Internships/Practica: WSPP has an on-site training clinic, the Psychology Center, which is designed to serve two purposes: to provide supervised training to students and to provide quality clinical services to an inner city multicultural disadvantaged population. The Center also maintains contracts and affiliations with a number of local service agencies to provide on-site services. Regardless of whether on- or off-site, all practica are supervised by WSPP faculty to ensure quality of supervision and communication with our DCT. Some 40 supervisors, all licensed and most National Register listed, are readily available. For assessment practica, WSPP maintains a library of psychological tests available for student use free of charge. Thus, all students are guaranteed ample practicum opportunities (the program requires 2,000 hours) without having to search for sites or supervisors. This high level of clinical training has led to our 100% internship placement rate to date. For those doctoral students for whom a professional internship is required prior to graduation, 4 applied in 2000–2001. Of those who applied, 3 were placed in internships listed by the Association of Psychology Postdoctoral and Internship Programs (APPIC).

Housing and Day Care: No on-campus housing and day care facilities are available.

Employment of Department Graduates:

Master's Degree Graduates: Of those who graduated in the academic year 2000–2001, the following categories and numbers represent the post-graduate activities and employment of master's degree graduates: Enrolled in a psychology doctoral program (6), enrolled in another graduate/professional program (0), enrolled in a post-doctoral residency/fellowship (n/a), employed in independent practice (n/a), employed in an academic position at a university (0), employed in an academic position at a 2-year/4-year college (0), employed in other positions at a higher education institution (0), employed in a professional position in a school system (0), employed in business or industry (research/consulting) (0), employed in business or industry (management) (0), employed in a government agency (research) (0), employed in a government agency (professional services) (0), employed in a community mental health/counseling center (0), employed in a hospital/medical center (0), still seeking employment (0), other employment position (0).

Doctoral Degree Graduates: Of those who graduated in the academic year 2000–2001, the following categories and numbers represent the post-graduate activities and employment of doctoral degree graduates: Enrolled in a psychology doctoral program (n/a), enrolled in another graduate/professional program (n/a), enrolled in a post-doctoral residency/fellowship (0), employed in independent practice (5), employed in an academic position at a university (0), employed in an academic position at a 2-year/4-year college (0), employed in other positions at a higher education institution (0), employed in a professional position in a school system (0), employed in business or industry (research/consulting) (0), employed in business or industry (management) (0), employed in a government agency (research) (0), employed in a government agency (professional services) (1), employed in a community mental health/counseling center (1), employed in a hospital/medical center (1), still seeking employment (0), other employment position (0).

Additional Information:

Orientation, Objectives, and Emphasis of Department: The Wisconsin School of Professional Psychology has as its goal the provision of a doctoral level education that emphasizes the acquisition of the traditional skills which defined the professional in the past, while staying open to new developments as they emerge. Our program balances theoretical and practical coursework, taking its impetus from the American Psychological Association's Vail Conference. The school's curriculum was developed in accord with APA norms and is continually evaluated to assure compliance with the requirements of that body. WSPP trains students toward competence in the following areas: self-awareness, assessment, research & evaluation, ethics & professional standards, management & supervision, relationship, intervention, respect for diversity, consultation, and social responsibility & community service. In its training philosophy, the school emphasizes clarity of verbal expression in written and oral communication, the development of clinical acumen, and an appreciation of the link between scientific data and clinical practice. Our program's small size and large faculty create abundant opportunities for mentorship with practicing psychologists in an apprentice-like setting.

Special Facilities or Resources: The Wisconsin School of Professional Psychology maintains a Training Clinic which includes facilities for research and practicum work associated with clinical courses. The Training Center houses an outpatient mental health clinic which serves a primarily inner city culturally diverse population, as well as provides opportunities for supervised experience with a wide range of clinical problems and populations. The center offers services to the community on a no-fee basis. Supervision provided by faculty.

Application Information:

Send to: Wisconsin School of Professional Psychology, 9120 W. Hampton Ave., Milwaukee, WI 53225. Students are admitted in the Fall, application deadline April 15; Spring, application deadline October 15. *Fee:* $75.

Wisconsin, University of, Eau Claire

School Psychology, Department of Psychology
Eau Claire, WI 54702
Telephone: (715) 836-5733
Fax: (715) 836-2380
E-mail: *frankewr@uwec.edu*
Web: *http://www.uwec.edu/*

Department Established:

Chairperson: Dr. Larry Morse. Number of Faculty: total–full-time 18, part-time 4; women–full-time 5; minority–full-time 1.

Programs and Degrees Offered:

Listed in the following order: Program area, degree type (T if terminal Master's), number awarded 7/00–6/01. School Psychology EdS (T) 8.

Student Applications/Admissions:

Student Applications

School Psychology EdS—Applications 2001–2002, 40. Total applicants accepted 2001–2002, 8. New applicants enrolled 2001–2002, 8. Total enrolled 2001–2002 full-time, 26, part-time, 1. Openings 2002–2003, 8. The Median number of years required for completion of a degree are 3. The number of students enrolled full and part-time, who were dismissed or voluntarily withdrew from this program area were 0.

Admissions Requirements:

Scores: Entries appear in this order: required test or GPA, minimum score (if required), median score of students entering in 2001–2002. Master's Programs: GRE-V 450, 500; GRE-V+Q+Analytical no minimum stated; overall undergraduate GPA 3.0, 3.3. Doctoral Programs: last 2 years GPA no minimum stated; psychology GPA no minimum stated; psychology GPA no minimum stated.

Other Criteria: (importance of criteria rated low, medium, or high): GRE/MAT scores, research experience medium, work experience medium, extracurricular activity medium, clinically related public service medium, GPA medium, letters of recommendation medium, interview medium, statement of goals and objectives medium.

Student Characteristics: The following represents characteristics of students in 2001–2002 in all graduate psychology programs in the department: Female–full-time 18, part-time 0; Male–full-time 8, part-time 0; African American/Black–full-time 0, part-time 0; Hispanic/Latino (a)–full-time 0, part-time 0; Asian/Pacific Islander–full-time 0, part-time 0; American Indian/Alaska Native–full-time 0, part-time 0.

Financial Information/Assistance:

Tuition for Full-Time Study: Master's: State residents per academic year $4,888; nonstate residents: per academic year $15,596.

Financial Assistance:

First Year Students: Research assistantships available for first-year. Average number of hours worked per week: 10. Apply by March 1. Fellowships and scholarships available for first-year. Apply by Varies.

Advanced Students: Research assistantships available for advanced students. Average number of hours worked per week: 10. Apply by March 1. Fellowships and scholarships available for advanced students. Apply by Varies.

Contact Information: Of all students currently enrolled full-time, 80% benefited from one or more of the listed financial assistance programs. For information on financial assistance, contact: Financial Aid Office, UW-Eau Claire, Schofield 115, Eau Claire, WI 54702, (715) 836-3373.

Internships/Practica: Internships are only available for students completing our school psychology program. Satisfactory completion of the first two years of training (which is comprised of the degree and certification phases of training) and recommendation of Graduate Review and Admissions Board are necessary for advancement to the internship phase of training. The Educational Specialist degree is awarded after completion of the internship phase.

Housing and Day Care: On-campus housing and day care facilities are available.

Employment of Department Graduates:

Master's Degree Graduates: Of those who graduated in the academic year 2000–2001, the following categories and numbers represent the post-graduate activities and employment of master's degree graduates: Enrolled in a post-doctoral residency/fellowship (n/a), employed in independent practice (n/a), employed in a professional position in a school system (8).

Doctoral Degree Graduates: Of those who graduated in the academic year 2000–2001, the following categories and numbers represent the post-graduate activities and employment of doctoral degree graduates: Enrolled in a psychology doctoral program (n/a), enrolled in another graduate/professional program (n/a).

Additional Information:

Orientation, Objectives, and Emphasis of Department: The primary goals of the school psychology training focus on preparation of a broadly skilled school psychology professional, one trained to meet the many and diverse challenges of practice in a rapidly changing work setting. Training in the delivery of evaluation and intervention (counseling, consultation, training, and research) services is eclectic, drawing heavily from behavioral (social learning, operant, and cognitive), clinical, developmental, and education (regular and special education) theoretical foundations. Professional training prepares the practitioner to work with individuals from early childhood/preschool through youth and adult ages providing services related to exceptional educational, at risk, and/or regular education initiative needs. Three training strands (diagnostic, research, and intervention) have been developed which make available extensive "applied training" or "hands on" learning opportunities. Twelve practica and a third-year internship have been structured to provide extensive supervised, professional training experiences (over 2000 hours), four practica beginning during the student's first semester of enrollment. Faculty supervisors have a training emphasis and appropriate professional license/certification in the areas of assigned supervision (for example, clinical, behavioral, school, counseling).

Special Facilities or Resources: Extensive on-campus and field site training opportunities are available. Three interdisciplinary clinics—The Human Development Center (Psychology-School Psychology; Special education-Learning Disabilities and Early Childhood; Communication Disorders; and Elementary Education-Reading), the Psychological Services Center (Psychology-School Psychology and Nursing), and the ADHD Behavioral Intervention Clinic—provide on-campus training in diagnostics, evaluation, and intervention. Area schools, residential facilities for developmentally disabled, emotionally disturbed youth and adults, and clinics offer and extensive array of additional supervised training settings.

Information for Students With Physical Disabilities: Facilities are accessible to individuals with physical disabilities.

Application Information:

Send to: Director, School Psychology Program, Department of Psychology, University of Wisconsin-Eau Claire, Eau Claire, WI 54702-4004. Students are admitted in the Fall, application deadline March 1. *Fee:* $45.

Wisconsin, University of, La Crosse
Department of Psychology/School Psychology
College of Liberal Studies
1725 State Street, 341 Main Hall
La Crosse, WI 54601
Telephone: (608) 785-8441
Fax: (608) 785-8443
E-mail: *dehn.milt@uwlax.edu*
Web: *http://www.uwlax.eduGraduate/index.html*

Department Established:

1967. Director: Milton Dehn. Number of Faculty: total–full-time 15, part-time 2; women–full-time 7, part-time 2; minority–full-time 1.

Programs and Degrees Offered:

Listed in the following order: Program area, degree type (T if terminal Master's), number awarded 7/00–6/01. School Psychology EdS new.

Student Applications/Admissions:

Student Applications

School Psychology EdS—Applications 2001–2002, 50. Total applicants accepted 2001–2002, 16. New applicants enrolled 2001–2002, 11. Total enrolled 2001–2002 full-time, 20. Openings 2002–2003, 12. The number of students enrolled full and part-time, who were dismissed or voluntarily withdrew from this program area were 0.

Admissions Requirements:

Scores: Entries appear in this order: required test or GPA, minimum score (if required), median score of students entering in 2001–2002. Master's Programs: GRE-V no minimum stated, 477; GRE-Q no minimum stated, 574; GRE-V+Q no minimum stated, 1021; GRE-Analytical no minimum stated, 625; GRE-V+Q+Analytical no minimum stated; overall undergraduate GPA 2.85, 3.5; last 2 years GPA no minimum stated, 3.65; psychology GPA no minimum stated, 3.62. Doctoral Programs: last 2 years GPA no minimum stated; psychology GPA no minimum stated; psychology GPA no minimum stated.

Other Criteria: (importance of criteria rated low, medium, or high): GRE/MAT scores medium, research experience medium, work experience medium, extracurricular activity medium, clinically related public service high, GPA high, letters of recommendation high, interview high, statement of goals and objectives high, Writing Sample high.

Student Characteristics: The following represents characteristics of students in 2001–2002 in all graduate psychology programs in the department: Female–full-time 17, part-time 0; Male–full-time 3, part-time 0; African American/Black–full-time 0, part-time 0; Hispanic/Latino (a)–full-time 0, part-time 0; Asian/Pacific Islander–full-time 1, part-time 0; American Indian/Alaska Native–full-time 0, part-time 0.

Financial Information/Assistance:

Tuition for Full-Time Study: *Master's:* State residents per academic year $2,322, $261 per credit hour; nonstate residents: per academic year $7,234, $807 per credit hour.

Financial Assistance:

First Year Students: No information provided.

Advanced Students: No information provided.

Contact Information: Of all students currently enrolled full-time, 20% benefited from one or more of the listed financial assistance programs. For information on financial assistance, contact: Financial Aid Office, University of Wisconsin-La Crosse, 1725 State St., La Crosse, WI 54601.

Internships/Practica: The School Psychology program prepares graduate students for certification as School Psychologists through academic coursework, 700 hours of supervised school practica, and a one year, 1,200 hour school internship. Graduate students are placed in local schools as early and intensively as possible. During their second, third, and fourth semesters students spend two days per week working in local schools under the direct supervision of experienced school psychologists. During these school practica students develop professional skills in assessment, consultation, intervention, counseling, and case management. Many of the core courses require projects which are completed in the schools during practica.

Housing and Day Care: On-campus housing and day care facilities are available.

Employment of Department Graduates:

Master's Degree Graduates: Of those who graduated in the academic year 2000–2001, the following categories and numbers represent the post-graduate activities and employment of master's degree graduates: Enrolled in a post-doctoral residency/fellowship (n/a), employed in independent practice (n/a).

Doctoral Degree Graduates: Of those who graduated in the academic year 2000–2001, the following categories and numbers represent the post-graduate activities and employment of doctoral degree graduates: Enrolled in a psychology doctoral program (n/a), enrolled in another graduate/professional program (n/a).

Additional Information:

Orientation, Objectives, and Emphasis of Department: The emphasis of this program is to train school psychologists who are effective teacher, parent, and school consultants. The program also emphasizes a pupil services model which addresses the educational and mental health needs of all children. The School Psychology knowledge base includes areas of Professional School Psychology, Educational Psychology, Psychological Foundations, Educational Foundations, and Mental Health. To provide psychological services in education, graduates of the School Psychology program must also have considerable knowledge of curriculum, special education, and pupil services. Graduates of the program are employed in public schools or educational agencies which serve public schools.

Special Facilities or Resources: Extensive fieldwork in local schools is a key to professional training. Faculty work closely with field supervisors and observe student performance in the field.

Application Information:

Send to: Office of Admissions, University of Wisconsin-La Crosse, 1725 State St., La Crosse, WI 54601. Students are admitted in the Spring, application deadline February 15. *Fee:* $45.

Wisconsin, University of, Madison

Department of Counseling Psychology,
  Counseling Psychology Program
School of Education
Education Building, Room 321, 1000 Bascom Mall
Madison, WI 53706
Telephone: (608) 262-0461 / 263-2746
Fax: (608) 265-3347
E-mail: *counpsych@education.wisc.edu*
Web: *http://www.education.wisc.edu/cp*

Department Established:

1964. Chairperson: Stephen Quintana. Number of Faculty: total–full-time 9, part-time 1; women–full-time 4, part-time 1; minority–full-time 4.

Programs and Degrees Offered:

Listed in the following order: Program area, degree type (T if terminal Master's), number awarded 7/00–6/01. Counseling, counseling psychology PhD 8.

APA Accreditation: Counseling PhD: full.

Student Applications/Admissions:

Student Applications

Counseling psychology PhD—Applications 2001–2002, 60. Total applicants accepted 2001–2002, 13. New applicants enrolled 2001–2002, 8. Total enrolled 2001–2002 full-time, 65, part-time, 1. Openings 2002–2003, 8. The Median number of years required for completion of a degree are 5. The number of students enrolled full and part-time, who were dismissed or voluntarily withdrew from this program area were 1.

Admissions Requirements:

Scores: Entries appear in this order: required test or GPA, minimum score (if required), median score of students entering in 2001–2002. Master's Programs: GRE-V no minimum stated; GRE-Q no minimum stated; GRE-Analytical no minimum stated; GRE-V+Q+Analytical no minimum stated, 1600; last 2 years GPA 3.0, 3.4. Doctoral Programs: GRE-V no minimum stated, 550; GRE-Q no minimum stated, 570; GRE-Analytical no minimum stated, 620; GRE-V+Q+Analytical no minimum stated, 1680; last 2 years GPA 3.0, 3.30; psychology GPA no minimum stated; psychology GPA 3.5, 3.70.

Other Criteria: (importance of criteria rated low, medium, or high): GRE/MAT scores medium, research experience medium, work experience medium, extracurricular activity high, clinically related public service high. GPA medium, letters of recommendation high, interview high, statement of goals and objectives high, Interest in multicultural high, For master's: research low, interview none. All other criteria the same.

Student Characteristics: The following represents characteristics of students in 2001–2002 in all graduate psychology programs in the department: Female–full-time 72, part-time 1; Male–full-time 33, part-time 1; African American/Black–full-time 8, part-time 0; Hispanic/Latino (a)–full-time 15, part-time 0; Asian/Pacific Islander–full-time 10, part-time 0; American Indian/Alaska Native–full-time 4, part-time 0; Multi-ethnic–full-time 5.

Financial Information/Assistance:

Tuition for Full-Time Study: *Master's:* State residents per academic year $7,360, $399 per credit hour; nonstate residents: per academic year $20,500, $1,282 per credit hour. *Doctoral:* State residents: per academic year $7,360, $399 per credit hour; nonstate residents: per academic year $20,500, $1,282 per credit hour.

Financial Assistance:

First Year Students: Teaching assistantships available for first-year. Average amount paid per academic year: $7,000. Average number of hours worked per week: 13. Apply by January 5. Tuition remission given: full. Research assistantships available for first-year. Average amount paid per academic year: $7,000. Average number of hours worked per week: 13. Apply by January 5. Tuition remission given: full. Fellowships and scholarships available for first-year. Average amount paid per academic year: $7,000. Average number of hours worked per week: 13. Apply by January 5. Tuition remission given: full.

Advanced Students: Teaching assistantships available for advanced students. Average amount paid per academic year: $7,000. Average number of hours worked per week: 13. Tuition remission given: full. Research assistantships available for advanced students. Average amount paid per academic year: $7,000. Average number of hours worked per week: 13. Tuition remission given: full. Fellowships and scholarships available for advanced students. Average amount paid per academic year: $7,000. Average number of hours worked per week: 13. Tuition remission given: full.

Contact Information: Of all students currently enrolled full-time, 35% benefited from one or more of the listed financial assistance programs. For information on financial assistance, contact: Maureen Garity, counpsych@education.wisc.edu, 608-262-4807.

Internships/Practica: Both master's and doctoral students are required to take at least two semesters of practica. For doctoral students (and some master's students), local sites include Dane County Community Mental Health Agency, Mendota Mental Health Institute, University of Wisconsin Counseling and Consultation Services, Veteran's Administration Hospital, and Family Therapy, Inc. Master's students may pursue practica in three types of settings: public schools, student services offices and counseling centers in higher education, and community mental health agencies and private clinics. The majority of practicum placements are in the Madison area but some are placed in nearby metropolitan areas in Wisconsin such as Milwaukee and Green Bay, as well as in rural communities served by regional mental health clinics. For those doctoral students for whom a professional internship is required prior to graduation, 8 applied in 2000–2001. Of those who applied, 5 were placed in internships listed by the Association of Psychology Postdoctoral and Internship Programs (APPIC); 5 were placed in APA accredited internships.

Housing and Day Care: On-campus housing and day care facilities are available.

Employment of Department Graduates:

Master's Degree Graduates: Of those who graduated in the academic year 2000–2001, the following categories and numbers represent the post-graduate activities and employment of master's degree graduates: Enrolled in a post-doctoral residency/fellowship (n/a), employed in independent practice (n/a).

Doctoral Degree Graduates: Of those who graduated in the academic year 2000–2001, the following categories and numbers represent the post-graduate activities and employment of doctoral degree graduates: Enrolled in a psychology doctoral program (n/a), enrolled in another graduate/professional program (n/a).

Additional Information:

Orientation, Objectives, and Emphasis of Department: The master's and doctoral programs are intended to provide a closely integrated didactic experimental curriculum for the preparation of counseling professionals. The master's degree strongly emphasizes service delivery and its practica/internship components reflect that emphasis. The doctoral degree emphasizes the integration of counseling and psychological theory and practice with substantive development of research skills in the domains encompassed by counseling psychology. The PhD program in counseling psychology is APA-accredited utilizing the scientist-practitioner model. Students are prepared for academic, service-delivery, research, and administrative positions in professional psychology. The Department infuses principles of multiculturalism throughout the curriculum.

Special Facilities or Resources: The department possesses excellent computer facilities including multimedia production. Also, two counseling psychologists employed at the University Counseling Service are adjunct professors in the department and provide us with on-going linkage with that service for practica and internships. We also have very up-to-date computer software assessment resources. The department, together with departments of Rehabilitation Psychology, Special Education, and School Psychology, utilizes an interdisciplinary training center that provides professional training practices.

Information for Students With Physical Disabilities: Students with physical disabilities may obtain information about learning aides, parking, building access, housing, library, and other services from the McBurney Disability Resource Center at 905 University Ave., Madison, WI 53706. Phone: 608-263-2741 (TDD 608-263-6393).

Application Information:
Send to: Counseling Psychology, Graduate Admissions, UW-Madison, 321 Education Bldg., 1000 Bascom Mall, Madison, WI 53706. Students are admitted in the Fall. For the Fall, application deadline is PhD—January 5, Master's—February 15. For the Summer, application deadlines are the same. *Fee:* $45.

Wisconsin, University of, Madison
Department of Educational Psychology,
  School Psychology Program
1025 West Johnson Street
Madison, WI 53706-1796
Telephone: (608) 262-3432
Fax: (608) 262-0843
E-mail: *edpsych@facstaff.wisc.edu*
Web: *http://www.education.wisc.edu/edpsych/index.html*

Department Established:
1960. Chairperson: Leonard Abbeduto. Number of Faculty: total–full-time 20, part-time 3; women–full-time 6, part-time 1.

Programs and Degrees Offered:

Listed in the following order: Program area, degree type (T if terminal Master's), number awarded 7/00–6/01. School Psychology PhD 12.

APA Accreditation: School PhD: full.

Student Applications/Admissions:

Student Applications

School Psychology PhD—Applications 2001–2002, 33. Total applicants accepted 2001–2002, 13. New applicants enrolled 2001–2002, 8. Total enrolled 2001–2002 full-time, 32. Openings 2002–2003, 9. The number of students enrolled full and part-time, who were dismissed or voluntarily withdrew from this program area were 1.

Admissions Requirements:

Scores: Entries appear in this order: required test or GPA, minimum score (if required), median score of students entering in 2001–2002. Doctoral Programs: GRE-V no minimum stated, 560; GRE-Q no minimum stated, 628; GRE-V+Q 1000, 1188; GRE-Analytical no minimum stated; overall undergraduate GPA 3.00; last 2 years GPA no minimum stated; psychology GPA no minimum stated; psychology GPA no minimum stated.

Other Criteria: (importance of criteria rated low, medium, or high): GRE/MAT scores medium, research experience medium, work experience medium, extracurricular activity low, clinically related public service medium, GPA medium, letters of recommendation high, interview high, statement of goals and objectives high.

Student Characteristics: The following represents characteristics of students in 2001–2002 in all graduate psychology programs in the department: Female–full-time 48, part-time 13; Male–full-time 25, part-time 5; African American/Black–full-time 2, part-time 0; Hispanic/Latino (a)–full-time 7, part-time 0; Asian/Pacific Islander–full-time 3, part-time 0; American Indian/Alaska Native–full-time 0, part-time 0; students subject to the Americans with Disabilities Act–full-time 1.

Financial Information/Assistance:

Tuition for Full-Time Study: *Master's:* State residents per academic year $6,361, $398 per credit hour; nonstate residents: per academic year $20,498, $1,281 per credit hour. *Doctoral:* State residents: per academic year $6,361, $398 per credit hour; nonstate residents: per academic year $20,498, $1,281 per credit hour.

Financial Assistance:

First Year Students: Teaching assistantships available for first-year. Average amount paid per academic year: $10,476. Average number of hours worked per week: 14. Apply by January 10. Tuition remission given: full. Research assistantships available for first-year. Average amount paid per academic year: $13,379. Average number of hours worked per week: 20. Apply by January 10. Tuition remission given: full. Traineeships available for first-year. Apply by January 10. Tuition remission given: full. Fellowships and scholarships available for first-year. Average amount paid per academic year: $13,446. Average number of hours worked per week: 0. Apply by January 10. Tuition remission given: full.

Advanced Students: Teaching assistantships available for advanced students. Average amount paid per academic year: $10,476. Average number of hours worked per week: 14. Apply by January 10. Tuition remission given: full. Research assistantships available for advanced students. Average amount paid per academic year: $13,379. Average number of hours worked per week: 20. Apply by January 10. Tuition remission given: full. Traineeships available for advanced students. Apply by January 10. Tuition remission given: full. Fellowships and scholarships available for advanced students. Average amount paid per academic year: $13,446. Average number of hours worked per week: 0. Apply by January 10. Tuition remission given: full.

Contact Information: Of all students currently enrolled full-time, 67% benefited from one or more of the listed financial assistance programs. For information on financial assistance, contact: Graduate Admissions Coordinator, Department of Educational Psychology, 1025 West Johnson St., Madison, WI 53706-1796.

Internships/Practica: The School Psychology Program admits students interested in obtaining a PhD. Students working toward this goal complete a two-semester clinical practicum experience during year two (200-hour minimum) and a two-semester field practicum during year three (400-hour minimum). This practicum experience is provided by the department. After the master's, students are required to complete either an APA approved internship or establish one of their own in a school (public or private), clinic, or hospital, that is approved by the program (minimum 200 hours) to complete their PhD requirements. The Wisconsin Internship Consortium in Professional School Psychology (WICPSP) is also administered through the School Psychology Program. The primary focus of the pre-doctoral internship program is to provide advanced training for graduate students from a wide variety of cooperating sites where an internship is provided over several rotations. This internship is implemented according to Ethical Principles of Psychologists (APA, 1992), and the criteria published by the National Register of Health Service Providers and the National Association of School Psychologists are also followed. Criteria endorsed by the Council of Directors of School Psychology are also met. For those doctoral students for whom a professional internship is required prior to graduation, 4 applied in 2000–2001. Of those who applied, 4 were placed in APA accredited internships.

Housing and Day Care: On-campus housing and day care facilities are available.

Employment of Department Graduates:

Master's Degree Graduates: Of those who graduated in the academic year 2000–2001, the following categories and numbers represent the post-graduate activities and employment of master's degree graduates: Enrolled in a psychology doctoral program (5), enrolled in a post-doctoral residency/fellowship (n/a), employed in independent practice (n/a).

Doctoral Degree Graduates: Of those who graduated in the academic year 2000–2001, the following categories and numbers represent the post-graduate activities and employment of doctoral degree graduates: Enrolled in a psychology doctoral program (n/a), enrolled in another graduate/professional program (n/a), employed in a professional position in a school system (6).

Additional Information:

Orientation, Objectives, and Emphasis of Department: The department moved to a completely remodeled building in September

1985, which contains a separate research laboratory for each member of the faculty; specifically designed quarters for teaching advanced laboratory courses in cognitive psychology, perception, physiological psychology, social psychology, experimental personality, child psychology, and learning; and a computing laboratory with links to the campus computer for teaching statistics and experimental design. Faculty have microcomputers in their offices, as well as in their laboratories, and these are also connected to the mainframe and to the World Wide Web. Special construction, air conditioning, and ventilation were included in the teaching and research laboratories to accommodate work with animal and human subjects. There is also a mechanical and woodworking shop and an excellent electronics shop, supervised by a full-time technician. The department training clinic is housed in a separate wing of the building with its own offices, clerical staff, research space, clinic rooms, and full-time director.

Special Facilities or Resources: The Educational and Psychological Training Center serves advanced graduate students in educational psychology. It provides diagnostic and treatment services for children and adolescents experiencing a variety of learning and behavior problems. The Laboratory of Experimental Design provides assistance to students and faculty in the design and analysis of research. Members of the laboratory include graduate students and faculty in the quantitative area.

Application Information:
Send to: Graduate Admissions Coordinator, Education Psychology, 1025 W. Johnson St., Madison, WI 53706-1796. Students are admitted in the Fall, application deadline December 1. *Fee:* $45.

Wisconsin, University of, Madison
Department of HD&FS
School of Human Ecology
1430 Linden Drive
Madison, WI 53706
Telephone: (608) 263-2381
Fax: (608) 265-1172
E-mail: *hdfs@mail.sohe.wisc.edu*
Web: *http://sohe.wisc.edu/hdfs*

Department Established:
Chairperson: William Aquilino. Number of Faculty: total–full-time 13; women–full-time 8; minority–full-time 2.

Programs and Degrees Offered:
Listed in the following order: Program area, degree type (T if terminal Master's), number awarded 7/00–6/01. Human Dev & Family Studies MA, Human Dev & Family Studies PhD.

Student Applications/Admissions:
Student Applications
Human Dev & Family Studies MA Openings 2002–2003, 12. The number of students enrolled full and part-time, who were dismissed or voluntarily withdrew from this program area were 1. Human Dev & Family Studies PhD.

Admissions Requirements:
Scores: Entries appear in this order: required test or GPA, minimum score (if required), median score of students entering

in 2001–2002. Master's Programs: GRE-V no minimum stated; GRE-Q no minimum stated; GRE-Analytical no minimum stated; overall undergraduate GPA no minimum stated. Doctoral Programs: GRE-V no minimum stated; GRE-Q no minimum stated; GRE-Analytical no minimum stated; overall undergraduate GPA no minimum stated; last 2 years GPA no minimum stated; psychology GPA no minimum stated; psychology GPA no minimum stated.

Financial Information/Assistance:
Tuition for Full-Time Study: No information provided.

Financial Assistance:
First Year Students: No information provided.
Advanced Students: No information provided.
Contact Information: No information provided.

Internships/Practica: No information provided.

Housing and Day Care: On-campus housing and day care facilities are available.

Employment of Department Graduates:
Master's Degree Graduates: Of those who graduated in the academic year 2000–2001, the following categories and numbers represent the post-graduate activities and employment of master's degree graduates: Enrolled in a post-doctoral residency/fellowship (n/a), employed in independent practice (n/a).
Doctoral Degree Graduates: Of those who graduated in the academic year 2000–2001, the following categories and numbers represent the post-graduate activities and employment of doctoral degree graduates: Enrolled in a psychology doctoral program (n/a), enrolled in another graduate/professional program (n/a).

Application Information:
Send to: Graduate Admissions, Human Development & Family Studies, Graduate Program, University of Wisconsin—Madison, 1430 Linden Drive, Madison, WI 53706. Students are admitted in the Fall, application deadline January 12. *Fee:* $45.

Wisconsin, University of, Madison
Department of Psychology
W. J. Brogden Psychology Building
1202 West Johnson Street
Madison, WI 53706
Telephone: (608) 262-2079
Fax: (608) 262-4029
E-mail: *jefoxand@facstaff.wisc.edu*
Web: *http://psych.wisc.edu*

Department Established:
1888. Director of Graduate Studies: Lyn Y. Abramson. Number of Faculty: total–full-time 33, part-time 2; women–full-time 12, part-time 1; minority–full-time 2, part-time 1.

Programs and Degrees Offered:
Listed in the following order: Program area, degree type (T if terminal Master's), number awarded 7/00–6/01. Biological PhD,

clinical PhD 2, cognitive and perceptual PhD 1, developmental PhD 1, Individualized Graduate Major PhD, social PhD 2.

APA Accreditation: Clinical PhD: full.

Student Applications/Admissions:

Student Applications

Biological PhD—Applications 2001–2002, 29. Total applicants accepted 2001–2002, 1. New applicants enrolled 2001–2002, 1. Total enrolled 2001–2002 full-time, 13. The number of students enrolled full and part-time, who were dismissed or voluntarily withdrew from this program area were 0. *Clinical PhD*—Applications 2001–2002, 102. Total applicants accepted 2001–2002, 6. New applicants enrolled 2001–2002, 2. Total enrolled 2001–2002 full-time, 26. The Median number of years required for completion of a degree are 8. The number of students enrolled full and part-time, who were dismissed or voluntarily withdrew from this program area were 1. *Cognitive and perceptual PhD*—Applications 2001–2002, 39. Total applicants accepted 2001–2002, 6. New applicants enrolled 2001–2002, 6. Total enrolled 2001–2002 full-time, 10. The Median number of years required for completion of a degree are 8. The number of students enrolled full and part-time, who were dismissed or voluntarily withdrew from this program area were 1. *Developmental PhD*—Applications 2001–2002, 34. Total applicants accepted 2001–2002, 6. New applicants enrolled 2001–2002, 2. Total enrolled 2001–2002 full-time, 9. The Median number of years required for completion of a degree are 7. The number of students enrolled full and part-time, who were dismissed or voluntarily withdrew from this program area were 0. *Individualized Graduate Major PhD*—Applications 2001–2002, 6. Total applicants accepted 2001–2002, 2. New applicants enrolled 2001–2002, 2. Total enrolled 2001–2002 full-time, 5. *Social PhD*—Applications 2001–2002, 47. Total applicants accepted 2001–2002, 6. New applicants enrolled 2001–2002, 2. Total enrolled 2001–2002 full-time, 11. The Median number of years required for completion of a degree are 7. The number of students enrolled full and part-time, who were dismissed or voluntarily withdrew from this program area were 0.

Admissions Requirements:

Scores: Entries appear in this order: required test or GPA, minimum score (if required), median score of students entering in 2001–2002. Doctoral Programs: GRE-V no minimum stated; GRE-Q no minimum stated; GRE-V+Q 1200, 1290; GRE-Analytical no minimum stated; overall undergraduate GPA 3.00, 3.78; last 2 years GPA no minimum stated; psychology GPA no minimum stated; psychology GPA no minimum stated. GRE Subject test is strongly recommended, but not required.

Other Criteria: (importance of criteria rated low, medium, or high): GRE/MAT scores high, research experience high, work experience low, clinically related public service low, GPA high, letters of recommendation high, interview high, statement of goals and objectives high.

Student Characteristics: The following represents characteristics of students in 2001–2002 in all graduate psychology programs in the department: Female–full-time 42, part-time 0; Male–full-time 32, part-time 0; African American/Black–full-time 2, part-time 0; Hispanic/Latino (a)–full-time 1, part-time 0; Asian/Pacific Islander–full-time 2, part-time 0; American Indian/Alaska Native–full-time 0, part-time 0.

Financial Information/Assistance:

Tuition for Full-Time Study: *Doctoral:* State residents: per academic year $3,180; nonstate residents: per academic year $10,250.

Financial Assistance:

First Year Students: Teaching assistantships available for first-year. Average amount paid per academic year: $10,476. Average number of hours worked per week: 20. Apply by Jan. 5. Tuition remission given: full. Research assistantships available for first-year. Average amount paid per academic year: $13,379. Average number of hours worked per week: 20. Apply by Jan. 5. Tuition remission given: full. Traineeships available for first-year. Average amount paid per academic year: $13,379. Average number of hours worked per week: 20. Apply by Jan. 5. Tuition remission given: full. Fellowships and scholarships available for first-year. Average amount paid per academic year: $13,379. Apply by Jan. 5. Tuition remission given: full.

Advanced Students: Teaching assistantships available for advanced students. Average amount paid per academic year: $13,800. Average number of hours worked per week: 20. Tuition remission given: full. Research assistantships available for advanced students. Average amount paid per academic year: $13,379. Average number of hours worked per week: 20. Tuition remission given: full. Traineeships available for advanced students. Average amount paid per academic year: $13,379. Average number of hours worked per week: 20. Tuition remission given: full. Fellowships and scholarships available for advanced students. Average amount paid per academic year: $13,446. Tuition remission given: full.

Contact Information: Of all students currently enrolled full-time, 91% benefited from one or more of the listed financial assistance programs. For information on financial assistance, contact: Student Financial Services; 432 N. Murray St., Rm. 231, Madison, WI 53706.

Internships/Practica: Clinical psychology graduate students are required to complete a minimum of 400 hours of practicum experience, of which at least 150 hours are in direct service experience and at least 75 hours are in formally scheduled supervision. Each student will complete a 160-hour clerkship at a preapproved site which is designed to expose students to diverse clinical populations and the practice of clinical psychology in an applied setting. Also, a one-year internship is required. For those doctoral students for whom a professional internship is required prior to graduation, 5 applied in 2000–2001. Of those who applied, 5 were placed in APA accredited internships.

Housing and Day Care: On-campus housing and day care facilities are available.

Employment of Department Graduates:

Master's Degree Graduates: Of those who graduated in the academic year 2000–2001, the following categories and numbers represent the post-graduate activities and employment of master's degree graduates: Enrolled in a post-doctoral residency/fellowship (n/a), employed in independent practice (n/a).

Doctoral Degree Graduates: Of those who graduated in the academic year 2000–2001, the following categories and numbers represent the post-graduate activities and employment of doctoral degree graduates: Enrolled in a psychology doctoral program (n/a), enrolled in another graduate/professional program (n/a), enrolled in a post-doctoral residency/fellowship (1), employed in an academic position at a university (2), employed in other positions at a higher education institution (2), employed in business or industry (research/consulting) (1).

Additional Information:

Orientation, Objectives, and Emphasis of Department: The psychology PhD program is characterized by the following goals: emphasis both on extensive academic training in general psychology and on intensive research training in the student's particular area of concentration, a wide offering of content courses and seminars permitting the student considerable freedom in working out a program of study in collaboration with the major professor, and early and continuing commitment to research. Students are expected to become competent scholars and creative scientists in their own areas of concentration.

Special Facilities or Resources: The department has an extraordinary array of research facilities. Virtually all laboratories are fully computer controlled, and the department's general-purpose facilities are freely available to all graduate students. The Brogden and the Harlow Primate Laboratory have special facilities for housing animals, as well as for behavioral, pharmacological, anatomical, immunological, and physiological studies. We are well-equipped for studies of visual, auditory, and language perception and other areas of cognitive psychology. In addition, the Psychology Department Research and Training Clinic is housed in the Brogden Building. Many of the faculty and graduate students are affiliated with the Institute of Aging, the Waisman Center on Mental Retardation and Human Development, the Wisconsin Regional Primate Research Center, the Health Emotions Center, the Neuroscience Training Program, the Keck Neuroimaging Center, the Hearing Training Program, the Institute for Research on Poverty, the NSF National Consortium on Violence Research, and the Women's Studies Research Center. There are strong ties to the departments of Anatomy, Anthropology, Communicative Disorders, Educational Psychology, Entomology, Immunology, Industrial Engineering, Ophthalmology, Psychiatry, Sociology, Wildlife Ecology, Zoology, the Mass Communication Research Center, the Institute for Research on Poverty, and the Survey Research Laboratory.

Information for Students With Physical Disabilities: Contact Mcburney Disability Resource Center, 905 University Avenue, University of Wisconsin, Madison, WI 53706.

Application Information:
Send to: Admissions Office: Department of Psychology, University of Wisconsin, 1202 W. Johnson Street, Madison, WI 53706. Students are admitted in the Fall, application deadline January 5. Contact the Graduate School, 500 Lincoln Drive, 228 Bascom Hall, Madison WI 53706. *Fee:* $45.

Wisconsin, University of, Milwaukee

Department of Psychology
P.O. Box 413
Milwaukee, WI 53201
Telephone: (414) 229-4747
Fax: (414) 229-5219
E-mail: *mundo@csd.uwm.edu*
Web: *http://www.uwm.edu/Dept/Psychology*

Department Established:
1956. Chairperson: Raymond Fleming. Number of Faculty: total–full-time 20, part-time 9; women–full-time 5, part-time 5.

Programs and Degrees Offered:
Listed in the following order: Program area, degree type (T if terminal Master's), number awarded 7/00–6/01. Clinical PhD 5, experimental PhD 4, experimental behavior analysis MA (T), experimental health psychology.

APA Accreditation: Clinical PhD: full.

Student Applications/Admissions:
Student Applications

Clinical PhD—Applications 2001–2002, 59. Total applicants accepted 2001–2002, 5. New applicants enrolled 2001–2002, 5. Total enrolled 2001–2002 full-time, 36. Openings 2002–2003, 5. The number of students enrolled full and part-time, who were dismissed or voluntarily withdrew from this program area were 0. *Experimental PhD*—Applications 2001–2002, 12. Total applicants accepted 2001–2002, 5. New applicants enrolled 2001–2002, 5. Total enrolled 2001–2002 full-time, 18. Openings 2002–2003, 5. The number of students enrolled full and part-time, who were dismissed or voluntarily withdrew from this program area were 0. *Experimental behavior analysis MA*—Applications 2001–2002, 2. Total applicants accepted 2001–2002, 2. New applicants enrolled 2001–2002, 2. Total enrolled 2001–2002 full-time, 2. Openings 2002–2003, 6. The number of students enrolled full and part-time, who were dismissed or voluntarily withdrew from this program area were 0.

Admissions Requirements:

Scores: Entries appear in this order: required test or GPA, minimum score (if required), median score of students entering in 2001–2002. Master's Programs: GRE-V no minimum stated, 437; GRE-Q no minimum stated, 543; GRE-Analytical no minimum stated, 493; GRE-Subject(Psych) no minimum stated, 532; overall undergraduate GPA 3.0, 3.27; last 2 years GPA no minimum stated, 3.44; psychology GPA no minimum stated, 3.52. Doctoral Programs: GRE-V 550, 568; GRE-Q 550, 584; GRE-Analytical no minimum stated, 657; GRE-Subject(Psych) no minimum stated; overall undergraduate GPA 3.00, 3.56; last 2 years GPA no minimum stated, 3.63; psychology GPA no minimum stated, 3.73; psychology GPA no minimum stated, 3.76. For the Experimental Doctoral Program: GRE V+Q minimum is 800.

Other Criteria: (importance of criteria rated low, medium, or high): work experience low, extracurricular activity low, interview medium, statement of goals and objectives high. No interview is required for admission to the Doctoral Program in Experimental Psychology.

Student Characteristics: The following represents characteristics of students in 2001–2002 in all graduate psychology programs in the department: Female–full-time 16, part-time 0; Male–full-time 2, part-time 0; African American/Black–full-time 0, part-time 0; Hispanic/Latino (a)–full-time 0, part-time 0; Asian/Pacific Islander–full-time 0, part-time 0; American Indian/Alaska Native–full-time 0, part-time 0.

Financial Information/Assistance:

Tuition for Full-Time Study: No information provided.

Financial Assistance:

First Year Students: No information provided.
Advanced Students: No information provided.
Contact Information: For information on financial assistance, contact: Chairperson, Graduate Admissions Committee, Department of Psychology, University of Wisconsin-Milwaukee, P.O. Box 413, Milwaukee, WI 53201.

Internships/Practica: Seventeen training sites in the Greater Milwaukee Area are used for clinical training practica, providing students with excellent training in Neuropsychology and Health Psychology. These training experiences equip students to compete for nationally recognized pre-doctoral internships in clinical psychology.

Housing and Day Care: No on-campus housing and day care facilities are available.

Employment of Department Graduates:

Master's Degree Graduates: Of those who graduated in the academic year 2000–2001, the following categories and numbers represent the post-graduate activities and employment of master's degree graduates: Enrolled in a post-doctoral residency/fellowship (n/a), employed in independent practice (n/a).

Doctoral Degree Graduates: Of those who graduated in the academic year 2000–2001, the following categories and numbers represent the post-graduate activities and employment of doctoral degree graduates: Enrolled in a psychology doctoral program (n/a), enrolled in another graduate/professional program (n/a).

Additional Information:

Orientation, Objectives, and Emphasis of Department: The department has a PhD program in experimental and clinical psychology. The experimental program provides specialization in neuroscience, physiological, conditioning and learning, cognition social, and developmental. Regardless of the specialty area, the goal of the program is to provide the students with an understanding of psychology as a scientific discipline and to prepare them for careers in research and teaching. The clinical program follows the Boulder model, in which students are trained as both scientists and practitioners through integration of research, practical experience, and coursework in personality theory, psychopathology, assessment, and psychotherapy. A predoctoral internship is required. Although a clinical student may emphasize either the basic or applied aspect of psychology, the goal of the program is excellence in both areas. Students in the clinical as well as the general program are directly involved in research under the direction of their major professor, during each semester in the department.

Special Facilities or Resources: The department moved to a completely remodeled building in September 1985, which contains a separate research laboratory for each member of the faculty; specifically designed quarters for teaching advanced laboratory courses in cognitive psychology, perception, physiological psychology, social psychology, experimental personality, child psychology, and learning; and a computing laboratory with links to the campus computer for teaching statistics and experimental design. Faculty have microcomputers in their offices, as well as in their laboratories, and these are also connected to the mainframe and to the World Wide Web. Special construction, air conditioning, and ventilation were included in the teaching and research laboratories to accommodate work with animal and human subjects. There is also a mechanical and woodworking shop and an excellent electronics shop, supervised by a full-time technician. The department training clinic is housed in a separate wing of the building with its own offices, clerical staff, research space, clinic rooms, and full-time director.

Information for Students With Physical Disabilities: UWM has a Student Accessibility Center (SAC) that offers academic accommodation services to students with documented disabilities. Through the diagnostic reports and professional consultation, the SAC maximizes the success of disabled students.

Application Information:

Send to: Chairperson, Graduate Admissions Committee, Department of Psychology, P.O. Box 413, Milwaukee, WI 53201. Students are admitted in the Fall, application deadline December 31. *Fee:* $45. Application fee for foreign students is $75. Under rare circumstances, one-half of foreign application fee will be waived.

Wisconsin, University of, Milwaukee

Educational Psychology
Education
2400 E. Hartford IP0413
Milwaukee, WI 53211
Telephone: (414) 229-4767
Fax: (414) 229-4939
E-mail: *dmickels@uwm.edu*
Web: *http://www.uwm.edu/Dept/EdPsych*

Department Established:

1965. Chairperson: Douglas J. Mickelson. Number of Faculty: total–full-time 20, part-time 14; women–full-time 11, part-time 12; minority–full-time 3, part-time 2.

Programs and Degrees Offered:

Listed in the following order: Program area, degree type (T if terminal Master's), number awarded 7/00–6/01. Counseling MA 95, school.

APA Accreditation: Counseling PhD: full. School PhD: full.

Student Applications/Admissions:

Student Applications

Counseling MA—Applications 2001–2002, 220. Total applicants accepted 2001–2002, 133. New applicants enrolled 2001–2002, 110. Total enrolled 2001–2002 full-time, 50, part-time, 180. Openings 2002–2003, 50. The Median number of years required for completion of a degree are 4.

Admissions Requirements:

Scores: Entries appear in this order: required test or GPA, minimum score (if required), median score of students entering in 2001–2002. Master's Programs: overall undergraduate GPA 2.75, 3.45. Doctoral Programs: GRE-V+Q 1050; overall undergraduate GPA 3.00; last 2 years GPA no minimum stated; psychology GPA no minimum stated; psychology GPA 3.50. 40th percentile GRE-V, 30th percentile GRE-M.

Other Criteria: (importance of criteria rated low, medium, or high): GRE/MAT scores medium, research experience medium, work experience medium, clinically related public service medium, GPA high, letters of recommendation medium, interview medium, statement of goals and objectives medium, writing test high.

Student Characteristics: The following represents characteristics of students in 2001–2002 in all graduate psychology programs in the department: Female–full-time 72, part-time 28; Male–full-time 24, part-time 36; African American/Black–full-time 10, part-time 12; Hispanic/Latino (a)–full-time 6, part-time 9; Asian/Pacific Islander–full-time 8, part-time 6; American Indian/Alaska Native–full-time 3, part-time 3.

Financial Information/Assistance:

Tuition for Full-Time Study: Master's: State residents per academic year $3,090, $535 per credit hour; nonstate residents: per academic year $9,741, $1,366 per credit hour. Doctoral: State residents: per academic year $3,090, $535 per credit hour; nonstate residents: per academic year $9,741, $1,366 per credit hour.

Financial Assistance:

First Year Students: Teaching assistantships available for first-year. Average amount paid per academic year: $9,796. Average number of hours worked per week: 20. Apply by Rolling. Tuition remission given: full. Research assistantships available for first-year. Average amount paid per academic year: $13,454. Average number of hours worked per week: 20. Apply by Rolling. Tuition remission given: full. Fellowships and scholarships available for first-year. Average amount paid per academic year: $8,825. Average number of hours worked per week: 20. Apply by Rolling. Tuition remission given: full.

Advanced Students: Teaching assistantships available for advanced students. Average amount paid per academic year: $12,695. Average number of hours worked per week: 20. Apply by Rolling. Research assistantships available for advanced students. Average amount paid per academic year: $13,879. Average number of hours worked per week: 20. Apply by Rolling. Fellowships and scholarships available for advanced students. Average amount paid per academic year: $11,639. Average number of hours worked per week: 20. Apply by Rolling.

Contact Information: Of all students currently enrolled full-time, 65% benefited from one or more of the listed financial assistance programs. For information on financial assistance, contact: Office of Doctoral Studies and/or Department of Educational Psychology.

Internships/Practica: Students are placed in a variety of educational, business, and , community settings as part of their graduate training. For those doctoral students for whom a professional internship is required prior to graduation, 6 applied in 2000–2001. Of those who applied, 6 were placed in internships listed by the Association of Psychology Postdoctoral and Internship Programs (APPIC); 4 were placed in APA accredited internships.

Housing and Day Care: On-campus housing and day care facilities are available.

Employment of Department Graduates:

Master's Degree Graduates: Of those who graduated in the academic year 2000–2001, the following categories and numbers represent the post-graduate activities and employment of master's degree graduates: Enrolled in a psychology doctoral program (8), enrolled in another graduate/professional program (6), enrolled in a post-doctoral residency/fellowship (n/a), employed in independent practice (n/a), employed in an academic position at a university (0), employed in an academic position at a 2-year/4-year college (9), employed in other positions at a higher education institution (7), employed in a professional position in a school system (33), employed in business or industry (research/consulting) (2), employed in business or industry (management) (2), employed in a government agency (research) (0), employed in a government agency (professional services) (2), employed in a community mental health/counseling center (14), employed in a hospital/medical center (7), still seeking employment (5), other employment position (0).

Doctoral Degree Graduates: Of those who graduated in the academic year 2000–2001, the following categories and numbers represent the post-graduate activities and employment of doctoral degree graduates: Enrolled in a psychology doctoral program (n/a), enrolled in another graduate/professional program (n/a), enrolled in a post-doctoral residency/fellowship (1), employed in independent practice (3), employed in an academic position at a university (2), employed in an academic position at a 2-year/4-year college (1), employed in other positions at a higher education institution (0), employed in a professional position in a school system (2), employed in business or industry (research/consulting) (1), employed in business or industry (management) (0), employed in a government agency (research) (0), employed in a government agency (professional services) (1), employed in a community mental health/counseling center (3), employed in a hospital/medical center (2), still seeking employment (0), other employment position (1).

Additional Information:

Orientation, Objectives, and Emphasis of Department: The PhD programs in School Psychology and Counseling Psychology follow the model of training outlined by the American Psychological Association. The programs are based on the scientist-practitioner model, in which students are trained as psychological scientists with specializations in school or counseling psychology. A strong multicultural perspective undergirds the programs, with an emphasis on the contextual factors in students' work. The programs are housed under the umbrella of the Urban Education Doctoral Program, providing unique training in the psychological, social, and educational needs of multiethnic populations within an urban psychosocial context. Students gain the knowledge, skills, and attitudes to work in a heterogeneous environment. Students are prepared to work in academic, service delivery, research. and administrative positions.

Special Facilities or Resources: The department possesses excellent computer facilities. The department enjoys a strong collaborative relationship with the Department of Psychology, working together in an on-campus psychology clinic. We also have strong linkages to urban community and school partners, which provide students with a diverse set of research and practice opportunities.

Information for Students With Physical Disabilities: The Student Accessibility Center provides significant support for students with physical disabilities. The campus is in compliance with ADA guidelines and the department is committed to ensuring access to its programs and facilities.

Application Information:
Send to: Department of Educational Psychology, UW-Milwaukee, P.O. Box 413, Milwaukee, WI 53201 (Master's applications), March 1 deadline, Director, Urban Education Doctoral Program; School of Education, U.W.-Milwaukee, P.O. Box 413, Milwaukee, WI 53201 (PhD applications), January 15 deadline. Students are admitted in the Fall, application deadline January 15; Spring, application deadline March 1; Summer, application deadline March 1. Admission once per academic year. *Fee:* $45.

Wisconsin, University of, Oshkosh
Department of Psychology
College of Letters and Science
800 Algoma Boulevard
Oshkosh, WI 54901
Telephone: (414) 424-2300
Fax: (414) 424-1204
E-mail: *psychology@uwosh.edu*
Web: *http://socsci.uwosh.edu*

Department Established:
1959. Chairperson: Susan H. McFadden. Number of Faculty: total–full-time 11; women–full-time 4; minority–full-time 1.

Student Applications/Admissions:
Admissions Requirements:
Scores: Entries appear in this order: required test or GPA, minimum score (if required), median score of students entering in 2001–2002. Master's Programs: GRE-V no minimum stated; GRE-Q no minimum stated; GRE-V+Q no minimum stated; GRE-Analytical no minimum stated; GRE-V+Q+Analytical no minimum stated; overall undergraduate GPA 2.75; last 2 years GPA 2.90. The GRE subject test in Psychology is desired but not required. Doctoral Programs: last 2 years GPA no minimum stated; psychology GPA no minimum stated; psychology GPA no minimum stated.
Other Criteria: (importance of criteria rated low, medium, or high): GRE/MAT scores medium, research experience medium, work experience low, extracurricular activity low, GPA medium, letters of recommendation medium, interview medium, statement of goals and objectives medium. Students in

the Industrial/Organizational emphasis are required to submit a 2–page personal statement covering the origins of their interest in working in Industrial/Organizational Psychology, relevant experience (work or volunteer) in this field, and any other relevant personal information. Students in the Experimental emphasis are required to submit a personal statement at least a page or two in length. This statement should include reasons for wanting to come to UW Oshkosh and areas of research interest. The admissions committee is particularly interested in details about research experience, including class projects, assistantships, presentations, or other research experiences. If there were any extenuating circumstances leading to low performance in any aspect as an undergraduate or on GRE exams, it would be appropriate to comment on these in the personal statement.

Student Characteristics: The following represents characteristics of students in 2001–2002 in all graduate psychology programs in the department: Female–full-time 16, part-time 0; Male–full-time 4, part-time 0; African American/Black–full-time 0, part-time 0; Hispanic/Latino (a)–full-time 0, part-time 0; Asian/Pacific Islander–full-time 1, part-time 0; American Indian/Alaska Native–full-time 0, part-time 0.

Financial Information/Assistance:
Tuition for Full-Time Study: *Master's:* State residents per academic year $4,472.

Financial Assistance:
First Year Students: Research assistantships available for first-year. Average number of hours worked per week: 15. Tuition remission given: partial. Fellowships and scholarships available for first-year.
Advanced Students: Research assistantships available for advanced students. Average number of hours worked per week: 15. Tuition remission given: partial. Fellowships and scholarships available for advanced students.
Contact Information: Of all students currently enrolled full-time, 48% benefited from one or more of the listed financial assistance programs. For information on financial assistance, contact: Financial Aid Office, University of Wisconsin Oshkosh, 800 Algoma Blvd., Oshkosh, WI 54901.

Internships/Practica: Industrial/Organizational students participate in practica in year two. Some students also have the opportunity to do internships.

Housing and Day Care: No on-campus housing and day care facilities are available.

Employment of Department Graduates:
Master's Degree Graduates: Of those who graduated in the academic year 2000–2001, the following categories and numbers represent the post-graduate activities and employment of master's degree graduates: Enrolled in a post-doctoral residency/fellowship (n/a), employed in independent practice (n/a).
Doctoral Degree Graduates: Of those who graduated in the academic year 2000–2001, the following categories and numbers represent the post-graduate activities and employment of doctoral degree graduates: Enrolled in a psychology doctoral program (n/a), enrolled in another graduate/professional program (n/a).

Additional Information:

Orientation, Objectives, and Emphasis of Department: The program offers a master's degree in psychology with emphases in industrial/organizational and general experimental psychology. Students are required to take core courses dealing with psychological methods. The program emphasizes practical experience leading toward a master's degree or continued study leading to a PhD.

Special Facilities or Resources: Practicum placements are available for research in local agencies and industries. Animal and human laboratories are also available.

Application Information:

Send to: Graduate School and Research, Univ. of WI, Oshkosh, 800 Algoma Blvd., Oshkosh, WI 54901. Students are admitted in the Spring, application deadline April 1. *Fee:* $45.

Wisconsin, University of, River Falls
Graduate Department of Counseling & School Psychology
University of Wisconsin River Falls
410 S. Third Street
River Falls, WI 54022-5001
Telephone: (715) 425-3399
E-mail: *john.e.lecapitaine@uwrf.edu*

Department Established:

Professor: Donald Stovall. Number of Faculty: total–full-time 6, part-time 1; women–full-time 2, part-time 1; minority–full-time 1; faculty subject to the Americans with Disabilities Act 1.

Programs and Degrees Offered:

Listed in the following order: Program area, degree type (T if terminal Master's), number awarded 7/00–6/01. Counseling MA (T), School Psychology MA (T).

Student Applications/Admissions:
Student Applications
Counseling MA. School Psychology MA.

Admissions Requirements:

Scores: Entries appear in this order: required test or GPA, minimum score (if required), median score of students entering in 2001–2002. Master's Programs: overall undergraduate GPA 2.75. Doctoral Programs: last 2 years GPA no minimum stated; psychology GPA no minimum stated; psychology GPA no minimum stated.

Other Criteria: (importance of criteria rated low, medium, or high): research experience medium, work experience high, extracurricular activity high, clinically related public service medium, GPA high, letters of recommendation high, statement of goals and objectives high.

Financial Information/Assistance:
Tuition for Full-Time Study: No information provided.

Financial Assistance:
First Year Students: No information provided.
Advanced Students: No information provided.

Contact Information: No information provided.

Internships/Practica: No information provided.

Housing and Day Care: On-campus housing and day care facilities are available.

Employment of Department Graduates:

Master's Degree Graduates: Of those who graduated in the academic year 2000–2001, the following categories and numbers represent the post-graduate activities and employment of master's degree graduates: Enrolled in a post-doctoral residency/fellowship (n/a), employed in independent practice (n/a).

Doctoral Degree Graduates: Of those who graduated in the academic year 2000–2001, the following categories and numbers represent the post-graduate activities and employment of doctoral degree graduates: Enrolled in a psychology doctoral program (n/a), enrolled in another graduate/professional program (n/a).

Wisconsin, University of, Stout
Psychology Department/Applied Psychology
College of Human Development
Human Services 317
Menomonie, WI 54751-0790
Telephone: (715) 232-2478
Fax: (715) 232-5303
E-mail: *franklint@uwstout.edu*
Web: *http://www.uwstout.edu*

Department Established:

1982. Program Director: Richard Tafalla. Number of Faculty: total–full-time 18, part-time 5; women–full-time 6, part-time 2; minority–full-time 2, part-time 1.

Programs and Degrees Offered:

Listed in the following order: Program area, degree type (T if terminal Master's), number awarded 7/00–6/01. Applied MA (T) 13.

Student Applications/Admissions:
Student Applications

Applied MA—Applications 2001–2002, 20. Total applicants accepted 2001–2002, 14. New applicants enrolled 2001–2002, 12. Total enrolled 2001–2002 full-time, 19, part-time, 2. Openings 2002–2003, 30.

Admissions Requirements:

Scores: Entries appear in this order: required test or GPA, minimum score (if required), median score of students entering in 2001–2002. Master's Programs: overall undergraduate GPA 3.0, 3.5. Doctoral Programs: last 2 years GPA no minimum stated; psychology GPA no minimum stated; psychology GPA no minimum stated.

Other Criteria: (importance of criteria rated low, medium, or high): research experience high, work experience high, extracurricular activity medium, clinically related public service high, GPA high, letters of recommendation high, statement of goals and objectives high, applied experience high.

Student Characteristics: The following represents characteristics of students in 2001–2002 in all graduate psychology programs in the department: Female–full-time 12, part-time 0; Male–full-time 8, part-time 0; African American/Black–full-time 0, part-time 0; Hispanic/Latino (a)–full-time 0, part-time 0; Asian/Pacific Islander–full-time 1, part-time 0; American Indian/Alaska Native–full-time 0, part-time 0.

Financial Information/Assistance:

Tuition for Full-Time Study: *Master's:* State residents per academic year $4,194; nonstate residents: per academic year $12,552.

Financial Assistance:

First Year Students: Teaching assistantships available for first-year. Average amount paid per academic year: $5,000. Average number of hours worked per week: 13. Apply by none. Research assistantships available for first-year. Average amount paid per academic year: $4,000. Average number of hours worked per week: 10. Apply by none.

Advanced Students: Teaching assistantships available for advanced students. Average amount paid per academic year: $5,000. Average number of hours worked per week: 13. Apply by none. Research assistantships available for advanced students. Average amount paid per academic year: $4,000. Average number of hours worked per week: 10. Apply by none.

Contact Information: Of all students currently enrolled full-time, 50% benefited from one or more of the listed financial assistance programs. For information on financial assistance, contact: Financial Aid Office, UW-Stout, Menomonie, WI 54751, (715) 232-1363 For assistantships contact Richard Tafalla, Program Director, (715)232-1662.

Internships/Practica: UW-Stout has a reputation for its experiential-based curriculum. Approximately 700 students annually are in co-op or internship placements. The institution has an extensive network of business and industry contacts for the internship experience that is organized through the Placement and Co-op Services office. Students are encouraged to seek out placement sites early in their program work.

Housing and Day Care: On-campus housing and day care facilities are available.

Employment of Department Graduates:

Master's Degree Graduates: Of those who graduated in the academic year 2000–2001, the following categories and numbers represent the post-graduate activities and employment of master's degree graduates: Enrolled in a psychology doctoral program (2), enrolled in another graduate/professional program (0), enrolled in a post-doctoral residency/fellowship (n/a), employed in independent practice (n/a), employed in an academic position at a 2-year/4-year college (1), employed in other positions at a higher education institution (3), employed in business or industry (research/consulting) (27).

Doctoral Degree Graduates: Of those who graduated in the academic year 2000–2001, the following categories and numbers represent the post-graduate activities and employment of doctoral degree graduates: Enrolled in a psychology doctoral program (n/a), enrolled in another graduate/professional program (n/a).

Additional Information:

Orientation, Objectives, and Emphasis of Department: The MS in applied psychology is a two-year program designed around a core of appropriate psychological theories and principles, with three applied concentration areas of industrial/organizational psychology, program evaluation, and health psychology. It is designed to provide students with the knowledge, experience, skills, and abilities to apply the theories and methods of psychology to the identification and solution of a variety of real-world problems. What distinguishes the applied psychologist are the competencies in accessing the vast resources of psychological theories, research methods, and research findings as a base for developing new and more effective approaches to the solution of these problems. The goal of the applied psychology program is to produce competent professionals with broad knowledge of the field of psychology. They will have the skills to apply this knowledge to the complex people problems of the 1990s and the 21st century, and to act as role models in the domains of organizational development, problem-solving, interpersonal interaction, personal growth, and evaluation. Business, health, and community service and other settings in which the applied psychologist will work have a critical need for educated and responsible professionals who can participate in the solution of complex individual and organizational problems.

Special Facilities or Resources: The university has recently opened a new computer facility that is used for instruction and individual research. Several facilities/labs within the College of Human Development and the Department of Psychology will receive or will have received lab modernization funds. These labs will utilize the latest multi-media hardware and software. The experimental psychology lab is currently undergoing a major renovation.

Information for Students With Physical Disabilities: The Disabled Student Services program provides assistance with educational and vocational planning, academic adjustment, self-advocacy training, reader/taping services, testing accommodation, and general issues related to accommodation and accessibility. A local carrier provides reasonably priced transportation for the immediate community. UW-Stout houses the Stout Vocational Rehabilitation Institute, one of the major rehabilitation research facilities in the nation.

Application Information:

Send to: Program Director, MSAP and Graduate College. All students applying to the MSAP program must be accepted by the graduate college. *Fee:* $45.

Wyoming, University of
Department of Psychology
Box 3415 University Station
Laramie, WY 82071
Telephone: (307) 766-6303
Fax: (307) 766-2926
E-mail: *psyc.uw@uwyo.edu*
Web: *http://www.uwyo.edu/psyc*

Department Established:
1909. Chairperson: Narina Nunez. Number of Faculty: total–full-time 13, part-time 3; women–full-time 6, part-time 3; minority–full-time 1.

Programs and Degrees Offered:
Listed in the following order: Program area, degree type (T if terminal Master's), number awarded 7/00–6/01. Clinical PhD, developmental PhD 1, general PhD 1.

APA Accreditation: Clinical PhD: full.

Student Applications/Admissions:
Student Applications
Clinical PhD—Applications 2001–2002, 0. Total enrolled 2001–2002 full-time, 33. Openings 2002–2003, 6. The Median number of years required for completion of a degree are n/a. The number of students enrolled full and part-time, who were dismissed or voluntarily withdrew from this program area were 0. *Developmental PhD*—Applications 2001–2002, 8. Total applicants accepted 2001–2002, 2. New applicants enrolled 2001–2002, 1. Total enrolled 2001–2002 full-time, 8. Openings 2002–2003, 3. The Median number of years required for completion of a degree are 5. The number of students enrolled full and part-time, who were dismissed or voluntarily withdrew from this program area were 0. *General PhD*—Applications 2001–2002, 11. Total applicants accepted 2001–2002, 4. New applicants enrolled 2001–2002, 3. Total enrolled 2001–2002 full-time, 6. Openings 2002–2003, 2. The number of students enrolled full and part-time, who were dismissed or voluntarily withdrew from this program area were 0.

Admissions Requirements:
Scores: Entries appear in this order: required test or GPA, minimum score (if required), median score of students entering in 2001–2002. Doctoral Programs: GRE-V 500, 555; GRE-Q 550, 580; GRE-V+Q 1050, 1190; GRE-Analytical 500, 640; GRE-V+Q+Analytical 1600, 1750; GRE-Subject(Psych) 550, 600; overall undergraduate GPA 3.00, 3.65; last 2 years GPA 3.00, 3.73; psychology GPA 3.00, 3.58; psychology GPA 3.00, 3.85.
Other Criteria: (importance of criteria rated low, medium, or high): GRE/MAT scores high, research experience high, work experience low, extracurricular activity low, clinically related public service medium, GPA medium, letters of recommendation high, interview high, statement of goals and objectives high. Public Service is relevant to the Clinical Program only.

Student Characteristics: The following represents characteristics of students in 2001–2002 in all graduate psychology programs in the department: Female–full-time 2, part-time 0; Male–full-time 4, part-time 0; African American/Black–full-time 0, part-time 0; Hispanic/Latino (a)–full-time 0, part-time 0; Asian/Pacific Islander–full-time 1, part-time 0; American Indian/Alaska Native–full-time 0, part-time 0.

Financial Information/Assistance:
Tuition for Full-Time Study: *Master's:* State residents per academic year $3,386, $170 per credit hour; nonstate residents: per academic year $8,858, $474 per credit hour. *Doctoral:* State residents: per academic year $3,386, $170 per credit hour; nonstate residents: per academic year $8,858, $474 per credit hour.

Financial Assistance:
First Year Students: Teaching assistantships available for first-year. Average amount paid per academic year: $10,100. Average number of hours worked per week: 20. Tuition remission given: full. Research assistantships available for first-year. Average amount paid per academic year: $10,100. Average number of hours worked per week: 20. Fellowships and scholarships available for first-year. Average amount paid per academic year: $2,000. Average number of hours worked per week: 0.
Advanced Students: Teaching assistantships available for advanced students. Average amount paid per academic year: $10,100. Average number of hours worked per week: 20. Tuition remission given: full. Research assistantships available for advanced students. Average amount paid per academic year: $10,100. Average number of hours worked per week: 20. Tuition remission given: full.
Contact Information: Of all students currently enrolled full-time, 96% benefited from one or more of the listed financial assistance programs. For information on financial assistance, contact: Graduate Admissions Committee, Department of Psychology.

Internships/Practica: Given Wyoming's large geographic area (approximately 100,000 square miles) and small population (approximately 475,000), we arrange practica and clerkships for Clinical students in various settings throughout the state. Clerkships are typically conducted in the summer for extended periods of time. Practica and clerkships include a variety of clinical populations such as children, adolescents, adults, elderly, and incarcerated individuals. They occur in a range of placements including outpatient mental health centers, inpatient hospitals, VA Medical Centers, and residential programs. Specialty experiences include forensic evaluation, substance abuse training, and parent training. For those doctoral students for whom a professional internship is required prior to graduation, 2 applied in 2000–2001. Of those who applied, 2 were placed in internships listed by the Association of Psychology Postdoctoral and Internship Programs (APPIC); 2 were placed in APA accredited internships.

Housing and Day Care: On-campus housing and day care facilities are available.

Employment of Department Graduates:

Master's Degree Graduates: Of those who graduated in the academic year 2000–2001, the following categories and numbers represent the post-graduate activities and employment of master's degree graduates: Enrolled in a post-doctoral residency/fellowship (n/a), employed in independent practice (n/a).

Doctoral Degree Graduates: Of those who graduated in the academic year 2000–2001, the following categories and numbers represent the post-graduate activities and employment of doctoral degree graduates: Enrolled in a psychology doctoral program (n/a), enrolled in another graduate/professional program (n/a), employed in an academic position at a university (1), employed in business or industry (research/consulting) (1).

Additional Information:

Orientation, Objectives, and Emphasis of Department: The University of Wyoming is the only four-year university in the state of Wyoming. The psychology department has a broad undergraduate teaching mission and has one of the largest number of majors in the College of Arts and Sciences. The graduate curriculum provides breadth of training in psychology and permits specialization in various content areas. The Clinical Psychology PhD Program is based on the scientist-practitioner model with an emphasis on training in primary care. The goal is to provide students with the knowledge base and broad conceptual skills necessary for professional practice and/or research in a variety of settings. The PhD program in Experimental Psychology provides students with broad training that can be used in a variety of academic and applied settings. Students may concentrate in Developmental Psychology or they may complete their Experimental Psychology degree through research in social or cognitive psychol-

ogy. Students in any of the programs may have a Psychology and Law concentration. All programs contain opportunities for both applied and basic research training.

Special Facilities or Resources: The department has approximately 24,000 square feet of laboratory, office, and clinic space in a science complex with direct access to the university's science library; and various computer labs. Faculty laboratories range from wet laboratories designed for the biological aspects of human behavior to labs designed to assess mock jurors and jury decision-making. The Psychology Clinic has ample space for individual or small group assessment and treatment. These facilities also have observation mirrors and video tape-recording capability.

Information for Students With Physical Disabilities: University Disability Support Services is a branch of the Division of Student Educational Opportunity (SEO) at the University of Wyoming. Through institutional services and the Montgomery Technology Center (MTC), UDSS provides disability-related accommodations and services, technical assistance, consultations, and resource information for students, faculty, staff, and campus visitors with disabilities, and to University departments seeking to improve accessibility for individuals with disabilities. UDSS also sponsors (DAW) Disability Awareness Week every spring.

Application Information:

Send to: Graduate Admissions Committee, Department of Psychology, P.O. Box 3415, University of Wyoming, Laramie, WY 82071. Students are admitted in the Fall, application deadline January 15. *Fee:* $40. There is no fee for applying to the program. Only students who are accepted into and are officially entering the program are charged the fee.

Acadia University

Department of Psychology
Wolfville, NS B0P 1X0 Canada
Telephone: (902) 585-1301
Fax: (902) 585-1078
E-mail: *peter.horvath@acadiau.ca*
Web: *http://ace.acadiau.ca/science/psyc/home.htm*

Department Established:

1926. Head: Pat O'Neill. Number of Faculty: total–full-time 11, part-time 5; women–full-time 5, part-time 3.

Programs and Degrees Offered:

Listed in the following order: Program area, degree type (T if terminal Master's), number awarded 7/00–6/01. Clinical MA (T) 6.

Student Applications/Admissions:

Student Applications

Clinical MA—Applications 2001–2002, 40. Total applicants accepted 2001–2002, 5. New applicants enrolled 2001–2002, 5. Total enrolled 2001–2002 full-time, 10, part-time, 1. Openings 2002–2003, 5. The Median number of years required for completion of a degree are 2. The number of students enrolled full and part-time, who were dismissed or voluntarily withdrew from this program area were 0.

Admissions Requirements:

Scores: Entries appear in this order: required test or GPA, minimum score (if required), median score of students entering in 2001–2002. Master's Programs: GRE-V 500, 580; GRE-Q 500, 610; GRE-Analytical 500, 650; overall undergraduate GPA 3.50; psychology GPA 3.50. Doctoral Programs: last 2 years GPA no minimum stated; psychology GPA no minimum stated; psychology GPA no minimum stated.

Other Criteria: (importance of criteria rated low, medium, or high): GRE/MAT scores high, research experience high, work experience medium, extracurricular activity medium, clinically related public service medium, GPA high, letters of recommendation high, interview medium, statement of goals and objectives high, publications medium.

Student Characteristics: The following represents characteristics of students in 2001–2002 in all graduate psychology programs in the department: Female–full-time 7, part-time 1; Male–full-time 1, part-time 0; African American/Black–full-time 0, part-time 0; Hispanic/Latino (a)–full-time 0, part-time 0; Asian/Pacific Islander–full-time 0, part-time 0; American Indian/Alaska Native–full-time 0, part-time 0.

Financial Information/Assistance:

Tuition for Full-Time Study: *Master's:* State residents per academic year $4,645.

Financial Assistance:

First Year Students: Teaching assistantships available for first-year. Average amount paid per academic year: $8,000. Average number of hours worked per week: 8. Apply by Feb 1.

Advanced Students: Teaching assistantships available for advanced students. Average amount paid per academic year: $8,000. Average number of hours worked per week: 8.

Contact Information: Of all students currently enrolled full-time, 80% benefited from one or more of the listed financial assistance programs. For information on financial assistance, contact: elaine.schofield@acadiau.ca.

Internships/Practica: Two 150-hour internships are mandatory in intervention and assessment. Internship in community psychology is available.

Housing and Day Care: No on-campus housing and day care facilities are available.

Employment of Department Graduates:

Master's Degree Graduates: Of those who graduated in the academic year 2000–2001, the following categories and numbers represent the post-graduate activities and employment of master's degree graduates: Enrolled in a psychology doctoral program (4), enrolled in another graduate/professional program (0), enrolled in a post-doctoral residency/fellowship (n/a), employed in independent practice (n/a), employed in an academic position at a university (5), employed in a professional position in a school system (2), employed in a community mental health/counseling center (2), employed in a hospital/medical center (2).

Doctoral Degree Graduates: Of those who graduated in the academic year 2000–2001, the following categories and numbers represent the post-graduate activities and employment of doctoral degree graduates: Enrolled in a psychology doctoral program (n/a), enrolled in another graduate/professional program (n/a).

Additional Information:

Orientation, Objectives, and Emphasis of Department: The department's principal objective is to train MSc students in clinical psychology. The department's orientation is eclectic although there is an emphasis on cognitive approaches to problems in psychology. Master's-level registration as a psychologist is available in all Maritime Provinces in Canada. Our curriculum is also highly respected, and graduates going on to doctoral programs elsewhere have had full recognition of coursework in all instances. We are registered with CAMPP.

Special Facilities or Resources: The department is part of the cooperative clinical PhD program of Dalhousie University.

Application Information:

Send to: Admissions Office, Acadia University, Wolfville, NS, B0P 1XO. Students are admitted in the Fall, application deadline February 1. *Fee:* $50. Applied against fellowship. Note: All dollar amounts specified in this entry are Canadian dollars.

Alberta, University of
Department of Psychology
Biological Sciences Building
Edmonton, AB T6G 2E9 Canada
Telephone: (708) 492-5216
Fax: (708) 492-1768
E-mail: *douglas.grant@ualberta.ca*
Web: *http://www.psych.ualberta.ca*

Department Established:
1961. Chair: Douglas S. Grant. Number of Faculty: total–full-time 30, part-time 1; women–full-time 9; minority–full-time 1.

Programs and Degrees Offered:
Listed in the following order: Program area, degree type (T if terminal Master's), number awarded 7/00–6/01. Applied Developmental Science PhD 2, Behav, Systems & Cog Neuro. PhD 2, Cognition PhD, Comparative Cognition & Behav. PhD 1, Social & Cultural Psychology PhD.

Student Applications/Admissions:
Student Applications

Applied Developmental Science PhD—Applications 2001–2002, 7. Total applicants accepted 2001–2002, 2. New applicants enrolled 2001–2002, 1. Total enrolled 2001–2002 full-time, 7. Openings 2002–2003, n/a. The Median number of years required for completion of a degree are 6. The number of students enrolled full and part-time, who were dismissed or voluntarily withdrew from this program area were 0. *Behav, Systems & Cog Neuro. PhD*—Applications 2001–2002, 7. Total applicants accepted 2001–2002, 2. New applicants enrolled 2001–2002, 1. Total enrolled 2001–2002 full-time, 7. Openings 2002–2003, n/a. The Median number of years required for completion of a degree are 3. The number of students enrolled full and part-time, who were dismissed or voluntarily withdrew from this program area were 0. *Cognition PhD*—Applications 2001–2002, 5. Total applicants accepted 2001–2002, 3. New applicants enrolled 2001–2002, 2. Total enrolled 2001–2002 full-time, 4. Openings 2002–2003, n/a. The Median number of years required for completion of a degree are n/a. The number of students enrolled full and part-time, who were dismissed or voluntarily withdrew from this program area were 0. *Comparative Cognition & Behav. PhD*—Applications 2001–2002, 1. Openings 2002–2003, n/a. The Median number of years required for completion of a degree are 8. The number of students enrolled full and part-time, who were dismissed or voluntarily withdrew from this program area were 0. *Social & Cultural Psychology PhD*—Applications 2001–2002, 24. Total applicants accepted 2001–2002, 7. New applicants enrolled 2001–2002, 6. Total enrolled 2001–2002 full-time, 16. Openings 2002–2003, n/a. The Median number of years required for completion of a degree are n/a. The number of students enrolled full and part-time, who were dismissed or voluntarily withdrew from this program area were 2.

Admissions Requirements:
Scores: Entries appear in this order: required test or GPA, minimum score (if required), median score of students entering in 2001–2002. Master's Programs: GRE-V no minimum stated; GRE-Q no minimum stated; GRE-Analytical no minimum

stated; overall undergraduate GPA 3.0. Doctoral Programs: GRE-V no minimum stated; GRE-Q no minimum stated; GRE-Analytical no minimum stated; overall undergraduate GPA 3.0; last 2 years GPA no minimum stated; psychology GPA no minimum stated; psychology GPA no minimum stated.

Other Criteria: (importance of criteria rated low, medium, or high): GRE/MAT scores high, research experience high, work experience low, extracurricular activity low, clinically related public service low, GPA high, letters of recommendation high, statement of goals and objectives high.

Student Characteristics: The following represents characteristics of students in 2001–2002 in all graduate psychology programs in the department: Female–full-time 21, part-time 0; Male–full-time 13, part-time 0; African American/Black–full-time 0, part-time 0; Hispanic/Latino (a)–full-time 0, part-time 0; Asian/Pacific Islander–full-time 0, part-time 0; American Indian/Alaska Native–full-time 0, part-time 0.

Financial Information/Assistance:
Tuition for Full-Time Study: Master's: State residents per academic year $3,402; nonstate residents: per academic year $6,239. *Doctoral:* State residents: per academic year $3,402; nonstate residents: per academic year $6,239.

Financial Assistance:
First Year Students: Teaching assistantships available for first-year. Average amount paid per academic year: $17,520. Average number of hours worked per week: 12. Apply by Jan 15. Research assistantships available for first-year. Average amount paid per academic year: $17,520. Average number of hours worked per week: 12. Apply by Jan 15. Fellowships and scholarships available for first-year. Average number of hours worked per week: 12. Apply by Jan 15.

Advanced Students: Teaching assistantships available for advanced students. Average amount paid per academic year: $17,520. Average number of hours worked per week: 12. Apply by Jan 15. Research assistantships available for advanced students. Average amount paid per academic year: $17,520. Average number of hours worked per week: 12. Apply by Jan 15. Fellowships and scholarships available for advanced students. Average amount paid per academic year: $17,520. Average number of hours worked per week: 12. Apply by Jan 15.

Contact Information: For information on financial assistance, contact: Graduate Program Assistant: psygrad@ualberta.ca. Faculty of Graduate Studies and Research: gradmail@ualberta.ca or http://gradfile.fgsro.ualberta.ca/.

Internships/Practica: No information provided.

Housing and Day Care: On-campus housing and day care facilities are available.

Employment of Department Graduates:
Master's Degree Graduates: Of those who graduated in the academic year 2000–2001, the following categories and numbers represent the post-graduate activities and employment of master's degree graduates: Enrolled in a post-doctoral residency/fellowship (n/a), employed in independent practice (n/a).
Doctoral Degree Graduates: Of those who graduated in the academic year 2000–2001, the following categories and numbers

represent the post-graduate activities and employment of doctoral degree graduates: Enrolled in a psychology doctoral program (n/a), enrolled in another graduate/professional program (n/a).

Additional Information:

Orientation, Objectives, and Emphasis of Department: The department is oriented toward research, both basic and applied. Ongoing investigations span a wide range of topics. A major goal is to help graduate students develop skills that will enable them to pursue careers as research psychologists in academic or nonacademic settings. The department admits approximately ten graduate students per year. Students holding an undergraduate degree are admitted to the Master's Program in either arts or science; they may proceed to the PhD program upon successful completion of the Master's degree. Students with a qualifying Master's Degree are admitted directly to the PhD Program.

Special Facilities or Resources: Research facilities consist of numerous laboratories: for work with humans—rooms for interviews and personality testing; observation rooms and experimental areas for social and developmental psychology; laboratories for sensory and perceptual studies in vision, audition, tactile, and chemical senses; and laboratories for the study of cognitive processes. For work with animals—surgeries, physiological recording rooms, behavioral testing rooms, various kinds of programming equipment, and a histological laboratory.

Application Information:

Send to: Graduate Program Assistant, Department of Psychology. Students are admitted in the Fall, application deadline January 15. The department admits approximately ten graduate students per year. Students holding an undergraduate degree are admitted to the Master's Program in either arts or science; upon successful completion of the Master's degree they may continue in the PhD program. Students holding a qualifying Master's Degree are admitted directly to the PhD Program.

British Columbia, University of
Department of Psychology
2136 West Mall, Douglas Kenny Building
Vancouver, BC V6T 1Z4 Canada
Telephone: (604) 822-2755
Fax: (604) 822-6923
E-mail: *askus@psych.ubc.ca*
Web: *http://www.psych.ubc.ca*

Department Established:
1951. Head: Richard Tees. Number of Faculty: total–full-time 43, part-time 19; women–full-time 12, part-time 13.

Programs and Degrees Offered:
Listed in the following order: Program area, degree type (T if terminal Master's), number awarded 7/00–6/01. Biopsychology PhD 1, clinical PhD 7, cognitive science PhD 1, developmental PhD 2, environmental PhD, forensic PhD, perception PhD, psychometrics PhD, social/personality PhD 1.

APA Accreditation: Clinical PhD: full.

Student Applications/Admissions:
Student Applications
Biopsychology PhD—Applications 2001–2002, 7. Total applicants accepted 2001–2002, 3. New applicants enrolled 2001–2002, 1. Total enrolled 2001–2002 full-time, 6. Openings 2002–2003, 5. The Median number of years required for completion of a degree are 7. The number of students enrolled full and part-time, who were dismissed or voluntarily withdrew from this program area were 0. *Clinical PhD*—Applications 2001–2002, 107. Total applicants accepted 2001–2002, 7. New applicants enrolled 2001–2002, 7. Total enrolled 2001–2002 full-time, 39. Openings 2002–2003, 8. The Median number of years required for completion of a degree are 7. The number of students enrolled full and part-time, who were dismissed or voluntarily withdrew from this program area were 0. *Cognitive science PhD*—Applications 2001–2002, 11. Total applicants accepted 2001–2002, 4. New applicants enrolled 2001–2002, 3. Total enrolled 2001–2002 full-time, 12. Openings 2002–2003, 4. The Median number of years required for completion of a degree are 6. The number of students enrolled full and part-time, who were dismissed or voluntarily withdrew from this program area were 1. *Developmental PhD*—Applications 2001–2002, 6. Total enrolled 2001–2002 full-time, 6. Openings 2002–2003, 4. The Median number of years required for completion of a degree are 7. The number of students enrolled full and part-time, who were dismissed or voluntarily withdrew from this program area were 0. *Environmental PhD*—Applications 2001–2002, 0. Total enrolled 2001–2002 full-time, 1. Openings 2002–2003, 1. The number of students enrolled full and part-time, who were dismissed or voluntarily withdrew from this program area were 0. *Forensic PhD*—Applications 2001–2002, 39. Total applicants accepted 2001–2002, 3. New applicants enrolled 2001–2002, 3. Total enrolled 2001–2002 full-time, 12. Openings 2002–2003, 3. The number of students enrolled full and part-time, who were dismissed or voluntarily withdrew from this program area were 1. *Perception PhD*—Applications 2001–2002, 0. Openings 2002–2003, 1. The number of students enrolled full and part-time, who were dismissed or voluntarily withdrew from this program area were 0. *Psychometrics PhD*—Applications 2001–2002, 1. Total enrolled 2001–2002 full-time, 2. Openings 2002–2003, 2. The number of students enrolled full and part-time, who were dismissed or voluntarily withdrew from this program area were 0. *Social/personality PhD*—Applications 2001–2002, 36. Total applicants accepted 2001–2002, 8. New applicants enrolled 2001–2002, 5. Total enrolled 2001–2002 full-time, 14. Openings 2002–2003, 4. The Median number of years required for completion of a degree are 5. The number of students enrolled full and part-time, who were dismissed or voluntarily withdrew from this program area were 0.

Admissions Requirements:
Scores: Entries appear in this order: required test or GPA, minimum score (if required), median score of students entering in 2001–2002. Master's Programs: GRE-V+Q+Analytical 580; GRE-Subject(Psych) 580; last 2 years GPA 3.5. Doctoral Programs: GRE-V+Q+Analytical 580; GRE-Subject(Psych) 580; last 2 years GPA no minimum stated; psychology GPA no minimum stated; psychology GPA B.

Other Criteria: (importance of criteria rated low, medium, or high): GRE/MAT scores medium, research experience high, clinically related public service low, GPA high, letters of recommendation high, statement of goals and objectives high.

Student Characteristics: The following represents characteristics of students in 2001–2002 in all graduate psychology programs in the department: Female–full-time 59, part-time 0; Male–full-time 33, part-time 0.

Financial Information/Assistance:

Tuition for Full-Time Study: *Master's:* State residents per academic year $2,165; nonstate residents: per academic year $7,200. *Doctoral:* State residents: per academic year $2,165; nonstate residents: per academic year $7,200.

Financial Assistance:

First Year Students: Teaching assistantships available for first-year. Average amount paid per academic year: $8,800. Average number of hours worked per week: 12. Apply by February 15. Research assistantships available for first-year. Average amount paid per academic year: $5,000. Apply by February 15. Fellowships and scholarships available for first-year. Average amount paid per academic year: $16,000. Apply by February 15.

Advanced Students: Teaching assistantships available for advanced students. Average amount paid per academic year: $9,000. Average number of hours worked per week: 12. Apply by February 15. Research assistantships available for advanced students. Average amount paid per academic year: $5,000. Apply by February 15. Fellowships and scholarships available for advanced students. Average amount paid per academic year: $16,000. Apply by February 15.

Contact Information: Of all students currently enrolled full-time, 100% benefited from one or more of the listed financial assistance programs. For information on financial assistance, contact: Graduate Secretary, Department of Psychology, University of British Columbia, Vancouver, BC, V6T 1Z4.

Internships/Practica: A 4-month practicum in an approved agency is required of clinical students during the summer after the second or third year of the program or during the third year. A 1-year internship at a mental health agency accredited by CPA or APA is required for the PhD in clinical psychology. For those doctoral students for whom a professional internship is required prior to graduation, 7 applied in 2000–2001. Of those who applied, 6 were placed in internships listed by the Association of Psychology Postdoctoral and Internship Programs (APPIC); 7 were placed in APA accredited internships.

Housing and Day Care: On-campus housing and day care facilities are available.

Employment of Department Graduates:

Master's Degree Graduates: Of those who graduated in the academic year 2000–2001, the following categories and numbers represent the post-graduate activities and employment of master's degree graduates: Enrolled in a psychology doctoral program (10), enrolled in another graduate/professional program (0), enrolled in a post-doctoral residency/fellowship (n/a), employed in independent practice (n/a).

Doctoral Degree Graduates: Of those who graduated in the academic year 2000–2001, the following categories and numbers represent the post-graduate activities and employment of doctoral degree graduates: Enrolled in a psychology doctoral program (n/a),

enrolled in another graduate/professional program (n/a), enrolled in a post-doctoral residency/fellowship (2), employed in independent practice (1), employed in an academic position at a university (2), employed in an academic position at a 2-year/4-year college (1), employed in a government agency (research) (1), employed in a community mental health/counseling center (1), employed in a hospital/medical center (4).

Additional Information:

Orientation, Objectives, and Emphasis of Department: The department is organized into nine subject content areas with which faculty and graduate students are affiliated. Graduate training emphasizes a high degree of research competence and, from the beginning of the program, students are involved in increasingly independent research activities.

Special Facilities or Resources: The department is housed in an attractive building of about 90,000 square feet, designed for psychological research. The department has well-equipped research facilities including a psychology clinic, observational galleries, and animal, psychophysiological, perceptual, cognitive, and social/personality laboratories.

Information for Students With Physical Disabilities: The department is housed in a modern building that is completely accessible for students with physical disabilities. The university's Disability Resource Center provides a wide range of services and resources.

Application Information:
Send to: Graduate Secretary, Department of Psychology, University of British Columbia, Vancouver, BC V6T 1Z4. Students are admitted in the Fall, application deadline February 15. *Fee:* $65. Note: All dollar amounts specified in this entry are Canadian dollars.

Calgary, University of
Department of Psychology
2500 University Drive, N.W.
Calgary, AB T2N 1N4 Canada
Telephone: (403) 220-5561
Fax: (403) 282-8249
E-mail: *bhbland@ucalgary.ca*
Web: *http://psycgrad@ucalgary.ca*

Department Established:
1964. Chairperson: Dr. Brian H. Bland. Number of Faculty: total–full-time 31; women–full-time 9.

Programs and Degrees Offered:
Listed in the following order: Program area, degree type (T if terminal Master's), number awarded 7/00–6/01. Experimental Psychology PhD (T) 5.

APA Accreditation: Clinical PhD: full.

Student Applications/Admissions:
Student Applications

Experimental Psychology PhD—Applications 2001–2002, 55. Total applicants accepted 2001–2002, 12. New applicants enrolled 2001–2002, 12. Total enrolled 2001–2002 full-time, 12. Openings 2002–2003, 8. The Median number of years required for completion of a degree are 2. The number of students enrolled full and part-time, who were dismissed or voluntarily withdrew from this program area were 0.

Admissions Requirements:
Scores: Entries appear in this order: required test or GPA, minimum score (if required), median score of students entering in 2001–2002. Master's Programs: GRE-V no minimum stated; GRE-Q no minimum stated; GRE-Analytical no minimum stated; last 2 years GPA no minimum stated. Clinical Psychology, GPA of 3.7 (A-) over the last two years of study. Experimental Psychology, GPA of 3.2 (B+) over the last two years of study. Doctoral Programs: GRE-V no minimum stated; GRE-Q no minimum stated; GRE-Analytical no minimum stated; last 2 years GPA no minimum stated; psychology GPA no minimum stated; psychology GPA no minimum stated.
Other Criteria: (importance of criteria rated low, medium, or high): GRE/MAT scores medium, research experience high, work experience medium, extracurricular activity low, clinically related public service medium, GPA high, letters of recommendation high, interview medium, statement of goals and objectives high.

Student Characteristics: The following represents characteristics of students in 2001–2002 in all graduate psychology programs in the department: Female–full-time 27, part-time 0; Male–full-time 17, part-time 0; African American/Black–full-time 0, part-time 0; Hispanic/Latino (a)–full-time 0, part-time 0; Asian/Pacific Islander–full-time 0, part-time 0; American Indian/Alaska Native–full-time 0, part-time 0.

Financial Information/Assistance:
Tuition for Full-Time Study: No information provided.

Financial Assistance:
First Year Students: Teaching assistantships available for first-year. Average amount paid per academic year: $11,760. Average number of hours worked per week: 12. Apply by N/A. Fellowships and scholarships available for first-year. Average amount paid per academic year: $15,000. Apply by January 15. Tuition remission given: partial.
Advanced Students: Teaching assistantships available for advanced students. Average amount paid per academic year: $15,000. Average number of hours worked per week: 12. Fellowships and scholarships available for advanced students. Average amount paid per academic year: $15,000. Apply by January 15. Tuition remission given: partial.
Contact Information: Of all students currently enrolled full-time, 100% benefited from one or more of the listed financial assistance programs.

Internships/Practica: Internships are available at several settings, including Foothills Hospital and Children's Hospital. For those doctoral students for whom a professional internship is required prior to graduation, 6 applied in 2000–2001. Of those who applied, 6 were placed in internships listed by the Association of Psychology Postdoctoral and Internship Programs (APPIC).

Housing and Day Care: On-campus housing and day care facilities are available.

Employment of Department Graduates:
Master's Degree Graduates: Of those who graduated in the academic year 2000–2001, the following categories and numbers represent the post-graduate activities and employment of master's degree graduates: Enrolled in a psychology doctoral program (10), enrolled in another graduate/professional program (1), enrolled in a post-doctoral residency/fellowship (n/a), employed in independent practice (n/a).
Doctoral Degree Graduates: Of those who graduated in the academic year 2000–2001, the following categories and numbers represent the post-graduate activities and employment of doctoral degree graduates: Enrolled in a psychology doctoral program (n/a), enrolled in another graduate/professional program (n/a), employed in independent practice (2), employed in an academic position at a university (3), employed in other positions at a higher education institution (3), employed in a community mental health/counseling center (1), employed in a hospital/medical center (4).

Additional Information:
Orientation, Objectives, and Emphasis of Department: This is a research-oriented department with a strong focus on applied problems. We offer both a clinical and an experimental psychology program. Specific research programs in experimental psychology include: cognition and cognitive development (CCD), industrial/organizational psychology (I/O), social psychology, perception aging and cognitive ergonomics (PACE), theoretical psychology.

Application Information:
Send to: Graduate Director, Department of Psychology, 2500 University Drive NW, University of Calgary, Calgary, AB 1N4. Students are admitted in the Fall, application deadline January 15. *Fee:* $60. Note: All dollar amounts specified in this entry are Canadian dollars.

Calgary, University of (2001 data)
Division of Applied Psychology
2500 University Drive, N.W.
Calgary, AB T2N 1N4 Canada
Telephone: (403) 220-5651
Fax: (403) 282-9244
E-mail: *apsygrad@ucalgary.ca*
Web: *http://www.ucalgary.ca*

Department Established:
Associate Dean: Bryan Hiebert. Number of Faculty: total–full-time 20, part-time 6; women–full-time 10, part-time 3.

Programs and Degrees Offered:
Listed in the following order: Program area, degree type (T if terminal Master's), number awarded 7/00–6/01. Counseling Psychology PhD (T) 10, Development and Learning MSc 3, School Psychology MSc 3, Special Education MSc.

Student Applications/Admissions:
Student Applications
Counseling Psychology PhD—Applications 2001–2002, 59. Total applicants accepted 2001–2002, 9. New applicants enrolled 2001–2002, 9. Total enrolled 2001–2002 full-time, 9. *Development and Learning MSc*—Applications 2001–2002, 2. Total

applicants accepted 2001–2002, 1. New applicants enrolled 2001–2002, 1. Total enrolled 2001–2002 full-time, 1. *School Psychology MSc*—Applications 2001–2002, 13. Total applicants accepted 2001–2002, 8. New applicants enrolled 2001–2002, 8. Total enrolled 2001–2002 full-time, 8. *Special Education MSc*—Applications 2001–2002, 4. Total applicants accepted 2001–2002, 1. New applicants enrolled 2001–2002, 1. Total enrolled 2001–2002 full-time, 1.

Admissions Requirements:

Scores: Entries appear in this order: required test or GPA, minimum score (if required), median score of students entering in 2001–2002. Master's Programs: last 2 years GPA 3.0, 3.5. Doctoral Programs: last 2 years GPA 3.0, 3.5 ; psychology GPA no minimum stated; psychology GPA 3.5, 3.8.

Other Criteria: (importance of criteria rated low, medium, or high): research experience medium, work experience high, extracurricular activity low, clinically related public service low, GPA high, letters of recommendation high, statement of goals and objectives high, publications/presentation medium.

Student Characteristics: The following represents characteristics of students in 2001–2002 in all graduate psychology programs in the department: Female–full-time 27, part-time 11; Male–full-time 2, part-time 2; African American/Black–full-time 0, part-time 0; Hispanic/Latino (a)–full-time 0, part-time 0; Asian/Pacific Islander–full-time 0, part-time 0; American Indian/Alaska Native–full-time 0, part-time 0.

Financial Information/Assistance:

Tuition for Full-Time Study: *Master's:* State residents per academic year $4,219; nonstate residents: per academic year $8,438. *Doctoral:* State residents: per academic year $8,438; nonstate residents: per academic year $1,687.

Financial Assistance:

First Year Students: Teaching assistantships available for first-year. Average amount paid per academic year: $3,000. Average number of hours worked per week: 6. Apply by Nov/Feb/Apr. Fellowships and scholarships available for first-year. Average number of hours worked per week: 0. Apply by Feb 1.

Advanced Students: Teaching assistantships available for advanced students. Average amount paid per academic year: $3,000. Average number of hours worked per week: 6. Apply by Nov/Feb/Apr. Average number of hours worked per week: 0. Apply by Feb 1.

Contact Information: Of all students currently enrolled full-time, 50% benefited from one or more of the listed financial assistance programs. For information on financial assistance, contact: Graduate Administrative Assistant, Division of Applied Psychology, University of Calgary, Calgary, Alberta, Canada T2N 1N4.

Internships/Practica: Students in both Master's and Doctoral degree programs complete practica over a minimum of academic semesters. Practica settings include a wide range of community and education-based services and settings.

Housing and Day Care: On-campus housing and day care facilities are available.

Employment of Department Graduates:

Master's Degree Graduates: Of those who graduated in the academic year 2000–2001, the following categories and numbers represent the post-graduate activities and employment of master's degree graduates: Enrolled in a post-doctoral residency/fellowship (n/a), employed in independent practice (n/a).

Doctoral Degree Graduates: Of those who graduated in the academic year 2000–2001, the following categories and numbers represent the post-graduate activities and employment of doctoral degree graduates: Enrolled in a psychology doctoral program (n/a), enrolled in another graduate/professional program (n/a).

Additional Information:

Orientation, Objectives, and Emphasis of Department: The Division of Applied Psychology provides courses at both the undergraduate level and graduate degree programs which reflect the range of roles which applied psychologists now assume in Canadian schools and society. This commitment to breadth of programming reflects a belief in maintaining strong relationships with educational and mental health institutions outside the university. There are two major organizational areas in the department: the area of fundamentals in educational psychology, which focuses on specializations in human development and learning and special education; and the area of professional practice in educational psychology, which focuses on specializations in community rehabilitation, counseling psychology, and school psychology. The spectrum of work in the department stretches from the developmental progress of pre-schoolers to the social and educational needs of adults, and across the full range of individual needs and abilities. The philosophy of the department embodies the belief that university studies in educational psychology should be balanced, and should reflect in microcosm the interests and needs of society at large.

Special Facilities or Resources: The department also has a child development laboratory with video recording facilities, counseling laboratories with recording equipment, a psychoeducational clinic with reasonable inventory of test materials, a rehabilitation resource center housing curricular resources, a behavioral support unit for working with children and adults who have disabilities, and a specialized computer unit. All are linked with community facilities. The department has a Commmunity Services Centre which involves training, research, and skill development in a psychoeducational setting. Partnerships with community agencies have been established.

Information for Students With Physical Disabilities: The University of Calgary has a Disability Resource Center which provides technical and personal support to students with physical disabilities.

Application Information:

Send to: Graduate Administrative Assistant, Division of Applied Psychology, University of Calgary, 2500 University Dr., NW, Calgary, AB T2N 1N4. Students are admitted in the Fall, application deadline February 1. *Fee:* $60. Note: All dollar amounts specified in this entry are Canadian dollars.

Concordia University

Department of Psychology
7141 Sherbrooke Street West
Montreal, QC H4B 1R6 Canada
Telephone: (514) 848-2205
Fax: (514) 848-4523
E-mail: *black@vax2.concordia.ca*
Web: *http://www-psychology.concordia.ca*

Department Established:
1963. Chairperson: June Chaikelson. Number of Faculty: total–full-time 38, part-time 16; women–full-time 15, part-time 5; minority–full-time 2, part-time 2.

Programs and Degrees Offered:
Listed in the following order: Program area, degree type (T if terminal Master's), number awarded 7/00–6/01. Clinical MA 8, general MA 1.

APA Accreditation: Clinical PhD: full.

Student Applications/Admissions:
Student Applications
Clinical MA—Applications 2001–2002, 84. Total applicants accepted 2001–2002, 13. New applicants enrolled 2001–2002, 10. Total enrolled 2001–2002 full-time, 22. Openings 2002–2003, 10. The Median number of years required for completion of a degree are 2. The number of students enrolled full and part-time, who were dismissed or voluntarily withdrew from this program area were 0. *General MA*—Applications 2001–2002, 33. Total applicants accepted 2001–2002, 12. New applicants enrolled 2001–2002, 8. Total enrolled 2001–2002 full-time, 12. Openings 2002–2003, 10. The Median number of years required for completion of a degree are 2. The number of students enrolled full and part-time, who were dismissed or voluntarily withdrew from this program area were 2.

Admissions Requirements:
Scores: Entries appear in this order: required test or GPA, minimum score (if required), median score of students entering in 2001–2002. Master's Programs: overall undergraduate GPA 3.00, 3.71. GRE not required but highly recommended. Concordia = 4.30 grading scale. Minimum: 3.00 = B; Median: 3.71 = A. Doctoral Programs: overall undergraduate GPA 3.00, 3.37; last 2 years GPA no minimum stated; psychology GPA no minimum stated; psychology GPA 3.00, 3.84. Most students are admitted at the MA level. Not required, but highly recommended GRE. Concordia = 4.30 grading scale.
Other Criteria: (importance of criteria rated low, medium, or high): research experience high, work experience medium, extracurricular activity low, clinically related public service medium, GPA medium, letters of recommendation high, interview medium, statement of goals and objectives high, Thesis supervisor reqd. high. General does not require clinically related service.

Student Characteristics: The following represents characteristics of students in 2001–2002 in all graduate psychology programs in the department: Female–full-time 81, part-time 0; Male–full-time 22, part-time 0; African American/Black–full-time 1, part-time 0; Hispanic/Latino (a)–full-time 3, part-time 0; Asian/Pacific Islander–full-time 3, part-time 0; American Indian/Alaska Native–full-time 1, part-time 0; Multi-ethnic–full-time 0, part-time 0; students subject to the Americans with Disabilities Act–full-time 0, part-time 0.

Financial Information/Assistance:
Tuition for Full-Time Study: *Master's:* State residents per academic year $1,764; nonstate residents: per academic year $6,714. *Doctoral:* State residents: per academic year $1,764; nonstate residents: per academic year $6,107.

Financial Assistance:
First Year Students: Teaching assistantships available for first-year. Average amount paid per academic year: $5,400. Average number of hours worked per week: 10. Apply by August 1. Research assistantships available for first-year. Average amount paid per academic year: $5,400. Average number of hours worked per week: 10. Fellowships and scholarships available for first-year. Average amount paid per academic year: $14,000. Apply by October.

Advanced Students: Teaching assistantships available for advanced students. Average amount paid per academic year: $5,400. Average number of hours worked per week: 10. Apply by August 1. Research assistantships available for advanced students. Average amount paid per academic year: $5,400. Average number of hours worked per week: 10. Fellowships and scholarships available for advanced students. Average amount paid per academic year: $14,000. Apply by October.

Contact Information: Of all students currently enrolled full-time, 61% benefited from one or more of the listed financial assistance programs. For information on financial assistance, contact: http://graduatestudies.concordia.ca/awards.

Internships/Practica: Clinical students complete a variety of practica and internships while in program residence. All clinical students receive extensive practicum experience in psychotherapy and assessment in our on-campus training clinic, the Applied Psychology Center (APC), which is located on Concordia University's Loyola campus. APC clients are seen by graduate students under the supervision of clinical faculty. The types of services offered by the APC reflect the interests of clinical supervisors and students, and may include individual, family, or marital psychotherapy, behavior therapy for sexual or phobic difficulties, treatment of child disorders, and day care consultation. During the summer of their second year, students also complete a full-time practicum at a mental health facility in the Montreal area. During their final year in the program, students complete their full-time, predoctoral clinical internships. Recent students have undertaken predoctoral internships at a variety of mental health facilities across Canada and the United States. All students are encouraged to seek internship positions in settings accredited by either the Canadian or American Psychological Associations. For those doctoral students for whom a professional internship is required prior to graduation, 12 applied in 2000–2001. Of those who applied, 8 were placed in internships listed by the Association of Psychology Postdoctoral and Internship Programs (APPIC); 4 were placed in APA accredited internships.

Housing and Day Care: On-campus housing and day care facilities are available.

Employment of Department Graduates:

Master's Degree Graduates: Of those who graduated in the academic year 2000–2001, the following categories and numbers represent the post-graduate activities and employment of master's degree graduates: Enrolled in a psychology doctoral program (9), enrolled in another graduate/professional program (0), enrolled in a post-doctoral residency/fellowship (n/a), employed in independent practice (n/a).

Doctoral Degree Graduates: Of those who graduated in the academic year 2000–2001, the following categories and numbers represent the post-graduate activities and employment of doctoral degree graduates: Enrolled in a psychology doctoral program (n/a), enrolled in another graduate/professional program (n/a), enrolled in a post-doctoral residency/fellowship (4), employed in an academic position at a university (1), employed in a government agency (professional services) (1), employed in a hospital/medical center (5).

Additional Information:

Orientation, Objectives, and Emphasis of Department: Graduate education in both experimental and clinical psychology is strongly research oriented and intended for students who are planning to complete the PhD degree. The research program for all students is based on an apprentice-type model. An outstanding feature of graduate education at Concordia is that students pursuing only research studies and students pursuing research and clinical studies may conduct their research in the laboratory of any faculty member. A wide variety of contemporary research areas are available, ranging from basic infrahuman investigation to applied interventions with humans. Research findings from numerous areas are integrated in an effort to solve problems associated with appetitive motivation and drug dependence, memory and aging, human cognitive development, developmental psychobiology, adult and child psychopathology, sensory deficits, and sexual dysfunctions, to name several examples. Clinical training is based on the scientist-practitioner model. That is, clinical students meet the same research requirements as other students, and receive extensive professional training in the delivery of psychological services. Students may choose to specialize their clinical training with children or adults.

Special Facilities or Resources: The department has extensive animal and human research facilities that are supported by provincial, federal, and U.S. granting agencies as well as various internal and private sector funds. Most research laboratories are well equipped, and have microcomputers and/or local terminals to support faculty and student research. In addition to those in research laboratories, there are several microcomputers and terminals within the department specifically designated for student use; the university also has excellent mainframe computer facilities that run modern statistical packages. The department also contains 2 research centers that are jointly funded by the Government of Quebec and the University, the Center for Studies in Behavioral Neurobiology, and the Center for Research in Human Development. Both centers coordinate multidisciplinary research programs, provide state-of-the-art laboratory equipment, and sponsor colloquia by specialists from other universities in North America and abroad. All graduate students benefit from activities supported by the research centers.

Information for Students With Physical Disabilities: The Psychology building, Concordia libraries, and main university buildings are handicapped accessible, as is the inter-campus shuttle bus.

Application Information:

Send to: Director of Graduate Admissions, School of Graduate Studies, Concordia University, 1455 de Maisonneuve Blvd. West, Montréal, Québec H3G 1M8, Canada. Students are admitted in the Fall, application deadline January 8. *Fee:* $50. Note: All dollar amounts specified in this entry are Canadian dollars.

Dalhousie University (2001 data)
Department of Psychology
Life Sciences Centre
Halifax, NS B3H 4J1 Canada
Telephone: (902) 494-3839
Fax: (902) 494-6585
E-mail: *psychology@dal.ca*
Web: *http://www.dal.ca/psychology*

Department Established:

1863. Acting Chair: Donald Mitchell. Number of Faculty: total–full-time 28, part-time 2; women–full-time 8, part-time 1; minority–full-time 1.

Programs and Degrees Offered:

Listed in the following order: Program area, degree type (T if terminal Master's), number awarded 7/00–6/01. Clinical PhD 6, experimental-animal MSc, experimental-human MSc, neuroscience MSc.

APA Accreditation: Clinical PhD: full.

Student Applications/Admissions:

Student Applications

Clinical PhD—Applications 2001–2002, 150. Total applicants accepted 2001–2002, 7. New applicants enrolled 2001–2002, 5. Total enrolled 2001–2002 full-time, 32. Openings 2002–2003, 3. The number of students enrolled full and part-time, who were dismissed or voluntarily withdrew from this program area were 1. *Experimental-animal MSc*—Applications 2001–2002, 5. Total applicants accepted 2001–2002, 7. New applicants enrolled 2001–2002, 4. Total enrolled 2001–2002 full-time, 5. *Experimental-human MSc*—Applications 2001–2002, 5. *Neuroscience MSc*—Applications 2001–2002, 10. Total applicants accepted 2001–2002, 4. Total enrolled 2001–2002 full-time, 1.

Admissions Requirements:

Scores: Entries appear in this order: required test or GPA, minimum score (if required), median score of students entering in 2001–2002. Master's Programs: GRE-V 600; GRE-Q 600; GRE-Analytical 600. Doctoral Programs: GRE-V 600; GRE-Q 600; GRE-Analytical 600; overall undergraduate GPA 3.70; last 2 years GPA 3.70; psychology GPA 3.70.

Other Criteria: (importance of criteria rated low, medium, or high): GRE/MAT scores, research experience high, work experience low, extracurricular activity low, clinically related public service low, GPA high, letters of recommendation high, interview low, statement of goals and objectives high. Clinically related public service is high for clinical program.

Student Characteristics: The following represents characteristics of students in 2001–2002 in all graduate psychology programs in the department: Female–full-time 9, part-time 0; Male–full-time 1, part-time 0; African American/Black–full-time 0, part-time 0; Hispanic/Latino (a)–full-time 0, part-time 0; Asian/Pacific Islander–full-time 0, part-time 0; American Indian/Alaska Native–full-time 0, part-time 0.

Financial Information/Assistance:

Tuition for Full-Time Study: No information provided.

Financial Assistance:

First Year Students: No information provided.
Advanced Students: No information provided.
Contact Information: Of all students currently enrolled full-time, 68% benefited from one or more of the listed financial assistance programs. For information on financial assistance, contact: Registar's Office.

Internships/Practica: No information provided.

Housing and Day Care: No on-campus housing and day care facilities are available.

Employment of Department Graduates:

Master's Degree Graduates: Of those who graduated in the academic year 2000–2001, the following categories and numbers represent the post-graduate activities and employment of master's degree graduates: Enrolled in a post-doctoral residency/fellowship (n/a), employed in independent practice (n/a).
Doctoral Degree Graduates: Of those who graduated in the academic year 2000–2001, the following categories and numbers represent the post-graduate activities and employment of doctoral degree graduates: Enrolled in a psychology doctoral program (n/a), enrolled in another graduate/professional program (n/a).

Additional Information:

Orientation, Objectives, and Emphasis of Department: The Department of Psychology offers graduate training leading to MSc and PhD degrees in psychology and in psychology/neuroscience, and to a PhD in clinical psychology. Our graduate programs emphasize training for research. They are best described as "apprenticeship" programs in which students work closely with a faculty member who has agreed to supervise the student's research. Compared with many other graduate programs, we place less emphasis on coursework and greater emphasis on research, scholarship, and independent thinking. The graduate programs in psychology/neuroscience are coordinated by the Psychology Department and an interdisciplinary Neuroscience Program Committee with representation from the Departments of Anatomy, Biochemistry, Pharmacology, Physiology and Biophysics, and Psychology. Master's level students in psychology and psychology/neuroscience are expected to advance into the corresponding PhD programs. We do not have a "terminal" Master's program. The PhD program in clinical psychology is cooperatively administered by the Psychology Department and the Clinical Program Committee with representation from Acadia University, Dalhousie University, Mount Saint Vincent University, Saint Mary's University, and professional psychologists from the teaching hospitals. It is a structured five-year program which follows the "scientist-practitioner" model. The department does not offer a Master's degree in clinical psychology. During the first four years of the clinical psychology program, students complete required courses, conduct supervised and thesis research, and gain clinical experience through field placements. In the fifth year, students are placed in a full-year clinical internship.

Special Facilities or Resources: The department of psychology is located in the Life Sciences Centre which also contains the departments of biology, earth sciences, and oceanography. The psychology building contains very extensive laboratory areas, some with circulating sea-water aquaria, and is designed for research with a range of animal groups (humans, cats, birds, fish, invertebrates) using a range of research techniques in behavior, electrophysiology, neuroanatomy, immunocytochemistry, neurogenetics, and so forth. The department also houses an electronics and woodworking shop, an animal care facility, a surgical facility, a computer lab for word processing, communications, and access to a mainframe; specific neuroscience facilities are in close proximity to hospitals.

Application Information:

Send to: Graduate Program Secretary, Psychology Department, Dalhousie University, Halifax, NS B3H 4J1. Students are admitted in the Fall, application deadline January 1. *Fee:* $65. Note: All dollar amounts specified in this entry are Canadian dollars.

Guelph, University of
Department of Psychology
College of Social and Applied Human Sciences
5th Floor MacKinnon
Guelph, ON N1G 2W1 Canada
Telephone: (519) 824-4120 ext. 3508
Fax: (519) 837-8629
E-mail: *marmurek@psy.uoguelph.ca*
Web: *http://www.psychology.uoguelph.ca*

Department Established:

1966. Chairperson: Harvey Marmurek. Number of Faculty: total–full-time 25; women–full-time 7.

Programs and Degrees Offered:

Listed in the following order: Program area, degree type (T if terminal Master's), number awarded 7/00–6/01. Applied developmental PhD 6, applied social PhD 4, General and Experimental MA (T) 1, industrial/organizational PhD (T) 5.

Student Applications/Admissions:

Student Applications

Applied developmental PhD—Applications 2001–2002, 36. Total applicants accepted 2001–2002, 6. New applicants enrolled 2001–2002, 6. Total enrolled 2001–2002 full-time, 22, part-time, 1. Openings 2002–2003, 4. *Applied social PhD*—Applications 2001–2002, 23. Total applicants accepted 2001–2002, 1. New applicants enrolled 2001–2002, 1. Total enrolled 2001–2002 full-time, 9, part-time, 2. Openings 2002–2003, 4. *General and Experimental MA*—Applications 2001–2002, 7. Total applicants accepted 2001–2002, 2. New applicants enrolled 2001–2002, 2. Total enrolled 2001–2002 full-time, 4. Openings 2002–2003, 2. *Industrial/organizational PhD*—Applications 2001–2002, 30. Total applicants accepted 2001–2002, 6. New applicants enrolled 2001–2002, 6. Total enrolled 2001–2002 full-time, 21, part-time, 2. Openings 2002–2003, 4.

Admissions Requirements:

Scores: Entries appear in this order: required test or GPA, minimum score (if required), median score of students entering in 2001–2002. Master's Programs: GRE-V no minimum stated, 580; GRE-Q no minimum stated, 650; GRE-Analytical no minimum stated, 640; GRE-Subject(Psych) no minimum stated, 670; last 2 years GPA no minimum stated, 3.75; psychology GPA no minimum stated, 3.80. Doctoral Programs: GRE-V no minimum stated, 620; GRE-Q no minimum stated, 650; GRE-Analytical no minimum stated, 640; GRE-Subject(Psych) no minimum stated, 660; last 2 years GPA no minimum stated; psychology GPA no minimum stated, 3.8 ; psychology GPA no minimum stated, 3.8.

Other Criteria: (importance of criteria rated low, medium, or high): GRE/MAT scores medium, research experience high, work experience medium, extracurricular activity low, clinically related public service low, GPA high, letters of recommendation high, interview high, statement of goals and objectives high.

Student Characteristics: The following represents characteristics of students in 2001–2002 in all graduate psychology programs in the department: Female–full-time 46, part-time 4; Male–full-time 11, part-time 0; African American/Black–full-time 0, part-time 0; Hispanic/Latino (a)–full-time 1, part-time 0; Asian/Pacific Islander–full-time 5, part-time 0; American Indian/Alaska Native–full-time 0, part-time 0.

Financial Information/Assistance:

Tuition for Full-Time Study: Master's: State residents per academic year $4,891; nonstate residents: per academic year $7,248. *Doctoral:* State residents: per academic year $4,891; nonstate residents: per academic year $7,248.

Financial Assistance:

First Year Students: Teaching assistantships available for first-year. Average amount paid per academic year: $12,400. Average number of hours worked per week: 10. Fellowships and scholarships available for first-year. Average amount paid per academic year: $2,000. Tuition remission given: partial.

Advanced Students: Teaching assistantships available for advanced students. Average amount paid per academic year: $12,400. Fellowships and scholarships available for advanced students. Average amount paid per academic year: $2,000. Tuition remission given: partial.

Contact Information: Of all students currently enrolled full-time, 95% benefited from one or more of the listed financial assistance programs. For information on financial assistance, contact: Graduate Awards Clerk, Registrarial Office, University of Guelph, Guelph, ON N1G 2W1. Additional fellowships and scholarships are available from government sources.

Internships/Practica: For the applied developmental emphasis, practicum experience generally consists of two placements. During the fourth semester, students work two days per week with the psychological services staff at local public school boards. During a later semester, students are placed four days a week in a service facility for atypical children, (e.g., clinics, hospitals, residential treatment centers, special schools). For the applied social empha-sis, students select one practicum setting comprising the development of practice skills and one concentrating on training in applied research skills. Settings include community health facilities, correctional and medical treatment settings, school systems, crisis intervention agencies, and private consulting firms. Industrial/organizational practica take place in industrial, governmental, and military settings. Practica are supervised by both on-campus and field instructors. For those doctoral students for whom a professional internship is required prior to graduation, 1 applied in 2000–2001. Of those who applied, 1 were placed in internships listed by the Association of Psychology Postdoctoral and Internship Programs (APPIC); 1 were placed in APA accredited internships.

Housing and Day Care: On-campus housing and day care facilities are available.

Employment of Department Graduates:

Master's Degree Graduates: Of those who graduated in the academic year 2000–2001, the following categories and numbers represent the post-graduate activities and employment of master's degree graduates: Enrolled in a psychology doctoral program (10), enrolled in a post-doctoral residency/fellowship (n/a), employed in independent practice (n/a), employed in a professional position in a school system (1), employed in business or industry (research/consulting) (6), employed in a community mental health/counseling center (1), employed in a hospital/medical center (3), still seeking employment (1).

Doctoral Degree Graduates: Of those who graduated in the academic year 2000–2001, the following categories and numbers represent the post-graduate activities and employment of doctoral degree graduates: Enrolled in a psychology doctoral program (n/a), enrolled in another graduate/professional program (n/a), employed in an academic position at a university (1), employed in a professional position in a school system (1), employed in a government agency (professional services) (1), employed in a community mental health/counseling center (3), employed in a hospital/medical center (1).

Additional Information:

Orientation, Objectives, and Emphasis of Department: The Department of Psychology offers a graduate program leading to a Master of Arts and Doctor of Philosophy in psychology. The primary aim for students accepted into the MA general experimental concentration is the development of competence in conducting and evaluating research in experimental psychology. Emphases include learning, physiological, perception, cognition, and human factors. For students in the PhD applied concentrations, the primary aim is to integrate theory, research, and practice by providing a foundation in both basic and applied psychology. In addition to coursework, students complete practica. The applied developmental emphasis prepares students to use a developmental perspective in the assessment and remediation of childhood problems. The applied social emphasis trains students in the implementation of applied research, program planning, and practical skills for social problems. The industrial/organizational emphasis stresses competency-based training in personnel selection and organizational consulting. An MA degree in industrial/organizational psychology is also offered.

Special Facilities or Resources: Faculty offices and laboratories are located mainly in the MacKinnon Building and Blackwood

Hall. Graduate students have office space in Blackwood Hall. The department is well supported with computer facilities. These include a microcomputer laboratory and extensive microcomputer support for research, teaching, data analysis, and word processing. Facilities for animal research include a fully equipped surgery room and physiological recording equipment. For research with human subjects, the department possesses portable video-recording equipment, observation rooms, and experimental chambers. All of these facilities are supplemented by excellent workshop and technical support. The Centre for Psychological Services is a non-profit organization associated with the Department of Psychology at the University of Guelph. The Centre provides high quality psychological services at a reasonable cost, working with families and the community. The Centre also offers workshops and presentations to professionals in the community. G-CORI is a non-profit consulting and research organization that hires psychology graduate students, allowing them to utilize the knowledge gained in their courses.

Information for Students With Physical Disabilities: The university has a Disabled Students' Center to provide support for students with special physical and hearing needs.

Application Information:
Send to: Graduate Secretary, Department of Psychology, University of Guelph, Guelph, Ontario N1G 2W1, Canada. Telephone: (519) 824-4120, ext. 3508. Students are admitted in the Fall, application deadline January 21. All applications are considered in February. *Fee:* $75. Note: All dollar amounts specified in this entry are Canadian dollars.

Manitoba, University of (2001 data)
Psychology Graduate Office
P514 Duff Roblin Building
Winnipeg, MB R3T 2N2 Canada
Telephone: (204) 474-6377
Fax: (204) 474-7599
E-mail: *inglislf@ms.umanitoba.ca*
Web: *http://www.umanitoba.ca/faculties/arts/psychology*

Department Established:
1947. Head: Gerry N. Sande. Number of Faculty: total–full-time 38, part-time 3; women–full-time 11, part-time 1; minority–full-time 2.

Programs and Degrees Offered:
Listed in the following order: Program area, degree type (T if terminal Master's), number awarded 7/00–6/01. Applied Behavioral Analysis PhD (T), Behavioral Neuroscience PhD (T) 1, Clinical PhD (T) 5, Cognitive PhD (T) 1, Developmental PhD (T), Experimental PhD (T), General PhD (T) 1, Social/Personality PhD (T) 3.

APA Accreditation: Clinical PhD: full.

Student Applications/Admissions:
Student Applications
Applied Behavioral Analysis PhD—Applications 2001–2002, 5. Total applicants accepted 2001–2002, 3. New applicants en-

rolled 2001–2002, 3. Total enrolled 2001–2002 full-time, 3. Openings 2002–2003, 2. The number of students enrolled full and part-time, who were dismissed or voluntarily withdrew from this program area were 0. *Behavioral Neuroscience PhD*—Applications 2001–2002, 4. Total applicants accepted 2001–2002, 3. New applicants enrolled 2001–2002, 3. Total enrolled 2001–2002 full-time, 6. Openings 2002–2003, 3. *Clinical PhD*—Applications 2001–2002, 49. Total applicants accepted 2001–2002, 6. New applicants enrolled 2001–2002, 3. Total enrolled 2001–2002 full-time, 46. Openings 2002–2003, 5. The Median number of years required for completion of a degree are 7. *Cognitive PhD*—Applications 2001–2002, 3. Total applicants accepted 2001–2002, 1. New applicants enrolled 2001–2002, 1. Total enrolled 2001–2002 full-time, 6. Openings 2002–2003, 3. The number of students enrolled full and part-time, who were dismissed or voluntarily withdrew from this program area were 0. *Developmental PhD*—Applications 2001–2002, 2. Total enrolled 2001–2002 full-time, 6. Openings 2002–2003, 4. *Experimental PhD*—Applications 2001–2002, 1. Total enrolled 2001–2002 full-time, 7. Openings 2002–2003, 3. The number of students enrolled full and part-time, who were dismissed or voluntarily withdrew from this program area were 0. *General PhD*—Applications 2001–2002, 0. Openings 2002–2003, 1. The number of students enrolled full and part-time, who were dismissed or voluntarily withdrew from this program area were 0. *Social/Personality PhD*—Applications 2001–2002, 13. Total applicants accepted 2001–2002, 5. New applicants enrolled 2001–2002, 2. Total enrolled 2001–2002 full-time, 11. Openings 2002–2003, 4. The Median number of years required for completion of a degree are 4. The number of students enrolled full and part-time, who were dismissed or voluntarily withdrew from this program area were 0.

Admissions Requirements:
Scores: Entries appear in this order: required test or GPA, minimum score (if required), median score of students entering in 2001–2002. Master's Programs: GRE-V no minimum stated, 540; GRE-Q no minimum stated, 600; GRE-V+Q no minimum stated, 1140; last 2 years GPA 3.0, 3.95. Doctoral Programs: GRE-V no minimum stated, 510; GRE-Q no minimum stated, 610; GRE-V+Q no minimum stated, 1120; last 2 years GPA 3.0, 3.96; psychology GPA no minimum stated; psychology GPA no minimum stated, 4.12.
Other Criteria: (importance of criteria rated low, medium, or high): GRE/MAT scores high, research experience high, work experience medium, extracurricular activity low, clinically related public service medium, GPA high, letters of recommendation medium, statement of goals and objectives low.

Student Characteristics: The following represents characteristics of students in 2001–2002 in all graduate psychology programs in the department: Female–full-time 55, part-time 2; Male–full-time 17, part-time 0; African American/Black–full-time 0, part-time 0; Hispanic/Latino (a)–full-time 1, part-time 0; Asian/Pacific Islander–full-time 0, part-time 0; American Indian/Alaska Native–full-time 1, part-time 0; students subject to the Americans with Disabilities Act–full-time 0.

Financial Information/Assistance:
Tuition for Full-Time Study: No information provided.

Financial Assistance:

First Year Students: No information provided.

Advanced Students: No information provided.

Contact Information: Of all students currently enrolled full-time, 68% benefited from one or more of the listed financial assistance programs. For information on financial assistance, contact: Fellowships/Scholarships: Psychology Graduate Office; TAs Mary Kuzmeniuk.

Internships/Practica: Clinical students have access to practica at our Psychological Service Center. A limited number of practica within the community are available for senior graduate students. However, the department does not offer an internship program. For those doctoral students for whom a professional internship is required prior to graduation, 1 applied in 2000–2001. Of those who applied, 1 were placed in internships listed by the Association of Psychology Postdoctoral and Internship Programs (APPIC); 1 were placed in APA accredited internships.

Housing and Day Care: No on-campus housing and day care facilities are available.

Employment of Department Graduates:

Master's Degree Graduates: Of those who graduated in the academic year 2000–2001, the following categories and numbers represent the post-graduate activities and employment of master's degree graduates: Enrolled in a post-doctoral residency/fellowship (n/a), employed in independent practice (n/a).

Doctoral Degree Graduates: Of those who graduated in the academic year 2000–2001, the following categories and numbers represent the post-graduate activities and employment of doctoral degree graduates: Enrolled in a psychology doctoral program (n/a), enrolled in another graduate/professional program (n/a).

Additional Information:

Orientation, Objectives, and Emphasis of Department: The primary purpose of our program is to provide training in several specialized areas of psychology for individuals desiring to advance their level of knowledge, their research skills, and their applied capabilities. The MA program is designed to provide a broad foundation, as well as specialized skills, in the scientific approach to psychology. The PhD program provides a higher degree of specialization coupled with more intensive training in research and application. Specialized areas of training within the department include applied behavioral analysis, behavioral neuroscience, clinical, cognitive, developmental, experimental, general, and social/personality.

Special Facilities or Resources: Special facilities or resources of the department are as follows: animal research laboratories; avian laboratories; psychophysiology and psychobiology laboratories; sleep laboratories; electronics, computer, multimedia, and woodworking shops; a local area network devoted to research and teaching; and the Psychological Service Center and Elizabeth Hill Counseling Centre.

Information for Students With Physical Disabilities: There is a Disability Services Office on campus. Students may also contact the Psychology Department directly regarding special needs.

Application Information:
Send to: Linda Inglis, Psychology Graduate Office, P514 Duff Roblin Bldg., University of Manitoba, Winnipeg, MB R3T 2N2. Students are admitted in the Fall, application deadline January 15. *Fee:* $50. Note: All dollar amounts specified in this entry are Canadian dollars.

McGill University
Department of Educational and Counseling Psychology
Faculty of Education
3700 McTavish Street
Montreal, QC H3A 1Y2 Canada
Telephone: (514) 398-4241
Fax: (514) 398-6968
E-mail: *selma.abumerhy@mcgill.ca*
Web: *http://www.education.mcgill.ca/ecp*

Department Established:
1965. Chair: Susanne P. Lajoie. Number of Faculty: total–full-time 27, part-time 40; women–full-time 12, part-time 18.

Programs and Degrees Offered:
Listed in the following order: Program area, degree type (T if terminal Master's), number awarded 7/00–6/01. Counseling PhD (T) 3, educational PhD (T) 4, school/applied child PhD 6.

APA Accreditation: Counseling PhD: full. School PhD: full.

Student Applications/Admissions:

Student Applications

Counseling PhD—Applications 2001–2002, 12. Total applicants accepted 2001–2002, 3. New applicants enrolled 2001–2002, 2. Total enrolled 2001–2002 full-time, 20, part-time, 1. Openings 2002–2003, 3. The Median number of years required for completion of a degree are 7. The number of students enrolled full and part-time, who were dismissed or voluntarily withdrew from this program area were 4. *Educational PhD*—Applications 2001–2002, 13. Total applicants accepted 2001–2002, 9. New applicants enrolled 2001–2002, 8. Total enrolled 2001–2002 full-time, 41, part-time, 3. Openings 2002–2003, 12. The Median number of years required for completion of a degree are 7. The number of students enrolled full and part-time, who were dismissed or voluntarily withdrew from this program area were 2. *School/applied child PhD*—Applications 2001–2002, 15. Total applicants accepted 2001–2002, 11. New applicants enrolled 2001–2002, 9. Total enrolled 2001–2002 full-time, 43, part-time, 13. Openings 2002–2003, 10. The Median number of years required for completion of a degree are 7. The number of students enrolled full and part-time, who were dismissed or voluntarily withdrew from this program area were 0.

Admissions Requirements:

Scores: Entries appear in this order: required test or GPA, minimum score (if required), median score of students entering in 2001–2002. Master's Programs: GRE-V 500, 600; GRE-Q 500, 600; GRE-Subject(Psych) 500, 600; overall undergraduate GPA 3.0, 3.5; last 2 years GPA 3.0, 3.3; psychology GPA 3.0, 3.3. GREs are required only in School/Applied Child, Applied Developmental Psychology, and Counseling Psychology—there is no minimum cut-off. Doctoral Programs: GRE-V no minimum stated; GRE-Q no minimum stated; GRE-Subject(Psych) no minimum stated; overall undergraduate

GPA 3.0; last 2 years GPA no minimum stated; psychology GPA no minimum stated; psychology GPA no minimum stated. As for master's, no minimums

Other Criteria: (importance of criteria rated low, medium, or high): GRE/MAT scores, research experience medium, work experience medium, extracurricular activity medium, clinically related public service medium, GPA high, letters of recommendation high, interview medium, statement of goals and objectives high. Relative weight of these criteria varies across program areas.

Student Characteristics: The following represents characteristics of students in 2001–2002 in all graduate psychology programs in the department: Female–full-time 151, part-time 85; Male–full-time 28, part-time 12.

Financial Information/Assistance:

Tuition for Full-Time Study: *Master's:* State residents per academic year $2,692, $89 per credit hour; nonstate residents: per academic year $9,051, $301 per credit hour. *Doctoral:* State residents: per academic year $2,692, $89 per credit hour; nonstate residents: per academic year $8,241, $274 per credit hour.

Financial Assistance:

First Year Students: Teaching assistantships available for first-year. Average amount paid per academic year: $1,849. Average number of hours worked per week: 3. Apply by Sept. 1. Research assistantships available for first-year. Average amount paid per academic year: $4,000. Average number of hours worked per week: 5.

Advanced Students: Teaching assistantships available for advanced students. Average amount paid per academic year: $3,698. Average number of hours worked per week: 6. Apply by Sept. 1. Research assistantships available for advanced students. Average amount paid per academic year: $8,000. Average number of hours worked per week: 10.

Contact Information: Of all students currently enrolled full-time, 6% benefited from one or more of the listed financial assistance programs. For information on financial assistance, contact: Department Chair, Program Directors, Administrative Officer, Program Coordinators.

Internships/Practica: All students in the professional psychology programs, the MA (non-thesis) and PhD in counseling Psychology, the MEd, MA in Educational Psychology (Special Education and Gifted Education option), and the MA and PhD in Educational Psychology (School/Applied Child Psychology option) are required to complete internships. According to the program option these may be in mental health facilities, community social service agencies, schools, psychoeducational clinics, etc. In some internships, more than one setting is advised or required. New internship opportunities are regularly added, and students are welcome to seek out those which may especially suit their needs, subject to program approval. For those doctoral students for whom a professional internship is required prior to graduation, 10 applied in 2000–2001. Of those who applied, 4 were placed in internships listed by the Association of Psychology Postdoctoral and Internship Programs (APPIC); 4 were placed in APA accredited internships.

Housing and Day Care: No on-campus housing and day care facilities are available.

Employment of Department Graduates:

Master's Degree Graduates: Of those who graduated in the academic year 2000–2001, the following categories and numbers represent the post-graduate activities and employment of master's degree graduates: Enrolled in a psychology doctoral program (11), enrolled in another graduate/professional program (3), enrolled in a post-doctoral residency/fellowship (n/a), employed in independent practice (n/a), still seeking employment (7).

Doctoral Degree Graduates: Of those who graduated in the academic year 2000–2001, the following categories and numbers represent the post-graduate activities and employment of doctoral degree graduates: Enrolled in a psychology doctoral program (n/a), enrolled in another graduate/professional program (n/a), employed in an academic position at a university (2), employed in other positions at a higher education institution (2), employed in a professional position in a school system (2), employed in business or industry (research/consulting) (1), employed in a community mental health/counseling center (4).

Additional Information:

Orientation, Objectives, and Emphasis of Department: There are six broad areas of major graduate-level specialization: Counseling Psychology, Applied Developmental Psychology, Instructional Psychology, Applied Cognitive Psychology, Special Populations, and School/Applied Child Psychology. Minors are available in most of these; in topics which bridge the majors (e.g., computer applications, special/integrated education, gifted education, adult/professional, higher education, or psychology of gender); or topics proposed by students and approved by the department. A substantial base in research methods and statistics is provided and adjusted to students' entering competence. Graduate students in professional school psychology normally enter the Master's and are considered for transfer to the PhD (if that is their goal) after 3 semesters for a further 3 years of training. Graduate studies directed toward research, academic, and leadership careers follow a similar enrollment pattern except that the program normally requires one year less at the doctoral level. Students are welcome to take selected courses in other departments and at other Quebec universities.

Special Facilities or Resources: The University has the Laboratory for Applied Cognitive Science, Summer Program in Gifted Education, Summer Institute in Integrated Education, Centre for University Teaching and Learning, Early Childhood Infant/Parent Education Project, mainframe-terminal and microcomputer (DOS and MAC) computer labs, and the Educational Media Centre.

Information for Students With Physical Disabilities: The university has an active Office for Students with Disabilities. The Department welcomes applications from all students and is greatly assisted by early notification of special needs.

Application Information:

Send to: Diane Bernier, Program Coordinator, Professional Psychology Graduate Programs; Geri Norton, Program Coordinator, Professional Educational Psychology Graduate Programs. Students are admitted in the Fall, application deadline February 1; Winter, application deadline N/A; Spring, application deadline February 1; Summer, application deadline February 1. Special circumstances may be examined on an individual basis. *Fee:* $60. Special circumstances may be examined on an individual basis. Note: All dollar amounts specified in this entry are Canadian dollars.

McGill University

Department of Psychology
1205 Avenue Docteur Penfield
Montreal, QC H3A 1B1 Canada
Telephone: (514) 398-6124
Fax: (514) 398-4896
E-mail: *giovanna@hebb.psych.mcgill.ca*
Web: *http://www.psych.mcgill.ca*

Department Established:
1922. Chairperson: Keith Franklin. Number of Faculty: total–full-time 34, part-time 7; women–full-time 8, part-time 2; minority–full-time 2.

Programs and Degrees Offered:
Listed in the following order: Program area, degree type (T if terminal Master's), number awarded 7/00–6/01. Clinical PhD 6, experimental PhD 8.

APA Accreditation: Clinical PhD: full.

Student Applications/Admissions:
Student Applications
Clinical PhD—Applications 2001–2002, 130. Total applicants accepted 2001–2002, 7. New applicants enrolled 2001–2002, 4. Total enrolled 2001–2002 full-time, 43. Openings 2002–2003, 10. *Experimental PhD*—Applications 2001–2002, 84. Total applicants accepted 2001–2002, 26. New applicants enrolled 2001–2002, 16. Total enrolled 2001–2002 full-time, 55. Openings 2002–2003, 10.

Admissions Requirements:
Scores: Entries appear in this order: required test or GPA, minimum score (if required), median score of students entering in 2001–2002. Doctoral Programs: GRE-V+Q+Analytical no minimum stated; GRE-Subject(Psych) no minimum stated; overall undergraduate GPA no minimum stated; last 2 years GPA no minimum stated; psychology GPA no minimum stated; psychology GPA no minimum stated.
Other Criteria: (importance of criteria rated low, medium, or high): GPA high, letters of recommendation high, statement of goals and objectives high.

Student Characteristics: The following represents characteristics of students in 2001–2002 in all graduate psychology programs in the department: Female–full-time 63, part-time 0; Male–full-time 33, part-time 0; African American/Black–full-time 1, part-time 0; Hispanic/Latino (a)–full-time 0, part-time 0; Asian/Pacific Islander–full-time 4, part-time 0; American Indian/Alaska Native–full-time 0, part-time 0.

Financial Information/Assistance:
Tuition for Full-Time Study: *Master's:* State residents per academic year $2,800; nonstate residents: per academic year $9,700. *Doctoral:* State residents: per academic year $2,800; nonstate residents: per academic year $8,800.

Financial Assistance:
First Year Students: Teaching assistantships available for first-year.
Advanced Students: Teaching assistantships available for advanced students.
Contact Information: For information on financial assistance, contact: The above is only if you are accepted into the program. The Student Services Office number is 514-398-8238 or via Website http://ww2.mcgill.ca/StuServ/.

Internships/Practica: The majority of students in our clinical program complete their internships within Montreal, especially at McGill-affiliated hospitals. These include three large and two small general hospitals, a large psychiatric hospital, and a large children's hospital, where a wide range of assessment and treatment skills can be acquired. Specialized, advanced training is provided at other institutions in the areas of neuropsychology, hearing impairments, orthopedic disabilities, and rehabilitation. One advantage of having a local internship is that it facilitates the integration of the student's clinical and research activities. In addition, the department is able to monitor the quality of the training at the placements. All placements have active, ongoing commitments to research. Students have also completed internships at a wide variety of settings in other parts of Canada, the United States, and Europe. Settings outside Montreal must meet with staff approval. For those doctoral students for whom a professional internship is required prior to graduation, 13 applied in 2000–2001. Of those who applied, 3 were placed in internships listed by the Association of Psychology Postdoctoral and Internship Programs (APPIC); 13 were placed in APA accredited internships.

Housing and Day Care: No on-campus housing and day care facilities are available.

Employment of Department Graduates:
Master's Degree Graduates: Of those who graduated in the academic year 2000–2001, the following categories and numbers represent the post-graduate activities and employment of master's degree graduates: Enrolled in a post-doctoral residency/fellowship (n/a), employed in independent practice (n/a).
Doctoral Degree Graduates: Of those who graduated in the academic year 2000–2001, the following categories and numbers represent the post-graduate activities and employment of doctoral degree graduates: Enrolled in a psychology doctoral program (n/a), enrolled in another graduate/professional program (n/a).

Additional Information:
Orientation, Objectives, and Emphasis of Department: McGill University's Department of Psychology offers graduate work leading to the PhD degree. The program in experimental psychology includes the areas of cognitive science (perception, learning, and language), developmental, social, personality, quantitative, and behavioral neuroscience. A program in clinical psychology (accredited by APA) is also offered. The basic purpose of the graduate program is to provide the student with an environment in which he or she is free to develop skills and expertise that will serve during a professional career in teaching, research, or clinical service as a psychologist. Individually conceived and conducted research in the student's area of interest is the single most important activity of all graduate students in the department.

Application Information:

Send to: Giovanna LoCascio, Graduate Program Co-ordinator, Department of Psychology, 1205 Docteur Penfield Avenue, Montreal, Quebec H3A 1B1. Students are admitted in the Fall, application deadline January 15. *Fee:* $60. Note: All dollar amounts specified in this entry are Canadian dollars.

Memorial University of Newfoundland (2001 data)
Department of Psychology
Elizabeth Avenue
St. John's, NF A1B 3X9 Canada
Telephone: (709) 737-8495
Fax: (709) 737-2430
E-mail: *gradpsyc@play.psych.mun.ca*
Web: *http://play.psych.mun.ca/index.html*

Department Established:

1960. Head: Dr. John Evans. Number of Faculty: total–full-time 29, part-time 1; women–full-time 11, part-time 1.

Programs and Degrees Offered:

Listed in the following order: Program area, degree type (T if terminal Master's), number awarded 7/00–6/01. Applied Social, Experimental PhD, MSc in Experimental Psychology MA.

Student Applications/Admissions:

Student Applications

Experimental PhD. MSc in Experimental Psychology MA.

Admissions Requirements:

Scores: Entries appear in this order: required test or GPA, minimum score (if required), median score of students entering in 2001–2002. Master's Programs: GRE-V no minimum stated; GRE-Q no minimum stated; GRE-V+Q 1000. Doctoral Programs: GRE-V no minimum stated; GRE-Q no minimum stated; GRE-V+Q 1000.

Other Criteria: (importance of criteria rated low, medium, or high): GRE/MAT scores medium, research experience high, work experience medium, extracurricular activity low, clinically related public service low, GPA high, letters of recommendation medium, statement of goals and objectives medium. GPA is the most important criterion for all programs. Research experience is required for experimental programs. Work experience is important for the M.Sc. in applied social psychology.

Student Characteristics: The following represents characteristics of students in 2001–2002 in all graduate psychology programs in the department: Female–full-time 11, part-time 0; Male–full-time 3, part-time 0; African American/Black–full-time 0, part-time 0; Hispanic/Latino (a)–full-time 0, part-time 0; Asian/Pacific Islander–full-time 0, part-time 0; American Indian/Alaska Native–full-time 0, part-time 0.

Financial Information/Assistance:

Tuition for Full-Time Study: No information provided.

Financial Assistance:

First Year Students: No information provided.

Advanced Students: No information provided.

Contact Information: Of all students currently enrolled full-time, 100% benefited from one or more of the listed financial assistance programs.

Internships/Practica: No information provided.

Housing and Day Care: No on-campus housing and day care facilities are available.

Employment of Department Graduates:

Master's Degree Graduates: Of those who graduated in the academic year 2000–2001, the following categories and numbers represent the post-graduate activities and employment of master's degree graduates: Enrolled in a post-doctoral residency/fellowship (n/a), employed in independent practice (n/a).

Doctoral Degree Graduates: Of those who graduated in the academic year 2000–2001, the following categories and numbers represent the post-graduate activities and employment of doctoral degree graduates: Enrolled in a psychology doctoral program (n/a), enrolled in another graduate/professional program (n/a).

Additional Information:

Orientation, Objectives, and Emphasis of Department: There are active research groups in biopsychology, developmental, animal learning, and behavioral neuroscience. The Biopsychology Program is an interdisciplinary graduate program focused on animal behaviour and behavioural ecology. Thesis supervisors in this program are drawn from the Departments of Psychology, Biology, Biochemistry and Geography, the Ocean Sciences Centre and the Faculty of Engineering. The M.Sc. program in applied social psychology is a two-year co-operative program with one work-term per year in business, government, or health care organizations. There is no thesis requirement in the applied social program. Please note: Information on the number of applications and enrollment, and degrees awarded in each program, do not apply to the Biopsychology program, as it is administered separately.

Special Facilities or Resources: Biopsychology: Due to our location, we are able to provide unequalled access to sea bird populations and marine mammals for animal behavior studies. Developmental: Due to a cooperative attitude in the community we have had access to a variety of subject populations, e.g., newborns, children with learning disabilities. Two on-campus day care centers provide access to children from 3 to 8 years of age. Neuroscience: The presence of Memorial University School of Medicine on the same campus allows interaction with neuroscientists in that faculty, and Psychology graduate students can take courses in the School of Medicine. There is an active local chapter of the Society for Neuroscience.

Application Information:

Send to: Application forms can be obtained by contacting gradpsyc@play.psych.mun.ca or writing to: Department of Psychology, Memorial University of Newfoundland, St. Johns, Newfoundland, A1B 3X9, CANADA Apply online at http://www.mun.ca/sgs/. Students are admitted in the Fall, application deadline Feb. 1; Winter, application deadline July 1. *Fee:* $40. Note: All dollar amounts specified in this entry are Canadian dollars.

Montreal, University of

Department of Psychology
C.P. 6128, Succ. Centre-Ville
Montreal, QC H3C 3J7 Canada
Telephone: (514) 343-6503
Fax: (514) 343-2285
E-mail: grangerl@psy.umontreal.ca
Web: http://www.fas.umontreal.ca/psy

Department Established:

1942. Chairperson: Luc Granger. Number of Faculty: total–full-time 55, part-time 1; women–full-time 24.

Programs and Degrees Offered:

Listed in the following order: Program area, degree type (T if terminal Master's), number awarded 7/00–6/01. Clinical PhD 12, Experimental, Industrial PhD 2, Neuropsychology PhD 5.

Student Applications/Admissions:

Student Applications

Clinical PhD—Applications 2001–2002, 110. Total applicants accepted 2001–2002, 12. New applicants enrolled 2001–2002, 12. Total enrolled 2001–2002 full-time, 45. Openings 2002–2003, 12. The Median number of years required for completion of a degree are 4. The number of students enrolled full and part-time, who were dismissed or voluntarily withdrew from this program area were 3. *Industrial PhD*—Applications 2001–2002, 30. Total applicants accepted 2001–2002, 5. New applicants enrolled 2001–2002, 5. Total enrolled 2001–2002 full-time, 10. Openings 2002–2003, 5. The Median number of years required for completion of a degree are 4. *Neuropsychology PhD*—Applications 2001–2002, 40. Total applicants accepted 2001–2002, 8. New applicants enrolled 2001–2002, 8. Total enrolled 2001–2002 full-time, 25. Openings 2002–2003, 8. The Median number of years required for completion of a degree are 4. The number of students enrolled full and part-time, who were dismissed or voluntarily withdrew from this program area were 1.

Admissions Requirements:

Scores: Entries appear in this order: required test or GPA, minimum score (if required), median score of students entering in 2001–2002. Master's Programs: psychology GPA no minimum stated, 3.8. Doctoral Programs: last 2 years GPA 3.8/4; psychology GPA 3.8/4.

Other Criteria: (importance of criteria rated low, medium, or high): research experience high, GPA high, letters of recommendation low, interview medium, statement of goals and objectives medium.

Student Characteristics: The following represents characteristics of students in 2001–2002 in all graduate psychology programs in the department: Female–full-time 0, part-time 0; Male–full-time 0, part-time 0; African American/Black–full-time 0, part-time 0; Hispanic/Latino (a)–full-time 0, part-time 0; Asian/Pacific Islander–full-time 0, part-time 0; American Indian/Alaska Native–full-time 0, part-time 0.

Financial Information/Assistance:

Tuition for Full-Time Study: *Master's:* State residents per academic year $2,758; nonstate residents: per academic year $10,800.

Doctoral: State residents: per academic year $2,758; nonstate residents: per academic year $10,800.

Financial Assistance:

First Year Students: Teaching assistantships available for first-year. Average amount paid per academic year: $2,000. Apply by variable. Research assistantships available for first-year. Average amount paid per academic year: $2,000. Apply by variable. Fellowships and scholarships available for first-year. Average amount paid per academic year: $5,000. Apply by December.

Advanced Students: Teaching assistantships available for advanced students. Average amount paid per academic year: $2,000. Apply by variable. Research assistantships available for advanced students. Average amount paid per academic year: $2,000. Apply by variable. Fellowships and scholarships available for advanced students. Average amount paid per academic year: $5,000. Apply by December.

Contact Information: Of all students currently enrolled full-time, 68% benefited from one or more of the listed financial assistance programs. For information on financial assistance, contact: Luc Granger, Director.

Internships/Practica: The PhD programs offer internships in clinical, neuropsychology, and industrial/organizational psychology, in collaboration with general and psychiatric hospitals, correctional facilities, schools, industry, and governmental agencies. For those doctoral students for whom a professional internship is required prior to graduation, 15 applied in 2000–2001. Of those who applied, 2 were placed in internships listed by the Association of Psychology Postdoctoral and Internship Programs (APPIC); 2 were placed in APA accredited internships.

Housing and Day Care: On-campus housing and day care facilities are available.

Employment of Department Graduates:

Master's Degree Graduates: Of those who graduated in the academic year 2000–2001, the following categories and numbers represent the post-graduate activities and employment of master's degree graduates: Enrolled in a post-doctoral residency/fellowship (n/a), employed in independent practice (n/a).

Doctoral Degree Graduates: Of those who graduated in the academic year 2000–2001, the following categories and numbers represent the post-graduate activities and employment of doctoral degree graduates: Enrolled in a psychology doctoral program (n/a), enrolled in another graduate/professional program (n/a).

Additional Information:

Orientation, Objectives, and Emphasis of Department: In several subfields, the department offers a complete graduate curriculum that is oriented either toward scientific research (MSc and PhD programs), at both the human and animal levels, or toward professional training (MPs and PhD, clinical, neuropsychology, and industrial) programs. Because of its large faculty, the department presents most current theoretical perspectives and methodological approaches. The emphasis is placed on the development of the student's capacity for critical judgment, scientific analysis, and conceptual organization. With regard to professional training, the emphasis is placed on the integration of theory and practice, in both diagnosis and intervention.

Special Facilities or Resources: Because of the academic background of its faculty, our department provides the students with the opportunity of contact with both the North American and European scientific and professional traditions. The department has also organized clinical services for the general community; in this service several MPs and PhD students receive part of their professional training. Finally, the department lists on its web site the current research of the faculty.

Application Information:

Send to: Department Chair. Students are admitted in the Fall, application deadline February 1; Winter, application deadline October 15; Summer, application deadline February 1. *Fee:* $30. Note: All dollar amounts specified in this entry are Canadian dollars.

New Brunswick, University of

Department of Psychology
Bag Service #45444
Fredericton, NB E3B 6E4 Canada
Telephone: (506) 453-4707
Fax: (506) 447-3063
E-mail: *nick@unb.ca*
Web: *http://www.unb.ca/psychology*

Department Established:

1966. Chairperson: Richard Nicki. Number of Faculty: total–full-time 15; women–full-time 5; minority–full-time 2.

Programs and Degrees Offered:

Listed in the following order: Program area, degree type (T if terminal Master's), number awarded 7/00–6/01. Clinical PhD 3, experimental/general PhD 3.

Student Applications/Admissions:

Student Applications

Clinical PhD—Applications 2001–2002, 46. Total applicants accepted 2001–2002, 5. New applicants enrolled 2001–2002, 4. Total enrolled 2001–2002 full-time, 30, part-time, 3. Openings 2002–2003, 4. *Experimental/general PhD*—Applications 2001–2002, 12. Total applicants accepted 2001–2002, 3. New applicants enrolled 2001–2002, 3. Total enrolled 2001–2002 full-time, 6, part-time, 4. Openings 2002–2003, 1.

Admissions Requirements:

Scores: Entries appear in this order: required test or GPA, minimum score (if required), median score of students entering in 2001–2002. Doctoral Programs: GRE-V no minimum stated, 600; GRE-Q no minimum stated, 600; GRE-Analytical no minimum stated, 600; GRE-Subject(Psych) no minimum stated, 600; overall undergraduate GPA 3.7, 3.7 ; last 2 years GPA no minimum stated; psychology GPA no minimum stated; psychology GPA no minimum stated.
Other Criteria: (importance of criteria rated low, medium, or high): GRE/MAT scores medium, research experience high, work experience medium, extracurricular activity low, clinically related public service low, GPA high, letters of recommendation high, interview high, statement of goals and objectives high. More emphasis is placed on research experience for students admitted to experimental/general program. Interview is required for clinical program.

Student Characteristics: The following represents characteristics of students in 2001–2002 in all graduate psychology programs in the department: Female–full-time 29, part-time 2; Male–full-time 4, part-time 1; African American/Black–full-time 0, part-time 0; Hispanic/Latino (a)–full-time 0, part-time 0; Asian/Pacific Islander–full-time 1, part-time 0; American Indian/Alaska Native–full-time 0, part-time 0.

Financial Information/Assistance:

Tuition for Full-Time Study: *Doctoral:* State residents: per academic year $1,230; nonstate residents: per academic year $4,030.

Financial Assistance:

First Year Students: Teaching assistantships available for first-year. Average amount paid per academic year: $9,900. Average number of hours worked per week: 8. Apply by January 15. Fellowships and scholarships available for first-year. Average amount paid per academic year: $9,900. Average number of hours worked per week: 8. Apply by January 15.
Advanced Students: Teaching assistantships available for advanced students. Average amount paid per academic year: $10,750. Average number of hours worked per week: 8. Fellowships and scholarships available for advanced students. Average amount paid per academic year: $10,750. Average number of hours worked per week: 8.
Contact Information: Of all students currently enrolled full-time, 74% benefited from one or more of the listed financial assistance programs. For information on financial assistance, contact: School of Graduate Studies, University of New Brunswick.

Internships/Practica: Students in Clinical areas have completed internships in the following types of local agencies: mental health clinic, general hospital, university counseling services, psychiatric hospital, school system, and a mental retardation facility.

Housing and Day Care: On-campus housing and day care facilities are available.

Employment of Department Graduates:

Master's Degree Graduates: Of those who graduated in the academic year 2000–2001, the following categories and numbers represent the post-graduate activities and employment of master's degree graduates: Enrolled in a post-doctoral residency/fellowship (n/a), employed in independent practice (n/a).
Doctoral Degree Graduates: Of those who graduated in the academic year 2000–2001, the following categories and numbers represent the post-graduate activities and employment of doctoral degree graduates: Enrolled in a psychology doctoral program (n/a), enrolled in another graduate/professional program (n/a).

Additional Information:

Orientation, Objectives, and Emphasis of Department: The Department of Psychology offers an integrated MA/PhD degree designed to provide extensive specialized study in either Clinical Psychology or Experimental/General Psychology. The Clinical Program provides graduates both with sufficient skills in assessment, treatment, and outcome evaluation to initiate careers in service settings under appropriate supervision, and with the knowledge and training needed for an academic career. The Experimental/General Program emphasizes individual training and the development of skills to equally prepare the student for a research oriented career in applied and academic settings.

Special Facilities or Resources: The department occupies Keirstead Hall, which is well supplied with research equipment. The facilities include laboratories for research in animal and human learning, perception, developmental psychology, physiological psychology, and neuropsychology; a direct line to the computer center; a child-study center; a sleep laboratory; and space for research and teaching in community, clinical, mental retardation, behavior therapy, biofeedback, and other areas of applied or clinical psychology.

Application Information:

Send to: School of Graduate Studies, University of New Brunswick, P.O. Box 4400, Federicton, NB Canada E3B 5A3. Students are admitted in the Fall, application deadline January 15. *Fee:* $50. Note: All dollar amounts specified in this entry are Canadian dollars.

Ottawa, University of

School of Psychology
Lamoureux Hall, 145 Jean-Jaques Lussier
Ottawa, ON K1N 6N5 Canada
Telephone: (613) 562-5801
Fax: (613) 562-5147
E-mail: *jdpaquet@uottawa.ca*
Web: *http://aix1.uottawa.ca/academic/socsci/psych/*

Department Established:

1941. Director and Associate Dean: Pierre Mercier. Number of Faculty: total–full-time 39, part-time 45; women–full-time 13, part-time 30.

Programs and Degrees Offered:

Listed in the following order: Program area, degree type (T if terminal Master's), number awarded 7/00–6/01. Clinical PhD 16, experimental PhD 3.

APA Accreditation: Clinical PhD: full.

Student Applications/Admissions:

Student Applications

Clinical PhD—Applications 2001–2002, 134. Total applicants accepted 2001–2002, 17. New applicants enrolled 2001–2002, 9. Total enrolled 2001–2002 full-time, 64, part-time, 1. Openings 2002–2003, 12. The Median number of years required for completion of a degree are 7. The number of students enrolled full and part-time, who were dismissed or voluntarily withdrew from this program area were 1. *Experimental PhD*—Applications 2001–2002, 22. Total applicants accepted 2001–2002, 11. New applicants enrolled 2001–2002, 9. Total enrolled 2001–2002 full-time, 40. Openings 2002–2003, 10. The Median number of years required for completion of a degree are 5. The number of students enrolled full and part-time, who were dismissed or voluntarily withdrew from this program area were 1.

Admissions Requirements:

Scores: Entries appear in this order: required test or GPA, minimum score (if required), median score of students entering in 2001–2002. Doctoral Programs: overall undergraduate GPA

8.0, 8.5 ; last 2 years GPA no minimum stated; psychology GPA no minimum stated; psychology GPA no minimum stated.

Other Criteria: (importance of criteria rated low, medium, or high): GRE/MAT scores, research experience high, work experience low, extracurricular activity low, clinically related public service medium, GPA high, letters of recommendation high, interview medium, statement of goals and objectives high, bilingualism (English/Fre) medium.

Student Characteristics: The following represents characteristics of students in 2001–2002 in all graduate psychology programs in the department: Female–full-time 91, part-time 1; Male–full-time 12, part-time 0; African American/Black–full-time 0, part-time 0; Hispanic/Latino (a)–full-time 0, part-time 0; Asian/Pacific Islander–full-time 0, part-time 0; American Indian/Alaska Native–full-time 0, part-time 0; Multi-ethnic–full-time 0, part-time 0; students subject to the Americans with Disabilities Act–full-time 0, part-time 0.

Financial Information/Assistance:

Tuition for Full-Time Study: *Doctoral:* State residents: per academic year $4,773, $192 per credit hour; nonstate residents: per academic year $11,700, $385 per credit hour.

Financial Assistance:

First Year Students: Teaching assistantships available for first-year. Average amount paid per academic year: $7,657. Average number of hours worked per week: 10. Apply by June. Research assistantships available for first-year. Average amount paid per academic year: $7,657. Average number of hours worked per week: 10. Apply by June. Fellowships and scholarships available for first-year. Average amount paid per academic year: $6,500. Apply by March.

Advanced Students: Teaching assistantships available for advanced students. Average amount paid per academic year: $7,657. Average number of hours worked per week: 10. Apply by June. Research assistantships available for advanced students. Average amount paid per academic year: $7,657. Average number of hours worked per week: 10. Apply by June. Traineeships available for advanced students. Average amount paid per academic year: $22,000. Average number of hours worked per week: 30. Apply by October. Fellowships and scholarships available for advanced students. Average amount paid per academic year: $6,500. Apply by October.

Contact Information: Of all students currently enrolled full-time, 90% benefited from one or more of the listed financial assistance programs. For information on financial assistance, contact: Graduate Program Administrator, School of Psychology, University of Ottawa, Lamoureux Hall, 145 Jean-Jacques Lussier, Ottawa, Ontario, K1N 6N5.

Internships/Practica: Internships, required of all clinical program students, take place in accredited external settings in Canada and the USA as well as in local, approved training units. There are two units in the university: the Centre for Psychological Services, and the Career and Counseling Services. There are fourteen external units: Children's Hospital of Eastern Ontario, Ottawa General Hospital, Brockville Psychiatric Hospital, Centre Hospitalier Pierre Janet, Ottawa-Carleton Detention Centre, Rideau Correctional and Treatment Centre, Conseil des ecoles catholiques de langue francaise, Sister of Charity of Ottawa Health Service,

Center for Treatment of Sexual Abuse and Childhood Trauma, Crossroads Children's Centre, Centre Roberts/Smart, Royal Ottawa Hospital, The Rehabilitation Centre, The Children's Aid Society of Ottawa-Carleton. Internships for the Experimental Program within the University of Ottawa take place in the departments of Sociology, Physiotherapy, Epidemiology, Faculties of Education, and Administration. External internships for the Experimental Program are: Royal Ottawa Hospital, Ottawa General Hospital, Children's Hospital of Eastern Ontario, Department of Psychology at Carleton University, Communications Research Center of Canada, Federal Government of Canada (Animal Care), Canadian Armed Forces, ENAP, Ministry of Health, and NORTEL. For those doctoral students for whom a professional internship is required prior to graduation, 11 applied in 2000–2001. Of those who applied, 11 were placed in internships listed by the Association of Psychology Postdoctoral and Internship Programs (APPIC); 11 were placed in APA accredited internships.

Housing and Day Care: On-campus housing and day care facilities are available.

Employment of Department Graduates:

Master's Degree Graduates: Of those who graduated in the academic year 2000–2001, the following categories and numbers represent the post-graduate activities and employment of master's degree graduates: Enrolled in a post-doctoral residency/fellowship (n/a), employed in independent practice (n/a).

Doctoral Degree Graduates: Of those who graduated in the academic year 2000–2001, the following categories and numbers represent the post-graduate activities and employment of doctoral degree graduates: Enrolled in a psychology doctoral program (n/a), enrolled in another graduate/professional program (n/a), enrolled in a post-doctoral residency/fellowship (1), employed in independent practice (4), employed in other positions at a higher education institution (1), employed in business or industry (management) (1), employed in a government agency (professional services) (3), employed in a community mental health/counseling center (2), employed in a hospital/medical center (4), other employment position (3).

Additional Information:

Orientation, Objectives, and Emphasis of Department: The School of Psychology offers both experimental and clinical PhD programs. The objective of the experimental psychology program is to train researchers in experimental psychology with emphasis on one of the following areas: behavioral neurophysiology, psychopharmacology, psychophysiology, human and animal cognition, learning language, sleep and dreams, social, cognitive and emotional development, personality, intergroup relations, motivation, and the social psychology of health and work. Training in behavioral neuroscience may also be provided through the Behavioural Neurosciences Specialization program which is a collaborative program coordinated by the University of Ottawa and Carleton University. The purpose of the clinical psychology program is to provide doctoral training in the area of clinical psychology and prepare students to work with adults and the area of children in both applied and research settings. Professional training includes exposure to cognitive-behavioral, experiential and systemic/interpersonal, and community consultation approaches. Thesis supervisors within the clinical program have special expertise in areas such as social development of children, behavior problems in children, social-skills training, depression, psychotherapy, marital therapy, family psychology, correctional psychology, community psychology, and program evaluation.

Special Facilities or Resources: The physical facilities available at the school of psychology take the form of integrated units serving specific purposes. These include: 1) animal care facilities for housing rats, mice, pigeons, and bees (5,000 sq. ft.); 2) surgery-necropsy facilities for neuroscience research; 3) facilities for animal behavior research; 4) individual units for testing human participants in experiments on psychophysiological, perceptual, cognitive, developmental, or social processes; 5) Community Services Research Unit, for research related to evaluating and improving community agency programs; 6) a sleep lab with 2 bedrooms; 7) technical workshop facilities for building customized equipment, and computer maintenance with 2 electronic technicians, 1 programmer and 1 microcomputer specialist; 8) local area networks (LANs); and 9) more than 50 PCs and mainframe computer facilities for access to e-mail library search software, scientific graphics, computer language, compilers, mathematical software library, and so on. Faculty members and graduate students have access to rich library collections of books and periodicals in English and in French. One library also houses a collection of tests and evaluation instruments in these two languages. Because Ottawa is Canada's capital and has two full-service universities, this geographical area provides access to excellent libraries (e.g., the National Library, the library of the Canada Institute for Scientific and Technical Information), research and clinical training facilities in hospitals, academic settings, and government departments.

Information for Students With Physical Disabilities: The University of Ottawa has a Centre for Special Services which offers services to persons with mobility or visual disability, who are deaf, deafened or hard-of-hearing, with learning disability, physical or mental health problems.

Application Information:

Send to: Graduate Program Administrator, School of Psychology, University of Ottawa, Lamoureux Hall, 145 Jean-Jacques Lussier, Ottawa,, K1N 6N5, Canada. Students are admitted in the Fall, application deadline January 15. *Fee:* $35. Candidates with a GPA of at least 8.5 on a scale of 10 are usually awarded a fee waiver. Note: All dollar amounts specified in this entry are Canadian dollars.

Quebec at Montreal, University of

Department of Psychology
C.P. 8888, Succ. Centre-Ville
Montreal, QC H3C 3P8 Canada
Telephone: (514) 987-4804
Fax: (514) 987-7953
E-mail: *psycho@uqam.ca*
Web: *http://www.psycho.uqam.ca/*

Department Established:

1969. Chairperson: Louis Brunet. Number of Faculty: total–full-time 52; women–full-time 16, part-time 1.

Programs and Degrees Offered:

Listed in the following order: Program area, degree type (T if terminal Master's), number awarded 7/00–6/01. Behavioral PhD

2, Community PhD 4, Development PhD 5, Education PhD 6, I/O PhD 1, Neuropsychology PhD 4, Psychodynamic PhD 6, Social PhD 2.

Student Applications/Admissions:

Student Applications

Behavioral PhD—Applications 2001–2002, 41. Total applicants accepted 2001–2002, 20. New applicants enrolled 2001–2002, 19. Total enrolled 2001–2002 full-time, 19. *Community PhD*—Applications 2001–2002, 10. Total applicants accepted 2001–2002, 3. New applicants enrolled 2001–2002, 3. Total enrolled 2001–2002 full-time, 3. *Development PhD*—Applications 2001–2002, 31. Total applicants accepted 2001–2002, 16. New applicants enrolled 2001–2002, 15. Total enrolled 2001–2002 full-time, 15. *Education PhD*—Applications 2001–2002, 21. Total applicants accepted 2001–2002, 4. New applicants enrolled 2001–2002, 4. Total enrolled 2001–2002 full-time, 4. *I/O PhD*—Applications 2001–2002, 7. Total applicants accepted 2001–2002, 3. New applicants enrolled 2001–2002, 3. Total enrolled 2001–2002 full-time, 3. *Neuropsychology PhD*—Applications 2001–2002, 26. Total applicants accepted 2001–2002, 7. New applicants enrolled 2001–2002, 7. Total enrolled 2001–2002 full-time, 7. *Psychodynamic PhD*—Applications 2001–2002, 38. Total applicants accepted 2001–2002, 21. New applicants enrolled 2001–2002, 21. Total enrolled 2001–2002 full-time, 21. *Social PhD*—Applications 2001–2002, 11. Total applicants accepted 2001–2002, 2. New applicants enrolled 2001–2002, 2. Total enrolled 2001–2002 full-time, 2.

Admissions Requirements:

Scores: Entries appear in this order: required test or GPA, minimum score (if required), median score of students entering in 2001–2002. Doctoral Programs: last 2 years GPA no minimum stated; psychology GPA no minimum stated; psychology GPA no minimum stated.

Other Criteria: (importance of criteria rated low, medium, or high): research experience low, work experience low, extracurricular activity low, clinically related public service low, letters of recommendation high, statement of goals and objectives high, academic records, high.

Student Characteristics: The following represents characteristics of students in 2001–2002 in all graduate psychology programs in the department: Female–full-time 64, part-time 0; Male–full-time 11, part-time 0; African American/Black–full-time 0, part-time 0; Hispanic/Latino (a)–full-time 2, part-time 0; Asian/Pacific Islander–full-time 0, part-time 0; American Indian/Alaska Native–full-time 0, part-time 0.

Financial Information/Assistance:

Tuition for Full-Time Study: No information provided.

Financial Assistance:

First Year Students: No information provided.
Advanced Students: No information provided.
Contact Information: Of all students currently enrolled full-time, 20% benefited from one or more of the listed financial assistance programs. For information on financial assistance, contact: Service de l'aide financière, Section prêts et bourses: (514) 987-3135 ou 4242 Section bourses d'excellence: (514) 987-7871, Accueil des étudiants étrangers: (514) 987-3580.

Internships/Practica: Internship settings include about 12 Montreal general and psychiatric hospitals, 7 community settings, 6 Montreal school boards, 4 university study centers as well as a number of private centers or clinics. Internships typically cover about 1600–2000 hours of supervised clinical work, including assessment procedures, multidisciplinary seminars, and various types of therapy with various orientations. Some settings also provide training in clinical observation and research.

Housing and Day Care: On-campus housing and day care facilities are available.

Employment of Department Graduates:

Master's Degree Graduates: Of those who graduated in the academic year 2000–2001, the following categories and numbers represent the post-graduate activities and employment of master's degree graduates: Enrolled in a post-doctoral residency/fellowship (n/a), employed in independent practice (n/a).

Doctoral Degree Graduates: Of those who graduated in the academic year 2000–2001, the following categories and numbers represent the post-graduate activities and employment of doctoral degree graduates: Enrolled in a psychology doctoral program (n/a), enrolled in another graduate/professional program (n/a).

Additional Information:

Special Facilities or Resources: Our department offers the following technical support to staff and graduate students: a consultant statistician, a consultant computer programmer, and a resident visual artist who designs and creates professional quality visual stimuli for research. He also prepares graphics for articles, posters, and the thesis. All labs are equipped with personal computers. Students have access to these computers and the mainframe university computer. The university offers support services for handicapped students. Please note that the teaching language in our university is French, though the majority of the literature in psychology is English. Some professors may require the students to write papers in French. Students must obtain permission to write the thesis in English. Courses in French conversation and composition are offered by the university.

Application Information:

Send to: Registrariat Service de l'admission, Université du Québec à Montréal, Case postale 8888, succursale Centre-ville, Montréal (Québec), Canada, H3C 3P8. Students are admitted in the Fall, application deadline Feb, 15. *Fee:* $55. Note: All dollar amounts specified in this entry are Canadian dollars.

Queen's University
Department of Psychology
Kingston, ON K7L 3N6 Canada
Telephone: (613) 533-6004
Fax: (613) 533-2499
E-mail: *leachj@psyc.queensu.ca*
Web: *http://pavlov.psyc.queensu.ca*

Department Established:
1949. Head: A.W. MacLean. Number of Faculty: total–full-time 32; women–full-time 11; minority–full-time 3.

Programs and Degrees Offered:
Listed in the following order: Program area, degree type (T if terminal Master's), number awarded 7/00–6/01. Brain, Behavior, and Cognitive PhD 1, Clinical PhD 3, Developmental PhD, Social-Personality PhD 3.

APA Accreditation: Clinical PhD: full.

Student Applications/Admissions:
Student Applications

Brain, Behavior, and Cognitive PhD—Applications 2001–2002, 18. Total applicants accepted 2001–2002, 10. New applicants enrolled 2001–2002, 4. Total enrolled 2001–2002 full-time, 24. Openings 2002–2003, 8. The Median number of years required for completion of a degree are 4. The number of students enrolled full and part-time, who were dismissed or voluntarily withdrew from this program area were 0. *Clinical PhD*—Applications 2001–2002, 87. Total applicants accepted 2001–2002, 10. New applicants enrolled 2001–2002, 6. Total enrolled 2001–2002 full-time, 41, part-time, 3. Openings 2002–2003, 6. The Median number of years required for completion of a degree are 6. The number of students enrolled full and part-time, who were dismissed or voluntarily withdrew from this program area were 0. *Developmental PhD*—Applications 2001–2002, 0. Total enrolled 2001–2002 full-time, 11. Openings 2002–2003, 6. The number of students enrolled full and part-time, who were dismissed or voluntarily withdrew from this program area were 0. *Social-Personality PhD*—Applications 2001–2002, 45. Total applicants accepted 2001–2002, 6. Total enrolled 2001–2002 full-time, 11. Openings 2002–2003, 5. The Median number of years required for completion of a degree are 6. The number of students enrolled full and part-time, who were dismissed or voluntarily withdrew from this program area were 0.

Admissions Requirements:

Scores: Entries appear in this order: required test or GPA, minimum score (if required), median score of students entering in 2001–2002. Master's Programs: GRE-V+Q+Analytical no minimum stated, 68; GRE-Subject(Psych) no minimum stated, 80; last 2 years GPA no minimum stated. For last 2 years GPA, upper second class honours degree is the minimum. Median of students entering in 2001 was first class. Doctoral Programs: GRE-V+Q+Analytical no minimum stated, 75; GRE-Subject(Psych) no minimum stated, 90; last 2 years GPA no minimum stated; psychology GPA no minimum stated; psychology GPA no minimum stated.

Other Criteria: (importance of criteria rated low, medium, or high): GRE/MAT scores high, research experience medium, work experience low, extracurricular activity low, clinically related public service low, GPA high, letters of recommendation high, statement of goals and objectives high, Supervisor availability high.

Student Characteristics: The following represents characteristics of students in 2001–2002 in all graduate psychology programs in the department: Female–full-time 63, part-time 3; Male–full-time 24, part-time 0; African American/Black–full-time 0, part-time 0; Hispanic/Latino (a)–full-time 0, part-time 0; Asian/Pacific Islander–full-time 0, part-time 0; American Indian/Alaska Native–full-time 0, part-time 0.

Financial Information/Assistance:
Tuition for Full-Time Study: *Master's:* State residents per academic year $5,836; nonstate residents: per academic year $11,276. *Doctoral:* State residents: per academic year $5,836; nonstate residents: per academic year $11,276.

Financial Assistance:
First Year Students: Teaching assistantships available for first-year. Average amount paid per academic year: $4,784. Average number of hours worked per week: 8. Apply by N/A. Fellowships and scholarships available for first-year. Average amount paid per academic year: $14,000. Average number of hours worked per week: 0. Apply by Oct.

Advanced Students: Teaching assistantships available for advanced students. Average amount paid per academic year: $6,420. Average number of hours worked per week: 10. Apply by N/A. Fellowships and scholarships available for advanced students. Average amount paid per academic year: $14,000. Average number of hours worked per week: 0. Apply by Oct.

Contact Information: Of all students currently enrolled full-time, 90% benefited from one or more of the listed financial assistance programs. For information on financial assistance, contact: Coordinator of Graduate Studies.

Internships/Practica: Clinical Program students must complete a pre-doctoral internship in an approved setting under the primary supervision of a registered psychologist. Students are encouraged to seek placement in a CPA/APA approved site. For those doctoral students for whom a professional internship is required prior to graduation, 8 applied in 2000–2001. Of those who applied, 5 were placed in internships listed by the Association of Psychology Postdoctoral and Internship Programs (APPIC); 4 were placed in APA accredited internships.

Housing and Day Care: No on-campus housing and day care facilities are available.

Employment of Department Graduates:
Master's Degree Graduates: Of those who graduated in the academic year 2000–2001, the following categories and numbers represent the post-graduate activities and employment of master's degree graduates: Enrolled in a psychology doctoral program (12), enrolled in another graduate/professional program (0), enrolled in a post-doctoral residency/fellowship (n/a), employed in independent practice (n/a), employed in an academic position at a university (0), employed in an academic position at a 2-year/4-year college (0), employed in other positions at a higher education institution (0), employed in a professional position in a school system (0), employed in business or industry (research/consulting) (0), employed in business or industry (management) (0), employed in a government agency (research) (0), employed in a government agency (professional services) (0), employed in a community mental health/counseling center (0), employed in a hospital/medical center (0), still seeking employment (0), other employment position (1).

Doctoral Degree Graduates: Of those who graduated in the academic year 2000–2001, the following categories and numbers represent the post-graduate activities and employment of doctoral degree graduates: Enrolled in a psychology doctoral program (n/a), enrolled in another graduate/professional program (n/a), enrolled in a post-doctoral residency/fellowship (0), employed in independent practice (0), employed in an academic position at a university

(1), employed in an academic position at a 2-year/4-year college (0), employed in other positions at a higher education institution (0), employed in a professional position in a school system (0), employed in business or industry (research/consulting) (0), employed in business or industry (management) (0), employed in a government agency (research) (0), employed in a government agency (professional services) (3), employed in a community mental health/counseling center (0), employed in a hospital/medical center (3), still seeking employment (0), other employment position (0).

Additional Information:

Orientation, Objectives, and Emphasis of Department: All programs stress empirical research. The Brain, Behavior, and Cognitive Science program, the Developmental program, and the Social-Personality program emphasize research skills and scholarship, preparing students for either academic positions or for research positions in government, industry, and the like. The Clinical Program is based on a scientist-practitioner model of training that emphasizes the integration of research and clinical skills in the understanding, assessment, treatment, and prevention of psychological problems.

Special Facilities or Resources: Extensive computer and laboratory facilities are available to graduate students for research and clinical experience. Financial assistance is available in the form of federal, provincial, and university fellowships, scholarships and bursaries, and commonwealth fellowships. For 2001–02, incoming graduate students received a minimum of $15,000.

Information for Students With Physical Disabilities: The university provides a range of services to students with disabilities, including special exam and registration arrangements, notetakers, assistance with adaptive technology, learning support, counseling, referral services, library aids for print material, and liaison with faculty and staff.

Application Information:

Send to: School of Graduate Studies. Students are admitted in the Fall, application deadline January 15. *Fee:* $70. Note: All dollar amounts specified in this entry are Canadian dollars.

Regina, University of
Psychology
Department of Psychology, University of Regina
Regina, SK S4S 0A2 Canada
Telephone: (306) 585-4157
Fax: (306) 585-4827
E-mail: *william.smythe@uregina.ca*
Web: *http://www.uregina.ca*

Department Established:

1965. Department Head: William Smythe. Number of Faculty: total–full-time 15; women–full-time 5; minority–full-time 1.

Programs and Degrees Offered:

Listed in the following order: Program area, degree type (T if terminal Master's), number awarded 7/00–6/01. Clinical MA (T) 3, cognitive & behavioral science MA (T), general MA (T).

Student Applications/Admissions:
Student Applications

Clinical MA—Applications 2001–2002, 29. Total applicants accepted 2001–2002, 8. New applicants enrolled 2001–2002, 8. Total enrolled 2001–2002 full-time, 20, part-time, 8. Openings 2002–2003, 6. The number of students enrolled full and part-time, who were dismissed or voluntarily withdrew from this program area were 3. *Cognitive & behavioral science MA*—Applications 2001–2002, 3. Total enrolled 2001–2002 part-time, 1. Openings 2002–2003, 1. The number of students enrolled full and part-time, who were dismissed or voluntarily withdrew from this program area were 0. *General MA*—Applications 2001–2002, 1. Total applicants accepted 2001–2002, 1. New applicants enrolled 2001–2002, 1. Total enrolled 2001–2002 full-time, 1, part-time, 2. Openings 2002–2003, 1. The number of students enrolled full and part-time, who were dismissed or voluntarily withdrew from this program area were 0.

Admissions Requirements:

Scores: Entries appear in this order: required test or GPA, minimum score (if required), median score of students entering in 2001–2002. Master's Programs: GRE-V no minimum stated; GRE-Q no minimum stated; GRE-V+Q no minimum stated; GRE-Analytical no minimum stated; GRE-V+Q+Analytical no minimum stated; GRE-Subject(Psych) no minimum stated; overall undergraduate GPA no minimum stated; psychology GPA no minimum stated. Doctoral Programs: GRE-V no minimum stated; GRE-Q no minimum stated; GRE-V+Q no minimum stated; GRE-Analytical no minimum stated; GRE-V+Q+Analytical no minimum stated; GRE-Subject(Psych) no minimum stated; overall undergraduate GPA no minimum stated; last 2 years GPA no minimum stated; psychology GPA no minimum stated; psychology GPA no minimum stated.
Other Criteria: (importance of criteria rated low, medium, or high): GRE/MAT scores high, research experience high, work experience low, clinically related public service medium, GPA low, letters of recommendation high, statement of goals and objectives high.

Student Characteristics: The following represents characteristics of students in 2001–2002 in all graduate psychology programs in the department: Female–full-time 17, part-time 9; Male–full-time 2, part-time 1; African American/Black–full-time 1, part-time 0; Hispanic/Latino (a)–full-time 0, part-time 0; Asian/Pacific Islander–full-time 0, part-time 0; American Indian/Alaska Native–full-time 0, part-time 0; Multi-ethnic–full-time 0.

Financial Information/Assistance:

Tuition for Full-Time Study: *Master's:* State residents $110 per credit hour; nonstate residents: $220 per credit hour. *Doctoral:* State residents: $110 per credit hour; nonstate residents: $220 per credit hour.

Financial Assistance:

First Year Students: No information provided.
Advanced Students: No information provided.
Contact Information: No information provided.

Internships/Practica: A wide array of community resources is available and well utilized in providing practicum and internship training. The department cannot guarantee placement in these facilities, but our record of supplying these has been perfect in the past. For those doctoral students for whom a professional internship is required prior to graduation, 1 applied in 2000–2001. Of those who applied, 1 were placed in APA accredited internships.

Housing and Day Care: On-campus housing and day care facilities are available.

Employment of Department Graduates:
Master's Degree Graduates: Of those who graduated in the academic year 2000–2001, the following categories and numbers represent the post-graduate activities and employment of master's degree graduates: Enrolled in a psychology doctoral program (1), enrolled in a post-doctoral residency/fellowship (n/a), employed in independent practice (n/a), employed in a professional position in a school system (1).
Doctoral Degree Graduates: Of those who graduated in the academic year 2000–2001, the following categories and numbers represent the post-graduate activities and employment of doctoral degree graduates: Enrolled in a psychology doctoral program (n/a), enrolled in another graduate/professional program (n/a), employed in independent practice (1).

Additional Information:
Orientation, Objectives, and Emphasis of Department: Teaching and research are oriented toward clinical, social, and applied approaches. The majority of graduate students are in clinical psychology. Faculty orientation is eclectic. Cognitive behavioral and humanistic approaches are represented. Neuropsychology is also well represented.

Special Facilities or Resources: The department has clinical/counseling rooms for research purposes, a small testing library, permanent space for faculty research, and observation rooms and computer labs.

Application Information:
Send to: Dean, Faculty of Graduate Studies and Research University of Regina, Regina, SK S4S 0A2. Students are admitted in the Fall, application deadline February 15. *Fee:* $60. All dollar amounts specified in this entry are Canadian dollars.

Saskatchewan, University of
Department of Psychology
Arts and Science
9 Campus Drive
Saskatoon, SK S7N 5A5 Canada
Telephone: (306) 966-6657
Fax: (306) 966-6630
E-mail: *psychology@usask.ca*
Web: *http://www.usask.ca/psychology/*

Department Established:
1946. Head: Linda McMullen. Number of Faculty: total–full-time 27, part-time 21; women–full-time 11, part-time 8.

Programs and Degrees Offered:
Listed in the following order: Program area, degree type (T if terminal Master's), number awarded 7/00–6/01. Applied social MA (T) 3, basic behaviour science PhD 1, clinical PhD 4.

APA Accreditation: Clinical PhD: full.

Student Applications/Admissions:
Student Applications
Applied social MA—Applications 2001–2002, 27. Total applicants accepted 2001–2002, 4. New applicants enrolled 2001–2002, 3. Total enrolled 2001–2002 full-time, 7, part-time, 7. Openings 2002–2003, 3. The Median number of years required for completion of a degree are 3. *Basic behaviour science PhD*—Applications 2001–2002, 11. Total applicants accepted 2001–2002, 6. New applicants enrolled 2001–2002, 6. Total enrolled 2001–2002 full-time, 11, part-time, 3. Openings 2002–2003, 4. The Median number of years required for completion of a degree are 2. The number of students enrolled full and part-time, who were dismissed or voluntarily withdrew from this program area were 1. *Clinical PhD*—Applications 2001–2002, 52. Total applicants accepted 2001–2002, 5. New applicants enrolled 2001–2002, 5. Total enrolled 2001–2002 full-time, 20, part-time, 15. Openings 2002–2003, 5. The Median number of years required for completion of a degree are 5.

Admissions Requirements:
Scores: Entries appear in this order: required test or GPA, minimum score (if required), median score of students entering in 2001–2002. Master's Programs: GRE-V no minimum stated, 600; GRE-Q no minimum stated, 645; GRE-Analytical no minimum stated; GRE-Subject(Psych) no minimum stated, 686; last 2 years GPA no minimum stated. Doctoral Programs: GRE-V no minimum stated, 529; GRE-Q no minimum stated, 610; GRE-Analytical no minimum stated; GRE-Subject(Psych) no minimum stated, 641; last 2 years GPA no minimum stated; psychology GPA no minimum stated; psychology GPA no minimum stated.
Other Criteria: (importance of criteria rated low, medium, or high): GRE/MAT scores medium, research experience high, work experience medium, extracurricular activity low, clinically related public service low, GPA high, letters of recommendation high, interview high, statement of goals and objectives high, research interest medium.

Student Characteristics: The following represents characteristics of students in 2001–2002 in all graduate psychology programs in the department: Female–full-time 29, part-time 18; Male–full-time 18, part-time 4; African American/Black–full-time 1, part-time 0; Hispanic/Latino (a)–full-time 0, part-time 0; Asian/Pacific Islander–full-time 2, part-time 1; American Indian/Alaska Native–full-time 1, part-time 0; Multi-ethnic–full-time 1.

Financial Information/Assistance:
Tuition for Full-Time Study: *Master's:* State residents per academic year $4,014; nonstate residents: per academic year $4,014. *Doctoral:* State residents: per academic year $4,014; nonstate residents: per academic year $4,014.

Financial Assistance:
First Year Students: Fellowships and scholarships available for first-year. Average amount paid per academic year: $16,000. Average number of hours worked per week: 8.

Advanced Students: Fellowships and scholarships available for advanced students. Average amount paid per academic year: $16,000. Average number of hours worked per week: 8.

Contact Information: Of all students currently enrolled full-time, 100% benefited from one or more of the listed financial assistance programs. For information on financial assistance, contact: Department Head at the time of application for admission.

Internships/Practica: Full-time internships and practicum training concurrent with coursework are required at the MA and PhD levels in both clinical and applied social programs. In the clinical program, four-month MA internship placements are available at a number of hospital and outpatient clinics throughout the province. At the PhD level, 12-month internships have been arranged in larger clinical settings with diversified client populations in Canada and the United States. The applied social program requires four-month applied research internships at both the MA and PhD levels. Practicum and internship placements are arranged in a wide variety of government, institutional, and business settings. For those doctoral students for whom a professional internship is required prior to graduation, 4 applied in 2000–2001. Of those who applied, 4 were placed in internships listed by the Association of Psychology Postdoctoral and Internship Programs (APPIC).

Housing and Day Care: On-campus housing and day care facilities are available.

Employment of Department Graduates:

Master's Degree Graduates: Of those who graduated in the academic year 2000–2001, the following categories and numbers represent the post-graduate activities and employment of master's degree graduates: Enrolled in a post-doctoral residency/fellowship (n/a), employed in independent practice (n/a), employed in other positions at a higher education institution (2), employed in business or industry (research/consulting) (2), other employment position (1).

Doctoral Degree Graduates: Of those who graduated in the academic year 2000–2001, the following categories and numbers represent the post-graduate activities and employment of doctoral degree graduates: Enrolled in a psychology doctoral program (n/a), enrolled in another graduate/professional program (n/a), employed in a hospital/medical center (3).

Additional Information:

Orientation, Objectives, and Emphasis of Department: All graduate programs are small and highly selective. The clinical program focuses on PhD training, based on a scientist-practitioner model with an eclectic theoretical perspective. The goal is to train people who will be able to function in a wide variety of community, agency, academic, and research settings. The applied social program attempts to train people at the MA and PhD level for researcher consultant positions in applied (MA) or academic (PhD) settings. Areas of concentration include program development and evaluation, group processes, and organizational development. The basic behavioural programs are individually structured, admitting a few students to work with active research supervisors, most frequently in physiological, neuropsychology, or cognitive psychology.

Special Facilities or Resources: The Department has a Psychological Services Centre, an animal lab, a cognitive science lab with access to fMRI facilities. There are also numerous microcomputers, excellent mainframe computer facilities, and a good research library. The Women's Studies Research Unit promotes scholarly research by, for, and about women, providing a source of support for all women studying, teaching, researching, and working on campus.

Information for Students With Physical Disabilities: University Student Services, (306) 966-5673, provides services to help disabled students meet their academic needs.

Application Information:
Send to: Department Head, University of Saskatchewan, Department of Psychology, 9 Campus Drive, Saskatoon, Canada SKS7N 5A5. Students are admitted in the Fall, application deadline January 15. *Fee:* $50. After initial screening of their application, applicants who will be short listed for further consideration will be required to pay an application fee of $50 Canadian. Applicants will be informed when this payment is required. Note: All dollar amounts specified in this entry are Canadian dollars.

Sherbrooke, University of

Department of Psychology
2500 Boulevard de l'Universite
Sherbrooke, QC J1K 2R1 Canada
Telephone: (819) 821-7222
Fax: (819) 821-7925
E-mail: *cdubois@courrier.usherb.ca*
Web: *http://www.usherb.ca*

Department Established:
1967. Chairperson: Claude Charbonneau. Number of Faculty: total–full-time 14; women–full-time 9.

Programs and Degrees Offered:
Listed in the following order: Program area, degree type (T if terminal Master's), number awarded 7/00–6/01. Human Relations MA (T) 45.

Student Applications/Admissions:
Student Applications

Human Relations MA—Applications 2001–2002, 210. Total applicants accepted 2001–2002, 30. New applicants enrolled 2001–2002, 30. Total enrolled 2001–2002 full-time, 70. Openings 2002–2003, 40. The Median number of years required for completion of a degree are 2. The number of students enrolled full and part-time, who were dismissed or voluntarily withdrew from this program area were 0.

Admissions Requirements:
Scores: Entries appear in this order: required test or GPA, minimum score (if required), median score of students entering in 2001–2002. Master's Programs: overall undergraduate GPA 3.0, 3.7. Doctoral Programs: last 2 years GPA no minimum stated; psychology GPA no minimum stated; psychology GPA no minimum stated.
Other Criteria: (importance of criteria rated low, medium, or high): work experience medium, extracurricular activity

medium, GPA high, letters of recommendation low, interview high, statement of goals and objectives high.

Student Characteristics: The following represents characteristics of students in 2001–2002 in all graduate psychology programs in the department: Female–full-time 26, part-time 0; Male–full-time 4, part-time 0; African American/Black–full-time 0, part-time 0; Hispanic/Latino (a)–full-time 0, part-time 0; Asian/Pacific Islander–full-time 0, part-time 0; American Indian/Alaska Native–full-time 0, part-time 0.

Financial Information/Assistance:
Tuition for Full-Time Study: No information provided.

Financial Assistance:
First Year Students: No information provided.
Advanced Students: No information provided.
Contact Information: Of all students currently enrolled full-time, 0% benefited from one or more of the listed financial assistance programs. For information on financial assistance, contact: www.usherb.ca.

Internships/Practica: All internships or practica are limited to students enrolled in our graduate program.

Housing and Day Care: No on-campus housing and day care facilities are available.

Employment of Department Graduates:
Master's Degree Graduates: Of those who graduated in the academic year 2000–2001, the following categories and numbers represent the post-graduate activities and employment of master's degree graduates: Enrolled in a post-doctoral residency/fellowship (n/a), employed in independent practice (n/a).
Doctoral Degree Graduates: Of those who graduated in the academic year 2000–2001, the following categories and numbers represent the post-graduate activities and employment of doctoral degree graduates: Enrolled in a psychology doctoral program (n/a), enrolled in another graduate/professional program (n/a).

Additional Information:
Orientation, Objectives, and Emphasis of Department: Our department presents itself as a professional school of psychology. It offers an undergraduate program in general psychology and a graduate program (master's degree) in human relations' psychology. The program offers three distinct sectors in which students may choose to orient their training: intercultural relationships, health care systems, and individual counseling. The determinants of the program are: the desire to foster democratic interactions; the development of a systems approach; the belief in human potential and the need to involve an organization's human resources in change processes that affect them; the importance of recognizing and taking into account people's subjectivity; and a focus on cooperative relationships. Students are introduced to the human relations' approach and model as well as to the basic knowledge to be acquired in their chosen sector. They participate in workshops aimed at developing specific skills needed in interventions such as team building, mediation, or data feedback. They test their professional abilities in practicum situations and finally in a 5 day internship. The curriculum requires the production of an essay which contributes to the advancement of professional intervention in the area of human relations.

Special Facilities or Resources: Our department is a small one with 14 faculty teachers. The professorial resources are directly available to students and the training and supervision are highly personalized. The department offers a community service of individual counseling through its intervention center, which is also the ground for research. We are affiliated with the local center for health and social services as well as the geriatric institution where colleages from the department cooperate in research programs and where one of our teachers has a well structured laboratory for research on sleeping patterns.

Information for Students With Physical Disabilities: Our university is well equipped for students with physical disabilities (access ramps, elevators) and offers individualized aid to any student in need of being accompanied or tutored.

Application Information:
Send to: Bureau du registraire - Universite de Sherbrooke - Sherbrooke (Quebec) J1K 2R1. Students are admitted in the Fall, application deadline February 1. *Fee:* $30. Note: All dollar amounts specified in this entry are Canadian dollars.

Simon Fraser University
Department of Psychology
8888 University Drive
Burnaby, BC V5A 1S6 Canada
Telephone: (604) 291-3354
Fax: (604) 291-3427
E-mail: *kumpula@sfu.ca*
Web: *http://www.sfu.ca/psychology*

Department Established:
1965. Acting Chair: Kim Bartholomew. Number of Faculty: total–full-time 38, part-time 1; women–full-time 9, part-time 1.

Programs and Degrees Offered:
Listed in the following order: Program area, degree type (T if terminal Master's), number awarded 7/00–6/01. Cognitive and biological PhD, developmental PhD 3, law and forensic PhD 2, social PhD 3, theory and methods PhD.

APA Accreditation: Clinical PhD: full.

Student Applications/Admissions:
Student Applications
Cognitive and biological PhD—Total applicants accepted 2001–2002, 2. New applicants enrolled 2001–2002, 2. Total enrolled 2001–2002 full-time, 15. Openings 2002–2003, 4. *Developmental PhD*—Total applicants accepted 2001–2002, 2. New applicants enrolled 2001–2002, 2. Total enrolled 2001–2002 full-time, 18, part-time, n/a. Openings 2002–2003, 4. The Median number of years required for completion of a degree are 2. *Law and forensic PhD*—Total applicants accepted 2001–2002, 2. New applicants enrolled 2001–2002, 3. Total enrolled 2001–2002 full-time, 29. Openings 2002–2003, 4. The Median number of years required for completion of a degree are 2. *Social PhD*—Total applicants accepted 2001–2002, 3. New applicants enrolled 2001–2002, 3. Total enrolled 2001–2002

full-time, 16. Openings 2002–2003, 4. The Median number of years required for completion of a degree are 2. *Theory and methods PhD*—Applications 2001–2002, 2. Total applicants accepted 2001–2002, 1. New applicants enrolled 2001–2002, 1. Total enrolled 2001–2002 full-time, 3. Openings 2002–2003, 4.

Admissions Requirements:

Scores: Entries appear in this order: required test or GPA, minimum score (if required), median score of students entering in 2001–2002. Master's Programs: GRE-V no minimum stated; GRE-Q no minimum stated; GRE-Analytical no minimum stated; GRE-Subject(Psych) no minimum stated; overall undergraduate GPA no minimum stated; psychology GPA no minimum stated. GRE-subject (Psychology) required for clinical applicants only. Applicants with cumulative GPA less than 3.3 unlikely to be accepted. Doctoral Programs: GRE-V no minimum stated; GRE-Q no minimum stated; GRE-Analytical no minimum stated; GRE-Subject(Psych) no minimum stated; overall undergraduate GPA no minimum stated; last 2 years GPA no minimum stated; psychology GPA no minimum stated; psychology GPA no minimum stated. GRE-subject (Psychology) required for clinical applicants only. Applicants with cumulative GPA less than 3.3 unlikely to be accepted.

Other Criteria: (importance of criteria rated low, medium, or high): GRE/MAT scores medium, research experience high, work experience low, extracurricular activity low, clinically related public service low, GPA high, letters of recommendation high, interview high, statement of goals and objectives high.

Student Characteristics: The following represents characteristics of students in 2001–2002 in all graduate psychology programs in the department: Female–full-time 62, part-time 0; Male–full-time 28, part-time 0; African American/Black–full-time 0, part-time 0; Hispanic/Latino (a)–full-time 0, part-time 0; Asian/Pacific Islander–full-time 0, part-time 0; American Indian/Alaska Native–full-time 0, part-time 0.

Financial Information/Assistance:

Tuition for Full-Time Study: *Master's:* State residents per academic year $2,631; nonstate residents: per academic year $2,631. *Doctoral:* State residents: per academic year $2,631; nonstate residents: per academic year $2,631.

Financial Assistance:

First Year Students: Teaching assistantships available for first-year. Research assistantships available for first-year. Traineeships available for first-year. Fellowships and scholarships available for first-year.

Advanced Students: Teaching assistantships available for advanced students. Research assistantships available for advanced students. Traineeships available for advanced students. Fellowships and scholarships available for advanced students.

Contact Information: Of all students currently enrolled full-time, 100% benefited from one or more of the listed financial assistance programs. For information on financial assistance, contact: Lynn Kumpula, Graduate Program Assistant, Psychology

Department, Simon Fraser University, 8888 University Drive, Burnaby, BC V5A 1S6. 604-291-4367.

Internships/Practica: Under the direction of a faculty internship coordinator, students in the clinical program are placed in various agencies within the community or throughout North America. Placements are approved by the coordinator based on the following criteria: (a) Students receive direct personal supervision of their work amounting to not less than two hours weekly in a full-time practicum/internship, and (b) Agency supervision must be provided by a registered psychologist.

Housing and Day Care: On-campus housing and day care facilities are available.

Employment of Department Graduates:

Master's Degree Graduates: Of those who graduated in the academic year 2000–2001, the following categories and numbers represent the post-graduate activities and employment of master's degree graduates: Enrolled in a post-doctoral residency/fellowship (n/a), employed in independent practice (n/a).

Doctoral Degree Graduates: Of those who graduated in the academic year 2000–2001, the following categories and numbers represent the post-graduate activities and employment of doctoral degree graduates: Enrolled in a psychology doctoral program (n/a), enrolled in another graduate/professional program (n/a).

Additional Information:

Orientation, Objectives, and Emphasis of Department: The department has a mainstream, empirical orientation. The objectives of our undergraduate program are to produce majors who have a broad exposure to the various fields of psychology, and to produce honors students who, in addition, have received higher-level training in methodology and have completed an honors research project. The department offers graduate work leading to master's and doctoral degrees in clinical or experimental psychology. We subscribe to the scientist-practitioner model of clinical training. Within the clinical and experimental programs, specialization is available in cognitive and biological psychology, developmental psychology, law and forensic psychology, social psychology, and theory and methods. The clinical program also offers certificate specializations in child clinical psychology, clinical forensic psychology, and clinical neuropsychology. In conjunction with the University of British Columbia, a joint LLB/PhD program in Law and Forensic Psychology is also offered.

Special Facilities or Resources: Video conferencing facilities, dedicated computer laboratories, including a microcomputer lab (20 Pentium PC's and laser printers) and a dedicated graduate student workroom containing both Pentium and Mac computers and laser printers. A wide variety of software is available, including word processing software, statistics and math, spreadsheets, databases, graphics programs, e-mail, WWW, and other applications. A Perception/Sensation lab contains computerized perceptual testing equipment, and a psychophysiology lab is equipped with 3 digital polygraphs and other specialized equipment. Neuroscience labs at the Animal Care Facility are well-equipped for physiological and behavioural investigations of the nervous system, as well as advanced microscopy and image analysis. Supervised contact with clinical clients is offered through the large and well-appointed Clinical Psychology Centre, and the department maintains a comprehensive Test Library of assessment instruments.

The Mental Health, Law and Policy Institute contains extensive research and work space, and mock jury rooms and facilities.

Information for Students With Physical Disabilities: The Center For Students With Disabilities was established to improve the general accessibility at SFU by developing and updating University programs. The Center is also responsible for providing direct services to students with disabilities. These services include assistance with note taking; tutor support; access to adaptive technology; support for exam modifications; general advocacy; coordination of American Sign Language interpreters. Course materials in alternative formats are also available for students through Inter-Library Loans in the Bennett Library. The Center For Students With Disabilities also works with other university departments to ensure appropriate services are in place. Information of accessible on-campus housing and accessible parking is available.

Application Information:

Send to: Lynn Kumpula, Graduate Program Assistant, Psychology Department, Simon Fraser University, 8888 University Drive, Burnaby, BC V5A 1S6. Students are admitted in the Fall, application deadline January 1. *Fee:* $55. Note: All dollar amounts specified in this entry are Canadian dollars.

St. Mary's University
Department of Psychology
903 Robie Street
Halifax, NS B3H 3C3 Canada
Telephone: (902) 420-5846
Fax: (902) 496-8287
E-mail: *vic.catano@stmarys.ca*
Web: *http://www.stmarys.ca/academic/science/psych/*

Department Established:
1966. Chairperson: Victor Catano. Number of Faculty: total–full-time 14, part-time 10; women–full-time 4, part-time 5; minority–full-time 1.

Programs and Degrees Offered:
Listed in the following order: Program area, degree type (T if terminal Master's), number awarded 7/00–6/01. Applied MA (T) 6.

Student Applications/Admissions:
Student Applications
Applied MA—Applications 2001–2002, 32. Total applicants accepted 2001–2002, 8. New applicants enrolled 2001–2002, 8. Total enrolled 2001–2002 full-time, 12, part-time, 4. Openings 2002–2003, 8. The Median number of years required for completion of a degree are 2.

Admissions Requirements:
Scores: Entries appear in this order: required test or GPA, minimum score (if required), median score of students entering in 2001–2002. Master's Programs: GRE-V+Q+Analytical 500, 610; GRE-Subject(Psych) 500, 640; overall undergraduate GPA 3.00, 3.33. Doctoral Programs: last 2 years GPA no minimum stated; psychology GPA no minimum stated; psychology GPA no minimum stated.

Other Criteria: (importance of criteria rated low, medium, or high): GRE/MAT scores medium, research experience high, work experience low, extracurricular activity low, GPA high, letters of recommendation high, statement of goals and objectives high.

Student Characteristics: The following represents characteristics of students in 2001–2002 in all graduate psychology programs in the department: Female–full-time 5, part-time 0; Male–full-time 3, part-time 0; African American/Black–full-time 0, part-time 0; Hispanic/Latino (a)–full-time 0, part-time 0; Asian/Pacific Islander–full-time 0, part-time 0; American Indian/Alaska Native–full-time 0, part-time 0.

Financial Information/Assistance:
Tuition for Full-Time Study: *Master's:* State residents per academic year $2,772; nonstate residents: per academic year $4,035.

Financial Assistance:
First Year Students: Teaching assistantships available for first-year. Average amount paid per academic year: $4,500. Average number of hours worked per week: 15. Apply by February 1. Research assistantships available for first-year. Apply by No Deadline. Fellowships and scholarships available for first-year. Average amount paid per academic year: $3,000. Apply by February 1.

Advanced Students: Teaching assistantships available for advanced students. Average amount paid per academic year: $4,500. Average number of hours worked per week: 15. Apply by June 1. Research assistantships available for advanced students. Apply by June 1. Fellowships and scholarships available for advanced students. Average amount paid per academic year: $3,000. Apply by June 1.

Contact Information: Of all students currently enrolled full-time, 100% benefited from one or more of the listed financial assistance programs. For information on financial assistance, contact: Director of Admissions, Saint Mary's University, Halifax, NS B3H 3C3 Canada.

Internships/Practica: Students are required to complete a supervised practicum either full-time in the summer following their first year or part-time during their second year. Placements are available in a variety of hospitals, clinics, government agencies, and private consulting firms.

Housing and Day Care: On-campus housing and day care facilities are available.

Employment of Department Graduates:
Master's Degree Graduates: Of those who graduated in the academic year 2000–2001, the following categories and numbers represent the post-graduate activities and employment of master's degree graduates: Enrolled in a psychology doctoral program (4), enrolled in another graduate/professional program (2), enrolled in a post-doctoral residency/fellowship (n/a), employed in independent practice (n/a), employed in an academic position at a university (1), employed in other positions at a higher education institution (2), employed in business or industry (research/consulting) (8), employed in a government agency (research) (2), employed in a hospital/medical center (1).

Doctoral Degree Graduates: Of those who graduated in the academic year 2000–2001, the following categories and numbers

represent the post-graduate activities and employment of doctoral degree graduates: Enrolled in a psychology doctoral program (n/a), enrolled in another graduate/professional program (n/a).

Additional Information:

Orientation, Objectives, and Emphasis of Department: Students are expected to acquire a background in theory and research that is consistent with the scientist-practitioner model, keeping in mind the goal of preparing themselves for employment at the master's level of continued graduate education. Full-time students normally require two years to complete the program. Part-time students may take two to four years longer. All students are provided with financial support for two years.

Special Facilities or Resources: General experimental laboratories, graduate computer lab, small-group research space, observation rooms, and an extensive tests and measurements library that includes neuropsychological test batteries are available. Support systems include audiovisual equipment, computer facilities, and a technical workshop.

Application Information:

Send to: Director of Admissions, Saint Mary's University, Halifax, Nova Scotia, Canada B3H 3C3. Students are admitted in the Fall, application deadline February 1. *Fee:* $35. Note: All dollar amounts specified in this entry are Canadian dollars.

Toronto, University of
Department of Psychology
100 St. George Street
Toronto, ON M5S 3G3 Canada
Telephone: (416) 978-3404
Fax: (416) 976-4811
E-mail: *grad@psych.utoronto.ca*
Web: *http://www.psych.utoronto.ca*

Department Established:

1891. Chairperson: Lynn Hasher. Number of Faculty: total–full-time 65, part-time 33; women–full-time 16, part-time 13.

Programs and Degrees Offered:

Listed in the following order: Program area, degree type (T if terminal Master's), number awarded 7/00–6/01. Behavioral Neuroscience MA 5, Behavioral Neuroscience PhD 5, Cognition/Perception MA 3, Cognition/Perception PhD, Developmental MA 2, Developmental PhD, Social/Personality/Abnormal MA 5, Social/ Personality/Abnormal PhD.

Student Applications/Admissions:

Student Applications

Behavioral Neuroscience MA—Applications 2001–2002, 27. Total applicants accepted 2001–2002, 8. New applicants enrolled 2001–2002, 4. Total enrolled 2001–2002 full-time, 6. The Median number of years required for completion of a degree is 1. *Behavioral Neuroscience PhD*—Applications 2001–

2002, 6. Total applicants accepted 2001–2002, 3. New applicants enrolled 2001–2002, 2. Total enrolled 2001–2002 full-time, 39. The Median number of years required for completion of a degree are 5. *Cognition/Perception MA*—Applications 2001–2002, 36. Total applicants accepted 2001–2002, 12. New applicants enrolled 2001–2002, 4. Total enrolled 2001–2002 full-time, 6. The Median number of years required for completion of a degree is 1. *Cognition/Perception PhD*—Applications 2001–2002, 5. Total applicants accepted 2001–2002, 3. New applicants enrolled 2001–2002, 3. Total enrolled 2001–2002 full-time, 19. *Developmental MA*—Applications 2001–2002, 23. Total applicants accepted 2001–2002, 2. The Median number of years required for completion of a degree is 1. *Developmental PhD*—Applications 2001–2002, 3. Total enrolled 2001–2002 full-time, 10. Openings 2002–2003, 1. The number of students enrolled full and part-time, who were dismissed or voluntarily withdrew from this program area were 0. *Social/Personality/Abnormal MA*—Applications 2001–2002, 61. Total applicants accepted 2001–2002, 5. New applicants enrolled 2001–2002, 4. Total enrolled 2001–2002 full-time, 4. The Median number of years required for completion of a degree is 1. *Social/Personality/Abnormal PhD*—Applications 2001–2002, 7. Total applicants accepted 2001–2002, 1. Total enrolled 2001–2002 full-time, 14.

Admissions Requirements:

Scores: Entries appear in this order: required test or GPA, minimum score (if required), median score of students entering in 2001–2002. Master's Programs: GRE-V no minimum stated, 560; GRE-Q no minimum stated, 675; GRE-Analytical no minimum stated, 645; last 2 years GPA 3.7, 4. Doctoral Programs: GRE-V no minimum stated, 560; GRE-Q no minimum stated, 675; GRE-Analytical no minimum stated, 645; last 2 years GPA 3.7, 3.8 ; psychology GPA no minimum stated; psychology GPA 3.7, 4.

Other Criteria: (importance of criteria rated low, medium, or high): GRE/MAT scores high, research experience high, work experience low, extracurricular activity low, GPA high, letters of recommendation high, interview medium, statement of goals and objectives high.

Student Characteristics: The following represents characteristics of students in 2001–2002 in all graduate psychology programs in the department: Female–full-time 59, Male–full-time 39, American Indian/Alaska Native–full-time 1, Multi-ethnic–full-time 9.

Financial Information/Assistance:

Tuition for Full-Time Study: Master's: State residents per academic year $4,701; nonstate residents: per academic year $8,501. *Doctoral:* State residents: per academic year $4,701; nonstate residents: per academic year $8,501.

Financial Assistance:

First Year Students: Teaching assistantships available for first-year. Average amount paid per academic year: $6,000. Average number of hours worked per week: 10. Apply by June 1. Traineeships available for first-year. Average amount paid per academic year: $6,000. Apply by January 15. Fellowships and scholarships available for first-year. Average amount paid per academic year: $8,600. Apply by January 15.

Advanced Students: Teaching assistantships available for advanced students. Average amount paid per academic year:

$6,000. Average number of hours worked per week: 10. Apply by June 1. Traineeships available for advanced students. Average amount paid per academic year: $6,000. Apply by January 15. Fellowships and scholarships available for advanced students. Average amount paid per academic year: $8,600. Apply by January 15.

Contact Information: Of all students currently enrolled full-time, 100% benefited from one or more of the listed financial assistance programs.

Internships/Practica: No information provided.

Housing and Day Care: On-campus housing and day care facilities are available.

Employment of Department Graduates:

Master's Degree Graduates: Of those who graduated in the academic year 2000–2001, the following categories and numbers represent the post-graduate activities and employment of master's degree graduates: Enrolled in a psychology doctoral program (15), enrolled in a post-doctoral residency/fellowship (n/a), employed in independent practice (n/a).

Doctoral Degree Graduates: Of those who graduated in the academic year 2000–2001, the following categories and numbers represent the post-graduate activities and employment of doctoral degree graduates: Enrolled in a psychology doctoral program (n/a), enrolled in another graduate/professional program (n/a), enrolled in a post-doctoral residency/fellowship (2), employed in business or industry (research/consulting) (1), still seeking employment (2).

Additional Information:

Orientation, Objectives, and Emphasis of Department: The purpose of graduate training at the University of Toronto is to prepare students for careers in teaching and research. Teaching and research apprenticeships, therefore, constitute a large portion of such training. Research training is supplemented by courses and seminars. In some cases the courses are designed to provide up-to-date fundamental background information in psychology. The bulk of instruction, however, takes place in informal seminars; these provide an opportunity for the discussion of theoretical issues, the formulation of research problems, and the review of current developments in specific research areas. In the past, most of our graduates have entered academic careers. More recently, graduates have also taken research and managerial positions in research institutes, hospitals, government agencies, and industrial corporations.

Special Facilities or Resources: The department has modern laboratories at the St. George, Erindale, and Scarborough campuses, as well as a fully equipped electronic workshop. Students have access to an extensive computer system including the university's central computer, the department's Sun computer, and many advanced microcomputers. The department has close ties to several medical hospitals, as well as the Clarke Psychiatric hospital, Baycrest Center, and the Rotman Research Institute at the Center and the Addiction Research Foundation.

Application Information:

Send to: Graduate Studies, Department of Psychology, University of Toronto, 100 St. George Street, Toronto, Ontario, Canada M5S 3G3. Students are admitted in the Fall, application deadline January 15.

Fee: $85. Note: All dollar amounts specified in this entry are Canadian dollars.

Université Laval (2001 data)

Ecole de Psychologie
Pavillon F.A. Savard
Québec, QU G1K 7P4 Canada
Telephone: (418) 656-5383
Fax: (418) 656-3646
E-mail: *psy@psy.ulaval.ca*
Web: *http://www.psy.ulaval.ca*

Department Established:

1961. Chairperson: François Y. Doré. Number of Faculty: total–full-time 37; women–full-time 13.

Programs and Degrees Offered:

Listed in the following order: Program area, degree type (T if terminal Master's), number awarded 7/00–6/01. Psychology MA (T).

Student Applications/Admissions:

Student Applications

Psychology MA—Applications 2001–2002, 17. Total applicants accepted 2001–2002, 9. New applicants enrolled 2001–2002, 1. Total enrolled 2001–2002 full-time, 1.

Admissions Requirements:

Scores: Entries appear in this order: required test or GPA, minimum score (if required), median score of students entering in 2001–2002. Master's Programs: overall undergraduate GPA 3.22. Doctoral Programs: overall undergraduate GPA no minimum stated.

Other Criteria: (importance of criteria rated low, medium, or high): research experience high, work experience low, extra-curricular activity medium, clinically related public service low, GPA high, letters of recommendation high, statement of goals and objectives high.

Student Characteristics: The following represents characteristics of students in 2001–2002 in all graduate psychology programs in the department: No information provided.

Financial Information/Assistance:

Tuition for Full-Time Study: No information provided.

Financial Assistance:

First Year Students: No information provided.
Advanced Students: No information provided.
Contact Information: For information on financial assistance, contact: www.ulaval.ca/fes/aide.html.

Internships/Practica: At the master's level, facilities for 1080 hours of practicum are offered in clinical and school psychology. These practica can be completed at the outpatient clinic located at the School of Psychology or in a number of several hospital and school settings approved by the school. At the PhD level, a full year of internship is offered to those enrolled in the clinical sub-program.

Housing and Day Care: No on-campus housing and day care facilities are available.

Employment of Department Graduates:

Master's Degree Graduates: Of those who graduated in the academic year 2000–2001, the following categories and numbers represent the post-graduate activities and employment of master's degree graduates: Enrolled in a post-doctoral residency/fellowship (n/a), employed in independent practice (n/a).

Doctoral Degree Graduates: Of those who graduated in the academic year 2000–2001, the following categories and numbers represent the post-graduate activities and employment of doctoral degree graduates: Enrolled in a psychology doctoral program (n/a), enrolled in another graduate/professional program (n/a).

Additional Information:

Orientation, Objectives, and Emphasis of Department: The MPs program comprises two sub-programs: Type A is an applied one and emphasizes courses and a practicum. A monograph is required instead of a thesis. The areas covered are essentially in clinical and general psychology. Usually terminal, this sub-program aims at training the student to become a professional psychologist. The Type B sub-program is research oriented and requires the completion of a thesis. It also demands a minimum of 360 hours of practicum. The MA program is exclusively research oriented and requires the completion of a thesis. It also demands a minimum of 360 hours of practicum. The PhD program is research-oriented and requires the completion and defense of a dissertation. If accepted in the clinical subprogram, one also has to complete a one year full-time internship. The major areas of study and research are experimental (psychopharmacology, psychobiology, and cognitive psychology); clinical (behavioral modification, psychopathology, and mental health); developmental, psychology in educational context, cognitive development, and development of social skills); and community and social (nonprofessional group interaction, experimental, and applied social psychology).

Special Facilities or Resources: The School possesses sophisticated audiovisual equipment for research purposes. It is equipped with automatic data processing systems in the experimental area. It has full access to Laval University's modern computer facilities. The government of Quebec has already started the implementation of its 'technological conversion program' and Laval is taking full advantage of it to offer facilities in the computer training area. Laboratory facilities for human psychophysiological research are currently being updated. The experimental psychology laboratories are currently equipped with several microcomputers for experimental control and UNIX computers for simulation. Those computers form a local area network with access to Internet.

Application Information:
Send to: Bureau du registraire, 2400 Pavillon Jean-Charles-Bonenfant, Universite Laval, Sainte Foy (Quebec), G1K 7P4, reg@reg.ulaval.ca. Students are admitted in the Fall, application deadline February 1; Winter, application deadline November 1. *Fee:* $30. Note: All dollar amounts specified in this entry are Canadian dollars.

Victoria, University of
Department of Psychology
P.O. Box 3050 STN CSC
Victoria, BC V8W 3P5 Canada
Telephone: (250) 721-7525
Fax: (250) 721-8929
E-mail: *galambos@uvic.ca*
Web: *http://web.uvic.ca/psyc/*

Department Established:
1963. Chair: Nancy Galambis. Number of Faculty: total–full-time 24; women–full-time 12.

Programs and Degrees Offered:
Listed in the following order: Program area, degree type (T if terminal Master's), number awarded 7/00–6/01. Clinical lifespan developmenta PhD 1, clinical neuropsychology PhD 4, cognitive PhD 1, experimental neuropsychology PhD, lifespan developmental and agi PhD 1, social PhD 1.

APA Accreditation: Clinical PhD: full.

Student Applications/Admissions:

Student Applications

Clinical lifespan developmenta PhD—Applications 2001–2002, 60. Total applicants accepted 2001–2002, 2. Total enrolled 2001–2002 full-time, 12. Openings 2002–2003, 2. The Median number of years required for completion of a degree are 6. *Clinical neuropsychology PhD*—Applications 2001–2002, 39. Total applicants accepted 2001–2002, 3. New applicants enrolled 2001–2002, 3. Total enrolled 2001–2002 full-time, 30. Openings 2002–2003, 5. The Median number of years required for completion of a degree are 6. *Cognitive PhD*—Applications 2001–2002, 11. Total applicants accepted 2001–2002, 1. Total enrolled 2001–2002 full-time, 4. Openings 2002–2003, 2. The Median number of years required for completion of a degree are 6. *Experimental neuropsychology PhD*—Applications 2001–2002, 9. Total applicants accepted 2001–2002, 2. New applicants enrolled 2001–2002, 1. Total enrolled 2001–2002 full-time, 3. Openings 2002–2003, 2. The Median number of years required for completion of a degree are 6. *Lifespan developmental and agi PhD*—Applications 2001–2002, 16. Total applicants accepted 2001–2002, 4. New applicants enrolled 2001–2002, 2. Total enrolled 2001–2002 full-time, 8. Openings 2002–2003, 5. The Median number of years required for completion of a degree are 6. *Social PhD*—Applications 2001–2002, 7. Total applicants accepted 2001–2002, 3. New applicants enrolled 2001–2002, 2. Total enrolled 2001–2002 full-time, 17. Openings 2002–2003, 3. The Median number of years required for completion of a degree are 6.

Admissions Requirements:

Scores: Entries appear in this order: required test or GPA, minimum score (if required), median score of students entering in 2001–2002. Master's Programs: GRE-V no minimum stated; GRE-Q no minimum stated; GRE-Analytical no minimum stated; last 2 years GPA no minimum stated, 7.75. Doctoral Programs: GRE-V no minimum stated, 560; GRE-Q no minimum stated, 609; GRE-Analytical no minimum stated, 589;

last 2 years GPA 5.0, 7.44; psychology GPA no minimum stated; psychology GPA no minimum stated.

Other Criteria: (importance of criteria rated low, medium, or high): GRE/MAT scores medium, research experience high, work experience medium, extracurricular activity medium, clinically related public service medium, GPA high, letters of recommendation high, interview high, statement of goals and objectives medium. Interview for Clinical Programs only.

Student Characteristics: The following represents characteristics of students in 2001–2002 in all graduate psychology programs in the department: Female–full-time 58, part-time 0; Male–full-time 16, part-time 0.

Financial Information/Assistance:

Tuition for Full-Time Study: Master's: State residents per academic year $3,000; nonstate residents: per academic year $3,000. *Doctoral:* State residents: per academic year $3,000; nonstate residents: per academic year $3,000.

Financial Assistance:

First Year Students: Teaching assistantships available for first-year. Average amount paid per academic year: $3,400. Research assistantships available for first-year. Average amount paid per academic year: $3,500. Fellowships and scholarships available for first-year. Average amount paid per academic year: $14,000.

Advanced Students: Teaching assistantships available for advanced students. Average amount paid per academic year: $3,400. Research assistantships available for advanced students. Average amount paid per academic year: $3,400. Fellowships and scholarships available for advanced students. Average amount paid per academic year: $14,000.

Contact Information: Of all students currently enrolled full-time, 95% benefited from one or more of the listed financial assistance programs.

Internships/Practica: Internships and practica for students in the clinical program are arranged through the clinical program. For those doctoral students for whom a professional internship is required prior to graduation, 4 applied in 2000–2001. Of those who applied, 4 were placed in internships listed by the Association of Psychology Postdoctoral and Internship Programs (APPIC); 4 were placed in APA accredited internships.

Housing and Day Care: On-campus housing and day care facilities are available.

Employment of Department Graduates:

Master's Degree Graduates: Of those who graduated in the academic year 2000–2001, the following categories and numbers represent the post-graduate activities and employment of master's degree graduates: Enrolled in a post-doctoral residency/fellowship (n/a), employed in independent practice (n/a).

Doctoral Degree Graduates: Of those who graduated in the academic year 2000–2001, the following categories and numbers represent the post-graduate activities and employment of doctoral degree graduates: Enrolled in a psychology doctoral program (n/a), enrolled in another graduate/professional program (n/a).

Additional Information:

Orientation, Objectives, and Emphasis of Department: The graduate program in psychology emphasizes the training of research competence, and, in the case of neuropsychology and lifespan, the acquisition of clinical skills. The department's orientation is strongly empirical, and students are expected to develop mastery of appropriate methods and design as well as of specific content areas of psychology. The program is directed toward the PhD degree, although students must obtain a master's degree as part of the normal requirements. Formal programs of study, involving a coordinated sequence of courses, are offered for both experimental and clinical neuropsychology (up to but not including a clinical internship), lifespan development and aging, and clinical lifespan development. Individual programs of study may be designed according to the interests of individual students and faculty members in such areas as social psychology, environmental psychology, experimental and applied behavior analysis, psychopathology, cognition, and human psychophysiology.

Special Facilities or Resources: Fully equipped facilities are available including: a psychology laboratory operating as an outpatient service and teaching clinic; large observation rooms with audio and video recording equipment for the study of group interaction and other social-developmental processes; experimental rooms with one-way mirrors; electrophysiological recording rooms; and specialized facilities for the study of visual and auditory perception. The department also has access to teaching laboratory and a data analysis centre with state-of-the-art microcomputers and several time-sharing terminals that access the university's mainframe. The department also enjoys good community contact with local hospitals (general, rehabilitation, and extended care), schools, and private and government agencies.

Application Information:

Send to: Graduate Admissions, Faculty of Graduate Studies, University of Victoria, PO Box 3025, Victoria BC V8W 3P2 Canada. Students are admitted in the Fall, application deadline January 3. *Fee:* $50. Note: All dollar amounts specified in this entry are Canadian dollars.

Waterloo, University of
Department of Psychology
200 University Avenue West
Waterloo, ON N2L 3G1 Canada
Telephone: (519) 888-4567
Fax: (519) 746-8631
E-mail: *gradinfo.psych@uwaterloo.ca*
Web: *http://www.psychology.uwaterloo.ca/*

Department Established:

1963. Chairperson: Philip M. Merikle. Number of Faculty: total–full-time 34, part-time 18; women–full-time 12, part-time 7; minority–full-time 1.

Programs and Degrees Offered:

Listed in the following order: Program area, degree type (T if terminal Master's), number awarded 7/00–6/01. Behavioral neuroscience PhD 4, clinical PhD 3, cognitive PhD (T), developmental PhD 2, industrial/organizational PhD (T) 1, social PhD 4.

APA Accreditation: Clinical PhD: full.

Student Applications/Admissions:

Student Applications

Behavioral neuroscience PhD—Applications 2001–2002, 14. Total applicants accepted 2001–2002, 7. New applicants enrolled 2001–2002, 2. Total enrolled 2001–2002 full-time, 20, part-time, 1. *Clinical PhD*—Applications 2001–2002, 113. Total applicants accepted 2001–2002, 5. New applicants enrolled 2001–2002, 4. Total enrolled 2001–2002 full-time, 26, part-time, 2. *Cognitive PhD*—Applications 2001–2002, 16. Total applicants accepted 2001–2002, 3. New applicants enrolled 2001–2002, 2. Total enrolled 2001–2002 full-time, 7. *Developmental PhD*—Applications 2001–2002, 9. Total applicants accepted 2001–2002, 3. New applicants enrolled 2001–2002, 1. Total enrolled 2001–2002 full-time, 15, part-time, 1. *Industrial/organizational PhD*—Applications 2001–2002, 14. Total applicants accepted 2001–2002, 6. New applicants enrolled 2001–2002, 4. Total enrolled 2001–2002 full-time, 8. *Social PhD*—Applications 2001–2002, 25. Total applicants accepted 2001–2002, 6. New applicants enrolled 2001–2002, 3. Total enrolled 2001–2002 full-time, 12.

Admissions Requirements:

Scores: Entries appear in this order: required test or GPA, minimum score (if required), median score of students entering in 2001–2002. Master's Programs: GRE-V+Q+Analytical no minimum stated; GRE-Subject(Psych) no minimum stated; overall undergraduate GPA 3.00. Doctoral Programs: GRE-V+Q+Analytical no minimum stated; GRE-Subject(Psych) no minimum stated; overall undergraduate GPA 3.00; last 2 years GPA no minimum stated; psychology GPA no minimum stated; psychology GPA no minimum stated.

Other Criteria: (importance of criteria rated low, medium, or high): GRE/MAT scores high, research experience medium, work experience low, clinically related public service medium, GPA high, letters of recommendation high, interview medium, statement of goals and objectives high.

Student Characteristics: The following represents characteristics of students in 2001–2002 in all graduate psychology programs in the department: Female–full-time 66, part-time 0; Male–full-time 36, part-time 0; African American/Black–full-time 0, part-time 0; Hispanic/Latino (a)–full-time 0, part-time 0; Asian/Pacific Islander–full-time 0, part-time 0; American Indian/Alaska Native–full-time 0, part-time 0.

Financial Information/Assistance:

Tuition for Full-Time Study: *Master's:* State residents per academic year $5,389; nonstate residents: per academic year $13,704. *Doctoral:* State residents: per academic year $5,389; nonstate residents: per academic year $13,704.

Financial Assistance:

First Year Students: Teaching assistantships available for first-year. Research assistantships available for first-year. Fellowships and scholarships available for first-year.

Advanced Students: Teaching assistantships available for advanced students. Research assistantships available for advanced students. Fellowships and scholarships available for advanced students.

Contact Information: Of all students currently enrolled full-time, 100% benefited from one or more of the listed financial assistance programs.

Internships/Practica: The Applied Master's program requires a 4-month supervised Internship. The Clinical program requires a 4-month Practicum during the program of study and a 12-month Internship at the conclusion of the academic program. Most Practicum placements are with local hospitals, schools, or industries. For those doctoral students for whom a professional internship is required prior to graduation, 7 applied in 2000–2001. Of those who applied, 7 were placed in internships listed by the Association of Psychology Postdoctoral and Internship Programs (APPIC); 7 were placed in APA accredited internships.

Housing and Day Care: On-campus housing and day care facilities are available.

Employment of Department Graduates:

Master's Degree Graduates: Of those who graduated in the academic year 2000–2001, the following categories and numbers represent the post-graduate activities and employment of master's degree graduates: Enrolled in a post-doctoral residency/fellowship (n/a), employed in independent practice (n/a).

Doctoral Degree Graduates: Of those who graduated in the academic year 2000–2001, the following categories and numbers represent the post-graduate activities and employment of doctoral degree graduates: Enrolled in a psychology doctoral program (n/a), enrolled in another graduate/professional program (n/a).

Additional Information:

Orientation, Objectives, and Emphasis of Department: There is a strong emphasis on research in all six Divisions of the PhD program and MASc students are prepared for careers in Applied Psychology in a variety of areas. Students are involved either through participation in ongoing faculty research or through development of their own ideas; coursework is intended to provide students with general knowledge and intensive preparation in their area of concentration and for some of the programs, the blending of theory and practice is experienced in Internship and Practicum arrangements.

Special Facilities or Resources: Within a large 4-story building, extensive laboratory facilities are available for animal and human research. Additional educational and resource centers operate in conjunction with academic and research programs; Animal Care, Preschool, two Assessment Clinics and mechanical and electronics shops. Research requiring special populations is often carried out at community institutions under the supervision of faculty members. Considerable investment has been made to technical services including excellent computer facilities and consulting personnel who are available for student research and courses.

Information for Students With Physical Disabilities: The department is located in a building serviced by an elevator, on a campus which is designed for easy wheelchair access. In addition to University policies and procedures which guide and protect students, all students have equal access to the departments of Counseling Services and Persons with Disabilities.

Application Information:
Send to: Graduate Studies Office, University of Waterloo, 200 University Ave., West Waterloo, ON N2L 3G1. Students are admitted in the Fall, application deadline January 15. *Fee:* $75. Note: All dollar amounts specified in this entry are Canadian dollars.

Western Ontario, The University of

Department of Psychology
Social Science Centre, 1151 Richmond Street North
London, AL N6A 5C2 Canada
Telephone: (519) 661-2064
Fax: (519) 661-3961
E-mail: *psych-grad@uwo.ca*
Web: *http://www.ssc.uwo.ca/psychology*

Department Established:

1931. Chairperson: James M. Olson. Number of Faculty: total–full-time 41, part-time 4; women–full-time 10.

Programs and Degrees Offered:

Listed in the following order: Program area, degree type (T if terminal Master's), number awarded 7/00–6/01. Animal cognition PhD 1, behavioural and cognitive neur PhD 2, clinical PhD 6, cognition PhD 4, developmental PhD, educational PhD, industrial/organizational PhD, measurement PhD, personality PhD, sensation and perception PhD, social PhD 1.

APA Accreditation: Clinical PhD: full.

Student Applications/Admissions:

Student Applications

Animal cognition PhD—Applications 2001–2002, 5. Total applicants accepted 2001–2002, 2. Total enrolled 2001–2002 full-time, 3. Openings 2002–2003, 2. The Median number of years required for completion of a degree are 4. The number of students enrolled full and part-time, who were dismissed or voluntarily withdrew from this program area were 0. *Behavioural and cognitive neur PhD*—Applications 2001–2002, 18. Total applicants accepted 2001–2002, 11. New applicants enrolled 2001–2002, 7. Total enrolled 2001–2002 full-time, 16. Openings 2002–2003, 6. The Median number of years required for completion of a degree are 5. The number of students enrolled full and part-time, who were dismissed or voluntarily withdrew from this program area were 0. *Clinical PhD*—Applications 2001–2002, 124. Total applicants accepted 2001–2002, 11. New applicants enrolled 2001–2002, 5. Total enrolled 2001–2002 full-time, 30, part-time, 2. Openings 2002–2003, 4. The Median number of years required for completion of a degree are 7. The number of students enrolled full and part-time, who were dismissed or voluntarily withdrew from this program area were 0. *Cognition PhD*—Applications 2001–2002, 7. Total applicants accepted 2001–2002, 5. New applicants enrolled 2001–2002, 2. Total enrolled 2001–2002 full-time, 4. Openings 2002–2003, 3. The Median number of years required for completion of a degree are 5. The number of students enrolled full and part-time, who were dismissed or voluntarily withdrew from this program area were 0. *Developmental PhD*—Applications 2001–2002, 12. Total applicants accepted 2001–2002, 4. New applicants enrolled 2001–2002, 1. Total enrolled 2001–2002 full-time, 5. Openings 2002–2003, 2. The Median number of years required for completion of a degree are n/a. The number of students enrolled full and part-time, who were dismissed or voluntarily withdrew from this program area were 0. *Educational PhD*—Applications 2001–2002, 2. Total applicants accepted 2001–2002, 3. Total enrolled 2001–2002 full-time, 5. Openings 2002–2003, 2. The

number of students enrolled full and part-time, who were dismissed or voluntarily withdrew from this program area were 0. *Industrial/organizational PhD*—Applications 2001–2002, 28. Total applicants accepted 2001–2002, 3. New applicants enrolled 2001–2002, 1. Total enrolled 2001–2002 full-time, 14. Openings 2002–2003, 2. The number of students enrolled full and part-time, who were dismissed or voluntarily withdrew from this program area were 0. *Measurement PhD*—Applications 2001–2002, 0. Total enrolled 2001–2002 full-time, 1, part-time, 1. Openings 2002–2003, 2. The number of students enrolled full and part-time, who were dismissed or voluntarily withdrew from this program area were 0. *Personality PhD*—Applications 2001–2002, 7. Total applicants accepted 2001–2002, 1. Total enrolled 2001–2002 full-time, 2. Openings 2002–2003, 2. The number of students enrolled full and part-time, who were dismissed or voluntarily withdrew from this program area were 0. *Sensation and perception PhD*—Applications 2001–2002, 0. Total applicants accepted 2001–2002, 2. New applicants enrolled 2001–2002, 1. Total enrolled 2001–2002 full-time, 4. Openings 2002–2003, 2. The number of students enrolled full and part-time, who were dismissed or voluntarily withdrew from this program area were 0. *Social PhD*—Applications 2001–2002, 23. Total applicants accepted 2001–2002, 8. New applicants enrolled 2001–2002, 4. Total enrolled 2001–2002 full-time, 8. Openings 2002–2003, 6. The Median number of years required for completion of a degree are 4. The number of students enrolled full and part-time, who were dismissed or voluntarily withdrew from this program area were 0.

Admissions Requirements:

Scores: Entries appear in this order: required test or GPA, minimum score (if required), median score of students entering in 2001–2002. Doctoral Programs: GRE-V 530; GRE-Q 560; GRE-Subject(Psych) no minimum stated; last 2 years GPA 3.7; psychology GPA 3.75; psychology GPA no minimum stated. *Other Criteria:* (importance of criteria rated low, medium, or high): GRE/MAT scores high, research experience high, work experience low, extracurricular activity low, clinically related public service low, GPA, letters of recommendation high, interview, statement of goals and objectives medium.

Student Characteristics: The following represents characteristics of students in 2001–2002 in all graduate psychology programs in the department: Female–full-time 66, part-time 2; Male–full-time 26, part-time 2; African American/Black–full-time 0, part-time 0; Hispanic/Latino (a)–full-time 0, part-time 0; Asian/Pacific Islander–full-time 0, part-time 0; American Indian/Alaska Native–full-time 0, part-time 0.

Financial Information/Assistance:

Tuition for Full-Time Study: *Doctoral:* State residents: per academic year $5,600; nonstate residents: per academic year $11,000.

Financial Assistance:

First Year Students: Teaching assistantships available for first-year. Average amount paid per academic year: $9,048. Average number of hours worked per week: 10. Tuition remission given: partial. Fellowships and scholarships available for first-year. Average amount paid per academic year: $17,000. Tuition remission given: partial.

Advanced Students: Teaching assistantships available for advanced students. Average amount paid per academic year: $9,048. Average number of hours worked per week: 10. Tuition remission given: partial. Fellowships and scholarships available for advanced students. Average amount paid per academic year: $17,000. Tuition remission given: partial.

Contact Information: Of all students currently enrolled full-time, 85% benefited from one or more of the listed financial assistance programs. For information on financial assistance, contact: See our Website: http://www.ssc.uwo.ca/psychology/psych_grad/.

Internships/Practica: Clinical psychology students complete a one-year internship (APA/CPA accredited) near the end of their doctoral training. Students in other applied areas including educational and industrial/organization, typically meet professional training requirements through a combination of practica courses and placements. For those doctoral students for whom a professional internship is required prior to graduation, 1 applied in 2000–2001. Of those who applied, 1 were placed in APA accredited internships.

Housing and Day Care: On-campus housing and day care facilities are available.

Employment of Department Graduates:

Master's Degree Graduates: Of those who graduated in the academic year 2000–2001, the following categories and numbers represent the post-graduate activities and employment of master's degree graduates: Enrolled in a post-doctoral residency/fellowship (n/a), employed in independent practice (n/a).

Doctoral Degree Graduates: Of those who graduated in the academic year 2000–2001, the following categories and numbers represent the post-graduate activities and employment of doctoral degree graduates: Enrolled in a psychology doctoral program (n/a), enrolled in another graduate/professional program (n/a), enrolled in a post-doctoral residency/fellowship (4), employed in independent practice (1), employed in an academic position at a university (2), employed in other positions at a higher education institution (1), employed in a government agency (professional services) (1), employed in a community mental health/counseling center (3), employed in a hospital/medical center (2).

Additional Information:

Orientation, Objectives, and Emphasis of Department: The department is organized into 11 subject content areas, with initial graduate selection procedures administered by area committees. Applicants must indicate an area of interest. The department is research-intensive and is oriented toward training researchers. Graduate students are expected to be continuously involved in research, as well as to complete required courses and comprehensive exams. The clinical psychology program adopts the scientist-practitioner model, where both research and professional skills are developed.

Special Facilities or Resources: Facilities for experimental research in the nine-story research wing of the Social Science Center include animal laboratories, rooms specially designed for research with human subjects in perception, behavioural and cognitive neuroscience, learning, developmental, personality and social psychology and, in addition, a preschool for observation and research into child development, early childhood education,

curricula, materials, and teaching methods. A broad range of equipment is available, and additional special equipment necessary for a student's research may be obtained. Facilities to aid in running experiments include sophisticated general and dedicated laboratory computers. An engineering shop, an audiovisual unit, a workshop, and electronic consultants are available. The department also has easy access to the Social Science Computing Laboratory. In addition to the Student Development Centre and the Psychological Services in the University Hospital on campus, potential field settings (and sources of subjects for research) include a wide variety of schools, and a large number of psychiatric, general hospitals, and specialized centers for research and treatment with children, adolescents, and adults.

Application Information:
Send to: The Graduate Office, Department of Psychology, Social Science Centre, The University of Western Ontario, 1151 Richmond Street, London, Ontario, Canada N6A 5C2. Students are admitted in the Fall, application deadline January 15th. *Fee:* $50. Note: All dollar amounts specified in this entry are Canadian dollars.

Wilfrid Laurier University

Department of Psychology
75 University Avenue, West
Waterloo, ON N2L 3C5 Canada
Telephone: (519) 884-1970
Fax: (519) 746-7605
E-mail: *rsharkey@wlu.ca*
Web: *http://www.wlu.ca/~wwwpsych*

Department Established:
1956. Chairperson: Angelo Santi. Number of Faculty: total–full-time 25, part-time 10; women–full-time 9, part-time 5; minority–full-time 1.

Programs and Degrees Offered:
Listed in the following order: Program area, degree type (T if terminal Master's), number awarded 7/00–6/01. Community MA (T) 4, experimental-general MA (T) 8.

Student Applications/Admissions:
Student Applications

Community MA—Applications 2001–2002, 39. Total applicants accepted 2001–2002, 7. New applicants enrolled 2001–2002, 7. Total enrolled 2001–2002 full-time, 17, part-time, 3. Openings 2002–2003, 6. The number of students enrolled full and part-time, who were dismissed or voluntarily withdrew from this program area were 0. *Experimental-general MA*—Applications 2001–2002, 26. Total applicants accepted 2001–2002, 5. New applicants enrolled 2001–2002, 5. Total enrolled 2001–2002 full-time, 11. Openings 2002–2003, 8.

Admissions Requirements:
Scores: Entries appear in this order: required test or GPA, minimum score (if required), median score of students entering in 2001–2002. Master's Programs: last 2 years GPA 8.0, 10.0. GPA of 8.0 is the equivalent of a B, and 10.0 is the equivalent of an A-. Doctoral Programs: last 2 years GPA no minimum

stated; psychology GPA no minimum stated; psychology GPA no minimum stated.

Other Criteria: (importance of criteria rated low, medium, or high): GRE/MAT scores, research experience medium, work experience low, extracurricular activity low, clinically related public service low, GPA, letters of recommendation high, interview medium, statement of goals and objectives high, coursework and faculty interest high,

Student Characteristics: The following represents characteristics of students in 2001–2002 in all graduate psychology programs in the department: Female–full-time 21, part-time 3; Male–full-time 7, part-time 0; African American/Black–full-time 1, part-time 0; Hispanic/Latino (a)–full-time 0, part-time 0; Asian/Pacific Islander–full-time 0, part-time 0; American Indian/Alaska Native–full-time 0, part-time 0.

Financial Information/Assistance:

Tuition for Full-Time Study: *Master's:* State residents per academic year $5,157; nonstate residents: per academic year $11,139.

Financial Assistance:

First Year Students: No information provided.
Advanced Students: No information provided.
Contact Information: Of all students currently enrolled full-time, 0% benefited from one or more of the listed financial assistance programs. For information on financial assistance, contact: Graduate Studies Office, http://www.wlu.ca/~wwwgrads.

Internships/Practica: No information provided.

Housing and Day Care: No on-campus housing and day care facilities are available.

Employment of Department Graduates:

Master's Degree Graduates: Of those who graduated in the academic year 2000–2001, the following categories and numbers represent the post-graduate activities and employment of master's degree graduates: Enrolled in a psychology doctoral program (7), enrolled in another graduate/professional program (1), enrolled in a post-doctoral residency/fellowship (n/a), employed in independent practice (n/a), employed in a government agency (research) (2), other employment position (4).
Doctoral Degree Graduates: Of those who graduated in the academic year 2000–2001, the following categories and numbers represent the post-graduate activities and employment of doctoral degree graduates: Enrolled in a psychology doctoral program (n/a), enrolled in another graduate/professional program (n/a).

Additional Information:

Orientation, Objectives, and Emphasis of Department: Graduate students can obtain an MA in one of the three fields of: 1) Brain and Cognition, 2) Social and Developmental Psychology, and 3) Community Psychology. The objective of the MA program in the fields of Brain and Cognition and Social and Developmental Psychology is to develop competence in designing, conducting, and evaluating research in the fields of Brian and Cognition and Social and Developmental Psychology. These two fields replace the previous field of General Experimental Psychology. Four half-credit courses and a thesis constitute the degree requirements. The purpose of the program is to prepare students for doctoral studies, or for employment in an environment requiring research

skills. In the field of Community Psychology, the objective is to train scientist-practitioners with skills in community collaboration. Students receive training in theory, research, and practice that will enable them to analyze the implications of social change for the delivery of community services. Six half-credit courses and a thesis are required for the degree. The MA degree requirements can be completed in a 12-month period, but students have typically spread the requirements over a 2-year period. Students who complete this program are prepared for either doctoral level training or for employment in community research and service.

Special Facilities or Resources: The department has free unlimited access to the university computer, microprocessors, extensive electromechanical equipment, full-time electronics research associate, full-time field supervisor, and access to a wide variety of field settings for research and consultation. We moved to a brand new facility in December, 1994.

Application Information:
Send to: Wilfrid Laurier University, Waterloo, ON N2L 3C5. Helen Paret, Coordinator of Graduate Admissions and Records, Faculty of Graduate Studies. Students are admitted in the Fall, application deadline February 1. *Fee:* $50. Note: All dollar amounts specified in this entry are Canadian dollars.

Windsor, University of
Psychology
Faculty of Arts and Social Sciences
401 Sunset Avenue
Windsor, ON N9B 3P4 Canada
Telephone: (519) 253-3000, Ext. 2215
Fax: (519) 973-7021
E-mail: *towson@uwindsor.ca*
Web: *http://www.uwindsor.ca*

Department Established:
1944. Head: Shelagh Towson. Number of Faculty: total–full-time 29; women–full-time 11; minority–full-time 1.

Programs and Degrees Offered:
Listed in the following order: Program area, degree type (T if terminal Master's), number awarded 7/00–6/01. Applied Social PhD 2, Clinical PhD 12, Respecialization Diploma.

APA Accreditation: Clinical PhD: full.

Student Applications/Admissions:
Student Applications
Applied Social PhD—Applications 2001–2002, 21. Total applicants accepted 2001–2002, 12. New applicants enrolled 2001–2002, 2. Total enrolled 2001–2002 full-time, 20. Openings 2002–2003, 4. The Median number of years required for completion of a degree are 6. The number of students enrolled full and part-time, who were dismissed or voluntarily withdrew from this program area were 2. *Clinical PhD*—Applications 2001–2002, 115. Total applicants accepted 2001–2002, 20. New applicants enrolled 2001–2002, 11. Total enrolled 2001–2002 full-time, 76. Openings 2002–2003, 14. The Median

number of years required for completion of a degree are 7. The number of students enrolled full and part-time, who were dismissed or voluntarily withdrew from this program area were 5. *Respecialization Diploma*—Applications 2001–2002, 1. Total enrolled 2001–2002 full-time, 1. Openings 2002–2003, 1. The number of students enrolled full and part-time, who were dismissed or voluntarily withdrew from this program area were 0.

Admissions Requirements:

Scores: Entries appear in this order: required test or GPA, minimum score (if required), median score of students entering in 2001–2002. Master's Programs: Students are accepted directly into PhD program. See Doctoral Program requirements below. Doctoral Programs: GRE-V+Q+Analytical 60, 70; GRE-Subject(Psych) 60, 84; overall undergraduate GPA 3 3.; last 2 years GPA no minimum stated; psychology GPA no minimum stated; psychology GPA no minimum stated.

Other Criteria: (importance of criteria rated low, medium, or high): GRE/MAT scores high, research experience medium, work experience low, extracurricular activity low, clinically related public service medium, GPA high, letters of recommendation high, interview medium, statement of goals and objectives medium.

Student Characteristics: The following represents characteristics of students in 2001–2002 in all graduate psychology programs in the department: Female–full-time 76, part-time 0; Male–full-time 21, part-time 0; African American/Black–full-time 0, part-time 0; Hispanic/Latino (a)–full-time 0, part-time 0; Asian/Pacific Islander–full-time 7, part-time 0; American Indian/Alaska Native–full-time 0, part-time 0.

Financial Information/Assistance:

Tuition for Full-Time Study: *Doctoral:* State residents: per academic year $5,530; nonstate residents: per academic year $9,600.

Financial Assistance:

First Year Students: Teaching assistantships available for first-year. Average amount paid per academic year: $7,150. Average number of hours worked per week: 10. Apply by Jan. 15. Fellowships and scholarships available for first-year. Average amount paid per academic year: $5,000. Apply by Jan. 15.

Advanced Students: Teaching assistantships available for advanced students. Average amount paid per academic year: $8,000. Average number of hours worked per week: 10. Apply by n/a. Fellowships and scholarships available for advanced students. Average amount paid per academic year: $5,000. Apply by Dec. 15.

Contact Information: Of all students currently enrolled full-time, 77% benefited from one or more of the listed financial assistance programs. For information on financial assistance, contact: Graduate Studies & Research, Ext. 2109; Department of Psychology, Ext. 2215.

Internships/Practica: A wide variety of clinical practica are available in the Windsor-Detroit area, and clinical students obtain additional summer practicum positions across the country. Students are placed in predoctoral internships throughout Canada and the U.S. Applied Social students obtain practica and internships in business and industry, community and health-related agencies. For those doctoral students for whom a professional internship is required prior to graduation, 8 applied in 2000–2001. Of those who applied, 8 were placed in internships listed by the Association of Psychology Postdoctoral and Internship Programs (APPIC); 6 were placed in APA accredited internships.

Housing and Day Care: No on-campus housing and day care facilities are available.

Employment of Department Graduates:

Master's Degree Graduates: Of those who graduated in the academic year 2000–2001, the following categories and numbers represent the post-graduate activities and employment of master's degree graduates: Enrolled in a psychology doctoral program (9), enrolled in a post-doctoral residency/fellowship (n/a), employed in independent practice (n/a), still seeking employment (1).

Doctoral Degree Graduates: Of those who graduated in the academic year 2000–2001, the following categories and numbers represent the post-graduate activities and employment of doctoral degree graduates: Enrolled in a psychology doctoral program (n/a), enrolled in another graduate/professional program (n/a), employed in independent practice (1), employed in an academic position at a 2-year/4-year college (1), employed in a professional position in a school system (1), employed in a government agency (professional services) (1), employed in a community mental health/counseling center (3), employed in a hospital/medical center (4), still seeking employment (1).

Additional Information:

Orientation, Objectives, and Emphasis of Department: Graduate offerings are divided into two areas: clinical and applied social. Student applying for the clinical program apply directly into specialty areas of adult clinical, clinical/developmental (child clinical or developmental psychopathology), or clinical neuropsychology. Each of the areas combines theoretical, substantive, and methodological coursework with a variety of applied training experiences.

Special Facilities or Resources: Computer facilities include a microcomputer laboratory with remote terminals linked to a central computing facility. Applied training and research resources include the Psychological Services Centre, Neuropsychology Laboratory, the Child Study Centre, Emotion/Cognition Research Laboratory, and the Psycho and Neurolinguistics Laboratory. There are faculty-student research groups in the areas of suicidology, eating disorders, trauma and psychotherapy, problem gambling, feminist research, emotional competence, culture and diversity, health psychology, clinical assessment, psychodynamic processes, aging, and forgiveness.

Information for Students With Physical Disabilities: The university and the department are wheelchair accessible. The Student Affairs office offers assistance to students with special needs.

Application Information:

Send to: Applicant Services-Graduate Division, University of Windsor, 401 Sunset Avenue, Windsor, Ontario N9B 3P4. Students are admitted in the Fall, application deadline January 15. *Fee:* $55. Note: All dollar amounts specified in this entry are Canadian dollars.

York University

Graduate Program in Psychology
4700 Keele Street
Toronto, ON M3J 1P3 Canada
Telephone: (416) 736-5290
Fax: (416) 736-5814
E-mail: *drennie@yorku.ca*
Web: *http://www.yorku.ca/grads/cal/psy.htm*

Department Established:

1963. Director, Graduate Programme in Psychology: David Rennie. Number of Faculty: total–full-time 71, part-time 30; women–full-time 30, part-time 15.

Programs and Degrees Offered:

Listed in the following order: Program area, degree type (T if terminal Master's), number awarded 7/00–6/01. Brain, Behaviour and Cognitive S PhD 6, Clinical PhD 11, Clinical-Developmental PhD 10, Developmental and Cognitive Pr PhD 2, History & Theory PhD 1, Social Personality PhD 8.

APA Accreditation: Clinical PhD: full.

Student Applications/Admissions:

Student Applications

Brain, Behaviour and Cognitive S PhD—Applications 2001–2002, 19. Total applicants accepted 2001–2002, 4. New applicants enrolled 2001–2002, 4. Total enrolled 2001–2002 full-time, 28, part-time, 3. Openings 2002–2003, 6. The number of students enrolled full and part-time, who were dismissed or voluntarily withdrew from this program area were 2. *Clinical PhD*—Applications 2001–2002, 115. Total applicants accepted 2001–2002, 10. New applicants enrolled 2001–2002, 10. Total enrolled 2001–2002 full-time, 63, part-time, 3. Openings 2002–2003, 8. The Median number of years required for completion of a degree are 6. The number of students enrolled full and part-time, who were dismissed or voluntarily withdrew from this program area were 2. *Clinical-Developmental PhD*—Applications 2001–2002, 102. Total applicants accepted 2001–2002, 7. New applicants enrolled 2001–2002, 7. Total enrolled 2001–2002 full-time, 50, part-time, 6. Openings 2002–2003, 8. The Median number of years required for completion of a degree are 6. *Developmental and Cognitive Pr PhD*—Applications 2001–2002, 11. Total applicants accepted 2001–2002, 7. New applicants enrolled 2001–2002, 7. Total enrolled 2001–2002 full-time, 25, part-time, 2. Openings 2002–2003, 5. *History & Theory PhD*—Applications 2001–2002, 5. Total applicants accepted 2001–2002, 1. New applicants enrolled 2001–2002, 1. Total enrolled 2001–2002 full-time, 8. Openings 2002–2003, 3. *Social Personality PhD*—Applications 2001–2002, 24. Total applicants accepted 2001–2002, 5. New applicants enrolled 2001–2002, 5. Total enrolled 2001–2002 full-time, 28, part-time, 2. Openings 2002–2003, 6.

Admissions Requirements:

Scores: Entries appear in this order: required test or GPA, minimum score (if required), median score of students entering in 2001–2002. Master's Programs: GRE-V+Q+Analytical no minimum stated; GRE-Subject(Psych) no minimum stated; last 2 years GPA no minimum stated. Doctoral Programs: last 2 years GPA no minimum stated; psychology GPA no minimum stated; psychology GPA no minimum stated.

Other Criteria: (importance of criteria rated low, medium, or high): GRE/MAT scores high, research experience medium, work experience low, GPA high, letters of recommendation high, statement of goals and objectives medium.

Student Characteristics: The following represents characteristics of students in 2001–2002 in all graduate psychology programs in the department: Female–full-time 172, part-time 13; Male–full-time 33, part-time 5.

Financial Information/Assistance:

Tuition for Full-Time Study: *Master's:* State residents per academic year $4,599; nonstate residents: per academic year $1,123. *Doctoral:* State residents: per academic year $4,599; nonstate residents: per academic year $1,123.

Financial Assistance:

First Year Students: Research assistantships available for first-year. Average amount paid per academic year: $8,000. Average number of hours worked per week: 10. Fellowships and scholarships available for first-year. Average amount paid per academic year: $3,000.

Advanced Students: Teaching assistantships available for advanced students. Average amount paid per academic year: $10,329. Average number of hours worked per week: 10. Research assistantships available for advanced students. Average amount paid per academic year: $8,000. Average number of hours worked per week: 10. Fellowships and scholarships available for advanced students. Average amount paid per academic year: $3,000.

Contact Information: Of all students currently enrolled full-time, 90% benefited from one or more of the listed financial assistance programs. For information on financial assistance, contact: Graduate Studies, 416-736-5328.

Internships/Practica: Master's or doctoral internships are available; practicum work is done on a half-time basis during the academic year and, when possible, full-time during the summer. Research and teaching practica, and a clinical practicum as part of the Clinical Area's programme, are done on campus. Clinical internships are available in the York Counseling and Development Center and a variety of hospitals, clinics, and counseling centers in the city. Descriptions of the programme and of faculty research interests are available on the Web.

Housing and Day Care: On-campus housing and day care facilities are available.

Employment of Department Graduates:

Master's Degree Graduates: Of those who graduated in the academic year 2000–2001, the following categories and numbers represent the post-graduate activities and employment of master's degree graduates: Enrolled in a post-doctoral residency/fellowship (n/a), employed in independent practice (n/a).

Doctoral Degree Graduates: Of those who graduated in the academic year 2000–2001, the following categories and numbers represent the post-graduate activities and employment of doctoral degree graduates: Enrolled in a psychology doctoral program (n/a), enrolled in another graduate/professional program (n/a), enrolled in a post-doctoral residency/fellowship (3), employed in independent practice (4), employed in an academic position at a university

(4), employed in an academic position at a 2-year/4-year college (0), employed in other positions at a higher education institution (2), employed in a professional position in a school system (1), employed in business or industry (research/consulting) (2), employed in business or industry (management) (0), employed in a government agency (research) (2), employed in a government agency (professional services) (4), employed in a community mental health/counseling center (0), employed in a hospital/medical center (4), still seeking employment (0), other employment position (0).

Additional Information:

Orientation, Objectives, and Emphasis of Department: Strength and depth are emphasized in the areas of brain, behaviour, and cognitive science (learning, perception, physiological, psychometrics); clinical; clinical-development; developmental cognitive processes; history and theory; and social-personality. The department attempts to prepare students as researchers and practitioners in a given area. Most students admitted to the MA but are accepted on the assumption that they will continue into PhD studies.

Special Facilities or Resources: The department has a vivarium; wet laboratories; shop facilities for woodwork, electronics, metalwork, and photography; substantial computing facilities; audiovisual equipment including VCRs; and observational laboratories with two-way mirrors.

Application Information:

Send to: Admissions Office, York University, 150 Atkinson, 4700 Keele Street, Toronto, Ontario M3J 1P3. Students are admitted in the Fall, application deadline Jan 15. *Fee:* $60. Note: All dollar amounts specified in this entry are Canadian dollars.

A

Adolescence and youth ✗
Arizona State University (MA)
Boston College (MA—terminal, PhD)
California Lutheran University
  (MA—terminal)
Cornell University (PhD)
Houston, University of (PhD)
Maine, University of (MA)
Manitoba, University of (PhD—terminal)
Nebraska, University of, Lincoln (PhD)
New York University (PhD)
Ohio State University (PhD)
Peabody College of Vanderbilt University
  (PhD)
Stanford University (PhD)
Temple University (PhD)
Victoria, University of (PhD)
Virginia, University of (PhD)
Washington, University of (PhD)
Wisconsin School of Professional
  Psychology (PsyD)
Wyoming, University of (PhD)
Yale University (PhD)

Adult development
Boston College (MA—terminal, PhD)
Bowling Green State University (PhD)
Nebraska, University of, Lincoln (PhD)
Southern California, University of (PhD)
Temple University (MA—terminal)
Washington University (St. Louis) (PhD)
Washington, University of (PhD)

Aging
Adler School of Professional Psychology
  (MA—terminal)
Akron, University of (PhD, MA—terminal)
Alabama, University of, at Birmingham
  (PhD)
Alberta, University of (PhD)
Argosy University, Tampa (PsyD)
Arizona State University (PhD)
Benedictine University (MA—terminal)
Brandeis University (PhD)
Case Western Reserve University (PhD)
Claremont Graduate University
  (MA—terminal)
Colorado, University of, at Colorado
  Springs (MA—terminal)
Concordia University (MA)
Cornell University (PhD)
Georgia Institute of Technology (PhD)
Indianapolis, University of (PsyD)
Johns Hopkins University (PhD)
New Hampshire, University of (PhD)
North Carolina State University (PhD)
Purdue University (PhD)
Southern California, University of (PhD)
St. Louis University (PhD)
Stanford University (PhD)
Syracuse University (PhD)

Toronto, University of (MA, PhD)
Washington University (St. Louis) (PhD)
West Virginia University (PhD)
Xavier University (PsyD)

AIDS intervention or research
Connecticut, University of (PhD)
Fairfield University (MA)
Goddard College (MA—terminal)
Illinois, University of, at Chicago (PhD)

Applied
Antioch University, Seattle (CT,
  MA—terminal)
Appalachian State University
  (MA—terminal)
Auburn University at Montgomery
  (MA—terminal)
Augusta State University (MA—terminal)
Baltimore, University of (MA—terminal)
Claremont Graduate University
  (MA—terminal)
Clemson University (PhD—terminal)
Dayton, University of (MA—terminal)
Embry-Riddle Aeronautical University
  (MA—terminal)
Iona College (MA—terminal)
Kansas State University (PhD)
Louisiana, University of, Lafayette
  (MA—terminal)
Manitoba, University of (PhD—terminal)
Montana State University (MA—terminal)
Nevada, University of, Las Vegas (PhD)
North Carolina, University of, at
  Wilmington (MA—terminal)
Penn State Harrisburg (MA—terminal)
Southern Illinois University at Carbondale
  (PhD)
St. Mary's University (MA—terminal)
Teachers College, Columbia University
  (MA—terminal)
Texas A&M University - Commerce
  (MA—terminal)
Texas of the Permian Basin, The University
  of (MA—terminal)
Texas, University of, El Paso (PhD)
The Catholic University of America (PhD)
Valdosta State University (MA—terminal)
Virginia Commonwealth University (PhD)
West Virginia University (PhD)
William Paterson University
  (MA—terminal)
Wisconsin, University of, Stout
  (MA—terminal)
Yeshiva University (MA—terminal)

Applied developmental
Alberta, University of (PhD)
City University of New York, Graduate
  School and University Center (PhD)
Claremont Graduate University
  (MA—terminal)
Cornell University (PhD)

Fordham University (PhD)
George Mason University (PhD,
  MA—terminal)
Georgia State University (PhD)
Guelph, University of (PhD)
Houston, University of (PhD)
Indiana University South Bend
  (MA—terminal)
McGill University (PhD)
Miami, University of (Florida) (PhD)
Minnesota, University of (PhD)
New Orleans, University of (PhD)
New York University (MA—terminal)
Oklahoma, University of (PhD)
Pittsburgh, University of (PhD)
Portland State University (MA, PhD)
San Francisco State University
  (MA—terminal)
Stanford University (PhD)
Temple University (PhD)
Tufts University (MA—terminal)
Virginia, University of (PhD)
Wayne State University (MA—terminal)
Wyoming, University of (PhD)

Applied social
Arizona State University (PhD)
Ball State University (MA—terminal)
Brigham Young University (MS—terminal)
Fairleigh Dickinson University, Madison
  (MA—terminal)
George Washington University (PhD)
Georgia State University (PhD)
Guelph, University of (PhD)
Indiana University South Bend
  (MA—terminal)
Iowa State University (PhD)
Loyola University of Chicago (MA)
Massachusetts, University of, Lowell
  (MA—terminal)
Memorial University of Newfoundland
  (PhD)
Missouri, University of, Columbia (PhD)
Nebraska, University of, Lincoln (PhD)
North Carolina, University of, at Chapel
  Hill (PhD)
Northern Illinois University (PhD)
Oklahoma, University of (PhD)
Pittsburgh, University of (PhD)
Portland State University (MA, PhD)
San Francisco State University
  (MA—terminal)
Saskatchewan, University of
  (MA—terminal)
Southern California, University of, School
  of Medicine (PhD)
Vanderbilt University (PhD)
Virginia, University of (PhD)
Washington University (St. Louis) (PhD)
Windsor, University of (PhD)
Wright State University (PhD)

Toledo, University of (PhD)
Washington State University (PhD)
Washington University (St. Louis) (PhD)

Behavioral science—applied
Hawaii, University of (PhD)
Kean University (MA—terminal)
State University of New York, College at
   Brockport (MA—terminal)

C

Child development ✗
American University (MA—terminal)
Arizona State University (PhD)
Boston College (MA—terminal, PhD)
Bowling Green State University (PhD)
British Columbia, University of (PhD)
California State University, San Bernardino
   (MA—terminal)
California, University of, Davis
   (MS—terminal)
Connecticut, University of (PhD)
Cornell University (PhD)
Denver, University of (PhD)
Georgia State University (MSEd, PhD)
Illinois, University of, at Urbana-
   Champaign (PhD)
Iowa, University of (PhD)
Maine, University of (MA)
Manitoba, University of (PhD)
Minnesota, University of (PhD)
Missouri, University of, Columbia
   (MA—terminal)
Nebraska, University of, Lincoln (PhD)
New Hampshire, University of (PhD)
New York University (PhD)
North Carolina, University of, at Chapel
   Hill (PhD)
Ohio State University (PhD)
Oklahoma, University of (PhD)
Peabody College of Vanderbilt University
   (PhD)
Pittsburgh, University of (PhD)
Purdue University (PhD)
San Francisco State University
   (MA—terminal)
Southern California, University of (PhD)
Southern Methodist University (PhD)
St. Louis University (PhD)
Stanford University (PhD)
Temple University (PhD)
Texas, University of, Austin (PhD)
The Citadel (EdS)
Toronto, University of (MA, PhD)
Tufts University (PhD)
Utah, University of (PhD)
Victoria, University of (PhD)
Washington, University of (PhD)
West Virginia University (PhD)
Western Michigan University (EdS)
Wisconsin, University of, Madison (PhD)
Yale University (PhD)
York University (PhD)

Child psychopathology
City University of New York, Graduate
   School and University Center (PhD)

Hawaii, University of (PhD)
Humboldt State University (MA—terminal)
Kent State University (PhD)
Minnesota, University of (PhD)
Pittsburgh, University of (PhD)
Southern Methodist University (PhD)
Stanford University (PhD)
Syracuse University (PhD)
Temple University (PhD)
Virginia Commonwealth University (PhD)
York University (PhD)

Clinical ✗
Abilene Christian University
   (MA—terminal)
Acadia University (MA—terminal)
Adelphi University (PhD)
Adler School of Professional Psychology
   (PsyD)
Alabama, University of (PhD)
Alabama, University of, at Birmingham
   (PhD)
Alaska, University of, Anchorage
   (MA—terminal)
Alliant International University (PhD)
Alliant International University, San Diego
   (PhD, PsyD)
American International College
   (MA—terminal)
American University (PhD)
Antioch New England Graduate School
   (PsyD)
Antioch University, Santa Barbara
   (MA—terminal)
Argosy University (PsyD)
Argosy University, Honolulu (PsyD)
Argosy University, Illinois School of
   Professional Psychology, Chicago Campus
   (PsyD)
Argosy University, Illinois School of
   Professional Psychology, Chicago
   Northwest Campus (PsyD)
Argosy University, Phoenix (PsyD)
Argosy University, San Francisco Bay Area
   (PsyD)
Argosy University, Washington School of
   Professional Psychology, Seattle (MA)
Argosy University, Washington, DC (PsyD)
Argosy University, Twin Cities (PsyD)
Arizona, University of (PhD)
Arkansas, University of (PhD)
Augusta State University (MA—terminal)
Austin Peay State University
   (MA—terminal)
Azusa Pacific University (PsyD)
Ball State University (MA—terminal)
Baltimore, University of (MA—terminal)
Benedictine University (MA—terminal)
Binghamton University (PhD)
Biola University (PhD)
⊕ Boston University (PhD)
British Columbia, University of (PhD)
California Institute of Integral Studies
   (PsyD)
California Lutheran University
   (MA—terminal)
California School of Professional
   Psychology/AIU: Alameda (PsyD)

California State University, Dominguez
   Hills (MA—terminal)
California State University, Fullerton
   (MA—terminal)
California State University, Northridge
   (MA)
California State University, San Bernardino
   (MA—terminal)
California, University of, Los Angeles
   (PhD)
California, University of, Santa Barbara
   (PhD)
Carlos Albizu University (PhD)
Carlos Albizu University, Miami Campus
   (PsyD)
Case Western Reserve University (PhD)
Center for Humanistic Studies Graduate
   School (MA—terminal)
Central Florida, University of
   (MA—terminal)
Central Michigan University (PhD)
Chicago School of Professional Psychology
   (PsyD)
Cincinnati, University of (PhD)
City University of New York, Graduate
   School and University Center (PhD)
Clark University (PhD)
Cleveland State University (MA—terminal)
Colorado State University (PhD)
Colorado, University of, at Boulder (PhD)
Colorado, University of, at Colorado
   Springs (MA—terminal)
Colorado, University of, at Denver
   (MA—terminal)
Connecticut College (MA—terminal)
Connecticut, University of (PhD)
Dalhousie University (PhD)
Dayton, University of (MA—terminal)
Delaware, University of (PhD)
⊕ Denver, University of (PsyD)
⊕ DePaul University (PhD)
Detroit-Mercy, University of
   (MA—terminal)
Drexel University (PhD)
East Carolina University (MA—terminal)
Eastern Kentucky University
   (MA—terminal)
Eastern Washington University
   (MA—terminal)
Edinboro University of Pennsylvania
   (MA—terminal)
⊕ Emory University (PhD)
Emporia State University (MA—terminal)
Fairleigh Dickinson University, Teaneck-
   Hackensack (PhD)
Fielding Graduate Institute (PhD)
Florida Institute of Technology (PsyD)
⊕ Florida State University (PhD)
Fordham University (PhD)
Forest Institute of Professional Psychology
   (PsyD)
Fort Hays State University (MA—terminal)
Gallaudet University (PhD)
George Fox University (PsyD)
George Mason University (PhD)
George Washington University (PsyD)
Georgia Southern University
   (MA—terminal)

Rutgers—The State University of New Jersey, New Brunswick (EdD)
Saint Francis, University of (MA—terminal)
Saint Mary's University of Minnesota (MA—terminal)
Seton Hall University (MA—terminal)
Southern Methodist University (MA—terminal)
Springfield College (MS—terminal)
State University of New York at Buffalo (PhD)
State University of West Georgia (MA—terminal)
Temple University (MA—terminal)
Texas, University of, Tyler (MA—terminal)
The Citadel (MA—terminal)
The Sage Colleges (MA—terminal)
Towson University (MA)
Tufts University (MA)
Valdosta State University (MA—terminal)
Valparaiso University (MA—terminal)
Vanguard University of Southern California (MA—terminal)
Walden University (PhD)
Washington State University (MA—terminal)
West Virginia University (MA—terminal)
Western Michigan University (WMU) (PhD)
William Paterson University (MA—terminal)

Counseling and guidance
Antioch University, Santa Barbara (MA—terminal)
Auburn University (EdS)
Ball State University (MA—terminal)
Connecticut, University of (MA—terminal)
Geneva College (MA—terminal)
Indiana University (EdS)
Iona College (MA—terminal)
Kansas, University of (MA—terminal)
Lesley University (MA—terminal)
Lewis University (MA—terminal)
Marquette University (MA—terminal)
McGill University (PhD)
Middle Tennessee State University (EdD)
Missouri, University of, Columbia (EdS)
Missouri, University of, Kansas City (MA—terminal, EdS)
New Mexico State University (MA—terminal)
Northeastern University (MA—terminal)
Northern Colorado, University of (MA—terminal)
Nova Southeastern University (MA—terminal)
Springfield College (MS—terminal)
State University of New York at Buffalo (MEd)
Temple University (MA—terminal)
Tennessee State University (PhD, EdS)
Valdosta State University (EdS)
Vanderbilt University (MA—terminal)
Washington, University of (PhD)

Counseling psychology
Adler School of Professional Psychology (MA—terminal)
Akron, University of (PhD)
Alaska Pacific University (MA—terminal)
Andrews University (PhD)
Argosy University (EdD)
Argosy University, Illinois School of Professional Psychology, Chicago Campus (MA—terminal)
Argosy University, San Francisco Bay Area (MA—terminal)
Argosy University, Washington, DC (MA—terminal)
Arizona State University (PhD)
Assumption College (MA—terminal)
Auburn University (PhD)
Avila College (MA—terminal)
Ball State University (PhD)
Boston College (PhD)
Boston University (PhD)
Brigham Young University (PhD)
Calgary, University of (PhD)
California Institute of Integral Studies (MA—terminal)
Central Arkansas, University of (MA)
Central Oklahoma, University of (MA—terminal)
Chatham College (MA—terminal)
Chestnut Hill College (MA—terminal)
Cleveland State University (MA—terminal)
Denver, University of (PhD)
Fairleigh Dickinson University, Madison (MA—terminal)
Florida State University (PhD)
Florida, University of (PhD)
Frostburg State University (MA—terminal)
Gannon University (PhD)
Georgia State University (PhD)
Georgia, University of (PhD)
Georgian Court College (MA—terminal)
Goddard College (MA—terminal)
Hartford, University of (MA—terminal)
Houston, University of, College of Education (PhD)
Indiana State University (PhD)
Indiana University (PhD)
Iowa State University (PhD)
John F. Kennedy University (MA—terminal)
Kansas, University of (PhD)
Lehigh University (PhD)
Lesley University (MA—terminal)
Lewis & Clark College (MA—terminal)
Lousiana Tech University (PhD)
Loyola College (MA—terminal)
Marist College (MA—terminal)
Marquette University (PhD)
Maryland, University of (PhD)
Marymount University (MA—terminal)
McGill University (PhD)
Miami, University of (PhD)
Michigan State University (PhD)
Midwestern State University (MA—terminal)
Minnesota, University of (PhD)
Missouri, University of, Columbia (EdS)
Missouri, University of, Kansas City (PhD)

Morehead State University (Kentucky) (MA—terminal)
New Mexico State University (PhD)
New York University (PhD)
Northeastern University (MA—terminal)
Northern Arizona University (EdD)
Northern Colorado, University of (PsyD)
Notre Dame, University of (PhD)
Ohio State University (PhD)
Oklahoma State University (PhD)
Oklahoma, University of, College of Education (PhD)
Our Lady of the Lake University (PsyD)
Pacific University (MA—terminal)
Pennsylvania State University (PhD)
Rowan University (MA—terminal)
Rutgers—The State University of New Jersey, New Brunswick (EdD)
Seton Hall University (PhD)
Sherbrooke, University of (MA—terminal)
Southern Illinois University at Carbondale (PhD)
Southern Mississippi, University of (PhD)
Springfield College (MS—terminal)
St. Thomas, University of (MA—terminal)
Stanford University (PhD)
State University of New York at Buffalo (PhD)
Teachers College, Columbia University (PhD)
Temple University (PhD)
Tennessee, University of, Knoxville (PhD)
Texas A&M International University (MA—terminal)
Texas Tech University (PhD)
Texas Woman's University (PhD)
Texas, University of, Austin (PhD)
The University of Memphis (PhD)
Trinity International University (MA—terminal)
Utah State University (PhD)
Utah, University of (PhD)
Valdosta State University (MA—terminal)
Virginia Commonwealth University (PhD)
Walden University (PhD)
West Florida, The University of (MA—terminal)
West Virginia University (PhD)
Western Michigan University (WMU) (PhD)
Western Washington University (MA—terminal)
Wisconsin, University of, Madison (PhD)

Counseling—colleges and universities
Antioch University, Santa Barbara (MA—terminal)
Denver, University of (PhD)
Georgia State University (PhD, MSEd)
Iowa State University (PhD)
James Madison University (MA—terminal)
New York University (MA—terminal)
Southern Mississippi, University of (PhD)
Springfield College (MS—terminal)
Tennessee, University of, Knoxville (PhD)
Texas Tech University (PhD)
Washington State University (PhD)
West Virginia University (PhD)

Counseling—elementary school

Arcadia University (MA—terminal)
Auburn University (MA—terminal)
Boston College (MA—terminal)
Brigham Young University (MA—terminal)
Connecticut, University of (MA—terminal)
Georgia State University (MSEd)
Governors State University
   (MA—terminal)
James Madison University (EdS)
Lesley University (MA—terminal)
Lewis University (MA—terminal)
Marymount University (MA—terminal)
Middle Tennessee State University (EdD)
Nebraska, University of, Lincoln (MA)
New York University (MA—terminal)
Northern Colorado, University of
   (MA—terminal)
Pittsburg State University (MA—terminal)
San Francisco State University
   (MA—terminal)
Sonoma State University (MA—terminal)
Tennessee State University (PhD, EdS)
Texas, University of, Tyler (MA—terminal)
Valdosta State University (EdS)
Washington State University
   (MA—terminal)
Washington, University of (PhD)
Wisconsin, University of, Milwaukee (MA)

Counseling—marriage and family

Adler School of Professional Psychology
   (MA—terminal)
Antioch University, Santa Barbara
   (MA—terminal)
Argosy University, Honolulu
   (MA—terminal)
California Lutheran University
   (MA—terminal)
California Polytechnic State University
   (MA—terminal)
California State University, Sacramento
   (MA—terminal)
Chapman University (MA—terminal)
Denver, University of (MA—terminal)
Gonzaga University (MA—terminal)
Governors State University
   (MA—terminal)
Humboldt State University (MA—terminal)
James Madison University (EdS)
Pittsburg State University (EdS)
Seton Hall University (PhD)
Sonoma State University (MA—terminal)
St. Cloud State University (MA—terminal)
Temple University (PhD)
Texas A&M University (PhD)
Texas, University of, Tyler (MA—terminal)

Counseling—secondary school

Arcadia University (MA—terminal)
Auburn University (MA—terminal)
Boston College (MA—terminal)
Brigham Young University (MA—terminal)
Denver, University of (MA—terminal)
Georgia State University (MSEd)
James Madison University (EdS)
Lesley University (MA—terminal)
Lewis University (MA—terminal)

Marymount University (MA—terminal)
Middle Tennessee State University (EdD)
Nebraska, University of, Lincoln (MA)
New York University (MA—terminal)
Northern Colorado, University of
   (MA—terminal)
Pittsburg State University (MA—terminal)
Sonoma State University (MA—terminal)
State University of New York at Buffalo
   (MEd)
Tennessee State University (PhD, EdS)
Texas, University of, Tyler (MA—terminal)
Valdosta State University (EdS)
Washington State University
   (MA—terminal)
Washington, University of (PhD)
Wisconsin, University of, Milwaukee (MA)

Counseling—vocational

Antioch University, Santa Barbara
   (MA—terminal)
Denver, University of (PhD)
Illinois, University of, at Urbana-
   Champaign (PhD)
Minnesota, University of (PhD)
Southern Illinois University at Carbondale
   (PhD)
Stanford University (PhD)
Temple University (PhD)
Utah, University of (PhD)

D

Developmental

Acadia University (MA—terminal)
Alabama, University of, at Birmingham
   (PhD)
Alberta, University of (PhD)
Andrews University (MA)
Arizona State University (PhD)
Arkansas, University of (PhD)
Boston College (PhD)
Boston University (PhD)
Brandeis University (PhD)
British Columbia, University of (PhD)
Calgary, University of (MSc)
California, University of, at Berkeley (PhD)
California, University of, Davis (PhD)
California, University of, Irvine (PhD)
California, University of, Los Angeles
   (PhD)
California, University of, Santa Barbara
   (MA)
California, University of, Santa Cruz (PhD)
Carnegie Mellon University (PhD)
Case Western Reserve University (PhD)
Chicago, University of (PhD)
City University of New York, Graduate
   School and University Center (PhD)
Claremont Graduate University
   (MA—terminal)
Clark University (PhD)
Concordia University (MA)
Connecticut, University of (PhD)
Dalhousie University (MSc)
Denver, University of (PhD)
Duquesne University (PhD)

Eastern Michigan University
   (MA—terminal)
Emory University (PhD)
Florida International University (PhD)
Florida, University of (PhD)
Fordham University (PhD)
Georgetown University (PhD)
Georgia State University (PhD)
Georgia, University of (PhD)
Goddard College (MA—terminal)
Harvard University (PhD)
Hawaii, University of (PhD)
Houston, University of (PhD)
Howard University (PhD)
Illinois, University of, at Urbana-
   Champaign (PhD)
Indiana University (PhD)
Iowa, University of (PhD)
Johns Hopkins University (PhD)
Kansas State University (PhD)
Lehigh University (PhD)
Louisiana State University (PhD)
Loyola University of Chicago (PhD)
Maine, University of (PhD)
Manitoba, University of (PhD)
Maryland, University of (PhD)
Massachusetts, University of (PhD)
Miami University (Ohio) (PhD)
Michigan State University (PhD)
Michigan, University of (PhD)
Middle Tennessee State University
   (MA—terminal)
Missouri, University of, Columbia (PhD)
Missouri, University of, St. Louis (MA)
Montana, The University of (PhD)
Nebraska, University of, Omaha (PhD)
New Hampshire, University of (PhD)
New Mexico, The University of (PhD)
North Carolina State University (PhD)
North Carolina, University of, at Chapel
   Hill (PhD)
North Carolina, University of, at
   Greensboro (PhD)
Northern Colorado, University of (PhD)
Northern Illinois University (PhD)
Notre Dame, University of (PhD)
Ohio State University (PhD)
Oklahoma State University (PhD)
Oklahoma, University of (PhD)
Oregon, University of (PhD)
Peabody College of Vanderbilt University
   (PhD)
Pennsylvania State University (PhD)
Pittsburgh, University of (PhD)
Purdue University (PhD)
Quebec at Montreal, University of (PhD)
Queen's University (PhD)
Rhode Island, University of, Chafee Social
   Sciences Center (PhD)
Richmond, University of (MA—terminal)
Rochester, University of (PhD)
Rutgers—The State University of New
   Jersey, New Brunswick (PhD, EdD)
San Francisco State University
   (MA—terminal)
South Carolina, University of (PhD)
Southern Illinois University at Carbondale
   (PhD)

Southern Methodist University (PhD)
St. Louis University (PhD)
Stanford University (PhD)
Suffolk University (Respecialization
   Diploma, PhD)
Temple University (PhD)
Texas A&M University (PhD)
Texas Christian University (PhD)
Texas, University of, Austin (PhD)
Toronto, University of (MA, PhD)
Tufts University (PhD)
Tulane University (PhD)
Valdosta State University (EdS)
Virginia Polytechnic Institute and State
   University (PhD)
Virginia, University of (PhD)
Washington University (St. Louis) (PhD)
Washington, University of (PhD)
Waterloo, University of (PhD)
Wayne State University (PhD)
Wesleyan University (MA—terminal)
West Florida, The University of
   (MA—terminal)
West Virginia University (PhD)
Western Ontario, The University of (PhD)
Wyoming, University of (PhD)
Yale University (PhD)
Yeshiva University (PhD)
York University (PhD)

Developmental psychobiology
Dalhousie University (MSc)
Indiana University (PhD)
Iowa, University of (PhD)

Developmental—comparative
California, University of, Riverside (PhD)
Connecticut, University of (PhD)
Manitoba, University of (PhD)
Michigan, University of (PhD)
Washington, University of (PhD)
York University (PhD)

Developmental—exceptional
Claremont Graduate University
   (MA—terminal)
Michigan, University of (PhD)
Nevada, University of, Reno (PhD)
Notre Dame, University of (PhD)
York University (PhD)

E

Early childhood education
Kansas, University of (MA)
Kent State University (PhD)
Tufts University (PhD)

Ecological
Cincinnati, University of (PhD)
City University of New York, Graduate
   School and University Center (PhD)
Connecticut, University of (PhD)
Michigan State University (PhD)
Minnesota, University of (PhD)
Northern Colorado, University of (EdS)

Educational
American International College (MA)
Argosy University, San Francisco Bay Area
   (EdD)
Ball State University (MA—terminal)
Colorado, University of, Boulder (PhD)
Denver, University of (PhD)
Hawaii, University of (MEd)
Houston, University of, College of
   Education (PhD)
Illinois State University (EdS, PhD)
Indiana University (PhD)
Iowa, University of (PhD)
Kansas, University of (PhD)
Kentucky, University of (MA)
Lousiana Tech University (MA—terminal)
Marist College (MA—terminal)
Maryland, University of (PhD)
Massachusetts, University of (PhD)
McGill University (PhD)
Michigan, University of (PhD)
Minnesota, University of (PhD)
Missouri, University of, Columbia
   (MA—terminal)
New York University (MA—terminal)
Northern Arizona University (EdD)
Northern Colorado, University of (EdS,
   PhD)
Oklahoma State University (PhD)
Pittsburgh, University of (PhD)
Quebec at Montreal, University of (PhD)
Rutgers—The State University of New
   Jersey, New Brunswick (EdD)
Stanford University (PhD)
Temple University (MA—terminal)
Tennessee, University of, Knoxville (PhD)
Texas A&M University - Commerce (PhD)
Texas Tech University (EdD)
Texas, University of, Austin (PhD)
Utah, University of (PhD)
Washington State University (PhD)
Wayne State University (PhD)
Western Ontario, The University of (PhD)
Wisconsin, University of, Madison (PhD)

Educational administration
James Madison University (MA—terminal)

Educational measurement
Arizona State University (PhD)
Iowa, University of (PhD)
Pennsylvania State University (PhD)
Pittsburgh, University of (PhD)
Rutgers-The State University of New Jersey,
   New Brunswick (PhD)
Stanford University (PhD)
State University of New York at Buffalo
   (PhD)

Educational research and evaluation
Claremont Graduate University
   (MA—terminal)
Connecticut, University of (PhD)
James Madison University (PsyD)
Kansas, University of (PhD)
Kentucky, University of (MA)
Manitoba, University of (PhD)
Marquette University (MA—terminal)

Mississippi State University (PhD)
Pennsylvania State University (PhD)
Quebec at Montreal, University of (PhD)
Syracuse University (PhD)
Texas Tech University (EdD)
Texas, University of, Austin (PhD)
Utah State University (PhD)
Utah, University of (PhD)

Engineering
Clemson University (MA—terminal)
Georgia Institute of Technology (PhD)
Kansas State University (PhD)
New Mexico State University (PhD)
North Carolina State University (PhD)
Wright State University (PhD)

Environmental
Antioch University, Seattle
   (MA—terminal)
British Columbia, University of (PhD)
California State University, Northridge
   (MA—terminal)
City University of New York, Graduate
   School and University Center (PhD)
Utah, University of (PhD)

Experimental psychopathology
Harvard University (PhD)
Hawaii, University of (PhD)
Iowa, University of (PhD)
Minnesota, University of (PhD)
Nevada, University of, Reno (PhD)
San Diego State University/University of
   California, San Diego Joint Doctoral
   Program in Clinical Psychology (PhD)
Southern Methodist University (PhD)
Texas, University of, Austin (PhD)
Wisconsin, University of, Madison (PhD)

Experimental—animal behavior
Alberta, University of (PhD)
American University (MA—terminal)
Arizona, University of (PhD)
Dalhousie University (MSc)
Georgia Institute of Technology (PhD)
Hawaii, University of (PhD)
Illinois, University of, at Chicago (PhD)
Kansas State University (PhD)
Manitoba, University of (PhD)
McGill University (PhD)
Nebraska, University of, Lincoln (PhD)
New Hampshire, University of (PhD)
Ohio State University (PhD)
Oklahoma, University of (PhD)
State University of New York, University at
   Albany (PhD)
Tulane University (PhD)
Washington, University of (PhD)
Western Ontario, The University of (PhD)
Yale University (PhD)

Experimental—general
Alabama, University of, at Huntsville
   (MA—terminal)
American University (PhD)
Appalachian State University
   (MA—terminal)

Arkansas, University of (PhD)
Auburn University (PhD)
Austin Peay State University
    (MA—terminal)
California State University, Northridge
    (MA)
California State University, San Bernardino
    (MA—terminal)
California State University, San Marcos
    (MA—terminal)
California, University of, San Diego (PhD)
Central Michigan University (PhD)
City University of New York, Graduate
    School and University Center (PhD)
City University of New York: Hunter
    College (PhD)
Cleveland State University (MA—terminal)
Colorado, University of, at Colorado
    Springs (MA—terminal)
Connecticut, University of (PhD)
Cornell University (PhD)
Dartmouth College (PhD)
Dayton, University of (MA—terminal)
DePaul University (PhD)
East Carolina University (MA—terminal)
Eastern Washington University
    (MA—terminal)
Emporia State University (MA—terminal)
Fairleigh Dickinson University, Teaneck-
    Hackensack (MA—terminal)
Florida Atlantic University (PhD)
Fort Hays State University (MA—terminal)
Georgia Southern University
    (MA—terminal)
Georgia, University of (PhD)
Governors State University
    (MA—terminal)
Hartford, University of (MA—terminal)
Harvard University (PhD)
Humboldt State University (MA—terminal)
Idaho State University (MA—terminal)
Illinois, University of, at Urbana-
    Champaign (PhD)
Indiana State University (MA—terminal)
Iona College (MA—terminal)
Iowa State University (PhD)
Iowa, University of (PhD)
Johns Hopkins University (PhD)
Kansas State University (PhD)
Kentucky, University of (PhD)
Long Island University (MA—terminal)
Louisiana, University of, Lafayette
    (MA—terminal)
Maine, University of (MA)
Manitoba, University of (PhD)
McGill University (PhD)
Memphis, University of (PhD)
Minnesota, University of (PhD)
Mississippi State University
    (MA—terminal)
Mississippi, University of (PhD)
Morehead State University (Kentucky)
    (MA—terminal)
Nevada, University of, Las Vegas (PhD)
New Brunswick, University of (PhD)
New Hampshire, University of (PhD)
New Mexico Highlands University
    (MA—terminal)

New Mexico State University
    (MA—terminal)
New Mexico, The University of (PhD)
New York University, Graduate School of
    Arts and Science (PhD)
North Carolina State University (PhD)
North Carolina, University of, at Chapel
    Hill (PhD)
Northern Michigan University (MA)
Ohio State University (PhD)
Oklahoma, University of (PhD)
Penn State Harrisburg (MA—terminal)
Purdue University (PhD)
Radford University (MA—terminal)
Regina, University of (MA—terminal)
Rhode Island, University of, Chafee Social
    Sciences Center (PhD)
Rice University (PhD)
Saint Joseph's University (MA—terminal)
San Francisco State University
    (MA—terminal)
San Jose State University (MA—terminal)
Saskatchewan, University of (PhD)
Simon Fraser University (PhD)
South Alabama, University of
    (MA—terminal)
Southeastern Louisiana University
    (MA—terminal)
Southern Connecticut State University
    (MA—terminal)
Southern Illinois University Edwardsville
    (MA—terminal)
Southern Mississippi, University of (PhD)
St. John's University (MA—terminal)
State University of New York at Stony
    Brook (PhD)
Syracuse University (PhD)
Tennessee, University of, Knoxville
    (MA—terminal)
Texas Christian University (PhD)
Texas Tech University (MA)
Texas, University of, Arlington (PhD)
Texas, University of, Austin (PhD)
Texas, University of, El Paso
    (MA—terminal)
Texas, University of, Pan American
    (MA—terminal)
The Catholic University of America (PhD)
Towson University (MA—terminal)
West Chester University of Pennsylvania
    (MA—terminal)
West Texas A & M University
    (MA—terminal)
Western Illinois University (MA—terminal)
Western Washington University
    (MA—terminal)
Wilfrid Laurier University (MA—terminal)
William and Mary, College of
    (MA—terminal)
Wisconsin, University of, Milwaukee
    (MA—terminal)
Wyoming, University of (PhD)
Xavier University (MA—terminal)
York University (PhD)

F

Forensic
American International College (MA)
British Columbia, University of (PhD)

California School of Professional
    Psychology/AIU: Alameda (PsyD)
Castleton State College (MA—terminal)
Chicago School of Professional Psychology
    (MA—terminal)
City University of New York: John Jay
    College of Criminal Justice
    (MA—terminal)
City University of New York: Graduate
    Center (PhD)
Denver, University of (PsyD)
Marymount University (MA—terminal)
Nebraska, University of, Lincoln (PhD)
Nova Southeastern University (PhD, PsyD)
Pacific Graduate School of Psychology
    (PsyD)
Penn State Harrisburg (MA—terminal)
Queen's University (PhD)
Sam Houston State University (PhD)
Simon Fraser University (PhD)
The Sage Colleges (MA—terminal)

G

General
Adelphi University (MA—terminal)
Adler School of Professional Psychology
    (MA—terminal)
American University (MA—terminal)
Angelo State University (MA—terminal)
Appalachian State University
    (MA—terminal)
Austin Peay State University
    (MA—terminal)
Boston University (MA—terminal)
Brandeis University (MA—terminal)
Brigham Young University (PhD)
California State University, Bakersfield
    (MA—terminal)
California State University, Chico
    (MA—terminal)
California State University, Fullerton
    (MA—terminal)
California State University, Long Beach
    (MA—terminal)
Carlos Albizu University, Miami Campus
    (MS—terminal)
Central Connecticut State University
    (MA—terminal)
Central Michigan University
    (MA—terminal)
Central Washington University
    (MA—terminal)
Dayton, University of (MA—terminal)
Duquesne University (MA)
Fairleigh Dickinson University, Teaneck-
    Hackensack (MA—terminal)
Fort Hays State University (MA—terminal)
Goddard College (MA—terminal)
Governors State University
    (MA—terminal)
Humboldt State University (MA—terminal)
Illinois State University (MA—terminal)
James Madison University (MA—terminal)

Long Island University (MA—terminal)
Marshall University (MA—terminal)
Marywood University (MA—terminal)
Massachusetts, University of, at Dartmouth
(MA—terminal)
McGill University (PhD)
Memphis, University of (MA—terminal)
Michigan, University of (PhD)
Missouri, University of, Kansas City (MA)
Montana State University-Billings
(MA—terminal)
Murray State University (MA—terminal)
New School University (MA—terminal)
North Carolina, University of, at
Wilmington (MA—terminal)
North Florida, University of
(MA—terminal)
Northern Arizona University
(MA—terminal)
Old Dominion University (MA—terminal)
Oregon, University of (MA—terminal)
Pace University (MA—terminal)
Peabody College of Vanderbilt University
(PhD)
Pepperdine University (MA—terminal)
Pittsburg State University (MA—terminal)
Roosevelt University (MA—terminal)
Saint Francis, University of
(MA—terminal)
Sam Houston State University
(MA—terminal)
San Jose State University (MA—terminal)
Seton Hall University (MA—terminal)
Shippensburg University (MA—terminal)
Southern Connecticut State University
(MA—terminal)
Southern Illinois University Edwardsville
(MA—terminal)
St. Bonaventure University
(MA—terminal)
State University of New York at New Paltz
(MA—terminal)
State University of New York, University at
Buffalo (MA—terminal)
Teachers College, Columbia University
(MA—terminal)
Texas A&M International University
(MA—terminal)
Texas A&M University (PhD)
Texas, University of, Arlington (PhD)
The Catholic University of America
(MA—terminal)
Toledo, University of (MA—terminal)
Université Laval (MA—terminal)
Wake Forest University (MA—terminal)
Walden University (MA)
Washington College (MA—terminal)
Wesleyan University (MA—terminal)
West Chester University of Pennsylvania
(MA—terminal)
Western Washington University
(MA—terminal)
Xavier University (MA—terminal)

Group psychotherapy
Antioch University, Seattle
(MA—terminal)

Argosy University, Washington School of
Professional Psychology, Seattle (PsyD)

H

Health psychology
Alliant International University, San Diego
(PhD)
Antioch University, Seattle
(MA—terminal)
Appalachian State University
(MA—terminal)
Arizona State University (PhD)
British Columbia, University of (PhD)
California School of Professional
Psychology/AIU: Los Angeles (PhD)
California, University of, Irvine (PhD)
California, University of, Riverside (PhD)
Cincinnati, University of (PhD)
Concordia University (MA)
Dalhousie University (PhD)
Fielding Graduate Institute (PhD)
Finch University of Health Sciences, The
Chicago Medical School (PhD)
Florida, University of (PhD)
Hartford, University of (MA—terminal)
Hawaii, University of (PhD)
Illinois, University of, at Chicago (PhD)
Indianapolis, University of (PsyD)
Iowa State University (PhD)
Iowa, University of (PhD)
Jackson State University (PhD)
Kansas, University of (PhD)
Loma Linda University (PhD, PsyD)
Loyola University of Chicago (PhD)
Maryland, University of (PhD)
Miami University (Ohio) (PhD)
Miami, University of (Florida) (PhD)
Missouri, University of, Kansas City (PhD)
North Dakota State University (PhD)
Northern Arizona University
(MA—terminal)
Northwestern University Medical School
(PhD)
Nova Southeastern University (PhD, PsyD)
Ohio State University (PhD)
Ohio University (PhD)
Penn State Harrisburg (MA—terminal)
Philadelphia College of Osteopathic
Medicine (CAGS, PsyD)
Pittsburgh, University of (PhD)
Regent University (PsyD)
Rhode Island, University of, Chafee Social
Sciences Center (PhD)
Saint Joseph's University (MA—terminal)
Seattle Pacific University (PhD)
Southern California, University of (PhD)
Southern California, University of, School
of Medicine (PhD)
Southern Methodist University (PhD)
Southern Mississippi, University of (PhD)
Southwest Texas State University
(MA—terminal)
Stanford University (PhD)
State University of New York at Stony
Brook (PhD)
Syracuse University (PhD)

Texas Southwestern Medical Center at
Dallas, University of (PhD)
Texas, University of, Austin (PhD)
Texas, University of, El Paso (PhD)
Texas, University of, Pan American
(MA—terminal)
Utah, University of (PhD)
Virginia Commonwealth University (PhD)
Virginia Polytechnic Institute and State
University (PhD)
Walden University (PhD)
Washington State University (PhD)
Washington University (St. Louis) (PhD)
West Florida, The University of
(MA—terminal)
West Virginia University (PhD)
Wisconsin, University of, Milwaukee (PhD)
Wisconsin, University of, Stout
(MA—terminal)
Yale University (PhD)
Yeshiva University (PhD)

Helping services
Northern Colorado, University of (EdS)

History and systems
Brigham Young University (PhD)
New Hampshire, University of (PhD)
York University (PhD)

Human development and family studies
Andrews University (MA)
Antioch University, Santa Barbara
(MA—terminal)
California, University of, Riverside (PhD)
Georgia College & State University
(MA—terminal)
Kansas, University of (MA)
Maryland, University of (PhD)
Michigan State University (PhD)
Pennsylvania State University (PhD)
Pennsylvania, University of (PhD)
Pittsburgh, University of (PhD)
Texas A&M University (MA—terminal)
The Catholic University of America (PhD)
Vanderbilt University (MA—terminal)
Wayne State University (MA—terminal)

Human factors
Alabama, University of, at Huntsville
(MA—terminal)
California State University, Long Beach
(MA—terminal)
California State University, Northridge
(MA—terminal)
California, University of, Riverside (PhD)
Central Florida, University of (PhD)
Cincinnati, University of (PhD)
Clemson University (MA—terminal)
Connecticut, University of (PhD)
Dayton, University of (MA—terminal)
Embry-Riddle Aeronautical University
(MA—terminal)
George Mason University (PhD)
Georgia Institute of Technology (PhD)
Guelph, University of (PhD)
Illinois, University of, at Chicago (PhD)
Illinois, University of, at Urbana-
Champaign (PhD)

British Columbia, University of (PhD)
Denver, University of (MA—terminal)
Florida International University (PhD)
Georgia, University of (PhD)
Illinois, University of, at Chicago (PhD)
Pacific Graduate School of Psychology
  (PsyD)
Sam Houston State University (PhD)
Simon Fraser University (PhD)
Texas, University of, El Paso (PhD)
Tulsa, University of (MA—terminal)
Virginia, University of (PhD)
Wyoming, University of (PhD)

Learning
Andrews University (MA)
Arizona State University (PhD)
California State University, San Bernardino
  (MA—terminal)
California, University of, Los Angeles
  (PhD)
City University of New York, Graduate
  School and University Center (PhD)
Connecticut, University of (PhD)
Indiana University (PhD)
Middle Tennessee State University
  (MA—terminal)
Montana, The University of (PhD)
New York University, Graduate School of
  Arts and Science (MA—terminal)
State University of New York at Buffalo
  (PhD)
Tennessee, University of, Knoxville (PhD)
Texas A&M University - Commerce (PhD)
Texas Tech University (EdD)
West Virginia University (PhD)
Western Ontario, The University of (PhD)

Learning disabilities
City University of New York, Graduate
  School and University Center (PhD)
Emporia State University (MA—terminal)
Rutgers—The State University of New
  Jersey, New Brunswick (EdD)
Texas A&M University (MA—terminal)

Learning—animal
Alberta, University of (PhD)
American University (MA—terminal)
Boston University (PhD)
City University of New York, Graduate
  School and University Center (PhD)
Dalhousie University (MSc)
Illinois State University (MA—terminal)
Iowa, University of (PhD)
Kansas State University (PhD)
Massachusetts, University of (PhD)
Nebraska, University of, Lincoln (PhD)
Oklahoma, University of (PhD)
Purdue University (PhD)
Texas, University of, Austin (PhD)
Washington, University of (PhD)
Western Ontario, The University of (PhD)

Learning—human
Alberta, University of (PhD)
Arizona State University (PhD, MA)
City University of New York, Graduate
  School and University Center (PhD)

Hawaii, University of (MEd, PhD)
Illinois, University of, at Chicago (PhD)
Kansas State University (PhD)
Mississippi State University (PhD)
Nebraska, University of, Lincoln (MA)
North Carolina, University of, at Chapel
  Hill (PhD)
Pennsylvania State University (PhD)
Pennsylvania, University of (PhD)
Rutgers—The State University of New
  Jersey, New Brunswick (PhD, EdD)
Texas, University of, Austin (PhD)
Yale University (PhD)

Life-span development
Akron, University of (PhD)
Antioch University, Santa Barbara
  (MA—terminal)
Argosy University, Tampa (PsyD)
Bowling Green State University (PhD)
Brandeis University (MA—terminal)
British Columbia, University of (PhD)
California, University of, Riverside (PhD)
Cornell University (PhD)
Georgia, University of (PhD)
Kansas, University of (PhD)
Maryland, University of (PhD)
Massachusetts, University of, at Boston
  (PhD)
North Carolina State University (PhD)
Temple University (PhD)
Toronto, University of (MA, PhD)
Utah, University of (PhD)
Victoria, University of (PhD)
Virginia Commonwealth University (PhD)
Virginia, University of (PhD)
Washington University (St. Louis) (PhD)
Wayne State University (PhD)
Wisconsin, University of, Madison (PhD)

M

Marriage and family
Adler School of Professional Psychology
  (MA—terminal)
Argosy University, Twin Cities (MA)
California School of Professional
  Psychology/AIU: Los Angeles (PhD)
Chapman University (MA—terminal)
Denver, University of (PhD)
Forest Institute of Professional Psychology
  (PsyD)
Geneva College (MA—terminal)
Georgia State University (MSc)
Northern Colorado, University of (MA)
Pittsburg State University (EdS)
Seattle Pacific University (PsyD, PhD)
Seton Hall University (PhD)
St. Cloud State University (MA—terminal)
The Catholic University of America (PhD)
Victoria, University of (PhD)

Marriage and family therapy
Adler School of Professional Psychology
  (MA—terminal)
Antioch University, Santa Barbara
  (MA—terminal)

Antioch University, Seattle
  (MA—terminal)
Argosy University (MA—terminal)
Argosy University, Honolulu
  (MA—terminal)
Azusa Pacific University (PsyD)
California Lutheran University
  (MA—terminal)
California Polytechnic State University
  (MA—terminal)
California State University, Dominguez
  Hills (MA—terminal)
California State University, San Bernardino
  (MA—terminal)
Chapman University (MA—terminal)
Chestnut Hill College (PsyD)
Frostburg State University (MA—terminal)
Georgia State University (MSEd)
Miami University (Ohio) (PhD)
Our Lady of the Lake University (PsyD)
Pepperdine University (MA—terminal)
Regent University (PsyD)
San Jose State University (MA—terminal)
Saybrook Graduate School and Research
  Center (MA)
Seton Hall University (PhD, EdS)
Sonoma State University (MA—terminal)
Springfield College (MS—terminal)
Texas, University of, Tyler (MA—terminal)
Vanguard University of Southern California
  (MA—terminal)
Virginia Commonwealth University (PhD)
Virginia, University of (PhD)

Mathematical
Ohio State University (PhD)
Stanford University (PhD)

Medical psychology
Appalachian State University
  (MA—terminal)
Kansas, University of (PhD)

Mental health
Antioch University, Seattle
  (MA—terminal)
Argosy University, Washington School of
  Professional Psychology, Seattle (PsyD)
Austin Peay State University
  (MA—terminal)
Boston College (MA—terminal)
Cincinnati, University of (PhD)
Columbia University (EdD)
Florida International University
  (MS—terminal)
Georgia State University (MSc)
Indiana State University (PhD)
Kean University (MA—terminal)
Lesley University (MA—terminal)
Lewis University (MA—terminal)
Maryland, University of (PhD)
Marymount University (MA—terminal)
Minnesota, University of (PhD)
New Mexico State University
  (MA—terminal)
New School University (MA—terminal)
Nova Southeastern University
  (MA—terminal)

The Citadel (MA—terminal)
The Sage Colleges (MA—terminal)
Valparaiso University (MA—terminal)
West Florida, The University of
(MA—terminal)
Western Washington University
(MA—terminal)
Widener University (PsyD)

Mental retardation
Case Western Reserve University (PhD)
East Carolina University (MA—terminal)
Emporia State University (MA—terminal)
Kansas, University of (PhD)
Ohio State University (PhD)
Pittsburg State University (MA—terminal)
Rutgers—The State University of New
Jersey, New Brunswick (EdD)
Western Michigan University
(MA—terminal)

Minority mental health
Alaska, University of, Fairbanks
(MA—terminal)
Argosy University, Honolulu (PsyD)
Auburn University (PhD)
Boston College (PhD)
California School of Professional
Psychology/AIU: Los Angeles (PhD)
Gallaudet University (PhD)
Jackson State University (PhD)
Lehigh University (PhD)
Ohio State University (PhD)
Our Lady of the Lake University (PsyD)
Rutgers—The State University of New
Jersey, New Brunswick (EdD)
South Dakota, University of (PhD)
Utah, University of (PhD)
Wright State University (PsyD)

N

Neuropsychology
Alberta, University of (PhD)
American University (PhD)
Brigham Young University (PhD)
California, University of, Davis (PhD)
California, University of, Riverside (PhD)
City University of New York, Graduate
School and University Center (PhD)
Cornell University (PhD)
Denver, University of (PhD)
Florida, University of (PhD)
George Mason University (PhD)
Georgia State University (PhD)
Howard University (PhD)
Johns Hopkins University (PhD)
Montreal, University of (PhD)
Pacific Graduate School of Psychology
(PhD)
Pittsburgh, University of (PhD)
Quebec at Montreal, University of (PhD)
Rice University (PhD)
San Diego State University/University of
California, San Diego Joint Doctoral
Program in Clinical Psychology (PhD)

State University of New York at Stony
Brook (PhD)
State University of New York, University at
Buffalo (PhD)
Syracuse University (PhD)
Toronto, University of (PhD)
Tufts University (PhD)
Utah, University of (PhD)
Victoria, University of (PhD)

Neuroscience
Alabama, University of, at Birmingham
(PhD)
Alberta, University of (PhD)
Arizona State University (PhD)
Arizona, University of (PhD)
Baylor University (PsyD)
Boston College (PhD)
Boston University (PhD)
Brandeis University (PhD)
British Columbia, University of (PhD)
California, University of, Davis (PhD)
California, University of, Riverside (PhD)
Carnegie Mellon University (PhD)
Cincinnati, University of (PhD)
City University of New York, Graduate
School and University Center (PhD)
Cornell University (PhD)
Dalhousie University (MSc)
Delaware, University of (PhD)
Denver, University of (PhD)
Florida State University (PhD)
Georgetown University (PhD)
Hartford, University of (MA—terminal)
Houston Baptist University
(MA—terminal)
Illinois, University of, at Chicago (PhD)
Illinois, University of, at Urbana-
Champaign (PhD)
Maryland, University of (PhD)
Massachusetts, University of
(MA—terminal)
Michigan State University (PhD)
Missouri, University of, Columbia (PhD)
North Carolina, University of, at Chapel
Hill (PhD)
North Dakota State University (PhD)
Northern Illinois University (PhD)
Oregon, University of (PhD)
Princeton University (PhD)
Purdue University (PhD)
Quebec at Montreal, University of (PhD)
Richmond, University of (MA—terminal)
South Florida, University of (PhD)
Texas A&M University (PhD)
Texas, University of, Austin (PhD)
Toronto, University of (PhD)
Vanderbilt University (PhD)
Virginia Polytechnic Institute and State
University (PhD)
Virginia, University of (PhD)
Washington University (St. Louis) (PhD)
Wisconsin, University of, Milwaukee (PhD)
York University (PhD)

O

Organizational
Adler School of Professional Psychology
(MA—terminal)

Alliant International University, San Diego
(PhD, PsyD)
Antioch University, Santa Barbara
(MA—terminal)
Appalachian State University
(MA—terminal)
Baltimore, University of (MA—terminal)
California School of Professional
Psychology/AIU: Alameda (PhD, PsyD)
California School of Professional
Psychology/AIU: Los Angeles
(MA—terminal)
Carnegie Mellon University (PhD)
Central Washington University
(MA—terminal)
Chicago School of Professional Psychology
(MA—terminal)
Claremont Graduate University
(MA—terminal)
Clemson University (PhD—terminal)
Cleveland State University (MA—terminal)
Connecticut, University of (PhD)
Detroit-Mercy, University of
(MA—terminal)
Fairleigh Dickinson University, Madison
(MA—terminal)
Georgia Institute of Technology (PhD)
Goddard College (MA—terminal)
Guelph, University of (PhD)
Harvard University (PhD)
Houston, University of (PhD)
Illinois Institute of Technology (PhD)
Illinois State University (MA—terminal)
Illinois, University of, at Urbana-
Champaign (PhD)
John F. Kennedy University
(MA—terminal)
Maryland, University of (PhD)
Michigan State University (PhD)
Middle Tennessee State University
(MA—terminal)
Minnesota, University of (PhD)
Nevada, University of, Reno (PhD)
North Carolina State University (PhD)
North Carolina, University of, at Charlotte
(MA—terminal)
Oklahoma, University of (PhD)
Pacific University (MA—terminal)
Philadelphia College of Osteopathic
Medicine (MS—terminal)
Rice University (PhD)
Rutgers—The State University of New
Jersey, Graduate School of Applied and
Professional Psychology (PsyD)
San Francisco State University
(MA—terminal)
Saybrook Graduate School and Research
Center (PhD)
Sonoma State University (MA)
South Florida, University of (PhD)
Southern Mississippi, University of (PhD)
St. Louis University (PhD)
Temple University (MA—terminal)
Tulsa, University of (PhD)
Vanderbilt University (MA—terminal)
Virginia Polytechnic Institute and State
University (PhD)
Walden University (PhD)

West Florida, The University of
(MA—terminal)
Western Michigan University
(MA—terminal)
Wright State University (PhD)
Xavier University (MA—terminal)

P

Parent education
New York University (MA—terminal)

Pastoral counseling
Trinity International University
(MA—terminal)

Pediatric psychology
Case Western Reserve University (PhD)
Cincinnati, University of (PhD)
Lehigh University (PhD)
Peabody College of Vanderbilt University
(PhD)
State University of New York at Buffalo
(MA)
State University of New York at New Paltz
(MA—terminal)
Virginia, University of (PhD)
West Virginia University (PhD)

Personality
American University (MA—terminal)
Arizona State University (PhD)
British Columbia, University of (PhD)
Calgary, University of (PhD)
California, University of, Davis (PhD)
California, University of, Riverside (PhD)
California, University of, Santa Barbara
(MA)
City University of New York, Graduate
School and University Center (PhD)
Connecticut, University of (PhD)
Cornell University (PhD)
Fairfield University (MA)
Georgia, University of (PhD)
Howard University (PhD)
Illinois, University of, at Chicago (PhD)
Illinois, University of, at Urbana-
Champaign (PhD)
Iowa, University of (PhD)
Kansas State University (PhD)
Maine, University of (MA)
Manitoba, University of (PhD)
Michigan State University (PhD)
Michigan, University of (PhD)
Minnesota, University of (PhD)
Missouri, University of, Columbia (PhD)
Nebraska, University of, Lincoln (PhD)
New Hampshire, University of (PhD)
New York University, Graduate School of
Arts and Science (PhD)
Northeastern University (PhD)
Northwestern University (PhD)
Oklahoma, University of (PhD)
Oregon, University of (PhD)
Princeton University (PhD)
Rochester, University of (PhD)
Stanford University (PhD)

State University of New York, University at
Albany (PhD)
State University of New York, University at
Buffalo (PhD)
Syracuse University (PhD)
Texas, University of, Austin (PhD)
Toronto, University of (PhD)
Utah, University of (PhD)
Washington University (St. Louis) (PhD)
Washington, University of (PhD)
Western Ontario, The University of (PhD)
Wisconsin, University of, Madison (PhD)
Yale University (PhD)

Personnel and guidance
Andrews University (MA—terminal)
New York University, Graduate School of
Arts and Science (MA—terminal)
Oklahoma, University of (PhD)
San Francisco State University
(MA—terminal)
Springfield College (MS—terminal)
State University of New York at Buffalo
(MEd)

Phenomenological
Duquesne University (PhD)
Seattle University (MA—terminal)
State University of West Georgia
(MA—terminal)

Physiological
Alberta, University of (PhD)
American University (MA—terminal)
British Columbia, University of (PhD)
California, University of, Davis (PhD)
California, University of, Santa Barbara
(MA)
Connecticut, University of (PhD)
Dalhousie University (MSc)
Kansas State University (PhD)
Minnesota, University of (PhD)
Nebraska, University of, Lincoln (PhD)
New Hampshire, University of (PhD)
North Carolina, University of, at Chapel
Hill (PhD)
San Francisco State University
(MA—terminal)
Saskatchewan, University of (PhD)
St. Louis University (PhD)
Texas, University of, Austin (PhD)
Washington, University of (PhD)
Wayne State University (PhD)
Yale University (PhD)

Preclinical
Fort Hays State University (MA—terminal)
Northern Iowa, University of
(MA—terminal)

Primate behavior
Arizona, University of (PhD)
California, University of, Davis (PhD)
Georgia, University of (PhD)
Nevada, University of, Reno (PhD)
Wisconsin, University of, Madison (PhD)

Professional
Antioch New England Graduate School
(PsyD)
Argosy University, Washington, DC (PsyD)
Argosy University, Twin Cities (PsyD)
Chestnut Hill College (PsyD)
Massachusetts School of Professional
Psychology (PsyD)
Pacific University (PsyD)
South Florida, University of (PhD)
West Virginia University (MA—terminal)
Wright State University (PsyD)

Program evaluation
Arizona, University of (PhD)
Cincinnati, University of (PhD)
Claremont Graduate University
(MA—terminal)
Connecticut, University of (PhD)
Guelph, University of (PhD)
Houston, University of (PhD)
Houston, University of, College of
Education (PhD)
Marquette University (MA—terminal)
Utah State University (PhD)
Valdosta State University (MA—terminal)
Vanderbilt University (PhD)
Washington State University (PhD)
West Texas A & M University
(MA—terminal)

Psychobiology
Arizona, University of (PhD)
Boston College (PhD)
California, University of, Santa Barbara
(MA)
City University of New York, Graduate
School and University Center (PhD)
City University of New York: Hunter
College (PhD)
Connecticut, University of (PhD)
Cornell University (PhD)
Emory University (PhD)
Florida State University (PhD)
Florida, University of (PhD)
Georgia, University of (PhD)
Illinois, University of, at Chicago (PhD)
Illinois, University of, at Urbana-
Champaign (PhD)
Indiana University—Purdue University
Indianapolis (PhD)
Kansas State University (PhD)
Kent State University (PhD)
Manitoba, University of (PhD)
Maryland, University of (PhD)
Michigan, University of (PhD)
Missouri, University of, St. Louis (PhD)
New Hampshire, University of (PhD)
New Orleans, University of (PhD)
Northeastern University (PhD)
Northern Illinois University (PhD)
Northwestern University (PhD)
Ohio State University (PhD)
Oklahoma State University (PhD)
Purdue University (PhD)
Southern Illinois University at Carbondale
(PhD)
Southern Mississippi, University of (PhD)

State University of New York at Stony
Brook (PhD)
Texas, University of, Austin (PhD)
Tulane University (PhD)
Virginia Commonwealth University (PhD)
Virginia Polytechnic Institute and State
University (PhD)
Virginia, University of (PhD)
Western Ontario, The University of (PhD)
Yale University (PhD)

Psycholinguistics
Alabama, University of, at Birmingham
(PhD)
Alberta, University of (PhD)
Arizona, University of (PhD)
California, University of, Riverside (PhD)
Chicago, University of (PhD)
Illinois, University of, at Urbana-
Champaign (PhD)
Kansas State University (PhD)
Manitoba, University of (PhD)
New Hampshire, University of (PhD)
San Francisco State University
(MA—terminal)
Stanford University (PhD)
State University of New York at Stony
Brook (PhD)
Texas, University of, Austin (PhD)
Wisconsin, University of, Madison (PhD)
Yale University (PhD)

Psychological assessment
Andrews University (EdS)
Appalachian State University (CAGS)
Argosy University, Honolulu (PsyD)
Argosy University,Twin Cities (PsyD)
Auburn University (PhD)
Baltimore, University of (PsyD)
Chestnut Hill College (PsyD)
Denver, University of (PsyD)
Humboldt State University (MA—terminal)
Minnesota, University of (PhD)
Pacific Graduate School of Psychology
(PhD)
Temple University (Other, PhD)
Tennessee, University of, Knoxville (PhD)
Tufts University (MA)
Valdosta State University (EdS)
West Virginia University (PhD)

Psychology of women
Rhode Island, University of, Chafee Social
Sciences Center (PhD)
Wisconsin, University of, Madison (PhD)

Psychometrics
Bowling Green State University (PhD)
British Columbia, University of (PhD)
California, University of, Los Angeles
(PhD)
Fordham University (PhD)
Illinois, University of, at Urbana-
Champaign (PhD)
Minnesota, University of (PsyD)
North Carolina, University of, at Chapel
Hill (PhD)
Ohio State University (PhD)

Oklahoma, University of (PhD)
Pennsylvania, University of (PhD)
Pittsburgh, University of (PhD)
Rutgers—The State University of New
Jersey, New Brunswick (EdD)
Southern California, University of (PhD)
Texas, University of, Austin (PhD)
Utah, University of (PhD)

Psychopharmacology
Bowling Green State University (PhD)
California, University of, Santa Barbara
(MA)
Hartford, University of (MA—terminal)
Illinois, University of, at Urbana-
Champaign (PhD)
Iowa, University of (PhD)
Nova Southeastern University
(MA—terminal)
Oklahoma, University of, Health Sciences
Center (PhD)
Pittsburgh, University of (PhD)
State University of New York, University at
Buffalo (PhD)
Western Michigan University (PhD)

Psychotherapy and psychoanalysis
Auburn University (PhD)
Boston University (PhD)
Georgia State University (PhD)
Quebec at Montreal, University of (PhD)
Rutgers—The State University of New
Jersey (PsyD)
San Francisco State University
(MA—terminal)
The Catholic University of America (PhD)

Public policy
City University of New York, Graduate
School and University Center (PhD)
Claremont Graduate University
(MA—terminal)
Cornell University (PhD)
Georgetown University (PhD)
North Carolina State University (PhD)
Tufts University (MA—terminal)
Virginia, University of (PhD)

Q

Quantitative (including measurement)
Arizona State University (PhD)
Bowling Green State University (PhD)
California, University of, Davis (PhD)
City University of New York, Graduate
School and University Center (PhD)
Denver, University of (PhD)
Georgia, University of (PhD)
Illinois State University (MA—terminal)
Illinois, University of, at Urbana-
Champaign (PhD)
Johns Hopkins University (PhD)
Kansas, University of (PhD)
Middle Tennessee State University
(MA—terminal)
Minnesota, University of (PhD, PsyD)
Missouri, University of, Columbia (PhD)

Nebraska, University of, Lincoln (PhD)
North Carolina, University of, at Chapel
Hill (PhD)
Notre Dame, University of (PhD)
Oklahoma, University of (PhD)
Pittsburgh, University of (PhD)
Purdue University (PhD)
Texas, University of, Austin (PhD)
Tulane University (PhD)
Utah, University of (PhD)
Virginia, University of (PhD)
Western Ontario, The University of (PhD)
Western Washington University
(MA—terminal)

Quantitative methods
Arizona State University (PhD)
California, University of, Davis (PhD)
Cleveland State University (MA—terminal)
Denver, University of (PhD)
Illinois State University (MA—terminal)
Illinois, University of, at Chicago (PhD)
Illinois, University of, at Urbana-
Champaign (PhD)
Manitoba, University of (PhD)
Middle Tennessee State University
(MA—terminal)
Minnesota, University of (PsyD)
North Carolina, University of, at Chapel
Hill (PhD)
Notre Dame, University of (PhD)
Ohio State University (PhD)
Peabody College of Vanderbilt University
(PhD)
Rutgers—The State University of New
Jersey, New Brunswick (EdD)
Southern California, University of (PhD)
State University of New York at Buffalo
(PhD)
Syracuse University (PhD)
Virginia, University of (PhD)

R

Reading
Marquette University (MA—terminal)
New York University (PhD)
Washington, University of (Other)

Rehabilitation
Ball State University (MA—terminal)
California Lutheran University
(MA—terminal)
Gallaudet University (PhD)
Georgia State University (MSc)
Illinois Institute of Technology (PhD)
Indiana University—Purdue University
Indianapolis (PhD)
Missouri, University of, Columbia (EdS)
Northeastern University (MA—terminal)
State University of New York at Buffalo
(MS—terminal)
West Virginia University (MA—terminal)

Research methodology
Arizona State University (PhD)
California State University, Long Beach
(MA—terminal)

California State University, Northridge (MA)
California, University of, Riverside (PhD)
Claremont Graduate University (MA—terminal)
Cleveland State University (MA—terminal)
Eastern Illinois University (MA—terminal)
Georgia State University (PhD)
Massachusetts, University of, at Dartmouth (MA—terminal)
Minnesota, University of (PhD)
Missouri, University of, Kansas City (MA)
Nebraska, University of, Lincoln (MA)
New York University (PhD)
Penn State Harrisburg (MA—terminal)
Pennsylvania, University of (PhD)
Rhode Island, University of, Chafee Social Sciences Center (PhD)
Rutgers—The State University of New Jersey, Graduate School of Applied and Professional Psychology (PsyD)
Saybrook Graduate School and Research Center (PhD)
Temple University (PhD)
Texas, University of, El Paso (PhD)
Utah State University (PhD)
Xavier University (MA—terminal)

S

School
Adelphi University (PhD, Respecialization Diploma)
Alfred University (EdS, PsyD)
Andrews University (MA—terminal)
Appalachian State University (CAGS)
Arizona State University (PhD)
Auburn University (PhD)
Austin Peay State University (EdS)
Ball State University (PhD, EdS)
Brigham Young University (MA—terminal)
Bryn Mawr College (PhD)
Calgary, University of (MSc)
California, University of, at Berkeley (PhD)
California, University of, Riverside (PhD)
California, University of, Santa Barbara (PhD)
Central Michigan University (PhD, EdS)
Cincinnati, University of (PhD)
City University of New York, Graduate School and University Center (PhD)
Columbia University (EdD)
Connecticut, University of (PhD)
Denver, University of (PhD)
East Carolina University (MA—terminal)
Eastern Kentucky University (EdS)
Eastern Washington University (MA—terminal)
Emporia State University (EdS)
Fairleigh Dickinson University, Teaneck-Hackensack (PsyD)
Fort Hays State University (EdS)
Gallaudet University (EdS)
George Mason University (MA—terminal)
Georgia, University of (PhD)
Governors State University (MA—terminal)

Guelph, University of (PhD)
Hofstra University (PhD, PsyD)
Humboldt State University (MA—terminal)
Illinois State University (EdS, PhD)
Immaculata College (PsyD)
Indiana State University (PhD)
Indiana University (PhD)
Iowa, University of (PhD)
James Madison University (PsyD, EdS)
Kansas, University of (PhD, EdS)
Kent State University (PhD)
Kentucky, University of (MA)
Lewis & Clark College (MA—terminal)
Louisiana State University (PhD)
Louisiana, University of, Monroe (EdS)
Marist College (MA—terminal)
Maryland, University of (PhD)
McGill University (PhD)
Memphis, University of (PhD)
Middle Tennessee State University (EdS)
Midwestern State University (MA—terminal)
Minnesota State University Moorhead (EdS)
Minnesota, University of (PhD)
Minot State University (EdS)
Mississippi State University (PhD)
Missouri, University of, Columbia (MA—terminal)
Montana, The University of (MA—terminal)
Nebraska, University of, Lincoln (EdS)
Nebraska, University of, Omaha (EdS)
New Mexico State University (EdS)
New York University (PsyD, PhD)
North Carolina State University (PhD)
Northeastern University (PhD)
Northern Arizona University (EdD)
Northern Illinois University (PhD)
Ohio State University (MA—terminal)
Oklahoma State University (PhD)
Oregon, University of (MA)
Our Lady of the Lake University (MA—terminal)
Pace University (PsyD)
Pennsylvania State University (PhD)
Pennsylvania, University of (PhD)
Pittsburg State University (EdS)
Quebec at Montreal, University of (PhD)
Radford University (EdS)
Rhode Island, University of, Chafee Social Sciences Center (PhD)
Sam Houston State University (MA—terminal)
San Francisco State University (MA—terminal)
Seton Hall University (EdS)
Sonoma State University (MA—terminal)
South Carolina, University of (PhD)
South Florida, University of (PhD)
Southern Mississippi, University of (PhD)
St. John's University (PsyD)
St. Mary's University (Texas) (MA—terminal)
State University of New York, College at Plattsburgh (MA—terminal)
State University of West Georgia (EdS)
Temple University (PhD)

Tennessee, University of, Knoxville (PhD)
Texas A&M University (PhD)
Texas A&M University - Commerce (MA—terminal)
Texas Woman's University (PhD)
Texas, University of, Austin (PhD)
Texas, University of, Tyler (MA—terminal)
The Citadel (EdS)
Towson University (MA)
Tufts University (MA)
Tulane University (PhD)
Utah, University of (PhD)
Valdosta State University (EdS)
Wayne State University (MA)
Western Carolina University (MA—terminal)
Western Michigan University (PhD, EdS)
Wisconsin, University of, Eau Claire (EdS)
Wisconsin, University of, La Crosse (EdS)
Wisconsin, University of, Madison (PhD)
Wisconsin, University of, River Falls (MA—terminal)
Yeshiva University (PsyD)

School psychometry
Andrews University (EdS)
Auburn University (EdS, PhD)
Austin Peay State University (EdS)
Central Arkansas, University of (PhD)
Denver, University of (PhD)
Georgia State University (MSEd)
Illinois State University (EdS)
Minot State University (EdS)
Missouri, University of, Columbia (MA—terminal)
State University of New York at Buffalo (MA)
State University of New York at New Paltz (MA—terminal)

Sensation and perception
American University (MA—terminal)
Arizona State University (PhD)
Brandeis University (PhD)
British Columbia, University of (PhD)
California, University of, Davis (PhD)
California, University of, Santa Barbara (MA)
Chicago, University of (PhD)
Cincinnati, University of (PhD)
Concordia University (MA)
Cornell University (PhD)
Dalhousie University (MSc)
Illinois, University of, at Urbana-Champaign (PhD)
Iowa, University of (PhD)
Johns Hopkins University (PhD)
Kansas State University (PhD)
Loyola University of Chicago (PhD)
Maine, University of (MA)
Manitoba, University of (PhD)
Maryland, University of (PhD)
Minnesota, University of (PhD)
Nebraska, University of, Lincoln (PhD)
Nevada, University of, Reno (PhD)
New Hampshire, University of (PhD)
Northeastern University (PhD)
Ohio State University (PhD)

Princeton University (PhD)
Purdue University (PhD)
Queen's University (PhD)
State University of New York, University at
  Buffalo (PhD)
Texas, University of, Austin (PhD)
Toronto, University of (PhD)
Vanderbilt University (PhD)
Virginia, University of (PhD)
Washington State University (PhD)
Washington, University of (PhD)
Western Ontario, The University of (PhD)
Wisconsin, University of, Madison (PhD)
Wright State University (PhD)

Social
Alberta, University of (PhD)
American University (MA—terminal)
Arizona State University (PhD)
Arizona, University of (PhD)
Arkansas, University of (PhD)
Ball State University (MA—terminal)
Boston College (PhD)
Brandeis University (PhD)
British Columbia, University of (PhD)
Calgary, University of (PhD)
California, University of, Davis (PhD)
California, University of, Irvine (PhD)
California, University of, Los Angeles
  (PhD)
California, University of, Riverside (PhD)
California, University of, Santa Barbara
  (MA)
California, University of, Santa Cruz (PhD)
Carnegie Mellon University (PhD)
Case Western Reserve University (PhD)
Chicago, University of (PhD)
City University of New York, Graduate
  School and University Center (PhD)
Claremont Graduate University
  (MA—terminal)
Clark University (PhD)
Colorado, University of, at Boulder (PhD)
Connecticut, University of (PhD)
Cornell University (PhD)
Dayton, University of (MA—terminal)
Delaware, University of (PhD)
Denver, University of (PhD)
Eastern Michigan University
  (MA—terminal)
Fairfield University (MA)
Florida State University (PhD)
Florida, University of (PhD)
Georgia College & State University
  (MA—terminal)
Georgia State University (PhD)
Georgia, University of (PhD)
Harvard University (PhD)
Hawaii, University of (PhD)
Houston, University of (PhD)
Houston, University of, College of
  Education (PhD)
Howard University (PhD)
Illinois State University (MA—terminal)
Illinois, University of, at Chicago (PhD)
Illinois, University of, at Urbana-
  Champaign (PhD)
Indiana University (PhD)

Iowa State University (PhD)
Iowa, University of (PhD)
Kansas State University (PhD)
Kansas, University of (PhD)
Kent State University (PhD)
Lehigh University (PhD)
Loyola University of Chicago (PhD)
Maine, University of (MA)
Manitoba, University of (PhD)
Maryland, University of (PhD)
Massachusetts, University of (PhD)
Miami University (Ohio) (PhD)
Michigan State University (PhD)
Michigan, University of (PhD)
Minnesota, University of (PhD)
Missouri, University of, Columbia (PhD)
Nebraska, University of, Lincoln (PhD)
Nebraska, University of, Omaha
  (MA—terminal)
New Hampshire, University of (PhD)
New Mexico State University (PhD)
New Mexico, The University of (PhD)
New York University, Graduate School of
  Arts and Science (PhD)
North Carolina, University of, at Chapel
  Hill (PhD)
North Carolina, University of, at
  Greensboro (PhD)
Northeastern University (PhD)
Northern Illinois University (PhD)
Northern Iowa, University of
  (MA—terminal)
Northwestern University (PhD)
Ohio State University (PhD)
Ohio University (PhD)
Oklahoma, University of (PhD)
Oregon, University of (PhD)
Ottawa, University of (PhD)
Pennsylvania State University (PhD)
Pittsburgh, University of (PhD)
Princeton University (PhD)
Purdue University (PhD)
Quebec at Montreal, University of (PhD)
Queen's University (PhD)
Rhode Island, University of, Chafee Social
  Sciences Center (PhD)
Richmond, University of (MA—terminal)
Rochester, University of (PhD)
Saint Joseph's University (MA—terminal)
San Francisco State University
  (MA—terminal)
Saybrook Graduate School and Research
  Center (PhD)
Southern California, University of (PhD)
Southern Illinois University Edwardsville
  (MA—terminal)
St. Louis University (PhD)
Stanford University (PhD)
State University of New York at Stony
  Brook (PhD)
State University of New York, University at
  Albany (PhD)
State University of New York, University at
  Buffalo (PhD)
Syracuse University (PhD)
Temple University (PhD)
Texas A&M University (PhD)
Texas Tech University (PhD)

Texas, University of, Austin (PhD)
Toronto, University of (PhD)
Tulane University (PhD)
Vanderbilt University (PhD)
Victoria, University of (PhD)
Virginia Commonwealth University (PhD)
Virginia, University of (PhD)
Washington State University (PhD)
Washington University (St. Louis) (PhD)
Washington, University of (PhD)
Waterloo, University of (PhD)
Wayne State University (PhD)
Wesleyan University (MA—terminal)
Western Ontario, The University of (PhD)
Wisconsin, University of, Madison (PhD)
Wyoming, University of (PhD)
Yale University (PhD)
York University (PhD)

Sociocultural perspectives
Boston College (PhD)
California, University of, Santa Barbara
  (MA)
City University of New York, Graduate
  School and University Center (PhD)
Cleveland State University (MA—terminal)
Massachusetts, University of, at Boston
  (PhD)
North Carolina State University (PhD)
North Carolina, University of, at Chapel
  Hill (PhD)
Pennsylvania, University of (PhD)
Southern California, University of (PhD)
The University of Memphis (PhD)
Utah, University of (PhD)
Virginia, University of (PhD)
Washington State University (PhD)

Special education
Calgary, University of (MSc)
Emporia State University (MA—terminal)
Lehigh University (PhD)
McGill University (PhD)
Northeastern University (MA—terminal)
Rutgers—The State University of New
  Jersey, New Brunswick (EdD)
Temple University (PhD)
Texas A&M University (MA—terminal)
The Citadel (EdS)

Sports
Argosy University, Phoenix
  (MA—terminal)
Springfield College (MS—terminal)

Statistics
Arizona State University (PhD)
British Columbia, University of (PhD)
California State University, Northridge
  (MA)
Houston, University of (PhD)
Illinois State University (MA—terminal)
Illinois, University of, at Urbana-
  Champaign (MA—terminal)
Iowa, University of (PhD)
Nebraska, University of, Lincoln (MA)
Oklahoma, University of (PhD)
Pennsylvania, University of (PhD)

Rutgers—The State University of New
  Jersey, New Brunswick (EdD)
Southern California, University of (PhD)

Substance abuse
Adler School of Professional Psychology
  (MA—terminal)
Alabama, University of, at Birmingham
  (PhD)
Arizona State University (PhD)
Auburn University (PhD)
Cincinnati, University of (PhD)
Detroit-Mercy, University of
  (MA—terminal)
Frostburg State University (MA—terminal)
Lewis & Clark College (MA—terminal)
New School University (MA—terminal)
North Carolina, University of, at
  Wilmington (MA—terminal)
Purdue University (PhD)

Supervision
Auburn University (PhD)
State University of New York at Buffalo
  (PhD)

ALPHABETICAL INDEX OF INSTITUTIONS

NOTES

NOTES

NOTES

NOTES

NOTES

NOTES

NOTES

NOTES

NOTES

NOTES

NOTES

NOTES